THIRTIETH EDITION

KOVELS'

ANTIQUES & COLLECTIBLES

PRICE LIST

FOR THE 1998 MARKET

ILLUSTRATED

Three Rivers Press New York

This book is dedicated to YOU, part of our extended family. Since
1968 we have been collecting and writing and meeting many of you as
we all search for treasures. Earlier books have been dedicated to
friends, workers, and family but this—the thirtieth edition—is for our
fellow collectors and readers. Without you we couldn't have written
our books and recorded the prices and changes in collecting. Your
loyalty created the best known price book in America.

And of course to our family that has grown over the thirty years
to include Kim, Al, Zoe, Cloe, Lee, Jennifer, and Sophie.

To those of you who wish the prices listed were a bit lower when
buying and a bit higher when selling—so do we.

Published by Three Rivers Press, a division of Crown Publishers, Inc., 201 East 50th
Street, New York, New York 10022. Member of the Crown Publishing Group.

Random House, Inc. New York, Toronto, London, Sydney, Auckland

http://www.randomhouse.com/

THREE RIVERS PRESS and colophon are trademarks of Crown Publishers, Inc.

Printed in the United States of America
Library of Congress Catalog Card Number: 83-643618
ISBN 0-609-80142-2 (pbk.)
10 9 8 7 6 5 4 3 2 1

Books by Ralph and Terry Kovel

American Country Furniture 1780–1875

A Directory of American Silver, Pewter, and Silver Plate

Kovels' Advertising Collectibles Price List

Kovels' American Art Pottery: The Collector's Guide to Makers,
Marks, and Factory Histories

Kovels' American Silver Marks: 1650 to the Present

Kovels' Antiques & Collectibles Fix-It Source Book

Kovels' Book of Antique Labels

Kovels' Bottles Price List

Kovels' Collector's Guide to American Art Pottery

Kovels' Collectors' Source Book

Kovels' Depression Glass & American Dinnerware Price List

Kovels' Dictionary of Marks—Pottery & Porcelain

Kovels' Guide to Selling, Buying, and Fixing
Your Antiques and Collectibles

Kovels' Guide to Selling Your Antiques & Collectibles

Kovels' Illustrated Price Guide to Royal Doulton

Kovels' Know Your Antiques

Kovels' Know Your Collectibles

Kovels' New Dictionary of Marks—Pottery & Porcelain

Kovels' Organizer for Collectors

Kovels' Price Guide for Collector Plates, Figurines,
Paperweights, and Other Limited Editions

Kovels' Quick Tips—799 Helpful Hints on
How to Care for Your Collectibles

Look at us! This is the thirtieth edition of *Kovels' Antiques & Collectibles Price List*. The colorful cover is just part of our new, more modern look. Inside you will find special redesigned pages, larger logos, and larger computer-enhanced pictures. But we still have thousands of prices and hundreds of pictures of antiques and collectibles offered for sale in the past year.

READ THIS BEFORE YOU USE THIS BOOK—IT WILL HELP

This is a book for the average collector. All year we check prices, visit shops and shows, read our mail, check on-line computer services and the Internet, and decide what antiques and collectibles are of most interest. We concentrate on the average pieces in any category. We sometimes include one or two high-priced pieces in a category so you will realize that some of the rarities are quite valuable. For example, the Watt pottery listed this year includes an apple teapot, no. 505, for $4,000 and a tear-drop bean server for $25 to $35. Examples of furniture, silver, Tiffany, or art pottery may sell for more than $50,000; we list few of those examples. The highest price in this book is $41,800 for a Rookwood vase. The lowest price is 10 cents for an Old Red Eye bottle cap. Most pieces we list are less than $10,000. We even list the weird and wonderful, and this year you can find prices for a rhinestone-studded musical saw, a Melvin Purvis pocket knife, a purse made of Armadillo hide, ice harvesting shoes, a figural frog-shaped mailbox, and a case holding 25 glass eyes. The smallest object is a 5/8-inch political button printed "Impeach LBJ"; the largest, a carved oak backbar, 11 by 18 feet. Sometimes prices surprise us because they seem to have changed so much from earlier years. Is a 5-cent Lone Ranger Clark candy bar wrapper from 1938 actually selling for $650? Flow blue bowl and pitcher sets, Marblehead tiles, celluloid jewelry boxes, and crystalline-glazed Pisgah Forest pottery all seem much higher. Iron of all types—doorstops, frying pans, bookends, and figures—are selling higher. Vinyl lunch boxes are now in demand, often selling for more than the common metal examples. And the "Prayer Lady," a 1970s set that included a cookie jar, egg timer, soap dish, spoon holder, canisters, and other pieces, is in several different categories in this book. Not only are prices high, but there would have been few collectors who even knew the name "Prayer Lady" a year or so ago.

The book is changed slightly each year. Categories are added or omitted to make it easier for you to find your antiques. New this year are Chintz china, Dorchester pottery, and WPA-made items. The book is kept at about 800 pages because it is written to go with you to sales. We try to have a balanced format—not too much glass, pottery, or collectibles, not too many items that sell for more than $5,000. The prices are *from* the American market *for* the American market. Few European sales are reported. We take the editorial privilege of not including any prices that seem to result from "auction fever."

The computer-generated index is so complete it amazes us. Use it often. An internal alphabetical index is also included. For example, there is a category for "Celluloid." Most items made of celluloid will be found there, but if there is a toy made of celluloid, it will be listed under "Toy" and also indexed under "Celluloid." There are also cross-references in the listings and in the paragraphs. But some searching must be done. For example, Barbie dolls are found in the doll category; there is no Barbie category. And when you look at "doll, Barbie" you will see a note that tells you that Barbie is under "doll, Mattel, Barbie" because most dolls are listed by maker. All pictures and prices are new every year, except pictures that are pattern examples shown in "Depression Glass" and "Pressed Glass." The pictures have been computer-enhanced to make them as crisp as possible. Antiques pictured are not museum pieces but items offered for sale. We hate to waste space, so whenever computer-generated spaces appeared, we filled them with tips about care of collections, security, and other useful information. These tips are set in special type, a bit larger and easier to read. Leaf through the book and learn how to wash porcelains, store textiles, guard against theft, and much more. Don't discard this book when it is time to buy a new one next year. Old Kovels' price books should be saved for future reference, and for tax and appraisal information.

The prices in this book are reports of the general antiques market, not the record-setting examples. Each year, every price in the book is new. We do not estimate or "update" prices. Prices are actual asking prices, although a buyer may have negotiated a price to a lower figure. No price is an estimate. We do not ask dealers and writers to estimate prices. Experience has shown that a collector of one type of antique is prejudiced in favor of that item, and prices are usually high or low, but rarely a true report. If a price range is given, it is because at least two identical items were offered for sale at different times. The computer records prices and prints the high and low figures. Price ranges are found only in categories like "Pressed Glass," where identical items can be identified. Some prices in *Kovels' Antiques & Collectibles Price List* may seem high and some may seem low because of regional variations. But each price is one you could have paid for the object.

If you are selling your collection, do not expect to get retail value unless you are a dealer. Wholesale prices for antiques are from 20 to 50 percent less than retail. Remember, the antiques dealer must make a profit or go out of business.

THE RECORD PRICES HYPE

The media loves to report record prices, amazing auctions, and other events that really have little to do with the antiques and collectibles market of the average collector. There were a few major shows and auctions this year that influenced the prices in the average antiques show. A "doggie" doorknob sold at an auction of hardware for $3,600, causing many dealers to look again at the old doorknobs in their shops. An auction of a famous collection of robots set a record of $42,550 for a Machine Man robot, a 1960s toy made by Masudaya of Japan. Another auction with extremely high prices was the sale of the Hires Rootbeer collection in May. A record price of $106,700 for the Mettlach urn rootbeer dispenser surprised many.

The following section lists some record prices that might influence the everyday market for antiques.

ADVERTISING

- **Coca-Cola 1910 calendar:** $14,300 for a Coca-Cola calendar from 1910, "Happy Days, Drink Coca-Cola, Delicious and Refreshing," with a smiling girl holding a glass of Coca-Cola.
- **Porcelain sign of this size:** $11,825 for a porcelain Oilzum Motor Oil sign, 2 sides, 24-inch diameter, says "If Motors Could Speak We Wouldn't Need To Advertise. The Cream of Pure Pennsylvania Oil."
- **Typewriter ribbon container:** $1,540 for a Service typewriter ribbon tin, pictures Model T pickup truck advertising for Muncie Typewriter Exchange, Muncie, Indiana, on the front, and an early Woodstock typewriter on the back, 2 1/2 x 2 1/2 x 3/4 inches.
- **Hires Mettlach urn dispenser:** $106,700 for a Hires Rootbeer urn dispenser by Mettlach, pictures Hires boy, "Drink Hires Rootbeer 5¢," and "America's Health Drink, Luscious and Pure," 19 inches high, 11 inches diameter.

CLOCKS & WATCHES

- **Patek Philippe wristwatch:** $456,293 for a Patek Philippe "World Time," 18-karat yellow-gold, enamel gentleman's wristwatch, with two crowns, made in 1953.

FURNITURE

- **Chinese furniture:** $1,102,500 for a 7-ft.-high monumental standing screen with metal hinges, a large dreamstone marble panel inset and carved frame, 17th century.
- **Early 2-door Gustav Stickley bookcase:** $34,650 for a 1901, 2-door, Gustav Stickley bookcase with rare amber glass panes, keyed tenons, chamfered backboard, and miter-mullioned doors, 72 inches wide.
- **Gustav Stickley lady's desk:** $29,900 for a Gustav Stickley lady's desk, no. 724, with paneled lid, trimmed in handwrought iron, interior with 11 pigeonholes and drawers, signed with large Gustav Stickley red mark, 46 x 32 x 12 inches.
- **Newport, Rhode Island, dressing table:** $310,500 for a Queen Anne carved mahogany dressing table, thumb-molded long drawer over 2 short drawers, center carved shell, original brasses, attributed to John Goddard (1723–1785), 31 1/4 x 35 1/2 x 22 1/2 in.

GLASS

- **J.H. Johnston Target Ball:** $5,060 for an American, c. 1880–1890 target ball, embossed "From J.H. Johnson Great Western Gun Works 169 Smithfield Street Pittsburgh, Pa. Rifles Shotguns Revolvers Ammunition Fishing Tackle Chock Boring, Repairing & C. Write For Price List," in deep amber, 2 1/2 inches.
- **Taylor-Cornstalk portrait flask:** $41,250 for a brilliant sapphire blue flask, produced at the Baltimore Glass Works, McK G I-074.
- **Tiffany window:** $1,047,500 for Louis Comfort Tiffany's parakeets-and-goldfish-bowl window executed for the World's Columbian Exposition in Chicago, 1893.

LAMP

- **Tiffany lamp:** $1,100,000 for a Tiffany favrile glass and bronze lotus lamp on a rare mosaic lily-pad base, c. 1900.

METAL

- **Doorknob:** $3,600 for a Doggie doorknob with the mark "MCCC/ Boston," backplate dated June 7, 1869, designed by Ludwig Kruzinger in the late 1860s for the Metallic Compression Casting Company of Boston, knob 2 1/4 inches in diameter, plate 4 1/2 x 5 1/2 inches.
- **Gustav Stickley andirons:** $9,775 for a pair of wrought iron Gustav Stickley andirons, no. 315, impressed mark, 16 x 13 1/2 x 18 inches.

PAPER

- **Movie poster:** $453,500 for a one-sheet movie poster from Universal Studios's classic 1932 horror film *The Mummy,* starring Boris Karloff, billed as "a love story that lived 3,000 years."
- **Single comic book:** $61,900 for a copy of *Action Comics, No. 1,* issued June 1938. This issue marks the introduction of Superman.

PHOTOGRAPHY & PICTURES

- **Ambrotype street scene image:** $8,250 for a sixth-plate ambrotype street scene of the intersection of 6th Street and Central Avenue in Cincinnati, Ohio, taken between 1852 and 1858.
- **Shaker artifact:** $299,500 for a gift drawing by Shaker Hannah Cohoon, "Blazing Tree."

POLITICAL

- **Lincoln mourning ribbon:** $1,430 for an 1865 Lincoln mourning ribbon, worn by one of the honor guards on Lincoln's funeral train as it traveled from Alexandria, Virginia, to Washington, D.C.
- **Political flag:** $35,200 for an 1876 Hayes-Wheeler campaign flag, 27 x 45 inches, red, white, and blue, featuring portraits of Rutherford B. Hayes and William A. Wheeler.

POTTERY & PORCELAIN

- **Clarice Cliff sugar sifter:** $3,040 for a Clarice Cliff conical sugar sifter, "Orange Roof Cottage" pattern, 5 1/2 in.
- **Grueby Palm Tree frieze:** $24,150 for a four-tile Grueby Pottery architectural frieze of palm trees.
- **Lucie Rie piece:** $52,470 for a Lucie Rie stoneware covered pot, with vertical sgraffito design on the body, 1950–1952, 18 inches high.
- **Marblehead Pottery tile frieze:** $21,850 for a Marblehead Pottery tile frieze with incised lake scene in matte yellow, browns, and greens, impressed mark, paper label, in original frame with sticker marked "No. D-64 Tiles Poplars with Reflections, Dec. by A.E. Baggs, Price $10.00," tiles are 7 1/2 inches square.
- **Mettlach stein, no. 2001:** $5,635 for a Mettlach stein no. 2001, Cornell University, 0.5 liter.
- **Mettlach stein, no. 2074:** $3,335 for a Mettlach stein no. 2074, 0.5 liter.
- **Mettlach stein, no. 2730:** $4,485 for a Mettlach stein no. 2730, 0.5 liter.
- **Mettlach stein, no. 2831:** $5,290 for a Mettlach stein no. 2831, 0.5 liter.
- **Mettlach vase:** $46,000 for a Mettlach etched vase, decorated with a knight on one side and a maiden on the other side, signed C. Spindler, dated 1900, 48 inches.
- **Nippon Rose Tapestry plate:** $2,640 for a fine linen, rose tapestry plate, raised gold edge, pink roses, blue maple leaf mark, 12 inches.
- **Teacup & saucer:** $106,182 for a teacup & saucer from Vincennes, France, dating to 1752.
- **Weller tiles:** $22,000 for a set of six Weller tiles with a scene of barns in which pottery is being produced, bottom of tiles reads "The Weller Pottery, 1872," oak frame, signed by Timberlake, 9 x 14 inches.
- **Van Briggle toast cup:** $14,300 for a 1902 dated Van Briggle toast cup (chalice), designed by Artus Van Briggle, stylized mermaid embracing a fish, shape no. 1, matte green glaze, 11 1/2 inches (repaired).
- **Van Briggle vase, "Lady of the Lily":** $11,550 for a "Lady of the Lily" vase, nude female with long hair, resting against lily-shape vase, embossed flowers, shape no. 4, matte lime green, c.1904, 11 inches (repaired).

SILVER

- **Piece of silver:** $10,287,500 for a Louis XV royal silver tureen, cover and liner, made in 1733 by Thomas Germain, lid has vegetables, shellfish, and a bird, handles and feet in form of a boar, hammered, chased stand resembling a pool for swans and reeds in the four cartouches.
- **Silver wine coolers:** $3,960,000 for a pair of Louis XV royal silver wine coolers, made by Claude Ballin II.

SPORTS

- **Bait casting reel:** $31,350 for a c. 1820 brass bait-casting reel by George Snyder, Paris, Kentucky, 1 5/8 inches in diameter.
- **Fishing lure box:** $2,750 for an empty Heddon wooden lure box, original illustrated surface showing minnow flyer, marked "Heddon's Dowagiac Surface Minnow – White No. 302," on the end panels of the box, red Heddon lid markings.
- **Golf memorabilia:** $35,650 for a Park Royal gutty ball with hexagonal faces. Park's patent of March 1896 stated that the hexagonal facets were "to prevent the ball running too easily on very keen greens or downhill."
- **Trout fly reel:** $28,800 for a Hardy trout fly reel of 1891, nickel silver Bickerdyke line guide and ivory handle, from the collection of Graham Turner, author of *Fishing Tackle: A Collector's Guide.*

TOYS, DOLLS, AND GAMES

- **American teddy bear:** $13,800 for a light yellow mohair teddy bear, c.1905, 25 in.
- **Robot toy:** $42,550 for a 1950s robot toy, Machine Man, *Masudaya,* one of the Gang of Five series, green lighting eyes, ears, and mouth, bump-and-go action, moving arms, lithographed decorative panels, ON/OFF switch, battery powered, 15 inches high.

A NOTE TO COLLECTORS

You already know this is a great overall price guide for antiques and collectibles. Each entry is current, every picture is new, all prices are accurate.

But in the collecting world, things change quickly. Important sales produce new record prices. Rarities are discovered. Fakes appear. To keep up with these developments, there's a monthly newsletter, *Kovels on Antiques and Collectibles,* with up-to-date information on the world of collecting. It is now filled with color photographs, about forty to an issue. The newsletter reports prices, trends, auction results, and other pertinent news for collectors *as it happens.* For a free sample of *Kovels on Antiques and Collectibles,* fill out and mail the postage-paid postcard at the back of this book.

KEEP READING— HOW TO USE THIS BOOK

There are a few rules for using this book. Each listing is arranged in the following manner: CATEGORY (such as Pressed Glass or Furniture), OBJECT (such as vase), DESCRIPTION (as much information as possible about size, age, color, and pattern). Some types of glass are exceptions to this rule. These are listed CATEGORY, PATTERN, OBJECT, DESCRIPTION. All items are presumed to be in good condition and undamaged, unless otherwise noted. If a maker's name is easily recognized, like Gustav Stickley, we try to include it near the beginning of the entry. If the maker is obscure, the name may be at the end. Because the descriptions are part of actual reports, we do not edit to make everything consistent in each entry. We try to edit enough to be sure that two items are not actually two descriptions of the same piece.

Several special categories were formed to make the most sensible listing possible. For instance, "Tool" includes special equipment because the casual collector might not know the proper name for an "adze." Many of the glass entries are in special categories: "Glass-Art," "Glass-Contemporary," "Glass-Midcentury," and "Glass-Venetian." Major glass factories are still listed under the factory names, and well-known types of glass, such as cut, pressed, Carnival, and others, can be found in their own categories. The silver listings are also a bit different. You will find silver flatware in either Silver Flatware Plated or Silver Flatware Sterling. You will also find a section for silver plate, which includes coffeepots, trays, and other plated pieces. Solid or sterling silver is listed by country, so look for Silver-American, Silver-English, and so on. Pottery and porcelain are usually listed by factory name or item, but some are found in Art Pottery, American Dinnerware, Art Nouveau, Art Deco, Arts & Crafts, Kitchen, Pottery, or Porcelain.

Sometimes we make arbitrary decisions based on the number of entries or interest in a subject. Fishing has its own category, but hunting is part of the larger category called Sports. We have eliminated all guns except toy types. It is not legal to sell weapons without a special license, and so guns are not part of the general antiques market. Airguns, B-B guns, rocket guns, and others are listed in the "Toy" section. New categories have been added this year for Chintz china, Dorchester pottery, and items marked WPA. The index can help if you are searching for other unusual pieces.

Several idiosyncrasies of style appear because the book is printed by computer. Everything is listed according to the computer alphabetizing system. This means words such as "Mt." are alphabetized as "M-T," not as "M-O-U-N-T." All numerals are before all letters; thus 2 comes before "A." A quick glance will make this clear, as it is consistent throughout the book.

We made several editorial decisions. A bowl is a "bowl," not a "dish" unless it is a special dish, such as a pickle dish. A butter dish is a "butter." A salt dish is a "salt" to differentiate it from a saltshaker. It is always "sugar & creamer," never "creamer & sugar." Political collectors refer to "pinbacks," round celluloid or tin pins that are decorated with candidates' names and faces. "Button" is sometimes used in this book instead of the word "pinback." Of course, the word "button" is also used when referring to fasteners used on clothing. Where one dimension is given, it is the height; or if the object is round, the dimension is the diameter. The height of a picture is listed before width. Glass is clear unless a color is indicated.

Entries are listed alphabetically, but problems remain. Some antiques terms, such as "Sheffield" or "Pratt," have two meanings. Be sure to read the paragraph headings to know the meaning used. All category headings are based on the language of the average person at an average show, and we use terms like "mud figures" even if not technically correct.

This book does *not* include price listings of fine art paintings, antiquities, stamps, coins, or most types of books. *Big Little Books* and similar children's books *are* included. Comic books are *not* listed but original comic art and cels *are* listed in their own categories.

All pictures in *Kovels' Antiques & Collectibles Price List* are listed with the prices asked by the seller. "Illus" (meaning "illustrated nearby") is part of the description if a picture is shown.

There have been misinformed comments about how this book is written. We *do* use the computer. It alphabetizes, ranges prices, sets type, and does other time-consuming jobs. Because of the computer, the book is produced quickly. The last entries are added in June; the book is available in October. This is six months faster than would be possible any other way. But it is human help that finds prices and checks accuracy. We read everything three times, sometimes more. We edit from 80,000 entries to 50,000 the entries found here. We correct spelling, remove incorrect data, write category headings, and decide on new categories. We sometimes make errors. Information in the paragraphs is reviewed and updated each year. This year fifty-five corrections and additions were made in the category headings.

Prices are reports from all parts of the United States and Canada (translated to U.S. dollars at the rate of $1.40 U.S. to $1 Canadian) between June 1996 and June 1997. Prices are from auctions, shops, and shows. Every price is checked for accuracy, but we are not responsible for errors.

It is unprofessional for an appraiser to set values for unseen items. Because of this, we can't answer your letters asking for specific prices. But please write if you have any requests for categories to be included in future editions or any corrections to information in the paragraphs.

When you see us at the shows, stop and say hello. Don't be surprised if we ask for your suggestions for the next edition of *Kovels' Antiques & Collectibles Price List*. Or you can visit us at our Web site: www.kovel.com or write us at P.O. Box 22200-K, Beachwood, Ohio 44122.

RALPH & TERRY KOVEL
Accredited Senior Appraisers
American Society of Appraisers
July 1997

ACKNOWLEDGMENTS

SPECIAL THANKS SHOULD GO TO THOSE WHO HELPED US WITH PICTURES AND DEEDS: Albrecht Auction Service, Inc.; Alderfer Auction Company; Anderson Auction; Andre Ammelounx; Auctions Unlimited; Bill Bertoia Auctions; Block's Box; Christie's; Christie's East; Cincinnati Art Galleries; David Rago Auctions, Inc.; DeFina Auctions; DuMouchelle's Art Galleries; Dunbar Gallery; Fink's Off the Wall Auctions; Frank H. Boos Gallery; Frank's Antiques; Garthoeffner Gallery; Garth's Auctions, Inc.; Gary Kirsner Auctions; Gene Harris Antique Auction Center, Inc.; Glass-Works Auctions; Hake's Americana and Collectibles; Hunt Auctions; Hunter's Vault; Jackson's Auctioneers & Appraisers; James D. Julia, Inc.; John McInnis Auctions; Joy Luke; Ken Farmer Auctions; Kenneth S. Hays & Associates, Inc.; Kurt R. Krueger; L.H. Selman Ltd.; Lang's Sporting Collectables Inc.; Leland's; Leslie Hindman Auctioneers; Lloyd Ralston Gallery; Lynn Geyer Advertising Auctions; Mapes Auctioneers & Appraisers; McMasters Doll Auctions; Neal Auction Company; New Hampshire Antique Co-op; North Shore Sports; Pacific Glass Auctions; Postcards International; Richard Opfer Auctioneering Inc.; Riverbend Auction Co.; Robert C. Eldred Co., Inc.; Skinner, Inc.; Smith & Jones; Sotheby's; Strawser Auctions; Tea Leaf Club International; Theriault's the Dollmasters; Toy Scouts Inc.; Treadway Gallery, Inc.; William Doyle Galleries; Willis Henry Auctions; Winter Associates, Auctioneers & Appraisers; Wolf's; Woody Auction. An extra thank you for the special help given by Carmie Amata, Leon Dixon, Tony Fusco, Lee Markley, Darryl Rehr, and Geoff Sindelar.

To the others in the antiques trade who knowingly or unknowingly contributed to this book, we say "thank you!" We could not do it without you. Some of you are: 20th Century Vintage Telephones; A Chip Off the Old Block; A Touch of Glass Ltd.; David Aasum; Barry Abel; Dominick Abel; Jo Abrams; After Promotion Collectables; All That Glitters; America's Pride; American Pottery Auctions; Brian Anderson; Loretta Anderson; Annapolis Antique Gallery; Antique Elegance; Antique Train Auction; The Antique Junction; Antiques by Mah Jong; Arcade Auction; Florence Archambault; ARK Antiques; Rolf Armstrong; As We Were Antiques; Ashley's Antiques & Interiors; Attenson's Coventry Antiques; Don Bailen; Baker's Antiques & Collectibles; Barbara's Doll; Jim Barillaro Toy Train Auction; Charlie Barnette; Mary Bassett; Sandra Bauer; Carole A. Berk, Ltd.; Lauralee Best; Betty & Otto Antiques; G. Bindewald; Bischoff Galleries; Blue Willow Antiques & Collectables; Joan Bogart; Jim & Carol Boshears; Annetta M. Bosselman; Gil Bouley; Jo-Anne Bowen; Brandywine House Antiques; Betty Bresler Inc.; Don Brewer; Brown Auction & Real Estate; Charles & Prissy Brown; Buck's Antiques; Burmese Cruet; Alfred Cali; Pat Call; Cara Antiques; Michelle Carey; Molly Caron; Philip Chasen Antiques; Chicago Playing Card Collectors, Inc.; Chicago Old Telephone Co.; China Serendipity; Melissa Circle; Classic Plastic Dolls; Clintsman International; John Coates; Coffman's Country Antiques Market; Ron Colantonio; Ken Cole; James Coleman; Collector's Auction Service; Collector's Sales & Service; Collectors' Choice Antique Gallery; John Cook; Roland Coover; Darcia Antiques; Lila De Lellis; Deco Deluxe; Decodence; Dee's Antiques; Lila de Lellis; Den of Antiquity; Dennis & George Collectables; J.C. Devine, Inc.; Devonia Antiques For Dining; Richard Diehl; Dixie Sporting Collectibles; Door Antiques; Theresa Dryden; Dunhill Antiques & Restoration; Early Auction Co.; Eden West Antiques; Eric's Antiques; Sandy Ernst; Evia Antiques; Exo Antiques; William Fagan & Co.; Ron Faley; Bette Farrell; Greg Ferland; Fiesta Plus; Michael FitzSimmons Decorative Arts; Eileen Flaks; Flo-Blue Shoppe; Fox Auctions; Foxcroft Antiques; Franklin Auction Gallery; Full Circle Antiques & Design; Gallery 47; Tim Gaudet; Tom Geiger; Gemini Antiques, Ltd.; Gale Gerds; J.S. Gimesh; Danny Gipson; Glasstiques; Charles Golden Jr.; Good Golly Ms. Lolly; Dale Gordon; Ted Grachek; Grandpa's Trading Co.; Dan Graves; John F. Green Inc.; June Greenwald Antiques; Pauline Griscom; Hampton Antiques; Hanzel Galleries, Inc.; Happy Cats Collectibles; Viki Harman Antiques; Allan H. Harris; Bill Hermanek; Hesson Collectables; Hi De Ho Collectibles; Patricia Hildreth; Holly Hill; Historic Originals; John Holmes; Sue Horn; Hot Stuff; Jordan Husser; In Love With Nippon; Arlene Jaffee; Jan-Tiques; Howie Jenner; Steve Johnson; Robert Karnes; Kearsarge Lodge Antiques; Kellar & Kellar; Sandy Kightlinger; Janie King; Judy Knauer; Ted Kromer; Jerry Lamb; Lambertville Antique & Auction Center; Perry Lane; Sue Langley; Joe Langley; Lawson's Antiques & Collectibles; Mike LeMay; Kenneth Paul Lesko; Susan Levine; Kathy Libraty; Lion's Den Antiques; Maxie Lisman; Steve Littrell; Love of Past; David MacArthur; Betty Maddalena; Manion's International Auction House Inc.; Dick Marshall Collection; Ken Masterson; Matrix; Michael Peirce McDowell; McMurray Antiques & Auctions; Mello Antiques; Memory Collectibles; Ralph Meranto; Chris Meriwether; Dori Miles; Doug Miller; Frank Mills; Minnah's Antiques; Mr. Modern; Modernism Gallery; Joan Mogensen; Mondo Cane; Walter B. Moore; Bruce E. Moses; Motion Picture Arts Gallery; The Mouse Man, Ink; Marve Mulligan; National Antique Lamp Shop; Maxine Nelson; New Age Antiques; Mike Nickel & Cindy Horvath; Nikel Enterprises, Inc.; Walter & Edith Noftall; Gene Nordquist; North Country Bottle Shop; Rich O'Donnell; Old Barn Auction; Old Paperphiles; Olde Antiques Market; On the Road Again; Only Yesterday; Hal Overell; Bob Owens; Ozark Annies Tiques & Fleas; Paper Chaser; Papillon Gallery; Paradise Found Antiques Pascoe & Company; Barbara Paterson; Jackie Peay; Terry Perez; Mike Peterson; David B. Phillips; Pins Ltd.; PKE, Inc.; Plantation Galleries; Frank Poole; Pottery Peddler; Princeton Antiques; Dick Purvis; Radioart; T. Rehberger; Ray Reichard; Eugene & Ellen Reno; Replacements, Ltd.; Linda Richard; Faye & John Ridgecrest; Ritchie's; Ritzy Bitz; Linda Romberg; Ruthie Rosenfeld Antique Fancies; Sandy Rosnick Auctions; Laurie Rubinetti; Shirley Ruch; Nate Russell; Sam & Anna Samuelian; Savoia's Auction, Inc.; Lori Schmitt; Alice J. Schnabel; Ken Schneringer; Elizabeth Scott; Wendy Seamons; Seekers Antiques; Frank Shannon; Shelley China Island Net; Robert Shepard; Side Door; The Silver Queen; Skylark Antiques; Small Pleasures; Bill Smith; Smith House Toys; So Rare Galleries; Stein's Antiques; Jean Stepp; Stitches in Time; Michael Strand; Betty Stribling; Susanin's Auctioneers & Appraisers; Sussex Antique Toy Shop; Dianne Taulbee; Team's Tiffany Treasures; Temple's Antiques; Paul & Wilma Thurston; Timeless Memories; Tom's Cypress Inc.; Tradewinds Auction; Turn of the Century Antiques; Bettye Ungar; Scot Vermillion; Vicki & Bruce Waasdorp; Denise Walters; Eileen Warburton; Jack T. Weiss; D. Wells; Eden West; Grace Williams; Mark Wiskow; Richard Withington, Inc.; Richard Wright; Yankee Tools & Collectables; Yesterday's South, Inc.; Ruben Ben Yosef; David Zeidman.

A. WALTER made pate-de-verre glass under contract at the Daum glass-works from 1908 to 1914. He started his own firm in Nancy, France, in 1919. Pieces made before 1914 are signed *Daum, Nancy* with a cross. After 1919 the signature is *A. Walter Nancy.*

Figurine, Cowled Maiden Bearing An Amphora, Signed, c.1900, 9 In.	2530.00
Lamp, Tri-Petal Flowers, Cone Shape, Yellow, Brown, Pate-De-Verre, Signed, 8 In.	2200.00
Paperweight, Bee, Pate-De-Verre, Signed	2310.00
Paperweight, Green Grasshopper On Purple Grapes, Pate-De-Verre, 4 In. . . . . . .750.00 to 800.00
Tray, Black Beetle, Pate-De-Verre	2700.00
Tray, Frog On Pond Lilies, Pate-De-Verre	2900.00
Tray, Green Butterfly, Butterscotch Pine Needles, Cones, 7 In.	2200.00
Vase, Leaves, Stems & Berries, Green, Brown, 2 Handles, 5 In.	2310.00

ABC plates, or children's alphabet plates, were most popular from 1780 to 1860, but are still being made. The letters on the plate were meant as teaching aids for children learning to read. The plates were made of pottery, porcelain, metal, or glass. Mugs and other items were also made with alphabet decorations.

Cup, Stangl	70.00
Cup & Saucer, Pink Luster	37.50
Dish, Baby's, Children Scene, Germany	35.00
Dish, Braille, Pink	25.00
Dish, Feeding, 2 Dutch Children, 7 1/2 In.	85.00
Dish, Feeding, 2 Little Girls, Hanging Up Wash, Germany, 6 In.	95.00
Dish, Feeding, Animals, 2 Sections, Walker China	20.00
Dish, Feeding, House That Jack Built, Three Crown China, Germany, 7 1/4 In. . . . . .65.00 to 68.00
Dish, Feeding, Little Bopeep	75.00
Mug, Jungle Animals	48.00
Plate, 2 Soldiers On Horseback, 7 1/2 In.	110.00
Plate, 4 Union Generals, Staffordshire	345.00
Plate, B Is For Bobby's Breakfast	110.00
Plate, Baby Bunting & Dog, England, 8 In. . . . . .65.00 to 85.00
Plate, Boys, Pulled By Dog, Brown Transfer, Staffordshire	148.00
Plate, Braille, Pink	60.00
Plate, Brownies, Verse, Tin, 9 1/2 In.	75.00
Plate, Chicken In Middle, Glass, 6 In.	65.00
Plate, Christmas Morn, Frosted Center, Glass	300.00
Plate, Crusoe Finding Footprints, 7 1/4 In.	80.00
Plate, Ducks, Amber Glass	145.00
Plate, Elephant	95.00
Plate, English Polo Players, Soft Paste . . . . .40.00 to 60.00
Plate, Girl's Head, Amber Glass	35.00
Plate, Indians In Canoe, The Candlefish, Staffordshire, 8 3/8 In.	160.00
Plate, Jungle Animals, Porcelain	110.00
Plate, Men On Horses, Dogs, Raised Letters, Staffordshire, 7 1/2 In.	65.00
Plate, Riders Jumping Horses, Blue & White, Staffordshire	125.00
Plate, Santa Claus, Victorian Toys	345.00
Plate, Slaves Gathering Cotton, 6 In.	425.00
Plate, Who Killed Cock Robin, 8 In. . . . . .27.50 to 55.00

ABINGDON POTTERY was established in 1908 by Raymond E. Bidwell as the Abingdon Sanitary Manufacturing Company. The company started making art pottery in 1934. The factory ceased production of art pottery in 1950.

Bookends, Horse Head, Black	105.00
Bookends, Horse Head, Pink	75.00
Bowl, Scalloped, Pink, 11 In.	14.00
Bowl, Scroll, Medium Blue, 11 In.	26.00
Bowl, Shell, Green, 11 1/2 In.	25.00
Bowl, Shell, Medium Pink, 11 In.	20.00
Cookie Jar, 3 Bears	125.00

Cookie Jar, Adv. 74th Birthday McMahan's 75.00
Cookie Jar, Baby, Pink 295.00
Cookie Jar, Bopeep ....145.00 to 400.00
Cookie Jar, Choo Choo, White, Turquoise ....90.00 to 200.00
Cookie Jar, Hippo, Yellow Flowers 350.00
Cookie Jar, Humpty Dumpty ....110.00 to 375.00
Cookie Jar, Jack-In-The-Box ....200.00 to 575.00
Cookie Jar, Jack-O'-Lantern ....325.00 to 525.00
Cookie Jar, Little Miss Muffet 325.00
Cookie Jar, Man In The Moon, Alfano 165.00
Cookie Jar, Pineapple ....79.00 to 85.00
Cookie Jar, Rocking Horse 260.00
Cookie Jar, Wigwam 725.00
Cornucopia, White, Large 95.00
Cornucopia, Yellow 16.00
Figurine, Donkey Milk Wagon 85.00
Figurine, Duck, Aqua, 2 1/2 x 5 In. 45.00
Figurine, Humpty Dumpty 225.00
Figurine, Majorette 375.00
Figurine, Money Bag 75.00
Figurine, Sea Bag 175.00
Figurine, Tugboat 250.00
Figurine, Woman, Holding Basket, Gold Hair, Trim, 10 In. 200.00
Flower Holder, Deer 22.00
Tray, Acanthus Leaf, Rose, 12 In. 23.00
Vase, Abbey, White, 7 In. 15.00
Vase, Bird, 7 1/2 In. 40.00
Vase, Blue, 11 In. 30.00
Vase, Cattails, Panels, Green, Brown, Cream Base, Signed, No. 149 ....25.00 to 28.00
Vase, George & Martha Washington Transfer, Gold Trim, 10 1/2 In. 125.00
Vase, Mint Green Glaze, Marked, 9 1/2 In. 35.00
Vase, Ship Design, Blue, 7 In. 25.00
Vase, Swirl, Green, 9 In. 50.00
Vase, Swirl, Rose Decals, Gold Flowers, 11 In. 95.00
Vase, White, 9 In. 30.00
Vase, Yellow, Handle, 10 In. 38.00
Wall Pocket, Blue 35.00
Wall Pocket, Daisy, Yellow, 9 In. 60.00
Wall Pocket, Green 35.00
Wall Pocket, Morning Glory, Pink 20.00

ADAMS china was made by William Adams and Sons of Staffordshire, England. The firm was founded in 1769 and is still working. All types of tablewares and useful wares have been made through the years. Other pieces of Adams will be found listed under Flow Blue.

Bowl, Dessert, Chinese Bird, Blue, White 145.00
Bowl, Fairy Villas, Flow Blue, 10 In. 200.00
Bowl, Porridge, Saucer, Farmer's Arms, 1900, 2 Piece ....125.00 to 150.00
Casserole, Cover, Royal Ivory, Titian Ware, 11 In. 95.00
Coffeepot, Red & Green, White Ground, Black, 1910, 12 In. 675.00
Dish, Soup, Fern, Flow Blue 125.00
Pitcher, Tonquin, Flow Blue 1540.00
Pitcher, Top Handle, Green, Red & Blue, Soft Paste, 1830s, 9 1/2 In. 390.00
Plate, Kyber, Flow Blue, 10 In. ....125.00 to 135.00
Plate, Pastoral Scene, 8 In. 75.00
Plate, Shannondale Springs, Pink, 7 3/4 In. 115.00
Plate, Spongeware, Rose Cut 75.00
Platter, Red Transfer, 3 1/4 x 11 1/8 In., Pair 385.00
Platter, Royal Ivory, Titian Ware, 13 In. 95.00
Teapot, Flower Basket Design, Blue, White 143.00
Tureen, Sauce, Cover, Empress, Ladle, Tray, 4 Piece 340.00

ADVERTISING containers and products sold in the old country store are now all collectibles. These stores, with the crackers in a barrel and a potbellied stove, are a symbol of an earlier, less hectic time. Listed here are many of the advertising items. Other similar pieces may be found under the product name, such as Planters Peanuts. We have tried to list items in the logical places, so large store fixtures will be found under the Architectural category, enameled tin dishes under Graniteware, paper items in the Paper category, etc. Store fixtures, cases, and other items that have no advertising as part of the decoration are listed in the Store category.

Apron, 7-Up	15.00
Apron, Brucks Jubilee Beer, 2-Color, 1940s	37.00
Ashtray, Big Boy, Figural	295.00
Ashtray, Camels, Embossed Tin	8.00
Ashtray, Coors Lite Beer, Pottery	10.00
Ashtray, Firestone Tire	30.00
Ashtray, Firestone, Amber Glass	145.00
Ashtray, Fisk Tire, Ceramic, Different Advertising Each Side	98.00
Ashtray, Folgers, Tin Lithograph, Gold Lacquered Base, 1900s, 4 1/2 In.	135.00
Ashtray, Goodrich, Green Glass Tire	85.00
Ashtray, Goodyear Silvertone Tire	30.00
Ashtray, Hood Arrow, Spare Tire	105.00
Ashtray, Joe Camel	12.00
Ashtray, Kentucky's Finest Whiskies, Colonial Glenmore, Figural	25.00
Ashtray, Kool Cigarettes, Willy Penguin	123.00
Ashtray, Michelin Man	80.00
Ashtray, Old Faithful Beer, Painted Metal, Gallatin Brewing Co., Montana, 4 1/2 In.	44.00
Ashtray, Reddy Kilowatt	22.00
Bag Holder, Griffiths, Griffin & Hoxie, Stenciling, Red Paint	485.00
Banner, Dr. Morse's Indian Root Pills, Paper, Tomahawk, 63 x 9 In.	85.00
Banner, Gangway Of The SS United States, Blue Lettering, 92 x 28 1/2 In.	748.00
Banner, Premium Crackers, Dandy With Jam, N.B.C. Label	25.00
Banner, Schlitz Malt Liquor, Silk, 24 x 36 In.	12.00
Barrel, Liberty Root Beer, Decals, Metal Straps, Spigot, 27 x 26 In.	1210.00
Bill Clip, Peacocks Condom	30.00
Billhook, Walker R.P.D., Celluloid	20.00
Bin, Beech-Nut Chewing Tobacco, Slant Top, Yellow, 10 x 8 x 8 In.	150.00
Bin, Blanke's Coffee, Woman On Horseback Picture, 25 In.	660.00
Bin, Duke's Mixture Tobacco, 24 In.	1500.00
Bin, Fountain Tobacco, Tin, Red, Round	355.00
Bin, Johnson's Peacemaker Coffee, Log Cabin Shape, 1915 Calendar, 25 In.	1200.00 to 2250.00
Bin, Mail Pouch Tobacco, 15 x 12 x 10 In.	357.00
Bin, Pastime Plug Tobacco, 14 x 10 x 3 In.	467.00
Blotter, Ask For Edelweiss, Finest Ever To Bear The Name, 1926, 7 x 9 In.	12.00
Blotter, Blue Ribbon Malt Extract, Colorful	18.00
Blotter, Bond Bread, Fighter Plane Series, Grumman Avenger	14.00
Blotter, Culman Shoe Hospital, J.L. Vick Prop., Unused, 3 x 6 In.	3.00
Blotter, Earl Moran, Pinup	65.00
Blotter, Kellogg's Rice Krispies, Snap, Crackle & Pop Characters, 4 1/2 In.	9.00
Blotter, New Deal Dental Laboratory, Nude, 1936 Calendar	15.00
Blotter, People Coal Co., Lancaster, Pa., Changed To Blue Coal, 1930s, 4 x 9 In.	5.00
Blotter, Peterson & Dering, Scappose, Ore., Pink Rose Design, 1920s, 3 1/2 x 8 In.	3.00
Booklet, Alka-Seltzer, Our Presidents, 1935	35.00
Booklet, Kellogg's Corn Flakes Jungleland, 1909	42.00
Booklet, Woolworth, Anniversary, 5 & 10 Cents Store, Gold Cover, 1929, 50 Pages	20.00
Bookmark, Dr Pepper, Celluloid	10.00
Books may be included in the Paper category.	
Bootjack, Lee Riders, Wooden	45.00
Bottle Openers are listed in their own category.	
Bottle Rack, Orange Crush	192.00
Bottle Topper, 7-Up, Easter Fresh-Up, 1951, 5 1/4 x 10 In.	5.00
Bottle Topper, 7-Up, St. Patrick's Day, 1954, 5 1/2 x 9 1/2 In.	5.00

Bottles are listed in their own category.

Bowl, Betty Crocker, Yellow, 8 1/2 In.	24.00
Bowl, Post Cereals, Alphabet, Mickey Mouse, Beetleware, 1930s, 5 1/2 In.	27.00
Bowl, Ranger Joe, Milk Glass, Blue Lettering, 1951, 5 1/2 In.	35.00
Box, see also Box category.	
Box, Almond Joy, Early TV Shows, 1950s	48.00
Box, American Horse Tonic, Cardboard, 12-Dose Box, 4 1/2 x 2 In.	60.00
Box, American Sword Brand, Pocket Knives, Camillus Cutlery, 1905, 1/2 Doz.	60.00
Box, Bazooka Bubble Gum, Held 25 2-Cent Pieces, 1969	16.00
Box, Beechnut Peppermint, Large Pack Of Gum Shape	135.00
Box, Beechnut Tab Gum, Pulver, Contents	125.00
Box, Bull Of The Woods Tobacco, 25 x 13 x 7 In.	225.00
Box, Calonite Powder, Metal Ends, Top Becomes Shaker, 1 3/4 x 4 5/8 In.	5.00
Box, Capwell Horse Nails, Dovetailed, Wooden, 12 In.	25.00
Box, Cereal, Kellogg's Corn Flakes, Vanessa Williams, Miss America Front	100.00
Box, Cereal, King Rolled Oats, Early 1900s, 11 x 6 1/2 x 5 In.	45.00
Box, Cereal, Kix, 1947	75.00
Box, Cereal, Raisin Bran, Free Baseball Cards, 1960s, 7 x 9 In.	20.00
Box, Cereal, Wheaties, Black T-Shirt	25.00
Box, Cigar, Flor De Anson, Cap Anson Portrait, 7 x 5 x 3 In.	2900.00
Box, Cigar, Gay-Boy Cigars, Wooden, Holds 20 Cigars, 1901	175.00
Box, Cigar, Old Virginia Cheroots, Black Man Label, Wooden, 12 x 7 x 4 In.	85.00
Box, Cigar, Sugar Cane, 5 Black Boys In Tree, 1893	200.00
Box, Dow Ziploc Sandwich Bag, Goonies Movie Sticker, 1985	15.00
Box, Dr. Felix LeBrun's G & G Cure, For Gonorrhea & Gleet	160.00
Box, Dr. Legear's Fly & Insect Powder, Cardboard, Labels, Oval, Contents	40.00
Box, Dupont, Dynamite	38.00
Box, Duryeas Satin Gloss Starch, Wooden, Label, Stenciled, 1870, 6 Lb.	265.00
Box, Extra Strength Prickly Plaster, Wooden, 2 Doz., 6 1/2 x 9 1/2 In.	80.00
Box, Fatima Cigarettes, Pack, Harem Girl, 13 x 17 In.	150.00
Box, Federal Monark, 16 Gauge, 1 Piece	25.00
Box, Fiddle Faddle Popcorn, Bear, Sticker Insert, 1988	7.00
Box, Fun-To-Wash Soap Powder, Mammy Picture, Cardboard	35.00
Box, Gambles Hiawatha Ace, 12 Gal., 1 Piece	24.00
Box, General Douglas MacArthur Candy, Picture, Cardboard	195.00
Box, Gold Dust Washing Powder, Cardboard	65.00
Box, Good Enough Peanuts, 1 Cent, Cardboard	42.00
Box, Grants Hygienic Breakfast Food, Strawberries, 3 1/2 x 7 1/2 x 1 1/2 In.	12.00
Box, Harmonica, Oak, Compartments, Square, 12 In.	65.00
Box, Hercules Rubber Cement, Wooden, 7 1/2 In.	26.00
Box, Hercules, Blasting Powder	35.00
Box, Hoppy Ice Cream, Cardboard, 1 Qt.	75.00
Box, Ivory Snow, Marilyn Chambers With Baby, Cardboard, Contents	35.00 to 75.00
Box, Keene Nursing Bottle, Bullard & Shedd Co., Cardboard, 6 1/2 x 4 In.	110.00
Box, Lamp, Mazda, Toy Train, GE Edison, 1920s	35.00
Box, Lorna Doone, National Biscuit Company, Top Handle, Front Latch	20.00
Box, Mahogany, Heppenheimer, Princess, Nude, 24 x 9 x 5 In.	465.00
Box, McCormick U.S. Certified Food Colors, Plastic Tops, 3 In. ....*Illus*	2.00
Box, Mississippi Glass Co., Salesman's Sample, 2 x 3 In.	70.00
Box, Mr. Dee-Lish Pop Corn, Red, White, Cardboard, 1950s, 5 1/2 x 8 1/2 In.	1.00
Box, Old Noma Fuses, Card, Cardboard	25.00
Box, Ox-Heart Chocolates, Blue & White, Porcelain, 3 x 36 In.	230.00
Box, Peters Target, Flying Quail, Labels, 12 Gal.	108.00
Box, Pretzel Lady, Chocolate Wrapper, 1920s	20.00
Box, Super Hero Cookies, Batman On Box, Nabisco Brands, Cardboard, 1982	95.00
Box, Taylor's Strengthening Plasters, Cardboard, 2 Doz., 6 1/2 x 9 In.	35.00
Box, Winchester Brass Shot Shell, Dark Green, 12 Gauge, 2 Piece	89.00
Box, Winchester Ranger, 12 Gal., 1 Piece	21.50
Box, Wrigley's Juicy Fruit, Packs, Wax Wrapper, 1940s, Contents	425.00
Box, Yankee Girl Tobacco, Wooden	25.00
Box Opener, Cigar, Hammer, Charles Denby Cigars, 5 Cents	30.00
Bread Box, Schepp's Cocoanut, Tin, Pictures On 4 Sides, 11 x 13 x 14 In.	195.00
Brush, Altes Lager, Wood Handle, 2 x 7 In.	23.00

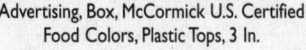

Advertising, Box, McCormick U.S. Certified
Food Colors, Plastic Tops, 3 In.

**Never wash a tobacco
"felt." The small flannel
flags and pictures that were
packed with cigarettes in
the early 1900s lose value
if washed.**

Buckle, Belt, Ritz Cracker, Brass, Uneeda Boy	20.00
Button, Schutter's Old Gold Candy, Andy Gump, Green Suit, White Ground, 7/8 In.	29.00
Button, Singer Sewing Machine Co., Authorized Representative, 1 1/4 In.	37.00
Cabinet, Boye Needles, Metal, Round, 3 1/4 x 16 In.	132.00
Cabinet, Boye Needles, Wooden	90.00
Cabinet, Corner, Humphrey Specifics, Triangular Shape	2420.00
Cabinet, Diamond Dyes, Children Skipping Rope, Mansion	1100.00
Cabinet, Diamond Dyes, Children With Balloon	1265.00
Cabinet, Diamond Dyes, Court Jester	770.00
Cabinet, Diamond Dyes, Maypole	2970.00
Cabinet, Diamond Dyes, Red Headed Fairy With Wand	2530.00
Cabinet, Diamond Dyes, Washer Woman	2640.00
Cabinet, Dr. Daniels' Veterinary Medicines, Oak, Tin Front	2860.00
Cabinet, Dr. Lesure's Famous Remedies, Horse Head, Oak, Tin Front	4620.00
Cabinet, Dr. Lesure's Famous Remedies, Triangular Shape	2420.00
Cabinet, GE Auto Bulbs, Plastic Drawers, 1950s, 18 In.	55.00
Cabinet, Kreso Dip No. 1, Protects Live Stock From Disease	2970.00
Cabinet, May's Seed, 4 Corner Decals, Revolving Wood Shelves, 23 In.	1980.00
Cabinet, P. Lorillard Tobacco, Etched Glass, Wooden, Fluted	6600.00
Cabinet, Putnam Dyes, Colonial Scene, Tin, 15 x 11 In.	176.00
Cabinet, Sovereign Remedies, Nurse Picture, Wooden, 4 Shelves	450.00
Cabinet, Spool, Brainerd & Armstrong, Brass Hardware, Mirrored Door, 40 In.	990.00
Cabinet, Spool, Clark's, O.N.T., Ruby Glass Front, 7 Drawers	2320.00
Cabinet, Spool, Clark's, O.N.T., Walnut, 2 Drawers, 21 3/4 In.	220.00
Cabinet, Spool, Clark's, O.N.T., Walnut, 5 Glass Front Drawers, 29 1/4 In.	2310.00
Cabinet, Spool, Clark's, Oak, 4 Doors	495.00
Cabinet, Spool, Corticelli-Braid, Oak, 2 Doors	295.00
Cabinet, Spool, Eureka Silk, 12 Levels, Mirror, Fluted & Carved, 3 Ft.	2750.00
Cabinet, Spool, Mah Star, 5 Doors	125.00
Calendars are listed in their own category.	
Camera, Charlie Tuna, Star Kist	55.00
Camera, DelMonte, Alvin & Chipmunks	15.00
Can, Carnation Malted Milk, Embossed, Aluminum, 8 1/2 In.	133.00
Can, Clicquot Club Ginger Ale, Cone Top, 1930s, 12 Oz.	65.00
Can, Nourse Oil Co., Graphite Axle Grease, Metal, 1 Lb., 4 1/2 x 3 1/2 In.	155.00
Can Opener, Schlitz Beer	40.00
Canisters, see introductory paragraph to Tins in this category.	
Canister, Defiance Mills Baking Powder, J. Rhodes & Co., Tin, 24 1/2 In.	467.00
Canister, Dunham's Concentrated Coconut, Black Paint, Tin, 12 In.	275.00
Car, Racing, Crisco, Ertl	20.00
Cards are listed in their own category.	
Carrier, Bottle, Dr. Wells Soda, Cardboard	27.00
Carrier, Egg, Reliable Egg Carrier, To Our Farmer Friends	120.00
Case, Boye, Crochet Hooks, Money Box, Glass Front, 8 In.	250.00
Case, Display, Johnny Walker Statue, 14 In.	40.00

Case, Dr. E.L. Wellbourn's Anti-Bilious Pills, 12 Tins 600.00
Case, Eli Lilly & Co. Soluble & Aseptic Hypodermic Tablets, Leather, 41 Vials 100.00
Case, Eureka Spool Silk, Windup Clock At Top, Wood & Glass, 24 x 23 In. 1430.00
Case, H.K. Mulford Co., Leather, 23 Amber Bottles, 24 Vials, With Key 260.00
Case, Hart's Seeds, 6 Trays, Casters Fit Into Case, Portable, 32 3/4 In. 350.00
Case, Heinz Pickles, Salesman's Sample, Painted Zinc Pickles, 6 Sizes, Leather 1840.00
Case, International Stockfood Tonic, 2 Sides, Canted, 52 In. 2035.00
Case, J. Riswig Gum, Chicago 400.00
Case, J.P. Primley Gum, Etched Curved Glass 550.00
Case, Johnson & Johnson, Red Cross, Blue Logo, Tin, 14 x 6 x 14 In. 132.00
Case, Magnetic Nervine, Nerve Tonic & Restorer, Tin, 12 Tins 1600.00
Case, Slidewell Collar 2750.00
Case, Trico Wiper Arms, Blades, Red, Black, White Face, Red Case, 16 In. 65.00
Case, Winchester-Simmons, Be Your Own Barber 550.00
Case, Winchester-Simmons, Safety Razor Blade 350.00
Change Receiver, Chiclets Chewing Gum 65.00
Change Receiver, see also Tip Tray in this category.
Charm, Schwinn Cycles, Plastic, Blue, Continents Other Side, Brass Loop, 1930s 14.00
Charm, Shoe, Ellet Kendell Shoe Co., Bakelite, Late 1800s 35.00
Chicken Feeder, Purina, Galvanized, Logo 27.00
Cigar Cutter, Black & White 5 Cent National Cigar 30.00
Cigar Cutter, Charles Denby, The Cigar You Want, Nickel Base 143.00
Cigar Cutter, Diamond, With Knife 95.00
Cigar Cutter, Indian Motorcycle 85.00
Cigar Cutter, Jules Frecht, The Columbia Cigar, Cast Iron, 1889 . . . . 100.00
Cigar Cutter, Pied Piper Tobacco, Seated, Thumbing Nose, Cast Iron . . . . .125.00 to 440.00
Cigar Cutter, Roi-Tan, Bronze Painted, 1916, 7 1/2 In. 440.00
Cigar Cutter, Topic, Othello Scene, Wooden Base 165.00
Clicker, Cheri-Suisse Chocolates, Tin, 1950s 10.00
Clicker, Weatherbird Shoes, Rooster Weathervane, Tin, 1920s 20.00
Clocks are listed in their own category.
Coaster, Eastern Airlines, Silver Fleet Deco, 1940s 15.00
Coaster, Valley Forge Special Beer, Metal, 1930s, 4 In. 66.00
Coaster Set, Reddy Kilowatt, Paper, Red & Black Graphics, 3 1/4 In., 4 Piece 12.00
Compass, Brooklyn Optician, Kodak Retailer, Magnetic Needle, Tin, 1 1/2 In. 18.00
Container, Chase's Ice Cream, Provo, Utah, Woman Skier, Paper, 1922, 1/2 Pt. 21.00
Container, Quinly's California Chocolate Shop, Grizzly Bear On Log, 10 x 18 In. 265.00
Cooler, 7-Up, Opener At Side, White, 18 In. 70.00
Cooler, Dr Pepper, Medium Size, 1940s 65.00
Crate, Egg, C.L. Major & Co., Stenciled 3 Sides, Blue Paint 200.00
Crate, Perfection Baking Powder, Wooden, Red, Yellow Label 82.00
Crate, Shipping, Winchester, Nublack, Stenciled, Dovetailed Wood 74.00
Cuff Links, Bon Ami Cleanser, Barbell Type, Enamel Over Sterling Silver, 1895 . . . . 160.00
Cuff Links & Tie Pin, Cadillac, Sterling Silver, Box 30.00
Cup, Baking, Kraft, Pottery, Yellow 9.00
Cup, Coffee, Red Tower 35.00
Cup, Coffee, Ritzee Hamburger 28.00
Cup, Coffee, Western Sizzlin' Steak House, Comical Cows 15.00
Cup, Collapsible, National Oats, Silver, Ornate, Early 1900s 100.00
Cup, Measuring, Hellick's Soap, Tin, Interior & Exterior Lithograph 150.00
Cup, Measuring, Stickley & Poors 30.00
Cuspidor, Red Skin Tobacco 30.00
Cutter, Paper, Chew Spearhead On Cutter Bar 85.00
Decanter, Old Crow, Royal Bayreuth 140.00
Dish, Britten & Bradshaw Chewing Gums, Glass 42.00
Dispenser, Bromo-Seltzer, Bottle On Top, Blue & White 330.00
Dispenser, Cardinal Cherry, Floral Design, Green Ground 6555.00
Dispenser, Cherry Chic, Floral Design, No Pump 6900.00
Dispenser, Cherry-Julep, Red, White Base 4025.00
Dispenser, Cigar, Tennyson, 5 Cent, Red Portrait, 8 In. 475.00
Dispenser, Cigarette, Elephant, Tail Crank, Bronze Finish, Ashtray Base, 1930 . . . . 650.00
Dispenser, Cigarette, Paris News Pillar, Lift Top, Flowers, Music Box 350.00
Dispenser, Coffee, Cup Tested Coffee, Miller Line, Tin, Counter Top 395.00

Dispenser, Drink Birchola, Red Letters, White Ground 1780.00
Dispenser, Drink Green River 935.00
Dispenser, Drink Hires, It Is Pure, White, Red Letters 1780.00
Dispenser, Grape Crush Syrup, Purple Glass, Pump 850.00
Dispenser, Grape Smash 5940.00
Dispenser, Hires Syrup, Medallions On Blue Porcelain Base, Stainless, 1940s 650.00
Dispenser, Hires Syrup, Trademark Smiling Boy, Villeroy & Boch 41400.00
Dispenser, Liberty Root Beer, White Ground, Replaced Pump 5865.00
Dispenser, Magnus Root Beer, Barrel Shape 575.00
Dispenser, Nesbitt's Syrup, Embossed, Paper Label 240.00
Display, Adams Chewing Gum, Metal 40.00
Display, Adams Gum, Wooden, Etched Glass, Countertop 150.00
Display, Alox Shoe Laces, Cardboard Shoe, 1930s, 14 In. 24.00
Display, Anola, Chocolate Flavored Sugar Wafer, N.B.C., 1918, 1 x 7 1/4 In. 50.00
Display, Bar, Johnnie Walker, 8 1/2 In. 58.00
Display, Beech Nut Coffee, Workers Picking Coffee, 28 x 48 In. 143.00
Display, Borax Soap Chips, Chest, Woman Demonstrating Uses, 12 x 60 In. 220.00
Display, Bottle, Steinhause Lager Beer, 1934, 20 In. 220.00
Display, Chiclets, Gum Counter, 8 x 10 In. 65.00
Display, Eveready Flasho-Scope, Store Window, Toys, 3-D, Die Cut, Early 1930s 350.00
Display, Eversharp Pen, 1 Drawer 35.00
Display, Firestone Tire, Enameled Steel, Wire Stand, 5 x 12 5/8 In. 75.00
Display, Gerber Baby, Die Cut Baby, 30 In. 48.00
Display, Giorgio Beverly Hills, Logo, Plastic, Stand, 6 x 7 x 5 In. 32.00
Display, Goebel's Beer, Rooster, With Bottle, Chalkware, 8 x 10 In. 150.00
Display, Hanley's Ale, Bulldog, Chalkware, 17 1/2 x 9 1/2 In. 175.00
Display, Klenzo Eraser Pencils, Pull String To Lengthen, Card, 1940s 27.00
Display, Lee Rider, Standee, 12 In. 125.00
Display, Longman & Martinez, Paint, 5 Stacked Cans, 19 In. ....*Illus* 325.00
Display, Mars Halloween Candy, Battery Operated, 1960 .... 350.00
Display, Mazda Lamp, Tin Lithograph, Wooden Base, Holds 11 Bulbs, 27 In. 450.00
Display, Mother Gray's Sweet Powders, Children, Cardboard, Box, 14 x 8 In. 60.00
Display, Nabisco Shredded Wheat, Embossed Glass On Wood Base 3750.00
Display, Napoleon Cigars, Napoleon Surrounded By Tobacco Leaves, 27 x 37 In. 193.00
Display, Parker Pen, 2 Towers, Black, Brass 2500.00
Display, Premium Crackers, Listen To Arthur Godfrey On CBS, 1950, 10 In. 450.00
Display, Remington Hi-Speed .22, Glass, Wooden, 13 x 12 In. 220.00
Display, Shaw & Tenney, Paddle, Canoe, Orono, Maine 65.00
Display, Spuds MacKenzie, Beer, Lighted, Name On Chest 135.00
Display, Squirt, Just Call Me Squirt, Red, Green, 13 x 8 In. 795.00
Display, Studebaker, Seat Covers, Box 145.00
Display, Sugar Corn Pops Cereal Box, Guy Madison Picture, 1940s 245.00
Display, Universal Headache Powders, Cardboard, With 8 Powders, Easel 120.00

**To untie knots in
ribbons or shoe laces
or necklaces, sprinkle
a little talcum power
on them.**

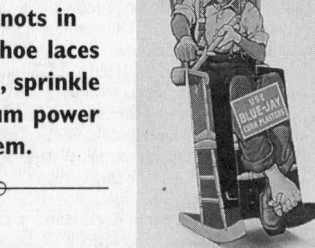

Advertising, Display, Longman & Martinez,
Paint, 5 Stacked Cans, 19 In.

Advertising, Display, Use Blue-Jay Corn
Plasters, A.M.D. Co., Tin, 6 x 13 In.

Display, Use Blue-Jay Corn Plasters, A.M.D. Co., Tin, 6 x 13 In. . . . . *Illus*   800.00
Display, Willie Kool, Cigarette Store, 1941, 10 1/2 x 15 1/2 In. 25.00
Display, Winchester, Horse With Rider, Bronze Finish, Counter 450.00
Display, Wrigley's Nips, 5 Cents, Gum Box 1200.00
Dolls are listed in their own category.
Door Push, 7-Up, Porcelain 7.00
Door Push, Bireley's 125.00
Door Push, Buckeye Beer, Tin, 3 x 14 In. 34.00
Door Push, Chesterfield Cigarettes, Porcelain . . . . .60.00 to 150.00
Door Push, Crescent Flour, Voigt Milling Co., Tin, 9 1/2 In. 440.00
Door Push, Dr. Caldwell's Syrup Pepsin, Porcelain, 6 1/2 x 3 3/4 In. 230.00
Door Push, Hires Root Beer, 1960s 80.00
Door Push, Ideal Bread, 1940s 135.00
Door Push, Junge's Bread, Porcelain, 9 1/4 x 3 3/4 In. 66.00
Door Push, Old Colony Beverages 75.00
Door Push, Orange Crush, Come In, Bottle Picture, Tin 342.00
Door Push, Orange Crush, Large 445.00
Door Push, Salada Tea, Red On Yellow, Reverse, Thank You-Call Again, 32 In. 66.00
Door Push, Thomas Bread, Porcelain, 8 x 4 In. 330.00
Door Push, Ward's, Orange Crush, Canada, 1920s 1300.00
Dose Cup, Daniel L. Cook Apothecary, Trenton, N.J., Machine Made, 2 In. 75.00
Dress, Campbell's, 1960 . . . .   100.00
Eraser, Wrigley's, Figural, Gum Pack 35.00
Fans are listed in their own category.
Figure, Blimp, Genesee Beer, Gold Beer, Blow-Up, 1970s, 14 x 30 In. 27.00
Figure, Boston Bulldog, Bryant Furnace, Papier-Mache, 22 In. 225.00
Figure, Budweiser, Budman, Aluminum, 13 In. 46.00
Figure, Budweiser, Budman, Sponge Rubber, 17 1/2 In. 145.00
Figure, Budweiser, Spuds MacKenzie, Bud Light, Plastic, 15 In. 65.00
Figure, California Raisins, Boy In Beach Chair 9.50
Figure, California Raisins, Broccoli 9.50
Figure, California Raisins, Hula Dancer, Wearing Blue Sunglasses 9.50
Figure, California Raisins, Michael Jackson 5.00
Figure, California Raisins, Piano 20.00
Figure, California Raisins, Rutabaga 9.50
Figure, California Raisins, Sax Player With Beret 10.00
Figure, California Raisins, Surfer Dude 9.50
Figure, California Raisins, Upright Surfboard 20.00
Figure, Charlie Tuna, Vinyl, Removable Hat, 1970s 95.00
Figure, Chester Cheetos, Stuffed, 20 In. 35.00
Figure, Chief Watta Pop, Store Display, Holes In Head For Pops 225.00
Figure, Dog, Frankenmuth Beer, Plaster, On Base, 1954, 6 In. 150.00
Figure, Drewry's Extra Fine Beer, Chalkware, 8 x 11 In. 100.00
Figure, Energizer Bunny, Box, 24 In. 30.00
Figure, Fruit Stripe Gum, Zebra, Promotional Bendy 30.00
Figure, Hanes, Merrichild Pajamas, 20 In. 375.00
Figure, Heinz 57, Tomato Head, Hard Rubber, 1940s, 3 x 3 x 5 1/2 In. 165.00
Figure, Hotel Marriott, Man, Head Is Globe 50.00
Figure, Jell-O Gelatin, Kids Love Jell-O, Old Lady In Shoe, Sebastian 295.00
Figure, Kentucky Whiskey, Snowman, Papier-Mache, 12 In. 65.00
Figure, Labatt's Pilsner, Tyrolean Man, Barrel, Plastic, 8 x 10 In. 29.00
Figure, Michelin Man, Swivel Head, 14 1/2 In. 85.00
Figure, Munsingwear, Penguin, 1971 . . . .   20.00
Figure, Nestle Quick Bunny, Bendable, 5 In. 5.00
Figure, Orange Crush, Man Holding Bottle, Dressed In Orange, Blue 250.00
Figure, Oreo Cookie Man, Bendable, Plastic, 4 1/2 In. . . . . *Illus*   10.00
Figure, Pepto Bismol, 24-Hour Bug, Vinyl 95.00
Figure, Reddy Kilowatt, 5 1/2 In. . . . . *Illus*   130.00
Figure, Rolling Rock Premium Beer, Horse, Chalkware, 11 In.   16.00
Figure, Ronald McDonald, Lego Block Figure, 1982, 18 In. 900.00
Figure, Smoke Edgeworth Tobacco, Jiggs The Clown 495.00
Figure, Thatcher Boilers, Ranges, Furnaces, Your Warm Friend, Iron, 3 1/2 In. 130.00
Figure, Waiter, Anheuser-Busch, Yellow Apron, White Shirt, Chalkware, 20 In. 210.00

Advertising, Figure, Oreo Cookie Man,
Bendable, Plastic, 4 1/2 In.

Advertising, Figure, Reddy Kilowatt,
5 1/2 In.

Figure, Westinghouse, Tuff Guy, Muscular Crossed Arms, Gold Paint, 1952, 5 In.	90.00
Figure, White Horse Whiskey	38.00
Flashlight, Captain Ray O Vac, Box	15.00
Flashlight, Li'l Green Sprout, Figural, Box	45.00
Flask, Coffee, Burns & Allen For Motorola TV On Box	40.00
Flip Book, Grape-Nuts Premium	11.00
Flip Book, See It Yourself RCA Victor Million-Proof Television, 1950s, 2 1/2 In.	18.00
Foam Scraper, Hulls Ale-Beer, Marbled Yellow, Beveled Edges	28.00
Foam Scraper, Iberts Supreme	45.00
Foam Scraper, Pickwick Ale, 2 Sides	37.00
Foam Scraper, Rheingold	10.00
Frisbee, McDonald's	22.00
Game, McDonald's, Ronald McDonald Flying Hamburger, 1960s	45.00
Glass, Arby's, Zodiac, Capricorn, 1976, 16 Oz.	5.00
Glass, Blatz Beer	20.00
Glass, Bob's Big Boy	8.00
Glass, Burger King, Star Wars, Darth Vader, Limited Edition, 1977	12.00
Glass, Burger King, Star Wars, R2D2, Coke, 1977	9.00
Glass, Cleaning Tissue, Curtiss Peppermint Gum, Stick Of Gum Picture, 1940s	50.00
Glass, Dick Bros., Beer, Etched	65.00
Glass, Dr Pepper, Stained Glass, Currier & Ives, Winter Scene, 1978	4.00
Glass, Dr Pepper, Star Trek, Enterprise, 1976	16.00
Glass, Eastern Airlines	5.00
Glass, Eastman Kodak, Measuring, Copper Handle	25.00
Glass, Erin Brew, Cleveland, Enameled, Post-Prohibition, 1951	370.00
Glass, I Hop, International House Of Pancakes	4.00
Glass, Jax Beer, New Orleans, Pilsner	80.00
Glass, Moxie, Amethyst, Flared, 4 In.	65.00
Glass, Nectar Beer, Pilsner	100.00
Glass, Old Crow, Glass, Morgantown	50.00
Glass, Old Silver Fox Beer	110.00
Glass, Pabst Beer, Enameled	20.00
Glass, Virginia Brewing, Jamestown Expo, Etched	95.00
Glass, Walkers Bourbon, Gold Rim	20.00
Glass, Welch's, Flintstones, Fred & Barney Bowl Duck Pins, 1962	4.00
Glass, Welch's, Yosemite Sam, Tweety Bird, Warner Bros., 1976	6.00
Glass, Wendy's, Dr Pepper, Cleveland Browns, Brian Sipe, 1981	3.00
Goblet, Puritan Beer, Etched, Pre-Prohibition, 6 In.	41.00
Gum Wrapper, Adams' Magic Trick, c.1890	110.00
Hanger, Keds Shoes, Fan, Woman On Reverse Side, 9 1/4 In.	93.00
Hat, Gold Rim Flour, Baker's	20.00
Hat, Kellogg's Tour, Tony The Tiger & Pop, Paper, 1960s	24.00
Hat, Mr. Salty Pretzel, Sailor Type, White	15.00
Holder, Tanglefoot, Destroying Flys, O & W Thum Co., Tin Lithograph	55.00
Hot Plate, Campbell's Soup, Metal Container, 1950s	175.00

Humidor, Culture Crush Cut Smoking Tobacco, Knob Top	280.00
Humidor, Old Glory Cigars, Eagle Picture	170.00
Ice Bucket, Bud Light, Spuds Mackenzie, 9 In.	35.00
Jar, Lorillard's Coarse French Rappee Snuff, Contents, 1900, 7 In.	235.00
Jar, Sunshine Biscuit, Loose-Wiles, Round, Lid	240.00
Jar, Yellow Kid Chewing Gum, 1 Cent	4500.00
Jug, LeGear's Fly Chaser, Contents, 1/4 Gal.	25.00
Jug Mixer, Ovaltine, Pottery, Woman, Holding Ovaltine Can, England, 1935	150.00
Keg, DuPont, Black Powder, FF, US Army & US Navy, Tin, Paper Label, 10 Lb.	100.00
Keg, Powder, Hercules, Tin, Dark Green Paint, Paper Label, 6 Lb.	85.00
Key Chain, BP, Yellow & Green Plastic Figure, 3 In.	12.00
Key Chain, Esso, Tiger Holding Esso Sign, Metal, 1966, 2 In.	22.00
Key Chain, Ford, Clear Plastic Tag, Logo, Dealership Other Side, 1940s	6.00
Label, Armour's Veribest Full Cream Cheese, 12 x 7 In.	6.00
Label, Aunty Citrus, Smiling Black Lady, Citrus Blossoms, 1920s, 9 x 9 In.	20.00
Label, Betsy Ross Cigar, Mild Pleasing Quality, 5 Cents	8.00
Label, Big John Plug Cut, For Smoke & Chew, John Weisert, 1970, 4 3/8 x 9 In.	2.00
Label, Big Pete Pipe Mixture, John Weisert, Chicago, 1950s, 19 x 4 1/2 In.	3.00
Label, Black Hawk Ginger Ale, Indian Trademark	1.00
Label, Bohemian, Mound City Beer Co., New Athens, 12 Oz.	15.00
Label, Briar Gold, Best Beer Co., Chicago, Illinois, 12 Oz.	20.00
Label, Bryn Mawr, Birk Bros. Beer Co., Chicago, Illinois, 1/2 Gal.	10.00
Label, Butterfly Brand Strawberry Beets, Butterfly Picture, 4 1/2 x 13 1/2 In.	4.00
Label, Butterfly Brand Stringless Beans, Beans On Vine, 1890s, 4 x 11 In.	5.00
Label, California Powder Works, Seal, Cannon, Flags, Muskets, Round	232.00
Label, Camel Cigar, Arab Riding On Camel, Pyramids, 9 x 7 In.	9.00
Label, Chautaugua Maid, Grape Juice, Girl & Grapes, 3 1/4 x 4 1/4 In.	1.00
Label, Christy Girl Cigar, 1930s, 3 1/2 x 4 1/4 In.	6.00
Label, Cigar Box, Tommix, 3 Piece	45.00
Label, Crescent City Citrus, Girl Sitting On Moon, 1920s, 9 x 9 In.	7.00
Label, Custom Blending Mixture, John Weisert, 1960s, 7 x 2 1/2 In.	2.00
Label, Dauntless Lima Beans, Boy In Suit Of Armor, 1930s, 4 1/4 x 11 In.	2.00
Label, Dunkirk, Deer Run A, Fred Koch Bry, 12 Oz.	13.00
Label, El Guado Cigar	25.00
Label, Eureka, Florida Citrus Fruit, Indian At River, 1940s, 9 x 9 In.	4.00
Label, First National Cigar	25.00
Label, Foot High Melons	2.00
Label, Frontier, Kern Beer Co., Bakersfield, California, 11 Oz.	20.00
Label, Gay Johnny, Texas Vegetable, Little Boy In Jeans, 1950s, 5 x 7 In.	2.00
Label, Hapsburg Bock, Best Beer Co., Chicago, Illinois, 1/2 Gal.	18.00
Label, Homer Orange, Flying Pigeon Picture, 1940s, 11 x 10 In.	2.00
Label, Honey Bee Sweet Potato, 2 Honey Bees, 1950s, 8 x 6 1/2 In.	2.00
Label, Jo Sole Grapefruit Juice, Black Boy, High Five, 1960s, 13 1/2 x 6 1/2 In.	2.00
Label, Koppitz Victory, Koppitz-Melcher's, Inc., Detroit, Michigan, 12 Oz.	11.00 to 20.00
Label, Levon, California Melons, Green-Eyed Lion, 1930s, 9 x 12 In.	4.00
Label, Lion Brew, Bakersfield Beer Co., Bakersfield, California, 11 Oz.	60.00
Label, Maryland Chief Stringless Beans, 8 x 4 In.	2.00
Label, Meteor Lemons, Falling Meteor, Branch Of Lemons, 12 x 9 In.	3.00
Label, Moonbeam Brand, Citrus Fruit, Orange Grove In Moonlight, 1910s, 8 x 8 In.	10.00
Label, My Choice Salmon, British Columbia, White Label	5.00
Label, Old Abe Cigar, Black, Gold, Gray, 2 x 6 In.	6.00
Label, Old Tavern Brew, Rock Island Beer Co., Rock Island, 12 Oz.	37.00
Label, On The Way To White House, Garfield's Boyhood Home, Cigar Box	75.00
Label, Paddler Salmon, Vancouver, Canada	5.00
Label, Pale Brave Valencia Orange, Indian Chief Picture, 1940s, 11 x 10 In.	4.00
Label, Penrod, June Peas, 1914, 10 x 4 In.	2.00
Label, Prince Of Pales, Ambrosia Beer Co., Chicago, Illinois, 1/2 Gal.	10.00
Label, Rainier Lime Rickey, Rainier Beer Co., San Francisco, California, 11 Oz.	25.00
Label, Repetition Apples, Boy Eating Apple Out Of Crate, 1920s, 10 1/2 x 9 In.	4.00
Label, Rose Leaf Golden Sweet Corn, Red Roses, 4 1/4 x 10 In.	1.00
Label, Rubaiyat Citrus, Arab With Girl, Tent, Palm Trees, 11 x 10 In.	4.00
Label, Santa Claus Plum Pudding, 4 x 12 In.	24.00
Label, Schaefer Dark Brew, F & M Schaefer Beer Co., New York	10.00

Label, Sea Robin Cigar, 4 x 4 In. 5.00
Label, Squaw Extra Small Peas 5.00
Label, Valley Brew, El Dorado Beer Co., Stockton, California 30.00
Label, Victor-Dewey, Multicolored, Cigar Box, 4 1/2 In. 50.00
Label, Victorious Louisiana Sweet Potatoes, Cowgirl, White Horse, 1950s, 9 x 9 In. 2.00
Label, Waitt & Bond Blackstone Cigar, Porcelain 175.00
Label, Wayne Carrots, Edgett-Burham Co. 2.00
Label, White Cat Cigar 5.00
Label, Winsom Whole Red Beets 2.00
Light, Cash Register, Miller High Life, Girl In Moon, 1930s, 8 x 9 In. 207.00
Lunch Boxes are listed in their own category.
Magazine, Uneeda Biscuit, 1926, Series Of Recipe Books 35.00
Malt Machine, Horlick's, Porcelain Base, White, Blue Lettering 575.00
Mask, Little Lulu, Kleenex Premium, Paper, 1948 .... 30.00
Mask, Pinocchio Face, Gillette Blue Blades Premium, Full Color Cardboard, 1939 ..... 25.00
Mat, Camel Cigarettes, Rubber, Spiked, Round 20.00
Match Strike, Bull Dog Cut Plug Tobacco 1980.00
Match Strike, Drink Orange Crush, Porcelain 1780.00
Match Strike, Orange Crush, French Language, Canada 960.00
Matchbook, Yellow Cab, The Thinking Fellow Call A Yellow, 1930s 14.00
Menu Board, Hendler's, Reverse Mirror Glass, 9 Cutout Flavor Strips, 24 In. 82.00

Advertising pocket mirrors range in size from 1 1/2 to 5 inches in
diameter. Most of these mirrors were given away as advertising pro-
motions and include the name of the company in the design.

Mirror, Angelus Marshmallow, Pocket, 1930 .... 175.00
Mirror, Bell's Imperial Coffee, Celluloid, 2 1/2 In. 55.00
Mirror, Borden's Milk, Pocket, 1930 .... 175.00
Mirror, Calox Tooth Powder, Pocket 60.00
Mirror, Carmen Complexion Powder, Celluloid, 1 3/4 In. 75.00
Mirror, Continental Cubes Tobacco, Oval 175.00
Mirror, Copper Clad Stoves, Pocket 45.00
Mirror, Dutch Java Coffee, Celluloid, Round, 2 1/8 In. 175.00
Mirror, Federal Express, Pocket 3.00
Mirror, Feigenspan's Beer, Beautiful Woman, Pocket 110.00
Mirror, Ford-Lincoln Zephyr, Clear Acetate Over Yellow Paper, Pocket, 1930-1940 ..... 24.00
Mirror, Girl, Bobbed & Windblown Hair, Naughty Images, Celluloid, Pocket 18.00
Mirror, Heel Hugger Ladies Shoes, Pocket 15.00
Mirror, Hibbard Hardware, Pocket 50.00
Mirror, Johnston Chocolates, Celluloid, 2 1/4 In. 75.00
Mirror, King Air Rifle, Markham Air Rifle Co., Pocket 66.00
Mirror, Klosed-Krotch Union Suits, Celluloid, Pocket, 2 1/2 In. 70.00
Mirror, Knerr's Ice Cream, Encased Thermometer & Barometer, Large 140.00
Mirror, Lemont's, Home Of Good Furniture, Fredericton, 10 x 14 In. 45.00
Mirror, Munsingwear, Silver, 2 1/4 In. 85.00
Mirror, New-Way Gasoline Engines, Image Of Engine, Celluloid, Pocket, 2 1/4 In. 235.00
Mirror, Pan-American Exposition, Pocket, 1901 .... 35.00
Mirror, Red Bull Dog Overalls, Pocket 95.00
Mirror, Skeezix Shoes, Pocket, 1920s 60.00
Mirror, Stoner Mfg., Fresh Candy, Coin-Operated Machine, 1960s, 20 x 20 In. 38.00
Mirror, Swan's Down Flour, Package Of Cake Flour, Celluloid, 4 In. 230.00
Mirror, Turner Motorcar, Overland, Pocket 1200.00
Mirror, White Cat Underwear, Copper, Oval, Pocket 95.00
Mirror, White Cat Union Suits, Celluloid, Pocket, 2 3/4 x 2 In. 110.00
Mirror, Williams Talc & Aftershave, Pocket 550.00
Mirror, Woolsey's Paint & Varnish, Pocket 40.00
Model, Store, Levis Man, Straus, Composition, 1940, 30 In. 4000.00
Model, Washing Machine, Oak, Natural, Double Washer Label, 17 1/2 In. 245.00
Moistener, Stamp, Store, S & H Green Stamps, Porcelain 25.00
Money Clip, Dutch Masters Ambassador 20.00
Money Clip, IBM, Gold 100.00
Money Clip, Signal Oil, Presentation 75.00
Mug, A & W Root Beer 9.00

Mug, Budweiser, Clydesdale, 1984, 8 In. 22.00
Mug, Cardinal Brewery, Scranton, Pennsylvania, Monk Portrait 75.00
Mug, Hires Root Beer, Child Holds Same Mug, 4 1/2 In. 85.00
Mug, Hires Root Beer, Early Drive In Style 15.00
Mug, Hires Root Beer, Hires Boy, White Glaze, Marked, 4 In. 77.00
Mug, Lash's Root Beer 50.00
Mug, Marlboro Man Cigarettes, Box 45.00
Mug, Monastery Beer, Ceramic, Pre-Prohibition, 5 In. 27.00
Mug, Ovaltine, Uncle Wiggily, 1924 .... 40.00
Mug, Pabst Brewery, Elves On Barrel, Pre-Prohibition 68.00
Mug, Piedmont Airlines Coffee, Red, Blue Stenciling, Heavy White China, 4 x 3 In. 23.00
Mug, Pillsbury Doughboy, Figural, Plastic, White, Child's, 1970 .... 18.00
Mug, Ranger Joe, White Milk Glass, Red Lettering, 1951 .... 35.00
Mug, Round Oak Stove, Doe-Wah-Jack Indian, Brown To Orange 295.00
Napkin Holder, Budweiser, Bar Mount 55.00
Napkin Holder, Chilly Willy, With Thermometer, Plastic 27.00
Necktie, Schlitz Beer, 1950s 18.00
Night-Light, Bob's Big Boy, Vinyl, 1960s, 6 1/2 In. 195.00
Note Pad, Union Electric Steel, Rolling Mill Shape, 10 In. 75.00
Opener, Cigar Box, Discriminator Cigar, 10 Cents 35.00
Opener, Cigar Box, Faust 10 Cent Cigar 35.00
Opener, Cigar Box, Hammer, Charles Denby Cigars, 5 Cents 30.00
Opener, Cigar Box, Laurel Stoves, Hatchet Shape .... .55.00 to 95.00
Opener, Cigar Box, R.B., 5 Cent Cigar 45.00
Opener, Cigar Box, San Felice Cigars 25.00
Pack, Cigarette, Black Cat, Virginia, Unopened 20.00
Pack, Cigarette, Lucky Strike, Green 50.00
Pack, Cigarette, Newport, 13 x 20 In. 149.00
Pack, Cigarette, Uncle Daniel's Paper Tobacco Pack, 1 Oz. 137.50
Pack, Fatima Cigarettes 35.00
Padlock, Lava Soap, Key, On Display 20.00
Pails are listed in the Lunch Box category.
Pan, Stick, Junior Krusty Korn Kob, 6 Corn, Wagner Ware, Registered July 6, 1920 ..... 125.00
Patch, Wings, Harley-Davidson Motorcycles, 1950s, 7 1/2 In. 85.00
Pencil Clip, 7-Up, Silver Metal, Red, White & Blue, 1940s 15.00
Pencil Clip, Edison Battery 25.00
Pencil Clip, Morton Salt 3.00
Pencil Clip, Star Brand Shoes 15.00
Pillbox, McGinty's Watch, Glass Bezel Case, Hinged Cover, Early 1900s 38.00
Pin, Elsie The Cow, For Today's Menu, 1940 .... 38.00
Pin, Harley-Davidson, Brass, Profile Motorcycle, 1950 .... 30.00
Pin, Kellogg's Toasted Corn Flakes, Child Picture, Celluloid, 1930s, 1 1/4 In. 145.00
Pin, Kids Ken-L Klub Member Button, Tin Lithograph, 1950s, 3 3/4 In. 40.00
Pin, Levis 501, Denim Jeans, Lapel 9.00
Pin, Miller High Life, Miller Girl On Moon, Celluloid, 1930s, 7/8 In. 115.00
Pin, Mobil Oil, Lapel 45.00
Pin, The Freshest Thing In Town Master Bread, Baby, Derby, Celluloid, 1 1/4 In. 10.00
Pin, Washburn Crosby Flour 10.00
Pin, Welch's Grape Juice, Celluloid, Metal Pin, 3/4 x 1/2 In. 110.00
Pitcher, Burke's Dublin Whiskey, Ceramic 82.00
Pitcher, Cutty Sark Blended Scotch Whiskey, 5 x 6 1/2 In. 5.00
Pitcher, Hershey's, Black & White Cow 24.00
Pitcher, Sunbright, Pale Yellow, Ring Style 40.00
Pitcher, White Satin Gin, Green Ceramic, 7 x 7 In. 11.00
Planter, Pillsbury Doughboy, Pottery, 1988 .... 7.50
Plaque, Barnum's Animal Cracker, Wooden 35.00
Plaque, Goodyear, 25 Years Friendly Relations, Cast Iron, 1920s, 12 x 17 In. 650.00
Plaque, Goodyear, Dealer, 10 Year Award, Cast Metal, 17 x 12 In. 175.00
Plaque, Neuweiler Beer, 12 x 10 1/2 In. 25.00
Plaque, Sky By Pfaltzgraff, Store, 3 5/8 x 6 1/2 In. 40.00
Plate, Armor Hosiery, Stand-Up, Die Cut Cardboard, 5 3/4 x 3 1/2 In. 33.00
Plate, Empire Bottling Co., Seasons Greetings, Vienna Art, 1909, 10 In. 225.00
Plate, Green's August Flower Patent Medicine, 8 1/2 In. 50.00

Plate, McDonald's, 4 Seasons, Ronald McDonald, Plastic, 1977, 10 In., 4 Piece 26.00
Plate, Quick Service Laundry Co., Tin, Early 1900s 30.00
Plate, Schenley Whiskey, Tin 20.00
Platter, Hillshire Farms, Pottery, Pfaltzgraff 38.00
Platter, Mobil Oil, Shenango China Co., Oval, 1938 .... 65.00
Pog, McDonald's, McPogs, Complete Set, 24 Piece 12.00
Pog, McDonald's, Power Ranger 50.00
Poster, Columbia Bicycle, Boy & Girl, Maxfield Parrish, 35 x 23 In. 35.00
Poster, Dupont Explosive Products, Greater Yellow Legs, 14 x 16 In. 90.00
Poster, Goodyear, Cars From 1915-1950, Colorful, Cardboard, Frame, 1951 .... 70.00
Poster, Ithaca Guns, Framed, Metal Bands At Top & Bottom, 27 x 19 In. 550.00
Poster, Jack & Jill Gelatin, 1950, 10 x 30 In. 8.00
Poster, Look At Our Model Department, N.B.C., Uneeda Boy On Sign, c.1918, 2 x 3 Ft. 475.00
Poster, Orphan Boy Tobacco, Die Cut, 1930s, 13 x 19 In. 15.00
Poster, Pangburn's Chocolates, Cowgirl, Rope & Candy Box, Elvgren 250.00
Poster, Philip Morris Cigarettes, 1940s, 18 1/4 x 23 1/2 In. 40.00
Poster, Red Devil Fire Cracker 20.00
Poster, Red Indian Cut Plug, Frame, 31 x 24 In. 785.00
Poster, Remington, Game Load Game, Lake & Animals, 1923, 23 1/4 x 17 1/2 In. 165.00
Poster, Safety First, Philip Morris, Indoor, Outdoor, 41 x 23 In. 275.00
Poster, Speed King Scooter Premium, Lansford Bottling Works, Pa., 8 x 11 In. 12.00
Poster, Sunbeam Bread, Die Cut, 1960s, 10 x 22 In. 7.00
Poster, Western, World's Champion Ammunition, Frame, 1924, 24 x 18 In. 33.00
Poster, Winchester Bird Buster II, Winchester Twins Picture, AA Shot Shells, 1983 ..... 90.00
Poster, Winchester, Model 94 Carbine, 34 x 13 In. 145.00
Poster, Winchester-Western, Squirrel In Tree, Hunter Below, Shrink Wrapped, 1955 .... 80.00
Pot Scraper, Sharples Cream Separator, Tin, 1909 .... 295.00
Print, Miss Rheingold, Pat Burrage, Frame, Signed, 22 x 22 In. 36.00
Push Bar, 7-Up, Porcelain, Bilingual, 1950s 50.00
Push Bar, Five Roses Flour, Porcelain 75.00
Push Bar, Orange Crush 95.00
Push Bar, Pure Spring Ginger Ale, Porcelain, England 65.00
Rack, Canada Dry, 3 Tiers, Metal, 43 x 24 In. 60.00
Rack, Kellogg's, Display, Restaurant, Red & White Metal, 29 x 19 In. 245.00
Rack, Lifesavers Candy, Bakelite 175.00
Rack, National Biscuit Company, 4 Shelves, Oak, 2 Ft. 600.00
Rack, Schrafft's, 5 Cents, Tin, Wire, 14 1/2 x 7 In. 65.00
Radio, California Raisins, AM/FM 85.00
Razor Bank, Listerine Frog 35.00
Ring, Carey Salt Co., Shadow, 1947 .... 356.00
Ring, Kellogg's, Rice Krispies Snap, Premium, 1950s 450.00
Rug, Red Goose Shoes, Green, Red & Black, 60 x 27 1/2 In. 412.00
Ruler, Glory Soap Chips, Swift & Co. Soap Dept., Celluloid, 1919, 5 3/8 To 12 In. 14.00
Ruler, Simon Pure Beer 20.00
Ruler, Try Bokes At Your Favorite Drive-In 85.00
Ruler, Valley Lumber, Decatur, Zigzag, 3 Ft. 60.00
Salt & Pepper Shakers are listed in their own category.
Saltshaker, Peerless Beer, Man With Beard, Plastic, 5 In. 8.00
Sample Case, Pacific Mills, Cotton Products, Wooden, 17 In. ....*Illus* 110.00
Scales are listed in their own category.
Sewing Kit, Lydia Pinkham 20.00
Sewing Kit, Peters Shoes 20.00
Sheet Music, Peerless March, Peerless Motorcar Co., 1916 .... 25.00
Shoehorn, Shinola Shoe Polish 35.00
Shopping Bag, Aunt Jemima, 8 x 18 In. 25.00
Shot Glass, 7-Up ....4.00 to 16.00
Shot Glass, Dr Pepper 4.00
Shot Glass, Old Man River Whiskey, Aluminum, Collapsible, Black Man, Banjo 45.00
Sign, 7-Up, Great With Food, 2 Bottles, 2 Glasses, Oak Frame, 1950, 26 x 23 In. 111.00
Sign, 7-Up, Preppies In Model A, Cardboard, 1958, 14 x 14 In. 25.00
Sign, Ada Olive Oil, Tin, 19 x 13 In. 165.00
Sign, Albis Barbershop, Pole Design, Red, White, Blue Stripes, 35 1/2 x 9 1/2 In. 172.00
Sign, Alpen Brau, Columbia Brewing Co., Reverse Glass, 1930s, 11 In. 77.00

Any lithographed can with a picture is of more value to the collector than a lithographed can with just names. Any paper-labeled can that can be dated before 1875 is rare. Any ad that pictures an American flag or a Black has added value. Known brand names are also of greater value.

Advertising, Sample Case, Pacific Mills, Cotton Products, Wooden, 17 In.

Sign, American 5 Cent Cigar, Red, White, Blue Painted Flag, Frame, 15 x 31 In. 2760.00
Sign, American Express, Metal, Black & Yellow Logo, 20 x 16 In. 135.00
Sign, Anheuser-Busch, Bare-Breasted Woman Protecting Her Glass, 27 x 21 In. 690.00
Sign, Anheuser-Busch, Young Lady In Barmaid Outfit, Frame, 14 x 24 In. 385.00
Sign, Approved Packard Service, Tin, Round, 23 In. 220.00
Sign, Arm & Hammer, Green-Winged Teal On Front, Cardboard, 11 x 14 1/4 In. 29.00
Sign, Armour's, Vintage Meat Market, Meek & Beach Co., Tin, 27 x 21 In. 5750.00
Sign, Ask For Wild Root, Barber, 12 x 39 In. 100.00
Sign, Aunt Jemima, Holding Pancakes, The Eaten'est Hot Cakes, 14 x 21 In. 110.00
Sign, Aunt Jemima, Holding Plate Full Of Pancakes, Cardboard, 20 x 16 In. 80.00
Sign, Ax, Hardware Store, Painted Wood, 53 In. 275.00
Sign, Bagley's Tobacco, 3-Dimensional, Papier-Mache, Wall Hanger, 25 In. 770.00
Sign, Balboa Beer, Metal, Nail Holes, 1933-1934, 54 x 18 In. 350.00
Sign, Ball Blue Washing Crystal, Women & Girls Doing Laundry, 19 x 25 In. 1035.00
Sign, Banner Brewery, Weyand Brewing Co., Paper Lithograph, Eagle At Top 4500.00
Sign, Barber Shop, Porcelain, Cast Iron Brackets, 24 x 18 In. 210.00
Sign, Becker Autoradio Service, Red, White, Black, 15 x 11 In. 253.00
Sign, Bickmore's Gall Cure, Horses, Farm Animals, 3-Panel Cardboard, 32 x 49 In. 250.00
Sign, Bieres Du Coq Hardi, Porcelain, Flange, 24 1/2 x 19 In. 715.00
Sign, Black Cat Cigarette, Black Cat With Mesmerizing Eyes, 36 x 24 In. 1035.00
Sign, Blacksmith, Horseshoe Form, J.J. Quinn, Suspended From Curved Bracket 465.00
Sign, Blackstone Cigars, Waitt & Bond Fine Cigars, Porcelain, 22 x 28 In. 45.00
Sign, Blackstone Cigars, Yellow & Blue, Porcelain, 22 x 28 In. 45.00
Sign, Blatz Beer, Bicycle Man Character, Round, 18 In. 190.00
Sign, Blatz Beer, Pheasant To Top With Brass Plate, Wood, 13 x 29 In. 58.00
Sign, Blatz Beer, Val Blatz Brewing Co., Canvas, Wood Frame, 27 x 35 In. 1430.00
Sign, BLT Tobacco, Red, White & Blue, Porcelain, 15 x 15 In. 38.00
Sign, Blue Bell Wranglers, Jeans Champions Wear, Wooden, 1960, 17 x 11 In. 235.00
Sign, Blue Coal, Better Heat, Less Attention, Red, White & Blue, Tin, 23 x 11 In. 95.00
Sign, Blue Grass Rye, Daniel Boone, Kentucky River, Tin, 19 1/2 x 15 In. 3300.00
Sign, Borden's, Elsie The Cow, Cardboard, 1950s, Round, 12 In. 38.00
Sign, Boschee's German Syrup, Framed, Tin Lithograph, 36 x 28 In. 825.00
Sign, Botl'O Grape Soda, Red, Blue, Green, Tin, Rectangular, 11 1/2 x 24 In. 22.00
Sign, Breen & Kennedy Distiller's, Frankfort, Kentucky, 24 x 35 1/2 In. 1265.00
Sign, British Oak Shag, Lambert & Butler, Frame, 25 x 21 In. 440.00
Sign, Budweiser, And They All Want Budweiser, Cardboard, 1950, 32 x 14 In. 102.00
Sign, Budweiser, Light, Pheasant, 2 Pheasants Eating Corn, 18 x 15 In. 64.00
Sign, Bull Durham Smoking Tobacco, Black Ground, Frame, 38 In. 688.00
Sign, Campbell's Tomato Soup, Die Cut, Porcelain, 22 1/2 x 13 In. 1322.50
Sign, Carling's Ale, Glass, Easel Back, 6 x 12 In. 25.00
Sign, Carling's Ale, Tin, 20 x 13 In. 95.00
Sign, Carry-Us-All Carousel, Horse, Jumping, Paper, 19 x 26 In. 632.00
Sign, Carter's Ideal Ribbons & Carbons, Portia's Choice, 13 x 19 In. 550.00
Sign, Case & Co., 3-D Carved Eagle, Papier-Mache & Composite, 1910, 27 In. 795.00

Sign, Cetacolor, Not A Soap, Black Ground, Frame, 37 x 25 In. 330.00
Sign, Champion Spark Plug, Yellow, Red, Blue, Cream, Gray, Tin, 27 3/4 In. 180.00
Sign, Chero-Cola Drink, Painted Tin, 14 x 19 1/2 In. 120.00
Sign, Chew Mail Pouch, Porcelain, Yellow, Blue & White, 11 x 36 In. 120.00
Sign, Collins & Co., Axes Of The World Are Collins, Hartford, Connecticut, 20 In. 55.00
Sign, Colonial Club 5 Cents Cigars, Black Ground, 8 1/2 x 18 In. 99.00
Sign, Columbia Records, Blue, White & Black, Porcelain, Round, 24 In. 28.00
Sign, Conoco, Danger High Pressure Gas Line, Porcelain, 8 x 15 In. 95.00
Sign, Cork Distilleries Co., Frame, Tin, 19 x 15 In. 220.00
Sign, Crawford's Tobacco 5 Cents Cigar, It's A Peach, Black Ground, 10 x 14 In. 110.00
Sign, Crescent Flour, Blue Cardboard, 6 x 20 In. 45.00
Sign, Crystaloid, International Grape Cream, Stand-Up, Lithograph, 13 In. 575.00
Sign, Cunard Steam Ship Company Limited, Beige Ground, 13 x 18 In. 920.00
Sign, De Laval Cream Separator, Bonneted Lass, Calf, Tin, Self-Framed, 38 x 29 In. 2970.00
Sign, De Laval Separator Co., Cream Separators, Tin, Frame, 25 x 19 In. 330.00
Sign, Dick's Pilsner, Gold Ground, Celluloid Over Tin, 1940s 75.00
Sign, Dino Gasoline, 4 x 20 In. 35.00
Sign, Dixie & Camillo Cigars, Young Woman, Wood Frame, 22 x 29 In. 176.00
Sign, Doe-Wah-Jack, Paper Lithograph, Embossed Oak Frame, 27 x 12 In. 825.00
Sign, Dolly Madison Cigars, Embossed Tin, 1930s, 5 x 20 In. 85.00
Sign, Dolly Madison Cigars, Embossed Tin, 1940s, 5 x 20 In. 70.00
Sign, Donnell's DeLuxe Ice Cream, Porcelain, 2 Sides, 24 In. . . . . *Illus* 495.00
Sign, Dr Pepper, Bottle Cap, Round, 36 In. 105.00
Sign, Dr Pepper, Porcelain, 9 x 20 In. 125.00
Sign, Dr Pepper, Thermometer, Tin, 5 x 17 In. 25.00
Sign, Dr Pepper, Warmer, Hot, Cardboard, 1960s, 15 x 25 In. 50.00
Sign, Dr. Caldwell's Syrup Pepsin, Cardboard, 21 x 11 In. 625.00
Sign, Dr. Clarke's Life Balsam, Cardboard, 9 1/2 x 14 In. 450.00
Sign, Dr. LeGears, Man On Horse, 1911, 14 x 16 In. 195.00
Sign, Dr. Livingston, Chiropractor, Phone 338, Yellow & Green, 12 x 24 In. 40.00
Sign, Dr. Pierce's Medical Discovery, World War I Battle Scene, 20 x 16 In. 375.00
Sign, Drink Grape Ola Fruit, Tin, 19 1/2 x 13 1/2 In. 85.00
Sign, Drink Hires, It Hits The Spot, Man In Suit Holding Bottle, Yellow, 9 x 17 In. 248.00 to 440.00
Sign, Drink Nehi Beverages, Tin, Bottle At Left, 29 x 11 1/4 In. 75.00
Sign, Drink Orange Blossoms, Painted Tin, 12 1/2 x 27 1/2 In. 105.00
Sign, Drink Smile, Painted Metal, Flange, 12 1/4 x 10 In. 467.00
Sign, Drink Sunny Isles, Pineapple Juice Drink, Paper, 10 x 9 In. 44.00
Sign, DuPont Paints, Ripple Glass Front, Light-Up, Plastic Frame, 9 x 24 In. 88.00
Sign, E & O Pilsner Beer, Tin Over Cardboard, 1930s, 11 x 9 In. 57.00
Sign, Eisenlohr's Cinco Cigars, Flange, Porcelain, Red, Blue, Yellow, 13 x 17 In. . .55.00 to 155.00
Sign, Ekhardt & Becker Beer, Pub Scene, 7 Men Drinking, Paper, 16 x 25 In. 690.00
Sign, Enameline Stove Polish, Young Girl, Cases Of Product, 1900, 12 x 20 In. 400.00
Sign, English Pub, King's Arms, Ind Coope, Tin, 2 Sides, Frame, 56 x 42 1/2 In. 950.00

Advertising, Sign, Donnell's DeLuxe Ice Cream,
Porcelain, 2 Sides, 24 In.

Advertising, Sign, Flora Fina Nicotine,
Embroidered, 1920, 24 x 24 In.

Sign, Enjoy Grapette Soda, Red, White, Blue, Label Design, 1950, 36 In. 132.00
Sign, Erickson's Whiskey, Tin, Self-Framed, 23 x 33 In. 550.00
Sign, Erin Brew The Standard Beer, Wooden, 3 1/2 x 10 1/2 In. 32.00
Sign, Fairbanks Gold Dust Washing Powder, Tin, Self-Framed, 38 x 26 In. 4400.00
Sign, Fairbanks Scale, Porcelain, 10 x 50 In. 110.00
Sign, Falstaff Beer, The Peacemaker, Tin, Frame, 31 x 23 In. 1430.00
Sign, Fatima Turkish Cigarettes, Egyptian Woman In Center, Yellow, 16 x 24 In. 94.00
Sign, Federal Land Bank Assn., White, Blue, Porcelain, 2 Sides, 18 x 36 In. 150.00
Sign, Feed Nutrena It Pays, Yellow, Red, Black, Metal, 1950, 46 x 36 In. 74.00
Sign, Fidelity Phoenix Fire Insurance, Glass, Metal, Early 1900s, 17 x 12 In. 125.00
Sign, Finest Old Scotch Whiskey, Reverse Painted, Mirror, 27 x 37 In. 195.00
Sign, Fish Bros., A Visit To Washington, Cardboard, 1900, 16 x 23 In. 259.00
Sign, Flanagan Brothers Hardware, Levers & Locks, Tin, 11 1/2 x 23 In. 95.00
Sign, Flora Fina Nicotine, Embroidered, 1920, 24 x 24 In. *Illus* 330.00
Sign, Florida Lottery, Neon, Pink Flamingo, Sun, Grass, 18 x 24 In. 250.00
Sign, Florsheim Shoe, 21 1/2 x 26 In. 60.00
Sign, Ford-Ferguson System Tractor, Masonite, Black, Yellow, 1940s, 11 x 22 In. 198.00
Sign, Francisco Auto Heater, Frame, Tin, 40 x 18 In. 715.00
Sign, Frank Fehr Brewing Co., Bock Beer, Frame, 26 x 36 In. 365.00
Sign, Franklin National Insurance Co., Metal, Frame, 16 1/2 x 28 In. 230.00
Sign, Frostie Root Beer, Embossed 4-Color Tin, Round, 11 In. 135.00
Sign, Gaucho, World's Smallest Horse, Canvas, 8 x 10 Ft. 1400.00
Sign, General Electric TV Service Master Tubes, Pressed Board, 8 x 6 In. 16.00
Sign, Globe Tobacco, Young Woman In Victorian Attire, 11 x 27 1/2 In. 187.00
Sign, Golden Glint Shampoo, Puts Sunshine In Your Hair, Black, Yellow, 8 x 7 In. 31.00
Sign, Goodyear, Porcelain, 1918, 2 x 6 Ft. 650.00
Sign, Grant's Hygienic Crackers, Constipated? Cardboard, 11 x 14 In. 30.00
Sign, Grape-Nuts, Family Saint Bernard Escorting Little Girl, Tin, 30 x 20 In. 3450.00
Sign, Great Heart Coal, Tin, Frame, 26 x 15 In. 192.00
Sign, Green River Whiskey, 24 In. 1000.00
Sign, Gund's Peerless Beer, Tin, Self-Framed, 24 x 31 In. 495.00
Sign, Hamm's Beer, Moving Waters, Light-Up, 1950s, 36 In. 675.00
Sign, Hamm's Beer, Revolving, Light-Up, Natural Setting, 1970, 31 x 18 In. 201.00
Sign, Hanford's Balsam Of Myrrh, Cardboard, 14 x 7 In. 70.00
Sign, Havoline Motor Oil, Red, White, Blue, 10 3/4 x 21 1/4 In. 88.00
Sign, Heinz Tomato Soup, Pickle Girl, Holding Soup, Die Cut, 1890, 1 3/4 x 5 In. 45.00
Sign, Hendler Creamery, Bronze, Painted Ground, 32 x 4 In. 385.00
Sign, Hershey's Ice Cream, Hanging, Light-Up, 15 x 29 In. 160.00
Sign, Hires Root Beer, Girl With Bottle, Boy With Glass, Stand-Up, 8 In. 250.00
Sign, Hires, Bottle Shape, Die Cut, 4 Ft. 285.00
Sign, Hires, Tin, 1940s, 18 x 30 In. 160.00
Sign, Holihan's Pilsner, Tin Over Cardboard, 1950, 9 In. 55.00
Sign, Honest Scrap Plug Tobacco, Terrier Dog & Black Cat 715.00
Sign, Horse Shoe Tobacco, Black Ground, White Lettering, Porcelain, 8 x 18 In. 121.00
Sign, Howe Scale, Black Lettering On White Ground, Pine, 13 1/2 x 39 1/4 In. 375.00
Sign, Hunt Club Shoes, Tin, Self-Framed, 20 x 24 In. 770.00
Sign, I.W. Harper Whiskey, The Parting Gift, Canvas, Frame, 1912, 34 x 46 In. 1650.00
Sign, Independent Lock Co., Fitchburg, Massachusetts, Key, Aluminum, 28 In. 523.00
Sign, Ivory Soap, Blue & White, Porcelain, 3 1/4 x 21 In. 247.00
Sign, J.B. Ford Company, Chief Wyandotte Shooting Bow, Arrow, Tin, 39 x 28 In. 460.00
Sign, Jefferson Brewing & Malting, Tin Over Cardboard, 13 x 19 In. 520.00
Sign, Kayo Chocolate Drink, Embossed Tin, 14 x 27 In. 60.00
Sign, Kellogg's Corn Flakes, Baby In Basket, Die Cut Sheet Steel, 1910 . . . . 3750.00
Sign, Key, Locksmith, Iron, 19th Century, 9 x 36 In. 950.00
Sign, King Korn, Black Lettering Both Sides, Metal, 1950s, 20 x 28 In. 45.00
Sign, Knickerbocker Beer, Cash Register, Reverse Glass, Light-Up, 9 x 10 In. 55.00
Sign, Knickerbocker Beer, White Ground, Light-Up, Gold Metal Frame, 25 x 10 In. 155.00
Sign, Kraft, Die-Cut Cow, Milk-Bank Boost From Kaff-A, Tin, 16 x 23 In. 192.00
Sign, Kraft, Die-Cut Pig, Tin, 12 x 18 In. 1375.00
Sign, L & M, Get Lots More From L & M, Red, White, Blue, Metal, 23 x 17 In. 51.00
Sign, La Palla, All Havana Cigar, Tin, Self-Framed, 1908, 14 x 17 In. 220.00
Sign, Lash's Bitters, Natural Tonic Laxative, Tin, Self-Framed, 25 x 20 In. 1980.00
Sign, Lee Tires, Flange, Green, Yellow, Red, Black, Metal, 27 1/2 x 18 1/4 In. 467.00

Sign, Lenox Soap, Burdick Sign Co., Porcelain, 6 x 10 In. 205.00
Sign, Liggett & Myers Tobacco Co., Cairo Hotel, Tin, 9 x 13 In. 28.00
Sign, Linseed Oil, Depicts Bail Handle Can, Rome, New York, 11 x 17 In. .... · 120.00
Sign, Lipton's Teas, Ceylonese Girl, Cardboard Lithograph, 19 1/2 x 16 In. 70.00
Sign, London Tavern, Eldorado Brewing Co., California, Cardboard, 18 x 21 In. 45.00
Sign, Longines Wittnauer, Pocket Watch Shape, 15 1/2 x 12 In. 1190.00
Sign, M.C.A. Cigars, Metal, Early 1900s, 14 x 10 In. 100.00
Sign, M.C.A. Cigars, Red, Yellow & Blue, Porcelain, 12 x 30 In. 50.00
Sign, Magnolia Gasoline Motor Oil, Red, White, Blue, 42 In. 60.00
Sign, Mail Pouch Tobacco, Indian Warrior, Full Headdress, Paper, 20 x 14 In. 2070.00
Sign, Mail Pouch Tobacco, Yellow, Blue & White, Porcelain, 11 x 36 In. 120.00
Sign, Maurice The Celebrated Concert Violinist, 1930, 14 x 22 In. 15.00
Sign, Mayo's Plug Tobacco, Cock O' The Walk, Porcelain, Frame, 15 1/2 x 9 In. 440.00
Sign, McCormick's Spices, Map Of World, 1960, 23 x 34 .... 35.00
Sign, McLean's Strengthening Cordial, Mammy Picture, Frame, 17 x 24 In. 1650.00
Sign, McVities, Mother & Children Feeding Parrot, 1930s, 14 x 19 In. 175.00
Sign, Meadow Gold Ice Cream, Reverse Painted, Light-Up, 4 1/4 x 14 1/2 In. 120.00
Sign, Meritorium Flour, Sleepy Eye, Tin, Self-Framed, 25 x 20 In. 2750.00
Sign, Michel Brewing, Stranger In His Native Land, Indian, Tin, 23 x 33 In. 685.00
Sign, Miller High Life, Champagne Of Bottle Beer, Flat Top, 1950, 8 x 4 In. 45.00
Sign, Missouri Pacific Lines, Route Of The Eagles, Calendar Pad, Tin, 19 x 13 In. ...... · 330.00
Sign, Mobil Regular Pump Plate, 12 x 14 In. 35.00
Sign, Moxie, Candy, Soda, Ice Cream, Polychromed Tin, Self-Framed, 30 x 54 In. 935.00
Sign, Munsingwear, 6 Children, Die Cut, Tin Lithograph, Stand-Up, 16 x 24 In. 3080.00
Sign, Murphy & Diebold Planning Mill, Street Car Scene, Oak Frame, 30 x 46 In. 1100.00
Sign, Murray's Warrior Plug Tobacco, Cardboard Lithograph, 29 1/2 x 21 In. 220.00
Sign, N. Shepard Inn, Central Indian Figure, Wooden, New England, 67 x 42 In. 4315.00
Sign, N.B.C. Sugar Cone, Stand-Up Cone, 1918, 10 In. 125.00
Sign, Nash Hardware Co., Established 1872, Brass, 12 x 18 In. 325.00
Sign, National Farm Loan Assn., Porcelain, 2 Sides, Cream, Green, 18 x 36 In. ....120.00 to 150.00
Sign, Nesbitt's Mileage Chart, West Fargo, North Dakota, Metal Frame, 7 x 31 In. 50.00
Sign, Newton's Pen & Ink Store, Hanging, Wooden, Frame, 29 In. 120.00
Sign, No Smoking, Black On White, Porcelain, 2 1/2 x 10 In. 44.00
Sign, Nu-Grape Soda, Bottle Of Soda With Sandwich On Plate, 13 x 10 In. 55.00
Sign, O.E. Ames & Son, Boat Builders, Wooden Frame, 21 x 72 In. 200.00
Sign, Old Crow Bourbon, Reverse On Glass, Tin Frame, 7 x 10 In. 28.00
Sign, Old Dad Chew, Old Black Man With Wild Cat, Red, Blue, 8 1/2 x 11 In. 20.00
Sign, Old Dutch Cleanser, Red Ground, Yellow Lettering, Tin Lithograph, 12 3/4 In. 176.00
Sign, Old Dutch Cleanser, Tin, 6 3/8 x 13 1/2 In. 65.00
Sign, Orange Crush, Bottle Cap, Tin, Round, 37 In. 110.00
Sign, Orange Crush, Molded, Plastic, 11 x 9 In. 45.00
Sign, Orange Drink, 10 Cents, Wooden Frame, 5 x 39 In. 110.00
Sign, Ovaltine, England, 18 x 12 In. 187.00
Sign, Owego Bridge Co., Port Jervis, New York, Tin, 19 x 13 In. 330.00
Sign, Pabst Blue Ribbon, 2 Bottles With Plate Of Oysters, 14 x 18 In. 178.00
Sign, Pabst Blue Ribbon, Window Bar, Turquoise, Plastic, 1970, 22 x 17 1/2 In. 173.00
Sign, Pabst Extracts, Victorian Woman, Stuart Travis, Early 1900s, 7 x 34 In. 150.00
Sign, Paul Jones & Co., Rye Whiskey, Tin, Frame, 1903, 22 1/2 x 28 1/2 In. 770.00
Sign, Pawn Shop, Money To Loan, Wooden, Wire, 6 x 7 Ft. 110.00
Sign, Pennzoil, 2 Sides, 18 x 22 In. 6.00
Sign, Pennzoil, Curb, Iron Frame, 23 1/2 x 21 In. 385.00
Sign, Pepsodent Toothpaste, Ain't Dis Sumpin!, Stand-Up, 1930, 54 x 21 In. 880.00
Sign, Peters Ammunition, Geese Gaggling Around Farmer's Pond, 21 x 15 In. 575.00
Sign, Philco Radio, Light-Up, Painted Wood, 35 In. 55.00
Sign, Picadilly Cigars, Tin Over Cardboard, Self-Framed, 21 1/4 x 13 In. 280.00
Sign, Pig Tail Crooks, Red Paper, 6 x 16 In. 30.00
Sign, Pine Tree Stores, Home Owned & Operated, Porcelain, 19 x 24 In. 295.00
Sign, Pipe, Stained To Simulate Briar, 1930, 19 In. 350.00
Sign, Plumber, Pointed Finger, Gold & Black Sandpaper, 2 Sides, 12 x 36 In. 350.00
Sign, Pocket Watch, Sheet Metal, Plexiglas Cover, 49 In. 550.00
Sign, Poll Parrot Shoes, Neon, Porcelain, 48 x 16 1/2 In. 1980.00
Sign, Postal Telegraph, 2 Sides, Porcelain, Oval, 24 x 30 In. 600.00
Sign, Poulson's Tours Of Russia & Trans-Siberian Railway, Painted, 47 x 26 In. 2415.00

Sign, Power Lube Motor Oil, Porcelain, 28 x 20 In. 770.00
Sign, Providence Washington Insurance, Tin Lithograph, 20 x 26 In. 550.00
Sign, Pure Rye Whiskey, Tin, Frame, 1903, 2 x 28 1/2 In. 990.00
Sign, Pyrex, You Can Be A Better Cook, Countertop, Light-Up, 9 1/2 x 19 In. 295.00
Sign, R. Roy, Pocket Watch Shape, Painted, Tin-Covered Wood, Maine 650.00
Sign, Railway Express Agency, Fiberboard, 2 Sides, Metal Handle, 25 x 19 1/2 In. 60.00
Sign, RCA, His Master's Voice, Porcelain, 2 Sides, 18 x 24 In. 2640.00
Sign, Reading Brewing Co., Tin Lithograph, Wooden Frame, 1900s, 36 x 48 In. 852.00
Sign, Reddy Kilowatt, 11 x 14 In. 210.00
Sign, Remington Chain Saws, Red, White, Gray, Sheet Metal, 1950, 8 x 3 In. 92.00
Sign, Remington Rifles, Let Us Show Your Remington Rifles, Cardboard, 25 x 5 In. 176.00
Sign, Rexall, Porcelain, 70 x 46 In. 225.00
Sign, Rock Island Lines, Rocky Mountain Limited, Tin Lithograph, 1907, 26 x 46 In. ... 330.00
Sign, Rolling Rock Premium Beer, Chateugay, Kentucky Derby Winner, 11 x 14 In. 45.00
Sign, Rooney's Malt Whiskey, We Challenge Them All, Tin, Self-Framed, 25 x 20 In. ... 1650.00
Sign, Rosenblatt Wine, Paper Lithograph, Lettered Frame, 18 x 25 In. 70.00
Sign, Royal Crown Cola, Beach Couple Holding Bottle, Cardboard, 28 x 11 In. 39.00
Sign, Royal Crown Cola, Best By Taste, Embossed, Red, Yellow, Tin, 22 x 52 In. 125.00
Sign, Royal Crown Cola, Die Cut, 2 Piece, 12 In. 365.00
Sign, Royal Crown Cola, Red, Blue, Blackboard, 20 x 28 In. 65.00
Sign, Royal Crown Cola, The Fresher Refresher, Red, White, Blue, 27 x 19 In. 78.00
Sign, Schlitz Beer In Bottles, Light-Up, Plastic, 1970, 11 x 11 x 1 3/4 In. 34.00
Sign, Schlitz, Reverse On Glass, 12 1/2 x 12 1/2 In. 70.00
Sign, Schmidt's Of Philadelphia, Light-Up, Plastic On Metal Frame, 20 x 13 In. 50.00
Sign, Schuco, Patent, 8 In. 95.00
Sign, Shaftoe Optician, Double-Sided Glass Globe, Wall Mount Sconce, 12 In. 410.00
Sign, Shoe, Wing Tip, Man's, Leather & Wood, Metal Studs, 71 1/2 In. 1150.00
Sign, Shredded Wheat, Straight Arrow Display, Cardboard, Easel Type, 1951, 66 In. 150.00
Sign, Silver Spring Ale, Canada's Best, Gold, Red, 11 x 17 1/2 In. 28.00
Sign, Skates Sharpened, Hanging, Painted Wood, 2 Sides, 70 In. 357.00
Sign, Smith Bros., 4 Gentlemen Enjoying Smith Bros. Beer, 15 x 21 In. 115.00
Sign, Smoke J.A. Cigars, Porcelain, Blue, Yellow & White, 16 x 16 In. 200.00
Sign, Smoke The Imperial Club 5 Cents Cigar, Tin, Black Ground, 10 x 13 3/4 In. 143.00
Sign, Smoke Victory, Cardboard, Black Ground, White Lettering, 6 3/4 In. 44.00
Sign, Snow King Baking Powder, Santa Claus In Sleigh, 36 In. 412.00
Sign, Sprite, Tin, Bottle, 1934, 45 In. 1100.00
Sign, Squire's, Pig With Sign Center, Self-Framed, Tin, 1906, 23 1/3 x 19 1/2 In. 1850.00
Sign, Stag Beer, Light-Up, Plastic, 1970, 16 1/2 x 14 x 5 1/2 In. 31.00
Sign, Standard Oil, Red Crown, Porcelain, 12 x 15 In. 85.00
Sign, Standard Sewing Machine Co., White Dove, 12 x 16 In. 83.00
Sign, Star Tobacco, Frame, Porcelain, 26 x 13 In. 440.00
Sign, Sterling Tobacco, Smoke & Chew, Yellow Ground, Porcelain, 12 x 36 In. 121.00
Sign, Stroh's Beer, Red Signal Lantern, Nautical Scene, 1970s, 20 x 9 1/2 In. 31.00
Sign, Stroh's Fire-Brewed Beer, Light-Up, Plastic, 1970s, 11 x 19 In. 35.00
Sign, Surge Milker, Metal, Painted, 12 x 18 In. 45.00
Sign, Swan Lager, 13 x 13 In. 5.00
Sign, Sylvania Radio & TV Tubes, 2 Sides, Tin, 31 1/2 x 42 In. 185.00
Sign, Tailor's, Large Shears, Forged Iron 431.00
Sign, Tavern, Black, Molded Frame, 1845 With Gilt Eagle, 43 x 44 In. 5750.00
Sign, Texaco Fire-Chief Gasoline, Porcelain, 12 x 18 In. 95.00
Sign, Texaco Motor Oil Lube, Red, White, Black, Green, 5 In. 357.00
Sign, Thompson's, Watch, 27 In. 1375.00
Sign, Titusville, Florida, Promoting Climate, Yellow Arrow, Black Lettering, 27 In. 69.00
Sign, To Hire, Wooden, 19th Century, 18 x 5 1/2 In. 350.00
Sign, Tom Moore, America's Favorite 10 Cents Cigar, Red Ground, Tin, 12 x 10 In. 908.00
Sign, Town Talk Bread, Porcelain, 14 x 22 1/4 In. 522.00
Sign, Trade, Eyeglasses, 2 Sides, Outdoor 1100.00
Sign, Tree Brand Shoes, Battreall Shoe Co., Red Ground, Tree In Center, 18 In. 275.00
Sign, True Fruit, Fresh Fruits On Table, Tin, 25 x 37 In. 115.00
Sign, U.S. Marine Cut Plug, Tin, Frame, 33 x 24 In. 2310.00
Sign, Use Perry Davis' Pain Killer, Paper On Canvas, Roll Down, 12 x 28 In. 425.00
Sign, Vacuum Oil, Horse, Paper Lithograph, 1878, 17 x 21 In. 99.00
Sign, Valley Forge Beer, Plastic Baseball Player, 8 x 14 In. 143.00

Advertising, Sign, Winchester Cartridges & Guns, Tin, 1914, 30 x 36 In.

Advertising, Sign, Winchester Rifles, 2 Mastiff Type Dogs, H.R. Poore, Frame

Sign, Vernor's, Chalkboard, 13 x 23 In. 175.00
Sign, Viceroy, Filtered Smoke With The Finest Flavor, Metal, 26 x 17 In. 35.00
Sign, Vintage Conductor Pointing To Yellow Car, Niagara Falls, 28 x 21 In. 230.00
Sign, Waitte & Bond Blackstone Cigar, Porcelain, 36 x 12 In. 100.00
Sign, Walk-Over Shoes, Brass, 2 x 15 In. 785.00
Sign, Wall Drug, Plastic, 12 x 21 In. 4.00
Sign, Waverly Cigarettes, Porcelain, 24 x 28 In. 225.00
Sign, We Sell Gold Seal Boots & Overshoes, Burnt Orange Ground, 18 1/4 In. 187.00
Sign, Welsbach Lights & Mantles, Tin, Self-Framed, 1905, 33 x 28 In. 660.00
Sign, Western Winchester, Hunter, Shooting At Running Rabbit, 40 x 26 In. 517.00
Sign, Whistle Soda Pop, 1930s, 15 x 36 In. 75.00
Sign, Whistle, Thirsty? Just Whistle Bottle Cap, Orange, Blue, White, 28 In. 30.00
Sign, Willie Kool, Cigarette Store, 1941, 10 1/2 x 15 1/2 In. 25.00
Sign, Willy's Jeep, Service, Porcelain, 42 In. 695.00
Sign, Winchester Cartridges & Guns, Tin, 1914, 30 x 36 In. ....*Illus* 1210.00
Sign, Winchester Loaded Shotgun Shells, Black Man, Skunks, Log, 1908, 32 x 39 In. ... 2206.00
Sign, Winchester Rifles, 2 Mastiff Type Dogs, H.R. Poore, Frame ....*Illus* 4675.00
Sign, Winchester Western Sporting Arms & Ammunition, 12 x 20 In. 210.00
Sign, Winchester, Bullet Heads For Rifle, Pistol, Tin, 17 1/2 x 11 1/2 .... 95.00
Sign, Winchester-Western, Phillip R. Goodwin, Enameled, 11 1/2 x 9 In. 105.00
Sign, Wonder Bread, Builds Strong Bodies 8 Ways, Tin, 13 x 20 In. 150.00
Sign, Woonsocket Rubbers, Boots, Shoes, Paper On Pasteboard, 33 x 23 1/2 In. 1595.00
Sign, Wrigley's, 1930s, 22 x 12 In. 98.00
Sign, X-Ray Headache Tablets, Orange Letters, Black Waxed Ground, 1910, 5 x 13 In. .. 37.00
Sign, Yankee Girl Tobacco, Light Blue Ground, 11 1/2 In. 60.00
Sign, Yankee Girl Tobacco, Pack Of Tobacco, Tin, 6 1/2 x 20 In. 192.00
Sign, Yeast Foam Makes Delicious Buckwheat Cakes, Girl, Paper, 10 x 15 In. ....120.00 to 145.00
Sign, Yellow Kid, Say! Get The High Toned 3 Cents Cigar, 8 x 17 In. 825.00
Sign, Yuengling Beer Ale & Porter, Tin On Cardboard, Horse, 20 x 22 In. 140.00
Sign, Yuengling Beer, Factory Scene, Mirror, Wooden Frame, 9 x 12 In. 13.00
Sign, Zenith, Glass, 13 x 19 1/4 In. 95.00
Sign, Zerolene Motor Oil, Diamond Shape, 2 Sides, Porcelain, 20 x 20 In. 600.00
Sign & Key Paddles, Texaco, Bathroom, Men & Women, 1974 .... 225.00
Silk, Cigarette, Northwestern University, Chicago, Flag, Seal, 1913, 4 x 5 1/2 In. 30.00
Silk, Cigarette, U.S. Naval Academy, Annapolis, 1913, 4 x 5 1/2 In. 30.00
Soap, Steamship Co. Fall River Line, New England 25.00
Soda Fountain, Bastian Blessing, Model 3554, Stainless Steel, 1950s 300.00
Soda Fountain, Clam Shell & Marble, 1932 .... 2000.00
Spoon, Howard Johnson, Pancake Man, Turner Turnpike, Holland, Oklahoma 45.00
Spoon, Jell-O, Girl Top 55.00
Spoon, Sterling Silver, Log Cabin Syrup, Towles 15.00
Stand, Gum, Clark's Teaberry, Clear, Gold Flashed Base 60.00
Stickpin, Moxie Man, Tin Lithograph, Die Cut, 1920s 78.00
Stickpin, Savage Arms Co., Indian Head, Metal, Enameled, 1935 .... 115.00
Stool, Fishing, Schlitz Beer, Metal, Vinyl, 1970 .... 20.00

Street Marker, Enjoy Grapette, Walk Safely, Brass, Unused . . . . .95.00 to 125.00
String Holder, Es-Ki-Mo Rubbers, 2 Sides 4400.00
String Holder, Holsum Bread, 2 Sides, Tin, 16 x 13 In. 440.00
String Holder, King Midas Flour, 2 Sides, Tin & Metal, Roll Of String, 20 x 15 In. 1540.00
String Holder, Red Goose Shoes 2090.00
Sugar & Creamer, Cover, Ken-L-Ration, Plastic 58.00
Sugar Bowl, For Cubes, Hody's Restaurants, Long Beach, Reed & Barton 19.00
Sugar Shaker & Creamer, Sugar Crisp Bear & Clown, F & F, 2 Piece 50.00
Table, Chrysler, Plymouth, Dodge & DeSoto Symbols Top, Wooden, 24 x 26 In. 360.00
Table, Monarch Foods, Wooden, 1920 . . . . 765.00
Table & Chair Set, 7-Up The Uncola, Unassembled, Child's, 1973, Box 30.00
Tablet Machine, W.T. Co., No. 25, Apothecary, Stenciled, Wooden, 1895, 10 In. 600.00
Tap Knob, Pabst, Ball Shape 25.00
Tape Dispenser, Star Kist, Charlie Tuna, Electric 10.00
Thermometers are listed in their own category.
Tie Bar, Reddy Kilowatt 35.00

Advertising tin cans or canisters were first used commercially in the
United States in 1819 and were called *tins*. The English language is
sometimes confusing. Today the word *tin* is used by most collectors to
describe many types of containers, including food tins, biscuit boxes,
roly poly tobacco containers, gunpowder cans, talcum powder sprin-
kle-top cans, cigarette flat-fifty tins, and more. Beer cans are listed in
their own category. Things made of undecorated tin are listed under
Tinware.

Tin, Admiral Rough Cut, Canister, Knob Top 220.00
Tin, All Nations Tobacco, Red Lettering, Burnt Orange Ground, 11 x 8 x 7 1/2 In. 525.00
Tin, American Rifle Team Coffee, 1 Lb. 125.00
Tin, Archer Oil, Red Indian Figure, Aircraft Grade, 1 Qt. 48.00
Tin, Atlantic Refining Co., Standard Household Lubricant, 5 In. 16.00
Tin, Avon, Smoker's Tooth Powder, Green, Blue, White, Chrome Top, 2 In. 34.00
Tin, Baker's Chocolate, Colonial Maid Serving Cocoa & Soda, 6 3/4 x 11 3/4 In. 198.00
Tin, Beech-Nut Cigars, 6 x 4 x 4 In. 35.00
Tin, Beech-Nut Coffee, Red, White, Blue, Green, 5 In. Diam. 34.00
Tin, Beech-Nut Coffee, Sample . . . . .50.00 to 55.00
Tin, Beehive Toffee, Figural, England 150.00
Tin, Ben-Hur Poultry Seasoning, 2 Oz. 6.00
Tin, Big Buster Yellow Popcorn, Contents, 10 Oz. 110.00
Tin, Biscuit, Huntley & Palmer, Book, Titled Literature 805.00
Tin, Black Cat Stove Polish, Round, Unopened 18.00
Tin, Blanke's Coffee Of St. Louis, Yellow, Green, Tin Cup, 1 Lb. 250.00
Tin, Blue Bird Coffee, 5 Lb. 275.00
Tin, Blue Parrot Coffee 5500.00
Tin, Bo-Kay Orange Blossom Talc, Brass-Colored Cap, Adopted 1936, 3 x 5 1/2 In. 25.00
Tin, Bond St. Pipe, Awning, Pocket 10.00
Tin, Bouquet Coffee, Red, 1 Lb. 100.00
Tin, Bowl Of Roses, Man, Fireplace, Pocket 125.00
Tin, Breakfast Cheer Coffee, Brown, Key, 1 Lb. 15.00
Tin, Buffalo Peanuts, Lithograph, 9 1/2 In. 203.00
Tin, Bulldog Cut Plug, Building, Vertical Pocket 360.00
Tin, Bunnie's Salted Peanuts, Red Ground, Lithograph, 11 1/4 In. 550.00
Tin, Bunte Marshmallow, Child Opening Can Of Marshmallows, 1914, 2 x 4 In. 105.00
Tin, Buster Brown Cigars, Can On Table, 6 x 4 In. 4500.00
Tin, Butter Nut Coffee, Red, Sample 50.00
Tin, Campbell's Horse Foot Remedy, Horse Picture, 1892, 3 3/4 x 7 In. 60.00
Tin, Capitol Mills Coffee, 5 x 3 In. 155.00
Tin, Capri Talc, Berries, Flowers, Brass Top, 3 x 1 1/2 x 5 3/4 In. 20.00
Tin, Captain John Orderley's, Owl Drug Co., Rectangular, Contents 110.00
Tin, Cardinal Cut Plug Tobacco, Bird, Vertical Pocket 3220.00
Tin, Cayenne Pepper, 2 Ladies On Sides, Lithograph, 7 1/2 In. 154.00
Tin, Chambly-Rose Perfumed Talc, White, Orange, Plastic Cap, 4 1/8 x 7 1/2 In. 15.00
Tin, Checker Strawberry Jam, Lithograph, 4 3/4 In. 176.00
Tin, Checkers Tobacco, Canister, Knob Top 485.00

Tin, Chef Peanut Butter, Chef On Front, Berdan Co., Toledo, Ohio, 4 In. 600.00
Tin, Chesterfield Cigarette, Flat 12.00
Tin, Coffee, Luzianne, White 185.00
Tin, Comfort Powder, Nurse On Side, Red Lettering, 3 1/2 In. 121.00
Tin, Comfort Powder, Smaller Picture Of Nurse On Side, 4 In. 275.00
Tin, Crawford's Biscuit, Bus, Figural, 1920s 3500.00
Tin, Crisco, Blue On White Ground, 50 Lb. 77.00
Tin, CXL Snap Shot Powder, Black Paint, Falling Duck In Circle, 1 Lb. 75.00
Tin, D'Jer Kiss Talcum 25.00
Tin, Dan Patch Cut Plug Tobacco, Yellow, Metal, Early 1900s, 6 x 3 1/2 x 3 In. 185.00
Tin, Dead Shot Powder, Brown Lacquer, Hunter & Dog Label, 1 Lb. 115.00
Tin, Delicious Oysters, 1 Pt. 65.00
Tin, Dill's Best Rubbed Cube Cut, Vertical Pocket 75.00
Tin, Dixie Queen Cut Plug Smoking Tobacco, Portrait, 1 Lb. 120.00
Tin, Doan's Pills, Miniature 20.00
Tin, Dr. David Roberts Badger Balm, Round, 2 3/4 x 3 1/2 In. 40.00
Tin, Dr. J.D. Kellogg's Asthma Remedy, Square, 2 1/2 x 5 In. 75.00
Tin, Dr. Legear's Udder Ointment, Round, 2 1/2 x 3 In. 50.00
Tin, Dr. Lyon's Toothpowder, Miniature 20.00
Tin, Dr. White's Cough Drops, Green & Black, 8 x 5 In. 125.00
Tin, Droste Cocoa, Holland, Sample 100.00
Tin, Duff's Peanut Butter, Red Lettering, Orange Ground, 1 3/4 In. 210.00
Tin, DuPont Ballistite Smokeless Powder, Label, Oval, 5 In. 90.00
Tin, DuPont Powder, 2 Dogs, Green Paper Label, 8 Oz. 65.00
Tin, Edgeworth Plug Slice, Larus Bros Co., 4 x 3 x 2 In. 38.00
Tin, Emeraude By Coty, Vines, Flowers, Slide Top, 3 x 1 x 4 3/4 In. 15.00
Tin, Evening In Paris, Talcum Powder, Blue Ribs, Label, 4 5/8 In. 15.00
Tin, Florient Talc, Sample 45.00
Tin, Folger's Coffee, 1931, 1 Lb. 18.00
Tin, Forest & Stream, 2 Men In Canoe, Pocket 525.00
Tin, Forest & Stream, Fisherman, Pocket 150.00
Tin, Fresher Refresher, Red, White, Blue, Gray Crown, Diamonds 125.00
Tin, Gold Circle Condom, Contents . . . . .10.00 to 20.00
Tin, Gold Dust Tobacco, 3 Prospectors, Vertical Pocket 4000.00
Tin, Golden West Coffee, Cowgirl, 3 Lb. 205.00
Tin, Granger Rough Cut Pipe Tobacco, Vertical Pocket 1100.00
Tin, Granulated 54 Sample, Tobacco Leaf In Center, Blue, Yellow, Pocket 220.00
Tin, H-O Cut Plug, 4 x 6 In. 44.00
Tin, Half & Half Tobacco, Red, White, Black, Green, Pocket, 4 1/2 x 3 x 1 In. 43.00
Tin, Half & Half, Sample 165.00
Tin, Hatchet Brand Coffee, 1 Lb. 35.00
Tin, Hi-Plane Tobacco, 4 Engine, Pocket . . . . .210.00 to 275.00
Tin, Hoffmann's Old Time Coffee, Since 1876, Screw Top 75.00
Tin, Home Run Cigars, Round 6500.00
Tin, Huntley & Palmer Biscuit, Book, Titled Literature 805.00
Tin, Huntley & Palmer Biscuit, Glasses 402.00
Tin, Huntley & Palmer Biscuit, Picnic Hamper 200.00
Tin, Huntley & Palmer Biscuit, Sentry, Box, 1909, 7 x 2 1/2 In. 247.00
Tin, Huntley & Palmer, Biscuit, Pair Of Books, 1870 . . . . 1050.00
Tin, Indian Premium Motorcycle Oil, Red, Yellow & White, 1 Qt. 100.00
Tin, Instant Postum Cereal, Postum Cereal Co., Battle Creek, Michigan, 2 In. 44.00
Tin, Jap Rose Talc 75.00
Tin, John A. Andrews & Co., Boston Tea Party Graphics, 1900, 5 x 6 In. 145.00
Tin, Jumbo Peanuts, 10 Lb. 350.00
Tin, June Knight Talcum, Coat Of Arms, Red & Yellow, Contents, 2 x 1 x 6 In. 12.00
Tin, Kamels Condom, Camel Cigarettes Look-Alike 150.00
Tin, Khush-Amadi Talc, Cluster Of Flower Petals 3410.00
Tin, Kibbs Salted Jumbo Peanuts, Springfield, Maine, 10 Lb. 125.00
Tin, Kingan's Lard, 1950s, 4 Lb. 20.00
Tin, Kiwi Boot Polish, Picture On Cover 20.00
Tin, Klein's Cocoa, White Lettering, Black Ground, Lithograph, 1 3/4 In. 209.00
Tin, Larkin Coffee, 3 Lb. 35.00
Tin, Light Sweet Burley Tobacco, Red Lettering, Orange Ground, 10 3/4 In. 242.00

Tin, Little Buster Popcorn 75.00
Tin, Long Run Lubricant 40.00
Tin, Lucky Strike Roll Cut, Canister, Knob Top 345.00
Tin, Lucky Strike, Roll Cut, Pocket, 4 In. 85.00
Tin, Mallard Cocoa, Embossed Child & Product 1300.00
Tin, Mammoth Peanuts, Picture Of Mammoth, 10 Lb. 185.00
Tin, Marcelle Talc, Teal, Baby Girl Picture 160.00
Tin, Martha White Coffee, 1 Lb. 22.00
Tin, Maryland Club, Clubhouse In Front, Orange Lithography, Pocket 220.00
Tin, Maxwell House Coffee, 1914, 3 Lb. 30.00
Tin, Maxwell House, Key Open, 1 Lb. 4.00
Tin, Mayflower, Silver Embossed, Flat, Pocket 95.00
Tin, Mayo's Cut Plug, Coffee, Hinged Lid, Round 155.00
Tin, Mocha Java Coffee, 1 Lb. 65.00
Tin, Monadnock Brand Coffee, Holbrook Grocery Co., Yellow, Black, 6 x 4 In. 77.00
Tin, Monarch Cocoa, 4 Sides, Mustard Center, Dark Green Ground, 3 In. 82.00
Tin, Monopol Cigarette, Flat Pocket 135.00
Tin, Montgomery Ward Japanese Tea, 1913, 5 Lb. 85.00
Tin, Mutton Tallow With Camphor, Yellow Sheep, 3 In. 15.00
Tin, Myrtle Tobacco, Lisley, Pocket 50.00
Tin, Nabisco, Boy & Girl At Lake, With Wagon, 1 Lb. 15.00
Tin, Natco Cream Of Tartar, Paper Label 4.00
Tin, National Biscuit Company, Green, Red Straps, Top Handle, 10 1/2 In. 65.00
Tin, Nature's Remedy Tablet, Doctor Picture, 3 x 2 In. 65.00
Tin, Navy Smoking Tobacco, Blue & Black, Trademark, G.W. Gail & Ax, 7 x 5 In. 165.00
Tin, Niggerhair Tobacco, Yellow, 7 x 5 In. 495.00
Tin, North Pole Cut Plug, Polar Bears, Oval Small Top, 6 x 4 x 4 In. 185.00
Tin, Old Dutch Cleanser, Dated 1907, Contents, Sample 67.00
Tin, Old Master Coffee, Master Wearing Fur Coat, Yellow, Green, 1 Lb. 44.00
Tin, Orcico Cigar, Indian Chief Front, Battlefield Back, 6 x 6 x 4 In. ... 300.00
Tin, Ovaltine, Wander Company, Switzerland, 4 Lb. 18.00
Tin, Peacocks, Condom 22.00
Tin, Penders Old Virginia Fruitcake, Mammy Serving Plantation Family 45.00
Tin, Pep Boys Motor Oil, Yellow, Blue & Green, 2 Gal. 105.00
Tin, Perfect Pipe Tobacco, Cobb, Bates, Xerxa, Boston, Pocket 350.00
Tin, Phonograph Needle, Alfred Friedrich Portrait, Plane, 2 1/2 In. 90.00
Tin, Pickaninny Peanut Butter 90.00
Tin, Pioneer Coffee, Conestoga Wagon, 1 Lb. 100.00
Tin, Pipe Major, Butler With Pipe, Pocket 250.00
Tin, Postum, Sample, Lithograph, 1 3/4 In. 27.00
Tin, Pow Wow Brand Peanuts, Indian In Center, Brown Ground, 8 1/2 In. 357.00
Tin, Prince Albert Tobacco, Pocket 5.00
Tin, Prize Winner Tobacco, Horses, Box, 4 x 3 x 1 In. 80.00
Tin, Pure As Gold Motor Oil, 1 Qt., 5 1/2 In. 275.00
Tin, Race Match, Barber Match Co., Black Paint, Red Striping, Transfer, 22 In. 220.00
Tin, Red & White Red Pepper, 1 1/4 Oz. 5.00
Tin, Red Bell Coffee, 1 Lb. 150.00
Tin, Rexall's Orderlies Laxative 4.00
Tin, Richmond Straight Cut, Chewing Tobacco, 4 1/2 x 3 x 1 In. 45.00
Tin, Rin Tin Tin, Chalk, 17 In. 55.00
Tin, Roly Poly, Business Man, 1980s 35.00
Tin, Roly Poly, Dutchman, Mayo ....435.00 to 605.00
Tin, Roly Poly, Mammy, Mayo ....400.00 to 860.00
Tin, Roly Poly, Satisfied Customer, Mayo 195.00
Tin, Roly Poly, Singer, 1980s 35.00
Tin, Roly Poly, Singing Waiter, Dixie Queen 400.00
Tin, Roly Poly, Singing Waiter, Mayo, 7 x 6 In. ....215.00 to 700.00
Tin, Roly Poly, Storekeeper, Navy Coat, Mayo 195.00
Tin, Roly Poly, Storekeeper, Teal Jacket, Mayo 260.00
Tin, Rose Leaf Chewing Tobacco, Bullfrog Holding Compass, Flat, Pocket 295.00
Tin, Royalty Assortment, Sugar Wafers Fit For A King, Paper Over Tin, 1923, 10 Oz. ... 75.00
Tin, Runkel's Cocoa, Dark Brown Ground, Lithograph, 1 3/4 In. 82.00

Tin, Salina Biscuit, Uneeda Bakers, Sailor Painted On Sides, 7 In. 65.00
Tin, Schepp's Coconut, Green, 5 1/2 x 3 x 3 In. 75.00
Tin, Sheik Condom, Man On Horse, Orange 77.00
Tin, Simmons Keen Kutter Paint, 1 Gal. 55.00
Tin, Sinclair Lighter Fluid 20.00
Tin, Stuart's Dyspepsia Tablets 15.00
Tin, Suisse Chocolate Clickers, 1950s 10.00
Tin, Sunshine Biscuit Co., Liberty Bell, Octagonal, 9 1/2 x 3 1/4 In. 175.00
Tin, Sweet Cuba Fine Cut Tobacco, Light Green, 2 x 8 In. 30.00
Tin, Sweet Cuba Tobacco, Lithograph, 10 3/4 In. 132.00
Tin, Sweet Georgia Brown, Hair Pomade 18.00
Tin, Swell Blend Coffee, 1 Lb. 75.00
Tin, Swift's Lard, 4 Lb. 10.00
Tin, T. & B. Tobacco, Canada, 6 x 4 x 3 In. 85.00
Tin, Tea Room Coffee, Marshall Field & Co., 1 Lb. 22.00
Tin, Teenie Weenie Toffees, Monarch, Round, 1 Lb. 175.00
Tin, Three Feathers, Pocket 375.00
Tin, Tidewater Motor Oil, 1960s 5.00
Tin, Tiger Chewing Tobacco, 5 Cents Packages, Red Ground, 11 In. 297.00
Tin, Tiny-Tot Bath Powder, Round, Contents 70.00
Tin, Tobacco, Sunflower Cut Plug, Square Corner 1595.00
Tin, Tom Sturgis Pretzel, Marked 35 Cents, 10 In. 50.00
Tin, Tooth Powder, California, Lithograph, 3 1/2 In. 121.00
Tin, Towle's Log Cabin Syrup, Frontier Inn, 6 x 6 In. 375.00
Tin, Towle's Log Cabin Syrup, Frontier Jail, 6 x 6 In. 325.00
Tin, Ultrex, Condom 5.00
Tin, Unica Torino Biscuit, Train Engine, Polychrome Design, 23 1/2 In. 203.00
Tin, Union Leader, Uncle Sam With Pipe, Yellow, Pocket ....60.00 to 100.00
Tin, Vantine's Talc Powder, Mother With Baby 1375.00
Tin, Vita Brand Marine Sprats, 5 Lb. 45.00
Tin, Voegele's, Lithograph, Red Lettering, 11 1/4 In. 165.00
Tin, Wells Richardson, Lithograph, 11 1/4 In. 187.00
Tin, Western Petro-Carbo Salve, Contents, 4 1/2 In. 25.00
Tin, Wild Cherry Sweet Scotch Snuff, Lithograph, Mustard Ground, 1 3/4 In. 82.00
Tin, Winchester Talc, Yellow Ground, Lithograph, 4 3/4 In. 187.00
Tin, Wing Coffee, Key Wind, Gift Box, 1 Lb. 200.00
Tin, Woolson's Vienna Coffee, Sample 85.00
Tin, Yankee Boy, Cut Plug, Boy With Blond Hair, Pocket 425.00
Tin, Yankee Boy, Cut Plug, Boy With Brown Hair, Vertical Pocket 650.00
Tin, Yucatan Gum, Green, 6 x 6 x 4 In. 475.00
Tin, Z.B.T. Baby Powder, Sample 18.00
Tin, Roly Poly, Mammy, Mayo 860.00

Advertising tip trays are decorated metal trays less than 5 inches in
diameter. They were placed on the table or counter to hold either the
bill or the coins that were left as a tip. Change receivers could be made
of glass, plastic, or metal. They were kept on the counter near the cash
register and held the money passed back and forth by the cashier.
Related items may be listed in the Advertising category under Change
Receivers.

Tip Tray, Arnholt-Schaefer Brewery, Philadelphia, 4 In. 82.00
Tip Tray, Bailey's Pure Rye, Philadelphia Distiller, Late 1800s, 4 In. 36.00
Tip Tray, Bartholomay Beer, In Kegs & Bottles, Rochester, New York, 4 3/4 In. 275.00
Tip Tray, Boston Herald, 3 1/2 In. 192.00
Tip Tray, Cottolene, Best For Shortening, Best For Frying, Tin Lithograph, 4 1/4 In. 104.00
Tip Tray, Crescent & Mapleine Syrup, Metal, 4 1/4 In. 49.00
Tip Tray, De Laval, Woman Utilizing A Cream Separator, 4 1/4 In. 287.00
Tip Tray, Doral Cigarettes, 4 In. 25.00
Tip Tray, Dubois Budweiser & Wurburger, Pre-Prohibition, American Made, 5 In. 200.00
Tip Tray, Evervess, Pepsi-Cola, Parrot 45.00
Tip Tray, Evervess, Sparkling Water, Parrot 50.00
Tip Tray, Eye-Fix, Red & Blue Edge, 4 1/4 In. 357.00

Tip Tray, Fairy Soap, Lithograph, Advertising On Reverse, 4 1/4 In. . . . . .65.00 to 145.00
Tip Tray, Ferro-Phos, Brown, Black, Blue & White, 4 1/2 In. 155.00
Tip Tray, Frank Jones Homestead Ale, 5 In. 82.00
Tip Tray, Gallagher & Burton Black Label Whiskey, Old Man In Center, 4 1/4 In. 43.00
Tip Tray, Gold Grain Belt Beers, Minneapolis Beer, 4 In. 55.00
Tip Tray, Gold Seal Champagne, 4 In. 69.00
Tip Tray, Gottfried Krueger High Grade Beer, 4 In. 35.00
Tip Tray, Greenfield Tap & Die Corp., Metal, 4 1/2 x 6 1/2 In. 330.00
Tip Tray, Gypsy Hosiery, Tin Lithograph, 6 In. 77.00
Tip Tray, Heptol Splits For Health's Sake, 4 1/4 In. 313.00
Tip Tray, Home Beer, Dallas Brewery, Dallas, Texas, 4 1/4 In. 137.00
Tip Tray, Hyroler Whiskey, Louis S. Adler & Co., 4 1/4 In. 60.00
Tip Tray, Incandescent Light & Stove Co., Tin Lithograph .75.00 to 100.00
Tip Tray, Jenny Aero Gasoline, Black, Orange, Cream, Metal, 4 In. 220.00
Tip Tray, King's Pure Malt, Pre-Prohibition, 4 1/2 x 6 In. .27.00 to 82.00
Tip Tray, Krueger Beer-Ale, Early 40s, 4 In. 16.00
Tip Tray, Lakeside Club 350.00
Tip Tray, Liberty Beer, American Brewing Co., 4 1/4 In. 330.00
Tip Tray, Lieber's Gold Medal Beer, Indianapolis Brewing Co., 5 In. 82.00
Tip Tray, Light Running Domestic Sewing Machine, 5 3/4 In. 275.00
Tip Tray, Mellwood Whiskey, Pre-Prohibition 55.00
Tip Tray, Monroe Brewing Co., Rochester, N.Y., 4 1/4 In. 77.00
Tip Tray, Old Reliable Coffee, Gold On Black Edge, 4 1/2 In. 175.00
Tip Tray, Old Reliable Liquor Dealers, Bust Of Woman, 1907 . . . . 45.00
Tip Tray, Old Scotch Whiskey, Porcelain, 6 x 4 1/2 In. 50.00
Tip Tray, Pippins 5 Cents Cigar, White Lettering, Red Ground, 5 1/2 In. 231.00
Tip Tray, President Suspenders, Early 1900s 75.00
Tip Tray, Red Raven, Little Girl, 6 x 4 In. 350.00
Tip Tray, Red Raven, Standing Over A Glass Of Red Raven, 6 1/4 x 4 1/4 In. 126.00
Tip Tray, Robert Burns Cigar, Round 25.00
Tip Tray, Rockford High-Grade Watches, Tin Lithograph, 3 1/4 In. 105.00
Tip Tray, Sears, 4 In. 50.00
Tip Tray, Stegmaier Brewing Co., Wilkes-Barre, 4 1/4 In. 120.00
Tip Tray, Terre Haute Brewing Co., Green & Blue Edges, 4 1/2 In. 170.00
Tip Tray, White Top Club Special Champagne, Early 1900s 45.00
Tip Tray, Zipp's Flavoring Extracts, 4 In. 110.00
Toothbrush, McDonald's, Good Morning 2.00
Toy, AC Spark Plugs, Sparkplug The Horse, In Bathtub, Die Cast, 1930s 195.00
Toy, Acrobat, Howel's Root Beer, Wooden 145.00
Toy, Airplane, Budweiser, Red, White, Blue, 9 In. 20.00
Toy, Bear, Maxwell Coffee-Loving, Bear Pours Coffee, Plush, Japan, 10 In. 40.00
Toy, Boat, Dairy Queen Banana Split, Plastic, Cone Top, 1950s 5.00
Toy, Bug, Raid, Remote Control 295.00
Toy, Bugs Bunny, McDonald's, Super Bugs, Looney Toons, 1991 . . . . 1.00
Toy, Hawaiian Man, Trader Vic's Restaurant, Vinyl, 3 In. 100.00
Toy, Kool-Aid Dancin' Man 22.00
Toy, Lark Walking Cigarette Pack, Windup, Unused 44.00
Toy, Lucky, 101 Dalmatians, McDonald's, 1991 . . . . 2.00
Toy, McNugget Buddies, McDonald's 1.00
Toy, Michelin Man, Windup, Box, 3 In. 25.00
Toy, Puppet, Crackle, Kellogg's Rice Krispies, Push 25.00
Toy, Sleepy Bear, Travel Lodge, Vinyl, 4 In. 200.00
Toy, Tasmanian Devil, McDonald's, Looney Toons, 1991 . . . . 1.00
Toy, Truck, Mr. Softee, Friction, Japan, 4 In. 45.00
Trade Stimulator, Bicycle, Wooden Base, 13 1/2 x 18 1/2 In. 4675.00
Tray, A-1 Pilsner Beer, 12 In. 18.00
Tray, Abe Freeman Liquor Dealer, Street Scene 4500.00
Tray, Baker's Chocolate, Product Boxes, Gold Ground, 13 1/2 x 16 1/2 In. . . . . . . .425.00 to 475.00
Tray, Barmann Beer, For Pure Pleasure, Red, White, Black, Metal, 12 In. 51.00
Tray, Bartels Beer, Round, 18 In. 40.00
Tray, Belmont Beer, 14 In. 182.00
Tray, Bevo Beer, Wood Grain Border, Horses Pulling Wagon, 10 1/2 x 13 1/4 In. 88.00

Tray, Black Horse Ale, Porcelain, 13 In. 25.00
Tray, Blatz Beer, Milwaukee's First Bottle Beer, Red, White, Blue, Gold, 12 In. 45.00
Tray, Burgomaster Beer, Red, White, Green, Fitzgerald Brewing Co., Metal, 13 In. 29.00
Tray, C. Ambrosius & Son Bottlers, Tin Lithograph, 13 In. 105.00
Tray, Crowell's Ice Cream, Children At Birthday Party 975.00
Tray, Dawes Black Horse Ale & Porter Beer, Porcelain, 13 In. 77.00
Tray, Derby Cream Ale, Red, White, Blue, Black, National Brewing Co., 12 In. 63.00
Tray, Fairy Soap, Round, 13 In. 85.00
Tray, Falstaff Beer, Tin Lithograph, Round, Box, 1960s, 24 In. 175.00
Tray, Fantan Gum 485.00
Tray, Fehr's Ambrosia, Nectar Of The Gods, Greek Scene, 13 In. 467.00
Tray, Fort Schuyzer Ales & Lager, Black, Red & White, 11 1/4 In. 45.00
Tray, Frank's Pale Dry Ginger Ale, Lithograph Of Bottle, 1930s 55.00
Tray, Fred Bauernschmidt's Brewery, 13 x 16 In. 1155.00
Tray, Golden Colorado Beer, Adolph Coors, Mountain Scene, 13 In. 242.00
Tray, Hanley's Peerless Ale, Red, White, Black, Metal, Rhode Island, 12 In. 36.00
Tray, Harvard Ale, Aluminum, 13 In. 10.00
Tray, Hellgate Brewery, 13 In. 85.00
Tray, Hensler Premium Dry Beer, 12 In. 110.00
Tray, Hires Root Beer, Victorian Woman, Logo At Corners, Haskell Coffin 248.00
Tray, Hyroler Whiskey Beer, Metal, Round, 12 In. 77.00
Tray, International Brewing Co., Lady In Center, Metal, 12 In. 75.00
Tray, J. Leisy Brewing Co., Factory Scene, Pre-Prohibition, 1900s, 16 x 14 In. 770.00
Tray, Jax Beer, 13 In. 25.00
Tray, Jenney-See Mineral Water, Meek Co., Tin Lithograph, 16 In. 220.00
Tray, Krueger Pilsner Beer, Aluminum, 12 In. 26.00
Tray, Labatt's Ale, Union Of U.B.C.F. & S.D.W. Of America, 13 In. 88.00
Tray, Loyal Friends, 12 In. 700.00
Tray, Molson's Ale, Porcelain, 13 In. 40.00
Tray, Moore's Ice Cream, Woman Serving Ice Cream To Children, 1920 . . . . 115.00
Tray, National Bohemian, Salutes Tall Ships, 1976, 16 1/2 In. 16.00
Tray, O.F.C. Bourbon, Tin, 12 In. 93.00
Tray, Old Catasauqua Dutch Beer, Red, White, Black, Metal, 13 In. 54.00
Tray, Rainier Beer, 1913, 13 In. 400.00
Tray, Rheingold-Gold Crown Beer, Red, White, Blue, Gold, 13 1/4 In. 29.00
Tray, Rock Island Brewing Co., Pre-Prohibition, 12 In. 560.00
Tray, Ruhstaller's Beer, Green Car, People, 13 1/4 x 13 1/4 In. 770.00
Tray, Schlitz Malt Liquor, 2 Sides, 13 In. 15.00
Tray, Schuster's Root Beer, Tin, 13 x 13 In. 385.00
Tray, St. Mary's Ale Beer, 12 In. 40.00
Tray, Taft's Velvet Ice Cream, 1913 . . . . 500.00
Tray, Tip, see Tip Trays in this category.
Tray, Trenton Old Stock Beer, 12 In. 50.00
Tray, Utica-Club Beer, Metal, 12 In. 16.00
Tray, Valley Forge Beer, 12 In. 88.00
Tray, Wm. C. Davis Bakery, Tin Lithograph, Pretty Woman, 16 In. 198.00
Tray, Wolverine Supply & Mfg. Co., Factory Bldg., 1920, 6 x 4 1/2 In. 46.00
Umbrella, Busch Beer, NASCAR Team 185.00
Umbrella, Gulf Oil, Baltimore Orioles, Original Sleeve 100.00
Vase, Anheuser-Busch, Budweiser, Label On Both Sides, 6 1/2 In. 497.00
Washtub, Iron Staves, Wooden, Color Label, Salesman's Sample, 1905, 10 In. 900.00
Whet Stone, Humble Gasoline, 1920s, Pocket 75.00
Whistle, Oscar Mayer Weiner 3.00
Whistle, Thirsty Just Whistle, Cardboard Tube, Orange & Blue, 1950, 2 In. 40.00
Yardstick, Berlin Brewing 12.00

AGATA glass was made by Joseph Locke of the New England Glass
Company of Cambridge, Massachusetts, after 1885. A metallic stain
was applied to New England Peachblow and the mottled design characteristic of agata appeared.

Toothpick, Tricorner, 2 1/2 In. 575.00
Tumbler, Dark Mottling, Gold Outlining 785.00

AKRO AGATE glass was made in Clarksburg, West Virginia, from 1932 to 1951. Before that time, the firm made children's glass marbles, which are listed in this book in the Marble category. Most of the glass is marked with a crow flying through the letter *A*.

Ashtray, Lincoln Hotel, Orange	80.00
Ashtray, Marbleized, Orange, Shell Shape, 4 x 2 7/8 In.	8.00
Ashtray, Marbleized, Red, Square, 4 x 2 7/8 In.	6.00
Candlestick, Green, 1 3/4 In.	75.00
Casserole, Creamware Relief, Goblet Form, Mask-Head Handles, 7 1/2 In.	402.50
Coaster, Marbleized, Green, 4 1/4 In.	55.00
Lamp, Marbleized, Green, Brown, Ribbed Base, 5 1/4 In.	95.00
Lamp, Marbleized, White, Brown, Shade	395.00
Pitcher, Stacked Disc, Blue	55.00
Planter, Orange, White Opalescent, Flowers, 5 1/4 x 3 In.	15.00
Plate, Octagonal, Pink, 4 3/8 In.	6.00
Powder Jar, Apple, Orange	300.00
Powder Jar, Colonial Woman, Medium Blue	80.00
Powder Jar, Colonial Woman, White	60.00
Powder Jar, Scotty, Blue	108.00
Powder Jar, Scotty, Lime Green	160.00
Smoker's Set, Marbleized, Maroon, Blue, Cup, Box, 4 x 9 1/2 In.	134.00
Tea Set, Child's, Turquoise, Open Handles, Octagonal, 3 Piece	75.00
Tie Back, Curtain, Pink	35.00
Vase, Brown, Tab Handle, 6 1/4 In.	40.00
Vase, Marbleized, Green, White, 4 3/8 In.	15.00
Water Set, Octagonal, Box	100.00

ALABASTER is a very soft form of gypsum, a stone that resembles marble. It was often carved into vases or statues in Victorian times. There are alabaster carvings being made even today. Because the alabaster is very porous, it will dissolve if kept in water, so do not use alabaster vases for flowers.

Bonbon, Footed, Ivory Color, 6 x 6 In.	40.00
Bookends, Owl, Glass Eyes, Italy, 7 3/4 In., Pair	60.00
Bust, Aphrodite, Circular Base, Italy, 19th Century, 18 In.	632.00
Bust, Beatrice, 16 In.	1072.50
Bust, Maiden, Smiling, High Lace Collar, 25 In.	115.00
Bust, Young Boy, 6 1/2 In.	60.00
Bust, Young Peasant Girl, Scarf Covered Head, 1880s, 12 1/2 In.	172.00
Bust, Young Woman, Faded Applied Collar, 7 1/2 In.	45.00
Bust, Young Woman, Feathered Hat, Lace Trimmed Blouse, Italy, 1880	805.00
Bust, Young Woman, Marble, Signed, G. Pedrini, Italy, 12 In.	745.00
Candlestick, Baluster, White Rim Wraps At Top, 10 In.	635.00
Chandelier, Domed Circular Shade, Fluted Edge, France, 1930, 29 In.	2990.00
Compote, Painted Fruit Ornaments, Pair	920.00
Figurine, 2 Young Lovers, Ferdinando Vichi, Late 19th Century, 36 In.	2860.00
Figurine, Child, With Bird, 15 In.	590.00
Figurine, Lions, Lying, Pair	575.00
Figurine, Middle Eastern Woman, Semidraped, 20th Century, 28 1/2 In.	4600.00
Figurine, Puma, Green Glass Eyes, 10 1/2 x 20 In.	575.00
Figurine, Water Nymph, Seated On Rock, Mask Head Fountain, 1880, 18 1/4 In.	1725.00
Figurine, Young Girl, Seated With Book & Flowers, Gernignani, 1880, 14 x 9 In.	632.00
Lamp, Table, Neoclassical, Carved Figures, 3 Graces, Columnar Support, 29 In.	2662.00
Pedestal, Turned, Leaf Carved Column, Octagonal Base, 39 1/2 In.	333.00
Plaque, Red Riding Hood & Wolf, I Am Going To Grandmama, 17 In.	2350.00
Urn, Neoclassical, Campana Shape, Applied Masks, Scroll Handles, 15 3/4 In.	968.00
Vase, Applied Cupped Black Foot, Mirror Black, Translucent Knop, 9 1/4 In.	575.00

ALEXANDRITE is a name with many meanings. It is a form of the mineral chrysoberyl that changes from green to red under artificial light. A man-made version of this mineral is sold in Mexico today. It changes from deep purple to aquamarine blue under artificial light. The Alexandrite listed here is glass made in the late nineteenth and twentieth centuries. Thomas Webb & Sons sold their transparent glass shaded from yellow to rose to blue under the name Alexandrite. Stevens and Williams had a cased Alexandrite of yellow, rose, and blue. A. Douglas Nash Corporation made an amethyst-colored Alexandrite. Several American glass companies of the 1920s made a glass that changed color under electric lights and this was also called Alexandrite.

Goblet, Amber Stem, 6 In.	850.00
Vase, Webb, 5 In.	2000.00

ALUMINUM was more expensive than gold or silver until the 1850s. Chemists learned how to refine bauxite to get aluminum. Jewelry and other small objects were made of the valuable metal until 1914, when an inexpensive smelting process was invented. The aluminum collected today dates from the 1930s through the 1950s. Hand-hammered pieces are the most popular.

Bowl, Notched Edge, Wendell August Forge, 10 In.	20.00
Butter, Cover, Glass Insert, Buenilum, Round	18.00
Child's Set, Coffeepot, Sugar & Creamer, 5 Piece	75.00
Coaster Set, Art Deco, Box	40.00
Crumber, Rodney Kent	22.00
Dish, Masonic, Arthur Armour, 1972, 6 1/2 In.	20.00
Gravy Boat, Ladle, Buenilum	18.00
Hitching Post, Black Jockey, Black, White, Light Blue, Pink, 31 In.	247.00
Ice Bucket, Looped Handle, Cromwell	20.00
Ice Bucket, Wendell August Forge	125.00
Pitcher, Wild Rose, Continental	27.00
Sugar & Creamer, Fluted Tray, Cromwell	25.00
Tray, Figural, Lobster, Signed, Bruce Fox	42.00
Tray, Floral, Unusual Twisted Handle, Round, 10 1/2 In.	17.00
Tray, Oak Leaves & Acorns, Leaf Design On Handles, Continental, 15 In.	35.00
Tray, Tile Insert, Cellini, Round	235.00

AMBER, see Jewelry category.

AMBER GLASS is the name of any glassware with the proper yellow-brown shading. It was a popular color just after the Civil War and many pressed glass pieces were made of amber glass. Depression glass of the 1930s–1950s was also made in shades of amber glass. Other pieces may be found in the Depression Glass, Pressed Glass, and other glass categories. All types are being reproduced.

Beaker, Enameled Eagle, Crown Crest, Egermann, 1890, 5 1/2 In.	72.00
Bottle, Encased In Open Work Pewter, Amber Stopper, 8 3/4 In.	165.00
Candlestick, Portieux, 3 1/2 In.	55.00
Celery, Diamond & Button With V Ornament, Scalloped Top	35.00
Decanter, Enameled Floral & Verse, Myers Neffee, 1890, 9 In.	290.00
Decanter, Wine, Inverted Thumbprint, Pewter Lace & Stopper, 10 1/2 In.	265.00
Goblet, Enameled Crest, Germany, 1890, 6 3/4 In.	110.00
Goblet, Medallion	38.00
Goblet, White Enameled Couple, Mary Gregory Style, Germany, 1890, 11 In.	275.00
Goblet, White Enameled Girl, Mary Gregory Style, Germany, 1890, 5 1/4 In.	44.00
Goblet, Wildflower	30.00
Pitcher, Overshot, Applied Prussian Blue Handle, Drip Rim & Spout, 8 3/4 In.	440.00
Pitcher, Water, Basket Weave	47.00
Pitcher, Water, Finecut & Block	85.00
Plate, Diamond Quilted, Leaf Shape, Ring Handle, 12 x 10 In.	42.00
Plate, Thousand Eye, Square, 8 In.	24.00
Salt, Christmas	95.00
Tazza, Baluster Stem, 6 x 6 1/2 In., Pair	130.00
Toothpick, Owl & Stump	75.00
Vase, Acorn & Leaf, Amber Edge, Ruffled Top, Amber Feet, Oak Leaf, 6 In.	145.00
Vase, Brown Floral Design, Signed, Cristallerie D'Art, 5 In.	373.00
Vase, Coralene Seaweed, Pink Ruffled Fold Down Rim, Camphor Edge, 5 In.	145.00

Vase, Enameled Flowers & Leaves, Applied Teardrops, 6 1/2 In. 145.00
Wine, Panel Cut Stem, Concave Hexagons, 4 3/4 In., 6 Piece 850.00

AMBERETTE pieces are listed in the Pressed Glass category under the pattern name Amberette.

AMBERINA is a two-toned glassware made from 1883 to about 1900. It was patented by Joseph Locke of the New England Glass Company, but was also made by other companies. The glass shades from red to amber. Similar pieces of glass may be found in the Baccarat and Plated Amberina categories. Glass shaded from blue to amber is called *Blue Amberina* or *Bluerina*.

Basket, Applied Amber & Ruffled Rim, Amber Thorn Handle, 6 3/4 x 5 1/2 In. 245.00
Bonbon, Persian Medallion, Multicolored Iridescent, Red 675.00
Bowl, Blue Swirl Bands, Flint, 2 3/4 x 4 1/2 In. 295.00
Bowl, Daisy & Button, Hobbs, Square, 7 1/8 In. 375.00
Bowl, Diamond-Quilted, 2 x 5 In. 215.00
Bowl, Diamond-Quilted, Ruffled Rim, 8 3/4 In. 467.00
Bowl, Light Ribbed, 1 1/2 x 5 In. 425.00
Bowl, Ruffled, Cranberry, Yellow Amber, Pontil, 3 3/4 In. 135.00
Bowl, Swirl, Amber Handles, Base, Oval, 11 3/4 x 6 1/2 x 6 3/4 In. 350.00
Bowl, Swirl, Cranberry To Yellow Amber, Ruffled, 3 3/4 x 5 3/4 In. 135.00
Bowl, Swirled Ribs, Libbey, 4 1/2 In. 125.00
Bowl, Venetian Diamond, Tricornered, 4 1/2 x 2 1/4 In. 325.00
Butter, Cover, Underplate, Inverted Thumbprint 350.00
Canister, Moon & Stars 45.00
Caster Set, 4 Bottles, 1 Stopper 985.00
Celery Vase, Diamond-Quilted, Scalloped Square Rim, 6 1/2 In. 300.00
Celery Vase, Inverted Thumbprint, Corset, Scalloped Rim, 7 In. 150.00
Celery Vase, Thumbprint, Ribbed, 6 3/4 In. 220.00
Centerpiece, Daisy & Button, Fuchsia, Boat Shape, Hobbs, Brockunier, 14 In. 950.00
Creamer, Amber Handle, 4 7/8 In. 135.00
Creamer, Clear Handle, Quilted, Ribbed Pattern, 3 3/4 In. 66.00
Cruet, Inverted Thumbprint, Dark Chocolate 425.00
Cruet, Inverted Thumbprint, Fuchsia, Amber Handle & Stopper, Tricorner Rim, 5 In. ... 385.00
Cruet, Thumbprint Pattern, Amber Handle, Faceted Stopper, 6 7/8 In. 143.00
Decanter, Wine, Amber Bubble Stopper, Amber Handle, 8 5/8 In. 225.00
Dish, Daisy & Button, Boat Shape, 8 3/8 In. 302.00
Dish, Diamond-Quilted, Libbey, 3 7/8 In. 192.00
Finger Bowl, Ruffled Rim, 2 1/2 x 5 In. 210.00
Globe, Lamp, Craquelle Glass, 6 1/2 x 6 1/2 In. 145.00
Goblet, Rose To Amber, Ribbed, 6 1/8 In. 125.00
Ice Bucket, Diamond Optic, Star Cut Base, Tab Handles, 5 x 6 3/4 In. 700.00
Ice Tub, Daisy & Button, 4 1/2 x 4 In. 65.00
Mug, Embossed Swirl, Gold Flowers, Cranberry Shaded To Amber, 5 1/2 In. 165.00
Mustard Pot, Hinged Metal Cover, Ribbed, 3 In. 495.00
Pitcher, Applied Amber Handle, 9 In. 110.00
Pitcher, Bulbous, 5 1/2 In. 145.00
Pitcher, Crackle, 7 3/4 In. 375.00
Pitcher, Daisy & Button, Fuschia Highlights, Hobbs, 5 In. 425.00
Pitcher, Diamond-Quilted, Clear Reeded Handle, Square Mouth, 6 In. 148.00
Pitcher, Inverted Thumbprint, 7 In. 425.00
Pitcher, Inverted Thumbprint, Amber Reeded Handle, Square Top, 4 1/2 In 325.00
Pitcher, Inverted Thumbprint, Clear Reeded Handle, Crimped, 5 1/2 In. 220.00
Pitcher, Inverted Thumbprint, Tricorner Top, 8 In. 475.00
Pitcher, Milk, Waffle, Handle 145.00
Pitcher, Opalescent White, Clear Handle, Ruffled, Petticoat, 8 x 5 In. 650.00
Pitcher, Thumbprint, Ribbed Handle, 7 In. 137.00
Plate, Inverted Thumbprint, 7 In. 160.00
Plate, Trinket, Diamond-Quilted, Flared Rim, Mt. Washington, 4 3/4 In. Diam. 95.00
Punch Cup, 18 Optic Ribs, 2 1/2 In. 185.00
Punch Cup, Diamond-Quilted, Amber Handle, 2 1/2 In., 4 Piece 265.00
Punch Cup, Diamond-Quilted, Reeded Handle, Libbey 192.50

Punch Cup, Inverted Coin Spot, 4 Piece 154.00
Sauce, Fuchsia, 1 1/4 x 4 In. 137.00
Spooner, Diamond Thumbprint, Petticoat Shape, Mt. Washington, 4 In. 850.00
Spooner, Diamond-Quilted, 4 1/2 In. 235.00
Tankard, 10 Panels, Applied Amber Reeded Handle, 6 3/4 In. 450.00
Tankard, Daisy & Button, Amber Handle, 5 In. 275.00
Tankard, Diamond-Quilted, Amberina Handle, 8 1/2 In. 850.00
Toothpick, Daisy & Button, Footed, 3 In. 300.00
Toothpick, Diamond-Quilted, Square Rim, 2 1/2 In. 192.00
Toothpick, Inverted Thumbprint, Pedestal Base 200.00
Tumbler, Floral, 4 In. 325.00
Tumbler, Inverted Thumbprint, 3 3/4 In. ....50.00 to 65.00
Tumbler, Juice, Cranberry, Amber, Gold Scrolls, Fans, 3 7/8 In. 65.00
Tumbler, Juice, Fuchsia, Libbey, 4 1/4 In. 236.00
Tumbler, Lemonade, Ribbed, Amber Reeded Handle, 3 3/4 In., 4 Piece 395.00
Tumbler, Swirl, Cranberry To Golden Amber, Bulging Base, 4 7/8 In. 45.00
Tumbler, Venetian Diamond, Fuchsia Color, 4 In. 135.00
Tumbler, Water, Inverted Thumbprint, Cranberry, Yellow Amber, 3 3/4 In. 45.00
Vase, Enameled Flowers, Cranberry To Olive Amber, Ruffled, 12 3/8 In. 350.00
Vase, Enameled Flowers, Gold Foliage, Crimped Ruffled Rim, Petal Feet, 12 3/8 In. 350.00
Vase, Flared Mouth, Ruffled, 4 In. 125.00
Vase, Fuchsia To Amber, Ribbed, Flared, Libbey, 11 1/2 In. 950.00
Vase, Jack-In-The-Pulpit, Libbey, 1917, 5 x 5 1/4 In. 1200.00
Vase, Libbey, 11 In. 750.00
Vase, Lily, 9 In. 385.00
Vase, Lily, Deep Ruby To Amber, 1880s, 15 In. 825.00
Vase, Lily, Ribbed, 10 In. 275.00
Vase, Lily, Silver Plated, 9 1/2 In. 5500.00
Vase, Rectangular Top, Flattened Bulbous Shape, 8 1/2 In. 235.00
Vase, Ribbed Stem, Round Foot, Red Pie Crust Rim, 7 In. 250.00
Vase, Ribbed, Fold-Down Top, Libbey, 6 1/2 In. 1210.00
Vase, Ribbed, Footed, Bottle Shape, Marked, Libbey, 9 In. 1155.00
Vase, Square Mouth, 6 1/2 In. 185.00
Vase, Stork, Joseph Loche, 4 1/2 In. 1925.00
Vase, Swirl, Amber Ruffled Rim, Petal Footed, 9 In. 77.00
Vase, Swirl, Cranberry To Amber, Enamel Flowers, Cylindrical, 6 7/8 In. 195.00

AMERICAN ART CLAY Company of Indianapolis, Indiana, made a variety of art pottery wares, especially vases, from about 1930 to after World War II. The company used the mark AMACO, as well as the company name. Do not confuse this company with an earlier art pottery firm from Edgerton, Wisconsin, called the American Art Clay Works.

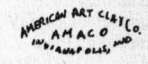

Figurine, Art Deco Woman, Celedon 125.00
Tile, Flowers, Green, 4 In. 25.00

AMERICAN DINNERWARE is the name used by collectors for ceramic dinnerware made in the United States from the 1930s through the 1950s. Most was made in potteries in southern Ohio, West Virginia, and California. Dishes were sold in gift shops and department stores, or were given away as premiums. Many of these patterns are listed in this book in their own categories, such as Autumn Leaf, Coors, Fiesta, Franciscan, Hall, Harker, Harlequin, Red Wing, Riviera, Russel Wright, Vernon Kilns, and Watt. For more information, see *Kovels' Depression Glass & American Dinnerware Price List.*

Ashtray, Amberstone 20.00
Ashtray, California Provincial, 8 1/2 In. 65.00
Ashtray, California Provincial, 10 In. 95.00
Bean Pot, Cover, Apple, Purinton, Individual ....50.00 to 75.00
Bowl, California Strawberry, Provincial, Metlox, Individual 90.00
Bowl, Daisy, Metlox, 7 In. 12.00
Bowl, Oatmeal, Virginia Rose, Homer Laughlin 5.00
Bowl, Orange Tree, Green, Homer Laughlin, 9 1/4 In. 45.00

Bowl, Orange Tree, Homer Laughlin 85.00
Bowl, Poppy Trail, Blue, Metlox, 6 In. 10.00
Bowl, Poppy Trail, Rose, Metlox, 6 In. 10.00
Bowl, Poppy Trail, Yellow, Metlox, 6 In. 10.00
Bowl, Salad, California Geranium, Metlox 60.00
Bowl, Salad, Homestead, Crooksville, 11 In. 75.00
Bowl, Serving, California Ivy, Round, Metlox, 9 In. 40.00
Bowl, Spaghetti, Normandy Plaid, Purinton 195.00
Bowl, Vegetable, California Geranium, Metlox, 10 In. 25.00
Bowl, Vegetable, California Ivy, 2 Sections, Metlox, 11 In. 45.00
Bowl, Vegetable, California Provincial, Metlox, 10 In. 80.00
Bowl, Vegetable, Cover, California Aztec, Metlox 175.00
Bowl, Vegetable, Cover, Rock Rose, Blue Ridge 95.00
Bowl, Vegetable, Golden Fruit, 2 Sections, Metlox 16.00
Bowl, Vegetable, Lu-Ray, Sharon Pink, Taylor, Smith & Taylor 20.00
Bowl, Vegetable, Poppy Trail, 2 Sections, Metlox, 12 In. 65.00
Bowl, Vegetable, Poppy Trail, California Provincial, Round, Metlox 55.00
Bowl, Vegetable, Provincial Blue, Metlox, 10 In. 35.00
Bowl, Yorkshire, Yellow, Metlox 45.00
Box, Cigarette, Homestead Provincial, Metlox 65.00
Bread Tray, Homestead Provincial, Metlox 38.00
Bread Tray, Los Angeles, California Original 22.00
Bread Tray, Provincial Blue, Metlox 65.00
Butter, Amberstone, Homer Laughlin 25.00
Butter, California Provincial, Metlox 55.00
Butter, Cover, Red Rooster, Metlox 55.00
Butter, Cover, San Fernando, Oval, Metlox 45.00
Butter, Cow's Head, Old MacDonald's Farm, Regal 180.00
Cake Plate, Fruit Fantasy, Handle, Blue Ridge 75.00
Cake Plate, Lu-Ray, Surf Green, Round, Taylor, Smith & Taylor, 11 In. 45.00
Cake Server, Kitchen Kraft, Floral Decals, Ivory, Homer Laughlin 18.00
Cake Server, Kitchen Kraft, Homer Laughlin 15.00
Candleholder, Blackamoor, Brayton 30.00
Canister, Flour, Apple, Purinton 35.00
Canister, Kitchen Kraft, Ivory, Decal, Gold Trim, Homer Laughlin 65.00
Canister Set, Red Rooster, Metlox, 8 Piece 200.00
Casserole, California Provincial, Individual 22.00
Casserole, Cover, Daisy, Metlox, 1 1/2 Qt. 90.00
Casserole, Cover, Intaglio, Brown, Purinton 45.00
Casserole, Cover, Virginia Rose, Homer Laughlin 50.00
Casserole, Town & Country, Peach, Zeisel, Individual 65.00
Celery, Pescado, Metlox 90.00
Chop Plate, Apple, Scalloped Border, Purinton, 12 In. 58.00
Chop Plate, California Provincial, Metlox, 12 In. 75.00
Chop Plate, Camellia Brown, Metlox 35.00
Chop Plate, Normandy Plaid, Purinton 25.00
Chop Plate, Provincial Blue, Metlox, 12 In. 35.00
Chop Plate, Red Rooster, Metlox 65.00
Chop Plate, Serenade, Pink, Homer Laughlin 40.00
Chop Plate, Serenade, Yellow, Homer Laughlin, 15 In. 35.00
Coffee Set, Della Robbia, Metlox, 9 Piece 100.00
Coffeepot, Amberstone, Homer Laughlin 40.00
Coffeepot, California Provincial, Metlox 115.00
Coffeepot, Colonial Heritage, Metlox 95.00
Coffeepot, Homestead Provincial, Metlox 65.00
Coffeepot, Ivy, Red Blossom, Drip Filter, 8 Cup, 11 In. 75.00
Coffeepot, Red Rooster, Provincial Shape, Metlox 95.00
Cookie Jar, Red Rooster, Cylinder, Metlox 75.00
Creamer, Amberstone, Homer Laughlin 10.00
Creamer, Daisy, Metlox 22.00
Creamer, Town & Country, Rust, Zeisel 55.00
Creamer, Virginia Rose, Homer Laughlin 12.00
Cup, California Apple, Metlox, After Dinner 5.00

Cup, California Aztec, Metlox 8.00
Cup, California Provincial, Metlox, 6 Oz. 12.00
Cup & Saucer, California Ivy, Metlox 4.00
Cup & Saucer, Currier & Ives, Royal 4.00
Cup & Saucer, Hacienda, Homer Laughlin 24.00
Cup & Saucer, Iroquois, White, Iroquois China 12.00
Cup & Saucer, Lady Alice, Homer Laughlin 6.00
Cup & Saucer, Lu-Ray, Surf Green, Taylor, Smith & Taylor, After Dinner .... 36.00 to 45.00
Cup & Saucer, Poppy Trail, Deep Sea Green, Metlox 7.00
Cup & Saucer, Ranchero, Chartreuse, W.S. George 8.00
Cup & Saucer, Rancho, French Saxon 20.00
Cup & Saucer, Red Rooster, Metlox 6.00
Cup & Saucer, Rhythm, Maroon, American Provincial, Homer Laughlin 9.00
Dinner Set, Cumberland, Blue Ridge, 34 Piece 295.00
Dinner Set, Museum Pattern, Ivory, Eva Zeisel, 1942, 58 Piece 2990.00
Dish, Feeding, Bo Peep, Divided, Hankscraft 75.00
Dish, Feeding, Clown, Turquoise, Divided, Hankscraft 85.00
Dish, Hen On Nest, California Provincial, Metlox 95.00
Eggcup, Lu-Ray, Persian Cream, Taylor, Smith & Taylor 25.00
Eggcup, Lu-Ray, Surf Green, Taylor, Smith & Taylor 45.00
Eggcup, Provincial Blue, Metlox 50.00
Ewer, Pink Clay, Green & Brown Spatter, Blue Ridge, 8 In. 25.00
Gravy Boat, Bouquet, Ladle, Zeisel 60.00
Gravy Boat, California Poppy, Blue Ridge 800.00
Gravy Boat, Lady Alice, Homer Laughlin 12.00
Gravy Boat, Oh Susannah, Metlox 30.00
Grill Plate, Apple, Purinton 60.00
Jar, Cover, Conchita, Large 350.00
Jar, Jam, California Provincial, Metlox 55.00
Jar, Range, Cover, Ivy, Purinton 45.00
Jug, Apple, Dutch, Purinton, 5 Pt. 75.00
Jug, Fruit, Dutch, Purinton, 2 Pt. 30.00
Jug, Fruit, Dutch, Purinton, 5 Pt. 85.00
Jug, Heather Plaid, Kent, Purinton 35.00
Jug, Ivy, Dutch, Red Blossom, Purinton, 2 Pt. 45.00
Jug, Rebecca, Mountain Rose, Purinton, 7 1/2 In. 45.00
Lazy Susan, 4 Sections, Pie Crust Cover, Wooden Base, Purinton 125.00
Lazy Susan, 5 Sections, Gray, Red Finial, California Originals, 18 In. 35.00
Mixing Bowl, Jubilee, Pastel Green, Kitchen Kraft, Homer Laughlin, 8 In. 100.00
Mixing Bowl, Rhythm Rose, Homer Laughlin, 6 In. 18.00
Mug, Apple, Purinton 20.00
Mug, Beer, Homestead Provincial, Metlox 15.00
Mug, Cocoa, California Provincial, Metlox 35.00
Mug, Cover, Homestead Provincial, Spout, Metlox 95.00
Mug, Flirtie Gertie, Pfaltzgraff 35.00
Mug, Herman & Gertie, Pfaltzgraff 35.00
Mug, Sleepy Sam, Mugsey, Pfaltzgraff 35.00
Mug, Strawberry, Provincial 20.00
Pie Plate, Amberstone, Homer Laughlin 25.00
Pie Plate, Oven Serve, Yellow, Homer Laughlin, 10 1/4 In. 25.00
Pitcher, Apple, Purinton, 2 Qt. 50.00
Pitcher, California Provincial, Figural, Rooster, Metlox 275.00
Pitcher, Chuck Wagon, Wallace, 64 Oz. 450.00
Pitcher, Hallcraft, Spring Flowers, Zeisel, 1 Qt. 37.00
Pitcher, Juice, Jubilee, Celadon, Homer Laughlin .... 180.00 to 225.00
Planter, Mountain Rose 50.00
Planter, Spice Box, Homestead Provincial, Metlox .... 55.00 to 70.00
Plate, American Provincial, Metlox, 7 1/2 In. 10.00
Plate, Apple, Purinton, 10 In. 20.00
Plate, Bread, Breakfast, Aqua, Catalina Pottery 35.00
Plate, Bread, Breakfast, Orange, Catalina Pottery 38.00
Plate, California Freeform, Metlox, 10 In. 22.00
Plate, Currier & Ives, Royal, 10 1/2 In. 4.00

Plate, Daisy, Metlox, 6 1/4 In.	8.00
Plate, Daisy, Metlox, 10 1/2 In.	13.00
Plate, Iroquois, White, Casual, Iroquois China, 10 In.	10.00
Plate, Jubilee, Gray, Kitchen Kraft, Homer Laughlin, 6 In.	3.00
Plate, Lady Alice, Homer Laughlin, 9 In.	8.00
Plate, Laurel Life, Pink, California Original, 7 In.	4.00
Plate, Mexicana, Deep, Homer Laughlin	15.00
Plate, Mexicana, Homer Laughlin, 10 In.	45.00
Plate, Orange, Catalina Pottery, 8 In.	48.00
Plate, Poppy Trail, Blue, Metlox, 10 In.	9.00
Plate, Poppy Trail, Deep Sea Green, Metlox, 10 In.	8.00
Plate, Poppy Trail, Green, Metlox, 6 In.	5.00
Plate, Poppy Trail, Green, Metlox, 10 In.	9.00
Plate, Poppy Trail, Rose, Metlox, 6 In.	5.00
Plate, Poppy Trail, Rose, Metlox, 10 In.	9.00
Plate, Poppy Trail, Yellow, Metlox, 6 In.	5.00
Plate, Poppy Trail, Yellow, Metlox, 10 In.	9.00
Plate, Proud Bear, Metlox	75.00
Plate, Rhythm, Maroon, American Provincial, Homer Laughlin, 6 1/2 In.	5.00
Plate, Serenade, Yellow, Deep, Homer Laughlin	18.00
Platter, Apple, 2 Sections, Purinton, 12 1/4 In.	35.00 to 55.00
Platter, California Freeform, Metlox	60.00
Platter, California Ivy, Oval, Metlox, 13 In.	50.00
Platter, California Provincial, Metlox	28.00
Platter, California Strawberry, Metlox	15.00
Platter, Daisy, Metlox, 14 1/2 In.	45.00
Platter, Daisy, Oval, Metlox, 11 In.	40.00
Platter, Eggshell Nautilus, Ferndale, Homer Laughlin, 11 1/2 In.	15.00
Platter, Homestead Provincial, Metlox, 22 1/2 In.	140.00
Platter, Lu-Ray, Sharon Pink, Oval, Taylor, Smith & Taylor, 14 In.	15.00
Platter, Mardi Gras, Blue Ridge, 11 1/2 In.	48.00
Platter, Poppy Trail, California Provincial, Oval, Metlox, 13 1/2 In.	55.00
Platter, Provincial Blue, Metlox, 13 In.	55.00
Platter, Provincial Rose, Metlox, 13 In.	45.00
Platter, Provincial Rose, Oblong, Metlox, 11 In.	45.00
Platter, Red Rooster, Metlox, 13 1/2 In.	25.00
Platter, Turkey, California Provincial, Metlox	495.00
Platter, Virginia Rose, Homer Laughlin, 11 1/2 In.	15.00
Punch Set, Tom & Jerry, Auld Lang Syne, Hazel Atlas, 7 Piece	40.00
Relish, Apple, 3 Sections, Purinton	50.00
Relish, Lu-Ray, Surf Green, 4 Sections, Taylor, Smith & Taylor	110.00
Relish, Lu-Ray, Windsor Blue, 4 Sections, Taylor, Smith & Taylor	75.00
Salt & Pepper, Apple, Jug, Purinton	25.00
Salt & Pepper, California Poppy, Blue Ridge	85.00
Salt & Pepper, Fruits, Jug, Purinton	16.00
Salt & Pepper, Homestead Provincial, Blue, Metlox	35.00
Salt & Pepper, Jubilee, Tango, Yellow, Homer Laughlin	13.00
Salt & Pepper, Lu-Ray, Windsor Blue, Taylor, Smith & Taylor	15.00
Salt & Pepper, Rhythm, Forest Green, Homer Laughlin	11.00
Salt Box, Green Rooster, Provincial	100.00
Sauceboat, Eggshell Nautilus, Ferndale, Homer Laughlin	15.00
Sauceboat, Stand, Rhythm, Gray, American Provincial, Homer Laughlin	30.00
Sauceboat, Virginia Rose, Liner, Homer Laughlin	25.00
Saucer, California Poppy, 6 3/8 In.	10.00
Snack Plate, Cup, Homestead Provincial, Metlox	85.00
Soup, Dish, American Provincial, Homer Laughlin	20.00
Soup, Dish, Indian Tree, Salem	5.00
Soup, Dish, Rancho Ware, Lug Handle, Turquoise, Catalina	20.00
Soup, Dish, Virginia Rose, Homer Laughlin	18.00
Spoon Rest, Rhythm, American Provincial, Homer Laughlin	125.00
Spoon Rest, Rhythm, Dark Green, Homer Laughlin	310.00
Sugar, Cover, Poppy Trail, Red Rooster, Red, Provincial Shape	20.00

Sugar & Creamer, Apple, Purinton	40.00
Sugar & Creamer, Cover, California Poppy, Blue Ridge	145.00
Sugar & Creamer, Cover, Provincial Rose, Metlox	65.00
Sugar & Creamer, Fruits, Purinton	25.00
Sugar & Creamer, Ranchero, Pumpkin, W.S. George	16.00
Syrup, Town & Country, Blue, Zeisel	110.00
Tea Set, Rust, Yellow, Ironstone, Eva Zeisel, 1928, 7 Piece	1035.00
Teapot, California Poppy, Blue Ridge	100.00
Teapot, Colonial, Yellow Nocturne, Blue Ridge	100.00
Teapot, Dutch, Purinton, 6 Cup	55.00
Teapot, Fruits, Purinton, 6 Cup	45.00
Teapot, Heather Plaid, Purinton	65.00
Teapot, Lu-Ray, Chatham Gray, Taylor, Smith & Taylor	145.00
Teapot, Mountain Rose, 2 Cup	45.00
Teapot, Oriental, Purinton	40.00
Teapot, Provincial, Tulip Stand, Brayton	125.00
Teapot, Red Rooster, Metlox	110.00
Teapot, Rhythm Rose, Homer Laughlin	55.00
Teapot, Rhythm, Forest Green, American Provincial, Homer Laughlin	40.00
Tray, Tropicana, Metlox, 21 In.	90.00
Tureen, Soup, Fruit Basket, Ladle, Metlox	250.00
Tureen, Soup, Hen, Provincial Blue, Ladle, Metlox	400.00
Tureen, Soup, Homestead Provincial, Ladle, Metlox	695.00
Vase, Blue Flowers, Oriental Design, Bulbous, California Originals	60.00
Vase, Bud, Lu-Ray, Windsor Blue, Taylor, Smith & Taylor	130.00
Vase, Tropicana, Pineapple, Teardrop, Metlox, 17 In.	95.00
Vase, York, Rose, Green, Pfaltzgraff, 4 In.	30.00
Vegetable, California Poppy, Blue Ridge, 8 1/2 In.	60.00

AMERICAN ENCAUSTIC TILING COMPANY was founded in Zanesville, Ohio, in 1875. The company planned to make a variety of tiles to compete with the English tiles that were selling in the United States for use in fireplaces and other architectural designs. The first glazed tiles were made in 1880, embossed tiles in 1881, faience tiles in the 1920s. The firm closed in 1935 and reopened in 1937 as the Shawnee Pottery.

Paperweight, Ram, Long Horns, Marked, 3 x 5 In.	65.00
Tile, Bird, Burgundy, Art Deco, Marked, 4 1/2 In.	125.00
Tile, Cavalier, Plumed Hat, Holding Flute, Frame	250.00
Tile, Grecian Woman & Large Pig, Square, 6 In.	160.00
Tile, Hunting Scene, Putti, Carrying Deer, Frame, 6 In.	275.00
Tile, Putto, In Woods, Dog, Olive Glaze, Frame, 6 In.	275.00
Tile, Winter, Goddess, 2 Putti, Amber, HM, 12 x 18 In.	1950.00
Trivet, Little Bopeep Front, Zanesville, Ohio, 1930	125.00

AMETHYST GLASS is any of the many glasswares made in the dark purple color of the gemstone called amethyst. Included in this category are many pieces made in the nineteenth and twentieth centuries. Very dark pieces are called *black amethyst* and are listed under that heading.

Bowl, 12 Molded Panels, Pittsburgh, 3 1/4 In.	195.00
Bowl, Persian Medallion, Purple, Aqua, Bronze Iridescent, 10 In.	295.00
Bowl, Wavy Rim, 10 In.	110.00
Dresser Set, Amethyst Cut To Clear, Spear Point Finial Cover, 7 In., 3 Piece	295.00
Dresser Set, Shaded To Clear, Cut Panels, 2 Bottles, Covered Box, 3 Piece	295.00
Lamp, Twinkle, Dark Amethyst Glass, Acorn Burner, 7 In.	2247.00
Pitcher, Water, 8 In.	150.00
Vase, Painted Bird, Floral Design, 10 In.	44.00
Vase, Urn Form, Late 19th Century, 16 1/2 In.	425.00
Vase, Walled Ridge, Purple, Facet Cut Panels, 8 1/2 In.	345.00

AMPHORA pieces are listed in the Teplitz category.

ANDIRONS and related fireplace items are included in the Fireplace category.

ANIMAL TROPHIES, such as stuffed animals, rugs made of animal skins, and other similar collectibles, are listed in this category. Collectors should be aware of the endangered species laws that make it illegal to buy and sell some of these items. Any eagle feathers, many types of pelts or rugs (such as leopard), ivory, and many forms of tortoiseshell can be confiscated by the government. Related trophies may be found in the Fishing category. Ivory items may be found in the Scrimshaw or Ivory categories.

African Antelope	630.00
Antlers, Rococo Style Carved Wooden Bracket, 24 In.	410.00
Black Bear, Full Mount	750.00
Bobcat, Head & Neck Mount	45.00
Dik-Dik, Mounted	200.00
Ermine Weasel, Full Mount	100.00
Red Fox, Full Mount	185.00
Robe, Lap, Black Bear Skin, Sleigh, 60 x 60 In.	125.00
Rug, Bear Skin, 1909	495.00
Rug, Bobcat Skin	185.00
Rug, Snow Leopard Skin, Government Stamps On Back, China	2200.00
Snake, Coiled On 4-Ft. Pole, Glass Eyes	1250.00
Water Buck	200.00

ANIMATION ART collectibles include cels that are painted drawings on celluloid needed to make animated cartoons shown in movie theaters or on TV. Hundreds of cels were made, then photographed in sequence to make a cartoon showing moving figures. Early examples made by the Walt Disney Studios are popular with collectors today. Original sketches used by the artists are also listed here. Modern animated cartoons are made using computer-generated pictures. Some of these are being produced as cels to be sold to collectors. Other cartoon art is listed in Comic Art and Disneyana.

Cel, 101 Dalmatians, Pongo, Happily Looking Out Window, 1961, 11 x 9 In.	1610.00
Cel, 101 Dalmatians, Pongo, Looking Up Sleepily, Walt Disney, 10 x 12 In.	1955.00
Cel, 101 Dalmatians, Pongo, Waiting For Birth Of Puppies, 8 x 11 In.	2875.00
Cel, 101 Dalmatians, Roger & Pongo, Walt Disney, 1961, 12 1/2 x 16 In.	1150.00
Cel, 1001 Rabbit Tales, Bugs Bunny Holding Book, Warner Bros., 9 x 12 In.	1035.00
Cel, Adventures Of Ichabod & Mr. Toad, Walt Disney, 1949, 8 x 5 1/2 In.	1495.00
Cel, Alice In Wonderland, Bust Of Alice, Walt Disney, 1955, 7 x 5 In.	575.00
Cel, Alice In Wonderland, Goliath Sniffing A Daffodil, Walt Disney, 6 x 5 In.	1035.00
Cel, Alice In Wonderland, Mad Hatter, Walt Disney, 1951, 12 1/2 x 16 In.	1955.00
Cel, Aristocats, Walt Disney, 1970, 11 x 14 1/2 In.	1725.00
Cel, Bambi, Great Prince & Bambi During Fire, 1942, 11 x 35 In.	10350.00
Cel, Bambi, Smiling At Adorable Bunny, Walt Disney, 10 x 14 In.	8050.00
Cel, Bambi, Thumper & Friends In Forest, Walt Disney, 1942, 7 x 9 In.	6670.00
Cel, Bambi, Thumper, Sliding On The Ice, Walt Disney, 1942, 7 x 9 In.	4025.00
Cel, Bambi, Thumper, Smiling At Each Other, 1980, 9 x 12 In.	1495.00
Cel, Bambi, Walking Along With 4 Bunnies, Walt Disney, 10 x 12 In.	4312.00
Cel, Bambi, With His Mother, Walt Disney, 1941, 5 x 3 1/2 In.	1380.00
Cel, Chip & Dale, Clarice Flirts With Chip & Dale, Walt Disney, 8 x 6 In.	1725.00
Cel, Chip & Dale, Dragon Around, Walt Disney, 1954, 7 1/2 x 9 1/2 In.	10350.00
Cel, Cinderella, Wearing Ballgown, Walt Disney, 1950, 7 1/2 x 9 In.	8625.00
Cel, Donald Duck, Donald Gets Drafted, Soldiers, Walt Disney, 1942, 5 x 4 In.	230.00
Cel, Donald Duck, Donald's Golf Game, Walt Disney, 1938, 10 x 12 In.	1150.00
Cel, Donald Duck, Donald's Penguin, Tootsie, Walt Disney, 1939, 5 x 5 In.	920.00
Cel, Donald Duck, Ducktales, Cowboy Scrooge, Walt Disney, 1987, 8 x 9 In.	920.00
Cel, Donald Duck, Dumb Bell Of The Yukon, Walt Disney, 1946, 8 x 11 In.	1150.00
Cel, Donald Duck, Hockey Champ, Fierce Concentration, Walt Disney, 7 x 8 In.	4025.00
Cel, Donald Duck, Saludos Amigos, In Peruvian Dress, Walt Disney, 7 x 7 In.	1840.00
Cel, Dumbo, 2 Kangaroos, Walt Disney, 1941, 8 x 10 In.	633.00
Cel, Dumbo, 6 Storks Fly With Sacks, Walt Disney, 10 1/2 x 13 1/2 In.	920.00
Cel, Dumbo, Casey Jr., Walt Disney, 1941, 8 1/2 x 8 In.	2760.00
Cel, Dumbo, Flies While Talking To Crows, Walt Disney, 1941, 7 x 9 In.	5175.00
Cel, Dumbo, Looking For His Mother, Walt Disney, 1941, 6 1/2 x 7 1/2 In.	3162.00

Cel, Dumbo, Sitting On Top Telephone Wire, Walt Disney, 1941, 8 x 10 In. 4025.00
Cel, Dumbo, Timothy, Walt Disney, 1941, 7 x 8 In. 1495.00
Cel, Fantasia, Mickey As Sorcerer's Apprentice, Walt Disney, 1940, 8 x 8 In. 1495.00
Cel, Fantasia, Pegasus Parents Gliding Along, White, Black, 1940, 2 x 4 In. 3450.00
Cel, Fantasia, The Broom, Walt Disney, 1940, 5 1/2 x 4 1/2 In. 3684.00
Cel, Ferdinand The Bull, 4 Matadors, Walt Disney, 1938, 9 x 11 In. 518.00
Cel, Ferdinand The Bull, Cow & The Bee, Walt Disney, 1938, 9 1/2 x 10 In. 1840.00
Cel, Ferdinand The Bull, Matador, Walt Disney, 1938, 7 x 9 In. 575.00
Cel, Ferdinand The Bull, Matadors & A Horse At A Wall, Walt Disney, 9 x 11 In. 1035.00
Cel, Ferdinand The Bull, Men Wearing Funny Hats, Walt Disney, 1938, 7 x 9 In. 690.00
Cel, Flying Mouse, Walt Disney, 1934, 11 1/2 x 11 In. 2875.00
Cel, Fun & Fancy Free, Bongo & Lulubell, Walt Disney, 1947, 8 x 10 In. 4025.00
Cel, Goofy, Art Of Skiing, Tries To Ski, Walt Disney, 1941, 7 1/2 x 9 In. 1495.00
Cel, Goofy, Californy Er Bust, Western Pioneer, Walt Disney, 7 x 10 In. 1265.00
Cel, Goofy, Knight For A Day, Goofy & Horse, Walt Disney, 1946, 8 x 10 In. 1150.00
Cel, Groucho, With Cigar, Brown Highlights, Warner Brothers, 8 1/4 x 10 In. 78.00
Cel, How The Grinch Stole Christmas, Grinch & Max On Sleigh, 6 x 6 1/2 In. 1150.00
Cel, How The Grinch Stole Christmas, MGM Studio, 1966, 5 1/2 x 6 In. 1610.00
Cel, Jungle Book, Baloo, Got Tiger By The Tail, Walt Disney, 11 x 15 In. 6900.00
Cel, Lady & The Tramp, Lady Stands On Hind Legs, Walt Disney, 1955, 9 x 6 In. 1265.00
Cel, Lady & The Tramp, Lady, Tramp & Jock, Walt Disney, 1955, 11 x 13 In. 6900.00
Cel, Lady & The Tramp, Looking To The Right, Walt Disney, 1955, 9 x 11 In. 1725.00
Cel, Lady & The Tramp, Tramp Smiling At Lady, Walt Disney, 1955, 8 x 12 In. 2185.00
Cel, Ludwig Von Drake, Walt Disney, 1960, 12 1/2 x 16 In. 632.00
Cel, Melody Time, Father Of Little Toot, Walt Disney, 1948, 10 x 12 In. 1093.00
Cel, Melody Time, Johnny Appleseed, Walt Disney, 1948, 10 1/2 x 14 In. 1610.00
Cel, Mickey & Minnie Mouse, The Whoopee Party, Walt Disney, 6 x 5 In. 19550.00
Cel, Mickey Mouse & Pluto, Smiling At Donald, The New Spirit, 1942, 4 x 7 In. 1955.00
Cel, Mickey Mouse, Brave Little Tailor, Walking Proudly Left, 1938, 5 x 7 In. 1265.00
Cel, Mickey Mouse, Fantasia, Sorcerer's Apprentice, Walt Disney, 10 x 12 In. 1380.00
Cel, Mickey Mouse, Mickey & The 3 Little Pigs, Walt Disney, 1935, 7 x 9 In. 1380.00
Cel, Mickey Mouse, Mickey Driving Steamroller, Walt Disney, 1934 . . . . 1495.00
Cel, Mickey Mouse, Mickey Gripping Shotgun, Walt Disney, 10 x 12 In. 517.00
Cel, Mickey Mouse, Mickey's Gala Premiere, Walt Disney, 9 1/2 x 12 In. 1265.00
Cel, Mickey Mouse, Mickey's Parrot, Walt Disney, 1938, 10 x 12 In. 747.00
Cel, Mickey, Minnie Mouse, Donald, Waving Farewell From Train, 8 x 11 In. 2300.00
Cel, Pepe Le Pew, Gestures With His Hands, Warner Bros., 1960, 8 x 11 1/4 In. 920.00
Cel, Peter Pan, Captain Hook, Walt Disney, 1952, 10 x 12 In. 2300.00
Cel, Peter Pan, Peter Takes Wendy's Hand As They Fly, 1953, 10 x 13 In. 1380.00
Cel, Peter Pan, Tiger Lily, Her Father, The Chief, Sitting In Circle, 11 x 13 In. 4600.00
Cel, Peter Pan, Tinker Bell Flies To The Left, Walt Disney, 1953, 9 x 13 In. 1150.00
Cel, Peter Pan, Tinker Bell Sits On Top Corked Bottle, Walt Disney, 8 x 9 In. 3162.00
Cel, Pinocchio, As A Boy, Walt Disney, 1940, 10 x 12 In. 633.00
Cel, Pinocchio, Cleo Looks Up Happily, Walt Disney, 1940, 6 x 6 1/2 In. 1840.00
Cel, Pinocchio, Drops To Bottom Of The Sea, Walt Disney, 8 x 6 In. 5175.00
Cel, Pinocchio, Figaro, Swipes At Unruly Fish, Walt Disney, 1940, 7 x 6 In. 1494.00
Cel, Pinocchio, Gideon, Listening To Fiendish Plots, Walt Disney, 7 x 9 In. 2300.00
Cel, Pinocchio, Jiminy Cricket, Happily Tips His Hat At Moth, 6 x 6 In. 3162.00
Cel, Pinocchio, Jiminy Cricket, Looking Up, Embarrassed Look, 7 x 11 In. 3162.00
Cel, Pinocchio, Jiminy Cricket, Perched On Tip Of Shoe, 13 x 15 In. 690.00
Cel, Pinocchio, Jiminy Cricket, Startled By Sea Horse, Walt Disney, 9 x 8 In. 3737.00
Cel, Pinocchio, Jiminy Cricket, Whistling, Walking Along, 1940, 5 x 4 In. 2587.00
Cel, Pluto & The Armadillo, Mickey & The Armadillo, Walt Disney, 7 x 7 In. 2530.00
Cel, Pocahontas, Protecting John Smith 2990.00
Cel, Pointer, Mickey & Pluto, Walt Disney, 1939, 8 x 11 In. 8625.00
Cel, Pooh & Rabbit, Walt Disney, 1980s, 10 x 12 In. 1150.00
Cel, Pooh, Sitting Against Tree Trunk, Walt Disney, 1980s, 11 x 13 In. 1725.00
Cel, Practical Pig, Fiddler, Fifer Pig Laughing, Walt Disney, 9 x 9 1/2 In. 3162.00
Cel, Prince And The Pauper, Goofy, Bucket As A Hat, 1990, 12 x 17 In. 1150.00
Cel, Puss In Boots, Casper, Playing With Kittens, Famous Studios, 10 x 13 In. 805.00
Cel, Reluctant Dragon, Goofy Tries To Ride A Horse, 1941, 10 x 12 In. 1955.00
Cel, Rescuers, Madame Medusa Clutching Her Staff, 12 x 16 In. 402.00
Cel, Robin Hood, Crocodile, Engage In Sword Duel, Walt Disney, 10 x 13 In. 3910.00

When the weather is bad,
the auction will probably
be good. Brave storms and
cold and attend auctions in
bad weather when the
crowd is small and the
prices low.

Animation Art, Cel, Snow White, 3 Dwarfs
In Kitchen, 1937, 9 x 9 1/2 In.

Cel, Robin Hood, Maid Marian Watches Robin, Walt Disney, 1973, 7 x 12 In. 1380.00
Cel, Robin Hood, Prince John Pointing His Finger, Walt Disney, 10 x 14 In. 1035.00
Cel, Simpsons, Homer, Marge & Maggie 258.00
Cel, Sleeping Beauty, Briar Rose, Sitting With Berry Basket, 1959, 12 x 15 In. 460.00
Cel, Sleeping Beauty, King Stefan Holding Goblet, Walt Disney, 12 x 9 In. 1150.00
Cel, Sleeping Beauty, Maleficent, Captured At Calm Moment, 12 x 15 In. 920.00
Cel, Sleeping Beauty, Maleficent, Walt Disney, 1959, 7 1/2 x 9 1/4 In. 3450.00
Cel, Sleeping Beauty, Maleficent, Walt Disney, 1959, 9 1/4 x 6 1/4 In. 2760.00
Cel, Snow White & Seven Dwarfs, Dopey, With Pick-Ax, 1937, 5 x 4 In. 3737.00
Cel, Snow White & Seven Dwarfs, Evil Queen In Hag Disguise, 9 x 11 In. 920.00
Cel, Snow White & Seven Dwarfs, Grumpy, Walt Disney, 1937, 7 x 6 In. 3220.00
Cel, Snow White & Seven Dwarfs, Grumpy, Walt Disney, 5 3/4 x 4 1/2 In. 220.00
Cel, Snow White & Seven Dwarfs, Sneezy, Walt Disney, 1937, 8 x 4 1/2 In. 2990.00
Cel, Snow White & Seven Dwarfs, Snow White Dancing, 10 x 13 In. 11500.00
Cel, Snow White & Seven Dwarfs, With 2 Squirrels, 1937, 8 x 6 In. 5750.00
Cel, Snow White, 3 Dwarfs In Kitchen, 1937, 9 x 9 1/2 In. .... *Illus* 7700.00
Cel, Song Of The South, Brer Rabbit, Eyes Wide Open, Walt Disney, 7 x 7 In. 4312.00
Cel, Sword & The Stone, Merlin Crowns Wart, Walt Disney, 12 x 16 In. 5175.00
Cel, Three Caballeros, Jose, Walt Disney, 1945, 7 x 7 In. 1380.00
Cel, Tigger & Rooh, Educational Series, Walt Disney, 1980s, 10 1/2 x 13 In. 1035.00
Cel, Tom & Jerry, Haunted Mouse, Various Drawings, MGM Studio, 1966 .... 3450.00
Cel, Ugly Duckling, Mother Duck Swims With Her Family, 10 x 12 In. 1265.00
Cel, Ugly Duckling, Smiling At Grasshopper, 1939, 7 x 8 In. 1610.00
Cel, Wendy, About To Tell The Children A Story, 1953, 7 1/2 x 9 1/2 In. 863.00
Cel, Who Framed Roger Rabbit? Touchstone, 1988, 10 x 17 In. 2587.00
Cel, Woody Woodpecker, Flies & Pecks Out His Name, 1952, 10 1/2 x 13 In. 1840.00
Cel, Wynken, Blynken & Nod, Walt Disney, 1948, 7 x 8 In. 805.00

ANNA POTTERY was started in Anna, Illinois, in 1859 by Cornwall and
Wallace Kirkpatrick. They made many types of utilitarian wares,
bricks, drain tiles, and giftware. The most collectible pieces made by *Anna Pottery*
the pottery are the pig-shaped bottles and jugs with special inscriptions, applied animals, and figures. The pottery closed in 1894.

Flask, Pig, World's Fair, 1893 .... 1800.00
Jug, Presentation, To William M. Brown, 1880s 5000.00

APPLE PEELERS are listed in the Kitchen category under Peeler, Apple.

ARC-EN-CIEL is the French word for rainbow. A pottery factory named
Arc-en-ciel was founded in Zanesville, Ohio, in 1903. The company
made art pottery for a short time, then became the Brighton Pottery in
1905.

Vase, Iridescent Gold, Purple & Green, Marked, 12 1/2 In. 65.00
Vase, Twisted Lobed Form, Gold & Yellow Glaze, Marked, 7 In. 55.00

ARCHITECTURAL antiques include a variety of collectibles, usually very large, that have been removed from buildings. Hardware, backbars, doors, paneling, and even old bathtubs are now wanted by collectors. Pieces of the Victorian, Art Nouveau, and Art Deco styles are in greatest demand.

Backbar, Apothecary, Mahogany, 5 x 8 Ft.	2200.00
Backbar, Cherry, Beveled Mirror, Marble Top, Stained Glass, Pillars, 9 x 8 Ft.	10500.00
Backbar, Oak, Glass & Panel Doors, Mirror, Columns, Carved, 1894, 11 x 18 Ft.	8000.00
Backbar, Saloon, Single Mirror, Wood Carving, Storage, Oak, 1890s	7500.00
Backbar, Soda Fountain, White Marble, Green Slag Glass, Oak, 105 x 100 In.	7000.00
Bar & Backbar, Art Deco, Mirrors, Lights, 8 x 14 Ft.	4500.00
Bathtub, Tin, Child's, Painted	495.00
Bathtub, Tin, Pears Soap, Adult, 1887	650.00
Cabinet, Drugstore, 6 Sliding Glass Doors, Oak, 8 x 10 Ft.	2500.00
Column, Corinthian, Baroque, Parcel Gilt, Acanthus Leaves, Bell Flowers, Pair	5175.00
Column, Corinthian, Neoclassical Style, Raised On Plinth Base, 21 In.	5750.00
Column, Corinthian, Wood, Various Leaves, Scrolls, 19th Century, 14 x 18 In.	488.75
Column, Faux Marble, Green, White Vases, Circular, 47 1/2 In.	1035.00
Column, Green Circular Marble, Faux White, 47 1/2 In., Pair	1035.00
Column, Louis XVI Style, Ormolu Laurel Wreath, Square Plinth, 44 3/4 In.	9200.00
Column, Neoclassical, Leaf Tipped Borders, Reeded Stem, Italy, 41 In., Pair	9200.00
Column, Painted, Fitted Screen, Dogs, Cows, Italy, 19th Century, 31 In.	4312.00
Column, Pedestal, Circular Foot, Chamfered Base, Deep Flutes, Faux Marble	977.00
Cornice, Rope Molded, Arched Center Over Hand Painted Floral Frieze	82.00
Counter, Marble Top, Pine, 8 Ft.	2850.00
Door, Barn Granary, Hand Forged Hardware	165.00
Door, Christ With Cross, Painted Carved Panel, 17 1/8 x 8 In.	690.00
Door, Double, Cherry, Half Leaded & Beveled Top, 36 x 80 In., Pair	7500.00
Door, Double, Oak, 3/4 Leaded & Beveled Top, Paneled Base, 6 x 7 Ft.	6500.00
Door, Louis XV, 1 Concave, 1 Convex, Fruitwood, 86 3/4 x 32 1/2 In., Pair	1330.00
Door, Stained Glass, Oak	450.00
Door Handle, Cutout Indian Head, Feather Headdress, Handwrought	1430.00
Door Knob, Cut Glass, 1910	95.00
Door Knocker, Striker Plate, Brass, England, 18th Century	550.00
Door Surround, Iron-Mounted, 4 Planks On 1 Side, Iron Rivets, 77 x 46 In.	1150.00
Doorbell, Pull, Greenfield, Patented 1865, Brass, 1870	155.00
Doorknob, Benjamin Franklin, Sulphide, Baccarat, 2 In.	1000.00
Doorknob, Black Porcelain, 3 Piece	15.00
Doorknob, Faceted Glass, Pair	20.00
Doorknob, Lafayette, Sulphide, Baccarat, 2 In.	1000.00
Doorknob, LaSalle Hotel, Chicago	185.00
Doorknob, Plumed Knight, Bronze, Metallic Compression Casting Co., 1870	660.00
Doorstop, Elephant, GOP, Original Paint, 11 In.	550.00
Fence, Grapevine Pattern, Patent May 10, 1876	8500.00
Finial, Turret, Victorian, 64 In.	1345.00
Fireplace Surround, Carved Oak, Over Mantel Mirror Frame, Victorian	6050.00
Fireplace Surround, Oak, Carved Demon Mask At Bow Of Mirror	6325.00
Fireplace Surround, Reverse Breakfront, Paneled Frieze, Painted White, 1810, 81 In.	690.00
Fireplace Surround & Fireboard, Painted Green & Cream, 1840s, 54 1/2 In.	2800.00
Gate, Iron, Black, Ornate, Victorian, 39 x 93 In., Pair	7500.00
Hitching Post, Horse Head, Black, Cast Iron, 62 In., Pair	605.00
Knob, Mirror, Brass, England, c.1785, 2 1/4 In., Pair	185.00
Lock, Drop Handles, Keeper & Key, All Brass, 1740s	295.00
Mantel, 14 Tiles, Ebonized Upper Mirror Frame, Chinese Export, 92 x 59 In.	9200.00
Mantel, Neoclassical Style, Inset Beveled Mirror, Oak, 79 x 56 In.	460.00
Mantel, Red & Black, c.1840, 62 x 52 In.	700.00
Mantel, Reeded Columns, Paterae Carving, Wooden	220.00
Mantel, White Marble, Black Veins, Side Vents, Black Marble Inset	8500.00
Newel Post, Bronze Lady, Roman Goddess, Gas Shade, 2-Color Bronze	4500.00
Ornament, Roof, Owl, Glass Eyes, Brown Paint, 19th Century, 27 1/2 In.	1063.00
Panel, Wallpaper, Classical Scenes, Frame, Zuber Et Cie, 72 x 43 In., Pair	2075.00
Pole Mount, Eagle Center, Brass Base, 19th Century	275.00
Post Office Unit, Cash Drawer	1045.00

Shelf, Eagle With Stars & Shield, Cast Plaster, 18 x 14 In. 550.00
Tile, Ceiling, Heart-In-Hand, Odd Fellows Lodge Pressed Tin, 23 x 47 In. 2500.00
Towel Bar, Glass, Pair 70.00

AREQUIPA POTTERY was produced from 1911 to 1918 by the patients of the Arequipa Sanitarium in Marin County Hills, California. The patients were trained by Frederick Hürten Rhead, who had worked at the Roseville Pottery.

Ewer, Florals & Blossoms, Pinched Spout, Green Ground, 10 In. 55.00
Vase, Band Of Stylized Flowers & Greek Key Pattern, Signed, 1910, 5 1/4 In. 1870.00
Vase, Embossed Leaves, Red Brown Matte Glaze, Tapered Rim, 8 x 5 In. 1045.00
Vase, Flower Design, Brown Matte Glaze, Signed, M.I.W., 5 1/2 In. 467.50
Vase, Morning Glories, Under Raspberry Pink & Gray Glaze, Signed, 6 1/2 In. 825.00
Vase, Stylized Flowers, Gold, Blue, Green Ground, Frederick Rhead, 1912, 3 x 3 In. 3080.00
Vase, Stylized Leaves In Squeezebag, Cobalt Blue, Frederick Rhead, 3 1/4 x 5 In. 3960.00
Vessel, Hand Tooled Jonquils Over Incised Stems, Blue Glaze, Signed, 4 1/2 In. 3630.00

ARGY-ROUSSEAU, see G. Argy-Rousseau category.

ARITA is a port in Japan. Porcelain was made there from about 1616. Many types of decorations were used, including the popular Imari designs, which are listed under Imari in this book.

Bowl, Crane, Marsh Grass Design, Blue, White, 5 3/4 In. 132.00
Vase, Birds On Branches, Black & White, 2 In. 405.00

ART DECO, or Art Moderne, a style started at the Paris Exposition of 1925, is characterized by linear, geometric designs. All types of furniture and decorative arts, jewelry, book bindings, and even games were designed in this style. Additional items may be found in the Furniture category or in various glass and pottery categories, etc.

Ashtray, Marble Finial 175.00
Card Case, Gold Wash, Filigree, 2 1/8 x 3 1/4 In. 100.00
Cigarette Holder, Bakelite, Pop-Up 125.00
Cocktail Shaker, Stainless Steel, WMF, Germany, Wagenfeld, 1959, 7 1/4 In. 230.00
Frame, Picture, Red, Blue, Catalin, 7 x 7 In. 45.00
Powder Box, Circular Marble, 6-In. Metal Figure Of Dancing Girl 175.00
Powder Box, Woman, Green Satin Glass 95.00

ART GLASS, see Glass-Art category.

ART NOUVEAU is a style of design that was at its most popular from 1895 to 1905. Famous designers, including Rene Lalique and Emile Galle, produced furniture, glass, silver, metalwork, and buildings in the new style. Ladies with long flowing hair and elongated bodies were among the more easily recognized design elements. Copies of this style are being made today. Many modern pieces of jewelry can be found. Additional Art Nouveau pieces may be found in Furniture or in various glass categories.

Box, Women's Face 4 Sides, Basket Weave, Lotus, Lilies, Bronze Finish 180.00
Cordial, Enamel, Green Stem, 1910, 5 3/4 In. . . . . .165.00 to 346.00
Ewer, Wheel Cut Floral, Green Glass, 1910, WMF Metalwork, 13 1/2 In. 990.00
Humidor, Lady's Head 240.00
Incense Burner, Neo-Egyptian, Partly Nude Woman, Reclining, Bird, Patina 375.00

ART POTTERY was first made in America in Cincinnati, Ohio, during the 1870s. The pieces were hand thrown and hand decorated. The art pottery tradition continued until the 1920s when studio potters began making the more artistic wares. American, English, and Continental art pottery by less well-known makers is listed here. Most makers listed in *Kovels' American Art Pottery,* such as Arequipa, Ohr, Rookwood, Roseville, and Weller, are listed in their own categories in this book. More recent pottery is listed under the name of the maker or in the Pottery category.

Bowl, Florals, Mottled Beige Ground, Charlotte Rhead, 3 1/2 x 10 In. 235.00

Bowl, Tulip, Chocolate Amber Drip Glaze, Van Briggle Mold, Dryden, 8 In. 50.00
Charger, Floral Design, Charles Rhead, 15 In. 60.00
Charger, Manchu Pattern, Rhead, 18 In. 450.00
Ewer, Fired-On Gold, Twig Handle, Cincinnati, 10 3/8 In. 305.00
Ewer, Floral Design, Buds, Blossoms, Blue, Caramel Centers, Cincinnati, 11 1/2 In. 230.00
Jug, Manchu Pattern, Charlotte Rhead, Large 375.00
Pitcher, Dark Green, Tan Glaze, Wannopee 150.00
Plate, Byzantine, Multicolored Florals, Charles Rhead, 9 1/4 In.   55.00
Vase, Blue Iridescent Lava Glaze, Marked, L.C.T., 4 1/2 In. 300.00
Vase, Floral Design, Blue, Brown, Black, Blossoms, Cincinnati Art Pottery, 10 In. 165.00
Vase, Flower Petal, Green Gloss, Brown Drip, Bretby, England, 5 1/2 In. 65.00
Vase, Gold, Orange, Yellow Iridescent, Brouwer, Squat, 3 x 4 1/4 In. 825.00
Vase, Indian Tree, Mottled Beige, Charlotte Rhead, 5 1/8 x 5 In.   175.00
Vase, Iridescent Oxblood Feathered, Bulbous, Alfred University, 1912, 7 3/4 In. 165.00
Vase, Olive, Green Matte Glaze, Zanesville, Oh., 1910, 21 In. 286.00
Vase, Scalloped Leaf, Blue Satin Gloss, Bulbous, 9 In. 95.00
Vase, Stylized Blossoms, Leaves, Gold Over Aqua, Cincinnati Art Pottery, 12 In. 220.00
Vase, Stylized Figures, Leaping Gazelle Borders, Jean Mayodon, 1925, 12 3/4 In. 1840.00
Vase, Stylized Monkeys Cavorting In Branches, Charles Catteau, 1925, 14 In. 9775.00
Vase, Tobacco Brown Matte, Raised Vertical Leaf Design, Chicago Crucible, 6 In. 495.00

ARTS & CRAFTS was a design style popular in American decorative arts
from 1894 to 1923. In the 1970s collectors began to rediscover
Mission furniture, art pottery, metalwork, linens, and light fixtures
from this period. The interest has continued. Today everything from
this era is collectible, including jewelry, graphics, and silverware.
Additional items may be found in the Furniture category, various glass
categories, etc.

Box, Enamel Cartouche Of Ship, Copper Lined, 6 x 12 1/2 In. 660.00
Vase, Raised Poppy Design, Brass, Hammered, Fayetteville, N.Y., 3 x 13 1/2 In. 286.00
Wall Sconce, Metal, Glass Insert, Signed, Moe Bridges, 14 In. 695.00

AURENE glass was made by Frederick Carder of New York about 1904.
It is an iridescent gold, blue, green, or red glass, usually marked   **AURENE**
Aurene or *Steuben*.

Basket, Iridescent Gold, Applied Loop Handle, Steuben, 6 3/4 In.   1750.00
Bowl, Blue Glass Body, Iridescent Surface, Signed, Steuben, 2 x 10 1/2 In. 575.00
Bowl, Flared Rim, Gold Interior, Calcite, Steuben, 2 5/8 x 6 In. 220.00
Bowl, Gold, Amber Flared Rim, Blue, Pink, Steuben, 1910, 12 In. 747.00
Bowl, Gold, Calcite, Steuben, 10 In. 175.00
Bowl, Gold, Steuben, 10 In. 400.00
Bowl, Iridescent Blue, Calcite Exterior, Steuben, 10 x 2 3/4 In. 805.00
Bowl, Rose, No. 2651, Ribbed, Scalloped Rim, Signed, 2 7/8 In. 450.00
Bowl, White, Gold Interior, Steuben, 10 x 3 1/2 In. 250.00
Candlestick, Blue, Purple, Green Highlights, Marked, Steuben, 8 1/4 In. 550.00
Centerpiece, Blue, No. 2586, Steuben, 10 x 1 1/2 In. 715.00
Centerpiece, Reddish Gold, 3 Button Feet, Steuben, 10 x 2 In. 385.00
Compote, Blue Gold, Hexagonal, Steuben, 3 1/2 In. 605.00
Compote, Blue, Calcite, Steuben, 6 1/4 In. 880.00
Compote, Blue, Raised On Round Domed Foot, Steuben, 6 x 2 3/4 In. 250.00
Compote, Gold Calcite, White Cut Easter Lilies, Flared, Steuben, 7 x 12 1/2 In. 1750.00
Compote, Stretched Rolled Rim, Gold Calcite, Steuben, 3 1/4 x 7 1/4 In. 575.00
Darner, Platinum Gold At Ball, Cobalt Blue, Signed, 9 In. 402.50
Decanter, Red Gold, Swirled Neck, Pinch Sided, Flame Stopper, Steuben, 10 In. 1375.00
Dish, Blue, Loop, Gold Ring Handle, Steuben, Signed, 4 x 1/2 In. 750.00
Fan, Gold, Flat Cone Design, Blue, White Vine Border, Hearts, Carder, Steuben, 8 In. . . .   2875.00
Goblet, Gold, Domed Foot, Short Stem, Steuben, 4 1/2 In. 235.00
Jar, Gold, Melon, Stopper, Steuben, Signed, 4 In. 715.00
Lamp, Oviform, Gold Shade, 5 In., Pair 57.50
Lamp, Pink Gold Entwined Veins, Floral Silk Shade, Bottle Shape, Steuben, 9 In. 1650.00
Lamp Base, Gold Purple, Gold Leafy Vine Design, Signed, 30 In. 2875.00
Sconce, Bell Shape, Butterscotch, Applied Border, Case Lining, Steuben, 9 1/2 In. 660.00
Sherbet & Underplate, Blue, Calcite, Paper Label, Steuben, 4 In. 825.00

Vase, 3-Part Trunk Design, Rust, Blue Iridescent Surface, Signed, 6 In. 862.50
Vase, 4 Green Eye Peacock Feathers, White, Gold, Green, Carder, Steuben, 12 In. 4600.00
Vase, Applied Cupped Foot, Swirled Ribbed Conical Shape, Blue, Signed, 12 In. 1955.00
Vase, Blue Gold Iridescence, Steuben, 1900, 11 In. 1955.00
Vase, Blue, 2 Snail Handles, Blue Surface, Steuben, 11 1/2 In. 990.00
Vase, Blue, Calcite Trumpet, Ruffled Rim, White Calcite, Carder, Steuben, 13 In. 1495.00
Vase, Blue, Steuben, 8 In. 1600.00
Vase, Flared Ruffled Top, Steuben, 7 1/4 In. 750.00
Vase, Gold, Blue, Pink Iridescence, Steuben, 1915, 8 1/4 In. 1090.00
Vase, Gold, Jack-In-The-Pulpit, Floriform, White Trumpet, Carder, Steuben, 10 In. 805.00
Vase, Gold, Jade Peacock, Acid Etched, Exotic Birds, Carder, Steuben, 12 In. 6325.00
Vase, Green, Platinum Gold Iridized Surface, Green Swirls Exterior, Steuben, 4 In. 1265.00
Vase, Stick, Iridescent Gold, Steuben, Signed, 8 1/4 In. 245.00
Vase, Threaded, Green Jade Iridescent, Trumpet Form, Carder, Steuben, 10 1/4 In. 2300.00
Vase, Tree Trunk, 3 Branches, 20 Thorns, Steuben, 6 1/2 In. 475.00
Vase, Trumpet, Gold Flared Rim, Tapered Shape, Gold Iridescence, Steuben, 10 1/4 In. . .   632.00

AUSTRIA is a collecting term which covers pieces made by a wide variety of factories. They are listed in this book in categories such as Kauffmann, Royal Dux, or Porcelain.

AUTO parts and accessories are collectors' items today. Gas pump globes and license plates are part of this specialty. Prices are determined by age, rarity, and condition. Signs and packaging related to automobiles may also be found in the Advertising category. Lalique hood ornaments will be listed in the Lalique category.

Battery Tester, Break Not, Box 25.00
Booklet, Alfa Romeo, Color, 1950, 20 Pages, 8 1/2 x 11 In. 25.00
Booklet, Chrysler, Color, 35 Pages, 11 x 13 In. 25.00
Box, Bulb Kit, Cadillac, Tin 140.00
Box, Gas Station, Crown Gas Coca-Cola, Tin 16.00
Bulb Kit, Packard, Tin, Complete 120.00
Catalog, Ford Motor Co., Detroit, Mi., 1917, 48 Page, 6 x 8 3/4 In. 22.00
Catalog, General Motors Corp., Detroit, Mi., 1949, 32 Page 5 1/2 x 7 1/2 In. 14.00
Clock, Oldsmobile, Early 1900s 145.00
Clock, Sweep Second Hand At 12, Crown At 6 O'Clock, 15 Jewels, 3 Adjustments 55.00
Gas Pump, Gilbert & Barker, 10 Gal. 1000.00
Gas Pump Globe, Bell Ethyl, Glass Body, Metal Base, 13 1/2 In. 825.00
Gas Pump Globe, Blu-Flame, Glass Body, Blue, Yellow & White Globe, 14 In. 550.00
Gas Pump Globe, Calso Gasoline, Gill Body, Silver Rings, Green Lens, 13 1/2 In. 852.00
Gas Pump Globe, Clark, Plastic Capolite Body, 13 1/2 In. 175.00
Gas Pump Globe, Frontier Gas, 3-Piece Glass Body, 13 1/2 In.   1980.00
Gas Pump Globe, Independent Gas, White Metal Body, 15 In. 385.00
Gas Pump Globe, Kerosene Diesel Fuel, Metal Body, Blue & White Lens, 15 In. 220.00
Gas Pump Globe, Richfield, Metal Body, West Coast Richfield, 15 In. 1100.00
Gas Pump Globe, Shamrock, White Plastic Body, 12 x 16 In. 247.00
Gas Pump Globe, Shell Diesoline, Seashell Shape, Milk Glass, 17 x 18 In. 880.00
Gas Pump Globe, Shell, Red Lettering, Milk Glass, 18 x 19 In.   357.00
Gas Pump Globe, Sinclair Diesel, No Lead, 1 Side 182.00
Gas Pump Globe, Sinclair Dino Supreme, White Plastic Body, 13 1/2 In. 165.00
Gas Pump Globe, Skelly Premium, Red & Blue On White, 13 1/2 In. 198.00
Gas Pump Globe, Tokheim, Flying A 795.00
Gas Pump Globe, White Eagle, Figural, Milk Glass, 21 In. 1200.00
Gas Pump Globe, Zephyr, 3-Piece Body, 13 1/2 In. 440.00
Gauge, Tire Pressure, Red, Black, Blue, White, Schrader Tire, 14 1/2 x 6 In. 357.00
Head Lamp, Rolls-Royce, Brass, Mounted To Frame, 1930s 300.00
Headlight, Model A Ford, Kerosene, Brass, 2 Lenses 37.00
Hood Ornament, Duesenberg, Brass, Chrome Plate, 1931 . . . .   357.00
Hood Ornament, Franklin, 1925 . . . .   100.00
Hood Ornament, Lincoln, Chrome Plate, 1933, 6 In. 302.00
Hood Ornament, Pontiac, Chrome Plate, Brass Face, 2 1/2 x 4 1/2 In. 82.00
Horn, Sparton Chime Bugle, Black, 16 In. 75.00
Jug, Esso Happy Motoring, Thermos 75.00

Knob, Gear Shift, Skull 60.00
Lens, Spreadlight, Essex Motor Cars, McKeen Glass, 1920, 8 In. 30.00
License Plate, AFI, American Forces, Italy 20.00
License Plate, Alabama, 1951 .... 15.50
License Plate, Alabama, National Guard, 1985 .... 5.50
License Plate, Alberta, Canada, 1966 .... 7.50
License Plate, Arizona, 1933, Copper 100.00
License Plate, Arkansas, 1988, Handicap 5.50
License Plate, California, 1930 .... 25.00
License Plate, California, 1963, Black 7.50
License Plate, Canal Zone, 1972 .... 28.00
License Plate, Hawaii, 1946 .... 75.00
License Plate, Illinois, 1912 .... 350.00
License Plate, Indiana, 1989, POW 15.50
License Plate, Indiana, 1983, Handicap 5.50
License Plate, Kansas, 1933 .... 65.00
License Plate, Maine, 1927, Pair 60.00
License Plate, Manitoba, Canada, 1950 .... 15.50
License Plate, Massachusetts, 1913, 5 1/2 x 14 In. 82.00
License Plate, Massachusetts, 1917 .... 35.00
License Plate, Michigan, 1947 .... 15.50
License Plate, New Jersey, 1916 .... 40.00
License Plate, New Mexico, 1972 .... 5.50
License Plate, New York, 1941 .... 10.50
License Plate, Ontario, Canada, 1918 .... 35.00
License Plate, Oregon, 1920 .... 30.00
License Plate, Pennsylvania, 1906 .... 700.00
License Plate, Pennsylvania, 1911 .... 350.00
License Plate, Pennsylvania, 1914, 6 x 14 In. 22.00
License Plate, Pennsylvania, 1915, Blue, White, 6 In. 100.00
License Plate, Pennsylvania, 1919 .... 25.00
License Plate, Pennsylvania, 1954, Dealer 330.00
License Plate, Quebec, Canada, 1962 .... 8.50
License Plate, Rhode Island, 1959 .... 17.00
License Plate, South Carolina, 1971 .... 4.50
License Plate, South Dakota, 1992, Mt. Rushmore 3.50
License Plate, Tennessee, 1946 .... 40.00
License Plate, Texas, 1958, Pair 18.50
License Plate, Texas, 1993, Lone Star 3.50
License Plate, U.S. Forces, Germany, 1953 .... 50.00
License Plate, Utah, 1939 .... 25.00
License Plate, Vermont, 1948 .... 10.50
License Plate, Virginia, 1970, Pair 15.50
License Plate, Washington, 1971 .... 3.50
License Plate, Washington, D.C., 1957, Inaugural, Pair 350.00
License Plate, West Virginia, 1964, Centennial 10.50
License Plate Attachment, California AAA 35.00
License Plate Attachment, Junior Chamber Of Commerce 50.00
License Plate Attachment, Shell, 3 Flags, 1930s, Unused 47.00
Manual, Chevrolet Corvette, All-American Sports Car, 1954, 7 1/2 x 12 In. 55.00
Manual, Franklin, 1925 .... 100.00
Oil Can, Adco, Easy Pour, Green, Yellow, 5 Gal., 14 1/2 In. 65.00
Oil Can, Amalie, 1952, 1 Qt. 30.00
Oil Can, Castrol Snowmobile Oil, 1 Qt. 15.00
Oil Can, Champlin, Easy Pour, Faded, 5 Gal. 95.00
Oil Can, Gargoyle Mobil, Chinese Writing, 1920s, 1 Gal. 130.00
Oil Can, Gargoyle Mobil, Ford, 1920s, 1 Gal. 125.00
Oil Can, Guardian Oil, 1 Qt. 12.00
Oil Can, Havoline Advanced Custom Made, 1 Qt. 20.00
Oil Can, Kendall, Round, 1 Gal. 25.00
Oil Can, Oilzum, Canco, 1 Qt. 180.00
Oil Can, Oilzum, Racing Oil, White, Orange Triangle, 1 Qt. 50.00
Oil Can, Remington, Powder Solvent, Label, Contents 55.00

Auto, Sign, Texaco Gasoline Filling Station,
Porcelain, 1915, 42-In. Diam.

A video inventory is being
offered in some cities. It is a
color video cassette recording
done in your home with your
voice describing the antiques.
Keep it in a safe deposit box
for a permanent record of
your collection.

Oil Can, Shell, 1 Qt.	12.00
Oil Can, Sinclair Opaline Motor Oil, Green, Display, 14 1/2 In.	110.00
Oil Can, Socony Vacuum Lubrite, 1930s, 1 Qt.	19.00
Oil Can, Veedol Grease Cans	15.00
Parking Meter, Duncan Miller, Model 50	45.00
Saltshaker, Quaker State Motor Oil, Can Shape	3.50
Shirt, Service Attendant's, Esso	65.00
Sign, Austin Service, White Background, Black Border, Porcelain, 17 x 36 In.	248.00
Sign, Chrysler, Plymouth, Round Center Band, Yellow, Red, Blue, Porcelain, 42 In.	523.00
Sign, Crosley Sales, White Background, Red Lettering, Porcelain, 42 In.	770.00
Sign, Desoto, Plymouth, Bright Red Center Band, Yellow, Blue, Porcelain, 42 In.	303.00
Sign, Dodge, Plymouth, Blue Ground, Red, White Lettering, Porcelain, 42 In.	660.00
Sign, Gas, Mobil, Flying Horse, Porcelain, Pump	85.00
Sign, Globe Gas, Blue Band Across Middle, Porcelain, 30 In.	605.00
Sign, GMC Trucks, Green, White, Porcelain, 24 x 48 In.	523.00
Sign, Good Gulf Gasoline, Porcelain, 10 In.	85.00
Sign, Hudson Parts, Red, White, Blue, White Lettering, Porcelain, 29 x 42 In.	220.00
Sign, Hudson Terraplane, White Background, Blue Trim, Porcelain, 42 In.	303.00
Sign, Magnolia Oil, Green Magnolias In Center, Motor Oil, Porcelain, 42 In.	253.00
Sign, McColl, Motor Oil, Red Indian, Porcelain, Round, 5 Ft.	2398.00
Sign, Mercury Sales & Service, Red, White, Blue, Porcelain, 30 x 48 In.	825.00
Sign, No Smoking, Porcelain, Standard, 1940s, 6 x 30 In.	325.00
Sign, Oldsmobile, Red, White, Blue Center Crest, Yellow Border, Porcelain, 42 In.	176.00
Sign, Pennzoil, Liberty Bell Logo In Center, Oval, Porcelain, 30 In.	110.00
Sign, Pontiac Goodwill, Red Ground, White Circle, Porcelain, 36 x 36 In.	209.00
Sign, Pontiac Service, Indian Bust In Center Logo, Red, White, Blue, Porcelain, 42 In.	990.00
Sign, Pump, Texaco Fire Chief, Porcelain	75.00 to 95.00
Sign, Quaker State, Porcelain, 2 Sides, Frame, 4 x 8 Ft.	700.00
Sign, Red Crown Ethyl, 2 Sides, Porcelain, 1920s, 30 In.	325.00
Sign, Sinclair Gasoline, Red Crown, Blue Border, Porcelain, 42 In.	275.00
Sign, Star Cars, Star In Center, Green, White Lettering, Porcelain, 24 x 36 In.	468.00
Sign, Texaco Gasoline Filling Station, Porcelain, 1915, 42-In. Diam. *Illus*	2750.00
Sign, Vacuum White Star, Red, White, Blue, Porcelain, 30 In.	880.00
Snowmobile, Polaris, 340TX, Chrome Skis, 1974	900.00
Tin, Texaco Lighter Fluid, New Logo, 4 Oz.	10.00
Tin, Texaco Water Pump Grease, 1930s-1940s	40.00
Tin, Yankee Grease, Red, White & Blue, New England Map, 5 Lb.	85.00
Tire Pump, Model T	35.00
Tire Rack, Armstrong, Rhino	35.00
Wheel, Ford, Wooden	175.00
Windshield Scraper, Philco, Advertising, Art Deco	20.00

AUTUMN LEAF pattern china was made for the Jewel Tea Company
beginning in 1933. Hall China Company of East Liverpool, Ohio,
Crooksville China Company of Crooksville, Ohio, Harker Potteries of
Chester, West Virginia, and Paden City Pottery, Paden City, West

Virginia, made dishes with this design. Autumn Leaf has remained popular and was made by Hall China Company until 1978. Some other pieces in the Autumn Leaf pattern are still being made. For more information, see *Kovels' Depression Glass & American Dinnerware Price List*.

Bean Pot, Handle	600.00
Bean Pot, No. 4	175.00
Bean Pot, No. 5	125.00 to 195.00
Berry Bowl, Hall, 5 1/2 In.	8.50
Bowl, 5 1/2 In.	5.00 to 6.00
Bowl, Hall, 6 1/2 In.	11.00
Bowl, Salad	18.00
Bowl, Vegetable, Divided	120.00
Bowl, Vegetable, Oval	20.00
Bowl, Vegetable, Round	110.00
Butter, Cover, Jewel Tea	350.00
Butter, Wings, Cover, 1/4 Lb.	1100.00
Cake Carrier, 1950	50.00
Cake Plate	10.00 to 20.00
Candy Dish	525.00
Candy Dish, Metal Base	490.00
Casserole, Cover, 6 1/2 In.	40.00
Clock, Electric	500.00
Coffee Maker, Drip, Metal	78.00
Coffeepot, 8 Cup, Hall	42.00
Coffeepot, Electric, Hall	285.00
Cookbook, Mary Dunbar, 1933	30.00
Creamer	8.00
Creamer, Ruffled	18.00
Cup & Saucer, Hall	8.00 to 9.50
Custard Cup	5.00
Gravy Boat	18.00
Holder, Sugar Packet, 1990	125.00
Mixing Bowl, Radiance	8.00
Mixing Bowl Set, Hall, 3 Piece	140.00 to 220.00
Mug, Conic	55.00
Mug, Irish Coffee	95.00
Pitcher, Breakfast, Hall, 9 In.	9.00
Pitcher, Ice Lip, Ball, Box, 1978	50.00
Plate, Hall, 6 In.	4.00 to 6.00
Plate, Hall, 7 1/4 In.	7.75
Punch Bowl Set	375.00
Salt & Pepper, Range, Hall	20.00
Sugar & Creamer, Cover, Hall	40.00
Tea For Two, Set	220.00
Teapot, Aladdin, Infuser	48.00 to 60.00
Teapot, Newport	100.00 to 120.00
Tin, Matching, Round, Low, Radiance	5.00
Tumbler, Frosted, 5 1/2 In.	27.00
Tumbler, Frosted, Hall, 14 Oz.	40.00
Vase, Bud, Hall, 6 In.	195.00
Vegetable, Round	75.00

AVON bottles are listed in the Bottle category under Avon.

BACCARAT glass was made in France by La Compagnie des Cristalleries de Baccarat, located 150 miles from Paris. The factory was started in 1765. The firm went bankrupt and began operating again about 1822. Cane and millefiori paperweights were made during the 1860 to 1880 period. The firm is still working near Paris making paperweights and glasswares.

Ashtray, Octagonal Geometric Design, Crystal, 4 1/2 In.	50.00
Beaker, Sulphide, 2 Hands Holding A Bouquet, 1860, 4 In.	808.00

Bowl, Gilt Oriental Design, Gilt Footed Base, Rectangular, 5 1/4 In. 287.00
Bowl, L'Ardrite Nuit, Corday, 3 3/4 In. 117.00
Candelabrum, 2-Light, Cut Glass, Prisms, 1850, 18 In., Pair 2850.00
Candlestick, Cut Glass, Hurricane Shade, Mid-19th Century, 27 In., Pair 1900.00
Candlestick, Oil Lamp Form, Swirl Molded Receptacle, Base, 19 1/2 In. 402.50
Decanter, Empire Pattern, Anthemion & Rosette, Paneled Baluster, 11 In., Pair 690.00
Decanter, Harcourt 150.00
Decanter, Louis XIII, Cognac, Queen's Visit To France In 1957 Scene, 5 In. 495.00
Decanter, Remy, Pinched, Spiked Sides 135.00
Decanter, Talleyrand 229.00
Decanter Set, Talleyrand, Silver Plate, With Tray, 8 Piece 550.00
Figurine, Cat, Seated, Grooming Itself, 4 1/4 In. 125.00
Figurine, Great Horned Owl, Bernard Augst, 1980, 11 1/2 In. 1900.00
Figurine, Horse's Head, Black Crystal, 7 In. 165.00
Figurine, Japanese Horse 80.00
Figurine, Owl, 4 1/2 In. 85.00
Figurine, Pelican 80.00
Figurine, Rabbit 90.00
Figurine, Squirrel, Signed 90.00
Inkwell, Crystal, Swag Design, Stamped, Glass Well, 5 1/2 In. 977.00
Lamp, Rose Teinte, Embossed Swirls & Scrolls, 8 1/2 In. 145.00
Paperweight, 4 Concentric Millefiori Rows, Pink, Blue, White, Green, 2 5/8 In. 201.00
Paperweight, Basket With Flowers, 1976 .... 500.00
Paperweight, Blue, Red, Green, White Millefiori Garland, Claret Ground, 2 3/4 In. 1495.00
Paperweight, Bouquet, Yellow Pompon, 1845-1860 ...._Illus_ 16500.00
Paperweight, Butterfly, Clematis, 1845-1860 ...._Illus_ 9350.00
Paperweight, Elephant 75.00
Paperweight, Lafayette 125.00
Paperweight, Lilies, 1977 .... 300.00
Paperweight, Pink Dog Rose ...._Illus_ 950.00
Paperweight, Rabbit 75.00
Paperweight, Silhouette Canes On Lace 3190.00
Paperweight, Starfish 70.00
Paperweight, Sulphide, Woodrow Wilson 75.00
Paperweight, Thousand Petal Roses 6600.00
Perfume Bottle, Coty, Scrolled Berry Vine Design, Frosted Square Stopper, 4 In. 805.00
Perfume Bottle, Frosted Floral Gray Stopper, Signed, 4 1/2 In. 450.00
Perfume Bottle, Guerlain Mitsouko, Original Label, 4 x 2 1/2 In. 65.00
Perfume Bottle, Jean Patou, Invitation, Label, 1932, 8 In. 795.00
Sculpture, Great Horned Owl, No. 767924, Bernard Augst, 1980 .... 1800.00
Sculpture, Large Bear, No. 764453 .... 2995.00
Sculpture, Polar Bear, Crystal, Stamped, 12 In. 1035.00
Toothpick, Swirl 225.00
Tumbler, Daisy, Amberina 60.00

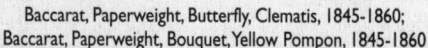

Baccarat, Paperweight, Butterfly, Clematis, 1845-1860;
Baccarat, Paperweight, Bouquet, Yellow Pompon, 1845-1860

Baccarat, Paperweight,
Pink Dog Rose

Vase, Allover Tendril Etch, 6 1/4 In. 195.00
Vase, Black & Gilt Serpent, Opalescent Rocky Base, Brass Ball Footed, Marked, 8 In. 1760.00
Vase, Blossoms & Berry Design, Translucent Pink, Cushion Foot, 1900, 15 1/2 In. 517.00

BADGES have been used since before the Civil War. Collectors search for examples of all types, including law enforcement and company identification badges. Well-known prison or law enforcement badges are most desirable. Most are made of nickel or brass. Many recent reproductions have been made.

Acme Wire Company 20.00
Berghoff Brewing Co., Plant, Employee Name, Black Letters, Yellow Ground 88.00
Braniff Pilot, Hat, Gold Wreath, White Enameled Details, 1960 .... 55.00
Buffalo New York Reserve Police, Stamped Eagle, Shield Design, 3 x 2 In. 29.00
Chauffeur, California, 1926 .... 50.00
Chauffeur, Illinois, 1928 .... 15.00
Chauffeur, Illinois, Set Of 4, 1930, 1933, 1934, 1935 .... 100.00
Chauffeur, New York, 1914, Brass, Enameled Details, 1 1/2 In. 24.00
Chauffeur, New York, 1927, 1 1/2 In. 23.00
Chicago International Livestock Exposition, 1922, Round 55.00
Clerk's, Christmas Shopping Reminder, Celluloid, Red & Green, White Ground, 1950s .. 18.00
Continental Aviation, Supervisor, Plant 40.00
Criminal Dep. Sheriff, Orleans Parish, La. 300.00
Deputy Sheriff, Bergen County, New Jersey 30.00
Deputy Sheriff, San Francisco, Name, Deputy's Initials, 1920s 995.00
Diamond Taxi, Black Engineer Title Below Sedan, Metal, 2 1/2 In. 37.00
Dixie Trailway's Sunshine, Hat, Bus Driver's, Red, White, Blue, Silver Finish, 3 1/4 In. 61.00
Dodge City, Pierced Star Center, White Metal Construction, Scalloped Shield, 1 3/4 In. . . 18.00
Doorman, The Roosevelt 45.00
Driver's, Keystone Pennsylvania, 1910 .... 600.00
Fire Inspector, SFFD, 16, 2-Digit Number 125.00
Fireman, 10, Exempt, Utica Fire Department, c.1885 .... 125.00
Fireman, Allentown Fire, 379, Department, Nickel, Copper Numerals, 1880s 110.00
Fireman, Bayside, Nickel, Applied Numbers 80.00
Fireman, Bethel, G.P., No. 1, C.G. Braxmar, New York City, c.1890 .... 75.00
Fireman, Black Enamel, Applied 2, Solid Gold, Hand Engraved, c.1870, 1 In. 82.00
Fireman, Breast, Portland Fire Department, c.1910 .... 40.00
Fireman, Cap, Maltese Cross, OFD, Numbers In Center, 1930s 100.00
Fireman, Cap, Steamer Center SFD, Wire Retainer, c.1900 .... 45.00
Fireman, Engraved King Phillip Steamer, Bristol, R.I., c.1895 .... 100.00
Fireman, John Duffy, 2, Steamer, Shield Shape, 1866 .... 100.00
Fireman, Member, Fire Department, Kansas City, Missouri, 56 .... 50.00
Fireman, Paramedic, Lucite 200.00
Fireman, President, Frank Cole, Cornalis Fire Dept., 1916 .... 375.00
Fireman, San Francisco Auxiliary, World War II 80.00
Fireman, State Fire Warden, California, c.1900 .... 125.00
Fireman, Union Hook & Ladder Co,, No. 1, Rutland, Vt., c.1885 .... 75.00
G.A.R., 1865 .... 75.00
G.A.R., Hat, Shell Wreath, Gold Finish, 2 1/4 In. 55.00
Hackensack Water Company 30.00
Kennedy Space Center, Visitor, Apollo 12 .... 68.00
Lincoln County Sheriff, 5-Point Star, White Metal, Ornate Stamped Design, 3 In. 18.00
M.G.M. Usher 65.00
North American Van Lines, Hat, Enameled Red, Green Details, Silver Finish, 2 3/4 In. 61.00
Police, Chicago, 1920 .... 150.00
Police, Clinton, Ornate Scrolling Design, Brass, 2 1/2 In. 89.00
Police, Indian, Crow, U.S. Center, Sterling Silver, Round 70.00
Police, Indian, White Metal Design, Raised Lettering, Crossed Arrows 18.00
Police, Nashville, Traffic, Officer, No. 7 .... 475.00
Police, Pennsylvania Tank Car Co., Kansas City, Missouri, 1922 .... 75.00
Pratt & Whitney Engines, Brass, Enameled Details, 2 1/4 In. 23.00
Radio City, Hat, Art Deco Style 135.00
Saloons Must Go, Engraved On Silver Metal, 1900s 60.00
Special Police, State Of Maine, 2 3/4 x 2 In. 85.00

Texaco Oil Co., Employee, 1930s 24.00
Texas Rangers Co., White Metal Design, Star Inside Outer Ring, 1 5/8 In. Diam. 18.00
U.S. Marshal Deputy, 5-Point Star, White Metal, Dark Patina, 2 3/4 In. 18.00
U.S. Post Office Dept., Eagle Above, Number Below, Oval 70.00
United States Marine Corps, Rifle Sharpshooter 4.00
Yellow Cab 125.00

BANKS of metal have been made since 1868. There are still banks, mechanical banks, and registering banks (those that show the total money deposited on the face of the bank). Many old iron or tin banks have been reproduced since the 1950s in iron or plastic. Pottery, glass, and plastic banks are also listed here. Mickey Mouse and other Disneyana banks are listed in Disneyana.

Abraham Lincoln, Bottle 14.00
Abraham Lincoln Bust, Lincoln National Life Insurance, Metal 75.00
Acorn Stoves, Acorn Shape, Stoneware, Blue Glaze 100.00
Admiral, Vinyl 20.00
Airplane, Continental Airlines, DC-3, Ertl 50.00
Airplane, Exxon Bi-Wing Tiger Spirit 40.00
Amish Boy, Black Overalls, Blue Shirt, Black Hat, John Wright, 1970s 65.00
Amoco 100 Anniversary, Model T, Painted Metal, Box, 3 1/2 x 6 In. 38.00
Andy Gump Savings Bank 550.00
Artillery Bank, 1960s, Cast Iron 125.00
Aunt Jemima, Cast Iron, 11 In. 23.00
Baba-Looey, Vinyl 35.00
Baby In Cradle, Rosettes, Cast Iron, 1890s, 3 1/4 In. 586.00
Bank Building, White, Red Roof, Cast Iron, 3 1/4 In. 140.00
Bank Of Industry, Kenton, Cast Iron 250.00
Barber Shop Pole, Painted Ceramic, 1940s 65.00
Bardahl Top Oil Can 25.00
Barney & Bambam 40.00
Bear, Begging, Brown, Pink, Blue & Black, Iron, 6 5/8 In. 95.00
Bear, Paddington 35.00
Bear, With Honey Pot, Hubley, 6 1/2 In. 240.00
Beehive, Cast Iron 375.00
Begging Bear, Cast Iron, 1910-1925, 5 5/8 In. 91.00
Betsy Ross House, Philadelphia 85.00
Big Boy, Figural, Soft Vinyl, Hands On Shoulder Straps, Copyright 1973, 9 1/2 In. 35.00
Billiken, Ceramic 145.00
Billy Brand Laxative, Cast Iron 245.00
Bismark Pig, J. & E. Stevens, c.1883 .... 3900.00
Black Sambo With Fruit, Nodder 40.00
Book, Singer, Simulated Leather Over Metal, American, 1930s, 3 x 3 1/2 In. 17.00
Bottle Shape, Spongeware, Blue Dots Top, J.W.B. Blue Stencil, 6 In. 740.00
Buffalo, Cast Iron 165.00
Building, Broadway National Bank, Denver, Metal 60.00
Building, Domed, Cast Iron 75.00
Building, Flat Iron, Cast Iron, 5 1/2 In. 215.00
Building, Howard Johnson Restaurant, Plastic 35.00
Building, Silver Dome, Window Holes, Cast Iron, 5 In. 65.00
Building, Skyscraper, Silver & Gold Paint, Cast Iron, A.C. Williams, c.1900, 6 In. 123.00
Building, South Main State Bank, Houston, Texas, Bronze, 2 3/4 x 6 1/2 In. 33.00
Building, State Bank, Kyser & Rex Co., Cast Iron, c.1897 .... 4500.00
Building, World's Fair Administration 2200.00
Bulldog, Ives, 1878 .... 4500.00
Bulldog, Mack Truck, Vinyl 40.00
California Raisins, Sun-Maid, Vinyl, Mailer Box 40.00
Canadian Prancing Horse, Cast Iron, 4 1/8 x 4 3/4 In. 375.00
Captain Crunch, Cereal Premium, Vinyl, 7 In. 65.00
Captain Marine, Vinyl 55.00
Car, 1914 Dodge, Metal, 5 1/2 In. 16.00
Car, Deluxe Yellow Cab, Arcade, 1921 .... 4800.00
Carnation Evaporated Milk, Tin 30.00

Cash Box, Tin, Chein, 3 1/2 x 2 3/4 In. 45.00
Casper, American Bisque 875.00
Cat, Kliban, On Stool, Sigma 150.00
Cat, Sitting, With Red Bow Tie, White, Cast Iron 48.00
Cat, Union Carbide, Plastic, 1981 . . . .   15.00
Charlie Tuna, Ceramic 75.00
Chef, With Dog, Sigma 95.00
Church Towers, Simulated Stained Glass 963.00
City Bank, Cast Iron, 4 x 3 x 2 In. 70.00
Clown, Bobs Head When Money Is Inserted, Nodder 45.00
Clown, Cast Iron, 6 1/4 In. . . . . .90.00 to 125.00
Clown, Figural, Tube, Plastic, Coin Holder Legs, 1 1/2 x 4 3/4 x 7 3/4 In. 18.00
Clown, Tin, Chein, 1930s 110.00
Coffin, Windup, Tin, Japan, 1960s 195.00
Colonel Sanders, Japan, Vinyl 195.00
Colonel Sanders, Plastic, Canada, 1970s . . . . .17.00 to 20.00
Coon Face 45.00
Cow, Cast Iron, Gold Paint, A.C. Williams, 5 1/4 In. 150.00
Cupola, Blue & Yellow, Cast Iron 265.00
Cutie, Hubley 100.00
Dandy Dan, Barber Shop, 1970s 55.00
Darth Vader, Sigma, 1977 . . . .   50.00
Dog, Cast Iron, Hubley 175.00
Dog, Mack Truck Bulldog, Vinyl 40.00
Dog, Spaniel, Cream & Brown, Cast Iron, 3 1/2 x 6 In. 50.00
Dog, Wirehaired Terrier, Seated, Hubley . . . . .135.00 to 165.00
Donkey, Cast Iron, 4 1/2 In. 65.00
Donkey, Laughing, ABC 75.00
Dow Scrubbing Bubble, Pottery . . . . .17.00 to 30.00
Dracula Castle 45.00
Dry Dock Savings, Ship's Wheel 33.00
Dutch Girl, Hubley 135.00
Eagle On Cupola, Cast Iron 935.00
Elephant, Cast Iron, 2 3/4 x 4 1/4 In. 85.00
Elephant, Republican, Nodder . . . . .60.00 to 125.00
Elephant, Swivel Trunk, Cast Iron, 2 1/2 x 3 1/2 In. 225.00
Elk, Cast Iron 65.00
Elmer Fudd, Holding Rifle, Iron, 11 In. 115.00
Elmer Fudd, Treasure Craft 58.00
En-Ar-Co, Red, Green & Cream, Metal, 3 1/2 x 2 In. 93.00
Entenmann's, Chef . . . . .75.00 to 95.00
Esso, Glass 125.00
Esso Tiger, Vinyl, 1960s 45.00
Eveready, Black Cat 10.00
Farmer Jack Savings, Vinyl 50.00
Federal Savings, Steamship Queen Mary, Model, 11 In. 20.00
Felix The Cat, Nodder 935.00
Felix The Cat, Pottery 45.00
Ferris Wheel, Hubley 6710.00
Fido, Cast Iron 135.00
Fido, Hubley 100.00
Fishing, The One That Got Away, Cast Iron, 1960s 175.00
Fisk Tire Boy, Ceramic 55.00
Florida Orange Bird, Hard Vinyl 35.00
Flowerpot, Bluebird 85.00
Fred & Wilma Flintstone, American Bisque Co. 275.00
Fred Flintstone, Vinyl, 13 In. . . . . .35.00 to 65.00
Furnace, Cast Iron, France, 8 1/2 In. 143.00
General Butler, Political Pamphlet, Cast Iron, J. & E. Stevens, 1884, 6 3/4 In. . .805.00 to 2185.00
General Pershing's Bust, Cast Iron, 1918, 8 In. 100.00
George Washington, Gold, Hubley 50.00
Girl, Piggy, Silver Dollar Large Slot, American Bisque, 1930-1940 . . . .   25.00
Glass, Pittsburgh Paints 45.00

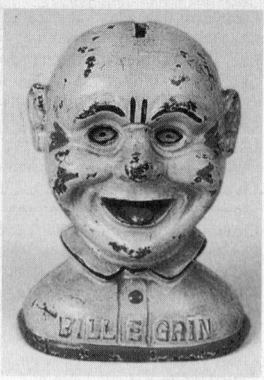

Bank, Massillon Tiger,   Bank, Mechanical, Acrobat,   Bank, Mechanical, Bill E. Grin,
Orange Shirt, Ceramic, 8 In.   Cast Iron, Pat. 1883   Cast Iron, J. & E. Stevens

Globe, Apollo Space Capsule Attached, Cast Iron, Gold Color 75.00
Globe, Tin Lithograph, Chein 20.00
Goose, Iron, Gold Traces, 5 In. 80.00
Grandma's Cookies, Blue & White, Vinyl, 6 In. 95.00
Grimace, McDonald's, 8 1/2 In. 30.00
Harley-Davidson, Side Car, Marble Base 475.00
Haunted House, Battery Operated, Tin, 1960s 150.00
Hen, With Bonnet, DeLee 30.00
Herky Iowa Hawkeye, Nodder 28.00
Hershey Bars, Plastic, Penny, Box 40.00
Hey Diddle Diddle, Copper Color Metal, 5 1/2 In. 45.00
Home Budget By Bank Book, Cast Iron, 6 x 2 1/2 In. 90.00
Horse, Prancing, Gold Finish, Cast Iron, 4 1/2 In. 99.00
Horse, Saddle, Cast Iron, A.C. Williams, c.1934, 3 In. 158.00
Horseshoe, Hubley 100.00
Hortense, Sigma 245.00
Hubert, Lion, Regal China . . . . .25.00 to 30.00
Humpty Dumpty, Chein, 1934, 6 In. 275.00
Icee Polar Bear, Advertising 28.00
Indian Head, Cast Iron, Large 42.50
Kangaroo, Orange, Wood, Nodder, Gimbels Store Sticker, 1940, 4 1/2 In. 10.00
Keebler, Elf, Red, White, Yellow & Peach, Pottery, Glazed, 10 In. . . . . .12.00 to 55.00
Kenton Radio, Green, 4 1/2 In. 425.00
Kliban Cat, Walking, Red Sneakers, Sigma 80.00
Kool-Aid 55.00
Kress Pig, Nodder 40.00
Laurel & Hardy, 1972, 12 In., 2 Piece 85.00
Li'l Abner, Tin Lithograph, 1953 . . . . 135.00
Liberty Bell, Marigold, Glass 35.00
Liberty Bell, Yoke, Cast Iron, Arcade Toys, c.1925 . . . . 125.00
Limousine, Green Cab, Steel Wheels 3200.00
Lincoln Top Hat, Hubley 75.00
Lion, Iron, Gold Paint, 5 1/4 In. 70.00
Little Audrey, ABC . . . . .525.00 to 550.00
Little Lulu, 1973, 10 In. 75.00
Magic Chef 25.00
Main Street Trolley, With People 175.00
Mammy, Cast Iron, Painted, Box, Hubley, 5 1/4 In. 373.00
Mammy, Chalkware, 6 1/2 In. 75.00
Man, With Mustache, Cleminson 35.00
Massillon Tiger, Orange Shirt, Ceramic, 8 In. . . . .*Illus* 400.00

Mechanical banks were first made about 1870. Any bank with moving parts is considered mechanical. The metal banks made before World War I are the most desirable. Copies and new designs of mechanical banks have been made in metal or plastic since the 1920s. The condition of the paint on the old banks is important. Worn paint can lower a price by 90%.

Mechanical, 2 Frogs, J. & E. Stevens, 8 1/8 In. 690.00
Mechanical, Acrobat, Cast Iron, Pat. 1883 ....*Illus* 4345.00
Mechanical, Artillery, Cast Iron, J. & E. Stevens, 8 In. 460.00
Mechanical, Artillery, Coin In Cannon, Coin Fired Into Fort, Book Of Knowledge 350.00
Mechanical, Bad Accident, Cast Iron, J. & E. Stevens, 10 1/8 In. 1093.00
Mechanical, Bank Of Education, Cast Iron 850.00
Mechanical, Bear & Tree Stump, Cast Iron 850.00
Mechanical, Bill E. Grin, Cast Iron, J. & E. Stevens ....*Illus* 4070.00
Mechanical, Birdie Putt, Richards, 1950s 375.00
Mechanical, Boy Milking Cow, 1960s 125.00
Mechanical, Boy On Trapeze, Spins When Coin Is Put In Cap, Book Of Knowledge 975.00
Mechanical, Boy On Trapeze, Spins, J. Barton & Smith Co., 1891 ....4500.00 to 8500.00
Mechanical, Boy Robbing Bird's Nest, J. & E. Stevens 7500.00
Mechanical, Boy Scout, Flag, Green Base, J. & E. Stevens 8700.00
Mechanical, Boys Stealing Watermelons, Kyser & Rex Co., 6 9/16 In. ....1495.00 to 6050.00
Mechanical, Bulldog, Book Of Knowledge, Cast Iron 350.00
Mechanical, Bulldog, Cast Iron, J. & E. Stevens, 1880, 5 9/16 In. 6325.00
Mechanical, Butting Buffalo, Book Of Knowledge ....235.00 to 350.00
Mechanical, Butting Buffalo, Book Of Knowledge, 1950s 350.00
Mechanical, Butting Buffalo, Kyser & Rex ....9900.00 to 18000.00
Mechanical, Cabin Bank, Book Of Knowledge, 1950s 325.00
Mechanical, Calamity, Football Action, Cast Iron, 1960s ....125.00 to 150.00
Mechanical, Cat & Mouse, Coin Flips Down As Cat Flips, Book Of Knowledge 375.00
Mechanical, Cat, Chasing Ball, Hubley 190.00
Mechanical, Cat, Sailboat, Richards Toys, 1950s 1250.00
Mechanical, Chief Big Moon, J. & E. Stevens, 10 In. ....2070.00 to 3080.00
Mechanical, Circus, Shepard Hardware Co., 8 In. 7475.00
Mechanical, Clown On Globe, Yellow Base, J. & E. Stevens, 9 In. ....4830.00 to 6325.00
Mechanical, Clown, Chein, 1930s ....90.00 to 110.00
Mechanical, Confectionery, Kyser & Rex 13200.00
Mechanical, Creedmoor, Confederate Version 850.00
Mechanical, Creedmoor, Man Firing Into Tree, 9 x 6 In. ....600.00 to 715.00
Mechanical, Creedmore, Book Of Knowledge, 1950s, Cast Iron 425.00
Mechanical, Cupola, J. & E. Stevens 12650.00
Mechanical, Darktown Battery, Baseball, J. & E. Stevens ....1400.00 to 4500.00
Mechanical, Dentist, Book Of Knowledge 310.00
Mechanical, Dentist, J. & E. Stevens 7500.00
Mechanical, Dinah, Gold Dress, Gold Earrings, Necklace 1700.00
Mechanical, Dinah, Wearing Yellow Shirt, Cast Iron 460.00
Mechanical, Dog On Turntable, Cast Iron, Judd Mfg. Co., 4 3/4 In. 402.00

Left: Bank, Mechanical, Speaking Dog, Shepard, Cast Iron, 1885, 7 1/8 In.
Bank, Mechanical, Punch & Judy, Shepard, Hardware, 1884, 7 1/2 In.

Right: Bank, Mechanical, I Always Did 'Spise A Mule, J. & E. Stevens, 10 1/16 In.

Mechanical, Dog, Speaking, Blue Dress, J. & E. Stevens 2750.00
Mechanical, Eagle & Eaglet, Glass Eyes 495.00
Mechanical, Eagle & Eaglets, Book Of Knowledge, 1950s .... .400.00 to 495.00
Mechanical, Eagle & Eaglets, J. & E. Stevens, 1883 .... 2400.00
Mechanical, Elephant, Man Pops Out Of Howdah, Elephant Eats Coin, Enterprise, 1884 . 1675.00
Mechanical, Elephant, Pull-Tail, Cast Iron, Hubley, 8 1/2 In. .... .402.00 to 525.00
Mechanical, Elephant, Trunk Flips Up, Depositing Coin Over Head, Cast Iron 230.00
Mechanical, Football, John Harper & Co., 10 In. 3220.00
Mechanical, Frog On Rock, Kilgore 57500.00
Mechanical, Frog, Round Base, J. & E. Stevens, c.1872 .... 1800.00
Mechanical, Girl, Skipping Rope, 9 x 8 In. 16100.00
Mechanical, Golfer, Cast Iron, John Wright, 1950s 350.00
Mechanical, Hall's Excelsior Bank, J. & E. Stevens, 1869 .... 1250.00
Mechanical, Hall's Excelsior, With Wooden Man, J. & E. Stevens, 6 In. 115.00
Mechanical, Hall's Excelsior, With Wooden Monkey, J. & E. Stevens ....115.00 to 230.00
Mechanical, Hall's Liliput, J. & E. Stevens, c.1877 .... 1800.00
Mechanical, Horse Race, Cast Iron, J. & E. Stevens, 1870s, 4 3/8 In. Diam. 24200.00
Mechanical, Horse Race, Hand Painted, Tin Horses, 1960s 325.00
Mechanical, Humpty Dumpty, Clown, 1970s 95.00
Mechanical, Humpty Dumpty, Shepard Hardware, 1884 .... .990.00 to 1800.00
Mechanical, I Always Did 'Spise A Mule, J. & E. Stevens, 10 1/16 In. ....*Illus* 3738.00
Mechanical, Indian Shooting Bear, 1950s 450.00
Mechanical, Indian Shooting Bear, J. & E. Stevens, 10 5/6 In. 1840.00
Mechanical, Jolly Nigger, Aluminum, 6 In. 55.00
Mechanical, Jolly Nigger, Harper & Co., 6 In. 230.00
Mechanical, Jolly Nigger, J. & E. Stevens, 6 1/2 In. 288.00
Mechanical, Jolly Nigger, Starkie, 1920s 650.00
Mechanical, Jukebox Band, Select-O-Matic, Windup, Tin, 1950s 250.00
Mechanical, Kick Inn, Melvisto Novelty Co., 9 1/2 In. 368.00
Mechanical, Las Vegas Jackpot, Cast Metal, Pennies, Nickels & Dimes, 1950s 65.00
Mechanical, Leap Frog, Book Of Knowledge .... .280.00 to 375.00
Mechanical, Leap Frog, Shepard .... .3000.00 to 7000.00
Mechanical, Lighthouse, 2 Coin Slots .... .5200.00 to 5720.00
Mechanical, Lion & 2 Monkeys, Kyser & Rex, 1883 .... .633.00 to 2400.00
Mechanical, Lion Hunter, J. & E. Stevens, 1911 .... 8050.00
Mechanical, Little Joe, Cast Iron, John Harper 400.00
Mechanical, Mama Katzenjammer, Cast Iron, Kenton 850.00
Mechanical, Mammy & Child, Kyser & Rex, Red Dress, Feeding Baby, c.1884 .... 4800.00
Mechanical, Mason, Building Wall, Shepard Hardware, Cast Iron, Key, 1887 .5500.00 to 10000.00
Mechanical, MBCA Convention, Tin Lithograph, 1970 .... 135.00
Mechanical, Modern Elephant Swinging Trunk, Cast Iron, Hubley, 5 In. 345.00
Mechanical, Monkey & Coconut, J. & E. Stevens, 5 In. 1610.00
Mechanical, Monkey & Parrot, Tin 450.00
Mechanical, Monkey, Tips Hat, Tin, Chein 125.00
Mechanical, Monkey, With Organ Grinder, Hubley 1155.00
Mechanical, Mosque, Rotating Gorilla, Woman Finial, Cast Iron, Judd Mfg., 9 In. 1035.00
Mechanical, Mule Entering Barn, Cast Iron, Painted, J. & E. Stevens, 8 1/2 In. . .200.00 to 1400.00
Mechanical, Novelty, J. & E. Stevens, Cast Iron, 4 1/4 In. 460.00
Mechanical, Organ Bank, Cat & Dog, Musical, Kyser & Rex, 1882 ....525.00 to 1500.00
Mechanical, Organ, Penny On Monkey's Tray, Boy & Girl Dance, Book Of Knowledge . 350.00
Mechanical, Owl, Turns Head, Cast Iron, Glass Eyes, J. & E. Stevens, c.1880 . . .495.00 to 1800.00
Mechanical, Paddy & Pig, Cast Iron, 1900s 125.00
Mechanical, Paddy & Pig, J. & E. Stevens, 7 1/8 In. 920.00
Mechanical, Pelican, Cast Iron, J. & E. Stevens, 1878 .... 2700.00
Mechanical, Penny Pineapple, Hawaii As 50th State Of Union, Richards, 1950s 650.00
Mechanical, Professor Pug Frog's Great Bicycle Feat, 1960s 250.00
Mechanical, Professor Pug Frog's Great Bicycle Feat, J. & E. Stevens, 1892 .... 15400.00
Mechanical, Punch & Judy, Cast Iron, Hand Painted, 1960s 350.00
Mechanical, Punch & Judy, Shepard Hardware, 1884, 7 1/2 In. ....*Illus* 1610.00
Mechanical, Rocket Ship, Cast Metal, 1950s 175.00
Mechanical, Santa Claus At Chimney, Cast Iron, 1960s 125.00
Mechanical, Santa Claus, Shepard Hardware, Cast Iron, 1889 .... 1600.00
Mechanical, Southern Comfort, Cast Metal, 1950s 95.00

To clean lithographed tin banks, try using Sani-wax and 0000-grade steel wool, but use with extreme caution.

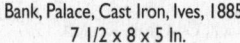

Bank, Palace, Cast Iron, Ives, 1885,
7 1/2 x 8 x 5 In.

Mechanical, Speaking Dog, Red Dress, Cast Iron, J. & E. Stevens, 7 1/8 In. 632.00
Mechanical, Speaking Dog, Shepard Hardware, 1885, 7 1/8 In. ....*Illus* 1610.00
Mechanical, Squirrel & Tree Stump, Mechanical Novelty Works, 1881 .... 2500.00
Mechanical, Stump Speaker, Shepard Hardware, 4 7/8 In. ....1380.00 to 2000.00
Mechanical, Tammany, Man, Nodding Head In Chair, J. & E. Stevens, 1873 .....467.00 to 675.00
Mechanical, Teddy & The Bear, J. & E. Stevens, 10 In. 1200.00
Mechanical, Toad On Stump, J. & E. Stevens, 1880s 1250.00
Mechanical, Toilet Bowl, Coin In Bowl, Press Lever, Flushes, Battery Operated, 1980s .. 24.00
Mechanical, Trick Dog, Hubley, 8 In. 115.00
Mechanical, Trick Pony, Cast Iron, Painted, Shepard Hardware, 1885, 7 In. .....862.00 to 2400.00
Mechanical, Uncle Sam, 1960s 125.00
Mechanical, Uncle Sam, Book Of Knowledge, 1950s 495.00
Mechanical, Uncle Sam, Shepard Hardware, 1886 ....1150.00 to 6500.00
Mechanical, Wild West, 1950s 175.00
Mechanical, William Tell, J. & E. Stevens, 1896, 10 In. ....374.00 to 950.00
Mechanical, Zoo, Cast Iron, Hand Painted, 1960s 650.00
Mechanical, Zoo, Cast Iron, Kyser & Rex, 4 1/4 In. 1150.00
Merry-Go-Round, Spinning, Red, Silver & Yellow, 4 1/2 x 4 1/2 In. 200.00
Miss Piggy, Blue Dress, Sigma 95.00
Money Sack, Terrace 45.00
Monkey, Airbrushed, Regal China 95.00
Monkey, Pink Glaze, Regal China 135.00
Monkey, Tin, Chein, 1930s 110.00
Monkey, Tin, Chein, 1940s 85.00
Moody & Sankey, Cast Iron 1155.00
Mosque, Cast Iron, Traces Of Gold, 3 1/2 In. 55.00
Mouse, Nodder 35.00
Mr. Fleet, Chrysler Cars, Vinyl, 1970s 395.00
Mr. Peanut, Planters Peanuts Advertising, Cast Iron, 1970s 95.00
Multiplying Bank, Hall Of Mirrors, J. & E. Stevens 8800.00
Mutt & Jeff, Cast Iron, 5 1/4 In. 175.00
Nipper The Dog, 1970s 95.00
Ocean Spray, Tin 20.00
Oliver Hardy, Vinyl 65.00
Orange Bird, Florida Orange Growers Association, Vinyl, Disney, 1970s 20.00
Oscar Mayer Wienermobile, Hard Plastic, 9 1/2 In. 95.00
Paddington Bear, Plastic, Box 30.00
Paddy And The Pig, Cast Iron, 1960s 125.00
Palace, Cast Iron, Ives, 1885, 7 1/2 x 8 x 5 In. ....*Illus* 10450.00
Panda, Porcelain, 3 1/4 In. 25.00
Pebbles On Dino, Vandor, 1985 .... 44.00
Pennsylvania Dutch Dowry Chest, Aluminum 50.00
Peppermint Patty, Ceramic, 7 In. 30.00

Piano, Detailed Casting Of Instrument, Cast Iron 1200.00
Pig, 2-Tone Brown Marbleized Glaze, 4 1/8 In. 28.00
Pig, 2-Tone Brown, Blue Marbleized Glaze, 6 1/2 In. 72.00
Pig, Blue Speckled On White, Curly Tail, Ceramic, 1980s, 5 x 6 In. 357.00
Pig, Diaper Pin, American Bisque 95.00
Pig, Gold Colored, I Made Chicago Famous, Raised Letters, 1902, 2 1/2 x 4 1/8 In. 75.00
Pig, Kreiss, Pink Pottery 55.00
Pig, Lying Down, Glass Eyes, Long Snout, Cast Iron, Duroc, 9 In. 250.00
Pig, Seated, Cast Iron, A.C. Williams, c.1910 .... 95.00
Pillsbury Poppin' Fresh 24.00
Pizza Hut Pete, Plastic, 1969 .... 55.00
Pluto, Plastic, Nodder 16.00
Princess Diana & Prince Charles, Copper Plated Cast Iron, 1981, 7 In. 88.00
Rabbit, Blue, Cast Iron, 4 In. 165.00
Rabbit, Upright, Gold, Cast Iron, 5 In. 33.00
Rabbit, White, Cast Iron, 4 1/2 x 4 1/2 In. 60.00
Radio, Turning Dial, Nickel Plated Door, Tin Sides & Back, Cast Iron, Kenton, 1937 .... 215.00
Red Goose Shoes, Cast Iron, 4 1/2 In. 175.00
Refrigerator, Electrolux, Painted White, 1930s 95.00
Register, Benjamin Franklin Thrift, Cash Register Shape, Tin, Dime, 1930s ...... .65.00 to 250.00
Register, Gem Registering 950.00
Register, Keep 'Em Rolling, Dime 285.00
Register, National Reserve Life Insurance Co., Dime, 1942 .... 38.00
Register, Penny Saver, Cast Iron, Pressed Steel, 5 In. 450.00
Register, Piggy, Dime 75.00
Register, Prince Valiant, Dime 265.00
Register, Tin, Hoge Manufacturing Co. 175.00
Register, Uncle Sam, 3 Coin, Cast Iron, Pressed Steel 195.00
Register, Uncle Sam, Dime .... .45.00 to 85.00
Robot, Radio Shack, Plastic 35.00
Ronald McDonald, Ceramic, Bust 35.00
Rumplestiltskin, Cast Iron, 1910, 6 x 2 5/16 In. 700.00
Santa Claus, Chalkware 75.00
Santa Claus, Holding Christmas Tree, Cast Iron, 5 1/2 In. 150.00
Santa Claus, Porcelain, 1960, 7 In. 65.00
Santa Claus, Tin 60.00
Save & Smile Money Box, Cast Iron, England, 4 1/4 x 4 In. 853.00
Seaman's Savings Bank, Sailor 40.00
Sharecropper, Black, Cast Iron, A.C. Williams, c.1901 .... 375.00
Sheep, Cast Iron, Grey Iron Co., 5 1/2 In. 300.00
Sheriff, Gonder 265.00
Signers Of Declaration Of Independence, Tin, Can Shape 27.00
Sinclair Aircraft, Oil Can Shape 22.00
Sinclair Dino, Gold, Black, Metal, 5 1/2 In. 240.00
Six Million Dollar Man, Figural, Steve Austin, Vinyl 45.00
Skyscraper, 12 Story, Cast Iron, c.1896 .... 95.00
Smokey The Bear, Pottery, White, Gold Trim 115.00
Snoopy, On Doghouse, Silver Plate, United Features, Copyright 1958, 6 In. ...... .18.00 to 35.00
Snoopy, On Food Bowl, Ceramic 45.00
Snoopy, Woodstock 20.00
Snowman's Head, American Bisque 55.00
Speedy Alka-Seltzer Man, Vinyl, 6 In. 50.00
Spiderman 25.00
Squirrel With Nut, Cast Iron 50.00
Star Wars, R2-D2, 1983 .... .25.00 to 35.00
Statue Of Liberty, Cast Iron, 6 1/4 In. 95.00
Stoneware, Silver Slip Glaze, Ohio 145.00
Sunoco, Gas Pump 150.00
Swee' Pea, American Bisque .... .850.00 to 875.00
Swee' Pea, Ceramic, Vandor, 1980, 6 In. .... .75.00 to 245.00
Theodora, Sigma 80.00
Thing, Addams Family, Original Photograph, Box, 1964 .... .75.00 to 195.00
Tiger, Esso, Vinyl, 1960s 45.00

Tootsie Roll, Canister, Heavy Paper, Metal End Caps, c.1970, 12 In. 12.00
Topo Gigio Mouse, Coveralls, Straw Hat, Plastic, Hand Painted, Roy Dee, 1970, 9 In. ... 25.00
Topo Gigio Mouse, Mr. & Mrs. 100.00
Topo Gigio Mouse, Sitting In Pineapple, Nodder, Box 50.00
Topo Gigio Mouse, With Apple, Nodder 35.00
Tower, Kyser & Rex, 1890, 6 7/8 x 2 1/2 In. ....1450.00 to 3520.00
Trader's Bank, Cast Iron, Canada, 8 1/2 In. 990.00
Truck, Hershey's Milk Chocolate, Model 1942 Chevy, Box 27.00
Truck, Tanker, Ford Motorcraft, Die Cast Metal 30.00
Truck, Texaco, Painted Metal, Box 60.00
Uncle Sam, Purinton 45.00
Westminster Abbey, Cast Iron, England, c.1908, 6 1/4 In. 475.00
Whitman's Candies 10.00
Wild West, Cast Metal, 1950s 95.00
Wilma Flintstone On Telephone, American Bisque Co. 875.00
Winnie The Pooh, Honey Jar Between Legs, Coin Slot At Top, 4 1/2 In. 50.00
Woodsy Owl, Pottery 75.00
Woody Woodpecker, Applause, Vandor ....25.00 to 30.00

BANKO, Korean ware, and Sumida are terms that are often confusing. We use the names in the way most often used by antiques dealers and collectors. Korean ware is now called *Sumida Gawa* or *Sumida* and is listed in this book in the Sumida category. Banko is a group of rustic Japanese wares made in the nineteenth and twentieth centuries. Some pieces are made of mosaics of colored clay, some are fanciful teapots. Redware and other materials were also used.

Wall Pocket, Geisha, Green Basket On Back, Blue, Red & Pink Costume, 9 In., Pair ... 125.00

BARBED WIRE was first patented in 1867. Collectors want eighteen-inch samples.

10 Point Spur Rowell, C.A. Holde, August 2, 1887, 18 In. 10.00
Dodge Rowell Wire, November 29, 1881, 18 In. 300.00
Hanging Star, December 27, 1881, 18 In. 200.00
Hart-McGlin Star, September 12, 1876, 18 In. 300.00
Stubbe Plate, Large & Small, October 3, 1883, 18 In. 3.00

BARBER collectibles range from the popular red and white striped pole that used to be found in front of every shop to the small scissors and tools of the trade. Barber chairs are wanted, especially the older models with elaborate iron trim.

Basin, Brass, c.1750, 10 1/4 In. 875.00
Basin, Pewter, Plain Rim, 1770, 13 1/2 In. 675.00
Chair, Double Shine, Oak, Marble 2400.00
Chair, Kochs, White Porcelain, Original Leather Seat, Wood, Child's, 43 x 19 x 31 In. 2127.00
Chair, Koken, Congress Pedestal, Hydraulic, No. 225 .... 1200.00
Chair, Koken, White Porcelain, Pair 600.00
Pole, Cast Iron, T.A. Kochs Co., Chicago, Electrified, 79 1/2 In. 1600.00
Pole, Modern Service Across Top, Red, White, Blue, Porcelain, 48 x 10 In. 402.50
Pole, Rayette GDT Dandruff Lotion Decal 75.00
Pole, Red & White Crackled Paint, 48 In. 375.00
Pole, Red & White, 18 In. 495.00
Pole, Stained Glass, Lighted Globe On Top, Electrified, Porcelain Base, 82 In. 2200.00
Sign, Barber Shop, Ask For Wildroot, Barber Pole, 1955, 13 x 40 In. 130.00
Sign, Curved, Red, White & Blue, Porcelain, 24 x 15 In. 165.00
Sign, Red, White & Black Crackled Paint, Square, 58 In. 225.00
Stool, Shine, Metal, Ice Cream Type Legs 250.00

BAROMETERS are used to forecast the weather. Antique barometers with elaborate wooden cases and brass trim are the most desirable. Mercury column barometers are also popular with collectors. It is difficult to find someone to repair a broken one, so be sure your barometer is in working condition.

Advertising, Okeefe's Beer, Button Sign, 9 In. 23.00

Advertising, Sunny Brook Whiskey, Button Sign, 9 In. 33.00
Andrews, Rosewood & Ivory, Buffalo, 19th Century 3200.00
B. Pike & Sons, Eagle Finial, Relief Of Washington 2860.00
Banjo, J.F. Williams, Rosewood Veneer, Brass Trim, Bristol, 38 1/2 In. 522.00
Banjo, Kiner Bros., Wheel Inlay, Black Paint, 39 3/4 In. 460.00
Banjo, Mahogany Veneer, Brass & Ebonized Trim, Mirror, Ivory Knob, 38 In. 528.00
Banjo, Mahogany, George III 345.00
Banjo, Mahogany, Inlaid With Shells, Signed, 19th Century, 39 In. 632.50
Banjo, Silvered Dial Under Mirror, Satin Wood Band, Mahogany, 42 1/2 In. 920.00
Banjo, Wheel, Mahogany, Swan's-Neck Cresting, 38 1/2 In. 402.00
Banjo, Wheel, Mother-Of-Pearl, Inlaid Rosewood, Foliage, 41 In. 402.00
Batwing Design, Patera Inlay, George III, 34 In. 150.00
Brass, Grow & Cuttle, Cutwork Frame, London, England 245.00
Brass Finial, Mahogany, Ebonized Trim, Ivory Knob, England, 42 In. 715.00
Brass Finial, Rosewood, Ivory Knob, England, 40 1/2 In. 550.00
Ciceri & Pini, Edinburgh, Mahogany, 19th Century, 36 In. 440.00
Clum & King, Agricultural, Oak, Ripple-Front, N.Y., 1860, 37 In. 460.00
Eastlake Style, Negretti & Zambra, Oak, Wheel, 1875, 43 In. 393.00
G. Lufft, Chromium Plated Metal, Glass, Black Paint, 1935, 6 5/8 In. 300.00
Georgian, Mahogany, Wheel, 19th Century, 39 In. 193.00
Giltwood, Circular Molded Frame, Floral Crest, Louis XVI, 40 1/2 In. 1598.00
Giltwood, Cream Painted Circular Dial, Pinecone Finial, Louis XVI, 49 In. 2587.00
Hughes-Owens Co., Brass, Leatherized Case, Montreal, 3 1/2 In. 165.00
J. Aprile, Sudbury, Mahogany Veneer, Crest, Finial, 38 1/2 In. 660.00
J. Lockwood, Mahogany Veneer Case, 19th Century 165.00
James Ayscough, Mahogany, Silver Plate, George II, 34 In. 2587.00
Mahogany, Wheel, 8-In. Silvered Dial, Scroll Pediment, Banjo Case, 1840 .... 920.00
Marine, Shock Absorbing Gimbal Mount, France 6325.00
Rosati & Co., Mahogany, Etched Steel Dial, Mid-19th Century, 38 In. 345.00
Round, Carved Oak Case, England 45.00
Scurr Thirsk, Silvered Dial, Mahogany Veneer, England, 38 1/4 In. 660.00
Stick, Adie & Sons, Mahogany, Bowfront Case, Molded Top, Scotland, 1840, 39 In. 6900.00
Stick, Alexander Adie, Mahogany, Molded Flat Top Crest, Scotland, 1840, 41 In. 2300.00
Stick, Chippendale, Mahogany, Signed Indicator Plate, London 825.00
Stick, Georgian Style, Swan's-Neck, Engraved Steel Face, 39 1/2 In. 287.00
Stick, I. Tessa, Walnut, Case With Floral Urn Crest, Holland, 1770, 48 In. 5750.00
Stick, J. Kendall & Co., c.1865, 35 1/2 In. 725.00
Stick, Joseph Crosa, Mahogany, Chevron Veneered Case, 1800, 37 3/4 In. 2300.00
Stick, Mahogany Case, Urn Finial Crest, Gadrooned Finials, 1775, 50 1/2 In. 6900.00
Stick, Mahogany, Ebony Urn Cistern, England, 1860, 39 3/4 In. 2875.00
Stick, Matthew Berge, Glazed Door, Mahogany Veneer 3900.00
Stick, Miner's, 2-Side Scale, Oak, England, Late 19th Century, 3 1/4 In. 220.00
Stick, Peter Caminada, Mahogany, Urn Finial, England, 1820, 38 1/4 In. 1840.00
Stick, Red Walnut, Ripple-Front, Molding, Cistern Cover, 1870, 40 In. 977.00
Stick, Swann & Co., Rosewood, Ripple-Molded Glazed Door, Rochester, 35 In. 1840.00
Stick, W. & S. Jones, Mahogany, Finial, Etched, London, c.1795, 39 In. 575.00
T. Littlewood, Arched Top, Walnut, Glazed Front, Glasgow, 43 1/4 In. 402.00
Thermometer, Arts & Crafts, England, 24 x 9 In. 15.00
Thermometer, Giltwood, Leaf Crest Above Pair Of Doves, France, 39 In. 302.50
Thermometer, W. Ward, Mahogany, Wheel, Conn., 37 1/2 In. 880.00
Torch-Shaped Shaft, Rope Carved, 1850s 7000.00
Wheel, Aitchison, Oak, London, 1880, 29 In. 88.00
Wheel, Ebonized, England, Oak, 19th Century, 36 In. 264.00
Wheel, J.E. Ames, Rosewood, Scrolled Pointed Crest, England, 43 In. 1090.00
Wheel, Rosewood, With Hydrometer, Thermometer, 1850, 37 In. 413.00

BASEBALL collectibles are in the Sports category, except for baseball cards, which are listed under Baseball in the Card category.

BASKETS of all types are popular with collectors. American Indian, Japanese, African, Shaker, and many other kinds of baskets can be found. Of course, baskets are still being made, so the collector must learn to tell the age and style of the basket to determine the value.

Buttocks, 16 Ribs, 4 1/2 x 8 In. 240.00

Buttocks, Splint, 28 Ribs, Bentwood Handle, Dark Green Paint, 11 x 13 In.	275.00
Buttocks, Splint, 44 Ribs, Bentwood Handle, 13 x 9 In.	110.00
Buttocks, Splint, Handle, 6 In.	125.00
Buttocks, Splint, Handle, 17 In.	250.00
Buttocks, Splint, Women, 11 Ribs, Dark Patina, 7 In.	247.50
Buttocks, Woven Splint, 26 Ribs, Bentwood Handle, 12 x 14 1/2 In.	100.00
Coiled, Bundled Grass & Rush, Lined Flat Bottom, 7 x 15 In.	525.00
Egg, Collapsible, 10 In.	28.00
Laundry, Splint, Bentwood Rim Handles, 17 1/2 x 25 1/2 x 12 In.	110.00
Lightship, Handle, Late 19th Century, 8 x 5 1/2 In.	1150.00
Melon, Handle, 8 x 5 In.	235.00
Nantucket, 20th Century, 12 x 11 1/2 In.	1150.00
Nantucket, Cane & Splint, Swivel Bentwood Handle, Wooden Base, 9 In.	165.00
Nantucket, Hinged Bail Handle, S.P. Boyer, 12 1/4 In.	1150.00
Nantucket, Pocketbook, Ivory Whale Carved, Signed, 1963, 7 In.	1495.00
Nantucket, Shoal Lightship, Oval, Isaac Hamblen, 12 1/2 In.	1610.00
Nantucket, Swing Handle, R. Folger, 11 In.	575.00
Nantucket, Work, Hinged Cover, Turned Final, 20th Century, 8 In.	1035.00
Nantucket, Work, Pivoting Cover, 20th Century, 4 1/4 x 5 3/4 In.	2990.00
Splint, 12 Melon Ribs, Round, Bentwood Handle, 9 1/2 In.	220.00
Splint, Bamboo, Boat Shape, Early 20th Century, 19 1/2 In.	187.00
Splint, Bamboo, Entwined Handle, Inverted Pear Shape, 16 In.	330.00
Splint, Bamboo, Entwined Handle, Pear Shape, 17 1/2 In.	385.00
Splint, Bamboo, Loop Handle, Egg Shape, 15 In.	495.00
Splint, Bamboo, Ring Handles, Early 20th Century, 9 In.	132.00
Splint, Bamboo, Tin Liner, Cylinder Form, 15 In.	154.00
Splint, Cane & Splint, Bentwood Swivel Handle, Varnish, Round, 8 In.	150.00
Splint, Eye Of God Handle, 1 1/8 In.	115.50
Splint, Gathering, 20 x 12 In.	175.00
Splint, Melon Ribbed, Eye Of God Design Handles, 11 x 12 1/2 x 5 1/2 In.	60.00
Splint, Swivel Handle, Round, 13 x 9 1/2 In.	65.00

BATCHELDER products are made from California clay. Ernest Batchelder established a tile studio in Pasadena, California, in 1909 and expanded until in 1916 he built a larger factory with a new partner. The Batchelder-Wilson Company made all types of architectural tiles, garden pots, and bookends. The plant closed in 1932. In 1936 Batchelder opened Batchelder Ceramics, also in Pasadena, and made bowls, vases, and earthenware pots. He retired in 1951 and died in 1957. Pieces are marked *Batchelder Pasadena* or *Batchelder Los Angeles*.

BATCHELDER LOS ANGELES

Bookends, Monk, Bisque . . . . .275.00 to 295.00	
Tile, Floral, Arts & Craft Style, Blue Glaze, 3 In.	75.00
Tile, Flower Design, 2 3/4 x 2 3/4 In.	125.00
Tile, Flowering Potted Plants, Pair Of Birds, 8 x 11 1/2 In.	625.00
Tile, Pomegranate Design, 2 3/4 x 2 3/4 In.	125.00
Tile, Potted Flowering Plant, 2 3/4 x 2 3/4 In.	125.00
Tile, Potted Plant, 5 3/4 x 5 3/4 In.	285.00
Tile, Rabbit, 5 3/4 x 5 3/4 In.	285.00
Tile, Vines & Birds, 12 x 12 In.	675.00
Vase, Brown Gunmetal Glaze, Bulbous Base, Incised Mark, 5 1/2 In.	176.00
Vase, Flared Rim, Blue, Turquoise, Pink, Square, 1950s, 6 In.	50.00
Vase, Maroon, Oblong, 6 x 7 1/2 In.	145.00

BATMAN and Robin are characters from a comic strip by Bob Kane that started in 1939. In 1966, the characters became part of a popular television series. There have been radio and movie serials that featured the pair. The first full-length movie was made in 1989. The third movie was made in 1995.

Ad, Newspaper, For Lunch Box, Aladdin, Thermos, 1966	18.50
Air Freshener, Joker, Superfriends, Package, 1970s	10.00
Bank, Batman & Robin, Pair	72.00
Banner, Batman & Robin, 1966	59.00

Batcycle, For 8-In. Figures, Mego, 1979 . . . . 150.00
Batmobile, Metal, Corgi, Box, 1973, 5 1/4 In. 159.00
Batmobile, With Rockets, Corgi, 1st Issue, Box 195.00
Batmobile Bubble Bath, Avon, Box 45.00
Batphone, Talking, Palitoy, Box 275.00
Batplane Launcher, Gordy Int., On Card, 1989 . . . . 22.00
Batscope, 1966 . . . . 75.00
Bicycle, AMF Decals, 1972 . . . . 295.00
Bowl, Batman & Robin, Batmobile, Washington Pottery, England, 1966, 6 1/2 In. 150.00
Box, Jewelry, Man's, Batmobile Shape, Pottery, 1966 . . . . 150.00
Button, Batman & Robin, White, Purple Ground, Heart Shape, 1960s 12.00
Candy Container, PEZ, Soft Vinyl Head, Gray Stem 110.00
Candy Container, Stick, Blue Cape 100.00
Clock, Alarm, Janex, 1974 . . . . 40.00
Clock, Batman & Robin, Alarm, Talking, 1974 . . . . .65.00 to 90.00
Colorforms, 1966 . . . . 50.00
Coloring Set, Hasbro, 1966 . . . . 200.00
Cookie Jar, Brush 100.00
Cookie Jar, Warner Bros. . . . . .70.00 to 95.00
Costume, Mask & Cape, Box, Ideal, 1966 . . . . 125.00
Costume, Mask & Cape, Official Playset, Ben Cooper, 1965 . . . . 60.00
Costume, Mask, Jumpsuit, 1966 . . . . 36.00
Cup, Sip-A-Drink, With Robin 20.00
Display, Wall, Full Color, Plastic, 48 x 24 In. 475.00
Doll, Batman Returns, Vinyl, 12 In. 20.00
Doll, Cloth, Vinyl, Applause, 15 In. 22.00
Doll, Mego, Box, 12 In. 90.00
Doll, Vinyl Face, 1966 . . . . 100.00
Figure, Mego, 1970s, 12 In. 85.00
Figure, Parachute, Metallic Blue, CDC, On Card, 1966 . . . . 70.00
Figure, Penguin, World's Greatest Super-Heroes, Action, Mego, Sealed, 8 In. 125.00
Figure, Robin, Mego, Pocket 8.00
Figure, With Videomatic Ring, 1967 . . . . 250.00
Figure, World's Greatest Super-Heroes, Bend N'Flex, Mego, Sealed, 5 In. 125.00
Game, Milton Bradley, 1966 . . . . 45.00
Game, Racing, Gordy Int., On Card, 1988 . . . . 22.00
Gum Card, Wrapper, Batman & Robin, Red Ground, Topps, 1966, 5 x 6 In. 32.00
Hat, Joker's, Movie, Felt, Purple, Nicholson Photograph Tag, 1989 . . . . 30.00
Key Chain, Figural, Batman, Robin & Joker, Poly Resin, 3 Piece 10.00
Lunch Box, Metal, Aladdin, 1966 . . . . .150.00 to 175.00
Magic Slate, 1966 . . . . 30.00
Mask, 2 Sides, Batman 1 Side, Robin On Reverse, Paper, 1960s 35.00
Mittens, Child's, Blue Vinyl, Batman & Logo, 1970s 12.00
Model Kit, Batmissile, Sealed, AMT, 1992 . . . . 24.00
Model Kit, Batmobile, Aurora, Shipper, 1966 . . . . 150.00
Model Kit, Batmobile, Movie, Kabaya, 1989 . . . . 15.00
Model Kit, Batmobile, Sealed, AMT, 1989 . . . . 24.00
Model Kit, Box, Aurora 50.00
Pencil, 1966 . . . . 15.00
Pennant, With Robin, 1966 . . . . 75.00
Periscope, Extendible To Look Around Corner, Shield On Side 80.00
Placemat, 1966 . . . . 55.00
Play Set, Batcave, Cardboard & Vinyl, TV Version, Mego, 1974, 15 x 11 1/4 In. 235.00
Play Set, Batmobile, Batcopter, Batboat & Trailer, Box, 3 Piece 450.00
Poster, Batman & Robin Movie, 1949, 1 Sheet 1995.00
Poster, Movie, Adam West, Burt Ward, Cesar Romero, 1966, 3 Sheet, 81 x 41 In. 688.00
Puppet, Hand, Cloth 20.00
Puppet, Hand, Original Package, 1960s 55.00
Puzzle, Riddler Posing In Front Of Batman & Robin, 1974 . . . . 29.00
Radio, Transistor, Figural, Box, 1973 . . . . 140.00
Record, The Catwoman's Revenge, Batman Being Attacked, 33 RPM 21.00
Ring, Flicker 15.00
Soaky, Vinyl . . . . .45.00 to 65.00

Thermos, 1966 .... 75.00
Utility Belt, Bat Cuffs & Bat Belt Buckle, 1966 .... 115.00
Van, Mobile Crime Unit, Mego 125.00
View-Master Set, 3 Reels, 1966 .... 36.00
Wastebasket, 1966 .... 65.00
Water Gun, MOC, 1989 .... 20.00

BATTERSEA enamels, which are enamels painted on copper, were made
in the Battersea district of London from about 1750 to 1756. Many
similar enamels are mistakenly called *Battersea.*

Box, Esteem The Giver, Bird On Nest, c.1780, 2 1/4 In. 295.00
Box, Hobbyhorse Scene On Hinged Cover, Pink & White Interior 187.00
Box, Man Fishing On River Bank On Hinged Cover, Pink & White Interior 210.00
Box, River & Garden Scene On Hinged Cover, White Enamel Interior 137.00
Box, Royal Crown, Washington King As King, 1780s 8500.00
Box, Sailing Ships In Port On Hinged Cover, Pink Enamel Interior 115.00
Box, Scene Of Sailing Ships In Port On Hinged Cover, Blue & White Interior 148.00
Box, Woman In Garden On Hinged Cover, Interior Mirror, Yellow, Oval 132.00
Plaque, Blue, Rose, Yellow, Green Sepia, Silver Metal Frame, 4 x 3 5/16 In. 3162.00
Plaque, Puce, Yellow, Green, Red, Purple Enamel, 1753, 4 x 4 3/16 In. 2587.00
Salt, Pastoral Scenes In White Ovals, c.1780, 2 1/2 In. 480.00
Tieback, Enameled Lady Leaning On Memorial, Gilt Metal, 2 1/2 In., 4 Piece 1035.00

BAUER pottery is a California-made ware. J.A. Bauer moved his
Kentucky pottery to Los Angeles, California, in 1909. The company
made art pottery after 1912 and dinnerwares marked *Bauer* after 1929.
The factory went out of business in 1962.

Ashtray, Ring, Orange, Round, 4 In. 75.00
Bean Pot, Yellow, 2 Qt. 125.00
Berry Bowl, Ring, Gray, 4 3/4 In. 10.00
Berry Bowl, Ring, Maroon, 4 3/4 In. 10.00
Bowl, Burnt Orange, 12 In. 155.00
Bowl, Ring, Black, 8 In. 65.00
Bowl, Ring, Green, 8 In. 55.00
Bowl, Ring, Light Blue, Low, 9 In. 65.00
Bowl, Ring, White, 12 In. 375.00
Bowl, Ring, Yellow, 12 In. 125.00
Box, Salt, Cobalt Blue & White Spongeware 325.00
Butter, Cover, Ring, Burnt Orange, Round ....145.00 to 150.00
Butter, Cover, Ring, Dark Blue, Round 145.00
Butter, Cover, Ring, Light Blue, Round ....125.00 to 225.00
Butter, Cover, Ring, Orange, Round ....150.00 to 165.00
Cake Plate, Monterey, Pedestal, Orange Red 375.00
Cake Plate, Monterey, Yellow ....185.00 to 195.00
Canister, Flour, Strawberries ....65.00 to 95.00
Carafe, Ring, Apple Green, California Exposition, San Diego, 1935 .... 95.00
Carafe, Ring, Burnt Orange, Copper Handle 125.00
Carafe, Ring, Dark Blue 75.00
Carafe, Ring, Green 30.00
Carafe, Ring, Light Blue, Copper Handle 275.00
Carafe, Ring, Orange, Copper Handle ....65.00 to 125.00
Carafe, Ring, White, Wooden Handle 350.00
Carafe, Ring, Yellow ....65.00 to 150.00
Casserole, Cover, Blue Tulip 40.00
Casserole, Cover, Blue Tulip, Handle, Individual 15.00
Casserole, Cover, Plainware, Light Green, 8 1/2 In. 80.00
Casserole, Cover, Ring, Burnt Orange, With Rack 255.00
Casserole, Ring, Orange, 9 1/2 In. 80.00
Casserole, Yellow, With Rack, 7 1/2 In. ....70.00 to 125.00
Chop Plate, Monterey, Dark Blue 45.00
Chop Plate, Monterey, Orange, 13 In. 45.00
Chop Plate, Monterey, Yellow 45.00
Chop Plate, Ring, Black, 12 1/2 In. ....195.00 to 250.00

Chop Plate, Ring, Burgundy, 12 In. 250.00
Chop Plate, Ring, Burnt Orange, 15 In. 95.00
Chop Plate, Ring, Dark Blue 85.00
Chop Plate, Ring, Green, 12 In. 65.00
Chop Plate, Ring, Green, 17 In. 265.00
Chop Plate, Ring, Ivory, 12 In. 145.00
Chop Plate, Ring, Orange, 12 In. ....40.00 to 65.00
Chop Plate, Ring, Orange, 14 1/2 In. 65.00
Chop Plate, Ring, Yellow, 12 In. 65.00
Coffeepot, Plainware, Yellow, Individual 150.00
Coffeepot, Ring, Green 120.00
Console, Black, Wavy Edge 45.00
Cookie Jar, Monterey Moderne, Chartreuse 100.00
Cookie Jar, Ring, Burnt Orange ....800.00 to 995.00
Creamer, Ring, Black 120.00
Creamer, Ring, Yellow 45.00
Cup & Saucer, Ring, Black 50.00
Dish, Pickle, Ring, Dark Blue 55.00
Ewer, Yellow, 10 In. 90.00
Figurine, Swan, Chartreuse ....85.00 to 95.00
Figurine, Swan, Turquoise 95.00
Flowerpot, Gardenware, Turquoise, 8 In. 65.00
Goblet, Ring, Burnt Orange 145.00
Goblet, Ring, Dark Blue ....140.00 to 225.00
Goblet, Ring, Green 225.00
Gravy Boat, La Linda, Pink & Green 35.00
Gravy Boat, Ring, Dark Blue 125.00
Gravy Boat, Ring, Maroon 145.00
Jar, Oil, White, 12 In., Pair 3000.00
Jar, Spice, Cover, Green 225.00
Jug, Ice Lip, Monterey, Marigold 125.00
Jug, Ice Lip, Monterey, Turquoise 325.00
Jug, Ice Lip, Yellow Speckled, 2 Qt. 55.00
Jug, Ice Water, Green 95.00
Jug, Ring, Orange 295.00
Mixing Bowl, Monterey, Yellow 150.00
Mixing Bowl, No. 9, Ring, Burnt Orange 155.00
Mixing Bowl, No. 9, Ring, Chartreuse 110.00
Mixing Bowl, No. 9, Ring, Yellow 125.00
Mixing Bowl, No. 12, Ring, Black 250.00
Mixing Bowl, No. 12, Ring, Green 50.00
Mixing Bowl, No. 24, Atlanta, Dark Blue ....150.00 to 165.00
Mixing Bowl, No. 30, Orange, 6 1/2 In. 25.00
Mixing Bowl, No. 36, Ring, Ivory 55.00
Mug, Ring, Burnt Orange 65.00
Mug, Ring, Maroon 40.00
Mug, Ring, Orange, Pair 75.00
Mug, Ring, Yellow 165.00
Mustard Jar, Ring, Yellow 525.00
Nappy, Ring, Curled Handle, Blue, 7 In. 16.00
Nappy, Ring, Yellow, 9 In. 50.00
Pie Plate, Ring, Green 45.00
Pitcher, Burnt Orange, 1 Qt. 75.00
Pitcher, Burnt Orange, 3 Qt. 225.00
Pitcher, Ring, Chartreuse, 2 Qt. 250.00
Pitcher, Ring, Light Blue, 1 Qt. 165.00
Pitcher, Ring, Light Blue, 2 Qt. ....250.00 to 275.00
Pitcher, Ring, Water, Burnt Orange 125.00
Place Setting, Ring, Ivory, 5 Piece 250.00
Planter, Light Brown, 9 In. 20.00
Plate, Plainware, Black, 8 In. 90.00
Plate, Ring, Burnt Orange, 11 In. 75.00
Plate, Ring, Green, 7 1/2 In. 12.00

Plate, Ring, Green, 10 1/2 In.	95.00
Plate, Ring, Ivory, 11 In.	75.00
Plate, Ring, Light Blue, 9 In.	36.00
Plate, Ring, Light Blue, 10 1/2 In.	95.00
Plate, Ring, Orange, 9 1/2 In.	15.00
Plate, Ring, Orange, 10 1/2 In.	95.00
Plate, Ring, Yellow, 9 1/2 In.	15.00
Plate, Ring, Yellow, 10 1/2 In.	95.00
Platter, Ring, Black, 13 In.	225.00
Punch Bowl, Ring, Dark Blue	1295.00
Punch Bowl, Ring, Pedestal, Chartreuse	450.00
Punch Bowl, Ring, Pedestal, White	2000.00
Punch Bowl, Ring, Pedestal, Yellow	995.00
Punch Cup, Light Blue	55.00
Punch Cup, Maroon	55.00
Punch Cup, Ring, Black	115.00 to 125.00
Punch Cup, Yellow	55.00
Relish, Ring, Dark Blue	225.00
Salt & Pepper, Ring, Barrel, Black	250.00 to 295.00
Salt & Pepper, Ring, Low	55.00
Salt & Pepper, Strawberries	95.00
Saucer, Ring, Light Blue	15.00
Stack Set, Cover, Ring, Green	95.00
Sugar, Cover, Ring, Orange	65.00
Sugar, Strawberries	95.00
Sugar & Creamer, Monterey, Orange	40.00
Sugar & Creamer, Ring, Burnt Orange	100.00
Sugar & Creamer, Ring, Ivory	350.00
Sugar & Creamer, Ring, Orange	125.00
Sugar Shaker, Ring, Green	350.00 to 395.00
Sugar Shaker, Ring, Orange, Low	15.00
Sugar Shaker, Ring, Yellow	15.00
Syrup, Ring, Chartreuse	120.00
Syrup, Ring, Yellow	85.00
Teapot, La Linda, Aladdin, Yellow	125.00
Teapot, Monterey, Dark Blue	95.00
Teapot, Monterey, Turquoise	60.00
Teapot, Ring, Burnt Orange, 6 Cup	125.00
Teapot, Ring, Dark Blue, 6 Cup	350.00
Teapot, Ring, Green	225.00
Teapot, Ring, Maroon	325.00
Teapot, Ring, Orange, 2 Cup	95.00
Teapot, Ring, Orange, 6 Cup	125.00
Teapot, Ring, Yellow, 2 Cup	225.00
Teapot, Ring, Yellow, 6 Cup	85.00
Teapot, Speckled, Yellow, 6 Cup	45.00
Teapot, Strawberries	45.00
Tumbler, Ring, Barrel, Handle, Burnt Orange	125.00 to 225.00
Tumbler, Ring, Barrel, Handle, Yellow	300.00
Tumbler, Ring, Blue, 6 Oz.	35.00
Tumbler, Ring, Dark Blue	45.00
Tumbler, Ring, Orange, 6 Oz.	20.00
Vase, Aqua, Ribbed, White, Matt Carlton, 4 x 8 In.	125.00
Vase, Atlanta, Blue, Rectangular, 9 In.	75.00
Vase, Atlanta, Light Blue, Cream, 7 In.	79.00
Vase, Black, Cylinder, 8 1/4 In.	225.00
Vase, Ipsen Swirl, 4 In.	100.00 to 125.00
Vase, Rebekah, Green, Matt Carlton, 18 In.	1650.00
Vase, Rebekah, Turquoise, 22 In.	1950.00
Vase, Ring, Dark Blue, 6 1/2 In.	75.00
Vase, Ring, Light Blue, Cylinder, 10 1/2 In.	80.00
Vase, Ring, Turquoise, Cylinder, 8 In.	85.00
Vase, Ring, White, Cylinder, 10 In.	110.00

Vase, Rust, Fred Johnson, 7 1/2 In.	90.00
Vase, Turquoise, Cylinder, 8 In.	95.00
Vase, Wavy Lip, Matt Carlton	375.00
Vase, White, Cylinder, 10 In.	195.00
Vase, White, Ribbed, Squatty, Matt Carlton, 4 x 8 In.	150.00

BAVARIA is a region in Europe where many types of porcelain were made. In the nineteenth century, the mark often included the word *Bavaria*. After 1871, the words *Bavaria, Germany*, were used. Listed here are pieces that include the name *Bavaria* in some form, but major porcelain makers, such as Rosenthal, are listed in their own categories.

Dresser Set, Pink Chevron Design, Women's Head Finials, 3 Piece	275.00
Pitcher, Lemonade, Fruit Motif, Blossoms, Gold Trim, Signed, Maxon	175.00
Pitcher, Water, Deep Pink Roses, Green Ground, Artist, Late 1800s	120.00
Sugar & Creamer, Demitasse	16.00

BEADED BAGS are included in the Purse category.

BEATLES collectors search for any items picturing the four members of the famous music group or any of their recordings. Because these items are so new, the condition is very important and top prices are paid only for items in mint condition. The Beatles first appeared on American network television in 1964. The group disbanded in 1971. Ringo Starr, George Harrison, and Paul McCartney are still performing. John Lennon died in 1980.

Book, Hard Days Night, Paperback, 1964	25.00
Book, The Real Story, 1968	9.00
Book, Yellow Submarine, Paperback, 128 Pages, 1968	35.00
Book Cover Set, Color Psychedelic Features, 1967	45.00
Booklet, Guitar Hits, 1964	28.00
Bookmark, Yellow Submarine, Cardboard, Marked King Features Syndicate, c.1968	8.00
Brunch Bag, 4 Heads On Side	250.00
Button, Yellow Submarine, 1 1/4 In.	9.50
Button, Yellow Submarine, 3 1/2 In.	14.50
Calendar, 1979, Rolled	25.00
Card, Fan Club Membership, 1964	40.00
Costume, Ringo Star, Ben Cooper, Box	300.00
Doll, Blow-Up, Box, 4 Piece	85.00
Doll, George Harrison, Remco, Instrument	75.00
Doll, Paul McCartney, 4 In.	85.00
Doll, Ringo Starr, 4 In.	85.00
Game, Flip Your Wig, Box, 1964	145.00 to 200.00
Glass Set, Red & Black Enamel, 4 Different Heads, NEMS Enterprises, 4 Piece	985.00

Beatles, Ornament, Christmas, Figural, Hand Blown Glass, 5 In., 4 Piece

Harmonica, Box 35.00
Kerchief, Leather Tie 75.00
Lunch Box, Yellow Submarine . . . . .135.00 to 425.00
Marble Set, 1 In., 4 Piece 10.00
Model, Ringo, Wildest Skins In Town, Revell, Box 85.00
Nodder Set, Cake, Package, 1964 . . . . 70.00
Ornament, Christmas, Figural, Hand Blown Glass, 5 In., 4 Piece . . . .*Illus* 550.00
Pin, Fan, NEMS, Small 80.00
Pin, Lapel, Enamel, 4 Beatles, Yellow Submarine Promotional Shot, c.1968 . . . . 25.00
Postcard, Times Takes, Ringo Starr 5.00
Poster, Hard Day's Night, Rolled, 1 Sheet 40.00
Record, Please, Please Me, Signed, 15 x 28 In. 2070.00
Ring, Flicker, 1960s 28.00
Ring Set, Gumball, 1960s, 4 Piece 20.00
Song Book, Illustrated, 1965 . . . . 20.00
Stationery, Sgt. Pepper's Lonely Hearts Club Band, 4 Envelopes, 4 Letterhead, 1968 . . . 20.00
Tin, Talcum Powder, 4 Portraits, Contents 395.00
Tour Guide, 1965 . . . . 80.00

BEEHIVE, Austria, or Beehive, Vienna, are terms used in English-
speaking countries to refer to the many types of decorated porcelain
bearing a mark that looks like a beehive. The mark is actually a shield,
viewed upside down. It was first used in 1744 by the Royal Porcelain
Manufactory of Vienna. The firm made porcelains, called *Royal
Vienna* by collectors, until it closed in 1864. Many other German,
Austrian, and Japanese factories have reproduced Royal Vienna wares,
complete with the original shield or *beehive* mark. This listing includes
the expensive, original Royal Vienna porcelains and many other types
of beehive porcelain. The Royal Vienna pieces include that name in the
description.

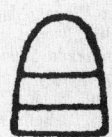

Chocolate Set, French Nobility Portraits, Beehive Mark, 20th Century, 15 Piece 490.00
Cup & Saucer, Scenic, Cobalt & Gold, Signed, Royal Vienna 175.00
Dish, Catherine II & Pierre LeGrande Portrait, Other Sovereigns Around, 13 In. 3680.00
Figurine, Boy, 6 In. 95.00
Plate, 2 Hunters & Dog, Gold Border, Signed, Wagner, 9 1/2 In. 924.00
Plate, Girl Holding Roses, Scarf Over Head, 8 In. 75.00
Plate, Napoleonic Man & Woman, Fence, Gilt Frame, Square, D'Amour, 9 In. 325.00
Plate, Portrait, Amicitia, Shadowbox Frame, Signed 300.00
Plate, Profile Portrait Of Bare Shouldered Young Woman, Signed, 9 1/2 In. 200.00
Plate, Venus & A Moor, Shield Mark, 9 1/2 In. 805.00
Plate, Woman & Basket, Man, Top Hat, Square, 9 In. 325.00
Potpourri, Finial Cover, Stand, 1840, 18 In. 3950.00
Stein, Man, Woman & Cupid, Cobalt Blue, Hand Painted, Marked, 1/5 Liter 2032.00
Teabowl & Saucer, Border Of Panels, Trellis Work, Ducks In Flight Interior, c.1735 . . . 3737.00
Tray, Gold Encrusted Border, Burgundy Band, Signed, 16 In. 1540.00
Urn, Cover, Gold & Blue, Underplate, Royal Vienna 235.00
Urn, Domed Cover, Continuous Classical Figural Scene, Shield Mark, 21 In. 3450.00
Urn, Maidens Dancing, Cherub, 8 In. 175.00
Urn, Polychromed Classically Attired Woman, Oval Reserve, Austria, 19 3/4 In. 275.00
Vase, Lebrun II Portrait, Purple Tiffany Finish, Gold Handles, Crown Mark, 9 In. 1700.00
Vase, People Gathered In Room, Eagle Handles, Cobalt Blue, 27 1/4 In. 5520.00

BEER BOTTLES are listed in the Bottle category under Beer.

BEER CANS are a twentieth-century idea. Beer was sold in kegs or
returnable bottles until 1934. The first patent for a can was issued to
the American Can Company in September of that year; and Gotfried
Kruger Brewing Company, Newark, New Jersey, was the first to use
the can. The cone-top can was first made in 1935, the aluminum pop-
top in 1962. Collectors should look for cans in good condition, with no
dents or rust. Serious collectors prefer cans that have been opened
from the bottom.

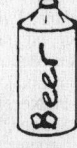

Acme, Flat Top, 12 Oz. 56.00

Ballantine's Export Beer, 1939 .... 40.00
Breidt's Pilsner Beer, Cone Top, 12 Oz. 100.00
Clyde Cream Ale, Cone Top 300.00
Eastside Beer, Cone Top 11.00
Edelweiss Light Beer, Cone Top, 12 Oz. 34.00
Effinger's Special Beer, 12 Oz. 34.00
Falstaff, Cone Top 25.00
Fort Pitt Beer, Cone Top, 12 Oz. 150.00
Goetz Country Club, Cone Top 45.00
Grain Belt, Cone Top 35.00
Gretz Beer, Cone Top, Contents, 12 Oz. 203.00
Kentucky Malt Liquor, Flat Top, 12 Oz. 23.00
Koehler's Beer, Cone Top, 12 Oz. 34.00

BELL collectors collect all types of bells. Favorites include glass bells, figural bells, school bells, and cowbells. Bells have been made of porcelain, china, or metal through the centuries.

Bicycle, Harold Lloyd, 1920s 295.00
Church, Brass, Buckeye Foundry, Van Duzon & Tift, 1889, 29 In. Diam. 2900.00
Door, Bronze, Spring & Bronze Spike Mount 85.00
Dutch Boy, Umbrella & Jug, Brass, 4 1/4 x 2 In. 55.00
Flute Player, Male, Luster, Porcelain, Japan, 6 In. 75.00
Gothic, Bronze, c.1530, 10 1/2 In. 1850.00
Hammered Silver Metal, Karl Gustav Hansen, 1935, 3 1/8 In. 150.00
Prayer Lady, Pink, Pottery 95.00
School, Metal, 12 x 8 In. 180.00
Sleigh, 21 Bells, Metal, New Leather Strap, 86 In. 385.00
Sleigh, Brass, 19 Graduated Bells, Leather Strap, 83 In. 335.00
Tap, Brass, Cherub Holding Up Bell, 10 x 3 1/2 In. 135.00

BELLE WARE glass was made in 1903 by Carl V. Helmschmied. In 1904 he started a corporation known as the Helmschmied Manufacturing Company. His factory closed in 1908 and he worked on his own until his death in 1934.

Vase, Multicolored Orchids, Beaded Rim, 6 In. 480.00

BELLEEK china was made in Ireland, other European countries, and the United States. The glaze is creamy yellow and appears wet. The first Belleek was made in 1857. All pieces listed here are Irish Belleek. The mark changed through the years. The first mark, black, dates from 1863 to 1890. The second mark, black, dates from 1891 to 1926 and includes the words *Co. Fermanagh, Ireland.* The third mark, black, dates from 1926 to 1946 and has the words *Deanta in Eirinn.* The fourth mark, same as the third mark but green, dates from 1946 to 1955. The fifth mark, green, dates from 1955 to 1965 and has an R in a circle added in the upper right. The sixth mark, green, dates after 1965 and the words *Co. Fermanagh* have been omitted. The seventh mark, gold, was used from 1980 to 1993 and omits the words *Deanta in Eirinn.* The eighth mark, introduced in 1993, is similar to the second mark but is printed in blue. The word *Belleek* is now used only on the pieces made in Ireland even though earlier pieces from other countries were sometimes marked *Belleek.* These early pieces are listed by manufacturer, such as Ceramic Art Co., Haviland, Lenox, Ott & Brewer, and Willets.

Cake Plate, Allover Green 3 Leaf Cover, Open Handle, 4th Mark, 10 1/4 In. 80.00
Cake Plate, Twig Handle, Basket Weave, 1890-1921, 10 1/2 In. 300.00
Creamer, Figural, Young Maiden, 2nd Mark, Black 75.00
Creamer, Neptune, 2nd Mark, Black 65.00
Creamer, Shell, 5th Mark, Green 30.00
Cup & Saucer, Limpet, 3rd Mark, Black 87.00
Cup & Saucer, Neptune, 3rd Mark, Black 85.00
Cup & Saucer, Shamrock, Basket Weave, 3rd Mark, Black 165.00

Cup & Saucer, Shell Shape, Pink, Blue, Gilt Handle	160.00
Cup & Saucer, Tridacna, 1st Mark, Black	55.00
Dish, Heart Shape, 3rd Mark, Black, 6 In.	.85.00 to 95.00
Figurine, Girl, Basket Bearer, 6th Mark, Green, 8 1/2 In.	145.00
Figurine, Pig, 5th Mark, Green, 4 In.	40.00
Figurine, Putto, Kneeling, Pink Coral Branches Bowl Form, Naturalistic Base, 14 In.	745.00
Figurine, Scotty, 3 1/2 In.	65.00
Figurine, Terrier, 6th Mark, Green, 3 1/2 In.	50.00
Honey Pot, 3rd Mark, Black, 2 Piece	225.00
Jug, Milk, Limpet, 3rd Mark, Black	395.00
Milk Pot, Thorn, Black, Gold Design, Impressed Mark, 1863-1890, 7 In.	500.00
Mug, Shamrock & Basket Weave, 6th Mark, Green	55.00
Plate, Tridacna, Tea Ware, 2nd Mark, Black 8 In.	90.00
Pot, Swirl, Applied Floral, 3rd Mark, Black, 3 2/5 In.	260.00
Salt & Pepper, Shamrock, 6th Mark, Green	70.00
Stein, Purple Grape Pods, Gold Rim & Handle, Yellow Luster Ground, A.R. Hadley, 7 In.	190.00
Sugar & Creamer, 3rd Mark, Black	120.00
Sugar & Creamer, Double Shell, 6th Mark, Green	95.00
Sugar & Creamer, Lotus, 3rd Mark, Black	150.00
Sugar & Creamer, Shamrock & Harp, 6th Mark, Green	145.00
Sugar & Creamer, Shamrock, 3rd Mark, Black	160.00
Tea Set, Overland, Laurel Wreath Decoration, 9 In., 3 Piece	287.00
Tea Set, Shell Pattern, 3rd Mark, Black, 3 Piece	402.00
Teapot, Pink Tint, 2nd Mark, Black	640.00
Vase, Aberdeen, 3rd Mark, Black	325.00
Vase, Sea Horse, 1st Mark, Black	578.00
Vase, Stump, 6th Mark, Green	135.00
Vase, Sunflower, 2nd Mark, Black	175.00
Vase, Tree Trunk, Nesting Birds, 1st Mark, Black, 12 1/2 In.	82.00
Vase, Tree Trunk, Shamrock, 6 In.	45.00

BENNINGTON ware was the product of two factories working in Bennington, Vermont. Both the Norton Company and the Lyman Fenton Company were out of business by 1896. The wares include brown and yellow mottled pottery, Parian, scroddled ware, stoneware, graniteware, yellowware, and Staffordshire-type vases. The name is also a generic term for mottled brownware of the type made in Bennington.

Bank, Flint Enamel, 1850-1860, 6 1/2 In.	862.00
Bottle, Coachman, Rockingham Glaze, 1849, 10 3/8 In.	247.00
Bowl, Brown Sponge, 10 1/2 In.	165.00
Candlestick, Flint Enamel, 1849-1858, 8 In.	920.00
Coffeepot, Flint Enamel, Tan, Deep Blue, Orange Glaze, 12 3/4 In.	1980.00
Crock, Stoneware, 1850s, 3 1/4 In.	550.00
Dish, Soap, Cover, Rib Pattern, Flint Glaze, 1849, 5 5/8 In.	880.00
Figurine, Boy, Parian, 1878	150.00
Figurine, Lion, Tongue Up, Flint Enamel, Coleslaw Mane, 7 1/2 In.	4312.00
Flask, Book, Bennington Battle Impressed On Spine, 5 3/4 In.	747.00
Flask, Book, Bennington Companion G Impressed On Spine, 8 In.	747.00
Flask, Book, Coming Thro' The Rye	287.00
Flask, Book, Dept. Spirits, Small	425.00
Flask, Book, Flint Enamel, 1849-1858, 5 3/4 In.	431.00
Flask, Book, Ladies Companion Impressed On Spine, Flint Enamel, 5 1/2 In.	690.00
Flask, Book, Rockingham Glaze, 11 In.	770.00
Flask, Book, Tan, Brown, Ocher, Pale Cream Glaze, 11 x 8 1/4 In.	3850.00
Flask, Shoe	225.00
Jug, Blue Butterfly, Julius Norton, Egg Shape, 2 Gal.	750.00
Jug, Gurgling, Rockingham Glaze, 10 In.	350.00
Marble, Blue-Green & Yellow, 11/16 In.	15.00
Marble, High Gloss, 1 3/16 In.	20.00
Pan, Bundt, Brown Spatterware	145.00
Paperweight, Spaniel, 1849-1858, 3 x 4 1/2 In.	805.00
Pie Plate, Yellow Highlights, Rockingham Glaze, 1849, 11 In.	715.00

Pitcher, Ear Of Corn, Blue & White, 9 In. 110.00
Pitcher, Flint Enamel, 1849 On Base, 13 In. 1093.00
Pitcher, Hound-Handle, Spout, 1852-1867, 9 1/2 In. 345.00
Pitcher, Hunting Scene, 1847-1858, 8 In. 172.00
Pitcher, Milk, St. George & The Dragon 390.00
Pitcher, Wash, Scroll Handle, Pale Cream Glaze, Yellow, Brown, 4 1/2 In. 4290.00
Teapot, Alternate Rib, Flint Enamel, 1844-1858, 7 1/2 In. 230.00
Tieback, Flint Enamel, Pale Cream Glaze, Brown, 4 1/2 x 4 1/2 In., Pair 440.00
Tumbler, Inverted Thumbprint 30.00

BERLIN, a German porcelain factory, was started in 1751 by Wilhelm Kaspar Wegely. In 1763, the factory was taken over by Frederick the Great and became the Royal Berlin Porcelain Manufactory. It is still in operation today. Pieces have been marked in a variety of ways.

Charger, Central Mythological Scene, Rape Of Europa, Floral Border, 27 3/4 In. 8625.00
Cup & Saucer, Battle Scene Reserves, Blue Ground, Gilt Borders, 4 In. 3220.00
Cup & Saucer, Grecian Maiden, Gilt, Pale Green, c.1810 .... 302.00
Figurine, Hercules & Omphale, Cupid Stands Behind Them, Signed, 11 1/2 In. 1610.00
Plaque, 2 Women, Classical Robes, 1st Woman Holds Greek Lekythos, Signed, 9 3/4 In. . 1600.00
Plaque, Fouruse De Mandolin, Peasant Woman, Framed, 6 1/4 x 4 1/4 In. 1650.00
Plaque, Full-Length Profile Of Woman, Carrying Tray, Rectangular.Signed, 9 x 6 In. 1300.00
Plaque, Girl Holding Candle, Gilt Frame, Rectangular, Signed, 9 3/4 x 7 In. 1700.00

BESWICK started making earthenware in Staffordshire, England, in 1936. The company is now part of Royal Doulton Tableware, Ltd. Figurines of animals, especially dogs and horses, Beatrix Potter animals, and other wares are still being made.

Ashtray, 3 Dogs In Front, Green 58.00
Ashtray, 5 Dogs, Figural 75.00
Creamer, Pickwick, No. 1119, 3 1/4 In. 60.00
Figurine, Alsatian, No. 969 .... 65.00
Figurine, Amiable Guinea Pig ....250.00 to 450.00
Figurine, Baltimore Oriole 56.00
Figurine, Barracuda 80.00
Figurine, Benjamin Bunny, No. 1105 .... 60.00
Figurine, Brindle Boxer, No. 1202 ....75.00 to 95.00
Figurine, Bull Terrier, White, No. 970 .... 125.00
Figurine, Bullfinch 20.00
Figurine, Cecily Parsley, No. 1941 ....40.00 to 125.00
Figurine, Cedar Waxwing, No. 2184 .... 65.00
Figurine, Cheshire Cat, Alice In Wonderland 590.00
Figurine, Christopher Robin 180.00
Figurine, Cocker Spaniel, Black, White, Miniature 29.00
Figurine, Cocker Spaniel, Tan, White, Miniature 30.00
Figurine, Cottontail 25.00
Figurine, Cousin Ribby 50.00
Figurine, Dachshund, No. 1460 .... 50.00
Figurine, Diggory Diggory Delvet 75.00
Figurine, Elephant, Gray, White Tusks Up, 10 1/2 x 14 In. 300.00
Figurine, Fisherman Otter, 6 In. 40.00
Figurine, Flopsy, Mopsy & Cottontail, c.1948 ....115.00 to 315.00
Figurine, Foal, Back Stamp, Label 25.00
Figurine, Fox 38.00
Figurine, Foxy Whiskered Gentleman, c.1948 .... 270.00
Figurine, Gentleman Pig, 6 In. 45.00
Figurine, Ginger 650.00
Figurine, Great Dane 65.00
Figurine, Hiker Badger ....40.00 to 45.00
Figurine, Hunca Munca, No. 1198 ....165.00 to 225.00
Figurine, Huntsman, No. 1501 .... 150.00
Figurine, Jemima Puddleduck, No. 3373, 6 In. ....50.00 to 60.00
Figurine, Jeremy Fisher, No. 1157 .... 65.00
Figurine, Jeremy Fisher, No. 3372, 5 1/2 In. 50.00

Figurine, Johnny Townmouse, No. 1276 ....45.00 to 100.00
Figurine, Labrador, Tan, No. 1548, Medium 55.00
Figurine, Lady Mouse 25.00
Figurine, Little Pig Robinson, 1st Version ....250.00 to 450.00
Figurine, Little Pig Robinson, No. 1104 ....65.00 to 75.00
Figurine, Mallard Duck, No. 750 .... 135.00
Figurine, Miss Doormouse, 1991 .... 45.00
Figurine, Miss Moppet, 1st Version 450.00
Figurine, Mr. Alderman Ptolemy 65.00
Figurine, Mr. Benjamin Bunny, No. 1940 .... 75.00
Figurine, Mr. Drake Puddleduck, No. 2628 ....25.00 to 70.00
Figurine, Mr. Jeremy Fisher, 1st Version ....175.00 to 180.00
Figurine, Mr. McGregor, No. 3056 ....35.00 to 40.00
Figurine, Mrs. Flopsy Bunny 60.00
Figurine, Mrs. Rabbit & Bunnies, No. 2543 ....25.00 to 75.00
Figurine, Mrs. Rabbit, 1st Version 450.00
Figurine, Mrs. Rabbit, Cooking, No. 3287 .... 20.00
Figurine, Nutkin 40.00
Figurine, Old English Sheep Dog, No. 453 .... 150.00
Figurine, Old Mr. Brown ....110.00 to 150.00
Figurine, Old Woman Who Lived In A Shoe ....25.00 to 100.00
Figurine, Owl, From Winnie The Pooh, Label, 4 In. ....75.00 to 100.00
Figurine, Peter In Bed, No. 3473 .... 55.00
Figurine, Peter Rabbit, 100th Anniversary, Box ....42.00 to 45.00
Figurine, Peter Rabbit, No. 1098 .... 70.00
Figurine, Peter, With Daffodils, Yellow Flowers, No. 3597 .... 33.00
Figurine, Peter, With Handkerchief, No. 3592, 6 In. 55.00
Figurine, Peter, With Postbag, Putting In Letter, No. 3591 .... 33.00
Figurine, Pheasant, No. 1225 .... 190.00
Figurine, Pickles 285.00
Figurine, Pig-Wig, Beatrix Potter 300.00
Figurine, Piggly Bland, No. 1365 .... 70.00
Figurine, Poorly Peter Rabbit, No. 2560 .... 65.00
Figurine, Rebecca Puddleduck, No. 2647 ....70.00 to 80.00
Figurine, Samuel Whiskers, No. 1106 .... 70.00
Figurine, Siamese Cat, 7 In. 68.00
Figurine, Siamese Kittens, No. 1296 .... 45.00
Figurine, Simpkin, Tailor Of Gloucester, 1975 ....550.00 to 900.00
Figurine, Sir Isaac Newton ....410.00 to 500.00
Figurine, Sleepytime 50.00
Figurine, Squirrel Nutkin, No. 1102 .... 65.00
Figurine, Strained Relations 60.00
Figurine, Susie Jamaica 290.00
Figurine, Tabitha Twitchet, No. 1676 ....70.00 to 99.00
Figurine, Tailor Of Gloucester, No. 1108 .... 70.00
Figurine, Thomasina Tittlemouse, No. 2668 .... 95.00
Figurine, Timmy Tiptoes, No. 1101 ....20.00 to 65.00
Figurine, Timmy Willie 95.00
Figurine, Tom Thumb, No. 2989 .... 70.00
Figurine, Tommy Brock, No. 1348 .... 70.00
Figurine, Uncle Sam 40.00
Figurine, Wire-Haired Fox Terrier, No. 963 .... 130.00
Mug, Christmas, 1971 .... 65.00
Mug, Christmas, 1972 .... 60.00
Mug, Christmas, 1973 .... 60.00
Mug, Christmas, 1974 .... 60.00
Pitcher, Blown-Out Palm Tree, c.1930 .... 65.00
Pitcher, Sairey Gamp 75.00
Salt & Pepper, Laurel & Hardy 175.00
Stand, Display, Stumps, Porcelain 155.00
Sugar & Creamer, Pecksniff ....54.00 to 75.00
Tankard, Christmas, 1972 .... 65.00
Tankard, Christmas, English Country Folk, Mrs. Rabbit Baking 32.00

Teapot, Peggotty, Rope Handle, No. 1116 .... 185.00
Teapot, Sairey Gamp, No. 671 .... 165.00
Wall Pocket, Palm Tree, Bongo, Maroon 100.00

BETTY BOOP, the cartoon figure, first appeared on the screen in 1931. Her face was modeled after the famous singer Helen Kane and her body after Mae West. In 1935, a comic strip was started. Her dog was named Bimbo. Although the Betty Boop cartoons ended by 1938, there was a revival of interest in the Betty Boop image in the 1980s and new pieces are being made.

Bank, Betty Boop 25.00
Bank, Figural, 1981, Vandor 95.00
Bank, Figural, Ceramic ....14.00 to 20.00
Bank, Head 35.00
Bank, Sock-It-Away, 1984 .... 15.00
Bookends, Betty & Dog, Jukebox 125.00
Box, Heart Shape, Ceramic 15.00
Clock, Alarm, Figural, Goodstuff 16.00
Cookie Jar, Betty Boop In Top Hat 110.00
Cookie Jar, Carmen Miranda, Vandor 525.00
Doll, Stuffed, King Features, Package, 18 In. 35.00
Doll, Trapeze, Celluloid, Windup, Japan, 1930 .... 1495.00
Doll, Vinyl, 5 In. 6.00
Doll, Wooden, Jointed, 1930s, 4 1/4 In. 185.00
Doll, Wooden, Jointed, Clothes, Crazed, 12 In. 1100.00
Doll, Wooden, Jointed, Hair & Eyes Touched Up, Black Dress, 11 In. 995.00
Earrings, Display Card 3.00
Figurine, 3-Dimensional, 3 In. 5.00
Figurine, 3-Dimensional, 6 In. 9.00
Figurine, Bonzo, Dog, Bisque, Japan, 1930s 68.00
Gift Bag, Betty 3.00
Key Chain, Heart Shape 7.00
Key Ring, Brass, 4 In. 7.00
Knife, Long Illustrated Handle, 6 In. 9.00
Light Bulb, Christmas 75.00
Mask, Pottery 20.00
Mug, Betty Picture, King Features Syndicate, 1981, 4 In. ... 23.00
Mug, Figural, Ceramic 10.00
Nodder, Celluloid, Pink Dress, Fleischer 575.00
Nodder, Hula Hip 175.00
Ornament, Christmas, Figural, Blown Glass 25.00
Pen Set, Figural Caps Of Betty, Box, 2 In. 13.00
Perfume Bottle, 3 1/2 In. 85.00
Ring, Metal, Adjustable 7.00
Salt & Pepper, Betty With Camera 30.00
Salt & Pepper, Betty With Christmas Presents 25.00
Salt & Pepper, Hollywood, Benjamin & Medwin 11.00
Spoon Rest, Box 10.00
Tambourine, 1960s 95.00
Teapot, Googly Eyed ....25.00 to 36.00
Tote Bag, Betty 10.00

BICYCLES were invented in 1839. The first manufactured bicycle was made in 1861. Special ladies' bicycles were made after 1874. The modern safety bicycle was not produced until 1885. Collectors search for all types of bicycles and tricycles. Bicycle-related items are also listed here.

Airflo, American, Headlights, Green & Yellow, 1930s 850.00
Bell, Crown Jewel, 1950s 65.00
Bowden, Spacelander, Fiberglass, 1960 .... 7500.00
Columbia, c.1890, 58 In. 1320.00
Columbia, Girl's, Green Metallic Handlebars, Chrome Fenders, Banana Seat 200.00
Elgin, Boy's, Blackhawk, c.1934 .... 2200.00

Bicycle, Tricycle, Fairy, Tiller Steering   Bicycle, Victor, 56-In. Front Wheel

Elgin, Twin 20, 1939	275.00
Evans-Colson, Girl's, Commander, Green & Cream, 26 In.	450.00
Firestone, Deluxe Cruiser, 26 In.	250.00
Fisca, Front Wheel, 54 In. Diam.	2090.00
H.B. Smith, Smithfield, New Jersey, Big Wheel In Back, c.1880, 48 In. Diam.	4675.00
Hawthorne, Girl's, 2 Speed, 26 In.	145.00
Horse, Wooden Wheels, Iron Handlebars, Horsehair Mane & Tail, 1880, 37 In.	3900.00
Huffy, Radiobike	2500.00
Iver Johnson Arms Co., Wooden Rear Fender, Chain Guards, Leather Tool Kit	715.00
J.C. Higgins, Boy's, Jeweled Tank, Batwing Headlight, 1952	880.00
J.C. Higgins, Woman's, Deluxe, c.1947	495.00
License Plate, Nashua, Metal, 2 1/2 x 4 In.	38.50
Monark, Silver King, All Aluminum, 1935	5000.00
Pin, Schwinn, Gold Luster, Enamel, Racing Bicyclist, 1930s	6.00
Remington, Tandem, c.1897	2310.00
Schwinn, Apple Krate	600.00
Schwinn, Boy's, Black Phantom	330.00
Schwinn, Boy's, Green & White	825.00
Schwinn, Girl's, Fiesta, Pink & White, 26 In.	150.00
Schwinn, Girl's, Panther, Chrome Trim, Pink & White	500.00
Schwinn, Hornet, 1957, 26 In.	300.00
Schwinn, Phantom, 1954	4500.00
Schwinn, Starlet, 1956, 26 In.	300.00
Schwinn, Stingray Centennial, Red, White & Blue	900.00
Schwinn, Stingray, Blue & White	150.00
Schwinn, Tornado, 1950s, 26 In.	250.00
Scorcher, Wooden Spokes & Rims, c.1894	1320.00
Sears, Spaceliner, 1960s, 26 In.	550.00
Shelby, Girl's, Donald Duck, c.1949, 24 In.	935.00 to 1760.00
Shelby, Girl's, Supreme, c.1940	220.00
Siren, Fire Chief, Hardware, Ranger-Steel Co., Box	45.00
Siren, Pato	15.00
Springfield Roadster, Springfield Bicycle Co., Boston, c.1889, 50 In.	7150.00
Starkley Simple, Metal	360.00
Tandem, Wooden Rims & Handlebars	632.50
Tricycle, Boneshaker, Wooden	450.00
Tricycle, Colson Company, Elyria, Ohio	425.00
Tricycle, Double Seat	150.00
Tricycle, Fairy, Tiller Steering	*Illus* 475.00
Tricycle, Fairy, Wicker Seat	2255.00
Velocipede, Horse, Crank & Chain Mechanism, Wooden, 38 In.	1210.00
Velocipede, Wooden-Horse Body, Hand Crank, Chain Drive, c.1890	1400.00
Victor, 56-In. Front Wheel	*Illus* 1550.00
Western Flyer, Buzz Bike, 1970s, 20 In.	150.00
Wolf-American, Woman's, c.1898	495.00

BING & GRONDAHL is a famous Danish factory making fine porcelains from 1853 to the present. Underglaze blue decoration was started in 1886. The annual Christmas plate series was introduced in 1895. Dinnerwares, stoneware, and figurines are still being made today. The firm has used the initials B & G and a stylized castle as part of the mark since 1898.

MADE IN DENMARK

Bell, Statue Of Liberty, 1976	60.00
Coffeepot, Sea Gulls In Flight With Dolphin Finial, Gold Trim, 7 1/2 In.	195.00
Compote, Sea Gull Pattern, 5 1/2 In.	125.00
Dish, Sea Gull Pattern, Leaf Shape, Foldover Handle	65.00
Figurine, Bird, Cuckoo, No. 1770, 8 In. ....100.00 to 160.00
Figurine, Bird, Titmouse, No. 1635, 3 1/2 In., Pair	150.00
Figurine, Bird, Tufted Duck, No. 1855, 2 3/4 In.	75.00
Figurine, Blacksmith At Anvil, No. 2225, 10 3/4 In.	550.00
Figurine, Boy & Girl Dancing, No. 1845, 8 1/2 In.	195.00
Figurine, Boy, Playing Trumpet, No. 179, 6 3/4 In.	38.00
Figurine, Cat, Sitting, No. 2256, 7 3/4 In.	108.00
Figurine, Catch, Girl, With Ball, No. 2391, 6 3/4 In.	120.00
Figurine, Child, Toothache, White, No. 2207, 4 1/2 In.	20.00
Figurine, Child, Tummyache, White, No. 2208, 4 1/2 In.	20.00
Figurine, Cobbler, No. 2228, 8 1/2 In.	325.00
Figurine, Dog, Fox Terrier, No. 1998	100.00
Figurine, Elsie, No. 1574, 6 1/2 In.	85.00
Figurine, Goose Girl, No. 2254, 9 1/4 In.	57.50
Figurine, Hans Christian Andersen, Seated, Girl, No. 2037, 8 3/4 In. ....185.00 to 325.00
Figurine, Ida, Girl, No. 2298, 5 1/2 In. ....68.00 to 100.00
Figurine, Lamb, No. 2171, 2 3/4 In.	50.00
Figurine, Little Builder, No. 2306, 4 In.	125.00
Figurine, Little Girl, No. 1526, 3 1/2 In.	48.00
Figurine, Love Refused, Boy & Girl, No. 1614, 6 3/4 In.	110.00
Figurine, Lovebird, Green, No. 2341, 3 In.	55.00
Figurine, My Balloon, Girl, With Arm Raised, No. 2273, 9 In.	135.00
Figurine, Ole Boy, Holding Puppy, No. 1747, 6 1/2 In.	117.00
Figurine, Penguin, No. 1822, 10 In. ....300.00 to 450.00
Figurine, Polar Bear, White, Black Nose, No. 1954, 18 In.	330.00
Figurine, School's Out, Boy, Seated On Book, No. 1742, 5 In.	158.00
Figurine, Sow & Her Young, 11 1/2 In.	264.00
Figurine, St. Bernard, No. 1926, 4 3/4 In.	65.00
Figurine, Titmouse, Bearded, No. 1633, 3 1/2 In.	50.00
Gravy Boat, Seahorse, Underplate	95.00
Plate, Christmas, 1919, Outside The Lighted Window, Friis	75.00
Plate, Christmas, 1923, Royal Hunting Castle, Friis	75.00
Plate, Christmas, 1924, Lighthouse In Danish Waters, Friis	75.00
Plate, Christmas, 1928, Eskimos Looking At Church, Friis	75.00
Plate, Christmas, 1956, Christmas In Copenhagen, Bonfils	90.00
Plate, Christmas, 1963, Christmas Elf, Thelander	60.00
Plate, Christmas, 1969, Arrival Of Christmas Guests, Thelander	25.00
Plate, Christmas, 1973, Country Christmas, Thelander	25.00
Plate, Christmas, 1974, Christmas In The Village, Thelander	14.00
Plate, Christmas, 1983, Christmas In The Old Town, Jensen	30.00
Plate, Jubilee, 1976, Statue Of Liberty	60.00
Plate, Mother's Day, Mare & Colt, 1972	75.00
Plate, Olympiad, 1972, Munich	25.00
Tea Caddy, Pale Green, Woman & Parasol Scene Panel, Denmark, 7 1/4 In.	140.00
Vase, Birds, Blue, 12 In., Pair	225.00

BINOCULARS of all types are wanted by collectors. Those made in the eighteenth and nineteenth centuries are favored by serious collectors. The small, attractive binoculars called *opera glasses* are listed in their own category.

Campoux, With Compass	70.00
Field, Civil War, Chevalier Opticien, Paris	95.00
Japanese Navy, X 20, 120 mm Diameter Objective Lenses, Brass Sun Shade	3000.00

Nanon, Deluxe Lenses, 8 In.	14.00
Naval Officer's, Burnished Brass, Original Leather Case, 19th Century, Pair	169.00
Nikon, Case, 8 In.	12.00
Stanhope, Green Glass	35.00
Stanhope, Miniature	85.00

BIRDCAGES are collected for use as homes for pet birds and as decorative objects of folk art. Elaborate wooden cages of the past centuries can still be found. The brass or wicker cages of the 1930s are popular with bird owners.

Arched Top, Oblong Base, Wire & Wood	27.00
Copper, Pierced	545.00
Hendryx, Brass	50.00
Hendryx, Brass, Platform, Perch & Porcelain Water Dish, 1905	95.00
Hendryx, Brass, Stand, 1876	450.00
Pagoda Style Zinc Dome, Mesh Case, Wrought Iron & Steel, 12 In.	2585.00
Victorian Style, Domed Top, Flattened Paw Feet, Metal, 1920s, 27 1/2 In.	115.00
Wirework, Inlaid Mahogany, Domed Form, Rectangular Base, c.1890, 17 x 17 In.	172.00
Wooden, Old Red & White Repaint, 11 3/4 x 19 1/2 x 20 1/2 In.	125.00
Wooden, Plywood, Duplex, Worn Orange Over Yellow Paint, 30 In.	75.00
Wooden, With Wire Bars, Turned Feet, Posts, Green Paint, Brown Glaze, 18 In.	313.00

BISQUE is an unglazed baked porcelain. Finished bisque has a slightly sandy texture with a dull finish. Some of it may be decorated with various colors. Bisque gained favor during the late Victorian era when thousands of bisque figurines were made. It is still being made. Additional bisque items may be listed under the factory name.

Bust, Woman, Blue Glazed Curly Hair, Square Mahogany Base, Baldelli, 12 x 7 In.	165.00
Cigar & Match Holder, Seated Black Boy, 8 1/2 In.	275.00
Figurine, 2 Owls, Black & Green Paint, England, 7 1/2 In.	95.00
Figurine, Alpine Boy & Girl, Gilt, Pastel, Germany, 12 1/2 & 12 3/4 In., Pair	50.00
Figurine, Boy, Eating Grapes, Mounted As Lamp, 26 In.	105.00
Figurine, Dog, Collie, Large Basket, 6 In.	25.00
Figurine, Googly-Eye Perfume Head, Cork, With Vile, 1920s	150.00
Figurine, Russian Man, Playing Concertina, Tan Overcoat, 7 In.	450.00
Figurine, Woman, Ball Gown, Man, Powdered Wig, Blue Clothes, France, 11 In., Pair	495.00
Lantern, Candle, Cat, Dog & Owl, 3 Faces, Glass Eyes	395.00 to 465.00
Match Holder, Skull	38.00
Sugar & Creamer, Smiling Cat	30.00
Sugar & Creamer, Smiling Pig	34.00
Tray, Austrian Imperial, Signed, 8 x 11 In.	65.00
Vase, Figural, Indian Chief Bust, Germany, 6 1/4 In.	125.00
Vase, Victorian Style, Figurines, UCAGCO, 7 In., Pair	150.00

BLACK memorabilia has become an important area of collecting since the 1970s. The best material dates from past centuries, but many recent items are also of interest. F & F is the mark used on plastic made by Fiedler & Fiedler Mold & Die Works, Inc. in the 1930s and 1940s. Objects that picture a black person may also be listed in this book under Advertising, Tins; Banks; Bottle Openers; Cookie Jars; Salt & Pepper; Sheet Music; etc.

Ashtray, Smoker, Figural, Black Man	45.00
Badge, Slave, Servant, No. 818, Charleston, S.C., Brass, 1 1/2 In.	1875.00
Bank, Nodder, Black Sambo	125.00
Banner, Aunt Jemima, 48 In.	350.00
Bell, Mammy, Red, White Dress	25.00
Bell, Mammy, Souvenir Of Texas	55.00
Birthday Card, Frame, 1924	22.00
Book, Golliwog Airplane, Rusty Tufty Flies High	40.00
Book, Little Black Sambo & Topsy, Reilly & Lee, 1908	275.00
Book, Little Black Sambo, 1917	185.00
Book, Little Black Sambo, Colored Pictures, 1919	75.00
Book, Little Black Sambo, Cupples & Leon Co., 1917	250.00

Book, Little Black Sambo, H. Bannerman, 1965 .... 65.00
Book, Little Black Sambo, Platt & Munk Co., 1935 .... 50.00
Book, Pop-Up, Little Black Sambo Story, McLoughlin, 1942 .... 75.00
Bottle, Mammy Soda 100.00
Bowl & Mug, Child's, Golliwog In Cart, Pig, Golliwog's Joy Ride, Poxon China 225.00
Box, Candy, Amos 'n' Andy Fresh-Air Taxi, 1930s 175.00
Box, Gold Dust Twins, Shipping Type, Large 160.00
Box, Old Virginia Cheroots, Etched Black Man Cover, Wooden, Late 1800s 100.00
Box, Recipe, Mah Bestest Recipes, Mammy Lithograph On Top, Pullout Drawer 155.00
Box, Recipe, Mammy, Red 265.00
Box, Sambo Flue Cleaner, Black Boy Chimney Sweep 45.00
Box, Solid Head Thumb Tacks, Outrageous Black Boy, Unopened 45.00
Candy Container, Figural, Loft, Black Boy 100.00
Canister, Sugar, Man Sitting On Bale Of Sugar Cane, England 125.00
Cigar Pack, Coon Heads, 4 Black Men Smoking, Peeking Over Fence 200.00
Cigarette Holder, Coon Chicken Inn, Signed M.L. Graham 495.00
Clothespin Holder, Mammy 495.00
Coffee Cup, Aunt Jemima 60.00
Coffee Cup, Sambo's 22.00
Comic Book, Uncle Tom's Cabin, 1940s 15.00
Condiment Set, 3 Heads, Bisque, Germany 800.00
Condiment Set, Mammy, Pushing Cart 350.00
Cookie Jar, Chef, Star-Burst 265.00
Cookie Jar, Gone With The Wind Mammy, Red Petticoat 395.00
Creamer, Mammy, Full Figure 145.00
Doll, Baby, Bisque, Jointed, 3 In. 35.00
Doll, Baby, Sascha, Tag, Box 250.00
Doll, Boy, Bisque, Black Original Wig, Hat, 13 1/2 In. 850.00
Doll, Celluloid, Flannel Dress, 5 In. 42.00
Doll, Character, Baby, Brown Sleep Eyes, Composition, 21 In. 375.00
Doll, Exaggerated Nose, Embroidered Face, Rings On Fingers, c.1860 .... 1950.00
Doll, Grace Drayton, Chocolate Drop, Black Girl, Cloth, Side Glancing Eyes, 11 In. 400.00
Doll, Jackie Robinson, Original Clothes, 13 In. 795.00
Doll, Mama, Smiling, Cloth Body, Composition Head & Arms, Molded Hair, 15 In. 495.00
Doll, Mammy, Cloth Stuffed, Vinyl, c.1930, 17 In. 85.00
Doll, Mammy, With Baby, Cloth, Large Hands & Feet, 14 In. 275.00
Doll, Rag, Tiny Feet, Pinched Nose, 1830s, 15 In. 465.00
Doll, Shoebutton Eyes, Earrings, Red Floral Dress, Bloomers, Headdress, 1940s 69.00
Doll, Sweetie Pie, Effanbee, Open-Close Eyes, Bent Knee, 1982, 17 In. 90.00
Doll, Topsy-Turvy, Rag, 1930s 60.00
Doll, Woman, Rag, Black Woolly Hair, Sculptured Nose, 13 In. 85.00
Fan, Man Wearing Top Hat, Use Darke Toothpaste, Paper, On Stick 55.00
Figurine, African Princess, Bisque, Turban, Blue Tunic, France, 11 In. 495.00
Figurine, Girl, Feeding Chickens, 6 In. 35.00
Figurine, Golliwog, Wooden, Japan, Box, 1950s, 5 In., Pair 12.50
Figurine, Jungle Imp, 7 In. 85.00
Figurine, Little Soldier Joe, Brayton Laguna 75.00
Figurine, Man, Carrying Woven Brass Basket, Metal, 1890, 5 3/8 In. 145.00
Game, Knock Down, Mammy, With 10-In. Figures On Plank, Pair ....*Illus* 660.00
Game, Old Maid, Jazzbo Jackson, Other Blacks, Box 40.00
Jelly Jar, Mammy, Red, White Apron, Brayton 700.00
Label, Dixie Boy Citrus, Black Boy, Eating Grapefruit, 1940s, 9 x 9 In. .... ‹ 4.00
Mirror, Boy, Watermelon, Southern Welcome Awaits You, Atlanta, 1909, Pocket 550.00
Mirror, Sheridan Coal Co., Mammy, Paperweight 175.00
Money Clip, Coon Chicken Inn, Brass, Black Man Under Dome 175.00
Night-Light, Mammy 1000.00
Nodder, Boy 125.00
Nodder, Sambo 45.00
Note Holder, Mammy, Wooden, Painted 50.00
Pad, Memo, Mammy 35.00
Pail, Aunt Dinah Molasses, Mammy, 1908 ..../...................100.00 to 125.00
Pen, Black Man In Turban, Jeweled 50.00

If you have a book or other small item that smells peculiar, put it in a large plastic bag with kitty litter. Seal it and let it stand for about a week.

Black, Game, Knock Down, Mammy,
With 10-In. Figures On Plank, Pair, 1 shown

Pencil Sharpener, Black Boy's Head, Exaggerated Features	60.00
Place Mat, Coon Chicken Inn	95.00
Place Mat, Fresh Up Freddie, Colorful, 1950s	15.00
Planter, Mammy's Head, Beige, Red Dots	125.00
Plaque, Black Face, Lane	35.00
Plaque, Pot Holder, Watermelon Boy	45.00
Plate, Bits Of The Old South, 1940-1950	250.00
Plate, Famous & Dandy, 10 In.	95.00
Plate, Sambo's, China, 9 3/4 In.	75.00
Platter, Coon Chicken, 10 In.	350.00
Postcard, Black Servants, Maid Whom We Must Live With, Photograph, 1906	60.00
Postcard, Camp Benj. Harrison, Colored Infantry Group, Rifles, Sept. '08, Unused	180.00
Postcard, Count Basie, At His Piano, Mutoscope Card, Black & White	25.00
Postcard, Let Dinah Black Tell You The Story, Triple Fold	75.00
Poster, Armstrongs America's Greatest Colored Magicians, 1911 Tour, 7 In.	140.00
Poster, Black Boy, Holding 3 Watermelons, Dated 1898	175.00
Poster, Slick Black Hair Straightener, Women & Products, 1940s	65.00
Poster, They Fight For You, Democratic Committee Men Pictures, 20 x 28 In.	150.00
Poster, Uncle Sam Needs You Nigger, Race-Baiting, Anti-Vietnam, 9 x 12 In.	75.00
Reel, Clothes Line, Mammy	45.00
Sign, Drinking Fountain, White-Colored	16.00
Sign, Public Swimming Pool, White Only	16.00
Sign, Rest Rooms, White-Colored	16.00
Skillet, Mammy Head, Cast Iron, 4 1/4 In.	75.00
Slave Neck Collar, Half-Moon Designs, Child's, 4 In.	430.00
Slave Restraints, Leg Shackles, Lock One End, Other End Loops To Ball, Forged Iron	470.00
Spice Rack, Mammy, White Plastic	125.00
Spice Set, Mammy, Red Plastic, 5 Piece	68.00
Spoon Rest, Mammy, Hanging	65.00
Sprinkler Bottle, Boy, Kerchief Around Neck	35.00
Sprinkler Bottle, Mammy, Standing, Hands Clasped In Front	35.00
Sprinkler Bottle, Mammy, Standing, Hands On Hips	35.00
String Holder, Chef's Head	25.00
String Holder, Cream Of Wheat Chef	30.00
String Holder, Flower Girl, Diamond	35.00
String Holder, Girl's Head, Big Eyes	35.00
String Holder, Mammy Face, Clay, Black Face, Red Polka Dot Scarf	450.00
String Holder, Mammy's Head, Pug Nose	35.00
String Holder, Mammy, Chalkware	275.00
String Holder, Mammy, Japan	35.00
String Holder, Mammy, National Silver	30.00
Sugar, Mammy, 2 Handles, Japan	300.00

Sugar & Creamer, Mammy 225.00
Syrup, Figural, Mandy ....95.00 to 165.00
Teapot, Golliwog With Girl, Green Luster 115.00
Teapot, Mammy, Googly-Eye 200.00
Teapot, Mandy 150.00
Thermos, Sambo's Restaurant 995.00
Ticket, Uncle Tom's Cabin, Topsy Picture, 1886, 2 1/2 x 5 In. 40.00
Tile, Mosaic, Mammy, Yellow 550.00
Timer, Egg, Standing Chef, Gold Trim 75.00
Toaster Cover, Mammy, 1940s 42.00
Tobacco Tag, Gravely & Millers Kids, Tin, Naked Black Babies 70.00
Toothpaste, Darkie, Box 35.00
Toothpick, Black Boy, Milk Glass 95.00
Toy, Alabama Coon Jigger, Tin 550.00
Toy, Aunt Jemima, With Basket, Windup, Gunthermann, 1900 .... 550.00
Toy, Black Man, Pull String & Eyes Roll, Tin, 1900s 250.00
Toy, Boy Runs With Watermelon, Dog Bites Seat Of Pants, Windup, Tin, Germany, 1920s   850.00
Tray, Cracker, Mandy 350.00
Tray, Serving, Calumet Baking Powder, Dixie Biscuit Baker, Mammy 40.00
Wall Plaque, Black Sambo, 12 In. 50.00
Whisk Broom, Mammy, Flat 75.00
Whisk Broom, Mammy, Round, Box 75.00
Whisk Broom, Mammy, Small 55.00

BLACK AMETHYST glass appears black until it is held to the light, then
a dark purple can be seen. It has been made in many factories from
1860 to the present.

Basket, Open Edge, 5 In. 200.00
Creamer, Ivy, Flint 135.00
Cup & Saucer, Clover Leaf 18.00
Cuspidor, Woman's 30.00
Salt & Pepper, Dog & Cat, Metal Heads 115.00
Vase, Applied Rainbow Entwined Vines, Loetz-Type, 10 1/2 In. 165.00
Vase, Corn, 8 In. 3000.00
Vase, Ruffled Edge, Enamel Daisies, Gold Trim, 7 1/2 In. 65.00
Vase, Young Girl, Standing In Bower Of Forget-Me-Nots, 10 7/8 In. 195.00

BLOWN GLASS was formed by forcing air through a rod into molten
glass. Early glass and some forms of art glass were hand blown. Other
types of glass were molded or pressed.

Baton, Blue Swirl, Clear, 65 In. 415.00
Beaker, Cut Design, Red, Yellow Stain, 5 1/2 In. 110.00
Beaker, Enameled, Man In Red Jacket, Pale Green, 6 In. 110.00
Bell, Opaque White, Red Looping, Applied Red Rim, 10 In. 275.00
Bottle, 20 Ribs, Swirled, Sapphire Blue, 4 7/8 In. 330.00
Bottle, 24 Swirled Ribs, Zanesville, Amber, 7 5/8 In. 330.00
Bottle, Applied Sloping Lip, Dark Olive-Amber, Pontil, 19 In. 105.00
Bottle, Bellows, Cranberry, White Opalescent Bands & Loops, 13 1/4 In. 330.00
Bottle, Condiment, 3-Piece Mold, 4 In. 250.00
Bottle, Flared Lip, Open Mouth, Olive Green, Pontil, 12 In. 165.00
Bottle, Half Post Neck, Pewter Top, Copper Wheel Engraved Floral Design, 6 In. 110.00
Bottle, Ludlow, Applied Collar, Olive-Amber, 9 In. 105.00
Bowl, Applied Foot, Knop Stem, Cut Star, Pittsburgh, 7 7/8 In. 495.00
Bowl, Cobalt Blue, Footed, 4 In. 110.00
Cake Stand, Dome, Applied Finial, Pittsburgh, 14 In. 300.00
Candlestick, Domed Foot, 11 1/8 In. 715.00
Candlestick, Pewter Insert, Applied Foot, Bulbous Socket, Pittsburgh, 9 3/4 In. 2585.00
Canister, 2 Applied Cobalt Blue Rings, Finial, Pittsburgh, 10 3/4 In. 495.00
Celery Vase, 8 1/4 In. 120.00
Compote, Cover, Applied Foot, Baluster Stem, Folded Rim, Pittsburgh, 11 3/4 In. 385.00
Compote, Cover, Baluster Stem, Applied Finial On Lid, Pittsburgh, 7 1/2 In. 195.00
Compote, Diamond Pattern, Cut Rollover Rim, Panel Cut Stem, 5 x 8 In. 495.00

Compote, Pillar Mold, Applied Foot, Stem, Gray, Amethystine, Pittsburgh, 9 1/4 In. 660.00
Creamer, 12 Vertical Rib, Handle, Pontil, 5 In. 990.00
Creamer, 4 1/2 In. 95.00
Creamer, Amethyst, Applied Handle, Folded Lip, 3 3/4 In. 110.00
Creamer, Applied Ribbed Handle, 3-Piece Mold, 2 7/8 In. 275.00
Creamer, Geometric, Clear Strap Handle, 3-Piece Mold 225.00
Creamer, Sapphire Blue, Applied Foot, Handle, 4 5/8 In. 385.00
Decanter, 3-Piece Mold, 3 Applied Rings, Stopper, 8 1/4 In. 165.00
Decanter, Applied Band, Chain Design, Underplate, 11 x 6 3/4 In. 1380.00
Decanter, Applied Handle, Pewter Jigger Cap, Pittsburgh, 7 3/8 In. 165.00
Decanter, Cut Design, Flutes, Panels, Mushroom Stopper, Pittsburgh, 9 3/8 In. 250.00
Decanter, Cut Design, Strawberry, Flower Cut Stopper, Pittsburgh, 8 In. 220.00
Decanter, Enameled, Parchment With Verse & Helmet, Pewter Rim, 14 In. 415.00
Decanter, Green, Tapered, 7 1/4 In. 140.00
Decanter, Ship's, Encased Air Twist, 8 In., Pair 165.00
Decanter, Tooled Mouth With Ring, Amethyst, Pontil, Cylindrical, 11 In. 250.00
Egg, Easter Greetings, Pink Flowers, 6 1/2 In. 45.00
Ewer, Engraved Tulips, Applied Handle, Cover, 9 7/8 In. 55.00
Figurine, Fly Catcher, Bamboo Motif Etch, 3 Scroll Feet, 8 3/4 In. 786.00
Goblet, Enameled Crest, Deep Green, 7 1/2 In. 135.00
Goblet, Enameled, Verse With Leaves, Amber, 11 1/2 In. 99.00
Goblet, Lincoln Drape, Flint 125.00
Goblet, Pale Green Tint Bowl, Engraved Hunt Scene, Hollow Stem, 11 3/4 In. 190.00
Jar, Apothecary, Ground Lid, Clear, 13 1/4 In. 137.00
Jar, Applied Base, Ring Near Lip, Folded Rim, 21 3/4 In. 660.00
Jar, Dark Green, Flared Lip, 11 3/4 In. 250.00
Jar, Pillar Mold, Applied Foot, Stem, Applied Finial, Pittsburgh, 17 In. 690.00
Lamp, Flint, Acanthus Font, Brass Collar, Burner, Square Base, 11 In. 220.00
Mug, Applied Handle, Floral Band, Lovebirds, 4 3/8 In. 330.00
Mug, Applied Handle, Flowers, Rooster, 5 In. 635.00
Pitcher, Applied Handle, 14 Vertical Ribs, 6 3/4 In. 50.00
Pitcher, Aqua, White Loops, South Jersey 660.00
Pitcher, Olive Amber, Applied Handle, 5 3/8 In. 50.00
Pitcher, Yellow To Red, Rainbow, 4 1/2 In. 26.00
Punch Cup, Diamond Quilted Bowl, Applied Foot & Handle, 3 1/4 In. 27.00
Salt, Hat Shape, 3-Piece Mold, Folded Rim, 2 1/4 In. .110.00 to 138.00
Sugar, Cover, 12 Vertical Ribs, Sapphire Blue, 7 1/2 In. 6000.00
Sugar, Galleried Rim, Funnel Shape Base, Pontil, 7 x 4 1/2 In.   1875.00
Tumbler, 3-Piece Mold, 5 1/4 In. 135.00
Tumbler, Basket Of Flowers, Engraved, Copper Wheel, 5 7/8 In.   132.00
Tumbler, Basket Of Flowers, Engraved, Copper Wheel, 7 1/2 In.   122.00
Tumbler, Floral Engraved, Birds, Copper Wheel, 7 In. 440.00
Tumbler, Flowers, Bird, 3 1/8 In. 138.00
Tumbler, Lovebirds On Heart, Engraved, Copper Wheel, Rayed Medallion, 7 In. 132.00
Tumbler, Man, On Horseback, Floral Design, 3 5/8 In. 635.00
Tumbler, Olive Green, Paper Label Marked Midwestern, 4 In. 715.00
Vase, Applied Blue, Brown Medallion, Diagonal Cut Lines, Signed, 8 7/8 In. 200.00
Vase, Canary, Bigler, Square Base, Scalloped Rim, Pittsburgh, 12 1/4 In. 1265.00
Vase, Elaborate Floral, Leaf Design With Butterfly, Pearl Finish, 8 In. 495.00
Vase, Floral, Engraved, Flared Lip, Applied Foot, Pittsburgh, 7 1/4 In. 3355.00
Vase, Flowers, Raised Enameled, 7 In. 38.00
Vase, Pillar Mold, Applied Foot With Star, Scalloped Rim, Pittsburgh, 8 7/8 In. 195.00
Vase, Pillar Mold, Applied Foot, Baluster Stem, Scalloped Rim, 9 1/4 In. 3750.00
Vase, Scene Of Woman, Rake, Musician, Enameled, Smoked Purple, 1900 . . . .   400.00
Vase, Trumpet, Applied Foot, Wafer Stem, 17 1/2 In. 495.00
Witch's Ball, Opaque White Looping, 7 In. 495.00
Witch's Ball, Pink & White Loopings, 1850-1880, 5 1/2 In. 300.00
Witch's Ball, Robin's Egg Blue, Milk Glass Base, 10 In. 300.00
Witch's Ball, Yellow Olive, Sheared Mouth, Smooth Base, 3 3/4 In. 265.00

BLUE GLASS, see Cobalt Blue category.

BLUE ONION, see Onion category.

BLUE WILLOW pattern has been made in England since 1780. The pattern has been copied by factories in many countries, including Germany, Japan, and the United States. It is still being made. Willow was named for a pattern that pictures a bridge, birds, willow trees, and a Chinese landscape.

Berry Bowl, Allerton, 5 Piece	16.00
Bowl, Crown Pottery, 8 In.	150.00
Bowl, Dessert, John Stevenson, 5 1/2 In.	10.00
Bowl, Fruit, Royal	5.00
Bowl, Vegetable, Cover, Allerton	125.00
Bowl, Vegetable, Green & Co., 8 1/2 In.	40.00
Bowl, Vegetable, Royal, 9 In.	25.00
Bread Plate, Staffordshire, 6 1/2 In.	9.00
Cake Plate, Royal	28.00
Canister, Flour, Square	150.00
Canister, Sugar, Square	125.00
Canister, Tea	95.00
Canister Set, Domed Cover, Regal China, 4 Piece	180.00
Carafe, Warmer	85.00
Coffeepot, Scalloped Rim, Allerton, 7 1/2 In.	250.00
Creamer, Cow, Staffordshire, Kent	985.00 to 1250.00
Creamer, Royal	8.00
Cup & Saucer, Grandpa Size, Johnson Bros.	35.00
Cup & Saucer, Richard Briggs, Boston	85.00
Cup & Saucer, Royal	5.00
Cup & Saucer, Staffordshire	18.00
Gravy Boat, Royal	23.00
Pitcher, Scalloped Rim, Allerton, 8 1/4 In.	250.00
Plate, Allerton, 9 In.	25.00
Plate, c.1850, 10 1/2 In.	50.00
Plate, Ridgway, 6 In.	10.00
Plate, Royal, 9 In.	10.00
Plate, Staffordshire, 10 In.	12.00
Platter, 1830-1840, 12 1/2 x 15 3/4 In.	225.00
Platter, Allerton, 11 x 9 In.	45.00
Platter, Ridgway, 10 1/2 In.	22.00
Platter, Ridgway, 11 1/2 x 9 In.	45.00
Platter, Ridgway, c.1927, 13 1/2 In.	150.00
Reamer, Moriyama	375.00
Salt & Pepper, Japan	45.00
Soup, Dish, Japan, 7 1/2 In.	50.00
Tea Set, Child's, 1940s, 16 Piece	110.00
Teapot, Footed, 7 x 9 In.	45.00
Warmer, Japan	65.00

BOCH FRERES factory was founded in 1841 in La Louviere in eastern Belgium. The wares resemble the work of Villeroy & Boch. The factory is still in business.

Jardiniere, Blue, Black Flowers, White Crackle Ground, 8 In.	247.00
Planter, Blue Crackled Persian Glaze, Footed, Rectangular, 11 3/4 In.	82.00
Vase, 4 Rows Of Stylized Flowers, Bulbous, Turquoise, Blue, Yellow, 9 1/2 In.	172.00
Vase, 8 Sides, Geometric, Orange, Gold, Brown, 9 In.	330.00
Vase, Abstract Floral Design, Turquoise, Black, Yellow, White Glaze, 10 x 8 In.	495.00
Vase, Art Deco, Lison, 12 In.	695.00
Vase, Art Deco, Rose Colored Handles, 7 In.	165.00
Vase, Blue, Yellow, Gold, Black Ground, Bulbous, 7 In.	522.50
Vase, Brown & Blue Stylized Flowers, Yellow, Green Ground, Marked, 6 In.	165.00
Vase, Bulbous, Blue Crackled Persian Glaze, 8 In.	82.00
Vase, Floral Design, Blossoms Amid Leaves, Black Ground, Ink Mark, 5 In.	230.00
Vase, Geometric Design, Brown, Gold, Yellow, White Ground, 12 In.	660.00
Vase, Green, Blue Flowers, White Crackled Ground, Catteau, 12 In.	247.00
Vase, Lamp, Floral Design, Gloss Glaze, Blue Ink Stamp, Black Slip, 8 3/8 In.	275.00

Vase, Stylized Design, Yellow, Black, Turquoise, Charles Catteau, 17 x 6 In. 1100.00
Vase, Stylized Flowers, Turquoise, Yellow, Blue Band, White Ground, 8 x 6 In. 220.00
Vase, Vertical Abstract Design, Gold, Charcoal, Light Blue Ground, 12 In., Pair 2860.00
Vase, White, Blue Grapes, Green Leaves, Green, Brown Flambe Ground, 10 x 5 In. 495.00
Vase, Yellow, Orange, Blue High Glaze, White Ground, Ink Mark, 18 In. 412.00

BOEHM is the collector's name for the porcelains of Edward Marshall
Boehm. In 1953 the Osso China Company was reorganized as Edward
Marshall Boehm, Inc. The company is still working in England and
New Jersey. In the early days of the factory, dishes were made, but the
elaborate and lifelike bird figurines are the best-known ware. Edward
Marshall Boehm, the founder, died in 1961, but the firm has continued
to design and produce porcelain. Today, the firm makes both limited
and unlimited editions of figurines and plates.

Figurine, American Eagle, Small, No. 428B 2000.00
Figurine, Black-Headed Grosbeak, No. 400-03 . . . . 1000.00
Figurine, Cocker Spaniel, Signed 495.00
Figurine, Common Tern, No. 497 . . . . 3000.00
Figurine, Dove With Cherry Blossom, No. 20238 . . . . 1800.00
Figurine, Emmett Kelly, A Hole In The Sole 350.00
Figurine, Fledgling Kingfisher, No. 449 . . . . 250.00
Figurine, French Poodle, Reclining, No. 133 . . . . 215.00
Figurine, Goldfinch, With Pink Violets, No. 400-39 . . . . 295.00
Figurine, Goldfinches, No. 457 . . . . 1200.00
Figurine, Green Jays, No. 486, Pair 2200.00
Figurine, Kestrels, No. 492, Pair 2300.00
Figurine, Little Blue Huron, Fledgling, No. 200-19 . . . . 275.00
Figurine, Madonna, Small 110.00
Figurine, Mallards, No. 406, Pair 1200.00
Figurine, Nonpareil Bunting, No. 466 . . . . 625.00
Figurine, Panda, Sitting, No. 400-54, 5 In. 125.00
Figurine, Parula Warblers, No. 484 . . . . 2000.00
Figurine, Pope Pius XII, No. 618 . . . . 135.00
Figurine, Ptarmigans, No. 463, Pair 1850.00
Figurine, Rabbit, Seated, 4 1/2 In. 50.00
Figurine, Road Runner & Toad, No. 493 . . . . 2000.00
Figurine, Snow Buntings, No. 400-21 . . . . 1250.00
Figurine, Snow Owl, 9 1/2 In. 250.00
Figurine, Truant, Boy With Apple & Sling Shot, On Tree Branch, 15 In. 82.00
Figurine, Tufted Titmice, No. 482 . . . . 1100.00
Figurine, Yellow Rose, 8 In. 30.00
Planter, Swan, White, 1950s, 7 In. 275.00
Plate, Bluebird, Box, 1972 . . . . 24.00
Plate, Goldfinch, No.1, 1971 . . . . 65.00
Plate, Hummingbird, Box, 1974 . . . . 24.00
Plate, Meadowlark, Box, 1973 . . . . 24.00
Plate, Rose, Box, 10 3/4 In., 8 Piece 185.00
Plate, Wood Thrush, 1970 . . . . 100.00

BOHEMIAN GLASS is an ornate overlay or flashed glass made during
the Victorian era. It has been reproduced in Bohemia, which is now a
part of the Czech Republic. Glass made from 1875 to 1900 is preferred
by collectors.

Basket, Amber, Enameled Floral, 1890, 11 1/2 x 7 1/4 In. 275.00
Beaker, Blue Over White, Cameo Cut Fawn Scene, 1850, 4 1/2 In. 1447.00
Beaker, Blue Over White, Enameled Floral, Opaline, 1840, 5 1/2 In. 935.00
Beaker, Clear Cut To Cranberry, Facets, 1870, 5 1/4 In. 88.00
Beaker, Clear Over Cranberry, 1870, 5 1/2 In. 126.00
Beaker, Cranberry Circles, 1870, 5 1/2 In. 181.00
Beaker, Cranberry Cut To Clear, Hunting Dog, 1890, 4 In. 170.00
Beaker, Cut, Birds, Hearts On Body, 1875, 5 1/2 In. 94.00
Beaker, Cut, Stag Scene, 1875, 5 In. 94.00

Beaker, Enameled, White Floral, Pink Variegated Interior, 1860, 4 3/4 In. 88.00
Beaker, Gold Ruby, 1840, 4 In. 187.00
Beaker, Opaline, Enameled Castle Scene, Beaded, 1860, 4 1/2 In. 275.00
Beaker, Pink Cut To White To Clear, Facets, 1860, 4 1/2 In. 210.00
Beaker, Pink Cut To White, 1875, 4 In. 170.00
Beaker, Ruby Over Clear, 1930, 5 1/4 In. 115.00
Beaker, Ruby Over Clear, Amber Panels, 1930, 5 3/4 In. 204.00
Beaker, Ruby Stained, Cut Commemorative Scene, 1860, 5 1/4 In. 225.00
Beaker, Ruby Stained, Cut Spa Panels, 1850, 5 In. 258.00
Beaker, Ruby Stained, Cut Stag & Animal Design, 1875, 7 1/2 In. 345.00
Beaker, Ruby Stained, Facet Cut, 1860, 4 1/8 In. 115.00
Beaker, Ruby, Amber, Cut, Floral Design, 1930, 5 1/2 In. 94.00
Beaker, Senate Building, German Senate, 1820-1845, 6 In. 253.00
Beaker, White Overlay, Cobalt Blue, Pocket, 1880, 4 In. 175.00
Bottle, Green, Enameled, Gentleman, Carrying Pistol On Horseback, 1689, 9 In. 1380.00
Chalice, Honey Amber Cut To Clear Panels, Gilt Garden Courting Scene, 6 In. 245.00
Champagne, Enameled Rose Design Interior & Foot, 1890, 4 1/4 In. 100.00
Compote, Amber, Cut Running Deer, Flared, Squatty, 10 In. 710.00
Compote, Cobalt Blue, Venetian Woman At Bath, On Horseback, 5 1/4 In. 201.25
Cordial, Floral Enamel, 1910, 4 3/8 In. 121.00
Decanter, Gold Design, White, 14 In. 177.00
Decanter, Green, Floral Enamel, 1890, 7 3/4 In. 462.00
Decanter Set, Blue Green, Doe & Stag Panels, Stopper, 10 In., 5 Piece 495.00
Goblet, Ruby Stained, Cut, Castle, 1890, 5 3/8 In. 110.00
Mug, Cut Scene, Bauhaus Segeberg, 1875, 4 3/8 In. 77.00
Mug, Ruby, Cut, Spa Scene, 1875, 4 3/4 In. 143.00
Mug, White Over Clear, 1860, 4 1/2 In. 193.00
Perfume Bottle, Cobalt Blue Cut To Clear, Facets, 1860, 8 3/4 In. 355.00
Perfume Bottle, Cobalt Blue Over Clear, Stopper, 1850, 5 In. 358.00
Pokal, Amber Cut To Clear, Birds, Leafy Vines, Faceted Knob, 16 1/2 In. 165.00
Pokal, Cover, Ruby, Cut Floral Design, Vermeil Silver Base, Rim, 1900, 13 In. 1760.00
Pokal, Cut, Amber, 1850, 7 In. 193.00
Pokal, Ruby Stained, Intaglio Cut, Stag Scene, 1860, 25 1/2 In. 7920.00
Vase, Amber Stained, Cut, Stag & Castle, 1910, 10 1/4 In. 220.00
Vase, Amber, Enameled Floral, Gold, 9 In. 495.00
Vase, Black, Green, Cut Inset Gold, 1900, 5 1/2 In. 56.00
Vase, Blue Cut To Clear, Deer Landscape, 19th Century, 13 In. 660.00
Vase, Cranberry, Gold Floral On Sandy Body, 1900, 7 1/4 In. 121.00
Vase, Cranberry, White Overlay, Bird Nest Scene, 1890, 7 1/2 In. 187.00
Vase, Green, Gold Floral Design, Applied Beads, Green, 1910, 10 1/2 In. 220.00
Vase, Green, Snail Shape, 1910, 8 In. 155.00
Vase, Green, White Overlay Panel, Enameled Floral, 1890, 12 1/2 In. 260.00
Vase, Red Amber Flashing, Peacock Design, 12 In. 137.00

BONE DISHES were considered a necessary part of a table setting for
the Victorian table. The crescent-shaped dish was kept at the edge of
the dinner plate so the bones removed from the fish could be stored
away from the uneaten food. Some bone dishes were made in more
fanciful shapes and many resemble fish.

Argyle, Wood & Son, 5 Piece 75.00
Different Flowers, 6 Piece 50.00
Floral, Porcelain, 6 Piece 60.00
Tea Leaf, Scalloped, Shaw, 7 In. 25.00

BOOKENDS have probably been used since books became inexpensive.
Early libraries kept books in cupboards, not on open shelves. By the
1870s bookends appeared, especially homemade fret-carved wooden
examples. Most bookends listed in this book date from the twentieth
century.

Adam & Eve, Nude, Brown Drip Glaze, Calico Pottery 395.00
Art Deco Floral, Copper, Rebaje 135.00
Basket Of Flowers, Pastel Paint, Cast Iron, 5 3/8 In., Pair 49.00

Charles Lindbergh, The Aviator, Bronze Finish, Cast Iron, 1929, 5 1/2 x 5 In., Pair 54.00
Classical Philosopher, Bronze, Germany, 7 In., Pair 575.00
Copper, Hammered, Apollo Studios, 4 x 6 In. 80.00
Copper, Hammered, Enamel Medallion, Orange Tree, R. Cauman, 1922, 6 In. 2860.00
Elephant, Dark To Light Maroon, Cliftwood 115.00
Fisherman, Bronze, Jennings Bros. 200.00
Galleon Ship, Lead 45.00
Garfield & Odie 90.00
George Washington, Blue, Red & Gold Painted, Brass, 1932, 7 3/4 In. 75.00
George Washington, Bronze, 6 1/4 In. 135.00
Horned Owl, On Book, Pyrography On Wood 85.00
Horse, Stylized, Metal Tubing, Brass, Von Nessen, 6 x 4 In. 470.00
Horse Head, Onyx, White 95.00
Indian Chief, In Headdress, Iron 80.00
John F. Kennedy, Pewter, FMC, 6 In. 30.00
Kate Greenaway Type Children, Bronzart 75.00
Leaf, Art Deco, Vermont Copper Co. 100.00
Lincoln, Bronze Color, 1928 .... 28.00
Lincoln, Bronze, 1925 .... 95.00
National Rifle Association, Figural, Jack Lambert, 1950s 150.00
Pelican, Stylized, Open Beak, Iron, Edgar Brandt, 1925, 7 In. 6030.00
Scotties, Onyx Base, 6 In. 75.00
Scotty, On Fence, Cast Iron, 5 x 4 1/2 In. 125.00
Scotty, Silver Over Cast Iron 50.00
Sea Captain At Wheel, Full Figure, Bronze Finish, 6 1/2 In. 100.00
Setter At Point, Bronze, Atmor 165.00
Ship, Galleon At The Time Of Elizabeth, Brass 65.00
Souvenir, Grand Tour, Lion Mask Above Cartouche, Marshall Cutler, Italy, 5 In. 345.00
Swashbucklers, Paul-Herzel, Bronze Finish, Pompeian Bronze Co., 7 3/4 In. 100.00
The Last Trail, 1930 .... 65.00
Todd Lincoln, Marked, Muller, 1922, 7 1/4 In. 85.00
Wheels, Ironsides, Material From U.S. Frigate Constitution, 1827, 6 5/8 In. 150.00
Whistler's Mother, Metal, White Face & Hands 75.00
Winnie The Pooh, Enesco 65.00
Wolfhound, Glass, 6 x 8 In. 210.00

BOOKMARKS were originally made of parchment, cloth, or leather.
Soon woven silk ribbon, thin cardboard, celluloid, wood, silver, tortoiseshell, and metals were used. Examples made before 1850 are
scarce, but there are many to be found dating before 1920.

Bell Blouse, Boy, Catching Baseball On Bell, Die Cut 60.00
Liberty Bell, Celluloid, Shield Shape, Bank, Flag, Sesquicentennial, 1926 .... 35.00
Old Nick Candy, 1946 .... 10.00
Palmer's Candy, Sioux City, Iowa, Beautiful Girl, 1910 .... 10.00
Snoopy, On Doghouse, Wearing Red Scarf, Soft Plastic 4.00
Summit Stoves, Embossed Lilac Flower, Die Cut, 1890, 6 1/4 x 2 In. 15.00
Texaco, Celluloid, 1 3/4 x 3 3/4 In. 2275.00
Uncle Sam & Salesman, Whitehead & Hoag Ad, Celluloid 125.00

BOSTON & SANDWICH CO. pieces may be found in the Lutz and
Sandwich Glass categories.

BOTTLE collecting has become a major American hobby. There are
several general categories of bottles, such as historic flasks, bitters,
household, and figural. Pyro is the shortened form of the word
pyroglaze, an enameled lettering used on bottles after the mid-1930s.
For more bottle prices, see the book *Kovels' Bottles Price List* by
Ralph and Terry Kovel.

Apothecary, Cobalt Blue, 10 In. 215.00
Apothecary, Cobalt Blue, Gold Gilt Label, Original Stopper, 8 In. 140.00
Apothecary, Ground Lid, Clear, 13 1/4 In. 138.00
Apothecary, Jar, Cobalt Blue, Applied Foot, 16 1/4 In. 1155.00

Avon started in 1886 as the California Perfume Company. It was not until 1929 that the name *Avon* was used. In 1939, it became Avon Products, Inc. Avon has made many figural bottles filled with cosmetic products. Ceramic, plastic, and glass bottles were made in limited editions.

Avon, American Belle, 1976	2.00
Avon, Blunderbuss Pistol, 1976	5.00
Avon, California Perfume Co., Concentrated Toilet Water, Crown Dabber, 5 5/8 In.	75.00
Avon, Charlie Brown & Lucy Character, Soap Containers, Plastic, 1970, 6 In.	55.00
Avon, Dutch Pipe, Box, 1973	8.00
Avon, First Mate's, Figural, Shampoo, Plastic, 1963, 5 In.	22.00
Avon, Goblet, Cape Cod, Wine	2.00
Avon, Hurricane Lamp, 1973	25.00
Avon, Mother's Love, 1981	5.00
Avon, Mrs. Albee, 1992	70.00
Avon, NAAC Club, 1975, Box	30.00
Avon, Picture Frame Cologne, 1970	3.00
Avon, Roll-A-Hoop, 1977	3.00
Avon, Six Shooter, Box, 1962-1963	18.00
Avon, Soaky, Pluto, Box, 1970	15.00 to 20.00
Avon, Soaky, Snoopy Snow Flyer, Box, 1972	20.00
Avon, Stein, Age Of Iron Horse, 1982	25.00
Avon, Stein, Tall Ships, 1978	25.00
Avon, Volkswagen, Red, Box, 1972	35.00
Avon, Watering Can, Box, 1962	10.00
Avon, Whistle Tots, Box, 1966	5.00
Avon, Wishful Thoughts, 1982	6.00
Barber, Amethyst, Enameled Flowers	175.00
Barber, Blue Opalescent, Hobnail, Polished Pontil	185.00
Barber, Clambroth Panel, Porcelain Top	90.00
Barber, Cranberry Opalescent Swirl, Hobnail, Pontil, 7 In.	125.00
Barber, Cranberry, Daisy & Fern	450.00
Barber, Cranberry, Enameled Floral, Ribbed	225.00
Barber, Cranberry, Enameled Flowers, Ribbed	225.00
Barber, Opalescent, White Seaweed	175.00

Beam bottles were made to hold Kentucky Straight Bourbon, made by the James B. Beam Distilling Company. The Beam series of ceramic bottles began in 1953.

Beam, Chevrolet Camaro, 1969 Model, Orange, Box, 1989	75.00
Beam, Chevrolet Camaro, 1969 Model, Pace Car, 1989	190.00
Beam, Chevrolet Corvette, 1953 Model, 1989	150.00
Beam, Circus Wagon, 1979	40.00
Beam, Fire Pump Truck, 1867 Model, Mississippi, 1978	150.00
Beam, Florida Shell, States Series, 1968	19.00
Beam, Harolds Club, Man In Barrel, No. 1, 1957	495.00
Beam, Harolds Club, Man In Barrel, No. 2, 1958	200.00
Beam, Mercedes Benz, 1974 Model, Dark Blue, Box, 1987	75.00
Beam, Montana, States Series, 1963	35.00
Beam, Pink Speckled Beauty, 1956	375.00
Beam, Red Fox, Collectors Edition, Vol. IX, 1978	900.00
Beam, Train, Caboose, Gray, 1988	65.00
Beam, Train, Caboose, Yellow, 1985	85.00
Beam, Train, Casey Jones, With Tender, 1989	50.00
Beam, Train, Coal Tender, No. 197	75.00
Beam, Train, Combination Car, 1988	45.00
Beam, Train, Flat Car, 1988	75.00
Beam, Train, General Locomotive	90.00 to 115.00
Beam, Train, Grant, Baggage Car, 1981	50.00
Beam, Train, Grant, Dining Room, 1982	85.00
Beam, Train, Grant, Locomotive, 1979	95.00
Beam, Train, J.B. Turner Locomotive, 1982	100.00 to 130.00
Beam, Train, Lumber Car, 1985	50.00

Beam, Train, Wood Tender, 1988 .... 95.00
Beer, A. Gettelman Brewing Co., Pre-Prohibition, Hands Holding Schooner 13.00
Beer, Calumet Brewery, Calumet, Mich., Amber, 1 Qt. 15.00
Beer, Conrad Original Budweiser 35.00
Beer, El Dorado Brewing Co., Stockton, Calif., Monogram, Amber, 1 Qt. 20.00
Beer, Enterprise Brewing Co., San Francisco, Yellow 80.00
Beer, Fredericksburg Brewery, San Jose, Calif., Amber, Round Slug, 1 Qt. 65.00
Beer, Fulton Street National Bottling Works, San Francisco, Amber, Blob Top, 1 Pt. 65.00
Beer, George Bechtel Brewing Co., Embossed Spanish Conqueror, Blob Top, 9 1/4 In. .. 80.00
Beer, Hoboken Brewing Co., A.H. Blob Seal, Olive Green, Blob Top, 11 In. 45.00
Beer, Indianapolis Brewing Co., Indianapolis, Ind., Aqua, 1 Pt. 10.00
Beer, Jacob Jockers, Philada., Aqua, Bail, Slug Plate, 10 In. 55.00
Beer, John Wagner Brewing Co., Sidney, Ohio, Amber, Round Slug, 1 Qt. 15.00
Beer, Jung Brewing Co., Milwaukee, Aqua, Blob Top, 1 Pt. 15.00
Beer, L. House, Orange Amber, Rochester Glass Works, Blob Top 38.00
Beer, McGovern, Gray Glaze, Stoneware, 1 Qt. 45.00
Beer, McGuiness, Utica, N.Y., Eagle, Aqua, 1 Qt. 50.00
Beer, Miniature, Carlsberg 2.00
Beer, Miniature, Moosehead 2.00
Beer, Paterson, N.J., Stoneware, Impressed 48.00
Beer, Schlitz, Red, 1 Qt. 26.00
Beer, Tengen & Thieme, Lafayette, Ind., Amber, Round Slug, 1 Qt. 25.00
Beer, Walter Raupfer Brewing Co., Columbia City, Ind., Eagle, Aqua, 1 Qt. 20.00
Bininger, A.M. & Co., Old Dominion, Wheat Tonic, Olive, 9 7/8 In. 135.00
Bitters, African Stomach Bitters, Spruance, Stanley & Co., Amber, 9 5/8 In. 60.00
Bitters, Atwood's Vegetable Dyspeptic Bitters, Aqua, Pontil, 1 Qt. 125.00
Bitters, Bagley's Stomach, Barrel, Yellow 185.00
Bitters, Baker's Orange Grove, Yellow Amber, Roped Corners, 3/4 Qt. 302.00
Bitters, Beggs' Dandelion Bitters, Amber, Rectangular, 7 3/4 In. 330.00
Bitters, Berkshire Bitters, Pig Shape, Golden Amber, 9 5/8 In. 1045.00
Bitters, Bischoff's, Charleston, S.C., Yellow Amber, Square, 9 1/2 In. 440.00
Bitters, Bismarck, W.H. Muller, New York, Amber, Tooled Lip, 6 1/8 In. 94.00
Bitters, Bissell's Tonic, Peoria, Ill., Amber, Whittled, Open Pontil, Square, 9 In. 225.00
Bitters, Boerhaves, Holland Bitters, B. Page Jr. & Co., Aqua, 8 In. 500.00
Bitters, Brown's Celebrated, Indian Maiden, Yellow Amber, 12 1/4 In. 415.00
Bitters, Burdock Blood, Foster Milburn Co., Buffalo, N.Y., Contents, Box, 7 1/2 In. 90.00
Bitters, C. Gates & Cos., Life Of Man, Rectangular, 8 In. 50.00
Bitters, Caldwell's Herb, The Great Tonic, Yellow Amber, Triangular, 12 3/8 In. 330.00
Bitters, Donnell Tilden & Co., St. Louis, Mo., Yellow Amber, Square, 8 3/4 In. 165.00
Bitters, Doyles Hop, Amber, Square, 10 In. 25.00
Bitters, Dr. Baxter's Mandrake Bitters, Aqua, 6 In. 15.00
Bitters, Dr. Bull's Superior Stomach, Amber, Square, 9 In. 135.00
Bitters, Dr. C.W. Roback's Stomach, Cincinnati, Ohio, Barrel, Amber, 10 In. ....175.00 to 185.00
Bitters, Dr. D.C. Kellinger, N.Y., Open Pontil, Cylinder, 6 1/4 In. 40.00
Bitters, Dr. De Andries Sarsaparilla, 10 In..................................... 1100.00
Bitters, Dr. F.F.W. Hogguers, Detroit, Amber, Square, 9 In. 150.00
Bitters, Dr. Fisch's, Fish Shape, Yellow Amber, 11 3/4 In. 180.00
Bitters, Dr. Geo. Pierce's Indian Restorative, Lowell, Mass., Aqua, 8 3/4 In. ....40.00 to 60.00
Bitters, Dr. Harter's Wild Cherry, St. Louis, Amber, 8 In......................... 40.00
Bitters, Dr. Henley's Wild Grape Root IXL, Oval, Olive Green, 12 1/2 In............ 1760.00
Bitters, Dr. Hoofland's German Liver Complaint, Aqua, 8 In. 15.00
Bitters, Dr. John Bull's Compound, Cedron, Olive Amber, 9 1/2 In................. 165.00
Bitters, Dr. Kaufman's Bitters, A.P. Ordway & Co., Label, 8 In. 35.00
Bitters, Dr. Langley's Root & Herb, Aqua, Open Pontil, 8 1/2 In. ....75.00 to 80.00
Bitters, Dr. Langley's Root & Herb, Boston, Amber, 7 1/4 In. 80.00
Bitters, Dr. Robinson, Cincinnati, Oh., Dark Aqua, Open Pontil, 5 3/8 In. 50.00
Bitters, Dr. Russell's Pepsin Calisaya, Green, 7 7/8 In. 65.00
Bitters, Dr. Stephen Jewett's Celebrated Health Restoring, Aqua, Open Pontil, 7 1/4 In. .. 160.00
Bitters, Drake's Plantation, 4 Log, Amber, 10 1/4 In..........................95.00 to 150.00
Bitters, Drake's Plantation, 4 Log, Lemon Apricot, 10 1/4 In. 245.00
Bitters, Drake's Plantation, 4 Log, Light Yellow, 10 1/4 In. 650.00
Bitters, Drake's Plantation, 4 Log, Yellow Topaz, Collared Mouth, 10 1/8 In. 325.00
Bitters, Drake's Plantation, 6 Log, Amber, 1870, 10 In......................*Illus* 250.00

Bottle, Bitters, Drake's Plantation,   Bottle, Bitters, Lutz's German   Bottle, Cosmetic, Vaseline Pomade,
6 Log, Amber, 1870, 10 In.   Stomach, Amber, 7 3/4 In.   Chesebrough Mfg. Co., 2 1/2 In.

Bitters, Drake's Plantation, 6 Log, Brilliant Yellow Olive, 10 In. 2420.00
Bitters, Drake's Plantation, 6 Log, Strawberry Puce, 1860-1880, 10 In. 145.00
Bitters, Drake's Plantation, 6 Log, Yellow Topaz, Square, 9 3/4 In. 250.00
Bitters, E. Baker's Premium, Richmond, Va., Cornflower Blue, Oval, 6 3/4 In. 770.00
Bitters, Fish, W.H. Ware, Amber, 1866, 11 1/2 In. 165.00
Bitters, Golden Seal, Light Yellow Orange, Rectangular, 9 In. 295.00
Bitters, Greeley's Bourbon Whiskey, Barrel, Puce, 10 Ring, 9 3/8 In. . . . . .425.00 to 440.00
Bitters, Greeley's Bourbon Whiskey, Medium Green, 9 3/8 In. 1400.00
Bitters, Hall's, New Haven, Barrel, Amber, 9 1/8 In. . . . . .200.00 to 350.00
Bitters, Holtzerman's Patent Stomach, Cabin, Amber, 9 5/8 In. . . . . .175.00 to 300.00
Bitters, Isham's Stomach, Amber, Square, 9 3/8 In. 250.00
Bitters, J. Walker's California Vinegar, Aqua, Label, 1 Pt. 55.00
Bitters, Johnson's Calisaya, Burlington, Vt., Honey Amber, 10 In. 85.00
Bitters, Keystone, Barrel, Amber, 9 3/4 In. 575.00
Bitters, Lash's Kidney & Liver, Amber, 9 In. 25.00
Bitters, Lutz's German Stomach, Amber, 7 3/4 In. . . . .*Illus* 900.00
Bitters, Moulton's Oloroso, Aqua, Cylindrical, Fluted Shoulder, 11 3/8 In. 220.00
Bitters, National, Ear Of Corn, Amber, 12 1/2 In. . . . . .300.00 to 465.00
Bitters, Old Dr. Warren's Quaker, Flint & Co., Providence, R.I., Aqua, 9 3/4 In. 60.00
Bitters, Old Homestead Wild Cherry, Amber, 9 7/8 In. 375.00
Bitters, Oxygenated Bitters For Dyspepsia Asthma General Debility, Aqua, 6 1/8 In. 75.00
Bitters, Pawnee Long Life, Aqua, Rectangular, 8 In. 305.00
Bitters, Pepsin Calisaya, Dr. Russell Med. Co., Green, 7 7/8 In. 75.00
Bitters, Peruvian, Amber, 9 1/4 In. 39.00
Bitters, Royal Pepsin Stomach, L & A Scharff, Amber, 3 7/8 In. 120.00
Bitters, Rush's Bitter, A.H. Flanders, M.D., N.Y., Honey Amber, Square, 8 7/8 In. 60.00
Bitters, S.O. Richardson's, Aqua, Rectangular, 6 7/8 In. 300.00
Bitters, Schroeder's, Louisville & Cincinnati, Lady's Leg, Amber, 5 1/4 In. 330.00
Bitters, Schroeder, Louisville, Ky., Lady's Leg, Amber, 8 7/8 In. 400.00
Bitters, Simon's Centennial, Geo. Washington Bust, Amber, 9 3/4 In. 1900.00
Bitters, Sunny Castle Stomach, Amber, Tooled Lip, Square, 9 In. 110.00
Bitters, W. & Co., Pontil, Pineapple, Amber 400.00
Bitters, W.F. Severa Stomach, Tooled Lip, Amber, Square, 9 5/8 In. 90.00
Bitters, W.L. Richardson's, Aqua, 7 In. . . . . .125.00 to 160.00
Bitters, Warner's Safe, Rochester, N.Y., Amber, Oval, 7 1/2 In. 525.00
Bitters, Yerba Buena, Amber, Rectangular, 9 1/2 In. 50.00
Bitters, Zoeller's Stomach, Amber, Label, Contents, 9 1/2 In. 120.00
Black Glass, Le Dandy, D'Orsay, Sealed, Cord, 4 3/4 In. 162.00
Coca-Cola bottles are listed in the Coca-Cola category.
Cordial, Blackberry, Back Bar 50.00
Cordial, J.N. Kline & Co., Sapphire Blue, Flattened Teardrop, 5 1/2 In. 275.00
Cosmetic, Circassian Hair Restorative, Cincinnati, Amber, Fancy Panels, 7 1/4 In. 200.00

Cosmetic, Dr. Campbell's Hair Invigorator, Aqua, Open Pontil, 6 3/4 In. 50.00
Cosmetic, Dr. D. Jayne's Hair Tonic, Aqua, Open Pontil 45.00
Cosmetic, J.W. Poland's Humor Doctor, Aqua 40.00
Cosmetic, Keasbey & Mattison Co., Ambler, Pa., Cylindrical, Sapphire Blue 15.00
Cosmetic, Lucky Tiger Shampoo For Men, 1951, 9 Oz. 5.00
Cosmetic, Lyons Kathairon For The Hair, New York, Aqua, OP, 6 1/8 In. 40.00
Cosmetic, Mrs. S.A. Allen's World's Hair, Yellow Olive, Beveled Corners, 7 1/4 In. 325.00
Cosmetic, Mrs. S.A. Allen's World's Hair Restorer, Orange Apricot, 6 1/8 In. 45.00
Cosmetic, Vaseline Pomade, Chesebrough Mfg. Co., 2 1/2 In. . . . .*Illus*   6.00
Cure, Brown's Celebrated, Light-Medium Amber 475.00
Cure, Burnett's Cod Liver Oil, T. Metcalf & Co., Boston, 8 In.   8.00
Cure, CCC Lightbody's Cough, Colds, Palmer Green, Rochester, N.H., 8 In. 70.00
Cure, Cities Safe Cure, Amber, 1 Pt. 105.00
Cure, Corbin's Rheumatic, John F. Corbin Proprietor, Aqua, Contents, Box, 7 1/2 In. 325.00
Cure, Dalby's Carminative, Aqua, Conical Shape, Open Pontil, 3 5/8 In. 25.00
Cure, Dr. Kilmer's Swamp Kidney Root Cure, Sample, 3 In. 8.00
Cure, Dr. Soule's, Yellow 175.00
Cure, Forestine Kidney, Amber, Contents, Box, 9 1/4 In. 800.00
Cure, Frankfort, Olive Green, 1 Pt. 525.00
Cure, Herb Medicine Co., Hot Drops, Large Eagle, Brown, Box 8.00
Cure, Kidney Liver Cure, Orange Amber 55.00
Cure, Laxative Worm Syrup, Box 10.00
Cure, London Safe Cure, Olive Green, 8 1/2 In. 105.00
Cure, Mulford's Digestive Malt, Amber, 4 1/2 In. 8.00
Cure, National Kidney & Liver, Amber, 9 In. 625.00
Cure, Paine's Celery Compound, 9 3/4 In. 8.00
Cure, Sanford's Radical Cure, Cobalt Blue, 7 1/2 In. 30.00
Cure, Taylor's Cherokee Remedy, Aqua, Box, 4 7/8 In. 25.00
Cure, Warner's Kidney & Liver Cure, Light Amber, 9 5/8 In. 175.00
Cure, Wyeth & Bros., Light Blue, 8 3/4 In. 27.00
Decanter, Blown, Flared Mouth, Pontil, 1 Pt. 150.00
Decanter, Cut Whiskey & Floral, 3-Ring Handle, Fluted Neck, Pontil 65.00
Decanter, Hamm's Beer, Bear Shape, Ceramarte, 10 1/4 In. 185.00
Decanter, Kentucky Derby 100th Anniversary, Stoneware, 1974, 12 3/4 In. 450.00
Decanter, Pillar Mold, Flint, Stopper, Pontil, 1850, 13 In. 165.00
Demijohn, Amber, Iron Pontil, 18 3/8 In. 190.00
Demijohn, Newman's Improved, Pacific Coast Glass Works, Aqua, Box, 3 Gal. 125.00
Ezra Brooks, Ford Thunderbird, 1956 Model, 1976 . . . .   60.00
Ezra Brooks, West Virginia, Mountain Man, 1970 . . . .   35.00
Figural, Balloon Captif 1878, Hot Air Balloon, Basket, No Stopper, 8 3/4 In. 1320.00
Figural, Bear, Kummel, Applied Face, Violet Blue, Pontil, 10 1/4 In. 2310.00
Figural, Black Person, 10 1/2 In. 60.00
Figural, Clydesdale Horses, Canadian Whiskey, 1978 . . . .   345.00
Figural, Cockatoo, Standing On Peg, Black Amethyst, Germany, 13 1/4 In. 355.00
Figural, Lighthouse, B. Schwartz, Pineapple, Yellow, 11 In. 2100.00
Figural, Moses, Poland Mineral Water, Amber, 10 1/2 In. 495.00
Figural, Policeman, Holding Club Above Head, Blue, White, Black, Red, 18 In. 140.00
Figural, Sandeman, Sherry, Wedgwood 70.00
Flask, 12 Diamond Pattern, Amethyst, Sheared Mouth, Pontil, 1930, 4 7/8 In. 90.00
Flask, 16 Ribs, Broken Swirl, Deep Grass Green, 6 5/8 In. 690.00
Flask, 16 Ribs, Swirled To Right, Cobalt Blue, Pontil, 3 3/4 In. 190.00
Flask, Army Officer, Large Flower, Light Blue Green, Pontil, 1 Pt. 180.00
Flask, Baltimore & Liberty & Union, Green 850.00
Flask, Chestnut, 16 Ribs, Vertical, Yellow Amber, 5 1/2 In. 385.00
Flask, Chestnut, 20 Ribs, Swirled To Right, Sapphire Blue, Pontil, 3 7/8 In. 300.00
Flask, Chestnut, 24 Ribs, Vertical, Aqua, Pontil, 8 In. 190.00
Flask, Clarke F. Hess, Druggist, Pure Grain Alcohol, Amber, Strap Side, 7 1/2 In. 90.00
Flask, Clasped Hands & Eagle, Light Yellow Green, 1/2 Pt. 160.00
Flask, Clasped Hands & Eagle, Orange Amber, Applied Mouth, 1 Qt. 220.00
Flask, Clasped Hands, Cannon & Flag, 1/2 Pt. 90.00
Flask, Clasped Hands, Cornflower Blue, 1 Qt. 605.00
Flask, Clasped Hands, Eagle & Shield, Reverse, Aqua, 1 Qt. 109.00
Flask, Corn For The World, Baltimore Monument, Golden Yellow, 1 Qt. 1210.00

Flask, Dan Donahue, Saloon, Marysville, Pumpkinseed, 1/2 Pt. 155.00
Flask, Double Eagle, Applied Mouth, Light Green, 1/2 Pt. 264.00
Flask, Double Eagle, Olive Amber, 8 In. 95.00
Flask, E.A. Buckhout's Dutch Liniment, Aqua, Rolled Mouth, 4 3/4 In. 230.00
Flask, Eagle & Cornucopia, Olive Green, 6 3/4 In. 140.00
Flask, Eagle & Shield, For Our Country, Aqua, 6 7/8 In. 60.00
Flask, Eagle, Medium Green, Sheared Mouth, Pontil, 1 Pt. 1100.00
Flask, Eagle, Willington Glass Co., Olive Green, Applied Collared Mouth, 1/2 Pt. 120.00
Flask, Eagle, Willington Glass Co., Yellow Olive, Sheared Mouth, 1 Pt. 110.00
Flask, Embossed Dewey Portrait, Hero Of Manila, Metal Cap, 5 1/2 In. 300.00
Flask, For Pike's Peak, Prospector, Aqua, Applied Mouth, 1860-1870, 1/2 Pt. 95.00
Flask, For Pike's Peak, Prospector, Hunter, Aqua, 1 Qt. 330.00
Flask, Gen. Taylor Never Surrenders, Apricot, 1 Pt. 3025.00
Flask, Geo. Riggins Wonderful Drug Store, Pure Whiskey, Amber, 1/2 Pt. 45.00
Flask, Granite Glass Co., Stoddard, N.H., Yellow Amber, Applied Collared Mouth, 1 Pt. .. 140.00
Flask, Masonic & Eagle, Kensington Glass Works, Aqua, 1 Pt. 100.00
Flask, Masonic & Eagle, Lebanon, Pennsylvania, Aqua, 7 1/2 In. 220.00
Flask, Masonic & Eagle, Olive Green, Applied Lip, 7 1/2 In. 3025.00
Flask, Masonic & Eagle, White Glass Works, Zanesville, Oh., Blue Green, Pontil, 6 In. ... 150.00
Flask, Masonic & Eagle, Yellow Amber, Sheared Mouth, Pontil, 1820-1830, 1 Pt. 176.00
Flask, Meincke & Ebberwlin Savannah, Cobalt Blue, 1882 .... 139.00
Flask, Pig, Railroad, 32 Cities & 7 Railroad Lines On Sides, Albany Slip Glaze, 1890 ... 6000.00
Flask, Pistol, Eagle With Shield, Arrows, Crossed Pistols, Pewter, 4 5/8 In. 165.00
Flask, Pitkin Type, 31 Ribs, Swirled To Right, Aqua, Pontil, 6 1/4 In. 120.00
Flask, Pitkin Type, 36 Ribs, Swirled At Neck, Olive Green, 7 1/4 In. 300.00
Flask, Pitkin Type, 36 Ribs, Swirled To Right, Sea Green, Pontil, 5 3/4 In. 415.00
Flask, Pitkin Type, Olive Yellow, 3 3/4 In. 2640.00
Flask, Saddle, Yellow Olive, Sheared Mouth, Long Neck, 13 In. 220.00
Flask, Sheaf Of Grain, Baltimore Glass Works, Aqua, Collared Mouth, 1/2 Pt. .... 100.00 to 130.00
Flask, Sheaf Of Wheat, Mechanic Glass Works, Philadelphia, Aqua, Pontil, 1 Qt. 100.00
Flask, Sheaf Of Wheat, Ravenna Glassworks, Calabash, Amber, 1 Qt. 275.00
Flask, Sheaf Of Wheat, Westford Glass Co., Red Amber, Collared Mouth, 1 Pt. 80.00
Flask, Sheaf Of Wheat, Westford Glass Co., Yellow Amber, 1 Pt. 110.00
Flask, Soldier & Dancer, Fanny, Lemon Yellow, 1 Pt. 2090.00
Flask, Soldier & Hound, Amber, 1 Qt. 302.00
Flask, Success Of The Railroad, Olive Amber, 1 Pt. 220.00
Flask, Success To The Railroad, Yellow Olive, Pontil, 1 Pt. 305.00
Flask, Summer & Winter, Aqua, Collared Mouth, 1 Pt. 90.00
Flask, Sunburst, Aqua, Pontil, 1/2 Pt. 160.00
Flask, Sunburst, Cornflower Blue, Pontil, 1/2 Pt. 550.00
Flask, Swirl, Aqua, Applied Pewter Mouth, Pontil, 8 1/2 In. 330.00
Flask, Traveler's Companion & Star, Ravenna, Yellow Amber, 1 Qt. 330.00
Flask, Traveler's Companion, Yellow Amber, Double Collared Mouth, Iron Pontil, 1 Pt. ... 880.00
Flask, Union, Clasped Hands & Eagle, Amber, 1/2 Pt. 220.00
Flask, Urn & Cornucopia, Olive Amber, 6 3/4 In. 105.00
Flask, Washington & Eagle, Green Aqua, Pontil, 1 Pt. 90.00
Flask, Washington & Taylor, Dark Yellow Olive, Pontil, 1 Pt. 400.00
Flask, Wheat, Price & Co., Wheeling, Va., Light Blue Green, Pontil, 1 Pt. 190.00
Food, Bunker Hill Pickles, Skilton Foote & Co., Aqua, 5 1/2 In. 20.00
Food, Burnett's Standard Flavoring Extracts, Aqua, 5 1/2 In. 8.00
Food, E. Condits Table Sauce, Geo. C. Ware Sole Mfg., Cincinnati, Oh., Aqua 25.00
Food, G. Vemard, Spice, San Francisco, Ice Aqua, Applied Top 25.00
Food, Gilchrest Bros. English Club Sauce, Aqua 20.00
Food, H.J. Heinz, Jar, Family Measuring 200.00
Food, John Wyeth & Co., Beef Juice, Amber, 3 1/4 In. 15.00
Food, Nonpareil Pickle Works, Jersey City, Aqua, 7 In. 55.00
Food, Obelisk Brand Pickles, Beach & Sherwood, N.Y., 6 In. 75.00
Food, Petal, Blue, Aqua, Iron Pontil, 1 Qt. 299.00
Food, White House Vinegar, Spout, Handle, 6 In. 40.00
Fruit Jar, Almey Glass Lid, 1 Qt. 150.00
Fruit Jar, Atlas, E-Z Seal, Blue, 2 Pt. 5.00
Fruit Jar, Ball Standard, Olive Green, Wax Seal, 1 Qt. 150.00
Fruit Jar, Blown Glass, Pale Green, Wide Mouth, Findlay Bottle Co., Ohio, 5 1/4 In. 60.00

Fruit Jar, Burger & Co., Flower On Front, Rochester, N.Y. 75.00
Fruit Jar, Burger & Co., Rochester, N.Y. 50.00
Fruit Jar, C.F. Spencer's Improved Jar, Aqua, Patent 1868, 1 Qt. 150.00
Fruit Jar, C.F. Spencer's, Rochester, N.Y., 1 Qt. 75.00
Fruit Jar, Champion, Patent Aug. 31, 1869, Glass Lid, Original Clamp, 1 Qt. 130.00
Fruit Jar, Eagle, Aqua, Iron Yoke Clamp, 1860-1880, 1/2 Gal. 132.00
Fruit Jar, Eureka, Aqua, Patent December 27, 1864, 1 Qt. 75.00
Fruit Jar, Fridley & Cornman's, Pat. Oct. 25th, 1859, Aqua, 1/2 Gal. 605.00
Fruit Jar, J.C. Baker's, Pat. Aug. 14, 1860, Aqua, Glass Lid, Clamp, 1 Qt. 550.00
Fruit Jar, Lyon & Bossard's, Aqua, Iron Yoke Clamp, 1880-1890, 1 Qt. 660.00
Fruit Jar, Mason's, CFJ Co., Pat. Nov. 30th, 1858, Citron, Zinc Lid, 1 Pt. 2530.00
Fruit Jar, Mason's, Light Green, 1 Qt. 110.00
Fruit Jar, Mason's, Pale Blue, Glass Lid, 1900-1910, 1 Qt. 88.00
Fruit Jar, Mason's, Patent Nov. 30th, 1858, Aqua, Zinc Lid, 1 Qt. 550.00
Fruit Jar, Millville Atmospheric, Whitalls Patent June, 1861, Lid, Clamp 50.00
Fruit Jar, Myers Test, Aqua, Clamp Lid, 1 Qt. 140.00
Fruit Jar, Newman's, Patent Dec. 20th, 1859, Ice Blue, Tin Lid, 1 Qt. 715.00
Fruit Jar, O K, Aqua, Wax Seal, Tin Lid, 1/2 Gal. 605.00
Fruit Jar, Quick Seal, Pat'd July 14, 1908, Blue, 1 Qt. 12.00
Fruit Jar, S.B. Dewey Jr., Aqua, Iron Stopple, 1 Qt. 825.00
Fruit Jar, Sun, Radiating Rays, Light Green, 1 Qt. ....80.00 to 125.00
Fruit Jar, Sun, Radiating Rays, Light Green, Glass Lid, Yoke Clamp, 1 Pt. 125.00
Fruit Jar, The Gem, Screw Sealer, 1 Qt. 10.00
Fruit Jar, Valve, Aqua, Ground Lip, Cylindrical, 1870-1880, 1 Pt. 715.00
Fruit Jar, Van Vliet, Aqua, Original Yoke, Thumbscrew & Wire, 1 Pt. 825.00
Fruit Jar, W.W. Lyman, Pat'd Feb. 9, 1864, 2 Qt. 15.00
Fruit Jar, Wm. McCully & Co., June 6th, 1866, Blue Aqua, 1 Qt. 440.00
Garnier, Sheriff, Cowboy, 1958 .... 60.00
Gin, Blown, Yellow Olive, Pontil, 1780-1800, 18 3/4 In. 770.00
Gin, Gilt Design, Stopper, 7 1/2 In. 195.00
Gin, W.S.C. Club House, Yellow Olive, 1860-1880, 9 1/4 In. 195.00
Gin, Yellow Olive, Short Applied Shoulder Handle, Cylinder, 10 1/4 In. 275.00
Household, Ammonia, Olive Green, 11 In. 75.00
Household, Clarke's Ammonia, Aqua, Octagonal, Light Haze, 9 In. 50.00
Household, Parsons' Ammonia, Aqua, Label, 1882 ....*Illus* 25.00
Ink, Black, Pyramid Form, Tooled Flared Mouth, Pontil, France, 1840-1860, 2 1/8 In. 90.00
Ink, Blown, Olive Amber, 3-Piece Mold, 2 3/4 In. 115.00
Ink, Carter's Diamond Red Ink, Cobalt Blue, Cork, 7 1/2 In. 250.00
Ink, Carter's, Cobalt Blue, 1 Qt ....*Illus* 95.00
Ink, Carter's, Hexagonal, Clover Leaf Design Panels, Sapphire Blue, 2 In. 150.00
Ink, Chas. M. Higgins & Co., Pour Spout, Master, 8 Oz., 5 3/4 In. 20.00
Ink, DeHalsey Patent, Dome Shape, Yellow Olive, Pontil, 2 7/8 In. 330.00

Bottle, Household, Parsons'
Ammonia, Aqua, Label, 1882

Bottle, Ink, Carter's,
Cobalt Blue, 1 Qt

Bottle, Ink, Stickwell & Co.,
Aqua, 3 In.

Ink, Harrison's Columbian, Blue, Rolled Lip, Open Pontil 440.00
Ink, Harrison's Columbian, Sapphire Blue, Cylindrical, Pontil, 2 In. 500.00
Ink, Laughin & Bushfield, Wheeling, Va., 8 Sides, Aqua, Open Pontil, 2 3/4 x 1 1/2 In. . . . 150.00
Ink, Sanford Mfg. Co., Square, 2 1/2 In. 10.00
Ink, Sanford's Inks & Library Paste, Amber, Round, 7 1/4 In. 35.00
Ink, Stafford's, Apple Green, Flared, Master, 7 1/2 In. 90.00
Ink, Stafford's, Cobalt Blue, Flared, 6 1/4 In. 40.00
Ink, Stickwell & Co., Aqua, 3 In. . . . . *Illus* 15.00
Ink, Umbrella, Lime Green, Octagonal, 2 5/8 In. 140.00
Ink, Umbrella, Medium Olive Yellow, Pontil, 2 1/2 In. 170.00
Ink, Umbrella, Yellow Amber, Octagonal, Pontil, 2 3/8 In. 120.00
Jar, Abbey Cigars, Counter, Embossed, 10 Cents 145.00
Jar, Farm Family, Globe, Honey Amber 8.00
Jar, Newman's Pure Gold Baking Powder, Fairport, N.Y. 30.00
Jar, Snuff, Olive Amber, Tooled Flared Mouth, 9 x 3 1/2 In. 550.00
Jar, Tobacco, Hetterman Bros. Co., Louisville, Ky., Orange Amber, 6 Sides, 6 3/4 In. 395.00
Jar, Tobacco, U.S.T. Co., Melon Shape, Sapphire Blue 230.00
Jar, Utility, Dark Yellow Olive, Square, Pontil, 6 1/8 In. 660.00
Jar, Utility, Mass Glass Co., Aqua, Tooled Mouth, Cylindrical, 5 1/4 In. 35.00
Jug, Bellarmine, Armorial Design, Germany, 1600-1650, 7 1/8 In. 1850.00
Medicine, A.H. Flander's, M.D., Sarsaparilla & Iron, Aqua, 1 Pt. 40.00
Medicine, Alvas Brazilian Specific Co., Cactus Shape, Pat'd 1890, Box, 9 1/4 In. 105.00
Medicine, Apothecary, AM Cole, Cary, Virginia, Nev. 35.00
Medicine, Apothecary, Jar, Cord & Beads, Puffy Blown Stopper, 14 In. 215.00
Medicine, Apothecary, Wm. H. Keith, Aqua, Double Roll Collar 65.00
Medicine, Barrel's Indian Liniment, Aqua, Applied Tapered Collar, 3 In. 25.00
Medicine, Bristol's Extract Of Sarsaparilla, Buffalo, Aqua, Pontil, Box, 5 5/8 In. 250.00
Medicine, Bromo-Seltzer, Aqua, 1906 . . . . 25.00
Medicine, Budd's Wound Nerve & Bone Liniment, Aqua, Flared, Pontil, 5 3/8 In. 355.00
Medicine, Butler's Effervescent, H. Butler Chemist, Pontil, 1790-1820, 5 x 1 In. 100.00
Medicine, C.W. Abbott & Co., Baltimore, Amber, Contents, Box, Round, 8 In. 120.00
Medicine, Cooper's New Discovery, Aqua, 9 In. 15.00
Medicine, Crafts Distemper & Cough Remedy, Amber, 5 1/16 In. 10.00
Medicine, Dr. A.C. Daniels' Disinfectant, Label, Contents, Box, 6 In. 45.00
Medicine, Dr. A.C. Daniels' Wonder Worker Lotion, For Man Or Beast, Box, 6 1/2 In. . . . 75.00
Medicine, Dr. Bells Universal Blood Purifier, Contents, 7 5/8 In. 70.00
Medicine, Dr. Curtis Cherry Syrup, Flint, 7 1/4 In. 75.00
Medicine, Dr. D. Kennedy's Favorite Remedy, Kingston, N.Y., Aqua, Labels, 9 In. 435.00
Medicine, Dr. Fahnestock's Vermifuge, Aqua, Open Pontil, 4 1/4 In. 30.00
Medicine, Dr. H.F. Peery's Dead Shot Vermifuge, Aqua, Open Pontil, 3 3/4 In. 80.00
Medicine, Dr. J.H. McLean's Liver & Kidney Balm, Aqua, Contents, Box, 8 3/4 In. 325.00
Medicine, Dr. J.N. Norwood, Naugatuck, Conn., Box, 5 In. 95.00
Medicine, Dr. Kennedy's Medical Discovery, Roxbury, Mass., Green, 8 1/2 In. 75.00
Medicine, Dr. Kilmer's Indian Cough Cure Consumption Oil, Aqua, 5 3/4 In. 80.00
Medicine, Dr. Kilmer's Kidney Liver Cure, Aqua, Sample 15.00
Medicine, Dr. Kilmer's Ocean Weed Heart Remedy, Aqua, 7 1/8 In. 40.00
Medicine, Dr. Langley's Root & Herb Bitters, Aqua, Open Pontil, 6 3/4 In. 85.00
Medicine, Dr. Le Roy's Mixture, Aqua, Iron Pontil, 7 1/2 In. 200.00
Medicine, Dr. Miles Remedy For The Heart, Aqua, Sample 15.00
Medicine, Dr. S.F. Stowe's Ambrosial Nectar, Amber, 7 7/8 In. 70.00
Medicine, Dr. S.S. Fitch, Aqua, Pontil, 6 In. 35.00
Medicine, Dr. Sanford's Invigorator Or Liver Remedy, Aqua, Open Pontil, 7 In. . . . .55.00 to 85.00
Medicine, Dr. Shoop's Family Medicines, Racine, Wis., Aqua, Booklet, Square, 7 In. . . . 95.00
Medicine, Dr. Steeling's Pulmonary Syrup, Bridgeton, N.J., Aqua, Open Pontil, 6 In. 160.00
Medicine, Dr. Wistar's Balsam Of Wild Cherry, Philadelphia, Aqua, 6 1/2 In. 15.00
Medicine, Druggist C.F. McGullough's Pharmacy, Reno, Nev. 30.00
Medicine, Elliman's Royal Embroction For Horses, Aqua, 7 3/8 In. 15.00
Medicine, Gargling Oil, Lockport, N.Y., Cobalt Blue, ABM, 5 9/16 In. 85.00
Medicine, Genuine Vernal Saw Palmetto, Aqua, 9 In. 35.00
Medicine, Gibson's Syrup, Emerald Green, Beveled Corners, 9 3/4 In. 275.00
Medicine, Grandma Perkins Cure-A-Pain, Aqua, Pamphlet, Box, 5 3/4 In. 450.00
Medicine, Great Dr. Kilmer's Swamp Root Kidney Liver & Bladder Cure Specific 15.00
Medicine, H. Bowman, Oakland, Citrate Of Magnesia, 1890s 220.00

Medicine, Helmbold's Compound Fluid Extract, Cork, Contents, 3 1/4 In. 170.00
Medicine, Homer's California Ginger Brandy, Full Label, 1 Qt. 55.00
Medicine, Hough's Vegetable Syrup Tribes, Hill, N.Y., 9 3/4 x 3 In. 50.00
Medicine, Humphrey's Homeopathic Veterinary Specific, Embossed Horsehead, Label . . 20.00
Medicine, Hunt's Liniment, Sing Sing, N.Y., Aqua, Pontil, 5 In. 45.00
Medicine, John Wyeth & Bros., Cobalt Blue, 6 1/2 In. 19.00
Medicine, Ka-Ton-Ka, The Great Indian Remedy, Aqua, 8 3/4 In. 30.00
Medicine, Laxol M. Calm & Brothers, N.Y., Green, 8 In. 30.00
Medicine, Lincoln Clarke's World Famous Blood Mixture, Blue, 7 1/4 In. 22.00
Medicine, Log Cabin Extract, Rochester, N.Y., 3 Embossed Panels, Amber, 8 1/8 In. 90.00
Medicine, Louden & Co. Indian Expectorant, Philadelphia, Aqua, Pontil, 5 1/4 In. 185.00
Medicine, Marine Drug Store, Cleveland, O., Aqua, 8 3/4 In. 75.00
Medicine, Medical Department, U.S. Army, Squatty, 4 1/2 In. . . . . .25.00 to 45.00
Medicine, Minard's Liniment, Framingham, Mass., Amethyst, 5 In. 25.00
Medicine, Mizpah Vegetable & Cancer Remedy 12.00
Medicine, Mrs. Kidder's Dysentery Cordial, Boston, Aqua, 7 1/8 In. 22.00
Medicine, Murine Eye Remedy Co., Chicago, Corkscrew, Box, 3 3/4 In. 85.00
Medicine, Otto's Cure For The Throat & Lungs, Aqua, 6 In. 15.00
Medicine, Radway's Sarsaparillian Resolvent, R.R.R., Act Of Congress, Aqua, 7 1/2 In. . 35.00
Medicine, Rokeach & Sons, Oil Refiners, Brooklyn, N.Y., Amethyst, Star & Crown 35.00
Medicine, Sanford's Radical Cure, Cobalt Blue, 7 5/8 In. 25.00
Medicine, Schenck's Pulmonic Syrup, Philad., Square, 7 1/4 In. 80.00
Medicine, Shaker Digestive Cordial, Aqua, 9 In. 60.00
Medicine, Silver Pine Healing Oil, Aqua, Label, Cork, 6 In. 40.00
Medicine, Sloan's Anti Colic, 4 7/8 In. 5.00
Medicine, Sloan's N & B Liniment, Dr. Earl S. Sloan, Boston, Mass., Aqua, 6 In. 10.00
Medicine, Smith's Green Mountain Renovator, Amber, Contents, Box, 7 1/2 In. 110.00
Medicine, Smith's Veterinary Remedy, Horse On Label, Aqua, 6 In. 45.00
Medicine, Syrup Rhubarb, Olive Green, Iron Pontil, 8 3/4 In. 70.00
Medicine, Vapo Cresoline Co., Aqua, 5 1/2 In. 20.00
Medicine, Vegetable Cancer Cure, Blood Diseases, Aqua, Label, Box, 10 In. 550.00
Medicine, W.W. Huff's Liniment, Blue Green, Cylindrical, 6 In. 1100.00
Medicine, Warner's Safe Diabetes Remedy, Rochester, N.Y., Amber, 9 3/4 In. 425.00
Medicine, Warner's Safe Kidney Cure, Amber, 5 1/2 In. 28.00
Medicine, Warner's Safe Nervine, Amber, 7 1/4 In. 40.00
Medicine, Wild Cherry Phosphate, Thompson's Pho's Co., Chicago, Aqua, 5 13/16 In. . . 20.00
Medicine, Wm. P. Funders Oregon Blood Purifier, Amber, Light Haze, 8 In. 75.00
Medicine, Yamara Female Remedy, Chicago, Ill., Square, Box, 4 1/2 In. 185.00
Milk, Alta Crest Farms, Cone Shape, Blue Pyro 210.00
Milk, Alta Crest Farms, Embossed SCA, 2 Breeds On Label 650.00
Milk, Brookdale Farm, Shrewsbury, Maine, Red Pyro, Baby Face, Square, 1 Qt. 110.00
Milk, Cloverdale Farms, Milk Is Your Best Food Buy, Cream Top, Spoon 17.00
Milk, Cloverleaf Farms, Blue Ribbon Farms, Grocery, Cream Top, 1 Qt. 28.00
Milk, Creamer, Delchester Farms, Edgemont, Pa., Gill 15.00
Milk, Creamer, Earl North Guernsey Farm, 3/4 Oz. 28.00
Milk, Creamer, Frank H. Cantwell, Clayton, N.Y., Gill 22.00
Milk, Creamer, Helfand Dairy Products, Dartmouth, Mass., 3/4 Oz. 20.00
Milk, Creamer, Land O' Pines, Lufkin, Texas, 1/2 Pt. 7.00
Milk, Creamer, Price Dairy, 3/4 Oz. 24.00
Milk, Creamer, Purity Maid Products Co., 3/4 Oz 20.00
Milk, Creamer, Roberts Brothers, Chef & Waiter In Circle, 3/4 Oz. 20.00
Milk, Creamer, Rosebud Creamery, Square, 3/4 Oz. 18.00
Milk, Creamer, Russ Collins, Adarns, N.Y., 1/4 Pt. 25.00
Milk, E.S. Dairy Magic, Unusual Neck Pourer, 1920, 1 Qt. 55.00
Milk, Farmer's Delight Dairy, Leechburg, Pa., Pasteurized, Pyro, 1 Qt. 20.00
Milk, Glenside Dairy, Deep Water, N.J., It Whips, Cream Top, 1 Pt. 80.00
Milk, Grafton State Hospital, Grafton, Maine, Pyro, Round, 1 Qt. 175.00
Milk, Greenwood Dairy, Worcester, Maine, 2-Color Pyro, 1 Qt. 400.00
Milk, Hycrest Farms, Sterling, Maine, 2-Color Pyro, 1 Qt. 55.00
Milk, Johnson Spruce Hill Farm, Hampton, N.Y., Embossed, 1 Qt. 7.00
Milk, Little Boss Dairy, Normal, Ill., Short, Square, 1 Qt. 8.00
Milk, Matuella's, Cop Top, 1 Qt. 90.00
Milk, Round Top Farms, Milkroom Picture, Cream Top, Maine Seal, 1 Qt. 25.00

Milk, Seneca Dairy, Indian, Syracuse, N.Y., Orange Pyro, 1/3 Qt. 20.00
Milk, Sunshine Dairy, Embossed Sunburst, Cream Top, 1 Qt. 35.00
Milk, Superior Dairy, Babyface, 1 Qt. 250.00
Milk, W.B. Brown, 2 Babyfaces At Neck, 1 Qt. 16.00
Milk, Washburg Dairy, Kane, Pa., Short, Square, 1 Qt. 7.00
Milk, Windermilk, Salt Lake City, Utah, Barnyard Scene, Short, Square, 1 Qt. 8.00
Milk, Worcester State Hospital, Worcester, Maine, Embossed, Round, 1 Pt. 65.00
Mineral Water, Alburgh Springs, Vermont, Yellow Amber, Cylindrical, 1 Qt. 230.00
Mineral Water, C & R Eagle Works, Sac City, Cobalt Blue, c.1860, 7 1/4 In. 1650.00
Mineral Water, C.A. Reiners, San Francisco, Olive Amber Striations, 1873 . . . . 715.00
Mineral Water, Clarke & White, New York, Yellow Olive, 1 Qt. 60.00
Mineral Water, D.A. Knowlton, Saratoga, N.Y., Yellow Olive, Cylindrical, 1 Qt. 185.00
Mineral Water, Deep Rock Spring, Oswego, N.Y., Blue Aqua, Cylindrical, 1 Qt. 210.00
Mineral Water, E. Durand's, Forest Green, Cylindrical, Pontil, 1 Pt. 3630.00
Mineral Water, Eureka Spring Co., Saratoga, N.Y., Yellow Green, Torpedo, 8 7/8 In. . . . 1045.00
Mineral Water, Imperial Nature Sparkling, Green, 12 In. 15.00
Mineral Water, Jackson's Napa Soda Springs, Green Striations, 1873, 7 In. 825.00
Mineral Water, John Clarke, N.Y., Olive Amber, Cylindrical, 1 Qt. 90.00
Mineral Water, L. Gahre, Bridgeton, N.J., Green 400.00
Mineral Water, Lincoln Water, Saratoga Springs, N.Y., Amber, 9 In. 35.00
Mineral Water, Middletown Healing Springs, Yellow Amber, Applied Mouth, 1 Qt. 75.00
Mineral Water, Mt. Clemens Mineral Spring Co., Embossed Base, 9 In. 145.00
Mineral Water, Saratoga Spring, Yellow Amber, Cylindrical, 4 In. 140.00
Mineral Water, Vermont Spring, Saxe & Co., Sheldon, Vt., Olive Green, 1 Qt. 80.00
Mineral Water, Welden Spring, St. Albans, Vt., Emerald Green, Cylindrical, 1 Qt. 3850.00
Mineral Water, William Allen's Congress, Blue Green 400.00
Miniature, Whiskey, David Netter & Co., Amber, 4 1/4 In. 95.00
Nursing, Boots The Chemists, Banana Shape, Openings Both Ends, 5 In. 28.00
Nursing, Favorite, Upright, 1890 . . . . 12.00
Nursing, H. Gilbertson & Son, Submarine Shape, Blown Glass, 8 3/4 In. 395.00
Nursing, Happy Baby, Baby Picture, 1930-1944, 4 In. 55.00
Nursing, Hygeia, Graduated Markings, Pat. Dec. 5, 1916, 5 1/2 In. 12.00
Nursing, Pear Shape, Flat, Embossed Star, Ring Neck, 2 1/2 In. 12.00
Nursing, Pottery, Cream Glaze, Flat, Upturned Neck, 1850, 6 In. 235.00
Nursing, S. Maw Son, Turtle, Threaded Neck, Stopper, Graduated Markings, 9 In. 48.00
Nursing, Staffordshire, Submarine Shape, Blue & White, 7 1/2 In. 675.00
Nursing, Submarine Shape, Victoria Bust, Stoneware, 1840, 7 3/4 In. 1950.00
Nursing, Sunny Babe, Baby's Head, Frosted Front, Graduated Markings, 2 3/4 In. 16.00
Oil, Gulf, Paper Label, 4 Oz. 42.00
Perfume bottles are listed in their own category.
Pickle, Cathedral, Light Green, Applied Mouth, Iron Pontil, 9 In. 240.00
Poison, Black Flag Insect Powder, Aqua, Cork, Front Label, Contents, 3 3/4 In. 30.00
Poison, D.C. Cameron Trade Mark, N.Y., Arm With Dagger, Aqua, 4 In. 50.00
Poison, Figural, Skull, Poison Embossed On Forehead, Cobalt Blue, 3 1/2 In. 1100.00
Poison, H.K. Mulford Co., Skull & Crossbones, Front & Back Labels 150.00
Poison, Iodine, Skull & Crossbones, Amber, 2 5/8 In. 27.00
Poison, Lattice, Stopper, 5 1/2 In. 130.00
Poison, Liquid Iodine, Skull & Crossbones, Amber, 2 1/2 In. 25.00
Poison, Poison Tincture Of Iodine, Skull & Crossbones, Amber, 3 In. 15.00
Poison, Quilted, Cobalt Blue, Stopper, 7 In. 130.00
Poison, Rochester Germicide Co., Rochester, N.Y., Amber, 9 In. 20.00
Poison, Smoky Yellow Olive Amber, Crosshatch, Beveled Corners, 12 Oz. 125.00
Poison, Sulpholine, Cobalt Blue, 4 1/2 In. 25.00
Poison, Tincture Iodine, Skull & Crossbones, Yellow Amber, 2 1/2 In. 20.00
Poison, U.S.P.H.S., Cobalt Blue, Crosshatch Design, Cylindrical, 13 3/8 In. 990.00
Sarsaparilla, Brown's Tomato & Sarsaparilla Bitters, Boston, Mass. 45.00
Sarsaparilla, Dewitt's, Chicago, Label, Contents, Part Box, 8 3/4 In. 110.00
Sarsaparilla, Dr. Cronk's, Stoneware, 12 Sides, Gray Glaze, 1 Qt. 60.00
Sarsaparilla, Dr. Guyscott's Yellow Dock, Oval, 10 1/4 In. 165.00
Sarsaparilla, Dr. Townsend's, Emerald Green 80.00
Sarsaparilla, Foley's, Chicago, USA, Amber, Contents, Box, 9 1/4 In. 40.00
Sarsaparilla, John Bull Extract, Louisville, Ky., Aqua, 9 In. 100.00
Seltzer, 12 Sides, Cobalt Blue, Czechoslovakia 35.00

Seltzer, Ambassador Hotel, Hollywood 195.00
Seltzer, H. Levin, Jersey City, N.J., Hatchet Picture 50.00
Seltzer, Hotel Commodore, N.Y., 1 Pt. 30.00
Seltzer, Irwin's Beverages, Phila., Pa., Deep Blue, Triple Filtered Water 65.00
Seltzer, White Star Beverage Co., Brooklyn, N.Y., Inside 5 Pointed Star, Light Blue 50.00
Snuff, Agate, 2 White Rabbits, Feasting On A Radish, Mongolian Stopper, 2 1/2 In. 465.00
Snuff, Agate, Banded Design, Mask, Mock Ring Handles, Porcelain Stopper, 1 7/8 In. 495.00
Snuff, Agate, Banded Design, Pudding Stone Stopper, 2 1/2 In. 195.00
Snuff, Agate, Cameo, Amber Horses, Cream Ground, Coral Stopper, 2 1/8 In. 330.00
Snuff, Agate, Goats Under Pine Trees, Light Brown, Mongolian Stopper, 2 In. 495.00
Snuff, Agate, Lappet Design At Foot, Agate Stopper, 19th Century, 2 1/4 In. 495.00
Snuff, Agate, Pine Tree Design, Spade Shape, Green Glass Stopper, 2 3/8 In. 165.00
Snuff, Agate, Quartz Carved, Foo Dogs, China, 3 In. 1150.00
Snuff, Agate, Scholar, Seated Under A Willow Tree, Jadeite Stopper, 2 1/4 In. 275.00
Snuff, Agate, White Horse, Gray Body, Coral Stopper, 19th Century, 2 In. 520.00
Snuff, Amber, Shou Lao & Goose, Liu Hai & Frog Other Side, Spade Shape, 2 1/2 In. 440.00
Snuff, Amethyst, Carved Squirrel, Grape, Fruit Form, Squirrel Stopper, 3 In. 305.00
Snuff, Amethyst, Fruit Form, Relief Leaves & Branches 66.00
Snuff, Carp, Swimming, Pale Lavender, Agate Stopper, 2 1/4 In. 195.00
Snuff, Chalcedony Agate, Floater, Ring Handles, Tiger's Eye Stopper, 2 1/4 In. 140.00
Snuff, Chalcedony Agate, Mask & Ring Handles, Coral Stopper, 2 1/2 In. 140.00
Snuff, Cloisonne, Allover Floral, Temple Jar Shape, Stopper, 2 3/4 In. 55.00
Snuff, Coral, Pink, Allover Incised Design, Handles, 1 5/8 In. 138.00
Snuff, Coral, Pink, Tree Stump Form, Carved Leaves & Birds, Bird Form Stopper, 3 In. . 121.00
Snuff, Enameled, Landscape, Temple Vase Shape, Bronze Stopper, 2 3/4 In. 110.00
Snuff, Figural, Shou Lao & Youthful Attendant, Amber Stopper, 2 1/4 In. 275.00
Snuff, Glass, Amethyst, Squirrel In Relief Form, Fruit Shape, Plastic Stopper, 2 1/4 In. .. 110.00
Snuff, Glass, Blue, Interior Painted, Battle Scene, Stopper, Egg Shape, 3 1/2 In. 75.00
Snuff, Glass, Brownatone Kenton Pharmacal Co., Covington, Ky., Amber, 4 5/8 In. 5.00
Snuff, Glass, Deep Olive, Flared Lip, 5 7/8 In. 385.00
Snuff, Glass, Deep Yellow, Dragon & Pearl Design, Temple Jar Shape, 2 1/2 In. 165.00
Snuff, Glass, Dr. Marshall's Catarrh, Aqua, 3 3/8 In. 10.00
Snuff, Glass, Forest Green, Flared Mouth, Pontil, Square, 4 1/4 In. 30.00
Snuff, Glass, Interior Painted, Warrior Design, Coral Stopper, Yun Shou-T'Ien, 3 1/4 In. . 135.00
Snuff, Glass, Opalescent White, Double Fish Shape, Green Stone Stopper, 2 3/4 In. 110.00
Snuff, Glass, Opalescent, Painted Boatman, Glass Stopper, 1900, 3 1/4 In. 55.00
Snuff, Glass, Painted Birds, Tree Landscape, Figure In Mountains, 4 In. 125.00
Snuff, Glass, Rose, Enamel, Bird & Floral, Coral Stopper, 1920, 2 3/8 In. 245.00
Snuff, Hornbill, Carp, Leaping, Pearl Stopper, Late 19th Century, 2 1/2 In. 440.00
Snuff, Hornbill, Phoenix, Rabbit Medallions, Double Gourd Form Handles, Stopper 635.00
Snuff, Ivory, Carved Landscape On 1 Side, Calligraphy On Other, 3 1/4 In. 80.00
Snuff, Ivory, Figural, Man & Woman, Pair 165.00
Snuff, Ivory, Relief Floral Design, Spade Shape, Conforming Stopper, 2 3/4 In. 220.00
Snuff, Jade, Black, Egg Shape, Agate Stopper, 2 1/4 In. 190.00
Snuff, Jade, Brown & Celadon, Rabbit & Kylin Carving, Glass Stopper, 2 In. 135.00
Snuff, Jade, Carved Crane, Green & White, Mask & Mock Ring Handles, 2 1/2 In. 4290.00
Snuff, Jade, Gray, Pebble Shape, Stone Stopper, 18th Century, 2 3/4 In. 220.00
Snuff, Jade, Pebble Form, Russet Inclusions, Jadeite Stopper, 2 1/4 In. 250.00
Snuff, Jade, Raised Double Character On Each Side, White, Egg Shape, 2 1/4 In. 515.00
Snuff, Jade, Red & White, Dragon Carved, Rectangular, 18th Century, 2 1/2 In. 960.00
Snuff, Jade, Relief Carved Willow Tree, Jadeite Stopper, 2 3/8 In. 192.00
Snuff, Jade, Sea Green, Carved Relief Flowers, Fruit Form 66.00
Snuff, Jade, Stone, Light Celadon, Egg Shape, 2 1/4 In. 172.00
Snuff, Jade, White, Landscape, Purse Form, Pietra Dura, Tiger's-Eye Stopper, 2 1/4 In. .. 2860.00
Snuff, Jadeite, Brown Bat Inclusions, Agate Stopper, 2 1/8 In. 825.00
Snuff, Jadeite, Foo Lion Finial, Loose Ring Handles, 19th Century, 2 1/4 In. 715.00
Snuff, Jasperware, Mottled Green, Pebble Form, Crystal Stopper, 2 In. 110.00
Snuff, Opal, Carved Dragon & Pearl, Spade Shape, Stopper, 2 In. 550.00
Snuff, Porcelain, Blue Horses, Jar Form, Mask & Ring Handles, Yung Cheng Mark, 2 In. 605.00
Snuff, Porcelain, Dragon Design, Blue, White, Cylindrical, 19th Century, 3 1/4 In. 121.00
Snuff, Porcelain, Figural, Blue, White, Jadeite Stopper, 3 1/2 In. 33.00
Snuff, Porcelain, Figural, Pale Blue Ground, White, 19th Century, 3 1/4 In. 66.00
Snuff, Porcelain, Relief Floral Design, Green Glaze, Ivory Stopper, 2 1/8 In. 55.00

Snuff, Porcelain, Shou Design, Jar Form, Ring Handles, Tiger's-Eye Stopper, 2 1/4 In. 110.00
Snuff, Quartz, Green, Applied Glass, Stone Flowers, Brass Base, Stopper, 4 In. 66.00
Snuff, Rock Crystal, Lion's Head & Mock Ring Handles, Egg Shape, 2 3/4 In. 330.00
Snuff, Sandstone, Mussel Shell Shape, Snail Stopper, 1900, 2 3/4 In. 120.00
Snuff, Staghorn, 2 Laughing Figures, Inset Ivory Panel, Gold Archaic Script, 2 1/8 In. 172.00
Snuff, Stone, Green & Black, Handles, Coral Stopper, Flattened Egg Shape, 2 In. 250.00
Snuff, Walnut, Silver Collar, Turquoise Stopper, 2 In. 300.00
Snuff, Wooden, Shark Skin Covering, Hardstone Top, 3 In. 195.00
Soaky, Alf 75.00
Soaky, Bambi 25.00
Soaky, Bamm Bamm, Purex, 1960s ....22.00 to 38.00
Soaky, Bugs Bunny 15.00
Soaky, Bullwinkle 35.00
Soaky, Casper The Ghost 30.00
Soaky, Deputy Dawg, 1960, 8 1/2 In. ....25.00 to 30.00
Soaky, Elmer Fudd, Elmer Goes Hunting, Red & Black, 1960s 20.00
Soaky, Felix The Cat, Blue Variations, 1960s 45.00
Soaky, Felix The Cat, Contents 95.00
Soaky, Fred Flintstone, Purex Corp., 6 In. 30.00
Soaky, King Kong 35.00
Soaky, Mighty Mouse, Cap On Head 25.00
Soaky, Mr. Magoo 38.00
Soaky, Peter Potamus, Light Blue 55.00
Soaky, Peter Potamus, Purple 55.00
Soaky, Porky Pig 25.00
Soaky, Skeleton, Masters Of The Universe 15.00
Soaky, Smokey The Bear, 1960s, 8 1/2 In. ....22.00 to 25.00
Soaky, Tennessee Tuxedo 35.00
Soaky, Top Cat, In Trash Can, Yellow, 1960s, 9 3/4 In. ....25.00 to 35.00
Soaky, Truck 35.00
Soaky, Winsome Witch 45.00
Soaky, Woody Woodpecker, 10 In. 25.00
Soda, Alden Bros., Battle Creek, Mich., Aqua, Hutchinson, Round Slug, 1 Qt. 35.00
Soda, Big Chief, On Horse, Red, White, 10 Oz. 65.00
Soda, Big G, Light Green, Dug, 9 1/2 In. 20.00
Soda, Bridge St., Paterson, N.J., Aqua, Hutchinson, Triangle Slug, 1 Qt. 40.00
Soda, Canada Dry Ginger Ale, Marigold Carnival Glass 3.00
Soda, Canada Dry, Miniature 2.00
Soda, Celro-Kola Co., Inc., Portland, Ore., Amber, 1910, 8 1/2 In. 35.00
Soda, Cha's Grove, Columbia, Pa., Emerald Green, Slug Plate 20.00
Soda, City Ice & Bottling Works, Georgetown, Tx., Aqua 20.00
Soda, Coos Bay Soda Works, J.A. Golden, Marshfield, Ore., Aqua 100.00
Soda, D.G. Hall, Deep Green, Collared Mouth, Iron Pontil, 7 1/4 In. 160.00
Soda, Donald Duck Pop 25.00
Soda, Dr Pepper, 10 Oz. 10.00
Soda, Dr Pepper, Cherokee Strip Stampede Rodeo, 4th Anniversary, 1994, 8 Oz. 5.00
Soda, Dr Pepper, Desert Storm, Long Neck, Tex., 1992, 12 Oz. 25.00
Soda, Dr Pepper, Display, Fiberglass, 48 In. 155.00
Soda, Dyottville Glass Works, Philadelphia, Pa., Green, Blue, Cylindrical, 1 Qt. 70.00
Soda, E. Ottenville, Nashville, Tenn., Cobalt Blue, Round Slug, Blob Top 140.00
Soda, Eight Ball, Amber, Blue & White Pyro, 7 Oz. 65.00
Soda, F. Snyder, Battle Creek, Mich., Aqua, Hutchinson, 1 Qt. 40.00
Soda, Family Pack Silver State Beverage, Reno, 1 Qt. 19.00
Soda, G. Norris & Co. City Bottling Works, Sapphire Blue, Hutchinson, 1 Pt. 140.00
Soda, George Allgair, South River, Aqua, Hutchinson, Round Slug, 1 Qt. 35.00
Soda, Gooch's Extract Of Sarsaparilla, Cincinnati, Oh., Aqua 75.00
Soda, H. Maillard Lead City, S.D., Aqua, Tombstone Slug 35.00
Soda, Haddock & Sons, Torpedo, Olive Green 2500.00
Soda, J.A. Dearborn & Co., N.Y., Cobalt Blue, Iron Pontil 135.00
Soda, J.F. Giering, Youngstown, Oh., Aqua, Hutchinson, 1 Qt. 35.00
Soda, J.J. Spitsley, Ionia, Mich., Aqua, Hutchinson, Round Slug, 1 Qt. 45.00
Soda, Jacksprat Root Beer, 8 Oz. 19.00
Soda, John Ryan, Savannah, Ga., Aqua, Torpedo, 8 1/2 In. 110.00

Soda, Kansas City Bottling Co., Kansas City, Mo., Aqua 25.00
Soda, L. Werrbach, Milwaukee, Wis., Blue Aqua, Blob Top 30.00
Soda, L.D. Clauss, Allentown, Pa., Hutchinson, Slug Plate, 7 In. 45.00
Soda, Lazy B Beverages, Cowboy, On Bucking Horse, Blue & White, 8 Oz. 15.00
Soda, Lynch & Clarke, N.Y., Olive Green, Pontil, 1 Pt. 150.00
Soda, Maumee Valley Beverages, Indian In Canoe, Red & White, 8 Oz. 35.00
Soda, Mountaineer Beverage, Mountain Man, With Gun, Blue & White, 9 Oz. 40.00
Soda, Negaunee Bottling Works, Negaunee, Mich., Aqua, Hutchinson, Oval Slug, 1 Qt. ... 40.00
Soda, Northwestern Bottling Co., Butte, Mont., Aqua, Hutchinson, 6 1/2 In. 20.00
Soda, Orange Crush, Ribbed, Cap, Label, 3 1/2 In. 50.00
Soda, Pacific Bottling Works, Tacoma, Wa., Aqua 20.00
Soda, Royal Crown Ginger Ale, Desert Scene, Camel, Contents 35.00
Soda, San Francisco Glass Works, California, Aqua, Blob Top, 1870 .... 70.00
Soda, Sands Genuine Sarsaparilla, New York, Aqua, Open Pontil, Large 165.00
Soda, South Bend Soda & Bottling Works, South Bend, Wa., Aqua, 6 3/4 In. 30.00
Soda, Spiffy Cola, Boy With Tongue, Yellow, Red & White Pyro, 12 Oz. 50.00
Soda, Tom Sawyer Root Beer, Red & White, 8 Oz. 50.00
Soda, Tom Tucker Beverage, Boy In Top Hat, Blue, White, 12 Oz. 30.00
Soda, Twin Springs Bottling Works, Kansas City, Mo., Blue Aqua 25.00
Soda, Vicksburg Steam Bottling Works, Aqua 20.00
Soda, Vincent Hathaway & Co., Boston, Green, Wire Bale, No Stopper 100.00
Soda, W. Eagle, Sapphire Blue, Tapered, Iron Pontil 425.00
Soda, W.H. Harrington, Stamford, N.Y., Aqua, Hutchinson, Stopper, Slug Plate, 7 In. 40.00
Soda, W.R. Chipman & Co., Registered, New London, Conn., Aqua, Round 20.00
Soda, Waring Webster & Co., Cobalt Blue, Octagonal, Iron Pontil, 1/2 Pt. 385.00
Soda, Wheaton's Beverages, Whale, Green, White, 8 Oz. 40.00
Stiegel Type, Cordial, Floral Design, 4 3/8 In. 165.00
Stiegel Type, Decanter, Bird & Heart Design, 7 1/4 In. 660.00
Stiegel Type, Enameled, 2 Lovebirds & Flowers, Pewter Collar, 5 1/4 In. 465.00
Stiegel Type, Woman, Carrying Buckets, 7 1/4 In. 355.00
Target Ball, Clear Blue, 1890 .... 165.00
Target Ball, Cobalt Blue, Fish Net Design, Bogardus Type 110.00
Target Ball, Cobalt Blue, Fish Net Design, Van Custem, A. St. Quenton 235.00
Target Ball, Jas. Bown & Son, Yellow Amber, Sheared Mouth, 2 1/2 In. 3300.00
Tonic, Betula Beer, Healthful Drink, Make 5 Gal., Camels, Men, Aqua, 4 3/4 In. 35.00
Tonic, C.C. Pendleton's, Red Amber, Square, 9 1/2 In. 50.00
Tonic, Dr. Warren's Tonic Cordial, Cincinnati & N.Y., Aqua, Square, 9 In. 90.00
Tonic, Ramsay's Virginia Tonic Bitters, Aqua, Hexagonal, Pontil, 8 1/4 In. 440.00
Tonic, Schenek's Seaweed, Aqua, Square, Contents, 8 1/4 In. 45.00
Whiskey, A.M. Bininger & Co., New York, Light Apricot, Square, 9 5/8 In. 1320.00
Whiskey, A.M. Bininger & Co., Urn, Yellow Amber, Handle, 8 3/4 In. 870.00
Whiskey, Bennett & Carroll, Chestnut, Yellow Amber, Iron Pontil, 8 1/4 In. 660.00
Whiskey, Brickwedel & Co., Yellow Amber, 1880s, 7 1/2 In. 605.00
Whiskey, Casper's Whiskey, Cobalt Blue 400.00
Whiskey, E & B Bevan, Pittston, Pa., Yellow Amber, Pontil, 1845-1860, 6 7/8 In. 1320.00
Whiskey, Fredericksburg Bottling, San Francisco, Leaf Green, 1 Qt. 35.00
Whiskey, Gaelic Old Smuggler Scotch, Olive Green, 1 Qt. 20.00
Whiskey, Golden Wedding, Orange Carnival Glass, Label, 1 Pt. 45.00
Whiskey, Hayner Distilling Co. Distillers & Importers, Fluted Shoulder, 12 In. 45.00
Whiskey, Jug, Durkins Whiskies & Wines, Spokane, Wash., Drum Shape, Brown Glaze . 245.00
Whiskey, Jug, Griffith Hyatt & Co., Baltimore, Olive Green, Handle, Pontil, 7 In. 1100.00
Whiskey, Jug, Moore Trimble & Co., Pear Shape, Yellow, Handle, 8 1/4 In. 385.00
Whiskey, Jug, O'Keefe's Pure Malt, Handles, Tan, Stoneware, 1 Qt. 60.00
Whiskey, Layfayette & Liberty, Coventry Glass Works, Yellow Olive, Pontil, 1/2 Pt. 400.00
Whiskey, Lilienthal & Co., Flask, Teardrop, Crosshatching Behind Shield, 1876 .... 770.00
Whiskey, Old Joe Gideon Bros., Flask, Amber, 6 In. 20.00
Whiskey, S.O.B. Bourbon, Stoneware, 11 In. 125.00
Whiskey, Sapphire Blue, Mushroom Mouth, Back Bar, Octagonal, 11 5/8 In. 525.00
Whiskey, Shaft & Globe, Olive Green, Long Shaft Neck, String Rim, England, 9 In. 2070.00
Whiskey, Swallow Bros., Norristown, Pa., Diagonal Script, 12 In. 95.00
Whiskey, Wild Turkey, Series 2, No. 4, Lore, 1982 .... 40.00
Wine, Columbian Exposition, 1892 .... 50.00
Wine, Old Jup, Applied Glass Seal, Dark Olive Green, 1760, 8 1/4 In. 1075.00

Zanesville, Flask, 24 Ribs, Aqua, Long Neck, 5 1/8 In. 70.00
Zanesville, Flask, 24 Ribs, Swirled, Aqua, 7 In. 195.00

BOTTLE CAP collectors search for the printed cardboard caps used during the past 80 years. Unusual mottoes, graphics, and caps from dairies
that are out of business bring the highest prices.
Old Red Eye, 1930-1950 10

BOTTLE OPENERS are needed to open many bottles. As soon as the
commercial bottle was invented, the opener to be used with the new
types of closures became a necessity. Many types of bottle openers can
be found, most dating from the twentieth century. Collectors prize
advertising and comic openers.

4-Eyed Woman, Cast Iron 40.00
Alligator, Cast Iron . . . . .40.00 to 55.00
Banjo Joe 35.00
Black Boy & Alligator, Cast Iron . . . . .55.00 to 300.00
Black Face, Brass 25.00
Black Man, Smooth Eyes, Chrome 55.00
Black Native, Girl, Nude, Kneeling, 1950s 68.00
Black Woman, Winking Eye 45.00
Buffalo, Bronze, Wall Mount 45.00
Bulldog, Cast Iron 25.00
Canada Goose . . . . .75.00 to 85.00
Cock Pheasant's Head, Painted 58.00
Cockatoo . . . . .150.00 to 180.00
Donkey's Head, Cast Iron 20.00
Drunk, Palm Tree 75.00
Elephant, Cast Iron 50.00
Elephant, Pink 60.00
False Teeth, Wall Mount 65.00
Goat, Aluminum 25.00
Guitar, Brass 10.00
Johnny Guitar, Cast Iron 22.00
Lobster 60.00
Mallard Duck's Head 55.00
Miller's Beer, Wooden 18.00
Monkey, Cast Iron 100.00
Nude, Brass, 3 1/2 In. 35.00
O'Keefe's Old Stack Ale, Wooden Handle 210.00
Parrot, Brass, 4 1/4 In. 30.00
Parrot, Bronze 30.00
Parrot, Seated 45.00
Pelican, Cast Iron 65.00
Pink Flamingo, Pot Metal 165.00
Pretzel 45.00
Quail, On Base 65.00
Risque Lady, Clothed On Front, Reverse, Ask For Fleck's, Since 1856 . . . .   45.00
Sailor, Leaning On Norfolk Va. Sign, Cast Iron 45.00
Spaniel, Cast Iron 45.00
Squirrel, Cast Iron 45.00
Straw Hat, Sign Post 50.00
Whale On Rock, Cast Metal, Painted, Scott Products Inc. 125.00

BOW is an English porcelain works started in 1744 in East London.
Bow made decorated porcelains, often copies of Chinese blue and
white patterns. The factory stopped working about 1776. Most items
sold as Bow today were made after 1750.

Candlestick, Currant Leaf Shape, Serrated Edge, Green, Yellow, 5 7/8 In. 1725.00
Dish, Chinese Water Scene, Blue, Rectangular, 1765, 10 5/8 In. 690.00
Dish, Pickle, Leaf Shape, Central Floral Spray, 3 Floral Sprigs, Serrated Rim, 4 In. 290.00
Dish, Pickle, Leaf Shape, Fluted, Puce Veins, Green Edge, 1760, 4 1/8 In. 632.00
Dish, White Cabbage Leaf, Blue Glaze, Curled Stem Handle, Ruffled Rim, 10 3/8 In. 632.00

Figurine, Bouquet Of Flowers, Rose, Yellow, Blue, Red, Green, White, 1765, 6 In. 805.00
Figurine, Jupiter, Red Enameled Billowing Drapery, Green Floral Sprigs, 1760, 7 In. 805.00
Figurine, Neptune & Jupiter, Pale Blue Billowing Drapery, 1760, 6 1/8 & 6 3/16 In. 1265.00
Figurine, Recumbent Pug Dog, White Coat, Brown On Muzzle, Blue Florette, 1755, 2 In. 230.00
Figurine, St. John The Baptist, Pale Blue Scallop Shell, Rococo Base, 1760, 8 1/4 In. ... 8625.00
Group, Birds In Branches, Pale Yellow Birds, Yellow Beaks, Red Flowers, 1755, 6 1/8 In. 460.00
Plate, Botanical, 3 Yellow, Purple Plums, Green, Turquoise Leaves, 7 5/8 In. 4315.00
Plate, Botanical, Green Leaf Sprig, Green Floral, Foliate Sprigs, Octagonal, 1756 ...... 3165.00
Platter, Botanical, Yellow Rose Blossoms, Gray Veined Green Leaves, 10 13/16 In. 5175.00
Sauceboat, Leaves, Floral Spray, Rose, Yellow, Blue, Red, Green On Sides, 7 In. 8660.00

BOXES of all kinds are collected. They were made of thin strips of
inlaid wood, metal, tortoiseshell, embroidery, or other material.
Additional boxes may be listed in other sections, such as Advertising,
Battersea, Ivory, Shaker, Tinware, and various Porcelain categories.
Tea Caddies are listed in their own category.

Alms, Country Gothic, Oak, Brown Grained, England, 10 3/4 x 16 In. 135.00
Apple, Poplar, Dovetailed, Lock, Removed Divider, Refinished, 13 x 13 x 3 1/2 In. 200.00
Ballot, 5 Sections, 5 Sliding Lids, Walnut, c.1870, 24 x 10 In. 1000.00
Ballot, Turned Handle, Old Nails, 4 1/4 x 6 3/8 x 10 In. 140.00
Band, Wallpaper Cover, Fox Hunting Scene, Late 18th Century, 15 3/4 x 12 In. 460.00
Band, Wallpaper, U.S. Capital, Flying American Flag, Man In Chariot On Lid, 15 In. ... 1540.00
Bentwood, Cover, Oval, Initials J.A., 23 1/2 In. 880.00
Bentwood, Finger Construction, Green Repaint, 3 Fingers, Oval, 7 3/4 In. 440.00
Bentwood, Nested, Varnish, Thos. Annette Jaffrey, Round, 9 3/4 In., 4 Piece 275.00
Bentwood, Old Varnish, Copper Tacks, W.E. Sawyer, Round, 14 3/4 In. 70.00
Bentwood, Overlapping Seams, Brass Tacks, Red Traces, Round, 13 3/4 x 6 1/2 In. 165.00
Bentwood, Pine, Blue Paint, Laced Seams, Oblong, 14 3/4 In. 247.00
Bible, Book Form, Oak, c.1900 .... 90.00
Bible, Chippendale, Walnut, Dovetailed Case, Bracket, 8 1/2 In. 907.00
Bird's-Eye Maple, Academy Painted, Floral & Shell, Compartments, c.1830, 6 1/2 In. .. 975.00
Book Form, 1 Piece Carved Pine, Blue, Red, Yellow, Black & White Paint, 7 7/8 In. ... 550.00
Book Form, Chip Carved Spruce, Sliding Lid 100.00
Bride's, Family Scene, Father Bouncing Child On Knee On Lid, Lithograph, c.1850 .... 775.00
Bride's, Hand Painted Paper Covering, 1779, Oval ....*Illus* 385.00
Bride's, Painted Sides, Blossoms, Man & Woman On Fitted Lid, 1820s, 18 1/2 In. 1495.00
Bride's, Tulips, Red Ground, Oval 675.00
Bristol-Type Glass, Cover, Enameled Hearts & Flowers, Blue Ground, Round, 3 1/2 In. 165.00
Candle, Chamfered Sliding Lid, Finger Grooves, Square Nails, 4 3/4 x 8 In. 125.00
Candle, Cherry, Sliding Lid, Dovetailed, Hanging, 19 In. 440.00
Candle, Exotic Inlays, Shaped Crest, Welsh, c.1840, 19 In. 2400.00
Candle, Poplar, Refinished, Hanging, 14 In. 110.00
Candle, Raised Panel Sliding Lid, Brass Pull, Red Paint, 1780s, 12 In. 235.00
Candle, Robin's-Egg Blue, Lift Top, Snipe Hinges, Fletcher, Whitewood, 1800, 16 3/4 In. 450.00
Candle, Sliding Lid, Arched Crest, 19th Century, 15 In. 575.00
Candle, Sunbursts & Resin Inserts, Hand Cut Nails, Walnut, 18 1/4 x 11 In. 385.00
Candle, Tombstone Form, Slide Top, 12 In. 195.00
Candle, Victorian, Milk Glass Studs, Hand Cut Pine, 23 7/8 x 12 1/4 In. 170.00
Candle, Wall, Original Hinges, American, Walnut, c.1780, 14 1/2 In. 585.00
Candy, Fish, White, Metallic Blue, Black, Red, Glass Eye, 12 In. 330.00
Card, Black Lacquer, Brass 35.00
Cardboard, Scenes, Pennsylvania, 1832, Oval, 17 x 14 x 13 In. 600.00
Chinoiserie, Lacquer Design, 2 Drawers, Oval, 21 1/2 In. 135.00
Chip Carved, Tulipwood, American, 19th Century, 8 x 10 3/4 In. 675.00
Cigarette, Allover Foliate & Figural Panels, Gilt Bronze, 2 1/4 x 6 In. 517.00
Collar, Celluloid, Pony Express Rider Scene Cover 160.00
Conestoga Wagon, Pine, Wrought Iron Fittings, 12 In. 275.00
Cutlery, Georgian, Mahogany, 3 Sections, Brass Loop Handle, 19th Century, 14 1/2 In. .. 145.00
Cutlery, Handle, Heart & Star Design, 13 In. 201.00
Cutlery, Maple, Dated 1925 .... 55.00
Document, Apple Green Paint, Sliding Lid, Iron Ball Handle, 1830s, 12 1/4 In. 395.00
Document, Brass Over Teak 165.00
Document, British Colonial, Serpentine Borders, Felt Lined, 1850s, 5 1/4 x 10 1/2 In. .. 230.00

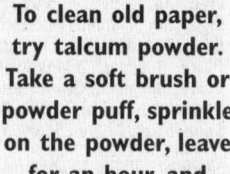

To clean old paper, try talcum powder. Take a soft brush or powder puff, sprinkle on the powder, leave for an hour, and brush it off.

Box, Bride's, Hand Painted Paper Covering, 1779, Oval

Document, Design On Side, Green Interior	395.00
Document, Dovetailed, Brass Handle, c.1790, 6 In.	110.00
Document, Dovetailed, Tiger Maple, c.1800, 8 1/2 x 22 In.	2500.00
Document, Heart Shape, Brass Lock With Key, Early 19th Century, 8 x 5 x 4 In.	165.00
Document, Incised Pinwheels & Geometric Designs, Iron Pin Hinges, 8 1/2 x 15 1/2 In.	950.00
Document, Mahogany, 19th Century	27.00
Document, Pine, Lion & Dome Top, England, 1800, 10 1/4 x 14 1/4 In.	210.00
Document, Poplar, Red Paint, Yellow, Olive Green Striping, 17 In.	110.00
Document, Salmon, Mustard & Black Paint Design, Pennsylvania, 14 x 9 x 6 In.	2250.00
Document, William & Mary, Hinges, Walnut, Oyster Veneer, Rectangular Top	1725.00
Dome Top, Bead Mosaic Inlay Of House & Building, England, Brass, 19th Century	518.00
Dome Top, Black, Green, Rustic Red Paint, Diamond Pattern, 24 1/4 x 13 x 9 3/4 In.	4830.00
Dome Top, Empire Style, Gilt Bronze Mounted, 20th Century, 10 1/2 x 9 In.	1840.00
Dome Top, Fish Scales Exterior, Battlefield Scenes, Porcelain, Germany, 4 1/2 In.	1610.00
Dome Top, Leather, England, Mid-18th Century, 9 In.	275.00
Dome Top, Mahogany Marquetry, Geometric Designs, 8 x 11 x 19 1/4 In.	770.00
Dome Top, Oil Cloth, 1822 Hallowell, Me., Newspaper Lined, Leather Hinges, 13 In.	355.00
Dome Top, Pine, 1-Finger Construction, Floral Scrolls, Initials T.V., 8 In.	190.00
Dome Top, Pine, Dovetailed, Carved Shoe Footed, Europe, 24 1/2 In.	275.00
Dome Top, Pine, Red & Cream Vinegar Painting, 12 x 24 x 13 In.	430.00
Dome Top, Poplar, Brown Flame Grained, Wrought Iron End Handles, 23 3/4 In.	460.00
Dome Top, Tooled Leather Cover, Wrought Iron Handle & Lock, 11 In.	135.00
Dome Top, Wooden, Birds & Flowers, Black Ground, 7 1/4 x 5 x 3 1/2 In.	415.00
Dough, 2-Board Top, Dovetailed, Splayed Feet, Pine, 19th Century	330.00
Dough, Nut Brown Finish, Square Nails, Pa., With Scraper, 19th Century, 26 In.	350.00
Dough, Pine, Stained, Trough Body, Square Legs, American	185.00
Dough, Pine, Trough Body, Circular Legs, American, 29 x 52 x 25 In.	430.00
Dresser, Hand Painted Courting Couple On Hinged Lid, France, c.1890, 9 1/2 In.	950.00
Game, Abacus & Playing Cards, Walnut, George W. Williams, N.Y., 12 In.	385.00
Game, Playing Board, Chess Pieces Inside, Inlaid Mahogany, 12 x 20 In.	305.00
Game, Playing Cards, Gaming Tiles & Counters, 19th Century	345.00
Glass, Cobalt Blue, Gold Fleur-De-Lis, Hinged Cover, 5 In.	325.00
Glass, Opalescent, Appliqued Flowers, Hinged, Footed, 4 1/2 x 5 1/2 In.	450.00
Glove, English Regency, 3 Frieze Drawers, Bracket Base, Mahogany, 13 x 8 1/2 In.	460.00
Hardwood, Primitive, Sliding Lid, Floral Design, Gray Ground, 4 x 6 1/4 x 6 1/4 In.	440.00
Hat, Black Kid Leather	50.00
Hat, Crolut & Knappy, Art Deco, Colorful	35.00
Hat, Leather, Circus & Winged Eagle Design, England, 19th Century, 14 In.	690.00
Hat, Military, Cardboard, Oval	12.00
Hat, Wallpaper Covered, Made By Hannah Davis, Newspaper Lined, 1835, 19 In.	460.00
Heart Shape, Wallpaper Covered, c.1830, 2 3/4 x 4 1/2 x 4 1/2 In.	920.00
Hidden Compartment, Brass Bail Handles, c.1840, 6 x 12 x 20 In.	230.00
Hide, Leather Trim, Brass Studs, J.G. On Lid, Iron Lock, 15 1/2 In.	50.00
Horn Powder, Battle Of Lake Erie, Lawrence & Perry Portrait, Engraved, 3 In.	75.00

Ivory, Silver Inlay & Fittings, Interior Mirror In Lid, Petit Point Lining, 3 5/8 In. 715.00
Jewelry, Brass, Ornate Angels, Doves & Stones, 14 In. 90.00
Jewelry, Lift Top, 2 Doors, Interior Drawers, Chinese Scenes, Decoupage, 10 x 11 1/2 In. . 805.00
Jewelry, Mother-Of-Pearl Inlay, Rosewood, England, 19th Century 345.00
Jewelry, Pierrot, Reclining, With Mandolin, Germany 75.00
Jewelry, Puzzle, Floral Marquetry Top, Mirror, Hidden Keyhole, 9 1/8 In. 500.00
Jewelry, Silhouette Of Couple, 11 x 9 In. 50.00
Jewelry, Traveling, Woman's, Mirror In Top, Fold-Out Sections, Rosewood 345.00
Knife, George III, Mahogany, Serpentine, Brass Mounted, Claw Feet, 14 1/2 In. 726.00
Knife, George III, Mahogany, Serpentine, Fitted Interior, Inlay, 14 x 9 In. 373.00
Knife, George III, Satinwood, Pair 3500.00
Knife, Hepplewhite, Mahogany Veneer, Inlaid, Interior Baffle, 15 1/2 In. 275.00
Knife, Mahogany, Inlaid At Corners, Star Inlay On Interior, England, c.1810 . . . . 660.00
Knife, Poplar, Divided, Many Blue Paint Layers, 13 1/2 x 21 1/2 In. 355.00
Knife, Walnut, Dovetailed, Hinged Lid, Ended Out Handle, 12 1/2 x 15 1/2 In. 245.00
Knife, Walnut, Dovetailed, Refinished, 4 Sections, 12 1/2 x 14 1/2 In. 95.00
Letter, Book Form, Victorian, Leather 460.00
Letter, Marquetry Inlay, Ship, British Flag, Rosewood, Bird's-Eye Maple, 12 1/2 In. 725.00
Letter, Regency Style, Mahogany, Courting Couple Painting, Frieze Drawer, 8 x 14 In. . . 320.00
Mahogany, Carved Design, Handles, 18th Century, Spanish Colonial, 20 x 9 In. 425.00
Mail, Walnut, Worn Finish, Scrolled, Hanging, 9 1/4 x 21 1/4 In. 105.00
Maple, Dovetailed, Ivory Inlay Of Crosses, Diamonds & Cannons 330.00
Maple, Rosewood, Geometric Design, Black Velvet Lining, 9 x 7 x 13 In. 1320.00
Marquetry, Mahogany Veneer, Classic Woman, Weaving, Zum Andenken, 11 In. 125.00
Painted, Floral Design, Child's, 17 5/8 x 25 1/4 x 12 3/4 In. 575.00
Pantry, Seeds, Dry Gray-Green Paint, 9 In. Diam. 235.00
Pantry, Wooden, Natural, Herkimer Co., Nov. 16, 1853, 6 3/4 In. 110.00
Patch, Cobalt Blue Cover, Ornate Gold & White Enameling, France 125.00
Pencil, Wooden, With Inlay 32.00
Pine, Dark Polychrome Painted, Sliding Lid, 2 7/8 x 5 1/2 x 5 1/2 In. 33.00
Pine, Geometric Tumbling Block Pattern, Red & Yellow, Lid, 12 x 13 x 15 In. 410.00
Pine, Grain Painted, 19th Century, 12 1/2 x 24 x 14 1/4 In. 316.00
Pine, Green Paint Traces, Sliding Lid, Primitive, 12 x 13 1/2 x 24 In. 80.00
Pine, Mahogany, Striped Satinwood, Shell Medallion, 8 x 10 x 16 In. 1760.00
Pine, Paper Lining, 12 x 2 x 4 In. 12.50
Pine, Red, Cream Flame Graining, England, Early 19th Century, 11 In. 747.50
Pine, Shaped Lid, Strap Hinges, Red Stain 220.00
Pink, Gold, Engine-Turned, Fluted Design, Udall & Ballou, 14K Yellow Gold 977.50
Pipe, Victorian, Crossband Mahogany, 19th Century, 18 In. 70.00
Poplar, Lift Top, 1 Dovetailed Drawer, Brown Finish, Brass Pull, 10 1/4 In. 82.00
Powder, Woman's, Screw Top, Incised Designs All Sides, 3 1/8 x 3 3/8 In. 110.00
Red Lacquer, Domed Cover, Welled Interior, Oriental Landscape, Chinese Export, 13 In. . 2645.00
Regency, Mahogany Inlaid, Piano Forte Case, Ivory, 1810 . . . . 495.00
Reverse On Glass, Painted Cover, 3-Masted Ship, Harbor Scene, 3 1/4 x 5 x 1 3/4 In. . . 85.00
Ring, Bisque, Molded & Applied Flowers, 1 1/2 x 2 1/2 x 3 1/2 In. 15.00
Rosewood, Dovetailed, Sea Captain, Whale Bone, Ebony, 5 x 7 x 14 In. 1650.00
Rosewood, Travel, Dressing, England, 1840 . . . . 950.00
Salt, Wooden, Painted Bird & Flowers, Hanging 5900.00
Sardine, On Cover, Underplate 880.00
Sardine, Pelican On Lid, Fish On Sides, Turquoise Underplate, George Jones 990.00
Sardine, Swan On Cobalt Water Lily, Underplate, Etruscan 2750.00
Schnitz, Bird's-Eye & Tiger Maple Designs Interior & Exterior, 12 3/4 x 10 3/4 In. 300.00
Scotty Shape, Sitting, Wood Carved 330.00
Slant Top, Hand Cut Nails, Brass Hinges, Tiger & Plain Maple, 9 1/2 x 8 7/8 In. 270.00
Snuff, Gold, Cover, Foliage Border, Matte, Rawlings, 18K, England, 1824, 3 In. 3450.00
Snuff, Gold, Cover, Sides, 2-Color Foliage, Shell Border, Oval, France, 1774, 3 In. 3162.00
Snuff, Gold, Rounded Corners, Leaf Border, Blue Enamel, Rectangular, 1810, 3 In. 4025.00
Snuff, Gold, Top Chased With Foliage, Matte, Rectangular, 1810, 3 1/2 In. 1840.00
Spice, Dome Top, Petal Shape, 5 Sections, Spain, 17th Century, 3 In. 175.00
Spice, Oak, Metal Fittings, 8 Containers, Round, Dated 1858, 9 In. 275.00
Spruce Gum, Carved From Solid Hard Pine, 3 7/8 x 3 5/8 In. 120.00
Storage, Arches Of Rust, Green & Gold Borders, Simulated Stringing, 11 x 24 In. 920.00
Storage, Carved Wood, Sliding Cover, Arched Handle, 12 In. 40.00

Storage, Putty Painted, New England, 1840s, 12 1/2 x 26 7/8 In. 402.00
Tea, Figural Scene, Painted Tin, Green Ground, China, 20 In., Pair 1495.00
Tea Caddy, Lacquerware, Pewter Inserts, Chinese Export, 19th Century, 6 x 9 x 6 In. . . . 400.00
Tin Straps, Red Over Gray Paint, 7 5/8 x 4 1/4 x 5 In. 75.00
Tobacco, Brass & Copper, Erotic Scenes, Dutch, c.1720, 7 In. 2850.00
Tobacco, Brass & Copper, Inscribed With Arms Of Holland & Provinces, 1750s 425.00
Tobacco, Brass & Copper, Polished, Engraved 4 Continents, Dated 1759, 5 3/8 In. 950.00
Tobacco, Brass, Couple, Dutch Inscription, Double Lid, Dutch, 1720, 5 In. 1035.00
Tobacco, Brass, Engraved Building Hinged Cover, Oval, 4 1/2 x 3 1/2 In. 95.00
Tobacco, Brass, Engraved Mythological Scenes, Dutch, c.1720, 7 In. 975.00
Tobacco, Brass, Lozenge Shape, Biblical Scenes, Holland, c.1760, 5 1/2 In. 500.00
Tobacco, Brass, Niello Inlaid Man Smoking Scene, Early 18th Century, Dutch, Oval 1350.00
Tobacco, Brass, Steam Frigate Scene, Mid-19th Century, 4 3/8 x 2 5/8 In. 95.00
Tobacco, Glass, Cylindrical, Oval, Brass, England, 3 In. 125.00
Toiletry, Drop Front, Lift Lid, Burl Walnut, Brass Pull, Tufted Satin Interior, Tray, 3 Vials 192.00
Toiletry, Velvet Patchwork Cover, Leather 385.00
Utility, Hinged Lid, Fitted Interior, Painted Clusters Of Fruit, c.1820, 13 7/8 In. 3162.00
Wall, Carved From Single Piece Of Wood, 11 x 4 1/2 In. 245.00
Wall, Lift Top, Walnut, Drawer, 12 x 12 3/4 In. 1900.00
Wall, Spoon Rack, With 6 Pewter Spoons, Painted Pine, Late 18th Century, 19 In. 2645.00
Wallpaper, Gettysburg Newspaper Liner, 1851, 21 x 13 1/2 In. 750.00
Wallpaper, Oval, 10 1/2 x 13 x 9 1/4 In. 135.00
Wallpaper Over Wood, Floral, Hannah Davis Label, Oval, 1835, 17 x 13 x 12 In. . . . 750.00
Wallpaper Over Wood, Ivy, Louisiana, Oval, 6 1/2 x 8 x 14 In. 295.00
Walnut, Oyster Veneer, Hinged Top, Divided Interior, William & Mary, 4 In. 2875.00
Walnut, Oyster Veneer, Hinged Top, Green Silk Lined Interior, William & Mary, 5 In. . . 1840.00
Walnut, Oyster Veneer, Hinged Top, Red Painted Interior, William & Mary, 3 1/4 In. . . . 517.00
Wooden, Painted Tulips Around Sides, Church On Lid, Bucher, Flat, Miniature 2600.00
Wooden, Sliding Lid, Geometric Design, 6 x 8 In. 2300.00
Wooden, Sliding Lid, Salmon Grained, 6 x 10 In. 3700.00
Wooden, Tom & Jerry, Mirror Inside, Spain, 1957 . . . . 75.00
Work, Black Lacquer, Cushion Shape, Figural Scenes, Chinese Export, 14 In. 258.00
Writing, 2 Iron Pots, Galleried Case, 3 Drawers, Japan, 8 x 9 In. 143.00
Writing, England, Pine, Slant Lid, Decoupage Top, 16 x 18 x 9 In. 285.00
Writing, Fitted Interior, Brass Mounted, Lion's Masks, Brass Ball Feet, 8 1/4 In. 2587.00
Writing, Walnut, Lift Top, Drop Front, Secret Drawers, Holland, 1675, 14 x 14 In. 2950.00

BOY SCOUT collectibles include any material related to scouting, including patches, manuals, and uniforms. The Boy Scout movement in the United States started in 1910. The first Jamboree was held in 1937. Girl Scout items are listed under their own heading.

Book, Bird Study, 1938 . . . . 12.50
Book, Gilcraft, 1928 . . . . 10.00
Brick, Winchester Boy Scouts Of America 75th Anniversary, Multicolored 92.00
Calendar, 1934, Hintermeister Border Art Work, Rockwell, 22 x 46 In. 650.00
Calendar, 1950, Norman Rockwell 30.00
Card, Boy Scouts Of America & Freedoms Foundation, Hanger, 1956, 7 1/2 In. 22.00
Catalog, Boy Scout Equipment, 12 Pages, 1937, 8 1/2 x 11 In. 24.00
Catalog, Boy Scouts Of America Scouting Equipment, Uniforms, 1927, 32 Page 75.00
Cookie Jar, Cub Scout, Metlox 850.00
Drum, Chein 35.00
Emblem, Bronze, 15 x 10 In. 395.00
Encyclopedia, 160 Pages, 1952 . . . . 15.00
Handbook, 448 Pages, 1959 . . . . 10.00
Handbook, For Boys, BSA Knife With Sheath, 1948 . . . . 26.00
Handbook, For Boys, Norman Rockwell Cover, Feb. 1938, 668 Pages 15.00
Handbook, Official, Norman Rockwell On Cover, 1933 . . . . 41.00
Kit, Fire Making, Box, 1930s 125.00
Kit, First Aid, 1950s 15.00
Kit, First Aid, Metal Box In Sheath 25.00
Kit, Rock & Minerals, 1930s 65.00
Knife, Remington, Medallion On Bone Grips, 4 Blades 35.00
Merit Badge, Archery, 1941 . . . . 9.00

Patch, First National Jamboree, 1937 .... 85.00
Pin, I'm A Camper 25.00
Plate, Baden-Powell, Portrait Center, Founder, Coats Of Arms, 9 In. 235.00
Postcard, Baden-Powell, Founder, Black & White, Photograph 50.00
Sheet Music, Boy Scouts March, J.C. Macy, Copyright 1911, 6 Pages 28.00
Sheet Music, March Of Boy Scouts, 1913 .... 15.00
Signal Set, Official Boy Scout, Twin, Box 30.00
Trophy, Silver, 1932 .... 25.00
Yearbook, Franklin K. Mathews, 240 Pages, 1927 .... 75.00
Yearbook, Hardcover, 1916 .... 40.00

BRADLEY & HUBBARD is a name found on many metal objects. Walter
Hubbard and his brother-in-law, Nathaniel Lyman Bradley, started
making cast iron clocks, tables, frames, andirons, lamps, chandeliers,
sconces, and sewing birds in 1854 in Meriden, Connecticut. The company became Bradley & Hubbard Manufacturing Company in 1875.
Charles Parker Company bought the firm in 1940. Their lamps are
especially prized by collectors.

Bookends, German Shepherd 68.00
Bookends, Horse 150.00
Desk Set, Inkwell, Square Base, Ball Feet 110.00
Doorstop, Sailing Ship, 1915 .... 110.00
Dresser Mirror, Curves, Plumes, Cattails, Lilies, 12 x 20 In. 345.00
Lamp, Banquet, Cupid On Base, Arms Around Pedestal, Etched Shade 645.00
Lamp, Banquet, Onyx Insert In Stem, Cast Iron, Electrified, 27 1/2 In. 330.00
Lamp, Bat, Dome Shade, Wing Spread Bats, Pressed Metal, 10 In. 1265.00
Lamp, Brass, Amber Tulip Slag Glass Shade, 13 In. 345.00
Lamp, Desk, Fish Swimming Design, Green Tulip Shade, 9 x 16 In. 412.00
Lamp, Desk, Tilt Shade, Green, Blue, Brown Arts & Crafts Border 460.00
Lamp, Floral, Bronze, Slag Glass, Art Nouveau, 20 In. 431.00
Lamp, Hanging, Store, Brass Repousse Font, Hammered Tin Shade 750.00
Lamp, Metal, Green & White Striated Glass Shade, 35 In. 978.00
Lamp, Oil, Free Standing, Original Shade, 1880-1920 .... 3200.00
Lamp, Oil, Green, Gray Metal, 6-Sided Metal Shade, 11 1/2 In. 770.00
Lamp, Ribbed Reverse Painted Shade, Table 1695.00
Lamp Base, Signed Slag Glass Shade, Table 632.00
Rack, Letter, Running Deer In The Woods, Double Sided 210.00

BRASS has been used for decorative pieces and useful tablewares since
ancient times. It is an alloy of copper, zinc, and other metals.
Additional brass items may be found under Bell, Candlestick, Tool, or
Trivet.

Alms Dish, Gothic Script, Floral Motif Rim, Germany, 16th Century, 15 In. 1150.00
Ashtray, Cover, Bail, Tripod, Harald Buchrucker, 1935, 19 3/4 In. 125.00
Bed Warmer, Brass Lid On Brass Pan, Wooden Handle, c.1800 .... 165.00
Bed Warmer, Engraved Rosette Design Cover, Treenware, England, 48 In. 230.00
Bed Warmer, Punched Design Lid, Turned Chestnut Handle, 42 In. 275.00
Bed Warmer, Punched Floral Design Lid, Maple Handle, Old Red Paint 190.00
Bed Warmer, Tooled Design, Turned Wooden Handle, Copper Rivets, 43 In. 495.00
Bed Warmer, Turned Wooden Handle, 46 1/4 In. 145.00
Bed Warmer, Walnut Turned Handle, Reticulated, England, 43 In. 150.00
Bowl, Gothic Revival, Brass, Pedestal 470.00
Bowl, Iron Handle, 10 3/4 In. 40.00
Brazier, Raised On 3 Legs, Flared, Round, 15 1/4 x 7 3/4 In. 85.00
Bucket, Bail Handle, England, 1780-1810, 9 In. 450.00
Bucket, Flaring Form, Wrought Iron Swing Handle, 19th Century, 9 x 14 In. 85.00
Bucket, Rolled, 1 Seam, Bail Handle, Ring Design, England, 1790-1800, 9 1/4 In. 425.00
Bust, Bearded Orthodox Priest, Floral Robes, Shaped Base, Russia, 30 In. 1610.00
Calendar, Perpetual, Figure Of Bird, Arts & Crafts Style, 6 In. 102.00
Card Tray, Indian Head, Feather Headdress, 5 x 5 1/2 In. 95.00
Card Tray, Monkey 135.00
Card Tray, Woman, Nude, 3 1/2 x 7 In. 125.00
Chalice, Cast & Turned, Scotland, Late 18th Century, 6 In., Pair 250.00

Chamberstick, Reflector, c.1790, 5 1/2 In.	165.00
Chamberstick, Snuffer, Wick Cutter, 19th Century, 5 1/4 In., Pair	200.00
Chocolate Pot, Engraved, France, c.1750, 7 In.	1650.00
Coffeepot, Acorn Finial, Dovetail Construction, England, c.1750, 9 1/2 In.	375.00
Coffeepot, Tin Interior, Scroll Handle, England, 1800, 10 3/4 In.	395.00
Coffeepot & Machine, Plastic Handle, Italy, 1930, 11 In. & 6 7/8 In., 2 Piece	630.00
Cross, Enameled Geometric Design, Evangelist Medallion, Continental, 15 In.	920.00
Cup, Wine, Stems Unscrew To Compact For Travel, c.1780, 3 3/8 In.	105.00
Cuspidor, Bull Dog Cut Plug, Label, 10 In.	27.00
Desk Set, Virginia Creeper, Arts & Crafts, Marshall Field & Co. Craft Shop, 6 Piece	795.00
Dish, Cross, Adjustable Frame, Footed, 1740, 12 1/2 In.	460.00
Door Knocker, Eagle	75.00
Humidor, Cigar, Walnut, Brass Flush Handles, 9 x 9 x 12 In.	825.00
Kettle, Water, On Stand, c.1892	148.00
Lamp, Floor, Turkey Foot, Amber Hobnail Font, Shade, P. & A. Duplex Burner, 45 In.	165.00
Lamp, Table, Mask, Open Work Floral Design, Early 20th Century, 43 In., Pair	425.00
Mold, Bullet, Colt, .31 Caliber, Makes Ball & Conical Bullets	190.00
Mortar & Pestle, 3 Cast Masks, Ring Turned Pestle, 17th Century, 7 1/4 In.	275.00
Obelisk, Art Deco, 20 1/4 In., Pair	350.00
Patch Box, Inscribed JMB To ES, January 1st, 1820, England, 3 In.	500.00
Samovar, Double Spigot, Russia, 1880s, 18 x 13 In.	800.00
Shoehorn, 1770, 8 1/2 In.	90.00
Shoehorn, For An Infant, England, 1750-1780, 2 3/4 In.	295.00
Snuffer, Stand, England, c.1740, 7 1/2 In.	1350.00
Spill Holder, Dutch, 18th Century, 8 1/2 In.	150.00
Spill Holder, Irish Shamrocks, England, c.1850, 7 In.	145.00
Spill Holder, Scottish Thistles, England, c.1850, 7 1/2 In.	145.00
Stand, Umbrella, Hammered, Dutch Style	260.00
Sugar Caster, Regency, Pierced Dome Lid, Urn Finial, 1720, 10 In.	1955.00
Teakettle, Pad Feet, Turned Handle, Scotland, c.1810, 8 In.	235.00
Teakettle, Swing Handle, Stepped Lid, Incised Design At Spout, 18th Century, 10 In.	350.00
Teapot, Amber Glass Handle, 8 1/4 In.	155.00
Tinderbox, Hinged Lid, Unpolished, Iron Striker & Flint, 19th Century	350.00
Tool, Artillery, Gauge & Angle Finder, Revolutionary War, c.1735, 6 7/8 In.	835.00
Toothpick, Cherubs	110.00
Tray, Clarence Crafters, 3 1/2 In.	80.00
Tray, Desk, 2 Inkwells, Letter Rack, Footed	550.00
Tray, Ebonized Stand, Shell Cast Loop Handles, Rectangular, 19th Century, 21 1/2 In.	3220.00
Urn, Tulip, Russia, 18th Century, 7 x 11 In.	365.00
Wall Sconce, England, 1720-1760, 10 1/2 In.	2850.00
Whistle, Steam, 13 In.	425.00
Writing Kit, Hinged Lid, Attached Pen Compartment, 1780s, 7 1/2 In.	175.00

BRASTOFF, see Sascha Brastoff category.

BREAD PLATE, see various silver categories, porcelain factories, and pressed glass patterns.

BRIDE'S BASKETS OR BRIDE'S BOWLS were usually one-of-a-kind novelties made in American and European glass factories. They were especially popular about 1880 when the decorated basket was often given as a wedding gift. Cut glass baskets were popular after 1890. All bride's baskets lost favor about 1905. Bride's baskets and bride's bowls may also be found in other glass sections. Check the index at the back of the book.

BRIDE'S BASKET, Delaware, Rose Design, Silver Plated Frame, 5 1/2 x 3 1/2 In.	245.00
Flared Ribbed Bowl, Shades From Red To Cranberry To Custard, 11 1/2 x 14 In.	350.00
Gold Design Interior, Silver Plated Frame, Handle	125.00
Inverted Honeycomb Insert, Enamel Daisies, Silver Plated Frame, Child's	375.00
Pleated & Ruffled Insert, Deep Pink, Ornate Silver Frame	295.00
Pumpkin Color, Ruffled, Raised White Enamel Beading, Silver Plated Frame	795.00
Sapphire Blue Glass Insert, Reticulated Frame, 10 x 14 In.	450.00
Satin Glass, Gold Design, Scalloped, Ornate Silver Frame	490.00

Scalloped Bowl, Red & Opal Looping, Silver Plated Frame, 12 x 9 1/2 In.	247.00
Scalloped Bowl, Salmon Pink, Silver Holder	250.00
BRIDE'S BOWL, Cased Glass, Raspberry, Ruffled Rim, 7 1/2 In.	92.00
Enameled, Pink Flowers, Cream Overlay, Maroon, 3 1/4 In.	195.00
Herringbone Pattern, Pink, Yellow Interior, Yellow Chrysanthemums	2380.00
Maroon To Cream Overlay, Embossed Rim, Enameled Floral, 3 1/4 x 11 In.	195.00
Opaque Pink Glass, Ruffled Rim, 12 In.	35.00
Peachblow, Crystal Edging, Silver Base, Open Chain Links, 5 x 12 In.	165.00
Peachblow, Diamond-Quilted, Blue Edge, Crimped, Silver Plated Holder, 13 In.	385.00
Purple To Pale Overlay, Orchids, Satin Glass, 3 1/4 x 10 1/4 In.	295.00
Ruffled, Pink, Footed Frame	225.00
White Satin, Blue Satin Interior, Pleated Rim, Frosted Edge, 10 1/2 In.	250.00
Yellow Cased Glass, Lavender Edge, Gold Lacy Design, 4 x 10 In.	295.00

BRISTOL glass was made in Bristol, England, after the 1700s. The
Bristol glass most often seen today is a Victorian, lightweight opaque
glass that is often blue. Some of the glass was decorated with enamels.

Biscuit Jar, Silver Top, Rim & Handle, Opaque Turquoise, Barrel Shape, 6 1/2 In.	175.00
Charger, Floral Design, Delft Manganese Powder Ground, 1740, 13 In.	1550.00
Decanter, Enameled Flowers, Butterfly, Ruffled Stopper, 1880, 11 1/2 In.	115.00
Finger Bowl, Blue, Faceted Sides, 4 3/8 In., 8 Piece	480.00
Jar, Cover, Gray, Floral, 8 In.	135.00
Mug, Enameled Floral, 1860, 4 1/4 In.	61.00
Teapot, Egret Scene, Opaque Cream, 5 1/2 In.	295.00
Vase, 3 Cupids Encircled In Oval Design, 10 In.	120.00
Vase, Birds & Leaves, Hand Painted Design, Victorian, 11 In.	85.00
Vase, Birds On Fuchsia Flowers, White Ground, 13 3/4 In., Pair	862.00
Vase, Enamel Neoclassical Figural Design, Pinkish Tan Ground, 14 3/8 In., Pair	115.00
Vase, Floral, Turquoise, 10 1/2 x 4 In.	225.00
Vase, Garniture, Animal Design, Pink Gilt, 13 In., Pair	330.00
Vase, Gold Flowers, Cream, 10 In.	92.00
Vase, Multicolored Floral Swag & Butterfly, Gray Ground, Brass Mount, 11 3/4 In.	115.00
Vase, Painted Stork, Flaring Rim, Baluster Form, 12 1/2 In., Pair	70.00
Vase, Pink, White Enameled Flowers, Leaves, Footed, 11 In.	70.00
Vase, Polychrome Enamel Floral & Foliate, 12 3/4 In., Pair	37.50
Vase, Yellow Swirl, Ribbed Design, Bulbed Foot, F. Carder, 10 In.	201.00

BRITANNIA, see Pewter category.

BRONZE is an alloy of copper, tin, and other metals. It is used to make
figurines, lamps, and other decorative objects. Pieces listed here date
from the eighteenth, nineteenth, and twentieth centuries.

Ashtray, Figural, Owl, 5 3/4 x 3 7/8 In.	135.00
Ashtray, Floor Model, 3 Fluted Rods, Tiffany Studios, New York, 1658, 24 In.	400.00
Ashtray, Mack Bulldog, Metal, Central Die Casting & Mfg. Co., 4 1/2 In.	55.00
Ashtray, Tereszczuk, Young Boy Drinking From A Large Shell, 6 In.	230.00
Bookends, Hunter Shooting Rifle, Signed	155.00
Bowl, Cover, Lotus Form, Wooden, 8 In.	154.00
Bowl, Cover, Sorenson, Verdigris, 6 1/2 In.	90.00
Bowl, Raised Cylindrical Sides, T'Ang Dynasty, China, 6 In.	115.00
Bust, Chaudet, Napoleon Bonaparte, Dark Brown Patina, Stand, 13 1/4 In.	1150.00
Bust, Marshal, Rope Twist Border, Foliate Scrolls, France, 12 In.	8625.00
Bust, Minerva, Continental, 19th Century, 27 1/2 In.	1900.00
Bust, Napoleon, Double Breasted Overcoat, Olive-Brown Patina, 24 In.	1265.00
Bust, Neoclassical, Floral Decorated Hair, Socle Black Marble Base, 17 In., Pair	1030.00
Bust, Robert, Of Woman, Silver Over Bronze, Signed, Tiffany Co., 23 In.	2300.00
Bust, Roman Senator, Gilt Metal Socle, Mid 19th Century, 23 In.	6050.00
Cachepot, Pagoda & The Mountains, Lion's Head Handles, 9 3/4 In.	110.00
Cauldron, Iron Handle, Hoof Feet, 7 1/4 In.	1250.00
Censor, Cover, Stylized Characters, Birds, Flowers, Pierced Bird On Lid	1150.00
Door Knocker, 2 Putti Supporting Medici Shield, Scrolled Strapwork, Italy, 8 3/8 In. . . .	920.00
Ewer, Wine, Bacchic Putti, 22 In.	100.00
Figurine, Amodio, M., Philosopher, Robed, Standing, 14 In.	172.00

Figurine, Ball, Daniel Webster, 1853, 29 1/2 In. . . . . .2875.00 to 6500.00
Figurine, Barrias, Jeanne D'Arc, Full Suit Of Body Armor, Golden Brown Patina, 26 In. . 1035.00
Figurine, Barye, Antoine, Walking Tiger, Green Patina, 20th Century, 17 In. 1610.00
Figurine, Bear, Standing On Naturalistic Base, Russia, 21 1/2 In. 1150.00
Figurine, Bergman, Rooster, Naturalistic Tones, Cold Painted, c.1920, 4 3/4 In. 1035.00
Figurine, Bouret, Mother & Child, Medium Brown Patina, France, 19 1/2 In. 575.00
Figurine, Bouret, Nymph, 28 1/2 In. 2875.00
Figurine, Bouter, Children, 1 Laughing, 1 Crying, Marble Base, 8 1/2 In., Pair 1265.00
Figurine, Brenner, Motherhood, Signed, 2 3/4 In. 80.00
Figurine, Canonica, Elena D'Orleans, Duchess Of Aosta, c.1904, 14 1/2 In. 1840.00
Figurine, Capado, Prowling Panther, Green Patina, 19th Century, 30 In. 2875.00
Figurine, Charpentier, Joan Of Arc, Gilt & Silvered, 29 In. 4900.00
Figurine, Chevre, Boy, Breaking Up Cockfight, 28 In. 2800.00
Figurine, Classically Robed Figure, Leaning Forward On Pedestal, Green, Red, 14 In. . . . 345.00
Figurine, Cormier, Kneeling Nude Maiden, 17 1/8 In. 4600.00
Figurine, Coulon, Crusader, Ivory Tipped Lance, 22 In. 6600.00
Figurine, Crab, Articulated, Meiji, Japan, 5 In. 1495.00
Figurine, Cupids, Rockwork Base, Continental, 22 In., Pair 1955.00
Figurine, Debut, Fisherwoman, 43 In. 1500.00
Figurine, Devrier, Dancing Faun, Cymbals, Concertina, Late 19th Century, 23 In. 2300.00
Figurine, Duret, Neapolitan Dancers, 22 In., Pair 5500.00
Figurine, Eagle, Upswept Wings, Claws Extended To Catch Prey, Wood Stand, 11 In. . . . 80.00
Figurine, Eriksen, Little Mermaid, Seated On Large Rock, Signed, 9 1/2 In. 2645.00
Figurine, Faguays, Nude Study, c.1925, 30 3/4 In. 5750.00
Figurine, Fat Comic Man On Donkey, 10 3/4 In. 360.50
Figurine, Feuchere, Muse, Standing, 16 1/4 In. 600.00
Figurine, Focht, Spirit Of Flight, Green, Brown Patina, 1919, 30 1/4 In. 6325.00
Figurine, Frishmuth, Harriet Whitney, Standing Nude Female, 12 In. 5175.00
Figurine, Gaudez, Armoursmith, 25 In. 2970.00
Figurine, Gaudez, Woman, Playing A Mandolin, Signed, 27 In. 1035.00
Figurine, Gerdago, Dancer, Ivory Face & Hands, 16 In. 5750.00
Figurine, Girl, With Birds, Marble Base, 5 In. 400.00
Figurine, Good Fairy, 1916, 11 1/2 In. 245.00
Figurine, Gori, Dancer, 24 1/2 In. 2760.00
Figurine, Gornik, Aquarium, Wrought Iron, Marble, Glass, 4 Ft. 11 In. 7475.00
Figurine, Gregoire, Captivity, Signed, 26 1/2 In. 690.00
Figurine, Guiraud-Riviere, Maiden, Carved Ivory, Gilt, 1881, 16 1/4 In. 7475.00
Figurine, Hanbury, Polo Player, On Lucite, Signed, 12 1/4 x 21 1/2 In. 172.00
Figurine, Hercules, Acanthus Leaves, Quatrefoil, Ormolu Base, 16 1/2 In. 4600.00
Figurine, Herzel, Arabian, On Rearing Horse, On Plaster, Signed, 11 In. 250.00
Figurine, Himmelstoss, Pearl Gatherer, Signed, Dated 1903, 12 1/2 In. 750.00
Figurine, Japan, Small Boy With Dog, 32 1/2 In. 1840.00
Figurine, Ladd, Naked Boy, Sitting, 18 1/2 In. 1595.00
Figurine, Lanceray, Bear, Standing, Oval Green Marble Base, 19th Century, 23 In. 6900.00
Figurine, Lanceray, Warrior On Horseback, 21 In. 5175.00
Figurine, Larche, Young Woman, Standing Barefoot, Medium Brown Patina, 12 In. 1955.00
Figurine, Laurent, Nymph, Kneeling, Holding Lamp, 9 In. 230.00
Figurine, Lavasseur, Standing Woman, Golden Patina, 1853, 34 In. 4600.00
Figurine, Le Normand, French Peasant Digging Soil, Wooden Shoes, 14 In. 315.00
Figurine, Lecourtier, Chained Mastiff, 1878, 17 In. 2645.00
Figurine, Levy, Faneur, 31 In. 2700.00
Figurine, Lion, Raised On Black Marble Stepped Plinth, 6 In. 2185.00
Figurine, Marochetti, Mounted Cavalier, No. 13, Brown Patina, 40 In. 9200.00
Figurine, Mene, Browsing Stag, 14 1/2 In. 2530.00
Figurine, Montagne, Young Hermes, Medium Brown Patina, France, 18 In. 4600.00
Figurine, Moreau, Winged Cherub, Hands To Mouth, Flowers At Feet, 26 In. 4025.00
Figurine, Obelisk, 11 1/2 In. 315.00
Figurine, Oury, Faun & Goat, Dark Brown Patina, 26 In. 1725.00
Figurine, Pandiani, Hunter, 20 In. 2300.00
Figurine, Peddler, Looks To His Right, Pack On Back, Italy, 17th Century, 4 3/4 In. 9200.00
Figurine, Peynot, Woman With Doves, Marble Base, 38 In. 2630.00
Figurine, Picault, Woman, With Raised Arm, Signed, 37 In. 3795.00

Figurine, Puech, Mermaid, Green Veined Marble Base, 19 In. 5450.00
Figurine, Ricci, Man's Head, 13 1/2 In. 165.00
Figurine, Rodin, Le Penseur, Cast After Model By Rodin, Barbedienne, Foundry, 32 In. . . 3450.00
Figurine, Sicard, Angel, Holding Sword & Flower, Gilt, Marble & Bronze Base, 17 In. . . . 690.00
Figurine, Verschneider, Gold Apples, 22 1/2 In. 1955.00
Figurine, Vienna, Donkey, Standing, Cold Painted, Brown Tones 1265.00
Figurine, Vonnoh, Nude Young Woman, Marble Base, 21 1/4 In. 8625.00
Figurine, Whistling Boy, Straw Hat, Barefooted, Hands In Pockets, 12 In. 245.00
Figurine, Woman, Dancer, Art Nouveau, France, 1901 . . . . 475.00
Figurine, Woman, Donning Her Tunic, Standing By Gnarled Tree Trunk, 23 5/8 In. 920.00
Figurine, Zach, Erotic Nymph, Signed, 6 3/4 In. 1495.00
Figurine, Zach, Snake Charmer, 20 In. 4600.00
Finial, Eagle, Spread Winged, Pedestal, Marble Base, Continental, 19th Century, 4 In. . . . 460.00
Group, Barye, Antoine, Lion Overcoming Antelope, Bronze, Green, Black Patina 920.00
Group, Belleophone, Taming Pegasus, 19th Century, 9 1/2 In. 140.00
Group, Chiparus, Ballet Dancer, Ivory, Gilt, 18 1/4 In. 9775.00
Group, Chiparus, Young Woman Standing With 2 Borzois At Side, 1925, 25 In. 6900.00
Group, Clodion, Bacchic Nymphs, Young Satyr, 22 In. 1955.00
Group, Clodion, Nymph & Child Satyr, 22 In. 2587.00
Group, Clodion, Woman, With Grapes & Satyr, Dark Brown Patina, Signed, 23 In. 2300.00
Group, Dubray, Napoleon, On Horseback, c.1880, 28 In. 8950.00
Group, Dubucand, Donkey & Tender, Signed, 13 x 13 In. 1085.00
Group, Hay Wagon, Horse Drawn, With Workers, Marble Base, Austria 3500.00
Group, King, Acrobats, Base, 16 3/4 In. 180.00
Group, Lanceray, Equestrian Group, 17 In. 4300.00
Group, Lund, 2 Choir Children, Wooden Base, 19 In. 1955.00
Group, Male, Female Figures, Seated On Bench Rolling Yarn, France, 6 x 6 1/2 In. 863.00
Group, Muller, Falconer Astride Rearing Horse, Marble Base, 17 1/2 In. 750.00
Group, Pautrot, Hounds With Game, Pair 4025.00
Group, Rauch, Man, Tricornered Hat, 2 Dogs, Black Marble Base, Painted, 12 In. 190.00
Head, Classical, Winged 1 Side, Verdigris Patina, 12 In. 515.00
Incense Burner, Cockatoo Shape, 19th Century, 22 1/2 In. 220.00
Incense Burner, Sage Riding A Mule, Black, Brown Patina, 5 1/4 In. 120.00
Jardiniere, Incised Dragon In Cloud Design, 11 In. 176.00
Jardiniere, Mermaid With Floral Swags, Gadrooned Border, France, 21 In. 2400.00
Jardiniere, Putti Surrounding Porcelain Cartouche, Floral Swags, France, 32 In. 5500.00
Jardiniere, Relief Bird, Floral Design, Meiji Period, 11 In. 154.00
Lamp, Semiclad Female Bearing Basket Of Fruit, Austria, 1910, 30 In. 4025.00
Lamp, Tereszczuk, Young Woman Crouching, Filling A Jar, Ivory, 13 In. 2185.00
Lamp, Water Lily, Mushroom Cap Shade, Applied Pond Lilies, 22 In. 1265.00
Mirror, Bach, Hammered, Arched Frame, Flower Filled Urn, 56 In. 2875.00
Mirror, Bach, Stylized Foliage, Frame, 1925, 26 3/4 In. 1725.00
Mirror, Crane, Pine, Calligraphy, Japan, 8 In. 50.00
Mortar, Band Of Cherubim Suspending Swags Of Drapery, France, 6 3/4 In. 805.00
Obelisk, Cleopatra's Needle, c.1900, 24 1/4 In. 1610.00
Paperweight, Figural, Man, Edison Co., 40 Years Of Service, 1882-1922, 4 3/4 In. 100.00
Pedestal, Putti Center Panel, Marble Top, Scrolled Legs, 4 Ft. 2 In. 4025.00
Planter, Floral, Cartouche Form, Raised On Feet, Gilt, France, Oval, 16 In. 950.00
Plaque, Dalou, Avenging Spirit, Brown Patina 5520.00
Sconce, Bach, Raised On Torch Form Support, Scrolled Foliage, 20 1/2 In. 3162.00
Sundial, Patina, England, 19th Century, 15 In. Diam. 3750.00
Tazza, Grand Tour, 3 Levels Of Existence, 19th Century, 8 1/2 x 12 3/4 In. 786.00
Teapot, Square Handle, China, 18th Century, 6 3/4 In. 275.00
Tray, Leaf & Berry Design, Arts & Crafts, Carence Crafters, 5 1/2 In. 143.00
Urn, Neoclassical, 2 Intertwined Maidens, Early 20th Century, 13 In., Pair 150.00
Urn, Relief Dragon, Tortoise Design, 1892, 26 1/2 In. 770.00
Vase, Aesthetic Movement Style, 2 Large Dragonfly Handles, Seal Mark, 8 In. 546.00
Vase, Amphora, Neoclassical Design Around Frieze, 21 1/2 In., Pair 3450.00
Vase, Baluster, Gilt Sun Spot Design, 4 Ring Handles, 18th Century, 9 1/2 In. 1815.00
Vase, Baluster, Lotus Design, Full Relief Dragon At Foot, 17 1/2 In. 1760.00
Vase, Bird, Dragon Design, Japan, 9 5/8 In. 154.00
Vase, Bird, Flower Design, Inlay, 4 1/2 In., Pair 220.00

Vase, Bird, Flying Among Branches, Concave Body, Brown Ground, Japan, 11 3/4 In. 201.00
Vase, Carp In Relief, Flared Rim, Footed, 20th Century, Japan, 15 1/2 In. 747.50
Vase, Cloud Form, Relief Kylin, Water Buffalo, Pig Design, 7 1/2 In. 2673.00
Vase, Club Shape, Relief Dragons On Neck, Lotus Petals At Base, Black, 14 In., Pair ... 825.00
Vase, Inlaid Bird Design, 19th Century, 15 In. 363.00
Vase, Inverted Pear Shape, Shakudo Dragon, Red Cloud Design, Body, 9 1/2 In. 825.00
Vase, Ledru, Nude Woman, Looking Into Nautilus Shell, Art Nouveau, 12 In. 1955.00
Vase, Mount Fuji Scene, 12 In. 209.00
Vase, Raised Bosses About The Body, Dragon Handles, 13 1/2 In. 181.50
Vase, Relief Bird, Floral Design, Meiji Period, 10 In., Pair 385.00
Vase, Relief Iris Design Feet, 3 Footed, Globular, Late 19th Century, 10 3/4 In. 220.00
Vase, Seed Shape, Dragon Handles, Black Patina, Signed, 19th Century, 12 In. 360.00
Vase, Silver Floral Design, Marked, Smaco, 9 3/4 In. 175.00
Vase, Teardrop Shape, Relief Phoenix Design, Signed, Meiji Period, 11 In. 470.00
Vase, Tree Stump Form, 18th Century, 5 1/4 In. 85.00
Vase, Trumpet Form, Floral Design, Meiji Period, 4 3/4 In. 120.00

BROWNIES were first drawn in 1883 by Palmer Cox. They are charac-
terized by large round eyes, downturned mouths, and skinny legs.
Toys, books, dinnerware, and other objects were made with the
Brownies as part of the design.

Card, Advertising, Dixon's Stove Polish, Palmer Cox Brownies, 1888, 5 x 3 1/2 In. 55.00
Creamer, Palmer Cox 75.00
Cup & Saucer, Brownies Playing Tug-O-War 95.00
Dish, 2 Brownies Walking With Golf Clubs 95.00
Dish, Palmer Cox, c.1900, 4 In. 45.00
Doll, Cap, Jacket, Vest, Molded, Painted Face, Jointed, Papier-Mache, 9 In. 450.00
Game, 10 Pins, Lithograph, Paper-On-Cardboard, McLoughlin Bros., c.1893 .... 1150.00
Game, Ring Toss, Lithographed Box, M.H. Miller, c.1920 .... 150.00
Game, Ten Pins, Palmer Cox 1150.00
Label, Crate, Pictures Palmer Cox Brownies, 1930s, 10 x 12 In. 14.00
Needle Case, 1893 World's Fair, Paper 35.00
Plate, Limoges, 9 In. 245.00

BRUSH Pottery was started in 1925. George Brush first worked in 1901
in Zanesville, Ohio. He started his own pottery in 1907, but it burned
to the ground and he joined McCoy in 1909. After a series of name
changes, the company became The Brush Pottery. It closed in 1982.
Collectors favor the figural cookie jars made by this company.

Cookie Jar, Cinderella's Pumpkin Coach .... .250.00 to 495.00
Cookie Jar, Circus Horse 675.00
Cookie Jar, Clock .... .125.00 to 150.00
Cookie Jar, Clown Bust .... .350.00 to 450.00
Cookie Jar, Clown, Brown Pants .... .225.00 to 235.00
Cookie Jar, Covered Wagon 750.00
Cookie Jar, Cow, Brown 1200.00
Cookie Jar, Cow, Purple .... .1200.00 to 1500.00
Cookie Jar, Crock With Praying Girl 75.00
Cookie Jar, Donkey With Cart, Brown .... .275.00 to 525.00
Cookie Jar, Donkey With Cart, Gray .... .425.00 to 625.00
Cookie Jar, Elephant .... .425.00 to 675.00
Cookie Jar, Formal Pig, Black Coat, Blue Vest .... .275.00 to 375.00
Cookie Jar, Gas Lamp 65.00
Cookie Jar, Granny 475.00
Cookie Jar, Happy Bunny Light 250.00
Cookie Jar, Hillbilly Frog 4200.00
Cookie Jar, House .... .135.00 to 175.00
Cookie Jar, Humpty Dumpty, Cowboy Hat .... .150.00 to 275.00
Cookie Jar, Little Boy Blue 925.00
Cookie Jar, Little Red Riding Hood .... .495.00 to 785.00
Cookie Jar, Old Shoe 140.00
Cookie Jar, Panda, Black & White 395.00

Cookie Jar, Peter Pan . . . . .650.00 to 700.00
Cookie Jar, Praying Girl, Pink 50.00
Cookie Jar, Pumpkin 135.00
Cookie Jar, Puppy Police . . . . .550.00 to 625.00
Cookie Jar, Raggedy Ann 300.00
Cookie Jar, Squirrel On Log 120.00
Cookie Jar, Squirrel With Top Hat . . . . .350.00 to 495.00
Cookie Jar, Stylized Owl . . . . .175.00 to 325.00
Cookie Jar, Teddy Bear . . . . .250.00 to 425.00
Cookie Jar, Teddy Bear, Feet Together . . . . .95.00 to 185.00
Cookie Jar, Touring Car . . . . .1300.00 to 1400.00
Cookie Jar, Treasure Chest 325.00
Figurine, Frog, 4 In. 30.00
Figurine, Frog, Reclining, 10 In. 65.00
Flower Frog, Sitting Up, 8 In. 100.00
Jardiniere, Amaryllis, Green, Pink, 6 In. 75.00
Jardiniere, Cobalt Blue, Orange, Green Floral Around Shoulder, 5 1/4 x 6 1/4 In. 75.00
Mug, Peter Pan 95.00
Planter, Boat 45.00
Planter, Raccoon, On Log 25.00
Planter, Squirrel, On Log 35.00
Vase, Blue Onyx, Art Vellum, 6 In., Pair 100.00
Vase, Brown Onyx, 6 In. 25.00
Vase, Green, Free Form, 10 x 6 In. 20.00
Vase, Zuniart, 4 In. 350.00
Wall Pocket, Fish . . . . .75.00 to 95.00
Wall Pocket, Roman, Green 145.00

BRUSH MCCOY, see McCoy category.

BUCK ROGERS was the first American science fiction comic strip. It started in 1929 and continued until 1965. Buck has also appeared in comic books, movies, and, in the 1980s, a television series. Any memorabilia connected with the character Buck Rogers is collectible.

Ad, Firecraft Kits, Colorful 20.00
Badge, Solar Scout Chief, Shield Shape, Pinback, 1934, 1 In. 385.00
Badge, Solar Scouts Member, Spaceship, Brass, Cream Of Wheat, 1935 . . . . 85.00
Book, Big Little Book, Buck Rogers & Doom Comet 60.00
Book, Big Little Book, Buck Rogers & The Depth-Men Of Jupiter, 1935 . . . . 65.00
Book, Big Little Book, Buck Rogers 25th Century, Coco Malt 45.00
Book, Pop-Up, Strange Adventures In Spider Ship, 1935, 8 x 9 In. 325.00
Box, Pencil, American Pencil Co., 1935 . . . . 100.00
Bucket, Halloween Candy, Plastic 40.00
Button, Solar Scout, Buck Holding 2 Ray Guns, Gold Colored, 1 1/4 In. 90.00
Casting Mold Set, 1935, 3 x 5 In. 350.00
Doll, Ardella, In The 25th Century, Original Bubble Pack, Mego Corp., 1979, 4 In. 40.00
Doll, Draco, In The 25th Century, Original Bubble Pack, Mego Corp., 1979, 4 In. 25.00
Doll, Mego, Box, 1970s, 12 In. . . . . .25.00 to 65.00
Gun, Atomic Pistol, Pops & Sparks, Box 655.00
Gun, Atomic, Gold, Sparking, Daisy, 1946 . . . . 150.00
Lunch Box, Thermos, Metal, 1979 . . . . .65.00 to 125.00
Pistol, Atomic, Daisy, 1930s . . . . .130.00 to 150.00
Puzzle, Frame, Space Station, John F. Dille Co., Milton Bradley, 1952 . . . . 100.00
Ring, Ring Of Saturn, Red Stone, Glow-In-The-Dark Crocodile Base, 1940s 750.00
Rocket Pistol Pop Gun, Model X-Z 31, Daisy, Pressed Steel, 1934, 10 In. 375.00
Rocket Ship, Windup, Marx, 1934 . . . . 425.00
Sonic Ray Gun, Signal Flashlight, Instructions.1950s 160.00
Space Ranger Kit, Unopened Envelope, All Pieces, Sylvania, 1952 . . . . 325.00
Space Ship, Windup, Painted, Marx 100.00
Toy, Robot, Twiki, Plastic, Box 60.00
Walkie-Talkie Set, Box, 1950s 195.00
Water Pistol, Liquid Helium, Daisy, Popsicle Premium, 1936, 7 1/2 In. 450.00

Always wash antique china in a sink lined with a rubber mat or towels. This helps prevent chipping. Wash one piece at a time. Rinse and let it air dry. If you suspect a piece has been repaired, do not wash it. Clean with a soft brush dampened in a solution of ammonia and water.

Buffalo Pottery Deldare, Pitcher, Dr. Syntax, Setting Out To Lakes, 1911, 8 3/4 In.

BUFFALO POTTERY was made in Buffalo, New York, after 1902. The company was established by the Larkin Company, famous manufacturers of soap. The wares are marked with a picture of a buffalo and the date of manufacture. Deldare ware is the most famous pottery made at the factory. It has khaki-colored or green background with hand painted transfer designs.

BUFFALO POTTERY, Dish, Feeding, Campbell Kids 80.00
Pitcher, Pilgrim, 9 In. 185.00
Pitcher, Pilgrim, Miles Standish, John Alden On Sides, 1908, 9 In. 880.00
Pitcher, Roosevelt Bears, Whimsical Scene, 5 In. 330.00
Pitcher, Sailor, 9 1/4 In. 495.00
Plate, Christmas, 1953 .... 55.00
Plate, Mallard Duck, 10 In. 55.00
Plate, Morgan's Red Coach Tavern, Rougeware, 11 1/2 In. 495.00
Plate, Windmill & Boat Scene, Albino, 1912, 10 In. 495.00
Platter, Buck & Deer, Gold Rim, Marked, 11 x 15 In. 60.00
Platter, Buffalo Hunting, 11 x 15 In. 300.00
Tile, Trivet, Little Boy Blue Come Blow Your Horn, 6 1/4 In. 120.00
Trivet, Hunting Scene 160.00
Trivet, Tea, Breaking Cover 425.00
BUFFALO POTTERY DELDARE, Bowl, Cereal, Ye Olden Days, 1908, 6 In. 275.00
Bowl, Fruit, Ye Village Tavern, 1908, 9 In. 355.00
Bowl, Vegetable, Village Scene, Oval, 1909, 1 x 8 In. 880.00
Candlestick, Town Scenes, Signed, 1925, 9 1/4 In., Pair 520.00
Charger, An Evening At Ye Lion Inn, Figural Design, 13 3/4 In. 282.00
Chop Plate, An Evening At Ye Lion Inn, 1908, 14 In. .... 280.00 to 550.00
Chop Plate, Fallowfield Hunt, The Start, 1908, 14 In. .... 770.00 to 795.00
Creamer, Dr. Syntax, With The Dairy Maid, 1911, 3 In. 165.00
Creamer, Fallowfield Hunt, Breaking Cover, 1908, 2 1/2 In. 330.00
Creamer, Scenes Of Village Life In Ye Olden Days, 1925, 2 3/4 In. 220.00
Cup & Saucer, Chocolate, Ye Village Street, 1909, 3 In. 660.00
Cup & Saucer, Tea, Ye Olden Days, 1909, 2 In. 220.00
Humidor, Ye Lion Inn, Dome Cover, 7 In. 1210.00
Jug, Mason, 1907, 8 1/4 In. 1465.00
Jug, Whaling City, 1907, 6 In. 785.00
Mug, At Three Pigeons, Tankard Style, 1909, 4 1/2 In. .... 275.00 to 550.00
Mug, Fallowfield Hunt, Breaking Cover, 1909 .... 225.00
Mug, Lion Inn, 4 1/2 In. .... 295.00 to 325.00
Pin Tray, Ye Olden Days, Village Scene Border, 6 1/2 x 3 1/2 In. 385.00
Pitcher, Dr. Syntax, Setting Out To Lakes, 1911, 8 3/4 In. ....*Illus* 2475.00

Pitcher, Fallowfield Hunt, Octagonal, 6 In. ....475.00 to 675.00
Pitcher, Fallowfield Hunt, Return, 1909, 8 In. 625.00
Pitcher, Telling Stories, 1923, 6 In. 412.00
Pitcher, The Great Controversy, 12 1/2 In.. .... 1100.00
Pitcher, Their Manor, 6 In. 595.00
Pitcher, To Demand Rent, 8 In. 750.00
Pitcher, Ye Lion Inn, Octagonal, 1908, 9 In. ....750.00 to 1035.00
Plate, An Evening At Ye Lion Inn, 13 3/4 In. 675.00
Plate, At Ye Lion Inn, Interior Scene At Inn, 6 1/4 In. 110.00
Plate, Fallowfield Hunt, The Start, 1908, 9 1/2 In. ....170.00 to 220.00
Plate, Misfortune At Tulip Hall, Signed, 8 1/2 In. 550.00
Plate, Ye Olden Times, 9 1/2 In. 400.00
Plate, Ye Village Street, Village Scene, 1908, 7 1/4 In. 140.00
Sugar, Ye Olden Days, Scenes Of Village Life, 3 In. 300.00
Tankard, Fallowfield Hunt, Hunt Supper, Logo, 1908, 12 1/4 In. 2475.00
Tankard, Ye Lion Inn, 12 1/4 In. 1200.00
Tankard Set, 3 Fallowfield Hunt Scene, Ye Lion Inn, 7 Piece 2400.00
Teapot, Ye Olden Days, Village Life, 6 Sides, 4 In. 550.00
Tray, Calling Card, Ye Lion Inn, Logo, 1909, 7 In. ....330.00 to 550.00
Tray, Card, Ye Lion Inn, 9 In. 210.00
Vase, King Fisher, Green, White, Olive Ground, Signed, 7 3/4 In. 1380.00
Vase, Stylized Foliate, Green, White, Olive Ground, 8 1/2 In. 805.00

BURMESE GLASS was developed by Frederick Shirley at the Mt.
Washington Glass Works in New Bedford, Massachusetts, in 1885. It
is a two-toned glass, shading from peach to yellow. Some pieces have
a pattern mold design. A few Burmese pieces were decorated with pictures or applied glass flowers of colored Burmese glass. Other factories made similar glass also called *Burmese*. Related items may be listed in the Fenton category, the Gunderson category, and under Webb
Burmese.

Berry Bowl, Diamond-Quilted, Mt. Washington, 1880s, 6 1/4 In. 225.00
Berry Bowl, Salmon To Bright Yellow, Ruffled, Mt. Washington, 9 In. 950.00
Biscuit Jar, Floral Cover, Pink Enameled Flowers, Mt. Washington, 6 1/2 In. 440.00
Bowl, Crimped Edge, Mt. Washington, 2 3/4 x 5 3/4 In. 250.00
Bowl, Ruffled, Mt. Washington, 9 In. 350.00
Bowl, Ruffled, Shell Footed, Mt. Washington, 7 1/4 x 6 In. 1500.00
Bowl, Scalloped, 2 1/2 x 4 3/4 In. 220.00
Creamer, 4-Fold Rim, Raspberry Pontil, Mt. Washington, 3 1/2 In. 770.00
Creamer, Tankard, Crimped, Mt. Washington, 5 1/2 In. 495.00
Cruet, Melon Ribbed, Mushroom Stopper, 6 3/4 In. 1085.00
Cruet, Mt. Washington 1100.00
Cruet, Salmon To Yellow, Blown Stopper, Mt. Washington 375.00
Epergne, Single, Fuchsia Flowers, 10 In. 165.00
Lamp, Fairy, Matching Underplate, Mt. Washington 325.00
Lamp, Pillar, Daybreak, 33 In. 550.00
Muffineer, Ostrich Egg, Arrow Form Lid, Mt. Washington, 4 In. 355.00
Mustard, Vertical Ribbed, Bail, Hinged Lid, 4 1/2 In. 375.00
Pickle Jar, Melon Ribbed, Enameled Flowers, Ornate Holder & Tongs, Barbour Bros. ... 770.00
Pitcher, Lemonade, Enameled Flowers & Hummingbirds ....*Illus* 605.00
Plate, Satin Finish, Gundersen, 9 In. 650.00
Rose Bowl, Crimped Top 100.00
Rose Jar, Cover, Allover Floral Sprays, Mt. Washington, 1880s, 4 1/4 In. 2250.00
Salt & Pepper, Holder, Pillar, Ribbed, Forget-Me-Nots, Mt. Washington 295.00
Salt & Pepper, Painted Flowers, Pairpoint Holder, Mt. Washington 300.00
Salt & Pepper, Ribbed, Silver Plated Holder, Mt. Washington, 2 In. 467.00
Sugar Shaker, Tomato, Silver Plated Cover, Mt. Washington, 3 x 3 1/2 In. 595.00
Toothpick, Blue Forget-Me-Nots, Mt. Washington, 2 7/8 In. 585.00
Toothpick, Diamond-Quilted, 2 5/8 In. 385.00
Toothpick, Diamond-Quilted, Squared Rim, Bulbous, 2 1/2 In. 330.00
Toothpick, Melon Ribbed, Alternating Bark Design, Enameled Flowers, 1 3/4 In. ... 825.00
Toothpick, Optic Diamond-Quilted, Mt. Washington, 2 1/2 In. 585.00
Toothpick, Tricornered, Mt. Washington, 2 In. 220.00

Remove stains from dishes with hydrogen peroxide or bicarbonate of soda, not with bleach, which was the suggested way years ago. The bleach may damage the finish.

Burmese, Pitcher, Lemonade, Enameled
Flowers & Hummingbirds

Tumbler, Diamond-Quilted, Lemonade, Low Loop Handle, 4 3/4 In.	575.00
Tumbler, Enameled Ivy Leaves & Vines, Mt. Washington, 3 3/4 In.	395.00
Tumbler, Mt. Washington, 3 3/4 In.	150.00 to 250.00
Tumbler, Yellow Roses, Mt. Washington, 3 3/4 In.	465.00
Urn, Crimped Foot, Mouth, 4 3/4 In.	143.00
Vase, Bamboo, Salmon To Yellow, Mt. Washington, 1880s, 11 1/2 In.	1875.00
Vase, Bulbous, Enameled Daisy Design, Mt. Washington, 3 x 3 1/2 In.	850.00
Vase, Bulbous, Mt. Washington, 1880s, 6 In.	350.00
Vase, Double Gourd Shape, Peach Colored Roses, Turquoise, 8 In.	1250.00
Vase, Double Gourd Shape, Roses & Turquoise Forget-Me-Nots, 8 In.	1250.00
Vase, Enameled Flowers, 6 In.	440.00
Vase, Enameled Flowers, 9 1/4 In.	1955.00
Vase, Enameled Flowers, Conical Form, 7 7/8 In.	402.00
Vase, Ginkgo Design, 2 Handles, Footed, 6 1/2 In., Pair	2100.00
Vase, Gourd, Mt. Washington, 5 1/4 In.	750.00
Vase, Jack-In-The Pulpit, Matte Finish, 13 3/8 In.	517.00
Vase, Jack-In-The-Pulpit, Mt. Washington, 13 In.	785.00
Vase, Jack-In-The-Pulpit, Pink To Yellow, Mt. Washington, 1880s, 15 In.	950.00
Vase, Lily, Deep Color, Mt. Washington, 12 3/4 In.	875.00
Vase, Lily, Matte, Mt. Washington, 6 x 3 In.	550.00
Vase, Lily, Mt. Washington, 23 1/2 In.	1250.00
Vase, Lily, Trumpet Form, Pink, Yellow Acid Finish, Mt. Washington, 12 1/2 In.	230.00
Vase, Melon Ribbed, Enameled Flowers, Brown Leaves, 2 1/4 In.	385.00
Vase, Pyramids, Sacred Ibis, Desert Oasis, Drilled For Lamp, 12 In.	2750.00
Vase, Stick, Enameled Floral, Bulbous, Mt. Washington, 1880s, 12 x 7 In.	3950.00
Vase, Top Flared, 6 In.	575.00
Vase, Tricornered Rim, Disc Base, Mt. Washington, 14 In.	825.00
Water Set, Egyptian, Square Handle, Mt. Washington, 1880s, 7 Piece	2250.00

BUSTER BROWN, the comic strip, first appeared in color in 1902.
Buster and his dog ,Tige, remained a popular comic and soon became
even more famous as the emblem for a shoe company, a textile firm,
and others. The strip was discontinued in 1920, but some of the advertising is still in use.

Bandanna, Orange, Green & White, Pictures TV Gang	90.00
Bank, Good Luck, Buster Brown, Horse, Horseshoe & Tige, Iron, 4 1/4 In.	150.00
Bazooka, Tin	65.00
Bill Hook	25.00
Book, Coloring, Pair	30.00
Book, Jolly Times, Buster Brown & Tige, R.F. Outcault, 30 Pages, c.1906	155.00
Bowl, Child's, Stop Smiling For Heaven's Sake, Come With Me	535.00
Button, Buster Brown & Tige, Advertising Shoes, Tin, 1900s	29.00
Button, Buster Brown Shoes, Buster & Tige	35.00
Cup & Saucer, Buster Brown Pouring Tea For Tige, Pottery	120.00
Felt Slippers, Tige	45.00
Game, Pin The Bow On Buster Brown, 10 Bows, Box	245.00 to 325.00

Hat, Child's, Wide Brimmed, Early 1900s, 11 1/2 In.	130.00
Hose Supporter, Tige, I Know It, Buster, 1920s	28.00
Kite, Buster Brown Shoes, Paper, 1940s	38.00
Periscope, Jiffy Kangaroo	15.00 to 18.00
Plate, Child's, Buster Brown & Tige, Gold Letters, c.1910, 7 1/4 In.	85.00
Postcard, Photograph	25.00
Postcard, Promotional, 1950s	4.00
Shoes, Buster Wearing White Hat Brim, Red Shoes, 1900s	85.00
Shoes, Tige & Buster Brown As Musician & Singer, Black Letters, 1930s	10.00
Sign, Buster Brown & Tige Bread, 28 x 22 In.	695.00
Sign, Hanging, Cellophane Over Pressed Board, Buster Brown & Tige, 1970s	75.00
Stretcher, Shoe, Green Plastic, 1940s, Pair	30.00
Watch, Buster Brown Shoes, Nickel Plate, U.S., Pocket, 1930s	488.00
Whistle, Tin, 1930s	45.00
Window Display, Figure Of Child Throwing Bone To Tige	325.00

BUTTER CHIPS, or butter pats, were small individual dishes for butter. They were the height of fashion from 1880 to 1910. Earlier as well as later examples are known.

Flowers, Limoges	15.00
Gold Trim	12.00
Ironstone, White, Wheat	20.00
Majolica, Each Different, 5 Piece	250.00

BUTTER MOLDS are listed in the Kitchen category under Mold, Butter.

BUTTON collecting has been popular since the nineteenth century. Buttons have been known throughout the centuries, and there are millions of styles. Gold, silver, or precious stones were used for the best buttons, but most were made of natural materials, like bone or shell, or from inexpensive metals. Only a few types are listed for comparison.

Chanel, Suit Set	24.00
Man's Blazer, Golfers In Knickers, 9 Piece	42.00
Mosaic, Tourist Scene, Corded Wire Bezel, 18K Gold, 10 Piece	1265.00
Virginia State Seal, Brass	135.00

BUTTONHOOKS have been a popular collectible in England for many years but only recently have gained the attention of American collectors. The buttonhooks were made to help fasten the many buttons of the old-fashioned high-button shoes and other items of apparel.

Bakelite, Green	35.00
Nude Mermaid	95.00
Sterling Silver, Nouveau, Woman's Face, 7 In.	45.00

CALENDARS made to hang on the wall or to be displayed on a desk top have been popular since the last quarter of the nineteenth century. Many were printed with advertising as part of the artwork and were given away as premiums. Calendars with guns, gunpowder, or Coca-Cola advertising are most prized.

1889, Clark's Spool Cotton, Full Pad	25.00
1894, Hood's Sarsaparilla, Beautiful Woman, Bonnet	80.00
1895, Hood's Sarsaparilla, 2 Little Girls, Full Pad	70.00
1898, Whittier, Die Cut, 3 Sheets	35.00
1899, John Belden Clothes	25.00
1901, Quaker Oats, American Cereal Co., 5 3/4 x 5 3/4 In.	750.00
1901, Swift's American Girl, Paper Lithograph, 15 x 32 In.	77.00
1903, Crosby & Buchanan Traver, Best Wishes, Frame, 30 x 26 In.	770.00
1903, Yale, Sports Illustrated	60.00
1906, Deering Cream Separators, Beautiful Woman	475.00
1906, National Stoves & Ranges, Child With Puppy, 9 3/4 x 13 In.	145.00
1906-1907, Wales Goodyear Rubbers, Woman, 9 1/2 x 11 In.	250.00
1907, January, Capewell Horse Nails, J. Kanerder & Shop, Canada, Matted, Frame	150.00
1907, Raphael Tuck, God Will Provide, Die Cut	35.00

1908, Yuengling & Son Brewery, Lithograph, Frame, 22 x 17 In. 175.00
1909, Pacific Brewing 195.00
1910, Easter Morning, F. Earl Christy, Unused 15.00
1910, Kelly's Famous Flour, Frame, 26 x 21 In. 430.00
1913, Diamond Salt Company, Lady Wrapped In Fox Stole, Bouquet 550.00
1914, Corticelli Thread Co., Desk Top, Die Cut, 5 1/2 In. 34.00
1914, Westinghouse Mazda, Woman 650.00
1915, Bromo-Seltzer, Booklet, Note Pad, 4 1/2 x 3 In. 8.00
1918, Hercules Powder Co., Not This Trip, Old Pal Band, 29 1/2 x 13 In. 275.00
1920, Federal Tires, Couple In Car, 17 1/2 x 13 1/2 In. 33.00
1920, Hercules Powder Co., Surprise Party Top Band, 29 1/2 x 13 In. 200.00
1922, Fox, Minnehaha Galls, 4 1/2 x 10 In. 35.00
1927, Rolf Armstrong, Beautiful Woman, Pompeian Creme, 7 x 24 In. 75.00
1929, Deering, Cream Separator 48.00
1929, Washday, Housewife, Cat, With Clothesline 175.00
1930, We're Going Home, Phillip Goodwin, 28 x 42 In. 250.00
1931, Gulbranson Baby, The Boss's Boss 65.00
1932, In Trouble, Phillip Goodwin, 28 x 42 In. 250.00
1932, Squire's Arlington Pork, Pig In Center, Pink Ground, 15 x 29 In. 170.00
1937, Vargas Girl, Salesman's Sample 121.00
1938, Little Watson Baby 45.00
1938, Lucky Strike 8.00
1939, Hercules, Young Chemist, December Sheet, 30 x 13 In. 84.00
1941, 7-Up 95.00
1941, Alka-Seltzer, Caricatures 45.00
1942, Esquire Vargas, Verse For Each Month Of Year, Phil Stack, 8 1/4 x 14 In. 160.00
1943, Geo. Ehrets Extra Beer, 8 1/2 x 10 In. 70.00
1943, Maas & Steffen Furs, Multicolored, Framed, 32 x 19 In. 175.00
1945, Esquire Girls, Vargas 85.00
1945, Mobil Oil, Armstrong Top 45.00
1946, Hercules 125.00
1946, Squirt Boy 125.00
1947, Esquire, Vargas, Envelope 85.00
1947, Nu-Grape 60.00
1948, Double Cola 60.00
1948, Esquire Glamour Gallery 75.00
1948, Sunoco Horoscope, Historical Lithographs, 12 Pages 15.00
1948, Vargas Girl, Pinup, 8 1/2 x 12 In. 55.00
1949, Zoe Mozert 125.00
1950, Irresistible, Pinup, Armstrong, 11 x 23 In. 95.00
1952, Keen Kutter 125.00
1952, Will Rogers 15.00
1953, Ambrosia Brewing Co., 19 x 14 In. 150.00
1953, Norman Rockwell Boy Scout, 32 In. 70.00
1953, Union Pacific Railroad, 16 Pages, 12 x 23 In. 27.50
1954, Esquire, 12 Page Pinup 15.00
1954, Fascination, Too Hot To Handle, Gil Elvgren 100.00
1954, Salvo Auto Parts, Marilyn Monroe, 23 In. 275.00
1954, Will Rogers 15.00
1955, Marilyn Monroe, Nude, Full Pad, 10 x 17 In. 25.00
1955, Will Rogers 15.00
1958, Girl In Pink Negligee, Elvgren, 16 x 33 In. 60.00
1958, National Life Insurance 15.00
1959, Marilyn Monroe, Salesman Sample, 8 1/4 x 11 In. 90.00
1960-1964, Pure Oil Co., Metal Clipboard, Gold & White, Sliding Scale 60.00
1962, Winchester 70.00
1964, Nude Sunbathing 30.00
1968, Horlacher Beer, Woman, Frame, 16 x 33 In. 65.00
1971, Winchester, Bird Scene, Spane, 21 1/2 x 28 In. 24.00
1972, Coke 20.00
1973, F & S Beer, Tin On Cardboard, Frame, 9 x 16 In. 9.00
1974-1976, Perpetual, Olin Chemical Co., Brass, 21 x 11 In. 72.00
1978, DuRee, Issued For 500th Birthday 150.00

1978, Winchester	35.00
1979, Ruger, Anniversary, Canoe Scene, Shrink Wrapped	22.00
1982, McDonald's	2.00
1992, Camel Joe	15.00
1992, Rocky & Bullwinkle	5.00
1993, Rocky & Bullwinkle	5.00

CALENDAR PLATES were very popular in the United States from 1906 to 1929. Since then, plates have been made every year. A calendar and the name of a store, a picture of flowers, a girl, or a scene were featured on the plate.

1909, Rose Center, Advertising, 8 1/2 In.	35.00
1911, Billiken, Store Ad	80.00
1915, Panama Canal	30.00
1928, Flowers, Store Ad, New York	30.00
1954, Fiesta, Ivory, Golding	30.00

CAMARK POTTERY started in 1924 in Camden, Arkansas. Jack Carnes founded the firm and made many types of glazes and wares. The company was bought by Mary Daniel. Production was halted in 1983.

Ashtray, Blue Splatter	45.00
Basket, Blue Iridescent	75.00
Bowl, Green, Drip, No. 315	55.00
Bowl, Pink Iris	125.00
Candlestick, Blue Iris, Stickers	75.00
Candlestick, Pink Iris	65.00
Cup, Admiral's, Blue Velvet, Paper Label, 5 In.	40.00
Dresser Tray, White	30.00
Ewer, Pink Iris, 13 In.	140.00
Ewer, Pumpkin, Green, 11 In.	175.00
Ewer, Turquoise, 8 1/2 In.	75.00
Figurine, Cat, Climbing, 15 In.	80.00
Figurine, Dog, Black	30.00
Figurine, Kitten, Wistful, Black	135.00
Figurine, Rooster, White	20.00
Figurine, Swan, Double	20.00
Figurine, White Stork Peering Into Fishbowl, 8 In.	100.00
Flower Frog, Butterfly	55.00 to 65.00
Flower Frog, Fish, No. 413	85.00
Flower Frog, Lady	50.00
Jug, Ball, Blue, Green Marble Glaze	80.00
Jug, Corn, Arkansas Ink Stamp, 6 In.	75.00
Mug, Dark Red Glaze, Die Stamp, 6 In.	45.00
Pitcher, Mottled Green, Die Stamp, 4 1/2 In.	85.00
Pitcher, Pelican, Maroon	75.00
Pitcher, Pointer & Setter, Pair	80.00
Planter, Brown Deer	45.00
Planter, Leaf, 17 In.	32.00
Plate, Oyster, Shells	225.00
Sugar & Creamer, No. 898	18.00
Tea Set, Flower, Swirl Design, Gold Trim	135.00
Vase, 3 Colors, Matte, Ring Handle, 5 In.	115.00
Vase, Art Deco, Rust Mottled, Matte, Side Handle, 6 In.	115.00
Vase, Blue Iris, Pitcher Shape	150.00
Vase, Cattail, 10 In.	25.00
Vase, Fan Shape, Green, 16 x 13 In.	45.00
Vase, Fan, Green, 13 x 16 In.	45.00
Vase, Flower, Green, 5 1/2 In.	60.00
Vase, Garland, Ram's Horn, Rose, No. 810, 6 In.	85.00
Vase, Gladiola, Black, Paper Label, 10 In.	45.00
Vase, Gladiola, Pumpkin, Matte, 3 Holes, 8 In.	55.00
Vase, Green, 5 1/2 In., Pair	65.00
Vase, Iris, 11 In.	95.00

Vase, Light Green, Die Stamp, 4 1/2 In. 50.00
Vase, Matte Blue & Green Gloss, Ring Handle, 6 In. 90.00
Vase, Matte Blue, Pinched Top, 5 In. 65.00
Vase, Morning Glory, Yellow & Purple, 8 In. 95.00
Vase, Olive, Gold Drip Glaze, Die Stamp, 6 In. 75.00
Vase, Orange & Green Drip, 3 In. 50.00
Vase, Orange & Green Drip, 8 In. 30.00
Vase, Pink & Green, Drip Glaze, 5 In. 75.00
Vase, Pink Glaze, Die Stamp, 8 In. ....65.00 to 85.00
Vase, Purple, Gloss, 5 In. 35.00
Vase, Ruffled Top, Pumpkin, Green, 8 In. 75.00
Vase, Rust Glaze, Die Stamp, 7 In. 70.00
Vase, Shell, 4 In. 28.00
Vase, Swan, Gold Trim, No. 521, 6 In. 50.00
Vase, Water Sprinkler 20.00
Vase, White, 14 In. 50.00
Wall Pocket, Bow 50.00

CAMBRIDGE GLASS Company was founded in 1901 in Cambridge, Ohio. The company closed in 1954, reopened briefly, and closed again in 1958. The firm made all types of glass. Their early wares included heavy pressed glass with the mark *Near Cut*. Later wares included Crown Tuscan, etched stemware, and clear and colored glass. The firm used a C in a triangle mark after 1920. Some Cambridge patterns may be included in the Depression Glass category.

Apple Blossom, Bowl, Yellow, 12 In. 90.00
Apple Blossom, Candy Dish, Yellow 75.00
Apple Blossom, Jug, Sterling Design, 76 Oz. 65.00
Apple Blossom, Plate, Pink, 8 1/2 In. 20.00
Apple Blossom, Plate, Yellow, 11 1/2 In. 30.00
Apple Blossom, Sherbet, Low, Yellow, 6 Oz. 35.00
Apple Blossom, Tumbler, 10 Oz. 22.50
Apple Blossom, Tumbler, 12 Oz. 32.00
Bashful Charlotte, Flower Frog, 6 In. 55.00
Caprice, Bonbon, Footed, Square, Blue, 6 In. 37.00
Caprice, Bowl, Fluted & Crimped Edge, Blue, 9 1/2 In. 92.00
Caprice, Bowl, Fluted & Crimped Edge, Blue, 12 1/2 In. 80.00
Caprice, Bowl, Footed, 13 1/2 In. 65.00
Caprice, Bowl, Footed, Blue, 10 1/2 In. 65.00
Caprice, Candlelight, Compote, 11 In. 320.00
Caprice, Candy Dish, Footed, Amber 45.00
Caprice, Champagne, Blue 45.00
Caprice, Coaster, Blue, 5 In., 6 Piece 39.50
Caprice, Cocktail, Oyster 12.00
Caprice, Cocktail, Oyster, Blue 35.00
Caprice, Compote, Alpine 179.00
Caprice, Compote, Blue 169.00
Caprice, Console Set, Blue, 3 Piece 135.00
Caprice, Cup & Saucer, Green 35.00
Caprice, Goblet, Blown, 3 1/2 In. ....18.00 to 20.00
Caprice, Ice Bucket, Alpine 299.00
Caprice, Ice Bucket, Blue Tongs 325.00
Caprice, Parfait, Blue, 5 Oz. 295.00
Caprice, Plate, 4-Footed, Amber, 14 In. 49.00
Caprice, Plate, Amber, 8 1/2 In. 35.00
Caprice, Plate, Blue, 8 1/2 In. 38.00
Caprice, Plate, Blue, 14 In. 110.00
Caprice, Plate, Oval, Blue, 9 In. 299.00
Caprice, Plate, Silver Trim, 12 In. 25.00
Caprice, Salt & Pepper, Sterling Silver Base & Top 65.00
Caprice, Salt & Pepper, Tray, Glass Lids, Blue 295.00
Caprice, Sugar & Creamer, 3 In. 35.00
Caprice, Tumbler, Blue, 5 Oz. 175.00

Caprice, Tumbler, Blue, 10 Oz.	37.00
Caprice, Tumbler, Blue, 12 Oz.	40.00
Caprice, Tumbler, Footed, Blue, 2 1/2 Oz.	295.00
Caprice, Tumbler, Footed, Blue, 12 Oz.	45.00
Chantilly, Candlestick, 2-Light, 5 1/2 In., Pair	180.00
Chantilly, Candlestick, 2-Light, Fleur-De-Lis, Pair	65.00
Chantilly, Centerpiece Bowl, 10 In.	75.00
Chantilly, Compote, 5 1/2 In.	60.00
Chantilly, Cruet, Glass Stopper, Sterling Silver Base, Pair	135.00
Chantilly, Lamp, Hurricane, Pair	195.00
Chantilly, Plate, 8 1/2 In.	24.50
Chantilly, Plate, Footed, Forest Green, 8 In.	42.00
Chantilly, Plate, Sandwich, 2 Handles, 12 In.	65.00
Chantilly, Tray, Olive, Farber Base, Fork, Forest Green, 7 In.	50.00
Chantilly, Vase, Sterling Silver Base, 10 1/2 In.	190.00
Cleo, Bonbon, Green	35.00
Cleo, Creamer, Footed, Pink	20.00
Cleo, Cup & Saucer, Blue	30.00 to 45.00
Cleo, Cup, Blue	25.00
Cleo, Plate, Blue, 8 In.	20.00
Cleo, Sandwich Server, Center Handle, Pink, 12 In.	100.00
Cleo, Tumbler, Pink, 10 Oz.	59.00
Cleo, Tumbler, Pink, 12 Oz.	50.00
Colonial, Sugar & Creamer, Child's	30.00
Crown Tuscan, Bowl, Salad, Seashell, 11 In.	80.00
Crown Tuscan, Bowl, Shell Shape, Shell Feet, Hand Painted Florals, 10 x 10 1/2 In.	125.00
Crown Tuscan, Box, Cigarette, Dolphin Feet	27.00 to 90.00
Crown Tuscan, Candlestick, Nude, 9 In.	210.00
Crown Tuscan, Compote, Nude Stem, Flowers, Gold Trim, 7 1/2 In.	225.00
Crown Tuscan, Compote, Sea Shell Scene, Roses, 7 In.	125.00
Crown Tuscan, Ivy Ball, Keyhole Stem, 8 In.	55.00
Crown Tuscan, Swan, Charleston Gardenia Design, Gold Trim, 8 1/2 In.	650.00
Crown Tuscan, Urn, Gold Chintz Pattern, 10 In.	350.00
Crown Tuscan, Vase, Cornucopia, Seashell, 9 1/2 In.	70.00
Dart & Ball, Mug, 1 7/8 In.	4.00
Decagon, Candlestick, Black, Pair	68.00
Decagon, Cup & Saucer, Pink	7.00
Decagon, Ice Bucket, Crystal Handle, Pink	35.00
Decagon, Plate, Blue, 6 In.	5.00
Decagon, Sandwich Server, Keyhole Handle, Blue	58.00
Decagon, Sugar & Creamer, Tray, Center Handle, 3 Piece	55.00
Decagon, Sugar, Scalloped Rim, Green	7.00
Decagon, Tumbler, Blue, 8 Oz.	18.00
Decagon, Tumbler, Blue, 10 Oz.	20.00
Dewey, Butter, Cover	78.00
Diane, Bowl, Console, 12 1/2 In.	40.00
Diane, Candlestick, 2-Light, Pair	35.00
Diane, Candlestick, Pair	110.00
Diane, Console, 12 1/2 In.	40.00
Diane, Cup & Saucer	39.00
Diane, Cup & Saucer, Demitasse	159.00
Diane, Goblet, 9 Oz.	45.00
Diane, Plate, 8 1/2 In.	9.00
Diane, Relish, 3 Sections	65.00
Diane, Relish, 5 Sections	85.00
Draped Lady, Flower Frog, Mandarin Gold, 8 1/2 In.	145.00
Eagle, Bookends	125.00
Elaine, Plate, 8 In.	15.00
Elaine, Plate, 13 1/2 In.	30.00
Inverted Feather, Toothpick, Near Cut, c.1910	30.00
Keyhole, Ivy Ball, Forest Green, 8 In.	45.00
Marjorie, Dish, Club Shape, Near Cut, 5 1/4 In.	15.00
Marjorie, Plate, Near Cut, 6 In.	15.00

Martha, Plate, Oyster, 10 1/2 In. 25.00
Martha Washington, Candy Box, Cover, 3 Sections, Amber, 7 1/2 In. 40.00
Mt. Vernon, Bowl, Label, 3 In. 50.00
Mt. Vernon, Candlestick, Clear, 8 In., Pair 110.00
Mt. Vernon, Compote, 2 Handles, 6 In. 50.00
Mt. Vernon, Relish, 10 In. 9.00
Mt. Vernon, Tumbler 15.00
Nude Stem, Box, Cigarette, Cobalt Blue, Silver Etching On Top 595.00
Nude Stem, Champagne, Amethyst 125.00
Nude Stem, Cigarette Holder, Emerald, Green 699.00
Nude Stem, Cocktail, Emerald, 3 Oz. 80.00
Nude Stem, Cocktail, Peachblow, 3 Oz. 110.00
Nude Stem, Cocktail, Pink 159.00
Nude Stem, Cocktail, Smoke 475.00
Nude Stem, Cocktail, Tulip, Cobalt Blue 499.00
Nude Stem, Compote, Sea Shell, Gold & Floral Design 150.00
Nude Stem, Goblet, Table, Smoke Crackle 679.00
Nude Stem, Ivy Ball, Carmen 150.00
Primrose, Atomizer, Black Enamel, Gold Trim 295.00
Primrose, Vase, Cylindrical, Footed, 10 1/4 In. 65.00
Pristine, Tray, Torte, 14 In. 425.00
Ribbon, Spooner, Double Handles, Saw Tooth Edge, Ruby Flashed 50.00
Rose Point, Bowl, 10 In. 60.00
Rose Point, Bowl, Crimped Edge, 11 In. 229.00
Rose Point, Bowl, Oval, Footed, Handle, 12 In. 175.00
Rose Point, Goblet 38.00
Rose Point, Plate, 9 1/2 In. 110.00
Rose Point, Plate, 10 1/2 In. ....145.00 to 169.00
Rose Point, Relish, 3 Sections, 3 Handles, 8 In. 45.00
Rose Point, Relish, 3 Sections, 9 1/2 In. 52.00
Rose Point, Sherbet, Low, 6 Oz. 20.00
Rose Point, Sherbet, Tall, 6 Oz. 22.00
Rose Point, Sugar & Creamer 42.00
Rose Point, Tray, 15 In. 229.00
Rose Point, Tumbler, Ice Tea, 12 Oz. 32.00
Rose Point, Wine, Cobalt Blue Bowl 165.00
Roselyn, Candlestick, 2-Light 35.00
Seagull, Flower Frog, 8 1/2 In. ....48.00 to 55.00
Swan, Ebony, 3 In. 55.00
Tally-Ho, Bowl, Salad Dressing, Underplate, Sterling Overlay, 2 Piece 45.00
Tally-Ho, Cocktail, Gold Trim 70.00
Tally-Ho, Goblet, Carmen, 8 Oz., Pair 70.00
Tally-Ho, Goblet, Platinum Band 32.50
Tally-Ho, Wine, Carmen 55.00
Wildflower, Epergne, Gold Trim 249.00
Wildflower, Salt & Pepper, Footed, Pair 89.00
Wildflower, Vase, Flip, 8 In. 115.00

CAMBRIDGE POTTERY was made in Cambridge, Ohio, from about
1895 until World War I. The factory made brown glazed decorated art
wares with a variety of marks, including an acorn, the name
Cambridge, the name *Oakwood*, or the name *Terrhea*.

Mug, Green, Brown, 5 In. 115.00
Vase, Pansies, Terrhea, 6 In. 140.00
Vase, Yellow, Green, Flowers, 24 In. 1500.00

CAMEO GLASS was made in much the same manner as a cameo in jewelry. Parts of the top layer of glass were cut away to reveal a different
colored glass beneath. The most famous cameo glass was made during
the nineteenth century. Signed cameo glass pieces are listed under the
glasswork's name, such as Daum or Galle.

Bottle, Snuff, Brown Dragon, Light Gray Ground, Stopper, 2 1/4 In. 550.00
Bowl, Citron To Clear, Flowers, Berries, Butterflies, England, 3 1/4 In. 250.00

Box, Autumnal Colored, Insects Over Foil, 1900, 5 1/4 In. 7820.00
Lamp, Conical Shade, Yellow Glass Overlaid In Red, Brown, 12 In. 4830.00
Perfume Bottle, Brown Raspberries, Blue Ground, Atomizer, Richard, 12 In. 770.00
Plate, Ruby Acanthus Leaves, Frosted Ground, 8 3/4 In. 75.00
Platter, Marine, Electric Blue Overlaid Milky Blue, White, 1900, 15 In. 5520.00
Rose Bowl, Morning Glory Flowers, White On Pink Leaves, Yellow Ground 1315.00
Rose Bowl, Rushes & Trees, Rose To White, 8-Crimp 695.00
Shell, Victory Woman, Flame Helmet, 5 x 2 1/4 In. 195.00
Vase, Banjo, Olive Green Seed Pods, Light Green & Pink Ground, 6 1/2 In. 770.00
Vase, Camellia Sprays, Yellow, Red, Brown, 1900, 10 3/4 In. 1725.00
Vase, Etched Mums, Leaves, Pink, Green, Gold Enamel Trim, 8 1/2 In. 8280.00
Vase, Floral On Blue Overlay Satin Glass, White Lining, 4 7/8 In. 895.00
Vase, Flowered Sprays Of Delphinium, Yellow, Purple, 1900, 17 In. 2645.00
Vase, Foliate & Seascape, Cut Floral, Christallerie De Pantin, 1910, 6 5/8 In. 545.00
Vase, Fruit On Vine, Tendrils, Blue, Brown, Conical, 1900, 18 In. 1955.00
Vase, Landscape, Mountain Lake With Tall Evergreens, Gray, 22 In. 4025.00
Vase, Landscape, Wooded Lake Scene, Brown, 1900, 14 1/8 In. 2300.00
Vase, Lavender Clematis, Vine, White & Lavender Ground, France, 7 1/2 In. 880.00
Vase, Maroon Overlay, Stylized Florals, Signed, Le Verre Francais, 1925, 28 In. 3737.00
Vase, Mulberry Iris, Leafy Stalks, Frosted Ground, Cressiere, 6 In. 440.00
Vase, Narcissus Etch, White, Amber, Green, 1900, 15 In. 1840.00
Vase, Oak Leaves, Acorns Sprays, Milky Yellow Overlaid In Mauve, 19 In. 2645.00
Vase, Purple Leaves & Floral Pods, Purple Pink Ground, St. Louis, 3 3/4 In. 740.00
Vase, Purple Morning Glories, Chartreuse & Frosted Ground, Arsall, 12 1/2 In. 880.00
Vase, Rampant Lion Holding Shield, Cranberry, White, Silver Plate Holder, 8 In. 1045.00
Vase, Red Poppies, Yellow Ground, Art Deco, Cameo, LeVerre, 13 1/2 In. 1100.00
Vase, Red, White Apple Blossoms, Branches, England, 7 1/4 In. 1100.00
Vase, Sailboats, Mountains, Green Satin Ground, Michel, 5 7/8 x 2 1/8 In. 650.00
Vase, Stick, Tangerine & White Morning Glory Cascade, Lemon Ground, 5 In. 2090.00
Vase, Water Lilies, Gray, Purple, Blue, 14 In. 2530.00
Vase, Wild Rose, White Over Pale Blue Ground, England, 5 1/2 In. 1320.00

CAMPAIGN memorabilia is listed in the Political category.

CAMPBELL KIDS were first used as part of an advertisement for the
Campbell Soup Company in 1906. The kids were created by Grace
Drayton, a popular illustrator of the day. The kids were used in magazine and newspaper ads until about 1951. They were presented again
in 1966; and in 1983, they were redesigned with a slimmer, more contemporary appearance.

Bowl, Girl Interior, Alphabet & Name Christine Base, 1940s 30.00
Clock, Kitchen, New Haven Clock Co., 1987 . . . . 25.00
Container, For Soup Game 38.00
Dish, Spoon & Fork, Child's 20.00
Display, Cardboard Cutout, 4 Ft. 35.00
Doll, Boy, All Composition, 12 In. 395.00
Doll, Composition Head, Black Painted Hair, Muslin Body, Horsman, 14 In. 675.00
Doll, Composition Head, Cloth Body, Sleeve Label, Horsman, 1910, 11 In. 300.00
Doll, Girl, All Composition, 12 In. 475.00
Doll, Scottish Clothes, Vinyl 35.00
Figurine, Vinyl, 1970s 125.00
Lunch Box 195.00
Mug, Kid, Orange Hair, Plastic, 1960s 20.00
Salt & Pepper, Plastic . . . . .45.00 to 75.00
Soup, Dish, Winter Olympics, Sarajevo, Pottery, 1984 . . . . 9.00
Spoon Rest, Campbell Girl 15.00
Thermometer, Figural, Plaster, 1940s, 7 In. . . . . .95.00 to 150.00

CAMPHOR GLASS is a cloudy white glass that has been blown or
pressed. It was made by many factories in the Midwest during the mid-
nineteenth century.

Vase, Stork, New England Glass, Square, 4 1/2 In. 175.00

CANDELABRUM refers to a candleholder with more than one arm to hold many candles; a candlestick is designed to hold one candle. The eccentricity of the English language makes the plural of candelabrum into candelabra.

2-Light, Art Deco, Aluminum, Hand Wrought, Pair	90.00
2-Light, Brass, Adjustable, Urn Finial, Flat Pans, Paw Footed, 16 In., Pair	690.00
2-Light, Charles X style, Patinated, Ormolu, Acanthus Baluster Stem, 13 In.	2300.00
2-Light, Empire Style, Gilt Bronze & Cut Glass, 20th Century, 16 /12 In., Pair	1150.00
2-Light, Louis XV Style, Blue Opaline, Bronze, 19th Century, 18 1/2 In.	172.00
2-Light, Louis XV Style, Foliate Scrolled Backplate, Pair, 17 In.	2587.00
2-Light, Ormolu, 3-Part Stem, Scallop Shells, Domed Base, 13 In.	3737.00
2-Light, Sconces, Square Marble Plinths, Bronze, France, 1810, 17 In., Pair	3450.00
2-Light, Scroll Branch Arms, Prism Drops, Hexagonal, 15 3/4 In., Pair	403.00
2-Light, Silver Plate, Georgian Style, Square Base, 8 In., Pair	950.00
3-Light, 2 Scrolled Branches, Turquoise Colored Drip Plates, Prisms, 25 In.	1955.00
3-Light, Brass, T Shape, Square Base, Bruno Paul, 1932, 9 3/4 In.	690.00
3-Light, Bronze, Female Figure Flanked By Candle Branches, 19 1/2 In., Pair	5175.00
3-Light, Charles X style, Ormolu, Baluster Urn, Scrolled Branches, 18 In., Pair	2875.00
3-Light, Empire Style, Brass, c.1930, 13 1/4 In., Pair	500.00
3-Light, Enameled Pink, Lavender With Gilt, 20 1/2 In., Pair	467.50
3-Light, Louis XV Style, Bras De Lumiere, Scrolled Arms, 29 1/2 In.	7475.00
3-Light, Louis XV, Dore Bronze, C-Scroll, Rocaille Base, 24 In., Pair	5980.00
3-Light, Rococo Style, Foliate Scrolled, Grape Design, 4 Ft. 1 In., Pair	5175.00
3-Light, Ruby Glass Column, Brass, Square Marble Base, 14 In., Pair	895.00
3-Light, Second Empire, Dore Bronze, Figural Cupid Trunk, 26 In., Pair	6810.00
3-Light, Silver Plate, Allover Floral, Shell Gadroon & Bead Design, 21 In.	1265.00
3-Light, Sterling Silver, 2 Reeded Scrolled Arms, George III, 14 In., Pair	490.00
3-Light, Sterling Silver, Gadrooned Border, Gorham, 6 3/4 In., Pair	165.00
3-Light, Sterling Silver, Gadrooned Border, Gorham, 14 1/4 In., Pair	632.00
4-Light, Empire, Ormolu, Candle Arms, Stepped Base, 25 In., Pair	13800.00
4-Light, Entwined Thick Chains, Electroplated, Jean Depres, 12 5/8 In., Pair	2875.00
4-Light, Female Figure Supporting 3 Branches, Flowers, 16 1/2 In., Pair	1650.00
4-Light, Figural, Bear, Standing, Holding Candelabrum, Carved Pine, 32 In., Pair	5750.00
4-Light, Gilt Bronze, Foliate & Floral Baluster, 19th Century, Russia, 17 In., Pair	4830.00
4-Light, Gilt, Each Has 3 Cherubs Holding Ivy Sconces, Bronze, France, 18 In.	2300.00
4-Light, Patinated, Classically Draped Female Figure Holding Aloft Urn, 25 In.	6900.00
4-Light, Silver Plate, Dolphin Candle Arms, Tripartite Acanthus, 28 In., Pair	1840.00
5-Light, Gilt, Patinated Bronze, Red Marble, Flower Design, Barbedienne, 27 In.	460.00
5-Light, Louis XV Style, Blue Opaline Glass, Late 19th Century, 26 1/2 In.	402.00
5-Light, Patinated, Bronze, Marble Stem, Scrolled Candle Branches, 26 In.	8050.00
5-Light, Silver Plate, International Silver, 9 5/8 In.	82.50
6-Light, Brass, Each With A Cockatoo Atop Candle Branch, 18 1/2 In.	5750.00
6-Light, Empire, Bronze, Patinated, Classically Draped Female Figure, Pair	14950.00
6-Light, Louis Philippe, Ormolu, Foliate Scrolled Branches, 27 In., Pair	2875.00
6-Light, Second Empire Style, Gilt Metal, Foliate Candle Arms, 28 1/2 In., Pair	2070.00
6-Light, Sterling Silver, Spikes Reflect Light, G. Benney, 1965, 19 1/2 In.	3450.00
6-Light, White Marble Standard, Bronze, France, 26 In.	350.00
7-Light, Iron, Black, Round Base, Leaf Dangle, Arts & Crafts, Sweden, 20 x 25 In.	250.00
7-Light, Louis Philippe, Ormolu, Patinated, Marble, Leaf Tip Cast, 36 In., Pair	6900.00
9-Light, Charles X, Ormolu, Leaf-Tip Gadrooned Tazza, Paw Feet, 20 In., Pair	12075.00
Cherubs, Holding Torch, Gilt Bronze, Lion's-Paw Feet, 1820-1850, Pair	3900.00
Girandole, Figural, Arabian, Prisms, Marble Base, 18 1/4 & 15 1/2 In., Pair	165.00
Louis XVI Style, Holding Aloft Curved Candle Branches, 35 In., Pair	6325.00
Sterling Silver, Baluster-Form, Removable Bobeches, Currier & Roby, 11 In., Pair	1495.00

CANDLESTICKS were made of brass, pewter, glass, sterling silver, plated silver, and all types of pottery and porcelain. The earliest candlesticks, dating from the sixteenth century, held the candle on a pricket (sharp pointed spike). These lost favor because in times of strife the large church candlesticks with prickets became formidable weapons, so the socket was mandated. Candlesticks changed in style through the centuries, and designs range from classic to rococo to Art Nouveau to Art Deco.

Black Basalt, 2nd Empire, Floral Molded Socket, Fitted As Lamp, 34 1/2 In. 2070.00

Brass, Bell Base, Knop-Form Stem, Continental, 17th Century, 7 1/4 In. 1500.00
Brass, C-Type Stem, Round Base, Arts & Crafts, Reimann, Chase, 8 1/2 In. 125.00
Brass, Charles II, Acorn Turned Stem, Medial Drip Pan, 17th Century, 9 In. 1380.00
Brass, Charles II, Square Stem & Plinth, 1680, 6 3/4 In., Pair 4830.00
Brass, Colonial Woman, Gilt, White Marble Base, 16 1/2 In. 242.00
Brass, Continental Rococo, Molded With C-Scroll, 18th Century, 9 In., Pair 747.00
Brass, Detachable Bobeche, French Restoration, 10 In., Pair 350.00
Brass, Diamond Princess, 19th Century, 10 3/4 In., Pair 220.00
Brass, Empire, Ormolu, Reeded Shaft With Laurel Leaf Design, 8 In., Pair 9200.00
Brass, England, 1785, 9 1/2 In., Pair 425.00
Brass, Engraved, St. Mildred's Church, Hartson, Peard & Co., England, 13 In., Pair 55.00
Brass, Filigree, Concave Glass Cover Petit Point Base, 1890, 5 In., Pair 65.00
Brass, Flared Square Base, Arts & Crafts, Kronheimer & Oldenbusch, 6 In., Pair 250.00
Brass, Footed Base, 18th Century, 11 1/2 In., Pair 395.00
Brass, Gargoyles, Ornate, Square Base, 6 1/2 In. 165.00
Brass, Hand Hammered, Red Glass Inserts, Impressed Mark, Dirk Van Erp, Pair 320.00
Brass, Heemskerk, Holland, 1670-1680, 9 1/2 In. 2400.00
Brass, Holland, 7 1/2 In. 3250.00
Brass, Neoclassical, Push-Up, 5 1/2 In., Pair 82.00
Brass, Porcelain Inserts, Cut Crystal Stems, Sockets, Prisms, 13 In., Pair 605.00
Brass, Pricket, Baluster-Form Stem, Domed Foot, 16th Century, 6 3/4 In., Pair 1955.00
Brass, Queen Anne Style, Square Base, Paw Feet, Pair 200.00
Brass, Queen Anne, 7 1/4 In., Pair 2200.00
Brass, Queen Anne, England, 1740, 7 1/4 In., Pair 1400.00
Brass, Queen Anne, Hexagonal Base, 6 In., Pair 330.00
Brass, Queen Anne, Mid-18th Century, England, 9 1/4 In., Pair 1150.00
Brass, Scalloped Base, Segmented Stem, Drip Pan, 9 In. 38.00
Brass, Spreading Foot Shape, 18th Century, 8 In., Pair 1150.00
Brass, Spring Loaded, Weighted Iron Base, 8 3/4 In., Pair 430.00
Brass, Square Base, Trefoil Footed, 10 1/2 In., Pair 110.00
Brass, Stamped, Boston, Early 19th Century, 9 3/4 In., Pair 595.00
Brass, Stepped Base, Gadroon, England, 1755-1765, 11 3/4 In. 2600.00
Brass, Trumpet Base, Medial Drip Pan, England, Mid-17th Century, 8 In. 2990.00
Brass, Tulip Candle Cups, Baluster, Continental, 4 1/2 In., Pair 165.00
Brass, Wide Flared Base, 11 3/4 In., Pair 385.00
Bronze, Charles X, Patinated, Baluster-Shape Acanthus Cast Stem, 10 3/4 In. 1150.00
Bronze, French Restoration Style, Detachable Bobeche, 10 In., Pair 275.00
Bronze, Pricket, France, 1745, Pair 3500.00
Champleve Enamel, Pitti Supporting Urn, Bronze, 12 In., Pair 1725.00
Giltwood, Carved, Pricket, 19th Century, 21 1/2 In., Pair 1150.00
Glass, Flint, Hexagonal, Pewter Insert, 9 5/8 In., Pair 275.00
Glass, Pressed Hexagonal Base, Pittsburgh, Mid-19th Century, 2 In. 195.00
Glass, Ruby, Garnet Cased, Cut Panels, 9 In., Pair 1400.00
Iron, Tinned Sheet Iron, Daffodil Form, 18 In., Pair 150.00
Lily Pad, Thumb Ring, 5 In., Pair 60.00
Marble, Napoleon III Style, Ormolu, Berried, Foliate Cast, Bun Feet, 11 In., Pair 1840.00
Marble, Photophores, Louis Philippe, Ormolu, White Marble Base, 12 In., Pair 4600.00
Onyx, Ormolu Fittings, Cloisonne Trim, White, 19 1/2 In. 247.50
Ormolu, Louis XVI Style, Leaf-Tip Cast, Fluted Stem, Fluted Dome Base, 11 In. 1610.00
Porcelain, Head Of Winsome Maiden, Gilt Borders, c.1910, 7 In. 145.00
Silver, Table, Fluted Baluster Form, Crested Bases, England, 1751, 9 1/4 In., Pair 4025.00
Silver, Table, Fluted Baluster Stems, Campana Sconces, England, 1750, 9 In., Pair 3737.00
Silver Plate, Gadrooned, Spreading Foot, Sheffield, 19th Century, 12 In., Pair 490.00
Silver Plate, Gorham, 9 1/2 In., Pair 95.00
Silver Plate, Leaf & Foliate Drip Pan, Spreading Foot, Sheffield, 13 In., Pair 805.00
Stainless Steel, Art Nouveau, WMF, W. Wagenfeld, 1952, 5 In. 65.00
Sterling Silver, 2-Light, Ribbed Baluster, Leafy Arms, France, 1750, 13 In., Pair 5750.00
Sterling Silver, Bailey, Banks & Biddle Co., Weighted Stems, 7 5/8 In., Pair 145.00
Sterling Silver, Baluster Form, Spiral Fluted, Dutch, J. Gilissen, 1772, 6 7/8 In. 3450.00
Sterling Silver, Bent Wire Form Centers, Ring Bases, W. Spratling, Mexico, 4 In. 18.50
Sterling Silver, Cluster Of Grapes, Twisted Stem, G. Jensen, 1918, 6 In., Pair 3450.00
Sterling Silver, Engraved Crest & Florals, Removable Bobeche, Dutch, 10 In., Pair 546.00
Sterling Silver, Figural, Charles & George Fox, England, 1846 . . . . 3737.00

Sterling Silver, Fluted Base, George II, John Cafe, 1756, 10 In., Set Of 4 . . . . 8625.00
Sterling Silver, Fluted Vase Form, Silver Plated Shades, 13 3/4 In., 4 Piece 4025.00
Sterling Silver, Ruby Glass Shade, Weighted, Gorham, 12 5/8 In., Pair 345.00
Telescoping, Mounts On Chair For Reading, c.1850, 14 1/4 In. 130.00
Tin, Hog Scraper, Push-Up, Lip Hanger, 5 1/4 In. 60.00
Tin, Hog Scraper, Push-Up, Lip Hanger, 6 1/2 In. . . . . .110.00 to 165.00
Tin, Hog Scraper, Push-Up, Lip Hanger, 7 In. 165.00
Tin, Hog Scraper, Push-Up, Lip Hanger, 10 1/4 In. 220.00
Twisted Iron, Hammered Copper Leaves, Arts & Crafts, Tall, Pair 120.00
Wood, Altar, Gilt, Cartouche-Shape Tripod, Paw Footed, Italy, 22 3/4 In., Pair 2185.00
Wrought Iron, Spiral Push-Up, Lip Hanger, Wooden Base, 7 1/4 In. 250.00
Wrought Steel, Spiral Push-Up, Wooden Base, 7 1/4 In. 275.00

CANDLEWICK items may be listed in the Imperial and Pressed Glass categories.

CANDY CONTAINERS have been popular since the late Victorian era. Collectors have long favored the glass containers, but now all types, including tin and papier-mache, are collected. Probably the earliest glass container sold commercially was the Liberty Bell made in 1876 for sale at the Centennial Exposition. Thousands of designs were made until the cost became too high in the 1960s. By the late 1970s, reproductions were being made and sold without the candy. Containers listed here are glass unless otherwise described. A Belsnickle is a nineteenth-century figure of Father Christmas.

Airplane, Spirit Of St. Louis, Green Glass, Metal Wings & Propeller, 3 In. 385.00
Angel, Bisque Head, Glass Eyes, 8 In. 3410.00
Barney Google & Ball, Glass 450.00
Basket, Glass 90.00
Bear, On Circus Tub 90.00
Belsnickle, 21 1/2 In. 4500.00
Belsnickle, Beard, Stern-Looking Santa Claus, Crown 1925.00
Belsnickle, Dated 1891, 21 In. 4620.00
Belsnickle, Gold, 10 In. 950.00
Belsnickle, Red, 4 1/2 In. 450.00
Belsnickle, Teal Blue, 7 1/2 In. 950.00
Belsnickle, White, 7 In. 800.00
Belsnickle, White, 11 1/2 In. 1400.00
Belsnickle, White, 13 In. 3520.00
Boat, Glass 90.00
Camera, On Tripod 605.00
Caroler, Papier-Mache 38.00
Carpet Sweeper, Dolly Sweeper 110.00
Casper The Friendly Ghost 110.00
Cat, Black, Pumpkin On Back, Plastic 18.00
Cat, On Box For Candy 70.00
Cat, Sailor, Removable Head, 5 1/4 In. 695.00
Chick, In Shell Auto, Glass 350.00
Chicken, Feathers, Metal Legs, 8 In. 65.00
Chicken, On The Nest, J.H. Millstein Co., 1946, 4 5/8 In. . . . . .30.00 to 75.00
Chicken, Papier-Mache, Germany, 4 1/4 In. 22.00
Chicken, Papier-Mache, Wax Face, Brown Eyes, Mohair Covered Body, 6 In. 687.50
Child, Boy, Bisque Head, Blue Inset Eyes, Blond Hair, Germany, 1900, 8 In. 2100.00
Clarinet, Glass 145.00
Clock, Alarm, No. 1, Penny Toy 210.00
Clown, On Rocking Horse, Glass 175.00
Crystal Palace 145.00
Derby, In Brown Hat Box 95.00
Dirigible, Los Angeles, Wheels 210.00
Dog, Bulldog 78.00
Dog, Circus, Hat, Candy 30.00
Dog, Salon, Papier-Mache, Removable Head, White Fur, Bead Eyes, 8 In. . . . . . . .400.00 to 650.00
Dog, Scotty, Black 85.00
Duck, Germany, 14 In. 125.00

Dutch Girl, Heubach	630.00
Egg, Paper Lithograph, W. Germany	15.00
Father Christmas, Brown Clothing, 15 In.	2860.00
Father Christmas, Display Figure, Clockwork, 32 In.	935.00
Father Christmas, Papier-Mache	1760.00
Felix, Glass	217.00
Fire Engine, Stough, 1914	78.00
Flask, Glass	90.00
George Washington, Sitting On Tree Stump, Papier-Mache	295.00
Gnome, Papier-Mache	225.00
Goblin Head	816.00
Gun, Flintlock	170.00
Gun, Indian Head Revolver	102.00
Happifats, On Drum	225.00
Jackie Coogan	145.00
Jeep, Original Belly Closure, 1940	35.00
Jeep, Willys	30.00
Lady, Draped, Cambridge, Yellow	225.00
Lamp, Christmas	30.00
Lamp, Kerosene	90.00
Lantern, Tin Bottom & Top, Bail	6.00
Lawn Swing	157.00
Liberty Bell, Perforated Top	78.00
Little Miss Washing Machine	302.00
Mailbox, Painted Stamps In Window	513.00
Megaphone	41.00
Military Hat	78.00
Mr. Duck, Papier-Mache, c.1920, 8 In.	175.00
Mule, Pulling 2-Wheeled Barrel, Driver	133.00
Naked Child, 2 1/2 In.	85.00
Naked Child, 3 5/8 In.	60.00
Nursing Bottle, Lynne Doll Nurser	40.00
Old Woman, Bisque Face & Hands, Straw Filled, Original Clothes, 8 In.	295.00
Pencil, Baby-Jumbo	85.00
Penguin, Papier-Mache	130.00
PEZ, Baloo	15.00 to 65.00
PEZ, Barney Bear	15.00
PEZ, Batman, Black Cape	400.00
PEZ, Camel, Melody Maker	40.00
PEZ, Camel, Whistle Head	25.00
PEZ, Captain America	80.00
PEZ, Captain Hook	25.00 to 40.00
PEZ, Casper The Friendly Ghost	100.00
PEZ, Cool Cat, Orange	25.00
PEZ, Dog, Melody Maker	15.00
PEZ, Donkey, Melody Maker	5.00
PEZ, Dumbo	15.00 to 30.00
PEZ, Easter Bunny, 1950s	275.00
PEZ, Engineer	47.50
PEZ, Fireman	65.00
PEZ, Green Hornet	225.00
PEZ, Ice Bear	5.00
PEZ, Indian Chief	100.00
PEZ, Indian, Melody Maker	10.00
PEZ, Jerry	5.00
PEZ, King Louie	15.00
PEZ, Merlin The Mouse	10.00
PEZ, Mowgli	15.00
PEZ, Pal Pirate	35.00
PEZ, Panda, Melody Maker	5.00
PEZ, Papa Smurf, 1989	6.00
PEZ, Petunia Pig	15.00
PEZ, Pirate	45.00

PEZ, Policeman 35.00
PEZ, Pony-Go Round, Caramel Head, Black Bridle 60.00
PEZ, Practical Pig 15.00
PEZ, Roadrunner 10.00
PEZ, Robot 60.00
PEZ, Silver Glow .... .12.00 to 15.00
PEZ, Smurf & Papa 5.00
PEZ, Smurfette 5.00
PEZ, Space Robot 5.00
PEZ, Spiderman, Package 25.00
PEZ, Spike 5.00
PEZ, Tarzan 5.00
PEZ, Tiger, Melody Maker 5.00
PEZ, Tom, 1970s, 4 In. .... .5.00 to 15.00
PEZ, Truck 45.00
PEZ, Tuffy 5.00
PEZ, Tweety Bird 10.00
PEZ, Uncle Sam 75.00
PEZ, Webb 5.00
PEZ, Yellow Caw 57.00
PEZ, Yosemite Sam, Short Mustache 5.00
Pickle, Papier-Mache, 4 1/2 In. 45.00
Police Car, Tin, 1930s 275.00
Potato, Papier-Mache, 3 1/2 In. 40.00
Rabbit, In Egg Shell, Glass 85.00
Rabbit, On Rocket, Yellow & Green Hard Plastic, Hole In Head For Lollipops 50.00
Rabbit, Papier-Mache 75.00
Rabbit, Sitting, 6 1/2 In. 30.00
Reindeer, Composition, 8 In., Pair 412.00
Reindeer, Glass Eyes, Germany, 5 x 5 In. 250.00
Reindeer, Heads Come Off, 5 1/2 In., 6 Piece 1540.00
Rolling Pin 217.00
Rooster, Metal Feet, Pull-Off Head, Germany, 4 1/2 In. 325.00
Rooster, Papier-Mache, 7 In. 225.00
Rooster, Papier-Mache, Glass Eyes, Wing Lifts, Germany, 1900s, 17 In. 725.00
Santa Claus, Bag Over Shoulder, Composition Face & Hands, Japan, 10 In. 235.00
Santa Claus, Double Cuff, Papier-Mache 48.00
Santa Claus, Fur Beard, Wicker Basket On Back, Feather Tree, 1920s, 12 In. 595.00
Santa Claus, Germany, 1920s, 9 1/2 In. 325.00
Santa Claus, On House, Cotton 95.00
Santa Claus, Papier-Mache, Fur Beard, Cloth Coat, Germany, 7 1/2 In. 65.00
Santa Claus, Papier-Mache, Fur Beard, Wire Neck, Germany, 9 In. 25.00
Santa Claus, Seated On Wood Pile 325.00
Santa Claus, Walking, Basket On Back For Candy, On Platform, 8 In. ... 865.00
Santa Claus Head, Rabbit Fur Beard, Felt Hat, West Germany 95.00
School Bell, Hand 66.00
Snow Baby, Bisque, Ivy, Holly Berries Design On Base, Germany, 7 In. 800.00
Snowman, Papier-Mache, 12 In. 125.00
Snowman, With Cap, Papier-Mache, Germany, 5 1/2 In. 16.00
Snowman, With Umbrella, Papier-Mache, Germany, 6 1/2 In. 36.00
Soldier, With Sword 1028.00
Spark Plug, Horse, 1923 .... 155.00
Stocking Darner 78.00
Submarine, Glass, Borgfeldt 450.00
Top Hat, Kerr's Kandy Kitchen, Cardboard 60.00
Trumpet, Souvenir York Springs, Pennsylvania, Milk Glass 363.00
Turkey, Tom, Papier-Mache, Germany, 2 In. 16.00
Wee Soup Kettle, Wire Bail 29.00
Windmill, Candy Guaranteed 120.00
Witch, Black Pot & Broom, Papier-Mache 193.00
Woman, Old, Bisque Head & Hands, 10 In. 315.00
World Globe, On Stand 575.00

CANES and walking sticks were used by every well-dressed man in the nineteenth century, but by World War I the style had changed. Today canes are used by few but the infirm. Collectors prize old canes made with special features, like hidden swords, whiskey flasks, or risqué pictures seen through peepholes. Examples with solid gold heads or made from exotic materials, such as walrus vertebrae, are among the higher priced canes.

Ball, Blue Handle, Tan Hardwood Shaft, Silver Collar, Marked, Sterling, 1900, 33 In. . . .	495.00
Bamboo, Carved, Natural Root Handle, 4 Figures In Costume On Handle, 35 1/4 In.	300.00
Blow-Gun, Nickel Silver, Horn & Ivory, Cap Unscrews, Reveals Mouth Piece, c.1890 . . .	1815.00
Brass Ball Knob, Dark Hardwood Shaft, 1870, 34 In.	825.00
Chinese Man, Raise Queue & Stream Shoots Out His Mouth . . . . .4500.00 to 4950.00
Dog Head, Open Mouth, Teeth, Tongue, Glass Eyes, Worn Shaft	145.00
Fireman's, Carved Conifer Wood, 2 Ball Chamber Whimsies, 1888, 33 1/2 In.	635.00
Flag Parade, Reversible Knob, Painted Shaft, Metal Ferrule, Silver Collar, 36 In.	990.00
Gold Head, Engraved Comdr. W.J. Kramer, G.A.R., Nov. 26, 1879, Ebonized	300.00
Goldstone Ball Handle, Ebony Shaft, Iron Ferrule, c.1900, 36 3/4 In.	495.00
Gun, 22 Caliber, Dog Head	6490.00
Gun, 32 Caliber, Dog Head, February, 1858	7370.00
Gun, 38 Caliber, Painted Black, Steel, 33 3/4 In.	862.00
Ivory Handle, Carved Mice On Ear Of Corn, Japan	3620.00
Ivory Handle, Dense Wood Shaft, Gold Collar, 1880, 38 In.	2750.00
Ivory Handle, Exotic Wood Shafts, Late 19th Century, Pair	363.00
Ivory Handle, Masonic, Silver Rimmed Glass Top, Horn Collar, Malacca Shaft, 35 In. . . .	1100.00
Ivory Handle, Mastiff, Brass Ferrule, Sterling Collar, 1894, 36 In.	2310.00
Ivory Handle, Mermaid	2200.00
Ivory Handle, Pistol Grip, With Lion, Gold Collar, White Metal, Iron Ferrule, 36 3/4 In.	578.00
Ivory Handle, Shibayama, Japan	235.00
Ivory Handle, Spaniel, Glass Eyes, Whalebone Ferrule, 34 1/2 In.	1100.00
Ivory Handle, Spitting Chinaman Head, Silver Collar, 1880, 36 1/2 In.	4950.00
Ivory Handle, Sterling Silver, Rosewood Shaft, Brass Ferrule, 1890, 37 1/2 In.	440.00
Ivory Handle, Thousand Faces, Sterling Collar, Rosewood Shaft, 35 In.	935.00
Ivory Handle, Warrior, Gold Gilt Collar, Malacca Shaft, Brass, Iron Ferrule, 1830, 37 In.	3740.00
Ivory Insert Of Golf Design, Swaine & Adenley, Ltd., London, Walnut, 39 1/2 In.	365.00
Malacca, Brass, Iron Ferrule, Spike Flicks Out When Used, 1830, 36 In.	990.00
Malacca, Initials On Top, Platinum Fleur-De-Lis Circumference, Tiffany, 35 3/4 In.	6050.00
Mechanical Retriever, Hand Grip, Metal Claw At Bottom Opens, Closes, 1910, 37 In. .	495.00
Nautical, Whale Ivory Eagle, Black Tropical Wood Shaft, 1850, 33 3/4 In.	1870.00
Nautical, Whale Ivory, Lady's Leg, Buttoned Boot, Whalebone Shaft	990.00
Nautical, Whale Ivory, Whalebone Shaft, Silver Inlays, Scrimshaw, c.1850, 36 In.	2640.00
Noisemaker, McKinley Slogan, Peace, Protection & Prosperity, 33 1/2 In.	660.00
Silver, 800, Open-Rail At Underside, Hardwood Shaft, Art Nouveau, 37 1/4 In.	522.00
Silver Canister Head, Civil War Veterans, Battle Scene, Horsemen, Cannon, 1888	1350.00
Silver Handle, Duck, England, 1902	700.00
Silver Handle, Owl, Monkey, Monkey Has Copper Face, Ears, 1890, 37 3/4 In.	1210.00
Silver Handle, Peacock With Sapphire, Snakewood Shaft, Horn Ferrule, 1900, 33 In. . . .	3410.00
Silver Handle, Tau, Mahogany Shaft, Horn Ferrule, 1900, 37 1/2 In.	303.00
Silver Hat, Ivory Man, Silver Collar, Partridgewood Shaft, Iron Ferrule, 35 1/4 In.	825.00
Staghorn Handle, Woman's, 19th Century	175.00
Staghorn Head, Silver Plaque Inset, J.W.D. Md. Surgeon 14 Regt., Aug. 22, 1822	850.00
Sword, Indian Head Handle, 1860	275.00
Sword, Silver, Walnut, Spain	454.00
Tau, Silver, Overlaid Dragon, China Trade	275.00
Teddy Roosevelt, Presentation	3950.00
Walking Stick, Brass, Animal, Snake, Heart, Horseshoe, Bead Inlay, 34 In.	385.00
Walking Stick, C-Curving Silver Handle, Crouching Lion, Austria, 36 In.	430.00
Walking Stick, C-Curving Silver Handle, Geometric Engraved Design, Germany, 37 In. . .	105.00
Walking Stick, Carved Indian Head, Dartmouth, Class Of '29	200.00
Walking Stick, Ebony, Cut Glass Spherical Top, Silver Band, Ivory Tip, 35 3/8 In.	240.00
Walking Stick, Gold Handles, Whimsical Sampler, Signed, 1821	285.00
Walking Stick, Gold Quartz, Ebonized Hardwood Shaft, Horn Ferrule, 1870, 37 1/2 In. .	4290.00
Walking Stick, Gold Top, Hazelwood, Metal Base, Natural Bark Finish Shaft, 36 In. . . .	220.00

Walking Stick, Gold, Platinum, Black Horn Ferrule, Tiffany, 1902-1907, 35 3/4 In. 6050.00
Walking Stick, Ivory Handle, With 11-In. Dagger 575.00
Walking Stick, Ivory Inlaid Ebony, Turned Knob, Geometric Inlay, 19th Century 632.00
Walking Stick, Ivory, 7 Screw-In Sections, Scarab & Lotus Top, 39 In. 258.00
Walking Stick, Mushroom Form Handle, Hunter, Wearing A Wide Brimmed Hat, 43 In. .. 460.00
Walking Stick, Pewter Band, Benj. Wright, Born Aug. 23, 1760, Iron Tip 245.00
Walking Stick, Polar Bear Carved Handle 400.00
Walking Stick, Remington, Dog Head, Gutta Percha, Nickel Silver Collar 5940.00
Walking Stick, Schenley's Liquor, With Seat 25.00
Walking Stick, Sterling Silver Handle, C-Scroll, Floral Design, Engraved, 37 In. 120.00
Walking Stick, Sword, Hand Carved, Painted To Simulate Bamboo, Brass Tip, 26 7/8 In. 385.00
Walking Stick, Whalebone, Engraved, June 16th 1819, 47 1/2 In. 1495.00
Walking Stick, Whalebone, Ivory, 19th Century, 33 In. 460.00
Woman's, Stag Horn Handle, 1880s 145.00
Wood, Carved Buttocks & Legs On Root Handle, Painted & Carved 320.00
Wood, Carved Snake Spiral, 34 1/2 In. 185.00
Wood, Carved, Of 2 Gods, Natural Hazelwood, Crooked Handle, 1880, 35 1/4 In. 385.00
Wood, Carved, Skull, Brass Collar, Brass Ferrule, 1880, 34 1/8 In. 522.00
Wood, Carved, Wood, Carp With Glass Eyes, Mahogany Shaft, 35 1/4 In. 550.00

CANTON CHINA is blue-and-white ware made near the city of Canton,
in China, from about 1785 to 1895. It is hand decorated with Chinese
scenes. Canton is part of the group of porcelains known today as
Chinese Export Porcelain.

Basket, Fruit, 19th Century, 9 1/4 In. 690.00
Beaker, Barefoot Boy On Ladder Against Tree, Floral Spray, 3 1/8 In., Pair 1380.00
Bidet, 19th Century, 24 In. 575.00
Bottle, Garlic Neck, 19th Century 495.00
Bowl, Lobed, Gilt Rim, 19th Century, 9 3/4 In. 863.00
Bowl, Ruffled Edge, Blue, White, 9 1/2 x 2 1/4 In. 403.00
Bowl, Salad, 19th Century, 9 3/4 In. 805.00
Bowl, Triple Layered Jade, Japonesque Design, Scrolled Ground, 4 In. 2645.00
Chop Plate, Blue & White, 16 1/4 In. 630.00
Coffeepot, Cover, 19th Century, 7 1/4 In. 748.00
Compote, Floral Border, Interior Painted Oriental Maidens In Garden, 14 1/8 In. 517.00
Creamer, Flat Spout, Handle, 3 1/2 x 5 1/2 In. 97.00
Creamer, Helmet Form, 4 1/4 x 6 1/2 In. 200.00
Dish, Blue Cover, Oval, 8 1/2 In. 85.00
Dish, Leaf Shape, 7 1/2 In. 192.00
Dish, Tobacco Leaf, 8 x 6 In. 155.00
Jug, Milk, 19th Century, 7 3/4 In. 489.00
Jug, Milk, 19th Century, 8 1/4 In. ....345.00 to 517.00
Mug, Oriental Scene, Twisted Handle, 5 In. 695.00
Plate, 7 1/2 In. 50.00
Plate, 10 1/2 In. 145.00
Plate, Reticulated, 6 In. 48.00
Plate, Serving, 19th Century, 12 In. 431.00
Platter, 9 1/4 In. 105.00
Platter, 12 1/4 x 9 1/2 In. 115.00
Platter, 15 3/4 x 12 3/4 In. 402.00
Platter, 19th Century, 14 1/2 In. 345.00
Platter, 19th Century, 15 3/8 x 12 1/2 In. 355.00
Platter, Chicken Skin, 11 5/8 x 9 1/2 In. 165.00
Platter, Landscape, Water, 19th Century, 12 1/2 x 15 3/8 In. 290.00
Platter, Well & Tree, 19th Century, 17 1/4 In. 525.00
Platter, Well & Tree, 19th Century, 18 In. 635.00
Tank, Mahogany Veneer Stand, 19th Century, 7 1/2 In. 4315.00
Tea Caddy, Octagonal, 19th Century, 5 1/2 In. 2415.00
Teapot, c.1835, 6 3/4 In. 800.00
Teapot, Dome Top, 19th Century, 8 1/2 In. 550.00
Teapot, Dome Top, 8 x 9 1/4 In. 635.00
Teapot, Rain Cloud Border, Sea Urchin Finial 200.00
Tureen, Sauce, Cover, 19th Century, 8 1/2 In. 865.00

Tureen, Sauce, Undertray, Boar's Head Handles, Blue, White, 7 1/2 In. 495.00
Tureen, Soup, 19th Century, 12 In. . . . . .635.00 to 750.00

CAPO-DI-MONTE porcelain was first made in Naples, Italy, from 1743 to 1759. The factory moved near Madrid, Spain, reopened in 1771, and worked to 1834. Since that time, the Doccia factory of Italy acquired the molds and is using the N and crown mark. Societe Richard Ceramica is a modern-day firm often referred to as Ginori or Capo-di-Monte. This company uses the crown and N mark.

Bread Plate, Raised Baskets Of Flowers, Gilded, 1818, 7 In., 12 Piece 170.00
Bust, Napoleon I, Marked Crown & N, 5 1/8 In. 145.00
Centerpiece, 12 Dancing Neoclassical Maidens, With Planters, 11 In. 4600.00
Chest, Mythical Figures, With Cherubs 800.00
Cup & Saucer, Scene, Cherub & People, Porcelain, Hand Painted, 3 1/2 In. 185.00
Ewer, Satyr Form Shaft, Shell-Form Bowls, Marked Blue Crown & N, 10 In., Pair 630.00
Figurine, 3 Musicians, White, 8 1/2 x 8 1/2 In. 190.00
Figurine, Knife Sharpener At Sharpening Wheel, 6 x 6 In. 125.00
Figurine, Maiden, Water With Wheelbarrow & Water Keg With Jugs 125.00
Figurine, Older Couple In Horse Drawn Carriage, 21 x 19 In. 1900.00
Figurine, Vagabond Child, Playing Bagpipes, 6 x 6 In. 125.00
Figurine, Woman, Ruffled Blue & Red Bonnet, Holding Fan, 4 In. 200.00
Figurine, Young Man, 17th Century Costume, Rocaille Base, 5 3/4 In. 375.00
Lamp, Rose, Alabaster Base, Gilt, Cupids, Tassels, Matching Shade, 34 In. 395.00
Plaque, Olympian Scene Of Drunken Revelers, Gods, 9 x 16 3/4 In. 460.00
Plate, Floral & Crest Center, Multicolored Allegorical Border, 8 In., 4 Piece 745.00
Stein, Battle Scene, Painted Relief, Lion Finial On Lid, Marked Crown & N, 1/3 Liter . . 326.00
Stein, Battle Scene, Painted Relief, Lion Finial On Lid, Marked Crown & N, 1/5 Liter . . 529.00
Stein, Cherub Finial, Classical Scene, Elephant Head Handle, 14 In. 530.00
Stein, People Around Altar With Fire, Porcelain, Marked Crown & N, 1 Liter 465.00
Stein, People, Dancing Around Wine Barrel, Porcelain Lid, 1/5 Liter 630.00
Tea Caddy, Classical Figures, Square Form, 6 In. 100.00
Urn, Gilt Mythological Scenes, Hercules, Lions, Flowers, 15 In. 385.00

CAPTAIN MARVEL was introduced in February 1940 in Whiz comic books. An orphan named Billy Batson met the wizard, Shazam, and whenever he said the magic word he was transformed into a superhero. A movie serial was released in 1940. The comic was discontinued in 1954. A second Captain Marvel appeared in 1966, a third in 1967. Only the original was transformed by shouting *Shazam.*

Book, Little Golden Book, Shazam, Captain Marvel's Circus Adventure, 1977 . . . . 7.00
Comic Book, Mighty Midget, No. 11, 1942 . . . . 65.00
Magic Folder, Test, Illustrations, Red, Blue, Yellow, Fawcett, 1940s, 5 x 6 1/2 In. . . . .65.00 to 85.00
Paint Set, Sealed Box, 1967 . . . . 95.00
Photograph, Captain Marvel Club, 1941 . . . . 45.00
Pin, Captain Marvel Club, Shazam, Celluloid, Glossy, 1940s 45.00
Toy, Car, Racing, Tin, Windup, 1947, 4 In., Pair . . . . .175.00 to 225.00
Wristwatch, Image Of Captain Marvel, Yellow Numerals, Green Hands, 1948 . . . . 175.00

CAPTAIN MIDNIGHT began as a radio show in September 1940. The first comic book appeared in July 1941. Captain Midnight was really the aviator Captain Albright, who was to defeat the Nazis. A movie serial was made in 1942 and a comic strip was published for a short time. The comic book Captain Midnight ended his career in 1948. The radio premiums are the prized collector memorabilia today.

Badge, Secret Squadron Decoder 175.00
Badge, Weather Forecasting, Brass, Propeller Wing, Dark Luster, 1939 . . . . 38.00
Book, Joyce Of The Secret Squadron, Wander Co., 1942 . . . . 65.00
Cup, Red Decal . . . . .25.00 to 65.00
Decoder, Brass Badge, Gold Finish, 1945 . . . . 78.00
Decoder, Brass Finish, Red Plastic Wheel, 1949 . . . . 58.00
Medal, Midnight Medal Of Membership 14.00
Mug, Ovaltine, Shake Up, Red . . . . .30.00 to 50.00
Patch, 50th Anniversary 115.00

CARAMEL SLAG, see Chocolate Glass category.

CARDS listed here include advertising cards (often called trade cards), greeting cards, baseball cards, playing cards, valentines, and others. Color pictures were rare in the nineteenth century, so companies gave away colorful cards with pictures of children, flowers, products, or related scenes that promoted the company name. These were often collected and stored in albums. Greeting cards are also a nineteenth-century idea that has remained popular. Baseball cards also date from the nineteenth century when they were used by tobacco companies as giveaways. Gum cards were started in 1933, but it was not until after World War II that the bubble gum cards favored today were produced. Today over 1,000 cards are issued each year by the gum companies. Related items may be found in the Postcard and Movie categories.

Advertising, America Baking Powder, Columbia, Standing, Flag & Sword	115.00
Advertising, Arbuckle Coffee, S.C., Indians Attacking Whites, Conquistadores, 1892	7.00
Advertising, Atkins Saws, Metamorphic, Foldover	285.00
Advertising, Ayer's Sarsaparilla Purifies The Blood, Woman, Children, 5 x 2 3/4 In.	10.00
Advertising, B.T. Babbitt's Soap, American Revolutionary War Soldier, Flag, 1776	20.00
Advertising, Carnrick's Soluble Food, I Am Using, Baby In Good Health	15.00
Advertising, Clock, None-Such Mince Meat, Die Cut, Pumpkin Shaped Paper	660.00
Advertising, Columbia Coffee, St. Bernard Dog, Flower Basket, Portland, Ore., 1885	9.00
Advertising, Dr. D.B. Hand's Remedies For Children, 2 Sides, 1896	30.00
Advertising, Eagle Marble Works, Reading, Penna., Monuments, Tombs, Cameo	440.00
Advertising, Fairbank's Fairy Soap, Theodore Roosevelt, Rough Riders, 3 3/4 x 6 In.	125.00
Advertising, G.A. Schwarz, Toys Fancy Goods & Novelties, 4 x 4 In.	65.00
Advertising, Gargling Oil Liniment, Baseball Player	20.00
Advertising, Great Sanitary Fair, Live Eagle Portrait, Chicago, 1865, 3 3/4 x 2 1/4 In.	125.00
Advertising, Heckers' Perfect Baking Powder, Lawn Tennis Scene	15.00
Advertising, Hires Root Beer, Boy On Ladder, Adjusting Clock, 1893	32.00
Advertising, Hood's Sarsaparilla, ABC Class, 7 x 2 In.	10.00
Advertising, Household Ranges, Built To Bake, Soldier, Standing, Gun, Flag	25.00
Advertising, J. & P. Coats, Best Six Cord, Lion & Eagle 1879 Calendar On Back	40.00
Advertising, Kast's Stylish Footwear, Black Man Balancing Balls & Bottles, 1883	85.00
Advertising, Kugler & Co. Practical Upholsterers, Fall Flowers, 2 1/2 x 5 In.	7.00
Advertising, Maplecroft Ice Cream, Wine Of Farm, Black & White, 4 1/2 x 6 1/2 In.	25.00
Advertising, Merrick Thread Co., Circus Performer, High Wire, Flag, 1886, 4 x 3 In.	22.00
Advertising, Merrick Thread, Child, With Flag, Riding Eagle, 1880s	12.00
Advertising, Merrick's Spool Cotton, Patronize Home Industry, 1890s	28.00
Advertising, Mrs. Hugo Andersen, Designing, Dressmaking, Oakland, Calif., 1930s, 6 In.	7.00
Advertising, Ocean Steamship Co., Savannah, Ga., 1890s	125.00
Advertising, Optical Co., Eye Glass Case Shape, Multicolored	48.00
Advertising, Peckham Stoves, Saratoga Model, 1890s	28.00
Advertising, Pozzoni's Dove Complexion Powder, Woman With Dove, 6 x 10 In.	50.00
Advertising, Singer Sewing Machine, Statue Of Liberty, 1883	22.00
Advertising, Victor Mara Coffee, Santa Claus With Children	85.00
Advertising, Wamsutta Lamp Wick, Anthropomorphized Lamps Picture, Pre-1900	820.00
Advertising, Webber's Vegetable Bitters, Petroline, Woman, 1880s, 4 x 2 1/2 In.	15.00
Advertising, White Sewing Machine, The White Is King, Winter Scene, 3 x 5 In.	7.00
Baseball, Bob Avila, Dairy Queen, White, 1955	35.00
Baseball, Don Drysdale, Topps, No. 400, 1969	14.00
Baseball, Don Sutton, Topps, No. 216, 1969	5.00
Baseball, Ernie Banks, Topps, No. 20, 1969	16.00
Baseball, Hires Root Beer, Complete Set, 1958, 66 Piece	3300.00
Baseball, Johnny Bench, Topps, No. 95, 1969	40.00
Baseball, Lou Brock, Topps, No. 85, 1969	16.00
Baseball, Luis Tiant, Topps, No. 377, 1967	6.00
Baseball, Marty Marion, Rookie, Topps, St. Louis Cardinals, Bowman, No. 40, 1948	28.00
Baseball, Mel Ott, Goudey, Puzzle, No. 6, 1935	245.00
Baseball, Mickey Mantle, No. 95, 1957	550.00
Baseball, Mike Garcia, Cleveland Indians, Bowman, No. 7, 1952 ....*Illus*	10.00
Baseball, Pete Rose, Topps, No. 430, 1967	80.00
Baseball, Player Ready To Pitch, Cigarette Trolley, Blue Ground, Yellow, 9 x 19 In.	121.00

Card,
Baseball,
Mike Garcia,
Cleveland
Indians,
Bowman, No. 7,
1952

JOHN JOHNSON
CAVALIERS' GUARD-FORWARD

Card,
Basketball,
John Johnson,
Cleveland
Cavaliers,
Topps, No. 4,
1971

Baseball, Roberto Clemente, Arco, 1970, 8 x 10 In. 75.00
Baseball, Roberto Clemente, Best Wishes, Autographed, Topps, No. 350, 1970 .... 250.00
Baseball, Roberto Clemente, Topps, No. 400, 1967 .... 95.00
Baseball, Sam Zoldak, Bowman, No. 78, 1949 .... 60.00
Basketball, ABL Hawaiian Chiefs, Union Oil, 1961, 10 Piece 180.00
Basketball, John Havlicek, Rookie Boston Celtics, Topps, No. 20, 1969-1970 .... 120.00
Basketball, John Johnson, Cleveland Cavaliers, Topps, No. 4, 1971 ....*Illus* 1.50
Basketball, Lucius Allen, Topps, No. 6, 1969-1970 .... 5.00
Basketball, Tom Boerwinkle, Topps, No. 7, 1969-1970 .... 5.00
Basketball, Walt Wesley, Topps, No. 22, 1969-1970 .... 3.00
Boxing, Sullivan, Johnson, O. Nelson & Corbett, Joe Palooka Candy, 4 Piece 115.00
Calling, Man's, Floral Die Cut, Hidden Name, 1880s 5.00
Football, Bill Swiacki, Detroit Lions, Bowman, No. 132, 1951 ....*Illus* 8.00
Football, Chicago Bears, Team, Topps, 1962 .... 7.00
Football, Doak Walker, Bowman, No. 1, 1950 .... 155.00
Football, Frank Gifford Rookie, New York, Giants, Topps, No. 53, 1956 .... 45.00
Football, Gale Sayers, Chicago Bears, Topps, No. 70, 1970 .... 25.00
Football, Green Bay Packers Team, Topps, No. 75, 1962 .... 35.00
Football, Jim Brown, Cleveland Browns, Topps, No. 28, 1962 .... 90.00
Football, Jim Taylor, Green Bay Packers, Topps, No. 66, 1962 .... 40.00
Football, Joe Namath, Topps, No. 100, 1972 .... 300.00
Football, Len Dawson, Topps, No. 1, 1970 .... 18.00
Football, Playing, Rose Bowl, Super Bowl XXI, 1987 .... 3.00
Football, Rose Tournament, Set Packet, 1934 .... 38.00
Football, Steve Spurrier, Topps, No. 291, 1972 .... 85.00
Football, Ted Hendricks, Topps, No. 93, 1972 .... 40.00
Football, Vic Sears, Philadelphia Eagles, Bowman, No. 119, 1951 ....*Illus* 10.00
Playing, Bicycle No. 808, U.S. Playing Card Co., 4 1/2 x 7 In. 55.00
Playing, Bicycle, 1890, 3 1/2 x 2 1/2 In. 70.00
Playing, Burlington Railroad Dining Car Service 45.00
Playing, Canadian National Railroad, 1935 .... 45.00
Playing, Colt, Horse Center, Blue & Maroon, 150 Years, 1836-1886, 2 Decks 38.00
Playing, Esquire, Nude Playing Cards, Hong Kong, Box, 1950s, 5 x 7 In. 20.00
Playing, Felix The Cat 5.00
Playing, Gaiety, Nude Playing Cards, Hong Kong, Box, 1950s 10.00
Playing, Kool Cigarette 8.00
Playing, Marilyn Monroe, 1950s 175.00
Playing, Nile Fortune, Backs With Sphinx & Nouveau Flowers 15.00
Playing, Nite Fortune, U.S. Playing Card Co., 1897, Box, Complete 30.00
Playing, Reddy Kilowatt, Servant Of The Century, Twin Set 50.00
Playing, Tarot, Hand Painted, c.1920 .... 75.00
Playing, Tennis, Billie Jean King 3.00
Playing, Voyage To The Bottom Of The Sea, 1964 .... 65.00
Playing, Woman's, Dondorf, No. 163, Box 40.00

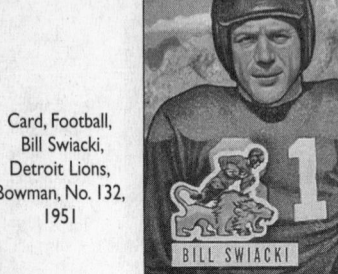

Card, Football,
Bill Swiacki,
Detroit Lions,
Bowman, No. 132,
1951

Card, Football,
Vic Sears,
Philadelphia Eagles,
Bowman, No. 119,
1951

Playing, Zenith Radio, Box, 1937 .... 25.00
Swimming, Johnny Weissmuller, Goudey Sport Kings, 1933, 9 x 5 1/2 In. 1610.00

CARDER, see Aurene and Steuben categories.

CARLSBAD is a mark found on china made by several factories in Germany, Austria, and Bavaria. Many pieces were exported to the United States. Most of the pieces available today were made after 1891.

Bone Dish, Floral, 6 Piece 55.00
Chocolate Pot, Portrait, Philippe Deo Orleans Regent, Cobalt Blue, 9 In. 475.00
Demitasse Set, Scene On Each Piece, Gold Trim, 20 Ounce 1500.00
Fish Set, 8 Plates, 20-In. Platter ....235.00 to 335.00
Plate, Imari Style, c.1895 .... 35.00
Vase, Pillow, Iris, Scrolls, Gold, 16 x 9 x 4 3/4 In. 260.00
Vase, Women & Cupid, In Garden, Maroon Ground, Gold Trim, 3 1/4 In. 45.00

CARLTON WARE was made at the Carlton Works of Stoke-on-Trent, England, about 1890. The firm traded as Wiltshaw & Robinson until 1957. It was renamed Carlton Ware Ltd. in 1958. The company went bankrupt in 1995, but the name is still in use.

Bank, Cat, Blue 65.00
Bowl, Apple Blossom, 5 In. 65.00
Bowl, Birds & Exotic Landscape, Vert Royale, 8 3/8 x 10 1/8 In. 235.00
Box, Luster, Bleu Royale, Spider Web Decor 185.00
Cookie Jar, Water Lily, 2 Handles, Marked, 6 1/2 In. 175.00
Cup, Walking Ware 35.00
Dish, Art Tree Scene, Orange Luster Foot & Handles, 7 1/4 x 12 1/4 In. 375.00
Dish, Cheese, Cover 120.00
Dish, Jam, Apple Blossom, Spoon 100.00
Dish, Jam, Hazelnut Design, Spoon, Box 110.00
Dish, Leaf, Australia 30.00
Dish, Leaf, With Spoon, Box 95.00
Dish, With Spoon, Apple Blossom, 5 In. 85.00
Jar, Cover, Mottled Ground, Branches & Leaves, Pink Flowers, 8 1/4 In. 395.00
Jar, Foo Dog Finial, Chinoiserie, 6 Sides, 9 In. 475.00
Jar, Ginger, Enamel Oriental Homes, Bridges, Birds, Gold Trim, 10 3/8 In. 895.00
Jar, Gold Finial On Cover, Chinoiserie Scene, Gold Base Trim, Signed, 9 3/8 In. 395.00
Mug, Drinkers Verse 45.00
Mug, Pilgrim Hanging From Gallows 55.00
Pot, Aladdin Type, Chinese Figure, 4 x 7 In. 65.00
Tazza, Floral, Gold Outlining, Green Ground, 7 1/4 x 2 1/2 In. 225.00
Teapot, Walking Ware 75.00
Vase, Blue Luster, Oriental Man & Woman, Mother-Of-Pearl Lining, 12 1/2 In. 395.00
Vase, Exotic Landscape & Long Tailed Birds, Blue, Gold Trim, Marked, 7 In. 450.00

Vase, Exotic Trees & Bird, Fairyland Luster, Mother-Of-Pearl Lining, 5 7/8 In. 450.00
Vase, Flowers & Hummingbirds, Blue Luster, Bulbous, 7 In. 295.00
Vase, Flowers, Hummingbirds, Blue Pedestal, 7 In. 295.00
Vase, Food Dog Finial Cover, Pink Flowers, Mottled Blue, Handcraft, 9 In. 395.00
Vase, Landscape, Long-Tailed Birds, Mother-Of-Pearl Luster, Signed, 7 In. 450.00
Vase, Oriental Man & Woman Scene, Blue Luster, 12 1/2 In. 395.00

CARNIVAL GLASS was an inexpensive, iridescent, pressed glass made
from about 1907 to about 1925. More than 1,000 different patterns are
known. Carnival glass is currently being reproduced. Additional pieces
may be found in the Northwood category.

Acanthus, Bowl, Marigold, 8 In. 30.00
Acorn, Bowl, Marigold, 7 1/2 In. 50.00
Acorn, Bowl, Ruffled, Blue 55.00
Acorn Burrs, Butter, Cover, Purple 473.00
Acorn Burrs, Creamer, Purple 171.00
Acorn Burrs, Punch Cup, White, Inscribed 80.00
Acorn Burrs, Spooner, Purple 225.00
Acorn Burrs, Sugar, Cover, Purple 281.00
Acorn Burrs, Water Set, Marigold, 7 Piece 1800.00
Acorn Burrs & Bark pattern is listed here as Acorn Burrs.
April Showers, Vase, Green, 11 1/2 In. ....85.00 to 95.00
April Showers, Vase, Marigold, 13 1/2 In. ....40.00 to 50.00
Banded Medallion & Teardrop pattern is listed here as Beaded Bull's Eye.
Basket, Bushel, Ice Green 310.00
Basketweave, Candy Dish, Open Lace Rim, Marigold, 6 In. 20.00
Battenburg Lace No. 1 pattern is listed here as Hearts & Flowers.
Battenburg Lace No. 2 pattern is listed here as Captive Rose.
Beaded Bull's Eye, Vase, Marigold, 10 In. 165.00
Beaded Bull's Eye, Vase, Marigold, 11 1/4 In. 65.00
Beaded Cable, Rose Bowl, Green ....95.00 to 175.00
Beaded Medallion & Teardrop pattern is listed here as Beaded Bull's Eye.
Beaded Shell, Creamer, Marigold 95.00
Blackberry, Plate, Marigold, Open Lace Edge, 7 1/2 In. 550.00
Blackberry A pattern is listed here as Blackberry.
Blackberry B pattern is listed here as Blackberry Spray.
Blackberry Spray, Hat, Amberina 400.00
Blackberry Spray, Hat, Marigold, 6 1/2 In. 30.00
Blackberry Wreath, Bowl 77.00
Blackberry Wreath, Bowl, Purple, 8 1/2 In. ....145.00 to 195.00
Broken Arches, Punch Cup, Amethyst 30.00
Bushel Basket pattern is listed here as Basket.
Butterfly, Bonbon 85.00
Butterfly & Berry, Berry Set, Marigold, 7 Piece ....160.00 to 300.00
Butterfly & Berry, Bowl, Footed, Marigold, 8 1/4 In. 55.00
Butterfly & Berry, Butter, Cover, Marigold 125.00
Butterfly & Berry, Tumbler, Blue 70.00
Butterfly & Berry, Water Set, Marigold, 7 Piece 395.00
Butterfly & Berry Spooner, Marigold 65.00
Butterfly & Fern, Pitcher, Amethyst 375.00
Butterfly & Grape pattern is listed here as Butterfly & Berry.
Butterfly & Plume pattern is listed here as Butterfly & Fern.
Butterfly & Stippled Rays pattern is listed here as Butterfly.
Cactus Leaf Rays pattern is listed here as Leaf Rays.
Captive Rose, Bowl, 3-In-1 Edge, Marigold, 8 In. 55.00
Captive Rose, Bowl, Ruffled, Blue 120.00
Captive Rose, Plate, Green 325.00
Cattails & Water Lily pattern is listed here as Water Lily & Cattails.
Cherries & Holly Wreath pattern is listed here as Cherry Circles.
Cherry, Bowl, Ball Footed, Purple, 9 In. 240.00
Cherry, Bowl, Footed, Peach Opalescent 95.00
Cherry, Bowl, Ruffled, 3-Footed, Marigold, 8 In. 235.00
Cherry Circles, Bonbon, Red ....*Illus* 5600.00

Carnival Glass, Cherry Circles,
Bonbon, Red

**If two tumblers get stuck
when stacked, try putting cold
water into the inside glass,
then put both into hot water
up to the lower rim.**

Cherry Wreathed pattern is listed here as Wreathed Cherry.
Christmas Cactus pattern is listed here as Thistle.
Chrysanthemum, Bowl, Ice Cream Shape, Marigold 82.00
Chrysanthemum, Bowl, Ruffled, Amberina, 9 In. 1980.00
Chrysanthemum Wreath pattern is listed here as Ten Mums.
Coin Dot, Bowl, Amethyst, 8 3/4 In. 38.00
Coin Dot, Bowl, Green, 6 In. 22.00
Coin Dot, Bowl, Marigold, 8 1/2 In. 30.00
Coin Dot, Bowl, Ruffled, Green, 7 3/4 In. 50.00
Coin Spot, Compote, Peach Opalescent .... 80.00 to 90.00
Coral, Plate, Marigold, 9 In. 1600.00
Corinth, Vase, Amethyst, 8 In. 50.00
Crackle, Vase, Marigold 20.00
Curved Star, Compote, Marigold, 7 In. 50.00
Daisy & Drape, Vase, Aqua Opalescent 800.00
Daisy & Plume, Bowl, 3-Footed, Green, 8 In. 60.00
Daisy & Plume, Rose Bowl, Amethyst 62.50
Daisy Band & Drape pattern is listed here as Daisy & Drape.
Dandelion, Tankard, Marigold 200.00
Dandelion Variant pattern is listed here as Panelled Dandelion.
Diamond Point, Vase, 11 1/2 In. 80.00
Diamond Point Column, Vase, Blue, 10 3/4 In. 70.00
Diamond Point Column, Vase, Green, 10 3/4 In. 70.00
Dogwood & Marsh Lily pattern is listed here as Two Flowers.
Double-Stem Rose, Bowl, Dome-Footed, Peach, 8 1/4 In. 30.00
Dragon & Lotus, Bowl, Collared Base, Green, 8 3/4 In. 125.00
Dragon & Lotus, Bowl, Marigold, 9 In. 100.00
Dragon & Lotus, Bowl, Ruffled, Blue, 9 In. .... 93.00 to 115.00
Dragon & Lotus, Bowl, Ruffled, Marigold, 9 In. 85.00
Dragon & Lotus, Bowl, Ruffled, Red, 9 In. 1650.00
Drape & Tie pattern is listed here as Rosalind.
Egyptian Band pattern is listed here as Round-Up.
Embroidered Mums, Bowl, Ice Blue, 9 In. .... 675.00 to 1000.00
English Hob & Button, Tray, Marigold, 8 x 11 1/2 In. 22.00
Fan & Arch pattern is listed here as Persian Garden.
Fantasy pattern is listed here as Question Marks.
Fashion, Pitcher, Water, Marigold 95.00
Fashion, Punch Bowl Set, Marigold, 12 Piece 350.00
Fashion, Punch Bowl, Base, Marigold 175.00
Fashion, Punch Bowl, Marigold 160.00
Fashion, Punch Cup, Marigold 24.00
Fashion, Sugar & Creamer, Marigold 100.00
Feather & Heart, Tumbler, Marigold 75.00
Feathers, Vase, Blue, 13 In. 90.00
Feathers, Vase, Green, 13 In. 90.00
Fenton's Butterfly pattern is listed here as Butterfly.
File & Fan, Bowl, Marigold, 7 In. 25.00

Fine Cut & Roses, Rose Bowl, Green . . . . .225.00 to 265.00
Fine Cut & Roses, Rose Bowl, Purple 165.00
Fine Rib, Vase, Amethyst, 9 1/2 In. 100.00
Fine Rib, Vase, Blue, 11 1/2 In. 125.00
Fine Rib, Vase, Green To Marigold Top, 7 1/2 In. 30.00
Fine Rib, Vase, Red, 9 In. 420.00
Finecut & Star pattern is listed here as Star & File.
Fish Net, Epergne, Amethyst 345.00
Fisherman's Net pattern is listed here as Tree Bark.
Fishscale & Beads, Bowl, Peach Opalescent, 9 1/2 In. 85.00
Floral & Diamond Point pattern is listed here as Fine Cut & Roses.
Floral & Grape, Tumbler, Amethyst 15.00
Floral & Grape, Water Set, Marigold, 5 Piece 185.00
Floral & Grapevine pattern is listed here as Floral & Grape.
Floral & Wheat, Bonbon, Footed, White 110.00
Floral & Wheat Spray pattern is listed here as Floral & Wheat.
Flowering Almonds pattern is listed here as Peacock Tail.
Fluffy Bird pattern is listed here as Peacock.
Flute, Toothpick, Marigold . . . . .35.00 to 40.00
Garland, Rose Bowl, Blue 55.00
Golden Grapes, Bowl, Marigold, 7 1/2 In. 28.00
Golden Honeycomb, Bowl, 2 Turned Up Sides, 7 1/2 In. 35.00
Good Luck, Bowl, Amethyst, 8 1/2 In. 395.00
Good Luck, Bowl, Marigold, 8 1/2 In. . . . . .175.00 to 195.00
Good Luck, Bowl, Ruffled, Green, 8 1/2 In. 400.00
Grape & Cable, Banana Boat, Blue 750.00
Grape & Cable, Banana Bowl, Purple . . . . *Illus* 260.00
Grape & Cable, Bonbon, Handles, Marigold 65.00
Grape & Cable, Bowl, Amethyst, 7 1/2 In. 85.00
Grape & Cable, Bowl, Amethyst, 9 In. 70.00
Grape & Cable, Bowl, Basketweave Exterior, Marigold, 7 1/2 In. 50.00
Grape & Cable, Bowl, Blue, 7 1/2 In. 70.00
Grape & Cable, Bowl, Footed, Green, 8 In. 85.00
Grape & Cable, Bowl, Footed, Marigold 85.00
Grape & Cable, Bowl, Footed, Marigold, 8 In. 70.00
Grape & Cable, Bowl, Fruit, Purple 800.00
Grape & Cable, Bowl, Green, 8 1/2 x 2 1/4 In. 75.00
Grape & Cable, Bowl, Ruffled, Footed, Purple, 8 In. 275.00
Grape & Cable, Bowl, Ruffled, Marigold 150.00
Grape & Cable, Butter, Cover, Purple 245.00
Grape & Cable, Cracker Jar, Amethyst 375.00
Grape & Cable, Hatpin Holder, Green 300.00

Carnival Glass, Grape & Cable,
Banana Bowl, Purple

Carnival Glass, Grape & Cable,
Plate, Pastel Marigold, 9 In.

Grape & Cable, Hatpin Holder, Marigold 302.00
Grape & Cable, Hatpin Holder, Purple 325.00
Grape & Cable, Humidor, Green 150.00
Grape & Cable, Pitcher, Purple 275.00
Grape & Cable, Plate, Amethyst, 7 1/2 In. 175.00
Grape & Cable, Plate, Footed, Amethyst 165.00
Grape & Cable, Plate, Footed, Marigold, 8 In. 175.00
Grape & Cable, Plate, Pastel Marigold, 9 In. ....*Illus* 170.00
Grape & Cable, Plate, Purple, 9 In. 175.00
Grape & Cable, Punch Bowl, Purple 880.00
Grape & Cable, Punch Cup, Amethyst 40.00
Grape & Cable, Punch Cup, Purple 32.00
Grape & Cable, Spooner, Purple 110.00
Grape & Cable, Sweetmeat Jar, Cover, Amethyst 150.00
Grape & Cable, Tumbler, Marigold 38.00
Grape & Cable, Water Set, Marigold, 5 Piece 250.00
Grape & Cable, Water Set, Purple, 7 Piece 550.00
Grape & Gothic Arches, Creamer, Blue 95.00
Grape Arbor, Water Set, Marigold, 7 Piece 700.00
Grape Delight pattern is listed here as Vintage.
Greek Key, Bowl, Footed, Green, 7 In. 150.00
Greek Key, Plate, Marigold, 9 1/2 In. 900.00
Greek Key, Tumbler, Green 195.00
Heart & Vine, Bowl, Blue, 8 1/2 In. ....50.00 to 95.00
Heart & Vine, Plate, Amethyst, 8 In. 300.00
Hearts & Flowers, Bowl, Ruffled, Ice Blue 455.00
Hearts & Flowers, Compote, Marigold 250.00
Heavy Grape, Chop Plate, Purple 375.00
Heron & Rushes pattern is listed here as Stork & Rushes.
Hobnail pattern is listed in this book as its own category.
Holly, Bowl, Amberina, Ruffled, 8 In. 675.00
Holly, Bowl, Blue, 9 In. ....80.00 to 90.00
Holly, Bowl, Green, 8 In. 80.00
Holly, Bowl, Marigold, 8 1/2 In. 50.00
Holly, Bowl, Marigold, 9 In. ....60.00 to 135.00
Holly, Bowl, Purple, 9 In. 85.00
Holly, Plate, Marigold, 9 In. 400.00
Holly & Berry pattern is listed here as Holly Carnival.
Holly Carnival, Bowl, Marigold, 8 In. 35.00
Holly Spray pattern is listed here as Holly Sprig.
Holly Sprig, Bowl, Amethyst, 9 In. 135.00
Holly Sprig, Bowl, Ruffled, Amethyst, 9 1/2 In. 200.00
Honeycomb & Clover, Bonbon, 2 Handles, Marigold 22.00
Honeycomb Collar pattern is listed here as Fishscale & Beads.
Horn Of Plenty pattern is listed here as Cornucopia.
Horse Medallions pattern is listed here as Horses' Heads.
Horses' Heads, Bowl, Ruffled, Marigold, 7 In. 75.00
Horses' Heads, Rose Bowl, Blue 375.00
Horses' Heads, Rose Bowl, Marigold 500.00
Imperial Grape, Bowl, Green, 9 In. 23.00
Imperial Grape, Bowl, Ruffled, Collared Base, Marigold, 8 In. 48.00
Imperial Grape, Bowl, Ruffled, Footed, Marigold, 11 In. 55.00
Imperial Grape, Bowl, Ruffled, Purple, 8 In. 100.00
Imperial Grape, Carafe, Water, Amethyst 225.00
Imperial Grape, Decanter, Stopper, Purple 250.00
Imperial Grape, Goblet, Purple 120.00
Imperial Grape, Plate, Marigold, 6 1/2 In. 25.00
Imperial Grape, Tumbler, Amethyst 45.00
Imperial Grape, Water Set, Marigold, 7 Piece 155.00
Imperial Grape, Wine, Green, Pair 18.00
Inverted Strawberry, Bowl, Amethyst, 10 1/2 In. 295.00
Inverted Strawberry, Tumbler, Marigold 300.00

Irish Lace pattern is listed here as Louisa.
Jeweled Heart, Tumbler, Marigold 110.00
Kittens, Cup & Saucer, Marigold 250.00
Kittens, Cup, Marigold 175.00
Kittens, Toothpick, Marigold 265.00
Labelle Rose pattern is listed here as Rose Show.
Lattice & Grape, Tankard, Marigold 225.00
Lattice & Grape, Water Set, Blue, 7 Piece 660.00
Lattice & Grapevine pattern is listed here as Lattice & Grape.
Leaf & Beads, Bowl, Footed, Marigold, 7 In. 30.00
Leaf & Beads, Candy Dish, 3-Footed, Marigold, 8 1/4 In. ....55.00 to 60.00
Leaf & Beads, Rose Bowl, Aqua Opalescent 400.00
Leaf Chain, Plate, Marigold, 7 In. 150.00
Leaf Medallion pattern is listed here as Leaf Chain.
Leaf Pinwheel & Star Flower pattern is listed here as Whirling Leaves.
Leaf Rays, Nappy, Handle, 6 In. 38.00
Leaf Rays, Nappy, Peach Opalescent 65.00
Lion, Bowl, Marigold, 6 1/2 In. 120.00
Little Flowers, Bowl, Amethyst, 5 In. 65.00
Little Flowers, Bowl, Marigold, 9 In. 65.00
Long Thumbprint, Creamer, Marigold 9.00
Lotus & Grape, Bowl, Footed, Marigold, 7 In. 125.00
Louisa, Bowl, 3-Footed, Green, 8 In. 50.00
Louisa, Plate, Footed, Teal 120.00
Lustre Rose, Bowl, Amber 165.00
Lustre Rose, Spooner, Marigold 35.00
Lustre Rose, Sugar, Cover, Marigold 40.00
Lustre Rose, Water Set, Marigold, 4 Piece 300.00
Magnolia & Poinsettia pattern is listed here as Water Lily.
Maple Leaf, Bowl, Peacock Tail Interior, Amethyst, 9 In. 115.00
Maple Leaf, Sherbet, Amethyst 30.00
Maple Leaf, Tumbler, Purple 42.00
Melinda pattern is listed here as Wishbone.
Memphis, Punch Cup, Marigold 25.00
Morning Glory, Vase, Purple, 7 In. 95.00
Mums & Greek Key pattern is listed here as Embroidered Mums.
Oak Leaf & Acorn pattern is listed here as Acorn.
Octagon, Bowl, Marigold, 8 1/2 In. 25.00
Octagon, Decanter, Stopper, Marigold 95.00
Ohio Star, Vase, Marigold, 9 In. 385.00
Open Rose, Bowl, Amber, Ruffled, 8 In. 55.00
Orange Tree, Bowl, Marigold, 9 In. 55.00
Orange Tree, Compote, 3-Footed, Blue 295.00
Orange Tree, Compote, Marigold 25.00
Orange Tree, Compote, Marigold, 4 1/2 In. 35.00
Orange Tree, Mug, Blue, 3 1/2 In. 130.00
Orange Tree, Mug, Marigold ....45.00 to 70.00
Orange Tree, Mug, Marigold, Small 27.00
Orange Tree, Plate, Tree Trunk Center, White 325.00
Orange Tree, Punch Bowl Set, Base, Marigold, 8 Piece 200.00
Orange Tree, Punch Cup, Blue 30.00
Orange Tree, Sauce, Pedestal, Cobalt Blue, 4 1/2 In. 35.00
Oriental Poppy, Tumbler, White 165.00
Oriental Poppy, Water Set, Tankard, Purple, 6 Piece ....*Illus* 1376.00
Panelled Dandelion, Water Set, Blue, 6 Piece 675.00
Pansy, Creamer, Marigold ....25.00 to 35.00
Pansy, Nappy, Handle, Amethyst, 5 1/2 In. ....40.00 to 42.00
Pansy, Sugar, Cover, Marigold 13.50
Panther, Bowl, Marigold, 5 1/4 In. 50.00
Peacock, Bowl, Marigold, 9 In. 253.00
Peacock, Bowl, Ruffled, Aqua, 9 In. 1695.00
Peacock, Plate, Ice Green, 9 In. 400.00

Peacock & Grape, Bowl, Amber, 8 3/4 In. 140.00
Peacock & Grape, Bowl, Footed, Green, 7 3/4 In. 125.00
Peacock & Grape, Plate, Marigold, 9 In. 750.00
Peacock & Urn, Bowl, Marigold, 8 1/2 In. ....160.00 to 175.00
Peacock & Urn, Bowl, Mystery, 3 In 1 Edge, Purple, 8 In. 750.00
Peacock & Urn, Dish, Ice Cream, Marigold, Large 500.00
Peacock & Urn, Plate, Blue 550.00
Peacock & Urn, Plate, White, 9 In. ....475.00 to 500.00
Peacock At The Fountain, Butter, Blue 290.00
Peacock At The Fountain, Pitcher, Marigold 325.00
Peacock At The Fountain, Punch Bowl, Base, Purple 800.00
Peacock At The Fountain, Punch Cup 45.00
Peacock At The Fountain, Spooner, Blue 190.00
Peacock Eye & Grape pattern is listed here as Vineyard.
Peacock On Fence pattern is listed here as Peacock.
Peacock Tail, Bowl, Amethyst, 7 1/4 In. 45.00
Peacock Tail, Bowl, Green, 9 In. 250.00
Peacock Tail, Candy Dish, Tricornered, Green, 6 In. 75.00
Persian Garden, Plate, White, 7 In. 155.00
Persian Medallion, Bonbon, Blue ....100.00 to 120.00
Persian Medallion, Plate, Blue, 6 In. 145.00
Pine Cone, Bowl, Blue, 7 In. 140.00
Pine Cone, Plate, Amethyst, 6 3/8 In. 200.00
Pine Cone Wreath pattern is listed here as Pine Cone.
Plate, Cherry, Purple, 6 In. 300.00
Plume Panels, Vase, Flared, Green, 13 1/2 In. 75.00
Polo, Ashtray, Marigold, 5 3/4 In. 45.00
Premium, Candlestick, Marigold, Pair 50.00
Princess Lace pattern is listed here as Octagon.
Question Marks, Bonbon, Handle, Marigold 35.00
Question Marks, Compote, Marigold, 6 1/4 x 3 3/4 In. 35.00
Rainbow, Compote, Amethyst 115.00
Raindrops, Bowl, Ruffled, Peach Opalescent 150.00
Raspberry, Tumbler, Green ....40.00 to 45.00
Raspberry, Water Set, Green, 7 Piece 550.00
Rays, Bowl, Fluted, Green, 9 In. 35.00
Ripple, Vase, Funeral, Marigold, 17 In. ....175.00 to 195.00
Ripple, Vase, Green, 8 1/2 In. 75.00
Ripple, Vase, Green, 9 In. 175.00
Ripple, Vase, Green, 10 3/4 In. 65.00
Ripple, Vase, Green, 12 In. 45.00

Carnival Glass, Oriental Poppy, Water Set,
Tankard, Purple, 6 Piece

**Store glass right side up to protect
the rims.**

**To clean wax from glass candle-
sticks, scrape with a wooden stick,
then wash off the remaining wax
with rubbing alcohol.**

Ripple, Vase, Marigold, 7 In. 11.00
Ripple, Vase, Purple, 9 In. 45.00
Rosalind, Bowl, Purple, 10 In. 200.00
Rose & Ruffles pattern is listed here as Open Rose.
Rose Show, Plate, Dark Marigold, 9 In. 2000.00
Rose Show, Plate, White, 9 In. 650.00
Roses & Loops pattern is listed here as Double-Stem Rose.
Round-Up, Plate, Marigold, 9 In. 95.00
Sailboat & Windmill pattern is listed here as Sailboats.
Sailboats, Sauce, Marigold, 6 In. 30.00
Sailboats, Wine, Marigold 35.00
Singing Birds, Mug, Marigold 85.00
Singing Birds, Tumbler, Green 125.00
Singing Birds, Tumbler, Purple 40.00
Single Flower, Bowl, Ruffled, Peach Opalescent, 8 In. 150.00
Stag & Holly, Bowl, Blue, 7 1/2 In. 225.00
Stag & Holly, Bowl, Footed, Blue, 7 1/2 In. 325.00
Stag & Holly, Platter, Red, Spade Footed 135.00
Star & File, Bowl, Marigold 35.00
Star & File, Decanter, Marigold 75.00
Star & File, Sugar, 2 Handles, Marigold 60.00
Star & File, Wine Set, Marigold, 7 Piece 300.00
Star Of David & Bows, Bowl, Purple, 7 1/4 In. 200.00
Star Of David Medallion pattern is listed here as Star of David & Bows.
Stippled Diamond & Flower pattern is listed here as Little Flowers.
Stippled Leaf & Beads pattern is listed here as Leaf & Beads.
Stippled Petals, Banana Boat, Dome-Footed, Peach Opalescent, 9 In. 100.00
Stippled Rays, Bowl, Amethyst, 10 In. 42.00
Stippled Rays, Bowl, Ruffled, Red, 6 In. 450.00
Stork, Vase, Marigold 30.00
Stork & Rushes, Tumbler, Purple 22.00
Strawberry pattern is listed here as Wild Strawberry.
Strawberry, Bonbon, 2 Handles, Amber 50.00
Strawberry, Bowl, Pie Crust Edge, Amethyst, 9 In. 125.00
Strawberry, Bowl, Stippled, Ruffled, Marigold, 8 1/2 In. 300.00
Strawberry, Plate, Green, 9 In. 275.00
Strawberry, Plate, Purple, 9 In. 325.00
Swirl Hobnail, Vase, Green, 9 3/4 In. 250.00
Teardrops pattern is listed here as Raindrops.
Ten Mums, Tumbler, Blue 55.00
Thistle, Banana Boat, Blue ....300.00 to 385.00
Thistle, Bowl, 3-In-1 Edge, Amethyst, 8 1/2 In. 115.00
Thistle, Bowl, Green, 9 In. 120.00
Thistle, Bowl, Ruffled, Green, 9 In. 100.00
Three Fruits, Bowl, Amethyst, 9 In. 135.00
Three Fruits, Bowl, Dome-Footed, Marigold, 8 In. 48.00
Three Fruits, Bowl, Green, 9 In. 140.00
Three Fruits, Bowl, Stippled, Blue, 9 In. 350.00
Three Fruits, Plate, Amethyst, 9 In. 300.00
Three Fruits, Plate, Basketweave Exterior, Stippled, 9 In. 450.00
Three Fruits, Plate, Marigold, 9 In. ....270.00 to 275.00
Three Fruits, Plate, Plain Back, Purple, 9 In. 600.00
Three Fruits, Plate, Stippled, Purple, 8 In. 425.00
Three Fruits Medallion, Bowl, Meander Exterior, Amethyst, 9 In. 150.00
Tree Bark, Water Set, Amethyst, 7 Piece 140.00
Tree Of Life, Basket, High Handle, Marigold, 6 In. 17.00
Tree Trunk, Vase, Green, 11 In. 150.00
Two Flowers, Bowl, Footed, Marigold, 10 1/2 In. 55.00
Two Flowers, Bowl, Marigold, 8 1/2 In. 65.00
Two Flowers, Rose Bowl, Marigold, Large 350.00
Two Fruits, Bonbon, 2 Sections, Marigold 50.00
Vineyard, Pitcher, Marigold 95.00

Vintage, Bonbon, Green, 5 1/2 In. 28.00
Vintage, Bonbon, Handle, Amethyst, 7 In. 80.00
Vintage, Bowl, Green, 5 1/2 In. 30.00
Vintage, Bowl, Green, 9 In. 85.00
Vintage, Plate, Amethyst, 7 1/2 In. 450.00
Vintage, Plate, Blue, 7 1/2 In. 275.00
Vintage, Powder Jar, Amethyst 60.00
Vintage, Rose Bowl, Amethyst 60.00
Vintage, Rose Bowl, Blue 125.00
Waffle Block, Basket, Teal 110.00
Water Lily, Bonbon, 2 Handles, Marigold 26.00
Water Lily, Bowl, Footed, Marigold, 5 In. 50.00
Water Lily & Cattails, Berry Bowl, Small 18.00
Water Lily & Cattails, Tumbler, Marigold .... 78.00 to 95.00
Whirling Leaves, Bowl, Flared, Marigold, 9 3/4 In. 50.00
Wide Panel, Plate, Marigold, 11 1/2 In. 35.00
Wide Panel, Vase, Green To Marigold Top, 9 1/2 In. 35.00
Wild Strawberry, Bowl, Green, 10 In. 135.00
Windflower, Bowl, Marigold, 9 In. .... 45.00 to 50.00
Windflower, Plate, Blue, 9 In. 225.00
Windmill, Pitcher, Milk, Marigold 75.00
Windmill Medallion pattern is listed here as Windmill.
Wishbone, Bowl, Footed, Ice Blue, 8 1/2 In. 1150.00
Wishbone, Bowl, Ruffled Edge, Footed, Marigold, 7 1/2 In. 82.00
Wishbone, Plate, 3-Footed, Purple 485.00
Wishbone, Tumbler, Amethyst 150.00
Wreathed Cherry, Bowl, Oval, Amethyst, 9 x 12 In. .... 115.00 to 120.00
Zipper Stitch, Cordial Set, Marigold, 7 Piece 1450.00

CAROUSEL or merry-go-round figures were first carved in the United
States in 1867 by Gustav Dentzel. Collectors discovered the charm of
the hand-carved figures in the 1970s, and they were soon classed as
folk art. Most desirable are the figures other than horses, such as pigs,
camels, lions, or dogs. A jumper is a figure that was made to move up
and down on a pole; a stander was placed in a stationary position.

Camel, Stander, E. Joy Morris 10450.00
Donkey, Herschell-Spillman 3850.00
Horse, Bucking Bronco, Jewels, Herschell-Spillman 8250.00
Horse, Flag, Herschell-Spillman 6325.00
Horse, Jumper, C.W. Parker 2475.00
Horse, Jumper, Illions 9075.00
Horse, Jumper, Metal, Parker 660.00
Horse, Jumper, Middle Row, Flowing Mane, Armitage Herschell, c.1895, 46 x 53 In. ... 4600.00
Horse, Jumper, Muller 8800.00
Horse, Jumper, Stein & Goldstein 8470.00
Horse, Merry-Go-Round Co., Detachable Mane & Tail, 46 In. 8500.00
Horse, Painted Wood, Dentzel, 50 In. 7920.00
Horse, Prancer, Herschell-Spillman 12100.00
Horse, Wooden, Iron Horseshoes, Gray, 63 In. 2420.00
Lion, Ortega, Mexico 1430.00
Panel, Mirrors, Clown's Face Center, Carved, Polychrome, c.1900, 28 x 16 In. 1500.00
Pig, Carved & Painted Wood, 50 In. 797.00
Pig, Muller, c.1920 .... 5800.00
Pig, Red, Blue & Yellow 6800.00
Rooster, Full Round, Carved Feathers, Saddle Blanket, Comb, Wattle, Pine, 48 x 52 In. .. 8050.00
Rooster, Pine, Carved & Painted, Orange & Yellow, 32 3/4 In. 4600.00

CARRIAGE means several things, so this category lists baby carriages,
buggies for adults, horse-drawn sleighs, and even strollers. Doll-sized
carriages are listed in the Toy category.

Baby Buggy, Haywood-Wakefield, Wooden, Enameled Metal, Chrome, 37 x 43 In. 825.00
Baby Buggy, Wicker, Wakefield Rattan Co., 1890 .... 4500.00

Baby Buggy, Wicker, Wooden Base, Frame, Wheels, 24 In. 160.00
Buggy, Amish, Single Horse, Sliding Glass Doors 1750.00
Cart, Governess, 1 Horse, 1900 . . . .   900.00
Sleigh, 2 Seater, Burgundy, Blue Upholstered Seats, Raised Side Panels, 1920s, 40 In. . . .   1500.00
Sleigh, Push, Maroon Paint, Striping & Stenciling 1430.00
Sleigh, Push, Red Paint, Yellow Striping, All Wooden, 45 In. 385.00
Sleigh, Village & Landscape Scenes, Upholstered Seat, Scroll Rails, 45 x 57 In. 3255.00
Sleigh, Wooden, Varnished, Striping, Painted Bird, 32 In. 770.00
Stroller, Heywood-Wakefield, Victorian, Twin 1150.00
Stroller, Wicker, Brown, Wooden Wheels, 19 x 19 In. 135.00
Wagon, Goat, Green 1100.00
Wagon Seat, Country, Refinished, Splint Seat, 28 3/4 x 33 In. 440.00

CASH REGISTERS were invented in 1884 because an eye on the cash was a necessity in stores of the nineteenth century, too. John and James Ritty invented a large model that resembled a clock and kept a record of the dollars and cents exchanged in the store. John Patterson improved the cash register with a paper roll to record the money. By the early 1900s, elaborate brass registers were made. About World War I, the fancy case was exchanged for the more modern types.

J.C. Cox, Mahogany, England, c.1840 . . . .   1915.00
National, 8 Drawers, Floor Model, Oak 1450.00
National, Brass, Original Metal Tag, 21 x 10 x 16 In. 517.00
National, Model 9, Fleur-De-Lis 1800.00
National, Model 18, Wooden, Burl & Gold Filled Carving On Cylinder 2090.00
National, Model 36, Scroll Case 1500.00
National, Model 47, Marble & Glass, Amount Purchased Sign, c.1896 . . . .   820.00
National, Model 225 . . . .   900.00
National, Model 313, Candy Store 1395.00
National, Model 441 . . . .   1000.00
National, Oak, Cabinet, 8 Drawers, 4 Ft. 11 In. 1700.00
St. Louis, Brass 350.00

CASTOR JARS for pickles are glass jars about six inches in height, held in special metal holders. They became a popular dinner table accessory about 1890. Each jar had a top that was usually silver or silver plate. The frame, also of a silver metal, had a handle that arched above the jar and a hook that held a pair of tongs. By 1900, the pickle castor was out of fashion. Many examples found today have reproduced glass jars in old holders. Additional pickle castors may be found in the various Glass categories.

Pickle, Coreopsis Insert, White Flowers, Footed Frame, Tongs 395.00
Pickle, Crackle Glass, Silver Plated Pickle Finial 35.00
Pickle, Cranberry Glass Container, Silver Plate, 11 1/2 In. 275.00
Pickle, Cranberry Insert, Nautical Style, Inverted Thumbprint 450.00
Pickle, Cranberry Insert, Silver Plate Holder, 10 3/4 In. 467.00
Pickle, Cranberry Paneled Sprig Insert, Footed Frame, Tongs, 10 3/4 In. 570.00
Pickle, Diamond-Quilted, Mother-Of-Pearl, Insert, Empire Holder, Fork, 9 3/4 In. 850.00
Pickle, Double, Clear Inserts, Vertical Panels, Engraved Vines, William Rogers Frame . . .   825.00
Pickle, Frosted Panel, Flowers, Double Silver Plated Handles & Frame, 4 1/2 In. 275.00
Pickle, Frosted, Enameled, Silver Holder, Mt. Joy Style 395.00
Pickle, Inverted Thumbprint, Amber, Enamel Blue Berries, Meriden Frame 525.00
Pickle, Mt. Washington Design, Diamond-Quilted, Cathedral Style Frame, 12 3/4 In. 695.00
Pickle, Mt. Washington Insert, Opalescent Swirled Stripes, Frame 350.00
Pickle, Open Heart Arches, White Satin, Complete 350.00
Pickle, Ram's Head, Silver Plated Holder 125.00
Pickle, Rubina Honeycomb, Coralene Type Florals, Bluebells Finial 425.00
Pickle, Rubina Insert, Inverted Thumbprint, Coralene, 10 1/2 In. 920.00
Pickle, Ruby Glass Insert, Enamel Millefiori Design, Multicolor, Frame & Tongs 435.00
Pickle, Sapphire Insert, Daisy & Button With V Ornament, Silver Frame, Tongs 375.00
Pickle, Sapphire Insert, Swirled Mold, Enamel, Ornate Tongs, Silver Plated Frame 475.00
Pickle, Zipper & Beading, Birds At Fountain At Base, Emerald Green 285.00

CASTOR SETS holding just salt and pepper castors were used in the seventeenth century. The sugar castor, mustard pot, spice dredger, bottles for vinegar and oil, and other spice holders became popular by the eighteenth century. These sets were usually made of sterling silver. The American Victorian castor set, the type most collected today, was made of silver plated Britannia metal. Colored glass bottles were introduced after the Civil War. The sets were out of fashion by World War I. Be careful when buying sets with colored bottles; many are reproductions. Other castor sets may be listed in various porcelain and glass categories in this book.

6 Bottles, Call Bell Finial, Silver Plated Frame, 17 In.	275.00
Cranberry Thumbprint, Silver Frame	540.00
Salt & Pepper, Cupid Finial, Repousse, Vermeil, Silver Plate, Sheffield, 7 In., Pair	403.00

CATALOGS are listed in the Paper category.

CAUGHLEY porcelain was made in England from 1772 to 1814. Caughley porcelains are very similar in appearance to those made at the Worcester factory. See the Salopian category for related items.

Dish, Gilt Trim, Oriental Scene, 18th Century, 7 7/8 In.	405.00
Tureen, Dessert, Oriental Design, 1780	500.00

CAULDON Limited worked in Staffordshire, Great Britain, and went through many name changes. John Ridgway made porcelain at Cauldon Place, Hanley, until 1855. The firm of John Ridgway, Bates and Co. of Cauldon Place worked from 1856 to 1859. It became Bates, Brown-Westhead, Moore and Co. from 1859 to 1862. Brown-Westhead, Moore and Co. worked from 1862 to 1904. About 1890, this firm started using the words *Cauldon* or *Cauldon ware* as part of the mark. Cauldon Ltd. worked from 1905 to 1920, Cauldon Potteries from 1920 to 1962. Related items may be found in the Indian Tree category.

Cup & Saucer, Flowers, Leaves	25.00
Cup & Saucer, Thistle	14.00
Plate, Center Floral, Gold Edge Trim, 10 In.	35.00
Plate, June Garden, 10 In.	22.00

CELADON is the name of a velvet-textured green-gray glaze used by Chinese, Japanese, Korean, and other factories. The name refers both to the glaze and to pieces covered with the glaze. It is still being made.

Bowl, 2 Dragons, Around Pearl, Early 20th Century, 10 1/2 In.	176.00
Bowl, Double Fish, 6 5/8 In.	275.00
Bowl, Everted Rim, Central Incised Flower Interior, Olive Glaze, 13 1/2 In.	630.00
Bowl, Fish, 10 1/2 In.	145.00
Bowl, Flower Shape, Phoenix, 8 In.	395.00
Bowl, Gray Crackle Glaze, 19th Century, 9 In.	575.00
Bowl, Relief Peony, Footed, 10 In.	908.00
Candlestick, Yi Dynasty, 7 In.	35.00
Charger, Incised Peony, Peacock, 22 In.	2300.00
Dish, Crackled Glaze, Ribbed Exterior, Song Dynasty, 12 In.	288.00
Dish, Incised, Flower, Gold Lacquer, Pale, 5 1/2 In.	180.00
Dish, Peony, 10 In.	150.00
Jar, Oxblood Splash, Globular, 4 In.	217.00
Teapot, Paneled Sides, Hexagonal, 5 In.	272.00
Vase, 9 Applied Bearded, Robed Figures Beneath Dragons, 12 1/2 In., Pair	495.00
Vase, Baluster, Peony, Ming Dynasty, 17 1/2 In.	908.00
Vase, Crackled, Double Gourd Shape, 7 3/4 In.	102.00
Vase, Crackleware, Ring Handles, Gray, Blue, 18th Century, 4 1/2 In.	72.00
Vase, Flowered Peony, Raised On Flared Foot, Olive Green Glaze, 8 1/2 In.	632.00
Vase, Foo Lion Handles, Baluster Shape, Blue, White, 23 1/2 In.	300.00
Vase, Raised Seal Mark On Base, Phoenix, Fret Designed, 14 In.	785.00
Water Dropper, Relief Lotus, Teapot Shape, Pale Glaze, 3 In.	275.00
Wine Pot, Pale, Globular, 4 1/2 In.	275.00

CELLULOID is a trademark for a plastic developed in 1868 by John W. Hyatt. Celluloid Manufacturing Company, the Celluloid Novelty Company, Celluloid Fancy Goods Company, and American Xylonite Company all used Celluloid to make jewelry, games, sewing equipment, false teeth, and piano keys. Eventually, the Hyatt Company became the American Celluloid and Chemical Manufacturing Company, the Celanese Corporation. The name *Celluloid* was often used to identify any similar plastic. Celluloid toys are listed under Toys.

Back Scratcher, Parrot Handle	12.00
Box, Floral, Round, Dennison	32.00
Box, Jewelry, Lovers Center, Allover Repousse, Cream, Interior Mirror	60.00
Figure, Sailor, 8 In.	28.00
Manicure Rack, Drawer Base, Amber & Green Marbelized, 9 Piece	75.00
Power Jar & Hair Receiver, Gold Trim, 2 Piece	24.00
Rattle, Man In The Moon, Winking	160.00
Ring, Carved	40.00

CELS are listed in this book in the Animation Art category.

CERAMIC ART COMPANY of Trenton, New Jersey, was established in 1889 by J. Coxon and W. Lenox and was an early producer of American Belleek porcelain. It became Lenox, Inc. in 1906. Do not confuse this ware with the pottery made by the Ceramic Arts Studio of Madison, Wisconsin.

Mug, Colonial Drinkers, Fred Littell Christmas, Pallet Mark, 1907, 5 In.	125.00

CERAMIC ARTS STUDIO was founded in Madison, Wisconsin, by Lawrence Rabbett and Ruben Sand. Their most popular products were expensive molded figurines. The pottery closed in 1955. Do not confuse these products with those of the Ceramic Art Co. of Trenton, New Jersey.

Bank, Mrs. Blankety Blank, 4 1/2 In.	85.00
Figurine, Alice In Wonderland, 4 1/2 In.	95.00
Figurine, Archibald The Dragon, 8 In.	185.00
Figurine, Beth & Bruce, Light Green	65.00
Figurine, Blythe, Black, White, 6 1/2 In.	90.00
Figurine, Bright Eyes Cat, 3 In.	35.00
Figurine, Chipmunk, Brown, 2 In.	40.00
Figurine, Dutch Love Girl, Blue, 5 In.	25.00
Figurine, Dutch Love Girl, Yellow, 5 In.	25.00
Figurine, Fawn, 4 1/4 In.	45.00
Figurine, Fawn, Stylized, Chartreuse, 2 In.	35.00
Figurine, Fighting Cocks, Green	50.00 to 60.00
Figurine, Flute Girl, 4 1/2 In.	45.00
Figurine, Gay '90s Couple	75.00
Figurine, Gay '90s Man, Gray Coat, Hat, Dog	45.00
Figurine, Hans & Katrinka, Blue, 5 In., Pair	85.00 to 110.00
Figurine, Inky Skunk, 2 1/4 In.	25.00
Figurine, Leopards, Fighting, Pair	200.00
Figurine, Little Bopeep, 5 1/2 In.	22.00 to 42.00
Figurine, Little Boy Blue, 4 1/2 In.	25.00 to 35.00
Figurine, Lu Tang & Wing Sang	45.00
Figurine, Lucindy, Blue, 7 In.	50.00
Figurine, Miss Muffet Stirring Food, 4 1/2 In.	50.00
Figurine, Mo-Pi, Chubby Woman, 6 In.	16.00
Figurine, Pete & Polly Parrots, Maroon, 7 1/2 In.	110.00
Figurine, Pioneer Sam & Suzie, Green	85.00
Figurine, Polish Girl, 6 1/2 In.	40.00
Figurine, Rhumba Woman, Green, 7 In.	45.00
Figurine, Ting-A-Ling & Sung-Tu, Pair	40.00
Figurine, Wing Sang, 6 In.	20.00
Jug, Adam & Eve	48.00
Plaque, Arabesque Ballerina, 9 1/4 In.	35.00
Plaque, Comedy Mask, 5 In.	150.00

Plaque, Greg & Grace, Black, Gold Trim, Pair . . . . .125.00 to 150.00
Plaque, Harlequin, Red & Black, 8 In. 75.00
Plaque, Wall, Shadow Dance, Pair 90.00
Salt & Pepper, Calico Cat & Gingham Dog 95.00
Salt & Pepper, Chipmunk, Brown, 2 In. 40.00
Salt & Pepper, Democratic Donkey, Republican Elephant, 4 1/4 In. 395.00
Salt & Pepper, Dutch Boy & Girl, 4 In. . . . . .25.00 to 30.00
Salt & Pepper, Fox & Goose 145.00
Salt & Pepper, Frog & Toadstool . . . . .35.00 to 52.00
Salt & Pepper, Kangaroo, Mother & Joey 85.00
Salt & Pepper, Kitten & Creamer 195.00
Salt & Pepper, Man & Woman 125.00
Salt & Pepper, Mother & Baby Bear, Brown . . . . .45.00 to 65.00
Salt & Pepper, Mouse & Cheese, Snuggle . . . . .25.00 to 30.00
Salt & Pepper, Oakie Straddling Spring Leaf 85.00
Salt & Pepper, Parakeets, Pudgie & Budgie, Metal Cage, 5 In. 90.00
Salt & Pepper, Pete & Polly Parrot, Maroon 110.00
Salt & Pepper, Sabu Elephant, Boy, Sitting In Trunk . . . . .145.00 to 225.00
Salt & Pepper, Seahorse & Coral, Snuggle 95.00
Salt & Pepper, Wee Chinese Boy 25.00
Salt & Pepper, Wee Eskimo Boy 35.00
Salt & Pepper, Wee Scottish Boy 35.00
Shelf Sitter, Banjo Girl, 4 In. 40.00
Shelf Sitter, Boy With Dog, 4 1/4 In. 45.00
Shelf Sitter, Canary, 5 In. 15.00
Shelf Sitter, Dance Moderne Man, Chartreuse 60.00
Shelf Sitter, Farm Girl, Blue, 4 3/4 In. . . . . .35.00 to 45.00
Shelf Sitter, Greg & Grace, Pair 150.00
Shelf Sitter, Jack & Jill, Pair 40.00
Shelf Sitter, Maurice, Dark Green, 7 In. 45.00
Shelf Sitter, Persian Mother Cat, Pair . . . . .65.00 to 95.00
Shelf Sitter, Pioneer Sam & Suzie, Green 85.00
Shelf Sitter, Pixie Girl, Kneeling, 2 1/2 In. 35.00
Shelf Sitter, Pixie, Riding Snail, 2 3/4 In. 35.00
Shelf Sitter, Sun-Li & Sun-Lin, 5 1/2 In. 40.00
Shelf Sitter, Tom Cat, 4 3/4 In. 50.00
Toby Mug, 2 3/4 In. 50.00

CHALKWARE is really plaster of Paris decorated with watercolors. One type was molded from Staffordshire and other porcelain models and painted and sold as inexpensive decorations in the nineteenth century. Figures of plaster, made from about 1910 to 1940 for use as prizes at carnivals, are also known as chalkware. Kewpie dolls made of chalkware will be found in their own category.

Bank, Dove, Brown & Green, 11 1/2 In. 950.00
Figurine, Boy, Fisher, 8 In. 35.00
Figurine, Brenda Starr, 12 In. 85.00
Figurine, Cat, Red, Mustard & Black, 9 1/2 In. 3500.00
Figurine, Christ On Cross 20.00
Figurine, Colonial Couple, Hand Painted, 11 In. 150.00
Figurine, Dog, Bulldog 20.00
Figurine, Dog, Rin Tin Tin, 17 In. 55.00
Figurine, Dog, Rin Tin Tin, Standing On Rock, 21 In. 150.00
Figurine, Dog, Rin Tin Tin, Yellow Jeweled Eyes, Marked, 1930s, 19 In. 250.00
Figurine, Dog, Seated, Black & White, Red Collar, Oval Base, 5 1/4 In., Pair 220.00
Figurine, Dog, Spaniel, White, 8 1/2 In. 28.00
Figurine, Dog, Yellow, Red, Black, Green, 7 1/2 In. 220.00
Figurine, Dove, Standing, Polychrome, 6 In. 325.00
Figurine, Ewe With Lamb, Recumbent, 8 1/2 In. 675.00
Figurine, Ferdinand The Bull 24.00
Figurine, Indian Boy, 14 In. 25.00
Figurine, Jiminy Cricket, 14 In. 135.00
Figurine, Kitten, Recumbent, 2 1/4 In. 395.00

Figurine, Mutt, Brass Coin In Base, Mark Hampton Co., 1911, 9 1/2 In.	125.00
Figurine, Rooster, Red Comb, Red & Mustard Tail, Green Base, 6 1/2 In.	450.00
Figurine, Rooster, Red, Yellow, Black Paint, 5 1/4 In.	485.00
Figurine, Sailor Girl, 1930s, 14 In.	20.00
Figurine, Sheep, With A Lamp	115.00
Figurine, Sioux Chief, 12 1/2 In.	75.00
Figurine, Squirrel, Holding Nut, Orange Tail, Green Base, 7 In.	650.00
Figurine, Uncle Sam, Rollin' 'Em Up, Red, White & Blue, Painted, 12 In.	35.00
Hutch-Shrine, Wax Mother & Child Behind Glass, Dated 1817, 15 In.	290.00
Ornament, Mantel, Fruit, Foliate Design, 19th Century, 12 1/2 In., Pair	460.00
String Holder, Chef	40.00
String Holder, Girl With Flower, Red Hat	65.00

CHARLIE CHAPLIN, the famous comic and actor, lived from 1889 to 1977. He made his first movie in 1913. He did the movie *The Tramp* in 1915. The character of the Tramp has remained famous, and in the 1980s appeared in a series of television commercials for computers. Dolls, candy containers, and all sorts of memorabilia picture Charlie Chaplin. Pieces are being made even today.

Box, Pencil, Signed H. Clive	75.00
Candy Container, Borgfeldt	130.00
Chaplin Cavalcade, 1940s, 1 Sheet	40.00
Doll, Dancing Charlie Illusion, Jointed, Box, 13 In.	175.00
Doll, Little Tramp Wearing Costume, Hat, 1990, 9 In.	36.00
Doll, Sitting, Wooden, Metal Chair, Cane, 25 1/2 In.	250.00
Doll, Windup, Black, Removable Cane, Reliable, Canada, 1950s, 7 1/2 In.	295.00
Figurine, Celluloid, Holding Cane, Prewar, 3 3/4 In.	157.00
Figurine, Lead, 2 1/2 In.	95.00
Mold, Candy	120.00
Pencil Box, Figure Of Charlie Chaplin, Tin, Signed, H. Clive	75.00
Toy, Dancing Charlie Illusion, Jointed	145.00
Toy, Walks, Iron Feet, Windup, 1920s	950.00
Watch, Pocket	70.00

CHARLIE MCCARTHY was the ventriloquist's dummy used by Edgar Bergen from the 1930s. He was famous for his work in radio, movies, and television. The act was retired in the 1970s.

Car, Marx, Box	1150.00
Doll, 20 In.	895.00
Doll, Composition, Head, 13 In.	395.00
Doll, Mortimer Snerd, Composition, Brown Suit & Tie, 1930s, 13 In.	300.00
Figure, Walking, Mouth Opens & Closes, Marx, 1930s, 8 In.	585.00
Game, Flying Hat	38.00
Pencil Sharpener, Bakelite, 1930, 1 3/4 In.	68.00
Pencil Sharpener, Catalin	40.00
Pin, Black, White Enamel, Moveable Mouth	518.00
Puppet, Composition Head, Cloth Body, Monocle, Juro Novelty Co., 1977	50.00
Ring, Metal, Gold Finish, 1940s	270.00
Sheet Music, Radio Show, 1940	40.00
Toy, Car, Benzine, Red & White Wheels	700.00
Toy, Drives Bensine Buggy, Windup, Marx, 1930s	485.00
Toy, Figure, 12 In.	125.00
Toy, Mortimer Snerd, Tin, Windup, Lithograph, 1939, 9 In.	350.00 to 850.00

CHELSEA porcelain was made in the Chelsea area of London from about 1745 to 1784. Some pieces made from 1770 to 1784 may include the letter *D* for *Derby* in the mark. Ceramic designs were borrowed from the Meissen models of the day. Pieces were made of soft paste. The gold anchor was used as the mark but it has been copied by many other factories. Recent copies of Chelsea have been made from the original molds. Do not confuse Chelsea porcelain with Chelsea Grape, the next category.

Beaker, Kakiemon, 2 Panels, Iron Red Poppies, Iron Red Flowerhead, 1750, 3 In.	1380.00

Beaker, Kakiemon, Chinese Pheasant, Iron Red Crest, Tail, 1747-1749, 2 3/4 In. 865.00
Beaker, Tea Plant, White Lobed, 4 Blossoming Plants, Scalloped Rim, 1745, 2 In. 4310.00
Bottle, Fruit Cluster, Puce Cherry, Purple Plum, White Blossom, Stopper, 3 In. 2185.00
Bottle, Peach Form, Fruit Shade, Pale Yellow To Pale Pink, Rose, 3 In. 3450.00
Bowl, Peach Shape, Scattered Sprigs, Insects, Brown Edge Rim, 4 3/16 In. 4600.00
Clock, Sunflower, Flowers, Leaves, Scroll Base, Gilt Metal Frame, 1761, 11 In. 2185.00
Dish, Basket Molded, Yellow Wheat Ears, Chartreuse Stems, Oval, 11 3/4 In. 575.00
Dish, Green Leaf Puce Center, Red Floral Sprigs, Oval, 1754, 10 13/16 In. 1495.00
Dish, Orange, Gray Winged Moth Interior, 6 Sprigs On Exterior, Oblong, 1755, 11 In. . . . 345.00
Dish, Peony, Black Dotted Center, Puce, White Petals, Stem Handle, 1755, 8 In. 2600.00
Dish, Vine Leaf, 2 Overlapping Leaves, Butterfly, Stem Handle, 1757, 9 1/16 In. 1265.00
Dish, Vine Leaf, 2 Overlapping Leaves, Puce, Emerald Green Edge, 1760, 9 1/4 In. 690.00
Figurine, Sportsman, Wearing A Black Hat, White Waistcoat, Green Base, 10 In. 920.00
Jug, Milk, Pear Shape, Twig Form Handle, Chartreuse, Yellow, 3 1/4 In. 400.00
Plate, Fruit, Brown Branch Bearing 2 Peaches, Green, Yellow Leaves, 1758, 8 3/8 In. . . . 290.00
Plate, Fruit, Sprig Of Blackberries & Peaches, Brown Edge Rim, 1760, 8 1/2 In. 1725.00
Plate, Mazarine Blue, Floral Cluster, Scattered Sprigs, Scalloped Rim, 9 1/8 In. 1725.00
Plate, Peacock, Gold Anchor Period, 10 In. 820.00
Plate, Scalloped, 6 Exotic Birds Amidst Shrubbery, Brown Edge, 8 1/2 In. 400.00
Platter, Brown, Gray Bird In Flight, Green Leaves, Shrubbery, Giles, Oval, 11 In., Pair . 3335.00
Platter, Rose, Blue, Yellow, Brown, Red, Gray, Floral Cluster, Chocolate Brown Edge . . 2600.00
Sauceboat, Strawberry Leaf, Pink Strawberry Vine, 2 Red Berries, 1755, 7 3/8 In. 3165.00
Sauceboat, Strawberry Leaf, Vine Issuing 2 Red Berries, 1755, 6 In. 1035.00
Teabowl & Saucer, Kakiemon, Standing Oriental Woman By Pavilion, 1752, 4 In. 1600.00
Teapot, Cover, 2 Butterflies, 1 Ladybird, Floral Sprigs On Cover, Hexagonal, 5 In. 5500.00
Tureen, Carp, Cover, Yellow Scales, Brown Eyes, Head, Back, Fin, 14 11/16 In. 2300.00
Tureen, Cover, Artichoke, White, Overlapping Leaves, 1755, 3 11/16 In. 2100.00
Vase, Salmon & Brown Butterfly, Blue Botanical Sprig, 1753, 5 7/8 In. 9775.00

CHELSEA GRAPE pattern was made before 1840. A small bunch of
grapes in a raised design, colored with purple or blue luster, is on the
border of the white plate. Most of the pieces are unmarked. The pattern is sometimes called *Aynsley* or *Grandmother*. Chelsea Sprig is
similar but has a sprig of flowers instead of the bunch of grapes.
Chelsea Thistle has a raised thistle pattern. Do not confuse these
Chelsea patterns with Chelsea Keramic Art Works, which can be found
in the Dedham category, or with Chelsea porcelain, the preceding category.

Creamer, Child's, Paneled Grape, 3 1/2 In. 220.00
Pitcher, Hexagonal, Luster Design 280.00
Tea Set, Teapot, Sugar & Creamer, Waste Bowl, 9 Cups & Saucer, 12 Plates 600.00

CHINESE EXPORT porcelain comprises all the many kinds of porcelain
made in China for export to America and Europe in the eighteenth,
nineteenth, and twentieth centuries. Other pieces may be listed in this
book under Canton, Celadon, Nanking, and Rose Medallion.

Bottle, Famille Rose, Protruding Frog, 19th Century, 4 In. 325.00
Bowl, Cloud Design, Purple Diapered Border, 1880s, 9 1/2 In. 245.00
Bowl, Court Landscape, Famille Rose, Porcelain, 1790, 2 1/2 x 4 3/8 In. 82.50
Bowl, Famille Rose, Mandarin Palette, Figures Of Nobles & Landscape, 10 In. 423.00
Bowl, Family Scene In Lakeside Garden, 1785, 10 1/4 In. 800.00
Bowl, Figural Design, Blue, White, Globular, 8 In. 605.00
Bowl, Flower Shape, Dragon Design, Green, Yellow Glaze, 5 In. 1515.00
Bowl, Glazed Florets, Brown, Cream Ground, 3 1/4 In. 58.00
Bowl, Green Fitzhugh Pattern, 10 In. 400.00
Bowl, Hand Painted Floral, 9 1/4 In. 57.00
Bowl, Incised Butterfly Design, 6-Petal Flower Form, 6 3/4 In. 357.00
Bowl, Incised Passion Floral, Cloud Design, Imperial Yellow Glaze, 4 1/2 In. 1694.00
Bowl, Landscape, Blue & White, 9 1/4 In. 40.00
Bowl, Lotus Form, Famille Rose, 9 In. 198.00
Bowl, Mandarin Paneled Scenes, 9 1/4 x 3 3/4 In. 460.00
Bowl, Ocher Band Over Floral & Foliate Clusters, 1880s, 9 In. 552.00
Bowl, Passion Flower Design, Lime Green Ground, Famille Rose, 4 1/8 In. 580.00

Bowl, People Scene, Mandarin, Floral Border, 10 x 3 3/4 In. 460.00
Bowl, Ringed Foot, Peach, Flower Design, Blue, White, Porcelain, 4 1/4 In. 690.00
Bowl, Salad, Green Fitzhugh, Square, 9 1/2 In. 742.00
Bowl, Women, Mythical Beast, Enameled Ware, 11 5/8 x 3 3/4 In. 250.00
Burner, Dragon On Stem, Phoenix, Patterned Border, Round, 7 In. 375.00
Coffeepot, Berry Finial, Flower & Leaf, Handle, Medallions Of Geese, 9 1/8 In. .880.00 to 1100.00
Coffeepot, Fruit Finial, Landscape, Intertwined Handle, Flowers, Foliage, 9 In. 550.00
Cup, Carp Design Interior, Gilt Foo Lion Design Exterior, Black, 3 In. 66.00
Dish, Armorial Design, Leaf Shape, Orange Peel Glaze, 1773, 8 3/4 In. 495.00
Dish, Center Figures, County House, Landscape, c.1790, 16 x 13 In. 575.00
Dish, Flower Basket Design, Famille Verte, 5 1/8 In. 455.00
Dish, Vegetable, Fitzhugh Pattern, Oval Scalloped Form, 10 3/4 x 8 1/2 In. 430.00
Garden Seat, Famille Rose, Celebration Scene, Barrel, Borders, 18 In., Pair 5520.00
Ginger Jar, Brass Base, Famille Verte, 29 1/2 In. 155.00
Ginger Jar, Cover, Provincial Blue, White, Early 19th Century, 7 In. 65.00
Ginger Jar, Woman, Seated In A Garden, Globular, Green, 9 1/4 In. 85.00
Humidor, Working Men, Pewter Lined, Black Lacquer, 1870s, 5 5/8 In. 750.00
Hutch, Watch, Porcelain, c.1770 . . . . 2500.00
Jar, Court Scene, Gilt Highlight, Famille Verte, 17 1/2 In. 8625.00
Jar, Peony Design, Globular Shape, Famille Verte, Early 19th Century, 6 In. 300.00
Jar, Temple Base Shape, Floral Design, Blue, White, 16 1/2 In. 665.50
Jardiniere, Undulated Rim, Gourd Shape, Lotus Blossoms, 10 In. 9775.00
Jug, Cream, Blue Armorial, 5 1/2 In. 80.00
Jug, Cream, Brown Floral, 5 In. 46.00
Jug, Milk, Hand Painted Floral Sprays, 5 1/2 In. 42.00
Lamp, Baluster Turquoise Glaze, Wooden Foot, 19 1/2 In. 430.00
Meat Platter, Famille Rose, 15 x 10 In. 725.00
Mug, 3-Panel Floral Scenes, Blue Design, 5 In. 400.00
Mug, Figural Landscape, Dragon Handle, Silver, F. Coit, 1866, 4 1/4 In. 900.00
Plate, Coates Family, c.1800, 7 3/4 In., Pair 550.00
Plate, Indian Figure, Riding Elephant, 19th Century, 9 3/8 In. 635.00
Plate, Kutani Figural Center, Porcelain, Famille Rose, 8 3/4 In. 120.00
Plate, Landscape Design, Blue, White, Meiji Period, 12 1/4 In. 605.00
Plate, Passion Flower Design, Blue, White, 5 1/2 In. 135.00
Plate, Puce Floral Design, Porcelain, Early 19th Century, 9 1/4 In. 55.00
Plate, Warming, Chinese Figures, 11 In., Pair 2650.00
Platter, Blue, White, Floral Design, Early 19th Century, 13 x 16 1/2 In. 385.00
Platter, Center Floral Spray, 2 Borders, 16 x 13 1/2 In. 834.00
Platter, Famille Rose, 1765 . . . . 747.00
Platter, Mandarin, 11 1/2 In., Pair 2200.00
Punch Bowl, Armorial, Monogrammed Outside, 18th Century, 15 3/4 In. 363.00
Punch Bowl, Mandarin Palette, Shell, Flowers, Butterflies, 1785, 15 In. 1725.00
Punch Bowl, Palace Vignettes, Chain Quilted Border, 10 1/2 In. 545.00
Punch Bowl, Paneled Scenes Of Birds, People, Famille Rose, 15 x 6 In. 1380.00
Punch Bowl, Rose Mandarin, 19th Century, 14 1/2 In. 1840.00
Tankard, Mandarin, 18th Century, 5 1/2 In. 650.00
Tea Caddy, Fruit Finial, Urn & Floral Borders, 5 1/4 In. 440.00
Tea Caddy, Love Birds In Sunburst Medallion, 5 In. 65.00
Tea Caddy, Scholars, Attendants In Garden Setting On Sides, Green 546.00
Tea Caddy, Silver Plated Lid, Medallions Of Woman & Dog, 5 1/4 In. 440.00
Tea Set, Thousand Butterfly, c.1820, 11 Piece 850.00
Teapot, Domed Cover, Stand, Loop Handle, Mid-18th Century, 5 In. 3450.00
Teapot, Floral, Seed Pod Finial, 6 In. 65.00
Teapot, Gold, Strap Handle, Strawberry Knob, 6 In. 250.00
Teapot, Hand Painted Floral & Bird, Orange Scale Ground, 5 1/2 In. 115.00
Temple Jar, Bird, Flowering Landscape, Blue, White, Globular, 15 3/4 In. 877.00
Trivet, Bamboo Design Top, Lotus, Scroll Design On Sides, Blue, White, 7 x 1 In. 90.00
Tureen, Cover, Armorial, Fitzhugh Border, Undertray, 18th Century, 8 x 12 In. 4830.00
Tureen, Cover, Stand, Scroll Finial, Shell Handles, 1760, 14 1/4 In. 8050.00
Tureen, Soup, Foo Dog Finial, Underplate, Stand, Late 18th Century, 9 x 12 In. 7740.00
Vase, 2 Opposing Dragons Chasing Flaming Pearl, Lappet Border, 7 1/2 In. 635.00
Vase, Baluster, Bird, Landscape & Floral Panels, 16 In. 847.00
Vase, Baluster, Coral Red Dragon Handles, Turquoise Glaze, 10 In. 363.00

Vase, Baluster, Horse Medallions, Yellow Ground, 14 In. 75.00
Vase, Baluster, Mandarins & Consorts, 23 In. 258.00
Vase, Bottle Shape, Ormolu Mounted, Famille Rose, 19th Century, 8 In., Pair 1495.00
Vase, Floral, Butterfly, Red Enameled, C-Scroll Ground, Famille Rose, 9 In. 259.00
Vase, Landscape Panels, Butterflies, Flowers, Green, 16 1/4 In. 797.00
Vase, Mounted As Lamp, Famille Rose, 19th Century, 20 In. 440.00
Vase, Peacocks, Floral, Foliate Design, Green, White Ground, 16 1/2 In. 690.00
Vase, Rouleau, Landscape Design, Blue, White, 7 1/8 In. 455.00

CHINTZ is the name of a group of china patterns featuring an overall design of flowers and leaves. The design became popular with English makers about 1928. A few pieces are still being made. The best known are designs by Royal Winton, James Kent Ltd., Crown Ducal, and Shelley.

Banana Boat, Cromer, Royal Winton 275.00
Banana Boat, Hazel, Royal Winton 340.00
Bowl, Sweet Pea, 2 Handles, Royal Winton 180.00
Butter, Cover, Spring Glory, Black, Royal Winton 265.00
Butter, Springtime, Royal Winton 250.00
Cake Plate, On Stand, Royal Winton 185.00
Cup & Saucer, Summertime, Royal Winton 85.00
Cup & Saucer, Sweat Pea, Royal Winton 125.00
Fruit Cake Set, Ivory, Crown Ducal 90.00
Jam, Sweet Pea, Royal Winton, 3 Piece 295.00
Mustard, Summertime, Royal Winton, 2 Piece 185.00
Pin Tray, Marguerite, 4 1/4 x 4 1/4 In. 55.00
Plate, Flowers & Birds, Blue Ground, Octagonal, Crown Ducal, 6 Piece 180.00
Plate, Old Cottage, Royal Winton, 9 In., 4 Piece 75.00
Platter, Dubarry, Oval, James Kent 250.00
Sugar & Creamer, Hazel, Royal Winton 310.00
Sugar & Creamer, Royal Winton 135.00
Sugar & Creamer, Welbeck, Royal Winton 135.00
Tea & Toast Set, Orient, Royal Winton 95.00
Tennis Set, Marguerite, Royal Winton 115.00

CHOCOLATE GLASS, sometimes mistakenly called caramel slag, was made by the Indiana Tumbler and Goblet Company of Greentown, Indiana, from 1900 to 1903. Fenton Art Glass Co. also made chocolate glass from about 1907 to 1915. More recent pieces have been made by Imperial and others.

Berry Set, Geneva, Oval Master & Sauces, 5 Piece 425.00
Bowl, Cactus, 6 In. 75.00
Butter, Leaf Bracket, Greentown ....90.00 to 150.00
Compote, Cactus, 5 1/2 In. 120.00
Compote, Geneva, 8 In. 135.00
Compote, Scroll, Challinor, Taylor, 8 In. 350.00
Cracker Jar, Cactus, Greentown, Cover 230.00
Creamer, Dewey 75.00
Creamer, Shuttle 90.00
Cruet, Wild Rose With Bowknot, Greentown 350.00
Dish, Jelly, Geneva, Greentown 135.00
Dish, Mallard Cover 32.00
Dish, Rabbit Cover 150.00
Lamp, Wild Rose With Festoon, Clear Font, 8 In. 130.00
Mug, Herringbone 50.00
Mug, Outdoor Drinking Scene, 5 1/2 In. 85.00
Nappy, Cactus, Greentown ....95.00 to 125.00
Nappy, Leaf Bracket, Greentown 65.00
Nappy, Masonic, Greentown 135.00
Pitcher, Water, Wild Rose With Bowknot 375.00
Plate, Serenade, Greentown, Large ....150.00 to 175.00
Sauce, Geneva, Round, 4 1/2 In. 85.00
Spooner, Child's, Wild Rose With Scrolling 325.00

Syrup, Cactus, Greentown, 2 1/2 In. 95.00
Syrup, Cord Drapery, Greentown 225.00
Toothpick, Cactus, Greentown 125.00
Tumbler, Cactus, Greentown 40.00
Tumbler, Iced Tea, Cactus, Greentown 70.00
Tumbler, Shuttle, Greentown .... .75.00 to 95.00

CHRISTMAS collectibles include not only Christmas trees and ornaments listed below, but also Santa Claus figures, special dishes, and
even games and wrapping paper. A Belsnickle is a nineteenth-century
figure of Father Christmas. A kugel is an early, heavy ornament made
of thick blown glass, lined with zinc or lead, and often covered with
colored wax. Christmas collectibles may also be listed in the Candy
Container category and in the Paper category under Greeting Card.
Christmas trees are listed in the section below.

Candlestick, Figure, Holly Leaves, Cast Iron, Green & Red, Low 75.00
Candy Container, Santa Claus, Plastic, Irwin 8.00
Card, Coree, Red Design, Paul Jacoulet 330.00
Card, Frankoma, 1974 .... 30.00
Card, Greeting, Kusai, Red Design, Original Envelope, Paul Jacoulet 91.00
Card, Le Bonze Errant, Yellow Design On Cover, Paul Jacoulet 121.00
Card, Longevite, Red Design On Cover, Original Folder, Paul Jacoulet 242.00
Charm, Figure, Santa Claus, Lantern, Celluloid, Japan, 1930s 20.00
Figure, Santa Claus, Black Boots, Rushton Co., 1950s 125.00
Figure, Santa Claus, Celluloid, Japan, 1940s, 3 3/4 In. 28.00
Figure, Santa Claus, Composition, Flannel Suit, Oil Cloth Boots, 1930s, 20 In. 475.00
Figure, Santa Claus, Hangs On Wall, Papier-Mache, England, 11 In. 278.00
Figure, Santa Claus, Papier-Mache .... *Illus* 110.00
Figure, Santa Claus, Red Flannel Coat & Hat, Pressed Face, 4 1/2 In. 95.00
Figure Set, Santa's Band, Cotton, Crepe Paper, France, 1930s, 4 In., 5 Piece 275.00
Lamp, Santa Claus, U.S. Glass 500.00
Mirror, Santa Claus Portrait, Celluloid, Pocket, 1930s 38.00
Mold, Cake, Santa Claus, Griswold, Erie, Pa. 450.00
Nodder, Elf, Gray Mittens, Trade Stimulator, Clockwork 1100.00
Nodder, Santa Claus, Clockwork, Papier-Mache, Cardboard & Wood, Gray Mittens 990.00
Nodder, Santa Claus, Clockwork, Red Robe, Beard 910.00
Nodder, Santa Claus, Clockwork, With Tree, 25 In. 1650.00
Nodder, Santa Claus, Electrified 525.00
Nodder, Santa Claus, Papier-Mache, Sheepskin Hair, Germany, 1930s, 25 1/2 In. 1265.00
Nodder, Santa Claus, Tree 990.00
Ornament, Lucy, Holding Football, Peanuts 20.00
Ornament, Santa's Sleigh, Red Wicker, 1930s 8.00
Pin, Meet Me At Black's Santa, Portrait, 1940s, 1 1/2 In. 35.00
Pin, Merry Christmas Santa, Portrait, Blue Ground, Silver Letters, 1900s 120.00
Pin, Santa Claus, Chenille, Plastic Face, 1950s 30.00
Pin, Smith's Ice Cream Santa, Portrait, White Ground, 1920-1930 .... 65.00

**Do not stack boxes of Christmas
ornaments. The weight may break
some of the glass ornaments.**

Christmas, Figure, Santa Claus,
Papier-Mache

Plate, Santa Claus, Green Luster Border, Porcelain, Germany 95.00
Plates that are limited editions are listed in the Collector Plate category or in the correct
factory listing.
Stocking, Santa Claus Printed On Cloth 440.00
String Holder, Santa Claus 30.00
Toy, Bell Ringer, Santa Claus, Box, 13 In. 225.00
Toy, Lantern, Santa Claus, Spring Arms & Legs, Celluloid 115.00
Toy, Panorama, Visit Of Santa Claus, Crank Turns Paper Roll, Milton Bradley 632.50
Toy, Pip-Squeak, Santa Claus, Straw Stuffed, Composition Face, Germany 475.00
Toy, Pip-Squeak, Santa Claus, Wooden, On Wood, 1930s 65.00
Toy, Rocking Santa, Battery Operated, Box 750.00
Toy, Santa Claus, Beats Drum, Rings Bell & Walks, Battery Operated, 1950s 275.00
Toy, Santa Claus, Eyes Light, Rings Bell, Battery Operated, 1950s 750.00
Toy, Santa Claus, Holding Toys, Iron, 1890, 5 1/2 In. 225.00
Toy, Santa Claus, On Helicopter, Battery Operated, Box, 9 1/2 In. 450.00
Toy, Santa Claus, On Reindeer, Tin Lithograph, Windup, Japan, 1950s 100.00
Toy, Santa Claus, Rings Bell, Tin In Celluloid, Windup, Box, 1950s 85.00
Toy, Santa Claus, Roly Poly, Composition, Schoenhut, 6 1/4 In. 485.00
Toy, Santa Claus, Shakes Bell, Eyes Light, Battery Operated, Box 125.00
Toy, Santa Claus, With Log Sled & Reindeer, Germany 1275.00
Toy, Santa Claus, With Reindeer, Metal Sleigh, Windup, Celluloid 100.00
Toy, Sled, Santa Head On Front, Germany, 1930s 195.00
Toy, Train, Lionel, No. 6-18403, Hand Car, Mr. & Mrs. Santa Claus 70.00

CHRISTMAS TREES made of feathers and Christmas tree decorations of
all types are popular with collectors. The first decorated Christmas tree
in America is claimed by many states, including Pennsylvania (1747),
Massachusetts (1832), Illinois (1833), Ohio (1838), and Iowa (1845).
The first glass ornaments were imported from Germany about 1860.
Dresden ornaments were made about 100 years ago of paper and tin-
sel. Manufacturers in the United States were making ornaments in the
early 1870s. Electric lights were first used on a Christmas tree in 1882.
Character light bulbs became popular in the 1920s, bubble lights in the
1940s, twinkle bulbs in the 1950s, plastic bulbs by 1955. In this book
a Christmas light is a holder for a candle used on the tree. Other forms
of lighting include light bulbs. Other Christmas memorabilia is listed
in the section above.

Aluminum, 3 Ft. 30.00
Aluminum, 6 Ft. 50.00
Bottle Brush, Blue, 6 Ft. 25.00
Color Wheel, For Aluminum Tree ....25.00 to 40.00
Feather, Green, Red & Green Base Design Base, Ornaments, 38 In. 300.00
Feather, White Wooden Base, Rewrapped Trunk, Reinforced Wire, 72 In. 275.00
Figure, Santa Claus, Light Bulb Eyes, 30 In. 385.00
Light, Stiegel Type, Diamond Design, Clear, 18th Century 110.00
Light, Stiegel Type, Diamond Design, Cobalt Blue, 18th Century 110.00
Light Bulb, Baby In Stocking 10.00
Light Bulb, Bear, Large 40.00
Light Bulb, Bubble, Noma, Box, Set Of 8 ....45.00 to 50.00
Light Bulb, Cat With Fiddle, Large 12.00
Light Bulb, Cottage, Snow Covered 8.00
Light Bulb, Ear Of Corn 35.00
Light Bulb, Girl, 2 Faces 20.00
Light Bulb, Lantern 6.00
Light Bulb, Santa Claus 40.00
Light Bulb, Scrappy Cartoon, Box 225.00
Light Bulb, Tadpole 50.00
Ornament, Angel, Dresden Wings, Blown Glass, Clip-On, 4 In. 150.00
Ornament, Angel, Flying, Wax, 4 In. 75.00
Ornament, Angel, On Glitter Star, Celluloid 12.00
Ornament, Bell, Embossed Santa Claus, 1920s, 2 1/2 In. 85.00
Ornament, German Soldier, Holding Dresden Rifle, Clip-On 990.00
Ornament, Girl, Bisque Head, Crepe Clothes, Holding Riding Crop, England 310.00

Ornament, Graf Zeppelin, 1920s, 5 In.	200.00
Ornament, Kugel, Berry Type, Glass, Silvered Amber, Germany, 3 1/4 In.	275.00
Ornament, Kugel, Grapes, Brass Caps	250.00
Ornament, Little Red Riding Hood & Wolf	522.00
Ornament, Man In The Moon, Crescent Form, c.1930, 3 1/2 In.	75.00
Ornament, Mushroom, Blown Glass	12.00
Ornament, Owl, Full Figured, Pearl White, Pink Blush	20.00
Ornament, Parakeet, Spun Glass Tail, Clip-On, c.1930	40.00
Ornament, Peanuts, Ice Hockey Holiday, Hallmark, 1979	125.00
Ornament, Raggedy Andy, 1974	5.00
Ornament, Raggedy Ann, Cloth	25.00
Ornament, Santa Claus Face, Hanging, 3 1/2 In.	35.00
Ornament, Skier, Composition Face, Cotton, Japan, 5 In.	80.00
Ornament, Snowman, Top Hat, Glass Eyes, 5 1/2 In.	28.00
Ornament, Snowman, With Umbrella, 6 1/4 In.	36.00
Ornament, Swan, Celluloid	40.00
Ornament, Uncle Sam, Papier-Mache, 6 1/2 In.	550.00
Stand, Adjustable, 2 Prongs, Figures Around Base, Iron, 1891	185.00
Stand, Crown, North Bros. Mfg. Co., Philadelphia, Penna.	70.00
Stand, Ornate, Cast Iron	90.00
Tree Topper, Angel, Blown Glass, 5 In.	125.00

CHROME items in the Art Deco style became popular in the 1930s. Collectors are most interested in high-style pieces made by the Connecticut firms of Chase Brass and Copper Company, and Manning Bowman.

Bookends, Chase, Walter Von Nessen, Die-Stamped Mark, Metal, Pair	165.00
Cocktail Shaker, Dumbbell, Red Catalin Knob	220.00
Cocktail Shaker, Krome Kraft, Alternating Plain & Hammered Panels, Farber	45.00
Coffee & Tea Set, Spigot Urn, Black Bakelite Handles, Manning Bowman, 4 Piece	300.00
Pitcher, Sparta, 2 Qt.	60.00
Pitcher, Water, Art Deco, Ice Lip, Lucite Handle, 2 Qt.	45.00
Rack, Newspaper	75.00
Syrup, Sparta	60.00
Tea Set, Chase, Startime Tray, 4 Piece	395.00
Tray, Triple, Folding, Chase	40.00
Tureen, Beehive Lucite Handle, Leehman Bros., 14 In.	75.00
Vase, Ring, 8 In.	70.00

CIGAR STORE FIGURES of carved wood or cast iron were used as advertisements in front of the Victorian cigar store. The carved figures are now collected as folk art. They range in size from counter type, about three feet, to over eight feet high.

Bust, Indian, Countertop, c.1880	11500.00

If you have to pack or store an oddly shaped antique, a footed bowl, or an unsteady figurine, try this trick: Dampen a polyurethane sponge, preferably the two-layer type with a stiffer bottom layer. Put the antique piece on the wet sponge. It will make the proper shaped indentation and when the sponge dries, the piece will be held safely in one position.

Cigar Store Figure, Indian,
Woodlands Brave, 22 In.

Indian, Browns, Green Trim, 7 Pine Laminated Planks, 1890, 42 In. 4400.00
Indian, Carved, Pine, Indian Squaw, Standing On Partial Step, 77 In. 29900.00
Indian, Countertop, Allover Black Paint, Feathers 5500.00
Indian, Woodlands Brave, 22 In. ....*Illus* 13200.00
Indian, Zinc, Wooden Base, Original Label, 62 In. 7370.00

CINNABAR is a vermilion or red lacquer. Pieces are made with tens to
hundreds of thicknesses of the lacquer that is later carved. Most
cinnabar was made in the Orient.

Bottle, Snuff, Foo Lion & Peony Design, Egg Shape, Coral Stopper, 3 In. 330.00
Bottle, Snuff, Red, 2 1/4 In. 50.00
Bottle, Snuff, Scholars, Boys In Pavilion, Red, Conforming Stopper, 3 In. 230.00
Box, Baluster Shape, Floral Ground, 15 In. 165.00
Box, Carved, 4 1/4 x 3 x 2 In. 65.00
Box, Carved, Matching Tray, 4 In. 99.00
Box, Carving Of Men, Mountains & Trees, Cover, 3 1/4 x 3 In., Pair 177.00
Box, Double Gourd Form, 8 In. 195.00
Box, High Relief Figural Design, Cylindrical, 19th Century, 3 In. 85.00
Box, Paste, Black, Red Lacquer, Floral Design, Round, 2 3/4 In. 180.00
Box, Red Cover, Small, 2 In. 25.00
Cigarette Box, Lid, Carved Figures In Front Of Pagoda, 2 In. 57.00
Hat Stand, Domed Base, Top, Bands Of Lotus Relief, Dragon & Patterning, 11 In. ... 1265.00
Planter, Scrolled Lotus, Quatrefoil White Jade Panels On Each Side, 9 1/2 x 15 In. 1850.00
Vase, Lacquer, Baluster Shape, Floral Design, 15 In. 215.00

CIVIL WAR mementos are important collector's items. Most of the
pieces are military items used from 1861 to 1865. Be sure to avoid any
explosive munitions.

Bandanna, Jackson, Beuregard, Lee, Nashville Buildings, Cotton, 1897, 16 x 18 In. 950.00
Banner, Welcome G.A.R., Eagle, Flag & Star Medal, Oilcloth, 28 1/2 x 48 1/2 In. 170.00
Belt Plate, Confederate Officer's, Army Of Northern Virginia, 2 Piece 895.00
Belt Plate, Eagle, 13 Stars, Date On Back, 1862 .... 895.00
Belt Pouch, Straps, Marked, Watertown Arsenal, 1864 .... 145.00
Bucket, Tar, Artillery, Riveted Sheet Metal, 10 In. 220.00
Bugle 485.00
Button, G.A.R, 40th Encampment, Galesburg, Illinois 35.00
Canteen, Bull's-Eye, Painted White 84.00
Canteen, Bull's-Eye, Splotched Red, Blue Sky, Irregular Bands, 7 1/4 In. 185.00
Canteen, G.A.R., Eagle Decal, We Drank From The Same Canteen, 1900 .... 215.00
Canteen, G.A.R., Nickel Plated, Brass Inserts, 26th Grand Encampment, 1892 .... 250.00
Canteen, Medical Type, Oval & Curved To Fit Body, Tin, 6 1/2 x 9 7/8 In. 60.00
Canteen, Wooden, Issued To F. Burr 1000.00
Certificate, Honorable Service, Private Jourdan H. Wells, 133 Regiment, 1864 .... 105.00
Chair, Camp, Folding, Original Carpet Seat ....90.00 to 135.00
Coat, Frock, Infantry, New York Buttons 350.00
Coat, Militia, New Jersey, 45 Sewell Guard Buttons, Dated 1864 .... 900.00
Cornet, 6 Maine Infantry, Brass, B-Flat, German Silver Keys, Europe 1725.00
Desk, Traveling, Walnut, With Inkwell 135.00
Drum, Blue Paint Traces, Calf's Skin Heads, 15 1/2 x 9 In. 550.00
Drum, Snare, Attached Metal U.S. Emblem, Rosewood Body, 14 1/2 x 16 1/2 In. 525.00
Drum, Snare, Black Paint & Varnish, J.C. Haynes, 10 x 14 3/4 In. 635.00
Drum, Stenciled Co. B. 3, Red & White Lines, 12 3/4 x 17 In. 2100.00
Fife, Brass Ends, Tin Mouthpiece 190.00
Foot Locker, Hinged Lid, Strap Iron Hardware, Wisconsin Calvary, 20 3/4 x 36 In. 735.00
Hat, Campaign, Cast Iron, Federal Tunnels, Petersburg, Va. 325.00
Hat Maker's Form, Military, Stitching Forage Caps, Plaster, Yellow Glaze 295.00
Holster, Colt Army Flap, Snake Buckle Belt, 1860 .... 800.00
Jacket, Shell, Cavalry, Belt Pillows Intact, 1854 .... 3000.00
Keg, Powder, Paper Label, Lafkin & Rand Powder Co., 10 x 8 In. 170.00
Knife, Bowie, D-Guard, Stars, C.S. On Blade, Marked Macon, Ga., 16 1/2 In. ....800.00 to 895.00
Knife, Cavalry, Bone Handle, B. Barber 180.00
Leg Irons, U.S. Navy, Towers Patent, 20 1/2 In. 240.00
Medicine Kit, Handwritten Labels, Felt Lined Leather, 2 x 4 1/4 x 9 1/2 In. 160.00

Medicine Kit, Vials & Packages, Original Labels, Brown Leather Case, 9 1/4 In. 185.00
Photograph, U.S. Grant, Signed 2000.00
Pouch, Ammo, Model 1855, U.S. Plate On The Front 300.00
Pouch, Ammo, Model 1864 .... 350.00
Powder Kit, Silver Plated Canister, Ivory Handles, 1775-1825, 3 x 3 1/4 In. 195.00
Print, 16th Regiment, N.Y. Artillery, Battle Scenes, Wood Frame, 22 x 27 In. 143.00
Print, 27th Regiment Mass. Vol. Infantry, Black Wood Frame, 21 1/2 x 17 In. 192.00
Print, Camp Scene Of Soldiers, Women, 1 Child, Wood Frame, 24 x 20 In. 330.00
Ribbon, Funeral, General W.T. Sherman, Ohio Legislature, 1891, 3 1/4 x 13 In. 120.00
Rifle Sighting Device, To Calibrate Rifle Sights, Cast Iron, 30 In. 275.00
Saber, Scabbard, Militia Belt 750.00
Scissors, Folding, Officer's 60.00
Shako, Officer's, Engineer, Engineers Front Plate, Massachusetts Militia Buttons 595.00
Shave Cup, Side Mount Slot For Strop, Eagle Engraved Blade, Tin 115.00
Spurs, U.S. Officer's, Eagle Form, Iron, Brass Trim 690.00
Stein, Brass Heart In Center, Red Cedar Wear, Brass Straps, Handle, 1/5 Liter 258.00
Sword, Ames, N.C.O., Leather Scabbard, Marked U.S. 1863 .... 420.00
Sword, Blade Marked U.S. D.F.M., 1863 .... 183.00
Sword, Foot Officer's, Engraved Blade 235.00
Table, Camp, Officer's Folding, Pine, Pegs, Square Nails, Screws, 43 x 15 x 20 In. 220.00
Telescope, Naval, 4-Draw, 36 In. 1200.00
Tool, Hoof Cleaner, Brass 85.00
Wrench, Armorer's Breech Plug, Marked, U.S., 12 In 185.00

CKAW, see Dedham category.

CLAMBROTH glass, popular in the Victorian era, is a grayish color and
is somewhat opaque, like clam broth. It was made by several factories
in the United States and England.

Bowl, Ice Cream, Fashion, 9 In. 48.00
Lamp, Acanthus, Blue Font, Satin Finish, 13 In. 770.00
Lamp, Acanthus, Brass Collar, 11 3/4 In. 55.00
Lamp, Acanthus, Lime Green Font, Brass Collar, 12 5/8 In. 715.00
Lamp, Blue Font, White Match Holder Center, White Milk Glass Base, 12 3/4 In. 1320.00
Lamp, Tulip, Blue Font, Mid-19th Century, 12 1/2 In., Pair 1840.00
Plate, Orange Tree 250.00
Saltshaker, Cathedral Panel 125.00
Sugar & Creamer, Diamond-Quilted 66.00
Toothpick, Buttons & Arches, Mother, Pink 25.00

CLARICE CLIFF was a designer who worked in several English factories
after the 1920s. She is best known for her brightly colored art deco
designs. She died in 1972.

Ashtray, Bizarre 245.00
Bowl, Autumn Crocus 225.00
Bowl, Crocus, Bizarre, Orange, Blue, Purple, Green, Marked, 3 x 6 1/2 In. 374.00
Charger, Rhodanthe, Orange, Yellow, Brown, Marked, 13 In. 862.00
Coffeepot, Autumn Crocus 350.00
Console Set, Geometric Design, Orange, Yellow Blue, Circular, 3 x 5 3/4 In. 440.00
Cup & Saucer, Fantasque, Wedge Handle 495.00
Gravy Boat, Tonquin, Underplate, Individual 40.00
Honey Jar, Crocus, Yellow, Orange Crocuses, Green Field, Wilkinson, 3 x 3 In. 345.00
Jam Jar, Celtic Harvest, Chrome Lid, Signed 66.00
Jam Jar, Crocus, Blue, Orange, Lavender, Green Stems, Brown Ground, 3 x 3 In. 402.00
Jam Jar, Hydrangea, Bizarre 200.00
Jug, Bizarre, Blue, Red, Yellow, Purple, Green, Black, Marked, 11 1/2 In. 747.00
Jug, Bizarre, Secrets, Yellow, Green, Blue Landscape, Marked, 10 In. 1035.00
Jug, Viscaria, Green, Red, Yellow Flowers, Brown Stems, Cream Ground, 7 In. 805.00
Pitcher, Bizarre, Visceria, Blue, Yellow, Brown, Marked, 10 x 7 1/2 In. 690.00
Pitcher, Celtic Harvest 650.00
Pitcher, Crocus, Blue, Orange, Lavender, Brown, Green Ground, Marked, 7 In. 258.00
Pitcher, Grapes & Leaves, Drip Glaze, Marked, 9 1/2 In. 297.00
Pitcher, Sliced Fruit, Bizarre, Yellow, Orange, Red, Marked, 7 x 7 In. 1380.00

Planter, Parakeet, 10 x 4 1/2 In. 750.00
Plaque, Eagle, Marked, 9 In. 410.00
Plate, Blue Chintz, Blue, Green, Red Flowers, Marked, 9 In. 215.00
Plate, Crocus, Blue, Yellow, Red, Green Ground, Ink Stamp, Newport, 9 In. 215.00
Plate, Geometric, Oranges & Blues, 8 3/4 In. 345.00
Plate, Inspiration, Lily, White Flowers, Blue Stems, Green Ground, Wilkinson, 9 In. 747.00
Plate, Secrets, Bizarre, Green, Yellow, Orange, Marked, 8 3/4 In. 172.00
Plate, Wall, My Garden, 9 1/4 In. . . . . .175.00 to 210.00
Platter, Tonquin, 12 In. 90.00
Sugar Shaker, Crocus, Bizarre, Yellow, Blue, Orange, Purple, Marked, 5 In. 517.00
Sugar Shaker, My Garden, Bizarre 300.00
Sugar Shaker, Viscaria, Bizarre, Yellow, Green, Brown, Marked, 4 3/4 In. 575.00
Tankard, Sliced Fruit, 7 In. 1200.00
Teapot, Bizarre, Banded, Etched, Turquoise, Pink & Green 350.00
Tureen, Odilon Shape 170.00
Vase, Bizarre, 8 In. 725.00
Vase, Blue Chintz, Blue, Green, Red Flowers, Bands At Top, Marked, 7 3/4 In. 977.00
Vase, Inspiration, Bizarre, Mottled Blue, Green, Purple, Marked, 7 1/2 In. 747.00
Vase, Inspiration, Blue, White Floral, Blue, Green Ground, Wilkinson, 7 1/4 In. 805.00
Vase, Pansies, Yellow, Blue, Red, Purple Pansies, Yellow Ground, 10 1/2 In. 575.00
Wall Pocket, Double, Rhodanthe, Flowers, Marked, 6 1/2 In. 460.00
Wall Pocket, Victorian Lady 375.00

CLEWELL ware was made in limited quantities by Charles Walter
Clewell of Canton, Ohio, from 1902 to 1955. Pottery was covered with
a thin coating of bronze, then treated to make the bronze turn different
colors. Pieces covered with copper, brass, or silver were also made.
Mr. Clewell's secret formula for blue patinated bronze was burned
when he died in 1965.

Ashtray, Copper Clad, Fowler Simpson Co., Cleveland, Oh., 4 In. 80.00
Bowl, Copper Clad, Brown, Green, Incised Mark, 9 1/2 x 3 1/2 In. 770.00
Mug, Copper Clad, Original Patina, Impressed Mark, 4 In. .88.00 to 143.00
Mug, Copper Clad, Rivet & Panel Design, Marked, 4 1/2 In. 100.00
Mug, Copper Clad, Rivet & Panel Design, MPA 1908, 4 1/2 In. 132.00
Mug, Copper Clad, Twisting Vines & Leaves, Bronzed Patina, Incised Mark, 5 In. 230.00
Vase, Black, Green Patina, 7 1/4 In. 605.00
Vase, Bronze Clad, 6 In. 750.00
Vase, Bud, Copper Clad, Green, Brown, 10 In. 303.00
Vase, Bud, Copper Clad, Green, Brown, Incised Mark, 7 1/2 In. 198.00
Vase, Bud, Copper Clad, Green, Brown, Tapered, 6 1/2 In. . . . . .220.00 to 286.00
Vase, Copper Clad, Broad Shouldered, Green Patina, Incised Mark, 11 In. 935.00
Vase, Copper Clad, Brown, Green, No. 466, 5 In. 412.00
Vase, Copper Clad, Brown, Light, Dark Green, 5 In. 385.00
Vase, Copper Clad, Bud, Flared Rim, Green Patina, 7 1/2 In., Pair 522.00
Vase, Copper Clad, Floral Design, Brass, Original Patina, Etched Mark, 4 1/2 In. 1045.00
Vase, Copper Clad, Green Over Orange Patina, 6 3/4 In. 550.00
Vase, Copper Clad, Green, Blue, Brown, Incised Mark, 5 In. 467.00
Vase, Copper Clad, Green, Brown, 16 In. 2640.00
Vase, Copper Clad, Green, Brown, No. 459, 8 In. 522.00
Vase, Copper Clad, Light Green, Blue, Brown, 7 In. 880.00
Vase, Copper Clad, Patinated In Brown To Blue To Light Green, 8 In. 330.00
Vase, Copper Clad, Patinated In Green To Gray To Brown, Incised Mark, 6 1/2 In. 297.00
Vase, Copper Clad, Rivet & Panel Design, Impressed Mark, 1 1/2 x 4 In. 77.00
Vase, Copper Clad, Verdigris Patina Around Base, Tapered, Marked, 8 1/4 In. 575.00
Vase, Dark Brown, Green Patina, Broad Shouldered Form, Incised Mark, 5 1/2 In. 605.00
Vase, Dark Orange, Verdigris Patina, Bulbous, 10 3/4 x 6 In. 522.00
Vase, Enameled Copper, 8 1/4 In. 460.00
Vase, Flared Lip, Broad Shouldered, Green & Brown Patina, Marked, 15 1/2 In. 1650.00
Vase, Green, Brown Patina, Tapered, Incised Mark, 6 1/2 In. 467.00
Vase, Orange Brown, Frothy Green Patina, 13 1/2 x 5 1/2 In. 770.00
Vase, Pottery Over Bronze, 6 1/2 In. 650.00
Vase, Striated Blue Green Patina Over Bronzed Ground, Signed, 6 1/2 In. 895.00
Vase, Turquoise, Green Over Brown Copper, 6 5/8 In. 550.00

CLEWS pottery was made by George Clews & Co. of Brownhill Pottery, Tunstall, England, from 1806 to 1861. Additional pieces may be listed in the Flow Blue category.

Cup & Saucer, Dark Blue Transfer, Shepherd & Sheep, Staffordshire	80.00
Pepper Pot, Urn Shape, Dark Blue, 4 1/2 In.	550.00
Pitcher, Mt. Vernon, Washington's Seat, Dark Blue, 6 3/4 In.	1980.00
Platter, America & Independence, Dark Blue, 12 7/8 In.	770.00
Platter, Dr. Syntax Amused At Pat In The Pool, 19 x 14 1/2 In.	650.00
Platter, Fisherman, On Shore, Castle, Scroll Border, 9 In.	80.00
Platter, Landing Of General Lafayette, 9 In.	185.00
Platter, Stylized Chinese Landscape, c.1830, 12 1/2 x 14 5/8 In.	242.00
Platter, Windsor Castle, Scroll Borders, Blue, 13 x 17 In.	575.00
Vase, Chameleon Ware, Corset, Blue, 6 In.	89.00 to 100.00
Vase, Chameleon Ware, Rust Mottled, 6 In.	100.00

CLIFTON POTTERY was founded by William Long in Clifton, New Jersey, in 1905. He worked there until 1908 making a line called *Crystal Patina.* Clifton Pottery made art pottery. Another firm, Chesapeake Pottery, sold majolica marked *Clifton ware.*

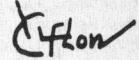

Bookends, Elephant, Dark To Light Maroon, Morton	110.00
Pitcher, Indian Ware, 5 3/4 In.	170.00
Teapot, Crystalline Glaze, Muted Yellow, Marked, 5 1/2 In.	120.00
Teapot, Geometric Design, Brown & Brick Red, Marked, 8 1/2 In.	65.00
Teapot, Oil Lamp Shape, Crystal Patina, Open	100.00
Vase, Crocus, Brown Matte Glaze, Marked, 8 1/2 In.	297.00
Vase, Drip Glaze, Dated & Signed, 7 1/2 In.	400.00
Vase, Embossed Fish, Olive Green Patina Glaze, Bulbous, 1906, 3 1/2 x 3 1/2 In.	715.00
Vase, Swirl Design, Zig Zags, 6 x 6 In.	50.00
Vase, Tafoya Tulip, Handles, Blue Ridge, 7 3/4 In.	75.00
Vase, Yellow, Celadon Matte Flambe, Organic Form, 1906, 10 x 7 1/4 In.	412.00

CLOCKS of all types have always been popular with collectors. The eighteenth-century tall case, or grandfather's clock, was designed to house a works with a long pendulum. In 1816, Eli Terry patented a new, smaller works for a clock, and the case became smaller. The clock could be kept on a shelf instead of on the floor. By 1840, coiled springs were used and even smaller clocks were made. Battery-powered electric clocks were made in the 1870s.

Advertising, 7-Up, Pop Art	75.00
Advertising, 7-Up, Real 7-Up Likes You, Red, Black, 1940, 15 1/2 x 15 1/2 In.	415.00
Advertising, 7-Up, Uncola, Scalloped Edge, Blue Field, Green Numbers, 17 In.	60.00
Advertising, 7-Up, You Like It, It Likes You, 18 1/4 In.	370.00
Advertising, Abington Mutual Fire Insurance Co., 75th Year, 1856-1931, Electric	125.00
Advertising, American Express, Metal Case, Plastic Face, Light-Up, 24 1/2 x 4 1/2 In.	80.00
Advertising, Arrow Beer, Paper Decal On Tin Face, Quartz Movement, 15 In.	245.00
Advertising, Atlantic Ale, Plastic, Frame, Square	100.00
Advertising, Atlas Tires, Round, Dated 1958, Light-Up	350.00
Advertising, Big Boy, Centered Figure, Aluminum Case, Light-Up, 1950s	295.00
Advertising, Black Label Beer, Electric, Wall	30.00
Advertising, Budweiser Beer, Gold Figure Of Horses & Wagon, Light-Up	95.00
Advertising, Burpee's Seeds, Electric	55.00
Advertising, Busch Beer, Bottle Cap Face, 1991, 14 In.	70.00
Advertising, Carling Beer, Plastic, 18 x 25 In.	82.00
Advertising, Celestial Seasonings, Sleepy Time Bear, Alarm, Box	35.00
Advertising, Chocolate Revillon, Windup, Key, Painted Tin, 23 In.	522.00
Advertising, Crown Jewelers, Bangor, Maine, Metal & Glass, Light-Up, 1940s	160.00
Advertising, Dixie Boy, Lux, 1930s	695.00
Advertising, Dr Pepper, Telechron, 1940s	225.00 to 325.00
Advertising, Drink Sun Crest Beverages, 16 x 19 In.	295.00
Advertising, Foremost Ice Cream, Light-Up, 26 x 9 In.	135.00
Advertising, Forst's Foremost Franks, Reverse Painted Glass Front, Round, 15 In.	120.00
Advertising, Frostie, Root Beer	195.00

Advertising, Heckers Flour, Glass Face, Bubble Front, Black & Red Hands, 15 In. 185.00
Advertising, Indian Motorcycles, Light-Up 660.00
Advertising, Iroquois Beer & Ale, Double Bubble, Light-Up 495.00
Advertising, Keen Kutter, Electric 295.00
Advertising, Kelly Tire, Set Into Tire Ring, Electric 75.00
Advertising, Kendall Motor Oil, Oil Derrick Face, Round, Light-Up, 14 In. 225.00
Advertising, Kendall, 2000 Mile Oil, Neon, Spinner, Light-Up, 1930-1940, 19 1/2 In. . . . 1100.00
Advertising, Lord Calvert, Distilled For Men Of Distinction, Wooden Case, 11 x 12 In. . . 70.00
Advertising, McCord Motor Gasket, Metal & Glass 95.00
Advertising, Michelob Beer, Revolving, Light-Up 80.00
Advertising, Miller, Ice Bucket, Animated 135.00
Advertising, Monroe Shocks, Double Bubble 195.00
Advertising, Narragansett Beer, Plastic, Metal, 7 x 10 In. 35.00
Advertising, Nu-Grape, Plastic, Round 120.00
Advertising, Old Mr. Boston Liquors 55.00
Advertising, Oldsmobile Service, Neon, Metal Face, Glass Front, 18 x 18 In. 770.00
Advertising, Orange Crush, Light-Up 75.00
Advertising, Orange Crush, On Front Of Dial, Wood, Round, 16 In. 400.00
Advertising, Orange Crush, Pam 115.00
Advertising, Ortlieb's Beer, Dome Glass Face, Round, Light-Up, 15 In. 110.00
Advertising, Peterson's Celebration, Renaissance Revival Style Case, Electric, 32 In. . . . 60.00
Advertising, Phillips 66, Double Bubble 625.00
Advertising, Piel's Light Beer, Plastic, 1959 . . . . 55.00
Advertising, Prestone Anti-Freeze, 8-Day, Key, Blue & Silver, Round, 10 In. 120.00
Advertising, Purina, Light-Up 125.00
Advertising, Quaker State, Alarm, Traveling 18.00
Advertising, Quaker State, Green & Black On White, Wall, 16 x 16 In. 40.00
Advertising, Quaker State, Neon, With Spinner 1300.00
Advertising, Raytheon Expert TV & Radio Service, Glass Face, Bubble Front, 15 In. . . . 130.00
Advertising, Regulator, Calumet Baking Powder, 38 x 17 In. . . . . .595.00 to 825.00
Advertising, Ritz Cracker, Windup 350.00
Advertising, Ronald McDonald, Windup, Alarm 35.00
Advertising, Royal Crown Cola, Me & My RC . . . . .65.00 to 95.00
Advertising, Royal Crown Cola, Pam 245.00
Advertising, Ruger, 30th Anniversary, Clock At Right Bottom Of Large Square, 1979 . . . 115.00
Advertising, Sauer's Flavoring Extracts, 42 x 16 In. . . . . .1650.00 to 1705.00
Advertising, Sauer's Flavoring Extracts, Regulator, Pendulum, 14 3/8 x 40 In. 825.00
Advertising, Schlitz, Rotating Globe, Box 125.00
Advertising, Schmidt's Beer & Ale, Plastic, Light-Up, 13 x 14 In. 75.00
Advertising, Sears Roebuck, Frog 45.00
Advertising, Sinclair Gasoline, Neon, Spinner, Glass & Metal, 20 1/2 In. 1760.00
Advertising, Snap-On Tools, Swimsuit 40.00
Advertising, Squibb Vitamins 65.00
Advertising, Sun Crest, Glass Front, Metal Edge, 16 1/4 x 13 1/4 In. 75.00
Advertising, Sweet Lassey, Light-Up 120.00
Advertising, Tadcaster Beer, Glass Dome, Round, Light-Up, 15 In. 100.00
Advertising, Tetley Tea Time, Metal Box, Glass Front, 1950s, 3 x 14 In. 75.00
Advertising, Tetley Tea, Tin 950.00
Advertising, Time To Buy Caterpillar, Glass Face, Bubble Front, Light-Up, 15 In. 357.00
Advertising, TV & Radio Service, Round, Light-Up 155.00
Advertising, Use Gulf Tires, Glass Face, Bubble, Round, 15 In. 385.00
Advertising, W.W. Appel, Lancaster, Reverse Painted, 27 In. 285.00
Advertising, Wear-Ever, Frying Pan Shape, Electric, 14 3/4 x 8 1/2 In. 90.00
Advertising, Winchester, Quartz Movement, Wall, 1970s, 18 x 12 In. 170.00
Advertising, Winston Cigarettes, Cigarette Pack Inside, Light-Up 45.00
Alabaster, Eagle Star Banners, Cornucopia, France, 22 In. 2530.00
Alarm, Bugs Bunny, Box, 1970 . . . . 75.00
Alarm, James Bond, 2 Bells, United Kingdom . . . . .40.00 to 75.00
Alarm, Mighty Mouse, Bradley 95.00
Alarm, Snoopy, Blessing, 1970 . . . . 250.00
Alarm, Star Wars, Talking, Battery Operated, 9 In. 75.00
Alarm, Tom & Jerry, Bradley 95.00
Alarm, Winnie The Pooh, Bradley 60.00

Alarm, Woody Woodpecker, Woody On Face, Box, 1959 .... 220.00
Alarm, Woody Woodpecker, Woody's Cafe, White, Metal Case, 1950 .... 30.00
Animated, Big Bad Wolf, 3 Little Pigs, Wolf, Red, Ingersoll, Alarm, 1930s, 4 In. .580.00 to 680.00
Animated, Blacksmith, Mastercrafters 85.00
Animated, Carousel, Onyx, Mastercrafters 275.00
Animated, Church Bell Ringer 100.00
Animated, Cowboy, Twirling Lasso, Bronze Finished, United 175.00
Animated, Fireplace, Mastercrafters, 1950s .... .65.00 to 115.00
Animated, Fishing Boy, Gold Metal, United 225.00
Animated, Frying Pan, Chef, United 75.00
Animated, Gold Poodle, Electric 125.00
Animated, Granny Rocking In Chair Next To Fireplace, Haddon .... .100.00 to 175.00
Animated, Guitar, Band Leader, U.S. Clock Co. 325.00
Animated, Huckleberry Finn, Fishing 225.00
Animated, Majorette Twirling Baton, United, 1950s 135.00
Animated, Snoopy, Alarm, Windup, Metal, 1950-1960, 4 1/4 In. 160.00
Animated, Statue Of Liberty, United 350.00
Animated, Swinging Canary, Mastercrafters 225.00
Animated, Swinging Girl, Mastercrafters, 1950s ....200.00 to 250.00
Animated, Swinging Playmates, Onyx Case, Electric, Mastercrafters 240.00
Animated, Teeter-Totter, Electric, Haddon 225.00
Animated, Waterfall, Mastercrafters 65.00
Animated, Woody Woodpecker, Columbia Time Products, c.1950, 7 In. 145.00
Ansonia, Arabic Numerals, Hour & Half-Hour Strike, Delft Case, 11 1/4 In. 400.00
Ansonia, Beveled Glass & Brass Case, Pendulum & Key, 8 7/8 In. 220.00
Ansonia, Enameled Face, Brass Works, Ironstone China Case, 10 3/4 In. 300.00
Ansonia, Mantel, Cast Metal, Gold Repaint, Pendulum, French Style, 15 x 18 In. 370.00
Ansonia, Mantel, Green Borders, Red Flowers, 11 1/2 x 14 In. 550.00
Ansonia, Mantel, Rococo Form, Floral Design, Porcelain, 15 In. 360.00
Ansonia, Marbleized, Enamel Face, Open Escapement, Brass Works, Iron, 17 3/4 In. 200.00
Ansonia, Regulator, Wall, Pendulum & Key, Ebonized Trim, Gilded Moldings, 31 In. ... 495.00
Ansonia, Rococo Revival, Scrolled Foliate, 18 1/2 In. 1380.00
Ansonia, Rosalind, c.1890 .... 250.00
Ansonia, Shelf, Gothic Revival, Brass Pendulum, Frosted Glass Door Panel, 19 In. 250.00
Ansonia, Wall, Gilt Bronze, Raised Face, Enamel Roman Numerals, Round, 3 1/2 In. ... 170.00
Astral, Coventry, Gallery, Single Fusee, England 775.00
Atkins, Rosewood, 8-Day, Time & Strike, Dog Chasing Birds Tablet, 1870s, 17 In. 495.00
Automaton, Industrial, Cyclist, Thermometer, Barometer, Marble Base, 15 1/2 In. ... 11500.00
Banjo, Boston, Federal, Mahogany, 8-Day Weight Driven Movement, 1820, 33 In. 3105.00
Banjo, Cummens, William, Eagle Finial, Reverse Painted Eagle, Mahogany, 1830 ..... 3160.00
Banjo, Curtis & Dunning, Federal, Mahogany, 19th Century, 33 In. 1380.00
Banjo, Curtis, Lemuel, Gilded Facade, Brass Trim, Mahogany Case, 41 In. 3300.00
Banjo, Dunning, J.L., 8-Day, c.1820, 30 3/4 In. 2300.00
Banjo, Foliate, Drapery Design, Gilt Metal, Enamel Dial, 11 1/2 In. 345.00
Banjo, Gilbert, 8-Day, Early 20th Century, 27 In. 99.00
Banjo, Howard & Davis, 8-Day, Rosewood Grained, c.1842, 31 3/4 In. 1955.00
Banjo, Hubbard, Daniel, Cherry Wood, 7 1/2-Inch Painted Dial, 1820, 41 1/2 In. 3450.00
Banjo, Ingraham, Pendulum, 33 In. 250.00
Banjo, Mahogany, 7 3/4-Inch Painted Dial, Acorn Finial, Convex Molding, 1840, 33 In. . 1150.00
Banjo, Mahogany, 8-Day, Skeletonized Front Plate, Gilt Eagle Finial, 1820, 43 In. 3737.00
Banjo, Mahogany, Reverse Painted Chariot In Sky, Brass Eagle Finial, 32 3/4 In. 1265.00
Banjo, New Haven, Willard Model, 30-Day 1050.00
Banjo, Willard, Simon, 8-Day, Mahogany, 30 In. 2200.00
Banjo, Willard, Simon, Giltwood, Eglomise, Acorn Finial, Floral Dial Band, Mahogany .. 3450.00
Banjo, Williams, David, Eagle Finial, Reverse Painted Dancing Women, 1815, 40 In. ... 3450.00
Banjo, Williams, Mahogany, Painted Dial, Brass Eagle, Ball Finial, 1830, 35 In. 2875.00
Behrens, 2 Sides, Electric, Black Painted Metal, 1910, 14 3/8 In. 5520.00
Birge, Mallory & Co., Shelf, Basket Of Fruit Crest, 30-Hour Brass Movement, 26 In. ... 260.00
Birge, Peck, & Co., Empire, Mahogany, Half Pillar, 8-Day, 1840 .... 630.00
Birge & Fuller, Shelf, Double Steeple, Mahogany, 8-Day, c.1845, 27 In. 860.00
Birge & Fuller, Shelf, Mahogany, Steeple, Wagon Spring, 1845, 26 In. ....*Illus* 2185.00
Birge & Fuller, Shelf, Rosewood, Steeple, Wagon Spring, 1845, 27 In. ....*Illus* 1840.00
Bishop & Bradley, Pillar & Scroll, Painted Wood Dial, Wood Movement, 31 1/4 In. 1955.00

Clock, Birge & Fuller, Shelf,
Mahogany, Steeple,
Wagon Spring, 1845, 26 In.;
Clock, Boardman, Rosewood,
Steeple, Fusee, 1847, 19 3/4 In.;
Clock, Birge & Fuller, Shelf,
Rosewood, Steeple,
Wagon Spring, 1845, 27 In.

Blinking Eye, Continental, Soldier, Bradley & Hubbard, Cast Iron, Patent 1885, 16 In. ... 750.00
Blinking Eye, Organ Grinder, 18 In. 1430.00
Blinking Eye, Toby, 17 In. 1100.00
Boardman, Rosewood, Steeple, Fusee, 1847, 19 3/4 In. ....*Illus* 575.00
Boardman & Wells, Wooden Works, Carved Columns, Reverse Painted Glass 995.00
Boston Clock Co., Regulator, Weight Driven 1350.00
Boudoir, Cut Glass, Large Tulip, Allover Leaves & Geometric, 6 1/4 In. 225.00
Bracket, Ebonized, Bronze Ormolu, 8 Bell Chiming Movement 4125.00
Bracket, George II, Brass Dial, Matte Center, Roman, Arabic Numerals, 16 1/2 In. 4310.00
Bracket, George III, Inlaid Satinwood, Bronze, Roman, Arabic Numerals, 27 1/2 In. 14950.00
Bronze, 3-Piece, Cut Glass Bodies, Swags, Foliage, France, 10 1/2 In. 3220.00
Bronze, Pedestal, Bronze, Gilt, Arabic Numerals, Victorian, 37 In. 8050.00
Bronze, Regency, Brass Mounted, Arch Dial, Inlaid Mahogany, England, 1815 .... 4025.00
Caldwell, J.S., Cloisonne On Dial, Mercury Pendulum, Glass Case, Brass, 12 In. 1250.00
Calendar Paper, Black Marble, France, 1875, 13 1/4 In. 1495.00
Calendar Paper, Black Marble, France, 1880, 14 1/2 In. 1100.00
Calendar Paper, Red, Black Marble, Perpetual, France, 1870, 15 3/4 In. 1725.00
Camerer, Kuss & Co., Victorian, Wall, Walnut 460.00
Carriage, Alarm, Half-Hour Repeat, Brass, Fitted Leather Case, France, 4 1/2 In. 660.00
Carriage, Brass, Beveled Glass Panels, Bail Handle, c.1900, 4 3/4 In. 145.00
Carriage, Brass, Beveled Glass Sides, Enamel Dial, Leather Case, 6 In. 430.00
Carriage, Glass & Brass, Stamped H & H, France, 1920s, 4 1/4 In. 200.00
Carriage, Moser, Henry, Alarm, Rococo Style, Gilt Metal, Paris 805.00
Carriage, Sterling Silver, Art Nouveau, Round Dial, Leather Case 375.00
Cartel, Foliate, Floral, Beveled Glass Door, Round Dial, 20 In. 260.00
Cartel, Louis XV Style, Enamel Dial, Foliate Frame, Gilt Bronze, 28 3/4 In. 2530.00
Cartier, Desk, Gilt-Metal, Red Matte Dial, Arabic Numerals, Rectangular, 1950 .... 1495.00
Catalin, Digital, Streamline Design, Chrome 220.00
Champion Regulator, 8-Day, Pewter Inlay, 1880s, 27 In. 1500.00
Charles II, Brass, Striking, Roman Chapter Ring, 15 In. 5750.00
Cottage, Reverse Painted Lower Panel, 19th Century, 7 x 3 1/2 x 9 In. 70.00
Couple On Swing, Globe, Blue Sphere, Arched Branches, France, 1900, 32 3/4 In. 8050.00
Cowan, James, Desk, Ebonized, 7-Inch Dial, Rococo Spandrels, Scotland, 18 In. 5175.00
Cronier, Mantel, Figural, Louis XVI, Diana With Bird, Glass Dome, c.1790, 14 1/2 In. ... 3105.00
Drum, Time & Strike, Bull's-Eye, French Bell, 5 In. Diam. 850.00
Dunster, Roger, Desk, Ebonized, 7-Inch Dial, Leaf Spandrels, England, 18 1/4 In. 4025.00
Econolite, Revolving Paper Tree, 1950s, 10 1/2 In. 75.00
Empire, Column, Ebonized, Bronze Mounts, 19th Century 495.00
Fattorini & Sons, Mantel, Automatic Repeating Alarm, England, 11 x 25 1/2 In. 75.00
Figural, Double-Headed Spread-Winged Eagle, Carved Giltwood, Austria, 20 x 29 In. ... 1495.00
Figural, Girl With Flowing Hair, Sunburst In Ground, 1898-1904 .... 275.00
Figural, Porcelain, Nymphenburg Mark, 14 1/2 In. 495.00
Figure, Snoopy, Talking Doghouse, Japan 100.00
Forrestville, Mahogany, Double Ogee, 8-Day, Time & Strike, Etched Tablet Glass 650.00

Francis, A., Mantel, Chinoiserie, Lacquer, London, 10 In. 230.00
Georges Briard, Wall, Foil Backed Glass, Walnut Frame, 24 x 8 In. 55.00
Gilbert, Kitchen, Crystal Palace, Corner, Oak, 8-Day, Time & Strike 1250.00
Gilt Metal, Faux Diamond, Loop Handle, Pierced Ribbon, Round, Victorian, 5 In. 800.00
Glasham, George, Double Fusee, 8-Day, Hour Strike, Matching Shelf, Mahogany, 34 In. . 5500.00
Herman Miller, Desk, Chrome Casing, Brass Face, Gilbert Rohde, 6 In. 400.00
Herman Miller, Desk, Chrome, Base, Square Face, Gilbert Rohde, 6 In. 460.00
Hoadley, Silas, Shelf, Pillar & Scroll, Wood Movement, Brass Finials, 1820, 31 In. 1610.00
Hodges, Erastus, Shelf, Half-Pillar & Scroll, Gilt Cresting, Paw Feet, c.1830, 27 3/4 In. . 1380.00
Howard, Astronomical Regulator 7750.00
Howard, Bank, White, Black Numerals, 1900-1910 .... 2500.00
Howard Miller, Asterisk, White Enamel Metal Body, George Nelson, 10 In. 550.00
Howard Miller, Ball, Brass Center, Radiating Arms, George Nelson, 14 In. 410.00
Howard Miller, Ball, Wood Body, White, Brass Rods, George Nelson, 13 In. 430.00
Howard Miller, Bird's-Eye Maple & Black Wood, Footed, Decal, 5 x 10 1/2 In. 220.00
Howard Miller, Cork Outer Ring, White Face, Nelson Hands, 12 In. 80.00
Howard Miller, Desk, Ball, Brass Ring, Black Face, George Nelson, 7 x 5 1/2 In. 220.00
Howard Miller, Table, Walnut, Circular Brass Stand, George Nelson, 6 1/2 In. 190.00
Howard Miller, Wall, Black Leather Face, Aluminum Numerals, Hands, 15 In. 175.00
Howard Miller, Wall, Black Masonite Face, Wooden Rim, George Nelson, 10 1/4 In. ... 305.00
Howard Miller, Wall, Black Metal Harps Around, Blond Wooden Dial, Decal, 17 In. ... 435.00
Howard Miller, Wall, Chrome Slats, Center Black Dial, Decal, 24 In. Diam. 660.00
Howard Miller, Wall, Metal Arms Around Blond Wooden Dial, Decal, 13 In. Diam. 470.00
Howard Miller, Wall, Plastic, Round, Marked, 12 In. 110.00
Howard Miller, Wall, Star, Blue, Green, Orange & Black Arms, White Center, 19 In. ... 470.00
Howard Miller, Wall, Star, Wooden, Dark Finish, Round, Decal, 17 1/2 In. 1320.00
Howard Miller, Wall, Sunburst, Orange Balls On Brass Rods, George Nelson, 40 In. ... 525.00
Howard Miller, Wall, Sunburst, Wooden Balls On Brass Rods, George Nelson, 13 1/2 In. 440.00
Howard Miller, Wooden Spheres, Round, Brass Rods, Signed, 14 In. 345.00
Howard Miller, Wooden, Semicircular Shape, 8 Ball Feet, Metal Tag, 5 x 9 In. 55.00
Hurley & Elliott, Seahorse Base & Finial, Gold Face, Bronze, Signed, 8 x 5 In. 990.00
Industry Beam Engine, France 2750.00
Ingraham, Brass Works, Separate Alarm Movement, Reverse Painted Glass, 21 1/2 In. . 190.00
Ingraham, Carved Portrait Of General Fitzhugh Lee At Top, Cannons, Oak, 23 In. 1125.00
Ingraham, Grecian, 8-Day, Burled Butternut, 14 1/2 In. 550.00
Ingraham & Co., Battleship, The Maine, Gingerbread 300.00
International Time, Recorder, Oak, Metal, Bell Ring Key Wind, 1908, 48 x 70 In. 1100.00
International Time, Regulator, Oak, 34 In. 250.00
Ithaca, Gothic Revival, Walnut Case, 28 3/4 In. 770.00
Ithaca, Zero Bank, Calendar 3850.00
Ives, Joseph, Shelf, Mahogany Veneer, Ogee, Pendulum, Weights, 30 x 17 In. 630.00
James Dean, Neon, Light-Up 200.00
Japy Freres, Mantel, Black Onyx & Bronze, 15 x 24 In. 1175.00
Jennings Bros., Desk, Art Deco, Bronzed 135.00
Jerome, Chauncy, Shelf, Mahogany Veneer, Ogee, Pendulum, Weights, 26 x 15 In. 220.00
Jeromes & Darrow, Pillar & Scroll, Wooden Face, Brass Works, Mahogany Case 300.00
Kienzle & Co., Glass, Chromium-Plated Metal, Wall, 1930, Round, 15 3/4 In. 1495.00
Kitchen, Pressed Oak, Brass Works, Pendulum, Key, 22 In. 165.00
Lawson Time, Zephyr, Digital, Copper, Plastic, 1934, 8 In. 1150.00
Leavenworth, Pillar & Scroll, c.1810 .... 2070.00
LeCoultre, 8-Day, Windup, Square Case, Square, 7 x 7 In. 400.00
LeCoultre, Perpetual Motion, Box & Papers, 8 3/4 In. 795.00
LeCoultre, Swinging Balloon, Industrial, Silvered Basket, Balloonist, 1900, 27 1/2 In. .. 7760.00
LeCoultre, Travel, 2 Day, Silk Case, Printed Instructions 95.00
Liberty & Co., Sterling Silver, Enameled Face, Mother-Of-Pearl Inlay 8250.00
Limoges, Desk, Enamel, Gilt-Brass, Running Stag, Forest Scene, 1900, 2 1/2 In. 5460.00
London, James, Skeleton, Lyre Style, Dial, Striking, Round Dome, 1886 .... 1700.00
Louis Philippe, Bronze & Sienna Marble, Draped Male Figure, Marble Base, 25 In. 4150.00
Louis Philippe, Gilt & Patinated Bronze, Boy Seated With Scrolls & Books, 13 1/4 In. .. 630.00
Louis XV Style, Dore Bronze, Chinoiserie Figures, 19th Century, 21 1/2 In. 6900.00
Louis XVI Style, Silver Gilt, White Enameled Dial, Signed, Sunburst Frame, 21 1/4 In. . 4025.00
Lux, Cat, Pendulum Tail 325.00

Lux, Dixie-Boy, 1930s 590.00
Lux, Metal, Stirrup, Hanging Leather & Clock 95.00
Lux, Schmoo, White 225.00
Mantel, 4-Glass, Enamel Dial, Black Marble Top, Base, Gilt-Brass Case, 18 3/4 In. 3160.00
Mantel, Adams, E.W., 8-Day, Mahogany, c.1830, 37 1/2 In. 1495.00
Mantel, Amorous Couple Under Arbor On Crest, White Enamel Dial, 18 In. 150.00
Mantel, Art Deco, Marble, Malachite, Rectangular Clock Center, Continental, 3 1/2 In. . . . 125.00
Mantel, Balance Wheel, Miniature 225.00
Mantel, Bowfront Door, Mercury Filled Pendulum, France, 10 In. 375.00
Mantel, Brass, Cut Glass Cover, Wooden Base, Germany, 14 x 6 x 9 1/2 In. 30.00
Mantel, Brass, Temple Form, Ornate, Hour, 1/2 Hour Chimes, c.1898, 16 In. 725.00
Mantel, Bronze, Female Figure Reclining Against White Clock Face, 1860, 26 In. 3910.00
Mantel, Bronze, Young Woman In Classical Dress, France, 11 x 4 x 14 In. 650.00
Mantel, Champleve Enamel, Flower Design On Enamel Dial, Gilt Brass Case, 12 In. 4885.00
Mantel, Classical, Mahogany, Carved, 8-Day, c.1830, 31 1/2 x 17 1/2 In. 3565.00
Mantel, Depicting Explorer Hudson, Gilt & Patinated Bronze, 1835, 24 x 15 In. 2415.00
Mantel, Diana With Hound, Brass Cylinder Movement, Gilt, 12 x 5 x 14 In. 250.00
Mantel, Dovetail Top, Brass Face, Brass Pendulum, 8 x 5 x 14 In. 8800.00
Mantel, Empire, Ormolu, Marble Pedestal Mounted With Ormolu Swan, 18 In. 17250.00
Mantel, Empire, Ormolu, White Enamel Dial, Bronze, 17 In. 5750.00
Mantel, Female, Lounging On Pedestal Footed Base, White Face, 22 x 19 In. 430.00
Mantel, French Empire Style, Gilt Bronze, Silver, Figural, 1880, 23 In. 8165.00
Mantel, Gilt, Enamel Dial, Roman, Green, White Marble Base, 12 In. 4600.00
Mantel, Gilt-Brass, Bell Striking Movement, France, 1875, 19 In. 2070.00
Mantel, Louis XVI Style, Gilt Bronze, Face Inscribed, c.1880, 14 1/4 In. 2185.00
Mantel, Louis XVI, Enamel Dial, Black Arabic Numerals, Fluted Columns, 14 In. 2300.00
Mantel, Louis XVI, Ormolu, Black Roman, Arabic Numerals, Drum Shape Base, 20 In. . 9200.00
Mantel, Louis XVI, Ormolu, White Enamel Dial, Black Roman Numerals, 13 In. 5750.00
Mantel, Louis XVI, Ormolu, White Enamel Dial, Laurel Wreath Base, 26 In. 5460.00
Mantel, Mahogany, Gothic Arch Case, Boxwood Leaves, Checkered Borders, 15 In. 1035.00
Mantel, Marble, Black & Red, Drum Shaped Movement, Mercury Pendulum, c.1890 . . . 345.00
Mantel, Marble, White Enamel Dial, Roman Numerals, Calendar Ring, 25 In. 20700.00
Mantel, Mother-Of-Pearl Trim, 8-Day, Time & Strike, Papier-Mache, 27 1/2 In. 1650.00
Mantel, Neoclassical, Black Marble, Gilt Floral Design, 13 x 5 x 16 1/2 In. 500.00
Mantel, Neoclassical, Classical Maiden On Base, White Marble, 1880, 15 In. 420.00
Mantel, Neoclassical, Domed Top, Mahogany, 13 x 8 x 16 In. 175.00
Mantel, Neoclassical, Gilt Floral, Black Marble, 19th Century, 14 x 5 x 12 In. 225.00
Mantel, Neoclassical, Giltwood, Circular Cream Painted Enamel Dial, 33 1/4 In. 3335.00
Mantel, Neoclassical, Goddess Mounted On Case, 1885, 16 1/2 In. 665.00
Mantel, Neoclassical, Mahogany, Fruitwood, Circular White Enamel Dial, 22 1/2 In. 5175.00
Mantel, Neoclassical, Rosewood, Double Glazed Door, White Face, 16 In. 85.00
Mantel, Neoclassical, White Enamel Dial, Black, Italy, 18th Century 30.00
Mantel, Ormolu, Enamel Dial, Black Roman Numerals, Rectangular Base, 17 In. 6325.00
Mantel, Ormolu, Serpent Design, Foliate Spray Design, Ebonized, 21 1/2 In. 6900.00
Mantel, Porcelain, Pink, White, Pastel Floral, Gilt, Pendulum, Germany, 10 1/2 In. 190.00
Mantel, Round Face, Red Marble, c.1900, France 345.00
Mantel, Venus Playing With Eros, Ormolu, Marble, Black Base, Charles X, 17 1/2 In. . . . 9200.00
Mantel, White Marble, Gilt Bronze, 1900, 13 1/4 In. 1380.00
Mantel, Whiting, Pillar & Scroll, 8-Day 850.00
Mystery, Swinging, In Arm Of Soldier, Bronzed Spelter & Bronze, 27 In. 2875.00
New Haven, Steeple, Rosewood Veneer, Brass Works, Reverse Transfer, 20 In. 200.00
Newark Co., Kitchen, 8-Day, Pendulum, Art Deco 85.00
Nu-Grape, Telechron, Light-Up, Round 450.00
Petal Form Pendulum, Swan Lyre, 8-Day, Hour & Half Hour Strike, 1860s, 19 3/4 In. . 895.00
Pewter, Incense, Brass Bandings, 6 In. 110.00
Regulator, Austria, Divided Glazed Door, Enamel Dial, 1860s, 38 3/4 In. 3737.00
Regulator, Ebonized, Enameled Face, Brass Weight, Pendulum, Key, 33 In. 410.00
Regulator, France, 14-Day, Crystal, Mercury Pendulum 610.00
Regulator, Oak, Brass Works, Pendulum, Key, 37 3/4 x 18 1/2 In. 190.00
Regulator, Vienna, Enamel Face, Brass Weight, Pendulum & Key, Ebonized Case, 33 In. 435.00
Regulator, Vienna, Walnut, Roman Numeral Dial, Molded, 19th Century, 35 In. 125.00
Rotary, Cupid At Top, Enamel Dial, Fruiting Foliage, 3 Graces Support, 1870s, 24 In. . . . 9775.00

Ruppelwerk, Black & White Painted Metal, Key, Germany, 1930, 5 5/8 In. 690.00
Sessions, Catalin, Yellow, Electric 130.00
Sessions, Chef's Head 125.00
Sessions, Faux Marble, Column Form, Metal Mounts, Time, Strike & Alarm, 10 1/2 In. . 100.00
Sessions, Swimming Angelfish, Light-Up 175.00
Sessions, Wall, Regulator, Oak Case, 38 1/2 x 18 In. 170.00
Seth Thomas, Calendar Paper, Double Dial 990.00
Seth Thomas, Desk, Art Deco, Wooden, Rounded Edge, Metal Label, 6 1/4 x 9 In. 30.00
Seth Thomas, Dial Marked U.S.L.H.E., Wooden Case, 36 In. 2530.00
Seth Thomas, Faux Marble, Late 19th Century, 18 x 7 x 11 1/4 In. 85.00
Seth Thomas, Mantel, 8-Day, Gothic Style Case 30.50
Seth Thomas, Mantel, Faux Marble, Temple Form, 1890, 12 In. 130.00
Seth Thomas, Mantel, Gothic Style, Mahogany Veneer, Brass Works, 13 1/4 In. 125.00
Seth Thomas, Mantel, Inlaid Wooden Case, 14 In. 175.00
Seth Thomas, Mantel, Mahogany Veneer, Brass Works, Bird Transfer, Key, 16 In. 165.00
Seth Thomas, Mantel, Mahogany, Sonora Chimes, 10 3/4 x 6 3/4 x 9 1/2 In. 145.00
Seth Thomas, Mantel, Sonora Chimes 500.00
Seth Thomas, Office, Perpetual Calendar Paper, Weight Driven, 1860, 36 In. . .2100.00 to 2200.00
Seth Thomas, Rebecca At The Well, Porcelain Dial, Sonora Bell Chime, 1876, 16 In. . . . 850.00
Seth Thomas, Regulator, No. 2, Oak 1100.00
Seth Thomas, Reverse Painted Glass, Brass Works, Key, Rosewood Veneer, 16 1/2 In. . . 135.00
Seth Thomas, Rosewood, Roman Numerals, 19th Century, 11 x 3 3/4 x 16 1/2 In. 110.00
Seth Thomas, School, Oak, Roman Numeral Dial, 16 x 5 x 24 In. 150.00
Seth Thomas, Shelf, Calendar, Walnut, 2 Dials, Key, Pat. Feb. 15, 1876, 20 x 13 In. 385.00
Seth Thomas, Shelf, Mahogany Case, 13 In. 170.00
Seth Thomas, Shelf, Ogee, Figured Veneer, Weights, Pendulum, Key, 25 x 15 In. 220.00
Seth Thomas, Shelf, Rosewood Veneer, Brass Works, Alarm, Pendulum, 16 In. 190.00
Seth Thomas, Shelf, Rosewood Veneer, Pilasters, Brass Works, Pendulum, 33 In. .220.00 to 250.00
Seth Thomas, Shelf, Scroll, Mahogany, Brass Works, Wooden Face, Beehives, 31 In. . . . 1210.00
Seth Thomas, Walnut, Roman Arched Top, Fluted Corner Columns, 8 1/2 x 5 x 10 In. . . 50.00
Shelf, Aluminum Case, Verichron Quartz, Smoky Glazed Front, Wood Base, 9 3/4 In. . . 70.00
Shelf, Carved Leaf, Mahogany, Shell Splat, 12-Inch Painted Wood Dial, 1840, 36 In. . . . 1090.00
Shelf, Empire, Brass, Rosewood Veneer, Metal Face, 32 1/2 In. 550.00
Shelf, Foliate Cartouche Form, Phoenix Incised Design, Glass Dome Case, 7 In. 115.00
Shelf, Mahogany, 2-Weight, Carved Eagle Crest, c.1830-1845, 38 1/4 In. 910.00
Shelf, Mahogany, Chippendale, Brass Bail Handle, Finials, Feet, 18 1/2 In. 2070.00
Shelf, Mahogany, Engraved Brass Face, Silver Trim, Chiming, Brass Pendulum, 4 In. . . 300.00
Shelf, Mahogany, Kitchen, Roman Numeral Dial, Gilt Door, 13 1/2 x 4 3/4 x 20 In. 110.00
Shelf, Mahogany, Thumbmolded Crest, Gilt Spandrels, 17 x 5 x 30 In. . . . . .100.00 to 125.00
Shelf, Rosewood Facade, Brass Works, Paper Label, 9 In. 105.00
Shelf, Walnut, Chippendale, Bracket, Domed Top, Brass Finials, Silvered Dial, 19 In. . . 17250.00
Shelf, Whiting, Riley, Empire, Mahogany Veneer, Ebonized, Wooden Works, 35 In. 525.00
Skeleton, Architectural Style, Round Dome, Striking 2250.00
Skeleton, Brass Frame & Works, Glass Domed Case, 19th Century, 16 1/2 In. 1725.00
Skeleton, Chinoiserie, Dragon Spire Finials, Brass, c.1855, 21 In. 2875.00
Skeleton, Gilt, Griffins & Rosettes, Y Frame, France, c.1800 . . . . 8250.00
Skeleton, Gothic Style, Chain Fusee, Strike, Marble Base, Oval Dome, 20 1/2 In. 3150.00
Skeleton, Great Exhibition, Mahogany Base, Oval Dome, Signed 950.00
Skeleton, Great Exhibition, Porcelain Dial, Ebonized Base, Silk Thread Suspension 1150.00
Skeleton, Ivy Leaf Style, White Marble Base, Oval Dome, 18 In. 2700.00
Skeleton, Lyre Style, Chain Fusee, 5 Spoke Wheel, Oval Dome, 14 In. 2650.00
Skeleton, Stylized Gothic Arch, Roman Numerals, Mahogany, England, 16 3/4 In. 2070.00
Skeleton, White Enamel Chapter Ring, Red Date Ring, Swags Of Ivy, 20 In. 8625.00
Smokey The Bear, Plastic, Box 165.00
Sommer, Art Deco, Green Glass, Birds, Germany 150.00
Starr, Theodore, Figural, Cupid Ormolu Mount, France 1400.00
Steeple, Rosewood, Alarm, Roman Numeral Dial, 19th Century, 10 x 4 x 19 1/2 In. 150.00
Stow, Solomon, Shelf, Half-Pillar & Splat, Wood Movement, Gilt Columns, 1830, 28 In. . 805.00
Tall Case, 14-In. Painted Dial, Painted Figures Representing Countries, 85 1/2 In. 2070.00
Tall Case, A. Jacobs, Regulator, Gothic, Mahogany, 102 In. 6325.00
Tall Case, Arched Door, Moon Phases, Walnut, 1780, 87 1/4 In. 7475.00
Tall Case, Baddy, Benjamin, Japanned, 8-Day, English Brass Dial, Lead Weights 2310.00

Tall Case, Carruthers, Walnut & Oak, 1800-1855 .... 1525.00
Tall Case, Cherry, 30-Hour, Wooden Pull Up, Weight Driven Movement, 1820, 91 In. 2990.00
Tall Case, Cherry, Bird's-Eye Maple Veneer, Raised Star Rosettes, 96 1/4 In. 4675.00
Tall Case, Chippendale, Arched Molded Hood, Spire Finials, Bombe Base, 101 In. 17250.00
Tall Case, Chippendale, Enamel Dial, Arched Top, Pierced Fret, Plinth Base, 94 In. 18400.00
Tall Case, Colonial Mfg., Bonnet, 9 Tubes, 1920 .... 7800.00
Tall Case, Curly Maple, Dovetailed Bracket Feet, 90 In. 5610.00
Tall Case, Daniel Oyster, Chippendale, 8-Day Movement, Walnut, 94 In. 7370.00
Tall Case, Domed Door, Reeded Columns, Second Hand, Time & Strike, 85 In. 2185.00
Tall Case, Dovetailed Bonnet, Paneled Base, Turned Feet, 91 1/2 In. 3850.00
Tall Case, Elisha Smith, Brass Works, Painted 6900.00
Tall Case, Elisha Smith, Incised Carving, 88 1/2 In. 2070.00
Tall Case, Enameled Brass Dial, Brass Pendulum, Pine, 89 In. 770.00
Tall Case, Federal, 8-Day, Brass Movement, Butternut & Maple, c.1810, 85 In. 4140.00
Tall Case, Federal, Inlaid Mahogany, Reeded Columns, 94 In. 25300.00
Tall Case, French Provincial, Oak, Domed, Floral, Plinth Base, 97 In. 1610.00
Tall Case, French Regulator, 8-Day, Pinwheel Escapement 2310.00
Tall Case, George III, Mahogany, Broken Arch, 18th Century, Scotland, 85 In. 2175.00
Tall Case, George III, Oak, Roman Numerals, Bracket Feet, Plinth Base, 78 In. 745.00
Tall Case, Georgian, Brass Dial, Oak, Roman Numerals, Columns, Domed Door, 83 In. . 600.00
Tall Case, Georgian, Oak, Swan Neck Pediment, Glazed Door, Late 19th Century, 96 In. . 1750.00
Tall Case, Grain Painted, Molded Cornice, Gilt Vines, Pink Swags, 86 In. 1380.00
Tall Case, Gustav Becker, Oak, 76 In. 300.00
Tall Case, Hand Painted Face, Masonic Symbols At Crest, Wooden Works, Pine 660.00
Tall Case, Inlaid Walnut, Calendar, Moon Phase Dial, 99 In. 8470.00
Tall Case, Iron Moon Phase Dial, J. Bliss, Cherry, 87 1/2 In. 9200.00
Tall Case, Jacob Fertig, Chippendale, Walnut, c.1811 .... 9500.00
Tall Case, James Cole, Maple, c.1810, 82 1/2 In. 5850.00
Tall Case, John Carmichael Greenock, Scotland, Mahogany, 1780s, 93 3/4 In. 4140.00
Tall Case, Luman Watson, Hepplewhite, Cherry, Bonnet, Masonic Designs, 92 In. 1870.00
Tall Case, Mahogany Veneer, Bonnet, Brass Works, Scotland, 85 In. 2145.00
Tall Case, Mahogany, 12-In. Painted Dial, Fan Spandrels, 1815, 96 In. 4890.00
Tall Case, Mahogany, Black Arabic Numerals, Rectangular Glazed Door, 78 In. 400.00
Tall Case, Mahogany, Brass Dial, Claw Feet, Early 20th Century 1840.00
Tall Case, Mahogany, Chippendale, White Painted Dial, Roman Numerals, 96 In. 17250.00
Tall Case, Mahogany, Westminster & Whittingham Chimes, Herschede, 125 In. 3700.00
Tall Case, Mahogany, With Music Box, Sun, Moon Face Design, H. Muhr & Sons, Pa. .. 5500.00
Tall Case, Mission Oak, Marked Quaint 750.00
Tall Case, Model, Dutch Delft, Panels Of Figural Landscape, Foliate Borders, 17 1/2 In. . 315.00
Tall Case, Nathan Howell, Chippendale, Cherry, c.1741, 81 1/2 In. 6325.00
Tall Case, Neoclassical, Birch, Mahogany, Roman, Arabic Numerals, Green, 91 In. 1495.00
Tall Case, Oak, Brass Works, Chimes, Pendulum Bob With Dutch Scene, 78 In. 275.00
Tall Case, Oak, Mahogany, Arch Crest, Brass Finial, Rosettes, Bracket Feet 1510.00
Tall Case, Oak, Overhanging Cornice, Brass Spandrels, England, 81 In. 1330.00
Tall Case, Oak, Painted Wood Dial, Gilt Spandrels, Plinth, 1800, 87 In. 2300.00
Tall Case, Riley Whiting, 98 In. 1210.00
Tall Case, Riley Whiting, Pine, Red, Floral, Foliate, Gold, Black Stringing, 83 In. 4890.00
Tall Case, Samuel Hofford, Federal, 8-Day, Movement, 93 In. 4840.00
Tall Case, Silas Hoadley, Arched Hood, Brass Finials, Sweep Second Hand, Pine, 85 In. . 2300.00
Tall Case, Silas Hoadley, Pine, Eagle Design Dial, Dark Finish, 83 x 18 In. 920.00
Tall Case, Silas Hoadley, Pine, Scrolled Crest, Brass Finials 2300.00
Tall Case, Silas Hoadley, Wooden Works, Pewter Hands, Wooden Face, 80 1/2 In. 1650.00
Tall Case, Thomas Norton, Chippendale, 8-Day, Mahogany, 97 1/2 In. 4640.00
Tall Case, Tulipwood, 8-Day, Broken Arch, Brass Works, Delaware Valley, 1795, 99 In. . 8525.00
Tall Case, Walnut, Foliage Arch, Square Dial, Roman, Arabic Numerals, 102 In. 5460.00
Tall Case, William A. Kelley, Brass Dial & Fittings, New Bedford 5500.00
Telechron, Electric, Black Catalin Hexagonal Case 75.00
Telechron, School, Round, 14 In. Diam. 35.00
Terry, Eli, Polychrome Flower, Reverse Painted House, Mahogany Veneer, 31 In. 520.00
Terry, Eli, Shelf, Mahogany, Half Pillar, 8-Day, 1825 .... 1035.00
Terry, Eli, Shelf, Pillar & Scroll, 30-Hour Wooden Movement, Mahogany, 30 In. 920.00
Terry, Eli, Shelf, Pillar & Scroll, Mahogany Veneer, Wooden Works, 31 In. 880.00
Terry, Eli, Shelf, Pillar & Scroll, Reverse Painted, Curly Maple Inlay, 1830, 30 1/2 In. 1725.00

Terry, Samuels, Shelf, Empire, Mahogany Veneer, Paper Label, c.1820, 32 In. 190.00
Terry, Theodore, Steeple, Double Acting Torsion Balance & Escapement, 13 In. 2750.00
Terry & Son, Shelf, Scroll, Mahogany, Birch, Plymouth, Ct., 31 1/4 In. 1380.00
Tiffany clocks are listed in the Tiffany category.
Travel, Thick Beveled Glass Face, Heavy Brass, Circa, 1870 . . . .   275.00
Triple Fusee, 8-Day, Westminster Chime, Carved Walnut, 27 In. 8500.00
United, Stagecoach, Brass 60.00
Vacheron & Constantin, Desk, Sterling, Enamel, Bronze, 8-Day, c.1920 . . . .   3850.00
Wag-On-Wall, Brass Gears, Pendulum, 1 Hand, 12 1/2 x 9 1/4 In. 460.00
Wall, Black Forest, Hunter With His Dog On Face, Rectangular Case 105.00
Wall, French Poodle, Eyes & Tail Move, Purple, Rhinestones 125.00
Wall, Raised Floral Corners, Square Ebonized Case, France, 23 x 23 In. 225.00
Wall, Reverse Painted Panel Opens To Dial, Giltwood Frame, c.1820, 30 1/2 In. 1840.00
Wall, Trunk-Dial, Mahogany, Applied Scrolled Sides, Off-White Face, England, 28 In. . .   300.00
Waterbury, Mantel, Faux Marble, Late 19th Century, 16 1/2 x 7 x 11 1/4 In. 60.00
Waterbury, Mantel, Ironstone Case, Rococo Form, Roman Chapters, 10 5/8 In. 260.00
Waterbury, Shelf, Rosewood Veneer, Ogee, Reverse Painted Scene, 18 5/8 x 12 In. 165.00
Waters, John, Primitive, Chip Carved, Brass Fittings, Name Plate, 29 In. 715.00
Welch, Rosewood, 30-Hour, Beveled Glass 295.00
Westclox, Alarm, Tin Can Shape 55.00
Whiting, Riley, Shelf, Empire, Mahogany Veneer, Pilasters, Eagle Crest, c.1820, 29 In. . .   190.00
William, Gilbert, Shelf, Mahogany Veneer, Ogee, Reverse Painted Base, 30 x 16 In. 190.00
Windmill, With Barometer & Thermometer, Brass & Silvered Metal, c.1895, 17 In. 2415.00
With Thermometer & Barometer, Hardwood Case, Brass Works, 36 1/4 In. 360.00
Wright Kay & Co., Mantel, Mahogany, Domed Top, Detroit, Mi., 21 x 6 x 12 In. 100.00

CLOISONNE enamel was developed during the tenth century. A glass
enamel was applied between small ribbons of metal on a metal base.
Most cloisonne is Chinese or Japanese. Pieces marked *China* are twentieth-century examples.

Basin, 7 Foo Lions On Interior, Chasing Ball, Reverse Floral Design, Wood Stand 431.00
Box, Cover, Bird, Floral Design, Enamel, 5 x 2 In. 110.00
Box, Cover, Butterfly, Flower Design, Trefoil Form, Black Ground, 3 1/2 In. 110.00
Box, Cover, Silver Wire Work, Black Goldstone Ground, Japan, 3 1/2 In. 395.00
Box, Duck Shape, Red Ground, Polychrome, 7 3/8 In. 190.00
Candlestick, Blues, Greens, Late 19th Century, 5 In., Pair 175.00
Charger, Roosters, Florals, 19th Century, 14 In. 170.00
Charger, Songbirds, Flying Among Flowers, Patterned Border, Pink Ground, 28 In. 1725.00
Cup, Cover, Flower Design, Copper Bronze Body, Pale Blue Ground, 5 In. 960.00
Figurine, Crane, Archaic Style Design, Blue Ground, 7 1/2 In., Pair 175.00
Figurine, Eagle, Perched On Base, 13 1/2 x 17 In. 425.00
Ginger Jar, White Flowers, Cobalt Blue Cover & Band, Teakwood Base, 8 1/2 In. 135.00
Jar, Allover Floral, Greens, Amber, Brown Ground, Wooden Stand, 9 In., Pair 115.00
Jar, Butterfly, Floral Design, Black Ground, Globular, 5 In. 120.00
Jar, Cover, Butterfly, Flower Design, Red Ground, Globular, 9 In. 165.00
Jar, Cover, Stylized Floral Body, Phoenix On Cover, Bead Finial, 5 1/2 In. 140.00
Jar, Floral Design, Purple Ground, Globular, 3 3/4 In. 120.00
Jar, Floral Rondels, Silver Blue Metallic Ground, Globular, 4 1/4 In. 120.00
Jar, Hinged Floral Cover, Multicolored Floral & Bird, Fan-Shaped Panels, 4 1/2 In. 660.00
Lamp, Colorful Bands Of Animals & Designs, 75 In. 690.00
Lamp, Flowers, Yellow Ground, 7 1/2 In., Pair 350.00
Plate, Birds & Lantern, Yellow Globular, 12 In. 275.00
Plate, Doves, Flower, Blue Ground, 9 3/4 In. 90.00
Plate, Geese, Landing On A Pond, 12 In. 175.00
Plate, Quail & Grasses, 12 In. 165.00
Plate, Squirrel, Grapes Amidst Fall Foliage, 14 1/2 In. 220.00
Table, Exotic Birds On Top, Foliate Pierced Gallery, Bronze, 19th Century, 30 In. 2970.00
Table Screen, Boat Scene, Anchored Beside Country Temple, 19th Century, 16 In. 4310.00
Teapot, Chrysanthemum Central Band, Pink Ground, 3 Raised Feet, 3 x 4 In. 4025.00
Teapot, Shou, Passion Flower Design, Blue Ground, 5 In. 205.00
Tureen, Cover, Scrolled Foliate Designs, Surrounding Characters, 14 1/2 In. 460.00
Urn, Cover, Floral Design, Waisted Base, Bulbous Body, Late 19th Century 130.00
Vase, 3-Clawed Dragon, Black Enamel Ground, Flared Neck, 6 In. 115.00

Vase, Baluster Shape, 5-Claw Yellow Dragon Design, Black Ground, 12 In. 300.00
Vase, Baluster, Floral Design, Turquoise Blue Ground, 9 1/2 In. 1210.00
Vase, Baluster, Gold Vine, Bird, Flowering Shrub Design, Blue Ground, 4 1/2 In. 4510.00
Vase, Baluster, Melon Ribbing, 5 1/8 In., Pair 360.00
Vase, Baluster, Pheasant, Flower Design, Midnight Blue Ground, 7 1/2 In. 1375.00
Vase, Bird, Flower Design, Inverted Pear Shape, Black Floral Ground, 12 In., Pair 630.00
Vase, Birds, Dark Blue Ground, Meiji Period, 3 1/2 In., Pair 200.00
Vase, Blooming Flower Design, Dark Blue Ground, Meiji Period, 6 In. 170.00
Vase, Cover, 2 Doves, Sitting Amid Autumnal Vine, Light Blue Ground, 5 1/4 In. 515.50
Vase, Crane Design, Black Ground, Wood Stand, 2 1/2 In. 140.00
Vase, Floral Band, 6 Sides, Dragon, Phoenix Design, Flecked Blue Ground, 6 In. 460.00
Vase, Floral, Avian Design, Egg Shape, 7 In., Pair 150.00
Vase, Floral, Wave Banding, Blue Ground, 15 In. 60.00
Vase, Flower Design, Inverted Pear Shape, Red Transparent Ground, 8 1/2 In. 145.00
Vase, Flowers & Butterflies, Blue, 7 In. 95.00
Vase, Green Floral Design, 6 In. 110.00
Vase, Inverted Pear Shape, Dragon On Red Design, 4 3/4 In. 220.00
Vase, Inverted Pear Shape, Gold, Silver Carp Disappearing In Sea, 6 1/4 In. 3740.00
Vase, Phoenix, Dragon Lappets, Gray Ground, 3/4 In. 190.00
Vase, Phoenix, Dragon, Floral Bands On Neck, Meiji Period, 12 In., Pair. 630.00
Vase, Phoenix, Floral Design, Seed Form, Beige Brocade Ground, 9 3/4 In. 100.00
Vase, Pink Cherry Blossom Design, Inverted Pear Shape, Green Ground, 9 In. 165.00
Vase, Pink Peonies, Iris, Mums, Blue Ground, Black Flared Rim, 13 In., Pair 440.00
Vase, Polychromed Dragon & Geometric Design, Mounted As Lamp, China, 20 In. 200.00
Vase, Seed Shape, Birds, Pale Blue Ground, 9 3/4 In. 250.00
Vase, Seibo On Back Of Rain Dragon, Blue Ground, Meiji Period, 7 In. 230.00
Vase, Single Yellow Rose, Green Ground, Ando Jubei, 12 7/8 In. 1100.00
Vase, Songbirds, Multicolored Fruit Branches, White Ground, 7 1/4 In. 1035.00
Vase, Tall Green Lappets With Lotus Flower Design, Blue Floral Ground, 13 In. 630.00

CLOTHING of all types is listed in this category. Dresses, hats, shoes,
underwear, and more are found here. Other textiles are to be found in
the Coverlet, Movie, Quilt, Textile, and World War I and II categories.

Apron, Laugh-In, Slogans From The TV Comedy Show, Copyright 1968 . . . . 25.00
Bathing Suit, Tunic, Self Belt, Red, Navy & Green Plaid, Claire McCardell, 1950s 1955.00
Bell-Bottoms, Mini Skirt & Jacket, Orange, Plaid, 1970s, 3 Piece 35.00
Belt, Woman's, Gilt Metal, Green & Carnelian Stones, 1980s 230.00
Belt Buckle, Silver Foliate Acorn Design, Round, Art Nouveau 488.00
Belt Buckle, Wood, Black Jade, Dragon's Head Clasp, 4 3/4 In. 242.00
Bikini, Red Wool, Rudi Gernreich 2760.00
Boots, Cowboy, Polychrome & Appliqued, Red, White, Yellow, Black Ground, Size 9A . 46.00
Boots, Cowboy, Toddler's, 1950s 30.00
Boots, Go-Go, Faux White Leather, Zipper Sides, Italian, Eskipets By Durham, Box 80.00
Boots, Riding, Leather, Hobnail Soles, Bottle Laces, Tan Patina, Boot Trees 245.00
Boots, White Bucks, Pointed Toes 118.00
Boots, Woman's, Lace-Up, Black 125.00
Breeches, Riding, Detachable Overskirt, Charcoal Wool, Late 19th Century 110.00
Camisole & Pantaloons, Black 45.00
Cap, Baby's, White Embroidered, Pink, Gold Thread, Lace, Ribbon Ties, 17th Century . . 400.00
Cap, Chauffeur's, With State Of Illinois Badge 68.00
Cap, Jerry Mahoney, Figural Face, Mouth Moves 45.00
Cape, Cocoon, Black Silk Velvet, Crenelated Collar, Chiffon Lining, 1930s, Size 6 . . . . . 80.00
Cape, Evening, Black Velvet, Ermine Bands At Shoulder & Hem, S.H. Dick, 1920s 115.00
Cape, Woman's, Ermine 46.00
Chaps, Cowboy's, Winter, Black Woolies, 1920 . . . . 2150.00
Coat, Black Bear, 1890s 650.00
Coat, Black Fur Top, Serge Fabric Bottom, Bronxville, N.Y. 75.00
Coat, Brown Velvet, Floral Ribbon Striped Silk Lining, A. Guerin & Ferrier, 1890s 172.00
Coat, Brown Velvet, Fur Trim On Sleeves, Brown Silk Lining, Franklin Simon, 1920s . . . 110.00
Coat, Farm, Denim Jean, Lee, 1970, Size 40 . . . . 116.00
Coat, Ribbon Tie, Silk Panel Insets, Black Border, Wiener Platt, 1915 . . . . 4025.00
Coat, Short, Wool, Navy Blue, Charles James, c.1945 . . . . 9200.00

Coat, Short, Wool, Navy Blue, Charles James, 1940s 2760.00
Coat, Single-Breasted, Oversize Black Buttons, Red Wool, Nina Ricci, 1960, Size 6 .... 258.00
Coat, Vest & Hat, Man's, Black Wool, Amish, 3 Piece 125.00
Coat, Woman's, Leopard, Full-Length 1495.00
Coat, Woman's, Mutton Sleeve, Full-Length 375.00
Collar, Blouse, Mink, Brown, 18 In. 4.00
Collar, Raccoon, 36 In. 8.00
Collar, Reverse Set Rhinestones, Kenneth Jay Lane, 1960s 460.00
Cuff, Ermine, 3 1/2 In., Pair 30.00
Dress, Ball, Pale Peach, Salzburg, Christian Dior 2990.00
Dress, Bands Of Black Silk Satin, Tiered Cutaway Skirt, Herman Patrick Tappe, 1930 ... 690.00
Dress, Beaded, Beige Lace, Glass Beads, Rhinestones, 1920, Size 6 .... 45.00
Dress, Beaded, Sleeveless, Embroidered Tulle, Bugle Beads & Sequins, 1920s, Size 4 ... 200.00
Dress, Black Wool Jersey, Charles James 4600.00
Dress, Brown Satin, Lace Insert At Neck, 1920s, Size 8 .... 120.00
Dress, Checked Pattern, Lace Inserts, V Neck, Full Ruffled Skirt, 2 Piece 192.00
Dress, Crocheted Irish Lace Over Peach Ruffled Petticoat, Taffeta Lining, c.1905 ...... 2400.00
Dress, Dinner, Lace, Beaded Sleeves, 1914 .... 65.00
Dress, Drawn Work Panels, White Batiste, 1920s, Size 8 .... 230.00
Dress, Enos Pattern, Printed Silk, Patch Pockets, Stars & Stripes, M. Snischek, 1926 .... 1840.00
Dress, Evening, Bias Cut Construction, Ivory Satin, Rose Petal Sleeves, 1930s, Size 4 ... 690.00
Dress, Evening, Navy Blue Chiffon Over Pink Silk Satin, Beaded 355.00
Dress, Evening, Printed Flowers, Cutout Flowers At Low Back, Schiaparelli, 1930s 2070.00
Dress, Flapper, Beaded, Rust Color 65.00
Dress, Layers Of Lace Inserts, Yoked Lace Neckline, White Cotton, c.1904 .... 275.00
Dress, Panels Of Cream & Black Chiffon, Black Lace Over Cream, Jacket, Austrian 1725.00
Dress, Peach Silk, Lace Insets, Long Tunic Over Pleated Skirt, 1920s 110.00
Dress, Pewter Chiffon, Lowered Waist, Flared Skirt, Crystal Beading, c.1925, Size 4 .... 230.00
Dress, Printed Silk, V-Neck, Pine Needles & Spots, Navy Ground, 1920s 1150.00
Dress, Shirtwaist, Black Faille, Velvet Collar, Rhinestone Buttons, Adrian, 1940s, Size 8 . 2300.00
Dress, Tiers Of Net With Lace Panel Inserts, Embroidered Floral, Drop Waist, c.1920 ... 440.00
Dress, Wedding, Ivory Satin, All Original, 1890 .... 300.00
Dress, Wedding, Lace, 1930s 125.00
Dress, White Lawn, Tucks, Lace Inserts, Ribbons, 44 In. Long, Small 45.00
Dress, Yellow Tropical, Jacket, Long, 1970s, Size 12 .... 17.00
Duster & Leather Goggles, Automobile, Silk 105.00
Garter, Man's, Box, Paris, 1920s 12.00
Gloves, Crocheted, Multicolored Flowers & Leaves On Cuff 42.00
Gloves, Ladies, 1920s 18.00
Gloves, Leather, Elbow Length, Unworn 45.00
Handkerchief, B.E.P. Exposition, Alaska Yukon Pacific Exposition, Eskimo, Pipe 200.00
Handkerchief, Bluebirds, Printed, Cotton, Folded 35.00
Handkerchief, Embroidered Flowers, White Cotton, On Fruit Of Loom Card 3.00
Hat, Cloche, Gray Felt, Halston, 1970s 80.00
Hat, Peaked, Embroidered Flames Of Bronze Beads, Brown, Dachettes, 1950s 45.00
Hat, Pill Box, Evening, Black Satin, Balenciaga, 1950s 1955.00
Hat, Stetson, Premier, Box 45.00
Hat, Straw Boater, Man's, Black Band, White Center Strip, 7 1/2 In. 65.00
Hat, Tom Corbett, Space Cadet, Flip-Up Sunglasses, Box, 1950s 35.00
Hat, White Violets, Beaded Trim, 1890s 62.00
Hat, Woman's, Pilgrim, White Wool, White Satin Band, 7 1/4 In. 28.00
Jacket, Blue Denim, 2 Red Flowers, With Scroll, Lee, Size 38 .... 55.00
Jacket, Bolero, Elbow Length Sleeves, Black Lace, 1930s, Size 6 .... 115.00
Jacket, Continental Airlines, Red Logo On Black 65.00
Jacket, Evening, Turn-Down Shawl Collar, Black Crepe Lining, Schiaparelli, 1930s 1150.00
Jacket, Jean, Blue Denim, Snap Fasteners, Lee, 1950, Medium 172.00
Jacket, Man's, Big E Denim, Levi, 1960, Size 40 .... 346.00
Jacket, Man's, Shearling Lined, Mittens, Suede 295.00
Jacket, Penguin, Braid, 1914 .... 75.00
Jacket, Roadrunner Painted On Back, Toggle Leather Buttons, Green Suede 200.00
Jacket, Russian Cossack, Purple Velvet, Silver Cord Embroidery, Worth, c.1908 .... 373.00
Jacket, Silk Brocade, Swirling Plume Pattern, Hot Pink Lining, Scaasi, 1960s, Size 6 ... 143.00

Clothing, Tie, Jeweled
Horsehead, With
Bridle

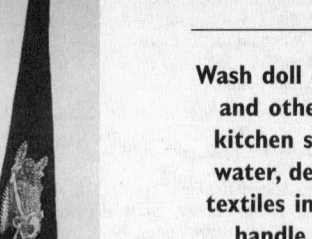

Wash doll clothes, handkerchiefs, and other small textiles in a kitchen salad washer. Put the water, detergent or soap, and textiles in the washer, spin the handle, empty, rinse, spin.

Jacket, Visor Cap, Man's, Greyhound Bus Driver, Gray Jacket, Blue Detail, Size 7	101.00
Jacket, Woman's, Black Denim, Stud Design, Size 14	45.00
Jeans, Man's, Blue Bell, Dungarees, Work, Blue Denim, 30 x 33 In.	124.00
Jeans, Man's, Blue Bell, Light Blue Denim, Wrangler, 1950, 36 x 34 In.	403.00
Jeans, Woman's, Added Embossed Stars Around Cuff, Blue Denim, Levi, 31 x 30 In.	23.00
Life Jacket, Canvas, Padded Orange Vest, S.S. United States, 1963	115.00
Mittens, Hooked, Sheared Wool, Red, Blue & Green, Camel Ground	430.00
Muff, Leopard, Purse	55.00
Nightgown, Butterfly Crochet Yoke	35.00
Nightgown, Crochet Bodice, Cotton, c.1910, 44 In.	25.00
Nightgown, Sleeveless, V Neck, Appliqued Embroidery, Black Tie At Waist, Ecru Silk	70.00
Nightgown, Smocking At Waist, Embroidered Bodice, Silk Chiffon, 1950s	70.00
Nightgown, Toddler's, Eyelet Trim	25.00
Nightgown, Yellow, Ribbon, Lace & Embroidery Trim	65.00
Pajama Bag, Linus	55.00
Pajamas, Girl's, Cotton, Blue Hearts, 1960	7.00
Petticoat, Embroidered Flowers & Foliage, White Organdy, Scalloped Hem, 1910s	287.00
Petticoat, Paisley Quilted Down Cotton, Horizontal Quilting, 40 In.	373.00
Purse, Brown Lizard	65.00
Purse, Red Barrel, Snakeskin	45.00
Raincoat, Brown & White Calvary Twill, Leather Buttons, Rivolia, 1930s, Size 6	373.00
Raincoat, Camel's Joe Cool	20.00
Robe, Woman's, Dragon, Court, Chinese	3450.00
Scarf, Silk Twill, Hand Painted Abstract, Balenciaga, 1960s	143.00
Scarf, White Silk Twill, Printed Fighting Cocks, Brown, Hermes, 1970s	172.00
Shawl, Paisley, 132 x 63 In.	302.00
Shawl, Paisley, 68 x 69 In.	115.00
Shawl, Paisley, Black & Red, Signed On Black Center, 144 x 66 In.	1250.00
Shawl, Piano, Long Fringe, Silk Embroidered Florals, Turquoise, 40 x 40 In.	145.00
Shawl, Polychrome Geometric Design, Brick Red Ground, Wool	137.00
Shoes, Black, Platform, High Heels, Heavy, 1970s, Size 6	5.00
Shoes, Child's, Suede Buckle, 1930s	36.00
Shoes, Converse, Canvas, Black High Top, Chuck Taylor, Size 12	98.00
Shoes, Girl's, Button Strap, Red Goose, 1950s	45.00
Shoes, Girl's, Patent Leather, Black, 1950-1960	10.00
Shoes, Kabuki, Glossy Black Wood Platforms, Beth Levine, 1960s, Size 7 1/2N	575.00
Shoes, Sandal, Toddler's, Open Toe	15.00
Shoes, Star Brand, Red Star Symbol On White Background, Dark Blue Rim, 1900s	10.00
Shoes, Star Brand, Yellow, 1900s	10.00
Shoes, Wedge Heeled, Black Suede & Gold Calf, Ferragamo, 1940s, Size 6AA	575.00
Shoes, Woman's, High Top, Leather, Brown, Lace-Up	75.00
Shoes, Woman's, Red, Heels, Open Toe, 1940s	40.00
Suit, Black Wool, Adrian, 1940s	2185.00
Suit, Blazer, Navy Wool, Tom Sawyer	42.00
Suit, Woman's, Silk, Peach, Black Trim, Peplum, Velvet Color, 1940s, Size 6	80.00
Swimsuit, Girl's, Cotton Print, Ruffles, 1950s	15.00

Tie, Jeweled Horsehead, With Bridle ....*Illus*   120.00
Tie, Man's, Rayon, Striped 50.00
Top Hat, Silk, Collapsible, Paris, 1800s 225.00
Uniform, Driver's, Coca-Cola Delivery, Dark Green Zippered Jacket, 1960s, Size 42 ....   113.00
Veil, Bobbin Lace Net, Belgian, 90 x 24 In. 545.00
Vest, Black Velvet, Victorian, Child's 40.00
Vest, Brocade, Turquoise & Taupe, High Flat Collar, 1910s 85.00
Vest, Man's, Velvet, Large Beaded 65.00

CLUTHRA glass is a two-layered glass with small air pockets that form
white spots. The Steuben Glass Works of Corning, New York, made it
after 1903. Kimball Glass Company of Vineland, New Jersey, made
Cluthra from about 1925. Victor Durand signed some pieces with his
name. Related items are listed in the Steuben category.

Vase, Blue, Clear Footed, Tapered, Kimball, 8 1/2 In. 330.00
Vase, Fan, Pink, Steuben, 8 In. 1320.00
Vase, Green, Mottled White, Yellow, Kimball, 10 In. 345.00
Vase, Pink, Opalescent M Handles, Steuben, 10 In. 2970.00
Vase, Pomona Green Stylized Flowers, Bubbles, Carder, Steuben, 14 In. 7700.00
Vase, Waisted Rim, Tapered, Kimball, 12 In. 465.00
Vase, Yellow Top, Rose Pink Bottom, Etched, F. Carder, 12 1/2 In. 3737.00
Vase, Yellow, Earth Tone Brown, Red, Elongated Oval, Kimball, 12 In. 374.00

COALBROOKDALE was made by the Coalport porcelain factory of
England during the Victorian period. Pieces are decorated with floral
encrustations.

Basket, Encrusted Polyanthus, Cowslips, Carnations, 1820, 7 In. 795.00

COALPORT ware has been made by the Coalport Porcelain Works of
England from 1795 to the present time. Early pieces were unmarked.
About 1810–1825 the pieces were marked with the name *Coalport*
in various forms. Later pieces also had the name *John Rose* in the
mark. The crown mark has been used with variations since 1881. The
date 1750 is printed in some marks but it is not the date the factory
started.

Box, Cover, Egg Form, Gilt, Turquoise Enameled Jeweled, Red, Blue, 3 In. 1725.00
Box, Cover, Landscape Reserve On Pink & Gilt Ground, 18th Century, 5 In. 1000.00
Cup & Saucer, Gilt, Turquoise Enameled Jeweled, England, 1900, 4 3/4 In. 258.00
Dinner Service, Fruit Tree Within Border, 4 Panels, 1810, 11 In., 26 Piece 7475.00
Dinner Service, Japan, Salmon Panels, Blue, Gold Stylized Design, 1805, 4 Piece 690.00
Dish, Gladiator & Insignia Panel, Family Crest, Off-White Ground, Square, 8 1/2 In. 230.00
Dish, Vegetable, Cover, Felt Spar, Floral Design, 19th Century, 8 x 4 In. 45.00
Ewer, Jeweled, Miniature 980.00
Perfume Bottle, Heart Shape, Turquoise, Red Enamel, Pink Ground, 1900, 4 In. 1495.00
Plate, Gilt Design, 9 In., 12 Piece 1725.00
Plate, Hand Painted Fruit, Scalloped Gold Border, Gosling, 9 In 150.00
Plate, Luncheon, Stylized Snowflake Reserve, Floral & Gilt Borders, 9 In., 6 Piece 288.00
Platter, Hong Kong 100.00
Platter, Japan, Vase Of Flowers On A Fenced Terrace, 1805, 10 5/8 In. 460.00
Powder Box, Birth Of Prince William 125.00
Powder Box, Charles & Diana Wedding 100.00
Soup, Dish, Cobalt Blue 100.00
Soup, Dish, Gold 100.00
Tea Caddy, Sedan Chair Form, Hand Painted & Gilt, c.1900, 6 1/2 In. 1550.00
Tea Canister, Cover, Turquoise Enamel, Gilt, Pink Ground, 1900, 5 3/4 In. 920.00
Tea Service, Exotic Birds In Flight, Salmon, Pale Yellow, John Rose, 1805, 16 Piece ...   1610.00
Tray, Scenic Medallions, Scalloped, Gold Trim, 12 1/4 x 9 1/2 In., Pair 375.00
Urn, Cover, Floral & Avian, Center Cartouches, 2 Handles, 1890s, 15 1/4 In. 460.00
Urn, Lake Scene, Cobalt Blue, Gold, 5 In. 350.00
Vase, Garden Flowers, Pale Blue Ground, Gilt Entwined Snake Base, 11 In. 544.00
Vase, Gilt Floral Sprays, Carnation Sprigs, Gilded Rim, 13 In., Pair 4025.00
Vase, Raised Gilt Foliate, Cobalt Blue Ground, England, 1900, 14 1/2 In. 1035.00
Vase, Swan Handle, Gilt, Turquoise Enameled Jeweled, Raised Gold Foliate, 8 3/4 In. 632.00

COBALT BLUE glass was made using oxide of cobalt. The characteristic bright dark blue identifies it for the collector. Most cobalt glass found today was made after the Civil War. There was renewed interest in the dark blue glass in the late 1930s and dinnerwares were made.

Blue, Applied Foot, Folded Rim, 9 3/4 In.	440.00
Bowl, Cut To Clear, 8 1/4 In.	60.00
Bowl, Footed, 19 Ribs, 3 7/8 In.	115.00
Box, Hinged, Enameled Flowers, Brass Rings & Footed, Round, 5 In.	275.00
Box, Hinged, White Enameled Leaves On Sides, Pink Flowers, 5 In.	275.00
Carafe, Water, Open Heart Arches	295.00
Compote, Cut To Clear, Deep Scalloped Edge, Hexagonal Base, 8 In., Pair	847.00
Creamer, Blue Glass, Cut To Clear, 4 In.	45.00
Creamer, Diamond Handle, 3 3/8 In.	60.00
Goblet, Crosscut To Clear, Bucket Shape, 1865, 7 3/4 In.	250.00
Lamp, Twinkle	125.00
Night-Light, Diamond Quilted, Ball Shape, Beaded Brass Trim, 6 1/2 In.	165.00
Pitcher, Applied Tooled Foot, Applied Handle, 6 1/2 In.	165.00
Salt, 12 Ribs, Applied Foot, 2 7/8 In.	247.00
Spooner, Open Heart Arches	150.00
Vase, Bird In Flight, White Outlining, 8 3/4 x 4 1/4 In.	110.00
Vase, Bulbous, Hand Painted Floral, Gold, 4 In.	35.00
Vase, Cornucopia, 8 3/4 In.	100.00 to 120.00
Vase, Cornucopia, Brass Hand Shaped Mount, Marble Base, 6 3/4 In.	80.00
Vase, Couple Strolling In Park, Gilt Foliate, Gold, White Acanthus, 11 In.	3737.00
Vase, Fruit Design Supports, Silver Plate, Neoclassical, 1900, 9 In., Pair	968.00
Vase, Iridescent, White Oil Spot Base, Palme Koenig, 1910, 7 In.	110.00

COCA-COLA was first served in 1886 in Atlanta, Georgia. It was advertised through signs, newspaper ads, coupons, bottles, trays, calendars, and even lamps and clocks. Collectors want anything with the word *Coca-Cola,* including a few rare products, like gum wrappers and cigar bands. The famous trademark was patented in 1893, the *Coke* mark in 1945. Many modern items and reproductions are being made.

Ashtray, New Home Of Coca-Cola, Bronze Finish, 1930, 8 x 7 x 4 In.	115.00
Bag, No-Drip, 1927	12.00
Bandanna, Kit Carson, 1953	48.00
Bank, Mechanical, Coca-Cola Santa, Cast Metal, Box, Ertl	95.00
Bank, Owl Still Savings, Crown Stores Fountain, 1970, 4 In.	29.00
Bank, Trolley Car	135.00
Blotter, 58 Million A Day	4.00
Book, Classic Cooking With Coca-Cola	6.00
Booklet, Coca-Cola Bottlers Regional Conventions, 1931	20.00
Bottle, Alexandria, Minn., Cola Clan, 1980, 10 Oz.	95.00
Bottle, Auburn Tigers, 1983 Sugar Bowl, Contents	8.00
Bottle, Baltimore Orioles, Cal Ripkin, Baseball, 6 Pack, Contents	45.00
Bottle, Big Bear 50 Years, Quality Supermarket Since 1934, 1984, 10 Oz.	10.00
Bottle, Coca-Cola Bottling Co. Of New London, Inc., Sapphire Blue, 12 1/8 In.	170.00
Bottle, Coke Technical Division Meeting, Saddlebrooke, Fl., 1982, 10 Oz.	125.00
Bottle, Crimson Tide, 315 Victories, Bear Bryant, Ala., 1981, 10 Oz.	10.00
Bottle, Elizabethtown, Ky., 75th Anniversary, 1976, 10 Oz.	8.00
Bottle, Gilleys In Pasadena, NSDA, Houston, Tex., 1983, 10 Oz.	60.00
Bottle, Grand Opening Springfield Coca-Cola Bottling Co., 1976	45.00
Bottle, Half Filled With Coke, Metal Cap, Glass, 3 In.	34.50
Bottle, Hobble Skirt, Smoke	150.00
Bottle, House For Coca-Cola, August 3, 1977, Amber, 10 Oz.	50.00
Bottle, Hygeia Bottling Works, Pensacola, Fla., Straight Sided, Aqua, 8 In.	75.00
Bottle, Introducing Diet Coke, New Orleans, La., 1983, 10 Oz.	25.00
Bottle, Jimmy Carter, 39th President Of U.S., Ga., 1985, 10 Oz.	250.00
Bottle, Knoxville, Tenn., Brown	65.00
Bottle, Los Angeles Olympics Commemorative, 1984	6.00
Bottle, Nashville, Tenn., 75th Anniversary, 1975, 10 Oz.	8.00
Bottle, North Dakota Centennial	8.00

Bottle, Olympic Winter Games, Lake Placid, N.Y., 1980, 10 Oz., 8 Piece 65.00
Bottle, Pumpkin Festival, Circleville, Oh., 75h Anniversary, 1981, 10 Oz. 8.00
Bottle, Republican National Convention, Houston, Tex., 1992 .... 425.00
Bottle, Rod Carew, Minnesota Twins, 1987, 10 Oz. ....25.00 to 50.00
Bottle, Ronald McDonald House, Ca., 1993, 8 Oz. 75.00
Bottle, Rose Bowl, Big 10 Champions, Iowa Hawkeyes, 1981, 10 Oz. 10.00
Bottle, Rose Bowl, Big 10 Football Champions, Iowa Hawkeyes, 1985, 10 Oz. 8.00
Bottle, Super Bowl XVII, Redskins, Washington, 1983, 10 Oz. 30.00
Bottle, Syrup, 1957, 1 Gal. 32.00
Bottle, Tom Mix Festival, 1985 .... 20.00
Bottle Opener, Cast Iron, Wall Type 5.00
Bottle Opener, Gold, 7 1/2 In. 5.00
Bracelet, Charm, Gold-Plated, 4 Charms, 1960s 25.00
Calendar Paper, 1910, Happy Days, Drink Coca-Cola, Pretty Woman 14300.00
Calendar Paper, 1925, Full Pad & Cover Page 2750.00
Calendar Paper, 1926, Frame, 18 In. 135.00
Calendar Paper, 1927, Girl Holding Glass, 12 1/2 x 6 1/2 In. 185.00
Calendar Paper, 1974, Girl With Glass & Bottle, 1927 Picture Reversed 20.00
Card, Nature Study, Complete Set In Box, 1930s 47.00
Card, Playing, Stewardess, 52 Cards, 1943 .... 45.00
Clock, 1950s, 64 In. 875.00
Clock, Alarm, 2 Bells 25.00
Clock, Alarm, Prism View, Seth Thomas, Box, 1970s 55.00
Clock, Bottle In Circle At Base, Neon Metal Frame, 1942 .... 900.00
Clock, Cleveland, Porcelain, Neon, 26 In. 1400.00
Clock, Fishtail, Green Face, Light-Up 250.00
Clock, Light-Up Sign, Square, 49 In. 440.00
Clock, Max Headroom, 1987 .... 20.00
Clock, Neon, Square 1000.00
Clock, Selecto, Wooden Frame, 1939, 16 In. 275.00
Clock, Things Go Better With Coke, Red, White, Green, Brown, 1970, 17 x 17 In. 159.00
Clock, Yellow Spot, Bottle, 1950s 400.00
Coaster Set, Santa's Faces, 6 Piece 20.00
Coin-Operated Machine, Cavalier, No. 27 .... 3750.00
Coin-Operated Machine, Vending, Jack Russell Co., Plastic, Japan, 8 x 3 x 1 In. 115.00
Coin-Operated Machine, Vendo, No. 44 .... 2398.00
Coin-Operated Machine, Vendolator, No. 33 .... 800.00
Comic Book, 1951 .... 6.50
Cookie Jar, Polar Bear 35.00
Cooler, Chest Type, Hinged Lid 600.00
Cooler, Junior, Floor Model 880.00
Cooler, Picnic, Ribbed, 1950s 150.00
Cooler, Serve Yourself, Please Pay The Clerk, Angle Iron Legs 993.00
Crate, Drink Coca-Cola In Bottles On Each Side, Yellow Plastic Dividers, 3 x 2 In. 56.00
Cuff Links, Toggle Closure, Box, Australia, 1970 .... 75.00
Dispenser, Counter, Glasses, Bottle, Child's 65.00
Dispenser, Fountain, Outboard Motor 350.00
Dispenser, Red, White Script, Dole Valve Co. 220.00
Display, Hot Dog, Drink Coca-Cola, Cardboard, Easel, 1920s, 10 x 14 In. 450.00
Doll, Aerobic, Wearing Coca-Cola Outfit, Carrying Dumbbells, Jointed, 1980, 11 In. 44.00
Door Push, Refreshing, New Feeling, Tin, 1960s, 3 x 20 In. 120.00
Fan, Ft. Myers, 1950s 25.00
Fly Swatter, Wooden Handle, Wire Mesh, 1942, Pair 10.00
Glass, Burger King, Star Wars, Coca-Cola, 4 Piece 35.00
Glass, Drink Coca-Cola 5 Cents, In Script 13.00
Glass, Popeye, Wimpy, Kollect-A-Set, 1975 .... 3.00
Glass, Soda, 1939, Small 35.00
Handkerchief, Kit Carson 48.00
Holder, 6 Bottles, Cardboard, 1930s 30.00
Jar, Pepsin Gum, Original Cover 550.00
Knife, Red Lettering On White Pearlized Sides 148.00
Lighter, Engraved Lettering, Red Enamel Details, Japan, 1950 .... 78.00
Lighter, Zippo, Red Enamel Details, Trademark On Front, Box 94.00

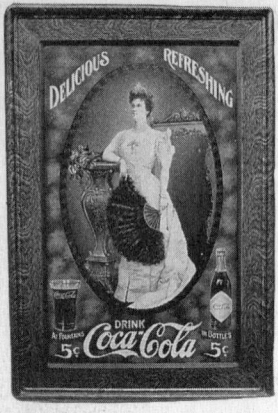

Coca-cola, Sign, Lillian Nordica, Tin, Self-Framed, 33 x 23 In.

Sunlight and heat can harm most antiques. Wood, paper, textiles, glass, ivory, leather, and many other organic materials will discolor, fade, or crack. Cover sunny windows with blinds or curtains or apply a sun-filtering plastic coating to the windows. These coatings can be found at hardware and window stores, or installed by special companies listed in the Yellow Pages. Information is available from museums or art conservators.

Marble, Coke, 1 In.	2.00
Marble, Coke, 5/8 In.	2.00
Match Striker, Red, Yellow, White & Black, Porcelain, 4 1/2 x 4 1/2 In.	275.00
Menu Board, 15 3/4 x 21 3/4 In.	20.00
Menu Board, Plastic, Racks Of White Plastic Letters, 14 x 13 1/4 In.	77.00
Menu Board, Round Button In Middle, 14 x 53 In.	650.00
Pencil, 1940s	65.00
Pencil, Clip, Drink Coca-Cola In Bottles, Red Ground, White Letters	45.00
Pencil Sharpener, Figural Bottle, Metal, Red Enamel, Germany, 1930s, 1 3/4 In.	38.00
Pin, Coca-Cola Air Meet, Cleveland Press, Red, White, 1940s	14.00
Plate, Bronze Medallion In Center, Liberty Bell & Honors, Gold, 1926.	25.00
Postcard, Holbrook, Ariz. Street Scene, Sign Over Drug Store, Photograph, Unused	11.00
Postcard, Main St., Bisbee, Ariz., Coke Sign On Building, Photograph, 1940	11.00
Poster, Betty, 41 x 26 In.	715.00
Punch Board, 1940, 7 x 8 In.	8.50
Punch Board, Dealer, 1940, 4 x 5 In., 3 Pair	20.00
Radio, Bottle Shape, Box	60.00
Radio, Cooler, Bakelite	495.00
Radio, Figural, Bottle, AM, Box	60.00
Record, Album, Coca-Cola Diner Woman, Hot Atlanta Home-Cookin'	35.00
Salt & Pepper, Coke Machine Shape	19.00
Scoop, Ice Cream, Bottle Shape, Gold, 8 In.	10.50
Shade, Hanging, Red, Green & White Slag Glass, c.1910, 16 In.	3500.00
Shot Glass	3.00 to 4.00
Sign, 50th Anniversary 1886-1936, Gold Wooden Frame, 1936, 50 In.	410.00
Sign, Betty, Self-Framed, Tin, 41 x 36 In.	1100.00
Sign, Bottle Shape, Porcelain, 16 In.	250.00
Sign, Bottle, Die Cut, 36 In.	300.00
Sign, Boy, Girl & Snowman, Sign Of Good Taste, Cardboard, 36 x 20 In.	186.00
Sign, Cap, Sign Of Good Taste, 18 In.	195.00
Sign, Cap, With Bottle, Tin, 24 In.	375.00
Sign, Drink Coca-Cola, Bottle, 1930s	50.00
Sign, Ice Cold Coca-Cola, Enjoy That Refreshing New Feeling, Tin, 1960, 20 x 28 In.	295.00
Sign, Lady In Bathing Suit, Lying On Bench, Holding Coke, 57 x 27 In.	676.00
Sign, Lillian Nordica, Tin, Self-Framed, 33 x 23 In. Illus	21275.00
Sign, Made In Canada, 2 Sides, 1941, 15 In.	110.00
Sign, Picture Of Bottle In Center, White Lettering, Red Ground, 36 1/2 In.	460.00
Sign, Policeman, Crossing Guard, 1950s	2500.00

Sign, Porcelain, 2 Sides, 28 In. 180.00
Sign, Red & White Lettering, Gold Wings, Pressured Fiber, Early 1940s, 9 1/2 In. 935.00
Sign, Santa & Little Girl Trimming Christmas Tree, 1960, 29 x 12 1/2 In. 80.50
Sign, Santa Claus, Holding Bottle Of Coke, Cardboard, 1950s, 26 x 18 In. 69.00
Sign, Sign Of Good Taste, Vertical Fishtail Above Bottle, 54 x 18 In. 160.00
Sign, Take Home A Carton, Tin, 1950s, 28 x 20 In. 290.00
Sign, Umbrella Girl, Cardboard, Frame, 1942 .... 876.00
Spigot, Fountain, Bakelite Handle, Chrome, Logo, Fisher Prod. Inc., 1940s, 6 In. 147.00
Stationery, Hold To Light, See Lady Holding Coke, 1959 .... 10.00
Sticker, Coke's 50th Anniversary, 1886-1936, Embossed 15.00
Syrup Urn, Box, 1970s 850.00
Thermometer, 1950s, 12 In. 135.00
Thermometer, Bottle, 16 In. 20.00
Thermometer, Bottle, 29 In. ....25.00 to 34.00
Thermometer, Christmas Date, Die-Cut Bottle Shape, 17 In. 154.00
Thermometer, Drink Coca-Cola, Be Really Refreshed, Plastic, 1960, 6 x 2 1/2 In. 92.00
Thermometer, Figural, Bottle 25.00
Thermometer, Green Double 95.00
Thermometer, Round Dial, 12 In. 29.00
Tie Clasp, Thermometer Shape, 1950s 80.00
Tip Tray, Girl, Hamilton King, 1910 ....350.00 to 700.00
Toy, Telephone, Bottle Shape, Box 60.00
Toy, Truck, Match Box, 1950s 75.00
Toy, Truck, With Bottles, Metalcraft 650.00
Toy, Truck, Yellow, Box, 1950s 425.00
Tray, 1909, Exhibition Girl, Oval, 13 1/2 x 16 1/2 In. 1500.00
Tray, 1914, Betty, Oval, 15 In. 220.00
Tray, 1916, Elaine, 19 In. 300.00
Tray, 1925, Party Girl, 13 x 10 In. 165.00
Tray, 1928, Girl, With Bobbed Hair, Bottle, Dark Green Ground, 13 1/4 x 10 In. 485.00
Tray, 1930, Fountain Sales, 13 x 10 In. 155.00
Tray, 1930, Telephone Girl, 13 1/4 x 10 In. 350.00
Tray, 1931, Farm Boy With Dog, Norman Rockwell 1100.00
Tray, 1934, Maureen O'Sullivan & Johnny Weissmuller, 13 x 11 In. 605.00
Tray, 1936, Hostess, Girl, Sitting, With Glass Of Coke, 13 3/4 x 10 In. ....128.00 to 355.00
Tray, 1938, Girl In Afternoon, Yellow Dress, Hat, 13 x 10 In. ....79.00 to 147.00
Tray, 1939, Springboard Girl ....275.00 to 350.00
Tray, 1940, Sailor Girl, Sitting On Dock, Coke In Hand, 13 x 10 In. 169.00
Tray, 1941, Girl, Ice Skater, 13 3/4 x 10 In. ....161.00 to 325.00
Tray, 1942, 2 Girls, 1 In Green Car, 13 3/4 x 10 In. ....80.00 to 153.00
Tray, 1950, Girl With Menu, 13 3/4 x 10 1/2 In. 55.00
Truck, Delivery, Buddy L, Accessories, Box 440.00
Truck, Delivery, Door Raises, Cases Of Bottles, 1950s, 10 1/2 In. 375.00
Truck, Delivery, Tin, Japan, 1950s, 8 In. 225.00
Truck, G.M.C. Tractor, Great Dane Trailer, Ertl, 1954 .... 85.00
Truck, Japan, 4 In. 225.00
Truck, Kenworth Bottle, Authentic Load Of Coca-Cola Bottle In Crates, 1925 .... 17.00
Truck, Kenworth, With Santa On Side, 1925 .... 22.00
Truck, Linemar, 5 In. 325.00
Truck, Painted, Metal Wheels, Lesney, England, Box, 1960 .... 55.00
Truck, Plastic, Marx, 11 In. 425.00
Truck, Stake Bed, Max 450.00
Wristwatch, Employee's, 1972 .... 125.00

COFFEE GRINDERS of home size were first made about 1894. They lost favor by the 1930s. Large floor-standing or counter-model coffee grinders were used in the nineteenth-century country store. The renewed interest in fresh-ground coffee has produced many modern electric and hand grinders, and reproductions of the old styles are being made.

Arcade, Art Deco Style, Crystal, Wall Mount 250.00
Arcade, No. 1, X-Ray 250.00

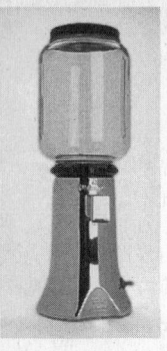

Clean aluminum with fine steel wool or steel wool soap pads. To remove discoloration boil 2 teaspoons cream of tartar and 1 quart water in the utensil. The acid from cooking tomatoes or rhubarb in the pot may also remove the stain.

Coffee Grinder, Kitchen Aid,
Hobart Mfg. Co., Electric, 23 3/4 In.

Arcade, Telephone	730.00
Enterprise, Cast Iron, Red, Black, 26 1/2 In.	412.50
Enterprise, Cast Iron, Worn Red & Blue Paint, Drawer, 10 1/2 In.	410.00
Enterprise, Mounted As Table Lamp, Early 20th Century, 31 In.	60.00
Enterprise, No. 2, Double Wheel, Pat. 1873	1050.00
Enterprise, No. 4, Mid-Size	610.50
Enterprise, Red, Blue Paint, Yellow, Black Striping, 35 In.	990.00
Enterprise, Wooden Block Mount, Cast Iron, 13 In.	245.00
Golden Rule, Cast Iron, Dovetailed Wooden, Wall Mount	220.00
Golden Rule Blend Coffee, Cast Iron On Wood Box, Bottle, 18 In.	155.00
Griswold, Grand Union Mill	750.00
Hoffmann's Old Time Coffee	1320.00
Kitchen Aid, Hobart Mfg. Co., Electric, 23 3/4 In. ....*Illus*	95.00
Landers, Frary & Clark, Double Wheel, Black Paint, Decals, 13 In.	950.00
Landers, Frary & Clark, No. 20, 8 1/2-In. Wheels, 12 In.	825.00
Lap, Ornate Iron Top, Side Handle, Wooden	145.00
Lap, Pine, Black Handle, Red Paint	45.00
Long Slab, 1 Drawer, Walnut & Brass	1500.00
Original Mustard Paint, Dovetailed, Wood, Brass & Iron, 1860, 9 1/2 In.	110.00
Premier, Wall Mount	85.00

COIN SPOT is a glass pattern that was named by the collectors for the spots resembling coins, which are part of the glass. Colored, clear, and opalescent glass was made with the spots. Many companies used the design in the 1870–1890 period. It is so popular that reproductions are still being made.

Cruet, Mother-Of-Pearl, Amber, Camphor Reeded Handle, Stopper, 7 In.	275.00
Pitcher, Cranberry, 5 3/4 In.	65.00
Pitcher, Milk, Opalescent, Cranberry	250.00
Pitcher, Ribbed Handle, Electric Blue Flowers, 7 1/4 In.	125.00
Sugar Shaker, Blue, 4 3/4 In.	175.00
Sugar Shaker, Rubena, Ring Neck	245.00
Syrup, Clear & Opalescent	225.00
Vase, Cranberry, 6 In.	85.00
Vase, Cranberry, 8 1/2 In.	125.00

COIN-OPERATED MACHINES of all types are collected. The vending machine is an ancient invention dating back to 200 B.C. when holy water was dispensed in a coin-operated vase. Smokers in seventeenth-century England could buy tobacco from a coin-operated box. It was not until after the Civil War that the technology made modern coin-operated games and vending machines plentiful. Slot machines, arcade games, and dispensers are all collected.

7-Up, Vendolator, Model 33	2500.00
Coin Changer, Label Under Glass Depicting Muriel Cigars Woman	85.00

Fortune Teller, Wizard, Wood 575.00
Gaming, Poker, Penny Line Pay Off, Oak Case, 1900 .... 6200.00
Gillette Blue Blade, Wall Mount, 18 x 7 In. 125.00
Gum, Adams Pepsin, Tutti Fruitti 2800.00
Gum, Lawrence Mfg. Co., Paper Wrapped Gum, 1 Cent, 5 Coin Slots 150.00
Gum, Peerless, White Lettering, Wood Frame, Blue Porcelain, 31 In. 4180.00
Gum, Pulver's Chocolate Cocoa & Gum, 1 Cent, 1889 .... 7500.00
Gum, Pulver, Cop Figure Inside, Porcelain On Steel, 1 Cent 580.00
Gum, Scoopy, Gaylord Manufacturing Co. 2500.00
Gum, Silver Queen, Dentyne, 5 Coin Slots 160.00
Gum, True Blue, 2 Column, Glass Dome, Cast Iron Base, 1906 .... 5500.00
Gum, Victor, Vending Glass Globe, 1954 .... 90.00
Gumball, Acorn, Key, Oak ....55.00 to 60.00
Gumball, Atlas Master, 1 Cent, 1950s 45.00
Gumball, Baby Grand, Victor, 1950s 65.00
Gumball, Baker Boy, With Indian 3500.00
Gumball, Columbus, Dart Gambling, Barrel Locks 1700.00
Gumball, Columbus, Glass Globe, Key, 16 1/2 x 9 In. 440.00
Gumball, Derby Confection Vendor, Colored Horses To Bet On 3800.00
Gumball, Ford, Original Placecard On Top, Lock 85.00
Gumball, Halfback, Victor, 1950s 50.00
Gumball, Masters, 1 Cent 55.00
Gumball, Northwestern, Red Porcelain, 16 In. 220.00
Gumball, Penny, Works With Key, Topper, Victor, 1954 .... 75.00
Gumball, Pillsbury Doughboy, Box 345.00
Gumball, Playball, 1 Cent 495.00
Gumball, Saturn 2000, Rocket, Red, White, Blue, Steel, 63 x 14 In. 175.00
Gumball, Supertest, Gas Pump Shape, 1970s 50.00
Gumball, Topper, Victor, 1954 .... 75.00
Gumball, White Rose, Gas Pump Shape, 1970s 50.00
Gumball, Yellow Kid, Clock Works, Animated, Pulver 800.00
Mills, Electricity Is Life 475.00
Nickelodeon, Coinola, Cupid, Walnut Case 6000.00
Nut, Almonds 125.00
Nut, Hot, Asco, Cast Iron 300.00
Nut, Hot, Challenger, Original Glass Jar, Stand, Set Up For Free Play 425.00
Peanut, Columbus, Model A, Cast Iron 275.00
Peanut, Master, White Porcelain Top & Base, Red, Glass, 1920s 300.00
Peanut, National 775.00
Peanut, Victor, Model V, 1 Cent, Cast Iron Base 100.00
Pinball, Bally, Glass, 1978 .... 1200.00
Pinball, Banko, Countertop 850.00
Pinball, Big Bertha, Battery Operated, Soldiers & Cannons, c.1932 .... 1500.00
Pinball, Coleco, Fonzie, Floor Model, 36 In. 150.00
Pinball, Rock-Ola, Jigsaw 1150.00
Polaris, Bowler, Chicago, 6 Players 695.00
Postage, Double Coin Slots, Enamel Finish 120.00
Quartoscope, Girlie Photos 2250.00
Slot, 5 Cent, Mills Dewey 7800.00
Slot, Bally Electro, Mechanical 8000.00
Slot, Bally, Heavy Hitter 495.00
Slot, Caille, 50 Cent, Centaur, Floor Model 23650.00
Slot, Caille, Superior, 5 Cent 1800.00
Slot, Jennings, 10 Cent, Restored, 1936 .... 1650.00
Slot, Jennings, Duchess, 5 Cent 1700.00
Slot, Jennings, Operator's Bell, Wooden Front, 25 Cent 1900.00
Slot, Maley, Eclipse 2100.00
Slot, Mills, Black Cherry, 25 Cent, 1940s 2700.00
Slot, Mills, Candy Dispenser 2000.00
Slot, Mills, Castle Front, 25 Cent 1475.00
Slot, Mills, Dewey Jackpot 6800.00
Slot, Mills, Dispenses Golf Balls ....4250.00 to 5800.00

Slot, Mills, Judge, Upright	6500.00
Slot, Mills, Nickel Finish, Diamonds On Both Sides, 27 x 16 x 15 In.	1320.00
Slot, Mills, Upright Perfection	1175.00
Slot, Mills, Wooden Sides, Base, Cast Iron Front, 27 x 16 x 15 In.	1320.00
Slot, Pace, Deluxe, Chrome, Dollar	975.00
Slot, Pace, Dollar	975.00
Slot, Rock-Ola, Princess	695.00
Slot, Rock-Ola, World Series	1250.00
Slot, Watling, Rol-A-Top, 10 Cent	2900.00
Slot, Watling, Rol-A-Top, 5 Cent	2800.00
Slot, Watling, Twin Jackpot, 5 Cent	1500.00
Stamp, 3 Stamps, 25 Cent	125.00
Stamp, Uncle Sam, Blue, White Porcelain Front Panel, 13 1/2 In.	120.00
Strength Tester, Clown Head, Metal Casing, 5 Cent, 54 In.	605.00
Trade Stimulator, Ace, 5 Reel	475.00
Trade Stimulator, Imperial, 3 Reel	425.00
Trade Stimulator, Joker's Wild	195.00
Vending, Baseball Cards, Premier	295.00
Vending, Light-Up Radio Hot Nut, Original Decals	195.00
Vending, Mills, O.K. Gum Vendor, 3 Reel, Left Hand Gum	5775.00
Vending, Stollwerck's Chocolate Confection	4070.00

COLLECTOR PLATES are modern plates produced in limited editions. Some may be found listed under the factory name, such as Bing & Grondahl, Royal Copenhagen, Royal Doulton, and Wedgwood.

American Greeting, Christmas, Holly Hobbie, 1978	25.00
Astri Holthe, Christmas, 1976, Pewter, Arendal, Norway, 7 1/4 In.	20.00
Astri Holthe, Christmas, 1979, Pewter, Arendal, Norway, 7 1/4 In.	20.00
Avon, Brightest Stars, 1989, Box	5.00
Avon, Mother's Day, 1981	5.00
Avon, Mother's Day, 1982	10.00
Knowles, A Young Girl's Dream	10.00
Knowles, The Professor	10.00
Kursar, Ashley, Gone With The Wind	50.00
Kursar, Scarlett, Gone With The Wind	75.00
Metlox, Christmas, 1977	75.00
Rockwell, Christmas Surprise	30.00
Rockwell, Dear Santy	20.00
Rockwell, Santa In Workshop	20.00
Schmid, Christmas, Snoopy, 1972, Box	55.00
Schmid, Christmas, Snoopy, 1975, Box	35.00
Schmid, Valentines Day, Snoopy, 1977, Box	25.00

COMIC ART, or cartoon art, is a relatively new field of collecting. Original comic strips, magazine covers, and even printed strips are collected. The first daily comic strip was printed in 1907. The paintings on celluloid used for movie cartoons are listed in this book under Animation Art.

Card, B.C. Picture, Johnny Hart, Signed, 3 x 5 In.	30.00
Drawing, Huey, Dewey & Louie, Baseball Scene, Jaymar Inc., 1950s, 10 x 12 In.	225.00
Layout Strip, Peanuts, Schulz, 1973, 5 1/4 x 27 In.	1500.00
Schmoo Flicker Picture, Al Capp, Photo-Move Inc., Plastic Frame, 5 x 7 In.	95.00

COMMEMORATIVE items have been made to honor members of royalty and those of great national fame. World's fairs and important historical events are also remembered with commemorative pieces. Related collectibles are listed in the Coronation and World's Fair categories.

Bell, Queen Elizabeth II, Metal, Police Helmet Shape	40.00
Book, In Honor Of Her Royal Highness Visit To Belfast, Miniature, 1885	45.00
Box, Tobacco, Queen Victoria, Gold, Sterling Silver, E. Smith, 1850, 4 In.	600.00
Button, Queen Elizabeth, Royal Visit Opening Of Seaway, Celluloid, 1 1/3 In.	50.00
Cards, Playing, King George VI, Elizabeth	3.00

Cards, Playing, Prince Charles, Princess Diana 3.00
Cards, Playing, William IV, Square Corner 5.00
Cup & Saucer, Princess Elizabeth & Duke Of Edinburgh To Canada, 1951 .... 30.00
Figurine, Queen Elizabeth Of Austria, Fur On Sleeves, Sitzendorf, 11 In. 350.00
Mug, Charles & Diana Marriage, July 29, 1981 .... 35.00
Mug, Prince Andrew & Sarah Marriage, Staffordshire Kiln Craft, 1986 .... 30.00
Mug, Queen Victoria's 60 Years As Queen, Burslem, 1837-1897, 4 In. 135.00
Plate, Admiral Nimitx, Flags Of Allied Nations 30.00
Plate, General Marshall, Surrounded By Flags Of Allied Nations 30.00
Plate, Prince Of Wales, Lady Diana, Hummel, 1981 .... 75.00
Spoon, King George VI & Elizabeth, Portrait, Silver Plated, 1937 ....45.00 to 65.00

COMPACTS hold face powder. A woman did not powder her face in public until after World War I. By 1920, the beauty parlor, permanent waves, and cosmetics had become acceptable. A few companies sold cake face powder in a box with a mirror and a pad or puff. Soon the compact was designed by jewelers and made of gold, silver, and precious materials. Cosmetic companies began to sell powder in attractive compacts of less valuable metal or plastic. Collectors today search for Art Deco designs, commemorative compacts from world's fairs or political events, and unusual examples. Many were made with companion lipsticks and other fittings.

Amere, Watch On Lid, Switzerland 135.00
Avon, Jewel Clasp, Goldtone 30.00
Avon, Tropical Scene 10.00
Bear, Schuco 750.00
Carryall, Powder, Coins, Bills, Cards, Wrist Chain, 2 x 3 1/2 In. 115.00
Der Kiss, Fairy Design 75.00
Dorset 10.00
Elgin, American Beauty 65.00
Elgin, American, White Enameled, Gold Filigree Disc Accent 30.00
Embossed Angels, Beaded Bottom, Change Purse 75.00
Enamel, Birds, Tassel 150.00
Enamel, Floral, Octagon Shape, Loose Powder 90.00
Enamel, Frolicking Putti, Gilt Metal, Italy, 3 1/2 In. 70.00
Enamel, Silver Pendants, France 75.00
Fluted Stippled Finish, Mirror, 14K Yellow Gold, 2 x 2 1/2 In. 650.00
Frisco Line, Vanity Box, Celluloid Top, Brass Box, Round, 2 In. 135.00
Illinois Watch Co. 150.00
Kigu, Enamel, Octagon Shape 30.00
Lentheric, Box 50.00
Marhill, Mother-Of-Pearl, Pouch 65.00
Mondaine, Enamel, Cameo With Filigree 85.00
Musical, Oriental Scene, Box 20.00
Rex 5th Avenue, Petit Point Under Lucite Top, Silver, Square 25.00
Silver, Raised Nude, 1920s, 2 In. 95.00
Silver Finish, Powder, 1 7/8 x 2 In. 95.00
Silver Metal, Enamel Floral Medallion, Wrist Chain, 1928 .... 45.00
Sterling Silver, With Attached Cigarette Case, Vanity, 4 In. 150.00
Stratton, Enamel & Goldtone 50.00
Suitcase, Emblems 135.00
Tiffany, Woman's Face On Cover, 1879 .... 450.00
Tortoiseshell, Round, Large 25.00
U.S.N. Academy Ring Dance, 1950 .... 60.00
Volupte, Cigarette Case, Mother-Of-Pearl 165.00
Volupte, Piano Form 95.00
Wadsworth, Fan Shape, Rose Bouquet 55.00
Wadsworth, Gold, Top Design, Round 20.00
Wadsworth, Sterling Silver Scroll Design 100.00
Weisner Of Miami, Box 85.00
With Lipstick & Coin Holder, Gold & Black Confetti 48.00
Wrist Chain, Sterling Silver, Hallmark, 2 In. 95.00

CONSOLIDATED LAMP AND GLASS COMPANY of Coraopolis, Pennsylvania, was founded in 1894. The company made lamps, tablewares, and art glass. Collectors are particularly interested in the wares made after 1925, including black satin glass, Cosmos (listed in its own category in this book), Martele (which resembled Lalique), Ruba Rombic (1928-1932 art deco line), and colored glasswares. Some Consolidated pieces are very similar to those made by the Phoenix Glass Company. The colors are sometimes different. Consolidated made Martele glass in blue, crystal, green, pink, white, or custard glass with added fired-on color or a satin finish. The company closed for the final time in 1967.

Bowl, Finger, Ruba Rombic, Smoky Topaz	175.00
Glass, Whiskey, Ruba Rombic, Green	125.00
Jug, Catalonian, Amethyst	160.00 to 175.00
Lamp, Five Fruits, Purple, Blue, Red, Yellow, Green, 10 In.	297.00
Lamp, Kerosene, Cosmos	110.00
Lamp, Olive	199.00
Plate, Swirl, Blue, Purple, Clear, 6 In., 8 Piece	120.00
Powder Jar, Hummingbirds	70.00
Toothpick, Sapphire Blue	85.00
Tumbler, Ruba Rombic, Smoky Topaz	175.00
Vase, Chickadee, Pink Blossoms, Green Leaves, 6 1/2 In.	100.00
Vase, Chickadee, Ruby Flash, 7 In.	225.00
Vase, Cockatoo, 4 Colors, 9 In.	375.00
Vase, Dragonfly, Green Satin, 5 In.	145.00
Vase, Dragonfly, Yellow Wash, 6 In.	100.00
Vase, Fan, Katydid, Frosted Ground, Whitewashed Pattern, 8 1/2 In.	250.00
Vase, Frosted Green, c.1930, 4 x 8 In.	140.00
Vase, Hummingbird, 5 1/2 In.	80.00
Vase, Katydid, Amber, Clear, 8 1/4 In.	185.00
Vase, Pinecone, Brown & Blue, Satin Milk Glass, Bulbous, 7 In.	100.00
Vase, Poppy, Ormolu Mounts At Top, 12 In.	250.00
Vase, Screech Owl, Green Wash, 6 In.	170.00
Vase, Seagull, Martele, 11 In.	325.00
Vase, Seagull, Rose, Blue Finish, 10 3/4 In.	325.00
Window Box, Nuthatch, Green Leaves, 10 x 5 In.	100.00

CONTEMPORARY GLASS, see Glass-Contemporary.

COOKBOOKS are collected for various reasons. Some are wanted for the recipes, some for investment, and some as examples of advertising. Cookbooks and recipe pamphlets are included in this category.

American Family, Wallace, 1950	17.00
Better Homes & Gardens Junior, Meridith Publishing Co., Ring Type, 1955	30.00
Bettina's Best Desserts, 194 Pages, 1923	25.00
Betty Crocker, For Boys & Girls, First Edition, 1957	40.00
Bisquick, Movie Stars, 1935	30.00
Boston Cooking School, 806 Pages, 1925	25.00
Breakfast, Dinner & Tea, 351 Pages, 1860	30.00
Campbell, Hard Cover	25.00
Clarke County, Georgia, 1951	22.00
Complete Menu Cookbook, 399 Pages, 1930	15.00
Escoffier, 1941	15.00
European, Brown, 1951	15.00
Every-Day, 316 Pages, 1889	45.00
Frigidaire Recipes, 77 Pages, 1928	8.00
Gold Medal Flour, 1917	24.00
Good Housekeeping, 1933	17.00
Good Meals & How To Prepare Them, Good Housekeeping, 1927	22.00
Grand Union Tea, 902 Pages	145.00
Hotel St. Francis, 432 Pages, 1919	100.00
Los Angeles Times, No. 2, 105 Pages, 1905	24.00
Mammy, New Orleans	28.00

Mary Dunbar, Green Silhouetted Factory	16.00 to 22.00
Mennonite Community, Mary Showwalter, Illustrated, 494 Pages, 1951	22.00
Mrs. Appelyard's Kitchen, Kent, 1942	15.00
New York Times, Craig Claiborne, Illustrated, 717 Pages, 1961	24.00
Pebeco Tooth Paste, Gone With The Wind, Black People, 48 Pages	35.00
Rumford Way Of Cookery & Household Economy, 1912	20.00
Savannah, Mammy Carrying Tray, Harriet Ross Colquitt, 1933	55.00
School Kitchen Textbook, Lincoln, 1915	15.00
Searchlight Recipe Book, Ida Migliario, Index, 320 Pages, 1958	23.00
Treasury Of Great Recipes, Mary & Vincent Price	25.00
Walter Baker Choice Recipes, 64 Pages, 1906	15.00

COOKIE JARS with brightly painted designs or amusing figural shapes became popular in the mid-1930s. Many companies made them and collectors search for cookie jars either by design or by maker's name. Listed here are examples by the less common makers. Major factories are listed under their own names in other categories of the book, such as Abingdon, Brush, Hull, McCoy, Red Wing, and Shawnee. See also the Black and Disneyana categories.

Alf	125.00
Alley Cat, Metlox	145.00
Anamaniacs, Warner Brothers	80.00
Apple, Metlox	95.00
Aramis Bear	50.00
Baby Elephant, American Bisque	155.00
Ballerina Bear, Metlox	70.00
Balloon Lady, Pottery Guild	185.00
Barn Happy Face, Starnes	295.00
Bart Simpson, With Cookie, Treasure Craft	55.00
Basket Of Eggs, Metlox	95.00
Bassett Hound, Metlox	450.00
Bear, Flasher, American Bisque	585.00
Bear, President's Choice Cookies	95.00
Bear, With Hat, American Bisque	95.00
Bear, With Yellow Sweaters, Metlox	65.00
Beau Bear, Metlox	50.00 to 55.00
Beaver, Metlox	145.00
Ben Franklin, Treasure Craft	185.00
Bert & Ernie Fine Cookies, California Originals	325.00
Blackboard Clown, American Bisque	250.00
Bloomers, Fitz & Floyd	65.00 to 150.00
Blue Bonnet Sue, Benjamin & Medwin	75.00
Blue Cat, Pink Dotted Cheeks, Tilso	78.00
Bluebird On Stump, Metlox	300.00
Bonnet Bunny, Fitz & Floyd	80.00 to 115.00
Boy Pig, American Bisque	125.00
Budweiser Wagon, 2 Horses, Metlox	850.00
Bunnies In Love Seat, California Originals	42.00
Bus, Piccadilly Circus, Double Decker, Marshall Field	275.00 to 950.00
C3PO, Roman Ceramics	425.00 to 450.00
Cactus, Green, Pink Flower, Treasure Craft	30.00
Calorie Sally, DeForest	175.00
Case Tractor, 1993	225.00
Castle, Sierra Vista	400.00
Century 21	650.00
Cheerleaders, Flasher, American Bisque	275.00 to 285.00
Chef Panda, Sigma	275.00
Chick, American Bisque	100.00
Christmas Tree, California Originals	900.00
Christmas Tree, Sigma	175.00
Churn Boy, American Bisque	155.00 to 210.00
Circus Tent, Brayton Laguna	275.00
Clown, American Bisque	110.00

Clown, Black & White, Metlox 175.00
Clown, Blue & White, Metlox 275.00
Clown, Cardinal ....210.00 to 245.00
Clown, Doranne Of California 200.00
Clown, Juggling, California Originals 75.00
Clown, Maddux Of California 175.00
Coach, Treasure Craft 850.00
Coffeepot, Speckled, American Bisque 45.00
Collegiate Owl, American Bisque 60.00
Cookie, Doranne Of California 40.00
Cookie Factory, Fitz & Floyd 85.00
Cookie Sack, Cardinal 75.00
Cookie Truck, American Bisque, 11 1/2 In. 75.00
Cookie Truck, American Bisque, 13 1/4 In. 85.00
Cookies & Milk, American Bisque 110.00
Corn, Metlox 125.00
Cow, Purple, Metlox 400.00
Cow, Yellow, Metlox ....195.00 to 300.00
Cow Jumped Over The Moon, Doranne Of California 175.00
Cow Jumped Over The Moon, Flasher, American Bisque 1275.00
Cow Painted Rex, Metlox 1200.00
Cowboy Boot, Treasure Craft 38.50
Cowboy Boots, American Bisque 250.00
Cowmen Moo-Randa, Vandor 395.00
Cupcake, Doranne Of California 20.00
Deer On Stump, Twin Winton 45.00
Diaper Pin Pig, Regal China 400.00
Dinosaur, Dino, Metlox 125.00
Dog, Black Scotty, Metlox ....100.00 to 175.00
Dog, Gingham, Blue, Metlox 220.00
Dog, On A Drum, Twin Winton ....100.00 to 175.00
Dog, On Quilted Base, American Bisque 135.00
Dog, Plaid, Blue & Red, Brayton Laguna 375.00
Dog, White Scotty, Metlox 165.00
Donkey, With Cape, Doranne Of California 85.00
Dragon, Doranne Of California 225.00
Drum, Children, Metlox 195.00
Drummer Boy, Metlox 750.00
Dutch Boy, American Bisque 60.00
Dutch Girl, Regal China ....225.00 to 995.00
Dutch Girl, Twin Winton 160.00
Elephant, With Baseball Cap, American Bisque 110.00
Elephant, With Hands In Pockets, American Bisque ....80.00 to 85.00
Elsie The Cow, In Barrel, Pottery Guild ....250.00 to 495.00
Emmett Kelly, On Circus Tent 450.00
Entemann's Chef 345.00
Fairy Godmother, Fitz & Floyd 90.00
Fat Cat, Sigma 350.00
Fire Hydrant, Doranne Of California 33.00
Flamingo, Metlox ....550.00 to 1150.00
Fluffy The Cat, American Bisque 45.00
Francine Duck, Metlox 95.00
Fred Flintstone, American Bisque ....900.00 to 1200.00
Freddy Frog, California Originals, 8 In. 40.00
Frog, Green, Doranne Of California 75.00
Frosty Penguin, Metlox ....95.00 to 100.00
Gigantic Clown, Maurice Of California 95.00
Gingerbread House, Cleminsons 95.00
Goldilocks, Regal China ....275.00 to 375.00
Graduate, Cardinal 65.00
Graduate Owl, Japan 11.00
Grandma, American Bisque 125.00
Granny's Cookies, Twin Winton 140.00

Green Giant Sprout, Benjamin & Medwin .... 55.00 to 75.00
Gumball Machine, California Originals 58.00
Gypsy Woman, Brayton Laguna 550.00
Halo Boy, DeForest .... 575.00 to 850.00
Harley-Davidson Gas Tank, Blue .... 65.00 to 85.00
Harpo Marx, White Hair, Regal China 1200.00
Haunted House, Fitz & Floyd 135.00
Hearts & Flowers, Sigma 275.00
Hen, On Nest, Twin Winton 45.00
Hen, With Bonnet, Chick Finial, Metlox 845.00
Hippo-Limpix, Fitz & Floyd 80.00
Hobby Horse, Sierra Vista 325.00
Holly Hobbie, Cookies Are For Sharing 75.00
Homer Simpson 1200.00
Hortense, Sigma 150.00
Humpty Dumpty, California Originals 100.00
Humpty Dumpty, Clay Arts 95.00
Humpty Dumpty, Purinton .... 295.00 to 425.00
Hydrangea Bear, Fitz & Floyd 80.00
Ice Cream Freezer, American Bisque 525.00
Jack-In-The-Box, American Bisque 145.00
Jazz Singer, Clay Art .... 165.00 to 195.00
Jazz'E Junque Shop, Kathy Wolfe 195.00
Jim Beam, Commemorative 115.00
Jolly Chef, Metlox .... 400.00 to 550.00
Katrina, Treasure Craft .... 415.00 to 425.00
Katy Cat, Metlox .... 45.00 to 60.00
Keebler Elf, Head, Plastic 125.00
Kermit On TV, Sigma 425.00
Kermit The Frog, Treasure Craft 55.00
Kitten On Beehive, American Bisque .... 50.00 to 65.00
Kittens, On Ball Of Yarn, American Bisque .... 70.00 to 90.00
Kittens Of Knightsbridge, Fitz & Floyd 75.00
Koala Bear, Metlox 200.00
Kraft-T Marshmallow Bear, Regal China 175.00
Lamb, American Bisque 55.00
Leprechaun, Doranne Of California 135.00
Lion, Metlox 195.00
Little Bopeep, Napco 250.00
Little Lamb, Twin Winton 55.00
Little Miss Muffett, Regal China .... 250.00 to 295.00
Little Red Riding Hood, Metlox 650.00
Little Red Riding Hood, Pottery Guild 125.00
Lucy Goose, Metlox .... 125.00 to 145.00
Magilla Gorilla, Twin Winton 300.00
Majorette, Regal China .... 350.00 to 375.00
Mammy, 4th Of July, Erwin Pottery 150.00
Mammy, Blue, Metlox 450.00
Mammy, Carol Gifford 275.00
Mammy, Ham 'n' Eggs, Gold Tooth, Erwin Pottery 150.00
Mammy, Pearl China .... 395.00 to 825.00
Marvin The Martian, Warner Brothers 75.00
Matilda, Brayton Laguna 395.00
Milk Wagon, American Bisque 125.00
Monk, Treasure Craft 25.00
Monkey, DeForest 70.00
Monkey, Doranne Of California 80.00
Monkey & Barrel, Starnes 95.00
Mother Goose, Doranne Of California 110.00
Mother Goose, Metlox 235.00
Mother Goose, Twin Winton 125.00
Mother Hen, Metlox .... 65.00 to 250.00
Mother Rabbit, Fitz & Floyd 65.00

Mouse Mobile, Metlox 175.00
Mr. Snowman, Fitz & Floyd 95.00
Mrs. Rabbit, Metlox 45.00
Night Before Christmas, Fitz & Floyd 175.00
Noah's Ark, California Originals 75.00
Noah's Ark, Treasure Craft 50.00
Noah's Ark, Twin Winton 95.00
Oaken Bucket With Dipper Finial, American Bisque 135.00
Old King Cole, Twin Winton ....325.00 to 350.00
Old Woman In The Shoe, Fitz & Floyd 85.00
Oliver Oink, Pastel, Treasure Craft ....35.00 to 38.00
Oscar The Grouch, California Originals 125.00
Owl, Green, Josef Originals 110.00
Paddington Bear, Santa At Fireplace, Eden Toys 650.00
Panda Bear, Metlox 75.00
Parking Garage, Cardinal China 60.00
Parrot, Metlox 250.00
Peasant Girl, American Bisque ....825.00 to 875.00
Peek-A-Boo, Regal China 495.00
Pennsylvania Dutch, Wooden Lid, Purinton 195.00
Peter Rabbit, Sigma 225.00
Pierre Mouse, Metlox 325.00
Pig, With Barrel, Doranne Of California 70.00
Pig In A Poke, Yellow, American Bisque 90.00
Pillsbury Doughboy, Benjamin & Medwin 35.00
Pineapple, Metlox 95.00
Pink Panther, Treasure Craft ....155.00 to 175.00
Pirate Captain, Omnibus 65.00
Plaid Dog, Brayton Laguna ....350.00 to 475.00
Polka Dot Witch, Fitz & Floyd 45.00
Poodle, American Bisque 85.00
Poodle, Gold Trim, American Bisque 450.00
Porky Pig, Warner Brothers 25.00
Puddles The Duck, Metlox ....30.00 to 75.00
Quaker Oats, Regal China ....90.00 to 165.00
R2D2, Roman Ceramics, Box, 1977 .... 375.00
Rabbit, On Cabbage, Metlox 150.00
Racoon Cookie Bandit, Metlox ....95.00 to 125.00
Rag Doll, Sierra Vista/Starnes 495.00
Raggedy Andy, Metlox ....100.00 to 150.00
Raggedy Ann, On Barrel, California Originals 75.00
Reclining Frog, California Originals 65.00
Red Pickup Truck, Treasure Craft 385.00
Rio Rita, Fitz & Floyd 80.00
Road Runner 800.00
Rocking Horse, Treasure Craft 25.00
Rollerskating Bear, Metlox ....80.00 to 100.00
Rooster, American Bisque 110.00
Rooster, California Originals 45.00
Rooster, Metlox ....75.00 to 185.00
Rooster, Pottery Guild 68.00
Rubbles House, American Bisque 595.00
Sack, Pepperidge Farm 85.00
Sailor Elephant, American Bisque 85.00
Sandman Cookies, Flasher, American Bisque 295.00
Santa, Winking, Napco ....95.00 to 225.00
Santa Claus, Bag Of Toys, Twin Winton 200.00
Santa Claus, California Originals ....175.00 to 250.00
Santa Claus, On Motorcycle, Fitz & Floyd ....350.00 to 450.00
Santa Claus, Spirit Of St. Nicholas, Fitz & Floyd, Small 185.00
Scarecrow, California Originals 365.00
Schoolhouse, Metlox 1100.00
Seal On Igloo, American Bisque 350.00

Sherman On The Mount, DeForest 280.00
Shoe House, California Originals 26.00
Sir Francis Drake, Metlox .... .25.00 to 45.00
Sitting Piggy, Metlox .... .150.00 to 175.00
Smokey The Bear, 50th Anniversary, Joyce Roerig 300.00
Smokey The Bear, Norcrest 900.00
Snoopy, Anchor Hocking 90.00
Snoopy Chef .... 195.00 to 225.00
Snoopy Chef, Small 75.00
Snowman, California Originals 375.00
Sock Hoppers, Fitz & Floyd 395.00
Soldier, Cardinal 425.00
Sombrero Bear, Metlox .... .70.00 to 85.00
Space Cadet, California Originals 95.00
Spaceship, American Bisque, 12 In. 290.00
Spaceship, Metlox 495.00
Spaceship, Sierra Vista/Starnes 795.00
Spuds MacKenzie 90.00
Squirrel, On Barrel Of Nuts, Metlox 350.00
Squirrel, On Stump, California Originals, Large 90.00
Squirrel, On Stump, California Originals, Small .... .28.00 to 50.00
Squirrel, With Cookie, Sierra Vista 110.00
Star Trek, U.S.S. Enterprise, Pfaltzgraff 45.00
Strawberry, Metlox 65.00
Sugar Plum Castle, Nutcracker Series, Fitz & Floyd .... .115.00 to 195.00
Tat-L-Tale, Helen Hetula, 1940s, 11 1/4 In. 1125.00
Taxi, California Originals 225.00
Teepee, Wisecarver 300.00
Telephone, Cardinal 125.00
The Count, Sesame Street, California Originals 395.00
Toby Cookies, Chef Head, Regal China .... .850.00 to 875.00
Tony The Tiger, Kellogg's, Plastic, 1968 .... .54.00 to 145.00
Toothache Dog, American Bisque 700.00
Topsy, Metlox .... 425.00 to 450.00
Toucan, Himark 35.00
Toy Soldier, American Bisque 100.00
Toy Soldier, Marsh 95.00
Train, Sierra Vista 225.00
Transformer, Roman Ceramics 65.00
Tug Boat, American Bisque 275.00
Tulip, Metlox .... .600.00 to 750.00
Turtle, Sitting, California Originals 25.00
Turtle, Sitting, Woodtone, California Originals 45.00
Umbrella Kids, American Bisque 170.00
Uncle Mistletoe, Regal China, 12 In. 1540.00
Uncle Sam Bear, Metlox 950.00
Victorian House, Fitz & Floyd 195.00
Victrola, California Originals 150.00
W.C. Fields, Cumberland Ware 795.00
Waitress, Diner, Liberty 250.00
Walrus, Doranne Of California 40.00
Whale, White, Metlox 115.00
Wildlife, Deer & Squirrel On Tree Trunk, Bird On Lid, Japan .... .30.00 to 85.00
Wilma, On Telephone, American Bisque 600.00
Winking Kitty, Enesco 365.00
Winky, Vallona Starr 895.00
Witch, Arms Around Pumpkin, Wolfe Studio 150.00
Witch, Fitz & Floyd 150.00
Witch, Polka Dot, Fitz & Floyd 250.00
Witch Head, Wolfe Studio 100.00
Woodstock, Benjamin & Medwin 550.00
Woody Woodpecker, In Stump, California Originals .... .240.00 to 925.00
Yarn Doll, American Bisque 95.00

Yogi Bear, American Bisque	.250.00 to 375.00
Yogi Bear, Head, Hanna Barbera	795.00
Ziggy On Stack Of Cookies	475.00

COORS ware was made by a pottery in Golden, Colorado, owned by the Coors Beverage Company. Dishes and decorative wares were produced from the turn of the century until the pottery was destroyed by fire in the 1930s. The name *Coors* is marked on the back. For more information, see *Kovels' Depression Glass & American Dinnerware Price List.*

Ashtray, Green, 1920s	65.00
Baker, Rosebud, Orange, Large	85.00
Bowl, Fruit, Coorado, Blue, Individual	20.00
Bowl, Mixing, Mello-Tone, 9 In.	70.00
Cake Plate, Knife, Rosebud, Red	.100.00 to 175.00
Cake Plate, Rosebud	35.00
Cake Plate, Rosebud, Orange	55.00
Casserole, Cover, Rosebud, Divided, Aqua	45.00
Cookie Jar, Rosebud, Orange	85.00
Cup & Saucer, Coorado, Blue	45.00
Honey Pot, Cover, Rosebud, Yellow	200.00
Pan, Loaf, Green, Sticker	200.00
Pitcher, Rock-Mount, Red	80.00
Pitcher, Rosebud, White	250.00
Pitcher, Water, Coorado, Orange	125.00
Teapot, Rosebud, Italian Red, Large	175.00
Tumbler, Rosebud, Handle	85.00
Vase, Golden Yellow, 8 In.	100.00
Vase, Golden, White Matte, Green Interior, Circular Handle, 8 In.	60.00
Vase, Handles, Orange, 10 1/2 In.	95.00
Vase, Lion, High Gloss Burgundy, 8 In.	70.00
Vase, Peach, 5 In.	45.00
Vase, Seven Falls, Matte Yellow, 8 In.	30.00

COPELAND pieces listed here are those that have a mark including the word Copeland used between 1847 and 1976. Marks include Copeland Spode and Copeland & Garrett. See also Copeland Spode and Royal Worcester.

Berry Set, Sugar & Creamer Wells, Strawberries, Leaves, Gold Trim, 10 In., 3 Piece	210.00
Bowl, Strainer Insert, White, Gold Trim, 8 In.	50.00
Bust, Alexandra, Parian, c.1860, 16 In.	625.00
Bust, Neoclassical Maiden, Crown, Pedestal, Bisque, 19th Century, 20 In.	755.00
Demitasse Set, Primrose, Register Mark, Cream, Black, 1855	135.00
Dessert Service, Gold, Cobalt Blue, Iron Red Floral Border, 8 1/2 In., 10 Piece	365.00
Figurine, Farmer, Seated, Holding Bagpipes, Impressed Mark, England, 1875, 11 In.	170.00
Figurine, Solitude, Classical Seminude, J. Lawlor, 1851, 20 1/2 In.	1550.00
Pitcher, Milk, White Hunt Scenes, Dark Putty Ground, Impressed Mark, 4 3/4 In.	190.00
Pitcher, Relief Hunt Scene	45.00
Plate, Blue, White, 1875, 7 In.	75.00
Plate, Rosette & Floral Swags, Turquoise Jeweled Rim, 10 In., 8 Piece	575.00
Platter, Blue Black Floral Transfer, Ironstone, 18 7/8 In.	105.00

COPELAND SPODE appears on some pieces of nineteenth-century English porcelain. Josiah Spode established a pottery at Stoke-on-Trent, England, in 1770. In 1833, the firm was purchased by William Copeland and Thomas Garrett and the mark was changed. In 1847, Copeland became the sole owner and the mark changed again. W. T. Copeland & Sons continued until a 1976 merger when it became Royal Worcester Spode. Pieces are listed in this book under the name that appears in the mark. Copeland Spode, Copeland, and Royal Worcester have separate listings.

Bowl, Vegetable, Tower, Pink, Rectangular, 9 3/4 In.	45.00
Breakfast Service, Blue Floral Design, Applied Toast Rack, 7 In.	60.00

Coffee Set, Sailing Scenes On River & Sea, 24 Piece 115.00
Cup & Saucer, Floral 25.00
Cup & Saucer, Tower, Pink 17.00
Egg Cup, Double, Tower, Pink 30.00
Figurine, Cries Of London 295.00
Invalid Feeder, Romantic Scenes, Cup Shape, Half Cover, 1850, 5 In. 240.00
Pitcher, Bulls On Dark Green, Jasper, 1891, 6 1/4 In. 125.00
Pitcher, Jasperware, Blue, 19th Century 150.00
Plate, Italy, 10 In. 40.00
Plate, Tower, Pink, 8 In. 16.00
Plate, Tower, Pink, 10 In. 29.00
Plate, Yellow Castle, Lilac Shading, Green Trees, 9 3/8 In. 125.00
Platter, Tower, Pink, 15 In. 80.00
Platter, Turkey Reserve, Blue Guilloche Border, Ironstone, 18 3/4 In. 345.00
Server, Pancake, Blue On White, Gold Trim On Handles, 1852, 11 1/4 In. 290.00
Soup, Dish, Tower, Dark Blue 60.00
Tray, Petal Shape Rim, Flat Interior, Purple, Yellow, 1835, 12 1/8 In. 3737.00
Vase, Apple Blossoms, Blue & White Relief, 5 1/4 In. 150.00
Vase, Italian Pattern, Ring Handles, Disc Feet, c.1890, 9 3/8 In., Pair 632.00

COPPER has been used to make utilitarian items, such as teakettles and
cooking pans, since the days of the early American colonists. Copper
became a popular metal with the Arts & Crafts makers of the early
1900s, and decorative pieces, like bookends and desk sets, were made.
Other pieces of copper may be found in the Arts & Crafts, Bradley &
Hubbard, Kitchen, and Roycroft categories.

Ashtray, Embossed Horse's Head, Hammered, Craftsman Co., 4 In. . . . . .120.00 to 125.00
Basket, Crescent Shape, Beaded Edge, Tapered Brown Handle, 1808, 26 3/4 In. 175.00
Bed Warmer, Floral Tooled Lid, Refinished Turned Maple Handle, 44 In. 165.00
Bed Warmer, Tooled Center Star Lid, Turned Wooden Handle, 43 1/2 In. 220.00
Bed Warmer, Tooled Lid, Wooden Handle, Black, Red Grain, 42 In. 355.00
Boiler, Cover, Handles, Spigot, Dovetailed, 13 x 13 1/2 In. 150.00
Bowl, Floriform, Red Patina, Dirk Van Erp, 16 In. 715.00
Bowl, Fluted Design, Handwrought, 12 x 3 In. 99.00
Bowl, Hammered, Crimped, Avon, Coppersmith, 10 x 1 In. 121.00
Bowl, Hammered, Original Patina, Impressed Mark, Dirk Van Erp, 12 1/2 x 3 In. 1650.00
Bowl, Handwrought, Red Patina, Round, Harry Dixon, 2 x 4 1/2 In. 470.00
Bowl, Lion Head Handles, Marked, Silver On Copper, 8 1/4 x 6 5/8 In. 55.00
Box, Brass Floral Design On Cover, Raised Garden Scenes & Dolphins, Footed 135.00
Box, Cover, Stylized Design On Top, Sides, Sweden, 3 In. 25.00
Box, Square Polished Abalone Shell On Lid, Arts & Crafts, 2 1/2 x 3 1/2 In. 97.00
Bucket, Round, Continental, 19 1/2 In. 375.00
Bucket, Wrought Iron Swing Handle, Bulbous Form, 9 x 11 In. 70.00
Chafing Dish, Hammered, Wooden Handles, Arts & Crafts, 3 Curled Legs, 15 x 15 In. . . .   880.00
Charger, Leaf, Scroll Stem Design, Hammered, Rebaje, 18 In. 175.00
Charger, Repousse Nude Figure, Hammered Rim, Rebaje, Stamped, 14 In. 55.00
Coal Scuttle, Cylindrical, Hinged Handle, 19th Century, 17 1/2 In. 345.00
Coffee Set, Perk Type Pot, Art Deco, Manning Bowman, 4 Piece 250.00
Coffeepot, Hammered, Hand Forged, Brass Handle, Dove Spout, 9 In. 160.00
Door Knocker, Handmade, Arts & Crafts, 7 In. 220.00
Finial, Architectural, Verdigris Surface, 19th Century, 73 1/2 In. 2875.00
Frame, Stone Inlays, Arts & Crafts, 13 x 16 In. 645.00
Jardiniere, Hammered Tapered Bottom, Rolled Rim, Arts & Crafts, 13 1/2 x 14 In. 412.00
Jardiniere, Hammered, Rolled Rim, Dark Brown Patina, Dirk Van Erp, 8 1/2 x 11 In. 440.00
Jug, Mother & Child Playing Badminton, Red, Yellow Ground, England, 5 3/4 In. .250.00 to 265.00
Kettle, Candy, Dovetailed, Wrought Iron Handle, 9 1/2 In. . . . . .250.00 to 265.00
Kettle, Cover, Handle, Wrought Iron Feet, 19th Century, 21 1/2 x 12 In. 1265.00
Kettle, Dovetailed, Iron Bale Handle, 25 In. 275.00
Lantern, Ship, Electric, 14 In. 135.00
Molds are listed in the Kitchen category.
Mug, Tavern Copper, Kettle, Candy, Dovetailed, Wrought-Iron Handle, 9 1/2 In. 265.00
Mug, Tavern, 18th Century, 1 Pt., 4 1/4 In. 195.00
Mug, Tavern, Dovetailed, Penna., Late 18th Century, 5 In. 265.00

Pitcher, Lamp Filler, Dovetailed, Penna., Late 18th Century, 4 1/2 In. 235.00
Pitcher, Riveted Handle, Hammered, Stove Pipe Neck, Stickley Brothers, 18 In. 1430.00
Plaque, 8 Crabs & A Starfish, Wood Frame, Nichols, 11 x 14 In.   4025.00
Plaque, Profile Bust Of Nelson, Pressed, Frame, 15 3/4 x 12 In.   103.00
Tankard, Barrel Form, Dovetailed Construction, Brass Bands, 1830s, 10 In. 175.00
Teakettle, Dovetailed, Gooseneck Spout, Fixed Handle, Brass Trim, 11 In. 180.00
Teakettle, Dovetailed, Swivel Handle, 6 In. 80.00
Teakettle, John W. Schlosser 1000.00
Teakettle, Lancaster, Pennsylvania, C. Kiefer, c.1830, 9 In. 750.00
Teakettle, Straight Spout, Bail Handle, Aldrich, Buffalo 65.00
Teakettle, W. Luckenbach, Bethlehem, c.1825 . . . .   295.00
Teapot, Brass Handle, 5 1/2 In. 28.00
Teapot, England, 1800, 6 In. 250.00
Tray, 2 Riveted Handles, Hammered, Signed G. Stickley, 11 1/4 In. 990.00
Tray, Hammered, Embossed Design, Original Patina, Impressed Mark, Benedict, 6 In. . . .   253.00
Umbrella Stand, Trumpet Form, Embossed Flower, Gustav Stickley, No. 382, 14 In. . . .   1650.00
Urn, Coffee, Universal, Dated 1914, Large 150.00
Vase, Hammered, Geometric Design, 3 Brass Handles, WMF, 5 x 8 In. 825.00
Vase, Hammered, Rolled Rim, Bulbous, Brown Patina, Dirk Van Erp, 7 1/2 x 7 3/4 In. . . .   1760.00
Vase, Hammered, Rolled Rim, Bulbous, Brown Patina, Dirk Van Erp, 8 x 6 In. 1430.00
Vase, Sharp Pointed Ribs Around Mid Section, Mottled Red & Brown, 12 In. 210.00
Vase, Wood Grain Hammered Panels, Raised Flowers, Arts & Crafts, I. Hixson, 8 In. 935.00
Wall Sconce, Hammered, Marked, Volk, 7 1/2 x 11 In. 245.00

COPPER LUSTER items are listed in the Luster category.

CORALENE glass was made by firing many small colored beads on the
outside of glassware. It was made in many patterns in the United States
and Europe in the 1880s. Reproductions are made today. Coralene-
decorated Japanese pottery is listed in the Japanese Coralene category.

Ewer, Orange, Gold Poppies On Brown, Stamped Mark, 4 In. 60.00
Rose Bowl, Flowers 200.00
Vase, Blue & White, Yellow Beads, 8 In. 850.00
Vase, Blue Satin Glass, Wheat Design, 12 In. 1250.00
Vase, Blue Satin, Seaweed, Irregular Rim, Amber Branch Footed, 6 1/2 In. 415.00
Vase, Diamond-Quilted, Blue, 6 1/2 x 7 1/2 In. 395.00
Vase, Diamond-Quilted, Blue, Yellow Stars, 5 1/4 In. 920.00
Vase, Green Beading, Gold Tracery, 8 1/2 In. 350.00
Vase, Mother-Of-Pearl, Opalescent White Diamond, Cross, Pink, Gold Rim, 6 In. 175.00
Vase, Mother-Of-Pearl, White Diamond, Gold Beaded, Pink Shade, 7 In. 489.00
Vase, Orange, Seaweed, Egg Shape, 9 In. 135.00
Vase, Peachblow, Rose To Pink, Yellow Seaweed Design, Wheeling, 1870, 7 1/2 In. 650.00
Vase, Peachblow, Seaweed Design, Gold Trim, c.1870, 7 1/2 In.   650.00
Vase, Raspberry, White, Bird, Leaves Design, 10 In. 57.00
Vase, Yellow, Seaweed, Bulbous, 10 1/2 In. 495.00

CORDEY China Company was founded by Boleslaw Cybis in 1942 in
Trenton, New Jersey. The firm produced gift shop items. In 1969 it was
acquired by the Lightron Corp. and operated as the Schiller Cordey Co.,
manufacturers of lamps. About 1950 Boleslaw Cybis began making
Cybis porcelains, which are listed in their own category in this book.

Box, Roses On Lid, 6 x 5 In. 55.00
Bust, Woman, Curls & Roses, 14 In. 275.00
Clock, Roses 275.00
Dresser Set, Tray, 2 Perfume Bottles, 3 Piece 285.00
Dresser Set, Tray, 5 Bottles, 6 Piece 170.00
Figurine, Bird, 9 1/2 In. 150.00
Figurine, Lady With Roses, No. 5054, 9 In. . . . . .115.00 to 119.00
Figurine, Lady, 16 In. 165.00
Figurine, Man & Woman, 10 In. 175.00
Figurine, Man, Tricornered Hat, French Provincial Type, Lace Gold Trim, 14 In. 165.00
Figurine, Oriental Duck, White, 14 1/2 In. 250.00
Figurine, Pilgrim, 7 In. 100.00

Figurine, Woman, Chinese, Frilly Dress, Roses, 12 In.	165.00
Lamp, Bird, Shade, 23 3/4 In.	135.00
Lamp, Colonial Man & Woman, 15 In., Pair	175.00
Vase, 2 Bluebirds, 9 In.	165.00
Vase, Cornucopia, 6 1/2 In.	135.00

CORKSCREWS have been needed since the first bottle was sealed with a cork, probably in the seventeenth century. Today collectors search for the early, unusual patented examples or the figural corkscrews of recent years.

Bottle Opener, 14K Yellow Gold, Monogram LFR	185.00
Carved Man's Head Handle	35.00
Double Twist, Green	25.00
Figural, Head, Red Cap Doorman, 1920	65.00
Keen Kutter	20.00 to 32.00
Lady's Leg, Brass, Celluloid	150.00
Man, Hat	20.00
Mr. Snifter, Chrome	25.00
Shakespeare, Brass, 1800s	65.00
W.C. Fields Sitting On Bench	75.00
Willow Springs Brewery Co., Stars, Stripes Bottled Beer, Omaha, Wooden Handle	55.00

CORONATION souvenirs have been made since the 1800s. Pottery, glass, tin, silver, and paper objects with a picture of the monarchs and date have been sold at many coronations. The pieces that mention King Edward VIII, the king who was never crowned, are not rare; collectors should be sure to check values before buying. Related pieces are found in the Commemorative category.

Ashtray, Elizabeth II, Wedgwood	30.00
Button, Queen Elizabeth II, 1958, Celluloid, 1 1/4 In.	50.00
Cards, Playing, Queen Elizabeth II	5.00
Cup, Queen Elizabeth, Lovatts, England	35.00
Figure Set, Royal Family, Queen Elizabeth II, Canada, Box, 6 Piece	185.00
Loving Cup, Edward VII, Royal Doulton, 1937	950.00
Loving Cup, King & Queen, Royal Doulton, 1937	900.00
Loving Cup, Queen Elizabeth II, Royal Doulton, 1953	1000.00
Mug, Queen Elizabeth, 1953	20.00
Plate, Elizabeth II, Cobalt Blue, Royal Staffordshire, 1953	20.00
Tumbler, Queen Elizabeth, Spode, 1953, 4 1/2 In.	36.00

COSMOS is a pressed milk glass pattern with colored flowers made from 1894 to 1915 by the Consolidated Lamp and Glass Company. Tablewares and lamps were made in this pattern. A few pieces were also made of clear glass with painted decorations. Other glass patterns are listed under Consolidated Lamp and also in various glass categories.

Butter, Cover	175.00
Butter, Cover, Pink Band	185.00
Creamer	160.00
Jug, Syrup, 6 In.	355.00
Lamp, Parlor, Half Shade, 8 In.	410.00
Lamp Base, Glass Chimney, 7 1/2 In.	155.00
Spooner	160.00
Syrup, Pink Band	155.00

COVERLETS were made of linen or wool during the nineteenth century. Most of the coverlets date from 1800 to 1860. Four types were made: the double weave, jacquard, summer and winter, and overshot. Later coverlets were made of a variety of materials. Quilts are listed in this book in their own category.

Jacquard, 4 Medallions, Vintage Border, Chesterfield, Ohio, 1858, 1 Piece, 70 x 90 In.	495.00
Jacquard, 4 Rose Medallions, D. Cosley, 1848, 82 x 94 In.	275.00
Jacquard, 4 Rose Medallions, Vintage Borders, Emanuel Etteiger, 1840, 72 x 88 In.	550.00

Jacquard, 9 Floral Medallions, Diamonds In Between, 82 x 90 In. 275.00
Jacquard, Central Birds Feeding Their Young, Town Border, 87 x 68 In. 1100.00
Jacquard, Floral Medallions, Border, Navy, White, J. & M. Ardner, 1852, 70 x 79 In. . . .   575.00
Jacquard, Floral Medallions, Eagle & Shield Borders, Initials F.B., 70 x 94 In. 275.00
Jacquard, Floral Medallions, Eagle Borders, John Hartman, Ohio, 1857, 78 x 88 In. 1017.00
Jacquard, Floral Medallions, Lion Border, Permela Gardner, 1838, 86 x 92 In. 1980.00
Jacquard, Floral Medallions, Navy, Teal, White, F. Yearous, Ohio, 1850, 71 x 85 In. 550.00
Jacquard, Floral Medallions, Rose & Vintage Border, 78 x 86 In. 137.00
Jacquard, Floral, Navy & White, Dated 1853, 2-Piece, 76 x 85 In. 275.00
Jacquard, Floral, Navy, Natural, 1850, 2-Piece, 78 x 92 In. 550.00
Jacquard, Floral, T. Marst Eller, L.S. 1845 Corner Block, 87 x 68 In. 230.00
Jacquard, Foliage Medallions, Busts Of Presidents Border, 82 x 86 In. 165.00
Jacquard, Geometric Floral Medallions, Emanuel Melly Lebanon, 1848, 84 x 96 In. 385.00
Jacquard, Geometric Floral Medallions, Trellis & Bird Border, 1854, 69 x 82 In. 412.00
Jacquard, Geometric Floral, Bird & Tree Border, 1846, 80 x 84 In. 385.00
Jacquard, Geometric Floral, Blue, White, 76 x 84 In. 220.00
Jacquard, Masonic, Corner Block Signed & Dated, E. Seely, 1824, 97 x 74 In. 230.00
Jacquard, Red, White, Floral Border, Foliage Wreath, 1875, 77 x 78 In. 82.00
Jacquard, Single Weave, Floral Medallion Center, Eagles, Natural, 81 x 84 In. 300.00
Jacquard, Snowflake, Pine Tree Borders, Red, White, Wool, 1-Piece, 63 x 100 In., Pair . .   385.00
Jacquard, Spread Wing Eagle, Blue & White, Fringed, Samuel Graham, Ind., 1847 . . . . .   750.00
Jacquard, Star Medallions, Borders, White, Navy, Fringe, J. Heeter, Ohio, 66 x 88 In. . . .   495.00
Jacquard, Summer, Winter, Pine Tree Border, 72 x 78 In. 546.00
Jacquard, Vining Flowers, Corner Labeled John Clark, 72 x 86 In. 165.00
Overshot, Dark Brown, Rust, White, 74 x 96 In. 115.00
Overshot, Dark Green, White, 78 x 104 In. 192.00
Overshot, Gold, Olive Green, White, 85 x 100 In. 137.00
Overshot, Optical Pattern, 68 x 86 In. 125.00
Overshot, Red, 2-Tone Blue, 76 x 94 In. 220.00

COWAN POTTERY made art pottery and wares for florists. Guy Cowan
made pottery in Rocky River, Ohio, a suburb of Cleveland, from 1913
to 1931. A stylized mark with the word *Cowan* was used on most
pieces. A commercial, mass-produced line was marked *Lakeware*.
Collectors today search for the Art Deco pieces by Guy Cowan, Viktor
Schreckengost, Waylande Gregory, or Thelma Frazier Winter.

Ashtray, Duck Shape, Green 50.00
Ashtray, Gazelle Center, Raised, Chinese Red Glaze, Marked, 5 1/2 In. 100.00
Ashtray, Ram Spans Triangular Base, Marked, 5 In. 330.00
Bookends, Elephant, Stylized, Push Me, Pull Me 1430.00
Bookends, Sunbonnet Girl, Antique Green . . . . .400.00 to 450.00
Bowl, April, Green, 4 x 9 In. 75.00
Bowl, Blue Luster, 5 1/2 In. . . . . .75.00 to 100.00
Bowl, Console, Sea Horse 40.00
Bowl, Larkspur Blue, Stand-Up, 10 In. . . . . .85.00 to 100.00
Bowl, Orange Matte Over Yellow, 9 x 4 In. 125.00
Candleholder, Diamond Shape, Black Matte, Pair 20.00
Candleholder, White 40.00
Candlestick, Blue Luster, 8 In., Pair 90.00
Candlestick, Fluted Body, Blue Luster, Marked, 10 1/2 In. 100.00
Candlestick, Fluted Cup & Base, Black Matte, 4 In., Pair 65.00
Candlestick, Ivory, No. 782, 3 In. 65.00
Candlestick, Larkspur Blue 75.00
Candlestick, Seahorse Design, Pink Luster, Marked, 4 1/2 In., Pair 45.00
Candlestick, Stylized Grape Clusters Form Open Handles, Marked, 7 1/2 In. 165.00
Charger, Stylized Birds, Guy Cowan Design, 15 1/2 In. . . . . .605.00 to 880.00
Charger, Turquoise Glazed, Guy Cowan, 1927, 14 1/2 In. 860.00
Compote, Seahorse, Yellow & White, 6 In. 75.00
Console Set, Etruscan, Oriental Red 395.00
Console Set, Verbena Glaze, 4 Piece 475.00
Decanter, Figural, King & Queen, Oriental Red, Pair . . . . .2795.00 to 2995.00
Figurine, Elephant, Block Base, Chinese Red Glaze, Marked, 4 1/2 In. 230.00

Figurine, Russian Peasant, Playing Tambourine, Beige Glaze, Signed, 9 1/2 In. 660.00
Flower Frog, 2 Female Figures, Dance On Stylized Ocean Base, Marked, 8 In. 660.00
Flower Frog, Nude Woman, Cream High Glaze, 11 7/8 In. 440.00
Flower Frog, Nude, Sitting On Tree Stump, Signed, 14 1/2 x 6 In. 2970.00
Flower Frog, Partially Clad Woman, Ivory Glaze, Signed, 10 x 4 1/2 In. 467.00
Flower Frog, Scarf Dancer, White Glaze . . . . .180.00 to 275.00
Jar, Gray Matte, Sage Green Highlights, Impressed Mark, 5 1/8 In. 121.00
Jar, Strawberry, 4 Openings At Shoulder, Underplate, Rose & Yellow, Marked, 7 1/2 In. . . .   495.00
Jar, Strawberry, Oriental Red 295.00
Jar, Strawberry, Plum, Underplate, 7 1/2 In. 400.00
Lamp, Chinese Red, Impressed Marks, 19 In. 165.00
Lamp, Dresser, Cream Luster, Fluted Body, Blue Shade, 15 1/2 In., Pair 230.00
Lamp, Pink Luster, Vase Shaped Base 125.00
Lamp, Twisted Stem, Orange Luster, Drilled Holes, 12 In., Pair 55.00
Match Holder, Sea Horse, Orange Luster 35.00
Paperweight, Elephant, Ivory, 4 1/2 In. 275.00
Tobacco Jar, Gourd Shape, Orange 325.00
Vase, Art Deco, Gunmetal & Silver Luster Glaze, Signed, 8 x 6 In. 605.00
Vase, Azure Luster, 8 1/2 In. 75.00
Vase, Blue Luster, 5 1/2 In. 95.00
Vase, Blue Luster, 9 5/8 In. 100.00
Vase, Bud, Pearl Luster, 7 In. 65.00
Vase, Chinese Red, 6 3/4 In. 150.00
Vase, Chinese, Red Ring, 5 In. 85.00
Vase, Larkspur Blue, 12 1/4 In. 150.00
Vase, Orange Luster, Logan Style, 6 1/2 In. . . . . .80.00 to 100.00
Vase, Orange Luster, Thin Neck, Bulbous Base, Marked, 14 In.   745.00
Vase, Oxblood Luster, 13 In. 125.00
Vase, Sea Horse, Ivory, 5 In. 90.00
Vase, Trumpet, Flower Frog, Mottled Green, 5 5/8 In. 110.00
Vase, Urn, Rust, Mottled Brown, 10 In. 150.00
Wall Pocket, Roaring Lion, Blue Luster, Marked, 10 x 10 In. 440.00

CRACKER JACK, the molasses-flavored popcorn mixture, was first
made in 1896 in Chicago, Illinois. A prize was added to each box in
1912. Collectors search for the old boxes, toys, and advertising materials. Many of the toys are unmarked.

Bookmark, Scotty Dog, Metal 35.00
Card, Magic Egg Trick, No. 18, 1930s 33.00
Card, Weight Puzzle, No. 1, 1930s 33.00
Card Set, Baseball, Factory, 1915 . . . .   46300.00
Coin, Cracker Jack Mystery Club, James Monroe, 5th President 10.00
Coin, Cracker Jack Mystery Club, Theodore Roosevelt, 26th President 10.00
Coin-Operated Machine, Vending, 1940-1950 . . . .   230.00
Fortune Wheel . . . . .45.00 to 55.00
Knife, Our Boy 65.00
Marble 10.00
Pin Set, Sports Figures, 1930, 25 Piece 400.00
Sign, Sailor Boy, 14 In. 250.00
Toonerville Trolley, Red Ground, Black Lettering, Tin, 1930, 2 In. 551.00
Uniform, Les Moss, Old Timers Day, Rawlings, Size 50, 1983 . . . .   330.00
Watch, Leather Band, Metal Case, Japan Movement, Box 42.00
Whistle, Metal, Green 25.00
Whistle, Tin, Flat Double, Reed, Silver Flashing, 1930s 18.00
Whistle, Tin, Single Tube, Reed, Name On Top Side, Silver Flashing, 1930s 18.00

CRACKLE GLASS was originally made by the Venetians, but most of the
ware found today dates from the 1800s. The glass was heated, cooled,
and refired so that many small lines appeared inside the glass. It was
made in many factories in the United States and Europe.

Vase, Amber, Rainbow Glass Company, 8 In. 38.00
Vase, Cranberry, Applied Glass Base & Trim, 8 In. 55.00

Vase, Enameled Flowers, Signed, A. Leopold, 10 In 95.00
Vase, Red, Rainbow Glass Company, 6 In. 35.00

CRANBERRY GLASS is an almost transparent yellow-red glass. It resembles the color of cranberry juice. The glass has been made in Europe and America since the Civil War. It is still being made, and reproductions can fool the unwary. Related glass items may be listed in other categories, such as Northwood, Rubena Verde, etc.

Basket, Crimped Rim, Twisted Twig Handle, Flowers, Pale Green, 5 x 4 In. 85.00
Bell, Diamond-Quilted, Clear Handle, 8 1/2 In. 145.00
Bottle, Clear Cut Stopper, 9 In., Pair 185.00
Bottle, Embossed Flowers, Bulbous, Cut Faceted Stopper, 6 3/4 In. 145.00
Bottle, Enameled Flowers, Clear Cut Stopper, 7 1/2 In. 165.00
Bottle, Gold Flowers & Leaves, Ground Pontil, Clear Stopper, 8 1/2 In. 165.00
Bottle, Wine, Gold Star Design, Bubble Stopper, 8 1/2 In. 165.00
Cordial, Enameled, Leaping Dogs, 1900, 2 1/2 In. 110.00
Cracker Jar, Silver Plated Cover, Bear Finial, Scroll, 1890, 10 In. 695.00
Cruet, Inverted Thumbprint 169.00
Cruet, Pinched Side, Flowers, Gold Enamel Centers, 11 1/2 In. 225.00
Cruet, Spun Rope Clear Handle, Controlled Bubble Stopper, Wafer Foot, 8 In. 120.00
Cruet, White Enamel, Ribbed Crystal Handle, Stopper, 7 1/2 In. 265.00
Decanter, 3 Dimples, Narrow Waist, Applied Handle, Clear Stopper, 11 In. 225.00
Decanter, Gold Roses, Leaf Design, Applied Handled, 13 In. 195.00
Decanter, Lacy Enameled Gold Design, Red Flowers, Applied Handle, 11 In. 198.00
Decanter, Lacy Gold Garlands, Blue Flowers, Pedestal Foot, 4 3/4 In. 195.00
Decanter, Ribbed, Cut Leaves & Stars, Controlled Bubble Stopper, 12 In. 295.00
Decanter, Wine, Controlled Bubble Stopper, Music Box In Base, 12 1/4 In. 295.00
Epergne, 3 Lilies, Yellow Vine & Green Flower, 16 In. 605.00
Epergne, Jack-In-The-Pulpit Shape, Center Trumpet, 19 1/2 In. 2075.00
Goblet, Floral Enamel, 1900, 7 1/4 In. 440.00
Jar, Gilt Design, Mary Gregory Type Figure On Lid 247.00
Lamp, Enameled Flowers, Inverted Thumbprint Shade, 17 In. 595.00
Lamp, Floral Enamel, White Overlay, Gold Trim, 11 1/2 x 5 3/4 In., Pair 175.00
Lamp, Herringbone Font, Ruffled Rubena Cut Shade, Flowers, 14 In. 395.00
Lamp, Night Light, Swirl, Crystal Pedestal Base, Pillar Shape, France, 7 3/8 In. 175.00
Lamp, Night Light, White Enamel Scallops, Grapes, Leaves, 6 1/4 In. 265.00
Lamp, Peg, Etched, Stippled Shade, Brass Diamond, 20 1/2 In. 335.00
Lamp, Ruffled Shade, Chimney, Enameled Scrolls, Brass, 10 1/2 In. 395.00
Liquor Set, Round Tray, Gold Bands, 8 Piece 275.00
Pickle Castor, Hobnail Insert, Silver Plate Holder, Victorian, 12 1/2 In. 495.00
Pitcher, Christmas Snowflake, Ribbed ....1500.00 to 1800.00
Pitcher, Clear Ice Lip, Bulbous, 10 In. 225.00
Pitcher, Enameled Diamond Design, Clear Base & Handle, 1 3/4 In. 125.00
Pitcher, Enameled Flowers 285.00
Pitcher, Hobnail, Light Pink 65.00
Pitcher, Lemonade, Ruffled 275.00
Pitcher, Spiral Optic, Applied Reed Handle, 3 1/2 In. 35.00
Salt, Clear Rigaree Around Top, 2 3/8 In. 75.00
Salt, Gold Dolphins, Venetian, Footed 30.00
Salt, Open, Silver Plate Holder, c.1880 .... 175.00
Saltshaker, Hobb's Windows, Swirled, Opalescent 135.00
Spooner, Reverse Swirl, Opalescent 175.00
Sugar Shaker, Diamond Cut, 5 3/4 In. 100.00
Sugar Shaker, Square, 5 3/4 In. 100.00
Tumbler, Swirl, Hobbs Glass Co. 150.00
Vase, Amethyst Base, Flared, 12 In. 190.00
Vase, Applied Ruffled Top, 4 5/8 In. 135.00
Vase, Bud, White Stripes, Bulbous, 8 In. 95.00
Vase, Herringbone, Satin, 8 In. 155.00
Vase, Jack-In-Pulpit, Translucent Pink, Ruffled, Goldstone, 7 3/4 In. 165.00
Vase, Mary Gregory Type Child, Basket Of Flowers, Gilt, 13 In. 360.00
Vase, Middletown Frame, Flowers & Butterflies, 10 1/4 In. 640.00
Vase, Ribbed, Marvered Threads, 6 In. 190.00

CREAMWARE, or queensware, was developed by Josiah Wedgwood about 1765. It is a cream-colored earthenware that has been copied by many factories. Similar wares may be listed under Pearlware and Wedgwood.

Basin, Barber's, Black Transfer Scene, 1780s	425.00
Bowl, Barber's, Late 18th Century, 11 1/2 In.	395.00
Bowl, Underplate, Foliage Rim, Handles, Reticulated, Oval, 9 1/4 In.	385.00
Dessert Service, Oval Sauce Tureen, Lozenge Shape Stands, 1810, 18 Piece	1610.00
Figurine, Greyhound, Dark Brown Spotted, White Coat, 1785, 4 1/2 In.	2415.00
Figurine, Highland Dancer, Puce Feathered Hat, Dress, Tartan Skirt, 6 1/4 In.	120.00
Figurine, Monkey, Brown Sponging, 2 1/2 In.	250.00
Figurine, Princess Alice & Prince Louis Of Hess, 11 In.	175.00
Jam Pot, All-White, 1760, 3 1/2 In.	225.00
Jug, Milk, Pearl Shape, Strap Handle, Floral Terminals, 1775, 5 5/8 In.	980.00
Mug, Remember The Maine, Transfer, Pair	385.00
Plaque, Brown Spotted Lion, Dark Brown Eye, Brown Mane, Round, 8 In.	1840.00
Plate, Turner, Staffordshire, c.1780, 7 In., Pair	850.00
Platter, Harvard University Scene, Foliate & Fruit Rim, 17 x 19 1/4 In.	145.00
Sauceboat, c.1760, 6 1/4 In.	195.00
Sauceboat, Duck Form, Molded Plumage, 1780, 8 In.	465.00
Strainer, Punch, Reticulation & Handle, 1780	235.00
Tea Caddy, Black & White Transfer, 1800	295.00
Teapot, Bird Finial, Allover Mottled Brown Glaze, 4 In.	690.00
Teapot, Bouquet On Filleted Sides, 1763, 4 3/8 In.	635.00
Teapot, Cauliflower, With Stand, 1790, 9 3/4 In.	1380.00
Teapot, Cover, Cauliflower, Green Overlapping Leaves, W. Greatbatch, 4 In.	1840.00
Teapot, Cover, Eliza Holding Parasol, Fence, 5 3/8 In.	1035.00
Teapot, Cover, Floral Bands, Purple Floral Sprigs, 1775, 5 In.	920.00
Teapot, Cover, Floral Bouquet, Sprigs, Beadwork Border, Handle, 4 5/8 In.	690.00
Teapot, Cover, Tortoiseshell Glaze, Grape Cluster, Foliage, W. Greatbatch, 4 In.	1725.00
Teapot, Molded Acanthus Spout	385.00
Teapot, Painted Dutch Design, Prince William V, 1787, 4 In.	865.00
Teapot, Pineapple, Floral Finial, 1770, 5 3/8 In.	1035.00
Toby Mug, Success To Lord Rodney, Brown, Green, Whieldon Type, 3 3/4 In.	400.00
Tureen, Cover, Swan Finial, Blue Border, France, 7 1/2 In.	45.00
Vase, Wall, Fluted, Bell Shape, Tortoiseshell Glaze, Teal Blue, Brown, Gray, 10 In.	9220.00

CROWN DERBY is the name given to porcelain made in Derby, England, from the 1770s to 1935. Pieces are marked with a crown and the letter *D* or the word *Derby*. The earliest pieces were made by the original Derby factory, while later pieces were made by the King Street Partnerships (1848–1935) or the Derby Crown Porcelain Co. (1876–1890). Derby Crown Porcelain Co. became Royal Crown Derby Co. Ltd. in 1890. It is now part of Royal Doulton Tableware Ltd.

Cup, Stirrup, Fox Head, Red, Salmon Head, Yellow Eyes, 1820, 3 7/8 In.	400.00
Ewer, Bird, Foliate Design, Iron Red, Mottled Blue Ground, 12 1/2 In.	690.00
Ewer, Terra-Cotta Glazed Bands, Pierced Handle, Yellow Ground, 1890, 13 In.	975.00
Figurine, Fox, Seated, Brown Coat, Pale Gray Paws, Black Eyes, 1785, 2 3/4 In.	750.00
Figurine, Goldfinches, Tan, Yellow Black Wings, 1770, 4 9/16 & 5 In., Pair	1150.00
Figurine, John Wilkes, Wearing Rose Cloak, White Costume, 1772, 12 In.	805.00
Figurine, Pug, Seated, Black Eyes, Ears, Turquoise Collar, Oval Base, 2 1/2 In.	920.00
Jar, Cover, Raised Gilt Floral, Vine Design, Pink Ground, 1894, 7 1/4 In.	805.00
Sauceboat, Serrated Edge, Yellow Center, Rose Florets, Green Leaves, 1760	460.00
Tureen, Sauce, Cover, Yellow, Rose, Green On 1 Side, Scroll Handles, 7 1/4 In.	805.00
Vase, Cover, 2 Handles, Raised Gilt Bird, Floral Design, Pink Ground, 1889, 4 In.	690.00
Vase, Gilt, Floral Designs, Scalloped White Enamel, 11 1/2 In.	805.00

CROWN DUCAL is the name used on some pieces of porcelain made by A. G. Richardson and Co., Ltd., of Tunstall and Cobridge, England. The name has been used since 1916.

Cake Plate, Allover Florals & Birds, Pedestal, Octagonal, 9 x 5 In.	325.00
Charger, Blue Floral, 17 In.	300.00

Charger, Manchu Dragon, C. Rhead, 17 In.	350.00
Mug, Pub Scene, 3 Piece	150.00
Plate, George Washington Bicentennial, 1732-1932, 10 1/2 In., 8 Piece	300.00
Vase, Poppies, Black, Orange Luster Interior, Art Deco, 7 3/4 In.	195.00

CROWN MILANO glass was made by Frederick Shirley at the Mt. Washington Glass Works about 1890. It had a plain biscuit color with a satin finish. It was decorated with flowers and often had large gold scrolls.

Biscuit Jar, Shadow Flowers, Leaves, Copper Outlining, Barrel Shape	815.00
Bowl, Cover, Multicolored Bouquets, Gold Floral, Red Wreath & Crown, 7 x 4 In.	685.00
Bowl, Diamond-Quilted, Painted Raspberry & Leaf Design, Square Top, 4 1/2 In.	495.00
Bowl, Flowers, Tricornered Rolled Edge, Gold Trim, 3 x 9 In.	1750.00
Candlestick, Woman's Portrait, Plated Base, 8 1/4 In., Pair	1750.00
Cologne Bottle, Black & Gold Apple Blossoms, Pink Shadow Scrolls, 5 In.	880.00
Cracker Jar, Allover Bamboo Design, Painted Burmese Ground, 6 In.	900.00
Cracker Jar, Enameled Tulip, Square, 6 x 5 In.	110.00
Cracker Jar, Gold Spider Mums, Leaves, Buds, Coiled Handle, Bulbous, 5 In.	1045.00
Dish, Sweetmeat, Jeweled Sea Urchins, Wheat Ground, Rope Double Bail, 3 In.	825.00
Dish, Sweetmeat, Jeweled, 3 In.	695.00
Pickle Castor, Pastel Pansies, Gold Tracing, Pairpoint Frame, Mt. Washington	1495.00
Pitcher, Floral Tapestry, Ivory Ground, Gold Swirls, Gilt Handle, 12 In.	1045.00
Pitcher, Grecian Woman, Sheep, Wreath Ground, Gilt Twisted Handle, 10 In.	3300.00
Rose Bowl, Chintz Design, White Ground, 3 1/2 x 4 In.	385.00
Shade, Umbrella Shape	1500.00
Sugar & Creamer, Cornflower, Beige Ground, Petticoat Shape, 4 1/2 In.	1250.00
Sugar & Creamer, Embossed, Ribbed, Blue Flowers On Pale Pink	800.00
Sugar & Creamer, Pansies, Yellow To White Ground	750.00
Tumbler, Amber Leaves, Coralene Outlining, Opalescent, Marked, 3 1/2 In.	575.00
Vase, 9 Gulls, Flying Over Salmon Colored Ground, Bulbous, Stick Top	2795.00
Vase, Allover Gold Fern, Beige, White, Ball Shape, 8 3/4 In.	1200.00
Vase, Applied Gold Roses, Beaded Border, Oval, Mt. Washington, 8 1/4 In.	1380.00
Vase, Beige Leaf Ground, Jeweled, Gold Trim, Bulbous, 5 x 7 In.	1400.00
Vase, Bud, Pink, White Blossoms Outlined In Gold, Mt. Washington, 9 In.	980.00
Vase, Bulbous Bottom, Beige Ground, Peony Design, Mt. Washington, 12 In.	550.00
Vase, Bulbous, 3 Pulled Petal Designs, Lavender Lilacs, Mt. Washington, 16 In.	1430.00
Vase, Dancing Couple, Red Crown In Wreath, Mt. Washington, 16 In.	805.00
Vase, Flower Shape Top, Turquoise Accents, Gourd Shape, 13 In.	1395.00
Vase, Flowering Cacti, Gold Outlining, Beige Ground, Gourd Shape, 9 1/4 In.	990.00
Vase, Gold Flora Design, White Interior, Blue Wash, Cylinder, 7 1/2 In.	450.00
Vase, Gold Outlined Pansies Design, Matte Gold Scrolls, Cup Pedestal, 9 In.	860.00
Vase, Gold Rose Blossoms Trailing, Stick Shape, Marked, 15 In.	990.00
Vase, Ivory Design, Gold, Tan, Green Highlights, Mt. Washington, 8 x 7 In.	400.00
Vase, Serpent Coiled Around Neck, Enameled Flowers, Jeweled, 10 3/4 In.	2035.00
Vase, Shield, Jeweled, Beige Ground, Shell Handles, 9 In.	985.00
Vase, Thistle, Beige Ground, 12 1/2 x 5 1/2 In.	1100.00
Vase, White Body, Pink, Amber Scroll, Mt. Washington, 9 In.	920.00

CROWN TUSCAN pattern is included in the Cambridge glass category.

CRUETS of glass or porcelain were made to hold vinegar, oil, and other condiments. They were especially popular during Victorian times and have been made in a variety of styles since the eighteenth century. Additional cruets may be found in the Castor Set category and also in various glass categories.

Amber Glass, Sapphire Blue Handle, Stopper, Pink, Gold Flowers Design, 6 3/4 In.	265.00
Amber Glass, Swirl, Decanter Type, Embossed Pewter Mount, 11 1/4 In., Pair	480.00
Cranberry Glass, Enameled Flowers, Blown, Victorian	245.00
Cranberry Glass, Swirl, Pewter Mount & Stopper, Clear Rigaree Base, 8 3/4 In.	195.00
Cut Glass, George III, 7 Bottles, Sterling Tops & Stand, William Abdy, 1818, 9 1/2 In.	950.00
Emerald Green Glass, Croesus, Fan Stopper, 6 1/2 In.	220.00
Glass, Pink Cut Velvet, Diamond-Quilted, Clear Handle, Stopper, Tricornered Spout, 6 In.	465.00
Glass, Sapphire Blue, Vinegar, Brass Openwork, Filigree Floral Band, Rope Handle, 7 3/4 In.	145.00

Millefiori, 6 In.	65.00
Mother-Of-Pearl Glass, Apricot, Diamond-Quilted, Camphor Handle, Stopper, 6 In.	410.00
Mother-Of-Pearl Glass, Blue, Diamond-Quilted, Camphor Handle, Stopper	440.00
Mother-Of-Pearl Glass, Herringbone, Camphor Handle, Ball Stopper, Squatty, 6 3/4 In.	275.00
Mother-Of-Pearl Glass, Pink, Camphor Handle, Tricorner Spout, 5 1/2 In.	440.00
Peachblow, Petticoat Shape, White Handle & Stopper, New England, 7 In.	1950.00
Pottery, Oel & Essig, Windmill Scene, Blue, 10 In., Pair	95.00

CUP PLATES are small glass or china plates that held the cup while a diner of the mid-nineteenth century drank coffee or tea from the saucer. The most famous cup plates were made of glass at the Boston and Sandwich factory located in Sandwich, Massachusetts. There have been many new glass cup plates made in recent years for sale to gift shops or limited edition collectors. These are similar to the old plates but can be recognized as new.

Glass, 9 Scallops, Green Tint	20.00
Glass, Eagle, Emerald, Sandwich	4675.00
Glass, George Washington, Gray Striations, Octagonal, Philadelphia	4400.00
Glass, Henry Clay	30.00
Glass, Lacy Opalescent, Sandwich Glass	200.00
Glass, Lacy, Eagle, Amethyst, Octagonal, Pair	275.00
Glass, Rope Shoulder Top & Bottom	50.00
Porcelain, Farm Scene, Royal Bayreuth	65.00
Pottery, 3 Figures By Water, Cow Grazing, Staffordshire, 4 In.	70.00
Pottery, Green, Napier, J. & G. Alcock, Staffordshire, 1830s	45.00
Pottery, Queen's Rose	185.00

CURRIER & IVES made the famous American lithographs marked with their name from 1857 to 1907. The mark used on the print included the street address in New York City, and it is possible to date the year of the original issue from this information. Earlier prints were made by N. Currier and use that name from 1835 to 1847. Many reprints of the Currier or Currier & Ives prints have been made. Some collectors buy the insurance calendars that were based on the old prints. The words *large*, *small*, or *medium folio* refer to size. The original print sizes were very small (up to about 7 x 9 in.), small (8.8 x 12.8 in.), medium (9 x 14 in. to 14 x 20 in.), large (larger than 14 x 20 in.). Other sizes are probably later copies. Other prints by Currier & Ives may be listed in the Card category under Advertising and in the Sheet Music category. Currier & Ives dinnerware patterns may be found in the Adams or American Dinnerware categories.

American Farm Scenes, Frame, 16 3/4 x 24 In.	1380.00
American Homestead Winter, Frame, 14 3/8 x 18 3/4 In.	1725.00
American Homestead Winter, Shadowbox Frame, 10 x 14 In.	455.00
American Winter Sports, Deer Shooting, Frame, 17 7/8 x 25 3/4 In.	4312.00
Battle Of Cedar Creek, Wood Frame, 12 x 6 In.	214.00
Battle Of Petersburg, Wood Frame, 18 x 15 In.	220.00
Branding Slaves On The Coast Of Africa, 1845, Small Folio	700.00
City Of New York, Frame, 21 1/8 x 33 1/2 In.	4312.00
Death Bed Of The Martyr President, Abraham Lincoln, April 15th, 1865	85.00
Fast Team Taking A Smash, Matted, Frame, 14 x 19 In.	275.00
Fast Trotters On Harlem Lane, N.Y., Frame, 18 1/4 x 28 1/2 In.	3450.00
Great West, Matted, Frame, 15 3/8 x 19 3/8 In.	300.00
Home Sweet Home, Matted, Frame, 16 1/4 x 20 1/4 In.	190.00
Hudson Near Coldspring, Frame, 10 x 14 1/8 In.	80.00
Lady Thorn, Matted, Frame, 17 x 21 1/4 In.	220.00
Lightning Express, Leaving The Junction, 17 5/8 x 27 3/4 In.	14950.00
Little Sisters, Tiger Maple Frame, 20 1/2 x 16 In.	395.00
Maple Sugaring, Matted, Frame, 15 1/4 x 19 1/4 In.	415.00
Miniature Ship, Red, White & Blue, 9 1/2 x 13 In.	138.00
Murder Of Miss Jane McCrea, Frame, 16 1/4 x 12 In.	137.00
My Boyhood's Home, Shadowbox Frame, 11 x 14 In.	137.50
Narrows, New York Bay To Staten Island, 1874, Frame, 12 x 16 1/4 In.	95.00

New England Home, Matted, Frame, 19 1/4 x 23 1/4 In. 190.00
Off For The War, 12 x 16 In. 275.00
Old Oaken Bucket, 8 1/4 x 12 1/2 In. 120.00
Squirrel Shooting, Matted, Frame, 9 7/8 x 13 7/8 In. 360.00
Steamship Alaska, Of The Guion Line, Wood Frame, 19 x 14 In. 50.00
Tick-Tick-Tickle, Frame, 19 1/2 x 16 In. 82.00
View Of Harper's Ferry, Va., Frame, c.1860.14 3/4 x 20 14 In. 1840.00
View On The St. Lawrence, Indian Encampment, Frame, 9 7/8 x 11 1/16 In. 220.00
Way To Happiness, Small Folio 35.00
Young Blood In An Old Body, Gilt Frame, 12 3/4 x 16 3/4 In. 127.00

CUSTARD GLASS is a slightly yellow opaque glass. It was first made in
the United States after 1886 at the La Belle Glass Works, Bridgeport,
Ohio. It is being reproduced. Additional pieces may be found in the
Cambridge, Fenton, Heisey, and Northwood categories.

Argonaut Shell, Creamer ....135.00 to 159.00
Argonaut Shell, Cruet 895.00
Argonaut Shell, Cruet, Gold Trim 975.00
Argonaut Shell, Cruet, Original Stopper, 6 1/2 In........................885.00 to 895.00
Argonaut Shell, Cruet, Plastic Stopper 500.00
Argonaut Shell, Pitcher, Water 475.00
Argonaut Shell, Planter 850.00
Argonaut Shell, Spooner ....125.00 to 159.00
Argonaut Shell, Sugar 225.00
Argonaut Shell, Toothpick, 3 In. ....330.00 to 495.00
Beaded Circle, Compote, Jelly 295.00
Beaded Circle, Creamer ....65.00 to 190.00
Beaded Circle, Spooner 190.00
Bee On Basket, Toothpick 65.00
Bell, Smocking, Blue 45.00
Cane, Celery Vase, Gold Trim 145.00
Cherry Chain, Tumbler 225.00
Chrysanthemum Sprig, Berry Bowl, Master ....295.00 to 525.00
Chrysanthemum Sprig, Berry Set, Blue, 7 Piece 1195.00
Chrysanthemum Sprig, Butter, Cover, Pagoda Style, Gilt, 5 1/2 In. 220.00
Chrysanthemum Sprig, Celery, Blue 1300.00
Chrysanthemum Sprig, Creamer ....125.00 to 250.00
Chrysanthemum Sprig, Creamer, Blue 350.00
Chrysanthemum Sprig, Cruet ....450.00 to 495.00
Chrysanthemum Sprig, Cruet, Blue 1200.00
Chrysanthemum Sprig, Cruet, Faceted Stopper, 6 3/4 In. 205.00
Chrysanthemum Sprig, Pitcher, 8 1/2 In. 485.00
Chrysanthemum Sprig, Spooner ....125.00 to 160.00
Chrysanthemum Sprig, Spooner, Gold 250.00
Chrysanthemum Sprig, Sugar, Blue 400.00
Chrysanthemum Sprig, Sugar, Cover 235.00
Chrysanthemum Sprig, Toothpick, 2 3/4 In. ....235.00 to 495.00
Chrysanthemum Sprig, Tray, Condiment 610.00
Chrysanthemum Sprig, Tray, Condiment, Footed, Gold, Round 275.00
Diamond Maple Leaf, Butter 350.00
Diamond Maple Leaf, Sugar, Gold, Dugan 275.00
Diamond With Peg, Pitcher, Ocean City, Roses, 7 In. 60.00
Diamond With Peg, Pitcher, Tankard, Gold 200.00
Diamond With Peg, Toothpick 125.00
Diamond With Peg, Toothpick, Roses 175.00
Garfield Drape, Butter, Cover 75.00
Geneva, Berry Bowl, 4 1/4 In. 60.00
Geneva, Toothpick 360.00
Geneva, Toothpick, Gold Trim 80.00
Geneva, Tumbler 38.00
Georgia Gem, Spooner 55.00
Georgia Gem, Toothpick ....50.00 to 65.00
Georgia Gem, Toothpick, Pea Green ....50.00 to 65.00

Georgia Gem, Toothpick, Souvenir 125.00
Grape Arbor, Vase, Hat Shape, 4 In. 55.00
Harvard, Toothpick ....25.00 to 50.00
Intaglio, Pitcher, Water 375.00
Intaglio, Tumbler, Green, Gold Design 65.00
Inverted Fan & Feather, Berry Bowl, Master ....295.00 to 365.00
Inverted Fan & Feather, Creamer 189.00
Inverted Fan & Feather, Dish, Jelly 495.00
Inverted Fan & Feather, Pitcher, Water 650.00
Inverted Fan & Feather, Punch Cup 295.00
Inverted Fan & Feather, Sugar & Creamer, Spooner 525.00
Inverted Fan & Feather, Tumbler 95.00
Inverted Fan & Feather, Tumbler, Gold 250.00
Ivorina Verde pattern is in this category under Winged Scroll.
Jefferson Optic, Berry Set, 7 Piece 350.00
Jefferson Optic, Creamer ....140.00 to 150.00
Jefferson Optic, Salt & Pepper, Warren, Ohio Souvenir 60.00
Jefferson Optic, Spooner 150.00
Jefferson Optic, Toothpick, Souvenir ....50.00 to 75.00
Little Gem, see Georgia Gem pattern in this category.
Louis XV, Banana Boat 110.00
Louis XV, Berry Set, 7 Piece 585.00
Louis XV, Butter, Cover, Northwood, 5 1/2 In. ....150.00 to 165.00
Louis XV, Creamer ....75.00 to 85.00
Louis XV, Pitcher 195.00
Louis XV, Sauce, Oval, Gold Trim 35.00
Louis XV, Spooner ....85.00 to 100.00
Louis XV, Sugar, Cover, Gold Trim 95.00
Louis XV, Water Set, 7 Piece 610.00
Maize is its own category in this book.
Maple Leaf, Butter, Cover 375.00
Maple Leaf, Butter, Gold 300.00
Maple Leaf, Creamer ....125.00 to 160.00
Maple Leaf, Spooner 160.00
Maple Leaf, Spooner, Gold Trim 135.00
Maple Leaf, Sugar, Cover 325.00
Maple Leaf, Tumbler 95.00
Maple Leaf, Water Set, 7 Piece 700.00
Peacock & Urn, Bowl, Ice Cream, Stippled, 10 In. 225.00
Ring Band, Toothpick ....75.00 to 95.00
Tiny Thumbprint, Berry, Master, Mums 260.00
Tiny Thumbprint, Creamer, Rose 110.00
Tiny Thumbprint, Salt & Pepper, Mums 225.00
Tiny Thumbprint, Tankard, Mums 370.00
Washington, Toothpick 120.00
Wild Bouquet, Cruet 525.00
Winged Scroll, Berry Set, 5 Piece 280.00
Winged Scroll, Creamer 100.00
Winged Scroll, Spooner ....45.00 to 100.00
Winged Scroll, Sugar, Cover 150.00
Winged Scroll, Tankard, 1/2 Gal. 160.00
Winged Scroll, Toothpick ....175.00 to 265.00
Winged Scroll, Toothpick, Green, Gold Trim 425.00

CUT GLASS has been made since ancient times, but the large majority of the pieces now for sale date from the brilliant period of glass design, 1880 to 1905. These pieces have elaborate geometric designs with a deep miter cut. Modern cut glass with a similar appearance is being made in England, Ireland, and the Czech and Slovak republics. Chips and scratches are often difficult to notice but lower the value dramatically. A signature on the glass adds significantly to the value. Other cut glass pieces are listed under factory names.

Banana Bowl, Cluster Variant, 11 1/4 x 8 1/4 In. 450.00

Banana Bowl, Propeller, Allover Cut, 11 1/2 x 7 3/4 In. 425.00
Basket, Hobstar, 3 x 4 1/2 In. 275.00
Basket, Hobstars, Notched Handle, Floral Design, 8 1/4 x 9 1/2 In. 440.00
Bonbon, Allover Cut, Center Stick Handle, Faceted Ball Handle, Meriden, Pair 295.00
Bonbon, Buzz Saw, 6 In. 50.00
Bonbon, Elk, Butterfly Shape, Irving Glass Co., 4 x 5 1/4 In. 325.00
Bottle, Bitters, Vixon, Sterling Silver Top, S. Cottle & Co., N.Y., 8 1/4 In. 300.00
Bottle, Cologne, Hindoo, Chain Of Hobstars, Notched Prisms, 7 x 4 1/2 In. 495.00
Bottle, Whiskey, Bull's-Eye & Prism 595.00
Bowl, Alhambra, Low, 10 In. 1350.00
Bowl, Alsatia, Maple City . . . . .45.00 to 65.00
Bowl, Banana, Royal, Hunt, 11 In. 575.00
Bowl, Byzantine, 4 Petal, 10 3/4 x 10 In. 900.00
Bowl, Carolyn, 6 Sides, Crimped, Hoare, 8 1/2 In. 450.00
Bowl, Comet, Swirls Of Cane & Strawberry-Diamond, 4 1/2, 10 In. 765.00
Bowl, Cosmos Flowers Body, Horizontal Leaves Base, Ray Cut Rim, Clark, 5 1/2 In. . . . 135.00
Bowl, Croesus, 9 In. 1500.00
Bowl, Diamond, Underplate, 19th Century, England, 2 Piece 345.00
Bowl, George V, Crosscut, Diamonds, Brilliant, London, 1912, 9 x 5 In. 1475.00
Bowl, Grecian, Square, 9 In. 1800.00
Bowl, Harvard, 3-Footed, 6 x 8 1/2 In. 330.00
Bowl, Hobstar, Notched Prism, 3 1/2 x 10 1/2 x 7 1/2 In. 365.00
Bowl, Hobstars Diamond, Orange, Petticoat Base, 9 x 10 In. 975.00
Bowl, Lilies Of The Valley, Hobstars, Floral Design, 2 Notched Handles, 4 In. 275.00
Bowl, Olga, Monroe, 8 In. 1250.00
Bowl, Pewter Cover, Enameled Green Finial, Green, R. Cauman, 4 3/4 In. 675.00
Bowl, Pineapple, 8 In. 66.00
Bowl, Prima Donna, Dental Edge, Clark, 4 x 9 1/3 In. 695.00
Bowl, Radiant Star, Rectangular, American Cut Glass Co., Large 950.00
Bowl, Russian, Ambassador, 8 In. 185.00
Bowl, Serving, Encore, Crimped Edge, Straus, 9 In. 285.00
Bowl, Star, Pedestal Foot, 5 1/2 x 8 In. 110.00
Box, Dresser, Hobstar Cover, Round, 5 In. 250.00
Box, Glove, Flowers, Leaves, Double Row Of Bulls-Eye Base, 11 In. 915.00
Box, Glove, Hobstar Design, 3 1/2 x 11 x 4 In. 1685.00
Bread Tray, 2 Large Hobstars, 11 1/2 x 7 1/2 In. 385.00
Bucket, Champagne, Diamond, Heart & Star, Silver Plated Liner, 9 1/4 x 10 In. 975.00
Butter, Cover, Hobstar Chain In Cluster, Brilliant 250.00
Candlestick, Colonial, Bergen, 9 1/2 In. 425.00
Candlestick, Lapidary Panels, Teardrop Stems, Rayed Base, 10 In., Pair 360.00
Carafe, Crisscross, Floral, Leaf Band, Star Base, 8 In. 105.00
Carafe, Drape, Straus, 6 1/4 x 7 In. 150.00
Carafe, Glenwood, Bergen, 8 1/2 x 4 1/2 In. 175.00
Celery, Concave Diamonds, Scalloped, French Stem, Star Cut Foot, 9 1/2 In. 550.00
Celery, Floral & Harvard, Boat Shape, 10 In. 95.00
Celery, Parisian Pattern, Dorflinger, 2 1/4 x 11 3/4 x 6 In. 310.00
Celery, Royal, Hunt, 11 1/2 x 5 1/2 In. 250.00
Celery, Strawberry-Diamond, 11 1/4 x 4 3/4 In. 75.00
Celery Vase, Full Hobstar Cut Base, Footed, 9 3/4 In. 985.00
Celery Vase, Miter Splits Divides Body Into Panels, Bucket Shape, Flared, 9 In. 325.00
Celery Vase, Rolled-In Sides, Scalloped Hobstar Foot, 6 1/2 x 11 3/4 In. 1980.00
Celery Vase, Strawberry-Diamond, Fans Alternating With Roundels, 7 3/4 In. 475.00
Champagne, Saucer, Double Prisms Cut Below Rim, 4 1/2 In., 6 Piece 850.00
Cheese Bell, Underplate, Ruby, Panel Cut & Knob Finial, 5 x 8 In. 550.00
Cheese Bell, Underplate, Spiked Argus Variant, 8 1/2 In. 450.00
Clock, Boudoir, Cut Geometrics & Leaves Allover, Tulip On Front, 6 1/4 In. 225.00
Compote, Carolyn, Ruffled Top, Petticoat Base, Hoare, 5 1/4 x 6 1/2 In. 145.00
Compote, Cover, Panels, Tooled Rim, Pontil, 8 In. 99.00
Compote, Panel, Band Of Russian, Clear Bottom, Teardrop Stem, Amber, 8 In. 2150.00
Compote, Rajah, Pitkin & Brooks, 8 x 6 1/2 In. 275.00
Compote, Shell, Satin Dolphin Stem, Lamp Shade Base, Bakewell, 1872, 9 In. 450.00
Cruet, Drape, Stopper, Rope Handle, Straus, 8 3/4 In. 230.00

Cruet, Pinwheels, Paneled Neck, Faceted Stopper 70.00
Decanter, Allover Baker's Gothic Pattern, Clark, 1900, 10 x 5 In. 320.00
Decanter, Allover Concave Hexagons, Blown Stopper, 12 In. 575.00
Decanter, Corn, Teardrop Stopper, Handle 695.00
Decanter, Du Barry, Double Gooseneck, Quaker City Glass Co., 12 In. 675.00
Decanter, Gooseneck, Cross Hatching, Faceted Stopper, 32 Point Base, 9 In. 348.00
Decanter, Green, Flute, Target Stopper, 1810-1820, 13 In., Pair 2500.00
Decanter, Hindoo, Hoare, 10 In. 475.00
Decanter, Hobstars, Fan & Notched Prism, 3 Ring Neck, Hobstar Base, 11 In. 635.00
Decanter, Lotus, 11 1/2 In. 425.00
Decanter, Orloff, Clark, 11 x 6 1/4 In. 1975.00
Decanter, Russian, Cut Stopper, 12 In. 1585.00
Decanter, Stars Inside Hexagons Inside Gothic Arches, Stopper, 13 In. 575.00
Decanter, Strawberry-Diamond & Fan, 3 Neck Rings, Stopper, 10 In. 625.00
Decanter, Strawberry-Diamond & Fan, Applied Loop Handle, Cut Stopper, 15 x 6 In. 415.00
Decanter, Triple Miter Trellis, Mt. Washington 950.00
Decanter Set, Argus, 4 Wines, New England Glass Co., 5 Piece 2995.00
Dish, Cheese, Allover Harvard, Hobstar Base, Underplate 750.00
Dish, Cheese, Cover, Royal, Dorflinger, 7 x 9 In. 745.00
Dish, Cut Quad Compartment, Triple-Notched Handle, J. Hoare, 9 In. 245.00
Dish, Gloria, Pitkin & Brooks, 7 In. 290.00
Dish, Hobstar, Center Handle, Heart Shape, 5 1/2 x 5 3/4 In. 165.00
Dish, Hobstar, Triangular, 6 In. 70.00
Dish, Ice Cream, Lotus, Egginton, 6 1/4 In. 150.00
Dish, Mayonnaise, Hobstar Centers, Oval, 7 x 5 In., 2 Piece 325.00
Dish, Olive, Allover Princess, Black, 7 x 1 1/2 In. 110.00
Dish, Olive, Royal, Hunt, 3 1/2 x 7 1/2 In. 95.00
Epergne, Thumbprint Edge, Crenelated Rim, Octagonal Base, 16 1/2 In. 484.00
Goblet, Argus, New England Glass Co., 5 3/4 In. 250.00
Goblet, Diamond, St. Louis 375.00
Ice Bucket, Russian, Persian Style, 24 Hobstar Base 275.00
Ice Cream Tray, Hoare, 18 x 10 1/2 In. 1320.00
Jar, Dresser, Allover Cut, Hunt, 3 1/2 x 4 In. 265.00
Jar, Dresser, Base Cut, Sterling Silver Cover, 4 x 5 In. 395.00
Jar, Dresser, Honeycomb, Silver Plate Art Nouveau Cover 45.00
Jar, Hobstars, Fans & Crosshatching, Cut Lid, 6 1/2 x 4 1/2 In. 450.00
Jar, Olive, Zipper, Hollow Mushroom Shaped Stopper, 8 In. 325.00
Jar, Pickle, Renaissance, Hollow Stopper, Dorflinger, 7 In. 325.00
Jug, Hobstar & Notched Prism Body, Triple Notched Handle, 8 In. 550.00
Jug, Rum, Hobstar Design, Triple Notched Strap Handle, 6 3/4 In. 875.00
Jug, Whiskey, Vertical Double Row Notched Prisms, Clear Tusks, 7 In. 350.00
Knife Rest, Honeycomb, Faceted Ball On Each End, 4 3/8 In. Diam. 150.00
Lamp, Harvard, Floral Design, Shade, 28 In. 2500.00
Lamp, Hobstar & Diamond, Mushroom Shade, Prisms, 20 1/2 In. 1840.00
Lamp, Strawberry Dome, Hobstar, Hoare, 17 3/4 In. 4950.00
Pitcher, Cane, Hobstars & Strawberry Diamond, Triple Notched Handle, 14 In. 1150.00
Pitcher, Champagne, Allover Cut, Brilliant, c.1890, 11 1/2 In. 625.00
Pitcher, Champagne, Chain Of Hobstars & Diamond Design, 14 In. 325.00
Pitcher, Champagne, Engadine, Dorflinger, 12 In. 595.00
Pitcher, Champagne, Hortensia, Mt. Washington, 12 In. 575.00
Pitcher, Chester, Full Hobstar Base, Cut Handle, Dorflinger, 12 In. 900.00
Pitcher, Diagonal Slashes, Horizontal Prism Steps, 7 1/2 x 7 In. 550.00
Pitcher, Feathered Stars & Other Cutting, Meriden Glass Co., 8 1/2 In. 395.00
Pitcher, Flashed Hobstar, Meriden, 13 1/4 In. 875.00
Pitcher, Greek Key, Meriden, 12 1/2 In. 2550.00
Pitcher, Hobstars, Triple Notched Handle, 7 3/4 In. 440.00
Pitcher, Lemonade, Ceska, 11 In. 125.00
Pitcher, Milk, Double Lozenge, Bull's-Eye Cut Handle, 6 3/4 In. 250.00
Pitcher, No. 41, Elmira, 8 In. 365.00
Pitcher, Pinwheel Diamond Front, 10 In. 100.00
Pitcher, Stylized Pinwheel Pattern, Triple Notched Handle, Libbey, 8 x 5 1/2 In. 385.00
Pitcher, Sunburst, Hobstar Base, 8 1/2 x 6 In. 295.00

Pitcher, Water, Cranberry To White, Applied Reeded Shell Handle, Wheeling, 8 In. 440.00
Pitcher, Wilmot, Bulbous, Quaker City, 7 3/4 In. . . . . .295.00 to 395.00
Plate, Seneca, Empire Glass Co., 7 In. 325.00
Plate, Star, Meriden, 7 In. 345.00
Plate, Strawberry-Diamond, Dorflinger, 7 In. 55.00
Punch Bowl, 32 Hobstars, Allover Cut, 1890-1900, 12 x 12 In. 1250.00
Punch Bowl, Half Spherical Form, Clark, 7 1/2 x 14 1/4 In. 352.00
Punch Bowl, Proto-Brilliant Pattern, 9 1/4 x 9 In. 1500.00
Punch Cup, Flute, 3 x 3 1/2 In. 75.00
Punch Cup, Greek Key, Meriden, 3 3/8 x 2 3/4 In. 450.00
Rose Bowl, Horizontal Leaves At Base, Vertical Leaves & Cosmos On Body, Clark 135.00
Rose Bowl, Mercede, Clark, 5 1/2 x 9 1/2 In. 1850.00
Salad Set, Alternating Diamonds, Crosscut Diamond, Hobstar Base, 12 In., 2 Piece 1175.00
Salt, Crosscut Diamond, Dorflinger, 1 3/4 x 3 1/2 In. 60.00
Shot Glass, Hobstar, Crosshatching 33.00
Spooner, Hobstars, Fans & Single Stars, 4 1/4 In. 70.00
Sugar, Drape, Triple Notched Handles, Straus, 5 x 7 In. 225.00
Sugar & Creamer, Acme, Footed, Hoare, 4 1/2 x 6 In. 475.00
Sugar & Creamer, Acme, Hoare 495.00
Sugar & Creamer, Arbutus Pattern, Clark, 3 In. 470.00
Sugar & Creamer, Hobstars & Diamond, Footed 325.00
Sugar & Creamer, Primrose Geometric, Petals At Base 350.00
Tankard, Hobstars, Cane & Diamond, 11 1/2 In. 525.00
Tankard, Oregon, Blackmer, 9 In. 175.00
Tankard, Pinwheels, Hobstars, 15 In. 1050.00
Tobacco Jar, Alternating Faceted Thumbprints, Star On Base, 9 x 6 In. 1150.00
Tray, Allover Strawberry-Diamond, Handles, 14 1/2 In. 450.00
Tray, Ellsmere, 12 In. 3000.00
Tray, Ice Cream, Allover Harvard, Canoe Shape, 14 In. 150.00
Tray, Ice Cream, Hobstar & Miter, Hoare, 14 1/2 x 8 In. 525.00
Tray, Ice Cream, Russian, 17 3/4 x 10 1/4 In. 690.00
Tray, Thumbprints, Vesicas, Scalloped, 16 Point Star Bottom, Round, 11 In. 155.00
Tumbler, Flute, 4 x 3 In. 80.00
Tumbler, Juice, Encore, Straus, 3 1/2 In. 45.00
Tumbler, Strawberry-Diamond & Roundels, Bakewell, 3 1/2 In., Pair 750.00
Vase, Alhambra, 20 Point Hobstar Base, Corset Shape, Meriden, 14 In. 1295.00
Vase, Allover Hobstars, Fans, Crosshatching & Cane, Step Cut Neck, 7 x 8 In. 490.00
Vase, Amethyst To Clear, 14 In. 115.00
Vase, Band Of Hobstars & Crosscuts, Engraved Leaves & Flowers, Hunt, 12 In. 410.00
Vase, Chain Of Hobstars, Corset Form, 16 In. 875.00
Vase, Chalice Shape, Teardrop Stem, Hobstar Base, 10 In. 310.00
Vase, Cranberry To Clear, Dorflinger, 10 In. 1350.00
Vase, Diamond, Brilliant, Tapering Cylindrical, 16 1/2 x 9 1/4 In. 490.00
Vase, Floral, Baluster Shape, 12 1/2 In. . . . . .77.00 to 150.00
Vase, Flower & Harvard, Sawtooth Rim, 24 Rays On Base, 16 1/4 In., Pair 450.00
Vase, Hobstars & Diamond, Cylinder, 12 In. 450.00
Vase, Hobstars, Square Foot, Hoare, 10 In. 215.00
Vase, Montrose, Green To Clear, Dorflinger, 8 In. 5250.00
Vase, Morning Glory, White Cut To Cobalt Blue, 14 In. 1350.00
Vase, Swirled Scrollwork, Gadroons, Flower Filled Cornucopia, Ormolu Rim, 15 In. 8050.00
Vase, Trumpet, Pluto, 24 Point Hobstar Base, Hoare, 10 In. 300.00
Water Set, Russian, Clear Buttons, Cut Handle, 11 In., 6 Piece 1950.00
Wine, Royal, 20 Point Hobstar Base, Dorflinger 55.00

CUT VELVET is a special type of art glass, made with two layers of blown glass, which shows a raised pattern. It usually had an acid finish or a texture like velvet. It was made by many glass factories during the late Victorian years.

Creamer, Diamond-Quilted, Pink, 5 1/2 In. 275.00
Lamp, Pale Blue Satin, Nutmeg Burner, 7 3/4 In. 550.00
Tumbler, Diamond-Quilted, Pink 195.00
Vase, Diamond-Quilted, Blue, 5 3/4 In. 600.00
Vase, Vertical Ribs, Pink, 8 3/4 In. 165.00

CYBIS porcelain is a twentieth-century product. Boleslaw Cybis came to the United States from Poland in 1939. He started making porcelains in Long Island, New York, in 1940. He moved to Trenton, New Jersey, in 1942 as one of the founders of Cordey China Co. and started his own Cybis Porcelains about 1950. The firm is still working. See also Cordey.

Figurine, Appaloosa Colt, No. 663	225.00
Figurine, Bear, No. 638, 6 In.	295.00
Figurine, Brown Bear, Walking, Dated 1968	175.00
Figurine, George Washington, Bisque, 10 In.	175.00
Figurine, Heidi, No. 432, 7 1/2 In. .... 188.00 to	295.00
Figurine, Madonna, With Bird, No. 2148, 11 In.	250.00
Figurine, Mushrooms, No. 521, 7 In.	195.00
Figurine, Owl On Branch, Marked, 4 1/2 In.	76.00
Figurine, Parakeet, Pair	950.00
Figurine, Rabbit	95.00
Figurine, Raccoon, On Tree Stump, No. 636, 7 1/2 x 9 In.	235.00
Figurine, Rapunzel, Lilac, No. 468L, 8 1/2 In.	650.00
Figurine, Turtle, Baron, No. 820	150.00
Figurine, Water Lily .... 99.00 to	160.00
Figurine, Wendy	175.00
Figurine, Wood Wren With Dogwood, No. 336, 5 1/2 In. .... 275.00 to	300.00

CZECHOSLOVAKIA is a popular term with collectors. The name, first used as a mark after the country was formed in 1918, appears on glass and porcelain and other decorative items. Although Czechoslovakia split into Slovakia and the Czech Republics on January 1, 1993, the name continues to be used in some trademarks.

CZECHOSLOVAKIA GLASS, Basket, Candy, Red, Black, Twisted Thorn Handle	185.00
Basket, Twist Handle, Blue, Yellow	175.00
Beaker, Cut Hunters Scene, Overlaid, 1930, 5 In.	195.00
Decanter, Amber, Ruby Stained, Wheel Cut Floral, 1920, 13 1/2 In.	200.00
Figurine, Alpine Boy, Glass, Multicolored, 1950, 6 In.	195.00
Figurine, Dentist, Glass, Multicolored, 1950, 8 1/2 In.	100.00
Figurine, Doctor, Multicolored, 1950, 7 1/2 In.	154.00
Figurine, Drummer, Glass, Multicolored, 1950, 5 1/2 In.	95.00
Figurine, Dutch Girl, With Tulips, Glass, Multicolored, 1950, 6 1/2 In.	230.00
Figurine, Dwarf Night Watchman, Multicolored, 1950, 5 1/2 In.	121.00
Figurine, Man, Working With Tool, Multicolored, 1950, 5 1/2 In.	215.00
Figurine, Trumpet Player, Multicolored, 1950, 8 1/2 In.	126.00
Figurine, Violin Player, Glass, Multicolored, 1950, 6 In.	95.00
Gravy Boat, Colonial Revival Style, Triple Ribbed Rim, Silver, 5 1/4 In., Pair	635.00
Lamp, Table, Blue Cut To Clear, Marble Base, Pair	330.00
Lamp, Table, Cranberry Cut To Clear Glass, Marble, 13 1/2 In.	143.00
Paperweight, Soldier, 1920, 3 1/2 In.	99.00
Perfume Bottle, Acid Etched Mark, Prism Stopper	80.00
Perfume Bottle, Amber, Art Deco, Pair	95.00
Perfume Bottle, Black Red Jeweled Base	650.00
Perfume Bottle, Blue, Signed	50.00
Perfume Bottle, Crystal, Silver Bands, Ball Stopper, 5 1/2 & 4 1/2 In., Pair	60.00
Perfume Bottle, Cut, Colored, Signed	155.00
Perfume Bottle, Long Stopper	95.00
Perfume Bottle, Purse, Filigree, Metal Spray, Rhinestone Flowers, 1 5/8 In.	100.00
Perfume Bottle, Purse, Jeweled Filigree, Blue, Dauber, 2 1/4 In.	75.00
Perfume Bottle, Woman, Plumed Hat Stopper, Blue Cut Glass Base	475.00
Perfume Lamp, Cut, Green	250.00
Pitcher, Brown Geometric Design, Ivory Ground, Art Deco, 7 x 6 In.	137.00
Powder Box, Yellow, 2 Dancing Harlequins On Cover, 4 1/2 In.	85.00
Toothpick, Gold, Green	75.00
Vase, Amber, Matte Iridescent Body, 1920, 12 In.	330.00
Vase, Amethyst, Handle, Orange, Yellow & Blue Mottling, 9 In.	125.00
Vase, Clear Speckles On White Ground, Black Base, Stamped, 10 In.	138.00
Vase, Glossy Rainbow Glass, Mottled, 10 1/4 In.	190.00

Vase, Jack-In-The-Pulpit, Orange, Signed, 7 In.	25.00
Vase, Orange, Black Rim, 1930, 7 1/2 In.	115.00
Vase, Orange, Cobalt Blue Rim, 1930, 9 In.	95.00
Vase, Orange, Enameled Star & Floral Pattern, 1930, 7 3/4 In.	85.00
Vase, Raised Rim, Red, Orange, Olive Green Design, Marked, 14 3/4 In.	517.00
Vase, Red, Black, Shoulder Handles, 8 1/4 In.	190.00
Vase, Red, Black Rim, 1930, 6 3/4 In.	95.00
Vase, Red, Hand Painted Black Leaves, Multicolored Jewels, 19 In.	250.00
Vase, Ruby Cut To Clear, 13 In.	143.00
Vase, Trumpet, Iridescent Amber, Blue Leaf Handles, Squatty, Signed	385.00
Vase, Wrought Iron Frame, Blue, Orange, Green, White, Marked, 9 In.	460.00
Vase, Yellow, Black Top Rim, 1930, 7 In.	85.00
Vase, Yellow, Dark Ruby Base, 1930, 8 1/2 In.	115.00
Wall Pocket, Bird On Branch, With Nest	48.00
CZECHOSLOVAKIA POTTERY, Basket, Rope Handle, Braided, Woven, Amphora, 9 1/2 x 7 In.	495.00
Bowl, Cover, Lobster, Large	95.00
Bowl, Underplate, Blue, Art Deco, 2 Piece	85.00
Box, Elephant, White Hi-Glaze, Blue, Orange, Gold, Dupoma, 7 In.	176.00
Centerpiece, Golden Crested, Porcelain, 6 1/4 In.	92.00
Creamer, Yellow Plaid	27.00
Cup & Saucer, Seminude Women Scene, Cobalt Blue, Demitasse	20.00
Dish, Elephant, White High Glaze, Standing, Dupoma, 8 In.	264.00
Ewer, Black Circle Face, White, Double Handles, Art Pottery, 5 In.	95.00
Ewer, White, Black Gloss Circle Face, Handles, 5 In.	95.00
Figurine, Ashtray, Western Man, Multicolored, 1950, 3 1/2 In.	88.00
Figurine, Boy, Walking In Snow, Multicolored, 1950, 6 In.	143.00
Flower Holder, Pottery Bird, 5 In.	25.00
Lamp, Bedside, Orange, Hand Painted Bird, Signed	145.00
Pitcher, Brown & Cream Mottled, Sea Horse Handle, 8 1/2 In.	225.00
Pitcher, Ditmar Urbach, 8 1/2 In.	225.00
Pitcher, Flowers, Yellow, Orange, Blue, Black Trim, 6 3/4 In.	60.00
Pitcher, Mrs. Gamp, 5 In.	85.00
Pitcher, Raised Fruit, Ditmar, 8 1/2 In.	150.00
Teapot, Art Deco Flowers	50.00
Teapot, Floral, Small	28.00
Vase, 2 Children Silhouette, Blue, Black Trim, 10 1/2 In.	70.00
Vase, Black Enamel Cupid, Floral, Yellow, 1930, 10 1/2 In.	110.00
Vase, Bopeep, 8 In.	60.00
Vase, White, 2 Gold Side Scrolls, 7 In.	85.00
Vase, White, Double Gold Side Scrolls, Art Pottery, 7 x 6 In.	85.00
Vase, Woman Nude Figure, Top Of White Base, Art Nouveau, 11 In.	285.00
Wall Pocket, Birds, Branches Design, Silver Overlay	135.00
Wall Pocket, Open Rose, 10 In.	125.00
Wall Pocket, Profile Of Woman's Face, c.1920	125.00 to 165.00

D'ARGENTAL is a mark used in France by the Compagnie des Cristalleries de St. Louis. The firm made multilayered, acid-cut cameo glass in the late nineteenth and twentieth centuries. D'Argental is the French name for the city of Munzthal, home of the glassworks. Later they made enameled etched glass.

Bowl, Field Of Tulips Design, Golden Yellow Overlaid In Forest Green, 1920	862.00
Burner, Perfume, Original Fittings	1400.00
Lamp, Table, Floral Design Shade, c.1920	8580.00
Vase, Amber Gold Ground, Brown, Red Raspberry, Leaf Design, 4 3/4 x 3 In.	330.00
Vase, Blue Flowers, Yellow Ground, Signed, 4 In.	385.00
Vase, Cabin In Woods, 18 In.	4500.00
Vase, Cherry Red Against Yellow Ground, Maple Leaves, 9 1/2 x 4 1/2 In.	770.00
Vase, Elongated Neck, Fruit, Leafage, Orange, Dark Green, Oviform, 12 In.	1150.00
Vase, Pink Roses On 2 Layers, 3 Acid Cuttings, Signed, 6 3/4 In.	880.00
Vase, Pink, Brown Fuchsia Blossoms, Yellow Amethysts, Brown Ground, 7 In.	605.00
Vase, Tan, Brown Flowers, Leaves, 2 5/8 In.	425.00
Vase, Trumpet Flowers, Red, Deep Yellow Ground, Signed, 13 1/2 In.	1100.00

DANIEL BOONE, a pre-Revolutionary War folk hero, was a surveyor, trapper, and frontiersman. A television series, which ran from 1964 to 1970, was based on his life and starred Fess Parker. All types of Daniel Boone memorabilia are collected.

Box, Novel Candy, Fighting Indians Picture, With Collector's Card, 1940s	60.00
Coloring Book, Daniel Boone Adventure, Lowe, 1965, 16 Pages, 11 x 8 In.	9.00
Coloring Book, Fess Parker On Cover, Color Chart On Top Border, 1951	91.00
Doll, Wilderness Scout, 24 Accessories, Marx, 11 In.	225.00
Mug, Harker	50.00
Whistle, Official Daniel Boone Fess Parker, Autolite, 1950s, Box, 6 In.	38.00

DAUM, a glassworks in Nancy, France, was started by Jean Daum in 1875. The company, now called *Cristalleries de Nancy*, is still working. The *Daum Nancy* mark has been used in many variations. The name of the city and the artist are usually both included.

Ashtray, Swirled, Crystal, Signed	395.00
Beverage Set, Pitcher, Yellow Mottled Glass, Orange, Brown Highlights, Signed, 8 In.	1595.00
Bowl, Dark Green Trees, Grasses, Gray Trees Ground, Cameo, Signed, 3 x 4 In.	1320.00
Bowl, Grapevine, Mottled Purple, Yellow, Trefoil Rim, Red, Blue, Green, 10 1/2 In.	3450.00
Bowl, Gray Green Branches, Fruit, Apricot & Frosted Ground, Cameo, 5 1/2 x 8 In.	1650.00
Bowl, Opaque Green, Butterscotch Highlights, France, 9 x 5 In.	440.00
Bowl, Orange, Imbedded Gold Leaf Pieces, Signed, 4 In.	350.00
Bowl, Orchid Plant Design, Allover Fern Pattern, Deep Purple, 1900, 13 3/4 In.	517.00
Bowl, Pate-De-Verre, Sheaves Of Wheat, Whiplash Design, Gray, Green, 1900, 8 In.	805.00
Bowl, Strawberry Vines, Floral Garland Rim, Circular, 1900, 8 3/4 In.	400.00
Bowl, Textured Leaves, Light Green, 7 1/2 In.	245.00
Box, Cover, Enamel Birds, Snow Mounded, Yellow, Tangerine, Silver Floral, 4 x 7 In.	2035.00
Box, Cover, Enameled Daisies, Yellow & Pink Ground, Cameo, Round, 2 x 3 In.	2090.00
Clock, Table, Wave Form Design, 8 In.	75.00
Cologne Bottle, Burgundy Orchids, Purple Ground, Ball Stopper, Cameo, 5 In.	2475.00
Goblet, Intaglio Cut Thistle Blossoms On Bowl, 5 1/2 In., 6 Piece	1020.00
Jigger, Cross Of Lorraine, Signed, 1906, 2 In.	400.00
Lamp, Gray Glass, Bright Orange, Yellow-Orange Shade, 1925, 31 In.	11500.00
Lamp, Hanging, Yellow, Signed, 8 In.	725.00
Lamp, Landscape, Leafy River, Mottled, Gray Glass, Yellow, 20 1/4 In.	10350.00
Lamp, Snowy Woodland Scene, 16 In.	14300.00
Lamp, Table, Conical Shape Shade, Spherical Base, Etched Glass, 18 In.	8050.00
Paperweight, Owl	90.00
Punch Bowl, Crossed Lily Sprig Border, Etched Ground, 1900, 15 1/2 In.	1035.00
Salt, Master, Etched Frosted, Cut Junko Leaf Design, Signed, 1 7/8 x 3 1/4 In.	545.00
Tea Set, Olympic, Enameled, 8 Piece	1000.00
Torchere, Wrought Iron, Gray Glass Shade, Maroon, Amber, 1925, 5 Ft. 6 In.	10925.00
Vase, Acid Textured Fluting, Flared Form, Purple Tinted, Signed, c.1925, 11 1/2 In.	920.00
Vase, Applied Angel Fish Design, Marked, 5 1/2 In.	160.00
Vase, Black Trees & Islands, Silhouetted, Multicolored Sky, Cameo, 6 1/4 In.	1375.00
Vase, Blossoms, Enameled Leaves, Gray Glass, Green, Yellow, Orange, 1900, 10 In.	3740.00
Vase, Brown Leaves & Branches, Art Deco Applied Beetles, Cameo, 13 In.	3025.00
Vase, Bud, Vine & Berry Design, Tangerine, Black Accents, Baluster, 1900, 6 1/4 In.	575.00
Vase, Daisies Above Leafage, Opalescent Gray Glass, Orange, Forest Green, 16 In.	6325.00
Vase, Dandelion, Pink, Green, Mottled, Opalescent, 1900, 4 3/4 In.	2300.00
Vase, Enameled With Flowering Nicotiana, Green Body, Yellow, 1900, 12 1/2 In.	4025.00
Vase, Enameled With Harebells, Milky White Glass, Blue, Green Base, Baluster, 9 In.	2990.00
Vase, Etched & Enamel Leaves & Berries, Signed, c.1905, 10 3/8 In.	2185.00
Vase, Etched Flowering Daisies, Martele Base, Signed, c.1905, 16 In.	6095.00
Vase, Etched Fruiting Olive Branches, Applied Olives, Signed, c.1900, 11 5/8 In.	2875.00
Vase, Etched Tall Sunflowers, Martele Ground, Signed, c.1900, 23 In.	7820.00
Vase, Etched, Gray Glass, Lime Green, Zigzags, Dots, 1925, 8 1/2 In.	5175.00
Vase, Etched, Gray Glass, Pale Salmon, Mottled, Black Speckles, 13 In.	3450.00
Vase, Flowering Poppies, Blue, White Interior, Cylindrical, 1900, 8 In.	6900.00
Vase, Gilded Thistles, Bronze Diamond Shape Base, Hourglass Shape, 5 In.	1500.00
Vase, Gilt Bronze, Chrysanthemums, Leaves, Gray Glass, Blue, 1900, 5 1/4 In.	3450.00

Vase, Landscape, Leafing Trees, Riverscape, Signed, c.1900, 4 3/4 In. 2415.00
Vase, Landscape, Leafy Trees Amidst Verdant Meadow, Gray Glass, Amber, 6 3/8 In. . . . 4025.00
Vase, Landscape, River Scene, Gray Glass, Tangerine, Charcoal Gray Ground, 19 In. 3450.00
Vase, Landscape, River Scene, Gray, Lemon Yellow, Salmon, Green Grass, 8 In. 2587.00
Vase, Landscape, Sailboats, Enamel, Mottled, Signed, 4 In. 1380.00
Vase, Landscape, Tall Conifers, Lemon-Yellow Glass, Opalescent White, 1900, 10 In. . . . 4140.00
Vase, Landscape, Woodland, Gray Glass, Orange, Cranberry, 1900, 14 3/4 In. 3737.00
Vase, Mottled Interior, Orange Pips & Leaves, Signed, 9 1/4 In. 4312.00
Vase, Mottled Interior, Random Bubbles, Geometric Bands, Signed, c.1925, 9 3/4 In. 3105.00
Vase, Mottled Yellow, White, Orange Ground, Purple Mottled Base, Red Flowers, 5 In. . . 1925.00
Vase, Pale Green Ground, 3 Chrysanthemums, Gold Trim, 5 1/2 In. 1870.00
Vase, Parrot Tulips, Leaves, Gray Glass, Mottled Salmon, Yellow, Orange, Green, 21 In. . 4312.00
Vase, Parrot Tulips, Leaves, Knopped Stem, Autumn Tones, Signed, 1905, 13 5/8 In. 2875.00
Vase, Scalloped Rim, Peach Ribbed Body, Signed, 5 1/2 In. 147.00
Vase, Scenic, Mottled Green, Sunset Red Orange, Trumpet, Brown, Black Layers, 11 In. . 1380.00
Vase, Stick, Enameled Red Berries, Gold To Purple Ground, Cameo, 9 In. 2090.00
Vase, Stick, Royal Blue Pencil Neck, Shaded To Light Blue Body, Signed, 6 In. 330.00
Vase, Thistle Pod, Thorny Stems, Red Striations, Enameled Burgundy Red, 4 1/2 In. 805.00
Vase, Towers, Royal Blue, Mottled To Frosted Chartreuse, Square, 28 1/2 In. 990.00
Vase, Trapezoidal Vessel, Cameo Etched Rows, Gold Dots, 7 1/2 In. 1090.00
Vase, Vase De Noel, Sprays Of Flowers, Small Gold Stars & Title, c.1900, 19 3/8 In. 4830.00
Vase, Verrerie Parlante, Fiery Peach Amber, Etched Iris Blossoms, 3 1/4 In. 375.00
Vase, White Mottled Glass, Orange Etched, Cameo, Baluster, 22 In. 2415.00
Vase, Wild Roses, Buds, Leaves, Cranberry, Emerald Green, 1900, 5 5/8 In. 3105.00
Vase, Yellow, Orange Ground, Applied Purple, Signed, 8 1/2 x 2 1/2 In. 1870.00

DAVENPORT pottery and porcelain were made at the Davenport factory in Longport, Staffordshire, England, from 1793 to 1887. Earthenwares, creamwares, porcelains, ironstone, and other ceramics were made. Most of the pieces are marked with a form of the word *Davenport.*

DAVENPORT
LONGPORT
STAFFORDSHIRE

Compote, Madras, Flow Blue, c.1841, 5 1/2 x 10 1/4 In. 345.00
Creamer, Child's, Rondeau 600.00
Cup Plate, Rondeau, 4 In. 140.00
Dessert Set, Botanical, 1840, 16 Piece 3737.00
Dish, Cover, Octagon Shape 270.00
Platter, Chinoiserie High Bridge, Blue & White, c.1810, 16 1/2 In. 430.00
Vase, Urn Shape, Cobalt Blue, Molded Floral, Gilt, Marked, 11 3/4 In. 235.00

DAVY CROCKETT, the American frontiersman, was born in 1786 and died in 1836. The historical character gained new fame in 1954 when the Walt Disney television show ran a series of episodes featuring Fess Parker as Davy Crockett. Coonskin caps and buckskins became popular and hundreds of different Davy Crockett items were made.

Bank, Bronze Color, 1950s 25.00
Bedspread, Scenes Of Alamo, Davy Figure, Single 225.00
Belt, Cowboy, Child's 15.00
Book, Little Golden Book, King Of The Wild Frontier, 1955 . . . . 14.00
Bowl, Indian Fighter, Milk Glass, Indians & Whites In Canoe, 5 In. 50.00
Box, Novel Candy, Davy Holding Musket, With Collector's Card, 1940s 60.00
Bracelet, Charm, Fess Parker, 7 Charms 95.00
Cap Gun, Cap, Plastic, Metal 55.00
Card Set, Color Photo, Orange Back, 1950s 260.00
Chair, Folding 150.00
Clock, Animated, Fighting Bear, Haddon 420.00
Cookie Jar, American Bisque 350.00
Cookie Jar, Boy, ABC 400.00
Cookie Jar, Brush . . . . 275.00 to 995.00
Cookie Jar, McCoy 500.00
Cup, Figural 60.00
Decal, 1950, Instruction Sheet, Unused, 3 Piece 15.00
Doll, Brown Wig, Blue Sleep Eyes, 7 In. 160.00
Flashlight . . . . 35.00 to 75.00

Guitar, Plywood, Bell Shape, Pick & Booklet, Box, 1955 . . . . 225.00
Gun, Clicker, Tin 65.00
Gun & Holster Set, Box 195.00
Hat, Coon Skin, Box 35.00
Jacket, Frontier Marshall, Copper Buttons 95.00
Knife, Pocket 50.00
Lamp, Figural, Copper 75.00
Lobby Card, Son Of Davy Crockett, Bill Elliot, 1941, 11 x 14 In. 30.00
Lunch Box, At Alamo, Adco, 1988 . . . . 110.00
Lunch Box, Canada 375.00
Lunch Box, Fess Parker 145.00
Lunch Box, Holtemp, 1955 . . . . 85.00
Moccasin Kit, Leather Soles, Box, Play-Learn 40.00
Mug, Brush . . . . .35.00 to 75.00
Neck Slide Set, Pearl 35.00
Pen, Ball-Point, 12 In. 12.00
Planter, Gold Trim, American Bisque . . . . .48.00 to 89.00
Play Set, Alamo, Directions, Marx 175.00
Pouch, Bisque 145.00
Puzzle, Whitman, 1955 . . . . 20.00
Record, Davy Crockett Ballad, Peter Pan Peanut Butter, Derby Foods Envelope 40.00
Record, Little Golden Records, Plastic, Yellow, 45 RPM 45.00
Rifle, Wooden, Metal 38.00
Ring, Character, Picture Of Davy Crockett, 1950s . . . . .5.00 to 25.00
Ring, Rifle, 1950s 75.00
Sheet Music, Farewell, Davy Crockett, Disney, 1954 . . . . 30.00
Tie Slide 30.00
Tumbler 10.00
Wristwatch, Davy Crockett On Face, Holding Gun, Green Plastic Case, Box . . . .285.00 to 350.00
Wristwatch, Davy Crockett On Face, Leatherette Band, 1950 . . . . 35.00

DE MORGAN art pottery was made in England by William De Morgan from the 1860s to 1907. He is best known for his luster-glazed Moorish-inspired pieces. The pottery used a variety of marks.

Tile, Blues, Brown & Green, Framed, 6 x 6 In., Pair 660.00

DE VEZ was a signature used on cameo glass after 1910. E. S. Monot founded the glass company near Paris in 1851. The company changed names many times. Mt. Joye, another glass by this factory, is listed in its own category.

Vase, 3 Stork-Like Birds, Standing In Water & Grass, Signed, 4 3/4 In. 650.00
Vase, Lake Scene, Blue Leaves Canopy, Mountains, Cameo, Signed, 8 In. 935.00
Vase, Sailboats & Rowboats On River, Leaves Top, Cameo, Signed, 6 In. 900.00
Vase, Sailboats On River, Trees, Grape Leaves At Top, 6 In. 900.00

DECOYS are carved or turned wooden copies of birds, fish, or animals. The decoy was placed in the water or propped on the shore to lure flying birds to the pond for hunters. Some decoys are handmade, some are commercial products. Today there is a group of artists making modern decoys for display, not for use in a pond.

Black & White Duck, 1930s 75.00
Black Duck, Hollow Carved, Smith Clinton Verity, c.1880 . . . . 220.00
Black Duck, Hollow, Glass Eyes, G. Crawford Hendrickson, 17 In. 375.00
Black Duck, M.M. Beam, 1930s 85.00
Black Duck, Original Paint, Balsa, Wooden Head, Glass Eyes, 14 1/2 In. 120.00
Black Duck, Wildfowler, 18 In. 200.00
Blue-Winged Teal Drake, 1930s 50.00
Blue-Winged Teal Drake, Mason-Type, Glass Eyes, Lead Weight, Dr. A.C. Wood 185.00
Blue-Winged Teal Drake, Ontario, c.1890 . . . . 350.00
Blue-Winged Teal Drake, Painted Eyes, Madison Mitchell Style, David Walker 90.00
Bluebill Drake, Painted Wood, 14 In. 70.00
Bluebill Hen, Painted Wood, Marked, Pirnie, 12 In. 430.00
Bufflehead Drake, Glass Eyes, Repainted, Flat Base, Flush Mounted Weight 55.00

Bufflehead Drake, Tack Eyes, Football Shape, Delbert Hudson, 1930s 2500.00
Canada Goose, Canvas Cover, Repainted, Bell Weight, John Lupton 110.00
Canada Goose, Hollow Carved, 3 Piece Construction, Weight, Joe King 1100.00
Canada Goose, Lloyd Johnson, Hollow, Carved Tail & Eyes, Original Paint 900.00
Canada Goose, Original Paint, Glass Eyes, Fishing Weight 365.00
Canada Goose, Original Paint, Signed, Stacy Bryanton 675.00
Canada Goose, Signed, Madison Mitchell, 1970 .... 450.00
Canvasback Hen, Glass Eyes, 1948, 17 In. 520.00
Canvasback Hen, Jim Currier 375.00
Canvasback Hen, Shot Scars, Havre De Grace, 15 In. 150.00
Duck, Carved, Painted, Vitreous Eyes, Steve & Lem Ward, 1967, 13 In. 750.00
Duck, No. 1 Glass Eye Grade, Mason, 16 1/2 In. 260.00
Fish, Louie Leech 150.00
Fish, Tin Fins, Wood, Red, Yellow, White, 6 In. 80.00
Goldeneye Drake, Glass Eyes, Center Board Keel, Herter, Pair 90.00
Goose, White Painted Breast, Dark Green Feathers, Signed, Ward, 1969, 24 In. 2185.00
Lapwing, New Hampshire, c.1910 .... 450.00
Mallard, Painted Eye, Mason, Pair 500.00
Mallard Drake, Glass Eyes, Signed Ken Coghill, 1986 .... 60.00
Merganser Hen, Mason Premier, 17 1/2 In. 170.00
Old-Squaw, A. Elmer Crowell, Circular Stamp, Miniature, 2 3/4 In. 430.00
Owl, Composition, Wire Legs, Glass Eyes, 18 In. 525.00
Pigeon, Carved, Painted, Brown, Gray, White, Black, Button Eyes, 20th Century, 17 In. . 145.00
Red-Breasted Merganser, Orran Hiltz, Nova Scotia, Pair 750.00
Red-Breasted Merganser Hen, Sam Toothacher, 16 1/4 In. 500.00
Redhead Drake, Glass Eyes, Repainted, Carved Bill 95.00
Redhead Drake, Replaced Brass Tack Eyes, 17 In. 55.00
Shelldrake, Tack Eyes, Repainted, Mason 145.00
Shore Bird, Carved, Painted, 13 In. 315.00
Shore Bird, Cork Body, Copper Bead, Legs & Feet, 12 1/2 x 17 1/2 In. 225.00
Shore Bird, Ephraim Hildreth 3800.00
Surf Scoter Drake, Carved Wing Tips, Hollow, Wendell Gilley, 20 In. 1725.00
Turtle, Ice Fishing, Weighted, 1930s................................. 150.00
Widgeon, James T. Holly, c.1900 .... 8800.00

DEDHAM Pottery was started in 1895. Chelsea Keramic Art Works was
established in 1872 in Chelsea, Massachusetts, by members of the
Robertson family. The factory closed in 1889 and was reorganized as
the Chelsea Pottery U.S. in 1891. The firm used the marks *CKAW* and
CPUS. It became the Dedham Pottery of Dedham, Massachusetts. The
factory closed in 1943. It was famous for its crackleware dishes, which
picture blue outlines of animals, flowers, and other natural motifs.

Ashtray, Raised Rabbits, Blue Ink Stamp, 1 x 6 1/4 In. 305.00
Bacon Rasher, Dolphin, Encircled By Waves, Blue Ink Stamp, 11 In. 1870.00
Bacon Rasher, Rabbit, White Ground, 9 x 6 In. 195.00
Bowl, Elephant, 3 x 8 In. 935.00
Bowl, Elephant, Blue Ink Stamp, 1932, 1 1/2 x 7 1/3 In. 770.00
Bowl, Rabbit, 2 1/2 x 5 1/2 In. 200.00
Bowl, Rabbit, Blue Ink Stamp, 3 In. 305.00
Bowl, Rabbit, Double Blue Ink Stamp, 2 x 5 1/2 In. 225.00
Bowl, Rabbit, Pinched In Sides, 1/2 x 4 1/2 In. 490.00
Bowl, Swan, 2 x 6 In. 525.00
Bowl, Whipped Cream, Rabbit, Blue Ink Stamp, 2 1/2 x 7 1/2 In. 357.00
Butter Pat, Petal Design, Cut Edge Form, Blue Ink Stamp, 3 1/4 In. 880.00
Candleholder, Elephant, Blue Ink Mark, 1 1/2 In., Pair 80.00
Charger, Rabbit, Blue Ink Stamp, 12 In. 660.00
Charger, Wolves & Owls, 12 In. 1725.00
Chocolate Pot, Rabbit, Blue Ink Stamp, 8 3/4 x 6 In. 1650.00
Creamer, Rabbit, Blue Ink Stamp, 3 1/2 In. 195.00
Cup & Saucer, Iris, Blue Ink Stamp, 2 1/4 In. 250.00
Cup & Saucer, Polar Bear, Blue Ink Stamp, 3 In. 345.00
Eggcup, Moth With Flower, Blue Ink Stamp, 3 In. 360.00
Eggcup, Rabbit, Blue Ink Stamp, 3 x 3 1/4 In. 220.00

Eggcup, Rabbit, Blue Ink Stamp, 4 1/4 x 4 1/2 In. 1540.00
Figurine, Flower Holder, Standing, Blue Ink Stamp, 1961 .... 1430.00
Mug, Child's, Blue Ink Stamp, 3 x 4 1/2 In. 2750.00
Nappy, Cover, Rabbit, 2 x 7 1/4 In. 470.00
Nappy, Rabbit, Flared Rim, 5 3/4 In. 195.00
Olive Dish, Rabbit, Flared Rim, 8 In. 715.00
Paperweight, Rabbit, Squatting, 3 1/2 x 1 1/2 In. 300.00
Paperweight, Turtle, Honeycomb Back, 3 1/2 x 2 1/4 In. ....460.00 to 575.00
Pitcher, Applied Leaves In Relief, Matte Sea Green, H.C. Robertson, CKAW, 6 x 5 In. ... 575.00
Pitcher, Mushroom, Blue Ink Stamp, 4 3/4 x 6 In. 1150.00
Pitcher, Night & Morning, 4 3/4 x 5 In. ....230.00 to 770.00
Pitcher, Oak Block, 6 In. 865.00
Plate, Azalea, 6 In. 110.00
Plate, Birds In Potted Orange Tree, Marked, 8 3/4 In. 465.00
Plate, Butterfly, Blue Ink Stamp, 9 In. 690.00
Plate, Crab, Blue Ink Stamp, 10 In. 550.00
Plate, Crab, Blue Ink Stamp, 1931, 7 1/2 In. 440.00
Plate, Crab, Rabbit Mark, 6 1/4 In. 165.00
Plate, Day Lily, Raised Lily Pads, Blue Ink Stamp, 6 In. 1430.00
Plate, Dolphin, 10 1/4 In. 250.00
Plate, Dolphin, Upside Down, Incised, CPUS, 6 1/4 In. 400.00
Plate, Duck, 9 In. 3375.00
Plate, Duck, 10 In. 400.00
Plate, Floral, 8 1/2 In. 175.00
Plate, Horsechestnut, 10 In. 275.00
Plate, Horsechestnut, Blue Ink Stamp, 8 In. 305.00
Plate, Horsechestnut, CPUS, 18 In. 345.00
Plate, Lady Reclining, Light Blue, 4 1/2 x 2 1/2 In. 545.00
Plate, Lobster, Blue Ink Stamp, 1931, 7 1/2 In. 440.00
Plate, Lobster, Blue Ink Stamp, 6 In. ....550.00 to 700.00
Plate, Lobster, Blue Ink Stamp, 8 1/4 In. 880.00
Plate, Lotus Leaf, Signed, 6 In., 6 Piece 715.00
Plate, Magnolia, 6 In. 200.00
Plate, Magnolia, 9 In. 235.00
Plate, Mushroom, 9 3/4 In. 1210.00
Plate, Mushroom, Rabbit Stamp, 8 In. 220.00
Plate, Owl, With Spaced Wing, 8 In. 1380.00
Plate, Polar Bear, Blue Ink Stamp, 10 In. 405.00
Plate, Polar Bear, Blue Ink Stamp, 1931, 8 1/8 In. 660.00
Plate, Pond Lily, Scenic Center, Impressed Rabbit, Blue Ink Stamp, 6 In. 975.00
Plate, Poppy, Rabbit Mark, 8 5/8 In. 715.00
Plate, Rabbit, 8 1/2 In. 125.00
Plate, Rabbit, 11 7/8 In. 140.00
Plate, Rabbit, Blue Ink Stamp, 7 1/2 In. 195.00
Plate, Raised Cherubs & Goats Border, Green Glaze, Blue Ink Stamp, 9 In. 430.00
Plate, Scotty Dog With Toad, 8 In. 1495.00
Plate, Scotty Dogs, 1931, 8 1/2 In. ....1495.00 to 1955.00
Plate, Snowtree, Blue Ink Stamp, 8 1/2 In. 495.00
Plate, Swan, Blue Ink Stamp, 8 1/2 In. 550.00
Plate, Turkey, 8 In. 325.00
Plate, Turkey, 10 In. ....230.00 to 260.00
Plate, Turkey, Blue Ink Stamp, 8 1/3 In. 360.00
Plate, Turtle, Blue Ink Stamp, 10 In. 1610.00
Salt & Pepper, Rabbit 360.00
Soup, Dish, Elephant & Baby Over Rabbit, Blue Ink Stamp, 8 1/2 In. 440.00
Spoon, Rabbit, Deep Blue, Arduous Form, Ladle Shaped, Diminutive Stamp, 4 In. 825.00
Stein, Rabbit, Floral Band Below Perimeter, Blue Ink Stamp, 4 x 5 1/4 In. ......425.00 to 470.00
Sugar & Creamer, Rabbit ....585.00 to 595.00
Tea Stand, Rabbit, Non-Scratch Surface, Round, Blue Ink Stamp, 6 In. 360.00
Tea Stand, Swan, Double Blue Band, Square Form, Blue Ink Stamp, 4 3/4 In. 600.00
Tile, Galleon In Full Sail, Ocher Glaze, Blue, White, Oak Frame, 1910, 8 In. 1495.00
Tile, Victorian Lady With Hat, Cobalt Blue, Low Art Tile Works, Chelsea, Mass, 1885 ... 145.00
Vase, Aqua Blue, H. Robertson, 5 1/2 In. 175.00

Vase, Blue Floral Design, Rabbit Mark, 7 1/4 In. 900.00
Vase, Dripping Flambe Glaze, Signed, Chelsea Keramic Art Works, 9 x 7 In. 770.00
Vase, Green, Gray, Yellow Glaze, Marked, 6 3/4 In. 375.00
Vase, Iris Blossoms, Cobalt Blue, 7 x 4 In. 1980.00
Vase, Pillow, Green, Brown, Footed, Chelsea Keramic Art Works, 1880, 6 In. 585.00
Vase, Sea Green Dripping Glaze, White Crackle, CKAW, 6 3/4 x 3 1/2 In. 1725.00

DEGENHART is the name used by collectors for the products of the
Crystal Art Glass Company of Cambridge, Ohio. John and Elizabeth
Degenhart started the glassworks in 1947. Quality paperweights and
other glass objects were made. John died in 1964 and his wife took
over management and production ideas. Over 145 colors of glass were
made. In 1978, after the death of Mrs. Degenhart, the molds were sold.
The D in a heart trademark was removed, so collectors can easily recognize the true Degenhart piece.

Dish, Hen On Nest Cover, Green, 3 In. 30.00
Owl, Brown 50.00
Plate, Cobalt Blue, 8 In. 75.00
Salt, Chicken, Amber 25.00
Toothpick, Shoe, Hobo 15.00

DEGUE is a signature acid-etched on pieces of French glass made in the
early 1900s. Cameo, mold blown, and smooth glass with contrasting
colored rims are the types most often found.

Vase, Art Deco, Geometric Design, Acid Etched, Mottled Pink Ground, 9 1/4 x 6 1/4 In. . 220.00
Vase, Brown Stylized Flowers, Spiked Leaves, Mottled Pink, Frosted, Cameo, 20 In. 2860.00
Vase, Orange, Amethyst Sunflowers, Leaves, White Ground, 8 3/4 In. 495.00
Vase, Pale Amethyst Ground, Green Floral, Leaf Design, Signed, 3 1/2 x 4 1/4 In. 165.00

DELATTE glass is a French cameo glass made by Andre Delatte. It was
first made in Nancy, France, in 1921. Lighting fixtures and opaque
glassware in imitation of Bohemian opaline were made. There were
many French cameo glass makers, so be sure to look in other appropriate categories.

Vase, Orange Mottled Ground, Purple Highlights, Art Deco, 16 1/2 In. 330.00

DELDARE, see Buffalo Pottery Deldare.

DELFT is a tin-glazed pottery that has been made since the seventeenth
century. It is decorated with blue on white or with colored decorations.
Most of the pieces sold today were made after 1891, and the name
Holland appears with the Delft factory marks. The word *delft* also
appears on pottery from other countries.

Bottle, Water, Figure & Floral Design, c.1760, 8 In. 1450.00
Bottle, Windmill Scene, Children, Ships, Blue, Ceramarte, Dutch, 12 In. 360.00
Bowl, Attached Strainer, Floral Design, 3 1/2 x 8 3/4 In. 465.00
Bowl, Floral, England, 1750 .... 225.00
Canister Set, Blue & White, Germany, 1920 .... 225.00
Charger, Adam & Eve, Bristol, c.1720, 11 3/4 In. 2500.00
Charger, Blue & White, England, 1720-1760, 12 In. 2100.00
Charger, Bowl Of Flowers, Yellow Rim, 12 5/8 In. 825.00
Charger, Chinese Landscape In Panels, Late 18th Century 300.00
Charger, Dutch, Blue & White, Johannes Van Duyn, c.1764, 13 1/2 In. 1200.00
Charger, Floral, Birds In Tree, Monogram Mark, 16 1/2 In. 715.00
Charger, Floral, Drill Ring For Hanger, 16 5/8 In. 770.00
Charger, Landscape, Floral Rim, 12 In. 190.00
Charger, Peasant Shepherds, Crossing River, Polychrome Border, 24 1/2 In. 800.00
Charger, Sign Of The Claw, L. Sanderus, c.1764, 11 1/4 In. 545.00
Charger, White Armorial, Embossed, Tylers' Crest, Blue, White, 1755, 13 1/2 In. 6900.00
Dish, Bird In Flight Perched Above Plants, Blue Edge, Polychrome, 12 In. 1955.00
Dish, Chinese Pheasant Perched On Tree, Blue, Green, Red, Yellow, Polychrome, 1740 .. 1725.00
Dish, Fazackerley Colors, England, c.1740-1760, 8 1/2 In. 450.00
Dish, Fishing Lady Amid River Landscape, Octagonal, England, c.1740, 8 3/4 In. 400.00
Drainer, Cheese, Netherlands, Early 18th Century, 4 In. 495.00

Figurine, Cow, Blue, White, Small 115.00
Figurine, Egg, Trailing Leaves, Dutch, 10 In. 80.00
Figurine, Hippopotamus, Polychrome, 19th Century, 4 1/2 In. 125.00
Figurine, Man, Polychrome, 19th Century, 7 In. 145.00
Jug, Pine, Willow Tree Design, Blossom Border, Flared Rim, Blue, White, 10 3/8 In. 690.00
Mug, Satyr, Blue & White, 19th Century, 4 In. 235.00
Plate, Blue & White, England, 1760, 8 3/4 In., Pair 365.00
Plate, Blue Center Scene, Marbleized Edge, Dutch, c.1760, 8 3/4 In. 395.00
Plate, Fazackerley Design, Iron Red, Yellow & Manganese, Polychrome, 9 In. 165.00
Plate, Fazackerley, Polychrome Colors, Liverpool, 1760, 8 7/8 In. 395.00
Plate, Tin-Glazed, Blue, White Scalloped Edge, 1760-1770, 8 3/4 In. 495.00
Plate, Woman, With Torch, Green Spatter Ground, 8 1/4 In. 410.00
Pot, Posset, Cover, White Blossoms, Scrolled Leaves, Loop Handles, 10 1/2 In. 2415.00
Pot, Trinket, Cover, 2 Handles, 5 1/4 In. 485.00
Punch Bowl, Ribbed, Floral, c.1740, 10 5/8 In., Pair 3200.00
Salt Cellar, Stylized Floral Sprig Center, Everted Rim, Blue Border, 3 In. 635.00
Strainer, Berry, c.1800, 9 In. 1400.00
Strainer Bowl, White Floral, 12 3/8 In. 520.00
Tankard, Dutch, Marked ARK, c.1775, 10 In. 450.00
Tankard, Garden Scene, 4 Figures Beneath Trellis, Diaper Border, Blue, White, 5 In. ... 750.00
Tankard, Landscape, Couple Strolling, Cottage, Hills, Blue, White, Cylindrical, 6 In. ... 5462.00
Tea Caddy, Floral, Scalloped Bottom Rim, Marked MVS, 1750, 5 7/8 In. .. 550.00
Tea Caddy, Gentleman, Standing, Holding Walking Stick, Blue, White, 1760, 4 1/8 In. .. 7475.00
Tile, Bearded Farmer Standing Behind Tree, Wheat Field, Scrollwork Border, 1760, 5 In.. 750.00
Tile, Boat Scene, Black, Caramel, Moored, Near Tan Land, Impressed Mark, 4 In. 275.00
Tile, Sailing Ship, Blue, White, 1750 .... 30.00
Tile, Urn With Flowers, Square, 10 1/2 In., 4 Piece 500.00
Tile, Various Animals, Square, 10 1/4 In., 4 Piece 500.00
Tile, Viking Ship, Birds & Water, Marked, 5 x 9 In. 385.00
Tobacco Jar, Indians, Brass Stepped Lid, 10 In. 1870.00
Vase, Amorous Couple Within Coastal Landscape, Blue & White, 20 In. 1035.00
Vase, Cover, Keyser & Pynaker, 9 1/4 In., Pair 575.00
Vase, Cover, Oriental Scene, Scroll Borders, Bobbin Knop, Dutch, 19 1/4 In. 980.00
Vase, Flower & Tree Design, Ribbed Body, Blue, White, 18th Century, 15 1/2 In. 290.00
Wall Pocket, Cornucopia, Cherub Head, 7 3/4 In. 1100.00

DENTAL cabinets, chairs, equipment, and other related items are listed
here. Other objects may be found in the Medical category.

Cabinet, Golden Oak, Marble, Brass Fittings, Swing Out Trays, 1880, 61 x 25 x 18 In. ... 4500.00
Cabinet, Oak, 156 Drawers 2000.00
Cabinet, Oak, Beveled Mirror, Brass Hardware 3500.00
Cabinet, Oak, Carved Top, Tall 3025.00
Cabinet, Ranson & Randolph, Quartersawn Oak 6900.00
Cabinet, Walnut, Graduated Drawers, Gray Marble Shelf, 1875-1880, 23 In. 1330.00
Chair, Oak, Black Leather Upholstery 2000.00

DENVER is part of the mark on an American art pottery. William Long
of Steubenville, Ohio, founded the Lonhuda Pottery Company in 1892.
In 1900 he moved to Denver, Colorado, and organized the Denver
China and Pottery Company. This pottery, which used the mark
Denver, worked until 1905 when Long moved to New Jersey and
founded the Clifton Pottery. Long also worked for Weller Pottery,
Roseville Pottery, and American Encaustic Tiling Company.

DENVER
C T &
P Co

Vase, Beige, 6 In. 220.00
Vase, Black, Blue, Green, 5 In. 150.00

DEPRESSION GLASS was an inexpensive glass manufactured in large
quantities during the 1920s and early 1930s. It was made in many colors and patterns by dozens of factories in the United States. The name
Depression glass is a modern one. For more descriptions, history, pictures, and prices of Depression glass, see the book *Kovels' Depression
Glass & American Dinnerware Price List*.

Adam, Ashtray, Green, 4 1/2 In. ....22.50 to 25.00

Adam, Ashtray, Pink, 4 1/2 In. 30.00
Adam, Bowl, Green, 4 3/4 In. 18.00
Adam, Bowl, Green, 5 3/4 In. ....37.50 to 46.00
Adam, Bowl, Pink, 4 3/4 In. 19.00
Adam, Cake Plate, Footed, Green, 10 In. ....30.00 to 73.00
Adam, Candy Jar, Cover, Pink ....85.00 to 105.00
Adam, Coaster, Green 20.00
Adam, Creamer, Green 17.50
Adam, Grill Plate, Green 18.00
Adam, Grill Plate, Pink 24.00
Adam, Plate, Pink, 6 In. 7.00
Adam, Saucer, Green ....4.50 to 7.00
Adam, Saucer, Pink 7.00
Adam, Sherbet, Pink 15.00
Adam, Sugar & Creamer, Green 39.00
Adam, Tumbler, Footed, Green, 4 1/2 In. 27.50
Adam, Tumbler, Green, Footed, 5 1/2 In. ....48.00 to 52.00
Adam, Tumbler, Pink, Footed, 4 1/2 In. ....28.00 to 30.00
Alice, Plate, White, 8 1/2 In. 10.00
American, Ashtray, Square, 2 7/8 In. 7.50
American, Goblet, Hexagonal Footed, 4 3/4 In. 7.00
American, Plate, Crystal, 9 1/2 In. 25.00
American Sweetheart, Bowl, Pink, 6 In. 15.00
American Sweetheart, Bowl, Pink, 9 In. ....45.00 to 50.00
American Sweetheart, Console, Red, 18 In. 2250.00
American Sweetheart, Creamer, Monax ....8.00 to 10.00
American Sweetheart, Cup & Saucer, Monax ....12.50 to 25.00
American Sweetheart, Cup & Saucer, Pink 20.00
American Sweetheart, Plate, Monax, 10 In. ....22.00 to 25.00
American Sweetheart, Plate, Monax, 9 In. 11.00
American Sweetheart, Plate, Pink, 6 In. 5.00
American Sweetheart, Plate, Pink, 8 In. 12.00
American Sweetheart, Saltshaker, Pink 225.00
American Sweetheart, Sherbet, Monax ....16.00 to 18.00
American Sweetheart, Sherbet, Pink 17.00
American Sweetheart, Sugar, Footed, Monax 7.00
American Sweetheart, Tumbler, Pink, 5 Oz., 3 1/2 In. 85.00
Apple Blossom pattern is listed here as Dogwood.
Aurora, Bowl, Cobalt Blue, 4 1/2 In. 47.50
Aurora, Creamer, Cobalt Blue 18.00
Aurora, Cup & Saucer, Cobalt Blue 20.00
Avocado, Bowl, Green, 7 1/2 In. 53.00
Avocado, Bowl, Handles, Green, Oval, 8 In. 30.00
Avocado, Cup, Pink 30.00
Avocado, Sherbet, Footed, Green 53.00
Avocado, Sugar & Creamer, Footed, Green 75.00
Avocado, Water Set, Green, 5 Piece 1950.00
Ballerina pattern is listed here as Cameo.
Banded Rib pattern is listed here as Coronation.
Baroque, Salt & Pepper, Blue 120.00
Basket pattern is listed here as No. 615.
Block pattern is listed here as Block Optic.
Block Optic, Bowl, Green, 4 1/4 In. 10.00
Block Optic, Bowl, Green, 5 1/4 In. 14.00
Block Optic, Bowl, Green, 8 1/2 In. 22.00
Block Optic, Cup & Saucer, Green 12.00
Block Optic, Cup, Curly Handle, Green 5.00
Block Optic, Cup, Green 5.50
Block Optic, Ice Bucket, Green 44.90
Block Optic, Pitcher 16.00
Block Optic, Pitcher, Water, Bulbous, Green, 68 Oz., 7 5/8 In. 70.00
Block Optic, Plate, 9 In. 20.00

Depression Glass,
Adam

Depression Glass,
Block Optic

Depression Glass,
Bubble

Block Optic, Plate, Green, 6 In. 2.50
Block Optic, Plate, Green, 8 In. ....4.00 to 5.00
Block Optic, Salt & Pepper, Footed, Green 38.00
Block Optic, Shaker, Footed, Green 15.00
Block Optic, Sherbet, Green, 3 1/4 In. 4.50
Block Optic, Sherbet, Pink, 4 3/4 In. 12.50
Block Optic, Sugar & Creamer, Footed, Green 25.00
Boopie, Sherbet 4.00
Bubble, Bowl, 4 1/2 In. 4.00
Bubble, Bowl, Blue, 4 In. 9.00
Bubble, Bowl, Blue, 5 1/4 In. 10.00
Bubble, Bowl, Red, 8 3/8 In. 35.00
Bubble, Bowl, White, 4 In. 4.00
Bubble, Creamer & Sugar, Blue 9.00
Bubble, Creamer, White 4.00
Bubble, Cup & Saucer, Blue 12.00
Bubble, Cup & Saucer, Red ....9.50 to 12.00
Bubble, Cup, Blue 2.25
Bubble, Plate, Blue, 6 3/4 In. ....2.00 to 5.00
Bubble, Plate, Blue, 9 3/4 In. ....5.25 to 6.00
Bubble, Plate, Green, 9 3/4 In. 20.00
Bubble, Plate, Red, 9 3/4 In. ....19.00 to 20.00
Bubble, Sugar & Creamer, Blue ....40.00 to 55.00
Bubble, Tumbler, Red, 12 Oz., 4 1/2 In. 10.50
Bubble, Water Set, Red, 1950s, 7 Piece 50.00
Bullseye pattern is listed here as Bubble.
Buttons & Bows pattern is listed here as Holiday.
Cabbage Rose pattern is listed here as Sharon.
Cameo, Bowl, Green, 7 1/2 In. 55.00
Cameo, Bowl, Green, 8 1/4 In. 35.00
Cameo, Bowl, Vegetable, Green, Oval, 10 In. ....30.00 to 35.00
Cameo, Cake Plate, Footed, Green, 10 In. ....19.00 to 22.00
Cameo, Candy Jar, Cover, Green ....65.00 to 70.00
Cameo, Compote, Green, 5 In. 32.00
Cameo, Creamer, Green 20.00
Cameo, Cup & Saucer, Green 17.00
Cameo, Cup & Saucer, Yellow ....7.00 to 10.00
Cameo, Cup, Fancy, Green 12.00
Cameo, Cup, Green 17.00
Cameo, Cup, Plain, Green 13.00
Cameo, Cup, Yellow ....6.00 to 8.00
Cameo, Decanter, Stopper, Green ....150.00 to 175.00
Cameo, Dish, Mayonnaise, Footed, Green ....27.50 to 35.00
Cameo, Goblet, Green, 6 In. ....55.00 to 68.00
Cameo, Grill Plate, Yellow 6.00
Cameo, Grill Plate, Yellow, 10 1/2 In. 4.50

Cameo, Pitcher, Green, 56 Oz., 8 12 In. 52.00
Cameo, Plate, 9 In. 3.00
Cameo, Plate, Green, 8 In. 10.00
Cameo, Plate, Yellow, 6 In. 2.50
Cameo, Plate, Yellow, 9 1/2 In. 10.00
Cameo, Platter, Green, Oval, 12 In. ....21.00 to 24.00
Cameo, Platter, Yellow, 12 In. 43.00
Cameo, Sherbet, Footed, Green, 3 1/8 In. ....13.00 to 14.00
Cameo, Sherbet, Footed, Green, 4 7/8 In. ....30.00 to 38.00
Cameo, Sherbet, Yellow 40.00
Cameo, Soup, Dish, Green, 9 In. 35.00
Cameo, Sugar 20.00
Cameo, Sugar & Creamer, Green 42.90
Cameo, Sugar, Green 19.90
Cameo, Tumbler, Footed, 5 In. 20.00
Cameo, Tumbler, Footed, Green, 3 3/4 In. 27.00
Cameo, Tumbler, Footed, Green, 5 In. ....29.00 to 30.00
Cameo, Tumbler, Green, 3 3/4 In. ....27.00 to 29.00
Cameo, Tumbler, Green, 5 In. 30.00
Candlewick pattern is listed in the Imperial Glass category.
Cape Cod, Tumbler, Footed, 5 Oz. 10.00
Caprice pattern is included in the Cambridge Glass category.
Caribbean, Bowl, Blue, 9 In. 65.00
Caribbean, Bowl, Liner, Blue, 12 1/2 In. 58.00
Caribbean, Candy, Cover, Blue 90.00
Caribbean, Celery, Blue 35.00
Caribbean, Cigarette Box, Tray, Blue 75.00
Caribbean, Cocktail Shaker, Blue 170.00
Caribbean, Cruet, Stopper, Blue 80.00
Caribbean, Cruet, Tray, Blue 195.00
Caribbean, Finger Bowl, Blue 32.00
Caribbean, Ice Bucket, Blue 125.00
Caribbean, Nappy, Handles, Blue, 6 In. 12.00
Caribbean, Pitcher, Blue, 8 1/4 In. 895.00
Caribbean, Plate, Blue, 6 In. 10.50
Caribbean, Plate, Blue, 8 12 In. 100.00
Caribbean, Relish, 5 Sections, Blue 85.00
Caribbean, Sugar & Creamer, Blue 45.00
Caribbean, Tumbler, Footed, Blue, 9 Oz. 41.00
Caribbean, Vase, Flared, Blue, 6 In. 48.00
Caribbean, Vase, Straight Side, Blue, 8 In. 68.00
Charm, Cup & Saucer, Azurite 3.00
Charm, Saucer, Azurite ....1.00 to 2.00
Charm, Sugar, Azurite 4.00
Cherry Blossom, Bowl, Green, 4 3/4 In. 18.00
Cherry Blossom, Bowl, Green, 8 1/2 In. 58.00
Cherry Blossom, Bowl, Pink, Handle, 9 In. 45.00
Cherry Blossom, Coaster, Green 15.00
Cherry Blossom, Creamer, Delphite 19.00
Cherry Blossom, Creamer, Pink 40.00
Cherry Blossom, Cup & Saucer, Delphite 23.00
Cherry Blossom, Cup & Saucer, Pink 24.00
Cherry Blossom, Cup, Delphite, Child's 30.00
Cherry Blossom, Cup, Pink 18.00
Cherry Blossom, Grill Plate, Green, 9 In. ....22.00 to 26.00
Cherry Blossom, Grill Plate, Pink, 9 In. ....24.00 to 25.00
Cherry Blossom, Mug, Green 185.00
Cherry Blossom, Pitcher, Delphite, 8 In. 90.00
Cherry Blossom, Plate, Green, 9 In. 18.00
Cherry Blossom, Platter, 2 Sections, Green, 13 In. ....30.00 to 45.00
Cherry Blossom, Saucer, Delphite, Child's 7.00
Cherry Blossom, Saucer, Green 6.00
Cherry Blossom, Sherbet, Green 18.00

Depression Glass,
Cherry Blossom

Depression Glass,
Cubist

Cherry Blossom, Sherbet, Pink	20.00
Cherry Blossom, Sugar & Creamer, Cover, Green	52.00
Cherry Blossom, Sugar, Cover, Pink	43.00
Cherry Blossom, Sugar, Pink	40.00
Cherry Blossom, Tray, Sandwich, Delphite, 10 1/2 In.	20.00
Cherry Blossom, Tray, Sandwich, Green	29.00
Cherry Blossom, Tumbler, Footed, Delphite, 4 1/2 In.	20.00
Chinex, Plate, Ivory With Decal, 6 1/4 In.	4.00
Chinex, Soup, Dish, Ivory With Decal	8.00
Christmas Candy, Plate, Sandwich, Teal Blue, 11 1/4 In.	40.00
Christmas Candy, Sugar, Footed, Teal Blue	20.00
Circle, Goblet, Green, 4 1/2 In	15.00
Colonial, Bowl, Green, 4 1/2 In.	15.00
Colonial, Bowl, Vegetable, Oval, Green, 10 In. . . . . .10.00 to 25.00
Colonial, Butter, Green	85.00
Colonial, Celery, Green	125.00
Colonial, Goblet, Green, 8 1/2 Oz., 5 3/4 In.	25.00
Colonial, Plate, Green, 10 In.	45.00
Colonial, Tumbler, Pink, 9 Oz., 4 In.	18.00
Columbia, Bowl, 8 1/2 In.	14.50
Columbia, Butter, Cover	16.50
Columbia, Cup & Saucer	15.00
Columbia, Sugar & Creamer, Cover	20.00
Coronation, Bowl, Ruby Red, 4 1/4 In.	4.50
Coronation, Bowl, Ruby Red, 6 1/2 In.	10.50
Coronation, Bowl, Ruby Red, 8 In.	14.00
Cube pattern is listed here as Cubist.	
Cubist, Bowl, Pink, 4 1/2 In.	5.50
Cubist, Butter, Cover, Pink	57.00
Cubist, Candy Jar, Cover, Green	25.00
Cubist, Pitcher, Water, Green, 45 Oz., 9 In.	25.00
Cubist, Plate, Green, 8 In.	12.00
Cubist, Salt & Pepper, Pink	25.00
Cubist, Saltshaker, Green	25.00
Cubist, Sugar & Creamer, Green, 2 5/8 In. . . . . .9.50 to 14.00
Cubist, Sugar, Green, 2 5/8 In.	6.50
Dancing Girl pattern is listed here as Cameo.	
Dewdrop, Snack Plate, Cup	35.00
Diamond Pattern is listed here as Miss America.	
Diana, Console, Pink, 11 In.	40.00
Diana, Creamer, Pink	20.00
Diana, Platter, Pink, Oval, 12 In.	30.00
Diana, Salt & Pepper, Crystal	20.00
Diana, Soup, Cream, Pink	25.00

Depression Glass,
Diana

Depression Glass,
Dogwood

Depression Glass,
Doric

Dogwood, Bowl, 8 1/2 In. 65.00
Dogwood, Bowl, Pink, 5 1/2 In. 6.00
Dogwood, Creamer, Thick, Pink 20.00
Dogwood, Pitcher, Design, Pink, 80 Oz., 8 In. .... 220.00 to 230.00
Dogwood, Plate, 8 In. 8.00
Dogwood, Plate, Pink, 6 In. 6.50
Dogwood, Plate, Pink, 8 In. 5.50
Dogwood, Plate, Pink, 9 1/4 In. 35.00
Dogwood, Sherbet, Pink, Low .... 30.00 to 35.00
Dogwood, Sugar & Creamer, Thick, Footed, Pink 35.00
Dogwood, Sugar & Creamer, Thin, Pink 32.00
Dogwood, Sugar, Thick, Pink 18.00
Dogwood, Sugar, Thin, Pink 15.00
Dogwood, Tumbler, Pink, 12 Oz., 5 In. 58.00
Doric, Bowl, Pink, 8 1/4 In. 17.00
Doric, Butter, Cover, Green 500.00
Doric, Cake Plate, Footed, Pink 22.00
Doric, Candy, Cover, Pink 39.00
Doric, Creamer, Pink 12.00
Doric, Cup & Saucer, Pink 12.00
Doric, Grill Plate, Pink 20.00
Doric, Sugar & Creamer, Cover, Pink 38.00
Doric, Sugar, Cover, Pink 13.00
Doric, Tray, Handle, Pink, 10 In. 16.00
Doric, Tumbler, Pink, 9 Oz., 4 1/2 In.. .... 66.00
Doric, Tumbler, Pink, 10 Oz., 4 In. 60.00
Doric & Pansy, Butter, Cover, Ultramarine 300.00
Doric & Pansy, Cup & Saucer, Ultramarine 21.00
Double Shield pattern is listed here as Mt. Pleasant.
Dutch Rose pattern is listed here as Rosemary.
Early American Rock Crystal pattern is listed here as Rock Crystal.
Fine Rib pattern is listed here as Homespun.
Fire-King, Bowl, Blue, 5 1/2 In. 12.00
Fire-King, Casserole, Knob Handle, Cover, Blue, 1 Qt. .... 11.00 to 15.00
Fire-King, Casserole, Knob Handle, Cover, Blue, 2 Qt. 15.00
Fire-King, Creamer, Fluerette, White 3.00
Fire-King, Cup & Saucer, Anchor, Ivory, St. Dennis 7.00
Fire-King, Cup & Saucer, Ivory, White, Blue Trim 8.50
Fire-King, Custard Cup, Blue, 5 Oz. 3.25
Fire-King, Jar, Grease, Tulip, White .... 20.00 to 25.00
Fire-King, Loaf Pan, Blue, 9 1/8 x 5 1/8 In. 18.00
Fire-King, Measuring Cup 40.00
Fire-King, Mixing Bowl Set, Apple, 4 Piece 100.00
Fire-King, Mixing Bowl Set, Red Dot, 4 Piece 100.00
Fire-King, Mixing Bowl, Blue Gazelle, Large 35.00

Depression Glass,
Doric & Pansy

Depression Glass,
Florentine No. I

Depression Glass,
Georgian

Fire-King, Percolator, Top, Blue, 2 1/8 In. 5.00
Fire-King, Pie Plate, Blue, 8 3/8 In. 7.00
Fire-King, Pie Plate, Blue, 9 In. . . . . .8.00 to 9.00
Fire-King, Pie Plate, Juice Saver, Blue 170.00
Fire-King, Skillet, Jadite 20.00
Floragold, Bowl, Ruffled, 5 1/2 In. 6.90
Floragold, Candlestick 20.00
Floragold, Candy, Cover, 6 3/4 In. 50.00
Floragold, Creamer 22.00
Floragold, Cup & Saucer 13.00
Floragold, Pitcher, 64 Oz. 40.00
Floragold, Plate, 13 1/2 In. 60.00
Floragold, Platter, Oval, 11 1/4 In. 22.00
Floragold, Sherbet 15.00
Floragold, Sugar, Cover 22.00
Floragold, Tumbler, Pink, 10 Oz., 4 3/4 In. 15.00
Floral, Bowl, Vegetable, Cover, Green, 8 In. 42.00
Floral, Lemonade Set, 6 Piece 425.00
Floral, Plate, Green, 9 In. 12.00
Floral, Tray, Closed Handles, Square, Pink, 6 In. 75.00
Florentine No. I, Grill Plate, Pink, 10 In. 18.00
Florentine No. I, Sugar & Creamer 50.00
Florentine No. 2, Ashtray, Yellow, 5 1/2 In. 35.00
Florentine No. 2, Bowl, Yellow, 8 In. 32.00
Florentine No. 2, Grill Plate, Green, 10 1/4 In. 12.00
Florentine No. 2, Pitcher, Cone-Footed, Green, 28 Oz., 7 1/2 In. 32.00
Florentine No. 2, Plate, Green, 8 1/2 In. 8.50
Flower & Leaf Band pattern is listed here as Indiana Custard.
Flower Rim pattern is listed here as Vitrock.
Forest Green, Cup & Saucer, Square 4.00
Forest Green, Plate, 6 3/4 In. 3.00
Forest Green, Plate, 8 3/8 In. 5.00
Fruits, Cup & Saucer, Green 13.50
Georgian, Bowl, Green, 4 1/2 In. 7.00
Georgian, Butter, Cover 70.00
Georgian, Creamer, Footed, Green, 4 In. 15.00
Georgian, Cup & Saucer, Green 12.00
Georgian, Sherbet, Footed, Green 11.00
Hairpin pattern is listed here as Newport.
Harp, Cake Stand, 9 In. 16.00
Harp, Coaster, Gold Trim 4.00
Hex Optic pattern is listed here as Hexagon Optic.
Hexagon Optic, Tumbler, Footed, Iridized, 7 In. 7.00
Hobnail pattern is listed in the Hobnail category.
Holiday, Butter, Cover, Pink 40.00

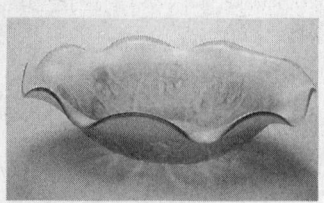

Depression Glass,
Iris

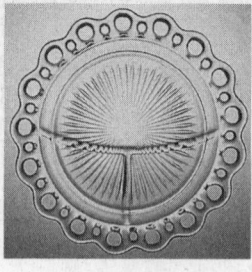

Depression Glass,
Lace Edge

Depression Glass,
Miss America

Holiday, Cup	7.00
Holiday, Pitcher, Milk, Pink, 16 Oz., 4 3/4 In.	48.00
Holiday, Plate, Pink, 9 In.	12.00
Holiday, Platter, Oval, Pink, 11 3/8 In.	16.00
Holiday, Soup, Dish, Pink, 7 3/4 In.	40.00
Homespun, Butter, Cover	35.00
Honeycomb pattern is listed here as Hexagon Optic.	
Horseshoe pattern is listed here as No. 612.	
Indiana Custard, Butter, Cover, Ivory	45.00
Iris, Bowl, 5 In.	110.00
Iris, Bowl, Ruffled, 9 1/2 In.	11.00
Iris, Candlestick	20.00
Iris, Candy Jar, Cover	150.00
Iris, Cup & Saucer, After Dinner	200.00
Iris, Goblet, 4 Oz.	20.00
Iris, Nut Set	75.00 to 90.00
Iris, Sherbet, Footed, 4 In.	22.50
Iris & Herringbone pattern is listed here as Iris.	
Jadite, Bowl, 4 1/2 In.	5.00
Jadite, Bowl, 5 7/8 In.	16.00
Jadite, Bowl, Batter, Green	20.00
Jadite, Cup	5.00
Jadite, Cup & Saucer	5.00
Jadite, Cup, Restaurant	5.00
Jadite, Mug	3.00 to 4.00
Jadite, Plate, 7 In.	5.00
Jadite, Shaving Mug, 8 Oz.	8.00
Jadite, Water Dispenser, 11 x 4 1/2 In.	325.00
Jane-Ray, Cup	3.00
Jane-Ray, Plate, 9 1/8 In.	7.00
Jane-Ray, Platter, 9 x 12 In.	9.00
Jane-Ray, Saucer	2.00
Jane-Ray, Soup, Dish, 8 In.	8.00
Jubilee, Bowl, Handles, Topaz, 9 In.	50.00
Jubilee, Candlestick, Pink, Pair	50.00
Jubilee, Cup & Saucer, Yellow	20.00
Jubilee, Plate, Sandwich, 2 Handles, Yellow, 11 In.	45.00
Jubilee, Plate, Yellow, 7 In.	12.00
Jubilee, Plate, Yellow, 8 3/4 In.	14.00
Jubilee, Sugar & Creamer, Yellow	40.00
Jubilee, Tumbler, Footed, Yellow, 10 Oz., 5 1/2 In.	35.00
Knife & Fork pattern is listed here as Colonial.	
Lace Edge, Bowl, 3-Footed, Pink, 10 1/2 In.	100.00
Lace Edge, Plate, Crystal, 7 1/4 In.	15.00
Lace Edge, Platter, 5 Sections, Pink, 12 3/4 In.	26.00
Lace Edge, Relish, 3 Sections, Pink, 7 1/2 In.	50.00

Laurel, Bowl, Vegetable, White Opalescent, 9 3/4 In. 14.00
Laurel, Cup, White Opalescent 4.00
Laurel, Saucer, White Opalescent 3.00
Lorain pattern is listed here as No. 615.
Louisa pattern is listed here as Floragold.
Lovebirds pattern is listed here as Georgian.
Madrid, Bowl, Amber, 9 In. 30.00
Madrid, Cake Plate, Amber, 11 1/4 In. 10.00
Madrid, Console, Amber, 11 In. 15.00
Madrid, Tumbler, Amber, 5 1/2 In. 20.00
Martha Washington pattern is included in the Cambridge Glass category.
Mayfair Open Rose, Bowl, Blue, 7 In. 50.00
Mayfair Open Rose, Bowl, Pink, 5 1/2 In. 20.00
Mayfair Open Rose, Cup, Pink ....15.00 to 18.00
Mayfair Open Rose, Decanter, Stopper, Pink, 32 Oz. 170.00
Mayfair Open Rose, Pitcher, Pink, 37 Oz., 6 In. 52.00
Mayfair Open Rose, Plate, Blue, 5 3/4 In. 25.00
Mayfair Open Rose, Plate, Blue, 8 1/2 In. 55.00
Mayfair Open Rose, Plate, Blue, 9 1/2 In. 75.00
Mayfair Open Rose, Plate, Pink, 8 1/2 In. 25.00
Mayfair Open Rose, Server, Sandwich, Green 38.00
Mayfair Open Rose, Sherbet, Footed, Blue, 4 3/4 In. 77.00
Mayfair Open Rose, Sherbet, Footed, Pink, 3 In. 16.00
Mayfair Open Rose, Soup, Cream, Pink, 5 In. 42.50
Miss America, Celery, Pink, 10 1/2 In. ....25.00 to 30.00
Miss America, Creamer, Footed 40.00
Miss America, Pitcher, 65 Oz., 8 In. 35.00
Moderntone, Creamer, Cobalt Blue 35.00
Moderntone, Cup & Saucer, Cobalt Blue ....15.00 to 16.00
Moderntone, Cup, Amethyst 9.00
Moderntone, Grill Plate, Cobalt Blue 8.00
Moderntone, Little Hostess Paarty, Tea Set, Pastels, 16 Piece 245.00
Moderntone, Little Hostess Party Set, Cup & Saucer, Gold 16.00
Moderntone, Little Hostess Party Set, Plate, Green 12.00
Moderntone, Plate, Cobalt Blue, 6 3/4 In. 5.00
Moderntone, Plate, Cobalt Blue, 7 3/4 In. 12.00
Moderntone, Plate, Cobalt Blue, 8 7/8 In. 17.50
Moderntone, Plate, Cobalt, 10 1/2 In. 50.00
Moderntone, Plate, Sherbet, Cobalt Blue, 5 7/8 In. 6.50
Moderntone, Salt & Pepper, Cobalt Blue ....30.00 to 37.50
Moderntone, Sherbet, Cobalt Blue ....10.00 to 20.00
Moderntone, Soup, Cream, Amethyst, 4 3/4 In. 15.00
Moderntone, Soup, Cream, Cobalt Blue, 4 3/4 In. 20.00
Moderntone, Sugar & Creamer, Amethyst 16.00
Moderntone, Sugar, Amethyst 7.00
Moderntone, Tumbler, Cobalt Blue, 9 Oz. 37.50
Moonstone, Bonbon, Heart Shape, 7 3/4 In. 13.00
Moonstone, Bowl, Cloverleaf 10.00
Moonstone, Bowl, Crimped, 9 1/2 In. 17.00
Moonstone, Bowl, Crimped, Handle, Blue, 6 1/2 In. 15.00
Moonstone, Candleholder, Pair 14.00
Moonstone, Plate, 8 In. 15.00
Moonstone, Relish, Divided, 7 3/4 In. 12.00
Moonstone, Sherbet, Footed ....5.00 to 7.00
Moonstone, Sugar, Cover, Footed 9.00
Moonstone, Vase, Bud, 5 1/2 In. 12.00
Mt. Vernon pattern is included in the Cambridge Glass category.
No. 601 pattern is listed here as Avocado.
No. 612, Plate, Salad, Yellow, 8 3/8 In. 7.00
No. 612, Plate, Sandwich, Yellow, 11 1/2 In. 15.00
No. 615, Bowl, Oval, Green, 9 3/4 In. 40.00
No. 615, Cup & Saucer, Yellow 20.00

Depression Glass,
No. 615

Depression Glass,
Moderntone

Depression Glass,
Patrician

No. 615, Cup, Green 11.00
No. 615, Plate, Green, 7 3/4 In. 10.00
No. 615, Tumbler, Footed, Green 20.00
No. 618, Bowl, Oval, 10 In. 12.00
No. 622 pattern is listed here as Pretzel.
Old Colony pattern is listed here as Lace Edge.
Old Florentine pattern is listed here as Florentine No. 1.
Open Lace pattern is listed here as Lace Edge.
Open Rose pattern is listed here as Mayfair Open Rose.
Oyster & Pearl, Bowl, Heart Shape, Handle, 5 1/4 In. 7.00
Oyster & Pearl, Plate, Sandwich, 13 1/2 In. 20.00
Parrot pattern is listed here as Sylvan.
Patrician, Bowl, Green, 8 1/2 In. 30.00
Patrician, Plate, Green, 9 In. 9.00
Patrician, Platter, Oval, Green, 11 1/2 In. 23.50
Patrician, Salt & Pepper, Green 60.00
Patrician, Sherbet, Footed, Amber 13.00
Patrician, Sherbet, Footed, Green 14.00
Peach Lustre, Bowl, 8 1/2 In. 7.00
Peach Lustre, Cup & Saucer 3.00
Peach Lustre, Plate, 9 1/8 In. 6.50
Peach Lustre, Sugar & Creamer, Footed 7.00
Petal Swirl pattern is listed here as Swirl.
Petalware, Bowl, Cremax, 5 3/4 In. 8.00
Petalware, Bowl, Pink, 5 3/4 In. 10.00
Petalware, Plate, Cremax, 9 In. 5.50
Petalware, Plate, Monax, 8 In. 10.00
Petalware, Plate, Monax, 9 In. 4.00
Petalware, Sherbet, Monax, Low Footed, 4 1/2 In. 8.00
Petalware, Soup, Cream, Pink 10.00
Pineapple & Floral pattern is listed here as No. 618.
Poinsettia pattern is listed here as Floral.
Poppy No. 1 pattern is listed here as Florentine No. 1.
Poppy No. 2 pattern is listed here as Florentine No. 2.
Pretty Polly Party Dishes, see also the related pattern Doric & Pansy.
Pretzel, Celery, 10 1/4 In. 1.50
Primrose, Cup, White, 8 Oz. 2.00
Primrose, Plate, White, 7 3/8 In. 2.50
Primrose, Saucer, White 1.50
Primrose, Snack Set, White, 8 Piece 20.00
Primrose, Sugar, Cover, Pink 5.00
Princess, Bowl, Octagonal, Pink, 9 In. ....35.00 to 40.00
Princess, Bowl, Oval, Green, 10 In. ....24.00 to 28.00
Princess, Bowl, Oval, Pink, 10 In. 30.00
Princess, Bowl, Pink, 4 1/2 In. 32.00
Princess, Butter, Cover, Green 80.00

Depression Glass,
Princess

Depression Glass,
Royal Ruby

Princess, Cake Stand, Green, 10 In.	25.00
Princess, Candy Dish, Cover, Green	60.00
Princess, Cookie Jar, Cover, Green	35.00
Princess, Cup, Green	8.00
Princess, Cup, Pink	12.00
Princess, Pitcher, Green, 60 Oz., 8 In.	55.00
Princess, Pitcher, Pink, 37 Oz., 8 In.	50.00
Princess, Pitcher, Pink, 60 Oz., 8 In.	55.00
Princess, Plate, Green, 9 1/2 In.	26.00
Princess, Plate, Pink, 8 In.	14.00
Princess, Plate, Pink, 9 1/2 In.	25.00
Princess, Platter, Closed Handles, Green, 12 In.	20.00
Princess, Sharon, Candy Dish, Cover, Pink	49.00
Princess, Sherbet, Footed, Topaz	35.00
Princess, Sugar, Cover, Green	42.00
Princess, Tumbler, Footed, Green, 10 Oz., 5 1/4 In.	30.00
Princess, Vase, Green, 8 In.	35.00
Princess, Vase, Pink, 8 In.	50.00
Princess Feather, Plate, 8 In.	65.00
Prismatic Line pattern is listed here as Queen Mary.	
Provincial pattern is listed here as Bubble.	
Queen Mary, Cup, Pink, Large	6.00
Radiance, Cup & Saucer, Ice Blue	25.90
Radiance, Salt & Pepper, Red	75.00
Rock Crystal, Goblet, Footed, 8 Oz.	9.00
Rock Crystal, Sundae, Footed, Low, 6 Oz.	6.00
Royal Lace, Bowl, Green, 10 In.	30.00
Royal Lace, Bowl, Oval, Cobalt Blue, 11 In.	70.00
Royal Lace, Bowl, Ruffled, 3-Footed, Green, 10 In.	65.00
Royal Lace, Bowl, Straight Edge, Cobalt Blue, 3-Footed, 10 In.	59.00
Royal Lace, Candlestick, Ruffled, Pink	25.00
Royal Lace, Cookie Jar, Cover, Green	85.00
Royal Lace, Creamer, Cobalt Blue	55.00
Royal Lace, Pitcher, Straight Sides, Green, 48 Oz.	115.00
Royal Lace, Pitcher, With Lip, Cobalt Blue, 8 1/2 In.	325.00
Royal Lace, Plate, Cobalt Blue, 8 1/2 In.	47.00
Royal Lace, Plate, Cobalt Blue, 9 7/8 In.	45.00
Royal Lace, Plate, Green, 9 7/8 In.	28.00
Royal Lace, Plate, Sherbet, Green, 6 In.	10.00
Royal Lace, Platter, Oval, Green, 13 In.	35.00 to 37.50
Royal Lace, Salt & Pepper, Pink	70.00
Royal Lace, Saltshaker, Green	65.00
Royal Lace, Saucer, Cobalt Blue	12.00 to 14.50
Royal Lace, Sherbet, Blue	42.50
Royal Lace, Sherbet, Cobalt Blue, Metal Holder, 5 Piece	125.00
Royal Lace, Soup, Cream, Cobalt Blue, 4 3/4 In.	45.00

Royal Lace, Soup, Cream, Green, 4 3/4 In. 32.00
Royal Lace, Sugar & Creamer, Cover, Green 95.00
Royal Lace, Sugar & Creamer, Green . . . . .30.00 to 45.00
Royal Lace, Sugar, Cobalt Blue 35.00
Royal Lace, Tumbler, Cobalt Blue, 5 Oz., 3 1/2 In. .35.00 to 55.00
Royal Lace, Tumbler, Cobalt Blue, 9 Oz., 4 1/8 In. .42.00 to 45.00
Royal Lace, Tumbler, Cobalt Blue, 12 Oz., 5 3/8 In. 100.00
Royal Ruby, Punch Bowl Set, 10 Piece 100.00
Royal Ruby, Tumbler, 9 Oz., 4 1/8 In. 5.00
Royal Ruby, Tumbler, 13 Oz., 5 3/8 In. 9.00
Royal Ruby, Water Set, 6 Piece 50.00
Sandwich Anchor Hocking, Pitcher, Ice Lip, 1/2 Gal. 90.00
Sandwich Anchor Hocking, Punch Bowl, 9 3/4 In. 60.00
Saxon pattern is listed here as Coronation.
Sharon, Bowl, Pink, 5 In. 12.00
Sharon, Butter, Green 125.00
Sharon, Cake Plate, Footed, Pink, 11 1/2 In. . . . . .25.00 to 36.50
Sharon, Cup & Saucer, Pink 225.00
Sharon, Sherbet, Pink . . . . .12.00 to 15.00
Sharon, Soup, Dish, Pink 50.00
Sharon, Sugar & Creamer, Cover, Pink 225.00
Sharon, Sugar, Pink 10.00
Sharon, Tumbler, Footed, Pink, 15 Oz., 6 1/2 In. 48.00
Spoke pattern is listed here as Patrician.
Swirl, Bowl, Pink, 9 In. 12.00
Swirl, Cup, Pink 4.00
Swirl, Plate, Sandwich, Ultramarine, 12 1/2 In. 40.00
Swirl, Saucer, Pink 1.00
Swirl, Sugar, Cover, Delphite 12.50
Swirl Fire-King, Bowl Set, Jadite, 6, 7, 8 & 9 In., 4 Piece 45.00
Swirl Fire-King, Cup, Ivory 2.50
Swirl Fire-King, Plate, Ivory, 9 1/8 In. 5.00
Swirl Fire-King, Plate, Jadite, 9 1/8 In. 11.00
Swirl Fire-King, Sugar, Cover, Jadite 49.00
Sylvan, Sugar, Green 30.00
Tea Room, Candlestick, Pink, Pair 50.00
Tea Room, Pitcher, Pink, 64 Oz. 135.00
Tea Room, Tumbler, Pink, 8 Oz., 4 3/16 In. 32.00
Tea Room, Water Set, Green, 48-Oz. Pitcher, 13 Piece 800.00
Tear Drop, Candy Dish, Heart Shape, 7 1/2 In. 23.50
Tear Drop, Sugar & Creamer 21.00
Tom & Jerry, Ivory, Red Snowflake, 9 Piece 60.00
Turquoise Blue, Bowl, 8 In. 8.00
Turquoise Blue, Bowl, Mixing, Tear Shape, 1 Qt. 18.00
Turquoise Blue, Egg Plate, Gold Trim, 9 3/4 In. 20.00
Turquoise Blue, Mug 4.00
Turquoise Blue, Plate, 10 In. 27.50
Turquoise Blue, Relish, 3 Sections, Oval, 11 1/8 In. 8.00
Vernon pattern is listed here as No. 616.
Vertical Ribbed pattern is listed here as Queen Mary.
Vitrock, Cup, White 4.00
Vitrock, Plate, White, 8 3/4 In. 5.00
Waffle pattern is listed here as Waterford.
Waterford, Tumbler, 10 Oz., 4 7/8 In. 10.00
Waterford, Tumbler, Footed, Pink, 10 Oz., 4 7/8 In. 20.00
Wild Rose pattern is listed here as Dogwood.
Windsor, Bowl, Boat Shape, Pink, 7 x 11 3/4 In. 15.00
Windsor, Candy, Cover Jar, Pink, 6 1/2 In. 25.00
Windsor, Chop Plate, 13 5/8 In. 32.00
Windsor, Compote, Pink 15.00
Windsor, Plate, Sandwich, Handle, Pink, 10 1/4 In. 18.00
Windsor, Sherbet, Footed, Pink 8.00

Windsor, Tumbler, Pink, 9 Oz., 4 In. 12.50
Windsor Diamond pattern is listed here as Windsor.

DERBY has been marked on porcelain made in the city of Derby, England, since about 1748. The original Derby factory closed in 1848, but others opened there and continued to produce quality porcelain. The Crown Derby mark began appearing on Derby wares in the 1770s.

Basket, 2 Birds On Branches Of Small Tree, Brown, Yellow, Green Center, 4 In. 1265.00
Dinner Service, Floral, Gilt Edge Rim, Lozenge Shape, 1825, 95 Piece 7877.00
Dish, Leaf, Blue, White, Floral Sprigs, Stem Handle, England, 1760, 8 3/4 In. 805.00
Dish, Peony, Sepia Center, Small Petals, Yellow Edge, Serrated Leaf Edge, 8 1/4 In. 3450.00
Figurine, Bacchus, Allegorical, Autumn, Rose, Turquoise Grape Clusters, 1760, 9 In. ... 575.00
Figurine, Minerva, Yellow Lines Iron Red Drapery, Gilt Scalework, 1765, 15 3/16 In. ... 805.00
Figurine, Shepherdess, 19th Century, 9 In. 242.00
Plate, Overlapping Serrated Leaves, Rose Veins, Chartreuse Edge, 7 1/8 In. 1840.00
Sweetmeat Stand, Shell Form, Floral Sprigs, Bands, Blue, White, 1765, 7 3/8 In. 1150.00
Tureen, Sauce, Pink Roses, Gilt Paw Feet, Lion Mask, Stand, 1815, 8 1/2 In., Pair 1400.00
Vase, Baluster Form, Double Looped Handles, Marked, 6 In. 70.00
Vase, Gilt Foliage, Birds & Insects On Base, Loop Handles, 1876, 6 1/4 In., Pair 725.00

DICK TRACY, the comic strip, started in 1931. Tracy was also the hero of movies from 1937 to 1947 and again in 1990, and starred in a radio series in the 1940s and a television series in the 1950s. Memorabilia from all these activities is collected.

Badge, Detective Club, With Leather Belt Pouch 65.00
Book, Big Little Book, Dick Tracy & Bicycle Gang 30.00
Book, Comic, No. 58, Harvey, 1952 .... 19.50
Book, Pop-Up, Capture Of Boris Arsoin, 1935 .... 325.00
Bracelet, Girl's Dick Tracy Club, Silvered Brass, Red Enamel Paint Shield, c.1939 ..... 135.00
Camera, Box 175.00
Camera, Candid, Black, Plastic, Graf 50mm Lens, 1940s 69.00
Car, Police 175.00
Car, Squad, Friction, Marx 180.00
Decoder, Red Cardboard, 1940s 50.00
Doll, Bonny Braids, Box, 13 In. 450.00
Game, Crime Stoppers Set, J. Henry Prod., On Card, 1940s 88.00
Game, Crime Stoppers, Ideal, 1963 .... 100.00
Game, Detective, 1937 .... 55.00
Game, Selchow & Righter, Board, 1961 .... 200.00
Game Board, 1933 .... 75.00
Gun, Junior Deputy, Plastic, Special 38 .... 295.00
Gun & Target Set, Marx 155.00
Handcuffs For Junior, Metal, J. Henry Prod., U.S., On Card, 1940s 80.00
Lunch Box 225.00
Model Kit, Space Coupe, Aurora 120.00
Paper Doll, Sparkle Plenty, Uncut 55.00
Pin, Detective, Celluloid 45.00
Pistol, Click, Steel, Decal, Marx, c.1935, 8 In. 300.00
Pistol, Water, Larami 45.00
Police Station, Tin, Box 35.00
Postcard, Teaching Boy About Crimes, Coca-Cola, 1942 .... 25.00
Puppet, Ideal, Box, 1961 .... 185.00
Puzzle, Box, 1940-1950 .... 25.00
Ring, Metal, Post Raisin Brand 48.00
Shotgun, Squad Gun, Power Jet, Mattel, 1961 .... 85.00
Soaky, Dapper Dick, Wearing Trench Coat, 1960s 69.00
Soaky, Dick Tracy Wearing Trench Coat, Fedora Hat, 1960s 80.00
Squad Car, Friction, Sparkling, Gun On Hood, Marx, Box, 11 In. 505.00
Suspenders, On Display Card 60.00
Thermos 45.00

Dionne Quintuplets, Doll, Dr. Dafoe, Madame Alexander, 13 In.;
Dionne Quintuplets, Doll, Babies, Swing, Madame Alexander, 7 In.

Toy, B.O. Plenty, Tin Lithograph, Battery Operated, 1940s 295.00
Wallet, 1961 .... 15.00
Wristwatch, Tracy On Face Holding Gun, Leather Band, New Haven, 1948 .... 110.00

DICKENS WARE pieces are listed in the Royal Doulton and Weller categories.

DINNERWARE, see American Dinnerware.

DIONNE QUINTUPLETS were born in Canada on May 28, 1934. The publicity about their birth and their special status as wards of the Canadian government made them famous throughout the world. Visitors could watch the girls play; reporters interviewed the girls and the staff. Thousands of special dolls and souvenirs were made picturing the quints at different ages. Emilie died in 1954, Marie in 1970. Yvonne, Annette, and Cecile still live in Canada.

Ashtray, Figural, Pastel-Colored Dresses, Sitting On Edge, 1930s, 2 x 3 In. 85.00
Book, Story Of Dionne Quintuplets, Authorized Edition, 1935 .... 35.00
Book, We're Two Years Old, 1936 .... 25.00
Bowl, Blue, 5 Girls 170.00
Cake Plate, With Server 300.00
Candy Box, Baby Ruth 190.00
Doll, Babies, Swing, Madame Alexander, 7 In. ....*Illus* 2300.00
Doll, Dr. Dafoe, Madame Alexander, 13 In. ....*Illus* 1600.00
Mug, 1 Girl 75.00
Paper Dolls, Palmolive Giveaway, Uncut, 1937 .... 155.00
Sign, Quaker Oats & Quints, 1935, 15 x 33 In. 125.00
Spoon Set, Figural, Silver, With Catalogs, 5 Piece 100.00

DISNEYANA is a collector's term. Walt Disney and his company introduced many comic characters to the world. Collectors search for examples of the work of the Disney Studios and the many commercial products modeled after his characters, including Mickey Mouse, Donald Duck, and recent films, like *Beauty and the Beast* and *The Little Mermaid.*

101 Dalmatians, Musical, Schmid 125.00
Ashtray, Mickey Mouse & Pluto, Figurine, Japan, 1930s 225.00
Ashtray, Mickey Mouse, Painted Wood, Wire Tail, 1930s, 5 3/4 In. 294.00
Bag, Pastry & Cake, Snow White, Rolling Pin, Paper, 1930s 18.00
Bag, Travel, Mickey Mouse Club 15.00
Bank, Donald Duck, Cash Register, Nickels, Dimes & Quarters 225.00

Bank, Donald Duck, Ceramic, 1950s	95.00
Bank, Donald Duck, Head	395.00
Bank, Donald Duck, With Blue Hat, Red Bow Tie, Large, 1971	31.00
Bank, Dumbo, Ceramic	35.00
Bank, Dumbo, Chalkware	55.00
Bank, Mickey Mouse, Figural, Red, 1991	25.00
Bank, Mickey Mouse, Head, Brechner	200.00
Bank, Mickey Mouse, Jar Of Honey, Beehive, Tin, 1932, 3 In.	1415.00
Bank, Mickey Mouse, Rubber, c.1920	230.00
Bank, Mickey Mouse, Still, Simulated Leather Over Metal, Zell Bros., 1930s, 4 x 3 In.	75.00
Bank, Pinocchio, Vinyl Head	28.00
Bank, Pluto, Pottery	34.00
Bank, Snow White On Wishing Well, Enesco	100.00
Beach Bag, Disney On Parade, Vinyl, 17 In.	38.00
Bell, Snow White, Treasure Craft	85.00
Billfold, Uncle Scrooge, Vinyl, 1950s	55.00
Block, Mickey Mouse & Pluto, Wood Lithograph, Japan, 1930s	150.00
Blotter, Mickey Mouse, Holding Spoon, Post-O-Wheat Cereal, 1930s, 3 1/2 x 6 In.	50.00
Book, Better Little Book, Donald Duck & Mystery Of Double X, 1949	10.00
Book, Better Little Book, Mickey Mouse In Treasure Hunt, 1941	30.00
Book, Big Little Book, Mickey Mouse Mail Pilot, Soft Cover, 1933	38.00
Book, Big Little Book, Snow White & Seven Dwarfs, 1938	35.00
Book, Little Golden Book, Donald Duck & The Mouseketeers, 1956	2.00
Book, Little Golden Book, Jiminy Cricket Fire Fighter, 1956	10.00
Book, Little Golden Book, Mickey Mouse's Picnic, 1950s	18.00
Book, Mickey Mouse & The Bat Bandit, Walt Disney, 1930, 3 x 4 In.	55.00
Book, Mickey Mouse Sails For Treasure Island, Walt Disney, 3 x 4 In.	55.00
Book, Mickey Mouse The Detective, Walt Disney, 1934, 3 1/4 x 4 In.	60.00
Book, Mickey Mouse Waddle, Blue Ribbon, 1934	1000.00
Book, Mickey Mouse, Blue Ribbon, Pop-Up, 1933, 8 3/4 x 7 3/4 In.	240.00
Book, Mickey Mouse, Cutout Doll, 1933	205.00
Book, Mickey Mouse, Silly Symphonies, Pop-Up, 1933	250.00
Book, Mickey Sees The U.S.A., Caroline D. Emerson, Illus., Disney Studio, 1944	7.00
Book, Minnie Mouse, Blue Ribbon, Pop-Up, 1933, 8 3/4 x 7 3/4 In.	55.00
Book, Minnie Mouse, Pop-Up, 1933	185.00
Book, Seven Dwarfs, Whitman, 1938, 20 Pages	125.00
Book, Snow White Music, Songs, Illustrations, 1955	40.00
Book, Story Of Grumpy, Whitman, 1938	80.00
Book, Walt Disney's Famous Seven Dwarfs, Whitman, 1938	65.00
Book, Walt Disney's Snow White & Seven Dwarfs, Whitman, 1957	15.00
Book, Winnie The Pooh, Now We Are Six, First Edition	100.00
Bottle, Donald Duck, Pictorial Bottle, 1951	15.00
Bowl, Fish, Fantasia, Green, 1940	395.00
Box, Mickey Mouse, Scuffy Shoe Polish, 1950s	22.00
Box, Pencil, Mickey Mouse Club, Hasbro, 1950s, 8 x 4 In.	30.00
Box, Pencil, Mickey Mouse, No. 2910, 2 Drawers, Tray, Czechoslovakia, 1930s	33.00
Box, Pencil, Mickey Mouse, Parade, Cardboard, Dixon, 1930s, 10 5/8 x 6 In.	81.00
Bracelet, Mickey Mouse, White Jacket, Red Pants, Metal Link Chain, 1960s	12.00
Brush, Grumpy & Dopey, Wooden, Metal, Hughes, 1938	85.00
Bulb, Donald & Pluto, Painted Glass, Japan, 1930s, 3 1/4 In.	45.00
Bulb, Mickey & Minnie Mouse, Painted Glass, Japan, 1930s, 3 1/4 In.	40.00
Candy Container, PEZ, Donald Duck	5.00 to 16.00
Candy Container, Snow White & Seven Dwarfs, Papier-Mache, Germany	425.00
Candy Container, Snow White, Composition, Painted, Germany, Pre-War, 5 1/2 In.	33.00
Cane, Dopey's Head, Metal Tip, 1939, 31 In.	125.00
Car, Mickey Dipsey, Tin, Windup, Linemar	495.00
Card, Birthday, Belated, Mickey Mouse, Walt Disney, 1934	35.00
Card, Birthday, Mickey Mouse, Figural, Hallmark, 1930s	65.00
Card, Birthday, Snow White, Doc & Dopey, Valentine & Sons, Ltd., 1930s	30.00
Card, Birthday, Snow White, Walt Disney, 1938	35.00
Card, Christmas, 101 Dalmatians Panorama, 1961 Calendar, 1960	85.00
Card, Greeting, Mickey Mouse, Enterprise	25.00
Card, Valentine, Seven Dwarfs, Mechanical, 1938	38.00

Card, Valentine, Sneezy, Mechanical, 1930s 22.00
Card, Valentine, Snow White, In Bed, Movable Heads Dwarfs, Mechanical, 1930s 30.00
Carpet Sweeper, Cinderella, Wooden Handle, Norstar Corp., 1940s 80.00
Cart, Minnie Mouse, Pluto, Celluloid, Tin, Windup, Japan, 1930s, 8 1/2 In. 1150.00
Case, Mini-Zippered, Tinker Bell, Vinyl, Blue, c.1970 .... 50.00
Cel, see Animation Art category.
Charm, Huey, Silver Color, Delta Mfg., On Card, 1/2 In. 35.00
Charm, Mickey Mouse, 1930s 85.00
Charm, Mickey Mouse, Brass Luster, Plastic, 1950s 8.00
Charm, Minnie Mouse, Sterling Silver, Cartier, 3/4 In. 50.00
Charm Set, Snow White & Seven Dwarfs, Celluloid, Japan, 1930s 185.00
Christmas Lights, Silly Symphony, Box, 1930s 225.00
Clock, Alarm, Bambi, Bayard 250.00
Clock, Alarm, Bugs Bunny, Talking, Battery Operated, Plastic, 1970s, 7 x 7 x 2 In. 53.00
Clock, Alarm, Mickey Mouse & Goofy, Bradley, Box 125.00
Clock, Alarm, Mickey Mouse, Avis 250.00
Clock, Alarm, Mickey Mouse, Bradley, Box 125.00
Clock, Alarm, Mickey Mouse, Talking, Box, Japan, 1970, 9 x 5 In. 135.00
Clock, Alarm, Mickey Mouse, Windup, Ingersoll, Box, 4 x 2 In. 2300.00
Clock, Alarm, Mickey Mouse, Windup, Phinney-Walker, W. Germany, 4 In. 75.00
Clock, Mickey Mouse, Radio, Walt Disney, Box, 1970, 12 x 5 x 5 In. 92.00
Coaster, Bulldog Insignia, 3rd Infantry, Cardboard, Walt Disney Prod., 1965, 4 In. 85.00
Colorforms, Robin Hood 29.00
Comic Book, Donald Duck & Pirates, Cheerios Premium, 1947, Pocket Size 24.00
Comic Book, Scamp, Dell, No. 703, 4 Color, Walt Disney 22.00
Comic Book, Scamp, Dell, No. 1204, 4 Color, Walt Disney 10.00
Comic Book, Snow White & Seven Dwarfs, Dell, 1944 .... 45.00
Cookie Cutter, Donald Duck, Figural, Plastic, Yellow, Grant Mfg. Co., 1953, 5 In. 20.00
Cookie Jar, Alice In Wonderland, 1940s, 9 In. 395.00
Cookie Jar, Donald Duck On Pumpkin, California Originals 225.00
Cookie Jar, Donald Duck, Hoan 40.00
Cookie Jar, Donald Duck, Walt Disney, Pair 90.00
Cookie Jar, Dumbo, Mouse Finial 135.00
Cookie Jar, Dumbo, Turnabout 220.00
Cookie Jar, Eyore 525.00
Cookie Jar, Genie, Sitting, Magic Lamp In Lap, Arms Folded, Treasure Craft 65.00
Cookie Jar, Mickey Mouse On Birthday Cake, Enesco 750.00
Cookie Jar, Mickey Mouse, Driving Car 350.00
Cookie Jar, Mickey Mouse, Leaning On Drum 275.00
Cookie Jar, Mickey Mouse, Treasure Craft, Box 65.00
Cookie Jar, Mickey Mouse, Turnabout, Leeds China ....220.00 to 450.00
Cookie Jar, Minnie Mouse, Treasure Craft, Box 65.00
Cookie Jar, Mrs. Potts, Beauty And The Beast, Treasure Craft 30.00
Cookie Jar, Pinocchio, Doranne Of California 225.00
Cookie Jar, Pinocchio, Hirsch 375.00
Cookie Jar, Pinocchio, Metlox ....225.00 to 325.00
Cookie Jar, Snow White, Treasure Craft, Box 45.00
Cookie Jar, Tigger, California Originals, 12 In. ....140.00 to 200.00
Cookie Jar, Winnie The Pooh, California Originals 110.00
Costume, Masquerade, Minnie Mouse, Box, 1950s 195.00
Costume, Mickey Mouse, Box, 1940s 100.00
Costume, Mickey Mouse, With Mask, Box, 1940s 195.00
Creamer, Figaro Handle, Climbing Over Pitcher Rim, Brayton Laguna Pottery 425.00
Cuff Links, Mickey Mouse, Box, 1934 .... 20.00
Cuff Links, Mickey Mouse, Box, 1940 .... 45.00
Cup & Saucer, Mickey Mouse, Artist, Gold Lusterware, Japan, 1930s 30.00
Cup & Saucer, Mickey Mouse, Tin 30.00
Cup & Saucer, Tinkerbell On Cup, Castle On Saucer, Gold Trim, 1960s ....30.00 to 35.00
Dexterity Puzzle, Mickey Mouse, Celluloid, 1930s, 7/8 In. ....*Illus* 165.00
Dish, Fantasia Flower, Dancing Mushrooms, Green, Vernon Kilns, 1940 .... 250.00
Display, Mickey Mouse Talking Watch, Mouth Moves, With His Voice 65.00
Doll, Alice In Wonderland, Bisque Head, Box, 14 In. 145.00
Doll, Donald Duck, Long Billed Cowboy, Knickerbocker, 1971, 10 In. 995.00

Disneyana, Dexterity Puzzle, Mickey Mouse,
Celluloid, 1930s, 7/8 In.

Disneyana, Doll, Snow White & Seven
Dwarfs, Knickerbocker, Box, 8 Piece

Doll, Donald Duck, Schuco	1450.00
Doll, Dopey, Original Clothes, 18 In.	550.00
Doll, Dwarf, Snow White & Seven Dwarfs, 1930s, Box, 9 In.	150.00
Doll, Ferdinand, Composition, Wire, Cloth Tail, Jointed Legs, Head, Ideal, 8 In.	55.00
Doll, Geppetto, Composition, Multi Products Co., 1940s, 5 1/2 In.	45.00
Doll, Mary Poppins, Open Close Eyes, Jointed, Effanbee, 1982, 12 In.	70.00
Doll, Mickey Mouse & Minnie Mouse, Charlotte Clark, 1940s, 22 In., Pair	295.00
Doll, Mickey Mouse & Minnie Mouse, Lenci, Pair	5500.00
Doll, Mickey Mouse, Stuffed Felt, Corduroy Hands, Feet, Pants, Gund, 1930s, 13 In.	168.00
Doll, Mickey Mouse, Stuffed Velvet, Metal Button Eyes, Dean's Rag Doll Co., 6 In.	50.00
Doll, Minnie Mouse, Cloth, Felt, Dean's Rag Doll Co., 4 1/2 In.	50.00
Doll, Minnie Mouse, Dean's Rag Doll, Metal Eyes, 1930s, 8 1/2 In.	585.00
Doll, Minnie Mouse, Original Clothes, Gund Mfg., 14 In.	800.00
Doll, Peter Pan, Composition, 7 In.	65.00
Doll, Pinocchio, Composition & Wood, Ideal, 20 In.	475.00
Doll, Pinocchio, Dakins, 1960s	22.00
Doll, Pinocchio, Open Close Eyes, Jointed, Effanbee, 1982, 12 In.	60.00
Doll, Pinocchio, Wood Jointed, Kreuger, 16 In.	385.00
Doll, Sleepy, Felt Clothes, Composition Face, Ideal, 1937, 12 In.	224.00
Doll, Snow White & Seven Dwarfs, Knickerbocker, Box, 8 Piece .... *Illus*	1800.00
Doll, Snow White, Composition, Hangtag, Canada	650.00
Doll, Snow White, Madame Alexander, 1982, 12 In.	80.00
Doll, Tinker Bell, Yellow Wig, Blue Open Eyes, Green Felt Suit, 1960, 12 In.	80.00
Doll, Winnie The Pooh, Steiff	650.00
Drum, Mickey Mouse Club, With Sticks, Chein	225.00
Ferdinand, Walt Disney All Star Parade, 1939, 4 3/4 In.	35.00
Figurine, Alice In Wonderland, Shaw Co., Label	900.00
Figurine, Bambi, Butterfly On Tail, Porcelain, Walt Disney Prod., Japan, 4 1/2 In.	85.00
Figurine, Cheshire Cat, Porcelain, Walt Disney Prod., Japan, 1960s, 4 In.	66.00
Figurine, Donald Duck, Bisque, 1930s, 4 1/2 In.	275.00
Figurine, Donald Duck, Bisque, Long Billed, 1930s, 1 3/4 In.	65.00
Figurine, Donald Duck, Chalkware, Airbrush, Glitter, 1930s	90.00
Figurine, Donald Duck, On Raft, Goebel	58.00
Figurine, Donald Duck, Porcelain, Japan, 1950s, 7 In.	33.00
Figurine, Donald Duck, Standing On Green Scooter, 3 1/4 In.	275.00
Figurine, Donald Duck, With Horn, Bisque, Japan, 1930s, 3 1/8 In.	35.00
Figurine, Dopey, Painted, England, 1930s, 4 In.	150.00
Figurine, Elephant, Fantasia, American Pottery, 1940s, 5 In.	145.00
Figurine, Ferdinand The Bull, Black, Rubber, Sieberling, 1937	65.00
Figurine, Figaro & Pinocchio, Walking, Pottery, American Pottery Co., 1940s	400.00
Figurine, Figaro, Disneykins, 1st Series, 1960s	22.00
Figurine, Grumpy, 1930s, 4 1/2 In.	40.00
Figurine, Ludwig Von Drake, Disneykins, Display Box, 1960s	90.00
Figurine, Mickey Mouse, Celluloid, Jointed Limbs, Japan, 1930s, 2 3/4 In.	110.00

Figurine, Mickey Mouse, Celluloid, String Tail, Jointed Arms, Japan, 1930, 4 In. 294.00
Figurine, Mickey Mouse, Painted Composition, 1930, 12 In. 236.00
Figurine, Mickey Mouse, Playing Saxophone, Bisque, Japan, 1930s, 3 1/2 In. 35.00
Figurine, Mickey Mouse, Waving Right Hand, Bisque, 1930s, 1 1/2 In. 75.00
Figurine, Minnie Mouse, American Pottery, Label, 1940s, 7 In. 250.00
Figurine, Minnie Mouse, Blue Bow, Broom, American Pottery, 1940s, 7 In. 265.00
Figurine, Minnie Mouse, Nurse's Kit, Bisque, 1930s, 3 In. 145.00
Figurine, Minnie Mouse, Playing Accordion, Bisque, Japan, 1930s, 3 1/2 In. 68.00
Figurine, Minnie Mouse, Playing Saxophone, Bisque, Japan, 1930s, 3 1/2 In. 68.00
Figurine, Minnie Mouse, Wooden, Fun-E-Flex, 7 In. 699.00
Figurine, Panchito, Three Caballeros, Pottery, Disney Shaw Pottery Co., 1945, Large . . . 200.00
Figurine, Pedro, Lady & The Tramp, Disneykins, 2nd Series, 1960s 75.00
Figurine, Pinocchio, Syroco, 1940s 75.00
Figurine, Pluto, By Guardhouse, Bisque, Japan, 1950s, 3 1/4 In. 220.00
Figurine, Pluto, Howling, Pottery, Brayton, 1940s 125.00
Figurine, Scrooge McDuck, With Cane, Hagen-Renaker, 1950s, 1 5/8 In. 350.00
Figurine, Snow White & Seven Dwarfs, Prewar, 6 & 7 In., 8 Piece 475.00
Figurine, Snow White, Porcelain, Japan, 6 In. 65.00
Figurine, Snow White, Schmid, 3 1/2 In. 15.00
Figurine, Three Caballeros, Donald Duck, Jiminy Cricket, American Pottery, 3 Piece 450.00
Figurine, Thumper, Open Eyes, Pottery, American Pottery, 1940s 90.00
Figurine, Thumper, Porcelain, American Pottery, 1950s, 4 In. 66.00
Figurine Set, Mickey Mouse, Donald Duck, Chalkware, 1940s, 3 To 4 In., 9 Piece 235.00
Fork & Spoon, Minnie Mouse, Silver Plated, c.1930, 4 1/4 In. 44.00
Fork & Spoon, Minnie On Fork, Mickey On Spoon, Silvercraft, 1940s, 2 Piece 29.00
Game, Bingo, Disney Characters 7.00
Game, Bowling, Donald Duck, Wooden Pins 95.00
Game, Disneyland Pinball, Tomy, Box, 1960s 175.00
Game, Donald Duck Bean Bag Party, Parker Brothers, 1939 . . . . 65.00
Game, Frontierland, Parker Brothers, Metal Pieces, Box, 1940s, 8 x 16 In. 50.00
Game, Mickey Mouse, Target, Guns, Darts, Target Stand, Marx, 18 x 18 In. 346.00
Game, Pinocchio, Parker Brothers. 125.00
Game, Pitfalls & Pinocchio, Marble, Box, Whitman 85.00
Game, Snow White & Seven Dwarfs, Board, Toothbrush, Johnson & Johnson, 1937 . . . . 50.00
Game, Snow White & Seven Dwarfs, Milton Bradley, 1937 . . . . 125.00
Game, Who's Afraid Of The Big Bad Wolf, Marx, 19 In. 231.00
Game, Who's Afraid Of The Big Bad Wolf, Three Little Pigs, Parker Brothers 145.00
Glass, Bashful, Libbey 45.00
Glass, Donald Duck, Blue, Bosco, 1930s, 3 1/2 In. 40.00
Glass, Donald Duck, Saying On Back, 1950s, 4 3/4 In. 20.00
Glass, Dopey, Snow White & Seven Dwarfs 20.00
Glass, Horace Horsecollar, Faded Red, 1930s, 4 3/4 In. 45.00
Glass, Mickey Mouse, Vertical Name, 1930s, 4 1/4 In. 40.00
Glass, Pinocchio, Red, Verse Back, 1940, 4 1/4 In. 24.00
Glass, Sleepy, Orange, Bosco, 1930s, 3 1/2 In. 35.00
Glass, Snow White, Black, 1930s, 3 1/23 In. 24.00
Glass, Three Little Pigs, 1930s 65.00
Glass Set, Snow White & Seven Dwarfs, Verse, 1930s, 4 3/4 In., 8 Piece 165.00
Greenhouse Kit, Fantasia Flowerland, With Tinkerbell, 1966 . . . . 15.00
Guitar, Mickey Mouse, Yellow, Black & Red, Plastic, 1950s, 15 In. 90.00
Handkerchief, Seven Dwarfs, 1930s, 9 x 9 In. 23.00
Hat, Conductor's, Disneyland 250.00
Hat, Mouseketeers, Official 25.00
Horn, Bicycle, Donald Duck, Battery Operated, Box 120.00
Invitation, Party, Pop-Up, Little Mermaid, Envelope 15.00
Kaleidoscope, Mickey Mouse, Tinplate, Linemar, 9 In. 230.00
Knife, Fork & Spoon, Pinocchio, Silver Plated, 1940s, 3 Piece 85.00
Label, Donald Duck Florida Blended Grapefruit & Orange Juice, 1942, 11 x 4 In. 65.00
Label, Dopey, Bread, Yellow, 1950s 7.00
Label, Jiminy Cricket, On Book, Says My Book, Official Conscience, 1939, 3 x 4 In. 12.00
Lamp, Donald Duck, With Cowboy Hat 175.00
Lamp, Mickey Mouse 35.00
Light Set, Walt Disney Silly Symphony, Box 335.00

Lighter, Mickey Mouse, Zippo 350.00
Lunch Box, Disney Express, Tin Lithograph, Original Tag 110.00
Lunch Box, Disney Fire Fighters, Dome Top 80.00
Lunch Box, Disney On Parade 28.00
Lunch Box, Disney School Bus, Dome Top, Metal, Aladdin, 1961-1973 .... .30.00 to 75.00
Lunch Box, Disneyland Monorail, Metal, Aladdin, 1960-1962 .... 175.00
Lunch Box, Ludwig Von Drake, Aladdin, 1962 .... 275.00
Lunch Box, Mickey Mouse & Donald Duck, 1954 .... 1250.00
Lunch Box, Mickey Mouse Club, Red 20.00
Lunch Box, Mickey Mouse, At Stop Crossing Guard & Bus, Yellow, Aladdin 54.00
Lunch Box, Pinocchio 55.00
Lunch Box, Robin Hood 25.00
Lunch Box, Snow White 45.00
Lunch Box, Snow White & Seven Dwarfs, 2 Handles, Tin, 1940s 2500.00
Lunch Pail, Cover, Pinocchio, Figaro, Coachman, Geppetto, Jiminy, Libbey, 6 1/2 In. ... 300.00
Lunch Pail, Cover, Pinocchio, Round, Libbey, 1940, 6 1/2 x 5 In. 250.00
Magazine, Disneyland Vacationland, Winter-Spring, 1969, 20 Pages 18.00
Marionette, Donald Duck, Beaver Hat, Cloth Label & Controls, Madame Alexander ... 850.00
Marionette, Donald Duck, Madame Alexander 650.00
Marionette, Minnie Mouse 110.00
Marionette, Minnie Mouse, Painted Gesso, Wire Arms, Legs, String Skirt, Japan, 7 In. ... 182.00
Marionette, Mouseketeer, Walt Disney, Box, 1945s, 15 In. 125.00
Mask, Geppetto, Paper, Gillette Blue Blade, 1939 .... 15.00
Match Safe, Three Little Pigs & Big Bad Wolf, Brass, 1930s, 1 5/8 x 1 1/8 In. 150.00
Melody Player, Rolls, Disneyland Characters, Chein 495.00
Mirror, Alice In Wonderland 650.00
Money Box, Mickey Mouse, Musical, Walt Disney, England, 6 In. 95.00
Mug, Aristocats, Gold Rim, Pottery, 1970s 30.00
Mug, Mickey Mouse Club, Glass, 1955 .... 12.00
Mug, Minnie Mouse, Silver Plated Metal, Gold Wash Interior, c.1930, 2 1/2 In. 60.00
Mug, Three Little Pigs, Patriot China, U.S., c.1930, 3 In. 55.00
Mug Set, Snow White, Doc, Grumpy & Dopey, Plastic, Soap Mfg., 1960s, 4 In., 4 Piece . 75.00
Night-Light, Mickey Mouse, Tin Lithograph, Mickey Decals, Soreng-Manegold, 7 In. .. 55.00
Nodder, Donald Duck, Celluloid, Metal Base, Japan, 1930s, 5 1/4 In. 302.00
Nodder, Mickey Mouse, Guitar, Metal Base, Lead Pendulum, 6 In. 1750.00
Nodder, Night-Light, Donald Duck, Vinyl 125.00
Nodder, Winnie The Pooh, Japan 95.00
Ornament, Christmas Tree, Mickey Mouse & Friends Around Christmas Tree 165.00
Pail, Donald Duck, Tin Lithograph, Playing Instruments, Ohio Art, 3 In. 164.00
Pail, Pig On Beach, Tin Lithograph, T. Cohn Inc., U.S., c.1940, 7 1/2 In. 55.00
Pail, Snow White, 2 Handles, Tin, 1940s 175.00
Pail, Treasure Island, Disney Characters, Tin Lithograph, Ohio Art, 1930s, 6 In. 385.00
Paint Set, Mickey Mouse, Tin Lithograph, England, c.1950, 9 3/4 x 6 3/4 In. 27.00
Paper Doll, Chitty Chitty Bang Bang, Whitman, Unpunched, 1968 .... 35.00
Paper Doll, Snow White & Seven Dwarfs, Box, 2 Uncut Sheets, Whitman, 1938 ...... 150.00
Pencil, Mickey Mouse, Automatic 115.00
Pencil Sharpener, Doc, Celluloid, Metal Sharpener, Japan, 1930s, 2 1/2 In. 350.00
Pencil Sharpener, Donald Duck, Bakelite, Decal, 1930s, 1 1/8 In. 45.00
Pencil Sharpener, Dopey, Bakelite, Decal, 1930s, 1 3/4 In. 110.00
Pencil Sharpener, Dumbo, Bakelite, Walt Disney, 1930, 1 3/4 In. 126.00
Pencil Sharpener, Mickey Mouse, Bakelite, 1930, 1 3/4 In. 94.00
Pencil Sharpener, Peter & Wolf, Bakelite, Circular 40.00
Pencil Sharpener, Pluto, Bakelite, 1940, 1 1/2 In. 68.00
Pencil Sharpener, Pluto, Bakelite, Circular 40.00
Pencil Sharpener, Snow White Playing A Mandolin, Bakelite, Decal, 1930s, 2 In. 135.00
Pencil Sharpener, Snow White, Figural, Mandolin, Bakelite, 1930s, 1 3/4 In. 135.00
Pencil Sharpener, Thumper, Catalin 40.00
Pepper Shaker, Mickey Mouse, Long Snout Mickey, Bisque, 1930, 3 In. 152.00
Photograph, Donald Duck, Happy Birthday Donald Duck, Blue Ground, 1984 .... 8.00
Pin, Bambi, Bakelite, Leather Ears 215.00
Pin, Mickey Mouse Globe Trotter, Eat Freihofer's Perfect Loaf, 1930s 65.00
Pin, Mickey Mouse, Figural, Cloisonne, Breier Mfg. Co., 1930s 125.00
Pin, Mickey Mouse, Globe Trotters Member, Eat Lucky Boy Bread, 1 1/4 In. 135.00

Pin, Mickey Mouse, Mickey Mouse Club, Blue Rim 8.00
Pin, Mickey Mouse, Orange Pants, Mickey Mouse Club, Red Lettering 88.00
Pin, Mickey Mouse, We Love Mickey Mouse 18.00
Pin, Minnie Mouse, Minnie As Astronaut 18.00
Pin, Minnie Mouse, Standing, Celluloid, Green, Black, Red, White, 1 1/4 In. 490.00
Pincushion, Tinkerbell 80.00
Pitcher, Cream, Donald Duck, Hat Spout, Leeds, 1940s, 6 1/2 In. 55.00
Pitcher, Dumbo, Leeds 95.00
Pitcher, Milk, Dumbo, Leeds, 6 In. 35.00
Place Mat, Various Characters, Laminated Plastic, 11 1/2 x 17 1/2 In., 4 Piece 33.00
Planter, Alice In Wonderland, Leeds 95.00
Planter, Bambi On Top, Figural, Green Base, Leeds, 1940s 45.00
Planter, Bambi, Figural, Green Base, Leeds, 1940s, 5 In. 45.00
Planter, Bambi, Standing Under Rim Of Tree Trunk, Leeds, 4 In. 35.00
Planter, Bambi, Tan, Pink & Green, Disney Productions, Leeds 40.00
Planter, Cinderella, Ball Dress, With Prince, Shaw Co. 300.00
Planter, Cinderella, Leeds, 1950s 45.00
Planter, Pluto, Gold Trim, Leeds 125.00
Planter, Thumper 42.00
Plaque, Minnie Mouse, Painted Masonite Board, 1930s, 11 1/4 In. 92.00
Plate, Disneyland, Castle, 1950s, 4 In. 40.00
Plate, Disneyland, Mickey Mouse, Tinkerbell, 4 In. 38.00
Postcard, Seven Dwarfs, Mine Entrance, France, 1930s 27.00
Poster, Alice In Wonderland, Standee, 1974 .... 100.00
Poster, Bambi, 1975, 1 Sheet 20.00
Poster, Chitty Chitty Bang Bang, Dick Van Dyke, 1969, 1 Sheet 30.00
Poster, Dumbo, Re-release, 1972, 1 Sheet 45.00
Poster, Old Yeller, Signed By Tommy Kirk, Re-release, 1974, 27 x 41 In. 35.00
Poster, Peter Pan, 1 Sheet 350.00
Poster, Snow White & The Seven Dwarfs, Re-release, 1975, 28 x 40 In. 30.00
Puppet, Hand, Dopey, Cloth Hat & Body, 1930s 125.00
Puppet, Hand, Wendy, From Peter Pan, Gund, 1960s 12.00
Puppet, Mickey & Minnie Mouse, Pressed-Card, 4 In. 75.00
Puppet, Mickey Mouse, Push-Up, Gabriel, 1977 .... 25.00
Puppet, Pinocchio, Hand, Gund, Box 75.00
Puppet, Push, Donald Duck, Kohner, Box, 1940s 275.00
Purse, Dopey On Front, Cloth, 1930s, 8 x 4 In. 40.00
Puzzle, Jiminy Cricket, Jaymar, Inlaid Wood, Box 65.00
Puzzle, Mickey Mouse & Bambi, Wood & Paper 30.00
Puzzle, Mickey Mouse & Minnie Mouse, 2 Nephews, Box, Whitman, 1967 .... 10.00
Puzzle, Mickey Mouse & Minnie Mouse, House Trailer, Jaymar, 1940s 40.00
Puzzle, Mickey Mouse Club, Jaymar, Box, 1950s 12.00
Puzzle Set, Dumbo, Ontex, Canada, Box, 1940s, 3 Piece 60.00
Radio, Mickey Mouse, 1960s 85.00
Radio, Mickey Mouse, Head 30.00
Record, Album, Book, Haunted Mansion, 33 1/3 RPM, 1969 .... 29.00
Record, Album, Three Cabelleros, Booklet, 1944 .... 55.00
Record, Mickey Mouse Newsreel Music, Mickey Mouse Club, 78 RPM, 1950s 12.00
Record, Songs From Annette, 33 1/3 RPM, Disney, 1960 .... 20.00
Record Album, Little Nipper Story, Pinocchio, RCA Victor, 78 RPM, Book, 1949 .... 50.00
Ring, Donald Duck, Living Toy, 1949 .... 67.00
Ring, Pinocchio, 3-D Magic, Weather Bird Shoes, Nose Grows, 1954 .... 15.00
Rug, Mary Poppins, WDP, Large 45.00
Rug, Mickey Mouse, Throwing Snow Ball At Donald, A. Smith, 42 x 26 1/2 In. 160.00
Ruler, Donald Duck, 1984 Commemorative, Clock & Adding Machine, Box 20.00
Salt & Pepper, Chilly Willy & Milly, Plastic, Pair 35.00
Salt & Pepper, Donald & Daisy, Japan, 1940s 65.00
Salt & Pepper, Donald Duck & Ludwig 135.00
Salt & Pepper, Donald Duck, Gold Trim, Leed's, 1940s 100.00
Salt & Pepper, Mickey Mouse & Minnie Mouse, Bisque, 1932, 2 3/4 In. ....300.00 to 400.00
Salt & Pepper, Mickey Mouse & Minnie Mouse, Leeds, 1940s, 3 In. 45.00
Salt & Pepper, Mickey Mouse & Minnie Mouse, On Bench 43.00
Salt & Pepper, Pinocchio, Japan 110.00

Salt & Pepper, Thumper	40.00
Sewing Set, Sleeping Beauty, Lithograph Cover, Transogram	75.00
Sheet Music, Der Fuehrer's Face, 1942	35.00
Sheet Music, Heigh-Ho, Snow White & Seven Dwarfs, 1937	17.00
Sheet Music, So This Is Love, Cinderella, France, 1958	16.00
Sheet Music, Whistle While You Work, Snow White & Seven Dwarfs, 1937	20.00
Sheet Music, World Owes Me A Living, Grasshopper & The Ants, 1934	45.00
Shovel, Pinocchio With Donkey Ears & Tail, Tin Lithograph, Italy, 1940s, 16 In.	85.00
Sleeping Bag, Snow White & Seven Dwarfs, Silk, Flannel Lining	25.00
Slippers, Pluto, Heavy Felt, c.1950, 7 In.	27.00
Soaky, Jiminy Cricket, W.D. Prod., 1960s, 7 In.	24.00
Soap, Dopey, Storybook, Walt Disney Ent.	60.00
Soap, Elmer Elephant, Figural, Lightfoot-Schultz Co., 1930s	25.00
Soap, Mickey Mouse, Box, 5 In.	345.00
Soap, Pluto Box, England, 1930s	195.00
Soap, Snow White, Ben Rickert, Inc., Box, 1980, 5 In.	45.00
Soldier Set, Gun, Metal, Wood Handle, Boston, 1930s, 18 1/4 x 8 1/2 In.	533.00
Spoon, Disneyland, Castle Top, Sterling Silver, 1970s, 4 In.	10.00
Spoon, Tinkerbell At Top, Enameled Shield Of Castle, Sterling Silver, 1960s, 3 5/8 In. ..	25.00
Spoon, Walt Disney World, Sterling Silver, Enameled Castle Shield, 1970s, 4 1/2 In.	10.00
Spoon Holder, Mickey Mouse	450.00
Spoon Rest, Mickey Mouse	15.00
Stickpin, Mickey Mouse, 1950s	65.00
Store Display, Mickey Mouse, Papier-Mache, 1930s, 16 In.	1600.00
String Holder, Mickey Mouse, Tin Lithograph, Decals, Soreng-Manegold, 4 In.	138.00
Suspenders, Donald Duck, Display Card, Detachable Puzzle, Metal Clips, Elastic	75.00
Tea Set, Mickey Mouse, Box, Japan, 1935	350.00
Tea Set, Mickey Mouse, Tin, Chein, 5 Piece	35.00
Tea Set, Snow White & Seven Dwarfs, 1937, 16 Piece	595.00
Teapot, Donald Duck, Wade	550.00
Telephone, Mickey Mouse, Tin, With Cardboard Figure, Walt Disney Studio, 5 In.	711.00
Telephone, Mickey Mouse, Western Electric, 1976	175.00
Telephone & Lamp, Mickey Mouse, 1970s	125.00
Thermometer, Goofy, Standing, Brass, 1940s, 6 In.	75.00
Thermos, Disneyland, 1959	25.00
Thermos, Mickey Mouse Club, 1962	20.00
Tie Rack, Mickey Mouse, Wooden, 1932, 9 1/2 In.	225.00
Tin, Mickey Mouse, Scuffy Shoe Polish, Box, 1950s	22.00
Toothbrush Holder, Donald Duck, Bisque, Japan, 1930s, 5 1/4 In.	297.00
Toothbrush Holder, Donald Duck, For Cup, Plaque, Porcelain, Evan K. Shaw, 1950s ..	445.00
Toothbrush Holder, Donald Duck, Long Billed, Bisque	400.00
Toothbrush Holder, Dopey, Maw, England, 1938	275.00
Toothbrush Holder, Mickey Mouse & Minnie Mouse, 4 1/2 In. ....290.00 to 325.00
Toothbrush Holder, Mickey Mouse & Minnie Mouse, Donald Duck	395.00
Toothbrush Holder, Mickey Mouse & Pluto, Bisque, Japan, 1930s, 4 1/2 In. .....220.00 to 295.00
Toothbrush Holder, Mickey Mouse, 1950s, Japan	95.00
Toothbrush Holder, Mickey Mouse, Bisque, Japan, 1930s, 5 In.	165.00
Toothbrush Holder, Mickey Mouse, With Toothbrush, Addis, England, Box	145.00
Toothbrush Holder, Three Little Pigs, Bisque, Japan, 1930s, 3 3/4 In. ....50.00 to 61.00
Toothbrush Holder, Three Little Pigs, Plaque, Evan K. Shaw, Porcelain, 1950s	445.00
Toothpick, Mickey Mouse, Japan	95.00
Toy, Cinderella, Dancing With Prince, Windup, Plastic, Irwin, Box	195.00
Toy, Disneykins, Hand-Painted Cartoon Characters, Display Box, Marx, 34 Piece	495.00
Toy, Donald Duck & Pluto, Car, Marx	140.00
Toy, Donald Duck & Pluto, Handcar, Lionel, No Tracks, 1934	850.00
Toy, Donald Duck, Binoculars, Squeak, Dell, 10 In.	90.00
Toy, Donald Duck, Fun Cycle, String Toy	95.00
Toy, Donald Duck, Handcar, Pressed Steel, Circle Track, Lionel, 1930s, 10 In.	460.00
Toy, Donald Duck, Jack-In-The-Box, Paper Lithograph, Dovetailed Box, Handmade	750.00
Toy, Donald Duck, Jack-In-The-Box, Spear, England, c.1940	190.00
Toy, Donald Duck, Quacking, Windup, Schuco	1200.00
Toy, Donald Duck, Schuco, Box, 6 In.	550.00
Toy, Donald Duck, Squeeze, Swivel Head, Sun Rubber Co., c.1950, 7 3/4 In.	80.00

Toy, Donald Duck, Sweeper, Wood & Tin, 1940 .... 98.00
Toy, Donald Duck, Tricycle, Linemar, Box, Marx 495.00
Toy, Donald Duck, Walker, Windup, Celluloid, Tin Feet, Japan 650.00
Toy, Donald Duck, Whirlybird, Box, 1958 .... 45.00
Toy, Donald Duck, With Cart, Fisher-Price 175.00
Toy, Donald Duck, Xylophone, Fisher-Price 180.00
Toy, Donald Duck, Xylophone, Tin, Box 160.00
Toy, Elliot The Dragon, Bendable, Box, 5 In. 20.00
Toy, Ferdinand, The Bull, Windup, Tin, Marx, 1939 .... 250.00
Toy, Ferris Wheel, Mickey Mouse, Box, Chein, 1950s 850.00
Toy, Flower, Friction, Tin Lithograph, Linemar, 1940s, 3 In. 75.00
Toy, Goofy, With Chipmunk On Tail, Windup, Marx 225.00
Toy, Ludwig Von Drake, Pip-Squeak, Rubber, Viceroy Of Canada, 7 In. 25.00
Toy, Mary Poppins, Plastic, Windup, Marx, Box, 1960s 150.00
Toy, Mickey Mouse & Minnie Mouse, Handcar, Lionel, No Tracks, 1934 .... 950.00
Toy, Mickey Mouse, Cardboard, Travels On String, Jointed, Dolly Toy Co., 1930s 475.00
Toy, Mickey Mouse, Handcar, Track, Lionel, No. 1101, Box 1150.00
Toy, Mickey Mouse, Jack-In-The-Box, Musical, Mattel, 1987 .... 15.00
Toy, Mickey Mouse, Krazy Kar, Box, Marx 175.00
Toy, Mickey Mouse, Loop The Loop Train, Battery Operated, Box, 14 x 11 In. 350.00
Toy, Mickey Mouse, Mechanical Tricycle, Linemar, Box ....*Illus* 660.00
Toy, Mickey Mouse, Playing Saxophone, Cymbals, Tin Lithograph, 5 1/2 In. 1100.00
Toy, Mickey Mouse, Playing Xylophone 750.00
Toy, Mickey Mouse, Projector, Tin, Decals, Keystone, 1930's, 9 x 9 1/2 In. 322.00
Toy, Mickey Mouse, Pull Toy, Fisher-Price, No. 798, 1939 .... 375.00
Toy, Mickey Mouse, Riding Tricycle, Illco, 1970s, 6 1/2 In. 75.00
Toy, Mickey Mouse, Roly Poly, Jointed, Sits On Ball, Celluloid, 1940, 4 In. 195.00
Toy, Mickey Mouse, Rubber, Seiberling, 1930s, 6 In. 250.00
Toy, Mickey Mouse, Scooter Jockey, Plastic, Windup, Mayco, 1960s 350.00
Toy, Mickey Mouse, Scooter, Card, Marx 75.00
Toy, Mickey Mouse, Squeeze, Rubber, Dell 25.00
Toy, Mickey Mouse, Sweeper, Walt Disney, 1930s 255.00
Toy, Mickey Mouse, Tractor, Sun Rubber 100.00
Toy, Mickey Mouse, Train, Lionel, Freight Car, Locomotive, Headlight 225.00
Toy, Mickey Mouse, Tricycle, Includes Bell Noise, Celluloid, 4 In. 609.00
Toy, Mickey Mouse, Trolley, Battery Operated, Tin, Japan, Box, 11 In. 280.00
Toy, Mickey Mouse, Xylophone, Pull Toy, Fisher-Price, 1939 .... 425.00
Toy, Mickey Mousketeers, Truck, Moving Van, Linemar 1750.00
Toy, Mickey's Delivery, Pluto, Celluloid, Tin Lithograph, Linemar, c.1940, 5 1/2 In. 431.00
Toy, Minnie Mouse, Acrobat, Trapeze, Clockwork, Celluloid, Japan, 1930s 780.00
Toy, Minnie Mouse, In Rocker, Linemar, Box 975.00
Toy, Minnie Mouse, Knitter, In Rocker, Clockwork, Box 1175.00
Toy, Minnie Mouse, Knitter, Rubber Ears, Tin, Windup, Linemar, 1950s, 7 In. 595.00
Toy, Pinocchio, The Acrobat, Marx, Box, 1939 .... 65.00
Toy, Pinocchio, Windup, Marx, 1935 .... 525.00
Toy, Pinocchio, Wooden, Composition, Ideal 225.00
Toy, Pluto, Drum Major, Mechanical, Box ....595.00 to 850.00
Toy, Pluto, Pop-Up, Fisher-Price 700.00
Toy, Pluto, Roll Over, Tin, Windup, Marx 275.00
Toy, Snow White, Kitchen, Disney Wolverine, 3 Piece 125.00
Toy, Thumper, Friction, Tin Lithograph, Linemar, 1940s, 3 In. 100.00
Toy, Zorro, Wrist Signal Light & Mask, Box 95.00
Tray, Peter Pan, Snow White, Pinocchio, Tin Lithograph, England, 1950s, 16 x 12 In. ... 45.00
Trivet, Mickey Mouse & Minnie Mouse 19.00
Trivet, Mickey Mouse, Ceramic, Metal Rim, 6 x 6 In. 40.00
Tumbler, Donald Duck, Walt Disney, 1939 .... 40.00
Tumbler, Dopey 20.00
Umbrella, Mary Poppins 95.00
Umbrella, Mickey Mouse Handle, Composition, 1930 .... 300.00
Umbrella, Mickey Mouse, 1950s 120.00
Wall Pocket, Bambi & Thumper 65.00
Wall Pocket, Bambi, Leeds 45.00
Wall Pocket, Pluto 55.00

Disneyana, Toy, Mickey Mouse,
Mechanical Tricycle, Linemar, Box

**Don't repaint old metal
toys. It lowers the value.**

Wallet, Mary Poppins, 1964 .... 28.00
Wallet, Mickey Mouse, Pie-Eyed Cowboy, Lariat, Leather, 1980s 25.00
Watch, Mickey Mouse, Pocket, Silver Plate Case, Paper Face, Ingersoll, 2 In. 433.00
Watch Fob, Mickey Mouse, Bradley, Box, 1970, 2 In. 144.00
Watering Can, Donald Duck, Tin, Ohio Art, 1938, 3 In. 265.00
Whirligig, Mickey Mouse, Celluloid, 7 In. 550.00
Wrapper, Mickey Mouse, Bubble Gum, GUM Inc., Philadelphia, 1930s, 7 x 5 In. 110.00
Wrapper, Mickey Mouse, Toasted Nut Chocolate, Paper, Redeem For Watch, 1930s 225.00
Wristwatch, 101 Dalmatians, Limited Edition 175.00
Wristwatch, Donald Duck, Metal Case, Blue Ground, Arms Point, Ingersoll, c.1947 .... 790.00
Wristwatch, Goofy Backwards, Lorus 25.00
Wristwatch, Mickey Mouse Medley 75.00
Wristwatch, Mickey Mouse, 7-Link Metal Band, Ingersoll US, c.1930 .... 358.00 to 475.00
Wristwatch, Mickey Mouse, Arms Move, Ingersoll 98.00
Wristwatch, Mickey Mouse, Birthday Cake Box, 1947 .... 700.00
Wristwatch, Mickey Mouse, Box, 1933 .... 700.00
Wristwatch, Mickey Mouse, Electric, Timex .... 50.00 to 150.00
Wristwatch, Mickey Mouse, Ingersoll, Box, 1930s 750.00
Wristwatch, Mickey Mouse, Metal, Simulated Leather Band, Ingersoll, 1950 .... 216.00
Wristwatch, Mickey Mouse, Stainless Steel, Ingersoll, c.1932 .... 1000.00 to 1100.00
Wristwatch, Mickey Mouse, Yellow Mickey, Medium Blue Leather Strap 112.00
Wristwatch, Minnie Mouse, Clear Plastic Band, Bradley 50.00
Wristwatch, Minnie Mouse, Display Case, Price Tag, Timex, 1958 .... 475.00
Wristwatch, Snow White 45.00

DOCTOR, see Dental; Medical

DOLL entries are listed by marks printed or incised on the doll, if possible. If there are no marks, the doll is listed by the name of the subject or country or maker. Notice that Barbie is listed under Mattel. G.I.
Joe figures are listed in the Toy section.

A.M., 255, Googly, Glass Eyes, 7 In. 895.00
A.M., 320, Bisque Head, Googly, Impish Smile, Papier-Mache Body, c.1925, 8 In. 425.00
A.M., 323, Googly, Blue Side Glancing Eyes, Chubby, Black Hat, 7 In. 925.00
A.M., 323, Googly, Boy, 10 In. 1295.00
A.M., 324, Googly, 7 In. 495.00
A.M., 341, Baby, Bisque Head, Soft Body, Porcelain Arms 195.00
A.M., 341, Dream Baby, Bisque Head, Blue Sleep Eyes, Composition, 16 In. 250.00
A.M., 341, Dream Baby, Bisque Head, Cloth Body, Jointed, c.1924, 23 In. 550.00
A.M., 351, Baby, Black, 15 In. 795.00
A.M., 351, Baby, Blue Eyes, 23 In. 800.00
A.M., 390, Bisque, Blue Eyes, Old Dress & Shoes, 29 In. 675.00
A.M., 390, Bisque, Brown Sleep Eyes, Human Hair Wig, 29 1/2 In. 625.00
A.M., 390, Composition Body, Sleep Eyes, Antique Outfit, 32 In. 900.00
A.M., 400, Bisque, Blue Sleep Eyes, Closed Mouth, Jointed, 1918, 15 In. 1800.00
A.M., 500, Baby, Boy, Bisque Head, 14 In. 950.00
A.M., 590, Bisque, Gray Sleep Eyes, Closed Mouth, Blond Mohair Wig, 19 In. 1900.00

A.M., 1894, Boy, Mohair Wig, Jointed Composition Body, Toreador Type Outfit, 14 In. ..   625.00
A.M., 1894, Sleep Eyes, Brown Composition Body, Antique Costume, 21 In. 1875.00
A.M., Baby Betty, Shoulder Head, Kid Body, 16 In. 675.00
A.M., Baby, Bisque, Blue Sleep Eyes, Cloth Body, 14 In. 285.00
A.M., Bisque, Blue Inset Eyes, Open Mouth, Blond Mohair Wig, 23 In. 750.00
A.M., Bisque, Composition Body, Sleep Eyes, Original Lashes, 27 In. 775.00
A.M., Floradora, 22 In. 550.00
A.M., Floradora, Blue Eyes, Mohair Wig, Original Clothes, 20 In. 425.00
A.M., Just Me, Composition Body, Mohair Wig, 10 In. 1495.00
A.M., Nobbikid, Blue Eyes, Nurse's Outfit, 7 In. 995.00
Advertising, Bell Telephone, Operator, Bell Box 50.00
Advertising, Blue Bonnet Sue, Cloth, Tag, 11 In. 25.00
Advertising, Buddy Lee, Overalls & Cap, 12 In. 475.00
Advertising, Burger King, Cloth, 13 In. 15.00
Advertising, Burger King, Knickerbocker, 1980, Box, 10 In. 50.00
Advertising, Chef, Cream Of Wheat, Envelope & Papers 145.00
Advertising, Chiquita Banana, Uncut Cloth, 1949 ....   30.00
Advertising, Cosmopolitan Ginger, Blond Wig, Blue Sleep Eyes, 1955 ....   160.00
Advertising, Cosmopolitan Ginger, Blue Nylon Dress, Tie Shoes, Box, 1957 ....   90.00
Advertising, Dig 'Em' Frog, Kellogg's Sugar Smacks, 1973, 17 In. ....*Illus*   10.00
Advertising, Dolly, Bob's Big Boy Girlfriend, Cloth, Large 16.00
Advertising, Eskimo Pie 35.00
Advertising, Humpty Dumpty Potato Chip, Inflatable, Cragstan, Package, 1950 ....   35.00
Advertising, Kool Aid Kid, Vinyl, 14 In. 16.00
Advertising, Mobil, Composition, Black, Ames Doll Co., Box, 1949, 12 In. 195.00
Advertising, Mobil, Composition, White, Ames Doll Co., Box, 1949, 12 In. 175.00
Advertising, Mr. Salty 10.00
Advertising, Nestles Chocolate, Hans, Bavarian 60.00
Advertising, Phillips 66, Composition, Painted, Ames Doll Co., 1940s, 12 In. .....175.00 to   295.00
Advertising, Ronald McDonald, Stuffed, Cloth, In Package, 13 In. 25.00
Advertising, Ronald McDonald, Whistle, Plastic Head, Hands & Feet, 1978, 20 In. 40.00
Advertising, Snap, Crackle & Pop, Kellogg's, Vinyl, Box, 3 Piece 85.00
Advertising, Swiss Miss, Stuffed 28.00
Advertising, Texaco Girl, Cheerleader, Box, 11 1/2 In. 35.00
Advertising, Tony Tiger, Plush 75.00
Advertising, Uneeda, Sleep Eyes, Shoes, Socks, Plastic, Vinyl 55.00
Alexander dolls are listed in this category under Madame Alexander.
Alt, Beck & Gottschalck, 698, Bisque, Set Eyes, Closed Mouth, Human Hair Wig, 17 In. .   350.00
Alt, Beck & Gottschalck, 698, Turned Shoulder Head, Paperweight Eyes, 16 In. 895.00
Alt, Beck & Gottschalck, Bisque, Blue Eyes, Scottish Costume, 1885, 19 In. 1200.00
Alt, Beck & Gottschalck, Bisque, Brown Inset Eyes, Jointed, 1890, 16 In. 1100.00
Alt, Beck & Gottschalck, Bisque, Closed Mouth, Blue Sleep Eyes, 17 In. 400.00
Alt, Beck & Gottschalck, Boy, Blue Eyes, Closed Mouth, Blond Hair, Wool Suit, 23 In. ...   250.00
Alt, Beck & Gottschalck, China Head & Hands, Open Mouth, Teeth, Kid Body, 21 In. 330.00
American Character, Sweet Sue, Brown Saran Wig, Green Sleep Eyes, 18 In. 325.00
American Character, Tiny Tears, Blue Sleep Eyes, Tosca Hair, Box, 1960, 12 In. 350.00
American Character, Tiny Tears, Plastic Head, Rubber, 1950s, 15 In. 40.00
American Character, Toodles, Blue Sleep Eyes, White Cotton Romper, 21 In. 425.00
Annalee, Santa Claus, Hot Air Ballooning, 1986, 23 In. 125.00
Armand Marseille dolls are listed in this category under A.M.
Arranbee, Little Angel, Blue Sleep Eyes, Polka Dot Sunsuit, 1958, 16 In. 150.00
Arranbee, Nancy Lee, Blond Floss Wig, Green Sleep Eyes, Plastic, 14 In. 600.00
Arranbee, Nancy Lee, Brown Floss Wig, Blue Sleep Eyes, Plastic, 14 In. 450.00
Arranbee, Nancy Lee, Skater, Blond Mohair Wig, Blue Sleep Eyes, 18 In. 825.00
Automaton, Bear, Plays Memories 225.00
Automaton, Boy On Tricycle, Iron Tricycle, Blue Eyes, Closed Mouth, 9 In. 3300.00
Automaton, Boy With Violin, Blue Paperweight Eyes, Open Mouth, 1890, 18 In. 3100.00
Automaton, Girl, Cobalt Blue Eyes, Open Mouth, Wax, Box, 1850, 12 In. 3500.00
Automaton, Girl, Playing Violin, Germany, 1880 ....   1100.00
Automaton, Jumeau, Girl, Musical, Earrings, Blue Eyes, Gown, Feather Fan, 18 1/2 In. ..   7800.00
Automaton, Piano Player, On Jewelry Box, Head & Hands Move, 3 Tunes, Marked 2995.00
Automaton, Rabbit, Knitting, Key Wind, Dekemps, 13 In. 978.00
Automaton, Woman, Gliding, With Fan, Bisque Head, France, 1890, 18 In. 3600.00

Doll, Advertising, Dig 'Em' Frog,
Kellogg's Sugar Smacks, 1973, 17 In.

Doll, Cloth, Mammy, Gingham, Torso On
Wooden Block, 13 1/2 In.

Averill, Bonnie Babe, Bisque, Blue Eyes, 22 In. 1800.00
Averill, Little Lulu, All Original, 1944, 15 In. 350.00
Averill, Raggedy Ann & Andy, 1918-1920, 19 & 20 In., Pair 300.00
Averill, Raggedy Ann, Original Clothes, 30 In. 695.00
Averill, Raggedy Ann, Strawberry Dress, Blue & Green Stripe, 18 In. 150.00
Averill, Uncle Wiggily, Nurse Jane Fuzzy Wuzzy, Cloth, 1943, 18 In., Pair 550.00
Bahr & Proschild, 204, Bisque, Blue Inset Eyes, Closed Mouth, 18 In. 1900.00
Bahr & Proschild, 204, Bisque, Brown Glass Eyes, Closed Mouth, 15 In. 1400.00
Bahr & Proschild, 204, Bisque, Hip Length Wig, Sailor Suit, 1880s, 13 In. 2000.00
Bahr & Proschild, 224, Bisque, Brown Glass Eyes, Closed Mouth, 12 In. 500.00
Bahr & Proschild, 277, Brown Bisque Head, Brown Inset Eyes, 11 In. 1100.00
Bahr & Proschild, 389, Bisque, Blue Sleep Eyes, Open Mouth, Jointed, 21 In. 850.00
Bahr & Proschild, 585, Baby, Bisque Head, Blue Sleep Eyes, Open Mouth, 12 In. 225.00
Bahr & Proschild, Baby, Brown Paperweight Eyes, Closed Mouth, 17 In. 2500.00
Bahr & Proschild, Bisque, Brown Sleep Eyes, Open Mouth, Composition, 29 In. 2300.00
Barbie dolls are listed in this category under Mattel.
Belton, 72, Composition, Closed Mouth, Paperweight Eyes, Jointed, 23 1/2 In. 2250.00
Belton, Bisque, Paperweight Eyes, Composition, Straight Wrists, 18 In. 3200.00
Belton, Bisque, Wood & Composition Body, Original Outfit, 11 In. 875.00
Belton, Composition Body, Paperweight Eyes, Mohair Wig, Straight Wrist, 15 In. 2495.00
Belton Type, 179, Black Bisque, Brown Set Eyes, Black Wool Wig, Costume, 15 In. ... 2550.00
Belton Type, Bisque, Closed Mouth, Straight Wrist, Composition Body, 18 In. 3200.00
Belton Type, Black Paperweight Eyes, Composition Body, Molded Shoes, 6 In. 550.00
Belton Type, Closed Mouth, Bisque Socket Head, Brown Paperweight Eyes, 16 In. 1600.00
Belton Type, Paperweight Eyes, Mohair Wig, Straight Wrist, Clothing, 15 In. ..2495.00 to 2995.00
Bergmann dolls are also in this category under S & H and Simon & Halbig.
Bergmann, Bisque Head, Blue Sleep Eyes, Open Mouth, Composition Body, 23 In. 300.00
Bergmann, Bisque, Socket Head, Blue Eyes, Synthetic Wig, Jointed, 24 In. 275.00
Bergmann, Brown Eyes, Blue Outfit, 24 In. 550.00
Bisque, Aged Woman, Brown Eyes, Gray Brows, Closed Mouth, Jointed, 18 In. 1250.00
Bisque, Blue Sleep Eyes, Blond Mohair Wig, Open Mouth, 1912, 15 In. 1400.00
Bisque, Brown Inset Eyes, Closed Mouth, Brown Mohair Wig, 1900, 12 In. 425.00
Bisque, Swivel Head, Cobalt Blue Eyes, Blond Mohair Wig, 7 In., Pair 2800.00
Bisque, Woman, Blue Inset Eyes, Turquoise Flowers, Closed Mouth, 14 In. 850.00
Black dolls are included in the Black category.
Borgfeldt, Girl, White Eyelet Flowered Hat, 25 In. 695.00
Boy, Lacmann, Papier-Mache, Cloth Body, Original Clothes, 12 In. 195.00
Bru Jne, Bisque, Amber Brown Enamel Eyes, Blond Wig, 1879, 11 In. 9000.00
Bru Jne, Bisque, Blue Enamel Eyes, Closed Mouth, 1880, 25 In. 9500.00
Bru Jne, Bisque, Blue Paperweight Eyes, Closed Mouth, 1895, 19 In. 4600.00
Bru Jne, Bisque, Brown Paperweight Eyes, Closed Mouth, Jointed, 19 In. 7200.00
Bru Jne, Bisque, c.1870, 12 In. 7360.00
Bru Jne, Fashion, Bisque Hands, Gusseted Body, Paperweight Eyes, Dressed, 14 In. 3450.00
Bru Jne, Fashion, Smiler, Wooden Articulated Body, Ball Gown, 15 In. 6950.00
Bru Jne, Nursing Baby, Mechanism, Nurses From Bottle, Curly Wig, Dressed, c.1898 ... 8500.00
Bru Jne, Walking, Kiss Throwing, Crying, 22 In. 3995.00
Bruckner, Muslin, Brown Complexion, Printed Features, Antique Costume, 13 In. 350.00

Bruno Schmidt, Bisque Head, Teeth, Composition, Wooden Jointed Body, 33 In. 1900.00
Bruno Schmidt, Bisque, Blue Eyes, Ringlets, Lavish Dress, Bonnet, 30 In. 1100.00
Bruno Schmidt, Blond Wig, Silk Shoes, Old Clothes, 16 In. ....905.00 to 950.00
Bruno Schmidt, Child, Ball-Jointed, Sleep Eyes, 28 In. 1450.00
Bye-Lo, Baby, Bisque Head, Blue Sleep Eyes, Closed Mouth, 13 In. 150.00
Bye-Lo, Baby, Bisque Head, Tan Hair, Blue Eyes, 1925, 4 In. 550.00
Bye-Lo, Baby, Bisque, Head, Brown Sleep Eyes, Closed Mouth, Dress, 11 In. ....200.00 to 220.00
Bye-Lo, Baby, Bisque, Head, Brown Sleep Eyes, Closed Mouth, Germany, 5 In. 300.00
Bye-Lo, Baby, Bisque, Tan Hair, Blue Sleep Eyes, Germany, 1923, 8 In. 650.00
Bye-Lo, Baby, Closed Mouth, Brown Sleep Eyes, Celluloid, 1923, 11 In. 425.00
Bye-Lo, Baby, Cloth Body, Sleep Eyes, Closed Mouth, Jacket, Cap, Bib, 12 1/2 In. 650.00
Bye-Lo, Bisque Head, Brown Hair, Bent-Limb, 1923, 13 In. 1350.00
Bye-Lo, Bisque Head, Brown Sleep Eyes, White Baby Dress, Bonnet, Germany, 4 In. ... 400.00
Bye-Lo, Sleep Eyes, Celluloid Hands, Antique Dress, 21 In. 1100.00
Cameo, Margie, Wood Segmented, Label, 1929, 10 In. 295.00
Captain Kangaroo, 1960s, 18 In. 150.00
Celluloid, Red Suit, Cotton Stuffed, 7 1/2 In. 20.00
Chad Valley, Princess Elizabeth, Felt & Velour, Trench Coat Outfit, 18 In. 1095.00
Character, Green Eyes, Jointed, High Knee Body, Homemade Clothes, 19 In. 1500.00
Charlie Brown, Cloth, 14 In. 25.00
Chase, Baby, Brown Hair, Original Paint, Antique Clothes, 25 In. 745.00
Chase, Baby, Fully Jointed, Weighted Body, Open Nostrils, Thermometer, 22 In. 895.00
Chase, Baby, Hospital, Composition Head, Cloth & Stockinet Body, 26 In. 375.00
Chase, Black Painted Eyes, Closed Mouth, 1900, 26 In. 8500.00
Chase, Blue Eyes, Closed Mouth, Jointed, 1900, 29 In. 850.00
Chase, Blue Eyes, Closed Mouth, Jointed, 1910, 22 In. 700.00
Chase, Brown Eyes, Closed Smiling Mouth, Blue Overalls, 12 1/2 In. 275.00
Chase, Painted Brown Eyes, Closed Mouth, Jointed, 17 In. 350.00
Chase, Painted Head & Limbs, Cotton Sateen Body, Brown Eyes, Blond Hair, 22 In. 345.00
Chase, Stockinet Head, Painted Blue Eyes, Closed Mouth, Painted Hair, 21 In. 275.00
China, Shoulder Head, Blue Eyes, Brown Human Hair, 1880s, 4 1/2 In. 90.00
China Head, Cloth Body, Blue Eyes, Floral Dress, S Stamp, Germany, 1840, 22 In. 360.00
China Head, Cloth Body, Molded Hair, Floral Dress, Germany, 20th Century, 19 1/2 In. .. 3300.00
Cloth, Blond Curly Hair, Blue Hair Ribbons, Lithographed, 1900, 22 In. 300.00
Cloth, Boudoir, Swivel Head, Blue Eyes, Closed Mouth, Jointed, 30 In. 275.00
Cloth, Little Red Riding Hood, Muslin, Uncut, 12 In. 145.00
Cloth, Mammy, Gingham, Torso On Wooden Block, 13 1/2 In. ....*Illus* 45.00
Cloth, Raggedy Ann & Andy, Cloth, Painted Face, Hang Tag, 1947, 18 In., Pair 165.00
Coleco, Cabbage Patch, Box, 1984 .... 50.00
Composition, World War I Doughboy, Jointed Arms & Legs, 12 In. 250.00
Dennis The Menace, 14 In. 100.00
DEP, 10, Bisque Head, Sleep Eyes, Kid Body, Black Ringlets, Dress, Lace, 24 In. 440.00
DEP, Bisque Head, Blue Sleep Eyes, Open Mouth, 23 In. 400.00
DEP, Bisque Head, Upper Teeth, Sleep Eyes, Jointed Body, Dressed, 14 In. 1100.00
DEP, Bisque, Blue Sleep Eyes, Open Mouth, Human Hair Wig, Jointed, 22 In. 495.00
DEP, Bisque, Jumeau Body, Silk & Lace Clothes, 26 In. 1495.00
DEP, Girl, Brown Eyes, Open Mouth, 19 In. 1200.00
DEP, Pierced Ears, Earrings, Aqua Satin Outfit, 12 In. 1095.00
DEP, Straight Legged Body, Brown Mohair Wig, Sleep Eyes, Open Mouth, 23 In. 1225.00
Eden Bebe, Pale Bisque, Paperweight Eyes, Long Human Hair Wig, Jointed, 27 In. 2350.00
Effanbee, Baby, Dy-Dee, Rubber Body, 15 In. 195.00
Effanbee, Betty Brite, Red Wig, All Composition, 16 In. 90.00
Effanbee, Brown Sleep Eyes, Brunette Saran Hair, Girl Scout Uniform, 8 In. 60.00
Effanbee, Composition Head, Sleep Eyes, Closed Rosebud Mouth, Velvet Hat, 14 In. 600.00
Effanbee, Flirty Eyes, Original Clothes, 19 In. 295.00
Effanbee, Groucho Marx, Sleep Eyes, Jointed, 1983, 17 In. 70.00
Effanbee, Honey, Cinderella, Blond Mohair Wig, Gray Sleep Eyes, 14 In. 650.00
Effanbee, Honey, Majorette, Auburn Mohair Wig, Blue Sleep Eyes, 1952, 17 In. 825.00
Effanbee, Honey, Prince Charming, Blond Mohair Wig, Gray Sleep Eyes, 14 In. 575.00
Effanbee, Honey, Walker, Hard Plastic, Trunk, Papers, Extra Outfits, 1949, 14 In. 695.00
Effanbee, Honey, Walker, Hard Plastic, Trunk, Rabbit Fur Coat, Muff, 1949, 14 In. 475.00
Effanbee, Ice Queen, 14 In. 595.00
Effanbee, John Wayne, Cavalry Uniform, Jointed, 1982, 17 In. ....60.00 to 85.00

Effanbee, Liberace, Box, 17 In. 550.00
Effanbee, Little Red Riding Hood, Sleep Eyes, Jointed, 1982, 12 In. 65.00
Effanbee, Lovums, All Original, 1928, 19 In. 325.00
Effanbee, Mae West, Legend, Open Close Eyes, Jointed, 1982, 17 In. 65.00
Effanbee, Mickey, Vinyl, 10 In. . . . . .35.00 to 95.00
Effanbee, Nicole, Grandes Dame, Sleep Eyes, Jointed, 1979, 19 In. . . . . .70.00 to 95.00
Effanbee, Patsy Ann, Composition Head, Tin Sleep Eyes, Molded Hair, 19 In. 225.00
Effanbee, Patsy Joan, Composition, Green Sleep Eyes, Closed Mouth, 17 In. 625.00
Effanbee, Patsy Joan, Composition, Original Bracelet, 16 In. 350.00
Effanbee, Patsy, Composition Head, Brown Sleep Eyes, Yellow Dress, 14 In. 600.00
Effanbee, Patsyette Boy, Paper Wrist Tag, 9 In. 350.00
Effanbee, Patsyette Girl, Paper Wrist Tag, 7 In. 275.00
Effanbee, Patsyette, Composition Head, Side Glancing Eyes, Dress, Hat, 9 In. 250.00
Effanbee, Patsyette, George & Martha Washington, Period Clothing, 9 In., Pair 290.00
Effanbee, Skippy, Composition & Cloth, Navy Outfit 275.00
Effanbee, Wee Patsy, Pin, Box, 6 In. 500.00
Eugenie Poir, Flapper, Felt, Green Dress, White Cloche Hat, 1920s, 16 In. 550.00
Fortune Telling, Cloth & Tin, Patented 1867, 8 1/2 In. .220.00 to 275.00
Foxy Grandpa, 18 In. 125.00
Franz Schmidt, Bisque, Flapper, 4 Teeth, Wooden Ball Jointed Body, c.1915, 18 In. 650.00
Franz Schmidt, Bisque, Toddler, Jointed Flirty Eyes, Wobble Tongue, 27 In. 2300.00
Franz Schmidt, Toddler, Skin Wig, 5 Piece Body, Star Fish Hands, 10 In. 690.00
French, Baby, Bisque, Crying Expression, Brown Hair, Blue Eyes, 7 In. 300.00
French, Bisque Head, Dark Blue Paperweight Eyes, Open Mouth, 26 In. 2000.00
French, Bisque, Blue Eyes, Closed Mouth, 2 1/4 In. 200.00
French, Bisque, Closed Mouth, Blue Eyes, Blond Mohair Wig, 18 In. 2600.00
French, Bisque, Wooden, Blue Eyes, Closed Mouth, Blond Mohair Wig, 18 In. 3600.00
French, Fashion, Bisque, Cloth Body & Limbs, Kid Boots, c.1880, 23 In. 1955.00
French, Fashion, Bisque, Socket Head, Cobalt Blue Eyes, Closed Mouth, 16 In. 1760.00
French, Fashion, Bisque, Swivel Head, Fixed Eyes, Kid Body, Dress, Jacket, 1875, 17 In. . 1840.00
French, Poupee, Venus, Paris, Molded Cloth Face, 1930s, 20 In. 450.00
Frozen Charlie, Painted Eyes, Molded Hair, Stiff Neck, Fists Clenched, 15 In. 270.00
Frozen Charlie, Pink Tint, Brown Color Hair, Badekinder, 1880, 16 In. 750.00
Frozen Charlotte, All China, Closed Mouth, Fists Clenched, Dress & Pinafore, 13 In. . . 320.00
Fulper, Bisque, Composition Jointed Body, 17 In. 595.00
Fulper, Ceramic Head, Real Hair, Signed, 18 In. 100.00
G.I. Joe figures are listed in the Toy category.
G.J. Edelweiss, Fashion, Bisque Swivel Head, Cloth Body, Leather Arms, Dressed, 19 In. 2995.00
Gaultier, Bisque Head, Composition & Wood Jointed Body, c.1882, 10 In. 4200.00
Gaultier, Bisque Head, Girl, Blond Skin Wig Over Cork Pate, Dress, Shoes, 16 1/2 In. . . 4025.00
Gaultier, Bisque Head, Open Mouth, Composition Body, Period Clothes, 16 In. 980.00
Gaultier, Bisque Swivel Head, Kid Body, Jointed, 17 In. 4885.00
Gaultier, Bisque Swivel Head, Kid Gusset-Jointed Body, c.1880, 19 In. 3700.00
Gaultier, Fashion, Bisque Swivel Head, Long Curls, Leather Body, Dress, 14 In. 1495.00
Gaultier, Swivel Head, Kid Body, Blue Eyes, Human Hair Wig, 1880, 25 In. 3800.00
Gebruder Heubach dolls are also in this category under Heubach.
Gebruder Heubach, 6871, Bisque, Blue Intaglio Eyes, Brown Hair, 16 In. 1000.00
Gebruder Heubach, 7959, Bisque, Pink Tinted Head, Bonnet, 1910, 14 In. 4200.00
Gebruder Heubach, 8420, Pouty Toddler, 9 Piece Body, Mohair Wig, 16 In. . .1800.00 to 1850.00
Gebruder Heubach, Bisque, Baby, Blue Flowered Bonnet, 1912, 11 In. 850.00
Gebruder Heubach, Bisque, Baby, Laughing, Blond Hair, 1910, 14 In. 3500.00
Gebruder Heubach, Bisque, Baby, Modeled Brown Hair, Brown Shoes, 4 In. 300.00
Gebruder Heubach, Bisque, Baby, Pouty Face, Dome Head, Composition Body, 6 In. . . . 235.00
Gebruder Heubach, Bisque, Baby, Seated In Green Tub, 1910, 4 In. 875.00
Gebruder Heubach, Bisque, Blue Intaglio Eyes, Composition, 14 In. 800.00
Gebruder Heubach, Bisque, Blue Sleep Eyes, Brunette Mohair Wig 900.00
Gebruder Heubach, Bisque, Boy, Naked, Brown Hair, Blue Eyes, Closed Mouth, 3 In. . 450.00
Gebruder Heubach, Bisque, Brown Inset Eyes, Blond Human Wig, 8 In. 950.00
Gebruder Heubach, Bisque, Girl, With Bonnet, Holding Basket, 1910, 4 In. 450.00
Gebruder Heubach, Bisque, Gray Spiral Eyes, Composition Body, 15 In. 1495.00
Gebruder Heubach, Bisque, Shoulder Head, Blue Intaglio Eyes, Knit Shirt, 10 In. 300.00
Gebruder Heubach, Bonnie Babe, Brown Sleep Eyes, Open Mouth, Jointed, 1923, 5 In. 1000.00
Gebruder Heubach, Dolly Dimple, Bisque, Brown Sleep Eyes, 1907, 21 In. 1800.00

Gebruder Kuhnlenz, Bisque, Spiral Eyes, Closed Mouth, Straight Wrist, 15 In. 1495.00
German, Bisque Head, Blue Sleep Eyes, Blond Mohair Wig, 16 In. 650.00
German, Bisque Socket Head, Open Mouth, Human Hair Wig, Jointed Body, 12 In. 285.00
German, Bisque, Bald, Black Side Glancing Eyes, Closed Mouth, 5 In. 350.00
German, Bisque, Blond Hair, Closed Mouth, Pouty, 1910, 24 In. 3000.00
German, Bisque, Blue Glass Eyes, Brown Mohair Wig, 1920, 6 In. 1200.00
German, Bisque, Blue Sleep Eyes, Blond Mohair Wig, Open Mouth, 9 In. 750.00
German, Bisque, Blue Sleep Eyes, Open Mouth, Composition, 11 In. 1600.00
German, Bisque, Brown Googly Eyes, Blond Mohair Wig, 4 1/2 In. 450.00
German, Bisque, Brown Googly Eyes, Brown Mohair Wig, 1915, 7 In. 500.00
German, Bisque, Character Head, Open Mouth, Brown Set Eyes, 23 In. 2100.00
German, Bisque, Child, Googly, Blue Sleep Eyes, Closed Mouth, 7 In. 700.00
German, Bisque, Googly, Blue Sleep Eyes, Blond Mohair Wig, 1920, 10 In. 850.00
German, Bisque, Gray Sleep Eyes, Open Mouth, Blond Mohair Wig, 10 In. 3100.00
German, Bisque, Shoulder Head, Cloth Body, Silk Dress, Early 20th Century, 14 In. 1995.00
German, Clown, Mustache & Goatee, Porcelain Head, Jointed Body, c.1880, 14 In. 500.00
German, Queen Louise, Bisque Socket Head, Open Mouth, Human Hair Wig, 27 In. 375.00
Gilbert, Honey West, Black Jumpsuit, Gold Trenchcoat, Books, 1965 .... 85.00
Gilbert, James Bond 007, Action, With Gun & Accessories, Box, 12 In. 450.00
Gilbert, Trudy, 3 Faces, Composition & Cloth, Smiling, Crying, Sleeping Face, 14 In. 225.00
Goebel, Baby, Crown Mark, 16 In. 375.00
Goebel, Bisque, Blue Sleep Eyes, Jointed, Box, 19 1/2 In. 275.00
Golliwog, Cloth, Yarn Hair, England, 18 1/2 In. 85.00
Googly, Bisque Head & Body, Our Fairy, Watermelon Mouth, Original Outfit, 11 1/2 In. . 2975.00
Googly, Bisque, Surprised Eyes, Open-Close Mouth, Orange Dress, Germany, 7 In. 412.00
Grace Drayton, Captain Kiddo, Cloth Body, Side Glancing Eyes, Smiling, 7 In. 350.00
Half Dolls are listed in the Pinchushion category.
Handwerck, 69, Child, Blue Almond Eyes, Blond Mohair Wig, 26 In. 1200.00
Handwerck, 79, Bisque Head, Teeth, Jointed Body, Brown Wig, Original Clothes, 16 In. . 978.00
Handwerck, 79, Little Girl Blue, Blond Mohair Wig, Blue Eyes, 17 In. 750.00
Handwerck, 99, Child, Blue Sleep Eyes, Brunette Wig, Victorian White Dress 1200.00
Handwerck, 99, Girl, 33 In. 1695.00
Handwerck, 109, Bisque, Brown Sleep Eyes, Open Mouth, Composition, 33 In. 1600.00
Handwerck, 119, Bisque, Child, Blue Inset Eyes, Peach Color, Straw Hat, 28 In. 1598.00
Handwerck, 297, Bisque, Blue Sleep Eyes, Open Mouth, 25 In. 400.00
Handwerck, 421, Bisque, Child, Blue Sleep Eyes, Open Mouth, Blond Wig, 20 In. 700.00
Handwerck, 421, Bisque, Sleep Eyes, Ball Jointed, Antique Clothing, 31 In. 875.00
Handwerck, Bebe Elite, Sleep Eyes, Human Hair, Ball-Jointed, Clothes, 19 1/2 In. 695.00
Handwerck, Bisque Head, Blue Sleep Eyes, Jointed, 25 In. 400.00
Handwerck, Bisque Head, Brown Sleep Eyes, Open Mouth, 24 In. 400.00
Handwerck, Bisque, Blue Eyes, Hair Wig, 23 In. 995.00
Handwerck, Bisque, Blue Sleep Eyes, Blond Mohair Wig, 17 In. 1300.00
Handwerck, Bisque, Blue Sleep Eyes, Brown Mohair Wig, 23 In. 1175.00
Handwerck, Bisque, Blue Sleep Eyes, Open Mouth, Brunette Mohair Wig, 18 In. 1050.00
Handwerck, Bisque, Blue Sleep Eyes, Pierced Ears, Human Hair Wig, Germany, 26 In. . 467.00
Handwerck, Bisque, Brown Sleep Eyes, Open Mouth, Composition, 10 In. 550.00
Handwerck, Bisque, Earrings, Straw Bonnet, 28 In. 895.00
Handwerck, Bisque, Sleep Eyes, Human Hair Wig, Jointed Body, Composition, 22 In. .. 488.00
Handwerck, Bisque, Sleep Eyes, Open Mouth, Human Hair Wig, 24 In. 316.00
Handwerck, Blue Paperweight Eyes, Human Hair Wig, Jointed, 32 In. 1700.00
Handwerck, Sleep Eyes, Ball-Jointed Body, Sleep Eyes, Dress & Bonnet, 25 In. 750.00
Handwerck, Sleep Eyes, Blond Wig, Ball-Jointed Body, 14 In. 625.00
Handwerck, Sleep Eyes, Curls, Ball Jointed Body, Long Dress, Matching Bonnet, 25 In. . 750.00
Handwerck, Socket Head, Girl, Synthetic Wig, Wood & Composition Body, 37 In. 1300.00
Hartmann, Baby, Sleep Eyes, Mohair Wig, Dress & Hat, 1910, 8 1/4 In. 420.00
Hasbro, Kate Jackson, Charlie's Angles, Poseable, Red Jumpsuit, 1977 .... 45.00
Herm Steiner, Ball Jointed, Original Clothes & Wig, 25 In. 470.00
Hertel Schwab, 99, Bisque, Sleep Eyes, Voice Box, 20 3/4 In. 375.00
Hertel Schwab, 150, Bisque, Baby, Open-Close Mouth, Human Hair Wig, 9 In. 330.00
Hertel Schwab, 151, Bisque, Baby, Brown Sleep Eyes, Open Mouth, 18 In. 135.00
Hertel Schwab, 151, Oily Bisque, Baby, Closed Mouth, Antique Gown, 15 In. 595.00
Hertel Schwab, 152, Boy, Toddler, Dimples, 20 In. 800.00
Hertel Schwab, 165, Blue Eyes, Blond Mohair Wig, Closed Mouth, 1912, 10 In. 4000.00

Hertel Schwab, 222/22, Bisque Head, Our Fairy Girl, Short Shirt, 8 1/2 In. 1840.00
Hertel Schwab, Googly, Bisque Head, Toddler Body, Wide Smile, c.1912, 14 In. 4200.00
Heubach dolls are also in this category under Gebruder Heubach.
Heubach, 1550, Tongue Sticking Out, Original Clothes, 14 In. 5400.00
Heubach, 6970, Soft Blue Sleep Eyes, Pouty, Composition, Hat, 14 In. 1895.00
Heubach, 7602, Character, Pouty, Intaglio Eyes, Original Clothes, 17 In. 995.00
Heubach, Bisque Head, Baby, Googly Eyed 4025.00
Heubach, Bisque, Girl With Seashell, On Pilings, Ruffled Sunbonnet, 7 In. 325.00
Heubach, Bisque, My Coquette, Intaglio Eyes, 15 In. 995.00
Heubach, Boy, Laughing, Original Wig & Clothing, Ball Jointed Body, 12 In. 1000.00
Heubach, Boy, Pouty, Fully Jointed Body, 3 Piece Velvet Costume, 12 In. 1900.00
Heubach, Sleep Eyes, Mohair Wig, Baby Clothes, 14 1/2 In. 495.00
Heubach Koppelsdorf, 250, Bisque, Composition Body, 15 In.   175.00
Heubach Koppelsdorf, 250, Composition, Lace Blue Ribbon Dress, 9 In. 245.00
Heubach Koppelsdorf, 399, Bisque, Character Baby, Grass Skirt, Ankle Bracelet, 13 In.   475.00
Horsman, Ella Cinders, Marked Outfit, 1925 . . . .   895.00
Horsman, Hee-Bee, She-Bee, Composition, Marked Outfits, 1925, Pair 1395.00
Horsman, Linda, 35 In. 120.00
Horsman, Poor Pitiful Pearl, Tosca Hair, Gray Sleep Eyes, Blue Dress, 11 In. 90.00
Horsman, Toddler, Dimples, Period Clothes, 10 In. 295.00
Houchen, Marilyn Monroe, 1980, 12 In. 1250.00
Ideal, Baby, Hard Plastic Head, Rubber Body, Tag, Box, 24 In.   125.00
Ideal, Betsy McCall, Ballerina, Red Dress, Ballet Slippers, Box 280.00
Ideal, Betsy McCall, Blond Wig, Floral Chemise, Box, 1958 . . . .   350.00
Ideal, Betsy McCall, Brunch Time, Pink Gingham Pajamas, Box 200.00
Ideal, Betsy McCall, Original Dress, Shoes, 8 In. 175.00
Ideal, Betsy McCall, Vinyl Head, Brown Sleep Eyes, Closed Smiling Mouth, 14 In. 440.00
Ideal, Betsy Wetsy, Cotton Print Romper, Matching Bonnet, 1957 . . . .   10.00
Ideal, Betty Big Girl, Moves Head Side To Side, Pigtails, Original Outfit, 1968, 31 In. . .   95.00
Ideal, Bonnie Braids, Box, 13 In. . . . .*Illus*   300.00
Ideal, Deanna Durbin, 1938, 21 In. . . . . .325.00 to 895.00
Ideal, Eddy Munster, 1965 . . . .   60.00
Ideal, Fanny Brice, Composition, 15 In. 175.00
Ideal, Harriet Hubbard Ayer, Hard Plastic Body, Vinyl Arms, Makeup Box, 15 In. 450.00
Ideal, Little Miss Muffet, Sleep Eyes, Jointed, 1984, 8 In. 25.00
Ideal, Little Miss Revlon, Brunette Wig, Green Sleep Eyes, Box, 1958, 10 In. 130.00
Ideal, Miss Curity, Plastic Head, Blue Sleep Eyes, Saran Wig, Box, 1950s, 14 In. .650.00 to 715.00
Ideal, Miss Revlon, 5 Piece Vinyl Body, Sleep Eyes, Box, 20 In. . . . .*Illus*   625.00
Ideal, Patti Playpal, Dark Blond Hair, 35 In. 350.00
Ideal, Peter Pan, Composition Head, Sleep Eyes, Bobbed Hair, 1928, 18 In. 325.00
Ideal, Pinocchio, Composition & Wood, 20 In. 395.00
Ideal, Rapunzel, Sleep Eyes, Jointed, 1984, 8 In. 25.00
Ideal, Sara Ann, Dark Blond Wig, Blue Sleep Eyes, Green Cotton Dress, 15 In. 400.00
Ideal, Saucy Walker, Pink Taffeta Dress, 22 In. 150.00
Ideal, Scarecrow, Wizard Of Oz, Box, 1970s 50.00
Ideal, Smokey The Bear . . . . .50.00 to 130.00
Ideal, Tammy, Doll You'll Love To Dress, Blond, Box, 1963 . . . .   95.00
Ideal, Thumbelina, Cloth Body, Painted Blue Eyes, Tosca Hair, 1961, 14 In. 350.00
Ideal, Toni, Blond Wig, Green Sleep Eyes, Red Polka Dot Organdy, Box, 14 In. 450.00
Ideal, Toni, Blond Wig, Pink Shirt, Aqua, Gold Skirt, White Shoes, 14 In. 300.00
Ideal, Toni, Blond Wig, Pink Waffle Weave Shirt, Green, Gold Skirt, 19 In. 350.00
Ideal, Toni, Blond, Sleep Eyes, Original Dress, Curlers, Box, 21 In. . . . .*Illus*   750.00
Ideal, Toni, Bride, Blond Wig, Gray Sleep Eyes, Cotton Petticoat, 14 In. 600.00
Ideal, Toni, Hard Plastic Head, Blue Sleep Eyes, Nylon Wig, Dress, Box, 21 In. 825.00
Ideal, Uneeda Kid, Character, Made For Uneeda Biscuit Co., 1914 . . . .   495.00
Indian dolls are listed in the Indian category.
J.D.K. dolls are also listed in this category under Kestner.
J.D.K., 221, Bisque, Googly, Plaster Pate, Dress, Shoes, Coat, 13 1/2 In. . . . . . . .5880.00 to 7600.00
Jackie Robinson, Original Clothes, 13 In. 795.00
Japanese, Samurai Warrior, Armor, Raffia Shoes, 19th Century, 15 In. 1610.00
Jiggs, Cloth, Velvet Face & Hands, Original Clothes, 15 In. 795.00
Jumeau, 1907, Bisque, Long Curls, Stationery Eyes, Open Mouth, Dress, 30 In. 2900.00
Jumeau, Angelic Portrait, Little Girl Look, 8 Ball Body, Satin Walking Suit, 15 In. 8500.00

Doll, Ideal, Bonnie Braids,   Doll, Ideal, Miss Revlon, 5 Piece   Doll, Ideal, Toni, Blond, Sleep Eyes,
Box, 13 In.   Vinyl Body, Sleep Eyes, Box, 20 In.   Original Dress, Curlers, Box, 21 In.

Jumeau, Bisque Head, Blue Eyes, Closed Mouth, 1886, 19 In. 5600.00
Jumeau, Bisque Head, Blue Eyes, Closed Mouth, Blond Mohair Wig, 1890, 5 In. 600.00
Jumeau, Bisque Head, Blue Paperweight Eyes, Closed Mouth, 1892, 13 In. 2600.00
Jumeau, Bisque Head, Brown Paperweight Eyes, Oriental Costume, 18 In. 4400.00
Jumeau, Bisque Head, Enamel Blue Eyes, Auburn Fleeced Wig, 12 In. 4400.00
Jumeau, Bisque Head, Girl, Cork Pate, Teeth, Fully Jointed, Clothes, Box, 24 In. 2300.00
Jumeau, Bisque Head, Glass Eyes, Upper Row Of Teeth, Long Curls, Dress, 34 In. 3200.00
Jumeau, Bisque Head, Open Mouth, Sleep Eyes, Jointed, Composition, 1910, 23 In. 2200.00
Jumeau, Bisque Head, Paperweight Eyes, Dressed, 23 1/2 In. 3450.00
Jumeau, Bisque Head, Paperweight Eyes, Human Hair, Jointed, Composition, 27 In. 2475.00
Jumeau, Bisque Socket Head, Jointed Wood & Composition Body, Dress, 20 In. 5400.00
Jumeau, Bisque, Almond Shape Brown Enamel Inset Eyes, Composition, 24 In. 11500.00
Jumeau, Bisque, Blue Enamel Eyes, Closed Mouth, Box, 1878, 13 In. 5000.00
Jumeau, Bisque, Blue Enamel Eyes, Composition, Antique Costume, 20 In. 8500.00
Jumeau, Bisque, Blue Paperweight Eyes, Brown Wig, 1907, 22 In. 1900.00
Jumeau, Bisque, Blue Paperweight Eyes, Closed Mouth, 1880, 18 In. 8250.00
Jumeau, Bisque, Blue Paperweight Eyes, Closed Mouth, 1885, Box, 23 In. 7750.00
Jumeau, Bisque, Blue Paperweight Eyes, Closed Mouth, 1892, Box, 11 In. 5750.00
Jumeau, Bisque, Blue Paperweight Eyes, Closed Mouth, 28 In. 14000.00
Jumeau, Bisque, Blue Paperweight Eyes, Jointed, 15 In. 3250.00
Jumeau, Bisque, Blue Paperweight Eyes, Open Mouth, 1892, 21 In. 3700.00
Jumeau, Bisque, Blue Paperweight Eyes, Wheat Blond Mohair Wig, 10 In. 3800.00
Jumeau, Bisque, Brown Enamel Eyes, Closed Mouth, 16 In. 7250.00
Jumeau, Bisque, Brown Eyes, Closed Mouth, 20 In. 9750.00
Jumeau, Bisque, Brown Eyes, Closed Mouth, Composition, 24 In. 3600.00
Jumeau, Bisque, Brown Paperweight Eyes, 16 In. 275.00
Jumeau, Bisque, Brown Paperweight Eyes, Brown Mohair Wig, 23 In. 7500.00
Jumeau, Bisque, Brown Paperweight Eyes, Closed Mouth, 11 In. 2300.00
Jumeau, Bisque, Brown Paperweight Eyes, Closed Mouth, 1885, 14 In. 6600.00
Jumeau, Bisque, Brown Paperweight Eyes, Closed Mouth, 1888, 9 1/2 In. 3700.00
Jumeau, Bisque, Brown Paperweight Eyes, Closed Mouth, 21 In. 3600.00
Jumeau, Bisque, Brown Paperweight Eyes, Closed Mouth, Jointed, 16 In. . . . . .3500.00 to 4500.00
Jumeau, Bisque, Brown Paperweight Eyes, Jointed, 1890, 14 In. 3900.00
Jumeau, Bisque, Brown Paperweight Eyes, Jointed, 1895, 12 In. 2600.00
Jumeau, Bisque, Brunette Mohair Wig, Open Mouth, 1900, 7 In. 525.00
Jumeau, Bisque, Child, Brown Paperweight Eyes, Jointed, 26 In. 7000.00
Jumeau, Bisque, Fixed Eyes, Upper Teeth, Cotton Dress, Socks & Shoes, 30 In. 2900.00
Jumeau, Bisque, Muslin, Red Flowered, Brown Eyes, 1895, 5 1/2 In. 1700.00
Jumeau, Bisque, Socket Head, Brown Eyes, Composition, 21 In. 3900.00
Jumeau, Blue Eyes, Closed Mouth, Box, 27 In. 6800.00
Jumeau, Blue Paperweight Eyes, Closed Mouth, Composition, 21 1/2 In. 1895.00
Jumeau, Blue Paperweight Eyes, Straight Wrist, Jointed, Mohair Wig, 11 In. 5500.00
Jumeau, Brown Inset Eyes, Blond Mohair Wig, Dress, Hat, France, 14 In. 3250.00
Jumeau, Fashion, Bisque Head, Wooden, Kid Arms & Legs, Paperweight Eyes, 25 In. . . . 7500.00

Jumeau, Fashion, Blue Eyes, Kid Body, Satin & Lace Bridal Gown, c.1880, 18 In. 5700.00
Jumeau, Fashion, Embroidered Wool Cape Over Lace Trimmed Aqua Dress, 22 In. 5500.00
Jumeau, Fashion, Skin Wig & Pate, Courtier Dress, Shoes, Bonnet, 18 1/2 In. 7700.00
Jumeau, Girl, Bisque Head, Jointed Wood & Composition Body, Dress, 15 1/4 In. 5175.00
Jumeau, Light Gray Paperweight Eyes, Solid Dome, Closed Mouth, 12 In. 975.00
Jumeau, Paperweight Eyes, Long Curls, Original Hat & Wig, Silk Dress, 26 In. 6550.00
Jumeau, Portrait, Girl, Bisque Head, Ball Jointed Wood & Composition Body, 14 In. ... 5750.00
Jumeau, Portrait, Pale Bisque, Brown Paperweight Eyes, 23 In. 11200.00
Jumeau, Portrait, Paperweight Eyes, Jointed Body, 16 In. 6800.00
Jutta, Bisque Head, Baby, 2 Teeth, Tongue, Auburn Wig, 18 1/2 In. 575.00
K * R, 22, Baby, Chubby Body, Blue Eyes, Christening Gown, 24 In. 1050.00
K * R, 22, Toddler, Bisque, Crier, 20 In. 1250.00
K * R, 50, Bride, Bisque Head, Jointed, Wood & Composition, 19 In. ....*Illus* 1700.00
K * R, 53, Bisque, Blue Sleep Eyes, Blond Mohair Wig, 1910, 21 In. 2700.00
K * R, 100, Baby, Brown Eyes, 15 In. 995.00
K * R, 101, Bisque, Blond Mohair Wig, Blue Eyes, Closed Mouth, 12 In. 2000.00
K * R, 101, Bisque, Blue Eyes, Brunette Mohair Wig, Ball Jointed, 12 In. 1400.00
K * R, 101, Bisque, Blue Eyes, Closed Mouth, Pouty, Jointed, 1910, 19 In. 5000.00
K * R, 101, Child, Pensive Look, Embroidered Whites, Crochet Socks, 12 In. 2700.00
K * R, 115A, Toddler, Jointed Body, Pleated Pinafore, Straw Bonnet, 13 In. 3800.00
K * R, 116, Bisque, Mold Face, Blue Sleep Eyes, Open-Close Mouth 3350.00
K * R, 116A, Bisque, Blue Eyes, Open-Close Mouth, Original Mohair Wig, 16 In. 2995.00
K * R, 117, Mein Liebling, Bisque, Oily Sheen, Antique Clothes, 19 In. 4900.00
K * R, 117A, Bisque, Mein Liebling, Sleep Eyes, Brunette Wig, Old Dress, 20 In. 7200.00
K * R, 117N, Bisque Head, Brown Sleep Eyes, Open Mouth, 1912, 30 In. 3200.00
K * R, 117N, Bisque, Mein Liebling, Flirty Eyes, Original Costume, 18 1/2 In. 2500.00
K * R, 121, Bisque, Blue Sleep Eyes, Blond Mohair Wig, 17 In. 1100.00
K * R, 121, Bisque, Blue Sleep Eyes, Open Mouth, Brown Mohair Wig, 15 In. 800.00
K * R, 126, Baby, Character, Flirty Eyes, Wobble Tongue, 17 In. 725.00
K * R, 126, Baby, Character, Red Head, Open Mouth, Happy Expression, 20 In. 825.00
K * R, 126, Baby, Chunky Body, Brown Eyes, Wobbly Tongue, 21 In. 800.00
K * R, 126, Bisque, Toddler, Bent Leg, Tiny Tongue, Original Wig, 10 In. 575.00
K * R, 192, Child, Bisque, Brown Sleep Eyes, Blond Mohair Wig, 1900, 15 In. 700.00
K * R, 403, Bisque, Sleep Eyes, Human Hair Wig, Flapper Body, Costume, 20 In. 1050.00
K * R, 403, Blue Sleep Eyes, Brown Mohair Wig, Jointed, 1915, 25 In. ....900.00 to 925.00
K * R, 403, Flapper Body, Blue Sleep Eyes, Closed Mouth, 26 In. 1500.00
K * R, 721, Baby, Socket Head, Brown Sleep Eyes, Mohair Wig, Baby Dress, 21 In. 200.00
K * R, 728, Toddler, Celluloid, Flirty Sleep Eyes, Open Mouth, Crochet Dress, 15 In. ... 360.00
K * R, Ball Jointed, No Clothes, 23 In. 490.00
K * R, Bisque Head, Blue Sleep Eyes, Dark Blue Dress, Open Mouth, 11 In. 400.00
K * R, Bisque Head, Blue Sleep Eyes, Open Mouth, 8 In., Pair 1050.00
K * R, Bisque Head, Brown Inset Eyes, Brown Mohair Wig, 1910, 6 In. 475.00
K * R, Bisque Head, Brown Sleep Eyes, Blond Mohair Wig, 1915, 11 In. 600.00
K * R, Bisque Head, Pale Blue Eyes, Blond Mohair Wig, Closed Mouth, 11 In. 1800.00
K * R, Bisque, Blue Flirty Eyes, Brown Mohair Wig, Composition, 14 In. 3900.00
K * R, Bisque, Blue Sleep Eyes, Brown Mohair Wig, Composition, 21 In. 900.00
K * R, Bisque, Blue Sleep Eyes, Open Mouth, Jointed, 1910, 23 In. ....900.00 to 1150.00
K * R, Bisque, Blue Sleep Eyes, Open Mouth, Wheat Blond Human Hair, 27 In. 1000.00
K * R, Bisque, Socket Head, Brown Sleep Eyes, Composition, Open Mouth, 6 In. 330.00
K * R, Human Hair Wig, Jointed Body, Victorian Dress, Shoes, 30 In. 1650.00
Kathe Kruse, Baby, Stockinet Body, Closed, Pouty Mouth, 1937, 19 In. 6000.00
Kathe Kruse, Brown Hair, Brown Eyes, Closed Mouth, Pouty, 1940, 18 In. 4000.00
Kathe Kruse, Du Mein, Awake, 16 In. 1950.00
Kathe Kruse, Gray Eyes, Closed Mouth, Jointed, 1911, 17 In. 4100.00
Kathe Kruse, Green Eyes, Stockinet Body, Closed Mouth, 1925, 17 In. ./........... 1300.00
Kathe Kruse, Oil Painted Face, Pouty, Jointed Arms, c.1920, 13 In. 2500.00
Kathe Kruse, Painted Blue Eyes, Rose Dress, Bonnet, 16 In. 1900.00
Kathe Kruse, Swivel Head, Flowered Frock, Closed Mouth, 1950, 20 In. 2000.00
Kathe Kruse, Swivel Head, Gray Eyes, Blue Dress, 1950, 14 In. 1600.00
Kathy Kruse, Girl, Green Shaded Eyes, Closed Mouth, Cloth, 14 In. 1400.00
Kestner dolls are also in this category under J.D.K.
Kestner, 26, Bisque, Baby, Dressed, 15 In. 700.00
Kestner, 102, Bisque, Swivel Head, Blue Eyes, Open Mouth, 8 1/2 In. ....2600.00 to 2800.00

Kestner, 143, Bisque Head, Sleep Eyes, Open Mouth, Mohair Wig, 12 In. . . . . . .690.00 to 990.00
Kestner, 150, Bisque, Brown Sleep Eyes, Closed Mouth, Mohair Wig, 6 In. 170.00
Kestner, 152, Bisque, Blue Sleep Eyes, Open Mouth, Antique Costume, 23 In. 1000.00
Kestner, 152, Bisque, Blue Sleep Eyes, Open Mouth, Jointed, 14 In. 1200.00
Kestner, 152, Bisque, Brown Sleep Eyes, Open Mouth, 23 In. 1350.00
Kestner, 152, Bisque, Human Hair Wig, Composition & Wooden Body, 1900, 16 In. 950.00
Kestner, 154, Bisque Hands, Riveted Leather Body, Sleep Eyes, 26 In. . . . . .695.00 to 795.00
Kestner, 154, Bisque, Blue Eyes, Brocade Clothes, 20 In. 625.00
Kestner, 154, Bisque, Brown Sleep Eyes, Open Mouth, 1910, 23 In. 950.00
Kestner, 154, Bisque, Shoulder Head, Brown Sleep Eyes, 20 In. 325.00
Kestner, 154, Bisque, Shoulder Head, Sleep Eyes, Blond Mohair Wig, 17 1/2 In. 275.00
Kestner, 156, Bisque, Turquoise Sleep Eyes, Jointed, 21 In. 1800.00
Kestner, 164, Bisque Head, Sleep Eyes, Human Hair, Wooden Body, c.1900, 16 In. 700.00
Kestner, 167, Bisque, Blue Threaded Eyes, Blond Mohair Wig, 20 In. 1195.00
Kestner, 167, Bisque, Clothes, 17 1/2 In. 850.00
Kestner, 168, Bisque, Sleep Eyes, Auburn Human Wig, Old Shoes, 24 In. 875.00
Kestner, 168, Bisque, Sleep Eyes, Open Mouth, Blond Mohair Wig, 19 1/2 In. 545.00
Kestner, 168, Nurse Nightingale, Brown Mohair Wig, 20 In. 700.00
Kestner, 171, Bisque, Blue Sleep Eyes, Open Mouth, Germany, 1910, 25 In. 850.00
Kestner, 171, Bisque, Brown Sleep Eyes, Blond Human Hair, 30 In. 1750.00
Kestner, 171, Bisque, Brown Sleep Eyes, Open Mouth, Composition, 22 In. 850.00
Kestner, 211, Baby, Blue Sleep Eyes, 21 In. 990.00
Kestner, 211, Baby, Open-Close Mouth, Original Wig & Body, 16 In. 850.00
Kestner, 214, Bisque, Blue Sleep Eyes, Brown Mohair Wig, 30 In. 950.00
Kestner, 214, Sleep Eyes, Open Mouth, Composition Body, 19 1/4 In. 630.00
Kestner, 221, Bisque Head, Googly, Sleep Eyes, Wooden Body, c.1912, 15 In. 7200.00
Kestner, 221, Bisque, Brown Googly Eyes, Closed Mouth, 1915, 13 In. 6500.00
Kestner, 221, Toddler Body, Googly, Sleep Eyes, 11 1/2 In. 6200.00
Kestner, 226, Blue Sleep Eyes, Blond Mohair Wig, 16 In. . . . . .895.00 to 995.00
Kestner, 243, Bisque Head, Oriental Baby, Teeth, Bent Limb Body, 1912, 16 In. 4400.00
Kestner, 245, Bisque, Hilda, Blue Sleep Eyes, Open Mouth, Blond Mohair Wig, 18 In. . . . 3400.00
Kestner, 247, Baby, All Original, 18 In. 1695.00
Kestner, 247, Bisque, Hilda, Bald Head, Factory Original Clothes, 15 In. . . . . .3300.00 to 3350.00
Kestner, 249, Character, Blue Sleep Eyes, Mohair Wig, 23 In. 1795.00
Kestner, 257, Bisque, Baby, Brown Sleep Eyes, Open Mouth, Baby Suit, 12 In. 750.00
Kestner, 260, Bisque, Blue Sleep Eyes, Lace Trimmed Dress, 20 In. 495.00
Kestner, 260, Bisque, Brown Sleep Eyes, Blond Mohair Wig, 1915, 10 In. 850.00
Kestner, 260, Toddler, Jointed Body, Sleep Eyes, 10 In. 1250.00
Kestner, Baby, Newborn, Crying, 12 In. 900.00
Kestner, Bisque Head, Blond Mohair Wig, 15 In. 1955.00
Kestner, Bisque Head, Blue Inset Eyes, Blond Human Hair, 1885, 8 1/2 In. 1800.00
Kestner, Bisque Head, Blue Sleep Eyes, Closed Mouth, 1900, 13 1/2 In. 2500.00
Kestner, Bisque Head, Blue Threaded Eyes, Closed Pouty Mouth, 25 In. 575.00
Kestner, Bisque Head, Brown Sleep Eyes, Open Mouth, Jointed, 11 In. 900.00
Kestner, Bisque Socket Head, Sleep Eyes, Human Wig, Jointed Body, 1890s, 32 In. 2970.00
Kestner, Bisque, Blue Inset Eyes, Closed Mouth, Antique Costume, 1890, 21 In. 550.00
Kestner, Bisque, Blue Inset Eyes, Open Mouth, Brown Human Hair, 8 In. 2200.00
Kestner, Bisque, Blue Sleep Eyes, Blond Mohair Wig, 1890, 23 In. 900.00
Kestner, Bisque, Blue Sleep Eyes, Closed Mouth, Composition, 24 In. 3100.00
Kestner, Bisque, Brown Eyes, Closed Mouth, Brown Wig, 19 In. 1000.00
Kestner, Bisque, Brown Sleep Eyes, Closed Mouth, 1890, 17 In. 2250.00
Kestner, Bisque, Brown Sleep Eyes, Jointed, 26 In. 875.00
Kestner, Bisque, Flange Head, Sleep Eyes, Closed Rosebud Mouth, Composition, 17 In. . . 605.00
Kestner, Bisque, Jointed, Composition Body, Sleep Eyes, Curly Wig, 26 In. 685.00
Kestner, Bisque, Shoulder Head, Set Brown Eyes, Closed Mouth, Velvet Dress, 18 In. . . . 495.00
Kestner, Bisque, Socket Head, Blue Sleep Eyes, Mohair Wig, 12 In. 330.00
Kestner, Bisque, Toddler, Original Wig & Clothes, 25 In. 950.00
Kestner, Bisque, Toddler, Wig & Clothes, 25 In. 950.00
Kestner, Child, Bisque, Swivel Head, Blue Eyes, Closed Mouth, 18 In. 6750.00
Kestner, Gibson Girl, Antique Bonnet, Heirloom Clothes, 19 1/2 In. 3200.00
Kestner, Jointed Body, Sleep Eyes, All Original, Marked L, 28 In. 1100.00
Kestner, O.I.C., Baby, Jointed Body, Antique Lace Dress, Leather Shoes, 7 1/2 In. 2850.00
Kestner, Painted Hair, Composition Jointed Body, 14 In. 165.00

Kestner, Pouty, Furrowed Brows, Blue Eyes, Original Clothes, 11 In. 650.00
Kestner, Pouty, Sleep Eyes, Powder Blue Dress, Leather Shoes, 22 In. 4200.00
Kestner, Straight Wrist, Composition Body, Mohair Wig, Closed Mouth, 19 In. 3495.00
Kewpie dolls are listed in the Kewpie category.
Kley & Hahn, 167, Baby, Brown Eyes, Crier Mechanism In Head, 20 In. 895.00
Kley & Hahn, 525, Bisque Head, Bent Limb Body, Dressed, 15 In. 700.00
Kley & Hahn, Bisque Head, Blue Intaglio Eyes, Open Mouth, Jointed Body, 15 In. 1050.00
Kley & Hahn, Bisque, Blond Hair, White Eye Dots, Closed Mouth, 21 In. 1500.00
Kling, Bisque Head, Sculpted Hair, Curls At Forehead, Muslin Body, c.1885, 19 In. 1100.00
Knickerbocker, Barney Rubble, Cloth, Box, 7 In. 25.00
Knickerbocker, Raggedy Ann & Andy, Bean Bag, 1971, 10 In., Pair 300.00
Kuhnlenz, Pale Iridescent Bisque, Gray Spiral Eyes, Composition Body, 15 In. 1495.00
Lenci, Girl, Cheerleader Outfit, Boy, Soccer Outfit, 1920s, 17 3/4 In., Pair 395.00
Lenci, Girl, Felt Swivel Head, Brown Eyes, Closed Mouth, 1930, 16 In. 850.00
Lenci, Girl, Felt Swivel Head, Side Glancing, Felt Body, Jointed Limbs, 1928, 16 In. 900.00
Lenci, Girl, Swivel Head, Blue Side Glancing Eyes, Brunette Wig, 1930, 14 In. 425.00
Lenci, Italian Boy, Felt Swivel Head, Brown Eyes, Closed Mouth, 1930, 17 In. 1100.00
Lenci, Oriental, Hand Stitched Rooted Wig, Widow's Peak, Kimono, Sandals, 14 In. 2000.00
Lenci, Pouty Girl, Felt Swivel Head, Blue Eyes, Closed Mouth, 19 In. 1300.00
Lenci, Salon Lady, Sultry Blue Eyes, Elongated Body, Cream Colored Gown, 19 In. 395.00
Lenci, Surprised Eyes, Holding Dog, Side Bustle On Dress, Long Curls, 22 In. 2200.00
Lenci, Woman, Long Limbs, All Original, 26 In. 1350.00
Limbach, Baby, Bisque, Jointed, 12 In. 595.00
Louis Amberg, Baby Peggy, Bisque Head, Brown Eyes, Kid Body, Human Wig, 20 In. ... 2500.00
Lucille Ball, Hollywood Walk Of Fame, Box, 20 In. 200.00
Madame Alexander, Agatha, 21 In. 400.00
Madame Alexander, Alice In Wonderland, 5 Piece Body, Box, 18 In. .... *Illus* 775.00
Madame Alexander, Alice, Blond Wig, Gray Sleep Eyes, 14 In. 400.00
Madame Alexander, Bride, 1958, 8 In. 850.00
Madame Alexander, Bunny, Original Clothes, Marked, 1930s, 16 In. 350.00
Madame Alexander, Butch, Composition & Cloth, 12 In. 225.00
Madame Alexander, Carmen, 1983-1986, 14 In. 90.00
Madame Alexander, Chatterbox, Blue Sleep Eyes, Blond Hair, 1961, 24 In. 325.00
Madame Alexander, Cissy, Plastic Head, Sleep Eyes, Jointed, Plaid Dress, 1955, 20 In. .. 160.00
Madame Alexander, Davy Crockett, 1955, 8 In. 1100.00
Madame Alexander, Degas Girl, 1967, 14 In. 95.00
Madame Alexander, Degas Girl, 1982, 14 In. 75.00
Madame Alexander, Denmark, No. 769, Box, 1970 .... 90.00
Madame Alexander, Dr. Defoe, 1938, 14 In. 1495.00
Madame Alexander, Elise Bride, 17 In. 175.00
Madame Alexander, Goldilocks, 1982, 12 In. 75.00
Madame Alexander, Goya, 1982, 21 In. 290.00
Madame Alexander, Groom, 7 1/2 In. 100.00
Madame Alexander, Holland, No. 391, Box, 1963 .... 220.00
Madame Alexander, Jane Withers, Name Pin, Clear Eyes, 15 In. 1250.00
Madame Alexander, Laurie, Little Women, 1982, 8 In. 80.00
Madame Alexander, Little Betty, All Composition, Tagged, 1930s, 9 In. 250.00
Madame Alexander, Little Red Riding Hood, Bent Knee, Walker, 8 In. 298.00
Madame Alexander, Little Women, 1982, 12 In., 6 Piece ....420.00 to 450.00
Madame Alexander, Marie, Composition Head, Brown Sleep Eyes, 1935, 11 In. 275.00
Madame Alexander, Mary Ann, Jointed, 1965, 14 In. 65.00
Madame Alexander, Marybel, The Doll Who Gets Well, Box, 1959 ....300.00 to 395.00
Madame Alexander, McGuffey Anna, 1981, 14 In. 75.00
Madame Alexander, Monet, All Tags, 1984, 20 In. 300.00
Madame Alexander, Prince Charles, 1957, 8 In. 1100.00
Madame Alexander, Princess Anne, 1957, 8 In. 1100.00
Madame Alexander, Princess Elizabeth, 16 In. 200.00
Madame Alexander, Princess Elizabeth, Composition, Marked, 17 In. 425.00
Madame Alexander, Puddin', Box, 14 In. 50.00
Madame Alexander, Pussy Cat, Black, Bent Knee, Crier, 1965, 19 In. 110.00
Madame Alexander, Queen Elizabeth II, 40 Year Celebration Of Coronation, 1992, 8 In. 135.00
Madame Alexander, Renoir, 1950, 14 In. 150.00
Madame Alexander, Rosamund Bridesmaid, 1951, 15 In. 350.00

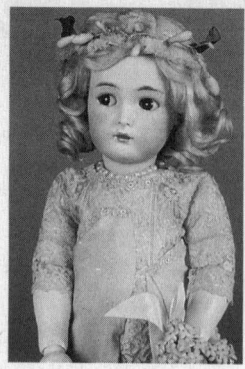

Doll, K * R, 50,
Bride, Bisque
Head,
Jointed, Wood
& Composition,
19 In.

Doll, Madame
Alexander, Alice
In Wonderland,
5 Piece Body,
Box, 18 In.;
Doll, Madame
Alexander, Sonja
Henie, Ski
Clothes,
Wooden Skis,
17 In.

Madame Alexander, Scarlett O'Hara, Green Velvet Dress, 1982, 21 In.	290.00
Madame Alexander, Scarlett O'Hara, White Dress, 1982, 14 In.	110.00
Madame Alexander, Snow White, Brown Sleep Eyes, Plastic, 8 In.	200.00
Madame Alexander, Sonja Henie, Composition, Brown Sleep Eyes, 1940, 18 In.	1000.00
Madame Alexander, Sonja Henie, Ski Clothes, Wooden Skis, 17 In. ....*Illus*	1250.00
Madame Alexander, Sweden, Chicken In Basket, No. 792	20.00
Madame Alexander, Treena Ballerina, All Original, 1952 ....600.00 to 650.00	
Madame Alexander, Victoria, 1954, 8 In.	1500.00
Mammy Yokum, Box, 1940s	165.00
Marionette, Baby Dragon, Pelham, Box, England	150.00
Marionette, Fred Flintstone, Dressed ....75.00 to 95.00	
Marionette, Indiana Jones, On Card, 3 3/4 In.	250.00
Marionette, Jambo The Jiver, Black Dancer, Wooden, 78 RPM Record, 1948	395.00
Marionette, Joonga From The Congo, Woman, 78 RPM Record, 1948	395.00
Marionette, Patty, With Skates, Box, 1950s	65.00
Marionette, Pinocchio, Composition, Moving Glass Eyes & Nose, Box, 1940s	275.00
Marionette, Sailor, Talking, Box, Hazelle's	125.00
Marionette, Wood & Composition, Tin Armor, 17 In.	550.00
Marotte, Bisque, Shoulder Head, Blue Eyes, Open Mouth, 13 In.	434.00
Martha Chase, Stockinet, Oil Painted Face, Dressed, c.1900, 20 In.	700.00
Mary Hoyer, Blond Curled Mohair Wig, Gray Sleep Eyes, Plastic, Box, 14 In.	425.00
Mary Hoyer, Brown Mohair Wig, Green Sleep Eyes, Plastic, Box, 14 In.	325.00
Mattel, Allan, Painted Red Hair, Beige Lips, Olive Green Jacket, 1964	60.00
Mattel, Barbie, 35th Anniversary	40.00
Mattel, Barbie, American Girl, Brown Hair ....*Illus*	450.00
Mattel, Barbie, Be My Valentine	75.00
Mattel, Barbie, Bubble Cut, Blue Swimsuit	125.00
Mattel, Barbie, Bubble Cut, Brunette, Pink Lips, Red Body Blouse	90.00
Mattel, Barbie, Career Girl, Black, White Tweed Jacket, Sheath Skirt	85.00
Mattel, Barbie, Cheerleader, White Sweater, Red Skirt, Red Tennis Shoes, White Socks	65.00
Mattel, Barbie, Czechoslovakian, Box, 1990	65.00
Mattel, Barbie, Drum Majorette, Red Velvet Jacket, Gold Trim, White Boots	60.00
Mattel, Barbie, Feelin' Groovy, 1986 ....100.00 to 140.00	
Mattel, Barbie, Golden Greetings, F.A.O. Schwarz, 1989	175.00
Mattel, Barbie, Happy Holiday, 1988 ....600.00 to 1000.00	
Mattel, Barbie, Happy Holiday, 1989	265.00
Mattel, Barbie, Happy Holiday, Black, 1990	160.00
Mattel, Barbie, Happy Holiday, Fuchsia Dress, Silver Design, 1990 ....165.00 to 200.00	
Mattel, Barbie, Hawaii, Grass Skirt, 2 Piece Red, White, Flower Lei, Plastic Pineapple	40.00
Mattel, Barbie, Kraft	50.00
Mattel, Barbie, Madison Avenue	150.00
Mattel, Barbie, Mexican, Box, 1988	20.00
Mattel, Barbie, Mexico, White Dress, Embroidered Trim, Green, Red Satin Skirt	20.00
Mattel, Barbie, Nigerian, Box, 1989	35.00

Mattel, Barbie, No. 1, Ponytail, Several Cards Of Clothing 4700.00
Mattel, Barbie, No. 3, Ponytail, Box .... *Illus* 1900.00
Mattel, Barbie, Nurse, Bubble Cut, Brown 185.00
Mattel, Barbie, Olympic Gymnast 20.00
Mattel, Barbie, Quick Curl, Box, 1972 .... 40.00
Mattel, Barbie, Rapunzel 48.00
Mattel, Barbie, Russian, Box, 1988 .... 45.00
Mattel, Barbie, Sapphire Dream 70.00
Mattel, Barbie, Savvy Shopper 95.00
Mattel, Barbie, Silver Screen 145.00
Mattel, Barbie, Snow Princess 95.00
Mattel, Barbie, Solo In The Spotlight, Box, 1990 .... 85.00
Mattel, Barbie, Sophisticated Lady, Box, 1990 .... 95.00
Mattel, Barbie, Spiegel's Shopping Chic 70.00
Mattel, Barbie, Star Trek 125.00
Mattel, Barbie, Starlight Waltz, Heather Dutton Signature 325.00
Mattel, Barbie, Summer Sophisticate 85.00
Mattel, Barbie, Swirl Ponytail, Medium Blond Hair, Beige Lips, 1964 .... 85.00
Mattel, Barbie, Talking, Original Clothes, 1971 .... 175.00
Mattel, Barbie, Twist'n Turn, Blond, Sunglasses, Pink & Orange Outfit, 1970 ..... 65.00
Mattel, Barbie, UNICEF, 1989 .... 40.00
Mattel, Barbie, Victorian Elegance 110.00
Mattel, Barbie, Walk Lively 95.00
Mattel, Barbie, Wedding Party Gift Set, 4 Dressed Dolls 1600.00
Mattel, Barbie, Wedding, White Taffeta & Lace, Box, 1960s 140.00
Mattel, Barbie, Winter Fantasy, Blue Earrings, Ring, F.A.O. Schwarz, 1990 .....155.00 to 205.00
Mattel, Barbie, Winter's Eve 30.00
Mattel, Buffy, Blond Character Doll, With Smaller Mrs. Beasley Doll, 1967 .... 210.00
Mattel, Captain Lazer 150.00
Mattel, Cecil Of Beany & Cecil, Plush, 1960s 35.00
Mattel, Francie, Black .... *Illus* 900.00
Mattel, Francie, Swimsuit, 1966 .... 125.00
Mattel, Julia, 1 Piece Nurse's Outfit, Box, 1968 .... 160.00
Mattel, Ken, 1962 .... 160.00
Mattel, Ken, Box, 1961 .... 80.00
Mattel, Ken, Dance Magic, Box, 1989 .... 35.00
Mattel, Ken, Holland, Box, 1961 .... 175.00
Mattel, Ken, Mexico, Brown Felt Jacket, Green Satin Cummerbund, Black Tie 115.00
Mattel, Midge, Black Hair, Box .... *Illus* 300.00
Mattel, Midge, Box, 1962 .... 450.00
Mattel, Midge, Brunette, Coral Lips With Teeth, 2 Piece Pink Outfit, Red Nylon, 1963 .. 105.00
Mattel, Midge, Brunette, Green Sheath Dress With Bow, Pink Lips, 1964 .... 80.00
Mattel, Mork & Mindy, Box, Pair 70.00
Mattel, Mork, Talking Space Pack, 1979 .... 28.00
Mattel, Neptune 850.00
Mattel, Skipper, Blond, Straight Leg, Box 100.00
Mattel, Skipper, No. 6, Bendable Legs, 1964 .... 300.00
Mattel, Twiggy, Original Clothes 125.00
Mego, Cher, Poseable, Plastic & Vinyl, Box, 1976, 12 In. ....50.00 to 75.00
Mego, Farrah, Box, Unused, 1977, 12 1/4 In. 75.00
Mego, Sonny Bono, 1976, 12 In. 45.00
Munich Art, Boy, Jointed, Knickered Dress Suit, Buckled Shoes, 13 In. 2950.00
Music Box, Singing Bird In A Gilded Cage, Metal, Windup 495.00
Nancy Ann Storybook, 151, Bridesmaid, Carrot Colored Wig, Box, 5 In. 30.00
Nancy Ann Storybook, 162, January Girl, Blond Wig, Blue Sleep Eyes, 5 In. 20.00
Nancy Ann Storybook, 162, January Girl, Carrot Colored Wig, Box, 5 In. 20.00
Nancy Ann Storybook, 9117, Little Bo Peep, Blond Wig, Box 30.00
Nancy Ann Storybook, Muffie, Blond Wig, Blue Sleep Eyes, Yellow Print Dress 160.00
Nancy Ann Storybook, Muffie, Blond Wig, White Cotton Panty, Red Shoes, Box, 8 In. 275.00
Nancy Ann Storybook, Muffie, Brown Sleep Eyes, Blond Wig, Plastic, 7 In. 110.00
Nancy Ann Storybook, Muffie, Brown Wig, Blue Sleep Eyes, 7 In. 250.00
Nancy Ann Storybook, Muffie, Brown Wig, Pink Nylon Panty, White Shoes, Box, 8 In. 260.00
Nancy Ann Storybook, Muffie, Pink Formal Lace Dress, Panties, Shoes, Box, 8 In. ... 210.00

Doll, Mattel,
Barbie,
American Girl,
Brown Hair

Doll, Mattel, Barbie,
No. 3, Ponytail, Box

Nancy Ann Storybook, Muffie, Red Hair, Blue Nylon Panty, White Shoes, Box, 8 In. . .	500.00
Nancy Ann Storybook, Muffie, Tosca Wig, Brown Sleep Eyes, Box, 7 In.	150.00
Nancy Ann Storybook, Style Show, Blond Saran Wig, Gray Sleep Eyes, 1950, 18 In. . .	475.00
Nippon, Baby, Orange Cap, Bisque, 4 In.	90.00
Norah Wellings, Black, 7 In.	85.00
Norah Wellings, Girl, West Indies, Tag, 8 In.	95.00
Ohlhaver, Coquette, Bisque Head, Molded Hair, Composition, Ball Jointed, 1915, 12 In. .	650.00
Ohlhaver, Revalo, Girl, Bisque Head, Open Mouth, Composition, Pale Blue Cap, 15 In. . .	495.00
Paper dolls are listed in their own category.	
Papier-Mache, Ballerina, Costume, France, Victorian, 10 In.	180.00
Papier-Mache, Black Enamel Eyes, Open Mouth, 1855, 23 In.	950.00
Papier-Mache, Black Sculpted Hair, Closed Mouth, Jointed, 1860, 19 In.	2300.00
Papier-Mache, Blue Eyes, Brunette Mohair Wig, 1900, 18 In.	1400.00
Papier-Mache, Cameo Face, Black Sculpted Hair, Wooden Limbs, 16 In.	1300.00
Papier-Mache, Enamel Eyes, Closed Smiling Mouth, 1893, 13 In.	850.00
Papier-Mache, Girl, Wax-Over, Blond Hair, Black Enamel Eyes, 20 In.	500.00
Papier-Mache, Glass Eyes, Closed Mouth, Mohair Wig, Muslin Body, Silk Gown, 25 In.	1500.00
Papier-Mache, Painted Brown Eyes, Closed Mouth, Wooden Arms, Legs, 8 In.	275.00
Papier-Mache, Shoulder Head, Painted Eyes, Closed Mouth, Plaid Dress, 32 In.	1000.00
Papier-Mache, Toddler, Dimples, Pug Nose, 14 In.	850.00
Parian, Blond, Dimple In Chin, 1880s, 27 In.	375.00
Parian, Fashion, Blond, Painted Eyes, Molded Neckline, Clothes, 24 1/2 In.	950.00
Parian, Fashion, Kid Body, Dress With Bustle & Train, 19 In.	2200.00
Parian, Kid Body, Blue Eyes, Closed Mouth, Blond Hair, Blue Ribbon, 15 In.	580.00
Pincushion dolls are listed in their own category.	
Pintel & Godchaux, Girl, Plump Cheeks, Velvet Jacket Over Lace Dress, 19 In.	3100.00
Pintel & Godchaux, Paperweight Eyes, Square Teeth, 16 In.	1395.00
Puppet, Bear Family, 3 Piece	1200.00
Puppet, Cindy Bear, Vinyl Head	65.00
Puppet, Hand, 101 Dalmatians, Plush	35.00
Puppet, Hand, Barney Google, Rubber Face	75.00
Puppet, Hand, Betty Rubble, Germany, 1960s	95.00
Puppet, Hand, Big Mac, McDonald, 1973	50.00
Puppet, Hand, Bozo The Clown, Cloth, Vinyl Head, Knickerbocker, 1962, 9 In.	20.00
Puppet, Hand, Dennis The Menace, Vinyl Head, 1950s	45.00
Puppet, Hand, Hoppy, Kangaroo From The Flintstones, Germany, 1960s	135.00
Puppet, Hand, Lion, Wizard Of Oz, 1960s	15.00
Puppet, Hand, Magilla Gorilla, Ideal, 1960s	75.00
Puppet, Hand, Mecki The Hedgehog, Steiff, 1940s	70.00
Puppet, Hand, Mr. Magoo	15.00
Puppet, Hand, Ricochet Rabbit, Ideal, 1960s	75.00
Puppet, Hand, Ronald McDonald, 1970	5.00
Puppet, Hand, Ronald Reagan, Boxing	35.00

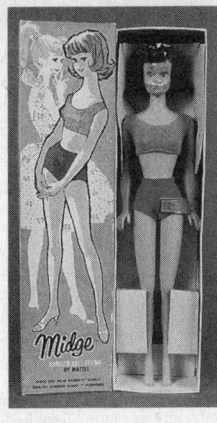

Doll, Mattel,
Francie, Black

Doll, Mattel,
Midge,
Black Hair, Box

Puppet, Hand, Talking Mister Ed, Vinyl, Cloth, Pull String, Mattel, 1962, 11 In.	40.00
Puppet, Hand, Thor, Super Hero, Imperial, Package, 1978	15.00
Puppet, Hand, Tin Man, Wizard Of Oz, Proctor & Gamble Premium, 1965	25.00
Puppet, Hand, Topo Gigio Mouse, Vinyl Head, Hair, Cloth Legs, 1960s	60.00
Puppet, Hand, Umbriago, Jimmy Durante, Box	195.00
Puppet, Hand, Woody Woodpecker, Talking Mechanism, Mattel, 1963	50.00
Puppet, Incredible Hulk, Cloth, 1970s	40.00
Puppet, Magilla Gorilla	95.00
Puppet, Mushmouse	75.00
Puppet, Push, Bugs Bunny, Label	30.00
Puppet, Push, Huckleberry Hound, Kohner, 1960s	30.00
Puppet, Push, Smurf, 1982	6.00
Puppet, Wizard Of Oz, Composition	1000.00
Puppet, Yogi Bear	50.00
Rabery & Delphieu, Bisque Head, Paperweight Eyes, Wooden Body, 1890, 23 In.	2900.00
Recknagel, Child, Bisque Head, Original Clothes, 13 In.	245.00
Recknagel, Googly, No. 49, 9 In.	795.00
Reliable, Indian Maid, Headband & Belt, 1940s, 11 In.	100.00
Revalo, Girl, Blue Sleep Eyes, Open Mouth, Mohair Wig, Peach Trimmed Dress, 18 In. .	225.00
Roni, Raccoon, Olympics, Lake Placid Winter Games, Stuffed, 1980	8.00
S & H dolls are also listed here as Bergmann and Simon & Halbig.	
S & H, 979, Lady, Bisque, High Cheekbones, Almond Eyes, Swivel Head, 27 In.	2500.00
S & H, Flapper Body, Ball Jointed, 13 In.	1350.00
S.F.B.J., 60, Brown Paperweight Eyes, Jointed, Silk Clothes, 14 In., Pair	650.00
S.F.B.J., 60, Enameled Blue Eyes, Closed Mouth, Molded Teeth, Redressed, 11 1/2 In. ...	295.00
S.F.B.J., 226, Bisque, Boy, Smiling, Dressed, Large	1995.00
S.F.B.J., 227, Bisque Head, Blue Eyes, Open Mouth, 21 In.	2000.00
S.F.B.J., 236, Bisque Head, Sleep Eyes, Bent Limb, Lace Gown, c.1915, 14 In.	1300.00
S.F.B.J., 236, Laughing, Original Wig, 26 In.	2600.00
S.F.B.J., 247, Bisque, Blue Sleep Eyes, Closed Mouth, 1910, 21 In.	2900.00
S.F.B.J., 247, Toddler, Sleep Eyes, Open Close Mouth, Upper Teeth, 20 In.	3950.00
S.F.B.J., 251, Bisque, Socket Head, Blue Sleep Eyes, Open Mouth, 14 In. ......1800.00 to	1870.00
S.F.B.J., 251, Toddler Body, Blue Sleep Eyes, 14 In.	1495.00
S.F.B.J., 252, Character, Pouty Toddler, Dressed, 13 In.	6820.00
Schoenau & Hoffmeister, 1078, Character, Sleep Eyes, 28 1/2 In.	1625.00
Schoenau & Hoffmeister, 1249, Santa Claus, Black, Child Body, 17 1/2 In.	2650.00
Schoenau & Hoffmeister, 1906, Bisque Head, Sleep Eyes, Jointed Body, 14 In.	400.00
Schoenau & Hoffmeister, 1906, Bisque Head, Sleep Eyes, Jointed Body, Girl, 30 In. ..	995.00
Schoenau & Hoffmeister, 1909, Bisque Head, Blue Sleep Eyes, 24 In.	300.00
Schoenau & Hoffmeister, 1910, Bisque Head, Brown Sleep Eyes, 23 In.	425.00
Schoenau & Hoffmeister, 1910, Oriental, Bisque Head, Straight Limb, 10 In.	810.00
Schoenau & Hoffmeister, 1912, Soldier, Bisque & Papier-Mache, 9 In.	410.00
Schoenau & Hoffmeister, Bisque, Blue Sleep Eyes, Open Mouth, 19 In.	550.00

Schoenau & Hoffmeister, Bisque, Swivel Head, Sleep Eyes, Open Mouth, Dress, 27 In. 550.00
Schoenhut, 114, Gretchen, Belted Drop Waist Dress, 17 In. 1695.00
Schoenhut, 204, Boy, Wooden Head, Closed Mouth, Pouty, 1911, 16 In. 2200.00
Schoenhut, 304, Girl, Wooden Head, Blue Eyes, White Eye Dots, Pouty, 16 In. 1050.00
Schoenhut, 309, Brown Intaglio Eyes, Jointed, Sailor Suit, 16 In. 2800.00
Schoenhut, Aged Man, Gray Hair, Beard, Closed Mouth, Jointed, 1910, 7 In. 275.00
Schoenhut, Auburn Mohair Wig, Brown Eyes, Open Mouth, Painted Teeth, 15 In. 2100.00
Schoenhut, Baby, Painted Hair, 14 1/2 In. 285.00
Schoenhut, Bisque, Pouty, Blue Intaglio Eyes, 18 In. 1250.00
Schoenhut, Circus Woman, Bisque Head, Brown Hair, Jointed Legs, 9 In. 650.00
Schoenhut, Farmer, Wooden Head, Gray Forelock Curl, Blue Eyes, 8 In. 425.00
Schoenhut, Milkmaid, Wooden Head, Brown Hair, Blue Eyes, Open Hands, 7 In. 450.00
Schoenhut, Ringmaster, Bisque Head, Brown Sculpted Hair, Blue Eyes, 9 In. 650.00
Schoenhut, Wooden Head, Miss Dolly, Brown Eyes, Brunette Mohair Wig, 22 In. 850.00
Schoenhut, Wooden Head, Pouty, Girl, Blue Eyes, Closed Mouth, Jointed, 14 In. 1000.00
Schoenhut, Wooden Head, Toddler, Blue Eyes, Tan Painted Hair, 1917, 11 In. 800.00
Schuetzmeister & Quendt, 101, Jeanette, 30 In. 995.00
Shari Lewis, With Lamb Chop, Box 25.00
Shirley Temple dolls are included in the Shirley Temple category.
Simon & Halbig dolls are also listed here under Bergmann and S & H.
Simon & Halbig, 120, Bisque, Blue Sleep Eyes, Brown Wig, Germany, 21 In. 4000.00
Simon & Halbig, 530, Bisque Head, Blue Sleep Eyes, Open Mouth, 20 In. 310.00
Simon & Halbig, 540, Baby Blanche, Bisque, 22 In. 595.00
Simon & Halbig, 550, Bisque Head, Composition Body, Redressed, 23 In. 360.00
Simon & Halbig, 719, 2 Faces, 1 Crying, 1 Smiling, Original Dress, 13 In. 4200.00
Simon & Halbig, 886, Bisque Head, Blue Sleep Eyes, Blond Mohair Wig, 5 In. 550.00
Simon & Halbig, 886, Bisque Head, Brown Sleep Eyes, Open Mouth, 8 In. 800.00
Simon & Halbig, 905, Bisque Head, Brown Inset Eyes, Jointed, 1890, 14 In. 1000.00
Simon & Halbig, 905, Bisque Swivel Head, Kid Body, Paperweight Eyes, 20 In. 2495.00
Simon & Halbig, 920, Bisque Head, Mohair Wig, Kid Gusset-Jointed Body, 1885, 16 In. 2000.00
Simon & Halbig, 920, Bisque, Paperweight Eyes, Mohair Wig, 18 In. 2995.00
Simon & Halbig, 949, Bisque, Oily, Brown Mohair Wig, Square Teeth, 32 In. 3200.00
Simon & Halbig, 950, Bisque, Brown Inset Eyes, Brunette Mohair Wig, 12 In. 1150.00
Simon & Halbig, 950, Dome Head, 15 In. 1150.00
Simon & Halbig, 979, Bisque, Brown Inset Eyes, Open Mouth, 13 In. 800.00
Simon & Halbig, 1004, Dancer, 5 Movements, Electric, Sleep Eyes, Lace Gown, 26 In. . 19000.00
Simon & Halbig, 1009, Character, Brown Paperweight Eyes, 19 In. 3100.00
Simon & Halbig, 1039, Kissing, Walking & Flirting, Brown Eyes, 22 In. 805.00
Simon & Halbig, 1078, Blue Sleep Eyes, Black Human Hair Wig, 30 In. 1250.00
Simon & Halbig, 1079, Bisque Head, Brown Sleep Eyes, 15 In. 1600.00
Simon & Halbig, 1079, Bisque, Blue Dress With Extra Lace, 25 In. 895.00
Simon & Halbig, 1079, Bisque, Blue Sleep Eyes, Blond Mohair Wig, 20 In. 950.00
Simon & Halbig, 1079, Bisque, Blue Sleep Eyes, Composition, 1900, 9 In. 700.00
Simon & Halbig, 1079, Bisque, Brown Sleep Eyes, Open Mouth, Jointed, 16 In. 550.00
Simon & Halbig, 1079, Bisque, Gray Sleep Eyes, Blond Mohair Wig, 8 In. 650.00
Simon & Halbig, 1079, Bisque, Jointed Body, Wig, Clothes, 11 1/2 In. 650.00
Simon & Halbig, 1079, Bisque, Sleep Eyes, Blond Mohair Wig, 17 1/2 In. 345.00
Simon & Halbig, 1079, Blue Sleep Eyes, Human Hair Wig, 21 In. 1225.00
Simon & Halbig, 1129, Bisque, Amber Head, Brown Sleep Eyes, 19 In. 4200.00
Simon & Halbig, 1129, Olive Tone Body, Slant Eyes, 21 1/2 In. 5900.00
Simon & Halbig, 1159, Woman, Bisque Head, Sleep Eyes, Fully Jointed Body, 23 In. ... 1840.00
Simon & Halbig, 1159, Woman, Blue Sleep Eyes, White Dress, 16 In. 1695.00
Simon & Halbig, 1199, Bisque, Brown Sleep Eyes, Open Mouth, 17 In. 1800.00
Simon & Halbig, 1249, Bisque, Blue Sleep Eyes, Jointed, 25 In. 1800.00
Simon & Halbig, 1249, Bisque, Santa, Large Amber Eyes, Hat, 20 In. 1300.00
Simon & Halbig, 1294, Toddler, Chubby, 2 Teeth, Starfish Hands, 8 In. 1100.00
Simon & Halbig, 1299, Character, Dimples, Blue Set Eyes, Human Hair Wig, 10 In. ... 775.00
Simon & Halbig, 1303, Bisque Head, Sleep Eyes, Wooden Body, Dressed, 22 In. 13250.00
Simon & Halbig, 1329, Bisque, Amber Head, Brown Sleep Eyes, 15 In. 1800.00
Simon & Halbig, 1329, Oriental, Bisque, 16 In. 2495.00
Simon & Halbig, 1388, Bisque, Jointed Body, Character, 23 In. 24000.00
Simon & Halbig, 1428, Freddie, Character, Sleep Eyes, 5 Piece Composition, 13 In. 1450.00
Simon & Halbig, 1428, Toddler, Closed Mouth, 14 1/2 In. 2500.00

Simon & Halbig, Bisque Head, Sleep Eyes, Open Mouth, Blond Wig, Kid Body, 18 In. .   905.00
Simon & Halbig, Bisque, Baby, Sleep Eyes, Closed Mouth, 13 In. 1265.00
Simon & Halbig, Bisque, Blue Sleep Eyes, Open Mouth, 1900, 23 In. 1000.00
Simon & Halbig, Bisque, Blue Sleep Eyes, Open Mouth, Brown Wig 800.00
Simon & Halbig, Bisque, Brown Eyes, Dressed As Scottish Lass, 21 In. 695.00
Simon & Halbig, Bisque, Brown Sleep Eyes, Open Mouth, Dress, Rosebuds, 21 In. 500.00
Simon & Halbig, Bisque, Character Boy, Painted Eyes, Mohair Wig, Suit, 16 In. 12000.00
Simon & Halbig, Bisque, Paperweight Eyes, Open Mouth, Human Hair Wig, 19 In. 2100.00
Simon & Halbig, Bisque, Socket Head, Brown Sleep Eyes, Open Mouth, 22 In. 2200.00
Simon & Halbig, Bisque, Swivel Head & Wrists, 4 Teeth, New Clothes, 22 In. 990.00
Simon & Halbig, Bisque, Swivel Head, Cobalt Blue Eyes, Closed Mouth, 10 In. 3300.00
Simon & Halbig, Bisque, Swivel Neck, Long Wig, 4 In. 1375.00
Simon & Halbig, Character, Fired Brown Color, Fixed Eyes, Original Wig, 16 In. 2750.00
Simon & Halbig, Sleep Eyes, Mohair Wig, Re-Dressed, 31 In. 2420.00
Skeezix, Oilcloth, King, 1924, 13 In. . . . . .95.00 to 100.00
Skookum, Indian Chief, 38 In. 900.00
Skookum, Indian, 14 In. 225.00
Sonneberg Taufling, Bisque, Blond Mohair Wig, Open Mouth, 16 In. 1250.00
Sorenson, Alice In Wonderland, Cotton Dress, c.1970, 28 In. 300.00
Steiff, Man, Caricature Features, Glass Eyes, Mohair Wig, Felt Body, 1910, 14 In. 1312.00
Steiff, Micki & Mecki, 6 1/2 In., Pair 100.00
Steiner, Baby, Crying, 17 1/2 In. 2530.00
Steiner, Bisque Head, Blue Paperweight Eyes, Closed Mouth, 1890, 10 In. 3800.00
Steiner, Bisque Head, Blue Sleep Eyes, Blond Mohair Wig, 8 In. 195.00
Steiner, Bisque Head, Blue Sleep Eyes, Brown Mohair Wig, 15 In. 4600.00
Steiner, Bisque Head, Blue Sleep Eyes, Open Mouth, 8 In. 195.00
Steiner, Bisque Head, Brown Sleep Eyes, Composition, 1910, 26 In. 800.00
Steiner, Bisque, Blue Enamel Eyes, Blond Lambs Wool Wig, 1882, 29 In. 4000.00
Steiner, Bisque, Blue Paperweight Eyes, Auburn Mohair Wig, 10 In. 2600.00
Steiner, Bisque, Blue Paperweight Eyes, Blond Mohair Wig, 1890, 16 In. 5000.00
Steiner, Bisque, Blue Paperweight Eyes, Brunette Human Hair, 18 In. 4200.00
Steiner, Bisque, Blue Paperweight Eyes, Closed Mouth, 1889, 11 In. 2900.00
Steiner, Bisque, Blue Paperweight Eyes, Closed Mouth, 25 In. 6200.00
Steiner, Bisque, Blue Paperweight Eyes, Lavender Lace, 16 In. 3900.00
Steiner, Fixed Paperweight Eyes, Jointed Papier-Mache Body, Ribbed Silk Suit, 29 In. . . 7360.00
Steiner, Girl, Fur Cape, Pocketbook, Glass Eyes, Stamped Back, 22 In. 7500.00
Steiner, Mechanical, Child, Says Mama, Open Mouth, Silk Smocked Dress, Bonnet 1200.00
Steiner, Walking, Bisque, Blue Enamel Eyes, Closed Mouth, 1889, 18 In. 3400.00
Steiner, Walking, Bisque, Paperweight Eyes, Outlined Mouth, c.1894, 22 In. . . .4000.00 to 5500.00
Stevens & Brown, Walking, Clockwork, Pushing Carriage, c.1872, 11 In. 1265.00
Swaine, Bisque, Curls, Glass Sleep Eyes, Closed Mouth, Bent Limb Baby Body, 16 In. . . . 1450.00
Terrene, Bisque Shoulder Plate, Head & Upper Arms, Wooden & Kid Body, 1860s 6500.00
Terri Lee, Bonnie Lu, Black, 16 In. 600.00
Terri Lee, Hard Plastic Body, Brown Eyes, Closed Mouth, Black Skin Wig, 16 In. 295.00
Terri Lee, Hard Plastic Body, Brown Eyes, Closed Mouth, Original Black Hair, 16 In. . .   630.00
Tete Jumeau, Bisque, Closed Mouth, Auburn Wig, Bulgy Eyes, Marked Shoes, 24 In. . . . 6650.00
Tete Jumeau, Bisque, Socket Head, Blue Eyes, Mohair Wig, Jointed, Dress, 20 In. 3630.00
Tete Jumeau, Brown Paperweight Eyes, Pink, Ecru Silk, Lace, 12 In. 4350.00
Topsy-Turvy, Composition, Brown Eyes, Painted Black Hair, Original Dress, 17 In. 137.50
Topsy-Turvy, Mammy, Rabbit 95.00
Troll, Voodoo, Black Plastic, White Fuzzy Hair, Ruby Eyes, 1960s 15.00
Ventriloquist Dummy, Farfel, Jimmy Nelson's TV Dog, With Record, Box, 1950s 150.00
Ventriloquist Dummy, Groucho Marx, Mouth Moves, Pull String, 30 In. 95.00
Ventriloquist Dummy, Pee-Wee Herman, Box, 1989 . . . .   100.00
Vogue, Ginny, Alaskan, Brown Wig, Blue Sleep Eyes, Brown Jacket, 8 In. 200.00
Vogue, Ginny, Beach, Blond Braided Wig, Blue Swimsuit Outfit, Plastic, 8 In. 450.00
Vogue, Ginny, Blue Sleep Eyes, Blond Braided Wig, Red Mouth, 1958, 8 In. 100.00
Vogue, Ginny, Brown Saran Hair, Blue Sleep Eyes, Red Mouth, 1957, 8 In. 170.00
Vogue, Ginny, Gretel, Yellow Braided Wig, Brown Sleep Eyes, Plastic, 1953, 8 In. 210.00
Vogue, Ginny, Gym Kids, Blond Braided Wig, Blue Eyes, Black Shoes, Box, 8 In. 180.00
Vogue, Ginny, Hansel, Blond Page Boy Cut Wig, Flowers In Cap, Plastic, 1953, 8 In. . . .   310.00
Vogue, Ginny, Indian, Black Braided Wig, Brown Sleep Eyes, White Outfit, 8 In. 190.00
Vogue, Ginny, Kindergarten, Blue Sleep Eyes, Blond Poodle Wig, 1952, 8 In. . . . .250.00 to 500.00

Doll, Volland, Raggedy Andy,
Cloth, 17 In.

**If you buy an old cloth doll, put it
in a closed box with an insect
strip for 48 hours to be sure
there are no insects. Be sure the
strip does not touch the doll.**

Vogue, Ginny, Skater, 8 In. . . . . .150.00 to 250.00
Vogue, Ginny, Skier, Brown Mohair Wig, Blue Sleep Eyes, Ski Outfit, 8 In. 130.00
Vogue, Ginny, Straight Leg, Painted Lashes, 8 In. 125.00
Vogue, Ginny, Tennis, Red Braided Wig, Brown Sleep Eyes, Box, 8 In. 275.00
Vogue, Ginny, Tiny Miss, Auburn Braided Wig, Blue Sleep Eyes, 1953, 8 In. 450.00
Vogue, Ginny, Tiny Miss, Auburn Curled Wig, Blue Sleep Eyes, 1953, 8 In. 475.00
Vogue, Ginny, Tiny Miss, Blond Braided Wig, Blue Sleep Eyes, 1953, 8 In. 425.00
Vogue, Ginny, Tiny Miss, Brown Braided Wig, Blue Sleep Eyes, Straw Hat, 7 In. 550.00
Vogue, Ginny, Walker, Blond Wig, Blue Sleep Eyes, Tagged Dress, 8 In. 130.00
Vogue, Jeff, Molded Black Hair, Gray Sleep Eyes, Aqua Outfit, 10 In. 80.00
Vogue, Jill, Blond Wig, Blue Sleep Eyes, Pink Strapless Dress, 10 In. 120.00
Vogue, Little Angel, Blue Sleep Eyes, Vinyl Head, Plastic, 1962, 11 In. 30.00
Vogue, Pixie, Red Caracul Wig, Blue Sleep Eyes, Red Shoes, Plastic, 7 In. 450.00
Volland, Raggedy Andy, Cloth Head, Black Shoebutton Eyes, Smiling Mouth, 17 In. 1870.00
Volland, Raggedy Andy, Cloth, 17 In. . . . .*Illus*   1700.00
Volland, Raggedy Ann & Andy, Muslin, Smiling Mouth, 1915, 15 & 16 In., Pair 1900.00
Walker, Mary-Lu, Green Sleep Eyes, Blond Braided Wig, Blue Skirt, 17 In. 80.00
Wax, Art Deco, Lavish Clothes, High Heeled Shoes, 10 1/2 In. 750.00
Wax, Baby, Pale Blue Eyes, Closed Mouth, Antique Christening Dress, 21 In. 1430.00
Wax, Baby, Rooted Hair, Glass Eyes, 19 In. 1150.00
Wax, Blond Wig, Tartan Wool Dress, Velvet School Clothes, 32 In. 695.00
Wax, Brown Eyes, Eyebrows, 17 In. 1100.00
Wax, Dark Brown Hair, Brown Glass Eyes, Open Mouth, Orange Dress, 28 In. 2000.00
Wax, Lucy Peck, White Dress, Straw Hat, Brunette Hair, Curled Fingers, 25 In. 2750.00
Wooden, Black Modeled Hair, Jointed Wooden Body, Germany, 1850, 7 In. 650.00
Wooden, Black, Pin Jointed, Late 19th Century, 18 In. 500.00
Wooden, Jointed, Original Paint, White Striped Dress, 16 In. 540.00
Wooden, Toy Peddler, Black Painted Hair, Jointed Limbs, 1830, 9 In. 1050.00
Wooden, Woman, Black Sculpted Braids, Blue Eyes, Jointed, 1840, 3 In., Pair 700.00

DONALD DUCK items are included in the Disneyana category.

DOORSTOPS have been made in all types of designs. The vast majority of the doorstops sold today are cast iron and were made from about
1890 to 1930. Most of them are shaped like people, animals, flowers,
or ships. Reproductions and newly designed examples are sold in gift
shops.

3 Geese, Cast Iron 650.00
Abe Lincoln, 7 3/4 x 5 5/8 In. 240.00
Amish Woman, Hubley 175.00
Aunt Jemima, Cast Iron 115.00
Baby, Crying, Cast Iron 60.00
Basket Of Flowers, Iron, Original Paint, 5 1/2 In. 85.00
Basket Of Flowers, Oval Frame, Albany Foundry, 8 In. 90.00

Bear, With Honey 3740.00
Bird In Box, Parrot, Hubley, 4 3/4 x 2 3/4 In. 330.00
Black Man On Cotton Bale, Pot Metal 3410.00
Blue Boy, Bradley & Hubbard 1250.00
Bobby The Cop, Cast Iron 350.00
Cat, Chase, Copper, Brass, Von Nessen 240.00
Cat, Scratching, Cast Iron 1870.00
Cat, Siamese, Bisque 40.00
Cat, Sitting, Black, Cast Iron 200.00
Cat, Sitting, Cast Iron, 12 In. 24.00
Charleston Dancers, Hubley 2970.00
Colonial Man, Waverly Studio, 4 1/2 x 2 3/4 In. 230.00
Colonial Woman, Waverly Studio, 4 1/2 x 2 3/4 In. 210.00
Cottage, Cape Cod, Hubley, 5 1/2 x 7 3/4 In. 415.00
Cottage, Casting, 4 5/8 x 7 1/2 In. 230.00
Cottage, National Foundry, 5 3/4 x 7 1/2 In. 220.00
Cottage, Whimsical Style, 7 1/4 x 8 1/2 In. 220.00
Dog, Airedale, Full-Figure, Black, Brown, Cast Iron, 8 1/2 In. 220.00
Dog, Boston Terrier, Original Paint, Cast Iron, 8 1/4 In. 95.00
Dog, Boston Terrier, Original Paint, Cast Iron, 9 3/4 In. 135.00
Dog, Boston Terrier, Standing, Full-Figure, Black & White, Leather Collar, 8 In. 60.00
Dog, Boston Terrier, Standing, Full-Figure, Black, White, Cast Iron, 9 1/2 In. 55.00
Dog, Boston Terrier, Standing, Full-Figure, Black, White, Hubley, 10 1/4 In. 220.00
Dog, Boxer, Bronze 633.00
Dog, Boxer, Full-Figure, Standing, Hubley, 8 1/2 x 9 In. 633.00
Dog, Bulldog Looking To The Left, Cast Iron 250.00
Dog, Bulldog, Painted, LAGS, Cast Iron, 7 3/4 In. 220.00
Dog, Cocker Spaniel, Full-Figure, Hubley, 6 3/4 x 11 In. 688.00
Dog, Dachshund, Full-Figure, Hubley, 5 1/2 x 9 1/2 In. 743.00
Dog, Doberman Pinscher, Full-Figure, Hubley, 8 x 8 1/2 In. 688.00
Dog, English Bulldog, Cast Iron, 8 In. 125.00
Dog, English Setter, Cast Iron, Late 19th Century, 9 x 16 In. 415.00
Dog, Fox Terrier, Painted, Black & White, Cast Iron, 7 3/4 In. 185.00
Dog, German Shepherd, Facing Sideways, Hubley 145.00
Dog, German Shepherd, Hubley 125.00
Dog, Pekingese 1980.00
Dog, Pointer, Standing, Full-Figure, Worn Paint, Iron, 15 1/4 In. 165.00
Dog, Scotty, Double, Cast Iron, 1920s, 6 x 9 In. 145.00
Dog, Scotty, Sitting, Full-Figure, Black, Cast Iron, 8 1/4 In. 105.00
Dog, Scotty, Standing, Hubley 170.00
Dog, St. Bernard, Hennessee Whiskey 155.00
Dog, Wirehaired Terrier, Cast Iron 165.00
Duck, Marked EMG, Cast Iron, 10 In. 195.00
Duck, White, Cast Iron, 9 1/2 In. 150.00
Dwarf, Full-Figure, Worn Polychrome Paint, Cast Iron, 10 In. 385.00
Eagle, No. 665, 1920s, 7 1/2 In. 125.00
Elephant, Cast Iron, 11 1/2 In. 150.00
Farm House, Bradley & Hubbard, 6 x 8 In. 3190.00
Floral Oval, Original Paint, 4 1/2 In. 160.00
Flower Basket, Bradley & Hubbard, 11 3/4 x 7 In. 360.00
Flower Basket, Cast Iron, Box, Hubley 1705.00
Flower Basket, Daisy Bowl, Hubley, 7 1/2 x 5 1/8 In. 190.00
Flower Basket, Iris, Hubley, 10 5/8 x 6 3/4 In. 415.00
Flower Basket, Jonquil, Wooden Base, Hubley, 7 x 6 In. 275.00
Flower Basket, Lilies Of The Valley, Hubley, 10 1/2 x 7 1/2 In. 385.00
Flower Basket, Marigolds, Pastel Colors, Hubley, 7 1/2 x 8 In. 210.00
Flower Basket, Poppies & Cornflowers, Hubley, 7 1/2 x 6 1/2 In. 358.00
Flower Basket, Poppies & Snapdragons, Hubley, 7 1/2 x 7 In. 305.00
Flower Basket, Poppies, Hubley, 10 5/8 x 7 7/8 In. 305.00
Flower Basket, Primrose, Yellow Flower Variation, Hubley, 7 3/8 x 6 1/4 In. 180.00
Flower Basket, Rose Vase, Hubley, 10 1/8 x 8 In. 275.00
Flower Basket, Tulip Vase, Hubley, 10 x 8 In. 330.00
Flower Basket, Zinnias, Hubley, 9 3/4 x 8 1/2 In. 305.00

Footmen, Fish, Cast Iron, 9 1/8 In. 1050.00
Footmen, Fish, Cast Iron, 12 1/8 In. ....1870.00 to 2200.00
Fruit Basket, Assorted Fruit, Multicolored, Albany Foundry, 10 1/8 x 7 1/2 In. 275.00
Fruit Basket, Cherries On Base, 11 1/2 x 10 In. 1155.00
Fruit Basket, Judd Co. 165.00
Fruit Cornucopia, Cast Iron, 8 1/2 In. 578.00
Giraffe, Hubley, 12 1/2 In. 4070.00
Golfer, Gold, Cast Iron 150.00
Golfer, Putting, Red Jacket, White Pants, Gray Socks, Cast Iron, 8 1/4 In. 357.00
Horse & Carriage, Cast Iron 125.00
Horse, 8 5/8 In. 135.00
Horse, King Genius, Signed, Iron, 1938, 12 x 12 In. ....110.00 to 140.00
Indian Head, Black Hair, Red, 7 /38 In. 190.00
Jack Rabbit, Painted, Cast Iron, 11 In. 70.00
Jonquils, Hubley 175.00
Lincoln's Cabin, Cast Iron 715.00
Little Red Riding Hood, Grace Drayton Design, Hubley, 9 1/2 x 5 In. 688.00
London Mail Coach, Cast Iron 145.00
Major Domo, Cast Iron 200.00
Man, Reading Book, Quaker Style Minister, 4 1/4 x 3 1/2 In. 358.00
Minuet Girl, Judd Co., 8 1/2 x 5 In. 210.00
Monkey, Sitting With Tail In Front, Cast Iron 250.00
Mutt & His Bone, Cast Iron 300.00
Narcissus, Hubley 175.00
Owl, Hubbard 2310.00
Parlor Maid, Fish, Cast Iron 1375.00
Parrot, Box, Hubley 330.00
Peacock On Fence, Greenblatt, Cast Iron 770.00
Pear, On Flower Backplate, 4 1/4 x 3 In. 245.00
Penguin, Taylor Cook, Cast Iron 2090.00
Peter Rabbit, Grace Drayton Design, Hubley, 9 1/2 x 4 3/4 In. 330.00
Pheasant, Hubley 425.00
Pillow, Beaded, Flowers On Fringe, Bird On Branch, Whimsy 120.00
Poppies & Cornflowers, Hubley, Cast Iron ....125.00 to 150.00
Potted Flower, Cast Iron 1020.00
Rabbit, Eating Carrot, Cast Iron, 1930, 8 In. 1155.00
Rabbit, Top Hat, Cast Iron, 9 7/8 In. 605.00
Ram, Worn Repaint, Cast Iron, 7 1/4 In. 300.00
Rooster, Cast Iron, Large ....195.00 to 259.00
Sailing Ship, Albany Foundry, 6 1/2 In. 90.00
Sailor, Blue Pants, White Shirt, Hat, 11 3/8 x 5 In. 825.00
Ship, Cast Iron, 11 x 10 1/2 In. ....65.00 to 100.00
Squirrel, Cast Iron 385.00
Stork, Hubley 475.00
Sun Face, Brass, 13 In. 145.00
Sunbonnet Baby, Cast Iron 125.00
Tulips, Cast Iron, 12 In. 175.00
Twin Kittens, Cast Iron 595.00
Urn, Grecian, Gray Paint, Cast Iron 40.00
Urn, With Flowers, Box, Hubley 275.00
Urn & Swan, Brass, 1930s 82.00
Whistling Boy, Black Figure, Pot Metal 880.00
Whistling Jim, Hubley 4290.00
Windmill, Greenblatt Studios, Boston, 1926, 9 7/8 x 11 1/2 In. 1020.00
Woman, Hoop Dress, Iron 75.00

DORCHESTER POTTERY was founded by George Henderson in 1895 in Dorchester, Massachusetts. At first, the firm made utilitarian stoneware, but collectors are most interested in the line of decorated blue and white pottery that Dorchester made from 1940 until it went out of business in 1979.

**DORCHESTER
POTTERY WORKS
BOSTON, MASS.**

Bowl, Apple, Cascading Brand, Leaf Design, White Glaze, 2 x 5 In. 55.00

Dorchester, Bowl, Floral, Dark Blue, Handles,
Charles Hill, 2 1/4 x 9 In.

Dorchester, Bowl, Pine Cone,
Charles Hill, 3 x 6 1/2 In.

Dorchester, Charger, Ship, Wave Border,
J. McCune, 12 1/4 In.

Dorchester, Charger, Whale, Waves,
Charles Hill, 11 1/3 In.

Bowl, Blueberry Pattern, Blue Swirl Center, 2 x 6 1/2 In.	385.00
Bowl, Floral, Dark Blue, Handles, Charles Hill, 2 1/4 x 9 In. ....*Illus*	415.00
Bowl, Pine Cone, Charles Hill, 3 x 6 1/2 In. ....*Illus*	100.00
Bowl, Teardrop, Light Blue Glaze, Charles Hill, 2 1/4 x 5 3/4 In.	165.00
Bowl, Whale Pattern, Mouth, Eye Design, Blue Swirl Underplate, 2 1/4 In.	99.00
Candy Dish, Whale Design, Deep Blue, Charles Hill, 5 1/2 In.	165.00
Casserole, Half-Scroll Pattern, Blue On White, Charles Hill, 4 3/4 x 7 1/4 In.	110.00
Casserole, Half-Scroll Pattern, Deep Blue, White Glaze, Charles Hill, 4 3/4 In.	110.00
Casserole, Pinecone, Pine Needle Design, Luster Finish, 2 3/4 x 5 1/2 In.	135.00
Charger, Blueberries	605.00
Charger, Ship, Wave Border, J. McCune, 12 1/4 In. ....*Illus*	385.00
Charger, Whale, Waves, Charles Hill, 11 1/3 In. ....*Illus*	330.00
Cheese Server, Half Scroll, Deep Blue Half Scroll Design, 2 x 6 In.	410.00
Dish, Star, Geometric Design, Blue On White Glaze, 7 1/4 In.	138.00
Jar, Cover, Sacred Cod Motif, Deep Blue, Charles Hill, 3 3/4 x 3 3/4 In.	135.00
Mug, Blue Clown & Stripe, Polka-Dot Costume, 4 1/2 In.	193.00
Mug, Clown & Stripe Motif, Clown Body Form, 4 1/2 In.	190.00
Mug, Clown, Happy Day, All Gone Inside, Blue On White, 2 3/4 In.	193.00
Mug, Grape Pattern, Swirling Vine Design, 4 1/2 x 5 In.	55.00
Mug, St. Patrick's Day Form, Charles Hill, 2 3/4 x 4 1/2 In.	165.00
Pitcher, Blue Glaze, Trumpet Shape, 8 1/2 x 9 In.	110.00
Pitcher, Cover, Colonial Lace, Medium Blue Glaze, Luster Finish, 2 x 5 In.	66.00
Pitcher, Cover, Pussy Willow, Incised Buds, 5 1/2 In.	193.00
Pitcher, Cover, Pussy Willow, White Glaze, 5 1/2 x 4 1/4 In.	192.00
Pitcher, Grapes, Charles Hill, 1776-1976, 5 1/2 x 7 1/2 In. ....*Illus*	250.00
Pitcher, Half-Scroll, Blue On White Band At Neck Band, Blue Base, 5 1/2 In.	193.00
Plate, Colonial Lace, Swirl Blue Interior, Charles Hill, 10 1/3 In.	138.00

Dorchester, Pitcher, Grapes, Charles Hill,
1776-1976, 5 1/2 x 7 1/2 In.

Be careful loading the dishwasher. Metal utensils that touch ceramic dishes may leave marks on the china. Dishes can also show black marks if rubbed against the stainless steel sink. The marks can be removed with a wet sponge and a bit of silver polish or other mild abrasive.

Plate, Farm Mill & Landscape Scene, K. Denisons, 7 1/2 In.	220.00
Toby Jug, Quaker Oats, Brown Glaze, Luster Finish, 8 x 7 1/2 In.	110.00

DOULTON pottery and porcelain were made by Doulton and Co. of Burslem, England, after 1882. The name *Royal Doulton* appeared on their wares after 1902. Other pottery by Doulton is listed under Royal Doulton.

Chamber Pot, Cover, Willow, Flow Blue, c.1891	143.00
Charger, Brown Leaves & Mums, 16 In.	125.00
Chess Piece, Mouse, Tinsmith, 4 In.	750.00
Cup, Siliconware, Gray, Flowers, Bisque	100.00
Decanter, Fruit Design, Slip Trailing, Arts & Crafts, 9 1/8 In.	110.00
Figurine, Elf, With Flute, Tinsmith, 6 In.	1000.00
Inkwell, Owl By Moon, Burslem, 4 In.	250.00
Jardiniere, Gold, 10 x 4 1/2 In.	800.00
Jug, Blue Willow, Dark Brown Top, Blue, Tan Lower, Strap Handle, Lambeth	395.00
Jug, Lord Admiral Nelson Shape, Salt Glazed, Trafalgar, England, 1805, 16 In.	460.00
Jug, Milk, Polychrome Stylized Flowers, Ring Handle, Lambeth, c.1882, 7 1/4 In.	70.00
Lamp, Flow Blue, 1891-1902	1800.00
Mug, Blue Willow	95.00
Mug, North American Indian	89.00
Pitcher, Iris Front & Back, Cobalt Blue, Gold Flowers, 10 1/2 In.	415.00
Plaque, 2 Little Girls Scene, With Pixie Man, 7 1/2 x 9 1/2 In.	1550.00
Plate, Madras, Flow Blue, 6 1/2 In.	60.00
Plate, Madras, Flow Blue, 10 1/2 In.	105.00
Plate, Persian Spray, Flow Blue, 10 1/2 In.	80.00
Soup, Dish, Madras, Flanged, Flow Blue, 5 Piece	95.00
Stand, Umbrella, Yellow Leaves, Mottled Blue Ground, 25 x 13 1/2 In.	1100.00
Tankard, Embossed Hunt Scene & Landscape, 10 1/4 In.	165.00
Tankard, Lambeth, Silver Rim, 9 1/2 In.	1250.00
Teapot, Madras, Flow Blue	700.00
Tobacco Jar, Lambeth	95.00
Tureen, Cover, Madras, Flow Blue	800.00
Vase, Art Deco Floral Design, Blue, 10 3/4 In.	295.00
Vase, Art Nouveau, Whiplash Curves, Mottled Purple, 8 In.	275.00
Vase, Babes In The Woods, Burslem, 16 In.	1450.00
Vase, Blue Green Flowers, Lambeth, 8 In.	75.00
Vase, Bud, Gold Leaf, Cobalt Blue Ground, Artist C.A., 1910, 5 In.	100.00
Vase, Cows, Grazing, Stylized Floral, Foliate Borders, England, 16 1/4 In.	630.00
Vase, Floral Garland Bands, Center Rosettes, Ring Foot, Lambeth, c.1875, 8 In.	144.00
Vase, Gray, All Around Blue Designs, Flared, 13 In.	200.00
Vase, Hand Painted Landscape, Signed J. Hancock, Marked, c.1900, 7 1/2 In.	485.00
Vase, Holly, Deep Blue Ground, Lambeth, Signed, A.S., 11 1/2 In.	275.00
Vase, Incised Goat Reserves, Lambeth, Hannah Barlow, 1891-1902, 20 In., Pair	5000.00
Vase, Raised Stylized Leaf, Floral Design, Cylindrical, 1900, 10 1/2 In.	259.00
Vase, Rochester Castle, Blue, White, Bulbous, 4 In.	66.00
Vase, Rust, Flowers, Nye, Lambeth, 7 In.	150.00
Vase, Slaters, Fluted, Miniature	75.00

Vase, Stanley Ware, Floral Design, Signed, England, 6 1/8 In., Pair 110.00
Vase, Stoneware, Brown & Green Design, Gray, Lambeth, 1887, 5 1/4 In. 195.00
Vase, Switzerland, Flow Blue, 14 In. 350.00

DRAGONWARE is a form of moriage pottery. Moriage is a type of decoration on Japanese pottery. Raised white designs are applied to the
ware. White dragons are the major raised decorations on the moriage
called *dragonware.* The background color is gray and white, orange
and lavender, or orange and brown. It is a twentieth-century ware.

Box, Gray, 4 In. 29.00
Plate, Brown, Blue, Orange, 8 In. 25.00
Saki Set, Red 55.00
Tea Set, 9 Piece 75.00
Tea Set, Gray & Black, 15 Piece 250.00
Vase, Gray, 4 In. 35.00

DRESDEN china is any china made in the town of Dresden, Germany.
The most famous factory in Dresden is the Meissen factory. Figurines
of eighteenth-century ladies and gentlemen, animal groups, or cherubs
and other mythological subjects were popular. One special type of figurine was made with skirts of porcelain-dipped lace. Do not make the
mistake of thinking that all pieces marked *Dresden* are from the
Meissen factory. The Meissen pieces usually have crossed swords
marks, and are listed under Meissen. Some recent porcelain from
Ireland, called *Irish Dresden,* is not included in this book.

Basket, Applied Rose, Forget-Me-Nots, 1920, 2 1/2 In. 45.00
Butter, Flower Design, 8 1/4 In. 16.50
Candlestick, Rose Shape, 10 In., Pair 50.00
Clock, Mantel, Enamel Dial, Encrusted Flowers, Landscape Scene, 20 1/2 In. 1840.00
Compote, Tiny Colored Florals, Basket & Base, Double Open Trellis, Gilt 400.00
Cup & Saucer, Floral Sprays, Watteau Scenes, Reticulated Saucer, c.1890, 5 1/2 In. 345.00
Figurine, Bird, No. 43 .... 1500.00
Figurine, Dog, Black, Gray Accents, Germany, 1900, 13 1/2 In. 575.00
Figurine, Musical Duo 245.00
Fish Set, Platter, 11 Piece 1100.00
Mirror, Vanity, 2 Putti Crest, Molded Flowers On Frame, Easel, 13 In. 230.00
Plaque, Comic Cook & Chef, Robert Lamb, 1900s, 9 In. 225.00
Plaque, Rebecca At The Well, Venetian Gilt Frame, 7 1/4 x 4 1/2 In. 800.00
Plate, Compliments Of Boston Store, Omaha, 1890, 8 1/2 In. ....50.00 to 75.00
Plate, Race Horse, Colin, 1905 .... 85.00
Urn, Cover, Ornate, 19th Century, 16 In., Pair 2500.00
Vase, Scenes, Flowers, Reticulated Neck, Footed, 6 1/2 In., Pair 375.00
Vase, Windmills & Sailboats, 16 In. 900.00

DUNCAN & MILLER is a term used by collectors when referring to glass
made by the George A. Duncan and Sons Company or the Duncan and
Miller Glass Company. These companies worked from 1893 to 1955,
when the use of the name *Duncan* was discontinued and the firm
became part of the United States Glass Company. Early patterns may
be listed under Pressed Glass.

Adoration, Sugar & Creamer, Sterling Silver Foot 35.00
Canterbury, Basket, Oval 75.00
Canterbury, Bottle, Oil, Stopper, 2 Oz. 45.00
Canterbury, Cocktail, 5 1/4 In. 14.00
Caribbean, Bowl, Tab Handle, 9 1/2 In. 35.00
Caribbean, Goblet, 3 Oz. 25.00
Caribbean, Relish, 5 Sections 40.00
Ellrose, Cruet 125.00
First Love, Ashtray, Green, Center Design 10.00
First Love, Goblet, Tall, 10 Oz. ....15.00 to 22.00
Heron, 7 In. 100.00
Hobnail, Bowl, Salad, Blue, Shallow, 12 In. 65.00
Hobnail, Relish, 3 Sections, 10 In. 20.00

Sandwich, Basket, 12 3/4 In.	150.00
Sandwich, Basket, 7 In.	94.00
Sandwich, Bowl, Crimped, 11 In.	55.00
Sandwich, Cake Stand, 13 In.	70.00
Sandwich, Candy Dish, Cover, 8 1/2 In.	55.00
Sandwich, Coaster, 8 Piece	50.00
Sandwich, Cocktail, 3 Oz.	6.00
Sandwich, Goblet, 9 Oz.	12.00 to 15.00
Sandwich, Plate, Cracker, Ring, 13 In.	30.00
Sandwich, Relish, 2 Sections, 7 In.	18.00
Sandwich, Salt & Pepper, Tray	32.00
Sandwich, Saucer, Champagne	10.00
Sandwich, Sugar & Creamer, Oval Tray	30.00
Sandwich, Vase, Footed, 10 In.	80.00
Sandwich, Wine	18.00
Spiral Flutes, Cup, Bouillon, Pink	15.00
Swan, Chartreuse, 13 3/4 In.	75.00
Swan, Red, 7 In.	75.00
Teardorp, Relish, 5 Sections, 12 In.	20.00
Teardrop, Ashtray	12.00
Teardrop, Cake Tray, Handles, 13 1/2 In.	35.00
Teardrop, Cup & Saucer	6.00 to 20.00
Teardrop, Mug, Handle, Green	20.00
Teardrop, Relish	6.00
Teardrop, Relish, 5 Sections, 12 In.	18.00
Teardrop, Relish, 5 Sections, Green, 12 In.	44.00
Teardrop, Tumbler, Juice, Footed, 4 1/2 Oz.	8.00
Teardrop, Wine, 3 Oz.	13.50
Terrace, Plate, Square, 9 In.	32.00
Terrace, Relish, 4 Sections, Round, 9 In.	22.00

DURAND glass was made by Victor Durand from 1879 to 1935 at several factories. Most of the iridescent Durand glass was made by Victor Durand, Jr., from 1912 to 1924 at the Durand Art Glass Works in Vineland, New Jersey.

Centerpiece, Iridescent Cobalt Blue, Wide Folded Down Rim, Marked, 2 1/2 x 14 In.	825.00
Compote, King Tut, Cobalt Blue, Clear Reeded Stem, 6 3/4 x 3 1/2 In.	525.00
Console Set, Cobalt Blue, Opalescent Pulled Feathers, Yellow Base, 3 Piece	1870.00
Creamer, Ruby, Opalescent Pulled Leaves, Applied White Handle, 4 In.	1430.00
Ginger Jar, Jade Green Ground, Purple, Blue King Tut Design, Amber Finial, 7 x 5 In.	1980.00
Lamp, Amber & Green Pulled Feathering, Gilt Metal Base, 6 Shell Feet, 7 In.	385.00
Lamp, Floor, Red, White, Crackled, Gold Iridescent Interior, 65 In.	1100.00
Lamp, Gold, Classic Form, Gold Feather & Threading, 10 In.	880.00
Lamp, Iridescent Gold, Allover Threading, Teakwood Base, No. 1710, 7 1/2 In.	770.00
Lamp Shade, Gold Hooked Feather, 12 In.	300.00
Rose Bowl, Iridescent Blue Black, Gold Base, Allover Blue Vines & Leaves, 5 In.	1815.00
Rose Bowl, Iridescent Gold, Iridescent Blue Gold Base, Globe, 5 1/4 In.	770.00
Rose Jar, Cover, King Tut, Jade, Oyster Lining, 7 1/2 x 6 1/4 In.	3500.00
Vase, 3 White Pulled Arches, Symmetrical Design, 6 3/4 In.	460.00
Vase, Blue, Purple, Green, Gold Iridescent, Silver Trailing, No. 1710, 7 In.	2300.00
Vase, Egyptian Craquelle, Red & White, Iridescent Gold Ground, Classic Form, 7 In.	575.00
Vase, Feather Design, Green & Milk Glass Ribbons, Cylinder, 8 In.	475.00
Vase, Gold Iridescent, Flared, Signed, 8 In.	770.00
Vase, Golden Threading, Marigold Over Yellow Body, Signed, 8 x 8 3/4 In.	440.00
Vase, Hearts & Vines, Blue, Signed, 9 1/2 In.	880.00
Vase, Hooked Feather, Amber, 6 1/2 In.	495.00
Vase, Iridescent Blue, Tapered, 5 In.	575.00
Vase, Iridescent Blue, Threaded, Iridescent Gold Footed, Marked, 8 1/2 In.	1375.00
Vase, King Tut, Green Ground, Blue, Silver-Purple Iridescent, Orange Interior, 10 In.	1320.00
Vase, King Tut, Iridescent Blue & Silver, White Ground, 12 1/4 In.	375.00
Vase, King Tut, Opalescent, Iridescent Blue, Caramel Inclusions, 7 In.	1100.00
Vase, Lady Gay, Rose Lining, Trumpet, Flared Top, Green Opal Rib, No. 1730, 6 3/4 In.	1150.00
Vase, Opalescent Leaves Dangle From Vertical Vines, Iridescent Blue, 7 1/2 In.	1320.00

Vase, Opalescent Pulled Feathers, Iridescent Gold Threading, Signed, 10 1/2 In. 1760.00
Vase, Orange, Gold Iridescent, Blue Highlights, 8 In. 520.00
Vase, Orange, Gold Surface, Green, Blue Heart Shaped Leaves, Oval, 7 3/4 In. 1095.00
Vase, Peacock Feather, Green To Clear Glass, Green, White Striped Feathers, 12 In. 747.50
Vase, Pilgrim, Iridescent Blue Gold, Marked, 1974, 16 In. 1540.00
Vase, Pulled Feather, Gold Threading, Signed, 7 In. 495.00
Vase, Silver, Gold, Blue, Purple, Luster Shading, Blue Iridescent, Oval, 3 3/4 In. 430.00

ELFINWARE is a mark found on Dresden-like porcelain that was sold in
dime stores and gift shops. Many pieces were decorated with raised
flowers. The mark was registered by Breslauer-Underberg, Inc. of New
York City in 1947. Pieces marked *Elfinware Made in Germany* had
been sold since 1945 by this importer.

Elfinware

Basket, Salts 15.00
Box, Jewel, Piano Form, 10 In. 275.00
Box, Trinket, Piano Form, 3 In. 40.00
Compote, Interior Flowers, Forget-Me-Nots, Hand Painted, 6 1/2 In. 235.00
Salt, 2 Handles, Basket Weave, Blue Forget-Me-Nots 35.00
Shoe, High Heel, Marked, 3 In. 85.00
Sugar & Creamer, Miniature 50.00

ELVIS PRESLEY, the well-known singer, lived from 1935 to 1977. He
became famous by 1956. Elvis appeared on television, starred in twen-
ty-seven movies, and performed in Las Vegas. Memorabilia from any
of the Presley shows, his records, and even memorials made after his
death are collected.

Balloon, With Cardboard Base, 1950s 78.00
Book, The Illustrated Elvis, 1976 . . . . 15.00
Boots, Black Leather, Square Toed, Comeback At Las Vegas, 1960s 6325.00
Bottle, Coca-Cola, Graceland, Tenn., 1995, 8 Oz. 6.00
Bracelet, With Letter, Silver, Turquoise 5500.00
Bracelet, With Photograph, Display Card, 1956 . . . . 85.00
Bust, Albany Slip Glaze, M. Rogers, 1980s, 9 3/4 In. 605.00
Calendar, Pocket, RCA, 1964 . . . . 40.00
Card Set, Gold Foil Trimmed Box, 660 Piece 160.00
Cologne, The King, 4 In. 13.00
Decanter, McCormick 125.00
Doll, Singing, Microphone & Guitar, Graceland, 1984, 12 In. 45.00
Figurine, Avon, 1987 . . . . 20.00
Guitar, Brown Plastic, 1970, 10 In. 28.00
Handkerchief, Portrait, Signed, Song Titles Around Edge, 1956, 13 x 13 In. 250.00
Jacket, Double Trouble, Red 6000.00
Lobby Card Set, Harum Scarum, 1965, 11 x 14 In. 105.00
Lobby Card Set, Loving You, 1957, 11 x 14 In. 275.00
Marble, 1 In., 1990s 2.50
Mirror, Celluloid, Photograph, White Ground, Memorial, 1970s 28.00
Photograph, Concert In Mobile, Al., 8 x 10 In. 50.00
Photograph, Elvis, Black, Yellow Ground, 1980s 15.00
Photograph, Elvis, Pink Ground, 1980s 15.00
Photograph, Vintage, Elvis In Uniform, Saluting, Color, 5 x 7 In. 10.00
Photograph, Vintage, Elvis Turban Outfit, With Actress, 5 x 7 In. 10.00
Photograph, Vintage, Elvis Wearing Cowboy Hat, Black & White, 8 x 10 In. 5.00
Postcard, Graceland Home, 1977 . . . . 10.00
Poster, Double Trouble, 1967, 3 Sheets 95.00
Poster, Elvis In Las Vegas, 1976, 24 x 36 In. 16.00
Poster, King Creole, Linen, 3 Sheets 725.00
Poster, Love Me Tender, 1 Sheet 425.00
Poster, Viva Las Vegas, 1 Sheet 175.00
Record, Any Way You Want Me 38.00
Record, Hound Dog, Gold Rim, 1956 . . . . 38.00
Record Case, Elvis Portrait Top 795.00
Sheet Music, Blue Suede Shoes, 1956 . . . . 30.00
Supplement, Detroit Newspaper, Picture, 1956 . . . . 175.00

Ticket, Concert, Memphis, September, 1977 . . . . 115.00
Wrapper, Gum Card, Donruss, Las Vegas-Era Elvis Singing, 1978 . . . . 7.00

ENAMELS listed here are made of glass particles and other materials heated and fused to metal. In the eighteenth and nineteenth centuries, workmen from Russia, France, England, and other countries made small boxes and table pieces of enamel on metal. One form of English enamel is called *Battersea* and is listed under that name. There was a revival of interest in enameling in the 1930s and a new style evolved. There is now renewed interest in the artistic enameled plaques, vases, ashtrays, and jewelry. Enamels made since the 1930s are usually on copper or steel, although silver was often used for jewelry. Graniteware is a separate category and enameled metal kitchen pieces may be included in the Kitchen category.

Beaker, Crest, Fritz Heckert, 1875, 3 1/2 In. 148.00
Bowl, Copper, Hammered, Iridescent Pearl Interior, Arts & Crafts, Marked HIB, 4 In. . . . 150.00
Bowl, Copper, Repousse Rose Interior, Society Of Arts & Crafts, 2 x 8 In. 725.00
Bowl, Silver, Blue & Ivory Grape Under Rim, Punched & Chased, M. Knight, 5 5/8 In. . . 2200.00
Box, Orange Plaque Cover, Copper, Hammered, Potter Mellen, 4 1/2 x 3 1/4 In. 375.00
Box, Peach Finial Cover, Copper, Hammered, Arts & Crafts, MW, 3 1/2 x 3 In. 60.00
Box, Peacock Plaque Cover, Copper, Hammered, Society Of Arts & Crafts, 6 In. 850.00
Cigarette Box, Wooden, Leather, Plaque, Cedar Lined, K. Drerup, 8 In. 625.00
Cup, Lobed Form, Leaves, Gilt Wash Interior, White, 20th Century, 3 1/4 In. 287.50
Cup, Silver-Gilt, Poppy Blossoms, Buds, Orange, Red, Green, Mucha, 1902, 1 7/8 In. . . . 3162.00
Epergne, Floral, Blue Overlay, White Opaque Top, 15 1/4 In. 395.00
Goblet, Clear, Cornell School Song, Ezra Cornell Seal, 13 In. 385.00
Humidor, Cut Star Base, 12 Sides, Enameled Peacock Sterling Cover, Marshall, 6 In. . . . 3200.00
Plaque, Copper, Grape Design, White Ground, Round, Arts & Crafts, 6 In. 235.00
Plaque, Copper, Lakeside Cottages, Wooden Frame, C. Camsla Faure, 10 x 12 In. 2200.00
Plaque, Young Satyr Blowing A Pipe, 1916, 2 7/8 In. 517.00
Salt, Red & White Rows Scale, Clear Lining, 3-Footed, Russia, 1940, 1 1/4 In. 110.00
Salt Cellar, Gilded Silver, Stylized Foliate, Vegetable Form, Blue, Green, 1910, Pair 7475.00
Vase, Cavalier Encampment, Baluster, 6 1/2 In. 85.00

ERICKSON glass was made in Bremen, Ohio, from 1943 to 1961. Carl and Steven Erickson designed and made free-blown and mold-blown glass. Best known are pieces with heavy ball bases filled with con-trolled bubbles.

Candleholder, Trapped Air Bubble Base, Pair 100.00
Vase, Green, Blue, 5 In. 150.00

ERPHILA is a mysterious mark found on 1930s Czechoslovakian and other pottery and porcelain. The mark was used on items imported by Eberling & Reuss, Philadelphia, a giftware firm that is still operating in Pennsylvania. The mark is a combination of the letters *É* and *R* (Eberling & Reuss) and the first letters of the city, Phila(delphia). Many whimsical figural pitchers and creamers, figurines, platters, and other giftwares carry this mark.

Box, Trinket, Silhouette Motif On Cover 49.00
Bust, Robert Burns, Ernst Bohe Sons, 5 1/8 In. 120.00
Card Holder, Figural 65.00
Dish, Leaf, Cream, 11 1/2 In. 30.00
Doll, Dresser, Madame Pompadour 90.00
Figurine, Dog, Airedale, Large 50.00
Figurine, Dog, Chow, Germany, 4 In. 34.00
Figurine, Dog, Fox Terrier, Large 60.00
Figurine, Dog, Long-Haired, 4 1/4 In. 30.00
Figurine, Dog, White, Brown, 4 1/2 In. 40.00
Figurine, Donkey, Foal 35.00
Ice Bucket 75.00
Pitcher, Dog 225.00
Pitcher, Ram 195.00
Plate, Grapes, Oranges, 8 In. 25.00

Teapot, Dachshund 110.00
Urn, White, Aqua, Interior Crazed, 10 In. 60.00
Wall Pocket, Young Woman, Tyrolean Hat, Signed, 11 In. 66.00

ES GERMANY porcelain was made at the factory of Erdmann
Schlegelmilch from 1861 to 1937 in Suhl, Germany. The porcelain,
marked *ES Germany* or *ES Suhl*, was sold decorated or undecorated.
Other pieces were made at a factory in Saxony, Prussia, and are
marked *ES Prussia*. Reinhold Schlegelmilch made the famous wares
marked *RS Germany*.

Bowl, Center Handle, Pink Roses, Divided, 10 In. 60.00
Creamer, Wing Mark 25.00
Plate, Classical Portrait, Maidens, Cupid 90.00

ESKIMO artifacts of all types are collected. Carvings of whale or walrus teeth are listed under Scrimshaw. Baskets are in the Basket category. All other types of Eskimo art are listed here.

Bowl, Coiled Basketry, Flat Base, 7 1/2 In. 270.00
Doll, Carved & Jointed, Trade Cloth Jacket, Hooded, 1920s, 11 In. 450.00
Figurine, Eskimo, Gray, Green Seal, Soapstone, 8 1/4 In. 85.00
Figurine, Hunter With Pouch & Tool, Alaskan Jade, 1706, 3 In. 99.00
Figurine, Kneeling Man, Stone, 4 3/4 In. 200.00
Figurine, Otter Man, M. Qiyuk, Stone, 7 1/4 In. 85.00
Figurine, Polar Bear, Baleen Inlay, Ivory, Red Pigment, 3 1/2 In. 265.00
Figurine, Polar Bear, Dancing, Ivory Teeth, Pauta Saila, Soapstone, 18 In. 8000.00
Figurine, Polar Bear, Dancing, Mottled Green, Pauta Saila, Soapstone, 9 In. 4000.00
Figurine, Seal Man, Stone, Davidee Aculiak, 8 1/2 x 9 In. 230.00
Figurine, Stylized Sea Lion, Stone, 5 In. 85.00
Figurine, Stylized, Man & Animals He Hunts, Stone, 14 In. 145.00
Jacket, Inuit, Sealskin, Man's, 1950 . . . . 750.00
Knife, Athabaskan, Copper, Cloth Wrapped Grip, 14 In. 2530.00
Mask, Inuit, Sealskin Beard, Pair 935.00
Model, Kayak With Man, Leather Covered, Man With Leather Clothing, 18 1/2 In. 288.00

FABERGE was a firm of jewelers and goldsmiths founded in St.
Petersburg, Russia, in 1842, by Gustav Faberge. Peter Carl Faberge,
his son, was jeweler to the Russian Imperial Court from about 1870 to
1914. The rare Imperial Easter eggs, jewelry, and decorative items are
very expensive today.

Beaker, Enameled, Gilded Silver, Translucent Strawberry Red, 1900, 2 1/4 In. 4600.00
Beaker, Gilded Silver, Enameled, Ribbon Tied Laurel Wreath, 1910, 2 3/8 In. 11500.00
Bellpush, Rabbit Form, Gold Mounted Cabochon, Ruby Eyes, 1900, 4 1/4 In. 11500.00
Bowl, Neo-Rococo Scrolls, Shellwork, Foliage, Silver, 3 Scroll Feet, 1890, 4 1/2 In. 4025.00
Box, Lilac Over A Guilloche Ground, Enameled, Silver, A. Gorianov, 1910, 1 3/4 In. . . . 9775.00
Box, Stylized Vegetable Forms, Hinged Cover, Green, White Ground, 1910, 1 3/4 In. . . . 2760.00
Cigarette Case, Brass, Copper, Hinged Cover, Rounded Sides, Rectangular, 3 3/4 In. . . 5462.00
Cigarette Case, Cover, Embossed With Leafy Branch, Cabochon Sapphires, 1900 . . . . . 3450.00
Cigarette Case, Enameled, Gilded Silver, Translucent Emerald Green, 1900, 3 In. 16100.00
Cigarette Case, Gold Mount, Rounded Sides, Rectangular, 1890, 3 3/4 In. 13800.00
Cigarette Case, Gold, Applied Imperial Eagle On Cover, St. Petersburg, 1890, 3 In. 4600.00
Cigarette Case, Gold, Enamel Etui, Gold Mounts, Hinged Cover, 1900, 3 3/4 In. 8050.00
Cigarette Case, Reeded, Applied With Enameled Flags, Red Stone, 1910, 3 5/8 In. 3737.00
Cigarette Case, Samorodok Gold Reserves Base, Gold Monogram, 1900, 4 In. 9775.00
Clock, Desk, Enameled Translucent Rose Pink, Acanthus Leaf Border, 1900, 5 In. 20700.00
Cup, Vodka, Silver, Eagle With Outstretched Wings, 1890, 1 3/4 In. 4025.00
Figurine, Bear Cub, Walking, Looking Directly Ahead, Obsidian, 1900, 1 3/4 In. 5750.00
Figurine, Bear, Standing In Attentive Posture, Ruby Eyes, Carved, Russia, 1900, 3 In. . . 3737.00
Figurine, Hippopotamus, Seated, Green, Head Projecting, 1900, 1 3/4 In. 7475.00
Figurine, Hippopotamus, Standing, Head Lowered, Cabochon Ruby Eyes, 1900, 1 In. . . . 5750.00
Figurine, Hippopotamus, Standing, Head Lowered, Red Stone Eyes, 1900, 1 7/8 In. 2990.00
Figurine, Piglet, Crouching Position, Curled Tail, Pink, Brown, 1900, 2 In. 9775.00
Flask, Scent, Gold, Hinged Dome Cover, Enameled Rust, Orange Ground, 2 1/2 In. 10062.00
Frame, Gold Inner Border, Gold Ribbon Bow, Workmaster, 1890, 2 3/8 In. 9487.00

Frame, Silver, Enameled Translucent Lilac, Ribbon Bows, Cabochon Ruby, 3 In.	16100.00
Holder, Tea Glass, Silver, Floral Swags, Bracket Handles, Cylindrical, 3 In.	1150.00
Kovsh, Enameled, Cathedral, Blue, Green, Cream, 1900, 4 1/2 In.	7475.00
Kovsh, Enameled, Floral, Scrolled Foliage, Blue Beaded Border, 1900, 6 1/2 In.	3737.00
Kovsh, Enameled, Foliage, White Beaded Border, Blue Ground, 1900, 3 3/4 In.	1495.00
Kovsh, Jeweled Cabochons, Monogram, Bracket Handle, 1912, 13 In.	9450.00
Letter Opener, Silver Serpent On Nephrite Blade, 1910, 6 1/2 In.	9200.00
Pendant, Easter Egg, Diamond Set Ribbon Bow, 1910, 1 3/4 In., Miniature	3450.00
Pendant, Easter Egg, Gold, Enameled White, Translucent Red Flashes, 1900, 5/8 In.	3162.00
Pendant, Easter Egg, Silver, Stylized Foliate Designs, F. Ruckert, Russia, 1900, 3 In.	8625.00
Sugar Tongs, Vermeil, Engraved Crest Handle, 1898-1917, 4 In.	630.00
Tea Kettle, On Stand, Silver, Knop Finial, Globular, Pre-1896, 10 In.	6880.00
Wine Decanter, Swirl Fluted Body, Silver Neck Mount, Scroll Handle, 1890, 9 In.	3335.00

FAIENCE refers to tin-glazed earthenware, especially the wares made in France, Germany, and Scandinavia. It is also correct to say that faience is the same as majolica or Delft, although usually the term refers only to the tin-glazed pottery of the three regions mentioned.

Bowl, Earthenware, Bird On Limb, Flowers, Chop Work Border, 1760, Pair	515.00
Charger, Central Floral Medallion, Stylized Flowerhead Border, Blue, White, 22 In.	3162.00
Clock, 2 Lions Rampant On Scrolled Base, Blue Glaze, 1895, 25 In.	6900.00
Dish, Angel Center, Pierced Border, Italy, c.1680, 9 1/2 In.	650.00
Dish, Chinoiserie Figure Amidst Rocks, Shrubbery, Everted Rim, Blue, White, 13 In.	690.00
Ewer, Applied Flowers & Leaves, Corset, 12 1/2 x 6 x 4 1/2 In.	160.00
Ewer, Wine, Hand Painted Grape Leaves & Clusters, 30 In.	385.00
Figurine, Bulldog, Yellow Glaze, Blue, White Spots, Hearts, 1895, 12 In.	2070.00
Figurine, Cows, Resting, Blue, White, 18th Century, 6 1/2 In., Pair	460.00
Figurine, Pig, France, 1880	225.00
Figurine, Saint Jeanne, Blue Robe, Holding Child, France, 9 5/8 In.	440.00
Jardiniere, Finialed Corners, Hand Painted Floral, 19th Century, 8 1/4 In.	430.00
Lamp, Brown & Yellow Design, White Ground, 25 In., Pair	66.00
Plate, Polychrome, Rose, Yellow, Purple, Blue, Green, Sprays, 1770, 9 In.	287.00
Sauceboat, Rose, Blue, Yellow, Green Exterior, 3 Green Leaf Sprigs, 1780, 9 In.	920.00
Snuff Bottle, Shield Design 1 Side, Ermine Tail On Other	335.00
Tankard, Bird, Floral Surrounded, Hinged Pewter Mounted & Lid, Continental, 7 In.	460.00
Tankard, Peacock, Floral Motif, Pewter Top, Germany, 10 1/4 In.	1380.00
Tile, Holy Family, Beneath Spread Winged Eagle, Continental, 19th Century, 8 In.	288.00
Tureen, Cover, Gilt Fern, Scroll, Paw Foot, Demi-Blossom Border, 14 1/8 In.	3740.00
Tureen, Rococo Revival, France, Marked D.P., c.1860, 26 1/2 In.	2600.00
Vase, Oriental Man About To Hit Gong, France, H. Boulegen, 10 In.	500.00

FAIRINGS are small souvenir china boxes and figurines that were sold at country fairs during the nineteenth century. Most were made in Germany. Reproductions of fairings are being made, especially of the famous *twelve months of marriage* series.

Box, Girl Shepherd, With Lamb, Staffordshire	155.00
Box, Pin, Greyhound On Pillow, Flowers, Cape, Polychrome Enamel, Gilt, 3 1/4 In.	110.00
Box, Printed Word Pins	35.00
Box, Spaniel On Couch	46.00
Box, Trinket, General Ulysses S. Grant, Next To Horse, 1860s, 4 In.	350.00

FAIRYLAND LUSTER pieces are included in the Wedgwood category.

FAMILLE ROSE, see Chinese Export category.

FANS have been used for cooling since the days of the ancients. By the eighteenth century, the fan was an accessory for the lady of fashion, and very elaborate and expensive fans were made. Sticks were made of ivory or wood, set with jewels or carved. The fans were made of painted silk or paper. Inexpensive paper fans printed with advertising were giveaways in the late nineteenth and early twentieth centuries. Electric fans were introduced in 1882.

Advertising, 3 Speed Banker's, 19 1/2 In.	700.00
Advertising, Cyco Ball Bearing Carpet Sweeper, Folding	10.00

Advertising, Dr. Thatcher's Compound, Senna & Rhubarb, 1920s 8.00
Advertising, Hoover & Gamble, Pretty Women, 4 Cards, Grommet Held, Diecut, 1889 .. 65.00
Advertising, Moxie Co., Eileen Percy 40.00
Advertising, Rexall Drugstore, Rex Ray 35.00
Advertising, Royal Cord Tires, Cardboard, 11 3/4 x 7 In...................... 143.00
Advertising, Schaefer Beer, Freedomland Advertising 24.00
Advertising, Women's Christian Temperance Union 10.00
Electric, Adams-Bagnall Electric Co., Ceiling, Gyrofan 2600.00
Electric, Emerson Electric Fan Co., Brass Case, 4 Blades, 8 1/2 In. 200.00
Electric, General Electric, Oscillating, Brass Blades, 16 In. 85.00
Electric, Hunter Fan & Ventilating Co., Ceiling, 4 Blades, 1940s 600.00
Electric, New York World's Fair 300.00
Electric, Table, Industrial, Dayton, 20 In..................................... 80.50
Electric, Winchester, 8 In. 425.00
Electric, Zephyr, Floor Model 2415.00
Feather, Ostrich, Ivorine Handle, Turquoise 65.00
Feather, Ostrich, Turquoise, Tortoiseshell Handle, 1890s 125.00
Feather, Peacock, Tortoiseshell Type Sticks, Opens To 10 1/2 In. 85.00
Figural Design, Shadowbox Frame, 1880s, 19 3/4 x 27 In. 180.00
Ivory, Silk, 22 x 26 In. 120.00
Lace, Hand Painted Roses, Mother-Of-Pearl Shadow Box Frame 145.00
Paper, Fabric & Needlework, Children At Play, Shadow Box Frame, 23 x 33 In. 220.00
Paper, Lithograph, Figures, In Landscape, Ivory Spokes, 19th Century, 22 3/4 In. 200.00
Satin, Red, Gold & Silver Embossed Sandalwood Sticks, 4-In. Ostrich Feathers 110.00

FAST FOOD COLLECTIBLES may be included in several categories, such
as Advertising, Coca-Cola, Toy, etc.

FEDERZEICHNUNG is the very strange German name for a pattern of
mother-of-pearl satin glass. The pattern had irregularly shaped sections
of brown glass covered with a pattern of gold squiggle lines. It was
first made in the late nineteenth century.

Vase, Gold Squiggles, Marked, Patent 9159, 5 1/2 x 4 1/2 In. 1925.00
Vase, Pearlized Scrolled Trails, Quadrafold Rim, Gilt Patterns, 8 1/2 In. 2310.00

FENTON Art Glass Company, founded in Martins Ferry, Ohio, by Frank
L. Fenton, is now located in Williamstown, West Virginia. It is noted
for early carnival glass produced between 1907 and 1920. Some of
these pieces are listed in the Carnival Glass category. Many other types
of glass were also made. Spanish Lace in this section refers to the pattern made by Fenton.

Aqua Crest, Basket, 8 1/2 In. 65.00
Cactus, Goblet, Topaz Opalescent 35.00
Cactus, Sugar, Cover, Topaz Opalescent 50.00
Coin Dot, Bottle, Barber, Cranberry 195.00
Coin Dot, Hat, Blue Opalescent 45.00
Coin Dot, Vase, Blue Opalescent, 6 In. 30.00
Coin Dot, Vase, Blue Opalescent, 8 In. 90.00
Coin Dot, Vase, Jack-In-The-Pulpit, Cranberry ....125.00 to 145.00
Daisy & Fern, Pitcher, Cranberry 225.00
Diamond Lace, Epergne, Opalescent, 3 Lily, Aqua Rim ....175.00 to 300.00
Diamond Optic, Cup, Topaz 35.00
Emerald Crest, Cruet, Stopper 125.00
Grape & Cable, Bowl, Amberina, 6 1/2 In. 650.00
Hobnail, Banana Stand, Rose Pastel ....65.00 to 75.00
Hobnail, Basket, Cranberry, 1940s, 10 In...................................... 110.00
Hobnail, Basket, Rose Pastel, 7 In. 45.00
Hobnail, Bowl, Pedestal, Ruffled, Green, 10 1/2 In. 60.00
Hobnail, Cruet, Stopper, Rose Pastel 65.00
Hobnail, Decanter Set, Stopper, 12 1/2 In., 7 Piece 125.00
Hobnail, Epergne, 3-Lily, Blue Opalescent 100.00
Hobnail, Pitcher, Water, Plum ....200.00 to 225.00

Hobnail, Punch Bowl, Blue Opalescent 275.00
Hobnail, Rose Bowl, Rose Pastel 35.00
Hobnail, Scent Bottle, Stopper, Blue Opalescent 35.00
Hobnail, Syrup, Pewter Cover, Blue Opalescent 345.00
Hobnail, Vase, Topaz Opalescent, Miniature 9.00
Ivory Crest, Plate, 12 In. 50.00
Ivory Crest, Vase, Tulip, 8 In. 75.00
Jade Green, Vase, 5-Toe Ebony Base, 9 In. 395.00
Jamestown, Vase, Blue, 5 In. 18.00
Lily-Of-The-Valley, Basket, Dusty Rose, Notched Handle, 7 In. 27.00
Mandarin Red, Compote, 7 1/2 In. 110.00
Mandarin Red, Flower Frog, Nymph, September Morn 220.00
Mandarin Red, Vase, Blue Back Ground, 8 In. 1760.00
Moonstone, Jug, Footed, 6 In. 175.00
Old Mosaic, Vase, Cobalt Blue Handles, 8 In. 1320.00
Peach Crest, Basket, 4 1/2 In. 35.00
Peach Crest, Vase, 8 In. 40.00
Peacock, Vase, Amethyst, 8 In. 70.00
Rib Optic, Vase, Green Opalescent, 11 In. 85.00
Rosalene, Vase, 9 In. 75.00
Silver Crest, Banana Bowl, 12 In. 65.00
Silver Crest, Banana Bowl, Low 40.00
Silver Crest, Basket, 13 In. 75.00
Silver Crest, Basket, Crystal Handle, 6 1/2 In. 25.00
Silver Crest, Bowl, 10 In. 45.00
Silver Crest, Bowl, 4 1/2 In. 10.00
Silver Crest, Bowl, 8 1/2 In. 30.00
Silver Crest, Bowl, Cupped Edge, 10 In. 40.00
Silver Crest, Bowl, Double Crimped, 11 In. 30.00
Silver Crest, Bowl, Fruit, Footed, Square 70.00
Silver Crest, Cake Plate, 13 In. ....35.00 to 40.00
Silver Crest, Cake Salver, 12 In. ....25.00 to 40.00
Silver Crest, Candy Dish, Footed, Cover 125.00
Silver Crest, Compote, 8 In. 30.00
Silver Crest, Mayonnaise Bowl, With Liner 40.00
Silver Crest, Plate, 6 In. 15.00
Silver Crest, Plate, 8 1/2 In. 20.00
Silver Crest, Plate, 12 In. 25.00
Silver Crest, Relish, Heart Shape, Handle 25.00
Silver Crest, Rose Bowl 10.00
Silver Crest, Sherbet 20.00
Silver Crest, Tidbit, 2 Tiers 40.00
Silver Crest, Tidbit, 3 Tiers, 6 In. 80.00
Silver Crest, Tidbit, 3 Tiers, 8 In. ....65.00 to 85.00
Silver Crest, Tidbit, 3 Tiers, 12 In. 80.00
Silver Crest, Vase, 8 In. 20.00
Silver Crest, Vase, Fan, 12 In. 90.00
Snow Crest, Vase, 9 In. 45.00
Spiral, Vase, Hat, Opalescent, Blue Ridge Crest, Triangular Top, 7 In. 145.00
Stretch, Bowl, Vaseline, 9 In. 35.00
Swirled Feather, Sugar Shaker, Cranberry 225.00
Thumbprint, Bowl, Colonial Blue, 12 In. 55.00
Thumbprint, Compote, Black 25.00
Thumbprint, Compote, Colonial Amber ....10.00 to 20.00
Thumbprint, Goblet, Colonial Blue, 10 Oz. 10.00
Thumbprint, Vase, Footed, Black 20.00
Water Lily, Bonbon, Green Opalescent 55.00
Water Lily, Tumbler, Marigold, Carnival 45.00
Water Lily & Cattail, Water Set, Marigold, Carnival, 5 Piece 295.00
Wide Rib, Vase, Aqua, 9 In. 115.00
Wild Rose, Rose Bowl, 6 In. 95.00

FIESTA, the colorful dinnerware, was introduced in 1936 by the Homer Laughlin China Co., redesigned in 1969, and withdrawn in 1973. It was reissued again in 1986 in different colors and is still being made. The simple design was characterized by a band of concentric circles, beginning at the rim. Cups had full-circle handles until 1969, when partial-circle handles were made. Harlequin and Riviera were related wares. For more information and prices of American dinnerware, see the book *Kovels' Depression Glass & American Dinnerware Price List*.

Ashtray, Cobalt Blue	65.00
Ashtray, Forest Green	65.00
Ashtray, Gray	95.00
Ashtray, Ivory	95.00
Ashtray, Light Green	45.00
Ashtray, Turquoise	65.00 to 70.00
Bowl, Cereal, Chartreuse, 5 1/2 In.	35.00
Bowl, Cereal, Forest Green, 5 1/2 In.	30.00 to 35.00
Bowl, Cereal, Gray, 5 1/2 In.	35.00 to 40.00
Bowl, Cereal, Ivory, 5 1/2 In.	35.00
Bowl, Cereal, Light Green, 5 1/2 In.	20.00
Bowl, Cereal, Medium Green, 5 1/2 In.	60.00
Bowl, Cereal, Red, 5 1/2 In.	35.00
Bowl, Cereal, Rose, 5 1/2 In.	35.00
Bowl, Cereal, Turquoise, 5 1/2 In.	15.00 to 30.00
Bowl, Cereal, Yellow, 11 3/4 In.	350.00
Bowl, Dessert, Forest Green, 6 In.	40.00
Bowl, Dessert, Gray, 6 In.	75.00
Bowl, Dessert, Green, 6 In.	35.00
Bowl, Dessert, Rose, 6 In.	35.00
Bowl, Dessert, Yellow, 6 In.	45.00
Bowl, Fruit, Chartreuse, 4 3/4 In.	25.00 to 30.00
Bowl, Fruit, Gray, 4 3/4 In.	30.00 to 40.00
Bowl, Fruit, Ivory, 4 3/4 In.	35.00 to 75.00
Bowl, Fruit, Light Green, 11 3/4 In.	365.00
Bowl, Fruit, Red, 4 3/4 In.	35.00
Bowl, Fruit, Rose, 4 3/4 In.	25.00 to 40.00
Bowl, Fruit, Turquoise, 4 3/4 In.	20.00 to 30.00
Bowl, Fruit, Yellow, 4 3/4 In.	20.00
Bowl, Fruit, Yellow, 5 1/2	25.00 to 30.00
Bowl, Mixing, No. 1, Red	175.00 to 275.00
Bowl, Mixing, No. 1, Turquoise	145.00
Bowl, Mixing, No. 2, Cobalt Blue	100.00 to 210.00
Bowl, Mixing, No. 2, Light Green	90.00
Bowl, Mixing, No. 2, Red	210.00
Bowl, Mixing, No. 2, Yellow	50.00 to 125.00
Bowl, Mixing, No. 3, Cobalt Blue	210.00
Bowl, Mixing, No. 3, Light Green	80.00 to 255.00
Bowl, Mixing, No. 3, Red	90.00 to 210.00
Bowl, Mixing, No. 3, Yellow	60.00
Bowl, Mixing, No. 4, Cobalt Blue	150.00 to 225.00
Bowl, Mixing, No. 4, Light Green	95.00
Bowl, Mixing, No. 4, Red	225.00
Bowl, Mixing, No. 4, Yellow	70.00
Bowl, Mixing, No. 5, Cobalt Blue	150.00 to 250.00
Bowl, Mixing, No. 5, Red	250.00
Bowl, Mixing, No. 5, Yellow	45.00 to 110.00
Bowl, Mixing, No. 6, Cobalt Blue	300.00
Bowl, Mixing, No. 6, Red	300.00
Bowl, Mixing, No. 7, Cover, Cobalt Blue	650.00
Bowl, Mixing, No. 7, Cover, Red	650.00
Bowl, Mixing, No. 7, Turquoise	150.00 to 350.00
Bowl, Mixing, No. 7, Yellow	175.00 to 350.00
Bowl, Nappy, Ivory, 9 1/2 In.	200.00

Bowl, Nappy, Yellow, 9 1/2 In. 50.00
Bowl, Salad, Footed, Ivory, 11 1/4 In. 350.00
Bowl, Salad, Footed, Light Green, 11 1/4 In. 215.00
Bowl, Salad, Footed, Yellow, 11 1/4 In. ....450.00 to 525.00
Bowl, Salad, Turquoise, Individual 85.00
Bowl, Salad, Yellow, 7 1/2 In. 65.00
Cake Plate, Cobalt Blue 950.00
Cake Plate, Yellow, Kitchen Kraft 50.00
Candleholder, Bulb, Cobalt Blue 70.00
Candleholder, Tripod, Cobalt Blue, Pair 225.00
Candleholder, Tripod, Ivory, Pair 700.00
Candleholder, Tripod, Red, Pair 500.00
Candleholder, Tripod, Turquoise, Pair 890.00
Carafe, Cobalt Blue ....325.00 to 350.00
Carafe, Ivory ....195.00 to 230.00
Carafe, Medium Green 185.00
Carafe, Red ....200.00 to 350.00
Carafe, Turquoise 265.00
Carafe, Yellow 185.00
Casserole, Cobalt Blue 175.00
Casserole, Cobalt Blue, Kitchen Kraft, Individual 45.00
Casserole, Cover, Chartreuse ....265.00 to 300.00
Casserole, Cover, Cobalt Blue 225.00
Casserole, Cover, Forest Green 300.00
Casserole, Cover, Gray ....265.00 to 375.00
Casserole, Cover, Medium Green ....1250.00 to 1500.00
Casserole, Cover, Red, Metal Holder, Kitchen Kraft, 8 1/2 In. 145.00
Casserole, Cover, Rose ....245.00 to 375.00
Casserole, Cover, Turquoise ....110.00 to 175.00
Casserole, Cover, Yellow 125.00
Casserole, Forest Green, Kitchen Kraft, Individual 45.00
Casserole, Turquoise, Kitchen Kraft, Individual 60.00
Casserole, Yellow, French 230.00
Chop Plate, Chartreuse, 13 In. 75.00
Chop Plate, Chartreuse, 15 In. ....140.00 to 150.00
Chop Plate, Cobalt Blue, 13 In. ....50.00 to 55.00
Chop Plate, Forest Green, 13 In. 95.00
Chop Plate, Forest Green, 15 In. ....95.00 to 150.00
Chop Plate, Gray, 15 In. ....110.00 to 135.00
Chop Plate, Ivory, 15 In. ....45.00 to 65.00
Chop Plate, Red, 13 In. 85.00
Chop Plate, Red, 15 In. ....60.00 to 140.00
Chop Plate, Rose, 13 In. ....60.00 to 95.00
Chop Plate, Rose, 15 In. 150.00
Chop Plate, Turquoise, 15 In. 45.00
Chop Plate, Yellow, 15 In. 35.00
Coffeepot, Cobalt Blue, After Dinner ....495.00 to 600.00
Coffeepot, Forest Green, After Dinner 795.00
Coffeepot, Gray, After Dinner 800.00
Coffeepot, Ivory, After Dinner 250.00
Coffeepot, Medium Green ....165.00 to 225.00
Coffeepot, Red ....50.00 to 75.00
Coffeepot, Red, After Dinner 650.00
Coffeepot, Rose, After Dinner 650.00
Coffeepot, Turquoise 185.00
Coffeepot, Yellow ....165.00 to 195.00
Coffeepot, Yellow, After Dinner 300.00
Compartment Plate, Cobalt Blue 35.00
Compote, Ivory, 12 In. 160.00
Compote, Red, 12 In. 155.00
Compote, Sweets, Cobalt Blue 95.00
Compote, Sweets, Yellow 85.00
Compote, Yellow, 12 In. 185.00

Cookie Jar, Green, Kitchen Kraft 315.00
Creamer, Chartreuse 35.00
Creamer, Cobalt Blue 30.00
Creamer, Forest Green 35.00
Creamer, Gray ....35.00 to 45.00
Creamer, Ivory ....30.00 to 40.00
Creamer, Light Green 30.00
Creamer, Medium Green, Box 110.00
Creamer, Red ....30.00 to 40.00
Creamer, Red, Individual ....200.00 to 350.00
Creamer, Rose ....30.00 to 45.00
Creamer, Stick, Turquoise 70.00
Creamer, Yellow 16.00
Creamer, Yellow Stick Handle 25.00
Cup, Cobalt Blue, After Dinner 60.00
Cup, Forest Green ....25.00 to 30.00
Cup, Tea, Chartreuse 25.00
Cup, Tea, Cobalt Blue 30.00
Cup, Tea, Forest Green 25.00
Cup, Tea, Light Green 20.00
Cup, Tea, Rose 35.00
Cup & Saucer, Cobalt Blue, After Dinner ....85.00 to 90.00
Cup & Saucer, Forest Green 55.00
Cup & Saucer, Gray 45.00
Cup & Saucer, Green, After Dinner 65.00
Cup & Saucer, Ivory 50.00
Cup & Saucer, Ivory, After Dinner ....85.00 to 90.00
Cup & Saucer, Light Green ....25.00 to 35.00
Cup & Saucer, Light Green, After Dinner ....75.00 to 80.00
Cup & Saucer, Medium Green ....45.00 to 65.00
Cup & Saucer, Red ....35.00 to 50.00
Cup & Saucer, Red, After Dinner ....85.00 to 100.00
Cup & Saucer, Rose ....35.00 to 55.00
Cup & Saucer, Tea, Turquoise 20.00
Cup & Saucer, Turquoise 25.00
Cup & Saucer, Turquoise, After Dinner ....65.00 to 75.00
Cup & Saucer, Turquoise, World's Fair, 1939 .... 65.00
Cup & Saucer, Yellow 30.00
Cup & Saucer, Yellow, After Dinner ....65.00 to 75.00
Eggcup, Chartreuse ....140.00 to 160.00
Eggcup, Cobalt Blue ....90.00 to 95.00
Eggcup, Forest Green 160.00
Eggcup, Gray ....105.00 to 160.00
Eggcup, Ivory 90.00
Eggcup, Light Green 50.00
Eggcup, Red ....60.00 to 100.00
Eggcup, Rose ....105.00 to 160.00
Eggcup, Turquoise 50.00
Eggcup, Yellow ....50.00 to 55.00
Jar, Marmalade, Red ....295.00 to 495.00
Jar, Marmalade, Turquoise ....300.00 to 350.00
Jug, Cover, Cobalt Blue, Kitchen Kraft 375.00
Jug, Cover, Orange, Kitchen Kraft, Small 100.00
Jug, Cover, Red, Kitchen Kraft 295.00
Jug, Water, Gray, 2 Pt. 160.00
Jug, Water, Ivory, 2 Pt. 115.00
Jug, Water, Red, 2 Pt. 150.00
Jug, Water, Rose, 2 Pt. 165.00
Lamp, Cobalt Blue, 13 In. 250.00
Lamp, Red, Original Shade 1500.00
Lamp, Rose, 13 In. ....150.00 to 175.00
Mug, Chartreuse ....65.00 to 90.00
Mug, Cobalt Blue 65.00

Mug, Gray ....45.00 to 95.00
Mug, Ivory 70.00
Mug, Light Green 50.00
Mug, Medium Green 145.00
Mug, Red 70.00
Mug, Rose 95.00
Mug, Tom & Jerry, Gray 90.00
Mug, Tom & Jerry, Ivory, Gold Letters 55.00
Mug, Tom & Jerry, Rose 90.00
Mug, Yellow 50.00
Mustard, Cobalt Blue 395.00
Mustard, Ivory 395.00
Mustard, Red ....170.00 to 350.00
Mustard, Turquoise ....300.00 to 395.00
Mustard, Yellow 125.00
Nappy, Chartreuse, 8 1/2 In. 40.00
Nappy, Cobalt Blue, 8 1/2 In. 40.00
Nappy, Cobalt Blue, 9 1/2 In. 70.00
Nappy, Gray, 8 1/2 In. 65.00
Nappy, Green, 8 1/2 In. 35.00
Nappy, Ivory, 8 1/2 In. ....25.00 to 60.00
Nappy, Ivory, 9 1/2 In. 70.00
Nappy, Red, 8 1/2 In. ....40.00 to 45.00
Nappy, Rose, 8 1/2 In. ....45.00 to 75.00
Nappy, Turquoise, 8 1/2 In. 30.00
Nappy, Turquoise, 9 1/2 In. 50.00
Nappy, Yellow, 8 1/2 In. ....35.00 to 40.00
Nappy, Yellow, 9 1/2 In. 45.00
Pie Plate, Light Green, 9 In. 50.00
Pitcher, Disk, Chartreuse ....260.00 to 275.00
Pitcher, Disk, Gray ....265.00 to 350.00
Pitcher, Disk, Ivory ....90.00 to 175.00
Pitcher, Disk, Light Green 185.00
Pitcher, Disk, Medium Green ....900.00 to 1600.00
Pitcher, Disk, Red 175.00
Pitcher, Disk, Rose ....225.00 to 325.00
Pitcher, Disk, Turquoise 90.00
Pitcher, Disk, Yellow ....55.00 to 115.00
Pitcher, Ice Lip, Cobalt Blue 180.00
Pitcher, Ice Lip, Red 195.00
Pitcher, Ice Lip, Turquoise ....100.00 to 175.00
Pitcher, Ice Lip, Yellow 90.00
Pitcher, Juice, Yellow ....30.00 to 35.00
Pitcher, Light Green 175.00
Pitcher, Syrup, Cobalt Blue 350.00
Pitcher, Water, Ivory 190.00
Plate, Calendar, Ivory, 1954, 10 In. 50.00
Plate, Calendar, Ivory, 1955, 9 In. 50.00
Plate, Chartreuse, 6 In. 10.00
Plate, Chartreuse, 9 In. ....25.00 to 30.00
Plate, Chartreuse, 10 In. 35.00
Plate, Cobalt Blue, 6 In. 10.00
Plate, Cobalt Blue, 7 In. ....10.00 to 15.00
Plate, Cobalt Blue, 9 In. 20.00
Plate, Compartment, Light Green, 10 1/2 In. 35.00
Plate, Compartment, Red, 12 In. 65.00
Plate, Deep, Chartreuse, 8 In. 65.00
Plate, Deep, Cobalt Blue, 8 In. 45.00
Plate, Deep, Forest Green, 8 In. 55.00
Plate, Deep, Gray, 8 In. ....50.00 to 55.00
Plate, Deep, Ivory, 8 In. ....45.00 to 50.00
Plate, Deep, Light Green, 8 In. 40.00
Plate, Deep, Medium Green, 8 In. ....95.00 to 145.00

Plate, Deep, Red, 8 In. . . . . .35.00 to 50.00
Plate, Deep, Rose, 8 In. . . . . .45.00 to 65.00
Plate, Deep, Turquoise, 8 In. . . . . .30.00 to 45.00
Plate, Forest Green, 6 In. . . . . .5.00 to 10.00
Plate, Forest Green, 7 In. 15.00
Plate, Forest Green, 9 In. 20.00
Plate, Gray, 6 In. . . . . .5.00 to 15.00
Plate, Gray, 7 In. 15.00
Plate, Gray, 10 In. . . . . .35.00 to 40.00
Plate, Green, 6 In. 5.00
Plate, Green, 7 In. 5.00
Plate, Green, 9 In. 10.00
Plate, Ivory, 6 In. 10.00
Plate, Ivory, 7 In. . . . . .10.00 to 15.00
Plate, Ivory, 9 In. 20.00
Plate, Ivory, 10 In. 45.00
Plate, Light Green, 6 In. 5.00
Plate, Light Green, 7 In. 10.00
Plate, Light Green, 9 In. 10.00
Plate, Light Green, 10 In. 30.00
Plate, Light Green, Sections, 12 In. 45.00
Plate, Medium Green, 6 In. 20.00
Plate, Medium Green, 7 In. 35.00
Plate, Medium Green, 9 In. . . . . .50.00 to 65.00
Plate, Red, 6 In. . . . . .5.00 to 10.00
Plate, Red, 7 In. 14.00
Plate, Red, 9 In. . . . . .15.00 to 20.00
Plate, Rose, 6 In. . . . . .10.00 to 15.00
Plate, Rose, 9 In. . . . . .10.00 to 20.00
Plate, Rose, 10 In. . . . . .35.00 to 55.00
Plate, Turquoise, 6 In. 6.00
Plate, Turquoise, 7 In. . . . . .5.00 to 10.00
Plate, Turquoise, 9 In. . . . . .5.00 to 10.00
Plate, Turquoise, 10 In. . . . . .25.00 to 30.00
Plate, Yellow, 6 In. 5.00
Plate, Yellow, 9 In. 15.00
Plate, Yellow, 10 In. 25.00
Platter, Chartreuse, 12 In. . . . . .55.00 to 65.00
Platter, Gray, 12 In. . . . . .60.00 to 80.00
Platter, Green, 12 In. 35.00
Platter, Ivory, 13 In. 40.00
Platter, Medium Green, 13 In. 95.00
Platter, Red, 12 In. 35.00
Platter, Rose . . . . .50.00 to 75.00
Platter, Turquoise, 12 In. 35.00
Platter, Yellow, 12 In. 45.00
Relish, Base, Ivory . . . . .55.00 to 60.00
Relish, Center, Ivory 45.00
Relish, Cobalt Blue 350.00
Relish, Cobalt Blue, Ivory Center . . . . .260.00 to 375.00
Salt & Pepper, Cobalt Blue 30.00
Salt & Pepper, Ivory 20.00
Salt & Pepper, Medium Green . . . . .95.00 to 270.00
Salt & Pepper, Rose 35.00
Saltshaker, Red 12.00
Sauceboat, Chartreuse 75.00
Sauceboat, Forest Green . . . . .75.00 to 90.00
Sauceboat, Gray . . . . .75.00 to 95.00
Sauceboat, Ivory 60.00
Sauceboat, Red . . . . .35.00 to 45.00
Sauceboat, Rose . . . . .75.00 to 95.00
Sauceboat, Turquoise 45.00
Sauceboat, Yellow 15.00

Saucer, Forest Green 5.00
Saucer, Light Green 3.00
Saucer, Medium Green 20.00
Saucer, Red 5.00
Saucer, Rose 75.00
Saucer, Yellow 2.50
Server, Cake, Medium Green, Kitchen Kraft 150.00
Soup, Cream, Chartreuse . . . . .40.00 to 95.00
Soup, Cream, Cobalt Blue 75.00
Soup, Cream, Forest Green . . . . .60.00 to 80.00
Soup, Cream, Gray . . . . .40.00 to 95.00
Soup, Cream, Ivory 69.00
Soup, Cream, Light Green . . . . .40.00 to 50.00
Soup, Cream, Red . . . . .60.00 to 80.00
Soup, Cream, Rose . . . . .85.00 to 95.00
Soup, Cream, Turquoise . . . . .40.00 to 50.00
Soup, Cream, Yellow . . . . .40.00 to 50.00
Soup, Onion, Cover, Cobalt Blue 400.00
Soup, Onion, Cover, Ivory . . . . .395.00 to 595.00
Soup, Onion, Cover, Turquoise, Professionally Restored 2000.00
Soup, Onion, Cover, Yellow 415.00
Soup, Onion, Ivory 550.00
Spoon, Cobalt Blue, Kitchen Kraft 125.00
Spoon, Red, Kitchen Kraft . . . . .120.00 to 175.00
Stack Set, Kitchen Kraft 48.00
Sugar, Amberstone 16.00
Sugar, Cover, Chartreuse 65.00
Sugar, Cover, Forest Green 75.00
Sugar, Cover, Gray 75.00
Sugar, Cover, Light Green 40.00
Sugar, Cover, Red 65.00
Sugar, Cover, Rose 75.00
Sugar, Cover, Turquoise 15.00
Sugar, Yellow, Individual 110.00
Sugar & Creamer, Medium Green 240.00
Sugar & Creamer, Red 15.00
Sugar & Creamer, Turquoise 25.00
Syrup, Light Green 245.00
Syrup, Medium Green . . . . .300.00 to 350.00
Syrup, Red . . . . .325.00 to 595.00
Syrup, Turquoise . . . . .550.00 to 595.00
Syrup, Yellow 425.00
Teapot, Chartreuse, 6 Cup . . . . .160.00 to 325.00
Teapot, Cobalt Blue, 8 Cup . . . . .190.00 to 320.00
Teapot, Cobalt Blue, After Dinner, 12 In. 500.00
Teapot, Forest Green, 8 Cup 395.00
Teapot, Gray, 8 Cup . . . . .350.00 to 495.00
Teapot, Ivory, 6 Cup . . . . .140.00 to 220.00
Teapot, Ivory, 8 Cup . . . . .195.00 to 260.00
Teapot, Light Green, 8 Cup 250.00
Teapot, Medium Green, 6 Cup 195.00
Teapot, Medium Green, 8 Cup 1000.00
Teapot, Red, 8 Cup . . . . .285.00 to 295.00
Teapot, Rose, 6 Cup 325.00
Teapot, Turquoise, 6 Cup 175.00
Teapot, Yellow, 6 Cup . . . . .80.00 to 175.00
Tom & Jerry Set, Ivory, Gold Letters, 9-In. Bowl, 9 Piece 850.00
Tray, Utility, Cobalt Blue 50.00
Tray, Utility, Ivory 45.00
Tray, Utility, Red . . . . .50.00 to 65.00
Tumbler, Juice, Cobalt Blue . . . . .35.00 to 50.00
Tumbler, Juice, Gray 425.00
Tumbler, Juice, Ivory . . . . .35.00 to 70.00

Tumbler, Juice, Light Green 30.00
Tumbler, Juice, Red . . . . .45.00 to 55.00
Tumbler, Juice, Rose . . . . .40.00 to 70.00
Tumbler, Water, Cobalt Blue . . . . .60.00 to 75.00
Tumbler, Water, Ivory . . . . .65.00 to 75.00
Tumbler, Water, Light Green . . . . .50.00 to 55.00
Tumbler, Water, Red . . . . .65.00 to 75.00
Tumbler, Water, Turquoise 55.00
Vase, Bud, Cobalt Blue . . . . .75.00 to 95.00
Vase, Bud, Ivory, 6 1/4 In. 55.00
Vase, Bud, Light Green, 6 1/4 In. 95.00
Vase, Bud, Turquoise, 6 1/4 In. 70.00
Vase, Bud, Yellow, 6 1/4 In. 85.00
Vase, Cobalt Blue, 8 In. . . . . .775.00 to 800.00
Vase, Cobalt Blue, 10 In. 1150.00
Vase, Ivory, 8 In. . . . . .450.00 to 895.00
Vase, Ivory, 10 In. 1150.00
Vase, Light Green, 10 In. 650.00
Vase, Orange, 8 In. 650.00
Vase, Red, 10 In. . . . . .325.00 to 395.00
Vase, Yellow, 8 In. 595.00
Vase, Yellow, 10 In. 850.00

FINCH, see Kay Finch category.

FINDLAY ONYX AND FLORADINE are two similar types of glass made by Dalzell, Gilmore and Leighton Co. of Findlay, Ohio, about 1889. Each piece was made using three layers of glass. Onyx is a patented yellowish white opaque glass with raised silver daisy decorations. A few rare pieces were made of rose, amber, orange, or purple glass. Floradine is made of raspberry or tan-colored opaque glass with opalescent white raised floral pattern. The same molds were used for both types of glass.

Cover, For Butter, Raspberry, 6 In. 550.00
Spooner, Floral, 4 In. 385.00
Sugar Shaker . . . . .395.00 to 450.00
Syrup, Silver Floral, Metal Fittings 985.00
Toothpick . . . . .225.00 to 375.00
Toothpick, Frosted, Floral, 2 1/2 In. 550.00
Tumbler, Ruby, 3 3/4 In. 12.00
Water Set, 4 Barrel Style Tumblers, 5 Piece 2400.00

FIREFIGHTING equipment of all types is wanted, from fire marks to uniforms to toy fire trucks. It is said that every little boy wanted to be a fireman or a train engineer 75 years ago and the collectors today reflect this interest.

Alarm, Gamewell, Brass, Register 200.00
Alarm, Pacific Fire Extinguisher Co., Interior Pull Box, Cast Iron, 1920s 75.00
Ax, Nickel Plating, Viking Style 275.00
Bell, Fire Engine, Chrome, 12 In. 450.00
Belt, Dress, Personalized 55.00
Belt, East Hartford 110.00
Belt, Fountain Hose, West Hartford 110.00
Box, Alarm, Cottage Style, Gamewell 275.00
Box, Alarm, Grand Central Terminal, Cast Iron Door, Gamewell 220.00
Box, Alarm, Telegraph Station, Gamewell 110.00
Bucket, Andw. Morton, Protection, Feeno, Leather, Original Handle, 6 1/2 In. 1700.00
Bucket, Black Leather, S. Buckius, Gold Letters No. 2 . . . . 675.00
Bucket, Black Paint, Gold Letters, B. & A., 12 In. 467.00
Bucket, Brass Bound, Bail Handles, 1800, 16 1/2 In., Pair 11500.00
Bucket, Calais F. Club, J.A. Lee, Maine, 1833, Pair 2530.00
Bucket, Green Leather, N. Call, Concord, Red Under Yellow Lettering, No Handle 775.00
Bucket, Leather, J.L. Watson, No. 1, J.L. Watson, No. 2, 1800, 13 In., Pair 770.00

Bucket, Leather, Mustard, Black Banner With Mustache Ends, 1821, 12 1/4 In. 1725.00
Bucket, Leather, Painted, 1806 . . . . 1200.00
Bucket, Leather, Painted, Inscribed United F.S., S.Y., 13 In. 460.00
Bucket, Leather, Strap Handle, Red, France, 11 In. 242.00
Bucket, Leather, Traces Of Red & White Paint, 10 In. 165.00
Bucket, Little Giant, Composition 450.00
Bucket, No. 37 Red Heart, Benj Marshall, Leather, 1827, 19 In. 460.00
Bucket, Polychromed English Royal Coat Of Arms, Red Leather, c.1825, 9 In. 375.00
Cape, Gold Leaf Monroe, 2, Linen, Gold Leaf & Maroon 1650.00
Coat, Rubber, Large Size 60.00
Extinguisher, Combined Universal, Red, Holder, Box, 13 1/2 In. 120.00
Extinguisher, Elkhart, Elk, Brass 75.00
Extinguisher, Fyr-Fyter, The Captain, Chase Brass, 22 In. 250.00
Extinguisher, Hand, Galvanized Steel, Marked CD, Post World War II, 4 Gal. 55.00
Extinguisher, Hand, Galvanized Steel, Post World War II, Gray 35.00
Extinguisher, Pacific Bear, San Francisco 25.00
Extinguisher, Quickaid, 1 1/2 Qt. 10.00
Extinguisher, Red Comet, Hanger 110.00
Extinguisher, Salesman's Sample, Burgundy, Gold, Yellow Decal, 1919, 6 In. 242.00
Extinguisher, Single Roll Collar, Partial Label, Pacific Glass Works 9350.00
Gong, Alarm, Gamewell, 8 In. 1750.00
Grenade, American, Allover Quilted, Bulbous, 1870-1900, 6 In. 357.00
Grenade, Harden Star, Turquoise, Contents 135.00
Grenade, Harden, Peacock Blue 55.00
Grenade, Melon, Vertical Ribs, Yellow Olive, Bulbous, 6 1/4 In. 605.00
Halberd, Tin, Parade, 1890, 35 1/2 In. 595.00
Hat, Leather, Engine 2, JFD, Cairns, 15 In. 220.00
Hat, Station, Assistant Chief's, Gold Button, Chin Strap, c.1900 . . . . 50.00
Hatchet, Engraved Chrome, Black Handle, Germany 577.50
Helmet, Active Hose Derby, 1870s 425.00
Helmet, Aluminum, 1889-1897, Small 176.00
Helmet, Aluminum, Henry Bratacap, N.Y., Mid-19th Century 165.00
Helmet, Cairns, Fireman's Fund 75.00
Helmet, Cataract 10, Boston, Matching Belt 350.00
Helmet, East Islip, Long Island, 1890s 325.00
Helmet, Engine 80 Frontpiece, World War II, FDNY Auxiliary, Yellow 200.00
Helmet, Fire, Cairns, Aluminum, Fireman's Fund 120.00
Helmet, Gadrooned Plume, Urn Plaque, Leather Chin Strap, Brass, France 430.00
Helmet, German Silver, Braided Chin Strap 245.00
Helmet, Junior 2, Reading, Pennsylvania, 1880s 375.00
Helmet, Needham, Massachusetts, 1950s 125.00
Helmet, New York City Officer, Engine 32 . . . . 250.00
Helmet, Parade, Plume, France 220.00
Helmet, Polished Nickel, Horsehair Plume, Cairns Brothers 330.00
Helmet, San Francisco Fire Department, Engine Company, Leather 200.00
Horn, Engraved Nickel Plated 770.00
Jacket, Dress, Mauch Chunk Badge, 1920s 100.00
Mark, Associated Firemen's Insurance Co., Of Baltimore, c.1847, 11 3/4 In. 316.00
Mark, BU153, Philadelphia, Pennsylvania, Cast Iron, Reproduction 33.00
Mark, BU490, Tin, Merchants Fire Firefighting, Sign, Norwich Union, British 27.50
Mark, Bulau 349, Oval, Zinc, North St. Louis Mutual, 1880s, 7 1/2 x 5 1/4 In. 605.00
Mark, Coat Hook, Miniature 5.00
Mark, County Fire Office, Copper, Britain 33.00
Mark, Eagle Insurance Company 695.00
Mark, Fire Association Of Philadelphia, c.1860, 11 3/4 In. 287.00
Mark, Green Tree Mutual Assurance Co., Oval, Cast Iron, 1884, 3 1/4 In. 125.00
Mark, Independence Hall, Grasshopper Weather Vane, Lead, c.1835, 9 In. 200.00
Mark, Merchants Assurance Corp., Chinese Characters 473.00
Mark, Mutual Of Philadelphia, Green Tree, Cast Aluminum 100.00
Mark, Sagre, Oval, Tin, Portugal 154.00
Mark, Tin, Russia 90.00
Mark, UF With Spread Eagle, Cast Iron, 19th Century, 11 In. 287.00
Mark, Valiant Hose No. 2, 19th Century, 10 5/8 In. 402.00

Mask, U.S. Navy	3850.00
Nozzle, Flow Control, McNab & Harlin, 12 1/2 In.	85.00
Nozzle, John Clark, Boston, 1869, 37 In.	250.00
Pin, Fireman, Saving Child, Ladder, Celluloid, 1 1/4 In.	10.00
Pitcher, Souvenir, St. Louis Convention, 1971	23.00
Plaque, Helmet, Presented To B.J. Galvin, Engine Co. No. 21, Feb. 1, 1899	50.00
Plaque, Imperial Order Of Red Men, Hanging Loop, 1904, 12 1/4 In.	275.00
Plate, Builder's, Newburg., New York, Steamer Engine	330.00
Ribbon, Convention, Brass Scroll, San Francisco, 1922	195.00
Ribbon, Firemen's Convention, August, 1882, John P. Kislingbaury, Treasurer	8.00
Ribbon, Montgomery H & L Co., Fonda, New York, Bullion Tassel	10.00
Ribbon, W.S. Northrup Hose Co., No. 2, Johnstown, New Jersey, Pink	10.00
Shirt, Parade, c.1880	100.00
Sign, Guardian Assurance Company, Papier-Mache, Britain, Frame, 18 x 14 In.	15.00
Trumpet, Brass, 18 In.	375.00
Trumpet, Speaking, Fire Dept., Silver Plate, 1880	1250.00

FIREGLOW glass is attributed to the Boston and Sandwich Glass Company. The light tan–colored glass appears reddish brown when held to the light. Most fireglow has an acid finish and enamel decoration, although it was also made with a satin finish.

Tumbler	125.00
Vase, 8 In.	120.00

FIREPLACES were used to cook food and to heat the American home in past centuries. Many types of tools and equipment were used. Andirons held the logs in place, firebacks reflected the heat into the room, and tongs were used to move either fuel or food. Many types of spits and roasting jacks were made and may be listed in the Kitchen category.

Andirons, Bell Metal, Early 19th Century, 15 1/2 In., Pair	115.00
Andirons, Brass, Ball Top, 19th Century, 15 1/2 In.	1092.00
Andirons, Brass, Bell Finial, Faceted Sphere, Molded Band, 18 3/4 In.	6325.00
Andirons, Brass, Belted Ball, Jamb Hooks, Shovel, Tongs, 19th Century, 14 In., Pair	400.00
Andirons, Brass, Belted Ball, Shovel, Tongs, Early 19th Century, 16 In., Pair	260.00
Andirons, Brass, Cannonball, c.1810	95.00
Andirons, Brass, Chased American Eagle Shafts, Spurred Legs, 1830s, 26 1/2 In.	605.00
Andirons, Brass, Chippendale, Ball Finial, Cabriole Legs, Penny Feet, 19 1/2 In.	4830.00
Andirons, Brass, Chippendale, Urn Top, Spurred Arch Supports, c.1780, 21 In., Pair	402.00
Andirons, Brass, Dolphins, Pair	2355.00
Andirons, Brass, Federal Style, Lemon Shape Finial, Claw & Ball Footed, 27 In.	60.00
Andirons, Brass, Federal, Ball Finials, Shod Slipper Feet, 1800, 14 1/2 In.	2300.00
Andirons, Brass, Federal, Double Urn Top, Snake Feet, c.1800, 15 1/2 In., Pair	920.00
Andirons, Brass, Federal, Urn Support, 2 Fire Tools, 17 3/4 In., Pair	345.00
Andirons, Brass, Federal, Wire Diamond, Iron Wire Screen, 17 In.	115.00
Andirons, Brass, Figural, George Washington, 21 In.	402.00
Andirons, Brass, Flame Finials, c.1920, 22 In.	225.00
Andirons, Brass, Flame Finials, Foliate Design, Scrolled Feet, French-Style, 27 In.	330.00
Andirons, Brass, Foliate Scrolls, Supporting Monkeys, Period Costume, 11 1/2 In.	4025.00
Andirons, Brass, Georgian Style, Swag, Acanthus Design, Hairy Paw Feet, 31 In., Pair	805.00
Andirons, Brass, Knife Blade, Doorknob Finials, c.1780, 11 3/4 In.	650.00
Andirons, Brass, Lemon Top, Brass, John Molineux, 1800, 19 1/2 In.	575.00
Andirons, Brass, Lemon Top, Late 18th Century, 19 In.	632.00
Andirons, Brass, Masks, Corinthian Column, Classical Style, With Screen, 26 In.	400.00
Andirons, Brass, Owl, Half Round, On Arched Branch, Glass Eyes, 14 1/2 In., Pair	690.00
Andirons, Brass, Pierced Foliate, Scroll Form, 16 In.	207.00
Andirons, Brass, Queen Anne, Ball & Pearl, Square Plinth, 18th Century, 16 In.	1495.00
Andirons, Brass, Queen Anne, Plinth, Arched Legs, Penny Feet, 16 In., Pair	1495.00
Andirons, Brass, Regency Style, Lion On Pedestal, c.1890, 9 In.	632.00
Andirons, Brass, Spherical Finial, Octagonal Medical Band, 1820-1830, 14 In., Pair	1028.00
Andirons, Brass, Steeple Top, Early 19th Century, 24 1/2 In.	977.50
Andirons, Bronze, Chained Slave Figures, Seated On Sphinx Base, 41 1/2 In.	4025.00
Andirons, Bronze, Cupid Standing On Pedestal, Dolphin Supports, 27 1/2 x 12 In.	2640.00

Andirons, Bronze, Empire Ormolu, Recumbent Lion, Plinth, Rectangular, 11 In. 3630.00
Andirons, Cast Iron, Baseball Player, Black Cap, White Uniform, 19 1/4 In., Pair 7475.00
Andirons, Cast Iron, Black Man, Half Round, Squatting, 16 3/4 In., Pr. 2645.00
Andirons, Cast Iron, Brownie, Half Round, Seated Cross-Legged, 18 1/4 In., Pair 287.00
Andirons, Cast Iron, Bulldog, 15 1/2 In. 1495.00
Andirons, Cast Iron, Comic Black Men, 16 1/2 In. 385.00
Andirons, Cast Iron, Cowboy, 19 In. 9200.00
Andirons, Cast Iron, Dachshunds, Sitting With Heads Down, 17 In., Pair 230.00
Andirons, Cast Iron, George Washington, Half-Round, 19th Century, 21 1/4 In. 2990.00
Andirons, Cast Iron, George Washington, Holding Book, Boots, 15 In., Pair 1495.00
Andirons, Cast Iron, Hammered, Bradley & Hubbard, 25 1/2 In. 75.00
Andirons, Cast Iron, Hessian Soldier, Looking Left, Holding Sword, 19 1/2 In., Pair 575.00
Andirons, Cast Iron, Hessian Soldier, Marching In Review, 20 In., Pair 345.00
Andirons, Cast Iron, Inverted Y, Ball Finial 195.00
Andirons, Cast Iron, Ladies, New England, c.1800 . . . . 395.00
Andirons, Cast Iron, Minerva Head Finials, 6 1/2 x 13 3/4 In. 220.00
Andirons, Cast Iron, Owl, 13 3/4 In. 450.00
Andirons, Cast Iron, Owl, Pat. Sept. 14, 1887, 15 1/2 In. 850.00
Andirons, Cast Iron, Owl, Perched On Arched Branch, 20th Century, 21 5/8 In., Pair 690.00
Andirons, Cast Iron, Owl, Seated, Glass Eyes, Claw Feet, 22 In., Pair 1380.00
Andirons, Cast Iron, Owl, Yellow, Black Glass, Twig Base, 15 In., Pair 1150.00
Andirons, Cast Iron, Santa Claus, Painted, 1920s, 15 In. 1475.00
Andirons, Cast Iron, Smiling Chubby Brownie, Splayed Legs, 15 In., Pair 115.00
Andirons, Cast Iron, Squirrel, Half-Round, Profile, Holding Nut, 15 3/4 In., Pair 2587.00
Andirons, Cast Iron, Wild West Gunfighter 2800.00
Andirons, Duck Form, Webbed Feet, Tail To Billet Bar, 9 1/4 x 23 In. 690.00
Andirons, Gilt & Patinated Bronze, Male & Female Asian Figure, 18 In. 4600.00
Andirons, Gilt Bronze, Cherub, Seated On Foliate Scrolled Base, 17 1/2 In. 1610.00
Andirons, Iron, Baroque Style, Ball Finial, Baluster Standard 400.00
Andirons, Iron, Black Butler 1800.00
Andirons, Stylized Floral Design, 4-Sided Column, Arts & Crafts, 20 In. 660.00
Andirons, Wrought Iron & Brass, Federal, Double Ovoid Finial, Mid Banding, 18 In. . . . 690.00
Andirons, Wrought Iron, Brass Ball Finial, 18 1/4 In. 135.00
Andirons, Wrought Iron, Gooseneck, Penny Feet, c.1760, 15 1/2 In. 295.00
Andirons, Wrought Iron, Knife Blade, Penny Feet, Brass Urn Finial, 19 In. 250.00
Andirons, Wrought Iron, Spherical Finial, Flat Penny Feet, 22 3/4 In. 157.00
Andirons, Wrought Iron, Swan's Neck, 19th Century, 15 In. 165.00
Andirons, Wrought Iron, With Crane, 19th Century, 32 1/2 In. 165.00
Basket, Log, Brass, U-Shape Form, 4 Scroll Legs, Rectangular, 20 x 15 In. 46.00
Bellows, Federal, Mahogany & Leather 200.00
Bellows, Overall Painted Floral & Chinoiserie, 19 In. 172.00
Bellows, Turtle Back, Stenciled & Free Hand Fruit, Brass Nozzle, 17 In. 440.00
Broiler, Rotary, Wrought Iron, 18th Century 295.00
Broom, Oven, Birch, Early 29th Century, 10 In. 175.00
Coal Box, Bronze, Lion's Head Mounts, Victorian, 21 In. 4312.00
Coal Box, Carved Oak Frame, Peasants Drinking In Tavern Plaque, 17 x 18 In. 172.00
Coal Grate, Attached Andirons, Brass Finials & Trim, Cast Iron, 23 1/4 In. 187.00
Coal Scuttle, Green, Gilt Apples, Lion Finial, Tole, France, 25 x 16 In. 690.00
Coal Scuttle, Grotesque Face, Bruxelles, Cast Iron, 23 In. 245.00
Fan, Peacock Mounted On Base, 3 Paw Feet, Cast Metal, 18-In. Peacock 172.00
Fender, Brass & Iron, Floral Finials, Running Floral Design At Base, 65 In. 495.00
Fender, Brass & Wire, 19th Century, 18 5/8 x 41 3/4 In. 1092.00
Fender, Brass & Wire, D-Form 230.00
Fender, Brass & Wirework, Banded Ball Finials & Feet, 39 3/4 In. 375.00
Fender, Brass, Cornucopia Design, Bosses, Paw Feet, 10 In. 290.00
Fender, Brass, Federal, Serpentine, Diamond, Star Pattern, 5 1/4 x 41 1/4 In. 1035.00
Fender, Brass, Leaf Cutouts, Sample, 1800-1830, 13 x 5 In. 1250.00
Fender, Brass, Pierced, D-Form, Victorian 260.00
Fender, Brass, Reticulated, Paw Feet, 35 In. 82.00
Fender, Bronze, Muses Of Poetry & Art, Adjustable Length, France, c.1870, 57 In. 2090.00
Fender, Cast Bronze, Art Nouveau, Curved, Ornate, 4 Ft. 9 In. 4500.00
Fender, Cast Bronze, Returns, France 7500.00
Fender, Georgian Style, D-Form, Pierced Brass . . . . .172.00 to 200.00

Fender, Steel Bow Front, Brass Feet, 37 1/2 In. 345.00
Fireback, Cast Iron, Arched Top, Raised Design, Man On Horseback, 24 In. 800.00
Fireback, Cast Iron, Noble Family Upper Part, 4 Figures Below, 33 x 31 In. 385.00
Fireback, Cast Iron, Seal Of United States, Spread-Wing Eagle, 1830s, 30 1/2 In. 3162.00
Flue Cover, Victorian Women 65.00
Footman, Plate Stand, Brass, c.1830, 5 In. 410.00
Fork, Cooking, Blacksmith Made, American, Late 28th Century, 29 In. 135.00
Fork, Curled Tines, 9 1/8 In. 35.00
Fork, Handle Twist, Iron, Tines 10 1/4 In., 42 5/8 In. 115.00
Fork, Toasting, Brass, England 18.00
Grate, Cast Iron, Fluted Flat Columns, Urn Finials, c.1840, 27 1/2 In. 605.00
Griddle, Hanging, Wrought Iron 375.00
Griddle, Hearth, Iron, Stubby Spider Footed, Keyhole Handle, 10 1/2 In. 195.00
Griddle, Holding Handle, Side Lock, 18th Century, 14 7/8 In. 240.00
Holder, Skewer, Hand Forged Shaping & Filing, 6 Skewers 675.00
Lifter, Log, Hand Forged, Iron, 29 1/4 In. 90.00
Log Holder, Riveted Straps, Flaring Feet, Arts & Crafts, 12 x 24 In. 247.00
Peel, 42 In. 150.00
Peel, 47 In. 95.00
Peel, Ram's Head Handle, Wrought Iron, 19th Century 30.00
Pot Lifter & Trivet Combination, Forged Iron, 14 5/8 In. 85.00
Roaster, Rotating, Serpentine Tines, Iron, c.1780, 25 In. 425.00
Salamander, Browning Cakes, Cast Iron, c.1820, 34 In. 500.00
Screen, Geometric Design, Wire Mesh Interior, 4 Panels, 27 1/2 In. 315.00
Screen, Georgian, Mahogany, Petit Point Floral Design, Baluster Pole, Square 365.00
Screen, Green, Arched Crest, Exotic Animals, Trees, 4 Panels, 69 In. 335.00
Screen, Griffin Figural Base, Scrolling Feet, Fan Form, Brass, 26 In. 200.00
Screen, Jacobean, Oak, Carved, 2 Panels, 1880-1809 .... 1330.00
Screen, Louis XV, Gilt Metal, Fan Shape 170.00
Screen, Mahogany, Floral Needlepoint, Acanthus Scrolled Legs, 39 1/2 In. 365.00
Screen, Mahogany, Spiral Motif, Foliage, Whippet, Victorian, 54 1/4 In. 1210.00
Screen, Moonlight Camp Scene, Painted Black Velvet, Oak Frame, 32 x 20 In. 48.00
Screen, Needlepoint, Country Estate, Mahogany Standard, Button Feet 412.00
Screen, Needlepoint, Scroll, Shell Rosewood Frame, 47 1/2 In. 1100.00
Screen, Needlepoint, Woman Playing Piano, Triangular Curving Plinth, Mahogany 742.00
Screen, Neoclassical, Brass, 6 Piece 2070.00
Screen, Neoclassical, Giltwood, Depicting Capriccio, 3 Panels, 44 x 19 In. 2070.00
Screen, Open Scroll Design, Wrought Iron, Raymond Subes, c.1940, 40 5/8 In. 517.00
Screen, Pivoting Needlepoint Panel, Wool, Colored Beads, 1870s, 51 x 30 1/2 In. 595.00
Screen, Pole, Acorn Finial, Mahogany Tripod Base, Embroidered Parrots, Walnut 400.00
Screen, Pole, Chippendale, Hinged Shelf, Petit Point Floral Panel, 63 1/2 In. 2070.00
Screen, Pole, George III, Mahogany, Crewel Work Panel, 3 Inlaid Arched Legs, 57 In. ... 435.00
Screen, Pole, Georgian Style, Tapestry, 18th Century 1725.00
Screen, Pole, Queen Anne, Needlework, Mahogany, c.1770, 57 In. 805.00
Screen, Pole, Rosewood, Armorial Cartouche, Baluster Standard, Tripod, 64 In. 865.00
Screen, Pole, William IV, Mahogany, Floral Needlepoint, Carved, 1835, 65 In. 600.00
Screen, Pole, Woolwork Parrot, c.1850 .... 2195.00
Screen, Renaissance, Mahogany, Carved & Pierced Crest, 1860, 50 x 33 x 17 In. 785.00
Screen, Rococo Style, Giltwood, Tapestry, Aubusson Tapestry Center, 39 x 25 In. 750.00
Screen, Shield Form, Framed Silk Fabric, Cherry Urn Form Standard 250.00
Screen, Spaniel Holding Riding Crop In Teeth, Arts & Crafts, 3 Panels, 42 x 39 In. 1045.00
Screen, Victorian, Fan Form 575.00
Scuttle, Coal, Brass, Repousse Lion Crest Back Plate, Cylindrical, Continental, 32 In. 405.00
Scuttle, Coal, Copper, Helmet Form, 22 In. 160.00
Scuttle, Coal, Hinged Cover, Brass, Mounted Ship Tile, Footed, 19th Century, 21 In. ... 430.00
Shovel, Ash, 21 1/2 In. 145.00
Shovel, Ash, Hooked Handle, Iron, 24 1/4 In. 130.00
Shovel, Ember, Blacksmith Made, Iron, 18th Century, 10 In. 215.00
Skimmer, Jessie Cornelius, Sunburst Touchmark, Copper 225.00
Skimmer, Tooled Initials A.H., Iron Handle, Brass, 21 3/4 In. 192.00
Spit, Key Wind, Tin & Iron, 19th Century 357.00
Spit, Roasting, Tinned Copper 345.00
Stand, Brass, Front Cover, 4 Legs 100.00

Stand, Napoleon III, Gilt Metal, Foliate Handle & Frame, Pierced Base, 28 In.	375.00
Stand, Wrought Iron, 4 Scrolled Feet, Candle Socket, 17 3/4 In.	412.00
Toaster, Rotating, Curlicue Design, Flat Shaped Handle, Iron, 19 In.	230.00
Toaster, Twisted Handle, Wooden Grip, Wrought Iron, 22 In.	110.00
Tongs, Live Coal, Forged Iron, 10 In.	60.00
Tongs, Log, Mechanical Gripping Action, Brass, 34 1/2 In.	58.00
Tools, Louis XVI, Dore Bronze, Iron, Basket Finial, 33 In., 3 Piece	1725.00
Trammel, Handwrought, c.1810, 28 In.	275.00
Trammel, Meat Hook, With Hanger, Hand Forged, 25 1/2 In.	185.00
Trammel, Sawtooth, Wrought Iron, 36 1/2 In.	140.00
Waffle Iron, B & S Cook, Chatham, Connecticut, Cast Iron, 1840s, 27 1/2 In.	295.00

FISCHER porcelain was made in Herend, Hungary, by Moritz Fischer. The factory was founded in 1839 and continued working into the twentieth century. The wares are sometimes referred to as *Herend* porcelain.

MF

Bowl, Blue Garden, Gold Trim, 4 1/2 x 7 In.	55.00
Bowl, Victoria Butterfly, Gold Trim, Signed, 9 1/2 In.	235.00
Cache, Pot, Floral Sideband, Gilt Ram's Head Handles, 6 1/2 In.	360.00
Cake Plate, Printemps, Handles, Square	236.00
Coffeepot, Rothschild Bird, 6 1/2 In.	135.00
Dish, Vegetable, Rothschild Bird Pattern, 10 In. Diam.	85.00
Figurine, Birds Among Flowers, 12 In.	150.00
Figurine, Duck, 3 3/4 In., Pair	125.00
Figurine, Gypsy Woman Dancer, No. 5881, 13 In.	368.00 to 375.00
Figurine, Russian Boy	275.00
Plate, Fruit & Flowers, Hand Painted, 9 3/4 In., 8 Piece	600.00

FISHING reels of brass or nickel were made in the United States by 1810. Bamboo fly rods were sold by 1860, often marked with the maker's name. Metal lures, then wooden and metal lures were made in the nineteenth century. Plastic lures were made by the 1930s. All fishing material is collected today and even equipment of the past thirty years is of interest if in good condition with original box. Other fishing equipment may be listed in the Sports category.

Bait, Case, Shurkatch Bass Baits, Salesman's Sample	275.00
Box, Fly, 5 Tray, Aluminum, Richardson	190.00
Box, Tackle, Carved, 18 x 10 x 10 In.	295.00
Box, Tackle, Pine, Nail Construction, Orange Shellac, 17 x 7 x 8 In.	98.00
Bucket, Bait, External Brass Air Pump, Air-Fed Mfg. Co., c.1926	35.00
Catalog, Shakespeare, Rods & Reels, 1964	30.00
Creel, Splint, Open Top, Leather Strap	95.00
Creel, Tight Weave, Leather Bound, Front Strap, Broken Buckle	100.00
Creel, Turtle Trademark, Wicker, Turtle Shaped Latch	715.00
Creel, Wicker, Close Weave, Small Center Hole	145.00
Creel, Woven Splint, Carved Lid, 1930s	325.00
Harpoon, 3 Barbless Tines, Papyrus Blossom Shape, Ideal, 15 1/2 In.	175.00
Harpoon, Eel, Winter, Hook Tined, J. Fordham, 14 3/4 In.	198.00
Harpoon, Hand Forged, Toggle Head, c.1850, 32 3/4 In.	300.00
Harpoon, Whaling Gun, E. Eggers, Brass	4620.00
Harpoon, Whaling, Wooden Pole, Canvas Covered Sheath	1540.00
Kit, Fly Tying, Noll, Custom Deluxe	35.00
License, Arkansas Resident, Metal Frame, Clear Plastic, 1941	18.00
License, Hunt & Fish, Washington, 1934 Duck Stamp	150.00
License, Hunt & Fish, Washington, 1938	25.00
Lure, Baby Chub Wiggler, Fish Scale Pattern, Glass Eyes, 2 Hooks, CCB, 2 3/4 In.	90.00
Lure, Baby Crawdad, Glass Eyes, 2 Treble Hooks, CCB, 2 1/4 In.	38.50
Lure, Baby Devon, Allcock, On Card	55.00
Lure, Beetle, Glass Eyes, Cup Rig Hardware, CCB, 2 1/2 In.	163.00
Lure, Black Sambo, Box	195.00
Lure, Cap'n Bill's Fish Flash, Blue, Box	75.00
Lure, Club Creek, Jigger	85.00
Lure, Fluted Spinner, Winchester, No. 9612, Feather Tail	82.00
Lure, Giant Pikie, Creek Chub, Jointed, Fish Scale Finish, Box, 11 In.	77.00

Lure, Glowurm, Oliver & Gruber, 3 Bait Sections, Red & White Stripes 105.00
Lure, Heddon Great Vamp, Musky Flaptail, Red Head, Glass Eyes, Toilet Bowl Rigs 150.00
Lure, Heddon Surface Minnow 300, Hook Digs To Belly 220.00
Lure, Heddon, 3-Hook SOS Yellow With Red Nose, Front & Rear Spinners 70.00
Lure, Holi-Comet 25.00
Lure, Injured Minnow, Creek Chub, Fish Scale Finish, 1950s 11.00
Lure, Injured Minnow, Heddon, Pearl Color, 2 Hooks, Painted Eyes, 2 1/4 In. 17.00
Lure, Meadow Mouse, Cup Hook, Glass Eyes, Heddon, 2 3/4 In. 118.00
Lure, Minnow, Neverfail, Pflueger . . . . .75.00 to 125.00
Lure, Multi-Wobbler, Glass Eyes, 2 Hooks, Winchester, 3 1/4 In. 261.00
Lure, Muskie, Wooden, Yellow, Orange, 8 In. 27.50
Lure, Paw Paw Wotta Frog, 3 In. 55.00
Lure, Popeye Frog, Heddon 35.00
Lure, Sea Sillinger, Eger Bait Co., 3 Hooks, 1940s 11.00
Lure, SOS, Silver Flake Finish, Rig Hardware, Heddon, 3 In. 35.00
Lure, Swimming Mouse Jr., Glass Eyes, Green, Shakespeare, 2 3/4 In. 28.00
Lure, Torpedo, 3 Hooks, Heddon, 4 1/2 In. 60.00
Lure, Vamp, Glass Eyes, Heddon, 4 1/2 In. 24.00
Lure, Wig-Wag, Glass Eyes, L Rig, Heddon, 4 1/2 In. 50.00
Lure, Winchester, 3 Hooks, Cup Hook Rig, 3 1/4 In. 400.00
Net, Trout, Willow, c.1920 . . . . 275.00
Patch, Jacket, Dupont, Fish & Game Association 48.00
Plug, Crazy Crawler, Heddon 25.00
Pole, Telescopes From Cane, Fiberglass, Ward's Hawthorne, 6 In. To 13 Ft. 200.00
Reel, Bait Casting, Heddon, No. 3-15 . . . . 302.00
Reel, Bait Casting, Winchester, Child's 85.00
Reel, Bait Casting, Winchester, No. 2237, Free Spool, Wooden Knobs 165.00
Reel, Cutty Hunk, Julius Vom Hofe, Pat. 1911, 5/0 Size 247.50
Reel, Edward Vom Hofe, No. 6/0, Pat. 1902 . . . . 192.50
Reel, Fits Around Kidney In Back, Attached To Game Reel, Gold Anodized Aluminum . . 687.00
Reel, Fly 7 Point Adjustable Drag, S Handle, Sliding Click, Leather Case 522.00
Reel, Fly, Perfect, Hardy, 2 7/8 In. 605.00
Reel, Fly, Perfect, Hardy, 3 3/8 In. 357.50
Reel, Fly, Pfleuger, Sal-Trout No. 1558, 5 1/4 In. 150.00
Reel, Fly, Side-Mount, Oil Reservoir Within Shaft, Pat. 1889 . . . . 4750.00
Reel, Fortune, Hardy Brothers, Monel & Bronze, Double Handle Knobs 495.00
Reel, Game Fish, Penn Senator, No. 117, Box, 14/0 Size 302.50
Reel, Hoosier, Shakespeare, 1922 . . . . 90.00
Reel, J.S. Coxe, Model 25-3, Original Leather Case 145.00
Reel, Model 504, V.J. & A., Les Colby On Reel, Leather Case 632.00
Reel, Pal, Heddon, Box 85.00
Reel, Penn Delmar 23.00
Reel, Pennell Supra, Brass, 1890s 27.50
Reel, Pflueger Supreme 22.00
Reel, Pflueger, Everlaster Surf Casting, Nickel Finish, Wooden Grips, 1902 . . . . 138.00
Reel, Star Logo Presentation, Marked, Edward Vom Hofe, 1883 . . . . 715.00
Reel, Trolling, Winchester, No. 2776, Free Spool, Some Nickel Plating 121.00
Reel, Trout, Fin-Nor No. 1, Wedding Cake, Gold Anodize Finish, 3 In. 1320.00
Reel, Winchester, Good As The Gun 150.00
Reel, Winona, Heddon, 1923 . . . . 75.00
Rod, Casting, Metal Bait, Gray Paint, Cork, Winchester, 5 1/2 Ft., 3 Piece 170.00
Rod, Fin-Nor Wedding Cake, No. 1, Box & Bag 990.00
Rod, Fly, 2 Tips, Grand Deluxe, St. Albans, 1950, 8 Ft. 175.00
Rod, Fly, Bamboo, Extra Tip, Cloth Case, Aluminum Tube, 7 1/2 In. 525.00
Rod, Fly, Split Bamboo, Hardy, Alnwick, England, Aluminum Case 225.00
Rod, Fly, Split Bamboo, Orvis Impregnated Battenkill, Aluminum Case 250.00
Rod, Fly, Tips, Original Case, F.E. Thomas, 1952, 9 Ft. 400.00
Rod, Granger, Goodwin, 7 1/2 Ft. 715.00
Rod, Orvis Bait Casting, Serial No. 654, Pat. May 15, 1906, 5 1/2 Ft. 175.00
Rod, Otto Zwarg, Model 300, 4/0 Size 1100.00
Rod, Payne, Model 208, Walnut Seat, 2 Tips, 3 Piece, 6 Ounce 797.00
Rod, Penn Senator, 16-0, Deep Sea, 81 In. 770.00
Rod, Spinning, Joe Bates Jr., No. 569, Light Action, 7 Ft. 110.00

Rod, Split Bamboo, Ocean City Reel, 73 In. 247.50
Rod, Trout, G.H. Howells, No. 4549, 2 Tips, No. 5 Line, 7 1/2 Ft. 1800.00
Rod, Trout, Intermediate Wraps, Ferrule Plugs, 2 Tips, Leonard, 1875, 9 1/2 Ft., 3 Piece . 200.00
Rod, Trout, Papyne, 9 Ft. 605.00
Sign, Pflueger's Fishing Tackle, Embossed Tin, 13 1/2 x 9 1/2 In. 1012.00
Sign, Warden Service, State Of Maine, Division D District, 4 x 11 1/2 In. 295.00
Spear, Eel, 3 Prongs, Serrated Teeth, Wrought Iron, 19th Century, 16 1/2 In. 962.50
Spear, Eel, 5 Prongs, 15 In. 225.00
Spear, Eel, 5 Prongs, 20 In. 200.00
Spear, Eel, 5 Prongs, 9 In. Wide 128.00
Spear, Eel, 5 Prongs, Wrought Iron, 18th Century, 21 In. 175.00
Spear, Eel, 8 Prongs, Hooked 115.00
Spear, Eel, Diamond-Shaped Central Head, Iron Band, Barbless Prongs, 19th Century ... 715.00
Spear, Eel, Single Central Barbless Prongs, 2 Side Pieces, 17 In. 688.00
Spear, Fish, 5 Prongs, 14 1/2 In. 192.00
Spear, Fish, 5 Prongs, Barbed, 10 1/2 In. 65.00
Spear, Fish, 5 Prongs, Hand-Forged Iron, 20 In. 85.00
Stove, Ice House, Cast Iron, 19th Century, 10 7/8 In. 125.00
Tag, Dip Net, Illinois, 1956 .... 45.00
Vise, Fly Tying, Herters 15.00

FLAGS are included in the Textile category.

FLASH GORDON appeared in the Sunday comics in 1934. The daily strip started in 1940. The hero was also in comic books from 1930 to 1970, in books from 1936, in movies from 1938, on the radio in the 1930s and 1940s, and on television from 1953 to 1954. All sorts of memorabilia are collected, but the ray guns and rocket ships are the most popular.

Book, Jungles Of Mongo 45.00
Book Cover, Proof, Adventures In Space, 1960s, 2 Piece ....*Illus* 135.00
Card, Don Moore, Mac Raboy, Flash & Dale, Black & White, KFS, 1949, 3 x 5 In. 55.00
Coloring Book, 1952 .... 100.00
Coloring Book, Adventures In Space, On Back & Front, 1960 .... 134.00
Compass, Wrist, 1950s 75.00
Doll, Full Costume, Box, Mego Corp., 1976, 9 In. 60.00
Figure, Flash Gordon With Ring, Videomatic, 1967 .... 225.00
Figure Set, On Card, Mego, 1976, 8 1/2 In., 4 Piece 150.00
Jumpsuit, Mask, Box, 1970s 40.00
Model Kit, Space Compass, On Display Card 125.00
Pistol, Signal, Green & Red 750.00
Poster, Buster Crabb Autograph, 24 x 36 In. 350.00

Flash Gordon, Book Cover, Proof, Adventures In Space, 1960s, 2 Piece

Puzzle, 1950s 60.00
Puzzle, Comic Slide, Also Popeye & Pink Panther, On Card, 1981, 4 x 5 In. 20.00
Spaceship, 5 Space Rocket, 1925 .... 675.00
Sparkler, Friction, 1950s 30.00
Toy, Rocket Fighter, Kingfisher Toys 450.00
Toy, Rocket Fighter, Windup, Marx 395.00

FLORENCE CERAMICS were made in Pasadena, California, from World War II to 1977. Florence Ward created many colorful figurines, boxes, candleholders, and other items for the gift shop trade. Each piece was marked with an ink stamp that included the name *Florence Ceramics Co.* The company was sold in 1964 and although the name remained the same the products were very different. Mugs, cups, and trays were made.

Ashtray, Rococo, Pink, Gold, 8 In. 20.00
Bowl, Merrymaid, Jane, Rosie, Shell Shape 425.00
Box, Powder, Diane 275.00
Figurine, Abigail, 8 1/2 In. ....85.00 to 175.00
Figurine, Adeline, Blue & Pink, 8 1/2 In. 295.00
Figurine, Amelia, Burgundy & Gray, 8 1/4 In. 195.00
Figurine, Amelia, Rust & Tan, 8 1/4 In. 265.00
Figurine, Angel, 7 3/4 In. 95.00
Figurine, Ann, Blue Dress, Hat, Carrying White Basket, 6 In. 60.00
Figurine, Annabel, Aqua, 8 In. 595.00
Figurine, Becky, Blonde Hair, White, Blue Trim, 5 1/2 In. 195.00
Figurine, Blue Boy & Pinkie, 12 In., Pair ....600.00 to 730.00
Figurine, Camille, 8 1/2 In. ....145.00 to 165.00
Figurine, Carmen, 12 1/2 In. 525.00
Figurine, Catherine, Purple, 6 3/4 x 7 3/4 In.In. 595.00
Figurine, Charmaine, Blue 195.00
Figurine, Charmaine, Green, 8 1/2 In. 460.00
Figurine, Choir Boys, 6 In. ....75.00 to 85.00
Figurine, Cindy, Purple, 8 In. 435.00
Figurine, Claudia, 8 1/2 In. 300.00
Figurine, Claudia, Articulated Hands, 8 1/4 In. 375.00
Figurine, Claudia, Burgundy, 8 1/4 In. 295.00
Figurine, Colleen, Articulated Hands, 8 In. 300.00
Figurine, David, White & Gold, 7 1/2 In. 180.00
Figurine, Edward, Green Chair, 7 In. 300.00
Figurine, Elizabeth, Seated, Maroon, 7 x 8 1/2 In. 275.00
Figurine, Ellen, 7 In. 95.00
Figurine, Gary, 8 1/2 In. 125.00
Figurine, Genevieve, 8 In. 175.00
Figurine, Irene, 6 In. 45.00
Figurine, Jeannette, 7 3/4 In. 170.00
Figurine, Jim, 5 1/2 In. 40.00
Figurine, John Alden & Priscilla, 9 1/4 And 7 1/4 In. ....375.00 to 545.00
Figurine, Joyce, 9 In. 225.00
Figurine, Julie, 7 1/4 In. 110.00
Figurine, Leading Man, 10 1/2 In. 275.00
Figurine, Louis XVI ....125.00 to 325.00
Figurine, Louise, Green, 7 1/4 In. 125.00
Figurine, Madonna & Child 40.00
Figurine, Marie Antoinette, 10 1/2 In. ....375.00 to 450.00
Figurine, Mary, 7 1/2 In. 500.00
Figurine, Matilda, 10 In. 145.00
Figurine, Melanie, Gray, Maroon, 7 1/2 In. 90.00
Figurine, Melanie, Pink, 7 1/2 In. 65.00
Figurine, Oriental Couple 75.00
Figurine, Our Lady Of Grace 175.00
Figurine, Portrait 800.00
Figurine, Princess, Green, 10 1/4 In. 400.00
Figurine, Priscilla, 7 1/4 In. 165.00

Figurine, Rebecca, Blue, 7 In.	175.00 to 180.00
Figurine, Rhett, Gray Suit, 9 In.	175.00 to 400.00
Figurine, Rose Marie, 9 1/2 In.	190.00
Figurine, Sarah, Gray & Maroon, 7 1/2 In.	75.00
Figurine, Scarlett, Pink, Gold Trim, 8 3/4 In.	125.00 to 145.00
Figurine, Stephen, 8 3/4 In.	325.00
Figurine, Story Hour, 8 x 6 3/4 In.	490.00
Figurine, Sue Ellen, 8 1/4 In.	110.00
Figurine, Sue, 6 In.	95.00
Figurine, Suzanna	275.00
Figurine, Tess, 7 1/4 In.	430.00
Figurine, Victor, Black & Gold, Ivory, 9 1/4 In.	195.00
Figurine, Victoria On Couch, 8 1/4 x 7 In.	285.00
Figurine, Vivian, With Umbrella, 10 In.	250.00
Figurine, Woman, Dahlia, 8 In.	95.00
Figurine, Young Girl, With Bird	110.00
Flower Holder, Ava, 10 1/2 In.	195.00
Flower Holder, Ava, Green & Gray, 10 1/2 In.	225.00
Head Vase, Violet	175.00
Plaque, Cameo	100.00
Vase, Cottage	80.00

FLOW BLUE, or flo blue, was made in England about 1830 to 1900. The plates were printed with designs using a cobalt blue coloring. The color flowed from the design to the white plate so that the finished plate has a smeared blue design. The plates were usually made of ironstone china.

Biscuit Jar, Floral, Barrel, England, 7 1/2 In.	195.00
Biscuit Jar, Floral, Barrel, Twig Handle, Copper Luster, Thomas Forrester & Sons	375.00
Biscuit Jar, Wood Nymph & Cherub, Gold	235.00
Bone Dish, Marechal Niel, W.H. Grindley	50.00
Bone Dish, Rose	65.00
Bone Dish, Touraine, Stanley Pottery Co.	195.00
Bowl, Astoria, New Wharf Pottery, 9 1/2 In.	150.00
Bowl, Duchess, Wood & Son, 17 1/2 In.	300.00
Bowl, Dundee, Ridgway, 6 1/4 In.	45.00
Bowl, Fairy Villas, 6 1/4 In.	65.00
Bowl, Florida, 6-Sides, Johnson Bros., 10 In.	100.00
Bowl, Fruit, Floral Sprig, H.C. Edmiston, 10 1/4 In.	225.00
Bowl, Garland, Oval, 12 x 9 3/4 In.	125.00
Bowl, Harvest, Sampson Hancock & Son, 15 1/4 In.	285.00
Bowl, Kenworth, Johnson Bros., 5 1/2 In.	10.00
Bowl, La Belle, Ruffled, Gold Trim, Wheeling Pottery, 12 In.	220.00
Bowl, Louise, 9 In.	90.00
Bowl, Madras, Cover, 8 In.	395.00
Bowl, Marechal Niel, Cover, W.H. Grindley, 8 In.	395.00
Bowl, Messina, 10 In.	110.00
Bowl, Montana, Johnson Bros., 5 In.	35.00
Bowl, Pekin, Staffordshire, 10 In.	195.00
Bowl, Touraine, Stanley Pottery Co., 1898, Round, 9 3/4 In.	58.50
Bowl, Touraine, Stanley Pottery Co., Oval, 9 3/4 In.	125.00
Bowl, Vegetable, Linda, Cover, John Maddock & Sons Ltd.	110.00
Bowl, Vegetable, Madras, Cover	350.00
Bowl, Vegetable, Nonpareil, Cover	375.00
Bowl, Vegetable, Touraine, Individual	85.00
Bowl, Watteau, New Wharf Pottery, 9 In.	125.00
Bowl, Watteau, Wilkinson, 6 3/4 In.	25.00
Butter, Cover, Argyle	495.00
Butter, Cover, La Francais, 2 Sections, French China Co.	195.00
Butter, Cover, Manhattan, W.H. Grindley, 1900	65.00
Butter, Cover, Scinde, Drainer	1100.00
Butter, Cover, Touraine	425.00 to 625.00
Butter, La Belle, Wheeling Potteries	40.00

Butter, Nonpareil 30.00
Butter Chip, Baltic, W.H. Grindley 55.00
Butter Chip, Conway, New Wharf Pottery 35.00
Butter Chip, Dunbarton, New Wharf Pottery 45.00
Butter Chip, Fairy Villas, Adams, 3 1/4 In., 8 Piece 165.00
Butter Chip, Floral Scalloped Border 35.00
Butter Chip, Florence, Wood & Son 45.00
Butter Chip, Hamilton, John Maddock & Son 45.00
Butter Chip, La Francais, French China Co. 22.00
Butter Chip, Linda, John Maddock & Sons Ltd. 55.00
Butter Chip, Lorne, W.H. Grindley .... 55.00 to 60.00
Butter Chip, Marechal Niel, W.H. Grindley 55.00
Butter Chip, Marlborough 55.00
Butter Chip, Nonpareil 30.00
Butter Chip, Togo, Hollins Head & Kirkham 55.00
Butter Chip, Touraine 125.00
Butter Chip, Vermont, Burgess & Leigh 55.00
Butter Chip, Virginia 55.00
Cache Pot, Margot, W.H. Grindley 395.00
Cake Plate, La Belle, Wheeling Pottery, 10 3/4 In. 175.00
Cake Plate, Pekin, Dimmock, 1845, 12 1/4 In. 172.00
Candy Plate, La Belle, Leaf Shape, Wheeling Pottery, 6 1/4 In. 110.00
Casserole, Cover, Turin, Johnson Bros. 225.00
Celery, La Belle, Wheeling Pottery 295.00
Chocolate Pot, Pansy, Warwick, 1893, 10 1/2 In. 345.00
Coffeepot, Scinde, Thom. Walker, 1845, 11 1/2 In. 1150.00
Compote, Cover, Pelew, Ed. Challinor, 8 In. 750.00
Compote, Whampoa, Looped Handles, Mellor & Venables, 1840, 12 1/2 In. 575.00
Creamer, Arabesque 695.00
Creamer, Chusan, Clementson, 1840, 5 In. 345.00
Creamer, Coburg, Pinched Neck, Gothic Shape, John Edwards, 1860, 5 In. ... 517.00
Creamer, Gothic, 16 Panel Broad Base 1380.00
Creamer, Indian Jar, Jacob & Thos. Furnival, 5 1/2 In. 750.00
Creamer, Indian, Inverted Diamond Shape, F. & R. Pratt, 5 In. 520.00
Creamer, Marguerite, W.H. Grindley 190.00
Creamer, Nonpareil, Johnson Bros. 75.00
Creamer, Temple, Podmore, Walker, 1850, 5 In. 515.00
Creamer, Touraine, Large 475.00
Creamer, Touraine, Small 425.00
Creamer, Waldorf, New Wharf Pottery 225.00
Cup, Touraine 35.00
Cup & Saucer, Hamilton, J. & G. Meakin 45.00
Cup & Saucer, Lancaster, New Wharf Pottery 65.00
Cup & Saucer, Oregon 130.00
Cup & Saucer, Punch & Judy 100.00
Cup & Saucer, Scinde, Set Of 4 .... 375.00
Cup & Saucer, Temple 225.00
Cup & Saucer, Touraine 115.00
Cup & Saucer, Waldorf 1210.00
Cup & Saucer, Watteau, Edge Malkin & Co., Ltd. 65.00
Dinner Set, Oakland, John Maddock, 72 Piece 3800.00
Dish, Japonica, 2 1/4 x 12 In. 85.00
Eggcup, Athol, Burgess & Leigh 125.00
Eggcup, Linda, John Maddock & Sons, Ltd. 125.00
Gravy Boat, Arabesque 475.00
Gravy Boat, Janette, W. H. Grindley 95.00
Gravy Boat, La Francais, Underplate, French China Co. 95.00
Gravy Boat, Marechal Niel, W. H. Grindley 140.00
Gravy Boat, Melbourne, Underplate, W. H. Grindley 195.00
Gravy Boat, Oxford 95.00
Gravy Boat, Touraine, Underplate, Stanley Pottery Co., c.1898 .... 115.00
Hot Plate, Cashmere, Ridgway & Morley 1210.00
Jardiniere, Silver Luster Band, Cauldon, 1900s, 6 1/4 In. 225.00

Jug, Milk, Watteau, New Wharf Pottery 288.00
Ladle, Sauce, Hamilton, John Maddock & Son 95.00
Pitcher, Bowl & Slop Jar, Festoon, W.H. Grindley, 3 Piece 2495.00
Pitcher, Brushstroke Gold, Cobalt Floral Design, England, 1893, 12 1/2 In. 350.00
Pitcher, Cashmere, Ridgway & Morley, 7 In. 1980.00
Pitcher, Florida, Floral, Gold Trim, New England Pottery, c.1890, 7 1/2 In. 150.00
Pitcher, Hot Water, Trilby, Wood & Son 175.00
Pitcher, La Belle, Wheeling Pottery, 3 Qt., 8 In. 795.00
Pitcher, La Belle, Wheeling Pottery, 7 In. 250.00
Pitcher, Milk, Oregon, T.J. & J. Mayer, c.1845, 6 1/4 In. 750.00
Pitcher, Milk, Touraine 1095.00
Pitcher, Milk, Touraine, Johnson Bros. 275.00
Pitcher, Milk, Watteau, New Wharf Pottery 320.00
Pitcher, Oxford, 7 In. 250.00
Pitcher, Pansy, Warwick, 8 1/2 In. 395.00
Pitcher, Touraine, 7 In. 625.00
Pitcher, Touraine, Stanley Pottery Co., c.1898, 8 In. 460.00
Pitcher, Vistas, Scenes On Sides, Ridgway, Square, 7 In. 295.00
Pitcher, Wash, Atlas, 19th Century, 13 In. 1200.00
Pitcher & Bowl, Amoy 3195.00
Pitcher & Bowl, Chapoo 2475.00
Pitcher & Bowl, Jeddo 2495.00
Pitcher & Bowl, Trilby, Wood & Sons 895.00
Plate, Argyle, 7 1/2 In. 30.00
Plate, Argyle, 10 In. 110.00
Plate, Argyle, W.H. Grindley, 9 In. 70.00
Plate, Chapoo, 9 1/2 In. 175.00
Plate, Chusan, Podmore, Walker, 8 1/4 In. 60.00
Plate, Clarence, W.H. Grindley, 9 In. 85.00
Plate, Clarence, W.H. Grindley, 10 In. 85.00
Plate, Conway, New Wharf Pottery, 10 In. 85.00
Plate, Fairy Villas, 8 3/4 In. 65.00
Plate, Fairy Villas, 10 1/4 In. 115.00
Plate, Formosa, 12 Sides, T.J. & J. Mayer, 7 1/2 In. 100.00
Plate, Formosa, T.J. & J. Mayer, 10 1/2 In. 125.00
Plate, Geisha, 9 In. 65.00
Plate, Geneva, New Wharf Pottery, 10 In. 85.00
Plate, Hong Kong, 8 In. 95.00
Plate, Iris, 7 In. 90.00
Plate, Iris, 9 In. 200.00
Plate, Kyber, 10 In. . . . . .110.00 to 125.00
Plate, La Belle, Wheeling Pottery, 9 1/2 In. 85.00
Plate, La Francais, 7 In. 45.00
Plate, La Francais, French China Co., 9 In. 35.00
Plate, Lonsdale, 8 In. 65.00
Plate, Madras, 6 In. 60.00
Plate, Madras, 8 3/4 In. 95.00
Plate, Messina, 8 1/4 In. 40.00
Plate, Nonpareil, 9 7/8 In. 85.00
Plate, Nonpareil, 10 In. 75.00
Plate, Nonpareil, Burgess & Leigh, 1900, 9 7/8 In. 170.00
Plate, Nonpareil, Burgess & Leigh, 6 3/4 In. 300.00
Plate, Nonpareil, John Edwards, 9 In. 40.00
Plate, Oregon, T.J. & J. Mayer, 7 1/2 In. . . . . .70.00 to 75.00
Plate, Oriental, 1850s, 9 1/2 In., Pair 190.00
Plate, Oriental, Alcock, 9 1/2 In. 120.00
Plate, Ormonde, Meakin, 9 In. 55.00
Plate, Oxford, Burgess & Leigh, 10 1/2 In. 65.00
Plate, Scinde, 10 1/2 In. . . . . .120.00 to 170.00
Plate, Shanghai, 6 In. 45.00
Plate, Shanghai, 7 1/4 In. 125.00
Plate, St. Louis, Johnson Bros., 7 In. 55.00
Plate, Tonquin, 9 In. 150.00

Plate, Touraine, 7 1/2 In.	65.00
Plate, Touraine, 8 3/4 In.	60.00
Plate, Touraine, 9 In.	80.00
Plate, Touraine, Alcock, 8 In.	65.00
Plate, Trilby, Wood & Sons, 10 1/4 In.	95.00
Plate, Troy, Charles Meigh, 8 In.	95.00
Plate, Waldorf, 9 In.	110.00
Plate, Warwick, 6 1/2 In.	38.00
Plate, Wheel, Brushstroke, 8 In.	50.00
Platter, Alaska, W.H. Grindley, 14 In.	185.00
Platter, Albany, 14 In.	165.00
Platter, Arcadia, Wood & Baggaley, 15 1/2 x 12 1/2 In.	382.00
Platter, Argyle, 15 In.	195.00 to 225.00
Platter, Belfort, John Maddock & Sons Ltd., 17 In.	195.00
Platter, Cashmere, Frances Morley, 1850, 15 x 11 In.	460.00
Platter, Chusan, Clementson, 13 3/4 x 10 1/2 In.	295.00
Platter, Chusan, Clementson, 1840, 15 3/4 x 12 1/4 In.	430.00
Platter, Chusan, Octagonal, 15 1/4 In.	172.00
Platter, Clayton, Johnson Bros., 14 1/2 In.	145.00
Platter, Conway, New Wharf Pottery, 10 In.	110.00
Platter, Dainty, John Maddock & Son, 17 In.	225.00
Platter, Gothic, 18 In.	895.00 to 975.00
Platter, Grace, W.H. Grindley, 15 1/2 In.	285.00
Platter, Hong Kong, 12 x 16 In.	295.00
Platter, Hong Kong, 15 In.	525.00
Platter, Hong Kong, Tree & Well, 22 In.	900.00
Platter, Iris, 16 1/2 x 12 In.	195.00
Platter, Iris, Arthur Wilkinson, 14 1/2 In.	210.00
Platter, Kaolinware, Podmore, Walker, 15 3/4 In.	248.00
Platter, Kenworth, Johnson Bros., 14 In.	250.00
Platter, La Francais, French China Co., 15 In.	165.00
Platter, Lorne, W.H. Grindley, 14 In.	225.00 to 295.00
Platter, Madras, Oval, 17 1/4 In.	795.00
Platter, Melbourne, W.H. Grindley, 14 In.	175.00
Platter, Melbourne, W.H. Grindley, 16 In.	475.00
Platter, Nonpareil, 13 x 16 In.	475.00
Platter, Oregon, T.J. & J. Mayer, c.1845, 17 3/4 x 13 3/4 In.	288.00
Platter, Paisley, Mercer Pottery, 14 In.	275.00
Platter, Persianna, Ashworth, 1862, 21 1/2 x 17 1/4 In.	460.00
Platter, Scinde, 10 1/2 x 13 In.	285.00 to 575.00
Platter, Scinde, 20 In.	1150.00 to 1795.00
Platter, Scinde, J. & G. Alcock, 15 1/2 x 12 In.	485.00 to 650.00
Platter, St. Louis, Johnson Bros., 10 1/2 In.	155.00
Platter, Tonquin, 13 In.	550.00
Platter, Touraine, 12 In.	150.00
Platter, Touraine, 16 In.	375.00
Platter, Vermont, Burgess & Leigh, 14 x 10 1/2 In.	65.00
Platter, Waldorf, 10 x 8 In.	85.00
Platter, Whampoa, Mellor & Venables, Well & Tree, 1840 .... *Illus*	1265.00
Punch Bowl, Lady In The Window	1100.00
Relish, Labelle, 8 In.	250.00
Relish, Melborne, Grindley	125.00
Relish, Oregon, Curled Handle, T.J. & J. Mayer, 9 In.	215.00
Relish, Scinde	395.00
Relish, Whampoa	375.00
Sauce, Scinde, 5 In.	55.00
Saucer, Argyle	55.00
Saucer, Dainty, John Maddock & Son	12.00
Saucer, Touraine	10.00
Shaving Mug, Jenny Lind	80.00
Soap, Dish, Petunia, 3 Piece	350.00
Soup, Dish, Duchess	95.00
Soup, Dish, Holland, Johnson Bros., 7 1/2 In.	45.00

**China can be washed in
warm water with mild
soapsuds. The addition of
ammonia to the water will
add that extra sparkle.**

Flow Blue, Platter, Whampoa, Mellor & Venables,
Well & Tree, 1840

Soup, Dish, Lancaster, W. & E. Corn, 8 3/4 In.	65.00
Soup, Dish, Milan, Ford & Sons, 9 1/2 In.	55.00
Soup, Dish, Regent, 8 3/4 In.	85.00
Spooner, Lily	75.00
Sugar, Arabesque, T.J. & J. Mayer, 1845	172.00
Sugar, Chapoo, Cover	595.00
Sugar, Chinese Ching, Cover	95.00
Sugar, La Belle, Cover, Wheeling Pottery, 5 1/4 In.	495.00
Sugar, Manilla, Cover, Lion's Head Handles, Podmore, Walker	615.00
Sugar, Marechal Niel, W.H. Grindley	195.00
Sugar, Scinde, Alcock, 1840	115.00
Sugar, Scinde, Cover	750.00
Sugar, Shanghai, Cover, Open Handles, Squatty	250.00
Sugar, Whampoa, Mellor & Venables, 1840	172.00
Sugar & Creamer, Berry 5 In.	35.00
Sugar & Creamer, Iris	50.00
Sugar & Creamer, Lorne, W.H. Grindley	365.00
Sugar & Creamer, Oriental	125.00
Sugar & Creamer, Waldorf	90.00
Sugar Shaker, Sprigs Of Holly, 5 In.	285.00
Syrup, La Belle, Wheeling Pottery, Hinged Silver Lid, 4 1/2 In.	395.00
Table Set, Touraine, Sugar & Creamer	1000.00
Tankard, Vistas, Forest Scenes, Ridgway, Square, 7 In.	295.00
Teapot, Carlton, Samuel Alcock	1095.00
Teapot, Cashmere	1430.00
Teapot, Daisy, Burgess & Leigh	525.00
Teapot, Gothic, Jacob Furnival, 1850, 9 3/4 In.	288.00
Teapot, Hong Kong, Podmore, Walker	1800.00
Teapot, Indian, F. & R. Pratt, 1840, 8 1/2 In.	745.00
Teapot, Kaolin, Podmore, Walker	895.00
Teapot, Manilla, Podmore, Walker, 1845, 9 1/4 In.	575.00
Teapot, Ning Po, R. Hall & Co., 1845, 8 1/2 In.	460.00
Teapot, Oregon, Podmore, Walker	975.00
Teapot, Pelew, Lighthouse Shape, Ed. Challinor, 1840, 10 In.	400.00
Teapot, Progress, W.H. Grindley	345.00
Teapot, Scinde, J. & G. Alcock, 1840, 9 1/2 In.	575.00
Teapot, Tonquin, Joseph Heath, Lighthouse Shape, 1850, 8 1/2 In.	575.00
Toothbrush Holder, Trilby, Wood & Sons	165.00
Tray, Abbey, George Jones & Sons, 11 1/2 In.	150.00
Tray, Pin, Tulip, Johnson Bros., Gold Branch	20.00
Tray, Rhone, Thom. Furnival, 1845, 12 x 8 1/2 In.	805.00
Tureen, Gravy, Cover, Dark Blue, Acanthus Handles, Wood & Sons, 6 3/8 In.	1045.00
Tureen, Sauce, Beauty Roses, Underplate, Grindley	125.00
Tureen, Sauce, Janette, W.H. Grindley, Pair	350.00
Tureen, Sauce, Melbourne, W.H. Grindley, 3 Piece	395.00
Tureen, Soup, Ning-Po, R. Hall & Co., 1841	1485.00

Tureen, Vegetable, Cover, Melborne, W.H. Grindley	275.00
Tureen, Vegetable, Dainty	250.00
Urn, Birds & Block, Gilt Design, Crescent, 11 In.	55.00
Vase, Bud, Polychrome Floral, Bulbous, 6 1/2 In.	110.00
Waste Bowl, Hong Kong, Octagonal	195.00
Waste Bowl, Sabroan, 3 1/4 x 6 In.	575.00
Waste Bowl, Scinde	500.00
Waste Bowl, Touraine	240.00

FLYING PHOENIX, see Phoenix Bird category.

FOLK ART is also listed in many categories of this book under the actual name of the object. See categories such as Box, Cigar Store Figure,
Paper, Weather Vane, Wooden, etc.

Band, Celebrating End Of World War II, Pipe Cleaners, 20 Piece	285.00
Bank, Chest Of Drawers, Coins Put In Upper Drawer Fall Into Lower Drawer	375.00
Baton, Wood, Carved Horsehead, With Ball In Cage, Dark Finish, 40 In.	140.00
Bird House, Martin, Mustard Paint, 34 In.	350.00
Bird House, Martin, White, 26 x 31 In.	380.00
Birdhouse, Arched Top, Feeding Trough, Water Holder At Sides, 14 1/2 In.	82.00
Birdhouse, Mounted On Bicycle Pedal, Red, Blue & Gray, Art Zeppelin, 40 In.	935.00
Birdhouse, Multi-House Combination, Red, White & Green, Large Dome Top, Large	1300.00
Birdhouse, Rusted Metal & Antlers	550.00
Birdhouse, Wood & Wirework, 3 Stories, Turrets, Bell Spire, Gold Trim, Russia, 81 In.	6800.00
Box, Birds, Flowers, Dated 1902	960.00
Box, Jewelry, House Shape, Wooden, 7 x 7 In.	250.00
Box, Matchstick, Dog Shape, Sides Decorated With Rabbit, Heart, Polar Bear, Cat, 4 In.	184.00
Chair, Plank Seat, Completely Covered With Postage Stamps, Pair	650.00
Church, Slices Of Walnut Shells	2400.00
Crucifix, Carved & Painted Figures, 1908, 34 In.	1320.00
Dollhouse, Furniture, Car, Cat & Dog, 48-Star Flag, 38 x 22 x 27 In.	750.00
Figure, Bell, Black Woman Shape, Hand Sewn Clothes, 6 In.	23.00
Figure, Blackamoor, Carnival Knock-Down, Male & Female, Painted Wood, 15 In.	5300.00
Figure, Bride & Groom, Painted, 11 In., Pair	2200.00
Figure, Cat, Light Brown, Black Accents, Green Eyes, Wood Carving, 2 x 5 In.	95.00
Figure, George Washington, Papier-Mache Head, Stuffed Limbs, Knees Bend, 23 In.	750.00
Figure, Reindeer, Horn, Antlers, Wood, Red Paint, 28 x 36 In.	172.00
Figure, Teeter Totter, Civil War Soldier, Teeters Up To 10 Minutes, 22 1/2 In.	210.00
Mirror, Applied Carved Grapes, Birds & Leaves, Rounded Top, 18 1/2 x 22 In.	1295.00
Planter, Pine, White Squiggles & Swirls, 13 x 31 In.	475.00
Retablo, Manger, Inset Shadow Box, Angel Holds Banner, Says Gloria	135.00
Snake, Twig, Green & Yellow Paint	300.00
Soldier, African Colonial, Carved, 1900, 19 In. ....*Illus*	495.00
Train Set, Wood, Wire & Nails, Tin, Painted, 29 Piece	1100.00

**Go outside and try to read your
house numbers from the street.
If you can't read them, get new,
larger ones. Police responding to
an emergency must be able to
see the numbers in your address.**

Folk Art, Soldier, African Colonial,
Carved, 1900, 19 In.

Whirligig, 2 Figures With Mule, Painted Wood, 21 In. 105.00
Whirligig, 2 Men Sawing Wood, Polychrome Paint, 20th Century, 43 In. 82.00
Whirligig, 4 Rowers, 2 Boats, Marked Harvard & Yale, Steel Pole, 43 In. 220.00
Whirligig, Acrobat, Red & Green Costume 2860.00
Whirligig, Airplane, 4-Ft. Wingspan 350.00
Whirligig, Ballerina, Windup, Celluloid, 1930s 155.00
Whirligig, Black Washer Lady 495.00
Whirligig, Donald Duck, Long Billed, Celluloid, Painted Tin 1200.00
Whirligig, Elephant, Windup, Celluloid, Platform, 1930s 195.00
Whirligig, Family Of 4, Crossbeams, Father, Mother, 2 Children, Full-Bodied 3190.00
Whirligig, Flying Geese, 1880 .... 3250.00
Whirligig, Hound Dog, Wooden 75.00
Whirligig, Indian, Wooden, Brown Body, Yellow Legs, War Paint, 11 1/2 In. 1450.00
Whirligig, Jack Tar, Sailor, 1870s 8200.00
Whirligig, Policeman, Hat With Tin Bill, Tin Hat Badge, Tacks For Buttons, 22 In. 440.00
Whirligig, Santa Claus, Painted Wood, 32 In. 175.00
Whirligig, Soldier, Wearing Red Tunic, Late 19th Century, 17 1/2 In. 862.00

FOOT WARMERS solved the problem of cold feet in past generations. Some warmers held charcoal, others held hot water. Pottery, tin, and soapstone were the favored materials to conduct the heat. The warmer was kept under the feet, then the legs and feet were tucked into a blanket, providing welcome warmth in a cold carriage or church.

Carriage, Copper, Hot Water, 19th Century 65.00
Eagle Design, Tin, Bail Handle 375.00
Heart & Diamond, Treen 495.00
Iron Handle, Tin Insert, Oak, c.1750 .... 350.00
Pierced Cover, Lifting Handles, Paw Feet, Brass, 11 In. 172.00
Punched Circle & Heart, Tin Cover, Walnut Frame, 7 3/4 x 9 In. 137.00
Punched Tin Cover, Hardwood Frame, Red Stain, 8 x 8 3/4 In. 180.00
Tin, Wooden Frame, Place For Coals, Square 225.00
Walnut, Sliding Front Door, Insert, 1820 .... 350.00

FOOTBALL collectibles may be found in the Card and the Sports categories.

FOSTORIA glass was made in Fostoria, Ohio, from 1887 to 1891. The factory was moved to Moundsville, West Virginia, and most of the glass seen in shops today is a twentieth-century product. The company was sold in 1983; new items will be easily identifiable, according to the new owner, Lancaster Colony Corporation. Additional Fostoria items may be listed in the Milk Glass category.

American, Basket, Reed Handle 75.00
American, Boat, Relish, Green, 9 In. 150.00
American, Bottle, Cordial, Stopper 70.00
American, Bowl, 3-Footed, 6 3/4 In. 13.00
American, Bowl, 3-Footed, 10 In. 38.00
American, Bowl, 4 1/2 In. 8.00
American, Bowl, 8 In. 10.00
American, Bowl, Shrimp 275.00
American, Bowl, Trophy, 2 Handles, Footed 115.00
American, Bowl, Wedding, 8 In. 85.00
American, Butter, Cover, Rectangular 35.00
American, Cake Stand, Round, 10 In. 65.00
American, Candy Dish, Footed 15.00
American, Centerpiece, Tri-Corner, Footed, 11 In. 65.00
American, Compote, Jelly, Cover, 6 3/4 In. 35.00
American, Cruet 20.00
American, Cup & Saucer 10.00
American, Decanter, Scotch & Rye, Pair 150.00
American, Goblet, 10 Oz. 10.00
American, Humidor, Cover, Walnut Base 350.00
American, Ice Bucket, Metal Handle 45.00
American, Ice Dish, Crab Meat Insert 45.00

American, Ice Tub	37.00
American, Jam Jar	50.00
American, Ladle, Punch	20.00
American, Mayonnaise, Underplate, Ladle	45.00
American, Pickle Jar	425.00
American, Pitcher, 1 1/2 Qt.	65.00
American, Pitcher, 1/2 Gal.	68.00
American, Pitcher, Ice Lip	67.50
American, Plate, 8 1/2 In.	10.00
American, Plate, Torte, 18 In.	90.00
American, Punch Bowl, 18 In.	265.00
American, Punch Bowl, Footed, Low	175.00
American, Punch Cup	10.00
American, Ring Holder	250.00 to 750.00
American, Rose Bowl, 5 In.	10.00
American, Rose Bowl, Slotted Silver Plate Cover	275.00
American, Server, Center Handle, 12 In.	28.00
American, Sherbet, Handle, 4 1/2 Oz.	150.00
American, Sherbet, Hexagonal Foot	10.00
American, Sugar & Creamer, Hexagonal Foot	1800.00
American, Sugar & Creamer, Oval Tray, 3 Piece	35.00 to 38.00
American, Sugar Cube Holder	325.00
American, Toothpick	30.00
American, Tray, 2 Handles, Oval, 10 1/2 x 5 In.	20.00
American, Tumbler, Flared, 4 1/8 In.	10.00
American, Vase, Flared, 8 In.	60.00 to 90.00
American, Vase, Flared, 9 In.	122.00
American, Vase, Flared, Swing, 9 1/2 In.	300.00
American, Vase, Footed, Square, 7 1/4 In.	35.00
American Lady, Goblet, Purple	25.00
American Lady, Sherbet	6.00
American Lady, Sherbet, Purple, 5 1/2 Oz.	20.00
American Lady, Wine	8.00
Aurora, Goblet, Label	10.00
Baroque, Bowl, 12 In.	40.00
Baroque, Bowl, Flared, 12 In.	58.00
Baroque, Candlestick, 3-Light, Blue	185.00
Baroque, Candlestick, 3-Light, Yellow, Pair	135.00
Baroque, Candlestick, Blue, 5 1/2 In., Pair	72.00
Baroque, Cruet	65.00
Baroque, Cup & Saucer	15.00
Baroque, Mayonnaise, Lido Etch	10.00
Baroque, Nappy, Footed, 2 Handles	20.00
Baroque, Nappy, Square, Azure, 6 In.	35.00
Baroque, Relish, 3 Sections, Amber	25.00
Baroque, Relish, 3 Sections, Blue	39.00
Baroque, Relish, 3 Sections, Chintz Etch	32.00
Baroque, Rose Bowl	15.00
Baroque, Sugar & Creamer	10.00
Baroque, Sugar & Creamer, Azure, After Dinner	60.00
Bookends, Lyre	125.00
Buttercup, Bowl, Lily Pond, 12 In.	55.00
Buttercup, Plate, Torte, 14 In.	45.00
Century, Cup, Footed, 6 Oz.	15.00
Century, Goblet, 10 Oz.	12.00
Century, Ice Bucket, Metal Handle	30.00
Century, Pitcher, Milk	48.00
Century, Sugar & Creamer, Tray, 3 Piece	20.00 to 35.00
Chintz, Bonbon, 7 5/8 In.	28.00
Chintz, Bowl, Flared, 12 In.	50.00
Chintz, Cake Plate, 2 Handles	35.00
Chintz, Celery, 11 In.	36.00
Chintz, Cocktail, Oyster, 4 Oz.	30.00

Chintz, Juice, Footed, 5 Oz. 27.00
Chintz, Plate, 9 1/2 In. 45.00
Chintz, Sugar & Creamer 28.00
Chintz, Wine, 4 1/2 Oz. 35.00
Coin, Ashtray, Amber, Round, 7 1/2 In. 20.00
Coin, Bowl, Frosted Coin, Amber, 8 1/2 In. 54.00
Coin, Candlestick, Amber, 8 In. 28.00
Coin, Candlestick, Ruby, 8 In., Pair 95.00
Coin, Candy Jar, Cover, Blue 85.00
Coin, Cigarette Jar, Olive Green 5.00
Coin, Compote, Ruby, Cover 200.00
Coin, Creamer, Amber 19.00
Coin, Cruet 95.00
Coin, Cruet, Amber 65.00
Coin, Jelly, Olive Green 14.00
Coin, Lamp, Oil, Electric Blue 150.00
Coin, Lamp, Oil, Patio, Shade 180.00
Coin, Pitcher, Water, Red 85.00
Coin, Punch Set, Bowl, 9 Cups, Glass Ladle 1000.00
Coin, Punch Set, Bowl, Base, 12 Cups 685.00
Coin, Salt & Pepper 25.00
Coin, Salt & Pepper, Amber 42.00
Coin, Sugar & Creamer, Ruby 25.00
Coin, Urn, Cover, Blue 135.00
Coin, Vase, Footed, Amber, 8 In. 30.00
Coin, Vase, Footed, Olive Green, 8 In. 24.00
Colonial, Toothpick 18.00
Colonial Mirror, Goblet, 9 Oz. 6.00
Colony, Candlestick, Pair 45.00
Colony, Cheese & Cracker Set 35.00
Coronet, Ice Bucket 80.00
Corsage, Cocktail, 3 1/2 Oz. 28.00
Diadem, Vase, Topaz, 8 In. 15.00
Dolphin, Ashtray 20.00
Fairfax, Ashtray, 4 In. 10.00
Fairfax, Bowl, Topaz, 12 In. 18.00
Fairfax, Candlestick, Green, Pair 42.00
Fairfax, Cup & Saucer, Green 6.00
Fairfax, Dish, Divided, Green 13.00
Fairfax, Grill Plate, Amber, 10 1/4 In. 28.00
Fairfax, Nut Cup, Pink 20.00
Fairfax, Pitcher, Amber 110.00
Fairfax, Plate, Torte, Amber, 13 In. 58.00
Fairfax, Platter, Oval, Amber, 10 In. 38.00
Fairfax, Platter, Oval, Amber, 12 In. 48.00
Fairfax, Platter, Oval, Amber, 15 In. 125.00
Fairfax, Relish, Green, 11 1/2 In. 28.00
Fairfax, Sherbet, Yellow 9.00
Fairfax, Sugar & Creamer, Ruby 40.00
Fairfax, Window Box, Black 95.00
Fairfax, Wine, Yellow 30.00
Flame, Bowl, Oval, 12 1/2 In. 5.00
Glacier, Candy Jar, 1/2 Lb. 35.00
Heirloom, Candlestick, Ruby 9.00
Hermitage, Salt & Pepper, Yellow 55.00
Hermitage, Tumbler, Juice, Footed, Blue 30.00
Holly, Cocktail, Oyster 13.50
Holly, Cordial 38.00
Holly, Goblet, Water, Low 16.00
Holly, Goblet, Water, Tall 18.00
Holly, Sherbet, Low 12.00
Holly, Sherbet, Tall 15.00

Holly, Tumbler, Juice, Footed 12.00
Indian Maiden, Vase, Painted, 6 In. 45.00
Jamestown, Goblet, Amber Stem, 9 1/2 Oz. 120.00
Jamestown, Goblet, Blue, 5 7/8 In. ....12.00 to 15.00
Jamestown, Sherbet, Amber Stem 7.00
Jamestown, Tumbler, Juice, Blue, 5 Oz. 26.00
June, Bonbon, Blue 30.00
June, Candlestick, Blue, Pair 139.00
June, Claret, Yellow 60.00
June, Tumbler, Footed, Yellow, 6 In. 35.00
Kashmir, Goblet, Yellow 30.00
Lafayette, Nut Cup, Pair 15.00
Lafayette, Pitcher, Wisteria, 7 1/2 In. 75.00
Lafayette, Plate, Torte, Empire Green, 13 In. 40.00
Lafayette, Relish, 2 Sections, Amber 24.00
Lafayette, Relish, 2 Sections, Red 34.00
Lafayette, Relish, 3 Sections, Fruit Design 20.00
Lafayette, Sauceboat, Red 28.00
Lido, Pitcher 130.00
Mayflower, Candlestick, Pair 65.00
Meadow Rose, Cordial 50.00
Meadow Rose, Cup & Saucer .... 23.00 to 25.00
Meadow Rose, Pitcher 375.00
Navarre, Champagne, Saucer, Blue 36.00
Navarre, Chop Plate, Green, 14 In. 43.00
Navarre, Claret, Blue, Signed, 6 1/2 In. 45.00
Navarre, Coaster, Green, 3 Piece 18.00
Navarre, Cup & Saucer 25.00
Navarre, Goblet, Water, Tall 28.00
Navarre, Plate, 7 1/2 In. 14.00
Navarre, Plate, 8 1/2 In. 22.00
Navarre, Plate, Green, 9 1/2 In. 23.00
Navarre, Relish, 3 Sections 25.00
Navarre, Tumbler, Green, 9 Oz. 300.00
Oak Leaf, Bowl, Footed, Green, 12 In. 80.00
Old English, Spooner 18.00
Orchid, Vase, 6 In. 45.00
Poppy, Cordial 30.00
Priscilla, Table Set, Green, Gold Trim, 4 Piece .... 295.00 to 360.00
Raleigh, Plate, 7 1/4 In. ....120.00 to 195.00
Regal, Toothpick 250.00
Richmond, Pitcher 95.00
Richmond, Pitcher, Needle Etch, c.1927 .... 145.00
Richmond, Plate, 7 1/4 In. 60.00
Rogene, Champagne, 5 Oz. 18.00
Romance, Candlestick, Trindle 38.00
Romance, Champagne, Saucer 15.00
Romance, Cup & Saucer 20.00
Romance, Pitcher 175.00
Romance, Relish, 3 Sections, 10 In. 32.00
Romance, Salt & Pepper, Glass Lids, Individual 15.00
Royal, Cake Plate, Amber, Gold Handle 45.00
Royal, Cocktail, Amber, 3 1/2 In. 10.00
Seville, Pitcher, Amber 235.00
Sunray, Relish, 4 Sections 10.00
Sunray, Sugar & Creamer, Individual 20.00
Sunray, Tumbler, Footed, 9 Oz. 7.00
Sylvan, Toothpick 25.00
Trojan, Candlestick, Scroll, Pink, 5 In., Pair 80.00
Trojan, Parfait 65.00
Trojan, Relish, 3 Sections, Yellow 30.00
Versailles, Bowl, Yellow, 5 In. 18.00

Versailles, Bowl, Yellow, 6 1/2 In. 23.00
Versailles, Compote, 7 In. 53.00
Versailles, Dish, Sweetmeat, Yellow 24.00
Versailles, Goblet, Low, Footed, 12 Oz. 30.00
Versailles, Plate, Yellow, 9 1/2 In. 65.00
Versailles, Sherbet, Yellow, Tall 24.00
Versailles, Sugar, Individual, Pink 28.00
Vesper, Console, Green, 11 1/4 In. 35.00
Vesper, Pitcher, Green 335.00
Vesper, Plate, Amber, 6 In. 7.00
Vesper, Platter, Green, 10 1/2 In. 35.00
Vesper, Sugar & Creamer, Amber 50.00
Victoria, Nappy, Tri-Corner 45.00
Virginia, Toothpick 60.00
Willowmere, Champagne, 6 Oz. ....20.00 to 22.00
Willowmere, Cocktail, 3 1/2 Oz. 17.00
Willowmere, Tumbler, 5 Oz. 20.00

FOVAL, see Fry category.

FRAMES are included in the Furniture category under Frame.

FRANCISCAN is a trademark that appears on pottery. Gladding, McBean and Company started in 1875. The company grew and acquired other potteries. They made sewer pipes, floor tiles, dinnerwares, and art pottery with a variety of trademarks. In 1934, dinnerware and art pottery were sold under the name Franciscan Ware. They made china and cream-colored, decorated earthenware. Desert Rose, Apple, El Patio, and Coronado were best-sellers. The company became Interpace Corporation and in 1979 was purchased by Josiah Wedgwood & Sons. The plant was closed in 1984 but a few of the patterns are still being made. For more information, see *Kovels' Depression Glass & American Dinnerware Price List.*

Ashtray, Apple 15.00
Ashtray, Apple, Individual, 3 Piece 15.00
Ashtray, Apple, Oval ....65.00 to 75.00
Ashtray, Apple, Square 75.00
Ashtray, Desert Rose, Individual 10.00
Ashtray, Desert Rose, Oblong ....65.00 to 80.00
Ashtray, Desert Rose, Oval 60.00
Ashtray, Wildflower, Yellow Poppy, 4 In. 55.00
Baking Dish, Apple 130.00
Baking Dish, Meadow Rose, Square ....90.00 to 165.00
Baking Dish, October, Square 80.00
Bank, Piggy, Desert Rose 350.00
Bell, Desert Rose, Danbury 50.00
Berry Bowl, Duet 10.00
Bonbon, Starburst 35.00
Bowl, Apple, 5 1/2 In. 15.00
Bowl, Apple, 6 In. 15.00
Bowl, Apple, 10 In. ....60.00 to 100.00
Bowl, Autumn, 5 1/2 In. 5.00
Bowl, Batter, Apple, 10 1/4 In. 495.00
Bowl, Cereal, Desert Rose 10.00
Bowl, Desert Rose, 8 In. 30.00
Bowl, Echo, 8 1/2 In. 20.00
Bowl, Fruit, Autumn 5.00
Bowl, Fruit, Jamocha 10.00
Bowl, Ivy, 6 In. 15.00
Bowl, Meadow Rose, 6 In. 10.00
Bowl, Salad, Desert Rose ....85.00 to 100.00
Bowl, Salad, Ivy, 10 In. 125.00
Bowl, Serving, Forget-Me-Not 45.00
Bowl, Starburst, Cover, 8 In. 50.00

Bowl,	Starburst, Divided	40.00
Bowl,	Starburst, Oval	35.00
Bowl,	Vegetable, Autumn, 2 Sections, Oblong	45.00
Bowl,	Vegetable, Daisy, 2 Sections, Oval	35.00
Bowl,	Vegetable, Desert Rose, 2 Sections, 10 3/4 In.	30.00
Bowl,	Vegetable, Desert Rose, 8 In.	30.00
Bowl,	Vegetable, Desert Rose, 9 In.	25.00
Bowl,	Vegetable, Desert Rose, Cover, 10 1/4 In.	200.00
Bowl,	Vegetable, Desert Rose, Round, 9 In.	35.00
Bowl,	Vegetable, Poppy, Round	80.00 to 85.00
Bowl,	Vegetable, Twilight Rose, 9 In.	105.00
Bowl,	Vegetable, Wildflower	195.00 to 350.00
Box,	Cafe Royal, Cover, Heart Shape	65.00
Box,	Cigarette, Apple, 4 1/2 x 3 1/2 In.	80.00 to 145.00
Box,	Cigarette, Coronado, Aqua	150.00
Box,	Cigarette, Desert Rose, 4 1/2 x 3 1/2 In.	150.00
Box,	Desert Rose, Heart Shaped	75.00
Bread Plate,	Coronado, Coral	2.00
Bread Plate,	Desert Rose	5.00
Bread Plate,	Starburst	10.00
Butter,	Apple	35.00 to 40.00
Butter,	Bountiful	55.00 to 70.00
Butter,	Coronado, Cover, Aqua	30.00
Butter,	Cover, Starburst	50.00
Butter,	Desert Rose, Cover	75.00
Butter,	Ivy, Cover	85.00
Cake Plate,	Autumn, Cover	20.00
Candleholder,	Apple, Pair	125.00
Candleholder,	Desert Rose	35.00
Canister,	Starburst, 5 In.	220.00
Canister,	Sugar, Duet	100.00
Canister,	Tea, Desert Rose	250.00
Casserole,	Apple, 13 3/4 x 8 3/4 In.	80.00
Casserole,	Apple, Cover	145.00
Casserole,	Apple, Individual	45.00 to 65.00
Casserole,	Duet, Small	45.00
Casserole,	Ivy, Cover	90.00 to 135.00
Casserole,	Madeira, 2 1/2 Qt.	75.00
Casserole,	Starburst, Cover, Large	65.00
Chop Plate,	Apple, 12 In.	40.00 to 85.00
Chop Plate,	Apple, 14 In.	65.00 to 125.00
Chop Plate,	Desert Rose, 12 In.	65.00
Chop Plate,	Desert Rose, 14 In.	85.00 to 110.00
Chop Plate,	Duet, 12 In.	26.00
Chop Plate,	El Patio, Coral, 14 In.	45.00
Chop Plate,	Ivy, 12 In.	60.00 to 95.00
Chop Plate,	Oasis, Blue, 12 In.	55.00
Chop Plate,	Poppy, 12 In.	150.00
Chop Plate,	Wildflower, 12 In.	175.00 to 325.00
Chop Plate,	Wildflower, 14 In.	275.00 to 425.00
Coffeepot,	Apple	75.00 to 175.00
Coffeepot,	Desert Rose	105.00
Coffeepot,	Desert Rose, After Dinner	250.00 to 350.00
Coffeepot,	Ivy	225.00
Coffeepot,	Small Fruit	175.00
Coffeepot,	Starburst	160.00
Compote,	Apple, 8 In.	75.00
Compote,	Desert Rose	60.00
Compote,	Ivy	75.00
Cookie Jar,	Apple	135.00 to 395.00
Cookie Jar,	Desert Rose	185.00 to 225.00
Cookie Jar,	Starburst	295.00 to 325.00
Cookie Jar,	Wheat	100.00

Creamer, Apple 15.00
Creamer, Apple, Individual ....10.00 to 20.00
Creamer, Desert Rose, After Dinner 40.00
Creamer, Ivy 30.00
Creamer, Jamocha 15.00
Creamer, October 15.00
Creamer, Poppy 60.00
Creamer, Starburst 80.00
Cup, Coffee, Desert Rose, 10 Oz. 28.00
Cup & Saucer, Apple ....7.00 to 15.00
Cup & Saucer, Apple, After Dinner ....40.00 to 50.00
Cup & Saucer, Cafe Royal 5.00
Cup & Saucer, Daisy 10.00
Cup & Saucer, Desert Rose ....8.00 to 15.00
Cup & Saucer, Desert Rose, After Dinner 35.00
Cup & Saucer, Desert Rose, Jumbo ....30.00 to 75.00
Cup & Saucer, Ivy 30.00
Cup & Saucer, Metropolitan 15.00
Cup & Saucer, October 10.00
Cup & Saucer, Platinum Band 25.00
Cup & Saucer, Poppy ....25.00 to 35.00
Cup & Saucer, Starburst, After Dinner 15.00
Cup & Saucer, Twilight Rose ....30.00 to 35.00
Cup & Saucer, Whirl-A-Gig 45.00
Cup & Saucer, Wildflower 130.00
Dish, Apple, 8 In. 20.00
Eggcup, Apple ....20.00 to 35.00
Eggcup, Desert Rose ....20.00 to 25.00
Eggcup, Oasis 40.00
Ginger Jar, Desert Rose 245.00
Goblet, Meadow Rose 175.00
Gravy Boat, Apple ....30.00 to 50.00
Gravy Boat, Desert Rose ....35.00 to 50.00
Gravy Boat, Ivy 45.00
Gravy Boat, Oasis, Underplate 20.00
Gravy Boat, Poppy 130.00
Gravy Boat, Small Fruit ....150.00 to 175.00
Gravy Boat, Starburst 40.00
Gravy Boat, Starburst, Ladle 75.00
Gravy Boat, Wildflower 300.00
Grill Plate, Apple, 11 In. 125.00
Grill Plate, Desert Rose, 11 In. 60.00
Hurricane Lamp, Cafe Royale 140.00
Jam Jar, Apple ....75.00 to 85.00
Jam Jar, Desert Rose 78.00
Mixing Bowl, Apple, Small 150.00
Mixing Bowl Set, Apple ....365.00 to 475.00
Mixing Bowl Set, Desert Rose ....365.00 to 395.00
Mug, Apple, 10 Oz. 85.00
Mug, Apple, 12 Oz. 45.00
Mug, Desert Rose, 7 Oz. 15.00
Mug, Desert Rose, 10 Oz. 80.00
Mug, Starburst, 7 Oz., Pair 30.00
Napkin Ring, Desert Rose 40.00
Napkin Ring Set, Cafe Royal, Box 100.00
Napkin Ring Set, Forget-Me-Not, Box, 4 Piece 125.00
Napkin Ring Set, Fresh Fruit, Box 130.00
Pepper Mill, Starburst 185.00
Pitcher, Apple, 1 Qt. 95.00
Pitcher, Apple, 2 Qt. ....100.00 to 125.00
Pitcher, Apple, Ice Lip 115.00
Pitcher, Ivy 175.00

Pitcher, Milk, Apple ....45.00 to 95.00
Pitcher, Milk, Desert Rose 75.00
Pitcher, Milk, Starburst ....80.00 to 82.00
Pitcher, October 135.00
Pitcher, Water, Apple 125.00
Pitcher, Water, Daisy 125.00
Pitcher, Water, Desert Rose 95.00
Pitcher, Water, Ivy 195.00
Pitcher, Water, October 110.00
Plate, Apple, 6 1/4 In. ....5.00 to 10.00
Plate, Apple, 7 3/8 In. ....15.00 to 30.00
Plate, Apple, 8 1/2 In. ....10.00 to 20.00
Plate, Apple, 10 3/4 In. 15.00
Plate, Autumn, 10 In. 8.00
Plate, Cafe Royal, 8 In. 7.00
Plate, Child's, Desert Rose 195.00
Plate, Child's, Starburst 45.00
Plate, Coronado, Burgundy, 9 1/2 In. 5.00
Plate, Coronado, Coral, 9 1/2 In. 5.00
Plate, Daisy, 10 1/2 In. 15.00
Plate, Desert Rose, 6 1/4 In. 4.00
Plate, Desert Rose, 8 In. 8.00
Plate, Desert Rose, 10 3/8 In. ....10.00 to 15.00
Plate, Duet, 10 3/4 In. 9.50
Plate, Forget-Me-Not, 8 In. 12.50
Plate, Forget-Me-Not, 10 3/4 In. 45.00
Plate, Ivy, 6 3/8 In. ....6.00 to 9.00
Plate, Ivy, 8 In. 18.00
Plate, Meadow Rose, 10 1/2 In. 18.00
Plate, October, 8 In. 8.00
Plate, Pink-A-Dilly, 10 1/2 In. 3.50
Plate, Platinum Band, 8 1/4 In. 18.00
Plate, Poppy, 10 1/2 In. 33.00
Plate, Rosette, 10 1/2 In. 12.00
Plate, Starburst, 8 In. 30.00
Plate, Starburst, 10 In. 12.00
Plate, TV, Ivy, 14 In. 125.00
Plate, Twilight Rose, 10 In. 30.00
Plate, Wildflower, 8 1/2 In. 45.00
Plate, Wildflower, 9 1/2 In. 105.00
Plate, Wildflower, 10 1/2 In. ....95.00 to 130.00
Platter, Apple, 12 In. ....35.00 to 55.00
Platter, Apple, 14 In. 45.00
Platter, Apple, 19 In. ....260.00 to 425.00
Platter, Arcadia Green, 16 In. 45.00
Platter, Daisy, 14 In. 45.00
Platter, Daisy, 16 In. 55.00
Platter, Daisy, 19 In. 125.00
Platter, Desert Rose, 12 1/2 In. 30.00
Platter, Desert Rose, 14 In. 35.00
Platter, Desert Rose, 19 In. ....245.00 to 395.00
Platter, Ivy, 19 In. 275.00
Platter, Meadow Rose, 14 1/2 In. ....40.00 to 55.00
Platter, October, 14 In. 45.00
Platter, October, Oval 50.00
Platter, Starburst, 13 1/8 In. 40.00
Platter, Twilight Rose, 12 In. 28.00
Porringer, Desert Rose 175.00
Relish, Apple, 3 Sections ....30.00 to 35.00
Relish, Desert Rose, 2 Sections 65.00
Relish, Desert Rose, 10 3/8 In. 165.00
Relish, El Patio, 3 Sections 10.00

Relish, Small Fruit, 3 Sections 75.00
Relish, Starburst, 2 Sections 20.00
Salt & Pepper, Apple, Jumbo ....70.00 to 185.00
Salt & Pepper, Apple, Tall 45.00
Salt & Pepper, Coronado, Aqua 20.00
Salt & Pepper, Desert Rose, Rose Bud 150.00
Salt & Pepper, Desert Rose, Tall 275.00
Salt & Pepper, Pepper Poppy 95.00
Salt & Pepper, Starburst 15.00
Salt & Pepper, Twilight Rose ....50.00 to 95.00
Salt & Pepper Mill, Apple, 6 In. 195.00
Salt & Pepper Mill, Desert Rose ....195.00 to 300.00
Sherbet, Apple 70.00
Sherbet, Desert Rose 25.00
Sherbet, Starburst 15.00
Snack Plate, October, Square 75.00
Soup, Bouillon, Desert Rose 105.00
Soup, Cream, Coronado, White 50.00
Soup, Dish, Apple 128.00
Soup, Dish, Footed, Cafe Royal 9.00
Soup, Dish, Meadow Rose 10.00
Soup, Ivy 39.00
Soup, Onion, Coronado, Burgundy 20.00
Soup, Onion, Coronado, Maroon 45.00
Sugar, Desert Rose, Cover 18.00
Sugar, October, Cover 20.00
Sugar, Poppy, Cover 80.00
Sugar, Wildflower, Cover 245.00
Sugar & Creamer, Bountiful 65.00
Sugar & Creamer, Desert Rose ....30.00 to 40.00
Sugar & Creamer, Ivy 65.00
Sugar & Creamer, October 8.00
Sugar & Creamer, Tulip 25.00
Syrup, Apple 75.00
Syrup, Desert Rose ....60.00 to 70.00
Syrup, Starburst ....35.00 to 55.00
Tea Canister, Desert Rose 175.00
Tea Set, Coronado, Aqua, 3 Piece 50.00
Teapot, Apple ....75.00 to 165.00
Teapot, Coronado, Coral 32.00
Teapot, Coronado, Ivory 50.00
Teapot, Desert Rose ....80.00 to 165.00
Teapot, Ivy 225.00
Teapot, Starburst 195.00
Teapot, Wildflower ....400.00 to 825.00
Tidbit, Bouquet, 2-Tier 45.00
Tidbit, Desert Rose, 2-Tier 140.00
Tidbit, Desert Rose, 3-Tier 85.00
Tile, Desert Rose 60.00
Tile, Fresh Fruit 80.00
Tray, TV, Apple 110.00
Tray, TV, Desert Rose 95.00
Tumbler, Apple ....25.00 to 30.00
Tumbler, Desert Rose, 6 Oz. 25.00
Tumbler, Ivy, 10 Oz. 35.00
Tumbler, Poppy 85.00
Tumbler, Wildflower, 10 Oz. 250.00
Tureen, Apple, Cover, Handles, Footed, Large ....450.00 to 850.00
Tureen, Apple, Leaf Handles 500.00
Tureen, Desert Rose, Flat Bottom ....495.00 to 550.00
Tureen, Soup, Ivy 995.00
Vase, Bud, Desert Rose, 6 In. ....55.00 to 110.00

FRANCISWARE is the name of a glassware made by Hobbs, Brockunier and Company of Wheeling, West Virginia, in the 1880s. It is a clear or frosted hobnail or swirl pattern glass with amber-stained rim. Some pieces were made by a pressed glass method, others were mold blown.

Bowl, Footed, Frosted, 9 In.	190.00
Pitcher, 7 1/2 In.	159.00
Sugar, Cover, Swirl	80.00

FRANKART, Inc., New York, New York, mass-produced nude *dancing lady* lamps, ashtrays, and other decorative Art Deco items in the 1920s and 1930s. They were made of white lead composition and spray-painted. *Frankart Inc.* and the patent number and year were stamped on the base.

Bookends, Antelope, Leaping	95.00
Bookends, Great Dane	95.00
Bookends, Horse, Rearing	65.00
Bookends, Nude With Frog	395.00 to 475.00
Bookends, Woman's Head, Stylized Chrome, 6 In.	80.00
Lamp, 2 Nudes, Hold Shade, Large	1400.00
Lamp, Silhouette	570.00

FRANKOMA POTTERY was originally known as The Frank Potteries when John F. Frank opened shop in 1933. The factory is now working in Sapulpa, Oklahoma. Early wares were made from a light cream-colored clay from Ada, Oklahoma, but in 1956 the company switched to a red burning clay from Sapulpa. The firm makes dinnerwares, utilitarian and decorative kitchenwares, figurines, flowerpots, and limited edition and commemorative pieces.

Ashtray, Leaf Form, Pair	18.00
Bank, Elephant, Walking	25.00
Bank, Piggy, Desert Rose	350.00
Billiken, Muskogee Court	125.00
Bookends, Charger Horse, Ivory	375.00
Bookends, Cowboy Boot	50.00
Bookends, Dog, Setter	175.00 to 220.00
Bookends, Mountain Girl, Black Glaze	65.00
Bookends, Puma, Stalking, Light Blue	420.00
Bookends, Sea Horse, Leopard Mark	400.00
Bowl, Cactus, Knobby, Red Clay, Round, No. 203	20.00
Bowl, Flat Rectangular, With Scalloped Attached Bowl, Ada Clay, 11 In.	25.00
Candleholder, Prairie Green, Ada Clay, Pair	45.00
Canister, Aztec	100.00
Canteen, Thunderbird, Brown Satin	30.00
Casserole, Cover, Green, Terra Cotta, Handle, Round, 11 1/2 x 4 In.	35.00
Cup, Wagon Wheel, Desert Gold	20.00
Cuspidor, Leaf Design Walls, Brown & Tan, 6 1/4 x 3 1/2 In.	45.00
Cuspidor, Vine Design, Brown, Green, 7 x 5 In.	30.00
Dish, Leaf Shape, Tan, 12 x 2 In.	25.00
Figurine, Cat, Reclining, Black Glossy Glaze, 4 1/2 x 9 In.	25.00
Figurine, Circus Horse	125.00
Figurine, Circus Horse, Prairie Green, Ada Clay	125.00
Figurine, Dreamer Girl, Blue	375.00
Figurine, Fan Dancer, Prairie Green	185.00
Figurine, Flower Girl, Ada Clay	85.00
Figurine, Gardener Boy, Blue Belted Pants	90.00
Figurine, Gardener Girl, Blue	80.00
Figurine, Herd Of Elephants, 1968, 12 Piece	210.00
Figurine, Indian Chief	75.00
Figurine, Ponytail Girl, Desert Gold	115.00
Figurine, Swan, Brown Glaze, 7 In.	18.00
Figurine, Turtle	28.50
Head Vase, Phoebe, Black	175.00

Jar, Indian, Ivory, Large 300.00
Jug, Texas Centennial, Ivory, 1936 .... 175.00
Jug, Texas Centennial, Leopard, 1936 .... 65.00
Juice Set, Guernsey, 5 Piece 65.00
Lazy Susan, Wagon Wheel 60.00
Mask, Peter Pan, Ivory, Ada 175.00
Mug, Baseball Player 12.00
Mug, Donkey, 1976 .... 30.00
Mug, Donkey, 1983 .... 20.00
Mug, Elephant, 1968, White ....65.00 to 75.00
Mug, Elephant, 1972, Prarie Green 20.00
Mug, Elephant, 1973, Desert Gold ....45.00 to 60.00
Mug, Elephant, Flame Glaze, 1969 .... 65.00
Mug, Uncle Sam, Red, White & Blue, 1976 .... 12.00
Napkin Holder, Butterfly, Blue 1500.00
Pitcher, Christmas Car, Red Bud, 1952 .... 78.00
Pitcher, Eagle, Red Clay, Ada Clay, No. 555 .... 20.00
Pitcher, Snail, No. 558 .... 33.00
Pitcher, Thunderbird, No. 551 .... 20.00
Pitcher, Thunderbird, Prairie Green, 2 1/2 In., Miniature 25.00
Pitcher, Wagon Wheel, Green, 7 In. 18.00
Pitcher, Wagon Wheel, Tan, 2 1/2 In., Miniature 25.00
Plate, Aztec, White, 10 In. 20.00
Plate, Bicentennial, 1972 .... 30.00
Plate, Christmas, 1965 ....150.00 to 250.00
Plate, Christmas, 1969 ....28.00 to 35.00
Plate, Christmas, 1971 .... 28.00
Plate, Christmas, 1972 .... 30.00
Plate, Christmas, 1977 .... 10.00
Plate, Conestoga, 1971 .... 150.00
Plate, Lazybones, Blue, 10 In. 20.00
Plate, Teenagers Of The Bible Set 125.00
Plate, Wagon Wheel, Prairie Green, 10 In. 20.00
Salt & Pepper, Bull, Yellow 75.00
Salt & Pepper, Cat, Sitting, Green 60.00
Salt & Pepper, Elephant 65.00
Salt & Pepper, Wagon Wheel 12.00
Sign, Brown Raised Letters, 1 1/2 x 7 In. 165.00
Sugar & Creamer, 1942 .... 125.00
Tile, World's Highest Bridge, Royal Gorge, Colorado, Tan, 6 1/2 In. ... 20.00
Trivet, Rooster 15.00
Trivet, Western Branding Iron Mark 15.00
Vase, Bird Handle, Royal Blue, 1936 .... 125.00
Vase, Bottle, Chinese Red, Limited Edition, No. 827, Signed, 1982 .... 225.00
Vase, Bud, 2 Squared-Off Handles, Tan, 6 1/2 In. 20.00
Vase, Cactus, Desert Gold, Red Clay, 6 3/4 In. 35.00
Vase, Flying Goose, Ada Clay, 6 In. 20.00
Vase, Grecian, Prairie Green, Ada Clay, 9 1/2 In. 65.00
Vase, Rams Head, Ada Clay, No. 38 .... 25.00
Vase, Ring, Beige, 1945-1950, 10 In. 48.00
Wall Pocket, Acorn, No. 190 ....20.00 to 35.00
Wall Pocket, Phoebe Head, Black, Semigloss 175.00
Wall Pocket, Wagon Wheel, Prairie Green 30.00

FRATERNAL objects that are related to the many different fraternal organizations in the United States are listed in this category. The Elks, Masons, Odd Fellows, and others are included. Furniture is listed in the Furniture category. Shaving mugs decorated with fraternal crests are included in the Shaving Mug category.

Eastern Star, Compact, Wadsworth, Enameled Cover 45.00
Eastern Star, Gavel, Gold, Enamel On Silver Sterling Band, 1938 ...... 25.00
Eastern Star, Necklace, Pendant, 10K Gold 30.00
Elks, Chip, Gambling, Tucson 10.00

Elks, Drum, 260 National Champion	450.00
Elks, Plaque, Burnt Wood, Elk's Head In Front Of Clock, Flemish Art	65.00
Elks, Plate, Atlantic City, 1911, Blue Carnival Glass	1600.00
Elks, Uniform, No. 260	35.00
Masonic, Apron, 3 Women & 2 Infants, Symbols, Silk	550.00
Masonic, Apron, Silk, Masonic Symbol Design, 19th Century, 15 x 18 1/4 In.	460.00
Masonic, Ashtray, Brass, Emblem Center, Eye, Hammer, Trowel On Rim, 5 1/2 In.	58.00
Masonic, Beaker, Glass, Wheel Cut Inscription, 5 In.	175.00
Masonic, Bottle Opener & Corkscrew, Figural, Man, Pair	50.00
Masonic, Bottle, Masons 200th Anniversary, Prince Hall, Coca-Cola, 1984, 10 Oz.	8.00
Masonic, Decanter, Cut & Wheel Etched, Europe, 19th Century, 11 In.	170.00
Masonic, Door Knocker, Gravel Metal	150.00
Masonic, Firing Glass, Masonic Symbols, Carl Ahlert, 1865, 4 3/4 In.	345.00
Masonic, Flask, Blown Molded, Olive Amber, Keene, 19th Century, 7 3/8 In.	200.00
Masonic, Loving Cup, Knights Templar, Syracuse, New York, June 1909	50.00
Masonic, Pitcher, Lodge No. 9, 1910, 11 In.	175.00
Masonic, Plate, 1973 Centennial, Gold, White, Blue	17.00
Masonic, Plate, Lodge No. 9, 1902, 8 1/2 In.	75.00
Masonic, Poster, Color, 1872, 20 x 26 In.	125.00
Masonic, Sword, Bayonet, Etched Blade, Brass Scabbard, France	130.00
Masonic, Sword, Belt, Ornately Etched Blade, Orange Commandery, Roy A. Ward	60.00
Masonic, Sword, Ceremonial, Knights In Armor, Horseback	130.00
Masonic, Sword, Chivalric Etched Blade, Clauberg, 19th Century	55.00
Masonic, Sword, Etched Blade Of Knights On Horseback, Horstmann, Pa.	55.00
Masonic, Tankard, Flow Blue, No. 25, F. & A.M., John Maddock & Sons, 12 1/4 In.	295.00
Masonic, Tile, Compass, Ruler & G, 6 x 6 1/2 In.	75.00
Masonic, Trivet, Cutout Symbols, Ladder Form, 3 Feet, Cast Brass, 8 1/2 In.	165.00
Masonic, Trivet, Hanging, Pierced Brass & Iron, 14 In.	160.00
Modern Woodsman Of America, Ax, Aluminum Head, 34 3/4 In.	25.00
Odd Fellows, Ax, Parade, Paint Decorated, Wood, 19th Century, 33 In.	862.00
Odd Fellows, Book, Official History & Manual Of Grand United Order, Brooks, 1902	30.00
Odd Fellows, Cornucopia, Carved Polychrome Wood, 19th Century, 21 In.	4200.00
Odd Fellows, Door, Lodge, Mustard Graining, Black & Green Lettering, 63 x 32 In.	195.00
Odd Fellows, Lectern, Poplar, Red Flame Grain, Blue Center Panel, 34 In.	1045.00
Odd Fellows, Lectern, Star, Interlocking Ovals	1045.00
Odd Fellows, Ring, Man's, 19K Gold, Engraved Heart In Hand, 3 Circles	250.00
Shriner, Champagne, New Orleans, 1910	82.00 to 125.00
Shriner, Dish, Los Angeles, May 1906, Syria, Pittsburgh, With Knife, 6 In.	58.00
Shriner, Lighter, Boise, Idaho, Wilson, Shriner's Hat, 1956	20.00
Shriner, Red Hat With Tassel, Jointed, 4 In.	110.00
Shriner, Ticket, East West Shrine All Star Football Game, Hospital, 1944, 2 1/2 In.	13.00

FRY GLASS was made by the H. C. Fry Glass Company of Rochester, Pennsylvania. The company, founded in 1901, first made cut glass and other types of fine glasswares. In 1922, they patented a heat-resistant glass called *Pearl Oven glass*. For two years, 1926–1927, the company made Fry Foval, an opal ware decorated with colored trim. Reproductions of this glass have been made. Depression glass patterns made by Fry may be listed in the Depression Glass category. Some pieces of cut glass may also be included in the Cut Glass category.

FRY, Bowl, Amber Ivy, Crystal Swirl Connector	85.00
Bowl, Americana, 8 In.	275.00
Bowl, Golden Glow, Ivy	40.00
Candlestick, Dark Amber, No. 25002	35.00
Casserole, Chrome Stand, Ebony Handle, Pearl Oven Ware, 8 In.	45.00
Casserole, Crystal Lime, Oval, No. 1932, 8 In.	45.00
Casserole, Lime Glass, Oval, 1932	50.00
Casserole, Oval	60.00
Clock, Signed	325.00
Pitcher, Green & Pink	45.00
Plate, Canape, Emerald Green	10.00
Plate, Diamond Quilt, Emerald Green, 7 1/2 In.	15.00
Ramekin	30.00

Reamer, Grapefruit	30.00
Teapot, All Pearl, Ground	85.00
Vase, Golden Glow, Straight Sides, 12 In.	150.00 to 195.00
Vase, Reeded, Black Threading, 10 In.	145.00
Vase, Trojan, Signed, 14 In.	800.00
Water Set, Crackle Glass	199.00
Water Set, Pershing, 6 Piece	400.00
FRY FOVAL, Bowl, Fruit, Pearl White, Raised On Delft Blue Foot, 5 1/4 x 9 7/8 In.	515.00
Candlesticks, Pearl White, Jade Green Threading, Trim, 12 In., Pair	1380.00
Cup & Saucer, Gold Overlay, Demitasse	195.00
Loaf Pan, Child's, Opalescent	55.00
Tea Set, Green Spout & Handle, 15 Piece	495.00
Vase, Sterling Overlay, Cone Shape, 10 In.	195.00

FULPER is the mark used by the American Pottery Company of Flemington, New Jersey. The art pottery was made from 1910 to 1929. The firm had been making bottles, jugs, and housewares from 1805. Doll heads were made about 1928. The firm became Stangl Pottery in 1929. Fulper art pottery is admired for its attractive glazes and simple shapes.

Basket, White, Sculptured Rose, Horizontal Ribs, Twisted Rope Handle, 15 x 7 1/4 In.	350.00
Bookends, Ladies In Full Skirts, Holding Flowers, Marked, 7 In.	230.00
Bookends, Liberty Bell, Matte Green	400.00
Bowl, Aladdin Style, Scalloped Edge Handles, Footed, Blue, 6 X12 In.	129.00
Bowl, Artichoke, Leopard's Skin Flambe Glaze, Signed, 5 1/2 x 8 In.	1760.00
Bowl, Blue Flambe Over Green Brown, 2 Loop Handles, 10 x 7 1/4 x 3 1/4 In.	195.00
Bowl, Chinese Blue Flambe, 3 Feet, Incised Mark, 12 In.	300.00
Bowl, Chinese Blue Flambe, Signed, 7 1/2 In.	210.00
Bowl, Cobalt Blue, Cream Flambe, Deep Pink Underglaze, 9 x 2 In.	295.00
Bowl, Effigy, 3 Figures Support Rolled Rim, Mirrored Black, Marked, 7 x 10 1/2 In.	750.00
Bowl, Effigy, 3 Figures, Frothy Butterscotch Flambe Glaze, Signed, 10 3/4 In.	880.00
Bowl, Effigy, Caramel Flambe Glaze Interior, Mustard Matte Exterior, 7 3/8 In.	1210.00
Bowl, Effigy, Dark Matte Blue Over Gray Glaze, 7 1/2 x 10 In.	825.00
Bowl, Flower, Scalloped Edge, Built-In Flower Frog, Gun Metal Flambe, 11 3/4 In.	150.00
Bowl, Handkerchief, Blue, Green Flambe, 11 1/2 x 6 1/2 x 6 In.	190.00
Bowl, Lily Pad Flower Frog, Gunmetal Glaze, 8 In.	55.00
Bowl, Turned Edge, Chinese Blue Flambe Over Mustard Matte, 4 Flaring Feet, 14 In.	550.00
Bowl, With Flower Frog, Blue & Yellow	260.00
Candleholder, Browns, 2 Handles, 3 1/2 x 5 In.	90.00
Candlestick, Cream Brown, Dark Blue Drip Glaze Over Blue Flambe Glaze, 10 1/2 In.	143.00
Candlestick, Mission Matte Brown Glaze, Rectangular Vertical Logo, 2 3/8 In., Pair	190.00
Candlestick, Turquoise, Crystalline, 3 Low Handles, 1 1/2 x 6 In.	150.00
Chamberstick, Light Blue Crystals	175.00
Chamberstick, Open Handle On Tall Heat Shield, Gunmetal & Tan Glaze, 7 In.	220.00
Cider Set, Cat's-Eye Flambe, Vertical Mark, 7 Piece	995.00
Compote, Pedestal, Blue, Caramel, 3 1/4 x 8 In.	115.00
Compote, Snowflake Flambe Crystalline Glaze, 6 1/8 In.	220.00
Ewer, Mauve, Green, 4 1/4 In.	140.00
Flower Frog, Crouched Frog On Lily Pad, Olive & Aqua Glaze, Marked, 2 x 4 1/2 In.	22.00
Flower Frog, Duck, Blue Crystalline	200.00
Flower Frog, Flemish Green	220.00
Flower Frog, Seated Nude Woman, White, Light Green & Yellow, Marked, 5 1/2 In.	230.00
Jar, Cover, Gunmetal Black, Stamp, 7 In.	330.00
Jardiniere, Yellow, Lavender Drip Glaze, 1930, 5 1/2 x 4 1/2 In.	325.00
Jug, Cat's-Eye, Musical, How Dry I Am, 9 x 5 In.	175.00
Jug, Copper Dust Crystalline Glaze, Signed, 12 x 9 In.	1320.00
Jug, Musical, Elephant's Breath Glaze	150.00
Jug, Musical, Stopper, Browns, Handle, 9 1/2 In.	125.00
Jug, Silver Overlay Of Sailing Ships, Billowing Sails, Gulls, Gunmetal Glaze, 9 1/2 In.	55.00
Lamp, Lady Ballerina, Green, White, 1930	185.00
Lamp, Mushroom, Shade, Gunmetal, Olive Green Glaze, Olive Green Ground, 16 In.	11500.00
Lamp, Perfume, Cytharia, Orange, 14 In.	950.00
Lamp, Perfume, Masked Woman, Hoop Skirt, 14 In.	900.00
Lamp, Perfume, Parrot, Marked, 11 In.	410.00

Lamp, Perfume, Parrot, Sitting On Stump, 9 1/2 In. 2200.00
Lamp, Toadstool, Helmet Shaped Shade, Amber Leaded Glass Set In Base, 16 In. 4400.00
Lamp Base, Copper Over Mustard, 2 Handles, 8 In. 295.00
Plate, Deviled Egg, Hen 125.00
Powder Box, Woman, Art Deco, Small 150.00
Tile, Camelia, 4 x 4 In. 20.00
Tile, Spruce, Oak Leaves, 4 x 4 In. 45.00
Urn, Covered In Cat's-Eye Flambe Glaze, Handles, 12 1/2 In. 770.00
Vase, 5 Buttresses, Brown, Green Mottled Glaze, Bulbous, Rolled Rim, Stamp, 5 In. 170.00
Vase, Blue Crystalline Glaze, 2 Handles, Bulbous, Vertical Ink Mark, 6 In. 231.00
Vase, Blue Crystalline, Trumpet, 9 In. 275.00
Vase, Blue Matte Glaze, Black Interior, 1930, 4 1/2 x 5 1/2 In. 195.00
Vase, Blue Snowflake Crystalline Glaze, Ink Stamp, 2 Handles, 6 1/4 In. 770.00
Vase, Blue, Green, Cream Flambe Over Mustard Matte Glaze, 3 7/8 In. 440.00
Vase, Brown Matte Glaze, Bulbous, Vertical Ink Stamp, 4 1/4 In. 230.00
Vase, Brown, Caramel, Green High Glaze, Vertical Ink Mark, 11 In. 385.00
Vase, Brown, Green Flambe, Incised Vertical Mark, Original Label, 5 In. 209.00
Vase, Caramel Flambe Over Mirrored Black Glaze, 13 1/4 In. 935.00
Vase, Caramel High Glaze, Blue, Tan, Green, 16 In. 1540.00
Vase, Caramel, Tan Crystalline Glaze, Vertical Ink Mark, 3 In. 165.00
Vase, Cat's-Eye Flambe Glaze, 2 Handles, 6 In. 330.00
Vase, Cat's-Eye To Mahogany Glaze, Mushroom, 2 Open Windows, Signed, 9 3/4 In. ... 1210.00
Vase, Copper Dust Glaze, Vertical Oval, Ink Stamp, 4 1/8 In. 355.00
Vase, Copperdust Crystalline To Black Flambe, Sloping Sides, Marked, 9 1/2 In. 600.00
Vase, Dark Blue, Green Drips Over Brown, 7 1/4 In. ....150.00 to 160.00
Vase, Double, Royal Blue Velvet, Bow-Tie, Vertical Mark, 6 x 9 In. 95.00
Vase, Elephant's Breath Flambe Glaze, Small Round Opening, 11 1/2 In. 550.00
Vase, Famille Rose Glaze, Bulbous, Fluted Neck, Vertical Mark, 12 In. 231.00
Vase, Famille Rose Over Crystalline Gray Matte Glaze, 8 1/4 In. 410.00
Vase, Flemington Green Flambe Glaze, Pilgrim Flask, Scrolled Handles, 10 x 8 In. 825.00
Vase, Flemington Green Flambe, Signed, 13 1/2 In. 935.00
Vase, Flemington Green, 17 In. 1100.00
Vase, Flemington Green, Mirrored Black, Rectangular Vertical, Ink Stamp, 4 1/2 In. 190.00
Vase, Flemington Green, Over Copper Dust, 2 Handles, 9 1/2 In. 410.00
Vase, Gray-Green & Tan Glaze, Squared Open Handles, Marked, 3 x 6 1/2 In. 55.00
Vase, Green & Blue Over Rose Glaze, Beehive Form, Marked, 3 1/2 In. 65.00
Vase, Hammered Texture, Handles, Mirrored Black Glaze, Signed, 12 In. 1210.00
Vase, Metallic Chinese Blue Flambe Over Green, Bulging Neck, Marked, 15 1/4 In. 950.00
Vase, Metallic Flemington Green Glaze, Signed, 8 1/4 In. 275.00
Vase, Metallic Trailing Blue Snowflake Crystalline Base, 2 Ring Handles, 13 In. 1320.00
Vase, Mirrored Black Glaze, Bulbous, 4 7/8 In. 275.00
Vase, Mirrored Black, Cat's-Eye & Mahogany Flambe Glaze, 11 1/2 In. 1430.00
Vase, Mouse Gray Over Wisteria Matte Flambe, Flared Rim, Paper Label, 11 1/2 In. 700.00
Vase, Mushrooms In Relief At Base, Elephant's Breath Flambe Glaze, Signed, 10 In. 990.00
Vase, Narrow Cylindrical Neck, Mirrored Black Flambe, Bulbous, Marked, 6 1/4 In. 375.00
Vase, Oatmeal Flambe Over Mirrored Black Glaze, 2 Square Chinese Handles, 9 In. 1320.00
Vase, Oriental Style, Brown Drip Over Famille Rose Mirrored Glaze, Signed, 10 1/2 In. .. 645.00
Vase, Ribbed Form, 2 Handles, Mottled Matte Green, Charcoal Glaze, 9 In. 220.00
Vase, Rose Matte, 8 In. 200.00
Vase, Rose, Olive Green Drip Glaze, Olive Green Matte Ground, 2 Handles, 6 x 6 In. ... 330.00
Vase, Rose, Purple, 9 1/2 In. 395.00
Vase, Rouge Gray Flambe Glaze, Tapering Body, Vertical Mark, Label, 12 In. 475.00
Vase, Rust Colored Crystalline Matte Glaze Over Cream Glaze, 11 In. 715.00
Vase, Silver Mirror Black Glaze, Oval Mark, Paper Label, 8 1/2 In. 575.00
Vase, Silvery Cucumber Crystalline Glaze, 2 Flat Handles, Signed, 11 1/2 In. 555.00
Vase, Vase, Frog Skin Glaze, 3 Handles, Bulbous, 7 /14 In. 450.00
Vase, Venetian Blue Crystalline Glaze, 4 Shoulder Handles, Signed, 13 In. 1540.00
Vase, Yellow Glaze, Blue, Brown, Deep Purple, 9 1/2 In. 319.00
Vase, Yellow, Beige, Brown Drip Glaze, 1930, 9 In. 245.00
Wall Pocket, Corner, Raised Fruit Relief, Cream Ground, 8 1/2 x 5 In. 280.00
Wall Pocket, Fruit On Cream, 8 1/2 In. 280.00
Wall Pocket, Geometric Design, Cafe Au Lait 700.00
Wall Pocket, Raised Geometric Design, Light & Dark Blue Glaze, Marked, 7 1/2 In. ... 132.00

FURNITURE of all types is listed in this category. Examples dating from the seventeenth century to the 1950s are included. Prices for furniture vary in different parts of the country. Oak furniture is most expensive in the West; large pieces over eight feet high are sold for the most money in the South, where high ceilings are found in the old homes. Condition is very important when determining prices. These are NOT average prices but rather reports of unique sales. If the description includes the word *style*, the piece resembles the old furniture style but was made at a later time. It is not a period piece. Garden furniture is listed in the Garden Furnishings category. Related items may be found in the Architectural, Brass, and Store categories.

Armchairs are listed under Chair in this category.

Armoire, Belle Epoque, Brass Mounted, Fluted Columns, 95 x 43 x 24 In.	2475.00
Armoire, Biedermeier, Birch, Ebonized, Plinth, Block Feet, 19th Century	4600.00
Armoire, Classical, Mahogany, Bronze Mounted, Half-Columns, Medial Shelf	4400.00
Armoire, Curved Top, Double Burl Walnut Paneled Doors, 77 In.	1300.00
Armoire, Double Door, Golden Oak, Beveled Mirror Door, 3 Drawers, 48 In.	770.00
Armoire, Landscape Of Inlaid Wood, Copper Pulls, Arts & Crafts, L. Wyburd, 78 In.	2970.00
Armoire, Louis XV Style, Oak, Floral Design, 20th Century, 84 In.	2875.00
Armoire, Louis XV, 2 Paneled Cupboard Doors, Undulating Apron, Miniature	2070.00
Armoire, Louis XV, Fruitwood, 2 Doors, Cavetto Cornice, 89 x 56 x 26 In.	3025.00
Armoire, Louis XV, Fruitwood, Shelf & Drawer Interior, 1852, 76 3/4 In.	5445.00
Armoire, Louis XV, Fruitwood, Single Door	1725.00
Armoire, Louis XV, Oak, 1780s, 83 x 56 In.	3735.00
Armoire, Louis XV, Oak, 19th Century, 84 x 51 1/2 In.	3100.00
Armoire, Louis XV, Provincial, Oak	3735.00
Armoire, Mahogany, 2 Doors, Cornice, 106 x 64 x 26 In.	3930.00
Armoire, Mahogany, Arched Cornice Above Gothic Paneled Doors, c.1830	5445.00
Armoire, Mahogany, Double Mirror Door, Carved Crests, 2 Drawers, 98 In.	4535.00
Armoire, Mahogany, Mirrored Door, Carved Crest Of Ribbon & Leaves	440.00
Armoire, Maple, Bird's Eye, Cornice, Beveled Glass Mirror, 86 In.	1020.00
Armoire, Neoclassical, Fruitwood, Marquetry, Bottom Drawer, 83 x 39 x 20 In.	990.00
Armoire, Oak, 2 Doors, 2 Drawers, Crest, Shelf With Hooks ....*Illus*	605.00
Armoire, Painted Floral Design, Pale Green, Ivory, Italy, 78 x 59 x 20 In.	2180.00
Armoire, Pine, 2 Doors, Broken Arched Pediment, Germany, 72 In.	2530.00
Armoire, Renaissance Revival, Walnut Paneled Doors, Victorian, 88 In.	990.00
Armoire, Renaissance Revival, Walnut, Ebonized, 1 Door, Crest, 110 x 57 x 30 In.	3630.00
Armoire, Rococo, Rosewood, 1 Door, Shaped Shell, Scroll, 8 Ft. 2 In.	3630.00
Armoire, Rococo, Rosewood, 2 Doors, Foliate Frieze, 2 Drawers In Base, 1850	3270.00
Armoire, Rococo, Rosewood, Ogee Cornice, Floral Cartouche, 1850-1860, 100 In.	3850.00
Armoire, Rosewood, Molded Cornice, Plinth Base, Victorian, 80 x 45 x 22 In.	1870.00
Armoire, Rosewood, Ogee Cornice, 2 Arch Panel Doors, Plinth Base, 93 In.	2665.00
Armoire, Satinwood, 3 Beveled Mirrored Doors, Putti Medallions, France, 88 In.	1430.00
Armoire, Sunflowers Inlay, Floral Hardware, Signed Galle, c.1895, 90 In.	6325.00
Armoire, Walnut, 2 Doors, Stepped Cornice, Stepped Plinth Feet, 1830	3740.00
Armoire, Walnut, 2 Paneled Doors, Stepped Cornice, 1840, 85 x 58 In.	1150.00
Armoire, Walnut, Beveled Mirror Door, Floral, Garland Design, France, 85 In.	1200.00
Armoire, Walnut, Door, Arched Crest, Beveled Plate, France	1100.00
Armoire, Walnut, Door, Mirror, Crest Top	4400.00
Armoire, Walnut, Double Door, Arched Burl Walnut Panels, 97 x 66 In.	3740.00
Armoire, Walnut, Molded Crest, 2 Paneled Doors, France, 52 x 78 In.	2070.00
Bar, Neoclassical, Mahogany, Marquetry, Paneled Front, Open Rear, 56 1/2 In.	690.00
Bar, Portable, Walnut, Folding Wings, Bar Mart, 1940s, 20 x 57 x 41 In.	445.00
Bed, Arts & Crafts, Oak, Paneled Headboard, Molded Posts, 25 x 74 x 46 In.	110.00
Bed, Belle Epoque, Mahogany, Brass Mounted, 53 x 47 In., Pair	2200.00
Bed, Biedermeier, Mahogany, Rectangular Headboards, Footboards, 37 In., Pair	1100.00
Bed, Birch, Pencil Posts, Dark Brown Grain, 84 In.	770.00
Bed, Campaign, Regency, Mahogany, Slatted Frame, 1810, 76 x 78 In.	2680.00
Bed, Canopy, Brass Fixtures, Reeded Columns, Gargoyle Heads, 1890	3250.00
Bed, Charles X, Boat Shape, Mahogany, Scrolled Head, Block Feet, 42 In.	4598.00
Bed, Classical, Four-Poster, Mahogany, 1840-1850, 92 In.	4675.00
Bed, Curly Maple Posts, Poplar Head & Footboards, Rope, Youth Size	660.00
Bed, Day, Louis XVI, Fluted Supports, 78 In.	4025.00

Bed, Directoire, Walnut, Carved Rosettes & Fluting, 42 x 43 x 80 In., Pair 845.00
Bed, Empire, Mahogany, Ormolu, Cupid Holding Love Birds 2185.00
Bed, Federal, Mahogany, Arched Tester, Ring & Baluster Turned, 70 x 39 In., Pair 1840.00
Bed, Federal, Mahogany, Reeded Foot Posts, 1810, 83 x 56 x 76 In. 2420.00
Bed, Federal, Mahogany, Vasiform Reeded & Swag Carved Foot Posts 1695.00
Bed, Field, Federal, Mahogany, Shaped Arched Headboard, 60 x 54 1/4 In. 920.00
Bed, Field, Federal, Mahogany, Tapering Posts, Arched Headboard, 60 In. 920.00
Bed, Four-Poster, Carved, West Indian Mahogany, Reeded Headboard, c.1830 .... 4125.00
Bed, Four-Poster, Mahogany, Canopy, 19th Century 2660.00
Bed, Four-Poster, Mahogany, Reeded, Acanthus Post, Arched Canopy, 64 x 53 In. 2420.00
Bed, Four-Poster, Mahogany, Waterleaf Carved, 1830s, 92 x 69 In. 2875.00
Bed, Four-Poster, Onion Finials, Paneled Headboard, Rails, Rope, 72 x 50 In. 275.00
Bed, Four-Poster, Poplar, Elongated Ball Finials, Rope, 1842, 57 In. 275.00
Bed, Four-Poster, Poplar, Red, Cannonball Finials, Rope, 53 In. 660.00
Bed, Galle, Burl Walnut Flowers & Leaves, Macassar Ebony, Signed, 62 x 81 In. 4400.00
Bed, Half-Tester, Carved, Walnut, c.1870, 119 x 63 1/2 In. 4850.00
Bed, Half-Tester, Renaissance Revival, Walnut, Burl Walnut Veneer, 1875-1880 .... 2660.00
Bed, Half-Tester, Rococo, Cluster Columns, 1850, 114 x 83 x 65 In. 13200.00
Bed, Hired Man's, New England, Ash, Early 19th Century, 31 x 69 In. 345.00
Bed, Hired Man's, Olive Green Paint, 35 3/4 x 71 In. 260.00
Bed, Jenny Lind, Cherry, Poplar, Old Finish, Single, 34 x 72 x 39 In. 55.00
Bed, Louis XVI, Ivory, Pale Green Headboards, Twin, Pair 1210.00
Bed, Low Post, Mahogany, Turned Posts, Pineapple Finials, 48 In., Pair 2200.00
Bed, Maple, High Post, Carved Bell & Ball, Rope, Double 400.00
Bed, Maple, Ring Turned Posts, Spade Feet, 88 x 77 In. 1725.00
Bed, Murphy, Oak 12750.00
Bed, Nakashima, Slab Headboard, 2 Platform Boxes, 37 x 115 In. 5610.00
Bed, Oak, High Back, Carved, c.1894 .... 875.00
Bed, Opium, Carved Teak, Tongue & Groove, Tenons, c.1900 .... 600.00
Bed, Pencil Post, Hardwood, Pine Headboard, Canopy, 60 x 80 In. 440.00
Bed, Pencil Post, Tester, Late 18th Century, 3/4 Size 1495.00
Bed, Plantation, Four-Poster, Mahogany, Mid-19th Century 4598.00
Bed, Red Lion, Blond, Headboard, 2 Nightstands & Platform, King Size 660.00
Bed, Rococo, Walnut, Portugal 5175.00
Bed, Rope, Bulbous Turned Posts, Ball Finials, Maple & Pine, 3/4 Size 110.00
Bed, Rope, Cherry, Maple, Curly Maple Panels, 50 x 75 x 47 In. 330.00
Bed, Rope, Cherry, Poplar, Scrolled Headboard, 51 In. 330.00
Bed, Rope, Goblet Finials, Scrolled Head & Footboards, 62 3/4 x 70 1/2 In. 770.00
Bed, Rope, Maple, Steel Rails, Refinished, 76 x 47 In. 220.00
Bed, Rope, Poplar, Olive Brown Paint, 47 In. 82.50
Bed, Rope, Reddish Brown Graining, Resembling Curly Maple, 71 3/4-In. Rails 440.00
Bed, Rope, Sheraton, Pine Headboard, Arched Canopy, 3/4 Size 1200.00
Bed, Rosewood, 3 Inset Panels, Foliate Spandrels, Dark Finish, 106 x 65 In. 7865.00
Bed, Second Empire, Mahogany, Parcel Gilt, Carved Putti, Twin, 53 x 48 In., Pair 7475.00
Bed, Sheraton, Four-Poster, Carved Floral Design, 62 In. 475.00
Bed, Sheraton, Pine Headboard, Maple, Curved Canopy Frame, 54 x 77 In. 1650.00
Bed, Sheraton, Tall Post, Rope Rails, Scrolled Headboard, 71 1/2 x 78 1/2 In. 600.00
Bed, Sleigh, Carved, Early 1900s 1100.00
Bed, Sleigh, Mahogany, Scroll Ends, Carved Dolphins, 44 1/2 In. 4235.00
Bed, Southern, Figured Mahogany, Vase Form Posts, 98-In. Posts, 1830 .... 4840.00
Bed, Tall Post, Empire Style, Mahogany, Paneled Head Board, 71 x 85 x 81 In. 550.00
Bed, Tall Post, Maple, Birch, Rails Fitted For Roping, Red Stained, c.1815, 83 In. 1725.00
Bed, Tall Post, Walnut, Canopy Frame, Refinished, Rope, 76 x 82 x 55 In. 275.00
Bed, Tester, Mahogany, 4 Octagonal Posts, Shell Design, Gold Canopy, 1840 .... 7700.00
Bed, Tester, Mahogany, Shaped Leaf Headboard, Baluster Turned, Victorian, 60 In. 6220.00
Bed, Tester, Pine, Painted Panel Scene Back, Floral Spray Cartouche, Austria 2530.00
Bed, Tester, Rosewood, Foliate, Oval Medallions, C. Lee, 1850-1860 .... 9680.00
Bed, Tester, Walnut, Raised On Fluted Leaf Carved Supports, 6 Ft. 2 In. 2875.00
Bed, Thin Edge, Birch, White Metal Legs, G. Nelson, 53 x 79 x 34 In. 3190.00
Bed, Trundle, Green Paint, c.1800, 36 x 70 In. 350.00
Bed, Trundle, Pine, Low Head & Footboards, 1850s 132.00
Bed, Turned Posts, Curly Maple, Trumpet Finials, Rope, 54 x 76 x 57 In. 1100.00
Bed, Turned Posts, Low Shaped Hardboard, Rope, Child's 110.00

Furniture, Armoire, Oak,
2 Doors, 2 Drawers, Crest,
Shelf With Hooks

Furniture, Bench, Nakashima,
Black Walnut, 105 In.

Bed, Turned Posts, Poplar, Acorn Finials, Crest, Refinished, Rope, 74 x 62 In. 165.00
Bed, Victorian, Walnut, Molded Frame, Continental, Pair 715.00
Bed Steps, Oak, Carved Date, Victorian, 1887 .... 145.00
Bed Steps, Wooden, Place For Chamber Pot 130.00
Bedroom Set, Aesthetic Revival, Walnut, Brown Marble, 88 x 59 x 83 In. 4400.00
Bedroom Set, Aesthetic Revival, Walnut, Carved Birds, Bird's Nest, 86 In. 9900.00
Bedroom Set, Art Deco, Walnut Veneer, Mahogany, Rounded, 5 Piece 825.00
Bedroom Set, Classical Revival, Mahogany, 7 Piece 3300.00
Bedroom Set, Cottage, Maple, Stenciled, Mirror, Worn Finish, 2 Piece 470.00
Bedroom Set, Cottage, Oak, Double Bed, Dresser, Beveled Mirror, Wash Stand 1045.00
Bedroom Set, Faux Bamboo, 6 Piece 8500.00
Bedroom Set, Heywood-Wakefield, Double Bed, Black Ink Mark, 4 Piece 1325.00
Bedroom Set, Mahogany, Flame Veneer, Carved, c.1930, 3 Piece 385.00
Bedroom Set, Victorian, Italy, 9 Pieces 5900.00
Bedroom Set, Walnut, High Back Bed, Dresser, Double Door Armoire, 1870 .... 3585.00
Bench, American Restauration, J & W Meeks, Mahogany, Upholstered, 1840s 2075.00
Bench, Arts & Crafts, L. & J.G. Stickley, Quartersawn Oak, Label, 72 In. 3300.00
Bench, Baby Guard, Rockers, Yellow Striping, Floral On Crest, 45 In. 715.00
Bench, Baroque Style, Walnut, Gros Point & Petit Point Upholstered, 34 In. 632.00
Bench, Black Wrought Iron Base, Branded Mark, 61 x 15 x 19 In. 330.00
Bench, Bucket, 2 Coats Yellow Paint, Lower Shelf 2900.00
Bench, Bucket, Birch & Pine, 5 Shelves, Cutout Ends, Red Stain, 52 1/4 x 64 In. 1435.00
Bench, Bucket, Poplar, Green Paint, Cutout Ends, Ohio, 38 x 9 3/8 x 36 In. 440.00
Bench, Bucket, Square Nail Construction 495.00
Bench, Conservatory, Bronze & Iron, Openwork Panels, c.1890, 49 1/4 x 18 In. 1650.00
Bench, Deacon's, Yellow Paint, 8 Ft. 2 In. 795.00
Bench, Double Chair Back, Outscrolling Down Curving Arms, Rush Seat, 39 In. 525.00
Bench, Fireside, Pine, Curved Paneled Back, Natural, England, 73 x 73 In. 825.00
Bench, Fireside, Sheridan, Mahogany, Tall Back, Upholstered, Inlaid Stripes 900.00
Bench, Fruitwood, Scrolling Ends, Rectangular Form, Tapering Curved Legs, 35 In. 105.00
Bench, Fruitwood, Shell Carved Apron, Floral Upholstery, 60 1/2 In. 720.00
Bench, G. Stickley, 4 Splayed Legs, Rectangular Top, 48 x 15 x 16 In. 4400.00
Bench, George II, Walnut, Scroll, 36 In. 770.00
Bench, Georgian Style, Gilt, Cane Seat, 39 In. 345.00
Bench, Georgian, Mahogany, Carved, Needlepoint 430.00
Bench, Gothic, Oak, Foliage Back Frame, Shaped Arms, c.1850, 72 1/2 In. 3630.00
Bench, Grain Painted, Horizontal Slat Back, Central Floral Medallions 165.00
Bench, Italian Baroque, Walnut, Scrolled Apron, Trestle Base, 19 x 58 In. 1150.00
Bench, Lift Seat, Arts & Crafts, Horizontal Leather Back Slat, Rose Tacks, 50 In. 105.00
Bench, Lift Seat, Mortised Construction, 30 x 34 In. 495.00
Bench, Light Wood, Black Enameled Legs, G. Nelson, 14 x 48 x 48 In. 605.00
Bench, Limbert, No. 95, Flip-Top, Leather Back Panel & Seat, 47 3/4 In. 1980.00

Bench, Louis XV, Fruitwood, Shell Carved Apron, Upholstered, 18 x 60 x 19 In. 725.00
Bench, Lyre Shape, Carved Frame, Paw Feet, Maroon Velvet, 51 1/2 In. 700.00
Bench, Mahogany, Foliate Carved Legs, Ball & Claw Feet, Velvet 275.00
Bench, Mammy's, Black Repaint, 2 Baby Guards, 79 In. .330.00 to 795.00
Bench, Mammy's, Windsor, Grain Paint, Stenciled, c.1840, 28 x 47 x 14 In. 460.00
Bench, Mammy, Black Paint, Gold Stenciled, Gate, 5 Ft. 1100.00
Bench, Mill River Methodist Church, 1810s, 7 Ft. 1250.00
Bench, Nakashima, Black Walnut, 105 In. . . . .*Illus* 7700.00
Bench, Narrow Plank Seat, Spindle Back, Worn Refinishing, Arms, 108 In. 355.00
Bench, Neoclassical, Fruitwood, Gilt Swan, 19th Century, 33 In. 3150.00
Bench, Oak, Plank Backrest, Early 18th Century, 9 Ft. 11 In., Pair 3740.00
Bench, Oak, Spindle Back, Late 19th Century 475.00
Bench, Painted Design, Pennsylvania, 1860, Arms, Child's 375.00
Bench, Piano, Cane Seat, Stop Fluting 39.00
Bench, Pine, Cutout Ends, 18 1/2 In. 470.00
Bench, Pine, Dark Finish, 66 In. 220.00
Bench, Pine, Gray Paint, Bootjack Ends, Mortised, Weathered Top, 68 In. 135.00
Bench, Pine, Spindle Back, Shaped Plank Seat, 19th Century, 75 In. 575.00
Bench, Pine, Yellow Over Red, Square Corner Posts, Scrolled Arms, 72 In. 600.00
Bench, Polychrome Stylized Fruit & Flowers, J. Swift, Chair Maker, 77 3/4 In. 1540.00
Bench, Prayer, Needlepoint & Bead Cover 1495.00
Bench, Prayer, Pine, 19th Century 27.50
Bench, Pulls Out For Storage Or Day Bed, Sweden, c.1830 . . . . 1770.00
Bench, Regency, Curule, C-Scroll Frame, Ivory Damask, 17 1/2 x 20 x 20 In. 665.50
Bench, Renaissance Revival, Oak, Splayed Turned Legs, Stretcher, 85 In. 495.00
Bench, School, Pine, Dark Finish, Shoe Feet, Low Seat, 72 x 21 In. 190.00
Bench, Settle, Arrow Back, Blue Repaint, 78 In. 220.00
Bench, Sleeping, Colonial, Caned, Scalloped Apron, 42 In. 1330.00
Bench, Stuart, Oak, Rectangular Seat, Raised On Turned Supports, 17 In. 4312.00
Bench, Wagon, Rush Seat, 19th Century, 36 In. 1265.00
Bench, Walnut, Cutout Feet, 17 3/4 In. 368.50
Bench, Water, Lower Cupboard, 1850s 1000.00
Bench, Water, Pine, Original Brown Paint, Curved Sides, 1870 . . . . 950.00
Bench, Water, Pine, Yellow Wash, 3 Shelves, Cutout Foot, 34 x 42 In. 440.00
Bench, Water, Poplar, Red Color, 2 Shelves, 18 x 37 x 29 In. 715.00
Bench, William & Mary, Oak, Plank Seat, Trestle Base, 18 1/2 x 84 In. 315.00
Bench, Window, Classical, Carved Mahogany, c.1830 . . . . 545.00
Bench, Wood Arm Rests, 4 Loose Cushions, Chrome, Vinyl, Upholstered, 44 In. 90.00
Bench, Wooden Carved, Central Heart Form Flanked With Scrolls, Turkey, 86 In. 575.00
Bench, Yellow Paint, Brown, Black Strips, Floral, Angel Wings, 78 In. 9900.00
Bin, Storage, Lift Lid, Paneled Top & Sides, Tin Lined, Incised Carving 357.00
Book Press, Oak, Spiral Turned, Drawer, England, Late-18th Century, 71 In. 920.00
Book Trough, Stickley Bros., Cutout Handles, Shelves Mortised Through Sides 715.00
Bookcase, Arts & Crafts, Oak, 3 Glazed Doors, 1910, 57 x 72 x 14 In. 1760.00
Bookcase, Barrister, Oak, Per Section 165.00
Bookcase, Bibliotheque, Louis XV, Tulipwood, Cornice, Plinth Base, 72 x 51 In. 9200.00
Bookcase, Brooks, Cutout Sides, Original Glass Panes, 2 Shelves, 53 x 18 In. 1430.00
Bookcase, Charles X, Ebonized, Glazed Doors, Plinth Base, 8 Ft. 3 In. 6325.00
Bookcase, Cherry, 4 Paneled Doors, Dovetailed Cornice, 91 In. 3850.00
Bookcase, Chippendale, Cherry, Glass Doors, Locks, c.1875 . . . . 2000.00
Bookcase, Classical, Flame Mahogany, 2 Glazed Doors Over 3 Wood Doors, 1825, 86 In. 2425.00
Bookcase, Classical, Mahogany, 2 Glass Crossbanded Doors, 1890, 57 x 48 In. 2250.00
Bookcase, Classical, Mahogany, Cornice, 2 Glazed Doors, 19th Century, 92 In. 7260.00
Bookcase, Double Glazed Doors, Lower Drawers, Walnut, 1850s, 94 3/4 In. 2055.00
Bookcase, Eastlake, Walnut, 61 1/2 x 30 In. 715.00
Bookcase, Empire, Mahogany, Gilt Metal, 3 Sections, 69 In. 2175.00
Bookcase, Federal, Mahogany, 2 Doors, Compartments, Drawers, c.1820, 54 In. 2070.00
Bookcase, G. Stickley, Door, 3 Leaded Panes, Over Vertical Panes, 58 In. 9350.00
Bookcase, G. Stickley, No. 715, Gallery Top, 16 Panes, 56 x 36 In. . . . . .4675.00 to 7150.00
Bookcase, G. Stickley, No. 717, D Door, 8 Panes Per Door, V Pulls, 55 In. 4125.00
Bookcase, George III, Mahogany Inlay, Ogee Bracket Feet, 11 In. 6900.00
Bookcase, George III, Mahogany, 4 Long Drawers, Bracket Feet, 84 In. 3450.00
Bookcase, George III, Mahogany, Peach Moire Interior, Bracket Feet, 89 In. 2299.00

Furniture, Bookcase, Limbert, No. 602,
Oak, 2 Doors, 3 Shelves, 52 x 34 In.

Furniture, Bookcase, Mahogany, 2 Glass
Doors, Columns, Claw Feet

Bookcase, Georgian, Mahogany, 2 Glazed Doors, 69 x 48 x 20 In. 1980.00
Bookcase, Georgian, Mahogany, 2 Glazed Doors, Cornice, 19th Century, 90 In. 2780.00
Bookcase, Georgian, Mahogany, Breakfront, 4 Glazed Doors, 85 In. 4235.00
Bookcase, Golden Oak, Quartersawn, 2 Glass Doors, 14 x 46 x 57 In. 340.00
Bookcase, Gothic Revival, Mahogany, 2 Glazed Panels, 1840-1850, 102 In. 8140.00
Bookcase, Hepplewhite, Birch, 4 Dovetailed Drawers, Bracket Feet, 81 In. 4400.00
Bookcase, Heywood-Wakefield, Corner, Champagne Finish, 32 x 28 In. 330.00
Bookcase, L. & J.G. Stickley, 2 Doors, 12 Panes, 1905, 55 In. 4025.00
Bookcase, Lawyer's, Oak, 5 Glass Door Shelf Sections, c.1890, 74 In. 970.00
Bookcase, Limbert, No. 358, Double Door, 4 Glass Panes, 3 Shelves, 57 In. 4675.00
Bookcase, Limbert, No. 602, Oak, 2 Doors, 3 Shelves, 52 x 34 In. ....*Illus* 1870.00
Bookcase, Mahogany, 2 Glass Doors, Columns, Claw Feet ....*Illus* 1210.00
Bookcase, Mahogany, 2 Top Glazed Doors, Molded Cornice, 1845, 90 x 50 In. 2660.00
Bookcase, Mahogany, 3 Glazed Doors, Carved Columns, Claw Feet, 55 x 72 In. 1100.00
Bookcase, Mahogany, Bowfront, 2 Shelves Behind Glass Doors, Paw Feet, 62 In. 400.00
Bookcase, Mahogany, Glass Front Doors, Adjustable Shelves, 58 x 49 x 15 In. 520.00
Bookcase, Mahogany, Tuned Side Supports, Lower Drawer, 5 Shelves, 48 In. 1495.00
Bookcase, Neoclassical, Black Faux Marble Top, 2 Drawers, Bun Feet, 51 In. 1980.00
Bookcase, Oak, Carved, Front Columns, Leather Fringe, 61 In. 4025.00
Bookcase, Oak, Step Back, 6 Doors With Locks, 6 Drawers, 120 In. 3500.00
Bookcase, Oak, Victorian, 75 x 37 In. 345.00
Bookcase, Queen Anne, Walnut, Seaweed Marquetry, 93 In. 5750.00
Bookcase, Regency, Mahogany, Glazed Doors, Plinth, 90 In. 6900.00
Bookcase, Revolving, 2 Tiers, Oak, Square, 32 x 12 In. 440.00
Bookcase, Rococo, Mahogany, Bonnet Top, Leaf Carved Crest, 2-Drawer Base 4235.00
Bookcase, Rococo, Rosewood, Wavy Mold, 4 Shelves, 48 In. 970.00
Bookcase, Satinwood, Brass Feet On Casters, Turned Legs, 15 In. 8050.00
Bookcase, Sheraton, Mahogany, Turned Legs, 1850 .... 2800.00
Bookcase, Victorian, 2 Glass Doors, Base Drawer, 3 Shelves ....*Illus* 1100.00
Bookcase, Victorian, Standing, Fluted Pilasters 300.00
Bookcase, Walnut, 3 Bottom Drawers, 4 Doors, Portrait Medallions, 54 x 96 In. 1450.00
Bookcase, Walnut, 4 Doors, Burl Walnut Panels, Adjustable Shelves, 56 x 70 In. 1435.00
Bookrack, G. Stickley, Expanding, Tabletop, 7 x 12 In. 825.00
Bookrack, G. Stickley, No. 74, Oak, Keyed Tenons, Shelf, Label, c.1910, 31 x 30 In. 1725.00
Bookshelf, Victorian, Mahogany, 3 Shelves, Baluster Supports, 45 x 41 x 19 In. 2530.00
Bookshelf, Walnut, 3 Shelves, Cornice, 11 x 41 x 42 In. 155.00
Bookstand, Arts & Crafts, 4 Shelves, Pyrography, Slag Glass, Ladder Shape 395.00
Bookstand, G. Stickley, Revolving, 4 Sections, Base Covered In Leather, 12 3/4 In. 2200.00
Bookstand, George II, Mahogany, Revolving 8250.00
Bookstand, Roycroft, Mahogany, Little Journeys, 2 Shelves, Trestle Sides, 26 In. 525.00
Bookstand, Stressed Pine, Drawer, 2 Shelves, Portable, 19th Century, 47 1/2 In. 920.00
Bookstand, Victorian, Walnut, Easel Back, Rectangular Form, England 125.00

Box, Blanket, Lift Top, Snipe Hinges, Square Head Nails, Drawer, Salesman's Sample ... 950.00
Breakfront, English Regency, 2 Base Drawers Each Side, 6 Doors, 1820 .... 7475.00
Breakfront-Bookcase, George III, Mahogany, Cornice, 17 1/2 In. 4600.00
Breakfront-Bookcase, Gothic Glazed Doors, Shelves, c.1840, 89 x 64 3/4 In. 7260.00
Breakfront-Bookcase, Mahogany, 4 Glazed Doors, 4 Panel Doors, 1850s, 97 In. 4535.00
Breakfront-Bookcase, Mahogany, 4 Upper Doors, Lower Drawer, 4 Cupboards 2000.00
Breakfront-Bookcase, Walnut, Marquetry, Gilt Metal Mounted, 1880s, 87 In. 6900.00
Buffet, French Provincial, Burl Walnut, Serpentine Front, Glass Top, 78 x 20 In. 2200.00
Buffet, French Provincial, Walnut, Cabriole Legs, Ball Feet, 37 In. 2300.00
Buffet, Heywood-Wakefield, Tambour, Champagne Finish, 32 x 50 x 19 In. 220.00
Buffet, Jacobean, Oak, Geometric Design, Recessed Central Panel, 45 In. 485.00
Buffet, Louis XV Style, Carved Oak 1265.00
Buffet, Louis XV, Pine, Wire Door, Provincial 1610.00
Buffet, Oak, Walnut Grip Handles, Open Shelf, 1930 .... 1325.00
Buffet, Provincial, Oak, 2 Drawers Over 2 Arched Doors, 36 In. 4140.00
Buffet, Robsjohn-Gibbings, Walnut, Medium Brown, 3 Drawers, 30 x 60 In. 660.00
Buffet, Rococo Style, Rosewood, Victorian 3200.00
Bureau, Art Deco, Lucite, 5 Drawers, Chrome Pulls, 29 x 40 In. 1320.00
Bureau, Chippendale, Ash, Bowfront, 4 Drawers, 1780, 34 In. 2990.00
Bureau, Classical, Cherry, Mahogany, Carved Columns, 1830, 54 In. 1430.00
Bureau, Classical, Mahogany, Cherry, 1825, 51 In. 635.00
Bureau, Dressing, Classical, Mahogany, 2 Short & 3 Long Drawers, 19th Century 485.00
Bureau, Dressing, Classical, Mahogany, Carved, 1825, 60 In. 800.00
Bureau, Dressing, Classical, Mahogany, Leaf Carved, N.Y., 1810, 15 1/2 In. 345.00
Bureau, Dressing, Classical, Mahogany, Scroll Arm, Supports, 2 Drawers, Paw Feet 970.00
Bureau, Dressing, Jos. Meeks, American Classical, Mahogany, 1830, 69 x 39 In. 4850.00
Bureau, Dressing, Mahogany, Scrolled Arm Supports, Tiered Drawers, c.1830 .... 900.00
Bureau, Dressing, Parquetry, Bronze Mounted, Marble Top, Kingwood 2060.00
Bureau, Empire, Mahogany, Green Tooled Leather Inset Top, 4 Drawers, 33 In. 2900.00
Bureau, Federal, Cherry, Cock-Beaded Drawer, Mass, 1810, 34 1/2 In. 1725.00
Bureau, George I, Burl Walnut, Slant Front, 41 In. 9775.00
Bureau, George III, Oak, Slant Front, 3 Drawers, Bracket Feet, 10 In. 2100.00
Bureau, Jamestown Sterling House, Cherry, 20th Century 85.00
Bureau, Louis XV Style, 2 Drawers, Scalloped Apron, Cabriole Legs, 37 In. 1100.00
Bureau, Louis XV, Marquetry Gilt, Rosewood, Scalloped Apron, 49 x 29 In. 725.00
Bureau, Louis XV, Ormolu, Banded Top, Cabriole Legs, 19th Century, 30 In. 1210.00
Bureau, Louis XVI Style, Parquetry, Cylinder, Francois Linke, 40 x 33 In. 9680.00
Bureau, Louis XVI, Mahogany, Black Tooled Leather Top, Fluted Legs, 31 In. 3960.00
Bureau, Louis XVI, Mahogany, Tilt Metal Mounted, Kneehole, 38 x 51 x 26 In. 1936.00
Bureau, Louis XVI, Walnut, Green Leather Writing Surface, 2 Drawers 1045.00

Furniture, Bookcase, Victorian,
2 Glass Doors, Base Drawer,
3 Shelves

Furniture, Bureau-Bookcase,
Peter Hunt, Floral, Signed
Ovince, 1943, 80 In.

Furniture, Cabinet, China, Oak,
Curved Glass, Mirrored
Backsplash, 79 In.

Bureau, Mahogany Veneer & Mahogany, 3 Short Over 3 Long Drawers 275.00
Bureau, Neoclassical, Gilt Metal, Green Tooled Leather Top 825.00
Bureau, Oak Veneer & Oak, Attached Mirror, 2 Short Over 32 Long Drawers 148.00
Bureau, Plat, Napoleon III, Gilt Bronze Mounted Ebonized, 1870s, 29 x 55 In. 460.00
Bureau, William & Mary, Oak, Slant Front, 2 Drawers, 1700, 39 In. 7475.00
Bureau, William & Mary, Oak, Slant Front, Molded Top, 1700, 41 In. 3740.00
Bureau-Bookcase, Bombe, 2 Arched Glass Doors, 3 Door Base, Paw Feet, 84 In. 3740.00
Bureau-Bookcase, Oak, Shelves, Slant Front Lid, Document Drawer, 1820s, 77 In. 2530.00
Bureau-Bookcase, Peter Hunt, Floral, Signed Ovince, 1943, 80 In. ....*Illus* 3520.00
Bureau-Bookcase, Walnut, Glazed Cupboard Doors, Shelves Over 3 Drawers, 90 In. 6900.00
Butler's Press, Sheraton, Mahogany 3850.00
Cabinet, 2 Cupboard Doors, 2 Long Over 3 Short Drawers, 17 1/8 In. 1840.00
Cabinet, Aesthetic Movement, Ebonized, Open Side Shelves, Mirrors, 48 x 73 In. 3500.00
Cabinet, Baroque Style, Walnut, Marquetry & Paint Design, Dutch, 33 In. 460.00
Cabinet, Baroque, Walnut, 6 Small Drawers, Bun Feet, 63 In. 5750.00
Cabinet, Beveled Glazed Doors, Mirrored Back, Satinwood Inlay, 70 x 42 In. 1725.00
Cabinet, Biedermeier, Fruitwood, Block Feet, 19th Century, 68 In. 6900.00
Cabinet, Black Lacquer, 5 Drawers, Gold Design, Chinese Export, 1820s, 17 1/2 In. 1800.00
Cabinet, Center, Gothic, Mahogany, Arched Doors, 1830, 43 x 48 x 31 In. 3390.00
Cabinet, China, Drexel, Cavetto Molded Top, 3 Doors, Doors Either Side, 72 1/2 In. 230.00
Cabinet, China, Elizabethan Revival, Oak, Leaf Carved Cornice, Apron, 72 In. 1320.00
Cabinet, China, G. Stickley, 2 Doors, 4 Adjustable Shelves, Brass Pulls, 55 1/4 In. 6600.00
Cabinet, China, G. Stickley, Dark Finish, 64 x 42 x 15 In. 6325.00
Cabinet, China, Mahogany, Curved Glass Sides, Ball & Claw Feet 770.00
Cabinet, China, No. 727, L. & J.G. Stickley, Door, 9 Glass Panes, 55 In. 5225.00
Cabinet, China, Oak, Curved Glass, Mirrored Backsplash, 79 In. ....*Illus* 1595.00
Cabinet, China, Oak, Serpentine Front, Carved Lions' Heads 4180.00
Cabinet, China, Renaissance Revival, Oak, Carved Paw Feet, Curved Glass 1600.00
Cabinet, China, Renaissance Revival, Oak, Curved Glass, 19th Century, 97 In., 2 Piece . 5445.00
Cabinet, China, Robsjohn-Gibbings, Walnut, 3 Glass Doors, 69 In. 1430.00
Cabinet, China, Serpentine Front, Attached Mirror, Carved Knees, 20th Century 715.00
Cabinet, China, Victorian, Oak, Breakfront Type, Carved, Bowed Glass Sides, 80 In. ... 3450.00
Cabinet, China, Walnut Veneer, Cupboard Door, Interior 3 Shelves 305.00
Cabinet, Chippendale, Mahogany, Hanging, 2 Doors, Cornice, 19th Century, 26 In. 545.00
Cabinet, Copper Panels, Painted Old Testament, Mirrored Interior, 53 1/2 In. 13800.00
Cabinet, Corner, Birch, Drop Brass Handles, 1870 .... 2185.00
Cabinet, Corner, Birch, Paneled Door, Inner Shelves, Russia, 1860s, 80 In. 5460.00
Cabinet, Corner, Cherry, Arched Glass Door, c.1830 .... 3500.00
Cabinet, Corner, Cherry, Glass, Mortise & Pegged, Turnip Feet, 1800s, 2 Piece 4895.00
Cabinet, Corner, Federal Style, Mahogany, 3 Shelves, Drawer, 2 Doors, 30 x 73 In. 247.00
Cabinet, Corner, George III, Oak, Glazed Door, Inner Shelves, Base Doors, 88 In. 1265.00
Cabinet, Corner, Gold Floral Design, Birds, Insects & Duck, Continental, 13 In. 275.00
Cabinet, Corner, Gothic Style Cornice, Mirrored Side Shelves, 1870s, 90 In. 4600.00
Cabinet, Corner, Reeded Walnut, 87 x 44 In. 5800.00
Cabinet, Corner, Rosewood, Wooden Trellis Above Drawers, Turned Legs, 73 In. 2550.00
Cabinet, Corner, Satinwood, Mullion & Glazed Door, Inlaid Lower Door, 80 In. 5750.00
Cabinet, Corner, Walnut, Cavetto Tops, 2 Mullioned Doors, Lower Doors, 75 1/4 In. 345.00
Cabinet, Curio, Corner, Gold Interior, Mirrored Back, 3 Glass Shelves, 64 In. 550.00
Cabinet, Curio, Oak, Curved Glass Side, Flat Glass Door, 60 x 37 1/2 In. 495.00
Cabinet, Curio, Paneled Front, Gold Enamel Design On Glass, Mirrored Back, 45 In. ... 195.00
Cabinet, Curio, Serpentine Door, Molded Gilt Fleur-De-Lis, Mirror Back, 48 In. 1045.00
Cabinet, Curio, Vernis Martin, Bowfront, Mirror Back, Floral Garnitures, 72 In. 1650.00
Cabinet, Curio, Walnut, 3 Sections, Woman's Bust On Crest, Mirrored, 53 In. 1380.00
Cabinet, De Velde, Pine, White Painted, Grip Handle, 1902, 33 x 15 In. 2185.00
Cabinet, Display, Frosted Domed Top, Chromium Plated Bronze, 1930, 56 1/2 In. 3450.00
Cabinet, Display, Walnut, Glass Door, Shelves, Drawer, Louis Philippe, 76 In. 1495.00
Cabinet, E. Wormley, Mahogany, Steel Rods, 61 x 18 x 37 In. 1045.00
Cabinet, Eames, Birch Drawers, Painted Panel, 33 x 47 In. ....*Illus* 3190.00
Cabinet, Ebonized Walnut, Ivory Inlay, Italy, 19th Century, 69 In. 8050.00
Cabinet, Ebonized Wood, Ivory Marquetry, Italy, 1880s 6900.00
Cabinet, Ebonized, Ivory Inlay, Italy, 19th Century, 78 In. ....*Illus* 9200.00
Cabinet, Empire, Tortoiseshell, Gilt Bronze Putti, Scrolled, 44 In. 2300.00
Cabinet, Empire, Walnut, 2 Drawers, Columnar Supports, 47 In. 2587.00

Furniture, Chest, Eames, Iron, 1950
35 x 24 x 16 In.

Furniture, Cabinet, Eames,
Birch Drawers, 33 x 47 In.

Cabinet, Fall Front, Cupboard Doors, 3 Drawers, Grotesque Carving, 70 1/2 In.	6900.00
Cabinet, File, Mahogany, Paneled Sides, 4 Drawers, 51 1/2 x 19 1/4 In.	220.00
Cabinet, Folio, Aesthetic Movement, Ebonized & Parcel Gilt, 1880s, 61 In.	1380.00
Cabinet, G. Nelson, Oak Veneer, 40 x 19 x 37 In.	415.00
Cabinet, G. Nelson, Rosewood, Thin Edge, 4 Drawers, White Pull, 31 In.	2090.00
Cabinet, G. Nelson, Walnut, Open Sections Over 4 Closed Sections, 43 x 81 In.	1650.00
Cabinet, G. Rohde, Sliding Glass Doors, 2 Base Drawers, 50 x 33 x 16 In.	1540.00
Cabinet, G. Stickley, Arched Top, 1912, 64 1/2 In.	5750.00
Cabinet, George II, Walnut, Parcel Gilt Display, 89 1/4 In.	5750.00
Cabinet, George III, Mahogany, 2 Mullion Glazed Doors, 2 Base Doors, 96 x 72 In.	8050.00
Cabinet, George III, Mahogany, Gallery Top, Drawer, Door	517.00
Cabinet, Georgian Style, Vitrine, Gilt, Floral, Cabriole Legs, 21 x 50 In.	800.00
Cabinet, Gothic, Pine, Stylized Foliage, 77 3/4 x 22 1/4 x 13 In.	1725.00
Cabinet, Hand Painted, 2 Hinged Doors, 4 Stacking Drawers	495.00
Cabinet, Herman Miller, Oak, 2 Drawers Over 2 Doors, 40 x 40 x 18 In.	1045.00
Cabinet, Hoosier Type, Enamel Top	495.00
Cabinet, Huang Huali, Red Lacquer, 2 Panel Doors, 39 In.	3105.00
Cabinet, Jacobean Style, Figural Panels, Painted & Parcel Gilt, 39 x 62 In.	6900.00
Cabinet, Jacobean, Oak, Carved, 19th Century, 39 In.	290.00
Cabinet, Jewelry, Papier-Mache, Lift Top, Fitted Interior, Interior Drawers, 12 In.	518.00
Cabinet, Kitchen, White Porcelain Shop, Gray Repaint, Child's, 23 x 16 x 39 In.	200.00
Cabinet, Knoly, Oak Veneer, 5 Drawers, Marble Top, Metal Legs, 26 x 37 x 18 In.	440.00
Cabinet, Lacquer Panel Inset Doors, Bronze Mounted, 83 In.	5175.00
Cabinet, Liquor, Elam Williams, Table Top, c.1810, 1 In.	5800.00
Cabinet, Liquor, Walnut, Carved, Decanters & Cordials, England, 19th Century	1610.00
Cabinet, Louis XIV, Walnut, Molded Cornice, 2 Paneled Doors, 71 1/2 In.	1035.00
Cabinet, Mahogany, 2 Sliding Doors, 1950, 27 x 48 x 17 In.	137.00
Cabinet, Mahogany, Humidor, Hinged Lid, Interior Trays For Cigars, 19 1/2 In.	4115.00
Cabinet, Majorelle, Divided Gallery, Center Door, Open Middle Shelf, 58 1/2 In.	8800.00
Cabinet, Marble Top, Floral Central Panel, Parquetry Doors, 43 In.	2200.00
Cabinet, Marble Top, Marquetry, England, 44 x 33 1/2 In.	1320.00
Cabinet, Marble Top, Serpentine Front, Yellow Paint, Floral Design, 32 In.	490.00
Cabinet, Marriage, Pine, Painted Peasant Scenes, 2 Doors, Continental, 75 In.	8280.00
Cabinet, Music, Cherry, Marquetry Urns Of Flowers & Instruments On Door, 40 In.	330.00
Cabinet, Music, Eastlake, Mirrored Backsplash, Lower Shelf, Carved Instruments	1150.00
Cabinet, Music, Gilt, Landscape Design, 2 Drawers, Cabriole Legs, 46 In.	635.00
Cabinet, Music, Gold Paint, Mirrored Top, Garden Scenes On Doors	360.00
Cabinet, Napoleon III, Marble Top, Gilt Bronze Birds In Nest, c.1860, 52 In.	18400.00
Cabinet, Napoleon III, Rosewood, Marquetry, Bronze Mounted, 1870s, 41 1/2 In.	2415.00
Cabinet, Napoleon III, Walnut, Beveled Mirror, 72 x 44 In.	1610.00
Cabinet, Neoclassical Style, Polychrome Painted, Italy, 65 x 35 1/4 In.	8050.00
Cabinet, Neoclassical, Mahogany, 2 Drawers, Turned Brass Feet, 36 In.	3450.00
Cabinet, Peter Hunt, Women Picking Grapes, 2 Doors, 61 In. ....*Illus*	3300.00
Cabinet, Pine, Stenciled Panel, 3 Recessed Compartments, 3 Drawers, 1870s, 62 In.	2185.00

Furniture, Cabinet, Ebonized, Ivory
Inlay, Italy, 19th Century, 78 In.

Furniture, Cabinet, Peter Hunt,
Women Picking Grapes, 2 Doors, 61 In.

Cabinet, Porcelain Columns, 1 Drawer Over Cupboard, Porcelain Mounted, 45 In. 6325.00
Cabinet, Queen Anne, Japanned, Shaped Dome Cornice, 2 Doors, 73 x 43 x 18 In. 1150.00
Cabinet, Revolving, Octagonal, Square Base 850.00
Cabinet, Rococo, Rosewood, Bowfront, White Marble Top, 35 1/4 In. 935.00
Cabinet, Rococo, Walnut, Arched Top, 3 Serpentine Drawers, Bun Feet, 72 In. 8625.00
Cabinet, Rococo, Walnut, Bowfront, Cabriole Legs, 36 In. 920.00
Cabinet, Rococo, Walnut, Floral, Foliate Spray, Giltwood Border 23000.00
Cabinet, Rosewood, Black Lacquer, Double Hinged Lid, Brass Inlay, 10 1/2 In. 825.00
Cabinet, Satinwood, 2 Doors Pastoral Scene, Saber Legs, 32 1/4 x 28 x 18 In. 485.00
Cabinet, Side, Biedermeier, Walnut, Cornice, Glazed Doors, 69 In. 2300.00
Cabinet, Side, Louis XVI, Mahogany, Paneled Cupboard Doors, Plinth Base 6325.00
Cabinet, Side, Renaissance Style, 2 Drawers Above 2 Doors, 44 1/2 In. 1320.00
Cabinet, Spice, Madder Red Graining, 30 Graduated Drawers, 20 x 48 In. 4025.00
Cabinet, Spice, Mahogany, 8 Various Sized Drawers, England, 20 In. 1155.00
Cabinet, Spice, Oak, Poplar, Porcelain Knobs, Crest, Hanging, 10 x 4 x 25 In. 170.00
Cabinet, Spice, Walnut, 10 Drawers, Brass Pulls, 1880, 13 x 10 x 16 In. 1600.00
Cabinet, Stand, Paul McCobb, Mahogany, Brass Tag, 76 x 59 x 20 In. 970.00
Cabinet, Tulipwood, On Stand, Domed Hood, Drawer, Sliding Surface, 61 In. 9200.00
Cabinet, Upper Cupboard Door, 2 Side Doors, 3 Drawers, Ivory Panels, Italy, 78 In. 9200.00
Cabinet, Victorian, Hinged Door, Ormolu Mounts, France, 60 x 30 In. 800.00
Cabinet, Victorian, Parlor, Beveled Glass Mirrors, Carved, c.1900, 62 x 27 1/2 In. 377.00
Cabinet, Wall, E. Wormley, Walnut, 3 Drawers, Metal Tag, 48 x 15 x 26 In. 660.00
Cabinet, Wall, Pine, Leaf Carved Doors, Continental, 40 x 25 x 13 In. 2300.00
Cabinet, Walnut, Carved Panels, Beveled Mirrored Panels, England, 78 1/2 In. 450.00
Cabinet, Wheat Finish, Pier, 3 Drawers, 1953, 33 x 18 x 16 1/2 In. 825.00
Candlestand, American Aesthetic, Ebonized, Gilt, Glass Over Needlepoint, 1870 ...... 425.00
Candlestand, Cherry & Maple, Ring Turned Column, 1-Board Figured Top, 26 In. 137.00
Candlestand, Cherry, New Hampshire, c.1810, 28 1/2 x 14 3/4 In. 920.00
Candlestand, Cherry, Tiger Maple, Dish Top, Vase & Ring Post, c.1820, 26 1/2 In. 545.00
Candlestand, Cherry, Tripod, Snake Feet, 1-Board Top, 14 5/8 x 15 x 25 In. 525.00
Candlestand, Chippendale, Birch, Dished Top, Snake Feet, 25 3/4 In. 1155.00
Candlestand, Chippendale, Birch, Tripod, Snake Feet, 1-Board Top, 14 In. 440.00
Candlestand, Chippendale, Maple, Tripod, 1-Board Top, 17 x 25 In. 225.00
Candlestand, Chippendale, Maple, Tripod, Snake Feet, 18 x 19 In. 660.00
Candlestand, Chippendale, Tilt Top, Mahogany, Birdcage, 1760, 27 In. Diam. 3450.00
Candlestand, Chippendale, Tilt Top, Mahogany, Tripod, Cabriole Legs, 73 In. 5175.00
Candlestand, Chippendale, Walnut, Tilt Top, Tripartite Birdcage, 28 x 23 In. 1035.00
Candlestand, Curly Maple, Tripod, Snake Feet, Cut Corners, 16 x 20 x 27 In. 880.00
Candlestand, Federal, Cherry, Circular Top, Snake Feet, Cabriole Legs, 24 In. 8050.00
Candlestand, Federal, Cherry, Round Dish Top, Pedestal, 18th Century, 26 In. 2300.00
Candlestand, Federal, Mahogany, Birch, Oblong Top, Tripod Base, 28 In. 425.00

Candlestand, Federal, Mahogany, New York, 1815, 30 In. 440.00
Candlestand, Federal, Maple, Birch, Curved Legs, New England, 1800, 28 1/2 In. 1495.00
Candlestand, Federal, Maple, Tilt Top, Spade Feet, New Hampshire, 28 In. 1150.00
Candlestand, Federal, New England, 19th Century, 26 1/2 x 15 x 14 1/2 In. 920.00
Candlestand, Federal, Octagonal, Cherry, c.1790, 27 x 15 x 15 1/2 In. 3000.00
Candlestand, Federal, Tilt Top, 3 Out-Swept Legs, 19th Century 330.00
Candlestand, Federal, Tilt Top, Mahogany, Inlaid & Veneered, Octagonal, 26 In. 2450.00
Candlestand, Federal, Tilt Top, Mahogany, Square Top, Tripod, c.1800, 28 1/2 In. 1265.00
Candlestand, George II, Mahogany, Vase-Form Standard, Tripod Base, 26 In. 300.00
Candlestand, George III, Mahogany, c.1890s, 29 In. 172.50
Candlestand, Georgian, Mahogany, Sampson Porcelain Around Top, 3 Legs, 12 In. 235.00
Candlestand, Georgian, Tilt Top, Bird Cage Support, Ball, Claw Feet, 25 In. 138.00
Candlestand, Georgian, Tilt Top, Oak, Down Scrolled Tripod, Dark Finish, 27 In. 275.00
Candlestand, Hepplewhite, Cherry, Turned Column, 28 3/4 In. 600.00
Candlestand, Hepplewhite, Pine & Maple, Tripod Base, Spider Legs, 29 1/4 In. 275.00
Candlestand, Hepplewhite, Tilt Top, Birch, Tripod Base, 28 1/2 In. 440.00
Candlestand, Hepplewhite, Tilt Top, Cherry, Tripod Base, Spider Legs, 28 3/4 In. 440.00
Candlestand, Horseshoe Form Tilt Top, Russia, 19th Century, 30 1/2 x 22 In. 765.00
Candlestand, Mahogany, Adjustable, England, 1790, Miniature 270.00
Candlestand, Mahogany, Georgian, Tilt Top 805.00
Candlestand, Mahogany, Tilt Top, Down Scrolling Trifid Base, 29 1/2 In. 545.00
Candlestand, Mahogany, Tilt Top, Inlaid Panel, Oval, 18th Century, 26 x 16 In. 1035.00
Candlestand, Mahogany, Tilt Top, Oval, Tripod Legs, England, 18th Century, 22 In. 920.00
Candlestand, Maple & Birch, Dish Top, Vase & Ring Turned Shaft, c.1800, 28 In. 2500.00
Candlestand, Maple, Adjustable, 2-Light, Tripartite Base, 19th Century, 44 In. 805.00
Candlestand, Maple, Tilt Top, 1760-1780, 15 1/2 In. 432.00
Candlestand, Oblong Tilt Top, Mahogany & Cherry, Cut Corners, c.1810 . . . . 137.00
Candlestand, Octagonal Tilt Top, Mahogany, Vase-Form Standard, 28 1/2 In. 800.00
Candlestand, Oval Tilt Top, Mahogany, Tripod Legs, England, 18th Century, 22 In. 920.00
Candlestand, Painted, Polychrome Floral, Dart Border, c.1790, 30 x 14 x 15 In. 1725.00
Candlestand, Queen Anne Style, Mahogany, Cabriole Snake Feet, 26 x 19 In. 575.00
Candlestand, Queen Anne Style, Square Tilt Top, Line Inlay, Snake Feet, 27 In. 140.00
Candlestand, Queen Anne, Black Paint, Octagonal Top, Cabriole Leg, 27 x 15 In. 1600.00
Candlestand, Queen Anne, Mahogany, Dish Top, Snake Feet On Pads, c.1770 . . . . 1595.00
Candlestand, Queen Anne, Tilt Top, Mahogany, Satinwood Inlay, c.1790, 28 In. 4025.00
Candlestand, Rosewood, Tilt Top, Adjustable, c.1760, 12 x 8 1/2 In. 600.00
Candlestand, Round Top, Vase & Ring Turned Post, Tripod Base, Painted, 27 In. 800.00
Candlestand, Spiral Carved Pedestal, Scroll Feet, Carved Design, 28 In. 290.00
Candlestand, Tiger Maple, Octagonal Top, Slipper Feet, New England, Small 935.00
Candlestand, Tiger Maple, Tilt Top, Baluster Support, Tripod Feet, 29 1/2 In. 2060.00
Candlestand, Tilt Top, Urn Turned, 21 3/4 In. 550.00
Candlestand, Walnut, Tiger Maple & Cherry, c.1820, 26 3/4 In. 290.00
Candlestand, Walnut, Tilt Top, Turned Column, 26 3/4 In. 330.00
Candlestand, Windsor, Black Paint 745.00
Candlestand, Wrought Iron, Brass, Drip Pans, 18th Century, 57 1/4 In. 8050.00
Canterbury, Georgian Style, Mahogany, Square Tapered Legs, 18 In. 790.00
Canterbury, Mahogany, 4 Downcurving Transverses, Drawer, Brass Casters, 1810 . . . . . 4600.00
Canterbury, Mahogany, Arched Transverses, Center Hand Hold, 1810, 19 1/2 In. 1495.00
Canterbury, Mahogany, Drawer, Carved & Pierced, Casters, 1840, 21 x 26 In. 985.00
Canterbury, Mahogany, Drawer, Turned Legs, Brass Casters, 24 In. 1150.00
Canterbury, Maple, Asymmetrical Serpentine Dividers, Drawer, 20 In. 1380.00
Canterbury, Rosewood, Drawer, Bulbous Legs, 20 1/4 x 20 x 15in. 1150.00
Canterbury, Rosewood, Drawer, Lyre Ends, 1854, 17 1/2 x 15 1/2 In. 1495.00
Canterbury, Rosewood, Pierced Carved Lyres On All Sides, Drawer, 21 x 23 In. 1150.00
Canterbury, Sheraton, Mahogany, Drawer, On Casters, 19 1/2 In. 245.00
Canterbury, Walnut, Burl Walnut, Carved, 1870, 28 x 17 x 14 In. 600.00
Case, Amberg Letter File, Walnut, 3 Drawers, 1870 . . . . 475.00
Case, Chrome & Glass, Swing-Out Glazed Doors, Contemporary, 89 x 31 In. 460.00
Case, Decanter, Regency, Mahogany, Reeded Edge, Paw Feet, 14 1/2 In. 10350.00
Case, Map, Pine, 8 Dovetailed Drawers, Officers Of England, 45 x 46 1/2 In. 3410.00
Case, Map, Quartersawn Oak, 8 Drawers, 2 Doors, 1920s 750.00
Cellarette, Arts & Crafts, Milk Glass Shelf, 1 Drawer, 4 Compartment Cabinet, 40 In. . . 1540.00
Cellarette, Edwardian, Satinwood, Cross Banded Top, 32 In. 1450.00

Cellarette, George II, Mahogany, Inlaid, Octagonal, 19th Century, 17 In. 1100.00
Cellarette, George III, Brass Banded, Octagonal Top, 1840s 2785.00
Cellarette, Mahogany, Arched Lid, Fitted Interior, Stand, England, 26 In. 1035.00
Cellarette, Mahogany, Lion's Head Handles, Ball Feet, England, 15 x 17 In. 1600.00
Cellarette, Mahogany, Sarcophagus Form, Winged Eagle Front Feet 3750.00
Cellarette, Mahogany, String Inlay, Brass Bail Handles, Drawer, c.1790, 29 In. 1695.00
Cellarette, Pumpkin Over Red, Divided Interior, 2 Faux Drawers, c.1850 . . . . 1800.00
Cellarette, Sheraton, Mahogany, Turned Legs, Brass Casters, 24 x 21 x 26 In. 6050.00
Cellarette, Stand, George III, Mahogany, Shell Inlaid Lid, 25 x 15 x 11 In. 605.00
Chair, Aalto, Birch Sides, Upholstered Seat, 25 In. 1210.00
Chair, Aalto, Birch, Dovetailed Arms, 30 x 21 x 26 In., Pair 445.00
Chair, Aalto, Lounge, Bent Laminated Wood, Lacquered Seat, 1931 . . . . 5520.00
Chair, Adams Style, Satinwood, Floral Top Rail, Lyre Form Splat, Upholstered Seat 230.00
Chair, Adirondack, Lawn, Wooden, Arms, Child's, 27 In. 75.00
Chair, Adirondack, Lawn, Wooden, Round Back, Arms, Child's, 20 1/2 In. 65.00
Chair, Aluminum, Leather Chanel Upholstered, Swivel, Arms, 35 x 27 In., Pair 1100.00
Chair, American Restauration, Mahogany, Arms, c.1840 . . . . 485.00
Chair, Arched Crest, Carved Arm Supports, Knees, Hand Rests, Upholstered 470.00
Chair, Arrow Back, Bamboo Stretchers, c.1835, Child's 525.00
Chair, Arrow Back, Maple, Rabbit Ear, Plank Seat, Pair 290.00
Chair, Art Deco, Rosewood, Leather, Arms 800.00
Chair, Arts & Crafts, Bookshelf Sides, Brass Fittings, Dutch, 41 x 30 In. 550.00
Chair, Arts & Crafts, Oak, 4-Slat Back, Slat Under Shelf, 38 x 24 In. 120.00
Chair, Arts & Crafts, Upholstered Seat, Turned Legs, 1880 . . . . 865.00
Chair, Augustus Eliaers, Carved Mahogany, Upholstered, Arms 5500.00
Chair, Ballroom, Bentwood, Gilt, 1930s 28.00
Chair, Banister Back, Black Finish, Rush Seat, 1700, 44 In. 660.00
Chair, Banister Back, Black Paint, Mushroom Finials, Rush Seat, 1740s, Pair 1955.00
Chair, Banister Back, New England, Splint Seat, Turned Posts & Finials, 42 1/2 In. 440.00
Chair, Banister Back, Split Baluster Uprights, Rush Seat, Arms, 1740s 2015.00
Chair, Baroque Revival, Walnut, 1850s, 42 1/2 In. 175.00
Chair, Baroque Style, Beechwood, Arms, Needlepoint Upholstery, 1890s, 46 1/2 In. 1495.00
Chair, Baroque Style, Carved Ram's Heads, Upholstered, Armrests, Pair 1380.00
Chair, Baroque Style, Walnut, Carved Putto & Fruit Back, Carved Legs, 37 3/4 In. 490.00
Chair, Baroque, Gilt, Arched Back, Leather, Pair 3737.00
Chair, Baroque, Mahogany, Needlepoint Back & Seat, Cabriole Legs, Pair 3450.00
Chair, Baroque, Walnut, Acanthus Finials, Block Feet, Arms, Italy 3165.00
Chair, Baroque, Walnut, Continental, 18th Century, 47 In. 2185.00
Chair, Baroque, Walnut, Padded Seat, Scrolled Legs 2300.00
Chair, Barrel, Swivel Base, Arms 100.00
Chair, Beechwood, Foliage, Voluted Supports, Upholstered Arms 4600.00
Chair, Beechwood, Leather Upholstered Back & Top Rail, Horseshoe Shaped Seat 2875.00
Chair, Beechwood, Upholstered Backrest, Foliate Top Rail, Padded Armrests 2100.00
Chair, Behrens, White Paint, Tapestry Seat, 1903 . . . . 2760.00
Chair, Belter, Rococo, Rosewood, 1850-1860, Pair 2450.00
Chair, Belter, Rococo, Rosewood, Laminated Side, 1850-1860 . . . . 1510.00
Chair, Bentwood, Backrest, Caned Seats, Austria, Child's, 25 In. 460.00
Chair, Bergere, Beechwood, Upholstered Backrest, Flower Heads, Pair 9200.00
Chair, Bergere, Empire, Mahogany, Cut Velvet, 37 In. 1955.00
Chair, Bergere, French Style, Fruitwood, Carved Frames, Cabriole Legs, Pair 635.00
Chair, Bergere, Giltwood, Bowfront Seat, Tapered Legs 690.00
Chair, Bergere, Louis XV Style, Flower Heads, Cabriole Legs, Pair 7475.00
Chair, Bergere, Louis XV Style, Upholstered Backrest, Cabriole Legs, Pair 2590.00
Chair, Bergere, Louis XV, Arched Back, Cabochon Crest, Bowed Seat 3220.00
Chair, Bergere, Louis XV, Beechwood, Floral Crest, Celadon Bowed Seat 2550.00
Chair, Bergere, Louis XVI, Beechwood, Arched, Tapered Legs 1150.00
Chair, Bergere, Louis XVI, Gilt, Floral, Beaded, Acanthus Design Frame, 39 In. 970.00
Chair, Bergere, Louis XVI, Giltwood, Needlepoint Seat, Caned Back, Child's 1955.00
Chair, Bergere, Louis XVI, Giltwood, Tub Back, Bowfront Seat, Cushion, Pair 6655.00
Chair, Bergere, Louis XVI, Walnut, Leather, Late 18th Century, Pair 1955.00
Chair, Bergere, Neoclassical, Mahogany, Palmette Arm Rail, 19th Century 1650.00
Chair, Bergere, Regency, Walnut, Carved 1150.00
Chair, Bergere, Rosewood, Slung Back Upholstery, Cabriole Legs, 1840 . . . . 660.00

Chair, Bertoia, Diamond, Wool Upholstered, Tag, 1960, 31 x 33 In. 165.00
Chair, Bertoia, Lounge, Diamond, Naugahyde Covers, Pair 330.00
Chair, Bertoia, White Finish, Red Pads, 31 x 21 x 22 In., Pair 137.00
Chair, Bertoia, White Wire, Brown Seat, 30 x 21 x 21 In., Pair 165.00
Chair, Biedermeier, Fruitwood, Provincial, Arms 375.00
Chair, Biedermeier, Mahogany, Scrolled Armrest, Saber Legs, Arms, Pair 5460.00
Chair, Biedermeier, Pierced Backsplat, Upholstered Seat, 19th Century 250.00
Chair, Billiard, Arts & Crafts 715.00
Chair, Birch, Slat Back, Mother-Of-Pearl Inlay, Cane Seat, Triangular, 1903 . . . . 4375.00
Chair, Birthing, Folding, 19th Century 2500.00
Chair, Bootjack Splats, Painted Designs, Plank Bottom 150.00
Chair, Bowditch & Son, Grape Carved, Victorian, Pair 400.00
Chair, Breuer, Tubular Steel, Broad Canvas Back & Seat, 1926, 33 In., Pair 4025.00
Chair, Bugatti, Hammered Metal, Circular Back, Brass Inlay 2300.00
Chair, Burl Walnut Veneer, Walnut, Hip Rests, Carved Crest, Velvet, 37 In., Pair 110.00
Chair, Camp, Mahogany, Buttoned Leather, Padded Buttoned Leather Arms 4900.00
Chair, Campeachy, Mahogany, Scrolled Crest, Arms, Green Backing 3932.50
Chair, Caned Back, Needlework Upholstered Seat, Open Arms, Pair 345.00
Chair, Cartouche Back, Trapezoidal Seat, Painted Vines, Austria, Child's 230.00
Chair, Carved Floral Design, Open Arms, Spain, Pair 260.00
Chair, Carved Gold Gilt Surface, Shell Carving On Stretcher, 50 1/4 In., Pair 3950.00
Chair, Carved, Scrolled Feet, Upholstered, Open Arms 143.00
Chair, Cast Iron, Scroll & Drapery Back Splat, Pierced Seat, Arms, 35 1/2 In. 315.00
Chair, Center Tablet, Pierced Splat With Urn, Trapezoidal Seat, 36 1/2 In., Pair 1850.00
Chair, Charles II, Walnut Caned Seat, 17th Century 5175.00
Chair, Charles II, Walnut Caned, Richard Price, 17th Century 8050.00
Chair, Charles X, Rosewood & Satinwood, Inlaid, c.1820 . . . . 1450.00
Chair, Cherner, Bent & Laminated Cherry, Upholstered, 1956, 31 In. 600.00
Chair, Cherry, Turned, Carved, Pierced Splat, Upholstered Seat, 41 In. 805.00
Chair, Chinese Chippendale, Ebonized, Bamboo, Slip Seat, Open Arms, Pair 690.00
Chair, Chinese Chippendale, Mahogany, Carved, Pair 1265.00
Chair, Chippendale, 3 Ornate Splats, Crest Rail, Marlboro Legs, 16 1/2 In. 1150.00
Chair, Chippendale, Carved Sabacu, Scalloped Crest Rail, Slip Seat, 38 In., Pair 2550.00
Chair, Chippendale, Cherry, Rush Seat, Ring Legs, 1760-1780, 39 1/2 In. 690.00
Chair, Chippendale, Cherry, Serpentine Crests, Pierced Strap Work Splats, Pair 2100.00
Chair, Chippendale, Ladder Back, Mahogany, 1780, 37 1/4 In. 980.00
Chair, Chippendale, Mahogany, Bowed Crest Rail, Trapezoidal Slip Seat, 40 In. 4025.00
Chair, Chippendale, Mahogany, Brocade, 20th Century, 39 1/4 In. 330.00
Chair, Chippendale, Mahogany, Cabriole Legs, Ball & Claw Feet, 38 In., Pair 6325.00
Chair, Chippendale, Mahogany, Carved Splat, Serpentine Front, 20th Century, 37 In. 315.00
Chair, Chippendale, Mahogany, Gothic Foliate, Cabriole Legs, Scroll Feet, 39 In. 2070.00
Chair, Chippendale, Mahogany, Molded Corners, Slip Seat, 38 1/2 In. 550.00
Chair, Chippendale, Mahogany, Oxbow Crest, Claw, Ball Feet, 20th Century 245.00
Chair, Chippendale, Mahogany, Ribbonback, Slip Seat, 1770-1790, 38 1/2 In. 260.00
Chair, Chippendale, Mahogany, Serpentine Crest, Rush Slip Seat, 37 x 16 In. 490.00
Chair, Chippendale, Mahogany, Slip Seat, Cabriole Legs, 36 In. 440.00
Chair, Chippendale, Mahogany, Wm. Kennedy, c.1760 . . . . 1895.00
Chair, Chippendale, Maple, Mass, 1760-1790, 17 In., Pair 2530.00
Chair, Chippendale, Maple, Pinned Stretchers, Woven Splint Seats, 37 In., Pair 770.00
Chair, Chippendale, Maple, Refinished, Pierced Splat, Rush Seat 190.00
Chair, Chippendale, Oak & Butternut, c.1760 . . . . 395.00
Chair, Chippendale, Pierced Backsplat, Acanthus Carved Ears, c.1780, 38 In. 850.00
Chair, Chippendale, Red Brown Paint, Yellow Line, Pair 2500.00
Chair, Chippendale, Ribbonback, Rush Seat, 37 3/4 In. 120.00
Chair, Chippendale, Stained Maple, Baluster Splat, Slip Seat, Arms, 40 In. 460.00
Chair, Chippendale, Walnut, Serpentine Crest, Ball, Claw Feet, 1760, 39 In. 9200.00
Chair, Classical, Black Paint, Gilt Stenciled, Cane Seat, 1810-1820 . . . . 1200.00
Chair, Classical, Curly Maple, Cane Seats, 1830, Pair 300.00
Chair, Classical, Faux Bois, Gilt Stencil, 1830, Pair 970.00
Chair, Classical, Faux Bois, Rush Seat, Early 19th Century, Pair 330.00
Chair, Classical, Figured Maple, Ring-Turned Crest Rail, Rush Seat, 31 In., Pair 1035.00
Chair, Classical, Green Paint, 1840, 38 In. 935.00
Chair, Classical, Mahogany, Brass Mounted, Slip Seats, Phila., Pair 3950.00

Chair, Classical, Mahogany, Crest Rail, Saber Legs, 33 In., Pair 970.00
Chair, Classical, Mahogany, Curved Rails, Down Curved Legs 1485.00
Chair, Classical, Mahogany, Philadelphia, 1820, Pair 545.00
Chair, Classical, Maple, Bird's Eye Maple Crest, Cane Seat, 1840, 33 1/2 In. 3875.00
Chair, Club, Chippendale, Mahogany, Lattice Back, Guilloche Apron, White, 31 In. 635.00
Chair, Club, Oak, Upholstered, c.1930, 25 x 29 In. 8050.00
Chair, Club, Victorian, Leather, Tufted Back, Apron, 36 In. 600.00
Chair, Continental, Mahogany, Cane Seat, 19th Century 200.00
Chair, Corey, Bowed Crest, Trapezoidal Cane Seat, Tapered Legs, 33 1/2 In., Pair 58.00
Chair, Corner, Ash, Woven Leather Seat, c.1860, 33 In. 1900.00
Chair, Corner, Black Paint, Vase & Ring-Turned Stiles, 18th Century, 29 In 546.00
Chair, Corner, Chippendale, Cherry, Upholstered Seat, c.1780, 31 x 18 In. 1840.00
Chair, Corner, George II, Mahogany, Concave Rail & Crest, Pierced Splats 920.00
Chair, Corner, Georgian, Mahogany, Rush Seat 1915.00
Chair, Corner, Leather Seat, Center Leg, 18th Century 5500.00
Chair, Corner, Mahogany, Carved Floral & Leaf, Arms Ending In Eagles, 34 1/2 In. 750.00
Chair, Corner, Mahogany, Chippendale, Strapwork Splats, Concave Arms, c.1760 . . . . . . 1725.00
Chair, Corner, Mahogany, Floral Carving, Arms Supports, Carved Splats, 32 In. 560.00
Chair, Corner, Mahogany, Needlework Seat, 20th Century 190.00
Chair, Corner, Mahogany, Pierced Strapwork Splats, Slip Seat, Carved Rails 1725.00
Chair, Corner, Mahogany, Upholstered, Stenciled Leather, Brass, Arms, Pair 6325.00
Chair, Corner, Queen Anne, Maple & Ash, Rush Seat, c.1770, 30 In. 230.00
Chair, Corner, Queen Anne, Maple, Horseshoe Crest Rail, Rush Slip Seat, 1740 . . . . 6325.00
Chair, Corner, Yoke Back, Lion Mask Grips, Cherub On 3 Stiles, Slip Seat, 1880s 450.00
Chair, Cowhorn, Bow Shape, D-Shape Seat, Horn Legs, Arms, 35 1/4 In. 5175.00
Chair, Dantesque, Renaissance Revival, Bracket Feet, Italy, Pair 3450.00
Chair, De Velde, Beech, Woven Cane Back & Seat, 1904 . . . . 3220.00
Chair, Deck, Adjustable Form, Blond Wood, Late 19th Century, Child's 605.00
Chair, Deco Style, Scrolled Arms, Button Tufted Upholstery, Pair 290.00
Chair, Desk, Cast Iron, Centripetal Spring, 19th Century 725.00
Chair, Desk, L. & J.G. Stickley, Mahogany, Spindled Back, Rush Seat, 41 1/2 In. 2200.00
Chair, Desk, Victorian, Oak, Carved Back Splat, Casters 225.00
Chair, E. Dieckmann, Beech, Red & Cream Paint, 1928, Child's, 25 3/8 In. 1495.00
Chair, Eames, Aluminum, Stem Base, Arms, 33 x 22 x 22 In. 825.00
Chair, Eames, Bentwood, Blond, LCW, Marked, 26 1/2 x 22 x 23 In. 600.00
Chair, Eames, Birch, Dowel Leg, Gray Shell, Black Metal Struts, 31 In. 995.00
Chair, Eames, Channeled Vinyl, 33 x 22 1/2 In. 250.00
Chair, Eames, DCW, Black Aniline Dyed Molded Plywood, 28 In., Pair 750.00
Chair, Eames, Fiberglass, Gray, Cross Base, Zenith Label, 30 x 24 x 23 In. 250.00
Chair, Eames, Low Wire, Gun Metal Low Strut Base, 19 x 17 x 26 In. 330.00
Chair, Eames, Office, Wool, 36 x 21 x 20 1/2 In. 275.00
Chair, Eames, Plywood Seat, Red Aniline, 22 x 23 x 27 In. 1200.00
Chair, Eames, Shell, Fiberglass, Aluminum Rod Base, 31 x 24 In. 440.00
Chair, Eames, Walnut, Chrome Tube Base, 30 x 19 x 21 In. 137.00
Chair, Eastlake Style, Walnut, Swivel, Leather Back & Seat, Casters, Arms 1000.00
Chair, Eastlake, Burl Walnut Panels, Trumpet Turned Legs, Arms, Tapestry 400.00
Chair, Easy, Leaf & Rosette Design, Down-Scrolling Arms, Cane Back & Seat 605.00
Chair, Easy, Louis XV Style, Black Lacquer 1610.00
Chair, Easy, Louis XV Style, Fruitwood, Pair 1380.00
Chair, Easy, Louis XVI Style, Beechwood, Upholstered, 1880s, 35 In., Pair 1610.00
Chair, Elephant, Cut From 1 Piece Of Wood, Wooden Tusks, 32 In. Diam. 495.00
Chair, Elizabethan Style, Oak, Carved, Arms 400.00
Chair, Empire Style, Painted Rectangular Panel, Turned & Tapered Legs, Arms 230.00
Chair, Empire, Caryatid Busts Mount, Black Leather, 19 1/8 In. 385.00
Chair, Empire, Deep Tufted Barrel Back, Arm Trim, Velvet, 41 1/2 In. 770.00
Chair, Empire, Mahogany, Parcel Gilt, Damask, 19th Century, France 1935.00
Chair, Empire, Mahogany, Scroll Arms, Baluster Splat, 35 x 23 x 20 In. 240.00
Chair, Empire, Scalloped Tablet Crest Rail, Swags, 33 In. 1035.00
Chair, Ernest Gimson, Walnut, Ladder Back, Strung Seat, Arms, c.1905 . . . . 4150.00
Chair, Federal, Mahogany, Carved, New York, c.1800, 35 1/2 In. 690.00
Chair, Federal, Mahogany, Carved, Shield Back, Upholstered Seat, c.1790, 40 In. 920.00
Chair, Federal, Original Red, Black Grain, Cane Seat, 31 In. 520.00
Chair, Fiberglass, Blue, Stamped Mark, Panton, 19 x 21 x 32 In. 440.00

Chair, Fiddleback, Dark Brown Paint, Rush Seat, Conn., 1810, 16 In. 290.00
Chair, Fiddleback, Yoke Crest, Turned Stiles & Legs, Rush Seat, Late 18th Century 110.00
Chair, Flared Back, Round Seat, Upholstered, Turkey, Mid-19th Century 395.00
Chair, Folding, Hunzinger, Upholstered Arms, 34 1/2 In. 5850.00
Chair, Folding, Thonet, Laminated Wood, Chromium Tubular Steel, 30 7/8 In. 390.00
Chair, Frank Lloyd Wright, Oak, Leather Seat, 1901, 30 In. 9775.00
Chair, French Style, Carved Mahogany Frame, Shell Carved Knees, Upholstered 115.00
Chair, Fruitwood Base, Tapered Fluted Legs, Arms, Silk, Pair 55.00
Chair, Fruitwood, Sheaves Of Wheat Backsplat, Rush Seat, Italy 115.00
Chair, Fruitwood, Shell, Scroll Arms, Apron, Bellflower Design, 47 In. 2540.00
Chair, G. Stickley, 2 Horizontal Back Slats, Rush Seat, 36 x 17 1/2 In. 600.00
Chair, G. Stickley, H-Back, 1 Vertical Back Slat, Drop-In Seat, 39 In. 195.00
Chair, G. Stickley, Ladder Back, Heavy Slats, Tacked-On Leather Seat, 37 In. 375.00
Chair, G. Stickley, No. 15, V-Back 920.00
Chair, G. Stickley, No. 88, Wicker, Flat Arms, Loose Seat Cushion, 39 In. 1430.00
Chair, G. Stickley, No. 328, Cube, 1 Vertical Slat Each Side, Loose Cushion, 30 In. 3300.00
Chair, G. Stickley, No. 348, Ladder Back, 3 Horizontal Back Slats, Rush Seat, Pair 470.00
Chair, G. Stickley, No. 2578, Chalet, Leather Seat, 15 x 16 x 29 In. 440.00
Chair, G. Stickley, U-Back, 3 Horizontal Back Slats, Rush Slat, Decal, Pair 5225.00
Chair, G. Stickley, Willow, Arms, Pair 4315.00
Chair, Gehry, Corrugated Cardboard & Masonite, Easy Edges, Pair 3737.00
Chair, Gentleman's, Victorian, Carved Walnut, Arms 550.00
Chair, George I, Elm, Vase Shaped Splat, Cabriole Legs, Pad Feet 360.00
Chair, George I, Walnut, Shaped Back, Vase Form Splat, Serpentine Seat 1150.00
Chair, George II, Mahogany, Eagle Head Crest, Serpentine Slip Seat, Open Arms 1265.00
Chair, George II, Mahogany, Prince Of Wales Plume Crest, Paw Feet 275.00
Chair, George II, Mahogany, Square Upholstered Back, Floral Linen, Arms 600.00
Chair, George II, Walnut, Needlepoint Seat, Back & Open Arms, Serpentine 3225.00
Chair, George II, Walnut, Rectangular Drop Seat, Pad Feet, Arms 4600.00
Chair, George III Style, Mahogany, Crest, Saddle Seat, Upholstered, Arms 365.00
Chair, George III Style, Ribbonback, Late 19th Century, 40 In. 345.00
Chair, George III, Cherry, Crest Rail, Slip Seat, Marlborough Legs 635.00
Chair, George III, Lattice Back Splat, Chinaman Crest Rail, Caned Seat, Arms 800.00
Chair, George III, Mahogany, Bargello Needlepoint, 39 In. 2060.00
Chair, George III, Mahogany, Cabriole Legs Ball, Claw Feet 2090.00
Chair, George III, Mahogany, Crest, Upholstered, Arms, 18th Century 2650.00
Chair, George III, Mahogany, Curved Crest, Gothic Splat, Pair 600.00
Chair, George III, Mahogany, Foliage, Needlepoint Seat, Cabriole Legs 2600.00
Chair, George III, Mahogany, Ladder Back, Serpentine Crest, Arms, 1790 . . . . 6900.00
Chair, George III, Mahogany, Pierced Splat Back, Serpentine, Square Legs, Arms 900.00
Chair, George III, Mahogany, Pierced Splat Shield Back, Needlepoint, Arms 695.00
Chair, George III, Mahogany, Serpentine Backrest, Cabriole Legs, Arms 8050.00
Chair, George III, Mahogany, Serpentine Crest Rail, Slip Seat, Arms 435.00
Chair, George III, Mahogany, Serpentine Seat, Square Legs, 1780 . . . . 7475.00
Chair, George III, Mahogany, Wheel Back, 2 Over 3 Beaded Drawers, 39 In. 1430.00
Chair, George III, Mahogany, Wheel Back, Central Rosette Medallion, Pair 600.00
Chair, Georgian Style, Leather Upholstered Back & Slip Seat, Open Arms 850.00
Chair, Georgian, Mahogany, Carved Crest, Armorial Motif Fabric 1100.00
Chair, Georgian, Mahogany, Fretwork Frieze, Ball Feet, 44 In. 290.00
Chair, Georgian, Mahogany, Pierced Splat, Needlepoint Seat, 18th Century 175.00
Chair, Georgian, Mahogany, Plain Crest, Ribbon Splat 1980.00
Chair, Georgian, Mahogany, Saddle Seat, Red Leather, Out-Scrolled Arms 470.00
Chair, Georgian, Mahogany, Scrolled Crest Rail, Cabriole Legs 345.00
Chair, Georgian, Mahogany, Shield Back, Pair 575.00
Chair, Georgian, Mahogany, Square Upholstered Back & Seat, Arms, Pair 4150.00
Chair, Georgian, Provincial, Elm, Pair 345.00
Chair, Girard, Aluminum Legs, Wool Upholstered, U-Shape Seat, Arms 535.00
Chair, Gold Metal Frame, Arrows Forming Back, Italy, 18 x 35 In. 72.00
Chair, Goshen Manut, Mission, Signed, Child's 200.00
Chair, Gothic Revival, Carved Crest, Plank Seat, Arms 110.00
Chair, Gothic Revival, Mahogany, American, Mid-19th Century, Pair 725.00
Chair, Gothic Revival, Mahogany, Serpentine Crest, 4 Painted Arches, Arms, Pair 1495.00
Chair, Gothic Revival, Mahogany, Triple Arched Crest, Padded Seat, 1840, 44 In. 300.00

Chair, Gothic Revival, Scrolled Hip Rests, Carved Back, Upholstered 165.00
Chair, Gothic Revival, Walnut, Damask, 55 x 17 In. 1452.00
Chair, Gothic Revival, Walnut, Serpentine Seat, Velvet, 54 In. 550.00
Chair, Grain Painted, 3 Arrow Back Slats, Fruit Stenciling, Pair 115.00
Chair, Gray Paint, Arched Upholstered Back & Armrests, Arms, 1770s 2875.00
Chair, Greene & Greene, Leather, Cloud-Lift Pattern, 33 1/2 In. 4675.00
Chair, Grotto, Swan Form, Walnut, 19th Century, 26 In. 1150.00
Chair, Hall, Limbert, No. 79, Leather Back, Tripod Wood Seat, Dutch, 42 In. 1200.00
Chair, Hall, Mahogany, Pierced Cartouche Circular Inset, Plank Seat, Victorian 260.00
Chair, Hall, Regency, Mahogany, Shield Back, Painted Armorial, Plank Seat 1495.00
Chair, Hall, Rosewood, Laminated Inset Back Panel, 1850-1860 .... 990.00
Chair, Hardwood, Leaf Design, Floral Upholstery, 19 1/2 In. 1030.00
Chair, Hardwood, Worn Finish, Vase Form, Yoke Crest, Rush Seat, Arms 225.00
Chair, Hepplewhite, Mahogany & Maple, Shield Back, Fluted Legs, 1790, 37 In. 995.00
Chair, Hepplewhite, Mahogany, Arched Crest, Carved Splat, Upholstered Seat, Pair 200.00
Chair, Hepplewhite, Mahogany, Carved Crest Rail, Leather Seat, c.1790 .... 850.00
Chair, Hepplewhite, Mahogany, Mid Square Rosettes, Castor Feet, 16 In. 115.00
Chair, Hepplewhite, Mahogany, Prince Of Wales Feather Swags, Upholstered 550.00
Chair, Hepplewhite, Mahogany, Shaped Seat, Red Floral Damask, 35 In. 2750.00
Chair, Hepplewhite, Mahogany, Shield Back, Molded Legs, c.1800, 37 In. 200.00
Chair, Herman Miller, Compass, Birch, Arms, 27 1/2 x 20 x 20 In. 225.00
Chair, Herman Miller, Gray Fiberglass, Wire Strut Base, Label, Arms, 29 1/2 In. 665.00
Chair, Herman Miller, Walnut, Plywood Seat, Back, 22 x 23 x 27 In. ....550.00 to 715.00
Chair, Herter Bros., Curule, Renaissance, Rosewood, Embroidered, Arms, 1870 .... 2175.00
Chair, Herter Bros., Sewing, Rosewood, Maple, Leaf Legs 1155.00
Chair, Herter Bros., Walnut, Upholstered Back, Arms, Braided Fringe, 1860 .... 3650.00
Chair, Heywood-Wakefield, Corset Horizontal Back Slats, 32 x 19 In. 467.00
Chair, Heywood-Wakefield, Pressed Seat, 35 In. 175.00
Chair, High Back, Medallion, Carved Grape Leaves, Upholstered Half Arms 290.00
Chair, Hitchcock, Painted, Pair 870.00
Chair, Hunzinger, Adjustable Back & Arms, 1866 .... 395.00
Chair, Hunzinger, Ebonized, Medallion Back Ball Finials, 1859 .... 330.00
Chair, Ice Cream, Child's, 14 In. 50.00
Chair, J. & J.W. Meeks, Laminated Rosewood, Victorian 2200.00
Chair, Jack & Jill, Red Metal Seat, Chrome Legs, Arms & Back 70.00
Chair, Jacobean Style, Lattice Work Back, Upholstered Seat, Arms, 64 In. 85.00
Chair, Jacobean Style, Open Arms, Floral Crewel Work Upholstery 150.00
Chair, Jacobsen, Egg, Upholstered, 40 x 36 In., Pair ....*Illus* 1695.00
Chair, Jacobsen, Plywood Seat, Tripod Base, Stacking, 29 x 16 x 19 In. 990.00
Chair, Jacobsen, T-Shape Backs, 4 Black Metal Legs, 31 x 15 x 18 In. 665.00
Chair, Jacobson, Swan, Shell On Cast Aluminum Base, 29 x 20 x 32 In. 600.00
Chair, Jelliff, Walnut, Burl Walnut, Mid-19th Century 850.00
Chair, Jens Risom, Woven Red Straps, 26 x 24 x 29 In. 220.00
Chair, Kagan, Lounge, Plexiglas Rockers, Wool 200.00
Chair, Kammerer, Bentwood, Paneled Back, Leather Covered, Arms, 1905 .... 2300.00
Chair, Karpin, Cube, Square Cutouts On Flat Sides, Leather, 36 In. 1100.00
Chair, Kittenger, Tufted, Fluted Square Legs, Leather Upholstered, Pair 230.00
Chair, L. & J.G. Stickley, Long Corbels Under Open Arms, Label, 40 1/4 In. 935.00
Chair, L. & J.G. Stickley, Tacked-On Hard Leather Back & Seat, Arms, 36 1/2 In. 2090.00
Chair, Ladder Back, 4 Slats, Rush Seat, Brown Paint, 18th Century, 43 In., Pair 1725.00
Chair, Ladder Back, Arts & Crafts, Leather Seat, 34 1/2 In. 190.00
Chair, Ladder Back, Black Paint, Gold Accents, Splint Seat, Arms, 47 In. 1600.00
Chair, Ladder Back, Curly Maple, 5 Slats, Ball & Ring Front Stretcher 5600.00
Chair, Ladder Back, Hardwood, 4 Slats, Sausage Turning, Rush Seat, 43 In. 95.00
Chair, Ladder Back, Maple & Hickory, Rush Seat, Acorn Finials, Child's 247.00
Chair, Ladder Back, Maple, Splint Seat, Arms, 41 In. 430.00
Chair, Ladder Back, McHugh, Rush Seat, 36 x 18 In. 660.00
Chair, Ladder Back, Mixed Woods, Rush Seat, New England, Arms, c.1770 .... 355.00
Chair, Ladder Back, Pine, Arms, Canada, 19th Century 145.00
Chair, Ladder Back, Rabbit Ear Posts, Woven Splint Seat, 36 In., Pair 145.00
Chair, Ladder Back, Scrolled Hand Rest, Rush Seat, Added Rockers, 1780s 360.00
Chair, Ladder Back, Shaker, Turned Finials, Splint Seat, 16 In. 290.00
Chair, Ladder Back, Stained Oak, Mushroom Cap Finials, Rush Seat, Pair 320.00

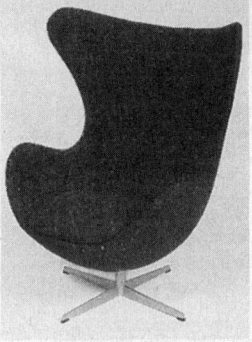

Furniture, Chair,
Jacobsen, Egg,
Upholstered,
40 x 36 In., Pair,
1 shown

Furniture, Chair,
Queen Anne,
Upholstered,
Arms

Chair, Ladder Back, Stained Oak, Rush Seat, Turned Legs, Child's 46.00
Chair, Ladder Back, Triple Slat Stretchers, Rush Seat, Arms 55.00
Chair, Ladder Back, Walnut, Black Leather Seat, England, Pair 845.00
Chair, Ladder Back, Woven Splint Seat, Arms, Child's, 21 In. 85.00
Chair, Laminated Pierced Back, Leaf & Acorn Design, Belter, Upholstered, 36 In. 3450.00
Chair, Laverne, Champagne Lucite, Red Seat Cushion, Arms, 32 x 23 In. 275.00
Chair, Leather Insert Of Woman's Head On Crest Rail, 7 Splats, Arms 85.00
Chair, Levantine Bone Inlay, Arms, 1920s, 35 In. 575.00
Chair, Library, Reclining, Walnut, Allegorical Scenes, Brown Leather, 46 In. 5225.00
Chair, Limbert, Curved Top Rail, Original Finish, 25 x 20 x 38 In. 460.00
Chair, Limbert, No. 911, Vertical Back Slat, Tacked On Leather Seat, 37 In. 385.00
Chair, Lolling, Chippendale, Velvet Brocade, 39 3/4 In. 1450.00
Chair, Lolling, Federal, Carved, Mahogany, Barrel-Back, Arms, c.1810, 43 In. 9775.00
Chair, Lolling, Federal, Mahogany, Serpentine Crest, Upholstered, Arms, 42 In. 1850.00
Chair, Lolling, Federal, Mahogany, Upholstered Back & Seat, Arms, 1790-1810 .... 6325.00
Chair, Lolling, Hepplewhite, Cherry & Birch, Back Splats, Open Arms, 44 1/4 In. 1875.00
Chair, Lolling, Mahogany Frame, 43 1/2 In. 1100.00
Chair, Lolling, Petit Point Padded Upholstered Back & Seat, Open Arms, 35 1/2 In. 805.00
Chair, Louis XIII, Walnut, Tapestry Back, Muslin Seat 1540.00
Chair, Louis XIII, Walnut, Twist Turned Supports, Pair 5750.00
Chair, Louis XIV, Walnut, Carved, High Back, Arms 630.00
Chair, Louis XV Style, Gilt Design, Child's 125.00
Chair, Louis XV Style, Oak, Caned Back, Slip Seat, 36 1/2 In., Pair 1840.00
Chair, Louis XV, Beechwood, Gondola Back, Velvet, 27 1/2 In. 1210.00
Chair, Louis XV, Beechwood, Upholstered Backrest & Seat, Padded Armrests 4312.00
Chair, Louis XV, Floral, Scroll Frames, Whorl Feet, 44 3/4 In. 1936.00
Chair, Louis XV, Giltwood, Needlepoint & Petit Point, Arms, 18th Century, Child's 785.00
Chair, Louis XV, Provincial, Walnut, Carved 460.00
Chair, Louis XV, Rose, Shell Motif, Foliate Sprays, Upholstered Arms 9200.00
Chair, Louis XV, Walnut, Floral Crest, Burgundy Damask, Geometric Design 770.00
Chair, Louis XVI Style, Antique White Paint, Carved Frame, Pair 1935.00
Chair, Louis XVI Style, Giltwood, Silk, Oval Back 330.00
Chair, Louis XVI Style, Green Paint, Upholstered, Arms 720.00
Chair, Louis XVI, Beaded, Acanthus Frame, Banded Back, 39 In., Pair 3870.00
Chair, Louis XVI, Beech, Lyre Design, Arms, 41 x 17 In. 725.00
Chair, Louis XVI, Beechwood, Baluster Supports, Upholstered Arms 2875.00
Chair, Louis XVI, Beechwood, Painted, Upholstered Back & Seat, 19th Century 345.00
Chair, Louis XVI, Bowed Seat Frame, Leaf Design, Velvet 1270.50
Chair, Louis XVI, Giltwood, Fluted Supports, Upholstered Arms 8625.00
Chair, Louis XVI, Horseshoe Shape Backrest, Fluted Legs 345.00
Chair, Louis XVI, Incurved Supports, Beaded Borders, Padded Armrests 2875.00
Chair, Louis XVI, Mahogany, Oval Back, Serpentine Seat Rail, Fluted Legs 485.00
Chair, Louis XVI, Urn Form Finials, Fluted Legs, Horseshoe Seat, 36 In. 175.00
Chair, Lounge, Victorian, Crest Shape, Tufted Back, Open Arms, 36 x 26 In. 485.00
Chair, Mahogany Veneer, Arched Crest, Vertical Splat, Saber Legs, 1850s 82.00

Chair, Mahogany, Downswept Arms, Ball & Claw Feet, Upholstered, 40 In. 1150.00
Chair, Mahogany, Pierced Splat, Slip Seat, Arms, Downswept Supports, 1800, Pair 1850.00
Chair, Mahogany, Pine Cones & Needles, Gold Brocade, 1900 . . . . 600.00
Chair, Mahogany, Red Plush, Ebonized, X-Shaped Legs, Arms, 1870 . . . . 2070.00
Chair, Mahogany, Ribbonback, Pierced Ribbon Crest, 3 Splats, 38 1/2 In. 1150.00
Chair, Mahogany, Upholstered Back Within Scrolled Frame, Sphinx Formed Arms 4900.00
Chair, Mahogany, Writing Arm With Drawer, Padded Back & Seat 400.00
Chair, Majorelle, Art Nouveau, Cane Back & Seat, Arms, Pair 3000.00
Chair, Majorelle, Art Nouveau, Carved Fruitwood, Floral Upholstery, 37 In., Pair 990.00
Chair, Maple, Carved, Lyre Back, Flame Maple Splat, Caned Seat, c.1830 . . . . 63.00
Chair, Maple, Shaped Crest Above Vasiform Splat, Woven Seat, Red, 1740s 575.00
Chair, Marcel Breuer, Wassily, Chrome Tubing, Leather Slings, 1960s, 28 In. 465.00
Chair, Marquetry, Griffins & Cornucopia On Top Rail, Arms, 1840 . . . . 725.00
Chair, McCobb, Spindles, Black Lacquered, Arms, Pair 385.00
Chair, Moravian, Pine, Mustard Paint Over Red, 17 1/4 In. 85.00
Chair, Moravian, Walnut, Pine, Tapered Legs, 36 3/4 In. 100.00
Chair, Morris, G. Stickley, Swing Seat, Loose Pillows, Flat Arms, 38 In. 6050.00
Chair, Morris, Harden, Slat Sides, Exposed Tenons, Arched Front Stretcher 3300.00
Chair, Morris, J.M. Young, Slats To Floor, Long Corbels, Spring Seat, 40 In. 2860.00
Chair, Morris, L. & J.G. Stickley, Drop-In Spring Seat, Slanted Arms, 40 In. 8750.00
Chair, Morris, L. & J.G. Stickley, No. 471, Spring Cushion, Flat Arms, 41 x 32 In. 4400.00
Chair, Morris, L. & J.G. Stickley, No. 473, Spindles To Drop-In Seat, Flat Arms 2750.00
Chair, Morris, L. & J.G. Stickley, No. 498, Drop-In Spring Seat, 41 x 32 In. 6050.00
Chair, Morris, L. & J.G. Stickley, No. 768, Slats Under Arms, Loose Cushions 1430.00
Chair, Morris, Limbert, Cutout On Sides, Drop-In Seat, Slanted Arms, 38 In. 3575.00
Chair, Morris, Oak, Lazy Boy, Early 1900s, Arms 495.00
Chair, Morris, Shop Of Crafters, No. 333, Inlaid 7700.00
Chair, Mushroom, Arrow Form Arms, Rush Seat 357.00
Chair, Music, Renaissance Revival, 34 In. 3200.00
Chair, Music, Walnut Marquetry 775.00
Chair, Napoleon III, Mid-19th Century 1100.00
Chair, Napoleon III, Oak, Ribbon-Tied Crest, Round Back, Serpentine Seat, Pair 690.00
Chair, Napoleon III, Rosewood, Carved Shells & Flowers, Aubusson Upholstered 2070.00
Chair, Natural Wood, Early 18th Century, 42 In. 625.00
Chair, Nelson, Coconut, Black Vinyl Triangular Seat, 33 x 38 In. 2650.00
Chair, Neoclassical, Back Scrolled Rail, 4 Slats, Rush Seat, Shaped Arms, Pair 1725.00
Chair, Neoclassical, Carved, Green Paint, Gesso Frame, 1790 . . . . 2970.00
Chair, Neoclassical, Fruitwood, Swan Carved Lyre Splats, c.1840, Pair 1030.00
Chair, Neoclassical, Giltwood, Scrolled Supports, Fluted Legs, Arms, Italy 1610.00
Chair, Neoclassical, Mahogany, 6 Sides, Padded Seat, Black Legs, 35 In. 1760.00
Chair, Neoclassical, Mahogany, Stylized Foliage, Scroll Arms 805.00
Chair, Neoclassical, Parcel Gilt, Cream Ground, Italy, 38 In., Pair 1430.00
Chair, Neoclassical, Walnut, Padded Back, Fluted Legs, Open Arms 2300.00
Chair, Oak, Eagle Head Crest, Turned Legs, Paw Feet, 40 In. 513.00
Chair, Oak, Tall Back, Needlepoint, Arms, England, 17th Century, Pair 3390.00
Chair, Oliver Morgue, Upholstered, 2-Dimensional Body Shape, 45 x 61 In. 1200.00
Chair, Opens Into Ironing Board 105.00
Chair, Organ, Walnut, Lion Heads 895.00
Chair, P. Paulin, Lounge, Tweed, 27 x 32 x 27 In. 165.00
Chair, P. Paulin, White Base, Ribbonback, Purple Fabric, 28 x 38 x 30 In. 1045.00
Chair, Parchment & Leather, Square Legs, 28 x 17 In., Pair 3450.00
Chair, Patriotic Stars & Stripes, Stars, Arms, Child's, 22 1/2 In. 605.00
Chair, Pedro Friedeberg, Left Hand & Right Hand Form, c.1970, Pair 4066.00
Chair, Pierced Heart, 4 Banister Slats, Rush Seat, Black Paint, Shaped Arms 1600.00
Chair, Pierced Splat & Yoke Crest, Carved Crosshatching & Ears, 38 In. 4950.00
Chair, Pine, Painted, Pierced Cartouche Back, Floral On Plank Seat 140.00
Chair, Plycraft, Bikini, Laminated Walnut, Upholstered, Arms, 31 x 25 In., Pair 825.00
Chair, Plywood, Rosewood Veneer, Upholstered, 34 x 32 In. 385.00
Chair, Porter's, Louis XVI Style, Fruitwood 690.00
Chair, Prince's, Africa, 1930s, Child's 1100.00
Chair, Queen Anne Style, Cherrywood, 41 In. 275.00
Chair, Queen Anne Style, Walnut, Duck Feet, Cabriole Legs, 39 In., Pair 6600.00
Chair, Queen Anne, Black Japanned, Serpentine Seat, Trellis Work 2875.00

Chair, Queen Anne, Durand Type, Brown Paint Over Red, Rush Seat, Arms, 1790 ...... 3575.00
Chair, Queen Anne, Gilt, Yoke Crest, Trapezoidal Rush Seat, 1740, 40 In. 230.00
Chair, Queen Anne, Grain Painted, Carved Crest, Rush Seat, 41 1/2 In. 1840.00
Chair, Queen Anne, Green Lacquer, Floral Painted, Cabriole Legs, 38 In. 360.00
Chair, Queen Anne, Hardwood, Red Paint Traces, Vase Form, Rush Seat 550.00
Chair, Queen Anne, Mahogany, Bargello Upholstery, Cabriole Legs, 36 In., Pair 725.00
Chair, Queen Anne, Maple, Molded Yoke Crest, Splat, Slip Seat, 1740-1760 .... 920.00
Chair, Queen Anne, Maple, Sausage Turned Legs, Vase-Form, Splint Seat 165.00
Chair, Queen Anne, Maple, Turned Legs, Carved, Spanish Feet, 41 1/2 In. 630.00
Chair, Queen Anne, Maple, Worn Dark Finish, Spanish Feet, Rush Seat 1200.00
Chair, Queen Anne, Maple, Yoked Crest Rail, Rush Seat, Arms, Child's, 23 In. 1150.00
Chair, Queen Anne, Maple, Yoked Crest Rail, Rush Seat, c.1770, 41 In. 575.00
Chair, Queen Anne, Oxbow Top, Leather Seat 1045.00
Chair, Queen Anne, Red Stained Finish, Turned & Carved, 41 In. 4025.00
Chair, Queen Anne, Rush Slip Seat, c.1750, Pair 7200.00
Chair, Queen Anne, Tiger Maple, Spanish Foot 550.00
Chair, Queen Anne, Upholstered, Arms ....*Illus* 1320.00
Chair, Queen Anne, Walnut, Arched Crest, Vase-Form Splat, Cushioned Seat, 1750s 6900.00
Chair, Queen Anne, Walnut, Balloon Seats, 1730-1760, 39 1/2 In., Pair 13800.00
Chair, Queen Anne, Walnut, Cabriole Legs, Out Scrolled Armrests 3160.00
Chair, Queen Anne, Walnut, Commode, Roundabout, 1740-1760, 30 In. 920.00
Chair, Queen Anne, Walnut, Dutch Marquetry 425.00
Chair, Queen Anne, Walnut, Molded Yoke Crest, Vase-Form Splat, Slip Seat 4370.00
Chair, Queen Anne, Walnut, Needlework Seat, Eagle Design, 38 3/4 In., Pair 865.00
Chair, Queen Anne, Walnut, Slip Seat, England, 30 1/2 In. 660.00
Chair, Queen Anne, Walnut, Vase-Form Splat, Trapezoidal Slip Seat, 1730s 3795.00
Chair, Reading, William IV, Mahogany, Tufted Leather, 58 In. 1650.00
Chair, Reclining, Victorian, Walnut, 19th Century 220.00
Chair, Regency, Beechwood, Caned Back & Seat, Serpentine Front, Arms, 1740s 2070.00
Chair, Regency, Black Paint, Painted Urn & Flowers, Stamped TS, Pair 600.00
Chair, Regency, Mahogany, Carved Crest, Reeded Legs, Burgundy Needlepoint 2650.00
Chair, Regency, Mahogany, Reeded Stiles, Ball Feet, 1830s 725.00
Chair, Regency, Mahogany, Rolled Crest, Slip Seat, 1815 .... 395.00
Chair, Regency, Mahogany, Scrolled Crest, Saber Legs, Arms, 34 In. 1935.00
Chair, Regency, Rosewood Tub, U-Shape Crest, Cane Backrest, 1820 .... 4900.00
Chair, Regency, Upholstered Back & Seat, Turned Legs, Scrolled Inlaid Arms 920.00
Chair, Renaissance Revival, Oak, Figural Carved Back, Cushion, Arms, Pair 1210.00
Chair, Renaissance Revival, Oak, Pierced Gothic Arched Back, Plank Seat, Pair 316.00
Chair, Renaissance Revival, Walnut, Burl Walnut, Crest, Arms, Pair 1320.00
Chair, Renaissance Revival, Walnut, Folding 100.00
Chair, Renaissance Revival, Walnut, Pierced Arms, Upholstered, 19th Century 1450.00
Chair, Renaissance Revival, Walnut, Shell Crest, Tuft Upholstery, Pair 520.00
Chair, Renaissance Revival, Walnut, Square Back, Gryphon Supports, 1870, Pair 1760.00
Chair, Ribbon & Acanthus Design, Carved Frames, Needlepoint Back, Arms, Pair 6450.00
Chair, Riemerschmid, Beech, Pearwood, Upholstered Seat, Open Arms, 1902 .... 3450.00
Chair, Rietveld, Militar, Gray, Black, Yellow & White Wood, 1930 .... 6440.00
Chair, Robsjohn-Gibbings, Black Boucle Wool, Wooden Legs 220.00
Chair, Robsjohn-Gibbings, Vinyl, High Back, 43 x 24 In., Pair 85.00
Chair, Robsjohn-Gibbings, Walnut, Webbed Seat, Linen, 31 In. 825.00
Chair, Rocker, is listed under Rocker in this category.
Chair, Rococo, Beechwood, Upholstered Seat, Cabriole Legs, Arms 2100.00
Chair, Rococo, Giltwood, Leaf Design Back, Serpentine Seat 3700.00
Chair, Rococo, Green Paint, Gilt Design, Needlework, Italy 290.00
Chair, Rococo, Rosewood, Floral Carved Crest, Pair 1210.00
Chair, Rococo, Rosewood, Fruited Crest, Tapestry Seat & Back, 1850 .... 2660.00
Chair, Rococo, Rosewood, Leafy Roses, Grapes, Carved Daisies, 1850 .... 3400.00
Chair, Rococo, Stanton Hall, Rosewood, Upholstered, 1850, Pair 2750.00
Chair, Rococo, Walnut, Foliate Design, Upholstered, 1850, 37 In. 1200.00
Chair, Rococo, Walnut, Leaf Carved Pierced Back, 19th Century 880.00
Chair, Rococo, Walnut, Open Shield Shape Back, 1860-1870, 36 In. 790.00
Chair, Rococo, Walnut, Pierced Back, Mid-19th Century 545.00
Chair, Rod Back, Black Paint, Pierced Crest Rail, Plank Seat, 35 In. 400.00
Chair, Rohde, Walnut Legs, Vinyl, 32 x 16 x 20 In. 495.00

Chair, Root, Pennsylvania, Arms, Pair 3850.00
Chair, Rope Carved Crest, Turned Spindles, Upholstered 85.00
Chair, Rosewood, Gothic Carved, Original Muslin, c.1840-1850, Pair 1100.00
Chair, Rosewood, Horizontal Slat Back, Cane Seat, Scrolled Arms, 19th Century 605.00
Chair, Rosewood, Spiral Turned Stiles, Crest, Upholstered, Floral 195.00
Chair, Roycroft, No. 25, 2 Horizontal Back Slats Under Elbow Rests, 34 In., Pair 1100.00
Chair, Rustic, Indiana, c.1935, Pair 695.00
Chair, Saarinen, Brown, Beige Boucle, Black Rod Legs, 36 x 38 In. 605.00
Chair, Saarinen, Chrome Tube Legs, Wool Fabric 660.00
Chair, Saarinen, Womb, Sand Colored Vinyl, 26 x 39 In. 600.00
Chair, Salmon Paint, White, Black Strips, Floral, 6 In. 715.00
Chair, Samuel Gragg, Painted, Bentwood, Arms 5225.00
Chair, Savonarola, Walnut, Carved, Gilt Crest, Upholstered, X-Form Base, Italy, Pair 3450.00
Chair, Second Empire, Serpentine Crest, Pierced Cartouche, Ribbon Splat, Pair 1600.00
Chair, Sedan, Center Glazed Door, Glazed Side Panels, Leather Veneer, 61 In. 3100.00
Chair, Shaker, 2 Arched Slats, Rush Seat, 19th Century, Child's, 29 3/4 x 12 In. 750.00
Chair, Shaker, 5 Slats, Rush Seat, Arms, 1930s 600.00
Chair, Shaker, Ladder Back, Mt. Lebanon Label, 3 On Top Slat, Tape Seat, 33 In. 470.00
Chair, Shaker, Mt. Lebanon, No. 3, 3 Slats, Rush Seat, Decal, Pair 1870.00
Chair, Shaker, Mt. Lebanon, Web Back, Decal, Arms, 1880-1900, Child's, 28 In. 1100.00
Chair, Shaker, New Lebanon, Bird's-Eye Slats, Tilters 2400.00
Chair, Shell, Wave Motif Foliate, Upholstered Arms, 18th Century 4312.00
Chair, Sheraton Style, Mahogany, Upholstered Seat, Cane Back, Arms, 33 In., Pair 385.00
Chair, Sheraton, Black Paint, Yellow Striping, Cane Seat, 35 1/2 In., Pair 385.00
Chair, Sheraton, Curly Maple, Yellow Striping, Stencil, 34 In., Pair 110.00
Chair, Sheraton, Floral Silk Brocade, Spade Feet, George III, 38 1/2 In. 1980.00
Chair, Sheraton, Red & Black Grained, Stenciled, Rush Balloon Seat, Child's 440.00
Chair, Sheraton, Triple Backrest, Square Tapered Legs, England, 57 In. 3250.00
Chair, Sheraton, Walnut, Arms 345.00
Chair, Sheraton, Worn Dark Paint, Gilt Design, Rush Balloon Seat, 34 In., Pair 240.00
Chair, Shield Back, Caned Seat, Foliate Swag Rail, Arms, 1780s, Pair 4600.00
Chair, Shield Back, Inlaid Fan, H Stretcher, Upholstered Seat, 37 3/4 In., Pair 2450.00
Chair, Slat Back, Black Paint, Gilt Stenciling, Needlepoint Seat, Sweden, Pair 750.00
Chair, Sling, Freeform Base, Leather Support, Mexico, 28 x 23 x 25 In., Pair 385.00
Chair, Slipper, Aesthetic Revival, Giltwood, 1880, 29 1/2 In. 2450.00
Chair, Slipper, Belter, Rococo, Rosewood, Oak Leaf, Acorn, 1850-1860 . . . . 3100.00
Chair, Slipper, Contemporary, Upholstered, Maroon, Wooden Legs, 30 In. 60.00
Chair, Slipper, Elizabethan, Rosewood, Gothic Design, Victorian, 46 In. 300.00
Chair, Slipper, Herter Bros., Greek Key Design, 1860s, Pair 2200.00
Chair, Slipper, Walnut & Oak, Mother-Of-Pearl, Copper & Pewter Inlay 3165.00
Chair, Slipper, Walnut, Button Tufted Upholstery, Fluted Legs, Victorian 300.00
Chair, Spratling, Wooden Frame, Fish Cutout, Leather Seat, Arms, 33 In. 415.00
Chair, Spratling, Wooden Frame, Heart Cutout, Leather Seat, 25 In. 121.00
Chair, Spring, Tufted, Velvet, Cord Fringe, 19th Century 176.00
Chair, Square Upholstered Back & Seat, Spiral Twist Arms & Legs, Pair 2185.00
Chair, Steel & Brass, Folding X-Form Base, Slung Leather Back & Arms 1610.00
Chair, Stickley Brothers, 5 Vertical Back Slats, Open Arms, Slat Seat, 38 1/2 In. 935.00
Chair, Stuart, Oak, Carved Backrest, Scrolled Arms, Square Seat 690.00
Chair, Swivel, Oak, Arrow Back, Leather Seat, Casters, Arms 750.00
Chair, Swivel, Victorian, Wicker, Brown, Casters, Arms 500.00
Chair, Tapered Legs, Ribbonback, 34 x 23 x 20 In. 770.00
Chair, Tapestry Upholstered Back & Seat, Carved Arms, 46 1/2 In. 430.00
Chair, Thonet, Bentwood, Laminated, Blond Finish, c.1955, 30 1/2 In. 185.00
Chair, Thonet, Bentwood, Orange Vinyl, Tapered Legs, 28 In. 140.00
Chair, Throne, Fruitwood, Circular Back, Medallion, Gourd-Shaped Legs, Russia 6325.00
Chair, Tub, Empire, Mahogany 1150.00
Chair, Tub, Faux Rosewood & Gilt Design, Pair 5175.00
Chair, Tub, Neoclassical Style, Caned, Upholstered Seat 165.00
Chair, Tub, Neoclassical, Padded Back, Cushion, Tapered Legs 3740.00
Chair, Turkey Work, Shirred Crest Rail, Upholstered Seat, Turned Feet, 38 In. 2070.00
Chair, Turned Spindles, Legs On Casters, Arms, England, Pair 175.00
Chair, Upholstered Back, Dolphin Tails And Dolphin Heads, Curved Arms, Pair 5500.00
Chair, Van Der Rohe, Barcelona, Black Leather Cushions, 29 x 29 In. 3300.00

Chair, Van Der Rohe, Barcelona, Steel x Frames, 29 x 26 x 28 In. 1210.00
Chair, Vanity, Metalform, Lucite Tube, Swiveling, Quilted Silk, 26 In. 495.00
Chair, Vanity, Round Shape, Scroll Design, Turned Legs, France, 26 In. 260.00
Chair, Victorian, Antler, Wooden Seat, Arms, Velvet Tufted Cushion 747.50
Chair, Victorian, Carved Walnut, Brocade, Spring Seat, Arms 220.00
Chair, Victorian, Carved Walnut, Upholstered, Minerva Head Arms, 43 1/2 In. 660.00
Chair, Victorian, Carved Walnut, Upholstered, Open Arms, 40 In., Pair 580.00
Chair, Victorian, Lady's, Walnut, Grape Carved Crest, Upholstered, Arms, 1860 .... 425.00
Chair, Victorian, Leather Upholster, U-Shape Tufted Backrest, Arms 4600.00
Chair, Victorian, Mahogany, Caned Circular Back, Scrolled Arms, Child's 805.00
Chair, Victorian, Mahogany, Floral Carved Crest, Upholstered, Arms 55.00
Chair, Victorian, Mahogany, Rose & Foliate Scroll Carved Crest, Child's 910.00
Chair, Victorian, Walnut, Red Leather, 38 1/2 In. 60.00
Chair, Victorian, Walnut, Rosewood, Ribbon Crests, 1860, 47 In. 440.00
Chair, Victorian, Wire, Ornate, Arms, Child's, 32 In. 200.00
Chair, Vinyl, Chrome, Wood Armrest, 23 x 19 In. 60.00
Chair, Walnut, Balloon Back, Finger Carving, Hip Rests 110.00
Chair, Walnut, Carved Lion's Heads, Trumpeted Legs 1090.00
Chair, Walnut, Gilt Incised, Upholstered, Fringe, N.Y., 19th Century 550.00
Chair, Walnut, Inlaid Lyre Form Crest, Carved Arms, Paw Feet, Child's 550.00
Chair, Walnut, Parcel Gilt, 2-Headed Eagle Splat, Continental, 18th Century 2300.00
Chair, Walnut, Saddle Seat, Dowel Legs, 37 1/2 x 18 1/2 x 16 1/2 In. 2310.00
Chair, Walnut, Shaped Apron, Velvet, Dog Head Arms 1430.00
Chair, Walnut, Woven Cane Seat, Italy, 1950, 32 x 28 x 27 In. .... ·165.00
Chair, Warren Planter, Wire 300.00
Chair, White Enameled, Bikini Shape, Dark Green Wool, 31 x 24 x 19 In. 275.00
Chair, Wicker, Green, Orange Trim, Victorian 225.00
Chair, William & Mary, Black Paint, Banister Back, Rush Seat, Arms, c.1710, 44 In. 1725.00
Chair, William & Mary, Black, Banister Back, Downswept Arms, 1730s 1725.00
Chair, William & Mary, Carved Beech, Acorn, Cane Back & Seat, 55 1/2 In. 3100.00
Chair, William & Mary, Crooked Back, Boston, 1730s, 40 3/4 In. 1150.00
Chair, William & Mary, Heart & Crown Crest, Rush Seat, New England 2990.00
Chair, William & Mary, Ladder Back, Ash, 5 Arched Slats, Rush Seat, Arms, 52 In. 690.00
Chair, William & Mary, Maple, Banister Back, Rush Seat, 18th Century, 41 In. 1035.00
Chair, William & Mary, Split Banister Back, Rush Seat, 1730-1750 .... 230.00
Chair, William & Mary, Walnut, Upholstered Back, Turned Legs, Pair 5750.00
Chair, Windsor, 9 Spindles, Bowed Crest Rail, Plank Seat, 37 1/2 In. 460.00
Chair, Windsor, 9 Spindles, Saddle Seat, William Russell, 1780s, Child's 1250.00
Chair, Windsor, Arrow Back, Painted Brown, Yellow & Red Foliate, c.1830, Pair 260.00
Chair, Windsor, Arrow Back, Writing, Pine, Painted, Bamboo Splayed Legs 260.00
Chair, Windsor, Ash, Pine & Maple, Continuous Arm, c.1780, 38 1/4 In. 980.00
Chair, Windsor, Bamboo Turnings, 34 1/2 In. 220.00
Chair, Windsor, Bamboo Turnings, Black Over Red, 34 In. 220.00
Chair, Windsor, Bamboo Turnings, Crest Rail, Refinished, 35 1/2 In., Pair 430.00
Chair, Windsor, Bamboo Turnings, Gold Paint, 1818, 28 1/2 In. 99.00
Chair, Windsor, Bamboo Turnings, Splayed Base, Continuous Arm 355.00
Chair, Windsor, Bamboo Turnings, Step-Down Crest, Plank Seat, 1840s 95.00
Chair, Windsor, Birch, Birdcage, Bamboo Turnings, Scroll Hard Rests 165.00
Chair, Windsor, Birdcage, Child's, Pair 695.00
Chair, Windsor, Bow Back, Arms, c.1800, 38 1/2 In., Pair 2100.00
Chair, Windsor, Bow Back, Bamboo Turnings Seat, 35 In. 195.00
Chair, Windsor, Bow Back, Bamboo Turnings, Repaint, Splayed, H-Stretcher, 35 In. 440.00
Chair, Windsor, Bow Back, Black Paint, New England, c.1810, 35 1/2 In. 230.00
Chair, Windsor, Bow Back, Braced, Black Paint 575.00
Chair, Windsor, Bow Back, Braced, Spindles, Saddle Seat, Painted, 1780 .... 1150.00
Chair, Windsor, Bow Back, Mahogany, Black Paint, Downscrolling Arms, 1830s 5400.00
Chair, Windsor, Bow Back, Saddle Seat, Spindle Back, 35 In. 825.00
Chair, Windsor, Bow Back, Saddle Seat, Splayed Base, Branded MB, 37 In. 275.00
Chair, Windsor, Bow Back, Shaped Arm Posts, Saddle Seat, 37 In. 495.00
Chair, Windsor, Bow Back, Shaped Spindle Back, Turned Arm Posts, 37 In. 440.00
Chair, Windsor, Bow Back, Spindle, Splayed, Bulbous Turnings, Arms, 39 1/2 In. 660.00
Chair, Windsor, Bow Back, Splayed Base, Oval Seat, Arms, Repaint 465.00
Chair, Windsor, Bow Back, Turned Legs, Child's 950.00

Chair, Windsor, Brace Back, 9 Spindles, Compass Shape Seat, 4 Splayed Legs 2760.00
Chair, Windsor, Brace Back, 9 Spindles, Continuous Arm, Late 18th Century 1495.00
Chair, Windsor, Brace Back, 9 Spindles, Continuous Arm, W. MacBride. 2530.00
Chair, Windsor, Brace Back, Dark Brown, Saddle Seat, Arm, 36 In. 3525.00
Chair, Windsor, Comb Back, Ash, Poplar, Maple, Arms, 18th Century, 40 In. 575.00
Chair, Windsor, Comb Back, Eared, Arm Terminals, Inturned Knuckles 2350.00
Chair, Windsor, Comb Back, Red Paint, Serpentine Crest Rail, Arms, c.1780, 38 In. 1495.00
Chair, Windsor, Elm Wood, Turned Legs, Scrolled Arms, England, 44 In. 750.00
Chair, Windsor, Esherick, Turned Legs, Woven Black Leather Seat, Arms 3190.00
Chair, Windsor, Fanback, 7 Spindles, Painted, Arched Crest Rail, 18th Century 3220.00
Chair, Windsor, Fanback, Black Over Old Red, B Greene, 18th Century 950.00
Chair, Windsor, Fanback, Brown Paint, 7 Tapering Spindles, Plank Seat, 1780s 345.00
Chair, Windsor, Fanback, Brown Paint, Baluster Turnings, Molded Seat 330.00
Chair, Windsor, Fanback, Hardwood, Curly Maple Post, Splayed, Yoke Crest 385.00
Chair, Windsor, Fanback, Maple, Ash, Pine, Vase & Ring Turnings, Saddle Seat, 37 In. .. 632.00
Chair, Windsor, Fanback, Painted, Bulbous Vase & Ring Turnings, c.1780, 36 1/2 In. 430.00
Chair, Windsor, Fanback, Painted, Gold Striping, c.1770-1790, 37 1/2 In. 1100.00
Chair, Windsor, Fanback, Traces Of Red Paint, J.C. Tuttle, 1780s, 36 In. 375.00
Chair, Windsor, Hoop Back, Braced, Pipe Stem Spindles, Saddle Seat, Arms, 38 In. 3200.00
Chair, Windsor, Hoop Back, Pierced Splat Back, Saddle Seat, Arms, England 605.00
Chair, Windsor, Low Back, Arms, c.1760 .... 3600.00
Chair, Windsor, Low Back, Black, Metal Brace, 28 In. 880.00
Chair, Windsor, Rod Back, Hickory, Maple & Poplar, c.1815 .... 195.00
Chair, Windsor, Rod Back, Painted, New England, Child's, 26 In. 200.00
Chair, Windsor, Sack Back, 1800-1808, 36 3/4 In. 920.00
Chair, Windsor, Sack Back, Arched Crest, Baluster Legs, 1780-1800, 37 In. 5520.00
Chair, Windsor, Sack Back, Bamboo Turnings, 1780, 36 In. 2415.00
Chair, Windsor, Sack Back, Continuous Arm, c.1790-1800, 38 In. 3000.00
Chair, Windsor, Sack Back, Dark Green, 1770, 17 1/8 In. 5175.00
Chair, Windsor, Sack Back, Silver Plaque On 1 Arm, Harvard, 1782, Pair 5800.00
Chair, Windsor, Spindle Back, Black Over Red, Saddle Seat, 33 1/2 In. 1100.00
Chair, Windsor, Steel, 1960s 475.00
Chair, Windsor, Step Back, Crest Stencil, Red Paint, c.1830, 35 1/2 In. 630.00
Chair, Windsor, Step Back, Stamped Halifax Warranted, Arms 475.00
Chair, Windsor, Step Back, White Repaint 110.00
Chair, Windsor, Triple Back, Combed Crest, Bar Harbor, Me., 44 In. 4150.00
Chair, Windsor, Wallace Nutting, No. 408, Bent Arms 1210.00
Chair, Windsor, Wallace Nutting, No. 440, Writing Arm, Pennsylvania 2800.00
Chair, Wing, Cherry, Serpentine Crest, Upholstered Scrolled Arms, c.1800 .... 3450.00
Chair, Wing, Chippendale, Mahogany Base, Frame, Molded Front Legs, 44 In. 300.00
Chair, Wing, Chippendale, Mahogany, Square Legs, 44 3/4 In. 2100.00
Chair, Wing, Chippendale, Upholstered, Claw Feet, Arms, 19th Century 600.00
Chair, Wing, Edwardian, Mahogany, Leather, Turned Legs 920.00
Chair, Wing, G. Stickley, Wicker, Tufted Seat Cushion, 42 1/2 In. 715.00
Chair, Wing, George I, Mahogany, Acanthus Cabriole Legs 880.00
Chair, Wing, George II, Walnut, Cushioned Seat, Cabriole Legs, Arms 3450.00
Chair, Wing, George III, Mahogany, Brown Leather, Tufted Back 1100.00
Chair, Wing, Hepplewhite, Mahogany, Tapered Legs, 45 In. 2550.00
Chair, Wing, Hepplewhite, Upholstered In Indian Crewel, Arms, 46 1/2 In. 495.00
Chair, Wing, Queen Anne Style, Cabriole Front Legs, 43 1/2 In. 230.00
Chair, Wing, Queen Anne, Beechwood, Cabriole Legs, Padded Arms 5750.00
Chair, Wing, Queen Anne, Walnut, Arms, 18th Century, 45 In. 750.00
Chair, Wing, Shell Carved Knees, Pad Feet, Outflaring Arms, 20th Century 192.00
Chair, Wormley, Mahogany, Caned Backs, Arms, 32 x 19 x 18 In. 1650.00
Chair & Ottoman, Eames, Swivel, Plywood Frame, Upholstered 85.00
Chair & Ottoman, Hans Wegner, Poppa Bear, Wing Back, Dowel Legs 1210.00
Chair & Ottoman, Herman Miller, Blond Wood Feet, Upholstered, Arms, 1954 .... 715.00
Chair & Ottoman, Knoll, Birdwool Upholstered, Wire Base, 40 x 38 x 33 In. 522.00
Chair & Ottoman, Warren Plattner, Wire, Corseted, Upholstered, 39 In. 465.00
Chair Set, American Restauration, Mahogany, New York, 1830, 6 .... 8170.00
Chair Set, Anglo Indian, Silvered Metal, Ram's Ears Back, 2 Armchairs, 6 .... 4600.00
Chair Set, Art Nouveau, Walnut, Pink Velvet, 40 In., 4 .... 220.00
Chair Set, Baker Co., French Empire, Rosewood Grained, Upholstered, Arms, 4 .... 1350.00

Chair Set, Balloon Back, Floral Carved Frames, Shaped Seat, 4 . . . . 85.00
Chair Set, Biedermeier, Fruitwood, Outscrolled Backrest, Pierced Back Splat, 6 . . . . 7475.00
Chair Set, Brass & Mother-Of-Pearl Inlaid, Mask Crest, Upholstered Back, Seat, 4 . . . . . 1575.00
Chair Set, Brown Paint, Vase Back, Red Floral Design, Plank Seat, 6 . . . . 395.00
Chair Set, Burnt Wax Inlay, Cane Seat, 6 . . . . 1700.00
Chair Set, Cane Back & Seat, Roman Key Inlays, England, 6 . . . . 1700.00
Chair Set, Captain's, Elm, England, 4 . . . . 1955.00
Chair Set, Central Splat, Carved Crest Rail, China, 20th Century, 6 . . . . 575.00
Chair Set, Cherner, Black Lacquered Wood, Vinyl Seat & Back, 2 Armchairs, 6 . . . . 1100.00
Chair Set, Chippendale Style, Ribbon Splat, Leather Seat, 2 Armchairs, 8 . . . . 5747.00
Chair Set, Chippendale, Leather Seat, 2 Eagle Armchairs, 8 . . . . 4000.00
Chair Set, Chippendale, Mahogany, Acanthus Carved Crest Rails, 37 In., 8 . . . . 8250.00
Chair Set, Chippendale, Mahogany, Pierced Back Splats, Upholstered, 8 . . . . 9075.00
Chair Set, Chippendale, Shaped Crest Rail, Pierced Splat, England, 1780, 6 . . . . 8400.00
Chair Set, Classical, Faux Bois, Gilt Stencil, Cane Seat, Baltimore, 1835, 5 . . . . 2055.00
Chair Set, Classical, Mahogany, Carved, Slip Seats, c.1820, 34 In., 4 . . . . 2415.00
Chair Set, Continental Classical, Fruitwood, 6 . . . . 2640.00
Chair Set, Directoire Style, Parcel Gild & Ebonized, Crossed Arrow Back, 4 . . . . 230.00
Chair Set, Eames, Molded Plywood Seat & Back, Tubular Frame, 29 In., 4 . . . . 600.00
Chair Set, Elizabethan Revival, Heraldic Carved Backs, 19th Century, 6 . . . . 2905.00
Chair Set, Elizabethan Revival, Heraldic Designs, Paw Feet, 40 In., 6 . . . . 2640.00
Chair Set, Empire Style, Mahogany, Gilt Design, 3 . . . . 3220.00
Chair Set, Faux Bois, Caned Seat, New England, 4 . . . . 1295.00
Chair Set, Federal, Mahogany, 2 Armchairs, 8 . . . . 1840.00
Chair Set, Federal, Stenciled Crest Rail, Painted, Cane Seat, 1810, 3 . . . . 230.00
Chair Set, Fiddleback, Mahogany, c.1845, 6 . . . . 925.00
Chair Set, Floral Design On Crest, Yellow & Green Striping, Rabbit Ear Posts, 4 . . . . . . 770.00
Chair Set, G. Stickley, Ladder Back, Skinned Finish, 36 1/2 In., 2 Armchairs, 6 . . . . 1760.00
Chair Set, G. Stickley, Ladder Back, Skinned Finish, Tacked-On Leather Seat 770.00
Chair Set, G. Stickley, No. 349 1/2, Ladder Back, Black Finish, Leather Seat, 6 . . . . 1100.00
Chair Set, G. Stickley, No. 804, Drop Seat, Decal, c.1910, 4 . . . . 1530.00
Chair Set, G. Stickley, No. 1297, 4 Slats, 4 . . . . 2415.00
Chair Set, George II Style, Mahogany, 40 In., 2 Armchairs, 6 . . . . 3450.00
Chair Set, George III Style, Mahogany, 38 In., 2 Armchairs, 8 . . . . 8050.00
Chair Set, George III Style, Mahogany, Interlaced Splats, 2 Armchairs, 6 . . . . 1090.00
Chair Set, George III Style, Upholstered, 37 In., 2 Armchairs, 8 . . . . 4200.00
Chair Set, George III, Fruitwood, Serpentine Crest, Slip Seat, 12 . . . . 4600.00
Chair Set, George III, Mahogany, Floral Carved Legs, Upholstered, 8 . . . . 2300.00
Chair Set, George III, Mahogany, Needlepoint Back & Seat, Cabriole Legs, 4 . . . . 6670.00
Chair Set, George III, Mahogany, Pierced Vasiform, Crewelwork Slip Seat, 6 . . . . 2900.00
Chair Set, George III, Mahogany, Ribbon Pierced Splat, Marlborough Legs, 8 . . . . 4600.00
Chair Set, George III, Mahogany, Satinwood, Reeded Legs, Upholstered Seat, 6 . . . . 1695.00
Chair Set, Georgian, Yew, 2 Armchairs, 6 . . . . 2645.00
Chair Set, Golden Oak, Refinished, Laminated Curved Back, 37 In., 4 . . . . 155.00
Chair Set, Gothic Revival, Mahogany, Upholstered Seat, c.1846, 34 In., 6 . . . . 4600.00
Chair Set, Gothic, Rush Seat, 19th Century, England, Arms, 6 . . . . 2035.00
Chair Set, Grain Painted, Painted Fruits On Crest Rail, Lyre Splat, Plank Seat, 4 . . . . . . 575.00
Chair Set, Green Paint, Yellow Striping, Gold Stenciled Floral, Plank Seat, 6 . . . . 3650.00
Chair Set, H. Miller, Gray Fiberglass, Metal Swag Leg Base, Arms, 35 In., 4 . . . . 3740.00
Chair Set, Half Spindle Back, Floral, Yellow & Black Striping, Plank Seat, 33 In., 6 . . . . 495.00
Chair Set, Hans Wegner, Wishbone Slat, Rush Seat, Dowel Legs, Arms, 6 . . . . 2750.00
Chair Set, Hardwood, Mahogany Finish, Saber Leg, Upholstered Slip Seats, 6 . . . . 330.00
Chair Set, Hepplewhite Style, Mahogany, Shield Back, Upholstered Seat, 2 Armchairs, 8 3450.00
Chair Set, Hepplewhite Style, Mahogany, Shield Back, Carved Splats, 2 Armchairs, 6 . . . . 455.00
Chair Set, Herman Miller, Stacking, Plastic, Green, Yellow & Dark Blue, 1960, 6 . . . . . . 1050.00
Chair Set, Howell, Smoked Lucite Back, 4 Prong, Swivel Base, 4 . . . . 120.00
Chair Set, Italian Rococo Style, Walnut, 4 . . . . 460.00
Chair Set, Jacobean Style, Carved, Escutcheon Crests, Lion's Head Ears, 5 . . . . 450.00
Chair Set, L. & J.G. Stickley, Ladder Back, 3 Horizontal Back Slats, 7 . . . . 3520.00
Chair Set, L. & J.G. Stickley, No. 804, Drop Seat, Decal, c.1910, 6 . . . . 1570.00
Chair Set, Ladder Back, Rush Seat, Turned Legs, Stretcher, American, 6 . . . . 520.00
Chair Set, Laminated Rosewood, Needlework Upholstery, c.1850, 2 Armchairs, 8 . . . . . . 6325.00
Chair Set, Late Classical, Mahogany, No Seat, Saber Legs, 1830, 6 . . . . 4355.00

Chair Set, Louis XIV, Bleached Walnut, Caned Back, Upholstered Brocade Seat, 4 . . . . . 2045.00
Chair Set, Louis XV Style, Cane Back, Painted, 10 . . . . 2990.00
Chair Set, Louis XVI Style, Blue Paint, Oval Caned Back, Upholstered Seat, 4 . . . . 450.00
Chair Set, Louis XVI Style, White Paint, 10 . . . . 4315.00
Chair Set, Mahogany, Carved Flower Form Backs, 2 Host, 10 . . . . 517.00
Chair Set, Mahogany, Ebonized, Table Crest, Russia, 19th Century, Arms, 4 . . . . 9000.00
Chair Set, Mahogany, England, 19th Century, 2 Armchairs, 4 . . . . 1035.00
Chair Set, Mahogany, Saber Leg, Upholstered Seat, American, 1830, 11 . . . . 3145.00
Chair Set, Mahogany, Volute Carved Crest Rail & Splat, Saber Legs, c.1825, 4 . . . . 1200.00
Chair Set, Maple, Molded Crested Splats, Plank Seat, 19th Century, 4 . . . . 260.00
Chair Set, Maple, Projecting Stiles, 3 Backrests, Polychrome Design, c.1820, 8 . . . . 2300.00
Chair Set, Maple, Shaped Back Scrolled Rail, Slat Back, Caned Seat, 4 . . . . 978.00
Chair Set, Neoclassical, Fruitwood, 35 In., 6 . . . . 2640.00
Chair Set, Oak & Walnut, Arched Upholstered Backrest, Tapestry Upholstered, 4 . . . . . . 4315.00
Chair Set, Oak, Cane Seat, Turned Legs, Molded & Pierced Back, 6 . . . . 287.00
Chair Set, Oak, Pressed Back, Acanthus Leaf Design, Case Seats, 6 . . . . 415.00
Chair Set, Oak, T-Back, 6 . . . . 550.00
Chair Set, Pine, Carved Black Forest Scene, Cartouche Back, 2 Armchairs, 4 . . . . 6440.00
Chair Set, Provincial, Fruitwood, Ladder Back, Rush Seat, American, 8 . . . . 460.00
Chair Set, Queen Anne Style, Walnut, Dark Varnish, Upholstered Slip Seat, 6 . . . . 530.00
Chair Set, Queen Anne, Fruitwood, 2 Armchairs, 6 . . . . 690.00
Chair Set, Queen Anne, Leather Seat, Cabriole Legs, 19th Century, 2 Armchairs, 8 . . . . . 4400.00
Chair Set, Queen Anne, Oak, Vase Back, Leather, 19th Century, 8 . . . . 4840.00
Chair Set, Queen Anne, Rush Seat, 4 . . . . 5600.00
Chair Set, Queen Anne, Yoke Crest, Rush Seat, c.1800, 4 . . . . 705.00
Chair Set, Red & Black Grained, New Cane Seat, 6 . . . . 1500.00
Chair Set, Regency, Horizontal Splat, Brass Inlay, Drop Seats, 33 In., 4 . . . . 1150.00
Chair Set, Regency, Tablet Back, Horizontal Splats, 1840s, 33 In., 4 . . . . 635.00
Chair Set, Renaissance Revival, Walnut, Carved, Italy, 19th Century, 6 . . . . 1100.00
Chair Set, Rococo, Gesso, Parcel Gilt, Pale Green Ground, Continental, 4 . . . . 1570.00
Chair Set, Rococo, Walnut, Marquetry, Continental, Mid-19th Century, 6 . . . . 3385.00
Chair Set, Rosewood, Carved Foliate Crest, Upholstered Back & Seat, 4 . . . . 977.00
Chair Set, Rosewood, Rose Carved, 6 . . . . 950.00
Chair Set, Rosewood, Satinwood Inlay, Carved & Pierced Splat, 1830s, 4 . . . . 3025.00
Chair Set, Shaped Crest Rail, Lyre Splat, Cane Seat, Painted Design, c.1840, 6 . . . . 978.00
Chair Set, Sheraton, Pillow Back, Eagle Head On Back Cross Splat, c.1817, 4 . . . . 1895.00
Chair Set, Sheraton, Red & Black Grained, Stenciled, Painted Rush Seat, 4 . . . . 240.00
Chair Set, Shield Back, Prince Of Wales Plume Over Upholstered Seat, 10 . . . . 1300.00
Chair Set, Stencil, Freehand Foliage, Worn Paint, Plank Seat, Penna., 4 . . . . 250.00
Chair Set, T-Back, Oak, 6 . . . . 425.00
Chair Set, Victorian, Mother-Of-Pearl Inlay, Carved Mask Crest, Arms, 1850s, 4 . . . . . . 1575.00
Chair Set, Walnut, Balloon Back, Damask, c.1880, 33 In., 4 . . . . 316.00
Chair Set, Walnut, Balloon Back, Overall Carved Designs, 6 . . . . 460.00
Chair Set, Walnut, Embossed Back & Seats, Explorers Of Western Hemisphere, 8 . . . . . 1570.00
Chair Set, William IV, Mahogany, 1 Armchair, 7 . . . . 1840.00
Chair Set, Windsor, Bow Back, Added Wire Braces, Turned Legs, Arms, 6 . . . . 825.00
Chair Set, Windsor, Bow Back, Black Paint, 19th Century, 37 In., 6 . . . . 8050.00
Chair Set, Windsor, Bow Back, c.1810, 6 . . . . 2750.00
Chair Set, Windsor, Dark Brown, Bamboo, Step-Down Crest, 2 Armchairs, 8 . . . . 925.00
Chair Set, Windsor, Grain Painted, Shaped Crest Rail, 5 Bowed Spindles, 1810, 5 . . . . . . 750.00
Chair Set, Windsor, Kitchen, Worn Brown Finish, 4 Spindles, Plank Seat, 4 . . . . 155.00
Chair Set, Windsor, Old Red Paint, 4 Spindles, Half Back, Plank, 2 In., 4 . . . . 230.00
Chair Set, Windsor, Painted Decorated Back, Yellow Paint, 1820-1830, 6 . . . . 2850.00
Chair Set, Windsor, Rod Back, Black Paint, Massachusetts, c.1820, 34 1/2 In., 6 . . . . 3105.00
Chair Set, Windsor, Rod Back, Mahogany, Plank Seat, 38 1/2 In., 6 . . . . 3450.00
Chair Set, Windsor, Rod Back, New England, 19th Century, 34 In., 6 . . . . 3450.00
Chair Set, Winged Crest, Brown, Yellow & White Striped, Penna., 1 Rocker, 7 . . . . 500.00
Chair-Table, Cherry, Molded Edge, Late 19th Century, 30 1/2 In. 990.00
Chair-Table, Green-Gray Paint Over Black, 2-Board Top, 35 1/2 x 36 1/2 In. 2860.00
Chair-Table, Jacobean, Oak 520.00
Chair-Table, Red Paint, 4-Board Top, Stretcher Base, New England 3520.00
Chaise Longue, Adirondack Style, Adjustable Back Wheeled, Splint Seat & Back 1380.00
Chaise Longue, Beige Wool Seat, Back, 1952, 33 x 27 x 29 In. 770.00

Chaise Longue, Classical, Vase-Form Splats, Saber Legs, Early 19th Century 420.00
Chaise Longue, Eames, Leather Pillows, Enameled Aluminum Legs, 76 In. 2090.00
Chaise Longue, Empire, Mahogany, Ormolu Mounted, Parcel Gilt, 32 In. 1955.00
Chaise Longue, Inset Basket Weave Leather, Scrolled Back, Animal Legs, 41 In., Pr. ... 5465.00
Chaise Longue, Louis XV, Beechwood, Serpentine Top, 72 In. 2300.00
Chaise Longue, Louis XV, Beechwood, Upholstered, 39 x 79 In. 1035.00
Chaise Longue, Louis XVI, Egg & Dart, Blue, Gray Gilt, 19th Century 1250.00
Chaise Longue, Mahogany, Art Deco, Reeded Legs, 1925, 52 In. 4025.00
Chaise Longue, Provincial, Louis XV, Walnut 2300.00
Chaise Longue, Richard Schultz, Vinyl Mesh Seat, White Aluminum Frame 495.00
Chaise Longue, Wicker, Late 19th Century 725.00
Chest, American Aesthetic, G. Vollmer, Mahogany, Parcel Gilt, 63 x 38 In. 1350.00
Chest, Amish, 3 Drawers, Porcelain Pulls, 1870, Miniature 695.00
Chest, Bachelor's, Baker Co., Mahogany, Flip Top, 4 Long Drawers, 29 x 13 x 31 In. ... 920.00
Chest, Bachelor's, George II, Mahogany, 4 Drawers, Bail Pulls, 31 x 34 In. 1815.00
Chest, Bachelor's, George II, Mahogany, 4 Graduated Drawers, Bail Pulls, 31 In. 1940.00
Chest, Bachelor's, George III, Mahogany, 4 Beaded Drawers, 35 In. 2060.00
Chest, Baker Co., Mahogany, 4 Graduated & 2 Silver Drawers, 24 x 15 In. 1150.00
Chest, Biedermeier, 3 Drawers, 1815-1830 .... 2000.00
Chest, Biedermeier, Bowfront, Walnut, 2 Drawers, Saber Legs, Miniature 425.00
Chest, Biedermeier, Cherry, 5 Drawers, Bracket Feet, 63 In. 1740.00
Chest, Biedermeier, Fruitwood, Long Overhanging Frieze Drawer, 33 x 44 In. 1700.00
Chest, Biedermeier, Mahogany, Bone Inlay, Bracket Supports, 34 In. 1600.00
Chest, Biedermeier, Mahogany, Top Narrow Drawer, 2 Deep Drawers, 37 In. 920.00
Chest, Birch, Red Paint, 4 Drawers, Brass Pulls, 19th Century, 37 1/2 x 38 In. 3450.00
Chest, Bird's-Eye Maple & Pine, Overhanging Drawer Over 3 Drawers, 1830 .... 1150.00
Chest, Blanket, Blue Paint, Mid-19th Century 525.00
Chest, Blanket, Cherry, Maple Colored Finish, Lid On Till, Ohio, 24 3/4 In. 250.00
Chest, Blanket, Chippendale, Walnut, 2 Overlapping Drawers, Penna., 50 x 24 In. 715.00
Chest, Blanket, Curly Maple, Iron Strap Hinges, 47 x 18 x 25 In. 550.00
Chest, Blanket, Drop Front, Carved Grapevine Center, Acanthus Scrolling, 64 1/2 In. ... 150.00
Chest, Blanket, Grain Painted, Red & Brown, Backsplash, Convex Drawers, 50 In. 900.00
Chest, Blanket, Grain Painted, Red, Black, Cutout Feet, 24 In. 330.00
Chest, Blanket, Mahogany Panel, Interior Till, 1 Drawer, 25 In. 245.00
Chest, Blanket, Mahogany, Carved, 3 Drawers, Ball & Claw Feet 2300.00
Chest, Blanket, Mahogany, Domed Top, Drawer, French Feet, c.1790, 11 x 14 In. 1250.00
Chest, Blanket, Maple, Bootjack Ends, 2 Drawers, E. Swan, 36 x 37 In. 3740.00
Chest, Blanket, Multicolored, 2 Pinwheels On Hinged Top, c.1790, 43 In. 5750.00
Chest, Blanket, Oak, Pine, Base Drawer, 1680-1700, 30 x 44 x 19 In. 6675.00
Chest, Blanket, Painted, Nova Scotia, Mid-19th Century 300.00
Chest, Blanket, Pine, Alligatored Red Stain, Interior Till, Ball Feet 385.00
Chest, Blanket, Pine, Black Paint, Ball Feet, Moldings, 1730-1750, 41 x 17 In. 4025.00
Chest, Blanket, Pine, Brown Grained, 3 Overlapping Drawers, Till, 49 x 23 In. 1430.00
Chest, Blanket, Pine, Grain Painted, Mustard & Black, c.1800, 42 x 42 x 18 In. 1150.00
Chest, Blanket, Pine, Hinged Top, Till, Landscape Design, Iron Handles, 42 1/2 In. 1050.00
Chest, Blanket, Pine, Lidded Till In Storage Cavity, Mass., 32 In. 635.00
Chest, Blanket, Pine, Poplar, Brown, Star In Yellow Panels, 32 x 16 x 22 In. 1700.00
Chest, Blanket, Pine, Red Paint, 19th Century, 45 x 42 x 18 3/4 In. 1955.00
Chest, Blanket, Pine, Red Paint, 2 Drawers, Cutout Feet, 37 x 38 In. 520.00
Chest, Blanket, Pine, Red, Blue Green Paint, New England, 24 1/2 In. 580.00
Chest, Blanket, Pine, Vinegar Graining, Lock & Key, Walnut Till, 27 1/2 x 49 In. 1450.00
Chest, Blanket, Pine, Yellow Paint, Brown Graining, Till, 44 x 22 x 24 In. 330.00
Chest, Blanket, Poplar, Basket Of Fruit Front, Red Paint, Gold Stenciling, 41 In. 3850.00
Chest, Blanket, Poplar, Brown Grained, Tulip Design, Green, Red, 22 In. 14300.00
Chest, Blanket, Poplar, Brown Grained, Yellow Ground, 38 x 19 x 24 In. 385.00
Chest, Blanket, Poplar, Cleaned To Original Paint, Reserves, Penna., 49 x 22 In. 2530.00
Chest, Blanket, Poplar, Dark Finish, Turned Legs, 20 In. 195.00
Chest, Blanket, Poplar, Dovetailed, Bracket Feet, Till With Lid, 44 x 19 x 19 In. 385.00
Chest, Blanket, Poplar, Imitation Graining Of Exotic Wood, Lid On Till, 37 1/2 In. 2200.00
Chest, Blanket, Poplar, Old Brown Finish, Till With Lid, Dovetailed, 44 x 22 x 26 In. ... 245.00
Chest, Blanket, Poplar, Red Grained, Yellow Ground, Paneled, 43 x 19 x 25 In. 165.00
Chest, Blanket, Poplar, Worn Blue Paint, Refinished Top, Dovetailed, 41 In. 220.00
Chest, Blanket, Quartersawn Oak, Dark, Handles, Escutcheon, Continental, 50 In. 415.00

Furniture, Chest, Blanket,
Scrolled Skirt

Furniture, Chest, Carved Cowboy &
Friend, 1935, 49 x 34 In.

Chest, Blanket, Queen Anne Hardware, Drawer, Woodstock, Vt. 1100.00
Chest, Blanket, Scrolled Skirt ....*Illus* 525.00
Chest, Blanket, Shaker, Red, H.B. Bear Stenciled On Back 775.00
Chest, Blanket, Smoke Design, Paper Label Of Moses Marchall, Ipswich 6050.00
Chest, Blanket, Sponged Design, Red & Black, Central Medallion, Corner Fans 450.00
Chest, Blanket, Tudor, Oak 1035.00
Chest, Blanket, Walnut, 2-Drawer Base, Tall Bracket Feet 900.00
Chest, Blanket, Walnut, Brown Grained, White Ground, 49 x 21 x 28 In. 440.00
Chest, Blanket, Walnut, Dovetailed Case, Drawers, Bear Trap Lock, Key, 28 In. 1650.00
Chest, Blanket, Walnut, Dovetailed Drawer, 28 x 11 x 13 In. 1100.00
Chest, Blanket, Walnut, End, Front Panels, 24 3/4 In. 415.00
Chest, Blanket, William & Mary, 2 Drawers Base, Penna., 24 x 27 x 50 In. 1200.00
Chest, Blanket, William & Mary, Original Red Paint, Trumpet & Ball Feet 7500.00
Chest, Bowfront, Mahogany, Satinwood Line, 2 Drawers, England, 37 1/2 In. 865.00
Chest, Burl Veneer, Locking Devise On Right, 6 Drawers, Ball Drop Pulls 1155.00
Chest, Campaign, Mahogany, Label From Bombay To London, Via Indus 2640.00
Chest, Camphorwood, Leather, Brass Bound, China, 19th Century, 19 1/2 x 42 In. 230.00
Chest, Carved Cowboy & Friend, 1935, 49 x 34 In. ....*Illus* 8050.00
Chest, Cedar, Bracket Base, 20th Century 135.00
Chest, Cedar, Square Nail Construction, Feet, Early American, 17 x 24 In. 270.00
Chest, Charles II, Oak, 3 Drawers, Brass Foliate, Ring Pulls, 34 In. 5465.00
Chest, Charles II, Oak, 4 Long Drawers, Molded Fronts, Bun Feet, 36 x 37 In. 860.00
Chest, Charles II, Oak, Molded Drawers, Bun Feet, 37 x 23 In. 3100.00
Chest, Charles II, Walnut, Oak, 4 Paneled Drawers, Straight Feet, 35 In. 6325.00
Chest, Cherry, 4 Dovetailed Drawers, 41 x 19 x 42 In. 165.00
Chest, Cherry, 4 Drawers, Lock, Turned Pillars 1100.00
Chest, Cherry, 4 Graduated Drawers, Ogee Bracket Feet, 37 In. 1380.00
Chest, Cherry, Half-Turn Columns, 2 Drawers, Floret Pulls, 1840, 10 In. 850.00
Chest, Cherry, Hinged Top, 2 Interior Drawers & Compartments, 13 x 25 x 13 In. 345.00
Chest, Cherry, Swell Front, Chestnut Banding, 4 Graduated Drawers, c.1800, 43 In. 5800.00
Chest, Chinese Export, Camphorwood, Brass Bound, 17 1/2 x 39 1/4 In. 575.00
Chest, Chippendale, 4 Drawers, Dovetailed, Reeded Columns, Ogee Feet 6050.00
Chest, Chippendale, Birch, Reverse Serpentine Front, c.1780, 34 In. 6900.00
Chest, Chippendale, Birch, Serpentine Front, 4 Graduated Drawers, 35 In. 4600.00
Chest, Chippendale, Block Front, Maple, 4 Graduated Drawers, 31 In. 2550.00
Chest, Chippendale, Cherry, 18th Century, New England, 37 In. 3000.00
Chest, Chippendale, Cherry, 4 Drawers, New England, 34 1/2 In. 1955.00
Chest, Chippendale, Cherry, 4 Graduated Drawers, Replaced Brasses, 39 x 41 In. 2200.00
Chest, Chippendale, Cherry, 5 Dovetailed Drawers, Cornice, Refinished, 36 x 50 In. 2640.00
Chest, Chippendale, Cherry, Pine, 4 Dovetailed Drawers, Bracket Feet, 42 In. 525.00

Chest, Chippendale, Cherry, Serpentine Front, Bracket Feet, 31 In. 3225.00
Chest, Chippendale, Curly Maple, 8 Dovetailed Drawers, 58 In. 7700.00
Chest, Chippendale, Curly Walnut, Dovetailed Case, 9 Overlapping Drawers, 61 In. 9350.00
Chest, Chippendale, Mahogany, 4 Dovetailed Drawers, 33 1/4 In. 3300.00
Chest, Chippendale, Mahogany, 4 Drawers, 18th Century, 33 1/2 x 38 In. 8050.00
Chest, Chippendale, Mahogany, 4 Drawers, Reverse-Serpentine, 1760, 32 x 37 In. 8050.00
Chest, Chippendale, Mahogany, 4 Graduated Drawers, Ogee Feet, 33 In. 1035.00
Chest, Chippendale, Mahogany, 5 Drawers, Chamfered Fluted Columns, 49 In. 315.00
Chest, Chippendale, Mahogany, Oxbow, 4 Graduated Drawers, 30 In. 9775.00
Chest, Chippendale, Pine, 4 Drawers, Western Mass., 44 1/2 In. 2100.00
Chest, Chippendale, Tiger Maple, Flame Maple, Bracket Base, 1780, 42 In. 8625.00
Chest, Chippendale, Walnut, 3 Small Over 5 Graduated Drawers, Penna., 67 In. 5775.00
Chest, Chippendale, Walnut, 4 Graduated Drawers, Brasses, Penna., 31 x 38 In. 3740.00
Chest, Chippendale, Walnut, Fluted Quarter Columns, Ogee Feet, 36 In. 5500.00
Chest, Classical, Gentleman's, Mirror, Philadelphia, 1840 . . . . 845.00
Chest, Classical, Mahogany, Brass Inlay, Scroll Supports, Paw Feet, 68 In. 1650.00
Chest, Classical, Mahogany, Marble Top, Brass Feet, 19th Century, 70 x 44 In. 7560.00
Chest, Classical, Mahogany, Ogee Frieze Drawer, Foliated Support, 50 In. 495.00
Chest, Classical, Mahogany, Pineapple Carved Columns, Paw Feet, 51 In. 450.00
Chest, Classical, Mahogany, Rosewood, Brass Inlay, Paw Feet, 45 x 38 In. 1090.00
Chest, Classical, Walnut, 4 Graduated Drawers, Reeded Panels, 40 1/2 In. 990.00
Chest, Continental, Green, 4 Serpentine Drawers, Maiden Foliate Border, 59 In. 770.00
Chest, Demilune, Mahogany, Concave Center Door, Tapered Legs, 1805, 35 In. 1850.00
Chest, Directoire Style, Marble Top, 2 Short Over 3 Long Drawers, Fluted Posts, 33 In. . . 250.00
Chest, Dower, Chippendale, Till, 3 Drawers, 18th Century, 23 x 53 In. 1495.00
Chest, Dower, Interior Secret Drawer, 18th Century, 54 x 24 1/2 In. 700.00
Chest, Dower, Parcel Gilt, Sarcophagus, Italy, 19th Century, 71 In. . . . . *Illus* 6325.00
Chest, Dower, Pine, Traces Of Green Paint, Late 18th Century, 48 5/8 In. 1725.00
Chest, Eames, Birch Veneer, 3 Drawers, Enameled Sides, 1950, 33 x 24 In. 2640.00
Chest, Eames, Birch, Iron, 1950, 35 x 24 x 16 In. . . . . *Illus* 2640.00
Chest, Edward Wormley, Dark Brier Finish, 3 Light Walnut Drawers, 30 x 35 In. 1100.00
Chest, Edward Wormley, Walnut, 3 Drawer, 30 x 34 x 18 In. 880.00
Chest, Empire, Backsplash With 2 Drawers, Carved . . . . *Illus* 660.00
Chest, Empire, Cherry, 4 Dovetailed Drawers, Castors, Refinished, 40 x 20 x 48 In. 745.00
Chest, Empire, Cherry, 4 Drawers, Cock-Beaded, Refinished, 40 x 45 In. 825.00
Chest, Empire, Cherry, 4 Drawers, Scrolled Feet, S Pilasters, Refinished, 49 In. 360.00
Chest, Empire, Cherry, 4 Tiger Maple Drawer Fronts, Pineapple Columns 450.00
Chest, Empire, Cherry, 5 Dovetailed Drawers, Half Columns, 44 3/4 x 44 In. 525.00
Chest, Empire, Cherry, Bird's-Eye Maple Facade, Carved Walnut Pulls, 42 x 46 In. 1265.00
Chest, Empire, Cherry, Bird's-Eye Veneer, 2 Over 3 Drawers, Crest, 22 x 52 In. 445.00
Chest, Empire, Cherry, Mahogany, 5 Dovetailed Drawers, 39 x 41 In. 360.00
Chest, Empire, Cherry, Turned Feet, 4 Dovetailed Drawers, 43 In. 495.00
Chest, Empire, Cherry, Veneer Facade, Scrolled Feet, 47 1/2 In. 275.00
Chest, Empire, Gothic, Mahogany Veneer, 4 Drawers, Adjustable Mirror, 77 In. 770.00

Furniture, Chest, Dower, Parcel Gilt, Sarcophagus, Italy,
19th Century, 71 In.

Furniture, Chest, Empire, Backsplash
With 2 Drawers, Carved

Chest, Empire, Grain Painted, Green, Yellow Trim, 3 Drawers, 45 In. 10925.00
Chest, Empire, Mahogany Figured Veneer, Mirror, 4 Drawers, 43 & 17 In., 2 Piece 250.00
Chest, Empire, Mahogany Flame Grain, Cherry & Maple, 4 Drawers, 40 1/2 In. 385.00
Chest, Empire, Mahogany, Pomfret, Vt., 51 x 53 In. 2100.00
Chest, Empire, Step Back, Mahogany Flame Veneer, Maple Trim, 4 Drawers, 60 In. 250.00
Chest, Federal, Birch & Maple, 4 Graduated Drawers, c.1800, 38 1/2 In. 2050.00
Chest, Federal, Birch, 2 Drawers, New England, 18th Century, 55 In. 2185.00
Chest, Federal, Bowfront, Mahogany Inlay, 4 Graduated Drawers, c.1800, 34 In. 2590.00
Chest, Federal, Bowfront, Mahogany, 3 Drawers, New York, 35 x 35 x 18 In. 1200.00
Chest, Federal, Bowfront, Mahogany, 4 Graduated Drawers, Turned Legs, 42 In. 6900.00
Chest, Federal, Cherry, Cock-Beaded Drawers, 1800, 37 In. 1500.00
Chest, Federal, Mahogany Veneer, 2 Short Over 3 Long Drawers, Brass Bail Pulls 670.00
Chest, Federal, Mahogany Veneer, Cherry, McConnellsburg, 1830, 9 x 6 x 7 In. 750.00
Chest, Federal, Mahogany, 2 Short Over 3 Drawers, Inlaid, 1790, 52 x 42 In. 3000.00
Chest, Federal, Mahogany, 4 Graduated Line Inlaid Drawers, 1840s 800.00
Chest, Federal, Walnut, Cornice, Reeded Sides, 5 Graduated Drawers, 66 In. 9350.00
Chest, Federal, Walnut, Inlaid, 2 Short Over 3 Long Drawers, 1790-1820, 33 In. 4235.00
Chest, Federal, Walnut, Molded Cornice, Graduated Drawers, Inlaid Sides, c.1800 . . . . . . 9350.00
Chest, French Provincial, Oak, Carved, 18th Century, 29 x 43 1/2 x 24 In. 1150.00
Chest, George I, Walnut, 2 Drawers, Bracket Feet, 15 1/2 In. 6325.00
Chest, George II, Mahogany, 2 Short Over 3 Long Drawers, 19th Century, 31 In. 1325.00
Chest, George II, Mahogany, Ogee Cornice, 6 Graduated Drawers, 59 In. 910.00
Chest, George II, Walnut, Burl Walnut Veneer, 3 Drawers, Bracket Feet, 37 x 44 In. 4600.00
Chest, George III, Chinoiserie, Parcel-Gilt Dome Top, 13 x 42 x 15 In. 750.00
Chest, George III, Mahogany Inlay, Serpentine, 30 In. 3740.00
Chest, George III, Mahogany, 3 Deep Drawers, Ivory Escutcheons, 38 In. 1155.00
Chest, George III, Mahogany, 3 Drawers, Bracket Feet, 20 1/2 In. 8050.00
Chest, George III, Mahogany, 3 Graduated Drawers, 43 In. 1450.00
Chest, George III, Mahogany, Bowfront, 2 Over 3 Drawers, 41 x 40 x 19 In. 865.00
Chest, George III, Mahogany, Drawer, Brass Castors, 19 x 16 x 17 In. 1210.00
Chest, George III, Mahogany, Satinwood Shell Inlay, Bracket Feet, 36 1/2 In. 1695.00
Chest, George III, Mahogany, Serpentine, 29 In. 1725.00
Chest, George III, Walnut, Herringbone Inlay, 5 Drawers, 18th Century, 37 In. 5750.00
Chest, Georgian, Bowfront, 2 Short Over 3 Long Drawers, England, 41 x 42 In. 1850.00
Chest, Georgian, Figured Walnut, 2 Short Over 3 Long Drawers, 34 x 37 In. 5800.00
Chest, Georgian, Mahogany, 2 Short Over 3 Long Drawers, 39 In. 775.00
Chest, Georgian, Mahogany, 2 Short Over 3 Long Drawers, Ogee Bracket Feet, 36 In. . . . 920.00
Chest, Georgian, Mahogany, Miniature 520.00
Chest, Georgian, Mahogany, Swell Front, Checkerboard, 4 Drawers, 1800, 33 In. 3145.00
Chest, Georgian, Oak, Molded Cornice, 3 Drawers, 69 1/2 In. 6325.00
Chest, Georgian, Walnut, 3 Short Over 3 Long Drawers, 19th Century, 39 1/4 In. 2550.00
Chest, Gray Paint Over Green, Dovetailed Construction, Feet, 1780s, 14 x 24 In. 975.00
Chest, Hepplewhite, 3 Over 3 Drawers, Reeded Quarter Columns, 39 x 23 x 39 In. 1325.00
Chest, Hepplewhite, 4 Drawers, Line Inlay, 38 1/2 x 41 x 22 In. 2860.00
Chest, Hepplewhite, 4 Graduated Drawers, Inlaid, 41 x 21 x 42 In. 2100.00
Chest, Hepplewhite, Bowfront, 4 Drawers, French Feet, 1800, 57 x 41 In. 1760.00
Chest, Hepplewhite, Bowfront, Cherry, Maple Veneer, 4 Drawers, 22 x 42 x 36 In. 1815.00
Chest, Hepplewhite, Cherry, 4 Beaded Graduated Drawers, French Feet, 42 In. 880.00
Chest, Hepplewhite, Mahogany, 2 Over 3 Graduated Drawers, 10 x 11 x 5 In. 400.00
Chest, Hepplewhite, Mahogany, 3 Drawers, 12 In. 1610.00
Chest, Hepplewhite, Mahogany, Serpentine Front, 5 Drawers, 19th Century 3000.00
Chest, Hepplewhite, Mahogany, Serpentine, 4 Dovetailed Drawers, 36 In. 3200.00
Chest, Hepplewhite, Maple, 4 Dovetailed Drawers, Scalloped Apron, 45 In. 4200.00
Chest, Hepplewhite, Walnut, 4 Dovetailed Drawers, French Feet, 27 1/4 In. 3575.00
Chest, Herman Miller, Rosewood, 4 Small Over 6 Large Drawers, 1956, 33 x 67 In. 3960.00
Chest, Heywood-Wakefield, Sculptura Birch, 4 Drawers, Flush Top, 40 x 38 In. 825.00
Chest, Immigrants, Mercer Co., Pennsylvania, Iron Strap Hinges, 3 Locks, 44 In. 115.00
Chest, Iron Bands, Punched Out Swastikas, Japan, 1800s, 34 x 30 In. 2500.00
Chest, Jacobean, Oak, 5 Dovetailed Drawers, Turned Bun Feet, 47 In. 3300.00
Chest, Jacobean, Oak, Stylized Leaves, 28 x 45 1/2 x 20 In. 575.00
Chest, Liquor, Captain's, Grain Painted, Fitted Interior, Bottles, England, 12 x 17 In. 488.00
Chest, Louis Phillipe, Walnut, Top Drawer Over 3 Graduated Drawers, 35 In. 747.00
Chest, Mahogany Veneer, Mahogany, Serpentine, Leather Top, 4 Drawers 275.00

Chest, Mahogany, 2 Cock-Beaded Drawers Over 3 Graduated Drawers, 44 In. 978.00
Chest, Mahogany, 2 Short, 1 Deep & 3 Graduated Long Drawers, c.1815, 43 In. 805.00
Chest, Mahogany, 3 Small Over 4 Long Drawers, Glass Pulls, Paw Feet, c.1830 . . . .   1210.00
Chest, Mahogany, 4 Cock-Beaded Graduated Drawers, Brass Pulls, 35 1/2 x 46 In. 635.00
Chest, Mahogany, 5 Graduated Drawers, Shell Inlay, Line Work, c.1850, 18 x 13 In. 3500.00
Chest, Mahogany, Blind Fretwork, 7 Drawers, Slide, 64 In. 1815.00
Chest, Mahogany, Cross Banded Border Top, 4 Graduated Drawers, 31 1/2 In. 925.00
Chest, Mahogany, Frieze With 6 Long Drawers, Foliate Marquetry, 55 In. 1955.00
Chest, Mahogany, Molded Cornice, 3 Drawers, 71 x 39 In. 4140.00
Chest, Mahogany, Serpentine, 2 Half-Width Drawers, 3 Full Drawers, Slide, 32 In. 4025.00
Chest, Maple Veneer & Maple, Drawers, Attached Mirror, Bowfront 165.00
Chest, Maple, 4 Drawers, Refinished, 37 3/4 In. 2425.00
Chest, Maple, Open Till, Shaped Sides, 6-Board, 18th Century, 27 x 47 x 19 In. 460.00
Chest, Maple, Painted, Bracket Feet, Graduated Drawers, 18th Century, 32 x 37 In. 3335.00
Chest, Mirror, Champagne Finish, 3 Drawers, Die Stamp Mark, 30 x 46 In. 467.00
Chest, Mother-Of-Pearl Inlay, Gadroon Bun Feet, Victorian, 13 In. 4315.00
Chest, Mule, Pine, 6-Board, 2 Faux & 2 Drawers, 40 x 18 x 37 In. 550.00
Chest, Mule, Queen Anne, Oak, Lift Top, 4 Faux Over 4 Long Drawers, 41 x 54 In. 3910.00
Chest, Mule, Queen Anne, Poplar, 2 Overlapping & 2 Faux Drawers, 43 In. 1540.00
Chest, Nelson, Herman Miller, Wooden Legs, 40 x 40 x 18 1/2 In. 415.00
Chest, New England, 4 Drawers, Red Paint, Ring Turned Legs, 41 1/2 In. 460.00
Chest, New England, Blue Over Blue Green Paint, 19th Century, 37 In. 6900.00
Chest, New England, Smoke Design, 6-Board, 1820, 27 x 47 In. . . . . *Illus*   3740.00
Chest, Oak, Chamfered Corners, Geometric, England, 90 1/4 In. 1935.00
Chest, Oak, Joined, Dated 1703, 27 x 47 In. 862.00
Chest, Oak, Paneled, Carved, Old Finish, Continental, 51 x 21 x 31 In. 495.00
Chest, On Frame, Walnut, 3 Long Drawers, Turned Legs 3300.00
Chest, Pine, 2 Drawers Over 4 Drawers, Mt. Pleasant, Canada, 1840 . . . .   1575.00
Chest, Pine, 3 Dovetailed Drawers, Apron, 42 x 21 x 35 In. 275.00
Chest, Pine, 4 Thumb-Molded Drawers, Dovetailed Feet, New England, 44 In. 520.00
Chest, Pine, Blue Sponge Over White, 6-Board, North Carolina 2530.00
Chest, Pine, Grain Painted, 6-Board, 1825-1840, 24 x 35 x 18 In. . . . . *Illus*   1035.00
Chest, Pine, Lift Top, Cutout Ends, Cotter Pin Hinges, Small 575.00
Chest, Pine, Painted, Cutout Ends, Tulip Border, 6-Board, 21 x 46 x 14 In. 3100.00

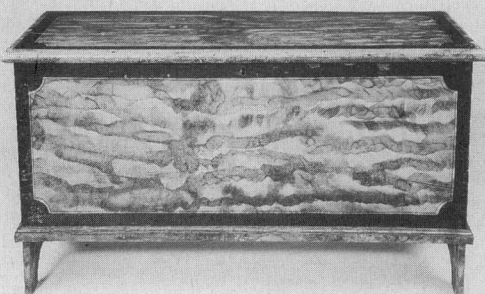

Left: Furniture, Chest,
New England,
Smoke Design, 6-Board,
1820, 27 x 47 In.

Right: Furniture, Chest,
Pine, Grain Painted, 6-Board,
1825-1840,
24 x 35 x 18 In.

Chest, Pine, Red Graining, Blue, 3 Overlapping Drawers, 45 x 48 In. 715.00
Chest, Pine, Red Paint, 3 Drawers, Hallowell, Me., 33 x 29 In. 900.00
Chest, Pine, Red Paint, Coastal Massachusetts, 1820, 26 1/2 In. 400.00
Chest, Poplar, Imitation Of Mahogany Graining, 4 Drawers, 46 In. 250.00
Chest, Pub, Mahogany, Crossbanded Top, Pullout Shelf Over 4 Drawers, 28 In. 1090.00
Chest, Queen Anne, Cherry, 4 Graduated Drawers, Pad Feet, 85 In. 8625.00
Chest, Queen Anne, Cherry, 5 Over 1 Long & 3 Short Drawers, 78 x 40 In. 6325.00
Chest, Queen Anne, Maple, New England, 18th Century 3220.00
Chest, Queen Anne, Pine, Dark Red Paint, 3 Dovetailed Drawers, 57 In. 7700.00
Chest, Red Paint, 2-Drawer Lift Top, 2 Base Drawers, 39 1/4 In. 885.00
Chest, Regency, Bowfront, Mahogany Veneer, 5 Dovetailed Drawers, 39 x 21 In. 415.00
Chest, Regency, Mahogany Inlay, 4 Graduated Drawers, 11 In. 2875.00
Chest, Regency, Mahogany, England, 1830 . . . . 600.00
Chest, Rococo, Walnut, Mahogany, Banded Borders, Bun Feet 4315.00
Chest, Rosewood Grained, 3 Drawers, Wishbone Mirror, Hankie Boxes, Victorian 275.00
Chest, Rosewood, 3 Drawers, Serpentine Front, Brass Pulls, Portugal, 35 In. 2875.00
Chest, Rosewood, Marble Top, Serpentine, 4 Drawers, 93 1/4 In. 1815.00
Chest, Rosewood, Mottled Gold Onyx Top, 3 Drawers, Kidney Shape, 34 1/4 In. 860.00
Chest, Sculptura, Champagne Finish, 4 Drawers, 39 x 38 x 19 In. 665.00
Chest, Semainier, Parquetry, Black Marble Top, 6 Drawers, Plinth Base, 59 In. 1980.00
Chest, Serpentine, 4 Drawers, Blind Fretwork, 19th Century, 34 In. 3630.00
Chest, Shaker, Red Stain, 5 Drawers, Breadboard Ends, Rectangular, 1820, 58 In. 27600.00
Chest, Sheraton, Cherry, 4 Dovetailed Drawers, Turned Feet, 45 In. 745.00
Chest, Sheraton, Cherry, Bowfront, Reeded Columns, 39 1/2 x 39 In. 2300.00
Chest, Sheraton, Cherry, Maple Veneer, Bowfront, 4 Drawers, 38 x 22 x 41 In. 1595.00
Chest, Sheraton, Cherry, Paneled Ends, 9 Drawers, Edge Beading, 66 3/4 In. 6600.00
Chest, Sheraton, Curly Maple, 3 Drawers Over 3 Graduated Drawers, Refinished 2530.00
Chest, Storage, Marine Scene, Farmyard Scene On Lid Interior 2590.00
Chest, Stuart, Walnut, Fruitwood, Ebonized Geometric Designs, 44 In. 8050.00
Chest, Swing Mirror, Ebony Handles, Coxwell Range, G. Russel, 1933, 36 In. 2070.00
Chest, Tailor's Counter, Shaker, Walnut Pulls, 6 Dovetailed Drawers 24150.00
Chest, Tiger Maple, 4 Drawers, Original Brasses 3900.00
Chest, Travel, Dome Top, Brass Tack Design, Wrought Iron Handles 55.00
Chest, Walnut, 3 Short Over 2 Short Drawers Over 4 Long Drawers, c.1780, 62 In. 6325.00
Chest, Walnut, 4 Drawers, Label, Fratelli Roiatiti/Milano, 42 x 50 In. 1150.00
Chest, Walnut, Drop Front, Lockside, 6 Drawers, Gallery Top, Victorian, 1870 . . . . 2750.00
Chest, Walnut, Hinged Top, 3 Graduated Drawers, Lemon Inlay, c.1790, 41 1/2 In. 6655.00
Chest, William & Mary, Maple, Pine, 3 Drawers, 1740, 36 x 33 x 19 In. 1380.00
Chest, William & Mary, Oak, 4 Drawers, 42 x 43 x 24 In., 2 Piece 1955.00
Chest, William & Mary, Walnut, 3 Drawers, Bun Feet, 18 In. 6325.00
Chest, William & Mary, Walnut, Oak, 3 Drawers, Bun Feet, 35 1/2 In. 7475.00
Chest-On-Chest, Charles II, Oak, 2 Long Drawers, Ivory Overlay Panel, 48 In. 3355.00
Chest-On-Chest, Cherry, 4 Base Drawers, 4 Drawers Under Top, Fan Carving, 84 In. . . . 3740.00
Chest-On-Chest, George III, Mahogany, 2 Short Over 6 Long Drawers, 1785 . . . . 6040.00
Chest-On-Chest, Georgian, Mahogany & Veneer, Inlaid Bracket Base, c.1790 . . . . 6850.00
Chest-On-Frame, Cedar, Rectangular Hinged Top, Molded Base, 1770, 33 In. 5175.00
Chest-On-Frame, Queen Anne, 9 Graduated Drawers, 3 Parts, 78 x 38 In. 6325.00
Chest-On-Frame, Queen Anne, Maple, 6 Overlapping Drawers Top, 1750s, 59 In. 9775.00
Chest-On-Frame, Queen Anne, Oak, Crossbanded Drawers, 61 3/4 In. 2900.00
Chest-On-Stand, Georgian, Burl Walnut, Oak, 18th Century, 62 x 40 x 22 In. 2300.00
Chippendale, Mahogany, Upholstered Seat, Arms, 20th Century, 36 In. 245.00
Coat Rack, 6 Hooks, Velvet Background, With Small Mirror 290.00
Coat Rack, Ebonized Wood, Central Sphere, Hooks, Brass Tray, K. Moser, 1905 . . . . 2100.00
Coffer, Brass Inlay, Iron Hinges, Bail Handles Sides, Black Finish, 35 In. 1485.00
Coffer, Oak, Charles II, Geometric Panels, Bun Feet, 1660, 29 In. 2300.00
Coffer, Oak, Jacobean, 4 Foliate Inset Panels, 28 In. 10925.00
Coffer, Stuart, Oak, 4 Inset Panels, Columns, Scrolled Foliage, 28 In. 1380.00
Coffer, Stuart, Oak, Demilune Upper Border, 3 Foliate Panels, 29 In. 1380.00
Coffer, Stuart, Oak, Flowerhead, Foliate Scrolls, 26 In. 1035.00
Coffer, Stuart, Oak, Paneled Top, Sides, Front, 27 x 45 In. 1495.00
Coffer, Stuart, Oak, Stylized Foliage, Scrolls, Hinged Lid, 29 In. 2600.00
Coffer-On-Stand, William IV, Mahogany, Hinged Top, 14 In. 1385.00
Commode, Baroque, 2 Drawers, Raised On Plinth, Outdoor Scene, 33 In. 2600.00

Commode, Bedside, Kingwood, Bronze Mounted, Parquetry 1200.00
Commode, Bedside, Renaissance Revival, Walnut, 3 Drawers, Marble, 29 x 21 In., Pair . 1450.00
Commode, Bedside, Rococo, Rosewood, Drawer, Marble, 1850, 35 x 19 x 16 In. 2300.00
Commode, Bedside, Rococo, Rosewood, Pumpkin Marble, 36 x 19 x 16 In. 1090.00
Commode, Bedside, Rosewood Marble Top, 1840 .... 910.00
Commode, Biedermeier, Fruitwood, Part-Ebonized, Parcel Gilt, 34 x 40 In. 3740.00
Commode, Bombe, Parquetry & Ormolu Mounted, Marble Top, 16 1/4 In. 485.00
Commode, Bombe, Rococo, Hardwood, Chinoiserie, Faux Marble, 34 x 43 x 20 In. 4600.00
Commode, Bombe, Serpentine Marble, Celadon Ground, Venetian, 40 x 19 In. 2300.00
Commode, Bowfront, Ebonized, 3 Drawers, Bracket Feet, France, 35 1/4 In. 1980.00
Commode, Chippendale, Mahogany, Green, Scalloped Aprons, 13 1/2 In. 660.00
Commode, Classical, Mahogany Marble Top, White, Black Mottled, 30 In. 910.00
Commode, Door, Walnut, 1 Long & 2 Small Drawers, Teardrop Pulls 300.00
Commode, Eastlake, Cherry, Paneled Door, 1 Drawer, 28 1/2 x 36 In. 300.00
Commode, Empire, Mahogany, Marble Top, 19th Century, 35 x 49 1/2 In. 1840.00
Commode, Empire, Mahogany, Marble, 3 Drawers, France, 19th Century, 48 In. 3630.00
Commode, Faux Parquetry, 3 Serpentine Drawers, Bun Feet, 50 In. 600.00
Commode, French Provincial, Walnut, 4 Drawers, 33 In. 1450.00
Commode, Fruitwood, Kingwood Inlay, 2 Drawers, Tapered Legs, 21 1/2 In. ....: 1150.00
Commode, George III, Satinwood, Floral Swag Design, Floral Bouquet, 31 In. 850.00
Commode, Georgian Style, Mahogany, Gallery Top, 31 In. 485.00
Commode, Georgian Style, Mahogany, Slide-Out Pot Stand, 31 In. 545.00
Commode, Italian Rococo, Marble Top, Bronze Mounts, Claw Feet, 38 In. 3910.00
Commode, Italian Rococo, Walnut Inlay, 2 Drawers, 34 In. 5750.00
Commode, Louis XV Style, Black Lacquer, Marble Top, Mazlow, Pair 865.00
Commode, Louis XV Style, Fruitwood, 3 Drawers 750.00
Commode, Louis XV Style, Serpentine Marble Top, Cabriole Legs, 35 In. 9350.00
Commode, Louis XV, Bombe, Fruitwood, 2 Drawers, Ormolu, 34 In. 7360.00
Commode, Louis XV, Bombe, Marquetry, 2 Drawers, Floral, 33 In. 4600.00
Commode, Louis XV, Demilune, Marquetry, Painted Flower Urn, 33 In., Pair 785.00
Commode, Louis XV, Fruitwood, Marble Top, 2 Drawers, 33 In. 9775.00
Commode, Louis XV, Fruitwood, Marquetry, Marble Top, 30 1/2 x 16 1/2 In. 825.00
Commode, Louis XV, Kingwood, Marble Top, 2 Inlaid Drawers, 33 x 38 In. 8050.00
Commode, Louis XV, Marquetry, Gilt Metal Mounts, Marble Top, 33 1/4 In. 1150.00
Commode, Louis XV, Oak, Serpentine Front, 3 Paneled Drawers, 1760s, 32 1/2 In. 3450.00
Commode, Louis XV, Ormolu, 4 Drawers, Cabriole Legs, 35 1/4 In. 6325.00
Commode, Louis XV, Pine, Stained, Pullout Candle Slides, Tambour, 27 x 12 In. 315.00
Commode, Louis XV, Walnut, 3 Drawers, Cabriole Legs, 37 1/2 In. 3960.00
Commode, Louis XVI Style, Parquetry & Marquetry, Marble Top, Drawers, 51 In. 1330.00
Commode, Louis XVI, Demilune, Variegated Marble Top, 36 In. 1330.00
Commode, Louis XVI, Fruitwood, Cupboard Doors, Stylized Flowers, 39 x 55 In. 4025.00
Commode, Louis XVI, Green Paint, Gray Mottled Marble Top, 32 In. 11500.00
Commode, Louis XVI, Ivory, Pale Green, 1 Drawer Above Cupboard Doors, Pair 1320.00
Commode, Louis XVI, Kidney Shape, 2 Drawers, Marble, 19th Century, Pair 1575.00
Commode, Louis XVI, Mahogany, Marble Top, Brass, Turned Feet, 32 In. 3450.00
Commode, Louis XVI, Marquetry, 2 Drawers, Cabriole Legs, 36 In. 3220.00
Commode, Louis XVI, Tulipwood, 3 Frieze Drawers, 4 Ft. 2 In. 5460.00
Commode, Louis XVI, Walnut, 4 Doors, Rectangular Top, 34 x 84 x 20 1/2 In. 660.00
Commode, Mahogany, Lift Top, Line Inlay, 4 Drawers, Casters, England, 29 x 26 In. ... 400.00
Commode, Mustard Ground, Serpentine, Faux Marble Top, Green Trim, 39 In., Pair 850.00
Commode, Neoclassical Style, 2 Drawers, Painted Design 4315.00
Commode, Neoclassical, Marquetry, Verde Antico Marble Top, 2 Drawers, 35 In. 3080.00
Commode, Neoclassical, Walnut, Marble Top, Italy, 30 In. 1100.00
Commode, Ogee Front, Step, Carpet Inset Lid, Chamber Pot, 17 3/4 x 19 In. 605.00
Commode, Painted Faux Marquetry, Serpentine Marble Top, Drawer Over Door 725.00
Commode, Parquetry & Ormolu Mounted, Marble Top, 36 x 49 In. 1935.00
Commode, Queen Anne, Walnut, Cabriole Legs, Trifid Feet, 41 In. 1980.00
Commode, Regency, Fruitwood, 3 Drawers, Gilt Bronze Handles, 35 In. 9680.00
Commode, Regency, Marquetry, Gilt Mounts, 2 Drawers, 34 In. 5445.00
Commode, Rococo, Kingwood, 3 Graduating Drawers, Splayed Legs, Italy, 34 In. 9200.00
Commode, Rococo, Ormolu, Mahogany, 4 Drawers, Bell Floral Design, 30 In. 9775.00
Commode, Rococo, Rosewood, Carved, White Marble Top, 32 In. 1150.00
Commode, Rococo, Walnut, Parquetry, Serpentine, Fire Gilt Mounts, Continental 1450.00

Furniture, Console, Hall, Rohde,
Burl Veneer, 1940, 49 In.

Commode, Rococo, Walnut, Serpentine Top, Cabriole Legs, 36 In. 3165.00
Commode, Venetian, Cabriole Legs, Tassel Feet, 18th Century, 32 In. 3575.00
Commode, Walnut, 3 Drawers, Incised Panel Design, France, 39 In. 4025.00
Commode, Walnut, Burl Panels, Marble Top, 2 Shelves, Victorian 525.00
Commode, Walnut, Marble Top, Carved Crest, Bracket, Continental, 62 In., Pair 935.00
Console, Biedermeier, Walnut, Ebonized, Downscrolled Supports, 37 In. 2185.00
Console, Classical, Mahogany, Green, 19th Century 1320.00
Console, Corner, Giltwood, Marble Top, Flower Filled Urn, Birds In Frieze, Pair 9200.00
Console, Empire, Mahogany, Marble Top 2070.00
Console, Empire, Marble, Columnar Supports, Leaf Tip Base, 33 In. 7475.00
Console, George III, Giltwood, Marble Top, Shaped Onyx, 30 1/2 In. 1935.00
Console, Hall, Rohde, Burl Veneer, 1940, 49 In. ....*Illus* 6050.00
Console, Louis XVI, Fruitwood, White, Gray Variegated Marble Top, 31 1/2 In. 3270.00
Console, Louis XVI, Giltwood, Carved Gesso, Marble, Floral Festoons, 43 x 19 In. 6200.00
Console, Louis XVI, Mahogany, Brass Mounts, 3 Drawers, 34 In. 7475.00
Console, Marble Top, Steel Scrolled Base, France, 50 In. 2200.00
Console, Neoclassical, Faux Marble Top, Scrolls, Tapered Legs, 32 In., Pair 10925.00
Console, Neoclassical, Green & Gold Painted Metal, Mirror, 2 Piece 1092.00
Console, Neoclassical, Rosewood, Marble, Pair 1845.00
Console, Painted, Marble Top, Leaf Tip & Grapevine Frieze, Sweden, 33 1/4 In. 3737.00
Console, Rococo Revival, Rosewood, Marble, Mirrored Base, Victorian, 22 x 54 In. 9500.00
Console, Rococo, Gray Mottled Marble Top, Serpentine, Pad Feet, 33 In., Pair 8050.00
Console, Rococo, Rosewood, Serpentine, White Marble Top, 29 1/2 In., Pair 1325.00
Couch, Fainting, Eastlake, Victorian, 66 In. 85.00
Cradle, Cast Iron, Swinging, 2 Scrolled Supports, 2 Brass Finials 275.00
Cradle, Cherry, Square Corner Posts, Turned Finials, 42 In. 185.00
Cradle, Cherry, Square Corner Posts, Turned Finials, Shaped Top Edge, 40 In. 110.00
Cradle, Curly Maple, Dovetailed, Scroll Edge & Rockers, Refinished, 42 In. 660.00
Cradle, Gilt, Stencil, Floral, Arch Headboard, 38 In. 275.00
Cradle, Grain Painted, Hood, Zoar, Ohio 275.00
Cradle, Heart Cutout, Unbroken Scrollwork, Lancaster County, Penna. 1200.00
Cradle, Mustard, Blue Sienna Design Interior, 22 In. 546.00
Cradle, Pine, Grain Painted, 47 x 26 In. 290.00
Cradle, Pine, Hood, Blue Paint, New England, 18th Century, 28 1/2 x 45 In. 430.00
Cradle, Pine, Hood, Reddish Brown Paint, Roseheaded Nails, 18th Century 675.00
Cradle, Poplar, Brown Grained Repaint, Dovetailed, Cutout & Scrolled Sides, 40 In. 150.00
Cradle, Poplar, Hood, Rounded, Green Interior, Refinished Exterior, 43 In. 165.00
Cradle, Red & Black Paint, Hood, Arched, Cyma Curve Supports, 1770s 225.00
Cradle, Red Paint, Stencil & Striping, Iron Wheels 500.00
Cradle, Walnut, Worn Green Paint, Reeded Side Panels, Cutout Hearts, 38 In. 205.00
Credenza, French Boulle, Black Lacquer, Red Tortoiseshell Inlay, Brass, 41 In. 1375.00
Credenza, Marble Top, Drawer Over 2 Doors, Side Columns, Dolphin Feet, 49 In. 400.00
Credenza, Renaissance Revival, Walnut 980.00
Credenza, Walnut, Baroque, 3 Drawers, Bracket, 34 x 31 x 13 1/2 In. 3165.00
Credenza, Walnut, Baroque, Molded Top, 3 Drawers, Bracket Feet, Pair 8625.00
Cupboard, Butternut, 6 Pane Doors, Pie Shelf, 2 Drawers, Cornice, 2 Piece, 84 In. 2530.00
Cupboard, Butternut, Paneled Doors, 2 Drawers, 48 x 88 In., 2 Piece 1870.00

Cupboard, Cant-Back, Plate Grooves On Top 4 Graduated Shelves, c.1850 . . . . 3500.00
Cupboard, Cherry, 4 Doors, Middle Drawer, Refinished, 73 In. 335.00
Cupboard, Cherry, Poplar, Repaint, 6 Pane Door, Cornice, 80 In., 2 Piece 3190.00
Cupboard, Chimney, Salmon Paint Traces, Cornice, Late 18th Century, 69 In. 1500.00
Cupboard, Chimney, Walnut, Yellow Pine, Bun Feet, 32 In. 8250.00
Cupboard, China, Walnut, Round Glazed Door, Ball Turned Legs, 61 x 42 In. 175.00
Cupboard, Corner, Black, White, Raised Chinoiserie Design, 33 1/2 In. 850.00
Cupboard, Corner, Brown Paint, Green Paint Interior, c.1850 . . . . 7200.00
Cupboard, Corner, Cherry Flame Grain, Original Hardware & Glass 7370.00
Cupboard, Corner, Cherry, 2 Doors, 6 Panes, Panels, 2 Base Drawers, 88 In. 4290.00
Cupboard, Corner, Cherry, 2 Doors, 6 Panes, Panels, c.1840, 89 1/2 In. 5200.00
Cupboard, Corner, Cherry, 2 Doors, 6 Panes, Panels, Cornice 6600.00
Cupboard, Corner, Cherry, 2 Doors, 8 Panes, Cornice, Lighted . . . . *Illus* 2650.00
Cupboard, Corner, Cherry, 2 Doors, 8 Panes, Grain Painted Yellow, c.1840 . . . . 3475.00
Cupboard, Corner, Cherry, Late 18th Century, 2 Piece, 91 x 56 In. 2300.00
Cupboard, Corner, Cherry, Reeded Frieze, 3 Shelves, 86 3/4 In. 6000.00
Cupboard, Corner, Cherry, Scrolled Apron, Bracket Feet, 95 1/2 In. 4450.00
Cupboard, Corner, Cherry, Upper & Lower Doors, Brass Thumb Latches, 82 1/2 In. 2000.00
Cupboard, Corner, Cherry, Upper Mullioned Glass Doors, c.1820, 87 In. 9200.00
Cupboard, Corner, Chippendale, Cherry, Glazed Doors Over 2 Doors, 1790, 88 In. 7475.00
Cupboard, Corner, Chippendale, Paneled Door, Shelves, 18th Century, 88 x 45 In. 4600.00
Cupboard, Corner, Classic, Mustard, 1900s, Child's, 30 In. 235.00
Cupboard, Corner, Dark Stain, Broken Arched Door, Glass Top, Mid-1800s, 93 In. 2750.00
Cupboard, Corner, Empire Style, Mahogany, 2 Piece 1875.00
Cupboard, Corner, Empire, Walnut, Paneled Doors, Drawers, 84 In. 1980.00
Cupboard, Corner, Federal, Walnut, Paneled Doors Below Shelves, c.1820, 87 In. 2185.00
Cupboard, Corner, Grain Painted To Simulate Mahogany, Rupp, 1850s, 78 x 50 In. 8500.00
Cupboard, Corner, Hanging, Oak, Inlaid Floral Medallion On Door, 40 1/2 In. 690.00
Cupboard, Corner, Hanging, Pine, Bowfront, Graduated Shelves, 42 x 19 14 In. 550.00
Cupboard, Corner, Heywood-Wakefield, Wheat, 2 Doors, 68 x 28 x 18 In. 885.00
Cupboard, Corner, Mahogany, 4 Upper Shelves, 2 Bottom Shelves, Middle Drawer 500.00
Cupboard, Corner, Napoleon III, Ebonized, White Marble Top, 41 1/2 x 32 In. 1331.00
Cupboard, Corner, Oak, Carved, Glass Door, Adjustable Shelves . . . . *Illus* 1540.00
Cupboard, Corner, Pine & Poplar, Paneled Doors, Wooden Knobs, 75 3/4 In. 880.00
Cupboard, Corner, Pine, 2 Doors, 6 Panes, 2 Piece, 84 In. 1760.00
Cupboard, Corner, Pine, Diamond Mullion Door, Refinished, England, 30 x 77 In. 1870.00
Cupboard, Corner, Pine, Paneled Door, 9 Panes, Drawer, 80 In. 3400.00
Cupboard, Corner, Pine, Paneled Door, Open Top, New York, 71 x 50 x 21 In. 1725.00
Cupboard, Corner, Pine, Red Paint, New England, 19th Century, 81 In. 1610.00
Cupboard, Corner, Poplar, 2 Doors Over 2 Raised Panel Doors 900.00
Cupboard, Corner, Poplar, 4 Blind Doors, 7 Ft. 4 In., 1 Piece 750.00
Cupboard, Corner, Poplar, Grain Painted, 4 Doors, Molded Cornice, 40 x 81 In. 2145.00
Cupboard, Corner, Salmon Grain Painted, 12 Pane Top Door, 2 Piece 4200.00

Furniture, Cupboard,
Corner, Cherry,
2 doors, 8 panes,
Cornice, Lighted

Furniture, Cupboard,
Corner, Oak, Carved,
Glass Door, Adjustable
Shelves

Furniture, Cupboard,
Peter Hunt, Painted
Grandfather Clock,
Door, 61 In.

Furniture, Cupboard,
Pine, Poplar,
2 Doors, 6 Panes,
2 Drawers

Cupboard, Corner, Tiger Maple, 2 Base Doors, 6 Panes, 90 In., 2 Piece 5800.00
Cupboard, Corner, Walnut, Glazed Doors Top, Spice Drawer, 19th Century, 92 In. 3025.00
Cupboard, Corner, Walnut, Scrolled Apron, Paneled Double Door Top, 81 3/4 In. 1215.00
Cupboard, Court, Oak, 2 Vine & Mask Carved Doors, Twist Columns, 59 x 40 In. 2070.00
Cupboard, Court, Walnut, 2 Doors, 2 Drawers, 62 x 48 1/2 In. 2100.00
Cupboard, Dutch, Grain Painted Over Red, 4 Doors, 3 Drawers, Cornice 2585.00
Cupboard, Empire, Cherry, Walnut, Rope & Ring Half Columns, 82 In., 2 Piece 1815.00
Cupboard, Federal, Pine, Poplar, 2 Drawers Over Doors, 52 In. 2070.00
Cupboard, Gothic, Oak, 2 Drawers, Coat Of Arms, 82 x 40 x 18 1/2 In. 2875.00
Cupboard, Grain Design, Shades Of Mustard & Yellow, 54 1/2 In. 1125.00
Cupboard, Hanging, 1 Panel Door, Rattail Hinges, Dentil Cornice 5100.00
Cupboard, Hanging, Elm, 5 Scalloped Shelves, England, 44 x 20 x 13 In. 600.00
Cupboard, Hanging, Painted Red Top, White Interior, Penna., 24 1/2 In. 345.00
Cupboard, Hanging, Pine, Dark Green Paint, Compass Star, 18 In. 385.00
Cupboard, Hanging, Pine, Poplar, Blue, Green Door Panels, 9 x 24 In. 1545.00
Cupboard, Hanging, Pine, Poplar, Red, Dovetailed Case, 24 In. 495.00
Cupboard, Hanging, Pine, Reeded Frame, Molded Cornice, 35 In. 770.00
Cupboard, Hanging, Pine, Repainted, Raised Panel Doors, Continental, 33 x 41 In. 300.00
Cupboard, Hanging, Poplar, Wood Burned Poppies, Red & Green, 27 x 9 x 29 In. 250.00
Cupboard, Hanging, Red Grain Paint, Blue Interior, 23 3/4 In. 495.00
Cupboard, Hanging, Walnut, Cherry, Dovetailed Case, 36 In. 335.00
Cupboard, Jacobean, Oak, Turned Legs, Rockford Co., 58 1/2 In. 330.00
Cupboard, Jelly, Grain Painted, 1750s 1200.00
Cupboard, Jelly, Pine, Raised Panel Sides & Doors, 1830, Child's, 23 In. 625.00
Cupboard, Jelly, Pine, Rattail Hinges, Scalloped Skirt, Paneled Door, 72 In. 4750.00
Cupboard, Jelly, Pine, Scrolled Apron, 4 Raised Panels, Rattail Hinges, 68 3/4 In. ... 4750.00
Cupboard, Jelly, Poplar, Top Drawer, Door, Scalloped Apron, 1-Board Top, 20 In. 600.00
Cupboard, Jelly, Walnut, 1-Board Doors, Drawer, 47 x 60 In. 1100.00
Cupboard, Jelly, Yellow Pine & Cherry, Paneled Doors, 2 Drawers, 57 /12 In. 885.00
Cupboard, Kitchen, Ash, Poplar, 2 Glass & 4 Doors, 3 Drawers, Refinished, 90 In. 600.00
Cupboard, Kitchen, Maple, Possum Belly, Drawers, 24 x 46 x 79 In. 775.00
Cupboard, Kitchen, Pine, Pane Glass Doors, Child's, 32 x 14 x 43 In. 245.00
Cupboard, Kitchen, Pine, Paneled Doors, 2 Drawers, 48 x 18 x 71 In. 385.00
Cupboard, Louis XVI, Elm, 2 Glazed Doors, Fluted Cornice, France, 83 x 43 In. 3350.00
Cupboard, Mahogany, Paneled Doors, Chamfered Legs, 32 In. 4025.00
Cupboard, Mahogany, Satinwood, Inlay, Victorian, 34 x 25 x 16 In. 525.00
Cupboard, Maple, Paneled Doors, Molded Cornice, Bracket, 77 In. 2850.00
Cupboard, Oak, 2 Glass Doors, 2 Drawers, 2 Paneled Doors, Carved, 41 x 80 In. 470.00
Cupboard, Oak, Jacobean, Foliage, Scroll, Geometric Design, 40 In. 3700.00
Cupboard, Peter Hunt, Painted Grandfather Clock, Door, 61 In. .... *Illus* 3300.00
Cupboard, Pewter, Cherry, Original Brass Hardware 3150.00

Cupboard, Pewter, Pine, Poplar, Open Shelves, Cutouts For Spoons, Rattail Hinges 6050.00
Cupboard, Pewter, Step Back, Paneled Doors In Beaded Frame, 84 In. 2000.00
Cupboard, Pewter, Walnut, 3 Shelves, Cutout Feet, 79 1/4 In. 2200.00
Cupboard, Pine, 15 Panes, 2 Drawers Over 2 Doors, 60 x 19 x 81 In., 2 Piece 5170.00
Cupboard, Pine, 4 Paneled Doors, 2 Drawers, Refinished, 54 x 80 In. 885.00
Cupboard, Pine, Poplar, 2 Doors, 6 Panes, 2 Drawers ....*Illus* 1200.00
Cupboard, Pine, Punched Tombstone Zinc Panel, Repainted, 66 In. 225.00
Cupboard, Pine, Wall, Door, Scalloped Apron, 81 1/2 In. 2860.00
Cupboard, Pine, Walnut, Drawer, Paneled Doors, Dark Finish, 17 x 11 x 22 In. 225.00
Cupboard, Poplar, Brown Grained, Paneled Doors, 2 Drawers, Cornice, 83 In. 1545.00
Cupboard, Poplar, Fluted Columns, Blind Doors, Penna., 72 x 48 In., 2 Piece 2300.00
Cupboard, Red & Gray Paint, 2 Raised Panel Doors, 4 Shelves, 1730s, 71 1/2 In. 2645.00
Cupboard, Shaker, 4 Doors, Quarter Round Molding On Doors, Old Finish 715.00
Cupboard, Step Back, Applied Carved Foliage, Nailed Construction, Child's, 42 In. 1100.00
Cupboard, Step Back, Butternut, Poplar Panels, 71 1/4 In. 775.00
Cupboard, Step Back, Cherry, Pie Shelf, Dovetailed Case & Drawers, 84 x 57 In. 4800.00
Cupboard, Step Back, Cherry, Upper Mullioned Doors, 3 Lower Drawers, 78 1/2 In. ... 1725.00
Cupboard, Step Back, Chestnut, Original Finish, Penna., 19th Century 1400.00
Cupboard, Step Back, Dark Paint Over Original Red, Vermont 4300.00
Cupboard, Step Back, Elm & Pine, Red & Gray, 3 Shelves, 3 Drawers, 70 1/2 In. 3740.00
Cupboard, Step Back, Oak, 2 Lower Doors, 17 x 22 In. 310.00
Cupboard, Step Back, Paint, 2 Doors, 6 Panes, 2 Drawers, New England, 2 Part 4350.00
Cupboard, Step Back, Pine, 2 Open Shelves, Lower Single Door, 72 x 42 1/2 In. 2300.00
Cupboard, Step Back, Pine, 6 Pane Glass Doors, 19th Century, Dutch, 38 x 19 In. 4700.00
Cupboard, Step Back, Pine, Gray Paint, 42 x 18 x 44 In. 385.00
Cupboard, Step Back, Poplar, Old Paint, Pie Safe Base, 48 x 83 In., 1 Piece 2300.00
Cupboard, Tudor, Oak, Metal Mounted, 5 Drawers, 52 In. 4600.00
Cupboard, Turkey Breast, Grain Painted, 2 Doors, 6 Panes, 2 Lower Doors 6100.00
Cupboard, Wall, Cherry, Paneled Doors, 2 Drawers, Refinished, 80 In. 385.00
Cupboard, Wall, Walnut, Glass & Paneled Doors, Cornice, Refinished, 43 x 79 In. 665.00
Cupboard, Walnut, 4 Doors, Pane & Paneled Doors, 2 Drawers, 86 In., 2 Piece 1870.00
Cupboard, Walnut, Ash, Drawer, Chamfered, Cornice, 91 3/4 In. 445.00
Cupboard, Walnut, Blue, Paneled Door, 75 In. 910.00
Cupboard, Walnut, Brown, Molded Corner, Va., 102 1/4 In. 5775.00
Cupboard, Walnut, Nailed Panel Doors, 2 Nailed Drawers, 45 x 84 In. 1650.00
Curio Cabinet, Oak, Glass, Original Finish, 41 x 63 In. 1195.00
Daybed, Arts & Crafts, Oak, Shaped Panel Ends, Fitted Cushions, c.1910, 82 In. 1695.00
Daybed, Charles Stickley, Oak, 6 Slat Panels, Leather Cushion, 29 x 79 In. 2300.00
Daybed, Chrome Metal Frame, Upholstered, 85 x 32 x 29 In. 2100.00
Daybed, Empire Style, Mahogany, Columnar Supports, 29 In. 7475.00
Daybed, Empire, Mahogany, Bronze Dore Mounts, 19th Century 1650.00
Daybed, Mahogany, Upright Gothic Ends, 1840-1850 .... 1450.00
Daybed, Nelson, Birch, Hairpin Legs, 75 x 33 x 28 In. 1870.00
Daybed, Oak, Black Naugahyde, Claw Feet 4000.00

Have an extra key made to fit doors and drawers in old furniture. Stick it to the bottom of the piece with a wad of gum or tape.

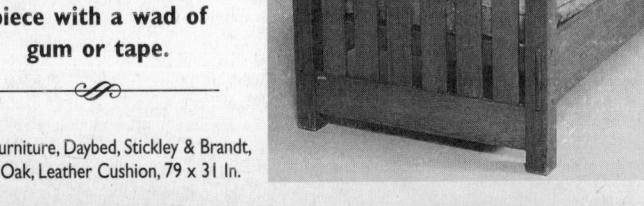

Furniture, Daybed, Stickley & Brandt,
Oak, Leather Cushion, 79 x 31 In.

Furniture, Desk, Carved Serpents, Scroll & Fruit

Daybed, Rosewood, Carved Shells, Rocaille Scrollwork, 40 In. 4600.00
Daybed, Spindle Turnings, Fitted Upholstered Cushions 150.00
Daybed, Stickley & Brandt, Oak, Leather Cushion, 79 x 31 In. ....*Illus* 2300.00
Daybed, Stickley Bros., Oak, Paper Label, 28 x 72 In. 300.00
Daybed, Walnut, Pine, Inverted Vase Shape Legs, Victorian, Child's, 20 In. 250.00
Daybed, Walnut, Turned Posts, Legs, 19th Century, 68 x 26 x 27 In. 100.00
Daybed, Wrought Iron, Greek Key Foot, Mesh Top, 75 x 30 x 14 In. 275.00
Desk, 3 Drawers, Leather Inset Panel Top, Brass Trim On Frieze, 29 x 60 In. 950.00
Desk, Art Deco, Rosewood, Chrome Pulls, 3 Tiers, Side Shelves, 59 x 28 In. 4250.00
Desk, Arts & Crafts, Full Tenon Construction, Copper Pulls, c.1920 .... 2100.00
Desk, Beechwood, 3 Drawers, Brass Pulls, Austria, 30 In........................ 9200.00
Desk, Biedermeier, Birch, Inlaid, 5 Drawers, 19th Century 5175.00
Desk, Biedermeier, Mahogany, Cherry, 2 Drawers, 31 In. 4315.00
Desk, Birch, Slant Front, 3 Drawers, Signed, 1810, 39 In. 5400.00
Desk, Butler's, Federal, Mahogany, Desk Drawer, Fitted Interior, c.1820, 49 x 46 In. 1380.00
Desk, Butler's, Mahogany, Cherry, Drop Front Drawer, Fitted Interior, 45 In. 1850.00
Desk, Carlton House Style, Walnut, Leather Writing Surface, 3 Drawers, 39 x 49 In. 1380.00
Desk, Carlton House, Mahogany, Line Inlay, England, 38 x 48 In. 3780.00
Desk, Carved Serpents, Scroll & Fruit ....*Illus* 3850.00
Desk, Chippendale Style, Mahogany, Block Front, Double Pedestal 1845.00
Desk, Chippendale Style, Walnut, Figured Veneer, Slant Front, 20th Century, 42 In. 385.00
Desk, Chippendale, 3 Drawers, Serpentine Interior, Back Feet 7150.00
Desk, Chippendale, Cherry, Slant Front, 2 Drawers, Bracket Feet, 39 In. 3000.00
Desk, Chippendale, Cherry, Slant Front, 4 Dovetailed Drawers, 31 In. 4950.00
Desk, Chippendale, Cherry, Slant Front, 4 Dovetailed Drawers, 45 In. 1650.00
Desk, Chippendale, Cherry, Slant Front, New England, 42 x 36 In. 1150.00
Desk, Chippendale, Cherry, Slant Front, Pigeonholes, Drawers, 1780s, 42 1/2 In. 1265.00
Desk, Chippendale, Cherry, Slant Front, Reeded Corner Columns, Penna. 3025.00
Desk, Chippendale, Cherry, Slat Front, 4 Graduated Drawers, c.1760, 45 x 40 In. 4600.00
Desk, Chippendale, Mahogany, Block Front, 4 Drawers, Hidden Drawers Interior 8800.00
Desk, Chippendale, Mahogany, Slant Front, 4 Drawers, Cabriole Legs, 44 3/4 In. 6325.00
Desk, Chippendale, Maple, Slant Front, 18th Century, 39 x 36 x 19 In. 2300.00
Desk, Chippendale, Maple, Slant Front, Compartments, 18th Century, 44 x 37 In. 3100.00
Desk, Chippendale, Maple, Slant Front, Late 18th Century ....*Illus* 4900.00
Desk, Chippendale, Maple, Slant Front, New England, 1760 ....*Illus* 3100.00
Desk, Chippendale, Maple, Slant Front, Pigeonholes, 1760, 41 x 36 x 19 In. 7475.00
Desk, Chippendale, Maple, Slant Front, Rhode Island, Late 18th Century 4900.00
Desk, Chippendale, Tiger Maple, Stand Front, 4 Drawers, 40 x 35 3/4 In. 5465.00
Desk, Chippendale, Walnut, Slant Front, 12 Drawers, Penna., 40 x 22 x 47 In. 2200.00
Desk, Chippendale, Walnut, Slant Front, 2 Thumb-Molded Drawers, 44 In. 5750.00
Desk, Chippendale, Walnut, Slant Front, 4 Graduated Drawers, Ogee Feet, 42 In. 2185.00
Desk, Chippendale, Walnut, Slant Front, Ogee Feet, 42 1/4 In. 1325.00
Desk, Chippendale, Walnut, Slant Front, Pigeonholes, 3 Drawers, 1965, 42 In. 2200.00
Desk, Chippendale, Walnut, Slant Front, Rhode Island, 1760, 44 In..............*Illus* 2300.00

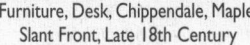

Furniture, Desk, Chippendale, Maple,
Slant Front, Late 18th Century

Furniture, Desk, Chippendale, Maple,
Slant Front, New England, 1760

Desk, Clerk's, Cherry & Walnut, Slanted, Pigeonholes, 2 Drawers, 36 In.	360.00
Desk, Clerk's, Walnut, Slanted, 3 Drawers, Gallery, 41 1/2 x 28 1/2 x 33 In.	220.00
Desk, Cylinder, Eastlake, Walnut, Burl Walnut, Gallery, 2 Drawers, 3 Base Drawers	1030.00
Desk, Cylinder, Neoclassical, Pine, Painted, c.1800, 44 1/2 x 49 In.	1725.00
Desk, Davenport, Burl Walnut, Victorian, England	2535.00
Desk, Davenport, Roll Top, Black Lacquer & Gilt Incised Design, Gothic Windows	1695.00
Desk, Davenport, Roll Top, Burl Walnut	1300.00
Desk, Demilune, 6 Small Drawers, Faux Book Facade, Secret Section, 1920s	3400.00
Desk, Deskey, Drop Front, 3 Drawers, Brass, Bronze Pulls, 1930	880.00
Desk, E. Barnsley, Hardwood, Center Drawer, 2 Fall Front Compartments, 1930s	4375.00
Desk, Edward Wormley, Walnut, L-Shape, Gallery, 3 Drawers, 36 x 60 x 30 In.	330.00
Desk, Empire, Cherry, Drop Front, Fitted, Refinished, 37 x 19 x 48 In.	775.00
Desk, Empire, Mahogany, Drop Front, 3 Drawers, Pigeonholes, Pilasters, 48 x 42 In.	925.00
Desk, Empire, Pedestal, Continental, 63 x 33 x 31 In.	1935.00
Desk, Federal Style, Mahogany, Tambour	800.00
Desk, Federal, Lady's, Mahogany Inlay, Tambour Doors, 2 Drawers, 43 x 40 In.	3000.00
Desk, Federal, Mahogany, Drawer In Base, Folding Top, 3 Drawers, 36 In.	330.00
Desk, Federal, Mahogany, Drop Front, 2 Drawers, 36 In.	1980.00
Desk, Federal, Mahogany, Stand-Up, Late 19th Century	5750.00
Desk, G. Stickley, No. 709, 5 Drawers, Decal, 30 x 48 x 29 In.	1200.00
Desk, G. Stickley, No. 728, Drop Front, Full Gallery Interior, 43 x 32 In.	1320.00
Desk, G. Stickley, No. 730, Paper Label, 40 x 42 In.	2300.00
Desk, George II Style, Walnut, 3 Drawers, Ball Feet, 30 In.	4600.00
Desk, George III, Floral, Ribbon Design, Fluted Legs, 29 1/2 In.	1650.00
Desk, George III, Mahogany, Knee-Hole, Late 18th Century, 30 x 36 x 18 In.	1495.00
Desk, George III, Mahogany, Kneehole, 9 Short Drawers, Recessed Cupboard, Small	1350.00
Desk, George III, Mahogany, Slant Front, 4 Graduated Drawers, 38 In.	3300.00
Desk, George III, Mahogany, Slant Front, Beaded Drawers, Bracket Feet, 41 In.	3300.00
Desk, George III, Mahogany, Slant Front, Quarter Column, Bracket Feet, 45 In.	4115.00
Desk, Georgian Style, Burl Walnut, 2 Pedestals	345.00
Desk, Georgian Style, Fruitwood, 2 Doors, Rectangular, 41 x 22 x 42 In.	345.00
Desk, Georgian, Mahogany, Leather Inset, 2 Pedestals	1600.00
Desk, Georgian, Mahogany, Leather Inset, Pedestal, 20th Century, 30 x 54 In.	575.00
Desk, Georgian, Mahogany, Slant Front, 2 Drawers Above 2 Long Drawers, 45 In.	1935.00
Desk, Georgian, Mahogany, Slant Front, Fitted, 4 Graduated Drawers, 70 In.	3875.00
Desk, Grain Painted, Traveling, c.1840	180.00
Desk, Hepplewhite, Cherry, Slant Front, 4 Drawers, Fitted Interior, 43 1/2 In.	1650.00
Desk, Hepplewhite, Tiger Maple, Mahogany Inlay, 53 1/2 In.	6325.00
Desk, Herman Miller, Pedestal, White Laminated Top, 29 x 60 x 30 In.	110.00
Desk, Herter Brothers, Burled Walnut, Drop Front, Marquetry, Bronze Medallion, 1875 . .	7500.00
Desk, Herter Brothers, Walnut, Walnut Burl, Mirror, Woman's	5775.00
Desk, Hinged Top, Leather Writing Surface, Trestle Supports, 46 In.	435.00

Desk, L. & J.G. Stickley, 2 Drawers, Copper Pulls, 29 1/2 x 36 In. 2200.00
Desk, Lap, Bird's-Eye Maple, Inlaid Top, 11 In. 145.00
Desk, Lap, Design On Top, c.1870, 10 x 14 In. 125.00
Desk, Lap, Mahogany, Brass Bound Case, Felt Surface, On Stand, 24 x 10 x 20 In. 690.00
Desk, Lap, Mahogany, Brass Mounted, England, 6 3/4 In. 200.00
Desk, Lap, Oak, Double Opening, Velvet Interior, Ink Bottle, Brass Trim 265.00
Desk, Lap, Rosewood, Brass Borders, Victorian, 15 1/4 In. 2185.00
Desk, Lap, Walnut, Blue Silk Interior, Victorian . . . . .165.00 to 185.00
Desk, Lap, Walnut, Fitted Interior, Tooled Leather, 1860s, 7 x 10 In. 230.00
Desk, Lap, Walnut, Marquetry, Hinged Front, c.1870, 12 x 10 In. 345.00
Desk, Limbert, Drawer, Flip Down, Book Storage On Sides, 29 In. 1265.00
Desk, Limbert, Drawer, Letter Holders On Backsplash, Caned Panel, 35 In. 2100.00
Desk, Limbert, Drawer, Refinished Brown, Marked 1165.00
Desk, Louis Philippe, Leather Surface, Trestle Support, 45 In.   750.00
Desk, Louis XVI, Burlwood, Bronze, Pedestal, Green Leather Inset, 29 1/2 In. 1045.00
Desk, Mahogany, Drop Front, Fitted Interior, Oxbow Front, 4 Drawers 192.00
Desk, Mahogany, Empire Style, Gilt Metal 1610.00
Desk, Mahogany, Kneehole, 2 Banks Of Short Drawers, c.1775, 33 1/2 In. 9775.00
Desk, Mahogany, Leather Top, Long Drawer, 2 Side Drawers, 2 Pedestals, 60 In. 1435.00
Desk, Mahogany, Ship Captain's, 3 Drawers, Downswept Legs, Metal Mounts, 51 In. 1800.00
Desk, Mahogany, Tambour Cylinder, 2 Drawers, Leather Inset, 29 1/2 In. 3450.00
Desk, Mahogany, Tambour Slide Opening, 4 Drawers, Russia, 1780s, 41 In. 8050.00
Desk, Mahogany, Woman's, Tambour Inlay, Pigeonhole Over Drawer, 44 1/2 In. 865.00
Desk, Maple & Cherry, Pigeonholes, 9 Drawers, c.1780, 35 x 41 In. 2600.00
Desk, Maple, Slant Front, Dovetailed Case, 3 Dovetailed Drawers, 19 In. 1430.00
Desk, Maple, Slant Front, Interior Drawers, 4 Graduated Drawers In Case, 41 In. 2750.00
Desk, Maple, Walnut, Slant Front, 8 Pigeonholes, 2 Short & 4 Long Drawers, 1780 . . . . .   4600.00
Desk, Mission, Oak, Pigeonholes, 31 In. 425.00
Desk, Mission, Quartersawn Oak, Drop Front, Fitted, 2 Drawers, 30 x 40 In. 495.00
Desk, Nelson, Drop Front, Pedestal, 3 Drawers, Metal Legs, 1946, 59 In. 990.00
Desk, Neoclassical, Fruitwood Marquetry, 2 Drawers, Tapered Legs, 39 In. 9200.00
Desk, Neoclassical, Walnut, Slant Front, 41 In. 3450.00
Desk, Oak & Parquetry, 2 Pedestals, Fitted, 19th Century, 49 x 44 x 27 In. 2300.00
Desk, Oak, Drop Front, Letter Compartments, Child's 275.00
Desk, Oak, Drop Front, Shell Carving, Gallery . . . .*Illus*   935.00
Desk, Oak, Kneehole, Top Above 1 Drawer, 3 Graduated Drawers, 2 Pedestals, Slide 175.00
Desk, Oak, Splayed Legs, Carved Acanthus Design, Victorian, 25 x 40 x 30 In. 99.00
Desk, Partner's, George III, Mahogany, Red Leather Top, 19th Century, 72 In. 3450.00
Desk, Partner's, Golden Oak, Quartersawn Top, Sides, 18 Drawers, 1890s, 84 In. 3500.00
Desk, Partner's, Mahogany, 9 Drawers, Leather Top, England, 72 x 48 In. 6500.00
Desk, Partner's, Mahogany, Scroll Design, Victorian, 30 In. 6655.00
Desk, Partner's, Oak, Lion's Head & Claw Feet, 54 x 36 In. 9750.00

Furniture, Desk, Chippendale, Walnut,
Slant Front, Rhode Island, 1760, 44 In.

Furniture, Desk, Oak, Drop Front,
Shell Carving, Gallery

Desk, Partner's, Oak, Raised Panels, Cabriole Legs, Leather, France, 72 x 44 In. 8500.00
Desk, Partner's, Oak, Woman's, Carved Banding 1650.00
Desk, Partner's, Quartersawn Oak, 9 Drawers, Leather Top, 59 x 50 In. 6000.00
Desk, Pine, Walnut, Slant Front, 2 Drawers, Cabriole Legs, 42 In. 4310.00
Desk, Plantation, Cherry & Walnut, Drop Front, 2 Drawers 850.00
Desk, Plantation, Cherry, Drop Front, c.1850, 76 x 39 In. 2400.00
Desk, Plantation, Cherry, Walnut, Turned Legs, 42 x 14 x 47 In. 775.00
Desk, Plantation, Drop Front Paneled Lid, 2 Drawers, H.A. Arnold, 91 1/2 In. 1320.00
Desk, Plantation, Lift Lid, Double Doors, Fitted Interior, Pine, Hardwood, 78 1/2 In. 995.00
Desk, Plantation, Poplar & Walnut, Drop Front Lid, Fitted Interior, 78 1/2 In. 1435.00
Desk, Plantation, Red, Black Paint, Mid-19th Century 1980.00
Desk, Queen Anne, Maple, Slant Front, New England, 18th Century 4885.00
Desk, Queen Anne, Maple, Slant Front, On Frame, Pigeonholes, 1740, 45 In. 4850.00
Desk, Red Paint, Slant Front, Interior Marked SSM 1743, 39 1/2 x 38 1/4 In. 4600.00
Desk, Regency, Satinwood, Trestle Base, Carlton House, 32 In. 1030.00
Desk, Roll Top, 2 Drawers, Animal & Trees Painted, Child's, 34 In. 1840.00
Desk, Roll Top, Cherry, Maple Interior, 5 Drawers, Pullout Shelves In Base, 50 In. 1000.00
Desk, Roll Top, D Roll, Paneled, 6 Drawers, Side Drop Leaf, 54 x 36 In. 1875.00
Desk, Roll Top, Mahogany, 9 Drawers, 8 Interior Drawers, Matching Chair, 40 In. 385.00
Desk, Roll Top, Oak, Kneehole, Fitted Interior . . . . *Illus* 1975.00
Desk, Roll Top, Oak, Raised Panels, Fluted Columns, 42 In. 1500.00
Desk, Roll Top, Oak, Smaller Roll Top Inside, American Case & Register Co. 2000.00
Desk, Roll Top, Quartersawn Oak, Raised Panels & Carved Pulls, 72 x 51 In. 10500.00
Desk, Roll Top, S Roll, Kneehole, Compartments, c.1900, 58 x 31 In. 1265.00
Desk, Roll Top, S Roll, Oak, 4 Drawer, Ledger Compartment, Pigeonholes, 48 x 48 In. . . 120.00
Desk, Roll Top, S Roll, Oak, 5 Drawers, Door, Typewriter Platform, 60 x 49 In. 2450.00
Desk, Roll Top, S Roll, Woman's, Pierced Galley Over 2 Drawers, Pullout Leather Inset . 770.00
Desk, Roll Top, Tambour, 2 Drawers, Apron Drawer, Rounded Legs, 32 In. 575.00
Desk, Roll Top, Walnut Paneled, 29 Pigeonhole Holes, 9 Drawers, Letter Rack, 1884 . . . . 4000.00
Desk, Roll Top, Walnut, Scrolled Tambour Slide, Burl Walnut Panels, 51 In. 3100.00
Desk, Schoolmaster's, Cherry, c.1840, Small 1050.00
Desk, Schoolmaster's, Federal, Walnut, Thumb-Molded Slant, 35 In. 865.00
Desk, Schoolmaster's, Pine, c.1860, Small 425.00
Desk, Schoolmaster's, Sheraton, Cherry, Drawer, 7 Pigeonholes, 38 In. 770.00
Desk, Shaker, Lift Lid, Box Stretcher, Alfred, Maine 4400.00
Desk, Shaker, Sewing, Central Panel Door, 3 Lip Drawers, Turned Legs, 28 In. 11500.00
Desk, Slant Front, 4 Drawers, Bracket Feet, 41 1/2 In. 1840.00
Desk, Slant Front, Lid Opens To Drawers, Pigeonholes, Shaped Skirt 275.00
Desk, Stephen Hedges, Mahogany, Patent, c.1885 . . . . 4887.00
Desk, Tiger Maple, Slant Front, 4 Graduated Drawers 4200.00
Desk, Walnut, Kneehole, Paneled, 6 Dovetailed Drawers, 23 x 48 x 30 In. 850.00
Desk, Walnut, Kneehole, Tooled Leather Top, 3 Short Drawers, 30 In. 2865.00
Desk, Walnut, Oak, Slant Front, 3 Drawers, Serpentine Case, 1860 . . . . 660.00
Desk, Walnut, Pedestal, Tooled Leather Top, Late 19th Century, 30 In. 3450.00
Desk, Walnut, Shopkeeper's, 108 In. 1300.00
Desk, Walnut, Slant Front, 3 Drawers, Pigeonholes, Victorian, 40 x 21 x 45 In. 440.00
Desk, Walnut, Slant Front, Fan Carved Door, French Feet 1850.00
Desk, Walnut, Slant Front, Interior Drawers & Compartments, 3 Drawers, 49 In. 7475.00
Desk, William & Mary, Cherry, Veneered Walnut Front, 40 x 32 In. 7500.00
Desk, William & Mary, Kneehole, Oyster-Shell Veneer 2315.00
Desk, William & Mary, Slant Front, Walnut, Inlaid, Boston, 40 In. . . . . *Illus* 4900.00
Desk, Woman's, Federal, Mahogany, Inlaid Tambour, c.1790, 43 1/2 In. 5750.00
Desk, Wooton, Queen Anne, Walnut, Burl, Gallery, 1884, 74 x 75 In. 16500.00
Desk, Wooton, Roll Top, Walnut, Wm. Sommerville's Son Escutcheon, 52 x 45 In. 7000.00
Desk, Wooton, Rotary, Oak, 1 Pier, Inset Panels, Leather Top, 1870, 54 x 32 In. 3500.00
Desk, Wooton, Walnut, Burl, Rotary, Slant Front, 1882, 78 x 56 In. 29500.00
Desk, Wooton, Walnut, Rotary, Flat Top, 2 Swing-Out Pedestals, Leather, 60 x 33 In. 6500.00
Desk Bookcase, Drop Front, 3 Drawers, Fitted Interior, Carved 1400.00
Desk Bookcase, Federal, Mahogany, 2 Mullioned Doors, Scalloped Apron, 86 In. 3450.00
Desk Box, Poplar, Table Top, Dovetailed, Refinished, 17 1/2 x 19 1/2 x 7 In. 190.00
Desk Cabinet, Arthur Miller, Oak, Drop Front, Gallery, 3 Drawers, 2 Doors, 60 In. 415.00
Dinette Set, Cherner, 4 Bentwood Chairs, 29 x 41 1/2 In., 5 Piece 880.00
Dinette Set, Rattan, Round Glass Top Table, 4 Chairs, 5 Piece 145.00

Furniture, Desk, Roll Top, Oak,
Kneehole, Fitted Interior

Furniture, Desk, William & Mary, Slant
Front, Walnut, Inlaid, Boston, 40 In.

Dinette Set, Rohde, Bentwood, Replaced Vinyl, Extension Table, 5 Piece 770.00
Dinette Set, Saarinen, Oval Top, 3 Side & 1 Arm Chair, All Pedestal, 5 Piece 425.00
Dinette Set, Wrought Iron, Rose & Leaf Design, Glass Top Table, 5 Piece 345.00
Dining Set, Arundel Clarke, Black Lacquered Top, White Base, 30 x 60 In. 770.00
Dining Set, Georgian Style, Paine Furniture, Leaves, Early 20th Century, 9 Piece 6900.00
Dining Set, Hans Wegner, Ash, Drop Leaf, X-Form Legs, Vinyl Seats, 5 Piece 1980.00
Dining Set, Heywood-Wakefield, 4 Chairs, 42 x 84 In., 5 Piece 1200.00
Dining Set, Heywood-Wakefield, Encore, Champagne Finish, Cabinet, 6 Piece 715.00
Dining Set, Hunzinger, Mahogany, Bronze Mounted Chairs, Lion Heads, 7 Piece 8000.00
Dining Set, Oak, Jacobean Style, 7 Piece 520.00
Dining Set, Rosewood, Walnut, Pedestal Table, China Cabinet, Austria, 10 Piece 2760.00
Dining Set, William & Mary Style, Walnut, 6 Upholstered Chairs, c.1935, 10 Piece 440.00
Display Case, Mahogany, Cherry, Glass, Tapestry Lined Stem, 3 Saber Legs, 1830 ..... 1090.00
Dresser, Belle Epoque, Brass Mounted, Early 20th Century, 80 x 48 In. 1045.00
Dresser, Burl Walnut, Marble Top, 3 Drawers, Silver Pulls, 96 In. 2500.00
Dresser, Charles II, Oak, 3 Drawers, Iron Pulls, 1660, 36 In. 10350.00
Dresser, Chestnut, Burl Inlay, Mirror 575.00
Dresser, Curly Ash Veneer, Mirror, Fruit Pulls, 2 Top & 3 Base Drawers, 68 In. 330.00
Dresser, Eastlake, Walnut, Marble Top, Child's, 13 1/2 x 27 x 53 In. 550.00
Dresser, Empire, Mahogany, Flame Veneer, 5 Drawers, Secret Base Drawer, 80 In. 600.00
Dresser, G. Stickley, No. 625, Oak, Mirror, 1902 ....*Illus* 4400.00
Dresser, George III, Oak, 5 Drawers, 2 Doors, Late 18th Century, 66 x 20 In. 4115.00
Dresser, Mahogany, Bowfront 2 Drawers Over 3 Drawers, 1840, 52 x 52 In. 935.00
Dresser, Mahogany, Original Red Paint, 2 Drawers Over 3 Drawers, Carved 1800.00
Dresser, Maple, Granite Top, 2 Short Over 2 Graduated Drawers, 1880s, 31 In. 300.00
Dresser, Maple, Princess Style, Mirror, Accessory Chest ....*Illus* 525.00
Dresser, McCobb, 10 Drawers 495.00
Dresser, Oak, 3 Shelves, England, Late 18th Century, 83 x 64 In. ....*Illus* 3300.00
Dresser, Oak, Attached Mirror, 2 Short Over 2 Long Drawers, Late 19th Century 330.00
Dresser, Oak, Beveled Glass Mirror, 4 Drawers, 19 x 40 x 66 In. 110.00
Dresser, Oak, Brass Pulls, Applied Design, 21 x 44 x 78 In. 415.00
Dresser, Pine, 3 Plate Shelves, 3 Drawers Over Open Cupboard, Ireland, 93 3/4 In. 1450.00
Dresser, Rococo, Mahogany, Marble Top, Crested Arch, 4 Graduated Drawers 3400.00
Dresser, Rosewood, Marble, 3 Graduated Drawers, 19th Century, 89 x 44 In. 1935.00
Dresser, Sheraton, Mahogany, Reeded Columns, Turned, 14 1/2 In. 1725.00
Dresser, Victorian, Walnut, Easel Mirror, 3 Drawers, 78 x 39 In. 350.00
Dresser, Victorian, Walnut, Mirror, Fruit Pulls, Marble Insert, 41 x 81 In. 330.00
Dresser, Walnut, Marble Top, 3 Drawers, Silver Pulls, Shelf Each Side, 44 x 28 In. 3000.00
Dresser, Walnut, Marble Top, Hand Carved Fruit Pulls, Secret Bottom Drawer 1800.00
Dresser, Welsh, Pine, Cavetto Frieze Over 2 Open Shelves, Plate Racks, 80 In. 800.00
Dresser, Welsh, Walnut, 3 Drawers Over 2 Paneled Doors, 77 x 56 In. 2100.00
Dry Sink, Amish, Doors Flanking 3 Drawers 925.00

Dry Sink, Ash, Poplar, 1 Door, 2 Paneled Doors, Top Shelf, 46 x 18 x 42 In. 600.00
Dry Sink, Blue Paint, 6 Drawers, Panel Door, Scalloped Apron, Secret Compartment . . . 1500.00
Dry Sink, Green Paint Over Mustard, Zinc Liner 1485.00
Dry Sink, Mustard & Red Combed Design, 19 x 18 In. 1875.00
Dry Sink, Pine & Poplar, Blue Gray Repaint, Crest, 14 x 36 In. 630.00
Dry Sink, Pine, Dovetailed, Beaded & Chamfered Paneled Doors 2500.00
Dry Sink, Pine, Drawer Over Shelf, Copper, Casters, 19th Century, 33 x 25 In. 290.00
Dry Sink, Pine, Paneled Door Over Shaped Skirt, Drawer 165.00
Dry Sink, Pine, Rectangular Well, Overhanging Sides, Cupboard Doors, 36 x 49 In. 1380.00
Dry Sink, Poplar, Copper Lined Top, 2 Wells, 1 Rectangular, 1 Round, 28 In. 300.00
Dry Sink, Walnut, Partly Removed Paint Layers, 2 Doors, 18 x 55 In. 1980.00
Dumbwaiter, George II, Mahogany, 2 Tiers, 3 Columnar Supports, Pad Feet 8625.00
Dumbwaiter, George II, Mahogany, 3 Tiers, Baluster Support, Tripod, 45 x 23 In. 845.00
Dumbwaiter, Georgian, Mahogany, Dish Shelves, 19th Century, 50 3/4 In. 800.00
Dumbwaiter, Mahogany, 3 Graduated Tiers, Tripod Base, Pad Feet, 40 In. 980.00
Dumbwaiter, Mixed Woods, Adjustable, Retractable Top, 3 Sections, 19th Century 775.00
Easel, Arts & Crafts, Cutout Handle In Back, Oak, 39 x 20 In. 60.00
Etagere, 4 Shelves, Joining Vase, Ring Supports, 2 Drawers, c.1825, 57 x 34 In. 1725.00
Etagere, Burl Walnut, 3 Tiers, Gallery, Serpentine, England, 46 x 24 In. 910.00
Etagere, Corner, Rococo Style, Rosewood, Carved, Victorian 1495.00
Etagere, Corner, Walnut, Scalloped Shelves, Turned Posts, 57 3/4 In. 165.00
Etagere, Ebonized, 2 Cylindrical Supports, White Finials, 51 In. 9200.00
Etagere, Faux Bamboo, Ebonized, 3 Tiers, 34 1/2 x 16 x 10 In. 195.00
Etagere, George III, Mahogany, 3 Tiers, Marble Top, 34 In. 3160.00
Etagere, Jeliff, Walnut, Ebonized Trim, Gold Gilding, 101 x 59 In. 9750.00
Etagere, Louis XVI, Gray Mottled Top, Fluted Legs, 33 In. 5175.00
Etagere, Mahogany, Gallery Top, Beaded Shelves, 40 1/4 In. 1695.00
Etagere, Mahogany, Satinwood, Drawer, Anglo-West Indian, 19th Century, 54 In. 965.00
Etagere, Oriental, Fretwork, Metal Mounts, 49 x 73 x 17 In. 845.00
Etagere, Rococo, Ebonized Gilt Metal, Mirrors, Upholstered Shelves, 74 In. 3650.00
Etagere, Rococo, Rosewood Grained, Marble, Mirror, Floral Cornice, 1850, 89 In. 3930.00
Etagere, Thomas Brooks, Walnut, Marble Top, c.1860 . . . . 5900.00
Etagere, Victorian, Walnut, 5 Shaped Shelves, Fretwork Galleries 475.00
Etagere, Victorian, Walnut, Carved, 88 x 47 1/2 In. 3850.00
Etagere, Victorian, Walnut, Marble Top Console, Mirror, Fretwork, 94 1/2 In. 3200.00
Footman, Brass, Steel, Serpentine Front, Engraved Shield, Leopard Heads, 1830, 9 In. . . .   950.00
Footstool, Aesthetic Revival, Ebonized, Gilt, Silk Damask, 1870-1880 . . . .   180.00
Footstool, Aesthetic Revival, Jeweler's, Leather, Metal Legs 395.00
Footstool, Arts & Crafts, Flaring Legs, Petit Point Upholstery, 7 x 17 1/2 x 12 In. 137.00
Footstool, Baroque, Walnut, Upholstered Seat, Italy, 19 x 19 x 15 In. 435.00
Footstool, Cherry Legs, Floral Upholstered, 1700 . . . .   195.00

Furniture, Dresser, Oak,
3 Shelves, England, Late 18th
Century, 83 x 64 In.

Furniture, Dresser,
G. Stickley, No. 625,
Oak, Mirror, 1902

Furniture, Dresser,
Maple, Princess Style, Mirror,
Accessory Chest

Footstool, Classical, Mustard Yellow, Black Design, 12 1/2 In. 1610.00
Footstool, Empire, Mahogany, Upholstered, 1840 . . . . 300.00
Footstool, Folke Ohlstrom, Teak, Doweled Legs, 13 x 23 x 12 In. 82.50
Footstool, G. Stickley, 7 Spindles Each Side, Leather Top, 15 1/4 x 20 1/2 In. 2200.00
Footstool, G. Stickley, Pyramidal Tacks, Uneven Stretchers, 15 x 20 In. 935.00
Footstool, G. Stickley, Red-Brown Finish 685.00
Footstool, Gilt, Iron, Upholstered Pansies, Red Ground 235.00
Footstool, L. & J.G. Stickley, Mahogany, Drop-In Spring Seat, 17 x 20 In. 220.00
Footstool, L. & J.G. Stickley, Original Leather Top, 18 x 19 In. 275.00
Footstool, Louis XV, Needlepoint Upholstered, Leaf Tip Carved Feet, Round, 14 In. . . . 800.00
Footstool, Mahogany, Brass Bun Feet, 10 1/2 In. 90.00
Footstool, Parsons, Square, 18 x 18 In., Pair 85.00
Footstool, Poplar, Floral Needlepoint, Black Ground, Refinished, 14 x 16 1/2 In. 70.00
Footstool, Red, Black Graining, Yellow Striping, Cane Seat, 12 1/2 In. 115.00
Footstool, Renaissance Revival, Walnut, Upholstered, Floral Carved Knees, 17 In. 80.00
Footstool, Rococo, Iron, Gilt, Victorian, 13 x 16 1/4 In. 287.00
Footstool, Rococo, Tufted Upholstery, Circular, 19 x 13 1/2 In. 100.00
Footstool, Rosewood, Carved, Serpentine Apron, Upholstered, 1840s, Pair 550.00
Footstool, Round Inlay, Floral Needlepoint, Pair, 11 In. 165.00
Footstool, Shaker, Mt. Lebanon, Dark Finish, Label, 11 3/4 x 11 1/2 In. 300.00
Footstool, Shaped Skirt, Bootjack Ends, 19th Century 50.00
Footstool, Stickley Bros., Mahogany, Arched Aprons, Drop-In Leather Seat, 24 In. 110.00
Footstool, Walnut, Floral Needlepoint Seat, Black Ground, 14 In. 250.00
Footstool, Walnut, Frieze Carved Flower Heads, Upholstered Top, 25 x 11 In. 690.00
Footstool, Walnut, Needlepoint Top, Bun Feet 65.00
Footstool, Walnut, Turned Legs, Rectangular, 8 In. 85.00
Footstool, Walnut, Turtle Shape, Carved Grape Clusters At Knees, Tapestry Seat, 23 In. . 230.00
Footstool, William & Mary, H-Stretcher, Upholstered, 15 x 19 x 17 In. 400.00
Footstool, Windsor, Dark Paint, Floral Design, 7 1/2 x 13 x 8 3/4 In. 135.00
Frame, Double, Walnut, Pedestal, Triple Shell Crest, 1840s, 12 3/4 In. 295.00
Gun Case, Oak, Brass, Tho.Elsworth Mortimer, Rifle, Gun & Pistol Maker, 30 In. 440.00
Hall Stand, Cast Iron, Mirror, Marble Shelf, Drip Pans, Rococo Revival, 1860s 1155.00
Hall Stand, Cast Iron, Oval Mirror, 4 Arms, Umbrella Tray, 84 In. 1815.00
Hall Stand, Gilt, Iron, Central Mirror, Over 2 Cherubs, Marble Shelf, 89 In. 6325.00
Hall Stand, Oak, Portrait Medallions, Wrought-Iron Hangers, 1910, 78 In. 1320.00
Hall Stand, Quartersawn Oak, Lift Lid Seat, Beveled Mirror, Hooks, 83 In. 880.00
Hall Stand, Renaissance Revival, Walnut, Mid-19th Century 1330.00
Hall Stand, Victorian, Oak, Beveled Glass Mirror, 1880 . . . . 1320.00
Hall Stand, Victorian, Walnut, Mirror, 7 Pegs, Oyster Shell Drip Pan 1795.00
Hall Stand, Walnut, Lift Top Seat, Beveled Mirror, Brass Bars For Umbrella 1500.00
Hall Tree, Gothic Revival, Walnut, Cast Iron Pan, Refinished, 35 x 91 In. 600.00
Hall Tree, L. & J.G. Stickley, Tapering Posts, Long Corbels Over Shoe Feet, 72 In. 2090.00
Hall Tree, Oak, Carved, England, c.1890 . . . . 1195.00
Hat Rack, Arts & Crafts, 3-Rail Gate Form, Motto, Friendship Hinges, 5 Pegs, 29 In. . . . 220.00
High Chair, Arrow Back, Red Paint, Thick Seat 80.00
High Chair, Ash, Rush Seat, England, 37 In. 575.00
High Chair, Curly Maple, Captain's Chair Back, Plank Seat, Turned Spindles, 31 In. 220.00
High Chair, Hardwood, Folds Into Play Station, Cane Seat, 37 1/2 In. 150.00
High Chair, Ladder Back, Splint Seat, 36 In. 195.00
High Chair, Maple, Hickory, Ball Finials, 3 Backrests, Splint Seat, Turned Arms, 1720 . . 920.00
High Chair, Pressed Wood, Cane Seat & Back, Adjustable Height, 39 3/4 In. 275.00
High Chair, Rod Back, Red Paint, Missing Footrest 550.00
High Chair, Windsor, Buttermilk Paint, Arms 275.00
High Chair, Windsor, Cherry, Bow Back, Arched Back, 6 Spindles, Green, Arms, 1830s . 1035.00
High Chair, Windsor, Painted, Thumb Back, Dover, N.H., c.1830, 35 In. 1095.00
Highboy, Queen Anne Style, Cherry, 4 Dovetailed Drawers, Carved Fan, 78 In. 5500.00
Highboy, Queen Anne Style, Mahogany, 3 Drawers, Cornice, 64 1/2 In. 9200.00
Highboy, Queen Anne Style, Walnut, 3 Drawers, Pad Feet, 64 1/2 In. 600.00
Highboy, Queen Anne, Cherry, Bonnet 8000.00
Highboy, Queen Anne, Cherry, Bonnet, Cabriole Legs, Pad Feet, Conn., 87 In. 13800.00
Highboy, Queen Anne, Maple, Scalloped Apron, Duck Feet, 72 In. 7700.00
Highboy, Queen Anne, Walnut, 4 Drawers, Hidden Drawer, 24 x 41 x 67 In. 3300.00
Highboy, Walnut, 2 Over 3 Drawers, 2 Side Drawers, Document Drawer, c.1710 . . . . 8500.00

Highboy, William & Mary, 8 Drawers, Hidden Drawer, 18th Century 4400.00
Highboy, William & Mary, Walnut, Pine, 5 Drawers, Teardrop Brasses, 61 In. 9350.00
Hoosier Cabinet, Oyster Oak, 1940s 595.00
Hoosier-Type Cupboard, 2 Glass Doors, 2 Drawers, 2 Bins, Breadboard, 64 In. 100.00
Huntboard, Mahogany, Bowfront, Line Inlaid Skirt & Legs, Spade Feet 2860.00
Huntboard, Oak, Rectangular Top Over 4 Drawers, Pad Feet, Welsh, 32 x 80 In. 3795.00
Huntboard, Regency Revival, Mahogany, Gadrooned Columns, Reeded Legs, 43 In. . . . 2750.00
Huntboard, Sheraton, Cherry, Reeded Posts, Turned Legs, 33 In. 2750.00
Hutch, Maple, Upper Shelves, Scroll Sides, 2 Short Over Long Drawer Top, 70 In. 230.00
Hutch, Pennsylvania House, Cherry, 2 Glazed Doors, Bracket Base 195.00
Hutch, Peter Hunt, 2 Shelves, 4 Base Drawers, Signed, 70 1/2 x 45 In. 5500.00
Hutch, Pine, Corner, Mullion Glazed Doors, Scalloped Shelves, 1760s, 88 1/2 In. 9200.00
Hutch, Pine, Upper Sliding Door, Shelves, 6 Lower Drawers, 85 x 45 1/2 In. 3740.00
Hutch, Watch, Cutout In Door For Display, Snipe Hinges, 18th Century 6500.00
Ice Cream Set, Table, 2 Chairs, Child, 3 Piece 200.00
Kas, 2 Drawers Below Double Paneled Doors 7560.00
Kas, Continental, Pine, 2 Drawer Base, Panels, Cornice, Carved Name & 1782, 76 In. . . . 165.00
Kas, Continental, Pine, Blue & Red Paint, Florals, 1819 . . . . 2760.00
Kas, Dutch, Faux Bois Graining, 3 Doors, Bun Feet, Medallions, 18th Century, 74 In. . . . 1700.00
Kas, Gumwood, Mid-Section Doors, 3 Shelves, Lower Long Drawer, 1730s, 80 In. 4600.00
Kas, Poplar, 2 Paneled Doors, Brass Thumb Latches, Pegs For Clothes, 73 In. 4950.00
Kas, Poplar, Floral Repaint, Ivory Panels, Cornice, 3 Sections, 56 x 68 x 71 In. 2750.00
Kas, Queen Anne, Poplar, Cornice, 73 1/2 In. 4730.00
Kitchen Set, Porcelain Top, Table, 4 Chairs 375.00
Ladder, Library, Mahogany, Joined By 2 Burgundy Ropes, Victorian, 78 In. 1725.00
Lectern, Poplar, Table Top, Alligatored Brown Graining, 19 3/4 x 17 1/2 In. 55.00
Lectern, Sheraton, Mahogany, 2 Shelves, Drawer, 49 1/2 In. 575.00
Lectern, Wrought Iron, Wood Support, Checkerboard Design, France, 67 In. 8050.00
Library Steps, Georgian, Mahogany, Square Upholstered Back & Seat, Arms, Pair 4140.00
Library Steps, Mahogany, 3 Leather Inset Treads, 57 In. 7762.00
Library Steps, Mahogany, 3 Tooled Leather Inset Steps, Balancing Stem 635.00
Library Steps, Mahogany, Crest, 2 Serpentine Treads, Square Legs 6900.00
Library Steps, Oak & Curly Maple, 20th Century, 22 x 24 x 18 In. 275.00
Library Steps, Regency Style, Mahogany, 22 x 19 1/4 In. 6565.00
Linen Press, Federal, Mahogany, 83 x 46 In. 9200.00
Linen Press, George II, Mahogany, Cornice, Bracket Feet, 96 In. 10350.00
Linen Press, Georgian, Oak, 2 Doors, Arched Panels, Square Feet, 72 x 54 In. 1760.00
Linen Press, Jackson, Cherry, Drawer, 2 Doors, Half Columns, Refinished, 42 x 56 In. . . 1155.00
Linen Press, Mahogany, 2 Doors, 4 Drawers, England, 19th Century, 77 x 46 In. 3585.00
Linen Press, Renaissance Revival, Walnut, Carved, Late 19th Century, 98 x 96 In. 3680.00
Linen Press, Sheraton, Mahogany, 3 Base Drawers, New York, 84 x 52 In. 10925.00
Love Seat, Carved Wooden Lion Heads, Extended Tongues, Tapestry Cover 1800.00
Love Seat, Knoll, Yellow, Wool, Black Rod Legs 1200.00
Love Seat, Saarinen, Boucle Upholstery, Black Rod Legs 1100.00
Love Seat, Walnut, Carved, Upholstered Back, Throw Cushion Seat, 52 In. 2885.00
Love Seat, Walnut, Slat Back, Dowel Legs, 31 x 51 x 30 In. 2475.00
Love Seat, Windsor, Maple, Thumb Back, Rush Seat, c.1820 . . . . 1500.00
Lowboy, Baker Co., Burl Walnut Fronts, Banded Border, 3 Drawers, 29 x 32 In. 1035.00
Lowboy, Colonial, Mahogany, 3 Short Drawers, Cabriole Legs, 28 x 27 x 18 In. 1815.00
Lowboy, George II, Red Walnut, Apron, Straight Cabriole Legs, 18th Century, 28 In. 5325.00
Lowboy, George III, Mahogany, 2 Short Over 1 Long Drawer, 28 x 33 x 18 In. 2425.00
Lowboy, Georgian Style, Oak, 3 Banded Drawers, Tapered Legs, 29 x 30 In. 775.00
Lowboy, Georgian, Oak, 3 Beaded Drawers, Cabriole Legs, 1780s, 27 1/2 In. 1815.00
Lowboy, Oak, Over Hung Top, 3 Banded Drawers, Pierced Apron, 27 x 33 In. 600.00
Lowboy, Queen Anne Style, Walnut, Drawer, 4 Cabriole Legs, Pad Feet, 1740 . . . . 6900.00
Lowboy, Queen Anne, Burl, 3 Beaded Drawers, Cabriole Legs, 30 1/4 In. 545.00
Lowboy, Queen Anne, Burl, Crossbanded, 3 Beaded Drawers, 30 In. 485.00
Lowboy, Queen Anne, Cherry, Cyma Curve Apron, Cabriole Legs, 31 In. 5445.00
Lowboy, Queen Anne, Maple, Cutout Skirt, 1770s 9800.00
Lowboy, Queen Anne, Maple, Scrolled Apron, 3 Dovetailed Drawers, 34 1/4 In. 2200.00
Lowboy, Queen Anne, Walnut, Walnut Veneer, Bleached Finish, 19 x 27 x 27 In. 1210.00
Lowboy, William & Mary, Walnut, Acorn Drops, 3 Drawers, 29 1/4 In. 11500.00
Mirror, Acanthus Crest, Medusa Medallion, Carved Finials, 1800, 55 x 24 In. 4200.00

Furniture, Mirror,
Chippendale, Mahogany
Veneer, 18th Century, 33 In.

Furniture, Mirror,
Chippendale, Mahogany, Parcel
Gilt, Crest, 1875, 45 In.

Furniture, Mirror, Federal,
Parcel Gilt, Inlaid,
New York City, 1800, 50 In.

Mirror, American Rococo, Gilt, Mantel, Late 19th Century, 72 x 72 In. 1840.00
Mirror, Arts & Crafts, Eagle Carved Oak Frame, Dark Finish, Branded R 1903, 11 In. . . .   165.00
Mirror, Baroque Style, Fruitwood, Wild Animal Border, 18th Century 5465.00
Mirror, Baroque Style, Giltwood, Carved, Shell & Floral Crest, 33 x 15 In. 120.00
Mirror, Baroque, Hardwood, Carved, Continental, 19th Century, 59 x 45 In. 1815.00
Mirror, Baroque, Scrolls, Mask Design, 18th Century, Italy, 36 In., Pair 230.00
Mirror, Beveled Glass, Carved Figural & Landscape Frame, China, 36 x 16 In. 60.00
Mirror, Beveled Glass, Floral Design, Octagonal, 34 1/2 In. 110.00
Mirror, Biedermeier, Ebonized, 2 Panels, Leafy Scrolls, Arch, 69 In. 2185.00
Mirror, Biedermeier, Mahogany, Ebonized, Turned Column, Austria, 51 x 30 In. 1980.00
Mirror, Biedermeier, Walnut, Inlaid, Molded Cornice, 19th Century, 67 x 26 In. 1725.00
Mirror, Bilboa, Giltwood & Marble Inset, Acorn Finial, c.1800, 24 x 7 1/2 In. 1150.00
Mirror, Bird's-Eye Veneer Ogee Frame, 23 1/2 x 27 In. 55.00
Mirror, Black & Gilt Design, Eglomise Upper Panel Castle, 31 1/2 x 16 1/4 In. 110.00
Mirror, Brass Rosettes, Corner Blocks, Reverse Painted, Child With Cat, 29 3/4 In. 445.00
Mirror, Carved Bracket Supports, Reverse Painted Flowers, c.1750, 72 In. 1495.00
Mirror, Cast Brass Easel, Beveled Mirror 100.00
Mirror, Cheval, Empire, Mahogany, Gabled Crest, Tapered Columns, 76 x 40 In. 3025.00
Mirror, Cheval, Empire, Mahogany, Ormolu 1725.00
Mirror, Cheval, Mahogany, Beveled, Brass Frame, Candleholders, 71 In. 1780.00
Mirror, Cheval, Mahogany, Rope Carved Swing Mirror, c.1830, 70 x 29 1/2 In. 3270.00
Mirror, Cheval, Pineapple & Eagle Finials, Brass Paw Casters, 69 1/2 In. 4600.00
Mirror, Cheval, Regency Revival, Mahogany, Beveled Plate, 1835, 62 1/4 In. 1150.00
Mirror, Cheval, Teak, Rosewood Cross Members, Anglo-Indian, 66 1/2 x 32 In. 1035.00
Mirror, Cheval, Walnut, Candleholders, Brass Inlaid, Paw Feet, 71 1/2 In. 1495.00
Mirror, Chinoiserie, 3 Sections, Beveled Plate, 19th Century, France, 12 x 10 In. 180.00
Mirror, Chippendale, Giltwood, Carved, Swan's-Neck Pediment, 43 x 24 In. 1035.00
Mirror, Chippendale, Mahogany Veneer On Pine, Carved Phoenix, 39 1/2 In. 1430.00
Mirror, Chippendale, Mahogany Veneer, 18th Century, 33 In. *Illus*   1035.00
Mirror, Chippendale, Mahogany Veneer, Gilt-Carved Frame, c.1740, 24 x 12 In. 460.00
Mirror, Chippendale, Mahogany Veneer, Parcel Gilt, Foliate Crest, 45 x 25 In. 2300.00
Mirror, Chippendale, Mahogany Veneer, Scroll, Dark Finish, 19 1/4 x 12 5/8 In. 465.00
Mirror, Chippendale, Mahogany, Gilt Heron On Crest, New England, 24 1/2 In. 690.00
Mirror, Chippendale, Mahogany, Gilt Leaf Scroll, Crest, 39 x 22 In. 345.00
Mirror, Chippendale, Mahogany, Gothic Border, Urn Design, 74 In. 1210.00
Mirror, Chippendale, Mahogany, Inlaid Reserve, Stylized Leaves, c.1790, 29 3/4 In. 460.00
Mirror, Chippendale, Mahogany, New England, c.1800, 18 x 11 1/2 In. 690.00
Mirror, Chippendale, Mahogany, Parcel Gilt, Crest, 1875, 45 In. . . . . *Illus*   1840.00
Mirror, Chippendale, Mahogany, Parcel Gilt, Scroll Carved, Pierced, 1760, 29 In. 1035.00

Mirror, Chippendale, Mahogany, Pine, Scroll, Gilt Eagle, 47 x 24 1/2 In.	580.00
Mirror, Chippendale, Mahogany, Scroll, Black, Gold Liner, 48 In.	440.00
Mirror, Chippendale, Mahogany, Scroll, Gilt Eagle, 31 In.	1155.00
Mirror, Chippendale, Mahogany, Scroll, Gilt Liner, Phoenix, 26 1/4 In.	335.00
Mirror, Chippendale, Mahogany, Scrolled Crest, England, 37 x 20 1/2 In.	750.00
Mirror, Chippendale, Maple, Scrolled Crest, Pendant Base, 39 x 17 In.	3450.00
Mirror, Chippendale, Tiger Maple, Cutout Top, New England, 1780, 17 In.	4800.00
Mirror, Chippendale, Walnut Veneer, Parcel Gilt Ruffles, 1750s, 35 1/2 x 20 In.	2300.00
Mirror, Chippendale, Walnut, Gilt Leaves, Phoenix Crest, 43 In.	990.00
Mirror, Chippendale, Walnut, Scalloped Crest, 22 1/2 In.	525.00
Mirror, Classical, Giltwood, 2 Cornucopia Form, Symmetrically Carved, 1840	5325.00
Mirror, Classical, Giltwood, Carved Colonettes, Boston, 1825, 47 x 31 In.	4355.00
Mirror, Classical, Giltwood, Frieze Panel, Spiral Columns, 1820, 54 In.	1100.50
Mirror, Classical, Giltwood, Overmantel, Tripartite, 1835	485.00
Mirror, Classical, Giltwood, Turned Half-Columns, Brass Roundels, 40 x 20 In.	220.00
Mirror, Classical, Mahogany, Cornice, Diamond Carved Spiral Columns, 52 In.	1090.00
Mirror, Classical, Mahogany, Ogee, 2-Part Plate, Gilt Inner Border, 53 1/2 In.	290.00
Mirror, Classical, Mahogany, Parcel Gilt, 2-Part, 19th Century, 49 3/4 In.	365.00
Mirror, Classical, Mahogany, Tripartite, Segmented Ogee Frame, 1840, 47 In.	360.00
Mirror, Classical, Pier, Giltwood, Rectangular Frame, Reeded Spindles, 61 In.	1955.00
Mirror, Courting, Reverse Painted Pot Of Flowers, Wooden Frame, 16 x 10 5/8 In.	385.00
Mirror, Dieppe Ivory, Carved Leaf Tops, Putti, Sea Creatures On Frame, 33 In.	2300.00
Mirror, Dressing, Federal, Mahogany, 1815, 15 5/8 In.	950.00
Mirror, Dressing, Ivory Banding, Sharkskin, Swing Mounted, c.1925, 16 3/4 In.	2300.00
Mirror, Dressing, Rosewood, Scrolled Supports, England, c.1840, 34 In.	455.00
Mirror, Edwardian, Mahogany, Carved Flower Basket Crest, 32 x 18 In.	150.00
Mirror, Eglomise Tablet, Woman & Child At Stream, 41 1/2 x 24 1/4 In.	1610.00
Mirror, Egyptian Revival, Gilt, Overmantel, Mid-19th Century, 72 x 70 In.	3105.00
Mirror, Empire, Ebonized, Trailing Flowers Frieze, Foliate, 53 x 44 In.	1265.00
Mirror, Empire, Gilt Bronze, Opposed Swans, Round, France, 10 1/2 In.	245.00
Mirror, Empire, Mahogany, Over Hanging Cornice, Half Columns, 76 x 47 In.	1155.00
Mirror, Empire, Red, White Striping, Black Corner, 29 1/2 In.	495.00
Mirror, Federal Style, Eglomise, Sailing Ship Top Panel, 20 x 11 1/2 In.	230.00
Mirror, Federal, Cherry & Mahogany Veneer, 36 3/4 x 19 1/4 In.	465.00
Mirror, Federal, Convex, Eagle Carved Crest, 19th Century, 38 x 21 In.	935.00
Mirror, Federal, Gilt Gesso, Eglomise, Tablet Scene, Riverbank, Fishermen, 42 In.	1150.00
Mirror, Federal, Giltwood, Convex, Oval Bosses, Stylized Flowers, 31 x 27 In.	2180.00
Mirror, Federal, Giltwood, Eagle Design With Spherules, New York, 55 In.	2185.00
Mirror, Federal, Giltwood, Eglomise, Church Scene, N.Y., 1800, 38 x 17 In.	1450.00
Mirror, Federal, Giltwood, Eglomise, Panel Inset, Cottage By River, 35 x 21 In.	402.00
Mirror, Federal, Mahogany Inlay, Swan's Neck Crest, c.1790, 53 x 23 In.	2070.00
Mirror, Federal, Mahogany, Carved, Molded Cornice, 1810-1820, 34 In.	635.00
Mirror, Federal, Mahogany, Gilt, Inlaid Crest, 1800, 50 1/2 In.	6325.00
Mirror, Federal, Mahogany, Inlaid Conch Shell, 1790-1810, 31 1/4 In.	460.00
Mirror, Federal, Mahogany, Overhanging Pediment, J. Barry, 29 x 21 3/4 In.	600.00
Mirror, Federal, Mahogany, Reeded Half-Columns, Cornice, Base, 31 3/4 In.	360.00
Mirror, Federal, Mahogany, Reverse Painted House & Trees, 37 7/8 In.	770.00
Mirror, Federal, Mahogany, Split Panel, Frieze, Phila., 19th Century, 30 In.	425.00
Mirror, Federal, Parcel Gilt, Inlaid, New York City, 1800, 50 In. ....*Illus*	6325.00
Mirror, Federal, Parcel Gilt, Tortoiseshell Paint, 19th Century, 29 x 14 In.	230.00
Mirror, Federal, Rope Spiral Pilasters, Acorn Drops, Reverse Painted, 24 In.	300.00
Mirror, French Style, Giltwood, Scrolling Acanthus, Rococo Frame, 52 x 35 In.	800.00
Mirror, Fruitwood, Molded Rectangular Frame, Mid-19th Century, 63 x 39 In.	330.00
Mirror, G. Stickley, Oak, Arched Top, Wrought-Iron Hooks, c.1909, 28 x 42 In.	2530.00
Mirror, George I, Walnut, Scroll Carved Crest, 18th Century, 34 In.	2300.00
Mirror, George II Style, Giltwood, Hinged Sides, Egg, Dart Border, 26 In.	375.00
Mirror, George II, Giltwood, Egg & Dark Cornice, Shell Cartouche, 67 x 30 In.	2300.00
Mirror, George III, Giltwood, Carved Leaves, Flowers, Oval, 43 In.	8600.00
Mirror, George III, Giltwood, Ribbon Tied Branches, Oval, 37 In.	7500.00
Mirror, Georgian Style, Gesso Wood, Eagle Crest, Pierced Scrolled Sides, 46 In.	250.00
Mirror, Georgian, Giltwood, Foliate, Phoenix, Oval, 68 x 40 In.	770.00
Mirror, Georgian, Mahogany, Phoenix Finial, Fruit, Leaf Design, 55 x 28 In.	3160.00
Mirror, Gilt & Black Pillar Frame, Upper Eglomise Cottage, Landscape, 20 x 11 In.	60.00

Mirror, Giltwood, 2-Part Plate, Applied Florets, Foliate, 48 x 27 In. 1375.00
Mirror, Giltwood, 2-Part, Foliate Inner Borders, 38 x 18 In. 220.00
Mirror, Giltwood, Beveled Plate, Foliage, Italy, 27 x 14 In., Pair 750.00
Mirror, Giltwood, Convex, Eagle Crest, Sphere Mounted Frame, 38 x 25 1/2 In. 690.00
Mirror, Giltwood, Convex, Ebonized Slip, Frame, Foliage, 45 In. 8050.00
Mirror, Giltwood, Crest, Urn, Swags At Sides, England, 48 In. 460.00
Mirror, Giltwood, Crown Above 2-Headed Eagle, Round, Continental, 32 In. 920.00
Mirror, Giltwood, Floral Frame, Boston, Mass., 1835, 49 x 27 In. 525.00
Mirror, Giltwood, Gesso, Floral Bouquets At Crest & Sides, Oval, 45 14 In. 1210.00
Mirror, Giltwood, Molded Cornice, Carved Scrolls, Acanthus, 1870, 88 In. 5175.00
Mirror, Giltwood, Molded Frame, Rectangular, 19th Century, 58 x 29 1/2 In. 495.00
Mirror, Giltwood, Overmantel, Ogee Form, 55 1/4 x 34 3/4 In. 565.00
Mirror, Giltwood, Overmantel, Rose Ground, 44 3/4 x 60 In. 770.00
Mirror, Iron, Pivoting, American Flag Base, 1860s, 20 1/2 x 14 In. 650.00
Mirror, Italian Baroque, Walnut, Gilt, Feather Crest, 60 x 31 In. 545.00
Mirror, Italian Rococo Revival, Carved Leaves, 24 In. 865.00
Mirror, Japanned, Reverse Painted, Peonies, Bird, China, 18th Century, 26 x 15 In. 4900.00
Mirror, Limbert, No. 21, Arched Bottom Rail, 3 Slats Either Side, 26 x 35 3/4 In. 1430.00
Mirror, Louis XIV, Boullework, Ormolu, Plaque, Paris, 19th Century, 78 x 50 In. 7260.00
Mirror, Louis XV Style, Walnut, Giltwood, Rococo Crest, 63 x 31 In. 1100.00
Mirror, Louis XV, Cartouche Shape Frame, Carved Flower Heads, 27 1/2 x 18 In. 2600.00
Mirror, Louis XV, Giltwood, Scroll Carve Moldings, Shell 3160.00
Mirror, Louis XV, Giltwood, Variegated Serpentine Marble Top, 36 1/4 In. 2200.00
Mirror, Louis XVI Style, Foliate Crest, Grape Filled Urn, 57 x 32 In., Pair 1760.00
Mirror, Louis XVI, Blue Green, Fluted Border, Eagle With Quiver Of Arrows 4315.00
Mirror, Louis XVI, Boiserie Panel, Carved Leaf Borders, 76 In. 1100.50
Mirror, Louis XVI, Parcel Gilt, White, Pair Of Birds On Crest, 54 x 29 In. 550.00
Mirror, Mahogany Veneer, Grained, Mt. Vernon Scene, 40 x 21 In. 1325.00
Mirror, Mahogany Veneer, Scrolled Crest, Leaf Carved, 1740s, 43 x 22 In. 6325.00
Mirror, Mahogany, Brass Mounted, Gray Marble, Tapered Legs, 30 In. 6050.00
Mirror, Mahogany, Eglomise, Floral Design Panel, 56 In. 21850.00
Mirror, Mahogany, Giltwood Front Cartouche, Rectangular, 20 1/2 In. 750.00
Mirror, Mahogany, Giltwood, Scrolled Frame, 1790, 26 In. 230.00
Mirror, Mahogany, Inlaid Frame, 30 x 17 1/2 In. 415.00
Mirror, Mahogany, Ogee Frame, 19th Century, 30 3/4 x 21 1/2 In. 70.00
Mirror, Mahogany, Plate Flanked By 2 Small Mirror Plates, Beveled, 50 In. 635.00
Mirror, Maple, Faux Bamboo, American, 19th Century, 23 x 18 In. 180.00
Mirror, Marquetry, Bellflower & Patera, Beveled, Late 19th Century, 41 In. 785.00
Mirror, Neoclassical Style, Bronze, Easel Form, Open Work Floral, 10 x 13 In. 50.00
Mirror, Neoclassical Style, Mahogany, Brass Mounted Borders, 5 Ft. 1 In. 2300.00
Mirror, Neoclassical Style, Shell, Scroll & Floral Design, 48 x 30 In. 400.00
Mirror, Neoclassical Style, Silver Plate, Leaf Border, 30 3/4 x 14 3/4 In. 850.00
Mirror, Neoclassical, Bronze, Champleve Crests, Russia, 40 1/2 x 16 In., Pair 1265.00
Mirror, Neoclassical, Giltwood, Cornucopia Crest, Beveled Glass, 55 In. 275.00
Mirror, Neoclassical, Giltwood, Overmantel, Beveled Plate, 44 x 52 In. 485.00
Mirror, Neoclassical, Giltwood, Ribbon, Flower Carved, Oval, 35 In. 2185.00
Mirror, Neoclassical, Overmantel, Gilt Bronze, Italy, 19th Century, 42 x 59 In. 485.00
Mirror, Oak Panel, 3 Graduated Mirrors, Columnar Form Supports, 51 In. 230.00
Mirror, Oak, Beveled Plate, 4 Bronze Hooks, 1900, 21 1/2 x 28 In. 440.00
Mirror, Oak, Overmantel, Beveled, Stained Glass, 105 x 90 x 18 In. 8500.00
Mirror, Oriental, Reverse Painted, Wise Old Man Scene, 19 x 27 In. 115.00
Mirror, Pier Trumeau, Giltwood, Oil On Canvas Top, Boy With Flute, 60 x 29 In. 1495.00
Mirror, Pier, Biedermeier, Mahogany, Divided Plate, Ionic Capitals, 116 In. 5750.00
Mirror, Pier, Classical, Giltwood, Cornice, New York, 1835, 64 x 38 In. 2300.00
Mirror, Pier, Eastlake, Marble Top On Base, Dark Varnish Stain Finish, 92 In. 715.00
Mirror, Pier, Federal, Ring Turned Pilasters, Eglomise Panel Of Ships, 43 x 22 In. 1265.00
Mirror, Pier, Giltwood, Molded Frame, Foliate Scrollwork, 82 1/2 x 29 3/8 In. 990.00
Mirror, Pier, Mahogany, Scrolled Pediment, Ogee Sides, England, c.1840 . . . . 665.00
Mirror, Pier, Neoclassical, Gilt, Blue Paint, Carved, 19th Century 1100.00
Mirror, Pier, Renaissance Revival, Walnut, Burl, Incised Carvings, 36 x 12 x 98 In. 5000.00
Mirror, Pier, Walnut, Stick & Ball Base & Gallery, Carved Half Columns, 95 In. 230.00
Mirror, Pine, Gold Stenciled Design In Corners, Beveled, 14 x 18 In. 275.00
Mirror, Pine, Ogee Form Frame, 19th Century, 34 1/2 x 24 1/2 In. 110.00

Early mirrors, those made before 1850, had thin glass. To judge the thickness of a mirror, hold a pencil point against the glass. The difference between the point and the reflection is the thickness.

Furniture, Mirror, Porcelain, Cherubs, Floral, Candelabra, 24 x 15 In.

Mirror, Pine, Red Paint, Crest, Stylized Leaves, Lower Pendant, 1740s, 18 x 12 In.	6325.00
Mirror, Porcelain, Cherubs, Floral, Candelabra, 24 x 15 In. ....*Illus*	1320.00
Mirror, Queen Anne Style, Mahogany, Scrolled Crest, 25 In.	690.00
Mirror, Queen Anne Style, Scrolled Crest, Stylized Shell Design, 26 In., Pair	660.00
Mirror, Queen Anne, Gilt Molding, Intaglio Carved Crest, c.1730, 16 x 10 In.	575.00
Mirror, Queen Anne, Mahogany Veneer, Pine, Crest, Scroll, 22 1/4 x 20 3/8 In.	165.00
Mirror, Queen Anne, Walnut, Parcel Gilt, Carved, Molded Frame, 36 1/2 x 14 In.	2530.00
Mirror, Queen Anne, Walnut, Parcel Gilt, Crest, 1730-1750, 32 In.	2070.00
Mirror, Rectangular, Ogee Frame, 19th Century, 39 x 26 In.	125.00
Mirror, Regency Revival, Giltwood, Arch Acanthus Frame, 67 In.	1955.00
Mirror, Regency Revival, Giltwood, Convex, Eagle Crest, Sconces, 44 x 32 In.	5445.00
Mirror, Regency Revival, Giltwood, Gesso, Urn Crest, Acorn, Oak Leaves, 51 x 28 In.	1575.00
Mirror, Regency, Giltwood, Overmantel, 3 Sections, Raised Garland, 29 In.	3005.00
Mirror, Renaissance Revival, Rosewood, Victorian, Late 19th Century	2100.00
Mirror, Renaissance Revival, Walnut, Scroll Carving, Rectangular, 19th Century	315.00
Mirror, Reverse Painted, Oriental, Wise Old Men Scene, 19 1/4 x 27 1/4 In.	115.00
Mirror, Rococo Revival, Giltwood, Gesso, Ornate Floral Crest, 66 x 33 In.	725.00
Mirror, Rococo Style, Giltwood, 2 Candle Arms, Leafy Surround, Italy, 33 1/2 In.	287.00
Mirror, Rococo Style, Giltwood, Scrolled Borders, Shells, 45 In.	860.00
Mirror, Rococo, Gesso, Floral, C-Scroll Crest, 34 x 26 1/2 In.	165.00
Mirror, Rococo, Giltwood Girandole, Foliate Scrolled Frame, 30 3/4 In., Pair	3450.00
Mirror, Rococo, Giltwood, Cartouche Crest, Floral, Fruit Clusters, 70 x 42 In.	1695.00
Mirror, Rococo, Giltwood, Elaborate Crest, Oval, 46 x 28 1/2 In.	330.00
Mirror, Rococo, Giltwood, Foliate Tendrils Entwined With S-Scrolls, 42 In.	2300.00
Mirror, Rosewood, Grain Painted, 19th Century, 15 3/4 x 11 3/4 In.	345.00
Mirror, Rosewood, Maple, Harlequin Design, Beveled Sides, 11 x 12 1/2 In.	215.00
Mirror, Russian Neoclassical Style, Mahogany, Beveled, 60 x 25 1/4 In.	2300.00
Mirror, Shadowbox Frame, Gilt Liner, Ebonized Stripes, 15 3/4 x 13 7/8 In.	60.00
Mirror, Shaving, Brown Paint Over Gray, Top Crest, 16 1/2 In.	55.00
Mirror, Shaving, Chippendale, Open Fret Crest, Drawer, England, c.1780, 29 In.	1650.00
Mirror, Shaving, G. Stickley, Inverted V Top, 21 1/2 x 23 1/2 In.	1520.00
Mirror, Shaving, Mahogany Veneer, Bun Front Feet, Bracket Rear Feet	350.00
Mirror, Shaving, Mahogany Veneer, Dovetailed Drawer, Adjustable Mirror, 16 In.	165.00
Mirror, Shaving, Mahogany, 2 Beaded Edge Drawers, Lion Pulls	850.00
Mirror, Shaving, Pine & Mahogany, Serpentine, 3 Dovetailed Drawers, 22 In.	495.00
Mirror, Sheffield, Silver Repousse Floral Frame, Prince Of Wales Crest Top, 37 In.	2300.00
Mirror, Spiral Twist Molding, Concave Gilt Frame, Claw Feet, 40 x 28 In.	385.00
Mirror, Stylized Figures In Frame, Mouse, Cat & Dachshund, 1930, 16 x 11 In.	3000.00
Mirror, Tabernacle, Eglomise Painting, Battling Sailing Ships, 1820, 29 x 15 In.	545.00
Mirror, Tabernacle, Mahogany, 2-Part Plate, Acanthus Carved, 1840, x 21 1/2 In.	485.00
Mirror, Urn Of Flowers Finial, c.1800, 50 1/2 In.	6325.00
Mirror, Venetian Glass, Reverse Painted, Segmented Rococo Border, 50 x 38 In.	885.00
Mirror, Walnut Veneer, Scrolled Crest, Pierced Flower, c.1875, 39 x 21 In.	1725.00
Mirror, Walnut, Overmantel, Carved Crest, 1870, 86 x 65 In.	2175.00
Mirror, White Leatherette, Chrome Studs, 1940s, 30 In.	88.00

Mirror, Wicker Frame, 36 1/2 x 24 In. 20.00
Mirror, William & Mary, Burlwood, Molded & Banded Frame, 31 x 29 In. 2660.00
Mirror, William & Mary, Eglomise, Crest, Reverse Painted, 18th Century, 18 In. 460.00
Mirror, William & Mary, Japanned, Birds & Floral, 1710-1730, 19 In. 1840.00
Mirror, William & Mary, Walnut, Cushion Molded Frame, 33 x 28 In. 4315.00
Mirror, William IV Style, Giltwood, Foliate Glass, 1840, 19 1/2 In. 395.00
Ottoman, Art Deco, Club Style, Maroon Segments, Leather, 17 In. 184.00
Ottoman, Frank Lloyd Wright, Suede, Mahogany, Hexagonal, 12 x 26 In. 825.00
Ottoman, Fruitwood, Upholstered Seat, Round, 17 In. 260.00
Ottoman, Robsjohn-Gibbings, Walnut, Webbed Seat, Angled Legs, 26 x 12 In. 415.00
Ottoman, Walnut, 4 Dowel Legs, 1960s, 11 x 24 In. 825.00
Parlor Set, Eastlake, Black Lacquer, Floral Basket & Scroll Upholstery, 4 Piece 460.00
Parlor Set, Eastlake, Walnut, Upholstered, 2 Piece 425.00
Parlor Set, Jeliff, Upholstered, Sofa, Chair & Armchair, 3 Piece 3995.00
Parlor Set, Louis XV, Rosewood, Floral Crest, Upholstered, 19th Century, 3 Piece 1450.00
Parlor Set, Mahogany, Settee, Chair & Platform Rocker, Carved, 3 Piece 1600.00
Parlor Set, Rococo, Rosewood, Mid-19th Century 4125.00
Parlor Set, Walnut, Carved, Upholstered, France, Early 20th Century, 5 Piece 880.00
Parlor Set, Walnut, Settee, 2 Tub Armchairs, Winged Monopodia Supports, 3 Piece 9200.00
Pedestal, Aesthetic Movement, Stork, Figural, Square Base 2365.00
Pedestal, Alabaster, Floral Brass Bands At Top & Bottom, 37 In. 600.00
Pedestal, Biedermeier, Fluted, Molded Column, Plinth, 46 In. 1610.00
Pedestal, Gilt Bronze & Porcelain, Portrait Of Napoleon & Josephine, 40 In. 9775.00
Pedestal, Gilt Incised, Marquetry, Marble Top, Ribbon Hung Trophy, 42 In. 1100.00
Pedestal, Giltwood, Carved, Oblong Top, Apron, Lion's Head, 19th Century, 40 In. 970.00
Pedestal, Green & Amber Onyx, Square Top, Convex Mid-Band, 41 In. 660.00
Pedestal, L. & J.G. Stickley, No. 27, Square Top, 4-Sided Column, Shoe Feet, 36 In. ... 1540.00
Pedestal, Mahogany, Carved, Carp Form, 20th Century, Pair 3165.00
Pedestal, Onyx, Column, Ionic Capital, Wreaths At Base, 43 1/2 In. 1200.00
Pedestal, Onyx, Gilt Bronze & Enamel Banding, 41 1/4 In. 3565.00
Pedestal, Rosewood, Marble Top, Floral Marquetry, France, 45 In. 575.00
Pedestal, Rouge Marble, Column, Revolving, 44 In. 1265.00
Pie Safe, 6 Tin Panels, Drawer At Bottom, Square Nails 425.00
Pie Safe, Cherry, 12 Tin Panels, 2 Doors, Refinished, 39 x 19 x 53 In. 1540.00
Pie Safe, Cherry, Vine & Flower Punched Tin Panels 3200.00
Pie Safe, Double Doors, Bootjack Ends, Brass Screening 1195.00
Pie Safe, Gray & Rose Paint, Combination Lock, Slotted Adjustable Shelves, 48 In. 395.00
Pie Safe, Mortised & Pinned Frame, Screen Covered Openings, Pine, 48 1/4 In. 415.00
Pie Safe, Oak, Pine, Screen Sides, Green Stain Over Red, Countertop, 19 x 30 In. 135.00
Pie Safe, Pine, 4 Doors, Screen, Peaked Roof, White Repaint, 34 x 17 x 38 In. 140.00
Pie Safe, Pine, 6 Punched Tin Panels, Base Drawer, 2 Doors, Worn Paint, 41 x 64 In. ... 880.00
Pie Safe, Pine, Poplar, 16 Punched Tin Panels, 37 x 63 In. 1700.00
Pie Safe, Poplar, 4 Sides Punched Tins, F.W. Sanner Hrdw., Hanging, 39 x 20 In. 1320.00
Pie Safe, Poplar, 6 Punched Tin Panels, 2 Drawers, Virginia, 53 x 47 In. 1650.00
Pie Safe, Poplar, Blue Repainted, 2 Doors, 16 Punched Tin Panels, 40 x 63 In. 1870.00
Pie Safe, Poplar, Masonic, Repainted, 12 Punched Tin Panels, Drawer, 39 x 57 In. 330.00
Pie Safe, Poplar, Old Red, 2 Punched Tin Doors, 2 Top Drawers, 19 x 54 In. 1650.00
Pie Safe, Poplar, Pine, Punched Tin Panels, Frame Grained, Gallery, 54 x 50 In. 1000.00
Pie Safe, Poplar, Red & Black Grained, Octagon Safe Pat'd 1870, 36 x 67 In. 1650.00
Pie Safe, Poplar, Red Repainted, 3 Punched Tin Panels, 15 x 23 x 49 In. 440.00
Pie Safe, Poplar, Stripped Paint, Red Wash, Punched Tin Panels, Ohio, 39 x 46 In. 1980.00
Pie Safe, Redwood, 8 Punched Tin Panels 2600.00
Pie Safe, Redwood, 8 Punched Tin, 2 Doors, Square Corner Posts, 36 x 48 In. 2860.00
Pie Safe, Screened, Black Graining Over Red Paint, Gold Stenciled Crest 750.00
Pie Safe, Walnut, 12 Punched Tin Panels, Refinished, Virginia, 40 x 58 In. 1200.00
Pie Safe, Walnut, 2 Dovetailed Drawers & 2 Doors, Floral Punched, 51 x 75 In. 3300.00
Pie Safe, Walnut, 6 Punched Tin Panels, 2 Doors, Square Corner Post, Cornice, 49 x 52 In. 2530.00
Pie Safe, Walnut, 6 Punched Tin Panels, Replacement Top Drawer 675.00
Pie Safe, Wooden, Punched Galvanized Panels, Hanging, 27 x 28 x 37 In. 95.00
Pie Safe, Yellow Pine, 6 Punched Tin Panels, Blue Paint Over Green, 19 x 39 x 55 In. ... 660.00
Planter, Arts & Crafts, Oak Box, Square Spindle Legs, Shaped Stretcher, 33 x 9 In. 385.00
Porch Set, Arts & Crafts Style, Wicker, Arms, Rocker, Magazine Pocket, 3 Piece 240.00
Porch Set, Heywood-Wakefield, Wicker, Desk & Chair, Sofa, Rocker, Armchair 2800.00

Infrequent waxing of furniture is best. Once a year is enough. Go heavy on elbow grease; light on wax. . . . We always knew lazy housekeeping with antiques is the best. Do as little as possible to clean and shine pieces and avoid creating problems.

Furniture, Rack, Magazine, Peter Hunt,
Heart & Flower Design, 38 x 23 In.

Rack, Boot, Mahogany, 19th Century, England, 36 1/2 x 24 1/2 In.	425.00
Rack, Candle Drying, Hardwood, Rotating Arms, Each With 32 Candle Wicks, 39 In.	770.00
Rack, Letter, Fretwork, Scene Of Man On Horse, 18 In.	115.00
Rack, Magazine, Cast Iron, Racing Hound Each Side, Art Deco	500.00
Rack, Magazine, Peter Hunt, Heart & Flower Design, 38 x 23 In. *Illus*	660.00
Rack, Plate, Continental, Pine, Brown Paint Trace, Scalloped, Hanging, 42 x 36 In.	475.00
Rack, Plate, Oak, Hand Carved, 2 Shelves	675.00
Rack, Plate, Pine, Georgian, Hanging	260.00
Rack, Portfolio, Walnut, Adjustable Vertical Slats, Trestle, Casters, 1870, 29 x 25 In.	3800.00
Rack, Sheraton, Green Paint, Yellow Line Design, Mortise, Tenon, 42 x 37 In.	2850.00
Rack, Towel, Hired Man's, Original Blue Paint	125.00
Recamier, Classical, Mahogany, Carved, Upholstered, 1820-1830	785.00
Recamier, Classical, Mahogany, Flame Veneer Frame, Paw Feet, 1830, 66 In.	1550.00
Recamier, Classical, Mahogany, Scroll Supports, Back, Box Shape, 1830, 33 In.	4115.00
Recamier, Dolphin Carved Arm, Fan Dolphin Carved Feet, 1830, 34 In.	2650.00
Recamier, Mahogany, Whorl, Berry Design, 1850, 34 3/4 In.	4000.00
Recamier, Rococo, Mahogany, Floral, Fruit Crest Rail, Velvet, 1860, 40 In.	2300.00
Recamier, Tufted Backrest, Curved Seat, Upholstered, Victorian, 16 x 71 x 31 In.	1100.00
Recamier, Wakefield, Rattan, Balls Inset At Criss Crosses, 1880s	6700.00
Rocker, 5 Vertical Back Slats, 3 Slats Under Arms, Springs, Buffalo Chair Works	600.00
Rocker, Acadian, Crackled Paint Over Green & Red Paint, Child's	175.00
Rocker, Adirondack Style, Bent Hickory Arms & Back Slats, 45 In.	230.00
Rocker, Adirondack Style, Bentwood, Brown Paint Over Blue, Child's, 25 In.	115.00
Rocker, Adirondack Style, Bentwood, Splint Seat, c.1930	225.00
Rocker, Adirondack Style, c.1900, Child's, 36 In.	285.00
Rocker, Alligatored Finish, Decal On Crest, Peek A Boo, Child's, 28 In.	190.00
Rocker, Arts & Crafts, Quartersawn Oak, 41 1/2 In.	220.00
Rocker, Boston, Mustard Grained, Stenciled, c.1840, Child's	975.00
Rocker, Carved Crests, Hip Rests, Cane Seat, 19th Century	50.00
Rocker, Centennial, Red, White & Blue	450.00
Rocker, Comb Back, Black, Early 19th Century, 42 1/2 In.	460.00
Rocker, Eames, Beige Fiberglass Shell, Zinc Wire Struts, 27 In.	715.00
Rocker, Eames, Bent Plywood, Tapered Legs, Dark Brown Finish, Arms	360.00
Rocker, Eames, Fiberglass, Shell, Yellow, 27 x 24 x 27 In.	660.00
Rocker, Folding, Hand Painted Finish, Upholstered, Adjustable Arm Rests, 1860s	575.00
Rocker, G. Stickley, No. 307, Drop-In Spring Seat, 17 x 21 x 35 In.	255.00
Rocker, G. Stickley, No. 309, 3 Horizontal Back Slats, Angular Arms	300.00
Rocker, G. Stickley, No. 319, 4 Horizontal Back Slats, Caned Base, 40 1/2 In.	1540.00
Rocker, G. Stickley, No. 365, 3 Vertical Back Slats, Leather Seat, Open Arms	300.00
Rocker, G. Stickley, Spindle	2500.00
Rocker, Grain Painted, Scroll Arms	135.00
Rocker, Harden, Wavy Vertical Back Slats, Spring Seat, Side Posts, 41 In.	1050.00

Rocker, High Plank Seat, Floral Design On Crest, Arms, Child's 350.00
Rocker, Hitchcock Style, Black Paint, Gold Floral Stencil, Arms, 20th Century 38.00
Rocker, J.M. Young, 4 Horizontal Back Slats, Spring Drop Seat, Open Arms, Pair 990.00
Rocker, L. & J.G. Stickley, 3 Horizontal Back Slats, Leather Spring Seat 470.00
Rocker, L. & J.G. Stickley, No. 823, Oak, Arms, 1912-1932 . . . . 625.00
Rocker, L. & J.G. Stickley, Sewing, 5 Vertical Back Slats, Loose Seat Cushion, 35 In. . . . 275.00
Rocker, Ladder Back, 4 Graduated Slats, Sausage Trimmings, Rush Seat, Arms 100.00
Rocker, Ladder Back, Acorn Turned Finials, Rush Seat, Painted Design 195.00
Rocker, Ladder Back, Hardwood, Chip Carved Turnings, Splint Seat, Arms 880.00
Rocker, Ladder Back, Maple, Red Paint, Woven Splint Seat, 46 3/4 In. 880.00
Rocker, Ladder Back, Maple, Turned Finials, Double Box Stretcher, 19th Century 115.00
Rocker, Ladder Back, Shaker, Shawl Bar, Mt. Lebanon Label, Arms, 7 On Top, 41 In. . . . 660.00
Rocker, Lifetime, Mission, Oak, 3 Vertical Slats, Arms, Signed 165.00
Rocker, Lincoln, Mahogany, Fruit Crest, Upholstered, Carved Arms, Victorian 230.00
Rocker, Mammy's, Half Arrow Back, Green, Stenciled Design, Baby Gate, Arms 725.00
Rocker, Mammy's, Stenciled Oak Leaves & Acorns, Arms 1375.00
Rocker, Maple, Slat Back, 42 3/4 In. 230.00
Rocker, Nakashima, Cherry & Ash, Free-Form Arm, 1966 . . . . 2875.00
Rocker, Oak, Wing Back, Child's, 28 1/2 x 19 1/4 In. 390.00
Rocker, Platform, Walnut, Reupholstered, Victorian, 38 1/2 In. 230.00
Rocker, Rattan, Child's, 1950s 75.00
Rocker, Rose Carved Crest, Upholstered, Victorian 137.00
Rocker, Roycroft, No. 39, Corseted Back Slat, Upholstered Seat, Orb Mark, 35 x 30 In. . 990.00
Rocker, Salem, Black & Gilt Paint, Ship On Headrest 350.00
Rocker, Shaker, 4 Slats, Black Paint, Tape Seat, Button Arms 1450.00
Rocker, Shaker, Maple, Mt. Lebanon, No. 5, Arms, c.1875, 38 1/2 In. 430.00
Rocker, Shaker, Maple, Mt. Lebanon, No. 7, Decal, 1875-1942, 42 In. 430.00
Rocker, Shaker, No. 6, Mushroom Caps 990.00
Rocker, Slate Blue Plush, Lane Action 85.00
Rocker, Stenciled Grape, Leaf & Daisy On Crest, Scrolled Hand Rests On Arms 55.00
Rocker, Stickley Bros., No. 280, Drop Seat Cushion, Leather, Child's 550.00
Rocker, Stickley Bros., Oak, Calfskin Seat, Label, 33 x 26 In. 300.00
Rocker, Stickley Bros., Sewing, Ladder Back, Rush Seat, 30 1/2 In. 275.00
Rocker, Victorian, Walnut, Cane Seat & Back, Child's, 26 In. 170.00
Rocker, Walnut, Caned Back & Seat, 1910s 110.00
Rocker, Walnut, Caned Back & Seat, Semi-Arms, 1920s 80.00
Rocker, William Hancock, Mahogany, 1830-1840, 40 1/4 In. 1330.00
Rocker, Windsor, 7 Spindles, Downswept Arms, Bamboo Turnings, 19th Century 575.00
Rocker, Windsor, Arrow Back, Beck, Comb Crest Extension, 1840, 45 In. 550.00
Rocker, Windsor, Black Paint, Bamboo Turnings, c.1810, 41 1/2 In. 230.00
Rocker, Windsor, Comb Back, Bamboo Turnings, Oval Seat Arms, 44 In. 180.00
Rocker, Windsor, Comb Back, Worn Paint, Bamboo Turnings, Shaped Arms 330.00
Rocker, Windsor, Fruit, Rosettes Design, Mustard, Yellow, Green, Black, 43 In. 290.00
Rocker, Windsor, Tiger Maple Seat, Bamboo Turnings 935.00
Rocker, Windsor, Yellow Paint, Black & Tan Striping, Bamboo Turnings, Child's 330.00
Rocker & Footstool, Horn, 2 Piece 895.00
Screen, 3-Panel, Art Nouveau, Floral Cloth Base, Glass Top 250.00
Screen, 3-Panel, Canvas Panels, Arts & Crafts, Oak, 66 x 59 In. 605.00
Screen, 3-Panel, Canvas, Villlage Scenes, Early 20th Century 490.00
Screen, 3-Panel, Dancing Figure On Each Panel, Black Ground, c.1930, 57 In. 9200.00
Screen, 3-Panel, Leather, Commemorating Christopher Columbus, 72 x 70 In. 1780.00
Screen, 3-Panel, Limbert, No. 53-L, Oak, Goat Leather, 73 x 68 In. . . . . *Illus* 3850.00
Screen, 3-Panel, Louis XV, Giltwood, Open Crest, Couple Tapestry, 69 x 66 In. 5520.00
Screen, 3-Panel, Louis XVI, Giltwood, Moire, Center Mirrored Panel, 75 x 72 In. 2300.00
Screen, 3-Panel, Mahogany, Silk Inset, 19th Century, 73 In. 2010.00
Screen, 3-Panel, Oil On Board, Hollyhocks, 69 1/2 x 72 In. 4875.00
Screen, 3-Panel, Painted Floral Design Each Panel, Roman Art, 68 x 54 In. 175.00
Screen, 3-Panel, Petit Point, Early 1900s 3900.00
Screen, 3-Panel, Satinwood, Portrait Medallions, 1900, 51 In. 4315.00
Screen, 3-Panel, Stained & Leaded Glass, 6 Colors, 57 x 48 In. 200.00
Screen, 3-Panel, Upper Fretwork, Embroidered Silk, Trees & Birds, 68 In. 6675.00
Screen, 3-Panel, Walnut, Carved, Mirrored Panels, 74 In. 805.00
Screen, 4-Panel, Allegorical Scenes, Foliate Scrolls, Medallions, 100 In. 3450.00

Screen, 4-Panel, Arts & Crafts, Linen, Stenciled, 66 x 70 In. 330.00
Screen, 4-Panel, Ink On Colored Paper, Quail & Flowers, Japan, 84 x 68 In. 200.00
Screen, 4-Panel, Lacquer, Figures In Pavilion, Birds On Reverse, Chinese, 72 In. 495.00
Screen, 4-Panel, Leather, Landscape, Figures, Chariot, Dogs On Reverse, 1780, 77 In. .. 4600.00
Screen, 4-Panel, Mahogany, Marquetry, Inset Fabric Panels, 1820s, 84 In. 4310.00
Screen, 4-Panel, Nobleman, Horse Continuous Scene, Victorian, 84 x 96 In. 4355.00
Screen, 4-Panel, Painted Paper, France, 19th Century, 68 x 80 In. 2185.00
Screen, 4-Panel, Parcel Gilt Canvas, Chinoiserie, 91 In. 4600.00
Screen, 4-Panel, Red Lacquer, Coromandel Design, Oriental, 72 3/4 In. 400.00
Screen, 4-Panel, Silk Avian & Floral Front, Avian & Floral Leather Back, 72 In. 145.00
Screen, 5-Panel, Oak, Black & White Engraved Top, Silk Panel Bottom, 61 In. 1380.00
Screen, 5-Panel, Zuber Et Cie, Classical Scene En Grissaille, France, 79 x 115 In. 3220.00
Screen, 6-Panel, Black Lacquer, Oriental, Carved, Applied Design, 72 In. 2475.00
Screen, 6-Panel, Chinoiserie, Shell & Floral Border, Continental, 26 x 144 In. 2175.00
Screen, 6-Panel, Coromandel, Lacquer, Garden Scenes, Exotic Birds, 72 In. 1080.00
Screen, 6-Panel, Eames, Undulating Birch, Veneered, 68 x 56 In. 2425.00
Screen, 6-Panel, Silk, Court Scenes, Japan, 36 x 114 In. 9000.00
Screen, 6-Panel, Wallpaper, Folk Scene, Turquoise Ground, 72 x 138 In. 978.00
Screen, 8-Panel, Eames, Undulating Birch, 68 x 76 In. 4400.00
Screen, 8-Panel, Rice Paper, Duck In Water Scene, Plants, Japan, 67 x 200 In. 2300.00
Screen, Candle, Cartouche Of 2 Reclining Female Terms, Carved Frame, 17 1/2 In. 4725.00
Screen, Limbert, Oak Panels Of Moroccan Goat Leather, Linen Back, 68 X73 In. 3850.00
Screen, Rosewood, Needlework Scene, c.1815, 17 In. 230.00
Secretary, Arts & Crafts, Hammered Metal, Drop Front, 2 Shelves 360.00
Secretary, Biedermeier, Ash, Ebonized, Oval Medallions, 70 In. 6950.00
Secretary, Biedermeier, Cherry, Mahogany, Stepped Cornice, 67 In. 5750.00
Secretary, Biedermeier, Drop Front, Mahogany, 13 Drawers, 41 x 20 x 59 In. 7200.00
Secretary, Biedermeier, Walnut, Fruitwood, Penwork, 4 Drawers, 62 In. 5750.00
Secretary, Burled Walnut, Slant Front, 2 Sliding Doors, Lower Drawers, 58 In. 4400.00
Secretary, Charles Guillaume Diehl, Drop Front, Louis Philippe, Marble Top, 50 In. 3000.00
Secretary, Chest, 3 Drawers, Bracket Feet, England, 39 In. 1035.00
Secretary, Classical Revival, Mahogany, 73 x 38 In. 3000.00
Secretary, Classical, Mahogany, Cornice, 2 Drawers, 1830, 55 In. 2900.00
Secretary, Eastlake, Walnut, Drop Front, 3 Base Drawers, Interior Shelves, 85 In. 1210.00
Secretary, Empire, Curly Walnut, Dovetailed, Mirror, Drawers, 44 x 81 In. 690.00
Secretary, Empire, Mahogany, 1860s, 55 1/4 x 39 In. 4900.00
Secretary, Empire, Mahogany, 3 Drawers, 35 3/4 x 64 1/2 In. 1700.00
Secretary, Empire, Mahogany, Black Marble Top, 57 x 39 In. 5775.00
Secretary, Empire, Mahogany, Molded Cornice, 4 Tiers Of Pigeonholes, 88 In. 1575.00
Secretary, Empire, Mahogany, Yellow, Orange Mottled Marble Top, 48 In. 5750.00
Secretary, George II, Mahogany, 2 Glazed Doors, Dentil Cornice, Fitted, 80 In. 4100.00
Secretary, Governor Winthrop Style, Mahogany, Curly Maple Veneer, 31 x 74 In. 330.00
Secretary, Louis XV, Kingwood, Marble Top, 42 In. 2875.00

To cover up cat or dog
scratches or other wood
cuts, use a wood stain, a
touch-up stick, or a colored
felt-tip pen. Color the scratch
to match the wood, then
polish the area with a paste
wax or furniture pollish.

Furniture, Screen, 3-Panel, Limbert,
No. 53-L, Oak, Goat Leather, 73 x 68 In.

Secretary, Louis XVI, Mahogany, Drawer, 55 In. 2300.00
Secretary, Louis XVI, Mahogany, Drop Front, Leather Surface, Block Feet, 55 In. 3740.00
Secretary, Louis XVI, Marble Top, Frieze Drawer, 53 1/2 In. 3737.00
Secretary, Mahogany Veneer, Empire, Woman's, Fold-Down Shelf, 60 In. 330.00
Secretary, Mahogany, Glazed Doors, Pigeonholes, 90 In. 8900.00
Secretary, Marquetry, Floral, Drop Front, Stepped Interior, 57 1/2 In. 1935.00
Secretary, Napoleon III, Ebonized, Drop Front, Green Marble Inset Top, 49 3/4 In. 1695.00
Secretary, Neoclassical, Mahogany, Gilt Bronze, Marble, 60 In. 5100.00
Secretary, Oak, Slant Front, 2 Drawers, Mirror, 1910 .... 2100.00
Secretary, Painted Doors, Flowers, Vases, Base Writing Surface, 69 In. 1850.00
Secretary, Parquetry, Marble Top, Leather Surface, Cupboard, 59 In. 1100.00
Secretary, Queen Anne Style, Mahogany, 2 Panel Doors, Ball Feet, 91 In. 5750.00
Secretary, Regency, Mahogany, Drop Front, Painted Medallion, Woman's, 43 x 21 In. .. 690.00
Secretary, Satinwood Inlay, Bowfront, Cornice, 6 Ft. 11 In. 9775.00
Secretary, Walnut Burl, Cylinder, Pigeonholes, Cornice, 2 Piece, 40 x 85 In. 1750.00
Secretary, Walnut, Drop Front, 3 Burled Front Drawers, 9 Pigeonholes, 52 x 37 In. 1850.00
Secretary, William & Mary, Drop Front, Walnut, 18th Century, 62 In. 7500.00
Secretary-Bookcase, Birch, Drop Front, Fitted, Mirror, 40 x 14 x 74 In. 715.00
Secretary-Bookcase, Burled Walnut Panels, Teardrop Hardware 1430.00
Secretary-Bookcase, Classical, Mahogany, 2 Doors, Foldover Desk, 1840, 103 In. 5500.00
Secretary-Bookcase, Classical, Mahogany, Bird's-Eye Maple Drawers, 90 In. 3740.00
Secretary-Bookcase, Empire, Mahogany, 3 Parts, Banded Top Drawer, 93 In. 3025.00
Secretary-Bookcase, Federal, Cherry, Slant Front, Paneled Doors, Interior Shelves 2100.00
Secretary-Bookcase, Federal, Mahogany, Drop Front, Upper Doors, c.1830, 62 In. 7755.00
Secretary-Bookcase, Federal, Mahogany, Mirror Doors, Drop Front 925.00
Secretary-Bookcase, Flame Grain Mahogany, Turned Feet, Ogee Cornice 1300.00
Secretary-Bookcase, George III, Mahogany, 3 Graduated Drawers, 2 Piece, 87 In. 3450.00
Secretary-Bookcase, George III, Mahogany, 4 Graduated Beaded Drawers, 84 In. 3300.00
Secretary-Bookcase, George III, Mahogany, Slant Front, 4 Drawers, 1790, 90 In. 6655.00
Secretary-Bookcase, Georgian, Mahogany, 15-Pane Doors, 1780, England, 92 In. 6900.00
Secretary-Bookcase, Gothic Revival, Mahogany Veneer, Marble Top, 82 In. 1450.00
Secretary-Bookcase, Hardwood, Campaign Brass, Bulbous Legs, 83 In. 1695.00
Secretary-Bookcase, Larkin, Oak, Curved Glass, Victorian 1950.00
Secretary-Bookcase, Mahogany, 2 Serpentine Drawers, 1830, 87 In. 1210.00
Secretary-Bookcase, Mahogany, Scalloped Door, 2 Ogee Drawers, 1840, 74 In. 1210.00
Secretary-Bookcase, Mahogany, Scroll Form Columns, Scroll Feet, 91 In. 1725.00
Secretary-Bookcase, Mahogany, Slant Front, Mullioned Doors, 4 Drawers, 88 In. 5175.00
Secretary-Bookcase, Oak, Drop Front, Drawer, Door, Beveled Mirror 465.00
Secretary-Bookcase, Pearwood, Slant Front, 3 Drawers, Dutch, 18th Century 11495.00
Secretary-Bookcase, Rococo, Floral Design, 2 Deep Drawers, Venetian, 97 In. 3850.00
Secretary-Bookcase, Rococo, Foliate Crest, 2 Drawers, 108 1/4 In. 4200.00
Secretary-Bookcase, Rosewood, Maple, 2 Glazed Doors, Beaded Cornice, 84 In. 1100.00
Secretary-Bookcase, Venetian Style, Green, 2 Doors Over Shaped Base, 88 In. 1150.00
Secretary-Bookcase, Walnut, 2 Glazed Doors, Flat Top, Reeded Columns, 81 In. 600.00
Secretary-Bookcase, Walnut, Arched Glazed Doors, Victorian, 97 In. 2100.00
Secretary-Bookcase, Walnut, Roll Top, Victorian, 83 In. 690.00
Server, Empire, Mahogany, 2 Long & 2 Short Drawers, Lyre Base, 34 x 44 In. 920.00
Server, Figured Olive Wood Veneer, Marble Inset, Continental, 2 Piece, 82 In. 825.00
Server, George III, Irish Pine, Late 18th Century, 50 x 84 x 23 In. 1380.00
Server, Georgian, Mahogany, Serpentine, Banded Top, 2 Drawers, 31 x 41 In. 495.00
Server, Jacobean Revival, Oak, Porcelain Top, Cover, 34 x 44 x 17 In. 600.00
Server, Mahogany, 2 Drawers, Slanted, 38 1/2 x 50 x 23 In. 825.00
Server, Mahogany, 3 Tiers, Porcelain Casters, England, c.1850, 43 x 41 In. 1605.00
Server, Oak, Barley Twist Legs, England 485.00
Server, Oak, Quartersawn, Bowed Glass Doors At Sides, Lion Paw Feet 925.00
Server, Sheraton, Birch & Bird's-Eye Maple, 4 Drawers, Scrolled Crest, 36 1/4 In. 825.00
Settee, Aesthetic Revival, Gilt, Guilloche Stiles, Arms, Paw Feet, 35 In. 1200.00
Settee, Biedermeier, Birch, Arched Backrest, Cornucopia, 94 In. 3737.00
Settee, Biedermeier, Walnut & Fruitwood, Floral Marquetry, 75 1/2 In. 3450.00
Settee, Carved, Swan's Head Arms, Upholstered, 2 Round Pillows, 56 In. 775.00
Settee, Classical, Mahogany Veneer, Carved, Scrolled Arms, 1810, 74 x 37 In. 1955.00
Settee, Classical, Mahogany, Carved Crest, Upholstered, Phila., 1820, 82 In. 910.00
Settee, Continental, Marquetry, 19th Century, 69 In. 1815.00

Settee, Empire, Mahogany, Crest Rail, Upholstered Back & Seat, Casters, 68 1/2 In. 460.00
Settee, Federal, Mahogany, Legs, Spade Feet, Reeded Downswept Arms, 34 In. 290.00
Settee, French Style, Walnut, Wing, Carved, Cabriole Legs, 61 In., Pair 1850.00
Settee, George II, Foliate Carved Legs, Paw Feet, 7 Ft. 8625.00
Settee, George III, Floral Painted Crest, Spade Feet, 18th Century 10925.00
Settee, George III, Mahogany, 4-Part Back, Upholstered Seat, 18th Century, 36 x 57 In. . .   1265.00
Settee, George III, Mahogany, Camelback, Chamfered Legs, 18th Century, 79 In. 1950.00
Settee, George III, Mahogany, Carved Acanthus & Rosettes, Serpentine, 53 In. 1390.00
Settee, Georgian Style, Velvet Upholstered, 36 1/2 x 58 In. 800.00
Settee, Georgian, Mahogany, Scalloped Crest, Cabriole Legs, 40 In. 2425.00
Settee, Giltwood, Acanthus Carved Scrolled Arms, Austria, 39 x 77 x 30 In. 4000.00
Settee, Hardwood, Velvet, Early 20th Century, 59 In. 275.00
Settee, Jacobean Style, Carved, 55 1/2 In. 200.00
Settee, Karelian Birch, Fluted Geometric Top Rail, Fluted Armrests, Russia, 56 In. 6325.00
Settee, Limbert, Ebony Oak, Drop-In Seat, Caned Paneled Back, 74 1/4 In. 3300.00
Settee, Louis XVI Style, Birch, Tufted Back, Floral, Squared Arms, 37 In. 195.00
Settee, Louis XVI Style, Fruitwood, Velvet Upholstered, 35 x 72 x 27 In., Pair 1325.00
Settee, Louis XVI Style, Giltwood, Plumed Finials, Tapered Legs, 39 In. 4600.00
Settee, Louis XVI Style, Giltwood, Velvet, Serpentine Seat 1320.00
Settee, Mahogany, Leaf Carved Supports, Casters, Scrolled Arms, 50 1/2 In. 1950.00
Settee, Mahogany, Leaf Carved Volutes, Acanthus Arms, 35 In.   2900.00
Settee, Mahogany, Paneled Rail, Acanthus Supports, Molded Arms, 78 In. 2530.00
Settee, Mahogany, Rosette Ends At Rail, Upholstered, Out Scrolled Arms, 90 In. 2415.00
Settee, Mahogany, Scrolled Rail, Leafage, Padded Seat, Back & Arms, 87 In. 1840.00
Settee, Mahogany, Spindle Sides & Back, 19th Century, 48 In. 460.00
Settee, Mahogany, Triple Back, Scrolled Splats, Tied Ribbons, 68 1/2 In. 4900.00
Settee, Maple, Cane Seat, Reverse Scrolling Crest & Scrolling Arms, 1815, 78 In. 7475.00
Settee, Neoclassical, Giltwood, Guilloche Apron, Tapered Legs, 7 Ft. 8625.00
Settee, Neoclassical, Mahogany, Gilt, Saber Legs, 8 Ft. 2 1/2 In. 2300.00
Settee, Neoclassical, Walnut, Foliate & Beaded Crest Rail, Swept Arms, 82 1/2 In. 3400.00
Settee, Oak, Paneled Back To Full Height, 43 In. 2990.00
Settee, Phail Bros., Slats, Weathered 2100.00
Settee, Queen Anne, Walnut, Outscrolled Arms, 56 In. 8625.00
Settee, Regency Revival, Rosewood, Gilt, Splayed Legs, Scrolled Arms, 30 In. 3025.00
Settee, Regency Revival, Upholstered Back, Loose Cushion, Sloping Arms, Mahogany .   525.00
Settee, Renaissance Revival, Ebonized, Tufted Back, 19th Century, 69 In. 2175.00
Settee, Renaissance Revival, Walnut, Burl Walnut Panel, 45 In.   3400.00
Settee, Rocker, Porch, Green, Slat Back, Caned Seat 700.00
Settee, Rococo, Giltwood, Scrolled Frame, Seat, Cabriole Legs, 66 In. 3450.00
Settee, Rococo, Rosewood, Triple Back, Pierced Crest, 19th Century, 71 In. 1200.00
Settee, Rococo, Rosewood, Velvet Upholstery, Gadroon Crest Rail, 1850, 56 In. 845.00
Settee, Rosewood, 3 Cane Panels, Stylized Tulips, 1891, 39 In.   5750.00
Settee, Serpentine Top Rail, Upholstered Backrest, Greek Key Apron, 92 In. 8625.00
Settee, Triple Back, Ribbon Form Splats, Shell Crest, Upholstered Seat, 57 In. 950.00
Settee, Walnut Frame, Finger Carved, Velvet, Victorian, 57 1/2 In. 330.00
Settee, Walnut, Arched Upholstered Back, Out Scrolled Armrests, 91 In. 3737.00
Settee, Walnut, Baroque Style, Printed Cotton, 44 1/2 x 48 In. 520.00
Settee, Walnut, Medallion Back, Burl Veneer Panels Crest, Victorian, 60 In. 415.00
Settee, Walnut, Rosewood Grained, Finger Carved, Upholstered, Victorian, 61 In. 275.00
Settee, Walnut, Triple Back, Upholstered Seat, Cabriole Legs, 65 In. 375.00
Settee, Walnut, Tufted Medallion Back, Carved, Velvet, 59 1/2 In. 440.00
Settee, Western Style, Burled Fir, Chimayo Wool, 59 x 36 In. . . . .*Illus*   8050.00
Settee, Windsor, Federal, Black Paint, Triple Back, Rush Seat, Arms, 56 In. 2070.00
Settee, Windsor, Maple, Pine & Ash, c.1800, 76 1/2 In. 1495.00
Settee, Windsor, Mixed Woods, Thumb Back, Bent Arrow, 8 Legs, 1850, 75 In. 885.00
Settee, Windsor, Poplar, 9 Spindles, Hickory Arms, Bamboo Turning, 78 In. 2850.00
Settle, Charles II, Oak, Cornice, Plank Seat, 70 x 41 x 20 3/4 In. 800.00
Settle, Grained, 3-Splat Back, Floral Design, Striping, Scrolled Arms, 80 In. 665.00
Settle, Gray Paint, Turned Legs, Light Gray Seat, 80 In. 2090.00
Settle, Hinged Lid, Shaped Sides, Scrolled Arms, Plank Seat, Pine, 65 x 48 In. 575.00
Settle, J.M. Young, Slatted Back, Upholstered Seat, Arms 2425.00
Settle, Jacobean, Oak, Paneled Backrest, Plant Seat, Box Frame, 59 In. 4025.00
Settle, L. & J.G. Stickley, No. 281, Oak, 16 Slats, 76 x 31 In. 6325.00

Furniture, Settee, Western
Style, Burled Fir, Chimayo
Wool, 59 x 36 In.

Settle, Mahogany, 2 Gothic Chair Back, Upholstered Seat, Shaped Arms, 44 In. 3400.00
Settle, Mustard Grained, Canada, 70 3/4 In. 1092.50
Settle, Oak, Curved Front, Flat Back, Storage Compartments, Arms, 57 x 59 In. 4675.00
Settle, Oak, High Paneled Back, Cutout Ends, Curved Seat, 69 In. 445.00
Settle, Pine, Curved Paneled High Back, 67 1/2 x 72 In. 825.00
Settle, Sheraton, Black Paint, Turned Legs, 82 In. 605.00
Settle, Stickley Bros., Mahogany, Tapering Posts, Loose Seat, Canvas Base, 60 In. 3850.00
Settle, Welsh, Elm, 4 Inset Panels, Hinged Seat, 43 In. 7475.00
Settle, Yellow Paint, Black Striping, Stencil, Plank Seat, Scrolled Arms, 72 In. 1328.00
Shelf, 3 Glass Shelves, Central Column Of Gilt Scrolls, R. Subaes, c.1940, 60 In. 1850.00
Shelf, Burl Walnut, Hanging, American, 1870, 43 In. 2665.00
Shelf, Butternut, 3 Shaped Shelves, 2 Drawers, Early 19th Century, 31 In. 1035.00
Shelf, Cherry, Hanging, 2 Shelves, Scrolled Termini, 20th Century, 24 In. 460.00
Shelf, Corner, Ceramics & Shells, Glass, Mosaic, 1880-1920, 48 x 15 In. 495.00
Shelf, Corner, Mahogany, Hanging, Fretwork Sides, 3 Graduated Shelves, 32 In. 250.00
Shelf, Corner, Mahogany, Hanging, Rococo Design, 4 Shelves, 34 1/2 In. 210.00
Shelf, Corner, Mahogany, Standing, Ogee Framed, 4 Shelves, c.1840, 73 3/4 In. 365.00
Shelf, Giltwood, Flower Head Form Supports, Scrolls, Italy, 8 In. 340.00
Shelf, Hanging, Gimson, Oak, Open Lattice Back, Side Cupboards, c.1905, 77 In. 4140.00
Shelf, Hanging, Green Paint, 3 Tiers, 19th Century, 27 7/8 In. 1385.00
Shelf, Hanging, Mahogany, Mirror Back, Shaped Gallery Top 45.00
Shelf, Hanging, Poplar, Old Black Paint, 36 In. 100.00
Shelf, Hanging, Regency Revival, Mahogany 750.00
Shelf, Louis XVI, Giltwood Bracket, Acanthus Design, 16 1/2 In. 365.00
Shelf, Louis XVI, Marble, Floral, Foliate Scrollwork, Bracket, 17 In., Pair 580.00
Shelf, Pine, Figural, Cherub, Shell Shelf, Continental, Bracket, 19th Century, 16 In. 725.00
Shelf, Pine, Step Back, Wire Nail Construction, Varnish, 36 x 12 x 16 In. 100.00
Shelf, Rococo, Walnut, Figural, Wheat Sheaf, Cock, Ivory Border, Bracket, 15 In. 910.00
Shelf, Victorian, Oak, Brass, 1890 .... 330.00
Shelf, Walnut, Shaped Sides, 3 Shaped Shelves, 27 1/2 x 24 3/8 In. 315.00
Sideboard, American Empire, Cherry, Maple, 4 Doors, 3 Drawers 6500.00
Sideboard, Baker Co., Mahogany, Long & Short Drawers, Doors, 57 x 19 In. 175.00
Sideboard, Bowfront, Mahogany, 3 Graduated Drawers, 39 In. 1650.00
Sideboard, Carved Crest, Mirror Sections, Refinished, 86 x 60 In. ....*Illus* 990.00
Sideboard, Chippendale Style, Carved, France, c.1910 .... 1600.00
Sideboard, Classical, Mahogany, Black Marble Top 2200.00
Sideboard, Classical, Mahogany, Broken Pediment Backsplash, 3 Drawers, 1820 ...... 3400.00
Sideboard, Classical, Mahogany, Columned Front, Paw Feet, 1825 .... 3100.00
Sideboard, Classical, Mahogany, Gilt, Marble, Phila., 1825, 43 x 60 x 23 In. 2300.00
Sideboard, Eastlake, Walnut, Brown Marble Top, 5 Drawers, 1885, 37 In. 1760.00
Sideboard, Empire, Mahogany, Carved Legs, Paw Feet, 58 In. 1035.00
Sideboard, Empire, Mahogany, Figured Veneer, 2 Drawers, 3 Doors, 61 In. 330.00
Sideboard, Federal, Mahogany, 3 Cock-Beaded Drawers, 1820, 40 In. 2425.00
Sideboard, Federal, Mahogany, 3 String Outlining Drawers, 40 3/4 In. 4900.50
Sideboard, Federal, Mahogany, Bird's-Eye Maple, Central Drawer, Side Doors, 71 In. ... 1725.00

Sideboard, Federal, Mahogany, Bottle Drawers, Brass Capped Feet, 1800, 49 In. 1600.00
Sideboard, Federal, Mahogany, Maple Banding, Bowfront 195.00
Sideboard, Federal, Mahogany, Serpentine Top, Square Legs, 39 In. 4700.00
Sideboard, Figural Painted, Gilt, Apron Crest, Cabriole Legs, England, 42 In. 1495.00
Sideboard, French Provincial, Oak, Carved Frieze, 2 Hinged Doors, 40 1/2 x 50 In. 300.00
Sideboard, G. Stickley, No. 814, Plate Rail, 66 x 24 x 49 In. .... *Illus* 11000.00
Sideboard, G. Stickley, Plate Rack, 2 Doors, 4 Drawers, Wooden Pulls, 40 1/2 In. 9900.00
Sideboard, George III Style, Mahogany, Inlaid Serpentine Front, 1920s, 78 In. 3450.00
Sideboard, George III, Mahogany, Banded Top, Bowfront, 1790, 37 x 78 In. 3260.00
Sideboard, George III, Mahogany, Bowfront, Square Tapered Legs, 60 x 24 In. 4355.00
Sideboard, George III, Mahogany, Inlay, 2 Drawers, Reeded Legs, 38 In. 4025.00
Sideboard, George III, Mahogany, Inlay, Serpentine Drawer, 36 In. 6325.00
Sideboard, George III, Mahogany, Serpentine Top, Cellerette Drawer, 36 In. 1700.00
Sideboard, George III, Mahogany, Serpentine, 2 Short Drawers, 35 x 54 In. 3950.00
Sideboard, Georgian, Satinwood, Mahogany, Bowfront, 1790 .... 14500.00
Sideboard, Grecian Backsplash, 3 Frieze Drawers, Center Doors, 1825 .... 2425.00
Sideboard, Hepplewhite Style, Mahogany, Serpentine Front, 4 Drawers, 4 Doors 2665.00
Sideboard, Hepplewhite, Mahogany Veneer, 3 Dovetailed Drawers, England, 74 In. 2000.00
Sideboard, Hepplewhite, Mahogany, Serpentine Double Curved Front 1955.00
Sideboard, Hepplewhite, Mahogany, Serpentine Front, 3 Drawers, 42 In. 5465.00
Sideboard, J.C. Dana, Birch Oval Inlays, Crotch & Banded Mahogany 6000.00
Sideboard, Jacobean, Oak, Turned Legs, 63 x 19 x 36 In. 440.00
Sideboard, Lacquered Case, Fiberglass Panels, Brass Handles 1870.00
Sideboard, Limbert, No. 457 1/2, Plate Rail, 2 Drawers, Linen Drawer, 45 In. 1550.00
Sideboard, Mahogany & Mahogany Veneer, Cock-Beaded Drawers & Doors 600.00
Sideboard, Mahogany Veneer, Carved, 1830s, 49 In. 865.00
Sideboard, Mahogany, 3 Drawers, 2 Doors, 45 x 48 x 18 In. 4400.00
Sideboard, Mahogany, 4 Star Reeded Columns, Ball Feet, 1825, 75 In. 3025.00
Sideboard, Mahogany, Center Mirror, Corinthian Columns, Paw Feet, 59 In. 200.00
Sideboard, Mahogany, Long Drawer, Faux Tambour Drawer, 67 In. 575.00
Sideboard, Mahogany, Profiles Of Man On Base Doors, Beveled Mirror, 94 1/2 In. 285.00
Sideboard, Mahogany, Scroll Supports, 2 Short, Tall Drawers, 57 x 73 In. 1100.00
Sideboard, Maple, 2 Cupboard Doors, Bracket Foot Base, 54 In. 140.00
Sideboard, McHugh, Oak, Railed Top 1100.00
Sideboard, Neoclassical, Mahogany, Marble Top, Fluted Case, 41 x 80 x 18 In. 1430.00
Sideboard, Oak, Beveled Mirrors, Claw Feet, Carved, 1840s 7500.00
Sideboard, Oak, Double Claw Feet, Mirror, c.1910 .... 1500.00
Sideboard, Oak, Mirror Back, c.1910, 56 1/2 x 48 In. 495.00
Sideboard, Oak, Quartersawn, Canopy, Bombe Front & Sides, Mirror, 67 x 72 In. 3750.00

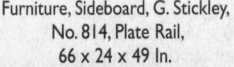

Furniture, Sideboard, G. Stickley,
No. 814, Plate Rail,
66 x 24 x 49 In.

Furniture, Sideboard, Carved Crest,
Mirror Sections,
Refinished, 86 x 60 In.

Sideboard, Pine, Cherry, 3 Drawers, Baluster Legs, American, 62 In. 1265.00
Sideboard, Regency, Mahogany, Bowfront, Inlaid, 2 Drawers, 36 In. 4850.00
Sideboard, Regency, Mahogany, Scroll Splashboard, 3 Drawers, 1820 . . . . 715.00
Sideboard, Renaissance Revival, Mitchell & Rammelsberg, Walnut, 58 x 100 In. 8500.00
Sideboard, Renaissance Revival, Walnut, 3 Base Doors, Philadelphia 7150.00
Sideboard, Rustic, 2500 Individual Pieces Of Wood Construction 3525.00
Sideboard, Sheraton, Cherry, 2 Flat Doors, 2 Curved Doors, 51 In. 3575.00
Sideboard, Sheraton, Mahogany & Tiger Maple, Miniature, 24 In. 7200.00
Sideboard, Sheraton, Mahogany, Bowfront, Reeded Legs, 41 1/2 In. 9150.00
Sideboard, Stickley Bros., Backsplash, Rail, Linen Drawer Over 3 Drawers, 60 In. 3300.00
Sideboard, Stickley Bros., No. 8604, 4 Drawers, 2 Doors, 63 x 70 In. 7700.00
Sideboard, Victorian, Mahogany, Marble, Bacchus Carved Crest, 60 In. 3935.00
Sideboard, Walnut, Marble Top, 3 Beveled Mirrors, Victorian 5750.00
Sideboard, Walnut, Marble Top, 4 Drawers, Carved Handles 690.00
Sideboard, Walnut, Marble Top, Bronze Handles, Tapered Legs, France, 42 In. 1120.00
Sideboard, Walnut, Mirrored Backsplash, Marble Top, 2 Drawers, 2 Doors 385.00
Sideboard, Walnut, Serpentine Front, Marble Top, Claw & Ball Feet, 1920s, 79 In. 460.00
Sideboard, Walnut, Walnut Burl, California Furniture Mfg. Co., San Francisco 2530.00
Sideboard, William IV, Mahogany, 3 Drawers, Secret Drawer, 6 Legs, 18 x 72 In. 5250.00
Sideboard, William IV, Mahogany, Architectural Backsplash, 1835, 33 In. 4400.00
Sideboard, William IV, Mahogany, Inlaid, Brass Splash Rail, 48 x 78 x 21 In. 4315.00
Sofa, 2 Square Wooden Support Legs, Brown Leather, 90 In. 1725.00
Sofa, American Empire, Mahogany, Silk, 83 In. 1325.00
Sofa, American Restauration, Mahogany, Scroll, Cyma Curved Arms, 1835, 83 In. 1815.00
Sofa, Arched Back, Plush, Cabriole Legs, Arms, 77 In. 520.00
Sofa, Art Deco, Majorelle, Cylinder Side Cabinets, Leather, Mother-Of-Pearl, 8 Ft. 6500.00
Sofa, Belter, Rosalie, Rosewood, Triple Crest, 1850-1860, 41 x 78 x 33 In. 4500.00
Sofa, Biedermeier, Mahogany Feet, Mohair, Cut Velvet, 7 Ft. 5 In. 9775.00
Sofa, Biedermeier, Mahogany, Shell Over Foliate Scrolls, 84 In. 2600.00
Sofa, Chesterfield, Leather, Tufted Back, 20th Century, 32 In. 2650.00
Sofa, Chippendale, Carved, Down Cushions, 1900s, 84 In. 2300.00
Sofa, Chippendale, Mahogany Base, Tapered Legs, 79 In. 990.00
Sofa, Chippendale, Mahogany, Serpentine Camelback, Tapered Legs, 35 1/4 In. 345.00
Sofa, Chippendale, Mahogany, Serpentine Crest, Padded Seat, 36 1/2 In. 635.00
Sofa, Chrome Base, Tufted Black Leather Back, 32 x 84 x 27 1/2 In. 1650.00
Sofa, Chrome Frame, Tubular, Upholstered, 1930, 70 x 26 x 27 In. 2860.00
Sofa, Classical, Mahogany, Box, 1830, 36 x 86 x 26 In. 665.00
Sofa, Classical, Mahogany, Box, Volute Arm Rests, Turned Legs, 1830 . . . . 770.00
Sofa, Classical, Mahogany, Carved, Philadelphia, 19th Century, 87 In. 3630.00
Sofa, Classical, Mahogany, Crest Rail, Acanthus, Reeded Frame, 1830, 33 In. 2060.00
Sofa, Classical, Mahogany, Reeded Crest Rail, Reeded Saber Legs, 32 1/2 In. 6325.00
Sofa, Classical, Mahogany, Reeded Crest, Vinery, Shell Arms, 1830, 36 In. 2180.00
Sofa, Classical, Mahogany, Rolled Over Crest, Shell Arms, 1830, 35 In. 1650.00
Sofa, Classical, Mahogany, Upholstered, 5 Scroll Feet, American, 1840 . . . . 1450.00
Sofa, Contemporary, 4 Cowhide Cushions, 30 1/2 x 79 In. 2530.00
Sofa, Directoire, Hardwood, Bowed Seat, Baluster Legs, 65 In. 3450.00
Sofa, Duncan Phyfe, Scrolled Arms, Swag Drapery Crest, Mahogany, 60 In. 12650.00
Sofa, Eames, Compact, Chrome Legs, Upholstered, 34 x 72 x 28 In. . . . . .715.00 to 1650.00
Sofa, Eastlake, Walnut, Ormolu Mounts, Upholstered, 77 In. 2200.00
Sofa, Elliptical Shape, Red Fabric, Black Cushions, 1950s 945.00
Sofa, Empire, Carved Central Panel, Cornucopia, 1840s, 74 In. 4600.00
Sofa, Empire, Mahogany, Flame Grain Veneer, 89 In. 1200.00
Sofa, Empire, Mahogany, Gilt Metal, Tapered Leg, Paw Feet, 38 In. 1200.00
Sofa, Empire, Needlework Upholstery, Claw Feet, 84 In. 775.00
Sofa, Empire, Walnut, Carved Lyre Frame, Paw Feet With Wings, 66 In. 2035.00
Sofa, Federal, Mahogany, Arched Crest Rail, Ring Arm Supports, 1790, 35 In. 2185.00
Sofa, Federal, Mahogany, Scrolled Arms, Serpentine, 1790-1810 . . . . 2300.00
Sofa, Federal, Mahogany, Upholstered Seat, Ring Turned Support, Legs, 35 In. 2185.00
Sofa, Federal, Scrolled Back, Hairy Paw Legs, Arms, 82 In. 1150.00
Sofa, Floral & Foliage Scrolls, 2 Birds, Nest Of Eggs On Crest, Upholstered, 71 In. 1700.00
Sofa, Frank Lloyd Wright Design, Corner, Suede, Mahogany Base, 1950s, 61 1/2 In. 825.00
Sofa, Freeform, Green Velvet, Black Trim, 1945, 30 x 55 x 41 In. 360.00
Sofa, Fruitwood, Floral Carved, Down Pillow, Upholstered, France 825.00

Sofa, Geometric Design, Stylized Flowers, Black, 28 In. 3900.00
Sofa, George III, Mahogany, Floral Brocade, Scrolling Crest & Arms, 79 In. 1755.00
Sofa, Grecian, Mahogany, Scroll Ends, Lion Paws Feet, Cornucopia, 31 x 84 In. 885.00
Sofa, Howard & Sons, Chesterfield, Mahogany Legs, Serpentine Front, 25 In. 2790.00
Sofa, J. & J.W. Meeks, Hawkin Pattern, Victorian 10000.00
Sofa, Louis XIV Style, Walnut, Curved Legs, 50 In. 6325.00
Sofa, Louis XV Style, Beechwood, Serpentine Leaf Top, 56 In. 1840.00
Sofa, Louis XV, Beechwood, Foliate, Cabriole Legs, 79 In. 2875.00
Sofa, Louis XV, Beechwood, Scrolled, Cabriole Legs, 78 In. 4600.00
Sofa, Louis XV, Beechwood, Serpentine Seat, Shell Design, 67 In. 9200.00
Sofa, Louis XV, Walnut, Scrolled Crest, Floral Brocade, 86 In. 1650.00
Sofa, Louis XVI Style, Walnut, Carved, Stop-Fluted Legs, 16 In. 970.00
Sofa, Louis XVI, Gilt, Crest Rail, Acanthus, Floral Design, 43 In. 1450.00
Sofa, Louis XVI, Giltwood, Carved, Moire Back & Seat, 19th Century, 60 In. 1200.00
Sofa, Mahogany, Acanthus & Floral Carved Arms, 8 Legs, 76 In. 9350.00
Sofa, Mahogany, Box Form, Anthemions Face, 32 In. 1330.00
Sofa, Mahogany, Camelback, 3 Cushions, 20th Century 860.00
Sofa, Mahogany, Carved & Shaped Back, Tufted Upholstery, Scrolled Arms 220.00
Sofa, Mahogany, Crest Rail, Acanthus, Shell Design, Cornucopia Legs, 40 In. 3150.00
Sofa, Mahogany, Stenciled Design, Box, c.1830, 89 In. 1800.00
Sofa, Mahogany, Wheat & Flower Carving, Curved Arms 1265.00
Sofa, Moderne, Blond Wood, 1940, 31 x 75 x 35 In. 935.00
Sofa, Moderne, Blond Wood, Ribbon Arms, 3-Piece Sectional, 31 x 25 x 29 In. 1215.00
Sofa, Napoleon III, Giltwood, Baluster Top Rail, Paw Feet, 100 In. 7475.00
Sofa, Oriental, Triple Panel Back, Mother-Of-Pearl Inlay, Silk Cushion, 73 In. 1035.00
Sofa, Renaissance Revival, Walnut, Circular Medallion, Serpentine, 1860, 78 In. 4025.00
Sofa, Rococo, Fruitwood, Serpentine Top Rail, 80 In. 4025.00
Sofa, Rococo, Mahogany, Carved Foliate, Dark Finish, 1850, 75 In. 1750.00
Sofa, Rococo, Rosewood, 1850, Child's, 47 x 33 In. 1375.00
Sofa, Rococo, Rosewood, Carved Roses, Upholstered, c.1850 . . . . 3250.00
Sofa, Rococo, Rosewood, Floral, Foliate Crest, Serpentine Apron, 15 In. 4600.00
Sofa, Rococo, Rosewood, Foliate Roses, Grapes, 1850, 40 1/2 In. 4850.00
Sofa, Rococo, Rosewood, Triple-Back, Serpentine Seat Rail, Velvet, 67 In. 495.00
Sofa, Rosewood Veneer, Carved & Pierced Crest, Striped Upholstered 275.00
Sofa, Rosewood, Carved, Damask Button Tufted Upholstery 2450.00
Sofa, Rosewood, Grapevine & Grapes Carved On Scrolled Ends, Victorian, 76 In. 6325.00
Sofa, Sheraton, Bird's-Eye Maple Panels, Scrolled Arms, 34 3/4 In. 4600.00
Sofa, Sheraton, Mahogany, Floral Upholstery, 76 In. 4400.00
Sofa, Sheraton, Mahogany, Rope Spiral Front Legs, Upholstered, England, 60 In. 1200.00
Sofa, Sheraton, Mahogany, Turned Legs, Beaded Frame, 72 In. 1200.00
Sofa, Sleeper, Lawson Type, 85 In. 430.00
Sofa, Techno, Osualdo Borsani, Folding, Italy, 1954, 33 x 73 x 29 In. 3000.00
Sofa, Triple Back, Carved Roses, Center Medallion, Velvet Apron, 69 In. 1865.00
Sofa, Victorian, Walnut, Carved Crest, Upholstered Back & Arms 515.00
Sofa, Victorian, Walnut, Finger Carved, Upholstered, 58 1/2 In. 275.00
Sofa, Victorian, Walnut, Fruit Crest, Upholstered, 56 In. 495.00
Sofa, Walnut, Arched Back, 4 Cabriole Legs, Scrolled Arms, Italy, 43 In. 2200.00
Sofa, Walnut, Caryatid On Crest, Upholstered, Carved Lion's Head On Arms 2700.00
Sofa, Walnut, Medallion Back, Carved, Damask, 57 In. 660.00
Sofa, Wicker, 3 Cushions, Upholstered, Springs 1100.00
Sofa, William & Mary Style, Mahogany, Upholstered, Rectangular Back & Seat 865.00
Stand, Arts & Crafts, Oak, Square Top, 4 Shelves, Keyhole Slat Sides, 42 In. 550.00
Stand, Bamboo, 5 Shelves, Spindles, Rear Gallery, Split Top Shelf, 42 x 16 x 12 In. 100.00
Stand, Basin, George III, Mahogany, Tripod, Early 19th Century, 31 x 11 1/4 In. 515.00
Stand, Basin, Mahogany, Original Brasses, c.1820 . . . . 968.00
Stand, Bedside, Oak, Sliding Tambour Door Over Drawer, 32 In, Pair 1100.00
Stand, Birch & Maple, 3 Drawers, Brass, New Hampshire, 29 1/4 x 18 In. 2300.00
Stand, Birch, Red Washed Paint, Drawer, 19th Century 690.00
Stand, Cast & Wrought Iron, Brass Trim, Plate Glass Top, 8 x 18 x 28 In. 110.00
Stand, Cherry, 2 Dovetailed Drawers, 2-Board Top, 19 x 22 x 29 In. 235.00
Stand, Cherry, 3 Tiers, Marquetry Musical Instruments On Top, Chain Swag, 33 In. 1045.00
Stand, Cherry, Dovetailed Drawer, 3-Board Top, Refinished, 17 x 20 x 29 In. 330.00
Stand, Cherry, Drawer, 2-Board Top, Turned Legs, 18 x 22 x 29 In. 190.00

Stand, Cherry, Drawer, 4-Board Top, Turned Legs, Refinished, 18 x 20 In.		300.00
Stand, Cherry, Drawer, Curly Maple Drawer Front		375.00
Stand, Cherry, Veneer Drawer, 1-Board Top, 38 x 18 5/8 x 29 In.		300.00
Stand, Chippendale, Cherry, Maple, Tripod Base, Snake Feet, 27 3/4 In.		1100.00
Stand, Chippendale, Walnut, Tripod Base, Snake Feet, 26 In.		150.00
Stand, Corner, Chippendale, Mahogany, Bamboo Legs, 32 In.		485.00
Stand, Curly Maple, Rounded Drawer Front, 1-Board Top, 30 x 22 1/8 In.		665.00
Stand, Dictionary, Adjustable Shelf, Webster's Dictionary, Cast Iron		250.00
Stand, Eastlake, Ash, 4 Carved Birds On Legs		185.00
Stand, Empire, Cherry & Maple, Drawer, 1-Board Top, Tripod, 18 x 20 In.		275.00
Stand, Empire, Cherry, 2 Dovetailed Ogee Drawers, Turned Legs, 28 In.		195.00
Stand, Empire, Cherry, Curly Maple, 3 Drawers, 1 Drop Leaf, 18 x 23 In.		600.00
Stand, Empire, Cherry, Mahogany, 2 Dovetailed Drawers, 10 3/4 x 19 x 28 In.		220.00
Stand, Empire, Mahogany, Drop Leaf, Figured Veneer, Square Pedestal, 2 Drawers		330.00
Stand, Empire, Mahogany, Gilt Bronze, Marble, 19th Century, 30 x 15 In.		1695.00
Stand, Empire, Walnut, Drop Leaf, Pedestal, 2 Drawers, 16 x 17 In., 8-In. Leaves		135.00
Stand, Faux Bamboo, 3 Tier, Black Lacquered, Gilt Design, 31 1/2 In.		300.00
Stand, Federal, Cherry Inlay, 2 Drawers, Tapered Legs, 28 In.		4375.00
Stand, Federal, Cherry, Bird's-Eye Maple, Mahogany, 29 In.		880.00
Stand, Federal, Cherry, Drawer, Apron, Square Top, 19th Century, 26 x 16 In.		920.00
Stand, Federal, Cherry, Veneered Drawer, Arrow Feet, 1815, 29 x 17 In.		575.00
Stand, Federal, Mahogany Veneer, Drop Leaf, Cock-Beaded Drawers, 30 x 18 In.		980.00
Stand, Federal, Mahogany, Drawer, Square Tapered Legs, c.1780, 29 x 16 In.		1380.00
Stand, Federal, Mahogany, Marble Top, Shelf With Drawer, c.1790, 31 x 16 In.		4025.00
Stand, Federal, Mahogany, Tilt Top, Urn Pedestal, 3 Leg Base, 1790, 28 In.		1955.00
Stand, Federal, Maple, 2 Graduated Drawers, Turned Legs, 28 In.		1600.00
Stand, Federal, Pine, 2 Drop Leaves, Drawer, Hinged Top, 1820, 30 x 19 In.		235.00
Stand, Federal, Walnut, Straight Apron, Splayed Legs, Square, 19th Century, 15 In.		575.00
Stand, Fern, Georgian Style, Mahogany, Stop-Fluted Column, 56 3/4 In.		520.00
Stand, Fern, Hardwood, Marble Inlay, Pierced Floral Apron, 12 1/2 In.		360.00
Stand, Fern, Neoclassical, Mahogany		115.00
Stand, Fern, Oak, Claw Feet, Glass Balls, Turned Legs, Square, 24 In.		105.00
Stand, Fern, Oriental, Rosewood, Pair		230.00
Stand, Fern, Walnut, Black, Gold, Turquoise, 19th Century		515.00
Stand, Galle, 2 Tiers, Inlaid Chestnut Leaves On Shelves, c.1900, 45 In.		2185.00
Stand, George III, Ribbons, Painted Flower Vines, 61 In.		4025.00
Stand, Giltwood, Scrolled Supports, Reeded Column Pedestal Base, 30 In.		1815.00
Stand, Hepplewhite, Birch, Square Tapered Legs, 1-Board Top, 27 3/4 x 15 1/4 In.		165.00
Stand, Hepplewhite, Cherry, Bird's-Eye Drawer, Tapered Legs, 28 In.		3905.00
Stand, Hepplewhite, Cherry, Bowfront Apron, 26 In.		2310.00
Stand, Hepplewhite, Maple, Tripod, 1-Board Rectangular Top, 15 x 22 In.		225.00
Stand, Hepplewhite, Pine, Poplar, Drawer, 1-Board Top, 21 x 29 x 30 In.		165.00
Stand, Hepplewhite, Walnut, Drawer, 1-Board Top, 21 x 21 x 29 In.		330.00
Stand, Hepplewhite, Walnut, Splayed Base, Scalloped Apron, 26 1/4 In.		1265.00
Stand, Heywood-Wakefield, Champagne Finish, Flared Base, Pair		550.00
Stand, L. & J.G. Stickley, No. 574, Drink, Second Tier Over Cross Stretchers, 29 In.		525.00
Stand, Louis XIV Style, Ebonized, Coffer Form, Gadroon Border, 5 1/2 In.		2300.00
Stand, Louis XV, Fruitwood, Marble Top, Carved Base, 16 x 20 1/2 In.		60.00
Stand, Louis XV, Provincial, Fruitwood Duet		700.00
Stand, Magazine, Champagne Finish, Ink Stamp, 22 x 28 x 15 In.		250.00
Stand, Magazine, G. Stickley, No. 72, 3 Shelves, 42 In.		2875.00
Stand, Magazine, L. & G. Stickley, No. 47, 4 Shelves, Arched Apron, 42 x 18 In.		2000.00
Stand, Magazine, L. & J.G. Stickley, 4 Shelves, Chamfered Back, 45 x 19 In.		2100.00
Stand, Magazine, L. & J.G. Stickley, No. 45, 4 Shelves, Stretchers, 45 In.		1650.00
Stand, Magazine, Stickley Bros., 5 Shelves, Slatted Sides & Back, 46 3/4 In.		885.00
Stand, Magazine, Stickley Bros., No. 4804, Slatted Back & Sides, 4 Shelves, 36 In.		935.00
Stand, Mahogany, Butler's Tray, Fold-Out Base, 30 x 21 x 29 In.		490.00
Stand, Mahogany, Frieze Drawer, Square Legs, England, 19th Century, 28 x 24 In.		520.00
Stand, Mahogany, Round Top, Green Marble Insert, Tripod Supports, 19 1/2 In.		2185.00
Stand, Maple & Cherry, Beaded Drawer & Skirt, 26 x 24 x 20 In.		2760.00
Stand, Maple, Tripod Base, S Curve Feet, 29 In.		250.00
Stand, Marquetry, Marble Top, 4 Drawers, Brass Sabots, France, 32 In.		650.00
Stand, Mottled Marble Top, Brass Gallery, Fluted Tapering Legs, 19 1/4 In.		95.00

Stand, Music, Oak, 1 Drawer, 2 Cabinet Doors	165.00
Stand, Music, Renaissance Revival, Walnut, Ebonized, Bronze Cherubs, 2 Sections	1750.00
Stand, Oak, Rectangular Top Over Drawer, Turned Legs, Continental	175.00
Stand, Oak, Stretcher Shelf, 24 In.	190.00
Stand, Oak, Tile Top, Straight Tapered Legs	85.00
Stand, Onyx & Brass, 2 Tiers, 4 Twisted Supports On Paw Feet, 38 1/4 In.	260.00
Stand, Pastry, Pear Wood, 3 Galleried Trays, Wooden Handle, 4 Legs, 25 In.	345.00
Stand, Pine, 3 Shelves, Crock, Layers Of Paint, Shoe Feet, Scalloped 39 x 22 In.	465.00
Stand, Pine, Hardwood, Red Over Blue, X Base, 17 1/2 x 18 x 29 In.	495.00
Stand, Pine, Poplar, 3 Drawers, Turned Legs, 18 3/4 x 28 x 26 In.	375.00
Stand, Pine, Red Finish, Drawer, 1-Board Top, 17 x 19 x 29 In.	100.00
Stand, Pine, Red Grained, Birdcage, Revolving 1-Board Top, 23 x 24 In.	880.00
Stand, Plant, Brass & Marble, 2 Tiers, Square, Victorian, 31 In.	625.00
Stand, Plant, Carved Serpent, 36 3/4 In., Pair	1350.00
Stand, Plant, G. Stickley, Tapering Legs, Red Finish, 28 x 12 In.	415.00
Stand, Plant, Limbert, Slatted, Flaring Sides, Signed, 32 1/4 In.	1760.00
Stand, Plant, Mahogany, Tripod Stand Base, Rectangular Top, 36 1/2 In.	115.00
Stand, Plant, Onyx, Gilt Brass, Lower Shelf, Victorian, 19th Century, 34 In.	785.00
Stand, Plant, Rosewood, Carved, Chinese	395.00
Stand, Plant, Twisted Wire, 3 Tiers, White Paint, 35 1/2 In.	275.00
Stand, Portfolio, Edwardian, Mahogany, Pierced Top, 3 Sections, 30 x 23 In.	3000.00
Stand, Portfolio, Mahogany Stained, Adjustable Side Shelf, 55 1/2 In.	920.00
Stand, Portfolio, William IV, Mahogany, 19th Century	2550.00
Stand, Queen Anne, Mahogany, Tripod, Cabriole Base, Pad Feet, 22 In.	1265.00
Stand, Quilt, Oak, Pine With Maple Ironing Board, 19th Century	85.00
Stand, Red Paint, Conforming Apron, Tapered Legs, 26 In.	800.00
Stand, Red Paint, Marble Top, 5 Drawers, 39 In., Pair	630.00
Stand, Regency Revival, Burled Elm, Fitted & Sectioned, c.1815, 34 1/2 In.	2725.00
Stand, Regency Revival, Sprays Of Flowers On Tray, Continental, 23 x 20 In.	195.00
Stand, Rosewood, Marble Top, Beaded Rim, Floral Carved Legs	300.00
Stand, Roycroft, Little Journeys, 2 Shelves, Trestle Sides, Metal Tag, 26 x 26 In.	660.00
Stand, Scroll Top, Tiered Shelves, Brass Capped Saber Feet	85.00
Stand, Shaker, Tiger Maple, 2 Drawers, Rectangular	4180.00
Stand, Shaped Gallery, Drawer, Stretcher Shelf, 19th Century	275.00
Stand, Shaving, A. Roux, Rosewood, Drawer, Mirror, Stenciled	3300.00
Stand, Shaving, Mahogany, Frieze Drawer, Inlay, England, 19th Century, 26 In.	260.00
Stand, Shaving, Oak, Quartersawn, Drawer, Door, Cabriole Legs, Mirror, 60 In.	575.00
Stand, Shaving, Regency Style, Satinwood, Painted, 3 Small Drawers, Feet, 26 In.	460.00
Stand, Shaving, Walnut, Carved Scrolled Feet, Swivel Lid, Adjustable Mirror, 61 In. . . .	385.00
Stand, Sheraton, Bird's-Eye Maple, 2 Drawers, Glass Pulls, 29 1/4 In.	1200.00
Stand, Sheraton, Cherry, 3 Tiger Maple Drawers, Sandwich Pulls	700.00
Stand, Sheraton, Cherry, Curly Maple Veneer, 2 Drawers, 16 x 21 x 28 3/4 In.	1045.00
Stand, Sheraton, Cherry, Drawer, 2-Board Top, Refinished, 19 x 22 x 28 In.	355.00
Stand, Sheraton, Cherry, Mahogany Veneer, 2 Drawers, Ogee, 18 x 20 In.	220.00
Stand, Sheraton, Cherry, Maple, Drawer, 2-Board Top, Splayed Base, 16 x 20 In.	660.00
Stand, Sheraton, Cherry, Red, Black Grained, Turned Legs, 28 3/4 In.	250.00
Stand, Sheraton, Cherry, Turned Legs, Dovetailed Drawer, 28 In.	415.00
Stand, Sheraton, Curly Birch, Drawer, 29 3/4 In.	288.00
Stand, Sheraton, Curly Maple, Drawer, Overlapping Top, Miniature	3950.00
Stand, Sheraton, Maple, 6 Dovetailed Drawers, Turned Legs, 32 In.	7425.00
Stand, Sheraton, Maple, Dovetailed Drawer, Turned Legs, 30 In.	660.00
Stand, Sheraton, Maple, New York, 1825	330.00
Stand, Sheraton, Shelf Drawer, Painted Swags, 30 x 22 1/2 In.	665.00
Stand, Sheraton, Walnut, Turned Legs, Dovetailed Drawer, 29 In.	385.00
Stand, Smoking, Arts & Crafts, Pine, 26 In.	40.00
Stand, Smoking, Hepplewhite, Mahogany, Tapered Legs, 28 1/2 In.	1325.00
Stand, Smoking, Log Cabin, Twig	80.00
Stand, Smoking, Mahogany, Cloverleaf Form, 2 Lift Doors, Tripod Base, 42 3/4 In.	115.00
Stand, Smoking, Metal, Parrot On Oak Tree, c.1930, 31 In.	805.00
Stand, Smoking, Wrought Iron, Indented Pottery Ashtray, 2 Shelves	125.00
Stand, Stickley Bros., No. 135, Drink, Square Overhanging Top, Scalloped Aprons	665.00
Stand, Sycamore, Open Folio, 7 Adjustable Shelves, 1928, 44 In.	2185.00
Stand, Telephone, Stickley Bros., Scalloped Apron, Blind Drawer, 30 x 15 3/4 In.	990.00

Stand, Tiger Maple, Drop Leaf, 2 Drawers 1450.00
Stand, Umbrella, Cast Iron, Black, c.1890, 24 x 19 1/4 In. 225.00
Stand, Umbrella, Iron, Foliate Scroll, Beaded, Mask Design, 30 1/4 In. 224.00
Stand, Umbrella, Lakeside Crafters, Tied With Oak Straps, 28 In. 330.00
Stand, Umbrella, Metal, Sailor, Painted, 17 In. 430.00
Stand, Umbrella, Oak, Drip Pan, 6 Sections 140.00
Stand, Umbrella, Putto Taming Snake Shape, Iron, Victorian, 31 In. 488.00
Stand, Umbrella, Stickley Bros., Wide & Narrow Slats, Tapered Posts, 32 In. 195.00
Stand, Urn Shape Drop Finials, Bird's-Eye Maple Drawer Fronts, 2 Drawers 900.00
Stand, Victorian, Walnut, White Marble Top, Fruit Drawer, 1875, 28 In. 495.00
Stand, W. Von Nessen, Art Deco, Scroll Design, Bakelite Handle, 19 In. 230.00
Stand, Walnut, Drop Leaf, 2 Drawers, Turned Legs, 17 x 18 x 29 In. 330.00
Stand, Wash, Mahogany, Triangular Drawer, 3 Feet, 31 In. 465.00
Stand, Wash, Sheraton, Mixed Woods, Dovetailed Drawer, 33 x 17 x 16 In. 295.00
Stand, Wig, Mahogany, Tripod Base, Snake Feet, 33 In. 290.00
Stool, Bar, Bertoia, White Wire, Green Vinyl Pad, 37 x 21 In. 55.00
Stool, Baroque, Walnut, Slanted Supports, Pierced Top, Italy 460.00
Stool, Black Japanned, Flower Apron, Cabriole Legs, 17 3/4 In. 9775.00
Stool, Breuer, Chrome Tubular Steel, Brown Eisengarn Seat, 1931, 18 In. 1150.00
Stool, Chippendale, Birch, Serpentine, Upholstered, H-Stretcher, 1760-1780 . . . . 920.00
Stool, Chippendale, Burl Wood, Cabriole Legs, Ball & Claw Feet, 20 x 17 In. 375.00
Stool, Chippendale, Mahogany, Carved Knees, Ball Feet 80.00
Stool, Classical Style, U-Shape Maple, Needlepoint Seat, 20th Century 110.00
Stool, Curule, Painted Maroon, Wrought Iron, Web Seat, Brass Finials, 27 1/2 In. 485.00
Stool, Empire, Mahogany, Needlepoint Cover 200.00
Stool, Federal, Mahogany, Carved Shields, 1840s 315.00
Stool, George II Style, Oak, Plain Frieze, Cabriole Legs, 20 In. 1850.00
Stool, Georgian, Oak, Brocade Slip Seat, Square Legs, 16 x 15 5/8 x 16 5/8 In. 150.00
Stool, Giltwood, Upholstered, Paw Feet, 1780s, 20 1/2 In., Pair 5175.00
Stool, Gout, Leather, Adjustable, Hospital Contacts Co., England, 22 In. 360.00
Stool, Gout, Regency Revival, Adjustable, Upholstered Leg & Foot Rest, 17 x 15 In. 365.00
Stool, Gout, Victorian, Walnut 460.00
Stool, Hardwood, Rouge Marble Top, Floral Apron, Median Stretcher, 16 In. 365.00
Stool, Jacobean, Oak, Rectangular Plank Seat, Foliate Frieze, 22 In. 2587.00
Stool, Limbert, No. 205, Slanted Sides, Cutouts, Padded Seat, 18 x 20 In. 825.00
Stool, Louis XV, Beechwood, Serpentine Seat, Floral Needlework, 16 In. 373.00
Stool, Louis XV, Shell Frame, Floral Upholstery, Scroll, 18 In., Pair 1210.00
Stool, Louis XV, Walnut, Velvet, Cabriole Legs 1725.00
Stool, Mahogany, Needlepoint Pad, Plinth Base, England, 6 x 45 x 10 In. 695.00
Stool, Milking, Pine, Clover Leaf Cutouts, Splint Seat, Carved & Pierced Base 110.00
Stool, Napoleon III Style, Giltwood, Gothic Apron, Saber Legs, 17 In. 1850.00
Stool, Neoclassical, Giltwood, Fan Carved Apron, 20 In., Pair 5465.00
Stool, Oak, 2 Drop Leaves, Spiral Turned Legs, England 520.00
Stool, Oak, Joint, Rectangular Top, Turned Legs, England, 17th Century, 16 x 17 In. 515.00
Stool, Organ, Eastlake, Needlepoint Cover 110.00
Stool, Piano, Duncan Phyfe, Mahogany, Brass Inset Lyre Splat, Adjustable, c.1810 . . . . . 1725.00
Stool, Piano, Mahogany, 4 Turned Legs, Claw & Glass Ball Feet 50.00
Stool, Piano, Mahogany, High Spindle Back, Victorian 150.00
Stool, Piano, Oak, 4 Turned Legs, Claw & Glass Ball Feet 80.00
Stool, Queen Anne Style, Walnut, Rectangular Seat, Cabriole Legs, 3 In. 1840.00
Stool, Queen Anne, Mahogany, Petit Point Slip Seat, Cabriole Legs, 17 x 19 In. 845.00
Stool, Regency Revival, Mahogany, X-Form, Ball Feet, 1810, 18 In. 9200.00
Stool, Renaissance Revival, Mahogany, Ebonized, Gilt, Needlepoint, 14 x 17 In. 195.00
Stool, Robsjohn-Gibbings, Wooden Frame, Webbed Seat, Brass Legs, 18 In. 880.00
Stool, Rosewood, Floral Carved Apron, Cabriole Legs, 15 1/2 In. 1350.00
Stool, Shaker, Tack Holes Top, Tin Patched 355.00
Stool, Victorian, Iron, Cabriole Legs, 14 In. 145.00
Stool, Walnut, Cabriole Legs Ending In Hoof Feet, Italy, 18th Century 1150.00
Stool, Walnut, Needlepoint, France, Pair 385.00
Stool, Walnut, Ribbon Carved Apron, Saber Legs, Needlepoint Top, 19th Century, Pair . . 550.00
Stool, Warren Plattner, Wire, Corseted, Wool Seat, Paper Label, 20 x 15 In., Pair 330.00
Stool, William & Mary, Oak, Turned Legs, 22 In. 86.00
Stool, William & Mary, Walnut, Rectangular Seat, Faceted Feet, 15 In. 8050.00

Stool, William IV, Giltwood, 4 Leaf Scrolled Legs, 1835, 7 1/2 In. 5460.00
Stool, William IV, Mahogany, Gilt Tooled Moroccan Leather, 18 In. 520.00
Stool, Windsor, Green Paint, Turned Legs, Round Seat, 28 1/2 In. 770.00
Stool, Windsor, Splayed Legs, Bamboo Turning, Shaped Seat, 15 In. 360.00
Table, Adirondack, Twig, Tree Of Life Design Top, 3 Legs, 1910 . . . . 165.00
Table, Aesthetic Revival, Burl Walnut, Carved, White Marble Top, 4 Legs, 29 In. 440.00
Table, Aesthetic Revival, Walnut, Marble Top, Anthemia Rim, 1875, 33 In. 1650.00
Table, Altar, Rectangular Top, Square Legs, China, 20th Century, 31 x 74 In. 400.00
Table, Altar, Rosewood, Carved, Oriental 900.00
Table, Altar, Teak, Frieze Carved With Precious Objects, China, 32 In. 2000.00
Table, Architect's, Chippendale, Maple, Square Legs, 30 In. 5175.00
Table, Architect's, Mahogany, Adjustable Top, Swing-Out Candleholder, Drawer 2665.00
Table, Art Deco, Rosewood, Brass, 4 Square Legs, 1935, 24 In. 4025.00
Table, Art Deco, Wrought Iron, Marble, Scalloped, Hammered Base, 29 In. 3450.00
Table, Arts & Crafts, Oak, Bamboo Turning, Tiles, 27 x 18 1/4 In. 290.00
Table, Arts & Crafts, Post Base, Mitered Step Design, 31 In. 460.00
Table, Baker's, Iron, Slab Top, Paint, France, 19th Century, 60 In. 1200.00
Table, Baker's, Steel, Rectangular Top, Scrolled Base, France, 47 In. 400.00
Table, Baker's, Tooled Leather Inset, Tripod Base, Snake Feet, 21 1/4 In. 115.00
Table, Banded Border, 3 Pedestals, Downswept Legs, Carved Leaves, 103 1/2 In. 8000.00
Table, Biedermeier, Fruitwood, Ebonized Single Drawer 750.00
Table, Black Lacquer, Gilt Figures, Pavilions & Foliage, Chinese Export, 50 In. 4600.00
Table, Black Marble, Mosaic Arch, Appian Way, Rondel Scene, Italy, 1844, 18 In. 4535.00
Table, Bone & Wood Inlay, Chinese Designs, 4 Supports, Japan, 33 In. 2070.00
Table, Brass Plate Mushroom Design, Laurel, 16 In., Pair 310.00
Table, Bread, French Provincial, Oak, Trestle, Drawer 605.00
Table, Brooks, Square Top, 4 Flaring Legs, Square Tier, 30 x 24 In. 2310.00
Table, Bugatti, Vellum Covered, X-Shaped Base, Brass, 1900, 25 In. 2875.00
Table, Card, Chippendale, Mahogany, Hinged Top, Block Legs, c.1770, 29 x 35 In. 8625.00
Table, Card, Chippendale, Mahogany, Opens To Fabric Top, 18th Century 2420.00
Table, Card, Chippendale, Walnut, Foldover, Cabriole Legs, Trifid Feet, 28 1/2 In. 3165.00
Table, Card, Chippendale, Walnut, Thumb-Molded Drawer, 1760, 30 In. 8625.00
Table, Card, Classical, Mahogany, D-Shape, Reeded Edge, Legs, 29 In., Pair 6655.00
Table, Card, Classical, Mahogany, Rectangular Top, Saber Legs, 28 1/4 In. 5750.00
Table, Card, Empire, Flip Top, Lyre Base, Incurving Plinth, 4 Scroll Feet 82.00
Table, Card, Empire, Walnut, Swivel Top, Lyre Base, Opens To 36 x 36 In. 360.00
Table, Card, Federal, Cherry, Maple Inlay, New Hampshire, 28 1/2 In. 1265.00
Table, Card, Federal, Mahogany Veneer & Mahogany, Demilune, c.1810, 28 1/2 In. 1380.00
Table, Card, Federal, Mahogany Veneer, Inlay, 1790, 29 1/2 In. 4025.00
Table, Card, Federal, Mahogany, Flame Birch, Hinged Top, 1790, 36 x 18 In. 9200.00
Table, Card, Federal, Mahogany, Inlay, Hinged Square Top, 1790, 29 1/2 In. 6900.00
Table, Card, Federal, Mahogany, Reeded Tapered Legs, Tapered Feet, N.Y., 29 In. 2300.00
Table, Card, Federal, Mahogany, Serpentine Top, Apron, Reeded Legs, 29 1/2 In. 970.00
Table, Card, Federal, Mahogany, Square Top, Reeded Legs, c.1800, 36 x 43 In. 2300.00
Table, Card, French Style, Foldover Top, Felt Interior, Storage, 29 3/4 In. 550.00
Table, Card, George III, Mahogany, Drawer, Marlborough Legs, 28 x 30 In. 330.00
Table, Card, Hepplewhite, Mahogany, Square Tapered Legs, 28 In. 1200.00
Table, Card, Mahogany & Mahogany Veneer, Swing Leg, Inlaid Banding On Skirt 330.00
Table, Card, Mahogany Veneer, Double Pedestal, Quadruped Base 190.00
Table, Card, Mahogany, Clover Shape Top, Reeded Legs, 29 In. 2300.00
Table, Card, Mahogany, Heart Shaped Pedestal, 1850 . . . . 1250.00
Table, Card, Mahogany, Oval Reserve On Drawer, Square Legs, c.1815, 28 1/2 In. 1600.00
Table, Card, Red & Black Grained, Pedestal, 1830-1845, Square, 36 In. Open 1450.00
Table, Card, Rococo Revival, Mahogany, Rosewood, Green Baize, Cabriole Legs, 31 In. . . 1200.00
Table, Card, Sheraton, Mahogany, Rope Twist Legs, 30 x 36 In. 600.00
Table, Card, Walnut, Chamfered Corners, Square Flared Stem, Plinth, 30 1/2 In. 660.00
Table, Carved, Lion's Mask, Drawer, Italy, c.1875, 30 x 58 In. 1840.00
Table, Center, Baroque, Wrought Iron, White On Black Slate Ground, 31 In. 9200.00
Table, Center, Belter, Rosewood, Marble Top, 1850s, 27 3/4 x 38 In. 8500.00
Table, Center, Charles II Style, Oak, Octagonal, Alternating Drawers, 30 x 52 In. 920.00
Table, Center, Classical, Circular Marble Top, Melon Feet, 1810, 29 In. 5750.00
Table, Center, Classical, Mahogany, Angular Scroll Feet Base, 1830, 28 In. 1200.00
Table, Center, Classical, Mahogany, Black Marble, 4 Scroll Feet, 28 In. 2750.00

Right: Furniture, Table, Dining, Mahogany, Pedestal, Leaves, Round

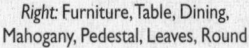

Left: Furniture, Table, Center, Ebonized, Ivory Inlay, Italy, 19th Century, 50 In.

Table, Center, Classical, Mahogany, Marble, 2 Supports, 1830, 37 x 26 In. 9075.00
Table, Center, Classical, Mahogany, Octagonal Base, Scrolled Legs, Round, 42 In. 4950.00
Table, Center, Classical, Mahogany, White Top, 4 Scroll Feet, 28 In. 2750.00
Table, Center, Classical, Rosewood, White Marble Top, 1840 . . . . 885.00
Table, Center, Cromwellian, Maple & Oak, Bead Turned Stretcher Base, c.1700 . . . . 825.00
Table, Center, Directoire Style, Mahogany, Brass Border, Paw Feet, 28 In. 6900.00
Table, Center, Eastlake, Maple, Victorian, 20 x 29 x 28 In. 85.00
Table, Center, Eastlake, Walnut Base, Burl Veneer, Marble Top, 28 In. 300.00
Table, Center, Eastlake, Walnut, Oval Marble Top, Victorian, 21 x 29 In. 415.00
Table, Center, Ebonized, Ivory Inlay, Italy, 19th Century, 50 In. . . . .*Illus* 5175.00
Table, Center, Empire, Mahogany, Gadroon Edge, Base, 32 In. 700.00
Table, Center, Georgian Style, Mahogany, Inlaid Trim, Oval Crossbanded Top, 41 In. . . . 925.00
Table, Center, Louis XV, Fruitwood, Marquetry, Floral, 26 In. 1100.00
Table, Center, Louis XVI, Gilt, Garland Design, Stretcher Shelf, 36 x 29 In. 1815.00
Table, Center, Louis XVI, Oak, Beveled Marble Top, Swag Apron, 33 x 57 In. 2700.00
Table, Center, Mahogany, Inlay, Paw Feet, Octagonal, 28 x 32 1/2 In. 1200.00
Table, Center, Mahogany, Marble Top, Pillar & Scroll, 1840, Rectangular 1030.00
Table, Center, Mahogany, Marble Top, Scroll Base, N.Y., 1830, 29 1/2 In. 2900.00
Table, Center, Mahogany, Marquetry, Dutch, 19th Century 2860.00
Table, Center, Marquetry, Mother-Of-Pearl Floral Top, Cabriole Legs, 29 In. 2200.00
Table, Center, Marquetry, Scroll Design Top, Cabriole Legs, 30 1/2 x 30 In. 2200.00
Table, Center, Neoclassical, Geometrical Design, Stepped Base, 28 1/4 In. 6325.00
Table, Center, Neoclassical, Mahogany, 4-Leg Plinth, 30 1/2 In. 8100.00
Table, Center, Neoclassical, Rosewood, White Marble Top, Bulbous, 29 In. 1100.00
Table, Center, Neoclassical, Travertine Top, Stylized Chariots, Italy, 28 In. 8625.00
Table, Center, Oval Marble Top, Carved Frieze, Trestle Base, 36 x 26 1/4 In. 700.00
Table, Center, Renaissance Revival, Ebonized, Inlay, Trumpet Legs, 41 x 25 In. 4400.00
Table, Center, Renaissance Revival, Walnut, Ebonized, Rectangular Top, 1865 . . . . 3650.00
Table, Center, Restauration, Mahogany, Marble, New York, 1835, 33 In. 2175.00
Table, Center, Rococo, Grained Rosewood, Scroll Shell Apron, Oval, 39 x 33 In. 2240.00
Table, Center, Rococo, Mahogany, Marble, Apron, Cabriole Legs, 1850, 41 In. 1815.00
Table, Center, Rococo, Rosewood, Marble, Fruit Carved Sides, 1850, 42 x 30 In. 1695.00
Table, Center, Rococo, Walnut, Bronze, 3 Bronze Dolphins, Shell Feet, 31 In. 9200.00
Table, Center, Victorian, Carrara Marble Top, Spiraled Legs, 1890s, 30 x 85 In. 980.00
Table, Center, Victorian, Fruitwood, Rosewood, Round Top, 5 In. 2875.00
Table, Center, Walnut, Burl Veneer, Marble Top, James Moriarty, 22 x 30 In. 325.00
Table, Center, Walnut, Burl Veneer, White Marble Top, 30 3/4 In. 440.00
Table, Center, Walnut, Burl, Turned Vase Form Pedestal, Victorian, 30 In. 2420.00
Table, Center, Walnut, Inset Marble Top, Paper Label, Victorian, 22 x 30 In. 715.00
Table, Center, Walnut, Marble Top, 3 Drawers, Door, Reeded Bands, 30 x 15 x 27 In. . . . 300.00
Table, Center, Walnut, Oval Marble Top, Applied Carvings, 29 1/4 In. 440.00
Table, Center, Walnut, Serpentine Top, 2 Drawers, Cabriole Legs, Italy, 31 In. 6325.00

Table, Center, William IV, Giltwood, Carved Apron, Embroidered Top, 32 In. 3650.00
Table, Center, William IV, Mahogany, Brass Inlaid, 19th Century 3100.00
Table, Charles X Style, Marquetry, Rosewood, Envelope, 1880s, 28 1/4 In. 1095.00
Table, Charles X, Mahogany, Marble Top, Trifid Base, 28 5/8 In. 365.00
Table, Charles X, Mahogany, Pedestal, Marble Top, Columns, Trifid Base, 16 3/8 In. 360.00
Table, Cherry, Drop Leaf, Cabriole Legs, Pad Feet 885.00
Table, Chip Carved, 1 Low & 2 Side Shelves, North Carolina, 1930 .... 2500.00
Table, Chippendale Style, Butler's Tray Top, 17 x 36 In. 100.00
Table, Chippendale, Cherry, Dovetailed Drawer, Square Legs, 27 In. 995.00
Table, Chippendale, Cherry, Drop Leaf, New England, 1750-1780, 28 1/2 In. 635.00
Table, Chippendale, Mahogany, Drop Leaf, Cabriole Legs, Claw Feet, 28 In. 690.00
Table, Chippendale, Mahogany, Tilt Top, Pie Crust Edge, Floral Standard, 30 1/4 In. 770.00
Table, Chippendale, Mahogany, Tilt Top, Williamsburg Reproduction, 27 1/4 In. 275.00
Table, Chippendale, Walnut, Tilt Top, Pa., 1750-1780, 28 3/4 In. 1100.00
Table, Classical, Mahogany, Drop Leaf, 3 Drawers, Tapered Legs, 29 x 20x 17 In. 920.00
Table, Classical, Mahogany, Drop Leaf, 4 Leaf Supports, 28 In. 715.00
Table, Classical, Mahogany, Drop Leaf, Pedestal, 1835, 41 1/2 In. 495.00
Table, Cocktail, Peter Hunt, Gambling Designs, Signed, 19 x 52 In. 1100.00
Table, Coffee, Black Lacquer, Glass Top, Curved Wood Segments, 17 In. 57.50
Table, Coffee, Brass Top, Chrome Base, Circular 83.00
Table, Coffee, Brass, Oval Glass Top, Hoof Feet, 16 In. 81.00
Table, Coffee, Breuer, Chrome Tubular Steel, Glass Top, 1930, Round, 31 In. 2100.00
Table, Coffee, Butler's Tray, Mahogany, Straight Legs, England, 19 In. 430.00
Table, Coffee, Eames, Black Laminated Top, 54 x 20 x 14 In. 550.00
Table, Coffee, Eames, White Laminated Top, Wooden Dowel Legs, 15 x 34 In. 550.00
Table, Coffee, Edward Wormley, Mahogany, 15 x 44 x 18 In. 495.00
Table, Coffee, Georgian Style, Milt Metal & Onyx, 37 x 20 x 17 In. 150.00
Table, Coffee, Herman Miller, Walnut Base, Freeform Glass, 1955, 15 x 48 In. 1650.00
Table, Coffee, Herman Miller, Walnut, Folding Chrome Legs, 1970, 58 x 24 In. 550.00
Table, Coffee, Kagan, Walnut Frame, 14 x 69 x 19 1/2 In. 220.00
Table, Coffee, Kittinger, Faux Tortoiseshell Top, Black Grid Base, 14 x 42 In. 440.00
Table, Coffee, McCobb, Maple, Turned Legs, 16 x 54 x 20 In. 85.00
Table, Coffee, Neoclassical, White Lacquered, Gilt Design, 2 Tiers 515.00
Table, Coffee, Paul Evans, Square Patchwork Glass Top, Metal Base, 15 x 42 In. 330.00
Table, Coffee, R. Subes, Marble, Green, Black, White, 21 1/4 In. 5175.00
Table, Coffee, Triangular Wooden Base, Metal Foot, 16 x 58 1/2 x 39 In. 165.00
Table, Coffee, Van Der Rohe, Barcelona, Steel X Base, 29 1/2 x 18 In. 470.00
Table, Coffee, Wooden Top, Iron Rod Base, 1950s, 13 x 48 x 24 In. 275.00
Table, Coffee, Wrought Iron & Verde Antico, Marble Top & Lower Shelf, c.1930 ...... 1495.00
Table, Console, Classical, Mahogany, Acanthus, Paw Feet, 1820, 29 In., Pair 3950.00
Table, Console, French Empire, Mahogany, Bronze Mounted, Marble Top, c.1810 ...... 3300.00
Table, Console, George III, Mahogany, Bellflower Inlay, Cuffs, 31 In., Pair 2100.00
Table, Console, Georgian, Satinwood, Pink Marble Top, Applied Ribbon Swag 1870.00
Table, Console, Hitchcock, Stenciled Backsplash & Skirt, Square Legs 165.00
Table, Console, Louis XVI Style, Giltwood, Demilune, Swag Apron, 35 In. 935.00
Table, Console, Louis XVI Style, Walnut, Tapered Legs, 32 x 33 x 16 3/4 In. 1100.00
Table, Console, Louis XVI, Faux Marble, Bowed & Carved, 42 x 24 In., Pair 1695.00
Table, Console, Louis XVI, Gesso, White Marble Top, Oak Leaf Design, 32 In. 1430.00
Table, Console, Neoclassical, Black Marble Top, Band Of Laurels, 30 In. 6615.00
Table, Console, Walnut, Grip Handles, Fluted, Scrolled Heads, 29 In. 4850.00
Table, Cypress, 19th Century, 30 1/2 In. 1330.00
Table, Dining, Baker Co., Mahogany, String Inlay, 4-Leg Base, 54 In. 690.00
Table, Dining, Burl, Fluted Frieze, Fluted Tapering Legs, Oval 300.00
Table, Dining, Cherry, 2 Parts, 1830-1840 .... 1815.00
Table, Dining, Chippendale, Walnut, Drop Leaf, Marlborough Legs, 15 x 47 In. 1850.00
Table, Dining, Classical, Mahogany, 2 Pedestal, Acanthus, Paw Feet, 28 1/2 In. 4785.00
Table, Dining, Classical, Mahogany, Drop Leaf, Acanthus Legs, 1820, 27 x 48 In. 990.00
Table, Dining, Classical, Mahogany, Pedestal, 4-Leg Base 1325.00
Table, Dining, Classical, Mahogany, Plinth Base, Scroll Feet, 1820, Pair 5775.00
Table, Dining, Duncan Phyfe, Mahogany, 2 Pedestals, 4 Leaves, 102 In. Open 600.00
Table, Dining, Empire, Gadrooned Edges, Mid-19th Century, 28 In. 2100.00
Table, Dining, Federal, 3 Ring Turned Pedestals, Mahogany, 129 In. 5175.00
Table, Dining, Federal, Cherry, Drop Leaf, Banded Border, 1800, 28 In. 490.00

Table, Dining, Federal, Mahogany, Beaded Edge, 3 Part, c.1820, 103 In. Extended 5460.00
Table, Dining, Federal, Mahogany, Inlay, Demilune End, 3 Part, 30 x 47 . . . . 1955.00
Table, Dining, G. Stickley, 4 Leaves, Round Top, 29 x 54 In. 4950.00
Table, Dining, George III Style, Mahogany & Yew, 2 Pedestal, 85 In. 2400.00
Table, Dining, George III Style, Mahogany, 2 Pedestal, 2 Leaves, 44 In. 3750.00
Table, Dining, George III Style, Mahogany, 3 Pedestal, c.1900, 48 x 64 In. 3750.00
Table, Dining, George III, Mahogany, 2 Pedestals, 2 Leaves, Paw Feet, 92 In. 2665.00
Table, Dining, George III, Mahogany, 3 Pedestals, Brass Paw Casters 4235.00
Table, Dining, George III, Mahogany, 4 Pedestals, Brass Paw Feet, 140 x 48 In. 6900.00
Table, Dining, George III, Mahogany, Baluster Stem, Brass Paw Casters, 91 In. 1955.00
Table, Dining, George III, Mahogany, Satinwood Top, Reeded Leg, 28 1/2 In. 910.00
Table, Dining, Georgian Style, Rosewood Banding, 2 Pedestal, 3 Leaves 3700.00
Table, Dining, Georgian, Mahogany, 2 Pedestals, 3 Leaves 2550.00
Table, Dining, Georgian, Mahogany, Double Pedestal Extension, 4 Leaves 460.00
Table, Dining, Georgian, Mahogany, Rosewood Banded, Pedestals, 2 Leaves 3700.00
Table, Dining, Hepplewhite Style, Mahogany, Line Inlaid, Leaves, 66 x 44 In. 315.00
Table, Dining, Herman Miller, Formica Top, Aluminum Base, Pedestal, 42 x 28 In. 230.00
Table, Dining, Heywood-Wakefield, Whale Bone Legs, 28 x 54 x 38 In. 440.00
Table, Dining, Jacobean, Oak, Carved Pedestal, 4 Grotesque Legs, 59 x 51 In. 1815.00
Table, Dining, John Widdicomb, Oak, Extension, Block & Spool Legs, 74 x 40 In. 345.00
Table, Dining, L. & J.G. Stickley, No. 713, Pedestal, 4 Leaves, 30 x 48 In. 3550.00
Table, Dining, Louis XVI, Faux Marble, Painted, Separate D-Ends, 51 In. Diam. 3650.00
Table, Dining, Mahogany, Crossbanded Satinwood, 2 Pedestal, 1910s, 51 In. 6900.00
Table, Dining, Mahogany, Pedestal, Acanthus Legs, England, Round, 19th Century 3150.00
Table, Dining, Mahogany, Pedestal, Gadroon Edge, Leaves, Flowers, 30 x 60 In. 4850.00
Table, Dining, Mahogany, Pedestal, Leaves, Round . . . . *Illus* 1325.00
Table, Dining, Meeks, Mahogany, 4 Leaves, Extension 3225.00
Table, Dining, Nelson, Birch, Drop Leaf, Gate Legs, 66 x 40 x 30 In. 600.00
Table, Dining, Neoclassical, Mahogany, Drop Leaf 290.00
Table, Dining, Oak, Pedestal, 4 Scroll Feet, Round, 48 In. 250.00
Table, Dining, Queen Anne Style, Walnut, Drop Leaf, Cabriole Legs, 1740, 48 In. 2750.00
Table, Dining, Regency Revival, Mahogany, Pedestal, England, 87 In., Open 3750.00
Table, Dining, Regency, Mahogany, Brown, 3 Pedestals, Reeded Legs, 29 In. 3850.00
Table, Dining, Rococo, Oak, Carved, 4 Leaves, American, 1850, 94 x 48 In. 5445.00
Table, Dining, Saarinen, Tulip, Flared Base, Round Top, 28 x 54 In. Diam. 600.00
Table, Dining, Sheraton, Drop Leaf, Turned Legs, Brass Casters, 29 x 42 In. 220.00
Table, Dining, Sheraton, Mahogany, Drop Leaf, Spiral Legs, 59 In. 640.00
Table, Dining, Victorian, Mahogany, Round Extension, 5 Leaves 1495.00
Table, Dining, Walnut, 3 Leaves, 2 Legs Pedestal Base Each End, 1860 . . . . 3330.00
Table, Dining, Walnut, Continental, 19th Century, 32 In. 1160.00
Table, Dining, William & Mary, Walnut, Gateleg, Drop Leaf, 1740s, 50 In. Open 3740.00
Table, Dish, Eames, Circular Birch, Plywood Legs, 34 x 15 In. 470.00
Table, Dish, Herman Miller, Walnut, Plywood, Chrome Metal Legs, 16 In. 550.00
Table, Dolphin Base, Variegated Marble Top, 21 In., Pair 2420.00
Table, Drafting, Federal, Mahogany, Fitted Interior, Fluted Legs 2650.00
Table, Drafting, Oak Shelf, Adjustable Arm, Cast Iron Frame, 21 x 26 In. 990.00
Table, Dressing, Beau Brummel, Mahogany, Inlaid, 2 Doors, Mirror, England, 33 In. 1150.00
Table, Dressing, Chinese Chippendale, Black Lacquer & Gilt Design 460.00
Table, Dressing, Classical, Mahogany, Marble, Hexagonal Mirror, 1840 . . . . 910.00
Table, Dressing, Duncan Phyfe, Reeded Curule Base 9200.00
Table, Dressing, Empire, Cherry, Black Marble Top, 49 In. 3450.00
Table, Dressing, Federal, Grain Painted Basswood, Red, Black, 35 In. 690.00
Table, Dressing, Federal, Mahogany, Bird's-Eye Maple, 1805-1820, 32 In. 4025.00
Table, Dressing, Federal, Mahogany, Reeded Legs, 1800, 36 In. 4600.00
Table, Dressing, George I, Oak Inlay, Border, 3 Drawers, 28 In. 7475.00
Table, Dressing, George II, Mahogany, Adjustable Mirror, 27 x 19 In. 900.00
Table, Dressing, Herter Bros., Mahogany, Satinwood, Durand Mirror 1650.00
Table, Dressing, Mahogany, 3 Frieze Drawers, Reeded Columns, 64 In. 1450.00
Table, Dressing, Mahogany, Bombe, Kneehole, Oval Mirror, Side Drawers, 72 In. 1450.00
Table, Dressing, Mahogany, Lyre Shaped Mirror & Legs, 19th Century, 63 In. 2175.00
Table, Dressing, Mahogany, Molded White Marble Top, Paw Feet, 54 In. 2200.00
Table, Dressing, Pine & Chestnut, Drawer, Removable Top Case, 44 3/4 In. 1875.00
Table, Dressing, Pine, Yellow Graining Over White Enamel, 40 1/2 x 30 1/2 In. 275.00

Furniture, Table, Dressing,
Rohde, Maccassar Ebony,
58 x 20 In.

Furniture, Table, Library,
G. Stickley, 3 Drawers,
54 x 29 In.

Table, Dressing, Queen Anne Style, Mahogany, 2 Drawers, Cabriole Legs, 29 In. 10350.00
Table, Dressing, Queen Anne, Cherry, Pad Feet, 20th Century 150.00
Table, Dressing, Queen Anne, Walnut, 1 Long Over 3 Short Drawers, 33 In. 4850.00
Table, Dressing, Queen Anne, Walnut, 3 Drawers, Cabriole Legs, 28 In. 6325.00
Table, Dressing, Rococo, Mahogany, Oval Mirror, Carved Crest, 19th Century 3630.00
Table, Dressing, Rococo, Mahogany, Serpentine Front, Cabriole Legs 2900.00
Table, Dressing, Rohde, Maccassar Ebony, 58 x 20 In. .... *Illus* 5225.00
Table, Dressing, Rosewood, Duchesse Form, Mirror, Carved, c.1850 .... 3145.00
Table, Dressing, Sheraton, Cherry, Scrolled Crest, 35 x 18 x 29 In. 465.00
Table, Dressing, Sheraton, Poplar, Red, Black Grain, 57 1/2 In. 4850.00
Table, Dressing, Sheraton, Walnut, Step Back, Figured Veneer, Spool Legs, 33 In. 335.00
Table, Dressing, Sheraton, Yellow Striping, Gold Stencil, 57 1/2 In. 4850.00
Table, Dressing, Walnut, 4 Drawers, Mirror, c.1820 .... 2800.00
Table, Dressing, Walnut, Lift Sides, Lift Easel Mirror, 2 Drawers, 28 x 30 In. 635.00
Table, Drop Leaf, Champagne Finish, 6 Legs, 29 x 40 x 28 In. 445.00
Table, Drop Leaf, Chippendale, Mahogany, Hoof Feet, 1770s 5750.00
Table, Drop Leaf, Classical, Mahogany, Scalloped Corners, American, 1815, 44 In. 4355.00
Table, Drop Leaf, Curly Maple, 1-Board Top, 21 x 42 x 29 In. 630.00
Table, Drop Leaf, Curly Maple, Striped & Scrubbed Top, 19 x 41 In. 495.00
Table, Drop Leaf, E. Wormley, Brown Walnut Top, 27 x 53 In. 1100.00
Table, Drop Leaf, Federal, Cherry, 4 Swell Reeded Legs, 1810, 28 1/4 In. 1035.00
Table, Drop Leaf, Federal, Mahogany, Reeded Tapering Legs, Ball Feet, 46 In. 400.00
Table, Drop Leaf, Federal, Maple, Tapered Legs, c.1800, 27 x 42 x 42 In. 400.00
Table, Drop Leaf, G. Stickley, Trestle Legs, Paper Label, 30 x 32 In. 1100.00
Table, Drop Leaf, George III, Mahogany, Extension, 28 x 36 x 60 In. 495.00
Table, Drop Leaf, Hepplewhite, Maple, Pine Breadboard Top, 23 x 37 1/2 In. 165.00
Table, Drop Leaf, Hepplewhite, Walnut, Square Legs, 12 3/4 In. 550.00
Table, Drop Leaf, Herman Miller, Blond Oak, No. 4656, 1948-1954, 30 x 66 x 40 In. 1375.00
Table, Drop Leaf, Mahogany, 2 D-Form Leaves, Square, 28 In. 690.00
Table, Drop Leaf, Mahogany, Brass Inlay, End Drawer, c.1815, 39 1/2 In. 2200.00
Table, Drop Leaf, Mahogany, Drawer, Molded Leg, Philadelphia, c.1790, 30 x 42 In. 1400.00
Table, Drop Leaf, Mahogany, Drawer, Rope Turned Legs, 36 x 16 1/2 x 30 In. 225.00
Table, Drop Leaf, Oak, Champagne Finish, Triple Arch 995.00
Table, Drop Leaf, Pembroke, Drawer, Pierced Cross Stretcher, Marlboro Feet 480.00
Table, Drop Leaf, Pembroke, Holland & Sons, Satinwood, Fitted Drawer, 39 In. 1100.00
Table, Drop Leaf, Pennsylvania House, Cherry, 4 Leaves, Sheraton Style 140.00
Table, Drop Leaf, Pine, c.1880, 43 3/4 x 42 1/4 In. 595.00
Table, Drop Leaf, Pine, Hardwood, Red Paint, 2-Board Top, 18 x 42 x 28 In. 110.00
Table, Drop Leaf, Pine, Red Paint, Tapered Legs, New England, 28 1/2 In. 431.00
Table, Drop Leaf, Queen Anne Style, Maple, Cabriole Legs, Pad Feet, 27 In. 1850.00
Table, Drop Leaf, Queen Anne, Cherry, Pad & Disc Feet, 1740, 36 In. 1850.00
Table, Drop Leaf, Queen Anne, Mahogany, Swing Legs, 18th Century, 44 x 53 In. 825.00
Table, Drop Leaf, Queen Anne, Mahogany, Swing Legs, Cabriole Legs, 19 x 53 In. 495.00
Table, Drop Leaf, Queen Anne, Mahogany, Swing Legs, Oval, England, 18 x 59 In. 715.00
Table, Drop Leaf, Queen Anne, Swing Legs, Duck Feet Tapered Legs, 15 x 42 x 28 In. ... 467.00

Table, Drop Leaf, Queen Anne, Walnut, Swing Leg Base, Cabriole Legs, 28 In. 1375.00
Table, Drop Leaf, Queen Anne, Walnut, Tapered Legs, 15 x 42 In. 470.00
Table, Drop Leaf, Red Chinoiserie, Kidney Form Top, Gilt, England, 24 1/2 In. 275.00
Table, Drop Leaf, Regency Style, Trestle Base, Brass Toe Caps, 28 x 37 In. 2875.00
Table, Drop Leaf, Regency, Mahogany, Line Drawers, Claw Feet, 30 x 42 In. 990.00
Table, Drop Leaf, Regency, Mahogany, Molded Top, 2 Beaded Drawers, 29 In. 600.00
Table, Drop Leaf, Sheraton, Birch, Shaped Leaves, Tiger Maple Drawer Each End 950.00
Table, Drop Leaf, Sheraton, Cherry, Rope Carved Legs, 29 1/2 In. 550.00
Table, Drop Leaf, Sheraton, Curly Maple, Swing Legs, 19 x 48 In. 1045.00
Table, Drop Leaf, Sheraton, Mahogany, Dovetailed Drawer, 28 In. 990.00
Table, Drop Leaf, Sheraton, Walnut, 6 Reeded Legs, 22 x 41 In. 195.00
Table, Drop Leaf, Stickley Bros., Hexagonal Top, Shoe Feet, 28 3/4 x 34 In. 935.00
Table, Drop Leaf, Sunderland, Mahogany, Scrolled Feet, 28 1/2 In. 3400.00
Table, Drop Leaf, Walnut, Drawer, 6 Legs, 30 x 45 In. 275.00
Table, Drop Leaf, Walnut, Panels, Over Drawer, Finial On Stretcher, 30 1/4 In. 8625.00
Table, Drop Leaf, Walnut, Square Tapered Legs, 36 x 18 x 28 3/4 In. 315.00
Table, Drop Leaf, Walnut, Swing Legs, 6 Turned Legs, 19 x 44 In. 330.00
Table, Drum, Georgian Style, Leather Inset Top 490.00
Table, Drum, Regency Revival, Mahogany, Down Swept Legs, 1800, 30 In. 11500.00
Table, Eastlake, Walnut, Granite Top, Burl Veneer, 29 1/2 x 32 In. 370.00
Table, Ebonized, Carved Top, Branched Apron, Figural Supports, 19th Century, 44 In. . . . 2060.00
Table, Edward, Mahogany, Floral Medallion Inlay, Columned Legs, 29 3/4 In. 665.00
Table, Eileen Grey, Adjustable, Chrome Rod, Glass, Round, 30 x 20 In. 550.00
Table, Elm, 1-Board Top, Drawer, 2 Long Benches, 30 x 32 In., 3 Piece 2850.00
Table, Empire Style, Mahogany, Marble Top, Ormolu Mounted, 1870s, 30 In. 8625.00
Table, Empire, Mahogany, Black Marble Top, Plain Frieze, 33 1/4 In., Pair 1200.00
Table, Empire, Mahogany, Marble Top, Lyre Supports, Medial Shelf, c.1830 . . . . 4025.00
Table, Empire, Mahogany, Round Top, Gadrooned Edge, Pedestal Base, 32 In. 700.00
Table, Empire, Winged Female Figures, Carved Masks, 72 x 27 x 32 In. 7000.00
Table, Exotic Hardwoods, Drop Leaf, West Indies, 29 x 48 In. 2200.00
Table, Federal, Cherry, Serpentine Top, Drawer, Tapered Legs, c.1800, 29 x 28 In. 9775.00
Table, Federal, Mahogany, Drawer, D-Shape Leaves, Inlay, 1790, 28 x 22-In. 8770.00
Table, Federal, Maple, Oval Top, Arched Legs, c.1800, 28 x 22 x 15 In. 460.00
Table, Frank Lloyd Wright Design, Mahogany, Triangular 715.00
Table, Frankl, Aluminum Band, 2-Tone, Drawer, 10 x 28 x 24 In. 550.00
Table, Frankl, Cork Top, Wooden Base, 24 x 24 x 26 In. 330.00
Table, French Provincial, Cherry, Square Tapering Legs, 29 x 76 x 34 In. 980.00
Table, Fruitwood, Drawer, 8 Tapered Legs, Paw Feet, 28 1/4 In. 690.00
Table, Fruitwood, Marquetry, Fern, Butterfly In Flight, 1900, 41 In. 1725.00
Table, G. Stickley, Splayed Legs, Round 7150.00
Table, Game, Charles X, Rosewood, Inlaid, Toile Lined Surface, 30 3/4 x 34 3/4 In. 1380.00
Table, Game, Classical, Foldover, Spiral Reeded Ball Pedestal, 4 Saber Legs 1450.00
Table, Game, Classical, Mahogany, Foldover Top, Faceted Pedestal, 31 In. 2200.00
Table, Game, Classical, Mahogany, Lyre Base, Phila., 1815, 29 x 36 x 17 In. 2660.00
Table, Game, Directoire Style, Mahogany, Retractable Leather Top, Backgammon 3160.00
Table, Game, Dutch Rococo, Mahogany, Satinwood Inlay, Triangular 800.00
Table, Game, Federal, Mahogany, Rope Turned Legs, 29 x 37 x 17 In. 880.00
Table, Game, Federal, Mahogany, Serpentine Front, Tapered Legs, 30 x 36 x 18 In. 825.00
Table, Game, French Provincial, Fruitwood, Cabriole Legs, 29 In. 1725.00
Table, Game, George III Style, Mahogany, Inlaid, Demilune, 28 3/4 x 32 3/4 In. 630.00
Table, Game, George III, Mahogany, Apron, Green Baize, Feet, 30 In., Pair 2100.00
Table, Game, George III, Mahogany, Foldover, Legs, 39 1/2 x 43 x 21 In. 2650.00
Table, Game, George III, Satinwood, Green Baize Interior, 30 x 36 x 17 In. 2060.00
Table, Game, Georgian Style, Mahogany, Slide Top, Inlaid Game Board, 36 x 30 In. 525.00
Table, Game, Georgian, Mahogany, Flip Top, Spade Feet, 29 In. 1265.00
Table, Game, Hepplewhite, Mahogany, Drawer, Opens To Cloth Diamond, 22 x 22 In. . . . 330.00
Table, Game, Louis XV, Green Paint, Playing Cards Design, Rectangular, 28 In. 4900.00
Table, Game, Louis XV, Kingwood, Fruitwood, Drawer, Cabriole Legs, 27 In. 4600.00
Table, Game, Louis XVI, Baize Top, Corner Candle Wells, 1780s, 34 3/4 In. 6900.00
Table, Game, Mahogany, Flip Top, Frieze Drawer, 18th Century, 28 In. 1325.00
Table, Game, Mahogany, Foldover, Acanthus Carved Support, 36 In. 1330.00
Table, Game, Mahogany, Foldover, Baize Surface, Drawer, 28 1/4 x 22 1/2 In. 1030.00
Table, Game, Mahogany, Foldover, Pillar Support, Bulbous Legs, 1830 . . . . 910.00

Table, Game, Mahogany, Rectangular, Block Feet, 29 In. 2300.00
Table, Game, Mahogany, Side Apron Drawer, Inlaid Medallion, 29 In. 977.00
Table, Game, Neoclassical, Black Lacquer, Barley Twist Legs, Italy, 30 3/4 In. 6325.00
Table, Game, Neoclassical, Mahogany, Satinwood, Floral Panels, 30 1/4 In. 790.00
Table, Game, Neoclassical, Walnut, Marquetry, Demilune, c.1800, 31 1/4 x 16 In. 2415.00
Table, Game, Queen Anne Style, Mahogany, Straight Legs, Pad Feet, 24 In. 1150.00
Table, Game, Queen Anne, Mahogany, Flip Top, Tapered Legs, 29 In. 1265.00
Table, Game, Queen Anne, Mahogany, Serpentine Folding Top, Square, 35 In. 1600.00
Table, Game, Regency, Mahogany, Brass Inlay, 1820s, 29 3/4 x 36 In. 575.00
Table, Game, Regency, Mahogany, Rosewood, Incised Frieze, Gadroon Base, 29 In. 600.00
Table, Game, Regency, Rosewood, Swivel Top, Brass Line Inlay, Star Design, 1815 . . . . 3150.00
Table, Game, Rococo, Serpentine Front, Green Baize, 27 1/2 In., Pair 4400.00
Table, Game, Sheraton, Mahogany, Flip Top, Serpentine Frieze, 29 x 25 In. 400.00
Table, Game, Victorian, Mahogany, Walnut Checkerboard 575.00
Table, Game, Walnut & Burl Walnut, Demilune c.1880, 31 x 34 In. 545.00
Table, Game, William IV, Rosewood, Incurvate Plinth, 1835, 28 x 36 x 18 In. 1935.00
Table, Gateleg, Colonial Revival, Walnut, Round Top, Drawer, 19th Century 845.00
Table, Gateleg, Drop Leaf, Huidt, Molgaard, 1958, 28 x 64 x 17 In. 660.00
Table, Gateleg, E. Garnsley, Walnut, Stepped Carved Flange Feet, c.1930, 40 In. 2760.00
Table, Gateleg, George II, Mahogany, Beaded Drawer, Pad Feet, 28 In. 715.00
Table, Gateleg, Walnut, Black Base, Turned Legs, 26 1/4 In. 1650.00
Table, George II, Mahogany, Demilune, Frieze Drawer, 29 1/2 In. 1380.00
Table, George III Style, Satinwood Inlay, 3 Drawers, Painted Flowers, 29 1/2 In. 545.00
Table, George III Style, Satinwood, Demilune, Garlands, Bellflowers, 30 In. 2200.00
Table, George III, Mahogany, 2 Tiers, Molded Edge, Square Legs, 26 x 19 In. 210.00
Table, George III, Mahogany, Baluster, Cabriole Legs, 27 In. 1725.00
Table, George III, Mahogany, Dish, Tilt Top, Tripod, 28 In. 6900.00
Table, George III, Mahogany, Foldover, Square Legs, Inlaid, c.1800 . . . . 545.00
Table, George III, Mahogany, Frieze Drawer, Tapered Legs, 29 3/4 In. 4900.00
Table, George III, Mahogany, Inlay, Gilt, Reeded Legs, 29 In. 8050.00
Table, George III, Mahogany, Oval Top, Reeded Edge, 28 1/4 In. 1980.00
Table, Georgian, Mahogany, 1 Drop Leaf, Tapering Legs, Pad Feet, 28 x 39 In. 485.00
Table, Georgian, Mahogany, 3 Out Swept Legs, Paw Feet, 53 In. 600.00
Table, Georgian, Mahogany, Brass Paw Feet, England, 19th Century, 29 In. 495.00
Table, Georgian, Mahogany, Crossbanded, 2 Piece 115.00
Table, Georgian, Mahogany, Drawer, Shell Inlay, 19th Century, Oval, 37 In. 2420.00
Table, Gilbert Rohde, Tubular Chrome, Round Top, 1934, 28 x 24 In. 440.00
Table, Giltwood, Malachite Top, Carved Parcel Gilt Shell Form Base, 58 1/2 In. 9200.00
Table, Giltwood, Rectangular Top, Lattice Work Apron, Flowers & Scrolls, 56 In. 6325.00
Table, Golden Oak, 4 Scrolled Legs, Turned Column, 29 1/2 In. 330.00
Table, Gothic Revival, Rosewood, Lyre Ends, Apron, Oval, 19 x 36 In. 165.00
Table, Handkerchief, 4 Hinged Leaves, Leather Surface, Bacchic Masks, 29 1/2 In. 3450.00
Table, Handkerchief, Mahogany, Louis XVI Style, Brass Bound, 30 x 21 1/2 In. 800.00
Table, Handkerchief, Mahogany, Triangular Leaf, Swing-Out Leg, 28 1/4 In. 1450.00
Table, Harvest, Birch Base, Poplar Top, Drop Leaf, 17 1/2 x 108 In. 3850.00
Table, Harvest, Black, Red Paint, Drawer, Turned Legs, 72 x 29 1/4 x 60 In. 9260.00
Table, Harvest, Federal, Red Stained Maple, Ringturned Legs, Vase Form, Feet, 71 In. . . 3450.00
Table, Harvest, Mahogany, Oblong Top, D-Shaped Drop Leaves 5175.00
Table, Harvest, Poplar, Turned Legs, 28 x 84 x 29 In. 825.00
Table, Harvest, Shaped Legs, 12 Ft. 6600.00
Table, Hepplewhite, Mahogany, Banded Inlay, Bowfront, 2 Drawers, 32 In. 14300.00
Table, Hepplewhite, Pine, Hardwood, Splayed Square Legs, 17 x 24 In. 190.00
Table, Hepplewhite, Walnut, Dovetailed Drawer, Tapered Legs, 28 In. 1155.00
Table, Herman Miller, Laminated Top, Pedestal, Flared Aluminum Legs, 22 x 17 In. 300.00
Table, Herman Miller, Oak Top, Brushed Chrome Base, 1938, 18 1/2 x 24 In., Pair 2970.00
Table, Hunt, George III, Mahogany, Bowed Ends, Straight Legs, 28 In. 6900.00
Table, Hunt, George III, Mahogany, Molded Edge, Square Legs, 28 x 64 In. 2185.00
Table, Hunt, Mahogany, Drop Leaf, 19th Century, 29 14 x 83 1/2 In. 2990.00
Table, Hutch, Pine, 3-Board Top, Refinished, 32 x 60 x 29 In. 600.00
Table, Hutch, Pine, Cutout Feet, 3-Board Top, Lift Seat In Base, 28 3/4 x 53 1/2 In. 935.00
Table, Hutch, Pine, Poplar, Black Paint, 3-Board Top, Bench Seat, 70 In. 1375.00
Table, Iron, Marble Top, White Paint, Round, 36 In. 250.00
Table, Kaufmann, Burl Walnut, Marquetry Allegorical Figures, 1918, 30 1/2 In. 8625.00

Table, Kitchen, Drop Leaf, Top Opens To Oval, 2 Leaves, 22 x 43 In.		250.00
Table, Knoll, Floriform Redwood Top, Enameled Metal Base, 19 x 16 In.		465.00
Table, Knoll, Rosewood Top, Star Chrome Base, Conference, 1954, 96 x 54 In.		935.00
Table, Knoll, Walnut Top, Bronzed Steel Rod Base, Label, 19 x 24 In.		415.00
Table, L. & J.G. Stickley, Encyclopedia		9350.00
Table, L. & J.G. Stickley, No. 541, Cross Stretcher Supporting Second Tier		3410.00
Table, L. & J.G. Stickley, Oak, Round Top, Lower Shelf		1000.00
Table, L. & J.G. Stickley, Pedestal, Decal, 4 Leaves, 30 x 54 In.		3335.00
Table, L. & J.G. Stickley, Round Top, Mortised Stretcher, 29 x 48 In.		1870.00
Table, Last Supper Inset Plaque, Enamel & Onyx, 29 1/4 In.		3737.00
Table, Leonard Furniture Co., Mahogany, Inlay, Serpentine, Extends To 78 In.		485.00
Table, Library, Arts & Crafts, 1 Drawer, Faceted Wooden Pulls, 30 x 40 x 26 In.		412.00
Table, Library, Arts & Crafts, Leather Top, 1 Drawer, Copper Pulls, 30 In.		725.00
Table, Library, Arts & Crafts, Oak, Drawer, Paper Label, 42 x 24 In.		525.00
Table, Library, Arts & Crafts, Oak, Keyed Tenon Stretcher Base		770.00
Table, Library, Arts & Crafts, Quartersawn Oak, 2 Drawers, Shelf, 30 x 54 x 29 In.		415.00
Table, Library, Baker Co., Drop Leaf, Drawer, Trestle Base, Oyster Shell, Walnut		650.00
Table, Library, English Baroque Style, Walnut, 66 In.		1150.00
Table, Library, Federal, Drop Leaf, Drawer At End, Medial Shelf, Hairy Paw Feet		800.00
Table, Library, G. Stickley, 3 Drawers, 54 x 29 In.	*Illus*	8800.00
Table, Library, G. Stickley, Drawer, Top Over Single Shelf, c.1907, 48 In.		1500.00
Table, Library, G. Stickley, No. 652, Drawer, Copper Pull, 30 x 48 In.		1200.00
Table, Library, G. Stickley, No. 659, Oak, 3 Drawers, Shelf, c.1909, 54 x 32 In.		6325.00
Table, Library, Horner Brothers, Quartersawn Oak, Griffin Legs, Oval, 54 x 36 In.		5500.00
Table, Library, Italian Renaissance Revival Style, Walnut, 19th Century, 84 In.		5750.00
Table, Library, L. & J.G. Stickley, No. 379, Keyed Through Tenons, 56 x 33 1/2 In.		3100.00
Table, Library, Louis Philippe Style, Walnut, Apron, Fluted Carved Legs, H Stretcher		460.00
Table, Library, Mahogany, Drop Leaf, 2 Drawers, S-Scroll Legs, 1830, 28 In.		25540.00
Table, Library, Mahogany, Griffin Carved Trestle, Italy, 19th Century		3500.00
Table, Library, Mahogany, Marble Top, 2 Pedestals, c.1840, 29 x 43 x 24 In.		2100.00
Table, Library, Maple, Rosewood, Veneered Top, Applied Roundels, Panels, 29 In.		4400.00
Table, Library, Maple, Short Drawer, Rectangular Top, Turned Legs, 31 x 54 In.		140.00
Table, Library, Mission, Oak, Bookcase At Each End, 28 x 42 x 29 In.		77.00
Table, Library, Mission, Oak, Long Drawer, Square Legs, 30 x 50 In.		115.00
Table, Library, Renaissance Revival, Mahogany, Carved Griffins Base		2300.00
Table, Library, Restauration, Rosewood, Marble, Pedestal, 4 Feet, 1840, 57 In.		3870.00
Table, Library, Stickley Bros., Overhanging Rectangular Top, Brass Pulls, 50 In.		1210.00
Table, Library, Walnut, Carved Female Figures, Winged Female Griffins On Base		4250.00
Table, Library, Walnut, Marquetry, Plum & Co., San Francisco		1955.00
Table, Limbert, No. 146, Overhanging Top, Oblong Cutouts, Oval, 44 3/4 In.		2860.00
Table, Limbert, No. 158, Oak, Shelf, Cruciform Base, 47 x 36 In.		8625.00
Table, Limbert, Slag Glass, Green, Hammered Copper, Acorn Pulls, 26 x 27 In.		885.00
Table, Limbert, Trapezoidal, 2 Drawers, Brass Pulls, Curved Apron, 66 In.		6050.00
Table, Louis XV Style, Brass Mounted Sevres Top		9200.00
Table, Louis XV Style, Red Marble Top, Carved, 21 x 18 In., Pair		660.00
Table, Louis XV, Kingwood, Raised On Cabriole Legs, 28 In.		2587.00
Table, Louis XV, Oak, Marble Top, 33 1/2 x 24 1/2 In.		2640.00
Table, Louis XV, Tulipwood Serpentine, 4 Drawers, 29 3/4 In.		2875.00
Table, Louis XV, Tulipwood, Marble, Drawer, Cabriole Legs, 26 In.		8050.00
Table, Louis XV, Tulipwood, Parquetry, 2 Drawers, Cabriole Legs, 17 In.		5175.00
Table, Louis XV, Tulipwood, Parquetry, 3 Drawers, Foliate Design, 28 In.		4600.00
Table, Louis XVI Style, Gilt Bronze, Ball Feet, Conference, 30 x 95 x 42 In.		2200.00
Table, Louis XVI Style, Parquetry, Square, 27 In., Pair		515.00
Table, Louis XVI, Bronze, Lapis Lazuli, Fluted Legs, 16 1/2 In.		5175.00
Table, Louis XVI, Fruitwood, Elm, Tooled Red Moroccan Top, 4 Cabriole Legs		1980.00
Table, Louis XVI, Gilt Metal, White Marble, Round, 27 In.		1840.00
Table, Louis XVI, Mahogany, Leather Inset Top, Tapered Legs, 29 In.		4600.00
Table, Louis XVI, Mahogany, Tambour, D-Shape, Marble		1150.00
Table, Louis XVI, Marble, 2 Tiers, Egyptian Masks, Hoof Feet, 28 In.		2300.00
Table, Louis XVI, Parquetry Top, Sunburst, Tapering Legs, 29 In.		960.00
Table, Macassar Ebony, Fruitwood, France, 1930, 25 In.		1725.00
Table, Mahogany Base, Marble & Micro Mosaic Top, Paw Feet, 29 1/2 In.		9775.00
Table, Mahogany, 2 Pedestal Base, Hairy Lion Paw Supports, c.1830, 8 Ft.		4950.00

Table, Mahogany, Agate Top, 4 Classical Supports, Leaf Carved Feet	495.00
Table, Mahogany, Bowfront, Brass Ring Handles, Tapered Legs, 34 In.	865.00
Table, Mahogany, Double-Shelf, Straight Legs, England, 16 1/4 In., Pair	920.00
Table, Mahogany, Flip Top, Tripod Stand, Cabriole Legs, Pad Feet, England, 27 In.	690.00
Table, Mahogany, Marble Top, 3 Scrolled Supports, Pedestal, c.1825	4850.00
Table, Mahogany, Marble Top, 3 Turned Antler Supports, Joined By Sphere, 29 In.	5175.00
Table, Mahogany, Marble Top, White, Stepped Base, 29 In.	1150.00
Table, Mahogany, Round Top, 41 1/2 In.	1495.00
Table, Mahogany, Scalloped, Central Medallion, Gallery, 19th Century	880.00
Table, Majorelle, Mahogany, Molded Edge, Twist Carved Legs, 30 In.	3750.00
Table, Majorelle, Marquetry Maple Pods, 2 Tiers, Giraffe Leg, 34 x 24 In.	3300.00
Table, Maple With Curl Top, Red Paint, Swing Leg, Corner Moldings, 45 1/4 In.	1000.00
Table, Marble Top, Marble Supports, 1920s, 40 3/4 x 96 In.	7565.00
Table, Marble Top, Over Frieze & Shelf, Square Legs, China	150.00
Table, Marcel Breuer, Chrome Tubular Steel, Painted, Wood, 1928, 35 x 35 In.	3450.00
Table, Marquetry Center, Marble Top, Inlaid Apron, Gilt Bronze Mounted, 31 In.	8625.00
Table, Marquetry Veneer, Tier, Ormolu Trim, Glass Insert, France, 21 x 32 In.	715.00
Table, McCobb, Maple Flush Top, Bamboo Shelf, 21 x 27 x 18 In.	360.00
Table, Mixing, George II, Mahogany, Marble, Cabriole Legs, 18th Century, 36 In.	4600.00
Table, Napoleon III, Cabinet, Boulle Marquetry, 1860, 63 In., Pair . . . . *Illus*	6900.00
Table, Napoleon III, Gilt Surface, Inset Mirror, Tripod Scrolled Legs, 1850s, 32 In.	425.00
Table, Nelson, Bubble Lamp, Zeppelin Shape, 36 x 16 In.	385.00
Table, Neoclassical, Cherubs Dancing Around Tree, Italy, 30 In.	1760.00
Table, Neoclassical, Mahogany, Satinwood, 3 Tiers, Galleried Trays, 28 x 21 x 9 In.	260.00
Table, Neogothic, Walnut, Scrolled Apron, 4-Legged Base	125.00
Table, Nesting, Bamboo, Black, Immortals, Strolling Front Of Temples, 28 In.	600.00
Table, Nesting, E. Wormley, Walnut Top, Ebonized Base, 20 x 26 x 16 In.	2090.00
Table, Nesting, Edwardian, Rosewood, Oval Inlaid Tops, c.1900, 3 Piece	750.00
Table, Nesting, Georgian, Mahogany, Crossbanded, 3 Piece	145.00
Table, Nesting, Georgian, Satinwood, Crossbanded, 24 x 22 x 14 In., 4 Piece	875.00
Table, Nesting, Georgian, Tooled Leather Tray Top, 42 x 22 x 17 In., 3 Piece	365.00
Table, Nesting, Heywood-Wakefield, Champagne Finish, 24 x 21 In.	495.00
Table, Nesting, Lacquered, Chinoiserie, Bamboo Legs, China, 21 In., 3 Piece	290.00
Table, Nesting, Mahogany, Fluted Legs, Oval, Imperial, Grand Rapids, 18 x 24 In.	350.00
Table, Nesting, Mahogany, Inlay, 20th Century, 11 x 16 x 24 In., 4 Piece	275.00
Table, Nesting, Rosewood, Leather Top, Gold Leaf Accents, 3 Piece	1950.00
Table, Oak, 5 Leaves In Holder, Leather Seat, 48 In.	1200.00
Table, Oak, Gothic Supports, Brass Floral Drop Handles, 31 In.	5520.00
Table, Oak, Quartersawn, Pedestal, 4 Part Base, 2 Leaves, Expands To 81 In.	440.00

Furniture, Table, Side, Parcel Gilt, Plaster,
Marble, Mirror, Italy, 40 In., Pair, I shown

Furniture, Table, Napoleon III, Cabinet,
Boulle Marquetry, 1860, 63 In., Pair, I shown

Table, Ormolu, Circular Marble Top, Hoof Feet, 31 In. 4600.00
Table, Papier-Mache, Mother-Of-Pearl Inlay, c.1850 . . . . 1290.00
Table, Parcel Gilt, Circular Brass Supports, 23 x 14 1/4 In. 1495.00
Table, Paul McCobb, Brass, Mahogany, Drawer, 2 Tiers, Glass Shelf, 24 x 32 In. 110.00
Table, Pear Wood, Floral Marquetry, Drawer, Cabriole Legs, 27 In. 430.00
Table, Pembroke, Bellflower Inlay, Tapered Legs 2425.00
Table, Pembroke, Cherry, Rectangular Top, Tapering Legs, 19th Century 725.00
Table, Pembroke, Chippendale, Cock-Beaded Drawers, Cherry, c.1765, 27 3/4 In. 3750.00
Table, Pembroke, Dutch Neoclassical, Satinwood, Marquetry 4600.00
Table, Pembroke, Federal, Mahogany, Crossbanded Top, Drawer, Inlay, 1795 . . . . 9775.00
Table, Pembroke, Federal, Mahogany, Faux Drawer, Tapered Legs, 27 1/2 In. 1150.00
Table, Pembroke, Federal, Mahogany, Tapered Legs, 27 x 17 x 28 In., Pair 175.00
Table, Pembroke, George III, Black Japanned, Landscape, Pagodas, 28 In. 7475.00
Table, Pembroke, George III, Mahogany, 2 Drawer, Pulls, 1800, 26 x 40 In. 550.00
Table, Pembroke, George III, Mahogany, Bowed Top, 28 In. 4315.00
Table, Pembroke, Georgian, Mahogany, Shaped Drop Leaves, Drawer, 18th Century 450.00
Table, Pembroke, Hepplewhite, Cherry, Dovetailed Drawer, 28 1/2 In. 715.00
Table, Pembroke, Mahogany, D-Shaped Leaves, 1 Drawer, Diamond Inlay, 1810 . . . . 1725.00
Table, Pembroke, Mahogany, Satinwood Inlay, Edwardian 2200.00
Table, Pembroke, Mahogany, Serpentine Leaves, Inlaid Apron, 30 3/4 x 39 In. 3950.00
Table, Pembroke, Mahogany, Serpentine Top, 27 1/2 In. 1380.00
Table, Pembroke, Marquetry, Satinwood, Dutch, Late 18th Century, 27 /12 In. 4600.00
Table, Pembroke, Sheraton, Mahogany, End Drawer, 28 1/2 In. 600.00
Table, Pier, Classical, Mahogany, Marble Top, Mirrored Back Panel, 41 In. 2200.00
Table, Pier, Classical, Mahogany, Marble, Blind Drawers, Mirror, 1840, 41 In. 970.00
Table, Pier, Classical, Mahogany, Marble, Scroll Supports, 36 x 41 x 18 In. 1100.00
Table, Pier, Classical, Mahogany, Mirror Back, Scroll Supports, 44 x 19 In. 3125.00
Table, Pier, Classical, Mahogany, Ogee Apron, Scroll Supports, 38 In. 1325.00
Table, Pier, Classical, Marble Top, Scrolled Supports, 1840, 36 x 42 x 17 In. 1450.00
Table, Pier, Classical, Marble Top, Serpentine Shelf, 36 1/2 In. 2475.00
Table, Pier, Classical, Marble, Scroll Supports, American, 1840 . . . . 1150.00
Table, Pier, Duncan Phyfe, Rosewood, White Carrara Marble Top, 1825 . . . . 2541.00
Table, Pier, Empire, Mahogany Veneer, Marble Top, Lyre Base, 17 1/2 x 34 x 32 In. 495.00
Table, Pier, Late Classical, Mahogany, Marble Top, Carved, Scroll Feet, 1840, 40 In. 2055.00
Table, Pier, Regency, Rosewood, Gothic Design, Paw Feet, 1825, 34 In. 3100.00
Table, Pier, Rococo, Mahogany, Black Marble Top, Shell Apron, Paw Feet, 32 In. 2100.00
Table, Pine, Demilune, Nailed Apron, Tapered Legs, 29 1/4 In. 470.00
Table, Pine, Demilune, Worn Refinishing, Triangular Apron, 15 x 36 In. 220.00
Table, Pine, Painted, Red Base, Drawer, Turned Pull, 28 1/2 x 41 x 27 In. 2760.00
Table, Plantation, Red Paint, Pullout Cutting Board 4200.00
Table, Polychrome, Stack Of Book Form, Early 20th Century, 16 In. 365.00
Table, Pub, Cast Iron, Marble Top 485.00
Table, Pub, Empire, Oak, Drop Leaf, England, 1920s 495.00
Table, Queen Anne Style, Maple, Drop Leaf, Rectangular Hinged Top, 27 In. 3000.00
Table, Queen Anne, Maple, Dark Red Finish, Pinned Apron, 28 1/2 In. 2200.00
Table, Red Paint, Straight-Sided Trapezoidal Apron, 29 In. 1150.00
Table, Refectory, Baroque, Wrought Iron, 29 3/4 x 157 x 34 1/2 In. 9775.00
Table, Refectory, Cherry, Honey Brown, Drawer, 31 In. 2750.00
Table, Refectory, Gothic, Oak, Trefoil Supports, 1875, 76 1/4 In. 4715.00
Table, Refectory, Pine, 3 Drawers, Tapered Legs, 29 In. 845.00
Table, Refectory, Walnut, Drawer, Bulbous Legs, Early 20th Century, 75 In. 700.00
Table, Regency Revival, Mahogany, Crossbanded Top, 28 In. 8050.00
Table, Regency Revival, Mahogany, Down Swept Legs, Casters, 28 x 43 3/4 In. 1150.00
Table, Regency, Mahogany, D-Shaped Ends, 29 1/2 In. 4150.00
Table, Regency, Mahogany, Paneled Octagonal Support, Bun Feet, Round, 41 In. 1270.00
Table, Renaissance Revival, Walnut, Open Shelf Over 2 Drawers, 28 3/4 In. 550.00
Table, Reverse Painted, Cut Crystal, Painted Scrollwork, Bronze Mounted, 28 In. 245.00
Table, Rosewood, Brass Nail Heads, 2 Tiers, Round, 28 In. 4600.00
Table, Rosewood, Fall River, Mass., 1850, 76 x 36 1/2 In. 5175.00
Table, Rosewood, Mahogany, 2 Drawers, Splayed Legs, 1815, 26 x 28 In. 5750.00
Table, Round Marble Top, Micro Mosaic, Italy 9775.00
Table, Saarinen, Tulip, Cream Marble Top, Pedestal, 24 x 18 In. 385.00
Table, Saarinen, Tulip, Vinyl, 29 x 54 In. 440.00

Table, Sawbuck, 1-Board Top, Rosehead Nail Construction, 27 x 60 In. 1000.00
Table, Sawbuck, Pine, Oval Scrubbed Top, X-Form Base, 18th Century, 23 x 30 In. 3740.00
Table, Sawbuck, Red Paint Base, 27 x 33 x 86 In. 5835.00
Table, Serving, Chippendale, Green Paint Apron, Skirt, 29 In. 1150.00
Table, Serving, Classical, Mahogany, Carved, Drawers, 35 x 18 In. 6900.00
Table, Serving, George III, Mahogany, Kneehole, Reeded Edge, 4 Drawers, 30 In. 1145.50
Table, Serving, Mahogany, Satinwood Banded, Bowfront, c.1800, 30 x 34 In. 1100.00
Table, Sewing, Biedermeier, Black Walnut, Cupboard Door, Paw Feet, 37 In. 10350.00
Table, Sewing, Biedermeier, Fruitwood, Hinged Top, Curved Legs, 1830 . . . . 1760.00
Table, Sewing, Bird's-Eye Maple & Mahogany, 2 Drawers, c.1825, 29 1/2 In. 490.00
Table, Sewing, Burlwood, Lift Top, Fitted Interior, Bronze Mounted, 28 1/2 In. 1380.00
Table, Sewing, Cherry, Drawer, Straight Tapered Legs, Brass Bail Pulls, 1830s 660.00
Table, Sewing, Classical, Mahogany Inlay, 2 Graduated Drawers, 1815, 49 In. 6900.00
Table, Sewing, Classical, Mahogany Inlay, Oval Top, 4 Tapered Legs, 28 In. 1380.00
Table, Sewing, Classical, Mahogany, 2 Drawers, Baltimore, 1830, 28 5/8 x 16 In. 845.00
Table, Sewing, Classical, Mahogany, Top Drawer Above 2 Drawers, 1830 . . . . 1210.00
Table, Sewing, Classical, Maple, Pedestal, 2 Drawers, 1830, 20 x 16 In. 1450.00
Table, Sewing, Drawer, Turned Legs, Penna., 19th Century, Square, 32 In. 345.00
Table, Sewing, Empire, Mahogany, 2 Convex Drawers, Wooden Pulls 245.00
Table, Sewing, Empire, Mahogany, Flip Top, 2 Drawers, Quadruped Pedestal, 30 In. 800.00
Table, Sewing, Empire, Maple, Mahogany Trim, Ball Feet, 28 1/2 In. 1430.00
Table, Sewing, Federal, Bird's-Eye Maple, Mahogany, 2 Drawers, Basket, 18 In. 5525.00
Table, Sewing, Federal, Mahogany, 2 Drawers, Twist Legs, 28 1/2 In. 1870.00
Table, Sewing, Federal, Mahogany, Birch Veneer, 27 In. 3000.00
Table, Sewing, Federal, Mahogany, Carved, Drop Leaf, 29 In. 2760.00
Table, Sewing, Federal, Mahogany, Drop Leaf, 3 Drawers, c.1800, 30 x 30 In. 1265.00
Table, Sewing, Federal, Mahogany, Pedestal, Paw Feet, Carved 900.00
Table, Sewing, Federal, Satinwood, Drawer, Cloth Bag, 1790, 29 x 19 x 14 In. 4025.00
Table, Sewing, Federal, Tiger Maple, 2 Drawers, Glass Pulls, c.1820, 28 x 19 In. 1495.00
Table, Sewing, Flame Mahogany Top, Drop Leaf, 2 Drawers, 9 x 29 In. 460.00
Table, Sewing, Fruitwood, Satinwood Inlay, 4 Tapered Legs, 1810, 27 1/2 In. 600.00
Table, Sewing, G. Stickley, No. 630, 3 Drawers, Wooden Knobs, 28 In. 2200.00
Table, Sewing, George III, Mahogany, Hinged Oval Top, X-Stretcher, 26 x 18 In. 845.00
Table, Sewing, George III, Mahogany, Inlay, Octagonal Lift Top, 1880, 28 In. 875.00
Table, Sewing, George III, Rosewood Inlay, Spade Feet, 30 In. 2100.00
Table, Sewing, Gothic, Mahogany, Flip Top, Tufted Yellow Interior On Stand, 27 In. 415.00
Table, Sewing, Hepplewhite, Mahogany Veneer & Mahogany, c.1790, 28 x 25 In. 4850.00
Table, Sewing, Hinged Top, Fitted Interior, Silk Bag, Russia, 1830s, 29 In. 4025.00
Table, Sewing, Late Federal, Cherry, Drawer, Tapered Legs, 19th Century 515.00
Table, Sewing, Louis XVI, Walnut, Hinged Compartment Stretcher Shelf, 28 In. 365.00
Table, Sewing, Mahogany, 2 Cock-Beaded Drawers, Gadroon Edge, 31 In. 3450.00
Table, Sewing, Mahogany, 2 Drawers, Acanthus Carved Legs, 1825 . . . . 910.00
Table, Sewing, Mahogany, 2 Drawers, Overhanging Top, Silk Basket, 1850 . . . . 970.00
Table, Sewing, Mahogany, 2 Lids, With 3 Sections, Basket, France, 27 x 18 In. 240.00
Table, Sewing, Mahogany, 3 Drawers, Stretcher Shelf, France, 19th Century, 119 In. 725.00
Table, Sewing, Mahogany, Allover Reeding, 2 Drawers, Divided Interior, 28 5/8 In. 2860.00
Table, Sewing, Mahogany, Door Over 1 Drawer, Carved, 19th Century 115.00
Table, Sewing, Mahogany, Drop Leaf, 2 Drawers, Ring Turned Legs, 1830 . . . . 600.00
Table, Sewing, Mahogany, Drop Leaf, Arched Legs, 1830s, 28 1/2 In. 747.00
Table, Sewing, Mahogany, Drop Leaf, Scrolled, 1840, 29 x 19 In. 1330.00
Table, Sewing, Mahogany, Empire, Barrel Shape Bottom Drawer 1050.00
Table, Sewing, Mahogany, Fruitwood, Pine, 3 Drawers, France, 18 In. 690.00
Table, Sewing, Mahogany, Turret Corners, Lyre Base, Brass Paw Feet 8625.00
Table, Sewing, Martha Washington Style, Mahogany 50.00
Table, Sewing, Papier-Mache, Gilt Design, Mother-Of-Pearl, Tripod, 1840 . . . . 1320.00
Table, Sewing, Pine, 2 Drawers, Turned & Faceted Legs, 1860s, 29 1/2 x 21 In. 200.00
Table, Sewing, Pine, Bennington Knobs, 1850s 425.00
Table, Sewing, Pine, Frieze With 2 Drawers, Square Legs, 30 x 41 In. 230.00
Table, Sewing, Poplar, Drawer, Turned Legs, Peg Feet, 27 1/4 x 18 x 18 In. 600.00
Table, Sewing, Queen Anne, Walnut, Scrubbed, 2 Drawers, 35 x 66 In. 440.00
Table, Sewing, Regency, Faux Tortoise, 2 Doors, Fitted, 9 1/2 x 8 3/4 x 6 In. 970.00
Table, Sewing, Regency, Faux Tortoise, Hinged Lid, 3 Drawers, 9 3/4 In. 1100.00
Table, Sewing, Regency, Mahogany, Rosewood, Lyre Support, 1815, 27 3/4 In. 2060.00

Table, Sewing, Regency, Rosewood, Brass Inlay, 2 Drawers, Trestle Base 970.00
Table, Sewing, Rococo, Rosewood, 2 Drawers, 1850-1860 .... 1350.00
Table, Sewing, Rococo, Rosewood, Sarcophagus Cover, Fitted Interior, 1850 .... 4235.00
Table, Sewing, Rosewood, Brass Inlay, Saber Legs, 1810 .... 485.00
Table, Sewing, Sheraton, Mahogany & Satinwood, 3 Drawers, c.1815 .... 3325.00
Table, Sewing, Walnut, 2 Drawers, Turned Legs, 22 x 18 x 29 3/4 In. 150.00
Table, Sewing, Walnut, Legs Fold For Storage, 1930s 70.00
Table, Sewing, Walnut, Pine, Drawer, Louisiana, 28 x 23 In. 665.00
Table, Sewing, Worn Blue Paint, Removable 3-Board Top, 30 x 50 x 31 In. 300.00
Table, Shaker, Cherry, Drop Leaf, Turned Legs, Small 4400.00
Table, Shaker, Tripod, Butternut, Circular Top, Pedestal, 3 Cabriole Legs, 24 3/4 In. 3220.00
Table, Shaker, Walnut, 2-Board Top, Mortised & Pinned Apron, 33 x 55 x 29 In. 440.00
Table, Shaker, Work, Pine Top, Mortised & Pinned Apron, Enfield, 27 x 48 3/4 In. 935.00
Table, Sheraton, Cherry, Drop Leaf, Brass Feet, 104 In., Open, Pair 2450.00
Table, Sheraton, Reeded Legs, Baluster Base, 29 1/2 x 35 1/2 In. 300.00
Table, Side, Art Deco, Burlwood, Rectangular Top, 22 x 29 In. 880.00
Table, Side, Champagne Finish, Black Ink Stamp, 21 x 28 In. 195.00
Table, Side, Classical, Marble Top, Drawer, Scrolled Supports, 1840, 29 In. 825.00
Table, Side, Dutch Rococo, Mahogany, Floral Marquetry 575.00
Table, Side, Girard, Swag Leg Aluminum Base, 16 x 20 x 16 1/2 In. 300.00
Table, Side, Late Regency, Mahogany, Bamboo Legs, 1840, 30 x 25 x 17 In. 970.00
Table, Side, Lifetime, Round Top, Original Finish, 18 x 29 In. 1045.00
Table, Side, Mahogany, Drawer, Lyre Supports, Octagonal Tray, France, 20 In. 600.00
Table, Side, Mahogany, Ring Turned Support, Brass Feet, 29 x 28 x 24 In. 495.00
Table, Side, McCobb, Marble Top, Brass Base, 14 x 20 In. 415.00
Table, Side, Neoclassical, Mahogany, Brass Border, Fluted Legs, 28 1/2 In. 2300.00
Table, Side, Neoclassical, Mahogany, Gray Marble Top, 30 In. 3740.00
Table, Side, Parcel Gilt, Plaster, Marble, Mirror, Italy, 40 In., Pair ....*Illus* 6325.00
Table, Stickley Bros., Cafe, Square Top, Straight Apron, 30 x 36 In. 715.00
Table, Tavern, Hepplewhite, Cherry, Pine, Breadboard Top, Drawer, 44 x 28 In. 590.00
Table, Tavern, Maple & Cherry, Drawer, Batwing Brass Over Hole For Pull, 28 In. 1000.00
Table, Tavern, Oak, Scalloped Apron, England, 19th Century, 30 x 45 In. 1265.00
Table, Tavern, Oblong Top, Drawer, Block & Vase Form Base 935.00
Table, Tavern, Pine Top, Maple Base, Frieze, Drawer, Pad Feet, 28 x 28 In. 2000.00
Table, Tavern, Pine, 18th Century, 9 x 66 In. 550.00
Table, Tavern, Pine, Drawer, Red Finish, Ring Turned Legs, Beaded Apron 5465.00
Table, Tavern, Pine, Frieze Drawer, Square Legs, Mid-19th Century, 56 In. 400.00
Table, Tavern, Pine, Frieze Drawer, Square Legs, Stretcher, Mid-19th Century, 56 In. 400.00
Table, Tavern, Pine, Hardwood, Red Paint Trace, 1-Board Top, 36 x 26 In. 520.00
Table, Tavern, Pine, Scrolled Apron, H Stretcher, Refinished, 22 x 30 x 27 In. 440.00
Table, Tavern, Queen Anne, Birch, Pine, Red Traces, Drawer, 26 x 40 In. 600.00
Table, Tavern, Queen Anne, Cherry, Oval Top, Apron, Pad Feet, c.1740, 28 x 27 In. 3450.00
Table, Tavern, Queen Anne, Maple, Rounded Inset Corners, Splayed Legs, 25 In. 575.00
Table, Tavern, Queen Anne, Maple, Splayed Legs, 19 x 30 In. 2420.00
Table, Tavern, Queen Anne, Pine, Walnut, Breadboard Ends, Drawer, 35 x 28 In. 2070.00
Table, Tavern, Queen Anne, Pine, Worn Paint, Apron, 2-Board Top, 23 x 34 In. 1100.00
Table, Tavern, Walnut, 2 Drawers, Removable Top, 1775, 30 1/2 In. 4315.00
Table, Tavern, William & Mary, Pegged Top, Breadboard Ends, Drawer, 42 In. 1075.00
Table, Tavern, William & Mary, Pine, Red Paint, Ring & Vase Turned Legs, 1730s 5460.00
Table, Tavern, Yellow Pine, Rectangular Top, Straight Frieze, Box Stretcher, 37 In. 370.00
Table, Tavern, Yellow Pine, Straight Frieze, Octagonal Legs, 19th Century, 27 In. 370.00
Table, Tea, Chippendale, Cherry, Birdcage Support, Vase Form Pedestal, 25 1/4 In. 920.00
Table, Tea, Chippendale, Cherry, Birdcage Mechanism, Cabriole Legs, 28 In. 1725.00
Table, Tea, Chippendale, Mahogany, Birdcage Support, Cabriole Legs, 29 In. 690.00
Table, Tea, Chippendale, Mahogany, Dish Tilt Top, Trifid Feet, 30 1/3 In. 3700.00
Table, Tea, Chippendale, Mahogany, Tilt Top, Birdcage, Ball & Claw Feet 2120.00
Table, Tea, Chippendale, Mahogany, Tilt Top, Tripod Base, Snake Feet, 27 In. 495.00
Table, Tea, Chippendale, Tilt Top, Walnut, Birdcage, 29 x 36 In. 137.00
Table, Tea, Chippendale, Walnut, Carved, Tilt Top, c.1760, 28 1/2 In. 800.00
Table, Tea, Chippendale, Walnut, Tilt Top, Birdcage, 18th Century, 29 x 33 1/4 In. 2300.00
Table, Tea, Chippendale, Walnut, Tilt Top, Tripod Base, 36 x 29 In. 3400.00
Table, Tea, Curly Maple, Tilt Top, Vase Form Standard, Tripod Base, 1780s 1842.00

Table, Tea, Federal, Cherry, Contrasting Compass Inlay, 18th Century, 30 In. 4315.00
Table, Tea, G. Stickley, No. 604, Overhanging Top, Mortised Through Legs, 26 In. 1650.00
Table, Tea, G. Stickley, No. 626, Corseted Cross-Stretchers, 30 x 40 1/4 In. 2100.00
Table, Tea, Georgian, Mahogany, Tilt Top, Acanthus Knees, Trifid, 28 x 33 In. 1450.00
Table, Tea, Georgian, Mahogany, Tilt Top, Cavetto Edge, 27 x 26 In., Pair 165.00
Table, Tea, Mahogany, Curule Legs, Folding, Late 19th Century, 27 In. 230.00
Table, Tea, Marquetry, 2 Tiers, Spray Of Flowering Shrub, 1900, 30 In. 2185.00
Table, Tea, Queen Anne, Cherry, Tilt Top, Tripod Base, Snake Feet, 28 x 34 In. 4400.00
Table, Tea, Queen Anne, Gateleg, North Shore, Mass., 1740, 25 1/4 In. 7000.00
Table, Tea, Queen Anne, Gumwood, Thumb-Molded Top, Pad Feet, c.1750, 29 In. 6325.00
Table, Tea, Queen Anne, Mahogany, Tray Top, Dark Gray Stain, 26 In. 2200.00
Table, Tea, Queen Anne, Maple & Pine, Cyma-Shaped Skirt, Button Feet, 28 1/4 In. 2875.00
Table, Tea, Queen Anne, Maple, Drop Leaf, Cutout Skirt, 36 x 25 In. 4025.00
Table, Tea, Queen Anne, Maple, Oval Top, Splayed Legs, 1760s, 28 1/4 In. 9775.00
Table, Tea, Queen Anne, Maple, Tilt Top, Tripod Cabriole Legs 920.00
Table, Tea, Queen Anne, Pine, Brown Finish, Red Grained, 26 1/2 In. 4125.00
Table, Tea, Queen Anne, Walnut, Tilt Top, Dish Top, Pedestal, 29 x 32 In. Diam. 2100.00
Table, Tea, Stickley Bros., Leather Top, Square Second Tier, 30 In. 770.00
Table, Tea, Walnut, Bentwood Support, Victorian, 30 x 35 In. 270.00
Table, Telephone, Rohde, Walnut, Asymmetrical, 32 x 12 x 28 In. 360.00
Table, Telephone, Walnut, Base Shelf, Square Legs, 34 1/2 In. 165.00
Table, Thomas Brooks, Round Marble Top, Pedestal, Casters, 39 x 26 x 30 In. 4000.00
Table, Thonet, Chromium Tubular Steel, 2 Tiers, Laminated Wood, 1932, 16 In. 200.00
Table, Tilt Top, Black Lacquer, Gilt Design, Chinese Figures, 28 In. 4025.00
Table, Tilt Top, Chippendale, Mahogany, Sun Bleached Top, Tripod, 22 x 28 In. 335.00
Table, Tilt Top, Chippendale, Walnut, Tripod, Cabriole Legs, c.1760, 28 x 31 In. 2300.00
Table, Tilt Top, Classical, Mahogany, Paw Feet, 1820, 29 1/2 In. 1485.00
Table, Tilt Top, Federal, Mahogany Inlay, Hexagon At Top, 29 x 15 3/4 x 23 1/2 In. 1495.00
Table, Tilt Top, Federal, Mahogany, Satinwood Inlay, Round 1495.00
Table, Tilt Top, George III, Mahogany, Baluster Support, 18th Century, 29 In. 660.00
Table, Tilt Top, George III, Mahogany, Tripod Base, Rectangular Top, 29 1/2 In. 330.00
Table, Tilt Top, Georgian, Mahogany, Carved Spiral Knob Shaft, Cabriole Legs 1200.00
Table, Tilt Top, Mahogany, Lafayette & Washington Portrait Inlays, 36 In. Diam. 3250.00
Table, Tilt Top, Mahogany, Leaf Carved Baluster, 4 Paw Feet, c.1830, 8 In. 2950.00
Table, Tilt Top, Mahogany, Molded, 3-Sided Concave Plinth, 5 3/4 In. 1150.00
Table, Tilt Top, Papier-Mache, Black Lacquer, Painted, Victorian 515.00
Table, Tilt Top, Papier-Mache, Mother-Of-Pearl Inlay, Tripod, Victorian, 28 In. 375.00
Table, Tilt Top, Queen Anne Style, Baluster Post, Cabriole Legs, 11 x 9 x 11 In. 575.00
Table, Tilt Top, Queen Anne Style, Mahogany, 1760, 29 In. 640.00
Table, Tilt Top, Queen Anne, Mahogany, New England, 18th Century, 29 In. 630.00
Table, Tilt Top, Regency Revival, Mahogany & Burlwood, 19th Century, 61 In. 2550.00
Table, Tilt Top, Regency, Exotic Bird, Foliage Design, 1830, 28 3/4 In. 1575.00
Table, Tilt Top, Regency, Mahogany, Rosewood, Brass Paw Feet, 1815 . . . . 4115.00
Table, Tilt Top, Regency, Mahogany, Turned Feet, 28 In. 800.00
Table, Tilt Top, Regency, Penwork, 1830s, 28 3/4 x 40 In. 7475.00
Table, Tray, 3-Sided Gallery, Marlborough Feet, 22 x 30 1/2 In. 745.00
Table, Tray, Black Lacquer, Gilt, Brass Handles, Stand, 1810, 32 In. 9775.00
Table, Tray, Black, Lacquer, Oriental Figures, Red & Gold Chinoiserie, 19th Century . . . 275.00
Table, Tray, Butler's, Georgian, Mahogany, Later Stand, 34 x 25 In. 545.00
Table, Tray, Decoupage, Gallery, Playing Cards, Collapsible Legs, Victorian, 27 In. 290.00
Table, Tray, George II, Mahogany, Stand 700.00
Table, Tray, George III, Mahogany, Brass Bound, 1890s, 22 1/2 x 36 In. 1265.00
Table, Tray, Georgian, Mahogany, Later Stand, Square Chamfered Legs 845.00
Table, Tray, Georgian, Mahogany, Turned Leg Stand, 1830 . . . . 695.00
Table, Tray, Herman Miller, Chrome Base, Laminate Top, Brown, 18 x 15 In. 415.00
Table, Tray, Lacquer, Oriental, Folding, Figural Designs, Stand, 19th Century 165.00
Table, Tray, Mahogany, Marquetry, Gallery, Brass Handles, 1920s, 25 x 16 In. 290.00
Table, Tray, Nelson, Laminated Walnut Top, Chrome Rod Base, 25 x 15 In. 385.00
Table, Tray, Nelson, Raised Edge, Chrome Frame, 15 x 21 In. 880.00
Table, Tray, Walnut, Collapsible Stand, England, 19th Century 440.00
Table, Trestle, French Provincial, Oak & Walnut, Slab Top, 28 x 94 1/2 In. 2415.00
Table, Trestle, French Provincial, Walnut, Cabriole Legs, 25 In. 690.00

Table, Trestle, Pine, Brown Paint, 2-Board Top, Cutouts, Continental, 25 x 79 In. 1000.00
Table, Trestle, Pine, Brown Paint, Removable 2-Board Top, Continental, 33 x 81 In. 495.00
Table, Trumpet Legs, Cross Stretcher With Urn, Inlaid Top 4400.00
Table, Tulip, Round Walnut Top, White Enameled Base, 20 x 20 In. 220.00
Table, Vertical Glass Cylinders, Frosted To Clear, Table, 1960s, 27 1/2 x 11 In. 275.00
Table, Victorian, Marble Top, Inlaid Stones, Checkerboard Design, 30 x 23 In. 3450.00
Table, Victorian, Walnut, Griffin Carved Supports, 27 In. 520.00
Table, Victorian, Walnut, Marble Top, Finger Carved, 19th Century, 20 x 29 In. 330.00
Table, W. Plattner, Rosewood Top, Knoll, Conference, 28 1/2 x 54 In. 1045.00
Table, Walnut, 2 Tiers, Italy, 22 3/4 In., Pair 220.00
Table, Walnut, Brass Casters, 4 Leaves, c.1875, Opens To 8 1/2 Ft. 1195.00
Table, Walnut, Burl Walnut, Marble Top, Mid-19th Century 970.00
Table, Walnut, Ebonized, Burl Walnut, Geometric Inlaid Border, 26 In. 550.00
Table, Walnut, Marble Top, Micro-Mosaic, Saint Peter's Square, 16 3/4 x 29 In. 4900.00
Table, Walnut, Oval Top, Floral Inlay, Down Swept Legs, 63 In. 1265.00
Table, White Marble Top, Cabriole Legs, Italy, 33 In., Pair 715.00
Table, William & Mary, Maple, Painted, Breadboard Ends, 1750, 26 x 17 In. 800.00
Table, William & Mary, Oak, Frieze Drawer, Brass Pull, 29 3/4 In. 2300.00
Table, William & Mary, Oak, Inlaid Drawer, Trumpet Turned Supports, 25 In. 7200.00
Table, William IV, Japanned, Chinoiserie Scene, 44 In. Diam. 5750.00
Table, Wine Tasting, Chippendale Style, Tripod Base, 20th Century, 21 In. 120.00
Table, Wine Tasting, Mahogany, Ring-Turned Pedestal, Trifid Legs, Slipper Feet, 25 In. . 485.00
Table, Writing, 2 Paper Binds At Top, Pine, c.1860 .... 145.00
Table, Writing, Ashford, Mahogany, Tooled Leather Top, 28 x 40 x 16 In. 600.00
Table, Writing, Biedermeier, Fruitwood, 3 Drawer 1610.00
Table, Writing, Biedermeier, Walnut, Columnar Supports, 30 In. 4315.00
Table, Writing, Burl Walnut, Gilt Bronze Edge, Serpentine, 28 In. 3450.00
Table, Writing, Chippendale, Mahogany, Leather, 3 Drawers, England, 66 x 33 In. 3750.00
Table, Writing, Empire, Mahogany, 63 3/4 In. 1095.00
Table, Writing, French Provincial, Fruitwood, Checkerboard, Fitted, 29 x 18 In. 1100.00
Table, Writing, G. Stickley, No. 459, 5 Drawers, Iron Pulls, Kneehole With Shelves 990.00
Table, Writing, Herter Bros., Walnut, Bird's-Eye Maple Writing Surface, 1874 .... 17600.00
Table, Writing, Louis XV, Black Paint, Gilt Leather Top, Scalloped Edge, 30 In. 1495.00
Table, Writing, Louis XV, Drawer, Leather, Ormolu, 19th Century, 39 In. 1575.00
Table, Writing, Mahogany, Leather Top, Drawer, Mounts Of Female Busts, 31 In. 100.00
Table, Writing, Mahogany, Marble Top, 2 Drawers, Winged Lion Supports, 45 In. 5465.00
Table, Writing, Mahogany, Slat Back, Leaf Design, 57 In. 2185.00
Table, Writing, Regency, Mahogany, Faded, Frieze Drawer, 31 x 17 3/4 In. 545.00
Table, Writing, Regency, Mahogany, Leather Top, Ball Feet, 31 x 36 x 18 In. 485.00
Table, Writing, Renaissance Revival, Mahogany, Red Tooled Leather Inset, 29 3/4 In. ... 1330.00
Table, Writing, Rosewood, Lattice Back, Pedestal Base, England, 33 In. 520.00
Table, Writing, Sleigh, Oval Top, Long Drawer, Circular Fluted Legs 180.00
Table, Writing, Walnut, Philadelphia, Daniel Pabst, 28 x 45 x 29 In. 1760.00
Table, Wrought Iron, Marble Top, Floral Frieze, Spiral Twist Legs, 33 1/2 In. 975.00
Table Set, Glass Top, Wrought Iron, 4 Folding Wood & Metal Chairs, 5 Piece 850.00
Table Set, Oak, Folding, Painted Scene, 22-In. Round Table, Child's, 3 Piece 350.00
Table Set, Pine, Trestle, 2 Carved Benches, Continental, 59 In., 3 Piece 980.00
Table Set, Quartetto, Edwardian, Mahogany, Trestle, Parquetry, 22 x 14 In. 330.00
Tabouret, Empire, Mahogany, Ormolu Mounted, Paw Feet, 21 In. 4315.00
Tabouret, G. Stickley, Mahogany, Round Top, Arched Cross Stretchers, 19 1/2 In. 825.00
Tabouret, L. & J.G. Stickley, Clip Corners, Cross Stretchers, 18 1/2 In. 880.00
Tabouret, Warren Planter, Wire 110.00
Tantalus, Boulle Style, Marquetry, 4 Crystal Decanters & 12 Cordials, 10 x 13 In. 750.00
Tea Cart, Aalto, Bent Laminated Birch, Lacquered, 1936, 35 x 18 In. 3450.00
Tea Cart, Eastlake, Walnut, Incised Design, Victorian, 18 x 28 x 30 In. 220.00
Tea Cart, Federal Style, Floral & Gilt Design, 28 x 28 In. 215.00
Tea Cart, Heywood-Wakefield, Bar Harbor, Wicker 495.00
Tea Cart, Mahogany, Brass, White Carrara Top, 29 1/2 x 36 x 19 In. 800.00
Tea Cart, Mahogany, Round Tray Top, 2 Lower Shelves, 20th Century 250.00
Tea Cart, McCobb, Brass Base, Drawer, 28 x 32 x 17 In. 165.00
Tea Chest, Chinoiserie Design, Red, Staved, Banded, Handles, 19th Century, 20 In. 450.00
Teapoy, Walnut, Coffer Form, Paw Feet, Mid-19th Century, 32 1/4 In. 2650.00
Tete-A-Tete, George III, Giltwood, Carved Crest, 59 In. 6900.00

Vanity, Art Deco, Gold & Silver Leaf, Mirror, Drum Pedestals, Glass Shelf, 72 In. 465.00
Vanity, L. & J.G. Stickley, No. 87, Swivel Mirror, 2 Drawers, Wooden Knobs, 54 In. 1540.00
Vanity, Marquetry, Flower Inlay, Sliding Mirror, Writing Slide, 30 1/2 In. 800.00
Vanity, Rohde, Wood Veneer, 3 Drawers, Asymmetrical, 1930, 65 In. 495.00
Vanity, Stool, Geddes, Yellow Enameled, Chrome, 30 x 49 x 17 In. 775.00
Vanity, Stool, McCobb, Caned, Brass, 28 x 44 x 18 In. 385.00
Vitrine, 3 Rounded Windows, Beaded Border, Courting Couple Scene, 55 In. 920.00
Vitrine, Baroque, Oak, Germany 1400.00
Vitrine, Biedermeier, Black Walnut, Pilaster, Wasted Feet, 5 Ft. 4 In. 8050.00
Vitrine, Biedermeier, Fruitwood, Hanging 545.00
Vitrine, Giltwood, Floral Swags, Putti Inset At Base, France, 72 In. 2100.00
Vitrine, Hardwood, Hanging, Scroll Carved, Glazed Door, 28 In., Pair 862.00
Vitrine, Louis XVI, Parquetry Panels, Brass Scroll At Frieze, 66 x 25 In. 1210.00
Vitrine, Oak, Carved Lion's Head Masks, Claw Feet 2750.00
Vitrine, Regency, Mahogany, Crossbanded Inlay, Brass Caps & Castors, 32 In. 990.00
Vitrine, Vernis Martin Style, Enamel, Courting Scene On Door, 2 Shelves, 10 In. 375.00
Wardrobe, Classical, Mahogany, Molded Cornice, Paw Feet, 1820, 87 In. 2990.00
Wardrobe, Poplar, Grain Painted, Paneled Door, Cover Molded Cornice, 84 1/2 In. 165.00
Wardrobe, Walnut, 2 Dovetailed Drawers, 2 Doors, Gallery Top, 18 x 53 x 87 In. 690.00
Washstand, American Rococo, Rosewood, Marble Backsplash & Top, 37 x 19 In. 2300.00
Washstand, Classical, Rectangular Top, Scrolled Support, 1830, 34 In. 365.00
Washstand, Corner, Curly Maple, Bowfront, 2 Shelves, Drawer, 43 1/2 In. 2970.00
Washstand, Corner, George III, Mahogany, Backsplash, Drawer, 43 x 22 x 15 In. 980.00
Washstand, Corner, Hepplewhite, Mahogany, Bowfront, Corner Drawer, 44 1/4 In. 965.00
Washstand, Corner, Sheraton, Poplar, Flame Graining, Gallery, Drawer, 31 x 22 In. 1485.00
Washstand, Empire, Cherry, Marble Top, Bottom Shelf, Drawer, 33 1/4 In. 550.00
Washstand, Federal, Mahogany, Bow Front, Medial Self, Baluster Spiral Legs, 36 In. 400.00
Washstand, Federal, Mahogany, Bowfront, 2 Faux Drawers, 1790, 38 1/4 In. 460.00
Washstand, Hepplewhite, Backsplash, Drawer, Hole Cutout, 37 x 15 1/2 In. 175.00
Washstand, Hepplewhite, Mahogany, Curved Feet, Square Legs, 41 In. 440.00
Washstand, Maple, Scrolled Backsplash, Drawer, c.1830, 37 1/2 In. 4600.00
Washstand, Marble Top, Colored Glass Backsplash, Door 220.00
Washstand, Oak, Thumb-Molded Gallery, Towel Racks, Drawer, 30 1/2 In. 175.00
Washstand, Painted, Scrolled Backsplash, Mid-Level Drawer, Thimble Feet, c.1825 . . . . 300.00
Washstand, Queen Anne Style, Mahogany, 3 Ring Supports, Slipper Feet, 30 In. 230.00
Washstand, Rosewood, Marble Top, 37 3/4 x 32 1/2 x 17 1/2 In. 910.00
Washstand, Rosewood, White Marble Top, Mirror, Drawers, Doors, Victorian 1200.00
Washstand, Sheraton, Gold Stenciled Florals, 2 Top Drawers, 36 x 40 In. 990.00
Washstand, Sheraton, Painted & Stenciled Backsplash, Corner Shelves, Drawer 230.00
Washstand, Sheraton, Stenciled Leaf & Vine, Corner Shelves, Brass Pull 470.00
Washstand, Walnut, Cutout Scalloped Feet, Raised Paneled Door, 32 In. 385.00
Washstand, Walnut, Green, Marble Top, White Backsplash, 47 x 36 x 18 In. 220.00
Washstand, Walnut, Marble Top, Backsplash, 1875, Victorian, 40 In. 550.00
Whatnot Shelf, Corner, Open Scroll Work Design, 27 x 15 x 62 In. 155.00
Whatnot Shelf, Corner, Walnut, Molded, 22 x 57 In. 75.00
Whatnot Shelf, Oak, Eagle Top Mirrored Back, Acorns, Oak Leaves, 37 In. 120.00
Whatnot Shelf, Walnut, 6 Shelves, Mid-19th Century, 67 x 21 x 16 In. 825.00
Whatnot Shelf, Walnut, Arched Crest, Mirrored Above, Italy, 42 x 26 In. 140.00
Window Seat, Burl Birch, Upholstered Outscrolled Sides, Scandinavian, 86 1/2 In. 7475.00
Window Seat, Classical Revival, Mahogany, Curule, Giltwood, 51 In. 12075.00
Window Seat, George III, Serpentine Seat, Scroll, Leaf Carved, 1775 . . . . 13800.00
Window Seat, Mahogany, Trapezoidal Form, Upholstered Seat, c.1825 . . . . 1515.00
Window Seat, Painted, Upholstered Sides, Seat, Fluted Cabriole Legs, 33 3/4 In. 3740.00
Wine Cooler, Mahogany, Hinged Domed Top, Victorian, 20 In. 2300.00

G. ARGY-ROUSSEAU is the impressed mark used on a variety of objects
in the Art Deco style. Gabriel Argy-Rousseau, born in 1885, was a
French glass artist.

G—ARGY—
ROUSSEAU

Bowl, Lierre, Cluster Of Berries, Purple Leaves, Signed, 1915, 3 1/2 In. 3450.00
Bowl, Pairs Of Birds On Rim, Rows Of Slashes, Signed, c.1927, 4 1/8 In. 3450.00
Bowl, Papillon, Moths Below Rim, Pate-De-Verre, 3 In. 4140.00
Lamp, Coupe Fleurie, Flower Heads, Iron Ring Base, Signed, 1923, 5 5/8 In. 6095.00
Lamp Base, Trumpet, Amber Glass Base, Red Ferns, Pate De Verre, 10 In. 2070.00

Vase, Bud, 2 Parakeets At Base, Signed, 5 x 5 In. 1870.00
Vase, Creamy White, Red, Maroon Blossoms, Pate-De-Verre, 5 In. 4025.00
Vase, Papyrus, Sprays Of Scrolled Egyptian Flower Heads, 1923, 10 In. 9430.00

GALLE was a designer who made glass, pottery, furniture, and other Art Nouveau items. Emile Galle founded his factory in France in 1874. After Galle's death in 1904, the firm continued to make glass and furniture until 1931. The name *Galle* was used as a mark, but it was often hidden in the design of the object. Galle glass is listed here. Pottery is in the next section. His furniture is listed in the Furniture category.

Beaker, Enameled, Floral Design On Foot, Tapered, Lavender Overlay, Signed, 5 In. 7130.00
Bottle, 2 Butterflies, Iris Blossoms, Gray, Amber, Caramel Brown, 3 1/2 In. 3680.00
Bottle, 4 Circular Panels, Enamel Meadow Scenes, Florals, Stopper, c.1895, 3 7/8 In. 2530.00
Bottle, Dresser, Red Floral, Pink, Green Ground, Heart Form Stopper, Signed, 8 In. 798.00
Bottle, Gladiola, Leaf Overlay, Red, Orange, Cameo Stopper, Signed, 4 In. 978.00
Bowl, Enameled Thistle, Crimped Triangular Design, Signed, 8 3/8 In. 1490.00
Bowl, Landscape, Blue Center, Boat Shape, Scroll Design, Scroll Feet, 4 x 5 x 3 In. 575.00
Bowl, Leaf Design, Amber, Cameo, Silver, Signed, 1910, 2 1/4 In. 1035.00
Bowl, Lily Pond, Floral Design, Purple, Blue Against White Ground, 6 1/4 In. 4830.00
Bowl, Marine Design, Seed Capsules, Swirled Ground, Squat, Cameo, 11 x 18 In. 12650.00
Bowl, Pink Floral Design, Leaves, Satin Opalescent, Squat, Cameo, 7 x 2 In. 287.00
Bowl, Stylized Leafy Plants, Mottled Green Gray, Pink, Mauve, Etched, 3 In........... 632.50
Box, Cover, Cherry Design, Deep Purple On Yellow, Brown, 3 1/2 x 4 1/2 In. 2145.00
Carafe, Enameled, Ribbed Topaz, Cruet Form, Twist Handle, 6 1/4 In. 865.00
Charger, 3 Crabs Against Bed Of Shells, Brown, Sand Overlay, Sea Blue, 15 In. 8740.00
Charger, Morning Glories, Gray Ground, Red, Yellow Mottled, Upturned Rim, 16 In. 1380.00
Compote, Cut Clematis Blossoms & Leaves, Gray To Yellow, Signed, 13 1/8 In........ 4600.00
Compote, Cut Strawberries & Leaves, Clear Foot, Red Overlay, Signed, 14 In. 7475.00
Decanter, Orange & White Grape Pods, Double Spout, Clear Stopper, Cameo, 8 In. 1320.00
Dish, Enameled, Topaz, 7 Plumes, Red, Black, White, Scalloped Tray, 5 3/4 In. 635.00
Figurine, Cat, Black Trimmed Blue Design, Glass Eyes, Signed, 13 In. 230.00
Fixture, Ceiling, 3 Colors, Original Chains, 14 In. 7000.00
Fixture, Ceiling, Brass, Gray Glass, Yellow, Burnt Sienna, Apple Blossoms, 35 In. 4890.00
Jar, Cover, Water Lily Pads, Dragonfly, Amber, Internal Shaded Turquoise, Signed, 7 In. . 3105.00
Jar, Hydrangea, Leafage Design, Green, Lavender, Peach, Egg Shape, 4 In. 1380.00
Lamp, 3 Bronze Arms, Exploding Mums, Leafage On Base, Blue, Conical Shade, 11 In. . 9860.00
Lamp, Boudoir, 4-Colored Shade, Silk Cord, 8 In. 8000.00
Lamp, Cherries & Foliage, Domed Shade, Yellow Ground, Cameo, 17 1/2 In. 440.00
Lamp, Landscape, Trees Against Mountain Tops, Brown, Purple Against Amber, 14 In. 3450.00
Lamp, Magenta Strawberries, Foliage, Yellow Ground, Domed Shade, Cameo, 6 In. 785.00
Lamp, Oriental, Yellow Floral Bonsai, Brown Designs, Triangular Shade, Cameo, 10 In. . 825.00
Pitcher, Napoleanic Soldiers, Blue, Gold, Signed, 10 1/2 In. 1045.00
Powder Box, Violets, Overlaid In White, Green, Amethyst, Pink Mottled, 5 1/2 In. 863.00
Tray, Etched Flower, Pod Emerald Green Shape, Engraved Galle Center, 6 In. 495.00
Tray, Floral & Bird Design, Pierced Gallery, Double Bow Handles, 20 1/2 x 12 1/2 In. 690.00
Tumbler, Enameled Mauve Orchid, Olive Stem, Amber & Cranberry Spatter, 4 In. 880.00
Vase, Allover Leaves & Blossoms, Yellow-Green Frosted Ground, 5 1/4 In. 850.00
Vase, Amber Clustered Pods, Long Stalks, Inverted Trumpet, Cameo, Signed, 18 In. 2750.00
Vase, Azaleas Design, Yellow, Russet Overlay, Gray, Cameo, 1900, 9 3/4 In. 575.00
Vase, Blossoms On Trailing Vines, Purple, Gray Ground, 10 1/2 In. 2760.00
Vase, Blue & Green Lotus Blossoms, Reeds, Citron & Frosted Sky, Cameo, 10 In. 1925.00
Vase, Blue Flowers, Green Leaves, Satin Cut To Brown, 14 In. 2500.00
Vase, Blue Mountains & Evergreens, Boulders, Yellow Sky, Cameo, 9 3/4 In. 1925.00
Vase, Branches With Pine Cones, Aqua, Yellow, 1900, 7 1/4 In. 3335.00
Vase, Branches, Leaves & Berries, Orange Satin Ground, Cameo, 5 1/2 In. 850.00
Vase, Branches, Lime Green, Yellow, Orange Bottom, Pink Lip, 11 1/8 In. 920.00
Vase, Brown Floral Pods, Chartreuse & Satin Ground, Tapered, Cameo, Signed, 5 In. ... 850.00
Vase, Brown Trees, Silhouetted Against Ginger Sky, Islands, Cameo, 8 In. 1100.00
Vase, Bud, Flowers, Leafage, Orange Over Pink Glass, Spherical, Signed, 5 In. 575.00
Vase, Bud, Hydrangeas, Green, Lavender, Cylindrical, Signed, 6 1/2 In. 978.00
Vase, Bud, Wild Rose, Leaves, Blue, Purple, Cameo, Etched, Trumpet Form, 8 3/4 In. ... 1380.00
Vase, Burgundy Floral, Leaf Motif, Rose Shaded To Peach, Signed, 1900, 4 In. 517.50

Vase, Burgundy Floral, Leaf Motif, Satin Cut To Amber, 1900, 6 In. 632.50
Vase, Chocolate Brown Trees, Yellow Sky, Birds, Banjo Shape, Signed, 6 1/2 In. 880.00
Vase, Chrysanthemum, Frosted Ground, Orange Overlay, Baluster Form, Signed, 9 3/4 In. 575.00
Vase, Clematis, Gray, Lemon Yellow, Lime Green, Mold Blown, 9 1/2 In. 8625.00
Vase, Cocoa Brown Trees, Lake, Pier, Apricot & Satin Sky, Cameo, 9 3/4 In. 2530.00
Vase, Commemorating Struggle For Lorraine, Fierce Faces, Signed, 1914, 11 In. 2875.00
Vase, Crocuses, Purple, Orange Stamens, Wheel Carved, Blue Body, 8 In. 15400.00
Vase, Cut Foliate Design, Yellow Ground, Ovoid, Flattened Sides, Signed, 5 1/2 In. 630.00
Vase, Cut Irises, Purple Overlay, Golden Yellow, 1900, 17 5/8 In. 3737.00
Vase, Daffodils, Leafage, White, Lime Green, Satin, Olive Green, 1900, 13 1/2 In. 5175.00
Vase, Enameled Iris, Green, Mushroom Mark, Signed, 8 1/2 In. 1430.00
Vase, Enameled, Bleeding Heart Blossoms, Pale Green, Leaves, White, Pink, Green, 9 In. 2760.00
Vase, Enameled, Flower, Pink, Lavender, Green, Pale Yellow, Signed, 24 In. 4140.00
Vase, Enameled, Pale Green, Ribbed Vessel, Etched Leaf Forms, Cameo, 9 1/2 In. 4025.00
Vase, Enameled, Wheel, Leaf, Stem Design, Orange, Red, Green, Gold Accents, 13 In. . . . 4600.00
Vase, Etched Chrysanthemum Blossoms, Topaz, Cameo, 12 1/2 In. 3220.00
Vase, Exotic Floral Leaf Design, Pale Pink Ground, Brown, 13 1/4 In. 1100.00
Vase, Fern Design, Green, Green Overlay, Brown, Frosted Gray Ground, 1900, 7 In. 805.00
Vase, Fish With Open Mouths Above Wavy Sea, 1900, 12 3/4 In. 3450.00
Vase, Floral, Foliate & Lily Pad, Frosted Green Ground, Flared, Conical, 9 3/4 In. 1435.00
Vase, Floral, Leaf Design, Satin Cut To Blue Brown, 1900, 4 In. 373.00
Vase, Flower Bud, Leaf Design, Amber Over Green, Signed, Cameo, 13 1/4 In. 1610.00
Vase, Flowered Plants, Brown, Cut To Lime Green, Gray Ground, 1900, 8 In. 1035.00
Vase, Flowers, Leaf Design, Amber Over Green, 12 1/2 In. 1840.00
Vase, Fruit Plant Design, Pale Brown, Cut To Light Green, White, Cameo, 1900, 9 In. . . . 862.00
Vase, Fruiting Vine, Etched & Mold Blown, Everted Neck, Signed, c.1900, 10 7/8 In. . . . 6900.00
Vase, Grapes, Leafage, Scrolled Vines, Red, Amber, Satin, 1900, 18 3/4 In. 5462.00
Vase, Green Leaves, Blue Flowers, Sea Green Ground, Signed, 6 1/2 In. 2750.00
Vase, Hydrangea, Leafage Design, Green, Lavender, Peach, Boat Shape, Signed, 2 In. . . . 1095.00
Vase, Indian Dancers Against Geometric Ground, Blue, Pink, Red, Signed, 12 In. 8050.00
Vase, Italian Man With Feathered Cap, Ring Handles, 4 Curled Feet, 8 1/4 In. 260.00
Vase, Landscape, Farmhouse, Leafy Trees, Gray Glass, Yellow, Brown, 1900, 10 In. 1840.00
Vase, Landscape, Mountainous Lake Scene, Lemon Yellow, Purple, Blue, 1900, 13 In. . . . 747.00
Vase, Lavender & Gray Green Phlox, Apricot & Lavender Ground, Stick, Cameo, 11 In. . 715.00
Vase, Lavender Violets & Leaves, Yellow & Blue Ground, Cameo, 3 1/2 In. 715.00
Vase, Leafy Plant Design, Lime Green Overlay, Cut To Pink, Cylindrical, 1900, 19 In. . . . 1840.00
Vase, Leaves, Berry Design, Yellow, Violet Overlay, Gray Ground, 1900, 11 In. 805.00
Vase, Magnolia Blossoms, Leafage, Silver, Purple Mounted, Silver Rim, 1900, 6 In. 2070.00
Vase, Maroon Fishing Harbor, Ships, Silhouettes, Cameo, Egg Shape, Signed, 7 3/4 In. . . 2750.00
Vase, Maroon Floral Clusters, Pink Ground, Cameo, Egg Shape, 5 3/4 In. 475.00
Vase, Marquetry, 2 Upright Flowers, White Petals, Purple Center, 8 1/2 In. 14300.00
Vase, Mocha Brown, Flowers, Yellow & Blue, Banjo Shape, Cameo, 6 3/4 In. 880.00
Vase, Molded Plums, Foliage, Gilt Bronze Base, Cylindrical, 15 1/2 In. 4140.00
Vase, Pansy Design, Leafage, Pink, Lavender Overlay, Gray Ground, Cameo, 8 In. 2300.00
Vase, Pink Apple Blossoms, Amber Branches, Almond Ground, Signed, 14 In. 10725.00
Vase, Pink, Olive Green, Dogwood Blossoms, Satin, Bright, 11 3/4 In. 2070.00
Vase, Poppies, Amber, Satin Ground, Cameo, Signed, 9 3/4 In. 770.00
Vase, Purple Flowers, Green Leaves, Cameo, 4 In. 595.00
Vase, Purple Foliaged Trees, Blue Mountain, Inverted Trumpet, 6 1/2 In. 715.00
Vase, Red Clematis, Mold Blown, 6 1/2 In. 7425.00
Vase, Sprays Of Flowers, Yellow Panels, Gilding, c.1890, 6 1/8 In. 2185.00
Vase, Sprays Of Thistles, Signed, Cross Of Lorraine, c.1900, 10 In. 3220.00
Vase, Sycamore Branch, Tangerine, White Overlay, Green, Gray Ground, 5 7/8 In. 690.00
Vase, Trailing Blossoms & Leaves, Purple Over White, Cameo, 17 In. 1725.00
Vase, Tulips, Burgundy, Salmon, Amber, Peach & Satin Ground, Cameo, 15 In. 6050.00
Vase, Water Lilies, Amber, Blue Water Against Ivory, Blue Sky, Signed, 11 In. 1980.00
Vase, Water Lilies, Lily Pads, Pink & Brown Overlay, c.1900, 7 In. 2580.00
Vase, Waterfall Running Into Mountain Lake, Signed, c.1900, 16 1/8 In. 4830.00
Vase, White, Yellow Ground, Floral Design, Flared Rim, 6 1/4 In. 275.00
Vase, Wisteria Design, Purple On Pink, Stick, Signed, Cameo, 13 1/4 In. 1610.00
Vase, Yellow, Red, Purple Design, 6 x 5 1/2 In. 1540.00
Wall Pocket, Gray Straw Bonnet, Blue Ribbon, Signed, 12 x 7 1/2 In. 770.00

GALLE POTTERY was made by Emile Galle, the famous French designer, after 1874. The pieces were marked with the initials *E. G.* impressed, *Em. Galle Faiencerie de Nancy*, or a version of his signature. Galle is best known for his glass, listed above.

Vase, 3 Gold & Blue Bamboo Shoots, Black Outlining, Ivory Ground, 6 In. 1100.00
Vase, Brown Leaves, Branches & Berries, Frosted Green Ground, 5 1/2 In. 850.00

GAME collectors like all types of games. Of special interest are any board games or card games. Transogram and other company names are included in the description when known. Other games may be found listed under Card, Toy, or the name of the character or celebrity featured in the game.

6 Million Dollar Man, Bionic Crisis, Parker Brothers, Board, Box, 1975 .... 29.00
6 Million Dollar Man, Mission Control Center, Parker Brothers, Board, Box, 1973 .... 145.00
12 O'Clock High, Milton Bradley, Card, Box, 1965 .... 50.00
Addams Family, Filmways, Box, 1965 ....70.00 to 125.00
Aerial Contest, J.W. Spear & Sons, Board ....*Illus* 145.00
Alice In Wonderland, Tea Party Scene, Box, Cadaco, 1984 .... 35.00
Alien, Board, Kenner, 1979 .... 50.00
All In The Family, Is There A Little Bit Of Archie In All Of Us?, Milton Bradley, 1972 . 23.00
All The Fun Of A Motor Ride, J.W. Speer & Sons, Board, 1910 ....*Illus* 290.00
Amos 'n' Andy, Board, Box, 1930 .... 90.00
Andy Gump Comic, Lithograph, Box, 1920s 65.00
Annie Oakley, Milton Bradley, Board, 1950s 28.00
Archie Bunker's Card Game, Milton Bradley, Box, 1972, 7 x 10 In. 17.00
Arithmetic, McLoughlin, 1887 .... 35.00
Around The World In 80 Days, Transogram, 1957 .... 65.00
Assembly Line, Car Assembly, Selchow 85.00
Astronaut, Tony The Tiger, Kellogg's, 1960 .... 20.00
Automobile Race, L.H. Mace & Co., Board On Box, 1905 ....*Illus* 635.00
Baseball, Hustler, Tin Lithograph, 1920s 185.00
Baseball, Lead Fielders, Lithographed Board, McLoughlin Bros., c.1886, 17 x 9 In. 1610.00
Baseball & Checkers, Lithographed, Wooden Pieces, Milton Bradley, c.1900 .....*Illus* 230.00
Baseball For Little League, Milton Bradley, Box, 1958 .... 65.00
Basketball, Tin Lithograph, Marx 35.00
Battle, Civil War, Box, Milton Bradley, 1961, 10 x 14 In. 38.00
Beany & Cecil, Ring Toss, Tin, 1961, 14 x 14 In. 110.00
Beat The Clock Game, Board, 1969 .... 12.50
Ben Casey, M.D., Board, Box 45.00
Beverly Hillbillies, Standard Toycraft, 1963 .... 15.00
Billboard The Brand Name Advertising Game, Harett-Gilmar American Toys, 1956 . 115.00
Bionic Crisis, Parker Brothers, 1975 .... 20.00
Black Cat Fortune Telling, Parker Brothers, Cards, Late 1940s 15.00
Board, Blue, Green & Black Painted Surface, 1880s, 12 x 13 In. ...:......... 375.00

Dust frequently if you live near the seashore. Salt air causes problems.

Game, Aerial Contest,
J.W. Spear & Sons, Board

Game, All The Fun Of A Motor Ride,
J.W. Speer & Sons, Board, 1910

Game, Automobile Race, L.H. Mace & Co.,
Board On Box, 1905

Board, Chess, Mahogany & Ivory Panels, Mother-Of-Pearl Star Form, Square, 17 1/4 In.   63.00
Board, Folding, Old Red, Black Squares 650.00
Board, Lap, Painted Checkerboard, Grained Surface, 18 x 36 1/2 In. 4025.00
Board, Rosewood, Ebony & Tinted Ivory, c.1643 . . . . 1940.00
Boy Scout In Camp, McLoughlin, Board, 22 Scouts On Wood Stand 220.00
Boy Scouts, Milton Bradley, c.1910 . . . . 115.00
Camp Granada, Milton Bradley, 1955 . . . . 30.00
Captain Gallant, Transogram, Board, 1955 . . . . 60.00
Castle Attack, Multiple Products, Drawbridge, Firing Catapult, 1964 . . . . 55.00
Cat & Mouse, Parker Brothers, Box Is Board, 1964 . . . . 15.00
Cattlemen, Selchow & Righter, Woman & Cowmen, Board Is Map Of West, Box, 1977 . 40.00
Charlie's Angels, Milton Bradley, Board, 1977 . . . . 25.00
Checkerboard, Birch, Worn Varnish & Black Paint, 18 3/4 x 28 1/2 In. 110.00
Checkerboard, Grain Paint, Shaped To Rest On Lap, 19th Century, 18 In. 4025.00
Checkerboard, Hardwood, Green & Black, Paint Traces, 18 1/2 x 29 In. 165.00
Checkerboard, Maple, Cherry, Walnut, Rosewood, Wooden, 17 1/4 x 17 1/4 In. 330.00
Checkerboard, Pine, Black, White & Gray Paint, 20 x 29 In. 95.00
Checkerboard, Pine, Olive-Gold & Black, 18 1/2 x 30 3/4 In. 275.00
Checkerboard, Pine, Worn Cream & Tan Paint, 3 Boards, 19 1/2 x 25 3/4 In. 245.00
Checkerboard, Poplar, Red & Black Paint, 19 x 27 1/4 In. 275.00
Checkerboard, Poplar, Walnut Edge Molding, Cream, Black, Green Border, 18 x 18 In. . . 247.50
Checkerboard, Red & Blue Paint, Rectangular, 20th Century, 15 x 14 In. 345.00
Checkerboard, Walnut, Ebony, Maple, Folding, Ivory Chess Pieces, 8 1/4 In. 33.00
Checkerboard, Walnut, Maple, Inlaid, Refinished, 21 x 21 In. 275.00
Checkerboard, Wooden, Blue & White, Silver Trim, Glass, Gilt Frame, 15 x 19 In. 165.00
Chess Set, Ivory, Carved, 1968, 4 1/8-In. King 3250.00
Chess Set, Ivory, Red & White, 2 5/8 In. 60.00
Close Encounters Of The Third Kind, Parker Brothers, Board, 1978 . . . . 12.00
Confucius Say, Milton Bradley, Card, 1937 . . . . 50.00
Coontown Shooting Gallery, 4 Target Heads, c.1920 . . . . 285.00
Cowboy Round Up, Parker Brothers, 1952 . . . . 35.00
Cribbage Board, Carved Bone, Reticulated Board With Hearts, Compass Stars, 7 In. . . . 215.00
Cribbage Board, Mahogany, Ivory Inlaid Heart Design, 1790-1820, 15 3/8 In. 475.00
Cribbage Board, Prisoner-Of-War Art, Carved Bone, France, 2 1/2 x 5 1/2 In. 950.00
Cross Country Race By Land, Air & Sea, Chicago Game Co., 1911 . . . . *Illus* 575.00
Dark Shadows, Box 100.00
Daytona, Marble, Wolverine, U.S.A. 95.00
Dennis The Menace, Stand Toykraft, 1960 . . . . 150.00
Dennis The Menace Tiddlywinks, Whitman 35.00
Detectives, Transogram, Board, 1961 . . . . 60.00
Dexterity Puzzle, Battleship, Paper Lithograph, Frame, Prewar, 1 5/8 In. 80.00
Dexterity Puzzle, Black Woman, Tin Lithograph, Metal Frame, Germany, 2 1/2 In. 67.00
Dexterity Puzzle, Boxers, Mirror Back, Tin Lithograph, U.S. Zone Germany, 2 In. 117.00

Dexterity Puzzle, Boy On Scooter, Metal Frame, Glass Front, c.1950, 1 7/8 In. Diam. . .   80.00
Dexterity Puzzle, Children Riding Sleigh, Paper Lithograph, Frame, Prewar, 1 1/2 In. . .   120.00
Dexterity Puzzle, Chinaman & Prussian, Paper Lithograph, Metal Frame, 2 In. 140.00
Dexterity Puzzle, Clown, Juggling, Europe, 1940s, 1 3/4 In. . . . .*Illus*   75.00
Dexterity Puzzle, Double, Bear, Rabbit Ring The Monkey's Tail, Japan, 2 3/4 In. 75.00
Dexterity Puzzle, Girl With Flowers, Paper Lithograph, Frame, Mirror Back, 2 1/8 In. .   128.00
Dexterity Puzzle, Man With Overcoat, D.R.G.M., Tin Lithograph, Frame, 1 5/8 In. 154.00
Dexterity Puzzle, Man, Bowtie, Europe, 1940s, 1 3/4 In. . . . .*Illus*   40.00
Dexterity Puzzle, Man, Hat, Europe, 1940s, 1 3/4 In. . . . .*Illus*   80.00
Dexterity Puzzle, Monkey, Cardboard Back, Metal Frame, 1950s, 1 3/4 In. Diam. 25.00
Dexterity Puzzle, Monkey, D.R.G.M., Tin Lithograph, Metal Frame, 1 5/8 In. 91.00
Dexterity Puzzle, Monks Drinking, Paper Lithograph, Frame, Prewar, 1 7/8 In. 102.00
Dexterity Puzzle, Mouse, Metal, Paper, Metal Frame, Japan, 1950s, 2 1/8 In. 22.00
Dexterity Puzzle, Skull, Paper Lithograph, Cardboard, Frame, Occupied Japan, 1940 . .   30.00
Dexterity Puzzle, Soccer Players, Europe, 1940s, 1 3/4 In. . . . .*Illus*   105.00
Dexterity Puzzle, Squirrel With Nut, Paper Lithograph, Frame, Prewar 55.00
Dexterity Puzzle, Woman In Kitchen, Paper Lithograph, Celluloid, 2 3/8 In. 154.00
Dice, Casino, Sealed, 1930s 50.00
Dino The Dinosaur, Transogram, Box, 1961, 15 x 8 In. 60.00
Down You Go, Selchow & Righter, 1954 . . . .   20.00
Dr. Kildare, Ideal, 1962 . . . .*Illus*   17.00
Dragnet, Target Game, Box 475.00
Dragnet, Transogram, Jack Webb, Unused, 1955 . . . .*Illus*   55.00
Fast Mail, Milton Bradley 195.00
Feeley Meeley, Milton Bradley, 1967 . . . .   15.00
Felix The Cat Rummy Card Game, Felix Prod., 1960 . . . .*Illus*   20.00
Flag Game, About The United Nations, Parker Brothers, 1961 . . . .   24.00
Flipper Flips, Mattel, 1965 . . . .   75.00
Football, Arcade, Chester Pollard, 1924 . . . .   2700.00
Football, Tudor, Electric, Box, 1949 . . . . .50.00 to 55.00
Fox & Geese, Painted Gray, Green, Board, Early 19th Century, 12 1/4 In. 295.00
G.I. Joe, Marine Paratrooper, 1965 . . . .   50.00
G.I. Joe, Milton Bradley, Board, 1986 . . . .   20.00
Game Of Baseball, McLoughlin Bros., Board, 1886 . . . .*Illus*   1610.00
Gang Busters, Marx, Tin, Board, Box, 1940 . . . .   375.00
George Of The Jungle, Parker Bros., Green Jungle, Board, 1968, 8 3/4 x 17 In. 35.00
Great Stampede West, Center Map Of West, Properties Outlined, Delight, 1981 . . . . .   50.00
Have Gun Will Travel, Board 95.00
Henry Fonda Deputy 40.00
Herb Shriner's TV Harmonica Jamboree, Instructions, Harmonica, c.1950 . . . .   157.00
Hialeah, Milton Bradley, 1940 . . . .   65.00
Hippety-Hop, Corey Games, Fairy Tale Characters, 1940 . . . .   75.00
Hollywood Squares, Western Publishing, 1967 . . . .   35.00
Home Run Baseball, McLoughlin, 1897 . . . .   2070.00

Game, Baseball &
Checkers,
Lithographed,
Wooden Pieces,
Milton Bradley,
c.1900

Game, Cross Country Race By Land, Air & Sea,
Chicago Game Co., 1911

Game, Dexterity Puzzle, Clown, Juggling, Europe, 1940s, 1 3/4 In.

Game, Dexterity Puzzle, Man, Bowtie, Europe, 1940s, 1 3/4 In.

Game, Dexterity Puzzle, Man, Hat, Europe, 1940s, 1 3/4 In.

Game, Dexterity Puzzle, Soccer Players, Europe, 1940s, 1 3/4 In.

Horse Racing, Horses On Outer Rim, Numbered Inner Rim, 2 Sides 3500.00
Horse Racing, Milton Bradley, Metal Dice, 1935 . . . . 100.00
Horseshoe Set, Rubber, Auburn, Box 20.00
Huggin' The Rail, Selchow & Righter, 6 Racing Cards, Lane Locator, Board 66.00
Ice Hockey, Gotham, Pressed Steel, Board 230.00
Innocence Abroad, Parker Brothers, Box, c.1888 . . . . 195.00
Jack & Beanstalk Adventure, Transogram, Box, 15 x 7 In. 20.00
Jan Murray's Charge Account, Lowell, TV, 1961 . . . . 20.00
Jeannette Horseshoe, Tin Lithograph, 3 Hard Rubber Shoes, Box 525.00
Jeopardy, Board, 1964 . . . . 40.00
Junior Combination, Milton Bradley, Board, 1905 . . . . 105.00
Kelly Pool, 9 Balls, Box, 10 x 18 In. 95.00
King Kong, Milton Bradley, Board, 1966 . . . . 15.00
Knockout Electronic Boxing, With Instructions, Box, 1950s 195.00
Kojak Stake Out Detective, Sealed 15.00
Laverne & Shirley, Parker Brothers, Board, 1977 . . . . 20.00
Leave It To Beaver, Rocket To Moon, Hasbro, Box 125.00
Li'l Abner, Parker Brothers 45.00
Lightning Express, Milton Bradley, Antique Train Engine On Cover, 1930s 85.00
Mah-Jongg, Ivory-Type, Case, 1920s 125.00
Mammoth Hunt, Cadeco, Board, 1962 . . . . 38.00
Mary Poppins, Illustration Of Mary & Friends On A Carousel 39.00
Missing Suspect, Perry Mason, Transogram, 1959 . . . . 40.00
Monopoly, Parker Brothers, Box, 1946 . . . . 20.00
Motor Race, Wolverine, Metal, Box 235.00
Mouse Trap, Ideal, 1970 . . . . 10.00
Mr. Magoo, Lowe, Box, 1961, 10 x 20 In. 80.00
Mr. President, 3M Company, Bookshelf Game Series, 1967 . . . . 30.00
Mrs. Potato Head, Hasbro 20.00
Musingo, Mattel, Crank-Operated Man, Music Box, 1962 . . . . 24.00
New Pretty Village, McLoughlin Bros., Board, Box, 16 x 11 3/4 In. 40.00
Newlywed, Hasbro, ABC TV Show, 1969 . . . . 15.00
Ocean, Parker Brothers, Box, c.1893 . . . . 175.00
Old Maid, Whitman, Cards, Box, Late 1950s 16.00
Operation, Milton Bradley, 1965 . . . . 20.00
Our Gang, Buckwheat, Mego, Board 25.00
Parlor Football, McLoughlin, 1891 . . . . 1380.00
Peanuts, Selchow & Righter, Box, 1959, 10 x 20 In. 80.00
Peter Rabbit, Pewter Playing Pieces 140.00
Philip Marlowe, Transogram, 1960 . . . . 65.00
Pigs In Clover, Wooden Bottom, Wooden Pen, 4 Clay Marbles, 6 In. 80.00
Pin The Nose On Pinocchio, Parker Brothers, Board, 1939, 14 3/4 x 17 In. 90.00
Pinball, Hanna Barbera, Japan 175.00
Pinball, Spider Man, Hasbro, 1976 . . . . 45.00
Pinky Lee, Who Am I, Ed-U-Cards, 1950s 20.00
Pirate & Traveler, Milton Bradley, Board, Box, 10 1/4 x 16 3/4 x 1 1/2 In. 40.00
Pitch-Em, Indoor Horseshoe, Walbeat, Complete 25.00

Game, Dr. Kildare, Ideal, 1962

Game, Felix
The Cat
Rummy Card
Game, Felix
Prod., 1960

Game, Dragnet, Transogram,
Jack Webb, Unused, 1955

Planet Of The Apes, Milton Bradley, Board, 1974	50.00
Poker Chips, 49'er Club, 25 Dollar Value	175.00
Poker Chips, Clay, Indian Chief, Walnut Hexagonal Chest, Key, 200 Piece	575.00
Poker Chips, Dunes, Las Vegas, Last Issue Includes Baccarat To 25,000.00	1250.00
Poker Chips, El Rancho Vegas Hotel, 25 Dollar Value	325.00
Poker Chips, Harrah's, Blackhawk, Colorado, 25 Dollar, 1993	100.00
Poker Chips, Regal Service Station, Green, Small Greek Key, 1 Dollar	18.00
Poker Chips, Silver Slipper, Las Vegas, Bicentennial	100.00
Poker Chips, Stardust, Hexagonal Mold, 25 Dollar Value	75.00
Poker Chips, Union Plaza Bicentennial, 5 Dollar, 1976	35.00
Poosh-M-Up Jr., Pinball, Table Top, Northwestern Products, Box, 1930s	45.00 to 98.00
Puck Luck Hockey, Schaper, Magnetic, 1950s	32.00
Puss In The Corner, Samuel Gabriel & Sons, Kitties & Kids, Kitty Markers, 1940s	85.00
Puzzle, Barney & Betty In A Car Getting Speeding Ticket, 1960	33.00
Puzzle, Bobbsey Twins, Box, 1958	18.00 to 22.00
Puzzle, Buster Crabbe As Tarzan, 1930s	85.00
Puzzle, Captain Crunch, Sticky Wicket, Cereal Premium, Box, 1970	85.00
Puzzle, Captain Kangaroo, Fairchild, 1956	15.00
Puzzle, City Of Worcester, McLoughlin, Box	715.00
Puzzle, Crusader Rabbit	30.00
Puzzle, Dale's Put-Away Puzzle, Whitman, Black Ink, 1950s, 9 1/2 x 14 In.	88.00
Puzzle, Dennis The Menace, Frame Tray, 1987	17.00
Puzzle, Dougan Club Rye Whisky, Colored Rings, Bar	35.00
Puzzle, Dr. Seuss, Esso Premium, 1930, 11 x 17 In.	183.00
Puzzle, Family Affair, Whitman, 1970	15.00
Puzzle, Flipper, Whitman, 1960s	20.00
Puzzle, Ghost At Large, Addams Family, Booklet	65.00
Puzzle, Jiminy Cricket, Jaymar, Inlaid Wood, Box	65.00
Puzzle, Journey To The Center Of The Earth, 1969	15.00
Puzzle, Kermitage Pigs, American Gothic, Colorforms No. 518, Box, 1986	35.00
Puzzle, Liberty, Wreath, White Sewing Machine, Factory, Morgan, 11 x 18 In.	300.00
Puzzle, Lord Of The Rings, Gandalf & Frodo Frame Tray	25.00
Puzzle, Mighty Mouse, 1940s	25.00
Puzzle, Outer Limits, Milton Bradley	75.00
Puzzle, Pink Panther, CFD, Box, Sealed, 100 Piece	10.00
Puzzle, Playboy, Tin Container, 1968	16.00
Puzzle, Punch & Judy, Lithographed, 4 Stage Scenes, Frame, Box	172.00

Puzzle, Raggedy Ann, Milton Bradley 55.00
Puzzle, Rainy Day & Balloon, Hood's, Reversible, Original Box, 1890s 150.00
Puzzle, Reddy To Serve, Reddy Kilowatt, Plastic 14.50
Puzzle, Sailing Steam Ship, McLoughlin 192.50
Puzzle, Sergeant Preston, Milton Bradley, Frame 75.00
Puzzle, Ship Pilgrim, Fall River Line, McLoughlin 522.50
Puzzle, Starsky & Hutch, Box 30.00
Puzzle, The Fall Guy, Lee Majors, Craft Master, Sealed Box, 1983 .... 25.00
Puzzle, Tom Corbet Space Cadet, Frame, Saalfield, 10 1/2 x 11 1/2 In. ....65.00 to 75.00
Puzzle, Vess Soda, Envelope, 9 Piece 20.00
Puzzle, Welcome Back Kotter, Frame Tray, 1977 .... 5.00
Quick Draw McGraw Magic Rub-Off, Whitman, Board 50.00
Quoits, Table, Box, 1910 .... 45.00
Ra-Sera, The Egyptian Fortune Telling Game, Pilgrim Products, Board, 1950s 50.00
Racing Greyhound, J.J. & Cie, France, 19th Century 137.50
Radio Game, Milton Bradley, 1920s 75.00
Rebel, Ideal, Board, 1961 .... 65.00
Rich Uncle, Parker Brothers, 1955 .... 65.00
Rin-Tin-Tin, Board, Transogram, 1955 ....25.00 to 35.00
Ring Toss, Ohio Art, Box 40.00
Roadrunner, Roadrunner On Cover, Board, Box, 1968 .... 63.00
Rock-A-Bye Birdies, Selchow & Righter, 1900s, 12-In. Board 75.00
Round The World With Nellie Bly, Pictures Statue Of Liberty, Board, c.1895 .... 125.00
Sgt. Bilko, Phil Silvers Picture 80.00
Skor-It, 11 x 17 In. ....*Illus* 70.00
Skunk, Schader, 1950s 20.00
Soldiers Cavalry, McLoughlin, 16 Mounted Cavaliers, Wood Stands, Board 165.00
Soldiers On Guard, McLoughlin, 24 Zouaves On Wood Bases, Board, Wooden Box ... 330.00
Solitaire Set, 28 Marbles, Box Depicting Bearded Man Playing Game, Board, 9 x 7 In. .. 200.00
Solitaire Set, 28 Marbles, Green Paint Around 9 Holes, Board, 7 3/4 x 1 1/2 In. 180.00
Spider Man, Ideal, Web Spinning Action, 1979 .... 45.00
Spin To Win, Time Tunnel, Pressman, Box 80.00
Spot-A-Plane, Toy Creations, Silhouette Cards, 1942 .... 225.00
Star Trek, Ideal, Shatner & Nimoy On Bridge Box, 1967 .... 130.00
Star Wars, Kenner 35.00
Steve Canyon, Lowell, 1959, 10 x 20 In., Box ....45.00 to 60.00
Story Cards, Ed-U-Cards, Box, 1947 .... 18.00
Submarine, Avalon Hill, 1977 .... 20.00
Susceptibles, A Parlor Amusement, McLoughlin, Board, 1891 .... 357.50
Sweeps Horserace, All Fair, 1943 .... 30.00
Tantalizer, Northern Signal Co., Pictures People Enjoying Game, Box, 1965, 16 x 10 ... 75.00
Target, Black Sambo, Board 125.00
Target, Gang Busters, Marx, P.H. Lord & Co., Tin, Box, 1940 ....295.00 to 375.00
Target, Gunfight At O.K. Corral, 2 Pine Trees, 1 Cactus Plant, Plastic, 2 1/2 x 14 1/4 In. .. 75.00
Target, Maxfield Parrish, Parker Brothers, Copyright 1913, 24 In. 623.00
Target, Sharp Shooters, Milton Bradley, Iron Gun 195.00
Tarzan To The Rescue, Milton Bradley, 1977 .... 20.00

**The best time to
buy an antique is
when you see it.**

Game, Game Of Baseball,
McLoughlin Bros., Board, 1886

Game, Skor-It, 11 x 17 In.

**If there are traces of glue
on the back of a label, soak
the label and carefully
scrape the glue off under
water. Then dry flat.**

Tell It To The Judge, Eddie Cantor Pictured, Board, 1930s	35.00
Thinking Man's Golf, 1967	60.00
Thunderball, Milton Bradley, 1965	60.00
Tiddlywinks, Huckle Berry Hound, 1960	23.00
Tortoise & Hare, Russell Mfg. Co., Multicolored Lithograph, Box, 1922, 10 x 6 In.	125.00
Touring, Parker Brothers, Card, 1926	48.00
Traffic Jam, Harett-Gilmar, 1954	75.00
Tree Tag, Girls, Chasing Each Other, Yellow, Orange, Board, Black Paper Label, 6 x 1 In.	61.00
Trik-Trak, Dare Devil, Transogram, Instructions, Box	40.00
Twilight Zone, Ideal, Board	125.00
Uncle Remus, Marble, Parker Brothers	100.00
Uncle Sam's Mail, McLoughlin Bros., c.1893	115.00
Uncle Sam's Postman, Bradley, Board Part Of Box Bottom, Letters, Spinner, 1890	393.00
Undersea World Of Jacques Cousteau, Parker Brothers, Box, 1968	25.00
Vince Lombardi, Research Games, Board, 1970	10.00
Voyage To The Bottom Of The Sea, Card, 1964	65.00
Welcome Back Kotter, Ideal, 1974	24.00
Wheel, Red, Black, Yellow & Green, 23 1/2 In.	195.00
Whirlpool, McLoughlin, Board Part Of Box Bottom, Spinner, Playing Pieces, 7 x 7 In.	130.00
Winnie The Pooh, Box, 1933	50.00
World's Educator Art & Science, W.S. Reed Toy Co., Questions, Answers, Box	82.00
Yacht Race Game, McLoughlin, Showing New York Harbor, Board, 1887	467.50
Zaxxon, Milton Bradley, 1982	15.00

GAME PLATES are plates of any make decorated with pictures of birds,
animals, or fish. The game plates usually came in sets consisting of
twelve dishes and a serving platter. These sets were most popular during the 1880s.

GAME PLATE, Elks, Deer, Moose, Mountain Goats, National China Co., 5 Piece	210.00
Lapwing, Gold Encrusted, Signed, 1893	245.00
Little Grebe, Gold Encrusted, Signed, 1893	245.00
GAME SET, Turkey Center, Brown Transfer Border, Platter, Royal Cauldon, 10 Piece	575.00
Wild Turkey, Brown Transfer, Border, Porcelain, Johnson Bros., 10 In., 12 Piece	260.00

GARDEN FURNISHINGS have been popular for centuries. The stone or
metal statues, wire, iron, or rustic furniture, urns and fountains, sundials, and small figurines are included in this category. Many of the
metal pieces have been made continuously for years.

Basin, Animal Bust Handles, Oval, Marble, India, 62 In.	9775.00
Basin, Roman Style, Double Welled, Center Cross, Marble, 1920s, 17 1/2 x 42 In.	3450.00
Basket, Fruit, Grapes, Apples, Pomegranates, Iron Loop Handles, Terra-Cotta, 29 In.	517.00
Bench, Fern Design, Cast Iron, Black, 59 1/2 In.	825.00
Bench, Intertwining Branches Supports, Dog Busts End Armrests, Iron, Wood, 58 In.	1725.00

Bench, Iron, Semicircular, Griffin Front Legs & Arms, White, 43 In.	150.00
Bench, Laurel, Black Paint, Iron, Hinderer's Iron Works, 1890, 33 x 43 In., Pair	2055.00
Bench, Moghul Style, Pierced Triple Back, Scrolled Sides, Marble, India, 66 In.	9200.00
Bench, Pierced Foliate Back & Sides, Lattice Seat, In-Scrolled Legs, Cast Metal	402.00
Bench, Plain Molded Rim, Concrete, 15 1/2 x 48 In.	55.00
Bench, Rectangular Seat, Scrolled Legs, Marble, 57 In.	5175.00
Bench, Reticulated Leaf Design, Cast Iron	220.00
Bench, Strapwork, Out Scrolled Crest & Arms, Wrought Iron, Painted Gray, 48 In.	907.00
Bench, White Paint, Cast Iron, Kramer Bros., Fdy Co., Dayton, Oh, 43 In.	1018.00
Bench, Wire, Lattice, Rusted White Paint, Victorian, 36 1/2 In.	165.00
Bench, Wire, Painted White	385.00
Birdbath, Figural Nude Pedestal, Cast Iron, 27 In.	143.00
Birdbath, Leaf Tip Carved Standard, Lotus Blossom Font, India, 47 In.	3450.00
Birdbath, Putto Upholding Fluted Bowl, Lead, 26 In.	725.00
Chair, Cast Iron, Painted White, c.1900, Pair	467.00
Chair, Foliate Circular Back, Pierced & Leaf Tip Seat, Cast Iron, Painted, Motts, Pair	460.00
Chair, Neoclassical, Cast Iron, White Paint, Pair	1430.00
Chair, Swivel Base, Iron, Arms, White Paint, 29 In., Pair	220.00
Chair, Winged Ornament Back Panel, Molded Arms Ending In Rams' Heads, Cast Iron	2175.00
Chair Set, Square Back Centered By Geometric Sunburst, Wrought Iron, 4 Piece	1955.00
Figure, Allegorical Woman, Cast Iron, 19th Century, 4 Ft., Pair .... *Illus*	7800.00
Figure, Allegorical, Crowned, Dressed In Renaissance Costume, Clay, 39 In.	3450.00
Figure, Apollo, Marble, Italy, 56 In.	3737.00
Figure, Armadillo, Glass Eyes, Limestone, William Kent, 1956, 29 In.	1495.00
Figure, Bird & Frog, Malachite, Turquoise Eyes, Limestone, William Kent, 1955, 20 In.	690.00
Figure, Capitoline Venus, Marble, 26 1/2 In.	2875.00
Figure, Cherub, Carrying Basket On Head, Lead, 19th Century, 30 In.	515.00
Figure, Classical Woman, Cast Stone, 60 1/2 In.	4312.00
Figure, Deer, Walking Forward, Cast Iron, 19th Century, 64 In.	7475.00
Figure, Elegant Woman, Holding Up Skirt, Carved Limestone, 19th Century, 52 In.	3795.00
Figure, Four Seasons, Lead, 19 1/2 In., 4 Piece	3450.00
Figure, Girl, With Goose, Green Matte Glaze, Weller, 22 In.	550.00
Figure, Hercules, Stone, Italy, 17th Century, 53 In.	3737.00
Figure, Hunter, Dog At Feet, Stone, Neoclassical Style, 60 In.	2500.00
Figure, Indian Maiden, Iron, 5 Ft. 3 In.	6050.00
Figure, Lion & Unicorn, Lying, Half Round Base, Iron, 15 & 27 1/2 In., Pair	1400.00
Figure, Lion, Roaring, Full Mane, Marble, 42 In., Pair	8050.00
Figure, Putti, 4 Seasons, Stone, Neoclassical Style, 61 In., 4 Piece	5520.00
Figure, Putto, Wide Sash & Hat, Plinth Base, Cement, Continental, 22 In.	547.00
Figure, Rabbit, Cast Iron, 11 In.	195.00
Figure, River God, On Rocky Base Beside Fish, Stone, 53 In.	4600.00
Figure, Sphinx, Stone, 31 In., 4 Piece	2587.00

Lead garden sculpture should not be cleaned. The dirt and discoloration adds to the beauty of the piece. Lead is so soft that most types of cleaning will harm the finish.

Garden, Figure, Allegorical Woman,
Cast Iron, 19th Century, 4 Ft., Pair

Figure, Swan, Bronze, 36 In. 2587.00
Figure, Whippets, Reclining, Cast Iron, White Paint, 1920s, 18 x 39 In., Pair 1610.00
Figure, Woman, Green, Cast Iron, Late 19th Century, 70 In. 3450.00
Fountain, Cherub, Zinc 1320.00
Fountain, Egret, Mouth Plumbed, Zinc, 46 In. 4887.00
Fountain, Figural, 2 Putti Holding Floral Swags, Plumbed In Basin, Cast Stone, 7 Ft. 6325.00
Fountain, Figural, Mermaid, Lead, Wheeler Williams, 1939, 62 In. 3450.00
Fountain, Masks, Foliate, Geometric Designs, Fiske Co., Cast Iron, 65 In. 1760.00
Fountain, Putto Holding Fish, Mouth Plumbed, Stone, 48 In. 3737.00
Fountain, Wall, Coat Of Arms Continuing To Basin, Nozzle At Back, Cast Iron, 29 In. . . . 460.00
Frog, Majolica, Green, c.1880 . . . . 1560.00
Gate, Foliate Scrolls, Wrought Iron, Painted, 60 x 38 In., Pair 2875.00
Gate, Pierced With Scrolls, Joined By Flower Heads, Painted Wrought Iron, 6 Ft., Pair . . 4887.00
Gate, Scrolled Cornice, Wreaths, Square Doors, Wrought Iron, 52 1/2 x 74 In., Pair 5750.00
Jardiniere, Alternating Bands With Cherub Masks & Rosettes, Terra-Cotta, 31 In. 805.00
Jardiniere, Egg & Dart Frieze, Lion Masks, Fruit & Garlands, 22 1/2 In. 690.00
Lantern, Baluster Form, Symbols, Carved Granite, China, 99 In. 8625.00
Planter, M. Murray, Baltimore, Cast Iron, c.1860, 19 In. 1500.00
Planter, Wire, Green Paint, 20th Century, 40 1/2 In. 374.00
Seat, Birds Amid Flowering Branches, Chinese Export, 18 1/2 In., Pair 805.00
Seat, Elephant, Green & Yellow, White Ground, 21 1/2 In. 105.00
Seat, Fern Pattern, Painted Cast Iron, James W. Carr, 19th Century, 38 In. 3737.00
Seat, Overall Scrolls & Flowers, Pink Ground, Porcelain, England, 20 1/2 In. 1380.00
Seat, Scallop Shell Design, Majolica, Blue & White, 14 1/2 In., Pair 115.00
Settee, Chairs, Rays Of Foliate Scrolls On Back & Seat, Painted Wire, c.1900, 3 Piece . . 3450.00
Settee, Fern Pattern, Cast Iron, Painted, 56 In. 1725.00
Settee, Grape Pattern, Cast Iron, c.1870 . . . . 675.00
Settee, Pair Of Armchairs, Pierced Foliate Back & Sides, Cast Metal 2587.00
Sprinkler, Alligator, Cast Iron 410.00
Sprinkler, Duck, Cast Iron 264.00
Sprinkler, Frog, Coppertone, Weller, 5 3/4 In. 850.00
Sprinkler, Lawn, Nelson, Tractor Style, Cast Iron, 16 x 18 In. 375.00
Stool, Pierced Circular Top, Cast Iron, Black Paint, 13 In., Pair 345.00
Sundial, Brass Gnomon, Slate, Octagonal, 5 Minute Divisions, Signed, 1835, 12 In. 1100.00
Sundial, Engraved For Italian Time, Ivory, Equino & Tiolos, 3 1/4 In. 633.00
Sundial, Iron, Manufacturer's Logo Bottom, Roman Numerals, 1870-1900, 12 In. 295.00
Sundial, Stone Pedestal, Bronze 1265.00
Surround, Tree, Regency Style, Wrought Iron, 19th Century 8625.00
Surround, Tree, Victorian Style, Intertwining Grapevines, Cast Iron 1495.00
Table, Baluster Decorated With Herons, Slate Blue, 28 1/2 In. 805.00
Table, Pierced Tilt Top, Astrological Figures On Trellis, Cast Iron, 1860s, 28 1/2 In. 2875.00
Table, Wrought Iron, Rouge Royale Marble Top, 20th Century, 22 In. 190.00
Trellis, Arched Top, Hinged Doors, Wrought Iron, 8 Ft. 6 In. x 4 Ft. 2 In. 805.00
Urn, Campana, Cast Lead Design, Black Body, Bows Each End, 24 x 17 1/2 In. 1500.00
Urn, Draping Cords, Bust Of Abraham Lincoln, Cast Iron 1000.00
Urn, Egg, Dart, Waist Knop Support, Cast Iron, Black, 29 In., Pair 1330.00
Urn, Figures Of Putti, Holding A Vessel, Cast Lead, 21 1/2 In. 785.00
Urn, Fish, 3 Part Base, Kramer Brothers, Iron, 26 In., Pair 2420.00
Urn, Foliate Swags, Cast Stone, 23 In., Pair 6325.00
Urn, Grape & Leaf Design, Fluted Pedestal, Cast Iron, 28 x 20 1/2 In. 275.00
Urn, Green, Cast Iron, 10 In., Pair 110.00
Urn, Kramer Bros. Co., Dayton, Oh, Dark Green Paint, 39 1/4 In. 660.00
Urn, Kramer Bros., Fdy Co., Dayton, Oh, Cast Iron, 32 1/4 In. 135.00
Urn, Plinth Base, Cast Iron, Victorian, 32 1/2 In. 847.00
Urn, Scroll Design, Cast Iron, Gray, 29 In. 200.00
Urn, Scroll Design, Square Pedestal Base, Cast Iron, 29 In. 200.00
Urn, Scrolled Handles, Cast Iron, 12 In., Pair 515.00
Urn, Square Plinth, Cast Iron, Black Paint, 25 In. 165.00
Urn, White Paint, C.E. Walbridge, Cast Iron, 1873, 34 1/4 In. 245.00
Urn, White Paint, Cast Iron, 58 1/2 In. 770.00
Urn, White Paint, Kramer Bros., Fdy Co., Dayton, Oh., Cast Iron, 23 In. 110.00
Urn, White, Cast Iron, 27 x 23 3/4 In. 190.00

GAUDY DUTCH pottery was made in England for America from about 1810 to 1820. It is a white earthenware with Imari-style decorations of red, blue, green, yellow, and black. Only sixteen patterns of Gaudy Dutch were made: Butterfly, Carnation, Dahlia, Double Rose, Dove, Grape, Leaf, Oyster, Primrose, Single Rose, Strawflower, Sunflower, Urn, War Bonnet, Zinnia, and No Name. Other similar wares are called *Gaudy Ironstone* and *Gaudy Welsh*.

Bowl, Carnation, 5 1/2 In.	165.00
Bowl, Dove, 5 1/2 x 2 5/8 In.	660.00
Bowl, Dove, 6 1/2 x 3 1/8 In.	1485.00
Cup & Saucer, No Handle, Rose	275.00 to 410.00
Cup Plate, Grape	850.00 to 1550.00
Cup Plate, Single Rose, 4 In.	2750.00
Cup Plate, War Bonnet, 3 1/2 In.	1950.00
Plate, Carnation, 7 3/8 In.	330.00
Plate, Rose, 9 7/8 In.	550.00
Plate, Toddy, Carnation, 6 1/2 In.	935.00
Plate, War Bonnet, 9 3/4 In.	550.00
Soup, Dish, Grape	1400.00
Soup, Dish, War Bonnet, 8 In.	1200.00
Soup, Dish, War Bonnet, 10 In.	2050.00
Teapot, War Bonnet, 5 3/4 In.	800.00
Waste Bowl, Dove, 3 1/4 x 6 1/2 In.	825.00
Waste Bowl, Rose, 5 1/2 In.	355.00

GAUDY IRONSTONE is the collector's name for the ironstone wares with the bright patterns similar to Gaudy Dutch. It was made in England for the American market. There may be other examples found in the listing for Ironstone or under the name of the ceramic factory.

Compote, Chinoiserie Garden Scene, 9 1/2 x 5 In.	143.00
Plate, Floral & Strawberry, 10 5/8 In.	385.00
Plate, Floral, 10 1/4 In.	75.00
Plate, Strawberry, Flowers, Marked, T. Walker, 9 7/8 In.	275.00
Plate, Vase Of Flowers, Polychrome Enamel, 8 5/8 In., Pair	385.00
Scent Bottle, Floral Design, Copper Luster On Blue Ground, 5 In.	95.00
Syrup, Metal Lid	140.00
Teapot, Red & Blue	95.00
Tureen, Undertray, Green, Red & Blue Flowers, 14 3/4 In.	135.00

GAUDY WELSH is an Imari-decorated earthenware with red, blue, green, and gold decorations. Most Gaudy Welsh was made in England for the American market. It was made after 1820.

Chocolate Pot, Cottageware, Kensington, England	110.00
Condiment Set, Cottageware, Kensington, England	55.00
Mug, Cider, Grape Pattern, c.1830, 5 x 4 1/2 In.	525.00
Mustard, Metal Cover, 3 In.	28.00
Pitcher, Face Under Green Handle, Blue, Orange Trim, Floral, 5 In.	178.00
Plate, Scalloped Edge, Square, 8 1/2 In.	75.00
Sugar, Cottageware, Kensington, England	38.00

GEISHA GIRL porcelain was made for export in the late nineteenth century in Japan. It was an inexpensive porcelain often sold in dime stores or used as free premiums. Pieces are sometimes marked with the name of a store. Japanese ladies in kimonos are pictured on the dishes. There are over 125 recorded patterns. Borders of red, blue, green, gold, brown, or several of these colors were used. Modern reproductions are being made.

Chocolate Set, 6 Piece	165.00
Creamer, Rectangular Underplate	22.00
Teapot	65.00

GENE AUTRY was born in 1907. He began his career as the *Singing Cowboy* in 1928. His first movie appearance was in 1934, his last in 1958. His likeness and that of the Wonder Horse, Champion, were used on toys, books, lunch boxes, and advertisements.

Badge, Deputy Sheriff, Brass, 12 Point	225.00
Big Little Book, No. 1414, 1930s	20.00
Book, Better Little Book, Gene Serenading, Whitman, 1943	54.00
Book, Songbook Deluxe, 1938	35.00 to 40.00
Book, Western Scrap, 50 Original Cards, 1942	225.00
Button, Gene Autry & Champ, Gene On Saddle, Yellow Ground, 1950	22.00
Button, Gene Autry, Black & White, Blue Ground, 1940s	24.00
Button, Pinback, Sunbeam Bread	20.00
Cap Gun, 1939	150.00
Cap Gun, Canton, Bright Finish	195.00
Cap Gun, Leslie-Henry, 44	150.00
Coloring Book, Whitman, 1950, 48 Pages, 11 x 14 In.	20.00
Comic Book, 1944	125.00
Cookie Jar, Limited Edition	195.00
Decals, Meyercord, On Card, 1950s	50.00
Game, Bandit Trail, Kenton, 10 x 19 In.	183.00
Guitar, Emenee, Box	225.00
Guitar, Handle, Metal, Original Box	245.00
Gun, Cast Iron, Pearl Grips, Kenton	150.00
Lobby Card, Back In The Saddle, Gene, With Guitar, 1941	25.00
Lobby Card, Comin' Round The Mountain, Title Card, 1936	165.00
Lobby Card, Under Blue Montana Skies, Gene & Smiley	15.00
Lobby Card Set, Stardust On The Sage, 1942, 11 x 14 In.	375.00
Outfit, Hat, Rope, Shirt, Vest, Chaps, Box	475.00
Program, Souvenir, 1941	25.00
Record, Christmas, 1978	24.00
Record, Gene Autry At The Rodeo, Columbia, 45 RPM, 1950s	8.00
Sheet Music, South Of The Border, 1939	10.00
Sheet Music, You're The Only Star, 1938	10.00
Shirt, Custom Made, 1940s	2000.00
Stencil Book	25.00
Wristwatch, Alligator Leather Strap, Wilane Watch Co., Box	358.00
Wristwatch, Animated	325.00
Wristwatch, Chrome Finish, Alligator Design, Wilane Watch Co., Box	330.00

GIBSON GIRL black-and-blue decorated plates were made in the early 1900s. Twenty-four different 10 1/2-inch plates were made by the Royal Doulton pottery at Lambeth, England. These pictured scenes from the book *A Widow and Her Friends* by Charles Dana Gibson. Another set of twelve 9-inch plates featuring pictures of the heads of Gibson Girls had all-blue decoration. Many other items also pictured the famous Gibson Girl.

Plate, A Quiet Dinner With Dr. Bottles	110.00
Plate, She Contemplates The Cloister	110.00
Plate, She Goes To Fancy Dress Ball As Juliet, 10 1/2 In.	85.00 to 155.00
Plate, Widow & Friends, She Finds Consolation, 10 1/2 In.	95.00

GIRL SCOUT collectors search for anything pertaining to the Girl Scouts, including uniforms, publications, and old cookie boxes. The Girl Scout movement started in 1912, two years after the Boy Scouts. It began under Juliette Gordon Low of Savannah, Georgia. The first Girl Scout cookies were sold in 1928.

Book, Songs, 1956, Pocket	20.00
Bookmark, Stamped Metal, Trefoil Shape, Silver Finish	29.00
Calendar, 1934, Hintermeister, 11 x 23 In.	225.00
Handbook, 1939	15.00
Handbook, Intermediate Program, 1953, 510 Pages	10.00 to 12.50
Hat, Leader's, Green & White Cotton, Satin Band, Size-21 1/2	30.00

Hatchet, Girl Scouts Of America, Plumb, 11 In.	45.00
Medal, National Capital Area Council, Brown, Yellow Ribbon, 1967	25.00

GLASS-ART. Art glass means any of the many forms of glassware made during the late nineteenth or early twentieth century. These wares were expensive and production was limited. Art glass is not the typical commercial glass that was made in large quantities, and most of the art glass was produced by hand methods. Later twentieth-century glass is listed under Glass-Contemporary, Glass-Midcentury, or Glass-Venetian. Even more art glass may be found in categories such as Burmese, Cameo Glass, Tiffany, Venini, and other factory names.

Beaker, Enameled Floral On Both Sides, Germany, 1860, 4 In.	75.00
Beaker, Enameled Landscape & Harbor Scene, Haida, 1875, 5 In.	695.00
Beaker, Family Group Transfer, Seated Around A Table, Purple, Russia, 19th Century	1035.00
Box, Blue, Cover, Silver Colored Metal, Black Enamel, G.A. Scheid, 1901, 2 1/2 In.	600.00
Box, Enameled Dancing Woman On 2 Sides, Haida, 1920, 3 3/4 x 2 1/4 In.	240.00
Candy, Dish, Pumpkin Shape, Crackled, Mold Blown, 5 1/2 In.	145.00
Chalice, Stem, Opalescent Trailing, Crimped Rim, James Powell & Sons, 12 In.	795.00
Champagne, Clear, Green Stem, Enameled, Art Nouveau, Theresienthal, 1910, 7 In.	285.00
Compote, Etched Nude Woman, Starry Sky, Amber, Footed, Salir, 1925, 8 1/2 In.	1100.00
Cordial, Cut, Panel, Gilded Design, 3 3/4 In., 10 Piece	400.00
Cup & Saucer, Latticinio, Rigaree	195.00
Cuspidor, Clear Over White Glass, Red Enamel Spatter, 2 3/4 In.	95.00
Goblet, Art Deco Enameled Design, Haida, 1930, 11 1/2 In.	460.00
Goblet, Clear, Blue Swirl Bowl, With Red Swirl Stirrer, Bimini, 1920, 3 3/8 In.	44.00
Goblet, Clear, Green Stem, Enameled Art Nouveau, Theresienthal, 1910, 9 In.	310.00
Jar, Biscuit, Allover Circle With Flower Inside, Turquoise, White Clear Cased Interior	350.00
Tumbler, Cobalt & Silver Feather, Large, Pair	65.00
Tumbler Set, Liquor, Different Color Bowls, Black Foot, 1930s, 6 Piece	110.00
Vase, Amber, Internal & External Applied Allover Design, Handles, 20 In.	245.00
Vase, Art Deco Enameled Design, Haida, 1930, 5 3/4 In.	310.00
Vase, Art Deco Enameled Design, Theresienthal, 1910, 5 3/4 In.	85.00
Vase, Blue Tinted, Wilhem Wagenfeld, Paris, 1936, 12 1/8 In.	1035.00
Vase, Clear, Internal Green & Ruby Design, WMF, 1920, 9 1/2 In.	345.00
Vase, Enameled Floral Design, Black, Josef Hoffmann, 1925, 5 3/4 In.	1380.00
Vase, Green To Blue, Enameled Lacy Gold Vine, Bulbous Bowl, Footed, 6 1/2 In.	235.00
Vase, Pink Cased, Flower Shape Top, Applied Clear Petals, 14 1/2 In.	395.00
Vase, Smoky, Cut Swallows & Waves, 9 x 8 1/2 In.	165.00
Vase, Topaz, Etched, Art Deco Vertical Arches, Flared Rim, Lorraine, France, 11 In.	460.00

GLASS-CONTEMPORARY includes pieces by glass artists working after 1975. Many of these pieces are free-form, one-of-a-kind sculptures. Paperweights by contemporary artists are listed in the Paperweight category. Earlier studio glass may be found listed under Glass-Midcentury or Glass-Venetian.

Figurine, Gaucho, Green, Solid, Italy, 12 In.	95.00
Figurine, Viking, Pukebergs	65.00
Sculpture, Orange, Red, White, Sea Green Interior, 1990, 27 3/4 In.	12650.00
Sculpture, The Female, Clear, Red Caning & Silver Leaf, R. Wilson, 15 In.	1100.00
Vase, Antares, Light & Dark Blue, Black Ovoid Base, Memphis, 20 In.	1980.00
Vase, Geometric Design, Sea, Free Form, Polychrome, J. Nowak, 16 In.	1900.00

GLASS-MIDCENTURY refers to art glass made from the 1950s to the 1980s. Some glass factories, such as Baccarat or Orrefors, are listed under their own categories. Earlier glass may be listed in the Glass-Art and Glass-Contemporary categories. Italian glass may be found under Venini and Glass-Venetian.

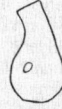

Ashtray, Blue & Brown Seaweed, Signed, Higgins, 5 In.	66.00
Ashtray, Blue Fish, Smoked Glass, Signed, Higgins, 10 x 14 In.	115.00
Ashtray, Green Pulled Feathers, White, Signed, Higgins, 14 x 10 In.	72.00
Champagne, Empire, Red, Morgantown	35.00
Charger, Geometric Design, Burgundy, Etched, Maurice Heaton, 14 In.	330.00
Figurine, Bird, Long Tail, Millefiore, 8 In.	100.00

If you move glass in cold weather, be sure to let it sit at room temperature for several hours before you try unpacking it. The glass will break more easily if there is an abrupt temperature change.

Glass-Midcentury, Plate, Design Encased
Between Layers, Sydenstricker, 6 In.

Goblet, Empire, Luncheon, Red, Morgantown 45.00
Plate, Amber & Gold Pulled Scroll, Signed, Higgins, 6 1/2 In. 60.00
Plate, Copper Forms, Mauve Ground, Signed, Higgins, In Gold, 10 x 6 In. 83.00
Plate, Design Encased Between Layers, Sydenstricker, 6 In. ....*Illus* 15.00
Plate, Turquoise, White, Gold Drawing, Signed, Higgins, In Gold, 14 x 12 In. 220.00
Tray, Gold Spiral Design, Yellow & Chartreuse Ray, Higgins, 14 x 17 In. 72.00
Vase, Brownish Blue Copper, Labino, 1967, 10 In. 465.00
Vase, Crackle, Blue, Blenko 40.00
Vase, Hobnail, Red To Smoky Topaz Rim, Labino, 1965, 7 In. 800.00
Vase, Iridescent, Blue, Green, Labino, 6 3/4 In. 517.00
Vase, Multicolored Iridescent, Overlay, Vandermark, 1970, 10 1/2 In. 230.00
Vessel, Petroglyph, Multicolored, Wm. Morris, 20 In. 6900.00

GLASS-VENETIAN. Venetian glass has been made near Venice, Italy, since the thirteenth century. Thin, colored glass with applied decoration is favored, although many other types have been made. Collectors have recently become interested in the Art Deco and 1950s designs. Glass was made on the Venetian island of Murano from 1291. The output dwindled in the late seventeenth century, but began to flourish again in the 1850s. Some of the old techniques of glassmaking were revived, and firms today make traditional designs and original modern glass. Since 1981, the name *Murano* may only be used on glass made on Murano Island. Other pieces of Italian glass may be found in the Glass-Contemporary, Glass-Midcentury, and Venini categories of this book.

Basket, 4-Color Aventurine Alternate With White Ribbons, Handle, 5 1/2 In. 50.00
Bottle, Blue Glass, Red Foil Label, Murano, 17 1/2 x 5 In. 1100.00
Bottle, Translucent Orange, Stopper, Murano, 10 1/2 x 3 1/2 In. 715.00
Bottle, Turquoise & Blue Striped, Ball Stopper, Fratelli Toso, 13 x 4 In. 715.00
Bowl, Amethyst With Gold Flecks, Stamped, 5 x 3 In. 325.00
Bowl, Bullicante, Cranberry Layer, Gold Leaf, Archimede Seguso, 9 x 3 In. 110.00
Bowl, Conch Shell, Luster Finish, Barovier & Toso, 1940, 7 x 15 In. 550.00
Bowl, Deep Blue, Acid Stamped, Paulo Venini, c.1950, 3 1/2 x 2 In. 209.00
Bowl, Deep Green, Acid Stamped, Venini, 1950, 3 1/2 x 2 In. 209.00
Bowl, Fish & Green Swirls, Clear, Alfredo Barbini, 1935, 4 x 9 1/2 In. 245.00
Bowl, Green, Black & White Caning, Clear, L. Tagliapietra, 1987, 8 x 11 In. 1045.00
Bowl, Silver Leaf Design, Murano, 5 1/2 In. 57.50
Bowl, Silver Leaf Inclusions, Amber Glass, Murano, 3 x 7 In. 34.50
Bowl, Snail Shape, White Glass, Gold Accents, Murano, 8 In. 57.50
Bowl, Tesuto, Red Caning On Blue Ground, Lino Tagliapietra, Murano, 8 x 9 In. 550.00
Bowl, Tesuto, Tapered Base, Green, Black, White Cane, Tagliapietra, 8 x 11 In. 935.00
Bowl, Tesuto, Yellow, Blue, Black Caning, Tagliapietra, 12 1/2 x 8 In. 1650.00
Bowl, Yellow Threads, Pale Amethyst, 6 1/2 In. 2300.00
Candlestick, Applied Grapes, Allover Foil, Barovier, 1940, 7 1/2 In., Pair 635.00
Centerpiece, Gold Foil, Clear, Allover Iridescent, Barovier, 1940, 6 x 18 In. 165.00
Chandelier, Scrolled Arms, Flaring Candle Cups, 42 In. 825.00
Chess Piece, Face, Red Features, Obelisk, Pawn, Cenedese, 11 In, 3 Piece 165.00

Compote, Amber, Aventurine, Salviati, 7 1/4 x 10 In. 550.00
Compote, Cover, Peaches, Leaves, Pink & Gold Spangles, Large Sundae Shape 180.00
Compote, Foliate Stem, Red Blossoms, Pale Green Leaves, Martinuzzi, 7 In. 1725.00
Compote, Iridescent, Footed, Barovier & Toso, 1940, 4 1/2 x 10 1/2 In. 55.00
Compote, Lemon-Yellow, Green Rim, Footed, Salviati, 6 3/4 x 8 3/4 In. 305.00
Compote, White Latticinio, Green Swirls, 1930, 5 x 11 1/2 In. 330.00
Decanter, Amber, Oval, Murano, 11 In. 80.50
Decanter, Black Designs, White, Fucina Degli Angeli, 11 1/2 In. 1320.00
Decanter, Yellow, Lattice White Stripes, Narrow Neck, Bulbous, Stopper, 9 In. 138.00
Dish, Serving, Pink & White Latticinio, Aventurine Rim, Salviati, 1920, 11 1/4 In. 330.00
Figurine, Bird, Blue & Green, Smoky Base, Vistosi, 10 1/2 x 6 In. 1650.00
Figurine, Bird, Clear, Gold Speckling, 13 1/2 In. & 12 3/4 In., Pair 275.00
Figurine, Dolphin, Sommerso Pedestal, Swirled Ribbed Surface, Green, 15 In. 770.00
Figurine, Duck, Blue, Murano, 6 1/2 In. 45.00
Figurine, Fish, Orange, Globular Base, Murano, 17 In. 161.00
Figurine, Longneck Bird, Amber To Blue, 21 In. 102.00
Figurine, Man, Kneeling With Head Bowed, 6 1/2 In. 115.00
Figurine, Pheasant, Blue, Green, White & Gold, 14 1/4 x 6 In. 90.00
Figurine, Pheasants, Blue, Green, Gold Speckling, Alfredo Barbini, 14 In. 275.00
Figurine, Sea Horse, Blue, Green & Amber, 13 In. 90.00
Figurine, Swan, White, Black Accents, Murano, 14 x 11 In. 225.00
Figurine, Woman Peasant, Alfredo Barbini, 7 In. 330.00
Figurine, Woman, Multicolored, White Threaded Twist Gown, 1950, 14 In. 270.00
Goblet, Dolphin Support, Gold Leaf, Blue Base, 7 3/4 x 5 In. 247.00
Goblet, Green, Red Stripes, Scalloped Rim, Fulvio Bianconi, 5 1/2 x 3 In. 770.00
Lamp, Clear, Internal Pink & Gold Flecked Design, 1950, 17 In., Pair 555.00
Night-Light, 2 Fish & Jellyfish, Cenedese, 8 1/2 x 7 In. 1760.00
Paperweight, Pear Form, Interior Gold Leaf, White Lines, Ercole Barovier 66.00
Paperweight, Silver Flex Interior, Blue Ground, 6 x 7 In. 95.00
Sconce, Flowers, Parrot Atop Shelf, 2 Sockets, Metal Vines, 23 In., Pair 1950.00
Sconce, Leaf Shape, Rigadoso, Barovier & Toso, 1940, 11 x 6 In, Pair 1650.00
Sculpture, Block, Aquarium, Molded Fish & Seaweed, Cenedese, 4 x 5 In., Pair 275.00
Vase, Allover Latticinio & Canes, Blue, A.V.E.M., 9 1/4 In. 573.00
Vase, Amethyst Shadow Base, Clear Ribbons, Ercole Barovier, 8 1/2 In. 187.00
Vase, Apple Green, Murano, 18 In., Pair 450.00
Vase, Applied Blue Glass Bowl, Amber, Tapered Neck, 10 In. 220.00
Vase, Applied Blue Grape Dots, White, Cylindrical, Salviati, 4 x 5 1/2 In. 303.00
Vase, Applied Crinoline Handles, Iridized Green, Seguso Vetri D'Arte, 12 In. 385.00
Vase, Blue Body, Gold Leaf, Rib Handles, Foot, Barovier & Toso, 1940, 7 In. 330.00
Vase, Blue Body, Gold Leaf, Rib Handles, Foot, Barovier & Toso, 9 1/2 In. 154.00
Vase, Blue Casing, Oval Windows, Toni Zuccheri, c.1968, 13 In. 2860.00
Vase, Blue Vertical Stripes, Broad Diagonal Stripe, Seguso Vetri D'Arte 192.00
Vase, Blue, Red & Clear, Salviati, 7 In. 165.00
Vase, Burnt Amber, 4 Sides, Foil Label, Cenedese, 7 1/2 x 5 In. 357.00
Vase, Controlled Bubbles, Ribbon Handles, Ercole Barovier, 1930s, 9 In. 440.00
Vase, Crimson Red, White Dots Arranged In Rows, Acid Stamp, 5 x 3 In. 2860.00
Vase, Deep Red, Red Handles, N. Martinuzzi, 9 1/2 In. 1045.00
Vase, Fazzoletto, Pale Blue Opaque Glass, Amethyst, Murano, 12 In. 247.00
Vase, Fazzoletto, Vertical Canes, Red, Blue, Amber, Green, Bianconi, 6 In. 440.00
Vase, Fazzoletto, Vertical Canes, White With Amethyst, Acid Stamp, 7 In. 660.00
Vase, Gold Foil, Green, Coronado Di Coro, Ribbed, Barovier & Toso, 13 x 7 In. 165.00
Vase, Gold Leaf Design, 2 Applied Bands, Pink Inclusions, T. Buzzi, 8 In. 805.00
Vase, Gourd Form, Vertical Canes, Earthtone, A. Seguso, 1950, 6 1/2 In. 286.00
Vase, Green Handles, Clear Body, Ercole Barovier, 6 In. 187.00
Vase, Handkarchief, Latticinio Cane Design, White, Pink, Fazzoletto, 7 1/2 In. 184.00
Vase, Handkarchief, Marbled Lattimo, Amethyst, Iridescent Interior, 15 In. 220.00
Vase, Horizontal Canes Of Blue, Green, Acid Stamp, Murano, 1950, 8 x 4 In. 935.00
Vase, Intarsia, Red, Blue Triangular Patches, Pillow Shape, Ercole Barovier, 14 In. 1430.00
Vase, Internal Plum Trails, Gold Leaf, Ercole Barovier, c.1960s, 10 In. 2090.00
Vase, Iridized Blue, Applied Clear Ribbons, Ercole Barovier, 8 In. 352.00
Vase, La Caccia, Floral, Avian & Zoomorphic Design, Amethyst, 20 1/4 In. 2175.00
Vase, Large Applied Green Teardrops, Fratelli Toso, 11 In. 1045.00
Vase, Marbleized Amber, Ercole Barovier, 8 In. 1320.00

Vase, Multicolored Patches, Gold Foil, Dimpled, 14 x 6 In. 415.00
Vase, Multicolored, Holding Twisted Stems, Moss Green, 1989, 24 In. 10350.00
Vase, Murrine, Grape-Type Clusters, Flowers, Maroon, Barovier, 6 1/2 In. 4840.00
Vase, Opaque Blue Swirl, Clear Ribbons, Ercole Barovier, 6 1/2 x 9 In. 221.00
Vase, Pale Yellow, Blue, Amethyst, 1950, 8 3/4 In. 5175.00
Vase, Pinched, 2 Bands Of Orange, Aureliano Toso, 11 In. 605.00
Vase, Pulegoso, Green, Light Iridescence, 16 In. 1870.00
Vase, Red Canes, Amethyst Base, Lino Tagliapietra, Murano, 13 x 9 1/2 In. 495.00
Vase, Red Over White Cased, Black Handles, Fratelli Toso, 11 1/2 In. 550.00
Vase, Red, Double Gourd, Salviati, 7 3/4 x 4 1/2 In. 220.00
Vase, Riffled Rim, Orange & White Latticinio, Fratelli Toso, 13 In. 192.00
Vase, Ruffled Top, Applied Foot, Orange, White Latticinio, Fratelli Toso, 13 x 7 In. 192.00
Vase, Shadow Ribs, Clear Ribbons, Ercole Barovier, 12 In. 440.00
Vase, Silver Leaf, Cobalt Ground, Clear Ruffled Sides, Barovier & Toso, 8 In. 220.00
Vase, Sommerso, Red & Blue Center, Clear Base, Murano, 1958, 11 1/2 In. 550.00
Vase, Striata, Alternating Vertical Rows Of Red, Blue, Canes, Ercole Barovier 220.00
Vase, Trumpet, Spiral Opaque Twist, Double Handles, Ring Foot, 11 5/8 In. 165.00
Vase, Vertical Canes, Red, Blue, Yellow, Amber, Green, Bianconi, 1950, 6 In. 440.00
Vase, Vertical Ribs, Pink Canes, Gold Layer, Murano, 12 In. 140.00
Vase, Whale Shape, Applied Murrhine Eyes, Smoked Glass, 1920, 7 x 10 In. 300.00

GLASSES for the eyes, or spectacles, were mentioned in a manuscript in 1289 and have been used ever since. The first eyeglasses with rigid side pieces were made in London in 1727. Bifocals were invented by Benjamin Franklin in 1785. Lorgnettes were popular in late Victorian times. Opera glasses are listed in their own category.

Chatelaine, Embossed Metal, Case, Clip 85.00
Spectacles, Original Lenses, Ribbon Loops, c.1770 .... 250.00
Spectacles, Original Lenses, Ribbon Loops, England, c.1750 .... 190.00

GOEBEL is the mark used by W. Goebel Porzellanfabrik of Oeslau, Germany, now Rodental, Germany. Many types of figurines and dishes have been made. The firm is still working. The pieces marked *Goebel Hummel* are listed under Hummel in this book.

Bank, Chimney Sweep 128.00
Bank, Friar Tuck 95.00
Bank, Penguin Savings, 6 1/2 In. 85.00
Bank, Piggy, Berry Red 100.00
Bell, Dinner, Glass 50.00
Bottle, Friar Tuck, 9 In. 60.00
Candleholder, Double, White Angel, c.1975, 6 In. 40.00
Cookie Jar, Friar Tuck 495.00
Creamer, Cat, Gray & White, Full Bee 80.00
Creamer, Cow, Sitting, Full Bee 25.00
Creamer, Cow, Standing, With Bell, Full Bee 38.00
Cup & Saucer, Harem Girl Face, Crown Mark 95.00
Cup & Saucer, Santa Claus, 1950s 85.00
Decanter, Friar Tuck 195.00
Egg Timer, Friar Tuck, Stylized Mark 125.00
Figurine, Bambi, Beside Tree, Bee Over Vee, 1950s, 4 In. 100.00
Figurine, Bambi, Standing On Base, Beside Tree Stump, V Over G, 4 In. 145.00
Figurine, Bambi, Standing, 1950s, 3 In. 80.00
Figurine, Bear Cub, Brown 20.00
Figurine, Bird, Nesting, Blue 15.00
Figurine, Boxer, Puppy, Brown 25.00
Figurine, Child In Pajamas, With Teddy Bear, Charlot Byj, 6 1/2 In. 115.00
Figurine, Child, Butterfly, White 20.00
Figurine, Clown, No. 3001-10, 4 In. 20.00
Figurine, Dog, Schnauzer, Seated, 11 In. 200.00
Figurine, Duckling, Swimming, No. 32004-05, 2 1/2 In. 30.00
Figurine, Horse, Palomino, Thoroughbred 125.00
Figurine, Mickey Mouse, Planting Garden 55.00
Figurine, Mickey Mouse, Sitting On Log, With Book, V Over G, 3 1/2 In. 300.00

Figurine, Nude, Ponytail, Striding, White, 10 x 6 In.	140.00
Figurine, Oriental Girl, Holding Flowers & Parasol, Crown Mark, 9 1/2 x 7 In.	95.00
Figurine, Parakeets, On Trunk, Color	100.00
Figurine, Persian Cat, No.12b	30.00
Figurine, Pigeon, No. 4247	85.00
Figurine, Polar Bear, Walking, No. 33517, 4 In.	25.00
Figurine, Praying Girl, Blond Braided Hair	50.00
Figurine, Puppy, Begging, Gray, No. 6406	40.00
Figurine, Puppy, Resting, No. 306	20.00
Figurine, Puppy, Standing, Brown	25.00
Figurine, Rabbit, Tan, No. 34829-04, 2 1/2 In.	15.00
Figurine, Raccoon, No. 3652	35.00
Figurine, Snowboy, Black Hat, No. 708-11, 4 In.	15.00
Figurine, Snowgirl, Red Hair, No. 708-12, 4 In.	15.00
Figurine, Tiger Cat, No. 3100, 4 In.	30.00
Figurine, Tiger On Rock, No. 36-025-17, 19 In.	250.00
Figurine, Zebra, Baby, 4 In.	50.00
Font, Holy Water, Art Deco, Pink Gloss, Full Bee	75.00
Mug, Friar Tuck, Mark No. 6	68.00
Mug, Owl	45.00
Ornament, Christmas, Angel, 1978	10.00
Perfume Bottle, Oriental Girl, Porcelain Head, Crown Mark	135.00
Perfume Lamp, Dog	295.00
Pitcher, Pickwick, Full Bee	78.00
Pitcher, Water, Friar Tuck, 7 In.	125.00
Plate, Annual, 1971, Box	450.00
Plate, Annual, 1980	42.00
Plate, Robin	16.00
Salt & Pepper, Angels & Devil	65.00
Salt & Pepper, Bonzo	60.00
Salt & Pepper, Bookworm	45.00
Salt & Pepper, Cat & Dog	50.00
Salt & Pepper, Chicks	30.00
Salt & Pepper, Friar Tuck, Full Bee	35.00 to 38.00
Salt & Pepper, Maggie & Jiggs	75.00
Salt & Pepper, Poddles, Black & White	35.00
Salt & Pepper, Tyrolean Boy & Girl	40.00
Sugar & Creamer, Friar Tuck, Pair	75.00
Wall Pocket, Hat, Cherries	45.00 to 50.00

GOLDSCHEIDER has made porcelains in three places. The family left
Vienna in 1938 and started factories in England and in Trenton, New
Jersey. The New Jersey factory started in 1940 as Goldscheider-U.S.A.
In 1941 it became Goldscheider-Everlast Corporation. From 1947 to
1953 it was Goldcrest Ceramics Corporation. In 1950 the Vienna plant
was returned to Mr. Goldscheider and the company continues in busi-
ness. The Trenton, New Jersey, business, now called *Goldscheider of
Vienna*, imports all of the pieces.

Ashtray, With Cigarette Holder, Dutch Girl	55.00
Bust, Madonna, Signed, 9 In.	145.00
Figurine, Balinese Dancer, 16 In.	275.00
Figurine, Blackamoors, Male & Female, B. Loveday, 15 In., Pair	650.00
Figurine, Chinese Musician & Woman, Pair	185.00
Figurine, Dancer, Butterfly, Marked, Austria, 17 1/2 In.	2000.00
Figurine, Dancer, Harem, Marked, Austria, 19 In.	2000.00
Figurine, Foal, Grazing, 4 1/2 x 4 1/2 In.	85.00
Figurine, German Shepherd	185.00
Figurine, Girl, With Hat Over Shoulder	45.00
Figurine, Horse, Box, 1940	125.00
Figurine, Madonna & Child, Blue Cream Crackle Glaze, 18 In.	51.00
Figurine, Salome, c.1920, 5 In.	3500.00
Figurine, Southern Belle, No. 800, 8 In.	65.00
Figurine, Woman, Christmas, White, 7 In.	90.00

Group, Spanish Dancer, No. 5775, Marked, 17 3/4 In.	1250.00
Music Box, Colonial Lady	100.00
Planter, Horse Head, Double	18.00
Vase, Geometric, Orange, Black, White, Austria, 6 x 9 In.	132.00

GOLF, see Sports category.

GONDER Ceramic Arts, Inc., was opened by Lawton Gonder in 1941 in Zanesville, Ohio. Gonder made high-grade pottery decorated with flambe, drip, gold crackle, and Chinese crackle glazes. The factory closed in 1957. From 1946 to 1954, Gonder also operated the Elgee Pottery, which made ceramic lamp bases.

Cookie Jar, Sheriff, Yellow	1600.00
Cookie Jar, Swirl Design, Speckled Drip Glaze	75.00
Figurine, Chinese Couple With Buckets, Dark Green	95.00
Figurine, Conquistador, Maroon, Hand Carved, 1950	65.00
Vase, Blue Velvet, 2 Handles, 7 1/2 x 6 In.	35.00
Vase, Chartreuse, No. 3710	25.00
Vase, Double Handle, Yellow, 9 1/2 In.	42.00
Vase, Pillow, Maroon, Foam Drip, 6 In.	30.00
Vase, Velvet, Blue, Handles, 7 1/2 In.	35.00

GOOFUS GLASS was made from about 1900 to 1920 by many American factories. It was originally painted gold, red, green, bronze, pink, purple, or other bright colors. Many pieces are found today with flaking paint, and this lowers the value.

Bowl, Jeweled Heart, Opalescent, 9 In	35.00
Bowl, Red Floral Design, Brown Painted, 10 In.	22.00
Bowl, Roses, 8 1/2 In.	20.00
Plate, Roses, 10 1/2 In.	18.00
Plate, Tulip, Opalescent Rim, 6 In.	18.00

GOSS china has been made since 1858. English potter William Henry Goss first made it at the Falcon Pottery in Stoke-on-Trent. The factory name was changed to Goss China Company in 1934 when it was taken over by Cauldon Potteries. Production ceased in 1940. Goss china resembles Irish Belleek in both body and glaze. The company also made popular souvenir china, usually marked with local crests and names.

W.H.GOSS

Bust, Shakespeare, 8 In.	75.00
Cuspidor, Woman's, Cranberry, Crimped	85.00
Ewer, Bideford	15.00
Figurine, Lady Godiva, Horse	400.00

GOUDA, Holland, has been a pottery center since the seventeenth century. Two firms, the Zenith pottery, established in the eighteenth century, and the Zuid-Hollandsche pottery made the brightly colored wares marked *Gouda* from 1880 to about 1940. Many pieces featured Art Nouveau or Art Deco designs.

Bowl, Art Nouveau Design, Peacock, Flowers On Black, 6 2/5 x 3 3/8 In.	155.00
Bowl, Cover, Floral Exterior, Emerald Interior, 5 Matching Bowls, 6 In.	195.00
Bowl, Florals, Bulbous Hip, Tapering To 4 1/2-In. Base, 4 3/4 In.	295.00
Bowl, Hand Painted Flowers, Round, Royal Zuid, 5 x 4 In.	125.00
Bowl, Stylized Flowers, Grapes, Black, 6 x 3 2/5 In.	150.00
Box, Trinket, No. 2614, Areo, 4 x 3 1/2 x 1 3/4 In.	90.00
Chamberstick, Blue Flowers, Gold, Rust, Brown Handle, House Mark, 2 1/4 x 6 1/2 In.	110.00
Dish, Cover, Signed, Anser A., Holland, 6 In.	145.00
Ewer, Regina Rosario, 7 1/2 x 7 In.	410.00
Figurine, Pipe, Dutch Shoe	55.00
Inkwell, Rodian House Mark	135.00
Jar, Cover, Stylized Floral, Black Gloss, 4 3/4 In.	135.00
Jar, Ginger, Art Nouveau Multicolored Design, Black Ground, House Mark, 10 In.	300.00
Jug, Liquor, Stopper, Floral Design, Black Ground	295.00
Jug, Stylized Florals, Ivory, 5 1/2 In.	250.00

Pitcher, Allover Floral & Vines, Bulbous, Glossy Glaze, Signed, 5 1/2 In. 375.00
Pitcher, Matte Green, Blue, White, Gold, Yellow, Brown, Art Nouveau Base, 9 1/4 In. .. 190.00
Plaque, Rural Autumn Scene, Mother, Children, Frame, 6 x 12 In. 425.00
Vase, Art Nouveau, Black, Tan, Yellow & Green, Marked, 12 In. 225.00
Vase, Art Nouveau, Flower Forms, 6 x 6 In. 145.00
Vase, Dark Blue, Olive, Orange, Mustard, Teal Design, Lime Highlights, 12 In. 700.00
Vase, Floral Sprays, Oyster White, Green Base, Mustard Top Rim, 2 2/5 x 3 In. 25.00
Vase, Lions, Vines, 12 In. 350.00
Vase, Matte Green, Floral, Silver Overlay, 7 In. 350.00
Vase, Stylized Eagles, Emerald Ground, Goedewaagen, 19 In. 475.00

GRANITEWARE is an enameled tinware that has been used in the kitchen
from the late nineteenth century to the present. Earlier graniteware was
green or turquoise blue, with white spatters. The later ware was gray
with white spatters. Reproductions are being made in all colors.

Bucket, Berry, Black Bakelite Lid Knob, White, Red Shield Label, 5 In. 55.00
Bucket, Water, Brown & White Swirl 150.00
Can, Cream, Gooseneck, Tin Lid, 10 In. 65.00
Can, Milk, Gray, 2 Qt. 75.00
Carrier, Food, 4 Stack 155.00
Coffee Boiler, 13 In. 275.00
Coffee Urn, Gray Mottled 100.00
Coffeepot, Gooseneck Spout, Brown & White Alternating Vertical Stripes, 8 In. 475.00
Coffeepot, Gooseneck Spout, Red & White Swirl, 8 In. 375.00
Coffeepot, Mottled Dark Gray, El-An-Ge, L & G Mfg., Co., 8 1/2 In. 95.00
Coffeepot, White, Black Trim, Balloon Gooseneck 18.00
Coffeepot, White, Pewter Trim 250.00
Colander, Footed, Gray 25.00
Colander, Handles, Pedestal Base, Blue Swirl, 9 1/2 In. 125.00
Cooler, Water, Blue & White Swirl, 3 Piece 985.00
Cup, Wide Strap Handle, Pair 44.00
Dish, Soap, High Back For Hanging, Cream, Green Trim 25.00
Dish, Soap, Scalloped Edge, Gray 70.00
Dish, Soap, Wall 85.00
Double Boiler, Blue & White Swirl 225.00
Egg Poacher Set, Buffalo, New York, World's Fair, 1890s, 16 Piece 750.00
Grater, Blue & White Speckled 1200.00
Grater, Ideal, Gray 485.00
Grater, Revolving 145.00
Holder, Sponge, Wall 68.00
Kettle, Blue & White Swirl, 12 In. 75.00
Kettle, Cover, Handle Lift, Bail Handle, Berlin, 5 In. 130.00
Kettle, Handle, Gray, 15 In. 35.00
Kettle, Preserve, Blue & White Swirl 260.00
Matchbox, White, Blue Trim, Embossed Allumettes 65.00
Measure, Oyster, Gray 285.00
Mold, Melon, Gray, Small 80.00
Mold, Rabbit, Gray 235.00
Mold, Ring, White, Cobalt Trim 45.00
Mold, Turk's Head, Gray 55.00
Mug, Black Strap Handle, Chrysolite, 3 In. 125.00
Mug, Iris, Large White Swirl 150.00
Mug, Light Blue Swirl, Black Trim, Handle 30.00
Pail, Brown, White, 9 x 11 1/2 In. 60.00
Pail, Cream, Tin Lid, Bail Handle, 7 1/2 In. 80.00
Pail, Milk, Chrysolite Green 895.00
Pan, Baking, White Interior, Granite Covered Riveted Handle, 10 x 15 In. 135.00
Pan, Bread, Blue & White Swirl, 11 In. 88.00
Pan, Muffin, Gray Mottled, 6 Large Shallow Cups 95.00
Pan, Muffin, Gray, 8 Cups 14.50
Pan, Riveted Tabs Either Side, 4 1/4 In. 45.00
Pan, Shallow, Gray, 11 In. 15.00
Percolator, White, Cobalt Blue Trim, 12 In. 50.00

Pie Plate, Gray, Child's 30.00
Pie Plate, Light Blue Swirl, Black Trim 35.00
Pitcher, Molasses, Gray 150.00
Platter, Lobster, White 30.00
Rack, Utensil, Red, Gold Trim, 7 x 12 In. 65.00
Roaster, Blue, Savory 30.00
Roaster, Cobalt Swirl, Oval, Insert Pan 235.00
Roaster, Gray 45.00
Salt Box, Wooden Cover, Cream & Green, Kockums, Sweden 95.00
Saucer, Belmont Ware, White, Black Trim 20.00
Sieve, Gravy, Kettle Hook 150.00
Spatula, Gray 85.00
Strainer, Gray, Handle 20.00
Strainer, Tea, Blue & White 190.00
Tea Kettle, Gooseneck Spout, Bail Handle, Sky Blue, 9 1/2 In. 45.00
Tea Set, Child's, White, Blue & Gold Bands, 7 Piece 195.00
Teapot, Brown, Germany 35.00
Teapot, Brown, Marked Germany, Child's 25.00
Teapot, Gooseneck, Aqua & White 275.00
Teapot, Gooseneck, Gray 55.00
Tray, Oval, Gray, 18 x 15 In. 175.00
Trivet, Tulip, Light Blue 55.00
Wash Basin, Cobalt Blue Windmill & Sailboats, White, Blue Trim 55.00

GREENTOWN glass was made by the Indiana Tumbler and Goblet Company of Greentown, Indiana, from 1894 to 1903. In 1899, the factory name was changed to National Glass Company. A variety of pressed, milk, and chocolate glass was made. Additional pieces may be found in other categories, such as Chocolate Glass, Custard Glass, Holly Amber, Milk Glass, and Pressed Glass.

Bowl, Cord Drapery, Footed 145.00
Butter, Cover, Dewey 295.00
Compote, Austrian, Tall 65.00
Creamer, Dewey, Amber 65.00
Cruet, Cord Drapery 85.00
Goblet, Diamond Prisms 75.00
Pitcher, Heron 165.00
Pitcher, Squirrel 350.00
Spooner, Herringbone Buttress 110.00
Tumbler, Brazen Shield, Cobalt Blue, 6 Piece 450.00
Tumbler, Cactus, Blue 75.00
Vase, Indiana, Embossed, 22K Gold, 6 x 18 In. 65.00
Wine, Cord Drapery, Amber 300.00

GRUEBY Faience Company of Boston, Massachusetts, was incorporated in 1897 by William H. Grueby. Garden statuary, art pottery, and architectural tiles were made until 1920. The company developed a matte green glaze that was so popular it was copied by many other factories making a less expensive type of pottery. This eventually led to the financial problems of the pottery.

Bowl, Applied Leaves, Matte Green Glaze, 5 1/2 x 2 In. 550.00
Bowl, Curdled Matte Blue Glaze, Green Gloss Interior, 8 In. 425.00
Bowl, Lotus, Stacked Leaves, Matte Green Glaze, Wilhemina Post, 7 1/2 In. 2970.00
Bowl, Matte Blue Glaze, Paper Label, Impressed Mark, 9 1/2 x 2 1/2 In. 715.00
Jardiniere, Applied Vertical Leaves, Buds, Matte Green Glaze, Bulbous, 10 In. 1760.00
Paperweight, Scarab Beetle Shape, Matte Yellow Glaze, 2 1/2 In. 495.00
Paperweight, Scarab, Gunmetal Glaze, Paper Labels, 1 1/4 x 4 In. 80.00
Paperweight, Scarab, Mustard Glaze, 4 x 2 3/4 In. 825.00
Tile, 4 Penguins On Iceberg, Paper Label, Square, 4 In. 660.00
Tile, Boat Scene, Purple, Golden Sail, Green Sea, Blue Sky, Oak Frame, 5 In. 412.50
Tile, Monk Series, 2 Matte Green Shades, Dark Red Clay, Artist Initials, 6 In. 875.00
Tile, Pelican, Red Clay, Oak Frame, Square, 4 In. 132.00
Tile, Rooster, Red Clay, Wide Oak Frame, Square, 4 In. 275.00

Tile, Stylized Cupid, Oatmeal Glaze, Green Ground, EROS On Front, Square, 6 In. 357.00
Tile, Stylized White Leaves, Matte Green Ground, 4 In. 35.00
Vase, 3 Elongated Handles At Top, Deep Green Matte Glaze, White Accents, 9 In. 2415.00
Vase, Alternating Leaf Pattern, Matte Green Glaze, Bulbous, 4 3/4 In. 4025.00
Vase, Alternating Leaves & Buds, Matte Green Glaze, White, Bulbous, 7 1/4 In. 2070.00
Vase, Applied Leaves Between Buds, Stems, Matte Green Glaze, 8 1/2 In. 465.00
Vase, Applied Leaves Buds, Flared Shoulder, Matte Green Glaze, 5 In. 220.00
Vase, Applied Vertical Leaf, Bud Design, 8 1/2 In. 1210.00
Vase, Applied Vertical Leaves, Green Matte Glaze, 9 x 5 In. 1980.00
Vase, Ascending Vines, Leaves At Base, Green Terra-Cotta Vase, Signed, 13 In. 860.00
Vase, Carved, Applied Vertical Leaves, Matte Green Glaze, Impressed Mark, 7 1/2 In. ... 1210.00
Vase, Crisp Leaves, Yellow Buds, Mottled Green Glaze, Marked, 11 1/4 In. 4600.00
Vase, Full Length Leaves, Buds, Curdled Green Glaze, Signed Ruth Erickson, 9 In. 1760.00
Vase, Green Matte Glaze, Marked, 6 In. 880.00
Vase, Leaf Design, Dark Green Matte Glaze, Baluster, 8 1/4 In. 345.00
Vase, Leaves & Flowers, Bulbous, 12 In. 8525.00
Vase, Matte Green Glaze, 3 In. 275.00
Vase, Matte Green Glaze, 5 In. 355.00
Vase, Overlapping Leaves, Vertical Stems, Matte Green Glaze, 12 1/2 In. 6050.00
Vase, Panel Design, Marked, 7 In. 660.00
Vase, Stacked Leaves, Broad Base, French Blue Glaze, Signed, 20 In. 8800.00
Vase, Stylized Flower & Leaf Pattern, Cucumber Green Matte Glaze, 7 3/4 In. ... 2300.00
Vase, Tooled & Applied Leaves, Buds On Tall Stems, Ruth Erickson, 1906, 13 1/2 In. ... 6600.00
Vase, Tooled & Applied Leaves, Matte Green Glaze, Signed, 4 1/2 x 3 1/4 In. 2640.00
Vase, Trefoils In Relief Under Rim, Ruth Erickson, 9 1/2 In. 2200.00
Vase, Vertical Ribs, Medium Blue Glaze, Baluster, 1905, 6 1/2 In. 1095.00
Vessel, Cover, Leaves At Top, Yellow To Cream, Light Blue Matte Glaze, 8 In. 2970.00

GUNDERSON glass was made at the Gunderson-Pairpoint Glass Works
of New Bedford, Massachusetts, from 1952 to 1957. Gunderson Peachblow is especially famous.

Bowl, Peachblow, Revere-Style, Pink To White, Light Pink Lining, 4 x 7 In. 325.00
Compote, Peachblow 250.00
Creamer, Paper Label, 5 In. 38.50
Cup & Saucer, Peachblow 275.00
Decanter, Peachblow, Raspberry To White, Ribbed Handle, Stopper, 10 In. 950.00
Decanter, Ruby Glass, Allover Flux & Canes, Enamel, Stopper, 12 In. 1450.00
Jug, Peachblow, Applied Loop Handle, Bulbous, 4 1/2 x 4 In. 450.00
Pitcher, Burmese, Ruffled Top, 4 In. 465.00
Vase, Burmese, Lily, 1940s, 9 1/2 In. 375.00
Vase, Peachblow, Cornucopia, Rose To White, Ruffled, 10 In. 525.00
Vase, Peachblow, Lily, 9 x 3 1/4 In. 425.00
Vase, Peachblow, Ruffled, Pinched-In, 5 x 6 In. 525.00
Wine, Peachblow, 5 In. 175.00

GUNS that may be classed as toys, such as BB guns, air rifles, and cap guns, are
listed in the Toy category.

GUSTAVSBERG ceramics factory was founded in 1827 near Stockholm,
Sweden. It is best known to collectors for its twentieth-century art   Gustafsberg
wares, especially a green stoneware with silver inlay called *Argenta*.

Bowl, Fish, Argenta, 6 In. ....250.00 to 275.00
Bowl, Gold Scroll Design, Green Exterior Glaze, J. Ekberg, 1930s, 5 In. 55.00
Bowl, Green Glaze, Silver Vine Design, K. Wilhem, Argenta, 1930s, 4 In. 287.50
Bowl, Silver Scalloped Border, Argenta, 7 x 2 In. 365.00
Box, Cover, Nude, Smoking Cigarette, Silver Inlay, Argenta, Signed, 1930 .... 550.00
Coaster Plate, Argenta, 3 1/2 In., Pair 45.00
Dish, Cover, Reds, Blues, 3 3/4 x 4 In. 110.00
Holder, Cigarette, Green Glaze, Silver Applique, K. Wilhem, Argenta, Square 46.00
Jug, Lion, 6 1/2 In. 450.00
Pitcher, Leaf Design, 3 In. 28.00
Plate, Argenta, 4 In. 45.00
Plate, Coaster, Argenta, 3 1/2 In. 45.00

Plate, Roman Figures At Center, Green Silver, Cream Ground, 11 In. 115.00
Tile, Stylized King, Blue, 9 x 9 In. 220.00
Vase, Blue & Turquoise Flowers, Signed JE, Dated 1925, 8 In. 425.00
Vase, Bud, Bellflower, 8 1/2 In. . . . . .150.00 to 200.00
Vase, Cameo Cut, Mottled Light Blue Ground, Floral, 4 1/2 x 6 1/4 In. 450.00
Vase, Carved, Blue & Turquoise Leaves, Signed JE, 6 In. 200.00
Vase, Floral Design, Heavy Slip, B.O. Mortensson, 1910, 6 1/2 In. 355.00
Vase, Green & Lime Leaves, High Glaze, 5 In. 325.00
Vase, Lily Of The Valley, Blue & Green, Argenta, 5 In. 200.00
Vase, Nude, Carved Blue Flowers, Signed, 1925, 8 In. 350.00
Vase, Sterling Fish, Argenta, 4 In. 175.00
Vase, Whimsical City Scene, Earthenware, Gray Ground, Lindberg, 16 x 3 1/2 In. 245.00

GUTTA-PERCHA was one of the first plastic materials. It was made from
a mixture of resins from Malaysian trees. It was molded and used for
daguerreotype cases, toilet articles, and picture frames in the nineteenth century.

Photograph Case, Bee Keeper, 1/9th Plate 85.00
Portrait, Young Woman, Amber 95.00

HAEGER Potteries, Inc., Dundee, Illinois, started making commercial
art wares in 1914. Early pieces were marked with the name *Haeger*
written over an *H*. About 1938, the mark *Royal Haeger* was used. The
firm is still making florist wares and lamp bases.

Ashtray, Clamshell, Turquoise Iridescent, Orange Lava Glaze, 13 1/2 x 7 In. 30.00
Ashtray, Earth Warp, Square, 7 In. 28.00
Basin, Lavabo Gold Tweed 38.00
Basket, Gypsy Girl, Holding Basket, Gold Tweed, 16 1/2 In. 70.00
Bowl, Daisy Flower 15.00
Bowl & Pitcher Set, White, Large, 2 Piece 37.00
Box, Desk, Wooden Knob Cover, Orange Gloss, 6 1/2 In. 40.00
Compote, Triangular Cutouts Cover & Foot, Brushed Gold Glaze 35.00
Cornucopia, Nude Nymph, Mauve Agate, 8 In., Pair 150.00
Figurine, Cat, With Fish Bowl, Charcoal, 1953, 8 In. 40.00
Figurine, Gazelle, Brown Streaks, Green, 13 In. 60.00
Figurine, Gypsy Girl, 16 In. 65.00
Figurine, Lion 35.00
Figurine, Orange Dog, Glass Eye, 9 In. 30.00
Figurine, Running Deer, Golden Brown, 15 1/4 In. 35.00
Figurine, Sailfish, Green, 9 In. 35.00
Figurine, Woman Holding Basket In Each Hand, Green, Paper Label, 17 In. 125.00
Flower Frog, Double Lady, 1920s 150.00
Lamp, TV, Black Panther, 1950s, 14 In. 30.00
Pitcher, Handle, Tall Thin Neck, Ebony Cascade, 18 3/4 In. 35.00
Planter, 3 Girls With Bonnets, Flared Skirts, Oyster White 25.00
Planter, Cat, 8 1/2 In. 45.00
Planter, Coral 10.00
Planter, Fawn, 1913 . . . . 45.00
Planter, Lion Face 35.00
Planter, Maiden 50.00
Planter, Mermaid, Holding Shell Bowl, White Hair, 22 1/2 x 13 1/2 In. 140.00
Planter, Red Rooster, 10 In. 50.00
Planter, Scalloped Edge, Caramel, Gray, 12 In. . . . . .49.00 to 70.00
Sign, Dealer's, Antique Gold 40.00
Sign, Dealer, Art Deco 50.00
Vase, Ballerina, 14 In. 75.00
Vase, Black, Gold, Rust, 11 1/2 In. 75.00
Vase, Fish, 8 In. 35.00
Vase, Gazelle, 13 In. 60.00
Vase, Leaf, Blue, 6 1/4 In. 12.00
Vase, Morning Glory, 3 Flowers Openings, Pale Pink & Blue, 16 1/2 In. 45.00
Vase, Morning Glory, Purple, 14 In., Pair 120.00
Vase, Orange Crystalline, Blue Ink Mark, 10 In. 39.00

Vase, Orange Crystalline, Twisted Form, 9 1/2 x 5 In. 50.00
Vase, Orange, 15 In. 95.00
Vase, Red Shaded To Black, Squatty Bottom, 1950s, 12 In. 50.00
Vase, Snakeskin, Orange Chocolate Matte, Bowl Shape, 9 In. 45.00
Vase, Twisted Form, Orange Crystalline, Blue Ink Mark, 10 In. 40.00
Vase, White Relief Curdles Over Green, Brown, 16 1/4 In. 28.00

HALF-DOLL, see Pincushion Doll category.

HALL CHINA Company started in East Liverpool, Ohio, in 1903. The
firm made many types of wares. Collectors search for the Hall teapots
made from the 1920s to the 1950s. The dinnerwares of the same period, especially Autumn Leaf pattern, are also popular. The Hall China
Company is still working. For more information, see *Kovels'*
Depression Glass & American Dinnerware Price List. Autumn Leaf
pattern dishes are listed in their own category in this book.

Ashtray, Palmer House 20.00
Blue Blossom, Creamer 50.00
Cactus, Cake Plate 30.00
Cameo Rose, Soup, Dish 12.00
Chinese Red, Canister, Cover 75.00
Chinese Red, Cookie Jar 85.00
Chinese Red, Salt & Pepper, Canister 110.00
Coffeepot, Percolator, Electric, Geese Decal 35.00
Forman, Casserole, Blue 22.00
Forman, Pitcher, Gold Trim, Black Matte 75.00
Heather Rose, Jug 22.00
Moderne, Sugar & Creamer 60.00
Moderne, Sugar, Cover 28.00
Morning Glory, Drip Jar, Pastel, Open 35.00
Mt. Vernon, Bowl, Vegetable, Oval 20.00
Mug, Town & Country, Rust, Eva Zeisal 40.00
New York, Sugar & Creamer 125.00
Old Crow, Punch Bowl, Cup Ladle, Box 275.00
Old Crow, Punch Set, 12 Piece 350.00
Poppy, Casserole, Cover, Oval 49.00
Poppy, Coffeepot 45.00
Poppy, Pretzel Jar ....110.00 to 145.00
Poppy, Spooner 65.00
Poppy, Sugar, Cover 25.00
Poppy, Vase 75.00
Poppy & Wheat, Bean Pot, No. 3 .... 195.00
Poppy & Wheat, Bean Pot, No. 5 .... 195.00
Poppy & Wheat, Coffeepot 375.00
Radiance, Cup & Saucer 17.00
Radiance, Jug 27.00
Red Poppy, Bowl, Radiance 10.00
Red Poppy, Coffeepot, Daniel 50.00
Red Poppy, Creamer 15.00
Red Poppy, Mixing Bowl 45.00
Red Poppy, Mixing Bowl, No. 5, Radiance 10.00
Red Poppy, Platter, Large 28.00
Red Poppy, Platter, Small 22.00
Red Poppy, Salt & Pepper 45.00
Red Poppy, Salt & Pepper, Teardrop 55.00
Rose Parade, Casserole ....25.00 to 50.00
Rose Parade, Teapot 60.00
Rose Parade, Teapot, Pert 35.00
Rose White, Bean Pot 25.00
Rose White, Syrup 17.00
Rose White, Teapot ....40.00 to 70.00
Royal Rose, Casserole 40.00
Royal Rose, Casserole, Blue, White Interior, Silver Rim, 8 1/2 In. 25.00

Royal Rose, Casserole, Polka Dot, Ivory, 2 Handles, Signed, 8 1/2 In. 25.00
Royal Rose, Jug 70.00
Royal Rose, Jug, Ball 125.00
Royal Rose, Pepper Shaker 20.00
Royal Rose, Saltshaker 20.00
Salt & Pepper, Red, Ribbed 18.00
Shaggy Tulip, Coffeepot, Kadota Drip, 4 Piece 115.00
Shaggy Tulip, Condiment Jar 395.00
Springtime, Coffeepot, 9 Cup 60.00
Springtime, Jug, Ball 90.00
Springtime, Plate, Dinner 8.00
Springtime, Soup, Dish 9.00
Sundial, Casserole, Chinese Red 40.00
Sundial, Casserole, Cobalt Blue . . . . .55.00 to 70.00
Sundial, Casserole, Yellow 35.00
Sundial, Jug, Batter, High Back 45.00
Sundial, Sugar, Cover, Yellow 30.00
Taverne, Leftover, Rectangular 45.00
Taverne, Teapot 65.00
Teapot, Airflow, Cobalt Blue 60.00
Teapot, Airflow, Red . . . . .85.00 to 125.00
Teapot, Aladdin, Black, Gold Trim 35.00
Teapot, Aladdin, Cobalt Blue, Gold 65.00
Teapot, Aladdin, Green, Gold Trim, 6 Cup 85.00
Teapot, Aladdin, Jewel Tea, Infuser 60.00
Teapot, Aladdin, Morning Glory, Blue Infuser 135.00
Teapot, Aladdin, Pink, Pastel Gloss, 4 Cup 80.00
Teapot, Aladdin, Red Poppy 45.00
Teapot, Aladdin, Serenade, Infuser 300.00
Teapot, Aladdin, Yellow, Gold Infuser 50.00
Teapot, Albany, Black 38.00
Teapot, Albany, Green, Gold Trim 45.00
Teapot, Automobile, Blue 725.00
Teapot, Automobile, Yellow 380.00
Teapot, Basketball, Black 325.00
Teapot, Basketball, Turquoise, Gold Trim 750.00
Teapot, Big Boy 45.00
Teapot, Boston, Blue 40.00
Teapot, Boston, Canary 40.00
Teapot, Boston, Poppy . . . . .175.00 to 200.00
Teapot, Boston, Red 150.00
Teapot, Crocus 65.00
Teapot, Donut, Chinese Red . . . . .250.00 to 350.00
Teapot, Donut, Delphinium 375.00
Teapot, French, 2 Cup 43.00
Teapot, French, Chinese Red 75.00
Teapot, Globe 75.00
Teapot, Globe, Ribbed, Red 350.00
Teapot, Hollywood, Red 200.00
Teapot, Los Angeles, Green, Gold Trim, 1920s 75.00
Teapot, Manhattan, Yellow 85.00
Teapot, McCormick, Maroon, Infuser 40.00
Teapot, McCormick, Turquoise, Infuser 40.00
Teapot, Melody, Red . . . . .250.00 to 350.00
Teapot, Melody, Turquoise, Gold Trim 125.00
Teapot, Nautilus, Maroon 245.00
Teapot, New York, 2 Cup 20.00
Teapot, New York, Yellow, Gold Trim 39.00
Teapot, Parade, 6 Cup 16.00
Teapot, Philadelphia, Red 150.00
Teapot, Radiance 325.00
Teapot, Ronald Reagan, 10 1/2 In. 45.00
Teapot, Streamline, Blue, Gold 75.00

Teapot, Streamline, Poppy	185.00
Teapot, Streamline, Red	125.00
Teapot, Teamaster, Twin Spout, Red	165.00
Teapot, Town & Country, Rust, Zeisel	130.00
Teapot, Windshield, Canary, Gold Trim	75.00 to 85.00
Teapot, Windshield, Game Birds Decal	195.00 to 300.00
Teapot, Windshield, Gold Dot	50.00
Teapot, Windshield, Maroon, Gold Trim	55.00
Trivet, Blue Rim, White Center, Signed, Gold Stamp, Round, 6 In.	30.00
Wild Poppy, Coffeepot, Washington	170.00
Wildfire, Ball Jug, Delphinium	50.00 to 60.00
Wildfire, Bowl, 5 1/2 In.	10.00
Wildfire, Bowl, Big Lip, 7 1/2 In.	45.00
Wildfire, Bowl, Blue, 6 In.	45.00
Wildfire, Bowl, Straight Sides, Blue, 6 In.	45.00
Wildfire, Casserole, Cover	40.00
Wildfire, Cup & Saucer	20.00
Wildfire, Gravy Boat	30.00
Wildfire, Jug, Yellow	50.00
Wildfire, Plate, 6 In.	7.00
Wildfire, Plate, 9 In.	15.00
Wildfire, Platter, 11 1/4 In.	28.00
Wildfire, Salt & Pepper, Teardrop	30.00
Yellow Rose, Salt & Pepper	45.00
Zeisel, Bouquet, Teapot	125.00
Zeisel, Buckingham, Soup, Onion, Cover	20.00
Zeisel, Cookie Jar	95.00
Zeisel, Cookie Jar, Casual Living	130.00
Zeisel, Plate, Dinner, Holiday	16.00
Zeisel, Salt & Pepper, Casual Living	48.00

HALLOWEEN is an ancient holiday that has been changed in the last 200 years. The jack-o'-lantern, witches on broomsticks, and orange decorations seem to be twentieth-century creations. Collectors started to become serious about collecting Halloween-related items in the late 1970s. The papier-mache decorations, now replaced by plastic, and old costumes are in demand.

Bucket, Wendy	40.00
Candy Container, Black Cat, Papier-Mache, Germany, 5 In.	22.00
Candy Container, Humpty Dumpty, Dancing, Wearing Witch's Hat, Germany, 4 In.	175.00
Candy Container, Jack-O'-Lantern, Germany, 1910, 2 1/2 In. ....*Illus*	355.00
Candy Container, Pumpkin, Papier-Mache, Germany, 6 In.	60.00
Candy Container, Witch On Pumpkin	40.00
Candy Container, Witch's Black Shoe, Papier-Mache, 3 x 7 In.	200.00
Candy Container, Witch, Celluloid, 1950s, 3 In.	15.00
Candy Container, Witch, Papier-Mache, Cone Shaped, Germany, 7 In.	60.00
Clicker, Witch	12.00
Cookie Cutter, Boxed Set	45.00
Costume, Blue Falcon, 1976	28.00
Costume, Bugaloo, Box	100.00
Costume, Casper The Friendly Ghost, 1960s	38.00
Costume, Casper The Friendly Ghost, Collegeville, 1950s	18.00
Costume, Clown, Child's, 1950s	20.00
Costume, Clown, Collegeville	50.00
Costume, Corporal Rusty, 101st Cavalry, Rin-Tin-Tin, TV, Pla-Master, Box, 1955	130.00
Costume, Cowboy, Maverick, Rifle & Guns, Box	750.00
Costume, Cowboy, With Gun, Yankeeboy	35.00
Costume, Elephants, Donkeys, Fabric, Crepe Paper Collar, 43 In., 1940s ....*Illus*	8.00
Costume, Evel Knievel, With Mask, Ben Cooper, Box, 1974	75.00
Costume, Fred Flintstone, Box	15.00
Costume, Garrison's Gorillas, Ben Cooper, Military Uniform, 1967	70.00
Costume, Incredible Hulk, Box, 1977	24.00
Costume, Indian Chief, Yankee Boy, 1930s, Box	125.00

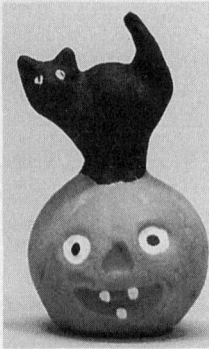

Halloween, Candy
Container, Jack-O'-
Lantern, Germany, 1910,
2 1/2 In.

Halloween, Costume,
Elephants, Donkeys, Fabric,
Crepe Paper Collar,
43 In., 1940s

Halloween, Jack-O'-Lantern,
Flapper, Die Cut, Germany,
1920s,
5 x 5 In.

Costume, Indian Suit, Leather Headdress, Moccasins, Hand Made, 1950s		65.00
Costume, John F. Kennedy, Mask, Halco, Box, Early 1960s		60.00
Costume, Kermit The Frog, Box		22.00
Costume, Li'l Abner & Daisy Mae, 1960s, Pair		50.00
Costume, Lone Rider, Cowboy Outfit, Chaps, Shirt & Vest, Child's, 1950s		50.00
Costume, Man From UNCLE, Box		65.00
Costume, Morticia Addams, Mask, Clothing, Box		95.00
Costume, Oswald Rabbit By Walter Lantz, Graphics On Orange Box		45.00
Costume, Popeye, Box		15.00
Costume, Skeleton, 1950s		85.00
Costume, Snoopy, Box		15.00
Costume, Spiderman, Ben Cooper, Package, 1978		12.00
Costume, Tarzan, 1975		50.00
Costume, The Fonz, Mask, 1980		28.00
Costume, Wonder Woman, Adult Size		30.00
Costume, Wonder Woman, Box, 1976		35.00
Costume, Woodstock, Collegeville, 1980s, Child's, Large		10.00
Costume, Yogi Bear, Ben Cooper, Box, 1960s		48.00
Costume, Zorro, Hat, Mask & Gun, Display Card, Marx, 1960		90.00 to 100.00
Figurine, Girl, Witch Hat, On Pumpkin, Pottery, Duncan Studios, 1949, 8 In.		35.00
Figurine, Scarecrow, Cardboard, Orange, Black, Honeycomb Tissue Arms, 7 3/4 In.		58.00
Fortune Boards, Gypsy Witch		25.00
Hat & Purse, Woman's, Orange Pumpkin		40.00
Incense Burner, Skull, Nodder Jaw, 4 In.		95.00
Jack-O'-Lantern, Cutout Eyes, Mouth With 3 Teeth		225.00
Jack-O'-Lantern, Flapper, Die Cut, Germany, 1920s, 5 x 5 In.	*Illus*	65.00
Jack-O'-Lantern, Garfield & Arlene, Salt & Pepper		90.00
Jack-O'-Lantern, Original Face, Papier-Mache, 4 In.		95.00
Jack-O'-Lantern, Original Face, Papier-Mache, 8 In.		160.00
Jack-O'-Lantern, Original Face, Papier-Mache, Germany, 5 In.		275.00
Jack-O'-Lantern, Papier-Mache, 5 1/2 In.		110.00
Jack-O'-Lantern, Plastic, 2 Faces, 4 In.		35.00
Jack-O'-Lantern, Plastic, 5 1/2 In.		45.00
Jack-O'-Lantern, Tin, Toledo Sign Company		880.00
Lantern, Candle, Black Graphic Of Large Cats, Marked, Orange, Germany, 18 In.		145.00
Lantern, Cat Head, Orange, Insert		195.00
Lantern, Cat, Devil, Owl & Witch, Orange Cardboard, 3 1/2 x 6 1/2 In.		78.00
Lantern, Devil, Insert		215.00 to 345.00
Lantern, Owl, Double Faced, Bail Handle, Tin, 6 In.		285.00
Lantern, Pumpkin, Papier-Mache		85.00

Lantern, Pumpkin, Pierced Tin, 6 In. 165.00
Lantern, Skull, Red Inserts, Germany 435.00
Magnet, Lucy, Witch 3.00
Mask, Alfred E. Newman, Real Hair, Rubber, 1981 .... 125.00
Mask, Boba Fett, Full Head 80.00
Mask, Bugaloo 45.00
Mask, Darth Vader 45.00
Mask, Darth Vader, Full Head 55.00
Mask, Darth Vader, Molded From Original 875.00
Mask, Emperor, Full Head 445.00
Mask, Jimmy From Pufnstuf 40.00
Mask, John Lennon 50.00
Mask, Mammy 295.00
Mask, Max Headroom, Paper, 1986 .... 12.00
Mask, Quick Draw McGraw, Envelope 45.00
Mask, Raptor, Jurassic Park, Head Mask 80.00
Mask, Ronald Reagan Monster, If You're Not Scared You Should Be 35.00
Mask, Sammy Davis Jr., 1960s 95.00
Mask, Satellite Scout Space, Vickers Gasoline Premium, 1950s 35.00
Mask, Spider Man, Ben Cooper 10.00
Mask, Storm Trooper, Hard Plastic, Smoked Lens Eyes 80.00
Noisemaker, 2 Black Minstrels, Germany 30.00
Noisemaker, Black Cat, Tin 40.00
Noisemaker, Black Cats On Fence, Tin 15.00
Noisemaker, Witch, Red & White Clothes, Composition Head, Germany, 8 In. 245.00
Nut Cup, Papier-Mache, 1930s, 2 3/4 In. 65.00
Pin, Jack-O'-Lantern, White Ground, 1930s, 1 3/4 In. 18.00
Place Mat, Textured Paper, Late 1940s, Set Of 4 .... 25.00
Poster, Ronald Reagan Monster Mask 25.00
Pumpkin, Metal, 6 In. 35.00
Pumpkin, Papier-Mache, Original Base, Paper Insert, Germany 70.00
Puppet, Hand, Black Cat, Ear Tag, Steiff, 1950s 255.00
Rattle, Witch Holding Pumpkin, Metal, Wooden Handle, T. Cohn, Inc., 2 1/2 x 5 In. 48.00
Tambourine, Metal 35.00

HAMPSHIRE pottery was made in Keene, New Hampshire, between
1871 and 1923. Hampshire developed a line of colored glazed wares
as early as 1883, including a Royal Worcester-type pink, olive green,
blue, and mahogany. Pieces are marked with the printed mark or the
impressed name *Hampshire Pottery* or *J.S.T. & Co., Keene, N.H.* Many
pieces were marked with city names and sold as souvenirs.

Bowl, Embossed Leaves, Buds, Matte Green Glaze, Lines To Inside Rim, 10 x 3 In. 385.00
Bowl, Foliate Form, Matte Green Glaze, 2 1/2 x 5 1/2 In. 316.00
Bowl, Incised Water Lily, Pink Interior, Signed, 5 1/2 In. 412.00
Bowl, Stylized Leaves Under Feathered Green Matte Flambe, Signed, 5 1/4 In. 357.00
Bowl, Swastika, Matte Green Glaze, 7 In. 285.00
Candlestick, Stippled Blues, Blacks & Grays, Handle, No. 82 .... 175.00
Chamberstick, Matte Green Glaze, Impressed Mark, 7 In. 297.00
Creamer, Souvenir, Laurel House, Catskill Mountains 40.00
Ewer, Luster, Floral, Matte Black Glaze, Signed, 8 In. 145.00
Lamp, Vertical Leaf Design, Flowers, Matte Green Glaze, 15 In. 2185.00
Mug, Taft Co., Keene, New Hampshire, Pair 385.00
Mug, Victorian Embossed Design, Capitol, Columbus, Oh. 125.00
Pitcher, Stein, Floral, 9 1/2 In. 275.00
Stein, Incised Design Under, Matte Jade Green Glaze, Signed, 8 1/4 In. 176.00
Tankard, Stylized Band, Marked, 7 In. 110.00
Tea Set, Rockingham Glaze, 1876, 16 Piece 495.00
Toothpick, Clear, F. Redig, Creamery Supplies, Seattle, Washington 30.00
Vase, 3 Handles, Matte Green Glaze, 5 In. 205.00
Vase, Calla Lilies, Green, 8 1/2 In. 595.00
Vase, Embossed Flowers, Collar Rim, Bulbous, Matte Green Glaze, 5 In. 770.00
Vase, Embossed Leaves, Vine Handles, Matte Green Glaze, 8 1/4 In. 575.00
Vase, Feathered Matte Blue Glaze, Cylindrical, 7 1/2 x 4 In. 515.00

Vase, Feathered Matte Green Glaze, 2 Handles, Cylindrical, 7 x 4 In. 431.00
Vase, Matte Green Glaze, 2 Handles, 4 In. 242.00
Vase, Matte Green Glaze, Cylindrical, 5 In. 145.00
Vase, Matte Leaves, Berry Glaze, Incised Mark, 4 In. 187.00
Vase, Matte Leaves, Green Raised Mark, 4 1/2 x 2 In. 88.00
Vase, Matte Mottled Blur, 6 In. 215.00
Vase, Overlapping Leaves, Matte Green Glaze, 8 1/2 In. 895.00
Vase, Plum & Green Glaze, 7 In. 450.00
Vase, Raised Leaf, Blossom, Matte Green Glaze, 4 1/2 In. 132.00
Vase, Raised Leaf, Matte Green Glaze, 7 1/2 In. 660.00
Vase, Raised Leaf, Matte Green Glaze, Bulbous, Marked, 10 In. 715.00

HANDEL glass was made by Philip Handel working in Meriden, Connecticut, from 1885 and in New York City from 1893 to 1933. The firm made art glass and other types of lamps. Handel shades were made not only of leaded glass in a style reminiscent of Tiffany but also of reverse painted glass. Handel also made vases and other glass objects.

Bookends, Roman Ruin Design, 3 Columns, Facade Of Building, Bronze, 7 1/2 In. 1045.00
Fernery, Opaline, White Glass, Painted Spider Mums, 4 x 9 In. 1800.00
Humidor, 3 Dogs, 2 Sitting, 1 Standing, Brown, Green Ground, 7 1/2 x 6 1/2 In. 1320.00
Humidor, Beige Ground, Green, Gold Bird, Wave Design, 7 1/4 x 5 1/2 In. 1210.00
Humidor, Golfing Scene, Man & Woman Playing Golf, Gray, Yellow Ground, 8 In. 1100.00
Humidor, Pond Lilies, Lily Pads, Dragonfly, Aqua Green Ground, Duck In Flight, 8 In. . . 1760.00
Lamp, 3-Light, Lily, Petals Attached To Sockets, Bronze, 21 In. 4600.00
Lamp, Base, Artichoke, Signed 450.00
Lamp, Boudoir, Butterflies, Pods, 7 In. 2200.00
Lamp, Boudoir, Reverse Painted Shade, Floral Bouquets, Pink, Blue Flowers, 7 In. 2145.00
Lamp, Conical Shade, Leaded Green Slag Panels, Green, Amber Ladderwork, 27 In. 2875.00
Lamp, Desk, Cylindrical Gold Shade, Gold Dore Finish To Base, 12 x 16 In. 330.00
Lamp, Desk, Green Teroma Glass, Case To White, Ribbed Base, 16 In. 1265.00
Lamp, Floral Filigree Shade, Green & Caramel Slag Inserts, Marked, 27 1/2 In. 605.00
Lamp, Hanging, Ball, Parrot On Rose Bush, Black, Green, Red, Blue Enamel, 6 In. 1650.00
Lamp, Harp Shape, Bronze, Label, 52 In. 520.00
Lamp, Leaded Stained Glass, Dogwood, Art Nouveau, 22 x 19 In. 4115.00
Lamp, Piano, Green Slag Apron, Granite Glass Segments, 9 x 22 x 7 In. 1265.00
Lamp, Reverse Painted Ice Conical Shade, Green Trees, Orange Ground, 18 x 26 In. 3850.00
Lamp, Reverse Painted Shade, Caramel, Green, Black, Rose, Bronze Metal Base, 28 In. . . 4400.00
Lamp, Reverse Painted Shade, Fall Woodland & Water Scene, 16 x 23 In. 3025.00
Lamp, Reverse Painted Shade, Pine Forest, Hills, Signed, c.1915, 23 In. 8625.00
Lamp, Reverse Painted Shade, Purple Mountains, Flowers, Blue Sky, 18 In. 4140.00
Lamp, Reverse Painted Shade, Seascape, Beach Front Tree Scene, 4 Handles, 23 In. 5750.00
Lamp, Reverse Painted Shade, Yellow Butterflies, Wild Rose Blossoms, 23 In. 14950.00
Lamp, Reverse Painted, Bell Formed Shade, 3 Stylized Wisteria, Leafage, 14 In. 3080.00
Lamp, Scenic Shade, Sunset, Leaded Pine Trees, Bronze Base, Floor Model 8750.00
Lamp, Stylized Foliate Band, Orange Amber Top, Teroma Shade, 24 In. 3335.00
Lamp, Table, 4-Panel Shade, Parrots, Frosted Cameo Glass, 24 In. 8050.00
Lamp, Teroca, Orange, Green Highlights, 8-Panel Shade, Palm-Like Trees, 18 1/2 In. . . . 3080.00
Lamp, Tropical Sunset Shade, 18 In. 7150.00
Shade, Mosserine, Green, 10 In. 1650.00
Shade, Reverse Painted, Intaglio Finish Exterior, Palm Trees Interior, 1910, 14 In. 2185.00
Vase, Teroma, Bailey, No. 4223, 6 1/2 In. 990.00

HARDWARE, see Architectural category.

HARKER Pottery Company of East Liverpool, Ohio, was founded by Benjamin Harker in 1840. The company made many types of pottery but by the Civil War was making quantities of yellowware from native clays. They also made Rockingham-type brown-glazed pottery and whiteware. The plant was moved to Chester, West Virginia, in 1931. Dinnerwares were made and sold nationally. In 1971 the company was sold to Jeannette Glass Company and all operations ceased in 1972. For more information, see *Kovels' Depression Glass & American Dinnerware Price List*.

Ashtray, Cameoware, Pink 15.00

Ashtray Set, Antique Auto, 4 Piece	25.00
Cake Plate, Dahlia	28.00
Cake Plate, Tulip Bouquet	20.00
Cake Set, Cameoware, Blue, 7 Piece	85.00
Casserole, Cover, Petit Point I, Stacking	55.00
Casserole, Cover, Petit Point II, Stacking	55.00
Casserole, Cover, Red Apple, 9 In.	75.00
Chop Plate, Corinthian, Handle, 10 In.	8.00
Cookie Jar, Dainty Flower, Cameoware, Blue	58.00
Cup & Saucer, Chesterton, Gray	5.00
Custard, Dahlia, 4 Piece	30.00
Custard, Mallow, 4 Piece	30.00
Mixing Bowl, Ivy	30.00
Pie Plate, Calico Tulip	25.00
Pitcher, Batter, Calico Tulip	40.00
Plate, Chesterton, Gray, 9 In.	8.00
Plate, Ivy Vine, 10 In.	18.00
Plate, Red Apple, 10 In.	18.00
Plate, Winter, Old Homestead, Currier & Ives, 9 In.	15.00
Plate, Winter, Old Homestead, Currier & Ives, 11 In.	15.00
Platter, Colonial Lady, 12 In.	20.00
Rolling Pin, Colonial Lady	150.00
Rolling Pin, Mallow	95.00
Rolling Pin, Modern Tulip, Cadet, White	80.00
Rolling Pin, Morning Glory	125.00
Salt & Pepper, Mallow	30.00
Salt & Pepper, White Clover, Meadow Green	40.00
Sugar, Cover, Corinthian	10.00
Sugar & Creamer, Cameoware, Rose	7.00

HARLEQUIN dinnerware was produced by the Homer Laughlin Company from 1938 to 1964, and sold without trademark by the F. W. Woolworth Co. It has a concentric ring design like Fiesta, but the rings are separated from the rim by a plain margin. Cup handles are triangular in shape. For more information, see *Kovels' Depression Glass & American Dinnerware Price List.*

Ashtray, Basket Weave, Mauve	50.00
Ashtray, Maroon	60.00
Ashtray, Red	50.00 to 90.00
Bowl, Forest Green	35.00
Bowl, Fruit, Rose	5.00
Bowl, Nut, Light, Green	125.00
Bowl, Oatmeal, Red	25.00
Bowl, Salad, Maroon, Individual	35.00
Bowl, Salad, Rose, Individual	20.00
Bowl, Yellow	15.00
Butter, Cover, Rose	75.00
Cake Plate, Blue	45.00
Cake Plate, Yellow	40.00
Candleholder, Rose	200.00
Casserole, Cover, Maroon	145.00 to 215.00
Casserole, Cover, Red	130.00 to 135.00
Casserole, Cover, Spruce Green	215.00
Casserole, Cover, Yellow	40.00
Creamer, Forest Green	60.00
Creamer, Gray	35.00
Creamer, Light Green	15.00
Creamer, Maroon	90.00
Creamer, Maroon, Individual	35.00
Creamer, Novelty, Blue	35.00
Creamer, Novelty, Gray	95.00
Creamer, Novelty, Spruce Green	40.00 to 45.00
Creamer, Spruce Green	60.00

Creamer, Spruce Green, Individual 125.00
Creamer, Tangerine 55.00
Cup, Spruce Green, After Dinner 95.00
Cup, Yellow, After Dinner 25.00
Cup & Saucer, Rose ....6.00 to 15.00
Cup & Saucer, Turquoise 10.00
Cup & Saucer, Yellow 10.00
Eggcup, Double, Maroon 40.00
Eggcup, Double, Rose ....30.00 to 45.00
Eggcup, Double, Spruce Green 30.00
Eggcup, Mauve, Individual 40.00
Eggcup, Spruce Green 40.00
Eggcup, Turquoise 20.00
Figurine, Cat, Maroon 225.00
Figurine, Cat, Maverick, White Gold Trim ....25.00 to 65.00
Figurine, Cat, Yellow 225.00
Figurine, Duck, Yellow ....85.00 to 195.00
Figurine, Fish, Yellow 225.00
Figurine, Lamb, Yellow 225.00
Gravy Boat, Forest Green 35.00
Gravy Boat, Mauve 20.00
Gravy Boat, Rose ....20.00 to 25.00
Jug, Gray, 22 Oz. 95.00
Jug, Maroon, 22 Oz. 100.00
Jug, Rose, 22 Oz. 80.00
Jug, Spruce Green, 22 Oz. ....40.00 to 120.00
Jug, Yellow, 22 Oz. ....35.00 to 45.00
Mixing Bowl, Yellow, 10 In. 55.00
Nappy, Spruce Green, 9 In. 10.00
Nappy, Turquoise, 9 In. 15.00
Pie Plate, Yellow, 10 In. ....40.00 to 55.00
Pitcher, Water, Gray, Ball 100.00
Pitcher, Water, Maroon, Ball 85.00
Pitcher, Water, Mauve, Ball 75.00
Pitcher, Water, Red, Ball 65.00
Pitcher, Water, Spruce Green, Ball 95.00
Plate, Forest Green, 9 In. 12.00
Plate, Gray, 10 In. 45.00
Plate, Maroon, 9 In. 8.00
Plate, Maroon, 10 In. 55.00
Plate, Mauve, 10 In. 35.00
Plate, Spruce Green, 7 In. ....10.00 to 34.00
Plate, Spruce Green, 9 In. 20.00
Plate, Turquoise, 7 In. 4.00
Plate, Turquoise, 10 In. 30.00
Plate, Turquoise, 11 In. 12.00
Plate, Yellow, 9 In. ....6.00 to 7.00
Plate, Yellow, 10 In. ....15.00 to 30.00
Platter, Rose, 11 In. 10.00
Soup, Cream, Chartreuse 40.00
Soup, Cream, Gray 20.00
Soup, Cream, Spruce Green ....35.00 to 40.00
Soup, Cream, Turquoise 25.00
Sugar, Chartreuse 60.00
Sugar, Cover, Maroon 45.00
Sugar, Cover, Turquoise 20.00
Sugar, Mauve 10.00
Sugar, Spruce Green 35.00
Sugar, Turquoise 30.00
Sugar, Yellow 20.00
Sugar & Creamer, Cover, Maroon 50.00
Sugar & Creamer, Forest Green, After Dinner 85.00
Sugar & Creamer, Maroon, After Dinner 110.00

Sugar & Creamer, Mauve, After Dinner 150.00
Sugar & Creamer, Red, After Dinner 130.00
Sugar & Creamer, Spruce Green, After Dinner 195.00
Sugar & Creamer, Tangerine 65.00
Syrup, Blue 110.00
Syrup, Yellow 300.00
Teapot, Blue 265.00
Teapot, Chartreuse ....75.00 to 125.00
Teapot, Gray 185.00
Teapot, Light Green 150.00
Teapot, Mauve ....95.00 to 125.00
Teapot, Red ....125.00 to 130.00
Teapot, Spruce Green ....95.00 to 140.00
Tumbler, Car Decal, Green 45.00
Tumbler, Red 50.00
Tumbler, Spruce Green ....45.00 to 55.00
Tumbler, Turquoise 40.00
Tumbler, Yellow 40.00

HATPIN collectors search for pins popular from 1860 to 1920. The long pin, often over four inches, was used to hold the hat in place on the hair. The tops of the pins were made of all materials, from solid gold and real gemstones to ceramics and glass. Be careful to buy original hatpins and not recent pieces made by altering old buttons.

Agate, Sterling Silver, Scotland 350.00
Cameo, Gutta Percha, 12 In. 95.00
Driver, Head On Tip, 9 In. 20.00
Gold Iridescent, Molded Flame, 7 1/2 In. 165.00
Sword Form, Pearl & Diamond, Enamel, 14K Gold 270.00

HATPIN HOLDERS were needed when hatpins were fashionable from 1860 to 1920. The large, heavy hat required special long-shanked pins to hold it in place. The hatpin holder resembles a large saltshaker, but it often has no opening at the bottom as a shaker does. Hatpin holders were made of all types of ceramics and metal. Look for other pieces under the names of specific manufacturers.

Egyptian Design, Brass, Benedict 96.00
Elk Scene, Sunset, Gold Design, Blue Mark 495.00
Figural, Pig, Black, Polychrome, 6 In. 77.00
Gold, With Daisies, Bavaria 78.00
Swirl, Niloak 700.00
White, With Roses, Germany, 7 In. 175.00

HAVILAND china has been made in Limoges, France, since 1842. The factory was started by the Haviland Brothers of New York City. Pieces are marked *H & Co.*, *Haviland & Co.*, or *Theodore Haviland*. It is possible to match existing sets of dishes through dealers who specialize in Haviland china. Other factories worked in the town of Limoges making a similar chinaware. These porcelains are listed in this book under Limoges.

HAVILAND & CO.

Berry Bowl, Blue Garland, 5 In. 5.00
Bowl, Rosalinde, Oval, 9 In. 45.00
Bowl, Salad, Drop Rose, Scalloped Rim, 9 In. 300.00
Bowl, Vegetable, Cover, Gold Trim, Handle, S Mark, 1903, 12 x 7 1/2 x 5 In. 110.00
Bowl, Vegetable, Cover, Red Rose Clusters, White Ground, Ribbon Finial, Handles 145.00
Bread Tray, Baltimore Rose, 13 3/4 x 7 1/2 In. 150.00
Butter Pat, Clover Leaf 15.00
Coffeepot, Blue Garland 85.00
Coffeepot, Moss Rose, Gold Trim 135.00
Creamer, Apple Blossom 45.00
Cup & Saucer, Apple Blossom 31.00
Cup & Saucer, Athena, White, Gold Trim 40.00
Cup & Saucer, Blue Garland 10.00

Cup & Saucer, Moss Rose, Black Mark 30.00
Cup & Saucer, Richmond 45.00
Dessert Set, Blackberry Pattern, H. & Co. 395.00
Dinner Set, Cobalt Blue Flowers, White Porcelain, Eva Ziesel, 80 Piece 595.00
Dinner Set, Pink, White Florals, Scalloped Rim, Gold Trim 1350.00
Figurine, China Lady's Cuspidor, White Bird, Pour Spout, 1880, 4 x 3 In. 225.00
Fish Set, Golden Yellow, With Sauce Pitcher, 7 Piece 1300.00
Game Set, Cobalt Blue, Gold Trim, Sauce Dish, 11 Piece 1850.00
Mustache Cup, With Saucer, Hand Painted Flowers, Butterflies 95.00
Plate, Athena, 8 In. 25.00
Plate, Berkeley, 6 1/2 In. 10.00
Plate, Blue Garland, 6 1/2 In. 5.00
Plate, Fish, Hand Painted, Gold Leaf With Gold Rim, 1880s, 9 In., 8 Piece 325.00
Plate, Gold Ribbon, Flower Wreath, 9 3/4 In. 25.00
Plate, Gold Scalloped Border, Gray, Pink, Roses 90.00
Plate, Grapes, 9 In. 100.00
Plate, Peonies, 9 In. 425.00
Plate, Roses, Traced In Gold, 9 In. 25.00
Plate, White Cat In Center, Green Eyes, Blue, Beige Ground, Scalloped Edge, 8 1/2 In. ... 85.00
Platter, Athena, 14 In. 185.00
Platter, Blue Garland, Oval, 13 In. 40.00
Platter, Blue Garland, Oval, 14 1/2 In. 50.00
Platter, Memphis, Well, 14 In. 95.00
Platter, Rosalinde, Oval, 14 In. .... 50.00 to 65.00
Salt & Pepper, Blue Garland 35.00
Sauceboat, Blackberries, Gold Trim, White Enameled Highlights 2195.00
Soup, Dish, Miramar 10.00
Sugar, Cover, Rope Handle, Large 150.00
Sugar, Cover, Rosalinde 45.00
Sugar, White, Gold Trim, Signed 20.00
Sugar & Creamer, Blossoms & Plumes, Gold Ribbon Handles 50.00
Tureen, Soup, Ranson 285.00
Tureen, Soup, Rose Garlands, Ribbon Handles 165.00
Tureen, Soup, White, Gold 295.00

HAWKES cut glass was made by T. G. Hawkes & Company of Corning, New York, founded in 1880. The firm cut glass blanks made at other glassworks until 1962. Many pieces are marked with the trademark, a trefoil ring enclosing a fleur-de-lis and two hawks. Cut glass by other manufacturers is listed under either the factory name or in the general Cut Glass category.

Berry Bowl, Valencian, Signed, 3 x 8 In. 325.00
Bottle Set, Oil & Vinegar, Etched Words, Floral, Silver & Crystal Stopper, 2 Piece 145.00
Bowl, Centauri, 8 In. 195.00
Bowl, Fruit, Classic, Intaglio Cutting, Signed 1500.00
Bowl, Hobstar, Blown Out, Signed, 9 1/2 x 6 1/2 In. 945.00
Bowl, Napoleon Pattern, 9 In. 450.00
Bowl, Pinwheel & Star, 3 x 8 5/8 In. 373.00
Breakfast Set, Sugar & Creamer, Sterling Silver Collars & Sugar Cover 1595.00
Butter Dish, 6 x 7 In., 2 Piece 247.00
Candlestick, Flute Cut, Rayed Star Base, Signed, 9 In., Pair 475.00
Candy Dish, Chrysanthemum, Leaf Shape, Signed, 7 1/2 x 6 1/2 In. 245.00
Carafe, Holland 295.00
Celery Dish, Hobstar, Blown Out, 11 3/4 x 6 In. 415.00
Celery Tray, Chrysanthemum, 11 1/2 x 6 In. 495.00
Cocktail Shaker, Signed 80.00
Compote, Candy, Green Teardrop Stem & Foot, Engraved Leaf, 6 1/2 In. 125.00
Compote, Geometric, Brilliant, Diamond Shape, 7 1/4 In., Pair 300.00
Compote, Strawberry & Fan, 8 1/2 In. 200.00
Cookie Jar, Hobstars Separated By Concave Tusks, Prisms, 9 1/4 In. 850.00
Cordial, Donisel, Signed, 10 Piece 375.00
Creamer, Pedestal Base, Engraved Satin Bands, Signed 125.00
Decanter, Brunswick, Signed Stopper & Decanter, 10 3/4 In. 545.00

Dish, Blown Out, 8 Swirling Leaf Shape, Signed, 10 In. 1285.00
Ginger Jar, Oriental Characters On Cover, Signed, 5 1/4 In. 345.00
Inkstand, Gravic, Polished Scroll Pattern, Hammered Copper, 5 In. 1725.00
Jug, Navarre, Ring-Shaped Handle, Signed, 11 1/2 In. 750.00
Nappy, Iris, Hawkes, 8 In. 225.00
Pitcher, Cider, Brunswick Pattern, Triple Cut Handle, Signed, 6 1/2 x 7 1/2 In. 695.00
Pitcher, Cider, Floral Cutting, Star Cut Design, Engraved Handle, 6 1/4 In. 275.00
Pitcher, Cider, Florence, 6 x 6 In. 425.00
Pitcher, Water, Floral, Green, 5 In. 350.00
Plate, Gladys Pattern, Marked, 6 In. 150.00
Punch Bowl, Pedestal, Hobstar & 5-Point Star, Signed 790.00
Rose Bowl, Grecian, 5 1/2 x 7 In. 1175.00
Rose Bowl, Persian Variation Of Russian, 5 3/4 x 7 1/2 In. 650.00
Sugar & Creamer, Geometric 225.00
Sugar & Creamer, Gracia, Cameo Panels, Stripe Cutting, Signed, 5 3/4-In. Sugar 750.00
Sugar & Creamer, Venetian, 3 Sides, Triple Notched Handle On Creamer 375.00
Tray, Pin, Key, Signed, 6 1/2 x 5 1/2 In. 55.00
Tray, Venetian, 12 In. 1400.00
Tumbler Set, Chrysanthemum, 6 Piece 275.00
Vase, Brunswick, 16 Point Hobstar Base, Signed, 8 In. 310.00
Vase, Corset, Brunswick, Cut Glass, 14 In. 950.00
Vase, Cut Flowers, Thick Blown, Signed, 10 3/4 In. 225.00
Vase, Engraved Flowers, Swags & Ribbons, Lemon Yellow, Signed, 8 1/2 In. 195.00
Vase, Gravic, Iris, Brilliant, 11 In. 495.00

HEAD VASES, generally showing a woman from the shoulders up, were used by florists primarily in the 1950s and 1960s. Made in a variety of sizes and often decorated with imitation jewelry and other lifelike accessories, the vases were manufactured in Japan and the U.S.A. Less elaborate examples were made as early as the 1930s. Religious themes, babies, and animals are also common subjects. Other head vases are listed under manufacturers' names and can be located through the index at the back of this book.

African Woman, Dorothy Kindell 60.00
Baby, Blue Bonnet ....38.00 to 45.00
Betty Lou Nichols, Sue 96.00
Bothwell, Hand Painted, Catalina 165.00
Carlotta, 4 In. 160.00
Carmen Miranda, Maroon & Yellow, 8 In. 300.00
Glamour Girl, Ivory, Gold ....38.00 to 45.00
Herman Kleiner, 1949 .... 55.00
Jane Wyman, Turban, UCAGCO 125.00
Manchu, Beige & Black Accents 75.00
Marilyn Monroe ....1500.00 to 2200.00
Marti Hollywood, Art Deco, 9 1/2 In. 250.00
Ornate Lady, Pinks & Blues, California Pottery, 10 14 In. 145.00
Parma, 8 1/2 In. 275.00
Polynesian Girl, Jane Payer, 11 In. 120.00
Poodle Head 8.00
Posegay & Wagner, No. 105 .... 75.00
Posegay & Wagner, No. 292, 7 In. 100.00
Puppy, Brown, Pink Bonnet 20.00
Raggedy Andy 25.00
Santa 100.00
Teen, Cole, 6 1/4 In. 110.00
Uncle Sam 25.00
Woman, Big Hat 25.00
Woman, Blond, Blue Eyes, 6 In. 40.00
Woman, Dorothy Kindell, 1950s 110.00
Woman, Glamour Girl, 6 1/2 In. 25.00
Woman, Green Eyes, Pearl Earrings 55.00
Young Girl, Bonnet, Singing, 7 In. 105.00

HEDI SCHOOP Art Creations, North Hollywood, California, started about 1945 and was working until 1954. Schoop made ceramic figurines, lamps, planters, and tablewares.

*Hedi Schoop
s*

Ashtray, Ballerina, Triangular Form, Gold Highlights, 10 In.	77.00
Basket, Boy, Girl, Oriental, Yellow, Black With Dragons	85.00
Bowl, Gold Sponge, Oval, Large	25.00
Bowl, Spider Web Design, Handles, Shallow, Marked	45.00
Cookie Jar, Darner Doll	195.00
Egg Dish, Darner Doll	150.00
Figurine, Angel, In Leaf Dish, Maroon, Gold	70.00
Figurine, Bali Dancer, Pair	115.00
Figurine, Cat, Turn-About, Male & Female	165.00
Figurine, Dancing Girl, Pink, Flowers, 11 In., Pair	195.00
Figurine, Dutch Boy	95.00
Figurine, Dutch Girl, 11 In.	65.00
Figurine, French Poodle, 12 In., Pair	425.00
Figurine, Girl, With Basket & Poodle, Gray & Blue, Signed, 10 In.	110.00 to 176.00
Figurine, Girl, With Ponytail, White, Pink Dress, Flower Basket, 9 1/2 In.	85.00
Figurine, Oriental Couple, Kneeling, Holding Branches For Basket, 7 1/2 In., Pair	165.00
Figurine, Oriental Woman, Green Head	135.00
Figurine, Oriental Woman, With Umbrellas, Gold	195.00
Figurine, Peasant Woman, Red Bandanna	95.00
Figurine, Peasant Woman, Red Scarf, With Basket, Signed, 13 In.	180.00
Figurine, Repose, Large	175.00
Figurine, Turnabout Cat, Woman & Man, Tooled Leather Look, 16 In.	150.00
Figurine, Woman Holding 2 Baskets, 12 In.	130.00
Figurine, Woman, Kneeling With Flared Skirt	125.00
Figurine, Woman, With Basket	85.00
Figurine, Woman, With Flowers, Yellow & Peach Glaze, Marked, 13 In.	110.00
Figurine, Woman, With Serving Bowl	135.00
Lamp, Woman, Green Gown, Gold Trim, Pair	595.00
Lamp Base, Jade, Figurines, 12 In.	70.00
Planter, Bali Dancer, Gold, Pair	150.00
Planter, Dutch Boy, Yellow, Purple, White, 10 1/2 In.	35.00
Planter, Fruit Basket, Yellow, Green Handles, Brown Stripes, 11 x 5 1/2 In.	35.00
Planter, Woman, Reading Book, 9 In.	50.00
Planter, Woman, With 2 Baskets, White, 14 In.	125.00
Tobacco Jar, Indian Head	42.00
Tray, Floral, 7 1/2 In.	25.00
Tray, Flowering Cactus, 14 x 9 In.	25.00
Vase, Butterflies, Bulbous, Pink Interior, 9 1/2 In.	85.00
Vase, Duck	75.00
Vase, Wedding, Indian Hills, Gold Fleck Glaze	64.00

HEINTZ ART Metal Shop made jewelry, copper, silver, and brass in Buffalo, New York, from 1906 to 1935, when a new company name was taken and the mark became *Silvercrest*. The most popular items with collectors today are the copper desk sets and vases made with applied silver designs.

Ashtray, Hunting Dog, Pheasant	85.00
Bowl, Floral, Silver Overlay, 3 3/4 x 7 1/4 In.	230.00
Bowl, Leaf, Berry Design, Green, Bronze, Silver Overlay, Brown Patina, 7 x 4 In.	330.00
Box, Cover, Geometric Design, Bronze, 8 1/2 x 3 1/2 x 3 In.	286.00
Box, Geometric Design, Bronze With Sterling Overlay, Impressed Mark, 8 x 3 In.	440.00
Candlestick, Leaf & Stem Overlay, Silver Wash, Signed, 5 1/2 In., Pair	440.00
Desk Set, Floral Design, Silver On Bronze, 3 1/2 x 4 1/2 In.	264.00
Desk Set, Silver Geometric Design On Brass, Signed, 5 Piece	385.00
Humidor, Pipe Ashtray & Matchbox Holder, Silver On Bronze, 3 Piece	375.00
Lamp, Boudoir, Silver On Bronze, Design On Front & Back	950.00
Lamp, Bronze, Verdigris Patina, Sterling Overleaf, Metal, 10 1/4 In.	805.00
Lamp, Cutout Shade, Floral Design, Silver On Bronze, 15 In.	880.00
Lamp, Cutout Shade, Floral Design, Silver On Bronze, 9 x 9 1/2 In.	990.00

Lamp, Cutout Shade, Floral Design, Silver On Bronze, Brass Finish, 11 In. 605.00
Lamp, Desk, Silver Weeds, Silver On Bronze, 10 1/2 x 7 3/4 In. 440.00
Lamp, Silver On Bronze, 2 Blue & White Cameos In Shade, Paper Label, 11 In. 1000.00
Smoking Set, Geometric Design, Impressed Mark, 11 In., 3 Piece 330.00
Smoking Set, Peacocks At Fountain, Humidor, 3 Ashtrays, Cigarette Box, Signed 412.00
Stamp Box, Geometric Design, Silver On Bronze, Insert 125.00
Vase, Applied Silver Tree Design, Bronze Patina, 8 x 3 1/2 In. 170.00
Vase, Bamboo Design, Silver On Bronze, Impressed Mark, 6 In. 355.00
Vase, Bulbous, Silver Foliate Design, 8 1/2 In. 400.00
Vase, Floral Design, Silver On Bronze, Impressed Mark, 4 In. 209.00
Vase, Floral Design, Silver On Bronze, Impressed Mark, 6 In. 330.00
Vase, Floral Design, Silver On Bronze, Impressed Mark, 7 1/2 In. 286.00
Vase, Landscape Design, Silver On Bronze, Impressed Mark, 5 In. 187.00
Vase, Landscape Design, Silver On Bronze, Impressed Mark, 8 In. 220.00
Vase, Mottled Bronze Patina, Sterling Overlay Of Florals, 11 In. 484.00
Vase, Poppy Design, Bronze With Sterling Overlay, Impressed Mark, 8 In. 297.00
Vase, Silver Blossoms, Tapered, Silver On Bronze, 14 1/4 x 4 In. 605.00
Vase, Silver Floral Design, Silver On Bronze, Trumpeted Footed, Signed, 16 In. 605.00
Vase, Silver Foliate Design, Bronze Patina, 8 x 5 In. 285.00
Vase, Silver On Bronze, Broad Leaf Design, 4 In. 286.00
Vase, Silver On Bronze, Pat. 1912, 4 1/2 In. 60.00
Vase, Silver Overlay, Bird Of Paradise, Green Patina, Art Nouveau Foliage, 6 In. 195.00
Vase, Silver Poppies On Verdigris Patinated Base, Silver On Bronze, 12 1/2 In. 770.00
Vase, Silver Weeds, Dark Brown Ground, Silver On Bronze, 9 x 4 1/2 In. 465.00

HEISEY glass was made from 1896 to 1957 in Newark, Ohio, by A. H.
Heisey and Co., Inc. The Imperial Glass Company of Bellaire, Ohio,
bought some of the molds and the rights to the trademark. Some
Heisey patterns have been made by Imperial since 1960. After 1968,
they stopped using the *H* trademark. Heisey used romantic names for
colors, such as *Sahara*. Do not confuse color and pattern names. The
Custard Glass and Ruby Glass categories may also include some
Heisey pieces.

H

Albemarle, Wine 22.00
Animal, Bunny, Head, Down, Yellow 65.00
Animal, Colt, Balking 70.00
Animal, Colt, Kicking 175.00
Animal, Colt, Standing ....55.00 to 95.00
Animal, Elephant, Small 215.00
Animal, Giraffe, Amber 425.00
Animal, Giraffe, Head Back, Marked 180.00
Animal, Giraffe, Head To Side ....220.00 to 260.00
Animal, Goose, Wings Half ....55.00 to 140.00
Animal, Mallard, Wings Up ....145.00 to 180.00
Animal, Plug Horse, Amber 595.00
Animal, Plug Horse, Oscar 105.00
Animal, Pouter Pigeon 850.00
Animal, Ringneck Pheasant ....135.00 to 145.00
Animal, Rooster, Fighting 190.00
Animal, Scotty, Amber 395.00
Animal, Sparrow 150.00
Banded Flute, Sauce, Marked 70.00
Bead Swag, Butter, Cover, Daisy Design 45.00
Bead Swag, Table Set, Daisy Design, 4 Piece 350.00
Bead Swag, Toothpick ....55.00 to 70.00
Bead Swag, Tumbler 35.00
Beaded Panel & Sunburst, Toothpick 135.00
Coarse Rib, Bowl, Marked, 9 1/2 In. 45.00
Colonial, Bowl, 8 1/2 In. 30.00
Colonial, Cordial 25.00
Colonial, Cup, Custard, Star Bottom, 4 1/2 Oz. 7.50
Colonial, Jug, 5 In. 25.00
Colonial, Mustard, Cover 35.00

Colonial, Pitcher, 40 Oz. 110.00
Colonial, Plate, 4 3/4 In. 4.75
Colonial, Sherbet, Low 10.00
Colonial, Sugar & Creamer 16.00
Colonial, Syrup, Floral Cut 60.00
Continental, Toothpick ....120.00 to 195.00
Crystolite, Ashtray, Square, Marked, 3 In. 10.00
Crystolite, Celery Dish, Marked, 12 In. 37.50
Crystolite, Nappy, Marked, 4 In. 45.00
Crystolite, Punch Set, Bowl, Underplate, 12 Cups 285.00
Crystolite, Relish, 3 Sections, 8 In. 15.00
Crystolite, Relish, 5 Sections 40.00
Empress, Celery Dish, Flamingo, 10 In. 20.00
Empress, Compote, Moongleam, Marked, 6 In. 160.00
Empress, Compote, Sahara 60.00
Empress, Cruet, Flamingo 155.00
Empress, Ice Bucket, Sahara 85.00
Empress, Plate, Chintz Etch, Square, Marked, 7 In. 55.00
Empress, Plate, Square, Moongleam, 7 In. 25.00
Empress, Sugar & Creamer, Dolphin, Footed, Sahara, Marked 80.00
Empress, Sugar & Creamer, Yellow 65.00
Fancy Loop, Celery Dish, C Shape, 12 In. 65.00
Fancy Loop, Salt, 12 Individual, Box 375.00
Fancy Loop, Salt, Gold Trim 75.00
Fancy Loop, Sugar & Creamer, Hotel, Gold Trim 130.00
Fancy Loop, Syrup 100.00
Fandango, Cake Salver 145.00
Fandango, Toothpick ....85.00 to 90.00
Fern, Candlestick, 2-Light 150.00
Fern, Plate, 2 Handles, 15 In. 50.00
Fish, Bookends ....100.00 to 185.00
Girandole Set, Cut Prisms, 15 In., 3 Piece 220.00
Girl's Head, Stopper, Amber 495.00
Greek Key, Celery Dish, Marked, 6 /38 In. 145.00
Greek Key, Punch Bowl, 15 In., 2 Piece 425.00
Ipswich, Cruet 60.00
Ipswich, Tumbler, Footed, 9 Oz. 25.00
Kohinoor, Chip & Dip Set, 11 In. 35.00
Kohinoor, Finger Bowl, 4 1/2 In. 295.00
Lariat, Bowl, Silver Overlay, Floral Design, Marked, 7 In. 8.00
Lariat, Butter, Etched 18.00
Lariat, Candlestick, 2-Light, 4 3/4 In., Pair 95.00
Lariat, Candlestick, Enameled Flowers 75.00
Lariat, Plate, Footed, 9 In. 65.00
Lariat, Platter, 13 1/2 In. 85.00
Lariat, Punch Set, Bowl, 19 Cups 200.00
Lariat, Relish, 3 Sections, 12 In. 30.00
Lariat, Serving Plate, Silver Overlay 85.00
Locket On Chain, Cake Salver 226.00
Mercury, Candlestick, 1-Light, Moongleam, Pair 75.00
Mercury, Candlestick, Blue Iridized, 3 In., Pair 45.00
Mercury, Candlestick, Orchid Etch, 3 In., Pair 60.00
Minuet, Goblet, Water, 9 Oz. 30.00
Minuet, Plate, 8 In. 20.00
Minuet, Sherbet 15.00
Minuet, Wine 65.00
Mug, Elephant Handle 250.00
Narrow Flute, Jug, Marked, 1/2 Gal. 95.00
Narrow Flute, Sugar, Cube Holder 20.00
Narrow Flute, Toothpick, Handles 50.00
New Era, Candlestick, 2-Light, Prisms 75.00
New Era, Cocktail 12.00
Old Colony, Champagne, Sahara 22.00

Old Colony, Cordial, Sahara . . . . .30.00 to 110.00
Old Colony, Sugar & Creamer, Sahara 65.00
Old Dominion, Cordial, Empress Etch, 1 Oz. 150.00
Old Williamsburg, Candlestick, 11 In., Pair 295.00
Orchid Etch, Bowl, 12 In. 110.00
Orchid Etch, Butter, Cover 165.00
Orchid Etch, Candlestick, Pair . . . . .80.00 to 129.00
Orchid Etch, Champagne, Tall 39.00
Orchid Etch, Cocktail Shaker, 1 Qt. 200.00
Orchid Etch, Cocktail Shaker, Stirrer, Sterling Silver Top & Bottom . . . . .225.00 to 395.00
Orchid Etch, Decanter, Sterling Silver Top, 1 Pt. 225.00
Orchid Etch, Goblet, Tall Stem 30.00
Orchid Etch, Plate, 7 In. 18.00
Orchid Etch, Plate, Sandwich, 16 In. 80.00
Orchid Etch, Plate, Torte 95.00
Orchid Etch, Sugar & Creamer 65.00
Orchid Etch, Tankard, Donna Shape, 1/2 Gal. 650.00
Orchid Etch, Tumbler, Footed, 5 Oz. 55.00
Orchid Etch, Water, Tall, 10 Oz. 49.00
Paneled Cane, Creamer 40.00
Paneled Cane, Toothpick 45.00
Patrician, Candlestick, 6 3/8 In., Pair 120.00
Patrician, Candlestick, 7 1/2 In., Pair 135.00
Peerless, Punch Cup 8.00
Petal, Sugar & Creamer, Hotel, Flamingo 50.00
Pied Piper, Cocktail, Oyster 20.00
Pied Piper, Goblet, Water, 10 Oz. 30.00
Pineapple & Fan, Spooner, Green, Gold Trim 60.00
Pineapple & Fan, Toothpick 80.00
Pineapple & Fan, Water Set, Emerald, 5 Piece 340.00
Plain Band, Banana Stand, Footed, 10 In. 65.00
Plantation, Candlestick, 2-Light, Pair 110.00
Plantation, Candlestick, Ivy Etch, 5 In., Pair 205.00
Plantation, Candy Dish, Cover 125.00
Plantation, Pitcher 425.00
Plantation, Punch Cup 38.00
Plantation, Sherbet, Ivy Etch 15.00
Plantation, Syrup, Metal Top 150.00
Pleat & Panel, Candy Jar, Cover, Flamingo 75.00
Pleat & Panel, Plate, Moongleam, 8 In. 45.00
Pleat & Panel, Sugar & Creamer, Cover, Flamingo 65.00
Prince Of Wales Plumes, Nappy, Gold Trim, 9 1/2 In. 55.00
Prince Of Wales Plumes, Punch Bowl, Base, 14 In. 200.00
Prince Of Wales Plumes, Sauce 18.00
Prison Stripe, Nappy, 8 In. 40.00
Prison Stripe, Toothpick 275.00
Provincial, Cocktail, Oyster 75.00
Provincial, Goblet, 10 Oz. 40.00
Provincial, Plate, 7 In. 70.00
Punty & Diamond Point, Vase, 8 In. 45.00
Punty Band, Bowl, Crimped Edge, 8 In. 40.00
Puritan, Bowl, Floral, Oblong, Cutting, 14 In. 25.00
Puritan, Relish, 9 In. 22.50
Queen Ann, Ashtray 15.00
Queen Ann, Bowl, 9 In. 50.00
Recessed Panel, Candy Dish, Flashed Amethyst Cover, Gold Trim, 10 In. . . . . . .120.00 to 125.00
Regency, Candlestick, 2-Light, Pair 85.00
Revere, Bowl, French Dressing, Oval Underplate, 7 In. 65.00
Ribbed Octagon, Sugar & Creamer 35.00
Ridgeleigh, Smoker Set, 4 Ashtrays, Covered Box 55.00
Ring Band, Syrup, Gold Trim . . . . .275.00 to 295.00
Ring Band, Tumbler 30.00
Rose Etch, Plate, Cake, Footed 275.00

Rose Etch, Relish, 3 Sections, 9 In.	85.00
Rose Etch, Relish, 4 Sections	110.00
Rose Etch, Sugar & Creamer	50.00
Rose Etch, Wine	115.00
Saturn, Bowl, Grapefruit, Footed, 5 In.	15.00
Saturn, Chip & Dip Set	35.00
Saturn, Cruet	40.00
Saturn, Sugar & Creamer	25.00
Sawtooth Band, Syrup, Hinged Lid	95.00
Sleeping Fox, Ashtray	175.00
Spanish, Cocktail, 5 1/4 In.	80.00
Spanish, Goblet, Floral Cutting	40.00
Stepped Octagon, Plate, Flamingo, 7 In.	40.00
Sunburst, Celery Dish, 12 In.	40.00
Sunburst, Punch Bowl, Stand	365.00
Thumbprint & Panel, Bowl, Floral, 11 In.	50.00
Twist, Bowl, 4 In.	12.00
Twist, Ice Bucket, Handle, Moongleam	140.00 to 160.00
Twist, Tumbler, Soda, Footed, Moongleam, 10 Oz.	60.00
Victorian, Goblet, 9 Oz.	15.00 to 17.00
Victorian, Plate, 8 1/2 In.	40.00
Victorian, Punch Cup	20.00
Victorian, Sherbet	17.00
Victorian, Tumbler, 8 Oz.	175.00
Wabash, Pitcher, Footed, 3 Pt.	150.00
Wabash, Sherbet, Hawthorne, 6 Oz.	110.00
Warwick, Vase, Horn Of Plenty, Cobalt Blue, 5 In., Pair	450.00
Waverly, Candlestick, 2-Light, Pair	100.00
Waverly, Candlestick, Orchid Etch, 8 In.	325.00
Waverly, Plate, Torte, Rolled Edge, Orchid Etch	35.00
Winged Scroll, Tumbler, Emerald, Gold Trim	65.00
Yeoman, Plate, Serving, Blue, Enameled, Fruit Pattern, 24K Gold, 12 In.	150.00
Yeoman, Powder Box, Cover, Moongleam, Crystal Insert	240.00
Yeoman, Sugar & Creamer, Hotel, Moongleam	55.00

HEREND, see Fischer category.

HEUBACH is the collector's name for Gebruder Heubach, a firm working in Lichten, Germany, from 1840 to 1925. It is best known for bisque dolls and doll heads, their principal products. They also manufactured bisque figurines, including piano babies, beginning in the 1880s, and glazed figurines in the 1900s. Piano babies are listed in their own category. Dolls are included in the Doll category under *Gebruder Heubach* and *Heubach*. Another factory, Ernst Heubach, working in Koppelsdorf, Germany, also made porcelain and dolls. These will also be found in the Doll category under Heubach Koppelsdorf.

Figurine, 2 Black Boys Sharing A Secret, A Dark Secret Incised On Base	500.00
Figurine, Baby, Standing, Lookout Pose, 4 In.	150.00
Figurine, Children, 12 In.	795.00
Figurine, Sailor, Stands At Wheel, 11 1/2 In.	450.00
Plaque, Indian, With Bow & Arrow, Bird Amid Foliage, Jasper, 8 In.	245.00
Vase, Dutch Woman, 6 In.	75.00
Vase, Iris Design Front & Back, Butterfly Front, Pearl Finish Inside & Out, 9 3/4 In.	310.00
Vase, Narcissus, Pate-Sur-Pate, c.1882, 7 In.	465.00
Vase, Wood Nymph, 7 In.	198.00

HIGBEE glass was made by the J. B. Higbee Company of Bridgeville, Pennsylvania, about 1900. Tablewares were made, and it is possible to assemble a full set of dishes and goblets in some Higbee patterns. Most of the glass is clear, not colored. Additional pieces may be found in the Pressed Glass category by pattern name.

Cake Stand, Child's	30.00
Cheese, Paneled Thistle, Square, 6 In.	20.00

HISTORIC BLUE, see factory names, such as Adams, Clews, Ridgway, and Staffordshire.

HOBNAIL glass is a style of glass with bumps all over. Dozens of hobnail patterns and variants have been made. Clear, colored, and opalescent hobnail have been made and are being reproduced. Other pieces of hobnail may also be listed in the Duncan & Miller, Fenton, and Francisware categories.

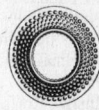

Basket, Opalescent, Medium To Pale Blue, Clear Applied Handle	95.00
Celery Vase, Peachblow, White To Rose, Sandwich, 7 In.	475.00
Cologne Bottle, Green, Stopper, England, 6 5/8 In., Pair	100.00
Cookie Jar, Heart Shape, Aqua	400.00
Cuspidor, Red, Carnival Glass	40.00
Pitcher, Blown, Milk Glass, 8 In.	150.00
Pitcher Set, Cranberry Opalescent, Square Mouth, Clear Handle, 8 In., 11 Piece	600.00
Toothpick, Amber	45.00
Toothpick, Blue	55.00
Vase, Cranberry Opalescent, Crimped, 4 In.	40.00
Water Set, Cranberry Opalescent, Square Mouth, Applied Clear Handle, 5 Piece	600.00

HOLLY AMBER, or golden agate, glass was made by the Indiana Tumbler and Goblet Company of Greentown, Indiana, from January 1, 1903, to June 13, 1903. It is a pressed glass pattern featuring holly leaves in the amber-shaded glass. The glass was made with shadings that range from creamy opalescent to brown-amber.

Butter, Cover	1100.00 to 1275.00
Cruet	2800.00
Dish, Sauce, Beads Around Center Circle, 4 1/4 In.	245.00
Pitcher, 4 1/2 In.	390.00
Relish, Table Handle, Oval, 9 In.	410.00
Toothpick	795.00

HOLT HOWARD was an importer who started working in 1949 in Stamford, Connecticut. He sold many types of table accessories, such as condiment jars, decanters, spoon holders, and saltshakers. The figures shown on some of his pieces had a cartoon-like quality. The company was bought out by General Housewares Corporation in 1969. Holt Howard pieces are often marked with the name and the year or HH and the year stamped in black. There was also a black and silver label.

Ashtray, Bartender	40.00
Ashtray, Cat	85.00 to 95.00
Ashtray, Rooster	28.00
Ashtray, Smoker, Man	45.00
Bowl, Cantaloupe, Green & Yellow, 1959, 6 In.	50.00
Candleholder, Huggers, Pixie, Pair	30.00 to 45.00
Candleholder, Rooster, Pair	75.00
Candleholder, Santa Claus, 2 Piece	25.00
Candleholder, Santa Claus, Mouse Climber	35.00
Candleholder, Santa In Car, Pair	15.00
Candleholder, Santa, With Sack	20.00
Cheese Keeper, Cats Cottage	35.00
Coffeepot, Rooster, Cover	110.00
Cookie Jar, Candy, Santa	250.00
Cookie Jar, Fig Newton Cookies	75.00 to 95.00
Cookie Jar, Rooster	75.00 to 175.00
Creamer, Rooster	12.00
Cup & Saucer, Rooster	20.00
Dish, Cottage Cheese	60.00
Dish, Pin, Cat, Tape Measure Tongue	55.00 to 175.00
Eggcup, Chick, Holds Salt & Pepper	45.00
Figurine, Cat	85.00
Figurine, Poodle	35.00
Figurine, Whale, 1960	28.00

Holder, Lipstick, Pixie 42.00
Holder, Razor, Barber Shape 15.00
Holder, Tea Bag, Rooster, 4 Piece 60.00
Jam Jar, Rooster 22.00
Jar, Christmas Treat, Santa Pops Out 150.00
Jar, Cocktail Onion, Pixie 75.00
Jar, Frog 85.00
Jar, Instant Coffee, Pixie ....160.00 to 275.00
Jar, Jam 'n Jelly, Pixie ....40.00 to 70.00
Jar, Jam 'n Jelly, Rooster 45.00
Jar, Ketchup, Pixie, Spoon 65.00
Jar, Ketchup, Rooster 22.00
Jar, Mustard, Pixie 55.00
Jar, Mustard, Rooster 22.00
Jar, Olive, 1958 ....35.00 to 79.00
Jar, Olive, Pixie 45.00
Jar, Olive, Spoon, 1958 .... 65.00
Jar, Relish, Pixie 125.00
Jar, Tiger 95.00
Ketchup, Pixie 55.00
Letter Holder, Cat 70.00
Mug, Rooster, Tapered 10.00
Napkin Holder, Rooster, Red ....45.00 to 55.00
Planter, Boy, On Shoe 18.00
Planter, Bull, Stylized 45.00
Planter, Doe & Fawn, Gold & White 28.00
Planter, Girl 14.00
Plate, Rooster, 8 1/2 In. ....10.00 to 14.00
Rack, Spice, Hang On, Cats 30.00
Salt & Pepper, Apple Slice 15.00
Salt & Pepper, Bird, Art Deco 25.00
Salt & Pepper, Blond Pixie 35.00
Salt & Pepper, Cat ....18.00 to 30.00
Salt & Pepper, Chicken 30.00
Salt & Pepper, Christmas Tree, Santa 35.00
Salt & Pepper, Mice 30.00
Salt & Pepper, Mice In Basket 35.00
Salt & Pepper, Raccoon, Large 32.00
Salt & Pepper, Rake 'n Spade, Box ....16.00 to 20.00
Salt & Pepper, Rooster 25.00
Salt Shaker, Strawberry With Face 30.00
Spoon Rest, Rooster 45.00
Spoon Rest, Santa's Face, 1964, Japan 80.00
String Holder, Cat ....38.00 to 65.00
Sugar, Cover, Pixie 65.00
Trivet, Tile, Design, Metal Holder 15.00
Tureen, Tomato Soup 165.00
Wall Pocket, Cat 145.00

HOPALONG CASSIDY was a character in a series of twenty-eight books written by Clarence E. Milford, first published in 1907. Movies and television shows were made based on the character. The best-known actor playing Hopalong Cassidy was William Lawrence Boyd. His first movie appearance was in 1919, but the first Hopalong Cassidy film was not until 1934. Sixty-six films were made. In 1948, William Boyd purchased the television rights to the movies, then later made fifty-two new programs. In the 1950s, Hopalong Cassidy and his horse, named *Topper,* were seen in comics, records, toys, and other products. Boyd died in 1972.

Badge, Sheriff, Star, Gold Metal, 1950s 20.00
Bag, Potato Chip 95.00
Bank, Hoppy, Plastic 65.00
Bedspread, Chenille, Green ....250.00 to 275.00

Binoculars, Black Metal, 2 Decals ....75.00 to 125.00
Binoculars, Red Metal, Silver, 2 Decals 145.00
Blotter, Hopalong Cassidy Movie, Illustrated 25.00
Book, Hopalong & His Young Friend Danny, TV, 1950 .... 97.00
Book, Pop-Up, Hopalong Cassidy Lends A Helping Hand, 1950 ....95.00 to 130.00
Bottle, Milk, Cloverdale Milk, 1/2 Pt. 250.00
Bottle, Milk, Dairylea, Illustration On Both Sides, 1 Qt. 145.00
Bottle, Milk, McClellan's Home Dairy, Lancaster, Ohio 135.00
Bottle, Milk, Melville, 1/2 Pt. 60.00
Bowl, Cereal, 1950s 55.00
Box, Hopalong Cassidy Chuck Wagon Set 15.00
Camera, Hoppy, Box, Large 145.00
Cap Pistol, Steel Gray, Silver Highlights, Wyandotte, 1950, 8 1/2 In. 285.00
Card, Good Luck, 3 x 5 In. 20.00
Chair, Official Bar 20 TV, Hoppy On Topper, Folding, Adjustable, 24 In. 920.00
Chaps, Shirt & Neckerchief, 3 Piece 375.00
Clock, Black 600.00
Coloring Book, Unused 25.00
Container, Ice Cream, Round, 1 Qt. 95.00
Cookie Jar, Decal 475.00
Dental Kit, Dr. West, Box 250.00
Figure, Topper, Ideal 95.00
Figure Set, Hoppy & Topper, Plastic, Ideal 125.00
Game, Canasta, Rotating Saddle Tray, 2 Decks Of Cards ....275.00 to 325.00
Game, Chinese Checkers, Box 185.00
Game, Milton Bradley, Board, Box, 1950 ....90.00 to 135.00
Glass, Juice 100.00
Glass, Red Hoppy 80.00
Glass Set, Western Series, 4 Piece 325.00
Gun, Medallion Holster, Black Bust On Grips, Pair 900.00
Gun & Holster Set, Deluxe 500.00
Holster, Single 185.00
Ice Cream Container, O'Fallon Dairy, 1 Qt. 30.00
Ice Cream Container, Rectangular, 1/2 Gal. 75.00
Knife, Black, 3 Blades, Hoppy On Topper Decals, Pocket ....55.00 to 75.00
Knife, Fork & Spoon, 3 Piece 35.00
Label, Bond Bread End, No. 19, 1950 .... 12.00
Lamp, Motion, Hoppy & Stagecoach, Econolite, 1950 ....350.00 to 450.00
Lobby Card, Renegades Of The Sage, 1949 .... 20.00
Lunch Box, Lithograph, Black, 1954 ....140.00 to 350.00
Lunch Box, Scallops, Red 75.00
Magazine, Life, June 12, 1950 .... 25.00
Marble, Black, 1 In. 2.50
Mirror, 1950 .... 45.00
Money Clip, Photograph 12.00
Mug, Hoppy With Guns Drawn, Cowboy Roping A Steer, Milk Glass, 1950s 42.00
Neckerchief Slide, Long Horn Steer, Red Glass Eyes, Silver Finish, 1 3/4 In. ......25.00 to 75.00
Neckerchief Slide, Raised Hoppy, Rope Design, Round, 1950s, 2 In. 70.00
Night-Light, Holster, Plastic ....250.00 to 375.00
Pamphlet, Jo-Mar Dairy Products, Hoppy & Mickey Mantle, 7 x 13 In. 119.00
Pen, Ball-Point, Figural Head, Hoppy's Name In White On Barrel 150.00
Pencil, With Light 60.00
Pencil Case, Hoppy Jumbo, With 2 Drawers 75.00
Pin, Ask Me About The Hopalong Cassidy Savings Club, 3 In. 38.00
Pin, Daily News 22.00
Pin, Ribbon & Hanging Gun, Photograph, 1950s, 1 1/4 In. 49.00
Place Mat, Hoppy Cloud, Plastic 120.00
Plate Set, Party, 1950s, 4 Piece 35.00
Poster, Hopalong Cassidy Bicycles, The Original Cowboy Bicycle 303.00
Poster, Rustlers Valley, Movie, 1 Sheet 150.00
Puzzle Set, Frame Tray, Box, Set Of 3 ....60.00 to 95.00
Radio, Red, Topper Rearing, Arvin ....575.00 to 675.00
Record Set, Capital, Singing Bandit, Autographed Photograph, 1950 .... 125.00

Ring, Bar 20, Metal, Copper & Silver Finish, 1950s 75.00
Ring, Hoppy & Initials HC, Metal, 1950s 24.00
Shoe Caddy, Yellow Vinyl, Multi-Pocketed 285.00
Suspenders, Bar 20, Bill Boyd Punch-Out, On Cardboard, 1940-1950, Box 400.00
Sweater, Child's, Button Down 275.00
Sweater, Plaid, Navy Trim, Image On Back 125.00
Thermos Only, 1973 .... 40.00
Tin, Potato Chip 200.00
Toy, Target Practice Sign, 1950 .... 250.00
Tumbler, Milk Glass 45.00
Tumbler, Plastic 100.00
Wood Burning Set, Graphic, Box ....195.00 to 275.00
Wristwatch, Hoppy, Original Band, U.S. Time, 1950s 65.00
Wristwatch, Western Band, Saddle Display Box ....375.00 to 498.00
Writing Pad, Graphics On Cover, 8 x 10 In. 55.00

HOWARD PIERCE has been working in Southern California since 1936. In 1945, he opened a pottery in Claremont. His contemporary-looking figurines are popular with collectors. Pieces are marked with his name. He stopped making pottery in 1991.

Howard Pierce

Figurine, 3 Owls 100.00
Figurine, African Head 120.00
Figurine, Bear 50.00
Figurine, Bear & Baby ....125.00 to 135.00
Figurine, Bird Family, White Chest, Gray Brown, 3 Piece 85.00
Figurine, Bobwhite, Mother & Baby, White, Brown Spots, Pair 60.00
Figurine, Cat, 11 In. 65.00
Figurine, Cat, Siamese, 10 In. & 8 In., Pair 135.00
Figurine, Cat, Stylized, Brown, White, 8 In. ....30.00 to 35.00
Figurine, Chipmunk ....50.00 to 55.00
Figurine, Coyote, Howling, 6 In. 45.00
Figurine, Dinosaur 85.00
Figurine, Dog, Dachshund ....60.00 to 70.00
Figurine, Dove, Blue, 6 In. ....65.00 to 70.00
Figurine, Doves, Wood Base 135.00
Figurine, Duck Family, Green Speckled Chests, Black, 3 Piece 80.00
Figurine, Duck, Seated, Green & White, 6 In. 25.00
Figurine, Fox, 1 Crouching, 1 Seated, Brown & White, Pair 110.00
Figurine, Girl, On Bench Holding Doll 95.00
Figurine, Girl, With Basket ....40.00 to 50.00
Figurine, Girl, With Book 85.00
Figurine, Goose & Baby Goose ....65.00 to 95.00
Figurine, Goose, 6 In. ....40.00 to 50.00
Figurine, Madonna, Blue, 8 1/2 In. ....65.00 to 75.00
Figurine, Monkey, Gray, Pair ....165.00 to 168.00
Figurine, Natives, Male & Female, Brown, Pair 145.00
Figurine, Owl, 2 1/2 In. 50.00
Figurine, Owl, 4 In. 70.00
Figurine, Owl, 5 In. 75.00
Figurine, Owl, Brown, 8 In. 85.00
Figurine, Owl, Gray 28.00
Figurine, Owl, Tan Speckled Glaze, 6 In. 65.00
Figurine, Partridge In Tree 65.00
Figurine, Partridge, Mother & Baby, Brown, Pair 55.00
Figurine, Peasant Woman, Feeding Chickens, 24K Gold, 8 1/2 In., 3 Piece 450.00
Figurine, Quail, Family Of 3, Brown & White ....60.00 to 75.00
Figurine, Rabbit, Pair 55.00
Figurine, Raccoon, Long Tail 125.00
Figurine, Roadrunner, 12 In. ....65.00 to 95.00
Figurine, Rooster & Hen, Charcoal 165.00
Figurine, Rooster & Hen, White & Brown, Pair 165.00
Figurine, Sparrow, 3 Piece ....50.00 to 65.00
Figurine, Turtle 75.00

Figurine, Water Bird, 14 In.	75.00
Figurine, Water Birds, Green, White, 5 1/2 In.	25.00
Figurine, Wolf	75.00
Figurine, Woman & Chickens, Gold Plated, Signed, 3 Piece	175.00
Figurine, Woman, Holding Basket	50.00
Planter, Deer	45.00
Planter, Owl	55.00
Vase, Gondola Style, Oval, 7 1/2 In.	40.00
Vase, Horse & Tree Insert, Green	85.00

HOWDY DOODY and Buffalo Bob were the main characters in a children's series televised from 1947 to 1960. Howdy was a redheaded puppet. The series became popular with college students in the late 1970s when Buffalo Bob began to lecture on campuses.

Bank, Figural Howdy, Small Smiling Pig, 7 In.	525.00
Bank, Head, Vandor	45.00
Bank, Standing, Front Of Box Base, Pottery, 1950s	80.00
Bath Mitt, Puppet Type	47.00
Belt Buckle, Metal	12.50
Bookends, Vandor	125.00
Boxing Gloves	300.00
Camera, Sun Ray	50.00
Can, Welch's Grape Juice	25.00
Clock, Alarm	100.00 to 125.00
Cookbook, Welch's	55.00
Cookie Jar, Howdy Doody On Pig Bank, Shawnee	450.00
Cookie Jar, With 5 Characters Riding Carousel Horses, Tin	175.00
Costume, Clarabel, Box	50.00
Doll, Composition, Pamphlet, Box	295.00
Dummy, Ventriloquist, 20 In.	65.00
Dummy, Ventriloquist, Goldberger, Box, 24 In., 1973	80.00 to 120.00
Figure, Bobbin' Head	39.00
Game, Bean Bag	175.00
Game, Howdy Doody's Electric Carnival	95.00
Game, TV Studio, Board, Box	75.00
Glass Set, Welch's, Howdy Doody Illustrations, 1950s, 7 Piece	125.00
Hat, Canvas	50.00
Head Vase	25.00
Lamp, Wall, Howdy With Santa Claus	350.00
Lunch Box	250.00 to 295.00
Marionette, Clarabell, 1950s	125.00 to 225.00
Marionette, Heidi, Box	575.00
Marionette, Howdy Doody, 1950s	120.00 to 130.00
Marionette, Mr. Bluster	148.00
Marionette, Summerfall-Winterspring, Necklace With 4 Seasons Charms	225.00
Mirror, It's Howdy Doody Time, 2 1/2 In.	2.00
Music Box, Playing Piano, Vandor	125.00
Necklace, Princess Summerfall-Winterspring, Composition	275.00
Necktie, NBC Radio, Howdy Doody Time	35.00
Night-Light, Howdy Doody Sitting On Round Wood Base, 1950, 6 In.	60.00
Pen, Moving Arms, Head, Leg, Vinyl, Japan, 6 1/2 In., Pair	10.00
Pencil, 6 Colorful Pencils, Picture	10.00
Pencil, Kargan	55.00
Pin, Howdy's Picture, Plastic, 1950s, 1 1/2 In.	45.00
Pin, Pictures Clarabell, 1 3/4 In.	7.50
Poster, Blue Bonnet Margarine, 1953, 12 x 40 In.	150.00
Puzzle, ABC	35.00
Puzzle, Circus Star, Frame, 1950, 9 x 11 In.	40.00
Puzzle, Tray, 1953	38.00
Ring, I'm For Howdy Doody, Doody For President, Post Cereals, 1948	125.00
Ring, Poll-Parrot Shoes, Brass, Parrot Head Top, 1950s	35.00
Ring, Poll-Parrot, TV, Blue Plastic, 1950s	125.00
Slate, 1950s	110.00

Spoon Holder, Vandor .... .35.00 to 45.00
Stationery, Pictorial Productions, Inc., c.1971, 18 Sheets & Envelopes 35.00
Sweatshirt, Cowboy, Paper Tag, 1948 .... 135.00
Swim Tube, Round, Unopened Package 90.00
Thermos, 1977 .... 45.00
Tin, Cookie, With Top Humidor 175.00
Toy, Acrobat, Composition Head, Tin Lithograph .... .375.00 to 395.00
Toy, Cookie-Go-Round, Tin 245.00
Toy, Driving Fire Truck, Windup, Tin 85.00
Ukulele, Box 100.00
Wall Plaque, Vandor 65.00
Wristwatch, Blue & White Dial, With Characters, Patent Watch Co. 225.00
Wristwatch, Eyes Rotate, 1950s 990.00

HULL pottery was made in Crooksville, Ohio, from 1905. Addis E. Hull bought the Acme Pottery Company and started making ceramic wares. In 1917, A. E. Hull Pottery began making art pottery as well as the commercial wares. For a short time, 1921 to 1929, the firm also sold pottery imported from Europe. The dinnerwares of the 1940s, including the Little Red Riding Hood line, the high gloss artwares of the 1950s, and the matte wares of the 1940s, are all popular with collectors. The firm officially closed in March 1986.

Hull
U.S.A.

Ashtray, Ebb Tide, Mermaid, Green & Pink 125.00
Ashtray, Serenade, Yellow, 13 x 10 1/2 In. 65.00
Bank, Corky Pig, Pink .... .35.00 to 55.00
Bank, Corky Pig, Seated, Brown 45.00
Bank, Corky Pig, Standing, Brown 45.00
Bank, Little Texan, Save At Graham Chevytown, Mansfield, Ohio 600.00
Bank, Porky Pig, Yellow 95.00
Basket, Blossom Flite, 8 1/4 x 9 1/4 In. 100.00
Basket, Bow Knot, Blue, 10 1/2 In. 750.00
Basket, Bow Knot, Pink, 6 1/2 In. 215.00
Basket, Butterfly, White Ground, 10 x 12 In. .... .55.00 to 75.00
Basket, Capri, Coral, 12 1/4 In. 45.00
Basket, Continental, Mountain Blue, 12 1/2 In. 75.00
Basket, Dogwood, Pink & Blue, 7 1/2 In. 245.00
Basket, Ebb Tide, Chartreuse & Wine, 16 1/2 In. 230.00
Basket, Granada, Pink & Tan, 8 In. 85.00
Basket, Magnolia Gloss, Pink, 10 1/2 In. 200.00
Basket, Magnolia Matte, 10 1/2 In. 250.00
Basket, Mardi Gras, 8 In. 85.00
Basket, Parchment & Pine, 8 In. 95.00
Basket, Parchment & Pine, 16 In. 125.00
Basket, Poppy, Pink & Cream, 12 In. 1350.00
Basket, Royal, Pink, 12 In. 75.00
Basket, Serenade, Pink, 6 3/4 In. 105.00
Basket, Sunglow, 6 1/2 In. 40.00
Basket, Tokay, Moon Shape, Pink, 10 1/2 In. .... .35.00 to 90.00
Basket, Tropicana, 12 3/4 In. 650.00
Basket, Tuscany, Green & Pink, 12 In. 155.00
Basket, Water Lily, Tan, 10 1/2 In. 395.00
Basket, Wildflower, Pink & Blue, 10 1/2 In. 340.00
Basket, Woodland, Chartreuse, 10 1/2 In. 175.00
Basket, Woodland, Hanging, 7 1/2 In. 160.00
Basket, Woodland, Twig Form Handle, 10 1/2 In. .... .585.00 to 725.00
Bookends, Orchid, 7 In. 1075.00
Bowl, Calla Lily, Blue Top, Pink Bottom, 8 In. 85.00
Bowl, Mixing, Cinderella, 5 1/2 In. 20.00
Butter, Cover, Little Red Riding Hood .... .395.00 to 450.00
Candleholder, Blossom Flite, 3 In. 35.00
Candleholder, Ebb Tide, 2 3/4 In., Pair 75.00
Candleholder, Magnolia, Blue & Pink, 4 In., Pair 50.00
Candleholder, Parchment, Pine Green, 2 1/4 In., Pair .... .10.00 to 25.00

Candleholder, Water Lily, 4 In. 25.00
Canister, Salt, Little Red Riding Hood 1000.00
Casserole, Cover, Debonair, Dutch Oven, Partitioned 35.00
Clock, Bluebird, Sessions . . . . .250.00 to 325.00
Coffeepot, Dripolator, Wildflower 45.00
Coffeepot, House & Garden, 8 Cup 20.00
Console, Blossom Flite, 6 3/4 In. 95.00
Console, Ebb Tide, Snail, 15 3/4 In. 160.00
Console, Magnolia, Pink Gloss, 13 In. 65.00
Console, Woodland, 14 In.. . . . . 140.00
Cookie Jar, Barefoot Boy, 13 In. . . . . .350.00 to 400.00
Cookie Jar, Daisy 85.00
Cookie Jar, Debonair, 12 1/2 In. 65.00
Cookie Jar, Gingerbread Man, Beige . . . . .125.00 to 295.00
Cookie Jar, Gingerbread Man, Gray . . . . .200.00 to 450.00
Cookie Jar, Little Red Riding Hood, Closed Basket 300.00
Cookie Jar, Little Red Riding Hood, Gold Stars, Roses .295.00 to 415.00
Cookie Jar, Little Red Riding Hood, Poinsettia, Large 825.00
Cookie Jar, Little Red Riding Hood, Red Shoes, Gold Bows 375.00
Cookie Jar, Plaidware 150.00
Cornucopia, Bow Knot, 7 1/2 In. 135.00
Cornucopia, Butterfly, 12 In. 70.00
Cornucopia, Dogwood, Pink & Blue, 4 In. 95.00
Cornucopia, Ebb Tide, Shrimp & Turquoise, 11 3/4 In. 105.00
Cornucopia, Magnolia Gloss, Pink, 8 1/2 In. 85.00
Cornucopia, Tokay, 11 1/2 In. 60.00
Cornucopia, Woodland, Pink, 11 In. . . . . .80.00 to 125.00
Cracker Jar, Little Red Riding Hood . . . . .725.00 to 800.00
Creamer, Bow Knot, 5 1/2 In. 165.00
Creamer, Little Red Riding Hood, Pantaloons 225.00
Creamer, Little Red Riding Hood, Tab Handle . . . . .425.00 to 625.00
Cup, Child's, House & Garden 65.00
Dish, Chip & Dip, House & Garden, Leaf Shape, 15 x 10 1/2 In. 12.00
Ewer, Blossom Flite, 13 1/2 In. 95.00
Ewer, Bow Knot, 5 1/2 In. . . . . .150.00 to 165.00
Ewer, Bow Knot, 13 1/2 In. 1200.00
Ewer, Dogwood, Pink & Blue, 8 In. 250.00
Ewer, Iris, 8 In. . . . . .115.00 to 145.00
Ewer, Iris, 13 1/2 In. 485.00
Ewer, Magnolia Matte, 4 1/2 In. 60.00
Ewer, Magnolia Matte, 13 1/2 In. . . . . .175.00 to 275.00
Ewer, Poppy, Pink & Blue, 13 1/2 In. 800.00
Ewer, Royal, Woodland, Pink, 13 1/2 In. 195.00
Ewer, Royal, Woodland, Turquoise, 13 1/2 In. 150.00
Ewer, Sunglow, Pink & Yellow, 5 1/2 In. 25.00
Ewer, Wildflower, 13 1/2 In. . . . . .450.00 to 900.00
Ewer, Woodland, 13 1/2 In. 325.00
Figurine, Dog, Dachshund, 14 In. 165.00
Figurine, Trumpet Player, Band Member 119.00
Flower Frog, Bird, Maroon, Green, 10 1/2 In. . . . . .100.00 to 120.00
Flowerpot, Tulip, Blue 100.00
Jar, Grease, Sun Glow, 5 1/2 In. 45.00
Jardiniere, Bow Knot, Pink & Blue, 7 In. 550.00
Jardiniere, Imperial, Speckled Orange, 10 In. 50.00
Jardiniere, Open Rose, Ram's Head Handles, 8 1/2 In. . . . . .125.00 to 250.00
Jardiniere, Orchid, 9 1/2 In. 350.00
Jardiniere, Poppy, 4 3/4 In. 80.00
Jardiniere, Tulip, Pink & Blue, 7 In. 295.00
Jardiniere, Water Lily, Pink & Turquoise, 5 1/2 In. 76.00
Jardiniere, Woodland, 9 1/2 In. . . . . .350.00 to 475.00
Jardiniere, Woodland, Matte, Pre-1950s, 5 1/2 In. 200.00
Lamp, Little Red Riding Hood 1500.00
Lavabo, Butterfly, 16 In. 175.00

Matchbox, Little Red Riding Hood, Hanging .... .400.00 to 800.00
Mixing Bowl, Bouquet, 7 1/2 In. 45.00
Mustard, Little Red Riding Hood, With Spoon, 5 1/4 In. .... .350.00 to 425.00
Pitcher, Blossom Flite, Pink, 12 1/2 In. .... .65.00 to 165.00
Pitcher, Butterfly, 8 3/4 In. .... .30.00 to 50.00
Pitcher, Dogwood, 13 1/2 In. 450.00
Pitcher, Ebb Tide, 6 In. 50.00
Pitcher, Ebb Tide, 13 In. 215.00
Pitcher, Ebb Tide, Shrimp & Turquoise, 13 In. 245.00
Pitcher, Magnolia Gloss, Pink, 13 1/2 In. 200.00
Pitcher, Magnolia Matte, 13 1/2 In. 240.00
Pitcher, Milk, Little Red Riding Hood, 8 In. .... .275.00 to 395.00
Pitcher, Open Rose, Pink & Blue, 13 1/2 In. 400.00
Pitcher, Rosella, 6 1/2 In. 1725.00
Pitcher, Woodland Gloss, 13 1/2 In. 200.00
Pitcher, Woodland, Pre-1950s, 13 1/2 In. 275.00
Pitcher, Woodland, Yellow & Green, 13 1/2 In. 400.00
Planter, Baby & Pillow .... .15.00 to 35.00
Planter, Bandanna Duck 20.00
Planter, Cat, Pink 24.00
Planter, Dancing Lady 65.00
Planter, Dog, Dachshund, 15 In. 70.00
Planter, Farmer Boy 300.00
Planter, Flying Duck, Hanging 45.00
Planter, Giraffe, 8 In. 60.00
Planter, Goose, Lime Green 35.00
Planter, Kitten, 7 1/2 In. 30.00
Planter, Knight On Horse 110.00
Planter, Lady & Basket 20.00
Planter, Lamb 45.00
Planter, Open Rose, Mermaid With Shell, 10 1/2 In. 1950.00
Planter, Parrot .... .35.00 to 50.00
Planter, Poodle Head, 6 1/2 In. 30.00
Planter, Siamese Cats 75.00
Planter, Water Lily, Tan & Salmon, 5 3/4 In. 125.00
Planter, Woodland Gloss, 10 In. 75.00
Plaque, Bow Knot, Yellow & Blue, 10 In. .... .1100.00 to 1375.00
Plate, Crestone, Turquoise, White Foam Edge, 10 1/2 In. 40.00
Plate, House & Garden, Gingerbread Man, Brown .... .35.00 to 45.00
Salt & Pepper, House & Garden 8.00
Salt & Pepper, Little Red Riding Hood, 3 1/2 In. .... .75.00 to 125.00
Salt & Pepper, Little Red Riding Hood, 4 1/2 In. 750.00
Salt & Pepper, Little Red Riding Hood, 5 1/2 In. .... .150.00 to 175.00
Serving Tray, Butterfly, 3 Section, 11 1/2 In. .... .75.00 to 125.00
Sugar, Cover, Woodland Gloss 35.00
Sugar & Creamer, Little Red Riding Hood, Open 150.00
Sugar & Creamer, Little Red Riding Hood, Side Pour 250.00
Sugar & Creamer, Magnolia 75.00
Teapot, Blossom Flight, 8 1/4 In. 95.00
Teapot, Bow Knot 600.00
Teapot, Little Red Riding Hood .... .275.00 to 375.00
Teapot, Parchment & Pine 40.00
Teapot, Royal, Blue 75.00
Teapot, Serenade, Blue .... .100.00 to 125.00
Teapot, Water Lilly, Pink & Green, 6 In. 170.00
Teapot, Woodland, Chartreuse .... .95.00 to 175.00
Teapot & Sugar, Parchment & Pine, 2 Piece 65.00
Teapot & Sugar, Water Lily, 2 Piece 175.00
Urn, Tokay, 5 1/2 In. 45.00
Vase, Bow Knot, Blue, 5 In. .... .145.00 to 165.00
Vase, Bow Knot, Pink & Blue, 8 1/2 In. .... .165.00 to 250.00
Vase, Bud, Sueno Tulip, 6 In. 75.00
Vase, Calla Lily, 6 1/2 In. 65.00

Vase, Continental, Orange, 15 In. 65.00
Vase, Crab Apple, Blue, 6 In. 80.00
Vase, Crab Apple, Yellow, 7 In. 125.00
Vase, Deer, Double, 12 In. 45.00
Vase, Dogwood, 8 1/2 In. 140.00
Vase, Ebb Tide, Angel Fish, 9 1/4 In. 120.00
Vase, Ebb Tide, Chartreuse & Wine, 9 x 10 1/2 In. 110.00
Vase, Ebb Tide, Fish, 11 In. ....95.00 to 130.00
Vase, Ebb Tide, Royal Blue, 6 1/2 In. ....65.00 to 140.00
Vase, Ebb Tide, Shrimp & Turquoise, 12 In. 175.00
Vase, Granada, Dancing Lady 50.00
Vase, Granada, White, 9 In, Pair 45.00
Vase, Iris, 7 In. 95.00
Vase, Lusterware, 8 1/2 In. 75.00
Vase, Magnolia Gloss, 10 1/2 In. 90.00
Vase, Magnolia Matte, Pink & Blue, 6 1/2 In. ....50.00 to 75.00
Vase, Magnolia, Yellow & Blue, 6 1/4 In. 50.00
Vase, Mardi Gras, 9 In. 95.00
Vase, Open Rose, White, Pink & Yellow, Handles, 6 1/4 In. 35.00
Vase, Orchid, Blue, 8 In. ....150.00 to 295.00
Vase, Orchid, Blue, 10 1/4 In. 300.00
Vase, Orchid, Ivory & Pink, 8 1/2 In. 145.00
Vase, Parchment & Pine, 7 In. 55.00
Vase, Parchment & Pine, 10 In. 50.00
Vase, Peacock, 10 In. ....30.00 to 50.00
Vase, Poppy, 8 1/2 In. 275.00
Vase, Royal Woodland, Pink & Gray, 1950, 9 In. 89.00
Vase, Serenade, Yellow, 8 In. 75.00
Vase, Sueno Tulip, Scalloped Rim, 2 Handles, 8 In. 185.00
Vase, Sun Glow, Pink, 6 1/2 In. 35.00
Vase, Sun Glow, Yellow, 8 In. 65.00
Vase, Thistle, Blue, 6 1/2 In. 90.00
Vase, Tokay, Pink & Green, 12 In. 70.00
Vase, Tulip, Blue, 6 In. ....135.00 to 200.00
Vase, Water Lily, 5 1/2 In. 105.00
Vase, Water Lily, 8 x 8 1/2 In. 75.00
Vase, Water Lily, Tan & Brown, 6 1/2 In. ....65.00 to 75.00
Vase, Wildflower, 6 1/2 In. 65.00
Vase, Wildflower, 9 1/2 In. 95.00
Vase, Wildflower, 10 1/2 In. 235.00
Vase, Wildflower, 12 1/4 In. 295.00
Vase, Woodland, Double, 8 1/2 In. 150.00
Vase, Woodland, Green, 5 1/2 In. 60.00
Wall Pocket, Bow Knot, Cup & Saucer, 6 In. 245.00
Wall Pocket, Bow Knot, Pitcher, 6 In. ....175.00 to 245.00
Wall Pocket, Bow Knot, Whisk Broom, Blue, 8 In. ....195.00 to 250.00
Wall Pocket, Bow Knot, Whisk Broom, Pink & Blue, 8 In. 143.00
Wall Pocket, Butterfly, 10 1/2 In. 50.00
Wall Pocket, Chinaman 95.00
Wall Pocket, Pitcher, Pink & Blue, 6 In. 195.00
Wall Pocket, Rosella, Heart Shape 38.00
Wall Pocket, Royal Woodland, Shell, Aqua, 1950 .... 69.00
Wall Pocket, Sunglow, Pitcher 40.00
Wall Pocket, Woodland Gloss, 7 1/2 In. 65.00
Wall Pocket, Woodland Gloss, Cream & Green 45.00
Wall Pocket, Woodland, Seashell, Yellow 100.00
Window Box, Parchment & Pine, Green 25.00
Window Box, Royal Woodland, Pink, Aqua Interior, 1950, 12 x 3 In. 48.00
Window Box, Scroll, 12 1/2 In. 35.00
Window Box, Serenade, Yellow 75.00
Window Box, Woodland Gloss, 10 In. 50.00
Window Box, Yellow Top, Blue Bottom 245.00

HUMMEL figurines, based on the drawings of the nun M.I. Hummel (Berta Hummel), are made by the W. Goebel Porzellanfabrik of Oeslau, Germany, now Rodenthal, Germany. They were first made in 1934. The mark has changed through the years. The following are the approximate dates for each of the marks: *Crown* mark, 1935 to 1949; *U.S. Zone, Germany*, 1946 to 1948; *West Germany*, after 1949. The company added the *bee* marks in 1950. The *full bee* with variations, was used from 1950 to 1959; *stylized bee*, 1960 to 1972; *three line mark*, 1968 to 1972; *vee over gee*, 1972 to 1979. In 1979 the V bee symbol was removed from the mark. The *Goebel, W. Germany* mark, called the *new mark* by some authors but now called the *missing bee* mark, was used from 1979 to 1991; *Goebel, Germany* was used from 1991 to the present. Porcelain figures inspired by Berta Hummel's drawings were introduced in 1997. These are marked BH followed by a number. They are made in the Far East, not Germany. Other decorative items and plates that feature Hummel drawings have been made by Schmid Brothers, Inc., since 1971.

Ashtray, No. 33, Joyful, Three Line Mark	125.00
Ashtray, No. 62, Happy Pastime, Vee Over Gee	210.00
Ashtray, No. 166, Boy With Bird, Stylized Bee	70.00
Bell, Annual, 1978, Let's Sing	25.00
Bell, Annual, 1979, Farewell	20.00
Bell, Annual, 1980, Thoughtful	30.00
Bell, Annual, 1981, In Tune	35.00
Bell, Annual, 1986, Sing Along	85.00
Bell, Annual, 1990, What's New?	125.00
Bell, Annual, 1991, Favorite Pet	20.00
Bookends, No. 14/A, Bookworm, New Mark	295.00
Bookends, No. 252/A & B, Apple Tree Boy & Girl, Stylized Bee	250.00
Candleholder, No. 37, Herald Angels, Stylized Bee	165.00
Candleholder, No. 38, Angel With Lute, Full Bee	200.00
Candleholder, No. 117, Boy With Horse	70.00
Figurine, No. 1, Puppy Love, Crown Mark	190.00
Figurine, No. 1, Puppy Love, New Mark	190.00
Figurine, No. 5, Strolling Along, Stylized Bee	165.00
Figurine, No. 7/L, Merry Wanderer, Double Base, Stylized Bee	660.00
Figurine, No. 9, Begging His Share, New Mark	165.00
Figurine, No. 10, Flower Madonna, Full Bee	895.00
Figurine, No. 10/1, Madonna, White, Full Bee	210.00
Figurine, No. 11/2/0, Merry Wanderer, Stylized Bee	95.00 to 125.00
Figurine, No. 12/2/0, Chimney Sweep, Stylized Bee	60.00
Figurine, No. 13/2/0, Meditation, Stylized Bee	125.00
Figurine, No. 15/0, Hear Ye, Hear Ye, Full Bee	165.00 to 200.00
Figurine, No. 15/II, Hear Ye, Hear Ye, New Mark	300.00
Figurine, No. 16/I, Little Hiker, Full Bee	350.00
Figurine, No. 16/I, Little Hiker, Stylized Bee	150.00
Figurine, No. 18, Christ Child, Full Bee	135.00
Figurine, No. 21/0, Heavenly Angel, Full Bee	198.00
Figurine, No. 21/I, Heavenly Angel, New Mark	250.00
Figurine, No. 23/I, Adoration, Stylized Bee	270.00
Figurine, No. 37, Herald Angels, Full Bee	210.00
Figurine, No. 43, March Winds, Full Bee	300.00
Figurine, No. 46/II, Madonna, Without Halo, Three Line Mark	125.00
Figurine, No. 47 3/0, Goose Girl, Crown Mark	200.00
Figurine, No. 47/3/0, Goose Girl, Stylized Bee	85.00
Figurine, No. 49/0, To Market, Stylized Bee	110.00
Figurine, No. 49/I, To Market, Stylized Mark	670.00
Figurine, No. 51/0, Village Boy, Full Bee	125.00
Figurine, No. 51/3/0, Village Boy, Stylized Bee	70.00 to 85.00
Figurine, No. 56B, Out Of Danger, Stylized Bee	165.00 to 200.00
Figurine, No. 57/0, Chick Girl, Crown Mark	185.00
Figurine, No. 57/0, Chick Girl, Stylized Bee	115.00

Figurine, No. 57/0, Chick Girl, Three Line Mark 95.00
Figurine, No. 58/0, Playmates, Crown Mark 200.00
Figurine, No. 59, Skier, Full Bee 220.00
Figurine, No. 63, Singing Lesson, Stylized Bee 85.00
Figurine, No. 67, Doll Mother, Full Bee 225.00
Figurine, No. 69, Happy Pastime, Full Bee 165.00
Figurine, No. 69, Happy Pastime, Stylized Bee 210.00
Figurine, No. 71, Stormy Weather, 1950, Full Bee 495.00
Figurine, No. 73, Little Helper, Stylized Bee 80.00
Figurine, No. 74, Little Gardener, Stylized Bee ....70.00 to 90.00
Figurine, No. 74, Little Gardner, Vee Over Gee 155.00
Figurine, No. 79, Globe Trotter, Stylized Bee 300.00
Figurine, No. 80, Little Scholar, Stylized Bee ....100.00 to 150.00
Figurine, No. 81/0, School Girl, Full Bee 250.00
Figurine, No. 82/0, School Boy, Full Bee 250.00
Figurine, No. 82/0, School Boy, Three Line Mark 100.00
Figurine, No. 82/2/0, School Boy, Stylized Bee 70.00
Figurine, No. 82/II, School Boy, Stylized Bee 730.00
Figurine, No. 85/0, Serenade, Full Bee 160.00
Figurine, No. 86, Happiness, Full Bee 100.00
Figurine, No. 86, Happiness, Stylized Bee 90.00
Figurine, No. 86/2, Happiness, Vee Over Gee 175.00
Figurine, No. 87, For Father, Green Radishes, Crown Mark 1250.00
Figurine, No. 87, For Father, Orange Radishes, Stylized Bee 1850.00
Figurine, No. 87, For Father, Stylized Bee 275.00
Figurine, No. 95, Brother, Stylized Bee ....135.00 to 140.00
Figurine, No. 99, Eventide, Stylized Bee 240.00
Figurine, No. 111, Wayside Harmony, Full Bee 185.00
Figurine, No. 111/I, Wayside Harmony, Stylized Bee 95.00
Figurine, No. 112/3/0, Just Resting, Full Bee 185.00
Figurine, No. 112/3/0, Just Resting, Stylized Bee ....75.00 to 112.00
Figurine, No. 119, Postman, Full Bee 220.00
Figurine, No. 119, Postman, Stylized Bee 155.00
Figurine, No. 119, Postman, Vee Over Gee 260.00
Figurine, No. 123, Max & Moritz, Three Line Mark 130.00
Figurine, No. 124/0, Hello, Green Pants, Full Bee 325.00
Figurine, No. 124/0, Hello, Green Pants, Stylized Bee 175.00
Figurine, No. 127, Doctor, Stylized Bee 110.00
Figurine, No. 129, Band Leader, Vee Over Gee 120.00
Figurine, No. 131, Street Singer, Crown Mark 350.00
Figurine, No. 132, Star Gazer, Stylized Bee 265.00
Figurine, No. 135, Soloist, Full Bee 200.00
Figurine, No. 136/I, Friends, Three Line Mark 135.00
Figurine, No. 141/3/0, Apple Tree Girl, Stylized Bee 180.00
Figurine, No. 141/3/0, Apple Tree Girl, Vee Over Gee 70.00
Figurine, No. 141/I, Apple Tree Girl, Stylized Bee 200.00
Figurine, No. 142/3/0, Apple Tree Boy, Full Bee 1875.00
Figurine, No. 142/3/0, Apple Tree Boy, Stylized Bee ....70.00 to 105.00
Figurine, No. 142/I, Apple Tree Boy, Stylized Bee 190.00
Figurine, No. 143/0, Boots, New Mark 130.00
Figurine, No. 143/I, Boots, Stylized Bee 430.00
Figurine, No. 151, Madonna, White, Full Bee 495.00
Figurine, No. 152/A, Umbrella Boy, Stylized Bee 1900.00
Figurine, No. 153/0, Auf Wiedersehen, Stylized Bee 190.00
Figurine, No. 154/0, Waiter, Full Bee 250.00
Figurine, No. 169, Bird Duet, Vee Over Gee 140.00
Figurine, No. 170/III, School Boys, Stylized Bee 1700.00
Figurine, No. 177, School Girls, Stylized Bee 2700.00
Figurine, No. 178, The Photographer, Three Line Mark 330.00
Figurine, No. 179, Coquettes, Vee Over Gee 205.00
Figurine, No. 182, Good Friends, Vee Over Gee 130.00
Figurine, No. 184, Latest News, Stylized Bee ....415.00 to 500.00

Figurine, No. 185, Accordion Boy, New Mark 120.00
Figurine, No. 186, Sweet Music, Stylized Bee ....140.00 to 270.00
Figurine, No. 195/2/0, Barnyard Hero, Stylized Bee 120.00
Figurine, No. 195/I, Barnyard Hero, Three Line Mark 175.00
Figurine, No. 196/0, Telling Her Secret, New Mark 200.00
Figurine, No. 196/0, Telling Her Secret, Three Line Mark 230.00
Figurine, No. 197/I, Be Patient, Stylized Bee ....225.00 to 380.00
Figurine, No. 198/2/0, Home From Market, Three Line Mark 95.00
Figurine, No. 200/0, Little Goat Herder, Three Line Mark 108.00
Figurine, No. 201/I, Retreat To Safety, Stylized Bee 220.00
Figurine, No. 201/I, Retreat To Safety, Three Line Mark 180.00
Figurine, No. 203/2/0, Signs Of Spring, Three Line Mark ....125.00 to 135.00
Figurine, No. 204, Weary Wanderer, Full Bee 175.00
Figurine, No. 204, Weary Wanderer, Stylized Bee 325.00
Figurine, No. 204, Weary Wanderer, Three Line Mark 150.00
Figurine, No. 214/C, Good Night Angel, Standing, Full Bee 95.00
Figurine, No. 217, Boy With Toothache, New Mark 138.00
Figurine, No. 217, Boy With Toothache, Stylized Bee 270.00
Figurine, No. 217, Boy With Toothache, Three Line Mark 147.00
Figurine, No. 226, Mail Is Here, New Mark 325.00
Figurine, No. 226, Mail Is Here, Three Line Mark 605.00
Figurine, No. 240, Little Drummer, Three Line Mark 85.00
Figurine, No. 257, For Mother, Three Line Mark 120.00
Figurine, No. 258, Which Hand?, Three Line Mark 115.00
Figurine, No. 300, Bird Watcher, Vee Over Gee 245.00
Figurine, No. 306, Little Bookkeeper, Stylized Bee 1000.00
Figurine, No. 308, Little Tailor, Vee Over Gee 680.00
Figurine, No. 311, Give Me A Kiss, Stylized Bee 500.00
Figurine, No. 311, Kiss Me, Stylized Bee 450.00
Figurine, No. 311, Kiss Me, Three Line Mark 350.00
Figurine, No. 317, Not For You!, Stylized Bee 875.00
Figurine, No. 321, Wash Day, Three Line Mark 205.00
Figurine, No. 322, Little Pharmacist Rizinusol, Stylized Bee 425.00
Figurine, No. 322, Little Pharmacist, Three Line Mark 275.00
Figurine, No. 327, The Run-A-Way, Three Line Mark ....550.00 to 850.00
Figurine, No. 333, Blessed Event, Three Line Mark 250.00
Figurine, No. 337, Cinderella, New Mark 285.00
Figurine, No. 337, Cinderella, Three Line Mark 950.00
Figurine, No. 340, Letter To Santa Claus, Three Line Mark 300.00
Figurine, No. 340, Letter To Santa Claus, Vee Over Gee 330.00
Figurine, No. 346, The Smart Little Sister, Three Line Mark 290.00
Figurine, No. 361, Favorite Pet, Three Line Mark 330.00
Figurine, No. 363, Big Housecleaning, New Mark 190.00
Figurine, No. 363, Big Housecleaning, Vee Over Gee 285.00
Figurine, No. 369, Follow The Leader, New Mark 1200.00
Figurine, No. 377, Bashful, Three Line Mark 750.00
Figurine, No. 378, Easter Greetings, Three Line Mark 750.00
Figurine, No. 383, Going Home, New Mark 204.00
Figurine, No. 384, Easter Time, Three Line Mark 750.00
Figurine, No. 384, Easter Time, Vee Over Gee 250.00
Figurine, No. 385, Chicken-Licken, Three Line Mark 850.00
Figurine, No. 386, On Secret Path, Three Line Mark 850.00
Figurine, No. 389, Girl With Sheet Music, New Mark 55.00
Figurine, No. 396, Ride Into Christmas, Vee Over Gee 230.00
Figurine, No. 396/I, Ride Into Christmas, New Mark 285.00
Figurine, No. 416, Jubilee, Three Line Mark 235.00
Font, No. 35/0, Good Shepherd, Full Bee 60.00
Font, No. 207, Heavenly Angel, Full Bee 175.00
Plaque, No. 48, Madonna, Crown Bee 950.00
Plaque, No. 93, Little Fiddler, Full Bee 150.00
Plaque, No. 93, Little Fiddler, Three Line Mark 170.00
Plaque, No. 187/B, Spring Dance, Vee Over Gee 150.00

Plate, Anniversary, No. 280, Stormy Weather, 1975 . . . . .65.00 to 185.00
Plate, Anniversary, No. 281, Ring Around The Rosie, 1980 . . . . .90.00 to 115.00
Plate, Annual, 1971, Heavenly Angel . . . . .350.00 to 475.00
Plate, Annual, 1972, Hear Ye, Hear Ye 45.00
Plate, Annual, 1973, Globe Trotter 120.00
Plate, Annual, 1974, Goose Girl . . . . .50.00 to 65.00
Plate, Annual, 1975, Ride Into Christmas 35.00
Plate, Annual, 1976, Apple Tree Girl . . . . .45.00 to 65.00
Plate, Annual, 1977, Apple Tree Boy . . . . .50.00 to 70.00
Plate, Annual, 1978, Happy Pastime 45.00
Plate, Annual, 1979, Singing Lesson . . . . .20.00 to 65.00
Plate, Annual, 1980, School Girl . . . . .35.00 to 50.00
Plate, Annual, 1981, Umbrella Boy 40.00
Plate, Annual, 1982, Umbrella Girl . . . . .75.00 to 95.00
Plate, Annual, 1983, Postman . . . . .115.00 to 165.00
Plate, Annual, Chick Girl, 1985 . . . .   70.00
Plate, Celebration Series, No. 737, Valentine Joy, 1987 . . . .   65.00
Plate, Celebration Series, No. 738, Valentine Gift, 1986 . . . .   65.00
Plate, Little Home Makers Series, No. 745, Little Sweeper, 1988 . . . .   40.00

HUTSCHENREUTHER Porcelain Company of Selb, Germany, was established in 1814 and is still working. The company makes fine quality
porcelain dinnerwares and figurines. The mark has changed through
the years, but the name and the lion insignia appear in most versions.

Chocolate Set, Oak Leaf Design, Gold Over Ivory, 13 Piece 275.00
Coffeepot, Coralle Viktoria Shape 200.00
Dinner Set, White, Silver Band, 12 Piece 950.00
Figurine, Apple Seller, 9 1/2 In. 40.00
Figurine, Cat, Recumbent, White, 7 In. 135.00
Figurine, Couple, Dancing, Signed, Werner, 11 1/2 In. 350.00
Figurine, Dancer, White Glaze, 12 In. 400.00
Figurine, Duck, 3 1/2 In. 50.00
Figurine, Eagle, 17 3/4 In. 110.00
Figurine, Elephant, 3 1/2 x 5 In. 125.00
Figurine, Finch, 3 1/2 In. 125.00
Figurine, Great Dane, Black, White, Harlequin, 7 1/4 In. 50.00
Figurine, Hawk, 15 3/4 In. 110.00
Figurine, Lady, Dancing Gown, Pale Yellow, Gray Shoes, 10 1/4 In. 250.00
Figurine, Maiden, With Fruit Basket & Fruit, 9 1/2 In. 165.00
Figurine, Nude, Standing On 1 Foot On Gold Ball, 9 In. 395.00
Figurine, Owl, 2 5/8 In. 125.00
Figurine, Panda, 2 x 3 1/2 In 125.00
Figurine, Rooster On Top Of Cat, On Top Of Dog, On Top Of Donkey, 6 In. 315.00
Figurine, Stallion, Rearing, Head Turned On Side, 14 x 16 In.   660.00
Plate, Dutch Woman, Harvesting Potatoes, Gilt Frame, 10 1/4 In. 195.00
Plate, Pink Florals, 8 3/4 In. 14.00
Sculpture, 5 Dolphins, Jumping, White, 27 In. 795.00
Vase, 3 Women, With Cherub, Beehive, 3 1/4 In. 75.00

ICONS, special, revered pictures of Jesus, Mary, or a saint, are usually Russian or Byzantine. The small icons collected today are made
of wood and tin or precious metals. Many modern copies have been
made in the old style and are being sold to tourists in Russia and
Europe.

3 Saints, Brass, Enameled Riza, Russia, 18th Century, 12 x 10 1/2 In. 1150.00
Alexander Nefski, 15th Century Defender Of Novgorad, Russia, 12 1/4 x 9 1/2 In. 115.00
Apostle Simon, 1680s, 21 x 44 In. 4400.00
Apparition Of Mary To St. Sergius, Oil On Wood, Gilded Metal Overlay, 9 x 11 In. . .   847.00
Archangel Gabriel, Gilded Silver Oklad, Engraved Robes, 14 1/2 x 11 3/4 In. 3220.00
Archangel Gabriel, Russia, 18th Century, 12 x 10 In. 3410.00
Baptism Of Christ, Figure Of Christ Immersed In The River Jordan, 21 x 17 1/4 In. . . .   1955.00
Baptism Of Christ, Outstretched Right Hand, Brass Border, 12 x 10 In. 1552.00

Baptism Of Christ, Tempera On Wood Panel, 19th Century, 8 3/4 x 10 1/2 In. 1270.00
Bearded Priest, Angels Each Side, Silver Repousse, Russia, 19th Century, 9 x 7 In. 748.00
Calendar, Month Of May, Various Saints & Feast Days, Blue Ground, 10 x 8 In. 1265.00
Christ, Enamel Halo, Silver By Pavel Ovchinnikov, Russia, 12 x 10 1/2 In. 9900.00
Christ Pantocrator, Enameled Silver Frame, Black Lacquer Backing, 12 x 10 1/2 In. .. 3737.00
Christ Pantocrator, Gilded Silver Oklad, Book Of Gospels, Russia, 1910, 8 3/8 x 7 In. . 1092.00
Christ Pantocrator, Gilded Silver Oklad, Russia, 1864, 13 1/2 x 11 3/4 In. 1955.00
Christ Pantocrator, Plain Silver Back, Border, Russia, 1900, 5 x 6 1/2 In. 2070.00
Christ Pantocrator, Repousse Silver Border, Shellwork, Scrolls, 12 1/2 x 10 3/4 In. ... 1725.00
Christ Pantocrator, Russia, Frame, 8 x 9 In. 275.00
Christ Pantocrator, Silver & Enamel Oklad, Russia, 1900, 10 1/2 x 8 3/4 In. 4025.00
Cross, St. George, Hinged Loop, Bronze, Byzantine, 4 3/4 In. 1150.00
Entry Into Jerusalem, Savior, Riding An Ass, Silver Border, 20 x 24 In. 4025.00
Hand Cross, Gilded Silver, Russia, 1890, 15 3/4 In. 1755.00
Holy Mother & Infant Jesus, Nickel Silver Riza, Russia, 19th Century, 15 x 13 In. ... 1210.00
Jesus With Angel, Rectangular, Russia, 12 1/4 x 10 1/2 In. 287.00
John The Baptist, Rectangular, Russia, 10 1/2 x 8 1/2 In. 345.00
Kazan Mother Of God, Gilded Silver Oklad, Chased With Foliage, 1884, 12 x 10 In. .. 5750.00
Kazan Mother Of God, Oil On Wood, Silvered Riza, Gilt Frame, Russia, 10 x 18 In. .. 742.00
Kazan Mother Of God, Silver Oklad, Monogram, Russia, 1900, 11 3/4 x 9 In. 1725.00
Kneeling Figure, Receiving Blessings, Gilt Metal Frame, Russia, 29 x 41 In. 4025.00
Korsun Mother Of God, Tempera, Gold Leaf On Wood, 19th Century, 14 x 12 In. 907.00
Life Of A Saint, Rectangular, Russia, 12 1/2 x 11 In. 431.00
Life Of Jesus, Rectangular, Russia, 12 1/4 x 10 1/4 In. 431.00
Madonna & Child, Silver & Faux Jeweled Oklad, Russia, 19th Century, 12 x 10 In. 1725.00
Madonna & Child, Silver Oklad, Jeweled Surround, Russia, 19th Century, 16 x 13 In. .. 6670.00
Mother & Child, Saints Surround, Brass, Painted, Oklad, Russia, 22 1/4 x 28 In. 8050.00
Mother Of God Of The Sign, 24 x 20 In. 8360.00
Mother Of God Of The Sign, Overlaid With Silver Gilt Rizza, 1817 .... 5225.00
Mother Of God Of The Sign, Rococo Shellwork, Russia, 18th Century, 12 In. 1380.00
Nativity Of Christ, Carved, Gilded Frame, Russia, 19th Century, 12 x 10 In. 2070.00
Nativity Of Virgin, Russia, 1600, 12 1/4 x 10 In. 1610.00
New Testament Trinity, Painted In 16th Century Style, 20th Century, 11 x 9 In. 605.00
New Testament Trinity, Silver Oklad, Russia, 19th Century, 16 x 13 3/4 In. 1840.00
Orthodox, Christ Surrounded By Saints, 16 x 12 In. 275.00
Our Lady Of Joy To Those Who Sorrow, St. Alexandra Border, Russia, 13 x 11 In. ... 1380.00
Painted Faces, Russia, 1880, 8 7/8 x 7 In. 165.00
Pokrov, Gilded Silver Oklad, Scrolled Foliage, Moscow, 1786, 13 x 11 In. 2760.00
Presentation Of Christ In Temple, Russia, Late 17th Century, 26 x 12 3/4 In. 1380.00
Presentation Of Christ In Temple, St. Simeon Holding Christ, Russia, 28 x 21 In. ... 1840.00
Prophet Zephaniah, Saint, Inclined To His Left, Russia, 1700, 23 1/2 x 16 1/4 In. 2185.00
Resurrection & Descent, Gold Leaf On Wood Panel, I. Gubkin, Russia, 12 1/2 x 11 In. 3630.00
Resurrection & Selected Saints, Descent Into Hell, 28 Scenes, 21 x 17 1/2 In. 1840.00
Resurrection With Feasts, Descent Into Hell, Russia, 19th Century, 21 x 17 In. 2070.00
Resurrection With Feasts, Gilded Silver Oklad, Leaf Border, Russia, 1830, 18 x 14 In. 2300.00
Saint, Rectangular, Russia, 12 3/4 x 10 1/4 In. 575.00
Smolensk Christ, Standing On A Cushion, Russia, 19th Century, 12 1/4 x 10 1/4 In. ... 2587.00
Smolensk Mother Of God, Oil On Wood, A. Feodorovic Golovin, 1882, 14 x 12 In. ... 2178.00
St. Elijah, Prophet On Upper Part Of Panel, Matted Ground, 12 x 11 1/4 In. 805.00
St. George, Slaying The Dragon, Rearing His Horse, Late 17th Century, 22 x 17 In. 17825.00
St. George, Slaying The Dragon, Saints Border, Russia, 19th Century, 17 x 15 In. 3162.00
St. John The Evangelist, Seated On Rocky Outcrop With Scribe, Russia, 19 x 16 In. ... 2300.00
St. Nicholas, Beaded Cover, Mounted With Jewels, Russia, 19th Century, 14 x 12 In. .. 1380.00
St. Nicholas, Beads, Silver Robes, Gold Threads, Fabric Cover, Russia, 9 x 7 1/4 In. 1265.00
St. Nicholas, Chased Metal Oklad, Carved, Gilded Frame, Russia, 1875, 12 x 10 In. 3737.00
St. Nicholas, Gilded Kiot, Russia, 19th Century, 31 1/2 x 25 1/4 In. 3105.00
St. Nicholas, Gilded Silver Oklad, Foliage, Russia, 19th Century, 13 x 11 In. 1725.00
St. Nicholas, Gilded Silver Oklad, Seed Pearl Robes, 19th Century, 12 x 10 In. 4600.00
St. Nicholas, Gilded Silver, Enameled Oklad, Russia, 1900, 8 7/8 x 7 1/8 In. 1150.00
St. Nicholas, Holding Bible, Floral Gilt, Wooden, Russia, 19th Century, 57 x 25 In. ... 2990.00
St. Nicholas, Silver Oklad, 19th Century, Russia, 10 5/8 x 9 3/8 In. 1955.00
St. Nicholas, Standing On Rocky Promontory Calming Waters, Russia, 12 x 10 1/4 In. .. 1380.00
St. Panteleimon, Oil Gold Leaf On Wood Panel, 19th Century, 8 3/4 x 7 In. 423.00

St. Peter, With Staff, Floral Gilt Leaf Ground, Painted, Russia, 19th Century, 14 x 11 In. 1725.00
Temple Of Archangel Michael, Temper On Wood, Silver & Gold Plated, 12 x 11 In. .. 1935.00
Tichvin Mother Of God, Female Saint Border, Russia, 13 5/8 x 11 3/4 In. 1092.00
Transfiguration Of Christ, Silver Gilded Oklad, Halo Of Christ, 1877, 14 3/4 x 11 In. . 1380.00
Triptych, St. Nicholas Flanked By Selected Saints, Christ Above, 5 1/4 x 10 In. 1840.00
Virgin & Child, Chased Gilded Silver Oklad, Russia, 1834, 12 1/2 x 11 In. 2990.00
Virgin Mary, Shrine, Reliquary Of St. Francis Di Girolamo, 12 x 9 1/2 In. 630.00
Virgin Of Tenderness, Gilded Silver Oklad, Moscow, 1850s, 11 1/2 x 8 3/4 In., Pair ... 977.00
Vladimir Mother Of God, Floral Border, Scrolled Foliage, Gilded Silver, 12 x 10 In. ... 1725.00
Vladimir Mother Of God, Gilded Silver Border, Halo, Scrolled Foliage, 11 x 8 1/4 In. .. 1840.00
Vladimir Mother Of God, Russia, 19th Century, 21 x 17 1/4 In. 1725.00
Vladimir Mother Of God, Tempera On Wood Panel, c.1800, 12 1/2 x 10 12 In. 1210.00
Washing Hands & Feet At Temple, Stylized Foliate Borders, Russia, 14 1/4 x 12 In. ... 690.00

IMARI patterns are named for the Japanese ware characteristically decorated with orange, red, green, and blue stylized designs. The bamboo,
floral, and geometric patterns on the Japanese ware became so familiar that the name *Imari* has come to mean any pattern of this type. It
has been copied by the Asian, European, and American factories since
the eighteenth century. It is still being made.

Biscuit Jar, Cover, Japan, 1900-1920, 7 1/2 In. 220.00
Bowl, 12 3/8 x 5 3/4 In. 440.00
Bowl, 3 Friends Center, Flower Form, 9 In. 176.00
Bowl, Black Ship, Figures & Ships In Typical Palette, 19th Century, 7 3/8 In. 575.00
Bowl, Brocade Design, Floral Center, 4-Lobed, 4 1/2 In. 27.00
Bowl, Carp Design, Mid-19th Century, 8 1/2 In. 135.00
Bowl, Dragon, Scalloped Edge, Ribbed Sides, 19th Century, 9 3/4 In. 495.00
Bowl, Fan, Scroll Design, 8 1/2 In. 77.00
Bowl, Farmer, Under Bamboo Tree, Karabitsu Shell Design, Early 19th Century, 10 In. .. 357.50
Bowl, Floral Reserves & Fan Design, Blue Ground, Pierced Turned Out Rim, 8 x 7 In. .. 2070.00
Bowl, Flower Basket Center, Flower Form, 10 In. 121.00
Bowl, Flower Form, Flower Basket Design, 12 In. 190.00
Bowl, Geometric Design, Japan, 19th Century, 8 3/4 In. 374.00
Bowl, Gold Floral Panels, Enclosing Vase Of Flowers, Oval, 10 1/4 x 9 1/4 In. 302.00
Bowl, Green & Coral, 10 In. 225.00
Bowl, Japan, 9 5/8 x 4 1/4 In. 330.00
Bowl, Peony Center Surrounded By Landscape, Flower Cartouches, Flower Mark 1870.00
Bowl, Scalloped Rim, 19th Century, Pair 130.00
Bowl, Scalloped Rim, Early 20th Century, 5 3/4 x 15 In. 220.00
Bowl, Shaving, Early 18th Century 412.00
Charger, Blue, Red, Green Glaze, White Ground, Japan, 18 1/4 In. 300.00
Charger, Crane, Peony Design, 12 In., Pair 55.00
Charger, Figural, Floral Design, 4 Character Mark On Base, 21 3/4 In. 1155.00
Charger, Floral Center, 16 1/4 In., Pair 550.00
Charger, Polychrome Scene Of 7 Figures, Orange Border, 26 1/2 In. 660.00
Charger, Red, Cobalt Blue, Green, Black, Japan, 18 1/2 In. 605.00
Charger, Stylized Green, Splash Of Colors, 1840s, 16 In. 1000.00
Dish, 3 Friends Center Surrounded By Crane, Flowers, Rectangular, 8 1/2 In. 66.00
Dish, Bamboo Surrounded By Seated Foo Lion, Iron Red, Gilt Scrolling, 8 7/8 In. 115.00
Dish, Fish & Turtle, 8 In. 105.00
Dish, Fish Form, Bamboo, Prunus Design, 9 In. 286.00
Dish, Lozenge Form, Flower Garden Design, 6 3/4 In. 66.00
Jar, Flower, Butterfly Design, 7 1/4 In., Pair 550.00
Jar, Inverted Pear Shape, Melon Ribbing, Flowering Tree Design, 1800, 6 1/2 In. 66.00
Jardiniere, Floral Design, Hexagonal Form, 6 In. 99.00
Plate, Birds & Flowers, Hand Painted, Gold, 9 In. 95.00
Plate, Chidori, Wave Design, 9 In., Pair 88.00
Plate, Chrysanthemum, Brocade Ball Design Surrounded By Karakusa, 9 1/2 In. 88.00
Plate, Fish, Flower Design, 9 1/2 In. 440.00
Plate, Floral, With Pheasant, Black Background, 8 In. 95.00
Plate, Gourd, Leaf Center Surrounded By Figural Landscape, 10 In. 143.00
Plate, Leaf Shape, Grapevine, Squirrel, Leaf Design, 9 In. 132.00
Plate, Passion Flower Center Surrounded By Butterflies, 8 1/2 In. 143.00

Plate, Passion Flower Design, 8 1/4 In.	66.00
Plate, Scalloped Edge, Octagonal, 13 In.	341.00
Plate, Symbolic Design, Blue, White, 7 In.	247.50
Platter, Fish Shape, Crane, Wave Design, 14 1/2 In.	742.50
Serving Dish, Carp Design, Oval, 14 1/2 In.	220.00
Stand, Umbrella, Bird & Floral Design, Iron Red & Blue, 1880s, 24 In.	690.00
Temple Jar, Figural Panels, Karakusa Ground, 27 1/2 In.	1210.00
Vase, Floral Cartouche, Serrated Rim, Foliate Handles, 19th Century, 27 1/2 In., Pair	1725.00
Vase, Floral Design, Fluted, 13 In.	1100.00
Vase, Fluted Tops, 6 In., Pair	600.00
Vase, Lobed Form With Branches, 19 In.	330.00

IMPERIAL GLASS Corporation was founded in Bellaire, Ohio, in 1901. It became a subsidiary of Lenox, Inc., in 1973 and was sold to Arthur R. Lorch in 1981. It was sold again in 1982, went bankrupt that same year, and some of the molds and assets were sold to other companies. The Imperial glass preferred by the collector is art glass, carnival glass, slag glass, stretch glass, and other top-quality tablewares. Tablewares and animals are listed here. The others may be found in the appropriate sections.

Animal, Asiatic Pheasant	250.00 to 350.00
Animal, Asiatic Pheasant, Amber	475.00
Animal, Bunny, Caramel Slag	45.00
Animal, Colt, Standing, Amber, 5 In.	165.00
Animal, Cygnet, Black	45.00
Animal, Swan, Blue	1750.00
Animal, Tiger, On Bust Off, Amber	395.00
Animal, Tropical Fish, Amber	2250.00
Beaded Bull's-Eye, Vase, Carnival Glass, Purple, 11 In.	75.00
Candlewick, Ashtray, Eagle, Pink, 6 In.	45.00
Candlewick, Ashtray, Match Holder, 6 In.	150.00
Candlewick, Ashtray, Patriotic, Blue V, 3 In.	35.00
Candlewick, Bowl, Chrome Pedestal, Blue, 5 In.	48.00
Candlewick, Bowl, Divided, 2 Handles, 6 In.	12.00
Candlewick, Bowl, Heart Shape, 5 1/4 In.	20.00
Candlewick, Bowl, Heart Shape, 9 In.	195.00
Candlewick, Candy Dish, Cover, 3 Sections, Cut & Mirror Finish	395.00
Candlewick, Candy Dish, Cover, 7 In.	150.00
Candlewick, Celery Dish, 13 1/2 In.	30.00
Candlewick, Celery Dish, Oval, 6 In.	40.00
Candlewick, Coaster	7.00
Candlewick, Cup & Saucer	12.00
Candlewick, Lamp, Hurricane, Pair	190.00
Candlewick, Lazy Susan, 3 Piece	195.00
Candlewick, Pitcher, 80 Oz.	150.00
Candlewick, Plate, 9 In.	18.00
Candlewick, Plate, Divided	10.00
Candlewick, Plate, Etched, 8 In.	10.00
Candlewick, Punch Bowl	275.00
Candlewick, Punch Set, Bowl, Tray, 11 Cups, 17 In.	150.00
Candlewick, Sherbet, 5 Oz.	14.00
Candlewick, Sherbet, Etch	35.00
Candlewick, Sugar, Blue, 2 1/2 In.	37.00
Candlewick, Tray, Center Handle, 8 3/8 In.	20.00
Candlewick, Tray, Pastry, Center Handle, Doeskin	155.00
Candlewick, Tray, Pastry, Center Handle, Red	700.00
Candlewick, Vase, 5 3/4 In.	75.00
Candlewick, Vase, Bud, 6 In.	40.00
Cape Cod, Bowl, 7 In.	65.00
Cape Cod, Butter, Cover, Handle	45.00
Cape Cod, Cake Plate, 11 In.	115.00
Cape Cod, Cake Plate, 4 Feet, Square	82.00

Imperial, Hattie, Chop Plate,
Amber, Carnival Glass, 10 1/2 In.

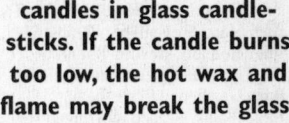

Be careful when burning
candles in glass candle-
sticks. If the candle burns
too low, the hot wax and
flame may break the glass.

Cape Cod, Cake Plate, 72 Birthday Candles	325.00
Cape Cod, Cake Stand, 10 In.	55.00
Cape Cod, Cordial, Red	20.00
Cape Cod, Decanter, Blue	50.00
Cape Cod, Decanter, Cobalt Blue	275.00
Cape Cod, Finger Bowl	15.00
Cape Cod, Goblet, 5 1/4 In.	6.00
Cape Cod, Goblet, 6 Oz.	8.00
Cape Cod, Goblet, Water	25.00
Cape Cod, Ice Bucket	100.00
Cape Cod, Nappy	45.00
Cape Cod, Parfait	8.00
Cape Cod, Plate, 10 In.	30.00
Cape Cod, Plate, 2 Handles, 8 1/2 In.	20.00
Cape Cod, Plate, 7 In.	35.00
Cape Cod, Punch Set, 14 Piece	155.00
Cape Cod, Salt & Pepper, Pewter Cone Tops	12.50
Cape Cod, Urn, Cover, 10 1/2 In.	45.00
Cape Cod, Wine	6.00
Cathay, Tray, Pavilion	250.00
Cathay, Urn, Cover, Bamboo, Satin Finish	150.00
Coin, Plate, President Kennedy, 1964	20.00
Grape, Salt & Pepper, Rubigold, Carnival Glass, Pointed Cover	50.00
Hattie, Chop Plate, Amber, Carnival Glass, 10 1/2 In. ....*Illus*	3850.00
Hawaiian Flowers, Platter, Maroon, 14 In.	125.00
Hobnail, Candleholder, 4 1/2 In.	25.00
Hobnail, Vase, 8 In.	80.00
Hobnail, Vase, Footed, 6 In.	45.00
Lei Lani, Creamer	20.00
Lei Lani, Platter, 12 In.	125.00
Octagon, Toothpick, Amber Carnival Glass	20.00
Plate, Marigold & Peacock, Lustre Rose, Milk Glass, 11 In.	110.00
Plate, Peacock, Lustre Rose, Milk Glass, 11 In.	220.00
San Marino, Tumbler	85.00
Shade, NuArt, Marigold, Pair, 4 1/2 In.	48.00
Shade, NuArt, White Opaque, 4 1/2 In.	28.00
Vase, Frosted Iridescent, Cobalt Blue Flared Rim, 8 In.	685.00
Vase, Gold Iridescent, Ruffled, Opalescent Swags, 10 1/2 In.	410.00
Vintage Grape, Plate, 10 In.	18.00
Vintage Grape, Punch Cup	8.00
Vintage Grape, Tumbler, 4 1/4 In.	16.00

Water Set, Field Flower, Sunset Ruby, Carnival Glass, 7 Piece 185.00
Water Set, Robin, Sunset Ruby, Carnival Glass, 7 Piece 198.00

INDIAN art from North America has attracted the collector for many
years. Each tribe has its own distinctive designs and techniques.
Baskets, jewelry, pottery, and leatherwork are of greatest collector
interest. Eskimo art is listed in another category in this book.

Bag, Great Lakes, Beaded Floral, Trade Cloth, Beaded Strands 10350.00
Bag, Hand Woven Hair, Beads, Shells, 1750s 650.00
Bag, Iroquois, Beaded Both Sides, c.1890, 5 x 5 1/2 In. 185.00
Bag, Nez Perce, Corn Husk, c.1860, 8 1/2 x 12 In. 775.00
Bag, Nez Perce, Corn Husk, c.1890, 12 x 11 1/4 In. 1850.00
Bag, Plains, Beaded & Fringed Hide, Thong Handles, Sinew Front & Flap, 9 1/2 In. 1842.00
Bag, Plateau, 2 Sides, With Fringe 750.00
Bag, Washo Tribe, Woven, Animal Design, 13 3/4 In. 3265.00
Basket, Apache, Coiled, Pictorial, 13 In. 1375.00
Basket, Apache, Geometric & Dog Design, c.1890, 8 x 8 In. 575.00
Basket, Apache, Geometric Pattern, Dark Brown, 15 x 4 In. 1610.00
Basket, Apache, Jar, Coiled, Polychrome, Willow Woven, Red Yucca Root, 6 1/4 In.! 575.00
Basket, Apache, Tray, Coiled, Flat Base, Dark Brown Devil's Claw, Willow, 10 In. 747.00
Basket, Apache, Tray, Coiled, Standing Human Figures, 11 1/2 In. 990.00
Basket, Apache, White Mountain, Human, Animal Figures, Black, 10 x 8 In. 2300.00
Basket, Cradle, Northwest Coast, 19th Century, 28 1/2 x 10 3/4 In. 575.00
Basket, Hopi, Bowl, Coiled, Pictorial Kachina Devices, 9 1/2 In. 462.00
Basket, Hopi, Coiled, Brown Step Design, 5 In. x 7 In. Diam. 49.00
Basket, Hopi, Wicker, Designs In Green, Yellow, Blue & Red, c.1900, 5 1/2 x 15 1/2 In. .. 850.00
Basket, Hupa, Bowl, Twined, Indented Base, Half-Twist Overlay, 7 1/2 x 11 In. 795.00
Basket, Navajo, Deep Dish, Black To Tan, 14 In. 295.00
Basket, Navajo, Tray, Red, Black & Natural, 13 In. 245.00
Basket, Northwest, Open Top ....*Illus* 1100.00
Basket, Northwest, Tlingit, Rattle-Top ....*Illus* 2750.00
Basket, Papago, Bowl, Coiled, 7 x 17 In. 395.00
Basket, Papago, Geometric Design, Devil's Claw & Yucca, 5 x 11 1/2 In. 49.00
Basket, Papago, Saguaro Cactus Design, 3 Women Harvesting Fruit, 4 x 9 In. 165.00
Basket, Passamaquoddy, Ash Splint, Painted, Circular Rayed Design On Lid, 6 7/8 In. ... 60.00
Basket, Pima, Bowl, Coiled, Pictorial, Trade Bead Trimmed Rim, 4 3/4 x 10 1/2 In. 362.00
Basket, Pima, Bowl, Flaring Rectangular Form, 5 1/2 x 13 In. 795.00
Basket, Pima, Tray, Geometric Pattern, Brown Center, 18 x 4 In. 1150.00
Basket, Pima, Tray, Geometric Pattern, Pinwheel Center, 14 In. 632.00
Basket, Pima, Tray, Man In Maze, c.1880, 5 In. 425.00
Basket, Pima, Tray, Whirling Fret Design, Martynia, Willow, 3 3/4 In. 440.00
Basket, Pomo, Bowl, Coiled, Compressed Form, 6 In. 362.00
Basket, Pomo, Bowl, Coiled, Shell Disc Design, 3 1/2 In. 115.00
Basket, Pomo, Treasure, Coiled, Feather, Glass Bead & Abalone, 5 1/4 In. 2382.00
Basket, Seneca, Ash Splint, Potato Stamp Design, 9 1/2 x 15 1/4 In. 242.00
Basket, Tlingit, Geometric Design, Black, Brown Running Horizontally, 5 1/2 x 6 In. ... 316.00
Basket, Tlingit, Geometric Design, Orange, Yellow Arrow, 8 3/4 x 10 In. 920.00
Basket, Wall, Northeast Woodland, Splint, Double Pocket, 40 x 37 In. 230.00
Basket, Washo, Bowl, Polychrome Coiled, Bracken Fern Root & Willow, 11 1/2 In. 5625.00
Beaded Boot, Iroquois, Owl, Flowers & Remember Me, 7 1/2 In. 175.00
Belt, Concho, 8 Butterflies, 7 Scalloped Edge, Silver, Turquoise, 40 In. 920.00
Belt, Navajo, 10 Wrought, Stamped Conchas, Sterling Silver, 51 1/2 In. 440.00
Belt, Navajo, Butterfly Shape, Silver Conchas, Turquoise Blue Stones, 38 In. 231.00
Belt, Navajo, Silver & Turquoise Concha, 1 Square Cut Stone, Open Buckle 530.00
Blanket, Navajo, 3-Ply Wool, Black, Violet & Ivory, Red Ground, 54 x 32 1/2 In. 3965.00
Blanket, Navajo, 9 Terraced Diamonds, Ivory Crosses Tipped In Red, 60 x 75 In. 5405.00
Blanket, Navajo, Alternating Bands Of Natural & Dark Brown, 67 x 49 In. 7187.00
Blanket, Navajo, Crystal Type, Red, Blue, White, Stripes, Gray Ground, 72 x 52 In. 3220.00
Blanket, Navajo, Multicolor Star Design, Gray Ground, 1970s, 27 x 38 In. 60.00
Blanket, Navajo, Saddle, Homespun Wool, Red, Black, White, Tan, 31 x 29 In. 230.00
Blanket, Navajo, Serrated Diamonds, Serrated Zigzags, 50 x 74 In. 1600.00
Blanket, Oregon City Woolen Mills, Olive, Green, Black, Red, 62 x 71 In. 105.00
Blanket, Sioux, Beaded, Block, Diamond, Apple Green, Navy, Yellow Beads, 59 x 27 In. 4312.00

Blanket Strip, Blackfoot, Sewn On Tent Cloth, Leather Drops, c.1920, 60 x 4 In. 2500.00
Bow, Blackfoot, Bone Backed With Red Painted Sinew 6037.00
Bowl, Dough, Pueblo, Geometric Design, Acoma Sky City, NM, 4 1/8 x 7 1/4 In. 82.00
Bowl, Hopi, Second Mesa, Umber, Red Ocher, White Cream, Corn Emblem, 5 1/4 In. ... 247.00
Bowl, Hopi, Stylized Parrot, Black, Blue, White, 8 1/4 In. 149.00
Bowl, Hopi, Wicker Work, 13 In. 165.00
Bowl, Northeast Woodland, Hand Cut & Carved Tree Trunk, 6 1/2 x 9 In. 175.00
Bowl, Polychrome, Creamy White Slip, Red Clay Body, Red, Orange, Brick Red, 11 In. .. 4312.00
Bowl, Southwestern, Fox Handle, Black Glaze, 20th Century, 8 In. 75.00
Box, Micmac, Domed Top, Quilled Birchbark, 6 x 5 3/4 In. 495.00
Bracelet, Navajo, 4 Inset Turquoise Pieces, Silver, 1 3/4 In. 172.00
Bracelet, Navajo, Geometric Design, 4 Inset Turquoise Pieces, 1 1/2 In. 258.00
Bracelet, Zuni, 4 Round Inset Turquoise, Sterling Silver, 3 1/4 In. 230.00
Canoe, Bark, Handwritten Supreme Chief Of Six Nations, 20th June, 1931, 30 x 11 In. .. 375.00
Canoe, Birchbark, Handmade, Cane Strip Tied, Gilbert On Side, 1900s, 27 x 8 In. 348.00
Cap, Micmac, Cloth, Allover Large Beaded Flowers, 19th Century 3450.00
Case, Needle, Apache, Sinew Sewn, c.1880, 5 1/2 In. 950.00
Comb, Woodland, Bird On Top, Wooden, Early 19th Century, 3 3/4 In. 285.00
Doll, Hide, Beaded, Fringed Hide Dress, Brass Belt, Navy, White, Teal, Yellow Beads ... 1495.00
Doll, Hopi, Kachina, c.1930, 5 1/2 In. 185.00
Doll, Hopi, Kachina, c.1930, 10 In. 500.00
Doll, Hopi, Kachina, c.1960, 6 In. 85.00
Doll, Hopi, Kachina, Cottonwood, Painted Mask, Tube Snout, 8 In. 495.00
Doll, Hopi, Kachina, Crow Mother, Green Yarn, Painted Mask, 12 In. 467.00
Doll, Kachina, Polychrome, 1950, 2 3/4 In. 315.00
Doll, Kachina, Zuni, c.1920, 9 1/2 In. 1200.00
Doll, Plateau, Hide, Beaded, 1920s, 6 1/2 In. 145.00
Doll, Seminole, Molded Face, Dress, 1920s, 7 In. 175.00
Dress, Sioux, Applied Shell Design, Turquoise, Red Bead Striping, Child's, 26 In. 575.00
Drum, Hide, Wood, Polychrome, Red, Yellow, Turquoise, Black Pigment, 6 In. 402.00
Earrings, Zuni, Silver & Turquoise, 3 1/4 In. 462.00
Effigy, Cherokee, Catlinite Fish, 18th Century, 3 1/4 In. 290.00
Fetish, Zuni, Frog Ring, Turquoise, c.1920, 3/4 x 1 In. 775.00
Figure, Zuni, Owl, Polychrome, 20th Century, 7 1/2 In. 460.00
Gauntlets, Cree, Multicolored Floral, c.1880 .... 400.00
Gauntlets, Sioux, Hide, Sinew Sewn, Cotton, Red, Orange, Purple, Blue Quill, 15 In. ... 1092.00
Hat, Yurok, Geometric Design, Maidenhair Fern, Beargrass, 3 1/4 x 6 1/2 In. 126.00
Jacket, Cree, Beaded, Fringed, Smoke Tanned Hide, Sinew & Cotton Thread, 34 In. 925.00
Jar, Acoma, Black On White, Punctuated Neck, Convex Base, c.1880, 4 1/2 x 7 In. 475.00
Jar, Acoma, Stylized Cloud, Sun, Star, Umber, Red Ocher, White Slip Ground, 7 In. 385.00
Jar, Blackware, Black-On-Black Matte, Tonita & Juan, 1896, 4 1/2 In. 862.00

Indian, Basket,
Northwest, Tlingit,
Rattle-Top;
Indian, Knife, Northwest,
Figural, Carved;
Indian, Basket,
Northwest, Open Top

Jar, Hopi, Seed, Dark Orange Body, 7 In. 1595.00
Jar, Santo Domingo, Blackware, Cream Slip, 8 3/4 In. 82.00
Knife, Made From Sheep Shearing Scissors, Buffalo Fur Sheath, 10 In. 700.00
Knife, Northwest, Figural, Carved ....*Illus* 6435.00
Knife Sheath, Plains, Beaded Hide, Deerskin Front, 9 3/4 In. 857.00
Knife Sheath, Sioux, Cotton, Sinew Stitched, Navy, Yellow, White, Red, Beads, 9 In. ... 517.00
Knife Sheath, Sioux, Sinew Sewn, c.1880, 7 1/2 In. 475.00
Knife Sheath, Woodlands, Beaded, Floral Motif, Wood Handle, 10 In. 258.00
Leggings, Cree, Shell Hangings, British Flag, Floral Ground, Single 895.00
Leggings, Plains, Beaded, Hide, Sinew Stitched, Hide Thong Closures, 16 1/2 In. 575.00
Mask, Iroquois, Ceremonial, Cherry, 19th Century, 40 In. 950.00
Moccasins, Algonquin, Red Velvet Uppers, Beaded Floral, Child's, 4 1/2 In. 88.00
Moccasins, Apache, Beaded, Sinew Stitched, Yellow, White, Green, Amber Beads 2415.00
Moccasins, Arapaho, Colored Beads, Woman's, c.1880, 9 1/2 In. 1090.00
Moccasins, Beaded, Sinew Sewn, Yellow Ocher, Pale Blue Ground, Child's, 6 In. 3335.00
Moccasins, Crown, Hard Soles, Sinew Sewn, Lined Cuffs, c.1870 .... 575.00
Moccasins, Eastern Woodlands, Iroquois, Beaded, Embossed, 10 In. 172.00
Moccasins, Huron, Baby's 125.00
Moccasins, Iroquois, Bead Stitched Floral On Toe & Cuff, 10 In. 265.00
Moccasins, Iroquois, Beaded Hide, Bead Stitched Toe & Cuff, 10 In. 265.00
Moccasins, Kiowa, Beaded, Sinew Sewn, Yellow, Red Ocher, 25 3/4 In. 7475.00
Moccasins, Northern Plains, Beaded, Hide, 8 Point Star, White Ground, 10 In., Pair 670.00
Moccasins, Plains, Beaded, Fringed Hide, Light Blue Ground, 10 In., Pair 1725.00
Moccasins, Plains, Beaded, Royal Blue, Green, White, Red, White Field, 9 In., Pair ... 431.00
Moccasins, Sioux, Beaded, Green, White, Blue, Yellow, White, 10 3/8 In. 247.00
Moccasins, Sioux, Fully Beaded Uppers, Youth 1200.00
Moccasins, Sioux, Geometric Patterns 1610.00
Necklace, Navajo, Squash Blossom, Silver, Coral, 36 In. 402.00
Necklace, San Ildefonso Pueblo, Fetish, Black Pottery 95.00
Necklace, Turquoise, Silver Sterling, With Bear Claw 75.00
Necklace, Zuni, Fly Bird Pendant, Coral & Turquoise Beads 45.00
Necklace & Earrings, Zuni, Silver & Turquoise, Kirk & Mary K. Eriacho, 16 In. 460.00
Olla, Acoma, Thin Walls, Signed, 8 x 9 In. 1800.00
Olla, Black & White, Bird, Small Design At Collar 4500.00
Olla, Multicolored Birds, On Branch ....*Illus* 8050.00
Olla, Southwestern, 7 3/4 In. 30.00
Pendant, Navajo, Turquoise, Sterling Silver 95.00
Pin, Mosaic, Knife-Throwing Man, Stone, Shell, Turquoise, 2 x 2 5/8 In. 345.00
Pin, Mosaic, Rainbow Man, Shell, Coral, Jet, Turquoise, 3 x 1 3/4 In. 4600.00
Pipe, Chippewa, Tomahawk Shape, c.1860 .... 7187.00
Pipe Bag, Cheyenne, Black, White Pony Beads, Maroon Red Trade Cloth, 20 In 82.00
Pipe Bag, Cree, Floral, Red, Orange, Green, Blue On Bottom, 15 In. 1150.00
Pipe Bag, Plains, Beaded, Quilled, Diamond Motif, Navy, Azure, White, Red, 23 1/4 In. .. 1955.00
Pipe Bag, Plains, Beaded, Sinew Stitched, Red Orange, Pink, Royal, Navy Blue Beads .. 1092.00
Pipe Bag, Sioux, Beaded, Sinew Sewn, Apple Green, Yellow, Navy, White Beads, 16 In. 632.00
Pipe Bag, Sioux, Narrow, c.1900 .... 2400.00
Plate, Curley Portrait, Red & Yellow Border, Beardmore, 1905, 10 In. 300.00
Plate, Hopi, Flat Rim, Dark Brown Design Over Yellow White Slip, 8 1/4 x 7/8 In. 690.00
Plate, San Ildefonso, Blackware, 6 1/4 In. 1035.00
Pot, San Ildefonso, Sea Serpent, Signed, 7 1/2 In. 180.00
Pot, Santa Clara, Black On Black, Stella Chavarria, 6 In. 595.00
Pot, Southwestern, Black On Black, Marie & Julian, 4 In. 500.00
Pouch, Cornhusk, Twined, Geometric, Hide Thong Closure, 5 1/2 x 6 1/2 In. 172.00
Pouch, Cree, Beaded Red Berries, Blue Flowers, Colored Flags, c.1880 .... 2650.00
Pouch, Plateau, Cornhusk, Geometric, 18 1/2 x 13 1/2 In. 287.00
Pouch, Sioux, Beaded Hide, Red Forked Triangular Design 1035.00
Pouch, Sioux, Hide, Beaded, Sinew Sewn, Tin Cone, Feather Suspensions, 5 3/4 In. 143.00
Pouch, Tobacco, Equestrian Figure Beaded, Holding Lance, Bonnet, Fringed 6325.00
Pouch, Tobacco, Geometric Beaded, Fringed 1610.00
Rug, Navajo, 2-Stepped Geometric Panels, Black Panel Center, 31 x 47 In. 630.00
Rug, Navajo, Angled Stripes, Serrated Edge, Red, Gray, White, 41 x 60 In. 460.00
Rug, Navajo, Ganado Cross, Terrace Design, Red, Brown, 1930, 48 x 64 In. 291.00

Take care of your old rug!
Be sure it lies flat, preferably with an underpadding
exactly the size of the rug.
Move furniture and clean
under legs to avoid moths.

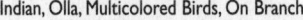

Indian, Olla, Multicolored Birds, On Branch

Rug, Navajo, Ganado Type, Gray Ground, Central Medallion, 77 x 61 In.	1150.00
Rug, Navajo, Ganado Type, Rows Of Cruciforms, Zigzag Border, 65 x 48 In.	1380.00
Rug, Navajo, Geometric Medallions, Gray, Brown Field, 40 x 68 In.	475.00
Rug, Navajo, Geometric Pattern, Gray & Black, 52 x 68 In.	1750.00
Rug, Navajo, Geometric Pattern, Terraced Triangular Border, 41 x 64 In.	575.00
Rug, Navajo, Germantown, Red, Green, Black, Gray & Ivory, 44 x 79 In.	6200.00
Rug, Navajo, Homespun Wool, Black, White, Gray, Brown, Red Ground, 52 x 31 In.	402.00
Rug, Navajo, Homespun Wool, Mustard, White, Black, Gray Ground, 48 x 32 In.	258.00
Rug, Navajo, Homespun Wool, Red, White, Sand, Gray, Brown Ground, 84 x 50 In.	920.00
Rug, Navajo, Homespun Wool, White, Mustard, Red, Black Field, 87 x 35 1/2 In.	488.00
Rug, Navajo, Moqui Diamond, 47 x 70 In.	1100.00
Rug, Navajo, Natural & Aniline Dyed Wool, Black, Gray & Ivory, 55 x 42 In.	530.00
Rug, Navajo, Overall Geometric Pattern, 51 x 86 In.	1265.00
Rug, Navajo, Overall Geometric Pattern, Feathers & Arrows, 43 x 65 In.	1380.00
Rug, Navajo, Overall Geometric Pattern, Feathers, Bessie Tsosie, 1983, 68 x 84 In.	3105.00
Rug, Navajo, Pine Tree Pattern, Beige, Tan & Brown, 43 x 72 In.	488.00
Rug, Navajo, Radiating Serrated Edge, Diamond Design, 47 x 57 In.	110.00
Rug, Navajo, Red Serrated Diamond, Gray Ground, 39 x 53 In.	330.00
Rug, Navajo, Regional, Homespun Wool, Muted Olive, Mustard, Gray, 62 x 35 In.	345.00
Rug, Navajo, Serrated Diamond Cross, Gray Ground, 41 x 68 In.	165.00
Rug, Navajo, Serrated Diamonds, Red, Dark Brown, 44 x 69 In.	880.00
Rug, Navajo, Serrated Diamonds, Red, Gold, Gray, Black, 1950s, 46 x 69 In.	214.00
Rug, Navajo, Serrated Stripes, Red, Black Border, 27 x 52 In.	275.00
Rug, Navajo, Stepped Diamond Design, Red, 32 x 43 In.	110.00
Rug, Navajo, Storm Pattern, Teec-Nos-Pas Type Border, c.1935, 36 x 56 In.	412.00
Rug, Navajo, Striped Bands Of Rhomboids, Red Border, c.1930, 30 x 51 In.	220.00
Rug, Navajo, Yei, 5 Figures, Cream Ground, 47 x 32 In.	632.00
Rug, Navajo, Yei, 5 Figures, Gray Ground, Black Border, 44 x 29 In.	405.00
Saddlebag, Beaded, U.S. Flags, Flap	2800.00
Snowshoes, Cree, Woven Babiche, c.1900	375.00
Snowshoes, Maine, Child's, 29 In.	75.00
Spoon, Northwest Coast, Goat Horn, Carved Handle, Abalone Shell Inlay, 13 In.	625.00
Spoon, Tlingit, Horn, Carved, Pierced & Incised Totemic Design, 9 1/2 In.	495.00
Tobacco Leather, Geronimo Portrait, Rifle, Brown, Red, Black & Gray, 10 x 12 In.	500.00
Totem Pole, Northwest Coast, Carved Birds, 1940s, 10 1/2 In.	72.00
Tray, Huron, Birchbark, Dyed Moose Hair, Porcupine Quill Floral Design, 5 1/4 In.	990.00
Trousers, Beaded, Boy's	5175.00
Trousers, Hide, Beaded, Sinew Sewn, Geometric, Teal, Navy, White, Child's, 12 In.	2185.00
Vest, Chippewa, Hide, Beaded Flowers, Brass Buttons, Steel Buckle, 1890s	450.00
War Club, Woodlands, 2 Edged Iron Blade, Green, Brown Pigment, 24 In.	3737.00
Weaving, Chimayo, Red, Black Design, 30 x 46 In.	137.00

INDIAN TREE is a china pattern that was popular during the last half of the nineteenth century. It was copied from earlier Indian textile patterns that were very similar. The pattern includes the crooked branch of a tree and a partial landscape with exotic flowers and leaves. Green, blue, pink, and orange were the favored colors used in the design.

Cup & Saucer, Fluted, Coalport	12.00
Pitcher, Coalport	25.00
Plate, 9 7/8 In.	15.00
Teapot, Coalport	30.00

INKSTANDS were made to be placed on a desk. They held some type of container for ink, and possibly a sander, a pen tray, a pen, a holder for pounce, and even a candle to melt the sealing wax. Inkstands date to the eighteenth century and have been made of silver, copper, ceramics, and glass. Additional inkstands may be found in these and other related categories.

Agate, Buff & Brown, 3 Quill Holders, Striped Panels, 1760, 4 1/4 In.	285.00
Brass, Alligator, Double Milk Glass Wells, Brass, 19th Century	245.00
Brass, Bell-Metal, Trefoil, Pounce Pot, Candlestick, 1760, 5 1/4 x 7 1/2 In.	1725.00
Brass, Buffalo, 2 Pen Wells, Ornate Stand, With Mother-Of-Pearl Handled Pen	225.00
Brass, Deer's Head, Antlers Form Pen Rack, Crystal Bottle, Branches, Acorns Base	245.00
Brass, Sander, England, Square, 1770-1790	595.00
Brass, Well, Arts & Crafts, Rococo Style, Cupids & Roses, 2 Twisted Glass Wells	145.00
Brass Lid, Cut Glass Wells, Brass Taper Stick, Regency, Drawer, Wooden, c.1815	2200.00
Copper, Silver Metal, Bull & Bear, Wavy Grasses Border, 1900, 13 3/4 In.	2875.00
Faience, Rococo Form, Exotic Birds, France, 9 1/2 In.	230.00
Iron, Revolving, 1 Blue & 1 Milk Glass Bottles, American, 3 1/2 x 4 1/2 In.	330.00
Silver, Oval Tray, Cut Bottles, Acanthus Leaf & Greek Key, London, 1878, 11 5/8 In.	747.00
Silver Plate, Glass Bottles, Sheffield, 1785-1800, 8 1/8 In.	500.00

INKWELLS, of course, held ink. Ready-made ink was first made about 1836 and was sold in bottles. The desk inkwell had a narrow hole so the pen would not slip inside. Inkwells were made of many materials, such as pottery, glass, pewter, and silver. Look in these categories for more listings of inkwells.

Brass, Cart, Pulled By Pug Dog, China, 4 1/2 In.	450.00
Brass, Made From Propeller, United Aircraft Club, 1923-1948, 8 x 5 x 5 In.	135.00
Brass, Quill Holder, Boy Holds Pitcher, Lids Lift Off Barrel, England, 4 1/2 In.	295.00
Brass, U.S. Post Office	80.00
Bronze, Cover, Acanthus, Scrolls, Berry Finial Center, Leafy Satyr Masks, 5 1/8 In.	4600.00
Bronze, Crab, Shell Hinged To Expose Brass Cup, Claws Hold Pen	200.00
Bronze, Dog	125.00
Bronze, Dog Head, Shaggy Head Hinged Cover, 1802, 6 x 9 In.	1150.00
Bronze, Dolphin Surrounding Platform, Rococo Base, Cherubs, 1860-1880, 3 x 4 In.	725.00
Bronze, Double, Bubble Thermometer In Center	125.00
Bronze, Elephant Head, Monkey On Head, c.1890	650.00
Bronze, Figurine, Encrusted Shells, Shell Dish, Ink Pot & Sander, Bronze, 7 In.	1035.00
Bronze, Man With Harp, Double Quill Holder, 5 In.	475.00
Bronze, Marble, Stag Figure Center, 18 1/2 In.	200.00
Bronze, Nude Figure, Atlas Kneeling, Head Tilted Upward, Brown Patina	9775.00
Bronze, Triton, Blowing Horn, Leafy Arabesques, 6 1/8 In.	9200.00
Bronze & Marble, Dolphin & Wheel Form, Painted, England, c.1800, 5 1/2 In.	1650.00
Copper, Pen Tray, Hammered, Arts & Crafts, 4 1/2 x 8 x 5 1/2 In.	467.00
Glass, 3-Mold, Coventry Glass Works, Medium Golden Amber, Pontil, 1 5/8 In.	190.00
Glass, 3-Mold, Disc Mouth, Dense Olive Amber, Pontil, Cylindrical, 2 1/4 In.	154.00
Glass, 3-Mold, Yellow Olive, Cylindrical, Coventry Glass Works, 1 1/2 In.	175.00
Glass, 36 Ribs, Swirled To Left, Yellow Olive, Pitkin Glass Works, Cylindrical, 2 In.	200.00
Glass, 7 Rings, Forest Green, 2 Piece Mold, New England, 1 3/8 x 2 3/8 In.	825.00
Glass, Amber, Hinged Top, Stippled, Dimpled Sides, Square, 4 1/8 x 2 5/8 In.	235.00
Glass, Black, U.S. Navy	50.00
Glass, Cut, Hinged Faceted Cover, Square, 2 x 3 In.	95.00
Glass, Floral Design, Applied Metal Collar, Cap, Green, Bulbous, Cylindrical, 3 1/4 In.	215.00

Glass, Green, Rippled, Brass Hinged Top, Ball Finial, Brass, 3 3/4 In. 235.00
Glass, Greenish Olive, Sheered Top, Open Pontil, Stoddard 330.00
Glass, Keene Marlboro Street Glassworks, Medium Yellow Olive, 1 1/2 In. 150.00
Glass, Locomotive, Aqua, 1860-1890, 1 7/8 x 2 1/8 In. 605.00
Glass, Pitkin Type, 36 Left Swirled Ribs, Olive, Funnel Mouth, Pontil, 1 1/2 In. 745.00
Glass, Pyramid Form, Applied Brass Collar, Blue, Green, Amethyst Iridescence, 4 3/4 In. 176.00
Glass, Teakettle, Blue, Hexagonal, Gilt Design, Brass Collar & Cap, 1 7/8 x 3 1/4 In. . . . 275.00
Glass, Teakettle, Cobalt Blue, Gilt, Brass Collar & Cap, 1 7/8 x 3 1/4 In. 275.00
Glass, Teakettle, Conical Octagonal Body, Spout, Amethyst, 2 In. 120.00
Glass, Teakettle, Medium Amethyst, Corseted Octagonal, 1830-1860, 2 1/8 In. 440.00
Glass, Teakettle, Teal, Hexagonal, c.1861, 2 x 3 1/8 In. 550.00
Glass, Umbrella, Rolled Lip, Open Pontil, Puce, Stretched Out Tapered Neck 1100.00
Iron, Tree Stump Form 110.00
Pottery, Dog, Whippet, Orange, Brown, White, Blue Glaze, Black, England, 5 In. 132.00
Pottery, Staffordshire, Dogs, 5 1/2 In. 500.00
Pressed Glass, Chandelier Pattern 125.00
Salt Glaze, Documentary Shape, Screw Finial, Staffordshire, 1745, 2 5/8 In. 2300.00
Satyr, Bronze, Kneeling, Scalloped Lid, 3 Scrolled Legs, Acorn Finial, 5 1/8 In. 2185.00
Silver, Mounted Horn, Whiting, 8 In. 317.00
Silver Plated, Arabs, On Camels, Palm Trees, Desert Landscape, 11 In. 1265.00
Stoneware, Blue & White, 2 1/4 In. 95.00
Wooden, Camel, Resting Position, Hinged Pack On Hump, Opens To Bottles 145.00
Yellowware, Cone Shape 200.00

INSULATORS of glass or pottery have been made for use on telegraph
or telephone poles since 1844. Thousands of different styles of insulators have been made. Most common are those of clear or aqua glass;
most desirable are the threadless types made from 1850 to 1870.

American Ins. Co., Light Blue, Embossed Base 24.00
American Telephone & Telegraph, Light Jade Green 10.00
Boston Bottle Works, Aqua, Pat. Oct. 15, 1972, Barrel . . . . : 620.00
Brookfield, Emerald Green, Yellow Swirls 20.00
Brookfield, No. 3, Transposition, Dark Blue-Aqua 10.00
Brookfield, No. 9, Blue, Bubbles & Snow 20.00
Cable, No. 2, Light Blue 10.00
Cable, No. 3, Dark Green, Bubbles 20.00
Cable, No. 4, Dark Aqua 80.00
Dominion, No. 42, Yellow Amber . . . . .65.00 to 85.00
Electrical Supply Co., Light Blue-Aqua 28.00
F.M. Locke, Victor, N.Y., No. 15, Yellow Green, Amber Streaks 35.00
F.M. Locke, Victor, N.Y., No. 16, Emerald Green, Yellow Tint 40.00
Hemingray, E-2, Light Yellow 65.00
Hemingray, No. 3, Bright Aqua, Cable 35.00
Hemingray, No. 3-512, Yellow Amber 20.00
Hemingray, No. 5, Dark Aqua, Pat. 1893 . . . . 10.00
Hemingray, No. 9, Aqua, Jade Green Swirl, Pat. 1893 . . . . 20.00
Hemingray, No. 12, Aqua Jade, Milk Swirls, Sharp Drip Points 25.00
Hemingray, No. 12, Dark Olive Green 90.00
Hemingray, No. 12, Jade Green 20.00
Hemingray, No. 12, Milk Swirls, Aqua 25.00
Hemingray, No. 19, Orange Amber, Round Drip Points 70.00
Hemingray, No. 23, Blue 25.00
Hemingray, No. 38, Aqua 14.00
Hemingray, No. 50, Blue Aqua 10.00
Hemingray, No. 54 A & B, Purple 58.00
Hemingray, No. 55, Blue 10.00
Hemingray, No. 60 . . . . 8.00
Hemingray, No. 62, Amber Flashed 40.00
Hemingray, No. 71, Blue 71.00
Hemingray, No. 109, Amber 30.00
Hemingray, TS-2, Carnival 25.00
Maydwell, No. 62, Light Green 22.00
McLaughlin, No. 9, Emerald Green, Round Drip Points 15.00

McLaughlin, No. 10, Ginger Ale 35.00
McLaughlin, No. 16, Dark Green 12.00
McLaughlin, No. 16, Deep Olive Green 13.00
McLaughlin, No. 16, Delft Blue 30.00
McLaughlin, No. 16, Green 25.00
McLaughlin, No. 16, Green, Round Drip Points 50.00
McLaughlin, No. 16, Light Yellow Lime Green 60.00
No. 100, Dark Aqua, Open Rim Bubbles 70.00
Prism, No. 2, Blue Aqua 28.00
Pyrex, No. 63 . . . . .20.00 to 25.00
Pyrex, No. 171, Carnival Glass 35.00
Pyrex, No. 662 . . . . 30.00
W. Brookfield, Blue, Bubbles, Pat. 1883-1884 . . . . 15.00
Whitall Tatum, No. 1 . . . . 15.00
Whitall Tatum, No. 2, Bright Yellow Green 20.00
Whitall Tatum, No. 3, Peach 4.00
Whitall Tatum, No. 9, Light Medium Purple 22.00

IRISH BELLEEK, see Belleek category.

IRON is a metal that has been used by man since prehistoric times. It is a popular metal for tools and decorative items like doorstops that need as much weight as possible. Items are listed here or under other appropriate headings, such as Bookends, Doorstop, Kitchen, Match Holder, or Tool. The tool that is used for ironing clothes, an iron, is listed in the Kitchen category under Iron and Sadiron.

Birdhouse, Gothic Revival Gabled House Form, 1870s, 11 x 15 In. 2070.00
Boot Scraper, Attached Cast Base, 19th Century 110.00
Boot Scraper, Dachshund, 14 In. 23.00
Boot Scraper, Dachshund, 22 In. 150.00
Bootjack, Beetle Shape, 10 1/8 In. 70.00
Bootjack, Floral Design, 11 1/2 In. 60.00
Bootjack, Tree Of Life, 14 7/8 In. 120.00
Chamberstick, Shell Form Ejector Lifter, Handle, Early 19th Century, 8 1/2 In. 185.00
Cigar Cutter, Pocket Scissors, End & V Cutter & Perforator 135.00
Cigar Cutter, Statesman, Key Wind, Store Model 325.00
Cigar Cutter, Table Top, Small 36.00
Cigar Cutter, Tail Is Cutter, Painted, 8 In. 302.00
Curling Iron, Forged, 18th Century, 23 In. 150.00
Cuspidor, Top Hat Shape, Worn Green & Black Paint, Over Gold, 7 In. 325.00

Iron, Door Knocker, Cottage In Woods, Judd Co., 3 1/2 x 2 1/2 In.
Iron, Door Knocker, Castle, Judd Co., 4 x 3 In.
Iron, Door Knocker, Cherub, Ribbon & Roses, Judd Co., 4 1/4 x 3 In.

Iron, Door Knocker, Cat, Black,
Rear View, 7 1/4 x 3 In.

**Nuts and bolts on old furniture
hardware should be removed
carefully. Wrap pliers with
masking tape to protect the
brass. Old brass is often soft.**

Cuspidor, Turtle, Step On Head, Raises Cover	795.00
Door Knocker, Basket Of Flowers, Painted	130.00
Door Knocker, Castle, Judd Co., 4 x 3 In. . . . .*Illus*	440.00
Door Knocker, Cat, Black, Rear View, 7 1/4 x 3 In. . . . .*Illus*	550.00
Door Knocker, Cherub, Ribbon & Roses, Judd Co., 4 1/4 x 3 In. . . . .*Illus*	1540.00
Door Knocker, Cottage In Woods, Judd Co., 3 1/2 x 2 1/2 In. . . . .*Illus*	580.00
Door Knocker, Hand Shape, 9 In.	105.00
Door Knocker, Little Girl, Knocking At Door, Worn Paint	300.00
Door Knocker, Parrot	65.00
Door Knocker, Rabbit, Eating Carrot	1705.00
Figure, Cat, Reclining, White, Blue Eyes, 6 x 11 In.	30.00
Figure, Clown, Shooting Gallery, 1912, 29 x 22 In.	1500.00
Figure, Dog, Seated With Free Standing Front Legs, Red Paint, 5 5/8 In.	110.00
Figurine, French Bulldog, Hubley	50.00
Figurine, Golfer, Orange & Black Paint, 3 1/2 In.	425.00
Figurine, Mammy, Green Dress, Hubley	100.00
Figurine, Sealyham, Hubley	40.00
Head, Man's, Mustache, Lead Filled, 2 Mounting Bolts, 8 1/4 In.	80.00
Hitching Post, Jockey, Hollow, Red, White & Black, 47 In.	880.00
Hitching Post, Jockey, Painted, 1920s, 35 1/2 In.	575.00
Hitching Post, Jockey, Painted, Late 1800s	1250.00
Leg Irons, Hand Forged, Slave, Takes T Wrench, Early 1800s, 16 1/2 In.	210.00
Mold, Candle, Makes Candles Up To 24 In., Drummond Candle Maker, 1846	375.00
Paperweight, Campaign Hat, 4 x 4	55.00
Seat, Tractor, Parlin & Orendorff	125.00
Seat, Tractor, Rock Island Plow Company	140.00
Silent Butler, Turtle, Press Down Head, Opens Shell, Bradley & Hubbard	395.00
Stand, Brass Trim, Plate Glass Top, 8 1/2 x 17 3/4 x 28 1/2 In.	110.00
Tobacco Cutter, Drummond, St. Louis	90.00
Trivet, Sadiron, Pottstown, Pa. & Mfg.	45.00
Umbrella Rack, Figure Of Sailor With Anchor, Paddle, 28 In.	495.00
Windmill Weight, Bobtail Horse, Dempster	195.00
Windmill Weight, Bobtail Horse, Dempster, Black Paint, 16 1/2 x 17 In.	110.00
Windmill Weight, Bull, Fairbury, Nebraska, Wooden Stand, 17 1/4 In.	920.00
Windmill Weight, E.W.P. & P. Co., Elgin, Ill., 11 3/4 In.	190.00
Windmill Weight, Eclipse A13, Fairbanks, Morse & Co., Chicago, 10 1/4 In.	190.00
Windmill Weight, Fairbury, 24 In.	1650.00
Windmill Weight, Full, Fairbury, Nebraska, Wooden Stand, 17 1/4 x 24 2/3 In.	920.00
Windmill Weight, Horse, Dempster Mill Mfg. Co., Black Paint, 16 1/2 x 17 In. . .300.00 to	385.00
Windmill Weight, Horse, Dempster Mill Mfg., Worn Paint, Wooden Base, 18 1/2 In.	415.00
Windmill Weight, Horse, Standing, Articulated Eyes, Mane & Tail, 15 1/2 x 17 In.	518.00
Windmill Weight, Horseshoe	1450.00
Windmill Weight, Letter W, Althouse Wheeler Co., 16 In.	355.00
Windmill Weight, Letter W, Althouse Wheeler Co., 17 In.	605.00

Windmill Weight, Rooster, Black, Red, Wooden Base, Elgin Wind, Power, Pump Co. .. 330.00
Windmill Weight, Rooster, Hummer 175.00
Windmill Weight, Star 875.00

IRONSTONE china was first made in 1813. It gained its greatest popularity during the mid-nineteenth century. The heavy, durable, off-white pottery was made in white or was decorated with any of hundreds of patterns. Much flow blue pottery was made of ironstone. Some of the decorations were raised. Many pieces of ironstone are unmarked, but some English and American factories included the word *Ironstone* in their marks. Additional pieces may be listed in other categories, such as Chelsea Grape, Chelsea Sprig, Flow Blue, Gaudy Ironstone, Moss Rose, Staffordshire, and Tea Leaf Ironstone.

Cake Plate, Verona, Signed, 10 In. 77.00
Carpet Ball, Spatter Design, Red, Blue, 3 In., Pair 308.00
Chamber Set, Floral, Maddock & Sons, Royal Vitreous, 3 Piece 185.00
Coffeepot, Gold Design, 10 3/4 In. 230.00
Coffeepot, Morning Glory, Richelieu Shape, Re-Glued Finial 550.00
Coffeepot, Rose Embossed Cover & Handle, Meakin, 10 In. 125.00
Coffeepot, Wreath Of Wheat Design, F. Jones & Co., 1868 .... 220.00
Compote, Square, Red Cliff 120.00
Creamer, Acanthus, Johnson Brothers 200.00
Creamer, Wheat In The Meadow, Copper Luster, Powell & Bishop 350.00
Cup & Saucer, Child's, Sayers 110.00
Cup & Saucer, Elsmore, Thomas 45.00
Cup & Saucer, Handleless, Copper Luster 150.00
Cup & Saucer, Laurel Wreath, Copper Luster, Elsmore & Forster 100.00
Dish, Cover, Fishhook, Meakin, 6 x 9 In. 80.00
Dish, Soap, Pagoda, Liner, Burgess 100.00
Gravy Boat, Cable Shape 50.00
Gravy Boat, Scallops, Walley 160.00
Jug, Imari Colors, Small 75.00
Lazy Susan, White, Scalloped Floral Border, Late 19th Century, 18 In. 575.00
Nappy, Iona, Gold, Powell & Bishop, 2 Sets 40.00
Pitcher, Black Transfer, Quail, Polychrome Enamel, J.M.P Bell, Scotland, 8 1/2 In. 100.00
Pitcher, Pulled Spout, Serpent Form Handle, England, 19th Century, 12 1/2 In. 35.00
Pitcher, White Glazed, Baluster, Flared Lip, C-Scroll Handle, 11 1/4 In. 60.00
Pitcher, Yeddo, Brown Transfer, 12 1/2 In. 60.00
Pitcher & Bowl, Raised Scrolling, Gilt Edges, 19th Century 80.00
Plate, Robert & Son, England, 1810 .... 165.00
Platter, Brown Spatter Border, Berry & Leaf Design, 16 1/4 In. 190.00
Platter, Cornucopia Reserve, Foliate Sprays, Octagonal, England, 18 3/4 In. 345.00
Soup, Dish, Laurel Wreath, Elsmore & Forster, 6 7/8 In. 200.00
Sugar, Morning Glory, Portland Shape, Elsmore & Forster 225.00
Tea Set, Black Transfer, Forget-Me-Not, c.1850, 6 Piece 310.00
Teapot, Pomegranate, Niagara Shape, Walley 400.00
Tureen, Soup, Undertray, Black Floral Transfer, Marked, 13 3/4 In. 465.00
Tureen, Underplate, Brown Transfer, Phileau, Turner, 13 1/4 In. 110.00
Vase, Cover, Black & Colored Landscape Panels, Fenton Stone Works, 58 1/4 In. 6325.00

IVORY from the tusk of an elephant is thought by many to be the only true ivory. To most collectors, the term *ivory* also includes such natural materials as walrus, hippopotamus, or whale teeth or tusks, and some of the vegetable materials that are of similar texture and density. Other ivory items may be found in the Scrimshaw and Netsuke categories. Collectors should be aware of the recent laws limiting the buying and selling of elephant ivory and scrimshaw.

Ball, Puzzle, Floral Motif, Concentric Balls In Interior, China, 5 In. 490.00
Bottle, Snuff, Figural Landscape, Temple Jar Form, Stopper, 19th Century, 4 1/8 In. 1100.00
Box, Hinged Cover, Coat Of Arms Eagle, Black, Green, Foliage Border, France, 4 In. ... 1610.00
Bust, Man, Shouting, Continental, 3 1/4 In. 402.00
Chest, Jewelry, Removable Lap Top Writing Desk, 12 x 13 1/2 In. 2450.00
Cigar Cutter, Tusk, Sterling Silver End Cap & Cutter, Table Top 450.00

Cigarette Holder, Carved, 3 1/2 In. 40.00
Cup, Cover, Putto On Cask Finial, Band Of Rowdy Putti, Foliate Carved Foot, 9 1/2 In. . . 1092.00
Figurine, Basket Seller, Etched Geometric Designs, 5 1/2 In. 805.00
Figurine, Boy, Seated On A Raft, 2 1/2 x 3 1/4 In. 150.00
Figurine, Daikoku Holding His Mallet, Signed, Early 20th Century, 4 1/4 In. 300.00
Figurine, Daikoku, Standing On Rice Bale Holding His Hammer, 3 3/4 In. 330.00
Figurine, Elephant Head, African Elephant One End, Silver Collar, c.1860, 2 x 6 In. 3400.00
Figurine, Elephants, Draped With Carved Harnesses, Blankets, Wood Bases, 5 In., Pair . . 860.00
Figurine, Elizabeth I, Hinged Skirt, Triptych Of Queen & Sir Walter Raleigh, 8 In. 546.00
Figurine, Empress, Standing On Raised Base, Dragons Among Clouds, 10 In. 1840.00
Figurine, Farmer, Holding Rooster With Magnificent Tail, Signed, 9 3/4 In. 495.00
Figurine, Fukurokuju, Standing, Staff In 1 Hand, Late Meiji Period, 8 1/2 In. 825.00
Figurine, God Figure, Seated On Lotus Base, 8 1/2 In. 460.00
Figurine, Hunter, Fabled, With Bow & Arrow Capturing Bird At Feet, Japan, 7 1/2 In. . . . 2530.00
Figurine, Jonah & Whale, Walrus, Silver Scalloped Collar, Horn Ferrule, 1830s, 5 1/4 In. 2000.00
Figurine, Man Carrying Water Pouch, Right Hand Holding Mask, Signed, 4 1/4 In. 82.00
Figurine, Man, With Monkey Standing On Shoulder, 6 In. 317.00
Figurine, Mermaid, Bare Breasted, Sleeping, Silver Collar, England, 1884, 4 1/3 In. 3600.00
Figurine, Musical Dragons With Grotesque Faces, 4 1/2 In., Pair 832.00
Figurine, Nativity & The Crucifixion, Gothic Arches, Dentilled Border, 2 x 1 3/4 In. 3220.00
Figurine, Nude, Woman, Seated On A Tiger's Back, Continental, 5 In. 345.00
Figurine, Our Madonna Of Milk, Black Hair, On Cloud Work Base, 11 1/4 In. 1840.00
Figurine, Peasant, Leaning On His Hoe, Signed, Masayuki, Meiji Period, 5 3/8 In. 330.00
Figurine, Penitent Magdalene, With Flowing Robes, Carved, Continental, 4 3/4 In. 1610.00
Figurine, Phoenix, Standing On Rookery, Peony Blossoms Below, 12 1/4 In., Pair 1035.00
Figurine, Prometheus And The Eagle, By Tree With Dog, Carved, 8 In. 805.00
Figurine, Sage, Holding Fruit Peach Branch, Wood Base, 18th Century, 9 1/2 In. 805.00
Figurine, Sage, Holding Peach, Signed, 20th Century, 7 1/8 In. 495.00
Figurine, Sage, Lying, Holding Gourd, Head Raised, Mouth Open, Wood Stand, 9 In. . . . 316.00
Figurine, Scholar, Enjoying Cup Of Wine, Japan, 6 1/4 In. 345.00
Figurine, Shao-Lu, Standing With A Crane, Peaches Of Immortality, 13 In. 316.00
Figurine, Woman, Holding A Floral Branch, Jeweled Crown, Jewelry, 13 In. 975.00
Figurine, Woman, Medicine, Japan, 11 In. 345.00
Figurine, Woman, Medicine, Japan, 12 In. 316.00
Figurine, Woman, Standing, Holding A Flowering Tree Branch, Meiji Period, 6 1/2 In. . . 605.00
Figurine, Woman, With A Folded Fan, Meiji Period, 7 3/4 In. 440.00
Figurine, Wood Cutter, Signed, Masamitsu, 20th Century, 5 1/4 In. 220.00
Figurine, Wood Cutter, With Bundle Of Sticks, Late Meiji Period, 8 In. 495.00
Group, Musicians, Standing In A Circle, 1 3/4 x 2 In. 253.00
Jagging Wheel, Elephant, Trojan Figurehead, England, 19th Century, 6 1/2 In. 515.00
Jar, Snuff, Cylinder Form, 19th Century, 1 3/4 x 1 1/4 In. 275.00
Magnifying Glass, Carved Knop Handle, Armorial, Gilt Metal, Continental, 12 In. 400.00
Ojime, Ball Of Ribbon Form, Meiji Period 66.00
Ojime, Relief Carved Flowers, Ball Form, 20th Century 44.00
Ojime, Wood Grain Design, Squat Globular Form, Early 20th Century 88.00
Page Turner, Chinese Carved, Allegorical Scene On Handle, 13 1/4 In. 151.00
Plaque, Coronation Of Josephine, Gilt Metal & Faux Pearl Frame, 8 1/2 In. 3450.00
Plaque, Walrus, Adoration Of The Magi, Gilt Beaded Border, 3 x 1 1/2 In. 9200.00
Ruler, Folding, Prolific Sheffield, 12 In. 165.00
Table Screen, 4-Panel, Relief Figural Panels, Early 19th Century, 10 5/8 In. 968.00

JACK ARMSTRONG, the all-American boy, was the hero of a radio se-
rial from 1933 to 1951. Premiums were offered to the listeners until
the mid-1940s. Jack Armstrong's best-known endorsement is for
Wheaties.

Comic Book, All American Boy, Nov. 1947 . . . . 125.00
Explore Telescope, Radio Premium 35.00
Flashlight, Torpedo, Premium 22.00
Hike-O-Meter, 1935 . . . . .50.00 to 75.00
Ped-O-Meter, Blue Rim, 1939, 2 3/4 In. 52.00
Pin, Gardenia, Glows In Dark, Plastic, 1939 . . . . 85.00
Secret Bombsight 145.00
Training Kit, Pre-Flight, How To Fly Manual, c.1945 . . . . 103.00

JACK-IN-THE-PULPIT vases, oddly shaped like trumpets, resemble the wild plant called jack-in-the-pulpit. The design originated in the late Victorian years. Vases in the jack-in-the-pulpit shape were made of ceramic or glass and the complete list of page references can be found in the index.

Vase, Iridescent Red, 16 In.	225.00
Vase, Marigold, Carnival Glass, 11 In.	35.00
Vase, White, Yellow Iridescent, Deep Red Interior, Green, Marked, 12 In.	324.50
White, Blown Glass, 8 In.	22.00

JADE is the name for two different minerals, nephrite and jadeite. Nephrite is the mineral used for most early Oriental carvings. Jade is a very tough stone that is found in many colors from dark green to pale lavender. Jade carvings are still being made in the old styles, so collectors must be careful not to be fooled by recent pieces. Jade jewelry is found in this book under Jewelry.

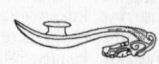

Bowl, Chrysanthemum, Radiating Petals, Dark Flecking, Spain, 8 1/2 In.	2300.00
Bowl, Cover, Animal Mask, Loop Handles, Flat Ribbed Lid, Carved Wooden Base, White	1495.00
Bowl, Yellow, Flared, Opaque Yellow Bulbed Integrated Foot, 5 1/2 x 16 In.	230.00
Box, Cover, Bird, Flower Design, Spinach Green, Wood Stand, 5 1/4 In.	242.00
Box, Gourd Form, Butterfly On Lid, Gourd Surrounded By Leaves, Tendrils, White	1840.00
Dish, Carved Relief Interior, Peony On Sides, Stylized Bracket Border, Green	3450.00
Figurine, 2 Mandarin Ducks, 2 3/4 In.	120.00
Figurine, Birds On A Branch, Carved Stands, 7 3/4 In., Pair	161.00
Figurine, Dragon-Type Beast, Finial On Back, Light Green Stone, 6 In.	460.00
Figurine, Frog Form, Lotus In His Mouth, White, Early 19th Century, 1 3/4 In.	154.00
Figurine, Lion, Reclining, Gray, Black, Ming Dynasty, 2 3/4 In.	357.50
Figurine, Phoenix, Tail Tucked Under Body, Blooming Flower, 6 1/2 In.	575.00
Figurine, Stylized Cabbage, Surmounted By 2 Grasshoppers, Teak Stand, 7 In.	34.50
Figurine, Water Buffalo, Reclining, Russet Inclusions, Yellow, 7 1/4 In.	3630.00
Plaque, Dragon, Passion Flower Design On Scrolled Ground, Pierced White, 3 x 2 In.	605.00
Teapot, Globular Shape, Stylized Dragon Design, Dragon Handle, White, 5 5/8 In.	7260.00
Vase, Baluster, Flowering Branch, China, 3 In.	103.50
Vase, Baluster, Mask Handles, Yellow, Late 19th Century, 5 In.	605.00
Vase, Bud, White Petals, Coral Flower Heads, Hardwood Stand, 9 In.	4600.00
Vase, Low Relief With Lappet, Leaf Borders, Phoenix Design, Cylindrical, 5 1/2 In.	18400.00
Vase, Scrolled Lotus Design On Body, Loose Ring Handles, White, 5 In.	2100.00

JAPANESE WOODBLOCK PRINTS are listed in this book in the Print category under Japanese.

JASPERWARE can be made in different ways. Some pieces are made from a solid colored clay with applied raised designs of a contrasting colored clay. Other pieces are made entirely of one color clay with raised decorations that are glazed with a contrasting color. Additional pieces of jasperware may also be listed in the Wedgwood category or under various art potteries.

Buttons, Blue, Cut Steel, White Classical Relief, 1 3/8 In., 12 Piece	5750.00
Jug, Liquor, Stopper, Green	125.00
Plaque, Boy, With Mandolin & Angels, 5 1/2 In.	135.00
Plaque, Continental, Frame, Oval, 4 1/2 & 5 In., Pair	20.00
Plaque, Cupid, With Bow & Hat, Target, Green, White, Germany, Round, 5 3/8 In.	65.00
Plaque, Old Fisherman, Smoking Pipe, Green, White, Germany, Round, 6 1/4 In.	55.00
Teapot, Blue, 1870, Miniature	575.00

JEWELRY, whether made from gold and precious gems or plastic and colored glass, is popular with collectors. Values are determined by the intrinsic value of the stones and metal and by the skill of the craftsmen and designers. Victorian and older jewelry have been collected since the 1950s. More recent interests are Art Deco and Edwardian styles, Mexican and Danish silver jewelry, and beads of all kinds. Copies of almost all styles are being made. American Indian jewelry is listed in the Indian category.

Beads, Gold Filled, 14 In.	50.00

Bracelet, Bakelite, Butterscotch, 3/4 In. 50.00
Bracelet, Bakelite, Butterscotch, Carved, 1 In. 115.00
Bracelet, Bakelite, Red Diamond Cut, 1 In. 110.00
Bracelet, Bakelite, Square Blocks, On Elastic, Wood & Brass 110.00
Bracelet, Bangle, 15 Diamonds, Yellow Gold 412.00
Bracelet, Bangle, 9 Diamonds, 14K Gold, 1960s 195.00
Bracelet, Bangle, Baguette, Geometric Motif, 14K Yellow Gold 1150.00
Bracelet, Bangle, Butterscotch Bakelite, Open Carved Leaves, 1 In. 110.00
Bracelet, Bangle, Carved Rope Twist 45.00
Bracelet, Bangle, Coiled Flexible Snake, Red Stone Eyes, England, 9K Yellow Gold ... 690.00
Bracelet, Bangle, Curb Link Design, Victorian, 18K Yellow Gold 402.50
Bracelet, Bangle, Red Bakelite, Deeply Carved, 1 In. 125.00
Bracelet, Bangle, Snake, Ruby Cabochon Eyes, Hinged Design, 18K Yellow Gold 977.00
Bracelet, Bangle, To Assemble, Bakelite, Yellow, Inner Rim Carved, Box, 22 Piece 125.00
Bracelet, Bangle, Tortoiseshell, 3/4 In. 50.00
Bracelet, Braiding & Hearts, 14K Gold, c.1930 .... 295.00
Bracelet, Center Channel Of Clustered Pearls, 18K Yellow Gold, France 920.00
Bracelet, Charm, Gold Filled, 14K Yellow Gold 1452.00
Bracelet, Charm, Household Items, Folk Tales, 14K Yellow Gold 488.00
Bracelet, Cherry Blossom Pattern, Sterling Silver, Pierced, Kalo Shop, 7 1/4 In. 695.00
Bracelet, Coiled Snake, Engraved Head, Ruby Eyes, Victorian, 9K Gold 485.00
Bracelet, Copper, Glass & Silver, Eagle Mark, Los Castillo 285.00
Bracelet, Cuff, Center Silver Coin, Profile Of Roman Man, Tapered Design 258.75
Bracelet, Diamond Line, Herringbone Mount, Tiffany & Co., 18K Yellow Gold 4715.00
Bracelet, Diamond, Geometric Design, 3 Marquise, Art Deco 8337.50
Bracelet, Flexible, Floral Repousse Sections, 14K Gold 565.00
Bracelet, Foliate Links, Cabochon Blue Stones, Evald Nielsen, 14K Yellow Gold ... 1092.50
Bracelet, Geometric Design, Openwork Links, Art Deco 10637.00
Bracelet, Gold, Pearls, Hinged, Florenza 45.00
Bracelet, Gold, Pearls, Trifari, 1950s 35.00
Bracelet, Gold, Pierced Swan, Foliate, 18K Yellow & White Gold 600.00
Bracelet, Gutta Percha & Gold Flexible Link, Geometric, England, c.1860 .... 285.00
Bracelet, Gutta Percha, Flexible Links, 15K Gold Studs, With Comb, England, 1860 ... 285.00
Bracelet, Honeycomb Design, Textured Florets, 18K Yellow Gold 920.00
Bracelet, Jade, 7 Oval Carved Pieces, 14K Gold Between, Hidden Clasp 275.00
Bracelet, Link, Gold, Opal Diamond, Turquoise Leafage, 1905, 7 In. 18400.00
Bracelet, Link, Sterling Silver, Openwork, Rectangular Plaques, Georg Jensen 350.00
Bracelet, Link, Suspending Gold Stone Fob, 18K Yellow Gold, 7 3/4 In. 603.00
Bracelet, Link, Woven Geometric, 18K Yellow Gold, 7 3/8 In. 700.00
Bracelet, Lucite, Beige, Rectangles On Elastic, Leah Stein 125.00
Bracelet, Lucite, Hinged, Gold Flecks, Pink Seashells 35.00
Bracelet, Man's, Rectangular Links, 14K Yellow Gold, 8 3/8 In. 1035.00
Bracelet, Marquise Diamond, Channel-Set Emeralds, Platinum Mount, Art Deco 14950.00
Bracelet, Matte Finish, Signed, Sixtar, 18K Yellow Gold 200.00
Bracelet, Micro Mosaic, Scenes Of Peasants, 18K Gold Corded Wire 3450.00
Bracelet, Moonstone, Stylized Floral Links, Georg Jensen, Sterling Silver 747.50
Bracelet, Onyx & Rectangular Links, France, 18K Yellow Gold, 1940 .... 690.00
Bracelet, Openwork Scrolling Links, Sterling Silver, Georg Jensen 350.00
Bracelet, Pearl & Diamond Link, 18K White Gold, Box, Marsh's Of California, 1940 ... 3680.00
Bracelet, Pearls, Cultured, 3 Bands Of Full Cut Diamonds, 14K White Gold 2760.00
Bracelet, Rectangular Links, Florentine Finish, 14K Yellow Gold 316.25
Bracelet, Rhinestones, Red, Weiss 20.00
Bracelet, Rhinestones, Robert, 1950s 50.00
Bracelet, Rope Twist, U.S. Gold 1904 20-Dollar Charm, 14K Yellow Gold 600.00
Bracelet, Rose Gold, 3 Wide Rows Of Lozenge-Shape Links, Retro, 14K Yellow Gold .. 1035.00
Bracelet, Ruby & Diamond, Double Row, S Link, 18K Yellow Gold, 7 In. 4600.00
Bracelet, Scrolling Ribbon Links, Collet-Set Sapphire, Sloan & Co., 14K Yellow Gold .. 2185.00
Bracelet, Silver Colored Metal, Hammered, Sam Kramer, 1935, 3 In. Diam. 205.00
Bracelet, Silver, Heavy Links, Turquoise Terminals, T Clasp, Antonio, Taxco, Mexico .. 490.00
Bracelet, Square-Cut Onyx, Platinum Box Links, Art Deco 805.00
Bracelet, Sterling Silver, 9 Panels, Siam 70.00
Bracelet, Sterling Silver, Amethyst, Marcasite, Art Deco, Theodor Fahrner, 1920 ... 2875.00
Bracelet, Sterling Silver, Art Deco, Amethyst, Bead-Set, Theodor Fahrner, 1920 .... 2875.00

Bracelet, Sterling Silver, Clear Chunky Stone, S. Eisenberg, 1930s 275.00
Bracelet, Sterling Silver, Cuff, Taxco, Los Castillo, Mexico 250.00
Bracelet, Sterling Silver, Hand, Tortoise, Silver Center, W. Spratling, Mexico, 8 In. 1495.00
Bracelet, Sterling Silver, Heavy Links, Turquoise Terminals, Signed Antonio, Taxco 490.00
Bracelet, Sterling Silver, Open Scrolling Links, Rectangular Plaques, G. Jensen 350.00
Bracelet, Sterling Silver, Stylized Geometric Design, Mexico 103.50
Bracelet, Woven, 1 Gold Aztec Charm, 18K Gold 660.00
Bracelet & Earrings, Navy Blue Bakelite, Light Blue Rhinestones, 3/4 In. 125.00
Brooch, Sterling Silver, Animal, Los Castillo 110.00
Brooch, Sterling Silver, Flower, Damaso Gallegos, Mexico 85.00
Buckle, Brass, Engraved Line Design, Karl Muller, 1930, 2 5/8 In. 645.00
Buckle, Gilded Open Work, Gray Marbleized Background, Czechoslovakia 25.00
Buckle, Head Of Mythological Creature In Repousse, Webb, 18K Yellow Gold 1840.00
Buckle, Pierced Whiplash Design, Colored Enamel, K. Moser, 1900, 2 3/4 In. 4025.00
Buckle, Sterling Silver, Circles Around, Arts & Crafts, Gorham, 3 1/2 x 2 1/2 In. 225.00
Buckle, Yellow Bakelite, Red Clothespins 125.00
Charm, Cuckoo Clock, Yellow Gold 132.00
Charm, Drum, Pearl Trim, 14K Gold 110.00
Charm, Princess Telephone, Sterling Silver 60.00
Charm, Spider, On Web, 14K Yellow Gold 55.00
Charm, Watch, Oval Links, Swivel Hook, 15K Yellow Gold, 19 In. 575.00
Chatelaine, 3 Original Pieces, Silver Plated 795.00
Chatelaine, 5 Appendages, Chased, Scrolled Motifs, Sterling Silver, Art Nouveau 1725.00
Chatelaine, Art Nouveau, Purse, Chain, Clip, Silver, Stones, Germany, 1900s 125.00
Chatelaine, Ivory & Silver Notepad, Purse, Pillbox, Penknife & Bird Form Pin 357.00
Chatelaine, Mesh Purse, Ball Trim, Chain Handle, 3 1/2 In. 90.00
Chatelaine, Needle Case, 14K Yellow Gold, 2 3/8 In. 175.00
Chatelaine, Purse, Sterling Silver, Germany 250.00
Chatelaine, Sterling Silver, Bird, Ruby Eye, Beak Flower, Emerald & Pearl Necklace ... 225.00
Chatelaine, Thimble Holder, Pincushion, Tape Measure, Sterling Silver, c.1880 .... 795.00
Chatelaine Ring, 4 Original Elements, Webster & Co., Sterling Silver, c.1900 .... 595.00
Cigarette Case, Sterling, Lighter Lights When Case Closes, Elgin 135.00
Cigarette Holder, 18K Gold, Sapphire Cabochon, Diamond, Black Stem, Cartier, 6 In. .. 2415.00
Cigarette Holder, Black, White Rhinestones 35.00
Cigarette Holder, Red Bakelite 35.00
Clip, 2 Prongs, Colored Stones, Sterling Silver, Eisenberg, 2 1/2 x 2 In. 425.00
Clip, Diamond, Openwork Design, Single-Cut, Platinum Mount, Art Deco 3335.00
Clip, Sweater, Sterling Silver, Enamel, Margot De Taxco 125.00
Cloak Fastener, Engraved John S. Pendleton, Sterling Silver, 18th Century 185.00
Cross, Amethyst, Square-Cut, Pierced Frame, 14K Yellow Gold 1725.00
Cross, Black Onyx, Seed Pearls, 9K Yellow Gold 195.00
Cross, Enamel, Yellow Gold 85.00
Cuff Links, Art Nouveau, Double Link Design, 2 Studs, Sterling Silver, G. Jensen 460.00
Cuff Links, Blue Enamel, 18K Yellow Gold 400.00
Cuff Links, Bon Ami Cleanser, Barbell Type Closure, Enamel Over Sterling, 1895 ..... 160.00
Cuff Links, Celluloid, Blue, Snap Link Brand, Mother-Of-Pearl Inset, Box, 1925 .... 60.00
Cuff Links, Celluloid, Faux Stone, With Tie Tack, Octagonal, 1925 .... 55.00
Cuff Links, Dice & Tie Tack, Removable Closure, Opens To Use Dice, c.1955 .... 90.00
Cuff Links, Double Oval Link, Circular Ruby & Sapphire, European, 18K Yellow Gold . 230.00
Cuff Links, Fleur-De-Lis, Silver & Blue, Swank, Square, 1960 .... 8.00
Cuff Links, Gold 2 1/2-Dollar Coin, 1905 & 1914 .... 345.00
Cuff Links, Hand, Peace Sign In Circle, Anson, 1970 .... 45.00
Cuff Links, Kumapart, Snap-On, Enamel, Mother-Of-Pearl 45.00
Cuff Links, Malachite, 14K Yellow Gold, Square 184.00
Cuff Links, Malachite, 18K Yellow Gold, Round 310.00
Cuff Links, Mother-Of-Pearl, 2 Faces, 4 Matching Studs, Krementz, Pouch, 1935 ...... 105.00
Cuff Links, Oil Rig Design, 14K Yellow Gold 230.00
Cuff Links, Onyx, Geometric Frames, Art Deco, 18K White Gold 1495.00
Cuff Links, Oval, Monogrammed, Yellow Gold 60.00
Cuff Links, Painting Of Italian Tourist Scene, 18K Gold Bezels 632.50
Cuff Links, Pewter Golf Bag & Club Design, c.1940 .... 15.00
Cuff Links, Presidential Seal, Reagan, Autopen Autograph, Box 200.00
Cuff Links, Rhinestone Studded, Black Plastic, Kenneth Jay Lane, c.1970 .... 40.00

Cuff Links, Ruby, 4 Diamonds Each Corner, 14K White Gold 805.00
Cuff Links, Senator Harry Darby, Official State Seal Of Kansas 25.00
Cuff Links, Separable, Mother-Of-Pearl Insert, Chance Brand, 1925 .... 100.00
Cuff Links, Soccer Balls, Barbell Shape, Sterling Silver, S & S Brand, 1902, 3/4 In. 150.00
Cuff Links, Tiger Eye, With Tie Tack, Swank, 1970 .... 30.00
Cuff Links, Turquoise Stone, Silver Colored Base, Swivel Closure, Shields, 1975 ...... 9.00
Cuff Links, Watch, 1 Watch, 1 Faux, Box, Sheffield 110.00
Cuff Links, Woman's High-Top Boots, Sterling Silver, 1890 .... 140.00
Earrings, Cherries, Bakelite 85.00
Earrings, Cherry Blossom Pattern, Screw Back, Sterling Silver, Kalo Shop 195.00
Earrings, Dangling, Gilt Metal Foliate Shape, Rhinestones, Hattie Carnegie, 1950s 85.00
Earrings, Diamond, Intaglio Moonstone, Classical Scene, Platinum Mount 4945.00
Earrings, Drop, 9 Small Cut Diamonds, Gold Tone 4125.00
Earrings, Flower Design, Open Kidney Bean Frame, Sterling Silver, Georg Jensen 175.00
Earrings, Flower Head, Pear Shape Aquamarines, Center Sapphire, 18K Gold 2070.00
Earrings, Flower Spray, Sterling, Coro Craft, 1930 .... 179.00
Earrings, Gold Flower, Stippled Center, Signed, Buccellati, 18K Yellow Gold 1610.00
Earrings, Gumdrop, Red & Cream Bakelite 175.00
Earrings, Hair, Open Weave, Gold Fittings, Acorn Design, Victorian 175.00
Earrings, Heart Dangles, Yellow Bakelite 45.00
Earrings, Hoop, Round-Cut Diamonds, 14K Yellow Gold Mounts 1380.00
Earrings, Jade, Carved Green Dangles, Screw Back 85.00
Earrings, Mabe Pearl Center, 14K Gold Rope Twist Frame 345.00
Earrings, Mabe Pearl, Diamond, Round, 14K Yellow Gold 862.50
Earrings, Melon Design, Textured, Nuovi Gioielli, 18K Yellow Gold 402.50
Earrings, Pendant, Yellow Gold, J.J. Marco 345.00
Earrings, Rock Crystal, Gilt Metal Free-Form Scrolls, Yves Saint Laurent, 1990s 345.00
Earrings, Rolling Style, 18K Tricolor Gold, Cartier, Box 1495.00
Earrings, Sea Horse, William De Lillo, Gold Tone 75.00
Earrings, Sterling Silver, Enamel, Margot De Taxco 129.00
Earrings, Sterling Silver, Hand, Tortoise, W. Spratling, Mexico, 1 1/4 In. 517.50
Earrings, Textured Flower, Gold Pistils, 18K Yellow Gold 287.00
Earrings, Textured Leaves, 14K Yellow Gold 258.00
Hatpins are listed in this book in the Hatpin category.
Key Chain, Carved Catalin, Polynesian Nude 75.00
Key Chain, Galloping Horse Form, 18K Gold, Buccellati 460.00
Lavaliere, Amethyst, Kite Shape Plaque, Links, Sloan & Co., 17 In. 1265.00
Lavaliere, Amethysts, 14K White Gold 50.00
Lavaliere, Openwork Plaque With Round Diamonds, Diamond Drop, Chain, 15 1/2 In. ... 373.00
Lipstick Mirror, Lip Shape, Metal Set With Rhinestones, Eisenberg, 1950s 175.00
Locket, Gold, Silver, Engraved Cabin Scene, Man & Woman Daguerreotype 175.00
Locket, Hair, Seed Pearls On Blue Ground, Crosshatched Design Hair On Reverse, 2 In. .. 600.00
Locket, Ivory, Carved Floral Pattern, Mid-1800s 500.00
Locket, Tintype Of Young Woman, Swatch Of Jacket Twill, Gold Filled Case, 1 5/8 In. .. 82.00
Locket, Woman In Naturalistic Setting, Round Diamond Accents, 14K Yellow Gold 517.00
Money Clip, Mother-Of-Pearl Stones, Sterling Silver 50.00
Money Clip, Nugget Design Dollar Sign, Hinged Top, 14K Gold 230.00
Money Clip, Rectangular Oscar Award Design, Cartier, 14K Yellow Gold 460.00
Money Clip, Repoussé, Sterling Silver, Kirk 75.00
Necklace, 6 Amber Bead Strands, Triple Closures, Miriam Haskell 175.00
Necklace, 14 Cherries, Bakelite 175.00
Necklace, 138 Pearls, Carved Jade Clasp, Set With 7 Small Diamonds 2990.00
Necklace, Amber, 18K Gold Bead Spacers, Graduated Beads, 25 In. 275.00
Necklace, Amber, Pressed Cut, Graduated Beads, 1920s, 35 In. 200.00
Necklace, Amethyst, 3 Strands, Graduated Beads, Large Amethyst Clasp 495.00
Necklace, Amethyst, Clasp, 18K Yellow Gold, 18 In. 5750.00
Necklace, Brass Chain, Red Rope Ties, Red Bakelite, 32 In. 23.00
Necklace, Chain, Curb Link, Swivel Hook, T-Bar, Victorian, 14K Gold, 14 In. 345.00
Necklace, Chain, Flat Curb Link Design, Marked, LD, 18K Yellow Gold, 17 1/4 In. 1150.00
Necklace, Chain, Georgian, Oval Trace Link Design, Turquoise Beaded Clasp, 30 In. ... 1265.00
Necklace, Chain, Rope, 20-Dollar Gold Piece, Rope Bezel, Yellow Gold, 24 In. 880.00
Necklace, Chain, Tassel, Wire Twist Connects Links, 14K Yellow Gold, 19 1/2 In. 402.50
Necklace, Chain, Twisted Rope, Swivel Hook, 14K Yellow Gold, 1900, 22 1/2 In. 287.50

Necklace, Cherry Amber, 15 In. 110.00
Necklace, Choker, Double, Pearl, Coral Clasp, Haskell 150.00
Necklace, Choker, Silver Metal, Oval Crystal Pendant, 1960, Georg Jensen, 8 3/4 In. ... 665.00
Necklace, Diamond, Foliate Plaques, Edward Oakes, 18K Yellow Gold 5175.00
Necklace, Filigree, 7 Flowers Of Filigree Petals, Gold Tassels In Center, 20 1/4 In. 3737.00
Necklace, Flexible Snake Design, 14K Yellow Gold, 15 In. 747.00
Necklace, Graduated Pearls, Cultured, Diamond & Sapphire Clasp, 18 In. 605.00
Necklace, Hair, 15K Gold, England, 1870, 46 In. 145.00
Necklace, Lapis Lazuli, 65 Graduated Beads, 18 In. 385.00
Necklace, Link, 14K Yellow Gold, 17 1/4 In. 200.00
Necklace, Locket, Art Nouveau, Swami, Rope Twist Chain, 14K Yellow Gold 230.00
Necklace, Marquise Emerald Stones, Gold Washed, Trifari, 1950s 50.00
Necklace, Mesh Design, 14K Yellow Gold, 18 In. 488.75
Necklace, Mosaic, Sterling, 1920s 100.00
Necklace, Mother-Of-Pearl, Aventurine, Grecian Scroll, 14K Yellow Gold, 1979 .... 1840.00
Necklace, Opal Beads, Victorian, 64 In. 550.00
Necklace, Pearls, Cultured, 2 Strands, Convertible, Screw Clasp, 50 In. 2875.00
Necklace, Pearls, Cultured, Graduated, Single Strand, 21 1/4 In. 310.00
Necklace, Red Cherries, Bakelite 750.00
Necklace, Rope Chain, 14K Gold, 32 In. 220.00
Necklace, Sautoir, Rope Twist Design, 2 Tassels, 14K Yellow Gold, 19 In. 488.75
Necklace, Silver, Labradorite, Alternating Links, Cabochons, G. Jensen, 1909, 15 In. ... 1495.00
Necklace, Slide Chain, 4 Opals On Side, Yellow Gold Filled 95.00
Necklace, Snake Chain, Tanzanite & Diamond, 18K Gold 8050.00
Necklace, Sterling Silver & Malachite, Chain, Enrique Ledesman 595.00
Necklace, Sterling Silver, Foliate Links, Signed, Los Castillo, Taxco, Mexico, 16 In. 520.00
Necklace, Sterling Silver, Hand, Tortoise, Ying-Yang, Mexico, W. Spratling, 5 In. 2300.00
Necklace, Sterling Silver, Onyx Stones, Eagle Mark, Taxco, Mexico 595.00
Necklace, Sterling, Danecraft 60.00
Necklace, Twisted, 18K Yellow Gold, 74 In. 1600.00
Necklace, Wheat, Amethysts & Pearl Drops, Krementz, 14K Gold, 1920, 14 In. 750.00
Necklace, Woven Hair, Small Brass Slide & Clip, 19th Century, 44 In. 185.00
Necklace & Earrings, Enamel Over Sterling, Box, Norway, 1930s 65.00
Necklace & Earrings, Sterling Silver, Silver Segments, W. Spratling, Mexico, 16 In. ... 747.50
Pendant, 22 Mine-Cut Diamonds 495.00
Pendant, Bezel-Set Moonstone, Paper Clip Chain, Sterling Silver, Kalo Shop, 19 In. 1100.00
Pendant, Butterfly, Rose-Cut Diamonds, 1910, 3 3/8 In. 6900.00
Pendant, Butterfly, Wheel Design, White Jade, 1900, 2 1/4 In. 120.00
Pendant, Cameo, 3 Putti Playing With 2 Dolphins, Gold Frame, 1 1/2 In. 6325.00
Pendant, Cameo, Hard Stone, Classical Male In Profile, 18K Gold Frame & Chain 805.00
Pendant, Cameo, Onyx, Profile Of Woman, Shield Shape Frame, Chain 230.00
Pendant, Carp, Lotus Form, White Jade, 2 1/8 In. 180.00
Pendant, Cloisonne, Heart Shape, Green With Flowers, 1 1/2 In. 60.00
Pendant, Copper, 2 Abstract Faces, Copper Chain, Rebajes, 17 In. 23.00
Pendant, Diamond, Pearl, 3 Leaves, Cluster Of Pearl Berries, Art Nouveau, 1900, 21 In. ... 2990.00
Pendant, Disk, Mother-Of-Pearl, Hand Painted Oriental Figures, Sterling Mount, Large . 28.00
Pendant, Enameled Portrait, Cobalt Blue Ground, Sterling Silver Chain 295.00
Pendant, Floral Form, Sterling Chain, Marked Sterling, Art Deco, 16 In. 34.50
Pendant, Ivory, Elephant, "R" Pendant 55.00
Pendant, Jade, Silver Mount, Silver Link Chain, 17 In. 1840.00
Pendant, Jasperware Medallion, Beads, Pearls, 14K Gold, Chain, E.E. Oakes, 16 In. 3600.00
Pendant, Pear-Shaped Faceted Citrine, 18K Yellow Gold 287.00
Pendant, Pink Coral Branches, Snake In Low Section, Turquoise, 1850, 3 1/4 In. 4312.00
Pendant, Pink Freesia Shape, Sterling Chain, Art Nouveau, Rokesley, 7 1/2 In. 1100.00
Pendant, Real Butterflies Under Glass, Sterling Silver, Large 35.00
Pendant, Rose Cut, Back Pin, Eyelet, White Gold Crown, 6 In. 650.00
Pendant, Round Citrine Center, Link Chain, Arts & Crafts, Theodor Fahrner, 16 In. 460.00
Pendant, Sprig Of Mistletoe On Crescent Moon, Ochre, Green, Cream, 2 5/8 In. 4600.00
Pendant, Starburst, 6 Pear-Shaped Opals, 7 Round Opals, Yellow Gold 247.00
Pendant, Stylized Winged Insect, Pink Sapphire, L. Gautrait, 1900, 3 1/8 In. 14950.00
Pendant, Tassel, Enamel, 14K Gold Link Chain, Edward Oakes, 18K Gold 3450.00
Pendant, Topaz, Marcasites, Silver Metal Chain, Theodor Fahrner, 1930, 14 In. 2300.00
Pendant, Turquoise Cabochon, Leaf Chain, Sterling Silver, Potter Studio, 16 In. 2100.00

Pendant & Earrings, Cameo, Gold Filled, Van Dell 45.00
Pin, 3 Birds Perched On Branch, Gemstone Eyes, 14K Gold, 1 In. 99.00
Pin, 3 Flower Spray, Sterling Silver, Corocraft, 1940, Large 165.00
Pin, 3 Flowers, Ruby Centers, Yellow Gold 275.00
Pin, 3 Sized Cultured Pearls, Gold Filigree, 14K Gold 247.00
Pin, 3-Color Hair Design, Seed Pearls, 1860 .... 735.00
Pin, 4 Sapphires, 26 Cultured Pearls, 14K Yellow Gold 258.75
Pin, AAF Lapel Wings, Screw Back, Silver Color, 1930s, 1 1/4 In. 25.00
Pin, Abstract Design, Bronze Element, Sterling Silver, Macchiarini, 1960s 258.00
Pin, American Flag, Sapphire & Diamond Stars, Ruby & Diamond Stripes, Platinum 5175.00
Pin, Arrow, Mine-Cut Diamonds, Ruby, Emerald, 14K Gold 1150.00
Pin, Art Deco, Silver Metal, Harry Bertoia, 1946, 2 3/8 x 1 1/2 In. 2530.00
Pin, Art Deco, Steel, Brass, Copper, Ebony, Macchiarini, 3 1/4 x 2 In. 875.00
Pin, Bagpipe, Sterling Silver, A. Cavines 50.00
Pin, Bakelite, 6 Cherries 135.00
Pin, Bar, 3 Cabochon-Cut Corals 2875.00
Pin, Bar, 3 Diamonds, 14K White Gold 192.00
Pin, Bar, Amethyst, Oval, Serpent Frame, Art Nouveau, 14K Gold 460.00
Pin, Bar, Arrow, 10K Gold, 7 Seed Pearls 50.00
Pin, Bar, Carved Red Bakelite 65.00
Pin, Bar, Conch, Rosette Drops, Wire Twist Top, Victorian, 18K Yellow Gold, Tiffany ... 1610.00
Pin, Bar, Diamond, Emerald, Scalloped Diamond Border, Platinum Mount, Art Deco 5405.00
Pin, Bar, Edwardian, 3 Diamonds, 14K White Gold, Pierced Gold Mount 1495.00
Pin, Bar, Lapis Lazuli Cabochon, Geometric, Sterling Silver, Kalo Shop, 2 1/4 In. 295.00
Pin, Bar, Pate-De-Verre Set In Gilt Metal, Rhinestone Insect Each End, Chanel 200.00
Pin, Bar, Sterling, Baroque Pearl, Beadwork, Arts & Crafts, CC Mark, 3/8 x 2 In. 195.00
Pin, Bar, Sterling, Baroque Pearl, Floral Around, Enameled, Rokesley, 5/8 x 2 In. 1100.00
Pin, Bar, Wishbone, Dangling Garnet Ball, 9K Gold 45.00
Pin, Bar, Zigzag Design, Square Sapphires, Baguette Diamond Center 1092.00
Pin, Begging Pooch, Leather Ears, Bakelite, c.1940 .... 575.00
Pin, Bezel-Set Quartz, 14K Green Gold, Flowers, E.E. Oakes, 1 1/4 In. 1350.00
Pin, Bird Of Paradise, Colored, Sterling Silver, Trifari 275.00
Pin, Bird Of Paradise, Sterling Silver, Multicolored Stones, Trifari, 3 1/4 x 2 In. 350.00
Pin, Bird, Collet-Set Amber & Malachite, Sterling Silver, Georg Jensen, 1915 .... 690.00
Pin, Bow, Brown Lucite, Round Dangles 95.00
Pin, Bow, Channel-Set Onyx, Platinum, Art Deco 1495.00
Pin, Bow, Gilt Metal, Large Faux Baroque Pearl Drop, Yves Saint Laurent, 1990s 115.00
Pin, Bow, Glass, Black Metal Leaves, Miriam Haskell, 2 1/4 In. 35.00
Pin, Bow, Jade, Front Borders, Panels Carved With Rabbits, 1935, 2 7/8 In. 2875.00
Pin, Brass, Egyptian Revival, Floral Design, Bakelite Centers, 4 1/2 In. 6.00
Pin, Brass, Rhinestones, Pearls, Green, Hattie Carnegie 96.00
Pin, Brass, Rose On Stem, Giovanni, 3 In. 45.00
Pin, Bug, Jade, Freshwater Pearl Body, Carved Wings, 14K Gold Antennae 632.50
Pin, Butterfly, Enamel Wings, Diamonds, Channel-Set Rubies, Sapphire Body, Silver ... 4025.00
Pin, Butterfly, Rose-Cut Diamond Wings, Emeralds, 14K Gold 1265.00
Pin, Butterfly, Rose-Cut Diamonds, Red Stones Edge, Pearl Body, Silver & Gold 1150.00
Pin, Butterfly, Sterling Silver, Coro 35.00
Pin, Butterfly, Sterling Silver, Siam 50.00
Pin, Camel, Jeweled Saddle, Joseff 350.00
Pin, Cameo, Black Bakelite 25.00
Pin, Cameo, Diamonds, 2 1/2 In. 325.00
Pin, Carnelian, Sterling Silver, Art Nouveau, Europe 225.00
Pin, Carved Ivory Scene, Gold-Filled Frame, 2 1/2 x 2 In. 310.00
Pin, Central Emerald, Foliate Scroll Openwork, Spain, 1700, 1 3/8 In. 862.00
Pin, Cheshire Cat, Blue Striped Enamel, Sterling Silver, Tiger-Eye Stone Eyes, 3-D 95.00
Pin, Chinese Man, Bakelite 125.00
Pin, Christmas Lantern, Glass, Enameled Mistletoe, Hollycraft 40.00
Pin, Christmas Tree, Tanfers 40.00
Pin, Circle, Beaded, Curled Blossom Design, Georg Jensen, 1 In. 121.00
Pin, Circle, Edwardian, Tapered, Accented By Snake, Platinum, Tiffany 1955.00
Pin, Clover, 4 Pearls, Gray Pearl, Center Diamond Petals, 14K White Gold 3565.00
Pin, Cocker Spaniel, Cini, 2 x 3 In. 85.00
Pin, Colored Cabochons & Rhinestones, Gilt Metal, Chanel, Box, c.1993 .... 287.00

Pin, Coral Cameo, Mercury, Within Open Beadwork Frame 920.00
Pin, Coral Tassel, Snake Chain Tassel, Wire Twist Frame, 15K Yellow Gold 1380.00
Pin, Cowboy Hat, Dangling Boots, Plastic 35.00
Pin, Crab, Black Onyx, Red Enamel Body, Diamond Eye, Tiffany, 18K Yellow Gold 1265.00
Pin, Crescent, Thief Of Baghdad, Filigree, Blue Stones, Pearls, Korda, 1940s, 3 1/2 In. ... 650.00
Pin, Donkey, Pulling Cart, Boy, Sterling Silver, Enameled, Margot, Detaxco 125.00
Pin, Double Horse Head, Colored Stones, Sterling Silver, Corocraft 150.00
Pin, Dove, In Wreath, Moonstones Around, Sterling Silver, G. Jensen 375.00
Pin, Dragonfly, Enamel Wings, Silver Gilt Body, Plique-A-Jour 488.00
Pin, Duck Design, 6 Brilliant-Cut Rubies, 14K Yellow Gold 138.00
Pin, Enameled Peacock Feather Eyes, Sterling Silver, Rokesley, 1 3/8 x 2 In. 1000.00
Pin, Face, Apple Juice, Tall Hat, 1 Red Earring, Art Deco, Bakelite 210.00
Pin, Fan, Shakudo, Gilt Overlay, Copper Ground, c.1880 .... 320.00
Pin, Feather, Open Work, Cabochon Opal, Art Nouveau, Riker Bros., 14K Yellow Gold. . 320.00
Pin, Floral Design, Black Bakelite Ring, 3 1/4 In. 23.00
Pin, Floral Spray, Goldtone, Faux Pearls & Rhinestones, Trifari, c.1955 .... 95.00
Pin, Floral Spray, Sapphire, 18K White & Yellow Gold 920.00
Pin, Flower & Leaf Design, Sterling Silver, Oval, Arts & Crafts, 1 5/8 x 2 1/4 In....... 125.00
Pin, Flower Shape, Cut Amber Center, White Jade, 2 1/8 In. 110.00
Pin, Flower, 13 Small Round-Cut Diamonds, 18K Yellow Gold, Preformed Parts, Inc. ... 345.00
Pin, Flower, 22 Round Rubies, 14K Yellow Gold 385.00
Pin, Flower, Amethyst Petals, Diamond Center, Silver Stem, 14K Yellow Gold 1380.00
Pin, Flower, Enamel Petals, Center Pearl, Pendant Loop, A.K. Jedges, 14K Gold 690.00
Pin, Flower, Rhinestones In Silver Tone Metal, Bead Center, Christian Dior 287.00
Pin, Frog, Green Enamel, Mine-Cut Diamond Eyes, 18K Yellow Gold, France 1035.00
Pin, Giraffe, Wood, Bakelite, 4 x 2 1/4 In.. 400.00
Pin, Golf Bag, Sterling Silver & Brass 225.00
Pin, Green Cabochon, Trapezoidal, Sterling Silver, Carence Crafters, 1 1/2 x 2 In. 2100.00
Pin, Greens Marker, Stylized Woman Golfer, Sterling Silver, Lonore Doskow 245.00
Pin, Hair, Double Bow Design, 2 Drops Off Gold Heart, Victorian 175.00
Pin, Hair, Memorial, Victorian 295.00
Pin, Half Circle, Acorns, Corals, Pearls, Victorian 65.00
Pin, Hard Stone Cameo, Woman In Profile, Tricolor Gold Frame, Pendant Loop 1150.00
Pin, Head, Josephine Baker, Bakelite, Reverse Tall Lucite Hat 480.00
Pin, Head, Silver, Black, Jade, Los Ballesteros 165.00
Pin, Horse, Red Wings 25.00
Pin, Horseshoe, 21 Graduated Diamonds, Yellow Gold 575.00
Pin, Horseshoe, Graduating Diamonds, 14K White Gold Mount 920.00
Pin, Huguenot Society Pendant, Suspended From Dove, 14K Yellow Gold 1100.00
Pin, Initial C, Green Bakelite, Silver Metal 55.00
Pin, Insect, Cast Silver, Sigi 125.00
Pin, Iowa State Fair, Red, White, Blue 25.00
Pin, Jade Cabochon, Oval, Sterling Silver, Charles B. Dyer, 1 1/2 x 2 1/2 In. 525.00
Pin, Jade, Freshwater Pearls, Foliate, Scrolled Frame, 14K Yellow Gold 862.50
Pin, Jade, Quatrefoil Design, Baguette Diamonds, 18K Yellow Gold 1380.00
Pin, Large Amethyst, 8 Full-Cut Diamonds, Florentine Finish, 14K Gold 302.00
Pin, Leaf Design, Brass, Glass Cabochon, George W. Frost, 2 1/4 x 2 1/2 In. 300.00
Pin, Maiden Encircled Within Iris Blossom, Violet, Cream, Green & Gold, 1900, 1 In. ... 2300.00
Pin, Minstrel, Black Lucite, Wooden, Leather Trim, Hand Painted 125.00
Pin, Moonstones, Dove In Wreath Frame, Sterling Silver, Georg Jensen 375.00
Pin, Mourning, Cameo Of Woman, Black Jet 80.00
Pin, Mourning, Cameo, Gutta Percha 90.00
Pin, Mourning, Center Oval Black Stone, Seed Pearls Surround, Gold Tone 92.50
Pin, Mourning, Daniel Webster, Lock Of Webster's Hair, Gold Chain, 14K Gold 907.50
Pin, Mourning, Picture Of Deceased In Center, Gold Plated 145.00
Pin, Owl, Lucite, 2 3/4 In. 50.00
Pin, Pale Amber Horn, Striated Deep Green, Amber Glass, Art Nouveau, 1900, 4 In. 1840.00
Pin, Pansy, Enamel & Mine-Cut Diamonds, 14K Yellow Gold 575.00
Pin, Pear Shape, Rhinestones, Enameled Leaves 25.00
Pin, Penguin, Sterling Silver 55.00
Pin, Portrait Of Woman, Plumed Hat, Hand Painted, Oval Porcelain, 1 5/8 In. 16.50
Pin, Profile Of Woman, Mine-Cut Diamond, Krementz, 14K Gold 1725.00
Pin, Puss 'n Boots, Chanel 1000.00

Pin, Ranch Sign, Dangling Horse, Plastic 35.00
Pin, RCA Victor, Bakelite 75.00
Pin, Red Peppers, Bakelite 450.00
Pin, Rhinestone, Lisner 30.00
Pin, Rhinestone, Pink, Judy Lee 45.00
Pin, Rhinestone, Starburst, Gold Tone, Green Glass Center, Sterling, 3 In. 57.50
Pin, Rhinestone, Weiss, 1 7/8 In. 45.00
Pin, Round Dangle, Norway, 1890 .... 35.00
Pin, Sapphire, Cushion Cut, Platinum Mount, Black Starr & Frost 20700.00
Pin, Scarab, Brass, Etched, Arts & Crafts, Carence Crafters, 1 3/4 x 2 5/8 In. 375.00
Pin, Scotty, Bakelite 75.00
Pin, Sea Horse, Sterling Silver, Lobel, 1950s 200.00
Pin, Serpent, Enamel & 18K Gold, Niki De Saint Phalle, 1971 .... 2185.00
Pin, Shell Cameo, Mythological Woman, Oval Frame, 18K Yellow Gold 2300.00
Pin, Shell Cameo, Woman's Profile, Classical Dress, 14K Yellow Gold 375.00
Pin, St. Peter, Micro Mosaic & Gilt Metal, Italy, 2 5/8 In. 690.00
Pin, Star, Faux Pearls & Rhinestones, Lisner, c.1960 .... 80.00
Pin, Sterling Silver, 2 Cabochon Stones, Los Castillo, Mexico, 2 1/2 In. 92.00
Pin, Sterling Silver, Dirk, Jasper, Bloodstone Agate, Citrons, Scotland, 1890, 5 In. 750.00
Pin, Sterling Silver, Owl, Cabochon Amethyst Eyes, W. Spratling, Mexico, 2 1/2 In. 747.50
Pin, Sterling Silver, Tartanware, Albert, Round, Scotland, 1880 .... 575.00
Pin, Studebaker, 10 Year Service 45.00
Pin, Stylized Horse, Sterling Silver, Paul Lobel, 1950 .... 375.00
Pin, Stylized Sea Horse, Paul Lobel, c.1950 .... 350.00
Pin, Stylized Swirl, Leaves, Brass, Green Highlights, Carence Crafters, 2 x 2 In. 88.00
Pin, Sunburst, Gilt Metal, Hermes 105.00
Pin, Sunburst, Seed Pearls, Clear Stone Center, 14K Yellow Gold 165.00
Pin, Sword, Edwardian, Scrolling Handle With Diamonds, Rubies, 14K Gold 345.00
Pin, Tennis Racket, Sterling Silver 25.00
Pin, Tortoise & Hare, Diamond In Platinum, Art Nouveau, 18K Yellow Gold, Contrau ... 1265.00
Pin, Tortoiseshell, Raised Woman's Head 290.00
Pin, Turtle, Bakelite 145.00
Pin, Victorian Scene, Limoges 90.00
Pin, Violin Shape, Opens To Reveal Watch, Brushed Dial, 14K Yellow Gold 632.50
Pin, Wishbone Design, Green Stone, Sigi Pineda, Mexico, 2 1/2 In. 115.00
Pin, Woman Front, Sterling Silver, Siam, 1930s 38.00
Pin, Zeppelin, Figural, Sterling Silver, 3 1/2 In. 475.00
Pin & Earrings, Free Form, Doppel, Sterling Silver, Georg Jensen, 1948 .... 595.00
Pin & Earrings, Jasperware, Green, White Classical Figures, Silver, Wedgwood 45.00
Pin & Earrings, Lemon, Yellow Rhinestones, Catalin 75.00
Ring, 3 Transitional-Cut Diamonds, Platinum 770.00
Ring, 7 Faceted Garnets, Flower Shape, Center Of 6 Petals 275.00
Ring, Belt Form, Buckle Set With Sapphires & Diamonds 350.00
Ring, Bloodstone, Oval, Gold Mount, Art Deco 275.00
Ring, Cameo, Coral, Classical Woman, 14K Yellow Gold 287.50
Ring, Cameo, Filigree Mounting, 14K Gold 165.00
Ring, Cameo, Full Figure, Wide Band, Victorian, Rose Gold 165.00
Ring, Cameo, Victorian, 14K Gold 185.00
Ring, Diamond Solitaire, European Cut Diamond, 14K Yellow Gold 1725.00
Ring, Diamond, 4 Faceted, Emerald-Cut, Bead-Set, 18K Yellow Gold, England 977.50
Ring, Diamond, Cluster, 1 Large & 12 Small Diamonds, Jabel, 18K White Gold 2005.00
Ring, Diamond, Cluster, Pear Shape, 10 Full-Cut Diamond Melee, Platinum 1035.00
Ring, Diamond, Collet-Set, Filigree Fleur-De-Lis Design, Art Deco 920.00
Ring, Diamond, Gold, Baby's 45.00
Ring, Diamond, Mine-Cut, Victorian, 14K Yellow Gold 192.00
Ring, Dome, Cluster Of Round Diamonds, 14K Gold 82.00
Ring, Emerald, Side Diamonds, 14K White Gold 275.00
Ring, Green Faceted Stone, 14K Yellow Gold 110.00
Ring, Heraldry Seal, Sterling Silver 300.00
Ring, Hunter College, Cabochon Amethyst, Tiffany, 1928 .... 225.00
Ring, Jade, Rose, Yellow Gold Foliate Mount, Oval 747.50
Ring, Man's, Mine-Cut Diamond, 18K White Gold Mount 2875.00
Ring, Moonstone, Cabochons, Silver Colored Metal, Friedrich Becker, 1960 .... 780.00

Ring, Mourning, Lock Of George Washington's Hair, Gold & Enamel 7475.00
Ring, Opal Doublet, Flower Petals, 14K Gold, E.E. Oakes, Size 4 1/4 .... 3400.00
Ring, Opal, Arts & Crafts, 18K Yellow Gold, Margaret Rogers, Box 2645.00
Ring, Opal, Diamond Bat, Cast In Relief, Charles Desrosiers, 1900, 1 3/8 In. 4887.00
Ring, Opal, Filigree Mount, Teardrop Shape, 15 Carats, 14K Gold 2500.00
Ring, Ruby, Diamond, 1950s, 3/4 Ct. 875.00
Ring, Ruby, Filigree, 14K Gold, 1920s 200.00
Ring, Shell Design, Sterling Silver, Patricia VonMusiln 95.00
Ring, Tourmaline, Domed Design, Orange Brown Center, 18K Yellow Gold, 1940s. 1265.00
Rosary, Emerald, Pearl, Wood Beads, Flower Head Form, 18th Century, 20 1/4 In. 2185.00
Set, Bracelet, Pin, Earrings, Studs, Cuff Links, Malachite, Box, c.1860 .... 6500.00
Stickpin, Indian Head, 1/2-Dollar Gold Piece, 1884 .... 125.00
Stickpin, John Deere 55.00
Stickpin, Mercedes Benz, Tire Gauge, 1955 .... 264.50
Stickpin, Profile Of Lady, Colored Stones, Europe, 18K Gold 575.00
Watches are listed in their own category.
Watch Chain, Ivory Links, T-Bar 120.00
Watch Chain, Paper-Clip Design, Bar & Swivel Hook, 18K Yellow Gold, 20 In. 1035.00
Watch Chain, With 1 1/2-In. Initialed Locket, Victorian, 14K Gold 75.00
Watch Chain, Woman's, Victorian, 14K Gold, c.1850, 60 In. 1210.00
Wristwatches are listed in their own category.

JOHN ROGERS statues were made from 1859 to 1892. The originals
were bronze, but the thousands of copies made by the Rogers factory
were of painted plaster. Eighty different figures were created. Similar
painted plaster figures were produced by some other factories. Rights
to the figures were sold in 1893 and they were manufactured for several more years by the Rogers Statuette Co. Never repaint a Rogers
figure because this lowers the value to collectors.

Group, Coming To The Parson, Painted, Signed, 11 x 16 In. ....230.00 to 300.00
Group, Fighting Bob, 21 1/2 x 7 1/2 In. 900.00
Group, Rip Van Winkle At Home 450.00
Group, Speak For Yourself John 600.00
Group, Uncle Ned's School, 20 1/2 x 13 1/2 In. ....450.00 to 750.00

JUDAICA is any memorabilia that refers to the Jews or the Jewish reli-
gion. Interests range from newspaper clippings that mention eigh-
teenth- and nineteenth-century Jewish Americans to religious objects,
such as menorahs or spice boxes. Age, condition, and the intrinsic
value of the material, as well as the historic and artistic importance,
determine the value.

Book, Haftarah Volume, Pull-Out Table Of Haftarah Readings, 1725 .... 7475.00
Book, Prayer, For Pentateuch Prophets, R. Estienne, 1544-1546, 5 Volumes 7475.00
Book, Psalms In Hebrew, Latin, Elias Hutter, 1586 .... 1495.00
Box, Charity, Tin Lithograph, Oval Windows, 1900 .... 250.00
Breast Shield, Torah, Lion-Topped Columns, Austria, Sterling Silver, 1806, 11 In. 7475.00
Decanter, Wine, Sterling Silver, Goldman Silversmiths Co., N.Y., c.1940 .... 395.00
Menorah, Oil, Baluster Form, Hebrew, Silver, 18 In. 1725.00
Scroll, Talmud, On Hide, 135 In. 120.00

JUGTOWN Pottery refers to pottery made in North Carolina as far back
as the 1750s. In 1915, Juliana and Jacques Busbee set up a training and
sales organization for what they named *Jugtown Pottery*. In 1921, they
built a shop at Jugtown, North Carolina, and hired Ben Owen as a potter in 1923. The Busbees moved the village store where the pottery
was sold to New York City. Juliana Busbee sold the New York store in
1926 and moved into a log cabin near the Jugtown Pottery. The pottery
closed in 1959. It reopened in 1960 and is still working near Seagrove,
North Carolina.

Bowl, Batter, Deep Blue Glaze 50.00
Bowl, Oriental, Frogskin 275.00
Bowl, Salt Glaze, Cobalt Blue Design Over Incised Scroll, 2 5/8 x 4 1/4 In. 104.50

Candlestick, Tapered Stem, Mottled Blue & Black, 4 1/2 In., Pair	120.00
Cup & Saucer, Salt Glaze, Cobalt Blue, Collar Rim, Ben Owen, 2 3/8 x 5 3/4 In.	71.50
Inkwell, Chinese Blue Glaze, Albany Slip, Ben Owen, 1930s, 3 In.	412.50
Jug, Frogskin, 8 3/4 In.	250.00
Mug, Ben Owen	185.00
Mug, Frogskin	95.00
Pitcher, Frogskin, 8 1/2 In.	195.00
Pitcher, Tobacco Spit, 8 In.	125.00
Vase, 4 Handles, Collar Neck, Creamy White Glaze, Impressed Mark, 10 x 7 In.	660.00
Vase, Chinese Blue Glaze, Green, Deep Rose, Tan, Light Blue, 4 In.	715.00
Vase, Chinese Blue Glaze, Impressed Mark, 4 1/2 In.	357.50
Vase, Chinese Blue Glaze, Impressed Mark, 5 1/2 In.	440.00
Vase, Chinese Blue Glaze, Marked, 7 In.	660.00
Vase, Gray, White High Glaze, Impressed Mark, 7 x 5 1/2 In.	253.00
Vase, Pinched & Flared Rim, 2 Nubby Handles, Oatmeal Glaze, Signed, 7 3/4 In.	302.00
Vase, Red, Blue Glaze, 5 In.	150.00
Vase, Thick White Glaze, 4 Handles, 7 In.	275.00 to 325.00
Vase, Thick White High Glaze, Impressed Mark, 5 x 4 In.	165.00
Vase, Thick White High Glaze, Impressed Mark, 7 In.	275.00

JUKEBOXES play records. The first coin-operated phonograph was demonstrated in 1889. In 1906 the *Automatic Entertainer* appeared, the first coin-operated phonograph to offer several different selections of music. The first electrically powered jukebox was introduced in 1927. Collectors search for jukeboxes of all ages, especially those with flashing lights and unusual design and graphics.

Capehart, Model 28A	3250.00
Rock-Ola, CM 39, Countertop, 1939	1760.00
Rock-Ola, High Fidelity 200, Model 1455-S, 57 1/2 In.	720.00
Seeburg, Model 100C	2700.00
Seeburg, Model 100JL	1500.00
Seeburg, Select-O-Matic, c.1957	550.00
Wurlitzer, Americana III, 3300 Series, Records, New Needle, Service Manual	1200.00
Wurlitzer, Model 41, Countertop	150.00
Wurlitzer, Model 61, Countertop	1595.00 to 4125.00
Wurlitzer, Model 71, Countertop, Stand	6050.00
Wurlitzer, Model 600, 1938	3200.00
Wurlitzer, Model 1015	5500.00 to 9900.00
Wurlitzer, Model 1100	4125.00
Wurlitzer, Model 1250, c.1950	1980.00
Wurlitzer, Model 1915	700.00
Wurlitzer, Model 2300	1800.00

KATE GREENAWAY, who was a famous illustrator of children's books, drew pictures of children in high-waisted Empire dresses. She lived from 1846 to 1901. Her designs appear on china, glass, and other pieces. Figural napkin rings depicting the Greenaway children may also be found in the Napkin Ring category under Figural.

Figurine, Child In Bonnet, Piggyback On Brother	65.00
Toothpick, Bisque	40.00

KAUFFMANN refers to porcelain wares decorated with scenes based on the works of Angelica Kauffmann (1741–1807), a Swiss-born painter who was a decorative artist for Adam Brothers, English furniture manufacturers, between 1766 and 1781. She designed small-scale pictorial subjects in the neoclassic manner and painted portraits as well as historical and classical pictures that were later reproduced on chinaware made across Europe. Most porcelains signed *Kauffmann* were made in the late 1800s. She did not do the artwork on the porcelain pieces signed with her name.

Plate, 2 Maidens, Cupid, Gold Rim, Royal Vienna, 7 1/4 In.	30.00
Plate, 3 Dancing Maidens, Cupid With Lute, Gold Rim, Royal Vienna, 5 1/2 In.	12.00

Plate, 3 Dancing Maidens, Gold Rim, Royal Vienna, 7 1/4 In. 30.00
Plate, 4 Maidens, Temple Of Venus, Gold Rim, Royal Vienna, 5 3/4 In. 12.00
Plate, Maidens, Chariot, Cherub, Burgundy, Gold, Royal Vienna, 9 1/2 In. 300.00
Vase, 3 Maidens, Men, Cobalt Blue, Scalloped, Handles, Royal Vienna, 7 1/4 In. 60.00
Vase, Dancing Maidens, Cupid, Cobalt Blue, Open Handles, Royal Vienna, 11 In. 80.00

KAY FINCH Ceramics were made in Corona Del Mar, California, from 1935 to 1963. The hand-decorated pieces often depicted whimsical animals and people. Pastel colors were used.

Kay Finch
CALIFORNIA

Ashtray, Dachshund 75.00
Bank, Pig, 5 1/2 In. 95.00
Candleholder, Scandie Girl, 5 1/2 In. 80.00
Figurine, Angel, No.114A 55.00
Figurine, Angel, White Gown, Blue Flowers & Wings, No. 114C 60.00
Figurine, Blue Rabbit & Baby Book 60.00
Figurine, Bride & Groom, No. 204, 1940s, 6 & 6 1/2 In. 150.00
Figurine, Cat, 8 In. 235.00
Figurine, Cat, Hannibal, No. 180 ....625.00 to 750.00
Figurine, Cat, Jezebel, No. 179 ....295.00 to 325.00
Figurine, Cat, Mehitable, No. 181, 8 1/2 In.. .... 450.00
Figurine, Cat, Reclining 75.00
Figurine, Cherub Head, No. 212 ....45.00 to 69.00
Figurine, Chicken, Biddy & Butch, White, No. 176 & No. 177, Pair ....175.00 to 250.00
Figurine, Chicken, Biddy, Ivory, Green, Tan, Yellow, No. 176 .... 125.00
Figurine, Choir Boy, Kneeling, No. 211 .... 150.00
Figurine, Choir Boy, No. 210 ....85.00 to 150.00
Figurine, Circus Monkey, 4 In. 125.00
Figurine, Court Lady, Gray, Silver & Burgundy Trim, 10 In. 125.00
Figurine, Dog, Cocker Spaniel, No. 5201, 8 In. 100.00
Figurine, Dog, Pekinese, No. 154, 14 In. ....420.00 to 595.00
Figurine, Dog, Poodle, Playful, Standing, Gray, No. 5203, 10 x 11 In. 750.00
Figurine, Dog, Yorkie, No. 4851, 5 In. ....175.00 to 325.00
Figurine, Dove, Gray & Black 85.00
Figurine, Dove, No. 5101 & No. 5102, Pair 100.00
Figurine, Draft Horse, No. 130 .... 135.00
Figurine, Duckling 75.00
Figurine, Elephant, Jumbo, No. 4805, 4 1/4 In. 185.00
Figurine, Elephant, Popcorn, No. 192, 6 3/4 In. 325.00
Figurine, Elephant, With Flowery Ears, No. 4626, 5 In. 95.00
Figurine, Elephant, With Vase, Yellow 125.00
Figurine, Grumpy Pig, No. 165, 7 1/2 In. ....125.00 to 300.00
Figurine, Hippopotamus, Flowers In Mouth, No. 5019, 5 3/4 In. 255.00
Figurine, Horse 135.00
Figurine, Kitten 50.00
Figurine, Lamb, Kneeling, No. 136 .... 45.00
Figurine, Lamb, Prancing, No. 168 .... 600.00
Figurine, Lamb, Rearing, No. 109 .... 145.00
Figurine, Mandarin, Mr. Foo, White, 22 In. 395.00
Figurine, Mr. Bird, No. 454, 4 1/2 In. 95.00
Figurine, Mrs. Bird, Brown, No. 453, 3 In. 75.00
Figurine, Muff The Kitten, No. 182, 3 1/4 In. 35.00
Figurine, Mumbo, No. 4804, 4 1/2 In. 185.00
Figurine, Oriental Sage & Maiden, No. 4854 & No. 4855, Pair 175.00
Figurine, Owl, Brown & Gold, No. 187, 8 3/4 In. 190.00
Figurine, Owl, Brown & Gray ....150.00 to 225.00
Figurine, Owl, Gray 225.00
Figurine, Owl, Gray & Pink 165.00
Figurine, Owl, Pink 225.00
Figurine, Owl, Tootsie, No. 188, 5 3/4 In. 75.00
Figurine, Owl, Tootsie, No. 189, 3 3/4 In. ....45.00 to 75.00
Figurine, Peasant Boy, No. 113, 6 3/4 In. 65.00
Figurine, Peasant Couple, No. 113 & No. 117, 6 3/4 In. 195.00
Figurine, Pig, Winkie, No. 185, 3 3/4 x 4 In. 95.00

Figurine, Rabbit	80.00 to 135.00
Figurine, Rooster & Hen, Green, Red Trim, White	175.00
Figurine, Rooster & Hen, Green, Turquoise	90.00
Figurine, Rooster, Gold Trim	195.00
Figurine, Sassy Pig, No. 166, 3 1/2 x 4 1/2 In.	95.00
Figurine, Scandie Girl, No. 126, 5 1/4 In.	38.00 to 52.00
Figurine, Squirrel, Brown, Other Gray, No. 108, 4 x 3 In., Pair	125.00
Figurine, Teddy Bear, Baby, No. 4906	125.00 to 295.00
Flower Bowl, Swan, No. 4956, 6 1/2 In.	150.00
Mug, Missouri Mule, Yellow	55.00
Mug, Santa, White	125.00
Planter, Baby Block	85.00
Planter, Baby Teddy Bear On Block, Aqua	90.00
Plaque, Butterfly, No. 5720, 14 In.	145.00
Punch Bowl, Santa Claus, 5 Mugs, No. 4950 & No. 4951, 5 3/4 & 4 In., 6 Piece	475.00
Toby Jub, Kitten Head, No. B5122	75.00
Vase, Monkey, Ivory, Yellow & Black	300.00
Vase, Moon, 17 In.	300.00

KAYSERZINN, see Pewter category.

KELVA glassware was made by the C. F. Monroe Company of Meriden, Connecticut, about 1904. It is a pale, pastel-painted glass decorated with flowers, designs, or scenes. Kelva resembles Nakara and Wave Crest, two other glasswares made by the same company.

KELVA

Box, Cover, Pink Poppies, Blue Ground, White Enamel, 8 1/2 In.	715.00
Box, Cover, Wild Rose, 4 1/2 In.	440.00
Box, Hinged Cover, Pink & Maroon Flowers, Green Ground, 3 x 5 1/4 In.	600.00
Box, Jewelry, Hinged Cover, Mottled Slate Blue, Pink Florals, Beading, 4 1/2 In.	570.00
Box, Marked Cigars In Gold, Pink Wild Roses, Blue Mottled Ground, Marked, 5 In.	550.00
Box, Pink Floral Cover, Dark Autumn Green Mottled Ground, Round, 2 1/2 x 4 1/2 In.	385.00
Fernery, Pink Wild Roses, Mottled Olive Green Ground, Marked, 8 In.	520.00
Planter, Pink Flowers On Body, Embossed Borders, Green Ground, 8 1/2 In.	875.00
Toothpick, White Flowers, Pink, Marked	325.00
Vase, Marbleized Green Ground, Pink Roses, 13 1/2 In.	795.00
Vase, Pink Flowers, Green Mottled Ground, Footed, 13 1/2 In.	795.00
Vase, Purple Tulips, Blue Ground, Ormolu Mounts, Marked, 11 In.	825.00

KEW BLAS is the name used by the Union Glass Company of Somerville, Massachusetts. The name refers to an iridescent golden glass made from the 1890s to 1924. The iridescent glass was reminiscent of the Tiffany glass of the period.

KFW-BLAS

Bowl, Rose, Scalloped Rim, Green Vertical Stripes, Orange Iridescent Interior, 4 In.	690.00
Compote, Flared Rim, Gold Iridescent, 3 1/2 x 4 1/2 In.	460.00
Decanter, Gold Iridescent, Ribbed, & Painted Stopper, Signed, 14 1/2 In.	1450.00
Goblet, Applied Baluster Stem, Cupped Disk Foot, Folded Rim, Golden Orange, 7 In.	200.00
Goblet, Gold Iridescent, Purple Highlights, 7 x 3 In.	330.00
Vase, Gold Iridescent, Feather Design, 6 3/4 In.	920.00
Vase, Green Hooked & Pull Feathers, Oyster Ground, Bulbous, Signed, 6 1/2 In.	1450.00
Vase, Green Pulled Leaves, Iridescent Gold, Cylindrical, Signed, 10 In.	770.00
Vase, Green, Gold Feathers, Swirled Gold Iridescent, 5 3/4 In.	1265.00
Vase, Iridescent Gold Leaves Base, Gold Opalescent, Bottle Shape, 4 In.	740.00
Vase, Jack-In-The-Pulpit, Gold Iridescent Flower Form, Amber, Gold, 12 In.	1495.00
Vase, Opalescent Pulled Feathers, Gold, Tapered, Signed, 6 In.	715.00
Vase, Ruffled Rim On Opal, Yellow, Gold Baluster Body, 6 In.	690.00

KEWPIES, designed by Rose O'Neill, were first pictured in the *Ladies' Home Journal*. The figures, which are similar to pixies, were a success, and Kewpie dolls started appearing in 1911. Kewpie pictures and other items soon followed. Collectors search for all items that picture the little winged people.

Bisque, Crawling, Military Gear	220.00
Bisque, Different Poses, Lefton, 4 1/2 In., 3 Piece	75.00

Bisque, Doll, Closed Mouth, Scottish Costume, 1910, 5 In. 900.00
Bisque, Doll, Label On Chest, Marked On Feet, 12 In. 1600.00
Bisque, Doll, Signed O'Neill, 8 1/2 In. 375.00
Bisque, Doll, Wings, Side-Glancing Eyes, Pink Taffeta, Krueger, 1935, 21 In. 525.00
Bisque, Doodle Dog, Closed Smiling Mouth, Blue Wings, Japan, 2 1/2 In. 330.00
Bisque, Reading Book, Sitting, Closed Smiling Mouth, Painted Tufted Hair, 2 In. 440.00
Bisque, Reclining, With Dog 132.00
Bisque, Seated, Eating 880.00
Bisque, Soldier, Lying On Tummy Aiming Gun, Red Military Cap, 3 In. 303.00
Bisque, Sweeperhead Turned Down, Closed Smiling Mouth, Jointed, 3 1/2 In. 270.00
Bisque, Traveler, Black Eyes, Dot Brows, Closed Smiling Mouth, 3 1/2 In. 250.00
Bisque, With Cat 230.00
Bisque Head, Doll, Kestner, 10 In. ....*Illus* 6400.00
Book, Paper Doll, 1963, Uncut 45.00
Book, Primer, Rose O'Neill, 1916 .... 195.00
Book, Rose O'Neill Autograph 295.00
Cameo, Doll, Jointed Shoulders, Red & White Heart Dress, 4 In. 165.00
Cameo, Doll, Skootles, 16 In. 795.00
Cameo, Doll, Skootles, All Original, Tag, 16 In. 995.00
Candy Container, By Barrel 60.00
Celluloid, Doll, Jointed Shoulders, 12 1/2 In. 150.00
Celluloid, Doll, Prewar, Japan, Box, 7 1/2 In. 850.00
Chalkware, Thinker, 6 In. 22.00
Cigarette Felt, 5 x 6 In. 50.00
Cigarette Felt, c.1914, 3 Piece 130.00
Clock, Bisque, Green Jasperware, 3 Frolicking Kewpies Along Base, Floral, 1915, 5 In. ... 350.00
Clock, Desk, Blue Jasperware, Arched Top, 2 Full-Bodied Kewpies, 5 In. 250.00
Clock, Upright, Green Jasperware, Arched Top, Floral Design, 1915, 4 In. 325.00
Composition, Doll, Rose O'Neill, 1920s, 11 1/2 In. 295.00
Composition, Doll, Rose O'Neill, 1930s, Box, 13 In. 525.00
Composition, Doll, With Heart Sticker, 12 In. 275.00
Cup & Saucer, Rose O'Neill 115.00
Dottie Darling, Doll, Dressed, Box, 9 In. 50.00
Hatpin Holder, Blue Jasperware, Rose O'Neill 385.00
Holder, Pencil 40.00
Jar, 3 Frolicking Kewpies On Lid, Garlands, Flower Border, 1915, 3 In. 275.00
Jointed, Doll, In Memory Of Joseph L. Kallus, 1894-1982, Rose O'Neill, 23 In. 275.00
Ladle, Porcelain, 5 In. 375.00
Nodder, Papier-Mache, Germany 95.00
Ornament, Wedding Cake, Huggers, Crepe Paper Dress 95.00
Paperweight, Brass, 3 In. 85.00

If you have an alarm system, program a strobe light attached to the outside of the house to go on if there is a break-in attempt. The light will frighten the burglar and will make it easy for the police to find the house.

Kewpie, Bisque Head, Doll, Kestner, 10 In.

Picture, Silk, Rose O'Neill, 1914 . . . . 60.00
Pitcher, Kewpie Jumping Over Kewpie, Royal Rudolstadt, 3 3/4 In. 125.00
Planter, Tumbling Kewpies, Green Jasperware, Rose O'Neill 325.00
Plate, Christmas, 1973 . . . . 20.00
Plate, Kewpies & Santa Claus 18.00
Porcelain, Doll, Cloth Dress, 1930s, 2 In. 55.00
Print, Lithograph, Halloween, Hendler Tag, Frame, 29 x 19 In. 990.00
Print, Lithograph, Happy New Year, Hendler Tag, Frame, 29 x 19 In. 415.00
Print, Lithograph, Indian, Hendler Tag, 29 x 20 In. 685.00
Print, St. Patrick's Day, No. 872, Frame, 30 x 20 In. 495.00
Print, Thanksgiving, Hendler Tag, 30 x 20 In. 532.00
Scootles, Composition, Jointed, Pink Dress, 1920s, 12 In. . . . . .300.00 to 375.00
Sign, Hendler's Ice Cream, Kewpie With Metal Spoon, 38 In. 2530.00
Sign, Hendler's Ice Cream, Kewpies & Blue Birds, Rose O'Neill, 21 x 28 In. 4400.00
Sign, Hendler's Ice Cream, Wooden Seated Figure, Fruit, 36 In. 1980.00
Soap, Box, 1940 . . . . 58.00
Tea Set, Doll's, Rose O'Neill, 21 Piece 1100.00
Tea Set, Doll's, Teapot, Sugar, Creamer, 4 Cups & Saucers, Germany, 1915 . . . . 900.00
Textile, 2 Kewpie Dolls, Target Shooting, Rose O'Neill, Frame, 8 1/2 x 7 1/2 In. 33.00
Tin, Candy, Black 45.00
Toothpick 165.00
Valentine, Hendler Tag, Framed, 29 x 19 In. 522.00

KIMBALL, see Cluthra category.

KING'S ROSE, see Soft Paste category.

KITCHEN utensils of all types, from eggbeaters to bowls, are collected today. Handmade wooden and metal items, like ladles and apple peelers, were made in the early nineteenth century. Mass-produced pieces, like iron apple peelers and graniteware, were made in the nineteenth century. Other kitchen wares are listed under manufacturers' names or under Advertising, Iron, Tool, or Wooden.

Ashtray, Griswold, No. 00, Quality Ware, Erie, Pennsylvania 75.00
Basket, Egg, Chicken Shape, Wire 18.00
Basket, Egg, Wire, Collapsible, 3 In. 45.00
Baster, Griswold, No. 11, Tite Top, Full Writing, Slant Logo 200.00
Batter Pail, Cover, Green, Square 325.00
Beater Jar, Wesson Oil 85.00
Blender, Hamilton Beach, Porcelain, Green 95.00
Board, Cutting, Chestnut, Primitive, New England, Late 18th Century, 17 1/2 In. 145.00
Board, Cutting, Lollipop Handle, American, Early 19th Century, 20 1/2 In. 295.00
Board, Cutting, Red & Black Checkerboard Top, Oval 190.00
Board, Noodle, Wooden, 1920s, Large 95.00
Board, Sleeve, Clamp-On Stand, Saves 1/2 Labor In Ironing Shirt Waists, Label 85.00
Bottle Warmer, Turquoise, Hankscraft 25.00
Bowl, Batter, White Glaze, Walter Cornelison, Bybee, 1960s, 2 3/4 x 7 1/4 x 9 1/4 In. 25.00
Bowl, General Electric, Cover, Gray, Pair 12.00
Bowl, Mixing, Plastic, Texasware 22.00
Box, Salt, Hanging, 1 Drawer, Lift Top Compartment, Poplar, 24 1/2 In. 357.00
Breadboard, Painted Cardinal On Branch, Round, 10 In. 25.00
Broiler, Wrought Iron, 5 Straight Cross Bars, 9 In. 165.00
Broiler, Wrought Iron, Rotary, Scrolled Design, 7 3/4 x 19 In. 190.00
Broiler, Wrought Iron, Wavy Cross Bars, 6 1/2 In. 85.00
Broom, Splint, Early 19th Century, 48 In. 185.00
Butter Mold, look under Mold, Butter in this category.
Butter Paddle, Burl, 9 1/2 In. 190.00
Butter Paddle, Carved Butter Stamp Handle, Fruit, Reverse Starflower, 11 3/4 In. 800.00
Butter Paddle, Curly Maple, 9 In. 170.00
Butter Paddle, Figure In Bowl, Ash, 8 1/2 In. 3002.00
Butter Paddle, Hook End, Curly Maple, 9 1/4 In. 170.00
Butter Stamp, 4 Hearts, Lollipop, 9 3/8 In. 275.00
Butter Stamp, Cow With Tree, Gray Finish, 1 Piece Handle, 4 5/8 In. 357.00

Butter Stamp, Cow, Turned Inserted Handle, Round, 4 In. 135.00
Butter Stamp, Dasher Style, Blue, Pair 632.50
Butter Stamp, Eagle, Gray Finish, 1-Piece Handle, 4 1/4 x 4 1/2 In. 715.00
Butter Stamp, Heart & Sunburst, Lollipop, 6 3/4 In. 215.00
Butter Stamp, Metal, 3 Gal., Dazey 225.00
Butter Stamp, Pineapple, Wooden, Miniature 40.00
Butter Stamp, Star Flower, Turned Handle, Round, 5 In. 410.00
Butter Stamp, Stylized Floral Design, Lollipop, 7 3/4 In. 245.00
Butter Stamp, Stylized Flower & Foliage, Whittled Handle, Round, 3 1/2 In. 115.00
Butter Stamp, Stylized Pineapple, Round, 4 1/2 x 4 3/4 In. 95.00
Butter Stamp, Swan 150.00
Butter Stamp, Tulip With Stars, Natural Growth Handle, 8 1/2 In. 148.00
Can Opener, Cow, Cast Iron, 6 In. 93.00
Can Opener, Keen Kutter 35.00
Can Opener, Winchester, Hand Held 75.00
Carving Set, Keen Kutter, Staghorn Handles, Sterling Trim, 3 Piece 55.00
Carving Set, Winchester, French Type Silver Butt & Bezels, 2 Piece 76.00
Cheese Preserver, Sanitary, Crystal 45.00
Cheese Press, Wooden Hoop 110.00
Cherry Pitter, Enterprise, Iron, 1903 .... 78.00
Cherry Pitter, Enterprise, No. 12 .... 87.00
Cherry Pitter, Goodell Co. 55.00
Chopper, Blade, Hand Forged, Crescent 35.00
Chopper, Food, Forged Steel, Side Wooden Handle, 19th Century 70.00
Chopper, Food, Forged Steel, Turned Handle, Brass Collar, 19th Century 80.00
Chopper, Food, Fox Form, England 1250.00
Churn, Davis Swing, Original Mustard Paint 350.00
Churn, Dazey, No. 4 .... 145.00
Churn, Egg, Cream, Blue, Tin 65.00
Churn, Ice Cream, Gem, Philadelphia, Salesman's Sample, 19th Century, 7 1/2 In. 450.00
Churn, Roseheaded Nails, Blue-Green Paint, 18th Century, 23 In. 925.00
Churn, Stave Construction, Blue Paint, Metal Bands, Turned Lid, 24 In. 330.00
Churn, Union Churn, No. 2 .... 475.00
Churn, Wooden Top & Plunger, A.P. Donaghho, Parkersburg, W.Va., 18 1/4 In. 240.00
Clock, Windmill Scene, Porcelain, Blue, White 160.00
Coffee Grinders are listed in their own category.
Coffeemaker, Chrome, Bakelite Handles & Spout, Art Deco 90.00
Coffeepot, Porcelain, Floral, Electric, Insert, 1940-1950 .... 150.00
Cookie Board, Beech, 4 5/8 x 21 In. 192.00
Cookie Board, Bird On A Branch, Dot Work, Cast Iron, 3 x 4 7/8 In. 165.00
Cookie Board, Maple, Cherry Finish, 6 1/8 x 11 1/4 In. 797.00
Cookie Board, Pineapple & Dot Work, Geometric Design, Cast Iron, 4 1/2 x 6 In. 150.00
Cookie Cutter, Deer, Leaping, Tin, 8 In. 192.00
Cookie Cutter, Deer, Stylized Antlers, Tin, 6 1/2 In. 159.00
Cookie Cutter, Gingerbread Man, Sheet Iron, American, 18th Century, 15 In. 675.00
Cookie Cutter, Man & Woman, Tin, 11 1/2 In., Pair 143.00
Cookie Cutter, Santa Claus, Flat Back, Germany, 4 In. 45.00
Cookie Cutter, Tom & Jerry, 1956 .... 90.00
Cover, For Skillet, Griswold, No. 3, Yellow 325.00
Cup, Measuring, Black Clown 50.00
Cup, Measuring, Fire-King, 1 Spout, Blue 19.00
Cup, Measuring, Kellogg's, Pink 38.00
Cup, Measuring, Presto Flour, 3 Spouts 29.50
Cutter, Cabbage, 3 Blades, Indianapolis Sanitary Kraut Cutter, Patent April 18, 1905 ... 50.00
Damper, Stove Pipe, Griswold 20.00
Dipper, Burl, Handle, 6 x 4 In. 275.00
Dipper, Ice Cream Sandwich, McLaren's 85.00
Dipper, Ice Cream, Indestructo, Brass, 1928 .... 48.00
Dough Box, 2-Board Lid, Splayed Turned Legs, Dovetailed, Poplar, 48 In. 1430.00
Dough Box, Blue, c.1850 .... 550.00
Dough Box, Dovetailed, Turned Legs, Ohio 795.00
Dough Box, On Stand, Ash 350.00
Dough Box, Walnut, Dovetailed, Breadboard Ends Lid, Splayed Base, 29 x 21 1/2 In. 385.00

DECODING
THE DATES ON
ANTIQUES

The old enameled ice cream sign says established 1884. Is it really more than 100 years old? The pencil sharpener pictured on page 8 was patented October 15, 1907. Is that the year it was made? Should I trust a date embroidered in my sampler, written on the bottom of my desk drawer, or printed on the bottom of my vase? Do the numbers tell the year my antique was made? Sometimes the date that appears on an antique is not what it seems. Common sense and a knowledge of the past will explain many dates. Look at this mark (right) from the bottom of a vase. At first it would seem that the vase was made in 1794. But the date refers to the first year the pottery was working. The vase and the mark are more recent. The mark was used by the Royally Privileged Porcelain Factory Tettau, called Royal Bayreuth by collectors.

"Est. 1884" can be seen on this sign for "Maine's I Scream" from Wakefield, R.I. It is an enameled sign 17½ by 13½ inches, probably used in the 20th century, long after the company was founded. The sign is worth $250.

Souvenirs are made even today to commemorate an exhibition, an election, or a special historic event or person. Sometimes antiques can be dated by the event that is part of the decoration or inscription. Coronation memorabilia, political campaign materials, and civic events—like the opening of a bridge or the building of a city hall—are often pictured on dishes or fabrics. It is usually safe to assume that there would be little demand for a souvenir of an event for many years after it takes place. But sometimes you can be fooled.

The Rowland & Marsellus Company of Staffordshire, England, made numerous dishes decorated with views of America to be sold in the United States from 1893 to the 1920s. They made a series of more than 100 plates that pictured scenes from cities and towns. They also made limited quantities of cups and

saucers and pitchers for special events and towns. This 7¼-inch pitcher has scenes from the American Revolution and the words "American Independence, 1776." At first glance one thinks the pitcher was a souvenir of the Philadelphia Centennial in 1876. But the bottom of the vase has the Rowland & Marsellus mark along with the English registry number 527015, which indicates the design was first made in 1908. Value, $125.

Soldiers in the Crimean war (1853–1856) bought souvenirs to send home to sweethearts to remind them of their love. This 7-inch creamware pitcher decorated with pink luster probably was made at the Sunderland factory in England during the war years. The decorations include British and French flags, an eagle, and a lion. The pitcher also has the verse "May they ever be united, Crimea, Vive l'Empereur, God save the queen."

Another decoration is a poem, "Women make men love,/ Love makes them sad,/ Sadness makes them drink,/ and drinking sets them mad." The back of the pitcher shows a woman, children, and a man going to sea. The well-known verse is "Sailors Farewell./ Sweet, oh Sweet is that Sensation,/ Where two hearts in union meet,/ But the pain of Separation,/ Mingles bitter with the Sweet." The pitcher is worth $300.

This silver plated shovel can be dated from the inscription on the blade. "In commemoration of Ground Breaking Exercises for the construction of Sixth Avenue Subway Route 101, Section 10 by Honorable Fiorello H. La Guardia, Mayor, and Honorable John H. Delaney, Chairman, Board of Transportation, March 23, 1936, Rosoff-Brader Construction Corporation Contractors." The 4½-by-18-inch shovel must have been part of the ceremony in 1936. The shovel, black but later cleaned to show the silver, was found at a flea market for $15.

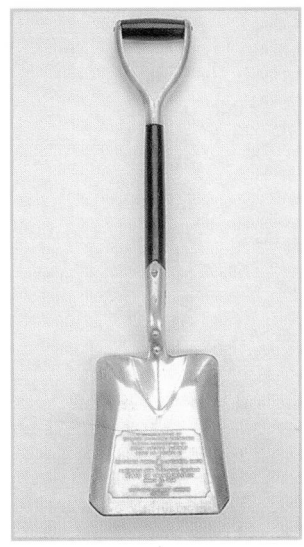

Sometimes souvenirs are made during demonstrations of crafts at World's Fairs. This 7-inch Homer Laughlin plate was made and sold at the New York World's Fair in 1939. Collectors can easily recognize it because it is stamped on the back "Joint Exhibit of Capital and Labor, the American Potter, New York World's Fair 1939." Value, $125.

This 2¾-by-5¼-inch brass lamp is marked with the impressed trademark of a satyr with a drawn bow. That is the mark used by Chase Brass Company of Waterbury, Connecticut, since 1928. Also on the bottom of the lamp are the words "Pat.87,543, Other Patents Pending." The lamp has a shade that pictures buildings and says "A Century of Progress Chicago 1934" across the front of the base. Collectors of both Chase and World's Fair memorabilia search for collectibles like this $150 lamp.

"World's Exposition Chicago. Admit the Bearer, 1st May to 30th Oct. 1893," says this paperweight. At the bottom it reads "American Bank Note Company, New York." On the other side it says "Good for one admission at pay gates." The 3¾-by-2¼-inch paperweight was a souvenir sold or given away at the exposition in 1893. Value, $50.

Perhaps the most interesting antiques for collectors are those one-of-a-kind pieces that are dated by the maker. Today it is unusual to add a date to a box, vase, or handkerchief. A child's piece of art from school or even a special craft project might be dated, especially if the artist is young. A few commercial artists sign and date paintings. But in the past, handcrafted pieces were often made with a date as part of the design. Most samplers, for example, were made with a date as well as the age of the young girl creating the needlework. These dates are almost always accurate. The history becomes part of the piece, making it a special treat for the collector.

Quill work is rare today. To make quills, small pieces of paper were rolled into short cigarettelike cylinders. Each cylinder was placed end out as part of a mosaic design. The end of each roll was painted, often gilded, so the finished design resembled metal filigree work. This hexagonal tea caddy was made with the paper rolls set in a glassed-in frame. At the back of the box, the artist has included the date 1800. The 8-by-5-by-5-inch box has a metal-lined interior to keep the tea leaves dry. A box like this sells for $1,000 today.

Satsuma pottery is made in Japan. In the United States during World War I the American china painters who had been using plain white German porcelain dishes searched for a new source of dishes. They were able to import undecorated Satsuma wares. The pieces were decorated by American painters with Art Nouveau and Art Deco inspired designs that were unlike the true Satsuma decorated pieces. These American wares are now called "American Satsuma." This extraordinary 11¼-inch example was decorated by one of the well-known artists. The vase has four vignettes showing seacoasts as well as an Art Nouveau gold border design. The bottom is signed "M.F. Mahoney 1918." The war years' date confirms the use of Oriental china blanks in the United States.

Edward Winter, an artist from Cleveland, Ohio, known nationwide for his enameled metal pieces, signed the back of this 11¾-inch plate with his name and the date 1936. This dated piece helps art historians to verify the type of work the artist was doing in his early years. Winter's style of enameling changed through the years, and by 1976, he was doing very abstract designs. An average Winter enamel sells today for $150. This dated, early example is worth $600.

"B.M.T.H.S.1904" is incised on the rim of this brown glazed pottery vase. The buff-colored clay vase was coated with brown glaze that outlined a floral design. The bottom of the 8¾-inch vase is marked "H.W.J." Could the letters on the rim stand for "Boston Massachusetts Technical High School" or some similar name? Was this a vase made in a school program? Or do the letters refer to an artist's society? Although we have owned this vase for twenty years, we have been unable to trace the maker. But the date makes us sure that this is a piece of 1904 pottery worth at least $100.

About 1880, American Indians began making bead-work souvenirs to sell to tourists. Pin cushions and decorative small hanging "pillows" often included the location and the date in the beaded design. This 4½-inch-square cushion is a souvenir of Toronto, Canada. The date 1935 is proof that the tradition of bead-work souvenirs lasted for more than fifty years. Because this cushion is considered an American Indian collectible, it is worth $65.

The inlaid wooden tabletop suggests the history of this table. The center design features the head of George Washington and an eagle flanked by "1776" and "1876." Other vignettes on the tabletop include the symbols for education, farming, seafaring, and industry, the themes of the centennial celebration in Philadelphia in 1876. The table design is in the Victorian Renaissance Revival style, with dark and light wood turnings, ebonized trim, and two bronze plaques picturing classic soldiers' heads. Was this a table made for the centennial as an example of the work of a talented cabinet-maker? Was it a gift to a special celebrity connected with the Philadelphia celebration? The 44½-by-30-by-26-inch table is worth more than $10,000, and the price goes higher if the history can be uncovered.

Anna Whitmore worked her name and the date 1832 into the design on her embroidered purse. She must have been proud of her accomplishment as a needlewoman. This 5-by-7-inch purse sold for $445. (Photograph courtesy of Paul and Karen Wendhiser, Ellington, Conn.)

Perhaps this is a square, lace-trimmed silk handkerchief, perhaps a doily meant for the center of a round oak table. It was sold as a tourist souvenir in Germany after World War I and is embroidered with the words "Andenken von Deutschland [souvenir of Germany] 1919." It was priced $10 in a box of assorted fabrics at a large flea market.

P atent and copyright dates can help to tell the age of an antique. However, there are several things to consider. The patent date tells when the piece was registered with the United States patent office, but it may have been made for many years with the same date appearing on each piece. It is only an indication of the earliest date the piece could have been made. Copyright and patent-pending dates will also give this same limited information. It is possible to trace a patent date through the patent office and learn who obtained the patent, how the piece was used, and what feature was the improvement that was patented. Some numbers are for inventions, some register designs.

Collectors of kitchen gadgets prize pieces with patent dates that help indicate the maker, the type of invention, and possibly the date of manufacture. This iron eggbeater has the words raised on the wheel "Dover Egg Beater, Pat'd May 6th 1873 Apr 3d 1888 July 9th 1889." The 9¾-inch-long beater is worth $25.

This lithographed tin stamp pad is printed with the words "Jumbo Excelsior trade mark, Self-Inking Stamp Pad, Always Ready for Use, No. 00." Along the bottom edge is the history, "Non-Collapsible Box Pat. Aug. 9-1910," and by the hinge, "The H.L. Hudson Co. Bklyn. N.Y." The 3¾-by-2¼-inch box cost $10.

"Niagara Falls" is shown on this motion lamp. The shade turns as the heat of the bulb creates air currents. The movement makes it appear as though the water is falling. The bottom of the shade is marked "Econolite Corp. © 1955 762 Oval," telling the collector that the piece is forty-three years old. The 11¼-by-5¾-inch lamp is a popular collectible selling for $150 in some parts of the country.

This strange 5-inch-high collection of gears, boxes, and blades is a pencil sharpener. The front is labeled so that its use and appropriate age are obvious, "U.S. Automatic Pencil Sharpener, Mfd. By Automatic Pencil Sharpener Co. Inc. Chicago, Ill. U.S.A., Pat. Oct. 2, 06.-Oct 15, 07. Foreign Patents Pending." Value, $100.

The mahogany revolving bookshelf has cast iron legs. Careful examination of the piece shows an ink stamp mark on a center post. It says "Danner's Revolving Book Case, Pat'd May 16 1876, Feb 20, Dec 11 1877, John Danner, Canton, Ohio." The top measures 19½ square inches. The bookcase is 33½ inches high. This design has become popular again, and modern adaptations are being made with slightly different dimensions so that the shelf will hold the standard paperback book. This signed-and-dated piece was a bargain at $500, less than the cost of a new one.

George Hunzinger of New York City worked in the 1860s and 1870s. He made chairs that sometimes resembled assembled plumbing pipes. He patented many folding, reclining, rocking, and other kinds of chairs. This chair with turned wooden parts is stamped on the back edge of the seat "Hunzinger, N.Y., Pat. March 30, 1869." Hunzinger chairs sell quickly to collectors. This one is worth $1,000. It is a solid chair and does not fold up even though it looks as if it should.

The patent date on this stoneware piece helps to identify it. The April 7, 1885, patent was for a chicken fountain. It was made by Akron Pottery Company of Akron, Ohio. The chicken fountain, with a 6½-inch diameter and 7½ inches long, has two small feet in the back that tip it so that the water flows into the trough and lets the chicken have a drink.

Although the car pictured on the poster tells a knowledgeable automobile collector that the poster was made in the late 1920s, it is reassuring to see the date also printed on this poster for the "Cleveland Automobile Show, January 21 to 28." In tiny print at the bottom it says "design © - by Courtesy Motor Magazine 1928." It is also marked "The Crane Howard Co. Cleveland." The 19½-by-25¾-inch poster is worth $150.

Souvenir spoons have been popular since the 1880s. They were made to be sold near the site of an event or building. Both silver and silver-plated spoons were popular. Most were marked with the patent date for the design and were made soon after that date. LEFT TO RIGHT: This demitasse spoon says "The Midnight Ride 1775" and pictures Paul Revere on his horse. On the back it says, "Sterling, Pat. Apl'd for Freeman & Taylor." The nut spoon with

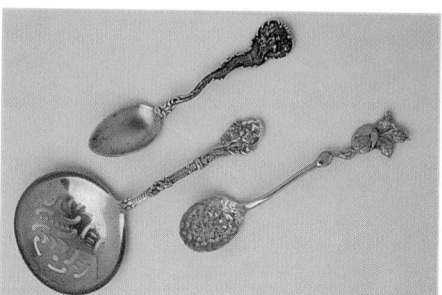

the cherub and urn on the handle says "Copyrighted '88, sterling." The teaspoon with the pierced bowl and flower-decorated handle is marked on the back "sterling, pat. Mar. 8 '91. H.S. & Co." An additional date is engraved, "Aug. 8th 92."

Sometimes the box for a collectible gives important information about the history of the piece. This plastic bowl has a box that says "Fruitbowl Centerpiece Set, Salt, Pepper & Sugarbowl, A Starke Design. At last a centerpiece that is truly decorative and functional. The realistic color and artistic arrangement will add charm and conversation to your table. The 4½" bowl holds an ample supply of sugar while the 4½" high fruit arrangement acts as a cleverly concealed base for the pineapple and grapefruit salt and pepper. To clean, simply use a damp cloth. Separates easily for filling or cleaning." The lower edge reads "Pat. Pend. ©1958-M.Gary Made in U.S.A." On the bottom of the bowl is "Starke Design Inc. Bklyn, N.Y. Pat. Pend. Made in U.S.A." The piece cost $12.

Advertising collectors know that dates on labels often tell the history of the company, not the age of the piece. This Heinz baked beans can has an old label, but the date "Established 1869" refers only to the company, not to the can. The medallion with the words "H.J. Heinz, Pure Food Products, Pittsburgh U.S.A" was used after 1896. The instructions on the side of the label tell the approximate age of the can—no word of microwaves but warnings about storage and cooking methods that were needed when canned goods were still unfamiliar, around the turn of the century: "Caution, Canned goods of every kind should be emptied into a glass or china receptacle immediately after being opened. Never allow them to remain in the can." On the back it adds "To serve hot, remove wrapper and place can in boiling water for twenty minutes." This can was sold for $45 last year. It was probably made before 1925.

This bottle was once the winner of a contest to find the oldest bourbon bottle in America. The proof is on the label that says "Bininger's Old Kentucky Bourbon, 1849 Reserve Distilled in 1848. A.M. Bininger & Co. Established 1778. Sole Proprietors, Nos. 19 & 21 Broad St. New York." Almost the same words are embossed on the sides and the back. The 9½-inch-high bottle sells for $95 at the bottle shows.

Kitchen equipment has become popular with collectors in the past fifteen years, and electric kitchen machines have sparked interest in the last five years. This electric milk shake machine is marked "Stevens Electric Co., Racine, Wis., U.S.A., Pat. No. 1300867" on the shaker. It also dates itself with the words "Pat'd. 4-19-33 No. 1927184." The 1933 machine with shaker top is 16 inches high. It's worth $125.

Printed fabrics are sometimes identified and dated at the edge of the fabric. Sometimes the date is a part of the design. This printed fabric was made to be cut and stitched into a stuffed doll. According to the words on the fabric, this is one of "Kellogg's Beautiful New Nursery Rhyme Dolls." It is obviously Little Red Riding Hood. There is a nursery rhyme in one panel and the Kellogg's version in another. "Little Red Riding Hood,/ Come to tea./ O Grandma, you've spread/ The white table for me./ What is this, Grandma,/ So crisp and so whole?/ Kellogg's Corn Flakes/ In a big white bowl." There are also instructions for making the doll and a note that this is one of four different dolls. At the bottom of the fabric is the date information, "#8116 © 1928 Kellogg Co., Battle Creek, Mich." The value of this fabric is $150.

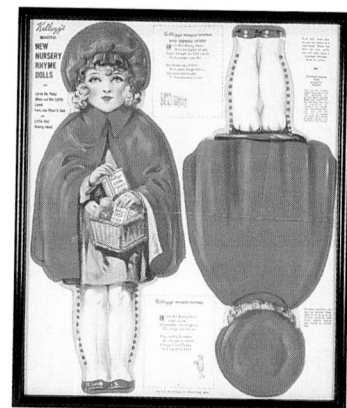

Sometimes the information printed on a collectible that gives its history is as compelling as the piece itself. Holt Howard was an importer who put his name and date on almost every piece. Most of the giftware pottery was whimsical, and collectors seem to like looking at shelves full of the comic figures. This bottle of "Russian Dressing" says "© 1959 Holt Howard" on the bottom. It is one of a set of three dressing bottles with heads that illustrate the names. The others are Italian Dressing and French Dressing. Each bottle is 7 inches high and sells for about $55.

Vienna Art plates are lithographed metal copies of expensive European Royal Vienna porcelain plates. They were made in Coshocton, Ohio, by J. F. Meeks Tuscarora Advertising Company and by another firm in the same city, H. D. Beach's Standard Advertising Company. The plates were often printed with a company name and given away as advertising premiums. The back of this 10-inch plate says "Vienna Art Plates Pat. Feb. 21st 1905." It is worth $85.

Some factories have their own date-marking codes that appear on each piece. One of the easiest dating systems to learn was used by the Rookwood Pottery of Cincinnati, Ohio. The company used its initials RP placed back to back starting in 1880, the year the company began production. Then a flame was added each year until 1900. After 1900, a Roman numeral was added each year. This vase has five flames, showing that it was made in 1885. The 6 1/4 - inch-high vase is worth $250.

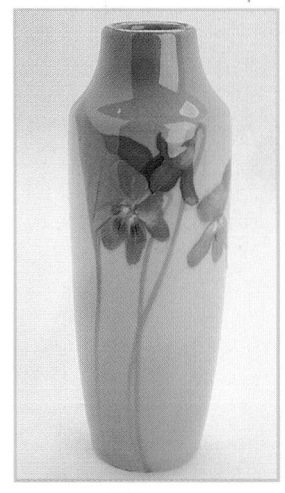

Another art pottery, Pisgah Forest, used a date in its mark. This vase with blue crystalline glaze is marked "1949 Stephen" in the familiar Pisgah Forest logo of a potter at the wheel. It is 5 ½ inches high, 5 ½ inches in diameter. The Pisgah Forest Company, located in North Carolina, was started in 1926 and is still working. The unusual glaze adds to the $250 value for the bowl.

Another pottery that used date marks was Van Briggle of Colorado Springs, Colorado. Only a few early pieces were marked with a year, although almost all had the company logo of A's in a rectangle. This 7 ¼ -inch vase has the date "1916" inscribed on the bottom. Because dated pieces are rare, the numerals add to the value. The vase is worth more than $500.

We bought this bowl primarily because of the date on the bottom. It is signed "EH" and incised with the date "Jun 27 1950," which is a wedding anniversary date in our family. Edith Harwell made this piece in "Pinewood, Fairhope, Ala." It is fun to think that this bowl was being thrown on a wheel at the exact time of our family's wedding ceremony. The 6-inch-diameter bowl cost $85.

Tins made by Somers Brothers are a "joy" for nearsighted tin collectors. Each tin is marked in very tiny type. Somers made some of the earliest lithographed tins in America. This one says "Monte Cristo. Filmy Cut, Superior Quality of Tobacco. A Mixture of Genuine Turkish Perique, Havana & Virginia, by Wm. S. Kimbell & Co. Rochester, N.Y." On one end is a barely legible notice about the manufacturer's compliance with the tobacco laws and the company's New York address. But what collectors like is the other information, "Somers Bros. Bklyn N.Y. Pat. Apl 29 1879." The box, made within a year or so of the patent date, is 1⅛ by 8½ inches and is worth $100.

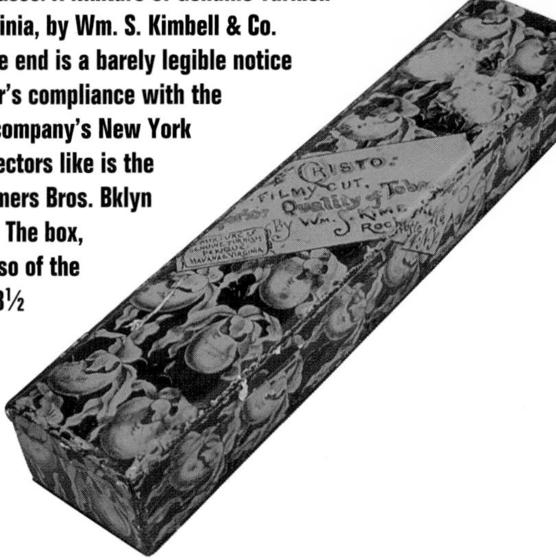

Look carefully at your antiques and collectibles. Sometimes dates appear in unexpected places. Silver pieces were often given as prizes at fairs or sports events and inscriptions were added. Class rings and pins are often dated. Autographed books, pictures, and baseballs often include a date.

Ever flatten a penny on a railroad track? Not a very safe hobby, but flattened pennies have attracted collectors for many years. The original date on the copper penny can be seen even when the coin has been pressed into a thin oval. The "squished" penny became a business at some of the fairs by the early 1900s. Machines were made that flattened the copper penny and formed a raised design on the surface. Special designs with pictures and dates were made, and the pennies were sold at many fairs. This souvenir was made from a penny and has the words "World's Fair, The Space Age, Seattle, 1962." There is also a picture of the Space Needle. An interesting souvenir, but only worth $1.

This gold charm bracelet looks as if it was worn by a child in the 1940s. Two of the charms are authentic 19th-century gold coins. The coins were from a family coin collection, and they were the first charms put on the link bracelet. But there is also a miniature gold ring with blue enamel and the date 1950. Research proved that the ring was a college class ring added to an existing charm bracelet. Charm bracelets often tell a story of events in the original owner's life. They are just interesting gold jewelry to others. This one is worth $750.

Sports trophies sometimes have inscriptions that tell a story and also include a date. These dates can almost always be trusted. This 9-inch, silver-trimmed, copper-colored loving cup is inscribed "Upper Saranac, 1916, Bang-and-go-back Race, First Prize." The bottom of the cup has the information about the maker. The letters HAMS in a diamond tell that it was made by the Heintz Art Metal Shop. " Sterling on bronze, Pat.Aug.27.12" gives the history of the materials used and the patents on the process of putting the silver on the bronze original. The trophy was cleaned too often and the dark brownish bronze finish was removed. Even so, it is worth $55, perhaps because collectors like to ponder questions such as "What was the 1916 Bang-and-go-back Race?"

This souvenir jug says "The Brown Jug, Delaware, Ohio" on the front. An impressed date on the back says "1947." It was probably bought at the Little Brown Jug horse race in Ohio about fifty years ago. It is 3¼ inches high. We found this jug in a box of stored "treasures" that had been put away in 1960 by a young boy. It may have nostalgic value but is probably worth less than $5.

Dutch Oven, Griswold, Red Porcelain 95.00
Dutch Oven, Red Enameled, Griswold, Table Service 75.00
Dutch Oven, Trivet, Griswold, Marked Glass Lid, No. 8 .... 35.00
Egg Coddler, Royal Worcester, Pair 25.00
Egg Cooker, Hankscraft, Orange 20.00
Egg Timer, Amish Girl, Cast Iron 35.00
Egg Timer, Humpty Dumpty, Plastic, England 95.00
Egg Timer, Lady On Phone 78.00
Egg Timer, Prayer Lady 55.00
Egg Timer, Winking Chef, Timer In Back 1195.00
Eggbeater, Bingo, Tin 16.00
Eggbeater, Coiled Wire Knob 30.00
Eggbeater, Dover, Tiny Wings, 1891 .... 125.00
Eggbeater, E.P. Munroe, Cast Iron 1550.00
Eggbeater, Jaquette, No. 2 .... 1000.00
Eggbeater, Taplin, 1903 .... 28.00
Flatiron, Cole Brookdale, No. 50 .... 25.00
Flue Cover, Victorian Women Picture 65.00
Food Press, Iron, Sensible, 2 Qt. 135.00
Fruit Press, Griswold, No. 110, Wood Slats 250.00
Fryer, Chicken, Griswold, No. 8, Hinged, Pattern No. 2528, No Lid 45.00
Frying Pan, Blacksmith Made, Walker, New England, 18th Century, 45 In. ... 365.00
Funnel, Canning, Handle 16.00
Grater, Cheese, Clamp On, Crank Handle 27.00
Grater, Cheese, Heavy Duty, 1903 .... 310.00
Grater, Engraved With Initials T. B. & A. B. At Top, Brass, Dutch, 1717, 9 1/2 In. 895.00
Grater, Nutmeg, All Tin, Crank 1 Side, Fingerhold On Other 210.00
Grater, Nutmeg, Edgar, Tin, Wooden 85.00
Grater, Nutmeg, Hinged Pocket, Tole 250.00
Grater, Nutmeg, Iron Bellows, Seymour, Connecticut 550.00
Grater, Nutmeg, Opens Top & Bottom, Tin Grater, Silver Plate 400.00
Grater, Nutmeg, Wire Handle, Cast Iron 275.00
Grater, Sliding Lid, Drawer, Pine Box, Wire Nail Construction, 9 5/8 In. . 93.00
Griddle, Griswold, Logo In Diamond 35.00
Griddle, Griswold, No. 7, Rectangular, Erie 25.00
Griddle, Griswold, No. 9, Cast Iron, Rectangular 40.00
Griddle, Griswold, No. 9, Hammered Handle, Chrome 65.00
Griddle, Guardian Service 25.00
Griddle, Wagner, No. 9, Handled 55.00
Grinder, Herb, Hand Carved, c.1800 .... 375.00
Grinder, Nutmeg, Iron 300.00
Grinder, Nutmeg, Tin, Wooden 55.00
Grinder-Grater, Fripu-Germany, Cast Iron, Aluminum, Clamp-On, 4 Inserts 28.00
Grisset, Copper, Collects Grease For Cooking, Wrought Iron Handle, 20 x 9 In. 375.00
Heater, Sadiron, Tripod, 1886 .... 245.00
Holder, Broom, Figural, Bear, Cast Iron, 4 In. 175.00
Holder, Measuring Spoons, Chinese Boy 16.00
Holder, Measuring Spoons, Flower Pot 14.00
Ice Box, Oak, Glass Front Doors, Center Mirrored Door, Gibson, Greenville, Mi., 7 Ft. ... 3800.00
Ice Shaver, Griswold, No. 1 .... 95.00
Ice Shaver, Mechanical, Snow King, 1920s 1350.00
Icebox, Alaska, Oak 750.00
Icebox, Brunswick, Oak, 84 x 32 In. 3250.00
Icebox, Oak, 1 Large & 2 Small Doors 650.00
Icebox, Oak, Top Loading, 35 x 18 In. 220.00
Icebox, Porcelain Interior, Leonard Cleanable Refrigerator, 46 3/4 In. .. 330.00
Icebox, Porcelain Lined, Golden Oak, 1920s, 52 In. 850.00
Icebox, Side Brass Towel Rack, 2 Vertical Doors, Oak, Sanitax, 1910s, 40 1/2 In. 230.00
Iron, Gas, Blue Enameled, Filler & Pump 35.00
Iron, Travel, Smoothie, Chromium Plated, Bakelite, Lucas Holder & Co., 1948, 4 In. 90.00
Ironing Board, Snow White, 1940s 95.00
Jagging Wheel, Hearts & Mariner's Compass, Bone 3300.00
Jar Rubbers, Good Luck Jar, Cold Pack Canning, Lot 195.00

Jug, Batter, Tin Lid, Cap & Handle, F.H. Cowden, Harrisburg, 9 1/2 In. 400.00
Juicer, Child's, Jack & Jill Bottom 40.00
Juicer, Daisy, Wall Mount, Metal 35.00
Juicer, Hamilton Beach, Black, Drugstore 250.00
Kettle, American Brass Kettle Mfg., Spun Brass, Iron Bale Handle, 15 In. 60.50
Kettle, Griswold, No. 7, Flat Bottom, Slant Erie 95.00
Kettle, Royal Worcester, Floral Design, Gilt U-Shaped Handle On Top, Cream Ground . .   175.00
Kettle, Sugar, Everted Rim, Iron, Louisiana, 19th Century, 26 1/2 x 60 In. 1935.00
Kettle, Wagner, 3 Legs, No. 6 . . . .   125.00
Ladle, Jessie Cornelius, Sunburst Touchmark, Copper 195.00
Lemon Squeezer, Arcade, No. 2, Black Paint, Porcelain Insert 55.00
Masher, Ash, Turned, New England, 18th Century, 14 1/2 In. 165.00
Match Holders can be found in their own category.
Match Safes can be found in their own category.
Meat Grinder, 3 Blades, Griswold, No. 4 . . . .   40.00
Meat Grinder, Keen Kutter 15.00
Meat Grinder, Winchester, No. 12, Nickel Finish, Wooden Handle 64.00
Meat Grinder, Winchester, No. W13, Extra Cutting Blades, Wooden Handle 93.00
Meat Grinder, Winchester, No. W32 . . . .   65.00
Meat Tenderizer, Carved Wood 22.00
Mincer, Keen Kutter, 6 Blades 40.00
Mixer, Hamilton Beach, Bowl & Accessories 50.00
Mixer, Hamilton Beach, Tan, Porcelain 95.00
Mixer, Malt, Arnold, No. 15 . . . .   125.00
Mixer, Malt, Hamilton Beach, Marble Base 225.00
Mixer, Mayonnaise, Universal 410.00
Mixer, Mayonnaise, Wesson Oil 48.00
Mixer, Mayonnaise, Wesson Oil, Glass 35.00
Mixer, Mixmaster Junior, Sunbeam, Chrome 18.00
Mixer, Nestle Chocolate Milk, Bunny Sits On Lid 25.00
Molds may also be found in the Pewter and Tinware categories.
Mold, Butter, 12 Houses Shape, Gray Scrubbed, 29 1/2 In. 75.00
Mold, Butter, Cow, Carved Wood, Round 150.00
Mold, Butter, Eagle, Wooden 105.00
Mold, Butter, House Shape, Chimney, Dormer, Wooden, Initials W.B., 6 In. 275.00
Mold, Butter, Leaf Design, Knob Handle, Scotland, 1 3/4 In. 55.00
Mold, Butter, Paddle Type, Wooden, 9 In. 30.00
Mold, Butter, Swan, Carved Wood, Round 200.00
Mold, Butter, Wheat, Wooden 105.00
Mold, Cake, Santa Claus, Hello Kiddies, Griswold, 12 In. 500.00
Mold, Cake, Swirling Turk's Cap Form, Redware, 1880 . . . .   75.00
Mold, Candle, see Tinware category.
Mold, Chocolate, Bear, Tin, Clips, 2 Part, 9 In. 220.00
Mold, Chocolate, Cat 45.00
Mold, Chocolate, Cat, Cartoon, Long Neck 295.00
Mold, Chocolate, Charlie Chaplin 255.00
Mold, Chocolate, Duck, Clamp & Hinge, Germany 68.00
Mold, Chocolate, Easter Bunny, Stoneware 55.00
Mold, Chocolate, Hen On Nest, Tin, 1920s, 7 1/2 x 8 In. 390.00
Mold, Chocolate, Lamb, Signed Kaiser, Germany, Large 65.00
Mold, Chocolate, Model T Ford, Germany, 7 1/2 In. 175.00
Mold, Chocolate, Pig & Fish 175.00
Mold, Chocolate, Rabbit 65.00
Mold, Chocolate, Rabbit With Basket, Tin, 12 In. 370.00
Mold, Chocolate, Rabbit, 3 Piece 40.00
Mold, Chocolate, Smokey The Bear, Metal, 8 1/2 In. 58.00
Mold, Chocolate, Triple Santa Claus, c.1900, 8 In. 345.00
Mold, Food, 4 Heart, Redware, Octagonal, 19th Century, 2 1/2 x 12 3/4 In. 805.00
Mold, Food, Green & Yellow, Footed, Redware, 19th Century, 3 3/4 x 11 x 7 1/4 In. 460.00
Mold, Food, Green & Yellow, Pinwheel Interior, Redware, 19th Century, 5 x 10 In. 345.00
Mold, Ice Cream, see Pewter category.
Mold, Pudding, Floral Bottom, Decorated Sides 35.00

Mold, Pudding, Jack-O'-Lantern, Storks, Etc., Ceramic, 11 Piece 100.00
Mold, Spoon, Bronze, 7 1/2 In. 275.00
Mold, Sugar Maple, Heart Form, Pine, 1830s, 3 In. 250.00
Mold, Turk's Head, Wagner, 6 Hole 20.00
Pan, 3 Mold, Folded Rim, 6 1/4 In. 165.00
Pan, Bread, Vienna, Griswold, No. 6958 .... 100.00
Pan, Breadstick, Wagner, EE Divided, Aluminum 40.00
Pan, Bridge, Little Slam, Wagner, No. 1340, Black Iron 145.00
Pan, Crispy Corn Stick, Griswold, No. 273 .... 50.00
Pan, Crusty Corn Cobs, Wagner Ware 40.00
Pan, French Roll, D, Wagner, Aluminum 20.00
Pan, Frying, Griswold 50.00
Pan, Griddle, Griswold, Slant, Iron 25.00
Pan, Muffin, 8 Cups, G.F. Filley, No. 5 .... 125.00
Pan, Muffin, Aluminum, Tea Size, Krusty Korn Kobs, Wagner Ware 75.00
Pan, Muffin, Griswold, No. 1 .... 275.00
Pan, Muffin, Griswold, No. 3 .... 550.00
Pan, Muffin, Griswold, No. 8 ....65.00 to 100.00
Pan, Muffin, Griswold, No. 11, Iron 45.00
Pan, Muffin, Griswold, No. 16, Vienna 160.00
Pan, Muffin, Griswold, No. 18 .... 75.00
Pan, Muffin, Griswold, No. 21 .... 135.00
Pan, Muffin, Griswold, No. 240 .... 425.00
Pan, Muffin, Griswold, No. 262 .... 55.00
Pan, Muffin, Griswold, No. 947, Golf Ball 150.00
Pan, Muffin, Griswold, No. 2700 .... 550.00
Pan, Pie, Wagner, No. 362 .... 15.00
Pan, Popover, 6 Cups, Aluminum, Griswold, No. 18, Aluminum 60.00
Pan, Vienna Roll, Griswold, No. 958 .... 150.00
Pastry Wheel, Made From Copper Penny, Iron Handle, Wooden Grip, 7 In. 165.00
Peel, Rams Horn End, Long Handle, Handwrought, Iron 145.00
Peel, Wrought Iron, 37 1/2 In. 135.00
Peeler, Apple, Amish Style, Bench, Patented June 25, 1889 .... 375.00
Peeler, Apple, Built-In Skin Shaver, Cog Driven, Wooden 300.00
Peeler, Apple, Goodell Company, Patent 1898, Cast Iron 125.00
Peeler, Apple, Goodell, 1898 .... 55.00
Peeler, Apple, Hudson, Cast Iron 55.00
Peeler, Apple, Sargent, Partial Label 155.00
Peeler, Apple, Signed Hudson Parer Co., Pat. 1882, Cast Iron 65.00
Peeler, Apple, Wooden Crank Handle, Pewter Ferrule, 18th Century, 22 In. 350.00
Percolator, Wagner, Aluminum, July 2, 1918, 5 1/2 Cup 20.00
Pie Bird, Bird, Cleminson 35.00
Pie Bird, Blackbird, White Base, Royal Worcester 55.00
Pie Bird, Blue, White, White Base, Royal Worcester 75.00
Pie Bird, Clown 12.00
Pie Bird, Flour Fred, England 45.00
Pie Bird, Frosty Snowman, Black & White 12.00
Pie Crimper, Whalebone, c.1820, 5 1/2 In. 295.00
Pie Crimper, Wooden Handle, Pewter Coin Wheel, 1798, 7 1/4 In. 195.00
Pie Crimper, Wrought Iron, c.1780, 6 In. 395.00
Pot Holder, Mammy, 12 In. 55.00
Rack, Plate Drying, Mortised & Pin Construction 445.00
Raisin Seeder, Crown, 1896 .... 60.00
Raisin Seeder, Gem 75.00
Reamers are listed in their own category.
Refrigerator, GE, Coil Top, 1926 .... 600.00
Ricer, Potato, Iron, Wm. Vogel, New York, Patent 1881 .... 75.00
Roaster, Coffee, Cylindrical, Griswold 1755.00
Roaster, Coffee, Herrington, 1849 .... 440.00
Roaster, Griswold, No. 5, Oval, Raised Letter Lid 290.00
Roaster, Trivet, Griswold, No. 3, Oval, Aluminum 90.00
Roaster, Wagner, No. 7, Oval, Full Writing 495.00

Roaster, Wagner, No. 10, Round, Nickel Knob 75.00
Rolling Pin, Blown Glass, Painted Flowers, Ships, Think Of Me When Far At Sea, 29 In. 192.00
Rolling Pin, Blown Glass, White & Pink Looping, 17 1/2 In. 82.00
Rolling Pin, Harker 85.00
Rolling Pin, Jadite 425.00
Rolling Pin, Porcelain, Green Wooden Handles 65.00
Sadiron, Chrome, Wooden, 3 7/8 In. 38.00
Salt & Pepper Shakers are listed in their own category.
Scissors, Winchester, Nickel Finish, 7 1/2 In. 34.00
Scissors, Winchester, Worn Finish, 7 In. 22.00
Scoop, Ice Cream, Conical Bowl, Squeeze Handle 350.00
Scoop, Ice Cream, Jeweled Copper, Brass Numerals At Top Of Bowl, 1-5 Cent, 48 In. 660.00
Scoop, Ice Cream, Key Wind, Cone Shape 40.00
Scraper, Ban, American-Maid Bread 75.00
Scrub Board, Wooden, Wire Staples, Pennsylvania 275.00
Shaker, Pancake, Aunt Jemima Face & Logo On Lid 75.00
Shaker, Pancake, Aunt Jemima, Yellow & White 100.00
Sieve, Foley Food Mill, Tin, 2 Wooden Handles 11.00
Sifter, Flour, Brite Pride, Aluminum, Red Handle 35.00
Skillet, Egg, Griswold, Square, Pat. 129 . . . . 30.00
Skillet, Griswold, 5 In 1 . . . . 165.00
Skillet, Griswold, No. 4 . . . . 80.00
Skillet, Griswold, No. 4, Large Block, Smooth Bottom 80.00
Skillet, Griswold, No. 5 . . . . 25.00
Skillet, Griswold, No. 6 . . . . 40.00
Skillet, Griswold, No. 7, Pattern Number 724 . . . . 35.00
Skillet, Griswold, No. 8, Cover, Small Logo 35.00
Skillet, Griswold, No. 9, Block Emblem, Smoke Ring 18.00
Skillet, Griswold, No. 10, Slant, Erie 55.00
Skillet, Griswold, No. 12, Large Logo 25.00
Skillet, Griswold, No. 15, Fish 300.00
Skillet, Griswold, No. 15, Oval 375.00
Skillet, Griswold, No. 20 . . . . 650.00
Skillet, Griswold, No. 42, Snack 40.00
Skillet, Griswold, No. 53, Square Egg 45.00
Skillet, Wagner, Bacon & Egg Breakfast, 3 Section 20.00
Skillet, Wagner, No. 9, 3 Hole Handle 55.00
Skillet, Wapak, No. 3, Indian Head Medallion 150.00
Skillet, Wapak, No. 11, With Indian 300.00
Skimmer, Heart & Circle Cutout, Rattail Handle, Copper & Iron 330.00
Smoothing Board, Chip Carved, Wooden, Dated Anno 1705 . . . . 895.00
Soap Saver, Wire 10.00
Spatula, Blacksmith Made, Iron, Signed 4 Times, D. Biehl, 1880s, 17 1/4 In. 250.00
Spatula, Iron, Heart End Handle, Signed, Penna., Late 18th Century, 16 In. 650.00
Spatula, Pancake, Aunt Jemima 45.00
Spatula, Rattail Handle, Iron, 11 1/8 In. 220.00
Spatula, Rumford Baking Powder, Green Handle 13.00
Spice Box, 6 Interior Canisters, Grater, Brown Japanning, Tole, 7 1/4 In. 93.50
Spice Box, Gold Leaf Designs, Cloves, Ginger, England, 8 1/2 x 7 1/4 In., Pr. 325.00
Spice Box, Hanging, Divided 6-Part Interior, Drawer, Lift Lid, Poplar, 14 1/4 In. 550.00
Spice Box, Sliding Lid, 6 Interior Compartments, Walnut, 10 In. 330.00
Spice Cabinet, 6 Drawers, Oak, Small 95.00
Spice Kitchen, Tin, Stenciled, Revolving Containers, Bins, Coffee Grinder, Palace 895.00
Spice Rack Set, Chef Master, Plastic, Box, 15 x 6 1/2 In. 45.00
Spoon, Tasting, Burly Maple, 18th Century, 6 In. 180.00
Spoon Rest, Mammy Face 95.00
Spoon Rest, Piglet 12.00
Sprinkler Bottle, Asian Man Holding Iron, Japan 140.00
Sprinkler Bottle, Cat, 7 1/2 In. 40.00
Sprinkler Bottle, Chinaman 55.00
Sprinkler Bottle, Clothespin, Yellow 145.00
Sprinkler Bottle, Dutch Boy 160.00

Sprinkler Bottle, Dutch Boy & Girl 295.00
Sprinkler Bottle, Dutch Girl 165.00
Sprinkler Bottle, Dutch Girl & Windmill, Multicolored, Tin, 6 In. 65.00
Sprinkler Bottle, Elephant, With Clover, White 150.00
Sprinkler Bottle, Gray Elephant 90.00
Sprinkler Bottle, Lady Ironing 85.00
Sprinkler Bottle, Siamese Cat ....80.00 to 145.00
Sprinkler Bottle, White Elephant, Leaves 90.00
Strainer, Cheese, Sheet Iron, R. Smith, Turnbridge, Vt., c.1820, 21 1/2 In. 165.00
Straw Holder, Bloomfield Industries 75.00
String Holder, Apple, Chalkware 43.00
String Holder, Bunch Of Bananas, Chalkware 25.00
String Holder, Cat, Chalkware, Box 60.00
String Holder, Cat, England 45.00
String Holder, Cat, With Scissors 50.00
String Holder, Cat-Snip 45.00
String Holder, Chef 35.00
String Holder, Dog Head 75.00
String Holder, Elephant, Sitting Up 35.00
String Holder, Elsie The Cow's Head 30.00
String Holder, Footed, Brass 95.00
String Holder, Girl In Bonnet 25.00
String Holder, Indian Head 40.00
String Holder, Mammy, Full-Bodied 175.00
String Holder, Mammy, Large Face, Ceramic 395.00
String Holder, Pear, Plums, Plaster 63.00
String Holder, Prayer Lady, Pink 375.00
String Holder, Seal, Nose Up, Green Glaze 60.00
String Holder, Strawberry 21.00
String Holder, Woman Sitting On Chair, Japan 55.00
String Holder, Woman's Head, Art Deco 168.00
String Holder, Woman, Green Dress 50.00
Sugar Nippers, Hand Wrought, Tooled Brass Detail, 10 1/4 In. 160.00
Swizzle Stick, Silver, Swedish Coin Each End 6.00
Swizzle Stick, Zulu, Plastic, On Card 18.00
Tea Cozy, Doll, Wicker Basket, Russia 135.00
Teakettle, Bail Handle, A. Kendrick & Sons, Iron, 2 Pt. 190.00
Teakettle, Griswold, Aluminum, 2 Qt. 70.00
Teakettle, Rice Pattern, Iron, Bronze Lid, 19th Century, 6 1/2 In. 247.50
Teakettle, Wagner Ware, 10 Oz. 115.00
Teakettle, Wagner Ware, No. 8, Aluminum, February 18, 1902, 6 Qt. 25.00
Teapot, Brass Cover, Chrysanthemum Design, Handle, Iron, 18th Century, 8 1/2 In. 132.00
Teapot, Cover, Electric, Chromium Plated Metal, Cane Handle, Bingwerke, 8 In. 975.00
Teapot, Electroplated Metal, Wooden Handle, Hans Ofner, Marked, 5 3/8 In. 595.00
Teapot, Wagner Ware, Colonial, 3 Pt. 50.00
Thermometer, Ice Cream, Puritan, Newark's Famous Ice Cream, c.1920 .... 95.00
Toaster, Excelsior, Hand Crank 200.00
Toaster, Merit Maid, Round 45.00
Toaster, Old Fostoria, No. 80, Plastic 94.00
Toaster, Son-Chief, Box 30.00
Toaster, Sunbeam, Deco 45.00
Toaster, Termax Landers, Frary & Clark, Electric 60.00
Toaster, Willowware 1320.00
Toaster, Wrought Iron, Wooden Handle, Scrolls, 31 In. 27.00
Tray, Cutlery, Cutout Heart, Honey Color, 1830s, 10 3/4 In. 450.00
Tray, Cutlery, Old Varnish, Heart Handle, 19th Century 225.00
Tray, Cutlery, Scalloped Edging, Dovetailed Construction, Flame Birch, 13 1/2 In. 450.00
Tray, Cutlery, Walnut, Dovetailed Design, Pa., 19th Century 325.00
Tray, Cutlery, Walnut, Pennsylvania, 19th Century, 13 3/4 In. 235.00
Trivet, Coffeepot, Griswold, No. 1739 .... 125.00
Trivet, Rooster, Iron, 9 In., Pair 25.00
Trivet, Star, Griswold 35.00

Tube, Pastry, Attachments, Tin, c.1875	75.00
Wafer Iron, Geometric Floral Designs, Cast Iron, 7 1/4 x 5 In.	175.00
Wafer Iron, Griswold, Patent June 29	300.00
Wafer Iron, J. Savery's Sons	150.00
Waffle Iron, Griddle & Fry Pan, Wagner-Ware, Cast Iron Child's, 4 Piece	115.00
Waffle Iron, Griswold No. 0, Cast Iron, Coil Handle	500.00
Waffle Iron, Griswold, No. 6	650.00
Waffle Iron, Griswold, No. 8, 1901	20.00
Waffle Iron, Griswold, No. 8-885, 1908	68.00
Waffle Iron, Griswold, No. 11	160.00
Waffle Iron, Griswold, No. 18, Heart & Star	175.00
Waffle Iron, Simmons	125.00
Waffle Iron, Wagner, No. 9	75.00
Waffle Iron, Winchester, Missing Cord, 8 In. Diam.	346.00
Waffle Iron, Wrought Handles, Iron, 34 In.	27.00
Warming Pan, Brass, Pierced Cover, King's Profile, Iron, 40 In.	287.00
Wash Stick, Weathered Gray Surface, 28 In.	11.00
Washboard, Little Queen	16.00
Washboard, National Washboard Company, No. 9, Signed, Child's	35.00
Washboard, Redware & Manganese, c.1899, 12 x 22 In.	425.00
Washboard, Soap Saver, Cobalt Blue Graniteware	75.00
Washboard, Wooden, Yellowware Insert, Gray Surface, 12 3/4 x 25 In.	55.00
Washboard, Zinc, National Washboard Co., Memphis, Tenn.	20.00
Washtub, Wooden, Legs On Wooden Rollers, Oval	210.00
Water Dispenser, Refrigerator, Royal Blue	12.00
Wringer, Clothes, Model, 1869	250.00
Wringer, Hand, Horseshoe Brand, Salesman's Sample	1500.00

KNIFE collectors usually specialize in a single type. In the 1960s, the United States government passed a law that required knife manufacturers to mark their knives with the country of origin. This seemed to encourage the collectors, and knife collecting became an interest of a large group of people. All types of knives are collected, from top quality twentieth-century examples to old bone- or pearl-handled knives in excellent condition.

Belt, Revolutionary War Era, Double Edge Spear Point, Stag Haft, 5 1/2-In. Blade	245.00
Bowie, Bone & Stag Handle, Crane Cutlery, Sheffield, England, Pre-1900, 6-In. Blade ..	115.00
Bowie, Brock, Sheffield, England, 7 1/2-In. Blade	275.00
Bowie, Confederate, Hand Made, Large Blade	1000.00
Bowie, Engraved Rorkes Drift, Zululand, Spear Point, 1879, 18 1/2 In.	1750.00
Bowie, German Silver, Flat Pommel, Rubber Scales, 7-In. Clip Point Blade, 11 1/2 In.	325.00
Bowie, Mexican War Era, A.E. Ganby, St. Louis, 1840	1800.00
Bowie, Southern & Richardson, Sheffield, England, Civil War, 6 In.	550.00
Bowie, Steel S-Guard, Bone Grip, Steel Pommel, 8-In. Blade, 12 In.	425.00
Butcher, Winchester, Logo, Wooden Handle, 14 In.	42.00
Cutter, Quill, Bone Handle, Blade, 3 3/8 In.	130.00
Dagger, Ornate Nickel Silver Handle	195.00
Folding, E.C. Works, Stag Grips, Brass Guard, 5 3/4-In. Clip Blade, 9 3/4 In.	425.00
Folding, Iron Retaining Spring, Brass Ferrule, Pipe Tamper, Bone Handle, 5 3/4 In.	350.00
Folding, Winchester, No. 1920, Bone Stag Handle, 4-In. Blade, 9 1/4 In.	635.00
Hook Blade, Bone Handle, 3 1/2-In. Blade	125.00
Hunting, George Butler & Co., Stag Horn Handle, 9 1/2-In. Blade	120.00
Hunting, Keen Kutter, Sheath	95.00
Hunting, U.S. Army, 1 Side Honed, Scabbard, 1880	450.00
Jack, Winchester, 2 Blades, Rosewood Handle, Small	135.00
Office, Remington, 2 Blades, Ivory Celluloid Handles	70.00
Patch, Bone Handle, Revolutionary War Era, 2 1/8-In. Blade	165.00
Pocket, Carved Bone Handle, 3 3/8-In. Blade	120.00
Pocket, Chevrolet, 3 1/2 In.	22.00
Pocket, Deer Foot Handle, Leather Sheath, Czechoslovakia, 11 In.	45.00
Pocket, Esso, Gas Pump Shape, Metal, 2 1/2 In.	110.00
Pocket, Esso, Gas Pump Shape, Metal, 3 In.	253.00

Pocket, Ford, Blue & Red, 3 1/2 In. 44.00
Pocket, German Electrician's, Black Walnut Grips, Gray Finish To Blade, 4 3/8 In. 70.00
Pocket, Marilyn Monroe, Nude 30.00
Pocket, Masonic, Marked 45.00
Pocket, Melvin Purvis Secret Operator, Blue Letters, Mother-Of-Pearl-Like Handle 225.00
Pocket, Mickey Mantle, Lists Baseball Statistics, 5 In. 10.00
Pocket, Powder Horn Pattern, Brown Celluloid Handles, Single Blade, 5 In. 145.00
Pocket, Purina 15.00
Pocket, Remington 300.00
Pocket, Schrade-Wostenholm Commemorative Set, 2 Blades, England, Box 55.00
Pocket, Scout, Stag Handles, A.W. Wadsworth 75.00
Pocket, Stag Handle, Blacksmith Made, Early 1800s, 17 In. 395.00
Pocket, Sterling, 2 Blades, Scissors, 1 3/4 In. 85.00
Pocket, Van Cleef & Arpels, 18K Yellow Gold, 2 Round Diamonds, Emerald 800.00
Pocket, Winchester, Swell Hunting Pattern, Blade Folder, Stag Handle, 5 1/2 In. 50.00
Remington, Bullet, Short Punch Blade, No. 4243 .... 895.00
Remington, Faux Mother-Of-Pearl Handle, 1-In. Blade 50.00
Rice, Trowel, Bayonet, U.S. Army, Sheath, 1873 .... 825.00
Sheath, Union Cutlery Co., Brown Handle, Marked KABAR 33.00
Survival, Air Force 250.00
Switch Blade, 1910 .... 250.00
Throwing, Case XX, 1940s 75.00
Trailmaker, Leather Wrapped Handle, Stag Pommel, 15 In. 765.00
Trench, U.S. Army, Sheath, 1917 .... 225.00
Utility, Remington, Box & Papers 20.00

KNOWLES, TAYLOR & KNOWLES items may be found in the Lotus Ware category.

KOREAN WARE, see Sumida.

KOSTA, the oldest Swedish glass factory, was founded in 1742. During
the 1920s through the 1950s, many pieces of original design were
made at the factory. The firm is still working.

KOSTA

Bowl, Figures, Vicke Lindstrand, 1952, 17 1/4 In. 2530.00
Bowl, Free-Form, Lindstrand, 11 In. 60.00
Paperweight, Father, 1971 .... 75.00
Paperweight, Mother, 1970 .... 75.00
Paperweight, Seaweed, Vicke Lindstrand 95.00
Plate, Christmas, 1972, Cobalt Blue, Signed 65.00
Vase, 3 Black Stripes, 2 Opalescent Stripes, 2 x 2 In. 125.00
Vase, Amber, Blue, Signed, 5 In. 99.00
Vase, Applied Trails Of Black, Red, White, Vicke Lindstrand, c.1950, 9 In. 242.00
Vase, Blue, Gray Body, Green Internal Layer, Vicke Lindstrand, 1958, 7 In. 275.00
Vase, Blue, Yellow Design, Flared Lip, Signed, 6 In. 195.50
Vase, Child Skipping, 6 In. 135.00
Vase, Diamond Shape Bubbles, Acid Stamp, Vicke Lindstrand, Hexagonal, 7 In. 220.00
Vase, Etched, Frosted Storks, Signed, 4 In. 45.00
Vase, Flattened Teardrop, Pedestal, Blue Interior, Vicke Lindstrand, c.1963, 6 In. 300.00
Vase, Green Internal Layer, Window Illusion, Vicke Lindstrand, c.1950, 6 1/2 In. 660.00
Vase, Green, Blue Vertical Bands, Bubbles, Pedestal Supported Basin, 10 In. 935.00
Vase, Linear Opaque Dot, Orange, White Ground, Nona Morales, 6 In. 259.00
Vase, Offset Basin, Green, Vicke Lindstrand, 6 In. 231.00
Vase, Pink, Red Enamel Pulled Feather Design, Barbil Vallien, 2 In. 250.00
Vase, Red Pulled Feather Design, Barbil Vallien, 2 In. 65.00
Vase, Smoky Blue, Slanted Rim, Oval, Signed, 4 5/8 In. 285.00
Vase, Squirrel, 5 1/2 x 7 1/2 In. 150.00
Vase, Thick Green, Blue & Clear Layers, Diagonal Lines, 6 In. 450.00
Vase, Vertical Lines Of Opaque White, Amethyst, Vicke Lindstrand, c.1954, 13 In. 253.00
Vase, White Concentric Swag Design, Deep Red Layer, Vicke Lindstrand, 5 In. 330.00
Vase, Winter, Black Trees, Frosted Ground, Vicke Lindstrand, 12 x 5 1/2 In. 3300.00
Vase, Yellow, Blue Rim, Footed, 5 In. 330.00

KPM refers to Berlin porcelain, but the same initials were used alone and in combination with other symbols by several German porcelain makers. They include the Konigliche Porzellan Manufaktur of Berlin, initials used in mark, 1823–1847; Meissen, 1723–1724 only; Krister Porzellan Manufaktur in Waldenburg, after 1831; Kranichfelder Porzellan Manufaktur in Kranichfeld, after 1903; and the Kister Porzellan Manufaktur in Scheibe, after 1838.

KPM

K.P.M

Bowl, Serving, Enamel Foliate Design, Gilt Border, Oval, 15 In.	200.00
Coffee Set, Armorial, Inscription, Baluster, Scroll Handle, 19th Century, 3 Piece	630.00
Dinner Set, Foliate Sprays, Molded Woven Border, Late 19th Century, 59 Piece	1840.00
Figurine, Slave, Young Maiden, Accompanied By Putto, Signed, 12 1/4 In.	575.00
Figurine, White Goose, Landing Position, Wings Up, 6 1/4 In.	95.00
Lithophane, see also Lithophane category.	
Mug, Floral Design	50.00
Plaque, 2 Water Sprites, Artist Signed, Leitz, 5 1/2 x 18 1/2 In.	3300.00
Plaque, 3 Children Crossing Stream, Berlin, 1898, 11 In.	5175.00
Plaque, Banishment Of Ishmael & Hagar, Berlin, 15 x 12 In.	4600.00
Plaque, Beer Drinker, Playing French Horn, Hand Painted, Signed, Marked, 8 In.	440.00
Plaque, Birth Of Venus, Rolling On Wave, Berlin, Late 19th Century, 7 3/4 x 13 In.	4600.00
Plaque, Bust Of Woman, Oval, Signed Wagner, 9 x 6 In.	4250.00
Plaque, Christ, Crown Of Thorns, Marked, 9 1/4 x 7 1/2 In.	1265.00
Plaque, Madonna & Child, Walther, Signed, 13 x 7 7/8 In.	1955.00
Plaque, Madonna Della Sistina, 10 x 7 1/2 In.	1495.00
Plaque, Maid In Bulrushes, Impressed Mark, 1900, 9 3/4 In.	3105.00
Plaque, Man, Sharpening His Pen, 12 x 10 In.	5060.00
Plaque, Marguerite, Daisies In Hair, Wagner, 9 1/2 x 6 1/2 In. . . . . *Illus*	6710.00
Plaque, Nude Maiden, Horse, Gold Frame, Marked, 12 x 16 In.	3300.00
Plaque, Penitent Mary Magdalene, Signed, c.1854, 10 1/4 x 15 3/4 In.	5175.00
Plaque, Portrait Of Lady, Oval, E. Volk, 9 x 6 3/4 In.	5175.00
Plaque, Portrait, Mother & Child, Porcelain, L.R. Wagner, c.1900, 4 In.	4950.00
Plaque, Portrait, Young Maiden, Plain White Headdress, Floral Gown, Marked, 11 In. . . .	1725.00
Plaque, Portrait, Young Prince, Blue, Black Hat, Ostrich Plume, Marked, 13 1/4 In.	4025.00
Plaque, Semi-Nude Huntress, Quiver Of Arrows, Reclining On Lion, Signed, 8 3/4 In. . .	6325.00
Plaque, The Rake, Gilded Frame, 13 x 10 3/4 In.	105.00
Plaque, Thread Of Life, 3 Fates, Berlin, 1870s, 9 1/2 x 6 1/4 In.	4025.00
Plaque, Viking Scene, R. Wagner, 10 1/2 x 12 1/2 In. . . . . *Illus*	3190.00
Plaque, Virgin Mary, Signed, Late 19th Century, 15 1/2 x 13 1/4 In.	3737.00
Plaque, Woman, Amidst A Den Of Lions, Marked, Late 19th Century, 9 1/4 x 6 1/4 In. . .	2185.00
Plaque, Woman, Profile, After Paul Thumann	862.00
Plaque, Young Maiden, After Bodenhauer, Impressed Mark, 12 x 6 In.	1495.00
Plaque, Young Maiden, Flowers In Hair, Signed, Late 19th Century, 11 1/2 x 9 In.	9200.00
Plaque, Young Woman, Daisies In Hair, Signed Wagner, 9 x 6 In.	6710.00

Above: KPM, Plaque, Viking Scene, R. Wagner, 10 1/2 x 12 1/2 In.

Left: KPM, Plaque, Marguerite, Daisies In Hair, Wagner, 9 1/2 x 6 1/2 In.

Platter, German Crest, Gilt Borders, Mahogany Bamboo Turned Stand, 21 In. 630.00
Sugar, Roses, Gold Design, Signed 45.00
Vase, Floral Designs, Ram's Head Handles, 7 In. 350.00
Vase, Floral Sprays, Turquoise Glazed Ground, Ram's Head Handles, 7 In., Pair 700.00
Vase, Tapered, 2 Women With Floral Garland, Gilt Floral Motif, Wagner, 20 In. 4255.00

KU KLUX KLAN items are now collected because of their historic
importance. Literature, robes, and memorabilia are available. The Klan
is still in existence, so new material is found.

Advertising, Movie, Both Sides Printed, 1920, 6 x 18 In. 115.00
Coin, 1922 . . . .   45.00
Figure, Bullfrog, Raised KKK Letters On Back, Iron, 2 1/2 In. 400.00
Hand Mirror, Photo 15.00
Jug, Brown Glaze, Klansman, Invisible Empire, Pottery, 5 1/2 In. 450.00
Magazine, World's Work, Why Klan Fights Smith, Jan. 1928, 7 x 9 1/2 In. 75.00
Medallion, Convention, May 11, 1907, Bristol, Tenn. 100.00
Medallion, Member In Good Standing, Michigan, 1919 . . . .   125.00
Photograph, Rally, Panoramic View, 1923 . . . .   415.00
Pin, KKK, Red, White Ground, Celluloid, 7/8 In. 66.00
Plate, Klansman On Horse, Red, White & Blue Border, Gilt, 1866, 6 In. 125.00
Postcard, Photograph, High School Students, Float, Hanford, Cal., 1920s 175.00
Postcard, Sepia Photograph, Coming Out Parade, Milo, Maine, 1923 . . . .   200.00
Sheet Music, Bright Fiery Cross, Our Song, 1913, 9 3/8 x 12 1/4 In. 165.00
Sheet Music, Ku Klux Klan Steppin' Blues, Klansmen On Horses, 1938 . . . .   165.00
Sheet Music, March Of The Klansmen, City Street, World War II Soldier, 1925 . . . .   165.00
Spinner, Brass, Red & Black Enameled, Burning Cross 100.00
Token, Honor, Imperial Symbol, Duty 60.00

KUTANI ware is a Japanese porcelain made after the mid-seventeenth
century. Most of the pieces found today are nineteenth-century.
Collectors often use the term *kutani* to refer to just the later, colorful
pieces decorated with red, gold, and black pictures of warriors, animals, and birds.

Bowl, Blooming Chrysanthemums, Blue Key Fret Border, Green Ground, 9 5/8 In. 172.00
Bowl, Geisha, Medallions, 1900, 6 1/2 In. 220.00
Bowl, Geishas, 1900, 13 In. 500.00
Bowl, Peacock, Peony, Pine Design, Rust Red, Meiji Period, 8 1/4 In. 121.00
Candlestick, Peony Design, Shishi, 9 In. 132.00
Dessert Set, Gilt & Dragon Design, 24 Piece 80.00
Pitcher, Six Scenic Medallions, 1885-1990, 3 1/4 In. 115.00
Tea Set, Bird, Bamboo Design, 19 Piece 357.50
Tureen, Cover, Rust Red, White Hawk On Cover, 14 1/2 In. 522.50
Vase, Daikoku, Karako Design, Pear Shape, Fuku Mark On Base, 13 In. 577.50
Vase, Dragon, Phoenix Design, Rust Red, Brocade Ground, Meiji Period, 18 In. 687.50
Vase, Floral Design, Rust Red, Marked, 8 In. 165.00

LACQUER is a type of varnish. Collectors are most interested in the
Chinese and Japanese lacquer wares made from the Japanese varnish
tree. Lacquer wares are made from wood with many coats of lacquer.
Sometimes the piece is carved or decorated with ivory or metal inlay.

Bottle, Snuff, Flattened Bell, Landscape Design, Malachite Stopper, Burgaute, 2 In. 120.00
Box, 2 Birds, Flying, Church Landscape, Seber, Russia, 5 1/2 x 6 1/2 In. 172.00
Box, 3 Peasants, Snowy Village Landscape, Mstera, Russia, 5 3/4 x 7 1/4 In. 115.00
Box, Cover, Black, Gold, Rookery, Fern Design, Meiji Period, 5 3/4 In. 605.00
Box, Gold, Ho Bird Design, Mashiji Ground, 19th Century, 5 1/4 In. 2530.00
Box, Gold, Letter, With Interior Tray, Pine Trees On Cover, 19th Century, 5 1/2 In. 935.00
Box, Peasant, With Peacock, Rural Landscape, Mstera, Russia, 6 1/2 x 6 1/2 In. 172.00
Box, Princess, Old Man, Exotic Temple Landscape, Russia, 10 1/4 x 6 In. 161.00
Box, Seal Paste, Phoenix, Paulownia Design, Black, Gold, Circular, 3 1/4 In. 143.00
Box, Tortoise, Wave Design, Black, Gold, Rectangular, 13 x 2 7/8 In. 44.00
Chest, Jewel, Black, Gold, Mother-Of-Pearl Inlay, Kingfisher, Lotus Design, 11 In. 231.00
Comb, Gold, Landscape, Brocade Design, Meiji Period, 4 In. 143.00
Comb, Gold, Maple Leaf, Butterfly Design, Meiji Period 440.00

Panel, Court Scenes, Grapevine Surround, Black, Converted Table, China, 27 x 67 In. 805.00
Sake Cup, Red, Gold, Chrysanthemum Design, 3 1/2 In. 275.00
Tray, On Wood, Gold, Fruit, Leaf Design, Circular, 14 1/2 In. 110.00
Tray, Serving, Bird, Prunus Design, Heart Shape, Gold, Wood, 10 3/4 In. 66.00

LADY HEAD VASE, see Head Vase.

LALIQUE glass was made by Rene Lalique in Paris, France, between the 1890s and his death in 1945. The glass was molded, pressed, and engraved in Art Nouveau and Art Deco styles. Pieces were marked with the signature *R. Lalique*. Lalique glass is still being made. Pieces made after 1945 bear the mark *Lalique*. Jewelry made by Rene Lalique is listed in the Jewelry category.

LALique

Ashtray, Cannes, 7 1/2 In. 120.00
Ashtray, Figural, Turkey, Dindon 325.00
Atomizer, Le Provencal, Molded Frieze, Dancing, Nudes, c.1929, 5 3/8 In. 920.00
Bonbon, Cyprins, School Of Swimming Carp, Gray Cover, Signed, 1921, 10 In. 2875.00
Bowl, Bacchantes, Clear & Frosted, Nude Females In Relief, Signed, 9 3/4 In. 4312.00
Bowl, Campanules, Graduated Horizontal Rows Of Tulips, Pink, Gray, 1932, 9 In. 1725.00
Bowl, Muguet, Lilies Of The Valley & Leafage, Signed, 12 In. 1092.00
Bowl, Nemours, Diminishing Rows Of Flower Blossoms, Signed, 4 x 10 In. 575.00
Bowl, Persepolis, Applied Stylized Floral Motifs, Signed, 7 1/2 In. 2645.00
Bowl, Shallow, Frosted Fish On Bottom, 6 1/4 In. 325.00
Bowl, Three Gazelles Prancing Amid Foliage, Opalescent, Signed, c.1925, 11 1/2 In. 1380.00
Bowl, Vases No. 1, Frosted Stylized Bouquets, Clear Urns, Signed, 3 1/4 In. 230.00
Bowl, Volubilis, No. 383, Yellow, 8 1/2 In. 200.00
Box, Cover, Primeveres, Floret Clusters, Frosted, Floret Handle Cover, Round, 6 x 4 In. . 850.00
Chandelier, Deux Sirenes, Two Sirens, Frosted Ceiling Cap, Signed, c.1921, 13 In. 10120.00
Chandelier, Masques, Four Masks, Brown Patina, Gray Glass, 1913, 18 In. 11500.00
Figurine, Caroline, Turtle, 1 3/4 In. 325.00
Figurine, Deux Poissons, 2 Fish, 11 1/2 In. 1265.00
Figurine, Gregoire, Frog, Green, 4 In. 325.00
Figurine, Luxembourg, 3 Cherubs, Holding Floral Swags, Signed, 8 In. 1955.00
Figurine, Moyenne Voilee, Female Bearing Wine Glass, Signed, Case, 1913, 5 1/2 In. ... 1955.00
Figurine, Salamandre, Salamander, Green, 7 1/2 In. 250.00
Figurine, Seated Nude, Frosted, Signed, 3 1/4 In. 103.50
Hood Ornament, Eagle 375.00
Hood Ornament, Rooster 475.00
Hood Ornament, Tete D'Epervier, Head Of Hawk, Chrome Holder, Signed, 2 1/2 In. .. 517.50
Hood Ornament, Vitesse, Kneeling Nude, 7 In. 7000.00
Hood Ornament, Vitesse, Nude Maiden, 1929, 7 1/4 In. 4025.00
Lamp, Hanging, St. Vincent, Silk Suspension Cords, Signed, 1920s, 25 x 14 In. 6500.00
Mirror, Eglantines, 6 Bronze Sections, Wild Roses, Thorny Branches, 1921, 17 In. 5175.00
Mirror, Narcisse Couche, Dressing Table, Male Nude Above Handle, Signed, 12 In. 977.00
Paperweight, Bison, 5 In. ....130.00 to 295.00
Paperweight, Elephant, Signed, 6 1/4 In. 258.00
Paperweight, Moineau Fier, Seated Sparrow, Signed, 1929, 3 1/4 In., Pair 575.00

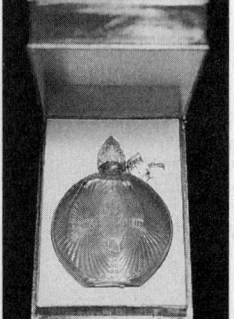

Dust mites are the subject of many articles today. The more humid the environment the more quickly they multiply. Dust mites eat dust particles, then will turn to paints and glazing materials on wooden pieces. The only way to avoid damage is to clean regularly.

Lalique, Perfume Bottle, Sergy
Ribbon, Stopper, Box

Paperweight, Tete D'aigle, Eagle Head, 5 1/2 In. 300.00
Pendant, Molded Acorn, Gilt Metal Cap, Frosted, 1 1/2 In. 489.00
Perfume Bottle, 4 Different Masks, Urn Form, 4 In. 1300.00
Perfume Bottle, Ambre, Draped Women In Corners, Square, 5 1/4 In. 1380.00
Perfume Bottle, Apple, Maison, 5 In. Diam. 405.00
Perfume Bottle, Bouchon Mures, Black Ribbing, Tiara Stopper, Signed, 5 1/2 In. 200.00
Perfume Bottle, Camille, 1932, 2 1/4 In. 1250.00
Perfume Bottle, Cinq Fleur, Clear & Frosted, Allover Molded Flowers, 1924, 4 In. 540.00
Perfume Bottle, Coty, Ambre Antique, Female Figures, 5 1/2 In. 488.00
Perfume Bottle, Cylindrique Fleurs, Clear, Frosted, Molded Floral, Atomizer, 1923 .... 475.00
Perfume Bottle, Duncan, 8 In. 275.00
Perfume Bottle, Epines, Signed, 1932 ....825.00 to 1395.00
Perfume Bottle, Hobnail, Black Tips, Round, France, 3 3/4 In. 325.00
Perfume Bottle, Lalique Worth France Molded In Base, 4 3/8 In. 100.00
Perfume Bottle, Molded Floral Garlands, Pierced Heart Form, 6 In. 920.00
Perfume Bottle, Molded With A Woman Smelling A Flower, Rectangular, 5 1/2 In. 5750.00
Perfume Bottle, Salamandres, Curving Lizards, Signed, 3 3/4 In. 1495.00
Perfume Bottle, Sergy Ribbon, Stopper, Box ....*Illus* 4675.00
Plate, Annual, 1968 .... 68.00
Plate, Dream Rose, Box, 1966, 8 1/2 In. 66.00
Plate, Figurine Et Fleurs, Nude Woman Amid Flowers, Amber, Signed, 7 In., 6 Piece ... 1100.00
Tray, Ring, Centennial 160.00
Vase, Actinia, Swirls, Signed, 8 1/2 In. 2200.00
Vase, Aigrettes, Flock Of Swooping Egrets, Bulrushes, Signed, 1926, 9 3/4 In. 2875.00
Vase, Avallon, Birds Perched On Fruiting Branches, Cylindrical, 1927, 6 In. 1265.00
Vase, Bacchantes, Dancing Nude Maidens, Signed, 1927, 9 5/8 In. 4600.00
Vase, Bacchantes, Frieze Of Cavorting Nude Maidens, Signed, 1927, 9 1/2 In. 4600.00
Vase, Baies, Branches Of Berries, Brown Enamel, Signed, 1924, 10 1/2 In. 8625.00
Vase, Borromee, Rows Of Peacock Heads, Signed, 1928, 9 1/4 In. 6900.00
Vase, Camaret, Four Rings Of Fish, Traces Of Blue, Signed, 1928, 5 3/8 In. 575.00
Vase, Chardon, Thistle Plant Design, Frosted, Red, Rounded Shoulder, 8 1/2 In. 6900.00
Vase, Dampierre, 4 7/8 In. 200.00
Vase, Domremy, Signed, 1926, 8 1/2 In. 2000.00
Vase, Domremy, Two Rows Of Thistle Form Blossoms, Signed, 1926, 8 1/2 In. 1495.00
Vase, Eglantines, Thorny Branches, Rose Blossoms, Signed, 4 1/2 In. 402.50
Vase, Ferrieres, 5 Rings Of Flowers, White Patina, Green, 1929, 6 3/4 In. 2645.00
Vase, Lagamar, Six Bands Of Geometric Devices, Enamel, Signed, 1926, 7 3/8 In. 6325.00
Vase, Lobelia, Flared Rim, Embossed Fern Fronds, Opalescent, 8 1/4 x 4 In. 165.00
Vase, Marisa, Fish, Green Patina, Clear & Frosted 2760.00
Vase, Montargis, Fern Fronds Spiraling From Neck, Signed, 1929, 8 1/8 In. 1725.00
Vase, Oran, Dahlias & Leafage, Signed, 1927, 10 1/4 In. 9430.00
Vase, Ormeaux, Frosted, Overlapping Leaves, Narrow Neck, Signed, 6 1/2 x 6 In. 850.00
Vase, Perruches, Pairs Of Lovebirds, Branches, Blue, Signed, 1919, 10 In. 11500.00
Vase, Perruches, Pairs Of Lovebirds, Leafy Branches, Gray, Signed, 1919, 10 In. 2875.00
Vase, Piriac, Fish Swimming Among Waves, Blue, Signed, 1930, 7 1/2 In. .....2070.00 to 2990.00
Vase, Raisins, Curved Branches, Blown-Out Berry Clusters, Frosted, 6 x 4 In. 700.00
Vase, Ronces, Thorns, White Opalescent Case, 9 1/8 In. 700.00
Vase, Ronces, Thorny Branches, Signed, 1921, 9 In. 2875.00
Vase, Sauterelles, Crickets Perched On Blades Of Grass, Signed, 1913, 10 3/4 In. 1955.00
Vase, Sauterelles, Grasshoppers Perched On Reeds, Blue, Green Patina, 1912, 11 In. 2760.00
Vase, Tulipes, Tulips On Stems, Closed Flower Heads, Signed, 1927, 8 1/8 In. 1035.00
Vase, Versailles, Clear & Frosted, 1939 .... 2300.00
Vase, Violettes, Violet Leaves Around Flaring Rim, Signed, 1921, 6 1/4 In. 230.00

LAMPS of every type, from the early oil-burning Betty and Phoebe lamps to the recent electric lamps with glass or beaded shades, interest collectors. Fuels used in lamps changed through the years; whale oil (1800–1840), camphene (1828), Argand (1830), lard (1833–1863), turpentine and alcohol (1840s), gas (1850–1879), kerosene (1860), and electricity (1879) are the most common. Other lamps are listed by manufacturer or type of material.

    Akari, Isamu Noguchi, Bamboo, 4 Sided Shade & Freeflowing Paper Sheets, 66 In. 465.00
    Aladdin, B-12, Colonial, Clear, All Original 150.00

Aladdin, B-26, Simplicity, Alacite, Decalmania, 1948-1953 .... 430.00
Aladdin, B-27, Simplicity, Gold Luster, Alacite, 1948-1953 .... 275.00
Aladdin, B-30, Simplicity, White, 1948-1953 .... 95.00
Aladdin, B-47, Washington Drape, Bell, Clear Stem, 1940-1941 .... 180.00
Aladdin, B-52, Washington Drape, Filigree Stem, Amber, 1940 .... 125.00
Aladdin, B-53, Washington Drape, Plain Stem, Clear, 1940-1948 .... 90.00
Aladdin, B-55, Washington Drape, Plain Stem, Amber, 1940-1942 ....90.00 to 140.00
Aladdin, B-60, Lincoln Drape, Alacite, 1939 .... 600.00
Aladdin, B-61, Short Lincoln Drape, Transparent Amber, 1939 .... 5000.00
Aladdin, B-70, Solitaire, White Moonstone, 1938 .... 3500.00
Aladdin, B-75, Tall Lincoln Drape, Alacite, Old Formula, 1940-1949 .... 160.00
Aladdin, B-80, Beehive, Clear Crystal, 1937-1938 .... 100.00
Aladdin, B-81, Beehive, Green, 1937-1938 .... 140.00
Aladdin, B-82D, Beehive, Amber, Dark, 1937-1938 ....170.00 to 190.00
Aladdin, B-82L, Beehive, Amber, Light, 1937-1938 .... 150.00
Aladdin, B-83, Beehive, Ruby Crystal, 1937 .... 495.00
Aladdin, B-83, Beehive, Ruby, 1937-1938 ....485.00 to 575.00
Aladdin, B-85, Quilt, White Moonstone, 1937 .... 325.00
Aladdin, B-87, Vertique, Rose Moonstone, 1938 .... 220.00
Aladdin, B-88, Vertique, Yellow Moonstone, 1938 ....550.00 to 575.00
Aladdin, B-90, Quilt, White Moonstone Font, Black Moonstone Foot, 1937 .... 350.00
Aladdin, B-91, Quilt, White Moonstone Font, Rose Moonstone Foot, 1937 ......300.00 to 375.00
Aladdin, B-92, Vertique, Green Moonstone, 1938 .... 350.00
Aladdin, B-93, Vertique, White Moonstone, 1938 .... 1200.00
Aladdin, B-96, Green, White Moonstone, 1937-1939 .... 375.00
Aladdin, B-101, Corinthian, Amber, 1935-1936 .... 130.00
Aladdin, B-102, Corinthian, Green, 1935-1936 .... 200.00
Aladdin, B-104, Corinthian, Clear, Black Foot, 1935-1936 .... 135.00
Aladdin, B-105, Colonial, Green, Table, 1933 .... 170.00
Aladdin, B-106, Colonial, Amber, Table, 1933 .... 170.00
Aladdin, B-111, Cathedral, Green Moonstone, 1934-1935 .... 275.00
Aladdin, B-112, Cathedral, Rose Moonstone, 1934-1935 .... 310.00
Aladdin, B-115, Corinthian, Green Moonstone, Jade, 1935-1936 .... 175.00
Aladdin, B-115, Corinthian, Green Moonstone, Pastel, 1935-1936 .... 215.00
Aladdin, B-116, Corinthian, Rose Moonstone, 1935-1936 ....210.00 to 295.00
Aladdin, B-120, Majestic, White Moonstone, 1935-1936 .... 180.00
Aladdin, B-121, Majestic, Rose Moonstone, 1935-1936 .... 500.00
Aladdin, B-124, Corinthian, White Moonstone Font, Black Moonstone Foot, 1935-1936 . 300.00
Aladdin, B-125, Corinthian, White Moonstone Font, Green Foot, c.1935 ....190.00 to 225.00
Aladdin, B-126, Corinthian, White Moonstone Font, Rose Foot, 1935-1936 .... 345.00
Aladdin, C-I, Hobnail 125.00
Aladdin, Double Candelabra, Electric 65.00
Aladdin, E-310, Green Vase, Straw Pattern 100.00
Aladdin, G-15, Boudoir, 1939 .... 120.00
Aladdin, G-24, Cupid, Alacite 195.00
Aladdin, G-33, Boudoir, Alacite, Pink 40.00
Aladdin, G-35, Boudoir, Alacite 50.00
Aladdin, G-36, Wreath Finial 115.00
Aladdin, G-65, Opalique Etched 90.00
Aladdin, G-66, Wreath Finial, Amber 70.00
Aladdin, G-202, Alacite, Student 65.00
Aladdin, G-282, Alacite, Table 55.00
Aladdin, G-311, Alacite, Table 55.00
Aladdin, G-315, Alacite, Table 85.00
Aladdin, G-333, Gray, Finials, Pair 165.00
Aladdin, G-375, Urn, Dancing Ladies 1100.00
Aladdin, No. 1254, Model B, Bronze & Gold, Floor, 1933-1935 .... 260.00
Aladdin, Nu-Lite, Model B, Honeycomb, Fluted Base, 23 In. 95.00
Aladdin, Planter, Alacite 125.00
Aladdin, Prince Edward, Opaque Green, Drilled, 9 1/2 In. 240.00
Aladdin, Prince Edward, Opaque White, 9 In. 460.00
Aladdin, Prince Edward, Pink Font, Clear Stem, 10 In. 870.00
Aladdin, Princess Feather, Opaque Green, 9 1/2 In. 890.00

Aladdin, Urn, Dancing Ladies 1150.00
Aladdin, V-116 .... 230.00
Argand, 2-Light, Pierced Foliate Edge, Blossom Form Arms, Frosted Shades, 20 In. 1450.00
Argand, Blown Glass, Green Latticinio, Metal Arms Terminating In Globes 195.00
Argand, Bronze, Label, Early 19th Century, 14 3/4 In. 450.00
Argand, Bronze, Urn Form Font, Greek Key Border, Foliate Support, Electrified, 32 In. . 905.00
Astral, Brass, Corinthian, Stepped Marble Base, Prisms, 29 3/4 In. 795.00
Astral, Brass, White Marble, Stepped Base, Blossom Form Shade, 19 In. 1090.00
Astral, Columnar, Blossom Form Shade, Etched Glass, Cut Prisms, Electrified, 30 In. ... 3145.00
Astral, Etched Glass Shade, Knopped Standard, Marble Base, c.1850, 29 1/2 In. 1330.00
Astral, Geometric, Floral Design, Silver Plated Column, Square Base, Electrified, 29 In. . 1400.00
Astral, Gilded Brass, Stepped Black Onyx Base, Cut Prisms, Electrified, 25 In. 80.00
Astral, Gilt Brass, Acid Etched Shade, Foliate, Stepped Marble Base, 23 In. 460.00
Astral, Gilt Brass, Blue Rim, Acid Etched Shade, Electrified, Cornelius & Co., 24 In. ... 630.00
Astral, Gilt Metal, Tapered Crest, Foliate Edge Base, White Marble Plinth, 47 In. 1695.00
Astral, Wheel Cut & Acid Finish Shade, 19th Century, 26 3/8 In. 460.00
Betty, On Stand, Tin, White Paint, Decoupage Top, Hanger, 11 In. 465.00
Betty, Open Font, Wrought Iron 100.00
Betty, Scrolled Adjustment Handle, Twisted Hook 135.00
Betty, Tin, Pan & Handle Base, Wick Pick On Chain, 7 1/4 In. 220.00
Betty, Wrought Iron, Bird Finial On Lid, Twisted Hanger, 4 In. 148.50
Betty, Wrought Iron, Heart Finial, Swivel Lid, Twisted Hanger, 4 1/4 In. 110.00
Betty, Wrought Iron, Heart Shape, Lid, Hanger, Pick, 1790 .... 150.00
Betty, Wrought Iron, Pear Shape, Hanger, Pick, 1790 .... 125.00
Bouillotte, 2 Candle Holders, Adjustable Tole Shade, France, 19th Century, 19 In. 1210.00
Bradley & Hubbard lamps are included in the Bradley & Hubbard category.
Candelabrum, 4-Light, Pendant Crystals, 23 In., Pair 700.00
Candelabrum, 5-Light, Foliate Design, Brass, 18 1/4 In., Pair 412.00
Candelabrum, 6-Light, Bronze, Putto Raising Cornucopia, Socle Base, 25 In. 544.50
Candelabrum, 6-Light, Charles X style, Bronze, Gilt, 19th Century, Pair 2185.00
Candelabrum, 6-Light, Napoleon III, Winged Victory Support, Bronze, 30 In. 1840.00
Candelabrum, 6-Light, Pricket Sticks, Swags, Pinecone Finial, Iron, 21 In., Pair 3737.00
Candelabrum, Brass, Georgian, Pair 315.00
Candelabrum, Curved Tapering Arms, Pewter, Electrified, G. Gareaiu, c.1928, 43 In. 6900.00
Candelabrum, Empire, Gilt & Patinated Metal 285.00
Candle, Night-Light, Crystal Cut Glass Insert, Hanging From Brass Base, France, 11 In. . 225.00
Chandelier, 3-Light, Etruscan Revival, Bronze, Cornelius & Baker, 1850s 2645.00
Chandelier, 3-Light, Iron, Brass, Electrified 55.00
Chandelier, 4-Light, Gas, 3 Classical Female Allegorical Figures, Bronze, 44 In. 4355.00
Chandelier, 5-Light, Georgian Style, Cut Glass, Curved Arms, Hung With Drops, 18 In. . 170.00
Chandelier, 5-Light, Silver Bronze, Early 19th Century 7150.00
Chandelier, 6-Light, Baluster, Floral Motif, 3-Tiered Finial, Golden Pine Cone, 25 In. ... 515.00
Chandelier, 6-Light, Brass, Early 19th Century, 27 In. 495.00
Chandelier, 6-Light, Candle, Gilt Frame, Clear & Amber Beads, 22 In. 700.00
Chandelier, 6-Light, Detachable Arms, Brass, 13 x 17 In. 1750.00
Chandelier, 6-Light, Empire Style, Flambeau Supports, Electrified, 24 x 23 In., Pair 1450.00
Chandelier, 6-Light, Enamel Floral & Foliate, Wrought Iron, 18 x 21 In. 80.00
Chandelier, 6-Light, Frosted Glass Globe, Art Deco, Electrified, France, 38 x 19 In. 2300.00
Chandelier, 6-Light, Louis XV Style, Gilt Metal & Crystal 1840.00
Chandelier, 6-Light, Neoclassical Style, Baltic, Curved Ormolu Sprays, 44 In. 18400.00
Chandelier, 6-Light, Neoclassical, Painted & Gilt Metal 1090.00
Chandelier, 6-Light, Victorian Style, 2 Tiers, Scrolled Design, Glass Mounted, 24 In. ... 1265.00
Chandelier, 6-Light, Wrought Iron, Hand Painted 302.50
Chandelier, 7-Light, Biedermeier Style, Cut Glass, Circular Corona, 41 In. 3735.00
Chandelier, 8-Light, 3 Putti Above Scrolling Gilt Bronze Arms, 38 x 26 In. 5300.00
Chandelier, 8-Light, Bronze, Gold Fabric Shade, Crystal Spears, France, 4 x 4 Ft. 9500.00
Chandelier, 8-Light, Candle Nozzles, Brass, Dutch, 19th Century, 32 In. 1725.00
Chandelier, 8-Light, Charles X, Ormolu, Stylized Anthemions, 35 In. 14950.00
Chandelier, 8-Light, Neoclassical, Painted Metal, Crystal, Prisms 805.00
Chandelier, 9-Light, Marble, Gilt Metal, Acanthus Form Corona, Scrolled Arms 1450.00
Chandelier, 10-Light, Neoclassical, Scalloped Tier, Cusped Skirt, Russia, 36 In. 6325.00
Chandelier, 10-Light, Ormolu Floral & Scrolling Vine, 1880s, 36 x 32 In. 495.00
Chandelier, 11-Light, George III, Giltwood, Late 18th Century 6900.00

Chandelier, 12-Light, Bronze, Crystal Beaded Basket, Flower Lights, France, 50 In. 7500.00
Chandelier, 12-Light, Louis XV Style, Ormolu, Cut Glass, Floral Sprays, 47 In., Pair ... 17250.00
Chandelier, 12-Light, Neoclassical, Ormolu, Collar Support, Sweden 4312.00
Chandelier, 24-Light, Gothic Foliage, Brass, 40 In. Diam. 2185.00
Chandelier, Anthemion Corona, S-Scrolled Chains, Winged Female, Bronze, 31 In. .. 4310.00
Chandelier, Canopied, Bronze, Leaded Glass, 36 x 36 In. 5500.00
Chandelier, Duffner & Kimberly, Leaded Glass, Pink & Red Slag Flowers, 30 In. 5775.00
Chandelier, Frosted Opalescent Shade, Pink Ruffled Rim, Scroll Frame, 26 In. 520.00
Chandelier, Neoclassical Style, Gilt Bronze, Carved Alabaster 7185.00
Chandelier, Peasant Form, Holding Lantern, Hardwood, Painted, Antlers, Austria, 26 In. . 4475.00
Chandelier, Slag Glass, Oak, Arts & Crafts 978.00
Electric, 2 Discs On Standard, Circular Base, Plaster-Of-Paris, White, 28 In. 1840.00
Electric, 3 Playful Cupids, Triangular Greek Key Base, Green, Gold Floral Vines, 20 In. . 235.00
Electric, 4 Arched Metal Leaf Lights, Hexagonal Lantern, Art Deco, 21 In. 450.00
Electric, Anheuser-Busch, Hanging, Rectangular, 1960s, Pair 160.00
Electric, Art Deco, Aquarium, Glass Block .... .95.00 to 250.00
Electric, Art Deco, Black Iron Leaping Woman, In Front Of Fiberglass Shade, 16 In. ... 195.00
Electric, Art Deco, Floral Design On Frosted Glass Shade, Brass Base, 17 In. 247.00
Electric, Art Deco, Frosted Glass, Pierrot, 11 In. 95.00
Electric, Art Deco, Mermaid, Bearing Fish, Bronze, c.1925, 43 In. 6900.00
Electric, Art Deco, Nude Woman Base, Chrome 40.00
Electric, Art Deco, Rembrandt, Bronze, 60 In. 135.00
Electric, Art Deco, Torchere, Chrome Reflector, Gold Flecked Glass Rod, 14 In., Pair ... 990.00
Electric, Art Deco, Woman, Kneeling, Multicolored Geometric Ball Above Head 375.00
Electric, Art Glass, 4-Sided Glass Column, Multicolor Geometric Patterns, 50 In. 1210.00
Electric, Art Nouveau, Banister, Figural, Classic Woman, Standing, 18 1/2 In. 750.00
Electric, Art Nouveau, Maiden, Wheel Shade, Bronze, 23 In. 1695.00
Electric, Banquet, Corinthian Column, Cranberry Font, Not Drilled, 33 In. 410.00
Electric, Bent Panel, Bronze Metal Shade, Green, White Slag Glass, 23 In. 630.00
Electric, Bigelow, Rose Blossom Shade, Leaded Glass Dome, Boston, 12 In. 5750.00
Electric, Blown Glass, Woman Shape, Clear, Amethyst, Gold Flecks, No Shade, 24 In. .. 40.00
Electric, Blue Glass, Frosted, Enameled Floral, 12 1/4 In. 395.00
Electric, Bowl Of Tendrils, Berries, Alabaster Shade, Wrought Iron, 1925, 16 3/4 In. ... 8625.00
Electric, Brass Standard, Applied Porcelain Vines, Victorian Style, 64 In. 750.00
Electric, Brass, Green Marble Rings At Base, Pair 30.00
Electric, Brass, Iron Carriage, Convex Front Lens, Flat Beveled Lens, 20 1/2 In. 725.00
Electric, Brass, Temple Bell Form, Stylized Animal Handle, Southeast Asian, 37 In. 55.00
Electric, Bronze, Empire Style, Ormolu, Leaf-Tip Baluster, Marble Base, 31 In. 3735.00
Electric, Bronze, Fluted Columns, Stepped White Marble Base, 30 In. 3390.00
Electric, Bronze, Owl's Head, Paperweight Eyes Light Up, Polychromed Leather, 7 In. .. 950.00
Electric, Budweiser, Clydesdale Horse Team & Wagon, Plastic, 15 x 10 In. 54.00
Electric, Bulldog, Animals Standing By Tree, Cold Painted White Metal, 15 In. 1265.00
Electric, Cathedral, Slag Glass, Yellow, Blue, 28 In. 3025.00
Electric, Ceiling, Domed, Carved Angels, Alabaster 275.00
Electric, Ceiling, Frosted Glass Panels, Floral & Grape Design, Brass Trim 137.00
Electric, Ceiling, Multicolored Metal Rods, Shade, 3 Frosted Glass, 1950, 21 x 39 In. ... 715.00
Electric, Cincinnati Artistic Wrought Iron Works, Leaf Shade, Bronze Trunk, 25 In. 3025.00
Electric, Cornelius & Co., Tin Column & Font, Marble Base, Brown Japanning, 12 In. .. 50.00
Electric, Cut Crystal, Onion Dome Form, Cane Pattern, Wheel Cut Flowers, 29 In. 2662.00
Electric, Cut Glass, Cast Stand, Vesica Form, 9 x 3 1/2 In., Pair 1100.00
Electric, Cut Glass, Domed Shade, Pinwheel Center, Cut Prisms, 20 In. 860.00
Electric, Desk, Copper, Tortoiseshell Shade, 9 In. 375.00
Electric, Desk, Metal, Flat Gooseneck, Signed Quezal Shade 165.00
Electric, Dirk Van Erp, Copper, Mica Shade 2395.00
Electric, Duffner & Kimberly, Colonial, White, Amber, Green Panels, 23 In. 8050.00
Electric, Duffner & Kimberly, Lead Shade, Orange, Yellow Shell Forms, 23 In. 11500.00
Electric, Duffner & Kimberly, Olive Green, Granite White Columns, 24 In. 4885.00
Electric, Edison Mazda, Tin, Painted 105.00
Electric, Emeralite, Stenographer's Model, Adjustable Arm, Desk Clamp 450.00
Electric, Empire Style, Ormolu, Baluster Shape Stem, Green Tole Shade, Pair 2070.00
Electric, Figural, Alabaster, Marble, Woman Holding A Basket, 53 In. 1650.00
Electric, Figural, Horses & Saddles, Porcelier 90.00
Electric, Figural, Owl, Brown, Gray, Green, Bisque, Foreign Burner, Blue Crown, 5 In. . 4400.00

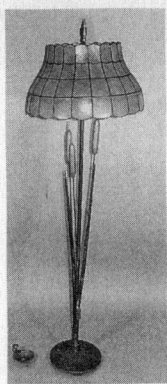

Never plug more than 1500 watts into any one circuit. You may have several plugs on one circuit. This is an easy mistake to make when decorating for the holidays. Don't encourage fires.

Lamp, Electric, McClelland
Barclay, Lily Pad, Cattails,
Mica Shade, 60 In.

Electric, Figural, Reclining Elephant Base, Milk Glass, Ball Top, 1880-1900, 7 1/2 In. . .	495.00
Electric, Figural, Scotty Dog, Plaster, 14 In.	60.00
Electric, Figural, Skeleton, White Bisque, Lavender, Blue Trim, Foreign Burner, 5 1/2 In.	4400.00
Electric, Figurine, Colonial Woman, Porcelain Shade, Finial, 1940s, Pair	585.00
Electric, Finger, Atterbury Head Pattern, Hornet Burner, 4 In.	275.00
Electric, G. Stickley, Copper Straps, Wicker Shade, Mahogany Shoe-Footed, 57 In.	3850.00
Electric, G. Stickley, Trumpeted Copper Base, Wicker Shade, Acorn Pull, 16 In.	1870.00
Electric, Gerrit Rietveld, Black Painted Wood, Glass, Hanging, 1920, 60 3/8 In.	8280.00
Electric, Gilt Metal, 2-Candle Arms, Porcelain Flowers Base, Victorian, 20 In.	175.00
Electric, Grecian Urn Shape, Bronze Patina, Marble Base, 12 In.	190.00
Electric, Hall, Neoclassical Style, Tole Shade	287.00
Electric, Henningsen, Opalescent Glass Shade, Brown Enameled Metal, 1927, 17 In. . . .	9775.00
Electric, Hexagonal Panel Shade, Rowboat Scene, Ornate Metal Armature, 22 In.	990.00
Electric, Hexagonal Slag Panels Shade, Grill Work, Cast Metal, 20 3/4 In.	190.00
Electric, Heywood Wakefield, Wicker Base & Shade, 16 In.	165.00
Electric, Horn, With Horn Shade, Table	185.00
Electric, Incandescent Lamp Co., Man & Dog Reverse Painted Shade, Gilt Base, 26 In. .	1485.00
Electric, Ken-L-Ration Pup, Original Shade	150.00
Electric, Lightolier, Triple-Shade, White, Black, Mauve, 21 In.	275.00
Electric, Limbert, Sailboats & Windmills, Cut Copper Shade, Yellow Slag Glass, 21 In. .	4400.00
Electric, Louis Philippe, Fluted Stem, Fox Masks, 22 In., Pair	5175.00
Electric, Manhattan Brass Co., Student, Brass, Green Ribbed Shade, 20 1/2 In.	220.00
Electric, McClelland Barclay, Lily Pad, Cattails, Mica Shade, 60 In. . . . .*Illus*	1980.00
Electric, Milk Glass, Enameled Landscapes With Mill, 14 In.	55.00
Electric, Miller, Copper, Brass Trim, 28 3/4 In.	95.00
Electric, Moe Bridges, Reverse Painted, Landscape, Bell Shape Shade, 15 In.	1980.00
Electric, Moe Bridges, Scenic, Signed, Boudoir	500.00
Electric, Motion, Antique Autos, Econolite, 1957, 11 In. . . . . .90.00 to 180.00
Electric, Motion, Aquarium	180.00
Electric, Motion, Christmas Tree, Box . . . . .50.00 to 75.00
Electric, Motion, Coach & Driver, Horses, United	135.00
Electric, Motion, Colonial Fountain, 1931	325.00
Electric, Motion, Dertel's Beer	95.00
Electric, Motion, Ducks Flying, Econolite	225.00
Electric, Motion, Fireplace, With Spinning Wheel, Econolite, 1958	200.00
Electric, Motion, Forest Fire, Deer In Stream, Goodman, 1956 . . . . .70.00 to 125.00
Electric, Motion, Forest Fire, Goodman	125.00
Electric, Motion, Fountain Of Youth	82.00
Electric, Motion, Japanese Twilight, Art Deco Frame, 1931	250.00
Electric, Motion, Marine, Scene In Action, 1931	275.00
Electric, Motion, Mayflower, Econolite, 11 In.	95.00
Electric, Motion, Mother Goose, Econolite . . . . .165.00 to 225.00
Electric, Motion, New York City Scene	135.00
Electric, Motion, Niagara Falls, Pink Sunset, Econolite	115.00

Electric, Motion, Old Mill, With Paddle Wheel, Waterfall, Econolite . . . . .135.00 to 150.00
Electric, Motion, Racing Trains, Goodman . . . . .145.00 to 190.00
Electric, Motion, Rainbow, Niagara, Econolite, 1960 . . . .   225.00
Electric, Motion, Robert E. Lee 195.00
Electric, Motion, Sailboats, Pedestal Base, Goodman 240.00
Electric, Motion, Sailing Ship 195.00
Electric, Motion, Sailing Ships, In Storm, Econolite, 1950s 250.00
Electric, Motion, Snow Scene, Econolite 175.00
Electric, Motion, Stream, Campfire 100.00
Electric, Motion, Train, Econolite 165.00
Electric, Motion, Volcano, Oriental Fantasy, Goodman 225.00
Electric, Motion, Warships, Sailing Vessels At War 125.00
Electric, Motion, Winter Scene 100.00
Electric, Motion, Yosemite Falls, Campers, Goodman 110.00
Electric, Murano Style, Clear, Turquoise, Shade, 40 In. 75.00
Electric, Opaque Lilies On Pink, 5 x 4 1/2 In. 25.00
Electric, Oscar Bach, Bronze, Iron, 4 Iron Legs, Bronze Straps, Mica Shade, 30 1/2 In. . . . 4025.00
Electric, Oscar Bach, Hammered Base, Parchment Shade, Bronze, Iron, 1925, 6 Ft., Pair . 6900.00
Electric, Overlay, Glass, Blue Cut To Clear, Stepped Marble Base, 16 1/2 In. 1760.00
Electric, Overlay, Glass, White Cut To Cranberry, Stepped Marble Base, 17 3/4 In. 440.00
Electric, Overlay, Star & Quatrefoil Font, Blue Cut To Clear, Tulip Blue Chimney 2240.00
Electric, Paris, Urn Shape, Transfer Of Man & Woman, Handles, Gilt 315.00
Electric, Piano, Cranberry Glass Shade, Floral Body On Brass Standard, 1920s, 24 In. . .   500.00
Electric, Piano, Roses On Ball Shade, Leaf & Scroll Design, Adjustable, Brass, 82 In. . .   720.00
Electric, Piano, Spherical Font, Floral Glass Shade, Spiral Support, Carved Legs, 61 In. .   305.00
Electric, Pink Flamingo, Shells, Chalkware Base 45.00
Electric, Pole, Shelf At Mid-Section, Adjustable Brass Risers, Mahogany, 1950s 575.00
Electric, Queen Anne, Columnar Standard, Japanned Medial Shelf, 58 In. 630.00
Electric, Raak Holland, Chrome Shaft & Tripod Base, Smoky Glass Globe, Floor, 49 In. .   250.00
Electric, Raggedy Ann, Cloth Doll, Plastic Blocks 25.00
Electric, Raised Dragon & Champleve Design, Copper, Oriental, 32 In. 45.00
Electric, Reverse Painted Shade, Geometric Pattern, Arts & Crafts, 22 In. 1100.00
Electric, Reverse Painted, Blue Summer Trees, Gold Sky, Dome Shade, Bronze, 21 In. . .   935.00
Electric, Reverse Painted, Maple Leaves, Yellow & Tan, Brown Bottle Base, 24 In. 1100.00
Electric, Reverse Painted, Peachblow Sky, Fall Trees, Floral Branches Urn Base, 18 In. . 2200.00
Electric, Reverse Painted, Waterway, Dark Ship, Peachblow, Art Deco Trim, 21 In. 1375.00
Electric, Rock-Crystal, Ormolu, Spiral Twist Baluster Shape Stem, 34 3/4 In., Pair 13800.00
Electric, Russel Wright, Brass, Conical Fiberglass Adjustable Shade, 53 x 15 In. 880.00
Electric, Schlitz Beer, Desk, Box 13.00
Electric, Second Empire, Gilt Metal, Column, Dolphin Footed, Tripod, 31 In., Pair 1380.00
Electric, Ship's Wheel, Bakelite, Green & Butterscotch 90.00
Electric, Silk Glass Globular Shade, Polychrome Floral, Brass Base, 1880s, 30 1/2 In. . .   165.00
Electric, Solar, Corinthian Column Form, Marble Base, Gilt Brass, 1843, 26 1/4 In. 1030.00
Electric, Solar, Gilt Brass, Pendant Flowers, Cabochons, Scrolled Legs, 26 1/2 In. 1452.00
Electric, Stiffel, Double Swing Arm, Brass Base, Leather Trim, 1940s, 40 In. 65.00
Electric, Student, Brass Adjustable Arm, White Glass Shade, Brass, 23 1/2 In. 258.00
Electric, Student, Emeralite 295.00
Electric, Student, Manhattan Lamp Co., Green Shades, Brass Base 7425.00
Electric, Stylized Scroll Design, Black Elliptical Wood Disks, Oval, Art Deco, 11 In. . . .   57.50
Electric, Television, Fish, Black, 1950s 45.00
Electric, Television, Gazelles, Tan, 11 1/2 In 35.00
Electric, Television, Mare & Foal, Japan, 1950s 30.00
Electric, Television, Oriental Figures 25.00
Electric, Television, Pink Flamingo, 1959, Lane 300.00
Electric, Vanity, Nodder, Oriental Lady, Blue 140.00
Electric, Veilleuse, Edgar Brandt, Band Of Berries & Leafage Above Glass Shade, 1925, 5 In. 2300.00
Electric, Walter Dorwin Teague, Polaroid, Bakelite, Aluminum, Flared Shade, 13 In. 935.00
Electric, Waylande Gregory, Peach Color, Sgraffito Polo Design, 1930s 350.00
Electric, White Metal, L'Echo, Figural, Nymph With Flutes Under Leafage, 23 1/2 In. . . .   300.00
Electric, Wicker Shade, Hammered Copper Base, Bottle Shape, Arts & Crafts, 19 In. . . .   880.00
Electric, Woman Kneeling On Pillow, Signed On Base, L.V. Aronson, 1923 . . . .   135.00
Electric, Woman, Sitting With Dog, Germany, 12 In. 75.00
Fairy, 3-Arm Candelabrum, Swirled Rib Base, Metal Arms, 14 In. 330.00

Fairy, 3-Arm Support, Signed, Clarke's Cricklite, 18 1/2 In. 990.00
Fairy, Amber Satin Finish Glass, Clarke Base, Pyramid, 3 1/2 In. 75.00
Fairy, Blue Shade, Base, Clarke Shade, 5 1/2 In. 250.00
Fairy, Brick Cottage Design, Open Windows, 6 3/4 In. 600.00
Fairy, Burmese Shade, Clarke's Pyramid Base, Acanthus Leaf Metal Stand, 2 1/2 In. 355.00
Fairy, Burmese Shade, Ruffled Base, Pyramid 110.00
Fairy, Burmese, Fenton 155.00
Fairy, Embossed, Mold Shade, Medium To Light Blue, Satin Finish, 6 x 6 In. 480.00
Fairy, Green Eye Winker 35.00
Fairy, Jeweled Religious Crosses & Trim, Pink Encrusted Ground, 4 In. 110.00
Fairy, Light House Shape, Blue Translucent Glass, 8 1/4 In. 320.00
Fairy, Nantucket Whalers 35.00
Fairy, Pink Satin Glass 30.00
Fairy, Red Nailsea, 5 1/2 In. 935.00
Fairy, Red Shade, Pyramid, Clarke Insert 75.00
Fairy, Swirl Pattern Shade, Foreign Burner, 6 1/4 In. 385.00
Fairy, Swirl Pattern, Cranberry, Pyramid, 4 1/4 In. 420.00
Fairy, White Spatter, On Chartreuse Encased Crystal, Swirled Rib Mold, 5 1/2 In. 580.00
Fairy, Yellow Coraleine Designs, White Shade, 7 In. 375.00
Fat, 4 Spout, Wick, Twist Hook & Wick Pick 135.00
Fat, Iron, 18th Century, 12 In. 395.00
Fluid, Domed Font, Opaque Fluted & Ribbed Standard, Olive Green, 1840, 13 In., Pair .. 402.00
Fluid, Figural Stem, Blue & White Porcelain, 10 In. 66.00
Fluid, Tapering Font, Hollow Baluster Stem, Hexagonal Base, 1847, 9 1/4 In., Pair 350.00
Fluid, Waterfall Base, Blown Font, Drop-In Burner 220.00
Gas, Gasolier, 1-Light, Leaves, Flower Buds, Cut & Frosted Shade, Gilt Bronze, 29 In. .. 2540.00
Girandole, Brass Urn, Clear Cut Prisms, 13 1/4 In., Pair 120.00
Girandole, Revolutionary War Soldier, Young Girl, Tricornered Hat, Marble Base, Pair .. 225.00
Grease, Hanging, Wrought Iron, Round Pan, Twisted Hanger, 21 In. 99.00
Grease, Wrought Iron, 5 1/4 In. 105.00
Handel Lamps are included in the Handel category.
Hanging, 4-Light, Brass, 4 Down Splaying Arms, Etch Glass Shades, Metal, 16 x 17 In. . 325.00
Hanging, Blue Hobnail Shade, Brass, Prisms ....*Illus* 1210.00
Hanging, Cranberry Bull's-Eye Shade, Brass, Prisms ....*Illus* 1045.00
Hanging, Cranberry Swirl Shade, Brass, Prisms ....*Illus* 1100.00
Hanging, Electric, Spherical Bubble, Howard Miller, 16 x 19 In. 110.00
Hanging, Frosted Francesware Shade, Brass Font, Prisms 1200.00
Hanging, Griffin, Scroll Motif, Bronze Frame, Victorian 110.00
Hanging, Hobnail Shade, Cranberry Opalescent, Bradley & Hubbard 935.00
Hanging, Iron, Brass Trim & Bird Finial, 8 In. 115.00
Hanging, Jeweler, Optician, Watchmaker, Milk Glass 605.00
Hanging, Raised Floral, Foliate, Geometric, Pink To Clear, White Striations, 21 In. 400.00
Hanging, Spout, Punchwork Design, 19th Century, 11 3/4 In. 295.00
Hanging, Store, Kerosene, Brass Font, Tin Shade, Moberly, Missouri 345.00
Hanging, Wells Fargo & Co., Virginia City, Nev., Oil, 1880s 1250.00
Kerosene, Amber Glass, Herringbone, Ruffled Shade, Brass Burner, Square Base, 18 In. . 395.00

Lamp, Hanging, Cranberry Swirl
Shade, Brass, Prisms
Lamp, Hanging, Blue Hobnail
Shade, Brass, Prisms
Lamp, Hanging, Cranberry
Bull's-Eye Shade, Brass, Prisms

Kerosene, Banquet, Column Style, 19th Century, Pair 3160.00
Kerosene, Banquet, Peachblow, Gilded Cast Iron, Brass Connector & Collar, 18 In. 245.00
Kerosene, Banquet, Terra Cotta Base, Brass, Peachblow Font, 17 1/4 In. 275.00
Kerosene, Blue Satin Finish, Frosted Petal Feet, Foreign Burner, 9 In. 495.00
Kerosene, Blue Satin Glass, Embossed Design, Foreign Burner, 9 In. 880.00
Kerosene, Blue Willow, 22 In. 45.00
Kerosene, Country Store Lamp, Embossed, Electrified 410.00
Kerosene, Cranberry Glass, Threaded, 12 1/2 In., Pair 1100.00
Kerosene, Cranberry Opalescent, Snowflake Stem, Clear Base, Metal Connector 395.00
Kerosene, Custard Glass, Sunset Pattern 270.00
Kerosene, Diamond In Line, Sawtooth Pattern, Frosted Glass Shade, 1890, 23 In. 60.00
Kerosene, Diamond-Quilted, Cherubs, Ruffled Shade, Griffin Metal Handles, 16 In. 395.00
Kerosene, Double Wick, Cherubs, Hand Painted Glass Globe, Crystal Prisms, England .. 750.00
Kerosene, Finger, Atterbury Head, Hornet Burner, 4 In. 205.00
Kerosene, Finger, Fern, Pedestal 48.00
Kerosene, Finger, Stippled Fishscale, Pedestal 48.00
Kerosene, Flute, White Opaque 110.00
Kerosene, Gone With The Wind, Floral Transfer, Metal Base, Electrified, 25 In. 330.00
Kerosene, Gone With The Wind, Floral, Marble Base, 1935 .... 38.50
Kerosene, Gone With The Wind, Gold, Magenta, White, Wired, 27 In. 225.00
Kerosene, Gone With The Wind, Owl, White Milk Glass, Ball Shade, 9 1/2 In. 220.00
Kerosene, Gone With The Wind, Painted Roses, Amber, 1940s 225.00
Kerosene, Gone With The Wind, Pink Glass Shade, Painted Reservoir, 24 In. 145.00
Kerosene, Gone With The Wind, Red Case Glass, White Lining, Ball Shade, 22 In. 1430.00
Kerosene, Gone With The Wind, Red Satin Glass, 1800s, 25 In. 895.00
Kerosene, Gone With The Wind, Red Satin Glass, Wreath, Pillar, Pebble Design, 25 In. .. 1182.50
Kerosene, Leaf & Berry, Etched, Frosted Glass Shade, 17 1/4 In. 60.50
Kerosene, Lincoln Drape, Draped & Gathered Frosted Font, Brass Base 135.00
Kerosene, Log Cabin, Amber, Hornet Burner, 3 5/8 In. 550.00
Kerosene, Nellie Bly, Miniature 45.00
Kerosene, Peacock Green, Bulbous Stem, Sandwich Glass, 1830, 8 1/8 In. 8250.00
Kerosene, Pink Opaline Base, White Milk Glass Shade, Olmsted Type Burner, 6 3/4 In. .. 165.00
Kerosene, Rochester Jr., Embossed, Electrified, 1886, 14 1/2 In. 350.00
Kerosene, Sapphire Blue, Hexagonal Stem, Base, Sandwich Glass, 8 1/2 In. 3300.00
Kerosene, Star & Quatrefoil Font, Blue To Clear, 16 1/2 In. ....*Illus* 2240.00
Kerosene, Student, Brass, Milk Glass Hobnail Shade, 19 1/2 In. 165.00
Kerosene, Tiny Juno, Embossed, Electrified, Handle, 11 1/2 In. 350.00
Kerosene, White Milk Glass, Acorn Burner, 5 3/4 In. 192.50
Lard, Wick Pick, Wide Saucer Base, Tin 290.00
Mercury, Jeweler's 225.00
Miner's, Autolite Caride 45.00
Miner's, Justrite, Brass ....20.00 to 30.00
Miner's, Wrought Iron, J.B. Wurtz, 3 1/2 In. 165.00
Oil, 3 Mold Font, Octagonal Base, 19th Century, 10 1/4 In. 750.00
Oil, Acorn-Shaped Font, Pewter, 1850s, 5 3/4 In. 230.00
Oil, Agate, Form Of Athenienne, Russia, 19th Century 2178.00
Oil, Amber & Opaline Glass Well, 3 Dolphin Form Feet, Gilt Bronze, 1884, 33 1/2 In. ... 575.00
Oil, Amber Cut Glass, Chimney, 15 In. 185.00
Oil, Atterbury, Milk Glass Base, c.1868 .... 175.00
Oil, Blue To Clear Overlay, Clambroth Base ....*Illus* 2240.00
Oil, Brass, Bracket Arm, Bell Shaped Foot, Victorian, Electrified, 24 In. 185.00
Oil, Bronze, Dragon Handle, 5 In. 270.00
Oil, Canary Pressed Glass, Loop Design, Hexagonal Base, Mid-19th Century, 8 In. 375.00
Oil, Coach, Amber, Fostoria 135.00
Oil, Cobalt Overlay, Reservoir On Milk Glass Base, Milk Glass Shade, 21 1/2 In. 287.00
Oil, Cranberry To Clear Overlay ....*Illus* 2700.00
Oil, Crusie, Double Valve, Signed, 18th Century, 12 1/2 In. 265.00
Oil, Eyewinker, Thumbprint With Oval Window Font 125.00
Oil, Feather Duster, Sawtooth Band 95.00
Oil, Figural, Little Girl, Slate Base, Blown White Banded Glass Font, 12 In. 250.00
Oil, Figural, Man In Cape Stem, Etched Font, Slate Base 125.00
Oil, Finger, Hand Painted Flowers, Custard Glass, 10 1/2 In. 185.00
Oil, Finger, King's Crown, Pressed Glass ....120.00 to 225.00

Lamp, Kerosene,	Lamp, Oil,	Lamp, Oil,
Star & Quatrefoil Font,	Blue To Clear Overlay,	Cranberry To Clear
Blue To Clear, 16 1/2 In.	Clambroth Base	Overlay

Oil, Finger, Little Buttercup, Amethyst 80.00
Oil, Frosted Glass Font, Gilded Figural Metal Stem, Metal Base, 13 In. 445.00
Oil, Georgian, Columnar Form, Silver Plated, Pair 690.00
Oil, Glass, Harp Pattern, 12 In., Pair 495.00
Oil, Green Ovals Cut To Clear, Fleur-De-Lis Band, Milk Glass Base, Sandwich Glass ... 595.00
Oil, Hanging, Wells Fargo & Co., Nevada Office, 1880s 1250.00
Oil, Heart With Thumbprint, Pressed Glass, Green 245.00
Oil, Lion & Baboon, Pressed Glass, Frosted Faces 450.00
Oil, Little Princess, Early Shade & Chimney, Brass, 14 In. 125.00
Oil, Malachite, Green, 10 In. 1600.00
Oil, Metal, Applied Band Of Flowers, Fruit Design, Scroll Feet, Etched, 15 In., Pair 1725.00
Oil, Metal, Circular Turned Bulbous Form, Floral, Foliate Design, Hurricane Shade, 28 In. 126.00
Oil, Milk Glass Base, c.1880, 13 1/2 In., Pair 590.00
Oil, Molded White Design On Shade, Prisms 175.00
Oil, Peacock Feathers, Pressed Glass, Blue, 12 In. 595.00
Oil, Pewter, Spout, Continental, 10 In. 55.00
Oil, Pressed Waisted Loop, Monument Base, Sandwich Glass, 1840-1860, 12 1/2 In. 295.00
Oil, Rouge Marble & Brass, Stamped 15 BEC ANNA, c.1860, 15 In. 1195.00
Oil, Sheldon Swirl, Opalescent Glass, Frosted Patterned Base, 15 3/4 In. 395.00
Oil, Silver Plate, Glass Fan & Diamond Bowl, Plinth, Electrified, Sheffield, 36 In., Pair .. 805.00
Oil, Skater's, 1880s 70.00
Oil, Spray Of Wild Flowers, Bronze & Painted Metal, 20 In., Pair 1150.00
Oil, Star & Quatrefoil Font, Brass Stem, Marble Foot, Sandwich Glass, 16 1/2 In. 1950.00
Oil, Washington Pattern, Cobalt Blue To Clear, Opaque Base, Sandwich Glass 1200.00
Pairpoint lamps are in the Pairpoint category.
Peg, Blue Satin Mother-Of-Pearl Glass, Swirl Pattern, Brass Candle Holder, 13 In. 55.00
Peg, Embossed, Ribbed Pattern, Deep Robin Egg Blue To Light Satin Blue, 15 In. 1480.00
Peg, Pink Shading To White Satin, Swirl Pattern, Foreign Burner, 12 x 7 3/4 In. 1210.00
Peg, Punty Design, Cut Amethyst, Pressed Brass Standard, Marble Base, 9 In. 345.00
Peg, Satin Glass, Blue To White Verre Moire, Ruffled, 10 In., Pair 265.00
Perfume Bottle, 2 Panels, Richard Hudnut 1450.00
Perfume Bottle, Cat, With Scarf, Irice 65.00
Rush & Candle, Wrought Iron, 3 Footed, 28 1/4 In. 465.00
Rushlight, Wrought Iron Holder, Crude Wooden Base, Pedestal 170.00
Sconce, 1-Light, Relief Floral Design, Brass, Swivel Arm, 8 1/2 In., Pair 110.00
Sconce, 2 Angled Arms, Gilt Bronze, Dominique, Electrified, c.1925, 10 In., Pair 2300.00
Sconce, 2-Light, Baroque Style, Scrolled Arms, Bronze, Electrified, 7 x 14 In., Pair 373.00
Sconce, 2-Light, Clear Cut Foliate, Fruit Design, Baluster, Brass, 14 x 14 In., Pair 575.00
Sconce, 2-Light, Empire Style, Bronze, Scroll, Swag Design, Electrified, 18 In., Pair 900.00
Sconce, 2-Light, Fluted Back Plate, Urn Above Ram's Head, Brass, 14 In., Pair 1725.00
Sconce, 2-Light, Louis XV Style, Wooden, Pair 1610.00
Sconce, 2-Light, Opalescent Glass Shade, Bronze, Jules Leleu, c.1935, 11 In., 4 Piece ... 3450.00
Sconce, 3-Light, Convex Reflector, Pressed Brass, Dutch, 18th Century, 26 1/2 x 23 In. ... 3600.00

Sconce, 3-Light, Crystal Drops, Bead & Gilt Design, 17 1/2 In., Pair 745.00
Sconce, 3-Light, Gilt, Metal, Flowering Branches Shape, 42 In. 970.00
Sconce, 3-Light, Louis XVI Style, Trumpet Form, Gilt Metal, Pair 1035.00
Sconce, 3-Light, Louis XVI, Lyre Form Cartouche, Scrolling Arms, 37 1/4 In. 630.00
Sconce, 3-Light, Ormolu, Love Birds Suspended From Bow Knotted Ribbon, 31 In., Pair 5750.00
Sconce, 3-Light, Pagoda Form, Rococo, Gilt Metal, Porcelain, 30 In., Pair 5272.00
Sconce, 3-Light, Rococo, Brass, Cut Glass, Teardrop, Prisms, 19 In. 3450.00
Sconce, 4-Light, Classical Figures In Relief, 4 Scrolled Arms, 34 In. 1495.00
Sconce, 5-Light, Brass, Neoclassical, Flambeau Backplate, Carved Arms, 28 In. 605.00
Sconce, 5-Light, Classical Female, On Sphere, With Wreath, Gilt Bronze, 24 In. 6325.00
Sconce, 5-Light, Louis XVI Style, Ormolu, 19th Century, 18 In., Pair 1570.00
Sconce, 5-Light, Louis XVI, Gilt Bronze, Prisms, Chains, 24 In., Pair 4370.00
Sconce, 5-Light, Neoclassical, Gilt Metal, Crystal, Pair 805.00
Sconce, 8-Light, Bronze, Electrified, 26 x 41 In., Pair 2500.00
Sconce, Art Nouveau, Blue & Iridescent Glass, 13 x 16 x 9 In., Pair 3500.00
Sconce, Candle, 2-Light, Cutouts In Reflector, Tin Under Glass, 9 1/2 In. 1815.00
Sconce, Candle, 2-Light, Gilded Brass Reflector, Dolphin Crest, Beveled Mirror, 21 In. .. 60.00
Sconce, Candle, 3-Light, Reflector Back, Tin, 10 1/2 x 14 In. 465.00
Sconce, Candle, Brass, Serpentine Support, Stepped Circular Wall Mount, 9 In. 2530.00
Sconce, Carved Gilt Wood Cornucopia, Electrified, 15 In., 6 Piece 2300.00
Sconce, Center Glass Parrot, 2 Scrolled Branches, Pendants, Electrified, 23 In., Pair 2700.00
Sconce, Embossed Tin, Wall Mounted, Round Dish, 1790, 12 3/4 x 9 1/2 In. 1725.00
Sconce, Gilt, Mirrored Back, Palladio, Italy, 25 In., Pair 245.00
Sconce, Tin, Hanging, Mirrored Reflector, 9 1/2 In. 165.00
Shade, Rayo, Milk Glass 40.00
Sinumbra, Cornelius & Co., Acid Etched Shade, Pewter, 1843, 21 3/4 In. 260.00
Sinumbra, Etched Glass Shade, Cut X's, Dots, Stylized Floral, Disc Feet, Brass, 29 In. ... 745.00
Sinumbra, Original Shade, Electrified 1300.00
Sinumbra, Wheel Cut & Acid Finish Shade, 19th Century, 27 In. 1380.00
Sinumbra, Yellow Brass, No Burner, No Shade, 21 1/2 In. 990.00
Tiffany lamps are listed in the Tiffany category.
Torchere, Baroque, Giltwood, Silver, Draped Putto, Foliate, Square Feet, 40 In., Pair ... 2990.00
Torchere, Bronze, Maiden, Standing A Torch Aloft, Faux Verde Marble, 72 In. 5142.00
Torchere, Chrome Stem, White Glass Bowl Shade, Floor, 70 x 19 1/2 In., Pair 880.00
Torchere, Cream Onyx Shade, Scalloped Rim, 1925, Edgar Brandt, 5 Ft. 11 In. 29900.00
Torchere, Edgar Brandt, Alabaster Shade, Wrought Iron, Leafage, Scrolls, 5 Ft. 7 In. 5462.00
Torchere, Female, Cast Iron, 64 1/2 In. 4600.00
Torchere, Louis XVI, Pierced Baluster, Acanthus Carved Top, Medallions, 46 In., Pr. 4310.00
Torchere, Oscar Bach, Bronze, Zigzag Shade, Stylized Foliage, 5 Ft. 8 In., Pair 5520.00
Torchere, Stylized Tulip Form Shade, Brass Coated, 65 In., Pair 402.50
Torchere, Wrought Iron, 63 In. 125.00
Torchere, Wrought Iron, Renaissance, Spiral Twist Branches, 55 In., Pair 6037.00
Whale Oil, 3 Fonts, Trimming Implements On Chain, 1700s, 22 In. 425.00
Whale Oil, Conical, Lemon Squeezer Base 120.00
Whale Oil, Cut Faceted Clear Glass, Sandwich Glass, 9 In., Pair 345.00
Whale Oil, Free Blown Font, Swags & Pendants, Colorless, c.1830, 11 In., Pair 517.00
Whale Oil, Giant Sawtooth, Drilled For Electricity 125.00
Whale Oil, Gimbal Ship's, Wood Handle, Iron 75.00
Whale Oil, Mold Blown, Expanded Aqua Font, Brass Supports, Marble Base, Pair 280.00
Whale Oil, Paneled Punty, Double Wicks, Attached Chain & Caps, 10 1/2 In. 250.00
Whale Oil, Pedestal Base, Sandwich Glass, 12 1/2 In. 425.00
Whale Oil, Peg, Pale Purple, Gold Ornaments, Brass Candleholder 375.00
Whale Oil, Pewter, G. Norris, New York 650.00
Whale Oil, Pewter, Ringed Holder, 8 In. 178.50
Whale Oil, Sandwich, 9 3/4 In. 265.00
Whale Oil, Single Burner, Saucer Base, Handle, Tin, 7 1/2 In. 230.00
Whale Oil, Star & Punty, Brass Angel Cradling Dove, Marble Base, 1845, 14 In., Pair .. 650.00
Whale Oil, Star & Punty, Clear, c.1840, 9 3/4 In. 450.00

LANTERNS are a special type of lighting device. They have a light
source, usually a candle, totally hidden inside the walls of the lantern.
Light is seen through holes or glass sections.

   Barn, Hinged Door, Wire Bale, Wooden, 11 1/2 In. 440.00

Barn, Leather Hinges, Pine & Chestnut, 15 1/4 In. 375.00
Barn, Wooden, Ash, Dark Patina, 3-Sided Glass, Wooden Panel, 10 3/4 In. 478.50
Barn, Wooden, Cherry, 3-Sided Glass, 11 3/4 In. 346.50
Brass, Chief's Style, Original Burner 245.00
Brass, Dome, Blown Globe, Whale Oil Burner, Tin, 13 1/2 In. 357.50
Candle, Attached Match Box, Original Glass, 14 In. 295.00
Candle, Half-Round Form, Tin, 16 x 8 1/2 In. 345.00
Candle, Iron Vent Cover & Handle, Wooden, American, 18th Century, 17 In. 695.00
Candle, Knob Feet & Finials, Sheet Metal, 17 1/2 In. 1430.00
Candle, Pierced Sheet Iron, c.1790, 15 In. 225.00
Candle, Wooden Frame, Punched Sheet Iron On Domed Top, 2 Glass Sides, 12 In. 550.00
Carriage, Beveled Glass Lenses, Brass, 19th Century 88.00
Copper, Green Patina, Wooden Post, 39 In. 550.00
Dietz, Convex, Ribbed Globe, Brass, 16 1/2 In. 375.00
Dietz, Fire King 295.00
Dietz, King, Nickel, 1907 .... 385.00
Dietz, Police 135.00
Dietz, Skater's, Scout 65.00
Dietz, Wagon, Bull's-Eye Globe 95.00
Dietz, Wagon, Wizard 100.00
Double Globe, Buckeye, Bell Bottom, 1880s 175.00
Electric, Civil Defense, Waterproof, Yellow, Post World War II 18.00
Fire Engine, Nickel Plated, Cut Glass Globes, Eagle Finial, 21 In., Pair 1380.00
Hanging, Blue Globe 195.00
Hanging, Hammered Copper, Stickley 9200.00
Oil, Pierced Tin, E. Miller & Co., 1870s, 16 1/4 In. 145.00
Punched Tin, Candle Socket, Burlington, 13 1/2 In. 715.00
Punched Tin, Conical Top, Looped Handle, 3 Smoke Holes, 12 In. 220.00
Punched Tin, Green Paint, Signed Ruth 395.00
Punched Tin Star & Eagle, Ring Handles, 29 In. 245.00
Skater's, Cobalt Chimney, Tin, c.1890, 7 1/4 In. 445.00
Stagecoach, Glass, Tiny Chimney, 1870 .... 495.00
Street, Copper, Electrified, England, 21 In. 303.00
Sulfur, Bulpitt & Sons, 1927 .... 150.00
Tavern, Copper, Glass Panels, Faceted Top, 32 x 15 In. Diam. 360.00
Tin, 3 Glass Sides, Font Chimney & Reflector, Painted Green, 22 x 13 In. 172.00
Tin, Clear Molded Shade, Pewter Collar, N.E. Glass Co., 17 1/4 In. 275.00
Tin, Onion Shaped Globe, Tin Wire Surround, 12 1/4 In. 40.00
Wall, Embossed Copper & Glass, Striated Panels, Arts & Crafts, 1915, 9 1/2 In. 1840.00
Whale Oil, Cobalt Blue Globe, Brown Japanning, Removable Font, Tin, 11 1/2 In. 495.00

LE VERRE FRANCAIS is one of the many types of cameo glass made in France. The glass was made by the C. Schneider factory in Epinay-sur-Seine from 1920 to 1933. It is a mottled glass, usually decorated with floral designs, and bears the incised signature *Le Verre Francais*.

Bowl, Green Mottled Ground, Pale Amethyst Blackberry, Vine, 8 1/2 In. 880.00
Lamp, Stylized Berries, Cameo Domed Shade & Base, Marked, 10 In. 3300.00
Vase, 3 Large Flowers, Mottled Pink, Purple, Cushion Foot, Globular, 7 In. 920.00
Vase, 3 Large Scarabs, Mottled Brown, Orange Ground, Ovoid, 1925, 16 In. 1610.00
Vase, 3 Stalks Blossoming, Mottled Yellow, Pink, Brown, Egg Shaped, 12 In. 865.00
Vase, 3 Stalks Of Leaves & Fruit, Mottled Yellow, Purple, Brown, 1925 .... 920.00
Vase, Bellflower Design, Mottled Red, Yellow, Brown, Gray Ground, 13 In. 1725.00
Vase, Floral, Orange To Brown, Yellow Ground, Egg Shaped, 6 In. 850.00
Vase, Flowering Lotus Plants, Yellow, Mottled Pink, Globular, 11 In. 2645.00
Vase, Geometric Flower Heads, Cobalt Blue, Mottled Orange, Yellow, 1925 .... 2300.00
Vase, Inverted Bell Form, Red, Mottled Brown, Yellow, 1925, 6 5/8 In. 1100.00
Vase, Maroon Over Clear Over Variegated, 5 x 7 1/2 In. 924.00
Vase, Orange Over Variegated Yellow, Acid Cut Floral Design, 8 In. 605.00
Vase, Pale Amethyst Ground, Orange, Purple Mottled Flowers, 5 In. 385.00
Vase, Stylized Blossoms, White, Mottled Brown, Orange, 1925, 12 In. 2185.00
Vase, Stylized Daisies, Mottled Pink, Purple, Gray Ground, 11 1/4 In. 635.00
Vase, Stylized Flowers, Purple Shading, Frosted, Signed, 5 In. 440.00

Vase, Stylized Leaf Design, Mottled Purple, Brown, Orange Streaks, 9 In. 1150.00
Vase, Stylized Pendant Leaves, Mottled Yellow, Green, Orange, 1925, 18 In. 2415.00

LEATHER is tanned animal hide and it has been used to make decorative and useful objects for centuries. Leather objects must be carefully preserved with proper humidity and oiling or the leather will deteriorate and crack. This damage cannot be repaired.

Bag, Canvas, Leather Bound, Hermes 400.00
Bag, Hunting, With Powder Horn & Small Priming Horn, 1830s 395.00
Belt, Woven Designs, Asian, 1920, 5 In. Wide 750.00
Box, Cartridge, Revolutionary War, Inner Wood Block Holds Cartridges 395.00
Case, Traveling, Stamped Crocodile, Leather Lined, Fitted Interior, 1950s 85.00
Cuffs, Cowboy's, Studded & Hand Tooled 390.00
Lederhosen, Child's 68.00
Luggage, Set, Amelia Earhardt, Woven Straw, Satin Lined, Tags, 11 To 17 In., 3 Piece ... 165.00
Pail, Wine, Farrow & Jackson, London, 18th Century, 7 In. 145.00
Saddle, Aluminum Pommel, 7 3/4 In. 126.50
Saddle, Child's, 1950s 400.00
Saddle, High Back, 1890s 300.00
Saddle, McClellan, 1885 .... 1500.00
Saddle, Military, Beveled To Carry Weapon, Heavy Equipment, c.1887 .... 365.00
Saddle, Officer's, McClellan, 1885 .... 2250.00
Saddle, Parade, Black 995.00
Saddle, Side, Woman's, 1 Horn 185.00
Saddle, Side, Woman's, 1800 .... 500.00
Saddlebag, Diamond Lattice, Hooked Diamonds, Kurd, 3 Ft. 4 In. x 1 Ft. 8 In. 402.00

LEEDS pottery was made at Leeds, Yorkshire, England, from 1774 to 1878. Most Leeds ware was not marked. Early Leeds pieces had distinctive twisted handles with a greenish glaze on part of the creamy ware. Later ware often had blue borders on the creamy pottery. A Chicago company named Leeds made many Disney-inspired figurines. They are listed in the Disneyana category.

LEEDS POTTERY.

Bowl, Creamware, Allegorical, Ship Motif, 8 3/4 In. 151.00
Creamer, 4 Colors 195.00
Cup & Saucer, Foliage Design, Pearlware, Handleless 180.00
Cup & Saucer, Leeds Enamel Type Apple Design, Pearlware, 8 Piece 1800.00
Cup Plate, Pearlware, Green Feather Edge, Floral, 4 1/2 In. 385.00
Dish, Footed, Twist Handle, c.1800, 5 1/2 In. 1050.00
Pitcher, Floral, Row Of Peacocks, 8 5/8 In. 275.00
Plate, Creamware, Eagle, Shell Edge 1100.00
Plate, Creamware, Oriental House, Free-Brushed, 8 In. 1700.00
Plate, Creamware, Pierced, 1790, 9 In. 195.00
Plate, Creamware, Tulip, 7 In. 1150.00
Platter, Oriental Design, Feather Edge, 20 3/4 In. 495.00
Sugar Caster, Dish, Brown, Green, Reticulated, Soft Paste, Monogram, 1792, 9 1/2 In. .. 400.00
Tankard, Blue Flowers, Mustard Stems, Green & Blue Designs 575.00
Tankard, Brown Bands, Red & Yellow Flowers, Green Leaves 675.00
Teapot, Enamel Portrait Of Prince Of Orange 440.00
Teapot, Flower Finial, Enameled Rose 3025.00
Teapot, Pearlware, Floral Design, Dome Top, 10 1/4 In. 300.00

LEFTON is a mark found on many pieces. The Geo. Zoltan Lefton Company has imported porcelains to be sold in America since 1940. The firm is still in business. The company mark has changed through the years; but because marks have been used for long periods of time, they are of little help in dating an object.

Bank, Bluebird 20.00
Bank, Devil 25.00
Bank, Grandmother In Rocking Chair, Retirement 24.00
Bank, Hubert The Lion ....25.00 to 40.00
Bank, Kangaroo ....25.00 to 75.00
Bank, Owl ....35.00 to 50.00

Bank, Pig, Smiling, Pink, With Flowers 24.00
Bank, Pocketbook 10.00
Bank, Snail 45.00
Biscuit Jar, Cat 45.00
Bookends, Poodle 40.00
Bookends, Siamese Cat 35.00
Bowl, Blue Cat, 5 1/2 In. 75.00
Clock, Owl 10.00
Compote, Green & Rose, Pierced 35.00
Cookie Jar, Angel 35.00
Cookie Jar, Bluebird ....190.00 to 255.00
Cookie Jar, Cat Head 120.00
Cookie Jar, Christmas Train 35.00
Cookie Jar, Daisy Head 195.00
Cookie Jar, Dutch Girl ....125.00 to 325.00
Cookie Jar, Graduate 20.00
Cookie Jar, Leprechaun 20.00
Cookie Jar, Little Lady, Blonde Hair 135.00
Cookie Jar, Little Lady, Gray Hair 325.00
Cookie Jar, Miss Priss, Cat ....85.00 to 125.00
Cookie Jar, Pixie Head With Butterfly 45.00
Cookie Jar, Sugar & Creamer, Miss Priss, Cat, 3 Piece 150.00
Cookie Jar, Thumbelina 250.00
Cookie Jar, Winking Santa 225.00
Cookie Jar, Young Girl, Plaid Hat ....125.00 to 195.00
Creamer, Bluebird 22.00
Creamer, Cow 40.00
Creamer, Dutch Girl ....32.00 to 35.00
Creamer, Thumbelina 30.00
Cup, Monk Decanter 35.00
Decanter, Santa 45.00
Dish, Compartment 175.00
Eggcup, Bluebird 40.00
Figurine, Angel, July Birthday 22.00
Figurine, Bloomer Girl 45.00
Figurine, Boy & Girl, Birds, No. 469, 7 1/2 In. 20.00
Figurine, Boy Fishing, No. KW227 .... 46.00
Figurine, Bull, Standing, Glossy Black 15.00
Figurine, Cherub, White Bisque, Wrapped Around Shell 38.00
Figurine, Chick, Yellow 35.00
Figurine, Christmas Girl 48.00
Figurine, Clarissa 55.00
Figurine, Colonial Woman 85.00
Figurine, Colonial Woman & Man, No. 3045 .... 125.00
Figurine, Dachshund, Brown, Glossy, Male, 8 1/2 In. 22.00
Figurine, Doberman 28.00
Figurine, Dove, White 55.00
Figurine, Drummer, No. 1796 .... 35.00
Figurine, Elephant 24.00
Figurine, Fancy Ladies, Bisque, 4 In. 20.00
Figurine, Fancy Ladies, Bisque, 7 In. 48.00
Figurine, General Washington 20.00
Figurine, Girl, Skater 25.00
Figurine, Kewpie 45.00
Figurine, Line Officer, No. 1779 .... 35.00
Figurine, Mrs. Goose, 3 In. 20.00
Figurine, Owl 10.00
Figurine, Puppy, Boxer 45.00
Figurine, Rabbit 25.00
Figurine, Red Robin 22.00
Figurine, Skunk On Log, 3 1/2 In. 6.00
Figurine, Spanish Dancer 65.00
Figurine, Tuesday's Child 30.00

Figurine, Wolfhound, Reclining, Black & White, 4 1/2 In. 12.00
Figurine, Woman, Pink, 6 In. 85.00
Figurine, Woman, White, 6 In. 85.00
Figurine, Woman, White, Gold 75.00
Head Vase, Angel Girl 45.00
Head Vase, Miss Priss, Cat 145.00
Head Vase, Miss Priss, Large 195.00
Jar, Condiment, Dutch Girl 85.00
Marmalade 65.00
Mug, Bluebird 65.00
Mug, Cat's Head 25.00
Mug, Miss Priss, Cat .... 60.00 to 85.00
Music Box, February Angel 29.00
Napkin Holder, Praying Angel 22.00
Planter, Antebellum Woman, 6 In. 16.00
Planter, Baby King 20.00
Plate, Deviled Egg, Hand Painted, Orange, Yellow & Green Floral 18.00
Relish, Hand Painted Violets, Oblong, Gold Trim 18.00
Salt & Pepper, Cat Head 20.00
Salt & Pepper, Dutch Girl & Boy .... 24.00 to 55.00
Salt & Pepper, Elf, Green 45.00
Salt & Pepper, Heritage, Green 15.00
Salt & Pepper, Ladybug, Blue 40.00
Salt & Pepper, Miss Cutie Pie 30.00
Salt & Pepper, Miss Priss, Blue Cat 23.00
Salt & Pepper, Owls, Signed, 1956 .... 30.00
Salt & Pepper, Thumbelina 45.00
Salt & Pepper, Toodles 25.00
Salt & Pepper, Woman, In Plaid Hat 25.00
Shaker, Cheese, Mammy & Chef 30.00
Spoon Holder, Mammy, Nodder Head 125.00
Sugar, Bluebird 30.00
Sugar, Thumbelina 38.00
Sugar & Creamer, Bluebird 65.00
Sugar & Creamer, Cat's Head 45.00
Sugar & Creamer, Grape 125.00
Sugar & Creamer, Heritage, Green 27.00
Sugar & Creamer, Miss Priss, Cat .... 33.00 to 65.00
Sugar & Creamer, Pixie 50.00
Sugar & Creamer, Prayer Lady, Pink 150.00
Tea Set, Cat Head, 3 Piece 150.00
Teapot, Bluebird 100.00
Teapot, Daisy Head 145.00
Teapot, Girl's Head 150.00
Teapot, Grape 125.00
Teapot, March Birthday Girl 25.00
Teapot, Miss Priss, Blue Cat 125.00
Teapot, Moss Rose 50.00
Teapot, Thumbelina, No. 1695 .... 295.00
Teapot, Toodles 85.00
Toby Jug, 4th Of July 24.00
Toby Jug, Grant 35.00
Toby Jug, Jackson 35.00
Vase, Leaf & Bird 10.00
Vase, Pink & Gold Wheat, 5 In. 20.00
Wall Pocket, Bluebird 65.00
Wall Pocket, Elf 85.00
Wall Pocket, Fish, With Bubbles 55.00
Wall Pocket, Grist Mill 15.00
Wall Pocket, Little Girl 45.00
Wall Pocket, Mermaid, Pair 55.00
Wall Pocket, Miss Priss, Cat 135.00
Wall Pocket, Violins, Pansies, Pair 45.00

LEGRAS was founded in 1864 by Auguste Legras at St. Denis, France. It is best known for cameo glass and enamel-decorated glass with Art Nouveau designs. Legras merged with Pantin in 1920 and became the Verreries et Cristalleries de St. Denis et de Pantin Reunies.

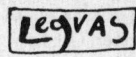

Bowl, Autumn Leaves, Frosted & Textured Clear Ground, Silver Plate Stand, 9 1/4 In. . . .	795.00
Bowl, Landscape Design, Enamel Green, Brown, Scalloped Rim, 2 1/2 In.	175.00
Rose Bowl, Silhouetted Trees, Tangerine Sky, Snowy Ground, Scalloped, 4 In.	440.00
Vase, Bud, Cameo, Fiery Opal, Olive Green Layers, Foliate Motif, 8 1/4 In.	635.00
Vase, Burgundy Florals Cascade, Frosted Ground, Cameo, Egg Shape, Marked, 8 In.	600.00
Vase, Elongated, Figure In A Forest, Signed, 14 1/2 In.	460.00
Vase, Enameled Mulberry Leaves, 11 In.	357.00
Vase, Enameled Mulberry Vines, Apricot To Frosted Ground, 9 In.	385.00
Vase, Enameled Serene Lake, Summer Trees, Cylindrical, Marked, 6 In.	415.00
Vase, Etched, Chartreuse Green Case, Mottled Brown, White, Stylized Fruits, 13 In.	977.00
Vase, Lake Front Scene, Men, Fishing In Boats, Yellow, Green, Brown, 11 In.	385.00
Vase, Landscape Design, Green, Red, Brown, Cylindrical, 10 1/2 In.	230.00
Vase, Leaf & Berry Design, Hourglass Form, Green, Yellow On Frosted Ground, 14 In. . . .	575.00
Vase, Mosaic, Cranberry Lining, Cream Spatter Outside, 10 1/2 In., Pair	395.00
Vase, Pink & Lilac Poppies, Emerald Green, Signed, 12 In.	330.00
Vase, Scenic, Etched, Acid Landscape, Flared Cylinder, 12 In.	690.00
Vase, Scenic, Etched, Tall Trees, Riverscape, Oval, 14 In.	977.50
Vase, Sea Plant Design, Amber, Beige Outer Lining, 7 1/2 In.	495.00
Vase, Winter Landscape, Enamel, Triangular Form, 5 3/4 In.	345.00
Vase, Woodbine Vine & Berries, Mottled Opal & Yellow Ground, Marked, 23 In.	1320.00

LENOX is the name of a porcelain maker. Walter Scott Lenox and Jonathan Cox founded the Ceramic Art Company in Trenton, New Jersey, in 1889. In 1906, Lenox left and started his own company called *Lenox*. The company makes a porcelain that is similar to Irish Belleek. The marks used by the firm have changed through the years and collectors prefer the earlier examples. Related pieces may also be listed in the Ceramic Art Co. category.

Bowl, Center, Crimped Rim, Oval, 12 x 5 1/2 In.	40.00
Bowl, Flower, White Interior, Turquoise Exterior, Green Mark, 10 In.	60.00
Bowl, Serving, Raised Vintage Design, 3 3/4 x 9 3/4 In.	27.00
Bowl, Silver Overlay, Footed, 1920, 5 1/2 In.	125.00
Bowl, Vegetable, Cover, Oak Leaf, Blue	195.00
Bowl & Plate Set, Child's, Gentle Friends, 2 Piece	40.00
Bust, Art Deco, c.1931, 4 In., Pair	350.00
Cigarette Holder, Matching Ronson Lighter	85.00
Creamer, Oak Leaf, Blue	35.00
Cup & Saucer, Brookline	34.00
Cup & Saucer, Demitasse, Mystic	25.00
Cup & Saucer, Harvest, Gold Mark	130.00
Cup & Saucer, Oak Leaf, Blue	38.00
Cup & Saucer, Springdale	18.00
Cup & Saucer, Wheat, 9 1/2 In.	12.00
Dish, Floral Design, Hand Painted, 6 In.	23.00
Dish, Footed, Pink, Fan Shape	110.00
Figurine, American Goldfinch, Matte	75.00
Figurine, Chipping Sparrow, Matte	70.00
Figurine, Eastern Bluebird, Matte	70.00
Figurine, Governor's Garden Party	85.00
Figurine, Hummingbird, Matte	75.00
Figurine, Red Breasted Nuthatch, Matte	65.00
Gravy Boat, Oval, Green Mark, 4 In.	10.00
Lamp, Table, Classical Style, Marble Globe, 18 In., Pair	140.00
Mustard Pot, Silver Overlay, Brown Glaze	150.00
Perfume Bottle, Swan	85.00
Plate, Belvidere, 10 1/2 In.	24.00
Plate, Flowers, c.1890, 9 1/2 In.	35.00
Plate, Ming, 8 1/4 In.	20.00

Plate, Springdale, 10 1/2 In.	18.00
Plate, W.H. Morley, 1906, 9 1/2 In.	165.00
Platter, Oak Leaf, 15 1/2 In.	175.00
Platter, Pavlova, 17 In.	85.00
Server, 3 Shell Shape Parts, Finial Center, 1920s	100.00
Server, Center, Acanthus Relief, Handle, Gold, 12 1/2 In.	125.00
Sugar, Cover, Oak Leaf, Blue	58.00
Sugar & Creamer, Washington, 1920s	.85.00 to 110.00
Tea & Coffee Set, Silver Overlay, Cobalt Blue, Late 1890s, 4 Piece	860.00
Teapot, Goose Neck Spout, White, Blue Band, Gold Trim Handle, Finial	110.00
Tile, Tea, Footed, Ming, 5 1/2 In.	45.00
Toby Jug, Benjamin Franklin	150.00
Toby Jug, William Penn, Green Mark	275.00
Vase, Coral Glaze, No. 27	110.00
Vase, Scarab, 6 Colors, 1920s, 7 1/2 In.	425.00

LETTER OPENERS have been used since the eighteenth century. Ivory and silver were favored by the well-to-do. In the late nineteenth century, the letter opener was popular as an advertising giveaway and many were made of metal or celluloid. Brass openers with figural handles were also popular.

Atlantic City Crescent Temple, Sword	30.00
B. & F. Oil Co., Germany	45.00
Bone Pen, Stanhope	49.00
Brass, Arts & Crafts, Bradley & Hubbard	65.00
Brass, Bust Of Woman	100.00
Brass Gilded, King Rex, 1910	95.00
Bronze, Airplane, Art Deco	95.00
Bronze, Red Gas Pump, Bowser Filtered Gasoline, 9 In.	170.00
Bronze Blade, Glass Handle, Iridescent Blue	195.00
Celluloid, Alligator, Black Pencil In Mouth	55.00
Crocodile, Crane & Breed Mfg. Co.	35.00
Duck, Avon	10.00
Eagle Handle	80.00
Eagle Pencil Company	25.00
Lucite, Hawaiian Girl	18.00
Mother-Of-Pearl, Sterling Silver Handle	245.00
Samurai Sword, Crescent Temple, Atlantic City, 1927	35.00
Sterling Silver, Elizabeth II, Churchill Coin At Top, Garrard & Co., Case	115.00
Sterling Silver, Foliate Gold Handle & Dagger Blade, Theodore B. Starr, 12 In.	207.00
Sterling Silver, Indian Head	79.00
Sterling Silver, Ivory, Ornate Scrolled Design	42.00
Sterling Silver, Woman's Head, Mother-Of-Pearl Blade	95.00
Walnut, Snake Handle, Carved	357.00
Yellow Kid	28.50

LIBBEY Glass Company has made many types of glass since 1888, including the cut glass and tablewares that are collected today. The stemwares of the 1930s and 1940s are once again in style. The Toledo, Ohio, firm was purchased by Owens-Illinois in 1935 and is still working under the name *Libbey* as a division of that company. Additional pieces may be listed under Amberina, Cut Glass, and Maize.

Basket, Intaglio, 12 In.	575.00
Bowl, 3-Sided, Wedgemere	1495.00
Bowl, Diana, Signed, 8 In.	550.00
Bowl, Oriena, Signed, 8 In.	185.00
Candlestick, Camel, 5 1/2 In.	250.00
Celery Dish, Rolled-In Sides, Signed, 11 1/2 In.	295.00
Champagne, Squirrel, 6 In.	200.00
Champagne, Squirrel, Opalescent, 4 In.	300.00
Claret, Bear, 5 1/2 In.	.165.00 to 170.00
Cocktail, Kangaroo, Ruby, Experimental, 6 In.	357.00
Compote, Cut Glass, Optic Ribbed, Dotted Green Internal Design, 6 3/4 In.	632.00

Console Set, Green & White Pulled Feather, Signed 825.00
Cordial, Whippet 175.00
Decanter, Flute, Green Cut To Clear, Teardrop Stopper, 8 1/2 In. 950.00
Decanter, Kimberly, Double Gooseneck, 12 1/2 In. 875.00
Goblet, Cat, Opalescent 200.00
Nappy, Glenda, 5 In. 165.00
Orange Bowl, Princess, Signed, 11 x 7 1/2 In. 310.00
Paperweight, Book Form, Line Cutting Allover, 3 7/8 x 3 In. 165.00
Pitcher, Corinthian, 7 1/2 In. 450.00
Platter, Hobstar, Feather Variant, Flower Bands, Marked, 1 1/2 x 12 In. 500.00
Punch Bowl, Hobstars, Acid Etched Stamp, 7 x 13 3/4 In. 632.00
Sherbet, Squirrel, Footed, 4 In. 125.00
Sugar & Creamer, Anita, Signed 110.00
Tankard, Verna, No. 300, Signed 275.00
Toothpick, Little Lobe, Signed 125.00
Tray, Delphos, Signed, 11 3/4 In. 2350.00
Tray, Ice Cream, Lorraine, Signed, 17 x 10 In. 1990.00
Vase, Bud, Cut Glass, Flowers & Stems, Signed, 12 In. 155.00
Vase, Clear Cut Floral Top, Signed, 6 x 7 1/2 In. 100.00
Vase, Trumpet Form, Zipper, Green Vertical Dots, 10 In. 373.00
Wine, Frosted Cat Stem, 6 Piece 750.00
Wine, Kangaroo, Signed, 6 In. 135.00
Wine, Opalescent, Monkey Stem, Signed, 5 In. 125.00

LIGHTERS for cigarettes and cigars are collectible. Cigarettes became popular in the late nineteenth century, and with the cigarette came matches and cigarette lighters. All types of lighters are collected, from solid gold to the first of the recent disposable lighters. Most examples found were made after 1940.

Airplane, Chrome 90.00
American Safety Razor, Ascot, Hidden Watch Swivels From Bottom 82.00
Beer Can, Canadian Ale, Cone Top, 1940s ....32.00 to 35.00
Bic, Denver Police Union, Butane, Holder, c.1978 .... 5.00
Big Boy, Holding Hamburger 25.00
Blue Bird, OU Initials Embossed On Front, White Letters, Silver Finish 25.00
Brass, World War I, With Magnifier 35.00
Brooklyn Dodgers, World Series, 1955 .... 800.00
Buccellati, Apple Form, Sterling Silver 575.00
Camel Cigarettes, Box 15.00
Canadian Pacific Railroad 25.00
Cigar, Dog, Plaster, Gold Repaint, 13 In. 120.00
Cigar, Gas, Risque Dancing Girl, Top, Ornate Pedestal, Table, 1880s, 15 In. 2950.00
Cigar, Musica, Otis Coiltroccs 125.00
Cigar, Navy, Silver, 1890s 450.00
Cigar, Wall Mount, Woman's Hand, Holding Rose-Tinted Globe, Brass 3250.00
Continental, Mother-Of-Pearl 25.00
Deep Turquoise Glass, 7 In. 15.00
Dixie Oils Gasoline, Orange, Blue & Silver, 1 1/2 In. 22.00
Dodge Trucks, Plastic Base, Black, Red, Tin, 3 In. 45.00
Dunhill, Corona, Gun Form, Chrome, Black 33.00
Dunhill, Pocket, 14K Gold 375.00
Dunhill, Rollagas, Diamond Pattern, Gold Plate 49.00
Dunhill, Silent Flame, Art Deco Woman 75.00
Dunhill, Sterling Rope 75.00
Dupont, Butane, Checkerboard Design, Gold Plate 95.00
Dupont, Butane, Gold Plate, 1960s 175.00
Dupont, Butane, Silver Plate, 1950s 50.00
Dynamite Triggering Device 40.00
Evans, Cowboy Boot 20.00
Evans, Golfer, Lucite, 2 1/2 In. 25.00
Evans, Hammered Chrome, Black Stripes, 1930s 42.00
Firestone, Metal 12.00
Flying A Service, Your Imprint Here, Dundee Bantam, Salesman Sample 100.00

Gas Pump, Red, Metal, 3 1/2 In. 187.00
Gold Club, Box, Table 40.00
Greyhound 40.00
Grossingers, Indoor Pool, Box 35.00
Gulf Service Station, Orange Reverse Side, Uniontown, Pa., 1 1/2 In. 93.00
Heart Design, Dan & Mary, Black Arrow, Gold Finish, Terraced Base, Table, 1980 .. 249.00
Honda Ski-Doo, Red, Black, Yellow On Silver, Dave Beriew Sales, Cortland, N.Y., 1 In. 11.00
Horse, Chromium, Butane, c.1988 .... 15.00
Horse Head, Occupied Japan 25.00
Jet 200, Torpedo, Black Plastic & Aluminum, Box 15.00
Johnson Wax Research, Tower Form, 5 3/4 x 2 1/2 In., Pair 440.00
Lays Potato Chips, Zippo Style 20.00
Matchomatic, Pistol, Box 25.00
Meb, Pull Apart, Austrian, 1912 .... 22.00
Musical, Blue Bird Deluxe, White Sides, Red Lettering, Box, 1950 .... 63.00
Newport, Continental, Box 5.00
Parker, Flaminaire 25.00
Parker, Flaminaire, Cobalt Blue, Gold, Limoges, Table, 3 1/2 In. 30.00
Parker, Flaminaire, Display Box, 1951 .... 55.00
Parker, Nude Figure, Peacock, Black Bakelite & Chrome 145.00
Pencil, Chromium & Bakelite, Occupied Japan, 1949 .... 40.00
Penguin, Kool, c.1930 .... 75.00
Pipe, Copper & Wood, Dutch, c.1720, 9 1/4 In. 385.00
Pipe, Copper & Wood, Dutch, c.1780, 4 1/2 x 5 In. 285.00
Playboy, Engraved Bunny .... .20.00 to 30.00
Poss Beef Stew Can 35.00
Rexxy, Chrome, 4 Hinge Mechanism, Switzerland, 1930s 37.00
Ronson, Butane Varaflame, Chrome Details, White Plastic Body 55.00
Ronson, Chromium, Standard, Box 45.00
Ronson, Comet, Maroon, Gold Tone, England 10.00
Ronson, Lighthouse Shape 30.00
Ronson, Master Case, Maroon Enamel 175.00
Ronson, Mayfair, Silver Plate Finish, 1950, 3 In. 60.00
Ronson, NRA, Green, Table, Pair 85.00
Ronson, Pal 45.00
Ronson, Queen Anne Style, Silver Plate Finish, 1950, 2 1/2 In. 60.00
Ronson, Silver, Crown, Table 25.00
Ronson, Standard, Sterling Silver Wrap, Picture Of Queen, England 85.00
Ronson, Sterling Silver, Siam 85.00
Ronson, Varaflame, Electronic, Chrome, Black Leather, England, Box 23.50
Saxophone, Butane, 1990 .... 10.00
Schlitz Beer, Dome Top, 1962 .... 28.00
Scotsman's Head 35.00
Scripto, Harley-Davidson, More Than A Machine, Plastic Compartment, 1960 ...115.00 to 125.00
Sedan, Chrome, 1940s 135.00
Spark-A-Matic, Midland, Cogar 425.00
Stock Broker's Ticker Tape 75.00
Universal, Peace Is Our Profession, Sac Shield On Front, Chrome, Box 22.50
Vulcan, Musical, Smoke Gets In Your Eyes 125.00
White Sewing Machine 25.00
Winston Cigarettes, Box 15.00
Woman's Head, Art Deco 285.00
Zippo, Acme Radiator Co. Embossed On Side, Brushed Finish, Box, 1963 ...... 32.00
Zippo, Air Force, Air Force Crest, Black Finish 16.00
Zippo, Army, Army Crest In Silver, Black Finish 16.00
Zippo, Boston Maine Railroad, Box, 1959 .... 45.00
Zippo, Bowling, Box, 1960 .... 88.00
Zippo, Commemorative, 60th Anniversary, Chromium, Tin Gift Box, c.1992 .... 20.00
Zippo, Engraved Caterpillar Trade Mark, Yellow Enamel, Box, 1958 .... 149.50
Zippo, Kingsford Pumps, Oswego, N.Y., 1869-1941, Brushed Finish 463.00
Zippo, Moose Lodge Emblem, Enamel, Brushed Finish, Box, 1947 .... 173.00
Zippo, Navy Aviator's Cigarette Lighter, Black Finish, Gold Tone, Plastic 16.00
Zippo, Navy, Flip Top Case, Gold Tone, Black Finish, Plastic 16.00

Zippo, Pinup Girl 30.00
Zippo, Plain Brush Finish, Fixed D-Ring At Hinge, Attached Elastic Black Cord, 1960 . . 81.00
Zippo, Polished Line Design, Box, 1976 . . . . 48.00
Zippo, Salem Cigarettes, Chromium, Box, 1991 . . . . 15.00
Zippo, Slim, No. 1615, 1977 . . . . 48.00
Zippo, U.S.A., Lifetime Guarantee, Chrome, Cased 13.00
Zippo, Venetian Scrolled Design On Both Sides, Brush Finish, 1978 . . . . 40.00

LIGHTNING RODS and lightning rod balls are collected for their variety
of shapes and colors. These glass balls were at the center of the rod that
was attached to the roof of a house or barn to avoid lightning damage.

Ball, Acorn Pendant, Flashed Red 500.00
Ball, Amber Ribbed, Light Shade, 5 1/2 . . . . 125.00
Ball, Barnett, Ribbed, Cobalt Blue 90.00
Ball, Chestnut, Medium Amber 150.00
Ball, D & S Co., Deep Red 275.00
Ball, D & S Co., Light To Medium Slag Swirling 165.00
Ball, Diddie Blitzen, Clear 45.00
Ball, Diddie Blitzen, Red 100.00
Ball, Doorknob, Amethyst 82.00
Ball, Doorknob, Slag 440.00
Ball, Electra, Cobalt Blue, Round 165.00
Ball, Electra, Cone 65.00
Ball, Electra, Cone, Embossed Pattern, Flashed Blue Over Clear 100.00
Ball, Electra, Round, Gold Mercury 335.00
Ball, Electra, Sun Colored Amethyst 35.00
Ball, Hawkeye, Sun Colored Amethyst 50.00
Ball, James F. Goetz, Cobalt Blue 95.00
Ball, Maher, Preston, Flashed Red 425.00
Ball, Moon & Star, Amber 100.00
Ball, Moon & Star, Gold Mercury 467.00
Ball, Moon & Star, White Milk Glass 30.00
Ball, National, Belted, Silver Mercury 418.00
Ball, Plain, Black 150.00
Ball, Plain, Blue Milk Glass 15.00
Ball, Quilt, Bright Red 330.00
Ball, Quilt, Flat, Amber 110.00
Ball, Quilt, Flat, Gray Green 95.00
Ball, Quilt, Flat, Teal Green 135.00
Ball, Quilt, Raised, Red 200.00
Ball, Ribbed, Red, Dated On Collar, 3 1/2 In. 225.00
Ball, Ribbed, Sun Colored Amethyst 275.00
Ball, S Co., Amber 135.00
Ball, Shinn System, Amber 95.00
Ball, Shinn System, Round 30.00
Ball, Shinn, Lincoln, Belted, Amethyst 60.00
Brass & Wrought Iron, 19th Century 225.00

LIMOGES porcelain has been made in Limoges, France, since the mid-
nineteenth century. Fine porcelains were made by many factories,
including Haviland, Ahrenfeldt, Guerin, Pouyat, Elite, and others.
Modern porcelains are being made at Limoges and the word *Limoges*
as part of the mark is not an indication of age. Haviland, one of the
Limoges factories, is listed as a separate category in this book.

Asparagus Set, Lavender Violets, Gold Rim, 15-In. Platter, 13 Piece 340.00
Biscuit Jar, Large Daisies & Foliage On Cream, Gold Trim, Handles 325.00
Bowl, Hand Painted Strawberries, 9 1/4 In. 110.00
Box, Courting Couple 90.00
Box, Lid, Gold, Old Fashioned Man & Woman, 5 In. 60.00
Box, Lid, Hexagonal, Enamel Geometric Design, Sarlandie 550.00
Box, Raised Cupid Scenes, Bisque, 9 x 3 In. 110.00
Box, White, Brick Red Flowers, Art Deco, Black Ground, Circular, 4 1/2 x 8 3/4 In. 440.00
Bust, Chopin, 8 1/8 In. 135.00

Butter, Cover, Pink Carnations All Around Base 75.00
Cake Plate, Floral, Signed, 12 In. 66.00
Celery Plate, Seashells, Gold Trim, 12 1/4 In. 65.00
Charger, Cobalt Blue, Gold Enameled Floral & Scrolls, 13 1/2 In. 250.00
Charger, Hand Painted Grape Clusters, Leaves, Vines, 14 In. 135.00
Chocolate Pot, Purple & Pink, Yellow Mums, Gold Handle & Finial 175.00
Chocolate Set, White Flowers, White Ground, Green & Gold Border, 9 Piece 200.00
Chop Plate, Hand Painted Fish, Signed, Dubois, 13 1/8 In. 247.00
Chop Plate, Purple & White Grapes, Signed, 13 In. 142.00
Clock, Mantel, Sedan Chair Form, Portrait Rondels, Bronze, Signed, 11 In. 3737.00
Cup & Saucer, Allover Gold Flowers, Yellow, Demitasse 28.00
Cup & Saucer, Brown, Tan, Orange Flowers, Demitasse 25.00
Demitasse Set, Iris Design, Gold Trimmed Creamer, 14 Piece 375.00
Dresser Tray, Powder, 1908 .... 130.00
Ewer, Pink, Yellow Roses, Hand Painted, Gold Handle, Base, Elite, 9 In. 85.00
Figurine, Pierrot Clown, Holding Cointreau Bottle 65.00
Fish Set, Different Hand Painted Water Lilies, 24-In. Platter, 5 Piece 295.00
Fish Set, Hand Painted Fish Platter, 8 Plates 750.00
Jar, Biscuit, Cover, Relief Scrolls, Blue, Gold Flowers, Scroll Handle, 7 x 5 1/2 In. 145.00
Jar, Potpourri, Cover, Florals Outlined In Gold, Gold Handles & Finial 295.00
Jardiniere, Tulips, Outline In Gold, 9 x 7 In. 325.00
Pitcher, Mistletoe Berries, Gray & Pink Ground, Art Deco, 6 In. 175.00
Pitcher, Printed Romantic Scenes, Pink Ground, c.1870, 13 In. 400.00
Plaque, Cavalier, Multicolored Garb & Banner, 7 5/8 In. 460.00
Plaque, Child, Embracing Mother, Signed, 10 In. 295.00
Plaque, Fish, Gold Rococo Edge 165.00
Plaque, Hand Painted Flowers, Frame, 14 In. 475.00
Plaque, Mediterranean Scene, Enameled, Early 20th Century, Frame, 10 x 14 In. .. 920.00
Plaque, Portrait Of Gypsy Woman, Beading On Earrings & Hair, 11 1/2 In. 495.00
Plaque, Seascape, Mother & Child, 10 In. 395.00
Plate, Country Scene, Church In Background, Gold Rim, 12 1/4 In. 185.00
Plate, Empress Josephine 38.00
Plate, Game Birds, Gold Border, L. Coudert, 10 1/4 In. 165.00
Plate, Game Birds, Gold Trim, Signed, Coronet 105.00
Plate, Game, Pheasant, Signed, 11 In. 95.00
Plate, Hand Painted Bird, c.1880, 12 Piece 700.00
Plate, Hand Painted Fruit, Pierced For Hanging, G. Rosier, 12 3/8 In. 210.00
Plate, Hand Painted Roses, Gold Rococo Edge, Green Leaves, Hanging, 10 In. 125.00
Plate, Joan Of Arc, With Flag At Altar, Signed, 9 3/4 In. 135.00
Plate, Peaches & Pear, Green & Beige Ground, Porcelain, 12 3/8 In. 235.00
Plate, Pink & Blue Flowers & Leaves On Gold Paint, Gilt Fluted Edge, 7 In. 20.00
Plate, Pink Floral, Gold Rococo, Felix, 10 In. 75.00
Plate, Purple Plums, Gold Rococo Borders, Pierced, 12 1/4 In. 245.00
Plate, Rococo Gold Edge, Blue, Tan, Cream, Pastel Ground, Hanging, 10 3/8 In. 125.00
Plate, Roses, Different Rose On Each Plate, 7 3/4 In., 6 Piece 325.00
Plate, Roses, Gold Trim, 8 1/2 In. 40.00
Plate, Scenic, Grassy Meadow, Pond & Trees, Irregular Edges, 12 1/4 In. 195.00
Plate, Vase Of Flowers Center, Gold Border, 15 1/4 In. 260.00
Plate, Woman, Young Nobleman, Gold Rococo Border, Hanging, 9 3/4 In. 78.00
Platter, Sage Green, Cream, Gold Roses 75.00
Punch Bowl, Green Interior, Purple Grapes Against Beige Ground, Roses, 15 1/2 In. ... 665.00
Punch Bowl, Hand Painted Grape Design, c.1900, 13 In. 1025.00
Punch Set, Stand, Hand Painted Pink & Red Roses, 6 Cups 800.00
Relish, Violet Pattern, Golden Roman Edge, Coronet 45.00
Salt, Pearlized Enamel Pinks, Gold & White Pearlized Swirls Edge, 4 1/2 In. 65.00
Sugar & Creamer, Gold Trim, Handle 430.00
Tankard, Cherries, 13 3/8 In. 325.00
Tankard, Grape Design, Leaves, 15 In. 500.00
Tile, Napoleon At Waterloo, Hand Painted, Frame 250.00
Toothpick, Gold Collar & Handle, Floral Upper, Black Lower Portion 35.00
Tray, Dresser, Allover Windmill, Cottage, Water Scene, Fisherman On Rock, 1870 ...... 165.00
Tray, Gold Design, Round, Signed, 13 1/2 In. 145.00
Tray, Gold Enamel, Handles, 13 1/2 In. 75.00

Vase, Profile Of Woman, Flowers In Hair, Gilt Foliate Scrolls, 10 In. 805.00
Vase, Scottish Child, Playing A Musical Instrument, Hand Painted, Marked, Pair 220.00

LINDBERGH was a national hero. In 1927, Charles Lindbergh, the aviator, became the first man to make a nonstop solo flight across the Atlantic Ocean. In 1932, his son was kidnapped and murdered, and Lindbergh was again the center of public interest. He died in 1974. All types of Lindbergh memorabilia are collected.

Button, Lindbergh's Spirit Of St. Louis, Bond Bread, Celluloid, 1 1/4 In. 40.00
Button, Welcome Lindy, Picture, Red, White & Blue, 1 1/4 In. 58.00
Card, Arcade, Lindy In Capital, Seated, Wicker Table, Outdoors, Govt. Air Service 12.00
Figurine, Cast Iron, 8 In. 75.00
Game, Lindy Hop-Off, New Airplane Game, Board, 13 x 26 In. 150.00
Game, Metal Spinner 195.00
Label, Airline, TWA First, Lindbergh Line, Color, 1930s, 3 1/2 x 3 3/4 In. 15.00
Model Kit, Spirit Of St. Louis, Metalcraft, Builds Over 15 Planes, Box 225.00
Pennant, Welcome Lindbergh, Oilcloth, Red & White, 15 In. 75.00
Photograph, Lindbergh Next To Spirit Of St. Louis 9.00
Pillowcase, Lindy, Face, Scenes, Fringed, 20 In. 135.00
Sheet Music, You Flew Over, Uncle Sam Takes His Hat Off To You 40.00

LITHOPHANES are porcelain pictures made by casting clay in layers of various thicknesses. When a piece is held to the light, a picture of light and shadow is seen through it. Most lithophanes date from the 1825–1875 period. A few are still being made. Many lithophanes sold today were originally panels for lampshades.

Cup & Saucer, Head Of Woman, Moriage Dragons All Around 28.00
Lamp, Heater, Porcelain Scenes, Square Brass Frame, Electrified, 5 1/2 In. 330.00
Lamp, Tin & Brass Pedestal, 9 In. 195.00

LIVERPOOL, England, was the site of several pottery and porcelain factories from 1716 to 1785. Some earthenware was made with transfer decorations. Sadler and Green made print-decorated wares from 1756. Many of the pieces were made for the American market and feature patriotic emblems, such as eagles, flags, and other special-interest motifs. Liverpool pitchers are always called Liverpool jugs by collectors.

Bottle, Landscape, 2 Fishermen On River Bank, Blue, White, 1760, 9 In. 3105.00
Bowl, Transfer, Ship, Sailing Motifs, Early 19th Century, England, 7 In. 345.00
Cup & Saucer, Handleless, Black Transfer, Washington, His Country's Father 330.00
Figurine, Nun, Seated, Yellow Veil, Purple, Blue, Yellow, Green Sprays, 1755, 4 3/4 In. . 1610.00
Jug, Children Of Bacchus, Hunter On Reverse, Sadler, 1800 .... 1100.00
Jug, Clipper Ships Flying American Flag, Transfer 1840.00
Jug, Courtship & Matrimony & Chip Off The Old Block, 9 In. 405.00
Jug, Masonic Symbols, Motto On Reverse, Creamware, 11 3/4 In. 575.00
Jug, Patriots, Polychrome Enamels, Creamware, England, 10 7/8 In. 1840.00
Jug, Portrait, Thomas Jefferson, President Of United States Of America 9350.00
Jug, Puzzle, Spherical, 2 Flowering Plants, Tubular Handle, Blue, White, 1765, 6 7/8 In. . 920.00
Jug, Puzzle, Spherical, Scalloped Edge Panel, Oriental Shrubbery, 1750, 7 1/8 In. 7475.00
Jug, Sailor's Return, Creamware, 1830s, 7 5/8 In. 632.50
Jug, Woman, Holding Early Federal Flag, Creamware, 9 3/4 In. 2090.00
Teapot, 3-Masted Vessel, British Flag, Black Transfer, Red, Blue, Yellow, Green, 5 In. . 990.00
Teapot, Spherical, Crabstock Spout, Plants, Bamboo, Rocks, Tin Glaze, 3 3/16 In. 8625.00

LLADRO is a Spanish porcelain. Juan, Jose, and Vicente Lladro opened a ceramics workshop in Almacera in 1951. They soon began making figurines in a distinctive, elongated style. In 1958 the factory moved to Tabernes Blanques, Spain. The company makes stoneware and porcelain figurines and vases in limited and unlimited editions. Dates given are first and last years of production.

Bell, 1987, Christmas ....45.00 to 175.00
Bell, 1988, Christmas ....15.00 to 45.00
Bell, 1991, Christmas ....15.00 to 60.00

Bust, Madonna, Hand Across Chest, No. 4649, 8 1/4 In. 100.00
Figurine, A Wintry Day, No. 3513, 1978-1988 .... .625.00 to 700.00
Figurine, Abraham, No. 5169, 1982-1985 .... 650.00
Figurine, All Aboard, No. 7619, 1992-1993 .... .220.00 to 440.00
Figurine, Andalucian Group, No. 4647, 1969-1990 .... 1100.00
Figurine, Angel With Lyre, No. 1321, 1976-1985 .... 500.00
Figurine, Architect, No. 5214, 1984-1990 .... 500.00
Figurine, At The Circus, No. 5052, 1979-1985 .... .1150.00 to 1250.00
Figurine, Attentive Dogs, No. 4957, 1977-1981 .... 1750.00
Figurine, Ballet First Step, No. 5094, 1980-1983 .... 325.00
Figurine, Basket Of Love, No. 7622, Retired .... .225.00 to 375.00
Figurine, Basket Of Margaritas, No. 1543, 1988-1991 .... 450.00
Figurine, Bat Mask No. 8, No. 1642, 1989-1991 .... 600.00
Figurine, Best Friend, No. 7620, 1993-1995 .... .250.00 to 345.00
Figurine, Billy Baseball Player, No. 5137, 1982-1983 .... 650.00
Figurine, Billy Football Player, No. 5134, 1982-1983 .... 650.00
Figurine, Bird Watcher, No. 4730, 1970-1985 .... 425.00
Figurine, Boy Clown Standing, No. 5057, 1980-1985 .... .415.00 to 1095.00
Figurine, Boy With Book, No. 1024, 1969-1975 .... 550.00
Figurine, Boy With Goat, No. 2009, 1970-1981 .... 750.00
Figurine, Bunny Girl, No. 5163, 1982-1985 .... 500.00
Figurine, Can Can, No. 5370, 1986-1990 .... .1100.00 to 1250.00
Figurine, Can I Play?, No. 7610, 1990-1992 .... .225.00 to 625.00
Figurine, Cat Eyes Mask No. 10, No. 1644, 1989-1991 .... 500.00
Figurine, Cat Girl, No. 5164, 1982-1985 .... 500.00
Figurine, Charlie The Tramp, No. 5233, 1984-1993 .... .695.00 to 745.00
Figurine, Chess Pieces, No. 4833.30, 1972-1985 .... 2000.00
Figurine, Christmas Carols, No. 1239, 1973-1981 .... 815.00
Figurine, Cinderella & Fairy Godmother, No. 7553, Retired 900.00
Figurine, Clown Thinking, No. 5058, 1980-1985 .... .450.00 to 1000.00
Figurine, Clown With Clock, No. 5056, 1980-1985 .... .640.00 to 1065.00
Figurine, Clown With Concertina, No. 1027, 1969-1995 .... .600.00 to 750.00
Figurine, Clown With Saxophone, No. 5059, 1980-1985 .... .450.00 to 1000.00
Figurine, Clown With Trumpet, No. 5060, 1980-1985 .... .450.00 to 685.00
Figurine, Cobbler, No. 4853, 1973-1985 .... 450.00
Figurine, Country Woman, No. 353.13, 1965 .... 1600.00
Figurine, Courting Time, No. 5409, 1987-1990 .... 500.00
Figurine, Cutting Flowers, No. 5088, 1980-1988 .... 1565.00
Figurine, Dancing Partner, No. 5093, 1980-1983 .... 400.00
Figurine, Daughters, No. 5013, 1978-1991 .... 845.00
Figurine, Daydream, No. 2062, 1977-1985 .... 1500.00
Figurine, Debbie & Her Doll, No. 1379, 1978-1985 .... .500.00 to 690.00
Figurine, Dog Playing Bongos, No. 1156, 1971-1978 .... 400.00
Figurine, Dog, No. 4642, 1969-1981 .... 295.00
Figurine, Dog, Poodle, No. 1259, 1974-1985 .... 200.00
Figurine, Donkey In Love, No. 4524, 1969-1985 .... .250.00 to 425.00
Figurine, Dutch Boy, No. 4811, 1972-1988 .... 265.00
Figurine, Fairy Queen, No 5068, 1980-1983 .... 900.00
Figurine, Fifa Trophy, No. 5133, 1982-1983 .... 600.00
Figurine, Flower For My Lady, No. 1513, 1987-1990 .... 1440.00
Figurine, Flower Peddler, No. 5029, 1979-1985 .... 1000.00
Figurine, Flower Song, No. 7607, 1988-1988 .... .330.00 to 750.00
Figurine, Flute Player, No. 1025, 1969-1978 .... 505.00
Figurine, For A Perfect Performance, No. 7641, Retired .... .420.00 to 565.00
Figurine, Fox & Cub, No. 1065, 1969-1985 .... 450.00
Figurine, Freedom, No. 5602, 1989-1989 .... 1000.00
Figurine, Garden Classic, No. 7911 .... .290.00 to 750.00
Figurine, German Shepherd With Pup, No. 4731, 1970-1975 .... 875.00
Figurine, Girl Singer, No. 4612, 1969-1979 .... 600.00
Figurine, Girl Tennis Player, No. 4798, 1972-1981 .... 400.00
Figurine, Girl Walking, No. 5040, 1979-1981 .... 750.00
Figurine, Girl With Bonnet, No. 1147, 1971-1985 .... 225.00
Figurine, Girl With Dice, No. 1176, 1971-1981 .... .198.00 to 300.00

Figurine, Girl With Dog, No. 4806, 1972-1982 . . . . 565.00
Figurine, Girl With Doll, No. 1083, 1969-1985 . . . . 250.00
Figurine, Girl With Flowers, No. 1088, 1969-1989 . . . . .600.00 to 750.00
Figurine, Girl With Lamp, No. 4507, 1969-1985 . . . . 625.00
Figurine, Girl With Milk Pail, No. 4682, 1970-1991 . . . . 275.00
Figurine, Girl With Motorcycle, No. 5143, 1982-1988 . . . . 1300.00
Figurine, Girl With Piglets, No. 4572, 1969-1985 . . . . 450.00
Figurine, Girl's Head, No. 1003.30, 1984-1985 . . . . 500.00
Figurine, Girls In The Swing, No. 1366, 1978-1988 . . . . 1900.00
Figurine, Good Bear, No. 1205, 1978-1981 . . . . 85.00
Figurine, Gothic Queen, No. 4689, 1970-1975 . . . . 750.00
Figurine, Hamlet, No. 4729, 1970-1980 . . . . 850.00
Figurine, Heavenly Harpist, No. 5830, 1991-1992 . . . . 95.00
Figurine, Hebrew Student, No. 4684, 1970-1985 . . . . 700.00
Figurine, Hunters, No. 1048, 1969-1976 . . . . 1375.00
Figurine, Idyl, No. 1017, 1969-1991 . . . . 600.00
Figurine, Jester's Serenade, No. 5932, Retired 1100.00
Figurine, Lady With Girl, No. 1353, 1978-1985 . . . . 700.00
Figurine, Lady With Greyhound, No. 4594, 1969-1981 . . . . .650.00 to 895.00
Figurine, Languid Clown, No. 4924, 1974-1983 . . . . .800.00 to 1250.00
Figurine, Little Ballet Girl, No. 5106, 1982-1985 . . . . 255.00
Figurine, Little Ballet Girl, Pink, No. 5105, 1982-1985 . . . . 240.00
Figurine, Little Eagle Owl, No. 2020, 1971-1985 . . . . 450.00
Figurine, Little Horse Resting, No. 1203, 1972-1981 . . . . 625.00
Figurine, Little Shepard With Goat, No. 4817, 1972-1981 . . . . 375.00
Figurine, Little Traveller, No. 7602, 1986-1986 . . . . 1195.00
Figurine, Lovers From Verona, No. 1250, 1974-1990 . . . . 1125.00
Figurine, Madonna, No. 4586, 1969-1979 . . . . 275.00
Figurine, Magic, No. 4605, 1969-1985 . . . . 265.00
Figurine, Magician's Mask No. 5, No. 1639, 1989-1991 . . . . 600.00
Figurine, Magistrates, No. 2052, 1974-1981 . . . . 750.00
Figurine, Male Equestrian, No. 4515, 1969-1985 . . . . 1000.00
Figurine, Male Tennis Player, No. 1426, 1982-1988 . . . . 300.00
Figurine, Milkmaid With Wheelbarrow, No. 4979, 1977-1981 . . . . 800.00
Figurine, Mother With Child & Donkey, No. 4666, 1969-1979 . . . . 845.00
Figurine, Music Time, No. 5430, 1987-1990 . . . . 600.00
Figurine, My Buddy, No. 7609, 1989-1990 . . . . .225.00 to 750.00
Figurine, Nude, No. 4511, 1983-1985 . . . . .625.00 to 750.00
Figurine, Old Folks, No. 1033, 1969-1985 . . . . 1500.00
Figurine, Old Man, No. 4622, 1969-1982 . . . . .790.00 to 800.00
Figurine, On The Beach, No. 1481, 1985-1988 . . . . 550.00
Figurine, Penguin, No. 5248, 1984-1988 . . . . 225.00
Figurine, Peter Pan, No. 7529, Limited Edition, 1993 . . . . .700.00 to 1200.00
Figurine, Pharmacist, No. 4844, 1973-1985 . . . . .1200.00 to 1300.00
Figurine, Picture Perfect, No. 7612, Retired . . . . .225.00 to 565.00
Figurine, Pleasantries, With Base, No. 1440, 1983-1990 . . . . 1500.00
Figurine, Precocious Courtship, No. 5072, 1980-1990 . . . . 995.00
Figurine, Pregonero, No. 1086, 1969-1975 . . . . 1250.00
Figurine, Princess Mask, No. 3, No. 1637, 1987-1991 . . . . 500.00
Figurine, Princess Sitting, No. 1381, 1978-1985 . . . . 595.00
Figurine, Professor, No. 5208, 1984-1990 . . . . .500.00 to 600.00
Figurine, Racing Motorcyclist, No. 5270, 1985-1988 . . . . 750.00
Figurine, Resting Nude, No. 3025, 1991-1992 . . . . 1250.00
Figurine, Ride In The Park, No. 5718, 1985-1990 . . . . 4250.00
Figurine, School Days, No. 7604, Retired . . . . .385.00 to 750.00
Figurine, Sitting Girl With Lilies, No. 4972, 1977-1995 . . . . 135.00
Figurine, Skye Terrier, No. 4643, 1969-1985 . . . . .350.00 to 500.00
Figurine, Snow White With Apple, No. 5067, 1980-1983 . . . . .835.00 to 1250.00
Figurine, Spanish Soldier, No. 5255, 1984-1985 . . . . 550.00
Figurine, Spring Blossom, No. 1631, 1989-1991 . . . . 500.00
Figurine, Spring Bouquets, No. 7603, 1987-1987 . . . . .565.00 to 875.00
Figurine, Storytime, No. 5229, 1984-1990 . . . . 825.00
Figurine, Summer Stock, No. 401, Retired . . . . .650.00 to 1125.00

Figurine, Summer Stroll, No. 7611, Retired ....175.00 to 500.00
Figurine, Swinging, No. 1297, 1974-1990 .... 1500.00
Figurine, Typical Peddler, No. 4859, 1974-1985 .... 1000.00
Figurine, Valencian Couple On Horseback, No. 4648, 1969-1990 .... 940.00
Figurine, Veterinarian, No. 4825, 1972-1985 .... 500.00
Figurine, Watchman, No. 5087, 1980-1983 .... 1000.00
Figurine, Woman Painting Vase, No. 5079, 1980-1985 .... 1125.00
Figurine, Wrath Of Don Quixote, No. 1343, 1977-1990 .... 1000.00
Figurine, Young Street Musicians, No. 5306, 1985-1988 .... 1065.00
Ornament, 3 Kings, No. 5729, 1990-1991 .... 110.00
Ornament, Mini Holy Family, No. 5657, 1989-1990 .... 80.00
Plate, 1971, Christmas, No. 7006 .... 250.00
Plate, 1972, Mother's Day, No. 7007 .... 180.00
Plate, 1979, Mother's Day, No. 7107 .... 550.00
Vase, Blue Tinge, Strobergshyttan, Sweden, 4 1/4 In. 90.00
Vase, Engraved Butterfly 90.00

LOCKE ART is a trademark found on glass of the early twentieth century. Joseph Locke worked at many English and American firms. He
designed and etched his own glass in Pittsburgh, Pennsylvania, starting in the 1880s. Some pieces were marked *Joe Locke*, but most were
marked with the words *Locke Art*. The mark is hidden in the pattern on
the glass.

Bowl, Console, Grape Design, Oval, 15 In. 75.00
Sherbet, Grape & Line, Saucer, Short Stem, 3 1/4 In. ....148.00 to 150.00

LOETZ glass was made in many varieties. Johann Loetz bought a glassworks in Austria in 1840. He died in 1848 and his widow ran the company; then in 1879, his grandson took over. Most collectors recognize
the iridescent gold glass similar to Tiffany, but many other types were
made. The firm closed during World War II.

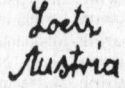

Berry Set, Green, Threaded, Gold, Rainbow Iridescent, 5 Piece 675.00
Biscuit Jar, Mottled Green On Pale Iridescent Green, Square, 7 3/8 In. 595.00
Bowl, Emerald Green, Oil Spot, Brass Floral Pierced Base, Handles, Squat, 7 In. 300.00
Bowl, Paperweight, Scalloped Rim, Gray & Green Exterior, 5 1/2 In. 660.00
Box, Hinged Cover, Cobalt Blue, Iridescent Chartreuse Vines, Round, 3 1/2 x 5 1/2 In. ... 495.00
Bride's Bowl, Gold, Iridescent, Hobnail, Ribbed, Ruffled, Brass Footed Stand, 10 1/2 In. ... 355.00
Compote, Amber Onionskin Bowl, Metal Base, 8 1/2 x 10 In. 550.00
Cracker Barrel, Oil Spots, Entwined Vines, Silver Bail & Cover, 5 1/2 In. 385.00
Inkwell, Emerald Green, Brass Pod, Hinged Cover, Peacock-Eye Pattern, Round, 5 In. ... 230.00
Inkwell, Green, Iridescent, Brass Devil, Hinged Cover, Art Nouveau, Square, 3 In. 605.00
Owl, Oil Spot Design, Blue, Iridescent, 5 x 6 In. 275.00
Rose Bowl, Emerald Green, Ribbed, Horizontal Threading, 3 1/4 In. 88.00
Vase, 3 Wavy Broad Green Iridescent Bands, Drop Shape Feet, Cylindrical, 5 7/8 In. 11500.00
Vase, Abstract Vine Design, Scalloped Rim, Blue, Green, Iridescent, 11 In. 690.00
Vase, Amber Glass, Silver Blue Heart Shape Leaves, Iridescent, 1900, 6 1/8 In. 3162.00
Vase, Amber Glass, Silver Blue Leaves, Horizontal Striations, 5 1/2 In. 2990.00
Vase, Amber Glass, Silver Blue Swirls, Teardrops, Iridescent, 1900, 8 1/4 In. 6900.00
Vase, Applied Bud & Stems, Green, Iridescent, 7 3/8 In. 175.00
Vase, Art Nouveau, Lily Pads & Blossoms, Dimpled, Metal Open Work, 2 3/4 x 4 In. 315.00
Vase, Blue, Iridescent, Applied Vine, 7 In. 295.00
Vase, Bud, Triple, Applied Leaves, Gold, Iridescent Overall, 6 In. 82.50
Vase, Clear Overspray, Pulled Striated Leafage, Amber Oil Spots, Signed, c.1900, 7 In. .. 3450.00
Vase, Corset Shape, Crimped Rim, Polished Pontil, Gold, Iridescent, 7 1/2 x 4 In. 275.00
Vase, Dimples, Bulbous, Green, Iridescent, Quatrefold Top, 5 1/2 In. 95.00
Vase, Double Gourd, Green Oil Spot, Pinched, 7 3/4 In. 225.00
Vase, Double Gourd, Red, Pinched, 11 3/4 In. 225.00
Vase, Embossed Design At Neck, Bulbous Bottom, 10 In. 395.00
Vase, Emerald Green, Iridescent, Pinched, Applied Coiled Serpent, 6 In. 160.00
Vase, Encased In Metal, Green, Iridescent, 1935, 5 x 6 In. 350.00
Vase, Everted Rim, Foliate Motif, Pink, Gold Iridescent Ground, 7 1/8 In. 4025.00
Vase, Flower Form, Cobalt Blue, Polished Pontil, 9 1/2 In. 375.00
Vase, Gold, Iridescent, Bronze Spots, Dimpled, Ground Pontil, 6 x 5 In. 750.00

Vase, Gray Green, Pulled Swirls, Allover Rainbow, Trefoil Rim, Cylindrical, 13 In.	330.00
Vase, Green Blue Swirls, Iridescent, Silver Ribbons, Leaves, 1900, 7 1/2 In.	3737.00
Vase, Green, Encased In Metal, 5 x 6 In.	350.00
Vase, Green, Iridescent, Bulbous, Waisted Neck, Lilac Threading, 8 In.	190.00
Vase, Green, Iridescent, Dimpled, 5 1/2 In.	90.00
Vase, Green, Iridescent, Melon, Extended Neck, 6 1/2 In.	330.00
Vase, Green, Pewter Frame, 6 1/2 In.	340.00
Vase, Hourglass Shape, Pulled Design, Pink, White, Yellow Glass, 10 In. .	207.00
Vase, Iridescent, Oil Spot, Cobalt Blue Vines, Dimpled Sides, Folded Down, 5 In.	110.00
Vase, Luster Tree Bark Design, Green, 1910, 8 In.	165.00
Vase, Metallic Luster, Amber, 1910, 9 1/2 In.	198.00
Vase, Metallic Luster, Green, 1910, 11 In.	330.00
Vase, Oil Spot, Gold, 8 1/4 x 6 1/2 In.	460.00
Vase, Oil Spot, Purples & Blue, 6 In.	595.00
Vase, Onion-Shape, Gold & Pink Background, 12 1/2 In.	4750.00
Vase, Pale Pink Opaque Top, Green Iridescent Waves, 7 1/2 In.	522.00
Vase, Peacock Feathers Half Way Up, Metal Fitted Flower Frog, 5 x 6 In. .	375.00
Vase, Pillow Style, Polished Pontil, Purple, Iridescent, 7 1/2 x 5 1/2 In.	575.00
Vase, Pinched Sides, Green, Purple, Red, Iridescent, 10 1/2 In.	172.50
Vase, Pulled Waves, Silver & Gold Luster, Green Pontil, 6 1/2 x 6 1/2 In.	300.00
Vase, Purple & Black Trailings On Edge, Silvery-Blue Dots, Signed, c.1902, 9 3/8 In. . . .	9775.00
Vase, Purple & Blue Concentric Waves, Purple Oil Spots At Base, 14 1/2 In.	425.00
Vase, Purple Thistles, Wide Mouth, Handles, Gold Tracery Encircles Bowl, 8 1/2 In.	525.00
Vase, Purple, Iridescent Ground, Green Amber Oil Spot, Cylindrical, 8 In.	990.00
Vase, Rainbow, Silver Overlay, Pale Pink, Green, Yellow Flowers, Scrolls, 5 x 2 3/4 In. . .	880.00
Vase, Raindrop Pattern, Shaded Rose, Bulbous, 4 1/2 In.	135.00
Vase, Raised Floral Design, Green, Gold & Blue, Glaze, Iridescent, Signed, 9 1/2 In.	259.00
Vase, Rib, Flared Mouth, Orange Random Threading, Polished Pontil, Iridescent, 8 x 8 In.	110.00
Vase, Rubina Verde, Bark Texture, Molded Rope Garlands, Bottle Shape, 11 3/4 In. . . .	190.00
Vase, Ruffled Trefoil Rim, Ambergris Body, Gold, Silver Iridescent Feathers, 6 1/2 In. . . .	862.50
Vase, Salmon Horizontal Lines, Random Placed Dots, Signed, c.1901, 5 7/8 In.	4600.00
Vase, Salmon, Silver-Blue Trailings, Overlapping At Middle, Signed, 1900, 9 In.	8625.00
Vase, Silver Blue, Iridescent, Pinch Sides, Cylindrical, 9 1/2 In.	190.00
Vase, Silver Green, Silver Lily Overlay, Corset, 4 1/4 In.	1100.00
Vase, Silver-Blue Waves, Ribbed, Squatty, 5 In.	1210.00
Vase, Striated Green, Amber, Purple Stringing, Mounted On Bronze Ring, 3 Legs, 9 In. . .	100.00
Vase, Swirling Cane & Medallion, Green, Iridescent, 24 x 8 In.	1650.00
Vase, Vines Top & Bottom, Iridescent, Bronze With Spots, 6 1/2 In.	750.00
Vase, Yellow & Red Trailings, Iridescent, Corset Form, 6 1/4 In.	165.00
Vase, Yellow Textured Base, Emerald Threaded Rim, Iridescent, Opalescent, 10 In.	175.00

LONE RANGER, a fictional character, was introduced on the radio in 1932. Over three thousand shows were produced before the series ended in 1954. In 1938, the first Lone Ranger movie was made. Television shows were started in 1949 and are still seen on some stations. The Lone Ranger appears on many products and was even the name of a restaurant chain for several years.

Badge, Deputy	35.00
Book, Better Little Book, The Great Western Span	35.00
Book, Big Little Book, Menace Of Murder Valley	25.00
Box, Empty, For Single Gun & Holster, 1938	135.00
Calendar, 1955, Merita Bread Fan Club	1000.00
Card, Official Outfit On Card, Black Fabric Mask, 1950s, 10 1/2 x 13 In.	145.00
Coloring Book, Whitman, 1957, 50 Pages, 7 x 8 In.	12.00
Costume, Suit, Mask, Gun, 1940s	375.00
Display, Cereal & Movie, Lone Ranger & Silver, Cardboard, 1958, 5 Ft.	2500.00
Figure, Hartland	150.00
Figurine, Chalkware, 1930, 16 In.	150.00
Figurine, Lone Ranger On Silver, Chalkware	165.00
Figurine, Lone Ranger, Standing, Chalkware	125.00
Flashlight, Box	125.00
Game, Board, Legend Of Lone Ranger	35.00
Game, Board, Lone Ranger & Tonto	35.00

Game, Board, Parker Brothers, 1938, 18 x 18 In. 25.00
Game, Horseshoe & Ring Toss Set 75.00
Game, Parker Brothers, 1938, 9 1/2 x 19 In. 33.00
Game, Ring Toss, Box 495.00
Game, Target Set, Frame, Marx, 35 x 24 In. 315.00
Game, Target Set, Round, Box, Marx, 1946 ....250.00 to 275.00
Glass, 1938 ....70.00 to 78.00
Hair Brush 20.00
Hartland Set, Cheyenne 175.00
Kit, First Aid, 1938 .... 25.00
Kit, Prairie Wagon, Plastic, Box, 1975, 6 x 10 1/2 x 15 1/2 In. 68.00
Knife, 2-Bladed Steel, Plastic Grip Panels, Camillus Cutlery Co., 1950s 900.00
Knife, Straight Shooter, Ralston 80.00
Lunch Box, Steel, 1950s 295.00
Map, Frontier Town, With 2 Cheerios Cereal Backs, 1948 .... 110.00
Model Kit, Aurora 280.00
Movie Poster, Lost City Of Gold, Promotional, 11 x 28 In. 100.00
Outfit, Chaps, Pants & Shirt 375.00
Paint Set 90.00
Pedometer ....25.00 to 40.00
Pin, Lone Ranger On His Horse, Celluloid, c.1959, 1 1/4 In. 38.00
Pin, Lone Ranger On Horse, Ribbon, With Indian Head End, Celluloid, 1 1/4 In. 80.00
Pin, Ranger On Silver, Green Ribbon, Horseshoe Charm, Celluloid, c.1939 .... 100.00
Play Set, Mysterious Prospector With Donkey, Box, Gabriel 35.00
Postcard, Bond Bread 45.00
Print Set, Picture, Box, 1939 .... 65.00
Punch Out Set 40.00
Ring, Atom Bomb, Kix Cereal, Metal, Gold & Silver Finish, 1946 ....75.00 to 83.00
Ring, Flashlight 75.00
Ring, Movie Film, Metal, Gold & Silver Finish, 1949 ....44.00 to 75.00
Ring, National Defenders, Look-Around, Metal, Gold Finish, 1941 .... 100.00
Ring, Weather, Metal, Gold Finish, General Mills, 1947 .... 83.00
Silver Bullet, Secret Compartment, 1947 ....40.00 to 45.00
Snow Dome 85.00
Tie 28.00
Toothbrush Holder, Ranger On Horse, 1938 ....120.00 to 125.00
Toy, On Silver, Moving Hand With Gun, Rotating Lasso, Tin, Marx, 1939 .... 350.00
Window Card, Movie, Color, 1951, 14 x 22 In. 195.00
Wrapper, Clark Candy Bar, 5 Cents, Certificate Toward Pocket Watch, 1938 .... 650.00
Wristwatch, On Horse, Yelling, Hi-Yo Silver, Chrome Finish, Tan Leather Strap 120.00

LONGWY Workshop of Longwy, France, first made ceramic wares in
1798. The workshop is still in business. Most of the ceramic pieces
found today are glazed with many colors to resemble cloisonne or
other enameled metal. Many pieces were made with stylized figures
and art deco designs. The factory used a variety of marks.

Bowl, 3 Swans, Trees, Mountains In Background, Saffron Ground, 15 In. 1100.00
Bowl, Archer, Hunting Deer On Horseback, Sea, Palm Trees, Gold Rim, 15 x 3 In. 1045.00
Bowl, Bird In Black, Blue Field, Incised Linear Design, 15 x 3 In. 440.00
Bowl, Birds In Flight, Flower Design, Green, Yellow, Dark Green Curled Handles, 3 In. .. 120.00
Bowl, Blue Circles, Triangles, Light Blue Ground, Flared, 2 Round Handles, 4 In. 360.00
Bowl, Blue Floral Design, White Interior, Marked, 15 x 5 In. 660.00
Bowl, Blue, Red Flowers In Center, Art Deco, Blue Footed Base, 4 In. 165.00
Bowl, Central Design Of Flowers, Stylized Floral Border, Turquoise Ground, 8 x 2 In. ... 110.00
Bowl, Cover, Flowers & Birds, Incised, Cobalt Blue Handles, 6 In. 125.00
Bowl, Cover, Oriental Design, Cobalt Blue Top, Knob, Side Handles, 9 In. 140.00
Bowl, Deer Scene, Foliage, Wide Purple Band, Art Deco, 10 In. 440.00
Bowl, Flower Design, Green, Yellow, Gold, Marked, 8 In. 275.00
Bowl, Flower Design, Vertical, 2 Handles, Blue, White Crackle Ground, 15 In. 605.00
Bowl, Pulled Vertical Design, Gold Square Exterior, Cream Crackle Ground, 15 In. 550.00
Box, Cover, Flowers In Deep Red, Black Corners, White Crackle Ground, 12 In. 385.00
Box, Flowers On Lid, Black Border, 8 x 2 1/2 In. ....275.00 to 330.00
Cache Pot, Black Circular Pattern, White Crackle Ground, 10 1/2 x 6 1/2 x 4 In. 185.00

Charger, Bird On Gilded Branch, Foliage, 14 3/4 In. 525.00
Charger, Blossoms, Light Blue Ground, Signed, Ink Mark, 14 In. 550.00
Charger, Stag In Forest, Circle Design, Blue, Black, Marked, 15 In. 440.00
Jar, Cover, Hunter, Ram, Bird Foliage, White Crackle Ground, 15 In. 715.00
Pitcher, Floral Design, Cobalt Blue Handle, Pink, Green, Blue Ground, 6 x 6 In. 295.00
Pitcher, Pink Roses, White Faience, Green Foliage, Impressed Mark, 5 In. 22.00
Plate, 2 Pheasants On Light Blue Ground, Marked, 12 1/2 In. 525.00
Plate, Art Deco Border, Blue, Turquoise, Gilt On Cream Crackle Glaze, 11 3/4 In. 230.00
Plate, Bird On Foliage, Blue, Border, Gold Rim, 10 In. ....145.00 to 245.00
Plate, Enameled Floral, Blossoms On Branches, Blue Bird On Panel, Marked, 8 In. 220.00
Plate, Floral Design, Black Ground, 12 In. 440.00
Plate, Flowers, Border, Blue Salamander On Handle, Scalloped, 10 x 7 In. 220.00
Tile, Bronze Stand, Swan Handles, Square, 2 x 8 1/4 In. 240.00
Tile, Woman, Garden, 8 In. 350.00
Tray, Bird Scenes, Red, White Floral Ground, Rectangular, 5 x 12 In. 385.00
Tray, Blue, Orange Art Deco Floral Design In Center, 8 Sides, 13 x 11 In. 285.00
Tray, Floral Design, Scalloped Edge, Green, Yellow, Gold Highlights, 9 1/2 x 11 In. 330.00
Tray, Flower Pattern, Brass Holder, Blue Ground, 16 x 8 x 3 In. 240.00
Trivet, 2 Birds In Nest, Wooden Frame, Square, 12 In. 155.00
Trivet, Deco Flowers, Cobalt Blue Edge, Saffron Ground, Square, 10 In. 255.00
Vase, 3-Tiered Tapered Form, Flared Rim, Floral Design, Yellow, Red, Blue, Gold, 15 In. 1650.00
Vase, Art Deco Design, Yellow, Red, Purple, Gilt Highlights, 8 Sides, 10 1/2 In. 770.00
Vase, Bird, Black, Yellow On White Crackle Ground, Flattened, 11 In. 253.00
Vase, Birds & Flowers, Flared Neck, Bulbous, White Crackle Ground, 9 In. 120.00
Vase, Black Pagoda, Incised, Flared Rim, Light Blue Ground, 13 In. 990.00
Vase, Circle Of Deer & Fawn, Foliage, White Crackle Ground, 11 1/2 In. 605.00
Vase, Deep Purple, Black Design, White Crackle Ground, 6 In. 525.00
Vase, Dragons, Flower Design, Metal Mount Base, White Ground, 8 In. 120.00
Vase, Fern In Pot Repeated Throughout, Cobalt Ground, Marked, 8 In. 78.00
Vase, Floral Design, Blue, Red, Teal, White, Orange, White Ground, Ink Mark, 9 In. 230.00
Vase, Floral Design, Outlined In Gold, Art Deco, Flattened, 6 x 7 1/2 In. 310.00
Vase, Flowers On Cream Crackled Ground, Bulbous, 5 x 7 In. 285.00
Vase, Flowers, Incised Art Deco, Blue, White, Red At Base, Orange Ground, 8 In. 660.00
Vase, Nudes, Ram, Bird With Exotic Foliage, Blue Ground, 13 In. 2310.00
Vase, Onion Shape, Black Line Design, Circles On Blue Ground, France, 12 In. . . .825.00 to 935.00
Vase, Red Fish & Seaweed, Black Ground, Applied Gold Elephant Handles, 13 In. 465.00
Vase, Red Floral Design, Cream Crackle, Green, Black Rim, 3-Footed, 7 1/2 In. 175.00
Vase, Tropical Landscape, Monkeys, Palms, Green Stamp, 11 x 3 1/2 In. 1045.00
Vase, Tropical Seascape, Nudes, Yellow, White Crackle Glaze, 4 x 5 In. 385.00
Vase, Vertical Purple, Brown Design, Cream Crackle Glaze, 11 In. 770.00

LONHUDA Pottery Company of Steubenville, Ohio, was organized in
1892 by William Long, W. H. Hunter, and Alfred Day. Brown underglaze slip-decorated pottery was made. The firm closed in 1896. The
company used many marks; the earliest included the letters *LPCO*.

Pitcher, Florals, Blossoms, Carmel & Brown Ground, Charles B. Upjohn, 9 1/2 In. 175.00
Pitcher, Indian, 3-Footed, 10 In. 695.00
Vase, Bulbous Bottom, Flaring Neck, Brown Ground, Jessie Spalding, 10 1/2 In. 250.00
Vase, Collie, Sitting On Grass, Flattened Footed Form, A.D.F., 7 1/2 x 8 In. 1650.00
Vase, Daises & Stems, 3 Handles, 3-Footed, 6 In. 440.00
Vase, Flared Rim, Golden Flowers, Brown & Yellow Ground, Jessie Spalding, 5 In. 175.00
Vase, Floral, Blossoms & Stems, Muted Purple & Gray Ground, Marked, 8 1/2 In. 2210.00

LOTUS WARE was made by the Knowles, Taylor & Knowles Company
of East Liverpool, Ohio, from 1890 to 1900. Lotus Ware, a thin porcelain which resembles Belleek, was sometimes decorated outside the
factory.

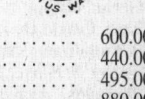

Bowl, Beaded Rim, Raised Flower Design, White, Columbia, 6 x 4 1/2 In. 600.00
Bowl, Netted, Gold Relief Floral & Leaf Panels, 3 3/4 In. 440.00
Bowl, Pink & Blue Cornflowers, Gold Beaded Rim, 4 1/2 In. 495.00
Bowl, Pink & Blue Floral, Royal Blue Ground, Reticulated Ornaments, 2 1/2 In. 880.00
Chocolate Pot, Gold Exotic Flowers, Lattice Base, Cream, Leaf Handle, 9 In. 385.00
Cracker Barrel, Netted Panels & Cover, Marked, 6 1/2 In. 605.00

Creamer, Gold Fish Net, Flowers, Bulbous, Squatty, 3 In. 295.00
Figurine, Banana Leaf, Aqua, 11 In. 35.00
Scent Container, Pierced Scrolled Center, Twig Handles, 3 1/2 In. 715.00
Syrup, Cover, White & Pink Morning Glory, Shaded Pink, Serpentine Handle, 3 In. 245.00
Tea Set, Relief Flowers, Gilt Cutout Rims, Individual, 2 1/2 In., 3 Piece 575.00
Vase, Tuscan, 4 Diamond Shaped Floral Panels, Green Ground, Ball Footed, 8 In. 920.00
Vase, Yellow & Pink Roses Top, Molded Mask Base, V-Cut Rim, Bulbous, 8 In. 465.00

LOW art tiles were made by the J. and J. G. Low Art Tile Works of Chelsea, Massachusetts, from 1877 to 1902. A variety of art and other tiles were made. Some of the tiles were made by a process called *natural*, some were hand modeled, and some were made mechanically.

J.&J.G.LOW

Tile, Benjamin Franklin, Blue, Osborne, 6 In. 425.00
Tile, Shylock, Blue, Osborne, 6 In. 250.00
Tile, Woman's Profile With Acanthus Leaves, Green, 6 In. 165.00

LOY-NEL-ART, see McCoy category.

LUNCH BOXES and lunch pails have been used to carry lunches to school or work since the nineteenth century. Today, most collectors want either early tobacco advertising boxes or children's lunch boxes made since the 1930s. These boxes are made of metal or plastic. Boxes listed here include the original Thermos bottle inside the box unless otherwise indicated. Movie, television, and cartoon characters may be found in their own categories.

LUNCH BOX, Adam-12, Embossed, Aladdin, 1972 . . . . 72.00
Addams Family, Cartoon Family On Vacation, Metal, King Seeley Thermos, 1974 .75.00 to 120.00
Aladdin Brunch Bag, With Sea Creatures, Vinyl, 1975 . . . . 40.00
Annie Oakley & Tagg, Metal, Adco Liberty 177.00
Astronaut, Dome, Metal, King Seeley Thermos, 1960-1966 . . . . 125.00
Astronauts, Metal, Aladdin, 1970 . . . . 85.00
Atom Ant, Metal, King Seeley Thermos . . . . .65.00 to 95.00
Banana Splits, Vinyl, King Seeley Thermos, 1970 . . . . 350.00
Barbie, Black, Tin, Canadian Thermos, 1962 . . . . 195.00
Barbie, Plastic, 1990 . . . . 12.00
Barbie & Francie, Vinyl, Copyright 1965, King Seeley Thermos Co., 1966-1970 . . . . . . 65.00
Battlestar Galactica, Metal, Aladdin, 1978 . . . . 25.00
Beany & Cecil, Cardboard Insert, Vinyl, King Seeley Thermos, 1962 . . . . 1200.00
Bee Gees, Maurice Gibb, Metal, King Seeley Thermos, 1979 . . . . .45.00 to 50.00
Bee Gees, Metal, King Seeley Thermos, 1978 . . . . .18.00 to 65.00
Beverly Hillbillies, Metal, Aladdin, 1963-1965 . . . . .95.00 to 495.00
Bionic Woman, Metal . . . . .20.00 to 80.00
Bonanza, Plastic Handle, Metal, Aladdin, 1960s . . . . .60.00 to 80.00
Boston Bruins 150.00
Bozo The Clown, Dome, Metal, Aladdin, 1964-1965 . . . . .65.00 to 100.00
Brady Bunch, Metal, King Seeley Thermos, 1970 . . . . .195.00 to 250.00
Buck Rogers, Original Paper Tag, Metal, Aladdin, 1979 . . . . 75.00
Bullwinkle, Blue, Vinyl, King Seeley Thermos, 1962 . . . . 395.00
Bullwinkle & Rocky, Metal, Universal, 1962 . . . . 300.00
California Raisins, Plastic . . . . .20.00 to 35.00
Campus Queen, Metal, King Seeley Thermos, 1967 . . . . 25.00
Captain Kangaroo, Vinyl, King Seeley Thermos, 1964-1966 . . . . 325.00
Care Bear, Plastic, 1983 . . . . .12.00 to 20.00
Care Bears Cousins, Metal, King Seeley Thermos, 1985 . . . . 15.00
Chitty Chitty Bang Bang, Metal, King Seeley Thermos, 1969 . . . . 45.00
Chuck Connors, Cowboy In Africa, Metal, King Seeley Thermos, 1968 . . . . 165.00
Circus Wagon, Dome Top, Metal, American Thermos, 1958 . . . . 150.00
Davy Crockett, Kit Carson, Metal, ADCO Liberty, 1955 . . . . 250.00
Deputy Dawg, Vinyl, King Seeley Thermos, 1961-1962 . . . . 200.00
Donny & Marie, Long Hair, Vinyl, Aladdin, 1977-1978 . . . . 85.00
Dr. Seuss, Metal, Aladdin, 1970 . . . . 85.00
Drag Strip, No Thermos, Metal, Aladdin, 1975 . . . . 55.00

Dudley Do Right, Metal, Universal, 1962 .... 350.00
Dukes Of Hazard, Tin Lithograph, Original Tag, Aladdin, 1980s 120.00
Early West, Indian, Metal, Ohio Art, 1982 .... 40.00
Empire Strikes Back, Ship, Metal, King Seeley Thermos, 1980 .... 20.00
Evel Knievel, Metal, Aladdin, 1974 .... 65.00
Family Affair, Metal, King Seeley Thermos, 1969 .... 55.00
Fashion Cut Plug 220.00
Fess Parker, Metal, King Seeley Thermos, 1965 .... 165.00
Fireball XL5, Metal, King Seeley Thermos, 1964 .... 135.00
Flintstones & Dino, Metal, Aladdin, 1962 ....95.00 to 115.00
Flipper, Metal, King Seeley Thermos, 1966 ....100.00 to 200.00
Flying Nun, Metal, Aladdin, 1968 .... 120.00
Fritos, Metal, King Seeley Thermos, 1975 .... 135.00
Frontier Day, Pony Express, Ohio Art, 1957 .... 145.00
G.I. Joe, Metal, King Seeley Thermos, 1967 ....63.00 to 95.00
G.I. Joe, Vinyl 25.00
Garfield, 1978 .... 12.00
George Washington Cut Plug, Bail Handle, 1 Lb. 75.00
George Washington Cut Plug, Blue, Red, Silver & Cream On Black, 7 1/2 In. 50.00
Globetrotter, Dome, Metal, Aladdin, 1959 ....140.00 to 200.00
Gomer Pyle, Metal, Aladdin, 1966 ....160.00 to 185.00
Green Hornet, Metal, King Seeley Thermos, 1967 .... 150.00
Grizzly Adams, Dome, Metal, Aladdin, 1978 ....80.00 to 100.00
Gunsmoke, Metal, Aladdin ....85.00 to 120.00
Hardy Boys, Metal, King Seeley Thermos, 1977 .... 45.00
Hee Haw, Metal, King Seeley Thermos, 1971 .... 65.00
Hogan's Heroes, Dome Top, Metal, Aladdin, 1966 ....235.00 to 245.00
Holly Hobbie, Vinyl, Aladdin, 1978-1980 .... 35.00
How The West Was Won, Metal, King Seeley Thermos, 1979 ....28.00 to 45.00
Huckleberry Hound & Friends, Metal, Aladdin, 1961 ....95.00 to 100.00
Hulk, Metal, Aladdin, 1978 .... 20.00
I Love A Parade, Vinyl, Ardee Industries, 1970s 125.00
Indiana Jones, Temple Of Doom, King Seeley Thermos, 1984 .... 35.00
Jetsons, Dome, Metal, Aladdin, 1963 ....200.00 to 300.00
Joe Palooka, Tin, Lithograph, Continental Can, 1949, 7 x 5 x 4 In. 220.00
Julia, Metal, King Seeley Thermos, 1969 .... 99.00
Junior Miss, Metal, Aladdin 20.00
Knight Rider, Metal, King Seeley Thermos, 1981 .... 30.00
Land Of The Giants, Metal, Aladdin, 1968 ....75.00 to 150.00
Land Of The Lost, Metal, Aladdin, 1975 .... 100.00
Laugh-In, Metal, Aladdin, 1968 ....45.00 to 75.00
Little House On The Prairie, Metal, King Seeley Thermos, 1978 .... 60.00
Little Kiddles, Metal, King Seeley Thermos, 1969 .... 250.00
Little Red Riding Hood, Metal, Ohio Art, 1982 .... 60.00
Loaf Of Bread, Dome Top, Metal, Aladdin, 1968 .... 40.00
Lost In Space, Dome, Metal, King Seeley Thermos, 1967 ....85.00 to 200.00
Ludwig Von Drake, Metal, Aladdin, 1962 .... 275.00
Man From U.N.C.L.E., Solo & Ilya, Metal, King Seelely Thermos, 1966 ....115.00 to 175.00
Marvel Super Heroes 20.00
Mary Poppins, Metal, Aladdin, 1965 .... 65.00
Mayo's Cut Plug, Tin 50.00
Mayo's Tobacco, Blue, Collapsible 110.00
Monkees, Vinyl, King Seeley Thermos, 1967 .... 295.00
Monsters, Universal Movie, Metal, Aladdin, 1980 .... 35.00
Munsters, Metal, King Seeley Thermos, 1965 .... 85.00
Muppet Show, Metal, King Seeley Thermos, 1978 .... 40.00
Muppets, Fozzie On Back, Metal, King Seeley Thermos, 1979 .... 40.00
NHL Players Assoc., Pictures Players, 1974 .... 75.00
Pac Man, Metal, Aladdin, 1980 ....25.00 to 80.00
Partridge Family, Metal, King Seeley Thermos, 1971 ....40.00 to 100.00
Peanuts, Vinyl, Green, King Seeley Thermos, 1971-1972 ....65.00 to 75.00
Pebbles & Bamm Bamm, Vinyl, Aladdin, 1972 .... 110.00

Pete's Dragon, Metal, Aladdin, 1978 . . . . 25.00
Pigs In Space, Metal, King Seeley Thermos, 1977 . . . . 15.00
Pink Panther & Sons, Metal, King Seeley Thermos, 1984 . . . . 40.00
Planet Of The Apes, Metal, Aladdin, 1974 . . . . .75.00 to 140.00
Pony Express, Metal, Ohio Art, 1982-1984 . . . . 195.00
Quarterbacks, Green Bay Packers & Chicago Bears, Metal, Aladdin, 1964 . . . . 65.00
Rainbow Bread Truck, Vinyl, Mold Mark Industries, 1984 . . . . 100.00
Rambo, Metal, King Seeley Thermos, 1985 . . . . 25.00
Red Barn, Open Doors, Dome, Metal, American Thermos, 1958 . . . . 85.00
Return Of Jedi, Wicket, Metal, King Seeley Thermos, 1983 . . . . .10.00 to 30.00
Rifleman, Metal, Aladdin, 1961 . . . . 245.00
Ringling Brothers, Barnum & Bailey Circus, Vinyl, King Seeley Thermos, 1970 . . . . . . 80.00
Road Runner, Metal, King Seeley Thermos, 1970 . . . . .15.00 to 35.00
Robin Hood, Green Border, Metal, Aladdin, 1956 . . . . 95.00
Ronald McDonald, Metal, Aladdin, 1982 . . . . 20.00
Rough Rider, Metal, Aladdin, 1973 . . . . 40.00
Six Million Dollar Man, Metal, Aladdin, 1974 . . . . 25.00
Smokey The Bear, Vinyl, King Seeley Thermos, 1965 . . . . 540.00
Snoopy & Woodstock, Sunglasses, Plastic, Thermos 10.00
Snow White & Seven Dwarfs, Tin, 2 Handles, Libby Glass Co., 1940s 250.00
Space 1999, Metal, King Seeley Thermos, 1976 . . . . 35.00
Space Shuttle, Metal, King Seeley Thermos, 1977 . . . . 80.00
Star Trek, Dome Top, Metal, Aladdin, 1968 . . . . .325.00 to 395.00
Star Trek, Motion Picture, Metal, King Seeley Thermos, 1980 . . . . 125.00
Star Wars, Metal, King Seeley Thermos, 1978 . . . . .45.00 to 75.00
Street Hawk, Metal, Aladdin, 1985 . . . . 60.00
Submarine, Metal, King Seeley Thermos, 1960 . . . . 125.00
Tarzan, Metal, Aladdin, 1966 . . . . .60.00 to 155.00
The World Of Barbie, Vinyl 40.00
Thundercats, Metal, Aladdin, 1985 . . . . 40.00
Tom Corbett, Space Cadet, Metal, Aladdin, 1952 . . . . 295.00
TV, Warner Brothers Cartoon Characters, 1950s 80.00
Twiggy, Vinyl, Strap & Zipper, Twiggy's Face, King Seeley Thermos, 1967 . . . . 245.00
U.S. Mail, Dome, Metal, Aladdin, 1969 . . . . .35.00 to 60.00
Voyage To Bottom Of Sea, Metal, Aladdin, 1967 . . . . 170.00
Wagon Train, Metal, King Seeley Thermos, 1964 . . . . 225.00
Washington & Lincoln On Lid, Tobacco 125.00
Welcome Back Kotter, Metal, Aladdin, 1977 . . . . 65.00
Western, Metal, King Seeley Thermos, 1963 . . . . 55.00
Wild, Wild, West, Metal, Aladdin, 1969 . . . . 140.00
Wild Bill Hickock, Metal, Aladdin, 1955 . . . . 135.00
Wild Frontier, Game Spinner On Back, Metal, Ohio Art, 1977 . . . . .80.00 to 110.00
Wonder Woman, Blue, Vinyl, Aladdin, 1978-1979 .110.00 to 190.00
World Of Barbie, Vinyl, Full Figure Images On 4 Sides, King Seeley Thermos, 1971 . . . 65.00
Yogi Bear, Metal, Aladdin . . . . .40.00 to 68.00
Yosemite Sam, Vinyl 40.00
Ziggy's Munch Box, Vinyl, Aladdin, 1979 . . . . 35.00
Zorro, Black Sky, Metal, Aladdin, 1966 . . . . .110.00 to 125.00
LUNCH PAIL, Beaver Brand Peanut Butter, Slant-Sided 1045.00
Central Union Cut Plug, 4 1/4 x 7 In. 115.00
Chicken In The Rough, Tin Lithograph, Copyright 1937 . . . . 100.00
Dinner Party Coffee 350.00
Dixie Kid Cut Plug, Black Child, Tin 495.00
Dixie Kid Cut Plug, Girl, Tin 385.00
Dixie Queen, Tin 275.00
Elsie Dairy, Metal, Ohio Art, 2 Qt. 30.00
F.W. Hinz & Sons Coffee 300.00
Frontenac Peanut Butter, Metal, 12 Oz. 33.00
Giant Peanut Butter 660.00
Gold Rod Coffee 450.00
Ground Hog Lard, Mustard Ground, Tin Lithograph, 4 1/2 In. 140.00
Jack Sprat Peanut Butter 550.00
Jackie Coogan Peanut Butter 275.00

Jumbo Peanut Butter, Vignette Of Barnum & Bailey Elephant	2420.00
Laurel Leaf Lard, 4 Lb.	35.00
Mayo's Milk, Bail Handle	225.00
Nigger Hair Smoking Tobacco	425.00
Ojibwa Fine Cut Chewing Tobacco, Bail Handle	395.00
Ox-Heart Peanut Butter, Oswego Candy Works, 3 1/2 x 4 In.	195.00
Scowcraft's Peanut Butter	1210.00
Snow White, Belgian, 1938	235.00
Sultana Peanut Butter, Open	35.00
Sunny Boy Peanut Butter, Brundage Brothers, Toledo, Ohio, 16 Oz.	132.00
Sweet Mist Fine Cut Chewing Tobacco	95.00
Uncle Wiggily Peanut Butter, Rabbit & Friends Playing At Beach	2750.00
Veribest Mince Meat, Armour & Co., Painted Tin, 4 x 3 1/2 In.	16.00

LUSTER glaze was meant to resemble copper, silver, or gold. It has been used since the sixteenth century. Most of the luster found today was made during the nineteenth century. The metallic glazes are applied on pottery. The finished color depends on the combination of the clay color and the glaze. Blue and orange luster decorations were used in the early 1900s. Tea Leaf pieces have their own category.

Blue, Pot, Demitasse	28.00
Blue, Tray, Orange Stylized Flowers	25.00
Copper, Creamer, Wheat In The Meadow, Powell & Bishop	350.00
Copper, Cup & Saucer, House Pattern	25.00
Copper, Pitcher & Bowl, Floral Design, 7 3/8-In. Pitcher, 5 1/4-In. Bowl	135.00
Copper, Pitcher, Blue & Mauve Bluebells, 6 In.	75.00
Copper, Pitcher, Cream, Couple Dancing, Wade, 6 1/2 In.	65.00 to 75.00
Copper, Teapot, Embroidered, Band, Burgess	150.00
Fairyland luster is included in the Wedgwood category.	
Orange, Tea Set, 13 Piece	55.00
Pink, Cup & Saucer	60.00
Pink, Cup & Saucer, Child's, Girl Feeding Chickens	30.00
Pink, Mug, Church, 4 3/4 In.	495.00
Pink, Pitcher, Buildings & Windmill, 7 1/4 In.	450.00
Silver, Pitcher, Floral, Blue, Squatty, Sadler, 4 1/2 In.	85.00
Silver, Teapot, Reeded Detail, 5 1/4 In.	135.00
Sunderland luster pieces are listed in the Sunderland category.	
Tea Leaf luster pieces are listed in the Tea Leaf Ironstone category.	

LUSTRE ART GLASS Company was founded in Long Island, New York, in 1920 by Conrad Vahlsing and Paul Frank. The company made lampshades and globes that are almost indistinguishable from those made by Quezal. Most of the shades made by the company were unmarked.

Spider Web Over Opalescent Feather, Gold Ground, Pair	450.00

LUSTRES are mantel decorations or pedestal vases with many hanging glass prisms. The name really refers to the prisms, and it is proper to refer to a single glass prism as a lustre. Either spelling, luster or lustre, is correct.

Bristol, Pale Aqua, Gold Ornaments, Prisms	220.00
Emerald Green, White Enameled Star Flowers, Beading, Prisms, 14 1/2 In., Pair	275.00
Georgian Style, Faceted, Pair	200.00
Ruby, Stag, Bohemia	800.00

MAASTRICHT, Holland, was the city where Petrus Regout established the De Sphinx pottery in 1836. The firm was noted for its transfer-printed earthenware. Many factories in Maastricht are still making ceramics.

Bowl, Soup, Timor	45.00
Plate, Blue, 6 In.	10.00
Teapot, Polychrome, Floral & Link Design, 7 In.	140.00
Tureen, Soup, Ladle, Ironstone, 12 1/2 x 13 1/2 In.	395.00

MAIZE glass was made by W.L. Libbey & Son Company of Toledo, Ohio, after 1889. The glass resembled an ear of corn. The leaves were usually green, but some pieces were made with blue or red leaves. The kernels of corn were light yellow, white, or light green.

Bowl, Green Enameled Leaves, 1818, 3 3/4 In.	49.00
Pitcher, Amber, 9 In.	600.00
Sugar Shaker, Gold Leaves, Custard	300.00
Sugar Shaker, Yellow Leaves	345.00

MAJOLICA is a general term for any pottery glazed with an opaque tin enamel that conceals the color of the clay body. It has been made since the fourteenth century. Today's collector is most likely to find Victorian majolica. The heavy, colorful ware is rarely marked. Some famous makers include Wedgwood; Minton; Griffen, Smith and Hill (marked *Etruscan*); and Chesapeake Pottery (marked *Avalon* or *Clifton*).

Bank, Figural, Child's Shoe, Mottled Green & Yellow	90.00
Berry Bowl, Shell & Seaweed	85.00
Bowl, Dead Game On Cover & Sides, Turquoise, Brownfield ....*Illus*	1430.00
Bowl, Fish, 1870	650.00
Bowl, Lion Mask Relief With Torso, Paw Feet, Triangular Base, 19th Century, 14 In.	975.00
Bowl, Shell, Seaweed, 7 3/4 In.	275.00
Box, Sardine, Fish Finial, Basket Weave, Seaweed, Attached Underplate, 9 1/4 In.	895.00
Box, Sardine, Swan On Pink Water Lily, Etruscan ....*Illus*	1540.00
Butter Chip, Lily Pad, Etruscan	70.00
Butter Chip, Pink Ribbon In Circles, Morning Glories	130.00
Butter Chip, Water Lily, Green	225.00
Caddy, Cigar & Match, Town Crier	95.00
Cake Stand, Green Fern, Mustard Yellow, Pedestal Base, 11 In.	175.00
Cake Stand, Shell Form, 3 Entwined Dolphins Support, c.1865, 7 3/4 In.	345.00
Candleholder, Deer Shape, 2 Sockets, Green & Brown Mottled, Continental, 11 In.	545.00
Charger, Cherubs Bands, Armorial Center, Cobalt Blue, Italy, 1888, 19 1/2 In.	850.00
Cheese Dish, Cover, Albino Lily, Etruscan	1540.00
Cheese Dish, Cover, Bird Cover, Water Lily, George Jones, 1875, 13 In. ....*Illus*	11000.00
Compote, Man & Woman, Reticulated, Floral Pedestal, 16 1/2 x 11 In.	780.00
Compote, Pink, Yellow Floral, Medium Blue Ground, Griffen, Smith & Hill, 9 x 5 In.	545.00
Compote, Young Woman Singing, Man Plays Lute, Floral Pedestal, 16 x 11 In.	875.00
Creamer, Fern Design, 3 1/4 In.	55.00
Cup, Bird, Large	105.00
Cup & Saucer, Shell & Seaweed, Pink Interior, 1875, American, 12 Piece	1610.00
Cuspidor, Sunflower, Etruscan	1800.00
Decanter, Wine, Continents, Oceans Delineated, Wrought Iron Holder	150.00
Dessert Set, Birds, Grapes, Turquoise Ground, Zell, Germany	295.00
Dish, Condiment, White Bird On Green Oak Leaf, Handle, 1861	1200.00
Dish, Continental Leaf, Incised, 7 x 7 3/4 In.	85.00

Majolica, Bowl, Dead Game On Cover
& Sides, Turquoise, Brownfield

Majolica, Box, Sardine, Swan On
Pink Water Lily, Etruscan

Dish, Grape Leaf, Triangle Shape, Brown, 8 1/2 x 8 1/2 In. 40.00
Dish, Leaf Shape, 9 In. 120.00
Dish, Leaf Shape, Acorns, 9 In. 110.00
Dish, Nut, Figural Singing Bird Handle, Turquoise, 6 x 11 In. 650.00
Dish, Shallow, Ferns Design, 1880 .... 90.00
Dish, Strawberry, Lily Pad & Blossoms, Branch Handle, G. Jones, 1876, 10 1/2 In. 1090.00
Figurine, Black Girl, Reclining, Aqua Hat, France, 1890s, 3 1/2 x 5 In. 95.00
Figurine, Colonial Man, Japan, 6 In. 85.00
Figurine, Elephant, Basket Top, Blue Blanket, 16 x 13 1/2 In. 575.00
Figurine, Polar Bear, 9 In. 300.00
Fish Server, Cover, Salmon On Fern Leaves Bed, George Jones 3220.00
Holder, Cigar, North African Tribesman Beside Well, Germany, 10 1/2 In. 275.00
Holder, Place Card, Holly 10.00
Humidor, Arab, 6 1/2 In. 295.00
Humidor, Bowler, 3/4 Figure Of Man, Blue & White, 6 In. 195.00
Humidor, Cover, Shell & Seaweed, Blue Cobalt Glaze, Etruscan 4000.00
Humidor, Floral Applied Pipe On Cover, Art Nouveau 160.00
Humidor, Irish Jockey, 5 In. 195.00
Humidor, Moroccan Type Man's Head 285.00
Humidor, Pipe Finial Cover, Floral Around, Art Nouveau 160.00
Humidor, Scotsman, Blue Coat, Marked, 6 1/2 In. 195.00
Humidor, Turkish Man, 3/4 Figure, Holding Pipe 95.00
Jardiniere, Spiral Design, Butterscotch, Yellow, Minton, 1882, 29 1/2 In. 450.00
Jug, Figural, Owl, 7 1/2 In. 210.00
Jug, Pug Dog, 7 1/2 In. 210.00
Match Holder, Small Basket 120.00
Mug, Floral Fence, Blue, Pink 125.00
Mug, Happy Hooligan 125.00
Napkin Holder, Strawberry, George Jones 895.00
Oyster Plate, Lavender, Yellow, White, Etruscan, 6 Shells, 10 In. .... *Illus*   6600.00
Pedestal, Lions' Heads, Swage, Portrait Medallions, Wedgwood, c.1877 .... 7500.00
Pitcher, Bamboo & Fern Leaf, 7 3/4 In. 375.00
Pitcher, Bamboo, Yellow, Cobalt Blue, Brown, Green, 7 In. 235.00
Pitcher, Bird Nest 250.00
Pitcher, Blackberry, 6 In. 100.00
Pitcher, Branch Handle, Leaf Spout, Yellow 65.00
Pitcher, Corn, English Registry Mark, 4 In. ....275.00 to 340.00
Pitcher, Deer ....95.00 to 110.00
Pitcher, Dog, 7 1/2 In. 275.00
Pitcher, Dogwood, Pink, 7 In. 195.00
Pitcher, Fish On Waves, 6 In. 295.00
Pitcher, Floral, Turquoise Basket Weave Ground, 6 In. 195.00
Pitcher, Flower & Leaves, Greens, Yellow & Rose, 5 In. 145.00

Majolica, Cheese Dish, Cover, Bird Cover,
Water Lily, George Jones, 1875, 13 In.

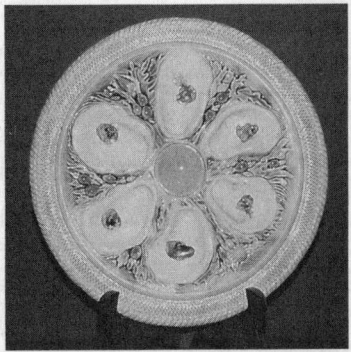

Majolica, Oyster Plate, Lavender, Yellow, White,
Etruscan, 6 Shells, 10 In.

Pitcher, Fruit Front, Back, Brown Ground, Pink Interior, 7 x 5 1/2 In. 85.00
Pitcher, Gargoyle Spout, Relief Drinking Scene, France, 8 1/2 In. 195.00
Pitcher, Gurgling Fish, 15 In. 495.00
Pitcher, Knights On Horseback, Butterscotch & Green, Magenta Interior, 10 In. 295.00
Pitcher, Lilies, 5 In. 155.00
Pitcher, Milk, Floral Design, 6 In. 30.00
Pitcher, Milk, Raised Pine Cones & Oak Leaves, Green & Brown Glaze, 7 1/4 In. 30.00
Pitcher, Monkey, 10 In. 495.00
Pitcher, Pansy Leaves, 19th Century, 6 In. ....175.00 to 195.00
Pitcher, Parrot, 9 1/2 In. ....165.00 to 275.00
Pitcher, Picket Fence & Floral, 4 1/4 In. 50.00
Pitcher, Pineapple Pattern, 7 3/4 In. 115.00
Pitcher, Pink Floral, 7 1/2 In. 165.00
Pitcher, Rooster, St. Clement, 10 In. 375.00
Pitcher, Shell & Seaweed, 6 3/4 In. 445.00
Pitcher, Water, Raised Floral Branch, Brown, Green Glaze, Yellow Base, 10 In. 220.00
Pitcher, Wild Rose, Tree Bark, 7 In. 95.00
Planter, Game, Stag's Head, Foliage, Rectangular, Continental, 10 x 14 x 8 In. 860.00
Plaque, Battle Scene & Scene Of Bacchanalian Revelry, Frame, 25 In., Pair 5750.00
Plaque, Group Of Men Leading Reluctant Maiden Onto Galleon, Frame, 17 1/2 In. 1840.00
Plaque, Madonna & Child, Pilasters Hold Roof, Nostra Signora Del Carmen, 16 In. 1150.00
Plate, 3 Birds On Fans, 7 1/2 In. 130.00
Plate, Basketweave, Berries, 8 In. 125.00
Plate, Bird In Fan, 7 1/2 In. 115.00
Plate, Birds, Blue Ground, 7 3/4 In., 9 Piece 170.00
Plate, Black Swallow, Red Breast, Letter In Beak, 9 In. 80.00
Plate, Blackberry, Basket Weave Ground, 8 In. ....125.00 to 135.00
Plate, Cauliflower, Etruscan, 9 In. 345.00
Plate, Fish, Green, Head, Tail & Fins Extended, 7 In. 75.00
Plate, Large Leaves, Scalloped Rim, Green & Tan, 10 In. 95.00
Plate, Lavender, Green, Yellow, Begonia Leaves, 8 1/2 In. 65.00
Plate, Leaf & Basketweave, Gien, France 30.00
Plate, Leaf, Begonia, Brownish Green, Incised 12, 11 x 8 1/2 In. 95.00
Plate, Maple Leaf On Basket, Cobalt Blue Rim, Etruscan, 9 In. 235.00
Plate, Morning Glory, 8 In. 95.00
Plate, Oyster, Pink, Blue Wells 200.00
Plate, Running Stag & Dog, Floral, Fence Rim, 8 In. 110.00
Plate, Strawberry, Blossoms, Leaves, 8 In. 95.00
Plate, With Bird, 8 In. 95.00
Platter, Blackberry, 13 In. 200.00
Platter, Fence & Vine Design, Wedgwood, 13 In. 305.00
Platter, Floral, Leaf & Belt Design, Center Circle With Fish Scales, 12 1/2 In. 140.00
Platter, Geranium, Etruscan, 12 In. 295.00
Platter, Ice Cream, Brown Seals & Seaweed, Wedgwood, 17 x 8 3/4 In. 1550.00
Platter, Leaves & Fern, 12 In. 180.00
Pot, Garden, Blossoming Branches, Water Lilies, Swimming Fish, c.1875 .... 1380.00
Pot, Garden, Underplate, Borders Of White Florets, Leaves, Minton, 1863 .... 1725.00
Salt, Scrolled Tripod Base, Impressed Marks, c.1865, 1 1/2 In. 345.00
Salt, Turquoise Blue Flower 70.00
Saltshaker, Owl, Green, Cork 95.00
Smoke Set, Figural Deer, Tree Stumps Form Holders For Matches, 6 x 6 In. 65.00
Sugar, Cover, Pineapple 110.00
Sugar, Cover, Wild Rose 90.00
Syrup, Daisy, Etruscan 375.00
Syrup, Sunflower, Cobalt Blue, Etruscan, 7 3/4 In. 385.00
Tea Caddy, Bamboo Motif, Yellow, Green, Brown, 1880, 5 1/2 In. 145.00
Teapot, Flying Crane, Flower Finial 175.00
Teapot, Open Ear Of Corn Design, Globular, 19th Century, 3 3/4 In. 460.00
Tile, Bird In Flight, Water, Floral Landscape, c.1877, 8 x 8 In. 375.00
Tile, Madonna & Child, Floral Cartouche, N.S. Do Perpetuo Socorro, 34 x 22 In. 345.00
Tray, Begonia Leaf Corners, Sunflower Center 195.00
Tray, Dessert, Apple Blossoms, George Jones 1840.00

Umbrella Stand, Flowers, Fielding 2650.00
Vase, Applied Duck, Water Plants In Full Relief, 11 x 5 1/2 x 4 In. 310.00
Vase, Art Nouveau Flowers, 12 In. 250.00
Vase, Bird In Flight, 9 In. 100.00
Vase, Chinese Man Figure Next To Vase, 6 In. ....90.00 to 95.00
Vase, Figure Of Black Child, 7 1/2 In. 335.00
Vase, Figure Of Chinese Woman Against Vase, 6 In. 90.00
Vase, Human Headed Chimera, Ribbons, Scrolls, Winged Chimera Handles, 30 In. 805.00
Vase, Raised Bird, Pilgrim Form, 12 In. 190.00
Vase, Rose Violet, 4 1/2 In. 85.00
Vase, Tree Trunk, Woman & Man, 12 1/2 In., Pair 185.00

MAPS of all types have been collected for centuries. The earliest known
printed maps were made in 1478. The first printed street map showed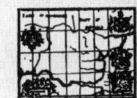
London in 1559. The first road maps for use by drivers of automobiles
were made in 1901. Collectors buy maps that were pages of old books,
as well as the multifolded road maps popular in this century.

Africa, S. Dunn, 1794 .... 250.00
Ancient Greece & Adjoining Islands, E. Bowen, Engineer, 14 x 16 In. 180.00
Ancient Italy, J. Blundell, Engineer, 14 x 16 In. 175.00
Arizona, Pictographic, Indians, Drums, Weaving, Teepees, Cowboys, 1937, 9 x 12 In. 25.00
Arkansas, Colton, Hand Colored, Orange Borders, Matted, 1855, 13 x 16 In. 105.00
Bear Mountain Bridge, West Point & Storm King Highway, 1924 .... 10.00
Chesapeake Bay Bridge Tunnel, 17 1/2-Mile, 1965 .... 6.00
Circuli Franconiae, J.B. Homann, 1720 .... 450.00
Coast Guard, Geodetic, Coastal Navigation, Stratford Shoal To New York, 1902, Large . 35.00
Colorado, Paramount, Station Photograph, 1920 .... 20.00
Denver, Paramount, Fold Up, 1920 .... 15.00
Eastern United States, Watercolor, Ink, Framed, Cynthia Beale, 1810, 11 1/4 x 12 In. . 690.00
Globe, Celestial, Cary's New Celestial Globe, 1800, 12 In. 3025.00
Globe, Celestial, Neoclassical, Tripod Stand, Holding Figure Of Atlas, 14 In., Pair 2590.00
Globe, Celestial, Wooden, Wooden Base, 1840s 4000.00
Globe, Lights Up, Walnut Frame, Butler, Late 1950s 75.00
Globe, Terrestrial & Celestial, Cary, 1830, 12 In., Pair 4140.00
Globe, Terrestrial, 19th Century, 12 1/2 In. ....690.00 to 695.00
Globe, Terrestrial, 3 Turned Ebonized Legs, Floor Model, c.1880, 42 x 22 In. 7475.00
Globe, Terrestrial, 4 Legged Stand, Foliate Carved, 1830, 18 In., Pair 4310.00
Globe, Terrestrial, Andrews, Cast Iron Base, 12 In. 1705.00
Globe, Terrestrial, Bacon, No. 6, School, Ebonized Stand, 1870s, 12 x 6 In. 1035.00
Globe, Terrestrial, Brass Meridian, Horizon Ring, Brass, Spain, 1850s, 13 In. 1495.00
Globe, Terrestrial, Brass Meridian, J. Schedler, c.1868, 24 1/2 In. 920.00
Globe, Terrestrial, C. Abel-Klinger, Nurnberg, Circular Box, 2 1/2 In. 1840.00
Globe, Terrestrial, Continental, Faux Fishskin Case, R. Cashee, 3 In. 2990.00
Globe, Terrestrial, Double Brass Meridian, G. Joslin, Iron Turntable, c.1880, 9 In. 4025.00
Globe, Terrestrial, Double Meridian, Fitz, Ginn & Heath, 1870, 16 In. ....*Illus* 2990.00
Globe, Terrestrial, Ebonized Stand, Mahogany, J. Wyld, c.1835, 12 x 6 In. 1725.00
Globe, Terrestrial, Fitz Globe, Ginn & Heath, c.1870, 16 x 12 In. 2990.00
Globe, Terrestrial, Franklin, Meriam, Moore & Co., Iron Tripod Base, c.1852, 6 In. 2415.00
Globe, Terrestrial, G. Joslin, Green Wrought Iron Stand, Boston, 1860, 18 In. 750.00
Globe, Terrestrial, George Phillip & Son, London, 19th Century, 17 In. ....*Illus* 2070.00
Globe, Terrestrial, Georgian Style, Stand, 40 In. 130.00
Globe, Terrestrial, Hand Colored, Rome, Holland, c.1744, 19 1/4 In. 10350.00
Globe, Terrestrial, Hour & Zodiac Rings, Wood & Paper, 1773, 40 1/2 In. 5520.00
Globe, Terrestrial, Lane's Of London, Case, 3 In. 2185.00
Globe, Terrestrial, Mahogany Stand, 6 In. Globe Raised On Iron Base, 19th Century, Pair 3740.00
Globe, Terrestrial, Metal Stand, Cast Iron, 19th Century, 20 In. 85.00
Globe, Terrestrial, Newton's New & Improved, Mid 19th Century, 12 In. 1035.00
Globe, Terrestrial, Phillips, Early 20th Century 275.00
Globe, Terrestrial, Raised On 3 Turned Ebonized Legs, 1880, 42 In. 7475.00
Globe, Terrestrial, Raised On 3 Turned Legs, Victorian, 1860, 10 In. 3737.00
Globe, Terrestrial, Raised On Ebonized Cast Iron Base, 1860, 18 In. 1840.00
Globe, Terrestrial, S. Chedler's Globe, Cast Iron Foliate Scrolled Legs, 1880, 40 In. 1380.00

Map, Globe, Terrestrial, George
Phillip & Son,
London, 19th Century, 17 In.;
Map, Globe, Terrestrial, Double
Meridian, Fitz,
Ginn & Heath, 1870, 16 In.

Globe, Terrestrial, Walnut Pedestal Base, Early 20th Century, 35 In. 1160.00
Globe, Terrestrial, William IV, Mahogany, J. Wyld, c.1835, 12 x 6 In. 1725.00
Gloucestershire, England, Uncolored, Dated 1712, 18 1/2 x 21 3/4 In. 225.00
Illinois, Hand Colored, Cowperthwait, 1850, 13 x 16 In. 105.00
Indiana, Hand Colored, Cowperthwait, Matted, 1850, 11 x 14 In. 100.00
Kingdoms Of Armenia, Engineer, 14 x 16 In. 175.00
Los Angeles To Washington DC, National Old Trails Road, 1922 .... 15.00
Mackinaw Bridge, Link Between Michigan's Upper & Lower Peninsulas, 1978 .... 5.00
Monk's Railroad & Telegraph, 1857 .... 440.00
N. & S. America, Engraved In French, Hand Colored, Frame, 1762, 12 x 18 In. 190.00
New Jersey, Esso, 1938 .... 10.00
New York, Folding, J.H. Colton, 1855 .... 200.00
North America, East Coast, French Engraved, Paper, Frame, 1755, 22 x 27 In. . .290.00 to 320.00
Oklahoma Turnpikes, 1966 .... 5.00
Oregon Highway, 1924 .... 10.00
Peace Bridge, Niagara River, Between Buffalo, N.Y. & Fort Erie, Canada, 1937 .... 10.00
Pennsylvania, Esso, 1938 .... 10.00
Pennsylvania, Hand Colored, Ornate, Matted, Cowperthwait, 1850, 11 x 14 In. 100.00
Pennsylvania Turnpike, 1949 .... 10.00
Portions Of 4 Counties, 2 Insert City Maps, English, 15 x 20 In. 230.00
Retreat Of Ten Thousand Greeks Under Xenophon, 14 x 16 In. 180.00
Route Which Hannibal Took Through Gaul & Over Alps, 14 x 16 In. 175.00
Routes To Lake Champlain, 1929 .... 8.00
Scandinavia, Hand Colored, City Crests Borders, France, 24 x 20 In. 405.00
Shell, United States Book, 50 States & Various Cities, 18 1/2 x 14 In. 30.00
Souvenir Map Of Pennsylvania Turnpike, 25 Cents, 1941 .... 15.00
Sunoco, Paper Lithograph Of Ontario, Quebec, Maritime Provinces, 1935, 1936, 7 Piece . 40.00
Surveyor's, Hamilton County, Ill., Pen, Ink, Watercolor, Crayon, 29 1/2 x 24 In. 115.00
Territory Of Alaska, Pictographic, Eskimos, Miners, Fish, Bears, 1937, 9 x 12 In. 25.00
Texas & Indian Territory, 1875 .... 30.00
The Hudson, Daylight Book, Fold-Out, 1878 .... 148.50
Topographical Atlas Of State Of Connecticut, Leather Binding, 1893 .... 82.00
Union Pacific Railroad, United States, Showing All Tracks, Wall, 1931 .... 225.00
United States, 1875 .... 30.00
United States, Paper Lithograph, Greyhound, November 1, 1934, 20 x 30 In. 40.00
Washington State Road & Recreation, 1924 .... 15.00
Welcome To Ohio Turnpike, 1956 .... 7.50

MARBLE collectors pay highest prices for glass and sulphide marbles.
The game of marbles has been popular since the days of the ancient
Romans. American children were able to buy marbles by the mid-eigh-
teenth century. Dutch glazed clay marbles were least expensive.
Glazed pottery marbles, attributed to the Bennington potteries in
Vermont, were of a better quality. Marbles made of pink marble were

also available by the 1830s. Glass marbles seem to have been made later. By 1880, Samuel C. Dyke of South Akron, Ohio, was making clay marbles and The National Onyx Marble Company was making marbles of onyx. The Navarre Glass Marble Company of Navarre, Ohio, and M. B. Mishler of Ravenna, Ohio, made the glass marbles. Ohio remained the center of the marble industry, and the Akron-made Akro Agate brand became nationally known. Other pieces made by Akro Agate are listed in this book in the Akro Agate category. Sulphides are glass marbles with frosted white figures in the center.

Agate, Gold Stone, Blue	8.00
Agate, Limeade Moss, Fluorescent, 7/8 In.	65.00
Akro Agate, Bag, 1930, 27 Marbles	89.00
Akro Agate, Bull's Eye, Carnelian, White, Black Lines, 3/4 In.	150.00
Akro Agate, Carnelian, White, Gray, Crystal Top, 3/4 In.	150.00
Akro Agate, Dark Brown, Cream, 15/16 In.	55.00
Akro Agate, No. 16, Slag, Cardboard Sleeve . . . . *Illus*	155.00
Akro Agate, Slag, Cardinal Red, Box, Cover, 25 Marbles	500.00
Banded Swirl, 2 Wide Opaque Yellow Bands, Red Accents, 1 1/16 In.	100.00
Banded Swirl, 3 Bands On Pink Opaque Base, Red, Pink, White Surface, 11/16 In.	40.00
Banded Swirl, Wide Yellow Bands, Pale Blue, Yellow Lines, Cobalt Blue Base, 9/16 In.	37.00
Christensen Agate, Transparent Striped, White Bands, White, 19/32 In.	37.00
Clambroth, 17 Blue Lines, Clambroth White Base, 5/9 In.	135.00
Clambroth, 18 Green Lines, Clambroth White Base, 5/8 In.	220.00
Clambroth, 19 Thin Purple Lines, Clambroth White Base, 9/16 In.	100.00
Clambroth, 20 White Lines, Black Opaque Base, 1 5/8 In.	80.00
Clambroth, Red, Blue Lines, Alternating, Clambroth White Base, Yellow Edge, 3/4 In. . .	230.00
Clambroth, Salmon Red Lines, Red On Black Base, 11/16 In.	200.00
Corkscrew, Cobalt Blue Band, Opaque White Lines, White Base, 1 In.	80.00
Corkscrew, Oxblood, 11/16 In.	75.00
Corkscrew, Tri-Color, Orange, Yellow, Green, Green Matrix, 11/16 In.	90.00
Corkscrew, Tri-Color, Red, Yellow, Blue, 5/8 In.	70.00
Guinea, Red, Orange, Blue, Green, White, Lavender, Purple, 9/16 In.	350.00
Guinea, Red, White, Blue, Yellow, Green, Orange, Lavender, 11 1/6 In.	170.00
Jasper, Amazon Valley	6.00
Latticinio, Core Swirl, Blue & White Outer Bands, Bubbles	25.00
Lutz, Onionskin, Blue, White Base, 5/8 In.	110.00
Lutz, Onionskin, White, 1/2 In.	150.00
Mica, Aqua Blue Matrix, 3/4 In.	41.00
Mica, Blue Core, Green, Transparent Green Lines, 7/16 In.	210.00
Mica, Peewee, Cyan Blue Matrix, 1/2 In.	36.00
Mica, Peewee, Yellow Matrix, 7/16 In.	65.00
Mica, Yellow, Smokey Yellow Matrix, 13/16 In.	56.00
Onionskin, 4 Panels, Blue, White Panels, Red, White Panels, 13/16 In.	65.00
Onionskin, 4 Panels, Red Streaks On Yellow, Blue Streaks On White, 1 In.	80.00
Onionskin, Green, Yellow Base, 3/4 In.	57.00
Onionskin, Orange, Green Accent Lines, Yellow Base, 5/8 In.	55.00
Onionskin, Red, Green Lines, Yellow Base, 9/16 In.	50.00
Orange Lace, Transparent Green Base, 5/8 In.	600.00
Peltier, Aqua Slag, Feathering, 19/32 In.	37.00
Peltier, Black Transfer Of Koko, White Base, Green Patch, 21/32 In.	95.00
Peppermint, 2 Blue Bands, White Ground, 2 Red Lines, 9/16 In.	85.00
Peppermint, 2 Wide Blue Bands, White Ground, 2 Red Lines, 11/16 In.	165.00

Marble, Akro Agate, No. 16, Slag,
Cardboard Sleeve

Peppermint, Beach Ball, Red, Blue Bands, Alternating, White Ground, 11/16 In. 80.00
Ribbon Swirl, Core, 3 Core Ribbons, 1 Band Of Green Aventurine In 1 Ribbon, 5/8 In. .. 90.00
Ribbon Swirl, Core, 4 Sets Of Yellow Outer Lines, 3/4 In. 45.00
Ribbon Swirl, Core, Orange, White, Blue, Yellow, 3 Outer Sets Of White Lines, 3/4 In. .. 28.00
Shooter, American Agate, 13/16 In. 95.00
Shooter, Ketchup & Mustard, 7/8 In. 95.00
Shooter, Swirl, Oxblood, 7/8 In. 50.00
Stoneware, Blue & White, 1 1/2 In. 82.00
Sulphide, Bunny, 1 In. 60.00
Sulphide, Cow, Standing, 1 7/8 In. 100.00
Sulphide, Deer, 1 1/4 In. 155.00
Sulphide, Dog, Seated, 1 1/16 In. 320.00
Sulphide, Elephant, Tusks, 1 5/16 In. 85.00
Sulphide, Girl With Basket, Wearing A Long Dress, 1 9/16 In. 110.00
Sulphide, Goat, 2 In. 85.00
Sulphide, Jenny Lind, 1 1/8 In. 110.00
Sulphide, Lamb, 1 3/4 In. ....155.00 to 195.00
Sulphide, Lamb, Lying Down With Head Held Up, 1 11/16 In. 56.00
Sulphide, Lion, Standing, 11/2 In. 75.00
Sulphide, Parrot, Sitting On Perch, 1 1/8 In. 51.00
Sulphide, Spread Wing Eagle, Head Turned To Right, 1 1/8 In. 91.00
Swirl, 8 Multicolor Bands, White Latticinio Core, 1 11/26 In. 100.00
Swirl, Broken, Red, White, Blue Bands, 7/8 In. 42.00
Swirl, Butterfly, White, Orange, Yellow, Blue, Translucent White Base, 1 1/4 In. 42.00
Swirl, Coral, Opaque Coral Swirls With Green, 9/16 In. 101.00
Swirl, End Of Cane, Red, White Bands, Alternating, Latticinio Co. 42.00
Swirl, Green Aventurine, 19/32 In. 10.00
Swirl, Green, Gooseberry, 3 Bands Of Yellow, Red, 11/16 In. 75.00
Swirl, Indian, 2 Bands, Red, Yellow, Blue, Green, Black Base, 11/16 In. 65.00
Swirl, Indian, 4 Bands, 2 Yellow, 2 White, Opaque Black Base, 11/16 In. 42.00
Swirl, Joseph's Coat, Orange, White, Blue, Yellow, Green, 4 Outer Bands, 11/16 In. 85.00
Swirl, Orange, 2 Red & White Bands, 1 Blue & White, 1 Green & White, 13/16 In. 100.00
Swirl, Ribbon Core, Yellow, Red Center Band, Green Edges, 1 3/8 In. 170.00
Swirl, Solid Core, Blue, Medium, Red, White Bands, Alternating, 11/16 In. 100.00
Swirl, Solid Core, Crackled Orange, 4 Outer Bands, 3/4 In. 31.00
Swirl, Solid Core, Mint Green, 4 Outer Bands, 11/16 In. 120.00
Swirl, Solid Core, Orange, 8 Outer Bands, Green, Purple, 11/16 In. 50.00
Swirl, Solid Core, White, Pink Stripes, 6 Outer Bands, 11/16 In. 47.00
Swirl, Solid Core, Yellow, Red, Pink, 3/4 In. 75.00
Swirl, Yellow, Green Tint, Latticinio Co., 7/8 In. 40.00

MARBLE CARVINGS, such as large or small figurines, groups of people or animals, and architectural decorations, have been a special art form since the time of the ancient Greeks. Reproductions, especially of large Victorian groups, are being made of a mixture using marble dust. These are very difficult to detect and collectors should be careful. Other carvings are listed under Alabaster.

Apollo, Victorian Style, Belvidere, 30 1/4 In. 770.00
Bookends, Eagle Form, 8 1/2 In. 50.00
Bust, Baron De Montesquieu & Wife, White, France, 1770, Pair 8050.00
Bust, Caesar, Studio O. Andreoni, Roma, 22 In. 2415.00
Bust, Caracalla, Gray Marble, Raised On Gray, White Socle, Italy, 34 In. 18400.00
Bust, Female, Pedestal, Signed, V. Luccardi, 1872, Italy, 27 In. 1540.00
Bust, Goddess, 13 In. 400.00
Bust, Handsome Maiden, White, Floral Spray On Her Bodice, Socle Base, 24 In. 365.00
Bust, Little Girl, Hair Wrapped In Bonnet, Marble Socle, 19 1/4 In. 2875.00
Bust, San Saens, Floral Drapery, Fluted Pedestal, 26 In. 5750.00
Bust, William Pitt, Classical Drapery, Carved Socle, 1807, 29 1/4 In. 4310.00
Bust, Young Boy, Raymond Roussel, 20th Century, 30 In. 4025.00
Chimney Piece, Louis XV Style, Serpentine Frieze, Scrolls, 58 In. 3450.00
Desk Set, Verte Antico, Foliate & Eagle Mounts, Gilt Bronze, 4 Piece 1035.00
Frame, Picture, Cloisonne, Enameled Brackets, Rectangular 865.00
Lamp, Urn Form, Marble Body Fitted With Scrolled Handles, 17 In. 4885.00

Obelisk, Green, White & Black, 20 In., Pair 275.00
Obelisk, Portoro Marble, Square Base, Italy, c.1930, 14 1/2 In., Pair 730.00
Pedestal, Bronze Mounted, Columnar Support, Octagonal Base, 39 In. 1575.00
Pedestal, Bronze, Applied Foliate, Berried Ring, Black Top, Base, 45 In. 1575.00
Pedestal, Carved Faces All Around, 40 x 20 In. 6000.00
Pedestal, Column Form, Purple Mottled Marble, Fluted, 34 In., 3 Part 1205.00
Pedestal, Columnar Form, Raised On Octagonal Base, Green Marble, 45 In. 660.00
Pedestal, Louis XVI, Onyx, 45 In. 1030.00
Pedestal, Mottled Green, White Marble Base, Circular, 44 In. 800.00
Pedestal, Mottled White, Fluted, Geometric Design, Circular, 40 3/8 In. 400.00
Pedestal, Overall Fitted With Gilt Bronze Foliate Mounts, 44 1/4 In., Pair 9200.00
Pedestal, Raised Floral, Foliate Design, Molded, 40 In. 150.00
Pedestal, Square, Inset Bronze Plaque, 13 x 12 In. 1090.00
Pedestal, Tapered Masks, Foliage, Plinth Base, 49 In. 1955.00
Pedestal, Verde Antique, Winged Goddess Holding Urn, 43 In. 1210.00
Planter, On Stand, Women & Children, Vine Of Grapes, 10 x 18 In., 4 Piece 2070.00
Statue, 3 Graces, Onyx Stepped Plinth, Italy, 11 1/2 In. 175.00
Statue, Fair Angler, Cipriani, 20th Century, 47 1/2 In. 9775.00
Statue, Madonna & Child, A. Canova, 58 In. 6900.00
Statue, Sleeping Lamb, On Base, Golden Ivory Patina, 14 x 6 In. 950.00
Statue, Woman, Face Leaning Forward During Conversation, White, 9 In. 345.00
Statue, Woman, Kneeling With Urn, 35 In. 6500.00
Statue, Woman, Neoclassical, Reclining, 19 In. 60.00
Statue, Woman, Seated On Rock Formation, White Marble, 24 In. 1100.00
Statue, Woman, With Cherubs, 30 In. 400.00
Statue, Young Boy & Cat, P.E. Fiaschi, 35 In. 8625.00
Tazza, Neoclassical Style, Everted Rim, Gadrooned Body, Beaded Base, 8 In. 4310.00
Urn, Charles X, Red, Bronze Dore, Pedestal, 13 In., Pair 1725.00
Urn, Continental, Baluster Shape, Flared Rim, 20 In., Pair 1150.00
Urn, Napoleon III, Floral Finial, Dore Bronze, Ram's Masks, 25 In., Pair 5750.00
Urn, Neoclassical Style, Campana Form, Classically Clad Figures, 13 In., Pair 1725.00
Urn, Neoclassical Style, Spiral Twisted, Domed Cover, Stepped Base, 30 In. 2875.00
Urn, Rococo, Foliate, C-Scroll Gadroon, White, 28 In., Pair 5460.00

MARBLEHEAD Pottery was founded in 1905 by Dr. J. Hall as a rehabil-
itative program for the patients of a Marblehead, Massachusetts, sanitarium. Two years later it was separated from the sanitarium and it continued operations until 1936. Many of the pieces were decorated with
marine motifs.

Bowl, Blue, Low, 9 In. 225.00
Bowl, Deep Blue Rim, Light Blue Interior, Flared, Impressed Mark, 14 x 2 1/2 In. 415.00
Bowl, Flower Frog, Matte Dark Green Glaze, 8 1/2 x 2 In. 230.00
Bowl, Flower Frog, Wisteria, Blue, 1 3/4 x 3 1/2 In. 165.00
Bowl, Glossy Green Interior, Matte Green, Impressed Mark, 9 In. 385.00
Bowl, Light Blue Glaze, Dark Blue Rim & Underside, Impressed Mark, 12 In. 275.00
Bowl, Matte Dark Blue, Impressed Mark, 8 1/2 x 2 In. 285.00
Bowl, Matte Green Glaze, Satin Finish Interior, Signed, 9 3/4 In. 495.00
Bowl, Olive Green Glaze, Marked, 6 1/2 In. 275.00
Bowl, Purple & Blue Blended Matte Glaze, Blue Interior, 9 x 4 1/2 In. 425.00
Bowl, Speckled Dark Blue Glaze, Light Blue Interior, 8 1/2 In. 330.00
Bowl, Turquoise To Blue Crystalline Glaze, Flared, Impressed Mark, 14 x 2 In. 495.00
Bowl, Violet Matte Glaze, Circular, 3 3/4 x 7 3/4 In. 330.00
Candlestick, Matte Yellow Glaze, Impressed Mark, 4 x 3 In. 230.00
Chamberstick, Blue Matte Glaze, Impressed Mark, 4 In. 285.00
Chamberstick, Matte Gray Glaze, Impressed Mark, 7 1/2 In. 440.00
Creamer, Dark Blue, Light Blue Interior, 3 In. 135.00
Pitcher, Blue Matte Glaze, A.E. Baggs, Impressed Mark, 1933, 8 In. 465.00
Pitcher, Wisteria, 4 3/4 In. 195.00
Tile, Basket Of Fruit, Flowers, 2 Parrots Perched On Handle, 6 x 6 In. 770.00
Tile, Embossed Design Of Spanish Galleon At Full Sail, 6 1/2 x 6 1/2 In. 525.00
Tile, Green Trees, Amber Ground, Quartered Oak Frame, Ship Mark, 4 1/4 In. 1200.00
Tile, Tea, Large Bowl Of Flowers, Blue, Green, Light Blue Ground, 5 In. 520.00
Trivet, Floral Basket, Blue, Red, Yellow, Green, Orange, Black Ground, 6 1/4 In. 430.00

Trivet, Stylized Flowers, Matte Blue, Green, Yellow, Red, Paper Label, 6 In. 875.00
Vase, Blue Flowers, Green Stems, Mauve Ground, Signed, 4 1/4 In. 1320.00
Vase, Blue, Black High Glaze, 4 In. 550.00
Vase, Broad Based Form, Blue Matte Glaze, Impressed Mark, 6 In. 385.00
Vase, Bulbous, Brown, 4 In. 275.00
Vase, Bulbous, Grapevines, Green, Blue Ground, Brown Speckled, Mark, 4 In. 1840.00
Vase, Bulbous, Rhythmic Stylized Grapevine, Green, Tinted Green, Mark, 3 In. 1840.00
Vase, Corset, Gray Matte Glaze, 4 3/4 x 2 In. 195.00
Vase, Cylindrical, Blue Matte Glaze, 8 1/4 x 3 3/4 In. 600.00
Vase, Cylindrical, Landscape, Trees On Mustard Ground, 10 In. 4180.00
Vase, Dark Blue Matte Glaze, Partial Paper Label, 5 In. 255.00
Vase, Dark Blue, Impressed Mark, 6 In. 550.00
Vase, Dragonflies, Light, Dark Brown, Green Ground, Signed, H.T., 6 In. 4675.00
Vase, Egg Shape, Dark Blue Matte Glaze, Impressed Ship Mark, 9 1/4 x 5 In. 880.00
Vase, Egg Shape, Green Leaves, Blue Grapes, Speckled Gray Ground, 3 x 3 In. 1320.00
Vase, Egg Shape, Medium Brown Pebbled Matte, 8 1/2 x 6 In. 1210.00
Vase, Fan, Embossed Rippled Design, Impressed Mark, Paper Label, 6 In. 385.00
Vase, Fan, Matte Blue Glaze, Impressed Mark, Paper Label, 6 1/4 x 8 In. 320.00
Vase, Flared Rim, Dark Blue Matte Glaze, Impressed Mark, 5 In. 360.00
Vase, Floral Design, Muted Lavender, Yellow Blossoms, Green Leaves, 3 1/2 In. 1320.00
Vase, Flowers, Blue, Pale Pink, Gray, Blue Ground, 9 In. 2100.00
Vase, Foliage, Deep Green, Red Highlights, Green Ground, 6 In. 11000.00
Vase, Foliage, Light Blue, Dark Blue Ground, 6 1/2 x 5 1/2 In. 8000.00
Vase, Glossy Teal Green Glaze, Signed, 5 1/2 In. 220.00
Vase, Gray Matte, Blue Interior, Signed, 5 In. 245.00
Vase, Incised Black Dots & Lines, Speckled Green Ground, Signed, 3 3/4 In. 1430.00
Vase, Incised Greek Key, Dark Blue On Gray Speckled Ground, Signed, 6 In. 1320.00
Vase, Leaves, Gray, Mottled Dark Green Ground, 9 1/2 In. 5225.00
Vase, Light Purple Matte Glaze, 8 In. 440.00
Vase, Light Purple Matte Glaze, Impressed Mark, 5 In. 190.00
Vase, Matte Blue Glaze, Impressed Mark, Cylinder, 9 x 4 In. 860.00
Vase, Matte Blue Glaze, Impressed Mark, Paper Label, 5 In. 495.00
Vase, Matte Blue Glaze, Silver Lid, Impressed Mark, 4 In. 230.00
Vase, Matte Bluish-Gray Glaze, Impressed Mark, 6 1/2 In. 275.00
Vase, Matte Brown Glaze, Impressed Mark, 5 In. 65.00
Vase, Matte Mottled Green Glaze, Impressed Mark, 7 In. 935.00
Vase, Matte Mottled Green Glaze, Red-Brown, Cylindrical, 1910, 7 In. 375.00
Vase, Matte Yellow Glaze, Impressed Mark, 3 1/2 In. 440.00
Vase, Mottled Blue Glossy Glaze, Impressed Mark, 5 In. 255.00
Vase, Mustard Yellow, 8 1/2 In. 720.00
Vase, Pear Shape, Dark Green Matte, Impressed Ship Mark, 5 1/4 x 4 In. 520.00
Vase, Purple Grape Cluster, Brown Vine, Green Leaf Design, 5 1/2 In. 1870.00
Vase, Purple Matte Glaze, 7 1/2 In. 385.00
Vase, Red Iridescent Striations, Cream, White, Red High Glaze Ground, 3 In. 3450.00
Vase, Slinking Black Panthers, Forest Setting, Hannah Tutt, 7 1/8 In. 3850.00
Vase, Squatty, Gray, 3 1/2 x 5 In. ....275.00 to 295.00
Vase, Tapered Form, Purple Glaze, Marked, 4 In. 275.00
Vase, Trees, Charcoal Black Against Matte Green Ground, 8 x 8 In. 7700.00
Vase, Trees, Dark Brown Against Green Ground, 12 1/2 In. 410.00
Vase, Trees, Light Brown, Cream, White Ground, 6 1/2 x 6 In. 3450.00
Wall Pocket, Blue Matte Glaze, Impressed Mark, 5 x 4 In. 230.00
Wall Pocket, Fluted Rim, Blue Matte Glaze, Impressed Mark, 8 x 4 In. 300.00

MARTIN BROTHERS of Middlesex, England, made Martinware, a salt-glazed stoneware, between 1873 and 1915. Many figural jugs and vases were made by the three brothers. Of special interest are the fanciful birds, usually made with removable heads.

Figurine, Bird, Hand Sculpted, Blue, Brown, Oatmeal, 1893, 3 x 1/2 In. 1045.00
Figurine, Bird, Whimsical, Blue, Green, Black, Brown, England, 1913, 9 In. 8250.00
Figurine, Bird, Whimsical, Green, Brown, Blue, Signed, England, 1905, 12 In. 12100.00
Jug, Bulbous Face, 2 Smirking Faces, Gun Metal, Brown Glaze, 6 1/4 x 6 In. 1760.00
Jug, Humorous Face, 2 Sides, Brown, 1898, 7 1/4 In. 1495.00
Pitcher, Grotesque Fish, 4 Sides, Signed, 1903, 8 3/4 In. 900.00

Statue, Grotesque, Monster Scene, Oatmeal, Gun Metal, Light Green, 3 x 3 In. 1980.00
Tile, Incised Flowers, Brown & Black, Square, 5 3/4 In. 110.00
Vase, 2 Handles, Fern, Olive Green, Royal Blue, Oatmeal, 1876, 12 x 5 3/4 In. 600.00
Vase, Grotesque, Outline Blue, Gray Ground, Signed, 1901, 3 1/2 In. 825.00
Vase, Trailing Line Design, Graphite Glaze, 3 3/4 In. 175.00

MARY GREGORY is the name used for a type of glass that is easily identified. White figures were painted on clear or colored glass as the decoration. The figures chosen were usually children at play. The first
glass known as Mary Gregory was made about 1870. Similar glass is
made even today. The traditional story has been that the glass was
made at the Sandwich Glass works in Boston by a woman named Mary
Gregory. Recent research suggests that it is possible that none was
made at Sandwich. In general, all-white figures were used in the
United States, tinted faces were probably used in Bohemia, France,
Italy, Germany, Switzerland, and England. Children standing, not playing, were pictured after the 1950s.

Bell, Boy Fishing, Light Green 70.00
Bell, White Girl & Bird 195.00
Bottle, Barber, Girl, Croquet, Inverted Thumbprint, Cranberry, Metal Stopper, 8 In. 380.00
Bottle, White Girl, Enameled, Lavender Glass, Champagne Stopper, 9 1/2 In. 145.00
Box, Boy Holding Flower, Enamel Designs, Metal Feet, 5 1/2 x 5 3/4 In. 1065.00
Box, Boy On Hinged Cover, Golden Amber, 3 1/4 x 3 3/8 In. 265.00
Box, Dome Cover, Boy With Flowers, Cranberry, Metal Base, 6 x 6 In. 1065.00
Box, Girl Standing By Fence On Cover, Lime Green, 3 3/4 x 4 1/2 In. 325.00
Box, Glove, 4 Figures, Children Lawn Bowling, Floral Swags, Blue, 4 1/2 x 5 In. 2400.00
Creamer, Girl, Blue Wafer Foot, Sapphire Blue Handle, Amber, 8 In. 225.00
Cruet, Boy, Clear 250.00
Cruet, Children, Green 145.00
Cruet, Inverted Thumbprint, Cranberry 165.00
Decanter, Ribbed, Man, Pink Suit, Handle, Emerald Green, Acorn Stopper, 11 In. 165.00
Decanter, White Enameled Girl, Amber, Bubble Stopper, 9 1/2 In. 195.00
Dresser Jar, Cover, Girl Blowing Bubbles, Tall Tulip On Cover, Gold Trim, 8 In. 150.00
Figurine, Boy Blowing Horn, Cranberry 95.00
Goblet, Girl With Flower Spray, Amber, 5 1/8 In. 118.00
Lamp, Girl Fishing, Flowers On Shade, Blue & White Swirl, 16 1/4 In. 1500.00
Mug, Girl, Mother, Applied Handle, Polished Base, White Enamel, Amber, 3 In. 85.00
Paperweight, Black, White, Floral, Square, 2 In. 65.00
Perfume Bottle, Boy, Holding Leafy Branch, Faceted Stopper, 3 3/4 In. 285.00
Perfume Bottle, Girl, Cobalt, 8 In. 140.00
Pitcher, Girl With Tinted Hair, Design On Dress, Blue, 10 3/4 In. 395.00
Pitcher, Girl, Swinging, Reed Handle, Black Amethyst, 9 In. 530.00
Pitcher, Woman, Carrying Vase Of Flowers, Petal Rim, Prussian Blue, 9 1/2 In. 355.00
Pitcher, Woman, Long Dress, Ribbed, Crimped, Prussian Girl, 9 1/2 In. 360.00
Tea Warmer, Lavender Man, With Net, Running After Butterfly, Metal Frame, 4 In. 275.00
Tumbler, Boy & Girl, Cobalt 65.00
Tumbler, Child, Azure Blue 135.00
Tumbler, Girl With Flower, Turquoise Blue 145.00
Tumbler, Girl, Light Blue, 4 In. 95.00
Urn, Girl, Boy, Picking Apples From Tree, Black, Pedestal, 9 3/4 In. 300.00
Vase, Boy & Girl Under Trees, Green, Rigaree On Sides, 11 In., Pair 350.00
Vase, Boy & Girl, Carrying Bottle, Black Amethyst, 8 1/4 In. 350.00
Vase, Boy & Girl, Gold Bands On Bottom, Cranberry, 12 In. 295.00
Vase, Boy, Blowing Bubbles, Ruffled, Sapphire Blue, 10 In. . . . . .275.00 to 295.00
Vase, Boy, Carrying Tray Of Flowers, Bristol Green, Ruffled, 11 1/2 In. . . . . .210.00 to 225.00
Vase, Boy, On His Knee, Holding Out Hand To Girl, Sapphire Blue, 11 3/4 In. 460.00
Vase, Cut Scalloped Top, Pedestal Foot, White Figures, 13 In. 895.00
Vase, Girl With Parasol & Hat, Cranberry, 8 1/2 In. 395.00
Vase, Girl, Carrying Butterfly Net, Lime Green, Cylinder, 10 5/8 In. 180.00
Vase, Girl, Ruffled Top, Ruffled, 8 In. . . . . .125.00 to 150.00
Vase, Girl, Ruffled, Amber, 8 1/4 In. 175.00
Vase, Girl, Wearing Hat, Carrying Basket, Black Amethyst, 11 In., Pair 650.00
Water Set, 2 Boys, 2 Girls, Cranberry, 5 Piece 500.00

MASON'S IRONSTONE was made by the English pottery of Charles J. Mason after 1813. Mason, of Lane Delph, was given a patent for this improved earthenware. He usually called it "Mason's Patent Ironstone China." It resisted chipping and breaking so it became popular for dinnerwares and other table service dishes. Vases and other decorative pieces were also made. The ironstone was decorated with orange, blue, gold, and other colors, often in Japanese inspired designs. The firm had financial difficulties but the molds and the name Mason were used by many owners through the years, including Francis Morley, Taylor Ashworth, George L. Ashworth, and John Shaw. Mason's joined the Wedgwood group in 1973 and the name is still found on dinnerwares.

Basket, Fruit, Octagonal, 5 1/2 x 4 3/8 In.	20.00
Creamer, Mandarin, 5 1/4 In.	35.00
Dish, Cheese, Flow Blue	200.00
Jar, Lion Finials, Cobalt Blue, Gold Trim, c.1840, 8 1/2 In., Pair	1100.00
Pitcher, Oriental, Red, Blue, 9 In.	350.00
Plate, Oriental Landscape Transfer, 9 In., 4 Piece	150.00
Plate, Vista, Brown, 9 In.	20.00
Platter, Mandarin, 1818	425.00
Platter, Willow, Blue, 10 1/2 In.	125.00
Tureen, Black Oriental Transfer, Orange Enameled, Gilt, 13 1/2 In.	355.00
Tureen, Soup, Underplate, Ladle, Early 20th Century, 15 x 10 1/2 In.	800.00
Vase, Chartreuse Pattern, Round, Mason's, 5 In.	30.00

MASONIC, see Fraternal category.

MASSIER, a French art pottery, was made by brothers Jerome, Delphin, and Clement Massier in Vallauris and Golfe-Juan, France, in the late nineteenth and early twentieth centuries. It has an iridescent metallic luster glaze that resembles the Weller Sicard pottery glaze. Most pieces are marked *J. Massier*.

Bowl, Signed Bottom, 4 1/2 x 2 In.	350.00
Ewer, Stylized Floral Design, White, Gold, Pink, Yellow Iridescent, 1887, 12 In.	520.00
Plate, Poppies, Iridescent, 10 In.	625.00
Tile, Floral, Signed, Round, 6 In.	65.00
Vase, Grapes, 5 1/4 In.	550.00

MATCH HOLDERS were made to hold the large wooden matches that were used in the nineteenth and twentieth centuries for a variety of purposes. The kitchen stove and the fireplace or furnace had to be lit regularly. One type of match holder was made to hang on the wall, another was designed to be kept on a tabletop. Of special interest today are match holders that have advertisements as part of the design.

A. Hussey & Co., Cherub, Tin, Wall	1705.00
Adriance Farm Machinery, Adriance Corn Binder, Yellow Ground, Tin, Wall, 5 In.	470.00
Basket, Milk Glass, Pink Handles	35.00
Black Man On Stump, Cast Iron	520.00
Boot Form, On Stand, Black & Gold Paint, Cast Iron, 4 3/4 x 4 5/8 In.	65.00
Brass, Incised Design, Wall, 1860, 6 x 7 In.	75.00
Ceresota Prize Bread Flour, Embossed, Tin Lithograph, Wall, 6 1/2 In.	465.00 to 495.00
Cherries, Cleminson	30.00
Cockroach, Lift Wings & Striker On Bottom, Bradley & Hubbard, 3 5/8 In.	475.00
Daisy & Button, Double Compartment, Striker	95.00
De Laval Cream Separator, The World's Standard, Embossed, Tin, Wall, 6 In.	115.00 to 385.00
Doggie, Window, Brass	65.00
Eveready, Tin, Wall, 1922	45.00
Figural, Plumpish Club Member, Bisque, 3 x 3 1/2 In.	195.00
Glass, 3 Dolphin Pattern, Amber	95.00
Glass, 3 Dolphin Pattern, Clear	75.00
Gray, Graniteware	395.00
Havana Cigars, Embossed Knight On Horseback	45.00
Helpful Mandy, Metal, Hanging	89.00
Holsum, The Sanitary Bread, Black Ground, Tin Lithograph, Wall, 5 In.	176.00

Indian Bust, White, Striker Base, Porcelain, 2 In. 50.00
Keybrand Shoes, Tin Lithograph, Wall, 5 In. 200.00
King Of Hearts, Clubs, Diamonds & Spades, Porcelain, With Striker 48.00
Kirkman's Borax Soap For Laundry Work, Wash Woman, Tin, Wall, 7 In. 6270.00
Kunkel's Drug Store, Tin, Mortar & Pestle Picture, Wall 175.00
Learn To Drink Moxie, Very Healthful, Tin, Wall, 7 In. 550.00
Little Red Riding Hood, All White 500.00
Mammy, Plaid 475.00
Sharples, Tin, Wall 365.00
Skull, Bisque 38.00
Striker, Marshall Field, Bronze 80.00
Topsy Hosiery, Fred Kron, Mankato, Minn., Tin Lithograph, Wall, 5 In. 1155.00
Valentine, Sheet Iron, Hand Chased, 5 5/8 In. 575.00
Vaseline Glass, Daisy & Button Pattern 55.00
Winchester, Cast Iron 125.00
Wrigley's Juicy Fruit, With Striker, Metal, 5 x 3 1/2 In. ....95.00 to 100.00

MATCH SAFES were designed to be carried in the pocket. Early matches were made with phosphorus and could ignite unexpectedly. The
matches were safely stored in the tightly closed container. Match safes
were made in sterling silver, plated silver, or other metals. The English
call these *vesta boxes*.

Barrel Shape 95.00
Bass Violin Form, Silver Plate 165.00
Bawdy French Couple, Enamel Top & Inner Lid, Brass ....*Illus* 405.00
Blatz Beer ....65.00 to 75.00
Bust Of Man, Silver 425.00
Butterfly Design, Gorham, Sterling Silver 395.00
Cat In Hat 450.00
Dog's Head, Metal ....*Illus* 220.00
Embossed Woman & Flowers, Engraved Name & Date, Sterling Silver 275.00
Embossed Woman Amid Stars, Sterling Silver 300.00
Enameled Dore, Bronze, On Base, France 75.00
Eureka Fire Hose Co., Eagle On Hydrant, Hard Rubber 175.00
Figural, Columbus Portrait, Stack Of Gold-Colored Coins 95.00
Fish Form, Silver Plated 405.00
General Ulysses S. Grant, Nickel Plated Brass, 2 1/2 x 1 3/4 In. 850.00
Home Brewing Co., Factory & Logo, Celluloid, 1901 .... 125.00
Jamestown Expo., Pocahontas, Reverse Church, 1907 .... 100.00
Knights Of Pythias, Embossed Design Of Organization's Skull, Hinged Lid, Steel 75.00
Lucky Lindy, Charles Lindbergh, Aluminum, 1928, 2 1/2 x 5 x 7 3/4 In. 70.00
Mermaid, Nude, Sterling Silver 250.00

Match Safe, Bawdy French Couple,
Enamel Top & Inner Lid, Brass

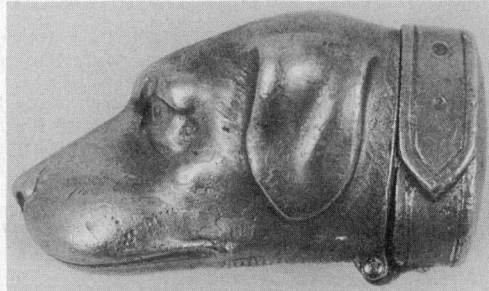

Match Safe, Dog's
Head, Metal

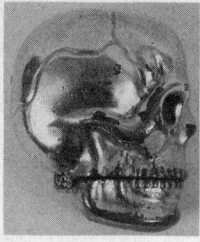

Match Safe, Pig, Brass, 2 1/2 In.

Match Safe,
Skeleton Head,
Silver Plate

Match Safe, Woman Arising, Waves,
Monogram, Sterling Silver

Monkey Smoking Pipe, Silver Plated	285.00
Moose, Brass	70.00
Ornate Floral Design, With Nude, Silver Plated	175.00
Pig, Brass, 2 1/2 In. ....*Illus*	220.00
Raised Anchor & Sailing Ship, Dated 1884	110.00
Raised Colored Scene, Indian With Spear, American Flag, Silver Plated	165.00
Schlitz Beer	90.00
Skeleton Head, Silver Plate ....*Illus*	220.00
Star Set With Mine-Cut Diamond, Schreve & Co., 14K Yellow Gold	287.00
United Cigar, Book	55.00
Val Blatz Brewing Co., Striker, Tin On Brass	70.00
With Cigar Cutter, St. Louis, 1904	64.00
Woman Arising, Waves, Monogram, Sterling Silver ....*Illus*	275.00
Woman In Field Of Flowers Lithograph, Silver Plated	250.00
Woman's Head, Horse's Head	135.00
Woman's Head Lithograph, Plated Color	195.00
Woman's Shoe, Striker Bottom, Gutta-Percha, c.1870	125.00

MATSU-NO-KE was a type of applied decoration for glass patented by
Frederick Carder in 1922. There is clear evidence that pieces were
made before that date at the Steuben glassworks. Stevens & Williams
of England also made an applied decoration by the same name.

Bowl, White, Diamond-Quilted, Brown Stems Support Rosette, 5 x 6 In. 600.00

MATT MORGAN, an English artist, was making pottery in Cincinnati,
Ohio, by 1883. His pieces were decorated to resemble Moorish wares.
Incised designs and colors were applied to raised panels on the pottery.
Shiny or matte glazes were used. The company lasted less than two
years.

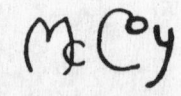

Vase, Floral, Bulbous Base, Open Handles, Incised Marks, 5 1/2 In. 143.00

MCCOY pottery was made in Roseville, Ohio. The J. W. McCoy Pottery
was founded in 1899. It became the Brush McCoy Pottery Company
in 1911. The name changed to the Brush Pottery in 1925. The word
Brush was usually included in the mark on their pieces. The Nelson
McCoy Sanitary and Stoneware Company, a different firm, was founded in Roseville, Ohio, in 1910. The firm made art pottery after 1926.
In 1933 it became the Nelson McCoy Pottery. Pieces marked *McCoy*
were made by the Nelson McCoy Company. Cookie jars were made
from the 1930s until December 1990, when the McCoy factory closed.
In 1990 the McCoy mark was put back on pottery by a firm unrelated
to the original company.

Ashtray, Double Frogs, 1945, 6 1/2 In.	65.00
Bank, Eagle, Immigrant Industrial Savings	35.00
Bank, Sailor, Seaman's For Saving, 1940s	125.00
Bank, Woodsey Owl, 1974 ....120.00 to 150.00

Bean Bowl, Heinz, Brown 5.00
Bean Pot, Cover, Bean Plant In Bas Relief Design, 1 Handle, Brown ....35.00 to 45.00
Bookends, Elephant Head, Matte Green, 1920s 395.00
Bookends, Lily, With Leaves 55.00
Bowl, Mixing, 1 Green, 1 Blue, Pair 42.00
Bowl, Mixing, Yellow 16.00
Caddy, Dresser, Lion, Swank 38.00
Coffee Server, El Rancho Bar-B-Que 85.00
Coffee Set, Sunburst Gold, 3 Piece 80.00
Cookie Jar, 2 Kittens In Low Basket, 1950s 600.00
Cookie Jar, Apple 40.00
Cookie Jar, Astronauts, Aqua, 1963 ....700.00 to 800.00
Cookie Jar, Baa Baa Black Sheep, Nursery Characters 210.00
Cookie Jar, Bananas, 1950s 65.00
Cookie Jar, Barnum's Animal Crackers, Nabisco Wagon 575.00
Cookie Jar, Barnums Animal Crackers 575.00
Cookie Jar, Bear & Beehive ....45.00 to 55.00
Cookie Jar, Betsy Baker 75.00
Cookie Jar, Bobby The Baker 40.00
Cookie Jar, Bronze Kettle, Metal Handle 40.00
Cookie Jar, Bugs Bunny, Cylinder 60.00
Cookie Jar, Chairman Of The Board ....550.00 to 760.00
Cookie Jar, Chilly Willy 65.00
Cookie Jar, Circus Horse 175.00
Cookie Jar, Clown Bust ....40.00 to 70.00
Cookie Jar, Clown, In Barrel, Green 100.00
Cookie Jar, Coalby Cat ....175.00 to 380.00
Cookie Jar, Coffee Grinder 40.00
Cookie Jar, Coke Can 95.00
Cookie Jar, Cookie Barrel 17.00
Cookie Jar, Cookie Bell 60.00
Cookie Jar, Cookie House 125.00
Cookie Jar, Cookie Log, Squirrel Finial 75.00
Cookie Jar, Cookstove, Ivory 45.00
Cookie Jar, Covered Wagon 45.00
Cookie Jar, Dalmations In Rocking Chair ....325.00 to 500.00
Cookie Jar, Early American Chest, 11 1/2 In. 110.00
Cookie Jar, Early American Frontier Family 25.00
Cookie Jar, Engine, Jupiter 60, Black ....100.00 to 175.00
Cookie Jar, Engine, Jupiter 60, Yellow ....135.00 to 150.00
Cookie Jar, Football Boy ....225.00 to 295.00
Cookie Jar, Forbidden Fruit, 1967 .... 50.00
Cookie Jar, Friendship 7, 1962-1963 .... 175.00
Cookie Jar, Gabled House 100.00
Cookie Jar, Garbage Can 45.00
Cookie Jar, Globe 200.00
Cookie Jar, Grandfather Clock 55.00
Cookie Jar, Happy Face, Have A Happy Day ....20.00 to 65.00
Cookie Jar, Harley-Davidson Hog, 1984 .... 115.00
Cookie Jar, Hillbilly Bear 30.00
Cookie Jar, Hobby Horse, Tan 175.00
Cookie Jar, Honey Bear, On Side Of Tree 125.00
Cookie Jar, Humpty Dumpty, Nursery Characters 120.00
Cookie Jar, Indian, Pontiac ....200.00 to 475.00
Cookie Jar, Jack-O-Lantern, Orange Cover 550.00
Cookie Jar, Keebler Tree House 40.00
Cookie Jar, Kitten On Basket Weave, Pink ....75.00 to 90.00
Cookie Jar, Lamb On Basket Weave 75.00
Cookie Jar, Lamp, Flame In Center Panel, 1962-1963 .... 75.00
Cookie Jar, Little Angel 75.00
Cookie Jar, Little Miss Muffet, Nursery Characters ....50.00 to 55.00
Cookie Jar, Little Red Riding Hood 250.00
Cookie Jar, Log Cabin 110.00

Cookie Jar, Mammy, Dem Cookies Shor Am Good 800.00
Cookie Jar, Mammy, With Cauliflower, 1939 .... 1200.00
Cookie Jar, Mr. & Mrs. Owl 125.00
Cookie Jar, Nabisco, 1974 .... 80.00
Cookie Jar, Pepper, Yellow, Green Cover 40.00
Cookie Jar, Picnic Basket 70.00
Cookie Jar, Puppy, Basketweave 35.00
Cookie Jar, Puppy, Holding Sign 35.00
Cookie Jar, Rag Doll, 1972-1975 .... 50.00
Cookie Jar, Red Barn, Cow In Door, 1963 .... 225.00
Cookie Jar, Snoopy On Doghouse, 1970 .... 295.00
Cookie Jar, Snow Bear, 1965 .... 120.00
Cookie Jar, Squirrel, Cracks Nut On Log, 10 1/2 In. 120.00
Cookie Jar, Stage Coach, White, Gold Trim 1050.00
Cookie Jar, Stagecoach, White ....950.00 to 1050.00
Cookie Jar, Strawberry .... 35.00 to 50.00
Cookie Jar, Strawberry, White, 1972-1979 .... 35.00
Cookie Jar, Teddy Bear & Friend, Bird On Teddy's Head 50.00
Cookie Jar, Teepee, Slant Cover 475.00
Cookie Jar, Teepee, Straight Cover 400.00
Cookie Jar, Traffic Light .... 55.00 to 60.00
Cookie Jar, Tug Boat, 1985 .... 50.00
Cookie Jar, Upside Down Bear, Panda 50.00
Cookie Jar, W.C. Fields, 1972-1974 .... 225.00
Cookie Jar, Wedding Jar, 22K Gold Trim 80.00
Cookie Jar, Winking Pig 200.00
Cookie Jar, Woodsy Owl ....200.00 to 395.00
Cookie Jar, Wren House, Brown Bird, 1958 .... 285.00
Cookie Jar, Wren House, Pink Bird, 1958 ....150.00 to 160.00
Cookie Jar, Yosemite Sam 225.00
Cuspidor, Brown-Gray Pattern, 1940s 50.00
Decanter, 1932 Pierce Arrow Sport Phantom 50.00
Decanter, Apollo, Missile, 1968 .... 40.00
Dish, Dog, Man's Best Friend 45.00
Dish, Shell, Pink 15.00
Ewer, Grape 35.00
Figurine, Black Cat 22.00
Figurine, Dog, Dachshund, Blue 85.00
Figurine, Duck, With Umbrella 80.00
Figurine, Shoe, Kicking Football 125.00
Flower Frog, Duck 125.00
Flowerpot, Bay Leaf Bas Design, Aqua, 3 x 4 In. 20.00
Flowerpot, Flower Blossom Shape, Leaves, Buds, Stem Handle, Light Blue, 6 x 4 In. 30.00
Flowerpot, Matte Green, 1935 .... 15.00
Flowerpot, White Embossed Roses 35.00
Jar, Cabbage Shape, 8 In. 35.00
Jar, Strawberry Shape, Green 70.00
Jardiniere, Basket 35.00
Jardiniere, Hand Painted, Footed, 1900, 5 x 5 1/2 In. 195.00
Jardiniere, Springwood, Green, 7 x 8 In. 75.00
Lamp, Boots, Small, 1956 .... 45.00
Lamp, Fireplace 30.00
Lamp, Smiley Face, White Shade, Plastic 45.00
Lantern, Patio, Owl, 10 In. 425.00
Mug, El Rancho, Bar-B-Que 20.00
Mug, Green Grape & Leaf Design, Stoneware 20.00
Mug, Happy Face ....8.00 to 14.00
Mug, Sabrina, Yellow 6.00
Pitcher, Brocade, Black & Aqua 50.00
Pitcher, Windmill & Tree, Blue & White 95.00
Pitcher, Woodland, Brown, Artist Initials 195.00
Pitcher, Woodland, Green 150.00
Planter, Brocade Artisan Pedestal, Pink 20.00

Planter, Butterfly, Pink 25.00
Planter, Calypso 65.00
Planter, Dove 30.00
Planter, Duck, Ringneck 45.00
Planter, Flying Ducks, Leaves At Base 120.00
Planter, Frog & Lotus 15.00
Planter, Grape Clusters, Leaves, Green 25.00
Planter, Hunting Dog, Large 145.00
Planter, Lamb, Black 20.00
Planter, Liberty Bell 245.00
Planter, Lion, Lying 30.00
Planter, Old Mill, 1953 .... 20.00
Planter, Panther, Black 40.00
Planter, Parrot, With Tub 70.00
Planter, Quail 50.00
Planter, Rocking Chair, 1954, 8 1/2 In. 30.00
Planter, Rodeo, Cowboy, 1950s 100.00
Planter, Springwood, Pink, Footed 25.00
Planter, Stork & Basket 30.00
Planter, Swan, White 35.00
Planter, Triple Lily, On Log ....30.00 to 50.00
Planter, Under The Spreading Chestnut Tree 35.00
Plate, Butterfly, White 50.00
Stein, Cowboy Boot 25.00
Sugar, Daisy 20.00
Sugar & Creamer, Rustic 26.00
Tankard, Buccaneer, Green Stoneware ....100.00 to 125.00
Tea Set, Pine Cone, Green, 3 Piece 85.00
Teapot, Brown, Small 20.00
Teapot, English Ivy, White & Green 50.00
Teapot, Painted Strawberries, White Ground 20.00
Teapot, Salada 25.00
Teapot, Yellow & Brown Blossom, Green Leaves, Black Glaze, 5 In. 77.00
Tureen, Soup, Pink & Blue Bands 65.00
Vase, Birdbath, Embossed Berries, Leaves, Yellow, 6 In. 15.00
Vase, Birds, Cherries, 8 In. 42.00
Vase, Blossomtime, 1946, 6 1/2 In. 20.00
Vase, Broad Green Leaves, Ivory Ground, Art Deco, 12 In. 145.00
Vase, Butterfly, Yellow, Cylinder, 7 In. 35.00
Vase, Fan, Grapes & Laves, Blue, Brown, 8 In., Pair 70.00
Vase, Flower, 2 Tulip, Cream High Gloss, 9 In. 85.00
Vase, Flower, 3 Lily, White High Gloss, 9 In. 58.00
Vase, Grape, 1951, 8 In. 30.00
Vase, Leaves Around Top, Green, 1945, 9 In. 55.00
Vase, Leaves, Red Berries, 9 In. 75.00
Vase, Lily, Label, 7 1/4 In. 60.00
Vase, Lizard Handles, 9 In. 75.00
Vase, Loy-Nel-Art, Flowers, Brown, 12 In. 500.00
Vase, Loy-Nel-Art, Iris Blossom, Brown & Green Ground, 8 In. 155.00
Vase, Loy-Nel-Art, Nasturtiums & Leaves, 12 1/2 In. 1500.00
Vase, Modern, Orange, 12 In. 50.00
Vase, Olympia, 5 1/2 In. 250.00
Vase, Ram's Head, Green 150.00
Vase, Sand Dollar, Matte White, 14 In. 125.00
Vase, Sunflower, Lime Green, 10 In. 85.00
Vase, Swan, Off White, 9 1/2 In. 15.00
Vase, Wheat, Florals, Turquoise, 2 Handles, 6 In. 35.00
Vase, White, 12 In. 50.00
Vase, Wild Rose, Yellow, 6 In. 25.00
Wall Pocket, Apple 45.00
Wall Pocket, Blossomtime, Yellow ....75.00 to 95.00
Wall Pocket, Cuckoo Clock 75.00
Wall Pocket, Grapes, 7 1/4 In. 55.00

Wall Pocket, Tan, Turquoise	40.00
Wall Pocket, Umbrella, Green, Yellow	40.00
Warmer, Food, El Rancho, Bar-B-Que	200.00
Water Set, El Rancho, Bar-B-Que, 5 Piece	1110.00
Watering Can, Turtle	40.00
Window Box, Grecian, 12 x 4 In.	125.00

MCKEE is a name associated with various glass enterprises in the United States since 1836, including J. & F. McKee (1850), Bryce, McKee & Co. (1850 to 1854), McKee and Brothers (1865), and National Glass Co. (1899). In 1903, the McKee Glass Company was formed in Jeannette, Pennsylvania. It became McKee Division of the Thatcher Glass Co. in 1951 and was bought out by the Jeannette Corporation in 1961. Pressed glass, kitchenwares, and tablewares were produced. Jeannette Corporation closed in the early 1980s. Additional pieces may be included in the Custard Glass category.

PRESCUT

Ashtray, Nude Girl Blowing Bubbles, Intaglio, 4 Piece	65.00
Bowl, Autumn, Skokie Green, 10 1/2 In.	47.00
Canister, Light Jade, Round	28.00
Canister, Sugar, Yellow, Round	65.00
Cup, Tom & Jerry, Jade, Black Letters, 12 Piece	225.00
Reamer, Delphite	650.00
Reamer, Delphite, Large	1000.00
Reamer, Jade ....65.00 to 80.00
Shaker, Flour, Yellow, Square	50.00
Syrup, Cover, Delphite	500.00
Syrup, Rock Crystal	150.00
Toothpick, Aztec	40.00
Tumble-Up, Jade	100.00
Tumbler, Jade, Footed	10.00
Tumbler, Nude, Bottoms-Up, Blue	55.00
Vase, Jade, 8 1/2 In.	250.00
Vase, Nude, Triangular, 8 1/2 In.	195.00
Vase, Vulcan, 8 In.	10.00
Vase, Vulcan, 12 In.	20.00

MECHANICAL BANKS are listed in the Bank category.

MEDICAL office furniture, operating tools, microscopes, thermometers, and other paraphernalia used by doctors are included in this category. Medicine bottles are listed in the Bottle category. There are related collectibles listed under Dental.

Apothecary Case, 24 Drawers, Pine, Poplar, Early 20th Century, 32 In.	550.00
Bag, Doctor's, Outfitted With 35 Files, 4 Large Bottles, Small	165.00
Bleeder, Brass & Iron, Civil War, 4 1/2 In.	220.00
Book, Hand Book Of First Aid, Johnson & Johnson, 3 Men, 1903	60.00
Bowl, Bleeding, John Williams, London, Pewter, 1729, 5 3/8 In.	575.00
Box, Smith's Pills, Tin Lithograph, Paper Instructions Inside, 3 In.	75.00
Breast Pump, Blown Glass, Cone, Globe Side Chamber, Rubber Bulb, 5 1/2 In.	30.00
Breast Pump, Blown Glass, Globe Base, Side Spout, 1850, 3 3/4 In.	315.00
Cabinet, Apothecary, 12 Deep Drawers, Pine, 36 1/2 x 36 In.	725.00
Cabinet, Doctor's, With Tools, 1900s	4500.00
Cabinet, Munyons Homeopathic Remedies, Tin Front, 24 x 16 In.	250.00
Case, Glass Eye, With 25 Eyes	200.00
Case, Specimen, Oak, 24 Mismatched Drawers, 2 Sections, 34 x 14 x 31 In.	165.00
Chest, 2 Doors, Fitted Interior, Lower Drawer, Brass Mounted, 15 x 13 In.	865.00
Chest, Apothecary, 72 Drawers, Mustard Paint	6300.00
Chest, Apothecary, Grain Painted, Square Legs, 47 In.	200.00
Chest, Apothecary, Pine, 9 Dovetailed Drawers, Turned Feet, 23 3/4 In.	1155.00
Chest, Apothecary, Walnut, 14 Drawers, Bracket Base, 16 x 18 In.	345.00
Chest, Ship Captain's, 1880	1500.00
Drill, Skull, Trephine	95.00
Eye Cup, John Bull, Cobalt Blue	65.00

Fleam, Veterinary, Brass & Iron, Leather Case, 4 3/4 In. 250.00
Generator, Violet Ray, 8 Applicators, Renulife Electric Co., Case, 1919, 14 1/2 In. 280.00
Glass, Dose, Embossed Buggies, 3 In. 15.00
Head, Phrenology, Scrolls, Foliage & Cranium, Glass Eyes, Ceramic, 9 1/4 In. 1610.00
Inhaler, Maw & Sons, Stoneware, 10 In., Pair 195.00
Invalid Feeder, Enamelware, White, Cup Shape, Loop Handle, 19th Century, 4 In. 85.00
Invalid Feeder, Pottery, Glazed, Embossed Flowers, Boat Shape, France, 6 1/2 In. 40.00
Invalid Feeder, Pottery, White Glaze, Cup Shape, Loop Handle, 1860, 3 1/4 In. 45.00
Kit, Instrument Sterilizing, Separate Burner, Brass Fittings, Copper, London, 15 1/4 In. . .   190.00
Kit, Military, Instrument, Scalpels, Bullet Probes, Forceps, Spanish-American War 2000.00
Kit, Optometrist, H. Beckmann, Tinted Glass Pieces, Opthalmoscope, Case, 12 In. 235.00
Kit, Optometrist, Oak Tray, 123 Lenses, Opthalmoscope, Leather Case, 15 3/4 In. 185.00
Kit, Surgeon's, Engraved, J.Wm. White MD, J.H. Gemrig, Philadelphia, 4 x 12 In. 1380.00
Kit, Violet Ray Aids & Life Process, Eneergex, Instructions, c.1920, 14 1/4 In. 100.00
Knife, Bleeding 75.00
Machine, Magnaeto Electric, For Nervous Diseases, Davis & Kidder 225.00
Mold, Suppository, Brass 75.00
Mortar & Pestle, American, Walnut, c.1780, 6 3/4 In. 285.00
Mortar & Pestle, Cherubic Faces On Mortar, Grasping Ridges, Brass 375.00
Mortar & Pestle, Walnut, England, c.1750, 6 3/4 In. 650.00
Mortar & Pestle, White Pottery, Gold Trim, 1930s, 5 1/2 In. 110.00
Mortar & Pestle, Wooden, American, c.1750, 7 1/2 In. . . . . .350.00 to 650.00
Nipple Shield, Blown Glass, Bun Shape, Slit On Side & Center 20.00
Pamphlet, Gargling Oil, 1881 . . . .   15.00
Pamphlet, Simmons Liver Regulator, 1902 . . . .   10.00
Pill Roller, Walnut, Brass, 7 3/4 x 16 In. 260.00
Premature Feeder, Glass Tube, Graduated, Nipple 1 End, Belcroy Feeder, 7 1/2 In. . . .   295.00
Saw, Surgeon's, Metacarpal, Ivory Handle, Civil War 285.00
Snare, Tonsil 65.00
Spoon, Feeding, Pewter, Elongated Bowl & Hinged Cover, A. Caron S.G.D.G., 9 In. 165.00
Spoon, Medicine, White Metal, Superost, 7 3/4 In. 50.00
Surgical Kit, Ivory & Ebony Handled Tools, J. & J. Arnold, Case, Civil War 1800.00
Syringe, Pewter 90.00
Thermometer, Oral, Case 15.00
Vaporizer, Vapo-Cresolene, Box & Bottle, 1894 . . . .   105.00
Wheel Chair, Oak, Woven Seat & Back 245.00

MEERSCHAUM is a soft white, gray, or cream-colored mineral named
magnesium silicate. The name comes from the German word for
seafoam, because it was sometimes found floating in the Black Sea and
people thought it was petrified seafoam. Pipes and other pieces of
carved meerschaum listed here date from the nineteenth century to the
present.

Cigar Holder, Celluloid, Case, 3 3/4 In. . . . .*Illus*   65.00
Pipe, American Eagle, Landing On Rock, Amber Holder, Case, 6 1/2 x 4 In. 150.00
Pipe, Boy On Horse, Spearing Lion, Case, 7 In. 440.00
Pipe, Bust Carved Of Ottoman, Fitted Case 34.50

**Never run an ad that says "Call
after 6 p.m." It is an announce-
ment that you are away from
the house during the day.**

Meerschaum, Cigar Holder,
Celluloid, Case, 3 3/4 In.

Pipe, Figure, Seated 750.00
Pipe, Head Of Cavalier, Case, 6 1/2 In. 215.00
Pipe, Horse Head, c.1880 .... 1200.00
Pipe, Victorian Woman 300.00

MEISSEN is a town in Germany where porcelain has been made since
1710. Any china made in the town can be called Meissen, although the
famous Meissen factory made the finest porcelains of the area. The
crossed swords mark of the great Meissen factory has been copied by
many other firms in Germany and other parts of the world. Pieces of
Meissen dinnerware in the Onion pattern are listed in their own category in this book.

Basket, Fruit & Flowers, Reticulated 3740.00
Bowl, Serving, Male, Reclining, Scalloped Edge, Gilt Floral Motif, Blue, 8 x 12 In. 1035.00
Centerpiece, 2 Handled Basket, Painted Sprays Of Flowers, Oval, 17 1/2 In. 6610.00
Centerpiece Bowl, Floral Motif, Cherub Finial, Floral Cornucopia, Gilt Handles, 12 In. . 1265.00
Chandelier, 6-Light, Pierced Basket Weave Baluster Form, Scrolled Branches, 28 In. 8625.00
Charger, Floral Design Center, Bird Perched, Crossed Swords, 17 In. 1540.00
Charger, Kakiemon, Polychrome, Crossed Swords, 17 In. ....*Illus* 1540.00
Clock, Boy, Seated, White Porcelain Dial, Black Arabic Numerals, Blue Glaze, 20 In. ... 5460.00
Clock, Cherub & Acanthus Leaf, Flowers, Lenzkirch Works, 20 In. ....*Illus* 5500.00
Clock, Dial Housed In Shaped Case, Figures & Flowers, 28 In. 7185.00
Clock, Flower Encrusted Rocky Form Case, Figure Of Zeus, Signed, 28 In. 6900.00
Compote, Hand Painted Polychrome Floral Sprays, Marked, c.1895, 6 1/2 In. 1050.00
Cruet, Indian Purple Pattern 195.00
Cup & Saucer, 3 Children In Classical Landscape, Scroll Handle 1265.00
Cup & Saucer, Floral 95.00
Cup & Saucer, Gilt, Floral Design, Transfer Decoration Of A Castle, Porcelain 35.00
Dish, Cherub Finial Cover, Blue Floral, Crossed Swords, 8 In. 200.00
Dish, Condiment, 2 Sections, Blue & White Floral, Marked, 8 x 9 1/2 In. 120.00
Dish, Floral & Fruit, Gilt Relief Border, Marked, 12 In. 150.00
Dish, Leaf Shape, Blue, Handle, 8 In., Pair 220.00
Dish, Leaf Shape, Hand Painted Flowers, 5 In. 30.00
Dish, Sweetmeat, Figural, Oriental, Foliate Scroll Panels, 1880s, 7 3/4 In. 4025.00
Figurine, 2 Musical Cherubs, With Horn, Tambourine, 5 In. 980.00
Figurine, 2 Putti Hauling Fishing Net, 1870s, 12 1/4 In. 3160.00
Figurine, Allegory Of Knowledge, Rockwork Base, Signed, 18 In. 5175.00
Figurine, Apple Boy, 10 In. 1800.00
Figurine, Bagpiper, 4 1/8 In. 550.00
Figurine, Beltrame, Standing On Flower Encrusted Pad Base, 5 1/8 In. 2875.00
Figurine, Bird, Brown Stripe, Black, White Plumage, 12 In. 920.00
Figurine, Blue Jay Chasing Squirrel, Open Beak, Signed, 15 3/8 In. 2645.00
Figurine, Boy & Girl, With Birdcage, 5 1/4 In. 1350.00
Figurine, Boy, Offering Flowers To Girl, 5 1/2 In. 860.00
Figurine, Boy, Picking Grapes, Crossed Swords, 1910, 4 In. 660.00
Figurine, Boy, Seated, Holding A Lamb In Lap, 9 In. 1610.00
Figurine, Boy, With Spade, Signed, 5 1/4 In. 400.00
Figurine, Canary, Perched On Tree Branch, 4 1/2 In. 330.00
Figurine, Cherub Musicians, Sheets Of Music, Signed, Late 19th Century, 5 1/2 In. 1495.00
Figurine, Colette & Collin, Pair 630.00
Figurine, Cupid Feeding Birds, Basket Of Feed, Quiver Of Arrows, Signed, 7 3/8 In. 1840.00
Figurine, Gardener, 7 1/2 In. 1295.00
Figurine, Gentleman, Purple Jacket, Gilt Waistcoat, Sword By Side, 6 In. 920.00
Figurine, Girl With Doll, Early 20th Century, Signed, 4 1/2 In. 920.00
Figurine, Girl With Spotted Dog, 20th Century, 5 In. 920.00
Figurine, Girl, Holding Pruning Knife, Watering Can, Gilt Rim, 4 In., Pair 1610.00
Figurine, Girl, Polishing An Apple With Her Dress, 5 1/4 In. 1840.00
Figurine, Girl, With Basket Of Flowers, Lace On Dress, 5 In. 795.00
Figurine, Green Parrot, Textured Plumage, Perched On Tree Stump, 16 3/16 In. 2585.00
Figurine, Harlequin With Bird, Seated Figure Playing Cards, c.1745, 5 1/8 In. 6900.00
Figurine, Kingfisher, Pale Russet Plumage On Breast, 1765, 9 1/4 In. 4310.00
Figurine, Man, With Green Bouquet, 6 In. 1090.00
Figurine, Map Seller, Wearing A Black Hat, Yellow Ribbon, 1746, 6 5/8 In. 4025.00

Figurine, Monkey Band, 20 Musicians & Conductor, 21 Piece 18400.00
Figurine, Monkey Band, Gilt Scroll Pad Base, Signed, 5 3/8 In. 3735.00
Figurine, Mounted Officer, Wearing White Trimmed Black Hat, 1755, 10 In. 1090.00
Figurine, Mute Swan, Signed, 4 In., Pair 2070.00
Figurine, Nesting Hen, 1920s, 1 1/2 In. 115.00
Figurine, Owl, Brown & Gray, Crossed Swords, 2 In. 145.00
Figurine, Parrot, 10 In. 1980.00
Figurine, Peasant Man, Wearing Tan Hat, Brown Coat, 1750, 3 1/16 In. 575.00
Figurine, Pug, Seated, Head Inclined To Right, Royal Blue Collar, Gilt Bells, 8 1/2 In. . . 2300.00
Figurine, Putto, Caught In A Bear Trap, 19th Century, 7 1/2 In. 1150.00
Figurine, Schnauzer, White Glaze, 20th Century, 6 3/4 In. 290.00
Figurine, Shepherdess, Seated On Rock, Long Floral Gown, Bonnet, Blue Glaze, 9 In. . . 975.00
Figurine, Song Bird, Perched On Tree Branch, Leafy Sprig, 5 1/2 In. 330.00
Figurine, Squirrel, Sitting, Russet Coat, Black Eyes, Chartreuse On Base, 8 1/4 In. 5750.00
Figurine, St. Hubertus, Stag, Pedestal, 34 In. 4600.00
Figurine, Tinker, Seated Before Anvil, Signed, 1880s, 7 1/4 In. 1380.00
Figurine, Woman In Country Dress, 9 In. 460.00
Figurine, Woman, With Floral Swag, 7 In. 745.00
Group, 3 Cherubs On Rocky Mound, Wooden Pedestal, 8 In. 1840.00
Group, 3 Children At Play, Boy Holding Drum, Girl On Seesaw, Blue Glaze, 10 3/8 In. . . 690.00
Group, 3 Putti, Scientific Instruments, Factory Mark, 7 x 7 In. 2875.00
Group, Bacchanalian Figure, & Maiden, With Frolicking Putti, 11 In. 4370.00
Group, Europa And The Bull, 3 Full Figures With Bull, Crossed Swords, 9 In. 1840.00
Group, Man, 2 Women, Baskets, 2 Have Candleholders, Marked, 5 7/8 In., 3 Piece 2750.00
Group, Neoclassical Seated Maidens, Putto, Natural Base, 13 In. 5520.00
Group, Oriental Couple & 2 Children With Dog, 6 1/2 In. 1955.00
Group, Putti, Sharpening Arrows On Whetstone, Basket At Feet, 8 1/4 In. 1095.00
Group, Seated Couple, Woman Playing Mandolin, Man Seated, Signed, 9 7/8 In. 2300.00
Group, Shepherd & Shepherdess, Girl With Basket Of Grapes, 1930s, 8 1/4 In. 1150.00
Group, Shepherd & Shepherdess, Seated Sheep, Signed, 7 1/2 In. 2415.00
Group, Tea Drinkers, 4 In. 1295.00
Plate, Bird & Insect Design, Gilded Border, 9 1/2 In., 11 Piece 1150.00
Plate, Gold & White Leaf, Beads 225.00
Plate, Ornithological, Center Bird On Branch, Insects, Bugs, 1890s, 9 7/8 In., 12 Piece . . 1840.00
Plate, Peasant Boy, Girl, Reticulated Border, Cobalt Blue Ground, Gilt, 9 In. 9200.00
Plate, Polychrome Flowers, Marked, 9 1/2 In. 105.00
Plate, Raised Grapevine Design, Pierced Border, White, Maroon, Gilt, 11 In. 170.00
Plate, Shepherd Boy, Cobalt Blue Ground, Reticulated Border, 9 1/2 In. 8910.00
Plate, Still Life Of Fruit, Pierced Borders, Gilded Edge, 9 3/4 In., Pair 690.00
Plate, Woman, Medieval, Cobalt Blue Ground, Gilt Frame, Rim, Blue Glaze, 9 1/2 In. . . 12075.00

Meissen, Charger, Kakiemon,
Polychrome, Crossed Swords,
17 In.

Meissen, Clock, Cherub &
Acanthus Leaf, Flowers,
Lenzkirch Works, 20 In.

Plate, Woman, Medieval, Cobalt Blue Ground, Gilt Rim, Blue Glaze, 9 In., Pair 8050.00
Platter, Fish, Gilt Edge, Floral Design, White Ground, 21 x 10 In. 500.00
Platter, Floral Pattern, Blue & White, Marked, 19 1/4 In. 330.00
Snuffbox, Cover, Floral Sprigs On Top Of Cover, Blue, Yellow, Puce, 1755, 3 1/8 In. . . . 5750.00
Sweetmeat, Neoclassical Maiden, Holding Boat Dish, Floral, Rocaille Base, 13 In. 1035.00
Tazza, Indian Purple Pattern, Signed, 12 1/2 In. 550.00
Tea Set, Tray Has Painted Town Scenes, Foliate Still Life, Yellow Ground 920.00
Teapot, Scantily Clad Figures, Compressed Onion Form, Gilt Bands, 4 3/8 In. 6900.00
Toothpick, Red Dragon 250.00
Tray, Puce, Purple, Red, Yellow, Blue, Brown, Green In Center, Oval, 1750, 17 13/16 In. . 1265.00
Tray, Serving, 4 Sections, Blue Floral, Center Handle, 15 In. 150.00
Tureen, Soup, Cover, Blue & White Floral, Marked, 13 In. 330.00
Vase, Enamel Floral, Gold Trim, c.1900, 7 1/4 In. 460.00
Vase, Floral, White Ground, Marked, 10 In. 375.00
Vase, Flower, Green Vine Bands On Top & Bottom, 9 3/4 In. 150.00
Vase, Hand Painted Flowers, Cobalt Ground, Handles, c.1920, 11 In. 1450.00
Vase, Trumpet Shape, Flower Design, Blue Underglaze, 16 3/4 In., Pair 2300.00
Waste Bowl, Panels Of Figures, Oriental Landscape, Interior Landscape, 7 1/8 In. 2875.00

MERCURY GLASS, or silvered glass, was first made in the 1850s. It lost
favor for a while but became popular again about 1910. It looks like a
piece of silver.

Compote, White Leaf Edge, Gilt Bowl Interior, 19th Century, 6 In. 105.00
Tieback, Flower Pattern, 3 3/4 In. Diam. 30.00
Vase, Beaker Form, Circular, 19th Century, 8 1/4 In. 135.00
Vase, Floral Spray, 10 In. 250.00
Vase, Gold Interior, Flowers Etched, 12 In. 900.00

MERRIMAC POTTERY Company was founded by Thomas Nickerson in
Newburyport, Massachusetts, in 1902. The company made art pottery,
garden pottery, and reproductions of Roman pottery. The pottery
burned to the ground in 1908.

Bowl, Tooled Lotus Blossoms, Spade Shape Leaves, Silvery Glaze, 8 3/4 In. 935.00
Vase, Cover, Green & Gunmetal Crystalline Glaze, Signed, 24 x 12 In. 3300.00
Vase, Mottled Green & Gunmetal Hi-Glaze, Flared Rim, 7 1/2 In. 230.00
Vase, Pale Green Matte Glaze, 6 In. . . . . .800.00 to 1000.00

METTLACH, Germany, is a city where the Villeroy and Boch factories
worked. Steins from the firm are known as Mettlach steins. They date
from about 1842. *PUG* means painted under glaze. The steins can be
dated from the marks on the bottom, which include a date-number
code. Other pieces may be listed in the Villeroy & Boch category.

Ashtray, Hunting Scene, 6 In. 715.00
Beaker, 6 Relief Panels, Pedestal, 5 3/4 In. 70.00
Beaker, Musician 85.00
Beaker, No. 2327, 1/4 Liter, Bavarian Crest 130.00
Beaker, No. 2327, 1/4 Liter, Berlin 115.00
Beaker, No. 2327, 1/4 Liter, Breslau 150.00
Beaker, No. 2327, 1/4 Liter, City Of Hamburg 115.00
Beaker, No. 2327, 1/4 Liter, Hannover 120.00
Beaker, No. 2327, 1/4 Liter, Kolan 170.00
Beaker, No. 2327, 1/4 Liter, Leipzig 135.00
Beaker, No. 2327, 1/4 Liter, Man Playing Violin, Handle 140.00
Beaker, No. 2327, 1/4 Liter, Man, With Pipe, Brown 185.00
Beaker, No. 2327, 1/4 Liter, Munchen 115.00
Beaker, No. 2327, 1/4 Liter, State Of Indiana 165.00
Beaker, No. 2781, 1/4 Liter, Couple, Etched 465.00
Beaker, No. 2788, 1/4 Liter, Eagle, With American Flag 220.00
Beaker, No. 2815, 1/4 Liter, Couple, Dancing, Brown Interior 330.00
Beaker, No. 2816, 1/4 Liter, Couple, Dancing 385.00
Beaker, No. 2904, 1/4 Liter, Repeating Design 285.00
Bowl, Dwarf Smoking Pipe Under Mushroom, 5 In. 355.00
Charger, No. 2548, Profile Of Woman, Surrounded By Flowers, 18 1/4 In. 690.00

Charger, No. 2561, Castle Scene, 17 1/4 In. 330.00
Figurine, Rooster, Red 550.00
Goblet, Gambrinus, Brown Tan, 7 In. 155.00
Mug, Brown Dot Band, Bearded Man Handle 125.00
Mug, No. 3361, Grapevine Design, Blue & Green 30.00
Pitcher, No. 535, Repeating Design, 10 In. 100.00
Planter, No. 2987, Art Deco, 3 3/4 x 10 1/4 In. 465.00
Plaque, No. 1044, Black Forest House On Hillside, 17 1/2 In. 600.00
Plaque, No. 1044, Jesus Christ, A. Lugo, 17 1/2 In. 825.00
Plaque, No. 1044/5042, Portrait, Delft, 12 In. 205.00
Plaque, No. 1108, Castle, Gilt Rim, c.1902, 17 In. 230.00
Plaque, No. 1365, Castle On The Rhine, Gold Border, 1908, 17 In. 895.00
Plaque, No. 1412, Bird On Branch, 7 1/2 In. 385.00
Plaque, No. 1413, Crane In Water, 7 1/2 In. 385.00
Plaque, No. 2322, Knight & Maiden, Cupid Shooting Arrow, Etched, 14 1/2 In. 825.00
Plaque, No. 2518, Town Scene Of Meissen, Signed PW, 1905, 17 1/4 In. 1035.00
Plaque, No. 2623, Waiter Serving Wine, Wine Jug & Glasses, 7 3/4 In. 200.00
Plaque, No. 2624, Cavalier Sitting At Table, Smoking Pipe, 1910, 7 1/2 In. 295.00
Plaque, No. 2898, Spring Scene, Girl With Flowers, Signed, c.1905, 17 1/2 In. .1500.00 to 2400.00
Plaque, No. 2899, Summer Scene, Girl In Wheat Field, 1905, 17 1/2 In. 1495.00
Plaque, No. 2997, Fall Scene, Girl Picking Fruit, 1904, 17 1/2 In. 1610.00
Plaque, No. 2998, Winter Scene, Girl, Snow-Covered Field, 1904, 17 1/2 In. 3220.00
Plaque, No. 3161, 2 Cavaliers Drinking, Polychrome Design, Stamp On Base, 17 In. 1250.00
Plaque, No. 3164, Maiden Coming Out Of Water, Knight, Etched, 17 1/2 In. 2200.00
Plaque, No. 7032, Bust Of Woman, White On Green, Phanolith, 1900, 9 In. .....325.00 to 395.00
Plaque, No. 7043, 3 Women, Dolphins, Ducks, Phanolith, Signed, Stahl, 21 In. 1270.00
Plate, Fish, Large, Oriental Type Design Edge, 10 1/2 In. 194.70
Punch Bowl, No. 2918, Art Nouveau Design, Sculpted Lid, Etched, 6 1/2 Liter 400.00
Salad Bowl, No. 1215, Floral Design, Silver Plated Top Rim, Etched, 4 In. 330.00
Stein, No. 1005, 1 Liter, 3 Tavern Scenes, Handle, Pink, Cream ....125.00 to 185.00
Stein, No. 1028, 1/2 Liter, Harvest, Tan, Brown, Inlaid Lid 70.00
Stein, No. 1037, 1/2 Liter, Man Drinking, Brown, Conical Inlaid Lid 125.00
Stein, No. 1154, 1 Liter, 4 Panels, Hunting Scene, Memoriam, Silver Lid 920.00
Stein, No. 1164, 1/2 Liter, Musician & Girl, Copper, Brass Lid 520.00
Stein, No. 1261, 1/2 Liter, Geometric Design, Etched, Glaze, Inlaid Lid 740.00
Stein, No. 1403, 1/2 Liter, Bowling Scene, Inlaid Lid ....375.00 to 405.00
Stein, No. 1403, 1/2 Liter, Man, Bowling In Tavern, Etched, 8 1/2 In. 258.00
Stein, No. 1467, 1/2 Liter, 4 Seasons, Marble Finish, Tan, Gray, Brown, Inlaid Lid 175.00
Stein, No. 1520, 1/2 Liter, Prussian Eagle, Soldiers, Original Pewter Lid 495.00
Stein, No. 1526, 1/2 Liter, Cavalier, Pewter Lid 120.00
Stein, No. 1526, 1/2 Liter, City Of Stuttgart, Flat Metal Lid 175.00
Stein, No. 1526, 1/2 Liter, Comically Dressed Man Smoking, Pewter Lid 115.00
Stein, No. 1526, 1/2 Liter, Dutch Children With Dog, Pewter Lid 410.00
Stein, No. 1526, 1/2 Liter, Festive Scene, Pewter Lid Depicting Barmaid 220.00
Stein, No. 1526, 1/2 Liter, Man & Woman Spinning Yarn, Pewter Lid 195.00
Stein, No. 1526, 1/2 Liter, Man, Playing Horn, Pewter Lid 215.00
Stein, No. 1526, 1/3 Liter, Falstaff, Pewter Lid 575.00
Stein, No. 1526, 1/3 Liter, Parade, Pewter Lid 345.00
Stein, No. 1533, 1 Liter, Man Drinking Beer, Pewter Lid 315.00
Stein, No. 1641, 1/3 Liter, Cavalier With Pipe And Jug, Pewter Lid ....310.00 to 350.00
Stein, No. 1654, 1/2 Liter, Mosaic Floral Design, Pewter Figural Lid, 10 In. 225.00
Stein, No. 1725, 1/2 Liter, Verse, Tan, Brown, Gray, Inlaid Lid 140.00
Stein, No. 1727, 1/2 Liter, Verse, Tan, Gray, Inlaid Lid Of Shell 150.00
Stein, No. 1727, 1/4 Liter, Figural Grape Vines, Gray, Tan 125.00
Stein, No. 1786, 1 Liter, St. Florian Extinguishing Fire, Dragon Handle 1230.00
Stein, No. 1856, 1/2 Liter, Eagle, Etched, Glazed, Pewter Lid 740.00
Stein, No. 1908, 1/2 Liter, Young Boy Hunter, Pewter Lid 330.00
Stein, No. 1909, 1/2 Liter, Dutch Children, Pewter Lid 630.00
Stein, No. 1909, 1/2 Liter, Dwarfs Bowling, H. Schlitt, Pewter Lid 360.00
Stein, No. 1909, 1/2 Liter, Falstaff, Pewter Lid ....200.00 to 345.00
Stein, No. 1909, 1/2 Liter, Hunter, Pewter Lid 330.00
Stein, No. 1909, 1/2 Liter, Men, Being Removed From Gasthaus, Pewter Lid 300.00
Stein, No. 1909, 1/2 Liter, Morning Rooster Meeting Night Watchman, Pewter Lid 245.00

Stein, No. 1909, 1/2 Liter, Owl, Shining Lantern On Drunken Man, Pewter Lid 385.00
Stein, No. 1968, 1/4 Liter, Lovers, Stork On Sides, Inlaid Lid 310.00
Stein, No. 1986, 1/2 Liter, 2 Women, Etched, 7 1/2 In. 490.00
Stein, No. 2001K, 5 Liter, Book, Stein For Banking Or Commerce 650.00
Stein, No. 2002, 1/2 Liter, Skyline Of Munchen, Verse, Etched ....430.00 to 650.00
Stein, No. 2035, 1/3 Liter, Bacchus Carousing, Inlaid Lid 265.00
Stein, No. 2036, 1/2 Liter, Owl 2040.00
Stein, No. 2057, 1/3 Liter, Peasants Dancing, Inlaid Lid 285.00
Stein, No. 2065, 2 1/4 Liter, Man & Barmaid, Inlaid Lid 770.00
Stein, No. 2068, 1/2 Liter, Men Drinking At Table, Etched, Inlaid Lid 410.00
Stein, No. 2090, 1/3 Liter, Man At Table, Verse, Etched, H. Schlitt, Inlaid Lid 575.00
Stein, No. 2094, 1/2 Liter, Musical Scene, Etched, Inlaid Lid 260.00
Stein, No. 2100, 1/3 Liter, Germans Meeting Romans, Etched, H. Schlitt 720.00
Stein, No. 2126, 5 1/2 Liter, Symphonia, Music & Composer Scene, Pewter Lid 5060.00
Stein, No. 2136, 1/2 Liter, Anheuser Busch Brewery 2110.00
Stein, No. 2140, 1/2 Liter, Brandenberg Jaeger, Battalion Number 3, 5 3/4 In. 575.00
Stein, No. 2181, 1/4 Liter, Barmaid, H. Schlitt, Pewter Lid 90.00
Stein, No. 2184, 1/2 Liter, Gnomes Drinking 290.00
Stein, No. 2204, 1 Liter, Prussian Eagle, Inlaid Lid 1430.00
Stein, No. 2222, 1/2 Liter, 75th Anniversary Of Student Society, Inlaid Lid 580.00
Stein, No. 2230, 1/2 Liter, Man & Barmaid, Inlaid Lid 605.00
Stein, No. 2246, 1/3 Liter, Peasants Dancing, Tan, Blue, Inlaid Lid 105.00
Stein, No. 2270, 3.3 Liter, English Soldier, Young Girl, Henrich Schlitt 575.00
Stein, No. 2271, 3/2 Liter, Barmaid, Before Large Group Of People 310.00
Stein, No. 2285, 1/2 Liter, Man Drinking Musician, Woman, Panels, Gray 295.00
Stein, No. 2303, Miniature, Bartholomay Brewing Co., Rochester, N.Y., 1911, 2 In. 195.00
Stein, No. 2327, 1/4 Liter, American Eagle With Flag 140.00
Stein, No. 2391, 1/2 Liter, Wedding March Of The Swan Knight, 1901 .... 630.00
Stein, No. 2402, 1/2 Liter, Courting Of Siegfried, Inlaid Lid 880.00
Stein, No. 2441, 1/2 Liter, Men, Playing Dice, Inlaid Lid 635.00
Stein, No. 2501, 1/2 Liter, Outdoor Drinking Scene, Inlaid Lid 520.00
Stein, No. 2530, 1 Liter, Boar Hunting Scene, Cameo 990.00
Stein, No. 2532, 1/2 Liter, Gasthaus Scene, Inlaid Lid 520.00
Stein, No. 2547, 1/2 Liter, Loving, Music Making, Drinking, Blue, Brown, Inlaid Lid ... 245.00
Stein, No. 2583, 1/2 Liter, Egyptian Design 850.00
Stein, No. 2632, 1/2 Liter, Bowling And Tavern Scene, Inlaid Lid 530.00
Stein, No. 2635, 1/2 Liter, Girl, With Bicycle, Etched, 8 In. 490.00
Stein, No. 2682, 1 1/4 Liter, Girl, Picking Grapes, Silver Plated Lid 450.00
Stein, No. 2717, 1/2 Liter, Venus Target 4620.00
Stein, No. 2718, 1 Liter, David & Goliath, Etched, Inlaid Lid 3595.00
Stein, No. 2765, 1/2 Liter, Knight, Riding A White Horse, Inlaid Lid 880.00
Stein, No. 2766, 1/2 Liter, Man, Sitting At Table With Beer, Inlaid Lid 440.00
Stein, No. 2778, 1 Liter, Carnival Scene, Etched, H. Schlitt 2020.00
Stein, No. 2778, 1/2 Liter, Carnival Scene, Etched, H. Schlitt 1270.00
Stein, No. 2780, 1 Liter, Man Serenading Woman, Etched, Inlaid Lid 850.00
Stein, No. 2808, 1/2 Liter, Girl Bowling, Inlaid Lid, 1903 .... 375.00
Stein, No. 2828, 1/2 Liter, Town Of Wartburg, Etched, Inlaid Lid 2540.00
Stein, No. 2832, 1/2 Liter, Woman, Watering Flowers In Window, Inlaid Lid 505.00
Stein, No. 2833B, 1/2 Liter, Hunters In Forest, Inlaid Lid ....400.00 to 575.00
Stein, No. 2833C, 1/2 Liter, Loreley River Scene, Inlaid Lid 635.00
Stein, No. 2833E, 1/2 Liter, Soldiers In Forest, Inlaid Lid 630.00
Stein, No. 2833F, 1/2 Liter, Students Toasting At Table, Signed MC 575.00
Stein, No. 2878, 1/2 Liter, Tyrolean Girls, Pewter Lid 385.00
Stein, No. 2942, 1/2 Liter, Verse In Center, Tan, Brown, Inlaid Lid 165.00
Stein, No. 2958, 2 4/5 Liter, Boy Bowling, 14 1/2 In. 700.00
Stein, No. 3119, 1 Liter, Prussian Eagle 7150.00
Stein, No. 3135, 1/2 Liter, American Flag, Inlaid Lid 360.00
Stein, No. 3202, 1/2 Liter, Car With Driver And Passenger ....3465.00 to 3520.00
Stein, No. 3282, 1/2 Liter, Barmaid, Pewter Lid 465.00
Stein, No. 3329, 1 Liter, 5 Cavaliers Gambling, Lady Luck, Devil 3630.00
Tray, No. 1328, Etched, Glazed, Repeating Design, 11 In. 135.00
Tureen, Underplate, Oval Panels On Opposing Sides, Scrolled Handles, 13 In. 2585.00
Vase, Brown, Cream, Early Style, 12 In. 120.00

Vase, Etched, 3 Glazed Feet, 5 1/2 In. 420.00
Vase, Floral Design, Terra-Cotta Yellow, Green, White, Signed, L. Payen, 14 In. 1760.00
Vase, Floral, Gold On Top Rim, 8 In. 385.00
Vase, Leaves, Berries, Marble Color, 6 1/2 In. 100.00
Vase, No. 1859, Spider Line On Underside Of Base, 7 1/2 In. 286.00
Vase, No. 1898, Angels, Bands, 3 Footed, 40 In., Pair 605.00
Vase, No. 3283, Cameo, Scene, Ladies & Gentlemen, Strauss & Lanner, 5 1/4 In. 325.00
Vase, Nouveau Pattern, Mosaic Style, Textured Rust Ground, Marked, 7 1/4 In. 500.00

MILK GLASS was named for its milky white color. It was first made in
England during the 1700s. The height of its popularity in the United
States was from 1870 to 1880. It is now correct to refer to some colored glass as blue milk glass, black milk glass, etc. Reproductions of
milk glass are being made and sold in many stores. Related pieces may
be listed in the Cosmos, Vallerysthal, and Westmoreland categories.

Basket, Cover, Child's 185.00
Bowl, Blackberry, Deep, 6 x 2 1/2 In. 35.00
Bowl, Hobnail, Ruffled, Blue, Square, 7 1/2 In. 50.00
Bowl, Hobnail, Tricorner, 7 1/4 In. 35.00
Box, Couch, Cover, Original Green Paint 200.00
Butter, Croesus, Pink, Gold Trim, Round 100.00
Cake Stand, Vintage, Anchor Hocking 30.00
Compote, Shell Shape, Dolphin Base 45.00
Compote, Square, Large 85.00
Creamer, Blue Swans 85.00
Cup, Swan Neck, Handle 25.00
Dish, Cat Cover, 1889 .... 125.00
Dish, Cat Cover, Westmoreland 45.00
Dish, Cat On Drum Cover, Blue, Portieux, 4 3/4 In. 75.00
Dish, Chick Cover, Basketweave Base, 5 1/4 In. 50.00
Dish, Crawfish Cover, Octagonal Base, Tab Handles 200.00
Dish, Cruiser Cover 70.00
Dish, Deer On Fallen Tree Cover, E.C. Flaccus Co., Wheeling W. Va., 7 In. 330.00
Dish, Dog On Carpet Cover, Blue, Vallerysthal 225.00
Dish, Dog, Cover, Half White, Half Blue, 5 1/2 In. 45.00
Dish, Duck Cover, Swimming, Blue, Vallerysthal, 6 1/4 In. 140.00
Dish, Fish Cover, 7 1/2 In. 195.00
Dish, Frog Cover, Split Rib Base, 5 1/2 In. 650.00
Dish, Hen On Nest Cover ....65.00 to 145.00
Dish, Hen On Nest Cover, Blue Head, Basketweave Base, 5 1/2 In. 35.00
Dish, Hen On Sleigh Cover 95.00
Dish, Leaf 30.00
Dish, Lion Cover, Ribbed Base, Marked Pat'd Aug. 6, 1889 .... 210.00
Dish, Melon Cover 135.00
Dish, Monkey On Grass Mound Cover, Leaf & Scroll Base, 6 1/4 In. 1800.00
Dish, Pheasant Cover 45.00
Dish, Prairie Schooner Cover 135.00
Dish, Rabbit Cover, Portieux 375.00
Dish, Royal Coach, L.E. Smith, 4 1/2 x 5 In. 65.00
Dish, Santa Claus On Sleigh, Cover 95.00
Dish, Sheep, Dome Cover 350.00
Dish, Soup, Cover, Cabbage 125.00
Dish, Squirrel On Acorn Cover 95.00
Dish, Swimming Duck Cover, Blue 125.00
Dish, Turkey Cover, 7 In. 200.00
Dish, Turtle, Knobby Backed, Cover 275.00
Eggcup, Double, Birch Leaf 20.00
Eggcup, Floral, Gold Trim 20.00
Epergne, Blue Trim, 4 Threaded Horns, 17 x 12 In. 350.00
Flask, Elks Tooth, Partial Label 120.00
Jar, Blue, Star Designs, 8 In. 40.00
Jar, Horsehead 25.00
Jar, Queen, Victoria, Cover, 8 In. 90.00

Match Holder, Basket, Rabbit & Rooster 165.00
Mustard, Bull's Head, Ladle, Atterbury 225.00
Perfume Bottle 45.00
Pitcher, Owl, Glass Eyes, Challinor Taylor, 7 1/4 In. 115.00
Pitcher, Persian, Blue Trim, 7 1/4 In. 75.00
Pitcher, Raised Flowers, Applied Handle, 8 1/2 In. 90.00
Planter, Snake Dance 35.00
Plate, Easter Day, Rabbit With Basket Of Eggs, Music Notes 80.00
Plate, Maine, White Ground, 5 In. 25.00
Plate, President Taft, Flags, Eagles, 7 In. 85.00
Plate, Rabbit, Clovers & Horseshoes 45.00
Plate, Raised Owls, Eagle, Frog On Pad, Gold Trim, 7 1/2 In. 65.00
Platter, Rock Of Ages, Clear Border, Pat'd Nov. 23, 1875 .... 75.00
Relish, Row Boat, Patented Feb. 17th, 1874, 9 1/2 In. 20.00
Sauce, Blackberry 20.00
Sugar & Creamer, Swan, Cover 75.00
Syrup, Netted Poppy, Metal Thumblift, 7 In. 90.00
Toothpick, Bees In A Basket 35.00
Toothpick, Beggar's Hand, Blue 65.00
Toothpick, Button & Bulge 35.00
Toothpick, Draped Beads 75.00
Toothpick, Pleat & Bow 35.00
Toothpick, Vermont 175.00
Tumbler, Flat, Imperial Grape, Marked 8.00
Vase, Bud, Hand Held Torch, 3 3/4 In., Pair 35.00

MILLEFIORI, see Paperweights.

MINTON china has been made in the Staffordshire region of England
from 1793 to the present. The firm became part of the Royal Doulton
Tableware Group in 1968, but the wares continued to be marked
Minton. Many marks have been used. The one shown dates from about
1873 to 1891, when the word *England* was added.

Bowl, Game On Cover, Basket Base, Majolica, 13 In. ....*Illus* 1540.00
Butter Tub, Drainer, Japanese Scroll, Flow Blue, c.1873 .... 95.00
Centerpiece, Giant Hunting Horns, Wrapped In Pine Cones 9775.00
Cistern, Wine, Stand, Grapevines, Masks & Neoclassical Borders, 1856 .... 6900.00
Coffeepot, Ancestral 250.00
Coffeepot, Spring Bouquet 180.00
Creamer, Ancestral 45.00
Creamer, Spring Bouquet 75.00
Cup & Saucer, Hand Painted Flowers In Scrolled Reserves, c.1900, 4 1/2 In. ... 295.00
Demitasse Set, Birds Of Paradise, Signed, 1863, 13 Piece 300.00
Dessert Set, Yellow Ground, Green Edge, 1830, 18 Piece 2415.00
Dinner Set, Ancestral, 5 Piece Place Setting, 1 Platter, Service For 12 .... 2000.00
Figurine, Boy, Standing, Foot On Drum, 7 In. 170.00
Figurine, Canova, Impressed Title, Circular Base, Impressed Marks, 1863, 15 In. 745.00
Game Dish, Cover, Basket Shape, 2 Bagged Birds & Rabbit 4140.00
Pitcher, Dancing Villagers In Medieval Dress, Impressed Marks, 12 In. 1035.00
Plate, Bird Center, Scrolled Reserves, Floral Sprays, c.1830, 9 1/2 In. 595.00
Plate, Chinese Red, Blue, Navy & Gold, 6 In. 10.00
Plate, Flower Encrusted, Forget-Me-Not Sprigs, Floral Border, 1845, 8 1/2 In. ... 1840.00
Plate Set, Polychromed Floral & Avian Design, Off-White Ground, 10 1/4 In., 12 Piece . 205.00
Plate Set, Ribbon & Floral Garland Edge, 20th Century, 10 1/4 In., 6 Piece 230.00
Platter, Ancestral, 12 1/2 In. 100.00
Platter, Anemone, Flow Blue, 17 x 22 In. 895.00
Sauce, Cover, Faux Bamboo Handle, Turquoise Ground, 5 1/8 In. 325.00
Sauce, Iron Red & Gold, White Ground, 7 1/2 x 8 In., Pair 575.00
Soup, Bouillon, Saucer, Hand Painted Chinoiserie Design, 12 Sets 80.00
Stand, Walking Stick, Stork, In Marsh, Cattails, Majolica ....*Illus* 18700.00
Sugar, Cover, Ancestral 75.00
Sugar, Spring Bouquet, Open 50.00
Tea Set, Birds Of Paradise, 1863, Signed, 15 Piece 300.00

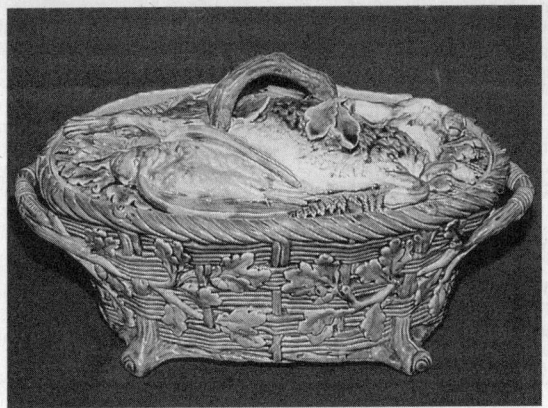

Minton, Bowl, Game On Cover,
Basket Base, Majolica,
13 In.

Minton, Stand, Walking
Stick, Stork, In Marsh,
Cattails, Majolica

Teapot, Ancestral	225.00
Teapot, Spring Bouquet	180.00
Tile, Black Bird Medallion, Ocher Ground, Floral Ground, 6 In.	55.00
Tile, Blue Stylized Flower, White Ground, Frame, Encaustic, Square, 6 In.	55.00
Tile Set, Shakespeare Scenes, 14 Piece	700.00
Vase, Pate-Sur-Pate, Flask Shape, Birds On Floral Branches, 1888, 16 3/4 In., Pair	3450.00
Vase, Secessionist, 5 In.	125.00 to 225.00

MIRRORS are listed in the Furniture category under Mirror.

MOCHA pottery is an English-made product that was sold in America during the early 1800s. It is a heavy pottery with pale coffee-and-cream coloring. Designs of blue, brown, green, orange, black, or white were added to the pottery and given fanciful names, such as *Tree*, *Snail Trail*, or *Moss*.

Bowl, Marbleized, 2 1/2 x 4 1/4 In.	375.00
Butter, Seaweed, Blue	235.00
Chamber Pot, 19th Century, 8 7/8 In.	315.00
Compote, Blue Feather Edge, 4 1/2 In.	395.00
Jug, Combed, Earthworm & Cat's-Eye, 6 In.	385.00
Jug, Measure, T.G. Green & Co., 1939, 7 1/2 In.	20.00
Jug, Seaweed	195.00
Measure, Black Seaweed, Green Band, Stripes, Leaf Handle, 6 In.	145.00
Mug, Blue Seaweed, White Band, Blue Stripes, 3 3/4 In.	220.00
Mug, Earthworm, On Orange, 1/2 Pt.	185.00
Mug, Green, Brown & Ivory, Engine Turned, c.1860, 5 1/2 In.	365.00
Mug, Ivory & Bittersweet Stripe, c.1800, 4 1/4 In.	750.00
Mug, Seaweed, Olive Gray Band, Black, Blue Stripes, 3 3/4 In.	100.00 to 150.00
Mustard, Cover, White Stripes, Leaf Handle, Dark Brown	30.00
Pitcher, Blue Seaweed, Cobalt Blue Bands	2395.00
Pitcher, Blue, Brown Seaweed, 6 3/4 In.	795.00
Pitcher, Brown Seaweed, Stripes, White Bands, Ribbed Handle, 7 5/8 In.	320.00
Pitcher, Earthworm & Cat's-Eye, Mustard Ground, Blue	5680.00
Pitcher, Earthworm, Blue Bands, Black, Tan Stripes, Molded Leaf Handle, 6 3/4 In.	1155.00
Pitcher, Oyster, In Center	1400.00
Pitcher, Seaweed, Blue, Pumpkin & Brown, c.1840, 5 3/4 In.	850.00
Pitcher, Seaweed, Ivory, Brown & Bittersweet, c.1820, 8 In.	750.00
Pitcher, Seaweed, Marked VR 32, 1 Pt.	195.00
Pitcher, Wide Bands Top & Bottom, 1800, 6 5/8 In.	650.00

MONMOUTH Pottery Company started working in Monmouth, Illinois, in 1892. The pottery made a variety of utilitarian wares. It became part of Western Stoneware Company in 1906. The maple leaf mark was used until 1930. If *Co.* appears as part of the mark, the piece was made before 1906.

Bowl, Blue	25.00
Cookie Jar, Wire Handle	35.00
Jar, Cover, Zeisel	65.00
Pitcher, Blue	40.00
Vase, Blue, 8 In.	150.00

MONT JOYE, see Mt. Joye category.

MOORCROFT pottery was first made in Burslem, England, in 1913. William Moorcroft had managed the art pottery department for James MacIntyre & Company of England from 1898 to 1913. The Moorcroft pottery continues today, although William Moorcroft died in 1945. The earlier wares are similar to the modern ones, but color and marking will help indicate the age.

Bowl, Cobalt Blue, Multicolored Violet, 5 3/4 In.	225.00
Bowl, Hibiscus Pattern, Paper Label, 6 1/4 In.	220.00
Bowl, Moonlit Blue, 5 In.	450.00
Bowl, Orchid Design, Cobalt Blue Ground, 7 3/8 In.	220.00
Bowl, Pansy, Blossoms Amid Leaves, Blue Ground, Marked, 2 1/2 x 7 In.	90.00
Bowl, Pansy, Deep Rose, Purple, Green, Yellow, Dark Blue Ground, 12 x 6 1/2 In.	220.00
Bowl, Red Poppy, Cobalt Blue, Footed, 6 In.	250.00
Box, Cover, Orchid, Marked, 4 1/4 In.	220.00
Box, Heart Shape, 2 1/4 In.	75.00
Candlestick, Footed, Low, Paper Label	100.00
Charger, Heron & Reed, Dark Blue Against Sunset, Walter Moorcroft, 14 In.	240.00
Compote, Hibiscus, 7 x 3 3/4 In.	150.00
Jar, Ginger, Cover, Eventide, 6 In.	3000.00
Jardiniere, Reeds At Sunset, 9 In.	595.00
Lamp, Anemone, 25 In.	350.00
Lamp, Orchid, Green Leaves On Blue Ground, Brass Base & Finial, 27 1/2 In.	355.00
Lamp Base, Leaves & Fruit, Flambe Glaze, Marked	470.00
Mug, Caribbean Lid, England, 6 1/4 In.	385.00
Nut Cup, Floral, Dark Blue	.65.00 to 70.00
Pitcher, Pansy, Deep Rose, Purple, Green, Pale Yellow, Dark Blue Ground, 7 1/2 In.	310.00
Pitcher, Pearlized, 5 In.	65.00
Plate, Moonlight Scene, 12 In.	550.00
Plate, White & Black Swans, Green Ground, Walter Moorcroft, 10 1/4 In.	90.00
Urn, Cigarette, White Flower On Green, Label, 2 1/2 In.	70.00
Vase, Alhambra, Pink, 4 Handles, MacIntyre, Early 20th Century, 3 3/4 In.	520.00
Vase, Aurelian, Poppy Design, Fired On Gold Trim, 6 In.	415.00
Vase, Blackberry, Marked W. Moorcroft, Potter To Queen, 4 1/2 In.	110.00
Vase, Blue & Yellow Fruit, Blue Ground, Marked, 12 3/4 In.	1210.00
Vase, Clematis, England, 6 In.	190.00
Vase, Cornflower, Blue, England, 1920, 6 1/8 In.	715.00
Vase, Florals, Dark Blue Glossy Glaze, Marked, 10 In.	210.00
Vase, Florals, Deep Blue Glossy Glaze, Marked, 5 In.	145.00
Vase, Florian Ware, Daisy, Blue, Yellow, Green, 2 Handles, Marked, 4 3/4 In.	935.00
Vase, Florian Ware, Green, Gold, MacIntyre, England, 8 3/4 In.	980.00
Vase, Florian Ware, Green, Gold, MacIntyre, England, 11 3/4 In.	490.00
Vase, Green, Gray Trees, Green Ground, Marked, 1913, 7 x 4 1/2 In.	1760.00
Vase, Hibiscus, Blossoms & Leaves, Green Ground, Paper Label, 3 1/2 In.	45.00
Vase, Hibiscus, Cobalt Blue, 5 3/4 x 3 5/8 In.	280.00
Vase, Hibiscus, Pea Green Ground, Marked, 7 In.	165.00
Vase, Landscape Scene, Trees, Mountains, Blue, Green, Red, Hammered Foot, 7 In.	315.00
Vase, Orange Luster, Burslem, 12 In.	195.00
Vase, Orchid, Flambe Glaze, England, 4 1/8 In.	330.00
Vase, Orchid, Marked, England, 3 In.	110.00

Vase, Orchids, Dark Blue Ground, Marked, 4 In.	125.00
Vase, Orchids, Red, Blue Irises, White Blossoms, Marked, 13 x 9 1/2 In.	1210.00
Vase, Pansy, 1930, 7 In.	395.00
Vase, Pansy, 4 In.	120.00
Vase, Pansy, Dark Magenta Flowers, Cobalt Blue Ground, 1930, 10 In.	595.00
Vase, Pears & Plums, Cobalt Blue, 11 1/2 In.	400.00
Vase, Pomegranate, Baluster Form, Marked, 4 x 7 1/4 In.	440.00
Vase, Pomegranate, Blue Ground, Marked In Green, 10 1/2 In.	950.00
Vase, Pomegranate, Cobalt Blue, 4 1/2 In.	30.00
Vase, Tulips, Green Glaze, 8 1/2 In.	1300.00
Vase, Wisteria, Cobalt Blue Ground, England, 3 1/2 In.	165.00
Vase, Yellow, Green Flowers, Cream Ground, 4 In.	200.00

MORIAGE is a special type of raised decoration used on some Japanese pottery. Sometimes pieces of clay were shaped by hand and applied to the item; sometimes the clay was squeezed from a tube in the way we apply cake frosting. One type of moriage is called *Dragonware* and is listed under that name.

Bowl, Nut, 3-Footed, Nippon, Pink	60.00
Bowl, Pink Shades, Gold, 7 1/2 In.	150.00
Bowl, Purple Flowers, Beading Around Flowers, 6 In.	75.00
Chocolate Pot, Gold Florals, Pink & Aqua Dots On Handle, 9 In.	325.00
Chocolate Set, Chinese Dragon, 13 Piece	125.00
Hair Receiver, Blue Flowers, Trim On Top & Lid	75.00
Jar, Ginger, Dots Allover Bottom, Roses At Top, Heart Shape	150.00
Rose Bowl, Jeweled, White Slip, Turquoise, 5 3/4 In.	250.00
Teapot, Enamel & Gold Design, Cobalt Blue	40.00
Teapot, Spiral Metal Handle, Brown	75.00
Vase, Dragon, 2 Handles, Noritake, Green Mark, 10 In.	125.00
Vase, Galle Scene, Hand Painted, 2 Handles, Nippon, Blue Maple Leaf, 8 In.	795.00
Vase, Spray Of Roses On Front & Back, Single Rose At Side, Handles, 9 1/2 In.	195.00

MOSAIC TILE COMPANY of Zanesville, Ohio, was started by Karl Langerbeck and Herman Mueller in 1894. Many types of plain and ornamental tiles were made until 1959. The company closed in 1967. The company also made some ashtrays, bookends, and related giftwares. Most pieces are marked with the entwined *MTC* monogram.

Ashtray	30.00
Baking Dish, Blue, Green, 11 x 7 x 1 1/2 In.	45.00
Bookends, Child, White	140.00
Figurine, Black Bear	250.00
Figurine, Buffalo, White Matte Glaze, 8 x 14 In., Pair	100.00
Figurine, Mammy, Blue	575.00
Tile, Lincoln Bust, Advertising	45.00
Tray, Card, Terrier Dog	165.00

MOSER glass is made by Ludwig Moser und Sohne, a Bohemian (Czech) glasshouse founded in 1857. Art Nouveau-type glassware and iridescent glassware were made. The most famous Moser glass is decorated with heavy enameling in gold and bright colors. The firm, Moser Glassworks, is still working in Karlsbad, West Czech Republic. Few pieces of Moser glass are marked.

Beaker, Green, Floral Enamel, 1900, 4 7/8 In.	115.00
Bottle, Gold Fern Design, Dagger Shape, Emerald Green, Chatelaine Top, 3 In.	260.00
Bowl, Blue, Enameled Fern Leaf Design, Signed, 1900, 2 5/8 In.	230.00
Bowl, Cover, Floral Enamel With Insects Design, Amberina, 1900, 8 x 7 1/2 In.	1565.00
Bowl, Enameled Child & Apple Design, 3 Applied Feet, Yellow, Blue, Gold, 2 x 8 In.	115.00
Bowl, Enameled Flowers, Applied Blue Rigaree & Feet, Amber, 4 In.	280.00
Bowl, Enameled Flowers, Scalloped Rim, Sapphire Blue, Brass Frame, 6 3/4 x 5 In.	245.00
Bowl, Geometric Cut Panels, Amazons On Horseback, Oval, Amber, 5 x 9 In.	350.00
Bowl, Geometric Cut Panels, Gold Cameo Amazon, 13 In.	495.00
Bowl, Rose, Amethyst, Flowers, 2 1/2 In.	60.00

Bowl, Rose, Green To Clear Shade, Intaglio Cut Lily, 2 1/2 In. 240.00
Box, Amber, Enameled Grape & Leaf , 1900, 3 1/8 x 3 In. 175.00
Box, Cover, Black Amethyst, Gold Etched Warriors Band, Round, Karlsbad, 3 x 6 In. ... 520.00
Box, Cover, Cranberry, Allover Gold Scrolled Leaves, Ruby Jewel, 10 x 3 In. 1100.00
Box, Cover, Green, Gold Floral Design, White Woman On Lid, 1890, 3 x 4 In. 300.00
Box, Cover, Prussian Blue, Amber Rib, Alligator With Amber Trim, 5 x 5 In. 155.00
Box, Cranberry, Acid Cut Flowers, 1920, 6 x 3 1/2 In. 815.00
Compote, Amethyst, Cut Glass, 5 1/4 x 5 In. 225.00
Cordial, Applied Purple, Green Wheel Cut Iris, 1910, 3 5/8 In. 715.00
Cordial, Gold Flowers On Cranberry, 1900, 3 5/8 In. 120.00
Cruet, Gold Enamel Oak Leaves, Applied Acorns, Ruby, 10 1/2 In. 1200.00
Decanter, Opaque Pink Cut, White, Faceted Stopper, 14 1/4 In. 250.00
Dish, Leaf Shape, Cranberry, Enameled Flowers, 1890, 7 1/4 x 6 1/2 In. 165.00
Dresser Jar, Center Medallion, Cupid With Box, Flowers, Emerald Green 375.00
Ewer, Enameled Flowers, Crimp Handles, Blue, 9 In., Pair 165.00
Ewer, Pewter Relief, Green, Germany, 1890, 14 In. 220.00
Garniture Set, Sapphire Blue, Clear, 1890, 21 In., 3 Piece 8000.00
Goblet, Enameled Crest, Green Stained To Clear, Prunts On Stem Knob, 1890, 18 In. ... 1485.00
Goblet, Enameled Flowers, Prunted Cranberry Stem, Signed, 1890, 7 1/4 In. 275.00
Goblet, Fern, Leaf Design, Cranberry, 4 5/8 In. 170.00
Goblet, Flowers, Green, Clear Faceted Stem, 1890, 7 3/4 In. 165.00
Goblet, Flowers, Leaves, 8 In. 325.00
Pitcher, Enameled Flowers, Green, Gold, Metal Spout, 1900, 10 In. 155.00
Plate, Etched Scene, Lavender Gilt Trim, 1970, 7 1/2 In. 300.00
Pokal, Amber, Applied Prunts & Rigaree, Acorns, Floral Beads, 1890, 20 1/2 In. 3850.00
Punch Bowl, Cover, Enameled Flowers, Insects, Cranberry 200.00
Punch Cup, Enameled Flowers & Vines, Blue, 4 Pinched-In Sides, Green Handle, 3 In. .. 75.00
Ring Tree, Green Leaves, Lacy Gold Foliage, Flowers, Black Amethyst, 4 In. 110.00
Shot Glass, Enameled Flowers, Rosettes 30.00
Tea Set, Flowers, Cranberry Glass, Gold Scrolls, 8 3/4 In, 5 Piece. 1210.00
Toothpick, Purple Enamel Scrolls, Multicolored Buds 55.00
Tumbler, Juice, Applied Acorns, Enameled Insects, Oak Leaves, 1900, 3 3/4 In. 380.00
Tumbler, Juice, Applied Glass Grape Clusters On Gold, 3 1/2 In. 395.00
Tumbler, Juice, Gold Flowers, Green, 1900, 3 1/2 In. 145.00
Tumbler, Nude Maiden, Flowing Hair, 4 In. 400.00
Vase, 2-Tone Gold Flowers, Diagonal Cut Body Band, 1900, 6 In. 205.00
Vase, Alexandrite, Signed, 4 1/2 In. 195.00
Vase, Allover Leaves & Flowers, Cranberry, 3-Sided Pedestal, 8 In. 990.00
Vase, Amethyst, Warrior Band, Signed, 1920, 7 1/2 In. 440.00
Vase, Art Nouveau Flowers, Amethyst Stained To Clear, Intaglio, Signed, 1910, 5 3/4 In. .. 250.00
Vase, Art Nouveau Flowers, Intaglio Cut, Signed, 1900, 5 3/4 In. 130.00
Vase, Enameled Branches, Citron, Cut Tulip Gold Rim, 4 In. 110.00
Vase, Enameled Chrysanthemums, Green, Signed, 10 In. 275.00
Vase, Enameled Flowers, Amber, 1890, 12 In. 265.00
Vase, Enameled Flowers, Birds, Blue Bark, Footed, Amber, Triangular, 3 3/4 x 3 In. 110.00
Vase, Enameled Flowers, Gold, 1900, 6 1/4 In. 150.00
Vase, Enameled Flowers, Green, Gold, 1900, 14 1/2 In. 250.00
Vase, Enameled Flowers, Insects, Blue, 1900, 7 1/2 In. 770.00
Vase, Enameled Flowers, Insects, Drapery Rim, Amber, Dripping Honey, 14 1/4 In. 5060.00
Vase, Floor, Silver Flowers, Gold, Cylindrical, 32 x 5 1/2 In. 1210.00
Vase, Flowers, Alexandrite, Stemmed, Marked, 8 1/2 In. 495.00
Vase, Gold Flowers, Egg Shape, Cranberry, 5 x 8 In. 395.00
Vase, Gold Mythological Band, Amethyst, Cut Panels, 7 3/4 In. 300.00
Vase, Gold Mythological Band, Emerald Green, Cut Panels, 9 In. 550.00
Vase, Intaglio Flowers, Amethyst To Clear, Cut Panels, Karlsbad, 7 1/2 In. 245.00
Vase, Intaglio Flowers, Cut Yellow Panels, Cylindrical, 10 1/2 In. 550.00
Vase, Multicolored Leaves & Flowers, Triangular, 8 In. 990.00
Vase, Pierced Floral Bands, Cutout Art Nouveau Woman Each Side, 6 In., Pair 495.00
Vase, Pink & White Chrysanthemums, Cranberry To Clear, 10 In. 190.00
Vase, Stylized Flowers, Amber, Applied Blue Rigaree Rim, Lizard, 4 1/2 In. 200.00
Vase, Wheel Cut Flower, Gold Clover, Leafage, Intaglio Handle, 8 1/2 In. 260.00
Water Set, Flowers In Sanded Gold, Blue & White Enamel, Crystal, 7 Piece 1000.00
Wine, Coralene Beaded Leaves, Cranberry 195.00

MOSS ROSE china was made by many firms from 1808 to 1900. It has a typical moss rose pictured as the design. The plant is not as popular now as it was in Victorian gardens, so the fuzz-covered bud is unfamiliar to most collectors. The dishes were usually decorated with pink and green flowers.

Bone Dish	30.00
Cup & Saucer, Handles, Footed	12.00
Gravy Boat, Meakin	35.00
Plate, 9 In.	25.00
Tea Set, Bridgwood & Son, Ironstone, 3 Piece	135.00

MOTHER-OF-PEARL GLASS, or pearl satin glass, was first made in the 1850s in England and in Massachusetts. It was a special type of mold-blown satin glass with air bubbles in the glass, giving it a pearlized color. It has been reproduced. Mother-of-pearl shell objects are listed under Pearl.

Basket, Diamond-Quilted, White, Rose Interior, Twisted Satin Handle, 9 In.	795.00
Bowl, Ribbon, Pink, White Lining, 5 1/2 In.	260.00
Creamer, 8-Crimp Top, Frosted Handle, White Lining, Blue, 2 3/4 In.	265.00
Creamer, Heart Shape, Frosted Handle, Wafer Foot, White Lining, 2 1/8 In.	245.00
Ewer, Herringbone, Rainbow, Frosted Handle, Folded Rim, 6 3/4 In.	440.00
Ewer, Pink, Herringbone, Melon, Tricorner Rim, Camphor Handle, 8 In.	190.00
Pitcher, Blue Raindrop, Frosted Reed Handle, 4 1/2 In.	195.00
Rose Bowl, Diamond-Quilted, Bruised Diamond, 2 1/2 In.	440.00
Rose Bowl, Diamond-Quilted, Cranberry, 5 In.	195.00
Rose Bowl, Satin Glass, 3 Crimped Top, Frosted Wafer Foot, 3 1/8 In.	175.00 to 185.00
Rose Bowl, Satin Glass, Avocado Ribbon, White Lining, Crimped, 3 x 3 1/2 In.	245.00
Rose Bowl, Satin Glass, Blue Ribbon, Frosted Foot, White Lining, 2 1/2 In.	185.00
Rose Bowl, Satin Glass, Blue Ribbon, White Lining, Crimped, 3 x 3 1/2 In.	245.00
Rose Bowl, Satin Glass, Diamond-Quilted, Yellow, White Lining, 3 1/2 In.	175.00
Rose Bowl, Satin Glass, Herringbone, Apricot, White Lining, Crimped, 3 3/4 In.	195.00
Salt & Pepper, Coin Spot, Blue, 3 1/2 In.	660.00
Shade, Diamond-Quilted, Ruffled, 6 1/4 x 9 1/4 In.	1250.00
Tazza, Diamond-Quilted, Red, Ruffled, Silver Plated Base, Handle, 10 In.	410.00
Tumbler, Water, Blue, White Gloss, White Lining, Air Traps, 3 1/2 In.	75.00
Vase, Diamond-Quilted, Apricot, Yellow Coralene Fleur-De-Lis, 5 In.	300.00
Vase, Diamond-Quilted, Pink, Ruffled & Camphor Rim, Handles, 9 1/2 In.	1100.00
Vase, Hobnail, Pink Top, Fades To Pale Pink Base, Folded-In Sides, 5 3/4 In.	500.00
Vase, Rose Ribbon, White Lining, Frosted Wafer Foot, 3 1/8 In.	195.00
Vase, Stick, Diamond-Quilted, Blue, Ribbed, 6 1/4 In.	105.00
Vase, Stick, Diamond-Quilted, Yellow, 10 In.	220.00

MOTORCYCLES and motorcycle accessories of all types are being collected today. Examples can be found that date back to the early years of the twentieth century. Toy motorcycles are listed in the Toy category.

BMW, 1937	7350.00
Clock, Harley-Davidson, Neon, Yellow, Black, White Logo, 18 In.	1540.00
Clock, Indian, Reverse Painted Glass Face, 1914, 20-In. Diam.	3575.00
Harley-Davidson, 1956	11000.00
License Plate, Arizona, 1971	6.00
License Plate, British Columbia, Canada, 1968	12.00
License Plate, Indiana, 1949	30.00
License Plate, Mississippi, 1976	10.00
License Plate, Ohio, 1966	10.00
License Plate, Texas, 1968	48.00
License Plate, Texas, 1985	6.00
License Plate, White On Green, Porcelain, 3 1/3 x 6 In.	198.00
Match Holder, Indian, Brass, Raised Lettering, 2 1/2 In.	605.00
Pamphlet, Indian, Paper Lithograph, 4 Pages, 8 1/2 x 6 In.	90.00
Pin, Indian, Indian Head Shape, Metal, Eastman Bros. Co., Rochester, 1 1/2 In.	75.00
Pin, Rider, 3/4 x 1 1/4 In.	90.00
Rainsuit, Harley Davidson	495.00

Saddle, Jumbo Fenders, Black, Silver Studs, Hess & Hopkins 400.00
Watch, Elgin, Harley Davidson, Second Hand, Leather Band, 1 1/2 x 1 1/4 In. 660.00
Watch Fob, Gold & Black, Metal, 2 x 1 1/2 In. 115.00

MOUNT WASHINGTON, see Mt. Washington category.

MOVIE memorabilia of all types is collected. Animation cels, games,
sheet music, toys, and some celebrity items are listed in their own section. Listed here are costumes and paper collectibles. A lobby card is 11
by 14 inches. A set of lobby cards includes seven scene cards and one
title card. A one sheet, the standard movie poster, is 27 by 41 inches. A
three sheet is 81 by 40 inches. A half sheet is 22 by 28 inches. A window card, made of cardboard, is 14 by 22 inches. An insert is 14 by 36
inches. A herald is a promotional item handed out to patrons. A press
book was sent to newspapers and magazines to promote a picture.

Ad Mat, The Caddy, Jerry Lewis, Dean Martin, 1953, 4 x 8 In. 19.00
Book, Screenplay, Gone With The Wind, Sidney Howard, 1964, 416 Pages 5.00
Bottle, Gotham Beer, Breakaway Prop, Used In Film 95.00
Box, Planet Of The Apes Model Kit, Dr. Zaius, Addar Products Corp., 1973 .... 50.00
Calendar, Marilyn Monroe, Nude, Framed, 1955 .... 525.00
Card, Arts & Entertainment, Whoopi Goldberg, Signed 7.00
Figure, James Bond, Moonraker, 1979, Box, 12 1/2 In. 170.00
Hot Water Bottle, Jayne Mansfield, 1957 .... 75.00
Lobby Card, A Night At The Opera, MGM, 1935 .... 575.00
Lobby Card, A Woman Of Affairs, Greta Garbo, 1928 .... 475.00
Lobby Card, Big Business, Laurel & Hardy, MGM, 1929 .... 920.00
Lobby Card, Bikini Beach, 1964 .... 20.00
Lobby Card, Blazing Frontier, Buster Crabbe, PRC Pictures, 1940s 10.00
Lobby Card, Blood Will Tell, Buck Jones With Pistol & Girl, 1927 .... 45.00
Lobby Card, Breakfast At Tiffany's, Audrey Hepburn, 1961 .... 75.00
Lobby Card, Casablanca, Warner Brothers, 1943 .... 2875.00
Lobby Card, Curse Of The Werewolf, Woman Feeding Werewolf, Hammer Films, 1961 . 29.00
Lobby Card, Dangerous Crossing, Jeanne Crain, Title Card, 1953 .... 20.00
Lobby Card, Fugitive Of The Plains, Buster Crabbe, 1943 .... 12.00
Lobby Card, Harry & Pearl Pureheart, Terrytoons 45.00
Lobby Card, Have Rocket Will Travel, Three Stooges, 1959 .... 65.00
Lobby Card, In The Navy, Abbott & Costello, 1942 .... 200.00
Lobby Card, It Happened One Night, Columbia, 1934 .... 575.00
Lobby Card, Kramer Vs. Kramer, 1979, 8 Piece 22.50
Lobby Card, Lady & The Tramp, Mexican, 1960s 50.00
Lobby Card, Mammy, Al Jolson, Warner Brothers, 1930 .... 920.00
Lobby Card, Ninotcka, Greta Garbo, 1939 .... 250.00
Lobby Card, Poster, Oregon Trail, King Of The Pecos, John Wayne, 1936 .... 805.00
Lobby Card, Private Lives Of Elizabeth & Essex, Flynn, Davis, 1939 .... 450.00
Lobby Card, Quiet Man, John Wayne, Maureen O'Hara, 1952 .... 150.00
Lobby Card, Red Dragon, Sidney Tolar As Charlie Chan, Monogram, 1945 .... 50.00
Lobby Card, Red-Headed Woman, Jean Harlow, 1932 .... 600.00
Lobby Card, Sabrina, Audrey Hepburn, 1954 .... 75.00
Lobby Card, Shaggy Dog, Fred MacMurray, Disney, 1967 .... 7.50
Lobby Card, Some Like It Hot, Marilyn Monroe, 1959 .... 100.00
Lobby Card, Son Of Frankenstein, Universal, 1938 .... 575.00
Lobby Card, Tall In The Saddle, John Wayne, 1953 .... 15.00
Lobby Card, The Idle Class, Charlie Chaplin Uncut Cards, First National, 1921 .... 2645.00
Lobby Card, There's No Business Like Show Business, Marilyn Monroe, 1954 .... 60.00
Lobby Card, Thief Of Bagdad, United Artists, 1924 .... 1725.00
Lobby Card, Wings, Clara Bow, 1927 .... 350.00
Lobby Card, Written On The Wind, Stack, Hudson, Malone, 1956 .... 35.00
Lobby Card Set, Father Of The Bride, Tracy, Taylor, 1950, 8 Piece 150.00
Lobby Card Set, Jet Pilot, John Wayne, 1957, 8 Piece 110.00
Lobby Card Set, Johnny Belinda, Jane Wyman, 1956, 8 Piece 60.00
Lobby Card Set, Ordinary People, 1980, 8 Piece 17.50
Lobby Card Set, Raging Bull, 1980, 8 Piece 17.50
Lobby Card Set, Wild River, Montgomery Clift, 8 Piece 40.00

Lobby Card Set, Without Honor, Dane Clark, 1949, 8 Piece 45.00
Loving Cup, To Miss Ray Gumpel From Warner Bros. Girls, Silver Plate, 1916 .... 250.00
Map, Hollywood, Addresses Of The Stars, Shaefer's, 1940s, 20 x 28 In. 22.00
Photograph, Betty Grable, Autographed, Sepia, 8 x 10 In. 245.00
Photograph, Charles Bronson, From Noon Till Three, Color, Signed, 8 x 10 In. 25.00
Photograph, Jane Wyman, Autographed, 3/4th View, 8 x 10 In. 25.00
Photograph, Jean Harlow, MGM 25.00
Photograph, Kirk & Funicello, Autograph, 1960s, 8 x 11 In. 20.00
Photograph, Robert Stack, Western Scene, Group, 8 x 10 In. 9.00
Photograph, Rudolph Valentino, Paramount Pictures, Walnut Frame, 26 x 32 In. 185.00
Poster, A Daughter Of The Mines, Edison, 1910, One Sheet 630.00
Poster, Allez-Oop, Buster Keaton, 1934, One Sheet 975.00
Poster, Babes & Boobs, A Larry Semon Comedy, Vitagraph, 1925, One Sheet 460.00
Poster, Bette Davis, Of Human Bondage, 1934, 14 x 17 In. 100.00
Poster, Breakfast At Tiffany's, Paramount, 1961, One Sheet 575.00
Poster, Buck Privates, Abbott & Costello, Re-release, 1953, One Sheet 75.00
Poster, Charlie Chan At The Opera, 20th Century Fox, 1937, One Sheet 920.00
Poster, Charlie Chan In Reno, 20th Century Fox, 1939, One Sheet 430.00
Poster, Citizen Kane, 1956, Half Sheet 225.00
Poster, Coal Miner's Daughter, Sissy Spacek, 1979, One Sheet 12.00
Poster, Cupid's Round Up, Fox, 1918, One Sheet 3335.00
Poster, Daddy, Jackie Cogan, First National, 1923, One Sheet 690.00
Poster, Doctor Zhivago, 1971, One Sheet 10.00
Poster, Elevating Father, Universal, 1916, Three Sheet 545.00
Poster, Escape From Alcatraz, Clint Eastwood, 1979, One Sheet 16.00
Poster, Fort Apache, John Ford, 1948, One Sheet 632.50
Poster, Garden Of Allah, Marlene Dietrich & Charles Boyer, 1936, 41 x 78 In. 430.00
Poster, Gold Rush, Charlie Chaplin, Spanish, 1940s 245.00
Poster, Gunsmoke Trail, Monogram, 1938, One Sheet 460.00
Poster, Harlem Globetrotters, All Black Cast, 1951, One Sheet 145.00
Poster, How To Stuff A Wild Bikini, Funicello, Hickman, 1965, One Sheet 45.00
Poster, Jean Harlow, Portrait, 1933, Half Sheet 400.00
Poster, King Kong, Orange & Black, Re-release Uncut Version, c.1969, One Sheet 150.00
Poster, King Of Kings, Pathe, C.B. De Mille, 1927, One Sheet 975.00
Poster, Kiss Them For Me, Cary Grant, 1957, One Sheet 45.00
Poster, Lana Turner Portrait, MGM, 1942, One Sheet 345.00
Poster, Leatherneck, Alan Hale, 1929, One Sheet 480.00
Poster, Lifeboat, Alfred Hitchcock, 20th Century Fox, 1943, One Sheet 1035.00
Poster, Lightning Carson Rides Again, Victory Pictures, 1938, Three Sheet 575.00
Poster, Live & Let Die, James Bond, Roger Moore, 1973, One Sheet 40.00
Poster, Looking For Trouble, 20th Century Fox, 1934, One Sheet 315.00
Poster, Love's Sunset, Vitagraph, 1913, Six Sheet 575.00
Poster, Mae West, Signed, 27 3/4 x 21 3/4 In. 143.00
Poster, Manhattan Melodrama, MGM, Sweden, 1934, One Sheet 805.00
Poster, Mary Poppins, Julie Andrews, 1964, One Sheet 150.00
Poster, Melody Trail, Republic, 1935, Three Sheet 485.00
Poster, Mummy, Realart, 1951, Half Sheet 690.00
Poster, Mutiny In The Big House, Charles Bickford, 1939, One Sheet 68.00
Poster, Mysterious Lady, Greta Garbo, J.H. Hooker Print Co., One Sheet 6210.00
Poster, On A Clear Day, Barbra Streisand, 1970, One Sheet 75.00
Poster, One-Eyed Jacks, Marlon Brando, Karl Malden, Paramount, 1959, One Sheet 65.00
Poster, Pillow Talk, Doris Day, Rock Hudson, 1959, Half Sheet 40.00
Poster, Pin Up Girl, 20th Century Fox, 1944, One Sheet 230.00
Poster, Pink Panther Strikes Again, Peter Sellars, 1976, Half Sheet 12.00
Poster, Prisoner Of War, Ronald Reagan, 1954, One Sheet 68.00
Poster, Rebecca Of Sunnybrook Farm, Artcraft, 1917, One Sheet 3450.00
Poster, Roman Spring Of Mrs. Stone, 1963, Insert 125.00
Poster, Scared To Death, Bela Lugosi, 1954, One Sheet 350.00
Poster, Sea Spoilers, John Wayne, Universal, 1936, One Sheet 1840.00
Poster, Secret Of Monte Cristo, Rory Calhoun, Half Sheet 15.00
Poster, Shane, Paramount, 1953, One Sheet 485.00
Poster, She-Wolf Of London, Universal, 1946, Six Sheet 805.00
Poster, Son Of Tarzan, The Last Episode, National, 1920, One Sheet 515.00

Poster, South Of The Rio Grande, Columbia, 1932, Insert 430.00
Poster, Starting Over, Burt Reynolds Autograph, 24 x 12 In. 40.00
Poster, Sun Valley Serenade, Glenn Miller, 1954, One Sheet 45.00
Poster, The Birds, Universal, 1963, Three Sheet 860.00
Poster, The Cure, Charlie Chaplin, 1923, One Sheet 1150.00
Poster, The Fan, James Garner Autograph, 24 x 42 In. 40.00
Poster, The Flying Deuces, MGM, 1939, Six Sheet 4025.00
Poster, The Man In The Mirror, Grand National, 1937, One Sheet 285.00
Poster, The Mysterious Lady, Greta Garbo, 1924, One Sheet 6210.00
Poster, The Searchers, Warner Brothers, 1956, Insert 430.00
Poster, The Sheriff Of Fractured Jaw, Jayne Mansfield, 1959, Insert 48.00
Poster, The Star Packer, John Wayne, Lone Star Western, 1934, Three Sheet 2587.50
Poster, The Timid Young Man, Buster Keaton, 1935, One Sheet 690.00
Poster, The Trail Of The Last Chord, American Film, 1914, Three Sheet 345.00
Poster, Three Faces Of Eve, Joanne Woodward, 1957, One Sheet 60.00
Poster, Three Texas Steers, John Wayne, 1939, One Sheet 1150.00
Poster, Times Have Changed, William Fox, 1923, One Sheet 570.00
Poster, Tip-Off Girls, Lloyd Nolan, 1938, One Sheet 68.00
Poster, Treasure Of The Golden Condor, Constance Smith, Fox, 1953, Three Sheet 50.00
Poster, Twilight For The Gods, Cyd Charisse, Universal, 1958, Three Sheet 50.00
Poster, Under The Yum Yum Tree, Jack Lemmon, Columbia, 1963, Three Sheet 35.00
Poster, Up In Daisy's Penthouse, The Three Stooges, Columbia, 1952 .... 400.00
Poster, Water, Water Everywhere, Samuel Goldwyn, 1920, One Sheet 430.00
Poster, Watusi, George Montgomery, MGM, 1958, Three Sheet 40.00
Poster, West Point Story, James Cagney, Warner Brothers, 1950, Three Sheet 80.00
Poster, Westward Ho, Republic, 1935, One Sheet 2300.00
Poster, What A Way To Go, Shirley MacLaine, 1964, Insert 7.00
Poster, While The City Sleeps, Dana Andrews, 1956, One Sheet 40.00
Poster, Will Penny, Charlton Heston, Paramount, 1968, Three Sheet 40.00
Poster, Zulu, Michael Caine, Embassy, 1964, Three Sheet 175.00
Press Book, Airport, 1975 .... 5.00
Press Book, Love Is News, Loretta Young, Oversize, 16 Pages, 1937, 16 x 22 In. 150.00
Press Book, Prince Of Foxes, 1949, 22 Pages, 11 x 14 In. 175.00
Press Book, Razor's Edge, Rockwell Color Cover, 1946, 68 Pages, 11 x 15 In. 250.00
Press Kit, Color Purple, 1985, 13 Stills 30.00
Press Kit, Empire Of The Sun, 1987, 4 Stills 10.00
Press Kit, Naked Spur, James Stewart, 1953 .... 15.00
Program, 50th Annual Academy Awards Presentation, 1978 .... 49.00
Program, 56th Annual Academy Awards, April 9, 1984, 9 x 12 In. 20.00
Program, Fantasia, Original Release 50.00
Program, House Of Rothschild, Geo. Arliss, 20th Century Fox, 1934, 9 x 12 In. 25.00
Program, King & I, Yul Brynner, 1956 .... 5.00
Program, Paint Your Wagon, P. Max Illustrations, Photographs, 1969, 30 Pages 35.00
Puzzle, Journey To The Center Of The Earth, 1969 .... 20.00
Scrapbook, Rock Hudson, 1957 .... 50.00
Script, Niagara, Starring Marilyn Monroe 295.00
Shoes, Tennis, Game Of Death, Bruce Lee, Worn 8500.00
Slide, Laurel & Hardy, Glass, Cardboard Mount, 3 1/2 x 4 In. 120.00
Slide, Marx Brothers, Color Glass, Cardboard Mount, 3 1/2 x 4 In. 45.00
Spoon, Different Movie Star Face & Autograph, Silver Plate, Onieda, 1925, 8 Piece 75.00
Tin, Rudolph Valentino, Sheik Of Araby, 1920s, 12 In. 65.00
Vest, Worn By Errol Flynn In Adventures Of Don Juan 1500.00
Wastebasket, Planet Of The Apes, Tin Lithograph, 1967 .... 25.00
Wastebasket, Return Of The Jedi, Tin Lithograph, Original, 1983 .... 25.00
Window Card, Absent Minded Professor, Fred MacMurray, Disney, 1961 .... 25.00
Window Card, African Queen, Humphrey Bogart, Katherine Hepburn, 1951, 14 x 18 In. ... 275.00
Window Card, Barbarella, Jane Fonda, 1969 .... 45.00
Window Card, Creature Walks Among Us, 1956 .... 150.00
Window Card, Here Comes The Navy, James Cagney, 1934 .... 500.00
Window Card, Invisible Man Returns, Sir Cedric Hardwicke, Universal, 1940 .... 650.00
Window Card, Jayne Mansfield, It Happened In Athens, 1962, 14 x 22 In. ... 48.00
Window Card, Lucky Me, Doris Day, 1954 .... 20.00
Window Card, Passage To Marseilles, Humphrey Bogart, 1944 .... 200.00

Window Card, Reap The Wild Wind, John Wayne, 1942 .... 125.00
Window Card, Red Badge Of Courage, Audie Murphy, 1951 .... 45.00
Window Card, Test Pilot, Clark Gable, Myrna Loy, Spencer Tracy, 1938 .... 150.00
Window Card, Three Stooges, Objective Venus & In Orbit, 1950s, 14 x 22 In. 375.00
Window Card, Till We Meet Again, Herbert Marshall, Paramount, 1936, 14 x 22 In. 45.00

MT. JOYE is an enameled cameo glass made in the late nineteenth and twentieth centuries by Saint-Hilaire Touvier de Varraux and Co. of Pantin, France. This same company made De Vez glass. Pieces were usually decorated with enameling. Most pieces are not marked.

Bowl, Enamel Lavender & White Iris, Spiked Leaves, Ruffled, Frosted, 5 1/4 In. 245.00
Tray, Enamel Lavender & White Iris, Spiked Leaves, Frosted, Marked, 11 1/2 In. 300.00
Vase, Amethyst, Ruffled, Thick Floral Enamel, 1900, 11 1/2 In. 460.00
Vase, Cameo, Leaf, Vine Motif, White, Purple, Gold Enameled, Cylindrical, 16 In. 430.00
Vase, Enameled Flowers, Red, Yellow, Green On Satin Finish, 10 In. 345.00
Vase, Enameled Purple Violet Blossoms, Gold Highlights, Etched, 6 In. 260.00
Vase, Floral Enamel, Amethyst, 1900, 10 In. 400.00
Vase, Floral Enamel, Amethyst, 1900, 12 In. 465.00
Vase, Floral Enamel, Cranberry, 1900, 7 3/4 In. 385.00
Vase, Gold Spider Mum, Green, Cameo, Square, Marked, 7 In. 355.00
Vase, Lavender Violets & Gilt Leaves, Frosted Ground, Dimpled & Ribbed, 4 3/4 In. 355.00
Vase, Mums & Leaves, Cylindrical Neck, White Opalescent Glass, 15 In. 425.00
Vase, Red, Enamel Floral, 1900, 11 In. 330.00
Vase, Stick, Green Textured, Enameled Violet Bouquet, Flat Sides, Marked, 7 In. 385.00
Vase, Trumpet, Enamel Violets, Gilt Leaves, Frosted Ground, 11 1/2 In. 385.00

MT. WASHINGTON Glass Works started in 1837 in South Boston, Massachusetts. In 1870 the company moved to New Bedford, Massachusetts. Many types of art glass were made there until 1894, when the company merged with Pairpoint Manufacturing Co. Amberina, Burmese, Crown Milano, Cut Glass, Peachblow, and Royal Flemish are each listed in their own category.

Biscuit Jar, Embossed Cover, Enameled Spider Mums, 7 1/2 In. 605.00
Biscuit Jar, Pink, Orchard Hydrangea, Green, Brown Leaves, 8 1/2 In. 295.00
Bowl, Blue Over White, Griffins, Ruffled, Cameo, Square, 8 x 4 In. 1475.00
Bowl, Bride's, Pale Mauve Interior, Deep Mauve Border, Paper Label, 11 In. 350.00
Bowl, Cranberry Cut Border, X Pattern, 4 x 8 In. 110.00
Bowl, Venetian Diamond, 3 3/4 x 9 1/2 In. 975.00
Box, Jewel, Monk, Opal Ware, Gold Washed, Lining, Schindler, 5 1/2 In. 550.00
Bride's Basket, Fluted Rim, Lyon Silver Co., 12 In. 625.00
Bride's Bowl, Square Bowl, Ruffled Rim, 2 Pink Cameos, Silver Plate Frame 1750.00
Celery Vase, Cut Velvet, Blue Over White, Diamond-Quilted, 6 1/2 In. 725.00
Cracker Jar, Leaf & Vine Design, Tan & Brown Ground, Bail Handle, 6 x 8 In. 440.00
Cracker Jar, Poppies, Leaves, Tan & Yellow, Raised Leaves, Bail, 5 In. 495.00
Cracker Jar, Puffy Cover, Cornstalks, Biscuit Ground, Gold, 6 1/2 In. 605.00
Cruet, Diamond-Quilted, Apricot, Satin, Frosted Twig Handles, Thorn Stopper 450.00
Cruet, Strawberry, Diamond & Fan 165.00
Cup & Saucer, Angular Design, Applied Yellow Handle, 5 1/4 In. 315.00
Egg Cup, Green To White, Pink & White Forget-Me-Nots 345.00
Ewer, Mother-Of-Pearl Herringbone Pattern, Apricot To Pink To White, 8 In. 110.00
Flower Frog, Toadstool Shape, 5 1/2 In. 295.00
Lamp, Cameo, Woman, Flowers, Yellow Over White, Brass Base, 21 In. 8500.00
Lamp, Kerosene, Nymph Sitting Amid Apple Blossoms, Base, Signed, 16 In. 770.00
Letter Holder, Opal Ware, Blown Out Floral, Cherub Head, Gold Washed 875.00
Muffineer, Ostrich Egg, Field Clover Design, Pale Blue Ground, 4 In. 300.00
Muffineer, Ostrich Egg, Flowers, Green Shaded Ground, 4 In. 190.00
Muffineer, Ostrich Egg, Pansies, Light Blue, 4 In. 385.00
Muffineer, Ostrich Egg, Pastel Nasturtiums, 4 In. 275.00
Muffineer, Tomato, Blue Flowers & Leaves, Biscuit Color, 2 1/2 In. 465.00
Perfume Bottle, Opal Ware, Nasturtiums, Sprinkler Top, 5 1/4 In. 375.00
Photo Box, Enameled Blue Forget-Me-Nots, Gold Scrolls, 5 x 3 3/4 In. 135.00
Pickle Castor, Seashell & Seaweed, Flowers, Aurora Frame, 9 1/2 In. 1150.00
Pitcher, Water, Cut Velvet, Sapphire Blue Over White, Blue Reeded Handle, 8 In. 355.00

Pitcher, Water, Spangled, 28 Swirl Ribs, Clear Handle, White Lining, 8 In.	575.00
Powder Box, Cover, Lusterless, Violets On Base & Cover	75.00
Rose Bowl, Herringbone, Mother-Of-Pearl Pink To Raspberry, 4 In.	195.00
Salt & Pepper, Colored Leaves, Biscuit Ground, Ribbed, 2 In.	295.00
Salt & Pepper, Melon Ribbed, Green Leaves, White Ground, 2 In.	300.00
Salt & Pepper, Tomato, Enamel Flowers, Green Ground, 1 3/4 In.	220.00
Saltshaker, Pansies, Tomato Shape	70.00
Saltshaker, Salt, Lay Down, Egg Shape, Hand Painted Violets	185.00
Saltshaker, Stand-Up Egg, Pecking Hen, 2 1/2 In.	350.00
Shaker, Pillar, Pewter Top	95.00
Sugar & Creamer, Opalware	195.00
Sugar Shaker, Fig, Pink & Blue Floral Clusters, Apricot Bark Ground	220.00
Sugar Shaker, Flowers, Opalescent, Pink Ground, Egg Shape, 4 3/4 In.	425.00
Toothpick, Baby Diamond-Quilted, Square Mouth	195.00
Toothpick, Diamond-Quilted, Squared Rim, Bulbous, 2 1/2 In.	220.00
Toothpick, Swirl Mold	295.00
Tumbler, Triple Triangle, Red	40.00
Tumbler, Yellow Roses, 3 3/4 In.	465.00
Vase, 8 Pulled-Up Ribs, Floral Petit Point, Beige Ground, 4 1/2 In.	875.00
Vase, Bud, Fireglow, Hand Painted Florals, Strawberries & Firefly, 5 3/4 In.	110.00
Vase, Corset, Crimped, 3 In.	355.00
Vase, Crimped Jack-In-The-Pulpit Rim, Pink, Yellow Foot, 10 In.	375.00
Vase, Gold Diamond-Quilted, Cut Velvet, Pumpkin Stem, 13 1/2 In.	650.00
Vase, Gold Stork, In Flight, Black Glass, Spoke Base, 8 In., Pair	550.00
Vase, Gourd Shape, Flowered Cacti, Gold, Beige Ground, Gold Scrolls, 9 In.	990.00
Vase, Lava, Black, Color Inclusions, Double Reeded Handles, Waisted, 4 In.	3190.00
Vase, Lily, Red Floral Sprays, White Trim, Pale Yellow, Crimped, 17 In.	660.00
Vase, Mother-Of-Pearl, Gold, Raindrop Lining, 1880s, 9 In.	285.00
Vase, Stick, Enamel Stylized Floral, Bulbous, 7 1/4 In.	715.00
Vase, Yellow Coralene, Geometric Patterns, Pink, White, Yellow Ground, 7 In.	740.00
Vase, Yellow Cut, Mother-Of-Pearl, Crimped Camphor Rib, 9 1/2 In.	325.00

MULBERRY ware was made in the Staffordshire district of England from about 1850 to 1860. The dishes were decorated with a reddish brown transfer design, now called *mulberry*. Many of the patterns are similar to those used for flow blue and other Staffordshire transfer wares.

Bowl, Cypress, Davenport, 14 x 16 In.	225.00
Casserole, Cover, 9 1/2 In.	110.00
Cup, Peruvian, Handleless	65.00
Dish, Cyprus	50.00
Dish, Honey, 5 In.	50.00
Pitcher, Athens, 6 1/2 In.	125.00
Pitcher & Bowl Set, Medina, J.P. & Co.	295.00
Plate, Athens, 10 1/2 In.	55.00
Plate, Hot Water, Rose Festoon, c.1850	500.00
Plate, Jeddo, 14-Sided, 9 1/2 In.	75.00
Plate, Susa, 10 1/2 In.	70.00
Platter, Cypress, 13 1/2 In.	175.00
Platter, Mogul, T. Meyer, 19th Century, 21 1/4 In.	287.00
Platter, Rose, 14 x 11 In.	225.00
Platter, Vegetable, Bochara	375.00
Platter, Vegetable, Cyprus, Cover	300.00
Soup, Dish, Washington Vase	45.00
Teapot, Calcutta	275.00

MULLER FRERES, French for Muller Brothers, made cameo and other glass from the early 1900s to the late 1930s. Their factory was first located in Luneville, then in nearby Croismaire, France. Pieces were usually marked with the company name.

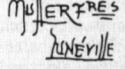

Bowl, African Native Aiming Spears At Elephant, Pastel Amethyst, 13 In.	316.25
Bowl, Flack Trees Silhouetted, Raspberry & Green Sky, Cameo, 3 3/4 In.	880.00
Lamp, Boudoir, Egg Shape, Amethyst, Pink, White Ground, Art Deco, 16 1/4 In.	1320.00

Lamp, Figural, Partially Dressed Girl, Signed, 1922	550.00
Lamp, Orange & Purple Shell Design, Blown-Out Shade, Signed	2500.00
Lamp, Purple Grape Pods, Orange Ground, Cameo, Egg Form Dome Shade, 8 In.	605.00
Vase, Gray, Amber, Blue, Orange Mottled, Enameled Cameo, 8 In.	3450.00
Vase, Landscape Scene, Stone Bridge Over Stream, Trees, Rocks, 16 1/2 In.	6050.00
Vase, Landscape, Dragonfly, Deep Purple, Mottled Blue Ground, 1910, 8 In.	977.00
Vase, Landscape, Gray, Pink, Lavender, Amber, Enameled Cameo, 8 In.	3450.00
Vase, Luneville, Mottled Yellow, Shading To Dark Purple, 6 In.	595.00
Vase, Northern Mountain Landscape, Yellow Sky, 5 Layers, Signed, 10 1/2 In.	4400.00
Vase, Poppies, Black Leafy Stems, Yellow, Blue & Satin Ground, Cameo, 5 In.	2310.00
Vase, Spherical Form, Everted Rim, Red, Brown Bottom, c.1920, 6 In.	1695.00
Vase, Tree Scene, Brown, Green, Lavender, Yellow, 1920, 10 1/4 In.	1265.00
Vase, Yellow Ground, Brown Enameled Leaves, Signed, 4 1/2 In.	1540.00

MUNCIE Clay Products Company was established by Charles Benham in Muncie, Indiana, in 1922. The company made pottery for the florist and giftshop trade. The company closed by 1939. Pieces are marked with the name *Muncie* or just with a system of numbers and letters, like *1A*.

MUNCIE

Basket, Hanging, Medium Matte Green	100.00
Bookends, Leda & Swan, Green & Rust Glaze, 5 x 7 In.	175.00
Bookends, Owl, Arts & Crafts, Purple, Blues, Single	165.00
Bowl, Console, Fluted Form, Marked, 10 In.	27.00
Creamer, Ruba Rombic, Pink & Green	225.00
Ewer, Pink, 9 In.	175.00
Lamp, Arches In Relief, Pale Green	250.00
Lamp, Dancing Nymphs	299.00
Lamp, Lovebird, Yellow	200.00
Lamp, Nude Panel, Stained Glass Shade, Matte Green	1450.00
Lamp, Octagonal, 10 In.	325.00
Pitcher, 2-Tone Blue, Triangular, 4 In.	68.00
Pitcher, Pink & Blue Drip Glaze, 8 In.	175.00
Pot, Strawberry, Dark Matte Green	100.00
Vase, Black, 5 In.	85.00
Vase, Blue & Turquoise, 9 In.	100.00
Vase, Canoe, Insert, 11 1/2 In.	170.00
Vase, Green Over Purple Drip, 8 1/2 In.	125.00
Vase, Orange Peel Glaze, 7 1/4 In.	80.00
Vase, Pink, 2 Handles, 5 In.	60.00

MURANO, see Glass-Venetian category.

MUSIC boxes and musical instruments are listed here. Phonograph records, jukeboxes, phonographs, and sheet music are listed in other categories in this book.

Accordion, Hohner, 3 Row Button, Red, Box	375.00
Accordion, Perfect Bellows	150.00
Banjo, 4 Strings, Mother-Of-Pearl Inlay On Tuning Head, Hardwood Back	110.00
Banjo, Dobro Tenortrope, Case, 1930s	1800.00
Banjo, Federal, Mahogany, 19th Century, 33 In.	2990.00
Banjo, Majestic, Tenor, 1930	550.00
Banjo, Vega, Style M	275.00
Bass, 3 Catgut Strings, Toledo, Ohio, German Immigrants	1500.00
Box, Criterion, Single Comb, Carved Case	4500.00
Box, Imperial Symphonion, Mahogany, Double Cone, 2 Doors, 15 1/2-In. Disc, 34 In.	4070.00
Box, Inlaid Rosewood, 8 Tunes, Switzerland, 19th Century, 35 In. *Illus*	4730.00
Box, Little Lulu, Windup, Revolving, Schmidt	195.00
Box, Mermod Freres, Interchangeable 4 Cylinders, Carved Oak Case, 11 x 31 In.	5900.00
Box, Mira, Double Comb, Mahogany	7000.00
Box, Mira, Regina Type Disk, Mahogany Case, 34 Discs, 21 In.	2420.00
Box, Mira, Table Model, Mahogany, 18 1/2-In. Disc	7000.00
Box, Nicole Freres, Print On Arched Door, Coin-Operated, 36 x 27 1/2 In.	7040.00
Box, Olympia, Gecophone, Upright Table Model	2495.00

Box, Paillard, Organ, Bells, Drum & Castanets, 5 Cylinders, c.1890 .... 39500.00
Box, Piccolo-Zither, Floral Inlaid Lid, Veneer Case, Cylinder, 11 In. 1035.00
Box, Polyphon, Twin Comb Movement, Walnut Case, Table Model, 15 1/2-In. Disc 4025.00
Box, Polyphon, Walnut & Ebonized Wood, Lift Top, 29 Steel Discs, 9 1/2 x 21 In. 2415.00
Box, Regina, Automatic, Disc Changer, 15 1/2-In. Disc 11500.00
Box, Regina, Corona, Upright, Mahogany, 27-In. Disc 22550.00
Box, Regina, Criterion, Carved Exterior, Mahogany, 39 Discs, 19 1/2 x 21 3/4 In. 3410.00
Box, Regina, Double Comb, Casket Model, Folding Top, 20 1/2 In. 8500.00
Box, Regina, Federal Style, Chime Clock, 14 Bells, Mahogany 7500.00
Box, Regina, Figured Veneer, Ebonized Finish, Walnut, 10 Discs, 17 x 19 In. 1980.00
Box, Regina, Hexaphone, 6 Cylinders 6500.00
Box, Regina, Lift Top Case, Oak, 12 Discs, 21 3/4 x 19 3/4 In. 1155.00
Box, Regina, Oak Case On Stand, 23 Discs 2875.00
Box, Regina, Rope Twist Trim, Oak Case, 34 Discs, 19 1/4 x 21 1/2 In. 4070.00
Box, Regina, Style No. 15, Oak, Double Cone, 15 1/2-In. Disc, 17 x 11 In. 4125.00
Box, Silver Plate, Blue Enameled, Singing Bird, Continental, 1 1/2 x 4 x 3 In. 1610.00
Box, Singing Bird, 1 Stops, Other Sings, Birdcage, Brass 895.00
Box, Singing Bird, Birdcage, 2 Feathered Birds, Worn Bellows, France, Key, 20 1/2 In. ... 1130.00
Box, Singing Bird, Birdcage, Brass, 1930s 675.00
Box, Singing Bird, Birdcage, Windup, Gesch 395.00
Box, Singing Bird, Mounted In Marquetry Commode, 19th Century, 4 In 1210.00
Box, Singing Birds, Brass, Mechanical, 21 x 9 In. 3950.00
Box, Singing Birds, Windup, Irwin, Box 62.00
Box, Sublime Harmony Pallard, 5 Interchangeable Cylinders, Mahogany 7500.00
Box, Swiss, Key Wind, 1840s 2500.00
Box, Symphonium, Periphery Drive Movement, Walnut Case, 24 Discs 1600.00
Box, The Brittania, B.H.A. St. Croix, Switzerland, 12-In. Disc, 9 1/2 x 24 In. 1210.00
Box, Troubadour, Hand Wind, Germany, 6 Discs, 1890-1915, 9 1/2 x 10 1/2 In. 1395.00
Box, Vanity, Mahogany, Burled Walnut, Mother-Of-Pearl Trim, 11 x 7 x 5 In. 795.00
Bugle, Brass Eagle With Shield On Breast, Holding Arrows & Branches, Civil War 125.00
Bugle, Co. A, Cavalry, Copper 45.00
Calliope, Tangley, Model CA43, Roll Operated Or Hand Played .... 7500.00 to 9500.00
Clavier, Tapered Folding Legs, Oak Case, 30 x 54 In. 55.00
Coinola, Cupid, Walnut Case 6000.00
Drum, Bass, Lettered For Grand Isle, Vermont 650.00
Flute, Presentation, Philipe Marcil, Sterling Silver, Case 700.00
French Horn, Carl Fisher, Brass, Extra Fittings 245.00
Graphophone, Columbia, Serpentine Case, Wooden Horn 3800.00
Guitar, Buck Jones, Message, Good Luck, Buck Jones & Silver 400.00
Guitar, Dual Head Harp 300.00
Harmonica, Bobby Breen, 1937, Box .. \ 175.00
Harmonica, Hohner, Echo, Box 85.00
Harmonica, Hohner, Little Lady, Box 25.00
Harmonica, Hohner, Man In Knickers Playing Harmonica, 1920s 235.00
Harmonica, Hohner, Model 683, Marine Band Echo, 4 Different Keys, 192 Reeds 165.00
Harmonica, Old Honer, Box, 1900 .... 95.00
Harp, Erard, France 3190.00
Harpsichord, Louis XVI, Mahogany, 1818, 36 In. 5750.00

Music, Box, Inlaid Rosewood, 8 Tunes,
Switzerland, 19th Century, 35 In.

**Never stop a music box
in the middle of a tune.
If the box is later moved,
there is more likely to be
damage to the spikes on
the cylinder if it is not at
the end of a song.**

The label of Antonius Stradivarius has been forged and appears in many 19th- and 20th-century violins of low value. One type of labeled violin was originally offered in the Sears catalog for $7.

Music, Violin, Inlaid Woman, American,
Late 19th Century, 24 In.

Melodeon, Ivory & Ebony Key Board, Dreher Kinnard & Co., Rosewood Veneer	605.00
Musical Saw, Copper, Rhinestones, 30 In.	125.00
Orchestrion, Lyon & Healy, Empress O-Roll	9500.00
Organ, Aolean, Player Golden Oak	2500.00
Organ, Band, Alan Pell, Computerized, Showman Harmonist, 25 Keys	4450.00
Organ, Band, Wurlitzer, Style 105, Pumps, Wind Chest, Spool Box	2000.00
Organ, Barrel, Cylinder Activates Hammers On String & Bells, Pine, Luis Casali, 48 In.	330.00
Organ, Chamber Barrel, Clementi, 17 Keys, England, 1810, 5 Ft. 9 In.	3500.00
Organ, Monkey, Cles Anciaume, Marquetry, 43 Keys	4500.00
Organ, Monkey, Molinan	4500.00
Organ, Monkey, O.G.M., 64 Keys	7500.00
Organ, Pipe, Seeburg, Paper Rolls	3500.00
Organ, Player, Pump, Wilcox & White, Rolls	1430.00
Organ, Pump, Stenciled Music Rack, Joseph M. Prescott, Early 19th Century	125.00
Organ, Reed, Aeolian Grand Player, Oak	3500.00
Organ, Reed, Mechanical, Gold Designs, 1 Paper Roll, 12 x 26 1/2 In.	495.00
Organ, Upright, Marshall & Wendall, Pump Action, Ampico A	2500.00
Piano, A. Bord, Pais, Ivory & Ebony Keys, Brass Fixtures, Candelabra	2500.00
Piano, Aeolian, Player, 65 To 88 Notes, Electrified	650.00
Piano, Aeolian, Player, Style 1500	1850.00
Piano, Arts & Crafts, Oak, Tree-Form Panels, 1900, 54 In.	690.00
Piano, Baldwin, Model SD-10, Ebonized Finish, Concert Grand	1495.00
Piano, Chickering, Rosewood Finish, Square, Grand, 1863	5800.00
Piano, Decker Brothers, Ivory & Ebony Keys, Square, Grand	5000.00
Piano, DuBois & Stodart, 2 Side Drawers, Silt Label, Rosewood, 1815	1430.00
Piano, Hayes & Rider, Rosewood Case, Square, Grand, 37 x 80 In.	520.00
Piano, Herbert, Player, Oak, 1920s	4750.00
Piano, Marshall & Wendall, Player, Foot Pumper, Ampico A, Upright	2500.00
Piano, Mills, Player, Expression, Rolls	6000.00
Piano, National, Coin-Operated, 5 Cents, 1917	4500.00
Piano, Netzow, Player, Walnut Case	3850.00
Piano, Putnam, Player, Upright, Cherry Finish, 88 Keys, Stool, 60 Rolls	1700.00
Piano, Regina Sublima, Player, Rolls	9800.00
Piano, Reproducing, Chickering, Ampico B, Grand	8500.00
Piano, Reproducing, Chickering, Ampico Player, Original Ivory Keys, Grand, 7 Ft.	14000.00
Piano, Reproducing, George Steck, Duo-Art, Model 68805, Model ZR, Walnut, 64 In.	4500.00
Piano, Reproducing, Knabe, Ampico, Model B, Mahogany, Rolls, 68 In.	5500.00
Piano, Reproducing, Steinway, Duo-Art, Upright, Mahogany, Rolls & Bench	9800.00
Piano, Reproducing, Stroud, Duo-Art, Model 87427, Style 593, Walnut	5000.00
Piano, Reproducing, Weber, Duo-Art, Model 77755, Model FR, Mahogany	5000.00
Piano, Schomacker, Carved Legs, Square, Grand, 1800s	7000.00
Piano, Schumann, Painted Design, Bench, Walnut Case, Grand, Apartment, c.1929, 58 In.	258.00
Piano, Shoninger, Baby Grand, Bench, 1923	6700.00
Piano, Spinet, Hardwood, Painted St. Hubertus & Leaves Panels, Contemporary, 56 In.	125.00
Piano, Stafford, Player, Green Art Glass, Foo Dog Carved Legs, 50 x 61 x 28 x 28 In.	5175.00

Piano, Steinway, Rosewood, Cabriole Legs, Square, Grand, Fretwork Music Stand 12500.00
Piano, Street, C. Maserati, 1850s 550.00
Piano, Stroud, Player, 76 Rolls 3000.00
Piano, Wheelock, Aeolian Harp, Walnut, Grand, Apartment, Bench, 58 In. 115.00
Piano, William Knabe, Ebonized Wood, Legs On Casters, Grand, 65 In. 4887.00
Piano, Yamaha, Mahogany, Bench, Grand, 37 x 72 In. 4312.00
Tambourine, Sheepskin, Wooden Handle, 1910s 595.00
Tuning Fork, European, Mahogany Case, c.1860, Pair 1150.00
Ukulele, Arthur Godfrey, Emenee 65.00
Ukulele, Martin Alto, 10 String, 27 In. 550.00
Violin, Carved Head Of Black Man, Casket Shaped Case, American, 1860, 28 x 7 1/2 In. 2100.00
Violin, Inlaid Woman, American, Late 19th Century, 24 In. ....*Illus* 1705.00
Violin, Johann Glass, Germany, 1926 .... 385.00
Violin, Wood, Bone Details, Tortoiseshell Veneer Neck, 18th Century, Italy, 13 3/8 In. 2185.00

MUSTACHE CUPS were popular from 1850 to 1900 when the large, flowing mustache was in style. A ledge of china or silver held the hair out of the liquid in the cup. This kept the mustache tidy and also kept the mustache wax from melting. Left-handed mustache cups are rare but are being reproduced.

2 Men In Canoe, Successful Hunters, Marked, Hampshire, 4 In. 45.00
Floral Pattern, Scalloped Gold Rim & Handle, Left Handed 150.00
Horse-Drawn Fire Truck, Porcelain 27.50
Saucer, Tea Leaf Ironstone, Cable, Shaw 950.00
Side-Wheeler Steamboat 60.00

MZ AUSTRIA is the wording on a mark used by Moritz Zdekauer on porcelains made at his works in Altrolau, Austria, from 1884 to 1909. The mark was changed to MZ Altrolau in 1909, when the firm was purchased by C.M. Hutschenreuther. The firm operated under the name Altrolau Porcelain Factories from 1909 to 1945. It was nationalized after World War II. The pieces were decorated with lavish floral patterns and overglaze gold decoration. Full sets of dishes were made as well as vases, toilet sets, and other wares.

MZ Austria

Cracker Jar, Pink Flowers, Green, 2 Handles, Marked 125.00
Vase, Deco Flowers, 12 In. 200.00

NAILSEA glass was made in the Bristol district in England from 1788 to 1873. It was made by many different factories, not just the Nailsea Glass House. Many pieces were made with loopings of either white or colored glass as decoration.

Bowl, Aqua, White Loops, c.1850, 7 1/4 In. 175.00
Decanter, Cobalt Blue, White Spiral Loopings, Flared Mouth, Pontil, 8 3/8 In. 412.00
Decanter, Yellow Olive, White Loopings, Handle, Inverted Conical, Pontil, 8 1/4 In. 550.00
Fairy Lamp, Blue Satin, Ruffled, Triangular Base, 8 x 6 1/2 In. 660.00
Fairy Lamp, Red, Ribbed Base, Domed Shade, Applied Camphor Footed, 6 In. 495.00
Finger Bowl, Amber, Pink Horizontal Threading, Clear Scroll Footed, Berry Pontil 275.00
Flask, Medium Red Swirl, 8 In. 125.00
Flask, Opalescent Looped Design, Cranberry, Pontil, 7 In. 675.00
Flask, Pink Swirl, 8 In. 125.00
Flask, Swan Design, Applied Punty, Red & White, 8 In. 176.00
Lamp, Fairy, Green, White, 5 In. 99.00
Perfume Bottle, Red & White Ribbon Design, 5 In. 88.00
Perfume Bottle, Ribbons, Red, White Spiral 190.00
Rolling Pin, Cobalt, White Flecks, 18 In. 195.00

NAKARA is a trade name for a white glassware made about 1900 by the C. F. Monroe Company of Meriden, Connecticut. It was decorated in pastel colors. The glass was very similar to another glass made by the company called *Wave Crest*. The company closed in 1916. Boxes for use on a dressing table are the most commonly found Nakara pieces. The mark is not found on every piece.

NAKARA

Bonbon, Handle, Hexagonal, 3 3/4 In. 250.00

Box, 2 Cupids Before Palette & Easel, Painting Portrait, 8 In. 2315.00
Box, Bishop's Hat Mold, Enamel Florals, Lined, Marked, 4 1/2 x 5 3/4 In. 825.00
Box, Collars & Cuffs, Ladies In Greco-Roman Garden, Pink Shading To Blue, 7 1/4 In. ... 2500.00
Box, Molded Pansy Lid, Green Ground, 7 In. 765.00
Box, Portrait Of Children On Cover, Beading, Blue, Round, 5 In. 595.00
Box, Portrait, Young Woman With Flowing Hair Surrounded By 3 Pink Flowers, 4 In. ... 495.00
Hair Receiver, Cover, Gold, 5 1/2 In. 685.00
Humidor, Cigars Cover, Indian, Headdress, Brass Holder Interior, Marked, CFM 525.00
Humidor, Indian, Full Headdress, Cigars On Cover, Moistener Inside Cover 525.00
Humidor, Indian, In Headdress, Red Brown Ground, Brass Lid 1270.00
Toothpick, Pink & White Flowers 325.00
Vase, Flowers, Shaded Green Ground, 15 3/4 In. 1910.00
Vase, Pink Roses, Green Ground, 16 In. 1495.00

NANKING is a type of blue-and-white porcelain made in Canton, China, since the late eighteenth century. It is very similar to Canton, which is listed under its own name in this book. Both Nanking and Canton are part of a larger group now called *Chinese Export* porcelain. Nanking has a spear-and-post border and may have gold decoration.

Candlestick, c.1835, 9 1/2 In. 850.00
Cider Jug, Cover, 19th Century, 11 In. 920.00
Posset Pot, Gilded Fruit Finial, Intertwined Handle 93.00
Saucer, Snuff, Blue & White, 4-Lobed Shape, Early 19th Century, 3 In. 165.00
Teapot, 19th Century, 7 In. 345.00

NAPKIN RINGS were in fashion from 1869 to about 1900. They were made of silver, porcelain, wood, and other materials. They are still being made today. The most popular rings with collectors are the silver plated figural examples. Small, realistic figures were made to hold the ring. Good and poor reproductions of the more expensive rings are now being made and collectors must be very careful.

Bakelite, Elephant 35.00
Bakelite, Schnauzer, 3 In. 55.00
Figural, 2 Dogs, Satchel-Shaped Ring, Scrolls 265.00
Figural, 2 Eagles, Silver Plated, Rogers Bros. 55.00
Figural, Boy With Butterfly Wings, Wilcox, No. 2206 .... 220.00
Figural, Bulldog Chases Cat To Top Of Ring, Silver Plate, Derby 275.00
Figural, Butterfly On Fan 195.00
Figural, Cherub Holding Grapes, Silver Plate, Simpson 450.00
Figural, Chick & Wishbone, Derby Silver Co. 120.00
Figural, Dog On Pillow 325.00
Figural, Engraved, Christmas, 1871, Coin Silver 53.00
Figural, Greenaway, Kate, Muff, Silver Plate, Simpson 450.00
Figural, Kate Greenaway, Silver Plate 48.00
Figural, Lion, Resting, Ring On Back 155.00
Figural, Oriental Fans, Butterfly, Ball-Footed Base 200.00
Figural, Owl On Leafy Branch 135.00
Figural, Owl, Glass Eyes, Wilcox 395.00
Hammered, Rectangular, Block Letter M, Arts & Crafts, Sterling, Lebolt, 3 In. 65.00
Hammered, Rectangular, Marshall Field & Co. Craft Shop, Sterling, 2 3/4 In. 68.00
Hammered, Ring Concave Band, Arts & Crafts, Sterling, Lebolt, 1 1/2 In. 75.00
Hammered, Round, Marked, Sterling, Randahl, 3 In. 184.00
Hammered, Round, Sterling, Cellini, 3 In. 126.00
Lucite, Orange, Square, 6 Piece 30.00

NASH glass was made in Corona, New York, from about 1928 to 1931. A. Douglas Nash bought the Corona glassworks from Louis C. Tiffany in 1928 and founded the A. Douglas Nash Corporation with support from his father, Arthur J. Nash. Arthur had worked at the Webb factory in England and for the Tiffany Glassworks in Corona.

NASH

Centerpiece, Gold Iridescent, Molded Veins, Footed, 11 x 3 1/2 In. 410.00
Compote, Aquamarine, Red Flat Rim, Gray, Green Strip, 4 1/2 In. 862.50
Plate, Chintz, Lavender & Green, 6 1/2 In., 4 Piece 195.00

Vase, Chintz, Pastel Orange Alternating Yellow Chintz Design, 5 1/2 In. 172.00
Vase, Polka Dot Red, 16 Ribbed Design With White Opal Dots, Signed, D.N., 9 In. 1092.00
Vase, Red, Black, Brown, Gray Striped Design, Chintz, Signed D.N., 5 1/2 In. 862.50

NAUTICAL antiques are listed in this category. Any of the many objects
that were made or used by the seafaring trade, including ship parts,
models, and tools, are included. Other pieces may be found listed
under Scrimshaw.

Barometer, Marine, Kelvin & James White, Cushion Molded Crest, 1860, 37 In. 3737.00
Barometer, Marine, Rosewood, Brass Gimbal Wall Mount, Dolphin, 1860, 36 In. 5750.00
Barometer, Marine, Rosewood, Brass Gimbal Wall Mount, England, 36 3/4 In. 2875.00
Barometer, Marine, Rosewood, Button Turned Crest, Gimbal Wall Mount, 38 In. 4025.00
Barometer, Marine, Rosewood, Leaf Carved Crest, Brass Gimbal Wall Mount, 40 In. . . . 4025.00
Barometer, Marine, Rosewood, Mahogany, Leaf Carved Base, 1860, 39 3/4 In. 6325.00
Binnacle, Brass, Mahogany, 18 In. 895.00
Binnacle, Kirk Habicht Co., Baltimore, Brass 748.00
Boat, Chris-Craft, Runabout, 6-Cylinder Engine, 95 Horse Power, Trailer, 1942, 17 Ft. . . 7700.00
Boat, Chris-Craft, Utility, 6-Cylinder Engine, Trailer, 1952 . . . . 1210.00
Brochure, Anchor Line, New York City, Ireland, Scotland, Ship's Interiors, 1920s 50.00
Candleholder, Brass, 6 3/4 x 5 7/8 In. 145.00
Canoe, Kennebec, Canvas On Wood, 1932, 16 Ft. 1540.00
Cards, Playing, Red Star Line, Box 40.00
Chest, Ship Builder's, Ship Joseph Holmes, 1851 . . . . 715.00
Chronometer, 2-Day, Earnshaw Spring Detent, 2-Tier Mahogany Box, Brass Handles . . 1955.00
Chronometer, 2-Day, Earnshaw Spring Detent, 3-Tier Brass Mahogany Box 1840.00
Chronometer, 2-Day, Spring Escapement, J. Sewill, Liverpool, No. 3052, Box, 5 In. . . . 3450.00
Chronometer, 2-Day, Up & Down 56 Hours, M.F. Dent, London, Box, 5 In. 2587.00
Chronometer, 8-Day, Brass Bowl Case, 3-Tier Mahogany Box, England, 1850, 8 In. . . . 2875.00
Chronometer, Gimbaled Negus, 3-Tier, Mahogany Case 2750.00
Chronometer, Negus, Brassbound Case, Flush Handles 2750.00
Chronometer, Thomas Mercer, Rosewood Mantel, 6-Inch Silvered Dial, 1920, 11 In. . . . 6325.00
Chronometer, Waltham, Brassbound Mahogany Box, 8-Day, 5 x 5 In. 695.00
Clock, Chelsea Clock Co., Boston, 24-Hour, 10 In. 660.00
Clock, Chelsea, 8-Day, Time & Strike, Presentation, J.E. Caldwell, 17 1/2 x 14 1/2 In. . . . 2200.00
Clock, Seth Thomas, External Bell Struck Proper Ship's Bells, Nickel Finish 412.00
Compass, 8-Point Direction, Em. Scherman, All Brass, Walnut Box, 14 x 14 In. 265.00
Compass, Fitted With Gimbal, Mahogany Box 93.00
Compass, Riggs & Bros., Standing, Brass 1100.00
Compass, S. Thaxter, Boston, 8 In. 1430.00
Deep Sea Diving Outfit, Mark V Morse Helmet, Weight Belt, Shoes, Hose 4125.00
Desk, Lap, Schooner On Top, Pen & Inkwell 350.00
Diorama, Ship, Crusty Paint, 12 x 29 In. 575.00
Display, Pacific Coast Steamship Co., Totem Pole Shape, Alaska, Menu, 1912 . . . . 45.00
Figurehead, From The Ship Pocahontas, Carved & Painted, 51 In. 2300.00
Figurehead, Maiden, Orange Dress, Carved Wood, England, 40 In. 1380.00
Figurehead, Osceola, Seminole Indian Chief, Carved, Painted, 35 In. 5750.00
Fireplace, Ship's, Murdock Parlor Grate Co., Brassbound, Ceramic Tiles, 27 1/2 In. 1320.00
Flare Gun, Emergency, Webley & Scott, Brass Flared Barrel, England, 9 1/2 In. 225.00
Flare Gun, Webley & Scott, No. 50, Brass, British 355.00
Fog Horn, Brass, Wooden Base, 1930s, 23 In. 165.00
Fog Horn, Tyfon, Sweden 325.00
Glass, Sundance Cruises, Steamship 6.00
Harpoon, Whaling, Wrought Iron, 45 In. 275.00
Lantern, Ship's Red Ribbed Globe, Iron Handles, Wire Guards, 15 x 18 1/2 In. 200.00
Lantern, Ship's, Brass, Bracket Handle, Cylindrical Chimney, Ribbed Globe, 23 In. 403.00
Lantern, Ship's, Brass, Cylindrical Chimney Above Globe, Electrified, England, 27 In. . . 430.00
Light, Bridge, Signal 325.00
Lock, Naval, Mail Bag, Anchor, Stars & Secure, Brass, 4 5/8 In., Pair 110.00
Model, 1-Masted, Painted Maroon, Gold & Blue Hull, Glass Case, 23 In. 385.00
Model, 2-Masted Transitional Steamship, Working Live Steam Engine, 30 x 60 In. 1320.00
Model, Cabin Cruiser, Mahogany, Fitted Wooden Case, 28 In. 110.00
Model, Canoe, Canvas Covered, Signed & Dated 1946, 36 In. 1800.00

Model, Canoe, Old Town, Wood & Canvas, c.1920, 49 In. 2200.00
Model, Clipper Ship, Full Sail, Scene Painted Background, Case, 25 1/2 x 12 In. 460.00
Model, Ferry Boat, Port Of Rose Hill, Painted Metal, 4 Ft. x 16 In. 517.00
Model, Frigate, Constellation, Case, Table, 29 x 40 x 13 1/2 In. 3960.00
Model, Half, Clipper, Cutty Sark, Fully Rigged, Shadowbox Frame, England, 20 x 11 In. 450.00
Model, Jylland, 3-Masted, Fully Rigged, 28 Guns, Plexiglass Case, 40 1/2 In. 632.00
Model, Lapstrake Rowboat, Mahogany Deck, Pine Hull, 42 In. 1595.00
Model, Malang, Burr Atwood, Scale, 1920s 600.00
Model, Prinz Eitel Friedrich, World War I, Metallic, 5 Ft. 990.00
Model, Rattlesnake, Fully Rigged, Glass Case, 28 In. 330.00
Model, Rigged 3-Masted War Ship, Painted, 31 x 39 In. 690.00
Model, River Boat, Red, White & Gray, Painted Wood, Dorchester, 90 In. 770.00
Model, Sailboat, Boy Percy, Stand, 21 x 25 In. . . . . *Illus* 2020.00
Model, Sailing Ship, English Warship, Canvas Sails, 19th Century, 36 In. 1500.00
Model, Sailing Ship, W.S. White, Great Lakes, 45 In. 2475.00
Model, Side-Wheeler, Mt. Washington, 44 1/2 In. 2860.00
Model, Superbe, 3-Masted, Canvas Sails, Brass Cannon, Painted Wood, 7 Ft. 6900.00
Model, Training Naval Vessel, USS Wolverine 900.00
Model, Tugboat, Painted Wood, Late 19th Century, 12 1/4 In. 517.00
Model, Whaling Schooner, Late 1800s, 17 x 16 In. 595.00
Model, Whaling Ship Morgan, Year 1841, 15 x 19 In. 150.00
Model, Whaling Ship, D.H. Bennet, Fully Rigged, Cased, 45 x 54 In. 3220.00
Motor, Wisconsin Row Boat, Brass, Nickel Plated Flywheel, 1913 . . . . 3500.00
Octant, Ebony, Brass & Ivory, C. Hutchison, Boston 495.00
Octant, Hemsly Tower Hill Longon, Ebony & Brass, Case, Label, 19th Century, 12 In. . . 440.00
Octant, Swing Arm, Mahogany Frame 4125.00
Passenger List, SS President Polk, Marseilles, N.Y., Dollar Steamship, 1927, 8 Pages . . 15.00
Passport, Hawaiian Island, Issued To Bark Fortune, Frame, 1856, 12 7/8 x 8 3/8 In. 85.00
Porthole, Bronze, Chris Craft, 1936, 11 x 18 In. 95.00
Quadrant, Brass, Edmund Gunter, 1618, 3 3/4 x 5 1/4 In. 3300.00
Sailor's Valentine, Shellwork, Home Again 3250.00
Sailor's Valentine, Shellwork, Love The Giver On Left, Heart On Right, 9 x 18 In. 3080.00
Sea Chest, Carved Handles, Shield Design Within Wreath, 19th Century, 16 x 33 In. 488.00
Sewing Kit, Basket Weave, 5 1/2 x 8 1/2 In. 148.00
Sextant, Brass, F.W. Lincoln Sr., Massachusetts, Case, 19th Century 460.00
Sextant, Brass, Heath & Co., London 440.00
Sextant, Brass, Signed Owen Owens Liverpool, Case, England, 19th Century, 9 In. 525.00
Sextant, Eugene F. Medinger, Wooden Case 475.00
Sextant, Negus, Brass, Mahogany Case, New York, 5 x 11 x 10 1/4 In. 230.00
Ship Model, see Nautical, Model.
Sign, Cunard Line, Mauritania, Self-Framed, Tin, 1907, 27 1/2 x 39 In. 1430.00
Sign, Trade, Shape Of Ship's Binnacle, Guillaume Bossineau, 52 x 42 In. 550.00

Lacquered wood can be
damaged by a sudden
change in humidity. Keep
lacquer away from heat
sources, preferably in a
room with high humidity.

Nautical, Model, Sailboat,
Boy Percy, Stand, 21 x 25 In.

Spyglass, Brass Pull, Mahogany, Late 1700s, 36 In. 375.00
Sticker, Baggage, Grace Line, Black, Gold, Unused, 1940, 4 x 4 In. 4.00
Taffrail Log, Finned Metal Bullet Shape, Towed To Determine Speed, Box 450.00
Telescope, C. Dollard, Finder's Scope, Rack-And-Pinion Focusing 2420.00
Telescope, C. Dollard, London, Day Or Night, Collapsing, Brass & Wood, c.1880 ...... 395.00
Tool, Docking, To Cut Rope & Tails Of Animals, Iron Hinge & Cutter, Pine, 1820s, 20 In. 110.00
Trumpet, Speaking, Pewter, Early 19th Century, 16 1/2 In. 225.00
Wheel, Ferry, New York City, 1900 .... 630.00
Wheel, Ship, 49 In. Diam. 770.00

NETSUKES are small ivory, wood, metal, or porcelain pieces used as toggles on the end of the cord that held a Japanese money pouch. The earliest date from the sixteenth century. Many are miniature, carved works of art.

Bone, Boy, Sitting With Dog, Signed, Japan, 1 5/8 In. 30.00
Boxwood, Fox, Curled Up Asleep On Walnut, Meiji Period, 1 5/8 In. 270.00
Boxwood, Horse, Grazing, Sash Tied Around His Midsection, 19th Century, 2 In. 285.00
Boxwood, Horse, Lying Next To Foal, Signed, Tomochika, Meiji Period 1150.00
Burl, Fungus, 3 In. 70.00
Elk Horn, Dragon Form, Signed 82.00
Ivory, 2 Farmers, Struggling Under Weight Of Large Sacks, Hideyuki, 1 1/4 In. 920.00
Ivory, 2 Men Helping Third Man Climb Onto Elephant 105.00
Ivory, 2 Men, Squatting, Abutting Form, 1 In. 460.00
Ivory, Boy Lying On Leaf, Signed, Japan, 2 1/4 In. 130.00
Ivory, Boy Sitting With Dog, Signed, Japan, 1 5/8 In. 130.00
Ivory, Boy With Walnut, 2 1/4 In. 45.00
Ivory, Buffalo With Human Form Head, Signed, 1 1/4 x 2 In. 160.00
Ivory, Carved Chicken In Egg Form, Signed, Seal Marked, Mitsuhiro, Meiji Period 250.00
Ivory, Fisherman, With His Catch, Signed, 2 In. 345.00
Ivory, Fukurokuju, Standing Holding Fan, Signed, Meiji Period 245.00
Ivory, In Demon Form, 1 1/2 In. 80.00
Ivory, Man With Mask 80.00
Ivory, Manju, Woman, Flying Demon Opposite Side With Cloth On Barrel, Signed 460.00
Ivory, Monkey Trainer, Meiji Period, Joso, 1 5/16 In. 1150.00
Ivory, Monkey, With Large Chestnut, 19th Century 605.00
Ivory, Moraya Eel, Signed, 2 1/2 In. 66.00
Ivory, Peasant, Dancing With Fishing Pole, Basket Stares Skyward, 18th Century 715.00
Ivory, Recumbent Tiger, Signed, 1 3/4 In. 45.00
Ivory, Revolving Head, Signed 48.00
Ivory, Samurai On Horse, Signed, 3 1/8 x 1 1/2 In. 103.00
Ivory, Shoki, Standing Holding Halberd, Signed, 20th Century 137.00
Ivory, Skull, Climbing Mouse, Signed, 19th Century 700.00
Ivory, Snake Form, 1 3/4 In. 185.00
Ivory, Sparrow, Carved, Signed 172.50
Ivory, Sparrow, Wings Outspread, Tail Raised, 19th Century, 2 In. 1380.00
Mother-Of-Pearl, Cat & Kitten, 1 15/16 In. 275.00
Staghorn, Boy Atop Octopus, 4 3/8 In. 70.00
Staghorn, Rat, Crawling, Inset Black Stone Eyes, Signed, Gyohuran, 3 In. 632.00
Wood, 2 Pigs Huddled Together, Signed 110.00
Wood, 3 Men Dressed In Chinese Costumes, 19th Century 330.00
Wood, Baboon Carrying Young Baboon, Signed 38.00
Wood, Benkei & Shojo Dancer, Ivory Head & Hands, Coral Mask, 1 11/16 In. 1610.00
Wood, Buddhist Monk, Emerging From Alms Bowl, Meiji Period, 1 3/16 In. 575.00
Wood, Dragon Figure, Signed 70.00
Wood, Foreigner, Standing Holding Jui Scepter, Signed, 2 1/2 In. 440.00
Wood, Gama Sennin, Standing Holding Staff, Balancing Frog On Shoulder 687.50
Wood, Man, Falling Asleep Atop Drum, 19th Century 143.00
Wood, Mask, Demon, Laughing, 19th Century 187.00
Wood, Polished, Skull Form, Deeply Carved Eyes, 1 1/4 In. 125.00
Wood, Puppy With Pillow, Signed, 2 In. 33.00
Wood, Stag, Kneeling Priest Presenting Offering, 1 1/2 In. 110.00
Wood, Water Buffalo, Inlaid Eyes, Meiji Period 742.50
Wood, Wolf, Pawing Decaying Skull, Ivory, Horn Inlaid Eyes, 19th Century 357.50

NEW HALL Porcelain Manufactory was started at Newhall, Shelton, Staffordshire, England, in 1782. Simple decorated wares were made. Between 1810 and 1825, the factory made a glassy bone porcelain sometimes marked with the factory name. Do not confuse New Hall porcelain with the pieces made by the New Hall Pottery Company, Ltd., a twentieth-century firm.

New Hall

Cup & Saucer, Oriental Figures, Pagoda	125.00
Teapot & Stand, Mandarin Palette, Early 19th Century	665.00

NEW MARTINSVILLE Glass Manufacturing Company was established in 1901 in New Martinsville, West Virginia. It was bought and renamed the Viking Glass Company in 1944 and is still producing fine glasswares.

Basket, Janice, Ice Blue, 12 In.	275.00
Berry Set, Old Colony, Red Flashed, 7 Piece	150.00
Bowl, Fluted, Flared, 2 1/2 x 6 1/2 In.	25.00
Bride's Bowl, Peachblow, Ribbed, Crimped Edge, 10 1/2 x 4 1/2 In.	245.00
Cake Plate, Radiance, Ice Blue	175.00
Candlestick, Janice, 6 In., Pair	25.00
Candy Dish, Cover, Janice, Ice Blue	225.00
Creamer, Janice	10.00
Creamer, Prelude	10.00
Decanter, Ruby Moondrops, Beehive Stopper, 9 In.	45.00
Figurine, Baby Bear	40.00
Figurine, Borzoi	95.00
Figurine, Mama Bear	225.00
Figurine, Piglet, Standing	150.00
Figurine, Rooster	65.00
Figurine, Tiger, Head Up	195.00
Perfume Bottle, Deco Green, Triangular	120.00
Pitcher, Prelude	175.00
Pitcher, Radiance, Amber	300.00
Punch Bowl, Radiance, Amber	425.00
Punch Set, Forest Green	500.00
Soup, Dish, Moondrops, Cobalt, 6 3/4 In.	75.00
Soup, Dish, Moondrops, Red, 6 3/4 In.	75.00
Sugar & Creamer, Eagle, Red, 18 In.	75.00
Syrup, Cover, Cobalt Blue	200.00
Syrup, Vining Rose	65.00
Toothpick, Florene	50.00
Toothpick, Frontier, Gold Trim	50.00
Tumbler, 2 3/4 In.	50.00
Vanity Set, Green & Crystal, 3 Piece	95.00
Vanity Set, Pink & Crystal, 3 Piece	185.00
Vase, Prelude, 11 In.	125.00
Vase, Radiance, Crimped, Red, 10 In.	125.00

NEWCOMB Pottery was founded by Ellsworth and William Woodward at Sophie Newcomb College, New Orleans, Louisiana, in 1895. The work continued through the 1940s. Pieces of this art pottery are marked with the printed letters *NC* and often have the incised initials of the artist as well. Most pieces have a matte glaze and incised decoration.

Bowl, Blossoms At Shoulder, Frances Devereaux Jones, 1910, 8 In.	18040.00
Bowl, Raised Design Of Flowers, Leafage, Tapered, Anna Frances Simpson, 9 In.	375.00
Jar, Coffer, Stylized Flowers, Henrietta Davidson Bailey, 7 In.	8000.00
Mug, Stylized Pine Cones, Ada Wilt Lonnegan, 1904, 4 1/4 x 5 In.	825.00
Pitcher, Stylized Vines, Leaves, Green, Dark Blue Against Tan Ground, 5 1/2 In.	3850.00
Plaque, Painted Tree Scene, Field, Blue, Green Shades, Yellow Moon, 6 x 9 1/2 In.	8250.00
Syrup, Lidded, Stylized Flowers, Light Green Ground, E.H.P., 1907, 4 3/4 In.	1540.00
Tile, White Flowers At Corner, Vine Border, Semimatte Blue Glaze, Marked, 1911	485.00
Toothpick, Floral, High Glaze, May Louise Dunn, 1908	1600.00
Trivet, White & Yellow Flowers, Corinna Margiana Luria, 1916, 5 3/4 In.	1210.00
Vase, Aurelia Coralie Arbo, 9 In.	3520.00

Vase, Aurelia Coralie Arbo, 10 In. 3520.00
Vase, Band Of Crocuses, Mottled Ground, Marie De Hoa LeBlanc, 1905, 8 In. 6050.00
Vase, Band Of Flowers In Relief, Circular, 5 3/4 In. 865.00
Vase, Bayou Scene, Oak Trees, Spanish Moss, Anna Frances Simpson, 1921, 12 In. 4950.00
Vase, Bayou Scene, Sadie Irvine, 1932, 14 In. 7700.00
Vase, Blue Paperwhites, Celadon Stems, Henrietta Davidson Bailey, 1915, 7 In. 3520.00
Vase, Carved & Painted Landscape, Trees, Moss, Blue, Green Matte, 5 In. .....2200.00 to 2420.00
Vase, Carved Bayou Scene, Signed, Anna Frances Simpson, 1927, 10 In. 4400.00
Vase, Daffodils & Leafage At Shoulder, Alma Florence Mason, c.1914, 6 1/4 In. 4600.00
Vase, Floral Design, Blue, Pale Yellow Blossoms, 6 In. 1210.00
Vase, Floral Design, Pink Blossoms, Buds, Vertical Green Leaves, Blue Ground, 9 In. ... 2750.00
Vase, Floral, Blue Cream, Green, Sadie Irvine, 4 In. 2200.00
Vase, Floral, Blue Cream, Green, Sadie Irvine, 8 In. 2200.00
Vase, Floral, Blue Ground, Artist, 6 1/2 In. 1980.00
Vase, Flowers, Blue, Cream, Green Leaves, Blue, Green Ground, Sadie Irvine, 12 In. ... 3575.00
Vase, Flowers, Blue, White Band, Bulbous, Signed, C. Pugh, 1915, 6 1/2 In. 1850.00
Vase, Full Moon Behind Oaks, Spanish Moss, Semimatte Glaze, 1927, 5 3/4 In. 970.00
Vase, Landscape, Blue Trees, Yellow Moon Against Light Blue, Green Ground 2310.00
Vase, Landscape, Green, Dark Blue Trees, Yellow Moon, Light Blue Ground 2750.00
Vase, Live Oak Trees, Hanging Spanish Moss, Semimatte Blue Glaze, 9 In. ....3630.00 to 3870.00
Vase, Moon, Moss In Moonlight, Blue Tones, Semimatte Glaze, 5 x 6 In. 2100.00
Vase, Moss & Trees, 5 In. 1500.00
Vase, Pine Cones, Red, Brown, Green, Impressed Mark, Henrietta Bailey, 5 1/2 In. 1325.00
Vase, Pine Cones, Rose, Green, Blue Matte Glaze, Blue, Henrietta Bailey, 10 In. 3100.00
Vase, Pink Blossoms At Shoulder, Joseph Meyer & Sadie Irving, 1929, 8 1/2 In. 850.00
Vase, Pink Floral Border, Blue Matte Body, 1924, 4 1/4 In. 970.00
Vase, Pink Flowers, Blue & Pink Ground, Leona Fischer Nicholson, 1917, 4 3/4 In. 1450.00
Vase, Pink Fruit, Leaves On Lavender Vines, Blue Ground, Sadie Irvine, 5 1/2 In. 2200.00
Vase, Spanish Moss Tree Scene, Distant Hills, Moon, Blue, Tan, Cream, 5 In. 3850.00
Vase, Stylized Blossoms, Leaves, Purple, Yellow, Dark Pink, Lavender Ground, 7 In. 2530.00
Vase, Swamp Lilies, Green, Blue, Ivory, Impressed Mark, Emma J. Urquhart, 7 In. 8250.00
Vase, Swirled Floral Design, Pink, Green, Blue Ground, Sadie Irving, 3 x 2 In. 935.00
Vase, Tooled Palm Trees, Serrated Trunks, Sabina Elliot Wells, 1902, 9 3/4 In. 5500.00
Vase, Tree Scene, Yellow Moon, Pale Blue, Green Brush, Anna F. Simpson, 8 In. 3850.00
Vase, Weeping Willow Trees, Blue, Purple, Green, Against Lavender Sky, 5 In. 1850.00
Vase, Weeping Willow, White Moon, Blue, Green Highlights, 6 In. 2850.00
Vase, White Roses, Blue Ground, Henrietta Davidson Bailey, 1923, 6 1/2 In. 2090.00
Vase, White Wild Roses, Thorny Stems, Bulbous, 1904, 6 1/4 In. 9080.00
Vase, Yellow, Pale Blue, White Daffodils, Dark Blue Ground, Anna F. Simpson, 8 In. ... 4125.00
Vessel, Floral Design, Blue, White, Marked, Maude Robinson, 1907 .... 3000.00

NILOAK Pottery (Kaolin spelled backward) was made at the Hyten
Brothers Pottery in Benton, Arkansas, between 1909 and 1946.
Although the factory did make cast and molded wares, collectors are
most interested in the marbleized art pottery line made of colored
swirls of clay. It was called *Mission Ware.*

Ashtray, Swan, 5 In. 40.00
Candlestick, Marbleized, Brown, Tan & Blue, 9 3/4 In. 155.00
Cigarette Humidor, Cover, Brown, Art Mark, 4 1/2 In. 275.00
Creamer, Bird, Pussy Willow Design, Green, 2 1/2 In. 60.00
Ewer, Pink 16.00
Lamp, Marbleized, 10 In. 275.00
Pitcher, Art Deco, Bright Blue, Clay Stopper 45.00
Pitcher, Ozark Dawn, Ball, 7 1/2 In. 85.00
Pitcher, Swan, 5 1/2 In. 45.00
Planter, Clown, Blue, 7 1/2 In. 30.00
Planter, Dove, White, 9 In. 100.00
Planter, Keystone Cop, 7 In. 30.00
Planter, Parrot, 4 1/2 In. 45.00
Planter, Polar Bear, Brown, 3 1/2 In. ....30.00 to 40.00
Planter, Rabbit, Maroon Matte, 3 In. 55.00
Planter, Seal, White, 4 3/4 In. 20.00
Planter, Squirrel, Yellow & White 30.00

Rose Bowl, Marbleized, 5 x 6 In. 200.00
Vase, Blue Matte Glaze, Impressed Mark, 3 1/2 In. 60.50
Vase, Deep Red Matte Glaze, Impressed Mark, 3 1/2 In. 60.50
Vase, Fan, Ozark Dawn, 14 In. 125.00
Vase, Marbleized, 4 3/4 In. 100.00
Vase, Marbleized, 7 In. 125.00
Vase, Marbleized, 8 1/2 In. 160.00
Vase, Marbleized, Blue, Brown, Dark Brown, Cream, Bulbous, 14 x 6 1/2 In. . . . 880.00
Vase, Marbleized, Blue, Cocoa, Beige, Rust, Brown Clay, Impressed Mark, 5 1/2 In. 165.00
Vase, Marbleized, Blue, Cream & Brown, 5 In. 65.00
Vase, Marbleized, Blue, Light, Dark Brown Clay, Impressed Mark, 9 1/2 In. 231.00
Vase, Marbleized, Blue, Tan, Cream, Light, Dark Brown Clay, Impressed Mark, 12 In. 660.00
Vase, Marbleized, Brown & Orange Clay Body, Signed, 12 In. 450.00
Vase, Marbleized, Brown, Art Mark, 10 In. 330.00
Vase, Marbleized, Brown, Blue, White Clay, Impressed Mark, 6 1/2 In. 121.00
Vase, Marbleized, Brown, Red, Blue, Cream, Impressed Mark, 8 In. 176.00
Vase, Marbleized, Brown, Tan Clay, Dark Brown Spots, Impressed Mark, 9 In. 121.00
Vase, Marbleized, Gray, Dark Brown, Beige, Brick Red Clay, Impressed Mark, 4 In. 77.00
Vase, Marbleized, Red, Blue, Green, Brown, Cream, Impressed Mark, 10 1/2 In. 412.00
Vase, Marbleized, Red, Brown, Blue, Impressed Mark, 4 1/2 In. 385.00
Vase, Marbleized, Scroddled Bisque Fired Clay, Signed, 10 In. 495.00
Vase, Marbleized, Signed, H.K. Tunstall, 8 1/2 In. 70.00
Wall Pocket, Marbleized, 6 1/4 In. 350.00

NIPPON porcelain was made in Japan from 1891 to 1921. *Nippon* is
the Japanese word for *Japan*. A few firms continued to use the word
Nippon on ceramics after 1921 as a part of the company name more
than as an identification of the country of origin. More pieces marked
Nippon will be found in the Dragonware, Moriage, and Noritake
categories.

Ashtray, Bird, Blue & Green, Green Wreath 150.00
Ashtray, Nile Scene, Hand Painted, Green Wreath, 4 3/4 In. 66.00
Berry Set, Cherries, Hand Painted, Pre-1891, 7 Piece 70.00
Biscuit Jar, Cover, Floral, Gold Beading, Hand Painted, 8 In. 154.00
Biscuit Jar, Cover, Gold Design, Hand Painted, Blue Maple Leaf, 8 In. 165.00
Bowl, 3 Boys Playing Baseball, 4 In. 38.00
Bowl, Blown Out Hazel Nuts, 2 Handles, Oval, 8 In. 145.00
Bowl, Child's Face, 8 In. 120.00
Bowl, Floral Band, Gold Handles, 7 1/2 In. 85.00
Bowl, Purple Flowers, Gold Looped Edges, 8 In. 75.00
Bowl, Red Roses, Cobalt Blue, Gold, 4-Lobed, Pre-1891, 10 1/2 x 2 1/2 In. 195.00
Bowl, Scenic, Pierced Handles, Hand Painted, Green Wreath, 6 In. 27.50
Cake Plate, Sailboat, Trees, Lavender Tones, Bisque, Handle, Green Wreath, 10 In. 50.00
Candlestick, Palm Trees, Foliage, Gold Trim, Sea & Mountains On Back, 8 In., Pair . . . 375.00
Candy Dish, 2 Handles, Violets, Gold, Green, Maple Leaf, 6 1/2 In. 35.00
Celery Dish, Leaves & Grapes, Gold On White, Green Mark, 12 x 5 1/2 In. 40.00
Celery Dish, Pink Roses, Gold Swags, Blue Maple Leaf, 11 3/8 x 4 7/8 In. 38.00
Charger, Rose Tapestry, 12 In. . . . .*Illus* 2600.00
Cheese Dish, Cover, Gold, Floral, Hand Painted, Blue Maple Leaf, 8 In. 55.00
Chocolate Set, Gold Flowers, Cream, 10 Piece 125.00
Chocolate Set, Park Scene, Bell-Shaped Pot, Cobalt Border, Gold Overlay, 8 Piece 300.00
Chocolate Set, White Flying Swans, Turquoise Border, 9 Piece 175.00
Compote, Sampan Scene, 8 x 6 In. 150.00
Cracker Jar, Cobalt Blue, Gold, Beaded, Hand Painted 350.00
Creamer, Child's, Flowers 95.00
Cup & Saucer, Gold, Geometric Trim 65.00
Dish, Leaf Shape, Acorns, Blown Out, 8 In. 85.00
Dish, Peanut, Footed, Gold Trim 135.00
Dish, Pin, Coralene 266.00
Dresser Set, Gold, Pink, Blue, Hair Receiver, Compote, Hatpin Holder, Marked, 3 Piece . . 120.00
Dresser Tray, Scene, Jewel Rim, Cobalt, Oval 475.00
Egg Warmer, Pink Roses 125.00
Ferner, Pink Roses, 4 Scroll Feet, Square, Blue Maple Leaf, 5 5/8 In. 140.00

Hatpin Holder, Floral 80.00
Hatpin Holder, Gold Swan Design, Attached Underplate 160.00
Hatpin Holder, Red & Pink Roses, Gold, Beaded, Green Jewels 85.00
Humidor, Camels In Band, 5 1/2 In. 485.00
Humidor, Cherries, Gold & Brown Ground 495.00
Humidor, Deer Front, Green Mark, 6 1/2 In. 575.00
Humidor, Man Riding Camel, Green Wreath, 7 1/2 In. 770.00
Humidor, Scenic, Tray, Marked 350.00
Jug, Wine, Flowers, Raised Gold, Jeweled, Blue Maple Leaf, 7 1/2 In. 395.00
Lamp, Floral, Cobalt Blue 350.00
Lemonade Set, Geometric Design, Cherries, 5 Piece 155.00
Lemonade Set, Stylized Flowers, 6 Piece 295.00
Mayonnaise Set, Floral, Hand Painted, Underplate, Blue Mark, 2 Piece 22.00
Nut Set, Bowl, Blown Out 69.00
Pancake Server, Gold Banded 400.00
Pancake Server, Roses, Gold Trim 120.00
Perfume Bottle, Gold Trim, Beaded 85.00
Perfume Bottle, Raised Gold Grapes & Leaves, White 125.00
Pin Tray, Lilac Flowers, Gold Trim, 5 1/2 x 7 1/2 In. 55.00
Pitcher, Roses Over Meadow Scene, Maple Leaf, 6 1/2 In. 150.00
Plaque, Birds, Hanging, 7 3/4 In. 90.00
Plaque, Buffalo Grazing, 10 1/2 In. 1300.00
Plaque, Castle Scene, Floral & Rams' Heads Border, Pierced, Wreath Mark, 10 In. 185.00
Plaque, Deer, At Stream In Forest, 10 In. 225.00
Plaque, Egyptian Boat, Sphinx Type Head Mast, Jeweled Border, 10 In. 275.00
Plaque, Egyptian Scene, Men On Camels, Palm Trees, Maple Leaf, 10 In. 275.00
Plaque, Elk, Blown Out, 10 1/2 In. 400.00
Plaque, Fall Scene, House & Meadow, Green Wreath, 10 In. 180.00
Plaque, Kingfisher, 10 1/2 In. 200.00
Plaque, Moose, 8 3/4 In. 150.00
Plaque, Moose, 9 1/2 In. 95.00
Plaque, Pheasant Game Scene, 11 In. 350.00
Plaque, Squirrel, Eating Nuts, Relief, Molded, 10 3/4 In. 790.00
Plaque, Swans, Trees, Pond Scene, Bisque, Green Wreath Mark, 10 In. 125.00
Plate, 3 Dutch Women On Dock, 10 In. 325.00
Plate, Autumn Scene, 8 In. 250.00
Plate, Buffalo, Blown Out, Green Mark, 10 1/4 In. 650.00
Plate, Gristmill Pastoral Scene, 12 Reserves Various Shapes & Sizes, 8 1/2 In. 125.00
Plate, Lion & Lioness, Blown Out, 10 In. 800.00
Plate, Trees, House, Green Mark, 6 In. 28.00
Relish, Windmill Scene, Oval 125.00
Salt, Roses, Gold Beading 65.00
Salt & Pepper, Floral 40.00
Sauce Boat, Underplate, Floral, Gold, Hand Painted, Blue Maple Leaf, 7 1/2 In. 165.00
Shaving Mug, Desert Scene, Man With Camel 225.00
Stein, Sampan Scene, 6 In. 375.00
Sugar & Creamer, Red Roses, Cobalt Blue 75.00
Sugar & Creamer, Stylized Floral, Footed, Green Mark 150.00
Sugar & Creamer, Violets 30.00
Sugar Shaker, Border Of Flowers, Gold Handle, White Ground, 3 3/4 In. 125.00
Tankard, Cobalt Blue, 18 In. 2420.00
Tankard, Gold Scroll & Lattice, 6 Roses Circle Center, Fluted, 16 In. 2420.00
Tankard, Roses, Cobalt Blue, Gold, 13 In. 125.00
Tankard Scene, Green Mark, 10 3/4 In. 348.00
Tea Set, Child's, Circus Scene, Service For 4 .... 225.00
Tea Set, Rose, Medallions, Gold Trim, 15 Piece 345.00
Toothpick, Hills & Palm Trees, Green Mark 42.00
Tray, Sailboat, Handle, 7 1/4 In. 20.00
Urn, Rococo Florals, Bolted Pedestal, JMDS, 18 In. ...._Illus_ 7700.00
Urn, Scenic Medallion, High Handles, Green Wreath, 14 5/8 x 7 In. 315.00
Vase, Blown Out, Man, Hand Painted, 11 In. ...._Illus_ 1760.00
Vase, Cartoon, Raised Enamel, Hand Painted, Imperial Mark, 12 In. 302.00
Vase, Coralene, 10 1/2 In., Pair 495.00

Nippon, Charger,
Rose Tapestry,
12 In..

Nippon, Urn,
Rococo Florals, Bolted
Pedestal, JMDS, 18 In.

Nippon, Vase, Blown Out,
Man, Hand Painted,
11 In.

Vase, Country Scene, Handles, 16 In.	1500.00
Vase, Daisies, Lavender, 9 In.	195.00
Vase, Desert Scene, Gold Handles, Gold Beading, 11 In.	295.00
Vase, Floral, Gold, Hand Painted, 2 Handles, Blue Maple Leaf, 9 In.	385.00
Vase, Floral, Griffins, Hand Painted, Blue M In Wreath, 13 In.	770.00
Vase, Floral, Hand Painted, 2 Handles, Footed, Blue M In Wreath, 10 In.	319.00
Vase, Floral, Hand Painted, 2 Handles, Green M In Wreath, 12 In.	467.00
Vase, Flying Geese, Floral Motif, Blue, 2 Handles, Bulbous, 9 1/4 In.	195.00
Vase, Gold Beading, 8 3/4 In.	100.00
Vase, Gold Trim, Cobalt Blue, 3 1/2 In.	350.00
Vase, Hand Painted, 4 3/4 In.	80.00
Vase, Hounds Chasing Stag Scene, Moriage Trim Handles, Base, 7 In.	795.00
Vase, Lavender Roses, Gold, Outlining Brown, 7 In., Pair	325.00
Vase, Lily-Of-The-Valley, Elephant Head Handle, Pair	550.00
Vase, Multicolored Floral, Gold Handles & Feet, Oval, Pair, 6 In.	450.00
Vase, Ostrich, Cobalt Handle, 8 In., Pair	950.00
Vase, Pastoral Scene, 7 1/2 In.	150.00
Vase, Peonies & Branches, Gold Outlining, Corner Handles, Green Wreath, 13 x 4 In.	245.00
Vase, Plate Shape, Water Scene, With Cranes, 12 In.	325.00
Vase, Plushy Roses, 10 In.	250.00
Vase, Poppy, Baluster Form, Enamel Handles, 7 1/2 In.	225.00
Vase, Raised Enamel, Hand Painted, 2 Handles, 11 In.	192.00
Vase, Red & Pink Roses, Gold Trim & Jewels, 14 1/2 In.	445.00
Vase, Roses, Gold Trim, 4 Footed, 2 Handles, 5 1/2 In., Pair	150.00
Vase, Roses, Raised Beading, Hand Painted, 6 In.	80.00
Vase, Scenic Panels, Cobalt Blue, Raised Red Cherries, Green Enameled Leaves, 9 In.	395.00
Vase, Scenic, Hand Painted, Gold Trim, 2 Handles, Green Wreath Mark, 10 In.	330.00
Vase, Scenic, Raised Beading Form Grapes & Leaves, 9 3/4 In.	375.00
Vase, Sunflowers, Gold Rim, 15 In.	325.00
Vase, Swan Scene, Cobalt Blue, Gold Trim, 11 In.	550.00
Vase, Yellow Flowers, Matte Brown, 8 In.	850.00

NODDERS, also called nodding figures or pagods, are porcelain figures with heads and hands that are attached to wires. Any slight movement causes the parts to move up and down. They were made in many countries during the eighteenth, nineteenth, and twentieth centuries. A few Art Deco designs are also known. Copies are being made. A more recent type of nodder is made of papier-mache or plastic. These often represent sports figures or comic characters.

4-Eyed Couple In Barrel	110.00
Ashtray, Girl, Legs Move	55.00

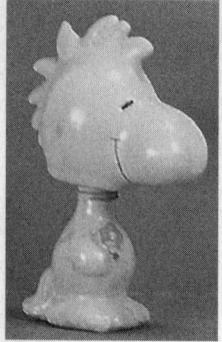

Take off your rings and bracelets before you start to wash figurines or dishes.

Nodder, Woodstock, Peanuts, Holding
Flower, Composition, 4 In.

Bambi, Germany, Tiny	25.00
Bear	19.00
Beetle Bailey	65.00
Beetle Bailey, Zero	135.00
Ben Casey, Composition, Box	100.00 to 185.00
Birds On Tree Stump, Pottery, Hand Painted, Japan, 4 In.	40.00
Boston Bruins, Japan, 1960s, Box, 4 1/2 In.	30.00
Bowler, Box, 1950, Small	20.00
Bunny, Full Figure, Pink, Plastic, Hong Kong, 1950, 4 3/4 In.	10.00
Buttercup, Bisque	95.00
Charlie Brown, Lego	75.00
Chinese Coolie, Red, Green, 6 In.	20.00
Clown, Pottery	45.00
Colonel Sanders, 1960s, 7 In.	75.00 to 85.00
Comical Man, Smoking Cigarette, Shofu China	175.00
Cow, Pink, Gray, Japan	15.00
Cowboy & Cowgirl, Pair	65.00
Detroit Tigers, Mascot Head, Composition	190.00
Dog, Dalmatian	82.00
Dog, German Shepherd, 10 1/2 In.	35.00
Dog, Snoopy	45.00
Donkey, Chalkware, Colored, 6 In.	45.00
Dr. Kildare, Box	150.00
Felix The Cat, Papier-Mache	500.00
Goofy, Composition Head, 7 1/2 In.	125.00
Gypsy	65.00
Hank Aaron, Milwaukee Brewers, Box	135.00 to 198.00
Hippie	75.00
Houston Astro	25.00
Hula Girl, Dancing	30.00 to 45.00
I May Never Smile Again, Composition	55.00
Icey The Ice Capades, 1960s	185.00
Irish Couple	175.00
Mammy	205.00
Man, Sour Puss, Corks In Ears	50.00
Martian, Brain Exposed, Plastic, 1960s	150.00
Mule, Cast Iron, 12 In.	550.00
Oriental, Couple, Kissing	55.00
Oriental Woman, With Fan, Bisque, 8 In.	350.00
Peanuts Gang, Charlie Brown, Lucy, Linus, Snoopy, Set Of 4	350.00
Phil, Gasoline That Won The West, Composition, Hand Made, Phillips 66, Box, 7 In.	155.00
Player, Detroit Lions, 1960s	198.00
Player, Detroit Pistons, 1969	198.00
Player, New Orleans Saints, Japan, 1960s	75.00
Player, Philadelphia Eagles, Japan, 1968	85.00
Player, St. Louis Cardinals, Miniature	315.00

Policeman, Pottery	75.00
Rabbit, 1950s	25.00
Rabbit, Celluloid, Japan, 7 1/2 In.	135.00
Reindeer, Large	1017.50
Russian Soldier, Bisque	145.00
Salt & Pepper Shakers are listed in the Salt & Pepper category.	
Santa Claus, Bisque, 3 1/4 In.	75.00
Santa Claus, Composition, Japan	50.00
Sea Captain, Pottery	65.00
Smokey The Bear	275.00
Snoopy, Red Baron	58.00
Snoopy Astronaut	48.00
Ugly Troll, Plastic, 1973	20.00
Washington Senator, Papier-Mache	105.00
Windmill, Turning, Blue White	13.00
Woodstock, Peanuts, Holding Flower, Composition, 4 In. ....*Illus*	30.00

NORITAKE porcelain was made in Japan after 1904 by Nippon Toki Kaisha. The best-known Noritake pieces are marked with the M in a wreath for the Morimura Brothers, a New York City distributing company. This mark was used until 1941. Another famous Noritake china was made for the Larkin Soap Company from 1916 through the 1930s. This dinnerware, decorated with azaleas, was sold or given away as a premium. There may be some helpful price information in the Nippon category, since prices are comparable.

Ashtray, Figural, Art Deco	85.00
Ashtray, Figural, Bulldog, Red Mark	50.00
Biscuit Jar, Light Green Flowers, Dark Green Ground, Gold, Signed	250.00
Bowl, Fruit, Biltmore, 5 1/2 In.	6.00
Bowl, Pheasants, Painted, Handle, Footed	225.00
Bowl, Squirrel, Blown-Out Peanuts, Luster, 7 In.	225.00
Bowl, Vegetable, Bluebell, Oval, 9 1/4 In.	20.00
Bowl, Vegetable, Cover, Baroda, Oval	25.00
Butter, Flower & Bud Finial	37.00
Butter Chip, Azalea, Red	115.00
Butter Tub, Azalea, Insert	45.00
Cake Plate, Azalea, 9 3/4 In.	40.00
Candy Dish, Girl Feeding Parrot	115.00
Casserole, Cover, Azalea, Gold Finial	315.00
Celery Dish, Colonial Couple, Pastel, Gold Trim	110.00
Celery Dish, Swan	36.00
Chocolate Set, Pink Poppy, Gold Trim, 11 Piece	125.00
Cigarette Holder, & Playing Cards, Lady With Fan, Orange Luster, Red Mark, 4 In.	200.00
Coffeepot, Tree In Meadow, After Dinner ....250.00 to	275.00
Condiment Set, Azalea, 5 Piece	60.00
Creamer, Biltmore	14.00
Creamer, Bluebell	13.00
Cup, Art Deco Woman, 3 Handles	95.00
Cup & Saucer, Tree In Meadow	90.00
Dish, Cracker & Dip, Blue Tree In Meadow, Red Mark	35.00
Eggcup, Azalea	55.00
Finger Bowl, Azalea	25.00
Fish Set, Green Rim, Gold Overlay, Platter, 7 Piece	800.00
Gravy Boat, Bluebell	31.00
Honey Pot, Hydrangeas, Orange Luster Hive, Bees On Outside, 4 In.	75.00
Humidor, Figural, Elk, Orange, Black, 3 1/2 In.	175.00
Humidor, Golfer Scene, Hand Painted, Green M In Wreath, 7 In.	825.00
Luncheon Set, Gold Floral, 21 Piece	750.00
Mayonnaise, Floral, Gold Luster	25.00
Mayonnaise Set, Azalea, 3 Piece	65.00
Mayonnaise Set, Windmill River Scene, Underplate, Spoon, Green Mark, 3 Piece	50.00
Mustard Jar, Cover, Art Deco, Spoon	20.00
Napkin Ring, Art Deco Man	55.00

Plate, Azalea, 6 1/2 In.	15.00
Plate, Azalea, 7 5/8 In.	12.50
Plate, Azalea, Larkin Co., 8 1/2 In.	20.00
Plate, Azalea, Larkin Co., 9 3/4 In.	24.00
Plate, Baroda, 10 1/4 In.	12.00
Plate, Bluebell, 6 1/2 In.	4.00
Plate, Bluebell, 9 3/4 In.	9.00
Plate, Egyptian Man, 7 1/2 In.	65.00
Plate, Lemon, Azalea, Ring, Handle, 5 1/2 In.	24.00
Plate, Pheasant, 7 1/2 In.	25.00
Plate, Portrait, Maidens, Cobalt Blue, Gold, 11 In.	85.00
Plate, Tree In Meadow, 7 1/2 In.	150.00
Plate, Tree In Meadow, 8 1/2 In.	200.00
Plate, Tree In Meadow, Rounded Triangular, 7 1/8 x 7 1/4 In.	35.00
Platter, Azalea, 16 In.	425.00
Platter, White & Gold, Oval, Marked, 16 In.	70.00
Powder Box, Bird Of Paradise, Gold	175.00
Powder Box, Woman In Blue, Gold Bow	275.00
Relish, Azalea, 4 Sections, 10 In.	110.00
Relish, Pheasant, Orange, 2 Sections, 4 x 6 In.	75.00
Salt, Fish, Yellow Rose	28.00
Salt & Pepper, Bluebell	15.00
Salt & Pepper, Chick, Luster, With Tray	32.00
Sauce Set, Minuet, 3 Piece	40.00
Soup, Dish, Azalea, Larkin Co., 7 3/8 In.	20.00
Spooner, Azalea	95.00
Spooner, Blue Iridescent	45.00
Sugar, Cover, Baroda	12.50
Sugar, Cover, Biltmore	19.00
Sugar & Creamer, Azalea, Gold Finial	135.00
Sugar Shaker, Parrots, 6 1/2 In.	35.00
Sugar Shaker, Roseara, 6 1/2 In.	35.00
Tea Set, Gold Birds, Pearlized White	75.00
Tea Set, Yellow, Black, White	150.00
Tray, River Scene, 14 In.	40.00
Trivet, Large Sailing Ship, Square, 5 In.	30.00
Vase, Parrot, 5 1/2 In.	45.00
Vase, Sailing Ship, Palm Trees, Black Elephant Head Handles, 8 3/4 In.	150.00
Vase, Squirrel, Foliage, Dark Gold Luster, Green, Red, 5 In.	115.00
Vase, Tree On Lake, 2 Handles, Green Mark, 6 1/2 In.	68.00
Vase, Trees, Foliage, Rowboat On Lake, Signed, 5 1/2 In.	95.00
Wall Pocket, Peacocks, Relief Mold	135.00

NORSE Pottery Company started in Edgerton, Wisconsin, in 1903. In 1904 the company moved to Rockford, Illinois. The company made a black pottery, which resembled early bronze relics of the Scandinavian countries. The firm went out of business in 1913.

Vase, Geometric, Shoulder Design, Black To Gold Matte Glaze, 4 1/2 In.	121.00
Vase, Lizard Crawling On Shoulder, Gold Traces, 12 1/4 In.	1210.00

NORTH DAKOTA SCHOOL OF MINES was established in 1892 at the University of North Dakota. A ceramic course was included and pieces were made from the clays found in the region. Students at the university made pieces from 1909 to 1949. Although very early pieces were marked *U.N.D.*, most pieces were stamped with the full name of the university.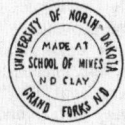

Bookend-Planter, Ivy, Signed	375.00
Bookends, Cable, Signed	350.00
Bowl, Black, Green Stylized Flowers, 1 1/4 x 7 1/4 In.	1045.00
Bowl, Florals, Checkerboard Design, Ruth Rudser, 3 1/2 In.	121.00
Bowl, Incised Leaf Design, Green, 1951, 7 x 4 In.	286.00
Carafe, Sioux Calendar, Turquoise, Julia Mattson	525.00
Lamp, Adjustable Height, Tapered Form, 9 1/2 In.	310.00

Plate, Carved Blue Morning Glories, M. Jacobson, 8 In.	595.00
Vase, Blossoms, Leaves, Tan Ground, Marked, 2 x 4 In.	200.00
Vase, Blue Slate, Signed, Julia Mattson, 4 x 4 1/2 In.	215.00
Vase, Daffodils, Mustard Leaves, Cream, Julia Mattson, 7 In.	775.00
Vase, Deer In Forest Scene, Matte Brown, Ink Mark, 8 In.	360.00
Vase, Floral Design, Brown, Blue Blossoms, Blue Ground, 3 In.	360.00
Vase, Floral Design, Yellow Blossoms, Brown Ground, 4 In.	285.00
Vase, M. Cable, 5 In., Pair	350.00
Vase, Matte Glaze, 9 In.	295.00
Vase, Pale Yellow, Blue Interior, 3 3/4 In.	125.00
Vase, Pilgrim Figures Around, Signed Masser	2450.00
Vase, Pink Blossoms, Green Leaves, Pale Peach Ground, 2 In.	231.00
Vase, Prairie Rose, 8 x 6 In.	295.00
Vase, Ships At Sea, Light Blue Glaze, Ink Mark, 6 In.	286.00
Vase, Stylized Leaves, Signed, D. O'Brien, 8 1/2 In.	550.00
Vase, Tulip Design, Light Green, 1933, 9 In.	357.50
Vase, Tulips, Purple, Brown, Huckfield, 5 x 4 In.	935.00
Vase, Violet, White Ground, Huckfield, 3 1/2 x 3 3/4 In.	495.00
Vase, Wheat Design, 2 1/4 In.	90.00
Vessel, Carved Flowers, Lemtuick, 5 1/2 In.	715.00

NORTHWOOD Glass Company was founded by Harry Northwood, a glassmaker who worked for Hobbs, Brockunier and Company, La Belle Glass Company, and Buckeye Glass Company before founding his own firm. He opened one factory in Indiana, Pennsylvania, in 1896, and another in Wheeling, West Virginia, in 1902. Northwood closed when Mr. Northwood died in 1923. Many types of glass were made, including carnival, custard, goofus, and pressed. The underlined N mark was used on some pieces.

Berry Set, Block, Ruby Red, 7 Piece	65.00
Bowl, Chinese Coral, 9 1/2 In.	75.00
Bowl, Chinese Coral, Orange, Black Footed, No. 678	55.00
Bowl, Ice Cream, Peacock & Urn, Custard	330.00
Bowl, Lattice Medallions, Opalescent, Green, 3-Footed, 9 In.	30.00
Butter, Cover, Leaf Mold, Lime Green	150.00
Celery Dish, Alaska, Green	125.00
Celery Vase, Block, Opalescent Blue Top, 6 In.	45.00
Celery Vase, Block, Opalescent Green Top, 6 In.	25.00
Compote, Wildflower, Green, 6 1/2 In.	45.00
Creamer, Leaf Mold, Spatter	195.00
Creamer, Opalescent, Vaseline	245.00
Creamer, Posies & Pods	70.00
Dish, Fruit, Grape Frieze, 11 In.	150.00
Pitcher, Leaf Umbrella, Mauve	425.00

Never put hot glass in cold water, or cold glass in hot water. The temperature change can crack the glass.

Northwood, Punch Bowl, Memphis, Ice Green, Carnival

Pitcher, Water, Peacock At The Fountain, Marigold, Clear Base 225.00
Plate, Beaded Drapery, Opalescent, Blue, 8 1/4 In. 48.00
Punch Bowl, Memphis, Green Iridescent, Green Base, 11 x 10 In. 330.00
Punch Bowl, Memphis, Ice Green, Carnival . . . . *Illus* 15000.00
Rose Bowl, Beaded Drapery, Blue Opalescent 48.00
Rose Bowl, Leaf Mold, Pink, Yellow, Crimped Top 110.00
Rose Bowl, Royal Ivy, Cranberry To Clear 230.00
Salt & Pepper, Leaf Mold, Vaseline 150.00
Spooner, Leaf Mold, Lime Green 150.00
Sugar, Cover, Leaf Mold, Lime Green 165.00
Sugar Shaker, Blue Opalescent 295.00
Syrup, Leaf Mold, Vaseline 475.00
Toothpick, Leaf Mold, Vaseline 125.00
Tumbler, Memphis, Green, Gilt 45.00
Tumbler, Peach, Green, Gold Trim 18.00
Vase, Basket Weave, Cut Velvet, Satin, Rose To Pale Pink, Pale Yellow Lining, 7 In. 495.00
Vase, Chartreuse & Aqua Swirls, White Lining, Pulled Up, 4 1/4 x 3 5/8 In. 175.00
Vase, Double Gourd, Camphor Leaf Handles, Pink, Yellow & White, 8 1/2 In. 355.00
Vase, Lattice Medallions, 4 In. 45.00
Water Set, Leaf Mold, Vaseline, 5 Piece 550.00

NU-ART see Imperial category.

NUTCRACKERS of many types have been used through the centuries. At
first the nutcracker was probably strong teeth or a hammer. But by the
nineteenth century, many elaborate and ingenious types were made.
Levers, screws, and hammer adaptations were the most popular.
Because nutcrackers are still useful, they are still being made, some in
the old styles.

Admiral Count Von Luckner, Steinbach, 15 1/2 In. 75.00
Dog, Black Paint 38.00
Dog, Black, Green Eyes, Graniteware 95.00
Dog's Head, Glass Eyes, 7 7/8 In. 440.00
Eagle, 19th Century 220.00
Legs, Woman's, Brass 32.00
Man's Head At Top, Painted Red & Gold, Brass Pin, 7 In. 125.00
Perfection, Cast Iron, 1909 . . . .   35.00
Rooster's Head, Brass 45.00
Squirrel, Cast Iron 175.00
Wolf's Head, Chrome, Wooden Base, June 1920 . . . .   80.00

NYMPHENBURG, see Royal Nymphenburg

OCCUPIED JAPAN was printed on pottery, porcelain, toys, and other
goods made during the American occupation of Japan after World War
II, from 1945 to 1952. Collectors now search for these pieces. The
items were made for export.

Ashtray, Chubuchina, Curled Leaf, Gold Trim, 3 In. 60.00
Ashtray, Indian 25.00
Bowl, Bamboo, 10 x 12 In. 20.00
Bowl, Pink Floral Design, Latticed Rim, 6 3/4 In. 20.00
Creamer, Cow, Brown & White 18.00
Creamer, Indian Head 45.00
Eggcup, Humpty Dumpty, Salt Top, Cup Body 120.00
Figurine, Black Baseball Player, 8 In. 95.00
Figurine, Boy & Girl, Porcelain, 6 In. 60.00
Figurine, Boy, Dog, 2 3/4 In. 12.00
Figurine, Colonial Man & Woman, 4 In., Pair . . . . .9.00 to 26.00
Figurine, Colonial Man & Woman, Hands To Head, Bisque, 6 1/4 In., Pair 28.00
Figurine, Colonial Man, 4 In. 8.00
Figurine, Colonial Man, 8 In. 50.00
Figurine, Colonial Woman, 4 In. 14.00
Figurine, Dancers, Pair, 4 In. . . . . .11.00 to 12.00

Figurine, Dutch Girl, Black & White Dog, 3 3/4 In. 8.00
Figurine, Dutch Girl, With Dog, 5 In. 8.00
Figurine, Girl, With Flowers, 2 3/4 In. 12.00
Figurine, Girl, With Puppy & Kitten, 5 3/4 In. 40.00
Figurine, Man, Pipe, 4 1/4 In. 15.00
Figurine, Mermaid, Nude, 4 In. 50.00
Figurine, Newsboy, 5 1/2 In. 40.00
Figurine, Oriental Girl In Pajamas, 3 In. 12.00
Figurine, Roseart, 6 In. 5.00
Figurine, Russian Man Pushing Woman In Sleigh, Dog, 8 In., Pair 125.00
Figurine, Scotty, 3 In. 55.00
Figurine, Uncle Sam, Porcelain, 1940s, 4 1/2 In. 38.00
Hand Warmer, Chrome, Stainless Steel, Blue Cloth Carrying Bag 50.00
Lamp, Colonial Man & Woman, Pair 60.00
Lamp Base, Boy & Girl, 12 In., Pair 75.00
Lighter, Cigarette, Pistol Form, Chrome, Black Handle & Barrel Cover, 3 1/8 In. 75.00
Mug, Indian Chief Head, Handle, 3 In. 45.00
Mug, MacArthur 65.00
Mug, Man, Sulky, Cap & Horse, Gold, Floral Design On Sides 325.00
Pitcher, Little Toby 15.00
Planter, Jack & The Beanstalk 35.00
Plaque, Ducks, 5 1/2 x 3 In. 45.00
Plaque, Shadow Box, Sitting Figures, 5 1/2 x 3 1/2 In., Pair 25.00
Plate, Trees & Brook Scene, 8 In. 22.00
Sake Set, 6 Piece 50.00
Shelf Sitter, Mandarin Girl ....11.00 to 13.00
Shelf Sitter, Oriental Girl In Pajamas 12.00
Strainer, Tea, Metal 10.00
Toby Mug 30.00
Toothpick, Boy, Basket, 4 1/2 In. 25.00
Vase, Dragon, 5 1/2 In. 50.00
Vase, Dragon, 6 1/2 In. 75.00

OHR pottery was made in Biloxi, Mississippi, from 1883 to 1918 by
George E. Ohr, a true eccentric. The pottery was made of very thin clay
that was twisted, folded, and dented into odd, graceful shapes. Some
pieces were lifelike models of hats, animal heads, or even a potato.
Others were decorated with folded clay *snakes*. Reproductions and
reworked pieces are appearing on the market. These have been
reglazed, or snakes and other embellishments have been added.

Bowl, Crimped, 4 Lobed, Speckled Green Glaze Over Orange Clay, Signed, 3 3/4 In. 935.00
Inkwell, Cabin Shape, Quill Hole, Gray Green Glaze, 2 5/8 x 3 3/8 In. 1330.00
Mug, Joe Jefferson, Here's To Your Good Health, Signed, 4 1/4 In. 495.00
Pitcher, Cutout Handle, Interior, Raspberry Glaze, Curdled Blue & Amber, 4 1/2 In. 9350.00
Pitcher, Frog Skin, Green Glaze, Bird-Like Pinched Form, Cutout Handle, 3 In. 855.00
Pitcher, Leathery Raspberry Glaze, Dimpled, Cut-Out Handles, Signed, 4 1/4 In. 210.00
Pitcher, Raised Floral Design, Black, Green Mottled Glaze, 7 x 8 In. 880.00
Pitcher, Red Flambe Glaze, Bulbous, Signed, 5 1/4 x 6 In. 1875.00
Pitcher, Thumbprint Design, Mottled Glaze, Bulbous, Signed, 2 3/4 In. 425.00
Vase, Black, Brown, Crimped Middle, Impressed Mark, 4 x 3 1/2 In. 1000.00
Vase, Brown Exterior Glaze, Cylindrical, Stamped, 4 3/4 x 4 1/2 In. 750.00
Vase, Buff Clay, Folded Rim, Dimpled Body, Squat, Bulbous, Signed, 4 x 5 1/4 In. 775.00
Vase, Egg, Spotted Green, Blue & Purple Glaze, Signed, 10 3/4 In. 10000.00
Vase, Green, Brown Glaze, Flared Form, Signed, 3 In. 260.00
Vase, Matte White Glaze, 4 Deep Dimples At Base, Signed, 4 x 5 1/2 In. 550.00
Vase, Mottled Brown, Green Glaze, Bulbous Base, 6 In. 1850.00
Vase, Mottled Red & Brown Glossy Glaze, Amber Ground, Signed, 4 x 6 1/2 In. 2200.00
Vase, Random Red Spots, Corseted, Looping Ribbon Handles, Signed, 7 3/4 In. 4125.00
Vase, Ruffled & Pinched Rim, Squeeze Pockets, Mirrored Finish, Signed, 6 3/4 In. 3025.00
Vase, Spotted Glaze, Green, Brown, Yellow Interior, Signed, 5 1/2 In. 800.00
Vase, Twist Design, Dark Gray, Black Exterior Glaze, Speckled Red, Tan Interior, 4 In. .. 1035.00
Vase, Volcanic Glaze, Green Over Pink Ground, Dimpled, Signed, 5 x 5 1/4 In. 5500.00

OLD IVORY china was made by Hermann Ohme in Silesia, Germany, at the end of the nineteenth century. The ivory-colored dishes have flowers, fruit, or acorns as decoration and are often marked with a crown and the word *Silesia*. Some pieces are also marked with the words *Old Ivory*. The pattern numbers appear on the base of each piece.

Berry Set, No. 27, Ohme, Silesia, 9 1/2-In. Master, 11 Piece	300.00
Biscuit Jar, No. 16, 8 In.	500.00 to 525.00
Bowl, No. 22, 9 1/2 In.	225.00
Chocolate Pot, No. 16	85.00
Chocolate Set, Clarion, 7 Piece	595.00
Chocolate Set, Silesia, 13 Piece	750.00
Cocoa Set, Syracuse, 3 Piece	40.00
Mustache Cup, Underplate	85.00
Plate, No. 17, Holly, 6 1/2 In.	135.00
Sugar & Creamer, No. 16, Silesia	150.00
Sugar & Creamer, No. 75	165.00
Toothpick, No. 16	195.00

OLD PARIS, see Paris category.

OLD SLEEPY EYE, see Sleepy Eye category.

ONION PATTERN, originally named *bulb pattern*, is a white ware decorated with cobalt blue or pink. Although it is commonly associated with Meissen, other companies made the pattern in the late nineteenth and the twentieth centuries. A rare type is called *red bud* because there are added red accents on the blue-and-white dishes.

Bone Dish, Meissen, 6 Piece	100.00
Bowl, Reticulated, Meissen, 19th Century, 8 1/2 In.	295.00
Compote, 2 Tiers, Blue, Meissen, c.1860, 14 x 9 1/2 In.	1050.00
Compote, Blue, Floral Design, Meissen, 5 x 14 In.	402.00
Cup & Saucer	85.00
Dish, Serving, Blue, Triangular, Meissen, Marked, 11 1/2 In.	150.00
Jar, Condiment, Labeled Oil, Wedgwood, 4 1/2 In.	475.00
Meat Tenderizer, Wooden Handle	200.00
Platter, Blue, Meissen, Crossed Swords, 15 x 21 In.	320.00
Tray & Coaster Set, Windmill Scenes, Blue, Reticulated Rim, Round, 1914, 9 In.	85.00
Tureen, Soup	85.00
Urn, Figural Flower On Cover, Meissen, 15 In.	425.00

OPALESCENT GLASS is translucent glass that has the tones of the opal gemstone. It originated in England in the 1870s and is often found in pressed glassware made in Victorian times. Opalescent glass was first made in America in 1897 at the Northwood glassworks in Indiana, Pennsylvania. Some dealers use the terms *opaline* and *opalescent* for any of these translucent wares. More opalescent pieces may be listed in Hobnail, Northwood, Pressed Glass, Spanish Lace, and other glass categories.

Banana Boat, Jewel & Fan, Blue	38.00
Banana Boat, Jewel & Fan, Green, Opalescent Top	38.00
Basket, Diamond-Quilted, Red, Green Leaves, Crystal Arched Handle, 7 1/4 In.	300.00
Basket, Vaseline Handle & Upright Leaves At Top, 6 In.	115.00
Berry Bowl, Jewel & Flower, Blue	190.00
Berry Bowl, Jewel & Flower, Vaseline, Master	175.00
Berry Bowl, Jewelled Heart, White	45.00
Berry Bowl, Swirl, Blue	295.00
Berry Set, Wreath & Shell, 7 Piece	200.00
Bottle, Bitters, Seaweed, Blue	250.00
Bowl, Alaska, Blue, Ruffled Rim	295.00
Bowl, Crimped Edge, Medallions, Cranberry, 3 3/4 x 7 1/2 In.	150.00
Bowl, Daisy & Plume, Clear To Opalescent Top, 3 Footed, 9 In.	20.00
Bowl, Drapery, Blue Crimped, 8 1/2 In.	45.00
Bowl, Drapery, White Rose, Button Panels	30.00

Bowl, Fan, Green, Square Dome Base, 7 In.	25.00
Bowl, Fluted Scrolls, Vaseline, 3 Footed, 7 1/2 In.	38.00
Bowl, Jackson, 3 Footed	40.00
Bowl, Many Loops, Green, Tricornered	50.00
Bowl, Palm & Scroll, Green To Opalescent Top, 3 Footed, 8 1/2 In.	38.00
Bowl, Roulette, Clear To Opalescent, Dome Footed, 8 1/2 In.	24.00
Bowl, Swirl, Rose, White, Cranberry	65.00
Bowl, Tokyo, Footed, 8 In.	22.00
Bowl, Wheel & Block, Green To Opalescent Top, 6 1/2 x 4 In.	25.00
Bowl, Wild Bouquet, White, 9 1/2 In.	49.00
Bowl, Winter Cabbage	59.00
Butter, Basketweave, Blue	190.00
Butter, Cover, Fluted Scrolls, Blue	260.00
Butter, Cover, Fluted Scrolls, Vaseline	120.00
Butter, Cover, Frosted Leaf & Basketweave, Blue	190.00
Butter, Cover, Iris With Meander, Vaseline	260.00
Butter, Cover, Jewel & Flower, Vaseline	295.00 to 320.00
Butter, Cover, Regal, Blue	245.00
Butter, Cover, Swag With Brackets, Blue	250.00
Butter, Cover, Swag With Brackets, Yellow	275.00
Butter, Cover, Wild Bouquet, Blue	450.00
Butter, Fan, Blue	275.00
Butter, Flora, Blue	275.00
Butter, Iris With Meander, Blue	225.00
Butter, Jewel & Flower, Blue	275.00
Butter, Jewel & Flower, Vaseline	320.00
Butter, Swag With Brackets, Blue	175.00
Butter, Swag With Brackets, Green	60.00
Candy Jar, Hobnail, Green	70.00
Celery Dish, Beatty Honeycomb, Blue	145.00
Celery Dish, Fern, Clear	125.00
Celery Dish, Fern, Cranberry	295.00
Celery Dish, Hobnail, Cranberry	225.00
Celery Dish, Wreath & Shell, Blue	180.00 to 450.00
Celery Vase, Flora, Blue	175.00
Celery Vase, Gonterman Swirl, Blue Crimped, Opalescent Base, Hobbs, 5 5/8 In.	150.00
Compote, Jelly, Circled Scroll, Green	125.00
Compote, Jelly, Diamond Spearhead, Cobalt Blue	180.00
Compote, Jelly, Scroll With Acanthus, Green	38.00
Compote, Loop, Flint, 4 3/4 x 7 In.	95.00
Creamer, Alaska	190.00
Creamer, Alaska, Blue	75.00
Creamer, Beatty Honeycomb, Blue, 3 In.	75.00
Creamer, Dot, Cranberry	85.00
Creamer, Jewel & Flower, Blue	165.00
Creamer, Jewel & Flower, Vaseline	130.00
Creamer, Ribbed Opal Lattice, Cranberry	295.00
Creamer, Wild Bouquet, Blue	135.00
Cruet, Circled Scroll, Green	450.00
Cruet, Intaglio, Blue	130.00
Cruet, Seaweed, Blue, Clear Ball Stopper, 6 In.	220.00
Cruet, Wild Bouquet, Blue	425.00
Epergne, 5 Floral Vases, Chartreuse, Pinched Rigaree Trim, 20 In.	550.00
Epergne, Pink, Coiled Snakes Around Trumpet, Brass Fittings, 24 In.	1250.00
Goblet, Nail, Ruby Stained	95.00
Goblet, Wildflower, Blue	35.00
Jam Jar, Hobnail, Blue	100.00
Lamp, Brass Plated, Electric, Coin Spot Globe	140.00
Lamp, Optic Seaweed, Beaumont Glass Co., c.1890, 7 1/2 In.	1150.00
Lamp, Painted Mermaids Swimming, Waves, Vase Form, 16 1/4 In., Pair	2875.00
Lamp, Student, Wild Rose & Bow Knot, Aqua	150.00
Nappy, Seaweed, Green	45.00
Pitcher, Drapery, Blue To Opalescent Top, 8 In.	100.00

Pitcher, Hobnail, Cranberry 295.00
Pitcher, Inverted Thumbprint, Blue, 9 1/2 In. 200.00
Pitcher, Satin Swirl, Star Crimp, Cranberry 575.00
Pitcher, Seaweed, Cranberry, Triangular Crimped Top 995.00
Pitcher, Tankard, Poinsetta, Blue To Opalescent, 13 In. 360.00
Pitcher, Water, Coin Spot, Cranberry, Crimped 240.00
Pitcher, Water, Intaglio, Blue 325.00
Plate, Spokes & Wheels, Blue, 8 1/2 In. 35.00
Plate, Waterlily With Cat Tails, Clear To Opalescent, 11 In. 45.00
Punch Set, Hobnail, Blue, 15 Piece 475.00
Rose Bowl, Ruffled Top, Button Panels, Blue, Pedestal, 4 1/4 In. 75.00
Salt, Pink, Flared Fluted Top, Striped, Gold Interior, Monot Stumpf, France, 1 1/8 In. ... 65.00
Salt & Pepper, Reverse Swirl, Blue 135.00
Salt & Pepper, Reverse Swirl, Cranberry 175.00
Salt & Pepper, Seaweed, Blue, Bulbous 400.00
Saltshaker, Windows, Cranberry 135.00
Sauce, Argonaut Shell, Blue 40.00
Sauce, Jewelled Heart, Blue To Opalescent Top, 5 1/2 In., 6 Piece 110.00
Sauce, Wreath & Shell, Vaseline 45.00
Spooner, Acorn, Oak Leaf Base 35.00
Spooner, Alaska, Blue 55.00
Spooner, Beatty Swirl, Blue 85.00
Spooner, Diamond Spearhead, Green 140.00
Spooner, Drapery, Blue 95.00
Spooner, Fluted Scrolls, Blue 65.00
Spooner, Hobnail In Square, White 70.00
Spooner, Jewel & Flower, Vaseline 100.00
Spooner, Reverse Swirl, Cranberry 175.00
Spooner, Wreath & Shell, White 55.00
Spooner, Wreath & Wheel, Blue 120.00
Sugar, Cover, Alaska 165.00
Sugar, Cover, Jewel & Flower, Blue 145.00
Sugar, Cover, Palm Beach, Blue 180.00
Sugar, Cover, Reverse Swirl, Blue 185.00
Sugar, Cover, Windows, Cranberry 395.00
Sugar Shaker, Daisy & Fern, Cranberry 395.00
Sugar Shaker, Daisy & Fern, Parian Swirl Mold, Blue 250.00
Sugar Shaker, Reverse Swirl, White 150.00
Sugar Shaker, Ribbed Opal Lattice, Blue 195.00
Sugar Shaker, Ribbed Opal Lattice, Cranberry 250.00
Sugar Shaker, Ribbed Pillar, Cranberry 295.00
Sugar Shaker, West Virginia's Optic, Rose 85.00
Syrup, Coin Spot & Swirl, Blue 200.00
Syrup, Coin Spot & Swirl, White 115.00
Syrup, Daisy & Fern, Blue 245.00
Syrup, Reverse Swirl, Blue 225.00
Syrup, Reverse Swirl, Cranberry 895.00
Syrup, Ring Neck Coin Spot, Blue 200.00
Syrup, Sunk Honeycomb, Ruby Stained 220.00
Table Set, Circled Scroll, Blue, 4 Piece 650.00
Table Set, Circled Scroll, Green, 4 Piece 575.00
Table Set, Fiora, Blue, 4 Piece 610.00
Table Set, Jewel & Flower, Blue, 4 Piece 750.00
Table Set, Tokyo, Blue, 4 Piece 495.00
Table Set, Tokyo, Green, 4 Piece 250.00
Table Set, Wreath & Shell, Blue, 4 Piece 590.00
Toothpicks are listed in the Toothpick category.
Tumbler, Everglades, Blue 70.00
Tumbler, Fluted Scrolls, White 45.00
Tumbler, Hobnail, Cranberry 40.00
Tumbler, Iris With Meander, Vaseline 45.00
Tumbler, Jewel & Flower, Vaseline 70.00

Tumbler, Lattice Medallions, Cranberry 90.00
Tumbler, Swag With Brackets, Vaseline 35.00
Tumbler, Waterlily & Cattails, Blue 40.00
Tumbler, Windows, Cranberry 90.00
Tumbler, Wreath & Shell, Blue 100.00
Vase, Applied Amber Ruffled Leaves, Rose Top, White, 5 3/4 In. 165.00
Vase, Applied Cire Perdu Heads, Chain Band, Yellow, 11 1/2 x 9 7/8 In. 165.00
Vase, Applied Flower & Leaves Front, Green, 15 In. ....425.00 to 450.00
Vase, Applied Flowers, Amber, Pink, White, 6 3/4 In. 77.00
Vase, Applied Flowers, Green To Vaseline, Footed, 10 3/4 In., Pair 425.00
Vase, Boggy Bayou, 11 In. 25.00
Vase, Coin Spot, Vaseline, Lamp Shade Shape, 8 In. 85.00
Vase, Diamond & Oval Thumbprint, White, 14 In. 30.00
Vase, Hobnail, Cranberry, 8 1/2 In. 240.00
Vase, Windows, Ruffled, Cranberry, 5 1/3 In. 295.00
Water Set, Circled Scroll, Blue, 6 Piece 650.00
Water Set, Coin Spot, Blue, 4-Leaf Clover Top, 5 Piece 235.00
Water Set, Everglades, White, 7 Piece 650.00
Water Set, Seaweed, Cranberry, 7 Piece 975.00
Water Set, Tokyo, Green, 7 Piece 250.00

OPALINE, or opal glass, was made in white, green, and other colors.
The glass had a matte surface and a lack of transparency. It was often
gilded or painted. It was a popular mid-nineteenth-century European
glassware.

Bowl, Gilt Monogram, France, 5 In. 46.00
Box, Parcel Gilt Floral Sprays, France, 4 1/2 x 7 1/2 x 4 1/2 In. 430.00
Candlestick, Blue, Gilt Metal Mounted, Pair 430.00
Centerpiece, Trumpet Vase, Alabaster Pink, France, 1860, 27 x 10 1/2 In. 1995.00
Chalice, Lime Green, Gold Design, France, 9 x 6 In. 240.00
Condiment Set, Silver Plated Holder & Lid, England, 6 3/4 x 5 1/4 In. 225.00
Dresser Box, Random Scrolled Edge 85.00
Goblet, Wheel Cut Floral Gold Design, White Enamel Dot Design, 1890, 5 1/2 In. 385.00
Hat Stand, Pink & White, 5 Piece 315.00
Jardiniere, Empire Style, Gilt Bronze, Square, Tasseled Chains, Paw Footed, 5 In., Pair . 1610.00
Lamp, Hanging, Flowers, Brass Chains & Scrolls, Blue Ground, 12 1/4 In. 295.00
Lamp, Oil, Baluster Turned Standard, Blue, Electrified, 22 In., Pair 635.00
Lamp, Oil, Dolphin Form, Clear Glass Oil Well, Frosted Shade, 24 In. 460.00
Perfume Bottle, Blue, Gilt Metal Mounted, 3 Piece 1265.00
Pitcher, High Looped Handle, Bulbous Body, Blue, 12 1/4 In. 230.00
Powder Jar, Blue, Gilt, 6 3/4 x 3 1/4 In. 95.00
Powder Jar, Jade, Pastel Floral, France, 1870s, 7 In. 125.00
Ring Tree, Green, Opaque Edge Around Ruffle, Lacy Gold Scrolls, 5 1/8 In. 110.00
Stein, Floral Enamel, Gold Trim, Blue, 6 In. 2750.00
Tumble-Up, Cut Glass, Panels, Floral, Enamel, 9 In. 495.00
Vase, Blue Threaded Design, 6 In. 260.00
Vase, Portraits Of Dogs, Blue, Pair 460.00

OPERA GLASSES are needed because the stage is a long way from some
of the seats at a play or an opera. Mother-of-pearl was a popular decoration on many French glasses.

Enameled, Hand Painted Floral, Blue Jewels, France 345.00
Lemaire, Multicolored Floral Wreath & Swag Enamel, Case, 3 1/2 In. 345.00
Lemaire, Paris, Mother-Of-Pearl, Brass, Leather Case 75.00
Marchand, Mother-Of-Pearl 120.00
Mignon, Mother-Of-Pearl, With Handle 45.00
Mother-Of-Pearl, 2-Tone 125.00
Mother-Of-Pearl, France 95.00
Mother-Of-Pearl, LaReinee 100.00
Mother-Of-Pearl Inlay, Theaus 50.00
Pearl-In-Gold, Lorgnette Handle, Draw String Silk Case, Colmont, Paris, France 260.00
Scenic Lorgnette 325.00

ORPHAN ANNIE first appeared in the comics in 1924. The redheaded girl and her friends have been on the radio and are still on the comic pages. A Broadway musical show and a movie in the 1980s made Annie popular again and many toys, dishes, and other memorabilia are being made.

Badge, Decoder, Star & Wreath Design, 1938, 2 In.	29.00 to 50.00
Bank, Annie With Sandy, Wooden	45.00
Bank, Wood Lithograph, 5 x 3 1/2 In.	145.00
Book, Drawing & Tracing, McLoughlin, 1932	75.00
Book, Pop-Up, Jumbo The Circus Elephant, 1935, 8 x 9 In.	220.00
Book, Pop-Up, Little Orphan Annie & Jumbo	425.00
Box, Paint & Color, Milton Bradley, Box, 1934, 9 1/2 x 14 1/2 In.	115.00 to 120.00
Bracelet, Identification, 1934	35.00
Bubble Set, Box	75.00
Candy Container, PEZ	50.00 to 60.00
Cup, Ovaltine, Beetleware, Pair	40.00
Decoder Badge, Brass, 1936	38.00
Doll, Annie & Sandy, Composition, Box, 12 & 6 In., Pair	3500.00
Doll, Annie & Sandy, Composition, Jointed, Pair	650.00
Doll, Annie, Knickerbocker, With Book, 1982, 11 In.	40.00
Doll, Composition, Blue Eyes, Original Red Dress, White Collar, 10 In.	280.00
Figurine, Sandy, Bisque, 2 In.	65.00
Game, 12 Standup Character Pieces, Board, Bradley, 1927, 9 x 17 In.	237.00
Game, Dexterity Puzzle	35.00
Game, Treasure Hunt, Board, 1933	25.00
Handbook, Little Orphan Annie Secret Guard	75.00
Lamp, Little Orphan Annie & Sandy, Lights Top & Bottom	95.00
Map, Simmons Corners, Paper, Envelope, 1940s, 19 x 24 In.	55.00
Mug, Orphan Annie & Sandy, Ovaltine	62.00
Mug, Shake-Up, Ovaltine, Beetleware, With Flyer For Shake-Up Game, 1940s	112.00
Mug, Shake-Up, Ovaltine, Leapin' Lizards	31.00
Sheet Music, Ovaltine, 1920s	25.00
Sheet Music, Published By Ovaltine, 1931	45.00
Stand, Tin, Cracker Jack, Small	50.00
Stove, Electric, Marx, 1930s, Box	225.00
Stove, Little Orphan Annie, Non-Electric	85.00
Toothbrush Holder, Orphan Annie & Sandy On Couch	250.00
Toothbrush Holder, Skippy	195.00
Toy, Windup, Marx, Box	650.00
Watch, Sun, Brass, Movable Sundial Pointer, Egyptian Symbols, 1938	75.00
Whistle-Badge, Tin Lithograph, Red, White & Blue, Radio Premium	45.00
Wristwatch, On Watch Face, Tan Leather Strap, New Haven Watch Co.	165.00

ORREFORS Glassworks, located in the Swedish province of Smaaland, was established in 1898. The company is still making glass for use on the table or as decorations. There is renewed interest in the glass made in the modern styles of the 1940s and 1950s. Most vases and decorative pieces are signed with the etched name.

Orrefors

Bowl, Maroon Radiating Stripes, Ariel Footed, E. Ohrstrom, 2 3/4 x 4 1/2 In.	413.00
Bowl, Pinched Spiral Form, Lobed Mouth, Blue, Signed, 4 1/2 In.	115.00
Bowl, Princess, Sven Palmquist, 7 In.	70.00
Bowl, Tooth Ring Design, Amber, Gold Against Blue Ground, Edwin Ohrstrom, 3 In.	575.00
Candlestick, Centerpiece, Double, 7 x 5 3/4 x 3 1/2 In.	65.00
Decanter Set, Engraved Ship, Stopper, Marked, 12 Cordials, 7 1/4 In.	165.00
Dish, Engraved Nude, 6 Sides, Palmquist	295.00
Figurine, Bird On Stump, Olle Alberius, 9 1/2 In.	115.00
Ice Bucket, Chrome Plated Tongs	35.00
Perfume Bottle, Birds In Flight, 4 In.	30.00
Perfume Bottle, Nude Eve With Apple	225.00
Vase, 4 Swimming Fish, Sea Plants, Edward Hald, 7 In.	1100.00
Vase, Apple, Gray Top, Applied Black Neck, Ingeborg Lundin, 1959, 13 x 12 In.	1210.00
Vase, Apple, Yellow Globe Base, Green Top, Ingeborg Lundin, 1955, 13 3/4 In.	3220.00
Vase, Bare Breasted Woman, Reaching High With Flower, Sven Palmquist, 10 1/2 In.	115.00

Vase, Bird, Edvin Ohrstrom, 1944, 5 1/2 In.	1495.00
Vase, Bucket Form, Bright Blue Powders, Applied Black Rim, Signed, 9 3/4 In.	230.00
Vase, Bud, Topaz Interior, Bulbous, 8 1/4 In.	259.00
Vase, Clear Over Circular, Semicircular Design, Cylindrical Form, Signed, 7 3/4 In.	200.00
Vase, Fish, Green, Brown, Graal, Edward Hald, Oval, 5 1/2 In.	575.00
Vase, Girl, With Flower Basket, Etched, Signed, 7 1/2 In.	115.00
Vase, Internal Chameleons & Foliate, Egg Form, Signed, 1951, 6 1/2 In.	2817.00
Vase, Internal Design Of Blue Heads, Girl & Boy, Signed, 1939, 8 1/4 In.	3450.00
Vase, Internal Green Fish & Plant Life, Spherical, Graal, 4 1/4 x 4 In.	495.00
Vase, Kantara, Light Blue Basin, Disk Foot, Nils Landberg, 1950s, 5 x 2 1/2 In.	220.00
Vase, Kantara, Red, Sven Palmquist, 1950s, 5 1/2 x 3 In.	33.00
Vase, Nude Woman By The Sea, Square, 1930, 6 1/2 In.	285.00
Vase, Nude Woman Sitting On Blanket, 7 x 5 In.	195.00
Vase, Nude Woman, Bow, Pheasant & Doe At Feet, Lindstrand, 9 1/4 In.	215.00
Vase, Nude, Woman, Etched, Tapered Body, Lindstrand, 13 1/2 In., Pair	935.00
Vase, Pale Blue, Graduated Squares Design, Signed, 6 1/2 In., Pair	550.00
Vase, Paneled, Cylindrical, Signed & Numbered, 10 In.	145.00
Vase, Paperweight, Underwater Scene, 10 Fish, 4 1/2 In.	585.00
Vase, Peacock, Baluster Shape, Signed, 5 In.	575.00
Vase, Pinched Rim, Cylindrical, Signed, 8 In.	129.00
Vase, Seaweed & Fish Design, Green, Spherical, Edward Hald, 5 In.	460.00
Vase, Slip Graal, Basin, Swirl Pattern Rim, Applied Black Disk Foot, E. Hald, 3 x 3 In.	245.00
Vase, Vertical Bubbles, Applied Clear Foot, Deep Blue, Cylindrical, 1959, 2 1/2 In.	165.00
Vase, Vertical Stripes, Vessel Form, Narrow Neck, Maroon Ground, 1940, 6 In.	750.00
Vase, Young Girl, Looking At Crescent Moon & Stars, 4 1/4 x 6 3/8 In.	70.00

OTT & BREWER Company operated the Etruria Pottery at Trenton, New Jersey, from 1863 to 1893. They started making belleek in 1882. The firm used a variety of marks that incorporated the initials *O & B*.

Cake Plate, Tridacna, Gold Trim, 9 1/2 In.	300.00
Cup & Saucer, Flowers	200.00
Plate, Luster, Gold Rim, 8 In.	150.00
Vase, Butterflies, Leaves, Gold, 7 In.	650.00

OVERBECK pottery was made by four sisters named Overbeck at a pottery in Cambridge City, Indiana. They started in 1911. They made all types of vases, each one-of-a-kind. Small, hand-modeled figurines are the most popular pieces with today's collectors. The factory continued until 1955, when the last of the four sisters died.

Figurine, Large-Footed Strutting Rooster, Red, White & Brown, 3 1/4 In.	275.00
Figurine, Man, With Top Hat & Woman, Flowery Dress, Hat, 5 In.	410.00
Vase, Birds, Feeding In A Vine & Berry Patch, 6 3/4 In.	4400.00
Vase, Carved Bird Medallions, Glossy Gray, 6 1/2 In.	2455.00
Vase, Floral Design, Pink Birds, Blossoms, Brown, White Glossy Glaze Ground, 3 1/2 In.	440.00
Vase, Landscape, 3 Panels, Light Rose Matte Glaze, 5 1/2 In.	4950.00
Vase, Stylized Wooded Landscape, Rose, Dark Brown Lunettes, 5 3/4 In.	2420.00

**Try not to immerse figurines in water.
Many have small holes in the bottom that
will let water get inside. It is difficult to
remove the water and it may drip out and
stain a wooden table or figurine.**

Overbeck, Vase, Trees & Leaves,
Elizabeth & Mary Frances, 11 7/8 In.

Vase, Trees & Leaves, Elizabeth & Mary Frances, 11 7/8 In. . . . .*Illus* 13750.00
Vase, Wizards, Wearing Striped Robes With White Over Green Stars, 7 1/2 In. 5225.00

OWENS Pottery was made in Zanesville, Ohio, from 1891 to 1928. The first art pottery was made after 1896. Utopian Ware, Cyrano, Navarre, Feroza, and Henri Deux were made. Pieces were usually marked with a form of the name *Owens*. About 1907, the firm began to make tile and discontinued the art pottery wares.

Bowl, Aborigine, 12 x 3 In.	165.00 to 195.00
Ewer, Utopian, Floral, 8 In.	100.00
Jug, Corn, Utopian, Signed	295.00
Lamp, Floral, Shaded Brown Ground, 23 In.	88.00
Lamp Vase, Floral, Brown, 8 In.	220.00
Mug, Utopian, Blackberry, Tot Steel, 5 1/4 In.	110.00
Mug, Utopian, Cherries, 5 In.	165.00
Mug, Utopian, Red Cherries, Green Leaves, Virginia Adams, 6 7/8 In.	190.00
Pitcher, Leaves, Berries, Green, Orange Shoulder, Brown, Green Ground, 5 1/2 In.	80.00
Pitcher, Lotus, Stork In Water, Gray To Cream Ground, 6 In.	165.00
Pitcher, Purple Grapes, Green Leaves, Black Ground, 3 1/8 In.	220.00
Pitcher, Wild Roses, Gussie Berwick, 4 In.	175.00
Tankard, Cherries, Spout, 9 1/2 In.	165.00
Tile, Floral, 6 x 6 In.	75.00
Tile, Gnome, Holding Barrel, Arts & Crafts Style Frame, 8 1/4 x 8 1/4 In.	1650.00
Tile, Scenic, 4 Trees, Green Grass, Green Ground, Arts & Crafts, 11 3/4 x 8 3/4 In.	1760.00
Vase, Aborigine, Jug, 9 1/2 In.	315.00
Vase, Feroza, Raised Floral Design, Stylized Blossoms, Gunmetal Glaze, Marked	230.00
Vase, Fruit & Leaves, Dark Brown & Tan Ground, Artist's Initials, 10 1/2 In.	33.00
Vase, Leaf Design, Green, Bronze, Cylindrical, 7 1/2 In.	115.00
Vase, Matte Green, 6 1/2 In.	325.00
Vase, Raised Design, Arts & Crafts, 13 In.	120.00
Vase, Sheaf Of Wheat, Dark Brown, 11 In.	145.00
Vase, Stylized Leaves, Tan Ground, Arts & Crafts, Marked, 7 In.	155.00
Vase, Sudanese, Lily Atop Broad Lily Pad, Dark Brown Glaze, Marked, 7 In.	2385.00
Vase, Transfer Of Young Woman, Pink & White, 11 3/4 In.	245.00
Vase, Utopian, Chrysanthemums, Brown-Gray Ground, Signed, 14 In.	412.00
Vase, Utopian, Grapes, Leaves & Vines, 11 In.	750.00
Vase, Utopian, Matte, Woman Surrounded By Apple Blossoms, 11 3/4 In.	660.00
Vase, Utopian, Red Tulips, Brown Slip, 13 1/2 In.	220.00
Vase, White Glossy Glaze Over Red Clay Body, Impressed Mark, 5 In.	55.00
Vase, Yellow, Brown, Green Flowers, Leaves On Green, Brown Ground, 10 In.	230.00
Wall Pocket, Greenware, 11 In.	775.00

OYSTER PLATES were popular from the 1880s. Each course at dinner was served in a special dish. The oyster plate had indentations shaped like oysters. Usually six oysters were held on a plate. There is no greater value to a plate with more oysters, although that myth continues to haunt antiques dealers. There are other plates for shellfish, including cockle plates and whelk plates. The appropriately shaped indentations are part of the design of these dishes.

5 Wells, Blue & Muted Flowers, Haviland	80.00
6 Wells, Porcelain, Enameled, Union Porcelain Works, Oval, 8 1/3 In., 12 Piece	1840.00
6 Wells, Rose, Turquoise Center, 9 In.	595.00
Bavarian, Grecian	125.00
Enamel Shell & Foliate Design, Gilt Rim, Limoges, Square, 7 3/4 In., 12 Piece	1150.00
Fish Design, Porcelain, 8 1/2 In., 5 Piece	410.00
Floral & Gold, Limoges	145.00
Gold Border, Shell, Carl Ahrenfeldt, c.1900, 9 1/4 In., 4 Piece	242.00
Grecian, Bavarian	125.00
Hand Painted, Violets, White Ground, Gilded Border, Limoges, 9 In.	715.00
Shell & Leaf Relief, Pink Luster, Gold Trim, 8 3/4 In.	50.00
Turkey Design, Limoges, 1880-1890, 8 1/2 In.	295.00
White Ground, Rock, Shell Mold, Stangl, 9 1/4 In. Diam.	500.00

PADEN CITY Glass Manufacturing Company was established in 1916 at Paden City, West Virginia. The company made more than twenty different colors of glass. The firm closed in 1951.

Ashtray, Tulip Green	25.00
Bowl, Black Forest Green, Handle, 9 In.	125.00
Bowl, Crow's Foot, 3-Footed, Red	190.00
Bowl, Crow's Foot, Cobalt Blue, 2 Handles, 9 3/4 In.	150.00
Bowl, Crow's Foot, Red, Square, 11 3/4 In.	100.00
Bowl, Maya Light Blue, Pedestal, 10 In.	85.00
Bowl, Peacock & Wild Rose, Pink, 14 In.	235.00
Candy Dish, Cover, Crow's Foot, Cobalt Blue	175.00
Candy Dish, Cover, Crow's Foot, Square	85.00
Cup, Tulip Green	19.00
Cup & Saucer, Black Forest, Red, 8 In.	295.00
Cup & Saucer, Domino	75.00
Cup & Saucer, Penny, Ruby	22.00
Figurine, Bunny, Ears Down, Frosted Pink	95.00 to 125.00
Figurine, Pheasant, Blue	165.00
Mayonnaise, Gazebo Etched, Footed	30.00
Plate, Sherbet, Tulip Green	12.00
Platter, Caliente, Yellow, 12 In.	15.00
Sherbet, Olive	25.00
Vase, Crow's Foot, Flared, Red, 10 In.	110.00
Vase, Fall Harvest Etched At Rim, Amber, 10 In.	75.00
Vase, Gothic Garden, Pink, 8 In.	190.00
Vase, Lela Bird, 12 In.	210.00
Vase, Lela Bird, Black, 10 In.	155.00 to 175.00
Vase, Peacock & Wild Rose, Pink, 10 In.	175.00
Vase, Utopia Black, 10 In.	195.00
Whiskey, Penny, Ruby	30.00

PAINTINGS listed in this book are not works by major artists but rather decorative paintings on ivory, board, or glass that would be of interest to the average collector. Watercolors on paper are listed under Picture. To learn the value of an oil painting by a listed artist you must contact an expert in that area.

Oil On Board, Arab Head, Malcolm Fraser, 23 1/2 x 16 In.	115.00
Oil On Board, Basket Of Fruit, Primitive, Frame, 18 1/4 x 22 1/4 In.	30.00
Oil On Board, Calm Autumn Day, Mari Lake, J. Wilton, 1909, 15 x 25 In.	77.00
Oil On Board, Farm Scene, A. Gammell, 14 x 18 In.	460.00
Oil On Board, Fox Hunt, Hugh Campbell, 1927, 16 x 18 In.	125.00
Oil On Board, Girl Sledding, G. Morrall, Frame, 14 1/2 x 8 1/2 In.	185.00
Oil On Board, Grandmother With Book, Gilt Frame, 17 1/4 x 13 In.	165.00
Oil On Board, Landscape, Autumn, Woods, Stream, E. Pritchard, 9 x 7 In.	110.00
Oil On Board, Landscape, Hudson River Valley, Gilt Frame, 21 1/2 x 27 1/2 In.	302.00
Oil On Board, Landscape, Impressionist, A. Munson, Gilt Frame, 12 1/2 x 15 1/4 In.	165.00
Oil On Board, Landscape, Road To Town, Marjorie Buel, 20th Century, 10 x 14 In.	110.00
Oil On Board, Landscape, Swamp, American School, 19th Century, 10 x 7 In.	58.00
Oil On Board, Water Nymph, Signed, Paul Swam, 1907, 29 x 17 In.	2860.00
Oil On Board, Winter Day, Marion Gray Travers, 22 x 28 In.	45.00
Oil On Canvas, 2 Men, Examining Shoes, Unsigned, 20th Century, 16 x 12 In.	28.00
Oil On Canvas, 2 Women Repairing Fishing Nets, J. McColvin, Frame, 19 1/2 x 23 In.	55.00
Oil On Canvas, Andreas Canyon, John A. Conner, Frame, 20 x 24 In.	2500.00
Oil On Canvas, Armorial, Col. Austin W. Hogle, Civil War, Gilt Frame, 32 x 27 In.	770.00
Oil On Canvas, Harvesters, Signed, R. Koelman, 38 1/2 x 60 In.	2640.00
Oil On Canvas, He Has Had Too Much Wine, Frame, England, 19th Century, 7 x 6 In.	115.00
Oil On Canvas, Horse & Colt In Barn, Frame, 20 x 24 In.	1100.00
Oil On Canvas, Landscape, Cottage & River, DeVoss, Frame, 31 x 43 In.	138.00
Oil On Canvas, Landscape, Cottage In Woods, Signed, W.H. Hillard, 24 x 16 In.	660.00
Oil On Canvas, Landscape, Dutch, Woman & Farmer, F.S. Sarslov, 1905, 20 x 33 In.	345.00
Oil On Canvas, Landscape, Maine, S.W. Steward, 1913, 21 1/2 x 37 In.	1090.00
Oil On Canvas, Landscape, Mountain, Cottage, American School, 9 3/4 x 13 In.	230.00

Pairpoint, Lamp,
Reverse Painted
Shade,
Controlled
Bubble Base,
14 In.

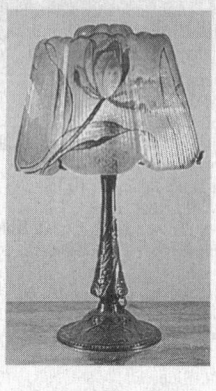

Pairpoint, Lamp,
Reverse Painted,
Tulips, Malta Shade

Oil On Canvas, Landscape, Mountain, Hudson River Valley, Gilt Frame, 19 x 23 In.	275.00
Oil On Canvas, Landscape, Mountains, Lake & Cows, Gilt Frame, 23 3/4 x 34 In.	880.00
Oil On Canvas, Landscape, River, Oval Frame, 22 x 25 3/4 In.	138.00
Oil On Canvas, Landscape, Swampscott Shoreline	935.00
Oil On Canvas, Landscape, Waves Breaking, Rocky Coast, Signed, Ehig, 35 x 45 In. . . .	220.00
Oil On Canvas, Landscape, Winter, Church, Gilt Frame, 16 x 21 In.	138.00
Oil On Canvas, Landscape, Winter, Processional, A. Baumgartner	2530.00
Oil On Canvas, Milking The Cow, A. Reibmayer, Frame, 1906, 12 1/2 x 19 In.	1200.00
Oil On Canvas, Paris Street Scene, Signed, Antoine Blanchard, 12 x 16 In.	4950.00
Oil On Canvas, Portrait, Boy, Holding Birdcage, Gilded Frame, England, 33 x 28 In. . . .	135.00
Oil On Canvas, Portrait, Boy, Pale Blue Coat, Walter Russell, Frame, 24 x 30 1/2 In. . . .	192.00
Oil On Canvas, Portrait, Girl, Blue Dress, Frame, 31 x 27 In.	770.00
Oil On Canvas, Portrait, Mrs. Harriet Young, 1831, 30 x 24 In.	2300.00
Oil On Canvas, Portrait, Old Man & Woman, Oval, 30 x 25 In., Pair	495.00
Oil On Canvas, Portrait, Woman, Black Dress, Bonnet, Gilt Frame, 42 x 34 In.	495.00
Oil On Canvas, Portrait, Young Woman, Baby, Frame, B.W., Dated '97, 20 x 15 In.	125.00
Oil On Canvas, Portrait, Young Woman, Red Hair, Winifred Stimpson, 18 x 14 In.	154.00
Oil On Canvas, Rooster & Hens, M.M. Testori, Frame, 1873, 10 x 16 1/2 In.	1800.00
Oil On Canvas, Seascape, Sailing Ships At Sea, E.K. Redmore, Frame, 18 x 30 In.	1610.00
Oil On Canvas, Seascape, Scene Of Rockport Harbor, Pauline Bliss, 14 x 16 In.	82.00
Oil On Canvas, Seascape, Seacoast, Crashing Waves, O. Merkel, 15 1/2 x 19 1/2 In.	515.00
Oil On Canvas, Seascape, Ship Entering Harbor, Signed H.T.M., Frame, 1891	2200.00
Oil On Canvas, Soldier, American Flag, Crazed, Regilded Frame, 36 x 31 In.	935.00
Oil On Canvas, Spring Love, Signed, Jane Bacon, 18 x 26 In.	1100.00
Oil On Canvas, Still Life, Bowl, Pitcher & Fruit, R. Stawn, Sep. 1878, 19 1/4 x 25 In. . .	192.00
Oil On Canvas, Still Life, Continental, Frame, 19th Century, 29 x 39 1/2 In.	545.00
Oil On Canvas, Still Life, Pansies, Gilt Frame, 13 3/8 x 16 3/8 In.	275.00
Oil On Canvas, Still Life, Pastel Flowers, Signed Eugene Bell, Gilt Frame, 28 x 34 In. . .	330.00
Oil On Canvas, Still Life, Roses In Pitcher, Gilt Frame, 21 x 24 In.	165.00
Oil On Canvas, Still Life, Vase Of Flowers, M.B. Holmboe, Frame, 42 x 36 In.	143.00
Oil On Canvas, The Beginning, Signed On Back, June Kingburne, 40 x 36 In.	230.00
Oil On Canvas Board, Landscape, Sawkill Creek, Winter, Signed, Samuel B. Wylie . . .	55.00
Oil On Panel, Portrait, Young Woman, Whitney Hubbard, 1906, 13 x 11 In.	110.00
On Celluloid, Portrait, Mozart, Handel, Haydn & Bach, Period Frame	1295.00
On Ivory, Madonna & Child, Raphaello, Frame, 4 x 3 1/4 In.	900.00
On Ivory, Portrait, Charlotte Hagn, Brass Frame, 2 7/16 x 3 5/16 In.	365.00
On Ivory, Portrait, Elegant Young Woman, Holding Portrait Of Her Beau, 3 In.	155.00
On Ivory, Portrait, Gentleman With High Collar Coat, Asstug, Brass Frame, 3 x 3 In. . . .	290.00
On Ivory, Portrait, Lady With Flowers, Doistcau, Brass Frame, 2 13/16 x 3 1/8 In.	385.00
On Ivory, Portrait, Lady With Rose In Hair, Brass Frame, Signed, Ross, 2 x 3 3/16 In. . . .	445.00
On Ivory, Portrait, Marie Louise, Signed AF, Wooden Frame, 1 3/16 In.	365.00
On Ivory, Portrait, Napoleon, Frame, 3 3/8 x 2 1/2 In.	350.00
On Ivory, Portrait, Napoleon, Gilt Bronze Shield Frame, Eagle, Continental, 3 In.	920.00
On Ivory, Portrait, Regal Woman, Gilt Brass Frame, 8 3/4 In.	319.00
On Ivory, Portrait, Sea Captain, Seated, Telescope In Hand, Brass Frame, 6 3/8 In.	1320.00

On Ivory, Portrait, Woman, Velvet & Gilded Metal Frame, Watercolor, 2 1/2 In., Pair ...   445.00
On Ivory, Portrait, Woman, With Flowers, Bronze Frame, Oval, 2 1/2 In. 300.00
On Ivory, Portrait, Woman, With Necklace, Oval, 2 1/2 In. 300.00
On Ivory, Portrait, Young Girl, Blond Hair, Red Dress, Memoriam, Gold Case, 2 In. 440.00
On Ivory, Portrait, Young Man With Stickpin, Wooden Frame, 1 7/8 x 2 1/4 In. 325.00
On Ivory, Portrait, Young Man, Gutta Percha Frame, Death, 1/17/58, Artist, 5 x 5 In. 298.00
On Panel, Seascape, Sailing Ship At Sea, British School, Frame, 5 x 7 1/2 In. 230.00
On Porcelain, Military Figure, Continental, 19th Century, 3 1/4 x 2 3/4 In. 3910.00
On Porcelain, Portrait, Josephine, O. Grun, Gilded Frame, 14 1/4 x 14 1/4 In. 1017.00
On Porcelain, Scene Of Women Digging Potatoes, Gilt Frame, Signed, 16 x 22 In. 550.00
On Tin, Madonna & Child, Surrounded By Halo Of Roses, 14 x 10 In. 231.00

PAIRPOINT Manufacturing Company started in 1880 in New Bedford,
Massachusetts. It soon joined with the glassworks nearby and made
glass, silver-plated pieces, and lamps. Reverse-painted glass shades
and molded shades known as *puffies* were part of the production until
the 1930s. The company reorganized and changed its name several
times but is still working today. Items listed here are glass or glass and
metal. Silver-plated pieces are listed under Silver Plate.

Basket, Art Nouveau Style, Cherry Fixed Handle, Ruffled Edge, Marked 66.00
Bowl, Green, Crystal Controlled Bubble Ball Connector, Footed, 10 In. 85.00
Bowl, Green, Footed, 10 In. 115.00
Bowl, Murillo, Leaves, Butterfly, Tulip, Crocus, 1910, 8 3/4 In. 165.00
Bowl, Myrtle, 9 3/4 In. 450.00
Box, Heart Shape, Crystal, 3 1/2 x 6 In. 595.00
Box, Jewelry, Gold Spider Mums, Green & White, Gold Trim, 1894, 5 In. 350.00
Bread Tray, Murillo, Large Butterflies On Ends, Flowers Fill Body, Oval, 9 x 6 3/4 In. ...   155.00
Cake Basket, Fretwork, Lovebirds, Center Cherries & Leaf, Floral Turned Feet 225.00
Candlestick, Blackberry Cut, Amber, 12 In., Pair 550.00
Candlestick, Grape Design, Cobalt Blue, Ball Connector, 10 3/4 In. 632.00
Candlestick, Hollow Stem, Green, 9 In. ....80.00 to 95.00
Candlestick, Peonies, Opal, Silver Overlay, Art Nouveau, 9 1/2 In., Pair 1250.00
Carafe, Sparkle 325.00
Compote, Canary Yellow, Clear, Controlled Bubble Ball Connector 110.00
Compote, Cover, Ruby, Controlled Bubble Ball Connector, Finial, 10 In. 195.00
Compote, Green, 6 1/2 In. ....40.00 to 55.00
Compote, Yellow, 4 1/2 In. 85.00
Console Set, Flambo, Red, Black Foot, 1915, 12-In. Bowl, 3 Piece 1950.00
Console Set, Potato Glass, Red, Green & White Flowers, 12-In. Bowl, 3 Piece 575.00
Cornucopia, Amethyst, Controlled Bubble Ball Connector, 11 In. 125.00
Cracker Jar, Gold Ivy Leaves, Beige Ground, Silver Plated Cover, 7 1/2 In. 750.00
Cracker Jar, Puffy Leaves, Spider Mums, Adolph Frederick, 7 3/4 In. 1150.00
Cracker Jar, Roses, Pistachio Top & Base, Silver Plated Cover & Bail, 6 3/4 In. 725.00
Decanter, Urn With Flame, Flame Stopper, Small 250.00
Gravy Boat, Scroll, Multicolored Dresden Flowers, Underplate, Handle, 2 Piece 175.00
Humidor, Scroll, Delft Design, Silver Plated, Hinged Cover, 5 1/2 In. 950.00
Lamp, 2-Light, Controlled Bubble Connector & Top, Marble Base, 13 1/2 In., Pair 605.00
Lamp, 3-Light, Directoire Shade, Tan Scrolls, Marble Base, Bobeches, 26 In. 2970.00
Lamp, Blue, Gray, Milk Glass, Acorn Burner, 8 1/4 In. 660.00
Lamp, Butterflies, Trees, 9 1/2 In. 2200.00
Lamp, Hurricane, Textured Glass Shade, Cylindrical, 17 In. 550.00
Lamp, Puffy, Chrysanthemums, Millefiori Scrolling, 16 In. 7475.00
Lamp, Puffy, Papillon Shade, Yellow, Pink Wild Roses Border, Blue, 16 In. 2990.00
Lamp, Puffy, Papillon, Butterflies, Red Rose Shade, Gilt Floral Swag Base, 14 In. 8050.00
Lamp, Puffy, Pilgrims, Blossom Wreaths, Red, Yellow, White Strips, 23 1/2 In. 9200.00
Lamp, Puffy, Red Rose Bouquet, Red Maroon Blossoms, Leafy Green, 21 1/2 In. 11500.00
Lamp, Puffy, Rose Bonnet, 14 In. 44000.00
Lamp, Puffy, Rose Tree, 8 In. ....4200.00 to 4500.00
Lamp, Reverse Painted River Town Shade, Urn Base, Signed, 10 In. 1540.00
Lamp, Reverse Painted Shade, Controlled Bubble Base, 14 In. ....*Illus*   1650.00
Lamp, Reverse Painted, 2 Peacocks, Floral Design, Black Ground, 20 In. 2200.00
Lamp, Reverse Painted, Etched, Shade, Iron Base, Electrified, Art Deco 960.00
Lamp, Reverse Painted, Flared Glass Shade, Green, Red, Yellow Amber Floral, 26 In. 2300.00

Lamp, Reverse Painted, Floral, Birds, Patinated Base, Signed, c.1900, 21 In. 3165.00
Lamp, Reverse Painted, John & Priscilla Alden 1 Side, Mayflower Other, 14 In. 9200.00
Lamp, Reverse Painted, Landscape Scene, Waterfront Building, 17 In. 2645.00
Lamp, Reverse Painted, Rose Bouquet Shade, Brass Base, c.1915, 13 In. 8625.00
Lamp, Reverse Painted, Rows Of Floral Medallions, Gilt Base, c.1915, 20 1/2 In. 2185.00
Lamp, Reverse Painted, Ships, Boston Harbor, Pink, Blue Frosted Ground, 22 In. 2000.00
Lamp, Reverse Painted, Summer Rural Landscape, Urn Base, C.Durand, 12 x 18 In. 1815.00
Lamp, Reverse Painted, Tulips, Malta Shade . . . .*Illus*   2550.00
Lamp, Reverse Painted, Venetian Harbor Scene, Beige Ground, Rim, Seville, 23 In. 1925.00
Lamp, Ribbed Puffy, Roses, Brass Base, 21 In. 3630.00
Lamp, Stylized Green Trees Against Red, Orange Ground, 14 In. 230.00
Lamp, Stylized Olive Green Leaves, Red Berries, Coraline Yellow Interior, 22 In. 2100.00
Lamp, Tourraine, Pink Wild Rose Design, Green Scrolls, Green Ground, 19 In. 3200.00
Lamp, Vassar Glass Shade, Floral Medallions, Square, 6 1/2 x 6 1/2 In. 1035.00
Lamp, Venetian Harbor Scene, 2 Handles, Vasiform Base, Bronze, Signed, 22 1/2 In. 3680.00
Paperweight, Rose Colored Serpent, Opalescent Footed Sphere, Signed 125.00
Paperweight, Rose Serpent, Footed, Signed 250.00
Sugar & Creamer, Murillo, Butterflies, Stylized Leaves, Handles, 6 In. 190.00
Toothpick, Buffalo 250.00
Toothpick, Girl On Turtle 595.00
Toothpick, This Is The Rat That Ate The Malt 110.00
Tray, Myrtle, Oval, 13 3/4 x 9 3/4 In. 1550.00
Urn, Marina Blue, 2 M Handles, 12 In. . . . . .195.00 to 295.00
Vase, 18th Century Garden Scene, Pale Blue, 11 In. 395.00
Vase, Black Enameled Sailing Ship, On Wavy Sea, 6 In. 385.00
Vase, Blue, Controlled Bubble Ball Connector, 17 In. 250.00
Vase, Bright Cut Floral Design, Trumpet Shape, Pedestal Base, 14 1/2 In. 488.00
Vase, Chalice, Fluted, Double Knob Stem, Burmese Glass, 1920s, 10 1/4 In. 850.00
Vase, Colias, Butterfly In Spider Web, Oval, 11 1/4 In. 345.00
Vase, Engraved, Controlled Bubble Ball Connector, Marble, Silver Base, 21 In. 1275.00
Vase, Irma, Puffy, 10 In. 295.00
Vase, Pink & White Poppies, Mottled Green Ground, 24 In., Pair 950.00
Vase, Ruffled Edge, Parrot Medallions, Black Amethyst, Trumpet Shape, 9 In. 517.50

PALMER COX, BROWNIES, see Brownies category.

PAPER collectibles, including almanacs, catalogs, children's books,
stock certificates, and other paper ephemera, are listed here. Paper calendars are listed separately in the Calendar Paper category.

Album, Pictorial, Ashbury Park, 1905 . . . .   25.00
Album, Pictorial, Hot Springs, Arkansas, 1904 . . . .   25.00
Album, Pictorial, Sevilla Exposition 20.00
Almanac, W.C.T.U., 1903 . . . .   20.00
Bond, Pittsburg Ice Co., Engraved Vignettes, Polar Bear 35.00
Bond, United States Confederate, With Coupons, Face Value 500.00, 34 x 22 In. 100.00
Book, ABC, Father Tuck's, Linen 35.00
Book, Big Little Book, Charlie Chan, Villainy On High Seas 35.00
Book, Big Little Book, Ellery Queen, Adventure Of Last Man Club 30.00
Book, Big Little Book, Houdini's Magic 40.00
Book, Big Little Book, Space Ghost, Hanna Barbera, 1968 . . . .   25.00
Book, Big Little Book, Tailspin Tommy 40.00
Book, Coloring & Activity, Brady Bunch 10.00
Book, Coloring, Barbie, Ballerina, Whitman 6.00
Book, Coloring, Bat Masterson, 1952, Pair . . . .*Illus*   63.00
Book, Coloring, Bing Crosby, 1951 . . . .   57.00
Book, Coloring, Bob Hope, 1954 . . . .   57.00
Book, Coloring, Bonanza, 1957 . . . .*Illus*   37.00
Book, Coloring, Bonanza, 1958 . . . .*Illus*   58.00
Book, Coloring, Bronco, 1959 . . . .   32.00
Book, Coloring, Cisco Kid, Saalfield, 1951 . . . .*Illus*   37.00
Book, Coloring, Colt .45, Cover Proof, 1950s, 9 x 11 In. 53.00
Book, Coloring, Fess Parker, Color Chart At Top Border, Cover Proof 92.00
Book, Coloring, John Wayne, Cover Proof, 1951 . . . .   184.00

Book, Coloring, My Little Margie, 1954 .... 35.00
Book, Coloring, Ozzie & Harriet, 1954 .... 48.00
Book, Coloring, Ozzie & Harriet, 1955 .... 42.00
Book, Coloring, Porky Pig, Saalfield, 1938 .... 69.00
Book, Coloring, Tom Corbett Space Cadet, 1952 ....*Illus* 130.00
Book, Golden Book, Mickey Mouse's Picnic 18.00
Book, Peter Pan & Wendy, 12 Mabel Lucie Attwell Color Plates, 1923 .... 135.00
Book, Pop-Up, Mother Goose 38.00
Book, Pop-Up, Nightmare Christmas 35.00
Book, Raggedy Ann, In The Deep Deep Woods, Dust Jacket 85.00
Catalog, Adriance Platt & Co., Poughkeepsie, N.Y., 1888, 16 Pages, 6 x 9 1/4 In. 63.00
Catalog, Ames & Frost Co., Imperial Bicycles, Chicago, Ill., 1897 .... 38.00
Catalog, Anheuser-Busch Brewing Co., St. Louis, Mo., 1914, 3 Pages, 5 1/2 x 8 1/2 In. .. 31.00
Catalog, Bausch & Lomb Binoculars, 1930, 30 Pages 18.00
Catalog, Bausch & Lomb Optical Co., Rochester, N.Y., 1911, 40 Pages, 6 1/2 x 9 3/4 In. .. 113.00
Catalog, Belcher & Taylor, 1910, 14 Pages 75.00
Catalog, Bella Hess, Full Line Fashion, Fall-Winter, 1922, 284 Pages 90.00
Catalog, Bradley Knitwear, Swimsuits, Sweaters, 21 Pages, Color, 1925 .... 18.00
Catalog, Calendar Sporting Goods Co., St. Paul, Minn., 48 Pages, 1938 .... 50.00
Catalog, Chicago & Erie Stove Co., Erie, Pa., 1890, 110 Pages, 5 3/4 x 8 1/4 In. 48.00
Catalog, Cleveland Bicycle, Lozier & Co., Cleveland, Oh. 38.00
Catalog, Columbian Planter Co., Springfield, Oh., 1923, 54 Pages, 4 x 9 In. 18.00
Catalog, Deering Farm Equipment Co., 1895, 32 Pages 60.00
Catalog, Ed Howes Greatest Bargain Book, Outdoor Equipment, 1939, 80 Pages 45.00
Catalog, F.A.O. Schwarz, Christmas 1960, 98 Pages, 11 In. ....*Illus* 50.00
Catalog, F.A.O. Schwarz, Christmas, 1962, Centennial Celebration, 102 Pages 35.00
Catalog, Gilbert Christmas Toy, No. 4, 1927 .... 45.00
Catalog, Goodell-Pratt Co., 1500 Good Tools, Illustrations, 1920 .... 30.00
Catalog, Guns Hunting Equipment, No. 1939, 32 Pages, 7 1/2 x 9 In. 50.00
Catalog, H.T. Cushman Mfg. Co., N. Bennington, Vt., Humidors & Tables, 1927 .... 44.00
Catalog, J.C. Christmas Sale, Clothing, Gifts, Toys, 1929, 32 Pages 50.00
Catalog, Kaywoodie, Pipe, 1937 .... 35.00
Catalog, Kresge's Christmas Gift Guide, Newsprint Type, 1957, 24 Pages 8.00
Catalog, Kyle & Co. Steel Products, Spiral Bound, 1947, 288 Pages 18.00
Catalog, L.L. Bean, Spring, Fishing Tackle, Clothing, 1940, 72 Pages 50.00
Catalog, Macy's Department Store, 1909, 446 Pages ....55.00 to 75.00
Catalog, Macy's, Spring, 1906 .... 60.00
Catalog, McCall, Dressmaker, 1903 .... 18.00
Catalog, McCormick Harvesting Machine Co., 1897, 42 Pages 200.00
Catalog, Medicinal Formulas, Henry Thayer Co., Cambridgeport, Ma., 1884, 276 Pages . 35.00
Catalog, Mighty Chrysler, 1957 .... 20.00
Catalog, Montgomery Ward & Co., Fall & Winter, Portland, Or., 1967, 1364 Pages 35.00
Catalog, Montgomery Ward, Christmas, 1953 .... 35.00

Paper, Book, Coloring, Bonanza, 1957
Paper, Book, Coloring, Bonanza, 1958
Paper, Book, Coloring, Bat Masterson, 1952, Pair, I shown

>
>
> **If old glue, paste, or even
> the new stick-on notes are
> left on paper items, stains
> will eventually appear.**

Paper, Book, Coloring, Tom Corbett Space Cadet, 1952
Paper, Book, Coloring, Cisco Kid, Saalfield, 1951

Catalog, Montgomery Ward, Sept.-Oct. Groceries, 1910, 74 Pages	40.00
Catalog, Montgomery Ward, Spring-Summer, No. 82, 1914, 272 Pages	100.00
Catalog, Pierce, Butler & Butler, Bathroom Fixtures, 1903, 60 Pages	80.00
Catalog, Pittsburgh Pump Co., Iron, Force, Wood, 1895, 100 Pages	75.00
Catalog, RCA Victor Phonograph Records, 1940, 612 Pages	50.00
Catalog, Richardson Manufacturing, Worcester, Ma., 1897, 14 Pages, 7 x 8 1/2 In.	31.00
Catalog, Ritter Dental Equipment, 1919, 110 Pages	75.00
Catalog, S & H Green Stamp Redemption, General Merchandise, 1975, 148 Pages	20.00
Catalog, Savage, 1932, Arms & Ammunition, 28 Pages, 7 1/2 x 9 1/2 In.	103.00
Catalog, Sears Roebuck, Concrete Machinery, 1920s	25.00
Catalog, Sears Roebuck, Your Grocery Store, Groceries, October, 1918, 66 Pages	40.00
Catalog, Sears, 1933, Spring & Summer	75.00
Catalog, Sears, 1935, Fall & Winter	85.00
Catalog, Sears, 1946, Spring & Summer	25.00
Catalog, Sears, 1960, Christmas Book, 482 Pages, 11 x 8 In. .... *Illus*	105.00
Catalog, Siegel Cooper Co., New York, N.Y., Clothes, 1909, 24 Pages, 6 3/4 x 9 In.	19.00
Catalog, Standard Oil Co., Oil Heaters, 1914, 16 Pages, 3 1/4 x 6 In.	11.00
Catalog, Stanley Tool Guide, 1941, 32 Pages, 11 x 12 In.	30.00
Catalog, Star Wars, Kenner, 1979	125.00
Catalog, Taylor Instruments Co., Rochester, N.Y., Barometer, 1911, 40 Pages	22.00
Catalog, Universal Electric Appliances, 1940, 40 Pages	22.00
Catalog, Victor Records, Phonograph Records, 3/4-In. Thick, 1924	50.00
Catalog, Victor Sarasqueta, Firearms, 72 Pages, 9 3/4 x 6 1/2 In.	56.00
Catalog, Wanamaker's, Summer, 1887, 500 Pages	250.00
Catalog, Wichita Sash & Door Co., Garden, Gates, Kitchens, Stairways, 1927, 356 Pages	25.00
Catalog, Wild-Flower Decoy, 20 Fold-Out Pictures, 1951	650.00
Catalog, Winchester Repeating Arms, No. 78, 212 Pages	200.00
Certificate, Ave Maria Gold Quartz Mine, English For California Mine, 1852	295.00
Check, Wells Fargo, Virginia City, Nev., 1863	75.00
Directory, Boston, Hard Cover, 1856	55.00
Family Register, Mary M. Rockwood, Frame, 1803, 19 x 23 In.	495.00
Fraktur, Birth & Baptism, Printed, Scheffer, Harrisburg, Pa., Frame, 18 x 14 In.	70.00
Fraktur, Birth Certificate, Watercolor, Chip Carved Frame, 1828, 9 x 7 In.	9775.00
Fraktur, Elias Hetterich, Born 1815, Pin Prick, Tulips, Birds, 12 x 15 In.	2860.00
Fraktur, Floral Wreath, 1791 Birth, Pen, Ink, Watercolor, Germany, Matted, 8 x 12 In.	770.00
Fraktur, Geburts & Tauf-Schein, Henrich Weiss, Hymn, Tulips, Frame, 1790, 12 x 16 In.	2860.00
Fraktur, Maria Schultz, Schwenkfelder, Tulips, Flowers, 6 1/2 x 7 7/8 In.	4180.00
Fraktur, Orange & Yellow Parrots, Tulips, Signed Krebs, 1807, 16 x 19 In.	4000.00
Fraktur, Pennsylvania Dutch, Maria Schultz, Flowers, 6 1/2 x 7 7/8 In.	4180.00
Fraktur, Watercolor On Laid Paper, Framed, Frederick Krebs, Birth, 1797, 16 x 19 In.	495.00
Geburts & Tauf-Schein, Samuel Keller, Born 1805, Montgomery Co., 13 x 16 In.	135.00
Greeting Card, 35th Anniversary, Henry & Edsel Ford, Photograph, 1938	14.00
Greeting Card, Valentine, 16 Verses, Folded, Frame	1760.00
Greeting Card, Valentine, Car, Riders, Accordion Crepe Paper, Fold-Out, 10 x 6 In.	33.00
Greeting Card, Valentine, Children, With Cameras, Embossed	24.00

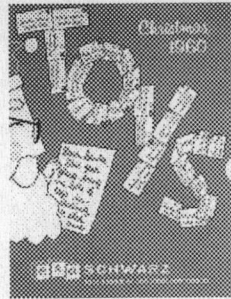

Paper, Catalog, F.A.O. Schwarz, Christmas
1960, 98 Pages, 11 In.

Paper, Catalog, Sears, 1960, Christmas
Book, 482 Pages, 11 x 8 In.

Greeting Card, Valentine, Cut Paper Hand, Silver Heart, Wedding Band, 8 x 6 In.	200.00
Greeting Card, Valentine, Dove Cottage, Accordion Fold	45.00
Greeting Card, Valentine, Fold-Out, Ship, House On Top, Boy & Girl, Germany, 1920s	140.00
Greeting Card, Valentine, Locomotive, Accordion Fold	95.00
Greeting Card, Valentine, Motorcycle With Sidecar, Accordion Fold	75.00
Greeting Card, Valentine, Popeye & Maggie, 1930s, Pair	45.00
Land Deed, Vellum, Red Wax Seals, England, 2 Pages, Dated 1707, 23 x 30 In.	175.00
Magazine, Life, Hawaii Edition, 1965	10.00
Magazine, Life, Marilyn Monroe On Cover, 1959	20.00
Magazine, Life, Raquel Welsh On Cover, 1972	12.00
Magazine, Look, Bob Hope, Bing Crosby On Cover, 1947	20.00
Manual, Technical, Star Trek, 1st Edition	70.00
Menu, Denver & Rio Grande Luncheon, Colorado Mountains, 1953	5.00
Program, Buffalo Bill Cody Wild West Show, 1885	250.00
Program, Globe Theatre, George White's Scandals, 1922	48.00
Program, Live Oak Union High School Commencement, Calif., June 10, 1926, 4 Pages	11.00
Stock Certificate, Bullfrog Mining, Nevada, Signed By Banker & John Cook, 1906	185.00
Stock Certificate, La France Copper Co., Gold Bond, 4 Corner Vignettes, 1905	20.00
Stock Certificate, Lake Copper Co., Woman On Pedestal, Men Behind Her, 1920s	130.00
Stock Certificate, Million Dollar Saloon, 3 Scantily Dressed Women, 1990s	30.00
Stock Certificate, Nevada, Goodman Gold & Silver Mining Co., 1877	145.00
Stock Certificate, Sperry Corp., Cockpit, Battleship & Biplane, 1950s	36.00
Ticket, Theater, Caruso, Dated May 22, 1911	20.00

PAPER DOLLS were probably inspired by the pantins, or jumping jacks, made in eighteenth-century Europe. By the 1880s, sheets of printed paper dolls and clothes were being made. The first paper doll books were made in the 1920s. Collectors prefer uncut sheets or books or boxed sets of paper dolls. Prices are about half as much if the pages have been cut.

3 Cheers, High School, Abbott, Uncut	15.00
4 Playmates, Lowe, 1940, Uncut	18.00
Amy Carter, Box	32.00
Annette Funicello, 1956, Cut	75.00
Archie, 1969, Uncut	35.00
Barbarino, Toy Factory, 1976	22.00
Barbie, Boutique, Whitman, 1973, Uncut	15.00
Barbie, Design A Fashion, Whitman, 1979	10.00
Barbie, Design A Fashion, Whitman, 1982	12.00
Barbie, Press-Out, Christmas, 1989	10.00
Barbie & Ken, Sun Valley Wardrobe, Whitman, 31 Piece, Uncut	15.00
Barbie & P.J., Fashion Photo, Whitman, Uncut	15.00
Barbie & Skipper, Campsite At Lucky Lake, Whitman, Playbook, 1980, Uncut	12.00
Betsy McCall, 16 Sheets, Uncut	55.00
Betsy McCall, 1971, Uncut	32.00

Blondie T.V. Show, 1958 .... 40.00
Book, Queens, Saalfield, 1944, Uncut 30.00
Brady Bunch, 1973 TV Show, Whitman, Uncut 45.00
Buffy 45.00
Carol Burnett, Cut 10.00
Charlie's Angels, Jill, Uncut 35.00
Chatty Twins, Cut 35.00
Circus, Uncut, 1974 .... 55.00
Dodi, Pepper's Friend, Uncut 45.00
Doris Day, Whitman Publishing Co., 1955, Cut 125.00
Elizabeth Taylor, 2 Dolls, Clothes, Whitman Publishing, 1955, Cut ... 125.00
Fluffy Ruffles, 1907, Cut 125.00
Gone With The Wind, 18 Dolls, 58 Outfits, 1920s, Cut 300.00
Imperial Granum Baby Food, Cloth, 1917, Uncut 85.00
Little Lulu, 1971, Uncut 32.00
Little Red Riding Hood, Grandma & Wolf, Lion Coffee, Envelope ... 55.00
Martha Washington's Doll Book, Whitman, Spiral Bound Book, 1945, Uncut ... 45.00
Mary Martin, Saalfield, 1944 .... 60.00
Mouseketeer, Book, 1957 .... 22.00
My Fair Lady, 1965, Uncut 30.00
Nancy, 1971, Uncut 32.00
Nancy & Sluggo, Whitman, 1974, Uncut 30.00
Nancy & Sluggo, Whitman, Book, 1979 .... 20.00
Natalie Woods, 1957, Cut 35.00
Navy & Marine Girls, World War II, Uncut 35.00
Opie Taylor, Cut 27.00
Partridge Family, Art Craft, 1972, Uncut 55.00
Partridge Family, Susan Dey, Saalfield, 1972, Uncut ....55.00 to 60.00
Platt & Munk, Early American, Box, 1963 ....25.00 to 30.00
Raggedy Ann, 1966, Cut 28.00
Raggedy Ann & Raggedy Andy, 1944, Uncut 73.00
Rhonda Fleming, With Coloring Book, Uncut 50.00
Sheet, Decalco Litho Co., Hoboken, N.J., 2 Dolls, 1912, 8 x 11 In. ... 18.00
Skookum, 7 In., Pair, Uncut 115.00
Star Trek, Crew, Control Room, Communicator, 1975, Uncut 90.00
That Girl, 1967, Uncut 38.00
Tricia Nixon, Book With White House Game, Saalfield, 1970, Uncut ... 35.00
Two-Gun Pete, Milton Bradley, Magnet, 1950s 36.00
Walter Lantz Cartoon Stars, 1963 .... 30.00

PAPERWEIGHTS must have first appeared along with paper in ancient
Egypt. Today's collectors search for every type, from the very expensive French weights of the nineteenth century to the modern artist
weights or advertising pieces. The glass tops of the paperweights
sometimes have been nicked or scratched, and this type of damage can
be removed by polishing. Some serious collectors think this type of
repair is an alteration and will not buy a repolished weight; others
think it is an acceptable technique of restoration that does not change
the value. Baccarat paperweights are listed separately under Baccarat.

Abrams, Black Buffalo Bill Figure, Standing, Milk Glass 325.00
Abrams, John Stetson Picture, Glass, Round, 4 In. 125.00
Advertising, Beck & Wheatley Insurance, Tarrytown, N.Y., Anvil, Brass, 3 In. .....35.00 to 45.00
Advertising, Boston Belting Co., Milk Glass, 1887 .... 65.00
Advertising, Disabled American Veterans, Iron, 4 x 4 In. 55.00
Advertising, First National Bank, Bangor, Me., Celluloid, 1 3/4 In. 25.00
Advertising, G.A.R., Pittsburgh, Glass, 1894 .... 55.00
Advertising, Golden Pheasant Gunpowder 35.00
Advertising, Grandpa's Wonder Soap, Cardboard Image Inside, Early 1900s 125.00
Advertising, Indian Motorcycles, Magnifier 75.00
Advertising, Lamb Club Whiskey, Pat. Nov. 25, 1892, Lowell, Mass. 125.00
Advertising, Luminal Paints, Cast Iron 20.00
Advertising, Mountain Dew, Glass, Hillbilly Shooting Prowler By Outhouse ... 25.00
Advertising, Neverslip Horseshoe, Figural, Horse Head Center 90.00

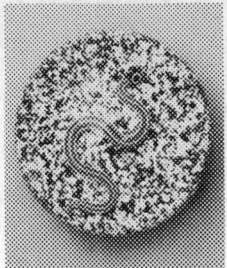
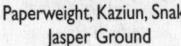

Paperweight, Kaziun, Snake,
Jasper Ground

Paperweight, Kaziun,
Yellow Rose

Paperweight, Lutz,
5-Petal Pansy, 3 In.

Advertising, Old Crow Whiskey, Glass	55.00
Advertising, Pan Am	50.00
Advertising, Reininger & Co., San Francisco, Cal., Octagonal	30.00
Advertising, Scott Baron Co., Figural, Dumbbell Shape, Iron	30.00
Advertising, Terrier, 1927, No. 2777	295.00
Advertising, U.S. Forest Service Dept. Of Agriculture, Brass, 3 1/2 x 2 3/4 In.	37.00
Advertising, Vermont State Building	50.00
Advertising, Zanesville, Ohio Sesquicentennial	40.00
American Bicentennial, 1776-1976, Red & Blue Star Symbol, Glass, 3 1/4 In.	10.00
Ayotte, Meadowlark, 1985	1210.00
Ayotte, Springtime In Manoraga, Almond Tree Blossoms, 3 5/8 In.	900.00
Billiken, Mosaic	150.00
Buzzini, Orchid, Signed	675.00
Clichy, Concentric Rings Of Millifiori Canes, Opaque Blue Ground	1695.00
Clichy, Millefiori On Latticinio, 2 1/2 In.	605.00
Clichy, Millefiori, Pastry Mold Canes, Pink, 2 3/4 In.	1150.00
Clichy, Red & White Flower	5390.00
Clichy, Roses, Moss Ground, c.1860.	14300.00
Floral, Flag Design, Early 20th Century, 4 In.	50.00
G.A.R., Washington D.C., Teddy Roosevelt Picture, 1902, 3 In.	175.00
Hansen, Blue & Green Flower, Orange Ground, Signed, 2 3/8 In.	120.00
Hansen, Flower, Brown Striated Ground, Ringed With Red Canes, 2 5/8 In.	275.00
Hansen, Green Snake, Beige Ground, H-Cane, 2 5/8 In.	110.00
John F. Kennedy, Cobalt Blue, White Profile	100.00
Kaziun, Pansy, Jasper Ground	1100.00
Kaziun, Pansy, Orange, Yellow Center Blossom, Chartreuse Ground, 2 1/4 In.	747.00
Kaziun, Red & Yellow Flower, 4-Part Green Leaves, 2 In.	522.00
Kaziun, Snake, Jasper Ground	*Illus* 1400.00
Kaziun, Yellow Rose	*Illus* 650.00
Louis Kossuth, Bust, Satin, 1825-1899, Cut In Base	55.00
Lundberg, Crown, Pink, Red Twists, White Ribbons In Laticinio, 3 In.	150.00
Lundberg, Flower, Orange Specks On Pink, Yellow Stamen, Green Leaves	1200.00
Lundberg, Flower, Purple, Heart Cane Center Sepal, 17 Petals, 2 3/8 In.	600.00
Lundberg, Winter Crown, Poinsettia Center, White, Green Rose Cane, 3 In.	180.00
Lutz, 5-Petal Pansy, 3 In.	*Illus* 775.00
Man's Head, Naughty Hidden Pictures, Bronze	35.00
Millefiori, Butterfly On Latticinio, Double Trefoil Garland, John Deacons, 3 In.	250.00
Millefiori, Butterfly, Over Fanciful Blossom, Buds, 2 3/4 In.	690.00
Millefiori, Raised Rim, Emerald Green Oval Vessel, Black, Tiffany, 3 3/4 In.	2645.00
Millefiori, White Flower Floats, Orange, Green Butterfly, John Deacons, 3 In.	295.00
Moses In Bulrushes, Satin	225.00
New England Glass, End-Of-Day, Multicolored Canes, Twists, 2 1/2 In.	172.00
Orient & Flume, Bee & Flower	200.00
Perthshire, Lampwork Flower, Lace Ground, Signed, 3 In.	285.00
Salazar, Art Glass, 1984	68.00
Snow Dome, Aloha	30.00

Paperweight, St. Louis,
Strawberry

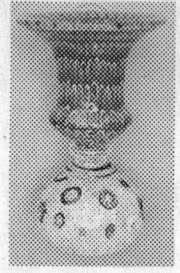

Paperweight, St. Louis,
With Pedestal Penholder

Paperweight, Ysart,
Butterfly & Flowers

Snow Dome, Atlantic City Steel Pier, Convention Hall 18.00
Snow Dome, Expo 86 Vancouver, Canada 22.00
Snow Dome, Faneuil Hall, Cradle Of Liberty, Boston 24.00
Snow Dome, Frog Prince, West Germany 29.00
Snow Dome, Gingerbread Castle 24.00
Snow Dome, Michelin Man, Mr. Bib 45.00
Snow Dome, New York City 14.00
Snow Dome, Pennsylvania Dutchland 18.00
Snow Dome, Snowman, Pottery Base 33.00
Snow Dome, South Of The Border 35.00
St. Clair, Apple Shape, Red Flowers, Controlled Bubbles ....55.00 to 125.00
St. Clair, Bell Shape, Dark Carnival 70.00
St. Clair, Joe Zimmerman, Weights 3 .... 135.00
St. Clair, Monarch Butterfly, 1977, 3 1/4 In. 57.00
St. Clair, Pear Shape, Green 65.00
St. Clair, Pear Shape, Marigold Carnival 70.00
St. Clair, Red, White, Blue, Green, Original Label 69.00
St. Clair, Woman, Sulphide 59.00
St. Louis, Bouquet On White Latticinio Ground, 2 3/4 In. 1440.00
St. Louis, Dahlia, Lemon Green, Star-Cane, 3 1/8 In. 287.00
St. Louis, Green Carpet, 5 Groups Of Silhouette Canes 4950.00
St. Louis, Red Double Clematis 1320.00
St. Louis, Strawberry ....*Illus* 1700.00
St. Louis, With Pedestal Penholder ....*Illus* 610.00
Stankard, Buttercup, Red Blossoms, 2 Green Leaf Clusters, 2 1/2 In. 747.00
Stankard, Floral, Window Cut, Cobalt Blue Ground, 1971, 2 In. 460.00
Stankard, Meadowreath, Yellow Blossom, Leafy Stem, 1973, 2 3/4 In. 1035.00
Stankard, Spring Beauty, Blue Center, White Blossom, 1971, 2 1/4 In. 805.00
Stankard, White Stylized Flower, 1972, 2 1/4 In. 632.00
Sulphide, Abraham Lincoln, 2 3/4 In. 675.00
Sulphide, Franklin Roosevelt, D'Albret 95.00
Tarsitano, Butterfly, Earth Life Series, 3 1/2 In. 950.00
Tarsitano, Dahlia, Yellow, Orange, Green Leaves, 2 1/2 In. 490.00
Tarsitano, Dragonfly, Sand Ground, Earth Life Series, 3 In. 805.00
Tarsitano, Millefiori, Concentric Rings Of Stars, Blossoms, 3 1/4 In. 1265.00
Whitefriars, Inkwell, Multicolored Concentric Millefiori, 1848, 4 1/2 In. 175.00
William Jennings Bryan & John W. Kern, 1908 .... 480.00
Ysart, Butterfly & Flowers ....*Illus* 625.00
Ysart, Clematis, Millefiori Center, Red, Green, White, Scotland, 3 1/2 In. 375.00

PAPIER-MACHE is made from paper mixed with glue, chalk, and other
ingredients, then molded and baked. It becomes very hard and can be
painted. Boxes, trays, and furniture were made of papier-mache. Some
of the nineteenth-century pieces were decorated with mother-of-pearl.
Furniture made of papier-mache is listed in the Furniture category.

Figurine, Black Baby Coachman, Nude, Germany, 1920s, 5 In. 125.00

Figurine, Easter Rabbit, Pulling Carrots In Cart	650.00
Figurine, Nativity, Joseph, Mary & Ox, Italy, 1930s, 3 Piece	300.00
Figurine, Swan, Painted, Large	80.00
Figurine, Turkey, Hen, 1950s, 5 1/2 In.	32.00
Figurine, Turkey, Tom, 1950s, 3 1/2 In.	24.00
Figurine, Turkey, Tom, Thanksgiving, 5 1/2 In.	42.00
Mask, Clown	300.00
Sake Cozy, Figural, Geisha Girl, Black, Reds & Ivory, 12 7/8 In.	185.00
Tray, Allover Floral & Foliate, Illidge Warranted, Stand, 20 1/2 x 30 1/4 In.	1155.00
Tray, Black Ground, Gilt Chinoiserie Design, Stand, 19th Century, 31 x 25 In.	805.00
Tray, Crumb, Shell Shape, Daisy Design, Black Ground, Victorian, 11 x 12 In.	65.00
Tray, Desk, Mother-Of-Pearl, Painted Roses, Black Lacquer	165.00
Tray, Floral & Foliate Sprays, Ebonized Bamboo Stand, Victorian, 18 x 16 In.	745.00
Tray, Floral Sprays Design, Black Ground, Victorian, Oval, 19th Century	862.00
Tray, Highland Scene, Ponies, England, 1869, 17 x 13 In.	2250.00
Tray, Painted & Gilt Chinoiserie Design, Black Ground, Stand, 19 x 25 In.	575.00
Tray, Table, Black Lacquered & Floral Design, Victorian	575.00
Wig Stand, Figural, Polychrome Repaint, 15 In.	660.00

PARASOL, see Umbrella category.

PARIAN is a fine-grained, hard-paste porcelain named for the marble it resembles. It was first made in England in 1846 and gained in favor in the United States about 1860. Figures, tea sets, vases, and other items were made of Parian at many English and American factories.

Bowl, Berry, Grape, Blue Ground, 10 x 7 In.	150.00
Bust, Apollo, Venus, 19th Century, 7 In., Pair	990.00
Bust, Charles Sumner, England, Mid-19th Century, 10 3/4 In.	650.00
Bust, John Milton, 7 1/2 In.	55.00
Bust, King Edward VII, Official Uniform, Medals, W.C. Lawton, 22 3/4 In.	1380.00
Bust, Maiden Wearing Bonnet, Neoclassical Base, Mid-19th Century, 18 In.	2300.00
Bust, Raleigh, England, 19th Century, 3 1/2 In.	402.00
Bust, Shakespeare, Holding Scroll, The Tempest, c.1865, 17 1/2 In.	968.00
Bust, Winter, Girl, With Scarf, 9 In.	95.00
Creamer, Game Keeper	65.00
Egg Holder, Rabbit, Standing In Front Of 2 Flowers, 3 1/4 In.	55.00
Figurine, Artist, Seated On Oil Lamp, Floral Design Base, France, 17 1/2 In.	460.00
Figurine, Child, 1 Reading & Other Writing, 13 1/2 x 6 In., Pair	170.00
Figurine, French Commander, Mid-19th Century, 9 1/2 In.	625.00
Figurine, Girl Holds Open Book While Boy Plays Flute, 11 1/2 In.	77.00
Figurine, Shakespeare, John Bell, 18 1/2 In.	231.00
Frame, 2 Oval Pictures, Ornate Carved Rococo	1540.00
Pitcher, Pewter Lid, England, 9 3/4 In.	55.00
Plate, Berry, Grape, Blue Ground, 8 In.	95.00
Urn, Cover, Hand Painted Medallions, Woman's Heads, 3 Sides, 1850, 22 In., Pair	12500.00
Vase, Bud, Woman, Kneeling While Playing Lyre, Metal, Continental, 19 1/2 In.	253.00

PARIS, Vieux Paris, or Old Paris, is porcelain ware that is known to have been made in Paris in the eighteenth or early nineteenth century. These porcelains have no identifying mark but can be recognized by the whiteness of the porcelain and the lines and decorations. Gold decoration is often used.

Basket, Rests On Heads Of Bisque Maidens, 1830s	9350.00
Basket, Wickwork, Frieze Of Cherub's Head, Paw Feet, Early 19 Century, 8 3/4 In.	1452.00
Bulb Pot, Floral Design, Octagonal Body, Painted Bouquets, 7 3/4 In.	1573.00
Compote, Pierced Center, Gilt Paw Feet, c.1820, 9 In.	70.00
Cup & Saucer, Love The Giver, Lacy Gold Interspersed With Floral Garland	85.00
Dinner Set, White, Magenta Trim	1320.00
Dish, Green & Gilt Border, Center Bouquet Of Flowers, Shell Shape, 9 1/2 In., Pair	485.00
Figurine, Turkish Lovers, Puce, Green & Yellow Glaze, 6 In.	57.00
Inkstand, Flowers, Gilt, 6 In.	403.00
Lamp, 2 Different Women's Scenes, Gold, Red Trim, 13 In.	295.00
Lamp, Battle Scene, Gilt Medallions, Pedestal Foot, c.1860, 12 In., Pair	2760.00

Platter, Portrait, 10 1/2 x 13 1/2 In. 225.00
Sauce, With Stand, Gold Trim, 7 In. 57.00
Tea Set, Floral Designs, Gilt Trim, Floral Panels, 20 Piece 287.00
Tete-A-Tete Set, Square Tray, Roses & Leaves, Gold Trim, 7 Piece 700.00
Urn, Floral & Gilt Design, Pair 3220.00
Urn, Garland Of Flowers, Gold Acanthus Loop Handles, Campaniform, Everted Rim 4025.00
Urn, Naturalistic Panel, Stag Hunt Scene, Gold Ground, Campaniform, 1835, Pair 6325.00
Vase, Children On Front, Floral Bouquet On Back, Rococo Revival, c.1840, 40 In., Pair . 725.00
Vase, Cornucopia, Swans, Green, Pink, Blue Foliate Scrolls, 1815, 10 7/8 In., Pair 4600.00
Vase, Figural, Nobleman, Gilt Vine Handles, c.1840, 11 1/4 In. 242.00
Vase, Figural, Woman, White Gown, Gilt, 10 1/2 In. 143.00
Vase, Gilt Vertical Lines, Biscuit Loop Handles, White, Green, Gold Ground, 15 In., Pair 3450.00
Vase, Landscape, 3 Figures In Classical Garb, Loop Handle, 12 In., Pair 4600.00
Vase, Landscape, Allegorical Scene, Reverse Painted, Heroic Swan Handles, 13 In., Pair . 2090.00
Vase, Landscape, Blue, Orange Sunset, Rustic Dwelling, Gold Ground, 13 1/4 In., Pair .. 4025.00
Vase, Leaf & Fruit Design, Side Handles, Gold Accents, 6 In. 185.00
Vase, Medieval Scene, Gilt Ground, Scroll Handles, Stand, c.1860, 22 3/4 In. 2415.00
Vase, Naturalistic Panel, Young Lady Writing At Table, Gold Ground, 13 1/4 In., Pair ... 4887.00
Vase, Painted Design, Egyptian Revival, 19th Century, 15 1/2 In. 372.00
Vase, Painted, Oval Figural Panels, 14 In. 770.00
Vase, Panels Of Amorous Couples, Swan Form Handles, c.1820, 15 1/2 In., Pair 2540.00
Vase, Panels With Agronomic Scene Of Figures Tilling, Gold, 1815, 13 In., Pair 5175.00
Vase, Serenade In Garden, Opposing Side, Mountain Landscape, Masks, 17 In., Pair 372.00
Vase, Winged Caryatid Supports, Lion Mask, Bronze Mounted, 15 3/4 In. 1265.00

PATE-DE-VERRE is an ancient technique in which glass is made by
blending and refining powdered glass of different colors into molds.
The process was revived by French glassmakers, especially Galle,
around the end of the nineteenth century.

Bowl, 3 Brown Scarab Beetles, Blue, Green, Yellow Center, Green Border, 9 In. 4600.00
Bowl, 3 Butterflies, Purple, Green, Red, Pale Gray Ground, 1915, 3 In. 8050.00
Bowl, Lizard, Detailed Deep Emerald, Red, Yellow, Green Flowers, 7 x 3 In. 5225.00
Bowl, Mermaid, Reclining, Purple Crab, Impressed, Decouchemont, 7 x 2 In. 4675.00
Box, Cover, Head Of Hydrangea Form, Purple, White Center, 4 In. 2875.00
Figurine, Fish, Rising From The Waves, Burnt Orange, Aqua, 1920 .... 1610.00
Figurine, Mermaid & Crab, Blue, Green, Orange, Red, 3 x 7 x 4 In. 3450.00
Figurine, Perched Sparrow, Pale Green, Emerald Glass, 4 In. 1150.00
Lamp, 2 Tigers Stalking Through Foliage, Pink, Purple, Fan Shaped Panel, 7 In. 16100.00
Paperweight, Gray Brown Field Mouse, Green, 1925, 2 In. 2070.00
Pendant, Cicada Relief, Green, Amethyst, Gray Glass, 1923, 2 1/2 In. 2070.00
Vase, 2 Heads Surrounded By Leaves, Gray, Green, Purple Ground, 4 In. 3300.00
Vase, Ivy Leaves, Berries, Gray, Red, Violet, Green, 1919, 3 1/2 In. 5462.00
Vase, Stylized Floral, Web Motif, Yellow, Red, Opaque Ground, 12 In. 7130.00

PATE-SUR-PATE means paste on paste. The design was made by painting layers of slip on the ceramic piece until a relief decoration was
formed. The method was developed at the Sevres factory in France
about 1850. It became even more famous at the English Minton factory about 1870. It has since been used by many potters to make both
pottery and porcelain wares.

Bowl, Reclining Maidens With Putti, Teal Blue Ground 5465.00
Box, Cover, Yellow Glaze Design, Cherub On Pink Ground, Marked, 3 In. 3795.00
Box, Female Portrait, Blue Ground, Limoges, 5 3/4 In. 690.00
Charger, Floral Design, Brown, Green, Genre Scenes, Signed, 1901, 19 1/4 In. 29900.00
Compote, Cover, White Enameled Foliate, Vine Design, Blue Ground, 9 1/2 In. 5175.00
Lamp Base, White Classical Relief, Brown Ground, F. Peyrat, 1875, 15 3/4 In. 1092.00
Plaque, 5 Armed Female Figures, Brown Ground, Wood Frame, 8 x 15 In. 9200.00
Plaque, Child, Reaching For Grapes, Blue Ground, White, France, 1874, 10 In. 1495.00
Plaque, Male Figure Holding Vessel, Brown, 3 3/4 x 6 3/4 In. 980.00
Plaque, Partially Clad Female, Holding Lantern, 1870, 11 x 16 In. 2760.00
Plaque, Phonograph, Woman & Child, Taxile Doat, 3 x 6 In. 4000.00
Plaque, Vomas & Okamas, Woman, Dancing, Blue Ground, Limoges, 7 In., Pair 1210.00
Stein, Seamen, On Sinking Ship, Woman Floating Through Air, 1/5 Liter 715.00

Tray, Elegant Lady, Cobalt Blue, 5 x 3 In.	75.00
Vase, Cherub With Floral Garland, Insect, Enamel & Gilt, Meissen, 4 In.	3450.00
Vase, Egrets Among Water Foliate, Cobalt Blue Stem, Gray Ground	747.00

PAUL REVERE POTTERY was made at several locations in and around Boston, Massachusetts, between 1906 and 1942. The pottery was operated as a settlement house program for teenage girls. Many pieces were signed *S.E.G.* for Saturday Evening Girls. The artists concentrated on children's dishes and tiles. Decorations were outlined in black and filled with color.

Bowl, Band Of Walking Ducks, Yellow, Black, Signed, S.E.G., 2 1/4 In.	517.00
Cake Set, Tree Design, Black Outline Scene, Blue Sky, S.E.G., 7 Piece	1840.00
Inkwell, Banded Landscape, Blue Ground, Original Liner, S.E.G., 2 x 4 In.	1870.00
Pitcher, Blue & Yellow Drip Glaze	550.00
Pitcher, Gray & Light Blue Glaze, Paper Label, 4 1/2 In.	120.00
Pitcher, Medallion Of Goose, French Blue, Signed, S.E.G., 4 1/2 In.	825.00
Pitcher, White Lotus Band, Speckled Blue Ground, S.E.G., 4 1/2 In.	550.00
Plate, Band Of Trees, Blue Sky, Ivory Ground, S.E.G., 8 1/2 In.	357.00
Plate, Duck Design, Blue, Black On White, S.E.G., 6 1/2 In.	220.00
Plate, Green, Tan Hi-Glaze, Ink Mark, S.E.G., 7 1/2 In.	110.00
Plate, Yellow Rooster, Brown, Black On Green, White Ground, S.E.G., 7 In.	385.00
Porringer, Convex Sides, Raised Center, Silver, Boston, 1725-1754, 2 In.	10350.00
Tile, Washington Street, Blue, White, Green, Brown, 3 3/4 In.	402.00
Trivet, Band Of Rabbits On White & Mauve Ground, S.E.G., 5 1/2 In.	467.00
Trivet, Bucolic Landscape, House, Trees & River, S.E.G., 5 1/4 In.	1760.00
Vase, Allover Drip Glaze, Gunmetal Brown Ground, Label, 10 1/2 In.	550.00
Vase, Band Of Tulips, Yellow, Green, Light Blue, Dark Blue Ground, S.E.G., 6 In.	1760.00
Vase, Black High Glaze, Marked, 3 1/2 In.	77.00
Vase, Blue, Dated Aug., 1923, 6 1/2 In.	195.00
Vase, Closed-In Rim, Banded Landscape, S.E.G., 8 1/2 x 7 In.	1870.00
Vase, Pale Lavender & Turquoise Glaze, 5 In.	138.00
Vase, Teal, Wide Rimmed, S.E.G., 6 1/2 In.	198.00
Wall Pocket, Flowing Sponge Design, Oval, Blue Ground, Signed, 6 3/4 In.	185.00

PEACHBLOW glass originated about 1883 at Hobbs, Brockunier and Company of Wheeling, West Virginia. It shades from yellow to peach and is lined with white glass. New England peachblow is a one-layer glass shading from red to white. Mt. Washington peachblow shades from pink to blue. Reproductions of all types of peachblow have been made. Some are poor and easy to identify as copies, others are very accurate reproductions and could fool the unwary. Related pieces may be listed under Gunderson and Webb Peachblow.

Bowl, Agata, Allover Blue Spots, Ruffled Edge, 5 1/4 x 3 In.	750.00
Bowl, Agata, Squat Bulbous Body, New England, 5 3/8 x 2 3/4 In.	546.00
Bride's Bowl, Gold Enameled Floral, Blue Casing, Amber Ruffled Rim	575.00
Chalice, Daisy, Bryden, 1970, 7 In.	275.00
Creamer, Applied Handle, Annealing Line, 2 1/2 In.	1320.00
Creamer, Applied White Handle, New England, 2 3/4 In.	250.00
Creamer, White Enameled Daisies, Leafy Stems, Ribbed, New England, 2 1/2 In.	605.00
Cruet, Wheeling	1100.00
Fairy Lamp, 3-Part, Enameled Floral Garland, 8 1/2 In.	690.00
Fairy Lamp, Ivy Shade, Glass Candle Cup, Signed, 5 In.	440.00
Pitcher, Amber Handle, Wheeling, c.1870, 7 1/4 In.	720.00
Pitcher, Dimpled, Square Top, Satin Handle, Sandwich, 6 3/4 x 7 1/2 In.	550.00
Punch Cup, Amber Loop Handle, Wheeling, 2 1/4 In.	415.00 to 440.00
Rose Bowl, 7-Crimp Top, New England, 2 3/4 x 2 7/8 In.	295.00
Rose Bowl, Crimped Edge	85.00
Rose Bowl, World's Fair, 1893, Scalloped, New England, 2 1/2 In.	630.00
Spooner, Square Top, New England	825.00
Toothpick, Tricorner	950.00
Toothpick, Wheeling, 2 1/4 In.	990.00
Tumbler, New England, 3 3/4 In.	190.00
Tumbler, Wheeling, 4 In.	275.00 to 485.00

Vase, Basket Weave, 5 In. 300.00
Vase, Bulbous Base, Broad Shoulder, New England, 6 x 3 In. 875.00
Vase, Bulbous, 4 In. 175.00
Vase, Bulbous, Wheeling, 2 1/2 In. 330.00
Vase, Bulbous, Wheeling, 9 In. 550.00
Vase, Coralene, Yellow Branches, Ruffled, Mt. Washington, 6 In. 795.00
Vase, Double Gourd, Satin, Mt. Washington, 7 In. 1870.00
Vase, Lily, New England, 6 1/2 x 3 In. 650.00
Vase, Lily, Wild Rose, New England, 15 1/2 x 6 In. 1450.00
Vase, Pinched-In Sides, New England, 14 In. 1800.00
Vase, Stick, Uneven Color, Glossy, Bulbous, Wheeling, 8 1/2 In. 440.00
Vase, Tapered, Wheeling, 6 1/2 In. 605.00
Vase, White Floral Spray Design, Mt. Washington, 8 x 3 1/2 In. 935.00

PEARL items listed here are made of the natural mother-of-pearl from
shells. Such natural pearl has been used to decorate furniture and small
utilitarian objects for centuries. The glassware known as mother-of-
pearl is listed by that name. Opera glasses made with natural pearl
shell are listed under Opera Glasses.

Fruit Set, 6 Knives, 6 Forks, Case 100.00
Knife, Fruit, Silver Sterling Blade, Carved Handle 165.00
Salt Spoon, 3 In. 15.00

PEARLWARE is an earthenware made by Josiah Wedgwood in 1779. It
was copied by other potters in England. Pearlware is only slightly different in color from creamware and for many years collectors have
confused the terms. Wedgwood pieces are listed in the Wedgwood category in this book.

Pearl

Bowl, 5 Colors, England, c.1810, 4 1/2 x 9 1/2 In. 1250.00
Bowl, Earthworm, Orange, Rust Slip Field, 9 In. 825.00
Butter Tub, Blue Dendritic Thistle Design, Yellow 220.00
Charger, Blue Floral Design, 20 1/2 In. 345.00
Coffeepot, Dome Top, Rose Design, Pink, Red, Green, 10 3/4 In. 550.00
Cream Jug, Herringbone Designs 385.00
Creamer, Cover, Cow, Brown, Ocher Spots, 1810, 5 1/16 In. 920.00
Creamer, Floral, Cup Shape, Leaf Handle, 3 1/4 In. 135.00
Cup, Hound Head Stirrup, Brown, White Coat, Brown Eyes & Collar, 6 In. 1610.00
Cup & Saucer, No Handle, Oriental Blue Transfer 110.00
Cup & Saucer, Peafowl, c.1830 .... 415.00
Dessert Service, Botanical, Floral Sprig On Each Piece, 1810-1815, 21 Piece 21850.00
Figurine, Autumn, Pink Flesh, 6 3/4 In. 330.00
Figurine, Bird, Yellow, Blue & Ocher Wings, England, 1800, 3 1/2 In. 635.00
Figurine, Boy, Feeding Spaniel, Enoch Wood, England, 7 1/4 In. 632.00
Figurine, Christ's Agony, Kneeling, In Garden, White, Black, Green Garden, 10 1/2 In. ... 1760.00
Figurine, Cybele, Classical Woman, Cornucopia, 1780, 5 3/8 In. 173.00
Figurine, Horse, Sepia Eyes, Rose-Edged Saddle, With Blue Dashes, 1820, 6 In. 3105.00
Figurine, John Liston, Wearing White Apron, Moss Green Jacket, E. Wood, 1826, 7 In. ... 345.00
Figurine, Jupiter, Bearded God, Pale Yellow, Tan Crown, Green Robe, 10 3/8 In. 1725.00
Figurine, King David, Wearing A Crown, Flowing Drapery Over Shoulder, 12 In. 402.00
Figurine, Lion, Funky, Mounted On Rectangular Base, Red Mouth, 5 x 5 In. 990.00
Figurine, Old Woman, Feeding Birds, Holding Loaf Of Bread, Green Bodice, 8 In. 1955.00
Figurine, Sleeping, Recumbent, Ocher Spots, Brown Stripes, 1820, 6 1/3 In. 1955.00
Figurine, Squirrel, With Nut, Collar With Ring, Orange Coat, 3 1/4 In. 632.00
Group, Peasant Couple, Woman In Flowered Dress, Man In Blue Waistcoat, 8 In. 207.00
Jug, Inlaid Agate, Checkered Bands, 1 Pt 660.00
Mug, Woman, Spaniel, Parrot, Copper Luster, Yellow, Strap Handle, 2 1/2 In. 345.00
Plaque, Bacchus, Venus & Ceres, 1810, 7 In. 1380.00
Plaque, Officer Wearing Black Hat, Red Coat, Green, 7 x 9 In. 1035.00
Plate, Eagle Design, Black, Blue, Green, Yellow Ocher, Green Feather Rim, 8 1/8 In. ... 660.00
Plate, Napoleon Bonaparte, 10 In. 150.00
Plate, Oriental Design, Impressed Turner, 7 3/4 In. 165.00
Platter, Molded Floral Rim, Blue Feather Edge, 17 In. 270.00
Tea Set, Blue Willow Transfer, 7 Piece 220.00

Teapot, Swan Finial, Oriental Transfer, Polychrome Enamel, Octagonal, 15 3/4 In. 412.00
Vase, Spill, 3 Openings, Cornucopia, Dolphins, 1780, 7 5/8 In. 1380.00

PEKING GLASS is a Chinese cameo glass first made popular in the eighteenth century. The Chinese have continued to make this layered glass
in the old manner, and many new pieces are now available that could
confuse the average buyer.

Bowl, Bell Shape, Butterfly, Floral Design, Red, White, 6 1/2 In. 210.00
Bowl, Bell Shape, Fluted Sides, Yellow, Early 19th Century, 4 3/4 In. 550.00
Bowl, Bell Shape, Red Bird, Floral Design, Milk White Ground, 7 In. 302.00
Bowl, Bird, Lotus Design, Yellow, 6 In., Pair 332.00
Bowl, Bright Yellow, Round, 19th Century, 11 3/4 In. 805.00
Bowl, Green Overlay, White, Crane Exterior Amid Lotus Plants, 5 3/4 In. 86.00
Bowl, Green Overlay, White, Flowered Lotus Exterior, Leaf Form Foot Rim, 7 In. 575.00
Bowl, Red Cut To White, 6 1/2 In., Pair 1350.00
Bowl, Red Overlay, White, Birds Among Lotus On Exterior, Leaf-Form Foot, 6 In. 1150.00
Cup, Red Overlay, Snowflake, Overlapping Dragons Beneath Cloud, 3 In. 2185.00
Jar, Stylized Bat Design, Yellow, 7 1/2 In. 392.00
Perfume Bottle, Red Overlay, White 340.00
Snuff Bottle, Blue Overlay, Snowflake, Prancing Deer On Sides, 2 1/2 In. 489.00
Snuff Bottle, Red Overlay, Snowflake, Serpent, Tortoise On 1 Side, 2 1/4 In. 1265.00
Snuff Bottle, Winged Creature Design, Multicolored Overlay Glass, 2 3/4 In. 70.00
Tazza, Multicolored Flowers, Blue Ground, Early 20th Century, 8 In. 316.00
Vase, Club Form, Grape, Squirrel Design, Imperial Yellow, 7 3/4 In., Pair 907.00
Vase, Female Figures In Garden, White, 8 In., Pair 1840.00
Vase, Flowers Carved In Relief, Hardwood Plaque, Yellow, 8 In. 330.00
Vase, Green Overlay, White, Ducks Swimming Among Lotus Plants, Pair 489.00
Vase, Monkey In Tree, Carved Yellow Scene On White, 10 In. 77.00
Vase, Pa Hua Design, Green, White Overlay, 13 1/2 In. 242.00
Vase, Red Dragon Design, Pear Shape, Blue Ground, 19th Century, 4 1/2 In. 880.00
Vase, Red Overlay, Snowflake, 2 Dragons, 2 Phoenix, 7 1/2 In., Pair 4600.00
Vase, Stick, Orange Finches, Floral, White Ground, Greek Key Rim, 8 In., Pair 450.00

PELOTON glass is a European glass with small threads of colored glass
rolled onto the surface of clear or colored glass. It is sometimes called
spaghetti, or shredded coconut, glass. Most pieces found today were
made in the nineteenth century.

Biscuit Jar, Colored Strands Over Jar, Blue Surface, 6 1/2 In. 785.00
Biscuit Jar, Multicolored Strands, Pink Ribbed Exterior, White Interior, Silver Plate 1070.00
Biscuit Jar, White, Yellow, Blue & Pink Strands, Pastel Blue Ground, 6 1/2 In. 785.00
Jar, Cover, Shredded Coconut, Melon Ribbing, 4 3/4 In. 440.00
Pitcher, Coconut Rainbow Strings, Clear Overshot, Squared Bulbous, Handle, 6 In. 165.00
Pitcher, Multicolored Pastel Strands, Overshot Surface, Square, 4 x 6 1/4 In. 355.00
Rose Bowl, 6-Crimp Top, Ribbing Around Outside, Coconut Strings, 2 3/4 In. 165.00
Vase, Tricorner Top, Coconut Rainbow Strings, White Cased, 4 x 4 3/4 In. 295.00

PENS replaced hand-cut quills as writing instruments in 1780 when the
first steel pen point was made in England. But it was 100 years before
the commercial pen was a common item. The fountain pen was invented in the 1830s but was not made in quantity until the 1880s. All types
of old pens are collected.

PEN, Blown Glass, Ink, Dark Green Swirled Stem, Reeded Nib, 5 1/4 In. 100.00
Eversharp, Doric, Art Deco, Fountain 220.00
George Burns, Tortoiseshell, Brass, Initials GB 977.00
Grieshaber, Swirled Pearl, Gold 90.00
Morrison, Gold Filled Filigree, Leaf Pattern, 14K Gold 400.00
Parker, Debutante, Box 55.00
Pelikan, Fountain, 1930s 65.00
Sheaffer, Basketball Team Photo, 1933 . . . . 30.00
Sheaffer, Italic M 10.00
Sheaffer, Jade, In Base, Original Box 105.00
Sheaffer, White Dot, Jade Green Bottom, Lighter Top 125.00
Ship, Floating In Oil, Tropical 8.00

Stanley Tools	5.00
Swan, Boy Playing Flute, Marble Base, Stand, Austria, 1930s	395.00
Wahl-Eversharp, Skyline, Fountain, 1940	50.00 to 75.00
Waterman, Filigree	125.00
Waterman, Ideal, No. 0512, 1912	300.00
Waterman, No. 454, Sterling Filigree	300.00
PEN & PENCIL, American Airlines, Gold, Box	40.00
Cross, Pepsi-Cola Logo On Clip, Box	20.00
Cross, Sunkist	45.00
Parker, Deluxe Challenger	125.00
Parker, Duofold Deluxe, Pearl Black	350.00
Parker, Sterling Silver	175.00
Sheaffer, Mother-Of-Pearl, Black	35.00
Sheaffer, Snorkel, Box & Tag, 1950s	110.00
Sheaffer, Woman's, Gold, French Ivory Case, Small	235.00
Wahl, Gold Filled	35.00

PENCILS were invented, so it is said, in 1565. The eraser was not added to the pencil until 1858. The automatic pencil was invented in 1863. Collectors today want advertising pencils or automatic pencils of unusual design. Boxes and sharpeners for pencils are also collected.

PENCIL, Mechanical, 7-Up, Floating Bottle	45.00
Mechanical, Sheaffer, Gold Filled, Green Marbleized, Chain, 1925	25.00
Wahl-Eversharp, Sterling Silver	35.00
PENCIL SHARPENER, Baker	40.00
Banjo, Metal, 2 1/2 In.	22.00 to 65.00
Black Boy Head, Exaggerated Features	60.00
Cowboy	90.00
Flintstones, Fred, Barney, Dino, Betty & Wilma, Plastic, 1983	75.00
French Poodle, Ceramic	45.00
Indian	90.00
Quick Draw McGraw	12.00
Snoopy, Battery Operated	75.00
Snoopy, Battery Operated, Box, General Mills, 1974	35.00
Typewriter, Germany	55.00

PENNSBURY Pottery worked in Morrisville, Pennsylvania, from 1950 to 1971. Full sets of dinnerware as well as many decorative items were made. Pieces are marked with the name of the factory.

Ashtray, Such Schmootzers	30.00
Bowl, Cereal, Red Rooster	5.00
Bowl, Figural, Rooster	95.00
Bowl, Pretzel, Quartet	55.00 to 65.00
Butter, Cover, Red Rooster, 5 x 4 In.	30.00 to 75.00
Cake Stand, Boy & Girl, 11 In.	90.00
Cake Stand, Family	125.00
Coffeepot, Black Rooster, 8 In.	115.00
Cookie Jar, Harvest, 8 In.	140.00
Cookie Jar, Red Barn	35.00
Cookie Jar, Red Rooster, 8 In.	45.00
Creamer, Hex, 4 In.	20.00
Creamer, Red Rooster, 2 1/2 In.	15.00
Creamer, Red Rooster, 4 In.	20.00
Cruet, Amish Head	40.00 to 80.00
Cruet, Vinegar & Oil, Amish Head, Pair	140.00
Cup, Red Rooster	30.00
Egg Plate, Rose & Rooster	65.00
Figurine, Barn Swallow, Teal Blue, No. 123, 6 1/4 In.	185.00
Figurine, Bird, Blue Bird, No. 103, 4 In.	175.00
Figurine, Bird, Blue Jay, No. 108, 10 1/2 In.	375.00
Figurine, Bird, Cardinal, No. 120, 6 1/2 In.	225.00
Figurine, Bird, Gold Finch, No. 102	195.00
Figurine, Bird, Magnolia Warbler, No. 112	200.00

Figurine, Bird, Nut Hatch, No. 110, 3 1/2 In. ....150.00 to 175.00
Figurine, Bird, Red Start, No. 113, 3 In. 55.00
Figurine, Bird, Scarlett Tanager, No. 105 .... 245.00
Figurine, Bird, Wren, No. 109, 3 In. 35.00
Figurine, Ducklings, Pair 295.00
Figurine, Rooster & Hen, 11 1/2 In., Pair 465.00
Figurine, Rooster, No. P 202, 12 In. 185.00
Mug, Beer, Amish, 5 In. 45.00
Mug, Beer, Barbershop Quartet, 5 In. ....30.00 to 45.00
Mug, Beer, Gay Ninety, 5 In. 45.00
Mug, Coffee, Black Rooster ....30.00 to 40.00
Mug, Coffee, Quartet, 3 1/4 In. 20.00
Mug, Coffee, Red Barn, 3 1/4 In. 35.00
Mug, Eagle, 3 1/4 In. 12.00
Mug, Sweet Adeline 23.00
Pie Plate, Amish Couple Picking Apples, 9 In. ....45.00 to 60.00
Pie Plate, Red Rooster, 9 In. 27.00
Pitcher, Amish, 2 1/2 In. ....35.00 to 45.00
Pitcher, Eagle, 6 1/4 In. ....60.00 to 70.00
Pitcher, Red Rooster, 10 In. 170.00
Plaque, Lafayette, Green Border 50.00
Plaque, Newark & Essex, Commemorative Ship, 1804-1954, 7 1/2 x 5 1/2 In. 20.00
Plate, Bread, 9 x 6 In. 35.00
Plate, Christmas Angel, 1970 .... 40.00
Plate, Christmas Is Giving, 1978 .... 35.00
Plate, Figural, Fish 195.00
Plate, Mother's Day, 1971 .... 35.00
Plate, Mother's Day, 1972 .... 42.00
Plate, Mother's Day, 1973 .... 100.00
Plate, Red Rooster, 8 In. 15.00
Plate, Red Rooster, 10 In. 35.00
Plate, Salad, Red Rooster 20.00
Platter, Red Rooster, 11 In. 30.00
Saucer, Red Rooster 15.00
Sugar, Cover, Rose & Rooster 40.00
Sugar & Creamer, Hex 40.00
Teapot, Black Rooster, 8 In. 37.00
Tray, Dutch Haven, Octagonal, 4 In. 30.00
Tray, Floral Design, 7 1/4 x 5 1/4 In. 25.00
Tureen, Soup, Ladle, Cover 215.00

PEPSI-COLA, the drink and the name, was invented in 1898 but was not trademarked until 1903. The logo was changed from an elaborate script to the modern block letters on the 1970 Pepsi label. Several different logos have been used. Until 1951, the words *Pepsi* and *Cola* were separated by 2 dashes. These bottles are called *double dash.* In 1951 the modern logo with a single hyphen was introduced. All types of advertising memorabilia are collected, and reproductions are being made.

Adventure Kit, Indiana Jones, Last Crusade, 6 Piece 125.00
Book, Salesman's Advertising Picture, 1964 .... 58.00
Bottle, Desert Storm, Long Neck, Tex., 1992, 12 Oz. 25.00
Bottle, GMC, 1952 ....30.00 to 39.00
Bottle, Ice Hockey, San Jose Sharks, Long Neck, 1994, 12 Oz. 6.00
Bottle, Richard Petty, Long Neck, 1991, 12 Oz., 4 Piece 30.00
Bottle, Stars & Stripes, Defense Of America's Cup, Long Neck, 1992, 12 Oz. 20.00
Bottle, SunBelt Agriculture Expo, Moultrie, Gal, 1988, 16 Oz. 15.00
Bottle Opener, Bottle Shape, Buffalo, N.Y., 1940 .... 75.00
Clock, Double Bubble, Think Young 950.00
Clock, Pepsi, Please, Red, White, Blue, Electric, Metal Frame, 13 x 13 In. 230.00
Clock, Say Pepsi Please On Front, Red, White, Pressed Steel, 1950, 15 x 15 In. 253.00
Coin-Operated Machine, Says Drink Pepsi-Cola Ice Cold, 1950s 685.00
Cooler, Blue Label Design, Carrying Handles On Side, Aluminum, 1960, 22 x 16 In. 172.00

Door Push, Red, Blue Lettering, Yellow Ground, Porcelain, 32 x 3 In. 121.00
Glass, Bugs Bunny, Elmer Fudd 12.00
Glass, Herfy's, 1962 Seattle World's Fair 20th Anniversary 7.00
Glass, Porky Pig & Petunia Mowing The Lawn 8.00
Glass, Super Series, Aquaman, 1976 .... 20.00
Glass, Underdog 18.00
Handle, Screen Door, 1930s 95.00
Pencil Clip, Red, White & Blue, Celluloid, Silver Metal, 1940s 18.00
Pin, Drink Pepsi Today, Red, White, Blue, Celluloid, 1 3/4 In. Diam. 75.00
Pin, Refresh Without Filling, Square 60.00
Poster, Listen To Counter-Spy Pepsi's Radio Thriller, 1950s, 8 x 19 In. 15.00
Push Bar, France, 1950s 75.00
Radio, Bottle Shape, 24 In. 495.00
Saltshaker, Bottle Shape 4.00
Shirt, Button Down, Long Sleeve, Knit, Arrow, 15 1/2 In. 37.00
Shot Glass ....3.00 to 4.00
Sign, Be Sociable Serve Pepsi, Bus, Blacks Drinking Pepsi, 1950s, 29 x 11 In. .. 100.00
Sign, Bottle Cap, Tin, 39 In. ....155.00 to 300.00
Sign, Bottle, 5 Cents, Tin, Early 1940s, 49 x 18 In. 400.00
Sign, Have A Pepsi, Red, White, Blue, Gold, Plastic, Cardboard, 1960, 13 x 8 1/2 In. 58.00
Sign, Man & Woman Holding Pepsi Bottles, 1960, 28 x 11 In. 98.00
Sign, Oak Frame, 15 1/2 x 32 In. 300.00
Sign, Red, White, Blue, Yellow, Black, Sheet Metal, Chalkboard, 1960s, 27 x 19 In. 58.00
Sign, Take Home A Carton Of Pepsi, Yellow, Red, White, Blue, Black, 1950, 20 x 8 In. .. 115.00
Sprint-Car, Knoxville National Championship, Long Neck, Iowa, 1993, 12 Oz. 7.00
Tape Measure, Key Chain 45.00
Thermometer, 27 In. 18.00
Thermometer, Round, 12 In. 16.00
Tip Tray, Coney Island, 1950s 50.00
Toy, Pick-Up, Ford, 1953 .... 45.00
Toy, Train, K-Line, Box, 1993 .... 165.00
Toy, Truck, Chevy, 1942 .... 33.00
Toy, Truck, Mack, B-61 ....55.00 to 95.00
Toy, Truck, Semi, Red, White & Blue, Mack T & T No. 9, 1960 .... 58.00
Toy, Van, Big Shot, Chevrolet, 1949 .... 65.00
Toy, Van, Ford, 1951 .... 39.00
Toy, Van, Ford, 1953 .... 30.00
Toy, Van, GMC, 1952 .... 38.00
Tray, Hits The Spot, Musical Notes On Front, 1940s 198.00
Watch Fob, Metal, Newbern, N.C. 12.00

PERFUME BOTTLES are made of cut glass, pressed glass, art glass, silver, metal, enamel, and even plastic or porcelain. Although the small bottle to hold perfume was first made before the time of ancient Egypt, it is the nineteenth- and twentieth-century examples that interest today's collector. DeVilbiss Company has made atomizers of all types since 1888 but no longer makes the perfume bottle tops so popular with collectors. These were made from 1920 to 1968. The glass bottle may be by any of many manufacturers even if the atomizer is marked *DeVilbiss*. The word *factice*, which often appears in ads, refers to store display bottles. Glass or porcelain examples may be found under the appropriate name such as Lalique, Czechoslovakia, etc.

Alexander Julian, Green Frosted 22.00
Amber, White Enameled Flowers, Blue Trim, Silver Plated Stand, 9 In. 295.00
Art Nouveau, Sterling Silver, 4 In. 100.00
Aurene, Iridescent Blue, Melon Ribbed, Pointed Stopper, Steuben, 6 In. 1430.00
Aurene, Iridescent Red Gold, Pointed Stopper, Dabber, Steuben, 6 In. 1100.00
Austen's, Forest Flower Cologne, Clear, Round, 1890, 1 1/2 x 3 3/4 In. 8.00
Baccarat, Flacon, Louis XV, Gold Trim, Marked 290.00
Baccarat, Roses, Hollow Stopper 95.00
Ball Shape, White Peacock Eye, Mother-Of-Pearl, Cologne, Stopper, 3 3/4 In. .. 485.00
Blown Glass, 3-Mold, Toilet Water, Medium Lilac, Cobalt Blue 190.00
Blue, Cut Panels & Concave Diamonds, Cologne, Stopper, 7 1/4 In. 550.00

Blue Opaline, White Powdered Glaze Pattern, Stopper, 1880, 10 In. 495.00
Boston & Sandwich Glass Works, Cobalt Blue, 5 3/4 In. 575.00
Brass, Filigree & Jeweled, Purse, 1 1/2 In. 68.00
Caithness, Blue Green, Atomizer, Signed, 5 1/2 In. 95.00
Chair Cane Pattern, Ruby Cut To Clear, Piston Atomizer, France, 3 1/2 In. 695.00
Chevalier Du Garde, Knight, Frosted, 2 1/2 In. 148.00
Christian Dior, Diorling, Baccarat 135.00
Christian Dior, Miss Dior, Box 115.00
Christmas Tree Shape, Germany, c.1920, 3 3/4 In. 70.00
Coax Me, Red Velvet Box 45.00
Cobalt Blue, Cut To Clear, Basket Of Flowers, Square Cut Stopper, 5 In. 160.00
Copper Blue, Cut Flutes & Lapidary Diamonds, Enamel, Cologne, 6 In. 395.00
Cranberry Glass, Gold Stars Design, Cranberry Bubble Stopper, 6 1/4 In. 165.00
Cube, Wooden, Unscrews For Cake Perfume, Paris, 1945 .... 28.00
Cupids & Flowers, Malachite 800.00
Cut Glass, Stars, Lay Down, Sterling Silver Collar & Cap, 5 In. 195.00
D'Orsay, Intoxication 25.00
DeVilbiss, Applied Rigaree, Opalescent 135.00
DeVilbiss, Art Deco, 1930s 65.00
DeVilbiss, Art Deco, Yellow Enamel, Atomizer, 4 1/2 In. 115.00
DeVilbiss, Black Atomizer, 6 1/2 x 6 In. 297.00
DeVilbiss, Cut Glass, Elongated 100.00
DeVilbiss, Gold Trim, Atomizer, 6 1/2 In. 350.00
DeVilbiss, Iridescent Gold, Atomizer, 6 1/2 In. 135.00
DeVilbiss, Iridescent Gold, Atomizer, Box 300.00
DeVilbiss, Kelly Green, Gold Design, Atomizer, 8 In. 385.00
DeVilbiss, Lenox, Penguin 225.00
Dralle, Illusion 75.00
Exotic Bouquet, Barrel Shape, Clear Glass, Embossed Hoops, 25 Cents, 2 1/4 In. 25.00
Farina, Cologne, Pontil, 6 Sides 75.00
Figural, Can-Can Girl, Luster, 1930s, Japan 65.00
Flask, Clambroth, Flowers, Sprays, Leaves, 3 7/8 In. 60.00
Flint White Foot, Blue Jade, Alabaster Stopper, Steuben 900.00
Free-Blown, White Nailsea Loopings, Sapphire Blue, 11 3/4 In. 550.00
Giorgio, Miniature 22.00
Givenchy, Display, 16 In. 225.00
Gold & Turquoise Top & Collar, Milk Glass, 3 1/8 In. 77.00
Gucci, No. 3 .... 15.00
Guerlain, Bee Design 44.00
Guerlain, Faux, Chamade Flashed Interior, 23 In. 450.00
Guerlain, Mitsouko, Paris, Heart-Shaped Stopper, 3 1/8 In. 25.00
Guerlain, Shalimar, Box 35.00
Guerlain, Shalimar, Display, Clear, Blue Flashed Stopper, 6 In. 135.00
Hand Painted Roses, Atomizer, Bavaria 25.00
Houbigant, Quelques Fleurs 20.00
Imperial Perfumery Co., Clear, Cork Stopper With Dabber, Round 10.00
Inlaid Wood, Hanging Brass Chain, Brass Stopper, Square, 1 In. 38.00
Iribe, Etched Stopper 150.00
Jean Patou, Amour Amour, Pineapple Stopper, 1929, Box, 3 1/2 In. 90.00
Jeanne Lanvin, Black, Raspberry Stopper, 3 In. 93.00
Latticinio, Pink, Bulbous Bottom, 5 1/2 In. 138.00
Light Blue Jade Stopper, Steuben 700.00
Light Green, Floral Design, Gold Outline, Sterling Screw Top, Satin Glass 385.00
Lithyalin, Green, Beige & Black Marbled, Bohemia, 1840, 3 1/2 In. 205.00
Lucien LeLong, Syroco, Twist, Label, 1/2 Contents, 3 In. 65.00
Lucien LeLong, Tailspin Cologne, Box, 8 Oz. 95.00
Malachite, Cupids & Flowers ....750.00 to 800.00
Malachite Stones, Purse, Metal 85.00
Mary Chess, Tapestry Toilet Water, Star Shape, Teardrop Stopper, 7 3/4 In. 40.00
Melliers, Musk, Label, 1890-1900, 2 1/4 x 6 1/2 In. 45.00
Melliers, Sweet Pea, Label Pictures Sweet Peas, c.1890-1900, 9 Oz. 45.00
Moon Gay, Frosted Cologne On Reverse, Pink Enamel, Brass Cap, 3 7/8 In. 40.00
Moorland, Made For Penslar Stores, Frosted, Fan Stopper, 5 3/4 In. 95.00

Moorland, Panel Grape, Pair 45.00
Narcisse, 2 Vertical Ribs, Cork, Frosted Glass Stopper, Neck Label, 5 x 2 In. 16.00
New England Glass, Free Blown, Amethyst, Cologne, 9 1/4 In. 595.00
Niki De St. Phalle, Gold Top, Sculptured Snakes, Enameled, Blue, 4 In. 75.00
Or-Blosco, Inc., Jasmine, Clear, Label, Plastic Box, Square, 1 x 2 7/8 In. 9.00
Paris Perfume Co., Clear, Embossed Vertically, 1890-1900, 2 x 1 x 5 1/4 In. 10.00
Phalon & Son, Barrel Shape, Clear, Crest On Lid, 1890, 3 3/4 In. 60.00
Piege, Grenoville, Box 85.00
Pink Glass, Cherubs & Woman Cut Stopper 55.00
Pink Glass, Cut Woman & Mythological Figures, Stopper 75.00
Pink Opaline, Enameled Design, Cologne, France, 1880, 9 1/2 In. 175.00
Prince Matchabelli, Crown Jewel 125.00
Prince Matchabelli, Crown Shape, Green Glass, Duchess Of York Label, 3 In. 100.00
Prince Matchabelli, Crown, 2 Oz. 195.00
Prince Matchabelli, Potpourri 20.00
Prince Matchabelli, Red & Black Velvet Box 250.00
Prince Matchabelli, Stradaveri, Gold & Black, Crown, 1/2 Oz. 50.00
Raphael Replique, 1 3/4 In. 60.00
Raphael Replique, Paris, Original Seal, Label, 5 x 2 1/2 In. 65.00
Ricksecker Cologne, Crock Shape, Stoneware, Tan, White, 3 3/4 In. 30.00
Ricksecker Cologne, Vines & Flowers, 2 Handles Near Top, Pottery, 8 3/8 In. 80.00
Ruby Over Clear, Cut Cane Pattern, Cologne, Pewter Atomizer, 4 In. 995.00
Schiaparelli, Sleeping, Candle, Red & Gold Flame Stopper, 5 1/2 In. 125.00
Shalimar, Baccarat Bottle, Etched Base, Marked, 4 3/8 In. 60.00
Shari, Langloi, Box 95.00
Teardrop Shape, Blue Milk Glass, Gold Metal Collar, Glass Stopper, 2 7/8 In. 45.00
Tinkerbell, With Atomizer, Box 38.00
Valois, Embossed, Ribbed, Amberina Stopper, 3 3/4 In. 40.00
Venetian, Faceted Stopper, Signed, Hawkes, 8 In. 495.00
Verre De Soie, Blue Teardrop Stopper, Tapered, Steuben, 7 1/2 In. 355.00
Vigny, Le Golliwogg Shape, Black Stopper, 4 In. 140.00
Yardley, Art Deco, Box, Small 30.00

PETERS & REED Pottery Company of Zanesville, Ohio, was founded by John D. Peters and Adam Reed in 1897. Chromal, Landsun, Montene, Pereco, and Persian are some of the art lines that were made. The company, which became Zane Pottery in 1920 and Gonder Pottery in 1941, closed in 1957. Peters & Reed pottery was unmarked.

Basket, Moss Aztec, Hanging, Red & Green Semimatte, 5 x 9 In. 120.00
Bowl, Futura, 9 In. 5525.00
Bowl, Landsun, 10 In. 95.00
Bowl, Landsun, Frog, 9 In. 125.00
Bowl, Landsun, Yellow, Tan, Brown, 3 x 8 In. 45.00
Bowl, Pereco, Dark Blue Glaze, Embossed Leaves, Vines, 9 In. 85.00
Candlestick, Wilse, Blue 125.00
Jardiniere, Matte Green 135.00
Jug, Cavalier, Swirled Form, 7 1/2 In. 55.00
Lamp Base, Yellow, 7 x 7 In. 175.00
Umbrella Stand, Maiden Strolling In A Glen, Ionic Columns, 19 In. 395.00
Vase, 2 Handles, Flowers On Front, Brown Glaze, 1900, 11 In. 165.00
Vase, Brown, Tripod, 6 In. 160.00
Vase, Bud, Landsun, 9 1/2 In. 85.00
Vase, Bud, Landsun, 10 In. 95.00
Vase, Chromal, Landscape, Blue & Brown Under Glaze, 7 In. 550.00
Vase, Flame, 6 1/2 In. 125.00
Vase, Gloss Drip, Cobalt Blue, Brown, 4 In. 105.00
Vase, Grape Clusters & Vines, Standard Glaze, 17 In. 450.00
Vase, Landsun, 9 In. 95.00
Vase, Landsun, Chocolate & Green Flames, Light Brown Base, 6 In. 125.00
Vase, Landsun, Flame, 3 3/4 x 3 1/2 In. 30.00
Vase, Marbleized, 9 In. 100.00
Vase, Moss Aztec, Pansies, 7 In. 140.00
Vase, Moss Aztec, Pedestal, Gray Green, 16 In. 200.00

Vase, Moss Aztec, Pinecones, Needles, 9 1/2 In. 330.00
Vase, Pereco, Floral Relief, Green, 8 1/2 In. 225.00
Vase, Raised Swirls, Muted Green, Brown, Tan & Blue, Paper Label, 4 1/2 In. 110.00
Wall Pocket, Moss Aztec, 9 x 6 1/2 In. 175.00

PETRUS REGOUT, see Maastricht category.

PEWABIC POTTERY was founded by Mary Chase Perry Stratton in 1903 in Detroit, Michigan. The company made many types of art pottery, including pieces with matte green glaze and an iridescent crystalline glaze. The company continued working until the death of Mary Stratton in 1961. It was reactivated by Michigan State University in 1968.

Bowl, Copper To Green To Lavender, Iridescent, 1930, 5 1/2 In. ....*Illus* 700.00
Bowl, Copper To Green To Lavender, Iridescent, 1940, 5 1/4 In. ....*Illus* 500.00
Bowl, Cover, Volcanic Brown Over Yellow Over Cream Glaze, 2 1/8 In. 210.00
Bowl, Flared Rim, Gunmetal Over Gold Finish, Impressed Mark, 10 1/2 x 6 1/4 In. 2650.00
Bowl, Yellow & Gray Rim, Iridescent Base, 3 x 5 1/2 In. 300.00
Candlestick, Iridescent Gray To Green Glaze, Ring Under Nozzle, c.1920, 15 In. 2070.00
Console, Green To Gold To Lavender, Turquoise Interior, 10 In. ....*Illus* 600.00
Console, Yellow, Stamp, c.1930, 4 1/2 x 11 In. 400.00
Pitcher, Green Matte Glaze, Early Maple Leaf Mark, 8 In. 330.00
Plate, Turquoise Rim, Blue To Lavender Interior, Stamp, c.1930, 9 1/4 In. 400.00
Tile, Fairy Tale Subjects, Surrounding Fireplace, Blue, Iridescent Teal, White, 12 x 9 In. . . 1200.00
Tile, Orange Turkey, Blue Ground, Square, 3 1/4 In. 125.00
Tile, Outline Of Michigan, Detroit Business Woman's Club, 1912, 4 In. 55.00
Vase, Blue Iridescent Dripping Glaze, 2 1/2 In. 225.00
Vase, Blue Matte Glaze, Incised Mark, 5 x 4 In. 415.00
Vase, Blue Metallic Glaze, Paper Label, Impressed Mark, 3 In. 330.00
Vase, Blue To Green, Sloped Base, Flared Neck, 10 1/4 In. 1955.00
Vase, Blue, Green Metallic, Impressed Mark, 2 1/2 In. 210.00
Vase, Egyptian Blue Glaze, Signed, 5 1/2 In. 825.00
Vase, Flared, Iridescent Turquoise, Gray, Impressed Mark, 5 1/4 In. 550.00
Vase, Flared Rim, Bulbous, Iridescent Glaze, Round Impressed Mark, 7 In. 870.00
Vase, Flared Rim, Tapered Foot, Turquoise Glossy Glaze, 7 x 5 In. 385.00
Vase, Flared Rim, Uneven Matte Brown Glaze, Paper Label, 5 1/4 x 6 3/4 In. 440.00
Vase, Gold To Blue, Iridescent, Egg Shape, 7 1/2 In. 1300.00
Vase, Green To Brown, Ribbed Neck, Egg Shape, c.1920, 7 3/4 In. 700.00
Vase, Iridescent Green & Purple Flambe Glaze, Hand Thrown, 6 3/4 In. 880.00
Vase, Light Green Metallic Glaze, Purple, Maroon, Paper Label, 6 1/2 In. 1450.00

Pewabic, Console,
Green To Gold
To Lavender,
Turquoise Interior,
10 In.

Pewabic, Bowl, Copper To Green To
Lavender, Iridescent, 1930, 5 1/2 In.

Pewabic, Bowl, Copper To Green To
Lavender, Iridescent, 1940, 5 1/4 In.

Vase, Turquoise Over Brown, 6 1/2 In. 650.00
Vase, Turquoise Over Luster Red Glaze, 3 1/2 In. 525.00

PEWTER is a metal alloy of tin and lead. Some of the pewter made after
1840 has a slightly different composition and is called *Britannia metal.*
This later type of pewter was worked by machine; the earlier pieces
were made by hand. In the 1920s pewter came back into fashion and
pieces were often marked *Genuine Pewter.* Eighteenth-, nineteenth-,
and twentieth-century examples are listed here.

Baptismal Bowl, Stamp Design Edge, Molded Inverted Dome, Round Foot, 3 5/8 In. 690.00
Basin, Single Reeded Rim, Late 18th Century, Germany, 12 1/2 In. 265.00
Basin, Thomas Danforth III, Connecticut, Marked Laughlin, c.1777, 9 In. 747.00
Basket, Kayserzinn, Art Nouveau, 11 In. 195.00
Beaker, Inside Bottom Stamped Touchmark, T.P., 1830s, 3 1/4 In. 395.00
Beaker, Oliver Trask, Massachusetts, c.1832-1847, 4 3/8 In., Pair 1150.00
Beaker, Tulip Shape, Incised Rim, England, 1825, 3 7/8 In., Pair 115.00
Beaker, Tulip Shape, Incised Rim, Footed, England, 1825, 4 In. 110.00
Bird Feeder, American, Early 19th Century, 3 1/2 In. 325.00
Bowl, Footed, Liberty, Turquoise, Large 1350.00
Bowl, Shallow, Thomas Danforth, Lion Touch, 13 1/4 In. 355.00
Bowl, Thomas Danforth, Philadelphia, 11 5/8 In. 385.00
Box, Engraved Eagle Scrolling & Floral Urn, America, 3 3/8 x 1 7/8 In. 85.00
Cache Pot, Hanging, Dutch, Raised Backs In Form Of Male & Female, 13 3/4 In., Pair . 720.00
Candlestick, Altar, Ring, Baluster Turned Stem, Cylindrical, 19 In. 58.00
Candlestick, Joshua B. & Henry H. Graves, Connecticut, c.1850, 9 3/4 In., Pair 632.00
Candlestick, Nekrassoff, Art Nouveau, 1940s, 9 1/4 In. 89.00
Chamberstick, Vanhauten, 7 In. 45.00
Charger, Gershom, Jones, Pitted, 13 1/2 In. 445.00
Charger, John Shovny, England, 15 In. 137.00
Charger, John Townsend & Reynolds, London, Oval, 1770, 22 3/4 In. 750.00
Charger, Nathaniel Austin, Engraved T.E. Back, 13 1/2 In. 550.00
Charger, S. Duncombe, Oval, England, 20 1/2 In.. .... 625.00
Charger, Thomas & Townsend Compton, 15 In. 260.00
Charger, Thomas Badger, 15 In. 520.00
Charger, Thomas Compton, England, 14 5/8 In. 220.00
Clock, Tudric, Copper Face, Hammered Numerals, Sloped Shaped Base, 1900, 12 In. 8050.00
Coffee & Tea Set, James Dixon & Sons, 1851, 5 Piece 1500.00
Coffeepot, Allen Porter, Westbrook, Maine, 1830, 11 3/4 In. 285.00
Coffeepot, H. Homan, Flower Finial, 8 3/4 In. 80.00
Coffeepot, J.H. Putnam, Malden, Mass., 1830, 11 In. 345.00
Coffeepot, James Dixon & Sons, Wooden Handle, 1848, 10 In. 200.00
Coffeepot, Lighthouse Form, Freeman Porter, 10 1/2 In. 125.00
Coffeepot, Melon, Fruit, Leaf Design Finial & Spout, Ivory Handle 375.00
Coffeepot, Rufus Dunham, Turned Body, c.1850 .... 110.00
Coffeepot, Triple-Belly, Boardman & Co., Connecticut, c.1830, 11 1/2 In. 862.00
Coffeepot, Wicker Handle, Porter Blanchard, 1930, 8 3/8 In. 205.00
Creamer, William Will, Beaded Spout, Spur Scroll Handle, Plinth Base, 4 1/2 In. 6900.00
Creamer, With Ear Handle, 4 5/8 In. 275.00
Dish, Continental, G. Voltlander, Angel Touch, 8 1/2 In. 220.00
Dish, Cover, Crown Finial, Continental, 11 1/2 In. 275.00
Dish, Cover, G. Voltlander, Angel Touch, Continental, 8 1/2 In. 220.00
Dish, Cover, Kayserzinn, Art Nouveau, 7 In. 95.00
Dish, Double, 11 1/2 In. 165.00
Dish, Engraved Inscription On Rim, Date 1693, 13 In. 550.00
Dish, Form Of Reclining Woman, Dress Forms Well, England, 13 1/2 In. 715.00
Eggcup, England, 18th Century 150.00
Flagon, Boardman & Hart, Connecticut, Marked, c.1830, 1 Qt. 430.00
Flagon, Double Scroll Handle, Finial, Scroll Thumbpiece, 12 3/4 In. 230.00
Flagon, Engraved Floral, Repeating Design, Pewter Cover, Berry Finial, 1814, 12 In. ... 180.00
Flagon, Thomas D. & Sherman Boardman, Connecticut, 3 Qt. 747.00
Humidor, Claw & Ball Feet, 7 1/2 In. 75.00
Jar, Potpourri, Geometric Pierced, Enameled Blue & Ivory Interior, 3 1/4 x 7 In. 695.00
Ladle, Boardman, Curved Handle, 13 In. 247.00

Lamp, Ear Handle, Burning Fluid Burner, American, 7 In. 110.00
Lamp, Ear Handle, Snuffer Caps, Fluid Burner, 5 3/4 In. 137.00
Lamp, Flange Foot, Whale Oil Burner, 8 1/2 In. 165.00
Lamp, Roswell Gleason, Burner, 5 1/2 In. 385.00
Lamp, Whale Oil Burner, 7 7/8 In. ....165.00 to 190.00
Lavabo, Arched Back Plate, Demilune Cistern, Mask Under Spout, Continental, 16 In. ... 285.00
Mold, Candle, 6 Tubes, Pine Frame, Varnish, 16 3/4 In. 825.00
Mold, Candle, 12 Tubes, Brass Top Plate & Tips, Poplar, A.D. Richmond, 6 x 15 In. 990.00
Mold, Candle, 12 Tubes, Pine Frame, 5 1/4 x 18 x 18 3/8 In. 605.00
Mold, Candle, 18 Tubes, Steel Rods For Tying Wicks, W. Webb, 17 1/2 x 22 In. 825.00
Mold, Candle, 21 Tubes, Pine & Poplar Frame, Worn Patina, 7 x 17 x 13 In. 825.00
Mold, Candle, 24 Tubes, Pine Frame, 6 1/2 x 22 x 18 In. 825.00
Mold, Candle, 24 Tubes, Varnished, W. Humiston 1375.00
Mold, Ice Cream, 5 Flowers, 5 In. 82.00
Mold, Ice Cream, Billiken 70.00
Mold, Ice Cream, Coffeepot 135.00
Mold, Ice Cream, E & Co. Rotary Club 27.00
Mold, Ice Cream, Eagle 135.00
Mold, Ice Cream, Elephant, 8 In. 242.00
Mold, Ice Cream, Fish, 14 In. 275.00
Mold, Ice Cream, Flower 45.00
Mold, Ice Cream, Football 48.00
Mold, Ice Cream, Fruit 45.00
Mold, Ice Cream, George Washington 60.00
Mold, Ice Cream, Heart, Love, Hinged 45.00
Mold, Ice Cream, Penguin 175.00
Mold, Ice Cream, Pretzel 45.00
Mold, Ice Cream, Seasonal, Turkey, Rabbit, Cupid & Washington Bust, 4 In. 55.00
Mold, Ice Cream, Squirrel, 2 1/2 In. 95.00
Mug, Boardman & Hart, New York, Cast Ear Handle, 3 1/8 In. 275.00
Mug, Boardman, Miniature 65.00
Mug, Stamped Quart, VR With Crown, Owner's Initials In Front, 6 In. 125.00
Nursing Bottle, Flask Shape, Narrow Neck, Removable Nipple, Japan, 6 1/4 In. 480.00
Pail, Market, Cherub Masks T-Handle Joints, Dutch, 1750s, 4 1/2 In. 350.00
Pap Boat, Scalloped Flat Handle, X & Crown & C.G., 1765, 5 1/2 In. 295.00
Pepper Pot, c.1820, 4 In. 75.00
Pitcher, Hinged Cover, 7 In. 70.00
Pitcher, Water, Boardman, Hinged Lid, 8 1/4 In. 245.00
Pitcher, Water, Cover, Thomas Boardman, c.1830, 11 In. 345.00
Plate, Ashbil Griswold Eagle Touch, 7 7/8 In. 160.00
Plate, Edward Danforth, Rampant Lion Touch, 8 In. 220.00
Plate, Frederick Bassett, N.Y., 8 1/2 In. 165.00
Plate, Jacob Eggleston, Eagle Touch, Middletown, Ct., 7 7/8 In. ....715.00 to 1210.00
Plate, Thomas Badger, Eagle Touch, 7 7/8 In. 275.00
Plate, Thomas Danforth, Eagle Touch, 6 1/8 In. 550.00
Porringer, Boardman, Old English Handle, Thomas Danforth, 4 In. 495.00
Porringer, c.1810-1830, 5 3/8 In. 690.00
Porringer, Cast Corn Handle, Marked I.G., 4 3/4 In. 137.00
Porringer, Cast Flowered Handle, 5 In. 145.00
Porringer, Crown Handle, New England, 19th Century, 5 1/2 In. 295.00
Porringer, Flower Handle, Marked, Rhode Island, 5 1/4 In. 295.00
Porringer, Tab Handle, Penna., 5 5/8 In. 975.00
Pot, Claw Feet, Loop Handles, Dutch, c.1780, 10 In. 650.00
Pot, Lighthouse, F. Porter, Westbrook No. 1, 10 3/4 In. 250.00
Pot, Tall, A. Griswold, Eagle Touch, 10 1/2 In. 357.00
Salt Cellar, James Dixon & Sons, 3 Bells, Bronze, Cast Metal, 1860 .... 33.00
Snuff Box, Embossed, With Knight & Horses On Both Sides, Me., 1800-1812 .... 140.00
Spice Box, 2 Compartments, Double-Hinged Lids, Paw Feet, c.1740, 4 3/4 In. 150.00
Spoon, Stuffing, Bright Cut Floral On Handle, Anchor Mark, 14 In. 110.00
Stein, Barrel Shape, Pewter Cover, 1840, 1/5 Liter 275.00
Sugar & Creamer, Puritan 125.00
Syrup, Hinged Cover, Hall & Cotton, 6 1/8 In. 660.00
Syrup, Hinged Lid, American, 4 1/2 In. 220.00

Tankard, Frederick Bassett, Thumbpiece, Crenellated Lip, Scroll Handle, 6 1/2 In. 575.00
Tankard, Hunting Scenes 85.00
Tankard, James Yates, 1/2 Pt. 85.00
Tankard, Silver Cross, 33 Whithall, Silver On Copper, 1/2 Pt. 60.00
Tankard, Thumbpiece, Dome Top, Scroll Handle, Molded Base, 7 In. 1495.00
Tea Set, Liberty & Co., Hammered, Bamboo Handle, Tray, 2 Handles 715.00
Teapot, Boardman, 7 3/8 In. 300.00
Teapot, E. Smith, Pear Shape, 7 1/4 In. 330.00
Teapot, Floral, Calligraphic Design, Jade Handles, 3 3/4 In. 33.00
Teapot, H. Yale & Co., 8 In. 192.00
Teapot, H.B. Ward, Wallingford, Ct., 8 1/2 In. 275.00
Teapot, Henry Graves, Middletown, Connecticut 345.00
Teapot, Incised Bamboo, Jade Handle, Spout, Finial, 19th Century, 4 In. 133.00
Teapot, James Dixon & Sons 85.00
Teapot, Melon Rib, Ivory On Handle, Eagle Head Spout, Marked 220.00
Teapot, Old Sheffield, Pumpkin Shape, Britannia 55.00
Teapot, Pear Shape, Continental, 8 1/2 In. 155.00
Teapot, R. Dunham, 8 In. 94.00
Teapot, Savage, No. 6 Touch, 6 3/4 In. 110.00
Teapot, Thomas Boardman 105.00
Teapot, Townsend & Compton, Pear Shape, 7 In. 415.00
Teapot, William Will, Pear Shape Body, Domed Lid, C-Shape Spur Handle, 7 1/2 In. ... 1380.00
Trophy, Liberty, Tudric, Glyn House Essay, Stylized Trees, 1922-1936, 8 x 7 In. 330.00
Urn, Coffee, Neoclassical, Eagle Head Handles, Bud Form Lid Finial, 1790 .... 665.00
Vase, 2 Greyhound Handles, 6 In., Pair 150.00
Vase, J. Despres, Pairs Of Glyphs, Hammered Balls At Tim, c.1930, 10 5/8 In. 6325.00
Vase, Kayserzinn, Clawed Rabbits Holding Fruit, Raised Mark, Footed 264.00
Vase, Osiris, Peacock Feather Design, Blue, Green Jewels, 4-Footed, 8 In. 355.00

PHOENIX BIRD, or Flying Phoenix, is the name given to a blue-and-
white kitchenware popular between 1900 and World War II. A variant
is known as Flying Turkey. Most of this dinnerware was made in Japan
for sale in the dime stores in America. It is still being made.

Casserole, Cover, Oval, 10 In. 185.00
Cup & Saucer 10.00
Pitcher, Bird, 2 1/2 In. 18.00
Plate, 6 In. 8.00
Plate, 10 In. 45.00
Sugar & Creamer 50.00

PHOENIX GLASS Company was founded in 1880 in Pennsylvania. The
firm made commercial products, such as lampshades, bottles, and glassware. Collectors today are interested in the "Sculptured Artware" made
by the company from the 1930s until the mid-1950s. Some pieces of
Phoenix glass are very similar to those made by the Consolidated Lamp
and Glass Company. Phoenix made Reuben Blue, lavender, and yellow
pieces. These colors were not used by Consolidated. In 1970 Phoenix
became a division of Anchor Hocking, then was sold to the Newell
Group in 1987. The company is still working.

Candlestick, Strawberry, Milk Glass, Tan Wash 75.00
Charger, Fishes, Shallow Bowl 295.00
Cologne, Cameo, Blue Lotus Blossoms, White Ground, Matching Stopper 395.00
Compote, Fish, Gray Wash, 3 x 6 In. ....80.00 to 135.00
Lamp, Dogwood, Pink, Metal Base, Shade, 22 In. 137.50
Shade, Art Deco, Reverse Painted Bell 250.00
Vase, Bluebell, Pink Wash, Pearlized Design, Label, 7 In. 125.00
Vase, Bluebells, Frosted Ground With Flowers, 7 In. 110.00
Vase, Cosmos, Milk Glass, Green Wash, 7 1/4 In. 120.00
Vase, Dancing Nymph, Blue Wash 390.00
Vase, Fern, Blue Wash, 7 1/2 In. ....60.00 to 100.00
Vase, Ferns, Tan Wash, Silver & Black, Label, 7 In. 150.00
Vase, Katydid, Amber Wash, 8 1/4 In. ....250.00 to 265.00
Vase, Philodendron, Blue Shadow, 11 1/2 In. 120.00

Vase, Pillow, Wild Geese, Paper Label, 9 In. 225.00
Vase, Primrose, Crystal, Cased Milk Glass, 9 In. 125.00
Vase, Starflower, Brown Wash, 7 In. 150.00
Vase, Thistle, Umbrella Shape, Opalescent, 9 In. 425.00
Vase, Wild Geese, Milk Glass, Pink Wash, 7 In. 195.00
Vase, Zodiac, 10 In. 655.00

PHONOGRAPHS, invented by Thomas Edison in the 1880s, have been
made by many firms. This category also includes other items associated with the phonograph. Jukeboxes and records are listed in their own
categories.

Bee Gees, Vanity Fair, Group Photograph Lid, 33 & 45 RPM, Strobe Light, 1979 ...... 139.00
Columbia, 17 1/2-In. Outside Red Horn 650.00
Columbia, Black & Gold Horn, Felt Turn Table, Oak, 19 Edison Records, 14 3/4 In. 522.00
Columbia, Graphophone, Model Q, Brass Bell, Horn 150.00
Doll, 2 Cylinders, Madame Hendron 750.00
Edison, Built-In Horn, 134 Edison Blue Amberola Cylinders, Oak Case, 32 1/4 In. 577.00
Edison, Diamond Disc, Mahogany, Floor Model 192.00
Edison, Fireside, Flowered Horn, 2-4 Minute Reproducer 600.00
Edison, Fireside, Horn, K Reproducer 750.00
Edison, Home, Black & Gold Horn, Oak Case, 25 Cylinders, 16 In. 577.00
Edison, Standard, Oak Case, Morning Glory Horn, Blue Japanning, 12 3/4 In. 577.50
Maestrofono, Beveled Glass Sides, Red Horn, Ornate Cabinet 2100.00
Multiphone, Coin-Operated, Cylinder, Multiphone Operating Co., N.Y., 1908 .... 30800.00
Needle, Cutter, Victor 95.00
Upright, Heywood Wakefield Cabinet, Perfektone Motor, Wicker 1450.00
Victor, Model VTLA No. 992, Internal Horn, 7 Albums, c.1906 .... 1955.00
Victor, Schoolhouse VXXV, Wooden Horn 2500.00
Victor IV, Mahogany, Horn, 1905-1915 ....2500.00 to 3600.00
Victor V, Oak Horn 3800.00
Victor VI, Mahogany ....5700.00 to 6000.00
Zon-O-Phone, Blue Horn, 1906 .... 2300.00

PHOTOGRAPHY items are listed here. The first photograph was a view
from a window in France taken in 1826. The commercially successful
photograph started with the daguerreotype introduced in 1839. Today
all sorts of photographs and photographic equipment are collected.
Albums were popular in Victorian times. Cartes de visite, popular after
1854, were mounted on 2 1/2-by-4-inch cardboard. Cabinet cards were
introduced in 1866. These were mounted on 4 1/4-by-6 1/2-inch cards.
Stereo views are listed under Stereo Card. The cases for daguerreo-
types are listed in the Gutta-Percha category.

Album, Photograph, Oriental Design, Black Lacquer 125.00
Albumen, Young Buffalo Bill, Floral Plastic Frame, 4 1/2 x 5 In. 450.00
Ambrotype, Carpenter, 6th Plate 605.00
Ambrotype, Civil War Officer, Musket, Revolver, 6th Plate 450.00
Ambrotype, Civil War Soldier In Jefferson Davis Hat, Camp Scene Case 175.00
Ambrotype, Civil War Soldier, New Hampshire, 1/9th Plate 95.00
Ambrotype, Corner Of 6th Street & Central Avenue, Cincinnati, 6th Plate 8250.00
Ambrotype, Lincoln, Hamlin, 6th Plate 8000.00
Ambrotype, Man, Bearded, Waist Up Seated View, 1/4 Plate 38.00
Ambrotype, Man, Begging Dog 65.00
Ambrotype, Union Cavalry Officer, Bearded, Holding 1850 Sword, 1/4 Plate 825.00
Ambrotype, Union Enlisted Man, Bearded, Leatherette Case, 1/6 Plate 105.00
Ambrotype, Union Enlisted Soldier, Wearing Kepi, 1851, 1/6 Plate 660.00
Ambrotype, Union Field Grade Officer, Sword, Seated, Whole Plate 880.00
Ambrotype, William A. Neer, Private, 66th Ohio Volunteer Infantry, 1/2 Plate 1430.00
Cabinet Card, 3 Apache Indians 250.00
Cabinet Card, Admiral Farragut, Full Dress, Sword, Sarony 225.00
Cabinet Card, Black Woman, With White Baby, 1875 .... 95.00
Cabinet Card, Buffalo Bill, Embossed Mount, Repro Photo Co., N.Y., 6 x 9 In. 1375.00
Cabinet Card, Clark Griffith, Portrait, Sporting Life 1600.00
Cabinet Card, Col. W.F. Cody, Buffalo Bill, Stacy 700.00

Cabinet Card, Fort Marion, St. Augustine, Florida, Oversized 45.00
Cabinet Card, G.A.R. Soldier, Illinois 65.00
Cabinet Card, General Tom Thumb & Wife, On Balcony, Signed By Both, 1881 ...... 125.00
Cabinet Card, Gold Miners, Placerville, Calif., 1892 .... 35.00
Cabinet Card, John L. Sullivan, 1889 .... 250.00
Cabinet Card, Lillian Russell, Max Platz, 1880s ....165.00 to 250.00
Cabinet Card, Little Boy, Sunday Outfit, With Baseball Bat & Ball, 1890s 125.00
Cabinet Card, Man, With Double Barrel Shotgun 32.00
Cabinet Card, Nagel's Photograph Studio, Lansford, Penna. 125.00
Cabinet Card, Sitting Bull, Biography On Reverse, Palmquist & Jurgens, 1884 .... 875.00
Cabinet Card, Soldier, Spanish-American War, 1898 .... 45.00
Cabinet Card, Winston Churchill, Young, Medals Bar, Elliott & Fry, 1901-1905 .... 200.00
Cabinet Card, Wrestler, John Hart, New York Illustrated News 55.00
Cabinet Card, Young Boy With Rocking Horse 35.00
Cabinet Card, Young Woman, Ornate Design On Back, J. Holler, San Francisco 15.00
Camera, Aircraft, World War II 250.00
Camera, Autographic Brownie, Case, Manual 45.00
Camera, Bell & Howell, 6 Lenses, 7 View Finders, Tripod, Case 275.00
Camera, Box, Rochester Optical Company, 11 1/2 x 7 In. 46.00
Camera, Ciroflex/Wollensak, Twin Lens 45.00
Camera, Contax 35mm, Zeiss Lens, Original Leather Case 220.00
Camera, Copy, Make Magic Lantern Slides, Folmer & Schwing, Stand, 1907 .... 800.00
Camera, Eastman, Brownie, No. 2, Box 115.00
Camera, Kodak, Beau Brownie 2A, Green Deco Faceplate 200.00
Camera, Kodak, Carrying Case & Cedar Lined Box, Walter Dorwin Teague 250.00
Camera, Kodak, Master Photoguide, Original Leather Case 33.00
Camera, Kodak, No. 5, Folding, Pneumatic Shutter, Focus Screen, Leather Case 80.00
Camera, Kodak, No. 100 Exposure, Factory Loaded 168.00
Camera, Kodak, Petite, Pink, Blush Compact Case 630.00
Camera, Leica III, Range Finder, 50 mm Lens, Leather Carrying Case 253.00
Camera, Mamiya, Super 16, Occupied Japan, Case 75.00
Camera, Vest Pocket, Leather Case, 1902 .... 65.00
Camera, Waterhouse Stops, Carrying Box, Rochester Optical Co., 1875 .... 995.00
Carte De Visite, Abraham Lincoln, Brady 1300.00
Carte De Visite, Admiral Farragut, Fredricks 75.00
Carte De Visite, Bearded Man In Civilian Dress, Identified As Mr. Chilton 5.00
Carte De Visite, Civil War Naval Officer, Seated, 1/6th Plate 165.00
Carte De Visite, Confederate Naval Office, Wearing Frock Coat 248.00
Carte De Visite, General George Armstrong 935.00
Carte De Visite, General George Custer, Whitehurst Gallery 1800.00
Carte De Visite, General John C. Fremont, Fredricks 55.00
Carte De Visite, General Phil Sheridan, Seated View 330.00
Carte De Visite, J.G. Barnard Bvt. Maj. Gen., Sword, Fassett, Autograph 400.00
Carte De Visite, John B. Dennis Bvt. Brig Gen., Jewett, Autograph 350.00
Carte De Visite, Lieutenant Colonel, Wearing Uniform Coat, Mustache 495.00
Carte De Visite, Pres. Lincoln's Farewell Address, Springfield Friends, 1865 .... 135.00
Carte De Visite, Robert E. Lee, Signed, c.1866 .... 6900.00
Carte De Visite, Sam Houston, Cane, Cloak, Hat, Fredricks, 1861 .... 1200.00
Carte De Visite, Sojourner Truth 1573.00
Carte De Visite, Soldier, Civil War Uniform, Signed B.J. Rhodes 75.00
Carte De Visite, Thomas Sully, 1860s 250.00
Carte De Visite, U.S. Grant, Signed Lt. Gen., U.S.A., Faded 460.00
Carte De Visite, Union General, Mutton Chop Whiskers & Mustache 192.00
Carte De Visite, Union Naval Officer, Mutton Chop Whiskers 165.00
Carte De Visite, Union Naval Officers, Seated With Swords 357.50
Carte De Visite, Union Navy Lieutenant Commander, Long Beard, Frock Coat 137.50
Carte De Visite, Union Officer, Waist Up Seated View, 1861 .... 275.00
Carte De Visite, Union Soldier, With Sword 55.00
Carte De Visite, Woman, Children, Wagon, Lions Pulling, St. Paul, 1879 .... 14.00
Carte De Visite, Young Girl, Doll In Buggy, Dog At Feet, Full Image 60.00
Daguerreotype, 3 Year Old Girl, Next To Table, 1/6th Plate 150.00
Daguerreotype, 3 Young Men, Gold Miners, Horizontal 1/2 Plate 550.00
Daguerreotype, American Indian Husband & Wife, Case 302.00

Daguerreotype, Bearded Gentleman, Leather Case, 1/2 Plate 350.00
Daguerreotype, Brick Federal House, Widow's Walk, Man In Yard, 1/4 Plate 1850.00
Daguerreotype, Cemetery Monument, 1/2 Plate 2610.00
Daguerreotype, Civil Soldier, High Collar Coat, Framed, Full Plate, 14 x 12 1/2 In. 155.00
Daguerreotype, Civil War Union Soldier, Leather Case Embossed, 3 x 3 3/4 In. 105.00
Daguerreotype, Clergyman, Big Bible 78.00
Daguerreotype, Couple, 1/4 Plate 85.00
Daguerreotype, Cross-Eyed Woman, 1/6 Plate 95.00
Daguerreotype, Family Scene, Baby In Mother's Arms, 1/2 Plate 775.00
Daguerreotype, Father, With Violin, Son, Cat On Lap, 1/6 Plate 605.00
Daguerreotype, Fireman, Saving Child, 1/6 Plate 200.00
Daguerreotype, Girl Holding Picture, Grandmother With Eyeglasses, 1/6 Plate 200.00
Daguerreotype, Group Of Miners, 1/2 Plate 25000.00
Daguerreotype, Horse-Drawn Buggy On Street, 1/2 Plate 385.00
Daguerreotype, Husband & Wife, 1/4 Plate 100.00
Daguerreotype, Indian Case, 1/16 Plate 300.00
Daguerreotype, Man In Suit, Leather Case, 1/9 Plate 85.00
Daguerreotype, Man With Daughter Holding Pocket Watch Up, 1/6 Plate 85.00
Daguerreotype, Portrait, Erastus Salisbury Fields, 1850, 1/6 Plate 490.00
Daguerreotype, Portrait, Joseph Davis, Leather Case, 1850, 1/6 Plate 920.00
Daguerreotype, Portrait, Of A Lady, Leather Case, 1850, 1/6 Plate 115.00
Daguerreotype, Pregnant 14 Year Old Sarah T. Mayo, 6th Plate 1200.00
Daguerreotype, Wedding Cake House, Kennebunk, Maine, 1/4 Plate 6600.00
Daguerreotype, Well Dressed Couple, 1/2 Plate 350.00
Daguerreotype, Woman In Lovely Dress, Beaded Purse, 3/4 Plate 550.00
Daguerreotype, Woman, Black Case, Mother-Of-Pearl On Front 70.00
Daguerreotype, Woman, Seated, Pale Blue Tint, 1/4 Plate 175.00
Daguerreotype, Young Child, Standing Blue Tinted Dress, 1/9 Plate 150.00
Daguerreotype, Young Woman, Dress & Bonnet, Holding Photo Case, 1/9 Plate 40.00
Developing Kit, Home, Kodak, 1913 .... 23.00
Lantern, Darkroom, Red Glass 45.00
Magic Lantern, 12 Slides, Box, c.1880 .... 130.00
Magic Lantern, Bausch & Lomb, Electric, Fitted Metal Case, 1930s 225.00
Photograph, Activities At Chicago Ship Building Co., Silver Gelatin, 1898 .... 770.00
Photograph, Child, Hoop, Landscape, Oil On Heavy Paper, Gilt Frame, 26 x 21 In. 80.00
Photograph, Civil War Soldier, Rossiter, 11 3/4 x 9 3/4 In. 66.00
Photograph, Civil War, U.S. Cavalryman, Long Coat, Tall Boots, 6 1/2 x 4 1/4 In. 122.00
Photograph, Engine, Body Of Pres. Lincoln, Leather Case, Full Plate ....*Illus* 1100.00
Photograph, Eskimos, In Front Of Trading Post, Pt. Barrow, 1920, 3 x 5 1/2 In. 12.50
Photograph, Impeachment Of Andrew Johnson, Brady, 1868, 9 1/2 x 11 In. 950.00
Photograph, John A. Logan, Civil War, Walnut Cross Frame, 11 x 14 In. 63.00
Photograph, John Wilkes Booth, Gothic Chair, 7 x 10 In. 2250.00
Photograph, Lincoln Memorial, Apple Trees Foreground, Tinted, 8 x 10 5/8 In. 65.00
Photograph, President McKinley, Full Masonic Outfit, 10 1/2 x 8 1/2 In. 110.00
Photograph, Seaman, Monument, Down To Sea In Ships, 1623-1923, 10 x 14 In. 75.00
Photograph, Workers Outside Redwood Brewery, Winnipeg, Canada, 10 x 12 In. 250.00
Projector, Opitica, Germany, Cased, 20 x 23 In. 85.00

**Never touch the surface of
a daguerreotype or an
ambrotype. The perspiration
will stain the image.**

Photography, Photograph, Engine,
Body Of Pres. Lincoln, Leather Case, Full Plate

Photography, Tintype,
Civil War Soldier & Wife

Photography, Tintype, Civil War
Soldier, Gun, Case, 1/4 Plate

Projector, Pathe, Films	195.00
Stanhope, Charm, Spy Glass, Atlantic City Scene	35.00
Stanhope, Opera Glass Shape, Mother-Of-Pearl, Trieste Views, 7/8 In.	110.00
Tintype, 2 Men, Shotguns & Pistols	125.00
Tintype, 5 Union Infantrymen, Leaning On Muskets, 2 5/8 x 4 In.	1320.00
Tintype, Bearded Union Infantryman, Holding Musket, 1/4 Plate	550.00
Tintype, Black Man With Cigar, 1/6 Plate	95.00
Tintype, Black Woman, Fancy Bustle Dress	65.00
Tintype, Civil War Era Musician, Wearing Kepi, 1/6 Plate	143.00
Tintype, Civil War Naval Officer, Engraved Sword, Leather Case	660.00
Tintype, Civil War Officer, On Horse, 6 Men With Handguns, 1/4 Plate	368.00
Tintype, Civil War Soldier & Wife . . . . *Illus*	2640.00
Tintype, Civil War Soldier, Bars On Shoulder, Cannons On Cap, Tinted, Full Plate	420.00
Tintype, Civil War Soldier, Death Certificate, Killed At Wilderness, 1864, 18 In.	835.00
Tintype, Civil War Soldier, Dressed In Gray, H On Cap, Leather Case, 1/4 Plate	95.00
Tintype, Civil War Soldier, Full Uniform, Bayonet Mounted Rifle, 1/6 Plate	420.00
Tintype, Civil War Soldier, Gun, Case, 1/4 Plate . . . . *Illus*	1760.00
Tintype, Civil War Soldier, Holding Fatigue Cap, McLaughlin, Full Plate	168.00
Tintype, Civil War Soldier, Uniform, Holding Cavalry Hat, Leather Case, 1/9 Plate	263.00
Tintype, Civil War Uniformed Soldier, Knives In Belt, Leather Case, 1/6 Plate	130.00
Tintype, Civil War Veteran, G.A.R., Small	100.00
Tintype, Civil War, 3 Boys Wearing Uniform Of Southern Enlisted Men	125.00
Tintype, Civil War, Cavalryman, Burnside Carbine, Revolver, Saber, 1/9 Plate	1070.00
Tintype, Jesse & Frank James, Another Man, Fort Smith, Ark.	6000.00
Tintype, John Wilkes Booth, Embossed CDV	850.00
Tintype, Man, Bowler Hat	9.00
Tintype, Men & Children, Henry I. Sundmaker's Building, Whole Plate, 1870s	825.00
Tintype, Soldier, Seated, 1860, 1/6 Plate	192.00
Tintype, Soldier, Uniform Jacket, Belt, 1850 Sword, 1/4 Plate	286.00
Tintype, Union Enlisted Soldier, British Belt, Snake Buckle, 1/9 Plate	192.00
Tintype, Union Enlisted Soldier, With Flag In Background, 1/4 Plate	44.00
Tintype, Union Infantryman, Frock Coat & Kepi, Musket, 1/4 Plate	700.00
Tintype, Union Infantryman, Kepi, Cap, 1842 Musket, 1/6 Plate	165.00
Tintype, Union Officer, Fatigue Cap, Jacket, Epaulets, Frame, 7 1/8 x 5 In.	95.00
Tintype, Union Officer, Holding Percussion Revolver, Red Sash, 1/6 Plate	220.00
Tintype, Union Officers & Their Wives Outdoors, 5 Wearing Kepis, 1/2 Plate	2695.00
Tintype, Will W. Harris, Musket At Side, Lock, 2 1/2 x 3 1/2 In.	125.00
Tintype, Young Girl, Only 1 Leg, Civil War Era, 1/6 Plate	25.00
Tintype, Young Lady, Seated, Waist Up, Gilt Leatherette Case, 1/6 Plate	65.00
Tintype, Young Man, Holding Shotgun, 1/6 Plate	25.00

Tintype, Young Soldier, Open Coat Shows Vest, From Va., 1/9 Plate 110.00

PIANO BABY is a collector's term. About 1880, the well-decorated home had a shawl on the piano. Bisque figures of babies were designed to help hold the shawl in place. They range in size from 6 to 18 inches. Most of the figures were made in Germany. Reproductions are being made. Other piano babies may be listed under manufacturers' names.

Lying On Back, Feet & Hands In Air, White Dress, Heubach, 10 1/2 In. 275.00
Lying On Back, Heubach, 10 In. 250.00
Lying On Stomach, Bisque, Head Down On Arms, Pink Bonnet, 4 1/2 In. 70.00
Lying On Stomach, Bisque, White Dress, 9 1/2 In. 115.00
Lying On Stomach, Crawling, Flowers On Dress, 10 In. 300.00
Lying On Stomach, Right Hand & Foot In Air, Thumb To Mouth, 7 In. 215.00
Seated, Arms Raised, Heubach, 4 1/2 In. 165.00
Seated, Crossed Legs, 5 In. 175.00
Sitting Up, Bisque, Left Hand Supports Him, Baby Dress, 4 In. 325.00

PICKARD China Company was started in 1898 by Wilder Pickard. Hand-painted designs were used on china purchased from other sources. In the 1930s, the company began to make its own china wares in Chicago, Illinois. The company now makes many types of porcelains, including a successful line of limited edition collector plates.

Basket, Roses, Trailing Vine, Cream, Ribbon Handle, Signed, Vobor, 1912, 6 x 6 In. 350.00
Bonbon, Chinese Pheasant, Double Handles, Samuelson, 8 1/2 In. .... 225.00 to 235.00
Bowl, Lotus Blossom, 5 In. 35.00
Bowl, Nut, Footed, Signed, 8 In. 265.00
Bowl, Painted Raspberries & Leaves, Footed, Artist, 7 1/4 In. 90.00
Bowl, Peaches Linear, Beutlich, Square, Marked, 8 1/4 In. 165.00
Bowl, Raspberries & Etched Gold, Signed, Coufall, 5 1/2 In. 132.00
Cake Platter, White Poppies, Marked, 11 In. 285.00
Candy Dish, Pale Pink Roses, Handles, Leach, 1903-1905 Mark, 8 1/4 In. 44.00
Celery Dish, Bell Flower 150.00
Chocolate Pot, Gold, Platinum, Marked, 7 In. 275.00
Compote, Orange Tree, Marked, 3 1/2 In. 150.00
Cup & Saucer, Encrusted Linear, Cup 1905-1910 Mark, Saucer 1912-1918 Mark 165.00
Cup & Saucer, Modern Conventional, Signed, P.G., 1912-1918 Mark .... 230.00 to 275.00
Cup & Saucer, Poppies On Gold, Signed, P.G., 1905-1910 Mark 275.00
Cup & Saucer, Roses, Cup 1903-1905 Mark, Saucer 1898-1903 Mark 248.00
Dish, Grape, Plum, Raspberries Design, Hexagonal Handle, Gold Trim, 8 1/4 x 4 In. 175.00
Dish, Poppy, Scalloped, Marked, 6 In. 250.00
Dish, Roman Garden Scene, 7 In. 195.00
Goblet, Currants, Gold, Marked, 6 In. 145.00
Jug, Apple Blossoms, Gold Highlights, F. Walters, 5 1/2 In. 530.00

Pickard, Pitcher, Crab Apples, Gold, Green, Signed Cou., 1905, 8 3/4 In.

Pickard, Pitcher, Lemonade, Gooseberries, Gifford, 6 1/2 In.

Pickard, Plate, Castle Mere, Challinor,
1912-1918, 8 1/2 In.

Pickard, Vase,
Cornflower,
1903-1905,
8 1/4 In.

Pitcher, Apples & Blossoms, Gifford, Marked, 8 In.	1211.00
Pitcher, Convolvulus, Hexagonal, Signed Fisher, 1912-1918, 8 In.	605.00
Pitcher, Crab Apples, Gold, Green, Signed Cou., 1905, 8 3/4 In. ....*Illus*	660.00
Pitcher, Lemonade, Carnations On Gold, Fisher, Marked, 6 1/4 In.	495.00
Pitcher, Lemonade, Daisy Multifloral, 1905-1910 Mark, 5 1/2 In.	303.00
Pitcher, Lemonade, Deserted Garden, Hexagonal, Gasper, 5 1/2 In.	990.00
Pitcher, Lemonade, Encrusted Linear, 1912-1918 Mark, 5 1/2 In.	495.00
Pitcher, Lemonade, Gooseberries, Gifford, 6 1/2 In. ....*Illus*	770.00
Pitcher, Modern Conventional, Signed, Hessler, 1905-1910 Mark, 7 3/4 In.	330.00
Pitcher, Poppies, Red, Signed, Wight, 1905-1910, 4 In.	285.00
Pitcher, Twin Tulips, Signed, 1905-1910 Mark, 7 3/4 In.	660.00
Pitcher, Wildwood, Signed, Challinor, 1912-1918 Mark, 7 3/4 In.	660.00
Plate, Castle Mere, Challinor, 1912-1918, 8 1/2 In. ....*Illus*	305.00
Plate, Children Of Christmas Past, 1983, Box	45.00
Plate, Classic Ruins By Moonlight, Square, Marked, 5 1/2 In.	275.00
Plate, Florida Moonlight, Signed, 1912-1918, 8 1/2 In.	215.00
Plate, Gold Embossed Flowers, Handles, No. 255	30.00
Plate, Gooseberries, F. Walter, 8 3/4 In.	145.00
Plate, Hand Painted, Mark, 8 1/2 In.	60.00
Plate, Nuts, Signed, Wight, 7 1/2 In.	45.00
Plate, Palm Trees, Orange Grove, Signed, Maley, 1912-1918, 8 3/4 In.	303.00
Plate, Peaches, Marked, 7 1/2 In.	65.00
Plate, Peacock, Marked, 8 1/2 In.	95.00
Plate, Plum, Signed, Leroy, 1905-1910, 6 In.	110.00
Plate, Red Cherries, Marked, 6 In.	55.00
Plate, Red, White Currant, Marked, 6 In.	60.00
Plate, Roses, Marked, 8 3/4 In.	95.00
Plate, Urn With Basket, Gold Trim, 8 In.	90.00
Plate, Wildwood, Signed, Challinor, 1912-1918 Mark, 8 1/4 In.	303.00
Plate, Yosemite, Signed, 1912-1918 Mark, 8 In.	303.00
Punch Bowl, Aura Argenta Linear, Signed, Hess, 10 In.	1640.00
Salt & Pepper, Floral Garlands, Gold Trim, c.1910	60.00
Salt & Pepper, Golden Clover, A. Richter, 1910 Mark	195.00
Salt & Pepper, Pink, Green	75.00
Salt & Pepper, Rose Band, Barrel Shape, c.1920	115.00
Saltshaker, Purple Pansies, Gold Trim, 1910	85.00
Sugar & Creamer, Peacock, Gold Etched	145.00
Sugar & Creamer, Tray, Gold Allover Pattern	150.00
Sugar & Creamer, Violet, Marked	95.00
Sugar & Creamer, Violets, Signed F.C., Marked	192.00
Sugar Shaker, Strawberries & Leaves, Artist Richmont	90.00
Teapot, Gold Allover Pattern	150.00

Tray, Italian Garden, Handles, Signed, Gaspar, 15 3/4 In. 385.00
Vase, China Twilight, Landscape, Mountain, Hand Painted, Marked, 8 In. 745.00
Vase, Cornflower, 1903-1905, 8 1/4 In. ....*Illus* 605.00
Vase, Encrusted Linear Pattern, Blue Bands To Bottom, 8 3/4 In. 650.00
Vase, Everglades, Signed, Challinor, 1912-1918 Mark, 12 In. 1595.00
Vase, Fall Birches, Scenic, Signed, Challinor, 1912-1918 Mark, 10 1/4 In. 990.00
Vase, Floral, With Birds & Butterflies, Etched, Gold Band, 8 1/2 In. 325.00
Vase, Italian Garden Band, Black Ground, 8 1/4 x 5 In. 875.00
Vase, Pond Lily, Keates, 7 In. 650.00
Vase, Purple Grapes, Luster Grapes & Leaves, Hess, 10 1/4 In. 302.00
Vase, Red Haired Sylph, Signed M, 1912-1918 Mark, 11 In. 1650.00
Vase, Rose & Daisy, Aqua Interior, Signed, 7 In. 120.00
Vase, Rose Basket, James, Marked, 11 In. 495.00
Vase, Vellum, Wildwood, Signed, E. Challinor, 7 13/16 In. 395.00

PICTURE FRAMES are listed in this book in the Furniture category under Frame.

PICTURES, silhouettes, and other small decorative objects framed to
hang on the wall are listed here. Sandpaper pictures are black and
white charcoal drawings done on a special sanded paper. Some other
types of pictures are listed in the Print and Painting categories.

Charcoal & Pencil On Paper, James M. Whistler, Walter Greaves, Frame, 12 x 8 In. ... 4025.00
Diorama, Castle Shaped Building, 9 3/4 x 178 x 17 3/4 In. 440.00
Engraving, Ashdown Coursing Meeting, Hand Colored, Matted, Frame, 28 x 50 In. 275.00
Engraving, Bonaparte, Matted, Frame, 19th Century, France, 29 x 17 In. 345.00
Engraving, Hand Colored, Live Bait Fishing For Jack, Frame, England, 25 x 27 In. 3800.00
Engraving, Sleeping Bloodhound, Hand Colored, Matted, Frame, 17 1/4 x 19 3/4 In. ... 60.00
Ink & Wash On Paper, Horn Player, Brown, Continental, 19th Century, 4 x 2 3/4 In. ... 400.00
Ink On Paper, Primitive Birds & Flowers, Watercolor, Frame, 6 x 7 3/8 In. 80.00
Needlework, Apollo, Seated, Castle, Silk Embroidered, Frame, 1660, 9 x 12 In. 8050.00
Needlework, Cornucopia, Vine Border, Silk On Linen, Frame, 1797, 14 x 13 In. 460.00
Needlework, Embroidery, Noble Persons At Castle Doorway, Silk Thread, 17 x 23 In. ... 460.00
Needlework, Embroidery, Panel, Wool Satin Stitch, Black Felt Ground, 43 x 52 1/4 In. ... 250.00
Needlework, Floral Still Life, Oval, 21 1/2 x 19 In. 525.00
Needlework, Girl, Dog & Puppies, Frame, 19th Century, 27 x 24 In. 115.00
Needlework, Madonna & Child, St. John The Baptist, Silk, Metallic Thread, 14 x 13 In. . 258.00
Needlework, Map Of England & Wales, Mary Downing, 1793, 23 1/2 x 21 In. 345.00
Needlework, Roses, Buds, Silk Chenille, Gold Leaf Frame, 16 1/2 x 20 In. 485.00
Needlework, Virgin Visitation, Silk Embroidery, Frame, 1660, 18 x 21 In. 3680.00
Needlework, Woman Spinning, Young Boy Feeding Pigs, England, 25 x 18 In. 402.00
Needlework, Wool-On-Linen, Lion, Standing In Tropical Landscape, 19 x 23 3/4 In. 9775.00
Needlework, Wool-On-Linen, Tiger, Stalking In Tropical Landscape, 19 x 24 In. 9775.00
Needlework & Stumpwork, Seated Lady At Spinning Wheel, Oval, 8 3/4 x 6 3/4 In. .. 460.00
Pastel On Paper, Girl On Swing, Jefferson Smith, 20th Century, 11 x 11 In. 27.50
Pen & Ink, Tree, Names & Banner, Merry Christmas, 1904, Happy New Year, 1905 .... 11.00
Pen & Ink Drawing, Little Birds, Home, On Lined Paper, Frame, 12 1/2 x 14 1/2 In. ... 95.00
Pen & Ink On Paper, Flowers & Birds Circle, J.W. Lanham Banner, Frame, 14 x 12 In. 120.00
Petit Point, Woman, Seated, Animals All Around, Frame, 1775, 17 x 19 In. 2300.00
Sandpaper, Landscape, Buildings, Frame, 16 1/2 x 22 In. 110.00
Shadow Box, Wax Flower, Mrs. B. Lewiston, N.Y., Verse, Oval, 1884, 25 x 21 In. 495.00
Shield, Pole, Floral, Needlework On Silk, Floral Frame, 1810, 16 In. 525.00
Silhouette, Caroline, Hollow Cut, Brass Frame, 1810, 4 x 2 1/2 In. 160.00
Silhouette, Children Skiing, Convex Glass, 4 x 5 In. 32.00
Silhouette, Elaborate Carriage Scene, Signed, 1800s 110.00
Silhouette, Elder Ladu, With Bonnet, Brass Over Wood Frame, 3 1/2 x 2 5/8 In. 155.00
Silhouette, Gentleman, Cut From Black Paper, Jacobus Ten Eyck, Age 19, Brass Frame . 220.00
Silhouette, George & Martha Washington, Gilt Frames, 3 x 3 3/4 In., Pair 430.00
Silhouette, Lady, Signed, Cooper, Oval, 3 1/4 x 2 3/8 In. 95.00
Silhouette, Man & Woman Bust, 1 Ink & Other Pencil, Gilt Frame, 5 1/2 x 8 1/4 In. ... 465.00
Silhouette, Man & Woman, Black, Yellow Paint, Gilt Frame, 4 7/8 x 3 3/4 In., Pair 220.00
Silhouette, Man & Woman, Hollow Cut, Cloth Backing, Frame, 5 1/4 x 8 In., Pair 135.00
Silhouette, Man, Bust Length, India Ink On White Paper, Brass Frame, 5 1/4 x 4 1/2 In. . 345.00

Picture, Theorem, Compote of Fruit,
Watercolor, Frame, 17 x 20 In.

Picture, Theorem, Compote Of Fruit,
Watercolor, Stencil, Frame, 14 x 18 In.

Silhouette, Man, Full-Bodied, Maple Frame, 10 1/4 x 6 In. 195.00
Silhouette, Man, High Collar, Hollow Cut, Brass Over Wood Frame, 2 7/8 x 2 1/4 In. .. 165.00
Silhouette, Noblewoman, Oval, 1 1/2 x 1 1/8 In. 200.00
Silhouette, Profile Of Young Woman, Black Cloth Ground, 1840s, 6 7/8 x 5 3/4 In. 230.00
Silhouette, Woman & Child, Hollow Cut, Eglomise Glass, 5 1/2 x 4 1/2 In., Pair 275.00
Silhouette, Young Girl, Half Length, Penciled-In Hair, Mahogany Frame 172.00
Silhouette, Young Man, Hollow Cut, Gold On Wooden Frame, 3 3/8 x 2 1/4 In. 160.00
Silhouette, Young Man, Ink, Hollow Cut, J.S. Smith On Frame, 5 3/4 x 5 1/8 In. 220.00
Silhouette, Young Woman, Dress & Collar Cut From Green Paper, Gilt Frame, 4 5/8 In. 248.00
Silhouette, Young Woman, In Bonnet, Hollow Cut, Brass Frame, 5 1/8 x 4 1/2 In. 220.00
Theorem, Compote Of Fruit, Watercolor, Frame, 17 x 20 In. ....*Illus* 690.00
Theorem, Compote Of Fruit, Watercolor, Stencil, Frame, 14 x 18 In. ....*Illus* 2585.00
Theorem, On Velvet, Basket Of Flowers, Frame, 1820-1830, 15 1/2 x 19 1/2 In. 2475.00
Theorem, On Velvet, Pink, Green, Blue, Yellow Roses, Gilt Frame, 8 1/4 In. 467.50
Theorem, On Velvet, Red, Yellow, Blue, Roses, Signed, L. Kellogg, Frame, 19 In. 495.00
Theorem, Watercolor, Bowl Of Fruit, Red, Yellow, Orange, Green, 10 3/8 In. 3150.00
Theorem, Watercolor, Fruit Basket, Foliage, Green, Brown, Blue, Red, 13 In. 1750.00
Watercolor, Cock Fight, Signed Coral Branch, Frame, 24 x 28 In. 82.00
Watercolor, Collage, Applied String, 8 People In A Boat, Frame, 23 1/2 x 46 1/4 In. 28.00
Watercolor, Country Scene, Man Plowing, F.F. English, Frame, 23 x 37 In. 880.00
Watercolor, Couple, Winter Landscape, F. Glyndon, Frame, 17 1/2 x 25 In. 275.00
Watercolor, Evening Of Twelfth Of August, Jas. Co., Frame, 11 x 9 In. 750.00
Watercolor, Fisherfolk, Low Tide, Graphite On Paper, Harold Hall, 20 x 28 In. 402.00
Watercolor, Interior, Mother & Infant, 19th Century, Frame, 19 x 15 In. 545.00
Watercolor, Landscape, Park, Path In Foreground, John LaValle, 1947, 13 x 19 In. 55.00
Watercolor, Parisian Cathedral, Joseph Margulies, Oak Frame, 12 x 17 In. 93.00
Watercolor, Pollywog, 2 Men In Boat, H.W. Shaylor, Frame, 13 x 16 1/2 In. 110.00
Watercolor, U.S. Bark, Vermont, E. Tufnell, 1866, 14 x 20 In. 895.00
Watercolor, View Of Fishkill, New York, 19th Century, 14 x 21 In. 240.00
Watercolor, Woman Bathing In Stream, Francis Humphrey Woolrych, 9 x 13 In. 55.00
Watercolor, Woman, Bonnet, Seated In Chair, J. Brewster Jr., 1808, 7 x 5 In. 220.00
Watercolor On Silk, Mountain Side, Figures In Boat, Bamboo Frame, 37 x 15 In. 137.00

PIERCE, see Howard Pierce category.

PIGEON FORGE Pottery was started in Pigeon Forge, Tennessee, in
1946. Red clay found near the pottery was used to make the pieces.
Molded or thrown pottery with matte glaze and slip decoration was
made. The pottery is still working.

Figurine, Black Bear 25.00
Vase, Blue Drip, Griffin, 7 In. 60.00

PILKINGTON Tile and Pottery Company was established in 1892 in England. The company made small pottery wares, like buttons and hatpins, but soon started decorating vases purchased from other potteries. By 1903, the company had discovered an opalescent glaze that became popular on the Lancastrian pottery line. The manufacture of pottery ended in 1937 but decorating continued until 1948.

Bowl, Royal Lancastrian, Stylized Shamrocks, 3 Closed Handles, Marked, 4 1/2 In.	357.00
Vase, Fruit Skin, Turquoise, 8 1/2 In.	175.00
Vase, Mottled Yellow Flowers, Blue Iridescent Ground, White Leaf Band, 4 3/4 In.	431.00
Vase, Orange Skin, 5 In.	235.00
Vase, Royal Lancastrian, Blue & Green Glaze, Marked, 5 In.	88.00
Vase, Sunstone, Flared Rim, Amber Flambes, Impressed Logo, 4 1/2 x 5 In.	550.00

PINCUSHION DOLLS are not really dolls and often were not even pincushions. Some collectors use the term *half-doll*. The top half of each doll was made of porcelain. The edge of the half-doll was made with several small holes for thread, and the doll was stitched to a fabric body with a voluminous skirt. The finished figure was used to cover a hot pot of tea, powder box, pincushion, whisk broom, or lamp. They were made in sizes from less than an inch to over 9 inches high. Most date from the early 1900s to the 1950s. Collectors often find just the porcelain doll without the fabric skirt.

Arms Away, Germany, 5 In.	145.00
Arms Away, Green, 3 7/8 In.	99.00
Bisque, Blond Hair, Blue Eyes, Germany, 1910, 3 In.	275.00
Child, Standing, Germany, 3 In.	100.00
Full-Figure, Art Deco, Lusterware, Germany, 8 In.	175.00
Half, Hands Away, China Head & Feet, Gray Hair, Cloth Body, 7 3/4 In.	145.00
Human Red Hair, Chalkware, 8 In.	75.00
Woman, Nude, Arms Out, Brown Hair, Volkstedt Rudolstadt, 6 In.	375.00

PINK SLAG pieces are listed in this book in the Slag category.

PIPES have been popular since tobacco was introduced to Europe by Sir Walter Raleigh. Carved wooden, porcelain, ivory, and glass pipes may be listed here. Meerschaum pipes are listed under Meerschaum.

African, Clay, Human Form Shape, Stem, Metal Insert, 21 In.	115.00
Bamboo, Opium, Ivory Mouthpiece, Late 19th Century, 23 1/4 In.	302.00
Calabash, Carved, Brown Patina, Horn Fittings, 18 In.	220.00
Case, Engraved Brass Mountings, Boxwood Body, Dutch, Dated 1759, 6 In.	550.00
Man's Head, Turban, Meer	75.00
Platform, Green & Gray Steatite, c.1900, 7 1/4 In.	325.00
Porcelain Bowl, Painted Landscape & Stag, Hair Tassels, 13 In.	115.00
Redware, Red Painted, Open Mouth, Covered Bowl, Late 19th Century, 42 1/2 In.	1725.00
Stoneware Bowl, Scene Of Man Playing Guitar, 1761	80.00
Water, Scenic, Arab Design, Gouda	150.00

PISGAH FOREST pottery was made in North Carolina beginning in 1926. The pottery was started by Walter R. Stephen in 1914, and after his death in 1941, the pottery continued in operation. The most famous kinds of Pisgah Forest ware are the cameo type with designs made of raised glaze and the turquoise crackle glaze wares.

Ewer, Crazed Turquoise, Pink Interior, Black Streaked Handle, 1936, 8 3/8 In.	195.00
Jar, Cover, Green, Turquoise, Pink Interior, 1936, 2 1/2 In.	65.00
Jar, Cover, Mottled Turquoise, 2 1/2 In.	30.00
Jar, Cover, Mottled Turquoise, Green, 3 In.	35.00
Jug, Turquoise, Purple, 1948, 4 1/2 In.	75.00
Mug, Clog Dancers, Cameo Design, Light Blue, Walter Stephen, 3 3/8 In.	110.00
Mug, Turquoise, Purple, Gray Interior, 3 1/2 In.	25.00
Pitcher, Maroon, Blue Crystalline Glaze, 8 x 4 In.	145.00
Pitcher, Pale Yellow, 9 In.	250.00
Pitcher, Pioneering Scene, White, Blue Matte Ground, 1953, 6 x 6 1/4 In.	415.00

Pitcher, Turquoise Exterior, Rose Interior Glaze, Stoneware, 1930-1940, 3 In. 50.00
Plate, Cameo, Green, White, Signed, Walter Stephen, 1915 .... 345.00
Pot, Blue & Tan, 3 Handles, 7 In. 45.00
Saucer, Pink, 1939 .... 12.00
Sugar & Creamer, Blue Crackle, 1949, 3 1/4 In. 65.00
Vase, Aqua, Pink, 9 1/2 In. 135.00
Vase, Aubergine, 7 1/2 In. 150.00
Vase, Blue, 3 Handles, 5 1/2 x 5 In. 25.00
Vase, Blue, Crystalline, 5 In. 300.00
Vase, Blue, Green, White Crystals, Pale Yellow Ground, Cameo Mark, 9 In. 550.00
Vase, Blue, Handles, 6 x 6 1/4 In. 125.00
Vase, Blue, White Crystalline Over White, Green Glossy Glaze, 7 1/2 In. 715.00
Vase, Broad Shouldered, Light Blue Glaze, 4 x 5 1/2 In. 55.00
Vase, Brown Brushed, 3 Handles, 5 x 5 In. 150.00
Vase, Celadon & Golden Crystalline Glaze, 1940, 9 3/4 In. 775.00
Vase, Covered Wagon, Blue, Walter Stephen, 8 1/2 In. 950.00
Vase, Crackle Pink Lining, Aqua, 1942, 4 In. 50.00
Vase, Flowing Crystalline Flambe Glaze, 1943, 6 In. 110.00
Vase, Green Crystalline Over Peach Glossy Glaze, Bulbous, Embossed Mark, 5 In. .. 665.00
Vase, Green, Handles, 6 1/4 x 5 3/4 In. 65.00
Vase, Green, Yellow, 1936, 4 1/2 In. 98.00
Vase, Scattered Blue Flecks, Ivory & Pink, 1935, 6 In. 375.00
Vase, Thick Brown, White, Caramel Glossy Glaze, Embossed Mark, 6 In. 176.00
Vase, Turquoise, Crackle Gray, Pink Interior, 5 1/2 In. 125.00
Vase, White Crystalline Glaze, Light Blue, Yellow, Raised Mark, 8 In. 825.00
Vase, White, Blue Crystalline Flambe, Bulbous, 1940, 9 x 6 1/2 In. 775.00
Vase, White, Blue Crystalline, Golden Ground, 5 1/2 x 3 1/2 In. 385.00
Vase, White, Blue Starburst Crystalline, Gold Ground, 1940, 4 x 4 1/2 In. 335.00

PLANTERS PEANUTS memorabilia is collected. Planters Nut and Chocolate Company was started in Wilkes-Barre, Pennsylvania, in 1906. The Mr. Peanut figure was adopted as a trademark in 1916. National advertising for Planters Peanuts started in 1918. The company was acquired by Standard Brands, Inc., in 1961. Standard Brands merged with Nabisco in 1981. Some of the Mr. Peanut jars and other memorabilia have been reproduced and, of course, new items are being made.

Bag, Graphics On Front, 1950s, 5 Lb. Bag 15.00
Bank, Figural, Mr. Peanut, Plastic, Green, Removable Hat, 1960, 8 1/4 In. 15.00
Bank, Mr. Peanut, Vendor, Red 550.00
Belt & Buckle, Dinah Shore Invitational Golf Tournament, Box 140.00
Book, Mr. Peanut, Paint, Original Mailer, 1929 .... 80.00
Book, Mr. Peanut, Parade Series, Holt, Rinehart & Winston, 7 x 10 In. 35.00
Box, Mr. Peanut, On Front, Bags On Sides, Box, 1940s 150.00
Box, Salted Peanuts, After Dinner B & L 450.00
Bracelet, 1939 World's Fair 30.00
Coloring Book, Mr. Peanut, 50 States 15.00
Coloring Book, Mr. Peanut, President Of U.S. 15.00
Cookie Jar, Mr. Peanut 50.00
Costume, Mr. Peanut, Parade 475.00
Coupon, Redeemable Towards Set Of Enameled Dishes, 1940 .... 35.00
Doll, Mr. Peanut Plush, Vinyl 35.00
Figurine, Mr. Peanut, Holding Piece Of Cake, In Party Hat 10.00
Figurine, Mr. Peanut, Pound-A-Ball 40.00
Glass, Mr. Peanut, Decal, 5 In. 50.00
Jar, Blown-Out Peanut Each Corner 250.00
Jar, Mr. Peanut, Decal, 4 Sides, Relief Lettering, 8 1/4 In. 308.00
Jar, Peanut Finial, Flattened Sides 95.00
Key Chain, Peanut, Tan 18.00
Knife, Fork & Spoon Set 130.00
Lighter, Cigarette, Yellow Plastic 22.00
Machine, Peanut Butter, Mr. Peanut 15.00
Marble, Mr. Peanut, 1950s, 5/8 In. 18.00
Marble Bag, Mr. Peanut, Pictorial, 1950s 14.00

Mug, Mr. Peanut, Decal, Glass, 5 1/2 In. 50.00
Nut Set, Metal, New York World's Fair, 7 Piece 55.00
Peanut, Papier-Mache, Hollow, 9 In. 110.00
Peanut Butter Maker, Box, 1970s 65.00
Pencil, Mechanical, Mr. Peanut 25.00
Pencil, Mechanical, Package, 1950s 12.00
Penlight, Mr. Peanut, Plastic 85.00
Pennant, Octagonal, 5 Cents, 7 Sides Embossed, Large 225.00
Pin, Mr. Peanut, 1950s, 1 In. 6.00
Pin, Mr. Peanut, Brass 10.00
Plate, Mr. Peanut, 40th Anniversary Collection, Applause 20.00
Potholder, Mr. Peanut 10.00
Punch Board, Mr. Peanut Picture, 5 Cents 125.00
Radio, Mr. Peanut, Figural, Box ....75.00 to 85.00
Salt & Pepper, Box, 1950s, 3 In. 50.00
Salt & Pepper, Mr. Peanut, Plastic, 4 In. ....15.00 to 20.00
Spoon, Measuring, Yellow Plastic 20.00
Spoon, Mr. Peanut, 1930s 20.00
Spoon, Mr. Peanut, 1950s, 6 In. 8.00
Straw, Plastic, With Figural Top, 1950s 8.00
Swizzle Stick, 1960s, 6 In. 5.00
Toothbrush, Mr. Peanut, Box 15.00
Toothpick, Mr. Peanut, 1960s, 3 In. 3.00
Vending Machine, Mr. Peanut 125.00
Whistle, Mr. Peanut, Plastic, Blue 15.00
Wristwatch, Mr. Peanut 75.00

PLASTIC objects of all types are being collected. Some pieces are listed in other categories; gutta-percha cases are listed in photography,
celluloid in its own category.

Cake Breaker, Lucite Handle, Silver, 1950s 85.00
Cigarette Holder, Bakelite, Red 45.00
Manicure Set, Tortoiseshell Color, 1920s 10.00
Memo Pad, Amber, Catalin, Carvecraft, England 95.00
Penholder, Modern Design, Bakelite 25.00
Server, 3 Coral Hinged Dishes, Gold Metal Armature, Jean Cocteau, 1950, 11 1/2 In. 385.00

PLATED AMBERINA was patented June 15, 1886, by Joseph Locke and
made by the New England Glass Company. It is similar in color to
amberina, but is characterized by a cream colored or chartreuse lining
(never white) and small ridges or ribs on the outside.

Bowl, Folded Quintet Rim, Red Ribbed & Swirled, 3 3/4 x 8 In. 6325.00
Tumbler, 3 3/4 In. 1870.00
Vase, Ribbed, Lavender Tones, Red To Yellow, New England, 3 1/2 In. 3520.00

PLIQUE-A-JOUR is an enameling process. The enamel is laid between
thin raised metal lines and heated. The finished piece has transparent
enamel held between the thin metal wires. It is different from cloi-
sonne because it is transparent.

Bowl, Floral Design, Bell Form, Pale Blue Fish-Scale Ground, Enamel, 4 In. 143.00
Bowl, Floral Design, Hemisphere Form, Pale Blue Fish-Scale Ground, 5 In. 220.00
Bowl, Petal Form, Floral, Native Wood Stand, 4 In. 40.00
Vase, Multicolored Flowers, Silver Rim, Base, Wood Box, Green Ground, 5 In. 285.00

POLITICAL memorabilia of all types, from buttons to banners, is collected. Items related to presidential candidates are the most popular,
but collectors also search for material related to state and local offices.
Many reproductions have been made. A jugate is a button with pho-
tographs of both the presidential and vice presidential candidates. In
this list a button is round, usually with a straight pin or metal tab to
secure it to a shirt. A pin is brass, often figural, sometimes attached to
a ribbon.

3 Dollar Bill, Jimmy Carter Front, Donkey Back, Presidential Campaign, 1976 .... 3.00

Badge, 2nd National Convention, Young Democrats Of America, Milwaukee, 1935 ..... 15.00
Badge, 44th Inauguration, Kennedy, Johnson, Celluloid, 1961, 6 In. 55.00
Badge, Franklin Roosevelt, Picture, Tinted, Celluloid, 1936, 6 In. 400.00
Badge, Honorary Sergeant At Arms, Republican Convention, Philadelphia, 1948 .... 50.00
Badge, Lincoln Funeral, Black & White Woodblock Engraving, Black Rosette, 8 In. 400.00
Badge, McKinley, Alternate Delegate, Philadelphia 125.00
Badge, National Progressive Convention, 1912 .... 60.00
Badge, Republican National Convention, Newsreel Operator, Philadelphia, 1948 ...... 60.00
Badge, Special Officer, Democrat National Convention, San Francisco, 1920 .... 60.00
Badge, Teddy Roosevelt At Top, Pennsylvania Progressive, Celluloid, 1916, 4 1/2 In. ... 625.00
Bag, Plastic, Carter, Mondale & 2 County Commissioners From Euclid, Ohio 10.00
Bandanna, Grover Cleveland & Thomas Hendricks, Frame, Square, 18 In. 300.00
Bandanna, Harrison, Morton 350.00
Bandanna, I Like Ike ....50.00 to 75.00
Bandanna, James Blaine & John Logan, Square, 18 In. 300.00
Bandanna, Jimmy Carter, With Peanut 50.00
Bandanna, McKinley & Teddy Roosevelt, Battle At The Polls, Musical 1208.00
Bandanna, William Harrison, On Horse, Scenes Of Tippecanoe, Harrison As Farmer ... 750.00
Bank, Douglas County Republican Party 65.00
Banner, Lincoln & Hamlin, Black Print, Muslin, 13 x 17 In. 1200.00
Banner, Our Next President Wendell L. Willkie, Satin, 5 1/2 x 7 In. 77.00
Book, Book Of Common Sense Etiquette, Eleanor Roosevelt, Macmillan, 1962 .... 5.00
Book, Memoirs Of Richard Nixon, Autographed 285.00
Book, Profiles In Courage, Senator John F. Kennedy, Signed 1650.00
Bracelet, Nixon, White Bakelite, Brass Letters, Blue Ground, Trifari 45.00
Button, 8 Years Is Enough, Black, White, 2 In. 4.00
Button, Admiral, William F. Halsey, 3 In. 7.00
Button, Al Smith Gave Us Sunday Movies, Picture, 1 In. 385.00
Button, Alfred Smith, Our Next President, Black & White, 7/8 In. 110.00
Button, All I Have Left Is A Vote For Willkie, Green, Yellow, 2 In. 4.00
Button, America Needs Kennedy, Johnson, 3 1/2 In. 38.00
Button, Back The President, Red, White & Blue, 2 In. 4.00
Button, Bryan & Bennett, Gubernatorial Candidate, Celluloid, 1 1/4 In. 1100.00
Button, Bryan & Davis, Nebraska, Black & White Jugate, Celluloid, 1 1/4 In. 10248.00
Button, Carter, Mondale, Carter Portrait, Celluloid, 1976, 2 1/4 In. 125.00
Button, Coolidge & Dawes, Sepia, Candidates, 1924, 1 1/4 In. 2400.00
Button, Coolidge Trigate, 1/4 In. 35.00
Button, Coolidge, Dawes, Mort Adams, Maine, Celluloid, 7/8 In. 1170.00
Button, Cox, Red, White & Blue, Celluloid, 1 1/4 In. 205.00
Button, Dewey, Figural, Elephant, Name Across Body, Wooden, 1 1/2 In. 26.00
Button, Dictator, Not For Us, Black, Yellow, 2 In. 4.00
Button, Don't Be A Third Term-Ite, 2 In. 3.00
Button, Down With The Capitalist Teapot Dome, Socialist Party 75.00
Button, Draft Roosevelt For '40, Celluloid, 7/8 In. 95.00
Button, Eleanor?, No Soap, Blue, Pink, 1 In. 8.00
Button, Elect John F. Kennedy, Vice President, Head Of Kennedy, 2 In. 785.00
Button, Elephant Printed On Body, Silver Color, 1 1/4 In. 13.00
Button, Elephant, Figural, Vote Republican, 1/2 In. 8.00
Button, Elk City Loves Jimmy Carter, 1 1/4 In. 150.00
Button, End Vietnam War Now, White Dove, Blue, Celluloid, 1 1/4 In. 35.00
Button, FDR & Wallace, Joint Picture, Celluloid, 7/8 In. 72.00
Button, For Carter-Mondale, Goober Peas, Peanut, Celluloid, 1 3/4 In. 14.00
Button, Franklin D. Roosevelt For President, Picture, Celluloid, 7/8 In. 40.00
Button, Franklin Delano Roosevelt, God Bless America, Yellow, 7/8 In. 75.00
Button, Franklin Delano Roosevelt, Vice President, Celluloid, 1920, 1 3/4 In. 2660.00
Button, Garner, Roosevelt, Stark, 5/8 In. 20.00
Button, George Washington Inaugural, Long Live The President, 1 1/4 In. 2250.00
Button, George Washington, Blue Illustration On White, St. Louis Button Co., 1930 .... 12.00
Button, Geraldine Ferraro, Celluloid, Autographed, 3 In. 55.00
Button, Goldwater, Indiana's Favorite Family, Yellow & Blue Lithograph, 3 In. 520.00
Button, Goldwater, Miller, Glow In The Dark, Celluloid, 1964, 1 1/2 In. 120.00
Button, Governor Rockefeller, Faux Diamonds & Sapphires, Autographed 65.00
Button, Grant, 1 1/2 In. 125.00

Button, Hall, White Name, Black Ground, 3/4 In. 12.00
Button, Harding & Coolidge, Color Lithograph, 2 In. 8.00
Button, Harry S Truman, Inauguration, January 1949, Celluloid, 1 3/4 In. 24.00
Button, Harry Truman, Nixon Is A Shifty-Eyed Liar, Celluloid, 3 1/2 In. 157.00
Button, Hoover, Curtis, Gray & White, Celluloid, 7/8 In. 60.00
Button, Hoover, Curtis, Heads Pictured, 1932, 1 1/4 In. 775.00
Button, Hoover, Curtis, Jugate, Pinback, 1 1/4 In. 1755.00
Button, Hoover, Elephant, GOP 25.00
Button, Hoover, Figural, Elephant, Bronze 52.00
Button, Hubert H. Humphrey For President, 4 In. 7.00
Button, Humphrey, Muskie, Multicolored, 1968, 2 In. 8.00
Button, Humphrey, Shriver, Celluloid, Purple, Black, White, 7/8 In. 13.00
Button, I Am A Democrat For Willkie, Black, White, 2 In. 7.00
Button, I Like Ike Eisenhower, 1971, 3 In. 4.00
Button, I Like Ike, Celluloid, Blue, White, 7/8 In. 13.00
Button, I'm For Barry Goldwater For Vice President.3 In. 20.00
Button, I'm For McGovern For Congress, South Dakota, Celluloid, 2 1/4 In. 627.00
Button, Ike, Tennessee, Blue, Gold & Red, Celluloid, 1 1/4 In. 75.00
Button, Ike, Texas, 1952, 1 1/4 In. 55.00
Button, Impeach LBJ, 5/8 In. 7.00
Button, In Memory Of F.D. Roosevelt, Memorial, Celluloid, 1 1/4 In. 28.00
Button, Jack Kennedy, 1960 .... 20.00
Button, Johnson, Humphrey, Vote Democratic, 9 In. 45.00
Button, Kennedy, Nebraska, Red, Center Picture, White & Black, 7/8 In. 710.00
Button, Kennedy, Peace, Center Picture, 1968, 5/8 In. 15.00
Button, Labor For Dewey & Bricker, 1 1/4 In. 40.00
Button, Labor Likes Ike, 1 1/8 In. 7.00
Button, Landon For Governor, Kansas, Celluloid, 7/8 In. 14.00
Button, Landon, Face Set In Floral Leaves, 1/2 In. 10.00
Button, Landon, Felt Flower Attached To Back, 7/8 In. 23.00
Button, Landon, West Virginia Republican State Convention, 1936, 2 1/4 In. 568.00
Button, LBJ For The USA, 9 In. 35.00
Button, McCarthy, Colorado, '76, Blue, White, 1 1/4 In. 24.00
Button, McGovern For President, Peter Max, Celluloid, 1972, 1 1/2 In. 660.00
Button, McGovern For Senator, Celluloid, 1960, 1 3/4 In. 110.00
Button, McGovern Grass Roots Club Of Marin, Celluloid, 1 1/2 In. 350.00
Button, McKinley Club, Grand Trunk Railroad, Picture, Sepia, 1 1/4 In. 450.00
Button, McKinley, Center Photograph, Red, White & Blue, Celluloid, 7/8 In. 24.00
Button, McKinley, Memorial, Multicolored, 1 3/4 In. 24.00
Button, McKinley, Picture In Sky Above Factories, Black, White, Brown, 7/8 In. 265.00
Button, Metal Derby, Smile With Al, A Century Of Progress, 1933 .... 125.00
Button, Missouri's Minute Men For Roosevelt, 1 1/4 In. 27.00
Button, My Choice Is For Kennedy & Johnson, 2 1/2 In. 18.00
Button, National Wheelman's, McKinley & Hobart, 2 In. 375.00
Button, National Women Suffrage Congressional Union, Gold, Lavender , 1 In. 1668.00
Button, Neely, Roosevelt, Kilgore, West Virginia, 7/8 In. 12.00
Button, Nevada Women Will Elect Clinton, Gore, 3/4 In. 50.00
Button, Nixon & Lodge, The Winning Team, Celluloid, Lithograph, 1960, 1 1/4 In. 11.00
Button, Nixon, Lodge, Jugate, 1 1/4 In. 200.00
Button, No More Fireside Chats, Red, White, 2 In. 3.00
Button, O.K. I Like Ike Club, Plastic, 1952 Sunflower Ordinance Works, 1 1/4 In. 270.00
Button, Official Press, MacArthur, Celluloid, 2 1/4 In. 93.00
Button, One Party Nation, Nothing Doing, Franklin, Black, White, 1 1/2 In. 3.00
Button, Our Next President, Adlai Stevenson, Center Photograph, 1 1/4 In. 5.00
Button, Peace & Freedom Party, Dove At Top, Green & Black, 1 1/2 In. 2.00
Button, Peace Now, Dove Center, Blue & White Lithography, c.1969, 2 1/4 In. 2.00
Button, Peanut, Carter, 5/8 In. 2.00
Button, Perhaps Roosevelt Is All You Deserve, Black, Yellow Ground, 3 In. 4.00
Button, Progressive Politics Become Law Under Wilson, 2 In. 35.00
Button, Prohibition, National Promotion Of America, 2 In. 18.00
Button, Quayle For Vice President, Center Picture, 7/8 In. 1.00
Button, Reagan For Governor, 3 In. 7.00
Button, Reagan, Bush, America's New Dawn, Sun Over Mountains, Celluloid, 2 In. 26.00

Button, Reagan, Bush, Friend In Pennsylvania, Celluloid, 1984, 4 In. 485.00
Button, Reagan, Hebrew Letters Above Name, Blue & White, 2 1/4 In. 3.00
Button, Richard Nixon, 1960, 3 In. 13.00
Button, Richard Nixon, Man Of Steel, Red, White, Blue & Black Celluloid, 3 1/2 In. ... 137.00
Button, Roosevelt, LaFollette, Jugate, 3/4 In. 225.00
Button, Roosevelt, Rough Riders Reunion, Las Vegas, N.M., Celluloid, 1899, 1 3/4 In. ... 950.00
Button, Saxophone, 1992, 1 3/4 In. 45.00
Button, Senator Robert Dole For President, Celluloid, 1988, 2 In. 43.00
Button, Speedy Recovery, Re-Elect Hoover, Lithograph, 2 In. 13.00
Button, Stop Nixon, Black Letters, White Ground, 3/4 In. 8.00
Button, Taft, Harding, Jugate, Ohio, 7/8 In. 235.00
Button, Taft, Sepia Portrait, Brown Border, Blue Ribbon, 2 1/4 In. 580.00
Button, Teddy Kennedy For President, Celluloid, 1980, 7/8 In. 10.00
Button, Theodore Roosevelt, On Horse, San Juan Hill, Celluloid, 1 1/4 In. 735.00
Button, Theodore Roosevelt, The American, 1912 .... 38.00
Button, There Is No Indispensable Man, Green, White, 2 In. 7.00
Button, Truman Memorial, Photograph, White Ground, 3 In. 4.00
Button, Truman, Barkley, 2 Ovals Connected, Celluloid, 1 1/4 In. 495.00
Button, Two Times Is Enough For Any Man, Black, Orange, 2 In. 7.00
Button, Unite The Country, McGovern, White Ground, 3 In. 7.00
Button, USC Aiken Pacers, Clinton, Gore, 1992, 3/4 In. 12.00
Button, Vietnam Moratorium, Blue Letters, White Ground, Celluloid, 1 1/4 In. 14.00
Button, We Want Mamie, White Ground, 3 In. 15.00
Button, William Haywood, 1907 .... 1065.00
Button, Willkie For President, Lithograph, Picture, 7/8 In. 14.00
Button, Willkie Not Royal, But Loyal, Purple, White, 2 In. 4.00
Button, Willkie, Elephant, Gold Color 13.00
Button, Willkie, I'd Give My Shirt For Willkie, Folded Shirt Form, Paper & Cloth 80.00
Button, Wilson & Pershing, Jugate, Victory, Celluloid, 1918, 1 1/4 In. 90.00
Button, Wilson & Senator Reed, Champions Of 8 Hour Day, Celluloid, 1 In. 1755.00
Button, Wilson Shield, Celluloid, Multicolored, 1 3/4 In. 1935.00
Button, Wilson, Flag, Gold Border, 2 1/4 In. 1205.00
Button, Wilson, Teacher-President, Portrait, Black & White, Celluloid, 1 1/4 In. 440.00
Button, Win In '56, Adlai, Estes, 3 1/2 In. 17.00
Button, Wm. H. Taft For President, Celluloid, 1 1/4 In. 40.00
Button, Women For Nixon Agnew, Lithograph, 4 In. 3.00
Button, Wyoming For Ike, Blue, Gold & Red, 1 1/4 In. 55.00
Button, Youth For Kennedy, Celluloid, Red, White & Blue, 2 1/4 In. 365.00
Button, Youth For Roosevelt, Lithograph, 2 In. 10.00
Button, Zachary Taylor Figure, Rough & Ready, Brass 275.00
Cards, Playing, We Still Like Ike 1.00
Certificate, Millard Filmore, American Colonization Society, Signed Henry Clay 1100.00
Charm, Wilson, Inaugural, 1913 .... 35.00
Cuff Links, Presidential Seal, Base Metal, Reagan Autograph, Box 200.00
Death Mask, Abraham Lincoln, Anna, Oct. 17, 1877, Stoneware 1750.00
Document, Signed By John Hancock As Governor Of Massachusetts, 1781 .... 1705.00
Fan, Hand, James Polk Campaign, First 10 Presidents, Bone & Paper, 20 x 10 In. 2750.00
Fan, Teddy Roosevelt Picture, Cardboard, St. Louis World's Fair, 1904 .... 85.00
Ferrotype, Lincoln & Hamlin, Brass Frame, No Beard On Lincoln, 1860, 15/16 In. 285.00
Figurine, John F. Kennedy, Rocking Chair, Porcelain 125.00
Flag, 40 Stars, Portrait, Rutherford B. Hayes & William A. Wheeler 35200.00
Flask, Bryan We Trust, Free Silver, Portrait Of Candidate, Embossed, Green 475.00
Flask, McKinley We Trust, Gold Standard, 1/2 Pint 450.00
Flask, McKinley, Genuine Distilled Protection, Raised Figures, Pewter Top 400.00
Flyswatter, Bush, Quayle, Jugate, Plastic 6.00
Fob, Coolidge, Blue & White Celluloid, 1 1/2 In. 1045.00
Handkerchief, Goldwater, Logo On 1 Side 10.00
Handkerchief, U.S.A. Likes L.B.J., Logo On 1 Side 10.00
Hat, Campaign, John F. Kennedy 25.00
Hat, Ike Paper Label On Crown, Mr. American, Official 45.00
Hat, Straw, Landon, Knox, Sunflower 150.00
Hat, Straw, Marked Roosevelt, Garner 140.00
Hat, Uncle Sam, Doodle Dandy Deal Days 25.00

You should not regild, resilver, or
repaint political buttons or badges.
It lowers the value.

Political, Match Safe,
President Benjamin Harrison,
Brass, Pat. 1888

Hat, We Like & We'll Stick With Ike & Dick, Paper, 3 1/2 x 11 In.	150.00
Key Chain, Destined To Become President, Pictures Robert Kennedy	18.00
Land Grant, Iowa City, Franklin Pierce, President, Land Office Seal, 16 x 10 In.	65.00
Lantern, Campaign, William Henry Harrison, Etched Eagle, C. Chapman On Banner	7700.00
Lantern, McKinley & Roosevelt, Tin, Pierced, Dinner Pail, 8 1/2 In.	1350.00
Letter, Barbara Bush, Autograph, 1971	65.00
License Plate, Inaugural, No. 21, District Of Columbia, 1937	500.00
License Plate, Vote Wallace	18.00
License Plate, Win With Roosevelt, Black, White	100.00
License Tag, I Like Ike & Dick	18.00
Lithograph, President McKinley, In Headstone, 1901, 16 x 20 In.	500.00
Magnet, Clinton, Gore	3.00
Mask, Donkey & Elephant, Papier-Mache, Findlay Mask Co., 22 In., Pair	145.00
Mask, LBJ & Willkie, Plastic, 1964	65.00
Match Safe, President Benjamin Harrison, Brass, Pat. 1888 ....*Illus*	250.00
Medal, Campaign, U.S. Grant, Bust, In Uniform, Reverse, For President, 1868	85.00
Medal, Indian Peace, Franklin Pierce, President Of The United States, 1853	5500.00
Medal, Indian Peace, President Abraham Lincoln, Silver, 1862	6800.00
Medal, McKinley, Eagle On Reverse	19.00
Medalet, Henry Clay, Brass, 1844	250.00
Mirror, Kennedy For President, Pocket, 1960	75.00
Mirror, McKinley Assassination Site, Celluloid, Pocket, 1901	45.00
Mug, FDR, New Deal, Silhouette, Yellowware, Barrel Shape	110.00
Mug, Nixon, Agnew, Amber Carnival Glass, Story Book, IG EWR	55.00
Mug, Reagan, Bush, Frankoma, 1981	39.00
Mug, Toby, Ike, White, 1956, 4 In.	40.00
Mustard, McKinley, Embossed Picture & Slogan, Clear Glass	40.00
Necklace, Re-Elect President Jimmie Carter	12.00
Necktie, Truman	32.00
Needle Book, Roosevelt, Prosperity	50.00
Nodder, Elephant, Donkey, Pair	165.00
Nodder, Nixon For President	200.00
Paperweight, Hoover	60.00
Pass, Employee, Republican National Convention, Chicago, July, 1960	4.00
Pass, News-Press, Democratic Convention, Metal, 1968, 3 3/8 x 2 1/8 In.	12.00
Pen Wiper, One Of Bears Teddy Didn't Get, Leather, Felt, 6 In.	200.00
Pencil, Al Smith For President, Wooden, Plastic Smith's Head On End, 1928	60.00
Pencil Clip, Douglas MacArthur, Celluloid, Red, White & Blue, Brown	75.00
Pendant, Republican National Convention, Elephant Head, Building, Chicago, 1952	25.00
Pennant, Barry Goldwater, Inset Picture, Red & White, 13 1/2 In.	20.00
Pennant, Franklin Delano Roosevelt, Head Of FDR & Capitol, 1941, 27 In.	38.00
Pennant, Inauguration, Truman, Red, White & Blue, 27 In.	75.00
Pennant, Nixon, Red, White & Blue, 29 1/2 In.	7.50
Pennant, Stevenson, Sparkman, White & Red, 1962	55.00
Photograph, Coolidge & Rickenbacker, Airplane, Sepiatone, 1925, 10 x 13 In.	425.00
Photograph, Samuel Jones Tilden, Democrat, Lost Presidential Race To Hayes	50.00

Pitcher, Raised Bust Of Garfield, Eagles With Shields, Ribbon Mark, 12 In. 850.00
Placemat, Nixon & Lodge, 1960 .... 10.00
Plaque, Roosevelt & Fairbanks, Parker & Davis, Stand-Up, 3 1/2 x 7 In., Pair 225.00
Plate, Harry Truman Picture, 9 In. 50.00
Plate, John F. Kennedy, 5 In. 14.00
Plate, President, Mr. & Mrs. John F. Kennedy 30.00
Plate, Taft & Sherman, Dark Blue 125.00
Plate, Taft & Sherman, Tin Lithograph, 1908 .... 250.00
Postcard, Christmas, Mr. & Mrs. George Bush, For Diplomats, 1989, 12 1/2 x 17 In. ... 100.00
Postcard, Christmas, Mr. & Mrs. Ronald Reagan, For Diplomats, 1988, 12 x 13 In. 95.00
Postcard, Davis, Homestead, Clarksburg, West Virginia, Multicolored 45.00
Postcard, Davis, Sepia, August, 1924 .... 93.00
Postcard, Nixon's The One, Record, 33 1/3 RPM, Nomination Speech, 1968 .... 40.00
Postcard, Nixon, Inauguration Day Commemorative, 1973 .... 6.00
Postcard, Suffrage Parade, Washington, D.C., Sepia, 1913 .... 40.00
Postcard, Taft & Sherman Campaign, Photograph, 1909 .... 15.00
Postcard, Taft & Sherman, Portraits, Nation's Choice, 1908 .... 16.00
Poster, 4 Freedoms, Roosevelt, 18 x 24 In. 45.00
Poster, Abraham Lincoln & Andrew Johnson, Frame, 21 1/4 In. 130.00
Poster, Coolidge, Dawes, 1924 .... 45.00
Poster, Eisenhower, Seated At Desk, Signing Paper, Facsimile Signature 8.00
Poster, Give Governor Wallace A Viable Alternative, 11 x 13 3/4 In. 15.00
Poster, Herbert H. Hoover, 12 x 22 In. 19.00
Poster, Jimmy Carter For President, Campaign, 1976 .... 10.00
Poster, Kennedy For President, Leadership For The '60s, 27 x 43 In. 45.00
Poster, Kennedy For President, Plastic, Red, White & Blue, 18 x 24 In. 40.00
Poster, Kennedy, Johnson, Leadership For The '60s, Shrink Wrapped, 18 x 24 In. 80.00
Poster, Nixon Portrait, 37 1/2 x 50 In. 35.00
Poster, Reconstruction Era, Grant & Lincoln, Rights Of Blacks, 36 x 28 In. 1100.00
Poster, Ronald Reagan, Law & Order, 20 x 28 In. 65.00
Poster, Roosevelt, V For Victory 250.00
Poster, Stevenson, Red, White & Blue, 10 1/4 x 14 In. 22.00
Poster, Truman, Barkley, Missouri 50.00
Poster, Willkie Wings, Red, White & Blue, 25 x 9 1/2 In. 32.00
Poster, Woodrow Wilson, Flag Ground, E. Renesch, 1919 .... 28.00
Print, Roosevelt, Artist Signed, Frame, 1933 .... 75.00
Print, Washington To McKinley, Old Government Whisky, 1902, 26 X22 In. 660.00
Program, Inaugural, Roosevelt & Garner Cover, 64 Pages, 1933 .... 35.00
Program, Republican Convention, Miami, 1972 .... 60.00
Puzzle, Nixon, Agnew, 1970 .... 40.00
Record, John F. Kennedy, Famous Speeches, 33 1/3 RPM, 1963 .... 10.00
Ribbon, 16 To 1, Bryan & Sewell, Metal Rooster At Top, 9 x 2 1/4 In. 180.00
Ribbon, Abraham Lincoln Beneath American Flag, Pink Silk, Brady Cooper 1210.00
Ribbon, Benjamin Harrison, Silk 65.00
Ribbon, Campaign, J.W. Garfield & Arthur Black, Picture Of Garfield, 1880, 5 1/4 In. ... 78.00
Ribbon, Campaign, Teddy Roosevelt For President, Picture 65.00
Ribbon, Colonel Teddy Roosevelt, Yellow & Black 58.00
Ribbon, For President, Howard Taft, Celluloid, 1 3/4 In. 85.00
Ribbon, For President, W.H. Taft, Sketched Head, 1 3/4 In. 40.00
Ribbon, Lincoln & Hamler, 1860 .... 1834.00
Ribbon, Logan Bushnell, Ohio, 1895 .... 115.00
Ribbon, McKinley Image On Attached Celluloid, Fabric 45.00
Ribbon, McKinley, Governor, Black & White 225.00
Ribbon, Silk, Henry Clay, Whig National Convention, May 2, 1884 .... 425.00
Ribbon, Vote For Lincoln, Silk, Red With Black Letters, 8 x 1 3/4 In. 315.00
Ribbon, Western Federation Of Miners 1170.00
Ribbon, William McKinley, Celluloid Image, Tied With Red Ribbons, 5 In. 65.00
Ribbon, Willing Workers Taft Club, Colored, Silk, 74 In. 495.00
Ribbon & Medal, Inaugural, 1965 .... 30.00
Ring, Flicker, Changes From John Kennedy's Face To American Flag 25.00
Serigraph Set, 32 Presidents, Bust Silhouette, Paul Dubosclard, 32 Piece 150.00
Sheet Music, Al Smith, Sidewalks Of New York 25.00
Sheet Music, Lincoln Mourning 50.00

Sheet Music, Roosevelt The Peace Victor, Portrait Cover, 1905	55.00
Sheet Music, Yellow Rose Of Texas, Dedicated To Pres. F. Roosevelt, 1936	15.00
Shield, Flag, Taft's Inauguration, Painted Tin	1800.00
Spoon, Kennedy, Gemini Space Spoon	12.00
Stickpin, McKinley, Red, White & Blue Flag	65.00
Stickpin, Taft, Multicolored	50.00
Stud, Bull Moose, Progressive, Pewter	37.00
Stud, Cox, Embossed Cox, Pewter	20.00
Stud, Rooster Shape, Cox, Silver Pewter, 7/8 In.	55.00
Tab Button, Agnew For Governor, 3/4 In.	28.00
Tab Button, Lapel, LaFollette, Wheeler, Brass, 1924	6.00
Tab Button, Roosevelt, Forward With UAW, CIO, Labor's Choice	20.00
Tab Button, Roosevelt, Truman	7.00
Tab Button, Stevenson, 2 In.	3.00
Textile, Protect Home Industry, Harrison, Marton, Framed, 1888, 22 x 24 1/2 In.	230.00
Ticket, Democratic National Convention, Roosevelt Inset, 1936	20.00
Ticket, Inaugural, Jan. 17, 1981, 3 1/2 x 6 1/2 In.	4.00
Tile, Abraham Lincoln, White Bust, Blue Ground	40.00
Tile, McKinley, Blue-Green High Gloss Glaze, Square, 3 In.	40.00
Toby Jug, Frank Delano Roosevelt, Royal Winton, 4 1/2 In.	250.00
Token, Abraham Lincoln, Memorial, Copper, 1860	157.00
Token, Clay, 1844-1861	180.00
Token, McClellan, Campaign Penny, 1864	45.00
Token, Stephan Douglas, Campaign Coin, 1860	30.00
Token, Stephen Douglas, Memorial, 1860-1861	80.00
Token, U.S. Grant, Painted Shell	285.00
Torch, Campaign, Harrison, Brass, 1841, 10 In.	1210.00
Tray, McKinley Portrait, Lithograph, 18 x 12 In.	118.00
Tray, McKinley, Frosted Bust, Star Border, Glass, Oblong	220.00
Tray, Teddy Roosevelt On Horse, Tin Lithograph, Oval, 16 In.	605.00
Tray, Theodore Roosevelt, Advertising On Back, Coshocton, Ohio, 13 5/8 x 16 1/2 In.	195.00
Tumbler, Teddy Roosevelt, Holly Berries In Wreath, Clear	240.00
Tumbler, William Henry Harrison, Glass	1600.00
Vase, William Henry Harrison, Etched Log Cabin & Other Designs, 8 1/2 In.	4000.00
Walking Stick, Bust Of McKinley Top, Wooden	275.00
Watch Fob, Bryan, 1908, 1 1/2 In.	36.00
Watch Fob, Howard Taft, Celluloid	60.00
Watch Fob, William Howard Taft	35.00
Watch Fob, Wilson, Pen Mightier Than Sword, Bronze, 1 1/2 In.	24.00
Watch Fob, Wilson, Right Man, Right Place, Enameled Red, White & Blue, Brass	165.00

POMONA glass is a clear glass with a soft amber border decorated with pale blue or rose-colored flowers and leaves. The colors are very, very pale. The background of the glass is covered with a network of fine lines. It was made from 1885 to 1888 by the New England Glass Company. First grind was made from April 1885 to June 1886. It was made by cutting a wax surface on the glass, then dipping it in acid. Second grind was a less expensive method of acid etching that was developed later.

Bowl, Cover, Amber Edge On Lid, Frosted Ribs	65.00
Bowl, Etched Cornflower, Blue, 2nd Grind, 5 1/4 In.	480.00
Bowl, Floral Pattern, Crimped Top, 4 Footed, Amber, Gray, Blue, 5 1/2 In.	245.00
Celery Dish, Inverted Thumbprint, Amber Scalloped Rim, 6 1/2 x 4 In.	110.00
Champagne, Amber Rim, 2nd Grind	140.00
Finger Bowl, Amber Ruffled Rim, 2 1/2 x 5 1/2 In.	50.00
Finger Bowl, Gold Stain, 1st Grind, 2 1/2 In.	75.00
Goblet, Amber Rim, 2nd Grind	150.00
Mug, Applied Handle, Gold Enamel, Pontil	75.00
Pitcher, Alternating Frosted & Iridescent Stained Ribs, White Enamel, 8 1/2 In.	600.00
Pitcher, Optic Diamond-Quilted Body, 1st Grind, 6 3/4 In.	385.00
Sugar, Ruffled, Double Handles, 2nd Grind	120.00
Sugar & Creamer, Amber, Ruffled Edge	485.00
Thumbprint, 3rd Grind, 7 1/2 In.	27.50

Tumbler, Cornflower, 2nd Grind 90.00
Tumbler, Cornflower, 4 1/2 In. 80.00
Tumbler, Water, Cornflower, Honey Amber, Leaves, Blue Flowers, 3 3/4 In. 145.00
Vase, Inverted Thumbprint, Amber Acorn Design, Square Top, 4 3/4 In. 77.00
Vase, Inverted Thumbprint, Crimped, 7 In. 225.00
Water Set, Luster Trim, 2nd Grind, 5 Piece 35.00

PONTYPOOL, see Tole category.

POPEYE was introduced to the Thimble Theater comic strip in 1929.
The character became a favorite of readers. In 1932, an animated car-
toon featuring Popeye was made by Paramount Studios. The cartoon
series continued and became even more popular when it was shown on
television starting in the 1950s. The full-length movie with Robin
Williams as Popeye was made in 1980.

Andirons, Standing Popeye, Half-Round, Incised ARK, Cast Metal, 14 1/2 In. 1380.00
Ashtray, 11 In. 30.00
Bank, American Bisque .... 365.00 to 395.00
Bank, Cast Iron, 9 In. 20.00
Bank, Daily Dime, Picture Of Popeye On Top, Yellow, 1956, 2 1/2-In. Diam. 20.00
Bank, Daily Quarter, Popeye With Spinach Can, Box, Kalon, c.1950, 5 In. 472.00
Bank, Dime Register, 1929, 2 1/2 x 2 1/2 In. .... 48.00 to 150.00
Bank, Dime Register, 1956 .... 110.00
Bank, Dime Register, K.F.S. Marked, 1929 .... 125.00
Bank, Jeep, Plastic 45.00
Bank, Popeye Sitting On Rope, Vinyl, PlayPal Plastics, 7 1/2 In. 90.00
Bank, Popeye's Head, Vandor 85.00
Bell, Figural Handle, Vandor 28.00
Bobbin' Head, Olive Oyl, France 350.00
Book, 1937 .... 60.00
Book, Big Little Book, Popeye Ghost Ship Treasure Island 9.00
Book, Popeye & The Pirates, Animated, 1945 .... 45.00
Box, Chalk Crayons, 1930s 95.00
Box, Popeye Candy & Prize, Phoenix Candy Co., 1979, 2 1/2 x 5 In. 12.00
Box, Trinket, Vandor, 1980 .... 50.00
Boxing Gloves, Original Display Wrapper, 1950s 145.00
Bucket, Plastic, 1950s, 14 In. 32.00
Button, Popeye Showing His Muscles To Swee'pea, 6 In. 10.00
Card, Popeye & Olive Oyl, In Boat, Corgi, Metal Painted, 1980 .... 29.00
Chalk Board, Alphabet Across Bottom, With Characters Around Board, 18 x 12 In. 35.00
Christmas Ornament, Figural, Blown Glass 25.00
Christmas Ornament, Swee'pea On Candy Cane 15.00
Christmas Ornament, Wimpy In Wreath, 1981 .... 15.00
Christmas Tree Lights, Box, 1930s 225.00
Coloring Book, Lowe, 80 Pages, 1964, 11 x 8 In. 20.00
Combat Target Set 20.00
Cookie Jar, Pipe, American Bisque .... 765.00 to 795.00
Cookie Jar, Popeye In Spinach Can, Cori Pottery Company 320.00
Cookie Jar, Popeye's Head, Vandor 395.00
Cup, Party, Wax Paper, Happy Birthday, Illustrations, Unused, 1950s, 3 In. 8.00
Doll, Cloth, Vinyl, Gund, 21 In. .... 135.00 to 184.00
Doll, Hard Rubber, 1934 .... 350.00
Doll, Olive Oyl, Wearing Usual Outfit, Boots, Presents, 1985, 11 In. 18.00
Doll, Uneeda Doll Co., Box, 8 In. 25.00
Figure, Popeye, Cast Iron, Painted, Spinach Wagon Toy, 1930s, 3 In. 300.00
Figure, Standing, Hard Rubber, Cameo, 14 In. 200.00
Flix Movie Cassette, Pocket, Package 15.00
Game, Bingo, 1929, 4 x 6 In. 75.00
Game, Dexterity, Popeye The Juggler, Balls In Holes, 1929 .... 60.00 to 125.00
Game, Jack Set, 16 Jacks, 2 Balls, Shimel Toys, 1960s 20.00
Game, Pearl Diving With Popeye, England, 1960 .... 75.00
Game, Pipe Toss, Popeye, With Pipe, Box .... 69.00 to 145.00
Game, Ring Toss, On Display Card, 1970s 8.00

Game, Roly Poly Popeye Target, Cork Gun, 6 Different Characters, 1940-1950 . . . . 275.00
Game, Spinach Toss 75.00
Kazoo, Corn Cob Pipe, Popeye & Wimpy Pictured, Tin, Cardboard, 1934, 3 1/2 In. 45.00
Knife, Folding, Photos Of Popeye, Olive & Swee'pea, 6 In. 8.00
Lamp, Original Shade 695.00
Light Covers, Christmas, Characters, Molded Plastic, 1930s 85.00
Lunch Box, Popeye Fighting, Universal, Metal, 1962 . . . . 95.00
Lunch Box, Schoolhouse, King Seeley Thermos, Metal, 1964 . . . . 80.00
Music Box, Popeye In Spinach Can, Mattel, Box 45.00
Paint Set, Popeye Paints, Tin, American Crayon Co., Sandusky, Ohio, 1933 . . . . 75.00
Pen Set, Figural Top Pens, Popeye, Olive & Swee'pea, Box 13.00
Pencil, Mechanical, Box, 1929 . . . . 45.00
Pencil Case, Popeye's Comic Strip Pals, 1929 . . . . 48.00
Pencil Holder, Tin Truck Has Holder Built Into Top, Box, 7 1/2 In. 12.00
Pencil Sharpener, Bakelite, K.F.S. Inc., 1930, 1 3/4 In. 89.00
Pin, Brass, Die Cut, 1950s, 1 1/2 In. 10.00
Pin, Wimpy, Lithograph, Color Portrait & Name, KFS Copyright, c.1936, 13/16 In. 45.00
Pipe, Lights Up, On Card, 1958 . . . . 45.00
Puppet, Hand, Swee'pea, Vinyl Head, Gund, 1950s 30.00
Puppet, Hand, Wimpy, Vinyl Head, Gund, 1950s 30.00
Puzzle, Jay Mar, Box 60.00
Puzzle, Popeye, Olive Oyl, Swee'pea, Popeye Playing Guitar Below Window, 1970 . . . . 24.00
Record, Album, Popeye The Sailor Man, 33 RPM 6.00
Ring, Flasher, 4 Different Rings, Vari-Vue, 1960s 8.00
Ring, Olive Oyl, Post Toasties Corn Flakes, 1949 . . . . 45.00
Ring, Wimpy, Post Toasties Corn Flakes, 1949 . . . . 20.00
Salt & Pepper, Popeye & Olive Oyl, Japan 165.00
Slate, Stow-A-Way, Popeye & Olive Oyl Top, Lowe, 1957, 12 x 8 In. 30.00
Tin, Licorice, Popeye With Ship's Wheel, Australia 357.00
Tin, Yellow Popcorn, 1949 . . . . 75.00
Toy, Boxing, Box, Chein 2640.00
Toy, Jigger, Marx, 1936 . . . . 850.00
Toy, Motorcycle, Spinach Delivery 2970.00
Toy, Nailing Set, Box, 1930s 125.00
Toy, Parrot Cages, Marx, Box 475.00
Toy, Playing Basketball, Windup, Chein, 7 1/2 In. 1955.00
Toy, Playing Basketball, Windup, Linemar 747.00
Toy, Popeye & Olive Oyl On The Roof, Windup, Marx, 1934 . . . . .1150.00 to 1925.00
Toy, Popeye Dances On Roof, Windup, Marx, 1930s 850.00
Toy, Popeye Does A Jig As Olive Rocks Back/Forth On Spinach Box, Tin, Marx 3150.00
Toy, Popeye Express, Tin . . . . .500.00 to 920.00
Toy, Popeye In Barrel, Chein, 7 In. 895.00
Toy, Popeye On Roller Skates, Tin, Windup, Linemar 880.00
Toy, Popeye The Champ, Tin Lithograph . . . . .895.00 to 1000.00
Toy, Popeye The Pilot, Marx, 8 x 5 In. 250.00
Toy, Popeye With Parrot Cages, Marx 920.00
Toy, Roller Skating, Windup, Linemar, 6 In. 925.00
Toy, Roller Skating, With Spinach Can, Tin, Windup, Linemar 450.00
Toy, Rollover Tank, Linemar 275.00
Toy, Roly Poly, Celluloid, 4 In. 3450.00
Toy, The Champ, Working Bell, Tin, Box, 7 In. 761.00
Toy, Waddler, Popeye Waddles Around, Tin, Windup, Chein, 1932, 6 In. . . . . 650.00 to 725.00
Toy, Walker, Windup, Chein, 1930s, 7 1/2 In. 220.00
Toy, Xylophonist, Noma, 10 1/2 In. 50.00
Tumbler, Popeye In Boxing Trunks Throwing A Punch, Printed Design, 1930s . . . .

PORCELAIN factories that are well known are listed in this book under
the factory name. This category lists pieces made by the less well-
known factories.

    Ashtray, Mayfair, Royal Winton 120.00
    Basin, Floral Design, Diapered Border, Sometsuke, 19th Century, 15 5/8 In. 275.00
    Basket, Sycamore Leaf, Bird In Flight In Center, Rose, Purple, Red, Longton Hall, 10 In. 1840.00
    Beaker, Lower Section Fluted, Military Transfer Trophy, Blue, Russia, 1825, 3 In. 2300.00

Bowl, Enameled, 3 Women Playing A Board Game In Garden, 3 x 6 In. 460.00
Bowl, Exotic Birds In Center, Leafy Gilt, Cobalt Blue, Green Edge, 1840, 8 In. 363.00
Bowl, Fruit, Applied Roses, Footed, Dresden Type, 12 In. ....*Illus* 330.00
Bowl, Tiger Pursing Dragon, Floral Design, Pewter Mounted, China, 10 In. 70.00
Box, Bunch Of Asparagus Tied By Ribbon, Green, Pink, Yellow, Russia, 5 3/4 In. 2070.00
Box, Hand Painted Bows, Fruit & Winged Creatures, Camille Naudel, Oval, 5 In. 125.00
Cache Pot, Gilt Birds & Insects, Floral Landscape, 1880s, 7 In., Pair 373.00
Cake Stand, Polychrome Scenes Of Birds, AR Mark, 9 3/8 x 9 1/4 In. 60.00
Celery Dish, Months Of The Year, Black Transfer, Yellow Border, 11 In. 575.00
Charger, Animal & Floral Reserves, Gilt Border, Imperial Russian Factory, 12 In. 1265.00
Charger, Double Headed Eagle Center, Floral Spray Border, Popov Factory, 18 In. 345.00
Charger, Polychrome Gilt, Coat Of Arms, Boat & Castle Scenes, 17 3/4 In. 275.00
Chocolate Set, Bunches Of Roses, Pink Shades, Royal Austria, 11 Piece 425.00
Coffeepot, Yellow, Lily Handle, Royal Winton 450.00
Cream Boat, Leaf Molded, Overlapping Vine Leaves, Stem Handle, Longton Hall 1840.00
Cream Boat, White Leaf Molded, Grape Clusters, Forked Stem Handle, Longton Hall .. 920.00
Creamer, Cow, Norway, 1930s 65.00
Creamer, George III Style, Bamboo Style Handle, John Scofield, 1783, 5 5/8 In. 2070.00
Creamer, Monogram, Crown, Raspberry Ground, Gilt, Russia, 5 1/4 In. 920.00
Cup & Saucer, Gilded Border, Russia, 1830, 6 7/8 In. 1150.00
Cup & Saucer, Peace After Napoleonic Wars, Gray, Green, 1816, 5 In. 285.00
Cup & Saucer, St. Cloud, White Coffee Cup, Artichoke Petals On Saucer, 2 In. 690.00
Cup & Saucer, Tea, Blue Cartouche Border, Spray Reserve, Kornilove Brothers, Russia . 430.00
Cup & Saucer, Tea, Monogram, Raspberry Ground, Gilt Bands, Imperial Factory, Pair .. 546.00
Desk Set, Dove On Pine Boughs, Removable Ink Pot & Sander, 7 1/4 In. 105.00
Dish, Floral Design, Gilt Border, Polychrome, 10 In. 220.00
Dish, Lettuce Leaf, 5 Overlapping Leaves, Pink Molded Veins, Longton Hall, 9 In. 3450.00
Dish, Squirrel, Gourd Vine Pattern, Squirrel, Crouched On Hedge, Brown Rim, 8 In. 747.00
Dish, Strawberry Leaf, Rose Veined, Green Strawberry Leaves, Longton Hall, 8 In. 3450.00
Dish, Strawberry Leaf, Twisted Stem Handle, Russet Fluted Rim, Longton Hall, 9 In. ... 747.00
Easter Egg, Figural Reserve, Wine & Gilt Banded, Blue Ground, Russia, 3 In. 260.00
Easter Egg, St. Anne Reserve, Cobalt Blue Ground, Imperial Por. Factory, 3 In. 3450.00
Eggcup, Fowl Footed Pedestal, Applied Flowers, Green, White, Gold 165.00
Ewer, Dragon Handle, Salmon Flowers, Leaves, Cream Ground, Red Stamp, 11 In. 200.00
Ewer, Flowers, Leaves, Dragon Handle, Red Stamp, 11 In. 200.00
Ewer, Salmon Color Flowers, Gold Dragon Mark, Red Stamp Mark, 11 In. 198.00
Figurine, African Dancers, Man Playing Cymbals, Girl With Tambourine, 26 1/4 In. 2590.00
Figurine, Blackamoors, Male & Female, Glazed Robes, Sitzendorf, 14 In., Pair 1840.00
Figurine, Cockerel, Red Comb, Pierced Brown Base, 19th Century, 15 In., Pair 1955.00
Figurine, Dog, Seated, Blue Eyes, Black Brows, Rocky Base, Mennecy, 1750, 4 In. 2415.00
Figurine, Drunken Innkeeper, Jacket, Red Breeches, Ludwigsburg, 1765, 5 1/4 In. 1150.00
Figurine, Frog, Green Speckled, Pink Shorts, On Lettuce Leaf, Umbrella, c.1890, 6 In. .. 525.00
Figurine, Googly-Eyed Boy, Next To Container, Germany, 7 In. 48.00

If you want to use a valuable porcelain punch bowl at a party, try this: Buy a piece of lightweight clear plastic hose at a hardware store. Slit the hose and use it to protect the rim of the bowl from the punch ladle.

Porcelain, Bowl, Fruit, Applied Roses,
Footed, Dresden Type, 12 In.

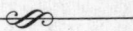

Rub salt inside old tea and coffee cups to remove stains.

Porcelain, Teapot, Parrot Shape,
Strainer Spout, 7 x 5 In.

Figurine, Guinevere, Blue Flowing Robe, Gold Crown, Signed, Ispanky	575.00
Figurine, Mallard Duck, Lettuce & Cabbage Leaves Surround, Continental, 11 In.	230.00
Figurine, Maria Foote, Wearing Black Cap, Gilt Collared Green Coat, 1831, 6 3/8 In.	345.00
Figurine, Mutt, Ceramic, Germany, 1912	190.00
Figurine, Napoleon, Black Hat, Green Uniform, 1850, 4 In.	225.00
Figurine, Pilgrim, Gilt Edged White Cap, Black Capelet, Buen Retiro, 1760	1380.00
Figurine, Sportsman's Companion, Wearing Yellow Hat, Longton Hall, 1755, 7 In.	1265.00
Figurine, Vintager, Wearing White Hat, Shirt, Gera, 1790, 6 3/16 In.	575.00
Ginger Jar, Bird, Flower Design, Blue, White, 7 3/4 In.	332.00
Ginger Jar, Canton Style Design, Blue, White, 6 3/4 In.	72.00
Group, Napoleon, Seated Beside Crib With Infant, Germany, 10 In.	290.00
Humidor, Comoy's Of London, Iridescent Emerald Glaze, Royal Winton	130.00
Jar, Figural, Cover, Figure Of A Sage, Buddha Figure On Side, Japan, 9 3/4 In.	260.00
Jar, Passion Flower Design, Blue, White, 4 3/4 In.	120.00
Lamp Base, Enameled, Gilt Birds, Floral Drapery, Dolphin Form Handles, Pink, Pair	3220.00
Mask, Smiling Muse, Curly Hair, Carpaux	550.00
Mug, Kakiemon, Sepia On 1 Side, Branches, Red, Green, Chantilly, 1740, 3 In.	920.00
Pitcher, Girl With Dove & Roses, Bacchante Mask Spout, Austria, 8 In.	575.00
Pitcher, Uncle Sam, Royal Winton	125.00
Plaque, Slave Girl Being Sold, H. Siemiradzki, 1878, 13 x 17 In.	5175.00
Plate, Gothic Spandrel Reserve, Gothic Tracery Rim, Gilt, Kuznetsova Factory, 11 In.	575.00
Plate, Leaf Molded, Rose, Purple, Red, Blue, Yellow, Green Bouquet, Longton Hall, 10 In.	1035.00
Plate, Strawberry Leaf, Floral Bouquet, Spray, Sprigs, Longton Hall, 1755, 12 1/16 In.	2875.00
Platter, Well & Tree, Stylized Chrysanthemum & Bamboo, Japan, 17 1/2 x 13 In.	660.00
Salt, Shell, ES Prussia, 1 In.	48.00
Sauceboat, Island Gazebo Beneath Flocks Of Birds, Loop Handle, Longton Hall, 7 In.	460.00
Sauceboat, Salt Glaze, Foliate Scrolls, S-Scroll Handle, Longton Hall, 7 1/2 In.	1035.00
Screen, 4-Panel, Lohans Scene, Late 19th Century, 13 1/2 In.	192.00
Serving Plate, Arch, Gilded Border, Black 2 Headed Eagle, Berlin Mfg., 10 In.	4900.00
Serving Plate, Blue Cipher Mark, Imperial Porcelain Mfg., 1825, 10 1/4 In.	4025.00
Shoe, Victorian, Sapphire Blue, Thimble Type	245.00
Sugar & Creamer, Luster, Royal Winton	65.00
Tea Bowl, Song Dynasty, Incised Design, 3-Character Mark, China, 6 1/4 In.	230.00
Teapot, Kanzi, Blue Lotus, 18th Century, 7 1/2 x 7 In.	1995.00
Teapot, Old Canada, Royal Winton	90.00
Teapot, Parrot Shape, Strainer Spout, 7 x 5 In. ....*Illus*	8.00
Toothbrush Holder, Cartoon Character, 7 In.	275.00
Tureen, Polychrome Floral Enameling, Oriental, 11 1/4 In.	115.00
Urn, Applied Cherubs, Flowers, Fruit Garlands, Polychrome, Thieme Mark, 21 In.	1375.00
Urn, Bulbous, Imperial Eagle On Both Sides, Domed Base, Russia, 1897, 16 3/8 In.	9775.00
Urn, Cobalt Blue Glaze, Ormolu Mount, France, 11 3/4 In., Pair	910.00
Urn, Cover, Eagle Finial, Couple Reserves, Reeded, Foliate Ground, Gilt, 12 In., Pair	2070.00
Urn, Figures, Clouds, Burgundy Bands, Gold Overlay, Royal Austrian, 15 In., Pair	515.00
Urn, Oval Cartouches Of Bawdy Peasant Scenes, Mask Handles, 15 In., Pair	3335.00
Urn, Panels Of Courting Couples & Landscape, Metal Mounted, c.1880, 16 In., Pair	2530.00

Vase, Bamboo & Heron Scene, Matte Finish Exterior, 9 3/4 In., Pair	660.00
Vase, Beehive, Dark Red On Gold, Gold Dust, Mountainside, 10 In.	150.00
Vase, Black Boy, With Banjo, Yellow, Black On Rust Red, Green Ground, 8 1/2 In.	135.00
Vase, Bulbous, Brown, Floral Design, Mountainside, 6 In.	75.00
Vase, Flared Rim, Black Curlicues, Glossy Brown Ground, Gres Mougin, 10 x 5 In.	495.00
Vase, Floral Arrangements Surrounded By Butterflies, Famille Rose Palette, 5 In.	920.00
Vase, Grain Of Rice Technique, Crystalline Glaze, Adelaide Robineau, 1903, 6 In.	5500.00
Vase, Lavender, Signed Rorstrand, 16 In.	600.00
Vase, Mask, Loose Ring Handles, Baluster Shape, Blue, White, 5 3/4 In.	363.00
Vase, Overall Green Glaze, Gourd Shape, Vine Like Finial On Cover, 6 1/4 In., Pair	515.00
Vase, Panel With Lonely, Jeweled & Rouge Luster Ground, c.1905, 21 3/4 In.	4600.00
Vase, Pear Shape, Black Glaze, 6 1/2 In.	100.00
Vase, Pine Branches, Flared, Egg Shape, Imperial Porcelain Factory, 1909, 12 In.	4180.00
Vase, Saturday Evening Girls, Landscape, Green, Brown, Light Blue, 1917, 6 x 4 In.	3190.00
Vase, Stick, Red Finch Flies, Mocha Bark Textured, Oriental, 5 In.	220.00
Vase, Teardrop Form, Turquoise Glaze, 11 In.	109.00
Vase, Teardrop Form, Yellow Crackle Glaze, 5 In.	109.00
Vase, Woman Portrait, Green Ground, Artist, Sonntag, 3 1/8 x 1 5/8 In.	110.00
Vase, Woman, Lounging At Base Looking Up At Putti On Lip, Violet Ribbon, 15 In.	834.00
Wall Pocket, Hawks, Crouching, Brown, Japan, 19th Century, 7 In., Pair	1610.00

POSTCARDS were first legally permitted in Austria on October 1, 1869. The United States passed postal regulations allowing the card in 1872. Most of the picture postcards collected today date after 1910. The amount of postage can help to date a card. The rates are: 1872 (1 cent), 1917 (2 cents), 1919 (1 cent), 1925 (2 cents), 1928 (1 cent), 1952 (2 cents), 1959 (3 cents), 1963 (4 cents), 1968 (5 cents), 1973 (8 cents), 1975 (7 cents), 1976 (9 cents), 1978 (10 cents), 1981 (12 cents), 1981 (13 cents), 1985 (14 cents), 1988 (15 cents), 1991 (19 cents), 1995 (20 cents).

Aitka, Eskimo Berry Sellers, Hand Colored, 1910	17.00
Auto, Packard, 1940s, Penny	12.00
Automobile Parade, Pulaski, N.Y., Old Home Week, Photograph	50.00
Bird's-Eye View Cleveland Municipal Stadium, Downtown............*Illus*	5.00
Brown Bear, Suede, I Can't Bear To Leave Berthoud Colo., 1906	10.00
Buster Brown, Yellow Kid, Over The Bounding Main	30.00
Cadbury's Cocoa, Raphael Tuck & Sons, Cecil Aldin	50.00
Camel Can Go 8 Days Without A Drink, Who Wants To Be A Camel	7.00
Cape Smythe Whaling & Trading Co., Eskimo Children, Photograph	19.00
Chesterfield Cigarettes, World War I Doughboy, Lyendecker	35.00
Chief Hiawatha, Photograph, 1904-1918	65.00
Clarkdale Smelter View, Ariz., Photograph, 1950	6.00
Columbia Exposition, Grover Cleveland, 1893	65.00
Coney Island, Steeplechase Park, Each Different, 1950s, 6 Piece	13.00
Crosley Field, Columbus, Ohio, White Border, Linen	18.00
David Bowie, Advertising TV Show, 1989, 7 x 5 In.	5.00
Dr Pepper, Free 6 Bottles, Red, Green & White, Government Card	15.00
Easter, Gold Rabbit, Standing, Shotgun Over Shoulder, Embossed, 1908	45.00
Easter, Mechanical Butterfly	22.00
Easter, Rose O'Neill, Kewpie	22.00
Economy King Cream Separators, Sears, Roebuck & Co., 1916, Large ....55.00 to 65.00	
Eisenhower Riding In Parade, Passing Margaret Truman Launderette, Key West	15.00
Ellis Island, Color, 1910s	5.00
Felix The Cat, Felix With Candlestick Phone, I'll Parley-Voo, 1920s, 3 x 5 In.	20.00
Fire Engine, F. Schmidt & Co., Chicago, Art Nouveau Series	35.00
Folder, Ford Auto Plant, Detroit, 20 Color Views Of Production, 1923	13.00
Grand Coulee Dam, Photograph, 1940s	6.00
Grateful Dead, Avalon Ballroom, San Francisco, 7 x 5 3/4 In.	12.00
Grateful Dead, Shea's Buffalo, Shea's Theatre, Buffalo, N.Y., 1980s, 5 x 7 In.	3.00
Grateful Dead, Without A Net, Rick Griffin On Cover, 6 x 4 In.	6.00
Green's Hotel, Philadelphia, Pa., Angora Cat, 1900	35.00
Greetings From Middletown, N.J., Floral Design, Embossed, 1909	8.00
Harding & Wife, Seated With Others In Background	22.00

Harley-Davidson 125, See & Ride This Sporty Lightweight, Text Back 45.00
Heinz Baked Beans, Greetings From Ocean Pier, Atlantic City 35.00
Hold-To-Light, Dreamland Coney Island, N.Y., L.J. Koehler 48.00
Hold-To-Light, Happy New Year, England, 1905 .... 35.00
Hold-To-Light, St. Louis World's Fair, 1904 .... 100.00
Horse Blankets, Stratton 10.00
Hot Springs, Ark., Maurice Baths, Art Nouveau Design, 1910 .... 18.00
House, Snow, C.E. Pike, Calif., 1913 .... 10.00
Ice Cream Parlor, Fountain, Los Angeles, Color, 1911 .... 10.00
Indian Motorcycle, Photograph, 20th Century Model 66.00
Jackson Brewing Co., Please Take Notice, 1902 .... 22.00
Jersey Dairy Herd, Araco-Coos Co., Ore., 41 Cows Produce 2200 Lbs. Of Milk, 1911 .. 12.00
Josephine Baker, Autographed 475.00
Kodak Camera, Pretty Woman 1 Side, Best Vacation Text Other Side, Photograph 50.00
Lithgow's Vaudeville, Penny 5.00
Maggie & Jiggs 35.00
Mardi Gras Material, Raphael Tuck Publisher, 6 Piece 120.00
Mechanical, Peacock, Dial On Side Moves Tail Feathers, Kaleidoscope Effect 75.00
Miss Alice Roosevelt, Hand Written On Front Picture 10.00
Montana Indians, Tribe Yankton Sioux, Photograph, J. Bjornson, 1909 .... 85.00
Presidential Campaign, Taft Riding Elephant To White House, 1908 .... 50.00
Raquel Welsh, 1967, Large 15.00
Red Cross Fund, Mobilize For Defense, March 1, 1931 .... 35.00
Royal Tailors, Chicago & N.Y., All World Loves A Royal Tailored Man, Lyendecker 50.00
Salmina's Resort, Cottage, Lake County, Calif., Photograph, 1930s 22.00
Sheridan Inn, Wyoming, Photograph 8.00
Silhouette Of Wilson, Quote From Josiah Holland 11.00
Sincerely Yours, Warren G. Harding, Black & White 25.00
Slow Dancing, Dolly Parton 3.00
Smith-Winchester Factory, 1915 .... 35.00
Somebody To Love, George Michael & Queen 5.00
Sportsmen's Park, St. Louis, 1920s 18.00
St. Anthony, Idaho, Chevron Gas Station, Photograph, 1940 .... 7.00
State Girls Series, Kansas In Silk, Red Silk Applied To Dress 32.00
Stay Sick, Ghoulardi, Horror Movie Host, Autographed, 1963 ....*Illus* 45.00
Stein Series, Indian, Fabric Art Co., 1908 .... 25.00
Suffragette Procession Moving Up Pennsylvania Avenue, Washington 15.00
Switzer's Dept. Store, Tucson, Drawing, Russell Wilson, 1940s 5.00
Titanic, Largest Ship In The World Remembrance, 1912 .... 600.00
Tobacco Field View, Marion, Leaves, Workers In Background, 1910 .... 4.00
Triumph Speed Twin, Motorcycle, Model 5T, Distributors Addresses Back 35.00
Tulare High School Banner, Calif., Embroidered, Yellow, Red, 1907 .... 8.00

Above: Postcard, Bird's-Eye View
Cleveland Municipal Stadium, Downtown
Right: Postcard, Stay Sick, Ghoulardi, Horror
Movie Host, Autographed, 1963

U.S. Olympic Team, Rome, Team Names Printed On Back, 1960 .... 35.00
Viewer, Keystone 38.00
Waldport, Oregon, Oregon Coast Highway, Sawyer Photo Street Scene, 1930s 5.00
Waring Aluron, For All You Iron 50.00
White Sulphur Springs, W.Va., Hotel Swimming Pool, Photograph, 1920 .... 15.00
Woodstock, Jimi Hendrix 5.00
World War I Soldier, Full Dress Uniform, On Stool 28.00
World's Fair, 1904 .... 7.00
Wrigley Field, White Border 18.00
Yankee Stadium, Linen 18.00
Young Queen Elizabeth & Family, England 12.00

POSTERS have informed the public about news and entertainment events since ancient times. Nineteenth-century advertising or theatrical posters and twentieth-century movie and war posters are of special interest today. The price is determined by the artist, the condition, and the rarity. Other posters may be listed under Movie, Political, and World War I and II.

Ace Of Spades, Adventure, 1925, 27 x 41 In. 515.00
Alfred E. Newman, Mad Magazine, Red, White, Blue, Black, Yellow, 4 x 2 In. 123.00
Borden Fudge Bar, 18 x 7 In. 10.00
Buy Coal Now, J.C. Leyendecker, 1917 .... 300.00
Calvert Whiskey, Baseball Game, 1950s 175.00
Clyde Beatty-Cole Bros., Full Color, Roland Butler, 36 x 21 In. 22.00
Evel Knievel, Snake River Canyon Jump, Sept. 8, 1974, 14 x 20 In. 195.00
Grand Celebration Of Soldiers & Old Settlers Reunion, Iowa, July 3, 1886 28 .... 120.00
Hanover Fair, Cotton & Banjo Picking, Steamship In Background, Frame, 1899 .... 325.00
Joey Chitwood & His Original Thrill Show, Cardboard, 1950s, 10 x 14 In. 195.00
Newsstand, The Flirt, Norman Rockwell, Framed, July 26, 1941, 28 x 22 In. 230.00
Ratification Of 15th Amendment, Scenes & Portraits, Frame, Civil War, 46 x 36 In. .. 420.00
Ringling Bros. Barnum Bailey Circus, Clown With Globe, Signed, 21 x 28 In. 210.00
Ringling Bros. Barnum Bailey Circus, Lithograph Of Clown, 28 x 41 In. 155.00
The Framing Of The Shrew, Sack Amusement, 1944, 27 x 41 In. 345.00
The Good Old Summertime, 1913, 27 x 41 In. 370.00
The Prince Of Darkness, 1914, 41 x 81 In. 575.00
The Tunnel, Supreme, 1940, 27 x 41 In. 1150.00
Uneeda Boy With Savings Bond, 18 x 23 In. 35.00
Western Ammunition, Saving The Day, Cardboard, 31 1/4 x 18 In. 386.00
Won In The Ninth, Chromolithograph, C.L. Wrenn, 15 x 20 In. 520.00

POTLIDS are just that, lids for pots. Transfer-printed potlids had their heyday from the 1840s to the early 1900s. The English Staffordshire potteries made ceramic containers with decorative lids for bear's grease, shrimp or meat paste, cold cream, and toothpaste. Printed advertising and pictures of historical events, portraits of famous people, or scenic views were designed in black and white or color. Reproductions have been made.

Children, With Pigeons, Color Lithograph Under Glaze, 4 In. 85.00
Cries Of London, Sandlane 65.00
Oliver Twist, England 55.00
Polychrome Scene, Grand International Building Of 1851, Pratt, 5 1/8 In. 80.00
Uncle Toby, Mahogany, 4 1/8 In. 145.00

POTTERY and porcelain are different. Pottery is opaque; you can't see through it. Porcelain is translucent. If you hold a porcelain dish in front of a strong light, you will see the light through the dish. Porcelain is colder to the touch. Pottery is softer and easier to break and will stain more easily because it is porous. Porcelain is thinner, lighter, and more durable. Majolica, faience, and stoneware are all pottery. Additional pieces of pottery are listed in this book in the Art Pottery category and under the factory name.

Ashtray, Dancers, Marc Bellaire, 1950s, 15 In. 85.00
Ashtray, Horse Head, Palanski Assault 15.00

Batter Jug, Cover, Brown, Handle, New Haven Pottery Co. 350.00
Biscuit Jar, Devon Ware, Windsor, Multicolored Flowers, Gold Trim, 8 In. 200.00
Bookend-Vase, Horn Of Plenty, Turquoise, Trenton Art, 6 x 4 In., Pair 90.00
Bowl, 4 Groups Of Stylized Nude Figures, Edouard Cazaux, c.1935, 10 1/4 In. 2875.00
Bowl, Banded Design, Turquoise Glaze, 8 In. 151.00
Bowl, Circle Of Life Design, Portrait Of Kwannon, Green, 7 In. 25.00
Bowl, Dark To Light Blue Glaze, Ink Mark, Natzler, 4 1/2 x 4 x 1 1/2 In. 520.00
Bowl, Green & Brown Matte, Flared, Natzler, 5 1/2 x 2 In. ....*Illus* 1760.00
Bowl, Green To Brown Glaze, Footed, Ink Mark, Natzler, 5 1/2 x 3 In. 385.00
Bowl, Half-Moon Crater, Yellow & Black Volcanic, Pillin, 4 x 5 1/4 In. 440.00
Bowl, Incised Design, Orange Semi-Gloss, Flared, Charles Harder, 11 In. 385.00
Bowl, Light Blue & Buff Over Brown Glaze, Scheier, 9 x 4 In. 350.00
Bowl, Oatmeal Glaze, Purple Highlights, Ink Mark, Natzler, 5 1/2 x 2 1/2 In. 1650.00
Bowl, Orange & Pink Geometric, Black Ground, Rudy Staffel, Flared, 11 1/2 In. 550.00
Bowl, Painted Nudes, White Ground, Straight Sides, Rudy Autio, 6 x 8 3/4 In. 2530.00
Bowl, Sheer Blue-Gray Satin Glaze, Folded, Beatrice Wood, 2 x 5 1/4 In. 605.00
Bowl, Turquoise & Black, Inscribed Base, Carl Walters, 1938, 1 7/8 x 4 1/4 In. 110.00
Bowl, White Fissure Glaze, Footed, Ink Mark, Natzler, 5 1/2 x 1 1/2 In. 1320.00
Bowl, White Glaze, Walter Cornelison, Bybee, 1960s, 2 3/4 x 7 1/2 In. 22.00
Candlestick, Peasant Girl, Bell, Blue, Yellow, Italy 50.00
Casserole, Cover, Chicken Of The Sea, Turquoise, Small 25.00
Charger, 3 Panels Stylized Figures, Yellow & Black Glaze, Scheier, 19 In. 2420.00
Coffeepot, Orange, Gooseneck, Art Deco, Perking Style, Chrome Trim, Marked 60.00
Crock, Brown Glazed, Everted Crimped, S. Bell & Sons, 9 1/4 x 7 In. 365.00
Figurine, Bird, Turquoise, Black, Carl Walters, 6 3/4 x 7 1/2 In. 440.00
Figurine, Blackamoor, Brayton, 14 In, Pair 350.00
Figurine, Cat, Salt Glaze, Buff, Brown, Blue Splashes, 1750, 4 5/8 In. 2530.00
Figurine, Cat, Seated, Brown Glaze, 19th Century, 7 1/2 In. 920.00
Figurine, Heron, Salmon, Metlox, 7 In. 45.00
Figurine, Hippopotamus, Turquoise, Black, Wooden Stand, Carl Walters, 16 x 7 In. 1375.00
Figurine, Siamese Cats, Sparkle Eyes, Roselane, 3 Piece 24.00
Flowerpot, Stamped, Willoughby Smith, 5 3/4 In. 145.00
Humidor, Woman, Child Harvesting Wheat, Hand Painted, Metal Rim, Burslem, 6 In. 429.00
Jar, Crosshatch Design, Loop Handles, 8 1/2 In. 270.00
Jardiniere, Basket Of Flowers, Brown, Yellow, Green, 9 1/2 x 8 In. 40.00
Jardiniere, Grapes, Brown Glaze, 6 1/4 In. 35.00
Jug, Brown Outer Glaze, Bluish Inner Glaze, Germany, c.1880 .... 300.00
Jug, Dewey, Olympia, Red, White & Blue, Flags, Eagle Spout, Cook Pottery, 4 In. 150.00
Jug, Puzzle, Blue Design, Gentlemen, Try Your Skill, England, 1790-1810, 7 In. 1650.00
Lamp, Mottled Matte Glaze, Morris Ware, England, 10 1/2 In. 100.00
Napkin Holder, Prayer Lady, Pink 32.00
Napkin-Toothpick, Woman, 1950s, 9 In. 43.00
Pan, White Glaze, Walter Cornelison, Bybee, 1960s, Oblong, 2 x 6 1/2 x 13 In. 22.00
Pap Boat, Cream, Glazed, Round Base, 1850, 4 1/2 In. 78.00
Pie Plate, Eby, Canada 1100.00
Pitcher, Dutch Boy & Girl Transfer, Blue, White, 8 3/4 In. 165.00
Pitcher, Green Glaze, Thos. Stahl, 1934, 6 1/8 In. 355.00
Pitcher, Letters Good Luck, Green & Brown Glaze, Wardle, 5 1/2 In. 88.00
Pitcher, Red Line Design, Tin Glazed, White, c.1750, 6 In. 110.00
Planter, Praying Nun Head, Betty Lou Nichols, 7 1/2 In. 175.00
Plate, 2 Women, Brown & Black Ground, Egg Shape, Pillin, 8 1/2 x 6 In. 220.00
Plate, 3 Women, Brown & Burgundy Ground, Signed, Pillin, 9 1/2 In. 440.00
Plate, Les Petits Orphelins, Le Cure E Compagne, Black Transfer, France, 8 In., Pair 190.00
Plate, Sgraffito, White Slip Birds & Star, Carrie Stahl, May 29, 1940, 9 3/4 In. 465.00
Platter, White Glaze, Walter Cornelison, Bybee, c.1964, 2 x 14 1/2 In. 49.50
Strawberry Server, Bird's Nest Form, Joseph Holdcroft 1725.00
Tea Set, Cottageware, England, 3 Piece 98.00
Teapot, Domed Lid, Handle, Blue, Green Panels, Green Ground, Shawsheen, 10 In. 805.00
Teapot, T-Form Body, Pink Glaze, Yellow Triangular, Red Ball Stopper, Shire, 7 In. 230.00
Tray, 3 Dancers, Brown Ground, Pillin, 8 x 6 1/2 In. 195.00
Tray, Turquoise Dot Ray, Divided, Signed Stickman, 7 x 14 In. 85.00
Urn, Etruscan Design, Gilt Metal Stand, Burnt Orange, Black Ground, Pair 7475.00
Urn, Serrated Rim, Bird & Plant Design, Gilt Scrolled Handles, Japan, c.1900, 49 1/2 In. . 1265.00

Pottery, Bowl,
Green & Brown Matte, Flared,
Natzler, 5 1/2 x 2 In.

Pottery, Vase, Orange Drip
Crystalline, Brown Clay, Natzler,
4 1/2 In.

Vase, 2 Handles, Red Glaze, Charlie Craven, North Carolina, 1930-1940, 19 In. 80.00
Vase, 2 Women & Birds In Pastel Tones, Pink, Orange Ground, Pillin, 11 3/4 x 5 In. 1540.00
Vase, Blue, Green Mottled, Square, Glidden, 8 3/4 x 5 In. 25.00
Vase, Bottle Shape, Yellow, White & Black Woman, Mottled Ground, Fantoni, 10 In. 220.00
Vase, Broad Leaf, Mottled Brown Glaze, Green Ground, Impressed WJW, Walley, 4 In. . . 1380.00
Vase, Canes Design, Flared, Cobalt Blue Ground, W.A. Hunting, 15 x 12 In. 330.00
Vase, Cherub On Large Seashell, 1 Hand Holds Vase, Antiqued, 23 x 17 In. 65.00
Vase, Chinese Red, Pillin, 9 In. 295.00
Vase, Cornucopia, White, Oval Base, Trenton Art, 6 In., Pair 70.00
Vase, Electric Blue, Danesbury Ware, 4 1/2 In. 100.00
Vase, Elongated Neck, Dripping Green High Glaze, Impressed Mark, Walley, 4 In. 345.00
Vase, Flared, Brown, Turquoise Glaze, Maija Grotell, 4 x 6 In. 220.00
Vase, Floral, Stylized Flower, Brown High Glaze, Green Ground, Impressed WJW, 8 In. . 805.00
Vase, Flower Frog, Lavender, Bybee, 4 1/4 x 5 In. 25.00
Vase, Geometric Circles, Blue, Green, Brown High Glaze, Grotell, 9 In. 825.00
Vase, Gray To Light Yellow Fissure Glaze, Bulbous, Natzler, 4 x 4 In. 2750.00
Vase, Green Cratered Drip Glaze, Coupe Shape, Footed, Natzler, 5 1/4 x 4 1/2 In. 5170.00
Vase, Gunmetal Squeezebag Design, Dark Green Ground, Heino, 1948, 5 In. 440.00
Vase, Lattice Handles, Medallions, Black, White, Green Glaze, Bulbous, Austria, 10 In. . . 460.00
Vase, Lavender, Flared, Bulbous, Rorstrand, 16 In. 750.00
Vase, Light Aqua Crackle Glaze, Robertson, 3 In. 110.00
Vase, Multicolored Florals, Gray Silk Ground, Birks, Paris, 5 In. 65.00
Vase, Olive Green Micro Crystalline Glaze, White Pines, 7 In. 715.00
Vase, Orange Drip Crystalline, Brown Clay, Natzler, 4 1/2 In. . . . . *Illus* 2090.00
Vase, Orange, Orange-Yellow Flambe, Bulbous, Pinched Neck, Pillin, 9 1/4 In. 220.00
Vase, Roosters, Yellow Ground, Bulbous, Pillin, Signed, 6 x 3 1/2 In. 195.00
Vase, Scrolled Bands, Orange, Lavender, Ring Handles, Western Han Dynasty, 13 In. 3737.50
Vase, Shell, Cream, Salmon Interior, Catalina-Gladding McBean, 6 In. 75.00
Vase, Smooth Gray Glaze, White Pines, Ralph Radcliffe Whitehead, 7 1/2 In. 825.00
Vase, Stylized Rising Suns, Brown, White Crackled Ground, Keramis, 13 x 6 In. 550.00
Vase, Swan, Drip Glaze, BMP, Canada, 7 In., Pair 50.00
Vase, Tapered Neck, 2 Angular Handles, Orange Glaze, Bulbous, 8 1/2 In. 92.00
Vase, White Specks, Black Matte Ground, Earl Hooks, 1950s, 7 x 7 1/2 In. 410.00
Vase, Woman Dancing Sgraffito, Blue, Art Deco, Waylande Gregory, 6 In. 275.00
Vase, Women & Birds, Pumpkin & Blue Ground, Bottle Shape, Pillin, 11 3/4 In. 465.00
Wall Pocket, Owl, Yellow Quarter Moon, Morton 20.00
Water Set, Aqua Foam Drip, Square Handle Pitcher, 6-In. Tumbler, 7 Piece 150.00
Whistle, Bird, Mottled Green Glaze, 19th Century, 3 1/8 In. 250.00

POWDER FLASKS AND POWDER HORNS were made to hold the gunpowder used in antique firearms. The early examples were made of
horn or wood; later ones were of copper or brass.

POWDER FLASK, Copper, Peace Pattern, Civil War, Marked Batty, 1853 . . . . 210.00
    Deer Pattern, Adjustable Charger, 4 Rings & Loops 60.00

Inlaid Wood, Bands Of Engraved Horn Tendrils, Bone Nozzle, 6 1/4 In. 1150.00
Inlaid Wood, Horn Pellets, Engraved Flower Heads, 1720-1730, 6 3/4 In. 1955.00
Ivory, Dieppe School, Mythological, Exotic Beasts, Carved Collar At Top, 10 In. 1150.00
Ivory, Dieppe School, Woodland Scene, Huntsmen, 7 7/8 In. 2070.00
Leather, AM Flask & Cap Co., Civil War 95.00
Leather, Spring Loaded Brass Dispenser, 1880 . . . . 65.00
Patina, Floral Design, Maker's Name 55.00
Pewter With Brass, Priming, Floral Design, 7 In. 245.00
Wooden Body, Keel-Like Border, Deer, Boar Hunting Scene, 20 1/2 In. 2875.00
POWDER HORN, Engraved, 3-Masted Ship Design, 16 In. 172.00
Engraved, Bird, Foliate & Geometric Designs, 9 3/4 In. 1150.00
Engraved, House, Vine With Leaves, Noah North, 6 5/8 In. 165.00
Engraved 2 Soldiers On Horseback, Guns Drawn, Civil War 300.00
Engraved 3-Masted Ship, Seaman, Cutlass & Harpoons, 12 In. 465.00
Engraved Ships At Sea, Serpents, Row Of Houses, 18th Century, 10 1/4 In. 2530.00
Flattened Horn, Flower Form Spout, Wooden Base, Revolutionary War, 10 In. 275.00
Leather, Brass, Hunting Hound Picture, 9 In. 58.00
Painted Red, Wood Plug, 4 3/8 In. 90.00
Repousse Cannon & Rifle, Late 19th Century 33.00
Silver, Engraved Leaf Design, Silver Bezel & Spout, Scotland, 1800, 11 In. 450.00
Texicans Unite, Signed Asa Good, Patriotic Themes, Texas Star, 1836 . . . . 2500.00
Top Unscrews To Use As Measure, RWT Carved On Side, 7 In. 265.00

PRATT ware means two different things. It was an early Staffordshire pottery, cream-colored with colored decorations, made by Felix Pratt during the late eighteenth century. There was also Pratt ware made with transfer designs during the mid-nineteenth century in Fenton, England. Reproductions of the transfer-printed Pratt are being made.

PRATT FENTON

Box, Dresser, Village Wedding, 4 1/4 In. 50.00
Clock, Flanked By 2 Children Wearing Yellow Crowns, Blue, Yellow, Orange Ocher 550.00
Dish, Lozenge Shape, Blue Feathered Edge, Yellow Pear In Center, 5 In., 3 Piece 575.00
Figurine, Bear, Muzzled & Chained, 1780s, 3 1/4 In. 675.00
Figurine, Horse, Brown Mane, Brown, Ocher Body, Brown Bridle, 1810, 6 1/16 In. 4312.00
Figurine, Summer, Pearlware, 5 1/2 In. 385.00
Group, Allegorical, Spring, Lady, Young Boy, Foliate Scroll, 8 1/2 In. 460.00
Plaque, Earthenware, Bacchanalian Scene, England, Late 18th Century, 10 1/2 In. 745.00
Plaque, Head Of Classical Youth Wearing Laurel Ocher Wreath, 1810, 10 3/16 In. 920.00
Plaque, Officer Wearing A Yellow-Edged Black Hat, Oval, 1800-1810, 7 1/8 In. 690.00
Pot, Elderly Man, Woman Playing Cribbage, Cover, 19th Century, 4 In. 121.00
Pot, Fallen Gentleman, Skaters On Ice, Cover, 19th Century, 3 1/2 In. 88.00
Pot, Gout-Struck Gentleman, Fishing In A Barrel, Cover, 19th Century, 4 1/4 In. 121.00
Pot, Group Of School Boys, Wolf & Lamb, Cover, 19th Century, 4 In. 121.00
Sauceboat, Fox Head Shape, Swan Handle, Yellow Green Acanthus Leaves, 5 In. 935.00
Tankard, Pagoda Beside A Willow Tree, Brown, Yellow, Ocher, Green, Cylindrical, 1790 . . . . 402.00
Tea Caddy, Glazed Floral Design, England, Early 19th Century, 5 1/4 In. 255.00
Toby Jug, Pearlware Glaze, Blue, Brown, Ocher Palette, England, 1800, 9 1/4 In. 402.00

PRESSED GLASS was first made in the United States in the 1820s after the invention of glass pressing machines. Hundreds of patterns of pressed glass were made in complete table settings. Although the Boston and Sandwich Works was the most famous of the pressed glass factories, there were about sixteen other factories making pressed glass from 1830 to 1850, and still more from 1850 to 1900, when pressed glass reached its greatest popularity. It is now being widely reproduced. The pattern names used in this listing are based on the information in the book *Pressed Glass in America* by John and Elizabeth Welker. There may be pieces of pressed glass listed in this book in other categories, such as Lamp, Ruby, Sandwich, and Souvenir.

101 pattern is listed here as One-Hundred-One.
1000-Eye pattern is listed here as Thousand Eye.
Acanthus pattern is listed here as Ribbed Palm.
Acorn, Saltshaker, Pink 45.00
Acorn Medallion pattern with beading is listed here as Beaded Acorn Medallion.

Actress, Celery Vase 140.00
Actress, Compote, Cover, 8 In. 145.00
Actress, Goblet 110.00
Alaska, Ashtray 90.00
Alaska, Berry Set, Blue Opalescent, 7 Piece 595.00
Alaska, Butter, Cover, Vaseline Opalescent 350.00
Alaska, Creamer 95.00
Alaska, Creamer, Blue Opalescent 75.00
Alaska, Spooner 85.00
Alaska, Spooner, Blue To Opalescent Top, 4 Footed 70.00
Alaska, Spooner, Green 60.00
Alaska, Table Set, Blue Opalescent, 4 Piece 750.00
Alden, Pitcher, Water, Ruby Stained 225.00
Almond Thumbprint, Champagne, Flint 85.00
Amberette, Celery, Amber Stained, 4 In. 175.00
Amberette, Goblet 795.00
Amberette, Jam Jar, Silver Plate Holder, 6 3/8 In. 135.00
Amberette, Pitcher 225.00
Amberette, Pitcher, Round 175.00
Amberette, Pitcher, Water ....1200.00 to 1250.00
Apple Blossom, Butter, Cover 265.00
Apple Blossom, Cruet 395.00
Apple Blossom, Sugar, Cover 1990.00
Ashburton, Goblet, Flint 25.00
Ashburton, Sugar 35.00
Ashman, Cake Stand, Blue, 8 3/4 In. 175.00
Atlanta, Syrup 190.00
Austrian, Compote, 4 In. ....45.00 to 65.00
Austrian, Goblet 55.00
Austrian, Nappy, Cover 75.00
Austrian, Nappy, Cover, Double Handles 45.00
Aztec, Toothpick 55.00
Baby Thumbprint pattern is listed here as Dakota.
Balder pattern is listed here as Pennsylvania.
Balky Mule pattern is listed here as Currier & Ives.
Baltimore Pear, Tray 35.00
Banded Portland, Bowl, Maiden's Blush 175.00
Banded Portland, Goblet 75.00
Banded Portland, Toothpick, Maiden's Blush 55.00
Banded Portland, Wine 35.00
Barberry, Butter, Cover 75.00
Barberry, Celery 30.00
Barley, Cake Stand 57.00
Barley, Compote, Cover, 8 In. 45.00
Barley, Goblet ....25.00 to 35.00
Barley & Oats pattern is listed here as Wheat & Barley.
Barley & Wheat pattern is listed here as Wheat & Barley.
Barrel Honeycomb, see also the related pattern Honeycomb.
Basket Weave, Pitcher, Blue 72.00
Bead & Scroll, Table Set, Blue, 4 Piece 375.00
Beaded Acorn Medallion, Goblet 28.00
Beaded Band, Goblet, Blue 65.00
Beaded Grape Medallion, Wine, Flint 70.00
Beaded Loop, Cake Stand, 10 In. 65.00
Beaded Loop, Compote, Cover, 6 In. 95.00
Beaded Loop, Goblet 25.00
Beaded Loop, Toothpick 65.00
Beaded Ovals In Sand, Table Set, Blue, 4 Piece 490.00
Beaded Swag, Berry Set, 7 Piece 250.00
Beaded Swag, Butter 120.00
Beaded Swag, Spooner 60.00
Beaded Tulip, Creamer, 6 1/8 In. 60.00
Bearded Head pattern is listed here as Viking.

Pressed Glass,
Actress

Pressed Glass,
Austrian

Pressed Glass,
Beaded Grape Medallion

Bearded Man pattern is listed here as Queen Anne.
Belladonna, Table Set, Blue, 4 Piece 450.00
Bellflower, Compote, Low, Flint 85.00
Bellflower, Eggcup, Flared 20.00
Bellflower, Eggcup, Flint 35.00
Bellflower, Salt, Master 45.00
Bellflower, Spooner, Flint .... .45.00 to 65.00
Bellflower, Tumbler 100.00
Bent Buckle pattern is listed here as New Hampshire.
Birch Leaf, Tumbler, Footed 25.00
Bird & Strawberry, Cake Stand, 9 In. ....48.00 to 65.00
Bird & Strawberry, Compote, Cover, 6 In. ....125.00 to 145.00
Bird & Strawberry, Creamer 45.00
Bird & Strawberry, Cup 25.00
Bird & Strawberry, Goblet 800.00
Bird & Strawberry, Spooner 45.00
Bird & Strawberry, Sugar, Cover 45.00
Bird & Strawberry, Tumbler, Gilt Trim 95.00
Bird In Ring pattern is listed here as Grace.
Bleeding Heart, Cake Stand, 11 In. 145.00
Bleeding Heart, Compote, Cover, 8 In. 125.00
Bleeding Heart, Goblet 42.00
Bleeding Heart, Mug, Child's 45.00
Bleeding Heart, Mug, Medium 30.00
Block, Pitcher, Red 165.00
Block & Star pattern is listed here as Valencia Waffle.
Bluebird pattern is listed here as Bird & Strawberry.
Branched Tree, Pitcher 90.00
Broken Column, Cake Stand, 10 In. 85.00
Broken Column, Celery Vase, Ruby Stained ....245.00 to 295.00
Broken Column, Compote, Cover, Ruby Stained, 8 In. 595.00
Broken Column, Cruet 95.00
Broken Column, Sugar Shaker, Ruby Stained 495.00
Bryce pattern is listed here as Ribbon Candy.
Bucket pattern is listed here as Oaken Bucket.
Buckle, Relish, Blue 65.00
Buckle, Wine 25.00
Bulging Loops, Toothpick 95.00
Bulging Loops, Toothpick, Blue 30.00
Bulging Loops, Toothpick, Red, Silver Collar 350.00
Bull's-Eye & Daisy, Berry Set, Green, 5 Piece 135.00
Bull's-Eye & Daisy, Butter, Cover, Green 135.00
Bull's-Eye & Daisy, Pitcher, Amethyst Medallions 55.00
Bull's-Eye & Daisy, Spooner 75.00
Bull's-Eye & Fan, Goblet 30.00

Bull's-Eye & Fan, Sugar, Cover, Blue 75.00
Bull's-Eye With Diamond Point, Celery, Flint 175.00
Bull's-Eye With Diamond Point, Sugar, Cover, Flint 35.00
Butterfly, Plate, Toddy 20.00
Butterfly & Fan pattern is listed here as Grace.
Button Arches, Toothpick, Souvenir, Ruby Flashed, 1907 .... 25.00
Button Band, Bowl, Cover, 8 1/4 In. 85.00
Button Panel, Tumbler, Ruby Stained 48.00
Buttressed Loop, Spooner, Vaseline 40.00
Buzz Star, Toothpick 40.00
Cabbage Leaf, Spooner, Amber 125.00
Cabbage Rose, Champagne 75.00
Cabbage Rose, Goblet 55.00
Cable, Compote, Low, Flint 56.00
Cable, Eggcup 60.00
California pattern is listed here as Beaded Grape.
Camel Caravan, Sauce Set, Footed, 4 1/2 In., 4 Piece 100.00
Cameo is listed here as Classic Medallion.
Canadian, Goblet ....55.00 to 60.00
Canadian, Wine 40.00
Candlewick as a pressed glass pattern is properly named *Banded Raindrop*. There is also a pattern called *Candlewick*, which has been made by Imperial Glass Corporation since 1936. It is listed in this book in the Imperial Glass category.
Candy Ribbon pattern is listed here as Ribbon Candy.
Cane, Pitcher, Amber 42.00
Cane, Spooner 42.00
Cannon Ball Pinwheel, Goblet 30.00
Cathedral, Cake Stand, Blue, 10 In. 58.00
Cathedral, Creamer 40.00
Cathedral, Cruet, Amber 85.00
Cathedral, Goblet, Canary 35.00
Cathedral, Relish, Fish Shape 53.00
Cathedral, Salt, Blue, Boat Shape 30.00
Centennial, see also the related patterns Liberty Bell, Viking, and Washington Centennial.
Chain With Diamonds pattern is listed here as Washington Centennial.
Chain With Star, Cake Plate, Open Handles, 13 1/4 In. 25.00
Chain With Star, Goblet 30.00
Champion, Tumbler, Amber Stained 45.00
Chrysanthemum, Sugar & Creamer 225.00
Chrysanthemum Sprig, Berry Bowl, Custard, Gold Trim 200.00
Chrysanthemum Sprig, Spooner 95.00
Church Windows pattern is listed here as Columbia.
Classic, Celery Vase, Footed 195.00
Classic Medallion, Compote, Low 28.00
Coin Spot pattern is listed in this book in its own category.

Pressed Glass,
Barberry

Pressed Glass,
Bellflower

Pressed Glass,
Bird and Strawberry

Colonial, Sugar & Creamer, Child's	20.00
Colonial, Table Set, Amethyst, 4 Piece	295.00
Colorado, Banana Boat, Blue	55.00
Colorado, Berry Bowl, Green, Gold Trim, Master	60.00
Colorado, Bowl, Green, 9 1/2 In.	30.00
Colorado, Cake Stand, Green, 11 In.	225.00
Colorado, Salt & Pepper, Green, Gold Trim	395.00
Colorado, Sauce, Footed, Green, Gold Trim	18.00
Colorado, Table Set, Green, Gold, 4 Piece	420.00
Colorado, Toothpick, Boot Shape, Souvenir, Gold Trim, 1901	25.00
Colorado, Toothpick, Green	20.00
Colorado, Toothpick, Souvenir, Omaha Exposition, 1899	35.00
Colorado, Vase, Green, 12 In.	275.00
Columbia, Toothpick	25.00 to 75.00
Columbian Coin, Compote, Cover, 8 In.	295.00
Comet, Saucer, Flint, 3 1/2 In.	28.00
Compact pattern is listed here as Snail.	
Cone, Spooner, Pink Case	65.00
Cord Drapery, Saltshaker	35.00
Cord Drapery, Syrup, Chocolate	250.00
Coreopsis, Creamer	180.00
Coreopsis, Syrup	350.00
Coreopsis, Table Set, 4 Piece	625.00
Cosmos pattern is listed in this book as its own category.	
Cottage, Cake Stand, Amber, 7 1/4 x 10 In.	104.00
Croesus, Butter, Purple	250.00
Croesus, Celery Vase, Green, Gold Trim	395.00
Croesus, Celery Vase, Purple, Gold Trim, 7 In.	195.00 to 425.00
Croesus, Compote, Jelly, Green, Gold Trim	185.00
Croesus, Pitcher, Purple	350.00
Croesus, Salt & Pepper, Green, Gold Trim	110.00
Croesus, Salt & Pepper, Purple, Gold Trim	265.00
Croesus, Toothpick, Amethyst	195.00
Croesus, Toothpick, Green	185.00
Croesus, Tray, Condiment, Purple, Gold Trim	95.00
Croesus, Tumbler, Purple, Gold Trim	75.00
Crown Jewels is listed here as Queen's Necklace.	
Crystal Wedding, Cake Stand	95.00
Crystal Wedding, Candy, Cover	75.00
Crystal Wedding, Compote, Cover, Pedestal, Square, 11 1/2 x 6 1/2 In.	85.00
Crystal Wedding, Compote, Cover, Pedestal, Square, 13 x 7 In.	110.00
Crystal Wedding, Creamer	85.00
Crystal Wedding, Spooner, Vaseline, Gold Trim	85.00
Crystal Wedding, Tankard, Etched, 1 Pt.	75.00
Cupid & Venus, Champagne	150.00
Cupid & Venus, Compote, 9 In.	65.00
Cupid & Venus, Jam Jar, Cover	150.00
Cupid & Venus, Mug, Child's	30.00
Cupid & Venus, Plate, Amber	125.00
Currant, Goblet	25.00
Currier & Ives, Cake Stand, Blue, 9 1/2 In.	195.00
Currier & Ives, Compote, Cover, Amber, 8 In.	155.00
Currier & Ives, Goblet, Blue	85.00
Currier & Ives, Pitcher, Amber	150.00
Currier & Ives, Pitcher, Blue	195.00
Currier & Ives, Salt & Pepper	65.00
Cut Log, Creamer, Individual	15.00
Cut Log, Cruet, Stopper, 5 1/2 In.	75.00
Cut Log, Mug	35.00
Cut Log, Salt & Pepper	150.00
Cut Log, Vase, 15 In.	48.00
Dahlia pattern is listed here as Square Fuchsia.	
Daisies In Oval Panels pattern is listed here as Bull's-Eye & Fan.	

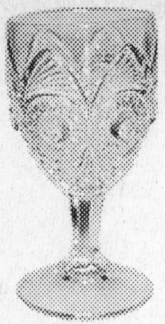

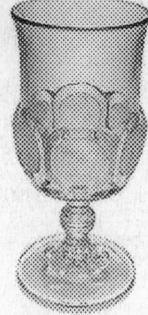

Pressed Glass,   Pressed Glass,   Pressed Glass,
Bull's Eye and Fan   Columbian Coin   Dakota

Daisy & Button,	Celery Dish, Boat Shape	40.00
Daisy & Button,	Celery Dish, Square Pedestal	30.00
Daisy & Button,	Celery Vase, Almond Band	30.00
Daisy & Button,	Celery Vase, Triangular, Green	45.00
Daisy & Button,	Cruet, Hobnail Stopper	75.00
Daisy & Button,	Goblet	20.00
Daisy & Button,	Plate, Vaseline, Square, 7 In.	10.00 to 21.00
Daisy & Button,	Toothpick, Amber	20.00
Daisy & Button,	Toothpick, Boot, Victorian, 5 1/2 In.	85.00
Daisy & Button With Crossbar,	Creamer, Amber	25.00
Daisy & Button With Narcissus,	Decanter Set, Amethyst, Gold Trim, 5 Piece	120.00
Daisy & Button With V-Ornament,	Celery Dish, Scalloped	35.00
Daisy & Button With V-Ornament,	Eggcup	25.00
Dakota,	Cake Basket	275.00
Dakota,	Cake Basket, Etched	350.00
Dakota,	Celery Dish, Etched, Fish	325.00
Dakota,	Compote, Cover, Etched, Oak Leaf, 8 In.	145.00 to 195.00
Dakota,	Compote, Etched, Oak Leaf, 8 In.	60.00 to 90.00
Dakota,	Cruet	55.00
Dakota,	Goblet, Souvenir, 1892	30.00
Dakota,	Spooner	30.00
Deer & Doe,	With Lily-Of-The-Valley, Goblet	190.00
Deer & Dog,	Creamer	95.00
Deer & Pine Tree,	Pitcher, Milk	165.00
Deer & Pine Tree,	Tray, 8 x 13 In.	225.00
Deer & Pine Tree,	Tray, Amber	145.00
Deer & Pine Tree,	Tray, Green	125.00
Delaware,	Banana Boat, Rose, Gold Trim	125.00
Delaware,	Bowl, Green, Gold Trim, 8 1/2 In.	40.00
Delaware,	Butter, Cover, Green, Gold Trim	125.00
Delaware,	Cup, Rose	40.00
Delaware,	Pitcher, Green, Gold Trim	295.00
Delaware,	Punch Cup, Green	10.00
Delaware,	Spooner, Green, Gold Trim	30.00 to 50.00
Delaware,	Table Set, Rose, Gold Trim, 4 Piece	375.00
Delaware,	Tankard Set, Rose, Gold Trim, 7 Piece	475.00
Delaware,	Tankard, Rose Trim	115.00
Delaware,	Toothpick	95.00
Delaware,	Toothpick, Cranberry Stained	85.00
Delaware,	Toothpick, Gold Trim	185.00
Delaware,	Tray, Pin, Rose, Gold Trim	65.00
Delaware,	Tumbler, Green, Gold Trim	135.00
Delaware,	Tumbler, Rose, Gold Trim	15.00
Delaware,	Water Set, Green, 6 Piece	450.00

Dewdrop & Star, Sugar, Cover 55.00
Dewey, Butter, Cover, Small 78.00
Dewey, Creamer, Cover, Small 75.00
Dewey, Pitcher ....80.00 to 145.00
Dewey, Salt & Pepper, Red 225.00
Dewey, Tumbler 90.00
Diamond & Bull's-Eye Band, Celery Vase, Etched 75.00
Diamond & Star, Cruet, 7 In. 125.00
Diamond Point, Compote, Cover, 9 x 14 In. 60.00
Diamond Point, Compote, Pedestal 115.00
Diamond Point, Goblet, Flint 65.00
Diamond Point, Spooner, Flint 55.00
Diamond Point, Wine, Flint 30.00
Diamond Quilted, Butter, Cover, Vaseline 75.00
Diamond Quilted, Champagne, Amethyst 40.00
Diamond Quilted, Decanter, 10 1/4 In., Pair 240.00
Diamond Quilted, Spooner, Vaseline 38.00
Diamond Spearhead, Compote, Jelly 95.00
Diamond Spearhead, Syrup, Vaseline Opalescent 495.00
Diamond Spearhead, Table Set, With Toothpick, Vaseline, 5 Piece 1050.00
Diamond Thumbprint, Cake Stand, Flint, 5 x 9 1/4 In. 240.00
Diamond Thumbprint, Celery Dish, Flint, 9 In. 105.00
Diamond Thumbprint, Compote, Footed, 8 In. 85.00
Diamond Thumbprint, Goblet, Flint 450.00
Diamond Thumbprint, Whiskey 195.00
Dog With Hat, Toothpick 95.00
Dog With Hat, Toothpick, Blue 125.00
Dog With Rabbit In Mouth, Pitcher, Water 550.00
Doric pattern is listed here as Feather.
Double Daisy pattern is listed here as Rosette Band.
Double Loop pattern is listed here as Ribbon Candy.
Double Wedding Ring pattern is listed here as Wedding Ring.
Dynast pattern is listed here as Radiant.
Egg In Sand, Spooner 50.00
Egyptian, Bowl, Footed, 7 In. 65.00
Egyptian, Goblet ....25.00 to 40.00
Egyptian, Pitcher 245.00
Egyptian, Plate, The Desert, Handles, 11 1/4 In. 75.00
Egyptian, Tray, Bread 68.00
Empress, Toothpick, Green, Gold Trim 225.00
Empress, Tumbler, Green, Gold Trim 55.00
English Hobnail Cross pattern is listed here as Amberette.
Esther, Cake Stand 95.00
Esther, Compote 60.00
Esther, Cruet, Green, Gold Trim 135.00

Pressed Glass,
Deer and Dog

Pressed Glass,
Fan With Diamond

Esther, Spooner, Green, Gold Trim	65.00
Esther, Sugar, Cover, Green, Gold Trim	115.00
Esther, Toothpick, Green, Gold Trim	50.00 to 95.00
Esther, Tumbler, Green, Gold Trim	85.00
Etched Dakota pattern is listed here as Dakota.	
Eureka, Toothpick	65.00
Everglades, Berry Set, Vaseline, Gold Trim, 7 Piece	595.00
Everglades, Compote, Jelly, Blue	140.00
Everglades, Salt & Pepper, Blue	295.00
Excelsior, Spooner, Flint	60.00
Excelsior, Sugar, Cover, Flint	100.00
Excelsior, Wine, Flint	60.00
Excelsior Variant, Tumbler, Flint	48.00
Eyewinker, Cake Stand, Low, 8 In.	80.00
Eyewinker, Compote, 7 In.	65.00
Eyewinker, Spooner	55.00
Fan, Bowl, Ice Cream, Blue, Gold Trim	175.00
Fan With Diamond pattern is listed here as Shell.	
Fancy Loop, Cracker Jar	175.00
Feather, Cake Stand	45.00
Feather, Cake Stand, Amber Stained, 11 In.	650.00
Feather, Pitcher, Green	195.00
Feather, Plate	55.00
Feather, Toothpick	90.00
Feather, Toothpick, Green	395.00
Feather, Wine, Scalloped	25.00
Feather Duster, Goblet	30.00
Festoon, Creamer	15.00
Fine Cut & Feather pattern is listed here as Feather.	
Fishscale, Mug	65.00
Fishscale, Pitcher	50.00
Flamingo Habitat, Celery Vase	50.00
Flamingo Habitat, Champagne	45.00 to 65.00
Flamingo Habitat, Wine	45.00
Fleur-De-Lis, Toothpick	95.00
Flora, Butter	150.00
Flora, Spooner	85.00
Flora, Tumbler	40.00
Florette, Syrup, Pink	225.00
Florida pattern pieces are listed here as Sunken Primrose if made of clear glass and as Emerald Green Herringbone if made of green glass.	
Flower Flange pattern is listed here as Dewey.	
Flower With Cane, Toothpick, Scalloped	65.00
Flute, Berry Set, Maiden's Blush, 7 Piece	125.00
Fluted Scrolls, Bowl, Cobalt Blue, 3 Footed, 8 In.	30.00
Fluted Scrolls, Salt & Pepper, Cobalt Blue	200.00
Flying Robin pattern is listed here as Hummingbird.	
Forget-Me-Not In Scroll, Pitcher, Stippled	100.00
Frosted patterns may also be listed under name of main pattern.	
Frosted Crane pattern is listed here as Frosted Stork.	
Frosted Dolphin, Creamer	145.00
Frosted Leaf, Celery Vase, Flint	135.00
Frosted Ribbon, Goblet	75.00
Frosted Stork, Bread Plate, Frosted Center	55.00
Galloway, Cracker Jar	150.00
Galloway, Goblet	95.00
Galloway, Pitcher, Maiden's Blush, Miniature	95.00
Galloway, Sugar, Cover	55.00
Garfield Drape, Bread Plate	30.00
Geneva, Spooner, Green, Gold Trim	47.00
Giant Baby Thumbprint, Goblet, Flint	85.00
Gonterman Swirl, Butter, Amber Stained, Frosted Base	225.00
Gonterman Swirl, Goblet, Amber Stained	295.00

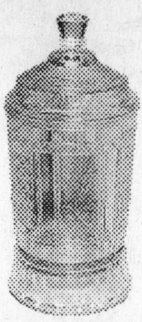

Pressed Glass,
Forget-Me-Not

Pressed Glass,
Fine Cut and Block

Pressed Glass,
Fleur-de-lis

Gonterman Swirl, Toothpick	225.00
Gonterman Swirl, Toothpick, Amber, Opalescent Swirl Base	325.00
Good Luck pattern is listed here as Horseshoe.	
Gooseberry, Mug	20.00 to 33.00
Gothic, Celery Vase, Flint	85.00
Gothic, Sugar, Cover, Stippled, Octagonal	150.00
Gothic, Sugar, Lacy, Deep Amethyst, 5 1/2 In.	3850.00
Gothic, Toothpick	25.00
Grace, Goblet	135.00
Grape, see also the related patterns Beaded Grape, Beaded Grape Medallion, Magnet & Grape, Magnet & Grape with Frosted Leaf, Paneled Grape, and Paneled Grape Band.	
Grape Band, Goblet	23.00
Grape With Vine, Mug	35.00
Grape With Vine, Table Set, 4 Piece	325.00
Grasshopper, Butter, Cover, Etched	60.00
Grasshopper, Celery Vase, Frosted	85.00
Hamilton, Eggcup	45.00
Hand, Compote, Electric Blue, Large	95.00
Hand, Goblet	90.00
Hand, Pitcher	95.00
Harp, Butter, Cover, Flint	100.00
Harp, Spill, Flint, 4 3/4 In.	45.00
Hawaiian Lei, Wine	25.00
Heart With Thumbprint, Cordial, 3 In.	135.00
Heart With Thumbprint, Mustard, Cover, Green	125.00
Heart With Thumbprint, Spooner	45.00
Hearts Of Loch Laven pattern is listed here as Shuttle.	
Heavy Paneled Grape, Wine	24.00
Heron, Pitcher	375.00
Herringbone Band, Goblet	35.00
Herringbone Band, Spooner	30.00
Herringbone Buttress, Spooner	95.00
Hexagon Block, Salt & Pepper, Ruby Stained	125.00
Hexagon Block, Syrup, Ruby Flashed	185.00
Hickman, Cake Stand, Low, 9 In.	65.00
Hickman, Toothpick	33.00
Hobnail pattern is in this book as its own category.	
Holly, Sugar, Cover	145.00
Honeycomb, Goblet	12.00
Honeycomb, Pitcher, Ruby Flashed, Bulbous	195.00
Horn Of Plenty, Bottle, Bar, Applied Bulbous Lip, 10 3/4 In.	137.50
Horn Of Plenty, Butter	140.00
Horn Of Plenty, Butter Chip	55.00
Horn Of Plenty, Champagne	150.00
Horn Of Plenty, Compote, 7 In.	100.00 to 105.00

Pressed Glass, Frosted Stork   Pressed Glass, Harp   Pressed Glass, Horseshoe

Horn Of Plenty, Compote, Flint, 8 1/2 x 11 In.	300.00
Horn Of Plenty, Cordial	140.00
Horn Of Plenty, Eggcup	40.00 to 58.00
Horn Of Plenty, Spill, Flint, 4 3/4 In.	45.00
Horn Of Plenty, Spooner	60.00
Horn Of Plenty, Sugar	60.00
Horn Of Plenty, Toothpick	25.00
Horn Of Plenty, Wine	130.00
Horseshoe, Cake Stand, 9 In.	95.00
Horseshoe, Celery Vase, Knob Stem	85.00
Horseshoe, Celery Vase, Round Stem	35.00
Horseshoe, Compote, Cover, 12 In.	60.00
Horseshoe, Compote, Low, 6 In.	100.00
Horseshoe, Creamer	15.00
Horseshoe, Goblet, Knob Stem	40.00 to 50.00
Horseshoe, Pitcher, 1 Qt.	45.00 to 60.00
Horseshoe, Pitcher, Milk	135.00
Horseshoe, Plate, 7 In.	55.00
Horseshoe, Spooner	20.00
Horseshoe, Sugar	5.00
Horseshoe, Tray, Bread, Double Horseshoe Handles	40.00 to 85.00
Horseshoe, Wine	250.00
Huber, Goblet	25.00
Huckle pattern is listed here as Feather Duster.	
Hummingbird, Celery Vase, Amber	95.00
Hummingbird, Goblet, Amber	65.00
Idyll, Butter, Cover, Green, Gold Trim	170.00
Idyll, Spooner, Green, Gold Trim	70.00
Idyll, Sugar, Cover, Blue	95.00
Idyll, Sugar, Green, Gold Trim	130.00
Illinois, Butter, Cover	75.00
Illinois, Holder, Straw	225.00 to 395.00
Illinois, Jar, Cover	195.00
Indiana Swirl pattern is listed here as Feather.	
Intaglio, Compote, Jelly, Green	110.00
Intaglio, Jam Jar, Blue Opalescent	55.00
Inverted Fan & Feather, Punch Cup, Pink, 2 1/2 In.	220.00
Inverted Fan & Feather, Saucer	75.00
Inverted Fern, Goblet, Flint	36.00
Inverted Thumbprint, Syrup, Amber, Applied Handle, Tin Lid, 7 In.	250.00
Inverted Thumbprint, Toothpick, Cranberry	85.00
Inverted Thumbprint, Wine, Blue	25.00
Iris With Meander, Butter, Cover	248.00
Iris With Meander, Toothpick, Amethyst	85.00
Iris With Meander, Toothpick, Green	95.00

Jacob's Ladder, Compote 35.00
Jacob's Ladder, Relish, Blue 65.00
Jefferson's Optic, Toothpick, Blue, White Design 95.00
Jewel & Dewdrop, Butter, Cover 75.00
Jewel & Dewdrop, Cake Stand, 9 1/2 In. 65.00
Jewel & Dewdrop, Celery Vase 85.00
Jewel & Dewdrop, Champagne 225.00
Jewel & Dewdrop, Tumbler 55.00
Jeweled Moon & Star pattern is listed here as Moon & Star.
Jubilee pattern is listed here as Hickman.
Jumbo & Barnum, Spooner 185.00
Kansas pattern is listed here as Jewel & Dewdrop.
Kentucky, Toothpick, Gold Trim 95.00
King's Crown, see also the related pattern Ruby Thumbprint.
King's Crown, Bowl, Amber, 10 1/2 In. 250.00
King's Crown, Castor Set ....110.00 to 225.00
King's Crown, Compote, 8 1/2 In. 85.00
King's Crown, Honey, Ruby Stained, Etched 325.00
King's Crown, Mustard, Cover 95.00
King's Crown, Plate, Square, 7 In. 60.00
King's Crown, Tankard, Etched, 13 In. 150.00
King's Crown, Tumbler, Cobalt Blue, 1950s 15.00
Klondike pattern is listed here as Amberette.
Knights Of Labor, Platter 175.00
Lacy Medallion, Toothpick, Souvenir 25.00
Ladder With Diamond, Toothpick ....35.00 to 40.00
Ladder With Diamond, Toothpick, Gold Trim 50.00
Ladder With Diamond, Water Set, Gold Trim, 6 Piece 450.00
Leaf Umbrella, Pitcher, Cranberry 395.00
Leaf Umbrella, Sugar Shaker, Blue 325.00
Leaf Umbrella, Toothpick, Cranberry, Top Polished Down 325.00
Liberty Bell, Bowl, Footed, 8 In. 100.00
Liberty Bell, Butter, Cover ....125.00 to 145.00
Liberty Bell, Goblet ....25.00 to 90.00
Liberty Bell, Pitcher 750.00
Lily-Of-The-Valley, Celery Vase 55.00
Lily-Of-The-Valley, Spooner 50.00
Lion, Celery Vase, Frosted 50.00
Lion, Creamer, Frosted 95.00
Lion, Goblet 90.00
Lion, Goblet, Frosted ....40.00 to 65.00
Lion, Paperweight, Frosted 350.00
Lion, Pitcher, Frosted 525.00
Lion, Sugar, Cover, Frosted 50.00

Press Glass,
Inverted Fern

Press Glass,
Inverted Thumbprint

Press Glass,
Jumbo

Pressed Glass,
Liberty Bell

Pressed Glass,
Moon & Star

Pressed Glass,
Medallion

Lion, Sugar, Frosted	125.00
Lion, Syrup, Frosted, 4 3/4 In.	600.00
Lion, Syrup, Frosted, 5 1/4 In.	650.00
Lion's Head, Relish, Square, 4 1/2 x 6 3/4 In.	55.00
Lion's Leg pattern is listed here as Alaska.	
Locket On Chain, Cake Stand	225.00
Log Cabin, Butter, Cover	425.00
Loop, see also the related pattern Seneca Loop.	
Loop, Celery Vase, Scalloped, Flint	65.00
Loop, Compote, Cover, Flint, 9 x 7 In.	85.00
Loops & Drops pattern is listed here as New Jersey.	
Louisiana, Cake Stand, 9 In.	65.00
Louisiana, Pitcher	85.00
Magnet & Grape, Pitcher, Buttermilk, Flint	50.00
Maine, Table Set, 4 Piece	195.00
Majestic, Toothpick, Ruby Stained	135.00
Manhattan, Toothpick, Gold Trim	65.00
Maple Leaf, Compote, Jelly, Gold	395.00
Maple Leaf, Compote, Leaf Finial, Cover	95.00
Mardi Gras, Cracker Jar	150.00
Marsh Fern, Butter, Cover, Pink	50.00
Marsh Fern, Compote, Cover, 7 In.	95.00
Maryland, Goblet, Ruby Stained	195.00
Maryland, Toothpick	135.00
Maryland, Wine	35.00
Mascotte, Spooner	50.00
Mascotte, Tumbler, Etched	20.00
Medallion, Creamer	28.00
Medallion, Goblet	60.00
Medallion, Spooner	26.00
Medallion Sunburst, Toothpick	20.00
Memphis, Sauce Set, Green, 6 Piece	190.00
Michigan, Bowl, Maiden's Blush, Gold Trim, 8 In.	175.00
Michigan, Butter, Cover, Maiden's Blush, Gold Trim	60.00
Michigan, Creamer, 3 In.	20.00
Michigan, Cruet	235.00
Michigan, Goblet	33.00
Michigan, Goblet, Maiden's Blush	85.00
Michigan, Pitcher, Maiden's Blush, Gold Trim	285.00
Michigan, Punch Cup, Yellow Flashed	30.00
Michigan, Toothpick	45.00 to 100.00
Michigan, Toothpick, Yellow Stained	65.00
Michigan, Tumbler	20.00
Minerva, Cake Stand, 9 In.	125.00

Minnesota, Bowl, Ruby Stained, 7 1/2 x 11 In. 375.00
Minnesota, Toothpick ....45.00 to 135.00
Missouri is listed here as Palm & Scroll.
Moon & Star, Cake Stand 50.00
Moon & Star, Goblet 17.00
Moon & Star, Sugar & Creamer, Cover, Red 30.00
Moon & Star, Syrup 450.00
Moose Eye In Sand, Cordial 18.00
Nail, Butter, Cover, Etched 75.00
Nailhead, Celery Vase 40.00
Nestor, Berry Set, Green, Gold Trim, 7 Piece 175.00
Nestor, Celery Vase, Blue 155.00
Nestor, Table Set, Blue, 4 Piece 650.00
Nestor, Toothpick 135.00
Nevada, Toothpick 65.00
New England Pineapple, Eggcup 65.00
New England Pineapple, Goblet, Flint 145.00
New Hampshire, Toothpick, Maiden's Blush 55.00
New Jersey, Goblet 48.00
New Jersey, Goblet, Gold Trim 25.00
New Jersey, Saltshaker 35.00
Nursery Tales, Butter, Cover, Child's 110.00
Nursery Tales, Pitcher 120.00
Oaken Bucket, Pitcher, Blue 120.00
Ohio Star, Syrup 900.00
One-Hundred-One, Toothpick, Blue 95.00
One-Hundred-One, Toothpick, Green 85.00
One-Hundred-One, Toothpick, Pink 75.00
One-O-One pattern is listed here as One-Hundred-One.
One-Thousand Eye pattern is listed here as Thousand Eye.
Open Rose, Tumbler 45.00
Oriental, Creamer 48.00
Orion pattern is listed here as Cathedral.
Oval Star, Pitcher, Child's 50.00
Owl pattern is listed here as Bull's-Eye with Diamond Point.
Palm & Scroll, Celery Vase 45.00
Palm Leaf, Toothpick, Green 65.00
Paneled 44, Pitcher, Maiden's Blush, Gold Trim, Bulbous 145.00
Paneled 44, Pitcher, Paneled, Platinum Stained 145.00
Paneled 44, Toothpick 65.00
Paneled Forget-Me-Not, Wine 75.00
Paneled Holly, Sauce Set, Green, 6 Piece 220.00
Paneled Sprig, Spooner, Cranberry 120.00
Paneled Stippled Scroll, Goblet 30.00
Paneled Sunflower, Toothpick 30.00
Paneled Thistle, Sugar & Creamer 50.00
Paneled Thistle, Toothpick 30.00
Paneled Thistle, Vase, 9 In. 45.00
Paneled Thistle, Vase, 12 In. 45.00
Parrot & Fan, Wine 135.00
Pavonia, Cake Stand, 10 In. 75.00
Pavonia, Goblet 50.00
Pavonia, Saltshaker, Etched, Leaf 35.00
Pavonia, Table Set, Etched, Leaf, 4 Piece 300.00
Pavonia, Tumbler 40.00
Pennsylvania, see also the related pattern Hand.
Pennsylvania, Goblet 15.00
Pennsylvania, Toothpick, Green 85.00
Pennsylvania, Wine, Green, Gold Trim 23.00
Pillar, Decanter 95.00
Pillar & Bull's-Eye pattern is listed here as Thistle.
Pinafore pattern is listed here as Actress.
Pittsburgh Fan, Plate 25.00

Pressed Glass,
Ohio Star

Pressed Glass,
Pleat and Panel

Pressed Glass,
Ribbon Candy

Pleat & Panel, Castor, Pickle, Cover 60.00
Pleat & Panel, Compote, Cover, 8 In. 145.00
Plume, Pitcher 85.00
Pointed Thumbprint pattern is listed here as Almond Thumbprint.
Portland, Cup 20.00
Portland, Goblet 20.00
Portland, Toothpick, Tab Handles 95.00
Portland With Diamond Point Band pattern is listed here as Banded Portland.
Powder & Shot, Eggcup 45.00
Powder & Shot, Goblet, Flint 60.00
Prayer Rug pattern is listed here as Horseshoe.
Pressed Diamond, Compote, Blue, 7 1/2 In. 38.00
Priscilla, Pitcher 135.00
Priscilla, Toothpick 55.00
Prism & Flattened Sawtooth, Spill, Flint 75.00
Prism & Thumbprint Band, Tumbler, Water, Flint 145.00
Prize, Cruet, Green 225.00
Prize, Toothpick 150.00
Prize, Toothpick, Ruby Stained 95.00
Prize, Wine, Ruby Stained 225.00
Queen, Cake Stand, Blue 45.00
Queen Anne, Butter, Domed, Cover, Finial 25.00
Queen Anne, Sugar 45.00
Queen Anne, Sugar & Creamer 85.00
Queen's Necklace, Toothpick 60.00
Racing Deer, Pitcher 650.00
Radiant, Water Set, Ruby Flash, 7 Piece 525.00
Reverse 44 pattern is listed here as Paneled 44.
Reverse Torpedo pattern is listed here as Diamond & Bull's-Eye Band.
Ribbed Grape, Compote, Bellflower Base, Flint, 8 In. 98.00
Ribbed Grape, Spooner, Flint 45.00
Ribbed Palm, Eggcup, Flint, Pair 35.00
Ribbed Palm, Pitcher, Flint . . . . .135.00 to 275.00
Ribbed Palm, Sauce, Vaseline 45.00
Ribbed Palm, Sugar 100.00
Ribbed Pineapple pattern is listed here as Prism & Flattened Sawtooth.
Ribbon Candy, Bread Plate, 8 1/2 In. . . . . .22.00 to 25.00
Ribbon Candy, Creamer 38.00
Rising Sun, Toothpick 20.00
Riverside's Victoria, Sugar, Cover, Amber 95.00
Robin Hood, Mug 20.00
Roman Rosette, Celery Vase, Ruby Stained 110.00
Roman Rosette, Goblet 35.00
Roman Rosette, Sugar & Creamer 45.00

Roman Rosette, Tray, Bread	30.00
Rose In Snow, Bread Plate, Blue, 9 1/2 In.	75.00
Rose In Snow, Mug	55.00
Rose In Snow, Sugar & Creamer, Cover	50.00
Rose Sprig, Celery Vase	55.00
Rose Sprig, Goblet	30.00
Rose Sprig, Goblet, Blue	68.00
Rosette Band, Compote, Cover, 7 In.	95.00
Royal Ivy, Pitcher, Rubina Handle	75.00
Royal Ivy, Salt & Pepper	75.00
Royal Ivy, Toothpick	125.00
Royal Ivy, Toothpick, Cased, Spatter	195.00
Royal Oak, Butter, Cover	86.00
Ruby Thumbprint, see also the related pattern King's Crown.	
Ruby Thumbprint, Goblet	30.00
Ruby Thumbprint, Spooner	65.00
Ruby Thumbprint, Tumbler	38.00
S-Repeat, Condiment Set, Green	425.00
S-Repeat, Punch Cup, Amethyst	95.00
S-Repeat, Salt & Pepper, Amethyst	65.00
S-Repeat, Wine, Blue, Gold Trim	38.00
Sandwich Star, Sugar	100.00
Sawtooth, Celery Vase	35.00
Sawtooth, Celery Vase, Flint . . . . .65.00 to 90.00	
Sawtooth, Compote, Cover, Cobalt Blue, 8 In., Pair	460.00
Sawtooth, Sugar, Cover, Cobalt Blue	90.00
Scalloped Lines, Goblet	20.00
Scalloped Lines, Spooner, Stemmed	20.00
Scroll, Bowl, Marigold, 9 In.	32.00
Scroll With Acanthus, Butter, Blue	100.00
Scroll With Cane Band, Spooner, Ruby Stained	45.00
Scroll With Cane Band, Toothpick	75.00
Scroll With Cane Band, Toothpick, Ruby Stained	35.00
Seneca Loop, Pitcher, Flint	175.00
Sheaf & Diamond, Compote, 7 1/2 In.	35.00
Sheaf Of Wheat pattern is listed here as Wheat Sheaf.	
Shell, Bowl	90.00
Shell, Bowl, Amethyst, 7 1/4 In.	60.00
Shell, Pitcher	100.00
Shell & Jewel, Banana Boat	70.00
Shell & Jewel, Butter, Cover	85.00
Shell & Jewel, Pitcher, Green	95.00
Shell & Jewel, Toothpick	23.00
Shell & Jewel, Toothpick, Gold Trim	30.00
Shell & Jewel, Tumbler	13.00
Shell & Tassel, Creamer, Square	65.00
Shell & Tassel, Pitcher, Water, Round	145.00
Shoshone pattern is listed here as Victor.	
Shrine, Butter, Cover	75.00
Shuttle, Cake Stand, 10 In.	125.00
Shuttle, Cordial	32.00
Shuttle, Nappy, Handle	135.00
Snail, Celery Dish	33.00
Snail, Syrup	165.00
Spanish Coin pattern is listed here as Columbian Coin.	
Square Fuchsia, Creamer	40.00
Square Fuchsia, Cup, Green, Small	85.00
Star & Punty pattern is listed here as Moon & Star.	
Star In Bull's-Eye, Toothpick	22.00
Star Of David, Water Set, 7 Piece	40.00
States pattern is listed here as The States.	
Stayman pattern is listed here as Rustic.	
Stippled Dahlia pattern is listed here as Square Fuchsia.	

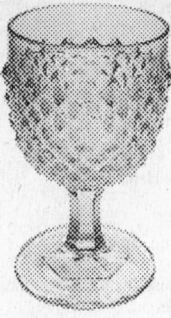

Pressed Glass,
Rose in Snow

Pressed Glass,
Sawtooth

Pressed Glass,
Sandwich Star

Stippled Fans, Toothpick	15.00
Stippled Forget-Me-Not, Plate, Baby In Tub Center, 7 In.	65.00
Stippled Forget-Me-Not, Plate, Kitten Center	58.00
Stippled Grape & Festoon, Celery Vase	35.00
Stippled Paneled Flower pattern is listed here as Maine.	
Stippled Scroll pattern is listed here as Scroll.	
Sunbeam, Toothpick	45.00
Sunburst On Shield, Butter	325.00
Sunk Honeycomb, Toothpick	40.00
Sunken Primrose, Spooner	35.00
Sunken Primrose, Sugar, Canary	60.00
Sunken Primrose, Tumbler, Blue	35.00
Sunrise pattern is listed here as Rising Sun.	
Swag With Brackets, Creamer	75.00
Swag With Brackets, Pitcher, Amethyst, Gold Trim	250.00
Swag With Brackets, Toothpick, Purple	70.00
Swan, Spooner	25.00
Tacoma, Table Set, Vaseline, 4 Piece	395.00
Tacoma, Toothpick	25.00
Teardrop pattern is listed here as Teardrop & Thumbprint.	
Teardrop & Tassel, Water Set, Sapphire Blue, 5 Piece	275.00
Teardrop & Thumbprint, Cake Stand, Scalloped, 6 x 4 In.	68.00
Tennessee, Pitcher, Milk	55.00
Tennessee, Toothpick	90.00
Tennessee, Wine	55.00
Texas, Cake Stand, 9 In.	95.00 to 125.00
Texas, Goblet	95.00
Texas, Pitcher, Water, Inverted Design	150.00
Texas, Saltshaker	65.00
Texas, Saltshaker, Maiden's Blush	195.00
Texas, Toothpick	20.00 to 30.00
Texas, Toothpick, Gold Trim	30.00
The States, Punch Bowl Base	55.00
The States, Toothpick	35.00
Theodore Roosevelt, Bread Plate, Bears Around Border	210.00
Thistle, Goblet	42.00
Thistle, Wine, Flint	85.00
Thousand Eye, Eggcup, Double	60.00
Thousand Eye, Syrup, Amber	125.00 to 150.00
Thousand Eye, Syrup, Green	175.00
Thousand Eye, Toothpick, Amber	65.00
Three Face, Butter, Cover	175.00
Three Face, Compote, Cover, 6 In.	175.00
Three Face, Pitcher, Etched	550.00

Three Face, Plate	35.00
Three Face, Spooner	110.00
Three Face, Sugar	155.00
Three Graces, see also the related pattern Three Face.	
Three Sisters pattern is listed here as Three Face.	
Thumbprint, Bowl, Waste, Amber	30.00
Thumbprint, Bowl, Waste, Blue	35.00
Thumbprint, Celery Dish, 7 1/2 In.	15.00
Thumbprint, Decanter, Thumbprint Stopper, Flint, 10 1/4 In.	182.00
Thumbprint, Pitcher, Amber	50.00
Torpedo, Decanter, Wine	125.00
Torpedo, Goblet	65.00 to 68.00
Torpedo, Syrup, Ruby Stained	160.00
Tree Of Life, Compote, Hand Stem, Blue, 9 x 9 In.	148.00
Triangular Prism, Celery Dish, Flint	50.00
Tulip Petals, Spooner, Rose	40.00
Tulip With Sawtooth, Celery, Flint	85.00
Tulip With Sawtooth, Compote, Pedestal, Flint	125.00
Tulip With Sawtooth, Decanter, Flint, 1 Pt.	125.00
Two Panel, Celery Vase, Vaseline	48.00
Two Panel, Spooner, Vaseline	28.00
U.S. Coin, Cake Plate, Pedestal, 1892	600.00
U.S. Coin, Tray, Frosted	365.00
Valencia Waffle, Syrup, Amber	135.00
Vermont, Goblet, Green	70.00
Vermont, Toothpick, Green, Gold Trim	45.00 to 50.00
Victor, Toothpick, Gold Trim	30.00 to 40.00
Viking, Compote, Cover, 9 In.	175.00
Waffle, Celery Vase	65.00
Waffle, Celery Vase, Flint	75.00
Waffle & Thumbprint, Celery, Flint	100.00
Waffle & Thumbprint, Champagne, Flint	135.00 to 150.00
Washington, Celery Vase, Flint	120.00
Washington Centennial, Celery Vase	58.00
Washington Centennial, Pitcher	225.00
Wedding, Compote, Candy, Cover	75.00
Wedding Ring, Cologne Bottle, Flint	175.00
Wee Branches, Butter, Cover	125.00
Westward Ho, Compote, Cover, Pedestal, 6 In.	250.00
Westward Ho, Compote, Cover, Pedestal, 7 In.	175.00
Westward Ho, Creamer	95.00 to 165.00
Westward Ho, Goblet	100.00
Westward Ho, Spooner	93.00 to 95.00
Wheat & Barley, Mug, Amber	55.00
Wheat & Barley, Sugar, Cover	35.00
Wheat Sheaf, Bread Plate	30.00

Pressed Glass, Thumbprint

In snowy weather, make tracks both in and out of your door. One set of tracks leaving the house is an invitation to an intruder. Or perhaps you could walk out of the house backward.

PRESSED GLASS, Wheat Sheaf 606 PRINT, Audubon

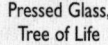

Pressed Glass,
Tree of Life

Pressed Glass,
Wheat Sheaf

Wheat Sheaf, Platter	24.00
Wildflower, Salt & Pepper, Blue	95.00
Wildflower, Tumbler, Blue	45.00
Willow Oak, Compote, Cover, 8 In.	125.00
Windflower, Compote, Cover, 8 In.	85.00
Wooden Pail pattern is listed here as Oaken Bucket.	
Wreath & Shell, Berry Set, Opalescent, 7 Piece	200.00
Wreath & Shell, Toothpick	225.00
Wyoming, Cake Stand, 8 In.	58.00
X-Ray, Berry Bowl, Gold Trim, Master	35.00
X-Ray, Berry Set, Gold Trim, 6 Piece	50.00
X-Ray, Bowl, Amethyst, Gold Trim, 7 In.	125.00
X-Ray, Butter, Cover, Marigold	125.00
X-Ray, Table Set, Green, Gold Trim, 4 Piece	255.00
X-Ray, Toothpick, Gold Trim	30.00
X-Ray, Toothpick, Green	50.00
X-Ray, Toothpick, Green, Gold Trim	45.00
Zipper Slash, Toothpick	45.00

PRINT, in this listing, means any of many printed images produced on paper by one of the more common methods, such as lithography. The prints listed here are of interest primarily to the antiques collector, not the fine arts collector. Many of these prints were originally part of books. Other prints will be found in the Advertising, Currier & Ives, Movie, and Poster categories.

2 Women, Trees, Pond, Field, Green, Red, Ridge Crafts, 1910, 5 x 3 In.	286.00
Ackerman, Doctor Syntax, Rowlandson, Matted, Frame, 8 1/8 x 11 1/8 In., 4 Piece	220.00
Aldin, Fallowfield Hunt Breaking Cover, Blue, Green, Frame, 11 x 18 1/2 In.	355.00
Aldin, Fallowfield Hunt The Kill, Blue, Gray Skyline, Frame, 11 x 18 1/2 In.	300.00

Audubon bird prints were originally issued as part of books printed from 1826 to 1854. They were issued in two sizes, 26 1/2 inches by 39 1/2 inches and 11 inches by 7 inches. The quadrupeds were issued in 28-by-22-inch prints. Later editions of the Audubon books were done in many sizes, and reprints of the books in the original size were also made. The bird pictures have been so popular they have been copied in myriad sizes by both old and new printing methods. This list includes originals and later copies because Audubon prints of all ages are sold in antiques shops.

J.W.Audubon

Audubon, Black & White Creeper, 19 1/2 x 12 1/4 In.	977.00
Audubon, Canada Jay, 39 x 25 1/4 In.	5462.00
Audubon, Carolina Pigeon, Frame, 31 1/2 x 24 5/8 In.	4025.00
Audubon, Great Horned Owl, Frame, 33 7/8 x 23 1/4 In.	3450.00
Audubon, Mississippi Kite, 26 3/8 x 21 In.	1150.00

Audubon,	Red Headed Woodpecker, 25 1/4 x 21 1/2 In.	5462.00
Audubon,	Towhe Bunting, 19 5/8 x 12 3/8 In.	1150.00
Audubon,	Whip-Poor-Will, 25 7/8 x 20 5/8 In.	5462.00
Audubon,	Winter Hawk, 26 x 38 1/4 In.	4025.00
Elvgren,	Bubbling Over, 1950s, 11 x 18 In.	27.00
Elvgren,	Some Help, Girl Painting Poodle, 8 x 11 In.	25.00
Fox,	Memories Of Home	90.00
Fox,	Political Argument, Calendar	75.00
Fox,	Warm Friends, Calendar, 1931	95.00
Frank E. English,	White Home, Horse & Buggies, 1959, 7 5/8 x 21 In.	770.00
Gally,	P. & P., Children's, Spring, Summer & Autumn, Winter, Frame, 6 x 8 In., Pair	180.00
Good Friends,	Child & Cat, Hand Colored, Frame, 25 1/2 x 21 1/2 In.	245.00
Gutmann,	Great Love, Woman & Baby, Lace, Ribbons, Signed On Dress, 12 x 16 In.	265.00
Gutmann,	Hillside Woods, Frame, 10 1/2 x 9 1/2 In.	2200.00
Gutmann,	In Disgrace, No. 794, Frame	125.00
Gutmann,	Love's Blossom, Frame, Convex Glass, Round, 9 In.	300.00
Gutmann,	Message Of The Roses	225.00
Gutmann,	Reward, No. 792, Frame	125.00
Haskell & Allen,	Great Race At Rochester, N.Y., Shadowbox Frame, 26 1/4 x 32 1/4 In.	245.00
Howard Chandler Christy,	B.S. Military Cadet, Frame, 1917, 12 x 8 In.	325.00
Icart,	Autumn, Purple	1350.00
Icart,	Bird Of Prey	2150.00
Icart,	Casanova, 1928, 20 1/4 x 13 3/8 In.	1500.00
Icart,	Charm Of Montmartre	2400.00
Icart,	Chestnut Vendor	1750.00
Icart,	Grande Eve, 1934, 30 1/4 x 19 3/4 In.	28500.00
Icart,	He Loves Me, 2-In. Margin, 1926	850.00
Icart,	Homage To Guynemere	2650.00
Icart,	Incident, 1920, 8 1/4 x 10 3/8 In.	1995.00
Icart,	Japanese Garden	2450.00
Icart,	Lady Of The Camelias	1650.00
Icart,	Laughing Buddha	950.00
Icart,	Love Letters	1925.00
Icart,	Mardi Gras, 1936, 18 5/8 x 18 1/4 In.	9600.00
Icart,	Miss Liberty, 1917, 19 1/4 x 12 5/8 In.	2500.00
Icart,	New Grapes	2400.00
Icart,	New Hat, 1924, 8 3/4 x 11 1/4 In.	1850.00
Icart,	Orchids, 1937, 27 x 18 3/4 In.	5700.00
Icart,	Puff Of Smoke, 1922, 19 1/4 x 13 5/8 In.	2250.00
Icart,	Spilled Jug Of Milk	1500.00
Icart,	Summer, Parasol, 1920, 9 1/4 x 7 3/4 In.	1450.00
Icart,	Symphony In Blue	2650.00
Icart,	The Dress Shop	1200.00
Icart,	Woman, Walking 3 Greyhounds, Sepia, Frame, 16 x 10 In.	295.00
Jacoulet,	Fan Seal, 15 1/2 x 12 In.	316.00
Jacoulet,	Fan Seal, Frame, Pencil Signed, 15 1/2 x 12 In.	431.00
Jacoulet,	Les Perles, 17 x 13 In.	341.00
Jacoulet,	Peach Seal, 15 1/2 x 12 In.	374.00

Japanese woodblock prints are listed as follows: Print, Japanese, name of artist, title or description, type, and size. Dealers use the following terms: Tate-e is a vertical composition. Yoko-e is a horizontal composition. The words Aiban (13 by 9 inches), Chuban (10 by 7 1/2 inches), Hosoban (12 by 6 inches), Oban (15 by 10 inches), and Koban (7 by 4 inches) denote size. Modern versions of some of these prints have been made.

Japanese,	Buildings In Heavy Snow, Frame, 15 1/2 x 19 1/2 In.	115.00
Japanese,	Entertainer & Monkey, Beauty & Boy, Matted, Frame, 22 x 15 In.	85.00
Japanese,	Floral Scenes, Multicolored, 14 x 9 1/2 In.	58.00
Japanese,	Hiroshige, Yabukoji Below Atago, Snow Scene, 15 x 10 In. ....*Illus*	1705.00
Japanese,	Hisashi Otsuka, Graceful Elegance, Matted, Frame, 37 1/2 x 49 1/2 In.	80.00
Japanese,	Hisashi Otsuka, The Dance Of The Lions, Matted, Frame, 33 1/2 x 47 1/2 In.	55.00
Japanese,	Joichi Hoshi, Winter Tree, Signed, 22 3/4 x 31 1/8 In.	2200.00

Left: Print, Nutting, View From Casino, Funchal

Right: Print, Nutting, Sheep At The Temple, Paestrum, 14 x 17 In.

Left: Print, Japanese, Hiroshige, Yabukoji Below Atago, Snow Scene, 15 x 10 In.

Japanese, Junichiro Sekino, Portrait, Actor Kichiemon, Pencil Signed, 22 x 18 In. 920.00
Japanese, Kawase Hasui, Night Rain At Maisaka In Soshu, 14 x 9 In. 245.00
Japanese, Kunisada, Samurai Watching Entertainment, Matted, Frame, 7 x 12 In. 85.00
Japanese, Miyaki, Figures On A Village Street, Frame, 17 x 11 1/2 In. 2990.00
Japanese, Oban Yoko-E, Snow Scene 95.00
Japanese, Parrot Tulips, Yellow, Pink, Quartered Oak Frame, 11 1/2 x 15 In. 357.00
Japanese, Tamami Shima, Cranes Flying, 16 x 22 In. 225.00
Japanese, Yoshida, T., Woman, Pencil Signed, 1953, 14 3/4 x 9 5/8 In. 230.00
Kellogg, A. Lincoln Being Shot, Frame, 1868 . . . . 50.00
Kellogg, A. Lincoln Dying, Family & Friends Around, Frame, 1868 . . . . 50.00
Kellogg, Words Of Daniel Webster, I Still Live, Hand Colored, Frame, 17 x 13 In. 95.00
Kellogg & Comstock, Happy Mother, Hand Colored, Frame, 14 x 10 In. 85.00
Kellogg & Comstock, Just Engaged, Frame, 17 1/4 x 13 1/4 In. 75.00
Maughan, Gone With The Wind, Tara, Signed, 32 x 38 In. 1000.00

Nutting prints are now popular with collectors. Wallace Nutting is known for his pictures, furniture, and books. Nutting *prints* are actually hand-colored photographs issued from 1900 to 1941. There are over 10,000 different titles. Wallace Nutting furniture is listed in the Furniture category.

Wallace Nutting

Nutting, 3 Ladies Having Tea, Dining Room Interior, Signed, 7 1/2 x 9 1/4 In. 110.00
Nutting, Meeting Place 2420.00
Nutting, Sheep At The Temple, Paestrum, 14 x 17 In. . . . . *Illus* 2200.00
Nutting, Tea In Yorktown Parlor, Matted, Full Size 275.00
Nutting, Teacup Talk, 2 Ladies, Fireplace 75.00
Nutting, View From Casino, Funchal . . . . *Illus* 1540.00

Parrish prints are wanted by collectors. Maxfield Frederick Parrish was an illustrator who lived from 1870 to 1966. He is best known as a designer of magazine covers, posters, calendars, and advertisements.

Maxfield Parrish

Parrish, Abstract Figural Brushstrokes, Light Brown Ground, Woodblock, 22 x 17 In. 115.00
Parrish, Daybreak, 11 x 7 In. 58.00
Parrish, Daybreak, Frame, 30 x 20 In. 245.00
Parrish, Daybreak, Wild Geese, Canyon, Triptych, 20 x 56 In. 1400.00
Parrish, Dream Garden 200.00
Parrish, Fisherman & Genie 175.00
Parrish, Florentine Fete, Frame 75.00
Parrish, Old King Cole 400.00

Parrish, Path To Home 275.00
Parrish, Rubaiyat, Seal, Verse On Back, Frame 450.00
Parrish, Twilight, Weidman, Dool & Green Co., Frame, 8 1/4 x 11 In. 135.00
Redoute, Pierre Joseph, Amaryllis Belladonna, Hand Colored, Engraving, 19 x 13 In. ... 3220.00
Redoute, Pierre Joseph, Rosa Damascena, Hand Colored, 13 x 9 In. 3220.00
Vargas, Nilene Entre Act, Nude, Color, 1919, 3 1/2 x 5 In. 45.00
Woodblock, Watson, Deer, Foliage, Blue, Brown, 12 x 12 In. 158.00
Woodblock, Watson, Grandpa's Barn, Red, Green, Blue, 9 1/2 x 15 In. 325.00

PURSES have been recognizable since the eighteenth century, when leather and needlework purses were preferred. Beaded purses became popular in the nineteenth century, went out of style, but are again in use. Mesh purses date from the 1880s and are still being made. How to carry a handkerchief and lipstick is a problem today for every woman, including the Queen of England.

Alligator, 1941 .... 50.00
Alligator, Black, Hermes 6325.00
Alligator, Brown, Rectangular 325.00
Alligator, Case, Fitted With 7 Covered Sections 350.00
Alligator, Complete Pelt 175.00
Alligator, Gilt Metal Dolphin Clasp, Beige, Signed, Judith Leiber, 1960s 977.00
Armadillo Hide 65.00
Beaded, Allover Black Bugle Beads, Mirrors, Regale Miami, 1950s 60.00
Beaded, Allover Seed Pearls, Evening Bag, Rhinestones On Clasp 40.00
Beaded, Czechoslovakia 45.00
Beaded, Drawstring Top, Open Winged Butterfly Design, 7 1/4 In. 172.00
Beaded, Floral, Gold & Silver Frame 110.00
Beaded, Indian Design, c.1880, 6 1/4 x 4 1/4 In. 125.00
Beaded, Indian Design, c.1900, 8 x 6 In. 125.00
Beaded, Indian, Crystal Leaves, Vines, Folds Over 190.00
Beaded, Landscape Scene, Germany 130.00
Beaded, Multicolored Landscape 175.00
Beaded, Oval, Imitation Tortoiseshell, Celluloid Frame, Mirror In Lid, Silk Cord Handle   155.00
Beaded, White Beads On Plastic, Germany 38.00
Beaded, White, 1950s 24.00
Beaded, Woven, Floral Design, Dark Blue Satin Lining, 1920, 5 x 7 In. 80.00
Black Silk, 14K Gold Frame & Chain, Diamond Clasp & Terminals, Cartier 2070.00
Boa Skin 60.00
Butterfly Shape, Comb, Coin Purse, Make-Up Mirror, Judith Leiber, 6 In. 2300.00
Calf, Brown, Kelly, Hermes, 12 In. 1400.00
Celluloid, Little Berry Kelly, 1920s 495.00
Chain Mail, Molded Roses & Scrolls, Chain Handle, Sterling Silver 143.00
Clutch, Spherical, Geometric, Green, Red, Blue, White, Gold, Signed, 1980, 3 1/2 In. ... 900.00
Cobra Snakeskin, Silver Frame, France 20.00
Coin, Alligator Foot 45.00
Coin, Girl's, Shell, Heart Shape, Christmas, Dorothy Thayer, 1912 .... 85.00
Coin, Sterling Silver 68.00
Coin, Tam O' Shanter, Cupid Design, Black Beaded Star Bottom 75.00
Crocodile, Black, Gilt Slide Clasp, Signed, Tiffany, 1950s 115.00
Crocodile, Black, Oval Box, Josef, Signed, c.1950 .... 315.00
Embroidered, Flame Stitch, Clutch, Initials E.H., 1751, 8 x 14 In. ....*Illus* 1760.00
Embroidered, Flame Stitch, Flap, Salmon Wool Edges, Magenta Silk Pocket, 5 x 8 In. ...   230.00
Embroidered, Scrolled Flowering Tendrils, Edges Of Green Wool, 4 1/2 x 9 In. 230.00
Faux Magazine Cover, Clutch, Elegance Paris, Hinged, 12 x 5 In. ....*Illus* 12.00
Flame Stitch, Drawstring, Red, Orange, Green, Pink, Blue & White 780.00
Flame Stitch, James Boyes, Londonberry Worked Into Pattern 2990.00
Gold, Turquoise Scarab, Red Roundels, Chain Handle, Sloan & Co., 12 In. 7475.00
Hammered Silver, Hinge Opening, Fitted, Chain, J.O. Bellis, 3 1/2 x 2 In. 1200.00
Leather, Bosco Nelson, 1890 .... 75.00
Leather, Embossed Design, Arts & Crafts Style, Reedcraft & Meeker, 7 x 8 In. 90.00
Leather, Gilt, Tooled, Envelope, Wiener Werkstatte, Box, 1910, 3 5/8 x 6 In. 1150.00
Leather, Gold, With Rhinestones, 2 Looped Handles, A. Scacci, 5 x 3 1/2 In. 60.00

Left: Purse, Embroidered, Flame Stitch, Clutch, Initials E.H., 1751, 8 x 14 In.
Above: Purse, Faux Magazine Cover, Clutch, Elegance Paris, Hinged, 12 x 5 In.

Leather, Hand Tooled, Saddle Top, Stirrups, Sheep Skin Under Saddle	135.00
Leather Pouch, Sporran, Metal Celtic Design, Horsehair, Tassels, Scotland, 1880	625.00
Linen, Embroidered, Carved Bakelite Tortoise Frame	85.00
Lucite, Amber, Brown Swirl, Handles, 4 1/2 x 8 1/2 In.	45.00
Lucite, Charles Kahn	45.00
Lucite, Gold Speckled, Gilli Original	75.00
Lucite, Hearts On Top	62.00
Lucite, Lighted Mirror, Caramel Swirl	85.00
Lucite, Lunch Box Shape, Shoulder Strap, Turtles, Saks Fifth Ave., Wilardy	85.00 to 135.00
Lucite, Rust Color, Scalloped, Yellow Carved Top	65.00
Lucite, Webbed & Silver Sides, Triangular Shape, Lucite Handles	85.00
Lucite & Cut Work Silver Metal, Gray Pearlized Top & Bottom	3950.00
Lucite & Wicker, Marbelized, Stylecraft	40.00
Mesh, 3 Sapphires, 2 Diamonds Hang From Frame, Oval Link Chain, 14K Gold	745.00
Mesh, Chatelaine, Spring Opening, Germany	75.00
Mesh, Circular Monogram Center, 14K Yellow Gold	285.00
Mesh, Enameled Frame, Whiting & Davis	145.00
Mesh, Enameled Red, Yellow Frame	85.00
Mesh, Enameled Salmon, Whiting & Davis	115.00
Mesh, Enameled, Ivory, Lavender & Green, Mandalian, 7 In.	242.00
Mesh, Gatetop, Goldtone, Whiting & Davis	95.00
Mesh, German Silver, Chain, Beaded Fringe, 3 x 4 1/2 In.	155.00
Mesh, Gold, Chased Frame, Blue Stones, Slide Mesh Handle, 14K Yellow Gold	920.00
Mesh, Gold, Clutch, Rhinestone Clasp, Whiting & Davis, 8 1/2 x 6 In.	50.00
Mesh, Gold, Rauf Co., 6 In.	40.00
Mesh, Gold, Whiting & Davis	75.00
Mesh, Hand Painted, Whiting & Davis	145.00
Mesh, Mandalian, 5 x 8 In.	160.00
Mesh, Mandalian, Pale Blue, 5 Beads Base	105.00
Mesh, Sapphire On Clasp, Whiting & Davis	145.00
Mesh, Scrolled Frame, 2 Cabochon Blue Stone Closures, 14K Yellow Gold	920.00
Mesh, Silver, 4-Beaded Fringe, Lined, Germany, 3 x 4 1/2 In.	130.00
Mesh, Silver, Compact Inset With Clasp, 6 x 5 In.	195.00
Mesh, Silver, Crochet Style Weave, Continental, 9 1/4 x 5 7/8 In.	250.00
Mesh, Silver, Floral, 6 x 6 In.	150.00
Mesh, Silver, Pierced, Griffins & Foliage Clasp, Round, 5 1/2 x 4 In.	195.00
Mesh, Silver, Whiting & Davis	110.00
Mesh, Sterling Silver, Chain, Nouveau Flowers On Frame, c.1880	365.00
Mesh, Sterling Silver, Engraved Bird's Head & Wings, Chain Handle, Spain, 1921	495.00
Mesh, White, Cream, Big Link Chain Handle & Trim, Whiting & Davis, Alumesh	80.00
Mesh, Whiting & Davis, Signed & Numbered	195.00
Mother-Of-Pearl, Glass, 1930s	16.00
Peacock Feather, 1940s	16.00
Petit Point, Carnelian Clasp, Vienna, 6 x 7 In.	75.00
Petit Point, Flowers, Cream Ground, Hand Made	65.00
Plastic, Beige, Box Type, 1940s	25.00
Plastic, Orange, Gold Crest Fashions, 4 x 7 x 3 In.	300.00
Satchel Shape, Floral Design, Judith Leiber, 5 1/2 In.	2300.00
Sequin, Gold, Chain	20.00

Sequin, Polychrome Design, Gold Lame Interior, Judith Leiber, 4 1/4 x 3 3/8 In. 1445.00
Silk, Black, George Washington Scene On Front, 6 x 9 In. 145.00
Sterling Silver, Pencil, Nickel & Dime Trolley Fare Space, Chain, R. Blackinton, 1916 . 165.00
Tapestry, Black & White Seed Pearls, 6 1/4 x 5 In. 20.00
Vanity, Gold Tone, Mondaine, 4 In. 65.00
Vanity, Lyric, Encrusted Pearls & Aqua Beads 90.00
Vanity, Wadsworth, Black Suede 80.00
Velvet, Expandable Round Metal Top, 7 1/2 x 8 In. 12.00
Wooden, Decoupage, Manselle, Escort, Octagonal 30.00

QUEZAL glass was made from 1901 to 1920 by Martin Bach, Sr., in Brooklyn, New York. Other glassware by other firms, such as Loetz, Steuben, and Tiffany, resembles this gold-colored iridescent glass. After Martin Bach's death in 1920, his son continued the manufacture of a similar glass under the name *Lustre Art Glass.*

Quezal

Bowl, Center, Flared Raised Rim, Ambergris, Silver Blue Iridescent, 11 1/4 In. 460.00
Bowl, Gold Iridescent, Square, 5 3/4 In. 575.00
Bowl, Gold Pulled Threads, Green Border, Gilt Interior, Signed, 12 x 2 3/4 In. 690.00
Bowl, Orange, Gold Iridescent, Purple, Blue, Pink Highlights, 11 x 2 3/4 In. 275.00
Chandelier, Herringbone, 3 Tiers, Green, Amber Segments, 40 In. 12650.00
Lamp, Boudoir, Opal Glass Shade, Leaf Design, Pulled Threads, 4 3/4 In. 230.00
Lamp, Desk, Pulled Feather, Brass, Gold Iridescent Shade, Sconce Design, 14 1/2 In. . . . 575.00
Lamp, Lily, 4-Light, Bronze Telescope Base Support, 24 In. 1925.00
Lamp, Morning Glory, Green Pulled Feathers, Opalescent Ground, 16 In., Pair 440.00
Perfume Bottle, Gold Iridescent, Purple, Blue, Green, Pink, Melba, 7 In. 600.00
Plate, Gold Iridescent, Purple Highlights, 6 1/2 In. 225.00
Plate, Orange, Gold Iridescent, Purple, Blue, Pink Highlights, Signed, 11 In. 330.00
Salt, Blue Iridescent, Signed, 1 3/8 In. 440.00
Salt, Gold Luster, Signed, 1 x 2 1/2 In. 110.00
Shade, Bell Form, Gilt Geometric, Signed, 4 1/2 In., Pair 500.00
Shade, Bell Form, Gold Lined, Yellow, Green Leaf Design, 5 1/2 In. 115.00
Shade, Chandelier, Bell Shape, Signed, 6 x 5 In., 4 Piece 700.00
Shade, Green Heart Design, Gold Threading Iridescent, Signed, 6 In. 275.00
Shade, Pulled Feather, White, Yellow Border, White Iridescent Ground, 1920, 6 In. 287.00
Shade, Pulled Petal Design, Gold Glass Threads, Flared, 5 1/2 In. 92.00
Sherbet, Iridescent Opal, Emerald Pulled Feathers, Gold Interior, Marked, 4 In. 1430.00
Vase, 3 Applied Glass Feet, Swirled Blue, Gold, Ivory Ground, 8 In. 2750.00
Vase, 5 Pointed Gold Iridescent Feathers, Gold Foot, 4 3/4 In. 575.00
Vase, Allover Green & Gold Feathers, Oyster Ground, Signed, 10 1/2 In. 1995.00
Vase, Ambergris, Blue Iridescent, Oval, 4 1/4 In. 400.00
Vase, Bell Form, Iridescent Rose, Metal, Art Nouveau Collar, Early 20th Century, 8 In. . . 110.00
Vase, Blue Iridescent, Purple Highlights, 8 x 4 1/2 In. 330.00
Vase, Blue Iridescent, Purple, Green Highlights, 7 1/2 In. 355.00
Vase, Bud, Floriform, Iridescent, Signed, 6 1/4 In. 345.00
Vase, Bud, Tubular, Scalloped Lip, 8 In. 275.00
Vase, Classic Form, Purple & Blue Luster, 9 1/2 x 5 1/2 In. 675.00
Vase, Floriform, Trumpet Blossom Form, Gold Amber Iridescent, 6 3/4 In. 2300.00
Vase, Gold Iridescent, Flared Rim, Cylindrical, 9 1/4 In. 92.00
Vase, Gold Iridescent, Flared, Purple, Green, Pink Highlights, Footed, 5 In. 715.00
Vase, Gold Iridescent, Ribbed, 6 In. 355.00
Vase, Gold, Rose, Green, Blue Iridescent Highlights, Silver Overlay, 8 1/2 In. 3300.00
Vase, Hooked, Pulled Gold Feathers, Medial Gold Band, Flared Rim, 4 5/8 In. 2070.00
Vase, Iridescent Gold Leaves, Pulled Top, Opalescent Ground, Flared Neck, 9 In. 2200.00
Vase, Iridescent Opalescent, Gold & Blue Leaves, Gold Threads, Signed, 6 1/2 In. 935.00
Vase, Iridescent Opalescent, Pulled Green Leaves Band, Tapered, Marked, 5 1/2 In. 935.00
Vase, Jack-In-The-Pulpit, Swirled Iridescent Blue, Purple, Green Ground, 1900, 11 In. . . . 1725.00
Vase, King Tut Pattern, Amber & Royal Blue, Iridescent Opalescent, 4 In. 1100.00
Vase, Lily, 5 Green Spiked Feathers, Gold, 5 In. 1035.00
Vase, Morning Glory, 5 Pulled Feathers, Flared Ribbed, Gold Iridescent, 7 3/4 In. 1265.00
Vase, Pulled Feather, Green, Gold Iridescent, 7 3/4 In. 5175.00
Vase, Purple Highlights, Blue Iridescence, Signed, 8 x 4 1/2 In. 605.00
Vase, Ruffled Rim, Pulled Feather Green Design, White Iridescent, 6 1/2 In. 467.50
Vase, Stylized Leaves, Flowers, Silver Overlay, Gold, Signed, 6 1/2 In. 1045.00

Vase, Stylized Leaves, Flowers, Silver Overlay, Gold, Signed, 10 In. 935.00
Vase, Trumpet, Green Pulled Feathers, Iridescent Gold Footed, 14 In. 1430.00
Vase, Yellow Feather, Green Trailing Around Shoulder, Amber Iridescent, 1920, 5 In. ... 1380.00
Vase, Yellow Satin, Gold Iridescent Lily Pads, Vertical Vines, 4 In. 1955.00

QUILTS have been made since the seventeenth century. Early textiles were very precious and every scrap was saved to be reused. A quilt is a combination of fabrics joined to a filler and a backing by small stitched designs known as quilting. An appliqued quilt has pieces stitched to the top of a large piece of background fabric. A patchwork, or pieced, quilt is made of many small pieces stitched together. Embroidery can be added to either type.

Amish, Appliqued, Diamond-In-Star, Magenta Corner Blocks, 83 x 83 In. 2990.00
Amish, Blue Lines, Gray Binding, 70 x 73 In. 110.00
Amish, Carpenter's Wheel, Red, Teal, Mustard Border, Red Cotton Binding, 80 x 80 In. . 4600.00
Amish, Diamond In The Square, Violet, Teal, Magenta, Cotton, Wool, 78 x 74 In. 1380.00
Amish, Patchwork, Bar Pattern, Velvet Binding, 80 3/4 x 75 1/4 In. 748.00
Amish, Red & Green Bar Pattern, Late 19th Century, 85 x 80 In. 690.00
Amish, Star Of Bethlehem, Red, Blue, Purple, Pink, Yellow Rainbow, 75 1/4 x 74 In. ... 1610.00
Amish, Sunshine & Shadow, Red, Green Cotton Border, Cranberry Binding, 78 x 76 In. . 2875.00
Appliqued, 25 Floral Circle, 8 Pointed Star Center, Vines, Red & Green, 97 x 97 In. 440.00
Appliqued, 48 Star Center, Red & White Surrounds, c.1885, 67 x 71 In. 1265.00
Appliqued, 9 Floral Medallions, Red, Green, Blue, White, 86 x 86 In. 412.00
Appliqued, 9 Medallions, Red & Green Calico, Floral Vining Border, 97 x 97 In. 660.00
Appliqued, 9 Squares, Rose Pattern, Red, Yellow, Green Calicos, 100 x 94 In. 4025.00
Appliqued, 9 Stylized Medallions, Red & Green, Oak Leaves, Vining Border, 87 x 87 In. 275.00
Appliqued, Album, 25 Cotton Blocks, c.1870, 82 x 82 In. 435.00
Appliqued, American Flags, Alternating Blocks, Shell Quilting, c.1920, 54 x 76 In. 2760.00
Appliqued, Anchor Flanked By 2 Stars, Blue, Yellow, 1944, 78 x 88 In. 2070.00
Appliqued, Central Wheel With Spokes, Red, Blue, Brown, 80 x 71 In. 2530.00
Appliqued, Diamond In The Square, Red, White, Calico Border & Binding, 80 x 81 In. . 1150.00
Appliqued, Dominant Green In Center, Green Border, c.1920, 108 x 89 In. 885.00
Appliqued, Double Irish Chain, Floral Scroll Borders, 72 x 84 In. 220.00
Appliqued, Drunkard's Path, Navy & White Print, 76 x 76 In. 330.00
Appliqued, Eagle Head Center, Corner Stars, Diamond Quilting, c.1940, 38 x 27 In. 2300.00
Appliqued, Evening Star, Red Sawtooth Binding, 82 1/2 x 83 In. 115.00
Appliqued, Floral Medallions, Swag Border, 82 x 90 In. 412.00
Appliqued, Floral Medallions, Vining Border, Calico, Dayton, Ohio, 1850, 76 x 90 In. .. 1265.00
Appliqued, Flowering Cacti, White Ground, Green & Red Borders, 76 1/2 x 69 1/2 In. ... 315.00
Appliqued, Flowers & Eagle, Teal, Yellow Calico, Red Backing, 80 x 94 In. 550.00
Appliqued, Geometric, Black, White, Embroidered Fish, Frogs, 1950s, 88 x 68 In. 175.00
Appliqued, Harvest Sun Pattern, Red, Green, Yellow, Sawtooth Border, 86 x 86 In. 1380.00

Quilt, Patchwork, Benjamin Harrison, Protection,
1880, 69 x 83 In.

Quilt, Patchwork & Appliqued, Bar
Pattern, Centennial, 1876, 75 x 55 In.

Quilt, Patchwork & Appliqued, Star Of
Bethlehem, 1865, 75 x 74 In.

Quilt, Trapunto, Rose & Wreath, Eagles, Penna.,
1885, 81 x 82 In.

Appliqued, Irish Chain Variant, Red & White, 64 x 80 In.	355.00
Appliqued, Irish Chain, Navy Blue, White, 76 x 79 In.	385.00
Appliqued, Lone Star, Reds & Greens, 75 x 81 In.	385.00
Appliqued, Martha & George Washington Portraits, Bars, c.1876, 75 x 55 In.	4600.00
Appliqued, Oak Leaf Pattern Variation, Stuffed Flowers, 89 1/4 x 89 1/4 In.	460.00
Appliqued, Princess Feather Variation, Green, Red, 94 x 93 1/2 In.	1295.00
Appliqued, Print Floral, Red & Green, 95 x 81 In.	950.00
Appliqued, Rose Wreath Pattern, Roses & Urns, 1858, 89 1/4 x 89 1/4 In.	1840.00
Appliqued, Spice Rose Pattern, Bud Vine Border, 76 1/3 x 75 1/4 In.	1035.00
Appliqued, Spread-Winged Eagles, Hand Stitched Near Initials J.A.S., 1878	8100.00
Appliqued, Star Of Bethlehem, Red, Olive Triple Border, Calico, 74 3/4 x 73 3/4 In.	1495.00
Appliqued, Star Of Bethlehem, Spread-Winged Eagles At Corners, c.1865, 75 x 74 In.	3450.00
Appliqued, Star Pattern, Embroidered Hexagonal Panels, Cotton, c.1830, 72 x 95 In.	2645.00
Appliqued, Star, Red Calico, White, 70 x 71 In.	410.00
Appliqued, Sunburst, Embroidered Peacock Reverse, Mary Tiffany, 1850, 79 x 74 In.	1150.00
Appliqued, Various Forms Of Transportation, 1939, 89 x 74 In.	3450.00
Linsey Woolsey, Beige, Overlapping Circles, 2 Corners For Bed Posts, 94 x 108 In.	220.00
Patchwork, 30 Stars, Red, White, 67 x 80 In.	440.00
Patchwork, American Flag Center, White Ground, Pink Binding, 79 1/2 x 66 1/2 In.	690.00
Patchwork, Benjamin Harrison, Protection, 1880, 69 x 83 In. ....*Illus*	4600.00
Patchwork, Blue, White, Blue Border, Crib, 38 x 46 In.	82.00
Patchwork, Bowtie, Navy, White Binding, 70 x 88 In.	275.00
Patchwork, Central Snowflake, Sawtooth Border, Cotton, 20th Century, 87 x 87 In.	165.00
Patchwork, Chimney Sweep, Hand Stitched, White Ground, 66 1/2 x 79 1/2 In.	165.00
Patchwork, Double Irish Chain, Sawtooth Border, Yellow Green Calico, 80 x 92 In.	180.00
Patchwork, Flower Garden, Multicolored Print, White Ground, 78 x 90 In.	192.00
Patchwork, Flying Geese, Goldenrod Grid, Feather Quilting, 82 1/2 x 82 1/2 In.	302.00
Patchwork, Grandfather, Dancing Tortoise, Man With Violin, c.1875, 88 x 90 In.	2200.00
Patchwork, Green Calico, Red Binding, 84 x 84 In.	770.00
Patchwork, Hearts & Gizzards, Surround Of Feather Circles, c.1910, 70 x 87 In.	220.00
Patchwork, Irish Chain, White Ground, Initials CK, 79 x 79 In.	605.00
Patchwork, Kansas Sunflower, Calico, 1883, 88 1/4 x 88 1/4 In.	1840.00
Patchwork, Log Cabin, Silk, 19th Century, 73 2/3 x 74 1/3 In.	230.00
Patchwork, Lone Star, 96 x 96 In.	1200.00
Patchwork, Maltese Cross Medallions, 66 x 84 In.	247.00
Patchwork, Multicolored Stars, White Squares, Red Calico Ground, 92 x 108 In.	440.00
Patchwork, Ocean Waves, Navy & White, Appliqued Border, 70 x 80 In.	275.00
Patchwork, Philadelphia Centennial Handkerchiefs, 76 x 84 In.	3500.00
Patchwork, Pinwheels, Pink, Multicolored Ground, 74 x 84 In.	55.00
Patchwork, Red, White & Blue Calico, Gingham Homespun Back, 72 x 72 In.	110.00
Patchwork, Red, White & Blue Flag, 1940, 89 1/2 x 62 3/4 In.	4125.00

Patchwork, Red, White & Blue, Flag Form, White Border, 73 x 83 1/2 In.	3680.00
Patchwork, Reverse Geometric Design, Pink & Gold Cotton Crepe, 73 x 73 In.	165.00
Patchwork, Rolling Stone, Multicolored, 88 x 88 In.	395.00
Patchwork, Scenes From Treasure Island, 24 Squares, Blue Binding, 63 x 43 In.	805.00
Patchwork, Soldier, Abstract Floral Landscape, Red, White Border, 88 x 74 1/2 In.	575.00
Patchwork, Star Of Bethlehem, Pink, Red, Blue, Green, 1845, 46 1/4 x 47 1/2 In.	2530.00
Patchwork, Star Of Bethlehem, Polychrome Patches, White Ground, 75 x 75 In.	385.00
Patchwork, Stars & Circles, Red, Grayish Blue & White, Polka Dots, 86 x 96 In.	247.00
Patchwork, Stylized Floral Medallions, Teal, Yellow Ground, Vine Border, 84 x 84 In. . .	247.50
Patchwork, Variation Of Old Maids, Rose Ground, 66 x 83 1/2 In.	192.00
Patchwork, Victorian Home Surrounded By Abstract Flowers, Red, Black, 86 x 78 In. . .	575.00
Patchwork & Appliqued, Bar Pattern, American Flags, Stars, 1920, 84 x 77 In.	805.00
Patchwork & Appliqued, Bar Pattern, Centennial, 1876, 75 x 55 In. . . . . *Illus*	4600.00
Patchwork & Appliqued, Star Of Bethlehem, 1865, 75 x 74 In. . . . . *Illus*	3450.00
Trapunto, Feather Wreaths Alternate With Wavy Lines, 72 x 76 In.	495.00
Trapunto, Rose & Wreath, Eagles, Penna., 1885, 81 x 82 In. . . . . *Illus*	1495.00
Trapunto, Wreath, Floral Center, All White, Crib, 31 x 42 In.	170.00

QUIMPER pottery has a long history. Tin-glazed, hand-painted pottery has been made in Quimper, France, since the late seventeenth century. The earliest firm, founded in 1685 by Jean Baptiste Bousquet, was known as HB Quimper. Another firm, founded in 1772 by Francois Eloury, was known as Porquier. The third firm, founded by Guillaume Dumaine in 1778, was known as HR or Henriot Quimper. All three firms made similar pottery decorated with designs of Breton peasants and sea and flower motifs. The Eloury (Porquier) and Dumaine (Henriot) firms merged in 1913. Bousquet (HB) merged with the others in 1968. The group was sold to a United States family in 1984. The American holding company is Quimper Faience Inc., located in Stonington, Connecticut. The French firm has been called Societe Nouvelle des Faienceries de Quimper HB Henriot since March 1984.

Bowl, Man, Scalloped Edge, 10 1/2 In.	200.00
Bowl, Peasant, Yellow	95.00
Butter Chip, Man In Center	55.00
Candlestick, Blue & Maroon Floral, Marked, 8 3/4 In., Pair	99.00
Charger, Woman Design, Scalloped Edge, 13 In.	200.00
Coffeepot, Woman Design, 10 In.	209.00
Demitasse Set, Cup & Saucer, Sugar, Cover, Floral, Marked, 8 Piece	550.00
Dish, Breton Peasant, Handle, Green Glaze, Scalloped Rim, 10 In.	195.00
Fish Set, Sponge Design, Wildflower Center, Platter & 12 Matching Plates, Signed	2200.00
Inkstand, Man, Orange Border, 2 Wells, Marked, 5 3/4 x 4 In. . . . . *Illus*	230.00
Inkwell, Blue & White, Square, Marked, 3 1/2 In.	110.00
Jug, Puzzle	145.00
Lavabo, Floral Design, Covered Dispenser, Yellow Ground, Marked, 3 Piece	245.00
Pin Tray, Couple, Salmon Leaf Border, 6 3/4 x 4 3/8 In.	110.00
Pitcher, Figural, Man Lighting Pipe, Signed, 8 In.	300.00
Pitcher, Man With Walking Stick, 8 In.	85.00
Pitcher, Woman Design, 6 1/2 In.	187.00
Plaque, Floral Center Medallion, Scallop Shell Shape, 6 In.	28.00
Plate, Breton Views, Scalloped Border, Marked, 9 1/2 In., 4 Piece	1705.00
Plate, Breton Woman, 9 In.	75.00
Plate, Man Design, Red, 8 1/4 x 8 1/2 In.	230.00
Platter, Fish, Peasant Couple, 23 x 11 1/2 In.	350.00
Platter, Peasant, 16 In.	175.00
Platter, Scalloped Edge, Salmon, Yellow Band Border, 13 x 8 1/2 In.	209.00
Platter, Woman Design, Scalloped Edge, 11 1/4 In.	88.00
Salt, Double, Figural, Woman Holding Salts, c.1877	180.00
Salt, Open, Pair Of Dutch Shoes	30.00
Soup, Dish, Cover, Breton Views, Attached Plate, Scalloped Finial, 5 x 6 3/4 In.	495.00
Teapot, Bird, Yellow, 5 1/2 In.	450.00
Teapot, Breton Man & Woman, Marked, 6 In. . . . . *Illus*	286.00
Teapot, Cover, Breton Woman, Marked, 8 1/4 In.	198.00
Tile, Man, Yellow, Blue Border, 6 x 6 In.	104.50

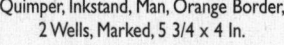

Quimper, Inkstand, Man, Orange Border,
2 Wells, Marked, 5 3/4 x 4 In.

Quimper, Teapot, Breton Man & Woman,
Marked, 6 In.

Tray, Man, Scalloped Edge, Oval, 4 3/4 In. 143.00
Vase, Floral Design, Blue-Green Bands, 6 1/2 In. 88.00
Vase, Man, Striped Pants, 2 Handles, 8 In. 225.00
Wall Pocket, Floral, 6 In. 65.00
Wall Pocket, Woman Figure, 9 3/4 In. 99.00

RADFORD pottery was made by Alfred Radford in Broadway, Virginia, Tiffin and Zanesville, Ohio, and Clarksburg, West Virginia, from 1891 until 1912. Jasperware, Ruko, Thera, Radura, and Velvety Art Ware were made. The jasperware resembles the famous Wedgwood ware of the same name.

RADURA.

Flask, Jasperware, White, Washington & Eagle, 1903, 7 In., Pair 400.00

RADIO broadcast receiving sets were first sold in New York City in 1910. They were used to pick up the experimental broadcasts of the day. The first commercial radios were made by Westinghouse Company for listeners of the experimental shows on KDKA Pittsburgh in 1920. Collectors today are interested in all early radios, especially those made of Bakelite plastic or decorated with blue mirrors. Figural advertising radios and transistor radios are also collected.

Addison, Catalin, Model 5E, Black Marbled, Vertical Grill Bar 1400.00
Addison, Model 5, Catalin, Marbleized, Black, Yellow, Vertical Grill Bar 1400.00
Admiral, AM Clock Radio, White Plastic Case, 1950, 11 x 6 x 4 In. 53.00
Advertising, Amoco, Silver, Red, Blue, White, Gold, Earphone In Box, 4 1/4 x 2 1/2 In. . 77.00
Advertising, Charlie Tuna, Star Kist, Figural . . . . .35.00 to 150.00
Advertising, Delco Battery, Plastic, Figural, 1960s 65.00
Advertising, Pabst, Beer Can, Figural 28.00
Advertising, Pratt & Lambert, Paint Can, Figural 25.00
Advertising, Ritz Crackers, Cathedral Type, c.1991 . . . . 40.00
Advertising, Tony The Tiger, Kellogg's, Figural, 1980 .35.00 to 48.00
Advertising, Woolite, Bottle Shape 55.00
Atlas, Battery, Figural 55.00
Atwater Kent, Model 10, Battery, 3 Dials, 1923 . . . . 990.00
Bulova, Art Deco, AM 45.00
Crosley, Amplifier, Black Front, Lift Top 412.50
Edison, Cathedral 350.00
Emerson, Tombstone, Table, 7 x 11 In. 105.00
Essentials, Push Button, 2 Dials, Maroon, 1940s, Table Model 125.00
Fada, Bullet, Maroon Catalin, 6 In. 805.00
Fada, Bullet, Red & Gold Catalin, Plastic, Table Model 935.00
Fada, Cloud, Red Knobs & Handle 750.00
Figural, Mork, Egg, Box 60.00
Figural, Peanut, Jimmy Carter, Box 40.00
Figural, Snoopy . . . . .20.00 to 25.00
Figural, Tune-A-Rabbit 30.00
Freshman, Masterpiece, With Tubes, 1925 . . . . 95.00
Galaxy, Transistor, Box 14.50

Ghostbusters, Blue, Symbol With Ghost 18.00
Karola, Coin-Operated, Wood & Metal, 25 Cents For 2 Hours 135.00
Kensington, Transistor, Globe 85.00
Lectrolab, Kit, 1959 . . . . 45.00
Majestic, Transistor 50.00
Marc, Art Deco, Globe Shape 115.00
Micronic, Ruby, Transistor 75.00
Motorola, AM Clock Radio, Beige Plastic Case, 1960, 11 x 6 x 4 In. 23.00
Muppets 5.00
Norelco, Kit, 1959 . . . . 45.00
Ozarka, Model Senior S-1 . . . . 27.50
Panasonic, Home Stereo Console Shape, 1950, Midget 35.00
Philco, Brown Bakelite, c.1950 . . . . 45.00
Philco, Chair Side, Art Deco Styling, Walnut, 15 x 24 1/2 In. 242.00
Philco, Model 500, Transistor 68.00
Philco, Model 511, c.1928 . . . . 11.00
Philco, Model C584, White, Black Grill 33.00
Philmore, Crystal Set . . . . .85.00 to 95.00
RCA Victor, Beehive, Arched Top 275.00
Scott, 26 Tubes, Phonograph In Chassis, 1937 . . . . 1595.00
Sentinel, No. 286PR, Portable 55.00
Silvertone, Beetle, Plastic 200.00
Silvertone, Model 4-233, Cowboy Design, Gun Pointer 275.00
Skyrover, Bakelite, Black, 4 x 7 In. 42.00
Solex, 5 Tubes, Guaranty Card, Dated 1925 . . . . 300.00
Sparton, Equasonne 340.00
Stewart-Warner, Marbleized Bakelite Casing, Knobs, Sonora Magic Antenna, 7 In. 11.50
Stromberg-Carlson, Black Front, Lift-Top, Art Deco 440.00
Sunoco Gas Pump, Transistor, 9 In., Box . . . . .100.00 to 125.00
Trav-Ler, Table Model, Burgundy Finish, 6 1/2 x 10 In. 35.00
Ward, Model 48, 6 Tubes, Friedman Unit 286.00
Washing Machine, Transistor, Box . . . . .70.00 to 75.00
Westinghouse, Model 26, Refrigerator Style 70.00
Westinghouse, Refrigerator Style, Bakelite, 1940s 150.00
Westinghouse, Tombstone, Restored 120.00
Zenith, Console 76, Inlaid Burl Banding, Black With Silver Accents 880.00
Zenith, FM, Bakelite, 1940s 55.00
Zenith, Model H-500, Trans-Oceanic . . . . .75.00 to 150.00
Zenith, Plastic, Gray, Flip Front, 1950s 45.00
Zenith, Win Charger, Wooden Blades, Roof To Battery Generator 440.00
Zephyr, Model AR-600, Case . . . . .100.00 to 135.00

RAILROAD enthusiasts collect any train memorabilia. Everything is
wanted, from oilcans to whole train cars. The Chessie system has
a store that sells many reproductions of their old dinnerware and
uniforms.

Ashtray, Denver, Black 110.00
Ashtray, Denver, Maroon 110.00
Ashtray, Northwestern, Cast Iron Base, Shaft, 26 In. 92.00
Bell, Locomotive, Yoke, Bronze, c.1890 . . . . 1400.00
Bond, Oklahoma Central Railway Co., 1905 . . . . 145.00
Bond, St. Joseph & Denver City Railroad Co., Unissued, 1870 . . . . 220.00
Book, B & O RR, World's Fair, 1893 . . . . 20.00
Book, Union Pacific Rules & Regulations, 1946 . . . . 40.00
Book, Union Pacific, Supplement No. 1, 1952 . . . . 25.00
Brochure, Lewis & Clark Centennial Exposition, Great Northern Railway, 1905 . . . . . . 36.00
Butter Chip, Milwaukee Traveler 40.00
Calendar, 1946, Great Northern Railroad, Indian, Incomplete Pad, 33 x 16 In. 50.00
Card, Playing, Santa Fe Railroad 2.00
Card, Playing, Southern Pacific RR, 52 Different Scenes, Map, Box 45.00
Chair, Smoking Car, Mahogany, 1900 . . . . 450.00
Chimes, Dining Car 90.00

Cup & Saucer, Southern Pacific, Prairie Mountain Wildflowers 65.00
Handkerchief, Chessie Cat, Cotton, Unused 55.00
Hard Hat, Palapsco, Back River Railroad 20.00
Lantern, Atchison Topeka & Santa Fe, Red 175.00
Lantern, Bell Bottom, C & NW, Green Cast 1100.00
Lantern, Caboose, Interior Side, Dressel, No. 525, C & O, 1920, Pair 400.00
Lantern, Kerosene, Dietz Victor, Red Globe, 13 1/4 In. 137.50
Lantern, Missouri Pacific, Brakeman, Red Globe, Marked 95.00
Lantern, MO PAC, Classic Pattern, Bale Handle, Gold Paint, Marked, St. Louis, Handlan 43.00
Lantern, MO PAC, Tall 190.00
Lantern, Railroad Inspector's, 1880s 175.00
Lantern, Switching, Handlan, St. Louis, Green & Red Reflectors 145.00
Lock, Switch, Brass, Utah & Pacific, 1898 .... 250.00
Map, Atlantic Coast Line, 1950s, Large 150.00
Nameplate, Chrome, Rebuilt By Long Island RR Morris Park Shop, 3 x 8 In. 20.00
Paperweight, Union Pacific, Engine & Tender, 10 1/2 In. 285.00
Pass, Chicago & Alton RR Co., Signed By President, 1909 .... 10.00
Plate, Baltimore & Ohio, Harper's Ferry Centenary 60.00
Plate, Pennsylvania RR, Mt. Laurel, 9 1/2 In. 40.00
Plate, Southern Pacific, Prairie Mountain Wildflowers, 9 1/2 In. 65.00
Plate, Union Pacific, 10 1/2 In. 60.00
Plate, Union Pacific, Harriman, Blue, 9 In. 65.00
Postcard, Bennington, Vt., Railroad Station, Black & White, 1906 .... 6.00
Postcard, Chicago Railroad Fair, 1948 .... 20.00
Postcard, Union Depot, Cheyenne, Wy., Train Scene, Unused, 1914 .... 5.00
Ruler, Chicago & Northwestern, Streamliners On Back, Wooden, 15 In. 22.00
Stock Certificate, Erie Railroad, 1950s 15.00
Stock Certificate, Gulf Mobile-Northern, 1935 .... 23.00
Stock Certificate, With Vignette, Over 100 Years Old 7.00
Teapot, Atlantic Coast Lines, Silver 100.00
Ticket Book, Texas-Pacific Railway, Eagles Route, Streamliner 16.00
Timetable, Baltimore & Ohio Railroad, 1927 .... 38.00
Token, Union Pacific Streamliner, 1940 .... 6.00
Torch, Engineer's, Dayton, 1895 .... 125.00
Tumbler, Pennsylvania RR, Highball 22.00

RAZORS were used in ancient Egypt and subsequently wherever shaving was in fashion. The metal razor used in America until about 1870 was made in Sheffield, England. After 1870, machine-made hollow-ground razors were made in Germany or America. Plastic or bone handles were popular. The razor was often sold in a set of seven, one for each day of the week. The set was often kept by the barber who shaved the well-to-do man each day in the shop.

Ace, Straight, Celluloid Handle, Case 150.00
Blade, Bank, Barber Figure, Stand Or Wall Hung 95.00
Blade, Bank, Cleminson Man Shaving 30.00
Blade, Winchester, Package, 3 Piece 95.00
Cattaraugus, Green Lizard 75.00
Christy, Box 10.00
Curvfit, Pat. 1913, Box 30.00
Dixie, Straight, Celluloid Off-White Handle, Marked, Union City, Ga. 80.50
Eagle, Word Eagle Cast In Handle, Flags At Ends, Large 90.00
Fairy, Safety, Brand, Tin Holder 2200.00
Gem, Micromatic, Goldtone, Plastic Case 12.00
Joseph Rodgers, Straight, Translucent Horn Handle, Blade, Etched, Henry Clay 500.00
Keen Kutter, Safety, Bakelite Handle, Box 40.00
Keen Kutter, Straight, Box 50.00
Minute Man, Straight 65.00
Star, Safety, Tin 160.00
Straight, 1893 Chicago Exposition Etched On Blade 100.00
Straight, Castle & Sailboat On Handle 95.00
Straight, Horn Handle, Gilt Label, Original Pipe Razor, Wooden Case, 8 In. 50.00
Straight, Ornate Gold Filled Handle 225.00

Straight, Set, Leather Case, 7 Day	275.00
Straight, Sterling Silver	275.00
Wilkinson, Straight, Single Edge, Wooden Box	85.00
Winchester, No. 8425	145.00
Winchester, Straight, Silver End Caps	95.00

REAMERS, or juice squeezers, have been known since 1767, although most of those collected today date from the twentieth century. Figural reamers are among the most prized.

Bird, Porcelain, Japan, 5 3/4 x 3 1/4 In. ....*Illus*	35.00
Blue Glass, 8 1/2 In.	18.00
Cambridge, Green	200.00
Clown, 8 In.	175.00
Clown, Cobalt Blue, 6 1/2 In.	160.00
Clown, Navy & Caramel, Medium, 8 In.	95.00
Clown, Painted	45.00
Clown, Pastel Colors, 8 In.	125.00
Clown, With Pitcher Set, Teal	85.00
Crisscross, Hazel Atlas, Cobalt Blue	245.00
Crisscross, Hazel Atlas, Large	10.00
Crisscross, Large	32.00
Crisscross, Lemon, Pink	325.00
Crisscross, Orange, Blue	375.00
Crisscross, Orange, Pink	275.00
Dazey Churn Co., Aluminum, Wooden Knob, Wall Mounted	17.00
Green & White, Shelley, 2 Piece	175.00
Hazel-Atlas, Cobalt Blue	200.00
Jadite	12.00
Jeanette, Pink	80.00
Jennyware, Jeanette Glass	120.00
Jennyware, Ultramarine	145.00
Lemon, Arcade	40.00
Lemon, Iron	20.00
Lemon, Wooden, 19th Century, 5 3/4 In.	195.00
Pelican, 2 Piece	145.00
Puddinhead	275.00
Sunkist, Black	800.00
Sunkist, Carmel	400.00
Sunkist, Chaline, Blue	275.00
Sunkist, Crown Tuscan	400.00
Sunkist, Custard	65.00
Sunkist, Green Milk Glass	25.00
Sunkist, Jadite	65.00
Sunkist, Light Gray	295.00
Sunkist, McKee	70.00
Sunkist, Tab Handle, Cobalt Blue	300.00

Reamer, Bird, Porcelain, Japan,
5 3/4 x 3 1/4 In.

For emergency repairs to chipped pottery, try coloring the spot with a wax crayon or oil paint. It will look a little better.

Sunkist, White Milk Glass . . . . .12.00 to 20.00
Wagner 65.00

RECORDS have changed size and shape through the years. The cylinder-shaped phonograph record for use with the early Edison models was made about 1889. Disc records were first made by 1894, the double-sided disc by 1904. High-fidelity records were first issued in 1944, the first vinyl disc in 1946, the first stereo record in 1958. The 78 RPM became the standard in 1926 but was discontinued in 1957. In 1932, the first 33 1/3 RPM was made but was not sold commercially until 1948. In 1949, the 45 RPM was introduced. Compact discs became available in the U.S. in 1982 and many companies began phasing out the production of phonograph records.

Advertising, General Electric, $25,000, Cash Press TV Service, 1940 . . . . 40.00
Album, A Rockin' Good Way, Priscilla Brown 40.00
Album, Best Of Elton John 10.00
Album, Bobby Rydell's Biggest Hits, Cameo, 33 1/3 RPM, 1960-1961 . . . . 18.00
Album, Captain Kangaroo, Peter & The Wolf, 33 1/3 RPM, Everest, 1960 . . . . 10.00
Album, Dr. Kildare, Richard Chamberlain Sings, 33 1/3 RPM, MGM, 1962 . . . . 8.00
Album, Drop By, Metallics 50.00
Album, Grateful Dead, The Music Never Stops, Rick Griffen, 1975 . . . . 25.00
Album, Hell Bent For Leather, Frankie Laine, Columbia, 1963 . . . . 8.00
Album, Judy In Love, Judy Garland, Capitol, 33 1/3 RPM, 1961 . . . . 8.00
Album, Lonely Island, Parliaments 200.00
Album, Marilyn Monroe 45.00
Album, McDonald's McRhythm, Negro College Fund, 33 1/3 RPM, 1985 . . . . 15.00
Album, My Plea For Love, Starlings 100.00
Album, My Son, The Nut, Allan Sherman, Warner Brothers, 33 1/3 RPM, 1963 . . . . . 15.00
Album, Punch & Judy, Twinkle Records, 1950s 5.00
Album, Richard Diamond TV Detective Series, 33 1/3 RPM, Mercury, 1959 . . . . 25.00
Album, Songs From Winnie The Pooh, 33 1/3 RPM, 1960s 10.00
Album, The Men In My Little Girl's Life, Mike Douglas, Epic, 1965 . . . . 8.00
Album, Thunderball, James Bond, Soundtrack, United Artists, 1965 . . . . .12.00 to 15.00
Album, Victory At Sea, Soundtrack, Spin-O-Rama, 1952 . . . . 10.00
Breaking In, Blues Burglars 12.00
Dionne & Friends, Picture Sleeve, 1985 . . . . 10.00
Elvis Presley, G.I. Blue 15.00
Elvis Presley, Roustabout 55.00
Great Radio Comedians, Original Broadcasts, 1976, 5 Records 70.00
Little Toot, 78 RPM, Story 55.00
MAD Magazine, Meet The Staff Of MAD 20.00
New Morning, Bob Dylan 10.00
Oh Mother Of Mine, Temptations 50.00
Queen Mary & King George V, Message To Girls & Boys Of British Empire, 78 RPM . 500.00
Radtzky March, Strauss, Needle Included, Black & White 30.00
Subterranean Homesick Blues, Bob Dylan 50.00
Swing Low, Sweet Spiritual, Jack Teargarden 200.00
Uncle Remus, 78 RPM, 1947 . . . . 65.00
Wagon Train Theme, Ward Bond Photograph, 45 RPM 20.00
Who's On First, Abbott & Costello, Nestle's Premium, Illustrated, Square, 7 1/2 In. 37.00

RED WING Pottery of Red Wing, Minnesota, was a firm started in 1878. The company first made utilitarian pottery. In the 1920s art pottery was made. Many dinner sets and vases were made before the company closed in 1967. Rumrill pottery was made for George Rumrill by the Red Wing Pottery and other firms. It was sold in the 1930s. For more information, see *Kovels' Depression Glass & American Dinnerware Price List.*

Ashtray, Fish 125.00
Ashtray, Maroon 395.00
Ashtray, Mosaic Tile 20.00
Ashtray, Pelican 75.00
Banana Boat, Purple 65.00

Bank, Hamm's Bear 575.00
Bean Pot, 1/2 Gal. 135.00
Bean Pot, Brown Glaze Top, Bail Handle, Red Wing Union Stoneware, 1 Qt. 50.00
Beverage Server, Bob White, 15 In. ....95.00 to 120.00
Bowl, Brittany, 5 In. 8.00
Bowl, Cobalt Blue, 10 1/2 In. 100.00
Bowl, Cover, Roundup Handles, Side Pour 95.00
Bowl, Fruit, Bob White 8.00
Bowl, Gray Line, Panel 75.00
Bowl, Leaf Design, Brown, Chartreuse, 11 In. 25.00
Bowl, Lotus, 8 1/2 In. 9.00
Bowl, Lute Song, 5 x 11 In. 25.00
Bowl, Magnolia, 5 In. 5.00
Bowl, Marmite, Cover, Village Green 8.00
Bowl, RoundUp, 5 1/2 In. 30.00
Bowl, Salad, Anniversary 45.00
Bowl, Salad, Bob White, 12 In. 50.00
Bowl, Salad, Tampico, 12 In. 75.00
Bowl, Salad, Town & Country, Honey Beige, 13 In. 125.00
Bowl, Vegetable, Crazy Rhythm 25.00
Bowl, Vegetable, Crazy Rhythm, Divided 40.00
Bowl, Vegetable, Lute Song, 5 In. 11.00
Bread Plate, RoundUp 150.00
Butter, Cover, Bob White, 1/4 Lb. 70.00
Butter, Cover, Brocade 15.00
Butter, Cover, Lute Song 48.00
Butter, Cover, RoundUp ....95.00 to 275.00
Butter Warmer, Cover, Bob White, 1/4 Lb. ....35.00 to 95.00
Carafe, Bob White 195.00
Casserole, Bob White, 2 Qt. 40.00
Casserole, Bob White, 4 Qt. ....50.00 to 52.00
Casserole, Cover, Bob White, 2 Qt. 45.00
Casserole, Cover, Smart Set, 2 Qt. 70.00
Casserole, Cover, Village Green 20.00
Celery Dish, Flight 175.00
Chicken Waterer, Eureka, 24 In. 195.00
Chop Plate, Salamina, 12 In. 265.00
Churn, Complete, 3 Gal. 525.00
Console, Deer, Eggshell Ivory, Brown, 2 Piece ....55.00 to 65.00
Cookie Jar, Bob White ....60.00 to 100.00
Cookie Jar, Chef Pierre, Blue 100.00
Cookie Jar, Chef Pierre, Yellow 185.00
Cookie Jar, Cover, King Of Tarts ....535.00 to 775.00
Cookie Jar, Drummer Boy 950.00
Cookie Jar, Dutch People, Dark Brown 75.00
Cookie Jar, Grapes, Green 275.00
Cookie Jar, Gypsy Trail, Red, 8 In. 195.00
Cookie Jar, Happy The Children 350.00
Cookie Jar, Jack Frost 495.00
Cookie Jar, Katrina, Green 350.00
Cracker Jar, Saffron 600.00
Creamer, Bob White 20.00
Creamer, Crazy Rhythm 20.00
Creamer, Tampico 25.00
Crock, Birch Leaves, Union Oval Bottom, Minnesota Stoneware Co., 4 Gal. 60.00
Crock, Cover, Wing, 6 Gal. 160.00
Crock, Double P, Salt Glaze, 3 Gal. 75.00
Crock, Wing, 6 Gal. 35.00
Cruet, Bob White 30.00
Cup, RoundUp 25.00
Cup & Saucer, Bob White ....10.00 to 25.00
Cup & Saucer, Brittany 9.00
Cup & Saucer, RoundUp 40.00

Cuspidor, Blue Spongeware 2750.00
Dish, Feeding, Clown, Blue, Hankscraft, 3 1/2 x 9 In. 75.00
Ewer, Black Leaves, Orange Gloss, Stamped, 14 In. 95.00
Figurine, Chef, Blue 100.00
Figurine, Cowboy & Cowgirl, Pair 495.00
Figurine, Man, With Derby, Crackle 175.00
Figurine, Oriental Man, Green, 9 1/2 In. 55.00
Flower Frog, Deer 90.00
Flower Frog, Fawn, 10 In. 30.00
Gravy Boat, Cover, Bob White 55.00
Gravy Boat, Magnolia, Ivory, Chartreuse Interior, Attached Liner 10.00
Gravy Boat, Tampico 40.00
Gravy Boat, Underplate, Tampico 60.00
Jug, Beehive, 5 Gal. . . . . .200.00 to 295.00
Jug, Beehive, Birch Leaves, 5 Gal. 310.00
Jug, Bob White, 60 Oz. 45.00
Jug, Fry's Hotel, Mineral Springs, Colfax, Iowa, 5 Gal. . . . .*Illus* 2860.00
Jug, Michigan-Minnesota, Who Will Win, Miniature 230.00
Jug, Small Wing, 5 Gal. 35.00
Lazy Susan, Bob White, 5 Piece 125.00
Mug, Bob White 80.00
Mug, Child's, Clown, Blue 20.00
Mug, Coffee, Village Green, 5 In. 10.00
Nut Bowl, Tampico, 5 Sections 125.00
Pitcher, Batter, Monk, Harp, Blue 250.00
Pitcher, Batter, Orange 25.00
Pitcher, Black Florals, Orange Ground, Handle, Marked, 9 In. 60.00
Pitcher, Bob White, 112 Oz. . . . . .25.00 to 60.00
Pitcher, Bob White, 6 3/4 In. 16.00
Pitcher, Bob White, 60 Oz. . . . . .38.00 to 60.00
Pitcher, Castle, Blue & Gray, 8 In. 195.00
Pitcher, Cherry Band, 2 Pt. 350.00
Pitcher, Cherry Band, 4 Pt. 160.00
Pitcher, Cherry Band, 6 Pt. 700.00
Pitcher, RoundUp, 12 In. . . . . .185.00 to 250.00
Pitcher, Tampico 90.00
Pitcher, Village Green, 7 In. 20.00
Planter, Flared, White Glaze, 5 In. 10.00
Planter, Leaf Design, Brushed Ware, 9 In. 45.00
Planter, Pink & Gray, Sticker 25.00
Planter, Seal, Blue 45.00
Planter, Swan, Matte White, Label 40.00
Plate, Blossom Time, 10 1/2 In. 5.00
Plate, Bob White, 6 1/2 In. . . . . .6.00 to 8.00
Plate, Bob White, 10 1/2 In. . . . . .10.00 to 14.00
Plate, Capistrano 10.00
Plate, Chuckwagon, 11 In. 80.00
Plate, Lotus, 4 1/4 In. 4.00

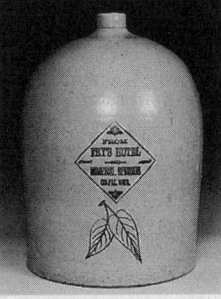

Red Wing, Jug,
Fry's Hotel,
Mineral Springs,
Colfax, Iowa,
5 Gal.

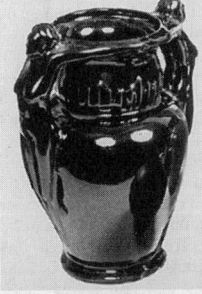

Red Wing, Vase,
Athenian Nude
Handles,
Cobalt Blue,
11 In.

Plate, Lotus, 10 1/2 In.	6.00
Plate, Lute Song, 7 In.	9.00
Plate, Random Harvest, Label	27.00
Plate, Tampico, 10 1/2 In.	12.00
Platter, Bob White, 13 In.	18.00 to 90.00
Platter, Bob White, 20 In.	100.00
Platter, Crazy Rhythm, 13 In.	30.00
Platter, Lotus, 12 3/4 In.	10.00
Platter, Tampico, 15 In.	90.00
Platter, Town & Country, Blue	75.00
Reamer, Gray Line	895.00
Relish, Bob White, 3 Sections	55.00
Relish, Chaps Shape	125.00
Salt, Hanging, Gray Line	1950.00
Salt & Pepper, Bob White	50.00
Salt & Pepper, Bob White, Bird Shape	32.00
Salt & Pepper, Bob White, Hourglass Shape, 6 In.	25.00
Salt & Pepper, Red Ice, Rumrill	20.00
Salt & Pepper, RoundUp	75.00
Salt & Pepper, Town & Country, Metallic Brown	80.00
Salt & Pepper, Village Green	15.00
Saucer, Lute Song	3.00
Service For 8, Lotus, 71 Piece	575.00
Sugar, Cover, Lotus	7.00
Sugar, Cover, Morning Glory	4.00
Sugar, Crazy Rhythm	20.00
Sugar & Creamer, Cover, Bob White	40.00
Sugar & Creamer, Cover, Smart Set	87.00
Sugar & Creamer, Lute Song	10.00
Syrup, Cover, Orange	18.00
Syrup, Town & Country, Blue	65.00 to 75.00
Teapot, Bob White	75.00
Teapot, Bob White, Stand	95.00 to 120.00
Teapot, Cover, Lady, Figural, Green	140.00
Teapot, Stand	140.00
Teapot, Town & Country, Blue	200.00
Tidbit, Normandy, 2 Tiers	10.00
Toothpick, Swan	45.00
Tray, Cocktail, Bob White	40.00
Tray, French Bread, Bob White, 24 In.	100.00
Tray, Home Plate Shape, All Star Home Baseball Game, 1965	250.00
Trivet, Minnesota Centennial, Tan Fleck	48.00 to 70.00
Vase, 2 Nudes In Sun, 11 In.	225.00
Vase, Antique Ivory, 8 In.	35.00 to 45.00
Vase, Athenian Nude Handles, Cobalt Blue, 11 In.	*Illus* 2900.00
Vase, Bronze, Green Interior	30.00
Vase, Brown Scalloped, Crystal Patina, 5 x 4 In.	60.00
Vase, Cornucopia, No. 1097, 5 In.	40.00
Vase, Fan, Camark, Maroon, Large	35.00
Vase, Fan, Shell, Ivory, 8 In.	50.00
Vase, Green & Tan, 2 Handles, Ink Mark, 7 In.	16.00
Vase, Green, Brushed Ware, 15 In.	125.00
Vase, Green, High Glaze, 12 x 12 In.	125.00
Vase, Ivory, Light Green Interior, 8 1/2 In.	125.00
Vase, Magnolia, 22 x 7 In.	265.00
Vase, Matte Green Leaves, Acorns, Union Stoneware	120.00
Vase, Pink, No. 1161, 9 In.	95.00
Vase, Ribbed, Stoneware, No. 637, 9 In.	145.00
Vase, Roses, 8 1/2 In.	30.00
Vase, Star, 10 In.	65.00
Vase, Trumpet, Turquoise, 9 In.	40.00
Vase, Yellow Panels, Tree Branch Design, Mocha, Ink Stamp, 12 In.	95.00
Wall Pocket, Rooster, Roses	90.00

Wall Pocket, Violin, Green	27.00
Wall Pocket, Violin, Pink	27.00
Wall Pocket, Violin, White	27.00
Water Cooler, Bob White, 2 Gal.	800.00
Water Cooler, Cover, Schoolhouse Type, 5 Gal.	500.00

REDWARE is a hard, red stoneware that originated in the late 1600s and continues to be made. The term is also used to describe any common clay pottery that is reddish in color.

Bank, Slip Designed Bird Top, Dorothy Long, 1985, 6 1/2 In.	65.00
Bank, Spaniel, Seated, Brown, Green & Orange Glazed, 1875, 6 1/2 In.	920.00
Basin, Shaving, Wheel-Thrown Form, 1790, 9 In.	995.00
Bowl, Agate Glaze, 19th Century, 14 1/2 In.	980.00
Bowl, Cover, Beaded, Brown Flecked, Applied Rope Twist Handles, 5 5/8 In.	205.00
Bowl, Fruit, Pierced, 1835	4200.00
Bowl, Glazed, Brown Incised Design Shoulders, 19th Century, 4 x 7 3/4 In.	345.00
Bowl, Mottled Brown Glaze, Strap Handles, 2 1/2 x 5 1/2 In.	175.00
Bowl, Sponged Design, Yellow, Green & Brown, 12 In.	375.00
Bowl, Squiggle Design Edges, Divided, 1840s, 12 3/4 x 10 1/4 In.	195.00
Bowl, Wavy Lines, Lehigh County, 8 In.	315.00
Canister, Tea, Agate, Dimpled Panels, Square, 4 In.	690.00
Chamberstick, Brown Glaze, Made By I.S. Stahl, 1938, 7 In.	27.00
Charger, Coggled Rim, Penna., 13 1/2 In.	275.00
Charger, Man On Horseback Center, Sgraffito Design, Dated 1714, 14 In.	2587.00
Charger, Pumpkin Color, Octagonal, 10 1/2 In.	125.00
Charger, Yellow Slip Ware, 15 1/2 x 9 1/2 In.	450.00
Coffeepot, Engine Turned Body, 1765, 9 In.	1400.00
Creamer, Strap Handle, 3 1/2 In.	198.00
Crock, Brown Glazed, Incised Line & Swag Shoulders, 19th Century, 8 1/2 In.	345.00
Crock, Green Glaze, Everted Rim, Shoulder Design, 19th Century, 7 In.	575.00
Crock, Jasper Gibbs, 1830-1850, 14 In.	695.00
Cup, Strap Handle, Incised J., 1850, 3 1/4 In.	160.00
Cuspidor	500.00
Custard Cup, Pair	75.00
Dish, Dark Glaze, Yellow Slip Spots, 7 5/8 In.	275.00
Dish, Loaf, Sgraffito Design Of Shrub In Urn, Birds, 1878	850.00
Dish, Loaf, Yellow Slip Ware, Beaded Rim, 19th Century, 18 x 11 In.	1100.00
Dish, Yellow Slip Ware Design, 8 In.	190.00
Figurine, Blacksmith, Fashioning Horseshoe On Anvil, 20th Century, 8 In.	258.00
Figurine, Cat, Seated, Brown & White Glazed, 19th Century, 2 3/4 In.	175.00
Figurine, Cat, Yellow Glass Eyes, Black Glaze, Impressed Mark, 10 7/8 In.	105.00
Figurine, Dog, Standing, Incised Coat, Brown & Yellow Glazed, 4 1/2 In.	2760.00
Flask, 2-Tone Brown Glaze, 6 3/8 In.	110.00
Inkwell, Grayish Glaze, 4 3/8 In.	83.00
Jar, Apple Butter, Tapered, Mottled Amber & Brown Glaze, Applied Strap Handle, 6 In.	125.00
Jar, Coffee, 2 Handles, 1792, 14 1/2 x 34 1/2 In.	605.00
Jar, Egg Shape	90.00
Jar, Green Glaze, Orange, 8 1/4 In.	220.00
Jar, Lamp Mounted, Incised Lines, Clear Glaze, Brown Splotches, Base, Shade, 23 In.	265.00
Jar, Mottled Glaze, 19th Century, Samuel Bell & Sons, 7 1/4 In.	690.00
Jar, Orange Glaze, Brown Splotches, Applied Shoulder Handles, 9 3/4 In.	360.00
Jar, Preserve, Green Beige Glaze, Brown Flecks, Red Highlights, 6 1/4 In.	50.00
Jar, Relief Dragon, Cloud Design, 19th Century, 11 1/2 In.	55.00
Jar, S. Bell & Son, Stasburg, White Slip, Shenandoah, Egg Shape, 8 3/4 In.	300.00
Jar, Storage, Ear Handles, Early 19th Century, 9 1/2 In.	395.00
Jug, Brown Glaze, Applied Strap Handle, 1842, 14 1/2 In.	150.00
Jug, Brown Manganese	440.00
Jug, Brown, Amber Glaze, Strap Handle, Wavy Lines, 4 7/8 In.	165.00
Jug, Green, Orange Glaze, Brown Highlights, Strap Handle, 8 1/4 In.	165.00
Jug, Mottled Green & Orange Glaze, Strap Handle, 19th Century, 5 1/2 In.	405.00
Jug, Olive Green Glaze, Strap Handle, Orange Spots, Globular, 6 In.	138.00
Jug, Orange Glaze, Strap Handle, Brown, 5 3/4 In.	275.00
Mortar, Lead Glaze, Wooden Pestle, 7 In.	75.00

Mug, Frog, Inscribed Sup It Off, 6 In. 230.00
Pan, Loaf 1350.00
Pan, Milk, Marked, F.T. Wright & Son, Mass., 19th Century, 15 In. 86.00
Paperweight, Lion, 1860, 3 1/2 In. 450.00
Pie Plate, 3 Line Yellow Slip, Coggled Rim, 10 In. 220.00
Pie Plate, ABC, Yellow Slip, Coggled Rim, 11 1/4 In. 195.00
Pie Plate, Yellow Slip, Coggled Rim, 12 1/4 In. 300.00
Pie Plate, Yellow Slip, Coggled Rim, Wavy Line, 8 5/8 In. 175.00
Pitcher, Brown, Red & Green Glaze, 8 1/2 In. 390.00
Pitcher, Mottled Brown & Orange Glaze, Strap Handle, 19th Century, 6 1/2 In. 690.00
Pitcher, New Geneva, 9 In. 725.00
Plate, 3 Line Yellow Slip, Coggled Rim, 11 1/4 In. 440.00
Plate, Green Slip, 8 3/16 In. 760.00
Plate, LBD, 13 1/2 In. 805.00
Plate, Toddy, Light Amber Glaze, Dark Brown, 4 7/8 In. 165.00
Plate, Toddy, Orange Glaze, Brown Highlights, 6 3/8 In. 72.00
Plate, Yellow Slip, 8 In. ....200.00 to 450.00
Plate, Yellow Slip, 9 In. 295.00
Plate, Yellow Slip, 9 3/8 In. 490.00
Pot, Hand Thrown, White Slip Turned Gold, Applied Spout, 5 7/8 In. 750.00
Saucer, Yellow Slip, 4 In., 4 Piece 2185.00
Shaving Mug, Terra-Cotta, Yellow & Green Link Design Top 125.00
Stand, Pot, Incised Tulips & Hearts, Mottled Olive Green Glaze, 1830, 8 1/4 In. 1035.00
Teapot, Incised Leaf Design, Egg Shape, 18th Century, 9 In. 132.00

REGOUT, see Maastricht category.

RIDGWAY pottery has been made in the Staffordshire district in
England since 1808 by a series of companies with the name Ridgway.
The transfer-design dinner sets are the most widely known product.
They are still being made. Other pieces of Ridgway are listed under
Flow Blue.

Bone Dish, Dundee, Flow Blue 50.00
Cake Plate, Capitol Washington, Blue, 10 1/4 In. 1840.00
Creamer, Dundee, Flow Blue 150.00
Gravy Boat, Underplate, Brown Transfer, Boat, Birds Scene, 1860-1870 .... 53.00
Mug, Burns & Highland Mary, Copper Luster 60.00
Pitcher, Coaching Days, 4 x 3 In. 45.00
Pitcher, Coaching Days, 5 1/2 In. 65.00
Pitcher, Coaching Days, Handle, 4 In. 75.00
Plate, Beaufort, 10 In. 20.00
Plate, Coaching Days, 9 In. ....30.00 to 75.00
Plate, Dickens Characters, Pickwick, 9 In. ....30.00 to 45.00
Platter, Chinese, Flow Blue, Large 300.00
Platter, Estrella, Gold Trim, Crazing, 16 1/4 In. 40.00
Platter, Flow Blue, 1838, 19 1/4 x 16 In. 875.00
Platter, Osborne, Flow Blue, c.1905, 17 1/2 x 13 In. 60.00
Sugar, Cover, Flow Blue, Large 250.00
Sugar, Peking, Rosebud Finial, Flow Blue, 1845 .... 288.00
Tankard, Dickens Characters, Mr. Pickwick 135.00
Teapot, Flow Blue, Large 300.00
Teapot, Josephine, Flow Blue 495.00
Tureen, Gravy, Cover, Dark Blue, Handles, Floral Finial, 6 1/4 x 8 1/4 In. 660.00
Tureen, Gravy, Dark Blue, Handle, Ladle, 6 In. 355.00

RIFLES that are firearms are not listed in this book. BB guns and air rifles are listed in the Toy category.

RIVIERA dinnerware was made by the Homer Laughlin Co. of Newell,
West Virginia, from 1938 to 1950. The pattern was similar in coloring
and in mood to Fiesta and Harlequin. The Riviera plates and cup handles were square. For more information, see *Kovels' Depression Glass
& American Dinnerware Price List*.

COLONIAL

Bowl, Oatmeal, Green 85.00

Bowl, Utility, Ivory 40.00
Butter, Cover, Turquoise, 1/4 Lb. 150.00
Butter, Green, 1/4 Lb. 65.00
Casserole, Cover, Green 95.00
Casserole, Cover, Mauve 110.00
Casserole, Cover, Yellow 110.00
Casserole, Ivory 65.00
Casserole, Mauve 85.00
Creamer, Ivory 10.00
Cup, Tea, Blue 10.00
Cup & Saucer, Ivory, Demitasse 45.00
Jug, Batter, Cover, Green 160.00
Jug, Batter, Cover, Ivory 160.00
Pitcher, Juice, Mauve ....325.00 to 350.00
Pitcher, Juice, Yellow ....75.00 to 160.00
Plate, Green, 10 In. 95.00
Plate, Yellow, 10 In. 95.00
Platter, Mauve, 13 x 10 In. 25.00
Syrup, Cover, Ivory 125.00
Syrup, Cover, Red 150.00
Teapot, Yellow 150.00
Tumbler, Handle, Green 80.00
Tumbler, Handle, Ivory 270.00
Tumbler, Handle, Yellow 55.00

ROCKINGHAM, in the United States, is a pottery with a brown glaze that
resembles tortoiseshell. It was made from 1840 to 1900 by many
American potteries. Mottled brown Rockingham wares were first
made in England at the Rockingham factory. Other types of ceramics
were also made by the English firm. Related pieces may be listed in the
Bennington category.

Bank, Chest Of Drawers, Glazed, Mid-19th Century, 3 1/4 x 3 3/4 In. 145.00
Boiler, Milk, Rapp Bros., 3 1/2 In. 75.00
Bottle, Hand Shape, Cork In Longest Finger, 6 In. 105.00
Bowl, 7 1/2 In. 65.00
Bowl, 8 1/2 x 2 1/4 In. 60.00
Bowl, 9 1/2 In. 80.00
Creamer, Cow, Mid-19th Century, 5 1/2 In. 115.00
Creamer, Figural, Mr. Toby, Hat Forms Spout, 5 In. 95.00
Cuspidor, Faces On Side, 1890 .... 165.00
Cuspidor, Molded Eagles, 6 In. 60.00
Figurine, Bull Dog, Glass Eyes, England, 18 1/2 x 36 1/2 In. 1980.00
Figurine, Cat, Seated, Green Streaks, England, 13 3/4 In. 3300.00
Figurine, Dog, Recumbent, White, Brown Markings, England, c.1810, 1 1/4 In. 350.00
Figurine, Dog, Seated, Free Standing Front Legs, England, 9 3/4 In. 95.00
Figurine, Dog, Seated, Spaniel, Redware, England, 12 In. 250.00
Figurine, John Liston, White Ruffled Shirt, White Waistcoat, England, 1826, 6 In. 1495.00
Flask, Mermaid 265.00
Jar, Cover, Molded Peacocks, 6 1/2 In. 110.00
Jar, Cover, Molded Ribs, 8 3/8 In. 110.00
Jug, Blue Glaze, Marked, D.C. McNicol, 8 5/8 In. 300.00
Jug, J.A. Garfield, Bust, Mottled Brown Glaze, 7 1/2 In. 650.00
Mug, Ringed Rim, C-Scroll Handle, Mottled, 3 3/4 In. 45.00
Pie Plate, Brown 140.00
Pitcher, Hunt Scene Design, Hound Form Handle, 6 3/4 In. 35.00
Pitcher, Hunt Scene, 19th Century, 8 1/2 In. 175.00
Pitcher, Molded Deer, Variegated Glaze, 9 In. 190.00
Pitcher, Paneled, Mask Spout, Brown, Green, 9 In. 190.00
Teapot, Rebecca At The Well, 7 In. 165.00
Tobacco Jar, 7 1/2 In. 220.00
Tub, Molded Cherub Heads, Variegated Glaze, 4 x 6 3/8 In. 195.00
Whistle, Figural, Frog 50.00
Whistle, Figural, Poodle 50.00

ROGERS, see John Rogers category.

ROOKWOOD pottery was made in Cincinnati, Ohio, from 1880 to 1960. All of this art pottery is marked, most with the famous flame mark. The R is reversed and placed back to back with the letter P. Flames surround the letters. After 1900, a Roman numeral was added to the mark to indicate the year. The name and some of the molds were purchased in 1984. A few new pieces were made, but these were glazed in colors not used by the original company.

Ashtray, Boss Kerosene Ranges, Blue High Glaze, 1947, 6 In.	88.00
Ashtray, Clown, Sitting, Multicolored, Sara Alice Toohey, 1928	895.00
Ashtray, Clown, Yellow, Blue, Orange, Black, Purple Glaze, S. Toohey, 1928, 4 In.	385.00
Ashtray, Dark Green, Logo, 1949, 4 In.	180.00
Ashtray, Fish	50.00 to 90.00
Ashtray, Fox, Cream High Glaze, 1950, 7 In.	110.00
Ashtray, Frog On Corner, Triangular, Wax Matte	275.00
Ashtray, Frog Shape, White, Green Tinted Mouth, 1929, 3 1/4 In.	195.00
Ashtray, Gargoyle	300.00
Ashtray, Gunmetal Glaze, Square, 1957, 9 In.	66.00
Ashtray, Pelican, Gun Metal Black Glaze, Yellow Lined Mouth, 1930, 4 In.	385.00
Ashtray, Rook, Clover, Dated, 1949, 6 In.	450.00
Ashtray, Stylized Initial On Center, Tobacco Brown Matte Glaze, 1922, 5 In.	55.00
Ashtray, Turquoise, Square, 9 In.	70.00
Bookends, Blue Jay On Oak Leaves, With Acorns, Caramel Drip Glaze, 1925, 5 In.	330.00
Bookends, Dutch Boy & Girl, Polychrome, S. Toohey, 1945, 5 5/8 In.	990.00
Bookends, Dutch Couple, Sallie Toohey, 1946, 6 x 4 1/4 In.	495.00
Bookends, Elephant, 1928	400.00
Bookends, Elephant, Avocado Matte Glaze, 1921, 5 In.	285.00
Bookends, Elephant, Dark Green Matte Glaze, 1925, 5 1/8 In.	600.00
Bookends, Elephant, Ivory, 1923	275.00 to 325.00
Bookends, Frog, Mottled Blue, Green Matte Glaze, 1924, 4 1/2 In.	1320.00
Bookends, Owl On Book, White Matte Glaze, 1936, 6 In.	242.00
Bookends, Owl, Tufted, Blue, Green Matte Glaze, Wm. McDonald, 1930, 4 x 7 In.	413.00
Bookends, Panther, Green Matte	231.00
Bookends, Peacock, Yellow Matte Glaze, 1925, 4 7/8 In.	495.00
Bookends, Rook, Black Matte	286.00 to 345.00
Bookends, Rook, Standing In Open Book, Green Glaze, 1924	520.00
Bookends, Sailing Ship, Green Matte Glaze, William McDonald, 1923, 7 1/2 In.	245.00
Bookends, Southern Belle, Blue	250.00
Bowl, Apple Blossom Design, Cameo, Harriet Wilcox, 1890, 9 3/8 In.	440.00
Bowl, Aqua, Black High Glaze, 1922, 9 1/2 x 4 1/2 In.	100.00
Bowl, Band Of Flowers, Interior, Brown Slip, V. Tischler, 1923, 12 In.	305.00
Bowl, Blue Ship, Blue, White High Glaze, 2 Handles, 5 x 2 In.	523.00
Bowl, Bulb, Blue, Green Glaze, 1921, 12 x 3 3/4 In.	110.00
Bowl, Cerulean Blue Matte Glaze, Incised Design, Logo, 1910, 7 1/2 In.	220.00
Bowl, Cover, Peacock Feather, Blue, Red Eye, Green Ground, S.E. Coyne, 1905, 6 In.	715.00
Bowl, Flowers, Blue, 1921, 6 In.	215.00
Bowl, Geometric Design, Brown Ground, A.M. Valentien, 1901, 4 1/2 In.	550.00
Bowl, Hibiscus, Red, Pink Ground, Green Leaves, S. Coyne, 1925, 6 1/2 x 4 1/2 In.	600.00
Bowl, Panel Design, Curdled Brown, Cocoa Matte Glaze, 1920, 6 x 4 In.	230.00
Bowl, Raised Cut-Out Fern Design, Green, Brown Matte Glaze, 1912, 7 x 3 In.	385.00
Bowl, Raised Holly, Blue, 1919, 7 1/2 x 3 In.	132.00
Bowl, Stylized Floral, Ivory, Pink Interior, Vellum, 4 In.	395.00
Bowl, Turquoise & Mirror Black, 1922, 9 1/2 In.	100.00
Box, Cover, Sprays Of Flowers, Multicolored, Lorinda Epply, 1925, 5 7/8 In.	770.00
Candlestick, Raised Floral Design, Light Blue Glaze, 1923, 2 In.	176.00
Candlestick, White Matte, 1956, 4 In., Pair	185.00
Charger, Russian Peasants, Yellow Ground, Jens Jensen, 1946, 13 In.	825.00
Chocolate Pot, Embossed Kingfisher & Oriental Plaque, 1883, 8 3/4 In.	220.00
Clock, White Matte Glaze, 1950, 8 x 7 1/2 In.	230.00
Compote, 3 Cherubs Holding Saucer Above Their Heads, Brown Matte, 1920	575.00
Creamer, Floral Design, Orange, Yellow, Standard Glaze, E.B. Cranch, 1894, 3 In.	165.00
Dish, Birds, In Flight, Green, Cream, Pale Blue Sky, M. Rettig, 1883, 7 x 5 x 1 In.	176.00

Dish, Cover, Stylized Open Design To Cover, Light Blue Matte Glaze, 1921, 3 In. 121.00
Dish, Floral, Yellow Against Yellow, Caramel Ground, Shell Shape, 5 1/2 In. 176.00
Dish, Grape Cluster, Olive Green Glaze, Leaf Shape, 1946, 6 x 7 In. 95.00
Dish, Reuben Menzel, 1958, 6 In. 230.00
Dish, Soap, Nude Figure, 1927, 1 3/4 In. 85.00
Dish, Swan, Sleeping, White Matte Glaze, 1929, 6 x 2 In. 176.00
Eggcup, Blue Ship, 1930, 3 3/4 In., Pair 358.00
Ewer, Flowers, Brown Blossoms, Caramel, Yellow, Standard Glaze, 8 1/2 In. 770.00
Ewer, Flowers, Caramel Blossoms, Brown, Yellow Ground, 6 1/2 In. 176.00
Ewer, Flowers, Sweep Handle, Standard Glaze, A. Valentien, 1889, 12 In. 1320.00
Ewer, Flowers, Yellow Blossoms, Buds, Green Stems, Standard Glaze, 9 1/2 In. 468.00
Ewer, Grape Design, Standard Glaze, Anna Valentien, 1892, 10 1/2 In. 660.00
Ewer, Jonquils, Yellow, Green Leaves, Sweep Handle, Standard Glaze, 1890, 16 In. 1540.00
Ewer, Nasturtium Design, Elizabeth Lincoln, 1895, 8 1/2 In. 220.00
Ewer, Silver Overlay Blossoms, Yellow, Olive, Tan, Standard Glaze, 7 In. 385.00
Ewer, Silver Overlay, Standard Glaze, Mary Nourse, 1893, 11 In. 9900.00
Ewer, Thistle, Standard Glaze, Sallie Toohey, 1897, 7 1/2 In. 330.00
Ewer, Yellow Iris, Standard Glaze, Amelia Sprague, 1890, 6 3/4 In. 550.00
Figurine, Bird, Tropical, Long Beak, Opaque Green High Glaze, 1952, 9 In. 110.00
Figurine, Black Crow, Black Glaze, William McDonald, 1922, 9 1/4 In. 1760.00
Figurine, Camel, Tan Matte Glaze, Louise Abel, 1930, 6 1/2 In. 1760.00
Figurine, Cat, Sitting, Brown, 1922, 5 1/4 In. 600.00
Figurine, Donkey, Carrying Empty Baskets, Yellow, 1935, 5 1/2 x 4 In. 358.00
Figurine, Duck, Yellow High Glaze, 5 In. 310.00
Figurine, Egret, Black, White High Glaze, 1953, 9 In. 176.00
Figurine, Flower Basket, Frog, Sitting On Lotus Blossom, Standard Glaze, 7 In. 6600.00
Figurine, Girl, Partly Nude, Reading Book, 6 1/2 x 5 1/2 In. 450.00
Figurine, Puppy, Anxious, Logo, 1930, 5 In. 270.00
Figurine, Rooster, Dark Blue Over Cocoa Matte Glaze, Wm. McDonald, 5 In. 265.00
Figurine, Woman, With Dog, 1918, 9 1/2 In. 500.00
Flower Frog, Blue High Glaze, 1926, 2 In. 245.00
Flower Frog, Blue, Dated 1921 .... 40.00
Flower Frog, Frog, Perched On Stump, Leaves, Black High Glaze, 1924, 6 In. 209.00
Flower Frog, Nude, Mirrored Black 245.00
Flower Frog, Woman, Nude, Kneels By Mushrooms, Light Blue Glaze, 6 In. 230.00
Flower Frog, Yellow Matte, 1914 .... 95.00
Gravy Boat, Blue Ship, Blue, White High Glaze, 9 1/2 x 4 In. 220.00
Humidor, Cigarette, Incised, Carved & Glazed, Sallie Coyne, 1905, 6 In. 715.00
Jar, Cover, Roman Warrior On Lid, White Matte Glaze, Scalloped Form, 3 1/2 In. 165.00
Jar, Cover, Tropical Birds, Violet, Blue, Peach Ground, Hurley, 1924, 9 1/2 In. .1980.00 to 2090.00
Jar, Lily Design, Aqua High Glaze, 1938, 5 x 2 In. 176.00
Jar, Potpourri, Blossom Design Interior, Outer Lid, Aqua High Glaze, 4 In. 286.00
Jar, Potpourri, Green Glaze, Black Opal Inner, Outer Lids, S. Sax, 1923, 9 In. 1045.00
Jardiniere, Matte Green, Blue Highlights, 1900, 7 1/2 x 9 In. 525.00
Jug, Corn Liquor, Corn Design, Silver Overlay Handle & Stopper, 8 1/2 In. 500.00
Jug, Ears Of Corn, Slip Painted, Leonore Asbury, 1903, 10 In. 605.00
Jug, Native American Chief, Brown Ground, Standard Glaze, Baker, 10 In. 4950.00
Jug, Whiskey, 2 Gourd, Silver Overlay, Standard Glaze, Sallie Toohey, 1896, 7 In. 1650.00
Lamp, Floral Panels, Green High Glaze, 17 In. 375.00
Lamp Base, Green Matte Glaze, Thistle Form, Arts & Crafts, 1905, 15 5/8 In. 1100.00
Medallion, Green Aventurine Glaze, Menzel, 1956, 5 5/8 In. 300.00
Mug, 2 Bug-Eyed Fairy-Like Creatures, Eating Watermelon, 4 1/2 In. 1045.00
Mug, 2 Fairy Type Creatures, 1 On Toadstool, Sallie Toohey, 1890, 4 1/2 In. 850.00
Mug, 3 Handles, Matte Glaze, 6 1/2 In. 575.00
Mug, Amused Black Man, 3 Handles, Label, Logo, O. Geneva Reed, 1899, 4 3/4 In. 880.00
Mug, Brown, Yellow, Cream Bee Among Green Pods, Standard Glaze, 6 In. 660.00
Mug, Commemorative, Railroad Mail Bag, Standard Glaze, Lindeman, 1905 .... 415.00
Mug, Figure, Walking, Green Hat, Standard Glaze, S. Toohey, 1892, 6 In. 935.00
Mug, Frog, Leaping, Iris Glaze, Broad Leaf, White Blossoms, White Ground, 4 1/2 In. ... 1650.00
Mug, Frog, Speckled Green, Coral Skirt, Green Ground, Standard Glaze, Daly, 6 In. 880.00
Mug, Grape Design, Standard Glaze, Edith Felten, 1903, 5 1/8 In. 415.00
Mug, Incised Pattern, Z-Z-Line 3 Handles, Signed, 6 1/2 In. 550.00
Panel, Classical Women, Dancing, Faience, Interlocking, Tan, Blue, 12 In., Pair 1750.00

Paperweight, Blue Jay, Louise Abel, 1931, 4 3/8 In. 600.00
Paperweight, Bunny, Turquoise Gloss 176.00
Paperweight, Dog, Blue, 1927 . . . . 225.00
Paperweight, Duck, Matte Green 180.00
Paperweight, Elephant & Clown, Gun Metal Black Glaze, 1921, 3 1/4 In. 605.00
Paperweight, Elephant, Matte Green, Initials WMD On Block, 1926, Pair 1000.00
Paperweight, Fish, Tan & Dark Blue 575.00
Paperweight, Kingfisher, Light Blue, 1924, BE 600.00
Paperweight, Lamb, Gun Metal Black, 1954, 5 1/8 In. 300.00
Paperweight, Large Dog, Metallic Brown, Louise Abel, 1929 . . . . 350.00
Paperweight, Mottled Brown Matte Glaze, 1921, 2 3/4 In. 360.00
Paperweight, Pup, Poised, Gunmetal Glaze, 1934, 3 1/2 x 5 In. 265.00
Paperweight, Pup, Poised, White Matte Glaze, 1928, 3 1/2 x 5 In. 245.00
Paperweight, Rose In Pink Matte Glaze, 1940, 5 1/2 In. 145.00
Paperweight, Seal, Sitting, Brown Matte Glaze, 1929, 3 In. 3520.00
Paperweight, Seal, Tan & Dark Blue 650.00
Paperweight, Zebra, Carmel & Blue Flecked Glaze, Able 295.00
Pin Tray, Fish, Swimming, Shell Shape, Blue Over Green Matte Glaze, 5 x 4 In. 250.00
Pin Tray, Nude, Sleeping, White Matte Glaze, 1927, 4 1/2 x 2 In. 150.00
Pin Tray, Owl, 1921 . . . . 275.00
Pin Tray, Peacock Feather Form, Green Matte Glaze, Blue Feather, 1905, 5 1/4 In. 193.00
Pitcher, Bird, Black, Gray, Soaring Among Pine Needles, Pink, Ivory Ground, 7 In. 175.00
Pitcher, Bird, Gray, Soaring Above Green Rushes, White, Tan, Rust Ground, 6 In. 175.00
Pitcher, Daisies Design, Ivory, Olive, Mustard Yellow Centers, Ribbed, Toohey, 4 In. . . . 110.00
Pitcher, Floral Design, Albert R. Valentien, 1888, 8 In. . . . . : 715.00
Pitcher, Pink Matte Glaze, 1943, 4 In. 55.00
Pitcher, Syrup, Yellow High Glaze, 1949, 5 In. 120.00
Pitcher, Yellow Matte, Dimpled, 1910, Small . . . . .90.00 to 100.00
Plaque, Black Trees, Cream Sky, Pale Pink, Vellum, 9 x 7 In. 4675.00
Plaque, Black, Brown Tree, Landscape, Green Grass, Water, Vellum, 8 x 6 In. 2310.00
Plaque, Dirt Road Running Through Tall Trees, Vellum, 1924, 7 x 4 In. 3850.00
Plaque, Gondolier Moving His Vessel Past Buildings, Vellum, 1919, 14 In. 8800.00
Plaque, Harbor At Dusk, Hulls, Calm Water, Vellum, Sara Sax, 1912, 10 x 8 In. 4125.00
Plaque, Scene, Birch Trees, Vellum, E.T. Hurley, 1946, 12 x 14 In. 11550.00
Plaque, Winding Stream, Cypress Trees, Ivory, Vellum, 7 1/2 x 5 1/2 In. 2200.00
Plate, Blue Ship, Blue, White High Glaze, 6 1/2 In., 8 Piece 440.00
Plate, Blue Ship, Blue, White High Glaze, 10 In., 8 Piece 523.00
Plate, Burgundy, Cecil Duell, 1909, 9 In. 395.00
Plate, Fruit Blossoms, Cameo, M.A. Daly, 1886, 10 1/4 In. 220.00
Sconce, Candle, Glasgow Roses, Blue Glaze, 1915, 8 1/2 x 4 1/2 In. 550.00
Sign, Dealer's, Drip Blue Matte, 1926 . . . . 1100.00
Stein, Wiedemann Brewing Co., Pewter Lid, Embossed Eagle Logo, 5 5/8 In. 600.00
Sugar & Creamer, Chartreuse Leaves, Yellow Ground, Standard Glaze, 4 x 3 In. 358.00
Sugar & Creamer, Pink High Glaze, 1949, 4 In. 77.00
Sugar & Creamer, Turquoise 145.00
Tea Set, Blue Ship, Blue, White High Glaze, 4 In. 445.00
Teapot, Virginia Creeper Design, Butterfly Handles, Standard Glaze, S. Toohey, 4 In. . . . 165.00
Tile, Architectural Faience, Coat-Of-Arms, Gold, Blue, Green, 14 x 8 In. 550.00
Tile, Embossed Grapes, Alternating With Leaves, Square, 6 In., 6 Piece 1430.00
Tile, Purple Grapes On Olive Green Leaves, Twisting Vines, Aqua Ground, 5 1/2 In. 550.00
Tile, Rolling Green Scene, Tan Hills, Green Trees, Lavender Sky, 6 In. 1100.00
Tile, Sea Gull, Blue, White, Green, 1922, 5 3/4 In. 220.00
Tile, Stylized Circle Design, Tan, Green, Impressed Mark, 4 In. 300.00
Tile, Stylized Flowers, Yellow, Purple Centers, Deep Brown Ground, 4 In. 255.00
Tile, Stylized Square Design, Dark Blue, Green, Impressed Mark, 3 3/4 In. 330.00
Tile, Tan Flowers, Purple Centers, Green, Deep Brown Ground, Oak Frame, 4 In. 255.00
Tile, Tea, Blue Ship, 1920s, 6 In. 330.00
Tile, Vellum, Polychromed, Square, 1929, 6 In. 245.00
Tray, Card, Lily, Green Ground, Anna Valentien, 1904, 9 5/8 In. 660.00
Tray, Carved Peacock Feather Design, 1905, 3 1/2 x 10 In. 176.00
Tray, Dark Blue Over Green, 1906, 5 1/2 In. 248.00
Trivet, 2 Rabbits, Sitting, Embossed Stylized Flowering Tree, 1918, 5 x 5 3/8 In. 413.00
Trivet, Carrot, Flowers, 1922, 6 x 6 In. . . . . .225.00 to 325.00

Trivet, Parrot, Lavender, Pink, White Face, Violet Morning Glories, Square, 6 In. 245.00
Trivet, Rook, Square, 5 1/2 In. 400.00
Trivet, Seagull, Aventurine Glaze Over Deep Purple, 1930, 5 3/4 In. 440.00
Trivet, White Duck, Low Relief, 1925, Square, 5 3/4 In. 55.00
Urn, Amber Tulips, Green Leaves, Sallie Toohey, 1900, 12 1/2 In. 880.00
Urn, Green, Pink Matte, 2 Handles, 1924, 4 1/2 In. 200.00
Urn, Large Pink Flower, Blue Glaze, Janet Harris, 1930, 8 In. 660.00
Vase, 2 Peafowl, Perched In Flowering Fruit Tree, Arthur Conant, 1919, 17 In. 24200.00
Vase, 3 Blue Panels, Soaring Birds, Silhouette, Charles Todd, 1911, 7 1/2 In. 1430.00
Vase, 3 Vertical Bands, Raised Bleeding Heart Flower, Blue, 1935, 5 1/2 In. 115.00
Vase, Acorn, Oak Leaf Design, Green, Brown, Deep Rose Ground, S. Coyne, 5 In. 600.00
Vase, Arts & Crafts Design, Medium Blue Matte Glaze, 1929, 4 1/2 In. 210.00
Vase, Arts & Crafts Design, Violet, Brown Matte Glaze, 1914, 4 1/2 x 2 1/2 In. 255.00
Vase, Autumn Scene, Vellum, E. Diers, 1922, 8 1/8 In. 1430.00
Vase, Band Of Wild Roses, Black Slip, Margaret McDonald, 1929, 4 3/8 In. 385.00
Vase, Banded Landscape, Winter Pond Scene, Fred Rothenbusch, 1912, 8 1/4 In. 1100.00
Vase, Birch Trees, Gray, Ivory Trunks, Vellum, McDermott, 8 In. 1540.00
Vase, Birds, Tufted, Black Spider, Gray, White, Black, A.R. Valentien, 1882, 14 1/2 In. .. 5225.00
Vase, Birds, Wild Foliage, Elizabeth Barrett, 1944, 8 3/4 In. 1000.00
Vase, Blue Blossoms, Buds, Fringed Petals, Pale Yellow Centers, Vellum, 13 In. 9350.00
Vase, Blue Flowers, Green Stems, Pink Ground, Vellum, H. Wilcox, 1921, 7 In. 1100.00
Vase, Blue Irises, Celadon Leaves, Gray To Pink Ground, Carl Schmidt, 1900, 8 In. 5775.00
Vase, Blue Jonquils, Green To Celadon Ground, Sallie Coyne, 1901, 10 In. 2300.00
Vase, Blue Leaves, Red Berries, Lavender Ground, Sara Sax, 1917, 9 3/4 In. 1870.00
Vase, Blue Matte Glaze, 2 Handles, 1927, 5 1/2 In. 190.00
Vase, Blue, Crackle, Rose Glaze, 1945, 5 3/8 In. 413.00
Vase, Branches Of Blossoms, Green Foliage, Olga G. Reed, 1907, 10 1/2 In. 3300.00
Vase, Bud, Pink, 7 1/2 In. 135.00
Vase, Bulb Flowers, Celadon Ground, Iris Glaze, Irene Bishop, 1906, 6 In. 825.00
Vase, Cattails, Blue, 1947, 4 3/4 In. 100.00
Vase, Cherry Blossom Design, Standard Glaze, E. Lincoln, 1903, 8 1/4 In. 300.00
Vase, Crocus, Covalenco, 1925, 7 In. 475.00
Vase, Daffodils, Vertical Leaves & Stems, Yellow Matte Glaze, 1929, 9 In. 440.00
Vase, Daisy Design, Elizabeth Lincoln, 1923, 9 1/2 In. 1540.00
Vase, Dogwood Blossoms, Leaves, Green Ground, Constance Baker, 1901, 8 In. 990.00
Vase, Dragonfly, 1920, 6 1/2 In. 275.00
Vase, Fan, Yellow, 1950, 8 In. 200.00
Vase, Fern At Base, Shirayamadani, 8 1/2 In. 1485.00
Vase, Fish, Swimming, Dark Green Water, White, E.T. Hurley, 1903, 6 In. 2750.00
Vase, Flower Design Around Top, Turquoise, 1919, 11 In. 985.00
Vase, Flowers, Around Top, Blue Drip Glaze, 1931, 4 1/2 In. 210.00
Vase, Flowers, Black Opal, S. Sax, 1929, 12 3/4 In. 8800.00
Vase, Flowers, Blue At Top, Pink Glaze, K. Shirayamadani, 1935, 6 In. 750.00
Vase, Flowers, Blue Matte, Bulbous, 7 1/2 In. 225.00
Vase, Flowers, Geometric Border, Brown Matte Glaze, Bulbous, 1928, 8 x 7 In. 220.00
Vase, Flowers, Green & Brown, Impressed Mark, 1892, 9 1/2 In. 605.00
Vase, Flowers, Green, Blue Matte Glaze, 5 Buttresssed Handles, 1932, 6 In. 330.00
Vase, Flowers, Impressed Mark, Vellum, F. Rothenbusch, 1930, 6 In. 715.00
Vase, Flowers, Iris Blossoms, White, Gray, Purple, Edward Diers, 1902, 9 1/2 In. 935.00
Vase, Flowers, Lavender Blossoms, Purple, Green Ground, 1935, 9 In. 2200.00
Vase, Flowers, Matte, John Wesley Pullman, 5 1/4 In. 800.00
Vase, Flowers, Matte, Maroon, Square, 1953, 6 In. 125.00
Vase, Flowers, Mint Green Blossoms, Sea Green Glaze, E. Lincoln, 1905, 6 In. 4125.00
Vase, Flowers, On Shoulder, Black Slip, Lorinda Epply, 1925, 4 7/8 In. 935.00
Vase, Flowers, Orange, Brown Zinnias, Sterling Overlay, Standard Glaze, Daly, 7 In. 3190.00
Vase, Flowers, Red, Green Stems, Leaves, Pink Ground, S. Coyne, 1931, 5 In. 550.00
Vase, Flowers, Tan Blossoms, Sea Green Glaze, L. Lindeman, 1901, 3 In. 1045.00
Vase, Flowers, Wax Matte Glaze, Jens Jensen, 1932, 4 1/2 In. 413.00
Vase, Flowers, Wax Matte, Jens Jensen, 1934, 4 In. 650.00
Vase, Flowers, Wax Matte, Kathy Jones, 1923, 4 3/4 In. 1350.00
Vase, Flowers, Whimsical Design, Aqua Matte Glaze, 1927, 4 1/2 In. 143.00
Vase, Flowers, White Matte Glaze, 1946, 10 In. 295.00
Vase, Flowers, White Matte, Rectangular, 1957, 6 In. 138.00

Vase, Flowers, White Stems, Violet, Blue, White, Olive, Blue Ground, Baker, 6 In. 1000.00
Vase, Flowers, Yellow, Brown, Sterling Overlay, Standard Glaze, Diers, 7 In. 4125.00
Vase, Forest Scene, Blue, Gray, Tan, Brown, 1917, 9 3/4 In. 1840.00
Vase, Frog, Broad Leaf, Sea Green Glaze, Green Ground, O. Reed, 1898, 6 In. 3300.00
Vase, Fruit Blossom Design, Standard Glaze, 2 Loop Handles, C. Baker, 1895, 5 In. 440.00
Vase, Fruit, Green Leaves, Yellow Ground, Pink, Yellow, Rose, 12 In. 2200.00
Vase, Fuschia Blossoms, Purple Ground, Louise Abel, 1922, 8 1/2 In. 715.00
Vase, Geometric Swirl, Yellow Matte Glaze, 1927, 6 In. 468.00
Vase, Geometric, Blue, 3 Handles, 1931, 5 1/2 In. 165.00
Vase, Geometric, Vivid Yellow Ground, Flared Rim, Sara Sax, 1930, 4 In. 990.00
Vase, Gold Vertical Swirl Bands Around, Blossoms, Teal Ground, 1883, 21 In. 3520.00
Vase, Green Irises, Yellow Flowers, Blue, Green Ground, C. Schmidt, 1923, 7 1/8 In. ... 3410.00
Vase, Holly Leaves & Berries, Burnt Amber Ground, Sallie Coyne, 1926, 8 In. 770.00
Vase, Horse, Leaping, Tall Flower, Gray, White, Black Slip, J. Jensen, 1946, 7 3/8 In. ... 660.00
Vase, Impressed Mark, Vellum, Albert Valentien, 1904, 13 3/4 In. 3850.00
Vase, Iris Glaze, Blue, Yellow Beards, Ed Diers, 1903, 8 3/4 In. 4400.00
Vase, Iris Glaze, Floral, Orchid Blossoms, Lavender, White, Valentien, 12 1/2 In. 8250.00
Vase, Iris Glaze, Fruit Blossoms, White, Peach Flowers, Shirayamadani, 9 3/4 In. 6875.00
Vase, Iris Glaze, Lakeside Landscape, Leonore Asbury, 1911, 7 1/2 In. 880.00
Vase, Iris Glaze, Lily-Of-The-Valley Design, White Glaze, Carl Schmidt, 1910, 9 In. 4510.00
Vase, Iris Glaze, Lily-Of-The-Valley Design, White, Carl Schmidt, 1912, 11 1/8 In. 3520.00
Vase, Iris Glaze, Mushroom Design, Pale Blue, Green Grass, Schmidt, 8 1/8 In. 4730.00
Vase, Iris Glaze, Night Blooming Cereus Flowers, Stems, Lenore Asbury, 1906, 9 In. 9625.00
Vase, Iris Glaze, Pink Wisteria, Carl Schmidt, 1909, 10 3/4 In. .... *Illus* 11550.00
Vase, Iris Glaze, Thistle, Carl Schmidt, 1907, 13 7/8 In. .... *Illus* 38500.00
Vase, Iris Glaze, Thistles, Leaves, Gray Ground, Fred Rothenbusch, 1903, 9 3/4 In. 1430.00
Vase, Iris Glaze, Thistles, White, Black Spots, Fred Rothenbusch, 1904, 8 5/8 In. 7150.00
Vase, Iris Glaze, White Petals, Black Iris Glaze, Brilliant Blue Ground, 8 1/2 In. 14300.00
Vase, Iris Glaze, Yellow Daffodils, Green Leaves, White, 9 1/8 In. 3850.00
Vase, Iris, Incised, Matte Glaze, 1920, 10 1/2 In. 770.00
Vase, Iris, White, Mauve, Blue Highlights, McLaughlin, 1919, 8 3/8 In. 1760.00
Vase, Iris, Wisteria, Carl Schmidt, 14 1/2 In. .... *Illus* 41800.00
Vase, Irises, Blue, Dark Blue Ground, C. Schmidt, 1923, 12 5/8 In. 10450.00
Vase, Lake & Reflecting Trees In Background, Vellum, Ed Diers, 1912, 16 1/4 In. 9350.00
Vase, Landscape, Summer, Blue Band At Top, Vellum, E. Diers, 1921, 10 In. 1650.00
Vase, Landscape, Trees & Ducks, Dusty Rose, Vellum, 8 1/2 In. 885.00
Vase, Lavender Wisteria, White Glaze, Carl Schmidt, 1908, 20 3/4 In. 33000.00
Vase, Leaf & Berry Design, Coromandel Glaze, M. McDonald, 1933, 8 In. 1430.00
Vase, Leaf Design, Yellow, Rust, Brown, Brown Ground, Standard Glaze, 4 x 2 In. 275.00
Vase, Leaves & Berries, Pale Green Over Pink Curdled Matte Glaze, 7 In. 155.00
Vase, Leaves & Berries, Yellow Matte Glaze, 1922, 7 In. 275.00
Vase, Leaves, Dark Brown To Golden Brown, 1893, 9 3/8 In. 175.00

Rookwood, Vase, Iris
Glaze, Pink Wisteria,
Carl Schmidt, 1909,
10 3/4 In.

Rookwood, Vase, Iris
Glaze, Thistle, Carl
Schmidt, 1907,
13 7/8 In.

Think about security when you landscape your house. Cut bushes low under windows. Don't plant trees or bushes near doors where prowlers could hide. Place decorative lights in the yard to illuminate windows and doors. You might try the early 19th-century style of landscaping in the Midwest farm areas—no shrubbery plantings, but flowers near the house.

Rookwood, Vase, Iris, Wisteria,
Carl Schmidt, 14 1/2 In.

Vase, Lion, Male, Mouth Slightly Open, Standard Glaze, Shirayamadani, 10 3/8 In.	3410.00
Vase, Magnolia Blossoms, Jens Jensen, 1944, 4 7/8 In.	715.00
Vase, Magnolias, Peach Ground, Impressed Mark, 1945, Jens Jensen, 7 1/2 In.	990.00
Vase, Molded Ducks In Flight, Sea Green High Glaze, 1955, 9 In.	260.00
Vase, Molded Flowers, Matte Green Glaze, Bulbous, 1923, 7 In.	285.00
Vase, Mustard Yellow Matte Glaze, 3 Handles, 1923, 3 1/2 In.	200.00
Vase, Orange Trumpet Creeper Flowers, Standard Glaze, Perkins, 1898, 7 1/4 In.	358.00
Vase, Pansies, 1897, 10 In.	2400.00
Vase, Peacock Feather Design, Pink, Blue, Green, Black Opal Glaze, Sara Sax, 12 In.	8800.00
Vase, Peacock Feather, Green & Rose, 1917, 5 In.	295.00
Vase, Peacock Feather, Tan, Blue, 1924, 5 In.	230.00
Vase, Peacock, Peahen, Surrounded By Lush Blossoms, Conant, 1919, 17 In.	24200.00
Vase, Pink & Green Matte Gaze, 1931, 8 In.	198.00
Vase, Pink Blossoms, Yellow, White, Slender Neck, S. Sax, 1918, 9 In.	1650.00
Vase, Pink Water Lilies, Leaves, Pale Green Ground, Vellum, 12 In.	1030.00
Vase, Pink, Green, 2 Handles, 1929, 7 1/2 In.	265.00
Vase, Poppy, 1930, 12 In.	400.00
Vase, Portrait, Native American, Standard Glaze, Grace Young, 1901, 8 7/8 In.	13750.00
Vase, Raised Blossoms In Panels, Purple Matte Glaze, 1921, 5 In.	525.00
Vase, Raised Geometric Design, Green, 3 Handles, 1906, 6 1/2 In.	290.00
Vase, Raised Poppy, Blue Leaves, Matte Glaze, 1930, 12 In.	360.00
Vase, Red Berries, Leaves, Raspberry Ground, Elizabeth Lincoln, 1926, 5 1/2 In.	660.00
Vase, Red Dragonflies, Brown Ground, Matte Glaze, W. Hentschel, 1912, 8 1/2 In.	660.00
Vase, Red Flowers, Green Leaves, Rust Ground, Elizabeth Lincoln, 1918, 10 In.	1760.00
Vase, Red Flowers, Green Leaves, Stems, Yellow Ground, C. Covalenco, 1924, 8 In.	770.00
Vase, Red Poppies Bending, Red, Standard Glaze, Shirayamadani, 1899, 15 In.	1430.00
Vase, Red Poppies, Green Leaves & Stems, 1907, 8 In.	825.00
Vase, Red Poppies, Pink To Pale Green Ground, Shirayamadani, 1943, 7 In.	1045.00
Vase, Red Poppies, Standard Glaze, Shirayamadani, 1899, 15 In.	12650.00
Vase, Red Trumpet Creepers Band, Brown Vines, Vellum, S. Sax, 9 5/8 In.	525.00
Vase, Rings On Each Side, Pale Green Matte, 1916, 8 In.	185.00
Vase, Robin's Egg Blue, Wilhelmine Rehn, 7 In.	250.00
Vase, Rose Matte Glaze, 2 Handles, 1926, 4 1/2 In.	175.00
Vase, Sailboat, Anchors, Birds, Water, Chartreuse Ground, W. Rehm, 1943, 5 In.	330.00
Vase, Sailing Ship, Leaping Fish With Gulls, High Glaze, Cocoa, 1944, 4 In.	175.00
Vase, Sailing Ships In Race, Sea Green, S. Laurence, 10 1/2 In.	5500.00
Vase, Scenic, Vellum, Diers, 9 In.	900.00
Vase, Scenic, Vellum, Frederick Rothenbusch, 1921, 7 1/2 In.	1650.00
Vase, Sea Horses, Seaweed, 1916, 8 In.	225.00
Vase, Seahorse Design, Brown Matte Glaze, 1919, 5 1/2 In.	255.00
Vase, Small Domed Building Scene, Green Ground, A. Conant, 1920, 15 In., Pair	26400.00
Vase, Stag & Does, Dark, Vellum, E.T. Hurley, 1947, 8 1/4 In.	2585.00

Vase, Stylized 3-Petal Flowers, Elizabeth Lincoln, 1920, 8 In. 600.00
Vase, Stylized Design, Blue Matte Glaze, 1930, 5 In. 235.00
Vase, Stylized Flowers Sprays, Pink Tint High Glaze, S. Sax, 1921, 9 1/2 In. 3300.00
Vase, Stylized Flowers Under Glaze, Arts & Crafts, 1926, 7 1/2 In. 210.00
Vase, Stylized Flowers, Leaf Design, Brown Matte Glaze, 1926, 11 1/2 In. 285.00
Vase, Stylized Flowers, Leaves, 3 Orange Birds In Flight, Epply, 1930, 11 In. 2425.00
Vase, Stylized Flowers, Matte Purple, Red & Green, E.N.L. Lincoln, 1919, 7 In. 800.00
Vase, Stylized Flowers, Rose Ground, Charles Todd, 1918, 5 In. 600.00
Vase, Stylized Flowers, Yellow High Glaze, 5 1/2 In. 65.00
Vase, Stylized Trees, Snowy Fields, William McDonald, 1905, 12 3/4 In. 2750.00
Vase, Sunset Landscape, Trees & Lake, Vellum Glaze, L. Epply, 8 3/4 In. 1005.00
Vase, Tan Pebble Glaze, Impressed Mark, 1925, 9 3/8 In. 215.00
Vase, Tree, Black Trunks, Tan, Gray, Leaves, Vellum, Diers, 1921, 8 In. 825.00
Vase, Trees, Brown Trunks, Green, Rose, Leaves, Vellum, S. Sax, 7 In. 1760.00
Vase, Trees, Gnarled Trunks, Black, Gray, Vellum, Rothenbusch, 9 1/2 In. 1650.00
Vase, Trees, Gold Fall Foliage, Distant Blue Trees, Vellum, E.T. Hurley, 10 1/2 In. 1980.00
Vase, Trees, Gray, Rose Trunks, Cream Sky, Vellum, Rothenbusch, 7 In. 1650.00
Vase, Tulips, Blue, 1926, 11 In. 350.00
Vase, Venetian Harbor Scene, Gray Ships, Blue, Green Sky, Vellum, Schmidt, 13 In. 12100.00
Vase, Vertical Leaves, Pod Design, Green, Pink Matte Glaze, 1914, 4 1/2 In. 155.00
Vase, Village Among Woods, Vellum, F. Rothenbusch, 14 In. 6050.00
Vase, Water Lilies, Blue, Green, 6 1/2 In. 275.00
Vase, Wax Matte, Shirayamadani, 9 1/2 In. 2575.00
Vase, White Geese In Flight Scene, K. Shirayamadani, 1910, 9 In. 4400.00
Vase, White Matte Glaze, 2 Handles, 1926, 9 In. 300.00
Vase, White Narcissus, Mauve To Ivory Ground, Sara Sax, 1911, 7 In. 1760.00
Vase, White Poppy Design, Vellum, K. Van Horne, 1913, 10 In. 935.00
Vase, Wild Roses, Shaded Brown Ground, Artus Van Briggle, 1890, 8 1/4 In. 880.00
Vase, Wine Madder, 1944, 4 1/2 In. 175.00
Vase, Wisteria Blossoms, Green Stems, Blue Matte, Albert Pons, 1907, 12 In. 1100.00
Vase, Woman & Man With Flowers, Birds, Green Ground, Barrett, 1934, 5 In. 2310.00
Vase, Woman, Long Robe Holding Flowers, Ariel Blue Glaze, Horsfall, 9 In. 6050.00
Vase, Woods & Small Village, Building, Castle, Vellum, Fred Rothenbusch, 15 In. 6050.00
Vase, Yellow Flowers, Blue, Green Ground, Shirayamadani, 1933, 7 3/8 In. 1325.00
Vase, Yellow Flowers, Green Leaves, Vera Tischler, 1923, 10 3/4 In. 1880.00
Vase, Yellow Flowers, Leaves, Blue Berries, Red, Blue Ground, L.N. Lincoln, 13 In. 1430.00
Vase, Yellow Flowers, Leaves, Yellow Ground, Red, Catherine Covalenco, 13 In. 715.00
Vase, Yellow Matte Glaze, 3 Small Handles, 1924, 9 In. 335.00
Vase, Yellow Thistle, Brown To Orange, Ribbon Handles, E.D., 1896, 17 x 6 In. 650.00
Wall Pocket, Gray Rook Eating Blue Grapes, On Twisted Vine, 1916, 12 In. 605.00
Wall Pocket, Lily Shape, Green Over Pink Matte Glaze, 1928, 15 1/2 In. 286.00
Wall Pocket, Locust, Matte Green, 1922, 7 3/4 In. 1200.00

ROSALINE, see Steuben category.

ROSE BOWLS were popular during the 1880s. Rose petals were kept in
the open bowl to add fragrance to a room, a popular idea in a time of
limited personal hygiene. The glass bowls were made with crimped
tops, which kept the petals inside. Many types of Victorian art glass
were made into rose bowls.

Button Panels, Blue 50.00
Button Panels, Candy Ribbon Rim, Dome Footed, Clear To Opalescent 30.00
Carnival Glass, White Ice, Tricorner 130.00
Cranberry, Oval Thumbprints, Threaded, 2 In. 135.00
Green, Ruffled, Footed, Levay, 1977 .... 45.00
Hobnail, Orange, Clear Applied Handle, White To Opalescent Lining, 4 x 5 1/2 In. 125.00
Hobstars, Cane & Strawberry Diamond, 4 3/4 x 6 In. 215.00
Moire Pattern, Chartreuse To Cranberry, Threaded, Crimped, 3 x 3 1/2 In. 110.00
Molded Vines, Crosshatching & Thumb Notches, Sterling Silver Mounted, 9 In. 345.00
Mother-Of-Pearl Satin Glass, Crimped Rim, 2 3/4 x 3 1/2 In. 245.00
Open Pattern, Vaseline To Opalescent Top 40.00
Pink, Herringbone, Mother-Of-Pearl, White Lining, Egg Shape, 3 7/8 In. 195.00
Pink Cased, Spangled Fernery, Scalloped, 3 3/4 In. 165.00

Purple To Lavender, White Spatter Applied Flower, Crimped, 3 7/8 x 4 In. 135.00
Sapphire Blue, White Spatter, Silvery Mica Flecks, 5 In. 135.00
Satin Glass, Pink & White Swirl, 3 3/4 In. 230.00

ROSE CANTON china is similar to Rose Medallion, except no people are
pictured in the decoration. It was made in China during the nineteenth
and twentieth centuries in greens, pinks, and other colors.

Bowl, Flower & Insect Panels, Pierced & Beaded Rim, Dragon Handles 3450.00
Teapot, Puzzle, Birds & Foliage, Blue Ground, Late 19th Century 145.00
Vase, Everted Rim, Allover Figural Landscape, Dogs & Dragons, 36 1/2 In. 3737.00
Vase, Figures In Interior, Gilt Flowers, Bronze Mounted, Lion Mask Handles, Pair 5750.00

ROSE MEDALLION china was made in China during the nineteenth and
twentieth centuries. It is a distinctive design picturing people, flowers,
birds, and butterflies. Pieces are colored in greens, pinks, and other
colors. It is similar to Rose Canton.

Bowl, 4 Scenic Panels, Figures & Birds, Dragon Handles, 11 1/2 In. 880.00
Bowl, Allover Floral, Figural Design, 19th Century, 15 1/2 x 6 3/4 In. 850.00
Bowl, Scalloped Rim, 10 1/4 In. 275.00
Bowl, Sugar, Cover 475.00
Box, Cover, Rectangular 975.00
Compote, 19th Century, 4 1/4 x 9 1/8 In. 230.00
Cup & Saucer, 1850 .... 295.00
Cup & Saucer, Demitasse 110.00
Dish, Sauce, Leaf Shape, 6 x 8 1/2 In. 350.00
Dish, Serving, Avian, Floral, Figural Design, Rectangular, 8 1/4 In. 150.00
Dish, Vegetable, Cover, Allover Floral, Figural Design, Oval, 9 In., Pair 375.00
Lamp, Fringed Shade 660.00
Mug, Twisted Handle, Mid-19th Century, 3 1/2 In. 295.00
Plate, Chamfered Corner, Porcelain, Square, 5 In. 35.00
Plate, Hot Water, 19th Century, 10 1/2 In., 4 Piece 2400.00
Plate, Medallion Center, Figural Cartouches, 19th Century, 9 1/2 In. 135.00
Platter, Allover Floral, Avian, Figural Design, Oval, 11 1/4 In. 250.00
Platter, Alternating Florals & Figures, Oval, 18 x 14 1/2 In. 650.00
Punch Bowl, 19th Century, 14 1/2 In. 1380.00
Punch Bowl, Early 19th Century, 15 5/8 In. 2800.00
Shrimp Dish, Butterflies, 19th Century, 10 1/4 In. 315.00
Tea Set, Teapot, 5 Cups, Red Silk Lined Woven Basket, c.1850 .... 375.00
Teapot, Allover Floral, Figural Design, Fitted With Wicker Caddy, 6 1/2 In. 100.00
Teapot & Cup, Original Fitted Basket, Early 20th Century, 5 1/4 In. 115.00
Tureen, Soup, Cover, Handles, Round, 11 1/4 In. 1150.00
Vase, 19th Century, 17 3/8 In., Pair 5950.00
Vase, Cylindrical, 19th Century, 12 3/4 In., Pair 980.00
Wine Pot, Cadogan, c.1880, 5 1/2 In. 375.00

ROSE O'NEILL, see Kewpie category.

ROSE TAPESTRY porcelain was made by the Royal Bayreuth factory of
Tettau, Germany, during the late nineteenth century. The surface of the
porcelain was pressed against a coarse fabric while it was still damp,
and the impressions remained on the finished porcelain. It looks and
feels like a textured cloth. Very skillful reproductions are being made
that even include a variation of the Royal Bayreuth mark, so be careful when buying.

Basket, Gold Trimmed, Rope Handle, Blue Mark, 4 In. 475.00
Biscuit Jar, Cover, Woman With Horse, Signed 850.00
Box, Powder, Cover, Woman & Prince 150.00
Box, Shell Shape, 2 x 5 1/4 In. 450.00
Box, White Rose, 5 In. 275.00
Creamer, Highland Goats Grazing In Field, Blue Mark, 5 In. 400.00
Creamer, Portrait 395.00
Creamer, Rose 185.00
Figurine, Basket Lady With Horse, 5 1/2 In. 595.00

Nappy, Leaf Shape, Royal Bayreuth	110.00
Nut Set, Rose Design, 5 Piece	490.00
Pitcher, Goats, Grazing In Field, Pinched Spout, 5 In.	400.00
Planter, Cottage By Waterfall	150.00
Plaque, Woman Leaning On Horse, No. 966, 9 1/2 In.	770.00
Powder Box, Royal Bayreuth, 3 1/4 x 2 In.	285.00
Relish, 2 Open Handles, Royal Bayreuth, Blue Mark	250.00
Teapot, Flowers	650.00
Tray, Dresser, Prince & His Lady, 9 1/4 x 7 In.	395.00
Vase, Bud, Woman & Prince, Thin Neck, Royal Bayreuth, 4 3/4 In.	120.00

ROSEMEADE Pottery of Wahpeton, North Dakota, worked from 1940 to 1961. The pottery was operated by Laura A. Taylor and her husband, R.I. Hughes. The company was also known as the Wahpeton Pottery Company. Art pottery and commercial wares were made.

Rosemeade

Ashtray, Blue Gill, Fish	200.00
Ashtray, Horse, Green	160.00
Ashtray, Indian, Pontiac	180.00
Ashtray, Minnesota, Green	60.00
Ashtray, Olson Supply, Larimore, North Dakota	90.00
Ashtray, Strutting Rooster	120.00
Bank, Buffalo, Brown, Jamestown, North Dakota	400.00
Bookends, Black Bear	1100.00
Bowl, Pink, Flared, 7 In.	45.00
Burner, Incense, Log Cabin	120.00
Figurine, Buffalo, 4 In.	55.00
Figurine, Coyote, Black, 4 1/4 In.	365.00
Figurine, Pheasant, Foil Label, 11 In.	125.00 to 175.00
Figurine, Pheasant, Rooster, 10 3/4 In.	250.00
Flower Frog, Bird	45.00
Flower Frog, Fish	45.00
Flower Frog, Frog	48.00
Flower Frog, Heron	80.00
Flower Frog, Leaping Deer	45.00
Flower Frog, Seahorse, 9 1/2 In.	80.00
Lamp, Pheasant, 13 In.	725.00
Planter, Cinnamon	165.00
Planter, Deer	55.00
Planter, Dove	85.00
Planter, Koala	120.00
Planter, Lamb, Pink, Blue, Pair	125.00
Planter, Squirrel	60.00
Plaque, Fish	115.00
Plate, Hors D'Oeuvre, Pheasant	65.00
Rose Bowl, Pink Matte	55.00
Salt & Pepper, Bears, Sitting, Brown, 3 In.	55.00
Salt & Pepper, Black Bears	55.00
Salt & Pepper, Blue Tulip, 4 Holes	35.00
Salt & Pepper, Bob White	50.00
Salt & Pepper, Boston Terrier	75.00
Salt & Pepper, Brussels Sprouts	30.00 to 45.00
Salt & Pepper, Buffalo	75.00
Salt & Pepper, Bull's Head, Paper Label	55.00
Salt & Pepper, Cucumber	25.00
Salt & Pepper, Dog Head	65.00 to 95.00
Salt & Pepper, Duck	50.00 to 95.00
Salt & Pepper, Elephant, Gray	85.00
Salt & Pepper, Elephant, Green	55.00
Salt & Pepper, Elephant, Pink	75.00
Salt & Pepper, Fawn, Lying Down	125.00
Salt & Pepper, Golden Pheasants	65.00
Salt & Pepper, Green Pepper	45.00
Salt & Pepper, Hen, Large	45.00

Salt & Pepper, Heron, White, On Black Rock 50.00
Salt & Pepper, Horse Head, Palomino .... .85.00 to 90.00
Salt & Pepper, Leaping Deer 150.00
Salt & Pepper, Mallard Duck, Drake & Hen .... .55.00 to 95.00
Salt & Pepper, Mice 40.00
Salt & Pepper, Pelicans 45.00
Salt & Pepper, Pheasant, Tail Down .... .95.00 to 110.00
Salt & Pepper, Pheasant, Tail Up 35.00
Salt & Pepper, Quail .... .35.00 to 70.00
Salt & Pepper, Raccoon 130.00
Salt & Pepper, Roadrunner 220.00
Salt & Pepper, Running Rabbit 95.00
Salt & Pepper, Sailboats 280.00
Salt & Pepper, Skunk, Large .... .45.00 to 65.00
Saltshaker, Begging Puppy 35.00
Saltshaker, Dalmatian 40.00
Saltshaker, Greyhound 38.00
Saltshaker, Penguin, Burgundy, 3 Holes 50.00
Sugar & Creamer, Corn 45.00
Sugar & Creamer, Tulip 50.00
Vase, Flared Edge, Hand Painted Violets & Roses, 5 In. 1700.00
Vase, Flared, Signed AK, 5 In. 1500.00
Vase, Lovebirds 45.00

ROSENTHAL porcelain was made at the factory established in Selb, Bavaria, in 1880. The factory is still making fine-quality tablewares and figurines. A series of Christmas plates was made from 1910. Other limited edition plates have been made since 1971.

Biscuit Jar, Gold Band, Donatello 75.00
Bowl, Burgundy Floral, Pleat Design Rim, White Ground, 9 1/2 In. 55.00
Butter Chip, Rose 15.00
Cake Plate, Gold Floral Border, Handle, 11 In. 75.00
Cake Plate, Roses, Burgundy, Gold Handles, 12 In. 62.00
Charger, Europa & The Bull, White, 12 1/2 In. 215.00
Chocolate Pot, Gold Band, Donatello 85.00
Dish, Gold, White, Picture Of Wagner, 1930 .... 25.00
Figurine, Bear, 7 1/2 In. 245.00
Figurine, Bird, No. 1647 .... 75.00
Figurine, Bird, On Branch, Signed, 6 In. 135.00
Figurine, Blackamoor, Dressed In White, Carrying Tray Of Fruit, 7 In. 245.00
Figurine, Boxer 325.00
Figurine, Boy, With Lamb 150.00
Figurine, Cat, Standing, 5 In. 90.00
Figurine, Cup & Saucer, Ivory, Linnie Lee 45.00
Figurine, Dachshund Puppy, Seated, 6 x 6 1/2 In. 195.00
Figurine, Goose, No. 788 .... 85.00
Figurine, Horse, Standing, Bisque, 18 In. 595.00
Figurine, Kitten, Seated, Black, White, 5 In. 130.00
Figurine, Line Foal, 6 In. 75.00
Figurine, Mouse, Begging, 1 3/4 In. 98.00
Figurine, Pan, Seated On Column, Playing Pipes, Lizard Around Base, 6 In. 345.00
Figurine, Polar Bear, On Round Ball, 3 3/4 In. 30.00
Figurine, Sleeping Cat, No. 1804 .... 295.00
Lamp, Owl, Yellow Glass Eyes, Brown & Gray Body, 7 In. 325.00
Lamp Base, Woman, Seated, Nude, Holding Torchere, White, 1925, 24 In. 1725.00
Pitcher, Poppies, Crossed Swords Mark, 1900, 6 1/2 In. 45.00
Plaque, Pysche & L'Amour, Pate-Sur-Pate, 1890 .... 300.00
Plate, Christmas, 1971, Christmas In Garmisch, 8 1/2 In. 93.00
Plate, Pastel Daisies, Marked, 8 In., 6 Piece 95.00
Plate, Pompadour, Gold Trim, 7 3/4 In. 10.00
Plate, Sweet Pea, Gold Trim, Versailles, 9 In. 75.00
Platter, Water Tureen, Ivory, White, Floral, Oval, 1900, 22 x 20 In., 2 Piece 415.00
Reamer, Juice, Lemon Design, White, Green Trim 45.00

Salt & Pepper, On Tray, Miniature 545.00
Tea & Dessert Set, Maria, 1908-1948 .... 350.00
Teapot, Cover, Floral 195.00
Vase, Brown, Tan Matte Glaze, Wafer Mark, 5 In. 165.00
Vase, Engraved Mermaid, Thick Walls, Bjorn Winblad, 6 1/4 In. 450.00
Vase, Gold Overlay, Gray Ground, Cylinder Shape, Label, Marked, 3 x 14 In. 132.00
Vase, Mermaid Design, Bjorn Winblad, 6 In. 450.00

ROSEVILLE Pottery Company was organized in Roseville, Ohio, in 1890. Another plant was opened in Zanesville, Ohio, in 1898. Many types of pottery were made until 1954. Early wares include Sgraffito, Olympic, and Rozane. Later lines were often made with molded decorations, especially flowers and fruit. Pieces are marked *Roseville*.

Roseville
U.S.A.

Ashtray, Donatello 125.00
Ashtray, Florentine .... 90.00 to 110.00
Ashtray, Hyde Park, 7 1/2 In. 25.00
Ashtray, Hyde Park, Burnt Orange 100.00
Ashtray, Magnolia, Green 75.00
Ashtray, Ming Tree, Blue 120.00
Ashtray, Ming Tree, Green 95.00
Ashtray, Snowberry, Blue 60.00
Basket, Bittersweet, Green, 1940, 10 In. 185.00
Basket, Bleeding Heart, Tan, 8 In. 410.00
Basket, Bushberry, Blue, 12 In. 425.00
Basket, Clematis, Blue, 7 In. 250.00
Basket, Clematis, Brown, 3 In. 100.00
Basket, Columbine, 10 In. 250.00
Basket, Columbine, Blue, 7 In. .... 250.00 to 275.00
Basket, Columbine, Brown, 8 In. 325.00
Basket, Columbine, Pink, 12 In. 165.00
Basket, Cosmos, 10 In. 440.00
Basket, Cosmos, Tan, Handles, 10 In. 285.00
Basket, Dogwood I, Green, 9 In. 225.00
Basket, Dogwood II, 6 In. 120.00
Basket, Freesia, Blue, 7 In. 125.00
Basket, Freesia, Brown, 7 In. .... 155.00 to 185.00
Basket, Freesia, Brown, 8 In. 295.00
Basket, Hanging, Antique Green Matte, 1916 .... 110.00 to 250.00
Basket, Hanging, Bittersweet, Green, 8 In. .... 245.00 to 275.00
Basket, Hanging, Bleeding Heart, Blue 270.00
Basket, Hanging, Bleeding Heart, Green 160.00
Basket, Hanging, Bleeding Heart, Pink .... 275.00 to 325.00
Basket, Hanging, Clematis, Green 185.00
Basket, Hanging, Columbine, Blue, 10 In. 365.00
Basket, Hanging, Cosmos, Green, 5 In. 275.00
Basket, Hanging, Egypto, Matte Green 250.00
Basket, Hanging, Foxglove, Blue, 12 In. .... 285.00 to 400.00
Basket, Hanging, Foxglove, Green 325.00
Basket, Hanging, Freesia, Green 250.00
Basket, Hanging, Fuchsia, Green 285.00
Basket, Hanging, Futura, Beige 450.00
Basket, Hanging, Futura, Terra-Cotta, 5 In. 450.00
Basket, Hanging, Gardenia, Green 195.00
Basket, Hanging, Gardenia, Tan 195.00
Basket, Hanging, Lombardy, Matte Blue 285.00
Basket, Hanging, Magnolia, Green, 10 In. .... 175.00 to 250.00
Basket, Hanging, Mock Orange, 6 In. 265.00
Basket, Hanging, Monticello, Brown, Label, 6 1/2 In. 695.00
Basket, Hanging, Mostique, Matte Pebbled Ground, 6 1/2 In. 350.00
Basket, Hanging, Peony, Green, 5 In. 140.00
Basket, Hanging, Pine Cone, Blue, 5 In. .... 450.00 to 600.00
Basket, Hanging, Primrose, Tan, 5 In. 245.00
Basket, Hanging, Rozane, Green, 6 In. 28.00

Basket, Hanging, Russco, Tan, 3 Handles, 7 In. 143.00
Basket, Hanging, Snowberry, Blue, 5 In. . . . . .195.00 to 250.00
Basket, Hanging, Snowberry, Green, 5 In. . . . . .195.00 to 225.00
Basket, Hanging, Snowberry, Pink, 5 In. . . . . .215.00 to 235.00
Basket, Hanging, Tourmaline 85.00
Basket, Hanging, Wincraft, Blue 145.00
Basket, Hanging, Wincraft, Green 165.00
Basket, Hanging, Zephyr Lily, Brown, 5 In. 200.00
Basket, Hanging, Zephyr Lily, Green, 5 In. . . . . .265.00 to 350.00
Basket, Imperial I, 9 In. 185.00
Basket, Imperial I, 11 In. 285.00
Basket, Iris, Pink, 8 In. 425.00
Basket, Magnolia, Blue, 12 In. 325.00
Basket, Ming Tree, Blue, 8 In. . . . . .165.00 to 250.00
Basket, Ming Tree, Blue, Gold Trim, 12 In. 375.00
Basket, Ming Tree, White, 8 In. 250.00
Basket, Monticello, 6 1/2 In. 695.00
Basket, Peony, Yellow, 7 In. 185.00
Basket, Pine Cone, Green, 10 In. . . . . .425.00 to 480.00
Basket, Rozane, Flowers, White, 8 In. 55.00
Basket, Silhouette, 10 In. 65.00
Basket, Snowberry, Green, 8 In. . . . . .175.00 to 225.00
Basket, Snowberry, Pink, 10 In. 225.00
Basket, Thorn Apple, Pink, 10 In. 225.00
Basket, Vista, 10 In. 565.00
Basket, White Rose, Blue, 8 In. 110.00
Basket, White Rose, Coral, 8 In. . . . . .200.00 to 225.00
Basket, White Rose, Coral, 10 In. 155.00
Basket, White Rose, Coral, 12 In. 200.00
Basket, White Rose, Green, 10 In. 195.00
Basket, Wincraft, Tan, Cactus In Bloom, 12 In. 325.00
Basket, Zephyr Lilly, 10 In. 275.00
Bean Pot, Cover, Raymor, Brown 70.00
Bookends, Apple Blossom, Green 245.00
Bookends, Burmese, Green 350.00
Bookends, Bushberry, Blue 300.00
Bookends, Bushberry, Brown 65.00
Bookends, Cosmos, Earth Tone 150.00
Bookends, Dawn, Yellow 200.00
Bookends, Foxglove, Blue 200.00
Bookends, Foxglove, Red 260.00
Bookends, Gardenia, Gray . . . . .100.00 to 135.00
Bookends, Magnolia, Blue . . . . .175.00 to 225.00
Bookends, Magnolia, Brown 165.00
Bookends, Pine Cone, Brown . . . . .175.00 to 425.00
Bookends, Snowberry, Blue 250.00
Bookends, Snowberry, Green 85.00
Bookends, Snowberry, Rose 265.00
Bookends, Thorn Apple, Brown 225.00
Bookends, Wincraft, Blue 150.00
Bookends, Wincraft, Chartreuse 155.00
Bowl, Apple Blossom, 7 In. 55.00
Bowl, Apple Blossom, Coral, 6 In. 135.00
Bowl, Apple Blossom, Green 235.00
Bowl, Bittersweet 95.00
Bowl, Carnelian, 6 In. 145.00
Bowl, Carnelian II, Oval Handles, 10 In. 155.00
Bowl, Cherry Blossom, Pink, 5 In. . . . . .400.00 to 450.00
Bowl, Clematis, 2 Handles, 14 In. 195.00
Bowl, Clematis, 6 In. 60.00
Bowl, Columbine, Brown, 6 In. 95.00
Bowl, Dahlrose, Mottled Beige, 10 In. . . . . .175.00 to 200.00
Bowl, Earlam, Tan, Flower Frog, 4 In. 300.00

Bowl, Florentine, Brown, 9 In. 75.00
Bowl, Florentine, Flower Frog, 10 In. 135.00
Bowl, Foxglove, Green, Flower Frog 135.00
Bowl, Freesia, Blue, Handle, 8 In. 75.00
Bowl, Gardenia, Brown, 14 In. 132.00
Bowl, Iris, Pink, 5 In. 150.00
Bowl, Jonquil, 9 In. 285.00
Bowl, Moss, 5 In. 150.00
Bowl, Mostique, 7 In. ....75.00 to 115.00
Bowl, Mostique, 8 In. ....90.00 to 140.00
Bowl, Peony, 10 In. ....75.00 to 80.00
Bowl, Peony, Brown, Footed, 10 In. ....185.00 to 235.00
Bowl, Rosecraft Black, 10 In. 90.00
Bowl, Rosecraft Blended, Blue, Footed, 7 3/8 In. 35.00
Bowl, Rozane, Tan, Glaze, 10 In. 60.00
Bowl, Silhouette, 8 In. 75.00
Bowl, Snowberry, 2 Handles, 6 In. 165.00
Bowl, Snowberry, Blue, 6 In. ....50.00 to 65.00
Bowl, Snowberry, Footed, 10 In. 175.00
Bowl, Sunflower, 9 In. 595.00
Bowl, Topeo, Pink & Green Raised Design, Oval, Silver Label, 13 In. 100.00
Bowl, Tuscany, Gray, Flower Frog 105.00
Bowl, Tuscany, Pink, Flower Frog, Oval, 15 1/2 x 9 In. 300.00
Bowl, Velmoss, Scroll, White, Oblong, 11 1/2 x 3 1/2 In. 198.00
Bowl, Wincraft, 12 In. 125.00
Bowl, Zephyr Lily, Tan, Green Interior, 6 In. 85.00
Box, Cigarette, Silhouette ....90.00 to 135.00
Bulb Bowl, Mostique, 7 x 3 In. 115.00
Candlestick, Baneda, 4 1/2 In., Pair 700.00
Candlestick, Bittersweet, Green, 3 In. 45.00
Candlestick, Burmese, Green, Pair 100.00
Candlestick, Clematis, 2 In. 55.00
Candlestick, Columbine, 4 1/2 In., Pair 210.00
Candlestick, Cosmos, Blue, 2 In., Pair 225.00
Candlestick, Cosmos, Earth Tone, 4 1/2 In. 75.00
Candlestick, Dogwood, Pair 63.00
Candlestick, Florentine, 3 In. 65.00
Candlestick, Good Night ....300.00 to 475.00
Candlestick, Ixia, Yellow, 3 In., Pair 145.00
Candlestick, La Rose, Pair 155.00
Candlestick, Luster, Purple, Paper Label, 8 In. 45.00
Candlestick, Magnolia, Green, 2 1/2 In., Pair 85.00
Candlestick, Pine Cone, Green, 4 1/2 In., Pair 225.00
Candlestick, Silhouette, Aqua, Pair 105.00
Candlestick, Silhouette, Ivory, 3 In., Pair 130.00
Candlestick, Silhouette, Turquoise, 3 In., Pair ....105.00 to 130.00
Candlestick, Snowberry, Blue, 4 1/2 In. 125.00
Candlestick, Snowberry, Rose, 4 1/2 In. 115.00
Candlestick, Tuscany, Pink, 4 In., Pair 125.00
Candlestick, Water Lily, Blue, 2 In. 100.00
Candlestick, White Rose, Pink, Double, Pair 125.00
Candlestick, Windsor, Brown, 4 1/2 In., Pair 165.00
Candlestick, Wisteria, Blue, 4 In., Pair 265.00
Candlestick, Zephyr Lily, Blue, Pair 75.00
Celery Dish, Raymor, Brown 60.00
Chocolate Pot, Persian, 7 In. 295.00
Cider Set, Bushberry, Green, 9 Piece 1300.00
Coffeepot, Wincraft, Blue 240.00
Coffeepot, Wincraft, Chartreuse 375.00
Compote, Donatella, 6 x 9 In. 135.00
Compote, Volpato, Ivory, Footed, 5 x 13 In. 150.00
Conch Shell, Magnolia, Blue, 8 In. 210.00
Conch Shell, Water Lily, Rose, 8 In. ....140.00 to 185.00

Console, Apple Blossom, Blue 185.00
Console, Baneda, Green, 13 In. 280.00
Console, Bittersweet, Green, 14 In. 150.00
Console, Bushberry, Blue, 10 In. 180.00
Console, Carnelian I, Scroll Handles, Blue Drip Pink, 12 In. 165.00
Console, Clematis, Blue 145.00
Console, Clematis, Brown 70.00
Console, Columbine, Blue, 10 In. 150.00
Console, Falline, Tan 275.00
Console, Foxglove, Pink 175.00
Console, Iris 175.00
Console, Luffa, Green, 13 In. 290.00
Console, Magnolia, 14 In. 250.00
Console, Magnolia, Green, 10 In. 120.00
Console, Peony, Pink, Footed, 10 In. ....295.00 to 325.00
Console, Poppy, Pink, Oval ....165.00 to 185.00
Console, Silhouette, 12 In. 75.00
Console, Tuscany, Gray, Octagonal, 12 In. 150.00
Cookie Jar, Clematis, Blue 450.00
Cookie Jar, Clematis, Brown ....350.00 to 450.00
Cookie Jar, Clematis, Green ....450.00 to 525.00
Cookie Jar, Freesia, Blue 300.00
Cookie Jar, Freesia, Green 450.00
Cookie Jar, Magnolia, Blue 450.00
Cookie Jar, Magnolia, Green 375.00
Cookie Jar, Water Lily, Brown ....550.00 to 650.00
Cookie Jar, Zephyr Lily, Tan 525.00
Cornucopia, Apple Blossom, Blue 115.00
Cornucopia, Apple Blossom, Pink 95.00
Cornucopia, Bushberry, Blue 130.00
Cornucopia, Capri, Maroon 75.00
Cornucopia, Columbine, Brown, 6 In. 115.00
Cornucopia, Foxglove 90.00
Cornucopia, Gardenia, Gray 85.00
Cornucopia, Gardenia, Gray, Double, 8 In. 130.00
Cornucopia, Magnolia, Green, 6 In. 185.00
Cornucopia, Mock Orange, Pink, 8 In. 100.00
Cornucopia, Silhouette, Pink, 8 In. ....75.00 to 95.00
Cornucopia, Snowberry, Rose, 6 In. ....85.00 to 97.00
Cornucopia, Water Lily, Rose, 6 In. ....115.00 to 145.00
Cornucopia, Woodland, Yellow 125.00
Creamer, Bittersweet, Gray 135.00
Creamer, Bushberry, Green 65.00
Creamer, Capri, Celadon 55.00
Creamer, Creamware, Sailing Ship Design, 2 7/8 In. 55.00
Creamer, Donatello 75.00
Creamer, Juvenile, Chicks 130.00
Creamer, Juvenile, Goose 350.00
Creamer, Juvenile, Rabbits, Side Spout 145.00
Creamer, Magnolia, Blue 75.00
Creamer, Zephyr Lily, Blue 50.00
Dish, Cover, Satin White Glaze, Fluted Sides, Silver Label, 4 3/4 x 5 1/4 In. 275.00
Dish & Bowl, Juvenile, Rabbits, 2 Piece 175.00
Ewer, Apple Blossom, 8 In. 195.00
Ewer, Bittersweet, Yellow, 8 In. 210.00
Ewer, Bleeding Heart, 6 In. 165.00
Ewer, Clematis, Blue, 15 In. ....290.00 to 350.00
Ewer, Clematis, Brown, 10 In. ....110.00 to 225.00
Ewer, Freesia, 6 In. 90.00
Ewer, Freesia, Brown, Pair 750.00
Ewer, Magnolia, Blue, 15 In. 195.00
Ewer, Ming Tree, 10 In. 185.00
Ewer, Peony, 6 In. 95.00

Ewer, Peony, Yellow, 10 In. . . . . .150.00 to 200.00
Ewer, Poppy, Green, 10 In. 180.00
Ewer, Poppy, Pink, 10 In. 295.00
Ewer, Rozane I, 9 1/2 In. 150.00
Ewer, Silhouette, Maroon 200.00
Ewer, White Rose, Blue, 10 In. 110.00
Ewer, White Rose, Brown, 15 In. 395.00
Ewer, Wincraft, Brown 110.00
Ewer, Zephyr Lily, Green, 10 In. 200.00
Figurine, Pine Cone, Pink 500.00
Flower Frog, Carnelian I 50.00
Flower Frog, Clematis, Brown 50.00
Flower Frog, Iris 135.00
Flower Frog, Magnolia, Green 95.00
Flower Pot, Cherry Blossom, Brown, 6 In. 150.00
Flower Pot, Clematis, Blue, 5 In. 115.00
Flower Pot, Columbine, Brown, 5 In. 165.00
Flower Pot, Cosmos, Green, 5 In. 150.00
Flower Pot, Cosmos, Green, 8 In. 225.00
Flower Pot, Freesia, Blue, 5 In. 95.00
Flower Pot, Hanging, Snowberry, Green, 5 In. 250.00
Flower Pot, Ixia, 5 In. 125.00
Flower Pot, Jonquil, Attached Frog, 5 1/2 In. 350.00
Flower Pot, Zephyr Lily, Brown, Saucer, 5 In. . . . . .195.00 to 200.00
Gravy Boat, Raymor, Brown 65.00
Jardiniere, Antique Matte Green, 4 x 6 In. 185.00
Jardiniere, Antique Matte Green, 8 In. 1200.00
Jardiniere, Apple Blossom, 10 In. 95.00
Jardiniere, Artcraft, Brown, 6 In. 275.00
Jardiniere, Aztec, Brown, Green Flowers, 7 3/4 In. 400.00
Jardiniere, Bleeding Heart, Blue, 18 In. 1200.00
Jardiniere, Bushberry, Brown, Pedestal, 8 In. 800.00
Jardiniere, Cameo, Brown, Band Of Dancing Women, 15 1/2 In. 600.00
Jardiniere, Cherry Blossom, Brown, 7 In. 500.00
Jardiniere, Cherry Blossom, Pedestal, 28 In. 2100.00
Jardiniere, Cherry Blossom, Pink, 4 In. 425.00
Jardiniere, Clematis, Brown, Pedestal, 8 In. . . . . .640.00 to 675.00
Jardiniere, Columbine, Pedestal, Red, 10 In. 2000.00
Jardiniere, Columbine, Red 75.00
Jardiniere, Columbine, Tan 185.00
Jardiniere, Donatello, Brown, 8 In. 225.00
Jardiniere, Florentine, Brown, 8 In. 90.00
Jardiniere, Florentine, Ivory 150.00
Jardiniere, Foxglove, Green, Pedestal, 10 In. 2000.00
Jardiniere, Fuchsia, Brown, 7 In. 175.00
Jardiniere, Futura, 6 In. 695.00
Jardiniere, Gardenia, Tan, 4 In. 95.00
Jardiniere, Green, Purple, Gray, 10 1/4 x 12 In. 546.00
Jardiniere, Imperial I, Pedestal, 10 In. 700.00
Jardiniere, Iris, Pink, 5 In. . . . . .115.00 to 135.00
Jardiniere, Jonquil, 6 In. 295.00
Jardiniere, Jonquil, 9 In. . . . . .275.00 to 450.00
Jardiniere, Jonquil, 14 In. 750.00
Jardiniere, Luffa, Green, 6 In. 250.00
Jardiniere, Luffa, Orange, Pedestal, 25 In. 800.00
Jardiniere, Mostique, 10 In. 55.00
Jardiniere, Mostique, Ivory, Pedestal, Clinton, 31 In. 550.00
Jardiniere, Mostique, Pedestal, 34 In. 800.00
Jardiniere, Persian . . . . .195.00 to 295.00
Jardiniere, Pine Cone, Blue, 6 In. . . . . .240.00 to 250.00
Jardiniere, Pine Cone, Brown, 6 In. 295.00
Jardiniere, Pink, Lavender Leaves, Gray Ground, 6 x 9 In. 405.00
Jardiniere, Snowberry, Green, Pedestal, 25 In. 750.00

Jardiniere, Snowberry, Rose, Pedestal, 8 In. 795.00
Jardiniere, Sunflower, 4 In. 475.00
Jardiniere, Sunflower, Pedestal 3500.00
Jardiniere, Thorn Apple 350.00
Jardiniere, Vintage, Brown Leaves, Mauve Grapes, Brown Ground, Marked, 9 In. 375.00
Jardiniere, Vista 595.00
Jardiniere, Water Lily, Pedestal, Rose 950.00
Jardiniere, White Rose, Green 75.00
Jardiniere, Wisteria, Blue, 8 In. 1400.00
Jardiniere, Zephyr Lily, Blue, 4 In. 75.00
Jug, Blackberry, 5 In. 455.00
Jug, Donatello, 8 In. 90.00
Jug, Egypto, Green, 3-Spouted Form, Open Handle, 5 x 7 1/2 In. 357.00
Jug, Thorn Apple 120.00
Jug, Tourmaline, 7 In. 75.00
Lamp, Cherry Blossom, Brown 600.00
Lamp, Clemana, Yellow-Beige 120.00
Lamp, Imperial II, Purple & Yellow, 6 In. 425.00
Lamp, Sunflower, 2 Handles, 23 In. 1210.00
Lamp, Tourmaline, 10 In. 125.00
Lamp, Tourmaline, Red, Foil Label, 24 In. 357.00
Lamp, Tulip, Pair 1500.00
Loving Cup, Bushberry, Green, 8 In. 375.00
Mug, Bushberry, Brown, 3 1/2 In. 95.00
Mug, Elk 135.00
Mug, Peony, Green, 3 1/2 In. . . . . .80.00 to 90.00
Mug, Wincraft, Brown, 4 1/2 In. 45.00
Pitcher, Bleeding Heart, Pink 275.00
Pitcher, Bridge 100.00
Pitcher, Cider, Bushberry, Brown 395.00
Pitcher, Cider, Magnolia 225.00
Pitcher, Donatello 250.00
Pitcher, Iris, 8 3/4 In. 150.00
Pitcher, Landscape 150.00
Pitcher, Magnolia 450.00
Pitcher, Medallion, Cream, Side Handle, 3 In. 45.00
Pitcher, Milk, Juvenile, Chick, 3 1/2 In. 75.00
Pitcher, Raymor, Brown, 10 In. 75.00
Pitcher, Raymor, Terra Cotta 165.00
Pitcher, Water, Acanthus, Brown 250.00
Planter, Apple Blossom, Blue, 12 In. 135.00
Planter, Artwood, Yellow, 10 In. 160.00
Planter, Bulb, Donatello, 2 1/2 x 10 In. 85.00
Planter, Bushberry, Oblong, 8 In. 195.00
Planter, Earlam, Green, 8 In. 235.00
Planter, Hanging, Freesia, Blue 195.00
Planter, Ivory Tint, Green Wash 225.00
Planter, Pine Cone, Green, 7 In. . . . . .225.00 to 235.00
Planter, Silhouette, 14 In. 60.00
Planter, Silhouette, Brown, 10 In. 50.00
Planter, Silhouette, Turquoise, 5 In. 75.00
Planter, Wincraft, Blue 110.00
Planter, Window, Ming Tree, Blue 65.00
Plate, Juvenile, Chicks, 8 In. 185.00
Plate, Juvenile, Nursery Rhyme, 6 In. 140.00
Plate, Juvenile, Rabbits, 6 In. 195.00
Plate, Pine Cone, Green, 7 1/2 In. 300.00
Punch Bowl, Rozane, Standard Glaze, Lemons On Branches, 13 1/2 In. 135.00
Relish, Raymor, Gray, 16 In. 45.00
Relish, Raymor, Terra Cotta, 16 In. 45.00
Rose Bowl, Columbine, Blue, 4 In. 110.00
Rose Bowl, Fuchsia, Blue, 4 In. 145.00
Rose Bowl, Pine Cone, Green, 7 In. 200.00

Rose Bowl, Zephyr Lily, Handles 60.00
Salt & Pepper, Raymor, Frogskin 30.00
Shell, Catalina, Turquoise, Green, 15 In. 75.00
Sign, Roseville Pottery, Self-Standing, Aqua Over Brown Glaze, 3 1/2 x 9 1/2 In. 2420.00
Stein Set, Dutch, Creamware, 6 Piece 750.00
Sugar, Cover, Magnolia, Blue, 2 In. 85.00
Sugar, Forget-Me-Not, Creamware 65.00
Sugar & Creamer, Cover, Magnolia, Blue 105.00
Sugar & Creamer, Freesia, Brown 110.00
Sugar & Creamer, Snowberry 80.00
Tankard, Dickinson 75.00
Tea Set, Apple Blossom, Pink, 3 Piece 535.00
Tea Set, Bushberry, Green, 3 Piece 395.00
Tea Set, Clematis, Blue, 3 Piece 220.00
Tea Set, Peony, Gold Trim, 3 Piece 375.00
Tea Set, Wincraft, Blue, 3 Piece 325.00
Tea Set, Wincraft, Chartreuse, 3 Piece 270.00
Tea Set, Zephyr Lily, Blue, 3 Piece 375.00
Teapot, Apple Blossom, Green 265.00
Teapot, Black 95.00
Teapot, Clematis, Brown 150.00
Teapot, Freesia, Green 90.00
Teapot, Juvenile, Goose 1250.00
Teapot, Peony, Green, 8 In. 225.00
Teapot, Snowberry, Green 210.00
Teapot, Snowberry, Rose 65.00
Teapot, Zephyr Lily, Blue 165.00
Tray, Foxglove, Blue, 11 In. 130.00
Tray, Foxglove, Green, 8 1/2 In. 125.00
Tray, Peony, 11 In. 150.00
Tray, Pine Cone, Brown, 12 In. 143.00
Tray, Pine Cone, Divided, Center Handle 315.00
Tray, Snowberry, 14 In. 125.00
Tumbler, Dutch 90.00
Umbrella Stand, Bushberry, Blue 550.00
Umbrella Stand, Donatello 350.00
Urn, Baneda, Green, 5 In. 500.00
Urn, Cherry Blossom, Blue, 8 In. 750.00
Urn, Cosmos, Blue, 4 In. 95.00
Urn, Freesia, Brown, 5 In. 115.00
Urn, Freesia, Tangerine, Handle, 8 In. 125.00
Urn, Gardenia, Tan 75.00
Urn, Iris 195.00
Urn, Russco, Blue, Footed, 8 In. 145.00
Urn, Silhouette, Aqua, Nude, 8 In. 375.00
Urn, Sunflower, Handle, 4 In. 475.00
Vase, Apple Blossom, Blue, 6 In. ....115.00 to 140.00
Vase, Apple Blossom, Green, 2 Branch Handles 125.00
Vase, Apple Blossom, Pink, 10 In. ....175.00 to 245.00
Vase, Artwood, Double Bud, 8 In. 150.00
Vase, Aztec, Art Nouveau Floral, 10 1/2 In. 165.00
Vase, Aztec, Gray, Raised Stylized Design, 10 In. 200.00
Vase, Aztec, Green, Stylized Flowers, 4 Sides, 9 x 11 In. 500.00
Vase, Baneda, 5 1/2 In. 250.00
Vase, Baneda, 7 In. 450.00
Vase, Baneda, Green, 7 In. ....495.00 to 535.00
Vase, Baneda, Green, 10 In. 775.00
Vase, Baneda, Green, Narrow Top, Handles, Squatty, 4 In. 295.00
Vase, Baneda, Red, 2 Handles, 6 1/2 In. ....340.00 to 420.00
Vase, Bittersweet, Double Bud 110.00
Vase, Bittersweet, Yellow, 7 In. 85.00
Vase, Blackberry, 4 In. 375.00
Vase, Blackberry, 5 In. ....425.00 to 495.00

Vase, Blackberry, 6 1/2 In. 595.00
Vase, Blackberry, 8 In. 700.00
Vase, Blackberry, 12 1/2 In. 2310.00
Vase, Blackberry, Handles, 5 In. 385.00
Vase, Bleeding Heart, Blue, Double Bud 155.00
Vase, Bleeding Heart, Brown, 2 Handles, 8 In. 187.00
Vase, Bleeding Heart, Pink, 18 In. 600.00
Vase, Blue, 9 In., Pair 550.00
Vase, Bushberry, 12 In. 275.00
Vase, Bushberry, Brown, 7 In. ....115.00 to 130.00
Vase, Bushberry, Green, 2 Handles, 9 In. 85.00
Vase, Bushberry, Green, 6 In. ....115.00 to 120.00
Vase, Carnelian I, Green, 9 1/2 In. 200.00
Vase, Carnelian II, Green, 7 In. 185.00
Vase, Carnelian II, Rose, Bud 135.00
Vase, Carnelian II, Rose, Handles, 7 In. 135.00
Vase, Cherry Blossom, 2 Handles, 8 In. 400.00
Vase, Cherry Blossom, 2 Handles, 10 In. ....305.00 to 500.00
Vase, Cherry Blossom, Brown, Handles, 5 In. 425.00
Vase, Clemana, Yellow-Beige, 7 In. 220.00
Vase, Clemana, Yellow-Beige, Handles, 6 1/4 In. 250.00
Vase, Clematis, 8 In. 120.00
Vase, Clematis, Blue, 7 In. ....85.00 to 95.00
Vase, Clematis, Brown, 8 In. 85.00
Vase, Clematis, Green, 6 In. ....80.00 to 90.00
Vase, Clematis, Green, 12 In. 250.00
Vase, Columbine, Blue, 12 In. 365.00
Vase, Columbine, Blue, 16 In. 350.00
Vase, Columbine, Brown, 7 In. 265.00
Vase, Columbine, Red, 6 In. 110.00
Vase, Columbine, Red, 7 In. 135.00
Vase, Corinthian, 6 In. 85.00
Vase, Cornelian, Blue, Green Drip Glaze, Fan, 2 Handles, 8 In. 198.00
Vase, Cosmos, Double Bud, Blue, 4 1/2 In. 155.00
Vase, Cosmos, Earth Tone, 15 In. 245.00
Vase, Cosmos, Earth Tone, Ball, 6 In. 185.00
Vase, Cosmos, Earth Tone, Handle, 3 In. 40.00
Vase, Cremona, Cream, Stylized Flowers, 7 3/4 In. 1000.00
Vase, Cremona, Pink, 7 In. ....95.00 to 125.00
Vase, Cremona, Pink, 10 In. 150.00
Vase, Dahlrose, 6 In. ....100.00 to 130.00
Vase, Dahlrose, 8 x 4 In. 325.00
Vase, Dahlrose, 2 Handles, 9 In. 285.00
Vase, Dahlrose, 10 In. 295.00
Vase, Della Robbia, 9 1/2 In. 2090.00
Vase, Della Robbia, 11 In. 2000.00
Vase, Della Robbia, F.H. Rhead, 11 3/4 In. ....*Illus* 14300.00
Vase, Dogwood II, Bud, 8 In. 135.00
Vase, Dogwood II, Green, 9 In. 225.00
Vase, Donatello, 12 In. 175.00
Vase, Donatello, Cylinder, 8 In. 125.00
Vase, Earlham, Tan Flambe, Flared Cylindrical Neck, 18 1/2 In. 1100.00
Vase, Egypto, 1 Handle, Ribbed & Beaded, 12 1/2 In. 495.00
Vase, Egypto, 10 1/2 In. 400.00
Vase, Egypto, 2 Open Handles At Neck, 5 12 In. 495.00
Vase, Falline, Beige, 8 In. ....375.00 to 575.00
Vase, Falline, Beige, Handles, Gold Foil Label, 6 1/4 In. 440.00
Vase, Ferrella, Brown, 6 In. 195.00
Vase, Ferrella, Brown, Handle, 9 1/4 In. ....500.00 to 595.00
Vase, Florentine, Top Handles, 8 In. 150.00
Vase, Foxglove, Blue, 2 Handles, 12 3/8 In. 305.00
Vase, Foxglove, Blue, 6 In. ....100.00 to 125.00
Vase, Foxglove, Blue, Pedestal, 8 In. 465.00

Roseville, Vase, Della Robbia,
F.H. Rhead, 11 3/4 In.

Many pieces of art pottery are porous.
To clean these pieces, soak the pottery
in a solution of $\frac{1}{3}$ quart of ammonia,
and $\frac{1}{2}$ cup of Spic and Span in a
bucket of water for several days. Then
soak it in hot water for a day, and
wash it with Soft Scrub or a similar
product using a nylon scouring pad.

Vase, Freesia, Blue, 10 In.	150.00
Vase, Freesia, Blue, Bud, 7 In.	75.00
Vase, Freesia, Brown, 2 Handles	150.00
Vase, Freesia, Brown, 6 In.	135.00 to 155.00
Vase, Freesia, Brown, Bud, 7 In.	110.00
Vase, Freesia, Fan, 6 In.	70.00
Vase, Freesia, Orange, Bud, 7 In.	85.00
Vase, Fuchsia, 12 In.	495.00
Vase, Fuchsia, Brown, 2 Handles, 6 In.	135.00 to 245.00
Vase, Fuchsia, Brown, 10 In.	275.00
Vase, Fuchsia, Brown, Sweeping Handles, Gold Foil Label, 12 In.	415.00
Vase, Fujiyama, Yellow, Pinched & Flared Rim, 10 1/4 In.	500.00
Vase, Futura, 5 In.	250.00
Vase, Futura, 7 In.	550.00
Vase, Futura, 10 In.	275.00
Vase, Futura, Green & Gun Metal Glaze, Michelin Tire, 6 x 10 1/4 In.	1200.00
Vase, Futura, Matte Green, 12 In.	50.00
Vase, Futura, Paper Label, 12 1/2 In.	1500.00
Vase, Gardenia, Gray, 6 In.	95.00
Vase, Gardenia, Gray, 10 In.	198.00
Vase, Gardenia, Gray, 12 In.	185.00
Vase, Gardenia, Tan, 8 In.	85.00
Vase, Imperial I, 5 1/2 In.	210.00
Vase, Imperial I, Violet, 6 In.	275.00
Vase, Imperial II, Green & Yellow Flambe, 5 1/4 In.	400.00
Vase, Imperial II, Red & Green Flambe, Trumpet, 8 1/4 In.	2400.00
Vase, Imperial II, Yellow & Violet, 6 In.	375.00
Vase, Iris, 2 Handles, 15 In.	300.00
Vase, Ixia, Green, Pillow, 8 In.	265.00
Vase, Ixia, Pink, 4 In.	90.00
Vase, Ixia, Pink, 12 In.	295.00
Vase, Jonquil, 4 1/2 In.	160.00
Vase, Jonquil, 6 In.	270.00
Vase, Laurel, Brown, 6 In.	265.00
Vase, Laurel, Green, Art Deco, Handles, 10 In.	250.00
Vase, Lotus, Pillow, 10 In.	235.00
Vase, Luffa, Brown, 6 In.	205.00
Vase, Luffa, Green, 6 In.	165.00
Vase, Luffa, Green, 7 In.	175.00
Vase, Luffa, Green, 8 In.	335.00
Vase, Magnolia, Blue, 2 Handles, 12 In.	395.00
Vase, Magnolia, Blue, 6 In.	135.00
Vase, Magnolia, Blue, 8 In.	225.00
Vase, Magnolia, Brown, 6 In.	85.00

Vase, Magnolia, Green, 8 In. 125.00
Vase, Magnolia, Green, 16 In. 495.00
Vase, Mayfair, Beige, 12 In. 200.00
Vase, Ming Tree, White, 12 In. 395.00
Vase, Moderne, Ivory, 9 In. 150.00
Vase, Moderne, Turquoise, Gold Trim, 3 Openings 495.00
Vase, Monticello, Blue, 4 In. 275.00
Vase, Monticello, Brown, Handles, 4 In. ....165.00 to 175.00
Vase, Monticello, Green & Ivory, 5 1/2 In. 295.00
Vase, Monticello, Green, 6 In. ....295.00 to 400.00
Vase, Morning Glory, 5 In. 350.00
Vase, Morning Glory, Green, 6 In. 350.00
Vase, Morning Glory, Green, 14 1/2 In. 1265.00
Vase, Morning Glory, Green, 2 Handles, Gold Foil Label, 5 In. 110.00
Vase, Morning Glory, Green, 2 Handles, Gold Foil Label, 7 In. 385.00
Vase, Morning Glory, Green, Fan, 7 1/2 In. 265.00
Vase, Moss, Peach To Blue, 8 1/4 In. 425.00
Vase, Moss, Pillow, 8 In. 285.00
Vase, Mostique, Gray, 6 In. 200.00
Vase, Mostique, Gray, 8 In. 200.00
Vase, Mostique, Gray, 10 In. 240.00
Vase, Mostique, Spade Design, 12 In. 345.00
Vase, Mostique, Tan, 10 In. ....110.00 to 165.00
Vase, Orian, 10 1/2 In. 235.00
Vase, Orian, Tan, Aqua, 2 Handles, 7 In. 100.00
Vase, Peony, 9 In. 135.00
Vase, Peony, Pink & Green, 8 In. 110.00
Vase, Peony, Yellow Flowers, 6 In. 165.00
Vase, Peony, Yellow Flowers, Floor, 18 In. ....245.00 to 475.00
Vase, Pine Cone, Blue, 4 In. 275.00
Vase, Pine Cone, Blue, 10 In. 425.00
Vase, Pine Cone, Brown, 6 In. ....175.00 to 225.00
Vase, Pine Cone, Brown, 10 In. ....225.00 to 450.00
Vase, Pine Cone, Green, 10 In. ....475.00 to 595.00
Vase, Primrose, Pink, 9 In. ....165.00 to 325.00
Vase, Primrose, Tan, 6 In. 95.00
Vase, Primrose, Tan, 8 In. 185.00
Vase, Raspberry, Green & Pink Glaze, 9 In. 750.00
Vase, Rosecraft Black, 8 In. 100.00
Vase, Rosecraft Hexagon, 7 3/8 In. 715.00
Vase, Rosecraft Hexagon, Brown, 5 1/4 In. 285.00
Vase, Rosecraft Hexagon, Double Bud, Blue High Glaze, 5 1/4 In. 550.00
Vase, Rosecraft Panel, Brown, Flowers, 10 In. 365.00
Vase, Rosecraft Panel, Brown, Flowers, 12 In. 185.00
Vase, Rosecraft Panel, Green, Pillow, 6 In. 275.00
Vase, Rosecraft Vintage, Brown, Tan Berries & Leaves, 10 In. 715.00
Vase, Rosecraft Vintage, Orange, Brown, 5 1/4 In. 330.00
Vase, Rozane Fudji, Tan, Stylized Flowers, 10 In. 935.00
Vase, Rozane Mara, Red Glaze, Squatty, Closed Handles, 7 1/2 In. 800.00
Vase, Rozane Royal, Brown Ground, 8 1/2 In. 225.00
Vase, Rozane Woodland, Cream, 8 In. 850.00
Vase, Rozane, Blue, 8 In. 125.00
Vase, Rozane, Brown, 10 In. 100.00
Vase, Russco, Gold Crystalline, 8 In. 125.00
Vase, Russco, Vertical Ribbing, Stacked Handles, 14 1/2 In. 200.00
Vase, Silhouette, Beige, Nude, Fan, 8 In. 575.00
Vase, Silhouette, Blue, Nude, 5 3/4 In. 750.00
Vase, Silhouette, Nude, Bulbous, 8 In. 500.00
Vase, Silhouette, Pink, Nude, Fan, 7 1/2 x 8 In. 350.00
Vase, Silhouette, White, Green Wheat Leaves, 6 In. 100.00
Vase, Snowberry, 7 In. 70.00
Vase, Snowberry, 9 In. 95.00
Vase, Snowberry, Handles, Pillow, 7 In. 140.00

Vase, Snowberry, Pink, 18 In. 265.00
Vase, Sunflower, 5 In. . . . . .450.00 to 600.00
Vase, Sunflower, 6 In 375.00
Vase, Sunflower, 8 In. 1150.00
Vase, Sunflower, 10 In. . . . . .795.00 to 2500.00
Vase, Sunflower, 2 Handles, Black Paper Label, 4 In. 415.00
Vase, Sunflower, Collar Rim, Bulbous, 7 1/4 x 8 1/4 In. 1500.00
Vase, Sunflower, Handles, 6 In. 450.00
Vase, Teasel, 6 In. 30.00
Vase, Teasel, 10 In. 165.00
Vase, Thorn Apple, Blue & Green, 6 In. 110.00
Vase, Thorn Apple, Blue, 15 In. 310.00
Vase, Thorn Apple, Pink, 4 In. 195.00
Vase, Thorn Apple, Pink, 7 In. 125.00
Vase, Topeo, Blue, 7 1/8 In. 140.00
Vase, Topeo, Red Glaze, 7 In. 145.00
Vase, Topeo, Red Glaze, 8 In. 295.00
Vase, Topeo, Red Glaze, Embossed Snail Design, Foil Label, 7 In. 175.00
Vase, Tourmaline, Blue, 6 In. 65.00
Vase, Tourmaline, Blue, Paper Label, 8 In. 185.00
Vase, Tourmaline, Yellow, 12 In. 275.00
Vase, Tuscany, Pink, Handles, 9 In. 125.00
Vase, Velmoss, Green, 6 In. . . . . .80.00 to 95.00
Vase, Vista, 10 In. 495.00
Vase, Vista, 15 In. 850.00
Vase, Water Lily, Brown, 9 In. 175.00
Vase, Water Lily, Rose, 8 1/4 In., Pair 275.00
Vase, White Rose, 8 In. 160.00
Vase, White Rose, Beige, Flared, Fan, 9 In. 200.00
Vase, White Rose, Blue, 9 In. 135.00
Vase, White Rose, Blue, Floor, 18 In. 500.00
Vase, Wincraft, Blue, Black Panther, 10 In. . . . . .165.00 to 265.00
Vase, Wincraft, Tulip, 8 In. 70.00
Vase, Windsor, Brown, 10 In. 575.00
Vase, Wisteria, 15 1/2 In. 1045.00
Vase, Wisteria, 8 In. . . . . .695.00 to 750.00
Vase, Wisteria, Blue, 5 In. 350.00
Vase, Wisteria, Blue, 6 In. 675.00
Vase, Wisteria, Brown, 7 In. . . . . .400.00 to 595.00
Vase, Wisteria, Brown, Handles, Sticker, 9 1/2 In. 350.00
Vase, Wisteria, Brown, Purple Flowers, 6 In. 600.00
Vase, Wisteria, Brown, Purple Flowers, 10 In. 650.00
Vase, Zephyr Lily, 7 1/2 In. 85.00
Vase, Zephyr Lily, Blue, 12 In. . . . . .125.00 to 250.00
Vase, Zephyr Lily, Blue, Floor, 15 In. 285.00
Vase, Zephyr Lily, Green, Floor, 15 In. 460.00
Vase, Zephyr Lily, Green, Floor, 18 1/2 In. 360.00
Vase, Zephyr Lily, Tan, 6 In. 140.00
Vase, Zephyr Lily, Tan, 8 In. 245.00
Vase, Zephyr Lily, Tan, Floor, 15 In. 395.00
Vase, Zephyr Lily, Tan, Green, 2 Handles, 7 1/4 In. 220.00
Vase, Zephyr Lily, Tan, Pillow 150.00
Wall Pocket, Apple Blossom, Green . . . . .195.00 to 265.00
Wall Pocket, Apple Blossom, Pink 275.00
Wall Pocket, Baneda, Blue, 8 1/2 In. 1400.00
Wall Pocket, Blackberry 995.00
Wall Pocket, Carmelian, Green 225.00
Wall Pocket, Carmelian II, Green, 7 In. 185.00
Wall Pocket, Corinthian, 12 In. . . . . .150.00 to 225.00
Wall Pocket, Dahlrose, 12 In. 235.00
Wall Pocket, Donatello, 9 In. 225.00
Wall Pocket, Florentine, 7 In. 225.00

Wall Pocket, Florentine, 9 In.	135.00
Wall Pocket, Florentine, 12 1/2 In.	245.00
Wall Pocket, Freesia, Blue	250.00
Wall Pocket, Freesia, Brown	170.00
Wall Pocket, Freesia, Orange	275.00
Wall Pocket, Fuchsia, Blue	495.00
Wall Pocket, Fuchsia, Brown	295.00
Wall Pocket, Iris, Pink	695.00
Wall Pocket, Luffa	1325.00
Wall Pocket, Magnolia, Tan	250.00
Wall Pocket, Mayfair, Beige	125.00
Wall Pocket, Mayfair, Brown, Beige Interior, Conar, 8 In.	100.00
Wall Pocket, Ming Tree, Green	375.00
Wall Pocket, Ming Tree, Turquoise	285.00
Wall Pocket, Poppy, Pair	1250.00
Wall Pocket, Rosecraft Panel	250.00
Wall Pocket, Rozane, White, Multicolored Flowers, 8 In.	110.00
Wall Pocket, Silhouette, Nude, 7 In.	495.00
Wall Pocket, Silhouette, Turquoise	235.00
Wall Pocket, Silhouette, White	90.00
Wall Pocket, Snowberry, Blue	1985.00
Wall Pocket, Snowberry, Green	195.00 to 230.00
Wall Pocket, Snowberry, Pink	255.00
Wall Pocket, Thorn Apple, Blue, 8 In.	550.00
Wall Pocket, Tuscany, Pink	345.00
Wall Pocket, Zephyr Lily, Blue, 8 In.	250.00 to 255.00
Wall Pocket, Zephyr Lily, Green, 8 In.	245.00
Window Box, Apple Blossom	85.00
Window Box, Cosmos, Blue	158.00
Window Box, Freesia, Green, 8 In.	135.00 to 150.00
Window Box, Gardenia, Gray, Handles	70.00
Window Box, Peony	85.00
Window Box, Pine Cone, Green	235.00
Window Box, Silhouette, Beige, 9 In.	55.00
Window Box, Silhouette, Turquoise	55.00 to 170.00
Window Box, Silhouette, White, 8 In.	45.00 to 50.00
Window Box, Snowberry, Rose	125.00 to 145.00

ROWLAND & MARSELLUS Company is part of a mark that appears on historical Staffordshire dating from the late nineteenth and early twentieth centuries. Rowland & Marsellus is the mark used by an American importing company in New York City. The company worked from 1893 to the 1920s. Some of the pieces may have been made by the British Anchor Pottery Co. of Longton, England, for export to a New York firm. Many American views were made. Of special interest to collectors are the blue and white plates with rolled edges.

Grill Plate, Blue Willow	22.00
Pitcher, 1776 Commemorative, 8 In.	400.00
Plate, Commemorative, Blue, White	100.00
Plate, Plymouth, Massachusetts, 10 In.	48.00
Plate, San Francisco Views, 10 In.	45.00

ROY ROGERS was born in 1911 in Cincinnati, Ohio. In the 1930s, he made a living as a singer; in 1935, his group started work at a Los Angeles radio station. He appeared in his first movie in 1937. From 1952 to 1957, he made 101 television shows. The other stars in the show were his wife, Dale Evans, his horse, Trigger, and his dog, Bullet. Roy Rogers memorabilia is collected, including items from the Roy Rogers restaurants.

Archery Set, Wooden Bow, Boy's Name On It, Box, 56 In.	275.00
Bank, Boot	45.00
Basket Bin, Comic Book Corral, Tin Lithograph, 1950s, 8 x 9 x 12 In.	130.00

If you're photographing antiques for insurance records, use a Polaroid camera. There will be no negative and no one else has to see your treasures.

Roy Rogers, Holster Set,
2 Guns, Box

Bedspread, Roy & Dale In Jeep	175.00
Bedspread, With Trigger, Double Size	300.00
Belt Buckle, Pouch, 50th Anniversary	15.00
Binoculars, With 2 Decals	125.00
Book, Better Little, 1947	35.00
Book, Bullet, Whitman, 1953	35.00
Book, Golden Book, 1953	35.00
Box, Roy Rogers Ring Offer, Quaker Oats, 1950s	69.00
Box, With Toy On Horse Picture, 1955	400.00
Box, Yo-Yo	65.00
Branding Iron Set, Ring Complete, With Cap	195.00
Button, Roy Roger's Ranch, 1/16 In.	50.00
Camera, With Trigger, Flash Attachment, Herbert George Co.	75.00 to 265.00
Cap Gun, Die Cast, Logo & Horse Head White Grips, 9 In.	95.00 to 170.00
Cap Gun, Kilgore, 1953	75.00
Chuck Wagon, Horses, 4 Figures, White Vinyl Cover, Ideal, 1950s, 13 In.	80.00
Clock, Alarm, Animated Roy On Horse	200.00 to 275.00
Comic Book, No. 5, Nov., 1948, Dell	16.00
Cup, Head Shape, 1950s	28.00
Figure, Bullet, Hartland	65.00
Figure, Dale Evans, Purple, Hartland	250.00
Game, Horseshoe Set, Cardboard Base, 1950s	200.00
Game, Horseshoe Set, Ohio Art, Bagged On Header Card	125.00
Game, Horseshoe Set, Tin Lithograph Base Inside Roy, Box	45.00
Guitar, Graphic, Orange, 30 In.	120.00 to 145.00
Guitar, Marked For Promotional Purposes Only, Not For Sale	204.00
Harmonica, With Instructions, Box	135.00
Holster Set, 2 Guns, Box	*Illus* 1980.00
Holster Set, Gun, Kilgore	575.00
Horse Trailer, Trigger & Trigger Jr., Ideal, 1950s, 15 In.	350.00
Jeep, Fix-It Stage Coach, With Nellie, Box, Ideal, 1950s, 13 In.	245.00
Lantern	45.00 to 93.00
Lantern, Ranch, Hurricane, Box, 1950s, 7 3/4 In.	225.00
Lobby Card, Don't Fence Me In, Roy & Gabby, 1945	25.00
Lobby Card, Heart Of The Rockies, Roy On Trigger, 1951	20.00
Lobby Card, Jesse James At Bay, Roy & Gabby, 1941	65.00
Lobby Card, Movie, Twilight In The Sierras	35.00
Lunch Box, Dale Evans, Double R Bar Ranch, Metal, 1955	85.00
Lunch Box, Roy Rogers & Dale Evans, Metal, American Thermos, 1950s	115.00
Lunch Box, Roy Rogers & Dale Evans, Metal, Canada	125.00
Lunch Box, Saddlebag, Vinyl	175.00 to 300.00
Lunch Box, Trigger, Metal, American Thermos, 1956	75.00

Mug, Figural, Face, Cowboy Hat, Plastic, Quaker Premium .... 45.00 to 63.00
Photograph, Mercury Outboard Motor 45.00
Photograph, Roy & Dale Evans, Color, Large 4.00
Pin, My Pal, Picture Center, 1 3/4 In. 7.00
Pin, Roy Rogers & Trigger, Black & White, Yellow Ground, 1950s 34.00
Poster, Socks With Pictures Of Roy Rogers & Mickey Mouse, Tin, 11 x 29 In. 250.00
Puzzle, Tray, Whitman, 1957 .... 35.00
Rifle, Carbine, Single Shot, Marx, 26 In. 75.00
Ring, Gabby Hayes, Cannon, Brass Barrel 185.00
Scarf, Silk, Roy, Trigger, Guns, Horseshoes, Red Border, 1950s, 23 x 24 In. 78.00
Shirt, Western, Roy Rogers Frontier, Size 6 .... 58.00
Spats, Box, Leather 275.00
Thermos, Roy & Dale, Thin 55.00
Watch & Fob 440.00
Wood Burning Set 385.00
Wristwatch, Dale Evans, Belt Buckle Strap 150.00
Wristwatch, Fossil 55.00
Wristwatch, Timex 95.00
Wristwatch, With Deputy Badge, Tin, Box 325.00
Yo-Yo, 1950s, 3 In. .... 10.00 to 19.00
Yo-Yo, Original Package, 1950s 35.00
Yo-Yo, Western Plastics Inc., Original Package, 1950, 2 1/2 In. 22.00

ROYAL BAYREUTH is the name of a factory that was founded in Tettau, Bavaria, in 1794. It has continued to modern times. The marks have changed through the years. A stylized crest, the name *Royal Bayreuth*, and the word *Bavaria* appear in slightly different forms from 1870 to about 1919. Later dishes may include the words *U.S. Zone*, the year of the issue, or the word *Germany* instead of *Bavaria*. Related pieces may be found listed in the Rose Tapestry, Sand Babies, Snow Babies, and Sunbonnet Babies categories.

Ashtray, Eagle 475.00
Ashtray, Fox Hunting Scene, Round 40.00
Ashtray, Lobster 85.00
Ashtray, Oyster & Pearl, Square 195.00
Bell, Musicians, Cello & Mandolin 215.00
Berry Set, Arabs On Horses, 5 Piece 80.00
Bowl, Corinthian, 4 In. 35.00
Bowl, Jack & Jill, 9 1/2 In. 245.00
Bowl, Little Boy Blue, Child's, 6 In. 225.00
Bowl, Little Miss Muffet, Child's, 6 In. 125.00
Bowl, Nut, Animal Pastoral Scenes, Pedestal, 7 Piece 450.00
Bowl, Radish, 5 In. 195.00
Bowl, Tomato, Leaf, Underplate, Marked, 5 1/2 In. 60.00
Bowl, Tomato, Salad 225.00
Bowl Set, Tomato, Leaf Stem, 4 Piece 395.00
Box, Cover, Woman On Horse Scene, 2 1/4 In. 200.00
Box, Dresser, Dark Green Satin, Medallions, Jasperware, Kidney Shape 225.00
Box, Dresser, Grapes, Cobalt Blue, Green & Gold, 3 x 4 1/2 In. 250.00
Box, Playing Cards, Ship Scene 195.00
Box, Tomato, 3 In. 49.00
Candleholder, Arabs On Horses 150.00
Candleholder, Fox Hunting Scene 60.00
Candy Dish, Art Nouveau Lady 950.00
Celery Dish, Spiky Shell 185.00
Coffeepot, Brittany Girl, Draft Horse, Trees & Meadow, Blue Mark, 8 In. 450.00
Creamer, 2 Children, 3 3/4 In. 40.00
Creamer, Alligator, Square Handle, 3 In. 325.00
Creamer, Apple .... 75.00 to 180.00
Creamer, Bird Of Paradise 795.00
Creamer, Black Crow 265.00
Creamer, Butterfly, Closed Wing 375.00

Creamer, Butterfly, Open Wing ....325.00 to 375.00
Creamer, Cat 180.00
Creamer, Chimpanzee, Marked 550.00
Creamer, Clown, Red ....385.00 to 475.00
Creamer, Coachman ....295.00 to 350.00
Creamer, Cockatoo 695.00
Creamer, Cows & Trees, 3 1/4 In. 175.00
Creamer, Cows & Trees, 3 7/8 In. 85.00
Creamer, Devil & Cards 195.00
Creamer, Duck ....185.00 to 325.00
Creamer, Elk ....70.00 to 95.00
Creamer, Fish Head ....200.00 to 295.00
Creamer, Frog ....155.00 to 160.00
Creamer, Girl With Basket ....525.00 to 550.00
Creamer, Grapes, Purple ....80.00 to 95.00
Creamer, Grapes, White ....80.00 to 100.00
Creamer, Highland Sheep Scene 125.00
Creamer, Hunting Scene 75.00
Creamer, Lamplighter 325.00
Creamer, Lobster ....95.00 to 110.00
Creamer, Monk 860.00
Creamer, Monkey 425.00
Creamer, Mountain Goat ....250.00 to 295.00
Creamer, Orchid 795.00
Creamer, Owl 375.00
Creamer, Oyster & Pearl ....175.00 to 225.00
Creamer, Pansy, Green Mark 300.00
Creamer, Parakeet 220.00
Creamer, Parrot ....325.00 to 395.00
Creamer, Peach 375.00
Creamer, Pear 350.00
Creamer, Pelican ....295.00 to 325.00
Creamer, Pig ....525.00 to 595.00
Creamer, Poodle ....125.00 to 200.00
Creamer, Poppy ....150.00 to 225.00
Creamer, Robin ....135.00 to 280.00
Creamer, Rose ....325.00 to 375.00
Creamer, Seal ....315.00 to 350.00
Creamer, Smoke 495.00
Creamer, Spiky Shell, Coral Handle ....120.00 to 165.00
Creamer, Spiky Shell, Lobster Handle 165.00
Creamer, Spiky Shell, Mother-Of-Pearl 95.00
Creamer, St. Bernard ....245.00 to 275.00
Creamer, Strawberry ....175.00 to 300.00
Creamer, Tavern Scene, Blue Mark 125.00
Creamer, Turtle, Green Mark 750.00
Creamer, Water Buffalo ....155.00 to 175.00
Cup & Saucer, Goat Scene 85.00
Cup & Saucer, Rose, Demitasse 425.00
Dish, Little Bo Peep 110.00
Fernery, Pink Roses, Gold Trim 325.00
Flower Holder, Hunt Scene, Frog Style Top, 3 3/4 In. 190.00
Hair Receiver, Hunter Shooting Ducks, Dog, 3 Footed 335.00
Hatpin Holder, Pelican 950.00
Match Holder, Arab On Horseback 275.00
Match Holder, Yellow 305.00
Mug, Beer, Elk 475.00
Mug, Children In Boat 170.00
Mug, Little Bo Peep, 3 1/2 In. 65.00
Pipe Holder, Basset Hound, Figural 275.00
Pitcher, Alligator 575.00
Pitcher, Apple, Marked 900.00

Pitcher, Arab On White Horse, Gold Rim, 4 In. 75.00
Pitcher, Babes In The Woods 485.00
Pitcher, Black Cat 425.00
Pitcher, Corinthian 48.00
Pitcher, Cottage & Waterfall, 5 In. 495.00
Pitcher, Cows In Pasture, Pinched Spout, Blue Mark, 7 1/4 In. 245.00
Pitcher, Devil & Cards, 7 In. 735.00
Pitcher, Devil Handle, 5 In. 625.00
Pitcher, Eagle, 5 In. 325.00
Pitcher, Fish Head, Marked, 5 1/2 In. 395.00
Pitcher, Hunting Scene, 5 In. 175.00
Pitcher, Lobster, 7 In. 425.00
Pitcher, Man, With Pipe, 7 In. 150.00
Pitcher, Oak Leaf, Pearlized Green 1300.00
Pitcher, Owl 475.00
Pitcher, Sheep Scene 125.00
Pitcher, St. Bernard 1300.00
Planter, Cottage By Waterfall, Handles 150.00
Plate, Arabs On Horses, 7 1/2 In. 40.00
Plate, Multicolored Flowers, Cream Ground, Gold Rim, Square, 9 In., 8 Piece 210.00
Plate, Pink & Yellow Flowers, Gold Rim, Marked, 8 In. 50.00
Salt, Lobster 45.00
Salt & Pepper, Grapes, Purple 165.00
Salt & Pepper, Tomato 110.00
Sauceboat, Poppy 135.00
Shaker, Radish 125.00
Shaving Mug, Elk 600.00
Smoking Set, Corinthian, Classic Figures, Black, White, 4 Piece 125.00
Sugar, Cover, Pansy, Purple 225.00
Sugar, Cover, Poppy, Red 225.00
Sugar, Little Miss Muffet 200.00
Sugar & Creamer, Cover, Lobster 110.00
Sugar & Creamer, Grapes, Purple 395.00
Sugar & Creamer, Poppy 250.00
Sugar Shaker, Orange & Gold Roses, Reticulated Base, 4 1/2 In. 500.00
Table Set, Empress, Green, 4 Piece 800.00
Teapot, Orange 375.00
Teapot, Pansy, Purple 625.00
Teapot, Poppy, Red 80.00
Teapot, Tomato, Gold Mark 195.00
Toothpick, Arab On Horse, Another Horse Beside Him, 3 In. 175.00
Toothpick, Elk, Blue Mark 250.00
Toothpick, Man & Donkey, 3 Handles 100.00
Toothpick, Man Fishing, In Boat, Marked 110.00
Toothpick, Musicians, Cylindrical, Marked 135.00
Toothpick, Musicians, Silver Top, Handles 65.00
Toothpick, Sheep 135.00
Tray, Girl With Geese, Gold Rim, 12 1/4 x 9 In. 320.00
Tray, Leaf Form, Pearlized, 12 3/4 In. 350.00
Vase, Babes In Woods, 4 1/2 In. 425.00
Vase, Bathers Scene, 8 1/4 In. 435.00
Vase, Boat Scene, Red Beads, Olive & Gray Ground, 4 In. 150.00
Vase, Bowl, Rose Design, Footed, 3 1/2 In. 75.00
Vase, Castle Scene, Nymphs Swimming, Marked, 6 In. 295.00
Vase, Girl, Holding Doll, Handles, 4 3/4 In. 500.00
Vase, Goose Girl, 4 In. 125.00
Vase, Hunt Scene Base, Green, 2 Handles, Bulbous, Blue Mark, 5 In. 95.00
Vase, Landscape, Maiden Herding Geese, 7 In. 245.00
Vase, Peacock, Open Work At Neck & Base, Scroll Handles, 9 1/2 In. 740.00
Vase, Roses, Hand Painted, 10 In. 285.00
Vase, Sailing Scene, 4 1/2 In. 135.00
Vase, Steamboat, 2 Handles, Sterling Rim, Blue Mark 85.00

ROYAL BONN is the nineteenth- and twentieth-century trade name for the Bonn China Manufactory. It was established in 1755 in Bonn, Germany. A general line of porcelain was made. Many marks were used, most including the name *Bonn*, the initials *FM*, and a crown.

Berry Set, Pedestal, 10 In., 7 Piece	150.00
Biscuit Jar, Flowers, Green Leaves, Silver Plated Top, Rim & Handle, 6 5/8 In.	195.00
Bowl, Cover, Underplate, Multicolored Flowers, Cobalt & Gold Rims, 5 3/4 In.	170.00
Clock, Ansonia, Green Tulips, Gold	625.00
Clock, Polychrome Flowers, Blue & White, Ansonia Brass Works, 14 1/4 In.	385.00
Ewer, Floral Tapestry, Brick Fence Scene, Gold Handle, 6 1/2 In.	150.00
Planter, Forest Scene, Stag & Doe, Standing, 30 x 18 In.	660.00
Punch Bowl, Florals, Hand Painted, Inside & Out, 13 In.	495.00
Urn, Palace, Cover, Roses In Bloom, Pedestal Base, Signed, 1900, 43 In.	4025.00
Vase, Flowers, Creamware, 10 In.	150.00
Vase, Portrait, Artist Signed, 8 1/4 In.	795.00
Vase, Portrait, Cavalier, Full Figure, Gold Rococo Trim, Hand Painted, Signed, 12 In.	525.00
Vase, Portrait, Peasant Girl, Rose Bush, Stream, Woods, 14 In.	1055.00
Vase, Portrait, Woman In Pink, Deep Blue Ground, 8 1/2 In.	625.00
Vase, Roses & River Scene, 1910, 9 1/2 In.	545.00

ROYAL COPENHAGEN porcelain and pottery have been made in Denmark since 1772. The Christmas plate series started in 1908. The figurines with pale blue and gray glazes have remained popular in this century and are still being made. Many other old and new style porcelains are made today.

Basket, Flora Danica, 9 1/4 In., Pair	4312.00
Basket, Fruit, Flora Danica, Gilt Border, Oval, 10 In.	4025.00
Bowl, Cover, Flora Danica, Double Twig Handle, 7 In.	3737.00
Bowl, Flora Danica, 8 3/4 In.	1150.00
Bowl, Salad, Flora Danica, 8 1/4 In.	805.00
Bowl, Salad, Flora Danica, 9 In.	1495.00
Bowl & Plate, Classical Reserve, Gray Ground, Gilt, Lichte, JEB, 10 In., Pair	300.00
Box, Trinket, Blue, White	45.00
Cake Stand, Flora Danica, Blue Design, Serrated Rim, 10 In.	805.00
Coffee Set, Blue Flower, Cup & Saucer	375.00
Coffee Set, Saxon Flower, After Dinner, 13 Piece	99.00
Coffeepot, Blue Flower	165.00
Coffeepot, Quaking Grass	78.00
Creamer, Blue, Fluted, 3 In.	45.00
Cup & Saucer, Flora Danica	595.00
Figurine, Boy, In Raincoat, No. 3556, 7 In.	225.00
Figurine, Cat, Siamese, Seated, No. 3281, 7 3/4 In.	185.00 to 220.00
Figurine, Dog, Airedale, No. 1652	220.00
Figurine, Dog, Brindle Boxer	225.00
Figurine, Dog, Bull Terrier, No. 3280, 5 1/2 In.	195.00
Figurine, Dog, Wire Terrier, No. 3165, 4 3/4 In.	175.00
Figurine, Foal, Lying Down, No. 5691	150.00
Figurine, Girl, Guarding A Goose, No. 528, 7 In.	190.00
Figurine, Girl, On Rock, 6 In.	69.00
Figurine, Girl, With Doll, No. 1938	250.00
Figurine, Lovebirds, No. 402	75.00
Figurine, Lunch Girl, No. 815, 9 In.	115.00
Figurine, Nude On Rock, No. 4027	125.00 to 198.00
Figurine, Pan On Stump, No. 1738	109.00
Figurine, Pan With Parrot, No. 752, 7 In.	428.00
Figurine, Pan, Rabbit On Gray Column, No. 456, 8 1/2 In.	295.00
Figurine, Pan, Studying Frog Sitting On Knees, No. 1713	225.00 to 245.00
Figurine, Parakeet, On Purple Eggplant	65.00
Figurine, Penguin, No. 3003, 2 3/4 In.	50.00
Figurine, Rabbit, No. 4705	45.00
Figurine, Sandman, No. 1145	140.00
Figurine, Sealyham, No. 2786, 4 x 6 In.	245.00
Figurine, Snowman	95.00

Figurine, Young Man With Cow, No. 772, 6 1/4 In. 83.00
Gravy Boat, Attached Underplate, Blue Fluted, 10 In. 65.00
Jardiniere, Anemones, 1890s, 13 In. ....275.00 to 350.00
Mustard Pot, White, Red, Green, Brown Design, Serrated Rim 3450.00
Plate, Birds, Mottled Green, Gilt, Artist, 11 In. 275.00
Plate, Christmas, 1908, Madonna & Child 2500.00
Plate, Christmas, 1909, Danish Landscape, 6 In. 150.00
Plate, Christmas, 1916, Shepherd At Christmas 115.00
Plate, Christmas, 1920, Mary With Child Jesus, 7 In. 75.00
Plate, Christmas, 1922, 3 Singing Angels 85.00
Plate, Christmas, 1925, Street Scene, Copenhagen 90.00
Plate, Christmas, 1929, Grundrvig Church 110.00
Plate, Christmas, 1955, Fano Girl 278.00
Plate, Christmas, 1958, Sunshine 60.00
Plate, Christmas, 1959, Christmas Night 55.00
Plate, Christmas, 1961, Training Ship 80.00
Plate, Christmas, 1964, Fetching The Tree 35.00
Plate, Christmas, 1965, Little Skaters 30.00
Plate, Christmas, 1966, Black Bird 70.00
Plate, Christmas, 1968, The Last Umiak 15.00
Plate, Christmas, 1970, Christmas Rose & Cat ....35.00 to 38.00
Plate, Christmas, 1971, Hare In Winter 15.00
Plate, Christmas, 1974, Winter Twilight 35.00
Plate, Christmas, 1977, Immervad Bridge 20.00
Plate, Christmas, 1979, Choosing Christmas Tree 35.00
Plate, Flora Danica, 9 In. 805.00
Plate, Flora Danica, Factory Mark, 10 In. 748.00
Plate, Flora Danica, Serrated Rim, 10 In. 1035.00
Plate, Hans Andersen Tales, 12 Piece 498.00
Plate, Ice Cream, Reticulated Cover, Florettes, Leafy Vines, 10 x 12 In. 9775.00
Plate, Mother's Day, 1972, Oriental Mother 15.00
Plate, Pickle, Flora Danica, 9 In., Pair 1150.00
Platter, Blue Onion Design, Rectangular, 13 1/2 In. 100.00
Platter, Fish, Lobster Among Marine Plants, Orange, Yellow, Green, 18 In. 8050.00
Platter, Flora Danica, 14 In. 1380.00
Platter, Flora Danica, Oval, 17 In. 3162.00
Platter, Flora Danica, Serrated Rim, Oval, 18 1/4 In. 2875.00
Sauceboat, Flora Danica, Brown Loop Handle, 9 In. 2875.00
Sauceboat, Flora Danica, Ocher Twig Handle, 9 1/8 In. 2300.00
Sauceboat, Helmet Shape, Blue Fish, Red, Green, Loop Handle, 9 In. 1495.00
Teapot, Blue Flower 135.00
Tureen, Cover, Flora Danica, 13 In. 5750.00
Tureen, Vegetable, Cover, Flora Danica 2875.00
Vase, Abstract Design, Brown, Blue, Tan, Ink Stamp, 7 In. 173.00
Vase, Abstract Fish, Faience, 11 In. 150.00
Vase, Abstract, Woman Design, Purple, White Ground, 7 x 11 In. 77.00
Vase, Apple Blossoms, No. 1752/47D, 9 In. 198.00
Vase, Blue Glossy Glaze, Bulbous, Impressed Mark, 6 x 9 In. 385.00
Vase, Floral Design, 10 3/4 In. 97.00
Vase, Floral, Pale Gray Ground, Gilt, Lichte, JEB, 9 7/8 In., Pair 255.00
Vase, Moderne, Faience, 11 1/2 In. 140.00
Vase, Stylized Cobalt Blue Flowers, 1950s, 10 In. 150.00
Wine Cooler, Flora Danica, 6 3/8 In. 3450.00
Wine Cooler, Pink, White Guilloche Border, Gilt Leafage, 4 x 5 In., Pair 6325.00

ROYAL COPLEY china was made by the Spaulding China Company of
Sebring, Ohio, from 1939 to 1960. The figural planters and the small
figurines, especially those with Art Deco designs, are of great collector interest.

Ashtray, Bird On Leaf, 5 In. 15.00
Bank, Bow Tie, Pig, 6 1/4 In. 15.00
Bank, Pig, 4 1/2 In. ....30.00 to 59.00
Bank, Pig, Brown Pants, 7 1/2 In. ....75.00 to 85.00

Bank, Pig, For My Mink 75.00
Creamer, Spaulding, Duck, 4 1/2 In. 22.00
Creamer, Spaulding, Pig, 4 1/2 In. . . . . .16.00 to 22.00
Figurine, Cat, Black, 8 In. 60.00
Figurine, Cockatoo, Big, 8 1/4 In. 38.00
Figurine, Cocker Spaniel, 6 In. . . . . .22.00 to 32.00
Figurine, Dancing Lady, 8 In. . . . . .15.00 to 22.00
Figurine, Deer Fawn, 8 1/2 In. 15.00
Figurine, Dove, 5 In. 13.00
Figurine, Flycatcher, 7 3/4 In. 25.00
Figurine, Girl, Oriental, 7 1/2 In. 13.00
Figurine, Goldfinch, On Stump, 6 1/2 In. .21.00 to 25.00
Figurine, Hen, White, Black, 6 1/2 In. 75.00
Figurine, Kinglet, Yellow, Blue & Green, 5 In. 25.00
Figurine, Mallard Duck, 7 In. 22.00
Figurine, Mallard Duck, Hen & Drake, 6 1/4 & 8 1/2 In., Pair . . . . .95.00 to 170.00
Figurine, Parrot, 5 In. 15.00
Figurine, Reclining Cat 89.00
Figurine, Seagull, 8 In. 35.00
Figurine, Spaulding, Pheasant, Pair 30.00
Figurine, Tanager, 6 1/4 In. . . . . .14.00 to 20.00
Figurine, Terrier, 8 In. 32.00
Figurine, Titmouse, 8 In. 22.00
Figurine, Woodpecker, 6 1/4 In. 20.00
Lamp, Water Lily, Deodorizing 50.00
Planter, Barefoot Boy & Girl, 7 1/2 In., Pair 45.00
Planter, Bear Cub, Clinging To Stump, 8 1/4 In. 18.00
Planter, Big Apple & Finch, 6 1/2 In. 16.00
Planter, Coach, 3 1/4 x 6 In. 16.00
Planter, Cockatiel 35.00
Planter, Cocker Head, 5 In. 35.00
Planter, Cocker Spaniel, 5 In. 16.00
Planter, Cocker Spaniel, 7 3/4 In. 26.00
Planter, Cocker Spaniel, With Basket, 5 1/2 In. 20.00
Planter, Colonial Woman Head, 8 In. . . . . .45.00 to 55.00
Planter, Deer & Fawn, 9 In. 26.00
Planter, Deer, Resting, Tin 25.00
Planter, Dog & Mailbox, 7 3/4 In. 20.00
Planter, Dog, Cocker Spaniel With Basket, 5 1/2 In. . . . . .20.00 to 30.00
Planter, Duck & Mailbox, 6 3/4 In. 35.00
Planter, Duck & Wheelbarrow, 3 3/4 In. 15.00
Planter, Elephant & Yellow Ball, 7 1/2 In. 30.00
Planter, Farm Girl, 6 1/2 In. 25.00
Planter, Finch On Tree Stump, 7 1/2 In. 12.00
Planter, Girl, Pigtail, 7 In. 35.00
Planter, Hen, 6 In. 16.00
Planter, Ivy, Footed, 4 In. . . . . .12.00 to 15.00
Planter, Kitten & Boot, 8 In. 38.00
Planter, Kitten On Stump, 6 1/2 In. 30.00
Planter, Mallard Duck, On Stump, 8 In. . . . . .30.00 to 38.00
Planter, Mature Wood Duck, Label, 7 1/4 In. . . . . .15.00 to 22.00
Planter, Oriental Boy 12.00
Planter, Oriental Boy & Urn, 4 3/4 In. 12.00
Planter, Oriental Boy, With Vase, 5 1/2 In. . . . . .12.00 to 15.00
Planter, Oriental, Girl, Basket On Ground, 7 3/4 In. 15.00
Planter, Peter Rabbit, 6 1/2 In. 75.00
Planter, Pirate, Head, 8 In. . . . . .40.00 to 45.00
Planter, Plaque, Fruit Plate, 6 3/4 In. 20.00
Planter, Pouter Pigeon, 5 3/4 In. . . . . .17.00 to 18.00
Planter, Ram Head, 6 1/2 In. . . . . .22.00 to 25.00
Planter, Rooster & Wheelbarrow, 8 In. . . . . .32.00 to 65.00
Planter, Running Gazelles, 6 In. 12.00
Planter, Running Horse, 6 In. . . . . .12.00 to 16.00

Planter, Salt Box, 5 1/2 In. 25.00
Planter, Star & Angel, 6 3/4 In. 28.00
Planter, Swallow, On Double Stump, 7 1/4 In. 30.00
Planter, Tony, 8 1/4 In. 50.00
Planter, Windsor Hen, 6 1/2 In. 25.00
Plate, Christmas, 1987 .... 38.00
Smoking Set, Mallard Duck, 4 Piece ....35.00 to 45.00
Vase, Carol's Corsage, 7 In. 15.00
Vase, Fish, Footed, 6 In. 10.00
Vase, Floral Elegance, 8 In. 30.00
Vase, Gazelle, 9 In. 16.00
Vase, Marine, 7 1/2 In. ....10.00 to 18.00
Vase, Pink Beauty, 6 3/4 In. 15.00
Vase, Pink, 6 3/4 In. 11.00
Vase, Spaulding, Rachel, 8 In. 25.00
Wall Pocket, Bird, Lavender Wings, Yellow & Gray Head 18.00
Wall Pocket, Boy & Girl, 6 1/4 In., Pair 48.00
Wall Pocket, Hat, 7 In. ....23.00 to 35.00
Wall Pocket, Oriental, Girl, Big Hat, 7 3/4 In. 35.00

ROYAL CROWN DERBY Company, Ltd., was established in England in
1890. There is a complex family tree that includes the Derby, Crown
Derby, and Royal Crown Derby porcelains. The Royal Crown Derby
mark includes the name and a crown. The words *Made in England*
were used after 1921. The company is now a part of Royal Doulton
Tableware Ltd.

Cup & Saucer, Coffee, Imari Pattern, 1899, 12 Sets 875.00
Jar, Medicine, Oxblood, 10 x 10 In. 300.00
Plate, Imari Pattern, 10 1/4 In., Pair 193.00
Plate Set, Fruit, 11 Piece 517.00
Plate Set, Japan Pattern, 8 1/4 In., 8 Piece 115.00
Soup, Cream, Snowflake, Gadrooned Scrolling Borders, 10 In., 7 Piece .. 345.00
Tea Set, Exotic Birds, Trees & Flowering Bushes, 27 Piece 288.00
Tea Set, Imari Pattern, 1883, 3 Piece 258.00
Tea Set, Imari Pattern, 1884, 19 Piece 2550.00
Tray, Imari Pattern, 8 x 11 x 2 In. 275.00
Tray, Imari Pattern, Scalloped, 1939, Round, 17 In. 550.00
Tray, Rose Floral, Scalloped Edge, White Ground, 12 In. 77.00
Vase, Cover, Gold, Orange, Blue, 2 Handles, 1899 .... 595.00
Vase, Flowers, Gilded Hand Painted, Cream Ground, Angle Handle, 8 In. . 495.00
Vase, Gilded Bird & Leaves, Blue Ground, 1889, 7 3/4 In. 575.00
Vase, Gilded Flowers & Leaves, Pink Ground, 8 1/2 In. 350.00
Vase, Gold Enameled Flowers, Pink Ground, 3 Gold Handles, 8 1/2 In. . 325.00

ROYAL DOULTON is the name used on Doulton and Company pottery
made from 1902 to the present. Doulton and Company of England was
founded in 1853. Pieces made before 1902 are listed in this book under
Doulton. Royal Doulton collectors search for the out-of-production
figurines, character jugs, vases, and series wares. Some vases and animal figurines were made with a special red glaze called flambe. Sung
and Chang glazed pieces are rare. The multicolored glaze is very thick
and looks as if it were dropped on the clay.

Animal, Cat, Flambe, 12 In. 350.00
Animal, Cat, Lucky The Cat, K 12 .... 125.00
Animal, Cat, Persian, HN 999, 5 In. 225.00
Animal, Dog On Back, HN 1098, 2 In. 140.00
Animal, Dog, Airedale, HN 1022, 8 In. 800.00
Animal, Dog, Airedale, HN 1023, 5 In. ....155.00 to 275.00
Animal, Dog, Airedale, K 5, 1 1/2 In. 295.00
Animal, Dog, Alsatian, HN 1115, 9 In. 695.00
Animal, Dog, Alsatian, HN 1116, 6 In. ....155.00 to 175.00
Animal, Dog, Boxer, HN 2643, 6 In. 125.00
Animal, Dog, Bull Terrier, HN 1100, 4 In. 68.00

Animal, Dog, Bull Terrier, K 14, 1 1/2 In. 350.00
Animal, Dog, Bulldog, HN 1044, 3 In. 200.00
Animal, Dog, Bulldog, HN 1074, 3 In. ....175.00 to 225.00
Animal, Dog, Bulldog, K 1, 2 1/2 In. ....75.00 to 150.00
Animal, Dog, Bulldog, Union Jack, HN 4607, 4 In. 350.00
Animal, Dog, Bulldog, Union Jack, HN 6406, 6 In. 250.00
Animal, Dog, Cairn, HN 1035, 3 In. 115.00
Animal, Dog, Chow, K 15, 2 In. ....100.00 to 130.00
Animal, Dog, Cocker Spaniel & Pheasant, HN 1028, 5 In. 190.00
Animal, Dog, Cocker Spaniel, HN 1002, 6 1/2 In. 450.00
Animal, Dog, Cocker Spaniel, HN 1020, 5 In. 145.00
Animal, Dog, Cocker Spaniel, HN 1036, 5 In. 150.00
Animal, Dog, Cocker Spaniel, HN 1037, 3 1/2 In. 110.00
Animal, Dog, Cocker Spaniel, HN 1078, 3 In. ....100.00 to 165.00
Animal, Dog, Cocker Spaniel, HN 1187, 5 In. 145.00
Animal, Dog, Cocker Spaniel, K 9, 2 In. 100.00
Animal, Dog, Cocker Spaniel, Pheasant, HN 1029, 4 In. 140.00
Animal, Dog, Collie, HN 1058, 5 In. 195.00
Animal, Dog, Dachshund, HN 1128, 4 In. ....135.00 to 150.00
Animal, Dog, Dachshund, HN 1140, 4 In. ....155.00 to 175.00
Animal, Dog, Dachshund, HN 1141, 3 In. 150.00
Animal, Dog, Dachshund, K 19, 1 1/2 In. 90.00
Animal, Dog, Dachshund, Seated, K 17, 2 In. 90.00
Animal, Dog, Dalmatian, HN 1113, 5 1/2 In. ....215.00 to 225.00
Animal, Dog, English Setter, HN 1050, 5 In. ....145.00 to 150.00
Animal, Dog, English Setter, HN 1051, 4 In. ....175.00 to 210.00
Animal, Dog, Fox Terrier, K 8, 2 1/2 In. ....75.00 to 100.00
Animal, Dog, Foxhound, Pup, K 7, 2 1/2 In. 90.00
Animal, Dog, French Poodle, HN 2631, 5 In. ....65.00 to 200.00
Animal, Dog, Irish Setter, HN 1055, 5 In. ....160.00 to 200.00
Animal, Dog, Pekinese, HN 1012, 3 In. ....135.00 to 160.00
Animal, Dog, Pekinese, K 6, 2 In. 100.00
Animal, Dog, Pointer, HN 2624, 5 In. 380.00
Animal, Dog, Rough-Haired Terrier, HN 1014, 4 In. ....125.00 to 165.00
Animal, Dog, Running With Ball, HN 1097, 2 In. 95.00
Animal, Dog, Scottish Terrier, Begging, K 10, 3 In. 110.00
Animal, Dog, Sealyham, HN 1030, 5 In. 775.00
Animal, Dog, Sealyham, K 4, 1 In. 295.00
Animal, Dog, Spaniel In Basket, HN 2585, 2 In. 80.00
Animal, Dog, St. Bernard, K 19, 1 1/2 In. 90.00
Animal, Duck, Floating, Flambe 325.00
Animal, Elephant, Flambe, HN 489a 125.00
Animal, Hare, Flambe 170.00
Animal, Horse, Chestnut Mare & Foal, HN 2522, 6 1/2 In. 425.00
Animal, Leopard On Rock, HN 2638, 9 In. 260.00
Animal, Owl, Flambe, 12 In. 350.00
Animal, Penguin, Flambe, HN 84 .... 100.00
Animal, Penguin, Head Down, K 23, 1 1/2 In. 200.00
Animal, Rabbit, Flambe 90.00
Animal, Rhinoceros, Flambe, HN 615 .... 875.00
Animal, Slinking Tiger, Signed, Noke 1150.00
Animal, Tiger On Rock, HN 2639, 11 1/2 In. 1500.00
Animal, Tiger, Flambe, HN 809, 6 In. 700.00
Animal, Tiger, Stalking, Flambe, 13 1/2 In. Long 645.00
Ash Pot, Dick Turpin 150.00
Ash Pot, Farmer John 150.00
Ash Pot, Parson Brown 150.00
Ashtray, Mr. Pickwick, Signed Noke 80.00
Ashtray, Parson Brown ....95.00 to 150.00
Bowl, Bill Sykes, Scalloped, Dickens Ware, Noke, 7 3/4 x 9 x 1 In. 150.00
Bowl, Cereal, Bunnykins 42.00
Bowl, Feeding, Bunnykins 17.00

Bowl, Golf, 6 In. 350.00
Bowl, Golf, 8 In. 400.00
Bowl, Group Of Golfers, Cream, Green, 3 x 4 In. 120.00
Bowl, Moreton Hall, 1915, 9 1/2 In. 225.00
Bowl, Vegetable, Pastorale, Oval 40.00
Bowl, Willow, Flow Blue, 3 7/8 x 8 1/2 In. 145.00
Bust, Mr. Pickwick, D 6049, 3 1/2 In. 75.00
Cake Plate, Coaching Days 30.00
Celery, Old English Scene, Brown, 6 x 10 In. 85.00

Royal Doulton character jugs depict the head and shoulders of the subject. They are made in four sizes: large, 5 1/4 to 7 inches; small, 3 1/4
to 4 inches; miniature, 2 1/4 to 2 1/2 inches; and tiny, 1 1/4 inches.
Toby jugs portray a seated, full figure.

Character Jug, 'Ard Of 'Earing, Large 1650.00
Character Jug, 'Ard Of 'Earing, Small 695.00
Character Jug, 'Arriet, Large 300.00
Character Jug, 'Arriet, Miniature 110.00
Character Jug, 'Arriet, Small ....125.00 to 150.00
Character Jug, 'Arriet, Tiny 150.00
Character Jug, 'Arry, Large 300.00
Character Jug, 'Arry, Miniature 95.00
Character Jug, 'Arry, Small 155.00
Character Jug, Abraham Lincoln, Large 155.00
Character Jug, Ahab, Large 80.00
Character Jug, Airman, Small 50.00
Character Jug, Albert Einstein, Large 150.00
Character Jug, Alfred Hitchcock, Large 175.00
Character Jug, Alfred Hitchcock, White, Black, Pink Handle, Large 1800.00
Character Jug, Angler, Small 50.00
Character Jug, Anne Boleyn, Large ....75.00 to 140.00
Character Jug, Anne Boleyn, Miniature 125.00
Character Jug, Anne Boleyn, Small 90.00
Character Jug, Anne Of Cleves, Large 300.00
Character Jug, Annie Oakley, Medium 115.00
Character Jug, Antique Dealer, Large 175.00
Character Jug, Antony & Cleopatra, Large, Pair ....125.00 to 170.00
Character Jug, Apothecary, Large 135.00
Character Jug, Apothecary, Miniature 80.00
Character Jug, Aramis, Large ....75.00 to 125.00
Character Jug, Aramis, Small ....70.00 to 75.00
Character Jug, Athos, 1991, Miniature 125.00
Character Jug, Athos, Large ....90.00 to 125.00
Character Jug, Auld Mac, Large ....120.00 to 140.00
Character Jug, Auld Mac, Miniature ....45.00 to 65.00
Character Jug, Auld Mac, Musical, Large 1000.00
Character Jug, Auld Mac, Tiny 295.00
Character Jug, Bahamas Policeman, Large 250.00
Character Jug, Barleycorn, Miniature 125.00
Character Jug, Barleycorn, Small 68.00
Character Jug, Beefeater, Large ....59.00 to 250.00
Character Jug, Beefeater, Miniature 50.00
Character Jug, Beefeater, Small 100.00
Character Jug, Beefeater, Tiny ....110.00 to 175.00
Character Jug, Benjamin Franklin, Small ....35.00 to 70.00
Character Jug, Bill Sykes, Large 275.00
Character Jug, Blacksmith, Miniature 80.00
Character Jug, Blacksmith, Williamsburg, Large ....68.00 to 91.00
Character Jug, Bootmaker, Large ....60.00 to 99.00
Character Jug, Buffalo Bill, Wild West, Mid 80.00
Character Jug, Busker, Large 89.00
Character Jug, Buz Fuz, Small 125.00

Character Jug, Captain Ahab, Large . . . . .80.00 to 115.00
Character Jug, Captain Cuttle, Small . . . . .125.00 to 135.00
Character Jug, Captain Henry Morgan, Large . . . . .100.00 to 135.00
Character Jug, Captain Henry Morgan, Miniature 65.00
Character Jug, Captain Henry Morgan, Small 75.00
Character Jug, Captain Hook, Large . . . . .325.00 to 525.00
Character Jug, Cardinal, A Mark, Small 100.00
Character Jug, Cardinal, Large . . . . .195.00 to 275.00
Character Jug, Cardinal, Miniature 100.00
Character Jug, Cardinal, Tiny 150.00
Character Jug, Catherine Howard, Large 225.00
Character Jug, Catherine Howard, Small 175.00
Character Jug, Catherine Of Aragon, Large 150.00
Character Jug, Catherine Of Aragon, Miniature 110.00
Character Jug, Catherine Of Aragon, Small 100.00
Character Jug, Cavalier, Large 95.00
Character Jug, Cavalier, Small 85.00
Character Jug, Cavalier, Without Goatee, Large 140.00
Character Jug, Charles Dickens, Large 450.00
Character Jug, Charles Dickens, Miniature 135.00
Character Jug, Charles Dickens, Small 115.00
Character Jug, Collector, Large 154.00
Character Jug, Confucius, Flambe, Large 220.00
Character Jug, Cyrano De Bergerac, Large 165.00
Character Jug, Dick Turpin, Horse Handle, Small 43.00
Character Jug, Dick Turpin, Miniature . . . . '75.00
Character Jug, Dick Turpin, Pistol Handle, Small 50.00
Character Jug, Doc Holiday, Wild West, Mid 80.00
Character Jug, Don Quixote, Large . . . . .80.00 to 100.00
Character Jug, Don Quixote, Miniature 65.00
Character Jug, Drake, Small 95.00
Character Jug, Earl Mountbatten Of Burma, Large 225.00
Character Jug, Eisenhower, Large 325.00
Character Jug, Falconer, Large 300.00
Character Jug, Falconer, Small 80.00
Character Jug, Falstaff, Large . . . . .75.00 to 120.00
Character Jug, Fat Boy, Miniature . . . . .70.00 to 75.00
Character Jug, Fat Boy, Small 160.00
Character Jug, Fat Boy, Tiny 190.00
Character Jug, Field Marshall, Montgomery, Alemein, Large 250.00
Character Jug, Fortune Teller, Large . . . . .440.00 to 462.00
Character Jug, Fortune Teller, Miniature 450.00
Character Jug, Gaoler, Williamsburg, Large 99.00
Character Jug, Gardener, Large 150.00
Character Jug, General Gordon, Large 175.00
Character Jug, George Tinworth, Small 100.00
Character Jug, George Washington, Large . . . . .89.00 to 180.00
Character Jug, Gladiator, Small 500.00
Character Jug, Golfer, Large . . . . .125.00 to 200.00
Character Jug, Golfer, Miniature 75.00
Character Jug, Gondolier, Large 800.00
Character Jug, Gondolier, Miniature 250.00
Character Jug, Gondolier, Small . . . . .185.00 to 550.00
Character Jug, Gone Away, Small 50.00
Character Jug, Granny, One Tooth, Small 40.00
Character Jug, Groucho Marx, Large 81.00
Character Jug, Guardsman, Large 699.00
Character Jug, Gulliver, Large 505.00
Character Jug, Gulliver, Small 525.00
Character Jug, Gunsmith, Large . . . . .63.00 to 81.00
Character Jug, Gunsmith, Miniature 85.00
Character Jug, Guy Fawkes, Large 105.00
Character Jug, Henry VIII, Small 50.00

Character Jug, Honest Measure, Tiny 75.00
Character Jug, Isaac Walton, Large 100.00
Character Jug, Jane Seymour, Miniature 150.00
Character Jug, Jockey, Large ....240.00 to 450.00
Character Jug, John Barleycorn, Large 225.00
Character Jug, John Barleycorn, Small 110.00
Character Jug, John Doulton, 2 O'Clock, Small 50.00
Character Jug, John Doulton, 8 O'Clock, Small ....53.00 to 100.00
Character Jug, John Peel, Large ....200.00 to 225.00
Character Jug, John Peel, Miniature ....44.00 to 158.00
Character Jug, John Peel, Small 155.00
Character Jug, John Peel, Tiny ....150.00 to 295.00
Character Jug, Johnny Appleseed, Large ....250.00 to 330.00
Character Jug, Lawyer, Small 50.00
Character Jug, Leprechaun, Large 99.00
Character Jug, Little Nell, Tiny 50.00
Character Jug, Lobster Man, Large 70.00
Character Jug, London Bobby, Miniature ....45.00 to 180.00
Character Jug, Lord Nelson, Large 130.00
Character Jug, Louis Armstrong, Large ....135.00 to 200.00
Character Jug, Mad Hatter, Large 200.00
Character Jug, Mad Hatter, Small ....152.00 to 250.00
Character Jug, Mae West, Large 172.00
Character Jug, Mark Twain, Large 100.00
Character Jug, Mephistopheles, Large 1775.00
Character Jug, Mephistopheles, With Verse, Small 970.00
Character Jug, Merlin, Large 68.00
Character Jug, Merlin, Small 50.00
Character Jug, Mine Host, Miniature 90.00
Character Jug, Mr. Micawber, Miniature 50.00
Character Jug, Mr. Micawber, Tiny 150.00
Character Jug, Mr. Pickwick, Large ....58.00 to 195.00
Character Jug, Mr. Pickwick, Miniature 45.00
Character Jug, Neptune, Large ....69.00 to 80.00
Character Jug, Night Watchman, Large 74.00
Character Jug, Night Watchman, Miniature 38.00
Character Jug, North American Indian, Large 60.00
Character Jug, Old Charley, Large 63.00
Character Jug, Old Salt, Large ....63.00 to 91.00
Character Jug, Paddy, Musical, An Irish Jig, Large 1000.00
Character Jug, Paddy, Small 50.00
Character Jug, Paddy, Tiny 85.00
Character Jug, Pearly Boy, Large 2200.00
Character Jug, Pearly Queen, Large 79.00
Character Jug, Pied Piper, Miniature 90.00
Character Jug, Pied Piper, Small 100.00
Character Jug, Piper, Large 300.00
Character Jug, Poacher, Miniature 40.00
Character Jug, Punch & Judy, Large 500.00
Character Jug, Queen Victoria, Large 220.00
Character Jug, Queen Victoria, Small 69.00
Character Jug, Red Queen, Miniature 175.00
Character Jug, Regency Beau, Large 1375.00
Character Jug, Regency Beau, Miniature 525.00
Character Jug, Regency Beau, Small ....450.00 to 950.00
Character Jug, Rip Van Winkle, Small 62.00
Character Jug, Robin Hood, Large ....77.00 to 115.00
Character Jug, Robin Hood, Miniature 100.00
Character Jug, Robin Hood, Small ....85.00 to 279.00
Character Jug, Robinson Crusoe, Large 175.00
Character Jug, Robinson Crusoe, Small 75.00
Character Jug, Romeo, Small 79.00
Character Jug, Sairey Gamp, Large 110.00

Character Jug, Sairey Gamp, Miniature 60.00
Character Jug, Sairey Gamp, Tiny 100.00
Character Jug, Sam Johnson, Large 475.00
Character Jug, Sam Weller, Miniature 100.00
Character Jug, Sam Weller, Small 265.00
Character Jug, Samson & Delilah, Two-Faced, Large ....180.00 to 200.00
Character Jug, Sancho Panca, Large 180.00
Character Jug, Santa Claus, Christmas Parcels Handle, Tiny 55.00
Character Jug, Santa Claus, Plain Handle, Small 50.00
Character Jug, Santa Claus, Plain Handle, Tiny 75.00
Character Jug, Santa Claus, Sack Of Toys Handle, Large 350.00
Character Jug, Scaramouche, Large 162.00
Character Jug, Scaramouche, Small ....425.00 to 650.00
Character Jug, Simon The Cellarer, Large ....185.00 to 190.00
Character Jug, Simon The Cellarer, Small 50.00
Character Jug, Sleuth, Small 200.00
Character Jug, Smuggler, Large ....95.00 to 205.00
Character Jug, Smuts, Large 2000.00
Character Jug, St. George, Large 175.00
Character Jug, St. George, Small ....220.00 to 225.00
Character Jug, Tam O'Shanter, Miniature 125.00
Character Jug, Toby Philpots, Miniature 70.00
Character Jug, Toby Philpots, Small 90.00
Character Jug, Tony Weller, Miniature ....45.00 to 65.00
Character Jug, Touchstone, Large 275.00
Character Jug, Town Crier, Miniature 90.00
Character Jug, Town Crier, Small 90.00
Character Jug, Trapper, Small 70.00
Character Jug, Ugly Duchess, Miniature ....255.00 to 450.00
Character Jug, Ugly Duchess, Small 450.00
Character Jug, Veteran Motorist, Large 95.00
Character Jug, Veteran Motorist, Miniature 100.00
Character Jug, Vicar Of Bray, Large ....143.00 to 300.00
Character Jug, W.C. Fields, Large ....109.00 to 138.00
Character Jug, Walrus & Carpenter, Large 240.00
Character Jug, Walrus & Carpenter, Miniature 135.00
Character Jug, Walrus & Carpenter, Small 140.00
Character Jug, Wild Bill Hickock, Small 80.00
Character Jug, William Shakespeare, Large 575.00
Character Jug, Winston Churchill, Large ....125.00 to 143.00
Character Jug, Yachtsman, Large ....80.00 to 145.00
Child's Set, Bunnykins 95.00
Creamer, Coaching Days 75.00
Creamer, Eglinton Tournament, 1902 .... 75.00
Cup, Coaching Days 25.00
Decanter, Old Crow Bourbon 110.00
Dish, Dark Blue Flowered Center, 8 x 10 1/2 In. 80.00
Ewer, Babes In Woods Series, Girl With Cape, 9 In. 1250.00
Ewer, John DeWar & Sons, 6 In. 95.00
Figurine, A' Courting, HN 2004 .... 675.00
Figurine, Ace, HN 3398 ....145.00 to 245.00
Figurine, Adele, HN 2480 ....125.00 to 150.00
Figurine, Adrienne, HN 2304 .... 110.00
Figurine, Afternoon Tea, HN 1747 ....395.00 to 575.00
Figurine, Alice, HN 3368 ....110.00 to 260.00
Figurine, Amy, HN 3316 ....550.00 to 725.00
Figurine, Angela, HN 1204 .... 1800.00
Figurine, Annabella, HN 1875 .... 535.00
Figurine, Anthea, HN 1527 .... 1750.00
Figurine, Ascot, HN 2356 .... 215.00
Figurine, Auctioneer, HN 2988 ....126.00 to 160.00
Figurine, Autumn (Automne), HN 3068 .... 440.00
Figurine, Autumn Breezes, HN 1913 .... 240.00

Figurine, Autumn Breezes, HN 1934 ....75.00 to 425.00
Figurine, Autumn Breezes, HN 2131 .... 300.00
Figurine, Autumn Breezes, HN 2147 ....275.00 to 350.00
Figurine, Autumn Breezes, Pink, HN 1911 .... 150.00
Figurine, Autumntime, HN 3231 .... 150.00
Figurine, Ballerina, HN 2116 .... 250.00
Figurine, Balloon Man, HN 1954 ....132.00 to 180.00
Figurine, Basket Weaver, HN 2245 .... 575.00
Figurine, Bathing Beauty, HN 3156 .... 325.00
Figurine, Beachcomber, HN 2487 .... 150.00
Figurine, Bedtime Story, HN 2059 .... 110.00
Figurine, Bell O' The Ball, HN 1997 ....250.00 to 450.00
Figurine, Belle, HN 2340 .... 75.00
Figurine, Bess, HN 2002 .... 110.00
Figurine, Bess, HN 2003 .... 525.00
Figurine, Beth, HN 2870 .... 300.00
Figurine, Biddy, HN 1513 ....150.00 to 190.00
Figurine, Bilbo, HN 2914 .... 100.00
Figurine, Blithe Morning, HN 2021 ....225.00 to 250.00
Figurine, Blithe Morning, HN 2065 .... 225.00
Figurine, Bluebeard, HN 2105 .... 260.00
Figurine, Bo-Peep, HN 1811 ....50.00 to 100.00
Figurine, Boy From Williamsburg, HN 2183 .... 150.00
Figurine, Breton Dancer, HN 2383 .... 950.00
Figurine, Bride, HN 1600 ....500.00 to 950.00
Figurine, Bride, HN 2166 .... 195.00
Figurine, Bride, HN 2873 ....115.00 to 150.00
Figurine, Bridesmaid, HN 2148 .... 250.00
Figurine, Bridesmaid, HN 2874 .... 75.00
Figurine, Bridget, HN 2070 ....215.00 to 250.00
Figurine, Broken Lance, HN 2041 .... 400.00
Figurine, Buttercup, HN 3268 .... 70.00
Figurine, Butterfly Girl, HN 1456 .... 3500.00
Figurine, Camellia, HN 2222 ....260.00 to 275.00
Figurine, Captain, 2nd New York Regiment, HN 2755 .... 1200.00
Figurine, Carmen, HN 1267 .... 2500.00
Figurine, Carolyn, HN 2974 .... 225.00
Figurine, Carpenter, HN 2678 .... 275.00
Figurine, Carpet Seller, HN 1464 .... 325.00
Figurine, Cavalier, HN 2716 .... 395.00
Figurine, Cellist, HN 2226 .... 425.00
Figurine, Charlotte, HN 3811 .... 200.00
Figurine, Chelsea Pensioner, HN 689 .... 900.00
Figurine, Child From Williamsburg, HN 2154 ....180.00 to 250.00
Figurine, Christine, HN 1840 .... 1300.00
Figurine, Christmas Morn, HN 1992 ....99.00 to 245.00
Figurine, Christmas Parcels, HN 2851 ....225.00 to 345.00
Figurine, Cissie, HN 1809 .... 120.00
Figurine, Coachman, HN 2282 .... 428.00
Figurine, Collinette, HN 1999 .... 650.00
Figurine, Cookie, HN 2218 .... 200.00
Figurine, Dancing Delight, HN 3078 .... 200.00
Figurine, Dancing Years, HN 2235 .... 250.00
Figurine, Daphne, HN 2268 .... 250.00
Figurine, Darling, HN 1985 .... 92.00
Figurine, Daydreams, HN 1731 .... 190.00
Figurine, Deauville, HN 2344 .... 250.00
Figurine, Debutante, HN 2210 .... 250.00
Figurine, Delight, HN 1772 .... 170.00
Figurine, Delphine, HN 2136 .... 260.00
Figurine, Detective, HN 2359 .... 395.00
Figurine, Dinky-Do, HN 1678 ....80.00 to 100.00
Figurine, Doctor, HN 2858 .... 250.00

Figurine, Donna, HN 2939 .... 200.00
Figurine, Dorcas, HN 1558 .... 220.00
Figurine, Dreamweaver, HN 2283 .... 200.00
Figurine, Easter Day, HN 2039 ....300.00 to 575.00
Figurine, Eleanor Of Provence, HN 2009 .... 775.00
Figurine, Elegance, HN 2264 ....155.00 to 200.00
Figurine, Enchantment, HN 2178 .... 175.00
Figurine, Ermine Coat, HN 1981 ....92.00 to 400.00
Figurine, Fair Lady, HN 2193 .... 85.00
Figurine, Fair Lady, HN 2832 .... 225.00
Figurine, Faith, HN 3082 .... 150.00
Figurine, Falstaff, HN 2054 .... 140.00
Figurine, Falstaff, HN 3236 .... 100.00
Figurine, Farmer's Wife, HN 2069 .... 470.00
Figurine, Father Christmas, HN 3399 .... 145.00
Figurine, Favourite, HN 2249 .... 220.00
Figurine, Fiona, HN 2694 .... 200.00
Figurine, First Steps, HN 2242 .... 385.00
Figurine, Fleur, HN 2368 .... 210.00
Figurine, Flora, HN 2349 .... 295.00
Figurine, Foaming Quart, HN 2162 ....80.00 to 93.00
Figurine, Folly, HN 1750 .... 1500.00
Figurine, Forget-Me-Not, HN 3388 .... 75.00
Figurine, Forty Winks, HN 1974 ....225.00 to 325.00
Figurine, Friar Tuck, HN 2143 ....275.00 to 375.00
Figurine, Frodo, HN 2912 .... 100.00
Figurine, Gardening Time, HN 3401 .... 185.00
Figurine, Gay Morning, HN 2135 .... 350.00
Figurine, Geisha, HN 3229 ....160.00 to 220.00
Figurine, General Robert E. Lee, HN 3404 .... 750.00
Figurine, Genevieve, HN 1962 .... 300.00
Figurine, Genie, HN 2989 .... 160.00
Figurine, George Washington At Prayer, HN 2861 .... 3200.00
Figurine, Giselle, HN 2140 .... 575.00
Figurine, Golfer, HN 2992 .... 300.00
Figurine, Golliwog, HN 2040 .... 140.00
Figurine, Good Catch, HN 2258 .... 170.00
Figurine, Good King Wenceslas, HN 2118 ....400.00 to 550.00
Figurine, Goody Two Shoes, HN 2017 .... 100.00
Figurine, Goody Two Shoes, HN 2037 ....120.00 to 140.00
Figurine, Grand Manner, HN 2723 .... 210.00
Figurine, Grandma, HN 2052 .... 250.00
Figurine, Guardsman, HN 2784 .... 180.00
Figurine, Gwendolen, HN 1570 .... 1600.00
Figurine, Hannah, HN 3369 .... 290.00
Figurine, Happy Anniversary, HN 3097 .... 150.00
Figurine, Harlequinade, HN 711 .... 1500.00
Figurine, Henrietta Maria, HN 2005 .... 700.00
Figurine, Her Ladyship, HN 1977 .... 350.00
Figurine, His Holiness, Pope John-Paul II, HN 2888 .... 250.00
Figurine, HM Queen Elizabeth II, HN 3440 .... 350.00
Figurine, Homecoming, HN 3295 .... 140.00
Figurine, Hornpipe, HN 2161 .... 595.00
Figurine, HRH Prince Of Wales, HN 2883 .... 700.00
Figurine, HRH Prince Philip, Duke Of Edinburgh, HN 2384 .... 500.00
Figurine, Indian Maiden, HN 3117 .... 200.00
Figurine, Invitation, HN 2170 ....140.00 to 160.00,
Figurine, Jack, HN 2060 .... 195.00
Figurine, Janet, HN 1916 .... 210.00
Figurine, Janice, HN 2022 .... 650.00
Figurine, Janine, HN 2461 .... 185.00
Figurine, Jean, HN 2032 .... 325.00

Figurine, Jester, HN 2016 . . . . .190.00 to 250.00
Figurine, Jester Mask, HN 1609 . . . . 850.00
Figurine, Jill, HN 2061 . . . . 150.00
Figurine, Joan, HN 3217 . . . . 250.00
Figurine, John F. Kennedy, White Suit 10000.00
Figurine, Joker, HN 3196 . . . . 145.00
Figurine, Jovial Monk, HN 2144 . . . . 180.00
Figurine, Judge, HN 2443 . . . . 250.00
Figurine, Karen, HN 1994 . . . . 485.00
Figurine, Karen, HN 2388 . . . . 300.00
Figurine, Kate Hardcastle, HN 2028 . . . . 975.00
Figurine, Kathy, HN 2346 . . . . 150.00
Figurine, King Charles, HN 2084 . . . . 1495.00
Figurine, Lady Anne Nevill, HN 2006 . . . . .775.00 to 795.00
Figurine, Lady Charmian, HN 1948 . . . . .235.00 to 290.00
Figurine, Lady Charmian, HN 1949 . . . . .75.00 to 212.00
Figurine, Lalla Rookh, HN 2910 . . . . .550.00 to 650.00
Figurine, Lambing Time, HN 1890 . . . . 175.00
Figurine, Last Waltz, HN 2315 . . . . 195.00
Figurine, Lavinia, HN 1955 . . . . 120.00
Figurine, Leisure Hour, HN 2055 . . . . 450.00
Figurine, Lilian In Summer, HN 3003 . . . . 125.00
Figurine, Little Bridesmaid, HN 1433 . . . . 135.00
Figurine, Lobster Man, HN 2317 . . . . 225.00
Figurine, Lorna, HN 2311 . . . . 150.00
Figurine, Lunchtime, HN 2485 . . . . 185.00
Figurine, Lydia, HN 1908 . . . . .50.00 to 140.00
Figurine, Lyric, HN 2757 . . . . 80.00
Figurine, Madonna Of The Square, HN 2034 . . . . 750.00
Figurine, Margaret Of Anjou, HN 2012 . . . . 900.00
Figurine, Marguerite, HN 1928 . . . . .72.00 to 325.00
Figurine, Marietta, HN 1341 . . . . 2000.00
Figurine, Mary, Countess Howe, HN 3007 . . . . 700.00
Figurine, Mary, HN 3375 . . . . .300.00 to 550.00
Figurine, Mary Mary, HN 2044 . . . . 225.00
Figurine, Mask Seller, HN 2103 . . . . 172.00
Figurine, Masquerade, HN 600 . . . . 950.00
Figurine, Masquerade, HN 2259 . . . . .270.00 to 290.00
Figurine, Maureen, HN 1770 . . . . .80.00 to 450.00
Figurine, May, HN 3251 . . . . 138.60
Figurine, Mayor, HN 2280 . . . . 400.00
Figurine, Megan, HN 3306 . . . . 120.00
Figurine, Mermaid, HN 97 . . . . 1500.00
Figurine, Midinette, HN 2090 . . . . .250.00 to 275.00
Figurine, Millicent, HN 1714 . . . . 1950.00
Figurine, Minuet, HN 2019 . . . . .200.00 to 265.00
Figurine, Miranda, HN 3037 . . . . 175.00
Figurine, Miss Demure, HN 1402 . . . . 168.00
Figurine, Miss Fortune, HN 1897 . . . . 495.00
Figurine, Miss Muffet, HN 1936 . . . . 140.00
Figurine, Miss Muffet, HN 1937 . . . . 285.00
Figurine, Monica, HN 1467 . . . . .100.00 to 225.00
Figurine, My Best Friend, HN 3011 . . . . 200.00
Figurine, My Love, HN 2339 . . . . .355.00 to 375.00
Figurine, My Pet, HN 2238 . . . . 175.00
Figurine, New Bonnet, HN 1728 . . . . .550.00 to 875.00
Figurine, Newsboy, HN 2244 . . . . 450.00
Figurine, Newsvendor, HN 2891 . . . . .176.00 to 225.00
Figurine, Noelle, HN 2179 . . . . .365.00 to 600.00
Figurine, Old Balloon Seller, HN 1315 . . . . .160.00 to 187.00
Figurine, Old Mother Hubbard, HN 2314 . . . . 375.00
Figurine, Once Upon A Time, HN 2047 . . . . 275.00

Figurine, Orange Lady, HN 1759 ....125.00 to 195.00
Figurine, Orange Lady, HN 1953 .... 108.00
Figurine, Orange Vendor, HN 72 .... 1400.00
Figurine, Organ Grinder, HN 2173 .... 850.00
Figurine, Paisley Shawl, HN 1988 ....200.00 to 325.00
Figurine, Parson's Daughter, HN 564 .... 475.00
Figurine, Past Glory, HN 2484 .... 172.00
Figurine, Patricia, HN 3365 ....175.00 to 425.00
Figurine, Patricia, M 7, Miniature 300.00
Figurine, Paula, HN 2906 .... 160.00
Figurine, Pearly Boy, HN 2035 ....140.00 to 175.00
Figurine, Pearly Boy, HN 2767 ....120.00 to 165.00
Figurine, Pearly Girl, HN 2769 .... 120.00
Figurine, Penelope, HN 1901 ....260.00 to 310.00
Figurine, Penny, HN 2338 .... 70.00
Figurine, Pied Piper, HN 2102 .... 250.00
Figurine, Piper, HN 2907 .... 285.00
Figurine, Please Keep Still, HN 2967 .... 150.00
Figurine, Poacher, HN 2043 .... 350.00
Figurine, Polka, HN 2156 .... 350.00
Figurine, Potter, HN 1493 ....305.00 to 350.00
Figurine, Pride & Joy, HN 2945 .... 275.00
Figurine, Prized Possessions, HN 2942 ....375.00 to 450.00
Figurine, Professor, HN 2281 .... 125.00
Figurine, Prue, HN 1996 .... 335.00
Figurine, Puppetmaker, HN 2253 .... 465.00
Figurine, Queen Elizabeth I, HN 3099 .... 600.00
Figurine, Queen Victoria, HN 3125 .... 1500.00
Figurine, Rag Doll, HN 2142 .... 95.00
Figurine, Rebecca, HN 2805 .... 375.00
Figurine, Rendezvous, HN 2212 .... 400.00
Figurine, Rhapsody, HN 2267 .... 215.00
Figurine, Rhythm, HN 1903 .... 3300.00
Figurine, River Boy, HN 2128 .... 115.00
Figurine, Rosamond, HN 1320 .... 3000.00
Figurine, Rose, HN 1368 .... 75.00
Figurine, Roseanna, HN 1921 .... 1000.00
Figurine, Rosebud, HN 1983 ....450.00 to 475.00
Figurine, Rowena, HN 2077 ....525.00 to 800.00
Figurine, Ruth, HN 2799 .... 275.00
Figurine, Ruth, The Pirate Maid, HN 2900 .... 250.00
Figurine, Sabbath Morn, HN 1982 .... 300.00
Figurine, Schoolmarm, HN 2223 .... 350.00
Figurine, Scottish Highland Dancer, HN 2436 .... 1000.00
Figurine, Sea Harvest, HN 2257 .... 125.00
Figurine, Secret Thoughts, HN 2382 ....175.00 to 195.00
Figurine, Shepherd, HN 1975 .... 200.00
Figurine, Shore Leave, HN 2254 ....177.00 to 231.00
Figurine, Shy Anne, HN 65 .... 3250.00
Figurine, Silks & Ribbons, HN 2017 .... 80.50
Figurine, Sir Walter Raleigh, HN 2015 .... 950.00
Figurine, Sleepy Darling, HN 2953 ....115.00 to 210.00
Figurine, Sleepyhead, HN 3761 .... 70.00
Figurine, Sophie, HN 3257 ....135.00 to 200.00
Figurine, Southern Belle, HN 2229 ....250.00 to 375.00
Figurine, Southern Belle, HN 3174, Miniature 100.00
Figurine, Spring Flowers, HN 1807 .... 400.00
Figurine, Spring Morning, HN 1922 ....250.00 to 350.00
Figurine, Spring Morning, HN 1923 .... 1400.00
Figurine, Spring, HN 2085 .... 500.00
Figurine, Springtime, HN 1971 .... 1650.00
Figurine, Springtime, HN 3033 .... 275.00

Figurine, St. George, HN 2051 . . . . .375.00 to 475.00
Figurine, Summer, HN 3067 . . . . 550.00
Figurine, Sunday Best, HN 3218, Miniature 110.00
Figurine, Sunday Morning, HN 2184 . . . . 325.00
Figurine, Suzette, HN 1487 . . . . 525.00
Figurine, Sweet & Twenty, HN 1298 . . . . .125.00 to 250.00
Figurine, Sweet Anne, HN 1318 . . . . 575.00
Figurine, Sweet Anne, HN 1496 . . . . .195.00 to 285.00
Figurine, Sweet Anne, M 27, Miniature 525.00
Figurine, Sweet Dreams, HN 3394 . . . . 50.00
Figurine, Sweet Lavender, HN 1373 . . . . 800.00
Figurine, Sweet Suzy, HN 1918 . . . . 275.00
Figurine, Teatime, HN 2255 . . . . 200.00
Figurine, Teeing Off, HN 3276 . . . . 125.00
Figurine, Teresa, HN 1682 . . . . 1450.00
Figurine, This Little Pig, HN 1793 . . . . 40.00
Figurine, Tiger On Rock, HN 2639 . . . . 1500.00
Figurine, Tinkle Bell, HN 1677 . . . . .90.00 to 100.00
Figurine, Tootles, HN 1680 . . . . 100.00
Figurine, Top O' The Hill, HN 1834 . . . . 270.00
Figurine, Top O' The Hill, HN 1849 . . . . 295.00
Figurine, Top O' The Hill, HN 2126, Miniature 140.00
Figurine, Top O' The Hill, HN 2127 . . . . 275.00
Figurine, Town Crier, HN 2119 . . . . .195.00 to 300.00
Figurine, Tumbler, HN 3183 . . . . 140.00
Figurine, Uncle Ned, HN 2094 . . . . .475.00 to 495.00
Figurine, Veronica, HN 1517 . . . . 525.00
Figurine, Veronica, HN 3205 . . . . 120.00
Figurine, Victoria, HN 2471 . . . . 225.00
Figurine, Wayfarer, HN 2362 . . . . 175.00
Figurine, Wimbledon, HN 3366 . . . . 350.00
Figurine, Windflower, HN 3077 . . . . 150.00
Figurine, Winston Churchill, HN 3433 . . . . 425.00
Figurine, Winter, HN 3069 . . . . 550.00
Figurine, Wintertime, HN 3622 . . . . 235.00
Figurine, Wizard, HN 2877 . . . . 300.00
Figurine, Young Master, HN 2872 . . . . 300.00
Figurine, Yvonne, HN 3038 . . . . 130.00
Humidor, Arabian Desert Scenes, 7 1/2 In. 400.00
Jug, Aladdin's Genie, Large 295.00
Jug, McCallum, Kingsware, Large 3000.00
Jug, Skater's 150.00
Lighter, Bacchus 350.00
Lighter, Beefeater 200.00
Lighter, Buz Fuz 325.00
Lighter, Falstaff 170.00
Lighter, Lawyer 300.00
Lighter, Mr. Pickwick 325.00
Lighter, Old Charley . . . . .190.00 to 220.00
Lighter, Rip Van Winkle 450.00
Loving Cup, Charles Dickens . . . . .425.00 to 450.00
Loving Cup, Henry VIII, Double Handle, Large .695.00 to 1200.00
Loving Cup, King & Queen Corona 900.00
Loving Cup, King Charles I 450.00
Loving Cup, King George V & Queen Mary Silver Jubilee, 1935 . . . . 1200.00
Loving Cup, Three Musketeers, 1955 . . . . 725.00
Loving Cup, Tower Of London, 1933 . . . . 1900.00
Loving Cup, Village Blacksmith, 1935 . . . . 1200.00
Loving Cup, William Wordsworth 145.00
Pitcher, Eglinton Tournament, Queen Victoria, 6 In. 285.00
Pitcher, Milk, Golf, 4 In. 750.00
Pitcher, Milk, Under The Greenwood Tree 395.00

Pitcher, Monks Standing At A Window, 6 Sided, 6 In. 325.00
Pitcher, Old Curiosity Shop 200.00
Pitcher, Quarreling Dogs, 1903 .... 450.00
Plate, Artful Dodger, Dickens Ware, 10 1/2 In. 110.00
Plate, Cap'n Cuttle, 10 In. 125.00
Plate, Fisherwoman, 1977 .... 50.00
Plate, Gallant Fisher, 10 1/4 In. 200.00
Plate, Gallant Fisher, 8 1/4 In. 250.00
Plate, George Washington, Blue, Garland Border, 1910, 9 1/2 In. 125.00
Plate, Golf, 10 1/2 In. 300.00
Plate, Golf, 6 In. 300.00
Plate, Handsome Is That Handsome Does, 10 1/2 In. 85.00
Plate, Hunting Man, 10 In. 95.00
Plate, Irish Setter 110.00
Plate, McCawber, Dickens Ware, 10 1/2 In. 98.00
Plate, Nursery Rhyme, Where Are You Going My Pretty Maid, 8 In. 95.00
Plate, Parson 60.00
Plate, Prince Of Wales, Lady Diana, Flowers, Commemorative, 1981 .... 75.00
Plate, Queen Elizabeth At Old Moreton, 10 In. 110.00
Plate, Sir Richard Greenville Revenge, Pastel, 10 1/2 In. 125.00
Plate, Valentine, 1975, Box 45.00
Plate, Valentine, 1981, Box 45.00
Plate, Watteau, 9 3/4 In. 50.00
Plate, William Wordsworth 50.00
Platter, Elegy, 13 In. 50.00
Platter, Forest Glade, 13 1/4 In. 60.00
Platter, Innocence, 13 In. 50.00
Porridge Set, Child's, Girls, In Long Dresses, D 3119, 3 Piece 220.00
Punch Bowl, Coaching Days 325.00
Sugar & Creamer, Coaching Days 200.00
Teapot, Dickens Ware, 7 In. 135.00
Teapot, Old Salt ....175.00 to 290.00
Teapot, Pastorale 125.00
Teapot, Sir Roger DeCoverly 345.00
Teapot, Tony Weller 1350.00
Tile, Tea, Old Lady In Bonnet, A Cup Of Tea That's Cheery 210.00
Toby Jug, Charlie Chaplin 10000.00
Toby Jug, Jolly Toby, Medium 120.00
Toby Jug, Old Charlie, Tiny 173.00
Toby Jug, Sairey Gamp, Tiny 173.00
Toby Jug, Sam Weller, Small ....75.00 to 95.00
Toby Jug, Sherlock Holmes, Large 180.00
Toby Jug, Sherlock Holmes, Tiny 80.00
Toothpick, Izaac Walton, Signed Noke 125.00
Tray, Dickens Ware, David & His Aunt, 4 1/2 In. 85.00
Vase, Arabian Scene, Outlined In Black, Red High Glaze, 13 x 8 1/2 In. 1210.00
Vase, Babes In Woods, 4 Children Playing Around Tree, Signed, 10 1/2 In. 595.00
Vase, Babes In Woods, 9 In. 1175.00
Vase, Babes In Woods, Pillow Shape, Girl Comforting Crying Toddler, 3 3/4 In. 600.00
Vase, Bud, Gold Leaf, Cobalt Blue Ground, 4 3/4 In. 95.00
Vase, Chang, Green & White Bleed Over, Chang, D 1152, Noke 850.00
Vase, Coaching Days, Ovoid, 2 1/4 x 3 1/4 In. 85.00
Vase, Fagin, Dickens Ware, Noke, 4 1/2 In. 95.00
Vase, Flambe Sung, Melon Shape Top, Fred Moore, 7 1/2 In. 550.00
Vase, Flambe, Bulbous, Red Swirl, Mottled Blue To Gray Glaze, 8 In. 495.00
Vase, Flambe, Country House, 8 In. 150.00
Vase, Flambe, Country House, 12 In. 150.00
Vase, Flambe, Scenic, Rural Church Surrounded By Flowers, Red, 5 In. 220.00
Vase, Flambe, Veined, Mottled Red, Blue, Green, Yellow Glaze, Printed Mark 172.50
Vase, Jackdaw Of Rheims, 1906-1930 .... 175.00
Vase, Persian, 14 In. 295.00
Vase, Roses In Wooden Pot, Blue, Green, 9 In. 125.00

Vase, Ruffled, Green, Beige, White Relief, Lambeth 170.00
Vase, Sung, Flambe, Mottled Blue, Signed, Allen, 11 1/4 In. 403.00
Vase, Sung, Red, Blue, Black Silver Flambe, C. Noke, 1920s, 9 1/4 In. 2420.00
Vase, Witch, Standing Over Her Cauldron, Crescent Moon Overhead, 5 1/4 In. 193.00

ROYAL DUX is the more common name for the Duxer Porzellan-
manufaktur, which was founded by E. Eichler in Dux, Bohemia, in
1860. By the turn of the century, the firm specialized in porcelain statuary and busts of Art Nouveau–style maidens, large porcelain figures,
and ornate vases with three-dimensional figures climbing on the sides.
The firm is still in business.

Bust, Woman, Adorned With Flowers, Czechoslovakia, c.1915, 18 1/2 In. 460.00
Bust, Woman, Early 20th Century, Czechoslovakia, 18 1/2 In. 1495.00
Figurine, Antelope, White, 4 x 3 In. 55.00
Figurine, Bathing Beauty 65.00
Figurine, Beetle 325.00
Figurine, Bird, On Stand, No. 359 .... 80.00
Figurine, Cat, Black, Art Deco 85.00
Figurine, Cat, Iridescent Black Glaze, Marked, 7 1/2 In. 57.50
Figurine, Cat, Modern, Black, No. 6278 ....75.00 to 125.00
Figurine, Cinderella 150.00
Figurine, Cockatoo, 15 1/2 In. 695.00
Figurine, Cockatoo, On Perch, Tan & Gray Glaze, Ink Mark, 15 In. 220.00
Figurine, Cockatoo, White, Pink Shading, Triangle Mark, 15 In. 185.00
Figurine, Dog, With Pheasant 350.00
Figurine, Elephant, 10 x 13 In. 195.00
Figurine, Elephant, Bisque 45.00
Figurine, Fish, In Plants, Brown 150.00
Figurine, Fish, Pike, Pink Triangle Mark 75.00
Figurine, German Shepherd, Reclining ....75.00 to 175.00
Figurine, German Shepherd, Sitting 45.00
Figurine, Lion, 4 In. 65.00
Figurine, Maiden, Barefoot, Flowing Gold Gown, Pink Triangle 250.00
Figurine, Man & Woman Dressed, Pink Triangle Mark, 14 In., Pair 414.00
Figurine, Man, Women Dancers, Blue, White, Gold, 1st Mark 450.00
Figurine, Owl, Modern, Bulbous, No. 613 .... 100.00
Figurine, Owl, White, No. 6890 .... 80.00
Figurine, Parrot, No. 329 .... 400.00
Figurine, Peacock, No. 642 .... 125.00
Figurine, Pig, White 30.00
Figurine, Ram, No. 694 .... 90.00
Figurine, Spaniel 45.00
Figurine, Tiger, 17 In. 325.00
Figurine, Woman, Seated, Sedan Chair, Gold, Signed, 14 x 8 1/2 x 15 1/2 In. 925.00
Figurine, Woman, Water Jug & Apples, Matte Natural Colors, 20 In. 495.00
Figurine, Young Maiden, Flowing Robe, Tragedy, 1920s, 16 5/8 In. 1035.00
Vase, Raised Blackberries, Vines & Leaves, Ivory Ground, 20 1/2 x 7 1/2 In. 300.00

ROYAL FLEMISH glass was made during the late 1880s in New Bedford,
Massachusetts, by the Mt. Washington Glass Works. It is a colored
satin glass decorated with dark colors and raised gold designs. The
glass was patented in 1894. It was supposed to resemble stained glass
windows.

Cracker Barrel, Cover, Roman Coins, Gold Lines, Floral, Rope Bail, 5 In. 1320.00
Pickle Castor, Blue Flower, Yellow Ground, Silver Holder, Victorian, 8 1/2 In. 495.00
Saltshaker 250.00
Vase, Duck, Frosted & Yellow Sections, Mocha Spirals, Marked, 16 In. 5500.00
Vase, Yellow & Orange Panels, Roses, Opaque, Ruffled Collar, 14 In. 3105.00

ROYAL HAEGER, see Haeger category.

ROYAL IVY pieces are listed in the Pressed Glass category by that pattern name.

ROYAL NYMPHENBURG is the modern name for the Nymphenburg porcelain factory, which was established at Neudeck-ob-der-Au, Germany, in 1753 and moved to Nymphenburg in 1761. The company is still in existence. Marks include a checkered shield topped by a crown, a crowned *CT* with the year, and a contemporary shield mark on reproductions of eighteenth-century porcelain.

Candelabrum, 5-Light, Foliate Branches, Grapes, 1980s, 23 1/2 In.	2300.00
Cup & Saucer, Classical Figurines, Landscape	920.00
Cup & Saucer, Mythological Scenes, Sprays Of Flowers	1610.00
Figurine, Bird, On Stump, 19th Century, 13 In.	23.00
Figurine, Miner, White Glaze, Crown, Shield Mark, 10 In.	805.00
Group, Wild Boar, Pursuing 18th-Century Clothed Figure, 9 1/2 x 18 In.	520.00
Soup, Dish, Beaded Border, Central Landscape, 9 1/2 In., 12 Piece	1150.00

ROYAL OAK pieces are listed in the Pressed Glass category by that pattern name.

ROYAL RUDOLSTADT, see Rudolstadt category.

ROYAL VIENNA, see Beehive category.

ROYAL WORCESTER is a name used by collectors. Worcester porcelains were made in Worcester, England, from about 1751. The firm went through many different periods and name changes. It became the Worcester Royal Porcelain Company, Ltd., in 1862. Today collectors call the porcelains made after 1862 *Royal Worcester*. In 1976, the firm merged with W. T. Copeland to become Royal Worcester Spode. Some early products of the factory are listed under Worcester.

Basket, Sugar, Gargoyle Heads, Hoof Footed, Ruby Glass Insert, 1873	200.00
Biscuit Jar, Melon	445.00
Bowl, Cover, Enamel Floral, Gilt, 1888, 8 1/2 In.	550.00
Bowl, Embossed Leaves, Basket Weave, Gold Trim, 1896, 9 In.	295.00
Bowl, Leaf Shape, 1899, 9 In.	375.00
Butter Pot, Drainer, Pine Cone Finial Cover, Acanthus Leaf Rim, 1890, 6 In.	525.00
Chocolate Pot, Red, Rose & Tan, Marked, 1894, 9 In.	125.00
Coffeepot, Floral Sprays, Tankardgold Bamboo Handle, Maroon Mark, 8 In.	200.00
Cup & Saucer, Bell Shape, Chrysanthemum Blossoms, 3 In.	630.00
Dish, Cover, Floral Design, Fluted, 1889, 6 1/4 In.	230.00
Ewer, Basket Weave Molded Body, Enamel Flowers, Shape No. 1028, 12 In.	490.00
Ewer, Enamel Landscape, Within Twig Frame, Gilt, 1888, 17 3/4 In.	750.00
Ewer, Floral, Reticulated Handle, 8 1/2 In.	210.00
Ewer, Parchment, Serpentine Handle, Salamander Shape, Puce Mark, 1889	770.00
Ewer, Tan & Gold Floral & Leaf Band, Bamboo Handle, Split Spout, 14 In.	190.00
Figurine, Baltimore Orioles & Tulip Tree, Dorothy Doughty, 1938, 10 1/4 In.	2300.00
Figurine, Blackbirds, Yellow Head, Dorothy Doughty, 11 In., Pair	520.00
Figurine, Blue Angel Fish, Signed, 1951, 18 In.	375.00
Figurine, Blue Tit, No. 3199, 1937, 2 1/4 In.	80.00
Figurine, Bridget, 1969	495.00
Figurine, Bullfinch, No. 3238, 1938, 2 7/8 In.	85.00
Figurine, Cairo Water Carrier, 1895, 8 3/4 In.	635.00
Figurine, Canyon Wren, Wild Lupin, No. 8939E, Dorothy Doughty, Pair	800.00
Figurine, Capt. Raimondo	995.00
Figurine, Classical Woman, Parian Glaze, England, c.1867, 16 In.	315.00
Figurine, Crowned Knights, Golden, No. 4260A, Dorothy Doughty, 7 In., Pair	800.00
Figurine, Galloping Horses, No. 3466, 1950, Marked, 16 1/4 In.	303.00
Figurine, Girl, Wales, No. 3103, 5 1/2 In.	690.00
Figurine, Girl, With A Basket, England, c.1887, 10 In.	259.00
Figurine, Goosey Goosey Gander, No. 3304, 5 1/2 In.	185.00
Figurine, Grandmother's Dress, No. 3435, 1960	95.00
Figurine, Marion Coates-Stroller	995.00
Figurine, Monday's Boy, No. 3519, 7 1/4 In.	127.00
Figurine, Napoleon, Commander	1995.00
Figurine, Orange Blossom & Butterflies, No. 2620, 8 In., Pair	800.00

Figurine, Percheron, French Draft Horse 1100.00
Figurine, Pheasants, Ring Necked, Standing On Branches, 14 1/2 In. 920.00
Figurine, Politician, White Glazed, Late 19th Century, 5 1/4 In. 290.00
Figurine, Red-Eyed Vireos & Swamp Azaleas, Dorothy Doughty, 1952, 7 In. 1330.00
Figurine, Robin, No. 3197, 1937, 2 3/4 In. 80.00
Figurine, Royal Artillery Officer, No. 2658, 10 3/4 In. 895.00
Figurine, Ruby Throated Hummingbirds & Fuchsias, 1950, 9 In. 1450.00
Figurine, Scarlet Tanager, No. 3534C, Dorothy Doughty, 12 In., Pair 1150.00
Figurine, Siamese Cat, 1961 .... 200.00
Figurine, Sister, No. 3149, 6 3/4 In. 345.00
Figurine, Sparrow, No. 3236, 1938, 3 3/8 In. 75.00
Figurine, Woodland Dance, No. 3076, 4 In. 150.00
Jug, Owl, On Tree Branch, Gold Serpent, Serpent Handle, 1885, 11 1/4 In. 930.00
Jug, Red Gold, Salamander Handles, 1883 .... 350.00
Jug, Tusk, 1885 .... 250.00
Mortar & Pestle 195.00
Mug, Wednesday's Child, Box 25.00
Pitcher, Beige, Horn Handle, 1880, 8 In. 169.00
Pitcher, Fern Design, 7 1/2 In. 187.00
Pitcher, Floral & Gilt Design, Cream Ground, Snake Handle, 7 In. 187.00
Pitcher, Flowers, Hand Painted, c.1880, 6 In. 140.00
Pitcher, Milk, Floral & Gilt Design, 6 1/2 In. 245.00
Pitcher, Painted Daisies & Field Flowers, Gold Handle, Maroon Mark, 6 In. 175.00
Pitcher, Pink Clematis, Gilt Vines, Pinched, Reed Handle, Maroon Mark, 8 In. ... 175.00
Pitcher, Raised Gold Floral, 9 In. 220.00
Pitcher, Tusk Handle, 1895, 10 In. 235.00
Plate, Scenic, Gold Edge, 1953, 10 3/4 In. 225.00
Platter, Black Transfer, Elephant Handles, Well, 21 1/4 In. 110.00
Platter, Pink & Floral Bouquet, Maroon Mark, Oval, 13 1/2 x 18 In. 165.00
Sugar & Creamer, Raised Wave Design, Green, Gold, 1894 .... 75.00
Tea Set, Floral, Dated 1890, 3 Piece 175.00
Teapot, Tankard, Assorted Flowers, Gold Bamboo Handle, Maroon Mark, 7 In. 165.00
Vase, Butterflies, Branched Flowers, Green Ground, Ball Footed, 5 In., Pair 440.00
Vase, Cover, Laurel Relief, 2 Tone Ivory Ground, Scrolled Ground, 17 In. 1495.00
Vase, Cover, Pierced Body Mounted To Back Of A Bird, 1908, 9 In. 400.00
Vase, Enamel Design Panel With Cows, Harry Stinton, 1909, 11 1/2 In. 1840.00
Vase, Floral Design, Gilt Trim, Reticulated, Printed Mark, 1891, 3 1/4 In. 115.00
Vase, Floral, Hand Painted, 20th Century, 9 1/2 In. 750.00
Vase, Foliate Panels To Neck, Ivory Ground, 2 Handles, 1888, 17 In. 980.00
Vase, Metallic Gold Trim, Yellow Ground, Late 19th Century, 5 3/4 In. 290.00
Vase, Nautilus Shell, 19th Century, 8 1/2 In. 230.00
Vase, Owls, Moon & Swallows, Handles, Artist, 1883, 12 1/2 In. 1150.00
Vase, Puffed Flowers, Dolphin Handles, Pedestal, 16 In. 875.00
Vase, Stick, Dark Owl, Gilt Branch, 2 Gold Handles, Green Mark, 6 1/2 In. 410.00
Vase, Swallows In Flight, Reticulated Color, Squatty, 1903, 7 1/2 x 3 In. 965.00
Vase, White & Gold Frog, Gold Trim, Square, 3 1/2 In. 325.00
Wall Pocket, Cornucopia, Cowherd Seated Under Tree, Blue, White, 8 3/4 In. 1265.00

ROYCROFT products were made by the Roycrofter community of East
Aurora, New York, in the late nineteenth and early twentieth centuries.
The community was founded by Elbert Hubbard, famous philosopher,
writer, and artist. The workshops owned by the community made furniture, metalware, leatherwork, embroidery, and jewelry. A printshop
produced many signs, books, and the magazines that promoted the say-
ings of Elbert Hubbard. Furniture by the Roycroft community is listed
in the Furniture category.

Ashtray, Nesting 100.00
Bookends, Brass Wash, Stylized Floral Design, Signed, 5 x 3 1/2 In. 220.00
Bookends, Copper, Dark Patina, Marked 150.00
Bookends, Copper, Embossed Owls, Hammered, 5 x 5 1/4 In. 330.00
Bookends, Copper, Embossed Owls, Hammered, Rectangular, 6 1/2 x 4 In. 330.00
Bookends, Copper, Embossed Seal Of Syracuse University, Hammered, 4 x 3 In. 385.00
Bookends, Copper, Galleon Riding Waves, Hammered, Brass Plated, 5 In. 148.00

Bookends, Copper, Hammered Finish, Marked, 4 3/4 In. 55.00
Bookends, Copper, Hammered, Brass Finish, Original Patina, Orb Mark, 2 x 3 In. 132.00
Bookends, Copper, Hammered, Orb Mark, 4 3/4 x 5 1/2 In. 345.00
Bookends, Copper, Not Hammered, Dark Patina 175.00
Bookends, Copper, Repousse Flowers, Hammered, Orb Mark, 8 1/2 x 5 3/4 In. 200.00
Bookends, Copper, Tree Design, Hammered, 4 x 7 In. 180.00
Bookends, Fleur-De-Lis, Brass Wash, Signed, 5 x 5 In. 192.00
Bookends, Poppy, Signed, 5 1/2 x 5 1/4 In. 550.00
Bookends, Tooled Leather, Girl With Ball, Applied Wirework, 4 3/4 x 4 1/2 In. 450.00
Bowl, Copper, 3-Footed, 7 1/8 x 3 1/8 In. 450.00
Bowl, Copper, Polished, 7 In. 140.00
Bowl, Incised Scrolls, Signed, 2 3/4 x 7 In. 440.00
Bowl, Presentation, To Boardie From The Squash Crowd, Original Dark Patina, 3 In. 201.00
Box, Brass, Hammered, Hinged Lid, Geometric Design, Brass Patina, 3 x 10 x 6 In. 1980.00
Candleholder, 8-Socket, Brass 400.00
Candleholder, Copper, Hammered, Twisted Stem, Round Base, Brown, 20 x 10 In. 520.00
Candlestick, Base, Princess, Double Stems, Pyramidal, Brass Patina, 7 x 3 1/4 In. 550.00
Candlestick, Brass Wash, Twisted Stem, 12 In., Pair 395.00
Candlestick, Copper & Brass, Hammered, Marked, 8 1/2 In., Pair 275.00
Candlestick, Copper, Hammered, 10 In., Pair 700.00
Chamberstick, Late Mark 75.00
Desk Set, Blossom Design, Curled Edge, Hammered Copper, Brown, 7 In. 715.00
Dish, Copper, Hammered, Applied Curled Handle, Orb Mark, Round, 6 x 3 In. 154.00
Frame, Nickel-Plated Copper, Hammered, Scalloped Edge, 9 x 11 In. ....165.00 to 187.00
Frame, Wooden, Orb Mark, 13 1/2 x 17 1/2 In. 1540.00
Jug, Stoneware, Brown, 5 In. ....27.00 to 50.00
Knife, Crumb, Tray, Copper, Hammered, Signed 220.00
Lamp, Helmet Shade, Copper, Hammered, 13 3/4 In. 2090.00
Lamp, Table, Copper, Hammered, Domed Shade, Wood Grain Base, 13 1/2 x 7 1/2 In. .. 1980.00
Lamp, Tapering Shade, 4-Sided Stem, Copper & Mica, 14 1/2 In. 1760.00
Plate, Copper, Hammered, Etched Silver Finish, Orb Mark, 7 In. 412.00
Sugar, Cover, Buffalo 75.00
Syrup, Brown 50.00
Tray, Copper, Hammered, Handles, Original Dark Patina, 1906-1910, 10 In. 290.00
Tray, Silver Over Copper, Embossed Floral Design, Signed, 21 1/2 x 9 1/2 In. 357.00
Vase, Copper, Bellflowers, Undulating Rim, Cylindrical, Signed, 9 1/2 In. 605.00
Vase, Copper, Hammered, Riveted Base, Dark Brown Patina, 5 x 2 3/4 In. 385.00
Vase, Jardiniere, Chrome, Green, 2 1/2 x 3 1/2 In. 395.00
Wall Sconce, Open Basket, Copper, Hammered, Mark, 10 1/2 In. 465.00

ROZANE, see Roseville category.

ROZENBURG worked at The Hague, Holland, from 1890 to 1914. The
most important pieces were earthenware made in the early twentieth
century with pale-colored Art Nouveau designs.

Vase, Cabinet, Eggshell, Pink, Violet, Yellow Blossoms, White Ground, 5 x 2 3/4 In. 550.00
Vase, Earthenware, Peacock, Stylized Flower Heads, Olive, Tan, Blue, 1899, 18 In. 2070.00
Vase, Exotic Bird, Lotus Blossoms, Scrolled Leafage, Yellow, Purple, 1905, 7 In. 1380.00
Vase, Fuchsia Blooms, Handles, 8 1/2 In. 200.00
Vase, Morning Glory Blossoms, Leafage, Handle, Mauve, Pink, Gray, 6 In. 3737.00

RRP is the mark used by the firm of Robinson-Ransbottom. It is not a
mark of the more famous Roseville Pottery. The Ransbottom brothers
started a pottery in 1900 in Ironspot, Ohio. In 1920, they merged with
the Robinson Clay Product Company of Akron, Ohio, to become
Robinson-Ransbottom. The factory is still working.

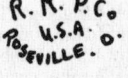

Cookie Jar, Dutch Boy 98.00
Cookie Jar, Frosty The Snowman 700.00
Cookie Jar, Sailor 115.00
Cookie Jar, Sheriff Pig 125.00
Cookie Jar, Whale 725.00
Pitcher, Green, Girl, 9 In. 125.00
Planter, Snail, Yellow, Green, 7 1/2 x 4 In. 60.00

RS GERMANY is part of the wording in marks used by the Tillowitz, Germany, factory of Reinhold Schlegelmilch from 1914 until about 1945. The porcelain was sold decorated and undecorated. The Schlegelmilch families made porcelains marked in many ways. See also ES Germany, RS Poland, RS Prussia, RS Suhl, and RS Tillowitz.

Basket, 3 Handles, 4 3/4 In.	250.00
Basket, Candy, Pink Roses, Gold Rim, 5 x 6 3/4 In.	65.00
Basket, Pheasants, Brown Tones, 6 1/2 In.	200.00
Basket, With Orchids, 6 In.	125.00
Bowl, Cabbage, Yellow Roses, 10 In.	260.00
Bowl, Chrysanthemums, Roses, Cream & Tan Ground, Pedestal, Blue Mark, 9 In.	100.00
Bowl, Floral, 6 In.	60.00
Bowl, Lilacs, Cream To Lavender Ground, Blue Wreath Mark, 9 In.	50.00
Bowl, Pink Tulips, Gold Trim, 10 In.	150.00
Cake Plate, Daisies, Green & Yellow Ground, Open Handles, 10 In.	40.00
Candlestick, Light Blue Flowers	90.00
Chocolate Set, Multicolored Roses, Green Ground, 13 Piece	350.00 to 375.00
Chocolate Set, White Roses, Ivory Ground, Marked, 9 1/2 In.	137.00
Cup & Saucer, Art Deco Dancing Woman, Marked, 2 1/4-In. Cup	90.00
Hatpin Holder, Calla Lily Design, Ribbed	145.00
Hatpin Holder, Floral	75.00
Lamp, Candle, White Owl, Orange Amber Eyes, 5 1/4 In.	110.00
Mug, Scuttle, Pink Poppies	95.00
Pitcher, Bison, 5 In.	75.00
Pitcher, Clown Head, Silver Overlay, 8 In.	425.00
Pitcher, Dogwood, Marked, 6 In.	145.00
Pitcher, Surreal Dogwood, Gold Stems & Trim, Blue Mark, 6 In.	120.00
Plate, Cloverleaf Shape, Orange & White Roses, 3 Sections	80.00
Plate, Embossed Frog Handle, 7 In.	35.00
Plate, Lake & Windmill Scene, 10 In.	125.00
Plate, White Shasta Daisies, Signed, 6 1/2 In.	20.00
Relish, White & Pink Carnations, Open Handle	28.00
Soap Dish, Acorn, Blue Mark	30.00
Toothbrush, Holder, Rose Design	125.00
Toothpick, Roses, Gold Trim, 2 Handles, Henke	60.00
Toothpick, White Daisies, Blue Ground, 3 Handles, Signed	95.00
Vase, Scantily Dressed Maidens, Handle, Tiffany Finish, 7 x 4 In.	245.00

RS POLAND (German) is a mark used by the Reinhold Schlegelmilch factory at Tillowitz from about 1946 to 1956. After 1956, the factory made porcelain marked PT Poland. This is one of many of the RS marks used. See also ES Germany, RS Germany, RS Prussia, RS Suhl, and RS Tillowitz.

Cup & Saucer, Chocolate, 4 Piece	90.00

RS PRUSSIA appears in several marks used on porcelain before 1917. Reinhold Schlegelmilch started his porcelain works in Suhl, Germany, in 1869. See also ES Germany, RS Germany, RS Poland, RS Suhl, and RS Tillowitz.

Bell, Ruffled Edge, White, Small Purple Flowers, Green Leaf, Twig Handle, 3 1/2 In.	285.00
Berry Bowl, Light To Dark Green, 5 1/2 In., Pair	230.00
Berry Bowl, Masted Schooner, 3 x 10 1/2 In.	750.00
Berry Bowl, Mill Scene, 5 1/4 In.	110.00
Berry Set, Forget-Me-Nots, 5 Lobed Floral Rims, Signed, 7 Piece	365.00
Berry Set, Icicle Mold, Pink & White Poppies, 5 Piece	280.00
Berry Set, Poppy Design, Iris Mold, 5 Piece	275.00
Berry Set, Quiet Cove, Red Mark, 7 Piece	1600.00
Bowl, Blue Edge, Gold Raised Flowers, 8 In.	195.00
Bowl, Cabbage Mold, Poppies, Blue & Cream, Star Mark, 10 In.	130.00
Bowl, Carnation Mold Variant, Pink & Yellow Roses, Green Ground, 10 1/2 In.	275.00
Bowl, Chinese Pheasant & Evergreens, Gold Trim, Medallion Mold, 7 In.	375.00
Bowl, Dice Players, 10 1/2 In.	1100.00

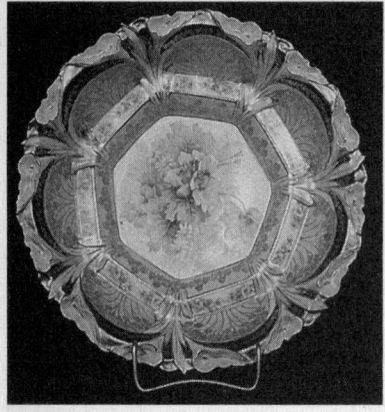

Don't store dishes for long periods of time in old newspaper wrappings. The ink can make indelible stains on china.

RS Prussia, Bowl, Floral Center, Gold Stencil, Lily Mold Border, 7 Sides

Bowl, Fall Season, Iris Mold, 9 1/2 In. . . . .*Illus*	1200.00
Bowl, Fish Scale Mold, White Lilies, Purple & Orange Luster, Signed, 11 In.	325.00
Bowl, Floral Center, Gold Stencil, Lily Mold Border, 7 Sides . . . .*Illus*	425.00
Bowl, Fruit Design, Mold 55, 10 1/2 In.	275.00
Bowl, Hidden Image, Floral, Teardrop Mold, 10 x 11 1/2 In.	1800.00
Bowl, Iris Mold, Fall Season, 9 1/2 In.	1200.00
Bowl, Jonquil, Cobalt Blue, 10 In.	595.00
Bowl, Nut, Roses, Point & Clover Mold, Gold Luster, Footed, 6 1/2 In.	185.00
Bowl, Pearlized, Multicolored Florals, 10 1/2 In.	275.00
Bowl, Pheasants Scene, Handle, Oval, 2 3/8 In.	165.00
Bowl, Pink & White Daisies, Ruffled Rim, Gold Trim, 3 x 10 In.	165.00
Bowl, Pink Poppy, Satin, 10 1/2 In.	350.00
Bowl, Pink Roses, Carnation Mold, Red Mark, 10 In.	310.00
Bowl, Pink Roses, Jewels, White Ground, Red Mark, 10 1/2 In.	100.00
Bowl, Pink, White Roses, Green Leaves, Satin, 10 1/4 In.	252.00
Bowl, Poppies, Silver Dome Sections, Scrolled Border, Red Mark, 10 In.	300.00
Bowl, Poppy Clusters, 3-Footed, 5 1/2 In.	175.00
Bowl, Poppy, Carnation Mold, Luster, 8 1/2 In.	220.00
Bowl, Reflecting Water Lilies, 10 3/4 In.	240.00
Bowl, Schooner, 11 In.	575.00
Bowl, Snowballs, 10 1/2 In.	175.00
Bowl, Watering Can, Green, 10 1/2 In.	975.00
Bowl, White Molded Floral, Mixed Floral Center, Pink Border, 10 In.	120.00
Bowl, Winter Season, 10 In. . . . . .525.00 to 625.00	
Bowl, Yellow & Red Roses, Blue Daisies, Gold Border, Lily Mold, 10 1/2 In.	225.00
Box, Portrait, Brass Hinged Lid, 2 x 10 1/2 In.	500.00
Cake Plate, Carnation Mold, Pink Roses, Teal, Green & Gold, 10 In.	225.00
Cake Plate, Leaf Wreath, Pink & Peach Roses, Circle Mold, 11 In.	75.00
Cake Plate, Pink & Red Roses, Carnation Mold, Red Mark, 10 1/2 In.	275.00
Cake Plate, Pink Roses, Autumn Portrait, Keyhole Frame, Red Mark, 9 1/2 In.	1100.00
Cake Plate, Pink, White Roses, 11 In.	350.00
Cake Plate, Poppies & Bell Lilies, 2 Handles, Green Mark	50.00
Cake Plate, Red Poinsettias, Iris Mold, Tiffany Highlights, Circle Mark, 10 3/4 In.	200.00
Cake Plate, Snapdragons, Pastel Mold, Signed, 11 1/2 In.	345.00
Cake Plate, Spring Season, 9 3/4 In.	1450.00
Cake Plate, Stag Scene, Pastel Ground, Satin, 9 In.	1395.00
Celery Dish, Lavender Satin, Pink Roses	350.00
Celery Dish, Pink Rose, Green Tiffany Border, 12 In.	175.00
Celery Dish, Pink Roses, Green Ivy Border, 12 In.	180.00
Celery Dish, Pink Roses, Jeweled, Satin, Red Tiffany Border, 12 In.	300.00
Celery Dish, Sitting Basket, Icicle Mold, 12 In.	50.00
Celery Dish, Surreal Dogwood, Pearlized Luster, Signed, 12 1/4 In.	200.00
Chocolate Pot, 4 Fleur-De-Lis Shaped Feet, Pierced Handles, 10 In.	385.00

Chocolate Pot, Lily, No. 508 .... 95.00
Chocolate Pot, Multicolored Roses, Gold Trim, Red Mark 395.00
Chocolate Pot, Pink Rose, Luster 200.00
Chocolate Pot, Roses, Cream To Brown Shaded Ground, Red Mark, 10 In. 225.00
Chocolate Pot, Snowballs & Poppies, Satin, Gold Handle, Red Mark, 10 1/2 In. 425.00
Chocolate Pot, Swans 150.00
Chocolate Set, Carnation Mold, Yellow & Green, 13 Piece 550.00
Chocolate Set, Floral, Pitcher, 13 Piece 675.00
Chocolate Set, Medallion Mold, Roses, Yellow & Green, 13 Piece 825.00
Chocolate Set, Multifloral, Rope Twist Handle, Sunflower Mold, 9 Piece 850.00
Coffeepot, Flowers & Leaves, Tiffany Iridescent, Jewels, 9 1/4 In. 600.00
Cracker Jar, Lilies, Mold 579 .... 295.00
Cracker Jar, Peasant Girl, Pink Roses, 8 x 6 In. 875.00
Cracker Jar, Pink Flowers, Red Mark, 5 1/2 x 8 1/2 In. 310.00
Creamer, Hidden Image, Star Mark, 4 1/2 In. 225.00
Creamer, Pheasant 140.00
Cup & Saucer, Chocolate, Satin Fish, Steeple Mark 80.00
Cup & Saucer, Egg Shape, Chocolate, Pink & White Poppies, Footed .... .95.00 to 110.00
Cup & Saucer, Magnolia 45.00
Cup & Saucer, Pink & White Poppies 125.00
Cup & Saucer, Rose 160.00
Cup & Saucer, Sunflower Mold 125.00
Demitasse Set, Mold 547, Gold Rims, 11 Piece 800.00
Ewer, Summer Season, 6 In. 700.00
Fernery, Lily-Of-The-Valley, Shaded Pastel, 6 Ribs, Signed, 8 1/4 In. 200.00
Hair Receiver, Salmon Roses, Scalloped, Tiffany Trim, 4 1/4 In. 185.00
Hatpin Holder, Magnolias 160.00
Hatpin Holder, Pink & White Roses, Yellow To Green Ground, Red Mark, 4 1/2 In. ... 225.00
Jar, Cover, Roses, Beaded Rim 155.00
Muffineer, Melon Eaters, 4 3/4 In. 725.00
Mustache Cup, Pierced 475.00
Mustard, Bell Lilies, Brown Ground 90.00
Mustard, Daisy, Green Ground 75.00
Mustard, Red & White Rose 250.00
Mustard, Roses, Spoon 70.00
Pin Tray, Green Bowtie Each End, Red Mark, 5 x 2 1/4 In. 170.00
Pitcher, Cider, Swans & Terrace, Brown & Rust Highlights 575.00
Pitcher, Fan Molded Floral, 7 In. 275.00
Pitcher, Floral Design, Allover Gilt Tracery, Cobalt Blue, Marked, 9 In. 750.00
Pitcher, Mixed Floral, Red Steeple Mark, 6 3/4 In. 160.00
Plaque, Wall, Woman Holding Flowers, Iridescent Finish, 11 x 17 In. 950.00
Plate, Barnyard, Raindrop Border, 8 1/2 In. 350.00

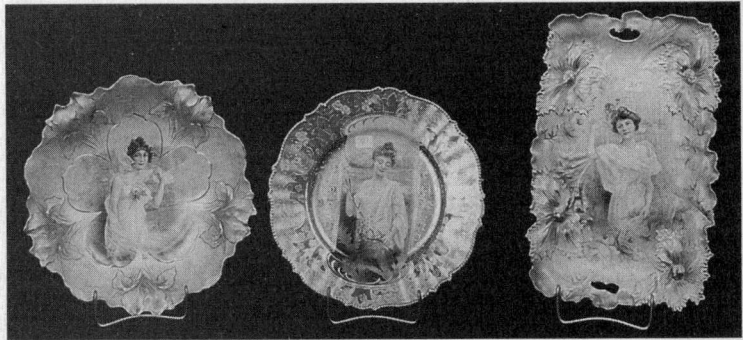

RS Prussia, Bowl, Fall Season, Iris Mold, 9 1/2 In.
RS Prussia, Plate, Spring Season, Keyhole, Gold & Red Border
RS Prussia, Tray, Dresser, Summer Season, Carnation Mold, Satin Finish

Plate, Carnation, Lavender, Pink Roses, Red Mark, 7 1/2 In. 225.00
Plate, Castle Scene, Fleur-De-Lis Mold, Handle, 10 1/4 In. 1100.00
Plate, Castle Scene, Mold 300, 8 3/4 In. 250.00
Plate, Dice Players, 8 In. 325.00
Plate, Hidden Image, Woman With Long Brown Hair, Green Ground, 9 1/2 In. 400.00
Plate, Lily-Of-The-Valley Mold, Open Handles, 10 1/2 In. ....85.00 to 95.00
Plate, Melon Eaters, Green Tones, Jewels, Gold, Red Mark, 11 1/2 In. 850.00
Plate, Pink Poppies, Green Border, 8 3/4 In. 150.00
Plate, Pink Roses & Snowballs, Gold Border, Jewels, Red Mark, 9 In. 175.00
Plate, Pond Lilies Over Water, Red Mark, 11 In. 650.00
Plate, Roses & Snowballs, Jewels, Gold Ornate Border, 8 3/4 In. 195.00
Plate, Roses, Scalloped Festoon Rim, Luster 95.00
Plate, Spring Portrait, 9 In. 1400.00
Plate, Spring Season, Keyhole, Gold & Red Border ....*Illus* 1250.00
Plate, Swan Scene, 7 1/2 In. 185.00
Plate, Yellow & Pink Roses, 6 Dome Sections, Tiffany Iridescent, Jewels, 12 In. 300.00
Plate, Yellow Roses On Pink Ground, Yellow Border, 8 3/4 In. 150.00
Relish, Basket Of Roses, Shadow Flowers, Fleur-De-Lis Mold 115.00
Relish, Dice Throwers, 9 1/2 In. 275.00
Relish, Mill Scene, 9 1/2 In. 225.00
Relish, Peacock, Icicle Mold, 8 In. 200.00
Relish, Sheepherders, 9 In. 225.00
Shaving Mug, Hidden Image, 3 1/2 In. 125.00
Shaving Mug, Poppy Design, Steeple Mold 200.00
Shaving Mug, Yellow Roses, Stippled Floral 75.00
Spooner, Surreal Dogwood, 2 Handles, Red Mark, 4 1/2 In. 175.00
Sugar & Creamer, Indian Runner, Duck & Bluebird, Pedestal 325.00
Sugar & Creamer, Pink & Yellow Roses, Off-White Ground, 5 1/2 In. 92.50
Sugar & Creamer, Pink Roses & Bows, Blue, Gold, Finial, Pedestal 245.00
Sugar & Creamer, Rose Vine Design, Blue Rims, Domed Pedestal Bases, 5 In. 155.00
Sugar & Creamer, Snowball & Roses 90.00
Sugar Shaker, Pink Roses, Garlands Of Gold, 4 3/4 In. 260.00
Syrup, Dogwood ....95.00 to 110.00
Syrup, Underplate 395.00
Syrup, Underplate, Cobalt Blue 275.00
Tankard, Floral, Yellow Roses, Gold Highlights, Steeple Mold, 13 1/8 In. 400.00
Tankard, Large Roses, Steeple Mold, 13 1/4 In. 625.00
Tankard, Lion & Lioness 9000.00
Tankard, Pink Poppies, Lily-Of-The-Valley, Plume Mold, 13 1/8 In. 500.00
Tankard, Red, Pink & Yellow Poppies, Gold Trim, Wheelock, 10 1/2 In. 400.00
Tankard, Roses, Steeple Mold, 13 1/4 In. 625.00
Tankard, Turkeys & Evergreens, Gold Stenciling & Trim, Icicle Mold, 14 In. 1300.00
Tea Caddy, Chocolate Girl, Reinhold Schlegelmilch, 6 In. 950.00
Tea Set, Child's, Beaded, Pink & White Roses, Gold Trim, 17 Piece 1200.00
Tea Set, Floral, Multicolored, Ball Footed, 3 Piece 425.00
Tea Set, Surreal Dogwood Design, Satin, Red Mark, 3 Piece 475.00
Tea Set, Swan & Water Lily, Satin Finish, 3 Piece 375.00
Teapot, Lily-Of-The-Valley, Red Mark, 6 1/2 In. 350.00
Teapot, Reflecting Water Lilies, Icicle Mold, Red Mark, 6 1/2 In. 575.00
Toothpick, Pink & Yellow Flowers, Green Border, Handle, Raised Star Mark 80.00
Toothpick, Roses, 2 Handles 275.00
Tray, Bun, Grape Leaves & Floral 60.00
Tray, Bun, Roses 150.00
Tray, Calling Card, Leaf Mold, Wing Mark 125.00
Tray, Dresser, Summer Season, Carnation Mold, Satin Finish ....*Illus* 2300.00
Tray, Dresser, Turkey, Icicle Mold, 11 1/2 In. 310.00
Tray, Full Blossom Red & Pink Roses, Pierced Handle, Marked, 11 1/8 x 8 In. 250.00
Vase, Game Birds, Cobalt Blue, Gold Stenciling & Trim, 6 In. 250.00
Vase, Gold Overlay, Steeple Mark, 9 In. 525.00
Vase, Large Roses, Lavender Ground, Satin, Red Mark, 8 In. 250.00
Vase, Melon Boys, Red, Gold Border, Purple Luster, Vienna Mark, 6 3/8 In. 325.00
Vase, Pillow, Sheepherder, Cottage & Swallows, 7 In. 675.00

Vase, Spring Season, 6 1/2 In. 800.00
Vase, Summer Season, Gold Beading Around Portrait, Red Mark 900.00
Vase, Urn, Dice Throwers, Jeweled, Gold, 2 Handles, 9 In. 1200.00

RS SUHL is a mark used by the Erdmann Schlegelmilch factory in Suhl, Germany, between 1900 and 1917. The Schlegelmilch families made porcelains in many places. See also ES Germany, RS Germany, RS Poland, RS Prussia, and RS Tillowitz.

Cup & Saucer, Man & Lady Scene On Front, Blue Beehive Mark, After Dinner 125.00

RS TILLOWITZ was marked on porcelain by the Reinhold Schlegelmilch factory at Tillowitz in from the 1920s to the 1940s. Table services and ornamental pieces were made. See also ES Germany, RS Germany, RS Poland, RS Prussia, and RS Suhl.

Chocolate Pot, Art Nouveau Design, Glossy Finish 55.00
Vase, Pheasants, Golden, 6 In. 260.00
Vase, Pheasants, White, Brown, 6 In. 260.00

RUBENA is a glassware that shades from red to clear. It was first made by George Duncan and Sons of Pittsburgh, Pennsylvania, about 1885. This coloring was used on many types of glassware. The pressed glass patterns of Royal Ivy and Royal Oak are listed under Pressed Glass.

Condiment Set, Cut Button & Daisy, 3 Bottles, Salt & Pepper, Mustard Pot, Oval Tray . 165.00
Cruet, Cranberry To Clear, Allover Gold Design, 11 3/8 In. 195.00
Cruet, Enameled Blossoms, 7 In. 375.00
Pitcher, Water, Melon Ribbed, Clear Handle, Bulbous, 8 5/8 In. 175.00
Saltshaker, Ring Neck 85.00
Toothpick, Ring Neck, Bulbous 85.00
Vase, Enameled Lilies-Of-The-Valley, 6 1/2 In. 75.00
Vase, Enameled Roses, 16 In. 200.00
Water Set, Floral Design, Gold, Enamel Scrollwork, Crystal Handle, 6 Piece 920.00

RUBENA VERDE is a Victorian glassware that was shaded from red to green. It was first made by Hobbs, Brockunier and Company of Wheeling, West Virginia, about 1890.

Bowl, Ruffled Edge, Square, 4 1/2 In. 165.00
Bowl, Thumbprint, 5 In. 33.00
Cup, Inverted Thumbprint, Enameled Flowers, 3 1/2 In. 65.00
Pitcher, Diamond-Quilted, White Enameled Flowers, Butterfly, 7 1/4 In. 550.00
Pitcher, Ribbed & Netted, Yellow Reeded Handle, 4 Folded Rim, Bulbous, 8 In. 190.00

RUBY GLASS is the dark red color of the precious gemstone known as a *ruby*. It was a popular Victorian color that never went completely out of style. The glass was shaped by many different processes to make many different types of ruby glass. There was a revival of interest in the 1940s when modern-shaped ruby table glassware became fashionable. Sometimes the red color is added to clear glass by a process called flashing or staining. Flashed glass is clear glass dipped in a colored glass, then pressed or cut. Stained glass has color painted on a clear glass. Then it is refired so the stain fuses with the glass. Pieces of glass colored in this way are indicated by the word *stained* in the description. Related items may be found in other categories, such as Cranberry Glass, Pressed Glass, and Souvenir.

Basket, Applied Flowers, 4 In. 68.00
Biscuit Jar, Florette 295.00
Biscuit Jar, Little Shrimp 325.00
Butter, Creamer & Spooner, Thumbprint, Stained, 3 Piece 315.00
Cake Stand, Miller, Stained 200.00
Celery Dish, Oregon 150.00
Creamer, Beaded Drape 150.00
Dish, Louis XVI Style, Ormolu, White Urns, Marble Base, Ball Feet, 10 1/4 In., Pair 3737.00
Pickle, Castor, Beaded Drape 595.00

Pickle, Castor, Open Heart Arches	375.00
Pitcher, Water, Coreopsis, Metal Top	400.00
Pitcher, Water, Millard	275.00
Syrup, Button Arches	125.00
Toothpick, Thumbprint, Stained	45.00
Tumbler, Bead Swag, Stained	25.00
Water Set, Carnation, Stained, 7 Piece	675.00
Water Set, Gloria, Stained, 6 Piece	550.00
Water Set, Ladder With Diamonds, Stained, 5 Piece	400.00
Wine Set, Loop & Block, Stained, 7 Piece	325.00

RUDOLSTADT was a faience factory in the Thuringia region of Germany from 1720 to about 1791. In 1854, Ernst Bohne began working in the area. From about 1887 to 1918, the New York and Rudolstadt Pottery made decorated porcelain marked with the RW and crown familiar to collectors. This porcelain was imported by Lewis Straus and Sons of New York, which later became Nathan Straus and Sons. The word *Royal* was included in their import mark. Collectors often call it *Royal Rudolstadt*. Most pieces found today were made in the late nineteenth or early twentieth century. Additional pieces may be listed in the Kewpie category.

Ewer, Floral Bouquet, Lion Mask Molded, Scroll & Pillar Handle, 16 In.	330.00
Ewer, Floral Design, Cream Ground, 11 In.	88.00
Figurine, Courting Couple, Ornate Bench, c.1900, 9 x 8 In.	375.00
Hatpin Holder, Green, White Roses	75.00
Ice Cream Set, Bluebird Design, Rectangular Tray, 6 Plates, Signed, 7 Piece	95.00
Pitcher, Insects, Leaves, Fruit, Cream Ground, 8 1/4 In.	88.00
Sauce, Sea Horses On Clamshell, Silver Overlay	475.00
Tray, Serving, Lilies, Handles, 11 In.	125.00
Vase, Freesia Design, Signed, 5 In.	75.00
Vase, Green & White, Gold Trim, Bulbous, 9 In.	45.00
Vase, Peach, Rococo Top & Bottom Border, Floral In Center, 9 3/4 In.	135.00

RUGS have been used in the American home since the seventeenth century. The oriental rug of that time was often used on a table, not on the floor. Rag rugs, hooked rugs, and braided rugs were made by housewives from scraps of material.

Afghan, 7 Columns Of Turkoman Style Guls, Ivory Border, 12 x 9 Ft.	862.00
Afshar, Boteh Rows, Red, Ivory Meander Border, 2 Ft. 6 In. x 2 Ft.	431.00
Afshar, Madder Medallion, Midnight Blue Ground, 3 Ft. 5 In. x 2 Ft. 10 In.	5750.00
Afshar, Medallion, Floral Sprays, Vine Border, 5 Ft. 2 In. x 4 Ft. 4 In.	920.00
Akstafa, Boteh Rows, Navy, Red, Tan, Black Border, 5 Ft. 5 In. x 2 Ft. 9 In.	1380.00
Anatolian, 4 Medallions, Stars, Coral, Red Field, 6 Ft. 4 In. x 4 Ft. 4 In.	1495.00
Anatolian, Concentric Diamonds, Gold, Orange Red, Red Field, 5 x 4 Ft.	2070.00
Anatolian, Floral, Geometric, Gold Border, 6 Ft. x 4 Ft. 4 In.	546.00
Anatolian, Hooked Diamonds, Rows Of Animal Designs, 8 Ft. 2 In. x 3 Ft. 2 In.	1150.00
Ardebil, Rust & Gold, Navy Ground, 7 Ft. 3 In. x 4 Ft. 6 1/8 In.	485.00
Art Deco, Tree & Bird Design, 13 Ft. 7 In. x 9 Ft. 7 In.	660.00
Aubusson, Center Oval Medallion, Floral Border, 14 Ft. 4 In. x 10 Ft.	3220.00
Aubusson, Charles X, 1825, France, 13 Ft. 4 In. x 10 Ft.1 In.	26500.00
Aubusson, Charles X, Band Borders, 1820, 11 Ft. 11 In. x 7 Ft. 6 In.	12075.00
Aubusson, Floral Medallion, Light Yellow Field, 14 Ft. 2 In. x 9 Ft. 10 In.	3162.00
Aubusson, Landscape, Birds, Floral Border, Blue, 10 Ft. 7 In. x 9 Ft. 2 In.	5462.00
Aubusson, Louis Philippe, Black Border, 16 Ft. 5 In. x 14 Ft. 2 In.	11500.00
Aubusson, Louis XV Style, 19th Century, 22 Ft. 7 In. x 14 Ft.	17250.00
Aubusson, Oval, Central Roundel, Cream Field, 14 Ft. 8 In. x 8 Ft. 6 In.	4600.00
Aubusson, Rose Red Medallion, Burgundy Field, 6 Ft. 10 In. x 6 Ft. 10 In.	2875.00
Bakhtiari, Blue, Red, Pink, Light Green & Ivory, Runner, 2 Ft. 6 In. x 10 Ft.	135.00
Bakhtiari, Geometric Designs, Ivory, Green, Red, Orange, 5 Ft. x 9 Ft. 8 In.	192.00
Baluchi, 2 Hooked Diamond Medallions, Red, 2 Ft. 6 In. x 1 Ft. 7 In.	690.00
Baluchi, 2 Octagonal Columns, Red, Sky Blue, 2 Ft. 2 In. x 1 Ft. 9 In.	259.00
Baluchi, 3 Palmettes, Red Hooked Diamonds, 5 Ft. 2 In. x 4 Ft. 3 In.	517.00
Baluchi, 4 Rust, Blue Hooked Diamonds, Brown Field, 4 Ft. 2 In. x 3 Ft.	345.00

Baluchi, Boteh Rows, Apricot Cross Border, 5 Ft. 6 In. x 3 Ft. 3 In. 1610.00
Baluchi, Diamond Medallions, Blue, Red, Brown Field, 5 Ft. 9 In. x 3 Ft. 2 In. 575.00
Baluchi, Olive Ground, Rust Borders, 2 Ft. 10 In. x 5 Ft. 2 In. 770.00
Baluchi, Red Diagonal Rows, Black Field, 6 Ft. 10 In. x 3 Ft. 8 In. 1725.00
Baluchi, Rows Of Birds, Serrated Leaf Border, 7 Ft. 4 In. x 4 Ft. 6 In. 747.00
Bidjar, 3 Rows Of Palmettes, Arabesque Leaves, Blue Field, 10 Ft. 6 In. x 5 Ft. 4 In. 2070.00
Bidjar, Blue Medallion, Flowering Vines, 7 Ft. 5 In. x 4 Ft. 8 In. 3335.00
Bidjar, Indigo Medallion, Ivory, 6 Ft. 9 In. x 4 Ft. 9 In. 2875.00
Bidjar, Indigo Spandrels & Border, Burgundy Ground, 4 x 8 Ft. 190.00
Bidjar, Light Brown Medallion, Camel Field, 7 Ft. 1 In. x 4 Ft. 4600.00
Bidjar, Stepped Medallion, Terra-Cotta Field, 5 Ft. 6 In. x 3 Ft. 10 In. 2070.00
Bokhara, Gray, Coral, Blue Ground, 9 Ft. 3 In. x 12 Ft. 5 In. 968.00
Bokhara, Multiple Tan Borders, Red Ground, 4 Ft. 2 In. x 6 Ft. 5 In. 165.00
Caucasian, 3 Linked Diamond Medallions, Indigo Field, 6 Ft. 3 In. x 3 Ft. 11 In. 1840.00
Caucasian, Arabesque Lattice On Green Field, Kufic Border, 5 Ft. 10 In. x 4 Ft. 5 In. ... 460.00
Caucasian, Flower Heads, Square Medallions, Georgian Border, 5 Ft. 4 In. x 3 Ft. 8 In. .. 920.00
Caucasian, Hexagonal Lattice, Diamonds, Gul Border, 19th Century, 4 Ft. 2 In. x 3 Ft. .. 230.00
Caucasian, Hooked Diamond, Running Dog Border, 9 Ft. 10 In. x 5 Ft. 4 In. 1610.00
Caucasian, Ivory Style S Dragons, Blue, 9 Ft. 4 In. x 6 Ft. 4 In. 8050.00
Caucasian, Polychrome Rosette Border, Open Brown Field, 4 Ft. x 3 Ft. 10 In. 800.00
Caucasian, Prayer, Fringed Camel Border, 5 Ft. 6 In. x 3 Ft. 10 In. 4312.00
Caucasian, Stylized Floral Lattice, 5 Ft. 5 In. x 3 Ft. 1 In. 2300.00
Caucasian, Tan Field, Blue Palmette Border, 3 Ft. 1 In. x 2 Ft. 11 In. 3162.00
Chinese, Florals, Temple Design, Beige & Pink Border, 9 Ft. x 11 Ft. 6 In. 220.00
Chinese, Flower Heads, Butterflies, Sky Blue, Gold, 11 x 9 Ft. 488.00
Derebend, Dark Blue, Shades Of Brown & Ivory, 3 Ft. 7 In. x 5 Ft. 1 In. 605.00
Ersari, Blue Plants, Rust Garden Field, 6 Ft. x 4 Ft. 8 In. 1150.00
Ersari, Columns Of Gulliguls, 9 Ft. 2 In. x 7 Ft. 2 In. 690.00
Ersari, Gulliguls, Madder Reserve, Indigo, Rust, 3 Ft. 3 In. x 3 Ft. 1 In. 1725.00
Ersari, Overall Floral Lattice, Rust Field, 4 Ft. 2 In. x 3 Ft. 4 In. 575.00
Ghiordes, Prayer, Backed With Fabric, 5 Ft. 6 In. x 4 Ft. 1495.00
Hamadan, Blue Border, Red Ground, 5 Ft. 2 In. x 7 Ft. 2 In. 300.00
Hamadan, Blue, Olive, Gold, Ivory, Red Ground, 7 Ft. 4 In. x 10 Ft. 165.00
Hamadan, Blue Spandrels, Blue Border, Red Ground, 5 Ft. 3 In. x 7 Ft. 3 In. 247.00
Hamadan, Boteh, Rust Ground, Beige Border, 4 Ft. 10 In. x 10 Ft. 3 In. 375.00
Herati, Blue, Red Turtle Border, 6 Ft. 4 In. x 4 Ft. 8 In. 1495.00
Heriz, Floral, Red, Navy, Green, Sand Ground, c.1890-1920, 11 Ft. 7 In. x 9 Ft. 2 In. ... 20700.00
Heriz, Gabled Square Medallions, Vines, Blue, Red, 12 Ft. 2 In. x 9 Ft. 2 In. 635.00
Heriz, Ivory Spandrels, Black Border, Red, Rose Ground, 7 Ft. x 9 Ft. 10 In. 500.00
Heriz, Ivory Spandrels, Blue Border, Red Ground, Runner, 2 Ft. 7 In. x 9 Ft. 9 In. 275.00
Heriz, Ivory Spandrels, Dark Blue Border, Red Ground, 2 Ft. 6 In. x 9 Ft. 203.00
Heriz, Overall Floral Lattice, Madder Field, 10 Ft. 4 In. x 8 Ft. 6 In. 6900.00
Heriz, Overall Palmettes, Blossoming Vines, Turtle Border, 10 x 8 Ft. 2645.00
Heriz, Overall Palmettes, Ivory Field, 11 Ft. x 8 Ft. 8 In. 4140.00
Heriz, Palmettes & Rosettes, Blue Field, Turtle Border, 11 Ft. 2 In. x 8 Ft. 10 In. 6900.00
Heriz, Rosette Medallion, Terra-Cotta Field, 10 Ft. 6 In. x 8 Ft. 4 In. 2415.00
Heriz, Rosettes, Flower Heads, Terra-Cotta Field, 11 Ft. 9 In. x 8 Ft. 8 In. 5462.00
Hooked, 2 Black Dogs, White Fence, Green, Red Flowers, Rag, 26 x 47 In. 330.00
Hooked, 2 Yellow Cats, Red Ground, Blue Border, 21 x 39 In. 275.00
Hooked, Angel Slaying Devil With Cross, Brown, Blue, Purple, Rag, 29 x 40 In. 495.00
Hooked, Basket Of Flowers, Striped Borders, Natural Ground, Wool, 1900, 26 x 54 In. ... 375.00
Hooked, Cat, Happy, Laszlo Zongor, Bedford, Pa., 1915, 16 x 24 In. 2400.00
Hooked, Cats, Scrolled Blossom Corners, Running Ovoid Border, 32 1/2 x 46 In. 1150.00
Hooked, Center Dog, 20 x 36 In. 1295.00
Hooked, Cobbler & Woman Spinning, Fireplace, Cat, 19 x 69 In. 580.00
Hooked, Deer Scene, Floral Cornucopias, Canvas, 27 x 62 In. 577.00
Hooked, Diamond Pattern, Alternating Waves, Stylized Flowers, 144 x 58 In. 55.00
Hooked, Dog On Shoes, Blue Edge, Multicolored, 37 x 18 In. 385.00
Hooked, Eagle With Shield, 31 1/2 x 63 In. 2200.00
Hooked, Family Members & Dog, 52 x 23 In. 690.00
Hooked, Fish, Birds, Flowers, White, Red, Fish Scale Edge, Wool, 22 x 43 In. 1925.00
Hooked, Floral Ends, 1920s, 38 x 20 In. 125.00
Hooked, Floral Spray, Black Oval, Gray Ground, Rag & Yarn, 15 x 41 In. 50.00

Hooked, Floral, 9 Squares, Pink Blossoms, Pinwheels, Green Ground, 51 x 37 In. 920.00
Hooked, Floral, Blooming Roses, Sand Field, Brown Border, 67 x 35 In. 345.00
Hooked, Floral, Green, Yellow Flowering Vines, 64 x 37 In. 750.00
Hooked, Folk Interior Scene With Cobbler, Yellow Ground, Rag, 19 x 69 In. 580.00
Hooked, Geometric, Floral, Olive Ground, 32 x 42 In. 170.00
Hooked, Geometric, Medallion, Arrow Design, Gray, Blue, Ocher, 78 x 53 In. 1400.00
Hooked, Geometric, Polychrome Yarns, 102 x 104 In. 4025.00
Hooked, Honeycomb Pattern, Red, Blue, Red Ground, 24 x 36 In. 575.00
Hooked, Horse & Carriage, Floral Border, 36 x 24 In. 55.00
Hooked, Horse With Oak Leaf Clusters, Beige, Blue, Tan, 46 x 34 1/2 In. 635.00
Hooked, Horse, Browns & Blues, Mounted, 25 5/8 x 39 In. 875.00
Hooked, Horse, Cart With Boy Driver, Black, Gray, Red, Purple, 17 x 33 In. 415.00
Hooked, Horse, Floral Border, Blue Ground, 34 1/2 x 38 1/2 In. 625.00
Hooked, Hunter, Dog & Deer, Blue, Brown & Beige, Orange Ground, 19 x 36 In. 275.00
Hooked, Indians At Camp, 23 x 37 1/2 In. 13800.00
Hooked, Leaping Lamb, 2 Red Flowers, Mottled Ground, Scalloped Edge, 23 x 39 In. ... 600.00
Hooked, Lion Center, Palm Trees, 1920s, 64 1/2 x 33 1/2 In. 585.00
Hooked, Log Cabin, 1930s, 58 x 27 In. 1275.00
Hooked, Owl, Mounted, 23 x 34 In. 425.00
Hooked, Pansies & Roses, Branch Border, 1920s, 34 1/4 x 23 3/4 In. 150.00
Hooked, Pictorial, Saltbox House, Fence, Wool, Cotton, 1930, 17 x 46 In. 375.00
Hooked, Raised Floral Design, Birds, Waldoboro Type, 1910, 21 x 37 In. 1430.00
Hooked, Rooster, Green Ground, Orange & Brown Border, Rag, 20 x 35 In. 190.00
Hooked, Roosters, Crowing, White, Brown, Yellow, Rag, 19 x 34 In. 495.00
Hooked, Rural Winter New England Landscape, 1910, 23 x 18 In. 300.00
Hooked, Seated Indian Chief, Holding Feathered Headdress, 24 1/2 x 38 3/4 In. 2990.00
Hooked, Spotted Dog Reclining On Tumbling Blocks Ground, 1880s, 30 x 50 In. 1840.00
Hooked, Squirrel & Leaf Design, White Ground, 51 x 84 In. 495.00
Hooked, Star Medallions, Blue, Green, Red, Gold, Navy Blue, 128 x 62 In. 1725.00
Hooked, Steamboat In Harbor, Scattered Cottages, Dog, 1870s, 23 1/2 x 39 1/2 In. 2300.00
Hooked, Stylized Maple Leaves, Vine Border, Red, Tan, Blue, 40 x 25 In. 145.00
Hooked, Symbols Of British Empire, Tudor Rose, Olive Field, 28 x 43 In. 345.00
Hooked, Tulip & Heart Design, 27 x 64 In. 995.00
Hooked, Wreath Of Poinsettias, Black Border, Rag & Yarn, 25 x 38 In. 360.00
Indo-Bidjar, Midnight Blue Border, 5 Ft. x 7 Ft. 2 In. 250.00
Indo-Bidjar, Midnight Blue Border, Red Ground, 4 Ft. x 5 Ft. 9 In. 192.00
Indo-Tabriz, Dark Red Border, 4 Ft. x 6 Ft. 2 In. 110.00
Joshaqan, Reds, Ivories & Blues, 2 Ft. 4 In. x 3 Ft. 373.00
Karabagh, 4 Diamond Medallions, Leaf Border, 10 Ft. 2 In. x 3 Ft. 8 In. 920.00
Karabagh, Eagle Medallions, 4 Ft. 4 In. x 8 Ft. 4 In. 4900.00
Karabagh, Geometric Design, Pomegranate, Rose Field, 10 x 14 Ft. 4887.00
Karabagh, Rectangular Medallion, Terra-Cotta Field, Gold Border, 6 x 3 Ft. 430.00
Kashan, Aubergine Medallion, Pearl Gray Field, 6 Ft. 10 In. x 4 Ft. 3 In. 4600.00
Kashan, Balcony Scene, Ivory & Green Ground, Border, 4 Ft. 7 In. x 6 Ft. 5 In. 2310.00
Kashan, Concentric Medallion, Rust Red Field, 6 Ft. 10 In. x 4 Ft. 4 In. 2415.00
Kashan, Diamond Medallion, Palmette Border, 16 Ft. 2 In. x 10 Ft. 8 In. 4887.00
Kashan, Diamond Medallion, Red, Rose Vines, 12 Ft. 2 In. x 8 Ft. 8 In. 4600.00
Kashan, Ivory Medallion, Black Ground, Roses At Corners, 6 x 9 Ft. 2185.00
Kashan, Lobed Arabesque, Floral Medallion, 6 Ft. 10 In. x 4 Ft. 4 In. 9775.00
Kashan, Overall Floral Design, Green, Blue, Brown, 6 Ft. x 8 Ft. 7 In. 330.00
Kashmir, Salmon Border, White Ground, 4 Ft. 2 In. x 6 Ft. 192.00
Kazak, 2 Diamond Medallions, Floral Border, 9 Ft. 2 In. x 4 Ft. 10 In. 1725.00
Kazak, 3 Stepped Hexagonal Medallions, Ivory Border, 7 Ft. x 5 Ft. 4 In. 3450.00
Kazak, 3 Stepped Medallions, Animal Design, 4 Ft. 2 In. x 2 Ft. 4 In. 2990.00
Kazak, 3 Stepped Medallions, Navy Blue, Ivory, 6 Ft. 4 In. x 3 Ft. 9 In. 1150.00
Kazak, 4 Octagonal Medallions, Red, Camel, 6 Ft. 9 In. x 4 Ft. 747.00
Kazak, Hexagonal Lattice, Gold Geometric Border, 6 Ft. 7 In. x 4 Ft. 1955.00
Kazak, Ivory Medallions, Red Field, 7 Ft. 8 In. x 4 Ft. 9 In. 3162.00
Kazak, Madder, Ivory Medallions, Ivory Border, 7 Ft. 3 In. x 4 Ft. 2 In. 1955.00
Kazak, Medallion, Geometric Design, Blue Field, 4 Ft. 8 In. x 7 Ft. 9 In. 375.00
Kazak, Palmettes, Red, Sky Blue, Brown Field, 6 Ft. 10 In. x 4 Ft. 3335.00
Kazak, Rust Ground, Abrash Blue Border, Signed, 3 Ft. 6 In. x 5 Ft. 6 In. 1650.00
Kazak, Rust Red, Medium Blue, 3 Ft. 2 In. x 6 Ft. 3 In. 2900.00

Kazak, Serrated Medallions, Rust, Teal, Ivory, Border, 1855, 6 Ft. 6 In. x 5 Ft. 4370.00
Kazak, Tomato Reserve, Latch-Hooked, 5 Ft. 6 In. x 4 Ft. 2 In. 2070.00
Kerman, Cream, Midnight Blue Cartouches, 19 Ft. 6 In. x 16 Ft. 4 In. 11500.00
Kerman, Deep Blue Medallion, Cream Field, 17 Ft. 3 In. x 10 Ft. 6 In. 14950.00
Kerman, Floral Bird Design, Royal Blue Field, Red Border, 4 x 6 Ft. 300.00
Kerman, Floral Medallion Design, Green Field, 2 Ft. 11 In. x 4 Ft. 11 In. 230.00
Kerman, Indigo, Dusty Rose Floral, Cream Field, 18 Ft. x 11 Ft. 1 In. 8050.00
Kerman, Ivory, Beige Medallion, Cream Field, 12 Ft. 1 In. x 9 Ft. 6 In. 9775.00
Kerman, Prayer, Tree Of Life Design, Cream Field, 4 Ft. 6 In. x 8 Ft. 6 In. 460.00
Kilim, Multicolored Concentric Diamonds, Camel Field, 6 Ft. x 3 Ft. 9 In. 286.00
Kurd, 5 Memling Guls, Navy, Sky Blue, Red, Brown, 6 Ft. 2 In. x 3 Ft. 4 In. 750.00
Kurd, Geometric Design, Ivory Field, Runner, 3 Ft. 5 In. x 8 Ft. 9 In. 105.00
Kurd, Hexagons, Red, Sky Blue, Gold, Rust, S Border, 12 Ft. x 2 Ft. 9 In. 517.00
Kurd, Serrated Diamonds, Red, Sky Blue, Gold, 7 Ft. 10 In. x 4 Ft. 10 In. 1725.00
Kurd Kazakh, Latch-Hook Diamond Medallions, Ivory Border, Cobalt, 4 Ft. x 3 Ft. 4 In. 920.00
Lillihan, Floral Design, Blue, Brown, Cream Border, 2 Ft. 6 In. x 4 Ft. 11 In. 175.00
Lillihan, Geometric Design, Multicolored Floral, Red Field, 3 Ft. 3 In. x 4 Ft. 9 In. 220.00
Lillihan, Overall Rosette Design, Red Field, 11 Ft. 4 In. x 8 Ft. 4 In. 3105.00
Mahal, Overall Gold Hennae, Rust Turtle Border, 13 Ft. 2 In. x 10 Ft. 4 In. 6900.00
Mahal, Overall Rosette Lattice, Red Field, 11 Ft. 10 In. x 9 Ft. 2 In. 4600.00
Mahal, Polychrome, Red Ground, Dark Blue Border, 12 Ft. x 16 Ft. 11 In. 5225.00
Mahal, Stylized Floral Design, Cream Ground, 2 Ft. 6 In. x 4 Ft. 4 In. 66.00
Makri, Elongated Medallion Insert, Radiating Diamonds, 4 Ft. 5 In. x 2 Ft. 10 In. 435.00
Malayer, Olive Spandrels, Burgundy Ground, Ivory Border, 4 Ft. 7 In. x 6 Ft. 5 In. 990.00
Malayer, Stepped Diamond Medallion, Rosette Border, 6 Ft. 8 In. x 4 Ft. 1265.00
Mosul, Dark Blue Ground, Ivory Border, 4 Ft. 5 In. x 6 Ft. 5 In. 330.00
Ning-Hsia, Fo-Dogs Design, Flowering Vines, 7 Ft. 8 In. x 5 Ft. 3 In. 4312.00
Ning-Hsia, Indigo Field, Peony Blossom Border, 7 Ft. 1 In. x 4 Ft. 3 In. 2070.00
Oushak, Cream Medallion, Palmettes, 14 Ft. 9 In. x 11 Ft. 1 In. 5750.00
Oushak, Ivory Medallion, Straw Field, 11 Ft. 3 In. x 9 Ft. 1 In. 4600.00
Oushak, Overall Palmettes Within Green Border, c.1910, 12 Ft. 7 In. x 12 Ft. 6 In. 1380.00
Penny, Red, Black Felt, Hexagonal Shape, 26 x 40 In. 235.00
Perpedil, 4 Octagons, Ram's Horn & Animal Design, 6 Ft. 8 In. x 4 Ft. 6 In. 1495.00
Persian, Beige, Camel Field, 1900, Runner, 16 Ft. 5 In. x 3 Ft. 4 In. 3737.00
Qashqai, Ivory Diamond Medallion, Leaves, Red, Gold, 7 Ft. x 4 Ft. 3 In. 1265.00
Qashqai, Staggered Filigree Style Boteh, Ivory Spandrels, 6 Ft. 2 In. x 4 Ft. 2 In. 2300.00
Sarouk, Central Rosette, Midnight Blue Ground, 6 Ft. 8 In. x 4 Ft. 4 In. 7475.00
Sarouk, Floral Design, Red Field, Red, Blue, Beige Border, 4 Ft. 4 In. x 5 Ft. 7 In. 1150.00
Sarouk, Floral Design, Red Field, Red, Blue, Floral Border, 2 Ft. 1 In. x 4 Ft. 2 In. 402.00
Sarouk, Floral Design, Red Field, Red, Blue, Floral Border, 2 Ft. 4 In. x 3 Ft. 10 In. 230.00
Sarouk, Floral Field, Maroon Ground, 2 Ft. x 2 Ft. 6 In. 450.00
Sarouk, Floral Field, Rose Ground, 2 Ft. 6 In. x 4 Ft. 10 In. 425.00
Sarouk, Floral Field, Rose, Maroon Ground, 4 Ft. 5 In. x 6 Ft. 4 In. 3200.00
Sarouk, Floral Sprays, Ivory Ground, 8 Ft. 1 In. x 10 Ft. 3 In. 2475.00
Sarouk, Floral, Red Field, Blue Border, 4 Ft. 10 In. x 3 Ft. 6 In. 862.00
Sarouk, Floral, Urn Design, Floral Border, 2 x 4 Ft. 325.00
Sarouk, Flowering Vines, Burgundy Field, Blue Border, 6 Ft. 6 In. x 4 Ft. 6 In. 575.00
Sarouk, Rosette Medallions, Palmette Border, 14 Ft. 9 In. x 11 Ft. 9 In. 7475.00
Sarouk, Vases Of Flowers, Midnight Blue Field, 7 Ft. 4 In. x 4 Ft. 9 In. 1035.00
Seishour, Roses, Flower Heads, Blue Georgian Border, 4 Ft. 8 In. x 3 Ft. 1725.00
Serab, 2 Medallions, 6 Triangles, Blue Border, 11 Ft. 2 In. x 4 Ft. 4 In. 1035.00
Serapi, Blue Gray Spandrels, Ivory Border, Deep Green Ground, 4 Ft. x 6 Ft. 2 In. 165.00
Serapi, Central Medallion, Stylized Vine & Floral Design, 6 Ft. 3 In. x 9 Ft. 4 In. 467.00
Shiraz, Ivory Border, Red Ground, 4 Ft. 10 In. x 9 Ft. 6 In. 192.00
Shirvan, 3 Palmettes, Dragon's Tooth Border, 5 Ft. x 3 Ft. 6 In. 1940.00
Shirvan, 3 Serrated Diamonds, Red, Royal Blue, 12 Ft. 10 In. x 6 Ft. 10 In. 4887.00
Shirvan, 4 Octagonal Medallions, Ivory Border, 9 Ft. 4 In. x 3 Ft. 7 In. 1955.00
Shirvan, 7 Palmettes, Red, Rust, Black, 7 Ft. 8 In. x 3 Ft. 10 In. 1495.00
Shirvan, Diamond Lattice, Blue Hook Border, 4 Ft. 8 In. x 3 Ft. 8 In. 1955.00
Shirvan, Ivory Hexagons, Royal Blue, Red, Gold, 9 Ft. 2 In. x 6 Ft. 5 In. 920.00
Shirvan, Ivory Medallion, Indigo Ground, 5 Ft. 3 In. x 3 Ft. 11 In. 2760.00
Shirvan, Latch-Hook Diamonds, Indigo Ground, Runner, 10 Ft. 7 In. x 46 Ft. 4600.00
Shirvan, Linked Diamond, Midnight Blue Reserve, 8 Ft. 2 In. x 4 Ft. 1 In. 8050.00

Shirvan, Staggered Palmette, Ivory Border, 4 Ft. 10 In. x 3 Ft. 8 In. 1035.00
Soumak, Indigo Palmettes, Sea Green, Deep Brick Field, 13 Ft. x 5 Ft. 5 In. 4025.00
Soumak, Medallion Design, Red Geometric Border, 5 Ft. 8 In. x 7 Ft. 9 In. 600.00
Soumak, Oxidized Browns, 1875, 9 Ft. x 8 Ft. 2 In. 5750.00
Sultanabad, Overall Floral Wreaths, Navy Blue Field, Vine Border, 16 Ft. 6 In. x 11 Ft. . 5462.00
Sultanabad, Overall Hennae Design, Terra-Cotta Red Field, 9 Ft. 10 In. x 8 Ft. 9 In. ... 2415.00
Sultanabad, Overall Palmettes, Rust Field, 17 Ft. 10 In. x 12 Ft. 10 In. 5175.00
Tabriz, Birds, Butterflies, Floral Sprays, 10 Ft. 6 In. x 7 Ft. 3 In. 7475.00
Tabriz, Multiple Borders, Burgundy Spandrels, Green Ground, 10 x 14 Ft. 3025.00
Tabriz, Overall Herati Design, Madder Field, 12 Ft. 5 In. x 9 Ft. 5 In. 12650.00
Tekke, 4 Columns, Ivory Guls, Rust Field, 9 Ft. x 7 Ft. 4 In. 4025.00
Tekke, 5 Rows Of Guls, Deep Brick Field, 10 Ft. 10 In. x 7 Ft. 6 In. 3450.00
Tekke, 25 Guls, Rust Field, 4 Ft. 2 In. x 2 Ft. 2 In. 517.00
Tekke, Diamond Flower Heads, Red, Blue, Rust Field, 2 Ft. 7 In. x 1 Ft. 862.00
Tekke, Floral, Rust Field, Pole Tree Border, 5 x 4 Ft. 460.00
Tekke, Prayer, Shades Of Red, Ivory & Blue, 3 Ft. 7 In. x 4 Ft. 6 In. 395.00
Yomud, Diagonal Rows, Ivory Cross Border, 2 Ft. 2 In. x 1 Ft. 690.00
Yomud, Kepse Guls, Ivory Curled Leaf Border, 9 Ft. 4 In. x 6 Ft. 4025.00
Yomud, Red Kepse Guls, Midnight Blue, 3 Ft. 3 In. x 2 Ft. 3 In. 230.00
Yomud, Rows Of Dyrnak Guls, Indigo, Blue, Green, 8 Ft. 11 In. x 5 Ft. 5 In. 2070.00
Yomud, Stylized Serrated Branches, Rust Border, 2 Ft. 6 In. x 3 Ft. 11 In. 2300.00
Yomud, Torba, Staggered Guls, Aubergine Field, 3 Ft. 2 In. x 1 Ft. 4 In. 285.00

RUMRILL Pottery was designed by George Rumrill of Little Rock, Arkansas. From 1933 to 1938, it was produced by the Red Wing Pottery of Red Wing, Minnesota. In 1938, production was transferred to the Shawnee Pottery in Zanesville, Ohio. Production ceased in the 1940s.

RumRill

Bowl, 4 1/2 x 6 1/2 In. 48.00
Bowl, Console, Handles, White, 14 1/2 In. 75.00
Bowl, Dutch Blue Flower 25.00
Bowl, Eggshell Ivory, Brown 50.00
Cornucopia, Double, 2-Tone, No. 416 .... 80.00
Cornucopia, Shell Form, Green Lining, Ivory 45.00
Ewer, Continental Group 85.00
Lamp, Peach 55.00
Pitcher, Ball, Orange 85.00
Pitcher, Fish On Handle & On Base, Floral, Reticulated Edge, Pair 145.00
Vase, Antique Blue, 7 In. 80.00
Vase, Aqua, 8 In. 45.00
Vase, Ball, Scarlet, Bay, 6 In. 120.00
Vase, Copper Dust Glaze, 5 3/4 In. 25.00
Vase, Double Handles, Cream Brown Interior, 5 In. 55.00
Vase, Grape, White, & Brown, 12 In. 75.00
Vase, Green, No. 570, 10 In. 350.00
Vase, Ivory, 8 In. 79.00
Vase, Mottled Orange, Elephant Handles, 8 In. 200.00
Vase, Neo-Classic, Green, 12 In. ....100.00 to 225.00
Vase, No. 239, Deep Blue, 8 In. 150.00
Vase, Orange Crystalline, 2 Handles, 6 In. 59.00
Vase, Orange Crystalline, Handle, 6 In. 50.00
Vase, Pink, 8-Sided, 5 In. 65.00
Vase, Pink, Green, Handles, 6 In. 50.00
Vase, Sunflower, Brown & Cream, 5 In. 85.00

RUSKIN is a British art pottery of the twentieth century. The Ruskin Pottery was started by William Howson Taylor, and his name was used as the mark until about 1899. The factory, at West Smethwick, Birmingham, England, stopped making new pieces in 1933 but continued to glaze and sell the remaining wares until 1935. The art pottery is noted for its exceptional glazes.

Bowl, Lavender Iridescent High Glaze, Pink, Gold, Blue Accents, 1925, 8 x 3 In. 77.00
Bowl, Red High Glaze, Purple, Gray, Impressed Mark, 1924, 5 x 1 1/2 In. 110.00

Pedestal, Red, Purple High Glaze, Gray, Impressed Mark, 4 x 2 1/2 In. 319.00
Tea Set, Mottled Blue, Tan Glaze, 4 Piece 55.00
Vase, Black Mottled High Glaze, Green, Tan, Impressed Marks, 1906, 7 In. 715.00
Vase, Cream, Blue Crystalline High Glaze, Impressed Marks, 1930, 5 In. 231.00
Vase, Iridescent Shades Of Green, Purple & Yellow, Marked, 1913, 9 In. 275.00
Vase, Light Blue Crystalline Over Tan Glaze, Orange, Mint Green, 1932, 5 1/2 In. 522.50
Vase, Light Blue Iridescent Luster Glaze, Pink, Yellow, Green Accents, 1925, 8 In. 319.00
Vase, Light Blue, Purple, Cream, Dark Green High Glaze, 1909, 3 In. 2530.00
Vase, Mottled Pink, Cream Luster Glaze, Impressed Mark, 7 In. 308.00
Vase, Mottled Yellow, Pink, Green, White Iridescent Luster Glaze, 1923, 10 In. 55.00
Vase, Orange Iridescent Luster Glaze, Gold, Green, Pink Accents, 1914, 11 In. 55.00
Vase, Purple High Glaze, White, Dark Green, Impressed Marks, 7 1/2 In. 825.00
Vase, Purple Mottled Glaze, Green, Light Blue, Impressed Marks, 1910, 6 3/4 In. 1980.00
Vase, Purple Mottled High Glaze, White, Blue, Impressed Marks, 1921, 8 In. 550.00
Vase, Red High Glaze, White, Gray, 1926, 6 x 3 1/2 In. 990.00
Vase, Red, Gray High Glaze, Impressed Mark, 6 1/2 In. 495.00
Vase, Red, White High Glaze, 1922, 9 1/2 In. 440.00
Vase, Red, White, Purple High Glaze, 1 Handle, 1933, 8 1/2 In. 253.00
Vase, Royal Blue Iridescent Luster Glaze, Purple, Green, Yellow Accents, 1910, 9 In. . . . 55.00
Vase, Shades Of Ivory, Green & Blue, Bulbous, Marked, 9 x 6 In. 155.00
Vase, Tapered Form, Blue Drip Over Gray, Marked, 9 1/2 In. 253.00
Vase, Trumpet, Oxblood, Marked 1921, 4 In. 150.00
Vase, White, Purple High Glaze, Impressed Marks, 1923, 7 1/2 In. 495.00
Vase, Yellow & Orange Luster Drip Over White Glaze, Marked, 10 In. 330.00
Vase, Yellow Iridescent Glaze, Pink, Green, Blue Accents, 1927, 7 x 6 1/2 In. 55.00
Vase, Yellow Luster Glaze, Impressed Marks, 1916, 14 In. 360.00

RUSSEL WRIGHT designed dinnerwares in modern shapes for many
companies. Iroquois China Company, Harker China Company,
Steubenville Pottery, and Justin Tharaud and Sons made dishes marked
Russel Wright. The Steubenville wares, first made in 1938, are the
most common today. Wright was a designer of domestic and industrial wares, including furniture, aluminum, radios, interiors, and glassware. Dinnerwares and other pieces by Wright are listed here. For
more information, see *Kovels' Depression Glass & American
Dinnerware Price List.*

Ashtray, Sterling, Straw Yellow 95.00
Bowl, Fruit, American Modern, Bean Brown, 1 Lug . . . . .18.00 to 20.00
Bowl, Gumbo, Iroquois, Ice Blue 25.00
Bowl, Salad, American Modern, Seafoam 100.00
Bowl, Vegetable, American Modern, Cedar Green, 2 Sections, 10 In. 100.00
Bowl, Vegetable, American Modern, Coral 18.00
Bowl, Vegetable, American Modern, Granite Gray, Divided 58.00
Bowl, Vegetable, Casual, Avocado Yellow 35.00
Bowl, Vegetable, Cover, American Modern, Seafoam, Round 5.00
Bowl, Vegetable, Iroquois, Avocado Yellow 40.00
Bowl, Vegetable, Iroquois, Ice Blue, Divided 20.00
Bowl, Vegetable, Iroquois, Lemon Yellow, 10 In. 35.00
Bowl, Vegetable, Iroquois, Pink Sherbet, 8 In. . . . . .20.00 to 32.00
Bread Plate, Iroquois, Sugar White, 6 1/2 In. 4.00
Butter, Casual, Avocado Yellow 25.00
Butter, Cover, American Modern, Granite Gray 175.00
Butter, Iroquois, Impromptu, Sugar White 20.00
Carafe, American Modern, Coral . . . . .135.00 to 145.00
Carafe, Iroquois, Avocado Yellow . . . . .125.00 to 140.00
Carafe, Iroquois, Ice Blue 110.00
Carafe, Iroquois, Nutmeg 125.00
Carafe, Iroquois, Pink Sherbet 125.00
Casserole, American Modern, Bean Brown 45.00
Casserole, Casual, Divided, Ice Blue, Round 20.00
Casserole, Casual, Ripe Apricot, 4 Qt. 85.00
Casserole, Cover, American Modern, Black Chutney 55.00
Casserole, Cover, American Modern, Granite Gray . . . . .45.00 to 55.00

Casserole, Cover, Casual, Ripe Apricot, Round 40.00
Casserole, Cover, Iroquois, Charcoal, 4 Qt. 145.00
Casserole, Cover, Iroquois, Ice Blue, 2 Qt. ....20.00 to 45.00
Casserole, Cover, Iroquois, Lettuce Green, 6 Qt. 95.00
Casserole, Cover, Iroquois, Sugar White, Divided, 4 Qt. 135.00
Casserole, Iroquois, Cover, Pink Sherbet, 4 Qt. 145.00
Casserole, Iroquois, Ice Blue, 2 Sections, 10 In. 70.00
Casserole, Iroquois, Nutmeg, 2 Qt. ....20.00 to 35.00
Celery Dish, American Modern, Bean Brown 45.00
Celery Dish, American Modern, Coral 30.00
Chop Plate, American Modern, Chartreuse, 13 In. 30.00
Chop Plate, American Modern, White 75.00
Clock, Lemon Spice, General Electric 60.00
Coffeepot, American Modern, Black Chutney 245.00
Coffeepot, American Modern, Seafoam, After Dinner 120.00
Coffeepot, Iroquois, Ice Blue, After Dinner ....75.00 to 135.00
Coffeepot, Iroquois, Impromptu, Sugar White, Ben Seidel 43.00
Coffeepot, Iroquois, Parsley, After Dinner 30.00
Creamer, American Modern, Granite Gray 9.00
Creamer, Iroquois, Ice Blue 11.00
Creamer, Iroquois, Parsley 12.00
Cup & Saucer, American Modern, Coral 24.00
Cup & Saucer, American Modern, Granite Gray 28.00
Cup & Saucer, American Modern, Seafoam 24.00
Cup & Saucer, American Modern, White 48.00
Cup & Saucer, Iroquois, Ice Blue 10.00
Cup & Saucer, Iroquois, Nutmeg 10.00
Cup & Saucer, Tea, Iroquois, Pink Sherbet 10.00
Fork & Spoon, Salad, American Modern, Chartreuse 85.00
Glass, Wine, American Modern, Smoky, 6 Piece 125.00
Gravy, Fast Stand, Iroquois, Avocado Yellow 75.00
Mug, Iroquois, Ice Blue 60.00
Mug, Iroquois, Pink Sherbet 65.00
Pitcher, American Modern, Coral, 7 1/2 In. 65.00
Pitcher, American Modern, Water, Granite Gray 70.00
Pitcher, American Modern, White, Ice Lip 195.00
Pitcher, Casual, Ripe Apricot, 5 1/4 In. 45.00
Pitcher, Cover, American Modern, Chartreuse 350.00
Pitcher, Cover, Iroquois, Sugar White 145.00
Plate, American Modern, Bean Brown, 8 In. 20.00
Plate, American Modern, Coral, 6 In. 5.00
Plate, American Modern, Granite Gray, 6 In. 5.00
Plate, Iroquois, Nutmeg, 7 1/2 In. 8.00
Plate, Iroquois, Sugar White, 10 In. ....9.00 to 15.00
Platter, American Modern, Bean Brown, 13 3/4 In. 38.00
Platter, American Modern, Coral, 13 3/4 In. 20.00
Platter, American Modern, Granite Gray, 13 3/4 In. 20.00
Platter, Iroquois, Chartreuse, 12 3/4 In. 15.00
Platter, Iroquois, Ice Blue, 12 3/4 In. 15.00
Platter, Iroquois, Ice Blue, Oval, 14 1/2 In. ....20.00 to 30.00
Platter, Iroquois, Oyster, Oval, 14 1/2 In. 45.00
Platter, Iroquois, Pink Sherbet, 12 3/4 In. 15.00
Platter, Sterling, Ivy Green, 7 1/2 In. 22.00
Relish, American Modern, Seafoam, Divided, Rattan Handle 185.00
Salt & Pepper, American Modern, Coral 20.00
Sherbet, American Modern, Seafoam Green 15.00
Soup, Dish, Casual, Nutmeg 20.00
Soup, Dish, Cover, Casual, Ice Blue 15.00
Sugar, Stacking, Iroquois, Ice Blue 20.00
Sugar, Stacking, Iroquois, Lettuce Green 20.00
Sugar & Creamer, Stacking, Iroquois, Avocado Yellow ....25.00 to 50.00
Teacup, Casual, Lettuce Green 3.00

Teapot, American Modern, Cedar Green 175.00
Teapot, American Modern, Chartreuse 85.00
Teapot, American Modern, Coral 75.00
Teapot, American Modern, Seafoam 135.00
Torchere, Spun Aluminum, Wood Switch Knobs, 1940, 65 In., Pair 715.00
Tray, Tidbit, Spun Aluminum, 2 Tiers, Rattan Handles, Small ....95.00 to 125.00
Tumbler, American Modern, Pinch, Chartreuse 28.00
Tumbler, Eclipse, Color Variation, 8 Piece 135.00
Tumbler, Iroquois, Pinched, Lettuce Green, Paper Label 38.00

SABINO glass was made in the 1920s and 1930s in Paris, France. Founded by Marius-Ernest Sabino (1878–1961), the firm was noted for Art Deco lamps, vases, figurines, and animals in clear, colored, and opalescent glass. Production stopped during World War II but resumed in the 1960s with the manufacture of nude figurines and small opalescent glass animals. The new pieces are a slightly different color and can be recognized.

Sabino
France

Figurine, Butterfly, Opalescent 115.00
Figurine, Isadora Duncan 650.00
Figurine, Stylized Leaping Animal, Opalescent Glass, 4 1/2 In. 69.00
Perfume Bottle, Raised Female, Nude, Circular, 6 In. 150.00
Vase, La Danse 1500.00

SALOPIAN ware was made by the Caughley factory of England during the eighteenth century. The early pieces were blue and white with some colored decorations. Another ware referred to as *Salopian* is a late nineteenth-century tableware decorated with color transfers.

Salopian

Bowl, Figures, Flowers, 6 1/2 In. 325.00
Bowl, Figures, Flowers, Scalloped Rim, 1780-1790, 7 In. 395.00
Cider Mug, Figures, Flowers, Initials, 1780-1790, 6 In. 650.00
Cup & Saucer, No Handle, Black Transfer Of Deer 105.00

SALT AND PEPPER SHAKERS in matched sets were first used in the nineteenth century. Collectors are primarily interested in figural examples made after World War I. *Huggers* are pairs of shakers that appear to embrace each other. Many salt and pepper shakers are listed in other categories and can be located through the index at the back of this book.

3-Face, Frosted, 2 1/2 In. 110.00
A-Nod To Abe, Regal China ....225.00 to 350.00
Alcatraz Figures, Ceramic, 1960s 45.00
Ale, Old Shay, Miniature 17.00
Alice In Wonderland, Regal China 295.00
Apple Jug, Purinton 25.00
Aqua, Roselane, Tall 30.00
Aunt Jemima, Large 85.00
Auntie Em, Treasure Craft 65.00
Baby & Stork 40.00
Ballantine Beer, Miniature 11.00
Bear, Huggers, Yellow, White, Van Tellingen ....20.00 to 45.00
Bear, Nodder 45.00
Bear, Sombrero, Metlox 40.00
Beau Bears, Metlox 30.00
Beer, Grain Belt, Miniature 23.00
Beer, Gunther, Miniature 27.00
Beer, Horlacher Pilsner, Miniature 15.00
Beer, Schlitz, Box 20.00
Betsy Ross & Bill Of Rights 15.00
Big Buttress, Red Flashed 110.00
Birds, In Nest, Vallona Starr 22.00
Black Boy, Hugging Puppy, Van Tellingen 175.00
Black Boy, Suitcase 55.00

Black Boy Eating Watermelon 125.00
Black Boys Eating Fruit 85.00
Black Chef & Maid, Japan 40.00
Black Children In Basket 95.00
Black Couple 32.00
Black Man With Alligator 150.00
Bluebird, Kreiss 35.00
Bottle, Heinz Ketchup 30.00
Bottle, Sealtest Milk, In Cow Holder 30.00
Bowling Ball, Tenpin 20.00
Boy & Dog, Van Tellingen 85.00
Boy & Girl, Old McDonald, Regal China 75.00
Bride & Groom, Sorcha Boru 175.00
Bunny, Huggers, Van Tellingen 22.00
Bus, Greyhound, Wheels Turn, 3 In. 70.00
Buster Brown & Puppy 20.00
Butler & Mammy, Flowers On Dress 125.00
Cat, Blue, Pink Dotted Cheeks, Tilso 45.00
Cat, Calico & Plaid Dog, Brayton Laguna, 4 In. 45.00
Cat, White, Gold, Vallona Starr 30.00
Chef & Mammy, Gold Trim, Large 195.00
Chef & Mammy, Yellow, Metlox 175.00
Chef Snoopy 40.00
Chinese Couple, Sitting 6.00
Conoco, Green, Red, White, Plastic, 2 1/2 In. 49.00
Couple In Barrel, Nodder, Japan, 1930s 45.00
Couple Shopping, Black 75.00
Cow, Jumped Over The Moon 15.00
Cow & Beach Ball, Vandor 30.00
Cowman Mooranda, Vandor ....25.00 to 29.00
Cut Glass, Notched Prisms, Metal Screw 35.00
Deep Sea Divers, 5 In. 50.00
Delphite, Blue 145.00
Dog, Little Mutt, Fitz & Floyd ....35.00 to 55.00
Dog & Cat, Brayton Laguna, 4 In. ....70.00 to 72.00
Dog & Cat, Ken-L Ration, Fiedler & Fiedler 12.00
Drunk, Against Lamppost 25.00
Duck, Nodder 45.00
Ducks, Metlox 20.00
Dutch Boy & Girl, Huggers, Van Tellingen 35.00
Dutch Boy & Girl, Shelf Sitters 12.00
Eeyore & Piglet, Winnie The Pooh 15.00
Fat Cat, Sigma 50.00
Figaro Cats, White, National Porcelain Co. 45.00
Flamingo, Nodder 57.00
Fox Head 400 Beer, Miniature 36.00
Frog, With Musical Instruments 25.00
Fruit Heads, Anthropomorphic, Napco 45.00
Gas Pump, Richfield, Beige, Blue, Plastic, 2 1/2 In. 82.00
Goetz Country Club, Box 20.00
Goldilocks, Regal China ....225.00 to 275.00
Goose & Egg, Vallona Starr, Large 45.00
Indian Couple, Nodder, 1930s 45.00
Indian Head, Nodder 55.00
Indiana & Race Car, Parkcraft 25.00
Jonah & Whale 75.00
Kanga & Roo, Enesco 235.00
Kangaroo With Child, Nodder 70.00
Kermit & Miss Piggy, Sigma 85.00
Kitchen Prayer, Pink 8.00
Kitten, American Bisque 12.00
Lobster Claws, With Label, Brad Keller 28.00
Log & Ax, Parkcraft 20.00

Love Bugs, Van Tellingen	70.00
Maggie & Jiggs, Canada	125.00
Maggie & Jiggs, Ceramic, Japan, 1930s	90.00
Mammy, Green & Yellow, Luzianne, 5 In.	160.00
Mammy & Butler, Plaid	135.00
Mammy & Chef, 8 1/2 In.	110.00 to 130.00
Mammy & Chef, Black & Yellow, Gold Trim, 8 In.	225.00
Mammy & Chef, Brayton	95.00
Mammy & Pappy, Regal	300.00
Man In Doghouse, Vallona Starr	85.00
Marilyn Monroe, Clay Art, 1985	32.00
Mary & Lamb, Yellow, Van Tellingen	40.00 to 48.00
Mason Jar, Ball, Handle	4.50
Matador & Bull, Nodder, Holder, Souvenir Of Mexico	145.00
Mickey McGuire, Toonerville Folks	95.00
Milk Churn, Old MacDonald, Red, Regal China	38.00
Mother Bear & Baby, Snuggle Pair	60.00
Mother Bird & Nest Of Eggs	15.00
Mother In The Kitchen, Pink, Van Tellingen	11.00
Mouse, With Garlic & Corn, Fitz & Floyd	12.00
Mr. & Mrs. Humpty Dumpty, Japan	22.00
New Orleans City Scenes, 3 In.	45.00
Nipper, RCA	18.00
Older Black Man In Suit & Hat	25.00
Papoose, Swaddled, 5 In.	25.00
Parrot, Fitz & Floyd	15.00
Paul Bunyan & Babe	25.00 to 50.00
Peasant Man & Woman, Nodder, Ireland	65.00
Piano & Bass Fiddle, Anthropomorphic, Sarsaparilla Deco Designs	15.00
Pig, American Bisque	12.00
Pig, Bendel, Huggers, Large	395.00
Pig, Formal Attire, Red, Japan	28.00
Pig, Pink, Kreiss	20.00
Piglet & Eeyore	15.00
Pillsbury Doughboy, 1988	55.00
Pillsbury Doughboy & Girl	30.00
Pineapple, Sitting In Multi-Leaved Planter	6.50
Pipe & Hat, McArthur's	20.00
Polka Dot Witch, Fitz & Floyd	45.00
Pooh & Hunny Jar, Winnie The Pooh	15.00
Pooh Bear & Rabbit, Enesco	175.00
Porter & Suitcase	185.00
Potbelly Stove, Twin Winton	18.00
Rabbit, Clover Finial, Metlox	275.00
Rabbit, Huggers, Green, Van Tellingen	15.00
Refrigerator, General Electric	45.00 to 65.00
Rooster, Hen, Brayton Laguna	120.00
Rooster, Nodder	45.00
Russian Generals, Old Imperial Characters, Signed	55.00
Sailor & Mermaid, Van Tellingen, Huggers	145.00 to 185.00
Sammy Seals, Metlox	100.00
Satin Glass, Bulbous, 3 3/4 In.	1870.00
Seahorse, Fitz & Floyd	35.00
Seal & Trainer	90.00
Shmoo, Cinnamon	65.00
Skeleton Head, Nodder, Gold, Purple Spatter Base	35.00
Skull, Nodder	25.00
Skunk, Sniffy & Snuffy, Paper Label	24.00
Smokey The Bear, 4 In.	75.00 to 85.00
Squirrel, On Stump, California Originals	50.00
Squirrel, Twin Winton	35.00
Stainless Steel, G. Jensen	16.00
Standard, Red Crown, White, Blue, Plastic, 2 1/2 In.	82.00

Sugar & Spice, Treasure Craft	30.00
Tastee Freeze	80.00
Taz & Bugs Bunny, Santa Claus Suits	58.00
Toothbrush & Toothpaste, Sarsaparilla Deco Designs	13.00
Tractor & Barn	25.00
Truck, Pick-Up, Beige, Treasure Craft	95.00
Tweedle Dee & Tweedle Dum, Fitz & Floyd	30.00
Vegetable Heads, Apple, Box	30.00
Washer & Dryer, Westinghouse	14.00
Watermelon Girl In Chair	175.00
Watermelon Head	40.00
Willie & Millie, Kool	30.00
Woman In Swimsuit, On Alligator	35.00
Woody Woodpecker & Girl Friend, Lantz	50.00 to 75.00

SALT GLAZE has a grayish white surface with a texture like an orange peel. It is a method of decoration that has been used since the eighteenth century. Salt-glazed pieces are still being made.

Bottle, Liquor, Applied Holly, Wicker Basket, Square, 1872, 8 3/4 In., Pair	800.00
Bowl, Undertray, Reticulated, Oval, 11 1/2 In.	1320.00
Crock, Butter, 3 Deer On Cover, Blue & Gray	395.00
Crock, Gray, Blue Designs, H.J. Heinz Co., Brown Albany Slip Interior, 6 3/4 In.	245.00
Flask, SP July 19, 1803, Reverse Side Flowering Tree, 5 1/4 In.	3220.00
Jar, Brown, 2 Loop Handles, Nottingham, 18th Century, 6 3/4 In.	175.00
Mug, Stroh's Beer, Detroit, Mich., 4 1/2 In.	485.00
Pitcher, Dutch Boy & Girl Kissing, Brown Glaze Figures, c.1860, 6 1/2 In.	875.00
Pitcher, King Sitting On Keg, Brown & Blue, Whites Utica, c.1880, 10 In.	200.00
Pitcher, Leaf & Rose On Bark Surface, Tavern Scene, 8 1/4 In.	145.00
Pitcher, Pierced Center, Dome Foot, Round, Germany, 13 In.	95.00
Pitcher, Tooled Pewter Lid, Star Design On Body, Blue Swag & Shields, 12 In.	160.00
Tankard, Cobalt Blue & Incised Floral Design, Cylindrical, Pewter Mounted, 7 In.	520.00
Tankard, Pewter Lid, Acorn Finial, 9 In.	125.00
Teapot, Red & Green Baskets Of Flowers, Holland, 1780, 4 1/2 In.	1600.00
Vase, Incised Daffodil & Butterfly, 10 1/2 In.	205.00

SAMPLERS were made in America from the early 1700s. The best examples were made from 1790 to 1840. Long, narrow samplers are usually older than square ones. Early samplers just had stitching or alphabets. The later examples had numerals, borders, and pictorial decorations. Those with mottoes are mid-Victorian. A revival of interest in the 1930s produced simpler samplers, usually with mottoes.

ABCDE

Adam & Eve, Standing Beside Apple Tree, Green, Yellow, 1805, 19 3/4 x 16 In.	460.00
Alphabet, 12 Herbs Listed With Plants, Red Stitching, Meifsen, 1822, 10 x 16 In.	150.00
Alphabet, Bertja Didensign, 1843, Cross-Stitched, 19th Century	385.00
Alphabet, Birds, Flowers, Blue, Green, Beige, Linen Homespun, Frame, 17 In.	412.00
Alphabet, Floral Borders, Pink, Red, Brown, Green, Linen Homespun, 16 In.	275.00
Alphabet, Jenny Glentz, ABC Frame, Germany, 1872, 20 x 20 In.	695.00
Alphabet, Martha West, 1810, Needlepoint, 11 1/2 x 14 In.	3450.00
Alphabet, Strawberry Border, Emily Miller, Homespun, Walnut Frame, 22 In.	1375.00
Alphabet, Verse, Floral Wreath, Charlotte Daggett, Needlepoint, 21 x 18 In.	3105.00
Alphabets, Flowers, Animals, Catherine Moylan, Silk, Wicker Frame, 7 x 7 In.	575.00
Alphabets, Framed, Annaline S. Barron, Washington City, Aged 9, 1837, 16 1/2 In.	412.00
Alphabets, Frances West Williams, 1824, Silk On Linen, Frame, 18 x 17 In.	220.00
Alphabets, Rachel Ann Bennets, 9 Years, Silk On Linen, Frame, 18 x 19 In.	605.00
Alphabets, Sheep, Agnes Roberts, Aged 9, Homespun, Frame, 18 x 9 In.	220.00
Animals, Flowers, Ann Brook, Aged 10, 1825, Silk On Linen, 16 1/2 x 25 In.	660.00
Ann Gay Is My Name & With My Needle I Work The Same, 11 Years, 1778	440.00
Betsey C. Converse, Aged 8 Years, AD 1828, Frame, 17 3/4 x 18 3/4 In.	2200.00
Climena Potter, Aged 11 Years, 1809, Silk On Homespun, Frame, 14 x 10 In.	412.00
Colonial America, Mary Waraken Kinsey, 1930, 12 x 18 In.	145.00
Eagle Emblem, J.A. Bartlet Her Sampler, May 27, 1829, 13 1/2 x 17 3/4 In.	4800.00
Elizabeth Dock Stader, Silk On Homespun Linen, Gilt Frame, 9 1/2 x 11 1/2 In.	225.00
Elizabeth Durrant, Aged 11, May 29, 1844, Silk On Linen, Frame, 16 x 13 1/2 In.	330.00

Family History, Paulina Talpey, York, Maine, c.1815, 7 1/2 x 10 1/2 In. 625.00
Family Register, Emily Dickinson Family, Diamond Border, 14 1/2 x 13 1/2 In. 920.00
Family Register, Felch Family, 20 1/2 x 16 1/2 In. 2645.00
Flower Basket, Wool, Burlin, S.R. Swenk, Aged 14 Years, 1934, 26 In. 550.00
Flower Border, Betsey C. Converse, Parkman, Ohio, 1828, 17 3/4 x 18 3/4 In. 2200.00
Flower Border, Catherine Margret Martens, Age 9, Silk On Linen, Frame, 18 x 18 In. . . 300.00
Flowering Plant In Urn, Red, Blue, Green, 1838, Silk On Linen, 22 1/4 x 21 In. 633.00
Flowers, Birds, Angela Nicholas, 9 Years, 1835, Silk On Linen, Frame, 17 x 19 In. 330.00
Flowers, Verse, Elizabeth Grant, May 30, 1812, Silk On Linen, Frame, 16 x 13 In. 385.00
Flowers, Vine Border, Hannah Coats & Jesse Carver, 1832, Frame, 17 x 17 1/2 In. 1100.00
Flowers Above Verse, Margaret A. Reed, 1835, Silk On Linen, 25 x 17 In. 805.00
Frances Emily Young, 12 Years Old, Born November 7, 1823, 12 1/2 x 25 In. 1650.00
Geometric Borders, M.A. Watkins 9th Year 1856, Silk On Linen, Frame, 21 x 12 In. . . 355.00
Hannah Tyson, Born 2nd Day Of June, 1815, Stylized, Frame, 17 1/2 x 17 In. 1540.00
House, Mansard Style, 7 Bays, Iron Fence, Ann Bush, 1834, 17 1/4 x 15 1/2 In. 950.00
House With Fence, Animal Surround, Elizabeth Beal, Age 9, 1806, 15 x 12 In. 345.00
House With Trees, Gold, Brown, Eufemea Moore, Silk On Linen, 21 In. 3685.00
Jane Newton, Aged 10 Years, July 28th 1827, 12 1/4 x 11 3/4 In. 488.00
Landing Of Columbus, Needlepoint, Metallic Threads, Boston, Mass., 19 x 20 In. 1380.00
Lincoln & Washington, Partially Printed, Colored Needlepoint, Frame, 9 x 21 In. 280.00
Mary Ann Plowman, 8 Years, 1822, Silk On Linen, Frame, 20 x 18 In. 605.00
Memorial, Felch Family, 16 x 17 In. 1725.00
Memorial, H. Nowell, 1790, Silk Threads With Watercolor, 15 x 20 In. 6325.00
Mrs. Rowson's Academy, Caroline Hull, November 8, 1803, 11 1/2 x 7 3/4 In. 1035.00
Peacock, Coat Of Arms, Connecticut Family, Betsy Hatch, 1799, Frame, 6 x 9 3/4 In. . . . 1095.00
Pheby Ann Bush, Aged 8 Years 1843, Wool On Linen, Frame, 19 x 20 In. 355.00
Rose Vines Around Verse, Margaret Shirmer, Wool On Linen, 1840, 17 x 16 In. 1093.00
Stitch Flowers, White, Blue, Green, Beige, Silk On Linen, Mahogany Frame, 12 In. . . . 715.00
Strawberries On Black Ground, 1785, 15 1/2 x 9 3/4 In. 2415.00
Strawberry Border, Mary Ann Tomlinsom, Flimby School, 1836, 22 x 17 In. 2650.00
Stylized Flowers, Buildings, Silk On Homespun, Dated 1797, Frame, 21 x 22 In. 465.00
Ten Commandments Verse, John Field & Dianna Field Married, 1799, 19 x 22 In. 825.00
Tulips, Dutch Design, Rebecca Parker, Aged 10 Years, Silk On Linen, 11 x 16 In. 550.00
Verse, Brick House, Silk On Linen, Frame, Inscribed, 1783, 19 x 15 In. 4250.00
Verse, Emily Dickinson, Lower Panel With Flowers, 19th Century, 16 x 12 In. 488.00
Verse, House, Birds, Rachel Mauger Age 12, Floral Border, 20 x 15 In. 460.00
Verses, Elizabeth Grave, 1760, Aged 14, Border, Linen, Gilt Frame, 16 x 13 In. 4370.00
Verses, Mary Collier, Aged 9, 1834, Frame, 14 1/2 x 12 In. 977.00
Vining Border, Linen Homespun, Stylized Trees, Frame, 16 3/4 In. 330.00
Vining Borders, Hannah Francia, 1817, Frame, 18 1/2 x 17 1/2 In. 962.50
Zigzag Border, Abigail Cool, Feb. 6th, 1796, Silk On Linen Homespun, 14 In. 2145.00

SAMSON and Company, a French firm specializing in the reproduction
of collectible wares of many countries and periods, was founded in
Paris in the early nineteenth century. Chelsea, Meissen, Famille Verte,
and Chinese Export porcelain are some of the wares that have been
reproduced by the company. The firm uses a variety of marks on the
reproductions. It is still in operation.

Bowl, Cover, Undertray With Square Rigged Ship, 5 1/4 In. 55.00
Figurine, Man, Costumed With Wine Cask & Goblet, Porcelain, Signed 250.00
Plate, Red, Green Floral Motif, Central Lion Crest, Ceramic, 9 In. 103.00
Supper Set, 6 Inserts, Florals, Mahogany Tray, Brass Handles, England, 1860 . . . . 750.00
Teapot, Porcelain, France, Late 19th Century, 5 1/4 In. 345.00
Urn, Baluster Form, Painted With Floral Swags, Sprays, 29 In. 58.00

SANDWICH GLASS is any of the myriad types of glass made by the
Boston and Sandwich Glass Works in Sandwich, Massachusetts,
between 1825 and 1888. It is often very difficult to be sure whether a
piece was really made at the Sandwich factory because so many types
were made there and similar pieces were made at other glass factories.
Additional pieces may be listed under Pressed Glass and in related categories.

Bottle, Cologne, 12-Sided Form, Sapphire Blue, Pontil, 4 In. 385.00

Keep your keys on a pull apart chain so the house keys and car keys can be separated when you leave the car in a parking lot.

Sandwich Glass, Decanter, Canary,
Engraved Harbor Scene, Stopper, 9 In.

Bowl, Beehive, Octagonal, 9 1/8 In. 44.00
Bowl, Flower, Green Glass Thread Applied To Ruffled Rim, 8 In. 295.00
Bowl, Peacock Feather, 7 1/2 In. 125.00
Candlestick, Canary Yellow, 1845, Pair 250.00
Candlestick, Dolphin, Double Step Base, 10 In. 225.00
Candlestick, Dolphin, Green & Gold, Prisms, 9 1/2 In., Pair 172.00
Candlestick, Electric Blue, Clambroth Base 590.00
Candlestick, Green Columnar Form, Petal Socket, 9 In., Pair 450.00
Candlestick, Hexagonal Base, Green Canary, Straw Marks, 7 1/8 In. 350.00
Candlestick, Loop Base, Canary, 7 In., Pair 375.00
Candlestick, Petal & Loop, Green Canary, 7 In. 350.00
Candlestick, Underplate, Handle, Canary, 3 x 6 In. 250.00
Centerpiece, Tortoiseshell, 9 1/2 In. 330.00
Cologne, Waisted Loop, Straw Marks, Sandwich, Mass., 5 1/8 In., Pair 172.50
Compote, Dolphin, Frosted, 4 1/2 In. 175.00
Decanter, Canary, Engraved Harbor Scene, Stopper, 9 In. . . . .*Illus* 6150.00
Dish, Honey, Sunburst, 3 1/2 In., 5 Piece 175.00
Dish, Sweetmeat, Cover, Princess Feather Variant Border, 5 1/4 x 7 In., Pair 890.00
Eggcup, Bull's Eye & Bar, Eggcup, Flint, 1850s 145.00
Hat, Black, Amethyst, With Opalescent Glass Baby, Compass Rose, N.Y. 1575.00
Spillholder, Star 68.00
Sugar Bowl, 3-Mold, Sapphire Blue, Pontil, Boston, 2 1/2 x 5 In. 3575.00
Tankard, Cranberry Overshot, Clear Reeded Handle, 6 3/4 In. 250.00
Vase, Amethyst, Applied Icicle Top, 8 1/4 x 8 1/4 In. 895.00
Vase, Trevaise, Triangular, Rainbow Swirl, Gray, Olive, Alton, 8 In. 1650.00
Vase, Trumpet, Flared Mouth, Emerald Green, Boston, 13 3/8 In. 2475.00

SARREGUEMINES is the name of a French town that is used as part of a
china mark. Utzschneider and Company, a porcelain factory, made
ceramics in Sarreguemines, Lorraine, France, from about 1775.
Transfer-printed wares and majolica were made in the nineteenth century. The nineteenth-century pieces, most often found today, usually
have colorful transfer-printed decorations showing peasants in local
costumes.

Basket, Textured Surface, Light Green Glaze, Marked, 9 In. 110.00
Candlestick, Silver Luster Glaze, Marked, 7 In., Pair 65.00
Ewer, Square Handled, Light Blue Glaze, Marked 55.00
Ewer, Stylized Blossoms & Wreaths, Gray & Tan Glaze, 11 1/2 In. 77.00
Pitcher, Blue Gray Glaze, 9 In. 225.00
Plate, Country Woman, 10 In. 100.00
Plate, Mischievous Children, 8 In. 100.00
Plate, With Tigers, Green Blue Background, 10 In. 125.00
Urn, Applied Dolphins, Over Sheaves Of Cattails, Majolica, 26 In., Pair 7185.00
Urn, Figural Handle, Modeled As Satyrs, c.1880 . . . . 2000.00
Vase, 4-Lobed Form, Blue Hi-Glaze, Purple, Gilt Outline, 4 Handles, 8 In. 55.00
Vase, Folded Tricornered Rim, Green Glaze, Marked, 5 1/2 x 6 1/2 In. 100.00

SASCHA BRASTOFF made decorative accessories, ceramics, enamels on copper, and plastics of his own design. He headed a factory, Sascha Brastoff of California, Inc., in West Los Angeles, from 1953 until about 1973. He died in 1993. Pieces made by Matt Adams after he left the factory are listed here with his name.

Sascha Brastoff

Ashtray, Alaska, Hooded	45.00
Ashtray, Covered Wagon Scene, 14 In.	165.00
Ashtray, Dancer, 6 1/2 In.	25.00
Ashtray, Freedom, 10 In.	75.00
Ashtray, Metal, Green With Abstract Design	36.00
Ashtray, Polar Bear, Brown, 7 1/2 In.	29.00
Ashtray, Rooftop, 5 1/2 x 7 In.	65.00
Ashtray, Rooftop, 14 1/2 In.	65.00
Ashtray, Rooftops, Large	95.00
Ashtray, Tulip, 17 In.	100.00
Ashtray, U.S. Borax Corp., 20 Mule Team Wagon Train, 1957, 13 x 5 In.	115.00
Ashtray & Table Lighter, Enamel On Metal	60.00
Bank, Pig	250.00
Beverage Set, Grizzly Bear, Brown, Matthew Adams, 7 Piece	223.00
Beverage Set, Polar Bear & Glacier, Matthew Adams, 5 Piece	170.00
Bookends, Horse	595.00
Bookends, Horse Head	495.00
Bowl, Cabin On Stilts, 7 In.	55.00 to 75.00
Bowl, Green, With Abstract Design, 7 In.	38.00
Bowl, Grizzly Bear, Free-Form, Brown, Matthew Adams, 6 1/2 In.	90.00
Bowl, Jeweled Bird, 5 3/4 In.	35.00
Bowl, Mosaic, 6 In.	30.00
Bowl, Persian Afghans, 13 In.	650.00
Bowl, Portrait Of Seal, Alaska Series, Oval	35.00
Bowl, Ram, Green, Free-Form, Matthew Adams, 7 In.	90.00
Box, Abstract, 5 1/2 In.	50.00
Box, Cover, With Fruit, 5 In.	55.00
Candlestick, Jeweled Bird, 8 In.	50.00
Charger, Circus Performer With A Horse, Pink, Gray, Blue, White, 17 In.	55.00
Charger, House Scene, Enamel On Copper, 15 In.	95.00
Chess Set, Collector's Encyclopedia	1600.00
Cigarette Box, Cover, Grapes, Gold Design, 5 3/8 In.	30.00
Cigarette Box, Star Steed	125.00
Compote, With Seal	35.00
Cup & Saucer, Surf Ballet, Blue	10.00
Dish, 3 Sections, Surf Ballet, Pink & Gold, 21 In.	80.00
Dish, Fish, Mosaic, 12 In.	165.00
Dish, Flounder Shape, 3-Footed, House, 8 1/2 x 8 1/4 In.	75.00
Dish, Freeform Bird, Jeweled, 10 In.	35.00
Dish, Horse, Green Ground, Square, 6 1/2 In.	28.00
Dish, Jeweled Bird, Free-Form, 10 In.	35.00
Dish, Nut, 7 In.	40.00
Dish, Nut, Bull's Eye, Signed	40.00
Figurine, Bear, Red Resin, 4 x 7 In. & 4 1/2 x 10 In., Pair	325.00
Figurine, Gold Egg	395.00
Figurine, Gregor Jeana	250.00
Figurine, Hippo, Blue Resin	450.00
Figurine, Musk Ox, Gold Resin	350.00
Figurine, Owl, Blue Resin	375.00
Figurine, Owl, Gold Resin, Tall	185.00
Figurine, Pelican	375.00
Figurine, Percheron Horse, 1950s	900.00
Figurine, Pintucks, 1982	500.00
Figurine, Rooster, Gold, Black Trim, 23 In.	750.00
Figurine, Rooster, Mosaic, 15 In.	395.00 to 450.00
Figurine, Sea Shell	165.00
Figurine, Whale, Blue, Resin	450.00
Figurine, Woodpecker, Green Resin	250.00

Lamp, Mosaic Tile, 27 In. 175.00
Lamp, Resin Votives 45.00
Pitcher, Stylized, 10 In. 75.00
Plaque, Wall, Grape Design, Enamel On Copper, 11 3/4 In. 75.00
Plate, African Dancer, Teal, Green, 12 In. ....596.00 to 650.00
Plate, Curled Houses, 10 1/2 In. 45.00
Plate, Serving, Star Steed, Silver & Gold, Signed, 1960, 10 In. 450.00
Plate, Strawberry, 8 In. 35.00
Textile, Resin, 10 Yards 1600.00
Textile, Star Steed, Frame, Pair 145.00
Tile, Erotic, Signed 395.00
Tray, Abstract, 15 In. 80.00
Vase, 3 Form, Misty Blue, 13 1/2 In. 95.00
Vase, Fruit, Brown, Rectangular, Signed, 9 3/8 In. 50.00
Vase, Green Grape, Resin, 10 In. 65.00
Vase, Mottled Bars Of Brown, Blue-Green, Rooster Logo, 13 1/2 In. 29.50
Vase, Star Steed, 9 1/4 In. 95.00
Vase, Swooping Rim, Stylized Incised Lion, Blue, 8 x 6 In. 135.00
Vase, Walrus, Blue, Matthew Adams, 10 In. 120.00
Wall Pocket, Crow, Black 45.00

SATIN GLASS is a late nineteenth-century art glass. It has a dull finish
that is caused by hydrofluoric acid vapor treatment. Satin glass was
made in many colors and sometimes has applied decorations. Satin
glass is also listed by factory name, such as Webb, or in the Mother-of-
Pearl category in this book.

Basket, Herringbone Pattern, Medium Blue Interior, White Exterior, 5 3/4 In. 365.00
Basket, Ruffled Edge, Blue Overlay, Melon Sectioned, White Outside, Blue, 7 In. 195.00
Biscuit Jar, Aqua To Pale Yellow, Cream Interior, Blue, Gold Bamboo, 4 x 9 In. 995.00
Biscuit Jar, Floral, Lavender Pink Overlay, Silver Plated Top, Handle, 6 5/8 In. 185.00
Biscuit Jar, Pink To White Shade, Yellow Flowers, Lavender Stems, Etched, 9 1/4 In. 525.00
Biscuit Jar, Rogers Silver Plated Handled Frame, 5 1/4 In. 615.00
Bowl, Internal Green Stripes, Ruffled Rim, 11 In. 95.00
Bowl, Rose, Pink, Pinched Mouth, 2 1/2 In. 60.50
Ewer, White, Raised Gold Floral Branches, Ruffled, Camphor Handle, 11 1/2 In. 130.00
Muffineer, Pink, Shouldered Base, 6 In. 110.00
Rose Bowl, Mother-Of-Pearl, Blue Herringbone, 4 In. 185.00
Rose Bowl, Seashell, Orange Enamel Florets, Yellow 85.00
Sugar & Creamer, Shell & Seaweed, Pink, Metal Spout & Scroll Handle 176.00
Syrup, Florette, Pink 395.00
Tumbler, Pink, White, 4 In., Pair 121.00
Vase, Apricot To Pink, Floral, White Lining, 20 1/2 In. 225.00
Vase, Blue Ribbon, Mother-Of-Pearl, Pinched Sides, White Lining, 4 1/2 In. 395.00
Vase, Blue, Diamond-Quilted Overlay, White Lining, Cut Velvet, 6 In. 125.00
Vase, Blue, Quilted, 5 1/2 In. 95.00
Vase, Bud, Pink Over White Interior, 6 1/4 In. 50.00
Vase, Butterscotch Raindrop, Mother-Of-Pearl, Jack-In-The-Pulpit, 7 3/8 In. 210.00
Vase, Butterscotch, Yellow To White, Ribbed, Oval, 9 x 5 x 3 1/4 In. 530.00
Vase, Crimped Top, Pink, 9 1/4 In., Pair 440.00
Vase, Floral Design, Green Ground, Globular, 3 In. 11.00
Vase, Floral Design, Yellow, Enameled, 2 7/8 In., Pair 264.00
Vase, Florentine, Yellow, White Bird, Field Grasses, Reverse Daisies, 3 1/2 In. 80.00
Vase, Flowers, Light, Medium Blue, Enameled, 10 1/2 In. 33.00
Vase, Green Webb, Cream Lining, Ground Pontil, 9 In. 395.00
Vase, Mother-Of-Pearl, Butterscotch Diamond, White Lining, 5 1/2 In. 195.00
Vase, Mother-Of-Pearl, Heavenly Blue Herringbone, Ruffled Top, 7 In., Pair 325.00
Vase, Mother-Of-Pearl, Pink, Art Deco Handles, Ruffled, 8 3/4 In. 200.00
Vase, Mother-Of-Pearl, White Lining, Diamond-Quilted, Pink, 10 3/8 In. 550.00
Vase, Pale Green, White Ground, Cut Velvet, 9 In. 350.00
Vase, Rainbow, Raindrops, Pink & Blue, Squared Dimpled Base, 10 In. 395.00
Vase, Ribbon, Fancy Metal Holders, Ruffled Top, Blue, 8 1/4 In. 240.00
Vase, Ruffled Opening, Blue Diamond Quilt, White Cased, 6 3/4 In. 125.00

Vase, Stick, Blue, Coralene Seaweed, Bulbous, 6 In. 165.00
Vase, Stick, Blue, Florentine, White Vine, Berries, Flowers, Bulbous, 9 In. 155.00
Vase, Stick, Gold Leaves, Berries, Vine, England, 8 1/2 In. 65.00
Vase, Stick, Yellow, White Interior, Bulbous, 7 1/2 In. 50.00
Water Set, Deep Apricot To White Shade, 7 Piece, 3 3/4 In. 1285.00

SATSUMA is a Japanese pottery with a distinctive creamy beige crackled glaze. Most of the pieces were decorated with blue, red, green,
orange, or gold. Almost all Satsuma found today was made after 1860.
During World War I, Americans could not buy undecorated European
porcelains. Women who liked to make hand painted porcelains at
home began to decorate plain Satsuma. These pieces are known today
as *American Satsuma.*

Bowl, Bird, Landscape Cartouches, 5-Lobed Floral Form, 1000 Floral Ground, 8 In. 385.00
Bowl, Birds Within Landscape, Late 19th Century, 4 7/8 In., Pair 373.00
Bowl, Figural Design, 5-Lobed Form, Red Mark, 6 In. 357.50
Bowl, Floral, Gilt, Multicolored, 2 In. 58.00
Bowl, Gilt & Enamel Immortals, River Landscape, Dragon Inside & Out, Signed, 6 In. .. 230.00
Bowl, Processional Scene, Signed, Seizan, Late Meiji Period, 9 1/2 In. 248.00
Bowl, Village Scene, Kwannon Design, 5 In. 355.00
Box, Cover, Fluttering Butterflies Above Leaf Border, Meiji Period, 3 1/2 In. 975.00
Brushpot, Floral Design, Bird, Flower Cartouches, Signed, Taizan, 3 1/2 In. 660.00
Censor, Continual River Landscape On Top, 2 Shaped Handles, 3 Cabriole Legs 2990.00
Censor, Flower Heads Amid Scrolled Tendrils, Gold Base, 3 Short Feet, 2 1/2 In. 1840.00
Charger, Woman & 2 Children Playing With Cat, 18 Figures In Rim, 19 In. 495.00
Dish, Gold Dragon On Gosu Blue Sea, Mid-19th Century, 7 In. 550.00
Dish, Male & Female Figures Gathered Around Goddess, Patterned Border, 14 In. 115.00
Dish, Sage Visited By Children, Diaper Pattern, Foliate Border, 10 In. 345.00
Dish, Woman, Butterflies In A Floral Landscape, Signed, 3 3/4 In. 121.00
Ewer, Gilt Dragon, Shagreen Ground, Ormolu Base, c.1820, 20 In. 1400.00
Figurine, Buddha, 10 In. 185.00
Figurine, Hotei, Seated On His Sack Holding Fan, 9 1/2 In. 63.00
Figurine, Hotei, With Boy On His Sack, 11 1/2 In. 92.00
Incense Burner, Figural Design, Elephant Handles, Signed, 5 1/2 In. 165.00
Incense Holder, Saints On Half, Ladies On Other Half, Gold, 2 1/4 In. 150.00
Jar, Cover, Mt. Fuji Roosters, Women With Children, Blue Ground, 3 In. 1495.00
Jar, Cover, Scholars, Teaching Children, Swag Ties At Neck, 8 1/2 In., Pair 718.00
Jar, Squat, Golden Weeping Cherry, Brown Ground, Impressed Mark, 3 1/8 In. 385.00
Pitcher, Allover Design, Multicolored, Bulbous, 6 In. 125.00
Plaque, Temple In A Rural Landscape, 20th Century, 7 x 9 1/2 In. 121.00
Plate, 100 Bird Pattern, 9 1/2 In. 143.00
Plate, Figural Cartouche Surrounded By Floral Brocade, Signed, Seizan, 7 1/2 In. 440.00
Plate, Floral Shape, Figural Center Surrounded By Flowers, Black Mark, 5 3/4 In. 135.00
Plate, Woman, Playing A Biwa, 5-Lobed Form, Signed, Meiji Period, 5 In. 440.00
Salt, 3 Holy Men, 4 Piece 27.00
Tea Set, Courtesans In Courtyard Settings, c.1900, 18 Piece 287.00
Tea Set, Dragon Design, Geishas, Gold Gilt, 1860s, 15 Piece 1150.00
Tea Set, Dragon Head Finials, Geisha Girl Scenes, Gold Trim, Meiji Period, 3 Piece 675.00
Teapot, Bird Design, Outlined In Gold, 3 1/4 In. 75.00
Teapot, Compressed Fluted Form, Raised Salamanders, 2 1/2 In. 265.00
Teapot, Cover, Dragon Head, Neck Spout, 8 1/2 In., 19 Piece 125.00
Teapot, Samurai Women With Boys, Blue Ground, Meiji Period, 3 In. 630.00
Urn, Cover, Lions On Handles & Lid, 49 x 29 In. 5500.00
Vase, Allover Gold Flowers, Red Leaves, 9 In., Pair 395.00
Vase, Artist Decorating Scrolls & Birds, Geometric Banded, Attached Base, 12 In. 258.00
Vase, Baluster, 1000 Butterflies Design, Red Mark, 4 In., Pair 415.00
Vase, Club Shape, Samurai Cartouches, Meiji Period, Black Mark, 7 1/2 In. 245.00
Vase, Cobalt Blue, Polychrome Enameled Scene, 10 1/4 In., Pair 577.00
Vase, Diamond Shape, Polychrome, Wisteria, Brass Cover, 6 In. 575.00
Vase, Double Gourd Form, Karako Design, Gold Brocade Top, 4 3/4 In. 440.00
Vase, Elephant Head Handles, Bamboo Chrysanthemum Design, Gosu Blue, 8 In. 1155.00
Vase, Figural Landscape, Signed, 3 1/4 In. 245.00

Vase, Fisherman, Immortal Amid Butterflies, 19th Century, 3 1/2 In. 1495.00
Vase, Fishermen Scene, Fishing In Water, Floral Lappet Border, Meiji Period, 4 In. 2070.00
Vase, Floral Design, Red Ground, 19 In. 55.00
Vase, Floral, Beaded, Raised Outlining, 12 In. 195.00
Vase, Gold Design, Baluster, Narrow Neck, Pierced Handles, 14 1/2 In., Pair 430.00
Vase, Gold Dragon Design, Baluster, Signed, Hozan, Meiji Period, 4 In. 200.00
Vase, High Relief Dragon Design, Gourd Form, Meiji Period, Signed, 11 1/2 In. 302.50
Vase, Landscape, Children In River With Flowering Trees, 8 In. 276.00
Vase, Raised Florals, 12 In. 89.00
Vase, Ribbon Handles, Weeping Cherry, Tortoise Ground, Brocade Rim, Globular, 6 In. . . 357.00
Vase, Samurai In Garden Setting, Blue Ground, 19th Century, 18 In. 6612.00
Vase, Seed Shape, Landscape Design, Black Mark, 7 3/4 In. 440.00
Vase, Teardrop Shape, Karako, Butterfly Design, 4 7/8 In., Pair 605.00
Vase, White Chrysanthemum, Blue Ground, 12 1/2 In. 475.00

SATURDAY EVENING GIRLS, see Paul Revere Pottery category.

SCALES have been made to weigh everything from babies to gold.
Collectors search for all types. Most popular are small gold dust scales
and special grocery scales.

Balance, Brass & Steel, Wooden Base With Drawer, 9 1/4 In. 93.00
Balance, Brass, Curved Support, Holding Tray, With Weights, England 127.00
Balance, Michigan Drug Co., Gold Weights, Black Wooden Case, Glass Top 140.00
Balance, Salter's Trade Spring, Round Brass Face, 9 1/2 In. 60.00
Balance, Tin Hopper, 3 Weights, Cast Iron, 26 In. 165.00
Balance, Troemner, Aluminum Top Plates, Case, 21 1/2 In. 137.50
Balance, W.W.S. Walkers, Manchester, Mahogany Base, Set Of Weights, 22 x 22 In. 192.00
Bathroom, Charlie Tuna, 1972 . . . . 95.00
Bushel, Winchester, Brass, 2 Sliding Bars, Pail 110.00
Candy, Black Iron & Brass 145.00
Candy, Detectogram 125.00
Dairy, Full-O-Pep, Red, White & Blue 85.00
Egg, Zenith, Earlville, New York 198.00
Hanging, Herbert & Sons, London, Weights Up To 200 Lbs., 32 3/4 In. 80.00
Merchant's, Newcombe, Cast Iron 195.00
Milk, Brass 95.00
Opium, Set 350.00
Postal, Brass & Mahogany, England, Late 19th Century 115.00
Postal, Mail, IDL Mfg. & Scales Corp., N.Y., 3 Cents 38.00
Postal, Mail, Pelozue, Evanston, Ill., Oz. To 2 Lbs., Oct. 1, 1953 . . . . 48.00
Postal, Metal, 1920, 6 In. 25.00
Postal, Star, Pat. 1899 . . . . 18.00
Store, Buffalo Co., Complete To 5 Lb. 30.00
Weighing, American Family, White Enameled Picture, Vegetables, Meat, Oz. To 25 Lbs. . 16.00
Weighing, Brass, Mahogany, 1900 . . . . 175.00
Weighing, Lollipop, Watling, Fortune Teller, Blue Porcelain 4000.00
Weighing, Walla Walla Gum Co., Knoxville, Tn., Indian Decal Back, Small 850.00
Weighing, Your Weight, Drop Penny, National Novelty Co., Green, Floor 1815.00
Weights, Travel Case, 19th Century, Signed & Stamped New York 225.00

SCHAFER & VATER, makers of small ceramic items, are best known for
their amusing figurals. The factory was located in Volkstedt-
Rudolstadt, Germany, from 1890 to 1962. Some pieces are marked
with the crown and R mark, but many are unmarked.

Bottle, A Wee Scotch, Child Imbibing From Whiskey Bottle 80.00
Bottle, Blue Glaze, Cork Stopper, Porcelain, 7 1/2 In. 440.00
Bottle, Don't Let Thy Nose Blush For Sins Of Thy Mouth, Red Nosed Man . . . . . . .40.00 to 80.00
Bottle, Figural, Bearded Man With Bowling Ball, 9 In. 340.00
Bottle, Flask, All Scotch 72.00
Bottle, Huntsman 110.00
Bottle, Man On Barstool 250.00
Bottle, Old Woman With Long Neck, Hands Clasped, 5 3/4 In. 125.00

Bottle, Professor 145.00
Bottle, St. Nick 175.00
Bottle Set, Skeleton, Tray & Cups 250.00
Box, Heart Shape, Green 45.00
Candy Container, Pink Pig Playing Flute, Bisque, 5 In. 395.00
Creamer, Figural, Welsh Woman, 4 3/4 In. 180.00
Creamer, Girl Holding Duck, 4 1/2 In. 150.00
Creamer, Maiden With Jug & Keys, Blue, Marked 68.00
Ewer, Pink Roses, Cork Stopper 100.00
Figurine, Dog, Comical, Green, White Eyes, White Rectangular Base, 5 1/2 In. 135.00
Figurine, Geese, We Want Our Vote, Suffragette 385.00
Hatpin Holder, Geisha Girl, Lavender 125.00
Holder, Stickpin, Cameo Type Face On Front 225.00
Humidor, Man With Pipe, Lavender 550.00
Jam Jar, Classical Women, Blue & White Jasper Ware, 5 1/4 In. 88.00
Jar, Grecian Relief Figures, Medallion Cover, 4 In. 125.00
Match Holder, Figural, Oversized Smiling Feet, 3 1/4 In. 255.00
Mug, Elk 45.00
Pitcher, Girl With Jug & Purse, Blue & White, 5 In. 135.00
Planter, Figural, Googly-Eyed Boy, Girl With Puppy, 3 3/4 x 4 1/2 In. 225.00
Powder Dish, Cherubs & Frog Dancing, Pink, Gold 38.00
Shaving Mug, Elk, With Brush 175.00
Vase, Blue Jasperware, White Embossed, Rectangular, 7 In. 110.00
Vase, Green Jasperware, Elliptical Shape, White Handles, 9 In. 125.00
Vase, Jasperware, 2 Women Cameo, Lavender, Green, 2 Handles, 4 1/2 In. 150.00
Vase, Pink & White, 4 3/4 In. 23.00

SCHNEIDER Glassworks was founded in 1903 at Epinay-sur-Seine, France, by Charles and Ernest Schneider. Art glass was made between 1903 and 1930. The company still produces clear crystal glass.   *Schneider*

Bowl, Mottled Orange & Cobalt Blue, Mottled Amethyst Foot, 8 x 6 1/4 In. 605.00
Bowl, Orange Design, Wrought Iron Holder Of Leaf, Scroll Design, France, 3 x 5 In. 175.00
Box, Cover, Green, Amethyst Glass, Orange Layer, Geometric, 2 5/8 In. 920.00
Charger, Amorphous Central Design, Orange, Brown, Green, Signed, 15 1/2 In. 400.00
Compote, Mottled Magenta To Opalescent, Ribbed, Amethyst Stem, 13 1/2 In. 600.00
Compote, On Wrought-Iron Stand, Tango Red, Mottled Blue, Black Rim, 8 1/2 In. 690.00
Compote, White Mottled, Burgundy Center, Iron Footed, Signed, 16 x 6 1/2 In. 600.00
Lamp, Hanging, Crimson Red Shade, Maroon Glass, Stylized Fruit, Oval, 8 1/2 In. 1600.00
Lamp, Hanging, From Ceiling Mount, Twisted, Knotted Cord, 15 1/2 In. Diam. 1380.00
Plate, Green, Yellow, Raised On Orange Pedestaled Foot, Signed, 3 In. 345.00
Vase, 2 Applied Handles At Neck, Mottled Royal Blue, Red, Orange, 1925, 10 1/2 In. . . . 860.00
Vase, Applied Clear Glass Trailings, Purple, Orange Base, 1925, 6 3/4 In. 460.00
Vase, Elongated Neck, Red Striations, Orange Body, Signed, 16 3/4 In. 515.00
Vase, Flared Lip, Lavender, Pink, Yellow, Burgundy Interior, Cylindrical, 19 In. 1725.00
Vase, Foliate Design, Mottled Pastel Blue Body, Royal Blue, Signed, 12 1/2 In. 1150.00
Vase, Green, Internal Bubbles, Marked, 1928, 3 3/8 In. 415.00
Vase, Orange, Red, Aubergine, Yellow Trailings, 23 1/2 In. 1840.00
Vase, Pale Topaz Ground, Abstract Floral Design, Petal Like Leaves, 8 1/4 In. 495.00
Vase, Purple, Orange Aubergine Highlights, Mottled White Glass, 15 1/2 In. 1725.00
Vase, Spherical, Flared Neck, Mottled Pale Blue, Turquoise, Violet, Orange, 10 In. 172.00
Vase, Stylized Floral Motif, Orange, White Field, Signed, 12 1/2 In. 860.00
Vase, Stylized Leaves, Berries, 2 Applied Purple Handles, Red, Yellow, 12 In. 1380.00
Vase, Stylized Leaves, Flowers, Etched, Mottled Red, Yellow, Signed, 11 In. 1265.00
Vase, Sunflower, Flared Rim, Pink, Amethyst, Purple, Etched, Signed, 4 In. 515.00
Vase, Sunflower, Pink Mottled Glass, Amethyst To Purple Shade, Signed, 10 In. 1035.00
Vase, Tricorn Rim, Crimson Red, Maroon Glass, Oval, 7 In. 630.00
Vessel, Yellow Pear Shape, Purple, Rose, Pink, Signed, 3 x 7 1/2 In. 374.00

SCIENTIFIC INSTRUMENTS of all kinds are included in this category. Other categories such as Barometer, Binoculars, Dental, Nautical, Medical, and Thermometer may also price scientific apparatus.

Adding Machine, Wolverine No. 39, Box 85.00

Air Flow Meter, Oxidized Brass Frame, Davis Of Darby, 14 x 12 In. 1380.00
Arithmometer, Crank-Operated Calculator, Mahogany Case, Tate, 22 In. 2850.00
Azimuth-Gyro Sensing Element, U.S. Military, 45 Lbs. 50.00
Calculator, Bowmar, 901B, Pocket 45.00
Calculator, Digital Displays, Friction Lever, Metal Case, Metal Stand, 34 In. 1380.00
Calculator, Hewlett Packard HP-67, Pocket 160.00
Calculator, Mechanical, Calculator Co., 1910, Box 35.00
Calculator, Sharp, EL-8, Pocket 45.00
Calculator, Texas Instrument, SR-50, Pocket 28.00
Check Writing Machine, Larry's, Paymaster, 7 Column 28.00
Chronometer, 8-Day, George Margetts, London, No. 123 . . . . 4600.00
Chronometer, Enamel Dial, George Margetts, No. 123 . . . . 9200.00
Chronometer, Up-Down Wind Indicator, 2-Tiered Box, Barraud 4600.00
Compass, Brass, William Helfericht 920.00
Compass, Bronze, WW1, Pocket, Marked, U.S. Engineer Corps. 65.00
Compass, Equinoctial, 6 Continents, Ducal Crest, Silver, 1760s, 3 In. 4370.00
Compass, Hand Drawn Dial, Red Ink, Walnut Case, 3 1/8 In. 145.00
Compass, Navigator's, Brass, Floral Design On Wood Box, 6 In. 332.00
Compass, Pocket, Brass Case, 18th Century, 1 3/4 In. Diam. 185.00
Compass, Silvered Ring, Black Matte, Fitted Wooden Case, Stoppani, 4 In. 70.00
Compass, Sundial, Brass Case, Sunburst On Cover, 1800 . . . . 300.00
Compass, Sundial, Hinged Bird Form Gnomon, Silver, France, 3 In. 1495.00
Compass, Surveying, 2 Sights, B.K. Hagger, Tripod, Pine Case, 16 In. 1955.00
Compass, Surveyor's, Brass, B.H. Hagger, 15 In. 316.00
Compass, Surveyor's, Brass, Wood Tripod, G.M. Pool, 14 3/4 In. 920.00
Compass, Taylor, White Metal, Pocket Watch Type 20.00
Compass, Wrist, Marbles, Brass Dial, Leather, Box 45.00
Compass & Sundial, Equinoctial, Brass, Korean & German Dial, 1765 . . . . 633.00
Compass & Sundial, Magnetic Time Keeper & Co., 1 5/8 In. 215.00
Compendium, Brass Lunar Volvelles, Iron Needle, Ivory, 3 1/4 In. 805.00
Cubic Precision Auto Ranger IIX, Velocity Of Light Measure 100.00
Dictaphone, Columbia Graphophone Co., Iron, Decal, 1915 . . . . 47.00
Geiger Counter, Civil Defense Decal, Cold War, 1950 . . . . 70.00
Hourglass, Blown Glass, Perfect Time, Hand Wrought, 15 In. 1150.00
Hydrometer, Sikes Type, 5 Weights, Brass Clasps, Mahogany Case, 8 In. 190.00
Magnifying Glass, Brass Frame, 18th Century, Case, 4 In. 185.00
Microscope, Bausch & Lomb, Baloptican Model D, Wooden Case 137.00
Microscope, Bausch & Lomb, Black Enamel, Crackle Finish, 13 In. 115.00
Microscope, Black Enamel, Brass, Tripod Stand, Mahogany Case 115.00
Microscope, Brass, Rack & Pinion Focusing, Mahogany Case 275.00
Microscope, Compound Monocular, R. & J. Beck, No. 8898, 16 1/2 In. 920.00
Microscope, Compound, Drawer, Culpepper, England, c.1730, 16 In. 5980.00
Microscope, Extra Eye Piece, Bausch & Lomb, Wooden Case 110.00
Microscope, Fine Screw Focusing, Brass Cased, Nachet Et Fils, 3 1/2 In. 4370.00
Microscope, Lacquered Brass, Triple Nose-Piece, Leitz, N.Y., 12 In. 115.00
Microscope, Slides, Tweezer, Hinged Case, 19th Century 175.00
Microscope, Spencer, 5 Pillar Supports, Y-Shape Stand, 11 In. 115.00
Microscope, Spencer, Brass, Black Enamel, Rack, Pinion Coarse, 13 In. 115.00
Navigational Computer, American Airlines, Case, Instructions, 1945 . . . . 60.00
Obergeometer, Box 415.00
Pantograph, Engraved Scales, Brass, J. Bennett, Mahogany Case, 27 In. 690.00
Polarimeter, Ivory Handle Adjustment, F. Schmidt & Heinch, Berlin 437.00
Quadrant, Mahogany Case, Ebony, Spencer, Browning & Co., England 635.00
Regulator, Balloon Table, Fruitwood, Thomas Ivory, 1800, 24 1/4 In. 4025.00
Saccharometer, Brass Float, Thermometer, Loftis, London, 1850s 225.00
Telegraph Apparatus, Key, Receiver & Sender, L.E. Knott Company 357.00
Telescope, Alignment Scope, Tripod Mounted 8000.00
Telescope, Brass, 2 Draw, Rack & Pinion Focus, Box, 44 3/4 In. 690.00
Telescope, Brass, Civil War, Pocket, Tube Case, 6 5/8 In. 150.00
Telescope, Brass, Lacquered Metal, Calfskin Sleeve, 5 1/2 In. 230.00
Telescope, Brass, On Table Stand, Japan, 30 x 40 In. 125.00

Telescope, Brass, On Wood Stand, France, 19th Century, 61 In. 1725.00
Telescope, Brass, Wooden, Collapses, Red Paint, 1880, 36 In. 325.00
Telescope, E. Vion, Paris, 19th Century, 50 In. 2750.00
Telescope, Refracting, 4 Eyepieces, Brass, Charles Chevalier, 36 1/2 In. 4025.00
Telescope, Refracting, Star Finder, Secretan A Paris, 51 In. 5520.00
Telescope, Short Brass Tripod, 53 In. Extended 2420.00
Telescope, Silver Dial, Cross-Wire Adjustment, Gurley, N.Y., 14 In. 575.00
Telescope, Stand, Oak Stand, Fitted Mahogany Case, E. Vion, France 7475.00
Telescope, Sunshade, 5 Sections, Brass, 36 In. 375.00
Transit, Surveyor's, Copper & Brass, Case, Eugene Dietzgen Co. 1275.00
Transit, Surveyor's, Starrett Co., Mass., Case, 1910 . . . . 145.00
Viewer, Optical, Stand, Mahogany Inlay, 1850s, 25 1/2 In. 373.00

SCRIMSHAW is bone or ivory or whale's teeth carved by sailors and others for entertainment during the sailing-ship days. Some scrimshaw was carved as early as 1800. There are modern scrimshanders making pieces today on bone, ivory, or plastic. Other pieces may be found in the Ivory and Nautical categories.

Basket, Whalebone, Allover Pierced Ring, Swing Handle, 19th Century, 10 In. 2990.00
Box, Document, Whaler's, Ivory Whale On Lid, Brass Hooks, 2 7/8 x 11 1/4 In. 285.00
Cigar Cutter, Violin Form, Silver Trim, Germany 350.00
Compass, Whalebone, Germany, 2 1/8 In. 185.00
Cribbage Board, Walrus Tusk, Late 1800s 850.00
Ditty Box, Whalebone, Carved, Ivory Feet, Knob, 8 5/8 In. 313.50
Glasses Case, Whalebone, Whaling Scene, Ship At Sea, 5 1/2 In. 172.50
Jagging Wheel, Whale Ivory, Crimper Fork, 19th Century, 6 In. 630.00
Rattle, Child's, Whalebone, Whistle Handle, Early 19th Century 385.00
String Holder, Turned Wood, 3 Ivory Feet & Insert, Brass Knob, 4 3/4 In. 110.00
Tooth, Whale, 3-Masted Ship Under Sail, 19th Century, 7 1/4 In. 4887.50
Tooth, Whale, American Eagle & Flag, Whaleboat Disaster, 5 3/4 In. 8625.00
Tooth, Whale, British Ship Under Full Sail, 19th Century, 7 1/2 In. 1265.00
Tooth, Whale, Fashionably Dressed Lady, 6 In. 920.00
Tooth, Whale, Frigate In Turbulent Waters, United States Seal On Reverse, 5 In. 460.00
Tooth, Whale, Frigate Under Full Sail, American Flag, 1850s, 6 1/2 In. 1150.00
Tooth, Whale, Harpooned Whale 1 Side, Ice Skating Scene Other, 5 1/2 In. 315.00
Tooth, Whale, Lighthouse Scene, Tacoma, Wash., 5 1/2 In. 258.75
Tooth, Whale, Man-Of-War Sailing Ship 1650.00
Tooth, Whale, Prince Of Wales, Black Swan, 6 In. 373.75
Tooth, Whale, Townscape Design Above 3-Masted Ship, 6 1/2 In. 2875.00
Tooth, Whale, View Of Nantucket Harbor, 1853, 8 1/4 In. 2587.00
Tooth, Whale, Whale Harpooner Scene, 8 In. 345.00
Tooth, Whale, Whaling Scene, Signed, Jones, 7 In. 316.00

SEBASTIAN MINIATURES were first made by Prescott W. Baston in 1938 in Marblehead, Massachusetts. More than 400 different designs have been made, and collectors search for the out-of-production models. The mark may say *Copr. P. W. Baston U.S.A.,* or *P. W. Baston, U.S.A.,* or *Prescott W. Baston.* Sometimes a paper label was used.

Corner Drugstore 58.00
Fisherman 95.00
Fisherman's Wife 95.00
John Alden 8.00
Lobsterman, Box 35.00
Mark Twain, Black & Silver Label 95.00
Mrs. Beacon Hill, 1947, 3 In. 125.00
Ride To The Hounds 35.00
Robert E. Lee, Black & Silver Label 95.00
Sign, Dealer 48.00
Swan Boat, Boston Public Garden, 1950 . . . . 150.00

SEG, see Paul Revere Pottery category.

SEVRES porcelain has been made in Sevres, France, since 1769. Many copies of the famous ware have been made. The name originally referred to the works of the Royal Porcelain factory. The name now includes any of the wares made in the town of Sevres, France. The entwined lines with a center letter used as the mark is one of the most forged marks in antiques. Be very careful to identify Sevres by quality, not just by mark.

Bowl, Flared Rim, Cobalt Ground, Bronze Mounted, 3 Paw Feet, 7 1/2 In.	575.00
Bowl, Nude Maidens Astride Gazelles, Jean Mayodon, c.1925, 5 1/2 In.	3450.00
Box, Polychrome Transfer, Scene Of Couple In Garden, Pink Ground, Signed, 7 3/4 In.	115.00
Bust, Woman, Holding Loosely Draped Cloth To Her Chest, White Biscuit, 19 In.	1495.00
Bust, Young Peasant Woman, Signed, 11 In.	165.00
Charger, Battle Of Pyramids, Leber D'Apres Gros, 18 In.	2300.00
Ewer, Ormolu Mounted, Inverted Pear Shape, Floral, Blue, White Body, 9 1/2 In.	266.00
Jar, Cover, Courtiers Scenes Alternating With Floral Panels, Marked, 21 In.	1090.00
Plaque, Figures Within Landscape, Signed, Round, 19th Century, 7 In., Pair	5175.00
Plate, Botanical Design, Signed, 10 In.	145.00
Plate, Cluster Of Pink Roses, Buds, Blue Cornflowers, 1790, 9 1/4 In.	1725.00
Plate, Hand Painted Floral & Gilt Design, 10 3/4 In., 11 Piece	1300.00
Plate, Pastel Fruit, Ivory Ground, 8 In.	95.00
Plate, Portrait, Queen Louise Of Austria, Gilt Rim, Signed, 10 In.	125.00
Plate, Stylized Flowering Vine Around Cavetto, Pink, Blue, Yellow, Green, 9 In.	920.00
Serving Dish, Enameled Cherubs, Gilt Metal, Powder Blue Ground, 13 In.	805.00
Urn, Allegorical Figures At Neck, Female & Scrolled Handles, 1880s, 25 1/2 In.	8050.00
Urn, Continuous Battle & Landscape Scene, Foliate Handles, Bronze Mounted, 37 In.	9200.00
Urn, Cover, Continuous Napoleonic Scene, Green Borders, Deprez, 38 In.	7475.00
Urn, Cover, Figural & Landscape Panel, Scrolled Handles, 27 3/4 In.	2760.00
Urn, Cover, Opposing Landscape Panels, Ring Handles, Laurel Wreath Base, 20 In.	4887.00
Urn, Cover, Portrait, Cobalt Blue, Gilt, 30 In., Pair	1750.00
Urn, Figural & Landscape Panels, Green Ground, F. Colibrot, 17 1/2 In.	3450.00
Urn, Figure Of Woman & Putto, Gilt On Blue Ground, c.1900, 31 In.	1955.00
Urn, Woman, Angel Above Head, Cobalt Blue, 19th Century, 38 In.	5000.00
Vase, Blackberry Blossoms & Leafage, Gray Ground, Signed, 1906, 16 In.	2875.00
Vase, Chestnuts & Leafage, Painted, Signed, 1906, 12 1/4 In.	2990.00
Vase, Couple, Landscape Scene, Scroll Border, Green, Pink, Gold, Gilt C-Scrolls, 22 In.	4600.00
Vase, Cover, Bronze, Figural, Floral Design, Yellow Ground, 24 In.	1380.00
Vase, Cover, Medallions, Figural Design, Ormolu Mounted, 22 1/2 In.	1445.00
Vase, Group Of Cavorting Nude Males & Females, c.1925, 8 In.	5760.00
Vase, Lovers, Landscape Scene, Fluted Cobalt Blue Ground, Acanthus Scroll, 17 In., Pair	2587.00
Vase, Lovers, Ormolu Mounted Celeste Body, Blue, 16 In.	330.00
Vase, Young Maiden, 3 Cupids, Landscape Scene, Fluted Neck, Domed Cover, 17 In.	977.00

SEWER TILE figures were made by workers at the sewer tile and pipe factories in the Ohio area during the late nineteenth and early twentieth centuries. Figurines, small vases, and cemetery vases were favored. Often the finished vase was a piece of the original pipe with added decorations and markings. All types of sewer tile work are now considered folk art by collectors.

Cat, Seated, 7 In.	165.00
Crow, On Stump	950.00
Dog, Seated, Flat Head, Tooled Coat, Collar & Face, 9 In.	415.00
Dog, Seated, Free Standing Front Legs, Tooled Coat & Face, 8 3/4 In.	165.00
Dog, Seated, Tooled Detail, 10 1/2 In.	150.00
Dog, Seated, With Free Standing Front Legs, 10 1/4 In.	220.00
Duck, 5 1/2 In.	125.00
Frog, 7 In.	105.00
Owl, Marked, Tim Gibson, 8 1/4 In.	140.00
Spaniel, Sitting	275.00
Squirrel, Mounting Holes For Nailing To Tree, Signed, E.A., 7 1/2 In.	150.00
Squirrel, Yellow Slip Eye, Signed, C.M., 1980, 6 3/4 In.	28.00

SEWING equipment of all types is collected, from sewing birds that held the cloth to tape measures, needle books, and old wooden spools. Sewing machines are included here.

Bag, Grenfell, Flying Ducks, Labels	80.00
Bird, With Brass Pincushion Top, Patent 1853	225.00 to 250.00
Book, Singer Sewing How To Book, 1930	12.00
Box, American Flags & Shield On Lid, Wood	385.00
Box, Ash Root, Hinged Top, Interior Kit, Well, Biedermeier, 5 3/4 In.	1725.00
Box, Baleen, Engraved, Stuffed Brocade Pincushion Lid, 19th-Century, 6 3/4 In.	1035.00
Box, Bird's-Eye Maple Veneer, Cluster Of Acorns, 1843, 6 x 7 x 11 3/4 In.	990.00
Box, Burl Walnut, Marquetry, Ship At Sail On Lid, Fitted Interior, Lift-Out Tray, 12 In.	605.00
Box, Carved Wood, Spool Rack, 19th Century, 14 In.	259.00
Box, Fitted, Original Implements, c.1890	595.00
Box, Mahogany Veneer, Dovetailed Drawer, Pincushion, Table Clamp, 5 3/4 In.	220.00
Box, Mahogany, Chest Of Drawers Shape, 4 Drawers, Pincushion Top, 8 In.	230.00
Box, Mahogany, Inlaid Ivory.Escutcheon, Beveled Edge Lid, Lift-Out Tray, 11 1/8 In.	95.00
Box, Mirror, Pincushions, 6 Gold Handled Utensils, Lock & Key	300.00
Box, Mother-Of-Pearl, Shell-Shape, Mirror, Lined, Contents, 5 1/2 In.	805.00
Box, Regency, Tooled Leather, Gilt Metal, 8 x 12 x 10 In.	1030.00
Box, Walnut, Pincushion Top, Drawer, Nail Construction, 7 1/8 In.	105.00
Cabinet, Spool, see Advertising category under Cabinet, Spool.	
Clamp, Hemming, Ribbed Design, Iron, 4 1/4 In.	60.00
Clamp, Pincushion & Needle Case, Ivory & Bone	300.00
Clamp, With Pincushion, Ivory	195.00
Clamp, With Spool, Ivory	345.00
Comb, Carding	13.00
Darner, Black, Ball Shape, Ornate Sterling Handle	65.00
Darner, Ebony, Sterling Handle	75.00
Darner, Egg, Vegetable Ivory	50.00
Darner, Glove	15.00
Darner, Sterling Silver, Handle	35.00
Dress Form, Maker's, J.R. Ballman, New York	165.00
Dress Form, Somerset Dress Form, Display Corset	1600.00
Egg, Darning, Mammy	45.00
Gauge, Hem, c.1910	35.00
Gauge, Hem, Sterling Silver	85.00
Gauge, Knitting Needle, Bell Shape	48.00
Kit, Hinged Nut Case, Gilded, 1 3/4 In.	220.00
Machine, B. Eldredge Automatic, Cast Iron, 10 3/8 x 8 1/2 In.	130.00
Machine, Child's, Ideal, Refinished Oak Top, 31 In.	1485.00
Machine, Elgin, Treadle	150.00
Machine, Empire, Hand, Boston	660.00
Machine, Featherlite	395.00
Machine, Florence, Table Model, Cast Iron Base, 2 Foot Pedals, Patent 1863	385.00
Machine, Frister & Rossmann, Hand Cranked, Gold Trim, Wooden Case	200.00
Machine, General Electric, Featherweight, Green, No. 11949	400.00
Machine, General Electric, No. 80185, Attachments, Case, 9 In.	60.00
Machine, Painted Gold Leaves, Flowers, Cast Iron	1980.00
Machine, Singer, Featherweight, Model 210, Attachments, Case	465.00
Machine, Singer, Featherweight, Model 221, Case & Attachments	365.00
Machine, Singer, Hand Crank, Dome Case, Portable, 1898	250.00
Machine, Singer, No. 3, Portable, Hand Crank, Domed Case, 1898	250.00
Machine, Wheeler & Wilson, c.1852	650.00
Machine, Winselmann, Titan, Gold Stenciling, Porcelain Knob .... *Illus*	1320.00
Needle Case, Inlaid Bone	265.00
Needle Case, Ivory, Umbrella Form, c.1800, 4 1/2 In.	250.00
Needle Case, Piccadilly Combination Sewing, Contents, 2 3/4 In. .... *Illus*	85.00
Needle Case, Tole, 19th Century	395.00
Needle Case, Umbrella Shape, Ivory, 4 In.	132.00
Needle Holder, 18K Yellow Gold	132.00

Sewing, Machine, Winselmann, Titan,
Gold Stenciling, Porcelain Knob

Sewing, Needle Case, Piccadilly
Combination Sewing, Contents, 2 3/4 In.

Needle Holder, Wooden, Painted, Box 50.00
Needle Threader, Threader, Tin Lithograph, J & P Coats, 1 1/2 In. 33.00
Pattern, Embroidery, Priscilla, 1930 .... 12.00
Pattern, Vogue, 1950s, 10 Piece 25.00
Pincushion, Blue, White Crochet, Red Satin Ribbon Intertwined, 5 1/2 x 7 In. 30.00
Pincushion, Carved Bone Buttons Top & Bottom, Scarlet Wool, 1780s, 6 In. 495.00
Pincushion, Dog, Luster, Japan 14.00
Pincushion, Elephant, Metal, Germany 45.00
Pincushion, Floral & Foliate Border, Fitted Cushion Interior, Sterling Silver, 3 1/2 In. 46.00
Pincushion, Lady's Shoe, Glass Beads In Floral Design, 4 x 2 1/2 In. 32.00
Pincushion, Shoe Shape, Plaid Laces, Metal 65.00
Pincushion, Swan, Metal, Victorian 70.00
Pincushion, Teddy Bear, Glass Eyes, 1920s 110.00
Pincushion, Thimble Holder, Wooden Boot, 1900 .... 60.00
Pincushion, Tinkerbell, Disney 30.00
Pincushion Dolls are listed in their own category.
Shears, Buttonhole, Keen Kutter 35.00
Shuttle, Tatting, Mother-Of-Pearl 95.00
Shuttle, Tatting, Sterling Silver 90.00
Sign, Singer Sewing Machine, Porcelain, Flange, 12 x 19 In. ....*Illus* 1100.00
Spool Cabinets are in the Advertising category under Cabinet, Spool.
Spool Holder, Acorn Form, Wooden, 11 In. 275.00
Spool Rack, 4 Levels, 23 Spools, Marquetry, 8 1/2 x 7 In. 150.00
Swift, All Wooden, Black Paint, Table Clamp, 29 In. 28.00
Swift, Walnut, Barrel Cage 225.00
Tape Loom, Colonial, Floor Model, Cherry, Butternut & Oak, c.1750, 39 3/4 In. 555.00
Tape Loom, Heart Cutout 1760.00
Tape Loom, Pine, American, 18th Century, 24 1/2 In. 395.00
Tape Loom, Signed & Dated WF 1776, 27 In. 850.00
Tape Measure, Alligator, Celluloid, Japan, 1950s, 2 1/4 In. 60.00
Tape Measure, Apple, Plastic ....25.00 to 45.00
Tape Measure, Armco Culverts, Celluloid, Canister, Iron, Cloth, 1930s 12.00
Tape Measure, Baseball Player, Celluloid 225.00
Tape Measure, Bavarian Man Dancing, Celluloid, Mechanical, Germany, 2 1/2 In. 180.00
Tape Measure, Black Cat On Base, Celluloid, Germany, Prewar, 2 In. 253.00
Tape Measure, Black Man's Head, Pull Cigar To Unroll, Celluloid, 1 1/2 In. 400.00
Tape Measure, Cat, In Boot, Metal 400.00
Tape Measure, Cat, With Ball Roly Poly, Celluloid, Germany, Prewar, 1 3/4 In. 286.00
Tape Measure, Covered Wagon, Disc Type, Celluloid 45.00
Tape Measure, Daisy, Dagwood's Dog, Celluloid 75.00
Tape Measure, Dog, Stuffed 20.00
Tape Measure, Doll, Skookum, Pinback Etui, Accessories 750.00
Tape Measure, Dressmaker Dummy 55.00

Tape Measure, Dutch Boy, Porcelain 145.00
Tape Measure, Egg, Pink, Fly Tab 75.00
Tape Measure, Eiffel Tower, Metal 375.00
Tape Measure, Elephant, Dumbo, Stuffed Cloth, Japan, 1950s, 4 1/2 In. 60.00
Tape Measure, Fab Detergent, Celluloid, 1919 . . . . .22.00 to 60.00
Tape Measure, Ferdinand, Painted Rubber, Sieberling Co., 1930s, 5 1/2 In. 68.00
Tape Measure, Fish, Celluloid 45.00
Tape Measure, Fly On Egg, Celluloid, Japan, Prewar, 1 1/2 In. 153.00
Tape Measure, Fruit Basket, Celluloid . . . . .60.00 to 120.00
Tape Measure, Golfer, Celluloid, Prewar, Germany, 3 1/4 In. 360.00
Tape Measure, Groom, Porcelain 225.00
Tape Measure, Hen With Chick On Its Back, Celluloid 45.00
Tape Measure, Indian Boy, Celluloid 40.00
Tape Measure, Indian Boy, In Headdress, Celluloid . . . . .105.00 to 115.00
Tape Measure, Indian Maiden 79.00
Tape Measure, Kangaroo, Baby, Celluloid 95.00
Tape Measure, Kangaroo, Celluloid 65.00
Tape Measure, Lewis Lye, Celluloid 25.00
Tape Measure, Little Red Riding Hood, Celluloid 195.00
Tape Measure, Lock, Nickel Plated Brass, Key Is Winder, Austria, 1920s, 1 3/4 In. 294.00
Tape Measure, Lydia Pinkham 75.00
Tape Measure, Man, Hitchhiking, Brass, Man Is Winder, England, 2 3/4 In. 218.00
Tape Measure, Man, With Fez, Celluloid, Germany, Prewar, 1 3/4 In. 253.00
Tape Measure, Man, With Hat & Scarf, Celluloid, Germany, Prewar, 2 1/2 In. 253.00
Tape Measure, Mantle Clock, Celluloid, Germany, Prewar, 1 1/2 In. 138.00
Tape Measure, Pablum, Celluloid 20.00
Tape Measure, Parrot, Celluloid, Glass Eyes, Germany, 1930s, 1 1/4 In. 180.00
Tape Measure, Pig, In Shoe 85.00
Tape Measure, Pig, Japan 65.00
Tape Measure, Pig, On Brass Die, Prewar, 1 1/2 In. 120.00
Tape Measure, Pig, Red-Eyed, Curly Tail, Pan-Am Exposition, 1901, 2 In. 350.00
Tape Measure, Pig, With Flowers, Celluloid 40.00
Tape Measure, Pincushion, Pink, Japan 22.00
Tape Measure, Sad Iron 35.00
Tape Measure, Scotty, Seated, Celluloid, Japan, 1950s, 2 1/4 In. 118.00
Tape Measure, Sewing Machine Form 32.00
Tape Measure, Ship 35.00
Tape Measure, Sitting Monkey, Celluloid, Prewar, 2 1/4 In. 436.00
Tape Measure, Spaniel, Sitting, Celluloid 60.00
Tape Measure, Spider, Painted Brass, Austria, Prewar, 1 1/4 In. 528.00
Tape Measure, Swordfish, Celluloid 95.00
Tape Measure, Topiary, Brass With Beads, Tree Spins As Tape Winds, Germany, 2 In. . . 138.00
Tape Measure, Turtle, Pull My Head Not My Leg, Brass, Prewar, 2 In. . . . . .90.00 to 120.00
Tape Measure, Turtle, The Moat Fortress, Sterling Top, Celluloid Head, Body, 2 In. 110.00
Tape Measure, Winking Pig 50.00
Tape Measure, Woman, Colonial, Celluloid, Prewar, 2 1/2 In. 80.00

Sewing, Sign, Singer Sewing Machine, Porcelain,
Flange, 12 x 19 In.

Tape Measure, Woman, In White Clingy Skirt, Celluloid, Occupied Japan, 3 In. 110.00
Tape Measure, Woman, Playing Mandolin, Celluloid, Germany, Prewar, 2 In. 253.00
Tape Measure, Woman, Playing Piano, Celluloid, Original Pull, 1930s, 1 1/2 In. 470.00
Thimble, Grant's Hygienic, Aluminum, Enamel Band, 1920 . . . . 20.00
Thimble, Silver, Red Coral 20.00
Yarn Reel, Geared Click, 31 1/2 In. 70.00
Yarn Reel, Tabletop, Handle, Blue Paint, 19 In. 165.00

SHAKER items are characterized by simplicity, functionalism, and
orderliness. There were many Shaker communities in America from
the eighteenth century to the present day. The religious order made furniture, small wooden pieces, and packaged medicines, herbs, and jel-
lies to sell to *outsiders*. Other useful objects were made for use by
members of the community. Shaker furniture is listed in this book in
the Furniture category.

Basket, Sewing, Woven Splint, With Small Rim Accessories Basket, 12 x 5 1/4 In. 70.00
Basket, Splint, Woven, Bentwood Rim Handles, Oblong, Thomas Moser, 5 In. 302.50
Basket, Splint, Woven, Blue Woven Bands, Oblong, 4 1/4 In. 93.50
Box, 1-Finger, Cover & Base, Oval, 3 1/2 x 1 7/8 In. 90.00
Box, 1-Finger, Light Brown Finish, 8 In. 175.00
Box, 3-Finger, Bentwood, Green Paint, Oval, 6 7/8 In. 60.50
Box, 3-Finger, Green, Oval, 9 1/4 x 7 In. 3450.00
Box, 3-Finger, Painted Design, Green Bordering, Rose On Lid, 6 1/2 In. 375.00
Box, 4-Finger, Bentwood, Green, Oval, 10 1/2 In. 1045.00
Box, Bentwood, Wooden Handle, Wire Bale, Enfield, 9 1/2 In. 522.00
Box, Bittersweet Paint, Oval, 4 5/8 In. 8800.00
Box, Blue Oxidized To Green, Oval, 8 3/4 In. 990.00
Box, Bonnet, Green Paint, 2 Interior Pegs For Hats 825.00
Box, Graduated, Fingered, Oval, 3 1/4 To 6 1/2 In., 4 Piece 1200.00
Box, Pumpkin Orange Paint, Oval, 7 In. 1870.00
Box, Pumpkin Red Paint, Oval, 5 In. 2090.00
Box, Sabbathday Lake, Signed, 19th Century, 7 1/2 In. 650.00
Box, Seed, Shakers Choice Vegetable Seeds, Mustard Paint Base, Mt. Lebanon 1550.00
Box, Seed, Shakers' Garden Seeds, New Lebanon, Leather Hinges, 14 3/4 In. 1100.00
Box, Sewing, Pincushion & Lift-Top Thread Compartment, Ivory Holes, 10 In. 245.00
Box, Sewing, Woven Poplar Needle Book, New Hampshire, 6 In. 525.00
Box, Swivel Handle, Copper Tacks, Bentwood, Varnish Finish, 7 1/4 In. 137.50
Box, Utility, Yellow Ocher Paint, 10 1/8 x 13 1/2 In. 750.00
Box, Yellow Paint Traces, Mugwort Label, New Lebanon, Oval, 11 3/4 In. 660.00
Box, Yellow, Presented To Eld'r Grove Wright To Martha Johnson, 3 3/16 In. 1840.00
Brush, Canterbury, 14 In. 1840.00
Bucket, Wooden Interlocking Bands, CB Carved In Lid, Handle 495.00
Carrier, Butternut, Dovetailed, Stationary Hickory Handle, 8 In. 1485.00
Carrier, Sewing, Tools, Sabbathday Lake 275.00
Cloak, Dorothy Label, Salesman's Sample, Canterbury 2400.00
Dipper, Wood, Turned Handle, Copper Tacks, 7 1/4 In. 287.50
Doll, Woman, Rubber, Poplarware Bonnet, Silk Dress, New Lebanon 275.00
Dust Pan, Signed 3680.00
Peg Board, Pine & Cherry, John Roberts, 38 3/4 In. 50.00
Spice Cabinet, 2 Middle Doors, 10 Small & 1 Base Drawer, Porcelain Pulls 275.00
Swift, Hancock, Massachusetts, 15 In. 220.00
Tankard, Tin, Civil War Era 45.00
Tape Loom, Marked, O.H. 1839 . . . . 5500.00
Teapot, Side Spout, Tin, 8 1/2 In. 165.00
Thread Caddy, Wooden, Worn Pincushion, Sabbathday Lake, Paper Label, 5 1/2 In. 220.00
Workbench, 1 Door, 7 Drawers, 2 Vices, Some Seed Labels, 9 Ft. 7 In. 3575.00

SHAVING MUGS were popular from 1860 to 1900. Many types were
made, including occupational mugs featuring pictures of men's jobs.
There were scuttle mugs, silver-plated mugs, glass-lined mugs, and
others.

Art Nouveau, Lilies, Leaves, Brush, Silver 225.00
Blue Opaline, France 125.00

Busts, Garfield & Mrs. Lucretia Randolph Garfield, Milk Glass, 6 1/4 In. 247.50
Fish, Open Mouth 90.00
Floral, 1910 .... 20.00
Floral, Brushwork 48.00
Floral Spray, Multicolored, Blue, White Design, Soap Tray Lid, 4 1/4 In. .... 28.00 to 40.00
Masonic, Emblem, Blue Flowers, Gold Trim 80.00
Occupational, Bartender 195.00
Occupational, Butcher, Gold Name, F.J. Bryant 180.00
Occupational, Cabinet Maker, Porcelain, Hand Painted, 3 1/2 In. 363.00
Occupational, Doctor In Carriage, Gold Lettering, 3 1/2 x 5 In. 40.00
Occupational, Duck Hunter, Dog, C.S. Garrett 375.00
Occupational, Fireman, Fire Wagon, Adila Brunette, c.1900 .... 295.00
Occupational, Fox Hunt Scene, Gold Band At Base, F.R. Maddell, 3 x 5 In. 460.00
Occupational, Grocer 350.00
Occupational, Ice Delivery Man, Porcelain, 3 1/4 In. 394.00
Occupational, Knight, Coat Of Arms 115.00
Occupational, Locomotive & Tender, Limoges, 1880s 180.00
Occupational, Mark Mertz, 3 3/4 x 5 In. 46.00
Occupational, Postman, Green Clothing, Gold Lettering & Trim, 3 1/2 In. 3850.00
Occupational, Railroad Engine 450.00
Occupational, Sea Serpent, Tail Handle, Brush Holder, 3 3/4 In. 39.00
Pig, With Tusks 150.00
Shriner, Symbol In Color, Name In Gold 275.00

SHAWNEE POTTERY was started in Zanesville, Ohio, in 1937. The
company made vases, novelty ware, flowerpots, planters, lamps, and
cookie jars. Three dinnerware lines were made: Corn, Lobster Ware,
and Valencia (a solid color line). White Corn pattern utility pieces were
made in 1945. Corn King was made from 1946 to 1954; Corn Queen,
with darker green leaves and lighter colored corn, from 1954 to 1961.
Shawnee produced pottery for George Rumrill during the late 1930s.
The company closed in 1961.

Ashtray, Monte Carlo, Pink & Black 35.00
Ashtray, Panther, 12 1/4 In. 20.00
Ashtray-Coaster 32.00
Bank, Bulldog, 4 1/2 In. 195.00
Bank, Gold 475.00
Bank, Howdy Doody On Pig, 6 3/4 In. 650.00
Bank, Smiley Pig, Chocolate 395.00
Bank, Winnie Pig, Butterscotch 495.00
Bank, Winnie Pig, Head 150.00
Bean Pot, Lobster 125.00
Bookends, Dog Head, White, 4 3/4 In. 55.00
Bookends, Flying Geese, 6 In. 45.00
Bowl, Fern Leaf, Aqua 35.00
Bowl, Mixing, Corn King, 6 1/2 In. 50.00
Butter, Corn Queen 55.00
Butter, Cover, Corn King 65.00
Cake Plate, Valencia, Red 300.00
Casserole, Corn King, 11 In. .... 60.00 to 70.00
Casserole, Corn King, Individual, 9 Oz. 125.00
Casserole, Lobster, 1 Qt. 30.00
Casserole, Lobster, Cover, Kenwood, 16 Oz. .... 30.00 to 35.00
Cookie Jar, Basket Weave, Turquoise, Yellow Flower 60.00
Cookie Jar, Carousel 145.00
Cookie Jar, Cottage .... 995.00 to 1200.00
Cookie Jar, Drum Major, Gold Trim 400.00
Cookie Jar, Dutch Boy, Blue Pants 95.00
Cookie Jar, Dutch Boy, Blue Stripe 150.00
Cookie Jar, Dutch Boy, Gold, Decals 550.00
Cookie Jar, Dutch Boy, Wildflowers, Gold Trim, Decals 220.00
Cookie Jar, Dutch Boy, With Crisscross 125.00
Cookie Jar, Dutch Boy, Yellow Pants .... 145.00 to 180.00

Cookie Jar, Dutch Girl, Gold, Decals ....250.00 to 300.00
Cookie Jar, Dutch Girl, Tulip & Flowers ....185.00 to 220.00
Cookie Jar, Dutch Girl, Tulip, Gold 295.00
Cookie Jar, Elephant, White 55.00
Cookie Jar, Jo Jo Clown, Gold Trim ....240.00 to 500.00
Cookie Jar, Jug, Blue 55.00
Cookie Jar, Little Chef Jar, Multicolored 90.00
Cookie Jar, Lobster 280.00
Cookie Jar, Muggsy, Gold Trim, Decals 600.00
Cookie Jar, Owl .... 75.00 to 120.00
Cookie Jar, Owl, Gold ....195.00 to 300.00
Cookie Jar, Pennsylvania Dutch, Yellow 145.00
Cookie Jar, Planter, Rickshaw, Gold Trim 16.00
Cookie Jar, Puss 'n Boots ....150.00 to 175.00
Cookie Jar, Puss 'n Boots, Gold ....395.00 to 550.00
Cookie Jar, Puss 'n Boots, Long Tail 175.00
Cookie Jar, Sailor, Decals, Gold Trim 695.00
Cookie Jar, Sailor, Plain, Black Trim 90.00
Cookie Jar, Smiley Pig With Plums 695.00
Cookie Jar, Smiley Pig, Chrysanthemum ....295.00 to 400.00
Cookie Jar, Smiley Pig, Chrysanthemum, Gold Trim 395.00
Cookie Jar, Smiley Pig, Clovers 185.00
Cookie Jar, Smiley Pig, Gold, Blue Bib 285.00
Cookie Jar, Smiley Pig, Green, Gold, Decals 250.00
Cookie Jar, Smiley Pig, Red Bandanna, Clover Bud, Marked USA 500.00
Cookie Jar, Smiley Pig, Roses, Gold Trim ....450.00 to 600.00
Cookie Jar, Smiley Pig, Shamrock, Gold ....225.00 to 300.00
Cookie Jar, Smiley Pig, Tulip ....295.00 to 400.00
Cookie Jar, Smiley Pig, Yellow Scarf, Gold 475.00
Cookie Jar, Snowflake, Blue 45.00
Cookie Jar, Winnie Pig, Blue Flowers & Collar ....275.00 to 425.00
Cookie Jar, Winnie Pig, Cloverleaf ....275.00 to 425.00
Cookie Jar, Winnie Pig, Green Collar ....240.00 to 350.00
Cookie Jar, Winnie Pig, Peach Collar 285.00
Cookie Jar, Winnie Pig, Red Collar, Clover, Gold Trim ....475.00 to 500.00
Cookie Jar, Winnie Pig, Shamrocks 175.00
Creamer, Corn King .... 25.00 to 40.00
Creamer, Corn Queen 40.00
Creamer, Elephant .... 30.00 to 50.00
Creamer, Elephant, Gold, Decals 110.00
Creamer, Flower, Fern & Ivory 9.00
Creamer, Pennsylvania Dutch ....35.00 to 65.00
Creamer, Puss 'n Boots, Gold Trim 275.00
Creamer, Puss 'n Boots, Green .... 40.00 to 85.00
Creamer, Puss 'n Boots, Yellow 40.00
Creamer, Smiley Pig, Peach Flower ....65.00 to 125.00
Creamer, Smiley Pig, Peach Flower, Gold Trim 140.00
Creamer, Snowflake, Blue 12.00
Figurine, Bear, Tumbling ....30.00 to 65.00
Figurine, Birds On Branch 28.00
Figurine, Donkey, Brown Spotted 10.00
Figurine, Dutch Boy & Girl 35.00
Figurine, Dutch Girl 20.00
Figurine, Fish USA, Burgundy 10.00
Figurine, Gazelle, Baby, Brown Glaze 60.00
Figurine, Lamb 35.00
Figurine, Owl 35.00
Figurine, Pekinese 65.00
Figurine, Puppy 55.00
Figurine, Queenie The Dog 22.00
Figurine, Rabbit 55.00
Figurine, Ram, Brown, White 24.00
Figurine, Rooster 30.00

Figurine, Squirrel 60.00
Figurine, Teddy Bear 65.00
Flower Frog, Dolphin 25.00
Flowerpot, Fawn & Fern, Black, Green 38.00
Hors D'Oeuvre, Lobster, Holder 1500.00
Jar, Grease, Kenwood, Sahara 45.00
Jar, Grease, Snowflake, Yellow 30.00
Jug, Coffee, Corn King 90.00
Jug, Cover, Sunflower, Ball, 7 1/4 In. 60.00
Jug, Snowflake, Blue, 7 1/4 In. 35.00
Jug, Snowflake, Green, 7 1/4 In. 35.00
Jug, Space Saver, Emblem Flower, 6 In. 17.00
Lamp, Elephant, With Ball, 7 1/2 In. 80.00
Lamp, Nautical 125.00
Lamp, Oriental Boy, Girl, 8 In., Pair 75.00
Lamp, Oriental Girl, 8 1/2 In. 20.00
Lamp, Oriental Girl, Leaf-Type Base, 12 In. 40.00
Lamp, Oriental Man, With Mandolin, 11 1/2 In. ....40.00 to 45.00
Lamp, Spanish Dancer, Man, 9 In. 60.00
Measuring Spoon Holder 15.00
Mug, Corn King ....50.00 to 55.00
Pie Bird, Pink, 5 In. ....45.00 to 50.00
Pitcher, Bo Peep, Blue Bonnet, Peach Coat Trim 135.00
Pitcher, Bo Peep, Decals, Red Lines, Gold ....170.00 to 260.00
Pitcher, Bo Peep, Flower Decals, Gold 250.00
Pitcher, Bo Peep, Green Hat, Gold, Decals 180.00
Pitcher, Bo Peep, White & Green 135.00
Pitcher, Chanticleer ....75.00 to 100.00
Pitcher, Chanticleer, Solid Gold ....125.00 to 475.00
Pitcher, Corn King, 40 Oz. 85.00
Pitcher, Fern, Batter, Blue 65.00
Pitcher, Fern, Batter, Yellow 65.00
Pitcher, Flower & Fern, Green 40.00
Pitcher, Fruit, Ball 68.00
Pitcher, Fruit, Gold Trim 100.00
Pitcher, Grecian, Turquoise ....5.00 to 10.00
Pitcher, Little Boy Blue 150.00
Pitcher, Little Boy Blue & Bo Peep, Pair 300.00
Pitcher, Smiley Pig, Large ....100.00 to 145.00
Pitcher, Smiley Pig, Red Flower, Gold Trim 205.00
Pitcher, Snowflake, Yellow 50.00
Pitcher, Water, Peach Flower 175.00
Planter, 3-Button Shoe & Dog 9.00
Planter, Alarm Clock ....15.00 to 25.00
Planter, Birds On Driftwood 85.00
Planter, Black Lamb, Gold Feet & Bow 3.00
Planter, Boy On High Stump 8.00
Planter, Buddha 30.00
Planter, Bull 25.00
Planter, Chick & Egg Cart 10.00
Planter, Children On Shoe 14.00
Planter, Chinese Rickshaw 14.00
Planter, Chuck Wagon 85.00
Planter, Circus Wagon 45.00
Planter, Clown 35.00
Planter, Clown, Gold Trim 48.00
Planter, Coal Bucket 10.50
Planter, Cocker At Doghouse 25.00
Planter, Coolie With Cart, Dark Green 10.00
Planter, Dachshund 16.00
Planter, Dog, Yellow 8.00
Planter, Donkey With Basket 16.00
Planter, Donkey, Pulling Cart ....10.00 to 20.00

Planter, Donkey, Sitting, With Basket 20.00
Planter, Dutch Children At Well 30.00
Planter, Elephant, Double-Leaf, Pink & Black 45.00
Planter, Elephant, With Howdah 20.00
Planter, Elf 18.00
Planter, Elf & Shoe 14.00
Planter, Farmer Pig 20.00
Planter, Fawn 25.00
Planter, Flying Geese 10.00
Planter, Gazelle 85.00
Planter, Geese, Square 20.00
Planter, Girl, Standing Against Fence ....8.00 to 13.00
Planter, Hound & Pekinese, Gold & Gray 12.00
Planter, House 40.00
Planter, Oriental Girl 30.00
Planter, Piano, Green 12.50
Planter, Pixie 28.00
Planter, Pony, Red 40.00
Planter, Poodle On Bike 20.00
Planter, Prairie Wagon 25.00
Planter, Puppy In Boat 25.00
Planter, Puppy, Brown 20.00
Planter, Queenie ....12.00 to 18.00
Planter, Rabbit With Turnip 30.00
Planter, Rickshaw, Gold Trim ....8.00 to 16.00
Planter, Southern Girl, Peach 125.00
Planter, Spanish Boy 35.00
Planter, Squirrel 12.00
Planter, Stagecoach, Bronzed Gun Metal 60.00
Planter, Tony The Peddler 20.00
Planter, Truck & Trailer 28.00
Planter, Wheelbarrow 15.00
Planter, Windmill, Green & White 20.00
Planter, Wishing Well, Dutch Boy & Girl 18.00
Plate, Corn King, 9 3/4 In. 31.00
Plate, Corn King, 10 In. 40.00
Platter, Corn King, 11 3/4 In. 41.00
Relish, Corn Queen 32.00
Salt & Pepper, Bo Beep & Boy Blue 35.00
Salt & Pepper, Bo Peep & Sailor, Gold Trim 125.00
Salt & Pepper, Chanticleer, 5 In. ....50.00 to 65.00
Salt & Pepper, Chef, Gold Trim ....25.00 to 45.00
Salt & Pepper, Corn King, Small 20.00
Salt & Pepper, Corn Queen, 5 In. ....35.00 to 48.00
Salt & Pepper, Cottage ....275.00 to 400.00
Salt & Pepper, Duck, 3 1/4 In. 35.00
Salt & Pepper, Dutch Boy & Girl, 5 In. ....45.00 to 60.00
Salt & Pepper, Dutch Boy & Girl, Gold ....130.00 to 165.00
Salt & Pepper, Dutch Boy, Single Stripe 150.00
Salt & Pepper, Dutch Girl, Blue Trim, 5 In. ....30.00 to 45.00
Salt & Pepper, Dutch Girl, Tulip 175.00
Salt & Pepper, Elephant, Teal ....30.00 to 35.00
Salt & Pepper, Farmer Pig ....14.00 to 20.00
Salt & Pepper, Fish 35.00
Salt & Pepper, Flower & Fern, Turquoise, 3 1/4 In. 10.00
Salt & Pepper, Flower & Fern, White 25.00
Salt & Pepper, Flowerpot 20.00
Salt & Pepper, Flowerpot, Gold Trim 46.00
Salt & Pepper, Fruit 30.00
Salt & Pepper, Huggers, Bendel 395.00
Salt & Pepper, Laurel Wreath, Blue 25.00
Salt & Pepper, Lobster 24.00
Salt & Pepper, Lobster Claw 50.00

Salt & Pepper, Milk Can ....16.00 to 25.00
Salt & Pepper, Muggsy, 3 1/4 In. ....65.00 to 110.00
Salt & Pepper, Muggsy, 5 In. ....150.00 to 165.00
Salt & Pepper, Muggsy, Gold Trim ....150.00 to 175.00
Salt & Pepper, Owl, 3 1/4 In. 35.00
Salt & Pepper, Owl, Gray Eyes 15.00
Salt & Pepper, Owl, Green Eyes ....20.00 to 45.00
Salt & Pepper, Pennsylvania Dutch 50.00
Salt & Pepper, Puss'n Boots ....25.00 to 45.00
Salt & Pepper, Sailor Boy & Bo Peep, Souvenir, Reading, Pennsylvania 17.00
Salt & Pepper, Smiley Pig & Winnie Pig, Cloverbud ....200.00 to 225.00
Salt & Pepper, Smiley Pig, 3 1/4 In. ....35.00 to 45.00
Salt & Pepper, Smiley Pig, Blue Neckerchief 60.00
Salt & Pepper, Smiley Pig, Green Neckerchief, Large 150.00
Salt & Pepper, Smiley Pig, Orange Neckerchief 75.00
Salt & Pepper, Snowflake, Yellow 18.00
Salt & Pepper, Sunflower, Small 30.00
Salt & Pepper, Swiss Boy & Girl ....45.00 to 52.00
Salt & Pepper, Swiss Boy & Girl, Gold 70.00
Salt & Pepper, Watering Can ....25.00 to 35.00
Saucer, Corn Queen, 5 1/2 In. ....11.00 to 20.00
Saucer, Valencia, Cobalt Blue, 6 1/2 In. 4.00
Shaker, Sugar, White Corn 60.00
Shaker, Sunflower, Large 60.00
Shaker, Valencia, Turquoise 15.00
Shaving Mug, Burgundy, 3 1/4 In. 40.00
Sugar, Cottage 295.00
Sugar, Cover, Corn King ....20.00 to 42.00
Sugar, Cover, Lobster 40.00
Sugar & Creamer, Corn King 75.00
Sugar & Creamer, Cover, Sunflower 60.00
Sugar & Creamer, Flower & Fern, Blue 12.00
Sugar & Creamer, Smiling Pig, Pair 33.00
Sugar & Creamer, Snowflake, Yellow 30.00
Syrup, Cover, Valencia, Yellow 95.00
Teapot, Corn King 125.00
Teapot, Corn King, Individual ....250.00 to 325.00
Teapot, Corn Queen 135.00
Teapot, Crisscross, Yellow 38.00
Teapot, Elephant, Blue 175.00
Teapot, Elephant, Yellow 225.00
Teapot, Embossed Rose 25.00
Teapot, Embossed Rose, Gold Trim 60.00
Teapot, Flower & Fern, Turquoise 25.00
Teapot, Granny Ann, Gold Trim 220.00
Teapot, Granny Ann, Lavender 110.00
Teapot, Granny Ann, Peach Apron ....105.00 to 120.00
Teapot, Paneled, Blue Daisy 55.00
Teapot, Pennsylvania Dutch, Blue ....27.00 to 45.00
Teapot, Pennsylvania Dutch, Individual 85.00
Teapot, Red Flower, Gold Trim 35.00
Teapot, Snowflake, Blue 30.00
Teapot, Snowflake, Yellow, 2 Cup 50.00
Teapot, Sunflower ....40.00 to 75.00
Teapot, Tom, Blue 125.00
Teapot, Tulip, Ribbed Top, Gold Spout & Handle 50.00
Teapot, White Corn, Gold Trim 195.00
Toby Mug, Burgundy 40.00
Toby Mug, Cream 40.00
Toby Mug, Sunflower, Ivory 38.00
Toby Mug, Teal 40.00
Vase, Cornucopia, Red Feather, 5 In. 9.00
Vase, Cornucopia, Yellow, Gold Trim, 5 In. ....8.00 to 12.00

Vase, Dove, Green, 9 In. 15.00
Vase, Hand, Blue, 8 In. 15.00
Vase, Leaf, Gold, 5 1/2 In. 11.00
Vase, Moor, Head, 8 In. 95.00
Vase, Philodendron, Green, 6 1/2 In. 12.00
Vase, Philodendron, Yellow, 6 1/2 In. 12.00
Vase, Swan, Dark Green, 5 In. 34.00
Vase, Swan, Gray & Burgundy, 5 In. 15.00
Vase, Swan, Light Green, 5 In. 34.00
Vase, Swan, Yellow, Gold, 5 In. 20.00
Wall Pocket, Bird On House .... 25.00 to 40.00
Wall Pocket, Birdhouse, Gold .... 22.00 to 35.00
Wall Pocket, Bowknot .... 20.00 to 25.00
Wall Pocket, Grandfather Clock, Gold Trim 40.00
Wall Pocket, Little Jack Horner 35.00
Wall Pocket, Mary & Lamb, Gold Trim 30.00
Wall Pocket, Telephone 25.00
Water Set, Stars & Strips, Maroon, 7 Piece 85.00

SHEARWATER pottery is a family business started by Mr. and Mrs. G. W. Anderson, Sr., and their three sons. The local Ocean Springs, Mississippi, clays were used to make the wares in the 1930s. The company is still in business.

Biscuit Jar, Blue & White 2640.00
Bowl, Blue Fulper Glaze, Pedestal, 9 1/2 x 3 1/2 In. 165.00
Bowl, Ducks In Water, Tapered, Blue, White, Black Glaze, 3 x 7 In. 115.00
Bowl, Raised Figural Design, Blue, Rust, Stamped, 11 1/2 In. 161.00
Cup & Saucer, Metallic Blue Drip Glaze, Circular Mark 60.00
Figurine, Black Men In Bib Overalls .... 45.00 to 50.00
Figurine, Cowboy 75.00
Figurine, Gull, Stylized Form, Tan Matte Glaze, Marked, 11 In. 77.00
Figurine, Horse, Prancing, Gunmetal Green 120.00
Figurine, Man, Seated On Horse, Black Glaze, Ink Mark, 6 1/2 In. 77.00
Figurine, Seagull 175.00
Mug, Bird Handle, Green, Signed 140.00
Mug, Strange Monkey Men On Handles, Turquoise, 3 In. 45.00
Mug, Woodpecker Handle, Green, Signed, 4 x 3 1/2 In. 125.00
Pitcher, Blue, Blue Green Glaze, 1/2 Moon Mark, 10 3/4 x 7 1/2 In. 100.00
Plate, Blue, Black Wave, High Glaze Cream Ground, Brown Glaze, 4 3/4 In. 968.00
Teapot, Blue Wave, High Glaze Cream Ground, Green Highlights, 6 In. 1694.00
Vase, Landscape Design, Blue, Yellow, Black, Tapered, 6 In. 184.00
Vase, Pelicans Swimming, Brown, Gray, Black, Deep Red, Yellow 330.00
Vase, Stylized Floral Design, Green On Yellow, 6 1/2 In. 161.00
Vase, Tapered, Black, White, Tan, 10 1/2 In. 218.50
Vase, Turquoise Over Cream Impressed Mauve, 6 x 8 In. 285.00

SHEET MUSIC from the past centuries is now collected. The favorites are examples with covers featuring artistic or historic pictures. Early sheet music covers were lithographed, but by the 1900s photographic reproductions were used. The early music was larger than more recent sheets, and you must watch out for examples that were trimmed to fit in a twentieth-century piano bench.

Ain't Dat A Shame, Bad Bill Bailey, Bill Clark, 1901 .... 9.00
Alabama Moon, Country Cottage, 1917 .... 9.00
At The Hop, Danny & The Juniors, 1957 .... 20.00
Autumn Leaves, Roger Williams 15.00
Bonanza, TV 10.00
Born To Be Kissed, Jean Harlow & Howard Dietz On Cover, 1935 .... 50.00
By The Watermelon Vine, Lindy Lou, 1904, 10 x 14 In. 30.00
Bye Bye Baby, Gentlemen Prefer Blondes, M. Monroe, R. Russell, 1949 .... 33.00
Calcutta, Lawrence Welk 15.00
California Gold Diggers, Hutchinson & Barker, Marsh, 1849 .... 250.00
Charlie My Boy, Andrews Sisters 20.00

Christy Minstrel, Black Band, Black Dancer & Actors, 1848 .... 250.00
Commence Ye Darkies All! Ethiopian Melodies, White's Serenaders, 1849 .... 36.00
Coon Coon Coon, Clarice Vance, 1900 .... 68.00
Cowboy & The Lady, Gary Cooper, Merle Oberon, 1938 .... 9.00
Darktown Strutter's Ball, Dancing, Con Conrad Photograph, 1917 .... 12.00
Dat's Harmony, Bert Williams Cover, Blackface, Ziegfeld Follies, 1911 .... 34.00
Dem Chickens Roost Too High, 1887 .... 46.00
Ev'ry Sammy Needs His Smokin' Over There, Doughboy, 1917 .... 21.00
Faithful Forever, From Gulliver's Travels 15.00
Falling In Love Again, Blue Angel, Marlene Dietrich, Emil Jennings, 1930 .... 43.00
Fire Brigade, Horsedrawn Fire Engine Picture, Going To Fire 55.00
For Me An' My Gal, Judy Garland 18.00
Freaks Of Blackville March, Caricature Type Figures, 1899 .... 55.00
Friendly Persuasion, Gary Cooper, 1956 .... 10.00
Girl Of Mine, Rolf Armstrong ....*Illus* 15.00
Gunsmoke 10.00
Happy Hannah Cake Walk, 1989 .... 23.00
High & The Mighty, John Wayne 10.00
I Hope The Band Keeps Playing, Abbott & Costello In Hollywood, 1945 .... 44.00
I'll Be Seeing You, Liberace 20.00
I'll Make Dat Black Gal Mine, George H. Primrose, 1896 .... 10.00
I'll Sing You A Song About Dear Old Dixie Land, Al Jolson, 1919 .... 34.00
I've Said My Last Farewell, 1906 .... 15.00
If You Just Must Go To War Bring Kaiser Back, Jazz Song 26.00
In The Good Old Summertime, Judy Garland 10.00
Jitterbug Waltz, Fats Waller 40.00
Juanita, The Palms, 1906 .... 400.00
Just Kiss Yourself Good-Bye, Rosalie Photograph, 1902 .... 15.00
King Cotton March, Sousa, 1895 .... 22.00
Klondike Annie, Mae West On Cover, 1936 .... 100.00
Learning The Blues, Frank Sinatra 40.00
Little French Mother, Goodbye, Rockwell Cover, 1919 .... 30.00
Me & My Old Banjo, Man On Porch, Jane P. Sousa, 1904 .... 10.00
Meet Me In St. Louis, Judy Garland 15.00
Monarch Of The Air, Man Portrait, Royal Blue Ground 35.00
Monkey Doodle-Doo, 1925 .... 36.00
More & More, Deanna Durbin 20.00
Mounted Police Two Step, Illustrated, 1909 .... 24.00
My Hawaii You Are Calling Me, Blue & Green Palms 11.00
My Sunshine Rose, Rolf Armstrong, Illustrator 12.00
My Sweetheart Went Down With The Ship, Titanic On Cover, Roger Lewis, 1912 .. 20.00
Nat Johnson's Rag, Black Couple Cake-Walking, 1911 .... 72.00
Nigger War Bride Blues, Black Doughboys March, 1917 .... 40.00
On Emancipation Day, Black Musicians, Pickaninnies, 1902 .... 50.00
Only Sixteen, Sam Cooke 40.00
Over There, Norman Rockwell Cover, Soldiers, Campfire, 1918 .... 35.00
Paul Revere's Ride, T.T. Paull, 1905 .... 45.00
Princess Pocahontas March, Full Figure On Cover 40.00
Rudy Vallee, Dancing With Tears In My Eyes, Autographed 75.00
Shop Worn Angel, Gary Cooper, 1928 .... 10.00
Slavery Days, 6 Pages, 1876, 10 x 13 In. 22.00
Sonny Boy, Al Jolson 18.00
Southern Snowballs Rag Two-Step, Black Playing Banjo, 1907 .... 40.00
Stewin' De Rice, Old Black Man, Aunt Jemima, 1918 .... 66.00
String Of Pearls, Glenn Miller Story, June Allyson, James Stewart, 1942 .... 19.00
Teenager's Romance, Ricky Nelson 35.00
Tell Me With Smiles, Al Jolson, 1923 .... 24.00
Tell That To The Marines, World War I, James Montgomery Flagg 45.00
Texas Teaser Wing Dance, Black Man, 1898 .... 55.00
Tickled To Death, Black Boys, Photograph, 1899 .... 15.00
Trolley Song, Judy Garland 15.00
Two O'Clock Jump, Harry James 25.00
Two Sleepy People, Bob Hope & Shirley Ross 17.00

U.S. Grand March, Gen. John Wool Comdr. East, East Div., 1843	30.00
Umbriago, Margaret O'Brien Picture	10.00
Utah Trail, Man, Wheat Fields, 1928	9.00
Valley Of Tears, Fats Domino	50.00
Walking After Midnight, Patsy Cline	20.00
Way Down On Tampa Bay	30.00
Wayward Wind, Gogi Grant	25.00
Wearing Of The Lei, Hawaiian Civic Club, Honolulu, Designs	10.00
When A Yankee Gets His Eye Down The Barrel Of Gun, 1918	28.00
When It's Nighttime Down In Dixieland, 1917	15.00
Won't You Let Me Call You Honey, Red Moon Co., 1911	28.00
You Can't Put Ketchup On The Moon, Ed Wynn, 1940	25.00
You Don't Know Me, Eddy Arnold	20.00
You're Sensational, Grace Kelly, Frank Sinatra, Bing Crosby On Cover	15.00
Zoot Suit, For My Sunday Gal, Black Man, With His Gal, 1942	22.00

SHEFFIELD items are listed in the Silver-English and Silver Plate categories.

SHELLEY first appeared on English ceramics about 1912. The Foley China Works started in England in 1860. Joseph Ball Shelley joined the company in 1862 and became a partner in 1872. Percy Shelley joined the firm in 1881. The company went through a series of name changes, and in 1910 the then Foley China Company became Shelley China. In 1929 it became Shelley Potteries. The company was acquired in 1966 by Allied English Potteries, then merged with the Doulton group in 1971. The name *Shelley* was put into use again in 1980.

Ashtray, Blue Rock, 3 3/4 In.	30.00
Ashtray, Harebell, 3 1/2 In.	33.00
Biscuit Plate	155.00
Bouillon, Underplate, Georgian, Gainsborough Shape	68.00
Bowl, Harmony, Dripware, Orange, 2 3/4 x 10 In.	130.00
Bowl, Yellow Luster, Suns, Palms, Multicolored, 13 In.	200.00
Butter, Cover, Blue Dripware	155.00
Butter, Cover, Sky Blue	135.00
Candy Dish, Dainty White, 5 In.	45.00
Cheese Dish, Rosebud, 6 Flute	325.00
Coffee Set, Cleopatra, 15 Piece	285.00
Creamer, Blue Rock	45.00
Creamer, Lilac	175.00
Creamer, Peony, 6 Flute	35.00
Creamer, Stocks	65.00
Creamer, Turquoise, Lavender & Green Interior, 1912	100.00
Creamer, Violets	65.00
Cup, Ludlow, White, Gold Trim, Demitasse	23.00
Cup, Rosebud, Demitasse	20.00
Cup & Saucer, Begonia, Dainty ....48.00 to 65.00
Cup & Saucer, Blue Flowers, Blue Interior	60.00
Cup & Saucer, Blue Rock ....50.00 to 65.00
Cup & Saucer, Blue Rock, Dainty	65.00
Cup & Saucer, Bridal Rose, Dainty	65.00
Cup & Saucer, Celandine, Dainty	60.00
Cup & Saucer, Children, Verse, Signed	85.00
Cup & Saucer, Dainty Blue	60.00
Cup & Saucer, Dainty Blue, Demitasse	85.00
Cup & Saucer, Dainty Yellow	125.00
Cup & Saucer, Daisy, Red	55.00
Cup & Saucer, English Rose, Black	70.00
Cup & Saucer, Floral, Demitasse	105.00
Cup & Saucer, Fluted, Demitasse	45.00
Cup & Saucer, Gainsborough, Sheraton	700.00
Cup & Saucer, Golden Broom	35.00
Cup & Saucer, Green, Chintz Interior, Gold Trim, Oleander Shape	75.00
Cup & Saucer, Heather	48.00

Cup & Saucer, Heavenly Blue . . . . .35.00 to 75.00
Cup & Saucer, Maytime 70.00
Cup & Saucer, Melody 70.00
Cup & Saucer, Old Mill 45.00
Cup & Saucer, Pansy 65.00
Cup & Saucer, Plate, Briar Rose, 3 Piece 95.00
Cup & Saucer, Polka Dot, Pink & White, Dainty 85.00
Cup & Saucer, Polka Dot, Red 60.00
Cup & Saucer, Primrose 60.00
Cup & Saucer, River Rock, Dainty 65.00
Cup & Saucer, Rock Gardens 78.00
Cup & Saucer, Rose & Pansy, Forget-Me-Nots, After Dinner 125.00
Cup & Saucer, Rose & Red Daisy 45.00
Cup & Saucer, Rose Spray, Dainty . . . . .60.00 to 65.00
Cup & Saucer, Rosebud 60.00
Cup & Saucer, Roses . . . . .70.00 to 90.00
Cup & Saucer, Roses, Pansy & Forget-Me-Nots, 14 Flutes 65.00
Cup & Saucer, Stocks . . . . .35.00 to 50.00
Cup & Saucer, Summer Glory 70.00
Cup & Saucer, Tropical Fish, Demitasse 85.00
Cup Plate, Dainty White, With Cup, 11 In. 180.00
Dish, Muffin, Swirl 175.00
Dish, Nut, Rose & Daisies, Scalloped Rim, Shell Pattern 45.00
Eggcup, Lily Of The Valley, 8 Flute 55.00
Eggcup, Shamrock 70.00
Figurine, Cheshire Cat, 3 1/2 In. 25.00
Figurine, Pixie, Mable Lucie Attwell, Child's 525.00
Gravy Boat, Underplate, Spring Flowers, Green Trim 80.00
Jar, Ginger, Swirl 180.00
Jardiniere, Florals, 8 x 9 In. 285.00
Place Setting, Rose Spray, Dainty, 5 Piece 175.00
Plate, Begonia, 9 1/4 In. 30.00
Plate, Blue Rock, 8 1/2 In. 40.00
Plate, Bread, Begonia 20.00
Plate, Chelsea Bird Center, 1914, 8 In. 95.00
Plate, Dainty Blue, 6 1/2 In. 55.00
Plate, Floral, 6 1/2 In. 50.00
Plate, Fox, English Limerick 45.00
Plate, Little Boy Blue, Cobalt Border, Signed, 8 In. 140.00
Plate, Mabel Lucie Attwell, 8 In. 168.00
Plate, Melody, Chintz, Green Trim, 8 1/4 In. 85.00
Plate, Primrose, 6 1/2 In. 50.00
Plate, Stocks, 6 1/4 In. 50.00
Plate, Stocks, 8 1/4 In. 32.00
Platter, Seashell, White, 12 In. 55.00
Platter, Spring Flowers, Green Trim, 15 In. 140.00
Reamer, Green & White, 2 Piece 195.00
Sauce, Dainty Mauve 12.00
Sauce, Dainty Mauve, Demitasse 120.00
Saucer, Dainty Blue 24.00
Soup, Cream, Bridal Rose, Underplate, 2 Piece 70.00
Sugar & Creamer, Begonia, 6 Fluted 45.00
Sugar & Creamer, Blue Rock 48.00
Sugar & Creamer, Dainty Blue 75.00
Sugar & Creamer, Dainty Orange & Rust, White Ground 125.00
Sugar & Creamer, Hedgerow 65.00
Sugar & Creamer, Rosebud, Demitasse 68.00
Teapot, Daffodil Time 175.00
Teapot, Dainty Blue, Large 295.00
Toothpick, Rosebud 40.00
Tray, Rambler Rose, 5 1/2 x 14 In. 110.00
Vase, Pink Carnations, Black, 1917, 7 In. 65.00

SHIRLEY TEMPLE, the famous movie star, was born in 1928. She made her first movie in 1932. Thousands of items picturing Shirley have been and still are being made. Shirley Temple dolls were first made in 1934 by Ideal Toy Company. Millions of Shirley Temple cobalt blue glass dishes were made by Hazel Atlas Glass Company and U.S. Glass Company from 1934 to 1942. They were given away as premiums for Wheaties and Bisquick. A bowl, mug, and pitcher were made as a breakfast set. Some pieces were decorated with the picture of a very young Shirley, others used a picture of Shirley in her 1936 *Captain January* costume. Although collectors refer to a cobalt creamer, it is actually the 4 1/2-inch-high milk pitcher from the breakfast set. Many of these items are being reproduced today.

Book, Big Little Book, Little Colonel, A.L. Burt, Illustrations Movie	20.00
Book, Big Little Book, Story Of Shirley Temple, Grace Mack, Saalfield	17.00
Book, Dimples, 20th Century Fox, 32 Pages, 1936	29.00
Book, Heidi, Saalfield Pub. Co., 31 Pages, 1937	23.00
Book, How I Raised Shirley Temple, By Her Mother	48.00
Book, Stowaway	95.00
Book, The Little Princess, 20th Century Fox, 25 Pages, 1939	29.00
Book, The Screaming Spector	25.00
Book, This Is My Crayon Book, Diecut Color Photo, Saalfield, 1935	25.00
Bowl, Cereal, Blue	60.00
Button, My Friend Shirley Temple, Black & White Photograph, 1930s	48.00
Card, Playing, Bridge, Shirley, Sunbonnet, Box, 1930	95.00
Carriage, Doll, Wooden With Oilcloth, Photograph On Both Sides, 1930	650.00
Creamer, Blue & White	15.00
Creamer, Cobalt Blue	48.00
Doll, Clear Eyes, Trunk, 10 Pieces Of Clothing, 2 Hats, 13 In.	1600.00
Doll, Composition, Clothes, 1930s, 18 In.	450.00
Doll, Composition, Hazel Sleep Eyes, Mohair Wig, Green Organdy Dress, Box	550.00
Doll, Composition, Vintage Trunk & Outfits, 11 In.	950.00
Doll, Curls, Green Pleated Dress, All Original, 20 In.	1400.00
Doll, Heidi, Box, 1972	42.00
Doll, Heidi, Vinyl, Flirty Eyes, 1950s, 17 In.	175.00
Doll, Ideal, 1957, 36 In.	995.00 to 1495.00
Doll, Ideal, Ballerina, Box, 1960s, 12 In.	65.00
Doll, Ideal, Brown Rooted Wig, Pink Bow, Hazel Sleep Eyes, 12 In.	150.00
Doll, Ideal, Brown Rooted Wig, Pink Bow, Hazel Sleep Eyes, 15 In.	180.00
Doll, Ideal, Captain January, Open-Close Eyes, Jointed, 1982, 12 In.	80.00
Doll, Ideal, Composition, Hazel Eyes, Pink, Organdy Dress, Socks, Box, 18 In.	660.00
Doll, Ideal, Composition, Original Wig, Blue Dress, Pink Bows, 18 In.	350.00
Doll, Ideal, Flirty Eyes, Original Clothes, 19 In.	450.00
Doll, Ideal, Littlest Rebel, Red Polka Dot Dress, 1972, 16 In.	145.00
Doll, Ideal, Plastic, Sleep Eyes, Hair, 1982, Box, 12 In.	39.00
Doll, Ideal, Ranger, Composition, Box, 17 In.	*Illus* 5000.00
Doll, Ideal, Rebecca Of Sunnybrook Farm, Jointed, 1982, 8 In.	65.00
Doll, Ideal, Stowaway, Open-Close Eyes, Jointed, 1982, 8 In.	65.00
Doll, Ideal, Vinyl Head, Hazel Sleep Eyes, Open-Close Mouth, 17 In.	280.00
Doll, Ideal, Wee Willie Winkle, Open-Close Eyes, Jointed, 1982, 8 In.	65.00
Doll, Little Colonel, Pin & Label, 13 In.	1350.00
Doll, Little Rebel Clothes, 13 In.	1200.00
Doll, Original Blue Dress, 1972, 12 In.	85.00
Doll, Pink, Yellow, 100th Anniversary, Montgomery Ward, Box, 1972, 15 In.	195.00
Doll, Wig, Promotional Photographs, Box, 16 In.	1500.00
Figurine, Chalkware, Baby Takes A Bow, Dancing Dress, 12 In.	275.00
Figurine, Wee Willie Winkle, 1937	50.00
Mirror, Celluloid, 1 3/4 In.	100.00
Mug, Cobalt Blue	50.00
Paper Doll, 1970s	16.00
Paper Doll, Full Color, 1930s, Cut	350.00
Pitcher, Milk, Cobalt Blue	30.00 to 40.00
Scrapbook, 1936	95.00
Scrapbook, Saalfield, 1930	98.00

Save your doll's packaging,
tags, and inserts. These can
triple the price when the
doll is sold.

Shirley Temple, Doll, Ideal, Ranger,
Composition, Box, 17 In.

Sheet Music, Bachelor & The Bobby-Soxer, Cary Grant, 1947	22.00
Sheet Music, Curly Top, 1935	15.00
Sheet Music, Laugh You Son-Of-A-Gun, Little Miss Marker, 1934	30.00
Sheet Music, Littlest Rebel	25.00
Sheet Music, Polly-Wolly-Doodle, Littlest Rebel, 1935	22.00
Sheet Music, Rebecca Of Sunnybrook Farm, 1938	30.00

SHRINER, see Fraternal category.

SILVER DEPOSIT glass was first made during the late nineteenth century. Solid sterling silver is applied to the glass by a chemical method so that a cutout design of silver metal appears against a clear or colored glass. It is sometimes called silver overlay.

Basket, Says Mohawk Trail, Handle, 5 1/2 In.	26.00
Bottle, Scent, Cobalt Blue	55.00
Bottle, Wine, 1909, 15 In.	585.00
Box, Crystal, Grape Design	125.00
Cruet, Amethyst Footed, Spout, Floral & Shield Pattern Stopper, 8 1/2 In.	175.00
Decanter, Allover Entwined Scrolls, Emerald Green Body, Stopper, 7 3/4 In.	1980.00
Decanter, Blue	150.00
Decanter, Green	135.00
Decanter Set, Liqueur, Cobalt Blue, Early 1900s, 6 Piece	60.00
Honey Pot, Bee Finial, 1910	325.00
Perfume Bottle, Alvin	135.00
Perfume Bottle, Bulbous, Gorham	195.00
Pitcher, Leaf Pattern, 8 x 5 In.	40.00
Pitcher, Scrolled Leaf, Berry, Cranberry, Monogram, 9 1/4 In. ....*Illus*	2645.00
Vase, Amethyst, Leaves & Vines, 4 In.	330.00
Vase, Bridge, Water & Figures, Blue, 6 1/2 In.	75.00
Vase, Trumpet, Floral & Scrolled Leaf, Green, 12 In. ....*Illus*	1495.00

SILVER FLATWARE PLATED includes many of the current and out-of-production silver and silver-plated flatware patterns made in the past eighty years. Other silver is listed under Silver-American, Silver-English, etc. Most silver flatware sets that are missing a few pieces can be completed through the help of one of the many silver matching services that advertise in many of the national publications.

SILVER FLATWARE PLATED, Alhambra, Cream Soup Spoon, International, 1907	3.00
American Rose, Jelly Spoon, International	1.00
Candleglow, Teaspoon, Towle, 1969	2.00
Clarendon, Pie Server, Reed & Barton, 1890	14.00

Silver Deposit, Pitcher,
Scrolled Leaf, Berry,
Cranberry, Monogram,
9 1/4 In.

Silver Deposit, Vase,
Trumpet, Floral &
Scrolled Leaf, Green,
12 In.

Commonwealth, Iced Tea Spoon, Reed & Barton, 1939	3.00
Emerson, Butter Spreader, Lunt, 1910	1.00
Fenway, Carving Knife, Oneida, 1937	7.00
Glenrose, Bouillon Spoon, Oneida, 1908	8.00
Melody, Teaspoon, Gorham, 1930	3.00
Modjeska, Dessert Fork, Oneida, 1916	5.00
Silhouette, Salad Fork, International, 1930	4.00
Queen's Pattern, Knife & Fork, Fish, Sheffield, 1926, 12 Piece	295.00
SILVER FLATWARE STERLING, Acanthus, Serving Spoon, Georg Jensen	150.00
Angelique, Demitasse Spoon, International	16.00
Angelique, Sugar Tongs, International	28.00
Antique Lily, Soup Ladle, Engraved, Whiting, c.1890, 12 In.	325.00 to 450.00
Armor, Dessert Spoon, Whiting	23.00
Armor, Nut Pick, Whiting	20.00
Armor, Pastry Fork, Whiting	45.00
Armor, Soup Ladle, Whiting	325.00
Armor, Teaspoon, Whiting	15.00
Baltimore Rose, Tea Caddy Spoon, Schofield	110.00
Belle Rose, Bonbon Spoon, Oneida	13.00
Bridal Rose, Demitasse Spoon, Alvin	25.00
Bridal Rose, Soup Spoon, Oval, Alvin	65.00
Buckingham, Demitasse Spoon, Gorham	14.00
Buttercup, Fruit Knife, Gorham	30.00
Buttercup, Gravy Ladle, Gorham	94.00
Buttercup, Roast Carving Set, Steiff	275.00
Cactus, Sauce Ladle, Jensen	120.00
Candlelight, Luncheon Knife, Towle	12.00
Chantilly, Olive Spoon, Gilt Bowl, Gorham	50.00
Chantilly, Soup Ladle, Gorham	275.00
Charmaine, Fork, International	23.00
Chased Acanthus, Fish Server, Whiting, 19th Century, 9 In.	375.00
Chased Diana, Seafood Fork, Towle	10.00
Chippendale, Butter Fork, Reed & Barton	24.00
Chippendale, Salad Fork, Reed & Barton	32.00
Chrysanthemum, Cold Meat Fork, Gorham	135.00
Chrysanthemum, Punch Ladle, Monogram, Tiffany, 12 Troy Oz.	1495.00
Chrysanthemum, Soup Spoon, 1880, Tiffany, 7 Troy Oz., Pair	345.00
Chrysanthemum, Stuffing Spoon, Monogram, Tiffany, 7 Troy Oz.	1035.00
Classic Rose, Sugar Spoon, Reed & Barton	12.00
Classic Rose, Teaspoon, Reed & Barton	11.00
Corinthian, Tablespoon, Shiebler	83.00
Corinthian, Teaspoon, Shiebler	32.00
Cromwell, Serving Spoon, Fluted, Gorham	75.00
Cupid, Dinner Fork	23.00
Damask Rose, Butter Knife, Heirloom	12.00

Damask Rose, Casserole Spoon, Lunt 48.00
Damask Rose, Jelly Server, Lunt 18.00
Damask Rose, Seafood Fork, Heirloom 10.00
Damask Rose, Tablespoon, Lunt 42.00
Damask Rose, Teaspoon, Heirloom 12.00
Dawn Star, Cold Meat Fork, Wallace 39.00
Dawn Star, Gravy Ladle, Wallace 42.00
Dawn Star, Sugar Spoon, Wallace 17.00
Dawn Star, Teaspoon, Wallace 15.00
Delacourt, Place Fork, Lunt 25.00
Delacourt, Teaspoon, Lunt 15.00
Dresden, Cracker Scoop, Enamel, Whiting 450.00
Dresden Scroll, Salad Fork, Lunt 24.00
Duke Of York, Teaspoon, Whiting 12.00
Edward VII, Berry Spoon, Gilt Bowl, Alvin, Large 125.00
Edward VII, Sauce Ladle, Alvin 80.00
Eloquence, Berry Spoon, Lunt 140.00
Eloquence, Gravy Ladle, Lunt 70.00
Eloquence, Luncheon Fork, Lunt 30.00
Eloquence, Luncheon Knife, Lunt 28.00
Eloquence, Pie Server, Lunt ....41.00 to 125.00
Eloquence, Sugar Spoon, Lunt 30.00
Eloquence, Tablespoon, Lunt 65.00
Eloquence, Teaspoon, Lunt 15.00
Eloquence, Tomato Server, Lunt 65.00
Eloquence, Tomato Server, Pierced, Lunt 81.00
Embassy Scroll, Salad Fork, Lunt 40.00
Empress, Dinner Fork, International 34.00
Empress, Gumbo Spoon, International 38.00
Enchanted Rose, Salad Fork, Century 24.00
Enchanted Rose, Teaspoon, Century 18.00
Enchanting Orchid, Butter Knife, Master, Westmorland 27.00
Enchanting Orchid, Luncheon Fork, Westmorland 20.00
Enchantress, Cream Soup Spoon, International 14.00
Enchantress, Dinner Fork, International 127.00
Enchantress, Gravy Ladle, International 44.00
Enchantress, Luncheon Fork, International 20.00
Enchantress, Teaspoon, International 12.00
Engagement, Cream Soup Spoon, Oneida 18.00
Engagement, Luncheon Fork, Oneida 20.00
English Chippendale, Lasagna Server, Reed & Barton 26.00
English Chippendale, Pasta Scoop, Reed & Barton 25.00
English Gadroon, Cream Soup Spoon, Gorham 26.00
English Gadroon, Gravy Ladle, Gorham 54.00
English Gadroon, Iced Tea Spoon, Gorham 24.00
English Provincial, Butter Knife, Master, Reed & Barton 21.00
English Shell, Carving Set, Lunt 61.00
English Shell, Teaspoon, Lunt 15.00
Esplanade, Luncheon Knife, Towle 24.00
Esprit, Cold Meat Fork, Gorham 51.00
Essex, Teaspoon, Durgin 13.00
Evening Mist, Luncheon Knife, Wallace 20.00
Evening Mist, Teaspoon, Wallace 16.00
Fairfax, Dinner Fork, Gorham 40.00
Fairfax, Salad Fork, Gorham 31.00
Fiorito, Fork, Potato, George Shiebler, 1902, Pair 225.00
Flora, Teaspoon, George Shiebler 45.00
Fontainebleau, Soup Ladle, Monogram, Gorham, 13 1/4 In. 517.50
Fontana, Teaspoon, Towle 13.00
Francis The First, Punch Ladle, Reed & Barton, 1907, 12 In. 345.00
French Provincial, Cheese Cleaver, Towle 20.00
French Provincial, Gravy Ladle, Towle 45.00
French Provincial, Letter Opener, Towle 20.00

French Provincial, Strawberry Fork, Towle 17.00
George & Martha, Iced Tea Spoon, Westmorland 15.00
George & Martha, Teaspoon, Westmorland 11.00
George & Martha, Tomato Server, Westmorland 50.00
Georgian, Carving Set, Towle, 2 Piece 51.00
Georgian, Ice Cream Fork, Towle 24.00
Georgian, Strawberry Fork, Towle 18.00
Georgian, Tomato Server, Towle 74.00
Gothic, Berry Spoon, George Shiebler 195.00
Grand Colonial, Demitasse Spoon, Wallace 16.00
Grecian, Gravy Ladle, Gorham 225.00
Heraldic, Gravy Ladle, Whiting 135.00
Heraldic, Punch Ladle, Whiting 375.00
Heraldic, Sardine Tongs, Whiting 185.00
Heraldic, Sauce Ladle, Whiting 65.00
Hindostanee, Crumber, Gorham 195.00
Hizen, Fish Slice, Dragon On Blade, Gorham, 1875, 12 In. 1150.00
Imperial Queen, Butter Knife, Flat, Whiting 18.00
Imperial Queen, Carving Set, Whiting 275.00
Imperial Queen, Dessert Spoon, Whiting 32.00
Imperial Queen, Gravy Ladle, Whiting 80.00
Imperial Queen, Pickle Fork, Whiting 45.00
Indian, Pie Server, Engraved Allover, Whiting, 1874 .... 125.00
Irian, Salad Set, Wallace, 2 Piece 475.00
Iris, Demitasse Spoon, Durgin 29.00
Ivy, Fish Fork, Gorham 50.00
Ivy, Fish Knife, Gorham 50.00
Ivy, Mustard Ladle, Gorham 75.00
Ivy, Soup Ladle, Whiting, 1880, 13 In. 259.00
Jenny Lind, Pastry Fork, Albert Coles, Pair 55.00
Joan Of Arc, Teaspoon, International 13.00
Josephine, Punch Ladle, Whiting 325.00
King, Dinner Fork, Dominick & Haff 60.00
King, Tablespoon, Dominick & Haff 50.00
King Cedric, Salad Fork, Oneida 16.00
King Cedric, Tablespoon, Oneida 27.00
King Richard, Letter Opener, Towle 25.00
Lady Baltimore, Salad Fork, Whiting 15.00
Lady Hilton, Luncheon Fork, Westmorland 20.00
Lady Hilton, Luncheon Knife, Westmorland 17.00
Lady Hilton, Teaspoon, Westmorland 11.00
Lafayette, Sandwich Fork, Towle 75.00
Legato, Bonbon Spoon, Towle 20.00
Legato, Cheese Cleaver, Towle 21.00
Les Cinq Fleurs, Teaspoon, Reed & Barton 18.00
Lily, Bouillon Spoon, Whiting 40.00
Lily, Salad Server, Engraved Script T, Whiting, 1902, Pair 430.00
Lily Of The Valley, Caviar Knife, Jensen 50.00
Lily Of The Valley, Gravy Ladle, Fluted, Gorham 325.00
Lily Of The Valley, Sugar Tongs, Whiting 125.00
Little Boy Blue, Fork, Baby's, Gorham 40.00
Livingston, Oyster Ladle, Whiting 100.00
Louis XIV, Cream Soup Spoon, Towle 15.00
Louis XIV, Iced Tea Spoon, Towle 11.00
Louis XIV, Jelly Spoon, Towle 15.00
Louis XV, Cold Meat Fork, Durgin 110.00
Louis XV, Cracker Scoop, Gold Wash Bowl, Durgin 345.00
Louis XV, Letter Opener 35.00
Louis XV, Lettuce Fork, Whiting 75.00
Louis XV, Olive Spoon, Gilt Bowl, Whiting 50.00
Louis XV, Tea Caddy Spoon, Whiting 125.00
Love Disarmed, Serving Spoon & Fork, Reed & Barton 345.00
Luxembourg, Mustard Ladle, Gorham 45.00

Madeira, Gravy Ladle, Towle 38.00
Madeira, Sugar Spoon, Towle 10.00
Maintenon, Olive Fork, Shiebler, 6 In. 35.00
Mansion House, Cold Meat Fork, Oneida 51.00
Mansion House, Sugar Spoon, Oneida 20.00
Mansion House, Teaspoon, Oneida 16.00
Marechal Niel, Sugar Tongs, Durgin 35.00
Marechal Niel, Teaspoon, Durgin 24.00
Margaret Rose, Dinner Fork, National 24.00
Margaret Rose, Dinner Knife, National 24.00
Margaux, Soup Spoon, Oval, Towle 37.00
Marguerite, Butter Knife, Master, Gorham 34.00
Marie Antoinette, Baby Fork, Dominick & Haff 30.00
Marie Antoinette, Serving Spoon, Gorham, 1900, Large 110.00
Marie Antoinette, Soup Ladle, Gorham 325.00
Marie Louise, Cold Meat Fork, Blackington 24.00
Marie Louise, Salad Server, Blackington 97.00
Marlborough, Dinner Knife, Reed & Barton 100.00
Marlborough, Luncheon Knife, Reed & Barton 25.00
Martha Washington, Pastry Server, Gorham 195.00
Martinique, Carving Set, Oneida 71.00
Martinique, Cold Meat Fork, Oneida 54.00
Martinique, Tablespoon, Pierced, Oneida 54.00
Mayflower, Beef Fork, Kirk 135.00
Mayflower, Fish Knife, Kirk 100.00
Mayflower, Tomato Server, Kirk 150.00
Mazarin, Berry Spoon, Dominick & Haff 269.00
Mazarin, Cold Meat Fork, Dominick & Haff 87.00
Mazarin, Ice Cream Spoon, Dominick & Haff 29.00
Mazarin, Sugar Spoon, Dominick & Haff 39.00
Meadow Song, Sugar Spoon, Towle 16.00
Michelangelo, Sugar Spoon, Oneida 26.00
Michelangelo, Tablespoon, Oneida 57.00
Michele, Knife, Wallace 26.00
Michele, Salad Fork, Wallace 24.00
Michele, Sugar Spoon, Wallace 21.00
Mignonette, Bonbon Spoon, Pierced, Lunt 34.00
Mignonette, Butter Knife, Master, Lunt 27.00
Mignonette, Cold Meat Fork, Lunt 64.00
Milburn Rose, Luncheon Knife, Westmorland 22.00
Milburn Rose, Salad Serving Spoon, Westmorland 91.00
Mille Fleurs, Luncheon Fork, International 34.00
Minuet, Carving Set, International 57.00
Minuet, Teaspoon, International 16.00
Minuet, Youth Set, International, 3 Piece 61.00
Modern Classic, Luncheon Fork, Lunt 24.00
Modern Victorian, Luncheon Knife, Lunt 28.00
Modern Victorian, Salad Knife, Lunt 28.00
Modern Victorian, Salad Serving Set, Lunt ....150.00 to 167.00
Modern Victorian, Tomato Server, Lunt 65.00
Monarch, Sugar Shell, Rogers & Hamilton 12.00
Mountjoy, Tongs, Sandwich, Bright Cut, Engraved 895.00
Newcastle, Lettuce Fork, Gorham 90.00
Newcastle, Mayonnaise Ladle, Gorham 60.00
Old Brocade, Salad Fork, Towle 23.00
Old Colonial, Nut Spoon, Towle 80.00
Old English, Punch Ladle, Shell Design, Dominick & Haff, 1913 .... 258.00
Old English, Sardine Fork, Towle 65.00
Old French, Cream Soup Spoon, Gorham 38.00
Old French, Gravy Ladle, Gorham 75.00
Old Lace, Teaspoon, Towle 10.00
Old Lace, Youth Set, Towle, 3 Piece 63.00
Old Master, Teaspoon, Towle 14.00

Old Newbury, Fish Set, Towle, 2 Piece 225.00
Old Orange Blossom, Luncheon Fork, Alvin 54.00
Old Orange Blossom, Tablespoon, Alvin 54.00
Old Tipt, Soup Ladle, Gorham 250.00
Orange Blossom, Cold Meat Fork, Alvin 195.00
Orange Blossom, Dinner Fork, Alvin 62.00
Orange Blossom, Fruit Spoon, Alvin 44.00
Orange Blossom, Teaspoon, Alvin 22.00
Orchid, Berry Spoon, Towle 110.00
Oval Twist, Cocktail Fork, Whiting, 6 Piece 120.00
Paul Revere, Pie Server, Towle 25.00
Pointed Antique, Carving Set, Reed & Barton, 3 Piece 141.00
Pointed Antique, Luncheon Fork, Reed & Barton 26.00
Pointed Antique, Pie Server, Sterling Blade, Reed & Barton 71.00
Pomona, Berry Spoon, Towle 75.00
Pomona, Cheese Knife, Towle 130.00
Pompadour, Gravy Ladle, Whiting-Gorham 61.00
Poppy, Cold Meat Fork, Gorham 75.00
Poppy, Cream Ladle, Gorham 28.00
Poppy, Luncheon Fork, Gorham 24.00
Poppy, Nut Spoon, Gorham 30.00
Portsmouth, Carving Set, Gorham 97.00
Portsmouth, Tablespoon, Gorham 81.00
Prelude, Fork, Baby's, International 22.00
Prelude, Luncheon Knife, International 15.00
Prelude, Teaspoon, International 11.00
Queen's Lace, Luncheon Fork, International 17.00
Radiant, Sugar Sifter, Gold Wash, Whiting 75.00
Radiant, Sugar Tongs, Whiting 30.00
Raleigh, Cheese Knife, Tines 85.00
Raphael, Berry Spoon, Gorham 195.00
Raphael, Luncheon Fork, Gorham 35.00
Raphael, Soup Ladle, Gorham . . . . .325.00 to 425.00
Renaissance, Ice Water Pitcher, Reed & Barton, 19 In. 287.50
Repousse, Berry Spoon, Kirk 85.00
Repousse, Fish Serving Fork, Kirk 125.00
Repousse, Mustard Ladle, Kirk 80.00
Repousse, Poultry Shears, Whiting 275.00
Repousse, Spoon, Condiment, Fruits & Flowers, S. Kirk & Son, 5 1/4 In. 50.00
Richmond, Salad Fork 25.00
Richmond, Teaspoon, Alvin 8.00
Rococo, Ice Cream Fork, Dominick & Haff 47.50
Romantique, Salad Fork, Alvin 15.00
Rose, Chowder Spoon, Stieff 25.00
Rose, Gravy Ladle, Stieff 59.00
Rose, Ice Cream Fork, Stieff 30.00
Rose, Lettuce Fork, Stieff 125.00
Rose, Teaspoon, Stieff 18.00
Rosette, Sugar Sifter, Gorham 85.00
Royal Danish, Gravy Ladle, International 79.00
Royal Danish, Luncheon Fork, International 20.00
Royal Danish, Pitcher, Water, International 650.00
Sir Christopher, Teaspoon, Wallace 18.00
Stieff Rose, Bacon Fork 65.00
Stieff Rose, Ice Cream Fork, Lunt 26.00
Stieff Rose, Iced Tea Spoon, 8 1/8 In. 28.00
Stieff Rose, Luncheon Knife 16.00
Stieff Rose, Pickle Fork 20.00
Stieff Rose, Preserve Spoon, 8 In. 55.00
Strasbourg, Punch Ladle, Gorham, 1897, 12 1/4 In. 259.00
Talisman Rose, Cocktail Fork, 5 1/2 In. 32.00
Talisman Rose, Gravy Ladle, Solid, 6 1/8 In. 89.00
Talisman Rose, Salad Fork, 6 1/8 In. 47.00

Talisman Rose, Soup Spoon, Round Bowl, 6 3/8 In. 40.00
Talisman Rose, Sugar Tongs, 3 5/8 In. 66.00
Talisman Rose, Teaspoon, 5 3/4 In. 28.00
Van Dyke, Asparagus Fork, International 110.00
Vassar Emblem, Pickle Fork 20.00
Versailles, Cocktail Fork, Gold Washed, Gorham, 12 Piece 600.00
Versailles, Nut Spoon, Gorham 125.00
Violet, Sugar Tongs, Whiting 125.00
William & Mary, Baby Fork, Lunt 16.00
William & Mary, Berry Spoon, Lunt 85.00
William & Mary, Cream Ladle, Lunt 22.00
William & Mary, Tablespoon, Lunt 32.00
Woodlily, Muddler, Frank Smith 135.00

SILVER PLATE is not solid silver. It is a ware made of a metal, such as nickel or copper, that is covered with a thin coating of silver. The letters *EPNS* are often found on American and English silver-plated wares. Sheffield is a term with two meanings. Sometimes it refers to sterling silver made in the town of Sheffield, England. In this section, Sheffield refers to a type of silver plate, usually English.

Biscuit Barrel, Floral Design, Floral Form Finial, Etched, Cylindrical, 5 x 5 In. 125.00
Biscuit Box, Acorn Finial, Victorian, Overall Floral & Swag, England, 6 3/4 In. 200.00
Biscuit Box, Ivory Finial Cover, England, Round, 8 1/2 x 9 1/2 In. 495.00
Bowl, Nut, Squirrel On Branch, Above Overlapping Leaves Bowl, Nutcracker, 7 In. 635.00
Butter, Mechanical, Swings Open On 2 Sides, Simpson, Hall & Miller, 1885 .... 525.00
Butter, Moose Head & Urn With Flowers, 12 x 6 In. 467.00
Butter, Shell Shaped, 13 In. 522.50
Cake Basket, Handle, Sheffield, 1785-1800, 12 In. 1350.00
Candelabrum is listed in its own category.
Candle Snuffer & Stand, Raised Foliate Design, T. Harwood, c.1816, 8 5/8 In. 127.00
Candle Snuffer & Tray, Chased Design, England, c.1815, 10 In. 695.00
Candlesticks are listed in their own category.
Cann, Sheffield, c.1780 .... 245.00
Card Holder, Cupid, Riding Goat 350.00
Carving Set, Simulated Ivory, Diamond Pattern, Victorian, Fitted Box 195.00
Case, Cigarette, Grid, Marked, WMF, 2 1/2 In. 46.00
Casserole, Cover, Eagle Finial, Pierced S-Scroll Footed, Rogers & Co., 14 In. 125.00
Centerpiece, Floral Relief Design, Art Nouveau, 8 In. 100.00
Centerpiece, Pedestal, Art Nouveau, Derby, 1900 .... 425.00
Chafing Dish, Rectangular Stand, Scrolled Handles, 4 Sections, George III, 19 In. 520.00
Coaster, Bottle, Grape & Vine Border, Pierced Floral Rim, Victorian, 9 In., Pair 690.00
Coaster, Bottle, Sheffield, c.1790, 5 7/8 In., Pair 550.00
Coaster, Wine Bottle, Flaring Rims, Scrolling & Floral Design, 7 1/2 In., Pair 200.00
Coffee Set, Grosvenor, 4 Piece 475.00
Coffeepot, Victorian, Quadruple Plate, Pairpoint 145.00
Cooler, Wine, Buffalo Form, Italian, 14 x 24 In. 660.00
Cooler, Wine, Gadrooned, Foliate Border, Handles, 9 x 10 In., Pair 100.00
Cooler, Wine, Regency, Campana, Liner, Sheffield, 19th Century, 10 1/2 x 9 In. 850.00
Cooler, Wine, Tub Shape, Lion Mask & Ring Handle, France, 8 3/4 In., Pair 2587.00
Cradle, Wine Bottle, Wickerwork, France, 10 In. 150.00
Cup, Child's, Little Girl Being Chased By Turkey, Forbes 95.00
Cup, Cylindrical Bowl, Engraved Scrolling, Medallion, Continental, 8 In. 219.00
Cup, Dot Pattern, Pierced Rim, Christofle, 2 1/2 In. 17.00
Decanter Stand, Floral, Shield Trefoil Design, Late 19th Century, 19 5/16 In. 288.00
Dish, Entree, Cover, Warming Stand, Steamer, Sheffield, 8 x 8 In., Pair 1100.00
Dish, Shell-Form, 3 Dolphin Feet, Beaded Handle 86.00
Epergne, Cut Glass Flower Insert, Cherubs, Flowers, Eastlake, Meriden, 28 3/4 In. 1440.00
Epergne, Grapevine Standard, 2 Stags Base, Continental, 19th Century, 25 In. 3220.00
Fish Set, Mother-Of-Pearl Handles, Fitted Case, English, 2 Piece 250.00
Fork, Little Miss Muffet, Child's 13.00
Frame, Crown Above C-Scroll Cartouche, Foliate Rocaille, Continental, 14 x 16 In. 288.00
Hunt Cup, Applied Elks Heads, Britannia, Ball Black & Co., 8 7/8 In. 465.00
Ice Bucket, Swing Handle, Italy, 7 1/2 In., Pair 109.00

Jug, Claret, Glass, Lion & Shield Thumb Piece Over Cover, Victorian, 17 In. 375.00
Knife, Fruit, Vermeil, Flared Reeded Handle, Fitted Box, France, 18 In. 230.00
Knife Rest, Figural, WMF, 1905, Box, Set Of 12 . . . .   3595.00
Ladle, Punch, Astoria, Wallace, 14 In. 98.00
Medallion, Nut Pick, Rogers 6.00
Mug, Shaving, Victorian, England, 1875 . . . .   275.00
Napkin Rings are listed in their own category.
Paperweight, Magnifier, Horse's Head Holding Sphere, France, Hermes 575.00
Pitcher, Insulated, Tilting Stand, Leaf & Floral Design, Meriden 175.00
Pitcher, On Stand, Ironstone Liner, Meriden, 14 1/4 In. 275.00
Pitcher & Bowl, Victorian, Simpson Hall Miller Co., 16 x 18 In. 525.00
Platter, Warming, Well & Tree, Shell Handle, Gadrooned Border, Sheffield, 24 In. 525.00
Salver, Scroll, Leaf & Flower Border, 3 Panel Supports, England, c.1830, 23 In. 1450.00
Spoon, Souvenir, see Souvenirs category.
Sugar & Creamer, Tapered Legs, Ovoid, WMF, 2 1/2 In. 35.00
Tankard, Open Cover, Boy Kisses Mermaid, Enid Yandell, 1890, 11 5/8 In. 5750.00
Tea & Coffee Set, Charter Oak 1850.00
Tea Set, Carved Ebony Handle, Stepped Feet, Graduated, Marked, Ziggurat 1725.00
Tea Set, James W. Tufts, 3 Piece 250.00
Tea Set, Knop Finial, Faceted, Globular, Floral Design, Reed & Barton, 3 Piece 185.00
Tea Set, Regency, Reed & Barton, 5 Piece 425.00
Tea Set, Victorian, Paneled Finish, Reed & Barton, 6 Piece 468.00
Tea Set, Winthrop, Reed & Barton, 6 Piece 385.00
Tea Urn, 2 Handles, Reed & Barton, 1870 . . . .   795.00
Tea Urn, Acanthus Leaf & Gadrooned Design, Walker & Hall, 19 In. 430.00
Tea Urn, Foliate Molded Edges, Shaped Feet, Sheffield, 18 In.   1265.00
Tea Urn, Georgian Style 345.00
Teapot, Bas Relief Flowers, Silva, Sheffield 125.00
Teapot, Quadruple Plate, Hand Chased, Repousse, Tufts 75.00
Teapot, Rococo Style, Melon Form Body, Chased Scrollwork, 9 In. 75.00
Teapot, Star, Floral Design, Scroll Handle, Reeded Oval Body, England, 6 In. 80.00
Toothpick, Aurora 95.00
Toothpick, Boy With Barrel, Meriden 250.00
Toothpick, Chicken & Wishbone 50.00
Toothpick, Figural, Woman Standing Next To Holder, Derby 125.00
Tray, Bacchus Mask, Gadrooned Rim, Double Handled, Gorham, 36 x 21 1/2 In. 860.00
Tray, Detailed Rim, International Silver Co., 21 1/2 In. 165.00
Tray, Foliate Border, Shell & Foliate Handles, Chased, Victorian, 29 In. 185.00
Tray, Grande Baroque, Oval, Footed, Wallace, 28 In. 375.00
Tray, Ornate Georgian Pattern, Wallace, 15 1/4 x 26 1/4 In. 138.00
Tray, Scrolled Foliage, Shaped Rim Handles, Early 19th Century, Sheffield, 29 In. 800.00
Tray, Tea, Gadroon Shell, Scroll Foliate Borders, Handle, Rectangular, 27 1/2 In. 200.00
Tray, Tea, Grape & Foliate Border, Bracket Handles, Victorian, Rectangular 320.00
Tureen, Chased Floral Design, Birmingham, 10 x 13 3/4 In. 300.00
Tureen, Cover, Classic, Handles, Pairpoint, 9 x 14 1/2 x 7 In. 375.00
Tureen, Game, Boar Finial, Domed Cover, Handles, St. Hubertus Lodge, 17 x 17 In. 4850.00
Tureen, Raised Gadroon Design, Reed & Barton, 7 x 14 1/2 In.   270.00
Tureen, Soup, Cover, Armorials Below Gadroon, Shell & Leaf, c.1815, 17 1/2 In. 3740.00
Vase, Neoclassical Figural Design, 2 Handles With Relief, Footed, 12 1/4 In., Pair 800.00
Vase, Trumpet, Fitted As Lamp, Sheffield, 32 In. 375.00
Waiter, Pierced Gallery, Georgian Design, Shell & Foliate Center 165.00
Warming Stand, Raised On 4 Scroll Legs, Wood Handles, 9 1/4 x 29 In. 150.00
Water Set, Pitcher With Bear Finial, Goblet, Gorham, 3 Piece 85.00
Wine Wagon, Crest Of Knight Commander Of Bath, Tray, c.1820, 15 1/4 In. 2750.00

SILVER, SHEFFIELD, see Silver Plate; Silver-English categories.

SILVER-AMERICAN. American silver is listed here. Most of the sterling
silver listed in this book is subdivided by country. There are also other
pieces of silver and silver plate listed under special categories, such as
Candelabrum, Napkin Ring, Silver Flatware, Silver Plate, Silver-
Sterling, and Tiffany Silver.

SILVER-AMERICAN, Ashtray, Smoking Lady, Unger 395.00

Basket, Reticulated & Engraved Design, Upright Handle, Gorham, 1919, 12 In. 230.00
Basket, Scroll Border, Handle, Reticulated, Black, Starr & Frost, 7 1/2 x 11 In. 285.00
Basket, Swing Handle, Claw Feet, Merrill Shops, New York 115.00
Beaker, Barrel Shape, Anthony Rash, c.1810, 3 1/2 In. 1100.00
Bell, Figure Of Man, Top Hat & Coat, Signed, Gorham 95.00
Birds, Dessert Spoon, Wendt 55.00
Bottle, Snuff, Temple Vase Shape, Tibetan Style Mounts, Stopper, 2 1/2 In. 130.00
Bowl, American Trap Assoc. Trophy, William Waldo Dodge, Jr., 1930, 9 1/2 In. 495.00
Bowl, Flared, Chased Stylized Lily, Arts & Crafts, Kalo Shop, 1 1/2 x 5 In. 875.00
Bowl, Fruit, Bas Relief Hollyhock Rim, Monogrammed, Unger Bros., 11 1/2 In. 488.00
Bowl, Grapevine, Paneled Body, Pierced Rim, Dominick & Haff, 1895, 10 In. 315.00
Bowl, Handle, 6 Fluted Groups Form Spiral, Ring Foot, K.C. Pratt, 2 x 8 1/2 In. 1700.00
Bowl, Lightly Hammered, Footed, Arts & Crafts, Gyllenberg, 4 1/2 x 9 In. 1350.00
Bowl, Marie Antoinette, Gorham, 11 In. 130.00
Bowl, Pierced Foliate Border, Half Spherical Form, Frank W. Smith, 8 5/8 In. 227.00
Bowl, Repousse Vintage Rim, H.W. Hess, 12 1/4 In. 300.00
Bowl, Reticulated Chrysanthemum Border, Black, Starr & Frost, 1899, 17 In. 1495.00
Bowl, Rococo Rim, Monogrammed, Bailey, Banks & Biddle Co., 10 3/4 In. 240.00
Bowl, Seafood, Overlapping Shells, Seaweed, Whiting, c.1885, 8 1/4 In. 4600.00
Bowl, Thumb Molded Edge, Paneled Sides, Crichton & Co., 6 1/4 In. 95.00
Bowl, Wedgwood Pattern, Monogrammed, International, 10 In. 100.00
Bowl, Wedgwood, 2 Handles, Pedestal, International, 12 In. 750.00
Bread Tray, Chantilly, Gorham 345.00
Bread Tray, Francis I, Reed & Barton 450.00
Breakfast Set, Square Rims, Dominick & Haff, 1879, 3 3/4 In., 3 Piece 4600.00
Butter Knife, Arrowhead End, Hammered, Master, Gaylord Craft, 7 In. 55.00
Cake Cutter, For Angel Food Cake, Hammered Handle, Allan Adler, 11 In. 265.00
Cake Stand, Fluted Pedestal, Wire Rim, Arts & Crafts, Lebolt, 5 x 8 3/4 In. 1100.00
Candelabrum is listed in its own category.
Candlesticks are listed in their own category.
Cann, Benjamin Burt 3680.00
Cann, John Burt, Boston, 1700s, 5 1/8 In. 3300.00
Card Case, Coin Silver, Gorham, 3 1/2 x 2 1/2 In. 110.00
Card Case, Coin, Engraved Scene, 1847-1850 . . . . 150.00
Case, Cigar, Elgin, Built In Lighter 175.00
Chocolate Pot, Repousse, Chased Floral Design, 8 In. 546.25
Cocktail Shaker, Hammered Surface, Shreve & Co., 1930s, 10 1/2 In. 445.00
Coffee Set, Lunt, 3 Piece 345.00
Coffee Set, Shreve & Co., 3 Piece 285.00
Coffee Set, Turkish Shape, Lotus Pattern, Porter Blanchard, 3 Piece 2100.00
Coffeepot, Floraform Rim & Foot, Monogrammed, Alvin, 9 1/2 In. 145.00
Compote, Holds Satsuma Bowl, Stemmed, Pierced, Shreve & Co., 7 1/2 In. 2100.00
Compote, La Paglia, Flared, Openwork Stem, International, 15 1/16 In. 520.00
Creamer, Classical, Gorham, 1917, 5 1/2 In. 275.00
Creamer, Coin Silver, Bailey & Kitchen, 1852 . . . . 175.00
Creamer, Gorham, Late 1800s 70.00
Cup, Applied Monogram & Engraved Date, Kalo Shop, 1916, 3 3/4 In. 425.00
Cup, Floral Rococo Repousse, Cast Handle, J.T. Bailey, 1848, 3 3/8 In. 110.00
Cup, Julep, Engraved Small Game Birds, Kirk, 3 5/8 In., 6 Piece 1935.00
Demitasse Set, Stylized Sunflowers, Dominick & Haff, 1884, 3 Piece 1495.00
Dish, Etched Carp, Dragonfly, Triangular, Whiting, 1890, 7 5/8 In. 2587.00
Dish, Pedestal, Grande Baroque, Wallace, 5 In. 45.00
Dish, Vegetable, Chippendale, Gorham, 10 1/4 In., Pair 175.00
Dish, Vegetable, Hammered, Oval, Scalloped Flange, A. Gunner, 11 1/2 In. 575.00
Ewer, Coin Silver Repousse, Pedestal, R. & W. Wilson, 15 In. 2750.00
Flask, Knight Head, Unger 795.00
Flask, Scent, Bird, Branch & Pipe Player, Suspension Chain, Gorham, 1879, 3 In. 460.00
Fork, Pickle, Hammered, Petterson Studio, 7 1/16 In. 135.00
Fork Set, Fish, Hammered, Applied F, Kalo Shop, 6 Piece 495.00
Garniture, Neo-Classical Frames, Crystal Bowls, Dominick & Haff, 8 Piece 5520.00
Goblet, Repousse Floral, Scroll Band, Andrew Ellicott Warner, c.1810, 5 In. 402.00
Gravy Boat, Repousse, Chased Landscape, Floral, S. Kirk & Son, 8 In. 633.00
Iced Tea Spoon, Teardrop Bowl, Geo. Porter Blanchard, 8 In. 68.00

Knife, Child's, Chased & Pierced Stork, Dominick & Haff, 5 1/4 In. 85.00
Knife & Server, Wedding Cake, Karen, 1966, Old Newbury Crafters, 2 Piece 375.00
Ladle, Baldwin Gardiner, c.1850 . . . . 175.00
Luncheon Knife, Stainless Blade, Engraved S., Arthur J. Stone, 8 3/8 In. 83.00
Matchbox, Ornate, Kirk 75.00
Mirror, Hand, Gourd Form, Spray Of Morning Glory, Whiting, c.1880, 9 1/2 In. 1840.00
Mug, Chased Floral Design, Engraved, Jones, Ball & Co., Child's 230.00
Mustard, L. Krider, c.1830, 3 1/2 In. 450.00
Napkin Rings are listed in their own category.
Nut Dish, Poppy, Shiebler 95.00
Nut Spoon, Long Bowl, Pierced C, Hammered Handle, Brochon, 3 7/8 In. 42.00
Pill Box, Domed Hinged Cover, Interlocking Monogram, A.J. Stone, 2 In. 695.00
Pitcher, 2 Goblets, Roman Soldier Bust On Handle, Wood & Hughes, c.1860 . . . . 4600.00
Pitcher, Baluster Form, Ribbed Design, Whiting, 9 In. 488.00
Pitcher, Chased Floral & Bow, Victor Siedman, 8 1/2 In. 373.00
Pitcher, Chased Floral & Leaf Design, Monogrammed, Kirk, 7 3/8 In. 1092.00
Pitcher, Ewer Shape, Reed & Barton, 9 7/8 In. 577.00
Pitcher, Federal, Embossed Acanthus Leaves, Stodder & Frobisher, 12 In. 3200.00
Pitcher, Japanese Style, Chased Iris, George W. Shiebler, 1890, 10 1/4 In. 2300.00
Pitcher, Milk, Scrolling Foliate Design, Center Oval Cartouche, Gorham, 1848 . . . . 373.00
Pitcher, Shaped Handle, Stepped Domed Foot, Frank W. Smith, 8 1/2 In. 287.50
Pitcher, Water, Broad Spout, Hollow Handle, Kalo Shop, 6 x 8 1/2 In. 2400.00
Pitcher, Water, Fluted, Panels, Arts & Crafts, Kalo Shop, 1928, 11 In. 2800.00
Platter, Meat, Well & Tree, 4 Acanthus & Fan Footed, Gorham, 22 In. 2800.00
Porringer, Pierced, Turned-In Sides, Keyhole Handle, Woolley, 8 In. 375.00
Punch Bowl, Shell & Scroll Border, Joslin & Park, Ladle, 8 1/2 x 12 In. 3500.00
Punch Ladle, Rounded Handle, Hammered, Block Letter S, Kalo Shop, 11 In. 375.00
Punch Ladle, Twig Stem, Encloses Spider's Web, P.L. Krider, 1870, 13 3/4 In. 3450.00
Punch Ladle, Wooden Handle, 1904, Leinonen, 15 1/4 x 5 In. 895.00
Punch Ladle, Wooden Handle, Handicraft Shop, 1903, 15 1/4 In. 895.00
Relish Bowl, Rose, Steiff, Oval, 9 In. 375.00
Salad Set, Fiddle Type, Smooth Finish, Porter Blanchard, 9 3/4 In., 2 Piece 450.00
Salad Set, Lotus Pattern, David Carlson, 8 1/4 In., 2 Piece 350.00
Salt & Pepper, Classic Colonial, Pedestal, Arts & Crafts, A.J. Stone, 4 In. 600.00
Salver, Shaped Molded Edge, 3 Claw Feet, Dominick & Haff, Round, 10 In. 200.00
Sauce Server, Crosshatch Pattern Handle, Allan Adler, 5 1/2 In. 58.00
Sauceboat, Double Lipped, Matching Tray, Gorham, 8 In. 92.00
Sauceboat, Georgian Style, Howard, 1880s, 8 In. 115.00
Server, Fish, Japanese Style, Fish & Seaweed, Gorham, c.1880, 11 1/4 In., Pair 1380.00
Servers, Fish Fork & Spoon, Carp In Net, Whiting, c.1880, 9 & 8 1/2 In. 1725.00
Serving Spoon, Floral, Art Nouveau Style, Monogram, Gorham, 10 In. 316.00
Serving Spoon, John Myers, Philadelphia, Late 18th Century 650.00
Serving Spoon, Square End, Hammered, Engraved, Potter Studio, 9 In. 120.00
Soup, Dish, Lenox Insert, Gorham 395.00
Soup Ladle, Beaded Edge, Pierced Attached Strainer, S.T. Crosby, 1850 . . . . 172.50
Spoon, Bird On Back Of Bowl, Initials Of Owners, J. Myers, 9 1/4 In. 220.00
Spoon, James Adams, Alexandria, Virginia, c.1775, 6 Piece 1380.00
Spoon, Martini, Arching Up To Point End, Shreve & Co., 12 In. 175.00
Spoon, Shell Back, Jacob Hurd, c.1760, 4 1/2 In. 350.00
Spoon, Shell Back, Samuel Minott, c.1760, 4 3/8 In. 295.00
Spoon, Tea Caddy, Leaf Bowl, Vine Handle, Katherine Pratt, 3 3/8 In. 250.00
Spoon Set, Iced Tea, Engraved Y, Porter Blanchard, 1 Large & 6 Small Piece 625.00
Spreader, Butter, Hammered, Lebolt, 6 Piece 475.00
Sugar, Cover, Bud Finial, Acanthus Leaves, J.B. Jones, Boston, c.1820, 8 In. 230.00
Sugar, Creamer & Waste, Harris & Shaffer, c.1930 . . . . 600.00
Sugar, Domed Cover, Acorn Knop, Foliate Handle, E. Lownes, c.1830, 9 In. 402.00
Sugar & Creamer, Band Of Birds & Branches, Gorham, 1873, 6 1/2 In. 460.00
Sugar & Creamer, Coin Silver, Federal, Harvey Lewis, 1811, 6 1/2 In. 440.00
Sugar & Creamer, Cover, Sanborn 395.00
Sugar & Creamer, Ovoid-Form, Scroll Feet, William B. Meyers Co. 460.00
Sugar & Creamer, Shore Birds, Pheasant & Owl, Gorham, 1880, 2 3/4 In. 2875.00
Sugar & Creamer, Talisman Rose, Individual 195.00
Sugar & Creamer, Vasiform, John Vernon, c.1800 . . . . 1035.00

Sugar Pail & Creamer, Lily Plants, Rushes & Bird, Gorham, 1879, 5 In. 3740.00
Sugar Sifter, Shiebler, 1874 . . . .   190.00
Sugar Spoon, Norman, Hammered, Engraved E, Shreve & Co., 5 7/8 In. 95.00
Tablespoon, Coffin End, T. Keeler, c.1805 . . . .   195.00
Tea & Coffee Set, Gale & Willis, 7 Piece 7475.00
Tea & Coffee Set, Ivory Insulators, Harris & Schafer, 1890s, 5 Piece 6000.00
Tea & Coffee Set, Repousse, Applied Rosettes, Gorham, 1875 . . . . 1695.00
Tea Ball, Teapot Form, Amcraft, Attleboro, Mass. 75.00
Tea Caddy, Squirrel, Exotic Bird, Spider Web, Dominick & Haff, 1880, 4 1/2 In. 2875.00
Tea Set, Chased Floral, Monogrammed & Cross, B. Gardiner, 3 Piece 1320.00
Tea Set, Francis 1st, Ivory Insets, Tray, Reed & Barton, 5 Piece 8500.00
Tea Set, Lobed Baluster Form, John B. Jones, c.1838, 3 Piece 1495.00
Tea Set, Louis XIV, Towle, 5 Piece 1320.00
Tea Set, Prelude, International, 5 Piece 1100.00
Tea Set, Queen Anne Style, Gorham, 1890, 3 Piece, Pot, 7 1/2 In. 1200.00
Tea Set, Shoulder Band Of Leaves, Acorns, Garrett Forbes, c.1825, 4 Piece 1380.00
Tea Urn, Pierced Repousse Supports, Ivory & Foliate Feet, 1835 . . . . 4715.00
Teapot, Chased Floral Design, Gorham, 8 1/4 In. 330.00
Teapot, Jennings Silver Co., c.1930 . . . .   525.00
Teapot & Sugar, Cover, Paneled Octagonal Form, Jones, Ball & Poor, c.1847 . . . .   635.00
Teaspoon, Applied Block R, Hammered, Lebolt, 5 3/4 In., 6 Piece 375.00
Teaspoon, Bright Cut Design, Jacob Perkins, 1790, 5 1/2 In., 4 Piece 425.00
Teaspoon, Bright Cut, Paul Revere, Pair 5175.00
Teaspoon, Spreading Tip & Handle, Edward H. Hill, 1840s, 6 In., 12 Piece 340.00
Tongs, Sugar Cube, Spade Shape End, Kalo Shop, 3 1/2 In. 195.00
Tongs, Sugar Cube, V Shaped Teeth, Pierced Initials, C.B. Dyer, 4 1/4 In. 110.00
Tray, Applied Scroll & Floral Rim, Monogrammed, Gorham, 14 3/8 In. 230.00
Tray, Bright-Cut Swags Of Flowers, William Forbes, c.1860, 31 In. 4315.00
Tray, Chippendale Scroll Rim, Black, Starr & Frost, 30 1/2 In. 3200.00
Tray, Chippendale, Round, Gorham, 12 In. 550.00
Tray, Gadroon Edge, Center Rococo Ornament, William Adams, 1850, 32 In. 4600.00
Tray, Greek Key & Classical Urn Border, Gorham, 1917, 10 1/2 In. 258.00
Tray, King Francis, Reed & Barton, 19 In. 1750.00
Tray, Molded Rim, Cut-Out Handles, Oval, Herbert Taylor, c.1930, 28 3/4 In. 2990.00
Tray, Scalloped Edge, Raised Shell & Scrolling, Redlich & Co., Round, 14 In. 520.00
Tray, Shell & Scroll Design, Handles, Durham, 27 In. 1610.00
Tray, Vermeil, Cartouche Form, Iris & Poppy Border, Reed & Barton, 18 In. 1725.00
Trophy, Wyoming Fairs, Horse, Dominick & Haff, 1889, 13 3/4 In. 5000.00
Tureen, Sauce, Cover, Leaf Finial, Gregor & Wilson, 1850s, 8 5/8 In. 2600.00
Vase, Bud, Ruffled Trumpet, Hammered, 1916, Kalo Shop, 5 1/2 In. 795.00
Vase, Chased Slender Leaves, Ruffled Rim, Martele, Gorham, 1898, 42 Oz. 8050.00
Vase, Indian Style, Exotic Flowers, Beads At Neck, Gorham, 1880, 8 1/2 In. 1840.00
Vase, Spiraled Leaves From Band Of Iris, Theodore B. Starr, c.1900, 11 1/2 In. 1840.00
Vase, Trumpet Form, Reticulated Border & Foot, Gorham, Gold Wash, 14 In. 550.00
Vase, Trumpet, Hammered, Fluted, Arts & Crafts, Gyllenberg, 7 1/2 In. 1100.00
Vase, Trumpet, Lightly Hammered, Ruffled, Arts & Crafts, Lebolt, 7 7/8 In. 775.00
Vase, Trumpet, Repousse Foliate, Border, Bell Footed, 21 In. 1090.00
Waiter, Chased Scroll Design, Presentation, S. Kirk, 25 1/2 In. 1430.00
SILVER-AUSTRIAN, Centerpiece, 4 Scrolled Acanthus Supports, Blue Glass Liner, 11 In. . 1495.00
Gravy Boat, Attached Tray, Double Lip, Rococo Design, 9 13/16 In. 550.00
Snuff Box, Ribbon Tied Laurel Wreath Design, Cover, 1900, 2 5/8 In. 747.00
Spoon, Coffee, Lapis Lazuli Cabochon, Wiener Werkstatte, 3 5/8 In. 630.00
SILVER-CHINESE, Cigarette Case, Figures In Boat, Bamboo & Foliage Ground, 5 1/2 x 3 1/2 In.   230.00
SILVER-CONTINENTAL, Chalice, Vermeil, Geometric Band, Last Supper, With Paten, 10 In.   800.00
Compote, Draped Female Figure Stem, 4 Handles Of Exotic Birds, 10 In. 2300.00
Holder, Place Card, Hapsburg Empress & Crest Coin, 12 Piece 430.00
Sauce Boat, Gadroon Rims, Gilt Interiors, Lion Mask Handles, 1820, 9 In. 3450.00
SILVER-DANISH, Bowl, Decorative Foot, Georg Jensen, 4 1/4 In. 770.00
Cocktail Set, 2 Spouted Shaker, 9 Cups, Tray, Georg Jensen, 1925, 11 Piece 4600.00
Decanter, Silver Mounts Design With Figures Tending Flowers, Silver, 9 3/4 In. 747.50
Fish Set, Georg Jensen 1725.00
Ice Bucket, Tapered Form, Engraved Lattice Design, Georg Jensen, 8 In. 1725.00
Pillbox, Filigree Top, Engraved Band, 1 1/2 In. 120.00

Salt, Cactus, Georg Jensen, Green Enamel Interior, 1 1/2 x 2 1/4 In., 4 Piece 660.00
Spoon, Serving, Figure Of Scandinavian Goddess, 1919 .... 55.00
Sugar Tongs, Blossom, Georg Jensen 150.00
Tazza, Clusters Of Grapes, Lobed Twisted Stem, Georg Jensen, c.1918, 10 1/2 In. 4370.00
Urn, Marriage, Faux Jeweled Crown Finial, Paneled Body, Jewels, 1877, 5 In. 468.00
Urn, Marriage, Faux Jewels, Teardrop Handles, Crown Finial, 5 1/2 In. 402.00
SILVER-DUTCH, Creamer, Chased Design, 4 In. 140.00
Tea Set, 12 Spoons, Strainer, Tongs, Tea Scoop, Fitted Case, 1837 .... 240.00
Teapot, Mermaid Finial, Duck Head Spout, Coats Of Arms Base, 1742, 5 1/2 In. 2300.00

SILVER-ENGLISH. English silver is marked with a series of four or five small hallmarks. The standing lion mark is the most commonly seen sterling quality mark. The other marks indicate the city of origin, the maker, and the year of manufacture. These dates can be verified in many good books on silver.

SILVER-ENGLISH, Basket, Cake, Swing Handle, Oval, William Smily, 1857, 14 In. 1265.00
Basket, Fruit, Applied Rim, Scrolled Leaves, Swing Handle, 1822, 12 In. 1150.00
Basket, Pierced Foliate, Ribbon Bail Handle, George III, Wm. Plummer, 13 In. 3910.00
Basket, Sweetmeat, Gadroon, Shell Rim, Swing Handle, 1760, 25 Oz. 2645.00
Basket, Sweetmeat, W. & P. Bateman, 1804; 5 1/4 x 6 In. 395.00
Basting Spoon, Cursive Monogram Stem, John Wm. Blake, 1824, 11 1/2 In. 350.00
Beaker, Raised Beaded Banding, Bright Cut Design, E. & J. Barnard, 4 1/8 In. 230.00
Box, Allover Chinoiserie Scenes, Velvet Interior, George V, 1918, 10 x 8 In. 1840.00
Breakfast Set, Victorian, Edward Barnard & Sons, 1871, 16 Piece 3450.00
Candelabrum is listed in its own category.
Candlesticks are listed in their own category.
Cann, Presentation, George II, Fuller White, 1757 .... 1380.00
Cann, Scrolled Handle, Baluster Form, George III, John Langlands, 1760, 5 In. 1000.00
Cann, Scrolled Handle, George III, Charles Hougham, 1784, 5 In. 1000.00
Champagne Bucket, Cover, Georgian, Chased Flutes, Handles, 1805, 9 5/8 In. 6325.00
Cheese Scoop, Carved Ivory Handle, William & Samuel Knight, 1814 .... 350.00
Cigarette Case, Russian Enameled Cross Pendant, Birmingham, 1876, 4 In. 575.00
Cigarette Case, Vermeil, 2 Headed Eagle Crest, Matchbox End, George V, 4 In. 488.00
Coaster, Wine, Openwork Gallery, Ruby Glass Liner, John Emes, 1801, 4 Piece 5750.00
Coffeepot, John Langlands, Newcastle, George II, 1757 .... 3105.00
Creamer, Helmet Form, Engraved Design, London Marks, 1796 .... 220.00
Creamer, Swirl Pattern, Floral Design, George III, Edward Reid, 1768, 4 1/2 In. 385.00
Cruet Set, Mushroom Stoppers, Cut Crystal Bottles, R. & S. Hannell, 1808 .... 750.00
Cruet Set, Salt, Pepper Pot, Mustard, Scrolled Wire, Silver Balls Below Rims 632.00
Cup, Cover, George III Style, Serpent Handles, Classical Foliage, Lambert & Co. 4600.00
Cup, Cover, Handles Rising From Grape Leaves, R. Emes & E. Barnard, 1819 .... 3105.00
Dish, Cover, Gadroon Borders, Coronet Handle, Emes & Barnard, 1822, 64 Oz. 5750.00
Dish, Cover, Gadroon Rims, Cushion Shape, Richard Cooke, 1803, 11 1/4 In. 9200.00
Dish, Vegetable, Cover, Straight Gadroon Rims, Handles, 1805, 108 Oz. 11500.00
Fish Service, Vine Engraved Blade, Ivory Reeded Handle, Box, Sheffield, 1863 .... 1150.00
Fish Slice, 1821, 4 Troy Oz. 132.00
Frame, Picture, Quadruple, Birmingham, 1904, 6 1/4 In. 950.00
Goblet, Urn Bowl, Repousse Hunting Scene, Footed, Robert Hennell, 8 1/4 In. 863.00
Gravy Ladle, King's Pattern, Hayne & Carter, 1854 .... 275.00
Gravy Ladle, King's Pattern, William Bateman II, 1824 .... 300.00
Inkstand, 2 Pen Wells, 2 Silver Covered Ink Pots, Paul Storr, 1813, 10 1/4 In. 7150.00
Inkstand, Center Seal Box, Taper Stick, Extinguisher, 2 Inserts, E. Barnard, 1843 ...... 2070.00
Inkstand, Foliate Scroll Borders, Cut Glass Ink Pot, 1905, 6 In. 127.00
Inkstand, George III, 2 Glass Wells, Paul Storr, 1813, 10 In. ....*Illus* 7150.00
Inkstand, Hinged Flat Cover, 3 Glass Liners, 1912, 12 1/2 In. 3450.00
Inkstand, Pierced Foliage, Taper Stick, R. & J. & S. Garrard, 1827, 15 In. 8050.00
Inkstand, Winged Cherub's Head Crest, 3 Bottles, John Roberts, 1814, 7 1/4 In. 1265.00
Jug, George II, William Shaw, 1757 .... 275.00
Jug, Hot Water, Urn Finial, Hester Bateman, 1785, 12 1/4 In. 3450.00
Kettle Stand, George III, Gadrooned Rim, Lion Paw Footed, Tripod, P. Storr, 24 In. ... 1725.00
Kettle Stand, Georgian, Chased Floral Design, John Schofield, 1791, 14 In. 1092.00
Knife, Cheese, George Adams, 1852, 8 In. 120.00
Ladle, Georgian, Fiddle Shell Pattern, Corrington, 13 In. 220.00

Silver-English, Inkstand, George III, 2 Glass
Wells, Paul Storr, 1813, 10 In.

Always dry silver immediately after using it. The chemicals in the water may stain.

Ladle, Sauce, George Wintle, 1813, Pair	450.00
Ladle, Toddy, George II Style, Vine Leaf Base, Paul De Lamerie, 1736, 12 3/4 In.	7475.00
Marrow Scoop, George I Style, Elongated Stem, Thomas Pierce, 1724, 12 In.	2590.00
Mug, Scroll Handle, Monogrammed, Thomas Evesdon, 1720, 3 3/4 In.	488.00
Mustard, Bombe Round Body, 3 Shell Feet, G.N. & R.H., 1923, 2 1/4 In.	150.00
Mustard, Repousse Design, A.E. Warner, 4 In.	395.00
Napkin Rings are listed in their own category.	
Page Turner, George III, Shell Finial, T. Devonshire, W. Watkins, 1760, 12 In.	747.50
Pepper Castor, George II, John Delmster, 1757	650.00
Pepper Shaker, Samuel Wood, 1747, 5 In., Pair	440.00
Pin, Kilt, Horn, Orange Cairngorm, Stamp, 1875, 3 3/4 In.	525.00
Pitcher, Claret, Grapes & Flowers, Presentation, Wilkinson, c.1836, 13 In.	2200.00
Platter, Meat, George III Style, Gadroon Rim, Foliage, William Brown, 20 In.	4312.00
Platter, Meat, Scalloped Gadroon Rim, Arms, Crest Border, 1810, 120 Oz.	5750.00
Platter, Tree, George III Style, Shell Rim, William Frisbee, 1806, 25 1/2 In.	4312.00
Porringer & Spoon, Clothed Cherub On Thorny Branch, Omar Ramsden, 1938	2300.00
Punch Bowl, Engraved Arms & Crest, Gilt Interior, William Keatt, 1717, 9 In.	9775.00
Punch Bowl, Lobed, Ribbed Pear Shape, Grapevine Handles, 1878, C.S. Harris	5175.00
Rose Bowl, Square, Incurved At Corners, William Comyns, 1914, 15 1/4 In.	6900.00
Salt, George III, Gilt Interior, Monograms, Paul Storr, 1800, 11 Oz., Pair	3450.00
Salt, George IV, Repousse, John Bridge, 1824, 2 1/2 x 3 In., Pair	725.00
Salt Spoon, Peter & Ann Bateman, 1799, 4 1/4 In., Pair	75.00
Saltcellar, Engraved Viscount's Coronet, Paul Storr, 1810, 5 1/2 In., 4 Piece	8050.00
Saltcellar, Vignettes & Clusters Of Flowers, Angell, Son & Angell, 1838, 6 Pc.	4315.00
Salver, Applied Openwork Rim, Scroll Feet, Samuel Courtauld, 1759, 33 Oz.	2415.00
Salver, Circular, Gadroon Shaped Rim, 4 Shell Design Feet, Hannam & Crouch	8050.00
Salver, Contemporary Arms Center, George Hindmarsh, 1735, 10 3/4 In.	4900.00
Salver, George II, Scalloped Edge, Armorial Center, George Wickes, 9 1/2 In.	1200.00
Salver, George III, Daniel Smith & Roger Sharp, 1782, Pair	1725.00
Salver, Scroll & Shell Rim, Bird Inside Cartouche Center, E. C. Monogram	1055.00
Salver, Shell & Scroll Rim, Center Arms, Hugh Mills, 1750, 23 In.	7475.00
Sauce Ladle, Shell Handle, William Chawner, 1821, 7 1/4 In., Pair	85.00
Serving Spoon, 1806, 12 In.	350.00
Serving Spoon, Fiddle, Lamb On End, Thomas Byne, 1849, Pair	450.00
Serving Spoon, George III, Long Handle, William Eley, 1801, 12 1/2 In.	365.00
Snuffbox, Mottled Yellow Frog Shape, Hinged Cover, Metal Mount, 2 In.	2300.00
Stuffing Spoon, Georgian, Shell & Foliate, Engraved Crest, 1820, 11 1/2 In.	145.00
Stuffing Spoon, Monogrammed, Wm. Eley & Wm. Fearn, 1807	175.00
Stuffing Spoon, Thomas Baker, 1818, 12 In.	55.00
Sugar Tongs, Bright Cut Engraving, G.W., George III	85.00
Sugar Tongs, Bright Cut Engraving, Hester Bateman, Georgian	148.00
Sugar Tongs, Bright Cut, P. & A. Bateman, George III, 1815	110.00
Sugar Tongs, Carousing Man On Barrel At Top, Foliate Tops, 1850s	88.00
Sugar Tongs, Engraved Wriggle Work & Leaves, Fiddle Handles, W. Bateman .....*Illus*	110.00
Sugar Tongs, Faceted Edge, W.B. Bateman, George IV	90.00
Sugar Tongs, Open Handles, C.H., Georgian, 18th Century ....*Illus*	110.00

Sugar Tongs, Open Handles, London, George III, 1808 .... 95.00
Sugar Tongs, Plain, Fiddle At Top, Peter & William Bateman, George II 110.00
Tablespoon, Bright Cut, Hester Bateman, 1781, 8 1/2 In., 5 Piece 1250.00
Tablespoon, King's Honeysuckle, William Eaton, 1823 .... 90.00
Tablespoon, King's, George Adams, 1840 .... 105.00
Tablespoon, Old English, Eley & Fearn, 1798 .... 105.00
Tablespoon, Old English, Hester Bateman, 8 3/8 In., Pair 513.00
Tankard, Edward Pocock, c.1732, 4 In. 630.00
Tankard, Scroll Handle, Domed Cover, Cylindrical, George I, 1722, 9 In. 2070.00
Tankard, Shooting Scene, Pond View, John Moore, 1843, 29 Oz. 2070.00
Tankard, Thomas Moore, George II, 1759, 7 7/8 In. 2300.00
Tea & Coffee Set, Teniers Scenes, Baluster, E. Farrell, 1837, 152 Oz. 7475.00
Tea & Coffee Set, Victorian, W.R. Smily, 1874, 4 Piece 3795.00
Tea Caddy, Sliding Base, Slip-On-Cap, Octagonal, 1710, 7 Oz. 3162.00
Tea Caddy, Sliding Cover, Slip-On Cap, Gundry Roode, 1726, 5 3/8 In. 3737.00
Tea Urn, Lobe-Form, Conical Cover, Ivory Handles, George III, 18 In. 1840.00
Teapot, Hinged Cover, Engraved Portcullis Crest, Edward Barnard, 1835 .... 2070.00
Teapot, Inverted Pear Form, Sprays Of Foliage, Scrolled Rim, T. Whipham, 1750 ...... 1840.00
Teapot, On Lampstand, Contemporary Crests, W. Burwash & R. Sibley, 1811 .... 1725.00
Teapot, Pineapple Finial, Linen Fold Top, Henry Cowper, 1791, 6 1/2 In. 863.00
Teapot & Stand, Foliate Borders, Oval, Samuel & Edward Davenport, 1795 .... 1980.00
Toast Rack, Cartouche 330.00
Tongs, Queen's Pattern, William Chawner II, 1830 .... 200.00
Tray, Bacon Warming, Septimus & Jones, 1770, 8 3/8 In. 300.00
Tray, Chased Design, Footed, Shreve Stanwood, Round, 9 1/4 In. 70.00
Tumbler Cup, Gilt Interior, John Payne, 1753, 2 3/8 In. 2530.00
Tureen, Cover, Georgian, Gadrooned Rim, Ovoid-Form, Paul Storr, 1811, 13 In. 4312.00
Tureen, Engraved Dog On Cover, Sheffield, 15 In. 385.00
Tureen, Sauce, Cover, Boat Form, Gadroon Borders, A. Peterson, 10 In., Pair 3450.00
Wine Coasters, George III, Reeded, Waisted Sides, Wood Base, T. Robins, 1812 ...... 3162.00
SILVER-FRENCH, Centerpiece, Boat Form, Putti Handles, 4 Acanthus Scroll Feet, E. Tetard, 76 Oz. 5750.00
Centerpiece, Shallow Boat Form, Scrolled Acanthus Grips, Keller, 1900, 99 Oz. 5750.00
Coffeepot, 3 Hairy Paw Feet, Ornament & Tassel Spout, Rennes, 1753, 9 1/2 In. 2645.00
Coffeepot, Chased Design Of Musical Instruments & Acanthus, 8 1/2 In. 605.00
Condiment Set, Openwork Frames, Masks, Grapevine, Box, 1870, 31 Oz. 1725.00
Creamer, Cow 400.00
Dish, Vegetable, Cover, Lobed, Fluted Form, Monogrammed, Circular, 10 In., Pair 3450.00
Ewer, Empire Style, Applied Figures, Masks, Female Caryatid Handle, 13 In. 2185.00

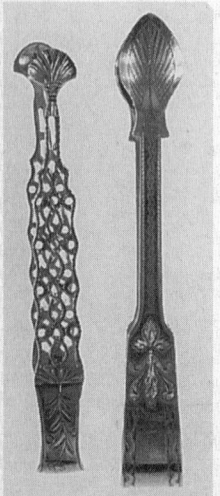

Discovered some old silver in the attic? Wash it with a brush in warm soapy water before you polish it. Dirt can scratch the silver.

Wrap a piece of white chalk in tissue paper and put it in your silver drawer. It will retard tarnish.

Silver-English, Sugar Tongs, Open Handles, C.H., Georgian, 18th Century
Silver-English, Sugar Tongs, Engraved Wriggle Work & Leaves,
Fiddle Handles, W. Bateman

Gilt Altar Set, Grapevine Border, Cruets With Stand, 9 5/8 In., Pair	3450.00
Ice Bowl, Pendant Icicle Rim, Rocky Surface, Mid-19th Century, 67 Oz.	4025.00
Tongs, Asparagus, Hinged, Christofle, Individual, 4 3/4 In. ....*Illus*	15.00
Tureen, Soup, Cover, Bud Finial, Bombe Oval Form, 1776, 13 In.	5462.00
Wine Cooler, Baluster Form, Trailing Flowers, Shell Grips, 1900, 11 3/4 In.	2587.00
SILVER-GERMAN, Beaker, Ribbon-Tied Swags, Sigmund Bierfreund, c.1680, 3 5/8 In.	1380.00
Box, Repousse Chased Design, Putti, Making Music, 19th Century, 6 In.	863.00
Bride's Basket, Cherub, Garland Of Roses, Swing Handle, Augsburg, 10 1/4 In.	745.00
Cake Basket, Pierced, Gilded Sides, Black Eagle In Center, 1775, 11 1/2 In.	8050.00
Casket, Frieze Of Dancing Cherubs, 4 Hoof Supports, 1870s, 10 1/2 In.	2875.00
Dish, Serving, Black Double Headed Eagle Holding Shields, 1775, 11 In.	6325.00
Ewer, Helmet Form, Harp-Shaped Handle, Hermannus Wilkin, 1741, 8 5/8 In.	5750.00
Figurine, Roosters, Head, Cast With Feathers, Applied Tail Feathers, 9 In., Pair	1035.00
Plate, Raised, Chased Leaf Form, 3-Dimensional Pond Lily, Art Nouveau, 10 In.	977.50
Pomander, Cruciform, 5 Sections, Piston Action, 1730s, 2 In.	2185.00
Tea & Coffee Set, Cartouches Of Putti, Birds On Foot, 6 In.	690.00
Tea & Coffee Set, Repousse Floral Design, Baluster, 8 In.	172.50
Tea Kettle, Stand, Domed Lid, Treen Handle, Sea Monster Spout, 15 In.	345.00
SILVER-HUNGARIAN, Horn Cigar Cutter, Mounted On Silver Boar's Head, 19th Century, 13 In.	4025.00
SILVER-IRISH, Jug, Beer, Pear Shape, Double Scroll Handle, John Laughlin, c.1760, 8 In.	3450.00
Jug, Engraved Armorials Within Cartouche, Matthew Walker, 1727, 9 1/4 In.	5750.00
Ladle, Sauce, Fiddle Thread Design, Engraved Dieu Ayde, T. Farnett, Pair	300.00
Serving Spoon, Slotted, Dublin, 1806, 13 In.	425.00
Stuffing Spoon, George IV, J. Buckton, 1820, Pair	287.00
Sugar Basket & Milk Jug, Dublin, G.W. Mark, 1799	1050.00
Tray, Coffee, Straight Gadroon Rim, Shamrock, Oak Spray Border, Le Bass, 1810	8050.00
SILVER-ITALIAN, Bowl, Shell Form, Dolphin Footed, 9 In.	195.00
Tea & Coffee Set, Lobed Body Baluster, Chased Leaf, 14 1/8 In.	2875.00
Tea & Coffee Set, Vase Form, Greyhound Handles, 98 Oz., 4 Piece	3450.00
Vase, Altar, Chased Foliage, Swags Of Flowers, G Over BB, 10 1/2 In., Pair	2300.00
Vase, Altar, Chased Stiff Leaves, Flutes & Lobes, 9 In., Pair	2875.00
SILVER-JAPANESE, Box, Relief Fan, Floral Design, Poetic Inscription On Interior, 2 1/2 In.	1705.00
Tea Set, Wrought, Gourd Form, Twisted Roots Handles, 1895, 3 Piece	2070.00
SILVER-MEXICAN, Bowl, Art Nouveau Style Feet, 6 1/2 In.	95.00
Bucket, Ice, Gadrooned Edge, Double Ring Handle, Tongs, Sterki, 7 1/2 In.	258.00
Caddy, Table, Carriage, L. Maciel, 17 In.	1290.00
Cocktail Shaker, Floral Band, L. Maciel, 11 1/2 In.	192.50
Coffee Set, Ball Finials, Oval, W. Spratling, 1940s, 44 Oz., 3 Piece	2875.00
Coffee Set, Colonial Revival, Heather Sterling, 62 Troy Oz., 3 Piece	315.00
Cup, Rosewood Base, Cylindrical, Demitasse, W. Spratling, 2 In.	460.00
Dish, Swan, Sterling Silver, 14 1/4 In.	137.50
Gong, Table, Mayan Symbols Make Frame & Base, 8 In.	300.00
Pitcher, Water, Spherical Body, Rosewood Handle, W. Spratling, 5 In.	1495.00
Plaque, Wall, Aztec Figures, Wood, W. Spratling, 4 In., Pair	690.00
Salt & Pepper, Men With Sombreros	39.00
Salver, Repousse Floral Rim, L. Maciel, Round, 16 1/2 In.	302.00
Sugar & Creamer, Angular Handles, Bulbous, W. Spratling, 1931-1945, 3 In.	1380.00
Sugar & Creamer, Aztec Design, Tane, 9 5/8 In.	210.00
Tea Set, A. G. F., 8-In. Coffeepot, 5 Piece	385.00
Tray, 2 Handles, Oval, 23 In.	795.00
Tray, Shaped Gadrooned Rim, Oval, 16 x 22 In.	605.00
SILVER-PERUVIAN, Tea Set, 5 Piece	1100.00

SILVER-RUSSIAN. Russian silver is marked with the Cyrillic, or Russian, alphabet. The numbers 84, 88, or 91 indicate the silver content. Russian silver may be higher or lower than sterling standard. Other marks indicate maker, assayer, or city of manufacture. Many pieces of silver made in Russia are decorated with enamel. Faberge pieces are listed in their own category.

SILVER-RUSSIAN, Basket, Sugar, Tongs, Blue, Green Foliage, Swing Handle, 1910, 5 In. Diam.	1955.00
Beaker, Rococo Shellwork, Scrolls, Foliage, 1760, 8 1/2 In.	2875.00
Bowl, Silver-Gilt, Cream Upper Border, Apple Green Lower Border, 6 3/8 In.	8625.00
Bowl, Silver-Gilt, Peacocks, Foliage Gilded Ground, White, 1900, 5 1/4 In.	4312.00

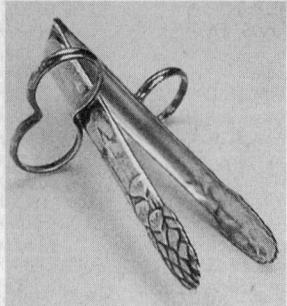

Cigar ashes, baking soda, and water mix into a paste that is good for cleaning silver.

Silver-French, Tongs, Asparagus, Hinged,
Christofle, Individual, 4 3/4 In.

Box, Cigarette, Bright Cut Florals & Birds On Hinged Cover, Vartan 345.00
Box, Gilded Silver, Hinged Dome Cover, Scrolled Foliage, 1900, 3 3/4 In. 2587.00
Bread Tray, Rope Twist Handles, Wire Footed, P. Ovchinnikov, 1874, 14 3/4 In. 5420.00
Case, Cigarette, Pan-Slavic Design, Gemstone Thumbpiece, c.1908, 4 1/4 In. 885.00
Case, Shell Shape, Engraved Russian Saying, 3 1/2 x 2 1/4 In. 75.00
Cigarette Case, Diamond Cross, Symbols, Vermeil, Rectangular, 4 In. 1950.00
Cigarette Case, Raised Fluted Design, Enamel Heraldic Device 460.00
Cigarette Case, Swan Floating On Pond, Blue Beaded Border, 1900, 3 In. 2070.00
Cup, 3 Handles, Enameled Floral, Chinese Red Ground, Cable Rim, 4 1/4 In. 8050.00
Fish Server, Engraved Fish Design, Monogram, Khlebnikov, 1879, 12 1/2 In. 320.00
Holder, Tea Cup, Pair 115.00
Holder, Tea Glass, Galloping Troika Front, Angular Handle, 1900, 5 In. 805.00
Holder, Tea, Enameled Monogram, Etched Glass, I. Khlebnikov, 4 In., 8 Piece 6210.00
Jewel Box, Red Fabric Interior, 4 Bun Feet, 1875, Rectangular, 3 1/2 In. 1265.00
Kovsh, Vermeil, Enameled Scrolling Foliate Design, Bracket Handle, 3 1/2 In. 1035.00
Mug, Rope Twist Rim, Bracket Handle, Engraved 1891-1916, 4 In. 250.00
Pitcher, Water, Cut Glass, Silver Neck Mount, Hinged Cover, 1900, 11 1/2 In. 1955.00
Samovar, Angular Handles, Ivory Grips, 1892, 122 Oz. 8625.00
Samovar, Campana Shape, Angular Handles, Pierced Spigot, 1900, 97 Oz. 9200.00
Snuffbox, Neo-Rococo Shell, Scroll Thumbpiece, Gold, 1845, 2 3/8 In. 2875.00
Spoon, Champleve Foliate Design, Monogram, Oval Bowl, 5 1/2 In., Pair 220.00
Tankard, Gilded Silver, Enamel, Panels Of Foliage, Geometric, 1877, 6 1/8 In. 7480.00
Tazza, Champleve, Shallow Bowl, P. Ovchinnikov, Pre-1896, 8 In. 2070.00
Tazza, Gilded Silver, Apron Enameled With Foliage, Domed Base, 1887, 7 In. 5465.00
Teapot, Enamel, Fish, Birds, Dolphin Design, Hinged Cover, Water Flowers, 5 In. 3162.00
Teapot, Enameled, Floral, Scrolled Foliage, Blue Beaded Border, 1890, 5 In. 4312.00
Teapot, Inlaid Enamel Floral Bouquets, Ovoid-Form, Khlebnikov, 4 1/2 In. 920.00
Tray, Silver, Grapevine Border, Openwork Scroll Handles, 1841, 18 1/4 In. 1035.00
Vodka Set, Enameled Foliage, Tray, M. Semenova, 1899-1908, 7 Piece 7130.00
Wine Cup, Globular Bowl, Foliate, Bracket Handle, Footed, 2 In., Pair 140.00
SILVER-SCOTTISH, Beaker, Band Of Grapes & Wheat Design, Shell, Scrollwork, 1762, 3 In., Pair 2875.00
Hash Spoon, Queen Anne Style, Curved Stem, Edward Penman, 1710, 13 In. 1725.00
Sauceboat, Gadrooned Body, Acanthus Scrolling Handle, Edinburgh, 1816 .... 200.00
Snuffbox, Mounted Horn, 19th Century, 2 & 3 In., Pair 230.00
Tea & Coffee Set, Water Urn, Handles, Mackay & Chisholm, 1878, 5 Piece 6800.00
Tureen, Soup, Cover, Rococo Ornament Arms, 4 Acanthus Feet, 1819, 74 Oz. 6325.00

SILVER-STERLING. Sterling silver is made with 925 parts silver out of
1,000 parts of metal. The word *sterling* is a quality guarantee used in
the United States after about 1860. The word was used much earlier in
England and Ireland. Pieces listed here are not identified by country.
Other pieces of sterling quality silver are listed under Silver-American,
Silver-English, etc.

SILVER-STERLING, Ashtray, Triple Shell, Footed, Art Nouveau, Marked, 4 1/4 x 4 1/4 In. . 95.00
Basket, Bread, Arched Handle 105.00
Bowl, Grape Design, 9 x 4 5/8 In. 495.00
Box, Engraved Foliage Arabesque On Lid, Wood Lined, 7 1/4 In. 220.00

Card Case, 1897, 5 5/8 x 2 1/2 In. 120.00
Case, Cigarette, Hammered 32.50
Chain, Watch, Mother-Of-Pearl Knife Fob 275.00
Clip, Bib, Chicks, Pair 30.00
Coffee & Tea Set, Fairfax, 5 Piece 1385.00
Coffeepot, Bird Finial, Spiral Fluted, Hoof Feet, Maltese, c.1800, 9 In. 4315.00
Comb, Hair, Male & Female Tops, Wooden Box, Louis McMillen, 1950s, Pair 1150.00
Creamer, Cow, Flip-Up Back, Embossed Beetle, 4 1/2 In. 258.00
Figurine, Pig, Sitting, Francis Randall Appleton, 1902 . . . . 3300.00
Fruit Set, Victorian, Mother-Of-Pearl Handles, Case 545.00
Holder, Bib, Rabbit 38.00
Jam Set, Acorn Design, Monogram, Crystal, Cover, Underplate, Spoon, 3 Piece 95.00
Mirror, Hand, Art Nouveau, Vines, Flowers, Ornate, Beveled, 11 x 7 In. 80.00
Pill Box, Turquoise Stone, Indian Symbols 42.00
Relish, Divided, Foliage Scroll Rim, Industria Perurna, Oval, 11 5/8 x 17 5/8 In. 165.00
Salt Basket, Enamel Bristol Insert, Pierced 40.00
Salt Dip, Mexican Design, With Spoon . . . . .35.00 to 60.00
Spoon, Souvenir, see Souvenir category.
Spoon-Straw, Heart Shape, 12 Piece 100.00
Tea Caddy, Spoon, Leaves & Vines Overlay 165.00
Tea Set, Chased Floral Design, 19th Century, 5 Piece 1725.00
Tea Set, Hand Chased, 5 Piece 3570.00
Tray, Classical Revival Urn & Swag Border, Center Date, 1917, 18 3/4 In. 490.00
Vase, Art Nouveau Floral, Frank Herschede, 20 In. 3740.00
Vinaigrette, Book Shape, 1851 . . . . 525.00
SILVER-SWEDISH, Box, Portrait, Enameled, Young Lady On Cover, Red Stones, 1820, 3 5/8 In. 6900.00
Wine, Tiered Stem, Hallmark, 1901, 2 1/2-In. Bowl 73.00

SINCLAIRE cut glass was made by H.P. Sinclaire and Company of
Corning, New York, between 1905 and 1929. He cut glass made at
other factories until 1920. Pieces were made of crystal as well as
amber, blue, green, or ruby glass. Only a small percentage of Sinclaire
glass is marked with the S in a wreath.

Bowl, Diamonds, Floral Panels, Silver Threads, Signed, 12 In. 1225.00
Candlestick, Threaded Stem & Foot, Celeste Blue Top, Topaz Bobeche, 9 In., Pair 250.00
Clock, Chain Of Hobstars & Fans, Moon Border, 5 1/4 In. 500.00
Compote, Engraved Garlands & Florals, Amber, Signed, 8 In. 75.00
Cruet, Gooseberries & Daisies On Body & Stopper, Signed, 7 3/4 In. 185.00
Decanter, Thistle & Grape, 6 1/2 In. 95.00
Pitcher, Prince Albert, Zipper Cut Handle, Signed, 8 In. 425.00
Plate, Stars & Pillar, 24 Point Star Center, Rayed To Band Of Hobstars, 10 In. 565.00
Tazza, Topaz, Cut & Engraved, Signed, 8 x 4 In. 110.00
Vase, Allover Honeycomb, Intaglio Engraved Ovals Of Flowers, Signed, 12 In. 650.00

SKIING, see Sports category.

SLAG GLASS resembles a marble cake. It can be streaked with different
colors. There were many types made from about 1880. Pink slag was
an American Victorian product made by Harry Barstow and Thomas
E.A. Dugan at Indiana, Pennsylvania. Purple and blue slag were made
in American and English factories. Red slag is a very late Victorian and
twentieth-century glass. Other colors are known but are of less importance to the collector. New versions of chocolate glass and colored slag
glass are being made.

Blue, Lamp, Birds, Flowers Motif, Early 20th Century, 21 In. 671.00
Blue, Sugar Shaker, Creased Teardrop 155.00
Caramel slag is listed in the Chocolate Glass category.
Pink, Cruet, Inverted Fan & Feather 1400.00
Pink, Toothpick, Inverted Fan & Feather . . . . .575.00 to 1100.00
Purple, Bowl, Ruffled 85.00
Purple, Celery, Jeweled Star, Challinor, Taylor, 1880 . . . . .55.00 to 125.00
Purple, Mug, Cat On Base 105.00
Purple, Plate, Lattice, 12 In. 85.00

Purple, Platter, Notched Daisy, Oval 75.00
Purple, Platter, Tam O'Shanter & Southbar Johnny, Oval 75.00
Purple, Toothpick, Imperial 30.00

SLEEPY EYE collectors look for anything bearing the image of the nineteenth-century Indian chief with the drooping eyelid. The Sleepy Eye
Milling Co., Sleepy Eye, Minnesota, used his portrait in advertising
from 1883 to 1921. It offered many premiums, including stoneware
and pottery steins, crocks, bowls, mugs, and pitchers, all decorated
with the famous profile of the Indian. The popular pottery was made
by Western Stoneware, Weir Pottery Company, and other companies
long after the flour mill went out of business in 1921. Reproductions
of the pitchers are being made today. The original pitchers came in
only five sizes: 4 inches, 5 1/4 inches, 6 1/2 inches, 8 inches, and 9
inches. The Sleepy Eye image was also used by companies unrelated
to the flour mill.

Barrel, Flour, Wooden, 1920s 2250.00
Box, Butter . . . . .25.00 to 35.00
Box, Pankako, Wooden 675.00
Clock, Sleepy Eye In Gold Letters 2850.00
Cookbook, Loaf Of Bread Shape 120.00
Crock, Indian Head On Side 550.00
Cup, Whitehall 550.00
Door Push Bar, Sign 675.00
Hot Plate, Blue On White 4100.00
Label, Barrel 250.00
Match Holder, Chalkware 185.00
Mug, Blue On White, 4 1/2 In. 230.00
Mug, Blue On White, Monmouth Mark, 4 1/4 In. 195.00
Mug, Monmouth Mark, 1976, 4 1/4 . . . .   25.00
Mug Set, Commemorative, 1976-1981, 6 Piece 250.00
Paddle, Canoe 200.00
Pie Plate, Hummer 325.00
Pitcher, Blue Floral, Vine Design, Gray Stoneware, 7 1/2 In.   115.00
Pitcher, Cream & Blue, 8 In. 350.00
Pitcher, Gray & Blue, 4 In. 200.00
Pitcher, Indian Among Trees, Cream & Blue 200.00
Pitcher, Indian Ceremony Scene, 8 In. 250.00
Pitcher, No. 1, Blue On Gray, 4 In. 200.00
Pitcher, No. 1, Blue On White, 4 In. 260.00
Pitcher, No. 2, Blue On White, 5 1/4 In. 225.00
Pitcher, No. 3, Blue On White, 6 1/2 In. 300.00
Pitcher, No. 3, Green, 6 1/2 In. 550.00
Pitcher, No. 4, Blue On Cream, 8 In. 350.00
Pitcher, No. 4, Blue On White, 8 In. 180.00
Pitcher, No. 4, Brown On Yellow, 8 In. . . . . .830.00 to 850.00
Pitcher, No. 4, Green On White, 8 In. 2200.00
Pitcher, No. 5, Blue On White, 9 In. . . . . .350.00 to 450.00
Pitcher, No. 5, Brown On White, 9 In. 5750.00
Pitcher Set, No. 5, 6 Large Mugs, Blue On White, 7 Piece 1750.00
Plate, Centennial, 1972 . . . .   30.00
Plate, Commemorative, 1976 . . . .   120.00
Plate, Commemorative, 1977 . . . .   40.00
Plate, Commemorative, 1979 . . . .   17.50
Plate, Commemorative, 1980 . . . .   15.00
Plate, Commemorative, 1981 . . . .   14.00
Plate, Commemorative, 1982 . . . .   16.66
Plate, Commemorative, 1984 . . . .   15.00
Plate, Commemorative, 1987 . . . .   35.00
Plate, Commemorative, 1988 . . . .   30.00
Plate, Commemorative, 1989 . . . .   45.00
Plate, Commemorative, 1990 . . . .   30.00

Postcard, Mill Scene 25.00
Sign, Flour, Self-Framed, Tin, 19 x 13 In. 2805.00
Sign, Old Sleepy Eye, Indian, Yellow Ground, Early 1900s, 14 x 24 In. 450.00
Sign, Paper, Red On Yellow 475.00
Stein, Blue On White, 7 3/4 In. 425.00
Stein, Blue, 7 3/4 In. ....525.00 to 1475.00
Stein, Brown On White, 7 3/4 In. 1300.00
Stein, Brown On Yellow, 7 3/4 In. ....1425.00 to 1850.00
Stein, Green On White, 7 3/4 In. 1750.00
Sugar Bowl, Blue On White ....310.00 to 575.00
Vase, Cattail, Blue On White, 8 1/2 In. ....350.00 to 725.00
Vase, Cattail, Blue, 8 1/2 In. 525.00
Vase, Cattail, Brown On Yellow, 9 In. ....500.00 to 900.00
Vase, Cattail, Green On White, 9 In. 8400.00
Vase, Cattail, Indian Portrait, Blue On White, 8 1/2 In. 420.00
Vase, Cattails, Gray On Blue, 9 In. 475.00
Vase, Indian, Cattails, Blue, Gray, 9 In. ....165.00 to 250.00

SLIPWARE is named for *slip*, a thin mixture of clay and water, about the
consistency of sour cream, which is applied to pottery for decoration.
It is a very old method of making pottery and is still in use.

    Charger, Blue, White Floral Edge, Trees & Fawn Center, 13 In. 285.00
    Cup, Fuddling, 3 Pear Shaped Vessels, Loop Handle, Yellow Glaze, 1739, 2 5/8 In. 3740.00
    Mug, Redware, 4-S Scrollneck Design, Handle, England, 4 In. 920.00
    Porringer, Brown Combed Design, Yellow Glaze, England, 18th Century, 5 1/16 In. 1380.00

SLOT MACHINES are included in the Coin-Operated Machine category.

SMITH BROTHERS glass was made after 1878. Alfred and Harry Smith
had worked for the Mt. Washington Glass Company in New Bedford,
Massachusetts, for seven years before going into their own shop. They
made many pieces with enamel decoration.   *Smith Bros. Co.*

Biscuit Jar, Blue Pansies On Cream, Swirled Rib Mold, Square, 8 3/4 In. 715.00
Biscuit Jar, Roses, Raised Gold Leaves & Outlining, Melon Ribbed, Handle, 7 In. 880.00
Bowl, Apple Blossom & Beaded Top, Melon Ribbed, 5 1/2 In. 355.00
Bowl, Cover, Young Girl's Head, Silver Bail, 3 3/4 x 4 In. 595.00
Bowl, Moss Rose Design, Beige Ground, Melon Ribbed, 4 x 9 In. 675.00
Bowl, Prunus Design, Allover Gold, Beaded Rim, Melon Ribbed, 6 x 3 In. 375.00
Cracker Jar, Cover, Pansies, Barrel Shape, Signed, 7 x 5 In. 750.00
Cracker Jar, Gold Leaf, Floral Design, Beige Ground, Pairpoint, 6 x 6 1/2 In. 330.00
Cracker Jar, Purple Wisteria Sprays, Leaves, Vines, Melon Ribbed, 8 1/2 In. 330.00
Humidor, Pansy Design, Cream Ground, Melon Ribbed, 6 1/2 In. 850.00
Jar, Ivory & Polychrome Floral, Melon Ribbed, Rampant Lion Mark, 4 In. 170.00
Plate, Santa Maria, Beige & Orange Ship, 7 3/4 In. 595.00
Rose Bowl, Daisy Sprays, Beige Ground, Beaded, Bulbous, 4 1/2 In. 325.00
Rose Bowl, Jeweled Prunus, Cream Ground, Beaded, Signed, 2 1/4 x 3 In. 285.00
Sugar & Creamer, Silver Plated Cover, Violets, 3 3/4 In. 750.00
Sugar Shaker, Jeweler's Cover, Shasta Daisy, Melon Ribbed, 5 1/2 In. 495.00
Sugar Shaker, Wild Rose & Blue Leaves, Pillar Ribbed, 5 3/4 In. 495.00
Toothpick, White Ground, Pale Pink, Green Floral Design, Blue Top 110.00
Toothpick, Wild Rose & Blue Leaves, Beaded, Pillar Ribbed, 2 1/4 In. 250.00
Vase, Clusters Of Wisteria Blossoms, Raised Gold Vine, 8 3/4 In. 750.00
Vase, Cover, Autumn Ivy Leaves, Raised Gold Vine, Melon, 3 1/2 In. 630.00
Vase, Daisies, Long Leafy Stems, Gilt & Enameled Rim, Marked, 4 1/2 In. 220.00
Vase, Pansies, Beaded Edge, 4 1/4 In. 250.00
Vase, Pink & Lilac Carnations, Gold Outlining, Dotted Rim, Global, 4 In. 165.00
Vase, Rampant Lion, Enameled Florals, Rope Rim, 6 In. 295.00
Vase, Stork, Pink Ground, Petticoat, Stamped, 5 1/2 In., Pair 850.00
Vase, Verona, Irises, Gold Trim, Interior Ribbed, 12 1/2 In. 550.00
Vase, White Pond Lily, Pink Ground, 1870s, 7 In., Pair 375.00
Vase, White Wisteria, Gold Trim, Apricot Ground, Pinched, 5 1/4 In. 375.00
Vase, Winter Scene, Petticoat Ring, Beige-Gray Ground, 8 1/2 In., Pair 1200.00
Vase, Wisteria Blossoms, Raised Gold Vine, 8 3/4 In. 750.00

SNOW BABIES, made from bisque and spattered with glitter sand, were first manufactured in 1864 by Hertwig and Company of Thuringia. Other German and Japanese companies copied the Hertwig designs. Originally, Snow Babies were made of candy and used as Christmas decorations. There are also Snow Babies tablewares made by Royal Bayreuth. Copies of the small Snow Babies figurines are being made today and can easily confuse the collector.

Dish, Sledding, Small, Marked	75.00
Figurine, 3 Babies On Sled, Germany, c.1910, 3 In.	225.00
Figurine, Dog, Licking Cheek, 2 In.	200.00
Figurine, Girl On Sled, Arms Out, 1 1/2 In.	145.00
Figurine, On Sled, Yellow, Bisque, 2 In.	200.00
Figurine, On Wooden Skis, 1 1/2 In.	115.00
Figurine, Riding Bear, 1 1/2 In.	115.00
Figurine, Sitting, Germany	120.00
Figurine, Standing, Germany	120.00

SNUFF BOTTLES are listed in the Bottle category.

SNUFFBOXES held snuff. Taking snuff was popular long before cigarettes became available. The gentleman or lady would take a small pinch of the ground tobacco or snuff in the fingers, then sniff it and sneeze. Snuffboxes were made of many materials, including gold, silver, enameled metal, and wood. Most snuffboxes date from the late eighteenth or early nineteenth centuries.

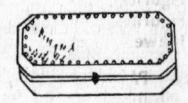

Brass, Double-Sided Compartments, Mirror, Th. Hallgren, 4 1/4 x 1 7/8 In.	175.00
Brass, Hinged Lid, Punched Design, J. Simpson, 18th Century, 2 3/4 In.	225.00
Burl, Tortoiseshell Interior, Banquet On Shipscene, France, 3 3/8 In.	220.00
Capo-Di-Monte, Putti Design, Shield Form, 2 1/2 In.	190.00
Cloisonne, Dragons, Blue Ground, 3 1/2 In.	85.00
Enamel, Allover On Exterior, Interior Of Cover, Puce Harbor Scene, 1750, 3 In.	2590.00
Enamel, Front Painted With Peasants, Rustic Settings, Gilt Mounts, Germany, 3 In.	1095.00
Gold, Enameled, Allegorical Figure Of Justice On Lid, Blue, Gray, White Border	5750.00
Gold, Enameled, Alpine Lake Scene On Lid, Gold Foliage, Switzerland, 1815, 4 In.	13800.00
Gold, Enameled, Cupid Looking Over Shoulder, Geometric Border, Switzerland	5750.00
Gold, Enameled, Foliate Scroll Design, Translucent Red, Europe	6900.00
Gold, Enameled, Lady In Forest Setting With 3 Doves, Pale Green Ground, Oval	4600.00
Gold, Enameled, Pearl Border, Translucent Red Inner Border, 1780, 2 1/2 In.	9200.00
Gold, Enameled, Spray Of Flowers, Translucent Red Ground, Green Sides, 4 In.	5750.00
Gold, Enameled, Stylized Foliage Border, Translucent Red, Switzerland, 3 In.	3450.00
Gold, Enameled, Waterfall Scene, Seed Pearl Border, Royal Blue, Switzerland, 3 In.	10925.00
Gold, Hinged Lid, Artichoke Design, Pierre Drais, 1731, 1 3/4 In.	4310.00
Gold, Hinged Lid, Scroll Border, Shellwork, Leaves, Faceted Topaz Quartz, 2 In.	2300.00
Gold, Purse Form, Tulip, Flowerhead Border, Switzerland, 1820, 2 3/4 In.	8340.00
Horn, Carved, Sterling Silver, Form Of Hedgehog, 18th Century	460.00
Inset, Bronze, Gilt, Burled Wood, Louis XVIII Profile On Cover, 2 3/4 In.	690.00
Inset, Burl, On Cover, Burl, Engraving Of Women, 2 In.	50.00
Iron, Black, Gold Design, Give Me Freedom, Give Me Love, Japanned, 3 1/2 In.	325.00
Papier-Mache, Guglielmo Pitt Brass Medallion, 3 3/4 In.	800.00
Papier-Mache, Lafayette Portrait, Blue Uniform, Mustard Ground	950.00
Papier-Mache, Painted Portrait On Lid, 3 1/4 In.	120.00
Papier-Mache, Scalloped Form, Red Marbleized Design, Black Ground, 4 x 2 In.	120.00
Papier-Mache, Transfer Design, Political Cartoon, Ebonized Case, 4 x 2 In.	145.00
Pewter, Farm Scene & Pheasants, 2 5/8 In.	90.00
Porcelain, Lovers, Venus & Cupid, Silver Border, Scrolled Feet, England, 3 3/4 In.	275.00
Silver, Regency, Vermeil, C-Scroll & Flower Border, John Lacy, 1834, 2 x 3 1/2 In.	980.00
Silver Plate, HCJ Monogram	65.00
Tole, Colorful Flower, Hinged Top, 1/2 x 1 1/2 In.	80.00
Tortoiseshell, Benjamin Franklin Painting On Ivory, France, 18th Century, 3 1/4 In.	8250.00
Tortoiseshell, Engraved Silver Lid, Georgian, Robert Gary & Sons, Scotland	315.00
Tortoiseshell, Ivory, Dyed Design, France, 3 3/4 x 1 1/16 In.	550.00
Tortoiseshell, Rectangular, 2 1/2 In.	120.00
Wood, Carved, Inlaid Brass, Mother Of Pearl, 3 3/8 In.	220.00

SOAPSTONE is a mineral that was used for foot warmers or griddles because of its heat-retaining properties. Soapstone was carved into figurines and bowls in many countries in the nineteenth and twentieth centuries. Most of the soapstone seen today is from China or Japan. It is still being carved in the old styles.

Bookends, Foo Dog, Signed	135.00
Bookends, Hoti, 7 1/2 In.	137.00
Brush Rest, Mountain Landscape Design, Pavilions, 1900, 6 In.	66.00
Figurine, 2 Fighting Lions, 6 1/4 In.	302.00
Figurine, 2 Toads, Chestnut, Light Green, 7 In.	460.00
Figurine, Buddha, On Base, 11 3/4 In.	80.00
Figurine, Dragon, 8 In.	40.00
Figurine, Hen, 3 Chicks, Early 20th Century, 7 In.	120.00
Figurine, Joss And Attendant In A Grotto, Tricolored, 7 1/2 In.	423.00
Figurine, Lohan, Standing With Scroll In Hands, With Foo Lion, 8 1/2 In.	302.00
Figurine, Oriental Men, Carrying Dragon, 6 x 6 In.	103.50
Figurine, Pagodas, Trees, 7 x 4 In.	35.00
Figurine, Seal, Mountain Shape, Lotus & Leaves, Low Relief, 19th Century, 2 In.	211.00
Figurine, Shou Lao And A Crane, 6 1/8 In.	133.00
Inkwell, Engraved F.R. Under Crown On Cover, Green, 1746	650.00

SOFT PASTE is a name for a type of pottery. Although it looks very much like porcelain, it is a chemically different material. Most of the soft-paste wares were made in the early nineteenth century. Other pieces may be listed under Gaudy Dutch or Leeds.

Basket, c.1785, 9 In.	525.00
Bowl, Castle Scenery, Medium Blue Transfer, 13 1/4 In.	357.00
Cup & Saucer, Handleless	395.00
Cup & Saucer, Strawberry, Allover Pattern Inside & Out, Handleless	195.00
Cup Plate, King's Rose, Luster, Floral & Vine, 4 1/2 In.	165.00
Dish, Leaf Form, Blue Feather Edge	195.00
Jardiniere, Country Scenes, Creil, Floral Border, Black Transfer, 6 1/8 x 6 7/8 In.	115.00
Plate, Imari Style, Tiger, France, 1700s, 8 In.	125.00

SOUVENIRS of a trip—what could be more fun? Our ancestors enjoyed the same thing and souvenirs were made for almost every location. Most of the souvenir pottery and porcelain pieces of the nineteenth century were made in England or Germany, even if the picture showed a North American scene. In the twentieth century, the souvenir china business seems to have gone to the manufacturers in Japan, Taiwan, Hong Kong, England, and America. Another popular souvenir item is the souvenir spoon, made of sterling or silver plate. These are usually made in the country pictured on the spoon. Related pieces may be found in the Coronation and World's Fair categories.

Ashtray, Jamaica, Triangular, Bellaire, 6 1/2 In.	65.00
Ashtray, Portofino, Redondo Beach, Calif., Aluminum	7.00
Bandanna, Buffalo Bill Picture Corner, Silk, Blue Ground, 1895-1910, 28 In.	1000.00
Bandanna, Memorial Hall, Centennial, 1876	98.00
Beanie, Air Races, Dayton, Oh., Yellow, Blue Felt Triangle Sections, 1930	67.00
Buttonhook, Shoehorn, Washington Irving	35.00
Coin, Amelia Earhart, Embossed Portrait, Aware City, Philadelphia, 1932	35.00
Cup & Saucer, Santa Catalina Island, Porcelain	10.00
Figurine, Boys Town, 7 In.	45.00
Figurine, Will Rogers, Metal, Small	50.00
Flashlight, Ringling Bros., Circus Tiger, Figural	20.00
Handkerchief, United Fruit Ship, Panama Canal, Silk	12.00
Jug, Ironstone, Cleveland, Ohio, Floral, Blue & Gray, Belgium	265.00
Knife, Statue Of Liberty, 1940s	15.00
Mask, Hawaiian, Body Size, 1950s	50.00
Pennant, Dog Land, Florida, 12 In.	65.00
Pillow Cover, New York City, Silk	20.00
Pin, National Western Stock Show, Ribbon, 1949	125.00

Souvenir, Pin, Soviet Battleship,
Star & Sickle, Missiles, Gold, Enamel

Pin, Second Annual National Livestock Convention, Ribbon, 1899	150.00
Pin, Soviet Battleship, Star & Sickle, Missiles, Gold, Enamel ....*Illus*	20.00
Pin, TWA, Junior Hostess, Brass, Winged	9.00
Pin, Well Done, Col. John Glenn, First American In Orbit, 1962	24.00
Plate, Hawaii, Hand Painted Figures, Color, 1950s	22.50
Plate, Statue Of Liberty, World Wide Art Studio, 1985, 8 1/2 In.	10.00
Program, Miss America Pageant, Atlantic City Steel Pier, 1954	75.00
Program, Miss America Pageant, L.L. Meade Cover, Royal Reunion, 1960	35.00
Ribbon, 20th Maine Vol. Infantry, 50th Anniversary, Little Round Top, 1913	275.00
Ribbon, Charles Lindbergh, Plane, Flag, Red, Blue, Black, Silk, 1927, 7 x 2 In.	112.00
Spoon, Apollo 11, White Metal, 1969, Demitasse	27.00
Spoon, Patrick Henry Bust, Cutout Handle	28.00
Spoon, Sterling Silver, Battle Of Manila, Commodore Dewey, 1898	17.00
Spoon, Sterling Silver, Billie Possum In Tree Handle	175.00
Spoon, Sterling Silver, Boston Public Library Bowl, Twisted Handle	19.00
Spoon, Sterling Silver, Brown Derby	9.00
Spoon, Sterling Silver, Catalina Island, Fish Handle, Gold-Washed Bowl	40.00
Spoon, Sterling Silver, Christopher Columbus, Santa Maria Bowl	28.00
Spoon, Sterling Silver, Frederick Douglass In Bowl, Chain Links, Date ....225.00 to 325.00
Spoon, Sterling Silver, Government Locks, Seattle, Enameled Bowl	16.00
Spoon, Sterling Silver, Lincoln, Nebraska	18.00
Spoon, Sterling Silver, Nevada, Rope-Entwined Handle, Spade Bowl, 5 1/4 In.	85.00
Spoon, Sterling Silver, Old Kentucky Home	18.00
Spoon, Sterling Silver, Old Woman Riding On Broom, Child's, Victoria Louis Handle	200.00
Spoon, Sterling Silver, Philadelphia, Liberty Bell In Bowl, Demitasse	30.00
Spoon, Sterling Silver, Salem Witch, Cat, Moon	55.00
Spoon, Sterling Silver, San Francisco, Bear Handle, Gold-Washed Sunrise Bowl	45.00
Spoon, Sterling Silver, Seattle, Washington	55.00
Spoon, Sterling Silver, Soldiers & Sailors Monument, Bright Cut, Gold-Washed Bowl	16.00
Spoon, Sterling Silver, Stuyvesant, Gold Chased Enameled Bowl, 6 1/8 In.	485.00
Spoon, Sterling Silver, Three Rivers, Pennsylvania	18.00
Spoon, Sterling Silver, University Of Mississippi	25.00
Spoon, Sterling Silver, Waco, Texas, Cutout Letters, Twisted Handle, Gold-Washed Bowl	35.00
Textile, Huzza For The Navy, War Of 1812, Scenes, Red & White, 25 x 29 In.	3000.00
Ticket, Theater, Caruso, Dated May 22, 1911	30.00
Tumbler, Chicago, Casino & Pier Scene, 1893	35.00

SPANGLE GLASS is multicolored glass made from odds and ends of colored glass rods. It includes metallic flakes of mica covered with gold, silver, nickel, or copper. Spangle glass is usually cased with a thin layer of clear glass over the multicolored layer. Similar glass is listed in the Vasa Murrhina category.

Basket, Overlay, White Lining, Clear Thorny Applied Handle, 6 1/4 In.	175.00
Bottle, Snuff, Red & Yellow, Green Glass Stopper, Pearl Shape, 3 In.	100.00
Bowl, English Blue, Mica, Crystal Floral Rigaree Collar, 4 In.	115.00

Ewer, Pink, Silver Spangles On White, Crystal Rim, Crimped Handle, 9 1/2 In. 250.00
Pitcher, Floral, Ribbed, Silver Mica, Clear Handle, 1883, Hobbs Brockunier, 8 In. 500.00
Pitcher, Wide Rib Blown Out, Heart Shape Pouring Spout, Silver Mica, 8 In. 500.00
Rose Bowl, 3 1/2 In. 80.00
Vase, Mica, Spatter, Chintz Type Pattern, 1930s, 6 1/4 In. 150.00

SPANISH LACE is a type of Victorian glass that has a white lace design.
Blue, yellow, cranberry, or clear glass was made with this distinctive
white pattern. It was made in England and the United States after 1885.
Copies are being made.

Bowl, Upturned Edge 95.00
Rose Bowl, Canary To Opalescent, 4 1/2 In. 50.00
Sugar Shaker, Wide Waist, Vaseline 175.00
Water Set, Blue, 7 Piece 235.00
Water Set, Riffled Rim Pitcher, White Opalescent, 7 Piece 185.00
Water Set, White Opalescent, Raised Pattern, 7 Piece 295.00

SPATTER GLASS is a multicolored glass made from many small pieces
of different colored glass. It is sometimes called *End-of-Day* glass. It
is still being made.

Basket, Applied Handle, Light Blue, White Glass, Ruffled Edge, 7 In. 85.00
Basket, Crimped, Triangular, Crystal Loop Branch Handle, 7 In. 110.00
Basket, Hobnail, Crimped, Clear Thorn Handle, Rectangular, 5 x 6 1/2 In. 135.00
Bowl, Fluted, 8 In. 130.00
Cruet, Pink, Applied Clear Handle, Stopper, Bulbous 165.00
Cruet, Royal Ivy, Clear Faceted Stopper & Handle, 6 In. 300.00
Mug, Peafowl, Blue, Child's 1050.00
Plate, Flower In Center, Blue Stick Spatter Flowers, 9 In. 115.00
Plate, Schoolhouse Center, Red Border, 8 1/2 In. 2750.00
Ring Tree, Orange & Off-White, Enameled Dots, Gold Trim, 3 1/2 x 3 1/4 In. 65.00
Tumbler, Water, Inverted Thumbprint, Orange, 3 3/4 In. 40.00
Vase, Pink & Yellow, Folded Ruffled Rim, White Spatter Interior, 5 1/4 In. 55.00
Vase, Rainbow, Square, Scalloped, 6 In., Pair 165.00
Vase, Yellow & Cobalt Blue, Silver Mica Flakes 195.00

SPATTERWARE is the creamware or soft paste dinnerware decorated
with colored spatter designs. The earliest pieces were made in the late
eighteenth century, but most of the spatterware found today was made
from about 1800 to 1850, or it is a form of kitchen crockery with added
spatter designs, made in the late nineteenth and twentieth centuries.
The early spatterware was made in the Staffordshire district of
England for sale in America. The later kitchen type is an American
product.

Bowl & Pitcher, Blue & White, Blue Stripes, 12 & 14 1/2 In. 330.00
Bowl & Pitcher Set, Tulip, Blue 3900.00
Cup & Plate, Blue, Rose Design, 2 5/8 & 3 3/4 In., 2 Piece 330.00
Cup & Saucer, Blue Design, 2 7/8 In. 120.00
Cup & Saucer, Castle, Blue 660.00
Cup & Saucer, Handleless, 4-Part Flower Design, Red & Green, Blue 95.00
Cup & Saucer, Handleless, Adam's Rose, Blue 93.50
Cup & Saucer, Handleless, Peafowl, Blue 165.00
Cup & Saucer, Peafowl, Green 550.00
Cup & Saucer, Peafowl, Red, 4 In. ....160.00 to 385.00
Cup & Saucer, Rose 185.00
Cup & Saucer, Starflower, Red, Blue 325.00
Cup & Saucer, Thistle, Yellow 2200.00
Cup & Saucer, Tulip Cluster, Red & Green Spatter Border 150.00
Cup & Saucer, Tulip, Red 150.00
Cup & Saucer, Tulip, Yellow 3000.00
Pitcher, Burnt Orange, Gold Mica, Clear Reeded Handle, Clear Edge, 9 In. 180.00
Plate, Bull's-Eye, Blue & Red, 7 3/8 In. 38.00
Plate, Floral Center, Green Border, 9 3/4 In. 245.00

Plate, Green & Red Design, 8 1/2 In. 35.00
Plate, Plum, Blue, 8 1/4 In. 55.00
Plate, Schoolhouse, Blue, Red, Yellow, Green, Black, 8 1/2 In. 220.00
Plate, Strawberry, Pink Band 1050.00
Plate, Thistle, Red, Purple, Green, 8 1/4 In. 330.00
Plate, Tulip Center, Purple, 10 In. 525.00
Platter, Adam's Rose, Blue, Red, Green, Black, 13 3/4 In. 495.00
Platter, Peafowl, Red, 15 3/4 In. 962.00
Platter, Yellow Tulip, Rainbow, Blue, Yellow Border, Red, Blue, 16 In. 15180.00
Soup, Dish, Strawberry 1300.00
Sugar, 2 Men On A Raft 2100.00
Sugar, Cover, Peafowl, Blue, 5 x 4 1/2 In. .... 300.00 to 850.00
Sugar, Paneled Tulip, Blue, 7 1/2 In. 275.00
Sugar, Red Tulip, Green Leaves, Purple & Pink 500.00
Tea Set, Child's, Peafowl, 19th Century, 6 Piece 575.00
Teapot, Willow Tree, Purple 2500.00
Washbowl, Rainbow, Blue, Purple, 12 1/2 x 4 1/4 In. 215.00

SPELTER is a synonym for a zinc alloy. Figurines, candlesticks, and other pieces were made of spelter and given a bronze or painted finish. The metal has been used since about the 1860s to make statues, tablewares, and lamps that resemble bronze. Spelter is soft and breaks easily. To test for spelter, scratch the base of the piece. Bronze is solid; spelter will show a silvery scratch.

Bust, Art Nouveau Lady, 12 In. 275.00
Clock, Mantel, White Alabaster, Gilt, Conical, Bronze, France, 1875, 23 In. 1610.00
Figurine, Girl, With Songbook, Wooden Base, Art Nouveau, 19th Century, 30 In. 795.00
Figurine, Hunter, France, 19th Century, 64 In. 9200.00
Figurine, La Melodie, Signed, Aug. Moreau, 21 In. 750.00
Figurine, Middle Eastern Woman, L. Hollot, 31 In. 4600.00
Lamp, Lighthouse, Keeper On Side 1900.00

SPINNING WHEELS in the corner have been symbols of earlier times for the past 100 years. Although spinning wheels date back to medieval days, the ones found today are rarely more than 200 years old. Because the style of the spinning wheel changed very little, it is often impossible to place an exact date on a wheel.

Black Paint, N. Wolf T., 21 1/2 In. 220.00
Flax, c.1820 .... 225.00
Hardwood, Dark Brown Patina, AK Brand, Distaff, 33 In. 165.00
Hardwood, Dark Finish, Slender Turned Legs, 46 x 62 In. 200.00
Hardwood, Red Stain, 34 In. 220.00
Mixed Softwood, Dark Brown Patina, 20 x 38 In. 192.00

SPODE pottery, porcelain, and bone china were made by the Stoke-on-Trent factory of England founded by Josiah Spode about 1770. The firm became Copeland and Garrett from 1833 to 1847, then W.T. Copeland or W.T. Copeland and Sons until 1976. It then became Royal Worcester Spode Ltd. The word *Spode* appears on many pieces made by the factories. Most collectors include all the wares under the more familiar name of Spode. Porcelains are listed in this book by the name that appears on the piece. Related pieces are listed under Copeland and Copeland Spode.

Bowl, Tower, View Of Bridge Of Salero, St. Angelo, c.1847, 10 x 7 In. 500.00
Bread Plate, Buttercup 10.00
Cake Stand, Florence, Footed 75.00
Coffeepot, Centurion, Blue & White, 10 In. 65.00
Compote, Cherub, Standing With Flowing Dress, Blanc Di Chin, 15 3/4 In. 230.00
Cottage, Cream, Pink, Blue Blossoms, Green Leaves, 1820, 4 3/8 In. 1840.00
Creamer, Bridal Rose 61.00
Cup, Tulip, White Petals, Striated In Rose, Marked, 1820, 2 11/16 In. 1494.00
Cup, Tulip, Yellow Petals, Striated In Purple, Marked, 1820, 2 3/4 In. 920.00
Cup & Saucer, Bridal Rose 42.00

Cup & Saucer, Cowslip Pattern, 8 In.	75.00
Cup & Saucer, Mayflower, After Dinner	195.00
Dessert Service, Animal Scenes, 4 Fruits, Floral Sprigs, Gilt Edged Rim, 1810, 12 In.	1437.00
Dessert Service, Botanical, Green Leaf Clusters, Twig Handles, 1820, 33 Piece	10350.00
Eggcup, Buttercup	35.00
Inkwell, Basket Form, Peasant, Seated On Riverbank Near Bridge, 1815, 5 3/8 In.	1035.00
Plate, Bridal Rose, 10 In.	37.00
Plate, Buttercup, 10 In.	20.00
Plate, Buttercup, Square, 9 In.	45.00
Plate, Castle Scene, Brown, 1894, 10 1/2 In., Pair	80.00
Plate, Christmas, 2nd, 1971	18.00
Plate, Florence, Square Handles, 9 In.	45.00
Plate, Gainsborough, 10 In.	25.00
Saucer, Buttercup, After Dinner	15.00
Server, Buttercup, 3 Tiers	60.00
Sugar, Cover, Bridle Rose	70.00
Tea & Coffee Service, Cluster Of Fruit Borne, Leafy Stems, Gild Border, 1810, 36 Piece	1035.00
Tea Set, Aster, 3 Piece	245.00
Tray, Forest Landscape I, c.1810, 10 x 7 In.	225.00
Tray, Gainsborough, 15 In.	135.00
Wine Pot, Cadogan, Applied Berries, Flowers, Leaves, Brown Glaze, 1860, 6 1/2 In.	175.00

SPONGEWARE is very similar to spatterware in appearance. The designs were applied to the ceramics by daubing the color on with a sponge or cloth. Many collectors do not differentiate between spongeware and spatterware and use the names interchangeably. Modern pottery is being made to resemble the old spongeware, but careful examination will show it is new.

Bean Pot, Blue & White, 4 5/8 In.	410.00
Bowl, Blue & White, Ears For Wire Bail Handle, 8 1/2 x 4 In.	70.00
Bowl, Blue & White, Molded Ribs, 9 x 3 1/2 In.	80.00
Bowl, Blue & White, Spout, Wire Bail, Straight Sides, 6 3/4 In.	330.00
Bowl, Blue & Yellow, 13 In.	135.00
Bowl, Dark Blue & White, 8 1/2 x 8 1/2 x 2 In.	355.00
Bowl, Relief Rose	85.00
Bowl, Rolled Lip, Allover Cobalt Blue On White, c.1850, 12 1/2 x 10 In.	650.00
Charger, Swan, Trees Border, Tin Glazed, 1690, 12 In.	1300.00
Cooler, Cover, Blue & White, Bung Hole, 14 3/4 In.	155.00
Cooler, Cover, Blue & White, Nickel Plated Spigot, Marked 8, 18 In.	340.00
Crock, Butter, Blue & White, 5 x 7 1/2 In.	200.00
Crock, Butter, Blue & White, Molded Pinwheels, Wire Bail, 5 3/4 In.	135.00
Crock, Butter, Blue & White, Molded Pinwheels, Wire Bail, 7 1/2 In.	220.00
Crock, Butter, Village Farm Dairy, Blue & White, 5 3/4 In.	165.00
Cuspidor, Blue Stripes, 3 1/4 In.	275.00
Dish, Cover, Blue & White, 3 1/4 In.	935.00
Figurine, Dog, Sitting, White Glaze, Dark Blue & Ocher, Ohio Clay, 6 1/2 In.	660.00
Jar, White, Blue Stripes, Cylindrical, 15 1/2 In.	770.00
Jug, Blue, White, Molded Leaf, Bail, Wooden Handle, F.H. Weeks, 5 1/2 In.	550.00
Jug, Dark Blue, Molded, F.H. Weeks, 7 3/4 In.	660.00
Jug, Grandmother's Maple Syrup, F.H. Weeks, 6 1/2 In.	465.00
Pitcher, Barrel Shape, Blue & White Spatter, 7 1/2 In.	165.00
Pitcher, Blue & White, 8 1/2 In.	290.00
Pitcher, Blue & White, 8 3/4 In.	340.00 to 355.00
Pitcher, Blue & White, 9 In.	195.00 to 330.00
Pitcher, Blue & White, Blue Flower, 9 In.	335.00
Pitcher, Blue & White, Child & Dog Molded Design, 8 7/8 In.	275.00
Pitcher, Blue & White, Flower, 9 In.	270.00
Pitcher, Blue & White, Molded Band, 11 1/2 In.	385.00
Pitcher, Blue & White, Molded Ribs & Band, 5 3/4 In.	220.00
Pitcher, Blue & White, Unusual Curved Shoulders, 8 1/4 In.	465.00
Pitcher, Green, Brown, 4 1/2 In.	75.00
Pitcher, Harples Rendering Works, Monterey, Embossed, 8 In.	100.00
Pitcher, Molded Swirled Ribs, Dark Gray Blue, 5 5/8 In.	415.00

Pitcher, Relief Rose Pattern 169.00
Plate, Pussy Willow Cut, 6 5/8 In. 150.00
Plate, Running Rabbit, 9 In. 445.00
Platter, Blue & White, 15 In. 300.00
Soup, Dish, Stick, 9 In. 295.00
Stand, Umbrella, Dutch Boy & Girl Transfer, Blue Stripes, 22 1/4 In. 825.00
Tea Set, Child's, Maroon, Staffordshire, 3 Piece 250.00
Tea Set, Child's, Red, Staffordshire, 16 Piece 357.00
Teapot, Blue & White, 6 3/4 In. 410.00
Teapot, Cream, Brown, Green 595.00
Water Filter, Cover, Blue & White, 22 1/2 In., 2 Piece 630.00

SPORTS equipment, sporting goods, brochures, and related items are
listed here. Items are listed by sport. Other categories of interest are
Bicycle, Card, Fishing, Sword, and Toy.

Auto Racing, Ashtray, Bronze, 1950s 200.00
Auto Racing, Glass, Indianapolis 500, 1970, Carton 8.00
Auto Racing, Glass, Indianapolis 500, 1972 .... 25.00
Auto Racing, Glass, Indianapolis 500, 1980, Carton 8.00
Auto Racing, Photograph, Bobby Unser, Bonneville, Autographed, 1993, 8 x 10 In. 12.00
Auto Racing, Photograph, Joe Amato, Color, Signed, 8 x 11 In. 5.00
Auto Racing, Pin, Soap Box Derby, Troy, Ohio, Booster, Optimist Club, Celluloid, 2 In. . 20.00
Auto Racing, Program, NASCAR, Photographs Of Herb Thomas, Lee Petty, 11 x 8 In. ... 55.00
Baseball, Ashtray, Los Angeles Dodgers, Stadium, Franciscan 145.00
Baseball, Ashtray, Minnesota Twins 135.00
Baseball, Ball, Autographed, Babe Ruth 5500.00
Baseball, Ball, Autographed, Brooklyn Dodgers, 23 Players, 1954 .... 700.00
Baseball, Ball, Autographed, Cecil Fielder 35.00
Baseball, Ball, Autographed, Jimmy Piersall, American League 20.00
Baseball, Ball, Autographed, Joe DiMaggio & Mickey Mantle, 1951 .... 615.00
Baseball, Ball, Autographed, Mickey Mantle, Upper Deck 350.00
Baseball, Ball, Autographed, N.Y. Mets, World Series, 1986, 28 Players & Coaches ... 300.00
Baseball, Ball, Autographed, N.Y. Yankees, Mantle, DiMaggio ....*Illus* 3060.00
Baseball, Ball, Autographed, Tommy Henrich, Don Larsen, Earl Battey 355.00
Baseball, Ball, Frosted Flakes, Tony The Tiger 35.00
Baseball, Bat Table, Black Painted Top, Straight Apron, Bat Legs, 33 1/2 In. . 690.00
Baseball, Bat, Display, Factory, Louisville, 1920-1930, 61 x 5 In. 650.00
Baseball, Bat, Harry Danning, Hillerich & Bradsby, Game Used, 1930s 642.00
Baseball, Bat, Joe DiMaggio, Miniature 125.00
Baseball, Bat, Lyman Bostock, Marks On Barrel, Game Used, 1977-1978 .... 195.00
Baseball, Bat, Ted Williams Model, Little League, Louisville Slugger 250.00
Baseball, Bat, Yogi Berra Model, Hillerich & Bradsby, 34-In. Special Power Drive ... 50.00
Baseball, Beer Mug, Mickey Mantle, Facsimile Signature, 12 Oz. 15.00
Baseball, Book, Chicago Cubs, 1934, Price 25 Cents 62.00
Baseball, Book, My 66 Years In Big Leagues, Connie Mack, 1st Edition, 1950 .. 30.00
Baseball, Book, Who's Who In Major Leagues, 1937 .... 50.00
Baseball, Booklet, Baseball For Boys, Prudential, Mathews, Snider, Kuenn, 1955 ... 10.00
Baseball, Button, Baltimore Orioles, League Champions, Team Photo, 1966 ..... 95.00
Baseball, Button, Cleveland Indians, Chief Wahoo, Celluloid, 1950s, 3 1/2 In. .. 35.00
Baseball, Button, Detroit Tigers, Embossed Tiger Head, Brass, 1940 .... 30.00
Baseball, Button, I Love Mickey, Mickey Mantle, Teresa Brewer 5.00
Baseball, Button, Jim Bunning, 1965, 3 1/2 In. 20.00
Baseball, Button, Mickey Mantle, At Echelon Mall, Dec. 1982, 2 In. 7.00
Baseball, Button, Schoolboy Rowe, Good Sports Enjoy Ward's Sporties, Celluloid, 1 In. . 45.00
Baseball, Button, St. Louis Cardinals, Cardinal Sitting On Bat Logo, 1940s, 1 3/4 In. ... 45.00
Baseball, Button, Ted Williams, Black & White, c.1948, 1 3/4 In. 20.00
Baseball, Button, Ted Williams, Boston Red Sox, Celluloid, 1 1/4 In. 20.00
Baseball, Button, Ty Cobb, Picture, Celluloid, Black, White, 3/4 In. 275.00
Baseball, Cartoon, Monte Ward, Drunken King Kelly, Laid Off Without Pay, 1893 ..... 550.00
Baseball, Cereal Box, Wheaties, Cal Ripken, Blank Shirt 85.00
Baseball, Cereal Box, Wheaties, Cal Ripken, No. 8 On Shirt 45.00
Baseball, Christmas Card, Babe Ruth's Personal, Addressed To Locker Boy, 1936 ...... 1250.00
Baseball, Clock, Alarm, Mickey Mantle 55.00

**Pen marks can be removed
from leather with a clear
gum eraser, not a pink one.**

Sports, Baseball, Ball, Autographed,
N.Y. Yankees, Mantle, DiMaggio

Baseball, Comic Book, Mickey Mantle, Color Photo Of Mickey On Cover	7.00
Baseball, Figure Set, Lead, 1920, 10 Piece	395.00
Baseball, Game, Big League Baseball, Artcraft-Saalfield, 1959	45.00
Baseball, Game, Electric Baseball, Tudor, Unused, Box	35.00
Baseball, Game, National Game, Card, 52 Different Players, Box, 1913	1650.00
Baseball, Glass, Baltimore Colts World Championship, 1959	20.00
Baseball, Glass, White Sox, American League, Comiskey Park	75.00
Baseball, Glove, Cy Young Model	900.00
Baseball, Glove, Joe DiMaggio Model	50.00
Baseball, Jersey, Waiter's, Mickey Mantle Restaurant, No. 7 On Back, Cotton, Gray	75.00
Baseball, Key Chain, Mickey Mantle, Pictures 1960 Topps Card	8.00
Baseball, Knife, Mickey Mantle, Lists Baseball Statistics, Pocket, 5 In.	7.00 to 10.00
Baseball, Label, Cigar, Handmade National League Perfectos	9.00
Baseball, Lunch Box, Boston Red Sox, Vinyl	75.00
Baseball, Lunch Box, Sports Skwirts	50.00
Baseball, Magazine, Life, Mickey Mantle Cover, June 26, 1956	35.00
Baseball, Marble, Mickey Mantle, 1 In.	4.00
Baseball, Matches, Mickey Mantle, Full Book Of Matches Of N.Y.C. Restaurant	2.00
Baseball, Menu, Mickey Mantle Restaurant, 14 x 11 In.	15.00
Baseball, Pen, Mickey Mantle, Bat Shape, Facsimile Autograph, 8 In.	12.00
Baseball, Pencil, Bat Shape, Mel Ott, Mechanical	40.00
Baseball, Pencil, Bat Shape, Oakland A's	20.00
Baseball, Pennant & Yearbook, L.A. Dodgers, 1959	100.00
Baseball, Photograph, Babe Ruth, Autographed, Barnstorming Tour Of Japan, 1930	4025.00
Baseball, Photograph, Babe Ruth, With Lou Gehrig	8.00
Baseball, Photograph, Brooks Robinson, Matted, Glass Frame, Signed, 11 x 14 In.	65.00
Baseball, Photograph, Lou Gehrig, Autographed, Iron Horse Not In Uniform, 1935	3450.00
Baseball, Photograph, Mickey Mantle, Mick In His Prime, Color, 8 x 10 In.	100.00
Baseball, Photograph, Roberto Clemente, Autographed, Frame	197.00
Baseball, Photograph, Ty Cobb, Autographed, Rounding Third Base	1725.00
Baseball, Photograph, Walter Johnson & Dazzy Vance, Autographed	748.00
Baseball, Picture, Silhouette, Boys Baseball Game, Frame, 1927	30.00
Baseball, Plaque, Baltimore Orioles, 1983 World Champions, Picture, Box, 12 x 16 In.	50.00
Baseball, Plate, Mickey Mantle, Dinner	65.00
Baseball, Press Pin, All-Star Game, Chicago Cubs, Box, 1962	295.00
Baseball, Press Pin, World Series, Brooklyn Dodgers, Game 3, Ebbetts Field, 1955	300.00
Baseball, Program, Chicago White Sox, Tour, Glove Shape, Charles Comiskey, 1912	980.00
Baseball, Program, St. Louis Cardinals, World Series, 1934	175.00
Baseball, Program, World Series, 1951	135.00
Baseball, Program, World Series, Boston Braves Vs. Philadelphia Athletics, 1914	1970.00
Baseball, Program, Yankees Old Timers, Mickey Mantle, 1975	15.00
Baseball, Punchboard, Play Ball, Jimmie Foxx & Lefty Grove, 1930s	95.00
Baseball, Puppet, Hand, Rootie Kazootie, Baseball Player, c.1952	175.00
Baseball, Ring, Mickey Mantle, Gold Metal, Adjustable	10.00

Baseball, Shot Glass, Mickey Mantle Restaurant, Central Park, 4 In. 12.00
Baseball, Sign, Enjoy Red Man, America's Best Chew, E. Slaughter, Cardboard, 15 In. ... 450.00
Baseball, Sketchbook, Cleveland Indians, 1963 .... 14.00
Baseball, Spoon, Mickey Mantle, Silver, 4 In. 10.00
Baseball, Stadium Seat Side, League Park, Cast Iron, Bat, Ball & Glove Design 495.00
Baseball, Stadium Seat, Arlington Stadium, Autographed, Nolan Ryan 450.00
Baseball, Tin, Chewing Tobacco, Chicago Cubs, Rock City Tobacco Co., 6 In. 150.00
Baseball, Umbrella, Baltimore Orioles, Gulf Oil, Original Sleeve 100.00
Baseball, Wallet, Boston Braves, World Series, Leather, Indian Head, Tomahawk, 1948 .. 185.00
Baseball, Wallet, Ted Williams, 1950s 225.00
Baseball, Watch, Mickey Mantle, Pocket 55.00
Baseball, Wooden Nickel, Mickey Mantle, 1 1/2 In. 4.00
Baseball, Wristband, Paul Mondesi, L.A. Dodger, Autographed, 1995 .... 35.00
Baseball, Yearbook, Boston Red Sox, 1959 .... 65.00
Baseball, Yearbook, L.A. Dodgers, 1958 .... 95.00
Baseball, Yearbook, N.Y. Mets, 1976-1995 .... 200.00
Basketball, Ball, Autographed, Grant Hill, NBA, Black Sharpie, Spalding 135.00
Basketball, Ball, Autographed, John Wooden, UCLA Coach 220.00
Basketball, Ball, Autographed, Rasheed Wallace, Spalding NBA Indoor-Outdoor 45.00
Basketball, Ball, Autographed, Shawn Kemp, Seattle Sonics, All Star 75.00
Basketball, Button, Michael Jordan, Phone Pass, Pinback 18.00
Basketball, Cap, Chicago Bulls, Visor 3.00
Basketball, Clock, World Champion Boston Celtics, Autographed, 1959-60 .... 330.00
Basketball, Goggles, Kareem Abdul-Jabbar, Game Worn, 1980s 550.00
Basketball, Jacket, Warm-Up, Calvin Murphy, Houston Rockets, Autographed, 1980s ... 255.00
Basketball, Jersey & Shoes, Larry Nance, Cleveland Cavaliers, Game Used, Signed 350.00
Basketball, Jersey, Bernard King, Washington Bullets, Game Used, 1990 .... 320.00
Basketball, Jersey, Harry Gallatin, No. 10 On Front, 1957 .... 2300.00
Basketball, Lunch Box, Sport Sqwirts 25.00
Basketball, Pendant, Boston Celtics, 10K Gold, Diamond, 1984 ....*Illus* 1320.00
Basketball, Pennant, Cleveland Cavaliers, NBA Logo, Pencil, 14 In. ....*Illus* 3.00
Basketball, Scoreboard, 8 Minute Time, Red & Black, 1940s 1500.00
Basketball, Shoes, Charles Barkley, Signed In Silver, Nike AirMax 303.00
Basketball, Shoes, Chuck Taylor, Black High-Top, Canvas, Size 12 .... 98.00
Basketball, Shoes, Pistol Pete Maravich, 1 White & 1 Gold Toe, 1970s 125.00
Basketball, Suit, Warm-Up, Marvin Webster, New York Knicks, 2 Piece 275.00
Basketball, Watch, Boston Celtics, World Championship, Omega ....*Illus* 605.00
Bowling, Badge, Ribbon, 1912 Tournament 75.00
Bowling, Ball Bar, Bakelite 150.00
Bowling, Clock, Wooden, Metal, 1950s, Large 85.00
Bowling, Photograph, Don Carter, Color, Signed, 5 x 7 In. 5.00
Boxing, 32nd Image Award, Mike Tyson, NAACP, Boxer Of The Decade, 1989 .... 3500.00
Boxing, Button, I Want To Go To The Louis-Nova Fight, Pinback, 3 1/2 In. 40.00
Boxing, Charm, Jose Velez's 1988 Golden Gloves, 10K Gold, 1/4 Ct. Diamond 795.00
Boxing, Check, Personal, Rocky Graziano, Signed, For $2500, Dated 1946 .... 70.00

Sports, Basketball,
Pendant, Boston
Celtics, 10K Gold,
Diamond, 1984

Sports, Basketball,
Watch, Boston Celtics,
World Championship,
Omega

Sports, Basketball, Pennant, Cleveland Cavaliers, NBA Logo, Pencil, 14 In.

Boxing, Glove, Roy Jones Jr., Autographed, Says Pound For Pound	45.00
Boxing, Gloves, Jack Dempsey, Everlast, Box, 4 Piece	375.00
Boxing, Head Protector, Box, 1940s	55.00
Boxing, Menu, Jack Dempsey's Broadway Restaurant, New York, 1947	25.00
Boxing, Pass, Official, Archie Moore Vs. Bobo Olson, 1955	40.00
Boxing, Photograph, Rocky Marciano, Autographed, Boxing Stance, Training Camp	805.00
Boxing, Photograph, Sugar Ray Leonard, In Ring, Inscribed, 8 x 10 In.	12.00
Boxing, Poster, Champions Forever, Ali, Frazier, Foreman, Holmes, 20 x 34 In.	75.00
Boxing, Poster, Fight, Roberto Duran, Sugar Ray Leonard, Autographed Nieman, 1989	265.00
Boxing, Poster, Muhammad Ali, As A Martyr, Multicolor, 1969, 20 x 25 In.	43.00
Boxing, Poster, Willie Langford, Oct. 8, 1915, 14 x 22 In.	190.00
Boxing, Print, Sting Like A Bee, Done & Signed By Muhammad Ali, 1979	500.00
Boxing, Prison ID Card, Mike Tyson, Wearing Gray Sweats, March 27, 1995	1100.00
Boxing, Program, Joe Louis Vs. Jersey Joe Walcott, June 23, 1948	165.00
Boxing, Program, Joey Maxim Vs. Ray Robinson, Yankee Stadium, Picture, 1952	110.00
Boxing, Robe, Joe Frazier, Smokin' Joe On Back, Green Terrycloth	2070.00
Boxing, Ticket & Membership Pass, John L. Sullivan Vs. James J. Corbett	1000.00
Boxing, Trunks, Rocky Marciano, 1948	6495.00
Football, Album, Uncut Stamps, 120 Pages, 1972	25.00
Football, Ashtray, Brass, Baltimore Colts World Champs, 1958-59	100.00
Football, Ball, Detroit Lions, 30 Autographs, 1980s	135.00
Football, Booklet, Tournament Of Roses Parade, 1948	12.00
Football, Bottle, Cowboys Barbeque Sauce, 7 In. ....*Illus*	8.00
Football, Bottle, Cowboys Mustard ....*Illus*	8.00
Football, Box, Paris Garters, Lithograph Of Game In Progress, c.1900	200.00
Football, Button, Cleve. Browns, Boys Back In Town, 1996, 2 1/2 In. ....*Illus*	1.00
Football, Cereal Box, Wheaties, Terry Bradshaw, Signed	25.00
Football, Comic Book, Baltimore Colts, Team Biographies & Photographs, 1950	400.00
Football, Doll, O.J. Simpson, Buffalo Bills Uniform, Early 1970s	125.00
Football, Figurine, Rod Jones, Tampa Bay Bucks, Starting Lineup, Package, 1988	40.00
Football, Glass, Vince Lombardi, Pizza Hut, 1970s	25.00
Football, Helmet, Dan Marino, Autographed	325.00
Football, Helmet, Denver Broncos, Latex, Designer Signed	125.00
Football, Helmet, Don Shula, Miami Dolphins, Autographed Miniature	125.00
Football, Helmet, Drew Bledsoe, Autographed Miniature	110.00
Football, Helmet, Face Mask, Atlanta Falcons, 1970s	140.00
Football, Helmet, Leather, Adjustable Forehead, 1920s	350.00
Football, Helmet, Oklahoma Outlaws, USFL, Used, 1985	395.00
Football, Jersey, Jim Everett, Los Angeles Rams, No. 11, Game Used	400.00
Football, Jersey, Kenny Anderson, Cincinnati Bengals, No. 14, Game Used, 1980s	440.00
Football, Lunch Box, NFL Quarterback, Metal, Plastic Handle, Aladdin, 1964	64.00
Football, Mug, Princeton, Porcelain, Dated 1905	485.00
Football, Mug, Sugar Bowl, Alabama Vs. Notre Dame, Jax Beer, 1973	75.00
Football, Pendant, University Of Penn, Girl & Player, 1908, 23 In.	325.00
Football, Photograph, Ernie Davis Appreciation Night, Autograph, Dec. 28, 1960	595.00
Football, Photograph, Four Horsemen Of Notre Dame, 1924	1495.00
Football, Photograph, Joe Theismann, Black & White, Signed, 8 x 11 In.	10.00

Sports, Football, Bottle,
Cowboys Barbeque
Sauce, 7 In.

Sports, Football,
Bottle, Cowboys
Mustard

Sports, Football, Button,
Cleve. Browns, Boys Back In Town,
1996, 2 1/2 In.

Football, Poster, Penn Central, Army-Navy, Train Service & Schedule, 1971, 22 x 36 In.	29.00
Football, Press Pin, Super Bowl III, Tie Bar, Bronze Colored, Jets Over Colts	920.00
Football, Program, Yale Vs. Harvard, 64 Pages, 1904, 10 x 12 In.	50.00
Football, Schedule, Baltimore Colts, 1967, Pocket	17.00
Football, Scorer, Wm. Read Sons, Boston, Football Shape	65.00
Football, Shoes, Dan Marino Autograph, Orange, Nike, Game Used, 1995	700.00
Football, Ticket, Yale, Harvard, This Ticket Will Not Admit A Lady, 1921	55.00
Football, Trophy, Argonauts, 1991 Grey Cup .... *Illus*	880.00
Football, Wastepaper Basket, New York Giants, Metal, 1971, 14 In.	35.00
Golf, Ball, Mesh Dunlop No. 1, England	100.00
Golf, Ball, Penfold Patented Dimple Balls, Felt Box, Unused, Set Of 6	550.00
Golf, Ball, Winchester, For Salesmen's Tournament, Spalding, 1970s	33.00
Golf, Banner, Bull Durham Tobacco, Linen	550.00
Golf, Book, Chick Evans' Golf Book, New York, Signed, 1924	1840.00
Golf, Book, East Loothian, Edinburgh, John Kerr, 1896	1725.00
Golf, Book, Golf In America, A Practical Manual, James P. Lee, 1895	1840.00
Golf, Book, Golf, A Royal & Ancient Game, Robert Clark, London, 1875	5175.00
Golf, Book, Mystery Of Golf, Boston, Arnold Haultain, 1908	1265.00
Golf, Book, Saint Andrews As It Was & As It Is, James Grierson, 1838	2875.00
Golf, Club, Niblick, Woman's, St. Andrews, R.B. Wilson, c.1890	275.00
Golf, Club, Putter, McGregor RA Model, Wooden Mallet Head, c.1925	330.00
Golf, Club, Putter, No. 55, Colt Golf Inc.	90.00
Golf, Club, Wood Shafted, Batchart-Nichols Co.	32.00
Golf, Decanter, 1930, 10 In.	300.00
Golf, Doorstop, Golfer, Figural, Bag For Doorstop, Cast Iron, 10 1/2 In.	24.00
Golf, Glove, Ben Hogan, Autographed, Unused	200.00
Golf, Glove, Billy Casper, Autographed	35.00
Golf, Label, Westwood Tomatoes, Golfer At End Of Back Swing, Unused	45.00
Golf, Paper Cutter, Figure Of Golfer At Bottom, Unger Bros., 1904	395.00
Golf, Photograph, Ben Hogan, On Course, Bag Of Clubs, Color, 8 x 10 In.	135.00
Golf, Photograph, Mildred Didrikson Zaharias, Signed	863.00
Golf, Photograph, Patty Berg, Swinging, Woman Champion, Autographed, 8 x 10 In.	15.00
Golf, Thermometer, Figural, Metal, c.1920, 10 In.	295.00
Gymnastics, Cap, Bart Conner & Nadia Comaneci, Signed	25.00
Hockey, Banner, Boston Bruins Stanley Cup, Logo Center, 1940-41, 9 x 15 In.	3575.00
Hockey, Book, Trail Of Stanley Cup, Charles L. Coleman, 3 Volumes, 1893-1967	695.00
Hockey, Doll, Mattel, Wayne Gretzky, Box	85.00
Hockey, Jersey, Luc Robitaille, No. 20, Los Angeles Kings, Game Used, 1990-91	725.00
Hockey, Jersey, Mario Lemieux, No. 66, Pittsburgh Penguins, 1991-92 Stanley Cup	300.00
Hockey, Jersey, Referee, Bruce Hood, Size 46	75.00

Hockey, Mask, Ed Belfour, Autographed, Metal, Graphics Goalkeeper Inc. 152.00
Hockey, Photograph, Wayne Gretzky, Autographed, Coca-Cola, Color, 8 x 10 In. 36.00
Hockey, Program, New York Rangers, First Season, February 24, 1927 . . . .   333.00
Hockey, Puck, No. 500 Goal, Mark Messier 90.00
Hockey, Puck, Wayne Gretzky, Autographed 100.00
Hockey, Skates, Bobby Orr Blue-Line Brand, Sears, Box Pictures Orr In Uniform, 1970 .   110.00
Hockey, Stick, Advertising Rolled Oats, 1930s 75.00
Hockey, Stick, Goalie, Felix Potvin, Autographed 165.00
Hockey, Stick, Guy Lafleur, Sher-Wood P.M.P., No. 503, Game Used 300.00
Hockey, Stick, Ray Bourque, Name & No. 77 On Side, Game Used, 1995 . . . .   225.00
Horse Racing, Broadside, Centennial Trot, July 4, 1876, 14 x 42 In. 90.00
Horse Racing, Game, Kentucky Derby, Whitman, 1961 . . . .   30.00
Horse Racing, Glass, Belmont Stakes, 1976 . . . .   40.00
Horse Racing, Glass, Belmont Stakes, 1977 . . . .   525.00
Horse Racing, Glass, Belmont Stakes, 1980 . . . .   100.00
Horse Racing, Glass, Belmont Stakes, 1982 . . . .   175.00
Horse Racing, Glass, Belmont Stakes, 1983 . . . . .200.00 to 245.00
Horse Racing, Glass, Breeders' Cup, 1985 . . . .   150.00
Horse Racing, Glass, Breeders' Cup, 1985, Box, 4 Piece 425.00
Horse Racing, Glass, Breeders' Cup, 1988 . . . .   15.00
Horse Racing, Glass, Kentucky Derby, 1940, Aluminum 425.00
Horse Racing, Glass, Kentucky Derby, 1950 . . . .   230.00
Horse Racing, Glass, Kentucky Derby, 1951 . . . . .330.00 to 450.00
Horse Racing, Glass, Kentucky Derby, 1952 . . . .   125.00
Horse Racing, Glass, Kentucky Derby, 1953 . . . .   90.00
Horse Racing, Glass, Kentucky Derby, 1957 . . . .   125.00
Horse Racing, Glass, Kentucky Derby, 1958 . . . .   115.00
Horse Racing, Glass, Kentucky Derby, 1964 . . . . .14.00 to 35.00
Horse Racing, Glass, Kentucky Derby, 1965 . . . .   50.00
Horse Racing, Glass, Kentucky Derby, 1966 . . . .   45.00
Horse Racing, Glass, Kentucky Derby, 1971 . . . .   40.00
Horse Racing, Glass, Kentucky Derby, 1974 . . . .   150.00
Horse Racing, Glass, Kentucky Derby, 1978 . . . .   14.00
Horse Racing, Glass, Kentucky Derby, 1992 . . . .   4.50
Horse Racing, Glass, Preakness, 1974 . . . . .160.00 to 225.00
Horse Racing, Glass, Preakness, 1975 . . . .   50.00
Horse Racing, Glass, Preakness, 1982 . . . .   45.00
Horse Racing, Program, Kentucky Derby, 1935 . . . .   275.00
Horse Racing, Program, Kentucky Derby, 1943 . . . .   400.00

**Always repair dented silver.
Repeated cleaning of a
piece with a dent can
eventually lead to a hole.**

Sports, Football, Trophy, Argonauts,
1991 Grey Cup

Hunting, Bullet Board, Winchester-Western, Horse & Rider, Frame, 20 x 13 In. 240.00
Hunting, Button, Ducks Unlimited, Blue Bill Duck, 1950 . . . . 55.00
Hunting, Button, Ducks Unlimited, Pintail Duck, 1948 . . . . 65.00
Hunting, Button, Dupont Golden Pheasant Gunpowder, Scene, 2 1/4 In. Diam. 345.00
Hunting, Crow Call, Lohman, All Walnut Construction 14.00
Hunting, Crow Call, Truetone, Walnut Barrel, Stamped, Plastic Bag, 5 1/4 In. 33.00
Hunting, Duck Call, Buford, Walnut Barrel, Maple Stopper, Metal Reed 45.00
Hunting, Duck Call, Dan Crooks, Walnut, 2 Panels & Carved Ducks, 5 7/8 In. 223.00
Hunting, Duck Call, Faulk's Pintail Whistle 25.00
Hunting, Duck Call, Glodo 1800.00
Hunting, Duck Call, Herder's 20.00
Hunting, Duck Call, Iverson, Cocobolo Barrel & Stopper, Metal Reed, Brass Ring 44.00
Hunting, Duck Call, John Asbille, Burl Walnut, Cocobolo Insert, Sticker, 6 5/8 In. 48.00
Hunting, Flask, Whiskey, Orvis, Nickel Finish, Engraved Dog 1 Side, Ducks Other 25.00
Hunting, Goose Call, Robert Etherton, Cherry Barrel, No Reed, 6 1/8 In. 24.00
Hunting, Gun Rack, Quarter-Sawn Oak, Keen Cutter Type, 27 1/2 x 24 1/2 In. 375.00
Hunting, Lapel Pin, Remington Shooting Star, Brass, Enamel, Round 6.50
Hunting, License, Arkansas, Paper, Clear Window Front 57.00
Hunting, License, New York Citizen-Resident, Hunting, Trapping, Fishing, Celluloid, 1934 28.00
Hunting, License, North Carolina County, Celluloid, 1928 . . . . 115.00
Hunting, License, Wisconsin Resident, 1932 . . . . 55.00
Hunting, Predator Call, Herter's, Walnut Barrel, Plastic Stopper, Box & Papers 23.00
Hunting, Quail Call, Thomas, No. 156, California Top Notch, Box 22.00
Hunting, Scorecard, Shooting, Remington, 1936, 1 Sheet 50.00
Hunting, Target Thrower, Remington, Cast Iron 125.00
Hunting, Trap Thrower, Hand, Winchester, Collapsible, For Mini Targets 110.00
Hunting, Trap Thrower, Peters Cartridge Co., Duvroc, Metal Mechanism 150.00
Hunting, Turkey Call, Herter's Plantation, Instructions, Box 50.00
Hunting, Turkey Call, Lynch's World Champion, Wooden 14.00
Hunting, Turkey Call, PS Olt, Box 28.00
Hunting, Vest, Browning Arms, Allover Patches, Joe Smith On Back 98.00
Ice Skating, Program, Shipstad & Johnson Ice Follies, 1941, 16 Pages 10.00
Ice Skating, Program, Sonja Henie, 1950, 16 Pages 25.00
Lacrosse, Stick, American Indian, 26 1/2 In. 220.00
Nodders are listed in the Nodder category.
Olympics, Pin, Woman Swimmer, 1940, Celluloid, 2 In. 50.00
Pool, Lithograph, Man Playing Pool On Early Style Pool Table, Color Lithograph 125.00
Pool, Phonograph Record, Minnesota Fats, Sealed 20.00
Pool, Table, Brunswick, Rosewood, Mother-Of-Pearl, Arcade Style, 1910, 9 x 5 Ft. 12500.00
Pool, Table, Oak Claw, Dorr, 46 x 27 In. 550.00
Snowshoes, Rawhide, Wooden, AFH Co., Wallingford, Vt., 57 In. 175.00
Tennis, Ball, Tin, Chemold, Championship Tennis Balls, Tony Roche, Australian Flag . . . 35.00
Tennis, Racket, Narragansett, Paper Wrapper, Labels, Victorian 185.00
Tennis, Racket, Pete Sampras, Wilson Pro Staff, Autograph On Grip 695.00
Tennis, Racket, Spalding Windermere, Flat Top, Original Gut Strings, 1885 . . . . 1010.00
Tennis, Racket, Winchester, Ranger, Varnish 405.00
Tennis, Shirt & Skirt, Monica Seles, Nike, Autographed, Game Used, 1990s 850.00
Weightlifting, Belt, Ultimate Warrior's, Autographed, Feb. 27, 1994 . . . . 85.00
Wrestling, Bandanna, Hulk Hogan 8.00
Wrestling, Box, Gold Bond Ice Cream Bar 10.00

STAFFORDSHIRE, England, has been a district making pottery and
porcelain since the 1700s. Hundreds of kilns are still working in the
area. Thousands of types of pottery and porcelain have been made in
the many factories that worked and still work in the area. Some of the
most famous factories have been listed separately, such as Adams,
Davenport, Ridgway, Rowland & Marsellus, Royal Doulton, Royal
Worcester, Spode, Wedgwood, and others. Some Staffordshire pieces
are listed under categories like Fairing, Flow Blue, Mulberry, Shaving
Mug, etc.

Basket, Fruit, Reticulated, Blue, Enoch Wood & Sons, England, 10 3/4 In. 1900.00
Biscuit Jar, With King Fisher 150.00

Bowl, 2 Insects Hovering Beside Flower Basket, Red, Green, Black Front, 7 In. 230.00
Bowl, Arms Of New York, Dark Blue Transfer, 10 7/8 x 4 5/8 In. 745.00
Bowl, English River Scene, Burgess & Leigh, 3 1/4 x 8 1/4 In. 145.00
Bowl, Pennsylvania Hospital Exterior, Charleston Exchange Interior, 9 In. 7700.00
Bowl, Salt Glaze, Wave Bands, Chain & Feather Design, 1760, 8 7/8 In. 3250.00
Bowl, Washington Crossing The Delaware, 1890 . . . . 150.00
Bowl, Waste, Enameled, Rose, Green, Purple, Blue, Yellow Exterior, 5 In. 400.00
Bust, Maria Foote, Gray Hair, Eyes, Ruddy Skin, Black Socle, 1825, 11 In. 2530.00
Bust, William Pitt, The Younger, Wearing A Blue, White Waistcoat, 1800, 9 In. 1095.00
Canister, Tea, Blue Inscription, Floral, Bovey Tracey, 1768, 5 1/2 In. 1995.00
Canister, Tea, Salt Glaze, Flowers, Inscribed, 1754, 3 1/2 In. 1495.00
Cheese Saver, c.1870 . . . . 425.00
Coffeepot, Dometop, Dark Blue, Enoch Wood, 10 1/2 In. 2760.00
Coffeepot, Hunting Scene, Hounds Chasing Rabbits, Dark Blue, 1830, 10 In. 600.00
Coffeepot, Lafayette At Tomb Of Franklin, 11 3/4 In. 1650.00
Coffeepot, Lafayette At Tomb Of Franklin, Blue, 10 1/2 In. 775.00
Compote, Boston State House, 3 Cows, Eagle Border, Joseph Stubbs, 11 1/2 In. 1430.00
Creamer, Cowl, Brown Spatter, 5 In. 415.00
Cup, Coffee, Coat Of Arms Above A Stag, Bird, 1745-1750, 2 In. 520.00
Cup & Saucer, Bird & Flowers, Dark Blue, Stone China 105.00
Cup & Saucer, Dark Blue Transfer, 3 Children, Dog In Basket 110.00
Dinner Set, Gem Pattern, Blue On White, Patriotic Design, 32 Piece 3700.00
Dish, Enameled, Leaf Shape, Green, Yellow, Green Loop Stem Handle, 7 In. 460.00
Dish, Hen On Nest Cover, 10 1/2 In. 715.00
Dish, Soap, Cover, Peruvian Horse Hunt 110.00
Figurine, Apollo, Holding Lyre, Pearlware, 1780, 8 1/2 In. 1850.00
Figurine, Benjamin Franklin, Blue Coat, Black Hat, Shoes, 14 1/4 In. 1210.00
Figurine, Boy, With Dog, Coaxing Squirrel With Nut, 18th Century, 6 1/4 In. 1100.00
Figurine, Cat, Black & White Spotted, Cushion Base, c.1890, 3 1/4 In., Pair 550.00
Figurine, Cat, Black Stripes On Cobalt Blue Base, England, 4 In., Pair 363.00
Figurine, Cat, Seated, Black & Yellow Splashes, Base, 1815, 3 1/2 In. 515.00
Figurine, Children Of Queen Victoria, On Sofa, 10 In. 650.00
Figurine, Cottage, 19th Century, 6 In. 380.00
Figurine, Cottage, 3-Story, Polychrome, 19th Century, 6 3/4 In. 100.00
Figurine, Cottage, 4 1/2 x 4 In. 175.00
Figurine, Couple, At Road Sign, London, 30 Miles, 11 In. 345.00
Figurine, Couple, With Flowers, Enameled, 10 3/4 In. 250.00
Figurine, Cow, Brown Hide, Black Eyes, Enoch Wood, 1820-1830, 6 1/2 In. 805.00
Figurine, Dappled Fawn, 19th Century, 3 In. 300.00
Figurine, Dog, Collie, 6 1/2 In. 55.00
Figurine, Dog, Dismal Hound, Liver Spotted, c.1820, 4 1/4 In. 475.00
Figurine, Dog, Pointer, Sitting, With Bird, 5 1/2 In. 85.00
Figurine, Dog, Poodle, Colored Features On White, 7 In., Pair 230.00
Figurine, Dog, Poodle, Gray Rough Coat, White, England, 7 3/4 In. 242.00
Figurine, Dog, Poodle, Seated, Heavy Coleslaw Trim, 5 1/2 In. 450.00
Figurine, Dog, Red Reclining, Front Legs Crossed, 5 In., Pair 1840.00
Figurine, Dog, Seated, Red, White, Gold, Black, Ocher, Marked, England, 13 In. 385.00
Figurine, Dog, Seated, With 2 Pups, White Sanded, Cobalt Blue Base, 7 1/8 In. 330.00
Figurine, Dog, Spaniel, Gold Collar, Padlock, 1830s, 4 3/8 In. 130.00
Figurine, Dog, Spaniel, Salt Glaze, 4 3/4 In., Pair 287.00
Figurine, Dog, Spaniel, White, Gilt Spots, Painted Eyes, 12 1/2 In. 137.00
Figurine, Dog, Spaniel, White, Rust Spots, Glass Eyes, Gold Collar, 11 In., Pair 300.00
Figurine, Dog, Spaniels, 9 1/2 In., Pair 272.00
Figurine, Dog, Whippet, Holding Rabbit In Mouth, Pillow Base, 12 In., Pair 900.00
Figurine, Dog, White, Black Nose, 12 In., Pair 240.00
Figurine, Dog, White, Gold Markings & Collar, Signed, 10 In. 95.00
Figurine, Dog, Wolfhound, Black & White, 11 In., Pair 385.00
Figurine, Dogs, Comforter, White, Glass Eyes, England, c.1870, 13 In. 215.00
Figurine, Dogs, Spaniel, Brown Curly Coats, 1790, 3 9/16 & 3 11/16 In., Pair 1380.00
Figurine, Fawn, Recumbent, Creamware, 1760, 2 3/4 In. 748.00
Figurine, Fox, With Tan Coat, Brown Eyes, 1815, 6 3/16 In. 575.00
Figurine, Gentleman, Seated, Book & Spectacles, 8 1/8 In. 275.00

Figurine, George Washington, Civilian Dress, Gold, Gray, Black, 14 In. 3850.00
Figurine, Girl, Pink Dress, Seated, Black & White Setter, c.1860, 4 1/2 In., Pair 375.00
Figurine, Girl, Riding Goat, Polychrome, 5 1/8 In. 300.00
Figurine, Harlequin, 19th Century 285.00
Figurine, Hen, On Nest, c.1830, 3 3/4 In., Pair 150.00
Figurine, Hen, On Nest, c.1830, 8 1/2 In., Pair 325.00
Figurine, House, Georgian, Polychrome, 19th Century, 3 3/4 In. 100.00
Figurine, Jockey On Horseback, 11 In., Pair 345.00
Figurine, Leopard, 1 White, Black Spots, 1 Reddish-Brown, Black Spots, 3 In., Pair 225.00
Figurine, Lion & Lioness, Recumbent, 19th Century, 8 1/2 In. 1350.00
Figurine, Milking Maid, 6 In. 80.00
Figurine, Parrot In Flight, 8 5/8 In. 70.00
Figurine, Pastille Burner In Cottage Form, Polychrome, 19th Century, 4 1/4 In. 100.00
Figurine, Rabbit, Black & White, Brown & Green Base, 3 1/4 In. 302.00
Figurine, Robin Hood, 15 In. 650.00
Figurine, Russian Fortress, Sebastopol, Gray With Red & Green, c.1854, 8 In. 525.00
Figurine, Scotsman, Dog & Gun, Enameled, 13 1/2 In. 275.00
Figurine, Shepherd Boy, Chalkware, 7 In. 125.00
Figurine, Shepherd Boy, Next To Tree Stump, Dog, 1780, 8 1/2 In. 1840.00
Figurine, William Penn & Child, Enameled, 10 1/4 In. 225.00
Figurine, Woman, Standing, Holding Fan, Plumed Hat, 1810, 4 3/4 In. 345.00
Figurine, Zebra, Coleslaw Design On Base, c.1850, 8 1/2 In., Pair 1100.00
Gravy Boat, Catskill Mountains, Hudson River, Blue, c.1840, 7 3/4 In. 565.00
Gravy Boat, Underplate, Liberty Blue 40.00
Group, Charity, Classical Woman Holding Baby, 1805, 7 15/16 & 8 5/8 In. 345.00
Group, Scuffle, 2 Little Girls & Boy, Grappling With Boy, 1810-1820, 7 1/2 In. 431.00
Group, Sheep, Tree Center, c.1860, 3 1/2 In. 350.00
Group, Tithe Pig, Farmer, Black Hat, Black Frocked Parson, 1825, 7 In. . . . . . .1115.00 to 1840.00
Humidor, Dog, Face On Back, White, Red & Brown, Pre World War II 425.00
Jar, Cover, Creamware, Mottled Gray Green, Blue Glaze, 2 In. 1265.00
Jar, Cover, Shaving Soap, A.G. Hackney 295.00
Jar, Salt Glaze, Blue Stylized Tulips, Flattened Spire Finial, 1755, 3 1/2 In. 805.00
Jar, Tobacco, With Ducks 70.00
Jug, Hot Milk, Acorn Finial Cover, Redware, Handle, 1740, 5 1/2 In. 270.00
Jug, Hunting Scene, Black Enameled Rose, Blue, Yellow, Green, Brown, 10 In. 345.00
Jug, Milk, Cover, Pear Shape Body, Salt Glaze, 1750, 4 5/8 In. 1725.00
Jug, Puzzle, Salt Glaze, Bluebirds, Applied Shells, 1760, 8 1/2 In. 6325.00
Mug, Immortal Shakespeare, Play Scenes Around Top, Blue, 4 3/4 In. 175.00
Mug, Mother Hubbard, Child's, Large 65.00
Mug, Need Tries Friendship, Blue & White 145.00
Mug, Punch & Judy, Soft Paste, Red, Green, Yellow & Blue 295.00
Mug, Ship, Sailor's Lament, Orange Luster, With Frog, 4 In. 165.00
Mustard Pot, Pink Flowers, Blue Border, 3 1/4 In. 35.00
Mustard Pot, Pink, Blue Flowers, Signed, 3 1/4 In. 45.00
Pap Boat, Blue Stylized Leaf Design, Oval, 1850, 4 3/4 In. 125.00
Pickle Dish, Leaf Shape, Stem Form Handle, 3 Conical Feet, 1765, 4 In., Pair 862.00
Pitcher, Black Transfer, Lafayette, Nation's Guest, 5 1/8 In. 220.00
Pitcher, Boston State House, Blue, 7 1/4 In. 545.00
Pitcher, Confederation, Indian Face, 1905, 7 In. 595.00
Pitcher, Corinth, Brown Transfer, 1840s, 12 In. 165.00
Pitcher, Cream, Young Person, With Sheep, Blue, White Transfer 69.00
Pitcher, Lambton Hall, Durham, Dark Blue, 6 3/4 In. 275.00
Pitcher, War Of 1812 Shape, Black Transfer, Buff Ground, 4 1/2 In. 1650.00
Plaque, Abraham Lincoln Birth Centennial, February 12, 1909, 9 x 6 In. 363.00
Plate, A Trifle For Charles In Center, Enoch Wood & Son, Dark Blue, White, 5 In. 185.00
Plate, American & Independence, Clews, Dark Blue, 10 5/8 In. 300.00
Plate, Boston State House, Reticulated Border, Rogers, 10 In. 950.00
Plate, Christ Rising From The Grave, 5 1/2 In. 120.00
Plate, City Hotel, New York, 8 1/2 In. 450.00
Plate, Dr. Franklin Little Strikes Fell Great Oaks, 5 1/2 In. 125.00
Plate, Exchange In Baltimore, 10 In. 550.00
Plate, Faulkbourn Hall, Stevenson, Dark Blue Transfer, 8 7/8 In. 105.00
Plate, For My Nephew, Blue Transfer, Colored Dots In Border, 6 1/4 In. 350.00

Plate, Fulham Church, Middlesex, R. Hall, Dark Blue Transfer, 8 1/2 In. 77.00
Plate, Gardener In Center With His Companion, Red, Green, 9 In. 1955.00
Plate, He That Will Not, When He May, Polychrome Transfer, 10 In. 485.00
Plate, Hollywell Cottage, Dark Blue Transfer, Impressed Riley, 10 In. 120.00
Plate, Italian Scenery, 5 3/4 In. 39.00
Plate, La Grange, Residence Of Marquis Lafayette, Blue Transfer, 10 1/4 In. . . . .135.00 to 300.00
Plate, Landing Of General Washington At Castle Garden, c.1825, 10 In. 450.00
Plate, Landing Of Lafayette, Dark Blue, Clews, 10 1/4 In. 330.00
Plate, Louise, New Wharf Pottery, 9 1/2 In. 25.00
Plate, Passaic Falls, A. Stevenson, Dark Blue, 10 1/4 In. 1090.00
Plate, Peace, Blue & White, 4 1/4 In. 450.00
Plate, Pine Orchard House, Catskill Mountains, Enoch Wood, Dark Blue, 10 In. 635.00
Plate, Sitting Up, 1800, 5 1/2 In. 120.00
Plate, Stevenson Fort, Gansevoort, N.Y., Dark Blue, 6 3/4 In. 800.00
Plate, Toddy, Catskill House, Hudson, Wood, 6 1/2 In. 520.00
Plate, Toddy, Hunter With Dog, Dark Blue Transfer, 5 In. 165.00
Plate, Union Line Pattern, Shell Border, Enoch Wood, 1820, 10 In. 375.00
Plate, View On Road To Lake George, A. Stevenson, Dark Blue, 8 3/4 In. 980.00
Plate, Washington, Praying At Valley Forge, Blue & White 165.00
Platter, Blue Pattern, Bourne & Leigh, 9 x 6 1/2 In. 25.00
Platter, Boston & Bunker's Hill, T. Godwin, 19th Century, 13 1/4 In. 373.00
Platter, Catskill Moss, Boston & Bunker's Hill, Blue, 1844, 19 In. 515.00
Platter, Dark Blue, A. Stevenson, 18 1/2 In. 4025.00
Platter, Donington Park, Building, Floral Border, White, 4 x 3 In. 144.00
Platter, Fairmount Near Philadelphia, Eagle Border, Kent & Stubbs, 20 In. 1925.00
Platter, French Scene, Dark Blue Transfer, 16 1/2 In. 990.00
Platter, Gem, Center Spread Eagle, Shield, R. Hammersley, 16 1/2 x 12 In. 315.00
Platter, Greek Coliseum Scene, Medium Dark Blue, 16 In. 125.00
Platter, Grosvenor, C.M. & S. Improved Stone China, Blue, White, 21 x 17 In. 55.00
Platter, Japan Pattern, Under & Overglazes Of Cobalt Blue, c.1820, 19 In. 350.00
Platter, Mendenhal Ferry, 16 1/2 In. 1320.00
Platter, Oriental Scenery Of Pagoda, Blue, White, 14 1/2 x 11 1/4 In. 431.00
Platter, Palestine, Stevenson, Dark Blue, 17 1/4 In. 715.00
Platter, Pastoral Genre Scene, Lavender, Signed, 1840, 16 In. 160.00
Platter, Pastoral Landscape, Strutting Turkey, Polychrome Transfer, 19 1/2 In. 375.00
Platter, Quadruped, Rhinoceros In Center Reserve, John Hall, 17 In. 1450.00
Platter, Sancho Panza & The Duchess, Dark Blue Transfer, 18 7/8 In. 385.00
Platter, State House Boston, Dark Blue, 19th Century, 11 1/2 In. 675.00
Platter, Upper Ferry Bridge Across Schuylkill River, Stubbs & Stubbs, 18 1/2 In. 1485.00
Platter, View Of Dublin Harbor, Seashell Border, Woods 590.00
Sauce, Figures, Grazing Cows By The Water, 1820, 6 In., Pair 200.00
Sauceboat, Salt Glaze, Blue Floral, Loop Handle, 1755, 6 In. 345.00
Saucer, Dark Blue Transfer With Shells, Impressed Mark, 5 5/8 In. 50.00
Snuffbox, Cover, 3 Floral Sprigs, Pale Blue Ground, 1765, 1 7/8 In. 2070.00
Stirrup Cup, Fox Head, Russet-Brown Coat, White Eyes, 1820, 5 1/4 In. 400.00
Stirrup Cup, Greyhound Head, Pale Mustard Coat, Black Edged Rim, 1825, 7 In. 1265.00
Strainer, Creamware, Mottled Gray, Yellow, Green Glaze, 1760, 2 5/8 In. 1380.00
Sugar, Floral, Gaudy, 4 7/8 In. 105.00
Sugar, Liberty Blue 15.00
Tankard, Salt Glaze, Blue Flowering Branches, Handle, 1755, 6 3/8 In. 345.00
Tea Caddy, Pineapple, Creamware, Cylindrical, Diamond, Green Leaves, 5 In. 2587.00
Tea Set, Blue & White, 4 Cups & Saucers, Teapot, Sugar Bowl, Miniature 375.00
Tea Set, Child's, C.A. & Son, 19th Century, 21 Piece 345.00
Tea Set, Cover, Form Of Woman, Victorian Dress 125.00
Tea Set, Creamware, Teabowl, Saucer, Mottled Brown, 1760, 6 Piece 2530.00
Teabowl & Saucer, Salt Glaze, Blue Lollipop Florals, 1765, 2 Piece 1035.00
Teabowl & Saucer, Salt Glaze, Blue Stylized Branches, 1750, 2 Piece 460.00
Teapot, Cauliflower, Early 19th Century, 4 1/2 In. 373.00
Teapot, Cover, Flowering Fruit Branch, Loop Handle, Salt Glaze, 3 13/16 In. 345.00
Teapot, Cover, Grapevines, Crabstock Spout, Handle, Spherical, 4 3/8 In. . . . . . .690.00 to 1840.00
Teapot, Cover, Indian Boy, Crabstock Spout, Handle, Red, 1745-1755, 3 7/8 In. 1265.00
Teapot, Cover, Liberty, Rope Twist Handle, Floral Sprigs, 3 In. 4887.00
Teapot, Cover, Pear Shape, 3 Graduated Scallop Shells, Green Branches, 5 In. 2875.00

Teapot, Cover, Tapered Cylindrical Spout, Loop Handle, Red, 1750-1760, 4 In. 805.00
Teapot, Cover, Tower Building Amidst Trees, Brown, Green, Blue, Black, 5 In. 1092.00
Teapot, Cover, Vine Leaf, Serrated Leaf Edge, Green, Ocher Glaze, 1765, 4 3/8 In. 2587.00
Teapot, Cover, White Pecten Shell, Shell Above Scalloped Foot, 1750, 5 In. 1380.00
Teapot, Redware, Allover Chevron Bands, Acorn Finial, 1755, 3 In. 365.00
Teapot, Redware, Black Glaze, Applied Vines, Bird Finial, 1770, 3 1/2 In. 460.00
Teapot, Wadsworth Tower 1550.00
Teapot, White Salt Glaze, Acorn Finial, Loop Handle, 1750, 4 1/2 In. 805.00
Toby Jugs are listed in their own category.
Tray, Figures By River, Border Of Flowers, Scroll Handles, c.1820, 8 In. 92.00
Tureen, Cover, Figures By The River, Floral Border, Handles, 7 1/2 In. 316.00
Tureen, Gravy, Dark Blue, 19th Century, 8 1/2 In. 575.00
Tureen, Leaves On Lid, Lion Head Scroll Handles, Dark Blue Transfer, Ladle, 12 In. . . . 2420.00
Tureen, Sauce, Stand, Blue Design, Octagonal, James Edwards, 1850s, 8 1/2 In. 350.00
Tureen, Soup, Liberty Blue 300.00
Vase, Cow & Feeding Calf, Flowing Stream, c.1860, 10 5/8 In. 440.00
Vase, Cow & Feeding Calf, Flowing Stream, c.1860, 11 3/8 In. 440.00
Vase, Figural, Deer & Tree Spill, Gray, Brown Curly Coat, 19th Century, 4 In. 345.00
Vase, Tree Trunk Form, Yellow, Pastel Ink & Blue Polychrome Trim, 10 In., Pair 2000.00
Vase, Tulip, Open Blossom, Bud Striated In Rose, 4 Green Leaves, 1835, 5 In. 3737.00
Vase, Tulip, Open Blossom, Small Bud, Striated In Puce, Purple, 6 1/4 x 6 In. 2875.00
Waste Bowl, Nest, R. Hall, Blue, 6 1/4 In. 190.00

STANGL Pottery traces its history back to the Fulper Pottery of New
Jersey. In 1910, Johann Martin Stangl started working at Fulper. He
bought into the firm in 1913, became president in 1926, and in 1929
changed the company name to Stangl Pottery. The pottery made dinnerwares and a line of limited-edition bird figurines. The company went
out of business in 1978. The numbers used by Stangl for the bird figures indicate two birds in one figure by adding the letter *D,* for double.

Ashtray, Canada Goose, Oval . . . . .35.00 to 55.00
Ashtray, Deer, Oval 70.00
Ashtray, Duck . . . . .40.00 to 45.00
Ashtray, Flying Duck, Large 30.00
Ashtray, Mallard, Square, 9 In. 80.00
Ashtray, Pheasant, Oval . . . . .30.00 to 45.00
Ashtray, Pig 60.00
Ashtray, Pink Elephant, Square 265.00
Ashtray, Pintail, Oval 35.00
Ashtray, Quail 40.00
Ashtray, Quail, Oval . . . . .35.00 to 60.00
Ashtray, Radiant, Oval 45.00
Ashtray, Redhead, Square, 9 In. 100.00
Ashtray, Woodcock, Oval 60.00
Bank, Piggy, Blue, Square Sticker 35.00
Basket, Terra Rose, Mauve, Rope Handle, 6 3/4 In. 50.00
Bird, Bird Of Paradise, No. 3408 . . . . 115.00
Bird, Black Poll Warbler, No. 3810 . . . . 55.00
Bird, Blue-Headed Vireo, No. 3448 . . . . 85.00
Bird, Bluebird, No. 3276 . . . . .50.00 to 100.00
Bird, Brewer's Blackbird, No. 3591 . . . . 88.00
Bird, Broadbill Hummingbird, No. 3629 . . . . 115.00
Bird, Cardinal, No. 3444, Revised . . . . .55.00 to 70.00
Bird, Chestnut-Backed, Chickadee, No. 3811 . . . . 120.00
Bird, Chestnut-Sided Warbler, No. 3812 . . . . 90.00
Bird, Chickadees, No. 3581 . . . . 200.00
Bird, Cock Pheasant, No. 3492 . . . . 100.00
Bird, Cockatoo, No. 3584 . . . . 300.00
Bird, Cockatoo, White, Medium, No. 3580 . . . . 325.00
Bird, Cockatoos, Double, No. 3405D . . . . .125.00 to 150.00
Bird, Duck, Standing, No. 3250A 85.00
Bird, Flying Duck, No. 3443 . . . . 300.00

Bird, Golden Crowned Kinglet, No. 3848 .... 120.00
Bird, Gray Cardinal, No. 3596 .... 50.00
Bird, Hen, No. 3286 .... 65.00
Bird, Hen, Pheasant, No. 3491 .... 275.00
Bird, Hen, Rooster, No. 3446 & No. 3445, Gray, Pair 300.00
Bird, Kentucky Warbler, No. 3598 .... 50.00
Bird, Key West Quail, 1 Wing Up, No. 3454 ....220.00 to 325.00
Bird, Kingfisher, No. 3406S 75.00
Bird, Kingfishers, Double, No. 3406D ....132.00 to 200.00
Bird, Lovebird, No. 3400 .... 55.00
Bird, Nuthatch, No. 3593 .... 44.00
Bird, Oriole, No. 3402S 100.00
Bird, Orioles, Double, No. 3402D ....95.00 to 100.00
Bird, Owl, No. 3407 .... 500.00
Bird, Painted Bunting, No. 3452 .... 143.00
Bird, Parakeets, Double, No. 3582D ....190.00 to 200.00
Bird, Parrot, No. 3449 .... 165.00
Bird, Parula Warbler, No. 3583 ....40.00 to 77.00
Bird, Passenger Pigeon, No. 3450 .... 1250.00
Bird, Pheasant, Feeding, Della Ware, Terra Rose, No. 3586 .... 500.00
Bird, Prothonatary, Warbler, No. 3447 .... 75.00
Bird, Red Faced Warbler, No. 3594 .... 55.00
Bird, Riefers Hummingbird, No. 3628 .... 22.00
Bird, Rooster, Blue, Gray, No. 3445 .... 185.00
Bird, Scarlet Tanager, No. 3749S 175.00
Bird, White-Crowned Pigeons, Double, No. 3518D 500.00
Bird, Wilson Warbler, No. 3597 .... 65.00
Bird, Wren, No. 3401S ....70.00 to 75.00
Bird, Wrens, Double, Revised, No. 3401D ....80.00 to 98.00
Bowl, Country Garden, Salad, 12 In. ....40.00 to 45.00
Bowl, Fruit & Flowers, Vegetable, 8 In. 35.00
Bowl, Golden Blossom, Vegetable, Divided 25.00
Bowl, Orchard Song, Salad, 15 In. 30.00
Bowl, Thistle, Mixing, 5 1/2 In. 10.00
Bowl, Thistle, Salad, 10 In. ....40.00 to 45.00
Bowl, Thistle, Salad, 12 In. 50.00
Bowl, Wild Rose, 5 1/2 In. 18.00
Butter, Orchard Song 35.00
Cake Stand, Florette, 10 In. 20.00
Candle Warmer, Dogwood, Pink, Green 12.00
Candle Warmer, Provincial 22.00
Carafe, Laurel 110.00
Carafe, Tropic Isle 135.00
Casserole, Caughley, Tiffany, 3 Qt. 75.00
Chop Plate, Bachelor Button, 12 1/4 In. 30.00
Chop Plate, Country Life, Farmhouse, 12 1/2 In. 450.00
Chop Plate, Garland, 12 1/2 In. 25.00
Chop Plate, Golden Harvest, 14 1/2 In. 25.00
Chop Plate, Magnolia, 14 1/2 In. 40.00
Chop Plate, Terra Rose, 12 1/2 In. 225.00
Chop Plate, Wild Rose, 12 1/2 In. 35.00
Chop Plate, Wild Rose, 14 1/2 In. 55.00
Cigarette Box, Blue Daisy, 4 1/2 x 5 1/2 In. 35.00
Cigarette Box, Fruit 50.00
Cigarette Box, Gladiola, 7 1/2 x 4 In. 45.00
Cigarette Box, Mountain Laurel 40.00
Coaster/Ashtray, Thistle 16.00
Coffee Server, Lyric 65.00
Coffee Warmer, Thistle ....25.00 to 40.00
Coffeepot, Blueberry, Individual, 4 In. 50.00
Coffeepot, Florentine 30.00
Coffeepot, Town & Country, Yellow 50.00

Creamer, Golden Blossom	8.00
Creamer, Town & Country, Blue	15.00
Creamer, Town & Country, Yellow, Black, 3 3/4 In.	10.00
Cup, Circus, Clown, Kiddieware	65.00
Cup, Ranger Boy, Kiddieware	95.00
Cup & Plate, Peter Rabbit, Kiddieware	250.00
Cup & Saucer, Magnolia	10.00
Cup & Saucer, Thistle	14.00
Dinner Set, Apple Delight, 50 Piece	200.00
Dish, Country Garden, Celery	25.00
Dish, Five Little Pigs, Kiddieware	145.00
Dish, Kitten Capers, Kiddieware	95.00 to 105.00
Dish, Our Barnyard Friends, Kiddieware	175.00
Dish & Cup, Our Barnyard Friends, Kiddieware	165.00
Dog, Sitting, No. 3280	275.00
Eggcup, Blueberry	15.00
Eggcup, Thistle	15.00
Figurine, Draft Horse, No. 3244	275.00
Figurine, Rabbit Cotton Holder	385.00
Flowerpot, Ringles, Large	55.00
Flowerpot, Yellow Tulip	12.00
Gravy Boat, Magnolia	15.00 to 18.00
Gravy Boat, Thistle, Stand	35.00 to 38.00
Mug, Flying, Duck	40.00
Mug, Pheasant	40.00
Mug, Terra Rose	59.00
Mug & Saucer, Florette, Stacking	12.00
Pitcher, Bittersweet, 2 Qt.	40.00
Pitcher, Fruit, 2 Qt.	40.00
Pitcher, Garden Flower, 1 Qt.	20.00
Pitcher, Tangerine, No. 1388, Miniature, 2 1/4 In.	55.00
Pitcher, Town & Country, Blue, 2 1/2 Pt.	65.00 to 95.00
Pitcher, Wild Rose, 1 Pt.	25.00
Planter, Gold, French Phone, No. 5303	150.00
Planter, Terra Rose	40.00
Plate, Colonial, White, Grill, 11 5/8 In.	25.00
Plate, Country Garden, 10 In.	15.00
Plate, Country Life, Rooster, 6 In.	45.00
Plate, Deviled Egg, Rooster	70.00
Plate, Florette, 8 In.	10.00 to 14.00
Plate, Little Bo Peep, Kiddieware, 9 In.	100.00 to 125.00
Plate, Little Boy Blue, Kiddieware, 9 In.	125.00
Plate, Little Quackers, Kiddieware, 9 In.	95.00 to 140.00
Plate, Magnolia, 8 In.	12.00
Plate, Magnolia, 10 In.	6.00 to 15.00
Plate, Provincial, 8 In.	12.00
Plate, Provincial, 10 In.	15.00
Plate, Provincial, Grill, 11 In.	25.00
Plate, Ranger, Boy, Kiddieware, 10 In.	145.00
Plate, Rooster, Hanging, 6 In.	29.00
Plate, Thistle, 6 In.	6.00 to 8.00
Plate, Thistle, 8 In.	8.00 to 12.00
Plate, Thistle, 9 In.	10.00 to 14.00
Plate, Thistle, 10 In.	18.00
Plate, Tulip, 11 In.	48.00
Plate, Wild Rose, 150th Anniversary, 5 In.	28.00
Plate, Wood Duck, 11 1/2 In.	125.00
Plate & Cup, Little Bo Peep, Kiddieware	200.00
Platter, Fruit, 14 In.	75.00
Relish, Golden Harvest, 11 In.	20.00 to 24.00
Relish, Thistle	20.00 to 22.00
Relish, Wild Rose	20.00

Salt & Pepper, Magnolia 20.00
Sign, Dealer, Black, Gold, White Gloss 125.00
Soup, Dish, Lug, Provincial 12.00
Soup, Dish, Lug, Thistle 10.00
Soup, Dish, Town & Country, Blue 48.00
Spoon Rest, Town & Country, Blue 48.00
Sugar, Country Life 30.00
Sugar, Cover, Lyric 22.00
Sugar, Cover, Magnolia 20.00
Sugar & Creamer, Provincial 28.00
Sugar & Creamer, Town & Country 30.00
Teapot, Flora, Footed, Individual, 5 3/4 In. 20.00
Tray, Bread, Country Garden 40.00
Tray, Condiment, Thistle 25.00
Vase, Double Side Hinge Handle, Tangerine Flambe, Egg Shape, 7 1/2 In. 110.00
Vase, Horsehead, Blue, Mauve Mane 695.00
Vase, Matte Crystalline, Double Long Side Loop Handles, 11 1/2 In. 190.00
Vase, Rainbow, 18 In. 450.00
Vase, Terra Rose, 5 In. 40.00
Vase, Terra Rose, Green, 10 In. 40.00
Vase, Terra Rose, Incised Tulip, 2 Handles, 6 In. 24.00
Vase, Tulip, Yellow, Early Penn 55.00
Wig Stand, Blond Head 325.00
Wig Stand, Brunette, Wooden Base, Marked .... .225.00 to 250.00
Wig Stand, Red Head 325.00
Wig Stand, White Head 175.00

STEINS have been used by beer and ale drinkers for over 500 years. They have been made of ivory, porcelain, stoneware, faience, silver, pewter, wood, or glass in sizes up to nine gallons. Although some were made by Mettlach, Meissen, Capo-di-Monte, and other famous factories, most were made by less important German potteries. The words *Geschutz* or *Musterschutz* on a stein are the German words for *patented* or *registered design*, not company names. Steins are still being made in the old styles. Lithophane steins may be found in the Lithophane category.

2 Women & Man, By Lake, Pewter Cover, Stoneware, 1/5 Liter 155.00
15th Germany Shooting Festival Muncheon, Pewter Lid, Stoneware, 1906, 1 Liter . 775.00
Amber, Hinged Pewter Lid, Embossed Ram's Heads, Glass, 15 1/4 In. 550.00
American Legion, Cincinnati, Ohio, Pottery, 1896 .... 20.00
Anheuser-Busch, Santa's Helper, Pewter Lid, Gerz, 1/2 Liter 120.00
Art Nouveau Pewter Lid, Stoneware, Signed, L. Hohlwein, 1/5 Liter 660.00
Baby, Beehive .... 1980.00 to 2200.00
Baker, Porcelain, Transfer & Enameled, Pewter Lid, 1/2 Liter 280.00
Bardwell's Root Beer, Hinged Pewter Lid, Bristol Blaze, 14 1/2 In. 605.00
Barmaid, Schierholz, 1/2 Liter 1485.00
Battle Of Lexington Relief Scene, Whites Utica, Stoneware, 8 1/2 In. 500.00
Bavarian Medical School 3300.00
Beehive, Inlaid Lid, 1/5 Liter 415.00
Bicycle Form, Lithophane Bottom, Musterschutz, 1/2 Liter 495.00
Bird Dressed In Vest & Shoes, Pewter Cover, Stoneware, 1/5 Liter 350.00
Bismark, Porcelain, Porcelain Lid, 1/2 Liter 360.00
Blown Glass, Applied Glass Prunts & Base Ruffle, Peach Coloring, Pewter Lid, 1/2 Liter 215.00
Blown Glass, Design, Germany, 1870, 3/10 Liter 90.00
Blown Glass, Eagle, Transfer & Enameled, Art Nouveau Pewter Lid, 1/2 Liter 220.00
Blown Glass, Girl In White Enamel, Ribbed, Green, Pink Inlaid Lid, 1/4 Liter 236.00
Blown Glass, Soccer Player, Transfer & Enameled, Silver Plated Lid, 1/4 Liter 165.00
Blue Glass, Mary Gregory Style, White Enameled Boy, Germany, 1890, 1/2 Liter 193.00
Blue To Clear Threaded, Dolphin Pewter Thumbpiece, Glass, 14 3/4 In. 495.00
Boar's Head, Figural, Schierholz, 5 Liter 3630.00
Brewery Burger Brau, Stoneware, 1 Liter 820.00
Budweiser, Bald Eagle 400.00

Budweiser, King Cobra 275.00
Budweiser, Osprey 400.00
Building In Forest Scene, Leaf Design, Engraved, Red, Glass, 1/5 Liter 277.00
Buildings, Faience, Pewter Cover, Base, Blue, 1960, 1 Liter 140.00
Buildings & Floral, Faience, Pewter Cover, Base, 1960, 1 Liter 180.00
Butcher, Barbell Painted Under Handle, Pewter Lid, 1/5 Liter 160.00
Butcher, Lines In Lithophane, Pewter Lid, 1/5 Liter 385.00
Butcher, Porcelain, Transfer & Enameled, 1/2 Liter ....'. 275.00
Carpenter, Lithophane, Enamel, 1/5 Liter 390.00
Carpenter, Pewter Lid, 1/5 Liter 300.00
Cat On Book, 1/2 Liter ....*Illus* 3190.00
Cat With Fish, Eckhardt & Engler, No. 420, 1/2 Liter 270.00
Cavaliers Having Good Time, Pewter Lid, Pottery, 1/5 Liter 360.00
Chauffeur 1595.00
Cheese Maker, Pewter Lid, 1/5 Liter 935.00
Comical Bowling Scene, Pewter Cover, 1/5 Liter 103.00
Couple Portrait, Porcelain Lid, Pewter Rim 75.00
Cucumber, Schierholz, 1/5 Liter 345.00
Cut Design, Pewter Cover, Base, 1/5 Liter ....92.00 to 182.00
Diesinger, Relief, Musicians, Flowers, Castle, Dwarfs, Pewter Lid, No. 742, 1/5 Liter ... 415.00
Dogs Attacking Deer Scene, Glass, Porcelain Inlaid Lid, 1/5 Liter 155.00
Eagle, Glass, Enameled, Pewter Lid, 1/5 Liter 270.00
Enameled City Scene, Tin Lid, Glass, Bohemian, 1900, 3/10 Liter 110.00
Enameled Man Drinking, Tin Lid, Glass, Bohemian, 1920, 4 1/2 In. 100.00
Enameled Verse & Yale University Seal, Glass, Germany, 1900, 1/2 Liter 165.00
Etched, Gasthaus Scene, Pewter Cover, Hauber & Reuther, 1/5 Liter 155.00
Etched, People In Boat, Pewter Cover, Hauber & Reuther, 1/5 Liter 225.00
Face, Pewter Lid, Pottery, Marked, Gerz, 1/5 Liter 200.00
Figure Of Man On Pewter Top, Pottery, Villeroy & Boch 275.00
Fish, Glass, Enameled, Pale Green, Crest, 1594, Fritz Heckert, 1/5 Liter 350.00
Foo Dog Finial, Burled Wood, 11 1/2 In. 2875.00
Forest Ranger Visiting Scene, Pewter Lid, Stoneware, M. Pauson, 1/5 Liter 352.00
Frogs In Suits, Lounging, Lizard Type Handle, Pewter Lid, Pottery, 1/5 Liter ....: 275.00
Funnel Man, Pottery, 1/5 Liter 90.00
Gentleman Boar, Beehive 3190.00
Gentleman Rabbit, Porcelain, Marked R.P.M., Inlaid Lid, 1/2 Liter 250.00
Gnomes Bowling, Inebriates, Heinrich Schlitt, 1/2 Liter 225.00
Hotel Bellman, Luggage Scene, Pewter Lid, 1/5 Liter 1155.00
Hunter, Faience, Pewter Cover, 1960, 1/4 Liter 110.00
Man Playing Mandolin, Faience, Pewter Cover, Base, 1960, 1 Liter 140.00
Man Riding High Wheel Bicycle, Pewter Lid, 1896, 1/5 Liter 495.00
Man With Beer & Radish, 1/5 Liter 360.00
Mettlach steins are listed in the Mettlach category.
Military Shooting Contest, No. 622, Relief, Pewter Cover, 1/5 Liter 75.00
Military-Ulanen Regiment, No. 1271, Pewter Cover, 1/5 Liter 68.00
Monk, Party Scene With Monks, Pewter Lid, Dumler & Breiden, 1/5 Liter 440.00
Monk, Strap Around Handle, 1/5 Liter 270.00
Monks In Cellar Scene, Pewter Lid, M. Pauson, 1/5 Liter 319.00
Monument In New Orleans, Seal Of Louisiana On Cover, 1/5 Liter 225.00
Munchner, Ceramic, 10 In. 15.00
Munchner Beer, Barmaid & Cavalier On Either Side, Pewter Lid, 1 Liter 1375.00
Munich Child, Inlaid Lid, J. Reinemann, 1/2 Liter 165.00
Musicians, Dwarfs & Floral On Sides, Pewter Lid, Diesinger, 1/5 Liter 360.00
Mythological Scene, Beehive, 1/4 Liter ....*Illus* 1980.00
Nurnberg Tower, Pewter Lid Forms Roof, Stoneware, Marked T.W., 1/2 Liter 290.00
People, Brown Marbleized Finish, Inlaid Cover, Villeroy & Boch, 1/5 Liter 173.00
People Riding Horseback Through Forest, Pewter Cover, Dumler & Breiden, 1 Liter ... 430.00
Rampant Lion Finial, Silver Collar, Jeweled Body, Sterling Silver, Germany, 7 1/4 In. .. 575.00
Regensburg, Gambrinus, Porcelain Cover, 1 Liter 120.00
Regimental, 2-Sided Scene, Eagle Thumblift With Star Pendant, 1/5 Liter 1070.00
Regimental, 2-Sided Scene, Griffin Thumblift, 12 In., 1/5 Liter ....515.00 to 645.00
Regimental, 2-Sided Scene, Wurttemberg Thumblift, 12 In., 1/5 Liter 565.00

Stein, Cat On Book,
1/2 Liter;
Stein, Mythological Scene,
Beehive, 1/4 Liter;
Stein, Regimental,
Luftschiffer, 1/2 Liter

Regimental, 4-Sided Scene, Floral Thumblift, 1910-1911, 1/5 Liter	140.00
Regimental, 4-Sided Scene, Lion Thumblift, Blue Glass Jewel In Center, 1/5 Liter	440.00
Regimental, 4-Sided Scene, Pewter Cover, 1 Liter	865.00
Regimental, 4-Sided Scene, Porcelain, 1/5 Liter	280.00
Regimental, 4-Sided Scene, Wurttemberg Thumblift, 12 In., 1/5 Liter	635.00
Regimental, 22nd Infantry, 2-Sided Scene, Lion Thumblift, 1/5 Liter	460.00
Regimental, 50 Field Artillery, Pewter Strap, Porcelain, 1/5 Liter	580.00
Regimental, 88 Infantry, 4-Sided Scene, Eagle Thumblift, 1/5 Liter	462.00
Regimental, 97th Signal, 1969-1970, 1/5 Liter	90.00
Regimental, Artillery, Lid, 1/5 Liter	85.00
Regimental, Artillery, Porcelain, 1/2 Liter	90.00
Regimental, Battle Scene From War, Pewter Lid, Dumler & Breiden, 1 Liter	495.00
Regimental, Field Artillery, Eagle Finial, Porcelain, Ludwigsburg, 1893-1895, 1/2 Liter	390.00
Regimental, Garde Field Artillery, Eagle Thumblift, Lines In Lithophane, 1/5 Liter	845.00
Regimental, Garde Grenadier, 2-Sided Scene, Eagle Thumblift In Beak, 1/5 Liter	1070.00
Regimental, Hussar Skull	2640.00
Regimental, Infantry, Lid, 1/5 Liter	90.00
Regimental, Infantry, Roster, Eagle Thumblift, Porcelain, Rastat 1903-1905, 1/2 Liter	555.00
Regimental, Lee Barracks, 1/5 Liter	110.00
Regimental, Luftschiffer, 1/2 Liter ....*Illus*	3410.00
Regimental, Soldier, Lion Thumblift With Prism, 1904-1906, 1/5 Liter	2145.00
Regimental, Tactical Air Force, 1955-1956, 1/5 Liter	130.00
Regimental, Third Field Artillery, Figural Pewter Top, Lithophane Base, 1899, 10 In.	345.00
Regimental, U.S. Army Hospital, 1965, 1/5 Liter	90.00
Regimentals, Eighth Wuerttemberg Infantry, Figural Pewter Lid, Lithophane Base, 11 In.	860.00
Roof Tile Manufacturer, Porcelain, Ceramic, Pewter Lid, 1/2 Liter	590.00
Ruby Glass, Gilded Wheel Cut Spa Scenes, Matching Lid, Bohemian, 1850, 1/2 Liter	990.00
Ruby Stained Glass, Cut Pattern, Inlaid Lid, Bohemian, 1860, 1/2 Liter	185.00
Rumph, Protruding Face, Blue Glaze, Pottery, 5 In.	225.00
Scene Of Cavaliers With Crossbows, Glass, Enameled, Brass Cover, Green, 12 In.	232.00
Schlitz Beer, 1971	25.00
Singing Pig, Inlaid Lid, Porcelain, Schierholz, 1/2 Liter	590.00
Skull, Inlaid Lid, Porcelain, E. Bohne & Sohne, 1/5 Liter	605.00
Skull, Inlaid Lid, Pottery, 1/5 Liter	330.00
Soccer, Scene Of Soccer Game, Soccer Ball Finial, Pottery Lid, 1 Liter	495.00
Soccer Ball Shape, 1/5 Liter	1550.00
Stoneware, Blue Figures, Bulbous, White's, Utica	295.00
Tailor, Elaborate Scene Around Front Of Body, Pewter Lid, 1/5 Liter	660.00
Tivili Lager, Pre-Prohibition, Germany, 6 1/2 In.	10.00
Town Scene, Trees, Hand Painted, Faience, Rastal, Pewter Cover, Marked, 1 Liter	225.00
U.S. Military Men, No. 1258, Relief, Pewter Cover, 1/5 Liter	115.00
Verse, Enameled, Pewter Cover, 1/5 Liter	86.00

Washington Crossing Delaware, Relief Scene, Blue-Gray, Stoneware, 11 1/2 In. 500.00
Washington Crossing Delaware, Utica, Stoneware 295.00
Woman, Seminude, Bowling, Pewter Cover, 1/5 Liter 155.00
Wrap Around Alligator, Porcelain, E. Bohne & Son, 1/4 Liter 220.00
Zither Player, Carved Horn Finial, Thumblift, Pewter Lid, Stoneware, 1/5 Liter 407.00

STEREO CARDS that were made for stereoscope viewers became popular after 1840. Two almost identical pictures were mounted on a stiff cardboard backing so that, when viewed through a stereoscope, a three-dimensional picture could be seen. Value is determined by maker and by subject. These cards were made in quantity through the 1930s.

Alaska, Pack Trains For Mines, Color, World Series Pub., 1889 .... 12.00
Chicago Fire, Close-Up View 18.00
Courtship & Marriage, Bride On Her Wedding Day, 3 1/2 x 7 In. 40.00
Dewey's Parade 8.00
Elevator Tower, Niagara Bridge 15.00
Indian, 1900s 25.00
Indian Beadwork 20.00
Picket Guard & Prisoners, Civil War 50.00
Scenes From Life Of Christ, Nativity To Resurrection, 3 1/2 x 7 In. 35.00

STEREOSCOPES were used for viewing stereo cards. The hand viewer was invented by Oliver Wendell Holmes, although more complicated table models were used before his was produced in 1859. Do not confuse the stereoscope with the stereopticon, a magic lantern that used glass slides.

Bates, Viewer 65.00
Keystone Eye Comfort, Brown, Wood 50.00
Pierced Metal, Wooden 65.00
Realist 25.00
Viewer, With 2 Girlie Cards 85.00

STERLING SILVER, see Silver-Sterling category.

STEUBEN glass was made at the Steuben Glass Works of Corning, New York. The factory, founded by Frederick Carder and T.G. Hawkes, Sr., was purchased by the Corning Glass Company. They continued to make glass called *Steuben.* Many types of art glass were made at Steuben. The firm is still making exceptional quality glass but it is clear, modern-style glass. Additional pieces may be found in the Aurene, Cluthra, and perfume bottle categories.

Ashtray, Commemorative, 1946 .... 1200.00
Bowl, Amethyst, Footed, Signed, 10 In. 210.00
Bowl, Aquamarine, Paper Label, 5 In. 150.00
Bowl, Blue, Pillar Shape, 4-Rib Design, Carder, 7 In. 4255.00
Bowl, Center, Gold Calcite, Black Glass Base, 3 1/2 x 13 1/2 In. 825.00
Bowl, Etched Acanthus, Leaf Design, Carder, 6 1/4 In. 1035.00
Bowl, Finger, Cintra, Opal, Blue & Pink 130.00
Bowl, George Thompson, Oval, 1949, 9 5/8 In. 225.00
Bowl, Gold Calcite, Rolled Stretch Rim, 2 1/2 x 5 1/2 In. 410.00
Bowl, Grotesque, Green, 12 In. 165.00
Bowl, Ivrene, Grotesque, 12 In. 450.00
Bowl, Jade, Black, Signed, 4 x 8 x 4 3/4 In. 440.00
Bowl, Pink Cintra, Tapered Shape, Mottled Pink, 10 In. 402.00
Bowl, Pomona Green, 11 In. 50.00
Bowl, Pomona Green, Flower, 4 Hollow Stems Around Central Opening, 5 x 10 In. 345.00
Bowl, Shell Form Handles, John Dreves, 1939, 7 In. 103.00
Bowl, Star Spangled, No. 8114, 10 1/2 In. 398.00
Bowl, Tapered Trumpet, Pink Cintra, Mottled, Bubble, 5 In. 405.00
Box, Dresser, Cover, Rosaline, Alabaster Knob & Base, 7 1/2 x 7 3/4 In. 385.00
Candleholder, Bowl Form, Triple Looped Base, 5 1/2 In., Pair 195.00
Candlestick, Double Twisted Stem, Amber, 10 In., Pair 495.00

Candlestick, Engraved, Ribbed Stem, Floral, Swag Wheel, Acid Stamped, 11 In., Pair . . 375.00
Centerpiece, Celeste Blue, Pear Shape, Floral Etched, Flanged Rim, 6 In. 385.00
Centerpiece, Oriental Jade, Ribbed, Scalloped Flanged Edge, 4 x 11 1/2 In. 795.00
Chandelier, 3-Light, Iridescent Gold, Squatty Shades, Flush Ceiling Mount, 30 In. 770.00
Charger, Acid-Cut Back, Deep Amethyst Over Crystal, 12 1/2 x 1 1/2 In. 440.00
Compote, Bluish Gold, Stretched Ruffled Rim, Half Twist Stem, 7 1/ 2 In. 880.00
Compote, Clear Bowl, Green Air-Twist Stem, Signed, 8 In. 110.00
Compote, Cover, Citron Yellow, Double Black Knobs, Rim & Foot, Pearl Finial, 12 In. . . 330.00
Compote, Gold Calcite, Rolled Rim, 3 1/4 x 7 1/2 In. 355.00
Compote, Green Jade, Swirl, Alabaster Footed, Fleur-De-Lis Mark, 4 x 7 In. 330.00
Compote, Raised On Air-Twist Stem, Carder, 8 1/2 In. 546.00
Console, Pomona Green, 11 In. 75.00
Cornucopia, Ivrene, Signed, 6 In. 425.00
Cornucopia, Jade, Domed Alabaster Foot, Ruffled, 8 1/4 x 4 1/2 In., Pair 1150.00
Decanter, Bulbous, Threaded Neck, Bull's-Eye In Stopper, Signed, 11 1/2 In., Pair 302.00
Figurine, Angelfish, Clear, 10 1/2 x 10 In. 750.00
Figurine, Duck, Incised Signature, 5 3/4 In., Pair 385.00
Figurine, Eagle, Outstretched Wings, On Ball, 6 1/4 In. 490.00
Figurine, Pheasant, Perched On Cushion Form Base, 1932, 11 In. 747.00
Finger Bowl, Underplate, Selenium Red, 6 1/2 In., 2 Piece 550.00
Goblet, Green Cut To Clear Thistles, Square Cut Base, Marked, 6 1/4 In. 260.00
Goblet, Green Jade, Twist Alabaster Stem, 7 In. 165.00
Goblet, Trumpet Shaped, No. 7737, 7 1/4 In., 12 Piece 1840.00
Lamp, Desk, Acid Etched Shade In Lappet, Scroll Border, Wood Base, 11 1/2 In. 315.00
Lamp, Metal Base, Profile Of Thomas Edison, 11 In. 1980.00
Lamp, Perfume, Hammered Copper Base, Gold Lustered Shade, Finial, 9 In. 990.00
Pendant, Gold Strawberry, Gold Hull Leafage, Red Leather Velvet, 18K Gold 1095.00
Pitcher, Pomona Green, Ribbed, Applied Amber Handle, Topaz, Carder, 8 1/2 In. 230.00
Plate, Flemish Blue, Reeded Bands, Bubble Center, Fleur-De-Lis, 8 1/2 In., 12 Piece . . . 365.00
Plate, Hibiscus, Carved Blossom With Bud, Marked, 8 1/4 In. 460.00
Plate, Pomona, Floral Garland Borders, 8 1/2 In., 6 Piece 198.00
Shade, Applied Teardrop Punts, Verre De Soie 150.00
Shade, Lamp, Bell Shape, Bronze, Green, Brown Rim, 7 1/2 In. 950.00
Shade, Pulled Feather, White, Green & Gold 250.00
Shade, Tulip & Floral Design, Gold Iridescent, Pair 495.00
Sugar & Creamer, Amethyst Handles, Celeste Blue, Signed 395.00
Sugar & Creamer, Snail Handle, Crystal, Signed 250.00
Tazza, Star Spangled, 10 1/2 In. 390.00
Urn, Black, Jade, 10 x 9 In. 1320.00
Urn, Green Jade, Alabaster M Handles, 9 3/4 In. 990.00
Vase, Amber Diagonal Rib, Signed, 10 In. 210.00
Vase, Amethyst To Clear, Swirl, Footed, 6 1/2 In. 355.00
Vase, Amethyst, Ruffled Rim, Disk Foot, Carder, 11 1/2 In. 400.00
Vase, Blown, Engraved, 7 1/4 In. 165.00
Vase, Blue Iridescent, Ribbed, Waisted Body, 6 In. 1210.00
Vase, Bud, Baluster Form, Circular, Foot, 4 3/4 In. 120.00
Vase, Calcite, Cornucopia Form, Circular, 8 1/4 In. 360.00
Vase, Cased Bubble Design, White To Gray, Carder, 13 x 12 In. 2070.00
Vase, Champagne Cooler, Applied Reeded Handles, Urn Form, 12 In. 375.00
Vase, Cluthra, Green, 10 In. 865.00
Vase, Cluthra, Mottled Apple Green, 1920, 10 1/4 In. 1610.00
Vase, Fan, Jade, Alabaster Stem & Foot, Vertical Ribbed, 11 x 9 In. 675.00
Vase, Fan, Yellow, Bristol, 8 1/2 In. 275.00
Vase, Flower, Crystal, Signed, 10 1/2 In. 176.00
Vase, Gold & Calcite, 4 1/2 In. 285.00
Vase, Gray To Blue, Controlled Bubbles, Carder, 1920s, 10 In. 2530.00
Vase, Green Jade, 6 In. 350.00
Vase, Green Jade, Global, Matzu, 7 In. 1375.00
Vase, Grotesque, Amethyst Top, Shaded To Clear, No. 7090, 1920, 11 In. 525.00
Vase, Grotesque, Cranberry, 5 1/2 x 9 In. 330.00
Vase, Grotesque, Ivory, 11 In. 300.00
Vase, Grotesque, Ivory, Raised Pillar Ribs, 6 x 10 In. 192.00

Vase, Grotesque, Ivory, Signed, 6 x 12 x 6 1/2 In. 275.00
Vase, Ivory Glass, Band Of Leaping Gazelles & Deer, Carder, 1920s, 10 1/2 In. 2875.00
Vase, Medium Green, 3 Parts, Signed, 10 1/2 In. 385.00
Vase, Opaque Cream Glass, Pedestal Form, 10 In. 110.00
Vase, Peacock Blue Iridescent, Pink, Purple Highlights, 7 1/2 In. 1760.00
Vase, Pomona Green, Air Trap, Diamond Pattern, Marked, Oval, 11 x 10 In. 488.00
Vase, Ruffled Rim, Ruby Red, Marked, Carder, 4 1/2 In. 402.50
Vase, Scalloped Flared Rim, Verre De Soie, Bulbous, 4 In. 150.00
Vase, Swirling Ribs, Green Base To Clear Top, Signed, 9 1/4 In. 605.00
Vase, Tapered, Air Bubbles, Acid Etched Mark, 7 In. 144.00
Vase, Topaz, Blown Optic Swirled Design, 11 In. 230.00
Vase, Tree Trunk, 3 Branches, Signed, 6 In. 295.00
Vase, Trumpet, Green Jade, Alabaster Footed, 8 In. 220.00
Vase, Urn Shape, Pedestal Base, Clear, Signed, 7 3/4 In. 110.00
Vase, Wisteria 3 Branches, Signed, 9 3/4 In. 990.00

STEVENGRAPHS

STEVENGRAPHS are woven pictures made like fancy ribbons. They were manufactured by Thomas Stevens of Coventry, England, and became popular in 1862. Most are marked *Woven in silk by Thomas Stevens* or were mounted on a cardboard that tells the story of the Stevengraph. Other similar ribbon pictures have been made in England and Germany.

Bookmark, Centennial, George Washington, Father Of Our Country, 1876, 9 1/2 In. 110.00
Bookmark, Centennial, George Washington, First In Peace, 6 3/4 In. 140.00
Bookmark, Centennial, George Washington, Star Spangled Banner 75.00
Bookmark, Father Of Our Country, Eagle & Trade Mark, 7 5/8 In. 120.00
First Train, Built By Geo. Stephenson, 1825, Blue, Yellow, Beige Black, 8 7/8 In. 135.00
Present Time, Lord Howe, Blue, Yellow, Green, Black, Frame, 8 3/4 In. ....110.00 to 135.00

STEVENS & WILLIAMS

STEVENS & WILLIAMS of Stourbridge, England, made many types of glass, including layered, etched, cameo, and art glass, between the 1830s and 1930s. Some pieces are signed *S & W*. Many pieces are decorated with flowers, leaves, and other designs based on nature.

Basket, Ruffled Leaf On Front, Pink Interior, Amber Handle, 7 1/2 In. 265.00
Biscuit Jar, Swirled Blue Stripes, White Narrow Rib, Handle, 8 In. 420.00
Bowl, Ruffled Rim, Strawberries, Green Leaves, Amber Glass, 7 x 12 In. 2475.00
Bowl, White, Applied Amber Trim & Prunts, Pink Interior, 4 x 10 1/2 In. 135.00
Centerpiece, Clear, Green Peacock Eyes, 10 In. 330.00
Cruet, Arboresque, Amber Handle & Cut Faceted Stopper, 8 In. 165.00
Decanter, Green, Cut Whiskey, Stopper, Silver Rim, 1900, 8 In. 460.00
Pitcher, Clear Over Peach, Enameled Dogwood, Blown Quilted, 1900, 6 In. 165.00
Powder Jar, Blue Swirl, Amber Finial 75.00
Rose Bowl, Bow Pleated Top, Blue Stripes, 4 1/2 In. 145.00
Rose Bowl, Diamond-Quilted Mother-Of-Peal, Box Pleated Top, 4 In. 225.00
Rose Bowl, Green Ribbon, Mother-Of-Pearl Lily Pad Underplate, 5 In. 400.00
Rose Bowl, Heavy Gold Prunus Design, Brown, Cream, 5 1/8 In. 425.00
Rose Bowl, Ruffled, Cranberry, Amber, Green, Berry Pontil, 3 1/4 In. 135.00
Vase, Cherry Tree Design, Bright Blue Overlaid In Opaque White, 4 In. 1265.00
Vase, Craquelle, Moss Agate, Applied Ring, Global, 4 1/2 In. 990.00
Vase, Cream Overlay, Amber Glass Leaves, Feet & Top, 6 1/2 In. 295.00
Vase, Crystal Leaves & Feet, Blue Overlay, White Lining, 7 1/4 In. 325.00
Vase, Floral Design In Glass, Scalloped Rim, Pearl Iridescence, Squatty 175.00
Vase, Gold Prunus, Box Pleated Top, Brown, Cream Lining, 5 In. 450.00
Vase, Jack-In-The-Pulpit, Blue & White Stripes, 12 1/4 In. 195.00
Vase, Opaque Overlay, Rose Lined, Ruffled Glass Leaves, Loop Feet, 6 1/2 In. 295.00
Vase, Pink Intaglio Cut To Cream, Floral, Wafer Foot, Ruffled, 4 1/2 In. 225.00
Vase, Pink, Crystal Rigaree, Matso-No-Ke Style, Cream Lining, 6 In., Pair 750.00
Vase, Rose, Amber, Ruffled Leaves, Loop Feet, 6 1/2 In. 295.00
Vase, Ruffed Top, Amber Leaves, Loop Feet, 6 1/2 In. 265.00
Vase, Ruffled Leaves, Cranberry, Green, Loop Feet, 5 1/2 In. 295.00
Vase, Silverina, 6 In. 3950.00
Vase, Stick, Butterscotch, Mother-Of-Pearl, Swirl, Bell Shape, 7 In. 495.00
Vase, Verre De Soie, Floral, Iridescent, 12 x 6 In. 245.00

STIEGEL TYPE glass is listed here. It is almost impossible to be sure a piece was actually made by Stiegel, so the knowing collector refers to this glass as *Stiegel type*. Henry William Stiegel, a colorful immigrant to the colonies, started his first factory in Pennsylvania in 1763. He remained in business until 1774. Glassware was made in a style popular in Europe at that time and was similar to the glass of many other makers. It was made of clear or colored glass and was decorated with enamel colors, mold blown designs, or etching.

Beaker, Woman Carrying Water, Enamel Decoration, 1800, 3 1/8 In.	347.00
Bottle, 12 Diamonds, Tooled Mouth, Deep Amethyst, Pontil, 1763-1774, 4 7/8 In.	1870.00
Bottle, White Polychrome Of Flowers, Hearts, Germany, 4 3/4 In.	525.00
Mug, Enameled Floral Design, Applied Handle, 6 3/8 In.	440.00
Tumbler, Engraved Floral, Off-Color, 4 7/8 In.	4500.00
Tumbler, Floral Enameled, Bird, 3 5/8 In.	415.00

STONEWARE is a coarse, glazed, and fired potter's ceramic that is used to make crocks, jugs, bowls, etc. It is often decorated with cobalt blue decorations. In the nineteenth and early twentieth centuries, potters often decorated crocks with blue numbers indicating the size of the container. A "2" meant 2 gallons. Stoneware is still being made.

Ashtray, Brick Center, Albany Slip, B.B. Craig, Impressed Mark, 1980s, 2 x 5 1/2 In.	93.00
Batter Bowl, Ears, Spout, 1880	45.00
Batter Bowl, Green, Brown Glaze, Walter Cornelison, Bybee, 3 x 10 x 12 In.	27.00
Bean Pot, Cover, Spirit Of 76 Bunker Hill, Bristol Glaze, 6 In.	363.00
Beater Jar, Wesson Oil	42.00
Birdhouse, Mottled Albany Glaze, Removable Wooden Bottom, c.1900	332.00
Bottle, Blue & Gray, Isaac Brownell, Bottle Not Sold, 9 3/4 In.	93.00
Bottle, Blue Accent Top Of Name, J.A. Wallis, 10 In.	120.00
Bottle, Brown Glaze Top, M.C. Heald, 10 In.	95.00
Bottle, Impressed J.P. Plummber, Marked 1853, 10 In.	157.00
Bottle, Impressed Label, Adams Allison & Co., Middleburg, Ohio, Tan Glaze, 6 7/8 In.	215.00
Bottle, Pebble Brown & Gray, J. Lamb, Root Beer, 9 7/8 In.	27.00
Bottle, Pinch, Lead Glaze, J.B. Cole, 1930-1940, 6 1/2 In.	115.00
Bowl, Chun Glaze, Lavender Highlights On Blue Ground, 4 3/4 In.	725.00
Bowl, Cover, Brown Glaze, Serrated Diamond Design, Zigzag Rim, 11 1/4 In.	440.00
Bowl, Milk, Cobalt Blue Brushed Flowers At Rim, Pouring Spout, 11 In.	575.00
Bowl, Milk, Diamond Point, Blue, White	125.00
Bowl, Molded Shells & Foliage Scrolls, Cobalt Blue, Gray Ground, 11 x 4 In.	80.00
Bowl, Soup, Cover, Alkaline Glaze, Deedie Cabell, 3 1/4 x 4 In.	220.00
Bowl, Wedding Ring, Blue, Gray, 5 In.	90.00
Butter, Cover, Daisy, White, 4 In.	395.00
Canister, Nutmeg, Blue Band, White	90.00
Canister, Tea, Wooden Lid, Blue & White	85.00
Canteen, Bail Handle, Bardwell's Root Beer, Deer Scene On Reverse, 11 In.	425.00
Canteen, Red Cross, Utica Commandery, Rochester, September 4, 1900, 2 3/4 In.	440.00
Casserole, Cover, Cherries, 6 x 10 In.	195.00
Chamber Pot, Alkaline, Crushed Glass Glaze, Rolled Handle, Vale, 7 x 8 3/4 In.	385.00
Chicken Feeder, 2 Protruding Chickens At Mouth, 19th Century	190.00
Chicken Waterer, Impressed 2, Cobalt Blue Trim, 13 3/4 In.	330.00
Churn, 2 Birds, S. Hart, 3 Gal.	1495.00
Churn, Bennington, Vt., 3 Gal.	650.00
Churn, Bennington, Vt., 4 Gal.	495.00
Churn, Cobalt Bird, E. & L.P. Norton, 16 3/4 In., 4 Gal.	690.00
Churn, Cobalt Blue Quill Work Flower, 5, Ovoid, 16 1/2 In.	140.00
Churn, Cobalt Blue Stenciled Label, 6 In Wreath, Ovoid, 18 In.	258.00
Churn, Cobalt Blue Tulips, Egg Shaped, Applied Shoulder Handles, 19 1/2 In.	220.00
Churn, Floral, Fort Edward, 5 Gal.	495.00
Churn, Grape Design, A.K. Ballard, Vermont, 5 Gal.	895.00
Churn, L. & F. Norton, Bennington, Vt., Blue Floral, Broken Dasher Handle, 14 In.	495.00
Churn, Large Paddle Tail, N.A. White	4500.00
Churn, Shoulder Handles, Cobalt Blue Flower, 3, J.C. Smith, 16 In.	905.00
Churn, Shoulder Handles, Incised Lines, P.H. Smith 4, Ovoid, 17 In.	70.00

Coffeepot, Blue, White, Spiral Stripes, Tin Base, Acorn Finial Cover, 9 3/4 In. 682.00
Coffeepot, Blue, White, Tin Base, Ball Finial Cover, 10 1/2 In. 1320.00
Cooler, Allen Germ Proof Filter, Toledo, Oh., Blue & White, Metal Cover, 14 In. 495.00
Cooler, Barrel Shape, Tooled Rings, Salt Glaze, Brown Highlights, Bung Hole, 15 In. . . . 80.00
Cooler, Barrel, Polar Bears 1 Side, Flowers Other, Nickel Plated Spout, 14 In. 495.00
Cooler, Blue Leaf Design, E. Norton & Co., c.1880, 12 3/4 In. 495.00
Cooler, Brookhill Sour Mash, Jockeys Riding Horses, Blue & Gray 1950.00
Cooler, Cheavin's World Renowned Filter, 20 1/2 In. 170.00
Cooler, Cobalt Blue Floral, Inverted Cone, Bung Hole, Shoulder Handles, 13 In. 220.00
Cooler, Filter Top, Water Leeched Out Of Holes Into Bottom Crock 4400.00
Cooler, Gate City Stoneware Cooler, Pat. 9, Gray Blue Floral, Wooden Lid, 14 In. 220.00
Cooler, Polar Bear Medallion, Ice Water, Bung Hole, 15 1/4 In. 385.00
Cooler, Woman At Well, Floral Spray, Robinson Clay Co., Blue & White, 14 1/2 In. 215.00
Crock, 2 Birds, Hubbell & Chesebro, 4 Gal. 950.00
Crock, 4 Bud Flower, M. Woodruff, c.1860, 3 Gal. 1090.00
Crock, Basket Of Flowers, F.B. Norton & Co., 4 Gal. 1695.00
Crock, Bird On Branch, Belmont Avenue Pottery, Impressed 3, 10 1/4 In. 190.00
Crock, Bird On Branch, Satterlee & Mory, Fort Edward, 4, Cobalt Quill Work, 12 In. . . . 72.00
Crock, Bird On Plume, Ovoid, Haxstun, Ottman & Co., c.1870, 2 Gal. 230.00
Crock, Bird On Stump, Dog Set To Pounce, Brady & Ryan, c.1880, 4 Gal. 545.00
Crock, Bird On Twig, Riedinger & Caire, c.1870, 2 Gal. 270.00
Crock, Blue Accents At Name & Ears, Goodwin & Webster, Ovoid, c.1860, 1 Gal. 392.00
Crock, Blue Flower, 3, W.T. Moore, Middleburg, Ohio, 11 1/4 In. 330.00
Crock, Blue Freehand Design, Small Ear Handles, 4 Gal., 15 In. 650.00
Crock, Blue Pittsburgh Advertising, 2 Gal., 10 1/2 In. 695.00
Crock, Blue Quill Work, Ohio, 6, Handles, 13 1/4 In. 1045.00
Crock, Brown Albany Slip, W.J. & E.G., Springfield, Ohio, 9 3/4 In. 935.00
Crock, Brush Flower & Flying Bird, Ovoid, Charlestown, c.1850, 3 Gal. 485.00
Crock, Brushed Cobalt Blue Design, R. Butt, 10 In. 1900.00
Crock, Butter, Blue & White, Molded Cherries, Wooden Handle, Cover, 7 x 4 In. 245.00
Crock, Butter, Blue & White, Molded Cows, Wire Bail, 7 1/4 x 4 1/2 In. 500.00
Crock, Butter, Blue Sponging, Stenciled Label, White, 9 1/4 In. 220.00
Crock, Butter, Brushed Cobalt Blue Foliage, R.C.R., Philadelphia, 6 1/2 x 12 In. 660.00
Crock, Butter, Dutch Boy & Girl, Blue Transfer, White, 7 1/4 In. 160.00
Crock, Cake, Bird On Stump, F.T. Wright & Sons, c.1860, 1 1/2 Gal. 575.00
Crock, Cake, Double Flower Design, Charlestown, c.1850, 7 In. 300.00
Crock, Cobalt Blue Design, Salt Glaze, Applied Handles, Brown Glaze, 11 1/4 In. 460.00
Crock, Cobalt Blue Design, Salt Glaze, Molded Handles, Brown Glaze, 7 In. 690.00
Crock, Cobalt Blue Floral, J. & E. Norton, 5 Gal. 1200.00
Crock, Cobalt Blue Grid, J.S. Taft, 2 Gal. 375.00
Crock, Cobalt Blue Hen, New York Stone Ware Co., 4 Gal. 275.00
Crock, Cobalt Blue Pecking Chicken, Applied Handles, Impressed 4, 11 In. 135.00
Crock, Cobalt Blue Stripes & Floral, A. & W. Boughneer 4, 12 3/8 In. 1485.00
Crock, Cobalt Design, White's Pottery, c.1865, 7 5/8 x 8 1/2 In. 115.00
Crock, Cover, 3 Eagles, S.S. Perry, Troy, Albany Slip, Branch Handle, 10 5/8 In. 195.00
Crock, Cross & Fuller, Fultonville, N.Y., Stamped In Blue, 7 In. 75.00
Crock, Dark Blue Iris, Ballard & Brothers, Ovoid, c.1860, 10 In. 270.00
Crock, Dotted Bird Perched On Branch, C.W. Braun, c.1860, 10 1/2 In. 815.00
Crock, Dotted Triple Flower, J. Morton, Ovoid, c.1870, 11 1/2 In. 580.00
Crock, Double Flower, Archibald & Collins, Grocers, c.1880, 2 Gal. 270.00
Crock, Double Flower, Macumber & Tannahill, c.1875, 3 Gal. 545.00
Crock, Dove On Branch, F.B. Norton Sons, 1 1/2 Gal. 575.00
Crock, Flag, House, Tree & Fields, A.O. Whittemore, 4 Gal. 7700.00
Crock, Freehand & Stenciled, Williams & Reppert, Greensboro, 2, 8 In. 495.00
Crock, Heinz English Prepared Mustard, 4 x 3 1/4 In. 175.00
Crock, Impressed 4, Running Rooster, Handles, 11 In. 247.50
Crock, Incised Bird & Flower, Goodwin & Webster, c.1840, 2 Gal. 485.00
Crock, Keller's Inks, Blue & White, 97 C 4 On Bottom, 8 1/2 In. 55.00
Crock, Large Fat Bird, Ottman Bro.'s & Co., c.1870, 5 Gal. 850.00
Crock, Leaf Design, Ear Handles, H. Myers, 1 Gal. 430.00
Crock, Man, Hair Standing Up, Wielding Knife, Decapitated Head, 12 In. 2145.00
Crock, Maxwell House Ice Tea, Blue & White, 5 Gal. . . . . .275.00 to 425.00

Crock, Myers, 2 Stamped Marks With Cross In Circle, 8 In. 300.00
Crock, New York Stoneware Co., Fort Edward, N.Y., Cobalt Blue Bird, 11 1/4 In. 465.00
Crock, Peace Dove, C.N. Mansfield, 2 Handles, 4 Gal. 440.00
Crock, Pecking Chicken, Impressed 3, Blue Quill Work, 10 3/4 In. 580.00
Crock, Salt, Hanging, Grapes On Basket Weave, 4 x 6 In. 145.00
Crock, Stenciled Label, H.C. Ward Stoneware Depot, Zanesville, Ohio, 7 3/4 In. 300.00
Crock, Tode Bros., 42 Bowery, New York, 4 In. 225.00
Crock, Tray, Goodwin & Webster, Converted To Lamp, c.1870 . . . . 105.00
Crock, W.J. & E.G. Schrop, Middlebury, O., Handles, 10 1/4 In. 300.00
Cup, Salt Glaze, Orange Peel, 1965, 3 1/4 In., Pair 44.00
Cup & Saucer, Crushed Glass Glaze, Blue Opaque, Tan, Cheever Meaders, 1960 . . . . . . 85.00
Cuspidor, Albany Slip, Hart Bro's., Fulton N.Y., Cobalt Blue Bands, 11 1/2 In. 467.00
Cuspidor, Basket Weave With Rose 85.00
Dish, Cobbler, Green Alkaline Glaze, Deedie Cabell, 2 1/4 x 9 In. 330.00
Dish, Soap, Lion's Head, Blue & White, 4 1/2 In. 175.00
Figurine, Baboon, Gray, Black Satin Glaze, Boulogne, France, 13 x 5 In. 360.00
Figurine, Chicken, Blue, White, Brown, Green Glaze, Edwin Meaders, 15 1/4 In. 715.00
Flask, Eagle, Threaded Neck, Screw Cap, Shield Shape, 3 1/2 In. 550.00
Flowerpot, Tanware, Hanging Rings 1700.00
Flowerpot, Unglazed, Manganese Splotches, Maryland, 7 1/2 In. 850.00
Jar, Bird On Flowering Branch, 2, Shoulder Handles, Whites Utica, 12 In. 550.00
Jar, Blue At Asymmetrical Shoulder Handles, I.M. Mead, Ovoid, 12 In. 140.00
Jar, Blue Polka Dots, 2, L. Marsilliot, Ovoid, 10 In. 880.00
Jar, Blue Swag At Top, Ovoid, Meyer, c.1830, 1/2 Gal. 145.00
Jar, Canning, Blue Basket Of Flowers, 1 Qt. 1095.00
Jar, Canning, Blue Brushed & Stenciled, John F. Thompson Jr., West Virginia, 10 In. 415.00
Jar, Canning, Blue Design, Orchard, 7 1/2 In. 695.00
Jar, Canning, Blue Stenciled Label, James Hamilton & Co., Greensboro, Pa., 8 In. 300.00
Jar, Canning, Blue Stenciled Label, Striping, J. & H., St. Clairsville, Ohio, 8 In. 300.00
Jar, Canning, Blue Triple Flower, Lyons, c.1860, 2 Gal. 2660.00
Jar, Canning, Brushed Floral, Handle, 8 3/4 In. 600.00
Jar, Canning, Cobalt Blue Brushed Flowers & Stripes, 8 1/4 In. 1650.00
Jar, Canning, Cobalt Blue Flower, Scheuter Bros., Yonkers, N.Y., 11 1/2 In. 115.00
Jar, Canning, Cobalt Blue Label, T.F. Reppert, Greensboro, Pa., Egg Shape, 9 1/2 In. 95.00
Jar, Canning, Cobalt Blue Stenciled Label, C.H. Dankwerth, Clarington, Ohio, 10 In. . . . 247.00
Jar, Canning, Cobalt Blue, S. Hamilton & Co., Greensboro, Pa., 9 1/2 In. 55.00
Jar, Canning, Dotted Design, O.L. & A.K. Ballard, Dotted 1862, 11 In. 450.00
Jar, Canning, Dotted Triple Flower, Edmands & Co., c.1870, 13 1/2 In. 230.00
Jar, Canning, Double Flower Design, Cortland, c.1870, 11 In. 245.00
Jar, Canning, Hamilton & Jones, Greensboro, Pa., Cobalt Blue Label, 9 3/4 In. 100.00
Jar, Canning, Leon Slip Glaze, Piedmont Salt Glaze, Fly Ash, 1890-1920, 8 3/16 In. 95.00
Jar, Canning, Stenciled Label, Barringer & McDad, Letart Falls, Ohio, 9 7/8 In. 580.00
Jar, Canning, Stenciled Label, Fred A. Blum, Wheeling, West Virginia, 6 In. 300.00
Jar, Canning, Stenciled Label, Striping, Wavy Line, Geo. H. Muth, Belleair, Ohio, 9 In. . . 690.00
Jar, Canning, Stenciled Label, Watson Boothover, Craysville, Ohio, 6 1/8 In. 797.00
Jar, Canning, Stenciled Name, A.P. Donaghho, c.1860, 1/2 Gal. 85.00
Jar, Canning, Wavy Scrolled Shoulder, Red Brown Glaze, 7 In. 770.00
Jar, Cobalt Blue & Freehand Label, Williams & Reppert, Greensboro, Pa., 3, 13 In. 190.00
Jar, Cobalt Blue At Label, L. Tracy, 2, Tuscarawas County, Ovoid, 11 3/4 In. 140.00
Jar, Cobalt Blue Brushed Flower, 2, Ovoid, Tooled Lip, 11 1/2 In. 275.00
Jar, Cobalt Blue Brushed X/S, Tree Shapes, 2, Shoulder Handles, 11 1/2 In. 605.00
Jar, Cobalt Blue Floral Design, Impressed Label, Applied Shoulder Handles, 12 In. 70.00
Jar, Cobalt Blue Floral, Impressed 4, Applied Handles, 15 In. 275.00
Jar, Cobalt Blue Flower, 2, Burger & Lang, Rochester, N.Y., Egg Shape, 11 1/2 In. 260.00
Jar, Cobalt Blue Label, R.W. Williams, New Geneva, Pa., 15 1/2 In. 165.00
Jar, Cobalt Blue Label, Shoulder Handles, S. Purdy, Portage Co., Ohio, 3, 12 1/4 In. 165.00
Jar, Cobalt Blue Stenciled & Freehand Label, Hamilton & Jones, 10 1/2 In. 1595.00
Jar, Cobalt Blue Stenciled Label, L. McCurdy, New Castle, Ohio 5, 16 In. 550.00
Jar, Cover, Blue Floral Design, Edmands & Co., c.1870, 12 In. 425.00
Jar, Floral Lip, S.S. Perry, Troy, Shoulder Handles, Egg Shape, 11 In. 85.00
Jar, Impressed A. DeHaven, Middlebury, Ohio, 3, Shoulder Handles, 14 1/2 In. 225.00
Jar, Impressed Label, Hall & Thomas, Springfield, Oh., 2, Ovoid, 11 In. 525.00

Jar, Incised Bird & Leaves, Shoulder Handles, T.F. Field, Utica, 10 1/2 In. 4290.00
Jar, Incised Bird On Flowering Tree, Blue At Shoulder Handles, Ovoid, 13 3/4 In. 3190.00
Jar, J. Weller Company Acme Pickles, Barrel Shape, Wooden Lid, 13 In. 145.00
Jar, Lid, Blue Quill Work, Shoulder Handles, F.N. Norton & Co., 10 1/2 In. 165.00
Jar, Quill Work Label, Floral On Reverse, H. Loundes Maker, A.D.1841, 12 1/4 In. 1735.00
Jar, Raised Cobalt Blue Slip Design, Ear Handles, B.C. Millburn, 11 1/2 In. 1100.00
Jar, Shoulder Handles, Cobalt Blue Floral, 13 1/2 In. 220.00
Jar, Shoulder Handles, H. Purdy, 2, Cobalt Blue At Handles & Label, 10 1/4 In. 192.00
Jar, Shoulder Handles, I.M. Mead & Co., 2, Blue At Handles & Label, 11 3/4 In. 165.00
Jar, Shoulder Handles, I.M. Mead & Co., 4, Blue At Label & Handles, 15 1/4 In. 115.00
Jar, Shoulder Handles, I.M. Mead & Co., Blue At Handles, 15 In. 275.00
Jar, Shoulder Handles, I.M. Mead & Co., Cobalt Blue At Handle & Label, 14 In. 115.00
Jar, Shoulder Handles, S. Purdy, Portage County, Ohio, Ovoid, 10 In. 300.00
Jar, Six Tulip Trees, 2, Brushed Cobalt Blue Slip, Handles, Ovoid, 11 1/2 In. 715.00
Jar, Stenciled Banner Held By Eagle, Spread Wings, Eagle Pottery, 1880, 3 Gal. 695.00
Jar, Storage, Alkaline Glaze, Freehand 4, 4 Gal. 325.00
Jar, Stripes, 2, Stenciled Label, Sel Vickers, Loydsville, Oh., 11 3/4 In. 770.00
Jar, Tooled Shoulder & Lip, Handles, Warne & Letts, S. Amboy, Ovoid, 9 In. 1240.00
Jar, Tooled Shoulder, Rim Bands, Leaf Design, S. Amboy, 12 5/8 In. 1595.00
Jardiniere, Green Design, Lion Head Handles, Solomon Bell, 13 In. 4200.00
Jug, 1 Framed In Brush Blue Plume, S. Hart, c.1870, 10 1/2 In. 157.00
Jug, 1876 In Blue Script, West Tray Pottery, c.1876, 12 In. 245.00
Jug, 316 On Front, Advertising, c.1825, 2 Gal. 245.00
Jug, Acorns & Oak Leaves, 2 Gal. 1800.00
Jug, Alkaline Glaze, Green Black Glaze, Handle, Daniel Seagle, 10 7/8 In. 220.00
Jug, Ancher & Durkee, Binghamton, N.Y., c.1870, 2 Gal. 230.00
Jug, Applied Handle, Gray Salt Glaze, Impressed Boston, Egg Shape, 12 In. 250.00
Jug, Batter, Feather & Flower, Blue & White, Wire Bail, Tin Cover On Spout 395.00
Jug, Bellarmine, Bearded Man, Germany, 1590, 6 1/2 In. 1150.00
Jug, Bird On Branch, 2, Strap Handle, N.A. White & Sons, Utica, N.Y., 14 3/4 In. 495.00
Jug, Bird On Stump, Cowden & Wilcox, 3 Gal. 1650.00
Jug, Bird On Twig, Haxstun Ottoman & Co., c.1870, 1 Gal. 360.00
Jug, Bird, Israel Seymour, 2 Gal. 797.00
Jug, Bird, Lamp Drilled, Wooden Base, Handle, G.W. Whittemare, Nashca, N.H., 26 In. .. 135.00
Jug, Black Stencil, Bail Handle, A.C. Trentman, 1 Qt. 175.00
Jug, Blue & White, Old Mill, 9 In. 120.00
Jug, Blue Accents At Handle, W.W. & D. Weston, c.1880, 12 In. 110.00
Jug, Blue Accents At Spout & Handle, Clark & Fox, c.1830, 1 Gal. 6897.00
Jug, Blue Bird On Stump, Fort Edward, 4 Gal. 825.00
Jug, Blue Floral, Norton & Fenton, 16 In. 1095.00
Jug, Blue Flower, 2, Gray Salt Glaze, Higgins & Co., Cleveland, Ohio, 14 1/4 In. 195.00
Jug, Blue Flower, 3, Applied Handle, Zoar Pottery, 15 In. 105.00
Jug, Brookfield Rye, The Geo. Bieler Sons Co., Upright Drum Shape, 12 3/4 In. 40.00
Jug, Brown Salt Glaze, Spherical Body, 6 Petaled Flower, 1785, 6 7/8 In. 1035.00
Jug, Brush Double Flower, Nichols & Boynton, c.1855, 12 In. 160.00
Jug, Brush Flower, P. Mugler & Co., c.1850, 12 1/2 In. 455.00
Jug, Brush Swag Design, C. Crolius, Ovoid, c.1840, 3 Gal. 755.00
Jug, Brushed 2, Blue Accent At Name & Handle, N.A. Seymour, c.1830, 2 Gal. 145.00
Jug, Brushed Flower & Label, Strap Handle, J. Heiser, Buffalo, N.Y., 11 1/2 In. 302.50
Jug, Cluster Of Cherries, Cowden & Wilcox, 1 Gal. 690.00
Jug, Cobalt Blue & Freehand Label, Laughlin Bros., Wheeling, W. Va., 15 In. 220.00
Jug, Cobalt Blue At Label, Applied Handle, H. Purdy, 3, Ohio, 17 In. 220.00
Jug, Cobalt Blue Bird, Applied Handle, West Troy Pottery, 12 In. 350.00
Jug, Cobalt Blue Design, Chevron Stripes Strap Handle, Egg Shape, 15 In. 55.00
Jug, Cobalt Blue Design, Strap Handle, G. Heiser, Buffalo, N.Y., 30 3/4 In. 360.00
Jug, Cobalt Blue Flower & Label, Handle, Wm. E. Warner, West Troy, 10 In. 130.00
Jug, Cobalt Blue Freehand Label, Williams & Reppert, Greensboro, Pa. 2, 13 1/2 In. 255.00
Jug, Cobalt Blue Label, Bernhardt Bros., Buffalo, N.Y., Applied Handle, 13 In. 190.00
Jug, Cobalt Blue Man, Hat & Jacket, Holding No. 3, Salt Glazed 5200.00
Jug, Cobalt Blue Quill Work Design, Flowers, Impressed Label, 18 In. 220.00
Jug, Cobalt Blue Quill Work, P. Fisher, Herbert Murray, Buffalo, N.Y., 11 1/4 In. 165.00
Jug, Cobalt Blue Scalloped Edge, Applied Top Handle, Filler Hole, 11 5/8 In. 250.00
Jug, Cobalt Blue Sitting Dog, 18 In. 2300.00

Jug, Cobalt Blue Slip Bird, 2, Strap Handle, Whites, Utica, 13 3/4 In. 685.00
Jug, Cobalt Blue Stylized Flower, —Gale, Gale-Ville, N.Y., 2, 14 1/2 In. 300.00
Jug, Cobalt Blue Tulip, Egg Shape, S.S. Perry & Co., 16 In. 220.00
Jug, Cobalt Blue X, Burger & Lang, c.1870, 2 Gal. 485.00
Jug, Cobalt Blue Zigzags, Strap Handle, Ovoid, Abraham Rhodenbaugh, 11 1/4 In. 330.00
Jug, Cobalt Flower Basket, Norton, 2 Gal. 1595.00
Jug, Cover, Turned Banding At Neck, Brown Wash, England, c.1800, 66 1/2 In. 520.00
Jug, Double Flower, Blue Accents, Cowden & Wilcox, c.1870, 2 Gal. 365.00
Jug, Double Flower, Blue Cobalt, G. Apley & Co., c.1860, 3 Gal. 365.00
Jug, Embossed 2, Beehive Shape, Applied Handle, W. Lewis, Milburn, 2 Gal. 95.00
Jug, Face, Albany Slip Glaze, Red, Brown, Black Luster, M. Rogers, 9 In. 358.00
Jug, Face, Alkaline Glaze, Shiny Green Upper Portion, Matte Green Lower, 8 In. 605.00
Jug, Field, Ovoid, 2 Shoulder Handles, Ohio, 10 Gal. 375.00
Jug, Floral, 3, Strap Handle, Norton & Fenton, East Bennington Vt., 15 In. 110.00
Jug, Handleless, Alkaline, Brown Over Yellow, 8 In. 250.00
Jug, Herman Carl, 139 Fourth St., Troy, N.Y., c.1880, 12 In. 135.00
Jug, Incised Floral Spray, A. States, 10 3/4 In. 467.00
Jug, James Hamilton, 2 Handles, 19 In. 995.00
Jug, Label I. Seymour, Troy, Cobalt Blue Label, Quill Work, 15 1/4 In. 192.00
Jug, Large Flower, C. Ark & Co., c.1840, 3 Gal. 665.00
Jug, New Geneva, 1869, 7 In. 295.00
Jug, Ohio, Cobalt Blue At Handle & Label, G. Baird, Huron County, 10 3/4 In. 165.00
Jug, Paul Cushman, Albany, c.1810, 12 In. 800.00
Jug, Peacock Design, I. Seymour, c.1850, 15 In. 725.00
Jug, Quill Work, Stylized Flower & 2, Strap Handle, Stetzenmeyer & Co., 14 1/2 In. 935.00
Jug, Stenciled Louis P.F.—, Wines & Liquors, Wheeling, W.Va., 14 In. 170.00
Jug, Storage, Albany Slip, Frogskin Color, 11 In. 82.00
Jug, Storage, Alkaline Glaze, 2 Handles, John H. Long, 1890s, 15 In. 99.00
Jug, Strap Handle, Brown Albany Slip, P.H. Smith 2, 12 1/2 In. 72.00
Jug, Swag Accent At Name, Ovoid, N. Clark, c.1825, 3 Gal. 195.00
Jug, Swan, 2 Gal. 2860.00
Jug, Swan, Cowden & Wilcox, 13 In. 4950.00
Jug, Triple Bud Flower, John Burger, c.1860, 3 Gal. 423.00
Jug, Triple Flower, Norton & Fenton, c.1860, 13 1/2 In. 302.00
Jug, Umber Design, Dyce Clarke, c.1820, 14 In. 1500.00
Jug, Water Jug For You To Get Full, Cream, Brown, 1 Gal. 145.00
Jug, Whiskey, S.T. Suit, MD, 1809 . . . . 425.00
Match Holder, Striker Between Top & Bottom Blue Stripes 110.00
Mold, Candle, 8 Tubes 70.00
Mold, Pudding, Floral, Scalloped 25.00
Mug, Brown Salt Glaze, 2 Branches Of Flowers, Leaves, Cylindrical, 1727, 4 In. 402.00
Mug, Burley & Winter, Marked 65.00
Mug, Leon Slip Glaze, Red, Brown, Green, Yellow, 1890-1920, 4 1/2 In. 16.00
Mug, Prohibition, Happy Days Are Here Again 25.00
Pitcher, Albany Slip, Black, Brown Glaze, Henrys, Alabama, 1890-1920, 13 In. 82.50
Pitcher, Albany Slip, Black, Brown Glaze, J.N. Roy, 1906, 9 3/4 In. 605.00
Pitcher, Alkaline Glaze, Matte Green Glaze, Handle, Deedie Cabell, 5 1/2 In. 303.00
Pitcher, Allover Design, Peter Perrine, 10 1/2 In. 1800.00
Pitcher, Blue Feather Design, Incised Bands, 10 3/4 In. 355.00
Pitcher, Blue On White Speck Glaze, Elongated Spout, V. Shelton, 1970, 6 1/4 In. 44.00
Pitcher, Blue Willow, Sterling Silver Rim, Lambeth, 5 1/2 In. 395.00
Pitcher, Cobalt Blue Design, 3 Gal. 950.00
Pitcher, Cobalt Blue Design, Handle, F.H. Cowden, Harrisburg, 8 3/4 In. 275.00
Pitcher, Cobalt Blue Floral Design, Strap Handle, Tooled Lines, 10 5/8 In. 880.00
Pitcher, Cobalt Blue Stenciled Label, Ovoid, Jas. Benjamin, Cincinnati, O., 11 In. 357.00
Pitcher, Cover, Brown Glaze, Otto Lindig, 1930, 7 1/8 In. 3105.00
Pitcher, Cow, Blue & White, 8 In. 240.00
Pitcher, Eagles & Shields In Ovals, Blue & White, 8 In. 385.00
Pitcher, Frogskin Glaze, Albany Slip, Morris Brown, 1965, 5 1/2 In. 100.00
Pitcher, Grape & Lattice, Star Pottery, 8 1/2 In. 190.00
Pitcher, Iced Beverage, Brown, Green, Spout, Cole, 1985, 5 1/2 In. 90.00
Pitcher, Indian Heads In Circles, Blue & White, 8 1/4 In. 410.00
Pitcher, Leaping Stags In Ovals, Blue & White, 8 In. 355.00

Pitcher, Long Neck, Green Over Brown Glaze, W.J. Gordy, 1960-1970, 6 3/4 In. 110.00
Pitcher, Molded Cattails, Blue & White, 7 In. 190.00
Pitcher, Molded Flying Swallows, Blue & White, 7 7/8 In. 570.00
Pitcher, Molded Pinwheels, Blue & White, 8 1/4 In. 190.00
Pitcher, Norton, Worcester, 1 1/2 Gal. 295.00
Pitcher, Rebekkah, Dark Blue Lead Glaze, M.L. Owens, 20 3/8 In. 275.00
Pitcher, Rebekkah, Pine Craft, M.L. Owens, 1950s, 10 3/4 In. 72.00
Pitcher, Reticulated Design, Westerwald, 6 In. 2860.00
Pitcher, Sponged Ware, Blue On White Double Dip Glaze, V. Shelton, 1989, 6 1/2 In. 60.00
Pitcher, Terra-Cotta Glaze, Otto Lindig, 1923, 7 3/8 In. 7130.00
Pitcher, Tulip, Burger & Lang, c.1870, 10 In. 335.00
Plate, Imari Design, Turner's Patent, 9 1/4 In., Pair 395.00
Pot, Cream, Blue Cobalt Cabbage Flower, John Burger, c.1865, 2 Gal. 725.00
Pot, Pansy, 2 Handles, Lead Glaze, Turquoise, Green Specks, W. Cole, 5 3/4 In. 40.00
Rum Pot, Man Picture Cover, Blue & Gray, Germany, Early 1900s, 4 In. 350.00
Salt Box, Hanging, Cover, Cherry 190.00
Soap Dish, Blue & White, Roses, 5 In. 70.00
Soap Dish, Floral, Blue & Gray 98.00
Soap Dish, Flower 120.00
Soap Dish, Lion Head, Blue & White 65.00
Teapot, Blue Exterior, Orange Interior, C.B. Craven, 7 x 9 1/2 In. 412.00
Teapot, Blue, White, Stripes, Bale, Wooden Handle, Acorn Finial Cover, 6 1/2 In. 705.00
Vase, Colonial Creme, Tan, Orange, Ink Stamp, Cole, 1950-1960, 2 1/2 x 4 1/2 In. 60.00
Vase, Lake Scene, Mottled Ground, Reissner, Stellmacher & Kessel, 1900, 11 In. 517.00
Vase, Mottled Brown, 2 Handles, De Velde, Marked, 3 1/2 x 10 5/8 In. 4025.00
Vase, Neck, Sky Blue Glaze, O.L. Bachelder, 6 1/2 In. 495.00
Vase, Oxblood Glaze, Dappled Spots Of Gray, Ernest Chaplet, c.1900, 6 5/8 In. 575.00
Vase, Sculptured Woman's Face, Flowing Hair, A. Stuchly, 12 In., Pair 192.00
Vase, Speckled Turquoise, 3 Handles, A.R. Cole, 5 1/8 In. 115.00
Whiskey, Jug, Brookhill, Merry Christmas, Dillinger Bros., Stoneware, 1 Qt. 450.00

STORE fixtures, cases, cutters, and other items that have no advertising
as part of the decoration are listed here. Most items found in an old
store are listed in the Advertising category in this book.

Adding Machine, Burroughs, Beveled Glass Sides 200.00
Barrel, Biscuit, Oak, Ceramic Interior, Chrome Trim, 7 x 6 In. 65.00
Bin, Pine, Blue Paint, 37 In. 385.00
Bin, Slanted Lid, Pine, Worn Paint, 1 Board Ends, 44 x 20 x 25 In. 330.00
Bin, Tin, Lithograph, Country, 20 1/4 x 12 1/2 x 20 1/2 In. 245.00
Cabinet, Hardware, Pine, Hardwood, 72 Drawers, Labels, Octagonal, 32 In. 1650.00
Cabinet, Nut & Bolt, Oak, 130 Drawer, Revolves 1395.00
Cabinet, Parts, 96 Drawers, With Contents 1500.00
Cabinet, Ribbon, Glass Front, 6 Drawers Each Side, 2 Side Drawers, 37 1/2 In. 935.00
Cabinet, Spool, Mahogany, 12 Glass Front Drawers, Victorian, 21 x 35 In. 340.00
Case, Bread, Oak, 2 Rear Doors, 2 Glass Shelves, 38 x 25 x 25 In. 290.00
Case, Display, Beveled Glass, Wooden Trim, Fluted Corner Columns, 38 x 45 In. 190.00
Case, Display, Candy, Slant Front, 2 Glass Shelves, 24 x 19 In. 302.00
Case, Display, Counter, Mahogany Inlaid, 19th Century, 11 3/4 In. 230.00
Case, Display, Oak Wood Trim, Collar, 25 x 19 x 6 1/2 In. 520.00
Case, Display, Walnut, Glazed Tops & Sides, Carved Cabriole Legs, 93 1/2 In., Pair 805.00
Case, Front Glass, Nickel Plate, 13 x 46 x 23 In. 460.00
Case, Oak, Retracting To Serve Customer From Front, 16 x 36 x 28 In. 460.00
Case, Slant Front Glass, 2 Side Panels, Glass Top, 22 x 47 x 26 In. 290.00
Cigar Cutter, Antler Handle, Tabletop, 3 Holes 165.00
Coffee Grinders are listed in their own category.
Cuspidor, Turtle Step On Head, Raises Cover, Tin 450.00
Cutter, Paper, Chew Spearhead On Bar 85.00
Dispenser, Butcher's Tape, Porcelain 28.00
Egg Crate, Cover, White, Handle, No Dividers 37.00
Jar, Cone Holder, Ice Cream, Clear Glass, Cover 350.00
Lighter, Cigar, Whale Oil, 2 Woven Dippers, Hand Painted Tank, Large 750.00
Machine, Wire Measuring, John J. Waldman, Tool 300.00
Mailbox, Figural, Frog, Hinged Mouth, Hinged Rear Flap For Retrieval, Tin, 21 In. 2420.00

Mannequin, Linen Over Wood Body, Freestanding, Wooden Shoes, Paris, 30 In. 1500.00
Straw Holder, Green Glass, Diamond Shape Base, Ribbed Panel 695.00
String Holder, Heart, Cleminson 65.00
Table, Drugstore, Iron, Swing-Out Seats, Center Pedestal, Claw Feet 1500.00
Tub, Coffee, Inside Cover, Bouquet Java, Tapers From 20 1/4 To 16 1/2 In. 420.00
Wagon, Popcorn, Sidewalk Model No. 2, Runs On Steam, Bottled Gas, Cretors, 1905 . . . 8500.00

STOVES have been used in America for heating since the eighteenth
century and for cooking since the nineteenth century. Most types of
wood, coal, gas, kerosene, and even some electric stoves are collected.

Cook, Chambers, Deluxe, Stainless Steel Top, Griddle, Deep Well Cooker, Cookbook . . . 675.00
Cook, Crosley, Electric, 1950s 275.00
Cook, Detroit Jewel, 4 Burners, Gas, 1926 . . . . 250.00
Cook, Hot Blast, Top Load, Chrome Trim, Wood, No. 158, Pat. 1897, Coles, 15 x 40 In. . 1000.00
Cook, Magee's Mystic, Wood-Burning, 6 Burners, 1891, 30 x 39 In. 1200.00
Cook, Magic Chef, 4 Burners, All Attachments, 1932 . . . . 2000.00
Cook, Magic Chef, Gas, Cream & Blue Gray, 1940s 2000.00
Cook, Monarch Malleable, Iron Stove Co., Graniteware, Warming Ovens, 58 x 48 In. . . . 950.00
Cook, Quickmeal, Blue 1800.00
Cook, Range, Magic Chef, 4 Burners, 1932 . . . . 2000.00
Cook, Southern Stove Works, Evansville, Indiana, 18 x 12 In. 5500.00
Heater, Space, Hot Point, Iron, Copper Disk, Cage, 1917 . . . . 95.00
Heating, Terra-Cotta, Flame Finial Above Domed Top, Brass Fender, Austria, 105 In. . . 6440.00
Parlor, Art Garland, Model 58J 8000.00
Parlor, Imperial Universal, Model 50 . . . . 4500.00
Parlor, Johnson, Cox & Fuller, 1850s 795.00
Parlor, Retort Oak 2600.00
Parlor, Wehrle 100, No. 14, Small 9000.00
Parlor, Westminster, Rare Art 22000.00
Roaster, Chestnut, English, 22 1/2 In. 165.00
Roasting, Operating Windup Rotisserie 450.00
Water Hob, Removable Plates, Lifter, Cast Iron, 1920s, 22 x 18 In. 550.00

STRETCH GLASS is named for the strange stretch marks in the glass. It
was made by many glass companies in the United States from about
1900 to the 1920s. It is iridescent. Most American stretch glass is
molded; most European pieces are blown and may have a pontil mark.

Bowl, Blue, Ribbed, 9 1/2 In. 45.00
Bowl, Green, Flared, 10 In. 35.00
Bowl, Orange, 9 In. 65.00
Candlestick 89.00

SUMIDA, or Sumida Gawa, is a Japanese pottery. The pieces collected
by that name today were made about 1895 to 1970. There has been
much confusion about the name of this ware, and it is often called
Korean Pottery. Most pieces have a very heavy orange-red, blue, or
green glaze, with raised three-dimensional figures as decorations.

Basket, Shaped Like Wishing Well, 6 In. 395.00
Bowl, Bell Shape, Green, 6 In. 425.00
Bowl, Black, White Flowers, Gray-Green Body, Green, Octagonal, 4 1/2 In. 395.00
Bowl, Child, 2 Animals, 7 In. 550.00
Bowl, Dragon, Blue, White, Signed, 6 3/4 In. 305.00
Bowl, Floral, Green, 8 In. 150.00
Bowl, Floral, Green, Octagonal, 4 1/4 In. 305.00
Bowl, Green, Conical, 7 In. 275.00
Bowl, Phoenix, Blue, White, 9 1/4 In. 180.00
Bowl, White Ware Cover, Signed, 3 1/2 In. 145.00
Coffeepot, Red Glaze, c.1900, 8 3/4 In. 300.00
Cup, Cover, Gray Stoneware, Conical Foot, 5 1/4 In. 180.00
Dish, Celadon, 3 1/2 In. 135.00
Jar, 2 Phoenix Flying Amid Clouds, Washed Blue Tones, White Ground, 16 1/2 In. 5750.00
Jar, Black Spotted Band, Gray Green, 3 1/4 In. 275.00
Jar, Loosely Drawn Fruiting Branch, Blue, White Glaze, 19th Century, 7 In. 1150.00

Jar, Oil, Pear Shape, Cupped Mouth, Green, 2 7/8 In.	574.00
Jar, Peony, Blue, White, 5 1/4 In.	245.00
Jar, Peony, Blue, White, Globular, 7 In.	365.00
Mug, Applied Monkey, Red-Orange, 4 1/2 In.	145.00
Mug, Red Glaze, Applied Male Figures, 4 3/8 In., 4 Piece	375.00
Pitcher, Lobster Form, c.1900, 8 In.	400.00
Pot, Wine, Shell Cover, Barnacles, 8 1/4 In.	250.00
Sauce Jar, Dragon Design, Blue Glaze, 10 1/4 In.	212.00
Teabowl, Grass Design, Cream, White Body, Blue Glaze, 6 1/4 In.	175.00
Teapot, 2 Character Ryosai Cartouche, Under Glaze Blue	325.00
Vase, Bottle, Pear Shape, Green, 9 1/2 In.	332.00
Vase, Boys Running, 12 In.	345.00
Vase, Central Pierced Woven Band, 4 White Cranes, Flying, Signed, Ovoid, 7 3/4 In.	805.00
Vase, Circular Ribs On Brick Red Ground, Enamel Drip At Top, Flower, 7 3/4 In.	125.00
Vase, Flaring Rim, Mother & Child, Red, Signed, 9 3/4 In.	500.00
Vase, Meiping Shape, Green, 6 1/4 In.	48.00
Vase, Protruding 3-Dimensional Wise Men, Orange Ground, 9 In.	287.00
Vase, Scholars & Attendants On Mountain, Red, 18 In.	530.00
Vase, White Ware, Pear Shape, Flared Rim, Pale Green, Blue Cast To Glaze, 12 1/2 In.	2420.00
Water Dropper, Relief Lotus, Tortoise Shape, Green, 5 In.	108.00

SUNBONNET BABIES were first introduced in 1900 in the book *The Sunbonnet Babies*. The stories were by Eulalie Osgood Grover, illustrated by Bertha Corbett. The children's faces were completely hidden by the sunbonnets. The children had been pictured in black and white before this time, but the color pictures in the book were immediately successful. The Royal Bayreuth China Company made a full line of children's dishes decorated with the Sunbonnet Babies. Some Sunbonnet Babies plates have been reproduced, but are clearly marked.

Basket, Vase, Babies In The Woods	310.00
Bell, Fishing	275.00
Candlestick, Cleaning, 4 1/8 In.	235.00
Creamer, Fishing	225.00 to 390.00
Creamer, Sweeping	225.00
Creamer, Washing, Pinched Spout, Bold Trim, 3 1/2 In.	250.00
Cup, Fishing	110.00
Dish, Feeding, Blue Mark	285.00
Jug, Washing, 4 1/4 In.	325.00
Pitcher, Sewing	195.00
Pitcher, Washing, Cream	250.00
Plate, Wash Day, 7 1/2 In.	100.00
Plate, Wash Day, Royal Bayreuth, 9 In.	238.00
Postcard, Days Of The Week, Ullman Mfg. Co., 1905, 7 Piece	120.00
Print Set, Days Of The Week, Matted, Frame	125.00
Saucer, Sweeping	60.00
Toothpick, Sewing, 3-Footed, Piecrust Edge, 2 1/2 In.	475.00

SUNDERLAND luster is a name given to a special type of pink luster made by Leeds, Newcastle, and other English firms during the nineteenth century. The luster glaze is metallic and glossy and appears to have bubbles in it. Other pieces of luster are listed in the Luster category.

Bowl, Great Eastern Steamship, Moore & Co., 10 1/4 In.	375.00
Cup & Saucer, Pink Luster	45.00
Jug, Dicken's Scene, Luster, 6 1/2 In.	60.00
Jug, Pink Luster Trim, Black Transfer, Bentley Ware, Borne, 6 1/2 In.	400.00
Mug, Boy With Sheep, A Present For Mary, Yellow, c.1830, 2 3/8 In.	345.00
Mug, Luster Seagoing Scene, 19th Century, 5 In.	90.00
Pitcher, Dickens Days	50.00
Pitcher, War Of 1812, Black Transfers Of Captain Hill Of Constitution	5500.00
Pitcher, War Of 1812, Black Transfers Of Sea Captains	5500.00
Plaque, Luster, Black Transfer, Prepare To Meet Thy God, 7 3/4 x 8 1/2 In.	275.00

Punch Bowl, Odd Fellows Design, 19th Century, 11 3/4 In. 1250.00
Vase, Luster, 8 In. 85.00

SUPERMAN was created by two seventeen-year-olds in 1938. The first
issue of *Action* comics had the strip. Superman remains popular and
became the hero of a radio show in 1940, cartoons in the 1940s, a television series, and several major movies.

Bank, Dime Register	385.00
Belt, Embossed Superman Breaking Chain, Gold Metal Buckle, Leather, 1940s	125.00
Belt Buckle, Red S, Vinyl	250.00
Billfold	45.00
Book, Pop-Up	10.00
Box, Clearfield Cheese Co., Superman Scenes, 1967, 8 x 2 1/2 x 2 In.	98.00
Card, Superman II, Wrapper, Display, 22 Stickers, 1981, 88 Cards	22.00
Card Set, Different Scene On Each Card, Gum Inc., c.1940, Set Of 72	2990.00
Club Card, 1966	30.00
Coloring Book, Superman In Action Poses On Front, 1955	160.00
Coloring Book, Superman Peering Into Pyramid, Whitman, 1979	20.00
Comic Book, No. 60, 1949	55.00
Comic Book, No. 61, 1949	115.00
Cookie Jar, Changing Clothes, Silver Phone Booth, California Originals, Box	595.00
Costume, 1940s	185.00
Costume, Ben Cooper, Package, 1978	12.00
Costume, Captain Action	250.00
Figure, Aurora No. 185, 1974	84.00
Figure, Clark Kent Superpowers, Box	60.00
Figure, Peppin, 1940s	12.00
Figure, Rubber, Advertising, 1973, 6 1/2 In.	45.00
Figure, World's Greatest Super-Heroes, Bend N' Flex, Mego, Sealed, 5 In.	150.00
Game, Inserts Of Lois, 3 Villains, Milton Bradley, Box, 1981	20.00
Game, Superman Flying Bingo, Box, 1966	28.00
Glass	10.00
Gum Card, 1941	24.00
Gum Card Pack, 1960s, Unopened	70.00
Gum Wrapper, 1966	40.00
Junior Horseshoe Set, Rubber, Box	85.00
Junior Horseshoe Set, Rubber, Instructions, 1940-1950, Box, 14 Piece	250.00
Knife	6.00
Lunch Box, 1967 . . . . .145.00 to 155.00
Lunch Box, Christopher Reeve, Steel, Aladdin, 1978 . . . . .24.00 to 35.00
Lunch Box, Metal, Universal, 1954	700.00
Marble, 11/16 In.	95.00
Marble, Peltier, 21/32 In.	235.00
Model Kit, Line Art, Aurora	360.00
Mug, Milk Glass	22.00
Mug, Raised Figure	30.00
Music Box, Box	125.00
Paints, Superman Sparkle, 1966, On Card	22.00
Pin, Man Of Steel, Red Rim, Yellow Lettering	12.00
Pin, Supermen Of America, Celluloid Pinback, 1961	85.00
Pin, This Is A Job For Superman, 1982	12.00
Plane, Rollover, Fighter, Windup, Tin, Marx, 5 In.	4987.00
Planter, Shazam	20.00
Planter, White Glazed Pottery, Superman, Super Plants Balloon, 1976, 3 In.	20.00
Poster, Superman, 1978, 1 Sheet	20.00
Puppet, In Package, 1960	55.00
Puzzle, Box, 1966	24.00
Ray Gun, Krypton	225.00
Record Player, D.C. Comics, 1978	125.00
Record Player, Portable, Electric, Card Stock Case, 45 & 33 RPM, 1978	78.00
Ring, Crusader, Metal, Silver Finish, 1940s	218.00
Ring, Pep Airplane, Metal, Gold Finish, Spring Loaded, 1940s	198.00

Rocket, Water, Krypton, Launcher, Box	1500.00
Soaky, 1950s	65.00
Soaky, 1978	35.00
Soap, Figural, Oh Dawn, Cellophane, 1979	10.00
Socks, 1949	250.00
Stardust, Sealed, 1960s	130.00
Swim Fins, 1940s	50.00
T-Shirt, Iron On Logo	10.00
Tank, Turnover, Superman Turns Tank Over, Windup, Tin, Lineman, 4 In.	1155.00
Tank, Windup, Marx	440.00
Telephone	995.00
Thermos	65.00
Toy, Figure, Energized, Remco, Box, 12 In.	150.00
Wallet, Yellow, Mattel, 1966	50.00
Wastebasket, 1978	50.00
Wristwatch, Lightning Bolt Hands, 1940s	295.00

SUSIE COOPER began as a designer in 1925 working for the English firm A.E. Gray & Company. In 1932 she formed Susie Cooper Pottery, Ltd. In 1950 it became Susie Cooper China, Ltd., and the company made china and earthenware. In 1966 it was acquired by Josiah Wedgwood & Sons, Ltd. The name Susie Cooper appears with the company names on many pieces of ceramics.

Butter, Cover, Light Blue Fan Tab Handle, Deer Mark	35.00
Coffee Set, Reverse Polka Dot, Green, White, Wedgwood, 11 Piece	295.00
Coffeepot, Drysten, Pink	130.00
Cup & Saucer, Bands, Red & Cream, 1930s	10.00
Cup & Saucer, Black Fruit, Wedgwood, Set Of 6	195.00
Plate, Narrow Turquoise Bands, 8 In.	200.00
Plate, Wide Yellow Bands, 8 In.	200.00
Ring Box, Floral Lustre	45.00
Service For 8, Diablo, Wedgwood	595.00
Service For 8, Floriana, Serving Pieces, c.1960, 48 Pieces	600.00
Soup, Dish, Red & Cream Shaded Bands, 1930s	10.00

SWANKYSWIGS are small drinking glasses. In 1933, the Kraft Food Company began to market cheese spreads in these decorated, reusable glass tumblers. They were discontinued from 1941 to 1946, then made again from 1947 to 1958. Then plain glasses were used for most of the cheese, although a few special decorated Swankyswigs have been made since that time. A complete list of prices can be found in *Kovels' Depression Glass & American Dinnerware Price List*.

Bustlin' Betsy, Brown, 3 3/4 In.	3.00 to 6.00
Carnival, Blue, 3 1/2 In.	4.00
Checkerboard, Red & White, 3 1/2 In.	16.00
Cornflower, No. 2, Dark Blue, 3 1/2 In.	2.00
Forget-Me-Not, Dark Blue, 3 1/2 In.	2.00
Forget-Me-Not, Red, 3 1/2 In.	4.00
Kid Kups	3.50
Posy, Jonquil, Yellow, 3 1/2 In.	6.00
Red Scotty, Black Fence, 3 1/2 In.	6.00
Stars, Black, 3 1/2 In.	2.00
Stars, Blue	5.00
Tulip, No. 1, Red, 3 1/2 In.	4.00

SWORDS of all types that are of interest to collectors are listed here. The military dress sword with elaborate handle is probably the most wanted. Be sure to display swords in a safe way, out of reach of children.

Bayonet, Musket, Winchester, No. 1873, Feather Brass Grip, 10-In. Blade	345.00
Bayonet, Remington, No. 1917, Leather & Metal Scabbard	50.00
Bayonet, Winchester, No. 1917, Leather & Iron Scabbard	230.00
French, Military, Artillery, 1830	350.00

Japanese, Brass Pierced Tsuba, Cloth Wrapped Handle, Tang Period, 24 1/4 In. 285.00
Japanese, Bronzed Pierced Tsuba, Skin Wrapped Handle, Metal Scabbard, 27 In. 185.00
Noncommissioned Officer's, Scabbard, Bone Grip, Helmet Pommel, 38 In. 145.00
Officer's, Army, Etched Blade, 3 Star General, Sterling, American 505.00
Officer's, Brass Hilt, Down Curved Boat Guard, French Revolution, 32 In. 750.00
Officer's, Dress, Tiffany & Co., 1863, Fleur-De-Lis Pattern, American, 32 In. 695.00
Officer's, Field, Tiffany & Co., Eagle 1 Side, US Other Side, 1862, 29 In. 690.00
Saber, Brass Wrapped Sharkskin Grip, Double Loop Symmetrical Guard, 29 In. 775.00
Saber, U.S. Cavalry, Brass, Leather Wire Grip, Mansfield & Lamb, 1860, 35 In. 400.00
Samurai, With Scabbard, Sharkskin & Cloth Wrapped Handle, Leather Covered 495.00
Whalebone Blade, Carved & Polychromed Wooden Shank, Sailor's Art 4000.00

SYRACUSE is a trademark used by the Onondaga Pottery of Syracuse,
New York. The company was established in 1871. It is still working.
The name became the Syracuse China Company in 1966. It is known
for fine dinnerware and restaurant china.

Bowl, Cereal, With Dog & Spinning Ball 70.00
Mug, With Horse & Elephant 125.00
Plate, Cardinal, 10 In. 30.00
Plate, Cedar Waxwing, 10 In. 30.00
Plate, With Clown Face, 10 In. 70.00

TAPESTRY, PORCELAIN, see Rose Tapestry category.

TEA CADDY is the name for a small box made to hold tea leaves. In the
eighteenth century, tea was very expensive and it was stored under
lock and key. The first tea caddies were made with locks. By the nineteenth century, tea was more plentiful and the tea caddy was larger.
Often there were two sections, one for green tea, one for black tea.

Blond Tortoiseshell, Double, Mixing Bowl, Silver Mounted, 5 x 11 3/4 In. 1265.00
Boxwood & Hardwood, 3 Foliate Inlaid Oval Panels, George III, 5 1/2 In. 315.00
Boxwood Inlay, 3 Porcelain Containers, France, c.1820 . . . .   4500.00
Brass, Partly Textured, Hans Przyrembel, Cylinder Shape, 1932, 4 1/2 In. 1035.00
Burl, Dome Top, Gothic Style Brass Mounts, England, 4 1/2 In.   180.00
Burl, Pale Sea Shell Inlay On Lid, 19th Century, 4 3/4 In. 484.00
Burl Veneer, Dome Top, Gilded Brass Strapping, 2 Sections With Lids, 9 In. 275.00
Burl Walnut, 2 Lidded Wells Interior, 19th Century 145.00
Burl Walnut, Domed Top, 2 Wells, Openwork Straps, Brass Mounted, Victorian 750.00
Burl Walnut, Hidden Drawer, Veneer, George III, 6 1/2 x 8 1/2 In. 1250.00
Chippendale, Zebra Striping, Original Brass, England, c.1780, 5 x 9 1/2 In. 880.00
Fruitwood, Melon Shape, Stem, Early 19th Century, 6 In. 6200.00
Fruitwood, Pear Form, Silvered Diamond Shape Escutcheon, 6 3/4 In. 3450.00
Inlaid Rosewood, Faux-Bois, Fitted Interior, Mixing Bowl, Regency, c.1815, 6 In. 545.00
Leather, Papier-Mache, Domed Lid, Continuous Landscape, 2 Bottles, 9 In. 2645.00
Mahogany, Brass Bale & Escutcheon, Interior Double Lids, 9 In. 495.00
Mahogany, Hinged Top, Brass Handle, Interior Compartments, 5 1/2 In. 1200.00
Mahogany, Inlaid Oval Reserve Of Shell, George III, 5 1/2 x 6 1/4 In. 460.00
Mahogany, Inlay, 2 Sections & 2 Covers, 8 In. 55.00
Mahogany, Inlay, Dome Lid, England, Early 19th Century, 5 In.   365.00
Mahogany, Inlay, Foliate Border, Fitted With 2 Compartments, 5 3/4 x 6 3/4 In. 2875.00
Mahogany, Inlay, Reserves Of Conch Shells, England, 19th Century, 4 7/8 In. 920.00
Mahogany, Stepped Case, 4 Lidded Wells, William IV, 9 x 14 1/2 In. 145.00
Mahogany, Stringing & Ivory Escutcheon, 2 Compartments 440.00
Mother-Of-Pearl Inlay, Black, 2 Sections 300.00
Papier-Mache, Double, Foil Exterior, Gilded Foliate Designs, 2 Wells, 8 In. 230.00
Papier-Mache, Mother-Of-Pearl, Serpentine Front, Fitted Interior, Floral Still Life 400.00
Penwork, Chinoiseries, 2 Lidded Compartments, Bun Feet, Regency 2600.00
Pewter, Fluted, Bright Cut, Oval, Owen & Bradford, 1770-1790, 3 5/8 In., Pair 675.00
Porcelain, Butterfly Design, Noritake 28.00
Porcelain, Chinese Export, Birds, Flowers, Blue, White, 1775, 4 In. 144.00
Porcelain, Chinese Export, Silver Top, Blue, White Floral Design, 1820 . . . .   600.00
Satinwood, Hardwood Inlay Of Garlands, Flowers, Oval, England, 1790 . . . .   2000.00
Satinwood, Old Patina Case, 2 Lidded Compartments, 1800, 6 In. 485.00

Sedan Chair Form, Gilt Porcelain, Coalport, c.1900, 6 1/2 In. 1550.00
Silver, Hinged Handle, Engraved, Double Headed Eagle Crest, Russia, 3 1/4 In. 1150.00
Silver, Spoon Inside Cover, England, Oval, 3 3/4 x 2 3/4 In. 275.00
Sterling Silver, Armorial On Front, Crest On Lid, Wm. & Aaron, 1771, 5 1/4 In. 1800.00
Sterling Silver, Stylized Bird & Flower Design, Marcolini Mark, 5 1/2 In. 740.00
Tortoiseshell, Plaque With Monogram, Regency, 6 1/2 In. 575.00
Walnut, 2 Sections, c.1780, 10 3/4 In. 650.00
Walnut, Bombe Exterior, Velvet Compartmentalized Interior, Regency, 12 In. 400.00
Walnut, Miniature Sideboard Form, Regency, c.1820, 18 In. 4500.00
Wood, Apple Shape, 19th Century, 4 1/2 In. 4300.00
Wood, Black Japanning, Gold Chinoiserie Design, Pewter Containers, c.1750 .... 575.00
Wood, Melon Shape, Marked, 19th Century, 5 1/4 In. 8625.00
Wood, Melon Shape, Segmented Body, Stemp, 19th Century, 6 In. 9200.00
Wood, Neoclassical Painting, George III, England, 1790, 10 3/4 x 6 x 7 In. 1950.00
Wood, Paper Scroll, Allover Scrolled Design, George III, Turnip Shape, 8 In. 575.00
Wood, Parquetry, George III, Sarcophagus Shape 1725.00
Wood, Pear Shape, Marbleized Surface, Wood Stem, 6 1/2 In. 9775.00
Wood, Pear Shape, Red Stain, Knopped Finial, 7 In. 5175.00
Wood, Pear Shape, Red Stain, Wood Stem, 19th Century, 6 3/4 In. 5750.00
Wood Veneer, Domed Cover, Colored Inlay, 2 Interior Lids, 7 5/8 In. 110.00

TEA LEAF IRONSTONE dishes are named for their decorations. There
was a superstition that it was lucky if a whole tea leaf unfolded at the
bottom of your cup. This idea was translated into the pattern of dishes
known as *tea leaf.* By 1850, at least twelve English factories were
making this pattern, and by the 1870s, it was a popular pattern in many
countries. The tea leaf was always a luster glaze on early wares,
although now some pieces are made with a brown tea leaf.

Baker, Chinese Shape, Oval, Shaw 160.00
Baker, Fan, Oval, Shaw, 6 x 7 1/2 In. 130.00
Baker, Lily-Of-The-Valley, Shaw, 7 1/2 x 10 In. 70.00
Baker, Tea Berry, Square, Clemenston, 6 x 7 5/8 In. 90.00
Bowl, Apple, Scalloped, Meakin 650.00
Bowl, Cereal, Copper Trim, Adams, 6 5/8 In. 30.00
Bowl, Dessert, 5 1/2 In. 25.00
Bowl, Fruit, Copper Trim, Adams, 5 3/8 In. 15.00
Bowl, Fruit, Scalloped, Shaw, 9 In. 220.00
Bowl, Gold, Meakin, 8 3/4 In. 45.00
Bowl, Vegetable, Cover, Adams, 9 3/4 In. 85.00
Bowl, Vegetable, Cover, Basket Weave, Shaw, 6 3/4 x 11 1/4 In. 200.00
Bowl, Vegetable, Cover, Chinese Shape, Shaw 400.00
Bowl, Vegetable, Cover, Gold, Rectangular, Meakin 45.00
Bowl, Vegetable, Cover, Golden Scroll, Powell & Bishop, 6 x 10 3/4 In. 20.00
Bowl, Vegetable, Cover, Oval 235.00
Bowl, Vegetable, Cover, Oval, Gold Design 220.00
Bowl, Vegetable, Cover, Tobacco Leaf, Elsmore & Forster 250.00
Bowl, Vegetable, Scroll, Meakin 200.00
Bread Plate, Adams 15.00
Bread Plate, Red Cliff, 6 1/2 In. 25.00
Butter Pat, Cloverleaf, Gold Luster, 4 Piece 5.00
Butter Pat, Meakin, Gold, 3 In. 15.00
Cake Plate, Fishhook, Meakin 35.00
Casserole, Rosebud Finial On Cover, Chinese Shape, 7 x 11 In. 235.00
Chamber Pot, Lily-Of-The-Valley, Shaw ....*Illus* 625.00
Chamber Pot, Maidenhair Fern, No Cover, Wilkinson 175.00
Coaster, Gold, Meakin, 4 1/4 In. 25.00
Coffeepot, Adams 140.00
Creamer, Gold Leaf In Center, Red Cliff 70.00
Creamer, Miniature 45.00
Cup & Saucer, Adams ....45.00 to 55.00
Cup & Saucer, Copper, Straight Sided, Shaw 55.00
Cup & Saucer, Flat, Copper Trim, Adams, 2 1/2 In. 50.00
Cup & Saucer, Gold Trim, Flintridge, 2 1/4 In. 60.00

Tea Leaf Ironstone, Teapot, Gothic Paneled, Furnival; Tea Leaf Ironstone, Chamber Pot,
Lily-Of-The-Valley, Shaw; Tea Leaf Ironstone, Jug, Milk, Fig Cousin, Davenport

Cup & Saucer, Handleless, Luster Band, Walley	15.00
Cup & Saucer, Handleless, Squatty, Meakin	70.00
Cup & Saucer, Luster Band, Livesley & Powell	140.00
Cup & Saucer, Luster Band, Walley	70.00
Cup & Saucer, Meakin	55.00
Cup & Saucer, Red Cliff, 2 7/8 In.	45.00
Cup & Saucer, Square, Ridged, Red Cliff	140.00
Cup Plate, Meakin	60.00
Cuspidor, Tobacco Leaf, Elsmore & Forster	650.00
Eggcup, Boston, Meakin	200.00
Eggcup, Meakin	275.00
Gravy Boat, Attached Underplate	160.00
Gravy Boat, Copper Trim, Adams	70.00
Gravy Boat, Copper Trim, Underplate, Adams	176.00
Gravy Boat, Glasgow Pottery, Moses, 1884	95.00
Gravy Boat, Gold, Meakin	180.00 to 195.00
Jug, Milk, Fig Cousin, Davenport	*Illus* 575.00
Luster, Copper, Mustache Cup & Saucer	950.00
Mixing Bowl, Gold Luster, Kitchen Kraft, 10 3/8 x 5 1/2 In.	55.00
Mug, Empress, Adams	120.00
Pitcher, Copper Trim, Adams, 6 3/4 In.	124.00
Pitcher, Gothic, Luster Band, Red Cliff, 8 1/4 In.	90.00
Pitcher, Hot Water, Maidenhair, Wilkinson	475.00
Pitcher, Milk, Hanging Leaves, Shaw, 7 1/2 In.	475.00
Pitcher, Peerless, Edwards, 10 In.	260.00
Plate, 6 3/8 In.	15.00 to 20.00
Plate, 8 3/8 In.	25.00
Plate, Copper Trim, Adams, 6 1/4 In.	15.00
Plate, Copper Trim, Adams, 7 3/4 In.	25.00
Plate, Copper Trim, Adams, 10 1/8 In.	50.00
Plate, Gold Leaf In Center, Red Cliff, 8 3/8 In.	15.00 to 30.00
Plate, Gold Leaf In Center, Red Cliff, 10 In.	50.00
Plate, Gold, Meakin, 7 7/8 In.	25.00 to 35.00
Plate, Gothic, Luster Band, 7 1/2 In.	60.00
Plate, Gothic, Luster Band, Walley, 9 In., 4 Piece	40.00
Plate, Meakin, 1880, 8 3/4 In.	115.00
Plate, Red Cliff, 8 3/8 In.	30.00
Plate, Red Cliff, 10 In.	50.00
Platter, Classic Gothic, Luster Band, Livesley & Powell, 12 x 15 1/2 In.	42.00
Platter, Gold, Rectangular, Meakin, 12 3/8 In.	165.00
Platter, John Edwards, 14 In.	55.00

Platter, Lily-Of-The-Valley, Shaw, 8 x 11 In. 95.00
Platter, Meakin, 8 x 10 3/4 In. 35.00
Platter, Serving, Gold, Oval, Meakin, 12 3/8 In. 160.00
Platter, Serving, Gold, Rectangular, Meakin, 10 In. 65.00
Platter, Serving, Gold, Rectangular, Meakin, 12 In. 125.00
Platter, Serving, Gold, Rectangular, Meakin, 13 1/4 In. ....70.00 to 85.00
Platter, Serving, Gold, Rectangular, Meakin, 14 In. 100.00
Platter, Tea Berry, Square, Clemenston, 9 1/4 x 12 7/8 In. 150.00
Posset Cup, Hanging Leaves, Shaw 400.00
Relish, Peerless, Edwards 110.00
Salt & Pepper 72.00
Salt & Pepper, Empress, Adams 150.00
Saltshaker 36.00
Saucer, Gold, Meakin 15.00
Saucer, Meakin 115.00
Shaving Mug, Basket Weave, Shaw 310.00
Shaving Mug, Chinese Shape, Shaw ....95.00 to 155.00
Shaving Mug, Eric Shape, Wells 150.00
Shaving Mug, Fishhook, Meakin ....135.00 to 155.00
Shaving Mug, Lily-Of-The-Valley, Shaw 225.00
Shaving Mug, Scroll, Meakin 180.00
Soap Dish, Daisy, Shaw, 3 Piece 250.00
Soup, Dish, Adams 45.00
Soup, Dish, Copper Trim, Adams, 8 In. 38.00
Soup, Dish, Daisy, Shaw 170.00
Soup, Dish, Meakin, 8 3/4 In. 45.00
Soup, Dish, Meakin, 9 In. 120.00
Sugar, Cover 60.00
Sugar, Golden Scroll, Powell & Bishop 80.00
Sugar, Meakin 90.00
Sugar, Red Cliff 90.00
Sugar, Tobacco Leaf, Fanfare, Elsmore & Forster 240.00
Tea Set, Child's, Mellor Taylor, 16 Piece 1000.00
Teapot, Beaded Handle, East End Pottery 100.00
Teapot, Chinese, Shaw 160.00
Teapot, Fishhook, Meakin 90.00
Teapot, Gothic Paneled, Furnival ....*Illus* 470.00
Teapot, Gothic Paneled, Teaberry Design, Professional Lip Repair 470.00
Tureen, Sauce, Cable Shape, Thomas Furnival 140.00
Tureen, Sauce, Ridged, Square, Red Cliff, 4 Piece 170.00
Tureen, Sauce, Scroll, Meakin 700.00
Tureen, Sauce, Stand & Ladle, Lion's Head, Mellor Taylor 400.00
Washbowl, Plain, Round, Shaw 90.00
Waste Bowl, Chinese Shape, Shaw 80.00

TECO is the mark used on the art pottery line made by the American
Terra Cotta and Ceramic Company of Terra Cotta and Chicago,
Illinois. The company was an offshoot of the firm founded by William
D. Gates in 1881. The Teco line was first made in 1885 but was not
sold commercially until 1902. It continued in production until 1922.
Over 500 designs were made in a variety of colors, shapes, and glazes.
The company closed in 1930.

Bowl, Matte Glaze, Green, Impressed Mark, F. Albert, 9 In. 360.00
Bowl, Shallow Form, Matte Glaze, Green, Double Stamp, 1 1/4 x 4 1/2 In. 1035.00
Bowl, Variegated Matte Glaze, Green, 6 3/4 In. 360.00
Candlestick, Squared Handle, Matte Glaze, Pink, Impressed Mark, 5 x 2 1/2 In. 320.00
Jardiniere, Broad Shouldered Form, Matte Glaze, Medium Green, 15 x 10 In. 770.00
Lamp, Pink, Matte Glaze, Green, Slag Glass Shade, 28 x 20 In. 8250.00
Paperweight, Pelican, Marked, 6 1/2 In. 165.00
Pitcher, Crystalline, 4 In. 550.00
Pitcher, Divided Handle, Matte Glaze, Light Green, 8 1/2 In. 600.00
Vase, 2 Buttressed Handles, Matte Glaze, Green, W.D. Gates, 7 In. 990.00
Vase, 2 Closed Buttresses At Shoulder, Matte Glaze, Green, Impressed Mark, 9 In. 1045.00

Vase, 2 Closed Handles, Caramel, Impressed Mark 525.00
Vase, 2 Closed Handles, Matte Glaze, Green, Impressed Mark, 6 In. 775.00
Vase, 2 Closed Squared Handles, Matte Glaze, Green, 7 In. 1045.00
Vase, 2 Handles, Matte Glaze, Green, Flared Lip, Heavy Charcoaling, 9 x 5 1/2 In. 715.00
Vase, 2 Handles, Matte Glaze, Green, Impressed Mark, 9 In. 880.00
Vase, 2 Open Buttresses At Shoulder, Matte Glaze, Green, Impressed Mark, 4 In. 1000.00
Vase, 2 Open Handles, Matte Glaze, Green, Impressed Mark, W.D. Gates, 8 In. 1450.00
Vase, 4 Buttressed Handles, Matte Glaze, Dark Green 3300.00
Vase, 4 Buttressed Handles, Matte Glaze, Green, Round, 13 x 10 In. 4600.00
Vase, 4 Buttressed Handles, Matte Glaze, Medium, Dark Green, 13 x 6 3/4 In. 3960.00
Vase, 4 Buttressed Handles, Matte Glaze, Rose, 7 1/8 In. 550.00
Vase, 4 Buttressed Handles, Matte Glaze, Brown, Signed, 7 1/2 In. 550.00
Vase, 4 Buttressed Handles, Matte Glaze, Green, Impressed Mark, 5 In. 1000.00
Vase, 4 Buttressed Handles, Matte Glaze, Green, Impressed Mark, 10 1/2 In. 1450.00
Vase, 4 Buttressed Handles, Matte Glaze, Green, Impressed Mark, W.D. Gates, 6 In. 1450.00
Vase, 4 Drop Shaped Columns, Matte Glaze, Brown, Impressed Mark, 9 In. 825.00
Vase, 4 Open Handles, Matte Glaze, Green, Circle Design, Impressed Mark, 6 In. 1540.00
Vase, 4 Open Handles, Matte Glaze, Green, Impressed Mark, 12 In. 880.00
Vase, 4 Panels, Matte Glaze, Blue, W.D. Gates, 7 In. 523.00
Vase, 4 Vertical Buttresses, Lily, Cup-Shaped Lotus Top, Trailing Stems, Signed, 12 In. . . 2640.00
Vase, Allover Embossed Bellflower Blossoms, Leathery Green Glaze, 17 1/4 In. 4675.00
Vase, Broad Shouldered Form, Green Glaze, Marked, 5 In. 440.00
Vase, Buttressed Handles, Floral Design At Shoulder, Lobed, Bulbous, Signed, 6 In. 1650.00
Vase, Buttressed, Matte Glaze, Green, 10 1/4 x 5 1/2 In. 2300.00
Vase, Cylindrical Handles, Matte Glaze, Green, Marked, Fritz Albert, 9 1/2 In. 635.00
Vase, Flared Rim, Matte Glaze, Green, 6 x 4 3/4 In. 400.00
Vase, Flared Rim, Matte Glaze, Rose, Impressed Mark, 6 In. 385.00
Vase, Long Fins At Base, Smooth Matte Glaze, Green, Signed, 9 In. 3850.00
Vase, Matte Glaze, Brown, Bulour, 3 3/4 In. 415.00
Vase, Matte Glaze, Dark Green, 9 In. 1200.00
Vase, Matte Glaze, Green, 3 Legs, 3 Protrusions, Impressed Mark, 5 x 3 In. 300.00
Vase, Matte Glaze, Green, Dimples To Sides, Impressed Mark, 3 In. 265.00
Vase, Matte Glaze, Green, Impressed Mark, 5 In. 415.00
Vase, Matte Glaze, Green, Impressed Mark, 5 1/2 In. 990.00
Vase, Matte Glaze, Green, Impressed Mark, W.D. Gates, 8 In. 4675.00
Vase, Matte Glaze, Green, Rounded Shape, Impressed Mark, 5 x 4 1/2 In. 330.00
Vase, Matte Glaze, Green, Triangular Tapered Form, 8 In. 545.00
Vase, Matte Glaze, Mustard, 7 In. 500.00
Vase, Narcissus In Relief, Matte Glaze, Light Pink Ground, 8 3/4 In. 550.00
Vase, Pinched Sides, Brown Glaze, Marked, 4 In. 470.00
Vase, Pompeian, Marked, W.D. Gates, 7 1/2 In. 600.00
Vase, Reticulated Rim & Body, Organic Design On Sides, Signed, 6 1/4 In. 2090.00
Vase, Vertical Columns At Side, Matte Glaze, Gray, 7 1/2 In. 470.00
Wall Pocket, Matte Glaze, Green, Raised Floral Design, Impressed Mark, 9 x 6 1/2 In. . . . 360.00

TEDDY BEARS were named for a president of the United States. The
first teddy bear was a cuddly toy said to be inspired by a hunting trip
made by Teddy Roosevelt in 1902. Morris and Rose Michtom started
selling their stuffed bears as *teddy bears* and the name stayed. The
Michtoms founded the Ideal Novelty and Toy Company. The German
version of the teddy bear was made about the same time by the Steiff
Company. There are many types of teddy bears and all are collected.
The old ones are being reproduced. Other bears are listed in the Toy
section.

Amber, Curly Plush, Swivel Neck, Jointed Limbs, Leather Collar, c.1925, 16 In. 350.00
American Electric Eye Bear, Mohair 675.00
Baseball, Uniform, Bat & Extra Suit, Germany 2600.00
Black Mohair, Metal Body, Jointed, Schuco, Box, 1950s, 2 1/2 In. 198.00
Concertina Mechanism, Curly Mohair, Purple, Articulated Limbs, Germany, 14 In. . . . 2530.00
Gund, Mohair, Straw Filled, Jointed 245.00
Ideal, Orange Brown, Swivel Head, Jointed Limbs, Felt Pads, 18 In. 58.00
Ideal, Swivel Head, Jointed Limbs, Black Boot Button Eyes, 13 In. 58.00
Knickerbocker, Growler, 1940s 450.00

Mohair, Articulated Limbs, Bead Eyes, Embroidered Detail, 12 1/2 In. 275.00
Mohair, Blond, Jointed, Button Eyes, Yarn Nose, 11 In. 165.00
Mohair, Brown, Excelsior & Kapok, Embroidered, Glass Eyes, 1920s, 30 In. 258.00
Mohair, Brown, Jointed Arms, Legs, Black Beaded Eyes, 1935, 29 In. 450.00
Mohair, Gold, Articulated Limbs, Beaded Eyes, 5 In. 135.00
Mohair, Gold, Articulated Limbs, Beaded Eyes, Ribbon, 7 In. 175.00
Mohair, Jointed, Cloth Pads, Black Eyes, Floss Nose, 20 In. 220.00
Musical Squeeze Box, Germany, 13 In. 1093.00
Petz, Max, Mohair, Blond, Built-In Music Box, 1920s, 17 In. 2185.00
Plush, Amber, Rounded Head, Snout Nose, Jointed Limbs, Bead Eyes, c.1930, 26 In. ... 1050.00
Plush, Beige, Swivel Head, Jointed, Brown Glass Eyes, 17 In. 375.00
Schuco, Cinnamon, 3 1/2 In. 145.00
Schuco, Perfume Bottle, Mohair, Gold, Jointed, 5 In. 825.00
Schuco, Perfume Bottle, Plush, Removable Head, Vial In Torso, 1935, 4 3/4 In. 850.00
Schuco, Yes/No Bear, Light Yellow, Glass Eyes, Embroidered, 1930s, 15 In. 920.00
Steiff, Anniversary, Mohair, Silver, Embroidered, Fully Jointed, Box, 1983, 12 In. 316.00
Steiff, Baby, In Crib, Seated, Germany, Box, 12 In. 143.00
Steiff, Boot Button Eyes, Elongated & Jointed Limbs, Red Sweater Outfit, 16 In. 1840.00
Steiff, Brown, 3 In. 75.00
Steiff, Glass Eyes, Brown Stitched Nose, Claws, Humpback, 1930s, 14 In. 690.00
Steiff, Luncheon Bear, Box, 10 In. 250.00
Steiff, Mohair, Apricot, c.1906 .... 3450.00
Steiff, Mohair, Black, Glass Eyes, Original Tags & Ear Button, 4 In. 165.00
Steiff, Mohair, Blond, Black Button Eyes, Nose, Felt Pads, 16 In. 2875.00
Steiff, Mohair, Blond, Excelsior Stuffed, Fully Jointed, Button Eyes, c.1905, 13 In. 977.00
Steiff, Mohair, Blond, Excelsior Stuffed, Glass Eyes, Embroidered, 1930s, 14 In. 460.00
Steiff, Mohair, Blond, Swivel Limbs, Black Button Eyes, Nose, Germany, 12 In. 805.00
Steiff, Mohair, Champagne, Black Button Eyes, Felt Paws, 1910, 14 In. 5100.00
Steiff, Mohair, Champagne, Black Shoebutton Eyes, 20 In. 10800.00
Steiff, Mohair, Cinnamon, Black Steel Eyes, 1906 .... 6325.00
Steiff, Mohair, Fully Jointed, Box, 7 In. 350.00
Steiff, Mohair, Gold, Brown Glass Eyes, Jointed, Black Floss Nose, 5 In. 550.00
Steiff, Mohair, Gray, Curly, Jointed, Button In Ear, 1950s, 30 In. 1955.00
Steiff, Mohair, Light Brown, Squeezable Concertina Music Box, Jointed, 13 In. 2760.00
Steiff, Mohair, Plush Body, Jointed, Black Eyes, Floss Nose, 16 In. 248.00
Steiff, Mohair, White, Black Shoebutton Eyes, 13 In. 2000.00
Steiff, Mohair, White, Turned Up Nose, 3 1/2 In. 350.00
Steiff, Mohair, Yellow, 1906, 14 In. 745.00
Steiff, Mohair, Yellow, Glass Eyes, Embroidered, c.1920, 24 In. 1150.00
Steiff, Ophelia, Brown Eyes, Gold Button In Left Ear, 17 In. 350.00
Steiff, Plush, Amber, Excelsior Filled, Swivel Head, Jointed Limbs, 13 In. 2000.00
Steiff, Plush, Gold, Jointed, Black Button Eyes, Beige Felt Pads, 9 3/4 In. 1725.00
Steiff, Plush, Gray, Jointed, Black Button Eyes, Off-White Felt Pads, 10 In. 575.00
Steiff, Plush, White, Jointed, Black Button Eyes, Cream Leather Pads, 13 In. 805.00
Twyford, Mohair, White, England, 10 In. 110.00

TELEPHONES are wanted by collectors if the phones are old enough or
unusual enough. The first telephone may have been made in Havana,
Cuba, in 1849, but it was not patented. The first publicly demonstrated phone was used in Frankfurt, Germany, in 1860. The phone made
by Alexander Graham Bell was shown at the Centennial Exhibition in
Philadelphia in 1876, but it was not until 1877 that the first private
phones were installed. Collectors today want all types of old phones,
phone parts, and advertising. Even recent figural phones are popular.

7-Up, Figural 125.00
Airplane Form, Yellow Plastic, Telcer, Italy, 1960s, 10 x 7 x 7 In. 187.00
American Electric Co., Hanging Hand Set Extension 75.00
Bart Simpson 65.00
Bear, Battery Operated, Box 200.00
Bells & Crank, Canada 25.00
Booth, Gray Granite Interior, Oak 1000.00
Booth, Pay Station, Gray/Western 600.00

Booth, Pay Station, Independent 616.00
Booth, White & Red Porcelain & Glass 1025.00
Cabbage Patch 95.00
Candlestick, Kellogg, Push To Talk Button, Jack Plug On Cord 40.00
Charlie The Tuna, Box, 1987 .... 75.00
Crank, Jydsk Telefon, Wall 192.00
Crest Toothpaste 95.00
Darth Vader, Speaker Phone 85.00
Desk, Automatic Electric Co., Model 40, Brass Dial & Bands, c.1930 .... 200.00
Desk, Metal Magneto, Federal Telephone & Radio Corp., Cradle 25.00
Ericophon, 1 Piece 25.00
Fido, Box 245.00
First Aid Kit, Bell, Scissors, Contents 45.00
First Aid Kit, Bell, Tin Suitcase 20.00
Garfield 65.00
Green Giant 85.00
Heinz Ketchup 65.00
Highboy, Magneto Desk Hand Set, Black, Erickson, Danish 125.00
Keebler Elf 50.00
Keebler Elf, Ernie, Premium, Box 125.00
Kellogg, Wall, 1-Piece Receiver, Cup-Shaped Mouthpiece, Oak 245.00
Kellogg, Wall, Switchboard Type, Oak 285.00
Kermit The Frog 95.00
Little Sprout, Push Button, 1984, 12 In. 75.00
Oscar Mayer, Foot Long Hot Dog 65.00
Pay Phone, Coin Chute, Single Slot 10.00
Pillsbury Dough Boy 325.00
Police, Call Box, Cannon Electric Development, Gamewell, 1915, 11 x 16 In. ....450.00 to 475.00
Pooh 250.00
Poppin' Fresh Doughboy, Push-Button ....250.00 to 325.00
Regal, Steel Body, Bakelite Hand Set, Internal Bells, Mute Button, Belfium, c.1926 ..... 150.00
Remco Dial Master, Battery Operated, Box, 1966 .... 25.00
Shoe, Sports Illustrated 35.00
Sign, Bell Public Telephone, Tin, Hand Painted, 1930-1940 .... 150.00
Sign, Bell System, Blue On White, Porcelain, Round, 7 In. 120.00
Sign, Public Telephone, 2 Sides, Flange, 1930s, 18-In. Diam. 160.00
Sign, Tele Mfg. Co., London, Dated 1944 .... 95.00
Sign, White On Blue, Porcelain, 3 3/4 x 20 In. 88.00
Single Box, Mercedes Dial, Oak 125.00
Snoopy, Rotary Dial, Box 250.00
Stromberg-Carlson, Crank, 2 Bells, Desk, Wooden, Wall, 1915, 18 In. 170.00
Stromberg-Carlson, Transmitter Arm Assembly, Steel Base, Slug & Socket 60.00
Telephone Mfg. Co., London, Wall Mounted Box, Light & Brass Hook, 1940s 125.00
U.S. Army Signal Corp., Wall, Wooden, Dial 175.00
Wall, Wooden, Brass Bells, Dial Crank, Bakelite Handset, 1920 .... 300.00
Western Electric, Block, Black Fiber Box, Black Plastic Phone, Hinged Lid, 1949 .... 52.00
Western Electric, Candlestick, Brass Bells, 1919 .... 550.00
Western Electric, Chrome, Turquoise, Cradle Style, 1962 .... 45.00
Western Electric, Dispatcher, Accordion Style, Metal Extension, Metal, 1909, 9 In. 225.00
Western Electric, Model 202, Metal Base, Bakelite Handset 330.00
Western Electric, Model 302, Molded Bakelite Hand Set, Internal Brass Bells, 1939 ... 160.00
Western Electric, Oak, Wall 340.00
Western Electric, Solid Brass Candlestick, Brass Bells, c.1919 .... 600.00

TELEVISION sets are twentieth-century collectibles. Although the first
television transmission took place in England in 1925, collectors find
few sets which pre-date 1946. The first sets had only five channels, but
by 1949 the additional VHF channels were included. The first color
television set became available in 1951.

Eversharp, CBS TV, Glass, Wood Display, 1940-1950 .... 200.00
Motorola, Bakelite, Tabletop, Circular Screen, 8 In. 230.00
Philco, Orange Plastic, Sculpted Casing On Swivel, Pedestal Base, 11 In. 92.00

Philco, Pedestal Base, Black, White Screen, Square, 10 In. 992.00
Predicta, Floor Model 750.00
Predicta, Table Model 450.00

TEPLITZ refers to art pottery manufactured by a number of companies in the Teplitz-Turn area of Bohemia during the late nineteenth and early twentieth centuries. The Amphora Porcelain Works and the Alexandra Works were two of these companies.

Basket, Basket Weave, Large Cluster Of Grapes, Vine, Leaves, Signed, 12 In. 185.00
Basket, Grape Draped Child, Art Nouveau, Amphora, 10 1/2 In. 325.00
Basket, Leaves, Vine, 9 x 6 In. 395.00
Bowl, Cover, Leaves, 4 Acorns, Tan, Footed, Austria, 1910 .... 110.00
Bust, Woman's Head, Pompadour, Lacy Gown, Signed, 14 In. 1800.00
Ewer, Gray Speckled, Dark Blue Interior, Austria, 1910 .... 115.00
Ewer, Purple Flower, Green Leaves, Serpent Handle 95.00
Jardiniere, Jeweled Cockerel, Cobalt Blue Trim, Amphora, 6 1/2 In. 195.00
Pitcher, Branch Handle, Floral, Gold, 7 In. 75.00
Vase, 2 Barn Swallows, Art Deco Flowers, Ink Stamp, Amphora, 12 In. 275.00
Vase, 2 Handles, Bulbous, Raised Leaf Design, Pink, Green, Blue, Amphora, 11 In. 469.00
Vase, 2 Handles, Multicolored Hi-Glaze Bird, Mottled Matte Ground, Amphora, 7 In. 143.00
Vase, 2 Women Gathering Wheat, Gloss Glaze, Impressed Crown, Amphora, 12 In. 330.00
Vase, 4 Masques Of Felines, Cream, Gold, Amphora Glaze, Earthenware, 17 In. 4600.00
Vase, Allover Leaf Forms, Folded & Twisted Body, Amphora, Signed, 7 1/2 In. 135.00
Vase, Art Nouveau, Blue, Glazed Jewels, Amphora, 9 In. 125.00
Vase, Bird In Flight, Checkerboard Pattern At Top, Amphora, 11 In. 231.00
Vase, Embossed Full Size Chicken In Center, Amphora, Gampini, 17 1/2 In. 850.00
Vase, Floral, Blue, 9 1/2 In. 70.00
Vase, Floral, Handle, 4 In. 150.00
Vase, Jeweled, Pedestal, Amphora, 6 1/4 In. 275.00
Vase, Orange Peel, 3-Dimensional Dragon, Gold, Silver, Red Tail, Amphora, 7 1/2 In. ... 550.00
Vase, Owl Design, Mosaic, Amphora, 15 1/2 In. 525.00
Vase, Pale Apple Green Rising To Darker Green, Fitted Base, Amphora 518.00
Vase, Pale Blue Flowers, Purple Ground, Red Ink Stamp, Amphora, 6 1/4 In. 193.00
Vase, Pink, Gold, Black, Amphora Glaze, Earthenware, 1900, 8 1/2 In. 4025.00
Vase, Portrait Of Woman, Wearing Gilt Helmet, Red, Nouveau Mark, 10 In. 1553.00
Vase, Portrait, Browns, Black, Gray, White, Gold Trim, Amphora, 5 In. 450.00
Vase, Relief Figural Design, Blue Lotus Ground, 8 1/2 In. 264.00
Vase, Stylized Art Deco Design, High Glaze Vertical Stripes, Amphora, 11 1/2 In. 220.00
Vase, Woman Portrait, Black Hair, Holding Flowers, Enamel, Jewels, Amphora, 6 In. ... 795.00

TERRA-COTTA is a special type of pottery. It ranges from pale orange to dark reddish-brown in color. The color comes from the clay, which is fired but not always glazed in the finished piece.

Bust, Court Of Louis XVI, France, 18th Century, 22 In. 1725.00
Bust, Female, Wearing Decollete Dress, Cloak, Signed, 1779, 28 1/2 In. 1380.00
Bust, Gentleman, Facing Right, Open Lace Shirt, Curly Hair, Continental, 23 In. 2587.00
Bust, Jeunesse, Marble Pedestal, Continental, Marked, 1775, 14 In. 968.00
Bust, Young Boy, Louis XV Style, 17 In. 575.00
Figurine, Balancing Pots On Head, Shoulder & Knee, G. Baudisch, 1920s, 10 In. 1840.00
Figurine, Young Man, Standing On Spade, 1920s, 51 3/4 In. 3450.00
Figurine, Young Woman, Basket Of Flowers, Continental, 49 1/4 In. 3450.00
Frame, 3 Stylized Heads, Fruit, Leaves, Ribbon Leaves, 1928, 11 1/4 In. 4370.00
Jardiniere, Polychrome Flowers, Glazed, Marked, 26 1/2 In. 157.00
Plaque, Apollo, Curly Tresses, Raised Circular Border, 28 In. 2057.00
Plum Pot, Swirled Green, Mustard, Brown Glaze, Applied Handles, 9 In. 172.00
Tobacco Jar, Munich Child On Cigar Box, Marked, 8 1/2 In. 452.00
Umbrella Receiver, Dragon Design, 24 In. 225.00
Urn, Campana, Medial Band Of Foliate Scroll Body, Loop Handles, 32 In. 1815.00
Urn, Garden, Low Loop Handle, 1904, 19 3/4 In. 4830.00
Urn, Neoclassical, Gadrooned Body, Foliate Scrolled Handles, Acorn Finial, Pair 17250.00
Vessel, Water, 2 Handles, Central America, 8 In. 55.00
Wall Pocket, Moriage 145.00

TEXTILES listed here include many types of printed fabrics and table and household linens. Some other textiles will be found under Clothing, Coverlet, Quilt, Rug, etc.

Bedspread, Chenille, Flower Design, Full Size, Unused	45.00
Bedspread, Crocheted, Heavy, 78 x 102 In.	175.00
Bedspread, Crocheted, Popcorn, White, Bertha Wilson LaRue, Ohio, 102 x 110 In.	100.00
Bedspread, Needlework, Horse Center, Border, Horse & Dog Corners, Red, 76 x 69 In. .	605.00
Bedspread, Six Million Dollar Man	35.00
Blanket, Donkey, Murphy The Hatter, Printing Both Sides, 40 x 40 In.	49.00
Blanket, Homespun Wool, Plaid, Red, Navy & Teal, Handsewn Hems, Seam, 72 x 96 In.	160.00
Blanket, Horse, Judge Day & Franklin Cigar, 68 x 68 In.	33.00
Blanket, Hudson Bay, Red, Black Stripes	145.00
Blanket, Indian Style, Green, Cream, Beacon, 70 x 70 In.	66.00
Drapes, White Linen, Picasso, 1950s, Pair	977.00
Flag, American, 12 Stars, White Painted, Red Painted Stripes, 27 3/8 x 47 1/2 In.	1265.00
Flag, American, 18 Stars, Hand Sewn Gauze, 1812, 66 x 93 In.	545.00
Flag, American, 34 Stars, Cotton, 22 x 33 In.	2310.00
Flag, American, 36 Stars, Garfield & Arthur, Block Lettering Logo, 6 x 10 In.	1320.00
Flag, American, 36 Stars, Place In Circular Design, Grant & Colfax Campaign	2750.00
Flag, American, 38 Stars, Glazed Cotton, 11 3/4 x 18 1/8 In.	210.00
Flag, American, 39 Stars, Dakota Territories Admitted Into Union, 1889, 24 x 33 In.	880.00
Flag, American, 39 Stars, Irregular Pattern, Printed Silk, Framed, 12 x 17 In.	170.00
Flag, American, 42 Stars, Blue Cotton Stars, Red Border, Binding, 46 1/2 x 69 In.	460.00
Flag, American, 42 Stars, Chenille, 19 x 23 In.	725.00
Flag, American, 45 Stars, Machine Sewn, Stars Both Sides, 72 x 120 In.	135.00
Flag, American, Battle Flag, Progressive, Roosevelt, Bandanna, 1912, 21 x 23 In.	395.00
Handkerchief Case, Orange Velvet, Beige Cord, 1920s, 7 1/2 x 8 1/2 In.	110.00
Kerchief, Celebrated United States Naval Victories, War Of 1812, 25 x 29 In.	1540.00
Lap Robe, Floral Band, Victorian	135.00
Panel, Embroidered, Garden Archway, Silk, Wool, Painted, Brussels, 1870s, 82 x 84 In. .	3300.00
Panel, Needlepoint, Boy With Stag, Frame, Victorian, 12 x 14 In.	230.00
Panel, Needlework, Landscape, Castle In Distance, 62 x 24 In.	517.00
Panel, Needlework, Muslin, Effe Nance Jones, Son, 1842-1865, 18 x 24 In.	4750.00
Panel, Tapestry, Verdure, Foliage & Birds, Landscape, Flemish, 77 x 57 In.	3105.00
Pillow, Aquatic Scene, Stork Among Cattails, Black Velvet, Down Filled, 15 x 15 In.	115.00
Pillow, Needlepoint, Edwardian Lady Reading, Giltwood Frame, 35 x 29 3/4 In.	181.00
Pillow, Wool, Embroidered Flowers Around, Stuffed, Round, 18 1/2 In.	190.00
Pillow Cover, Silk Embroidery, Egyptian Scarab, Art Deco, 18 x 14 In.	90.00
Pillow Sham, Crazy Quilt, Embroidered Pictorial Designs, Anne, '85, 26 x 26 In.	225.00
Printed Fabric, Whole Bear Family, Hand Colored, Matted, Frame, 20 3/4 x 23 3/4 In. .	195.00
Runner, Crocheted, God Bless Our Home, House & Trees, 9 x 16 In.	45.00
Runner, Filet Lace, Ecru, Grecian Woman Playing Lyre, Horn, Cherubs, 10 x 23 In.	78.00
Runner, Homespun, Cotton, Bird's Eye Weave, Red Stripes, 11 x 86 In.	72.00
Sack, Domino Sugar, NRA Logo, 25 Lb.	8.00
Sack, Flour, Indian Huntress Overlooking Vista, Yeager Milling Co., 18 x 10 In.	135.00
Scarf, Black Silk, 12-In. Fringe, 4 x 4 Ft.	195.00
Scarf, Piano, Large Pink Roses, Black Silk, Fringe, 48 x 48 In. . . . . .195.00 to 225.00
Scarf, Silk, Mocha Color Ground, Jewelry Design, Chanel, 50 x 50 In.	230.00
Shawl, Paisley, Black, Silver, Kashmir, 70 x 70 In.	195.00
Shawl, Paisley, Wool, Embroidered Border, Signed Center Medallion, 71 x 71 In.	715.00
Sheet, Homespun Wool, Natural, Red & Blue Stripe, 2-Piece Construction, 72 x 81 In. . .	95.00
Table Cover, Embroidered Dogsled, Grenfell, 36 x 36 In.	350.00
Tablecloth, Banquet, Inserts Of Drawn Work, 12 Napkins, 70 x 104 In.	145.00
Tablecloth, Banquet, Point De Venise, Flowers & Scrolls, 1930s, 154 x 70 In.	430.00
Tablecloth, Cafe Au Lait Lace, 12 Linen Napkins, 100 x 66 In.	247.00
Tablecloth, Cutwork, Filet Lace Inserts & Border, 12 Napkins, 102 x 70 In.	172.00
Tablecloth, Damask, White, 62 x 62 In.	25.00
Tablecloth, Embroidered Puppies, Fence, Floral, 43 x 13 In.	24.00
Tablecloth, Homespun, Cotton, Floral, Pink, Yellow, 35 x 36 In.	115.00
Tablecloth, Homespun, Diamond, Woven Bird's Eye, 52 x 74 In.	55.00
Tablecloth, Homespun, Geometric, 1843, 51 x 70 In.	71.00

Tablecloth, Homespun, Linen, Brown, Natural, 57 1/2 x 74 In. 137.00
Tablecloth, Lace, Cutwork, Cherubs, Flowers, White, Embroidered, 64 x 132 In. 585.00
Tablecloth, Lace, Linen, 12 Laced Trim Napkins, 63 x 102 In. 220.00
Tablecloth, Lace, Linen, Cutwork, Embroidery, Cherubs, 48 x 48 In. 275.00
Tablecloth, Linen, Cutwork, Embroidered, Ornate, 48 x 48 In. 275.00
Tablecloth, Linen, Damask, Hand Stitched Edges, 6 Napkins, 70 x 54 In. 65.00
Tablecloth, Paisley, 61 x 122 In. 225.00
Tablecloth, Point De Venise Lace, Birds, Animals, Italy, 12 Napkins, 69 x 138 In. 1900.00
Tapestry, 2 Birds Perched On Branches, 9 Ft. 5 In. x 8 Ft. 5 In. 8050.00
Tapestry, Animals, Birds Around Central Tree, 40 x 44 1/2 In. 270.00
Tapestry, Aubusson, Romantic Figures In Courtyard, 7 Ft. 9 In. x 7 Ft. 3 In. 7475.00
Tapestry, Birds, Flowering Scrolls, Italy, 9 Ft. 1/2 In. x 12 Ft. x 3 In. 3910.00
Tapestry, Distant Castle, Green, Tan, 61 x 89 In. 4598.00
Tapestry, Female Saint, Romanesque Style, 36 x 17 In. 90.00
Tapestry, Garden Scene, Ladies & Courtiers, 1 On Horseback, France, 55 x 61 In. 880.00
Tapestry, Kings & Queens, Norway, 19th Century, 52 x 29 In. 2995.00
Tapestry, Landscape, 8 Ft. 6 In. x 5 Ft. 4 1/2 In. 1725.00
Tapestry, Madonna & Child With Saint, 52 x 72 In. 1028.00
Tapestry, Polsterer, 4 Black Musicians, 1928, 71 1/4 In. 21275.00
Tapestry, Resurrection, Romanesque Style, 52 x 72 In. 605.00
Tapestry, Rose, Gold Ships, Oriental, 48 x 70 In. 50.00
Tapestry, Village Scene, Birds, France, 6 x 8 Ft. 3400.00
Tapestry, Western Ghost Town, 17 1/4 x 12 1/4 In. 150.00
Throw, Paisley, Stripes Overlaid With Florals, 108 x 54 In. 402.00
Towel, Show, Homespun, Cutwork, Star, 2 Women, 59 x 59 In. 357.00
Towel, Show, Homespun, Stylized Flowers, Birds, Olive, Red, 51 x 51 In. 412.50
Towel, Show, Homespun, White Woven, Star Flowers, Tulips, 53 x 53 In. 50.00
Towel, Tea, Mammy, Cotton 15.00

THERMOMETER is a name that comes from the Greek word for heat.
The thermometer was invented in 1731 to measure the temperature of
either water or air. All kinds of thermometers are collected, but those
with advertising messages are the most popular.

7-Up, Porcelain, French & English 70.00
A. Peja, Mahogany, Inlaid Shell, Checkered Banding, 1800, 48 In. 3450.00
AC Spark Plug, Metal, Blue, Cream, Orange, 21 In. 160.00
AGFA Photograph, Orange, Cobalt Blue & White, Germany, 39 x 8 3/4 In. 285.00
Antique, Tortoiseshell Case 70.00
Bee-Line Aligning, Tin, Bee Driving Car 100.00
Bireley's Noncarbonated Beverage, 1940s, 25 5/8 x 9 3/4 In. 95.00
Blue Coal, Wooden, Blue 35.00
Brass, 3 Sides, Hanging, 7 In. 50.00
C. Wilder, Maple Stick, Tapered Body, 1870, 40 3/4 In. 2185.00
Carter White Lead Paint, Porcelain, 27 1/2 In. 220.00
Champale Malt Liquor, Tin On Cardboard, 9 x 9 In. 10.00
Charles Wilder, Apple Wood, Silvered Plates, 1865, 38 1/4 In. 1725.00
Chesterfield, Tin Lithograph, 3-D Cigarette Pack, 1950s, 18 In. 200.00
Chew Mail Pouch Tobacco, 9 x 3 In. 165.00
Chew Mail Pouch Tobacco, Painted Blue, Yellow & White, Metal, 39 x 8 In. 28.00
Clipper Ship, California Souvenir, Metal 8.00
Cole's Liniment, Porcelain, 1920s 200.00
Desk, Brass, Ornate Gilt, Cast Iron, Bradley & Hubbard, c.1890, 11 In. 210.00
Doan's Kidney Pills, Die Cut, Wooden 165.00
Dr Pepper, 1960s 150.00
Dr Pepper, Bottle Cap, Plastic, 10 In. 40.00
Elz. Fortier & Cie, Porcelain, 1915, 27 1/2 In. 66.00
Ex-Lax, Drugs, Prescriptions, 39 In. 35.00
Ex-Lax, Keep Regular With Ex-Lax, Porcelain, 36 1/2 x 8 1/4 In. 75.00
Gold Bottle, Red Ground, Embossed Tin, 16 In. 198.00
Gulf, Old Style, 7 1/2 x 27 In. 195.00
Hendler's Ice Cream, Paper Face, 9 In. 143.00
Hires, Bottle Shape, 28 1/2 In. 125.00

Hutt's Creamilk, Black Lettering, Beige, Brown Ground, Porcelain, 14 x 38 In.	330.00
Ice Cream, Puritan, Newark's Famous Ice Cream, c.1920	95.00
International Motor Trucks, Porcelain	75.00
J. Casartelli, Angled Ceramic Plates, Crest, 1880, 40 1/2 In.	575.00
Jaeger Butter Tub Co., Blue, Red, Orange & Black, Round, 9 In.	44.00
Keen Kutter, 12 In.	150.00
Kist Soda, Round, 1950s	140.00
Labatt Biere 50 Ale, Y A Rien Qui, Metal, Glass, Round, 1950s, 10 In.	75.00
Lash's Bitters, Wooden, Black, Mustard, 21 In.	185.00
Mail Pouch Tobacco, 38 In.	90.00
Mail Pouch Tobacco, Porcelain, Yellow & White On Blue, 71 In.	135.00
Marathon, Red, White & Blue, Metal, 16 In.	98.00
Marble Columnar, Ormolu, 10 1/2 In.	205.00
Marquette Cement, Wood, Coal, Coke	140.00
Midway, 18 x 10 In.	35.00
Mobil Wall, Blue On White, Black Numbers, 1960, 16 1/2 In.	22.00
Moxie, A Great New Taste, c.1960, 16 1/8 x 6 7/8 In.	75.00
National Fibre Allentown Bobbin Works, 3 In.	45.00
Nesbitt's, Bottle Shape, Orange, 8 x 17 In.	55.00
O.L. Phipps Motor Co., Ford Products Since 1914, 7 In.	145.00
Old Schneider, Grand Prize Beverages, Tin, Box	25.00
Ortlieb's Beer, Glass Face, Round, 10 1/2 In.	30.00
Ortlieb's Famous Beer, Tin On Cardboard, 1960s	62.00
Pabst, Red, Gold, 20 1/4 x 9 In.	20.00
Pacific Oil, Glass, Metal, Red, Yellow, 12 In.	198.00
Packard Motors, Tin, 38 In.	225.00
Piels Real Draft Beer, Round, 12 In.	70.00
Prestone Anti-Freeze, Porcelain On Steel, Outdoor	70.00
Puritan Ice Cream, Newark's Famous Ice Cream, c.1920	95.00
RC Cola, Blue & White	35.00
Regal Beer, Aluminum, Picture, 10 x 26 In.	95.00
Royal Crown Cola, 1940s	115.00
Royal Crown Cola, Arrow Shape, 25 x 9 In. . . . . .45.00 to 65.00
Speedy Alka-Seltzer, No Glass, 1950s	495.00
Sprite Boy, Round, 12 In.	16.00
Texaco No Smoking, Red, Green, Black, White, 4 In.	357.00
Tums, Box, 1950s	180.00
Uneeda Boy, Green, Boy In Slicker, 100th Anniversary, 1876-1976	45.00
Vernor's Ginger Ale, Glass Front, Green & Yellow, Metal Edge, Round, 12 In.	88.00
Wall, Bubble Up, Domed Glass, Metal Frame, Red, White, Blue, 13 In.	161.00
Willard Batteries, Round	85.00
Winchester-Western, Tin, 26 1/2 x 7 1/4 In.	150.00
Windshield Shape, Tin, Glass Front, Trico Wiper Blades, 9 1/2 x 15 1/4 In.	143.00
Winston Tastes Good, Like A Cigarette Should, Metal, 13 x 6 In.	70.00
Winston Tastes Good, Like A Cigarette Should, Metal, Round, 9 In.	60.00

TIFFANY is a name that appears on items made by Louis Comfort Tiffany, the American glass designer who worked from about 1879 to 1933. His work included iridescent glass, Art Nouveau styles of design, and original contemporary styles. He was also noted for stained glass windows, unusual lamps, bronze work, pottery, and silver. Other types of Tiffany are listed under Tiffany Glass, Tiffany Pottery, or Tiffany Silver. The famous Tiffany lamps are listed in this section. Tiffany jewelry is listed in the jewelry and wristwatch categories. Reproductions of some types of Tiffany are being made.

Louis C. Tiffany

Ash Receiver, Artichoke, Dark Patina, Impressed Mark, 26 1/2 In.	375.00
Ashtray, Artichoke, Gilt Bronze, Gold Patina, Platform Base, Signed, 25 1/2 In.	1035.00
Ashtray, Bronze Trifid, Ribbed Triparte Shaft, Metal Ash Receiver, 24 1/2 In.	1265.00
Ashtray, Bronze, 3 Fluted Rods, 24 In.	400.00
Ashtray, Bronze, Gold Dore, 2 Handles, Round, Signed, 4 x 1 In.	135.00
Ashtray, Bronze, Green Wash, Dark Patina, Adjustable, Signed, 27 In.	345.00
Ashtray, Handle Each End, Ribbed, Bronze, Signed	135.00

Ashtray, Match Safe, American Indian, Signed, 6 1/2 x 3 1/4 In. 150.00
Ashtray, Match Safe, Pine Needle, Bronze, Gold Dore, 6 x 1 1/4 x 2 1/2 In. 250.00
Ashtray, Venetian, Gold Dore, Signed, 5 1/4 x 3 3/4 In. 250.00
Basket, Bronze Handle, Red & Gold Enamel Design, Bronze, Signed, 3 1/2 x 8 In. 1500.00
Basket, Bronze, Enameled, 2 Arms Form Handle, Round, 4 x 5 1/2 In. 250.00
Blotter, Hand, American Indian, Knob Handle, 5 1/2 x 3 In. 150.00
Blotter, Hand, Grapevine, Dark Patina, Green Glass, Beaded Edge, 3 x 6 x 2 In. 300.00
Blotter, Hand, Heraldic, Green Enameled, Hobnail Edge, 5 x 2 In. 300.00
Blotter, Hand, Venetian, Signed, 5 1/4 x 2 3/4 In. 250.00
Blotter Ends, Grapevine, Bronze, Dark Patina, 19 x 2 In., Pair 350.00
Blotter Ends, Venetian, Signed, 5 x 5 In., 4 Piece 250.00
Book Rack, Abalone Flower & Leaf Design, Bronze, Gold Dore, Extends To 24 In. 1800.00
Book Rack, Grapevine, Bronze, Green Slag Glass, 5 3/4 In. 1500.00
Bookends, Ninth Century, Bronze, Blue & Green Jewels, 14K Gold Plate, 4 x 6 In. 900.00
Bookends, Zodiac, Entwined Circle, Line Design, Bronze, Dark Patina, Signed, 6 In. . . . 550.00
Bowl, Reclining Nude Under Full Moon, Flying Owl, Irises, Bronze, Signed, 10 1/2 In. . . 935.00
Bowl, Relief Floral, Inlaid Mother-Of-Pearl Rim Design, Gilt Bronze, 9 In. 100.00
Box, American Indian, Hinged Cover, Bronze, Mask Center, 5 1/2 x 3 x 2 In. 450.00
Box, Bronze Repousse, Raised Star Design Top, Cedar Lining, 9 x 6 x 2 In. 3500.00
Box, Bronze, Twine, Grapevine, Green Slag Glass, Bronze Beaded Border, 3 In. 1500.00
Box, Dresser Top, Spider Web, Green Slag Glass, Bronze, Signed, Square, 7 In. 715.00
Box, Overlaid Grapevines, Pink Glass, Bronze Mounted, Hinged Lid, 6 5/8 In. 455.00
Box, Pine Needle, Bronze & Slag Glass, 3 3/4 x 12 1/2 In. 320.00
Box, Pine Needle, Bronze, Green Slag Glass, 9 1/2 x 7 x 3 In. 2000.00
Box, Stamp, Grapevine, Bronze, Green Slag Glass, Ball Feet, Tray, 3 Sections, 4 x 2 In. . . 550.00
Box, Stamp, Grapevine, Flange Top Opening, 4 x 2 1/4 In. 550.00
Box, Stamp, Venetian, Gold Dore, 3 Compartments, 4 x 2 x 1 3/4 In. 450.00
Box, Zodiac, Bronze, Gold Dore, Hinged Cover, 5 1/4 x 3 1/4 x 1 1/4 In. 350.00
Calendar, Daily, Modeled Pattern, Bronze, Gold Dore, Signed, 5 3/4 x 4 3/4 x 4 In. 650.00
Calendar, Desk, Pine Needle, Caramel Slag & Glass, Gold Dore, 4 1/2 x 3 1/2 In. 245.00
Candelabrum, Bronze, 4-Light, Center Tall Arm, Bobeches, 15 x 14 In. 2000.00
Candelabrum, Bronze, Favrile, Green Glass, 15 In. 3450.00
Candelabrum, Gilt Bronze, 3-Arm, Waisted Rib Shades, Amber Iridescent, 16 1/4 In. . . . 8050.00
Candlestick, Bronze, 2-Arm, Amber Iridescent, Green Glass, Brown, 11 In. 4025.00
Candlestick, Favrile, Beaded Bobeche, Pentagonal Handle, Brown Patina, 18 In. 5175.00
Candlestick, Favrile, Bronze Root Base, Floriform Shade, Green, Amber, 18 In. 4025.00
Candlestick, Favrile, Bronze, 3-Light, Amber Iridescent, Green Leaves, 23 In. 5465.00
Candlestick, Queen Anne's Lace, Favrile, Bronze Base, 19 1/2 In. 5750.00
Centerpiece, Bronze, Enamel Base, Floral, Leaf Design, 4 Paw Feet 1500.00
Centerpiece, Bronze, Enamel Footed, Gold Dore Finish, Enamel Blossoms, 4 1/2 In. . . . 1800.00
Centerpiece, Chased Floral Design, 1875, 21 5/8 In. 2645.00
Chandelier, Easter Egg, Slumped Glass, Wirework Leaves, Pendent Chains, 35 In. 9200.00
Clock, Black Slate & Marble Urn Finial, Lion Handles, 17 In. 750.00
Clock, Bracket, Napoleon III, Gilt Metal, Alabaster, Roman Numerals, 1900, 22 In. 4390.00
Clock, Desk, Adam, Bronze, Gold Dore Finish, 4 x 4 1/4 In. 1800.00
Clock, Desk, Double Dial, Bronze & Onyx, 1920s 1750.00
Clock, Desk, Gilt Brass, Enamel, Black Numerals, Metal Clock Face, 5 1/2 In. 1380.00
Clock, Mantel, Red Marble, French Movement, 19th Century, 9 x 9 In. 2100.00
Clock, Tall Case, Pierced Broken Arch, Gilt & Reeded Columns, Mahogany, 104 In. 5500.00
Clock, Travel, 8-Day, 2 5/8-In. Diam. 190.00
Clock, Zodiac, Bronze, Dark Dore, Key In Back Compartment, 4 x 2 x 5 1/2 In. 1800.00
Compote, 3 Enamel Scenic Medallions, Pink Flowers, Bronze, 9 In. 595.00
Compote, Bronze, Enamel, Gold Dore Finish, Center Well, Blue, Green, Yellow, 3 In. . . 450.00
Compote, Chinese Gold, Favrile, Ruffled, Ribbed Underside, Pedestal, 6 x 4 In. 650.00
Desk Set, Pine Needle, 2-Tier Letter Rack, Bronze, Green, White Striated Glass .750.00 to 1150.00
Desk Set, Zodiac, 11 Piece 3630.00
Dresser Set, Shoehorn, Buttonhook, Clothes Brush & Mirror, Silver & Ivory 800.00
Frame, Abalone, Bronze, Gold Dore Finish, Abalone Discs, Leaf, Floral Design, 7 1/4 In. 2800.00
Frame, Bronze, Easel-Style Frame, Dark Patina, Green Slag Glass, 12 x 14 In. 3500.00
Frame, Chinese, Bronze, Gold Dore, 8 3/4 x 7 1/4 In. 675.00
Frame, Grapevine, Beaded Edge, Green Striated Glass, Oval, 10 x 8 In. 1150.00
Frame, Grapevine, Bronze, Green Slag Glass, Oval Opening, 9 1/2 x 8 In. 1800.00
Frame, Grapevine, Gilt Bronze, Yellow, Green Mottled Iridescence, 9 x 7 In. 2300.00

Frame, Pine Needle, Bronze, Oval, Green & Red Slag Glass, 9 3/4 x 7 3/4 In. 850.00
Frame, Pine Needle, Gilt Bronze, Yellow, Green Mottled Slag Glass, 10 x 8 In. 2300.00
Frame, Spanish, Easel-Style Frame, Bronze, Gold Dore Finish, 8 x 11 3/4 In. 1800.00
Globe, Feather Line, Swirl, Gold Iridescent, Gold Dore Holder, 6 x 13 In. 2800.00
Hall Lantern, Favrile, Bronze, Teardrop Form Shade, Amber, Green Iridescent, 38 In. . . .   9200.00
Humidor, Abalone, Leaf Pattern, Bronze, Gold Dore Finish, Curve Line, 6 x 4 x 2 3/4 In.   1200.00
Humidor, Pine Needle, Dark Patina Finish, Bronze, Knob Handle 3200.00
Inkwell, American Indian, Hinged Cover, Bronze, Glass, 3 Tapered To 5 1/2-In. Base . . .   550.00
Inkwell, Byzantine, Gold Dore Finish, Coral Jewels On Top Cover, 2 3/4 In. 2500.00
Inkwell, Double, Venetian, Treasure Chest Style, Bronze Chain Latch, 2 1/2 x 5 In. 675.00
Inkwell, Favrile, Bronze, Gold Dore, Bell Shape, Signed, 3 1/4 x 4 1/2 In. 2000.00
Inkwell, Filigree Bronze, Branch & Leaf Design Over Green Slag Glass, 3 3/4 x 4 In. 440.00
Inkwell, Grapevine, Bronze, Green Slag Glass, 4 1/2 x 3 1/2 In. 650.00
Inkwell, Heraldic, Emerald Green Hinged Cover, Silver Finish, 3 In. 650.00
Inkwell, Nautical, Seashell Form Cover, 4 Dolphin Feet, Blossoms, Signed, 5 1/4 In. 1400.00
Inkwell, Turtleback & Jewel, 3 Curved Feet, Glass Insert, Bronze, 4-In. Body 2500.00
Inkwell, Venetian, Bronze, Double Well, Gold Dore, Signed, 5 x 3 x 2 1/2 In. 675.00
Inkwell, Zodiac, Hinged Lid, Sign Of Crab, Gold Dore Finish, 2 1/2 x 4 In. 250.00
Inkwell, Zodiac, Octagonal, No. 1075, 6 1/2 In. 590.00
Lamp, Abalone, Bronze, Gold Dore, White Favrile Paneled Shade 8500.00
Lamp, Acorn, Favrile, Dichroic Green, 10 In. 4300.00
Lamp, Acorn, Green Dome Shade, Acorn Border, Bronze, Favrile, Signed, 18 In. 10350.00
Lamp, Acorn, Medial Band Of Meandering Leaves, Vines, Favrile, Bronze, 21 In. 9775.00
Lamp, Adjustable Weight-Balance, Bronze, Feathered Peacock, c.1900, 16 In. 5520.00
Lamp, Apple Blossom, Bronze, Domed Shade, Pink, White Blossoms, 16 In. 13800.00
Lamp, Apple Blossom, Domed Shade, Mottled Pink, White Blossoms, 22 In. 17250.00
Lamp, Applied Glass Punts, Conical Shade, Iridescent Gray, Electrified, 14 In. 400.00
Lamp, Avocado Green, Turtleback Shade, Bronze Urn Stepped Base, 23 In. 6600.00
Lamp, Bamboo, Bronze Base, Dark Patina Finish, Emerald Green Shade, 14 1/2 In. 2500.00
Lamp, Bronze, Swirl Design, Green Iridescent Case Domed Shade, 17 1/2 In. 4025.00
Lamp, Bronze, Swirl Design, Green Ribbed Domed Shade, White, 13 1/2 In. 3737.50
Lamp, Candlestick, Gold Iridescent Glass, Ribbed Body, Red, Violet, Favrile, 12 In. 1400.00
Lamp, Candlestick, Lime Green Striated Feathered Edge, Amber, Favrile, 26 In. 8625.00
Lamp, Candlestick, Twisted Ribbed Body, Flange, Ruffled Shade, Favrile, 12 In., Pair . . .   3000.00
Lamp, Cat's Paw, Bronze Finished, Adjustable, 12 In. 880.00
Lamp, Chinese Pattern, Bronze, Octagon Shaped Shade, 17 In. 6000.00
Lamp, Chinese Pattern, Paneled Shade, Scrolled Lines, Brown, Favrile, Bronze, 16 In. . . .   4312.00
Lamp, Damascene, Blue Iridescent, Bronze Base, 16 In. 6600.00
Lamp, Dogwood Blossoms, Yellow Centered Pink, White Flowers, Favrile, 19 In. 20700.00
Lamp, Domed Geometric Shade, Mottled Green, Yellow Swirl, 26 In. 12650.00
Lamp, Favrile, 3-Arm, Bronze, Domed Shade, Emerald Green, Amber Swirls, 9 In. 4887.00
Lamp, Favrile, Bronze Bridge, Damascene Shade, Golden Amber, 4 Ft. 10 In. 8625.00
Lamp, Favrile, Bronze, Bell, Domed Caramel Shade, Wavy Lines, Green, 13 In. 4025.00
Lamp, Favrile, Bronze, Domed Shade, Lemon Yellow Iridescent, Amber, 18 In. 4312.00
Lamp, Favrile, Bronze, Domed Shade, Mottled Green, White Scrolls, 29 In. 9200.00
Lamp, Favrile, Bronze, Geometric, Domed Shade, Wavy Rows, Golden Amber, 21 In. 9775.00
Lamp, Favrile, Bronze, Greek Key Border, Domed Shade, Sea Green Tiles, 22 1/4 In. . . .   23000.00
Lamp, Favrile, Bronze, Jeweled Candle, Bell Form Shade, Green Leafage, 14 In. 4312.00
Lamp, Favrile, Bronze, Silver, Domed Shade, Vertical Panels, Blue Spongework, 15 In. . .   3450.00
Lamp, Favrile, Bronze, Spherical Shade, Mustard Iridescent, Bulbous, 14 7/8 In. 4312.00
Lamp, Favrile, Bronze, Swirling Leaf Border, Domed Shade, Emerald, Green, 26 In. 17250.00
Lamp, Favrile, Bronze, Vine Border, Domed Shade, Green, White Tiles, 23 In. 7475.00
Lamp, Favrile, Bronze, Vine Border, Domed Shade, Red Amber, Green Leaves, 19 In. 6325.00
Lamp, Favrile, Bronze, Vine Border, Domed Shade, Red Brick Striated, Leaves, 21 In. . . .   9200.00
Lamp, Favrile, Bulbous, Ribbed Shade, Amber Iridescent Glass, Blue, Kerosene, 21 In. . . .   5175.00
Lamp, Fishscale & Jewels, Rookwood Base, Bronze, 25 In. 15000.00
Lamp, Green & White Geometric Glass Shade, Bronze, 23 In.   9000.00
Lamp, Green Favrile Shade, 7 In. 7500.00
Lamp, Green Glass Base, Favrile, Green Shade, Gold Iridescent Zipper, 15 In. 3000.00
Lamp, Green Paneled Shade, 12 Sides, Projecting Feet, Bronze, c.1927, 26 In. 5445.00
Lamp, Hanging, Geometric, Pastel Greens, Blue, Yellow, Domed Shade, 14 In. 3630.00
Lamp, Leaf, Mottled Green, White Glass, Bronze Warty Base, 23 1/2 In. 25300.00
Lamp, Lily, 18-Light, Bronze Lily Pad Base, Amber Iridescent Shade, 21 In. 1265.00

Lamp, Lily, Favrile, Bronze, White, Green Leaf Shade, 10 In. 3335.00
Lamp, Linenfold, Favrile, Gilt Bronze, Abalone, 12 Amber Panels, 16 1/2 In. 8050.00
Lamp, Linenfold, Favrile, Gilt Bronze, Abalone, Paneled Shade, Amber, 18 3/4 In. 9200.00
Lamp, Mesh, Wire, Jeweled, Red Floral Design, Ribbon Border, 5 In. 1100.00
Lamp, Nautilus, Bronze Base, Patina, Bronze Ball Feet, 5 In. 7500.00
Lamp, Nautilus, Raised Ribs, 5 Ball Feet, White To Green Shade, Bronze, 13 1/2 In. 7500.00
Lamp, Pansy Blossoms, Multicolored Pansies, Green Ground, Favrile, 24 In. 24150.00
Lamp, Peony, Domed Shade, Mottled Pink, Fuchsia, Magenta Blossoms, 26 1/2 In. 68500.00
Lamp, Pine Needle, Bronze, Favrile, 4 Amber Panels, 8 1/2 In. 2070.00
Lamp, Pomegranate, Geometric Leaded Shade, 3-Light, Bronze, Signed, 21 In. 9000.00
Lamp, Poppies, Mottled Yellow, Red Conical Shade, Bronze, 24 1/4 In. 30000.00
Lamp, Poppy, Conical Shade, Mottled Orange Red Poppies, 21 In. 27600.00
Lamp, Raised Pagoda Rim, Green Dome Shade, Green Slag Ground, 25 In. 13800.00
Lamp, Sconce, 2-Light, Reticulated Chain Mail, 1899-1928, 9 In., Pair 9775.00
Lamp, Silver Acid Etched Base, Silver Patinated Shade, Floor 1650.00
Lamp, Swirling Leaf, Domed Shade, Mottled Spring Green, Amber Swirl, 25 In. 9200.00
Lamp, Turtleback, Favrile Bronze Shade, Brown Green Patina, 1899-1920, 15 In. 4470.00
Lamp, Turtleback, Favrile, Tile, Pivot Shade, Blue Cabochon Glass, Brown, 14 1/2 In. .. 5750.00
Lamp, Turtleback, Green Iridescent, Jeweled Bronze Base, 14 In. 6875.00
Lamp, Vine Border, Dome Geometric Shade, Emerald Green, 21 1/4 In. 8050.00
Lamp, Weight-Balance, Bronze, Green Iridescent Damascene Swirl Shade 6000.00
Lamp, Weight-Balance, Favrile, Bronze, Blue, Purple, Gold Wave, 54 1/4 In. 17250.00
Lamp, Weight-Balance, Favrile, Bronze, Domed Shade, Caramel, Pink Swirls, 15 In. 5750.00
Lamp, Weight-Balance, Favrile, Bronze, Pivot Domed Shade, Amber, White, 14 In. 4890.00
Lamp, Weight-Balance, Favrile, Bronze, Pivot Domed Shade, Gold Waves, 4 Ft. 4 In. ... 9200.00
Lamp, Woodbine Leaves, Favrile, Bronze, Domed Shade, Green Iridescent, 18 In. 6325.00
Lamp, Zodiac, Oil, Bronze, 2 1/4 In. 695.00
Lamp Base, Blue Cypriote, Favrile, Gilt Bronze, 24 In. 1150.00
Lamp Base, Blue Cypriote, Favrile, White Marked, 8 3/4 In. 1265.00
Lantern, Turtleback, Bronze, 4-Sided Frame, Favrile, Amber Opalescent, 9 In. 6900.00
Letter Holder, Grapevine, Green Slag Glass, Large Center Divider, 4 x 6 1/2 In. 650.00
Letter Holder, Indian, Bronze, 2 Sections, Side By Side, 6 1/2 x 2 3/4 x 4 1/2 In. 550.00
Letter Holder, Pine Needle, Caramel Slag, Gold Dore, 2 Sections 575.00
Letter Holder, Venetian, Bronze, Gold Dore, Side By Side, 4 1/2 x 6 x 3 In. 650.00
Letter Rack, Byzantine, Favrile, Blue Iridescent, 2 Compartments, 6 x 3 In. 1500.00
Letter Rack, Etched Metal, 2 Compartment Rack, Gold Dore Finish, 6 1/2 In. 950.00
Letter Rack, Geometric, Bronze, Gold Dore, 3 Compartments, 12 x 3 1/2 x 8 1/4 In. ... 750.00
Letter Rack, Grapevine, Bronze & Green Slag Glass 400.00
Letter Rack, Heraldic, Green Enamel Bronze, Silver Shield, Signed, 9 x 6 x 2 In. 750.00
Letter Rack, Spanish Pattern, 2 Compartments, Gold Dore, Design On Front, 8 x 10 In. .. 950.00
Magnifying Glass, Abalone, Gold Dore, Signed, 8 3/4 In. 750.00
Magnifying Glass, Bookmark Pattern, Gold Dore, Signed, 8 3/4 In. 650.00
Magnifying Glass, Graduate Pattern, Gold Dore, Signed, 8 3/4 In. 650.00
Magnifying Glass, Grapevine, Bronze, Green Glass In Handle, Signed, 8 In. 1200.00
Magnifying Glass, Zodiac, Gold Dore, Signed, 8 3/4 In. 650.00
Mirror, Hand, Grapevine, Bronze, Gold Dore, Curved Handle, Round, 11 3/4 In. 1800.00
Paper Clip, Geometric, Gold Dore Finish, Raised Indian Mask, 2 x 4 In. 250.00
Paper Clip, Grapevine, Gold Dore Finish, Amber Slag, 2 1/2 x 3 3/4 In. 350.00
Paper Clip, Zodiac, Bronze 250.00
Paperweight, Bronze, Favrile, Swirling Wave Design, Green Iridescent, 5/8 x 3 3/4 In. .. 2070.00
Paperweight, Pine Needle, Bronze, Gold Dore, Amber Slag Glass, Knob Handle, 4 In. ... 400.00
Pen Brush, American Indian, Bronze, Signed, 3 x 1 3/4 In. 250.00
Pen Brush, Pine Needle, Glass, Signed, 2 1/4 x 1 1/2 In. 300.00
Pen Brush, Venetian, Gold Dore, Octagonal, Signed, 3 x 2 1/4 In. 400.00
Pen Holder, Pine Needle, Green Glass, Bronze, 3 1/4 x 9 1/2 In. 325.00
Pen Tray, Grapevine, Bronze, Green Glass, 3 Sections, Ball Feet, 9 1/2 x 2 3/4 In. 250.00
Pen Tray, Pine Needle, 4 Bronze Ball Feet, 3 Sections, 9 1/2 x 3 In. 250.00
Sconce, Gold Favrile Shade, Purple, Green Highlights, 8 In., Pair 4510.00
Stand, Smoking, Enameled Bronze 750.00
Tray, Abalone, Floral & Line Pattern, Bronze, Gold Dore, Round, 9 In. 250.00
Tray, Art Nouveau, Bronze, Gold Dore, Round, Signed, 10 In. 250.00
Tray, Bronze, Gold Dore, Leaves & Berries Border, Signed, Round, 6 3/4 In. 150.00

Having trouble with stain in a glass bottle or vase? Sometimes this type of stain can be removed. Fill the bottle with water, drop in an Alka-Seltzer, and let it soak for about 24 hours. Then rub the ring with a brush or a cloth. If the stain is a chemical deposit, this treatment should remove it. If the ring is actually caused by etching of the glass, it cannot be removed unless the bottle is polished.

Tiffany, Vase, Intaglio Butterfly,
Favrile, Bronze Holder, Signed

Tray, Card, Pastel Green, Turned-Up Rim, Favrile, Signed, 6 In.	325.00
Tray, Geometric Design Edge, Short Pedestal, Bronze, 9 3/4 In.	225.00
Tray, Venetian, 2 Sections, Pattern In Center, Minks All Around, Signed, 10 In.	250.00
Tray, Venetian, Gold Dore, 2 Compartments, 10 x 3 3/4 In.	250.00
Urn, Cover, Japanese Figure, Scrolled Handles, Bronze & Porcelain, 14 In., Pair	1380.00
Vase, Bud, Gold Iridescent, Favrile, Green Enameled Bronze, 13 In.	1200.00
Vase, Floriform, Pulled Green Leafage, Knopped Stem, Favrile, Signed, c.1905, 15 In.	5750.00
Vase, Glazed Interior, Prunus Branches, Bronze, Favrile, 1910-1914, 6 1/4 In.	3450.00
Vase, Gold Favrile, Bronze, Gold, Amber Flower Holder Fitted Into Cup, 12 1/4 In.	550.00
Vase, Intaglio Butterfly, Favrile, Bronze Holder, Signed ....Illus	935.00
Vase, Pulled Feather Design, Favrile, Bronze Base, Pineapple Stem, 11 In.	1840.00
Vase, Trumpet, Bronze Base, 16 In.	1500.00
Vase, Trumpet, Gilt Bronze, Flared, Bronze Pedestal Foot, 15 In.	865.00
Vase, Trumpet, Gold Iridescent Pulled Feathers, Bronze Base, Marked, 14 In.	1650.00
Vase, Twisted Onion, Bulbed Base, 10 1/4 In.	690.00
TIFFANY GLASS, Bonbon, Emerald Green Pastel, Green Outer Edge, Opalescent, Favrile, 2 In.	550.00
Bonbon, Gold Iridescent, Blue & Violet Highlights, Favrile, 2 x 4 3/4 In.	275.00
Bonbon, Intaglio Cut Leaf Border, Golden Amber Bowl, Signed, 1 3/4 x 6 In.	865.00
Bowl, 8 Ribs, Scalloped, Golden Surface, Signed, L.C.T., 2 1/2 In.	430.00
Bowl, 10 Flared Ribs, Scalloped, Emerald Green Interior, Favrile, Signed, 4 In.	865.00
Bowl, Applied Floral, Scroll Handles, Round, 1938-1947, 2 5/8 In.	520.00
Bowl, Blue Iridescent, Purple Blue Iridized Luster, 1848, 3 3/4 In.	1380.00
Bowl, Fern, Arrow Root, 12 In.	1800.00
Bowl, Flared, Footed, Bluish Gold Iridescence, Favrile, Signed, 8 x 3 1/2 In.	750.00
Bowl, Iridescent Blue, Ribbed, Wavy Rim, Favrile, Marked, 3 x 6 1/2 In.	905.00
Bowl, Jar Form, 10 Pale Green Ribs, Gold Interior, Signed, 2 1/2 x 4 1/2 In.	316.00
Bowl, Ribbed Leaf Pattern, Iridescent Blue, Signed, 1925, 12 In.	2165.00
Bowl, Ruffled, Favrile, Gold Iridescent, Blue, Violet Highlights, 3 1/4 In.	650.00
Bowl, Scalloped Yellow Rim, White Opalescent Strips, 1 1/2 In.	402.00
Bowl, Wide Everted Rim, Amber Iridescent, Pink, 1925, 11 5/8 In.	1035.00
Candleholder, Opalescent Diamond-Quilted Foot, Pink Rims, 3 1/2 In., Pair	935.00
Candlestick, Favrile, Trefoil Base, Foliate Tripod, Green, Gold Iridescent, 9 5/8 In.	3680.00
Centerpiece, Favrile, Green Pastel Intaglio Cut, Signed, 10 x 3 1/2 In.	950.00
Compote, Crimped Flaring Form, Domed Foot, Favrile, Signed, 5 5/8 In.	1155.00
Compote, Diamond-Quilted, Dark Golden Amber Interior, 2 3/4 x 9 In.	635.00
Compote, Favrile, Diamond-Quilted, Gold Iridescent, Violet Highlights, 4 In.	650.00
Compote, Favrile, Textured Rim, Amber Iridescent, Pink, Blue, 1900, 8 In.	980.00
Compote, Flared, Purple Iridescent, Disk Foot, 4 1/2 In.	865.00
Compote, Iridescent Blue, Silver Shading, Favrile, Signed, c.1892, 5 In.	865.00
Compote, Iridescent Pink, Ribbed Opal, 1871, 2 1/4 In.	575.00

Compote, Irregular Rim, Short Standard, Circular Foot, Blue Iridescent, 5 In. 690.00
Compote, Opalescent Amber, Pulled Feathering Pale Green, Signed, 1892, 6 In. 2070.00
Compote, Quilted, Iridescent Butterscotch Yellow Rim, Signed, 2 x 6 In. 460.00
Compote, Ruffled Rim, Amber Iridescence, Pink, Circular Foot, 1903, 8 In. 1265.00
Decanter, Pulled Trailings To Base, Pale Chartreuse Iridescent, Favrile, 12 In. 1035.00
Decanter Set, Iridescent Gold, Pinched In Sides, Stopper, L.C.T., 7 Piece 2950.00
Finger Bowl, Underplate, Iridescent Gold, Etched Wreath, 5 & 6 In., 2 Piece 385.00
Finger Bowl, Underplate, Iridescent Gold, Signed, 5 & 5 3/4 In., 2 Piece 385.00
Globe, Diamond-Quilted, Gold Iridescent, Gold Chain Top Lip, 12 In. 1800.00
Goblet, Violet Blue, Turquoise, Flared Stem, Favrile, Round Base, 1900, 8 In. 460.00
Jam Jar, Amber, Green Leaf Design, Rim Handle, 6 In. 495.00
Nut Bowl, Iridescent Blue Gold, Ribbed, Signed, 1 x 2 3/4 In. 210.00
Paperweight, Pale Green Vines, Purple Blossoms, Everted Rim, 6 In. 7360.00
Paperweight, Red Applied Lappets, Baluster, Lemon Yellow, 4 In. 5750.00
Pitcher, Bluish Gold, Favrile, Cylindrical, 7 1/2 In. 1100.00
Plate, Card, Pastel Green, Signed 150.00
Plate, Jade Green Iridescent, 16 Exterior Ribs, 10 In. 605.00
Plate, Tel El Amarna, Favrile, Pulled Gold Design, Green Iridescent Rim, 8 In. 865.00
Salt, Gold Iridescent, Favrile, Ruffled, Flat Base, Violet & Blue Highlights 200.00
Salt, Gold Iridescent, Favrile, Silver Blue Tones, Raised Twists, 1 1/2 x 2 In. 375.00
Salt, Gold, Favrile, Ruffled 300.00
Salt, Iridescent Gold, Peg Footed, Signed, 1 1/2 In. 220.00
Salt, Iridescent Red-Gold, 8 Applied Stemmed Pods, Signed, 1 1/4 In. 275.00
Seal, 3 Scarabs, Gold Iridescent, Favrile, Triangular, Signed, 1 3/4 In. 450.00
Tile, Blue Iridescent, Textured Pattern, Square, 4 In. 400.00
Tile, Blue-Purple Iridescent, Raised Center Circular Pattern, Square, 3 3/4 In. 400.00
Tile, Favrile, Stylized Geometric Design, Opal, Green, Gold Tiles, 17 x 18 In. 1840.00
Toothpick, Pinched Form Pattern, 1 3/4 In. 145.00
Tray, Amethyst Rim, White Scalloped Plate, Signed, 3 /4 x 7 In. 400.00
Tumbler, Favrile, Gold Iridescent, Raised Twists, Blue Highlights, 3 In. 375.00
Tumbler, Gold Iridescent, Favrile, Pods & Vines Center To Base, 4 In. 275.00
Tumbler, Gold Iridescent, Favrile, Raised Twists Around Body, 3 x 4 In. 375.00
Tumbler, Iridescent Gold, Etched Vintage Wreath, Contoured, 4 In. 575.00
Urn, Gold Favrile, Applied Foot, Rolled Edge, Signed, 10 3/4 x 9 1/2 In. 2950.00
Vase, 5 Oval Quilted Depressions, Red, Yellow, Signed, 5 In. 4315.00
Vase, 10 Ribs, Gold Iridescent, Bulbous, Signed, 7 1/4 In. 520.00
Vase, 18 Ribs, Amber, Applied Disk Foot, Gold, Paper Label, 12 In. 865.00
Vase, Agate, Embedded Amber Flowers, Earthtone Ground, Marked, 6 In. 4400.00
Vase, Agate, Green Ground, Green Brown Stripes, Favrile, 2 1/4 x 1 1/2 In. 2500.00
Vase, Applied Purple Blossoms, Green Leaf Pads, Scrolls, Favrile, 4 3/4 In. 2530.00
Vase, Bean Pot Type, Pastel Oyster To Vaseline, L.C.T., 2 x 2 1/2 In. 575.00
Vase, Black Emerald Green, Iridescent Blue Pulled Feathers, Marked, 2 In. 1650.00
Vase, Blue, Bulbous Bottom, Iridescent, Favrile, Signed, 5 1/2 In. 550.00
Vase, Blue, Green, Gold, Pink, Blue Surface, 7 In. 2415.00
Vase, Blue, Urn Shape, Shell Handles, Pedestal, Favrile, 6 1/2 x 5 In. 1800.00
Vase, Chain, Favrile, Pulled Feather, Brown Iridescent, 4 1/2 In. 1610.00
Vase, Cobalt Blue, 16 Vertical Ribs, Favrile, 9 In. 920.00
Vase, Cypriote, Amber, Blue Shadings, Random Pitting, Signed, c.1919, 5 In. 2760.00
Vase, Cypriote, Blue Glass, Silver, Red Shadings, Random Pitting, 1904, 7 In. 5290.00
Vase, Dark Brown, Purple, 3 Swirls, Blue, Green, Yellow, Purple, Favrile, 4 1/4 In. 3500.00
Vase, Dark Emerald Green, Aventurine Flecks, Black Iridescent, Favrile, 6 In. 2875.00
Vase, Diatreta, Iridescent Gold Lattice, Flanged Rim, Favrile, Signed, 4 In. 2860.00
Vase, Double Gourd, Allover Iridescent Blue Hooked, Amber, Green, Signed, 5 In. 2310.00
Vase, Double Gourd, Green, Burgundy Iridescent, Favrile, 9 In. 3680.00
Vase, Egyptian, Gold Iridescent, Caramel Neck, Favrile, Marked, 4 1/2 In. 2530.00
Vase, Everted Rim, Stylized Floral Design, Baluster, 1902, 10 In. 865.00
Vase, Flared, Crimped Edge, Blue Iridescent, Favrile, Signed, 11 1/2 In. 2100.00
Vase, Floriform, Favrile, Gold Iridescent, Purple, Domed Circular Foot, 13 In. 1265.00
Vase, Floriform, Favrile, Inverted Rim, Amber Iridescent, 1905, 10 1/2 In. 1150.00
Vase, Floriform, Favrile, Ruffled Rim, Pale Amber Iridescent, Pink, 10 3/4 In. 1955.00
Vase, Floriform, Favrile, Scalloped Edge, White Iridescent, Pink Rim, 5 In. 1610.00
Vase, Floriform, Orange, Mahogany Blossom, Green Striation, 8 1/4 In. 3910.00

Vase, Flower Form, Feathered Bowl, Domed Foot, Favrile, 1900, 12 In. 2300.00
Vase, Gold Favrile, Jade Pulled Feather, L.C.T., 3 1/4 x 2 1/2 In. 1250.00
Vase, Gold Iridescent Foot, Pale Green Stem, Favrile, 4 1/2 In. 5000.00
Vase, Gold Iridescent, Brown Tones, Ruffled Rim, Border, 5 1/2 In. 3740.00
Vase, Gold Iridescent, Cylindrical, 9 1/2 In. 865.00
Vase, Gold Iridescent, Deep Green Heart Vine Design, 9 1/4 In. 745.00
Vase, Gold Iridescent, Trifold Shape, Purple, Blue, Green Body, Favrile, 2 In. 500.00
Vase, Grape Tumbler, Gold Iridescent, Wheel Cut Intaglio Border, 5 1/2 In. 460.00
Vase, High Black Gloss, Silver Iridescent Leaf, Vine Design, Favrile, Signed, 3 In. 3500.00
Vase, Inverted Rim, Amber Iridescence, Pink, Green Trailing Vine, Favrile, 4 In. 1035.00
Vase, Iridescent Gold, Green Leaves, Vines, Favrile, 6 In. 1650.00
Vase, Iridescent Green, Gold, Leaves & Vines, Favrile, Signed, 10 1/2 In. 4200.00
Vase, Iridescent Yellow, Pulled Leaf Feather Designs, Favrile 2300.00
Vase, Jack-In-The-Pulpit, Favrile, Gold, Signed, 15 1/2 In. 6050.00
Vase, Jack-In-The-Pulpit, Favrile, Pulled Green, White Leafage, Amber, 13 In. 2300.00
Vase, Jack-In-The-Pulpit, Gold, Flared, Ribbed, Pink, Gold Iridescence, 16 1/2 In. 6900.00
Vase, Jack-In-The-Pulpit, Vase, Gold Iridescent, Purple, Blue Highlights, 12 1/2 In. 1650.00
Vase, Leaf, Vine, Blue, Gold, Opalescent Interior, Heart, Vine Border, Favrile, 4 In. 865.00
Vase, Loop Rim, Engraved Woodbine Leaves, Stems, Signed, c.1918, 14 3/4 In. 5175.00
Vase, Millefiore, Gold, Green Heart Shaped Leaves, Amber Vines, Favrile, 5 In. 1150.00
Vase, Morning Glory, Yellow Iridescent, White Exterior, Signed, 4 3/4 In. 805.00
Vase, Pale Amber, Pink Morning Glory Design, Green Leaves, 6 x 5 In. 2200.00
Vase, Pastel Pink Rim, White Foot, Signed, 5 1/4 In. 805.00
Vase, Peach, 3-Color Iridescent Pulled Feathered, Favrile, 1900, 8 3/4 In. 3105.00
Vase, Peacock Blue, Violet Silver Cast, Favrile, 1 1/2 In. 1200.00
Vase, Pulled Feather, Gold, Green, Favrile, Signed, L.C.T., 1972, 5 x 7 1/2 In. 1150.00
Vase, Pulled Heart Design, Crimped, Iridescent Gold, Favrile, 6 3/4 In. 1840.00
Vase, Red Iridescent, Silver Blue-Gold Swirl Top, 1 1/2 x 2 1/2 In. 2500.00
Vase, Ribbed Form, Amber Iridescent, Pink, Favrile, 1917, 10 3/4 In. 1095.00
Vase, Ribbed Form, Gold Iridescent, Favrile, Signed, Paper Label, 15 In. 2070.00
Vase, Rows Of Iridescent Pulled Feathering, Favrile, Signed, c.1894, 6 In. 2645.00
Vase, Tan Opalescent, Olive Leaves, Vines, Yellow Floral, Corset, Signed, 6 In. 3850.00
Vase, Tel El Amarna, Turquoise Blue, Bulbous, Gold Iridescent Leafs, 6 3/4 In. 4600.00
Vase, Trumpet, Amber Iridescent, Pink, Green Trailing Vine, Favrile, 9 In. 1955.00
Vase, Trumpet, Gold Iridescent, Favrile, Knob Stem, Ribbed Foot, 13 1/2 In. 1265.00
Vase, Trumpet, Purple, Blue Iridescent Luster, Signed, 8 In. 920.00
Vase, Zipper, Gold Iridescent, Threaded Top, Corset, 6 1/2 In. 1000.00
Window, Leaded, Apple Blossoms, Crimson, Maroon, Pink, White, 43 x 29 In. 6325.00
TIFFANY GOLD, Cane, Platinum Fleur-De-Lis Around Top, 18K Gold, Tiffany & Co. 5500.00
Case, Cigarette, 14K Gold, 1930s 3000.00
Medal, Faithful Service, W/15 Year 18K Gold Suspension, No. 2026, New York 125.00
Pin, Leaves & Flowers, 7 Rubies, 18K Yellow Gold 220.00
TIFFANY POTTERY, Pitcher, Cat-O'-Nine Tails, Unglazed, Glazed Green Interior, 12 1/2 In. 1800.00
Vase, Artichoke Shape, Green Ivory Glaze, Signed, 11 1/4 x 5 In. 1650.00
Vase, Bud, Raised Vines, Pods, Yellow Green, Blue, Glazed, 5 x 1 1/2 In. 2200.00
Vase, Green & Black Textured, Purple Ground, Glazed, 4 1/4 x 2 In. 1500.00
Vase, Interlaced Leaves & Vines, Unglazed, Pale Green Interior, 9 1/2 In. 1800.00
Vase, Seafoam Green Glaze, 7 1/8 In. 1265.00
TIFFANY SILVER, Berry Spoon, Audubon, Pierced Gilt-Washed Bowl, 1871 . . . . 980.00
Bookmark, Eagle's Head At Top, 3 1/2 In. 230.00
Bowl, Applied Floral Rim, Deep Form, 1902-1907, 11 In. 920.00
Bowl, Dandelion & Clover Border, 1891-1902, 12 In. 1265.00
Bowl, Japanese Style, Dancers One Side, Flute Players Other, c.1870, 8 1/4 In. 1495.00
Bowl, Olive, Bright Cut Swag Design At Rim, 4 1/2 In., Pair 330.00
Bowl, Shallow, Short Footed, Signed, 10 3/8 In. 525.00
Bowl, Underplate, Child's, Flared, Vertical Panels, Arts & Crafts, 5 & 6 In. 1400.00
Bowl, Vegetable, Cover, Monogrammed, 12 5/8 In. 1155.00
Box, Hinged Cover, Oval 150.00
Box, Stamp, Floral Repousse 285.00
Candelabra, Rococo Revival Scrolling, 14 3/4 In., Pair 920.00
Candlestick, Corinthian Column, 8 1/2 In., 4 Piece 3450.00
Carving Set, Colonial 225.00

Castor, Salt & Pepper, Chrysanthemum, Baluster, 1902-1907, 5 1/2 In., Pair 750.00
Cheese Server, English King 70.00
Cocktail Fork, Chrysanthemum 85.00
Compote, Grapevine Edge, Thistle Sprays, Oval, c.1895, 10 In., Pair 3450.00
Crumb Knife, Chrysanthemum, Floral Bowl, Monogrammed, 11 1/2 In. 400.00
Cup & Saucer, Japanese Style, Copper Camellias On Leaves, Signed, 1878 . . . . 1380.00
Dish, Asparagus, Liner, Scrolled Acanthus Edge, Leaf-Headed Feet, c.1895, 13 In. 2645.00
Dish, Heart Shape, Signed, 6 In., Pair 198.00
Fish Server, Persian, 1872 . . . . 475.00
Flask, Allover Engraved Design, 4 1/2 x 7 In. 750.00
Fork, Asparagus, Grammercy 275.00
Fork, Cold Meat, Shell & Thread 120.00
Fork, Dinner, Marquise 47.00
Fork, Dinner, Saratoga 45.00
Fork, Fish, Shell & Thread 66.00
Fork, Luncheon, Colonial 35.00
Fork, Meat, Faneuil 65.00
Gravy Ladle, Grammercy 125.00
Gravy Ladle, Richelie 225.00
Gravy Ladle, Shell & Thread 120.00
Inkwell, Butterfly & Spray Of Gilt & Copper Leaves, Signed, 1885, 2 1/2 In. 1840.00
Knife, Luncheon, Audubon, 12 Piece 1760.00
Knife, Persian, 8 In., 6 Piece 450.00
Ladle, Japanese Style, 3 Fish Among Reeds, Frosted Ground, Signed, 1875, 11 In. 1380.00
Ladle, Renaissance, Pierced 295.00
Letter Opener, Monkey Form Handle, Outstretched Paws, c.1880, 12 1/4 In. 6325.00
Mustard, Repousse Floral Design, Gilt Wash Interior, 3 1/2 In. 330.00
Pitcher, Dragonfly On Lotus Plant, Spot Hammered, Signed, c.1877, 7 1/2 In. 4025.00
Pitcher, Gilt Bamboo & Prunus Spray, Spot Hammered, c.1880, 6 1/8 In. 4600.00
Pitcher, Japanese Style, 2 Lobsters, 2 Crabs, Spiral Bands, Signed, c.1879, 6 In. 9775.00
Pitcher, Repousse Band At Shoulder, Square Base, c.1875, 14 1/2 In. 7762.00
Porringer, Pierced & Scrolled Handle, Inscription On Base, 4 7/8 In. 230.00
Punch Bowl, Presentation, Inscribed & Dated 1917, 10 1/4 In. 2875.00
Punch Ladle, Beekman, 7 1/2 Oz. 220.00
Salt, Chrysanthemum, Out Curved Floral Repousse Border, 4 In., Pair 575.00
Scissors, Grape, Serpentine Form, Spot Hammered, Signed, c.1880, 8 In. 2645.00
Shoehorn, Lobster, Squirrel, Bird's Nest In Ovals, Signed, 1884, 10 In. 1035.00
Slice, Ice Cream, Lap Over Edge, Monkeys On Handle, Signed, c.1880, 12 3/4 In. 2415.00
Soup Ladle, Antique 875.00
Soup Ladle, Olympian, 1878 . . . . 747.00
Soup Ladle, Persian 950.00
Spoon, Bouillon, Shell & Thread 39.00
Spoon, Cream Soup, Shell & Thread 60.00
Spoon, Serving, Chrysanthemum 175.00
Spoon, Serving, Clinton 200.00
Spoon, Serving, Indian War Dance, Signed, c.1890, 9 3/4 In. 3740.00
Spoon, Sipping, Iced Tea, Mint Leaf Form, 8 Piece 125.00
Sugar & Creamer, Sprays Of Leaves, Dragonfly & Butterfly, c.1879, 2 3/8 In. 2587.00
Tablespoon, Colonial 50.00
Tablespoon, English King 95.00
Tea Caddy, Swirl Cap, Copper Cricket, Butterfly, Signed, 1878, 4 5/8 In. 5750.00
Tea Set, Geometric Design Overall, Marked, Monogrammed, c.1870, 5 Piece 5175.00
Teaspoon, Colonial 22.00
Teaspoon, English King 40.00
Teaspoon, San Lorenco 28.00
Tomato Server, Audubon 295.00
Toothpick, Damascene 400.00
Toy, Yo-Yo 175.00
Tray, Japanese Manner Design, Kidney Shape, 1870, 16 x 9 In. 4125.00
Tray, Pen, Heraldic, Green Enameled Finish, 3 Compartments, Silver, Signed 250.00
Tray, Tea, Serpentine Edge, Acanthus Intervals, Rectangular, c.1905, 30 3/4 In. 6325.00
Vase, Faceted Jewels, Foliate Strapwork, Enamel Ground, c.1895, 8 1/2 In. 8625.00
Vase, Relief Shell & Scroll Band At Base, Baluster Form, 1938, 10 9/16 In. 635.00

Vase, Trumpet, Drape Design, 20 In.	2150.00
Waffle Server, Faneuil	225.00
Waiter, Etched Pearling Technique, Fish Between Reeds, Signed, c.1885, 13 In.	6325.00

TIFFIN Glass Company of Tiffin, Ohio, was a subsidiary of the United States Glass Co. of Pittsburgh, Pennsylvania, in 1892. The U.S. Glass Co. went bankrupt in 1963, and the Tiffin plant employees purchased the building and the inventory. They continued running it from 1963 to 1966, when it was sold to Continental Can Company. In 1969, it was sold to Interpace, and in 1980, it was closed. The black satin glass, made from 1923 to 1926, and the stemware of the last twenty years are the best-known products.

Bowl, Cascade, 8 x 14 In.	45.00
Champagne, Cherokee Rose	18.00
Champagne, June Night	16.00
Cocktail, Cherokee Rose	22.00
Cocktail, June Night	18.00
Goblet, Flanders, Topaz	37.00
Goblet, June Night, 9 Oz.	25.00
Goblet, Water, Cherokee Rose	25.00
Pitcher, Flanders, Pink	475.00
Plate, Julia, Amber, 6 In.	5.00
Snack Set, King's Crown, Green	25.00
Tumbler, Footed, 12 Oz.	50.00
Tumbler, June Night, 6 1/2 In.	22.00

TILES have been used in most countries of the world as a sturdy building material for floors, roofs, fireplace surrounds, and surface toppings. Many of the American tiles are listed in this book under the factory name.

3 Birds, Perched On Branches, Green Glaze, Hamilton Ohio Tile, Square, 6 In.	60.00
Bird On Branch, Mustard Color, Art Pottery, Marked AE, 4 1/2 x 4 1/2 In.	85.00
Blue Bird & Flowers, Byrdcliffe, Square, 5 1/2 In.	165.00
Brocade Musicians, Multicolored, Moravian	175.00
Cherub, Noweta Advertising, Terra-Cotta, 5 1/4 x 3 7/8 In.	160.00
Chick, Running, Dark Green, Art Pottery, Marked MTC, 4 1/2 In.	75.00
Classical Woman Profile Portrait, Olive Green Glaze, Isaac Broome, 13 x 10 In.	1250.00
Fireplace Surround, Leaf, Pomegranate, Gargoyle, Ernest Batchelder, 4 In., 60 Piece	6900.00
Flying Dutchman Ship, Blue, Blush High Gloss, Red Clay, Moravian, 4 In.	75.00
Henry VIII & Queen Katherine, Transfer, Black, Gray & Gold, M. Smith, 6 In.	285.00
Lincoln Bust, Furniture Co. Advertising, Blue, White, Hexagonal, Mosaic Tile Co.	85.00
Little Miss Muffet, Polychrome Matte Glaze, 12 1/4 In.	1450.00
Madonna, Mosaic & Glass, Blue Ground, Gilt Frame, 24 1/4 x 20 1/3 In.	1610.00
Man, Planting Tree, Moravian Pottery	175.00
Mask, Painted & Partially Glazed, Picasso, No. 154/250, 1956, 7 7/8 In.	1610.00
Mayflower, Blue, White Matte, Moravian Pottery, 4 In.	65.00 to 90.00
Men, Drinking At Bar, Transfer, Earth Tones, Arts & Crafts Frame, Artist, 6 In.	195.00
Monkey, Looking In Hand Mirror, Multicolor, Gladding McBean	85.00
Old Woman Who Lived In A Shoe, Polychrome Matte Glaze, 12 1/4 In.	1450.00
Panel, Whimsical, Lion, Black Squeeze Bag Outlined, Harris Strong, 47 1/2 x 12 In.	700.00
Peasant Design, Carved, Moravian Pottery	65.00
Sailing Ship, Multicolored Glaze, Arts & Crafts, 6 x 6 In.	120.00
Ship, Moravian Pottery, La Perousa, 4 x 4 In.	75.00
Skier, Brocade, Orange, Yellow, Blue & White Matte, Moravian Pottery	125.00
Spanish Galleon, Blues, Browns & White, Matte & Gloss, California Faience, 5 1/2 In.	290.00
Steamboat, Green, Blush High Gloss, Red Clay, Moravian Pottery, 2 1/4 In.	45.00
Stylized Flowers & Curlicues, White, Green, Celadon Ground, Art Nouveau, 6 In.	125.00
Stylized Lotus Blossoms, Ivory, Brown, Green, Gold, Art Nouveau, England, 6 In.	85.00
Stylized Red Blossoms, Yellow Centers, Green Ground, Arts And Crafts, Square, 6 In.	440.00
Tea, Black Transfer, Mr. Pickwick & Mrs. Bardell, 1878	95.00
Victorian, Seashell, Amethyst Glaze	65.00
Western Scene, Harris Strong, 5 Tiles	245.00
Yellow Daffodil Among Narrow Green Leaves, Pale Pink Ground, Arts And Crafts, 6 In.	605.00

TINWARE containers for household use have been made in America since the seventeenth century. The first tin utensils were brought from Europe, but by 1798, tin plate was imported and local tinsmiths made the wares. Painted tin is called *tole* and is listed separately. Some tin kitchen items may be found listed under Kitchen. The lithographed tin containers used to hold food and tobacco are listed in the Advertising category under Tin.

Bed Warmer, Floral Engraving On Lid, Turned Handle, Copper, 45 1/2 In.	215.00
Bed Warmer, Pierced Lid, Brass Knob On Lever, Replaced Turned Handle, 36 In.	110.00
Box, Tinder, Striker, Flint, Damper, Early 1800s, 4 3/8 In.	270.00
Canister, Tea, Figure In Landscape, Mounted As Lamp, Painted Green, 20 In., Pair	980.00
Cigar Holder, Pocket	45.00
Coffeepot, Tapered Cylindrical Form, Domed Lid, Strap Handle, 10 3/8 In.	1725.00
Colander, Footed, Figural Star Punched	40.00
Cookie Cutter, Eagle Shape, 19th Century, 4 3/8 In.	175.00
Foot Warmer, Punched, Hardwood Frame, Tuned Corner Posts, 1800, 6 x 8 x 9 In.	225.00
Mold, Candle, 2 Tube, Ear Handle, 15 1/2 In.	302.50
Mold, Candle, 3 Tube, Round, 4 1/4 In.	220.00
Mold, Candle, 4 Tube, Oversized, 30 1/2 In.	140.00
Mold, Candle, 8 Tube, Ear Handle, 10 3/8 In.	247.00
Mold, Candle, 8 Tube, Ear Handle, Curved Footed, 10 7/8 In.	260.00
Mold, Candle, 10 Tube, Curved Foot, Ear Handle, 10 5/8 In.	110.00
Mold, Candle, 10 Tube, Hinged Top, Notches For Wicks, 10 3/4 In.	275.00
Mold, Candle, 10 Tube, Removable Conical Tip Ends, 15 In.	150.00
Mold, Candle, 12 Tube, Conical Finial, Ring Handle, 12 In.	495.00
Mold, Candle, 12 Tube, Curved Base, Conforming Feet, Ear Handle, 11 5/8 In.	190.00
Mold, Candle, 12 Tube, Rim Handles, 11 1/2 In.	95.00
Mold, Candle, 18 Tube, Double Ear Handles, Round, 10 1/2 In.	220.00
Mold, Candle, 18 Tube, Pine & Poplar Frame, 16 1/4 In.	495.00
Mold, Candle, 20 Tube, Pine Frame, Dark Finish, 5 3/4 x 26 1/4 x 12 1/2 In.	465.00
Mold, Candle, 24 Tube, Double Ear Handles, 9 3/4 In.	300.00
Mold, Candle, 24 Tube, Ear Handle, 10 In.	302.00
Mold, Candle, 24 Tube, Pine, Poplar, Wooden Frame, 18 In.	962.00
Mold, Candle, 24 Tube, Stenciled J. Walker	1595.00
Mold, Candle, 25 Tube, Ear Handles, 11 3/4 In.	180.00
Mold, Candle, 36 Tube, Ear Handles, 14 3/4 In.	135.00
Mold, Candle, 36 Tube, Wick-Tying Rods, Stenciled J. Walker	2255.00
Mold, Candle, 48 Tube, 4 x 19 x 11 In.	330.00
Mold, Chocolate, Easter Rabbit, Germany, 2 Part, 20 In.	170.00
Mold, Chocolate, Rabbit, Steel Frame, 13 1/2 In., 3 Sections	220.00
Nursing Bottle, Tapered Cylindrical, Cover, Loop Handle, Penna. Dutch, 4 In.	395.00
Pan, Spring Form, Heart Shape	45.00
Plate, Girl In Center, Children & Bears On Rim, Union Pacific Tea Co., 1907	65.00
Rolling Pin, Wooden Handles	120.00
Wood's Emergency Case, First Aid, J & J, 1926	90.00

TOBACCO CUTTERS may be listed in either the Advertising or Store categories.

TOBACCO JAR collectors search for those made in odd shapes and colors. Because tobacco needs special conditions of humidity and air, it has been stored in special containers since the eighteenth century.

Barrel Shape, Dog Cover, Terra-Cotta, Marked, Bohemia, 7 1/2 In.	179.00
Barrel Shape, Hoops, Shield-Shaped Cartouche, Black, Starr & Frost, 7 In.	920.00
Black Man, Straw Hat	450.00
Dog Shape, Full Bodied, Majolica, 7 3/4 In.	500.00
Geometric & Figural Landscape, Indian With Horse, Nippon, 7 1/4 In.	287.00
Horse & Jockey, Multicolored Cap, Black	495.00
Man, Drinking Beer On Cover, Terra-Cotta, Marked, Bohemia, 8 1/4 In.	223.00
Skull With Ivory & Bone Snake, Wooden	890.00
Stylized Chrysanthemums On Front, Porcelain, St. Cloud, White, 1740, 4 In.	920.00
Woman, Bandanna Covered Head, Bisque Finish, 4 3/4 In.	135.00

TOBY JUG is the name of a very special form of pitcher. It is shaped like
the full figure of a man or woman. A pitcher that shows just the top half
of a person is not correctly called a toby. More examples of toby jugs
can be found under Royal Doulton and other factory names.

Gentlemen Sitting, Wearing 18th Century Dress, Tricornered Hat, Staffordshire, 6 In. . . .	115.00
Man, Holding Mug & Pipe, Ceramic, 4 In.	23.00
Man, Holding Pitcher, Orange Jacket, Staffordshire, Late 18th Century, 10 1/4 In.	1800.00
Man, Polychrome Enamel & Luster, Allerton, Staffordshire, 9 1/4 In.	176.00
Man, Robert Edwin Peary, Arctic Clothing, Porcelain, 5 In.	135.00
Man, Sitting, Pale Brown Hat, Green Coat, Staffordshire, 1775, 9 1/2 In.	920.00
Man, Yorkshire Type, Palette With Sponged Base, Pratt, Early 19th Century, 4 5/8 In. . . .	230.00
Old King Cole, Staffordshire, 5 1/2 In.	55.00
Toby Philpot, 5 In.	55.00
Wellington, Staffordshire, 1840s	340.00
William Howard Taft, Porcelain	125.00

TOLE is painted tin. It is sometimes called *japanned ware, pontypool,*
or *toleware.* Most nineteenth-century tole is painted with an orange-
red or black background and multicolored decorations. Many recent
versions of toleware are made and sold. Related items may be listed in
the Tin category.

Basket, Black, Brass Handle, 10 In.	165.00
Bin, Store, English Walnuts, 20th Century	70.00
Box, Deed, Brass Lock, Handle, Ribbed Tin, Tan, 10 1/2 In.	165.00
Box, Deed, Dome Top, Black Paint, Floral, Red & Blue Striping, 10 In.	60.00
Box, Document, Black, Brass Handle, 9 1/2 In.	150.00
Box, Document, Black, England, c.1850, 11 1/4 In.	121.00
Box, Document, Blue & Red, Gold Stars, 19th Century	2450.00
Box, Document, Dovetailed, Red, Orange, A.J. Stout, Limington, Me., 12 x 7 x 5 In.	500.00
Box, Document, Red, Green, Yellow, White, 8 In.	195.00
Box, Document, Red-Orange Painted, Andrew J. Strout, Maine, 1849, 5 x 12 In.	350.00
Box, Dome Top, Beech, Dark Blue, Floral Design, Red, White Birds, 25 1/2 In.	357.00
Box, Dome Top, Dark Brown Japanning, Stylized Floral, Red, White, Green, 10 In.105.00 to	180.00
Box, Dome Top, Dark Brown Japanning, Stylized Floral, Red, White, Green, Yellow, 9 In.	105.00
Bucket, Foliate Design, Lion's Head Mounts, Gold Rim, Green	55.00
Canister, Tea, Chinoiserie Maidens, Green, Fitted As Lamps, Victorian, 29 In., Pair	2300.00
Canister, Tea, Gilt Stenciled, Painted Oriental Figures, Green, 35 In., Pair	2012.00
Canister, Tea, Painted Design, Pair	1265.00
Chamberstick, Floral, Dark Brown Japanning, 6 1/2 In.	1705.00
Coal Scuttle, Victorian, Painted	517.00
Creamer, Cover, Red, Yellow, Green & Blue Design	580.00
Jardiniere, 3-Tier Oval Shape, Chinoiserie Design, Cream, Teal Blue Ground, 13 In., Pair	920.00
Lamp, 3-Light, Green Adjustable Shade, Fluted Columnar Stem, Circular Base, 31 In. . . .	3450.00
Lamp, Painted Yellow, Electrified, 19th Century, 28 In.	365.00
Mug, White, Yellow, Red & Brown Design	500.00
Pipe Tongs, Wrought Iron, Tooled, 16 1/2 In.	220.00
Pot, Cache, Neoclassical Design, Black, Red Ground, 6 3/4 In., Pair	1725.00
Pot, Cache, Oval, Chinoiserie Design, Rose, Gilding, Cream Ground, 4 3/4 In., Pair	690.00
Rack, Cheese, Boat Form, Gilt Tracery & Flowers, France, 1830s, 4 1/4 x 13 In.	242.00
Spice Box, 6 Canisters Inside, Brown Japanning, Striping, 9 In.	55.00
Stand, Bulb, Empire, Gilt Metal, Putti, Chariot, 3 Demilune Tiers, France, 14 In.	575.00
Stand, Compote, Regency, Tiered Gilt Frame, Round Top, Pedestal, 9 x 22 In.	150.00
Teapot, Shield Design, Dark Red, 7 1/2 In.	175.00
Teapot, Stylized Floral, Red & Yellow, Dark Brown Japanning, 9 In.	357.00
Tray, Central Landscape Scene, Bamboo Turned Stand, Painted & Stenciled	412.00
Tray, Central Scene, Flight From Egypt, Fruiting Foliate Borders, 18 1/2 x 24 1/4 In.	287.00
Tray, Chippendale Shape, Central Floral Spray, Gold Foliate Border, Black, 23 x 29 In. . .	605.00
Tray, Chippendale, Original Painted Design, England, 19th Century, 30 1/4 In.	250.00
Tray, Courting Couple In Center, With 2 Putti, Oval, 19th Century, 30 x 23 In.	747.00
Tray, Empire Style, Oval, Provincial Landscape Scene, Cream Border, On Stand, 21 In. . .	2875.00
Tray, European Harbor Scene, 21 x 16 1/2 In.	207.00
Tray, Figural & Floral Cartouche, Conforming Wooden Stand, Oval, 25 x 18 3/4 In.	920.00

Tray, Figural Anterior Cartouche, Red & Gold Floral Border, Oval, France, 27 In. 1210.00
Tray, Figural Landscape Design, Red & Gold Floral Border, Oval, France, 19 In. 825.00
Tray, Floral Arrangement In Center, Gold Lappet Border, Rectangular, 22 x 30 In. 785.00
Tray, Floral Center Panel, Gilt Foliate Edge, Green Ground, 16 1/4 x 23 1/2 In. 430.00
Tray, Floral Design, 25 In. 88.00
Tray, Floral Design, 29 In. 165.00
Tray, French Scenes Of Events At Edge, Wrinkled Yellow Ground, 26 1/2 x 19 1/2 In. ... 200.00
Tray, French Soldiers Surrendering To British, 22 x 30 In. 60.00
Tray, Gallery, Landscape, Conforming Stand, Red, Circular, 19th Century, 23 3/4 In. 1650.00
Tray, Gallery, Landscape, Foliate Border, Conforming Stand, Yellow, 20 x 22 x 29 In. . 4125.00
Tray, George III, Ebonized Stand, 19th Century, 20 1/2 In. 2300.00
Tray, Gilt, Signed, Georges M. Briard, Early 20th Century, 24 1/4 x 12 1/2 In. 165.00
Tray, Grapevine Border, Raised On Turned Legs, Bun Feet, France, 20 1/2 In. 3450.00
Tray, Green Floral Design, 24 In. ...., 70.00
Tray, Green Leaf Border, Cranberry Red, 1830s, 24 x 17 1/2 In. 145.00
Tray, Painted Red Roses, Wood Folding Stand, Signed Pilgrim, Oval, 30 In. 125.00
Tray, Regency, Center Cartouche, Figures, Classical Landscape, Oval, 19 1/4 x 24 1/4 In. 860.00
Tray, Sailor Giving Bouquet To Mermaid, Sailing Ship & Whales, M. Cahoon, 20 x 15 In. 1435.00
Tray, Stenciled Exotic Landscape, Peacocks, Black & Gilt, 17 3/4 x 24 In. 395.00
Tray, White, Silver, Gilt, Pair Of Cherubs In Center, Leafy Border, Oval, 19 x 15 In. 275.00
Urn, Floral Spray Design, Songbirds, Chestnut, 15 In., Pair 1265.00
Urn, Gilt Design, Tapering Body, Plinth Base, Green, 9 1/2 In., Pair 1515.00
Wall Sconce, Gilt, Green, 19th Century, 12 In., Pair 1210.00
Washstand, Bird's-Eye Maple, Bamboo, Paw Feet, 45 x 33 x 25 In. 1320.00
Wine Cooler, Gold Grapevine, Flower Panels, Double 450.00

TOM MIX was born in 1880 and died in 1940. He was the hero of over 100 silent movies from 1910 to 1929, and 25 sound films from 1929 to 1935. There was a Ralston Tom Mix radio show from 1933 to 1950, but the original Tom Mix was not in the show. Tom Mix comics were published from 1942 to 1953.

Badge, Straight Shooter 90.00
Belt Buckle, Secret Compartment 95.00
Bottle, Coca-Cola, 6th Annual National Festival, Dubois, Penn., 1985, 10 Oz. 25.00
Branding Iron, With Ink Pad, Checkerboard, Original Mailer, 1930s 95.00
Certificate, Gold Ore 45.00
Comic Book, Mail Premium 250.00
Compass, Glow-In-The-Dark ....65.00 to 70.00
Cowboy Boots, Child's, Box 375.00
Flashlight, Bullet 50.00
Knife, Ralston, Pocket 25.00
Label, Cigar Box, Embossed, Picture, 5 In. 35.00
Light, 3-In-1 .... 50.00
Magnifying Glass, 1940 .... 75.00
Periscope, Straight Shooters, 1939 .... 60.00
Photograph, Frame, 5/8 x 3/4 In. 20.00
Pin, Tom Mix & Tony, Tony Is Brown, 1930 .... 28.00
Program, Sells Floto Circus, 1931 .... 35.00
Radio, Silver Badge, Ralston Premium, 1937 .... 80.00
Ring, Magnet, Metal, Gold Finish, Ralston, 1940s ....60.00 to 67.00
Ring, Signature, Metal, Copper Plating, 1942 .... 235.00
Ring, Sliding Whistle, Metal, Gold & Silver Finish, Ralston 90.00
Ring, Tiger Eye, 1950s 163.00
Spurs, Glow In Dark 75.00
Telescope, Bird & Call, Papers, Mailer 175.00
Tin, Make-Up, Checkerboard Design, 1940s 12.00
Watch Fob, Gold Ore, Miner's Pick, Gold Pan, 1940 .... 68.00

TOOLS of all sorts are listed here, but most are related to industry. Other tools may be found listed under Iron, Kitchen, Tinware, and Wooden.

Adze, Wooden Haft, Blacksmith Made, Initial W, 1740s, 16 In. 75.00
Apron, Nail, Bib Type, Shapleigh 75.00
Auger, Hook Nose Nave, France, 4 Piece 245.00

Auger, Water Pipe, Log-Boring Spoon Type Bit, 6-In. Diam. 105.00
Battery Tester, Atlas, 1941 . . . . 20.00
Battery Tester, Dry, Signal Corp., 1950 . . . . 75.00
Bellows, Blacksmith's, 6 Ft. 210.00
Bellows, Wig, For Blowing Powder, Leather, 2 1/8 x 6 1/2 In. 225.00
Bench, Work, Pine, Attached 2 Large Block Vises 1210.00
Bevel, Ship's, Lufkin, 12 In. 40.00
Bevel, Stanley, No. 25, Rosewood, 8 In. 25.00
Bit Set, Russell Jennings, Oak Box, 13 Piece 125.00
Blasting Machine, Fidelity 135.00
Box, Compartment, Inlay On Top, Original Lock, Hasp & Key, 1840s 350.00
Box, Conestoga Wagon, Cover, Hinged, Blue, Green Paint, Pennsylvania, 13 1/4 In. 950.00
Box, Conestoga Wagon, Traces Of Red Paint 1150.00
Brace, Alfred Ridge, Ultimatum 495.00
Brace, Beece, Pilkington, Pedigor & Storr 425.00
Brace, Pilkington, Pedigor & Storr 425.00
Brace, Sheffield, H. Brown & Sons, Brass Plated, 14 In. 140.00
Brace, Stanley, No. 112, Wood, Brown Patina Frame 40.00
Branding Iron, K 25.00
Cabinet, Nuts & Bolts, Pine, Many Drawers, Square Base, Hexagonal Top 1500.00
Cabinet, Typesetter's, Hamilton Mfg., Slanted Top, 38 Drawers, 60 In. 1050.00
Calculator, Mechanical, Brunsvega Midget, Wooden Base 375.00
Caliper Rule, C.S. & Co., No. 40, Folding, Ivory, 1 x 4 In. 225.00
Caliper Rule, Carpenter's, Stanley, No. 36 . . . . 22.00
Caliper Rule, Carpenter's, Stanley, No. 36-1/2 . . . . 35.00
Caliper Rule, Carpenter's, Stanley, No. 36-1/2R 18.00
Caliper Rule, Carpenter's, Stanley, No. 38, Ivory 265.00
Caliper Rule, Carpenter's, Stanley, No. 40, Ivory 170.00
Caliper Rule, Putnam's, Cloth Chart, 1896 . . . . 60.00
Candle Maker, Fill With Tallow, Attached Wick, Push-Up, Used As Chamberstick, 1846 750.00
Chain Drill, Millers Falls-Goodell Pratt, World War II 40.00
Check Writer, Paymaster 55.00
Check Writer, Speedrite 55.00
Chest, Carpenter's, Pine, Worn Finish, Mahogany Grained Lid, Compartments, 38 In. . . . 275.00
Chest, Carpenter's, Poplar, Fitted, Dovetailed, 48 x 23 x 23 In. 190.00
Chest, Hinged Lid, Sliding Tray, Dovetailed Corners, Wooden, 19th Century 55.00
Chest, Pine, Dovetailed, Added Feet, Till, Black Label, Omaha, Neb., 28 3/4 In. 210.00
Chisel, Carving, Greenlee, Beech Handles, Brass Ferules, Canvas Roll 265.00
Cigar Box, Opener, Hatchet Shape 30.00
Clothespin, Hand Carved, 1830s, 6 3/8 In., Pair 115.00
Cobbler's Bench, Complete With Tools, Shoes & Forms 440.00
Cobbler's Bench, Provincial, Stained Pine, Drawers, 19th Century, 50 x 22 In. 920.00
Cobbler's Bench, Tray On Top, 3 Bottom Drawers, 29 x 40 1/2 In. 258.00
Cobbler's Bench, Worn Patina, Replaced 2 Drawers, With Tools & Lasts, 49 In. 550.00
Compass, Dividers, Tightening Screw, Hand Cut, Walnut, 30 3/4 In. 90.00
Cork Press, Iron, Original Paint, 9 In. 100.00
Corn Sheller, A.F. Severance, Maine, Painted Green 187.00
Cultivator, Garden, Forged Iron, Wooden Handle, 1930s, 10 1/2 In. . . . . *Illus* 15.00
Curler, Mustache, Duke, 1890 . . . . 15.00
Cutter, Peat, Handmade, Irish 65.00
Cutter, Sugar, Iron & Brass, Mounted On Maple Block, Early 19th Century, 14 In. 460.00
Depth Gauge-Protractor, Millers Falls 20.00
Draftsmen's Set, Case, Germany 60.00
Drawing Board, Architect's, Washburn Shops Institute, Cast Iron Base, 2 Top Drawers . 1275.00
Drill, Eggbeater, Millers Falls, No. 2 . . . . .10.00 to 15.00
Drill, Hand, Stanley, No. 610 . . . . 210.00
Drill, Hand, Stanley, No. 803, England . . . . .15.00 to 20.00
Drill, Hand, Stanley, No. 1221 . . . . 20.00
Egg Candler, Tin, Brass Burner, 19th Century, 11 1/2 In. 165.00
Flashlight, Focusing, Winchester 40.00
Flashlight, Ringling Bros., Figural, Circus Tiger 20.00
Flashlight, Winchester, Nickel Plated, 7 In. 75.00
Gauge, Brown & Sharpe, No. 621 . . . . 30.00

Some collectors want tools in restored condition. Others think restoring lowers the value. To restore old tools, wash wood with Murphy's Oil Soap, dry, sand with steel wool, apply two coats of Minwax or other oil, then use paste wax and buff. Clean metal parts, then coat with clear lacquer.

Tool, Cultivator, Garden, Forged Iron,
Wooden Handle, 1930s, 10 1/2 In.

Gauge, Butt & Rabbet, Stanley, No. 95-1/2	75.00
Gauge, Height, Tumico, 24 In.	200.00
Gauge, Mortise, Stanley, No. 92	60.00
Gauge, Surface, Lufkin, No. 521, 5 In.	25.00
Gauge, Surface, Tool Maker's	95.00
Grain Measure Set, Pine, Poplar, Dovetailed, Nesting, 8 3/4 In., 3 Piece	165.00
Hackle, Cherry, All Wood, Including Tines, 27 1/2 In.	185.00
Hackle, Double-Ended, Wooden, Late 18th Century	275.00
Hackle, Punched Both Sides, Chip-Carved Design Ends, W.T., 1765	235.00
Hackle, Red Paint, Table Clamps, 1849, 21 In.	445.00
Hammer, Claw, Bell System, Stanley, 32 Oz.	15.00
Hammer, Jeweler's, Brass Head	70.00
Hatchet, Bell System Lineman, Slot In Blade For Turning Nuts & Bolts	70.00
Hatchet, Camp, Marbles, No. 5, Wooden Handle, Guard, Logos	165.00
Hatchet, Hammer Poll, 15 1/2-In. Shaft	180.00
Hatchet, Winchester	55.00 to 100.00
Hatchet, Winchester, Leather Case	100.00
Ice Pick, Winchester	85.00
Ice Tongs, Commercial Size	35.00
Ice Tongs, Cuero, Texas	25.00
Jack, Buggy, Wooden, Early 1800s	85.00
Jack, Keen Kutter, No. 5, Logo	72.00
Jig, Dowel, Stanley, No. 59, Box	60.00
Jig, Dowel, Stanley, No. 60, SR & L Box	160.00
Jointer, Cherry, Roman Style 1-Piece Back Handle, France, 33 1/2 In.	2475.00
Jointer, Razee, Standard Rule Co., No. 31, Transitional, 24 In.	100.00
Jointer, Stanley No. 7, Type 6, 1888-1890	60.00
Lathe, Craftsman, Atlas, Metal, On Tool Cabinet, 6 x 18 In.	950.00
Lathe, Edestall, Unimat, Metal, Wooden Box, Unused	850.00
Lathe, South Bend Steady Rest, 10 In.	125.00
Lathe, Taig, Metal, Unused, 4 x 8 In.	375.00
Lawn Mower, Cast Iron, Salmon Paint, Charter Oak Mfg. Co., 1875, 58 In.	1395.00
Lawn Mower, Monta Mower, 16 Spiked Discs, Rotate When Pushed	85.00
Level, Akron Eclipse, Brassbound	80.00
Level, Brass & Rosewood, Brass Case, England	125.00
Level, Engineer's & Plumber's, Starrett, No. 133, 1940s	100.00
Level, Favorite Farm, Keuffel & Esser, Manual & Tripod, Box, 1915	135.00
Level, Hockley Abbey, Brass Plated, 6 In.	50.00
Level, L.B. Watts, Mahogany, 29 In.	75.00
Level, Leitz, No. 16564, Wooden Box	125.00
Level, Millers Falls, Full Brassbound, Mahogany	145.00
Level, Stanley, No. 0, Cherry	30.00
Level, Stanley, No. 3	10.00 to 40.00
Level, Stanley, No. 03, Mahogany, 28 In.	30.00
Level, Stanley, No. 37, Iron, 6 In.	50.00

Level, Stanley, No. 43, Cast Iron & Brass 175.00
Level, Stanley, No. 104 .... 10.00
Level, Transit, Brass, T.F. Randolph, Cincinnati, Oh., Wooden Case, 12 In. 385.00
Level, Upson Nut, Cherry, 15 In. 40.00
Level, Winchester, No. 9802, Wooden, 12 In. 95.00
Level, Winchester, No. 9815, Brass, 28 In. 124.00
Level, Winchester, No. 9815, Wood, 28 In. 100.00
Level, Winchester, No. W104, Brass Hardware, 18 In. 125.00
Level Sights, Stanley, Original Box, c.1920 .... 65.00
Machine, Dowel & Rod Turning, Stanley, No. 77, 3/8 In. ....380.00 to 590.00
Measure, Haystack, Copper, Dovetailed, 11 1/2 In. 77.00
Measure, Liquid, Divided By Feet & Inches, Ring Top, Weighted Bottom, Brass, 4 Ft. .. 225.00
Measure, Surveyor's, Mahogany, England, 19th Century 460.00
Miter Box & Saw, Stanley, No. 2360 ....50.00 to 75.00
Mold, Bottle, Iron, For Pistol Candy Container, 10 x 9 x 11 In. 1650.00
Monkey Wrench, Coe's Pattern, No. 1003, 10 In. 85.00
Monkey Wrench, Coe's, Worcester, Ma., 8 In. 18.00
Monkey Wrench, Wooden Handle, Winchester, No. 1004, 12 In. 95.00
Nail Puller, Keen Kutter 65.00
Notcher, Diacro, 6 In. 250.00
Padlock, Standard Oil, Brass 38.00
Padlock, Winchester, No. 6, Logo, No Key 86.00
Paper Dispenser, Mr. Zig Zag 250.00
Picker, Apple, Iron 28.00
Plane, Adjustable, Boat Shape, Birmingham, 7 In. 220.00
Plane, Beltmaker's, Stanley, No. 11, 1907 ....110.00 to 120.00
Plane, Block, Adjustable, Dunlap 15.00
Plane, Block, Cabinet Maker's, Stanley, No. 9 ....1150.00 to 1200.00
Plane, Block, Double End, Ohio 90.00
Plane, Block, Double End, Stanley, No. 131, Adjustable Cutter 220.00
Plane, Block, Edge Trimming, Stanley, No. 95 .... 135.00
Plane, Block, Sargent No. 316, Handle, Oval Mark 375.00
Plane, Block, Stanley, No. 17, Nickel Plated 50.00
Plane, Block, Stanley, No. 100, Box 125.00
Plane, Block, Stanley, No. 9-1/4, Box 30.00
Plane, Block, Winchester, No. W-6, Logo, Rosewood Handles, 18 In. 130.00
Plane, Block, Winchester, No. W220 .... 25.00
Plane, Block, Winchester, Wooden, 15 In. 81.00
Plane, Block, Winchester, Wooden, Rear Logo, 9 In. 110.00
Plane, Box Maker's, Ohio Tool 1200.00
Plane, Cabinet Scraper, Stanley, No. 112, 9 In. ....150.00 to 175.00
Plane, Cabinet, Stanley, No. 9 .... 1200.00
Plane, Circular, Stanley, No. 13, 1888 ....180.00 to 185.00
Plane, Circular, Victor, No. 20 .... 180.00
Plane, Combination, Miller's Patent No. 41, Pine Box 4010.00
Plane, Combination, Stanley, No. 45, 22 Cutters, Aluminum, Made From 1926 To 1934 . 3500.00
Plane, Combination, Stanley, No. 45, Original Box, Type 14, c.1922 .... 295.00
Plane, Combination, Universal, Stanley, No. 55, Wooden Box ....525.00 to 650.00
Plane, Coping, Copeland, Double Sash 35.00
Plane, Dado, Stanley, No. 39-1/4 ....120.00 to 245.00
Plane, Dado, Stanley, No. 39-3/8, 1910 .... 125.00
Plane, Dado, Stanley, No. 39-7/8, Type 1 .... 150.00
Plane, Double Iron, Taber Patent, 1865 .... 275.00
Plane, Dovetail, Stanley, No. 444 .... 1350.00
Plane, Duplex, Stanley, No. 78, Box 45.00
Plane, Edge Trimming, Stanley, No. 95 .... 150.00
Plane, Floor, Stanley, No. 11-1/2 .... 645.00
Plane, Fore, B, Birmingham, No. 6 .... 95.00
Plane, Jack, Auto-Set, Sargent, No. 714 .... 145.00
Plane, Jack, Bed Rock, Stanley, No. 605-1/4 .... 660.00
Plane, Jack, Bed Rock, Stanley, No. 605C 110.00
Plane, Jack, Chaplin, No. 120, Corrugated Bottom, Hard Rubber Handle 165.00
Plane, Jack, Junior, No. 5-1/4 .... 60.00

Plane, Jack, Keen Kutter, No. 5 .... 72.00
Plane, Jack, Sargent, No. 414 .... 25.00
Plane, Jack, Siegley, No. 6, Corrugated Bottom, Pat. Dec. 5, 1893 .... 155.00
Plane, Jack, Stanley, No. 5 .... 25.00
Plane, Jack, Stanley, No. 5-1/4 .... 65.00
Plane, Jack, Vaughn & Bushnell, No. 905 .... 65.00
Plane, Jointer, Bailey, Stanley, No. 8, Marked U.S. Pat. April 1910 .... 45.00
Plane, Jointer, Ohio, No. 08C, Wood 90.00
Plane, Jointer, Siegley, No. 8C, Pat. 1893 .... 85.00
Plane, Jointer, Stanley, No. 7, 1888-1890 .... 60.00
Plane, Keen Kutter, No. 27 .... 75.00
Plane, Low Angle, Stanley, No. 164, Label On Handle 4970.00
Plane, Nosing, Sargent & Co. 20.00
Plane, Plow, H. Wells, Slide Arms, Depth Stop 100.00
Plane, Plow, Holbrook, Boxwood Scales .... 295.00 to 450.00
Plane, Plow, Siegly No. 2, 17 Cutters, Wooden Box 225.00
Plane, Plow, Union Factory, No. 239, Applewood 200.00
Plane, Plow, Weatherstrip, Stanley, No. 248 .... 75.00
Plane, Rabbet & Block, Stanley, No. 140 .... 95.00
Plane, Rabbet, Stanley, No. 90, Steel Case 125.00
Plane, Rabbet, Stanley, No. 181 .... 85.00
Plane, Rabbet, Weatherstrip, Stanley, No. 378 .... 135.00
Plane, Sargent, No. 407, 7 In. 185.00
Plane, Sargent, No. 2204, Steel, 4 1/4 In. 65.00
Plane, Scrub, Stanley, No. 40 .... 65.00
Plane, Scrub, Stanley, No. 40, Notched Logo Cutter, Rosewood Handles, c.1940 .... 325.00
Plane, Scrub, Stanley, No. 40-1/2, 10 1/2 In. 95.00
Plane, Smooth, Bed Rock, Stanley, No. 602 .... 635.00
Plane, Smooth, Bed Rock, Stanley, No. 604C 110.00
Plane, Smooth, Corrugated, Union 495.00
Plane, Smooth, Dunlap, Box, Instruction Sheet 46.00
Plane, Smooth, Millers Falls, No. 900, Box 50.00
Plane, Smooth, Stanley Handyman, No. H1203, Box 45.00
Plane, Smooth, Stanley, No. 2 .... 225.00
Plane, Smooth, Stanley, No. 2C, 1910 .... 450.00
Plane, Smooth, Winchester, No. 3005 .... 80.00
Plane, Tongue & Groove, Stanley, No. 48 .... 75.00
Plane, Transitional, Keen Kutter, No. 27 .... 75.00
Plane, Winchester, No. 3004 .... 140.00
Plane, Winchester, No. 3005 .... 80.00
Plane, Wood Block, Winchester, No. 3045, Logo, 15 In. 113.00
Plane, Wood Block, Winchester, No. 3050, Logo, 18 In. 113.00
Plant, Tongue & Groove, Keen Kutter, No, K76 .... 95.00
Pliers, Slip, Straight Nose, Winchester, 10 In. 48.00
Plow, Applewood, White, Handle, Buffalo 195.00
Plow, Boxwood, Howland & Co. 265.00
Plumb & Level, Stanley, No. 36, Iron, 24 In. 40.00
Plumb Bob, Iron, 16 Pounds, 8 1/2 x 5 In. 400.00
Post Grinder, Dumore, Model 14-011, Case 275.00
Potato Cutter, Bucher & Gibbs Plow Company, Sit Down, For Planting 4450.00
Protractor, Brass, Interpolation Grids, Mid-18th Century, 6 In. 325.00
Rack, Quilt, Folding, Mortised Construction, Folding, Red, 2 Sections, 37 x 62 In. ... 70.00
Rack, Quilt, Folding, Screw Construction, Poplar, 3 Sections, 30 x 76 In. 50.00
Rake, Clam, Iron, Fan-Type Form, 19th Century 110.00
Rake, Clam, Mounted On Steel Post & Plate, 34 In. 350.00
Rake, Cranberry, New England 150.00
Rake, Harvesting, Stencil C.R. King, Carlisle, Ky., Red 165.00
Rip Saw, Disston, No. 7, Refinished Handle, 28 In. 30.00
Rule, Boxwood, Stephens & Co., No. 46, 2 x 4 In. 35.00
Rule, Carpenter's, E.A. Sterns, No. 56B, 4-Fold, Ivory, German Silver, 2 Ft. 220.00
Rule, Carpenter's, Sliding, Stanley, No. 12 .... 75.00
Rule, Carpenter's, Sliding, Stanley, No. 27 .... 125.00
Rule, Combination, Stephens & Co., No. 036 .... 225.00

Rule, Farrand Rapid, Box, 1922 . . . . 50.00
Rule, Folding, Lufkin, Brass, 24 In. 64.00
Rule, Folding, Stanley, No. 26, With Slide, 24 In. 75.00
Rule, H. Chapin, No. 9, 4-Fold, Brass Clad, c.1850 . . . . 145.00
Rule, Lufkin, Brassbound, 2 x 4 In. 50.00
Rule, Lufkin, No. 781, Brassbound 30.00
Rule, Sliding, H. Chapin, 24 In. 145.00
Rule, Sliding, Metal, Picket, Box, 14 In. 15.00
Rule, Stanley, No. 32-1/2 . . . . 40.00
Rule, Stanley, No. 36-1/2R 18.00
Sander, Delta, Combination, 12-In. Disc, 4-In. Belt 450.00
Saw, Dovetail, Stanley, Brass Backed, 150th Anniversary 35.00
Saw, Frame, Hand-Filed Teeth, Blade Attached With Hand Forged Nails, 47 In. 275.00
Saw, Hack, Keller, No. 3 HD-HY-Duty, 3/4 H.P. 450.00
Saw, Hand, Winchester, W 10 . . . . 85.00
Saw, Ice, Horse Drawn 350.00
Saw, Rip, Disston, No. 7, 28 In. 55.00
Saw, Rip, KK, No. 88, 28 In. 65.00
Scraper, Cooper, C. Drew & Co. 23.00
Scraper, Stanley, No. 12, Rosewood Bottom & Handle 130.00
Scraper, Winchester, No. 3076, Handle, 10 In. 175.00
Screwdriver, Ivory Handle 125.00
Screwdriver, Spiral, Stanley, No. 130A 12.00
Screwdriver, Winchester, No. 7113, 4 In. 45.00
Scrubber, Clothing, Hand Carved Oak, 14 1/8 In. 85.00
Set, Yankee, No. 100, Box 95.00
Sharpener, Cudahy's Blue Ribbon Meat & Bone Scraper, Sharpening Stone, 2 3/4 In. . . . 55.00
Shears, Forged Iron, 18th Century, 8 In. 90.00
Shoe, Ice Harvesting, Pair 325.00
Shoe Measure, Lufkin, No. 8223 . . . . 85.00
Shoehorn, Bell Metal, c.1770, 6 In. 11500.00
Shoehorn, Blacksmith Made, American, 18th Century 165.00
Sorter, Apple, Vermont, Wooden, 20 x 40 In. 495.00
Spokeshave, Beech, Doremus, Newark, N.J., 19th Century 35.00
Spokeshave, Stanley, No. 62, B Casting Mark 135.00
Spokeshave, Stanley, No. 81, Rosewood 75.00
Square, Double Bevel, Stanley, No. 225 . . . . 175.00
Square, Stanley, Aluminum 12.00
Square, Stanley, No. 100, Aluminum 20.00
Square, Stanley, No. 500C, Handyman, Copper 25.00
Stool, Weaver's, Old Red Paint, New England, c.1780, 29 In. 200.00
Stretcher, Sock, Tulip Wood, 13 In. 50.00
Test Kit, Internal Revenue, 5 Hydrometers, Copper Cup With Thermometer, 1860 . . . . . . 200.00
Tongs, Goffering, Hand Forged, c.1750, 9 7/16 In. 75.00
Tool, Grinder, Craftsman/Atlas, Tool Post, 12 In. 800.00
Trammel, Lighting, All Wood, Adjusts From 38 In. 225.00
Trammel, Sawtooth, Wooden, 32 3/4 In. 137.00
Trammel, Stanley, No. 3, Brass 90.00
Trammel, Stanley, No. 4, Holder For Pencil . . . . 30.00 to 32.00
Trammel, Wooden, Dark Patina, 25 In. 275.00
Traveler, Wheelwright's, Pointer, Iron Handle 65.00
Tray, Type, Divided, 32 x 16 1/2 In. 25.00
Turning Set, Holtzapffel, Ornamental, Beech & Rosewood Handles, Case, 75 Piece 2825.00
Vise, Leather Worker's, 11 Brass Tools, Maple, 19th Century, 6 5/8 x 12 3/8 In. 170.00
Vise, Saw, Disston, No. 2, Unused 30.00
Vise, Woodworker's, Stanley, No. 700, Box 35.00
Wheelbarrow, Painted Red, Gold Stencils 220.00
Wheelbarrow, Paris Sled Co., Maine 325.00
Wheelbarrow, Ross Brothers, Worcester, Ma., Red Paint 275.00
Wrench, Adjustable, Athol Machine Co., 6 In. 110.00
Wrench, Adjustable, Indian, 1920s 100.00
Wrench, Adjustable, Keen Kutter, 4 In. 45.00
Wrench, Bolt, Brass, For Rope Bed 50.00

Wrench, J.L. Taylor Redman Mfg., Pipe & Nut 95.00
Wrench, Pipe, Beryllium, Ampco, No. W1150, 18 In. 45.00
Wrench, Pipe, Winchester, No. 1020, Wooden Handle, 6 In. 85.00

TOOTHPICK HOLDERS are sometimes called *toothpicks* by collectors.
The variously shaped containers used to hold small wooden toothpicks
are made of glass, china, or metal. Most of the toothpick holders are
Victorian. Additional items may be found in other categories, such as
Bisque, Silver Plate, Slag Glass, etc.

Amberina, Baby Inverted Thumbprint, Tricornered 275.00
Barrel, White, Opalescent, Coin Spot 150.00
Bead & Scroll, Ruby Stain 225.00
Bead Swag With Roses, White, Opalescent 45.00
Beaded Grape, Emerald Green 95.00
Beaded Swag, Ruby Stain 110.00
Beatty Honeycomb, White, Opalescent 30.00
Bees On A Basket, Blue 75.00
Box-In-Box, Green, Gold Trim 65.00
Bulging Loops, Pink, Opalescent 150.00
Burmese Glass, Pinecones, Branches, Mt. Washington, 1880s, 3 x 3 In. 675.00
Burmese Glass, Tricornered, Mt. Washington, 1880s, 2 1/4 In. 425.00
Carmen 38.00
Cat On A Pillow, Amber, D & B 165.00
Colorado, Green, Gold 57.00
Custard Glass, Aurora, Ind., The Plucky City 75.00
Diamond Spearhead, Green, Opalescent ....100.00 to 165.00
Diamond Spearhead, Vaseline, Opalescent 195.00
Double Faced Devil, 4 1/2 In. 245.00
Gonterman Swirl, Yellow, Opalescent 325.00
Hand Painted Floral, Purple, Scalloped Skirt, Gilt Rim 125.00
Hobnail, Allover Blue, Opalescent ....45.00 to 70.00
Hobnail, Blue, Opalescent 195.00
Iris With Meander, Blue, Gold Trim 70.00
Iris With Meander, Blue, Opalescent ....80.00 to 95.00
Iris With Meander, Green, Opalescent 55.00
Madame Bovary, Blue, Amber Rim & Foot 95.00
Michigan, Enameled Flower 165.00
Millifiori Blown 95.00
Monkey & Hat, Green 95.00
Owl, Standing On Branch, Egg Shaped Holder, Silver Plated 85.00
Panelled Sprig, Opalescent 125.00
Panelled Sprig, White, Opalescent 45.00
Pansy, Blue, Glossy 95.00
Pansy, Pink Glossy Cased 175.00
Pink Opalescent, Clear Leaves, 1 1/2 In. 50.00
Prayer Lady, Blue 25.00
Pug Dog, With Bag, Metal, 3 x 1 1/2 In. ....*Illus*   55.00

Toothpick, Pug Dog, With
Bag, Metal, 3 x 1 1/2 In.

**To clean tortoiseshell, rub it
with a mixture of jeweler's
rouge and olive oil.**

Ribbed Swirl, White, Opalescent	165.00
Scalloped Skirt, Hand Painted Florals, Jefferson Glass Co., Amethyst	90.00
Shoshone, Clear & Gold	30.00
Spinning Star	45.00
Sunbeam, Green, Gold	40.00
Sunset, Blue Opaque	115.00
Swag With Brackets, Blue, Opalescent	200.00
Swirl, White, Opalescent	195.00
Twisted Hobnail	25.00
Washington, Ruby Stained, Opalescent	120.00
Windows, Blue, Opalescent	80.00
Windsor Anvil, Blue	34.00
Wreath & Shell, Vaseline, Opalescent	225.00

TORQUAY is the name given to ceramics by several potteries working near Torquay, England, from 1870 until 1962. Until about 1900, the potteries used local red clay to make classical-style art pottery vases and figurines. Then they turned to making souvenir wares. Items were dipped in colored slip and decorated with painted slip and sgraffito designs. They often had mottoes or proverbs, and scenes of cottages, ships, birds, or flowers. The *Scandy* design was a symmetrical arrangement of brushstrokes and spots done in colored slips. Potteries included Watcombe Pottery (1870–1962); Torquay Terra-Cotta Company (1875–1905); Aller Vale (1881–1924); Torquay Pottery (1908–1940); and Longpark (1883–1957).

TORQUAY

Ashtray, Cottage, Watcombe	35.00
Bowl, Junket Motto Around Outside, Band Of Flowers, 5 1/4 x 6 3/4 In.	190.00
Chamberstick, Scandy Design, 7 3/4 In.	120.00
Cheese Dish, Cover, Scenic Blue Peacock, Trees, Eat Well Of The Bread	125.00
Eggcup, Cottage, Motto Ware, Fresh To-Day, 2 3/4 In.	35.00
Inkwell, Tray, Colored Cockerel	300.00
Jam Jar, Cover, Cottage, Handle	100.00
Jam Jar, Devonware, Cottage, Watcombe	40.00
Jam Jar, Handle	75.00
Jug, Cottage, Hot Water, Cover	135.00
Jug, Puzzle	70.00
Pitcher, Cottage, Motto Ware, From Gretna Green, Child's, 2 1/4 In.	40.00
Pitcher, Kingfisher, 8 In.	85.00
Plate, Black Cockerel, 7 1/4 In.	70.00
Plate, Motto Ware, Life Has No Pleasure Nobler Than Friendship	30.00
Tea Caddy	95.00
Teapot, Cottage, Motto Ware, Tak Cup Kindness For Auld Lang Syne, 7 In.	85.00
Teapot, Cottage, Motto Ware, Tea Seldom Spoils When Water Boils, 4 In.	85.00
Teapot, Cottage, Motto Ware, Watcombe, 6 In.	125.00
Teapot, Embossed Men, On Horse, Brown, 5 1/2 In.	125.00
Teapot, Shamrock Green, Motto Ware, O'er Earth, Devon	125.00
Tray, Dresser	110.00
Vase, 3 Handles, Motto Ware, If You Can't Be Aisy, Aller Vale, 1897-1901	180.00
Vase, 3 Handles, Parrot, Blue, 7 In.	66.00
Vase, Purple Tones, Stylized Flower Handles, Signed, 8 1/2 In.	110.00

TORTOISESHELL is the shell of the tortoise. It has been used as inlay and to make small decorative objects since the seventeenth century. Some species of tortoise are now on the endangered species list, and objects made from these shells cannot be sold legally.

Bottle, Snuff, Warriors On Horseback, Ivory Stopper, 2 In.	630.00
Box, Ornate Gild, Brass Fittings, Handle, 5 1/2 In.	357.00
Brush Holder, Landscape Design, Mountain, Scrolled Foot, 3 3/4 In.	453.00
Case, Bun Feet, 19th Century, 2 3/8 In.	968.00
Cross, Ivory Corpus, Christ Carved With Open Eyes, 1770, 35 x 22 1/2 In.	9200.00
Hairpin, Rectangular Form, Japan, 9 1/2 In.	46.00
Mirror, Standing, Art Nouveau, 7 1/2 x 5 In.	50.00
Tea Caddy, Ball Form Feet, Octagonal, England, 7 1/4 In.	1550.00

TORTOISESHELL GLASS was made during the 1800s and after by the Sandwich Glass Works of Massachusetts and some firms in Germany. Tortoiseshell glass is, of course, named for its resemblance to real shell from a tortoise. It has been reproduced.

Pitcher, 8 In.	90.00
Pitcher, Hand Blown, Polished Pontil, 10 In.	135.00
Vase, Crimped, Ruffled Top, 9 In.	69.00

TOY collectors have special clubs, magazines, and shows. Toys are designed to entice children, and today they have attracted new interest among adults who are still children at heart. All types of toys are collected. Tin toys, iron toys, battery operated toys, and many others are collected by specialists. Dolls, Games, Teddy Bears, and Bicycles are listed in their own categories. Other toys may be found under company or celebrity names.

Acrobat, Jolly Skipper, Clockwork, Prewar, 7 In.	540.00
Acrobat, Red, Blue, Yellow Plastic Body, Battery Operated, Tin, 9 1/2 In.	230.00
Acrobat, Windup, Tin, Chein	65.00
African Native, From Teddy Roosevelt Safari Set, Schoenhut, 7 1/2 In.	2750.00
Airplane, Air Control Tower, Battery Operated, Box, Cragstan	465.00
Airplane, Airmail, Kenton, 1920s, 10-In. Wingspan	950.00
Airplane, America, Trimotor, High Wing, Hubley, 13 In.	4400.00
Airplane, American Airlines, Battery Operated, 24-In. Wingspan	465.00
Airplane, American Airlines, Electra II, Battery Operated, 8 1/2 In.	245.00
Airplane, Aquaplane, Windup, Chein	225.00
Airplane, Army Bomber, Marx, 18-In. Wingspan	150.00
Airplane, Army Bomber, Windup, Tin, Marx	325.00
Airplane, B-36, Yonezawa, 1950, 36 In.	1995.00
Airplane, B-36-D Bomber, Friction, Tin, 1950, Large	1800.00
Airplane, B-50, Yonezawa, 19-In. Wingspan, Box	1095.00
Airplane, Biplane, Snoopy, Die Cast Metal, Aviva, 1965, 5 In.	35.00
Airplane, BOAC Constellation Sky Cruiser, Battery Operated, Marx, 7 In.	550.00
Airplane, Boeing Stratocruiser, Wyandotte	247.00
Airplane, Bomber, 4 Engine, Marx, 14 3/4 In.	150.00
Airplane, Bristol Britannia, Dinky Toy	340.00
Airplane, Buddy L, Pressed Steel, 27-In. Wingspan	295.00
Airplane, Buzzy, Pull Toy, Ideal, 7 In.	110.00
Airplane, Capital Airlines, Remote Control, Marx, 11 1/2 In.	135.00
Airplane, Cessna, Sky Lark, Friction Powered, Box, 11 In.	750.00
Airplane, China Clipper, Red, Blue, Wyandotte, 13 In.	125.00 to 160.00
Airplane, Circus Stunt, Yellow, Red, Die Cast, Green Box, Hubley, 1971	75.00
Airplane, Clockwork, Gunthermann, 8 1/2-In. Wingspan, 9 In.	2400.00
Airplane, Cox Corsair, F2G-1, Gas, Box	45.00
Airplane, Dogwood, Pilot, Windup, Marx	1300.00
Airplane, Fokker, Nickeled Wheels, Vindex, 8 1/4-In. Wingspan	6160.00
Airplane, Hell Cat, Hubley, 1950s	95.00
Airplane, Jet Fighter, Moving Wings, Battery Operated, Stop & Go Action, Grumman	175.00
Airplane, Jet, F6-761, Japan, Box, 12-In. Wingspan	395.00
Airplane, Keystone, Pressed Steel, 24-In. Wingspan	1275.00
Airplane, Lindy, Gray Underneath, Spring Wind Gear, Cast Iron, Hubley, 11 In.	880.00
Airplane, Loop The Loop, Battery Operated, Tin, Box	175.00
Airplane, Monoplane, Ikarus, Lehmann	6270.00
Airplane, Navy Jet, Box, Japan, 7-In. Wingspan	185.00
Airplane, North American F-86, Rocket X7, Tin, Box, Japan	110.00
Airplane, North American F-86, Sparking, Tin, Friction, Japan	140.00
Airplane, Northwest, DC-7C, Battery Operated, Box, 24-In. Wingspan	895.00
Airplane, Open Air, Wright Brothers, Muller & Kadeder	1485.00
Airplane, Pan Am, Airways China Clipper, Windup, Chein, 11-In. Wingspan	165.00
Airplane, Pan Am, Linemar, 18-In. Wingspan, Box	500.00
Airplane, Red Wings, Tan Body, Glossy Paint, Pressed Steel, Turer, 28-In. Wingspan	1400.00
Airplane, Roller, Pilot, Tin Lithograph, Plush, Schuco, 3 3/4 In.	810.00
Airplane, Rollover, Fighter, Windup, Tin, Marx, 6 In.	630.00

Airplane, Rollover, Prewar, Marx, Box	595.00
Airplane, Scout, Steelcraft, 2 Ft.	650.00
Airplane, Seaplane, Props Spin, Pilot, Passengers Lithograph In Windows, Chein, 1930s	265.00
Airplane, Seaplane, Spinning Propellers, Silver Tin Lithograph, Paya, 13 In.	165.00
Airplane, Spirit Of St. Louis, Friction, 12-In. Wingspan	295.00
Airplane, Spirit Of St. Louis, Gray, Silver, Wood, Unique Novelty Co.	140.00
Airplane, Spirit Of St. Louis, HTC, Japan, 12 In.	450.00
Airplane, Spirit Of St. Louis, Windup, Prop Turns, Tin, Girard, 13-In. Wingspan	985.00
Airplane, Spitfire, Hubley, 1950s	60.00
Airplane, Stingray, Friction, Tempest, Box, 1964	450.00
Airplane, Stunt, Pilot, Tin, Battery Operated, Marx	250.00
Airplane, Stunt, Pilot, Tin, Marx, Linemar, Box	195.00
Airplane, Stunt, Pilot, Windup, Marx, Box	195.00
Airplane, Super Sabre Navy Jet, Tin Bombs, Friction, Japan, 1950s	175.00
Airplane, Swallow, Fighter, Sparking, C-9, Battery Operated, Tin	175.00
Airplane, T.C.A., Japan, 15 1/2-In. Wingspan	145.00
Airplane, Tin Lithograph, Air Plane Go-Round, 8 1/2 In.	95.00
Airplane, Tin, Windup, England, 1940s, 10 In.	195.00
Airplane, TWA Constellation, Friction, 1960, 10 In.	185.00
Airplane, TWA, Boeing Super Jet, Battery Operated, 8 /12 In.	225.00
Airplane, TWA, DC-3, Stand, Ertl	50.00
Airplane, Twin Tail Cessna, Tin, Red & White Lithograph, Friction, W.S., 11 In.	175.00
Airplane, U.S. Mail, 22-In. Wingspan	852.50
Airplane, UN Freedom Plane, Plastic, Nosco, Box, 8 In.	135.00
Airplane, United Airlines, Super Main Liner, Wyandotte, 1930s, 12-In. Wingspan	175.00
Airplane, Windup, Tin, Prop Turns As Moved, Girard, 1920s, 9 In.	375.00
Airplane Set, Beechcraft, Starfire, Cutlass, Sabre Jets, Tootsietoy, Box, 4 In.	420.00
Airport, Tin Lithograph Hangar & Pylon, 3 Airplanes, Tootsietoy	770.00
Alf, Alien, Plush, Talking, 16 In.	24.00
Alligator, Jungle Pete, Clockwork, Box, 15 In.	450.00
Alligator, Snapping, Windup, Japan	225.00
Alligator, Steiff, 12 In.	75.00
Alligator, With Native, Tin, Chein, Windup	250.00
Alvin Chipmunk, Talking, Pull String, 19 In.	20.00
Ambulance, Bedford, Corgi	165.00
Ambulance, Cadillac, Matchbox Superfast, No. 54, Box	35.00
Ambulance, Canvas Sides, Keystone, 27 1/2 x 11 x 7 1/2 In.	660.00
Ambulance, Gunthermann, Box	1650.00
Ambulance, Military, Balloon Tires, Lift-Up Hinged Roof, France, c.1930, 7 In.	290.00
Ambulance, Pressed Steel, Wyandotte, 1930s	110.00
Ambulance, Schuco, Box	400.00
Ambulance, U.S. Army, Chevy Van, 1949	36.00
Ambulance, White Rubber Tires, Green Paint, 3 1/2 In.	25.00
American Flyer, Tank, Car, T-Slotted Couplers	25.00
Ant Farm, E. Joseph Cossman Co., Mid-1960s, 12 x 7 In.	30.00
Arty Trapeze Artist, Occupied Japan	220.00
Astronaut, Advances With Spark Action, Blue, Tin, Windup, 8 1/2 In.	995.00
Astronaut Space Helmet, Ideal, Box, 1960s	75.00
Auto Speedway, Automatic Toy Co.	125.00
Baby, Crawling, Bottle, Battery Operated, Japan, Box	100.00
Baby, Crawling, Crying Sound, Battery Operated, T.N. Japan, 12 In.	125.00
Baby, In Peanut, Celluloid, Japan, 5 In.	65.00
Baby Sandy, Child Star, Pull Toy, 1940	350.00
Badge, Arlene Airess Flying Club, Pinback	18.00
Badge, Space Patrol, Plastic, X-8 Spaceship, Gold Finish, Pin, 1 In.	75.00
Balky Mule, Lehmann, Box	495.00
Balky Mule, Tin, Windup, Marx, Postwar	165.00
Ball Shooter, Black Finish, Strauss, 8 1/2 In.	120.00
Balloon Blower, Gino Neopolitan, Box	165.00
Balloon Set, Hot Air, Raikes April & Johnnie, Cloth Clothing, 9 In., Pair	65.00
Barney Bear, Battery Operated, Box	140.00
Barney Google & Spark Plug, Scooter Toy, Tin	4200.00
Barrel Wagon, Horses, Black Driver, Cast Iron, Wilkins, 1895, 21 In.	1250.00

Bartender, Pours, Drinks, Lights Up, Smokes, Battery Operated, Box 95.00
Bears are also listed in the Teddy Bears category.
Bear, Baby, Clock Rings, Wakes, Yawns & Cries, Battery Operated, Box, Linemar 425.00
Bear, Beauty Parlor, Battery Operated, Box 1075.00
Bear, Bubble-Blowing Washing, Battery Operated, Box 475.00
Bear, Cashier, Battery Operated, Box 425.00
Bear, Clown, Windup, Gold Mohair, Red & Blue Felt, 12 In. 310.00
Bear, Coffee Time, Battery Operated, Box, Japan 395.00
Bear, Cubby, Reading, Windup, Box 125.00
Bear, Dancing, Glass Eyes, Tag, Box, Ideal, 11 In. 245.00
Bear, Dancing, Mohair, Glass Eyes, Metal Footed, Windup, 1930s, 5 1/2 In. 200.00
Bear, Dentist, Battery Operated, Box 650.00
Bear, Drumming, Windup, 1950s, Japan 95.00
Bear, Eating Corn, Windup, Tin Lithograph, Mouth Opens, Corn Spins, Japan, 1950 . . . 125.00
Bear, Fishing, String Of Tin Fish, Clockwork, Box, 5 In. 260.00
Bear, Golfer, Swings Club, Hits Ball Over Bridge Into Net, Windup, Tin, Japan, 4 In. . . . 325.00
Bear, Holding Tambourine, Red, Gray Stripe Pants, Metal Feet, 7 In. 35.00
Bear, Hoppie, Tin, Windup, Japan, Box, 4 1/2 In. 40.00
Bear, Log Rolling, Windup, Box 100.00
Bear, Mechanical, Red Fur, Ives 600.00
Bear, Mother Knitting, Battery Operated, Japan, Box 250.00
Bear, On Wheels, Brown Mohair, Voice Box, Steiff, 26 x 36 1/2 In. 742.00
Bear, Panda, Knitting, Windup, 1950s, Japan 775.00
Bear, Papa, Smokes Lit Pipe, Blows Smoke, Walks, Battery Operated, Japan . . . . . .75.00 to 145.00
Bear, Papa, Smoking, Battery Operated, Japan, 1950s 185.00
Bear, Plays Accordion, Windup 30.00
Bear, Sneezing, Eyes Light, Wipes Nose, Tin Kleenex Box, Battery Operated, Linemar . . 345.00
Bear, Walks & Growls, Brown, Windup 65.00
Bed, Doll's, 4-Poster, Curly Maple, Miniature 440.00
Bed, Doll's, 4-Poster, Mahogany 115.00
Bed, Doll's, 4-Poster, Maple, Walnut 330.00
Bed, Doll's, Wire Frame, 5 x 4 In. 24.00
Bed-Armoire, Doll's, Opens To Pull-Down Bed, Silk Quilt, Painted, c.1880, 25 In. 1200.00
Bell Ringer, Clown With Trick Poodle, 1890s 850.00
Bell Ringer, Frog Riding Turtle, 1890s 850.00
Bell Ringer, Little Nemo & Mr. Flip, Cast Iron, 1880s 650.00
Bellhop With Suitcase, Windup, Germany 95.00
Belt, Cowboy, Kid's Western, Leather, Topps, 1954 . . . . 14.00
Belt Buckle, Space Patrol, 1950s 125.00
Bicycles are listed in their own category.
Bicyclist, Kiddie, Unique Art 300.00
Big Parade, Battery Operated, Marx, Box 150.00
Big Parade, Key Wind, Marx 450.00
Billiard Players, 2 Men, Windup, Tin, 1920s, 7 x 13 In. 300.00
Billiard Table, Red Sides, Black Legs, Green Top, Yellow Accents, 15 In. 65.00
Binoculars, Tom Corbett . . . . .85.00 to 135.00
Bird, Canary, Singing, Celluloid, Occupied Japan, Box 225.00
Bird, Chirping, Windup, Germany, 1950s 185.00
Bird, Ostrich, Schoenhut 675.00
Birdcage, 2 Birds, Squeak, 1880s . . . .*Illus* 800.00
Black Boy, On Velocipede, Windup 2310.00
Blocks, Alphabet, Animals 1 Side, Girl Other Side, Schoenhut, Box, 1916, Set 1000.00
Blocks, Alphabet, Chromolithographed Paper, Wooden, Box, 24 Piece 75.00
Blocks, Building, Little Tots, Schoenhut, Wooden 75.00
Blocks, Building, Natural Brick, FAD Richter & Co., Box, 75 Piece 175.00
Blocks, Paper Covering, Different Scene Each Side, Set In Wagon, 3 3/4 x 12 In. 990.00
Boat, Aircraft Carrier, Plastic Airplanes, Renwal 260.00
Boat, Battleship, Indiana, Lithographed Paper On Wood 1375.00
Boat, Cabin Cruiser, Outboard, Langcraft, Box 100.00
Boat, Gunboat, Tin, Green & White Paint, Penny, Uebelaker 325.00
Boat, Hawk Speed, Clockwork, Green & White, Tin, Sutcliffe, Box, 12 In. 195.00
Boat, Hydroplane, Propeller, Wooden, 1950s, 22 In. 225.00
Boat, Impy Cabin Cruiser, Box, 16 In. 385.00

"Lead rot" is a disease of lead soldiers and other lead toys. Gray dust forms on the soldier and eventually the toy will disintegrate. It is not contagious but it often appears on a group of soldiers stored together because it is caused by oxidation brought on by the environment. It seems to appear if lead items are stored in new wooden cases (use metal cases). Old wooden cases that are sealed with latex paint seem safe.

Toy, Birdcage, 2 Birds, Squeak, 1880s

Boat, Jupiter Ocean Pilot Cruiser, Clockwork, Tin, Sutcliffe, 9 1/2 In.	195.00
Boat, Milky Way, Red, White, Blue, Tin, 1970, 8 3/4 In.	115.00
Boat, Navy, Metal L., Orkin, 16 In.	325.00
Boat, Ocean Liner, Bing	4025.00
Boat, Ocean Liner, Rotterdam, Travel Agent Model, Brass, 51 In.	2500.00
Boat, Ocean Liner, Windup, Tin, Paya, Spain, Box	220.00
Boat, P.T., Wooden, Japan, 22 In.	525.00
Boat, Paddlewheel, 13 In.	450.00
Boat, Paddlewheel, Clockwork, England, 1940s, 10 In.	185.00
Boat, Painted Tin, Clockwork, Fleishmann	575.00
Boat, Pond, S.S. Ettamog, 1935	3200.00
Boat, Pull Toy, Ocean Ware, Wooden	495.00
Boat, Queen Of The Sea, Battery Operated, Tin Lithograph, Box, 21 In.	575.00
Boat, Racing, Turnabout Racing Launch, Schuco, Box, 5 In.	325.00
Boat, Riverboat, New York, 3-Wheeler, Smokestack & Lifeboat, Cast Iron, 15 In.	3450.00
Boat, Sailboat, Hercules Peggy Jane, Chein	450.00
Boat, Sailboat, Tin Lithograph, Windup, France, c.1940, 5 In.	121.00
Boat, Silver Mariner, Cargo On Miniature Tanks, Battery Operated, Bandai, 15 In.	450.00
Boat, Speed King, Friction, Alps, 7 1/2 In.	185.00
Boat, Speed, Driver With Goggles, Helmet, White, Burgundy, Windup, Tin, Schuco	430.00
Boat, Speed, Lionel, No. 43, Original Figures, Flag, Box	1700.00
Boat, Speed, Pitt, Tin, Plastic, Schuco, Box	395.00
Boat, Speed, Windup, Japan, 7 1/2 In.	85.00
Boat, Static, Green, Hubley, 3 x 9 1/2 In.	3450.00
Boat, Troop Transport, Wooden, Tillicum, Milton Bradley, Box	350.00
Boat, Tug, Friction, Tin, Japan, 1950s	85.00
Boat, U.S. Cruiser Columbia, Lithographed Paper On Wood	3630.00
Boat, Windup, Ohio Art, 14 In.	160.00
Boat, Wood, Battery Operated, Japan, 17 In.	265.00
Bowling Alley, 10 Wooden Pins, Tin Lithograph, Ranger Steel Products, 30 In.	95.00
Box, Clothespins, Wooden, For Dolly's Clothes	16.00
Boxers, Hit & Miss, Windup, Kohner	95.00
Boy, Blowing Bubbles, Tin, Windup, 1950s, 8 In.	150.00
Boy, On Sled, Friction, Dayton	475.00
Boy, Traveling, Windup, Celluloid, Tin, Occupied Japan, Box	175.00
Brick Set, Build It Up	60.00
Bricks, Flexible Building, Auburn Rubber Co., Plastic, 1950s, 224 Piece	32.00
Bridge, Marklin, Embossed Texture, Hand Painted	50.00
Bucking Bronco, Windup, Celluloid, Japan, Box, 1950s	65.00
Buffalo Bill, On Horse, Metal, England, 1900-1910, 3 In.	385.00
Bugs Bunny, Plastic, Dakin, 1971, 10 In.	18.00
Building, Fire Department, Tin Lithograph, Toy Town	250.00
Bull, Fighting, Battery Operated	90.00
Bulldozer, 6 Wheels, Rubber, Auburn	45.00

Bulldozer, Battery Operated, Linemar, Box 230.00
Bulldozer, Orange, Red, Windup, Tin, Marx, 11 In. 375.00
Bulldozer, Orange, Teal Blue Robot Driver, Tin, 1950, 8 1/2 In. 575.00
Bullfighter, On Red Tin Wheels, Windup, Bull, Brown, Yellow Accents, Tin 175.00
Bunny, Eating Carrot, Windup, 1940s 55.00
Bunny, Pulling Tin Carrot, Babies, Celluloid, Windup, Box, Occupied Japan 155.00
Bus, Arcade Century Of Progress, White, Large 575.00
Bus, Arcade Century Of Progress, White, Small 375.00
Bus, BOAC, Plastic, Battery Operated, Remote Control, Box, Hong Kong, 6 In. 100.00
Bus, Century Of Progress, Cast Iron, Arcade, 10 1/2 In. 285.00
Bus, City, Red, Yellow, Chrome Radiator, Metal Wheels, Tin, 9 In. 143.00
Bus, Coast To Coast, Red & Blue, Wyandote, 21 In. 155.00
Bus, Cor-Cor, Metal, 6 Windows On Each Side, Black, 24 In. 100.00
Bus, Double-Decker, Cast Iron, Painted, Arcade, 1930s, 7 3/4 In. .... 230.00 to 400.00
Bus, Double-Decker, Driver, Kenton, 1933, 10 In. 750.00
Bus, Double-Decker, Inter-State, Mechanical, Strauss, 1930s 515.00
Bus, Double-Decker, Tin, Red, Yellow Gray, White Wheels, Germany, 4 In. 200.00
Bus, Fageol, Arcade, Cast Iron, 12 x 3 x 3 In. 345.00
Bus, G.M., Coach With Moving Passengers, Battery Operated, Blue, Silver, Box 400.00
Bus, Greyhound, 1933 Century Of Progress, Arcade, Cast Iron, 10 In. .... 245.00 to 440.00
Bus, Greyhound, Cruiser Coach, Arcade, 9 1/8 In. 300.00
Bus, Greyhound, Friction, Tin Lithograph, Japan, Box, 13 In. 75.00
Bus, Greyhound, Lithograph Of Passengers In Windows, Friction, Tin, 9 In. 65.00
Bus, Greyhound, No. 228, Pressed Steel, Windup, Painted, 1930s, 18 In. 230.00
Bus, Greyhound, Tin Lithograph, KTS, Box, 14 In. 275.00
Bus, Greyhound, Tin Lithograph, Plastic Wheels, Battery Operated, 7 In. 45.00
Bus, Greyhound, Tin, Friction, Buddy L, 1980s, 7 1/2 In. 40.00
Bus, Interstate, Windup, Strauss 295.00
Bus, Jitney, Straus, 1920s 600.00
Bus, Orange, Black Trim, Nickel Plated Wheels, Cast Iron, Dent, 8 x 3 x 2 1/2 In. 575.00
Bus, Pressed Steel, 6 Wheels, 2 Spares, 11 Open Windows, Buddy L, 29 In. 8050.00
Bus, Remote Control, Flashing Lights, Gray, Tin, 15 1/2 In. 395.00
Bus, School Line, Bonnet Style, Japan, 1950s, 7 In. 495.00
Bus, School Yellow, Friction, Tin Lithograph, Linemar, 1950s, 6 In. 85.00
Bus, School, Volkswagen, Box, 12 In. 85.00
Bus, Touring, Shanghai 516, Siren, Friction, Tin, China, 15 In. 27.00
Bus, Transportation, Buddy L 4285.00
Bus, Volkswagen, 2-Tone Green, Miniature, Corgi 175.00
Bus, Wolverine Express, Box, 14 In. 200.00
Bus, World's Fair, New York, Arcade, 8 1/4 In. 600.00
Busy Lizzy, Uses Carpet Sweeper, Tin Lithograph, Germany, 1915 .... 950.00
Butcher Shop, Paper, Wood, Composition, 30 Pieces Of Meat, 19th Century 1430.00
Butterfly, Windup, Tin 75.00
Cabinet, Kitchen, Hoosier Type, Zinc Service, 50 In. 775.00
Cable Car, San Francisco, Tin Lithograph, Friction, Bell Ringer, Japan, 7 In. 110.00
Cadet, Marching, Windup, Celluloid, Tin, Japan, Prewar, Box 295.00
California Raisins, Tambourine Girl, Yellow Shoes, Windup 55.00
Camel, Cast Iron Wheels, Button, Steiff, 1913, 16 In. 695.00
Camel, Steiff, 5 1/2 In. 80.00
Camel, Wrinkled Knees, Blue, Knickerbocker 95.00
Camera, Yogi Bear, Black, Plastic, Hanna-Barbera, Box, 3 1/2 In. 44.00
Canadian Mountie, Reliable Toy Co. 75.00
Cane, Bat Masterson 65.00
Cannon, Dive Bomber, Metal Cap, 72 Caps, Callen Mfg. Co., 1965, 5 In., Pair 25.00
Cannon, Iron, David N. Carlin, Highgrade Toys, 7-In. Barrel, 14 1/2-In. Carriage 80.00
Cannon, Mobile Artillery Unit, Revolving Radar Screen, Blinking Light, Tin, Box 225.00
Cannon, Shoots Caps, Cast Iron, 5 1/2 In. 325.00
Cannon, Young America Rapid Fire Gun, Copperplated, Marbles, 1907, 15 In. ... 300.00 to 395.00
Cannon & Caisson, Wooden, Reddish-Orange Pinstriping, Schoenhut 775.00
Cap Bomb, Bear & Black Boy, Wield Hammers, Cast Iron 2000.00
Cap Bomb, Devil's Head, Fires .22 Caliber Blank, Ives, 2 1/4 In. .... *Illus* 275.00
Cap Gun, Atomic Disintegrator, No. 270, Die Cast, Zinc Finish, Hubley, 1954 .... 425.00
Cap Gun, Best Butter, Dark Japan Finish, 5 3/4 In. 2090.00

Left to Right: Toy, Cap Gun, Butting Match, Animated, 2 Boys, Ives, 5 In.
Toy, Cap Gun, Shoot The Hat, Animated, Japan Finish, 4 3/4 In.
Toy, Cap Bomb, Devil's Head, Fires .22 Caliber Blank, Ives, 2 1/4 In.
Toy, Cap Strike, Sambo & Bear, Cast Iron, Black, Red & Blue Painted

Cap Gun, Butting Match, Animated, 2 Boys, Ives, 5 In. ....*Illus*	910.00
Cap Gun, Captain, Kilgore	85.00
Cap Gun, Challenge, Cast Iron	140.00
Cap Gun, Circle K, Falcon	22.00
Cap Gun, Colt 45, Gold Revolving Cylinder, Presentation Box, Hubley	295.00
Cap Gun, Detective, Silver Metal	16.00
Cap Gun, Echo	825.00
Cap Gun, Fanner 50, Mattel	39.00
Cap Gun, Federal Kilgore No. 1, Embossed Lettering, 5 1/4 In.	45.00
Cap Gun, Hubley Star, 7 In.	18.00
Cap Gun, Johnnie's Little Gun, Ives, 11 In.	1100.00
Cap Gun, Just Out, Animated, Cast Iron, Ives	5800.00
Cap Gun, Kit Carson	45.00
Cap Gun, Lightning Express, Animated, Broken Spring, U.S., 1913, 5 In.	240.00
Cap Gun, Locomotive, Animated, Kenton, 5 In.	715.00
Cap Gun, Me & My Buddy	135.00
Cap Gun, Mountie, Pop-Up Magazine, Plastic Grips, Kilgore, Box, 1950	45.00
Cap Gun, Paul Jones, Rubber Band Type, Stand-Up Indians & Soldiers, Box, 1920s	275.00
Cap Gun, Presto, No. 18, Pop-Up Cap Magazine, Kilgore, Cast Iron, Box	12500.00
Cap Gun, Punch & Judy, Animated, Ives, 5 1/4 In.	1320.00
Cap Gun, Ric-O-Shay, Revolving Cylinder, Fires Roll Caps, Box, Hubley	385.00
Cap Gun, Rifleman, Box, 1959	700.00
Cap Gun, Sea Serpent	750.00
Cap Gun, Shoot The Hat, Animated, Japan Finish, 4 3/4 In. ....*Illus*	1320.00
Cap Gun, Shootin' Shell .45, Die Cast, Mattel, 1960	225.00
Cap Gun, Texan Jr., Hubley, 1950s	55.00
Cap Gun, Texan Jr., Marble Grip, Hubley, Pair	110.00
Cap Gun, Texas Jack, Ives, c.1886	200.00
Cap Gun, Windup, Black Plastic, Steel, Mattel, 1960s, 13 In.	35.00
Cap Strike, Sambo & Bear, Cast Iron, Black, Red & Blue Painted ....*Illus*	850.00
Captain Kangaroo Magic Slate, 1960s	20.00
Car, 777 Hot Rod, Battery Operated, Marx, 11 In.	295.00
Car, Armored Command, Gerry Anderson, Sparks, No. 602, Dinky Toys, Box	145.00
Car, Army Staff, Windup, Marx, 1940s, 11 In.	260.00
Car, Batmobile, Battery Operated, Hard Plastic, 1989	350.00
Car, Batmobile, Firing Rockets, Chain Cutter, Batman, Robin, Metal, Corgi, 1973, 5 In. ...	150.00
Car, Bentley, 2 Door Convertible, Gray Paint Finish, Die Cast Metal, Dinky, 4 In.	41.00
Car, Black Beauty, Green, 1966, Corgi, 5 In.	386.00
Car, Bouncing Benny, Windup, Marx	135.00
Car, Buick, 1958 Model, Red & White, Bandai, 8 In.	235.00
Car, Buick, Century, Convertible, White, Yellow Interior, Plastic, 3 1/4 x 8 x 2 In.	85.00
Car, Buick, Coupe, Green, Black, Rubber, Metal Spare Tire, Arcade, 3 x 8 In.	6325.00
Car, Buick, LeSabre, Light Green, 8 In.	485.00

Car, Buick, Plastic Windshield, Tin Steering Wheel, Tin, 10 1/2 In. 1470.00
Car, Buick, Riviera, Giant Door-Matic, Haji, Box 375.00
Car, Buick, Sedan, 1927 Model, Arcade 2530.00
Car, Bump 'n Go Action, Girl Turning, Battery Operated, Tin, 12 In. 29.00
Car, Cable, HO Scale, Motorized, Accessories, Eheim 195.00
Car, Cadillac, Coupe, 1931, Tin, Windup, Marx 1075.00
Car, Cadillac, Linemar Friction, Tin Lithograph, Box, 1950s, 2 x 6 1/4 x 2 In. 160.00
Car, Cadillac, Musical, Battery Operated, Box 450.00
Car, Carette, Red, 9 In. 950.00
Car, Chevrolet, Bel Air, 2-Tone, Blue, Green, Plastic, 1956, 3 x 8 x 2 In. 85.00
Car, Chevrolet, Corvair, Corgi 320.00
Car, Chevrolet, Coupe, Arcade, Gray Body, Black Fender, 8 1/4 In. 4950.00
Car, Chevrolet, Linemar, Black, Gray, 1954, 11 In. 3300.00
Car, Chevrolet, Occupied Japan, Box, 5 In. 110.00
Car, Chevy Secret Agent, Battery Operated, 14 In. 250.00
Car, Chrysler, Airflow, Red, Electric Lights, Windup, Kingsbury, 14 x 4 In. 460.00
Car, Citroen Convertible, Green, Friction, Bandai, 1960s, 8 In. 375.00
Car, Convertible, Kaiser, Box, 10 1/2 In. 335.00
Car, Convertible, Windup, Red, Yellow Windshield, Plastic Masters, 7 In. 125.00
Car, Corvair, 1963 Model, Friction, Lithograph Interior, Tinted Windows, 8 In. 93.00
Car, Corvette, Die Cast, Hubley, 12 1/2 In. 195.00
Car, Corvette, Metal, Rubber Wheels, Dark Blue, Tootsietoy, 1950s, 1 1/4 x 4 x 1 In. 28.00
Car, Corvette, Split-Window, Battery Operated, Maroon, Ichiko, 1963, 12 In. 550.00
Car, Country Squire Wagon, Buddy L, Box 295.00
Car, Couple, No. 36C, Dinky Toy 80.00
Car, Cowboy Whoopie, Tin, Windup, Marx, 1932 .... 475.00
Car, Crazy, Driver, Tin, Windup, Mexican Version, Disney Lithograph, Marx, 6 In. 368.00
Car, DeSoto Diplomat, Dinky Toy 187.00
Car, Dora Dipsy, Red, Yellow, Striped Tin Wheels, Marx, 6 1/2 In. 105.00
Car, Electrimobile, Battery Operated, Japan, 8 1/2 In. 100.00
Car, Elektro Amphibio, Battery Operated, Schuco, Box 450.00
Car, Felix, Metal, 1930s, 2 1/4 In. 285.00
Car, Ferrari Berlinetta, Matchbox Superfast, No. 75, Box 40.00
Car, Ferrari, Servo, Schuco, Box 975.00
Car, Fire Chief, Blinking Red Light On Top, 2-Tone Red, White, Tin 95.00
Car, Fire Chief, Cortland 100.00
Car, Fire Chief, Friction Powered, Japan, Tin, Box 85.00
Car, Fire Chief, Kingsbury, 1930s 650.00
Car, Firebird, Indy Style, Inflatable Tires, Battery Operated, Box, 14 In. 1800.00
Car, Flivver, Coupe, Buddy L, Original Paint, 1920s ....575.00 to 700.00
Car, Flivver, Flintstone, Friction, Marx, 1962 .... 475.00
Car, Flivver, Pickup, Buddy L, No. 210, Bent Windshield Posts, 1920s ....805.00 to 1100.00
Car, Flivver, Tin, Windup, Bing, 1924, 6 1/4 In. 595.00
Car, Ford, 2-Tone, Pulling U-Haul, Tin 145.00
Car, Ford, Coupe, Cast Iron, Kilgore 495.00
Car, Ford, Coupe, Schuco, 1917 .... 150.00
Car, Ford, Fairlane 500, Skyliner, Battery Operated, Dark Blue, Box 495.00
Car, Ford, Galaxie, Red Plastic, 1963 .... 25.00
Car, Ford, Mustang, Engine Sound, Remote Control, Tin Lithograph Interior, Japan, 6 In. .. 165.00
Car, Ford, Mustang, Fastback, Corgi 220.00
Car, Ford, Pick-Up, Blue, White Lettering, Load Of Tires In Back, 1951 .... 25.00
Car, Ford, Pulling U-Haul, Kyow 145.00
Car, Ford, Sedan, Nickel-Plated Driver, Painted, Arcade, 1930s, 6 1/2 In. 220.00
Car, Ford, T-Bird, Convertible, Battery Operated, Tin, Cragstan, Box 265.00
Car, Ford, T-Bird, Promo, 2-Door, Light Green, 1964, 8 In. 53.00
Car, Ford, T-Bird, Slot, Yellow Body, 1960, 3 In. 362.00
Car, Ford, T-Bird, Yellow Polyethylene, Red, Wheels, Plastic, 1950, 12 In. 47.00
Car, Ford, Thunderbird, White, 1962 .... 25.00
Car, Ford, Torino, Radio Controlled TV's Starsky & Hutch, Box, 11 In. 50.00
Car, Ford, Yellow, California Or Bust, Hubley, 7 1/2 In. 225.00
Car, Friction, Clark, 1894, 10 1/2 In. 2310.00
Car, Funny Flivver, Driver In Red, Brown, Tin, Windup, Marx, 7 In. 350.00
Car, Golden Arrow Racer, Pressed Steel, Kingsbury, 1930s 920.00

Toy, Car, Horseless Carriage,
Naughty Boy, Windup, Lehmann, 1900

Toy, Car, Packard
Sedan, Turner

Car, Golden Jubilee, Man, Battery Operated, Tin, Japan, 1950s	185.00
Car, Gooney, Battery Operated, Alps	125.00
Car, Graham Paige, No. 3, Windup, Tin, Automatic Stopper, Japan, Box, 6 In.	187.00
Car, Green Hornet, Missile & Rocket	245.00
Car, Happy Chick, Rooster, Bouncing Up & Down, Tin, Yonezawa, 5 In.	230.00
Car, Highway Patrol Police, Blinking Red Light On Top, Tin, Battery Operated, Box	.75.00 to 95.00
Car, Hornby, Lumber, Box	15.00
Car, Horseless Carriage, Naughty Boy, Windup, Lehmann, 1900 ....*Illus*	660.00
Car, Hot Red, Nylint	55.00
Car, Issemayer, Lithograph, Red, Black, Tin Wheels	25.00
Car, Jaguar, Premate, Schuco, Silver	650.00
Car, Jaguar, S.K.E., Bandi	95.00
Car, Jalopy, Box, Marx	475.00
Car, Kingsbury Golden Arrow Racer, Gilt Paint, 21 In.	1540.00
Car, Knight Rider, 1982, 1/64 Scale	7.00
Car, Land Rover, Cast Metal, Dinky Toy, 1950s, 3 1/2 In.	58.00
Car, Limousine, Airport, Friction, 5 In.	155.00
Car, Limousine, Red, Black, Gold Lithograph, Tin, Battery Operated, Japan, 1960	82.00
Car, Lincoln Touring, Nickeled Wheels, A.C. Williams	825.00
Car, Lincoln, Zephyr, Cast Iron, Hubley, 6 In.	275.00
Car, Mercedes-Benz, Blinking Rear Window, Logo On Front & Wheels, Red, Tin	120.00
Car, Mercedes-Benz, Red, Black, 1950s	400.00
Car, Mercedes-Benz, Slot Cars, Marx, 5 In.	250.00
Car, Mercury Comet, Plastic, Silver, 1960 License Plates, 2 1/2 x 7 1/4 In.	45.00
Car, MG Midget, Convertible, 2 Seats, Light Green, Die Cast Metal, Dinky Toy, 3 In.	56.00
Car, MG, Convertible, Tin Lithograph, Japan, 6 1/2 In.	145.00
Car, MG, Magnette Mark III, Convertible, Box, Friction, Japan, 8 1/4 In.	360.00
Car, Milton Berle	550.00
Car, Model 1955 Convertible, Turquoise, Tin, Friction, Bandai, 11 In.	650.00
Car, Model 1958 Ford T-Bird, Convertible, Tin, Battery Operated, Japan, 11 In.	380.00
Car, Model 1959 Cadillac HT, Yellow, White, Friction, Bandai, 12 In.	225.00
Car, Model 1960s Porsche, Red, Battery Operated, Bandai, 10 1/2 In.	185.00
Car, Mr. Magoo, Battery Operated, Hubley, Box, c.1961	375.00 to 475.00
Car, Nutty Mad, Friction, Linemar, Box, 4 In.	260.00
Car, Old Jalopy, Windup, Marx	150.00
Car, Oldsmobile 98, Green, Black, 1959	89.50
Car, Open Touring, Fisher, 10 In.	1250.00
Car, Open Touring, Hubley	990.00
Car, Packard Sedan, Turner ....*Illus*	2640.00
Car, Packard Traffic, Tin, Friction, 6 In.	135.00
Car, Packard, Schuco, Box	2100.00
Car, Pedal, 3 Wheels, Chocolate Tin, France	9350.00
Car, Pet Mobile, Bronco, With Pets, Nylint	125.00
Car, Peter Rabbit, Crazy, Windup, Marx	125.00
Car, Police, Battery Operated, Alps, Box, 14 In.	260.00
Car, Police, Chevrolet Impala, Ichicko, Tin, Box, 7 1/2 In.	75.00

Car, Police, Ford Zephyr, White Painted Finish, Die Cast Metal, Corgi, 4 In. 50.00
Car, Police, Highway Patrol, Black & White, Blinking Light On Top 95.00
Car, Police, Mercedes-Benz, Ichicko, Tin, Box, 7 1/2 In. 95.00
Car, Police, Porsche, Battery Operated, Box, Asher Toys 75.00
Car, Police, Volkswagen, Battery Operated, 13 In. 650.00
Car, Police, Volkswagen, Schuco, Box 340.00
Car, Police, With Sidecar, Marx 300.00
Car, Porsche, Red Painted Finish, Chrome, Tin, Battery Operated, Japan, 10 In. 128.00
Car, Racing, 7-Up, Tin, Japan, Taiyo, 10 1/2 In. 595.00
Car, Racing, A.C. Williams, Cast Iron, Red Paint, c.1925, 5 1/2 In. 145.00
Car, Racing, Alfa Romeo, Cast Iron, 1929 .... 4000.00
Car, Racing, Asahi, Battery Operated, Box 295.00
Car, Racing, Aston Martin, Red Painted Finish, Die Cast Metal, Corgi, 3 1/2 In. 29.00
Car, Racing, Atom, 16 In. 395.00
Car, Racing, Battery Operated, Japan, 6 1/2 In. 165.00
Car, Racing, Bremer Whirlwind, Dennymite Powered 3295.00
Car, Racing, Corvette, Korris, Plastic, 13 In. 95.00
Car, Racing, Driver, Cast Iron, Painted, 1920s, 5 In. 150.00
Car, Racing, Ferraris, No. 2 .... 450.00
Car, Racing, Ferraris, No. 7 .... 450.00
Car, Racing, Ford, GT, Tin, Battery Operated, Blue Finish, Japan, 10 1/2 In. 55.00
Car, Racing, Gallop, Tin, Windup, Yellow, Blue, Red & Cream, Lehman, 1913, 6 In. 1090.00
Car, Racing, Hess Speedster, Red, Black, 8 In. 495.00
Car, Racing, International, Slot Cars, 1950s 225.00
Car, Racing, Maserati, Metal Hubs, Dinky 100.00
Car, Racing, Matra, Ready To Run, Schuco, Box 475.00
Car, Racing, Mercedes-Benz, 230, White, Box 550.00
Car, Racing, Mercedes-Benz, Schuco, Box .... 290.00 to 310.00
Car, Racing, Mercedes-Benz, Silver, Blue, West Germany, Box, 10 In. 750.00
Car, Racing, Mercedes-Benz, U.S. Zone, Metallic Blue 395.00
Car, Racing, Micro, Schuco, Box .... 225.00 to 325.00
Car, Racing, Porsche, Bandai, Box 295.00
Car, Racing, Renault, Steel, Windup, Composition Driver, Black, France, 14 In. 1295.00
Car, Racing, Rider, T.N. Toys 325.00
Car, Racing, Schuco Studio, Red, 2nd Edition, Box 650.00
Car, Racing, Schuco Studio, Yellow, 2nd Edition, Box 750.00
Car, Racing, Schuco, Original Nickel, 1950s 95.00
Car, Racing, Skoglund & Olsen, Black, Red Wheels, Cast Iron, 1930, 7 In. 3650.00
Car, Racing, Speed Of The Wind, Dinky Toy 59.00
Car, Racing, Starburst, Dual Cockpit, 11 In. 1200.00
Car, Racing, Super Hot Rod, Bulbs Flash, Battery Operated, Tin, Marx, 11 In. 435.00
Car, Racing, Thimble Drome Special, Gas-Powered, Blue 335.00
Car, Racing, Tin Lithograph, Metal Wheels, Windup, 11 1/2 In. 110.00
Car, Racing, Tyrel, Ready To Run, Schuco, Box 450.00
Car, Racing, U.S. Zone, Blue, Schuco, Box 700.00
Car, Racing, Windup, General Toy Of Canada, 4 3/4 In. 125.00
Car, Racing, Yellow, Orange, Windup, Tin, England, 7 In. 195.00
Car, Radio, Windup, Built-In Music Box, Schuco 290.00
Car, Rambler Station Wagon, Bandai 145.00
Car, Reo Coupe, 1931 Model 1870.00
Car, Roadster, Cast Iron, 6 In. 95.00
Car, Roadster, Dayton Friction Toy Co., c.1930 .... 750.00
Car, Roadster, Doepke 1954 MG, Red, Black Paint, Silver Trim, 15 In. 145.00
Car, Roadster, Monkey Driver, Key Wind, Schuco 9020.00
Car, Roadster, Red, Cast Iron Driver, Windup, Tin, Kingsbury, 10 x 4 x 3 In. 316.00
Car, Rocket Rover, Marx 975.00
Car, Rodeo Joe, Crazy, Windup, Unique .... 195.00 to 250.00
Car, Roll Over, Windup, Tin, 1940s 95.00
Car, Rollevox, Schuco 1250.00
Car, Rolls-Royce, Bandai, White Convertible 250.00
Car, Rolls-Royce, Convertible, Bandai, Box, 12 In. 750.00
Car, Rolls-Royce, Spot-On, Maroon 330.00
Car, Rumble Seat Sedan, Arcade, Cast Iron, 5 In. 195.00

Car, Sanyo Continental, III, White Top, Green, Box, 9 In. 675.00
Car, Sedan, Buick, Green, Black, Rubber Tires, Arcade, 3 1/2 x 8 1/2 In. 5175.00
Car, Sedan, Cadillac, 4 Door, Gray, 1950, Marusan, 12 x 3 x 5 In. 460.00
Car, Sedan, Champion, Delivery 525.00
Car, Sedan, Chevrolet, Arcade, Black Overall, Cast Iron, 1925, 7 In. 825.00
Car, Sedan, Driver & Screen Grill, Cast Iron, Original Paint, Arcade, 6 1/2 In. 775.00
Car, Sedan, LaSalle, Orange, Green, 1937, Kenton, 4 1/2 In. 850.00
Car, Sedan, O.J. Simpson, Friction 65.00
Car, Sedan, Pontiac, Green, Black, 1936, Kenton, 4 1/2 In. 395.00
Car, Sedan, With Opening Hood, Schuco 450.00
Car, Service Station, Pressed Board & Plastic, Station Folds Up, 9 1/4 x 22 In. 120.00
Car, Space Patrol, Blue, White, Battery Operated, Box, 1955 . . . . 1265.00
Car, Space Patrol, Red, Rotating Lights, Blue Car, 1950, 8 In. 3737.00
Car, Space, Friction, Japan 150.00
Car, Speed Boy Delivery, Marx 350.00
Car, Speed King, No. 16, 1950s, 8 In. 650.00
Car, Speedo, Schuco 325.00
Car, Stan & Ollie In Lizzie, 1974 . . . . 195.00
Car, Station Wagon, Buddy L, Teepee Camp Trailer 95.00
Car, Studebaker, Commander, Clockwork Motor, Blue, Germany, 1954, 5 1/2 In. 175.00
Car, Studebaker, Golden Hawk, Corgi 210.00
Car, Studebaker, Occupied Japan, Box, 5 In. 110.00
Car, Studebaker, World's Fair 1934, Gold, National Products 550.00
Car, Take Apart Roadster, Cast Iron, Hubley, 6 1/8 In. 262.00
Car, Tom & Jerry Comic, Battery Operated, Tin, Japan, Box, 11 1/2 In. 280.00
Car, Touring, 7 Passenger, Friction, 7 1/4 In. 375.00
Car, Touring, Black, Gold & Red, Metal Wheels, Lever Action, Tin, 1950s, 7 In. 33.00
Car, Touring, Dayton, Friction, Tin, Jewelry, 1900s, 13 1/2 In. 750.00
Car, Toyota, James Bond, Corgi 632.00
Car, Treasure Hunt, Hot Wheels 50.00
Car, Tricky Taxi, Windup, Black & White, Marx 75.00
Car, Volkswagen, Bandai, 7 In. 200.00
Car, Volkswagen, Battery Operated, Box, 9 1/2 x 4 x 3 3/4 In. 175.00
Car, Volkswagen, Battery Operated, Red, Japan, Box, 11 In. 100.00
Car, Volkswagen, Battery Operated, White, Tin, Japan, 10 In. 145.00
Car, Volkswagen, Coupe, Red Lithograph, Battery Operated, Japan 52.00
Car, What's Wrong, Windup, Distler, Germany, 1920s 1100.00
Car, Woody Station Wagon, With Camper, Clockwork, 6 In. & 8 In., 2 Piece 750.00
Car, Wyandotte, Pressed Steel, 1930s, 11 In. 295.00
Car Set, Dukes Of Hazzard, Die Cast, Photos Of The Cast, Box, Ertl, 1981, 4 Piece 54.00
Carnival Shooting Gallery, Ohio Art, Box 160.00
Carousel, 4 Horses, Tin Lithograph, Complete, 1953 . . . . 175.00
Carousel, Wyandotte, 1930s, 5 1/4 In. 295.00
Carriage, Doll's, Columbia Carriage & Rattan Co. 1100.00
Carriage, Doll's, Folding Leather Canopy, Wood Handle, Wilson Carriage Co., 32 In. . . . 365.00
Carriage, Doll's, Folding Steel Frame, Brown Leatherized Fabric Covering, 22 In. 50.00
Carriage, Doll's, Hood, Wicker 250.00
Carriage, Doll's, Joel Ellis, Wooden, Painted 385.00
Carriage, Doll's, Pull Toy, Blue Eyes, Closed Mouth, Tin, Goodwin, 11 In. 2000.00
Carriage, Doll's, Wicker, Shirley Temple 895.00
Carriage, Doll's, Wooden, Painted, Leatherized Cloth, Adjustable Shade, Fringe, 33 In. . . 355.00
Carrier, Car, Mack, Tootsietoy 275.00
Carrying Case, Tammy, Blue Vinyl, 1960s 25.00
Cart, Bunny & Carrot, Plastic, Tin, Japan 106.00
Cart, Donkey, Friction, Tin, Alps Japan, 4 1/2 In. 175.00
Cart, Mule, Gloomy Gus, Tin Cart, Cast Iron Mule, Removable Figure 325.00
Cart, Pig, Boy Driver, Bell, Cast Iron, 6 1/4 In. 287.00
Cart, Rooster, Pulls, Chick Jumps Up & Down, Tin, Windup, 1930, 7 1/2 In. 485.00
Cart, Wooden, Yellow Stenciled Dandy, Red Paint, Tongue, 33 In. 192.00
Case, Tinkerbell, Vinyl, 1970s, Miniature 25.00
Cash Register, Little Storekeeper, Red Crinkled Finish, Red, Tin, 1950-1960 . . . . 40.00
Cash Register, Tom Thumb, Bell Sound, Western Stamping Co., 1950s 65.00
Cat, Felix, Decal On Chest & Foot, Wood Jointed, Schoenhut, 1925, 4 In. 265.00

Cat, Felix, Mohair Stuffed, Jointed, Glass Eyes, c.1930, 13 In. 192.00
Cat, Felix, On Scooter, Gunthermann 1250.00
Cat, Felix, On Scooter, Orange Base, Nifty 1450.00
Cat, Felix, Squeaker In Chest, Glass Eyes, Metal Nose, 1920-1930, 15 In. 485.00
Cat, Felix, Wood Jointed, Decals, Schoenhut, 1920s, 8 In. 450.00
Cat, Felix, Wood Jointed, Decals, Schoenhut, 1925, 4 In. .... 165.00 to 260.00
Cat, Knitting, Holding 2 Knitting Needles, Windup, Box, Japan .... 95.00 to 125.00
Cat, Playful, Windup, Japan, Box, 1960s 60.00
Cat, Rag, Dark Brown Velvet, Glass Eyes, Embroidered, 12 In. 70.00
Cat, Roll Over, Windup, Marx, Box 165.00
Cat, Roll Over, Windup, Tin, Celluloid, Japan 60.00
Cat, Susi, Composition, Steiff, 13 In. 125.00
Cat, Turnover, Windup, Japan 60.00
Cat In The Hat, Dr. Seuss, 30 In. 42.00
Cement Mixer, Wonder, Cast Iron, Hubley, 3 5/8 In. 425.00
Chair, Doll's, Wooden, Black Over Brown, 1870, 13 In. 525.00
Chariot, Female Driver, Pulled By 3 Horses, Hubley 950.00
Charlie The Drumming Clown, Battery Operated, 6 Actions, Alps, Box 275.00
Charlie's Angels, Sabrina, Kris, Kelly, On Card, 8 In., 3 Piece 125.00
Chef, Skater, Windup, Cloth Pants, Japan, 1950s 300.00
Chicken, Egg-Laying, Metal, Red, Yellow, White, Chicken On Red Base, 8 In. 5.00
Chicken, On Wheels, Flaps Wings, Hand-Painted, Windup, Box, Bavaria 575.00
Child In Clown Costume, On Stick, Revolving Body, Bisque Head, 10 1/2 In. 245.00
Chimpanzee, Flipping, Windup, T.P.S., 4 1/2 In. 175.00
Circus, Overland With Lion, Kenton, 1940s 250.00
Circus, Schoenhut, 10 Piece 550.00
Circus, Three Ring, Pull Toy, Wonderblox, Box, 1950s 95.00
Circus, Wagon, 2 Bears And Flag, Plus Tongue, Steiff, 9 In. 220.00
Circus Acrobat, Mechanical, Irwin, Box 200.00
Circus Wagon, Arcade, Circus Pole, Red, Yellow, 28 In. 185.00
Circus Wagon, Cage, Schoenhut 2100.00
Circus Wagon, Driver, Lion & Tiger In Cage, Pressed Steel, 1830s, 13 x 9 3/4 In. ... 1095.00
Clarinet, Emanee, Box 20.00
Claw Digger, Table Model, Cast Iron 1900.00
Clown, Bisque Head, Pull Toy, Germany 850.00
Clown, Carnival, 3 Balls, Knock Off Hat, 10 Cents, 1950s 1950.00
Clown, Climbing, Battery Operated, Japan 1450.00
Clown, Clockwork, Chein, 8 In. 1450.00
Clown, Cloth & Celluloid, Tin Head, Moves On Hands While Juggling, Windup, 10 In. ... 360.00
Clown, Crazy, Windup Head, Box, Japan, 1960s 120.00
Clown, Drumming, Schuco, Box 650.00
Clown, Handstand, Key Wind, Chein .... 50.00 to 95.00
Clown, High Jinks Circus, Battery Operated, Alps For Cragstan, c.1950 .... 375.00
Clown, Hobo, Playing Cymbals, Windup, Japan 95.00
Clown, In Cart, Mule, Windup, Tinplate, Germany, Pat. 1/22/07, 7 1/2 In. 450.00
Clown, Jimmy The Acrobat, Box 275.00
Clown, Jointed At Shoulders, Hips & Neck, Blue Ribbon Shoe Co., 15 1/2 In. 250.00
Clown, On Cart, Clockwork, Unique Art, 7 In. 730.00
Clown, On Donkey, Tin, Windup, Germany, Prewar 450.00
Clown, On Motorcycle, Clockwork, Prewar, Japan, 6 In. 1375.00
Clown, Papier-Mache, Yellow Cap, Closed Smiling Mouth, 1885, Germany, 8 In. 50.00
Clown, Puncher, Flails At Celluloid Bag, Tin, Windup, Chein, 8 1/2 In. 770.00
Clown, Roller Skating, Tin & Cloth, Windup, Japan, Box .... 375.00 to 450.00
Clown, Roly Poly Circus, Box, 6 In. 350.00
Clown, Roly Poly, Composition, 11 In. 280.00
Clown, Scolding Donkey, Penny, Meir 475.00
Clown, Skipping, West Germany, 1950s 495.00
Clown, Tumbling, Schuco 1100.00
Clown, Uncle Joey, Battery Operated, Box, 16 In. 70.00
Clown, Violinist, Vibrates Around Playing Violin, Germany, 4 1/2 In. 190.00
Clown, Walking Happy, Windup, Box 115.00
Clown, Walking, Holding Rod, Satin Cloth Body, Tin, Japan, 10 In. 70.00
Clown, Walks On Hands, Celluloid, Windup, Occupied Japan 295.00

Clown, With Tumbling Monkey & Bell, Clockwork, Prewar, Japan, 10 In. 1550.00
Coach, Horse Drawn, Painted Wagon, Tin, 9 In. 225.00
Coach, Observation, Dinky Toy 165.00
Coatrack, Yogi Bear, 1979 . . . . 50.00
Cock Fight, Multicolored Tin Lithograph, Windup, Japan, 7 In. 140.00
Colorforms, Beetlejuice, Sealed 32.00
Colorforms, CHIPS, Box, 1981 . . . . 19.00
Colorforms, Munsters Cartoon Kit, Munsters' Home, Black & White, 1960, 12 x 8 In. . . 47.00
Colorforms, Play Set, Twiggy, Box, 1967 . . . . 45.00
Commando Joe, Ohio Art, Box 285.00
Construction Set, Bild-A-Set, Cardboard, Wood, D.A. Pachter Co., 1943, 170 Piece . . . 50.00
Cop, Motorcycle, Rubber, Auburn 30.00
Cornelius, Planet Of The Apes, Bend 'n Flex, Mego, On Card, 5 In. 30.00
Couch, Fainting, Doll's, Victorian 75.00
Couple In Bed, Naughty, Action, Adult Pull Toy, Box, 1970 . . . . 30.00
Cowboy, On Horse, Windup, 1938, Marx . . . . .145.00 to 175.00
Cowboy, On Rocking Horse, Windup, Japan 65.00
Cowboys & Indians Set, Plastic, Marx, 1964, 12 Piece 40.00
Cradle, Doll's, Brown Paint, Mustard Striping, Red Florals, 19th Century 275.00
Cradle, Doll's, Carved Cathedral Shaped Dome Over Back, c.1900, 16-In. Doll 345.00
Cradle, Doll's, Carved Side Slats, Painted, 13 3/4 x 24 In. 75.00
Cradle, Doll's, Grain Painted, 19th Century, 7 3/4 x 17 1/2 In. 230.00
Cradle, Doll's, Paint-Grained, Words Little Emiline On Back Of Hood 3400.00
Cradle, Doll's, Pink Wicker, Hangs On Frame, 1930s, 12 x 16 In. 98.00
Cradle, Doll's, Stenciled Floral & Scroll Design, Painted Black 220.00
Cro-Magnon Man, Lifelike, No. 383, 1973 . . . . 20.00
Croquet Set, Wooden, Rules Book, Box, 1893, 32 In. 165.00
Crystal Radio Kit, Remco, 1950s, Box 65.00
Cupboard, Doll's, Natural Finish, Open Top, Faience Dishes, France, 17 In. 450.00
Cyclist, Does Figure Eights, Rings Bell, Windup, 1930s 410.00
Cyclist, Nutty Mad, Black Hair, Mustache, Dinging Bell, Windup 165.00
Daisy, Dukes Of Hazzard, Mego, On Card, 8 In. 20.00
Dancer, Black Juba, Clockwork, Oak Dovetailed Case, Pair 2750.00
Dancer, Twist, On Pedestal, Windup, Japan 95.00
Dancers, Jubilee Platform, Ives, Box, 1876 . . . . 9570.00
Dandy Dobbin, Fisher-Price 185.00
Darth Vader, 12 In. 70.00
Daybed, Doll's, Napoleonic, High Rolled Sides, Scalloped Apron, Upholstered, c.1910 . . 300.00
Dennis The Menace, Playing Xylophone, Battery Operated, Box 185.00
Dino The Dinosaur, Tin, Windup, Marx 650.00
Dirigible, Windup, Tin, Germany, 1930s 350.00
Distillery, Steam, Grass, Tin & Wood, Ernest Plank, 1890, 13 x 15 x 6 In. 9350.00
Dizzy Donkey, Pop-Up Critter, Fisher-Price 65.00
Dog, Boxer, Standing, Chest Tag & Collar, Steiff, 4 In. 175.00
Dog, Bulldog, With Shoe, Windup, Tin Lithograph 135.00
Dog, Bully Bulldog, Chest Tag & Collar, Steiff, 4 In. 175.00
Dog, Carrying Briefcase, Pictures Orphan Annie, Tin 225.00
Dog, Chasing Butterfly, Brown Dog, Has Red Coat On, Red, White, Tin, Windup 25.00
Dog, Flippo, Windup, Marx, Box 225.00
Dog, Fox Terrier, Foxy, Mohair, 1950s, Steiff, 4 In. 85.00
Dog, French Poodle, Snobby, Black, Steiff, 6 In. 135.00
Dog, Gaylord, Walking, Bone, Leash & Collar, Battery-Operated, Ideal, Box 90.00
Dog, German Shepherd, Reclining, Tag, Steiff, 7 In. 150.00
Dog, Lassie, Poseable, Gabriel, Box, 1976 . . . . 85.00
Dog, Pluto, Plush Covered, Windup, Tin, Box, Marx 700.00
Dog, Poodle, Jumping, Battery Operated, Box 150.00
Dog, Riding, Or Pushed, Gray & White Plus, Steel Frame, Northern Ireland, 24 In. 165.00
Dog, Schnauzer, Tessie, Chest Tag & Collar, Steiff, 3 In. 125.00
Dog, Scotty, Black Mohair Plush, Does Tricks, Windup, Brochette Bone, c.1920 . . . . . . 65.00
Dog, Space, Red, Wobbly Eyes, Moving Ears, Tin, 1950s, 7 1/4 In. 402.00
Dog, Space, Silver, Red Ears, Nose, Tin, 1950s, 7 In. 1150.00
Dog, Squeak, Baby With Bunny & Dog, Baby, Seated, Brown Bunny, 1860, 3 In. 1100.00
Dog, Squeak, Boy With Basket Of Puppies, Papier-Mache, 1850, 3 1/2 In. 825.00

Dog, Terrier On Wheels, Metal Frame Base, Wooden Wheels, Steiff, 17 x 20 In. 345.00
Dolls are listed in their own category.
Doll Case, Tammy, Blue Vinyl, Covered Cardboard, Ideal, 1960s 25.00
Dollhouse, 2 Story, Germany, 1870s ....*Illus* 4400.00
Dollhouse, Barbie Country Living Home, With Furniture, 1970s 60.00
Dollhouse, Bliss, Door & Windows Open, Small 895.00
Dollhouse, Bliss, Wood & Paper Lithograph, Victorian, Early 1900s 900.00
Dollhouse, Bliss, Wooden, Paper Lithograph, Gingerbread Trim, 19 In. 2400.00
Dollhouse, Cass Grocery, Tile Floor, Store Counter, Velvet Candy, 8 x 7 In. 350.00
Dollhouse, English Half Timbered, Handmade, Doghouse, 18 x 36 x 22 In. 245.00
Dollhouse, Reed, 2 Stories, Open Back, Original Furniture, 1880s, 23 In. 1275.00
Dollhouse, Schoenhut, 2 Stories, Wooden Base, Fiberboard Furniture, 14 In. 450.00
Dollhouse, Tootsietoy, 6 Rooms, c.1927 .... 850.00
Dollhouse, With Furniture, Box, 1960s 275.00
Dollhouse Furniture, Bath Set, Renwal, 4 Piece 15.00
Dollhouse Furniture, Bathroom Fixtures, Cast Iron, Cream Enamel, 4 Pieces 135.00
Dollhouse Furniture, Bed, Eastlake 225.00
Dollhouse Furniture, Bedroom Set, Bliss 550.00
Dollhouse Furniture, Blue, Cream Bedroom, Living Room, Tootsietoy, 12 x 10 In. 575.00
Dollhouse Furniture, Chair, Orange & Black Paint, 18 In. 195.00
Dollhouse Furniture, Chest, Mahogany, Oak, 2 Drawers, Bracket Base, 15 In. 1495.00
Dollhouse Furniture, Chest-On-Chest 465.00
Dollhouse Furniture, Disneyland, Marx, 60 Piece 175.00
Dollhouse Furniture, Dresser, Attached Mirror 195.00
Dollhouse Furniture, Grand Piano, Princess Patti, Box 55.00
Dollhouse Furniture, Lavender, Green Bathroom, Tootsietoy, 12 x 10 In. 500.00
Dollhouse Furniture, Parlor Set, Metal, Columbus Landing Scene, Cushions, 4 Piece .. 375.00
Dollhouse Furniture, Rocker, Iron, Kilgore 55.00
Dollhouse Furniture, Sideboard, Oak 295.00
Dollhouse Furniture, Stove, Steel, Kitchen, Drawer, Oven, 1930s, 4 1/2 In. 85.00
Dolphin, Spouting, Battery Operated, Bandai, 1960s 95.00
Donkey, Pull Toy, Steel Frame, Mohair Coat, Button Eyes, Red Blanket, Steiff, 13 1/2 In. 300.00
Donkey, Velvet, Stuffed, Glass Eyes, Mohair Tail, Wooden Base, Pull Toy, 13 In. 300.00
Dr. Doodle, Fisher-Price, No. 477 .... 450.00
Dreadnaught, Flywheel Mechanism, Penny Toy, Germany, 4 In. 350.00
Dresser, Doll's, Wooden, Lift-Top Centered Mirror, 9 Drawers, 6 In. 550.00
Drinking Man, Coffee, Cup In 1 Hand, Percolator In Other, Windup, Japan 95.00
Drum, Baseball Scenes, 1910, 8 In. 425.00
Drum, Children, American Flag, Mid-19th Century 415.00
Drum, Felix The Cat, Tin, 1930s 225.00
Drum, Tin, Ohio Arts, 1940s 29.00
Drum Set, Spike Jones, Junior City Slickers, Tin Lithograph, 13-In. Drum .....100.00 to 115.00
Drummer Boy, Majorette, Tin, Windup, Chein, 1930s ....125.00 to 150.00
Drummer Boy, Tin, Cello Head, Windup, Japan, Prewar 350.00
Duck, Crank Handle, Turns Head, Opens Bill, Plush Cover, Carved Wood, 18 In. 300.00
Duck, Dancing, On Top Of Drum, Tin, White Box, Key Wind, 11 In., Pair 29.00
Duck, Family, Windup, Tin, Japan, 13 In. 50.00
Duck, Felt, Button Eyes, Iron Wheels, Steiff Button, Pull Toy, 10 1/4 In. 330.00
Duck, Sailor & Sailorette, Removable Shoes, Germany, 4 In. 157.00
Duck, Velvet Covered, Squeaks 165.00
Dune Buggy, Tonka, Box 360.00
Earth Man, Astronaut Design, Yellow, Tin, 1950, 9 1/2 In. 975.00
Elephant, Circus, Clockwork, Tin, Prewar, 5 In. 440.00
Elephant, Pulling Cart, Penny, Head Nods 295.00
Elephant, Steel Frame, Mohair Coat, Bead Eyes, Wooden Wheels, Pull Toy, Steiff, 16 In. 275.00
Elephant, Windy Juggling, Tin Lithograph Base, Box, Japan, 1959, 4 x 5 x 12 In. 165.00
Elvira, Plastic, Screaming, Sealed On Card 40.00
Emergency Medical Kit, CHIPS, Box 20.00
Erector Set, Gilbert, No. 5 1/2, Instructions 29.00
Explorer, Orbit, Tank Form, Box, 1955, 8 3/4 In. 635.00
Expressman, No. 12 On Breast Pocket, Lehmann, 5 x 6 In. 230.00
Farm Set, Earth Mover, Tractor, Disc Plow, 2 Mowers, Rake, Cast Iron, 1930s, 6 Piece . 287.00
Farm Wagon, Arcade, Green Paint, Red Spoke Wheels, Cast Iron, McCormick, 12 In. .. 360.00

Toy, Dollhouse,
2 Story,
Germany, 1870s

Toy, G.I. Joe,
Land Adventurer,
Hasbro, Box

Farm Wagon, Horse Team, Arcade, Green Men With Black, White Horses, 1939, 13 In. .   415.00
Ferdinand The Bull, Windup, Marx 250.00
Ferris Wheel, 6 Cars With Pictures Of Passengers, Tin, 16 1/2 In. 470.00
Ferris Wheel, 6 Ski Lift Seats, Ohio Art 275.00
Ferris Wheel, Double, Sand Operated 325.00
Ferris Wheel, Hercules, 1930s, Chein . . . . .375.00 to 450.00
Ferris Wheel, Tin Lithograph, Battery Operated, Ohio Art . . . . .275.00 to 395.00
Ferris Wheel, Tin Lithograph, Windup, J. Chein & Co., 1940s, Box, 17 In. 385.00
Fire Chief Hat, Microphone & Speaker, Texaco, 1960s 95.00
Fire Pumper, 2 Horses, Mechanical, Ives Blakeslee, Dovetailed Box 7475.00
Fire Pumper, 3 Horse Drawn, 2 Firemen, Late 19th Century, 20 In. 175.00
Fire Pumper, Buddy L, Nickel Plate Boiler, 23 x 11 x 9 In. 1035.00
Fire Pumper, Friction, 11 3/4 In. 525.00
Fire Pumper, Horses, Cast Iron, 14 In. 2450.00
Fire Pumper, Horses, Firemen, Cast Iron, Ives, Blakeslee & Williams, c.1890, 20 In. . . .   8337.00
Fire Pumper, Hose Carriage, No. 35, Horse Drawn, Carpenter 5465.00
Fire Pumper, Kenton, Cast Iron, 1930s, 10 In. 325.00
Fire Pumper, Ladders, Yellow On Red, Turner Ahrens Fox, 16 In. 975.00
Fire Pumper, No. 205A, Buddy L, 23 1/4 In. 690.00
Fire Pumper, No. 33, Horse Drawn, Carpenter 7245.00
Fire Pumper, Pressed Steel, Dayton Friction Works 300.00
Fire Pumper, Sturditoy, 20 In. 1800.00
Fire Pumper, Suburban, Tonka, No. 46 . . . .   150.00
Fire Pumper, Tonka, 1957 . . . .   345.00
Fire Pumper, Windup, Kingsbury, 9 In. 335.00
Fire Truck, 3 Ladders, Steel, Structo, 1940s 275.00
Fire Truck, Aerial Ladder, Big Boy, Kelmet 1995.00
Fire Truck, Aerial Ladder, Ford, Tonka, 1956 . . . .   595.00
Fire Truck, Aerial Ladder, Tonka No. 1125, 1983, Box, 11 1/2 In. 26.00
Fire Truck, Arnold Sparking, U.S. Zone, Germany, 4 1/2 In. 450.00
Fire Truck, Auburn, Rubber, 1920s 285.00
Fire Truck, Boiler Type, Kenton, 14 1/2 In. 1200.00
Fire Truck, Buddy L, With Ladder, Wood, 1943, 13 In. 125.00
Fire Truck, Dinky Toy, No. 250 . . . .   75.00
Fire Truck, Ford, White Truck, Blue Fenders, Red, White, Blue Logo, 1951 . . . .   38.00
Fire Truck, Gold Boiler, Bell, Red Body, Turner, 28 x 9 x 13 1/2 In. 632.50
Fire Truck, H. Yamada, Windup, Japan, 1930s, 11 In. 1250.00
Fire Truck, Hoist, Red & Green, Sheet Steel Winch, Arcade, 1932 . . . .   3960.00
Fire Truck, Hook & Ladder, Disk Wheels, Hubley, 16 In. 1760.00
Fire Truck, Hook & Ladder, No. 205, Buddy L, 1920s, 24 In. 490.00
Fire Truck, Hook & Ladder, Tootsietoy, 9 In. 95.00
Fire Truck, Hook & Ladder, Wyandotte, 23 In. 200.00
Fire Truck, Hubley, 8 1/2 In. 375.00
Fire Truck, Ladder Support, Dinky Toy 285.00
Fire Truck, Ladder, Aerial, Keystone, 31 In. 800.00
Fire Truck, Ladder, Climbing Fireman, Tin, Marx 275.00

Fire Truck, Ladder, Driver, Rubber Tires, Windup, Kingsbury, 10 x 5 x 3 In. 259.00
Fire Truck, Ladder, Rubber Tires, Cast Iron, Hubley, 13 1/4 x 5 x 3 1/2 In. 230.00
Fire Truck, No. 473, Cast Iron Driver, 3 Ladders, Kiddietoy, Hubley, 10 In. 145.00
Fire Truck, Pressed Steel, Nyint, 28 In. 55.00
Fire Truck, Republic Fire Ladder, Red, Green, 17 In. 295.00
Fire Truck, SSS Super, Box, 18 In. 450.00
Fire Truck, Swivel Action, Siren, Friction, Box, Japan 225.00
Fire Truck, Texaco, Buddy L, 25 In. 150.00
Fire Truck, Working Pump, Gunthermann, 1930s, 16 In. 3500.00
Fire Wagon, Hose, Fireman Pulled By Horse, Hubley, 1907, 11 In. 785.00
Fireman, 1950s, Tin 78.00
Fireman, Climbing, Windup, Tin & Celluloid, Marx ....115.00 to 125.00
Fish, Terror, Friction, Tin Lithograph, Garry Anderson 200.00
Flashlight, Yogi Bear, Vinyl, Squeeze 30.00
Fonzie, Mego, 8 In. 35.00
Frankenstein, Blushing, Vinyl Head, Tin, Battery Operated, Japan, 13 In. ....175.00 to 235.00
Fred Flintstone, Hopper, Windup, Marx, 1962 .... 425.00
Fred Flintstone, On Dino, Featuring Purple Dino, Battery Operated, 12 In. 1015.00
Fred Flintstone, On Dino, Windup, Tin, Marx, 1962, 8 1/2 In. ....215.00 to 425.00
Fred Flintstone, Train, Windup, Tin 435.00
Fred Flintstone, Turnover Tank, Fred Turns Tank Over, Tin, Linemar, 3 In. 450.00
Freddy Krueger, Screamin' Products, Vinyl, 1987, 18 In. 50.00
Frisbee, Big Boy 10.00
Froggie The Gremlin, Rubber, Squeaks, Rempel Mfg. Inc., 1950s, 10 1/2 In. .....95.00 to 110.00
G.I. Joe, Action Sailor, 30th Anniversary, Hasbro 100.00
G.I. Joe, Action Soldier, Dog Tags, Rifle, Box 150.00
G.I. Joe, Adventure Team Commander, Box 550.00
G.I. Joe, Annapolis Cadet, Parade Dress Jacket, M-1 Rifle 395.00
G.I. Joe, Astronaut, Space Suit, Talking, Box, 2969 .... 225.00
G.I. Joe, Astronaut, Talking 750.00
G.I. Joe, Black Soldier, 30th Anniversary 140.00
G.I. Joe, Black, Suit, Shoulder Holster, Gun 125.00
G.I. Joe, Blond Flocked Hair, Brown Eyes, Gray Flight Suit, Hasbro, 11 In. 160.00
G.I. Joe, Brazil Mission Force, Leatherneck, Kenner Bag 20.00
G.I. Joe, British Commando, All Accessories 395.00
G.I. Joe, Brown Flocked Hair, Blue Painted Eyes, Hasbro, Box, 11 1/2 In. 200.00
G.I. Joe, Command Headquarters, Box 60.00
G.I. Joe, Commando, Red Beret 20.00
G.I. Joe, Desert Patrol Adventure Jeep, Box 675.00
G.I. Joe, Freefall, Plastic, Jumpsuit, Oxygen Mask, 12 1/2 In. 240.00
G.I. Joe, French Resistance Fighter, All Accessories 350.00
G.I. Joe, German Soldier, All Accessories, 1970s 395.00
G.I. Joe, Green Beret, Beret With Emblem, Accessories 395.00
G.I. Joe, Grenadier Outfit, Hasbro, 1970s 128.00
G.I. Joe, High Voltage Escape, Hasbro 75.00
G.I. Joe, Jeep & Trailer, 1960s, Large 45.00
G.I. Joe, Jeep & Trailer, Accessories, 1965, 20-In. Jeep, 15-In. Trailer 800.00
G.I. Joe, Jouncing Jeep, Unique Toy 350.00
G.I. Joe, Land Adventurer, Hasbro, Box ....*Illus* 135.00
G.I. Joe, Man Of Action, Talking 550.00
G.I. Joe, Marine, Blond, 30th Anniversary, 12 In. 65.00
G.I. Joe, Mountie Outfit, Hasbro, 1970s 128.00
G.I. Joe, Official Sea Sled & Frogman Box 595.00
G.I. Joe, Parachutist, Red Devil 275.00
G.I. Joe, Radiation Detection, Hasbro 75.00
G.I. Joe, Rhino Jeep, Box 125.00
G.I. Joe, Russian Outfit, Hasbro, 1970s, ... 118.00
G.I. Joe, Scuba Gear, Fuzzy Hair, Box 100.00
G.I. Joe, Sky Diveto Danger, Hasbro 250.00
G.I. Joe, Space Capsule, Box 795.00
G.I. Joe, Space Capsule, Suit, Box 120.00
G.I. Joe, Talking Astronaut, Hasbro 250.00
G.I. Joe, Tank Commander, 1970s, Hasbro 148.00

G.I. Joe, With Footlocker, 2 Outfits & Skis 75.00
Games are listed in their own category.
Garage, Race Car, Lehmann 440.00
Garage, Schuco 325.00
Gardener, Happy, Moves Legs, Advancing Wheelbarrow, Windup, Tin, Marx, 8 In. 173.00
Gardener, Sam, Jointed, Pushing Wheelbarrow, Windup, Marx, Box 275.00
Gas Station, Firestone, Marx, 1950s 950.00
Gas Station, Texaco, Cars, Trucks, Signs 225.00
Giraffe, Ball Playing, Bounces Ball Up & Down A Wire, Tin, Windup, Box, 8 1/2 In. ... 262.00
Giraffe, Glass Inset Eyes, Leather Ears, Wooden, Schoenhut, 1905, 11 In. 525.00
Glider, Friction, Kayee 85.00
Go-Cart, Ludwig Von Drake, Friction, Tin, Marx, 1960s 270.00
Go-Cart, Tom & Jerry, Red Cart, Tom Steering, Friction, Plastic, Box, 3 x 4 x 5 In. 115.00
Goggles, Trail, Sgt. Preston, Puff Rice Box, 1952 .... 10.00
Gorilla, Roaring, Battery Operated, T-N Co. 150.00
Gorilla, Roaring, Battery Operated, Tin Lithograph 225.00
Grasshopper, Hand Panted Tin, Windup, c.1900, 7 In. 350.00
Green Hornet, With Videomatic Ring, 1967 .... 1500.00
Guitar, Bee Gees 85.00
Guitar, Wyatt Earp, Box 165.00
Guitarist, Jolly, Plush, Tin, Windup, Monkey Plays Guitar Moving Head, 9 In. 95.00
Gum, Machine, Play Boy, Box, Marx 70.00
Gumball Machine, Pillsbury Doughboy, Box 345.00
Gun, Air Pistol, Benjamin, Model 117, Swing Lever Plump Handle, Silver 105.00
Gun, Air Pistol, Benjamin, Model 312, Adjustable Sight, Metal Finish 65.00
Gun, Air Pistol, Crosman Model 130, .22 Cal. 40.00
Gun, Air Pistol, Crosman Model V-300, Lever Action 60.00
Gun, Air Pistol, Crosman, Model 160, Auto Safety, Standard Peep Sight 95.00
Gun, Air Pistol, Crosman, Model 160, Block Trigger 190.00
Gun, Air Pistol, Daisy, Chrome, 1937 .... 77.00
Gun, Air Pistol, Daisy, Model 25, Adjustable Front Sight, Blue 250.00
Gun, Air Pistol, Daisy, Model 41, Chrome, .177 Cal. 65.00
Gun, Air Pistol, Daisy, Model 118, Targeteer, Blue Finish 45.00
Gun, Air Pistol, Daisy, Model 853 .... 60.00
Gun, Air Pistol, Daisy, No. 177, Target Special, Slide Action 55.00
Gun, Air Pistol, Daisy, Red Ryder, Copper Bands 260.00
Gun, Air Pistol, Daisy, Targeteer, Chrome, 1946 .... 50.00
Gun, Air Pistol, Hy-Score, Brass Barrel, Ivory Colored Grips, .22 Cal. 75.00
Gun, Air Pistol, RWS Model M-10, Adjustable Grips, Box 350.00
Gun, Air Pistol, Walther, Model 55, Reblued, Beach Stock 300.00
Gun, Air Pistol, Webley Junior, Model 177, 1946-1950 .... 125.00
Gun, Air Pistol, Webley Nemesis, .177 Cal. 150.00
Gun, Air Rifle, Beeman, .177 Cal. 375.00
Gun, Air Rifle, Crosman, Model 73, Lever Action, Gas Operated 25.00
Gun, Air Rifle, Daisy, Model 94, All Metal 25.00
Gun, Astroray, Plastic, Ohio Art 75.00
Gun, Astroray, Remco 75.00
Gun, Atom Ray, Water, Aluminum, Hiller 495.00
Gun, Auto Pistol, Metal, Cork 28.00
Gun, BB, Daisy, Golden Eagle, 50th Anniversary Model, 1886-1936 .... 210.00
Gun, BB, Daisy, No. 11, Walnut, Chrome 58.00
Gun, BB, Daisy, No. 25, Pump Action 125.00
Gun, BB, Daisy, No. 177, Target Special 20.00
Gun, BB, Daisy, No. 195, Buzz Barton, Faux Scope, Blue Finish, Marked Special 305.00
Gun, BB, King Mfg., Model 5533, 1000 Shot, Blue Finish, Walnut 356.00
Gun, BB, Remington, Air Rifle, Pump Action, Walnut, Black Barrel 575.00
Gun, Colt 45, White Plastic Grips, Hubley, Box, 13 1/2 In. 60.00
Gun, Dan Dare, Planet, Plastic Gun, Shoots Missiles, Randell, England, 1953, 4 1/2 In. .. 178.00
Gun, Derringer, Secret Agent, Hide-A-Way, Original Colorful Box 85.00
Gun, Fire Cracker, Cast Iron 225.00
Gun, G-Man, Sparks, Label, Marx, c.1930, 4 In. 130.00
Gun, Machine Gun, Rapid Fire, Anti-Aircraft, Cast Iron, Painted, 1930s, 7 1/2 In. 143.00
Gun, Marshall 45, Stag Grips, Hubley, 10 In. 80.00

Gun, Rocket Dart, Daisy, 1 Dart 90.00
Gun, Semi-Automatic Gas, Daisy, No. 200, Plastic, 1960s, Box, 10 In. 20.00
Gun, Space, Atomic Disintegrator, Hubley, 1954 .... 325.00
Gun, Space, Jupiter, Remco, Box 80.00
Gun, Space, Sparking, Tin Lithograph, Box, China, 1970s 12.05
Gun, Stallion 45, Black Grips, Nichols, Box 40.00
Gun, Stallion 45, Mark II, Nichols, 12 In. 215.00
Gun, Texan Jr., Gold Dummy, Hubley, Box 175.00
Gun, Texan Jr., Hubley, 8 1/4 In. 65.00
Gun, Tom Corbett Space Cadet, Marx, 1950s 150.00
Gun & Holster Set, Leather, Red Jewels, Brass & Silver 225.00
Gun & Holster Set, Untouchables, Marx, On Card, Unused, 1960 .... 75.00
Gun Set, With Helmet, Lost In Space, Remco, Box 350.00
Gunfighter, Marx, 1964, 5 Piece 20.00
Gyro Copter, Tin, Friction, Haji, 8 In. 195.00
Harmonica, Figural, Underdog, Yellow, Green, Plastic, 1975 .... 81.00
Harmonica, Figural, Woody Woodpecker, Plastic, 6 In. 35.00
Harmonica, Swing-A-Tune, Magnus, Red & Green 48.00
Harold Lloyd, Walks, Cane, Face Changes, Windup, Tin, Marx, 1930s .... 450.00 to 750.00
Helicopter, Battery Operated, Piaseki, Box 125.00
Helicopter, Forest Ranger, Hubley, Box 175.00
Helicopter, N.A.S.A. Moon Scout, Windup, Japan, 10 1/2 In. 175.00
Helicopter, Police Sky Patrol, Battery Operated, 15 In. 210.00
Helicopter, Tin, Windup, J. Chein, 12 In. 230.00
Helmet, Dennis The Menace Crash, Ideal, Box, 1950s 75.00
Helmet, Space, Tom Corbett, Silver & Blue 95.00
Helmet, Steve Canyon, 1959 .... 135.00
Helmet, Texaco Firechief, Box 250.00
Hen, Egg Laying, Windup, Wyandotte 60.00
Henry On Elephant, Celluloid, Windup, Geo. Borgfeldt, Box, 8 In. 1280.00
High Chair, Doll's, Can Be Made Into Play Table 750.00
Hillbilly, With Guitar, Windup, Alps, 1950s, 4 In. 50.00
Hippopotamus, Green, Metlox, Miniature 70.00
Hobbyhorse, Cisco Kid, 1950s 75.00
Hobbyhorse, Pokey, Lakeside Ind., 1966 .... 25.00
Holster, Double, Jewels, Studded 65.00
Holster, Double, Wyatt Earp, Leather Jeweled, Hubley 68.00
Holster, Wyatt Earp Esquire, Double Deluxe Set With Gun & Bullets 425.00
Hoosier Cabinet, Doll's 400.00
Hopping Baraby Banana, Windup, Marx, Box 135.00
Horse, 2-Wheeled Cart Marked Daisy, Cast Iron, Pull Toy, Ives 600.00
Horse, Black Fabric Covering, Cast Iron Wheels, Pull Toy, 24 In. 440.00
Horse, Coal Wagon 695.00
Horse, Composition, Pull Toy, Germany, 1920s, 5 In. 71.00
Horse, Dapple Gray, Fiber Tail, Tin Wheels, Red, Black Base, Pull Toy, 10 In. 302.50
Horse, On Wheeled Platform, Polychrome Paint, 11 1/2 In. 1550.00
Horse, Papier-Mache, Wood, Black Spots On Red & Black Sponge, Pull Toy, 12 3/4 In. .. 325.00
Horse, Prancing, Mechanical, Wagon 995.00
Horse, Rocking, Ash, 2 Cutout Silhouettes, Seat Between, Varnish, Monogram, 37 In. ... 27.50
Horse, Rocking, Carved & Painted Wood, Leather Saddle, Horsehair Tail 110.00
Horse, Rocking, Carved Wood, Dapple Gray, Natural Rockers, Glass Eyes, Saddle, 52 In. 630.00
Horse, Rocking, Dapple-Gray On Red Base, 27 In. 1150.00
Horse, Rocking, Dapple-Gray Paint, Red Rockers, Wooden, Mane & Tail Traces, 42 In. . 440.00
Horse, Rocking, Dark Blue, Blue, Gray Ground, Roan, 42 In. 1265.00
Horse, Rocking, Painted Red-Brown With Blue, White & Red Designs, Carved, 43 In. .. 635.00
Horse, Rocking, Wooden, Dapple Gray Repaint, Harness, Blue Rockers, 45 In. 350.00
Horse, Standing, On Wooden Platform, Glass Eyes, Pull Toy, 1890, 12 In. 1050.00
Horse, Stick, Cisco Kid 22.00
Horse, Velocipede, Steel Frame, Wire Wheels, Racing Wooden Horse, Glass Eyes, 39 In. 550.00
Horse, Wheeled Platform, Papier-Mache 100.00
Horse, White Dappled, Amber Glass Eyes, Carved Mouth, Schoenhut, 1905, 9 In. 500.00
Horse, Wooden Platform, Iron Wheels, Felt, Leather Ears, Pull Toy, 1890, 23 In. 900.00
Horse, Wooden, Composition, Painted, Tail, Mane, Harness, Pull Toy, 9 In. 110.00

Horse, Wooden, Yellow, Red, Tin Wheels, France, Pull Toy, 1885, 13 In. 450.00
Horse & Cart, Canvas Covered Wooden Horses, Wooden Cart, Pull Toy, 31 In. 288.00
Horse & Wagon, Borden's, Driver, Wooden Box, 4 Milk Glass Bottles, 14 x 30 In. 1870.00
Horse & Wagon, Rider, Drop-Out Bottom, Stamped Sand & Gravel, Cast Iron, 15 In. . . 345.00
Horse & Wagon, Toytown Dairy, Marx, Box 475.00
Hot Diggity, Windup, Fisher-Price, c.1934 . . . . 995.00
Hot Mammy, Windup, Fisher-Price, c.1934 . . . . 995.00
House, Rabbit, Bear & Monkey On Seesaw, Tin, 6 In. 210.00
Hula Girl, Celluloid, Windup, 1930s, 7 In. 105.00
Humans, 1 Million BC, Mego, 8 In., 4 Piece 35.00
Ice Cream Fountain Set, Child's, Box 95.00
Ice Cream Store, Baskin-Robbins, Dolls & Freezer, Folds Into Own Case 40.00
Ice Skates, Leather, Steel Blade, 1894 . . . . 250.00
Ice Skates, Wooden, Steel Blades, Holland, Label, De Beste Freiche Schaats 250.00
Ice Wagon, Horse Drawn, Cast Iron, Painted, Hubley, c.1920, 15 1/2 In. 635.00
Indian, In Canoe, Hand Carved Wood, Box, 4 In. 80.00
Indian, Nutty, Plays Drums, Battery Operated, Marx 150.00
Indian Chief, Crawling, Windup, Ohio Art, 8 In. 75.00
Indian Warrior, Bendi, Brown Rubber, Lakeside, 1966, 6 In. 8.00
Indiana Jones, Kenner, 12 In. 195.00
Irish Mail, Iron, Wooden, Ride-On, 1910, All Original 695.00
Iron, Clothing, Sunny Suzy, Wolverine, Electric, Box 15.00
Iron, General Electric, Steam, 1959, Child's 35.00
Ironing Board, Snow White & 7 Dwarfs On Cover 55.00
Jack-In-The-Box, Cloth Costume, Printed Cardboard Head, Paper Covering, 6 1/2 In. . . . 465.00
Jack-In-The-Box, Clown, Mattel, Box 25.00
Jack-In-The-Box, Girl, Germany 225.00
Jack-In-The-Box, Snoopy, Mattel . . . . .45.00 to 75.00
James Bond, Aurora, No. 414, 1966 . . . . 475.00
James Bond, Moonraker, Box, 1979, 12 1/2 In. 170.00
Jazzbo Jim, Dances On Roof Of Tin Log Cabin, Windup, Unique Art, 10 In. 305.00
Jazzbo Jim, Dances With Banjo On Roof, Windup, Strauss, 1920s 450.00
Jeep, Desert Patrol, Battery Operated, Japan, Tin, Box, 11 1/2 In. 150.00
Jeep, Jolly Joe, Original Hat, Box, Marx 750.00
Jeep, Jouncing, Rodeo Joe, Unique Art 200.00
Jeep, Jumpin' Jeep, Tin, Marx, 1930s . . . . .265.00 to 375.00
Jeep, Nellybelle, Figures Of Pat Brady, Dale & Bullet, Pressed Steel, Marx, 11 In. 415.00
Jeep, Police, Friction, Tin, Japan, 1950s, 8 In. 80.00
Jeep, Radio, Battery Operated, T-N Co., 1950s 450.00
Jeep, Searchlight & Artillery, Battery Operated 200.00
Jeep, Trailer, U.S. Army, Plastic Soldier Driver, Radar Decal, Marx, c.1950, 21 In. 278.00
Jeep, U.S. Army, With Trailer, Marx, Box 350.00
Jelly Bean Dispenser, Doughboy & Sprout, Paper Lithograph Box 295.00
Jockey, Bunny, Windup, Japan 175.00
Johnny The Bellhop, Philip Morris, Jointed, Vinyl, Squeaks, 1940s 300.00
Kaleidoscope, Bush, Brown Leather, Wooden Stand, 1873, 14 In. 1150.00
King Kong, Pounds Chest While Walking, Windup 375.00
Kit, Insect Science, 6 Insects, Renwal, Box, 1960s 50.00
Kit, Motor Boat, Japan, Box 295.00
Kitchen Set, Tin Lithograph, Plastic Utensils, Superior Toy Co., 1950s 45.00
Kitchen Set, Waffle Iron, Griddle, Fry Pan, Pot, Wagner Ware, Child's, 4 Piece 115.00
Kitten, Papier-Mache, White Fur, Green Glass Eyes, Pink Nose, 1920, 10 In. 575.00
Kodiak Bear, Palmer Plastics, No. S22, 1950s 24.00
Krazy Kat, Chases Mice On Platform, Pull Toy, 1930s 975.00
Krazy Kat, Velveteen, Stuffed, Knickerbocker, 1930s, 10 1/2 In. 1265.00
Lady Bug, Tin, Windup, 1950s, Japan, 5 1/2 In. 75.00
Lady Bug, Tin, Windup, TPS, Box, Japan, 1950s, 12 In. 95.00
Lamb, On Wheels, Mohair, Glass Eyes, Steel Frame & Wheels, Steiff, c.1915, 20 In. 575.00
Lantern, Hansel & Gretel, 4 Sides, Die Cut, Germany 65.00
Lassie, Brown & White Plush, Vinyl Face, Knickerbocker, 1960s, 12 In. 12.00
Lawn Mower, Arcade, Cast Iron, 1920s 400.00
Lawn Mower, Bell, Gong Bell Toy Co., 1950s 85.00
Leopard, Silver Button, Steiff, 15 In. 185.00

Li'l Abner Dogpatch Band, Windup, Unique Art, 1945 .575.00 to 975.00
Limousine, Driver, Passengers, Germany . . . .*Illus* 2750.00
Lincoln Logs Set, Tongue, Groove Box, Label, 1920, 332 Piece 225.00
Lincoln Tunnel, Windup, Unique Art, 1930s 475.00
Lion, Circus, Place On Mat, Rises, Waving Front Legs, Plush, Tin, Battery, 10 In. 500.00
Lion, Mohair, Stuffed, Glass Eyes, Button, Steiff, 1950s, 11 In. 28.00
Lion, On Wheels, Steiff 495.00
Lion, Standing, Fully Jointed, Button, Steiff, 1920s, 12 In. 285.00
Llama, Ear Button, Steiff, 6 1/2 In. 75.00
Loop A Loop, Carnival 200.00
Magilla Gorilla, Pull Toy, Vinyl, Sits On Yellow Plastic Wagon, Red Wheels 125.00
Mammy, Sweeping, Danced As She Swept, Windup, Lindstrom 357.50
Mammy's Boy, Tin 350.00
Man, Musical, On Trapeze, Hand Crank, Mattel, Box 195.00
Man Drinking Coffee, Mr. Dan, Tin, Windup, T-N Co., Japan, Box, 7 In. 118.00
Man From U.N.C.L.E Target Set, Box, Ideal 295.00
Man Pushing Wheelbarrow, Windup, Strauss 425.00
Manure Spreader, Oliver Superior Manure, Charles Wright 2860.00
Map, Yukon Territory, Sgt. Preston, 1953 . . . . 45.00
Marionette Theater, Celluloid Figures Dance, 1920s 650.00
Marionette Theater, Clown & Girl, Clockwork, Japan, Prewar, 11 x 9 In. 1800.00
Marshall Wild Bill, Battery Operated, Box 425.00
Mary & Her Little Lamb, Tin, Celluloid Figures, Windup, Japan, Early 1950s 395.00
Mask, Zorro, Guy Williams, With Whip, Lariat & Ring, Sealed On Card 175.00
McGregor, Smokes, Battery Operated, T-N Co., Japan 195.00
Meat Grinder, Heavy Casting 85.00
Merry-Go-Round, 3 Bears In Cups & Saucers, Battery Operated, Japan 275.00
Merry-Go-Round, 3 Children Sitting In Teacups On Saucers . . . . .145.00 to 175.00
Merry-Go-Round, 3 Kids On Horses, Spinning, Country Fair, Tin, 7 In. 160.00
Merry-Go-Round, 3 Kids On Horses, Spinning, Tin, 8 In. 289.00
Merry-Go-Round, 4 Planes, 4 Flags, Wolverine, 1930s 550.00
Merry-Go-Round, 4 Seat, Marked V & R, 12 1/2 x 11 In. 5500.00
Merry-Go-Round, Airplanes, Windup, Wolverine, 1930s 500.00
Merry-Go-Round, Music Lithograph, Ohio Art, Box 145.00
Merry-Go-Round, Playland, Box, Chein 750.00
Merry-Go-Round, Sunny Andy, Musical, Lever Action, Wolverine, Box, 15 x 12 In. 525.00
Merry-Go-Round, Swan Seats, Chein, 1930 . . . . .995.00 to 1075.00
Merrymakers, 4 Mice, Piano Band, Marx, 1930s . . . . .747.00 to 1000.00
Microscope, Gilbert 25.00
Microscope Kit, Science Craft, 1953 . . . . 45.00
Mighty Mouse, Squeeze, Vinyl, Yellow, Red Felt Cape, 9 1/2 In. 75.00
Milk Wagon, Horse Drawn, Tin, Converse 425.00
Minstrel Musician, Black Man, Strums Banjo On Chair, Kicks Legs, Windup, 1890s . . . 1450.00
Minstrel Musician, On Chair, Shakes Bells, Crashes Cymbals 1250.00
Mischief Kit, Dennis The Menace, 1955 . . . . 35.00
Model, Paddle Boat, Billie K, Wood & Paper, Photograph Of Crew, 1890s, 26 In. 245.00
Model Kit, Airplane, DC8, United Airlines, 1969, Revell 30.00
Model Kit, Airplane, Flying Tiger, P40E, 1960s 35.00
Model Kit, Airplane, Painted Tin & Wood, 1930, 21 3/4 In. 545.00
Model Kit, Alien Creature & Vehicle, MPC, No. 1902, 1976 . . . . 74.00
Model Kit, Aliens, Ripley-Combat, AEF Designs, 1980s 40.00
Model Kit, Alphabet Blocks, BVOOP On Both Sides 150.00
Model Kit, Apollo Saturn 5 Rocket, Revell, No. 1843, 1969 . . . . 230.00
Model Kit, Aston Martin DB 5, Airfix, 1965 . . . . 250.00
Model Kit, Austin Healey, 100-Six, Plastic, Box, 1976 . . . . 45.00
Model Kit, Bertram The Stag Beetle, Silly Surfers, Hawk, No. 0516, 1959 . . . . 60.00
Model Kit, Black Falcon Pirate Ship, Aurora, No. 210, 1972 . . . . 44.00
Model Kit, Boat, California Battleship, Pine, Balsa, Strombecker, 1938-1940 . . . . 25.00
Model Kit, Boat, Maple Brand, Wooden, Battery Operated, Box 175.00
Model Kit, Boat, PT No. 211, Revell, 1974 . . . . 35.00
Model Kit, Boat, USS Franklin, Revell, 1967 . . . . 45.00
Model Kit, Boat, USS Nautilus Sub, Pine, Balsa, Strombecker, 1938-1940 . . . . 25.00
Model Kit, Brabham, Schuco, Box 450.00

Don't let plastic toys or dishes touch each other. Different types of plastic may react to each other and be damaged.

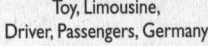

Toy, Limousine,
Driver, Passengers, Germany

Model Kit, Build Your Own Telephone Truck, Irwin	250.00
Model Kit, Captain America, Aurora, Box	50.00
Model Kit, Car, Model T, Depot Hack, Metal, 10 In.	125.00
Model Kit, Dinah Twin Engine Scout, Box, UPC, 12 In.	70.00
Model Kit, Dr. Jekyll, Movies, Aurora	590.00
Model Kit, Dracula's Dragster, Aurora	490.00
Model Kit, Dracula, Aurora, 1964	150.00
Model Kit, Dukes Of Hazzard, General Lee, Dodge Charger, MPC, Box, 1979	95.00
Model Kit, Enterprise, Space Lab, Revell, No. S200, 1978	14.00
Model Kit, Fire House, Fire Truck, Chair, Car, Firemen, 1930, Marx, Tin	551.00
Model Kit, Flying Saucer, Orange, Battery Operated, Tin, Japan	250.00
Model Kit, Fort Builder Set, Build Cardboard Castle, 1950, Box	50.00
Model Kit, Frankenstein, Aurora	400.00
Model Kit, Hawk Spaceship, Airfix, 1977	90.00
Model Kit, Johnny Service Station, Car, Box	75.00
Model Kit, King Kong, Aurora	590.00
Model Kit, Leaky Boat Louie, Hawk, No. 534, 1963	90.00
Model Kit, Little Buckeye Speedboat, Scientific, 12 1/2 In.	55.00
Model Kit, Model A Phaeton, Metal Car, Plastic Top, Box	27.50
Model Kit, Montage Matra, Ford, Schuco, Box	550.00
Model Kit, Motorcycle, Harley-Davidson Electra Glide, Unassembled, 1967	75.00
Model Kit, Mr. Potato Head, Funny Face Kit, Hong Kong, 1950s	35.00
Model Kit, Mrs. Potato Head, Funny Face Kit, Merritt, England, Box	195.00
Model Kit, My Mother The Car, TV, AMT, 1965	61.00
Model Kit, Police Station, Crooks Behind Bars, Marx, 1930	446.00
Model Kit, Rat Patrol, Aurora, 1967	75.00
Model Kit, Shogun Warriors, Plastic, Monogram, 1977	95.00
Model Kit, Space Fighter Raider, Monogram, No. 06026, 1978	130.00
Model Kit, Space Station, Plastic, Revell	345.00
Model Kit, Stagecoach Of England, Lifelike, No. 509670, 1970s	20.00
Model Kit, Stingray, G. Anderson, TV, Union, 1983	74.00
Model Kit, Trolley, Aristocraft, Box, 1954	195.00
Model Kit, USS Enterprise Command Bridge, Star Trek, AMT, Box, 1975	20.00
Model Kit, USS Enterprise, Star Trek VI, Movie, AMT, 1986	14.00
Model Kit, Vampire Van, Disney's Haunted Mansion, MPC, No. PA626, 1969	140.00
Model Kit, Walkie-Talkies, Box, Remco	50.00
Molding Set, Creeple People, Ideal	55.00
Molding Set, Fighting Men, Ideal	55.00
Monk, Drinking, Windup, Schuco, 5 1/2 In.	75.00
Monkey, Bar Tender, Windup	75.00
Monkey, Bellhop, Yes-No, Schuco, Large	995.00
Monkey, Bellhop, Yes-No, Schuco, Small	775.00
Monkey, Blowing, With Bubble Dish, Vinyl Face, Tin, Battery Operated, Japan	129.00
Monkey, Bombo, The Acrobatic Monkey, Box, Unique Art, 1930	250.00
Monkey, Brown Mohair, Character Felt Face & Hands, Jointed, 16 1/2 In.	250.00

Monkey, Chimp Banging Cymbals, Battery Operated 68.00
Monkey, Crap Shooter, Shakes Dice, Battery Operated, Japan .... .95.00 to 145.00
Monkey, Fur Covered, Eyes Light, Plays Cymbals, Windup & Battery Operated, 8 In. 45.00
Monkey, Glass Button Eyes, Felt Hands & Feet, Steiff, 1950s, 8 In. 100.00
Monkey, Hoppo, Waltzing, Windup, Marx 225.00
Monkey, Jolly Drummer, Mechanical, Box 125.00
Monkey, Juggling, Windup, Alps, 1950s 135.00
Monkey, Looping, Windup, Box 60.00
Monkey, Mighty Kong, Remote Control, Box 650.00
Monkey, On Scooter, Schuco 800.00
Monkey, Playing Guitar, Windup, Japan 95.00
Monkey, Playing Trumpet, Metal, Velvet Face, Ears, Battery Operated, Japan 65.00
Monkey, Plush, With Comb & Celluloid Mirror, Windup, Japan, 1950s 95.00
Monkey, Rock 'n' Roll, Battery Operated, Box .... .125.00 to 250.00
Monkey, Rock 'n' Roll, Holding Metal Guitar, Plush, Japan, 11 In. 90.00
Monkey, Shoeshine Joe, Lighted Pipe, Tin, Plastic, Plush Cover, Battery Operated, Japan 210.00
Monkey, Tumbling, Marx, Box 450.00
Monkey, With Compact & Mirror, Mohair, Schuco, 1920s, 3 1/2 In. 750.00
Moon Base Alpha, Space 1999, Gerry Anderson, TV, Mattel, No. 9592, 1976 .... 110.00
Moon Explorer, Gray, Battery Operated, Tin, 1950s, 14 In. 4255.00
Moon Face, Tin Lithograph, Penny, Germany 225.00
Moon Mullins & Kayo Handcar, Kayo Standing On Dynamite Box, Tin, Marx 190.00
Mortimer Snerd, Walker, Tin, Windup, McCarthy, Inc., 1938, 8 In. 400.00
Mortimer Snerd, Walker, Windup, Marx 450.00
Motor, Outboard, Johnson, 5 1/2 In. 175.00
Motor Scooter, Eagle, Cushman, Die Cast 36.00
Motorcycle, Balloon Tires, Tin, Penny Toy, 3 1/2 In. 295.00
Motorcycle, Champion, Cast Iron, Original Tires, 1930s, 7 In. 450.00
Motorcycle, Champion, Rider, Rubber Tires, Cast Iron, 7 In. 148.00
Motorcycle, Champion, White Rubber Tires, Cast Iron, 5 In. 325.00
Motorcycle, CHIPS, Free Wheeling Cycle, 1980 .... 35.00
Motorcycle, Circus, Cycle Advances, Makes U Turn, Windup, Tin, 6 In. 267.00
Motorcycle, Cop, Sidecar, Orange, Cast Iron, 1930s, 4 In. 195.00
Motorcycle, Curvo 1000, Windup, Schuco, Box 350.00
Motorcycle, Girl Rider, Vinyl Face, Rooted Hair, Friction, Box, Japan 285.00
Motorcycle, Harley-Davidson, Lockheed Vega Airplane 55.00
Motorcycle, Harley-Davidson, Pressed Steel, Friction 390.50
Motorcycle, Harley-Davidson, Rider With Goggles, Cast Iron 990.00
Motorcycle, Harley-Davidson, Travel Air Airplane, 1929 .... 90.00
Motorcycle, Indian, Black, Red, Black Beautiful Set 125.00
Motorcycle, Indian, Clown Rider 545.00
Motorcycle, Indian, Iron, Globe Solo, 1930s, 9 In. 875.00
Motorcycle, Monkey On Motorcycle, Japan, 9 In. 295.00
Motorcycle, Police Auto, Battery Operated, Bandai, Box 400.00
Motorcycle, Police Patrol, Engine Noise & Spark, Windup, Tin, 8 In. 190.00
Motorcycle, Police Rider, Rubber Tires, Wooden Hubs, Cast Iron, 6 In. 175.00
Motorcycle, Police, Sidecar, Windup, Headlight, Tin, Marx No. 3, 8 1/2 In. 575.00
Motorcycle, Police, Sidecar, Windup, Plastic, Japan, Box, 1970s 165.00
Motorcycle, Policeman, Cast Iron, Champion, 7 In. 175.00
Motorcycle, Policeman, Champion, Cast Iron, Green, Rubber Wheels, 1930s, 7 In. 400.00
Motorcycle, Policeman, Khaki Paint, Gold Trim, Rubber Tires, Cast Iron, Hubley, 9 In. .. 1760.00
Motorcycle, Policeman, Rubber, Auburn 75.00
Motorcycle, Racing, Tin, Windup, Sidecar, U.S. Zone, Germany 190.00
Motorcycle, Rider, Battery Operated Headlight, Iron, 1930s 510.00
Motorcycle, Roll Over, Tin Lithograph, Friction, Alps, Japan, c.1950, 5 In. 55.00
Motorcycle, Sidecar, Removable Driver, Cast Iron, Hubley, 9 In. 1100.00
Motorcycle, Sidecar, Rider, U.S. Zone, Germany, Tin, Windup 190.00
Motorcycle, Speed Boy Delivery, Marx, Box 690.00
Motorcycle, Speed King, With Rider, Tin 397.00
Motorcycle, Tricky, Moves To End Of Table & Turns, Key Wind, Marx, 1930s, 4 In. 315.00
Motorcycle, With Driver, Tin Lithograph, Friction, Technofix, 1940s, 7 1/4 In. 1760.00
Mouse, Wonder, Windup, Japan 50.00
Moving Van, Atlas Van Lines, 1957 .... 89.00

Moving Van, Black Cabin, Chassis, Red Body, Wheels, Keystone, 26 x 11 x 7 In. 750.00
Mr. Bubbles, Bubble Blowing Turtle, Box 125.00
Mr. Potato Head, Styrofoam Ball Head, Original Box, Hasbro, c.1950 .... 40.00
Music Box, Baby's Face With Bonnet Top, Swiss, 3 x 2 1/2 In. 75.00
Music Box, Cathedral Form, Pull String, Metal, Chein 90.00
Music Box, Penguin, Ceramic 145.00
Music Box, Snoopy, Astronaut 95.00
Music Box, Snoopy, Bowl On Head, Mattel, 1960s 35.00
Music Box, Snoopy, WWI Flying Ace, Wooden, It's A Long Way To Tipperary, 4 1/2 In. . 125.00
Mystery Section Satellite, Astronaut In Orbit, Cragstan, Box 850.00
Mysto Magic Set, Gilbert, Box, 1930 .... 145.00
Night-Light, Big Boy 110.00
Night-Light, Bozo The Clown, Head & Collar, Plastic, Gem, 1960s, 5 In. 15.00
Night-Light, Flintstones, Original Package ....20.00 to 22.00
Noisemaker, Chinaman, Lead Ball Hits Tin Lithographed Plate 85.00
Noisemaker, Golfer, Lead Ball Hits Tin Lithographed Plate 85.00
Noisemaker, Lead Ball Hits Tin Lithographed Plate, Penny Toy, Germany 85.00
Nu-Nu, Chinese Porter With Tea Chest, Box, Lehmann, 6 In. 1725.00
Omnibus, Hide-Covered Horses, Painted Wood, 32 In. 2200.00
Organ, Cathedral, Windup, Tin, Chein, 1930s, 10 In. 175.00
Ostrich, Pulling Cart, Tin Lithograph, Lehmann, 7 In. 290.00
Oven, Easy Bake, Accessories, Box, 1964 .... 35.00
Pail, Children, Playing With Beach Ball, Lobster Embossed Base, 1930s, 3 In. 75.00
Pail, Hanna Barbera Characters, All, Tin Lithograph, Shovel, 8 In. 50.00
Paint By Number, Bionic Woman, Box 35.00
Parrot, Pretty Peggy, Battery Operated, Box 295.00
Parrot, Red, Yellow Saddle, Plays Music & Rocks, Coin-Operated, 10 Cent 2000.00
Peacock, Walks, Windup, Ebo, 1920s 250.00
Pedal Car, Airplane, Fokker, Blue Streak, Toledo 2090.00
Pedal Car, Airplane, Large Wings & Tail Fin, Pressed Steel 2970.00
Pedal Car, Auburn, Blue 3080.00
Pedal Car, Blue Streak 675.00
Pedal Car, BMC Special, Derby Racer, Red, Original Decals, 1953 .... 750.00
Pedal Car, BMC, Red Crown, Die Cast, Lights, Red, White, Blue, 1948, Miniature 36.00
Pedal Car, Buick, Chrome Windshield, Murray, 1950, 38 x 20 x 17 In. 1092.50
Pedal Car, Bulldozer, 1950s 2975.00
Pedal Car, Cadillac, Steelcraft, 1925 .... 4995.00
Pedal Car, Champion, Murray 975.00
Pedal Car, Chrysler Airflow 3740.00
Pedal Car, Clipper, Chain Drive, Unassembled, Murray, 1959 .... 1595.00
Pedal Car, Comet, Murray, Red & Blue Trim, 1949 .... 1000.00
Pedal Car, Dump Truck, 1930s 2800.00
Pedal Car, Earth Mover, Murray, 1959 .... 595.00
Pedal Car, Fire Ball, Red & White Paint, Chrome Plated Trim, Murray, 40 In. 275.00
Pedal Car, Fire Chief, Twin Six, Gendron, 1925 .... 6820.00
Pedal Car, Fire Truck, Casey Jones 550.00
Pedal Car, Gendron, 1932, 28 x 50 In. 2530.00
Pedal Car, Gendron, Pneumatic Tires, 1930s, 28 x 53 In. 4400.00
Pedal Car, Lyon's Towing Service 425.00
Pedal Car, Pace Car, Murray, 1959 .... 995.00
Pedal Car, Packard 6050.00
Pedal Car, Packard 6 Roadster, Mustard Yellow Paint, 49 In. 9350.00
Pedal Car, Packard Coupe, Painted Dark Blue, Red Wheels 5500.00
Pedal Car, Plymouth, Arcade 450.00
Pedal Car, Pontiac, Yellow, Maroon Wheel Arches, Steelcraft, 1935, 36 In. 1725.00
Pedal Car, Pursuit Plane 3850.00
Pedal Car, Race, No. 8, Chain Drive, Murray, 1962 .... 395.00
Pedal Car, Racer, Matthews, Gas Powered, Restored, 1938 .... 1100.00
Pedal Car, Radio Sports Car, Murray, 1959 .... 795.00
Pedal Car, Ride-Em Fire Truck, Keystone, Late 1930s 745.00
Pedal Car, Ride-Em Steamroller, Keystone, No. 60, 1931 .... 745.00
Pedal Car, Spirit Of St. Louis 2200.00
Pedal Car, Station Wagon, Murray, 1953 .... 880.00

Pedal Car, Tractor, Hard Rubber Wheels, Red, White & Black, Farmall, 38 In. 88.00
Pedal Car, Willys-Knight, Steelcraft, 1920s 4485.00
Pekinese, Miniature 175.00
Penguin, Button, Tag, Steiff, 5 In. 80.00
Penguin, Metal, 3 In. 58.00
Penguin, Skiing, Windup, Wire Remote, Japan, Box, 1960s 65.00
Periscope, Electronic, Cragstan 95.00
Peter Pan Crayon Set, Box, 1950s 70.00
Pheasant, Windup, Tin Lithograph, G.N.K., Box, 1950s, 7 In. 70.00
Phonograph, Ding Dong School, RCA Victor, White Plastic, 1953, 8 x 10 x 4 In. .. 130.00
Photographer, Shutterbug, Camera Flash, 5 Actions, Japan, 1950s 645.00
Piano, Lodeon, Player, 26 Rolls, Chein & Co. 495.00
Piano, Schoenhut, 6 3/4 x 5 x 6 1/2 In. 85.00
Piano, Tiny Tot, Upright, 20 x 22 In. 150.00
Pianola, 6 Rolls, Chein 200.00
Pig, Madame Alexander, Original Tail 750.00
Pigs, Racing, Painted, Tin, Windup, Gunthermann, Germany, 5 In. 365.00
Pigs, Three Little, Tin, Thick Felt, Argentina, 1940s 675.00
Pinocchio, Holding Cymbals, Metal Body, Vinyl Head, Windup, Japan, 12 In. 50.00
Pip-Squeak, Cat, Flannel Coat, Glass Eyes, Opens Mouth, 7 In. 155.00
Pip-Squeak, Cat, Opens Mouth, Flannel, Button Eyes, Painted Pupils, 7 1/4 In. 110.00
Pip-Squeak, Pumpkin Head, Straw Filled Body, Wooden Arms & Legs, 30 In. 795.00
Play Family Farm, Fisher-Price 50.00
Play House, Log Cabin, Joel Ellis, c.1880 .... 575.00
Play Set, A-TEAM Action Corvette, Box 40.00
Play Set, Alaska, Marx, Box 425.00
Play Set, Captain Blood 40.00
Play Set, Charlie's Angels, Hideaway House 150.00
Play Set, Fort Apache 25.00
Play Set, Happy Days, Includes 1957 Chevy, Motorcycle, Hotrod, Box, 1976 .... 34.50
Play Set, Johnny Seven OMA Helmet, Walkie-Talkie, Box 195.00
Play Set, Rifleman Ranch, Box, Marx, 1950s 500.00
Play Set, Rin Tin Tin, Marx, 1950s 300.00
Play Set, Sears Service Center 45.00
Play Set, Star Wars, Empire Strikes Back, Imperial Attack Base, Kenner, 1980 ...... 33.00
Play Set, Starblazers, Bridge, 3 Flashing Console Lights, Voice Box, Japan 89.00
Play Set, Western Town, Box, Fisher-Price, 1982, 19 Piece 23.00
Playground, Mechanical, Windup, Metal, Box, Lee Toy 150.00
Polar Bear, Grenfell Label 375.00
Polar Bear, Mohair, Stuffed, Glass Eyes, Collar With Bell, Button, Steiff, 1950s 180.00
Policeman, Pull Toy, Mayflower, 1930s 75.00
Policeman, Traffic, Windup, Marx 400.00
Policeman & Traffic Sign, Tin, Bradford Co., 1914 .... 350.00
Pool Players, Tin, Windup, Germany, 1920s, 13 In. ....325.00 to 350.00
Porky Pig, Twirls Umbrella, Windup, Marx, 1939 .... 425.00
Porter, Celluloid, Windup, Occupied Japan 150.00
Preacher, Black Man, Ives 2310.00
Projector, 8mm, Battery Operated, Brumberger, Plastic Case, 1960s, 7 x 8 In. 24.00
Projector, Give-A-Show, Battery Operated, Plastic, 15 Slides, Kenner, Box, 1962 ...... 60.00
Puppy, Drumming, Musical, Battery Operated, Box, 10 In. 85.00
Rabbit, Boxing Bunny, Windup, Box, Japan 165.00
Rabbit, Busy Housekeeper, Battery Operated, Alps, Box 350.00
Rabbit, Celluloid, Dressed, 6 In. 38.00
Rabbit, Drumming, Rocks From Side To Side Playing Drums, Tin, Prewar, Alps, 8 In. ... 418.00
Rabbit, Glass Eyes, Tan Mohair, Jointed, Steiff, 9 In. 275.00
Rabbit, Lop Ear Louis, Fisher-Price, 1934 .... 275.00
Rabbit, Mohair & Fabric, Standing, Dressed, Open Felt Mouth, 16 In. 125.00
Rabbit, Mohair, Stuffed, Glass Eyes, Button, Steiff, 1950s, 8 In. 38.00
Rabbit, Peter Cottontail, Tin, Windup 60.00
Rabbit, Peter The Drumming Rabbit, Battery Operated, Box 189.95
Rabbit, Pulling Cart, Tin Lithograph, Chein 95.00
Rabbit, Pulling Tin Sled, Celluloid, Windup, With Ducks & Chicks 120.00
Rabbit, Running, On Wooden Wheels, Steiff 185.00

Ramp Walker, Circus Ringmaster, Marx 36.00
Ramp Walker, Hap & Hop Soldiers 20.00
Ramp Walker, Nanny Pushing Carriage 30.00
Ray Gun, Space Pilot Jet, Plastic, Futuristic Design, 8 1/2 In. 55.00
Reel, View-Master, Dells Of Wisconsin, No. 124 .... 8.00
Reel Set, View-Master, Peanuts, Lucy, Charlie Brown, Story, Sawyers, 1966, 3 Piece ... 22.00
Refrigerator, Steel, Monito, 2 Shelves, 1930s 145.00
Refrigerator, Steel, Wolverine, Box 85.00
Reindeer, Pulling Sleigh, Papier-Mache, Clockwork, Germany 4950.00
Reindeer, Tan Mohair, Felt Antlers, Glass Eyes, Embroidered, Steiff, 1950s, 9 3/4 In. ... 110.00
Ride A Rocket, Tin, Chein, 19 In. 775.00
Rifle, Agent Zero-M, Radio, Mattel, 1964 .... 120.00
Rifle, Tom Corbett Space Cadet, Box, 1950s 375.00
Ring, Face, Tom Corbett, Silver Finish, c.1950 .... 55.00
Ring, Green Hornet, Adjustable 18.50
Ring, Green Hornet, Brass 15.00
Ring, Green Hornet, Rubber Hornet 20.00
Ring, Holster, Removable Ring 36.00
Ring, Junior Fire Marshall, Metal, Silver Finish, Red Painted, Sealed, 1950s 22.00
Ring, Laugh-In, Don't Rush Me Big Boy, T.V., Metal, 1960s 60.00
Ring, Romper Room, Metal, Silver Fish, T.V. Premium, 1960s 50.00
Ring, Sky King, Glow In The Dark Stone, Brass, 1940s 85.00
Road Construction Set, Flatbed Truck, Dump Truck, Bulldozer, Grader, Tootsietoy ... 420.00
Robot, 2500, Red Light On Torso, Battery Operated, Box, 10 In. 80.00
Robot, Acrobat, Battery Operated, Blue & Red, 1960s 390.00
Robot, Astro-Scout, Light Metallic Blue, Red Arms, 1950, 9 In. 3105.00
Robot, Atom, Silver, Hinged Arms, Tin, 1950, 6 1/2 In. 805.00
Robot, Black, Red, Battery Operated, Tin, 1950s, 13 In. 2415.00
Robot, Bulldozer, Orange, Black, Red Design, Flag In Left Hand, Tin, 6 In. 488.00
Robot, Bump & Go Action, Flashing Light, Battery Operated, Marx, 6 In. 2500.00
Robot, Busy Cart, Black, Yellow, Battery Operated, Tin, 1960s, 12 In. 1265.00
Robot, Change Nab, Dinosaur Head, Remote Control, Horikawa, 13 In. ....*Illus* 3105.00
Robot, Clown, Lights & Sounds, Mouth Moves, Plastic, Box 150.00
Robot, Colonel Hap Hazard, Walking, Marx ....700.00 to 900.00
Robot, Commander, Windup, Red, Gray, Tin, Japan 550.00
Robot, Cragstan Astronaut, Red, Domed Helmet, Tin, 1950s, 9 1/2 In. 1725.00
Robot, Cragstan Astronaut, Red, Walks & Steps, Battery Operated, 1955, 14 In. 3565.00
Robot, Cragstan Great Astronaut, Red, Battery, Box, Japan, 1950, 11 In. 2530.00
Robot, Dino, Walks, Stops, Head Splits, Reveals Dinosaur Head, Battery Operated, 12 In. 552.00
Robot, Directional, Light Blue, Block Head, Red Flashing Light, 11 In. 1840.00
Robot, Directional, Multidirectional, Blue Tin, Yonezawa, Box, 10 In. 690.00
Robot, Gizmo The Peaceable, 1950s, 6 1/2 Ft. 11500.00
Robot, Go-Go, Figure & Plane, Red, Windup, Japan, Box 125.00
Robot, Golden, Light Bulb Eyes, Black Head, 1950s, 6 3/8 In. 1100.00
Robot, Great Garloo, Original Medallion, Battery Operated 475.00
Robot, High Wheel, Metallic Blue, Box, 1960s, 9 In. 1265.00
Robot, I-M-2, Radio Controlled, Box 110.00
Robot, Interplanetary Explorer Spaceman, Japan, 1950s, 7 7/8 In. ....*Illus* 1725.00
Robot, Jumping Rocket, Windup, Tin, Japan, 6 In. 185.00
Robot, Jumping, Windup, Tin, Hard Plastic Feet, Argentina 95.00
Robot, Jupiter, Red, Black Plastic Arms, Box, 1960s, 7 In. ....360.00 to 415.00
Robot, Lantern, Gray Cubical Torso, Red Lantern, Box, 1950s, 7 3/4 In. 4890.00
Robot, Lavender, Masudaya, 1950s, 15 In. ....*Illus* 8050.00
Robot, Lavender, Non-Stop, Box 8050.00
Robot, Light Metallic Blue, Tin, 6 In. 1150.00
Robot, Lilliput, Clockwork, Japan, 1940s, 6 In. ....*Illus* 8625.00
Robot, Lost In Space, Motorized, Remco, Box 375.00
Robot, Machine Man, 15 In. 42550.00
Robot, Mammy Spaceship 80.00
Robot, Mars Explorer, Red, Black Face, Black Rubber Tires, 1960, 10 In. 1380.00
Robot, Mighty Robot, With Spark, Clockwork, Box, 7 In. 310.00
Robot, Monster, Helmet Opens & Closes, Red Lighted Dragon, Walks 95.00
Robot, Moon Explorer, Box, 12 In. 210.00

Robot, Moon, Dark Gray, Pink Tinted Dome, Red Arms, Feet, 1950s, 10 In. 3740.00
Robot, Mr. Mercury 325.00
Robot, Mr. Robot, White Body, Red Arms, Cragstan, 1950s, 11 In. 400.00
Robot, Mr. Smash, Clockwork, Box, Marx, 6 In. 450.00
Robot, Musical Drummer, Silver Body, Cube Torso, Battery Operated, 8 In. 17250.00
Robot, Nonstop, Lavender, Lilac Purple, Battery Operated, 1950, 15 In. 8050.00
Robot, Radicon, Masudaya, 1950s .... *Illus* 21850.00
Robot, Red & Blue, Battery Operated, Japan, 11 1/4 In. 110.00
Robot, Robby, Planet, Blue Outline, Walks, Battery Operated, 1950s .....1265.00 to 2400.00
Robot, Robby, Sitting In Diesel Bulldozer, Holding Gear Shift, 1950s 275.00
Robot, Robert, Ideal Toy Co., Box, 1950s 150.00
Robot, Rock 'Em-Sock 'Em, Marx, Box 195.00
Robot, Rotate-O-Matic Super Astronaut, Red, Battery Operated, Box, 1980, 11 In. ... 170.00
Robot, Sir Galaxy, Radio Control, Box 110.00
Robot, Smoking, Linemar, 1950s 1000.00
Robot, Son Of Garloo, Tin Lithograph, Walking, Windup 275.00
Robot, Spaceman, Battery Operated, Box 1250.00
Robot, Spaceman, Silver, Red Arms, Legs, Astronaut Face, 1950, 9 In. 1265.00
Robot, Spaceman, Smoking, Gray Body, Red Feet, Battery Operated, 1950, 12 In. 1725.00
Robot, Sparking Mike, Silver, Blue Ears, Feet, Box, 1950s, 8 In. 1380.00
Robot, Sparky, Silver, Block Head Sparks, Red Feet, Tin, 1950, 8 In. 1035.00
Robot, Sparky, Silver, Red Feet, Ears, Japan, Box, 1955, 7 1/2 In. ......425.00 to 575.00
Robot, Speedboat, Red, Silver Helm, White, Blue, Tin, 1950s 2875.00
Robot, Super Gun, Robot Walks Forward, Battery Operated, Box, 12 In. 200.00
Robot, Swinging Baby, Yellow, Red, Blue Swing, Box, 1960-1965, 6 In. 400.00
Robot, Swivel-O-Matic Astronaut, Battery Operated, Box, Japan 195.00
Robot, Talking, Red, Silver Arms, Battery Operated, 1960s, 11 In. 430.00
Robot, Thunder, Battery Operated, Asakusa, 1950s, 11 1/4 In. .... *Illus* 2185.00
Robot, Visible Gear, Battery Operated, 11 1/2 In. 345.00
Robot, Walking, Tin, Windup, Linemar Toys, 6 In. 385.00
Robot, Wheel-A-Gear, Black Metal Torso, Head, 1960s, Box 1035.00
Robot, X-27 Explorer, Blue, Red, Space Suit, Tin, 1950s, 9 In. 2300.00
Robot, Yone, Battery Operated, Japan, Box 230.00
Robot, Zoomer, Burgundy Finish, Black Feet, Hands, Ears, 1950s, 8 In. 805.00
Robot, Zoomer, Windup, Key, 1950s 230.00
Robot Tractor, Marvelous Mike, Battery Operated, 1954 .... 350.00
Robot Tractor, Radar, Metallic Blue, Silver Robot, Tin, Box, 1950s, 7 1/2 In. 862.00
Robot Tractor, With Robot Driver, Gray, Red Detail, Battery Operated, Japan, 9 In. 345.00
Rocket Ride, Windup, Chein 650.00
Rocket Ship, Apollo Saturn, 3 Stage, Battery Operated, Japan 375.00
Rocket Ship, Automatic Docking, Blinking Lite, Battery Operated, 17 In. 175.00
Rocket Ship, Docking, Battery Operated, Box 250.00

Toy, Robot, Change Nab,
Dinosaur Head, Remote
Control, Horikawa, 13 In.

Toy, Robot,
Lavender, Masudaya,
1950s, 15 In.

Toy, Robot, Interplanetary
Explorer Spaceman, Japan,
1950s, 7 7/8 In.

Toy, Robot,
Lilliput, Clockwork,
Japan, 1940s, 6 In.

Toy, Robot,
Radicon, Masudaya,
1950s

Toy, Robot, Thunder, Battery
Operated, Asakusa, 1950s,
11 1/4 In.

Rocket Ship, Lunar Loop, Hard Plastic, Cragstan, Box, 1969	125.00
Rocket Ship, Silver, Seated On Top, Tin, Japan, 1960s, 6 In.	258.00
Rocket Ship, Tin Lithograph	210.00
Rocket Ship, Tom Corbett, Space Cadet, Marx	220.00
Rodeo Joe, Jeep, Crazy Action, Joe Jerked Out Of Seat, Unique Art, 7 In.	425.00
Roller Coaster, 2 Cars, Amusement Park Graphics, Ohio Art	275.00
Roller Coaster, 2 Cars, Windup, Tin, Technofix, Box	225.00
Roller Coaster, Big Dipper, Technofix, Box	575.00
Roller Coaster, Chein, 1930s, 2 Cars	450.00 to 595.00
Roller Skates, Adjustable, Chrome Plated, Leather, Winchester	23.00
Roller Skates, Adjustable, Nickel Plated, Red Wheels, Leather, Winchester	18.50 to 36.00
Roly Poly, Easter Bunny, With Chimes, Label, Gundy	20.00
Roly Poly, Policeman, Schoenhut	395.00
Roly Poly, Soldier, Schoenhut, c.1912	450.00
Roly-Poly Bear, Fisher-Price, No. 719, 7 1/2 In.	22.00
Rooster, Flaps Wings, Windup, Hand Painted, 10 In.	575.00
Rooster, On Platform, Tin, Iron Wheels, Gilt, Red, Green, 4 1/2 In.	275.00
Sailor, Dancing, Blue Sailor Suit, Molded Blue Hat, Germany, Lehman, 7 1/2 In.	375.00
Sand, Busy Mike With Monkey, Chein	135.00
Sand, Windmill, Tin, Japan, 1950s, 8 In.	75.00
Sand Sifter, Ohio Art, 1940s	200.00
Santee Claus, Windup, Strauss, 1920s	950.00
Sax-O-Fun, Spike Jones, 1950s	50.00
Scale, 5 Weights, Tin Scoop, Cast Iron, c.1900	250.00
Scene, Shoe Cobbler, Mechanical, Schoenhut	1500.00
Science Kit, Master Electrical, Remco, Box, 1950s	445.00
Scooter, Deliver, Tekno	363.00
Scooter, Eagle Motor, Die Cast, Black, Cushman, 6 1/2 In.	36.00
Scooter, Hamilton, 1949	60.00
Scooter, Krazy Kat, Nifty, 1932, 7 x 6 In.	450.00
Scooter, U.S. Mail, Gay Toy	10.00
Scrappy & Margie, Pull Toy, Columbia Pictures	450.00
Service Station, Tin Lithograph, Accessories, Box, 16 x 24 x 11 In.	360.00
Service Station Set, Texaco, Porcelain, Box, 5 1/2 x 9 1/2 In.	35.00
Sewing Kit, Dolly Dear, Doll Patterns, Suitcase, 1930	70.00
Sewing Machine, Artcraft Jr. Miss	95.00
Sewing Machine, Betsy Ross, Alligator Cover Case, Die Cast Metal, Gray	81.00
Sewing Machine, Betsy Ross, Electric, Carrying Case, 8 3/4 In.	95.00 to 135.00
Sewing Machine, Casige, Decals, British Zone	60.00 to 110.00
Sewing Machine, Durham, Plastic	25.00

Sewing Machine, Hollie Hobbie 25.00
Sewing Machine, Junior Miss, Artcraft Metal Products, Wooden Base, 6 1/2 In. 35.00
Sewing Machine, Little Mary Mix-Up, Hand Operated, Joseph Schneider, 7 In. 50.00
Sewing Machine, Little Modiste 20.00
Sewing Machine, Sew Perfect, Mattel 25.00
Sewing Machine, Singer, Black, Battery Operated ....50.00 to 85.00
Sewing Machine, Singer, Century Of Sewing Service, 1851-1951 .... 165.00
Sewing Machine, Singer, Tan 125.00
Sewing Machine, Snoopy, Japan, Box 120.00
Sewing Machine, Soezy, Bachelor Stenson, Patent 1900 ....1100.00 to 2900.00
Sewing Machine, Victoria, Ernst Plank, Germany, Metal, Hand Operated, Pre-1940 .... 130.00
Sewing Machine, Vulcan Countess, Box 65.00
Sewing Machine, W.A.C.O., Battery Operated, Tin, Japan, 6 In. 80.00
Sheriff's Set, Gabby Hayes, 1950s 80.00
Shoemaker, Windup, Alps, Box, 1950s 275.00
Shoeshine Joe, Lighted Pipe, Tin, Battery Operated, T-N Co. Works, Box, 9 In. 210.00
Shooting Gallery, Gun, Mechanical, Wyandotte, Box 180.00
Shooting Gallery, Tin Lithograph, Windup, Box, Wyandotte 175.00
Shotgun, Johnny Eagle Over & Under, Topper 95.00
Shovel, Sand, Pirate, Tin, J. Chein, 14 In. 45.00
Sideboard, Doll's, Poplar, 2 Doors, 3 Drawers, Crest, 26 x 12 x 21 In. 90.00
Sign, Don't Park Here, Cast Iron, White, 1920s, 4 3/4 In. 100.00
Siren, G-Man, Pocket, Tin Lithograph, Courtland 95.00
Ski Boy, Windup, Chein, No. 157 ....170.00 to 345.00
Sky Cycle, Evel Knievel, Metal, Plastic, Ideal, Box, 1976 .... 75.00
Sky Ringer, Prop Plane, Pilot, Zeppelin Revolving From Tower, Unique Art, Tin, 1933 .. 375.00
Sled, Bentwood Scrolled Runners, Steel Tipped, All Wooden, 44 In. 145.00
Sled, Box, Red Cutters, Green 415.00
Sled, Flexible Flyer, On Wheels, Box 295.00
Sled, Green Center Board, Flowers, Swan's Head Finials, Red Runners, 36 In. 380.00
Sled, Green, Red, Yellow & Mustard Flourishes, Gray Ground, Curled Runners, c.1900 .. 625.00
Sled, Painted Flowers, All Wood, Red 725.00
Sled, Red & Green Paint, Yellow Striping, Black Bird, Steel Tipped Runners, 32 In. 66.00
Sled, Stenciled Boy On Rocking Horse 350.00
Sled, Wabash, Red & Yellow Paint, 10 x 27 In. 185.00
Sled, Wooden, Red & Green Rose, Steel Tipped Runners, 36 In. 220.00
Sled, Wooden, Worn Red & Blue Paint, Black Striping, 35 In. 355.00
Smoking Grandpa, Battery Operated, Box 425.00
Sneezy, Belgium, Squeaks, 1937 .... 25.00
Snoopy, Cook & Flipping Action, Windup, Plastic, Box 25.00
Snoopy, My Friend Snoopy, Pull Arms Back & He Knocks Down Bowling Pins, 1955 ... 35.00
Soda Fountain Set, Mirro 195.00
Soldier, 22nd Cheshire Regiment Band, Britains, 10 Piece 155.00
Soldier, Babes In Toyland, Soldier Playing Drum, Windup, Box, Tin, 6 In. 313.00
Soldier, Black Watch Band, Ducal, 12 Piece 185.00
Soldier, Celluloid, 6 In. 17.00
Soldier, German Playing Cymbals & Drum, Tin Lithograph, Schuco, 1930s, 5 In. 440.00
Soldier, Mammoth Circus, Britains, Set 1650.00
Soldier, McLoughlin Bros., Lead Cavalry, 1900s 290.00
Soldier, On Black Horse, TPS, Tin, Japan, 5 1/2 In. 185.00
Soldier, On Horse, Babes In Toyland, Pull Toy, Wooden 275.00
Soldier, Royal Marine Band, Blue Uniforms, Britains 1540.00
Soldier, Scots Guard Fife & Drum Band, Ducal, 12 Piece 185.00
Space, Capsule No. 5, Battery Operated, Tin, Modern Toys, 1950s 125.00
Space Commando, Gray, Dome Over Head, 1 Hand Holds Gun, 1950, 4 In. 1955.00
Space Explorer, Tank, Blue, Red Metallic, Radar Dish, Japan, 1960s, 7 In. 805.00
Space Man, Light Blue, Orange Helmet, 1960, 6 In. 230.00
Space Rocket, Automatic Toy Co., 9 In. 80.00
Space Shuttle, Battery Operated, Corgi 230.00
Space Station, With Launching Satellite, Tin Crank Action, Marx, 1950s 145.00
Space Vehicle, Spaceman Pilot, Rear Lights, Battery Operated, Tin, 8 In. 315.00
Space Vehicle, With Astronaut In Center Cockpit, X-5 .... 95.00
Spaceman, Hard Plastic, Take-Apart, Blue & Yellow, Renwal 125.00

Spaceship, Flying Saucer Type, Battery Operated, 1960s 145.00
Spanish Conquistador, Palmer Plastics, No. 32, 1950s 76.00
Speakphone, Darth Vader 145.00
Speedboat, Tin, Windup, Lindstrom, 18 1/2 In. 435.00
Speedboat, Tin, Windup, Lionel 375.00
Speedboat, Tommy Boy, Wooden, Label, 18 In. 95.00
Spice Set, Child's, Green & White, 4 Piece 25.00
Spider Man, On Trike, Linemar, Windup 370.00
Spinning Wheel, Remco, Box, Unused 85.00
Squirrel, Perry, Steiff, 6 1/2 In. 55.00
Stamp Set, Sylvester & Tweety, Box 30.00
Star Wars, Action Play Set, Land Of Jawas, Kenner 150.00
Star Wars, Chewbacca, Green Crossbow 50.00
Star Wars, Droid Factory 80.00
Star Wars, Han Solo, 14 In. 215.00
Star Wars, Jabba The Hutt Throne Room, Action Scene, 12 x 18 In. 35.00
Star Wars, Princess Leia, 14 In. 75.00
Star Wars, R2-D2 Robot, Battery Operated With Movie Viewer, Takara, Box 250.00
Star Wars, Rebel Commander 12.00
Star Wars, Snaggletooth 10.00
Star Wars, Transfer Set, Presto Magix, Transtar 5.00
Star Wars, Twin-Pod Cloud Car, Kenner 65.00
Star Wars, Yoda 25.00
Star Wars, Zuckhuss 15.00
Station, Alpine, 2 Trolley Cars, Windup, Ohio Art, 1950s, 32 In. 175.00
Station, Filling, Box, Brightlite, Marx 1650.00
Steam Engine, Cast Iron, Weeden Steam, 7 In. 275.00
Steam Engine, Ride 'Em, Pressed Steel, Twentieth Century Limited 195.00
Steam Shovel, Riding, Keystone 275.00
Steamroller, Hubley 625.00
Steamroller, Keystone, Pressed Steel, 26 In. 410.00
Steamroller, Windup, Marx 200.00
Stove, Arcade Roper Stove, With Fry Pan 145.00
Stove, Cast Iron, Royal, Shelves, Lids, Stove Pipe, Kenton, 7 1/2 x 5 In. 195.00
Stove, Coal, Cast Brass, Salesman's Sample, 6 1/2 In. 280.00
Stove, Cook, Engman Matthews, Eternal Range, 30 In. 4250.00
Stove, Eclipse, Accessories 1980.00
Stove, Electric, Metal Ware Corporation, 8 x 15 x 15 In. 65.00
Stove, Empire, 2 Burners, Oven, Black & Green, 1930s 425.00
Stove, Karr, Speckled Blue On White, Nickel & Stainless Steel Trim 6000.00
Stove, Little Lady, Electric 40.00
Stove, Royal, Plated, 2 Side Shelves, 7 Stove Top Lids 335.00
Stove, Shelves, Lids, Stove Pipe, Kenton, 7 1/2 x 5 In. 195.00
Stove, Suzy Homemaker Kitchen Range 35.00
Stove, Tin, Brass, Pots & Pans 475.00
Street Scene, Lamp, Plastic Light Bulb, Tin, W. Germany, Schuco, 7 In. 78.00
Stroller, Doll, Faux Wicker, 2 Larger Wheels At Back, Footrest, Embossed Tin, 7 In. 1800.00
Stroller, Doll, Wicker, Black Paint, Leominster, Massachusetts, 1920s, 26 1/4 In. 115.00
Strutting Sam, Black, Dancing On Pedestal, Tin, Battery Operated, 1950s ......485.00 to 575.00
Stunt Kit, Stunt Plane, With Pilot, Tin, Marx 275.00
Submarine, Brass Gun, Windup, Wolverine, 1930s 145.00
Submarine, Cast Bronze, c.1940, 10 In. 290.00
Submarine, Sea Wolf Atomic, Tin, Windup, Sutcliffe, 1960s 225.00
Sulky Racer, Horse, Windup, Wolverine, Box 95.00
Sweeper, Carpet, Dopey, Musical 210.00
Sweeper, Carpet, Musical 90.00
Table, Doll's, Nursery Rhymes, Green Paint, 20 x 16 x 18 In. 50.00
Table, Sewing, Oak, Folding, Junior Seamstress, Ruler On Edge, 4 1/2 x 9 In. 125.00
Table, Tea, Doll's, Birch, Refinished, 20 x 17 In. 75.00
Table & Chairs, Doll's, Ice Cream, White Repaint, 5 Piece 135.00
Tank, Anti-Aircraft, Bump & Go, Battery Operated, Tin, Box, 8 1/2 In. 25.00
Tank, Climbing, Sparking, Blue, Orange, Red, Yellow, Tin, Windup, Marx 25.00
Tank, Climbing, Sparking, Windup, Marx 185.00

Tank, Doughboy, No Turrets, Windup, Marx 180.00
Tank, Doughboy, Tin Lithograph, Marx 215.00
Tank, Doughboy, Turrets, Windup, Marx 350.00
Tank, Fleishman's Oil, Windup, Tin, Germany, 1950, 20 In. 1250.00
Tank, General Lee M3, Green Finish, Metal Track, Die Cast, 1978, 5 In. 65.00
Tank, Green Finish, Rubber Track, Plastic Parts, Die Cast, Dinky Toy, 6 In. 57.50
Tank, Leopard, Green Finish, Die Cast, Dinky Toy, 5 In. 57.50
Tank, Maneuver, Accessories, Geoscha, Box, 8 In. 1450.00
Tank, Metal, Green, White Accents, Red Door Over Compartment, Windup, Marx 50.00
Tank, Milk, Corgi 230.00
Tank, Missile Firing, Windup, Gama, Germany, 1940s 45.00
Tank, Radar, Antenna, Blue, Red Light, Box, 1960s, 8 In. 402.00
Tank, Richfield, Blue, Yellow, 1957 . . . . 37.00
Tank, Space Patrol, Orange Clad Astronaut, Blue Metallic, 4 1/2 In. 287.00
Tank, Space, Mighty Explorer, Light Blue, Tin, 6 3/4 In. 488.00
Tank, Space, Super Robot, Light Metallic Blue, 1950s, 9 In. 1265.00
Tank, Turnover, Windup, Marx . . . . .65.00 to 90.00
Tanker, Chevron 38.00
Tanker, Exxon Aviation Gas, Marx, Box, 1993 . . . . 45.00
Tanker, Mobilgas, 1953 Model Ford, Red & White & Blue Graphics 37.00
Tanker, Standard Oil, No. 14, Buddy L 4025.00
Target, Shooting Gallery, 2 Spring Mounted Roosters, Iron, Concrete Base, 18 1/2 In. . . . 80.00
Target Board, Rudolph The Reindeer, Box, 1938 . . . . 65.00
Taxi, Amos 'n' Andy, Marx 675.00
Taxi, Checker, Driver In Uniform & Passengers In Windows, Tin, 6 In 290.00
Taxi, Driver, Yellow, Black, Windup, Strauss, 7 x 4 x 3 In. 345.00
Taxi, Dual Axle Wheels, 1930s Model, Black & Orange, Cast Iron, Arcade 690.00
Taxi, Friction, Yellow, Tin Lithograph, Toymaster, Box, 1960s, 3 1/4 x 9 1/4 x 2 In. 85.00
Taxi, Mercedes-Benz, Tin Lithograph Interior, Battery Operated, Japan, 10 In. 120.00
Taxi, Orange & Blue, Cast Iron, Arcade, 5 1/4 In. 495.00
Taxi, Tricky, Windup, Marx . . . . .90.00 to 125.00
Taxi, Yellow, Freidag, Cast Iron, Painted, c.1925, 5 In. 546.00
Taxi, Yellow, Rubber Tires, 1930s, Arcade, 8 1/4 In. 485.00
Tea Set, 25th Anniversary, Barbie, Gray Velvet Case, 1984, 14 Piece 50.00
Tea Set, Blue Willow, Metal, 16 Piece 100.00
Tea Set, Little Girl With Ducks, Tin, Ohio Art, 23 Piece 65.00
Tea Set, Little Hostess, Moderntone, Pink, Black, 12 Piece 200.00
Tea Set, Pink & Yellow Leaves, Butterflies & Roses, Gold Trim, 21 Piece 250.00
Teddy Bears are also listed in the Teddy Bear category.
Teddy The Artist, Battery Operated, 9 Patterns, Crayons, Instructions, Y Co. 450.00
Telegraph Set, A.C. Gilbert, Illustrated Manual 200.00
Telephone, Ernie Keebler, Box 125.00
Telephone, Playphone 600, Wooden, Dated 1922 . . . . 12.00
Telephone, Spider Man 67.00
Theater, Punch & Judy, Bell Toy, Lithograph Paper, Pat. Dec. 8, 1891, 9 x 6 x 2 In. 260.00
Theater, Punch & Judy, Crew Of Puppets, 36 In. 450.00
Thermos, Barbie, Pictured On Sides 90.00
Thresher, Cast Iron, Yellow, Arcade 750.00
Thresher, McCormick, Deering, Arcade 385.00
Tidy Tim, Street Cleaner, Lithographed Clothing, Windup 143.00
Tiger, Esso, Windup, 7 In. 35.00
Tiger, Stalking, Clockwork, Stenciled Dog Fur, Glass Eyes, DeCamps, 15 In. 517.00
Tinkertoy, Big Boy, Hardwood & Plastic, Toy Tinkers, 1950s, 318 Piece 30.00
Tom & Jerry, Rubber, Squeaks, Pair 51.00
Tom & Jerry, Walker, Marx, Pair 112.50
Tom & Jerry In Car, Battery Operated, Tin, Rico, 1970, 13 1/2 In. 475.00
Tool Chest, Big Boy, Gilbert, Some Tools 25.00
Tool Chest, Bliss Union, Paper Label, 12 Tools, Wooden Box, c.1890 . . . . 245.00
Toolbox, Finished Wood, Mason & Parker Mfg. Co., 11 1/4 In. 65.00
Toonerville Trolley, Red, Yellow & Black, Box, G. Borgfeldt, 1930s, 5 1/2 In. 1470.00
Toonerville Trolley, Tin, Windup, Germany, 1922 . . . . 1300.00
Top, 3 Little Pigs & Big Bad Wolf, Tin, Chein, 1940s . . . . .125.00 to 250.00
Top, Rainbow, Seneca Toy Co., 1930s 95.00

Tow Truck, Jeep, Wonka, White 75.00
Toy Chest, NFL Official Foot Locker, Bradshaw, Butkus, Others, 1971, 30 x 15 x 12 In. . 195.00
Track Set, Johnny Lightning 500, Box 150.00
Tractor, Caterpillar, Arcade, Cast Iron 3190.00
Tractor, Caterpillar, Windup, Marx, Box 325.00
Tractor, Cultivision, Arcade 2860.00
Tractor, Disk Harrow, Ertl Co., 4 1/2 In. 35.00
Tractor, Disk Harrow, Tru Scale, Red, Box 50.00
Tractor, Driver, Cast Iron 65.00
Tractor, Hi Loader, Shovel Lift, Mechanical Lifting Shovel, 15 In. 145.00
Tractor, Highboy, Climbing Tractor, Farmer Driver, Windup, Tin, Marx, 11 In. 262.00
Tractor, John Deere, Green, 8 1/4 In. 85.00
Tractor, McCormick Deering, Arcade, 7 In. 650.00
Tractor, Sparking, Rubber Treads, Farmer Driver, Windup, Tin, Box, Marx, 1950, 8 In. . . 210.00
Tractor, Tin Lithograph, Rubber Treads, 6 Wheels, Louis Marx, 1930s, 11 1/2 In. . . . 170.00
Tractor, With Shovel, Belt Driven, Cast Iron & Steel, Hubley 850.00
Tractor, With Shovel, Box, Matchbox, King Size 80.00
Tractor Trailer, Caterpillar, Sandy Andy, Wolverine, 1920s, 21 In. 750.00
Traffic Cycle-Car Delivery, Windup, Tin, Goggled Driver, Hoge, 1930 . . . . 3220.00
Traffic Light, Lights Flash, 30 In. 85.00
Trailer, Construction, Japan, Box, 13 1/2 In. 435.00
Train, American Flyer, Burlington Zephyr, No. 9900 Locomotive, Electric 120.00
Train, American Flyer, Passenger Station, No. 105, Box 150.00
Train, American Flyer, Piggyback Unloader & Car, No. 23830 . . . . 220.00
Train, Baggage Car, Ives, 8-Wheel, Green, Orange Lettering 25.00
Train, Bassett Lowke, Locomotive, Steam, Black Prince, 1902 . . . . 1000.00
Train, Bassett Lowke, Locomotive, Steam, Electric, Green, Black, Box, 1924 . . . . 3500.00
Train, Bassett Lowke, Locomotive, Steam, Lithograph, 6 Die Cast Wheels, 1927 . . . . 100.00
Train, Bing, Locomotive, Cowcatcher, Black Paint 145.00
Train, Bing, Snow Plow, O Gauge, Multicolors, 6 Spoke Cast Wheels 225.00
Train, Circus Car, Red Roof, Yellow Sides, Standard Gauge 200.00
Train, Disneyland Express, Marx 250.00
Train, Gerard, Handcar, Surface Pitting 300.00
Train, Hog Tom Thumb, Locomotive, Tin, Electric, Box 200.00
Train, Hornby, No. 4472, Flying Scotsman, Locomotive, Tender, Green, Electric 588.00
Train, Hornby, Tank Locomotive No. 6954, Maroon & Gray, Lithograph, Electric 935.00
Train, Ingersoll, Beggs Mfg. Co., Steam, c.1870 . . . . 2850.00
Train, Ives, Limited Vestibule Express, Saratoga Coach, No. 129 . . . . 350.00
Train, Ives, Locomotive, Clockwork Motor, Cast Iron, 1922 . . . . 95.00
Train, Ives, Locomotive, Clockwork, Steel Wheels, 1926 . . . . 25.00
Train, Ives, Locomotive, Clockwork, Tin Plated Wheels, 1927 . . . . 45.00
Train, Ives, No. 3251, Locomotive, Olive, Rubber Stamped 190.00
Train, Ives, Parlor Car, Light Green, Black Outline Letters 35.00
Train, Ives, Refrigerator Car, Medium Gray Roof, 9 In. 25.00
Train, Ives, Tank Car, Red, Green Top, Black Frame, Gold Stripes 55.00
Train, Jetson's, Tin, Marx 425.00
Train, Joyland Express, Friction, Tin, Japan, Box, 5 In. 65.00
Train, Lionel, Box Car, No. 2954, Semiscale, 1941 . . . . 122.00
Train, Lionel, Box Car, Sentinel, No. 6464-325 . . . . 300.00
Train, Lionel, Boxcar, No. 814 . . . . 225.00
Train, Lionel, Caboose, No. 2957, Semiscale, 1941 . . . . 300.00
Train, Lionel, Caboose, No. 6447 NSC 257.00
Train, Lionel, Cattle Car, Loading Platform, 6 Cows, Box 75.00
Train, Lionel, Fire Car, No. 52 . . . . 242.00
Train, Lionel, Handcar, No. 1107, Donald & Pluto 290.00
Train, Lionel, Harnischfeger Truck Crane, No. 6827, Dark Yellow 135.00
Train, Lionel, Hopper, No. 2956, Semiscale, 1941 . . . . 440.00
Train, Lionel, Inspection Car, No. 68, Red & Cream, Chrome 313.00
Train, Lionel, J.C. Penney, Locomotive, No. 8006, Display Case, Sealed 265.00
Train, Lionel, Life Savers Tanker, Five Flavor Life Savers, c.1978, 10 In. 150.00
Train, Lionel, Locomotive, No. 253 . . . . 165.00
Train, Lionel, Locomotive, No. 2056, Tender, No. 2040W 200.00
Train, Lionel, Milk Car, Automatic, Platform At 1 End, Box . . . . .35.00 to 40.00

Train, Lionel, Oil Derrick & Pumper, No. 455, Sealed 715.00
Train, Lionel, Packmaker Boxcar, No. 6464, No. 125, Metal Trucks 1210.00
Train, Lionel, Pullman, Peacock With Orange Trim, Roof 50.00
Train, Lionel, Rio Grande Snow Plow, No. 53, Metal Steps 198.00
Train, Lionel, Rutland Box Car, No. 6464, Unpainted Door, Metal Trucks 110.00
Train, Lionel, U.S. Army Switcher, No. 41 .... 325.00
Train, Lionel, Virginian NSC Caboose, No. 6427 .... 132.00
Train, Locomotive, Cable Pacific, Battery Operated, Tin, Japan, Box 120.00
Train, Locomotive, Clockwork Motor, Japanned Finish, 12 1/2 In. 465.00
Train, Locomotive, Old Timer, Tin, Japan, Box, 8 In. 180.00
Train, Locomotive, Push, Cast Iron Wheels, Gauged Steel, Brass Smoke Stack 250.00
Train, Locomotive, Steam, Duchess Of Montrose, Electric Motor, 6 Coaches 3850.00
Train, Marklin, Boxcar, Fruit Growers Express, Tin Lithograph 250.00
Train, Marklin, Crocodile Locomotive, No. CCS800, 1957 .... 1105.00
Train, Marklin, Locomotive, No. 12920, Tender, Black Lithograph, Gold Trim 2090.00
Train, Marklin, Locomotive, No. G800, Black & Red 175.00
Train, Marklin, Log, Iron Wheels, Cast Iron Log Brackets, Pressed Steel 250.00
Train, Marx, 333 Hudson, Coaches, Observation, Flat-Side Trucks 242.00
Train, Marx, Honeymoon Express, Tin, Windup 215.00
Train, Marx, New York Central, Steam Engine, No. 400, Tracks 150.00
Train, Santa Fe Locomotive, Electric, Western Germany, 1950 .... 25.00
Train, Steam Locomotive, No. 950, Penny Toy By JM, Germany 350.00
Train, Weeden, Stream Engine, No. 20 .... 150.00
Train Accessories, A Flyer, Dealer Sign, Paper, Stenciled, E.H. Scholl, 1955, 11 Ft. 4 In. 201.00
Train Accessories, A Flyer, Operating Hopper, No. 41, Red 230.00
Train Accessories, Hornby, Liner Diner, Brown, Gold Trim, Gray Roof 235.00
Train Accessories, House, Bing, Track Side, Mechanical Warning Bell, Windup, 10-In. Base 125.00
Train Accessories, Ives, Crossing Gates, 10 1/2 In., Pair 90.00
Train Accessories, Ives, No. 140, Crossing Gate, Iron Window Frame 290.00
Train Accessories, Ives, Ringing Crossing Signal, Red Base 418.00
Train Accessories, Ives, Ticket Station 100.00
Train Accessories, Lionel, Animated Newsstand 198.00
Train Accessories, Lionel, Bascule Bridge, No. 313 .... 320.00
Train Accessories, Lionel, Bridge, No. 103 .... 358.00
Train Accessories, Lionel, City Station, No. 123 .... 347.00
Train Accessories, Lionel, Dealer Sign, Plastic, Shipping Carton, 1980s 145.00
Train Accessories, Lionel, Derrick Platform Set, Boom Control, No. 462 .... 325.00
Train Accessories, Lionel, Freight Station, No. 155 .... 230.00
Train Accessories, Lionel, Freight Station, Trestle Bridges 210.00
Train Accessories, Lionel, Landscaped Bungalow, Yellow, Red Roof, Tan, No. 913 .... 470.00
Train Accessories, Lionel, Motorized Turntable, No. 375 .... 392.00
Train Accessories, Lionel, Oil Derrick, Red Top, No. 455 .... 253.00
Train Accessories, Lionel, Operator Saw Mill, No. 2301 .... 67.00
Train Accessories, Lionel, Rotary Snow Plow, No. 58 .... 320.00
Train Accessories, Lionel, Station, Mojave, Pea Green & Red 340.00
Train Accessories, Lionel, Tool Set, Tool Box, With Tools 216.00
Train Accessories, Lionel, Villa, Cream, Green Base, Gray Roof, Dormer Type, No. 189 550.00
Train Accessories, Wannatoy, Plastic, Box Folds Out To Track & Station 75.00
Train Set, American Flyer, Burlington Zephyr, Locomotive, No. 9900, 3 Coaches, Silver 121.00
Train Set, American Flyer, Locomotive, No. 420, Tender, Boxcar, Illuminated Caboose . 100.00
Train Set, Baxtoy, Fly-Over Railway, Battery Operated, 2 Coaches, Bridge, Track, England 145.00
Train Set, Fleischmann, Locomotive, No. 99221, Tender, Coaches, Tin, Plastic Roofs ... 436.00
Train Set, Fleischmann, Locomotive, No. 1366, Tender, 3 Banana Cars, BP Tank 156.00
Train Set, Lionel, Congressional, Vista Dome, Wm. Penn & Molly Pitcher Coach 560.00
Train Set, Lionel, Engine, Caboose, Cars, Track, 1973 .... 95.00
Train Set, Lionel, Flying Yankee, Locomotive, No. 616W, Observation, Gunmetal 418.00
Train Set, Lionel, Locomotive, No. 2037-500, Gondola, No. 6462, Girl's, Box 2805.00
Train Set, Lionel, Locomotive, No. 2046, Tender, No. 2046W 253.00
Train Set, Lionel, No. 136, Locomotive, No. 262, Cowcatcher, Tender, Pullman 980.00
Train Set, Lionel, No. 725, Boxcar, Gondola, Lumber Dump, Caboose, Transformer 120.00
Train Set, Lionel, No. 1599, Texas Special, No. 210, Red 448.00
Train Set, Lionel, No. 2245, Texas Special, 2 Newark Pullmans, Vista Dome 578.00
Train Set, Lionel, No. X736, Girl's, Sear's Box Set 1045.00

Train Set, Marklin, Locomotive, 3 Tanks, Goodswagon, Crane & Gondola 302.00
Train Set, Marklin, Locomotive, No. CM 800, Twinpacks 448.00
Train Set, Marx, Locomotive, No. 833, Tank Car, No. 553, Steel Wheels, Box 55.00
Train Set, Marx, Lumar Lines, Locomotive, Bell, 2 Hoppers, Pullman, Floor 78.00
Train Set, Marx, Mohawk Freight, No. 41850, Locomotive, Gondola, Exxon Tank 1094.00
Train Set, Marx, No. 333 Hudson, Tender, 2 Coaches, Flat Trucks 242.00
Train Set, Marx, No. 414S Mechanical General, Plastic Wheels 532.00
Train Set, Marx, Union Pacific, Diesel, No. M10005 Engine, Cars, Crossings, Tracks ... 200.00
Train Set, Remco, Mighty Mike, Astro, Box 50.00
Train Set, Weaver, No. 5511, Central, New Jersey Locomotive, 1986 .... 55.00
Train Set, Williams, Locomotive, No. 5601, Tender, Aluminum Cars 784.00
Train Set, Williams, No. 2702, PRR, 80-In. Scale, Madison, 5 Cars 187.00
Train Set, Williams, No. 4000, New York City, Hudson, Baggage, 3 Coaches, Aluminum 448.00
Train Set, Williams, San Francisco Alco, Aluminum Cars 395.00
Tram, Red, Spool Of Line, Tin, 4 In. 25.00
Tram, Windup, Japan, 1930s 395.00
Tree, Whistling Spooky Kooky, Battery Operated, Tin, Bump & Go, Marx, 14 1/2 In. ... 1985.00
Tricycle, Clown, Windup, Tin Lithograph, Vinyl, Japan 150.00
Tricycle, Monkey Riser, Tin, Arnold 199.50
Tricycle, Nutty Mad, Box, Marx 275.00
Tricycle, U-Haul, Small Size, 1970s 35.00
Trolley, 2 Wheel Gyro Action, Lehmann 1195.00
Trolley, Broadway, Chein, 8 1/2 In. 320.00
Trolley, City Hall Park, Tin, Converse 1045.00
Trolley, Electric, Tin Lithograph, Beige, Red & Blue, Friction, Box, Diaya, 15 In. 192.00
Trolley, Kingsbury, Windup, 14 In. 485.00
Trolley, Opening Doors, Green & Red, 20 In. 400.00
Trolley, Pridelines, Corrugated Box, Plastic Wrapper, 1979 .... 105.00
Trolley, Royal Express, Friction, Tin, Rubber Tires, Diaya, 13 1/2 In. 38.00
Trolley, Third Avenue R.R. Co., Marklin, No. 859 ....*Illus* 14500.00
Trolley, With Conductor, Wooden, Penny Toy 72.00
Trombone Golden, Emenee, Carrying Case 40.00
Truck, Ambulance, Pressed Steel, Wyandotte, 6 1/4 In. 100.00
Truck, American Railway Express, Keystone, 26 In. 825.00
Truck, Army, Keystone, 26 x 11 x 8 1/2 In. 520.00
Truck, Army, Steelcraft Mack, C-8, 26 In. 550.00
Truck, Bekins Van Lines, White, 1960 .... 50.00
Truck, Bell Telephone, With Tools, Hubley, c.1930, 9 In. 1430.00
Truck, Breyer's Ice Cream, Cast Iron, Dent 2500.00

Toy, Trolley,
Third Avenue R.R. Co.,
Marklin, No. 859

Toy, Truck, Car
Carrier, Austin Cars,
Cast Iron, A.C.
Williams, 1920, 13 In.

Toy, Truck, Dump, Bulldog Mack, Black Cab,
Red Body, Toledo

Toy, Truck, Huckster,
Buddy L

Truck, Buddy L, Battery Operated, Pressed Steel, 1950, 26 In.	127.00
Truck, Buddy L, Traveling Zoo, Orange, White Plastic, Yellow Finish, 13 In.	52.00
Truck, Burlington Truck Lines, White, Red Truck & Trailer, White Graphics, 1953	65.00
Truck, Car Carrier, 4 Cars, Ramp, Box, Japan	35.00
Truck, Car Carrier, Austin Cars, Cast Iron, A.C. Williams, 1920, 13 In. .... *Illus*	770.00
Truck, Cattle, Structo	95.00
Truck, Cement Mixer, Battery Operated, Plastic, Sears	50.00
Truck, Cement Mixer, Tonka	125.00
Truck, Circus, Paper Label, Animals In Removable Cages, Keystone, 26 1/2 In.	2750.00
Truck, Coal, Buddy L, Black Cab, Red Chassis, Black Coal Bin, 25 In.	1035.00
Truck, Coal, Cast Iron, Arcade	2800.00
Truck, Coal, Rubber Tires, Opening Doors, Buddy L, 26 In.	4850.00
Truck, Crane, Mechanical, Cortland, Box	375.00
Truck, D.A.F. Tipper Container, Matchbox, No. 47, Box	37.00
Truck, Delivery, Canadian Lincoln, Painted Pressed Steel, 1950s, 24 In.	295.00
Truck, Delivery, Country Good Soups, Painted Pressed Steel, England, 30 In.	395.00
Truck, Delivery, Kronenbourg Beer, Alligator Paint On Roof	363.00
Truck, Driver, Blue, Windup, Kingsbury, 9 x 4 x 3 In.	173.00
Truck, Dugan Brothers Bakery, Keystone, 26 In.	3300.00
Truck, Dump, 10 Wheel, Yellow, Smith Miller M.I.C.	995.00
Truck, Dump, 1923 International, Blue, Black Overall, Dugan Sand & Gravel, 10 1/2 In. .	275.00
Truck, Dump, All Chrome, 25th Anniversary, Tonka, Box	125.00
Truck, Dump, Arcade, Mack, 5 1/4 x 12 x 3 3/4 In.	9775.00
Truck, Dump, Automatic, Red, Windup, Tin, 14 1/2 In.	125.00
Truck, Dump, B61 Mack, Valley Asphalt, 1958	45.00
Truck, Dump, Boston Sand & Gravel, Red Truck, Yellow Dump Bed, 1960	50.00
Truck, Dump, Boycraft, 24 In.	225.00
Truck, Dump, Buddy L, 1950s	425.00
Truck, Dump, Buddy L, Piston Mechanism, 24 x 9 x 8 1/2 In.	460.00
Truck, Dump, Bulldog Mack, Black Cab, Red Body, Toledo .... *Illus*	1870.00
Truck, Dump, Clockwork, Kingsbury Type, Structo	295.00
Truck, Dump, Crank, Pulley Action, Buddy L, Decal, 1920s, 25 In.	1000.00
Truck, Dump, CW Brand Coffee, Black, Pressed Steel, Metal Disc Wheels, 10 In.	360.00
Truck, Dump, Electric Lights, Wyandotte, 10 In.	95.00
Truck, Dump, General Motors, Steelcraft, 26 In.	255.00
Truck, Dump, Hydraulic, Buddy L, c.1925, 25 In.	850.00
Truck, Dump, Hydraulic, Tonka	150.00
Truck, Dump, Hydraulic, Tonka, 1960	40.00
Truck, Dump, Key Wind, Marx	625.00
Truck, Dump, Lincoln, Pressed Steel, 1950s, 20 In.	145.00
Truck, Dump, Mack, Green Cab, Red Dump Box, 6 Tires, Hubley, 5 x 5 1/2 In.	715.00
Truck, Dump, Motor Fleet Hauling Service, Wyandotte, 1950, 17 1/2 In.	125.00
Truck, Dump, Ralph W. Coho Clean Coal, Kilgore Reo	1100.00
Truck, Dump, Richmond Scale Model, Pressed Steel, 12 In.	95.00
Truck, Dump, Sand & Gravel, Marx	80.00
Truck, Dump, Sand, Marx, Box	245.00
Truck, Dump, Sturditoy, 27 In.	765.00
Truck, Dump, Tin Lithograph, Tin Wheels, G.F. Germany, 1930s, 4 1/2 In.	33.00

Truck, Excavator, Pressed Steel, Clockwork Winch, Buddy L, c.1940, 20 In.	115.00
Truck, Express Line, Black, Green, Buddy L, 25 In.	635.00
Truck, Express Line, Black, Red, Green, Buddy L	2800.00
Truck, Express Service, Battery Operated, Corgi	310.00
Truck, Express, Gulf, Kenworth T & T, 1953	68.00
Truck, Fanny Farmer Candy, Box	195.00
Truck, Firestone, Red, White, Plastic Tools, Marx, 14 In.	675.00
Truck, Fork Lift, Operator On Seat Operating Gears, Red, Battery Operated	70.00
Truck, Gas & Motor Oil, Balloon Rubber Tires, Box, Champion	1760.00
Truck, Gas, Royal Oil Company, Red, White, Marx, 8 1/2 In.	695.00
Truck, Good Humor Ice Cream, Japan, 11 In.	1100.00
Truck, Green Giant Brands, Pressed Metal, Decals, Tonka, 9 x 24 In.	245.00
Truck, Hercules Coal, Chein	750.00
Truck, Hi-Way Express Van Lines, Marx	215.00
Truck, Highway Maintenance, With Lift, Structo, 12 In.	110.00
Truck, Hood's Ice Cream, Steelcraft, 1930s	400.00
Truck, Horse Van, Tonka, Box	195.00
Truck, Huckster, Buddy L . . . . *Illus*	4400.00
Truck, Hunting, Savage Beast, Japan, Box	160.00
Truck, Ice Cream Vendor, Tin Lever Action, Driver, White Suit, Bump & Go, Japan, 7 In.	425.00
Truck, Ice, Buddy L, 1928	1500.00
Truck, Ice, Buddy L, No. 602, Box, 1930s	690.00
Truck, International Harvester Sales & Service, Buddy L	2530.00
Truck, International Harvester, Winch, Dumping Action, Decals, Iron, Arcade, 10 3/4 In. .	840.00
Truck, Keystone, U.S. Army, Pressed Steel	700.00
Truck, Ladder, Cast Iron, Painted, Nickel Grill, Hubley, c.1930s, 6 1/2 In.	115.00
Truck, Lazy Day Farms, Tin, Marx, 17 1/2 In.	100.00
Truck, Livestock Trailer, Tin, Japan, Box, 7 1/4 In.	99.00
Truck, Livestock, Structo	125.00
Truck, Loader, Tonka Clamshell	100.00
Truck, Lumber, Buddy L, No. 103A, 1927	3680.00
Truck, Machinery Hauler, With Shovel, Structo	265.00
Truck, Mack Body, Nickel Plated Driver, Spoke Wheels, Arcade, 8 1/4 In.	1980.00
Truck, Mack Stake, Orange, Hubley	300.00
Truck, Mack, Lubrite Gas Tanker, Nickeled Spoke Wheels, Arcade, 13 1/2 In.	1075.00
Truck, Mack, Military Green, 1930s, Marx, 8 In.	200.00
Truck, Mack, U.S. Airmail Service, Tootsietoy	165.00
Truck, Meadow Brook Dairy, Red Wood Barrels, Blue Cart, Pressed Steel, 10 In.	95.00
Truck, Merry-Go-Round, Advances As Merry-Go-Round Spins, Bell Noise, Tin, 8 In. . . .	378.00
Truck, Merry-Go-Round, Black, Red, White, Friction, 1960s, Japan, 8 1/2 In.	375.00
Truck, Milk Delivery, Frankonia, 1960s, 7 In.	250.00
Truck, Milk, Borden's, With Milk Bottles, Buddy L	350.00
Truck, Milk, Cragstan Milk, Box, 4 1/2 In.	210.00
Truck, Milk-Cream, White, Cast Iron, 3 3/4 In.	450.00
Truck, Model A, Side Dump Trailer & Wagon , Arcade	2645.00
Truck, Motor Express, Trailer, Cab, Red, Green, 1950s, 12 In.	165.00
Truck, Moving Van, Lambert's, Cast Iron, Midnight Blue, Arcade, 13 In.	13225.00
Truck, Moving Van, North American Van Lines, Structo	150.00
Truck, Ohio Express, Tin, Friction, Daxie, Japan, 1960s	22.00
Truck, Panama Digger, Mack, Hubley, 12 In.	1300.00
Truck, Pickup & Delivery, Structo, 1950s	250.00
Truck, Pickup, Tonka, 1955	185.00
Truck, Pickup, Tru-Scale B Series, 5-Wheel, Blue	235.00
Truck, Plumbing & Heating, Irwin, 1960s, Box	125.00
Truck, Police Patrol, Black Paint, Red Wheels, White Tires, 28 In.	1210.00
Truck, Pure Oil, Metalcraft, Blue, 15 In.	1000.00
Truck, Ranchero, No. 5423, Buddy L, Box	295.00
Truck, REA Express, Buddy L, Box	285.00
Truck, Ready-Mix Cement, Structo	165.00
Truck, Robotoy, Red & Green, No. 72, Buddy L, c.1932, 21 In.	1265.00
Truck, Sand & Gravel, Kenton, 1940s	250.00
Truck, Sand, Buddy L, Gravel, Box, 1950	295.00
Truck, Schraffts Ice Cream, Tin, Japan, 1950s	55.00

Truck, Semi, Alka-Seltzer, Lionel, Box, 1982 .... 200.00
Truck, Semi, Motor Express, Die Cast, Hubley, 18 In. 85.00
Truck, Semi, Safeway, Tin, Japan, 16 1/2 In. 45.00
Truck, Semi, Tru-Scale S Series, Ryersons Steel 295.00
Truck, Semi, United Van Lines, Tonka, 1956 .... 120.00
Truck, Shell Motor Oil, Red & Yellow, Metalcraft 250.00
Truck, Shell, Friction, Tin, Sakai 60.00
Truck, Sprinkler, Keystone 1195.00
Truck, Stake, 1920s Ford, Cast Iron, Red 450.00
Truck, Stake, Cast Iron, Kilgore, 3 1/2 In. 125.00
Truck, Stake, Champion, 533/Champion, Geneva, Ohio, Cast Iron, 3 1/2 x 7 1/2 In. 310.00
Truck, Stake, Nickel Racks, White Rubber Tires, Cast Iron, Hubley, 5 In. 150.00
Truck, Stake, Rubber Tires, Green Paint, Nickel Side Rails, Hubley, 6 3/4 In. 375.00
Truck, Standard Oil, Tinplate, Windup, Marklin, 16 1/2 In. 4950.00
Truck, Street Sprinkler, Nylint 245.00
Truck, Street Sweeper, Elgin, 1932 .... 6270.00
Truck, Studebaker, Nestles Milk, Dinky 145.00
Truck, Super Market Delivery Truck, Pressed Steel, Painted, Buddy L, c.1940, 14 In. ... 150.00
Truck, T.P.S. Clown's Popcorn, Battery Operated, 1960s 250.00
Truck, Tank, GMC Mobil Oil & Gas, Smith Miller 375.00
Truck, Tank, Little Jim, Steelcraft, 26 x 9 1/2 x 8 1/2 In. 545.00
Truck, Tank, Mack, Tootsietoy 85.00
Truck, Tank, Mobiloil, Red, Logo, Smitty Toys, 14 In. 495.00
Truck, Tank, Steel, Steering Wheel Control, 1950s, Box 295.00
Truck, Tank, Water, Keystone, 24 x 10 x 8 In. 920.00
Truck, Telephone Maintenance Repair, Trailer, Ladder, Buddy L, No. 450, Box 345.00
Truck, Texaco, Buddy L 125.00
Truck, Texaco, No. 2, Ertl, Box 450.00
Truck, Tow, Black, Orange, 6 1/2 In. 425.00
Truck, Tow, Blue, 3 Tools, Buddy L 165.00
Truck, Tow, Cities Service, Hood Opens, Plastic, 9 1/2 In. 255.00
Truck, Tow, Cities Service, Tin Lithograph, Marx, 18 In. 225.00
Truck, Tow, Dave's Towing, Diamond T, Gum Metal Gray, Black Fenders, 1955 .... 39.00
Truck, Tow, Goodrich Silvertown Tires, Metal Craft 1850.00
Truck, Tow, Mack, Cast Iron, Red, Champion, 9 In. 650.00
Truck, Tow, Nickel Grill, Red & Black, Cast Iron, Hubley, 4 1/2 In. 170.00
Truck, Trailer, Mechanical Gasoline, Box, Marx 495.00
Truck, Trailer, Side Dump, Windup, Cragstan, Box 120.00
Truck, Trench Digger, Buddy L 4312.00
Truck, U-Haul Pickup, Ny-Lint 195.00
Truck, U.S. Army Troop Carrier, Lumar, Marx 125.00
Truck, U.S. Mail Airmail Service, Tootsietoy, No. 4645 .... 165.00
Truck, U.S. Mail, Black Cab, Red Chassis, Wheels, Green Body, Sturdi, 26 In. 805.00
Truck, U.S. Mail, Blue, White, Tin Lithograph, Marx, 12 1/2 In. 65.00
Truck, U.S. Mail, Buddy L 395.00
Truck, V-Room, Mattel, Box 125.00
Truck, Van, Smith & Wesson, GMC, Stake, 1952 .... 39.00
Truck, Van, Smith & Wesson, Mack, B-61 .... 75.00
Truck, Wrecker, Cities Service, Box, 4 1/2 In. 165.00
Truck, Wrecker, Ford, Weaver, Arcade 880.00
Truck, Wrecker, Nite-Day, Pressed Steel, Jack & Tools, Marx, 20 In. 385.00
Truck, Wrecker, Red Baby Weaver, Arcade 4400.00
Truck, Wrecker, Tonka, No. 518 .... 60.00
Truck, Wrecker, Tools & Jack, Box, Buddy L 1295.00
Trucker, Jeep Wrecker & Plow, Tonka, Box 295.00
Turtle, Rubber Shell, Paper Tag, Steiff, 5 In. 60.00
Turtle, Snuggy Slo, Steiff, Chest Tag, Mounted On Floor Coasters For Security 518.00
Typewriter, Simplex, 1903 .... 30.00
Typewriter, Tin Lithograph, Unique Art 85.00
Typist, Miss Friday, Battery Operated, Box 275.00
U.S. Navy Phantom, Dinky Toy 165.00
Ukulele, Tin, Box, Japan, 10 1/2 In. 95.00
Umbrella, Porky Pig 450.00

Umbrella, Raggedy Ann 20.00
Van, Arcade, Panel, Green, Black, Nickel Wheels, 4 x 8 1/4 In. 2015.00
Van, Bantam Lucozade, Corgi 540.00
Van, Buddy L, Mister Buddy Ice Cream 160.00
Van, Camera, Mobile, Battery Operated, Corgi 130.00
Van, Wall's Ice Cream, Corgi 450.00
Vanity Set, That's My Mamma, 5 Piece 45.00
View-Master, Babes In Toyland, Complete Package, 1961 . . . . 24.00
View-Master, Beverly Hillbillies, Booklet, 1964 . . . . 20.00
View-Master, Captain Kangaroo, 1957 . . . . 16.00
View-Master, Casper The Friendly Ghost, Package 10.00
View-Master, Dark Shadows, 1968 . . . . 65.00
View-Master, Flash Gordon, On The Planet Mongo, 3 Reels, 1979 . . . . 20.00
View-Master, Flipper-Dolphin Love, 1966 . . . . 12.00
View-Master, Happy Days, 1974 . . . . 21.00
View-Master, Junior Projector, Box 25.00
View-Master, Land Of The Giants, Booklet, 1968, Complete 35.00
View-Master, Mission Impossible, 3 Reels, 1968 . . . . 24.00
View-Master, Norfolk Southern Line 45.00
View-Master, Orkin Pest Control 45.00
View-Master, Popeye, Paint Ahoy, 3 Reels, 1970s 12.00
View-Master, Secrets Of Space, Tom Corbett, 1954 . . . . 65.00
View-Master, Top Cat, Belgium, 1962 . . . . 15.00
View-Master, Voyage To The Bottom Of The Sea, 3 Reels, 1966 . . . . 30.00
Waffle Iron, Griddle & Fry Pan, Cast Iron, Wagner Ware, 4 Piece 115.00
Wagon, Buckboard, Wire Wheels, Hard Rubber Tread, Red & Black Paint, 39 In. 660.00
Wagon, Coaster, Pioneer, Artillery Wheels 1295.00
Wagon, Comet, Dinky Toy 365.00
Wagon, Convertible, Sleigh Runners, Iron Wheel Tread, Wooden, Red, 41 In. 525.00
Wagon, Cover, Red, Wooden, 4 Silver Metal Wheels, Metal Axles, Gibbs, 18 In. 286.00
Wagon, Doll's, Tin, Green, Red Fenders, Wyandotte, 11 In. 95.00
Wagon, Express On Sides, Wooden Bed, Spoke Wheels, Large Rear Wheels, 26 1/2 In. . . 330.00
Wagon, Express, Iron Hardware, Flip-Down Tailgate, Wooden, 43 In. 520.00
Wagon, Goat, Studebaker Junior, Hand Pull, Sled Runners To Convert To Bobsled 4000.00
Wagon, Greyhound, Yellow, Red, Blue & Silver, 34 In. 305.00
Wagon, Hy-Speed, Red Metal, 14 In. 80.00
Wagon, Radio Flyer, 1939 World's Fair, Decals, 7 In. 195.00
Wagon, Radio Flyer, Steel, 1930s, 4 1/2 In. 95.00
Wagon, Railroad, Cast Iron, Whitehead & Kates 150.00
Wagon, Studebaker, Green Paint, Black & Gold Stenciling, Wooden 1595.00
Wagon, Victorian, Oval Scenic Vignettes On Sides, Red 2300.00
Wagon, Wooden, Express, Blue Gray Paint, Tongue, 29 In. 385.00
Wagon, Wooden, Solid Wooden Wheels, Spindle Sides, Painted, 49 In. 135.00
Walkie-Talkie, Green Hornet, Box, Instructions 400.00
Walkie-Talkie, Remco, Box, 1950s 35.00
Walkie-Talkie, Space Patrol, Plastic Figures, England, 1955, 5 In. 210.00
Walrus, In Zippered Knapsack, Plastic Tusks, Body Is Knapsack, Steiff, 30 In. 173.00
Walrus, Paddy, Steiff, 4 In. 65.00
Washboard, National Washboard Co., No. 9 . . . . 33.00
Washing Machine, 3 Little Pigs, Chain 115.00
Washing Machine, Modern Miss, Clear Rub, Side Wringer, Box 150.00
Washstand, With China Bowl, Tin, 1870s, 6 In. 125.00
Waste Can, Raggedy Ann, Metal, 1972 . . . . 28.00
Wastebasket, Huckleberry Hound & Friends, Chein, 1950s 75.00
Watercolor Set, Tin, 1931 . . . . 24.00
Western Ranch Set, Tin Lithograph, Marx, Box 75.00
Wheelbarrow, Black, Red, Yellow Striping, Marked, HCJ 395.00
Wheelbarrow, Stenciled Sides, Wooden 365.00
Whistle, Fire Chief Siren, Plastic, 7 In. 65.00
Whistle, Jack Webb, Dragnet, Plastic 10.00
Whistle, Papier-Mache Face, Tin, Wood, Germany 60.00
White Tail Deer, Aurora, No. DS 403, Sealed, 1972 . . . . 60.00
Whoopee Car, Tin, Windup, Marx 325.00

Toy, Zoetrope, Wheel Of Life

Whoopee Car, Yipee-I-Anny, Unique Art, Box 675.00
Windmill, Native, Ringing Bell, Tin Lithograph, Germany, Box, 9 In. 49.00
Winnie The Pooh Family, With Baby, Blue, Tan, 11 In. 48.00
Wire Riding Cyclist, Red Plaid Coat, Yellow Pants, Black Boots, Tin, 8 In. 85.00
Wyatt Earp, Horse, Famous Gunfighter Series, Hartland, 2 Piece 150.00
Xylophone, Lithographed Paper On Wood, Bliss 65.00
Xylophone Player, Windup, Box, Japan 210.00
Xylophone Players, Celluloid, Tin Lithograph, TM Japan, c.1950, 6 In. 145.00
Yo-Yo, Duncan, Paper Bag 25.00
Yo-Yo, Pee Wee Herman, On Card, 1988 .... 10.00
Zeppelin, Cast Iron, 9 In. 210.00
Zeppelin, Dewt, Cast Iron, 1930s, 6 In. 170.00
Zeppelin, Graf, Prop Spins, Propels Across Floor, Windup, Tin, Chein, 9 In. 765.00
Zeppelin, Pressed Steel, Painted, Steelcraft Graf, c.1930, 25 1/2 In. 230.00
Zeppelin, Transatlantic, Tin, Windup, Prop Spins Propelling In Circle, Max, 1930, 10 In. 550.00
Zilotone, Tin, Windup, Wolverine, 6 Interchangeable Disks, 7 1/2 In. 220.00
Zoetrope, Wheel Of Life..*Illus* 1210.00

TRAMP ART is a form of folk art made since the Civil War. It is usually made from chip-carved cigar boxes. Examples range from small
boxes and picture frames to full-sized pieces of furniture.

Bank, Chest Form, Porcelain Knobs, 5 1/4 x 4 1/2 x 7 3/4 In. 275.00
Bank, Green & Blue Paint, 1920s, 6 1/2 In. 250.00
Birdcage, Rounded Fretwork Panels, 26 In. 1100.00
Box, Cigarette 350.00
Box, Cross, Crown Of Thorns, 19 x 11 In. 475.00
Box, Newspapers 950.00
Box, Red Paint, 3 3/4 In. 69.00
Box, Sewing, 5 Layer, 15 x 10 x 10 In. 350.00
Box, Sides Fitted With Mirrors, 3 3/8 In. 35.00
Cabinet, Chromolithograph Children's Prints, Hanging, 21 x 6 1/2 x 11 1/2 In. 55.00
Chest, Blanket, Till, Central Vase With Flowers, Initials HM, 9 In. 250.00
Chest, Crown Of Thorns, Drawers 1045.00
Church, On 1-Drawer Stand, Triangle Banding, 65 x 22 In. 1500.00
Cross, 24 In. 175.00
Dresser, 2 Drawers, Mirror, 10 3/4 In. 245.00
Dresser Box, 10 x 10 In. 145.00
Dresser Box, 10 x 20 In. 165.00
Dresser Box, Cigar, 13 x 10 x 7 1/2 In. 395.00
Frame, 3 Tiers Of Star Form, Carved Wood Frame, 23 x 20 In. 230.00
Frame, Boy & Girl Eating Pie, 12 1/2 x 10 1/2 In. 120.00
Frame, Layered Outer Edges, Inlaid Center, 1900s, 8 x 10 In. 95.00
Frame, Patina, 1915, 18 x 14 In. 210.00
Frame, Pen & Pencil Drawing, T. Van Wyck, 1919, 14 1/2 x 18 1/2 In. 695.00
Frame, Porcelain Buttons, 8 x 6 In. ....65.00 to 75.00
Frame, Wood Cigar Box Lid Construction, Period Photographs, 28 x 31 In. 725.00
Lamp, Shade, Flat Sticks Style, Wooden 135.00
Mirror, Star Shape, Carved Painted Frame, 30 In. 460.00

TRAPS for animals may be handmade. One of the most unusual is the mousetrap made so that when the mouse entered the trap, it was hit on the head with a mallet. Other traps were commercially manufactured and often are marked with the name of the manufacturer. Many traps were designed to be as humane as possible, and they would trap the live animal so it could be released in the woods.

Bear, Grizzly Bear, No. 6, 1855, 43 In.	300.00
Puzzle, Horseshoe Form, 14 In.	46.00
Rat, Wire, 15 In.	35.00
Squirrel, Punched Tin	350.00
Squirrel, Well-Formed House & Runner, Indigo Paint	295.00
Wolf, Triumph, No. 415	145.00

TREEN, see Wooden category.

TRENCH ART is a form of folk art made by soldiers. Metal casings from bullets and mortar shells were cut and decorated to form useful objects, such as vases.

Club, Carved Wooden Head & Grip, World War I, 16 In.	210.00
Lamp, World War I	450.00
Letter Opener, 2 Rifle Bullet Heads For Handle, England, World War I	65.00
Nickeled German 8cm Cases, American Shield, European Shield, Pair	33.00

TRIVETS are now used to hold hot dishes. Most trivets of the late nineteenth and early twentieth centuries were made to hold hot irons. Iron or brass reproductions are being made of many of the old styles.

Brass, Fancy Cutouts, Wrought Iron Penny Legs, 11 7/8 In.	265.00
Brass, Georgian, Scrolled Apron, Cabriole Legs, Rectangular, England, 11 1/4 In.	545.00
Brass, Interlace Design, England, c.1780-1820, 7 1/2 In.	200.00
Brass, Iron, Applewood Handle, Steel Legs, Pad Feet, 10 x 15 x 6 In.	230.00
Brass, Steel Hearth, Cabriole Legs, 18th Century, 11 x 13 x 13 In.	431.00
Cast Iron, Horseshoe Shape, G.A.R. Medal & Eagle Top, Civil War	45.00
Iron, Adjustable Fork Rest, Twisted, Long Handle, 25 1/2 In.	95.00
Iron, Double Grate, Heart Pierced Front Frame, 18th Century, 11 In.	395.00
Iron, Griswold, Tassel & Grain	30.00
Iron, Heart Shape, Blacksmith Made, 1780s, 7 In.	295.00
Iron, Hearts & Scrolls, 3 Penny Feet, 31 x 16 In.	995.00
Iron, Round, Heart Feet	105.00
Iron, Round, Pad Feet	100.00
Iron, Triangular, Fretwork	100.00
Iron, Triangular, Heart Shaped Handle, Penny Feet	125.00
Silver, Overlay Lobed, Greek Key Design	90.00

TRUNKS of many types were made. The nineteenth-century sea chest was often handmade of unpainted wood. Brass-fitted camphorwood chests were brought back from the Orient. Leather-covered trunks were popular from the late eighteenth to mid-nineteenth centuries. By 1895, trunks were covered with canvas or decorated sheet metal. Embossed metal coverings were used from 1870 to 1910. By 1925, trunks were covered with vulcanized fiber or undecorated metal.

Bag, Louis Vuitton, Carry-On, Overnight	600.00
Bag, Louis Vuitton, Carry-On, Suit Size	600.00
Cloisonne, Yellow Silk Lining, 10 x 10 1/2 In.	950.00
Commemorative Ship, Hinged Top, Union Jack, Stars, Stripes, Black, Gilt, 22 x 43 In.	330.00
Dome Top, Dovetailed	375.00
Dome Top, Hand Dovetailed & Pegged, 29 x 46 In.	695.00
Dome Top, Immigrant's, Dovetailed Construction, Old Red Paint, Pine & Poplar, 43 In.	315.00
Dome Top, Painted, Lined With Newspaper, 1814, 11 In.	1495.00
Dome Top, Red Paint, Black Dots, New England, 1830	665.00
Folk Style Floral Scrolls, Brass Nailhead Trim, Leather Bound, 17 x 30 1/2 In.	345.00
Foot Locker, Leather, Louis Vuitton	1200.00
Immigrant's, Oak, Dovetailed, Dome Top, Wrought Iron Strapping, 45 3/4 In.	467.00
Leather, Handles, Red Handkerchief Folder, Straps, France, 1875, 9 x 5 In.	350.00

Louis Vuitton, Bag, Garment, Leather Mounts 287.50
Louis Vuitton, Cabin 2000.00
Louis Vuitton, Canvas, Edged With Monogrammed Leather, Steamship Label 977.00
Louis Vuitton, Case, Traveling, Brass Mounts, Leather Handle, 17 1/2 x 26 In. 748.00
Louis Vuitton, Case, Traveling, Brass Mounts, Leather Handle, 19 1/2 x 19 1/2 In. 690.00
Louis Vuitton, Case, Traveling, Brass Mounts, Leather Handle, 20 1/2 x 31 1/2 In. 805.00
Louis Vuitton, Shoe, Canvas Edge, Monogrammed Leather, Fitted Interior, Brass Catch . 1380.00
Louis Vuitton, Steamer, Brass, Wooden Bound, Lacquered Leather, 43 x 12 x 22 In. 1955.00
Louis Vuitton, Steamer, Leather Handles, Rectangular Case, 43 1/2 In. 2300.00
Louis Vuitton, Steamer, Pigskin Lining, 1920s, 21 3/4 x 45 In. 2070.00
Louis Vuitton, Steamer, White Star Line Baggage Tag, Rectangular, 29 3/4 In. 1955.00
Louis Vuitton, Suitcase, Canvas, Leather, Soft Back 800.00
Louis Vuitton, Wardrobe, Canvas, Orange Stripe, Wood & Metal, Signed 1380.00
Metal Strapping, Interior Till & Drawer, Pine 60.00
Pine, Dome Top, Blue, Green Paint, Floral Design, 11 x 12 1/2 x 27 In. 4620.00
Pine, Dome Top, Poplar, Brown, Red, Black, 13 x 13 1/2 x 24 In. 2750.00
Pine, Dovetailed, Original Brown Paint, Red Stripes, 1874, 6 x 10 x 13 1/2 In. 1100.00
Pine, Dovetailed, Red Grain, White Initials, Floral Design, Red, Black, 7 x 12 x 18 In. . . 2145.00
Stagecoach, Saratoga Type, 5 Band, Key, c.1840, 18 x 32 In. 750.00
Steamer, Kentucky Derby, Concessionaires Supplies To Derby, 1940s, 40 x 30 In. 660.00
Storage, Wicker, Contemporary, 15 x 30 x 21 In. 46.00
Suitcase, Leatheroid, Walton Trunk Co., Early 1920s, 22 x 12 x 8 In. 75.00
Travel, Stenciled E.B. Stoddard, King Street, Brass Tack Design, Wood 137.00
U.S.N., Confidential—Do Not Open, W.R. Brooks, Mine Disposal Officer, 16 x 32 In. . . 52.00

TUTHILL Cut Glass Company of Middletown, New York, worked from 1902 to 1923. Of special interest are the finely cut pieces of stemware and tableware.

Bowl, Intaglio Engraved, Triform Pattern, Hobstars, 4 x 8 In. 350.00
Bowl, Whipped Cream, Vintage & Brilliant Cut, 6 In. 450.00

TYPEWRITER collectors divide typewriters into two main classifications: the index machine, which has a pointer and a dial for letter selection, and the keyboard machine, most commonly seen today. The first successful typewriter was made by Sholes and Glidden in 1874.

Hammond, No. 1, Case 650.00
Hammond Multiplex, Index, Cover, 1920s 83.00
Oliver, Standard Visible Writer, Keyboard, No. 5 . . . . 65.00
Olivetti, Portable, Red, Valentine, Ettore Sottsass Case, 4 1/2 x 13 1/2 x 14 In. 330.00
Remington, Portable, White Keys 40.00

TYPEWRITER RIBBON TINS are now being collected. The lithographed tin containers have been used since the 1870s. Most popular with collectors are tins with pictorial graphics.

Tin, Bundy, Giant, Blue, White, Phily Co., 2 1/4 In. 75.00
Tin, Carter's Midnight Blue, Round 48.00
Tin, Crown Brand, Purple, Black, Square 80.00
Tin, Elk Brand, Blue, Round, 2 1/2 In. 114.00
Tin, Emerald Brand, Green, Smith & Corona Typewriter Co. 42.00
Tin, Everlasting, Pyramids, Palm Trees, Yellow, Black, Round 63.00
Tin, Just-Rite, Red, Black, Allen & Company, 2 1/2 In. 60.00
Tin, Kleen-Write 8.00
Tin, Perm-O-Rite, Old Dutch Carbon & Ribbon Co., 2 1/4 In. 56.00
Tin, Pure Silk, Woman, Red Gown, Round, 2 1/2 In. 57.00
Tin, Secretaire-Berry's, Red, Black, Round 32.00
Tin, Super Shell, Yellow, Red, Shell Petroleum Corp., 2 1/2 In. 183.00

UHL pottery was made in Evansville, Indiana, in 1854. The pottery moved to Huntingburg, Indiana, in 1908. Stoneware and glazed pottery were made until the mid-1940s.

Ashtray, Dog & Fire Plug, Brown 450.00
Ashtray, Pig, Pink 250.00
Bank, Pig, White 350.00

Bank, Piggy, Christmas Greeting, 1943	4160.00
Bean Pot, Blue, Boston Baked Bean Printed On Front, Large	250.00
Chicken Feeder	125.00
Coffee Maker, Stone Filter, Blue	925.00
Cookie Jar, Globe, Blue	60.00
Creamer, Pink, 1 Oz.	200.00
Flowerpot, Attached Saucer, Blue, 2 In.	200.00
Flowerpot, Green	75.00
Jar, Grease, Green	60.00
Jar, Strawberry, Hanging, Blue	60.00
Jar, Thieves, Black	90.00
Jug, Baseball	65.00
Jug, Canteen, Believe It Or Not, Miniature	200.00
Jug, Cat, Peach, Miniature	105.00
Jug, Christmas Cheer From Uhl Pottery, 1933	370.00
Jug, Christmas Shoulder, Paper Label, 1943	1100.00
Jug, Egyptian, Purple	100.00
Jug, Elephant, Tan	100.00
Jug, Evansville, 3 Gal.	60.00
Jug, Football	55.00
Jug, Harvest, 2 Gal.	275.00
Jug, Shoulder, Grandpa Meier's Label, Miniature	145.00
Mixing Bowl, Shouldered, Blue Glaze	250.00
Mug, Dillsboro Sanitarium, Tan	100.00
Pitcher, Barrel, Yellow	40.00
Pitcher, Blue & White Sponged, Ink Stamp, 1 Gal.	510.00
Pitcher, Blue & White Spongeware, Bulbous Base, 6 1/2 In.	770.00
Pitcher, Brown, 1/2 Gal.	80.00
Pitcher, Grape, Cover, Squat, Blue	375.00
Pitcher, Hill-Top Gift Shop, Canmer, Ky., Miniature	145.00
Planter, Kitten With Spool	50.00
Plaque, Abraham Lincoln	595.00
Rabbit Feeder, Yellow	70.00
Teapot, Blue, No. 143	280.00
Vase, Bud, Narcissus, 7 1/2 In.	60.00
Vase, Dark Green, 5 1/2 In.	60.00
Vase, Yellow, 8 In.	125.00
Water Cooler, White Glaze, Black & Green Finish, 2 Gal.	230.00

UMBRELLA collectors like rain or shine. The first known umbrella was owned by King Louis XIII of France in 1637. The earliest umbrellas were sunshades, not designed to be used in the rain. The umbrella was embellished and redesigned many times. In 1852, the fluted steel rib style was developed, and it has remained the most useful style.

Advertising, Music Store In Corinth, Orange & Cream	385.00
Lucite, Tree Handle, 1940	12.00
Parasol, Black Silk, Folding Handle, Small	75.00
Taffeta, Plaid, 1930	22.50

UNION PORCELAIN WORKS was established at Greenpoint, New York, in 1848 by Charles Cartlidge. The company went through a series of ownership changes and finally closed in the early 1900s. The company made a fine quality white porcelain that was often decorated in clear, bright colors.

Bowl, Shaker, Band Around Rim, 1887	115.00
Oyster Plate	150.00

UNIVERSITY OF NORTH DAKOTA, see North Dakota School of Mines category.

VAL ST. LAMBERT Cristalleries of Belgium was founded by Messieurs Kemlin and Lelievre in 1825. The company is still in operation. All types of table glassware and decorative glassware have been made. Pieces are often decorated with cut designs.

Beaker, Cranberry Stained, Circle Pattern, 4 3/4 In.	165.00

Bottle, Floral Acid Cut Body, Green, Stopper, 1910, 8 1/2 In. 275.00
Bowl, Lion On Base, 6 In. 26.00
Bowl, On Silver Pedestal 80.00
Bowl, Ruby Cut To Clear, Vertical Bull's-Eye & Bars, Signed, 5 1/2 x 12 In. 660.00
Bowl, Violet Bouquets, Gold Leaves, Emerald Green Textured, Signed, 5 In. 245.00
Candlesticks, Bird Design, Circular Form, Frosted, 10 3/4 In., Pair 60.00
Charger, Scalloped, Round, 13 1/4 In. 175.00
Cordial, Signed 20.00
Finger Bowl, Underplate 30.00
Obelisk, 6 1/2 In. 40.00
Ornament, Shelf, Wheel Cut Bull & Matador, Signed, 13 3/4 In., Pair 385.00
Paperweight, Centennial NWDA, 3 x 3 In. 35.00
Perfume Bottle, Green Stained, Acid Fruit Floral, Prism Cut Stopper, 1910, 7 In. 195.00
Tableware, Fruit Pattern, Crystal, 30 Piece 495.00
Tray, Pattern, Round, 6 In. 20.00
Vase, Cameo, Stylized Blossoming Trees, Ruby Red, Belgium, 7 In. 575.00

VALLERYSTHAL Glassworks was founded in 1836 in Lorraine, France.
In 1854, the firm became Klenglin et Cie. It made table and decorative
glass, opaline, cameo, and art glass. A line of covered, pressed glass
animal dishes was made in the nineteenth century. The firm is still
working.

Dish, Fish Cover 325.00
Dish, Reclining Camel Cover 150.00
Vase, Cameo, Thistle, Amber Highlights, Pastel Opal Pink, 11 1/2 In. 920.00
Vase, Flared, Burgundy Red Rim, Pale Green Body, Berry Bush On Front, 8 In. 489.00
Vase, Green Holly Leaves, Burgundy Ground, Cameo, Signed, 6 1/2 In. 410.00

VAN BRIGGLE pottery was made by Artus Van Briggle in Colorado
Springs, Colorado, after 1901. Van Briggle had been a decorator at
Rookwood Pottery of Cincinnati, Ohio. He died in 1904. His wares
usually had modeled relief decorations and a soft, dull glaze. The pottery is still working and still making some of the original designs.

Bookends, Owl, Blue Over Aqua Matte Glaze, Marked, 5 1/2 In. 100.00
Bookends, Owl, On Open Book, Mountain Craig Brown, Logo, Signed, 5 In. 180.00
Bookends, Poised Pups, Blue Over Aqua Matte Glaze, 5 In. 132.00
Bookends, Pug Dog, Mulberry Glaze 175.00
Bookends, Squirrel, Dark Blue Over Rose Matte, 6 1/2 In. 135.00
Bookends, Squirrel, Turquoise, 1940s, 7 In. 245.00
Bowl, Acorn, Leaf, Signed 75.00
Bowl, Cover, Flower Frog, 5-Sided, Persian Rose Matte Glaze, 5 1/2 In. 187.00
Bowl, Embossed Leaves, Light Green, 1912, 5 In. 450.00
Bowl, Robin's-Egg Blue Glaze, Closed-In, Signed, 6 3/4 In. 565.00
Bowl, Scalloped, Blue, 9 1/2 In. 60.00
Bowl, Turquoise, 1960s, 5 In. 30.00
Candleholder, Acorn On Oak Leaf 58.00
Candleholder, Purple, Black, 1918 .... 350.00
Candleshield, Matte Green, Dated 1914 .... 425.00
Conch Shell, Blue, 9 In. 55.00
Conch Shell, Turquoise, 9 In. 65.00
Console, Flower Frog, Pinecone, Moonglow, 4 Piece 265.00
Creamer, Stylized Geometric Design, Blue Over Burgundy Glaze, Marked, 4 In. 155.00
Cup, Toast, Matte Green Glaze, 1901 .... 14300.00
Figurine, Birds In Flight, No. 498, 1907 .... 4070.00
Figurine, Donkey, Seated, Violet & Blue Glaze, Marked, 15 1/2 In. 45.00
Figurine, Indian Maiden Grinding Corn, Turquoise, 1940, 5 1/2 In. ....90.00 to 200.00
Figurine, Indian Maiden, Grinding Corn, Persian Rose, 5 1/2 In. 165.00
Figurine, Indian Maiden, Grinding Corn, White, 5 1/2 In. 95.00
Figurine, Kneeling At The Well, Maroon 125.00
Figurine, Panther, Seated, Blue-Green Glaze, Marked, 10 1/2 In. 100.00
Figurine, Rabbit, Marked, 2 1/2 In. 143.00
Figurine, Swan, Anna, Brown, 4 In. 35.00
Flower Frog, Blue Mottled Glaze, 1920s, 4 1/2 In. 60.00

   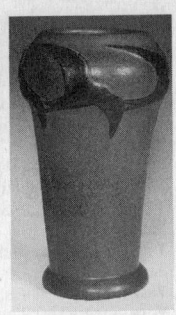

Van Briggle, Vase, 2 Bears, Molded, Brown, Blue, Marked, 1918, 14 1/2 In.; Van Briggle, Vase, Dos Cabezas, 2 Molded Nude Women, Mulberry, 1919, 7 3/4 In.; Van Briggle, Vase, Lady Of The Lily, Matte Green, Repaired, 1904, 11 In.; Van Briggle, Vase, Stylized Birds, Embossed, Blue Matte, 1901, 9 1/2 In.

Flower Frog, Mulberry & Blue, 1920s, 3 1/2 In.	24.00
Jug, Fire Water, Indian Design, Dark Green Glaze, Logo, 1902, 6 1/2 In.	2057.00
Jug, Red Brown Over Pale Green Matte Glaze, 1901, 4 5/8 In.	2310.00
Jug, Snake, Green Matte Glaze, Rust Highlights, 1902, 6 7/8 In.	3190.00
Lamp, 3 Handles, Maroon, Original Shades, 5 1/2 In., Pair	200.00
Lamp, 3 Handles, Turquoise, Pair	200.00
Lamp, Damsel Of Damascus, Persian Rose	340.00
Lamp, Day Dreamer, Original Shade	278.00
Lamp, Owl, Mulberry Glaze	350.00 to 400.00
Lamp, Squirrel Base, Turquoise	120.00
Lamp, Swirling Leaves & Stems, White Glaze, Marked, 21 In.	120.00
Paperweight, Rabbit, Brown, 1916	175.00
Paperweight, Rabbit, Moonglo Mist, 1 In.	65.00
Pitcher, Barrel, Black, White Drip, 6 Mugs	75.00
Pitcher, Black, 12 In.	50.00
Pitcher, Thick Pink Glaze, Marked, 1905, 4 1/2 In.	198.00
Planter, Crescent Moon, Persian Rose	80.00
Planter, Hanging, Green & Blue, 4 x 3 In.	110.00
Plaque, Big Buffalo, Indian Brave, Persian Rose	125.00
Plaque, Little Star, Indian Squaw, Persian Rose	125.00
Plate, Center Leaf, Turquoise & Blue, 1907, 6 1/4 In.	210.00
Plate, Grape Cluster & Leaves, Rose Color, c.1910, 8 1/2 In.	332.00
Salt & Pepper, Elephant	95.00
Salt & Pepper, Penguins, Blue Over Aqua Glaze, 4 In.	220.00
Sugar & Creamer, Blue Green	135.00
Vase, 2 Bears, Molded, Brown, Blue, Marked, 1918, 14 1/2 In. ...*Illus*	4675.00
Vase, 3-Headed Indian, Ming Turquoise Designs, 12 In.	240.00
Vase, Blue Green Shaded To Pale Blue, 4 In.	50.00
Vase, Bud, Blue Green, Whiplash Stems, 3 3/4 In.	225.00
Vase, Dirty Bottom, Maroon, 7 In.	250.00
Vase, Dos Cabezas, 2 Molded Nude Women, Mulberry, 1919, 7 3/4 In. ...*Illus*	3265.00
Vase, Dos Cabezas, 2 Reclining Women, Mulberry, Black, Logo, 1908, 7 In.	7700.00
Vase, Embossed Leaves & Violets, Mountain Craig Brown Glaze, 1914, 4 In.	357.00
Vase, Embossed Leaves, Gunmetal & Green Glaze, Signed, 1914, 5 3/4 In.	440.00
Vase, Embossed Peacock Feathers, Medium Green Ground, 1903, 12 In.	1980.00
Vase, Flamingo, Blue & Green, Paper Label, Incised Mark, 21 1/2 In.	357.00
Vase, Floral, Cobalt Blue, 4 1/2 In.	65.00
Vase, Gourd Form, Leaf Design, 1920s, 5 In.	88.00
Vase, Green To Blue Top, 6 In.	88.00
Vase, Gunmetal Black Over Green Glaze, 1916, 7 1/2 In.	2970.00
Vase, Lady Of The Lake, Kneeling, Looking At Turtle On Flower Frog, 16 In.	410.00
Vase, Lady Of The Lake, Turquoise & Blue, Logo, 11 x 15 In.	170.00
Vase, Lady Of The Lily, Matte Green, Repaired, 1904, 11 In. ...*Illus*	11550.00

Vase, Lady Of The Lily, Reclining Against Calla Lily, Turquoise, Marked, 14 1/2 In. 550.00
Vase, Leaf & Bud Design, Incised Marks, 1920s, 4 1/2 In. 55.00
Vase, Leaves, Blossoms, Mottled Green Matte Glaze, Bulbous, 9 1/2 In. 1093.00
Vase, Lorelei, Blue, 1970s, 11 In. ....165.00 to 225.00
Vase, Overlapping Leaves, Blue Over Burgundy, Marked, 1920s, 3 x 7 In. 165.00
Vase, Poppy Buds, Stems, Blue-Green, 3 3/4 In. 125.00
Vase, Poppy Design, Green Over Deep Red, Thick Matte Glaze, 1903, 9 In. 4675.00
Vase, Raised Leaf Design, 2 Handles, Blue, 1920, 7 In. 495.00
Vase, Raised Pointed Leaf Design, Rose Matte Glaze, c.1920, 4 1/2 In. 70.00
Vase, Siren Of The Sea, 1920s Logo, 13 x 15 In. 423.00
Vase, Stylized Birds, Embossed, Blue Matte, 1901, 9 1/2 In. ....*Illus* 4070.00
Vase, Stylized Flowers In Panels, Broad Waist, c.1907, 4 In. 550.00
Vase, Stylized Peacock Feathers, Mottled Light Blue Matte Glaze, 1903, 13 In. 3300.00
Vase, Stylized Stems, Powder White Matte Glaze, Oviform, 3 3/4 In. 690.00
Vase, Tree Bark, World's Fair, 1933, 6 In. 145.00
Vase, Turquoise, Horseshoe Handles, Marked, 3 In. 95.00
Vase, Yellow Thistles, Ocher Matte Finish, Corseted, Signed, 1906, 8 In. 1320.00
Vase, Yucca Blossoms Under Matte Purple Glaze, 17 In. 1760.00
Wall Pocket, Parrot, Blue & Green 700.00

VASA MURRHINA is the name of a glassware made by the Vasa
Murrhina Art Glass Company of Sandwich, Massachusetts, about
1884. The glassware was transparent and was embedded with small
pieces of colored glass and metallic flakes. The mica flakes were coated with silver, gold, copper, or nickel. Some of the pieces were cased.
The same type of glass was made in England. Collectors often confuse
Vasa Murrhina glass with aventurine, spatter, or spangle glass. There
is uncertainty about what actually was made by the Vasa Murrhina factory. Related pieces may be listed under Spangle Glass.

Basket, Embossed Ribs, Ruffled Rim, Clear Twisted Handle, 7 1/2 x 5 1/2 In. 135.00
Creamer, Embossed Swirl Design, Clear Handle, Blue, 4 3/8 In. 195.00
Rose Bowl, 8 Crimp Top, Mica Flakes, Deep Rose, White Lining, 3 3/4 In. ......100.00 to 110.00
Rose Bowl, Blue Spatter, White, 8 Crimp Top, 3 1/4 x 3 5/8 In. 85.00
Rose Bowl, Pink Spatter, Beige Ground, 8 Crimp Top, 3 3/4 x 3 3/4 In. 110.00
Rose Bowl, Pink Spatter, Ruffled, Clear Footed, 3 3/4 x 3 1/2 In. 110.00
Rose Bowl, Rose Overlay, White Lining, 8 Crimp Top, 3 3/4 x 3 3/8 In. 110.00
Rose Bowl, Satin, Ruffled, 3 In. 155.00
Vase, Aventurine Green With Blue, Fenton, 11 In. 45.00
Vase, Clear To Cranberry, White Spatter, Floral, Pedestal, 11 In. 295.00
Vase, Ewer Shape, Thorny Glass Handle, White Lining, Blue, 7 3/8 In. 115.00
Vase, Jack In The Pulpit, Blue Spatter, Mica Flakes, Swirled, 5 1/2 In. 250.00
Vase, Rigaree, 10 In. 325.00
Vase, Ruffled, Rose With Aventurine Green, Fenton 60.00
Water Set, Field Flowers, Marigold, 3 Piece 325.00

VASART is the signature used on a late type of art glass made by the
Streathearn Glass Company of Scotland. Pieces are marked with an engraved signature on the bottom. Most of the glass is mottled or shaded.

Vasart

Toothpick, Hat Form, Red Brim, Bluish Body, Signed, 2 1/2 In. 125.00

VASELINE GLASS is a greenish-yellow glassware resembling petroleum
jelly. Some vaseline glass is still being made in old and new styles.
Pressed glass of the 1870s was often made of vaseline-colored glass.
Additional pieces of vaseline glass may also be listed under Pressed
Glass in this book.

Bowl, Opalescent, Lily, 5 In. 115.00
Candlestick, Flint, 1890, 10 1/2 In. 140.00
Candy, William & Mary, Opalescent, 6 1/2 In. 38.00
Celery Vase, Yacht, Daisy & Button, Hobbs Brockunier, 14 x 2 In. 125.00
Compote, Clark's Teaberry Gum, Pedestal ....85.00 to 135.00
Compote, Cover, Medallion 33.00
Creamer, Ribbed Spiral, Opalescent, 4 In. 65.00
Figurine, Carousel Horse 30.00

Goblet, Inverted Thumbprint With Star 30.00
Goblet, Medallion 38.00
Knife Rest, Cut Honeycomb Ball Ends 125.00
Pitcher, Opalescent, 6 In. 500.00
Pitcher, Water, Reeded Handle 125.00
Rose Bowl, Pearles & Scales, Stemmed, Opalescent, 5 In. 45.00
Salt, Opalescent, 1 1/4 x 2 In. 55.00
Spooner 85.00
Toothpick, Chrysanthemum Base Swirl, Speckled 175.00
Vase, Ground Pontil, Large 145.00
Vase, Jack In The Pulpit, 6 1/2 In. 48.00
Vase, Nude Lady, 7 In. 30.00
Wine, Two Panel 35.00

VENETIAN GLASS, see Glass-Venetian category.

VENINI glass was first designed by Paolo Venini, who established his
factory in Murano, Italy, in 1925. He is best known for pieces of modern design, including the famous *handkerchief* vase. The company is
still working. Other pieces of Italian glass may be found in the Glass-
Contemporary, Glass-Midcentury, and Glass-Venetian categories of
this book.

Bookends, Red Glass, Radiating Bands, Ovoid, 5 In. 824.00
Bottle, Gray & White Vertical Caned, Round Ball Stopper 770.00
Bottle, Wide Vertical Canes, Stopper, 13 In. 1650.00
Bowl, Blue & Green, Signed, 8 In. 935.00
Bowl, Leaf Form, Internal Green Stripes, 7 In. 1093.00
Carafe, Bottle, Vertical Red Stripes 1 Side, Other, Opaque Pink Stripes, 12 1/2 In. 741.00
Charger, Green Abstract Design, Clear & Olive Border, Etched Mark, 16 1/2 In. 325.00
Compote, Green Cactus Leaf Stem, Red Blossoms, 7 In. 1725.00
Decanter, Blue Horizontal Band & Stopper, Green, 14 1/4 In. 1080.00
Decanter, Sommerso, Aquamarine, Free-Blown Stopper 248.00
Figurine, Bird, Clear Body, Applied Wings, Signed, 9 1/2 In. 880.00
Figurine, Dove, Tyra Lundgren, c.1951, 6 3/4 In. 1200.00
Figurine, Egret, Female, Chest Of Yellow & White Murrines, 11 In. 716.00
Figurine, Fish, Internal Design Of Orange Stripes, Clear, 14 1/2 In. 870.00
Figurine, Pigeon, Red Body, Applied Iridized Wings, 8 In. 1160.00
Goblet, Red & Green Vertical Stripes, 5 1/2 In. 770.00
Lamp, Rope Twist Form, Blue Opalescent, Cased In Bubbles, 18 In., Pair . . . . . . .550.00 to 695.00
Paperweight, Turquoise Band, Light Pink & Clear, Square, 5 In. 460.00
Screen, 4-Panels, Applied Amorphous Trailings, Iron Frame, c.1955, 5 x 6 Ft. 8050.00
Vase, Applied Prunts, Carlo Scarpa Design, c.1936, 10 3/4 In. 7475.00
Vase, Clear To Yellow, Blue & Amethyst Designs, Signed, 8 3/4 In. 5175.00
Vase, Colored Vertical Stripes, Flared, 9 In. 4943.00
Vase, Cylindrical, Long Vertical Bubbles, 10 1/2 In. 770.00
Vase, Cylindrical, Patchwork, Signed, c.1960, 9 1/2 In. 1380.00
Vase, Internal Gray String With White, Triangular, 1960s, 8 1/2 In. 1035.00
Vase, Internal Multicolored Bands, Everted Rim, Signed, 1953, 14 1/2 In. 1380.00
Vase, Latticinio Stripes Of Pink, White & Amethyst, 9 3/4 In. 2118.00
Vase, Latticino, Pink & Green, 6 1/2 In. 522.00
Vase, Red Exterior, White Cased, 3 1/2 In. 143.00
Vase, Topaz & Ruby, Signed, 11 1/2 In. 575.00
Vase, Vertical Canes, Goblet Form, Multicolored, 6 In. 440.00
Vase, Wide Horizontal Spiraling Strip In White, 7 1/2 In. 1059.00

VERLYS glass was made in France after 1931. It was made in the United
States from 1935 to 1951. The glass is either blown or molded. The
American glass is signed with a diamond-point-scratched name, but
the French pieces are marked with a molded signature. The designs
resemble those used by Lalique.

Bonbon, Cover, Butterfly, Topaz 175.00
Bowl, Cupidon 90.00
Bowl, Dragonfly 225.00

Bowl, Duck, Fish, Opalescent	250.00
Bowl, Floral Design, Opalescent Glass, Signed, France, 12 In.	288.00
Bowl, Orchid, 14 In.	150.00
Bowl, Pine Cone, 6 1/4 In.	65.00
Bowl, Poppy, Molded Blossoms, Raised Feet, Signed, 13 3/4 In.	201.25
Bowl, Poppy, Signed, Acid, 13 1/2 In.	175.00
Bowl, Tassel, 11 3/4 In.	105.00 to 150.00
Bowl, Thistle, 13 In.	150.00
Bowl, Water Lily, Dusty Rose	500.00
Cigarette Box, With Bird, Signed	145.00
Dish, 3 Moths & Glass Knob On Cover, 8 In.	220.00
Platter, Palm Leaves, Clear & Satin, 14 In.	145.00
Soap Dish, Figural, Duck	45.00
Vase, Alpine Thistle, Topaz, 11 In.	400.00
Vase, Eglantine, Opalescent, 9 1/2 In.	250.00
Vase, Gems, 6 3/4 In.	175.00 to 200.00
Vase, Gems, With Flower Frog, Amber, 6 3/4 In.	350.00
Vase, Grasshopper, 5 1/4 In.	125.00
Vase, Lovebird, 6 1/2 x 2 3/4 In.	125.00 to 150.00
Vase, Mandarin, 9 1/2 In.	400.00
Vase, Mermaid, Frosted Crystal, 10 In.	750.00 to 795.00
Vase, Mermaid, Topaz, Straight Top	1200.00
Vase, Thistle, 9 3/4 In.	110.00

VERNON KILNS was the name used after 1958 by Vernon Potteries, Ltd. The company, which started in 1931 in Vernon, California, made dinnerware and figurines until it closed in 1958. Collectors search for the brightly colored dinnerware and the pieces designed by Rockwell Kent, Walt Disney, and Don Blanding. For more information, see *Kovels' Depression Glass & American Dinnerware Price List*.

Berry Bowl, Calico	9.00
Bowl, Cover, Santa Anita, Pink	36.00
Bowl, May Flower, 9 In.	22.00
Bowl, May Flower, Tab Handle, 6 1/8 In.	8.00
Bowl, Mushroom, Fantasia, Pink	200.00
Bowl, Organdie, 5 1/2 In.	3.00
Bowl, Salad, Organdie	60.00
Bowl, Salad, Tam O'Shanter, Individual	25.00
Bowl, Serving, Organdie	18.00
Bowl, Sprite, Blue	235.00 to 325.00
Bowl, Winged Nymph	325.00
Butter, Organdie	22.00 to 30.00
Butter, Raffia	30.00
Candleholder, 3-Light, Jane Bennison, Yellow	75.00
Carafe, Homespun	42.00
Casserole, Cover, Gingham, Individual	28.00
Casserole, Cover, Raffia	20.00
Casserole, Desert Bloom	25.00
Casserole, Monterey, Individual	30.00
Chop Plate, 12 1/5 In.	100.00
Chop Plate, 14 In.	55.00
Chop Plate, Blue, 12 In.	85.00
Chop Plate, Dolores, 12 In.	25.00
Chop Plate, Floral Wreath, 17 In.	95.00
Chop Plate, Gingham, 12 In.	40.00
Chop Plate, Hawaiian Flowers, 12 1/2 In.	70.00
Chop Plate, Hawaiian Flowers, Blue, 14 In.	110.00
Chop Plate, Hawaiian Flowers, Maroon, 12 In.	135.00 to 145.00
Chop Plate, Hawaiian Flowers, Maroon, 14 In.	95.00
Chop Plate, Homespun, 12 In.	30.00
Chop Plate, Lei Lani, 14 In.	175.00 to 195.00
Chop Plate, Lei Lani, 17 In.	275.00 to 375.00
Chop Plate, May Flower, 12 In.	25.00

Chop Plate, Moby Dick, Blue, 12 1/2 In. ....125.00 to 150.00
Chop Plate, Organdie, 16 5/8 In. 425.00
Chop Plate, Our America, Brown, 17 In. 350.00
Chop Plate, Pan American Lei, 13 In. 60.00
Chop Plate, Raffia 20.00
Chop Plate, Salamina, 14 In. 375.00
Chop Plate, Santa Barbara, 14 In. 50.00
Chop Plate, Sierra Madre, Pink Border, 12 In. 20.00
Chop Plate, Winchester, 12 In. 100.00
Coffee Server, Modern California, Ivory, 10 Cup 45.00
Coffee Server, Organdie 25.00
Coffeepot, Tickled Pink 45.00
Creamer, Calico 20.00
Creamer, Early California, Turquoise 15.00
Creamer, Lei Lani, Short 35.00
Creamer, Nutcracker, Individual 195.00
Creamer, Organdie 9.00
Creamer, Our America, 2 In. 45.00
Creamer, Raffia 10.00
Creamer, Streamline 20.00
Creamer, Tickled Pink 12.00
Cup, Coral Reef, Maroon 45.00
Cup, Organdie, After Dinner 18.00
Cup, Winchester, 1973 .... 60.00
Cup & Saucer, Arcadia, After Dinner 16.00
Cup & Saucer, Calico 42.00
Cup & Saucer, Harry Bird, 2-Tone, After Dinner 25.00
Cup & Saucer, Homespun 6.00
Cup & Saucer, May Flower 15.00
Cup & Saucer, Moby Dick, After Dinner 50.00
Cup & Saucer, Raffia, Colossal 200.00
Custard Cup, Brown-Eyed Susan 35.00
Decanter, Penguin, 1930s 195.00
Dish, Divided, San Marino 85.00
Eggcup, Gingham 18.00
Eggcup, Raffia 20.00
Eggcup, Tam O'Shanter ....12.00 to 18.00
Figurine, Baby Weems 350.00
Figurine, Elephant, Dancing 350.00
Figurine, Unicorn 450.00
Flowerpot, Homespun, Small 35.00
Gravy Boat, Arcadia 22.00
Jug, Hawaiian Coral, Small 15.00
Mixing Bowl, Mojave, 5 In. 15.00
Mug, Organdie 15.00
Pitcher, Moby Dick, Brown, 2 Qt. 425.00
Pitcher, Organdie, 2 Qt. 65.00
Pitcher, Raffia, 2 Qt. 45.00
Pitcher, Salamina, 2 Qt. 825.00
Pitcher, Trade Winds, 2 Qt. ....40.00 to 45.00
Plate, Advertising, Moor Man's, 10 1/2 In. 45.00
Plate, Aircraft, Red 45.00
Plate, Aqua, 12 1/4 In. 12.00
Plate, Arcadia, 9 1/2 In. 12.00
Plate, Arizona 18.00
Plate, Bits Of Old South 45.00
Plate, Calico, 6 In. 9.00
Plate, Camelia, Brown Trim, 9 1/2 In. 12.00
Plate, Chicago 50.00
Plate, Gingham, 6 In. 8.00
Plate, Homespun, 6 In. ....1.25 to 4.00
Plate, Homespun, 9 1/2 In. ....8.00 to 9.00
Plate, Lei Lani, 7 In. 30.00

Plate, Lei Lani, 9 1/2 In. 40.00
Plate, Lei Lani, 10 1/4 In. ....55.00 to 65.00
Plate, Little Miss Muffet, 7 1/2 In. 32.00
Plate, May Flower, 7 1/2 In. 6.00
Plate, May Flower, 9 In. 12.00
Plate, Moby Dick, Blue, 6 1/2 In. ....35.00 to 40.00
Plate, Moby Dick, Blue, 10 1/2 In. ....55.00 to 95.00
Plate, Mt. Rushmore, Souvenir, 10 1/2 In. 15.00
Plate, My Maryland, 10 1/2 In. 15.00
Plate, Old Covered Bridge, 8 In. 50.00
Plate, Organdie, 6 In. 3.00
Plate, Organdie, 9 1/2 In. ....8.00 to 10.00
Plate, Our America, Brown, 10 1/2 In. 75.00
Plate, Pink, 12 1/4 In. 12.00
Plate, Salamina, 10 1/2 In. 125.00
Plate, St. Louis 15.00
Plate, Tam O'Shanter, 6 In. 4.00
Plate, Tam O'Shanter, 9 1/2 In. 8.00
Plate, Texas 18.00
Plate, Texas Bicentennial, Goliad, Tex., 1949 .... 24.00
Plate, Tickled Pink, 10 In. 4.00
Plate, Veiled Prophet 40.00
Plate, Virginia 15.00
Plate, Winchester, 6 In. 32.00
Plate, Wisconsin Transfer, Signed, Joyner 22.00
Platter, 8 1/2 In. 65.00
Platter, Frolic, 11 In. 15.00
Platter, Hawaiian Flowers, Maroon, 14 In. 125.00
Platter, Homespun, 12 1/2 In. 9.00
Platter, May Flower, 13 1/2 In. 20.00
Platter, Organdie, 12 1/2 In. 15.00
Platter, Oval, 14 In. 22.00
Salt & Pepper, Calico 35.00
Salt & Pepper, Hawaiian Flowers, Blue 45.00
Salt & Pepper, Hawaiian Flowers, Maroon 35.00
Salt & Pepper, Heavenly Days 12.50
Salt & Pepper, Homespun 10.00
Salt & Pepper, Hoplow Mushroom, Marked 200.00
Salt & Pepper, May Flower 15.00
Salt & Pepper, Organdie 10.00
Saucer, Gingham 4.00
Server, 2 Tiers, Organdie 20.00
Soup, Chowder, Chintz 13.00
Soup, Dish, Organdie, 8 In. 10.00
Sugar, Cover, Chatelaine, Platinum 50.00
Sugar, Cover, Moby Dick, Maroon 75.00
Sugar & Creamer, Cover, May Flower 25.00
Sugar & Creamer, Homespun 20.00
Syrup, Raffia Dripcut 45.00
Teapot, Brown Eyed Susan 55.00
Tidbit, Homespun, Metal Handle, 3 Tiers 26.00
Tumbler, Frontier Days 125.00
Tumbler, Heavenly Days 16.00
Tumbler, Homespun, 5 In. 18.00
Tumbler, Moby Dick 115.00
Tumbler, Mojave, 14 Oz. 18.00
Tumbler, Tickled Pink 18.00
Vase, Fantasia Goddess, All White 575.00
Vase, Rotary Club, Handle 110.00

VERRE DE SOIE glass was first made by Frederick Carder at the Steuben Glass Works from about 1905 to 1930. It is an iridescent glass of soft white or very, very pale green. The name means *glass of silk*, and it does resemble silk. Other factories have made verre de soie, and some of the English examples were made of different colors. Verre de soie is an art glass and is not related to the iridescent, pressed, white carnival glass mistakenly called by its name. Related pieces may be found in the Steuben category.

Bowl, Draped Florals, Etched, Yellow Glass Rim, 10 In.	125.00
Candlestick, 11 3/4 In.	395.00
Candlestick, 14 In.	395.00
Compote, Cover, Pear Finial, Frosted Celested Blue Twist Stem, Steuben, 7 In.	770.00
Compote, Fruit Finial, Celeste Blue, 6 1/2 In.	2600.00
Dresser Jar, Bulbous Iridescent Holder, Silver Cap, Floral Motif, 3 In.	230.00
Jar, Cover, Pear Finial, Orange Pear, Green Stem, Leaf, 4 1/4 In.	258.75
Jar, Undertray, Pink, Red Pear Finial, F. Carder, 5 In.	172.50
Perfume Bottle, Blue Threading, Blue Stopper	475.00
Vase, Blue Threading Around Flaring Edge, Flared Form, 4 1/4 In.	1150.00
Vase, Diamond-Quilted, Amethyst Reeded Rim, Flared, Steuben, 8 In.	330.00
Vase, Melon Ribbed Bottom, Rainbow & Ormolu Top, 9 In.	395.00

VIENNA, see Beehive category.

VIENNA ART plates are round metal serving trays produced at the turn of the century. The designs, copied from Royal Vienna porcelain plates, usually featured a portrait of a woman encircled by a wide, ornate border. Many were used as advertising or promotional items and were produced in Coshocton, Ohio, by J.F. Meeks Tuscarora Advertising Co. and H.D. Beach's Standard Advertising Co.

Plate, Anheuser-Busch, Madonna Della Sedia, Blue	98.00
Plate, Empire Bottling Co., Grecian Woman, Flowers, 1909	135.00
Plate, Perfection Beer, Pre-Prohibition, 1905	68.00

VILLEROY & BOCH Pottery of Mettlach was founded in 1841. The firm made many types of wares, including the famous Mettlach steins. Collectors can be confused because although Villeroy & Boch made most of its pieces in the city of Mettlach, Germany, they also had factories in other locations. The dating code impressed on the bottom of most pieces makes it possible to determine the age of the piece. Additional items may be found in the Mettlach category.

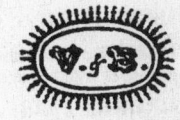

Charger, Fruit & Flowers, 17 In.	190.00
Dish, Juvenile, Divided, Birds, Blue	45.00
Paperweight, Dwarf Pressing On Seal At Envelope, 4 1/4 In.	330.00
Plaque, Story Book Rabbits Scene, 12 In.	275.00
Vase, Birds In Flight Above Waves, Brown, Blue, Cream Ground, 12 In.	176.00
Vase, Stylized Blossom Design, Dark Brown, Cocoa, Pale Green, 10 1/2 In.	55.00

VOLKMAR pottery was made by Charles Volkmar of New York from 1879 to about 1911. He was associated with several firms, including the Volkmar Ceramic Company, Volkmar and Cory, and Charles Volkmar and Son. Volkmar had been a painter, and his designs often look like oil paintings drawn on pottery.

VOLKMAR
Corona N.Y

Mug, Swollen Form, Covered In Green Glaze, Ink Mark, 4 In.	285.00
Pitcher, Bulbous Bottom, Ribbon Handle, Dark Green Glaze, Signed, 5 x 4 In.	82.00
Plaque, Mt. Vernon, Blue & White, 1890, 11 1/2 In.	300.00 to 325.00
Plaque, Tree Scene, Green, Tan, Rolling Hills, White, Pale Pink Sky, 8 x 9 1/2 In.	2750.00
Tile, Squeeze Bag Design, Stylized Duck, Green & Black Glaze, Signed, 8 x 8 In.	495.00
Vase, Pillow, Trumpet Flowers, Leaves, Textured Ground, Signed, 9 3/4 In.	660.00

VOLKSTEDT was a soft-paste porcelain factory started in 1760 by Georg Heinrich Macheleid at Volkstedt, Thuringia. Volkstedt-Rudolstadt was a porcelain factory started at Volkstedt-Rudolstadt by Beyer and Bock in 1890. Most pieces seen in shops today are from the later factory.

Candlestick, Applied Roses, c.1930, Pair	50.00
Figurine, 2 Young Men, 4 1/2 In.	40.00
Figurine, Amorous Couple, 16 In.	805.00
Perfume Bottle, Cupid, 1895, Pair	45.00

WADE pottery is made by the Wade Group of Potteries started in 1810 near Burslem, England. Several potteries merged to become George Wade & Son, Ltd. early in the twentieth century, and other potteries have been added through the years. The best-known Wade pieces are the small figurines given away with Red Rose Tea and other promotional items. The Disney figures are listed in this book in the Disneyana category.

Bank, Baby	25.00
Bank, Daughter	30.00
Bank, Natwest Piggy	30.00
Charger, Snow White, 1930s	185.00
Figurine, 3-Leaf Clover, Porcelain, Ireland	6.00
Figurine, Blynken, Green Mark	100.00
Figurine, Bunnies, Kissing	160.00
Figurine, Nod, Green Mark	100.00
Figurine, Penguin, Mother & Father	85.00
Figurine, Tortoise, 9 1/2 In.	145.00
Figurine, Whimsy Hippos Set, 3 Piece	75.00
Teapot, Copper Luster	85.00
Teapot, Festival	135.00
Teapot, Man, With Plaid Hat, Figural	65.00
Teapot, Paisley Chintz	70.00
Teapot, Scotty	200.00
Vase, Art Deco Style, Bulbous, 7 In.	175.00

WAHPETON POTTERY, see Rosemeade category.

WALLACE NUTTING photographs are listed under Print, Nutting. His reproduction furniture is listed under Furniture.

WALRATH was a potter who worked in New York City; Rochester, New York; and at the Newcomb Pottery in New Orleans, Louisiana. Frederick Walrath died in 1920. Pieces listed here are from his Rochester period.

Bowl, 3 Frogs Sitting On Leaves, Green Matte Glaze, 8 x 3 In.	825.00
Bowl, Floral Design, Gray Ground, Flaring Shoulders, 8 In.	175.00
Chamberstick, Gray, 5 In.	300.00
Chamberstick, Green, 7 In.	400.00
Mug, Foliate Design, Red, Brown, Brown Ground, 3 1/4 x 4 1/2 In., Pair	431.00
Vase, Stylized Leaf-Forms, Blue, Light Blue Matte Ground, 7 3/4 x 3 3/4 In.	1380.00

WALT DISNEY, see Disneyana category.

WALTER, see A. Walter category.

WARWICK china was made in Wheeling, West Virginia, in a pottery working from 1887 to 1951. Many pieces were made with hand painted or decal decorations. The most familiar Warwick has a shaded brown background. The name *Warwick* is part of the mark and sometimes the mysterious word *IOGA* is also included.

Bowl, Flow Blue, Scalloped Border, Gold Accents, 9 5/8 In.	125.00
Cuspidor, Flowers, Brown & Yellow, IOGA	150.00
Lamp, Moose, Large Antlers, 28 In.	120.00
Mug, Bulldog	36.00

Mug, Indian, 4 In. ....85.00 to 100.00
Pitcher, Chrysanthemum 165.00
Pitcher, Gold Trim, Flow Blue 375.00
Pitcher, Lemonade, Beech-Nut, Brown To Light Orange 150.00
Plate, Monk, Drinking Ale, Brown, Yellow, Ivory 65.00
Tankard, Champion Bulldog, Rodney Stone ....38.00 to 40.00
Tankard, Elks, 12 1/2 In. 195.00
Vase, Flamingos, Orchid & Gray, IOGA, 10 1/2 In............................. 125.00
Vase, Hibiscus, Twig Handles, Brown, 10 1/2 In. 125.00
Vase, Urn Form, Bronze, Twig Handles, Paw Feet, 12 In. 1850.00

WATCH pockets held the pocket watch that was important in Victorian times because it was not until World War I that the wristwatch was used. All types of watches are collected: silver, gold, or plated. Watches are arranged by company name or by style. Pocket watches are listed here; wristwatches are a separate category.

A.C. Cuendet, 22 Jewel, Independent Seconds, Enamel & Gold Dial, Key Wind, Gold .. 865.00
Audemars, 2 Train Wind, Jeweled, Gold Cuvette, Enamel Dial, c.1880 .... 5750.00
Automaton, Gold, Egyptian Motif, Gilt, Foliate Wreath, 1815 ....10350.00
Automaton, Repeating, Gold Quarter, Engine Silver Dial, 1810 .... 4025.00
Baume & Mercier, Riviera, Moon Face, Gold & Steel, Pocket 11200.00
Cartier, Open Face, 18K Gold, Red, Blue Enamel, Silvered Matte Dial 4025.00
Elgin, 14K Yellow Gold, Engraved Case Monogrammed J. G., 1 5/8 In. 385.00
Elgin, 17 Jewel, Railroad Grade, Ticket Case 100.00
Elgin, Engraved Indian On Horseback, Shooting Buffalo, Pocket 495.00
Elgin, Hunting Case, 17 Jewel, Gold, White Enamel Dial, Roman Numerals, 1900 ...... 4887.00
Elgin, Hunting Case, Gold Filled, Chain, Bell Shaped Gold Quartz Fob, 1880s 1750.00
Elgin, Hunting Case, Slider Chain, Presentation Box, c.1902 .... 600.00
Elgin, Let-Her-Buck, Cowboy, 19 Jewel 385.00
Elgin, Open Face, 14K Yellow Gold, Porcelain Dial, Seconds Dial 373.00
Hamilton, 14K White Gold, 3 Clusters Of Diamonds 75.00
Hamilton, 23 Jewel, 14K Gold, Masonic Dial, Box, c.1922 .... 1400.00
Hamilton, Military Hour, Black Porcelain Dial, Pair 1000.00
Hamilton, Platinum, 14K Gold, White Circular Dial, Art Deco 805.00
Illinois, Bunn Special, Railroad, Original Case 375.00
Illinois, Hunting Case, 15 Jewel, Gold Plated 75.00
Illinois, Hunting Case, Deer In Naturalistic Setting, Enamel Dial, Fob, Plated Chain 1610.00
Joseph Johnson, 3-Color Gold Dial, Gold Plated Chain, Key & 2 1/2 Gold Dollar 1100.00
Longines, 17 Jewel, 14K Yellow Gold, Pave Diamond, Rectangular Face 575.00
Longines, Open Face, Chronograph, White Enamel Dial, 1900 .... 1380.00
Movado, Sterling Silver Case, Chronometer, Coin On Back, 1908 .... 650.00
Niello, Hunting Case, Enamel Dial, Second Hand, Continental Hallmarks 230.00
Open Face, 18K Gold, White Enamel Dial, 1844 .... 3680.00
Open Face, 18K Gold, White Enamel Dial, 1875 .... 4600.00
Pendant, Lozenge Shape, Collet Set Diamonds, Diamond Set Platinum Chain, 16 In. 6325.00
Perret & Berthoud, Hunting Case, Floral Design, 18K Gold, c.1900 .... 1610.00
Picard, Hunting Case, Dust Cover, 18K Yellow Gold, Enameled Dial, Seconds Dial 805.00
Pocket, Open Face, White Enameled Face, Black Numbers, 1910, 2 In. 138.00
Repeating, Gun Metal, Champagne Matte Dial, Circular, 1900 .... 805.00
Repousse, Gilt Metal, Scrolls, Bird, White Enamel Dial, Roman Numerals, 1780 ...... 402.00
Rockford, Texas Confederate Flags, 1895 .... 325.00
Shreve & Co., Hunting Case, Gold & Platinum, Factory Engraved, O Size 1000.00
Shreve & Co., Open Face, 14K Gold, Porcelain Dial 450.00
Tiffany, 5 Minute Repeating, Pocket 2600.00
Tiffany, Chronograph, Second Hand, 18K Gold, Pocket 3200.00
Tiffany, Swiss Movement, Fitted Box, 18K Gold Case 635.00
Trail Blazer, Byrd's Antarctic Expedition, Nickel Plate, Not Running 185.00
Vacheron & Constantin, 17 Jewel, Gold, Champagne Matte Dial, Roman Numerals ... 2070.00
Vacheron & Constantin, 18 Jewel, 18K Gold, Champagne Matte Dial, 1930 .... 1380.00
Vacheron & Constantin, 18K Gold, Open Face, Pink Dial, Gold Baton Numerals, 1920 2645.00
Vacheron & Constantin, 18K Gold, White Enamel Dial, Roman Numerals, 1890 ..... 2185.00
Vacheron & Constantin, Woman's, Pendant, 14K Gold 750.00

Waltham, 14K Gold, Enameled Dial, Filigree Hands 225.00
Waltham, 17 Jewel, Silvered Matte Dial, Masonic Emblematic Numerals, 1950 .... 2645.00
Waltham, 23 Jewel, 10K Gold Filled, Stem Wind 187.00
Waltham, Chronometer, Gimbal Mounted Movement, Brassbound Case, 3 3/4 In. 748.00
Waltham, Hunting Case, 14K Yellow Gold, 2-In. Diam. 325.00
Waltham, Hunting Case, 14K Yellow Gold, Porcelain Enamel, Seconds Dial 230.00
Waltham, Hunting Case, 17 Jewel, 14K Gold, Enamel Dial, Seconds Dial, Dust Cover .. 488.00
Waltham, Hunting Case, Gold Filled, White Enamel Face, Roman Numerals 50.00
Waltham, Lapel, 14K Yellow Gold, Porcelain Enamel Dial, Blue Numerals 200.00
Waltham, Open Face, 17 Jewel, 14K Gold, Enamel Face, Chain, 14K Gold 275.00
Waltham, Railroad, 15 Jewel, Etched Train On Case 150.00
Waltham, Riverside, 14K Yellow Gold, Open Face, Enamel Dial, Seconds Dial 488.00
Washington Watch Co., Rose & Yellow Gold Inlay, Sterling Silver, 2 In. 275.00
Woman's, Ladybug Form Case, Rose Cut Diamonds On Wings, Oval, c.1900 .... 8050.00
Woman's, Scarab Form, Rose Cut Diamonds, Gold & Enamel, c.1900 .... 9200.00

WATCH FOBS were worn on watch chains. They were popular during
Victorian times and after. Many styles, especially advertising designs,
are still made today.

Abraham Fur Company, St. Louis, Arrowhead Shape 85.00
Attached Cigar Cutter, Gold 250.00
Attached Cigar Cutter, Sterling Silver 110.00
Avery Tractor 110.00
Buffalo Bill, Pawnee Bill 45.00
Caterpillar, Views In Nutshell, Strap 45.00
Caterpillar Tractor ....15.00 to 25.00
Central States Insurance 35.00
Cheyenne Days, Pin, 1909 .... 275.00
Dane Manufacturing Co., Ottumwa, Iowa 220.00
Fremont Brewing Co., Fremont, Nebraska, 1891-1917 .... 450.00
Gold Dust Twins 195.00
Gold Filled, Mesh Ribbon, Dated 1913 .... 45.00
Good Roads 125.00
Green River, 1904 .... 30.00
Hair, Victorian 75.00
Hastings Brewing Co., Hastings, Nebraska, 1908, Picture Of Cavalier, 1917 .... 530.00
Heiden Tractor 120.00
Hibbard Spencer Bartlett & Co., Padlock Shape, Our Very Best 85.00
International Harvester 60.00
John Deere, Centennial, Cast Bronze, 1937 .... 95.00
Keen Kutter, Ax Head, Ribbon 185.00
Kentucky Whiskey 80.00
Kienzler Prune Juice, Baudy Woman 60.00
Marion Steam Shovels 30.00
Mule's Head, Carved Ivory, Ornate Gold Filled Chain 375.00
N.A.R.D. Notes, Baudy Woman 60.00
National Cigar Stands, 5 Cent, Attached Cigar Cutter 85.00
National Sportsman Advertising, Buck Deer, Gun, Brass 47.00
Old Ben Coal, Cigar Cutter, Sterling Silver, 1902 .... 40.00
Oshkosh Brewing Co., Oshkosh, Wisconsin, 1864-1943 .... 95.00
OVB, Hibbard Spencer Barlett & Co., Padlock Shape 85.00
Peden Iron & Steel, Houston, San Antonio 60.00
Peru Brewing Co., Peru, Illinois, Eagle Center, 1868-1943 .... 95.00
Rock Island Plow 95.00
S. Silblerman Fur Co., Chicago, Ill., Brass 79.00
Southern California Automobile Club, Celluloid, 1 3/4 In. 45.00
St. Andrews Golf Club, Election Day, 1918, Sterling Silver 75.00
Sterling Silver, Cigar Cutter, Ornate 110.00
Teddy Roosevelt, Johnson, Metal, 1912 .... 180.00
U.C.V. Reunion, Little Rock, Cowboy, Pin, 1911 .... 225.00
U.S. Compass Co., Indian 65.00
Weatherbird Shoes 225.00

WATERFORD type glass resembles the famous glass made from 1783 to 1851 in the Waterford Glass Works in Ireland. It is a clear glass that was often decorated by cutting. Modern glass is being made again in Waterford, Ireland, and is marketed under the name *Waterford*.

Bowl, Geometric, Circular, 7 In.	60.00
Box, Crystal Cut, Cover, Etched Mark, 2 In.	60.00
Champagne, Saucer	50.00
Cordial, Alana	25.00
Decanter, 3 Spouts, Silver Trefoil Top, Stopper, 1912, 10 In.	330.00
Decanter, Kenmare	195.00
Decanter, Ovoid, 10 1/2 In.	110.00
Goblet, Alana	170.00
Goblet, Sheila	30.00
Jar, Cover, Pineapple Shape, Heavy Cut, 8 1/2 In.	90.00
Perfume Bottle, Colleen	68.00
Punch Set, Notched Diamond Cut Bodies, Laurel Leaf Band, Signed, 26 Piece	2585.00
Vase, Cut Crystal, Floral Edge, Diamond Sides, 6 1/4 In.	180.00
Vase, Geometric, Circular, Flared, 6 In.	65.00
Vase, Geometric, Narrow, Flared Neck, Circular, 10 1/4 In.	85.00
Vase, Scalloped Rim, Cutting, Signed, 9 1/2 In.	200.00 to 225.00
Wine, Kildare	35.00

WATT family members bought the Globe pottery of Crooksville, Ohio, in 1922. They made pottery mixing bowls and tableware of the type made by Globe. In 1935 they changed the production and made the pieces with the freehand decorations that are popular with collectors today. Apple, Starflower, Rooster, Tulip, and Autumn Foliage are the best-known patterns. Pansy, also called Rio Rose, was the earliest pattern. Apple, the most popular pattern, can be dated from the leaves. Originally, the apples had three leaves; after 1958 two leaves were used. The plant closed in 1965. For more information, see *Kovels' Depression Glass & American Dinnerware Price List.*

Baker, Apple, 3-Leaf, Rectangular, No. 85	1000.00
Baker, Cover, Apple, No. 67	140.00
Baker, Cover, Apple, No. 96	125.00
Baker, Cover, Double Apple, No. 96	275.00
Baker, Cover, Open Apple, No. 110	600.00
Baker, Cover, Rooster, No. 67	160.00
Baker, Cover, Starflower, No. 67	160.00
Baker, Cover, Tulip, No. 600	340.00
Baker, Rooster, Rectangular, No. 85	1400.00
Baker, Tulip, Ribbed, No. 601	150.00
Bean Pot, Apple, No. 76	90.00 to 200.00
Bean Pot, Autumn Foliage, No. 76	125.00 to 145.00
Bean Pot, Tear Drop, No. 76	95.00
Bean Server, Tear Drop, Individual, No. 75	25.00 to 35.00
Bowl, Salad, Apple, 2-Leaf, No. 74	30.00 to 40.00
Bowl, Salad, Tulip, No. 73	140.00
Bowl, Spaghetti, Apple, 3-Leaf, No. 24	85.00 to 175.00
Bowl, Spaghetti, Pansy, Crosshatch, No. 39	375.00
Bowl, Spaghetti, Pansy, Cut-Leaf, No. 39	60.00 to 70.00
Bowl, Spaghetti, Starflower, No. 24	100.00
Canister, Apple, Large, No. 72	600.00
Canister, Sugar, Apple, No. 81	650.00
Canister Set, Dutch Tulip, No. 81 & No. 82	2050.00
Canister Set, Esmond, 4 Sections, Wooden Base & Top, Swivel	225.00
Canister Set, Esmond, No. 81 & No. 82	145.00
Carafe, Orchard Ware, No. 115	125.00
Casserole, Apple, Green Band, Apple Bottom, No. 73	100.00
Casserole, Apple, Stick Handle, Individual, No. 18	150.00
Casserole, Cover, Apple, 2-Leaf, No. 05	60.00
Casserole, Cover, Apple, No. 73	190.00

Casserole, Cover, Moonflower, Tab Handles, Black, Individual, No. 18 .... 120.00
Casserole, Cover, Pansy, Cut-Leaf, Groove Handle, Individual, No. 18 .... 85.00
Casserole, Cover, Rooster, Individual, No. 18 .... 425.00
Casserole, Starflower, Tab Handles, Green-On-Brown, Individual, No. 18 .... 100.00
Chop Plate, Apple, No. 49 .... 100.00
Coffee Server, Cover, Apple, No. 115 ....300.00 to 350.00
Cookie Jar, Apple, No. 503 ....2350.00 to 3000.00
Cookie Jar, Esmond, Happy, Sad Face, No. 34 .... 495.00
Cookie Jar, Pansy, Cut-Leaf, No. 21 ....225.00 to 245.00
Cookie Jar, Starflower, No. 21 .... 70.00
Cookie Jar, Tulip, No. 503 .... 155.00
Cookie Jar, White Daisy, No. 21 ....280.00 to 450.00
Creamer, Apple, 2-Leaf, No. 62 .... 150.00
Creamer, Apple, 3-Leaf, No. 62 .... 115.00
Creamer, Autumn Foliage, No. 62 .... 130.00
Creamer, Double Apple, No. 62 .... 195.00
Creamer, Dutch Tulip, No. 62 .... 350.00
Creamer, Morning Glory, No. 62 ....180.00 to 295.00
Creamer, Rooster, No. 62 .... 425.00
Creamer, Starflower, No. 62 .... 295.00
Creamer, Tear Drop, No. 62 ....80.00 to 250.00
Creamer, Tulip, No. 62 ....295.00 to 350.00
Crock, Cheese, Rooster, No. 80 ....185.00 to 225.00
Cruet Set, Autumn Foliage, No. 126 .... 1500.00
Ice Bucket, Apple, No. 59 .... 625.00
Ice Bucket, Tear Drop, No. 59 .... 325.00
Jar, Grease, Apple, Commemorative, 1995 .... 235.00
Jar, Grease, Starflower, No. 01 .... 200.00
Mixing Bowl, Apple, 2-Leaf, No. 5 .... 350.00
Mixing Bowl, Apple, No. 64 .... 45.00
Mixing Bowl, Apple, Ribbed, No. 5 .... 60.00
Mixing Bowl, Apple, Ribbed, No. 6 .... 60.00
Mixing Bowl, Apple, Ribbed, No.7 .... 55.00
Mixing Bowl, Rooster, Ribbed, No. 5 .... 55.00
Mixing Bowl, Tulip, No. 63 .... 80.00
Mixing Bowl, Tulip, No. 64 ....65.00 to 110.00
Mixing Bowl Set, Tear Drop, 4 Piece 100.00
Mug, Apple, No. 121 .... 290.00
Mug, Apple, No. 501 ....175.00 to 200.00
Mug, Apple, No. 701 .... 265.00
Mug, Rooster, No. 701 .... 475.00
Mug, Starflower, No. 501 .... 1000.00
Mug, Starflower, White-On-Red, No. 121 ....75.00 to 90.00
Nappy, Apple Ribbed, No. 04 .... 1100.00
Nappy, Tear Drop, No. 7 ....60.00 to 70.00
Pepper Shaker, Starflower, Barrel, No. 46 .... 50.00
Pie Plate, Apple, No. 33 .... 65.00
Pie Plate, Pansy, No. 33 .... 160.00
Pitcher, Apple, 2-Leaf, No. 16 .... 80.00
Pitcher, Cherry, No. 15 .... 60.00
Pitcher, Cherry, No. 16 .... 145.00
Pitcher, Double Apple, Commemorative, 1994 .... 225.00
Pitcher, Double Apple, No. 15 .... 400.00
Pitcher, Dutch Tulip, No. 15 .... 200.00
Pitcher, Pansy, Cut-Leaf, No. 16 .... 250.00
Pitcher, Pansy, No. 17 ....175.00 to 210.00
Pitcher, Rooster, No. 15 .... 195.00
Pitcher, Starflower, 5-Petal, No. 15 .... 150.00
Pitcher, Starflower, Ice Lip, 4-Petal, No. 17 .... 85.00
Pitcher, Starflower, Ice Lip, No. 17 .... 110.00
Pitcher, Tear Drop, No. 15 ....120.00 to 175.00
Pitcher, Tulip, Ice Lip, No. 17 .... 62.00
Pitcher, Tulip, No. 16 .... 200.00
.... 225.00

Pitcher, Wood Grain, No. 613W	100.00
Plate, Dinner, Apple, No. 29	250.00
Platter, Starflower, Round, 15 In., No. 31	50.00
Salt & Pepper, Apple, Barrel	425.00
Salt & Pepper, Apple, Hourglass	150.00 to 225.00
Salt & Pepper, Rooster, Barrel	295.00
Salt & Pepper, Starflower, Barrel	135.00 to 185.00
Salt & Pepper, Starflower, Hourglass	295.00
Salt & Pepper, Tear Drop, Barrel, No. 45 & No. 46	250.00
Saltshaker, Cherry, Barrel	75.00
Sugar, Cover, Apple, No. 98	400.00
Sugar, Cover, Autumn Foliage, No. 98	140.00
Sugar & Creamer, Apple, 3-Leaf, No. 98 & No. 62	595.00
Sugar & Creamer, Morning Glory, No. 98 & No. 97	650.00
Teapot, Apple, No. 505	4000.00
Teapot, Autumn Foliage, No. 505	980.00

WAVE CREST glass is a white glassware manufactured by the Pairpoint Manufacturing Company of New Bedford, Massachusetts, and some French factories. It was decorated by the C.F. Monroe Company of Meriden, Connecticut. The glass was painted in pastel colors and decorated with flowers. The name *Wave Crest* was used after 1898.

WAVE CREST WARE

Ash Receiver, Blue, White Flowers, 3 1/4 In.	235.00
Biscuit Jar, Cover, Floral Design, Pairpoint Silver Mounts, 6 In.	275.00
Biscuit Jar, Egg Crate Shape, Floral, Silver Plate Lid & Handle, 8 1/2 In.	375.00
Biscuit Jar, Fern Design, Pale Yellow Ground, Metal, Handle, 10 1/2 In.	280.00
Biscuit Jar, Helmschmied Swirl, Arrow Leaves, Blue Ground, 2 3/4 In.	575.00
Biscuit Jar, Painted Daisies & Embossed Leaves, 7 1/2 In.	300.00
Biscuit Jar, Peach, Mixed Flowers	385.00
Biscuit Jar, Raised Floral, Beaded, Silver Plate, Bail Handle	285.00
Biscuit Jar, Rococo, Enamel Floral, Banner Mark, Square, 8 x 5 1/4 In.	385.00 to 413.00
Bowl, Glossy Brown Ground, Blue, Lavender Aster Type Floral Design, 5 1/2 In.	275.00
Box, Baroque Shell	495.00
Box, Black, Green Corners, Molded Scroll Sides, Ferns, Ormolu Footed, Round, 5 In.	495.00
Box, Cherubs, Cattails, Lake Scene, Hinged, Lined, Oval, 4 x 3 1/2 In.	385.00
Box, Collars & Cuffs, Blue Rococo Mold	1550.00
Box, Cover, Double Shell, Flowers, Signed, 3 In.	295.00
Box, Dresser, Cover, Fern Design, 7 1/2 In.	715.00
Box, Dresser, Cover, Helmschmied Swirl, Blossoms, Blue, White Ground, 5 1/2 In.	230.00
Box, Dresser, Hinged, Helmschmied Swirl, Blue Flower, Enamel, 7 In.	520.00
Box, Embossed, Robin's-Egg Blue, Pink Tea Rose, 5 1/4 x 3 1/2 In.	505.00
Box, Floral Design On Top, Spring Of Flowers, Powder Blue To White, 4 1/2 In.	165.00
Box, Floral Motif, Pink, White Beading, 4 1/2 x 3 In.	475.00
Box, Hand Painted Blue & White Asters, Scrolls, Silk Lining, 7 1/4 In.	675.00
Box, Handkerchief, Rococo, Daisies, Pink Flowers, 9 1/2 x 6 1/2 In.	1195.00
Box, Helmschmied Swirl, Flowers, Pale Blue, 3 x 4 1/2 In.	350.00
Box, Helmschmied Swirl, Hinged, Blue, White Floral, Pink Banner Mark, 3 x 3 In.	165.00
Box, Helmschmied Swirl, Pink, 5 1/2 In.	595.00
Box, Hinged Cover, Egg Crate Shape, Forget-Me-Nots, Lavender Scrolls, Square, 6 1/2 In.	770.00
Box, Hinged Cover, Egg Crate Shape, Maroon & White Daisies, Square, 7 1/2 In.	1100.00
Box, Hinged, Cherub In Cattails, Sailboat Scene, Lined, Oval, 4 x 3 1/2 x 3 In.	385.00
Box, Hinged, Helmschmied Swirl, Pink, Blue Floral Design, Spider Web, 7 x 6 In.	440.00
Box, Jewelry, Enameled Florals, 5 In.	525.00
Box, Jewelry, Hinged, Pale Yellow Ground, White, Blue Flowers, Oval, 5 1/4 In.	440.00
Box, Jewelry, Piecrust Edge, Floral Sides, Hand Painted Flowers, 5 In.	525.00
Box, Jewelry, Pink Floral Design, Lined, 3 x 3 In.	285.00
Box, Jewelry, Serene Lakeside Cottage Cover, Black Mark, 2 1/2 x 3 1/2 In.	250.00
Box, Orange & Yellow Floral, Beaded & Pink Edge Banner, 3 1/2 x 5 1/2 x 4 In.	715.00
Box, Small Flower Design On Top, Square, 3 1/2 In.	185.00
Box, Sprays Of Christmas Holly On Block Of Ice, 4 x 7 In.	950.00
Broom Holder, Blue, Lavender, Yellow Ground	1220.00
Card Holder, Pink Tea Roses, Light Blue, 4 x 2 3/4 x 1 1/4 In.	410.00
Cookie Jar, Floral, Embossed Medallion, Square	195.00

Cracker Jar, Blue Flowers, Tan Arabesque Design, Metal Rim & Cover, 7 In. 165.00
Cracker Jar, Helmschmied Swirl, Pale Yellow Floral Design, 10 1/2 In. 195.00
Cracker Jar, Pale Pink, Green Ground, Bird, Sitting Among Flowers 165.00
Cracker Jar, Pansies, Ribbed, Silver Cover, Bail Handle 495.00
Cracker Jar, Pink Clover, Leaf Design, Pale Blue Ground, Pink Banner Mark, 8 In. 440.00
Cracker Jar, Red, Yellow Carnations, White, Blue Ground, 8 In. 55.00
Cracker Jar, Tulip Molded, Wild Roses, Metal Rim, Bail & Cover, 8 In. 330.00
Creamer, Helmschmied Swirl, Mushroom Garden Design 75.00
Dish, Blown Out, Cobalt Blue, 5 1/2 In. 475.00
Fernery, Egg Crate Shape, Liner, 7 In. 295.00
Fernery, Enameled Floral, Blown Out, Beaded Twist, Banner Mark, 7 In. 220.00
Fernery, Yellow, Footed 650.00
Humidor, Cigar, With Lilacs, Leaf 1100.00
Jar, Powder, Floral Design, 5 In. 66.00
Key Box, Petticoat & Mushroom Mold, 7 1/2 In. 900.00
Match Holder, Beaded Top & Bottom, Flowers, 4 Gold Feet 195.00
Perfume Bottle, White Enameled Floral Design, Soft Blue Ground, 3 3/4 In. 522.00
Salt & Pepper, House Design, Original Lids 95.00
Salt & Pepper, Pale Blue Green Ground, Pink Flowers, Metal Tops, 3 In. 247.00
Salt & Pepper, Pearl, House Scene, Original Tops 95.00
Saltshaker, Chick On Pedestal 495.00
Saltshaker, Scroll Wave, Blue Flowers 75.00
Sugar & Creamer, Helmschmied Swirl, Beige, White, Pink Wild Rose Design, 5 In. . . . 165.00
Sugar & Creamer, Helmschmied Swirl, Blownout, Enamel Design, 3 1/4 In. 330.00
Syrup, Ribbed Skirt, Blue Florals 165.00
Tobacco Jar, Egg Crate Shape, 4 1/2 x 5 In. 695.00
Tobacco Jar, Pink, Polychrome Flowers, Word Tobacco, Marked, 5 3/8 In. 248.00
Toothbrush Holder, Cover 525.00
Tray, Jewelry, Rococo, Handles, Footed, Banner Mark, 2 3/4 x 6 In. 275.00
Vase, Daisies, Yellow Ground, Metal Footed, 6 In. 260.00
Vase, Embossed Hand Painted Florals, Beaded Rim, 5 1/4 In. 235.00
Vase, Light Blue, Pink Flowers Front & Back, Metal, 6 1/2 In. 480.00
Vase, Pink & Blue Florals Cascade From Gilt Rim, Ormolu Base, 6 1/4 In. 330.00
Vase, Pink Daisy, Enameled, Pale Yellow Ground, Gold Highlights, 13 3/4 In. 1210.00
Vase, Pink Flowers, 2 Ormolu Handles, 6 1/2 In. 550.00
Vase, White Daises, Rust, Gold, 12 1/4 In. 1850.00
Vase, White Orchid Blossoms, Bright Blue Band, Gold Ormolu, 12 1/2 In. 2450.00

WEAPONS listed here include instruments of combat other than guns,
knives, rifles, or swords. Firearms are not listed in this book. Knives
and swords are listed in their own categories.

Blackjack, Nautical, Cord Wrist Thong, 8 In. 195.00
Bow, Arrow, Quiver, Africa 50.00
Parrying Shield, Heavy Hide, 4 Flower Head Bosses, 18th Century, 12 3/4 In. 375.00
Pouch, Bullet, Doe Skin, Bone Neck, Revolutionary War 130.00

WEATHER VANES were used in seventeenth-century Boston. The direction of the wind was an indication of coming weather, important to the
seafaring and farming communities. By the mid-nineteenth century,
commercial weather vanes were made of metal. Today's collectors
often consider weather vanes to be examples of folk art, even though
they may not have been handmade.

3 Letters & Arrow Above Globular Finial, Pierced Foliate Silvered Iron, 46 In. 127.00
Angel Gabriel, Carved For One Plank, Mounted On Iron Rod, Pine 1875.00
Banner, Copper, Verdigris Surface, 37 1/2 In. 747.00
Banner, Cutout W, Copper, Verdigris Surface, Late 19th Century 315.00
Banner, Pierced Finial Designed, Directionals, 19th Century, 97 x 36 In. 1780.00
Biplane, Planks Joined By Iron Wires, Rotating Wheels, Pine, 1920, 19 In. 1150.00
Bull, Gilt Copper, Verdigris Surface, 19th Century, 24 In. 2070.00
Cockerel, Sheet Metal, Red Tin Tail, Cast Iron, Directionals, 31 In. 1725.00
Cow, Copper Spire, Standing With Applied Ears, Horn, Wooden Base, 17 In. 3910.00
Cow, Full-Bodied, Zinc Head, Copper, 1870s, 17 In. 2185.00
Cow, Gilded Copper, Standing, Applied Ears & Horns, Wooden Stand, 17 1/4 In. 4025.00

An old cotton sock is a good polishing cloth. So is an old cloth diaper.

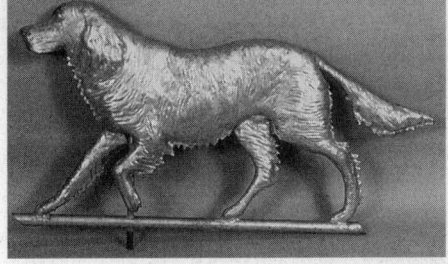

Weather Vane, Dog, Setter, Standing,
Copper, Regilded, 36 In.

Cow, Iron, Sliding, Turning Arrow, Cylindrical Shaft, Molded Globe, 33 In.	58.00
Cow, Silver, Copper, Sliding, Turning Arrow, Wooden Base, 24 In.	115.00
Cow, Solid Metal Head, Copper, 25 In.	550.00
Cow, Standing, Painted, Black, White, Late 19th Century, 20 1/2 In.	805.00
Cow, Swell Bodied, Sheet Copper Ears, Zinc Horns, Copper	2587.00
Cow, Zinc Head, Copper, Green Patina, 17 1/2 In.	3850.00
Dog, Setter, Standing, Copper, Regilded, 36 In. ....*Illus*	2970.00
Driver & Car, Verdigris Surface	675.00
Eagle, Copper, On Brass Orb, 25-In. Wingspan	1250.00
Eagle, Full-Bodied, 34-In. Wingspan	800.00
Eagle, Gilt Copper, 19th Century, 12 1/2 x 18 In.	1610.00
Eagle, Gilt Copper, 19th Century, 17 In.	920.00
Eagle, Gilt Copper, Late 19th Century, 38 x 44 In.	4025.00
Eagle, Hammered Copper & Tin, Sling Shot Dents, Fiske, 1860s, 68 x 32 In.	1925.00
Eagle, Spread Wings, Copper, Claw Feet, Molded Arrow, 19 In.	805.00
Ear Of Corn, 5 Bullet Holes	3375.00
Ear Of Corn, BB Ping On Side	650.00
Ewe, Zinc Lead, Verdigris Surface, Gold Leafing	5500.00
Fire Chief, Silhouette	935.00
Fish, Codfish, Articulated Gills, Tail, Yellow-Painted, Black Base, 15 1/2 In.	4600.00
Fleur-De-Lis, Red, Small	105.00
Gaggle Of Geese, Tin	3200.00
Horse, Black Hawk, Full-Bodied, 19th Century, 19 In.	1400.00
Horse, Black Hawk, Full-Bodied, Rod, Cardinal Points, Orbs, 16 1/2 In.	2800.00
Horse, Black Hawk, Running, Copper, 19th Century, 18 In.	2530.00
Horse, Copper, Gilt, Verdigris Surface, 19th Century, 37 In.	1725.00
Horse, Jockey, Articulated Hat, Beige Pedestal, Molded Copper, 17 1/4 In.	4025.00
Horse, Running, Articulated Mane, Tail, Black Base, Gilt Copper, 25 1/2 In.	3450.00
Horse, Running, Articulated Mane, Tail, Black Base, Zinc & Copper, 19 3/4 In.	920.00
Horse, Running, Articulated Mane, Tail, Molded Copper, Tan Pedestal, 23 3/4 In.	2070.00
Horse, Running, Copper, Cole Bros.	700.00
Horse, Running, Copper, Verdigris Surface, 19th Century, 31 1/4 In.	1380.00
Horse, Running, Full-Bodied, Copper, Mustard, Fiske, 38 In.	9200.00
Horse, Running, Full-Bodied, Mounted On Rod, 20th Century, 18 In.	1150.00
Horse, Running, Gilt Copper, 19th Century, 29 In.	747.00
Horse, Running, Gilt Copper, 19th Century, 42 In.	1610.00
Horse, Running, Gilt Copper, 28 In.	1100.00
Horse, Running, Jockey On Horse, Copper, 19th Century, 15 In.	1700.00
Horse, Running, Yellow, Articulated Mane, Tail, Painted Pine, 31 In.	4600.00
Horse, Sheet Metal, Blacksmith Riveted Construction, 1930s, 30 In.	137.00
Horse, Stallion, On Bar, A.B. Westervelt, Church, N.Y., 1883, 22 In.	6900.00
Horse, Standing, Copper Molded, A.L. Jewell & Co., 27 In.	7475.00
Horse, Sulky With Driver, Copper, 1900, 32 In.	6500.00
Indian, Shooting Arrow, Copper, 20th Century, 41 In.	165.00
Lightning Rod, Ribbed Ball & Zinc Car Directional, W.E. Shinn	1200.00
Locomotive, Sheet Metal, 19th Century	7700.00

Maltese Cross, Red, Large 195.00
Pig, Zinc, Cast Iron Arrow, 20 3/4 In. 412.00
Polar Bear, Molded Copper 5500.00
Quill Pen, Zinc, Gilt Copper, 19th Century, 24 x 36 1/2 In. 1265.00
Roadster Car, 1 Side Mint, 1 Side 1 BB Hole, Small 250.00
Rooster, 23 x 24 1/2 In. 1295.00
Rooster, Arrow, Cast Iron, Sheet Metal, 20 1/2 In. 150.00
Rooster, Copper, Cast Metal Feet, 20 x 20 1/2 In. 1495.00
Rooster, Molded Feather, Wing & Tail, Zinc Feet, Rod Over Orb, Copper, 26 In. 1955.00
Rooster, Sheet Iron 1950.00
Rooster, Standing, Molded Copper, Swelled Body, Spurred Legs, 30 In. 3450.00
Rooster, Swelled Body, Sheet Copper Tail, Comb & Wattle, 22 In. 1150.00
Rooster, Wooden, Old Paint, 18 In. 1870.00
Sailing Ship, Copper & Iron, 19th Century, 19 x 14 In. 1050.00
Sheep, Copper, Verdigris Surface, Bullet Holes, 19th Century, 29 1/2 In. 5750.00
Silhouette, Civil War Soldiers, Marching, 4 Full-Bodied, Black Base, 18 In. 4600.00
Sperm Whale, Articulated Mouth, Fins, Tail, Copper, 19 In. 2530.00
Stag, Articulated Mane, Tail, Molded & Gilt Copper, Black Base, 30 1/2 In. 4025.00
Stag, Running, Sheet Iron, 40 x 49 1/2 In. 1610.00
Swordfish, Wood & Cast Iron 1150.00
Windmill Whirligig, Weathered Old Paint 225.00

WEBB glass is made by Thomas Webb & Sons of Ambelcot, England.
Many types of art and cameo glass were made by them during the
Victorian era. Production ceased by 1991, and the factory was demol-
ished in 1995. Webb Burmese and Webb Peachblow are special colored glasswares of the Victorian era. They are listed at the end of this
section. Glassware that is not Burmese or Peachblow is included here.

Bonbon, Diamond-Quilted, Mother-Of-Pearl, White & Clear Ribbons, 8 1/2 In. 250.00
Bottle, Scene, Flattened Teardrop, Sapphire Blue Design, White Ferns, 4 In. 920.00
Bowl, Butterfly Hovering Over Branch, Foxglove Blossoms, 1 1/2 x 6 In. 750.00
Bowl, Satin Glass, Brown, Crimped, Cream Lining, Gold Reeded Feet, 3 5/8 In. 495.00
Bowl, Thistle Form, Bulbous Reeded Section, Engraved Florals, England, 2 7/8 In. 2587.00
Creamer, Frosted Handle, Cream Lining, 3 3/4 In. 245.00
Cruet, Allover Blue & White Designs, 4 Lobes, Amber Handle, Stopper, 6 In. 965.00
Decanter, Apricot Overlay, Amber Thorny Applied Handle, Brass Stopper, Square, 9 In. . . 225.00
Paperweight, Yellow Diamond Air Trap 175.00
Perfume Bottle, Cantaloupe, Ivory, Silver Onion Cap, Clear Plug Stopper, J.G. & S. 2200.00
Perfume Bottle, Forget-Me-Nots, Etched, 2 Butterflies On Shoulder, Gilt Screw Cap . . . 431.00
Pitcher, Blue Satin, Camphor Branch Handle, Enamel Beetle, Queen Ann's Lace 905.00
Pitcher, Brown Shaded, Cream Lining, Bulbous, Frosted Applied Handle, 3 3/4 In. 195.00
Plaque, Woman, Barefoot In Flowing Gown, Amethyst Glass, Woodall, 6 x 4 In. 12650.00
Plate, 3 Bands Scrolled Vines, Stylized Flowers, Ivory, Stamped, 9 In. 1430.00
Rose Bowl, 8 Crimp Top, Diamond-Quilted, Mother-Of-Pearl, Cream Lining, 3 x 3 In. . . 395.00
Rose Bowl, Red & White Clematis, Vine Cascades From Rim, Yellow, Cameo, 4 In. 1430.00
Vase, Amber Glass Leaves, Berries, Pair 185.00
Vase, Butterfly, Fuchsia Blossom, Red Ground, Shouldered, Cup Rim, Cameo, 6 In. 2200.00
Vase, Butterscotch Yellow, Turquoise Blue, White Opalescent Case, 7 In. 1955.00
Vase, Carved Lion Masks, Woodall Style Cutting, 6 1/2 In. 3025.00
Vase, Citron, 5 1/2 In. 795.00
Vase, Custard, Dimpled, Flowers & Butterflies, 5 x 5 3/4 In. 210.00
Vase, Gold & Black Wild Roses, Butterflies, Yellow To White, Satin, 18 In. 605.00
Vase, Gold Floral Design, Gold Butterfly In Flight, Bronze Handles, 7 1/2 In. 245.00
Vase, Gold Floral Design, Ivory, Gold Butterfly On Back Side, 4 In. 175.00
Vase, Gold Flowers, Vines & Foliage, Opaque Ivory, 2 3/8 In. 175.00
Vase, Gold Lotus Blossoms, Floral Cascades From Rim, Blue, 9 1/2 In. 245.00
Vase, Ivory, Silver Top Rim, Leaf Design, Brown Ground, T. Webb & Sons, 5 1/4 In. . . . 695.00
Vase, Leafy Bough Design, Blossom Clusters, Raisin Color, White, Linear Border, 4 In. . . 575.00
Vase, Leafy Branches With Applied Amber Pears, Green Fruits, Woodall, 6 In. 9200.00
Vase, Pink, Allover Cut To Opal, Floral Branches, Ribbed, Cameo, 8 In. 1210.00
Vase, Satin Glass, Brown, Heavy Gold Pine Needles, Prunus Floral, 5 1/2 In. 495.00
Vase, Sepia Design, Ivy Above Berries On Leaf Vines, Ivory, 7 In. 805.00
Vase, Stick, Blue Glossy, Allover Gold Seedlings, Enameled Flowers, 8 In. 302.00

Vase, Stick, Sunbursts, Floral Branches, Elephant Head Handles, Ivory, Cameo, 8 3/4 In. . . 1100.00
Vase, Tricolor, White Over Red Glass, Geraniums, Butterfly, Signed, 9 In. 2185.00
Vase, White Enamel, Lace Look, White Cased Pink Body, Bulbous, Signed, 10 1/4 In. 325.00
Vase, White Leaves & Floral, Citron Ground, Cameo, 3 1/4 In. 880.00
Vase, White Morning Glories Cascade Rim, Red, Egg Shape, Cameo, Marked, 8 In. 2475.00
Wine Cooler, Cut & Etched, Signed, c.1900 . . . . 375.00

WEBB BURMESE is a colored Victorian glass made by Thomas Webb
& Sons of Stourbridge, England, from 1886.

Candelabra, 6-Lights, Ivy, Leaf Design, Green, Brown Shades, 13 3/4 In. 2310.00
Epergne, 4 Trumpet, Petal Rim, Crystal Rigaree Leaves, Mirror, 11 x 12 In. 4400.00
Epergne, Clear Leaf, Molded Frog, Beveled Mirror, 7 Bowls, 14 x 8 In. 3850.00
Lamp, Fairy, Queens 2400.00
Nut Dish, Crimped Petal Top, Yellow Floral, 2 1/2 x 4 In. 275.00
Perfume Bottle, Lay Down, Rose Blossoms, Silver Top, 2 x 2 In. 875.00
Rose Bowl, Acid Finish, 8 Crimps Top, Salmon Pink, Yellow . . . . .195.00 to 210.00
Rose Bowl, Floral, Salmon Pink To Yellow, 8 Crimps Top, 2 3/8 In. . . . . .210.00 to 335.00
Vase, 5-Point Star Top, Ivy Design, 3 3/4 In. 165.00
Vase, 6-Lobed Crimped Rim, Floral Design, 3 3/4 In. 99.00
Vase, Crimped, Ruffled Rim, Ruffled Foot, 4 In. 250.00
Vase, Enameled Blue & White Floral, Ruffled, 3 3/4 In. 475.00
Vase, Enameled Flowers, Blue, Salmon Pink, Yellow, 3 1/2 In. 265.00
Vase, Green Shades Of Ivy, Ribbed, Flared, 3 3/4 x 4 1/4 In. 480.00
Vase, Ivy & Leaves, Signed, 1880s, 8 1/2 In. 1275.00
Vase, Ivy Design, Metal Holder, 6 In. 275.00
Vase, Japonesque, White To Pink, Oval, 7 1/4 In. 345.00
Vase, Petal Top, Queens, Stamped, 3 1/4 In. 330.00
Vase, Petal Top, Scalloped Foot, 4 In. 220.00
Vase, Salmon Pink To Yellow, Ruffled, Bulbous Base, 3 1/2 x 2 1/2 In. 225.00
Whiskey Taster, Matte, Marked, 1 7/8 x 2 1/2 In. 150.00

WEBB PEACHBLOW is a colored Victorian glass made by Thomas
Webb & Sons of Stourbridge, England, from 1885.

Biscuit Jar, Rose To Pink, Light Blue, White Daisies, White Interior 1850.00
Bowl, Amber Rigaree Trim, Square Top, 3 1/4 x 7 In. 160.00
Bowl, Raised Gold Floral Branch, Crimped Pinched Rim, 2 In. 220.00
Cruet, Amber Reeded Handle & Stopper, 6 3/4 In. 175.00
Cruet, Fall Leaves & Flowers, Amber Reeded Handle, Stopper, 6 1/2 In. 495.00
Finger Bowl, Gold Prunus, Butterflies, Ruffled, 6-In. Underplate 600.00
Plate, Crimped Rim, Gilt Design Of Insects, Prunus, 9 In. 220.00
Rose Bowl, Red Butterfly, Mustard Yellow Flowers, Camphor Leaf Footed 155.00
Sweetmeat, Cover, Gold Floral Branches, Silver Rim, Clover Handle, 2 1/2 In. 330.00
Vase, Club Form, Gilt, Green Floral Design, 8 1/4 In. 248.00
Vase, Gold Enameled, Flowers & Bee, 6 In. 375.00
Vase, Gold Flowers, Gold Butterfly On Reverse, Cream Lining, 3 1/4 In. 295.00
Vase, Gold Prunus Blossoms On Branches, Cream Lining, 3 3/4 In. 325.00
Vase, Gold Prunus, Red, Pink, Gold Branches, 3 3/4 In. 325.00
Vase, Lacy Allover Design, Silver Flower Blossoms, Cream Lining, 5 1/4 In. 295.00
Vase, Multicolored Crested Hummingbird, Branches, 9 In. 286.00
Vase, Pine Needles, Boughs, Butterflies, 11 1/4 In. 750.00
Vase, Red To Pink, Gold & Silver Leaves, White Lining, 5 1/8 In. 295.00
Vase, Rose Red Shade To Pink, Gold Leaves, Silver, Gold Flowers, 5 1/8 In. 295.00
Vase, Satin, Knob Neck, 8 In. 190.00
Vase, Stick, Blue & White Bird, Vines & Pine Cone Branches, 14 In. 410.00
Vase, Stick, Gold Prunus, Bulbous Bottom, 8 In. 295.00
Vase, Stick, Raspberry To Pink Base, Pinch Side, Bulbous, 8 1/4 In. 300.00
Vase, Thorny Base, Crystal Matsu-No-Ke Flowers, 4 3/4 In. 325.00
Vase, Yellow Outlined Branches, Flowers, Basket Weave, 8 In. 330.00
Vase, Yellow Roses, Brown & Green Foliage, Hexagonal, 13 In. 220.00

WEDGWOOD, one of the world's most successful potteries, was founded by Josiah Wedgwood, who was considered a cripple by his brother
and was forbidden to work at the family business. The pottery was

established in England in 1759. A large variety of wares has been made, including the well-known jasperware, basalt, creamware, and even a limited amount of porcelain. There are two kinds of jasperware. One is made from two colors of clay, the other is made from one color of clay with a color dip to create the contrast in design. The firm is still in business. Other Wedgwood pieces may be listed under Flow Blue, Majolica, or in other porcelain categories.

WEDGWOOD

Ashtray, Winston Churchill, Blue, 4 1/2 In.	35.00
Basket, Chestnut, Cover, Scrolled Foliate, Floral Finial, 1920, 8 1/2 In.	315.00
Biscuit Barrel, Jasperware, Blue, Hunters On Horseback, Hounds, Fox	275.00
Biscuit Barrel, Jasperware, Blue, Silver Plated Cover, Swing Handle, 8 1/2 In.	295.00
Biscuit Barrel, Silver Plated Cover, Black Fruit, Grapevine, Yellow, 5 1/4 In.	489.00
Biscuit Barrel, Silver Plated Cover, White Classical Relief, Green Ground	575.00
Biscuit Jar, Jasperware, Tricolor, Black Ground, White Classical Relief, 5 1/4 In.	490.00
Biscuit Jar, Jasperware, Tricolor, Central Green Frieze, White Classical Relief	750.00
Biscuit Jar, Jasperware, Tricolor, Light Blue Ground, White Classical Relief, 5 In.	230.00
Bowl, Black Basalt, Classical Figures, 1850, 6 In.	185.00
Bowl, Cover, Chapoo, Flow Blue, c.1850, 12 x 9 3/4 In.	920.00
Bowl, Fairyland Luster, Castle On A Road, Octagonal, 1920, 8 7/8 In.	1840.00
Bowl, Fairyland Luster, Fairy In Cage Interior, Castle Exterior, 9 In.	4625.00
Bowl, Fairyland Luster, Firbolgs II, Green, Gilt Outlined Figures, 6 1/4 In.	345.00
Bowl, Fairyland Luster, K'Ang Hsi, Woodland Bridge, 1920, 7 3/8 In.	2875.00
Bowl, Fairyland Luster, Leapfrogging Elves, Empire, 1920, 4 3/8 In.	920.00
Bowl, Fairyland Luster, Woodland Elves, 1920, 8 5/8 In.	2760.00
Bowl, Hummingbird Luster, Hummingbird Interior Center, 8 In.	805.00
Bowl, Jasperware, Green, 6 In.	195.00
Bowl, Jasperware, White Leaf Relief, Light Blue, 1800, 5 In.	546.00
Bowl, Lovebirds On Cover, Griffins Base, Majolica, 9 1/2 In. ....*Illus*	825.00
Bowl, Mother-Of-Pearl Ground, Orange Interior, 1920, 7 1/4 In.	290.00
Bowl, Poplar Trees, Black Exterior, Bell Branch Interior, 1920, 9 1/8 In.	2300.00
Bowl, Queensware, Boston, Black Transfer, Print Marks, 12 1/4 In.	86.00
Bowl, Rams' Heads, Cream, 6 x 11 In.	145.00
Box, Dresser, Jasper Dip, Blue, White Classical Design, 4 x 4 In.	33.00
Box, Jasperware, Gray, Round, 1 1/2 In.	45.00
Box, Sardine, Cover, Majolica, 8 x 7 1/4 In.	275.00
Breakfast Set, Creamware, Barlston Pattern, Grapevine Border	135.00
Bust, John Locke, Black Basalt, On Raised Base, Impressed Mark, 1865, 7 3/4 In.	520.00
Bust, Laughing Boy, Black Basalt, Raised Circular Base, England, 2 3/4 In.	115.00
Bust, Robert Burns, Black Basalt, Raised Round Base, Impressed Mark, 7 1/2 In.	375.00
Bust, Roman Male, Black Basalt, On Pedestal Base, 18th Century, 11 In.	195.00
Bust, Shakespeare, Black Basalt, Impressed Marks, England, 1964, 10 In.	375.00
Bust, Shakespeare, Moonstone, Impressed Mark, 20th Century, 11 In.	290.00
Bust, Sleeping Boy, Black Basalt, England, 19th Century, 4 5/8 In.	175.00
Cake Plate, Chapoo, Flow Blue, Pedestal, c.1850	2920.00
Candleholder, Applied Creamware Drapery Swags, Black Basalt Base, 6 1/2 In.	1495.00
Candlestick, Jasperware, Banquet, Pair	90.00
Candlestick, Jasperware, Green, 5 In., Pair	135.00
Chalice, Luster, Dragon, Cloud Border, Mottled Blue, 1920, 10 3/4 In.	545.00
Chamberstick, Jasperware, Green, White Classical Figures, 6 1/2 In.	110.00
Charger, Charles I, Creamware, Portrait, Enamel, c.1800, 16 In.	575.00
Charger, Queensware, Pink Luster, Enamel Floral Design, 14 7/8 In.	805.00
Cheese Keeper, Cobalt Blue Primrose, Basket, Majolica, 10 In. ....*Illus*	860.00
Clock, Enamel Dial, Garlands Of Flowers, Gilt Bronze Frame, Signed, 16 In.	2070.00
Compote, Queensware, Shell, Japonica Pattern, Triangular Base, 1872, 6 3/4 In.	345.00
Creamer, Cover, Cauliflower, Green Glazed Leaves, Cream Florets, 5 1/2 In.	1265.00
Creamer, Fallow Deer, Luster	60.00
Creamer, Jasperware, Blue, 4 1/4 In.	95.00
Creamer, Yellow With White, 4 In.	135.00
Cup, Custard, Jasperware, Blue, Latticework, Impressed Mark, 1790, 1 5/8 In.	488.00
Cup, Jasperware, Hunting Scene, England, 3 1/4 In.	80.00
Cup & Saucer, Gilt Band Rims, Handles, Pale Turquoise Interior, Olive Green, Pair	100.00
Cup & Saucer, Gilt Edge, Polychrome Botanical, Red, White Ground, 1812	100.00
Cup & Saucer, Jasperware, Green, Yellow Quatrefoils, White, 5 3/8 In.	1610.00

Wedgwood, Bowl, Lovebirds On Cover,
Griffins Base, Majolica,
9 1/2 In.

Wedgwood, Cheese Keeper,
Cobalt Blue Primrose, Basket,
Majolica, 10 In.

Cup & Saucer, Moonlight, Luster, England, c.1810, 5 1/2 In.	230.00
Cup & Saucer, Peter Rabbit	25.00
Cup & Saucer, Queensware, Countryside	15.00
Decanter, Sandeman, Black	38.00 to 45.00
Dish, Cheese, Cover, Jasperware, Dark Blue, White Classical Relief, 9 1/2 In.	460.00
Dish, Game Pie, Caneware, Fruit Grapevine Relief, Round, c.1820, 3 1/2 In.	632.00
Dish, Leaves On Basket, Majolica, 10 1/2 In.	305.00
Dish & Cup, Peter Rabbit	35.00
Eggcup, Jasperware, Black, White	65.00
Figure, William Beattie, Ireland, Impressed Mark, 1859, 12 3/4 In.	920.00
Figurine, Bulldog, Black Basalt, Glass Eyes, Impressed Mark, 1915, 4 3/4 In.	290.00
Figurine, Deer, Queensware, J. Skeaping	250.00
Figurine, Diana & Minerva, Seated, Holding Acanthus, Black Basalt, 13 In., Pair	1000.00
Figurine, Eros & Euphrosyne, Black Basalt, England, 19th Century, 16 1/4 In.	1610.00
Figurine, Kingfisher, Black Basalt, Tall Rocky Base, Ernest Light, c.1918, 7 1/4 In.	345.00
Figurine, Mercury, Seated On Freeform Base, Black Basalt, 1840, 18 1/4 In.	1265.00
Figurine, Poodle, Black Basalt, Ernest Light, England, c.1918, 3 In.	375.00
Figurine, Psyche, Nude, Seated On Freeform Rocks, Black Basalt, 8 1/2 In.	518.00
Figurine, Raven, Black Basalt, England, c.1913, 4 1/2 In.	175.00
Figurine, Reclining Baby, Black Basalt, England, 19th Century, 4 1/4 In.	430.00
Figurine, Squirrel, Black Basalt, England, c.1915, 5 1/4 In.	690.00
Figurine, Tiger & Buck, Black Basalt, Artist, 1927, 11 3/4 In.	860.00
Game Dish, Rabbit & Game On Cover, 10 In.	660.00
Humidor, Jasperware, Blue	375.00
Inkwell, Caneware, Black Basalt Foliate Relief, England, c.1800, 2 1/4 In.	375.00
Inkwell, Cover, Blue Luster, Gilt Dragon & Cloud, 1920, 4 In.	490.00
Jam Pot, Jasperware, Dark Blue, Figures & Horses, Impressed Mark, 8 3/8 In.	460.00
Jar, Biscuit, Jasperware, Black, Classical, Silver Cover & Handle, 5 3/8 In.	460.00
Jar, Cover, Lilac Jasperware, Trophies Between Floral Festoons, 1869, 5 In.	515.00
Jar, Sweetmeat, Jasperware, Blue & White, Silver Plated Top, Marked, 4 In.	145.00
Jardiniere, Jasperware, Dark Blue, White Classical Relief, England, 8 In.	230.00
Jardiniere, Jasperware, Garland Of Grapes, Blue, White, 4 1/2 In.	195.00
Jug, Commemorative, Queensware, Gilt Trim, Brown Transfer, 8 In.	175.00
Jug, Dip, Portland, Jasperware, Dark Blue, White Classical Relief, 1891, 7 3/4 In.	375.00
Jug, Etruscan, Green, 6 1/4 In.	125.00
Jug, Hinged Pewter Cover, Majolica, Japanese Style Florets, 1878, 6 1/2 In.	517.00
Jug, Lincoln & Washington, Profiles, U.S. Centenary, Majolica, 1876, 5 1/2 In.	402.00
Lamp, Reading, Black Basalt, Gilt, Acanthus, Bellflower Relief, 1875, 8 1/4 In.	1380.00
Medallion, Jasperware, Blue, Classical, 5 Colors, Oval, 19th Century, 3 1/8 In.	1650.00
Medallion, Jasperware, Blue, White Children, Oval, 18th Century, 2 5/8 x 3 In.	315.00
Mortar & Pestle, Stoneware, Wooden Handle, 1900, 4 In.	260.00
Mug, F.D. Roosevelt, Bust, Eagle, Blue, Black Letters Around, 4 1/4 In.	400.00
Mug, Floral Design, Silver Resist Luster, England, 1950, 3 3/4 In.	520.00
Mug, Jasperware, Blue & White, Royal Visit To Canada, 1939	75.00

Mug, Jasperware, Dark Blue & White, 3 Handles, 4 1/4 x 4 In.	295.00
Mustard, Cover, Jasperware, Sage	68.00
Perfume Bottle, Jasperware, Light Blue, Lay Down, 19th Century, 3 In.	295.00
Pin, Blue Grecian Woman, Gold Filled Frame	40.00
Pitcher, Black Basalt, 3 1/2 In.	245.00
Pitcher, Chapoo, Flow Blue, Bulbous, c.1850, 6 3/4 In.	805.00
Pitcher, Floral Design, Enamel, Black Basalt, Impressed Mark, 5 1/2 In.	230.00
Pitcher, Floral Design, Enamel, Impressed Mark, England, 1860, 6 1/2 In.	345.00
Pitcher, Green, Hound Handle, 7 In.	95.00
Pitcher, Jasperware, Crimson, White Classical Relief, England, 4 3/4 In.	635.00
Pitcher, Jasperware, Dark Blue & White, Man With Dog, Lady With Dog, 4 In.	195.00
Pitcher, Jasperware, Green, 2 1/2 In.	30.00
Pitcher, Jasperware, Yellow, White Classical Relief, England, 4 1/4 In.	488.00
Pitcher, Tankard, Jasperware, Grape Border, White Top Edge, 4 1/4 In.	88.00
Pitcher, Tankard, Jasperware, White Grape Border, Cupids, 3 7/8 In.	95.00
Pitcher, Women, Children, Cupids, White Relief On Green, 8 In.	275.00
Pitcher & Bowl, Blue Willow, 2 Piece	1450.00
Pitcher & Bowl, Chapoo, Flow Blue, c.1850	3210.00
Pitcher & Bowl, Wamba	1500.00
Placecard Holder, Jasperware, Blue, White Classical Relief, 2 1/2 In.	258.00
Plaque, Black Basalt, Allegorical, Bacchic Revelry, Walnut Frame, 22 1/2 In., Pair	2875.00
Plaque, Black Basalt, Death Of A Roman Warrior, England, 10 3/8 x 18 7/8 In.	3220.00
Plaque, Black Basalt, Scenes Of Bacchanalian Merriment, 8 1/2 x 20 In., Pair	805.00
Plaque, Fairyland Luster, Picnic By River, Frame, 1920, 4 1/2 x 10 1/2 In.	2990.00
Plaque, Jasperware, Bacchanalian Boys, Blue, Frame, 6 1/2 x 23 1/4 In.	1610.00
Plaque, Jasperware, Marriage Of Cupid & Psyche, Blue, White Relief, 7 x 11 In.	1840.00
Plaque, Jasperware, Portrait, Blue, T. Bentley & J. Wedgwood, 4 1/4 In., Pair	745.00
Plaque, Pan & Syrinx Relief, White, Terra-Cotta, Oval, 1775, 4 1/2 x 5 3/8 In.	1495.00
Plate, Bennett Hall, 1929, 10 1/4 In.	85.00
Plate, Cauliflower Pattern, Majolica, 9 In.	160.00
Plate, Christmas, 1969, Windsor Castle	110.00
Plate, Christmas, 1970, Christmas In Trafalgar Square	65.00
Plate, Commemorative, Simmons College, Anniversary, 10 1/2 In.	26.00
Plate, Constantine, 8 In.	16.00
Plate, Creamware, Tan, Sepia Scallop Border, Pale Cream Ground, 9 3/8 In.	600.00
Plate, Cupid, Jasperware, Pink, 9 1/2 In.	135.00
Plate, Dominion Of Canada, Coat Of Arms With Oak, Acorn Border, 1907, 9 1/2 In. ...	70.00
Plate, Fairyland Luster, Floral Border, Printed Mark, 1928, 9 1/4 In.	2875.00
Plate, Fairyland Luster, Imps On Bridge, Orange Border, 1920, 10 3/4 In.	2415.00
Plate, Jasperware, Cupid, Pink, 9 1/2 In.	135.00
Plate, Mercersburg Academy, 10 3/4 In.	65.00
Plate, Old London Scene, Buckingham Palace, 10 In.	45.00
Plate, Pavilion, 8 In.	16.00
Plate, Provost Tower, University Of Pennsylvania, 1929, 10 1/4 In.	85.00
Plate, Queensware, Landscape, Figural, Raised Oakleaf Border, 1872, 9 In.	316.00
Plate, Raised Floral Branch, Insect Design, Yellow Glaze, Majolica, 9 In.	70.00
Plate, Seafood, Chrysanthemum, Radiating Flowers, Pair	1495.00
Plate, South Cottage, 10 3/4 In.	65.00
Plate, Sugaring, New England Industries Series, Clare Leighton	75.00
Plate, Tea Leaf, 8 In.	25.00
Plate, Towne Scientific School, 1929, 10 1/4 In.	85.00
Plate, Trophy, Jasperware, Black, White Classical, Fruit Festoons, 8 5/8 In.	865.00
Plate Set, Different Harvard Views, Blue & White, 1927, 10 In., 12 Piece	500.00
Plate Set, Homes Of Famous Americans Center, c.1927, 12 Piece	2530.00
Platter, Blue Willow, 11 x 9 In.	45.00
Platter, Bullfinch, Transferware, c.1860	250.00
Platter, Chapoo, c.1850, 20 1/4 x 15 3/4 In.	1380.00
Platter, Columbia, Blue, Gold Trim, 14 In.	55.00
Platter, Columbia, Blue, Gold Trim, 15 1/2 In.	110.00
Platter, Harvard University, Maroon & White, 1941, 19 x 17 In.	500.00
Platter, Indiana, Flow Blue, 16 In.	475.00
Platter, Queensware, Bird, Floral Design, Polychrome, Oval, 1871, 15 3/4 x 20 In.	374.00
Pot, Jam, Jasperware, Blue, White, Silver, Handle, 4 In.	145.00

Pot, Jasperware, Blue, Classical Design, Underplate, 6 1/2 In. 145.00
Slop Pail, Cover, Queensware, Enamel Oak Leaf Border, c.1886, 11 In. 430.00
Sugar, Jasperware, Blue, 4 x 6 In. 130.00
Sugar & Creamer, Jasperware, Dark Blue, Pre-1920 . . . . 125.00
Sugar & Creamer, Salt Glaze, Geometric Design, Olive Green Ground, 4 In. 70.00
Tea Caddy, Jasperware, Blue, Shell Form Bowl, England, 2 1/8 In. 430.00
Tea Set, Black Basalt, 14 Piece 425.00
Tea Set, Black Basalt, Widow Finial, England, 19th Century, 3 3/4 In., 3 Piece 490.00
Tea Set, Drabware, Applied White Fruit & Floral Banding, 3 Piece 400.00
Tea Set, Jasperware, Green, Diceware, White Laurel Borders, 3 Piece 3335.00
Teapot, Black Basalt, Bamboo Design, England, 20th Century, 3 7/8 In. 260.00
Teapot, Black Basalt, Enamel Floral Design, England, c.1860, 2 1/8 In. 460.00
Teapot, Black Basalt, Floral Sprays, c.1850, 7 In. 632.00
Teapot, Black Basalt, Gilt Decorated Widow Finial, Scalloped Rim, 4 In. 635.00
Teapot, Drabware, Applied Blue Classical Reliefs, England, 4 1/2 In. 430.00
Teapot, Dragon Design 3450.00
Teapot, Glazed Caneware, Arabesque, Spaniel Finial, c.1820, 5 In. 230.00
Teapot, Ironwood, Raised Fruit, Miniature 135.00
Teapot, Jasperware, Black, Floral, Leaf Design, 19th Century, England, 10 In. 115.00
Teapot, Jasperware, Black, White Classical & Foliate, 19th Century, 4 1/2 In. 975.00
Teapot, Jasperware, Blue, 3 1/2 In. 550.00
Teapot, Jasperware, Blue, c.1924, 5 x 9 In. 240.00
Teapot, Jasperware, Blue, White, Raised Classical Figures Of Ladies, 4 In. 195.00
Teapot, Jasperware, Dark Blue, Green Quatrefoils, Diceware, 1800, 3 1/2 In. 1840.00
Teapot, Jasperware, Relief Trim, Impressed Marks, 18th Century, 5 1/4 In. 980.00
Teapot, Rhine, Flow Blue . . . . .600.00 to 675.00
Tile, Bone China, Medallions Of Birds Set In Turquoise, Gilt Dot Field, 8 x 8 In. 345.00
Tile, Calendar, Brown Transfer, Cathedral Church Of St. Paul, 1922, 3 x 4 In. 143.00
Tile, Midsummer Night's Dream, Etruria, Marked, Square, 6 In. 125.00
Tray, Dresser, Jasperware, Blue & White, 10 In. 35.00
Tray, Fairyland Luster, Jumping Faun, Lily, Mottled Green, Round, 1920, 9 In. 1495.00
Tray, Jasperware, Lilac, Green Stars, White Ribbon, 18th Century, 12 1/2 In. 460.00
Tray, Jasperware, Teal, Oval, 7 x 10 In. 170.00
Tray, Jasperware, With Flowers, Round 45.00
Tray, Pin, Jasperware, Green, Oval 20.00
Tureen, Sauce, Chapoo, Flow Blue, 1850, 3 Piece 575.00
Urn, Cover, Caneware, Crater, Rosso Antico Foliate Reliefs, Marked, 5 1/4 In. 575.00
Urn, Cover, Greco-Roman Taste, Parcel Gilt, c.1830, 9 In. 750.00
Urn, Jasperware, Blue, Base, Goat-Head Handles, Impressed Mark, 5 3/4 In. 200.00
Urn, Jasperware, Pale Blue, Glazed, 1800, Pair 2950.00
Urn, Jasperware, White Classic Figures On Lavender, Handle, 9 1/4 In. 1190.00
Vase, Beaker, Jasperware, Blue, White, 4 In., Pair 50.00
Vase, Black Basalt, Applied Cupid Reliefs, Leaf Loop Handles, Bulbous, 11 In. 1955.00
Vase, Black Basalt, Classical Medallions, Ram's Head Handles, 7 1/2 In. 490.00
Vase, Black Basalt, Classical Relief, Leaf Borders, England, 10 In. 1150.00
Vase, Black Basalt, White, Black, Iron Red Figural Design, Greek Key, 10 3/8 In. 2300.00
Vase, Blue, Green Foliate Glaze, White Beaded Relief, Plinth, 1775, 10 1/2 In. 2185.00
Vase, Butterfly Design, Powder Blue Luster, Mother-Of-Pearl Interior, 6 3/4 In. 345.00
Vase, Caneware, Enamel Foliate Design, Millicent Taplin, 1930, 7 7/8 In. 290.00
Vase, Caneware, Rosso Antico Leafy Vinework, Impressed Mark, 5 3/4 In. 115.00
Vase, Cover, Aubergine Glaze, Cream Ground, Laurel, Acanthus Border, 12 In. 980.00
Vase, Cover, Black Basalt Base, Applied Laurel Garlands, 1775, 6 3/4 In. 920.00
Vase, Cover, Black Basalt, Applied Drapery Swags, Squatty, 1775, 7 In. 1150.00
Vase, Cover, Black Basalt, Leaf Molded Handles, 18th Century, 10 1/2 In., Pair 2300.00
Vase, Cover, Fairyland Luster, Candlemas, Printed Mark, 1920, 11 In. 2300.00
Vase, Cover, Fairyland Luster, Coral, Bronze, 1923, 9 3/4 In. 4025.00
Vase, Cover, Fairyland Luster, Ghostly Wood, Printed Marks, 1920, 15 3/4 In. 8625.00
Vase, Cover, Fairyland Luster, Rainbow, Printed Marks, 1920, 9 In. 1955.00
Vase, Cover, Jasperware, Black, Diceware, Dancing Hours Frieze, 8 3/4 In. 1495.00
Vase, Cover, Jasperware, Black, White Classical, Foliate Border, 6 3/4 In. 980.00
Vase, Cover, Jasperware, Blue, Drum Pedestal, Children In Relief, c.1871, Pair 3450.00
Vase, Cover, Jasperware, Blue, Portland, White Relief Of Muses, England, 12 In. 1035.00
Vase, Cover, Jasperware, Blue, Ribbon, Fruit Vine, White Relief, 8 1/2 In. 489.00

Vase, Cover, Jasperware, Green, White Classical Relief, Impressed Marks, 11 In. 405.00
Vase, Cover, Queensware, Swagged Drapery, Bacchus Handles, 8 1/2 In. 375.00
Vase, Creamware, Floral, Reticulated, Red Glass Liner, 1912, 8 1/4 In. 515.00
Vase, Dragonware, Oriental Design, Blue Mottled Ground, 1920, 23 1/4 In. 747.00
Vase, Engine Turn Banding, Matte Gray Glaze, Bulbous, Keith Murray, 6 In. 405.00
Vase, Fairyland Luster, Castle On Road, Daylight Color, 1920, 7 1/4 In. 3335.00
Vase, Fairyland Luster, Firbolgs V, Green Ground, Gilt, 1920, 7 3/4 In. 575.00
Vase, Fish, Blue Ground, Printed Marks, 1920, 8 1/2 In., Pair 1380.00
Vase, Hummingbird, Mottled Blue Exterior, Orange Interior, 1920, 6 In., Pair 747.00
Vase, Jasperware, Black, Portland, White Classical Relief, 1900, 5 In. . . . . .375.00 to 600.00
Vase, Jasperware, Classical, Yellow, Black, 5 In. 275.00
Vase, Jasperware, Dark Blue, Portland, 10 1/2 In. 1675.00
Vase, Jasperware, Dark Blue, White Classical Relief, Impressed Mark, 8 3/4 In. 375.00
Vase, Jasperware, Light Green, White Classical Relief, Impressed Mark, 6 1/2 In. 635.00
Vase, Jasperware, Light Green, White Leaves, Shell Relief, Impressed Mark, 6 In. 489.00
Vase, Jasperware, Potpourri, White Classical Medallions, 13 1/4 In. 2530.00
Vase, Jasperware, Teal, Miniature 55.00
Vase, Jasperware, White, Classical & Leaves, Green & Lilac, 19th Century, 5 In. 460.00
Vase, Jasperware, White, Green Stripes, Basket Weave, 19th Century, 4 1/4 In. 860.00
Vase, Jasperware, Yellow, Blue Classical, Foliate Relief, 4 3/4 In. 545.00
Vase, Stylized Flowers, Leaves, Gold Luster, Louise Powell, c.1925, 13 3/8 In. 2070.00
Vase, Trumpet, Fairyland Luster, Butterfly Woman, Black, 1920, 6 1/8 In. 1840.00
Vase, Trumpet, Luster, Hummingbird, Blue, Orange Interior, 1920, 8 1/8 In. 375.00
Waste Bowl, Chapoo, Flow Blue, 1850, 3 x 5 1/4 In. 200.00

WELLER pottery was first made in 1873 in Fultonham, Ohio. The firm moved to Zanesville, Ohio, in 1882. Art wares were introduced in 1893. Hundreds of lines of pottery were produced, including Louwelsa, Eocean, Dickens Ware, and Sicardo, before the pottery closed in 1948.

LOUWELSA
WELLER

Ashtray, 3 Pigs On Bar Spanning Tray, 4 x 5 In. 110.00
Ashtray, Cream Matte Glaze, Friendly Whale, Gold Tail, Pink Tongue, 2 1/4 In. 440.00
Ashtray, Frog, Coppertone 325.00
Ashtray, Woodcraft, Oak Leaves, 1920, 3 In. 185.00
Basket, Copra, Floral Design, Blossoms, Green Matte Ground, Marked, 14 In. 88.00
Basket, Eocean, Daisies, 4 Small Feet, Mae Timberlake 468.00
Basket, Hanging, Barcelona, Geometric Design, Tan Ground, 9 In. 302.00
Basket, Hanging, Knifewood, Daisy Design, 6 x 8 1/2 In. 275.00
Basket, Oak Leaf, Green, Artist, 9 1/2 In. 195.00
Batter Bowl, Mammy . . . . .875.00 to 995.00
Bookends, Pinecone, Blue 200.00
Bottle, Ink, Louwelsa, Yellow Carnation, Handle, Bell Shape, 2 In. 135.00
Bowl, Claywood, 4 In. 40.00
Bowl, Coppertone, Chinese Form, 2 Square Loop Handles, 4 3/4 In. . . . . .138.00 to 165.00
Bowl, Coppertone, With Flower Frog, 15 In. 750.00
Bowl, Eocean, Floral, Handles, High Glaze, 8 In. 295.00
Bowl, Flower Frog, Lavonia, Figural, Girl, 2 Piece 325.00
Bowl, Flower Frog, Marvo, Green, 8 In. 225.00
Bowl, Marvo, Pink, 8 In. 150.00
Bowl, Sabrinian, 6 1/2 In. 275.00
Bowl, Seneca, Blue, 4 1/2 x 4 In. 60.00
Chalice, Woodcraft, 3 Handles, 9 In. 275.00
Charger, Louwelsa, Harvest Moon & Owl, 15 1/4 In. 975.00
Cigarette Holder, Frog, Coppertone 295.00
Clock, Aurelian, Jonquil Design, Josephine Inlay 1760.00
Clock, Louwelsa, Yellow, Wild Rose, Browns, Signed, 5 1/4 x 7 In. 400.00
Console, Wild Rose, Green, 6 x 18 In. 90.00
Console Set, Coppertone, Flower Frog & Lily Pad, 15 In. . . . . .550.00 to 700.00
Console Set, Silvertone, 4 Piece . . . . .675.00 to 900.00
Cookie Jar, Mammy . . . . .2450.00 to 2750.00
Cookie Jar, Pierre 95.00
Cornucopia, Oak Leaf 38.00
Creamer, 2 Trees, White Leaves, Green Trunk, Blue Ground, 4 In. 330.00

Weller, Garden
Ornament, Frog, Playing
Banjo, Coppertone,
12 1/8 In.

Weller, Vase, Sicardo,
Leaf & Berry,
Crashing Waves,
24 1/4 In.

Creamer, Mammy	550.00
Creamer, Zona, 4 1/2 In.	75.00
Ewer, Etna, Gray, Maroon Flowers, Hand Painted, 1890, 6 In.	185.00
Ewer, Louwelsa, Fluted Top, 1900, 4 x 5 In.	215.00
Ewer, Louwelsa, Pencil Neck, Golden Red Leaves, Black Ground, Artist, 4 1/2 In.	165.00
Figurine, Bird & Nest, Glendale, 4 In.	495.00
Figurine, Bumblebee, Brighton, Green & White Body, Gray Wings, 2 In.	245.00
Figurine, Butterfly, Brighton, Brown Body, Pink & Black Wings, 2 1/2 In.	187.00
Figurine, Butterfly, Brighton, Pair	150.00
Figurine, Dachshund, 6 In.	50.00 to 60.00
Figurine, Dog, Glass Eyes, 14 In.	2090.00
Figurine, Dog, Terrier, Brown, Signed	4000.00
Figurine, Dragonfly, Brighton, Green Body, Gray Wings, 3 In.	90.00
Figurine, Elephant, Muskota, Bug-Eyed, Yellow	145.00
Figurine, Frog, Bluebird, Brighton, 8 1/2 In.	195.00
Figurine, Frog, Coppertone, Fountain, Green, Brown Glaze, Marked, 5 1/2 x 6 1/2 In.	635.00
Figurine, Frog, Coppertone, Holding Lily Pad	250.00 to 265.00
Figurine, Frog, Coppertone, Yellow Chest, Marked, 2 In., Pair	660.00
Figurine, Muskota, Gate With Cats & Pots, 7 In.	550.00
Figurine, Nude On Rock, Muskota, 8 In.	295.00
Figurine, Parrot, Brighton, 7 1/2 In.	495.00
Figurine, Pheasant, Brighton, Marked, 7 x 10 In.	440.00
Figurine, Pop Eye Dog, 4 In.	600.00
Figurine, Rabbit, Crouching, Ink Mark, 7 1/2 In.	1870.00
Figurine, Rabbit, Standing, Gray, Yellow & Brown Glaze, 15 In.	3850.00
Figurine, Rooster, Brighton, Aqua, Cream, Red, Black, Tan, Marked, 13 In.	3250.00 to 3575.00
Figurine, Squirrel, Tree, Signed, 14 In.	1800.00
Figurine, Woodpecker, Brighton	200.00 to 250.00
Flower Frog, 2 Geese, Wings Spread Out, Marked, 6 x 8 1/2 In.	275.00
Flower Frog, Child, Holds Grapes, Round Base With Stylized Grape & Blossom, 9 In.	145.00
Flower Frog, Coppertone, 4 In.	325.00
Flower Frog, Coppertone, Emerging From Lily Pad, 4 1/2 In.	193.00
Flower Frog, Duck, Green, Yellow & Brown Glaze, 3 x 4 1/2 In.	175.00
Flower Frog, Fish, Surround Stump, Marked, 5 In.	110.00
Flower Frog, Kingfisher, 9 In.	332.00
Flower Frog, Muskota, Bee On Toadstool	145.00
Flower Frog, Pheasant, Brighton, 5 In.	550.00
Garden Ornament, Frog, Playing Banjo, Coppertone, 12 1/8 In. ....*Illus*	8800.00
Hair Receiver, Sicardo, Swirling Blossoms, Gold Dots, 3 1/2 x 5 In.	880.00
Jar, Cover, Claywood, Floral Design, Dark Brown Matte, 6 x 5 1/2 In.	176.00
Jar, Cover, Knifewood, Apple Finial	950.00
Jardiniere, 4 Buttresses & 4 Squares On Each Panel, Green Accents, 7 3/4 In.	431.00
Jardiniere, Aurelian, Marked, 11 In.	675.00
Jardiniere, Blue Ware, 10 In.	250.00
Jardiniere, Eocean, Stylized Grapes, Grape Leaves, Vines, Frank Ferrel, 11 1/8 In.	550.00
Jardiniere, Flemish, 10 In.	225.00
Jardiniere, Floretta, Embossed Florals, Glossy Glaze, Signed, 10 In.	110.00

Jardiniere, Forest, Brown Interior, 11 1/2 In. 1450.00
Jardiniere, Forest, Green, 4 1/2 In. 135.00
Jardiniere, Jap Birdimal, Stylized Landscape, Blue Ground, 13 In. 350.00
Jardiniere, Louwelsa, Floral, Orange, Brown, Green, Gold Buds, 9 In. ....130.00 to 179.00
Jardiniere, Marvo, 8 1/2 In. 125.00
Jardiniere, Marvo, Gray, 10 In. 225.00
Jardiniere, Pearl, 7 In. 225.00
Jardiniere, Pedestal, Brighton, Birds & Mums, Round Handle, Cream, 31 1/2 In. 850.00
Jardiniere, Pedestal, Sicard, Dandelions, Heavy Slip, 3 Dimensional, 1902, 31 3/8 In. 4180.00
Jardiniere, Rosemont, Pink Blossoms, Branches, Birds On Black Ground, 7 1/2 In. 175.00
Jardiniere, Woodrose, 9 In. 295.00
Jug, Dickens Ware II, Monk, 5 1/2 In. 285.00
Jug, Louwelsa, Berries, Brown Glaze, Pouring Lip, 6 x 4 1/2 In. 250.00
Jug, Whiskey, Louwelsa, M. Mitchell, 1904, 5 1/2 In. 242.00
Lamp, Cactus, Gnome, Orange Glaze, 11 In. 145.00
Lamp, Green, Brown, 11 In. 675.00
Lamp, Oil, Louwelsa, Lilies, M. Mitchell, 16 In. ....695.00 to 975.00
Lamp, Woodcraft, Trees With Berries, Paper Label, 30 In. ....495.00 to 660.00
Lamp, Zona, Dogs, Birds & Twisting Vines, Berries, 22 In. 520.00
Letter Holder, Rozane Ware, Pine Bough, Artist, Rectangular, 3 1/2 x 4 1/2 In. 190.00
Mug, Aurelian 250.00
Mug, Carnation Design, 5 1/2 In. 80.00
Mug, Dickens Ware, Indian Portrait Of Tame Wolf, Anna Dautherty, 6 In. 585.00
Mug, Dickens Ware, Painted Fish Underwater, E.P. Hunter 450.00
Mug, Dickens Ware, Young Circus Girl Picture, 5 3/8 In. 413.00
Mug, Eocean, Raspberries 175.00
Mug, Etna, Embossed Cherries, Gray Ground, Marked, 5 3/4 In. 125.00
Mug, Etna, Grapes, 6 In. 95.00
Mug, Etna, Pink, Gray Chrysanthemums, 6 In. 145.00
Mug, Louwelsa, Berries, Signed, 6 In. 210.00
Mug, Louwelsa, Cherry Cluster & Leaves, 6 In. ....175.00 to 190.00
Pitcher, Barcelona, Stylized Design, Tan & Ivory Ground, 6 In. 143.00
Pitcher, Coppertone, Fish Handle, Green Ground, 7 5/8 In. 770.00
Pitcher, Kingfisher, 10 In. 250.00
Pitcher, L'Art Nouveau, Embossed Nude, Green Bisque Ground, Marked, 21 3/4 In. 750.00
Pitcher, Louwelsa, Pansies, Low Handle, 5 1/2 In. 300.00
Pitcher, Pierre, Blue, 5 In. 30.00
Pitcher, Souevo, 11 1/2 In. 395.00
Pitcher, Zona, All Blue, Apple, 7 In. 175.00
Pitcher, Zona, Splashing Duck 185.00
Planter, Hudson, Floral Design, Squared Form, 4-Footed, 8 In. 385.00
Planter, Klyro, Green, Signed, 3 1/2 In. 55.00
Planter, Woodcraft, 3 Foxes, 5 1/2 In. 365.00
Planter, Woodrose, Signed, 9 In. 41.00
Plaque, Teddy Roosevelt, 1904 .... 135.00
Plate, Burntwood, Florals, Bird, 9 In. 187.00
Pot, Marblo Ware, Paper Label, 4 1/2 In. 150.00
Pot, Spider Web Pattern, Clay Wood, 4 In. 95.00
Sand Jar, Forest, 13 In. 605.00
Sugar, Cover, Mammy 995.00
Syrup, Mammy ....595.00 to 875.00
Tankard, Hand Painted Pear, Brown, 11 1/2 In. 475.00
Tankard, Louwelsa, 11 In. 395.00
Tankard, Louwelsa, Floral, Signed, 10 1/2 In. 215.00
Tankard, Rozane Ware, Cat Portrait, E. Steele, 14 1/2 In. 1980.00
Teapot, Open Rose, Pink & Blue, 8 1/2 In. 275.00
Teapot, Pierre, White, 6 1/2 In. 40.00
Tobacco Jar, Dickens Ware, Chinaman, Charles B. Upjohn, Marked, 5 x 6 In. 1430.00
Toothpick, Coppertone 325.00
Umbrella Stand, Baldin 750.00
Umbrella Stand, Bedford Matte, Embossed Tulips, Green Glaze, 20 In. 935.00
Umbrella Stand, Denton, 22 1/8 In. 2970.00
Umbrella Stand, Etna, Peacock, 22 In. 1595.00

Umbrella Stand, Ivory, Art Nouveau, Leaves & Blossoms, Cutouts, 23 In. 297.00
Umbrella Stand, Zona, Women Holding Garlands Of Flowers, Pastel, 20 In. 1100.00
Urn, Jap Birdimal, Moonlit Scene, 8 3/8 In. 275.00
Vase, Aladdin, Luster, Purple & Orange, 5 1/2 In. 225.00
Vase, Art Nouveau, 9 3/4 In. 245.00
Vase, Atlas, 5-Sided Star Form, Marked, 5 1/2 In. 45.00
Vase, Aurelian, 4 Blossoming Irises, High Gloss Glaze, Flared Rim, 24 1/2 x 13 In. 1955.00
Vase, Aurelian, Dark Brown & Black Ground, Artist C.T., 8 1/2 In. 155.00
Vase, Aurelian, Poppy Blossom, Bud & Leaves, Abstract Ground, Marked, 10 In. 175.00
Vase, Baldin, 9 1/2 In. 435.00
Vase, Baldin, Fruit, Leaves, Branches, 2 Closed Handles, Marked, 9 1/2 In. 210.00
Vase, Barcelona, 3 Strap Handles, 10 In. 475.00
Vase, Barcelona, 6 1/2 In. 175.00
Vase, Barcelona, 9 In. 225.00
Vase, Barcelona, Multicolored Florals, Yellow Ground, Signed, 7 In. 132.00
Vase, Beautiful Lady, Flowing Windblown Hair, Aqua, 8 In. 485.00
Vase, Besline, Berries, Leaves, 9 1/2 In. 300.00
Vase, Besline, Gold Luster, Etched Leaves, 7 In. . . . . .200.00 to 235.00
Vase, Besline, Grapevine, 3 Handles, Gold Luster, 9 1/2 In. 77.00
Vase, Blossom, Double Handles, 16 In. 350.00
Vase, Bonito, Handles, Marked, 6 1/2 In. 155.00
Vase, Bud, Baldin, 7 In. 95.00
Vase, Bud, Coppertone, Fish Stands On Lily Pad, Marked, 8 In. 1980.00
Vase, Bud, Woodcraft, 9 In. 95.00
Vase, Burntwood, Egyptian Figures, Columns, 9 1/2 In. 77.00
Vase, Burntwood, Florals, Cylinder, 6 In. 175.00
Vase, Camelot, 5 In. 275.00
Vase, Chengtu, Chinese Red Glaze, Black Glass Display Stand, Marked, 14 In. 245.00
Vase, Chengtu, Chinese Red Glaze, Signed, 5 3/4 In. 55.00
Vase, Chengtu, Chinese Red, 16 In. 645.00
Vase, Circle, Malverne, 8 In. 80.00
Vase, Clarmont, Beaded Design, Roses & Leaves, Marked, 7 1/2 In. 110.00
Vase, Clarmont, Handles, 5 In. 55.00
Vase, Clinton Ivory, Bulbous, Signed, 18 In. 440.00
Vase, Cloudburst, Pink, White, 9 3/4 In. 75.00
Vase, Coppertone, 13 1/4 In. 585.00
Vase, Coppertone, Flared, 6 In. 120.00
Vase, Coppertone, Handle, 9 3/4 In. 375.00
Vase, Cornish, Cover, Leaf & Berry Design, Marked, 8 In. 165.00
Vase, Creamware, Woman's Portrait, Footed, 8 1/2 In. 275.00
Vase, Dickens Ware II, Incised Golfer, Pink Shirt, Brown Ground, Marked, 8 3/4 In. 1100.00
Vase, Dickens Ware, Classical Figures Proceeding Through Forest, 10 1/8 In. 2090.00
Vase, Dickens Ware, Embossed Design, Blue Pansies, Signed, 5 1/2 In. 78.00
Vase, Dickens Ware, Indian Chief In Full Headdress 1400.00
Vase, Dickens Ware, Little Wound Chief Portrait, Charles Upjohn, 12 In. 1760.00
Vase, Dickens Ware, Monk, Blue, Olive, Brown, Artist Initials, 4 3/4 In. 250.00
Vase, Eocean, Flowers, Multicolored, 5 In. 193.00
Vase, Eocean, Holly Design, Spittoon Shape, 5 1/2 x 7 In. 600.00
Vase, Eocean, Magenta Floral, Pink & Gray, 12 In. 850.00
Vase, Eocean, Pink Daisies, 10 1/8 In. 550.00
Vase, Eocean, Rose, 6 1/2 In. 220.00
Vase, Eocean, Yellow Roses, Mae Timberlake, 8 3/8 In. 605.00
Vase, Etna, Floral Design, 2 Loop Handles, Pink Ground, 11 1/8 In. 275.00
Vase, Etna, Gray & Pink Floral At Top, 9 In. 325.00
Vase, Etna, Poppy Design, Olive To Gray Ground, Marked, 10 In. 385.00
Vase, Fan, Ardsley, Pussy Willows, Green Ground, 8 In. 90.00
Vase, Fan, Sabrinian, 7 1/2 x 8 In. 130.00
Vase, Fan, Sydonia, 6 1/2 In. 40.00
Vase, Flemish, Raised Floral Design, Brown & Yellow Glaze, 8 In. 65.00
Vase, Fleuron, Funnel Shape, 12 x 10 In. . . . . .595.00 to 750.00
Vase, Floral, White, 13 In. 285.00
Vase, Florenzo, 7 1/2 In. 185.00
Vase, Forest, 8 1/4 In. 350.00

Vase, Forest, 10 In. 298.00
Vase, Forest, 13 In. 225.00
Vase, Fudzi, 11 In. 1300.00
Vase, Fudzi, Floral Design, Marked, 8 In. 467.00
Vase, Glendale, 3 Birds, 9 In. 675.00
Vase, Glendale, Bird & Nest, 6 3/4 In. 495.00
Vase, Glendale, Marsh Scene Of Bird & Nest, Cattails, Ink Mark, 13 In. 467.00
Vase, Goldenglow, Leaf Design, Open Handles, Paper Label, Marked, 12 1/2 In. 187.00
Vase, Grapes, Green, Triangular, 1900, 6 1/2 In. 165.00
Vase, Greenbriar, Lavender, Green & Burgundy Glaze, 8 In. 198.00
Vase, Greora, Egg Shape, 5 In. 65.00
Vase, Hobart Girl, With Duck, Turquoise, 5 In. 55.00
Vase, Hudson, Autumn Scene, 7 In. 995.00
Vase, Hudson, Blue, Blue & Pink Flowers, 8 1/2 In. 195.00
Vase, Hudson, Blue, Green & White Flowers Around Top, 1900, 8 1/2 In. 485.00
Vase, Hudson, Blue, White & Pastel Flowers, 7 1/2 In. 275.00
Vase, Hudson, Dogwood Flowers, Leaves, Stems, Gray, 11 In. 220.00
Vase, Hudson, Hibiscus Flowers, Buds, Multicolored, Signed, Pillsbury, 12 In. 1760.00
Vase, Hudson, Hibiscus, White, Yellow, Red Centers, 13 7/8 In. 880.00
Vase, Hudson, Iris, White, Blue, Green, Blue Ground, 9 1/2 In. .... 546.00 to 900.00
Vase, Hudson, Red Clover Design, Sarah Reid McLaughlin, 7 In. 468.00
Vase, Hudson, Signed Pillsbury, 6 In. 400.00
Vase, Hudson-Light, Irises, Buds, Multicolored, 10 3/4 In. 660.00
Vase, Hudson-Light, Lily-Of-The-Valley Design, 7 In. 358.00
Vase, Ivory Scene, Chase Overlay, Dark Blue Ground, Marked, 5 1/2 In. 230.00
Vase, Ivory Scene, Chase Overlay, Dark Blue Ground, Marked, 10 1/2 In. 385.00
Vase, Jap Birdimal, Bubble-Blowing Fish At Slip Trail Sea, 3 Footed, 4 3/8 In. 770.00
Vase, Juneau, 8 In. 90.00
Vase, Kenova, Grape Leaf Vines, Signed, 11 1/2 x 10 In. 275.00
Vase, Kenova, Roses & Leaves On Branches, Branch Forms Open Handles, 9 1/2 In. 330.00
Vase, Klyro, Red Flowers, Green Leaves, 9 In. 78.00
Vase, Knifewood, 12 In. 245.00
Vase, Knifewood, Peacock & Tree Design, Marked, 9 In. .... 440.00 to 450.00
Vase, LaMar, Elm Trees, 6 In. 295.00
Vase, LaMar, Landscape, Trees & Windmills In Background, Dark Red, 7 1/2 In. 138.00
Vase, Landscape, Trees & Lake In Foreground, Gold, Red, Blue, Metallic Iridescent, 7 In. 303.00
Vase, LaSa, Black Palm Trees, Ivory, 13 1/2 In. 1800.00
Vase, LaSa, Conical, Panoramic Scene Of Evergreen Trees, Mountains, Lake, 9 In. 440.00
Vase, LaSa, Landscape, 7 In. 395.00
Vase, LaSa, Landscape, Brown, Cylindrical, 8 7/8 In. 415.00
Vase, LaSa, Landscape, Trees, Backed By Hills, Marked, 14 In. 230.00
Vase, LaSa, Palm Trees, Flared Lip, 9 1/2 In. .... 595.00 to 695.00
Vase, Lorbeek, 7 In. 100.00
Vase, Loru, 11 1/2 In. 115.00
Vase, Loru, Leaf Design, Ribbed Form, Tan Over Aqua Glaze, Script Mark, 8 In. 65.00
Vase, Louwelsa, Chrysanthemums, Butterworth, 9 In. 285.00
Vase, Louwelsa, Clover Design, Trefoil Rim, Brown Slip, John Butterworth, 3 1/8 In. ... 138.00
Vase, Louwelsa, Floral & Berries, Cylinder, Pinched, 6 In. 250.00
Vase, Louwelsa, Flowers, Hand Painted, 1880, 6 1/2 In. 185.00
Vase, Louwelsa, Genie Shape, Double Handles, Signed, 5 x 8 In. 695.00
Vase, Louwelsa, Green & Brown Ground, 11 1/2 In. 275.00
Vase, Louwelsa, Green & Brown Ground, M. Mitchell, 5 In. 215.00
Vase, Louwelsa, Lily-Of-The-Valley, Dark Brown Glaze, 3 Handles, 6 1/4 In. 245.00
Vase, Louwelsa, Nasturtium, Blue, 11 5/8 In. 1430.00
Vase, Louwelsa, Orange Poppy, Brown Ground, 9 1/4 In. 385.00
Vase, Louwelsa, Orange Poppy, Half Circle Seal, 11 3/4 In. 325.00
Vase, Louwelsa, Poppies, Hand Painted, 1890-1900, 12 In. 365.00
Vase, Louwelsa, Rounded Blossoms On Stems, Shades Of Blue, Marked, 7 In. 770.00
Vase, Louwelsa, Wild Rose Design, 2 Loop Handles, Red, 9 In. 935.00
Vase, Louwelsa, Yellow, Orange Peonies, Signed, Frank Ferrel, 14 In. 715.00
Vase, Malverne, 5 3/4 In. 40.00
Vase, Marengo Scene, With Tree Design, Shades Of Pink & Red, 7 In. 330.00
Vase, Monticello, White, Tan & Green Design, Blue Ground, 7 In. 440.00

Vase, Oak Leaf, Green, 12 In. 75.00
Vase, Panella, Gold, 13 In. 80.00
Vase, Paragon, Small Mouth, Tan, 7 In. 200.00
Vase, Pillow, Louwelsa, Brown, Head Of Man, Quill Pen Behind Ear, 4 In. 75.00
Vase, Raceme, Flaring Rim, Stylized Flowers & Leaves, Blue & Black Ground, 9 In. 300.00
Vase, Raydance, Floral Mold, Ivory, 10 In. 110.00
Vase, Rhead Faience, Geisha Playing Musical Instrument, 7 7/8 In. 825.00
Vase, Roba, 9 In. 60.00
Vase, Rochelle, Hop Design, Brown Ground, 6 In. 415.00
Vase, Rochelle, Pink & Yellow Roses, On Thorned Branches 1100.00
Vase, Roma, Signed, 9 In. 102.00
Vase, Rozane, Colored Thistle, Label, M. Mitchell, 19 1/4 In. 220.00
Vase, Selma, 5 In. 60.00
Vase, Selma, Daisies & Butterflies, Red, 5 In. 150.00
Vase, Sicardo, Applied Handles, Iridescent, Floral Ground, Signed, 7 In. 1600.00
Vase, Sicardo, Daffodils, 7 1/2 In. 1200.00
Vase, Sicardo, Daisy Flowers, Signed 700.00
Vase, Sicardo, Double Gourd, Iridescent, Floral Design, 7 In. 1600.00
Vase, Sicardo, Floral Design, 6-Lobed Globular Form, Marked, 6 7/8 In. 990.00
Vase, Sicardo, Floral Design, Iridescent, 2 Handles, 6 1/2 In. 1095.00
Vase, Sicardo, Floral Design, Iridescent, Random Spotted Design, 10 In. 920.00
Vase, Sicardo, Floral Design, Ribbed Form, Blue, Yellow, Gold Iridescent, 11 In. 750.00
Vase, Sicardo, Foliate Design, Iridescent Glaze, Circular, 7 x 6 In. 2415.00
Vase, Sicardo, Foliate Design, Iridescent Glaze, Triangular, Signed, 5 x 3 In. 489.00
Vase, Sicardo, Green Clover Design, 6-Ribbed Tapered Sides, Iridescent Glaze, 8 x 5 In. .. 1095.00
Vase, Sicardo, Leaf & Berry, Crashing Waves, 24 1/4 In. ....*Illus* 1045.00
Vase, Sicardo, Leaf Pattern, Shoulder Form, Iridescent, 4 In. 515.00
Vase, Sicardo, Stylized Peacock Feathers, Iridescent Glaze, 6 In. 1035.00
Vase, Sicardo, Twist Form, Signed, Marked, 5 In. 895.00
Vase, Silvertone, 2 Handles, 7 In. 250.00
Vase, Silvertone, 7 x 7 In. 320.00
Vase, Silvertone, 9 In. 175.00
Vase, Silvertone, Full Kiln Stamp, 6 1/4 In. 220.00
Vase, Tiger Lily, 14 In. 550.00
Vase, Ting, 2 Leaf & Ring Handles, Ivory Semigloss Glaze, 12 1/2 In. 325.00
Vase, Trailing Flowers On Top, 4 Sides, Blue, 9 3/8 In. 385.00
Vase, Trailing Flowers, White, 10 7/8 In. 523.00
Vase, Tulip, Lavender & Yellow, Blue Ground, Marked, 11 1/4 In. 121.00
Vase, Turkis, Green & Yellow Drip Over Rose Glaze, 2 Handles, Marked, 8 1/2 In. 132.00
Vase, Turkis, Scarlet & Lime Foam Drip, 2 Handles, 8 1/2 In. 245.00
Vase, Turkis, Scarlet, Lime Glaze, Side Handles, 4 In. 89.00
Vase, Tutone, 6 In. 140.00
Vase, Velva, Handles, Signed, 6 In. 85.00
Vase, Warwick, 4 In. 110.00
Vase, Warwick, 7 In. 195.00
Vase, Warwick, Floral, Black Branches, Mottled Ground, Ink Mark, 10 1/2 In. 132.00
Vase, White Roses, Etched Matte, 10 In. 375.00
Vase, Woodcraft, 9 In. 175.00
Vase, Woodcraft, Branches, Red Flowers, 10 In. 140.00
Vase, Woodcraft, Owl & Squirrel On Side, Tree Trunk Form, Marked, 17 In. .....748.00 to 770.00
Vase, Woodcraft, Owl, 16 In. 1200.00
Vase, Zona, Kingfisher, 8 In. 155.00
Wall Pocket, Double, Brighton, Woodpecker, On Branch, 12 In. 440.00
Wall Pocket, Fairfield, Cherub, Marked, 9 In. 230.00
Wall Pocket, Glendale, Birds On Branch, Marked, 12 In. 330.00
Wall Pocket, Marvo, Brown Fern, Green Ground, 4 1/2 x 7 1/2 In. 150.00
Wall Pocket, Oak Leaf, Blue & Green, Incised Mark, 8 1/2 In. 120.00
Wall Pocket, Roma, Floral, 6 In. 200.00
Wall Pocket, Triple, Brighton, Crow, On Branch With Grapes, 15 In. 1090.00
Wall Pocket, Woodcraft, Owl In Tree, 10 In. ....220.00 to 395.00
Wall Pocket, Woodcraft, Squirrel 300.00
Wall Pocket, Woodcraft, Wooden Bucket, 9 1/2 In. 195.00
Window Box, Forest, 17 x 7 1/2 In. 600.00

Window Box, Pale Green, White Matte, 1930	85.00
Window Box, Warwick, 8 1/2 In.	95.00

WEMYSS ware was made by Robert Heron in Kirkaldy, Scotland, from 1850 to 1929. It is a colorful peasant-type pottery that is occasionally found in the United States.

Figurine, Pig, Covered With Painted Thistles, Neckola, Large	3000.00
Figurine, Pig, Covered With Painted Thistles, Neckola, Small	1500.00

WESTMORELAND GLASS was made by the Westmoreland Glass Company of Grapeville, Pennsylvania, from 1890 to 1984. They made clear and colored glass of many varieties, such as milk glass, pressed glass, and slag glass.

Appetizer Set, Paneled Grape, Milk Glass, 3 Piece	70.00
Banana Boat, Ring & Petal, Lilac	130.00
Basket, Paneled Grape, 6 In.	22.00
Basket, Paneled Grape, Handle, 8 In.	85.00
Bonbon, English Hobnail, Milk Glass, Handle, Hexagonal	10.00
Bowl, Beaded Grape, Floral, Footed, 9 In.	45.00
Bowl, Cover, Beaded Grape, Square, 7 In.	40.00
Bowl, Cover, Paneled Grape, Footed, 11 In.	115.00
Bowl, Footed, Oval, 12 In.	95.00
Bowl, Old Quilt, Bell Footed, 5 1/2 In.	30.00
Bowl, Old Quilt, Round, 4 1/2 In.	30.00
Bowl, Paneled Grape, 4 1/2 In.	22.00
Bowl, Paneled Grape, Footed, Lip, 9 In.	55.00
Bowl, Paneled Grape, Footed, Oval Lip, 11 In.	115.00
Bowl, Paneled Grape, Footed, Scalloped, 11 In.	55.00
Bowl, Roses & Bows, 10 In.	80.00
Box, Cover, Beaded Grape, Square, 4 In.	35.00
Box, Puff, Paneled Grape, Cover	45.00
Butter, Cover, Checkerboard, Amethyst	55.00
Cake Salver, Doric	20.00
Cake Salver, Paneled Grape	65.00
Cake Salver, Paneled Grape, Milk Glass, Skirt, 11 In.	60.00 to 85.00
Canape Set, Paneled Grape, 9 In.	53.00
Candleholder, 2-Light, Paneled Grape, 8 In., Pair	20.00
Candleholder, Della Robbia, Light Luster	25.00
Candleholder, Doric, Dark Blue Mist	15.00
Candlestick, 4 In., Pair	30.00
Candlestick, American Hobnail, Milk Glass, Single, 5 In.	15.00 to 20.00
Candlestick, Paneled Grape, 4 In., Pair	15.00 to 25.00
Candy Dish, Cover, Beaded Grape	10.00
Candy Dish, Cover, Paneled Grape, 3 Footed	50.00
Candy Dish, Cover, Paneled Grape, Sawtooth	20.00
Candy Dish, Cover, Seashell & Dolphin, Green Mist	50.00
Celery Vase, Paneled Grape	45.00
Cocktail, Fruit, Paneled Grape, Milk Glass	12.00
Compote, Della Robbia	32.00
Compote, Doric, Milk Glass, Footed	40.00
Compote, Ruby, Hollow Blown Stem, Italy, 1950s, 20 In.	145.00
Cookie Jar, Cover, Maple Leaf	88.00
Creamer, Della Robbia, Milk Glass	15.00
Creamer, Old Quilt, 3 1/2 In.	15.00
Creamer, Paneled Grape, 5 1/4 In.	30.00 to 40.00
Cruet, English Hobnail, 4 Oz.	22.00
Cruet, Old Quilt	25.00 to 35.00
Cruet, Paneled Grape, Stopper	40.00
Cup & Saucer, American Hobnail, Milk Glass	10.00
Cup & Saucer, English Hobnail, Milk Glass	15.00
Cup & Saucer, Old Quilt, Milk Glass	40.00
Cup & Saucer, Paneled Grape	22.00 to 24.00
Dish, Cheese, Cover, Paneled Grape	60.00

Dish, Duck Cover, Red, Carnival Glass 98.00
Dish, Heart, Handle, Della Robbia, 8 In. 70.00
Dish, Rabbit Cover, Red, Carnival Glass 98.00
Dish, Ribbons & Bows 110.00
Dish, Sweetmeat, Doric 35.00
Dresser Set, White Daisies, Light Blue, Tray, 3 Piece 135.00
Epergne, Paneled Grape, 8 In. 175.00
Goblet, American Hobnail, Milk Glass 15.00
Goblet, Della Robbia, Milk Glass 17.00
Goblet, English Hobnail 9.00
Goblet, Water, American Hobnail, Milk Glass 20.00
Goblet, Water, Della Robbia, Milk Glass ....16.00 to 20.00
Goblet, Water, Della Robbia, Red 19.00
Goblet, Water, English Hobnail, Green 15.00
Goblet, Water, Paneled Grape 18.00
Goblet, Wine, American Hobnail, Milk Glass 12.00
Goblet, Wine, Della Robbia, Milk Glass 18.00
Gravy Boat, Paneled Grape, Liner 70.00
Jardiniere, Paneled Grape, 5 In. 30.00
Jardiniere, Paneled Grape, Footed, 6 1/2 In. 35.00
Ladle, Punch Bowl, Paneled Grape, Milk Glass 98.00
Mayonnaise, Paneled Grape, Footed, 4 In. 25.00
Pitcher, Old Quilt, 32 Oz. 35.00
Pitcher, Paneled Grape, 1 Qt. 37.00
Pitcher, Paneled Grape, 16 Oz. ....40.00 to 42.00
Pitcher, Paneled Grape, Milk Glass, 16 Oz. 25.00
Planter, Paneled Grape, 5 x 9 In. 35.00
Plate, 3 Cats, Milk Glass 40.00
Plate, Fruit, Beaded Edge 45.00
Plate, Paneled Grape, 8 In. 25.00
Powder Jar, Milk Glass 14.00
Punch Set, Light Blue Carnival, Signed, Mini Bowl & 6 Cups 50.00
Salt & Pepper, Della Robbia 65.00
Sauceboat, Tray, Paneled Grape 70.00
Sherbet, Paneled Grape 18.00
Sugar, Paneled Grape 40.00
Sugar & Creamer, Cover 25.00
Sugar & Creamer, Della Robbia ....22.00 to 25.00
Sugar & Creamer, Paneled Grape, Milk Glass ....27.00 to 30.00
Toothpick, Columned Thumbprints 65.00
Tumbler, Ice Tea, Della Robbia, Footed 17.00
Urn, Cover, Roses & Bows 125.00
Vase, Beaded Grape, 11 1/2 In. 40.00
Vase, Ivy Ball, Milk Glass 30.00
Vase, Paneled Grape, 6 In. 10.00
Vase, Paneled Grape, 11 In. 32.00
Vase, Paneled Grape, Footed, Bell Shape, 9 In. 30.00
Water Set, Checkerboard, Black, 7 Piece 275.00

WHEATLEY Pottery was established in 1880. Thomas J. Wheatley had
worked in Cincinnati, Ohio, with the founders of the art pottery movement, including M. Louise McLaughlin of the Rookwood Pottery.
Wheatley Pottery was purchased by the Cambridge Tile Manufacturing Company in 1927.

Bowl, Broad Vertical Leaves At Rim, Marked, 9 In. 495.00
Lamp, Vertical Pod & Leaf Design, Green, 3 Brass Arms, Coral Fabric, 14 In. ... 415.00
Pitcher, Raised Grape Cluster Design, Leaves, Vines, Green Matte Glaze, 8 In. 550.00
Plaque, Stylized Floral Design, Black Glossy Glaze Ground, Yellow Matte Glaze, 13 In. .. 550.00
Tile, Horse, Rearing, Light Brown, Yellow, Mauve, Gray, Light Blue Ground, 6 In. 300.00
Vase, Applied Flowers, Signed, Dated, 8 1/2 In. 2200.00
Vase, Applied Leaves, Matte Green Glaze, 12 1/2 In. 4400.00
Vase, Band Of Carved Curved Lines, Green Glaze, 6 1/2 x 8 1/2 In. 660.00
Vase, Cream Blossoms, Brown Centers Atop Green Stems, Leaves, 1880, 8 In. 310.00

Vase, Daisies, White, Yellow, Brown Centers, Teal Leaves, 1880, 7 1/2 In. 500.00
Vase, Embossed Leaves, Medium, Dark Green Matte Glaze, 12 x 9 In. 550.00
Vase, Floral Design, White, Green, Mottled Blue, Light Blue High Glaze, 1879, 12 In. . . . 865.00
Vase, Floral Design, White, Green, Mottled Brown, Green High Glaze, 1879, 13 In. 862.00
Vase, Floral Design, Yellow, Pink, Salmon, Green Ground, 1880, 12 1/2 In. 660.00
Vase, Geometric Design, Green Glaze, Rolled Rim, Signed, 8 3/4 In. 825.00
Vase, Pink, White Blossoms, Buds, Broad Green Leaves, Cobalt Blue, 13 In. 440.00
Vase, Silver Overlay, Green Matte Glaze, Waisted, 4-Lobe Top, 7 1/2 In. 1760.00
Vase, Stovepipe Neck, Frothy Dripping Matte, Signed, 11 x 9 1/4 In. 1100.00

WHIELDON was an English potter who worked alone and with Josiah
Wedgwood in eighteenth-century England. Whieldon made many
pieces in natural shapes, like cauliflowers or cabbages.

Bowl, Cover, Pineapple, Green, Yellow Translucent Glaze, 1765, 4 1/4 In. 800.00
Coffeepot, Cover, Creamware, Sinuous Vines Bearing Blossoms, Leaves, 1755, 6 In. . . . 515.00
Coffeepot, Tortoiseshell Glaze, Molded Spout, Strap Handle, 7 1/2 In. 467.00
Creamer, Cauliflower, Handle, Green & Clear Glaze, 4 1/4 In. 385.00
Plate, Brown, Green, Yellow, Tortoiseshell Glaze, Calloped Rim, 8 In. 375.00
Sugar, Cover, Cauliflower, Green & Clear Glaze, 34 5/8 x 4 3/8 In. 3245.00
Tea Caddy, Cauliflower, Green & Clear Glaze, 4 1/4 In. 550.00
Tea Canister, Cauliflower, Green Glazed Leaves, Cream Florets, Oval, 3 5/8 In. 230.00
Teapot, Cauliflower, Green Glazed Leaves, Cream Florets, Handle, 4 1/2 In. 800.00
Teapot, Cover, Apple Form, Tortoiseshell Glaze, Green Leaves, Creamware, 4 In. 1380.00

WILLETS Manufacturing Company of Trenton, New Jersey, began
work in 1879. The company made Belleek in the late 1880s and 1890s
in shapes similar to those used by the Irish Belleek factory. They
stopped working about 1912. A variety of marks were used, all including the name Willets.

Bowl, Roses, Leaves, 8 In. 300.00
Cup & Saucer, Demitasse 45.00
Stein, Drunken 18th Century Men, Castle, Gold Bands, Belleek, 5 1/2 In. 385.00
Vase, White & Mulberry Orchid Band, Multicolor Ground, Belleek, 30 In. 660.00

WILLOW, see Blue Willow category.

WINDOW glass that was stained and beveled was popular for houses
during the late nineteenth and early twentieth centuries. The old windows became popular with collectors in the 1970s; today, old and new
examples are seen.

Frame, Demilune, Fan Light, Tole & Cast Lead, Central Eagle, Pine, 11 x 33 1/2 In. 3162.00
Frame, Fan Light, Peacock Panes, c.1900 . . . . 375.00
Geometric Pattern, Green, Red, Clear & Blue Panels, 40 1/2 x 31 1/2 In. 110.00
Half-Round, Multi-Mullioned, 84 In. 825.00
Leaded, Diamond Design, Floral, Green, White, Prairie School, 17 x 38 In. . . . . . .385.00 to 550.00
Leaded, Dogwood Blossoms, Foliage, Wooden Frame, 92 1/2 x 35 3/4 In. 550.00
Leaded, Female Figure Perched Upon Lily Pad, Brown, Green, Pink, Blue, 77 In. 4887.00
Leaded, Foliate & Geometric Design, Oak Frame, Square, 15 1/2 In. 488.00
Leaded, Foliate Design, Amber, Blue, Gold, Red, Cherrywood Frame, 111 x 38 In. 3025.00
Leaded, Framed Stylized Sunrise Over Green Landscape, 34 x 12 In. 230.00
Leaded, Infant Jesus, Cross, Continental, Frame, 46 x 27 In., Pair 750.00
Leaded, Jeweled Center Design, Wooden Frame, 45 x 24 In., Pair 6000.00
Leaded, Panel, Woman With Hawk, Hunter, 6 1/4 x 22 In., Pair 1088.00
Leaded, Symmetrical Gothic Design, Amber, Blue, 32 x 27 In., Pair 440.00
Leaded, Vine & Trellis, Opalescent, c.1900, 68 x 92 In., 3 Piece Set 3600.00
Round Landscape & Fruit Foreground, Circle Border Of Jewels, Square, 27 In. 1435.00
Scrolled Florals, Cut Jewels, Slag Field, Wooden Frame, 51 x 19 In. 75.00
Stained Glass, Christ, Winged Angels, Gold & Blue Ground, 54 x 56 In. 7000.00
Wreath & Shield, Iced Textured Glass, Brass Frame, 29 x 20 In. 975.00

WOOD CARVINGS and wooden pieces are listed separately in this book.
Many of the wood carvings are figurines or statues. There are also
wooden pieces found in other categories, such as Kitchen.

American Eagle, Norman Narkon, Dated 1964 . . . . 165.00

Angel, Hand Outstretched, Classical Robes, Pine, Continental, 42 In., Pair 4370.00
Angel, Renaissance Clothes, Holding Cornucopia, Giltwood, Continental, 30 In. 4150.00
Apollo, Green Laurel Wreath On Tan Hair, Green Lined Drapery, 8 In. 805.00
Beer Wagon, 8 1/2 x 17 1/2 In. 165.00
Bird, Redheaded Duck, Glass Eyes, c.1900, 8 3/4 In. 275.00
Bishop, Miter & Vestments, Gesso, Giltwood, Continental, 39 In., Pair 4370.00
Black Bear, Stylized, Seated On Haunches, Head Forward, 30 x 36 In. 2300.00
Blackamoor, Typical, Arm Raised Supporting Torch, 49 3/4 In. 8625.00
Boot, 3-Dimensional, Pre-1900, 24 In. 4500.00
Bottle Stopper, Pull Lever & Man Tips Hat, Nods . . . . .50.00 to 75.00
Buddha, Standing With Crown, Gold Gilt, Lotus Blossom Pedestal Base, 13 In. 1035.00
Bust, George Washington, White Painted Face, Brown Vest, Yellow Coat, 15 In. 9775.00
Car, Railroad, Spoke Wheels, Early 1900s, 72 In. 1800.00
Casque, Masks, Griffin Footed, 15 In. 290.00
Chair, African, Inlaid, Applied Brass, White Metal, Golden Brown Patina, 29 In. 175.00
Eagle, On Lectern, 42-In. Wingspan, Continental, 1810, 51 In. 2700.00
Eagle, On Lectern, Outspread Wings, 1870, 69 In. 1840.00
Eagle, Signed & Dated 1912, 57-In. Wingspan 1265.00
Eagle, Wings Spread, Tail Down, Giltwood, 13 1/2 In., Pair 1330.00
Eve, Nude, Linden Wood, 33 In. 6469.00
Eve, Snake, Apple, Mahogany, Varnish, S.T. Terry, 22 1/2 In. 575.00
Fish, Bass, On Birch Painted Plaque, Lawrence Irvine 850.00
Foo Dog, Guardian, Male & Female, Gilt Paint, China, 29 1/2 In., Pair 1100.00
Humidor, Dog's Head, 10 In. 498.00
Man, African-American, Cotton Shirt, Blue Trapezoidal Base, 65 1/2 In. 11500.00
Man, Green Painted Uniform, Belt, Sash, Red Lips, 67 In. 4600.00
Man, Oriental, Ivory Eyes & Teeth, Large 90.00
Mask, African, Black Patina, Liberia, 7 3/4 In. 230.00
Mask, African, Polychrome, Brick, White Pigment, Brown Face, 17 1/2 In. 373.00
Mask, African, Polychrome, Wood, Goli Society, Ivory Coast, 20 In. 345.00
Mask, African, Wood Helmet, Animal, Bared Teeth, Metal Eyes, Brown, 11 In. 316.00
Mask, Demon Mounted On Frame, Japan, 19th Century, 3 3/4 In. 165.00
Mask, Tribal Face, Flat, Relief Carving, Painted, 15 1/2 In. 192.00
Mask, Tribal Figure, Cowrie Shell Eye, Dark Finish, 25 In. 38.00
Mask, Young Woman, Japan, 1954, 10 1/4 In. 770.00
Mountain Goat, Standing, Plinth, Fruitwood, Continental, 42 In. 2530.00
Ox, Glass Eyes, Brown, Cream Hide, Black Leather Collar, Brass Bell, 1910, 3 In. 175.00
Parrot, On Pedestal, Eyes Painted Black, Wire Legs & Feet 695.00
Plaque, Don Quixote, 12 x 30 1/2 In. 35.00
Plaque, Eagle, Solid Walnut, Civil War Era, 24 1/8 In. 210.00
Plaque, Madonna & Child, Frank Moran, Oval, 21 1/2 In. 425.00
Rebecca, Italy, 18th Century, 18 1/2 In. 500.00
Santos, Metal Chain, Plastic Cross, Polychrome, 13 In. 70.00
Shield, Candle, Acorn Finial, Bird's-Eye Maple, 18 1/2 In. 475.00
Shield, Stars Top, Stripes Bottom, Early 20th Century, 39 x 29 In. 595.00
Stork, Bearded Man, Hands To Chin, Signed, 22 In. 195.00
Tiger, Gold Paint, 19th Century, 25 x 32 In. . . . . *Illus* 5500.00
Train Set, Engine & Cars, Black, Red, Gray, Black Painted, Caboose, 75 1/2 In. 1265.00

**Don't keep identification on
your key ring. If it is lost, it's an
invitation for burglars to visit.**

Wood Carving, Tiger, Gold Paint,
19th Century, 25 x 32 In.

Vial, Gunpowder, Intertwined Wild Boar, Dogs & Deer, 4 1/2 In. 6038.00
Wall Pocket, Walnut, Gilded, Carved Griffin & Foliage, Crest, Hanging, 21 In. 385.00
Woman, Fertility Figure, 48 In. 484.00

WOODEN wares were used in all parts of the home. Wood was used for
many containers and tools. Small wooden pieces are called *treenware*
in England, but the term *woodenware* is more common in the United
States. Additional pieces may be found in the Advertising, Kitchen,
and Tool categories.

Bowl, Burl, 30 In. 1150.00
Bowl, Burl, Carved Wooden Handles, 16 In. 650.00
Bowl, Late 19th Century, 33 In. 750.00
Bowl, Pudding Grain, Ash Burl, c.1800, 12 1/4 In. 1800.00
Box, Sugar, Peaseware, Ohio, 6 1/2 x 7 1/2 In. 450.00
Bucket, Kerosene Oil, Red Paint, Stenciled 140.00
Bucket, Lift Top, Brass Straps, Lion Mask Ring Handles, Mahogany Base, 23 1/2 In. ... 190.00
Bucket, Piggin 250.00
Bucket, Staved, Old Varnish, 1840s, Large 225.00
Caddy, Bottle, Georgian, Oak, Brassbound, Shell Molded Footed, 11 x 11 1/2 In. .. 80.00
Case, Flatware, Georgian, Mahogany, Hinged Top, 2 Drawers, 12 x 22 x 16 In. 748.00
Casket, Cherub On Lid, Painted, Stained & Gilded, 6 3/8 In. 575.00
Cheese Press, Maple & Walnut, Dovetailed, 10 1/4 x 8 5/8 In. 225.00
Chest, Gilt Painted Design, Silver Lock & Hinges, Spanish Colonial, c.1750, 6 In. .. 1850.00
Chest, Yellow Striping, Polychrome Floral, Pine & Poplar, Lehnware, Miniature 6380.00
Comb, Boxwood, 18th Century, 5 In. 285.00
Container, Spice, Urn Finial, c.1790, 4 1/2 In. 275.00
Cup & Saucer, Yellow Strawberries, Red, Green, Blue Foliage, Lehnware, 1881 .... 2530.00
Dish, Pink Flowers, Green, Red, White Foliage, Lehnware, 1888, 2 7/8 In. 1045.00
Eggcup, Red, Pink With Tulips, Lehnware, 3 In. 880.00
Foot Warmer, Heart Shaped Holes On Top, Iron Bail Handle, New England, 1769 .... 295.00
Furkin, Cover, Blue Paint 135.00
Hair Receiver, Burl Walnut 175.00
Hair Receiver, Burl, Threaded Lid, Turned, 4 1/8 x 3 1/4 In. 220.00
Jar, Acorn Finial, Treen, Poplar, Footed, 6 1/2 In. 90.00
Jar, Cover, Polychrome Flowers, Strawberries On Lid, Red, Green, Lehnware, 4 In. 880.00
Jar, Cover, Polychrome Strawberries, Pink Ground, Lehnware, 5 1/8 In. 960.00
Jar, Cover, Red, Blue, Pink Strawberries, Foliage, Lehnware, 4 3/4 In. 1265.00
Jar, Strawberries On Lid, Polychrome Flowers, Peach Ground, Lehnware, 5 In. 715.00
Jar, Tobacco, Rosewood, Dutch, c.1720, 4 1/2 x 4 1/4 In. 385.00
Jardiniere, Pine, Worn Black Paint, Yellow Striping, Draining, Hexagonal, 6 1/4 In. 80.00
Jardiniere, Walnut, Louis XVI, Tapered Fluted Legs, 26 3/4 In. 1955.00
Keg, Powder, Black Metal, Painted Red Bands, 4 In. 160.00
Keg, Water, Pine Staves, Iron Hoops, Revolutionary War Era, 18 3/4 In., 5 Gal. 190.00
Mold, Hat, 2 Piece 55.00
String Holder, Barrel Shape, Lignum Vitae, c.1800, 6 1/2 In. 385.00
Tankard, Early 19th Century, 11 In. 230.00
Tray, Apple, Pine, Worn Pumpkin Colored Paint, 17 x 26 x 4 In. 250.00
Urn, Cover, Pear Wood, c.1820, 9 In. 1600.00
Urn, From Battleship Esmonth, Teak, c.1820. 14 In. 1100.00

WORCESTER porcelains were made in Worcester, England, from 1751.
The firm went through many name changes and eventually, in 1862,
became The Royal Worcester Porcelain Company Ltd. Collectors
often refer to *Dr. Wall, Barr, Flight,* and other names that indicate time
periods or artists at the factory. It became part of Royal Worcester
Spode Ltd. in 1976. Related pieces may be found in the Royal
Worcester category.

Bowl, Chinese Design, Floral, Blue, White, 1775, 7 1/2 In. 200.00
Bowl, Dr. Wall, Floral, Blue, White, Reticulated Rim, Crescent Mark, 7 1/2 In. 245.00
Bowl, Oriental Plants, Red Cell Diaper Border, 4 Floral Panels, Kakiemon, 8 In. 316.00
Compote, Triumphal Car, J. & M.P. Bell, 1850, 10 1/2 In. 675.00
Cream Boat, Crested Bird On Branch, Scalloped Rim, Blue, White, 5 In. 805.00
Cup & Saucer, Floral, Kakiemon, Blue Fret Mark, 18th Century, 3 In. 115.00

Cup & Saucer, Imari Design, Blue, Gilt, Square Mark 450.00
Dish, Floral Reserves, Blue Scale, Fluted, 18th Century, 7 3/4 In. 430.00
Dish, Leaf Shape, Floral Bouquet, Pale Yellow Scrolled Edge, 7 3/8 In. 4600.00
Dish, Leaf Shape, Floral Sprig, 2 Overlapping Leaves, Pale Puce, 13 15/16 In. 1150.00
Dish, Leaf Shape, Insect Hovering Over Shrubbery, Serrated Mulberry, 7 In. 4600.00
Figurine, Chinguin Indian, Beating Drum, Hadley, 1892, 13 1/4 In. 325.00
Mug, Dr. Wall, White Reserves, Birds & Insects, Square Mark, 4 7/8 In. 550.00
Mug, King Of Prussia, Black Transfer, Bell Shape, 4 5/8 In. 575.00
Mug, Walk In Garden, Blue, White, Bell Shape, 1758, 3 3/8 In. 920.00
Mustard Pot, Cover, Mansfield Pattern, Floral Spray, Border, 1770, 3 3/4 In. 633.00
Plate, Boy Portrait, Bust, Snake, Barr, Flight & Barr, 7 1/4 In. 345.00
Plate, Cathedral City Series, 1830, 10 1/2 In. 250.00
Plate, Cobalt Blue & Gilt Design, Crescent Mark, 18th Century, 8 1/2 In. 288.00
Plate, Grainger, Daisies Design, Gold Trim, 3 Shell Feet, Reticulated Rim, 10 In. 765.00
Plate, Hunter Shooting Ducks, Zoological Series, 1820, 10 1/2 In. 225.00
Plate, Sprigs, Swags, Yellow Flowers, Green Leaves, Yellow Border, 1775, 8 In. 632.00
Sauceboat, Exotic Bird Among Shrubbery, Green Floral Sprig, 1765, 8 In. 690.00
Sauceboat, Floral Sprigs, Leaf Shape, 18th Century, 9 In. 690.00
Sauceboat, Rose Flower Heads, Blue Foliage, Green, Red, Yellow, 6 In. 1600.00
Sauceboat, Scrolls, Yellow Floral Sprig, Scalloped Rim, 7 5/8 In. 1495.00
Sauceboat & Bowl, Landscape, Blue, White, 2 Handles, 7 1/2 In. 460.00
Soup, Dish, Crest, Banner, A Cruce Salus, Flight Barr & Barr, 9 1/2 In. 275.00
Strainer, Handle, 1785, 3 1/2 x 4 In. 395.00
Sweetmeat Dish, 2 Sprays, Yellow Tipped Green Rose Leaves, 1765, 6 In. 1265.00
Sweetmeat Dish, 4 Blossom Floral Spray Center, Handle, Shell Shape, 1760, 6 In. 805.00
Teapot, Cover, Feather Mold Floral, Flowering Branch, 5 3/8 & 2 5/16 In. 575.00
Teapot, Cover, Green Floral Sprig Knop, Floral Bouquet, Ribbed Handle, 5 In. 750.00
Teapot, Cover, Pleated Body, Leaf Sprigs, Floral Sprays, Blue, White, 5 1/4 In. 1840.00
Teapot, Floral Sprays, Gilt Border, Apple Green Ground, 5 In. 460.00
Teapot, Fruit & Butterflies, Gilt, Melon Shape, Crescent Mark, 18th Century, 8 In. 1035.00
Waste Bowl, Dr. Wall, Flowers, Fruit, Blue, White, Crescent Mark, 6 1/4 x 2 7/8 In. 355.00
Waste Bowl, Flowering Plants, Floral Sprig Interior, 1756, 5 1/8 In. 920.00

WORLD WAR I and World War II souvenirs are collected today. Be careful not to store anything that includes live ammunition. Your local police will tell you how to dispose of the explosives. See also Sword and Trench Art.

WORLD WAR I, Bell, S.S. Liberty Bell, Bronze 2350.00
Book, Sergeant York & His People, Inscribed, 1922, 294 Pages 375.00
Bottle, Sailing Ship In A Bottle, Metal Cap, Glass, 10 1/2 In. 30.00
Box, Safety Deposit, For War Bonds 40.00
Compass, Army, Marching, Leather Case 65.00
Compass, Pocket Watch Style 75.00
Frame, Poster, Alfred Everitt Orr, 20 x 30 In. 95.00
Grenade, Style Ball, Metal, Threaded Hole, Brass Fuse Fitting, 3 In. 38.00
Helmet, Germany 75.00
Knife, Trench, U.S. Army, Sheath, 1917 .... 225.00
Medal, Mothers, City Of Buffalo, New York 25.00
Medal, Service, Allen County, Kansas 40.00
Medal, Unity, Portrait Of King Vittorio Emanuele, Red, White, Green Ribbon, Italy 20.00
Mess Kit, Army 15.00
Pin, Australia Day, Brown, Yellow, White, Coo-Ee Bird, 1916 .... 18.00
Pin, Australian Carnival, Black & White, 1919 .... 28.00
Pin, Liberty Bond Owner, Red, White & Blue, Gray Ground, Celluloid, 7/8 In. 18.00
Pin, Mt. Gambier Red Cross, Scenic View 20.00
Pin, Red Cross, French Red Cross Nurse Holding Allied Flags, Yellow, 1918 .... 20.00
Poster, And They Thought We Couldn't Fight, Frame, 21 x 32 In. 105.00
Poster, Buy Liberty Bonds, Lend Him A Hand, Hold-To-Light, 12 x 21 In. 85.00
Poster, Carry On, Stamp, Stamp, Stamp, Frame, 29 x 40 In. 400.00
Poster, Food Is Ammunition, Frame, 21 x 29 In. 350.00
Poster, Hey Fellows, Frame, 1918, 20 x 30 In. 95.00
Poster, Home & Country, Frame, 1918, 20 x 30 In. 95.00
Poster, I Summon You, Frame, 21 x 29 In. 250.00

Poster, Join The Army Air Service, Be An American Eagle, C.L. Bull, 27 x 20 In. 495.00
Saddle, Army Officer's, Leather, Whitman, 1916 . . . . 750.00
Scabbard Cover, Marked, Brauer Bros., 1918 . . . . 12.00
Uniform, Navy 45.00
Uniform, U.S., 3rd Infantry, Machine Gun Patch, Wool, Overseas Cap, 4 Piece 225.00
WORLD WAR II, Backpack, Canvas Body, Black Leather Straps, Fur Back, Pockets, 1939 50.00
Badge, Eagle Brooches, National Defenders Of USA, Silver Tone, 1941 . . . . 10.00
Badge, Gray Metal, Eagle & Wreath, 1942 . . . . 7.00
Boots, Rubber, Red Inked, Wehrmacht Black, 1944, 16 In. 200.00
Bottle, Ink, V-Mail, Box 25.00
Clip, Brass, Tan Cloth Box, Japan 22.00
Compact, 1939, New York 60.00
Dagger, Commando, Fairbur-Sykes, England 125.00
Dagger, Patton Sword Blade 100.00
Flight Suit, Fur Collar, Luftwaffe, Cloth 600.00
Flight Suit, Pilot, Fleece-Lined Boots, Helmet, Nazi 950.00
Game, Victory Checkers, Leather Case, Mailer, Pocket 35.00
Gas Mask, Waterproofing Kit 5.00
Gloves, 5 Fingers, Fleece Lined, Air Force 85.00
Goggles, Dust, Sand, Clear Lens, Marked, BWZ, 1944 . . . . 10.00
Helmet, Flight, Air Force, With Headset, A-11 . . . . 200.00
Helmet, Flight, Leather, Army Air Force B-6 . . . . 125.00
Helmet, Flight, Throat Microphone & Earphones 300.00
Helmet, Nazi, Bread Bag Strap, Cotton With Leather Ends, Blue, Gray 15.00
Helmet, Soldier, Russia 20.00
Helmet, Spiked, Germany 190.00
Helmet, Tankers, Rawlings 155.00
Helmet, Transfer Of Wings, Swastika, Black Paint, Size 59 . . . . 207.00
Insignia, Officer's, Gen. Patton's Army Tank, Sterling Silver 110.00
Invitation Card, Adolph Hitler, Formal Party, 1942 . . . . 22.00
Jacket, Flight, Leather, Air Force, A-2 . . . . 595.00
Jacket, Pants & Helmet, Pilot, Sheepskin, 3 Piece 200.00
Jump Smock, German Paratrooper, Water Pattern 2200.00
Jump Suit, Camouflage, O.S.S. 600.00
Knife, Paratrooper, Switchblade, Presto, 3 In. 150.00
Knife, U.S. Medical Corp, Hospital, With Scabbard 135.00
Knife, U.S. Ulster, Ski Troop, Pocket 150.00
Lighter, Engraved Bombardier Wing & 5th AAF Patch, Ronson 141.00
Matchbook, V For Victory 15.00
Medal, American Campaign 10.00
Medal, Bronze Star, On Mounted Ribbon 17.00
Medal, Cross With Swords, Third Reich, Hanging Loop, Ribbon 15.00
Medal, Cross With Swords, Third Reich, Wreath Center, Hanging Loop, Ribbon 18.00
Medal, Distinguished Service Cross, Black 90.00
Medal, Eagle, Swastika Design, We Struggle Against Hunger & Cold 17.00
Medal, Hitler Youth 75.00
Medal, Purple Heart, Ribbon Bar, Lapel Device 45.00
Medal, The 50th Anniversary Of World War II, Presentation Case 20.00
Medal, Veteran, New York, City Of Rome 35.00
Medal, Wall, Reich West, Hanging Loop, Bronze, Oval 12.00
Medal, War Volunteer, Maroon Ribbon, Blue, Black Stripes, Bronze 20.00
Mess Kit, With Spoon 9.00
Paperweight, Hitler Profile, Cast Iron, Round 80.00
Periscope, 1942 . . . . 22.00
Pin, Abbott & Costello, Keep 'Em Flying, Blue, White, Pinback, 7/8 In. 45.00
Pin, Anti-Japan Slogan, Black Lettering On Yellow 28.00
Pin, Anti-Japan Slogan, Blue Lettering On White 35.00
Pin, Anti-Japan Slogan, White Lettering On Red Rim 35.00
Pin, Brass, Nickel Finish, Marked, 1936 . . . . 7.00
Pin, Down With Hitlerism, Black Letters, White Ground, Celluloid, 7/8 In. 25.00
Pin, General Patton, Black & White 48.00
Pin, Keep 'Em Flying, Red Aircraft Silhouette, White Rim 24.00
Pin, Keep Us Out Of War, Enamel, Brass Eagle, 1930s 18.00

Pin, Lapel, Ships For Victory, Silver Eagle, Patriotic Colors 20.00
Pin, Manhattan Project, A-Bomb, Building, Brass, Pin, Whitehead & Hoag, 1940s 125.00
Pin, Remember Pearl Harbor, Gold Luster, White Metal 18.00
Poster, Confidence, Over Picture Of FDR, 18 x 24 In. 9.00
Poster, Keep 'Em Flying, In Plane, Abbott & Costello, Linen, 28 x 38 In. 475.00
Poster, Red Cross Club, RAF Gang Show, Royal Air Force Concert Party, 1943 .... 100.00
Poster, Red Cross, War Fund, Douglass Signed, 1944, 16 x 22 In. 75.00
Poster, Special Services Section United Army, USO Camp Shows, 1943, 9 In. 200.00
Poster, Tell That To The Marines, 9th & Main St., J.M. Flagg, 30 x 40 In. 225.00
Poster, USO Camp Shows Presents Full Speed Ahead, Folded 125.00
Range Finder, Adjusting Lath, Original Tan Finish, Green Paint, 1944 .... 400.00
Ration Book 46.00
Ribbon, Merit Medal, Third Reich, 24 In. 12.00
Ribbon, Russian Front, Ribbon Bar Use, 1941, 16 In. 8.00
Saber, Nazi Officer, Scabbard, Horster, Soligen, 39 3/8 In. 450.00
Sign, Civil Defense, Shelter Area, Arrow, Metal, 2 1/4 x 18 In. 25.00
Smoke Kit, Dunhill Service Lighter, 3 Star Walnut Pipe, Pouch, Unused, 1945 ...... 60.00
Stationery, Keep 'Em Smilin', Cartoons, Envelopes, Wrapper, 1942, Pack Of 8 .... 35.00
Submarine Sight 250.00
Telephone, Field, Japan 100.00
Telephone, Field, Pair 110.00
Token, Red Meat, 1943 .... 1.00
Uniform, Army 125.00
Uniform, Buffalo Insignia, Tunic, Breeches & Cap, Dated 495.00
Uniform Tunic, Nazi, Pilot, 1938 .... 2500.00

WORLD'S FAIR souvenirs from all of the fairs are collected. The first fair was the Great Exhibition of 1851 in London. Other important exhibitions and fairs include Philadelphia, 1876 (Centennial); Chicago, 1893 (World's Columbian); Buffalo, 1901 (Pan-American); St. Louis, 1904 (Louisiana Purchase); San Francisco, 1915 (Panama-Pacific); Philadelphia, 1926 (Sesquicentennial); Chicago, 1933 (Century of Progress); Cleveland, 1936 (Great Lakes); San Francisco, 1939 (Golden Gate International); New York, 1939 (World of Tomorrow); Seattle, 1962; New York, 1964; Montreal, 1967; New Orleans, 1984; Tsukuba, Japan, 1985; Vancouver, B.C., 1986; Brisbane, Australia, 1988; Seville, Spain, 1992; and Genoa, Italy, 1992. Memorabilia of fairs include directories, pictures, fabrics, ceramics, etc.

Ashtray, 1939, New York, Glass, Communication Building, 4 In. 17.00
Ashtray, 1940, San Francisco, Homer Laughlin 75.00
Bank, 1893, Columbian Exposition, Mechanical, J & E Stevens 2800.00
Bank, 1964, New York, Dime Register, Octagonal 48.00
Bell, 1984, Louisiana Expo 12.00
Bell, Dinner, 1893, World's Columbian Exposition, Frosted Handle, Libbey, 5 3/4 In. 285.00
Bill Clip, 1933, Lincoln Exhibit 15.00
Book, 1904, Beauties Of The World & St. Louis 30.00
Book, 1933, Chicago, Century Of Progress, View, 32 Pages .... 25.00 to 30.00
Book, 1933, Sears Roebuck, Pop-Up 20.00
Book, 1964, New York, Pop-Up 40.00
Booklet, 1933, Chicago, Firestone Tire & Rubber Co. 25.00
Booklet, 1933, Chicago, International Harvester 30.00
Booklet, 1939, New York, American Art Today, National Art Society, Wrapper 75.00
Bowl, 1939, New York, Paden City Pottery, 10 In. 110.00
Box, Ring, 1904, St. Louis, Reverse Painting, Fine Arts Building Cover, Glass 145.00
Brick, 1893, Columbian Official Medal, RPCC, 9 x 5 x 4 In. 150.00
Camera, 1939, New York, Kodak, Black, Brass 374.00
Camera, 1940, Kodak Bullet, Trylon & Perisphere Medallion, Box 375.00
Cane, 1939, Blue Painted Wood 45.00
Cards, Playing, 1934, Chicago, 13 Different Scenes 2.00
Cigar Holder, 1901, Pan-American, Aluminum, 5 In. 20.00
Clock, 1893, Chicago 110.00
Clock, Alarm, 1933, Chicago, Section Of Hall Of Science 250.00
Coaster, 1964, New York 8.00

Compact, 1934, Century Of Progress 45.00
Compact, 1934, Chicago Exposition 75.00
Cookbook, 1933, Chicago, Durkee 15.00
Cup, 1901, Pan-American, Ruby Flashed 27.00
Decanter, 1965, Gilbey Scotch Whiskey 30.00
Emblem, 1939, Trylon & Perisphere, Blue, White, 1 1/2 In. 35.00
Glass Set, 1962, Seattle, Different Scenes & Colors, 6 1/2 In., 8 Piece 100.00
Guide, 1934, Chicago, Ford Motor Company, 18 x 23 In. 24.00
Handkerchief, 1901, Pan-American, Temple Of Music 15.00
Hot Plate, 1901, Pan-American, Indian Congress, 6 1/2 In. 75.00
Hot Plate, 1939, Aluminum, Felt Back, Diagonal Corners, 7 x 10 In. 60.00
Jar, Fruit, 1933, Chicago, Mason, Box 50.00
Kerchief, 1901 Pan-American Exposition Printed Flags 150.00
Key Chain, 1964, New York, Medallion Shape, Unisphere, Bronze 3.00
Key Holder, 1933, Chicago, Wooden, Ft. Dearborn, 9 In. 10.00
Lamp, 1962, Seattle, Econolite 350.00
Letter Opener, 1901, Pan-American, Bronze Buffalo On Top, 6 1/2 In. 40.00
Letter Opener, 1934, Art Deco 25.00
Locket Pin, 1939, New York 45.00
Map, 1939, New York, Official World's Fair Pictorial Map, Created By Tony Sarg 25.00
Map, 1939, San Francisco, Around The Ground, Greyhound Bus, Fold-Out 15.00
Matchbook, 1939, New York 1.00
Matchbook Holder, 1939, New York 30.00
Medal, 1962, Space Needle 6.00
Necklace, 1964, New York, Orange, Blue, Gold Base, Gold Color Chain 13.00
Pamphlet, 1939, New York, Heinz Exhibit, 57 Varieties, Aristocrat, 20 x 14 In. 29.00
Paperweight, 1876, Centennial, Independence Hall, Gillender, Oval 125.00
Paperweight, 1893, Columbian, Chicago, Lady, Hair Blowing 100.00
Paperweight, 1901, Pan-American, Pictures McKinley, Glass, Temple Of Music 17.00
Paperweight, 1939, New York, Underwood Typewriter 48.00
Pen, 1939, New York, Brass 45.00
Pennant, 1964, New York, Blue, 12 In. 9.00
Pillow Cover, 1933, Chicago, Various Fair Scenes, 16 x 16 In. 20.00
Pin, 1901, Pan-American Expo, Beaded Brass, Copper Luster ....18.00 to 28.00
Pin, 1904, St. Louis, Liberty Bell In White 8.00
Pin, 1904, St. Louis, World's Fair Missouri Day 24.00
Pin, 1905, Lewis & Clark Expo, Sighting The Pacific, 1805 .... 45.00
Pin, 1939, New York, I Have Seen The Future, Futurama Building 25.00
Pitcher, 1893, Columbian Exposition, Electrical Building, 3 In. 50.00
Plate, 1893, Columbian Exposition, Grant's Portrait, Libby Prison Museum, 8 In. 200.00
Plate, 1893, Columbian, Wedgwood Blue 55.00
Plate, 1904, St. Louis, Cascade Gardens 45.00
Plate, 1909, Alaska Yukon, Pacific Expo 75.00
Plate, 1939, American Potter, Turquoise 125.00
Plate, 1939, New York, Le Restaurante Francais, 4 In. 40.00
Plate, 1939, Plate, San Francisco, Homer Laughlin 85.00
Plate, 1939, Trylon & Perisphere, Blue & White, J & G Meakin, 10 3/4 In. 50.00
Play Set, 1939, New York, Build Your Own New York Fair, Standard Toykraft 300.00
Postcard, 1904, Greetings From Indianapolis Brewing Co., Machinery Bldg. 50.00
Postcard, 1904, Waterman Pen Co., St. Louis, Unused 37.00
Postcard, 1933, Century Of Progress, 16 Card Set 48.00
Postcard, 1939, Polish Pavilion, Jan Henryk DeRosen, Hand Colored 40.00
Program, 1933, Century Of Progress, Rodeo, Soldier's Field, 4 Pages, 4 x 7 In. 20.00
Program, 1933, Chicago, Century Of Progress 30.00
Program, 1939, New York, Billy Rose Aquacade, 32 Pages, Pinup Cover 30.00
Program, 1939, New York, Opening Day, April 30, 1939 .... 150.00
Punch Cup, 1893, Columbian Exposition, Pressed Glass, Petal Shape, Libbey 75.00
Purse, Coin, 1901, Panama-Pacific International Exposition 50.00
Purse, Coin, 1915 Panama-Pacific International Exposition 50.00
Razor, Straight, 1904, St. Louis, Etched Blade, Louisiana Purchase Exposition 100.00
Ring, 1939, New York, Metal, Gold Finish 22.00
Ring, Flasher, 1964, New York, Gold Ring Base 10.00
Salt, 1893, Columbian Exposition, Flat Side, Pink, Libbey 150.00

Salt & Pepper, 1901, Pan-American, Aluminum 15.00
Salt & Pepper, 1939, New York, Emeloid, One-Piece, 3 3/4 In. 40.00
Salt & Pepper, 1939, New York, Trylon & Perisphere, Orange & Blue 25.00
Scarf, 1939, New York, Silk 60.00
Serving Set, 1939, New York, Mr. Peanut, Tin 30.00
Sheet Music, 1904, St. Louis, World's Fair March, J. Fred Berry, Illustrated 45.00
Sheet Music, 1940, Treasure Island Memories, Fair Scene Cover 15.00
Shoe, 1904, St. Louis, Ceramic, Machinery Building, 4 In. 70.00
Spoon, 1904, St. Louis Fair, Palace Mines & Metallurgy, Sterling Silver 22.00
Spoon, 1915, Panama Pacific, Canal Locks, California, Sterling Silver 20.00
Spoon, 1915, Panama Pacific, Jewel Tower, Sterling Silver 11.00
Spoon, 1933, Century Of Progress Administration Building, Silver 10.00
Spoon Set, 1893, Columbian Exposition, Silver Plate, Exhibit Scene Bowl, 6 Piece 45.00
Sugar & Creamer, 1962, Seattle, Miniature 25.00
Sword, 1893, Chicago, Scabbard 295.00
Tape Measure, 1904, Jefferson, Napoleon, St. Louis, Celluloid 135.00
Ticket, 1934, Century Of Progress 5.00
Tie Bar, 1964, New York, Orange, Blue, Gold Base, Clip 9.00
Tie Clip, 1934, Chicago 18.00
Toy, 1939, New York, Greyhound Bus, New York World's Fair On Roof, Arcade 50.00
Toy, 1964, New York, Sinclair, Dinosaur 35.00
Tray, 1901, Pan-American, Change, Electric Tower, Metal 10.00
Tray, 1939, New York, Maxwell House 35.00
Tray, 1939, New York, Metal, Orange & Blue, Recessed, 11 1/2 x 17 3/4 In. .... .50.00 to 65.00
Umbrella, 1933, Chicago, Logo 100.00
Umbrella, 1933, Chicago, Paper, Wooden Handle, 19 1/2 In. 23.00
Vase, 1940, New York, Crystal, Bulb Design, Pink Center, Gold Lettering 15.00
View-Master, 1939, New York World's Fair Reels 40.00
Wall Pocket, 1939, New York, Wedgwood, Blue 75.00

WPA is the abbreviation for Works Progress Administration, a program created by executive order in 1935 to provide jobs for millions of unemployed Americans. Artists were hired to create murals, paintings, drawings, and sculptures for public buildings. Pieces are marked WPA and may have the artist's name on them.

Figurine, Lion, North Dakota, Black Gloss, 2 1/2 x 3 In. 750.00
Figurine, Tortoise & Hare, White & Brown, Blue Green Base, 4 x 9 In. 660.00
Print, Woodblock, Stag Beetle, Werner Drewes, 16 x 26 In. 242.00

WRISTWATCHES came into use during World War I. Wristwatches are listed here by manufacturer or as advertising or character watches. Pocket watches are listed in the Watch category.

Advertising, Chicken Of The Sea, Mail-A-Way, Box 30.00
Advertising, Elsie The Cow 100.00
Advertising, Ritz Crackers, Crackers Indicate Hours, Windup .... .700.00 to 750.00
Advertising, Royal Crown Cola, 17 Jewel, Helbros, W. Germany, 1960s .... .100.00 to 125.00
Advertising, Winston Cigarettes, Eagle 24.00
Agassiz, Square Cut Corner Case, 17 Jewel, Adjusted To Temperature, 1940s 410.00
Arnex, Peasant Scenes On Enameled Face, Switzerland, 2 In. 138.00
Audemars Piguet, Automatic, Thin Style 2750.00
Audemars Piguet, Back Wind & Set, Diamond Bezel & Lugs, Gold Bracelet, 1950 .... 1380.00
Audemars Piguet, Free Sprung Regulator, 20 Jewel, 18K Gold, Rope Twist Band 2300.00
Blancpain, Aqua Lung, Sweep Seconds, Black Matte Dial, 17 Jewel, 1965 .... 2645.00
Breguet, Chronograph, Moon Phases, 3 Dials, Signed, Gold, 1969 .... 9200.00
Breitling, Chronomat, Steel Case, Gold Appointments, Manual White Dial, c.1980 .... 1800.00
Bueche Girod, Elongated, 18K Yellow Gold, Black Roman Numerals, c.1960s 3800.00
Bueche Girod, Herringbone Design, 17 Jewel, Gold Bracelet, 1970 .... 3335.00
Bueche Girod, Mechanical, Yellow Gold 415.00
Bulova, 17 Jewel, Yellow Gold Plate, Expansion Band 85.00
Bulova, 21 Jewel, 14K Gold, Leather Band 195.00
Bulova, 21 Jewel, 14K Rose Gold, Rose & Ivory Dial, Blue Hands, 1940s 1150.00
Cartier, 18 Jewel, Adjusted To Temperature, 18K Gold Buckle, 1955 .... 2990.00
Cartier, 18K Gold, White Dial, Roman Numerals, Octagonal Case, 1985 .... 6615.00

Cartier, 18K Yellow Gold, Black Dial, Gold Hands, 14K Gold Bracelet, c.1950 . . . . 5900.00
Cartier, Gondola Model, 17 Jewel, Lever Movement, Sapphire Crown, 1 1/2 In. 1610.00
Cartier, Tank, 17 Jewel, 18K Gold Deployant Buckle, 1980 . . . . 2070.00
Cartier, Woman's, 18K Quartz, Off-White Dial, Roman Numerals, 1985 . . . . 4900.00
Cartier, Woman's, 18K Quartz, White Matte Dial, Roman Numerals, 1990 . . . . 5750.00
Character, Alice In Wonderland, U.S., 1950s 65.00
Character, Bugs Bunny, Stainless Steel, Carrot Hands, c.1951 . . . . .550.00 to 900.00
Character, Charlie Tuna 85.00
Character, Cinderella, Box 95.00
Character, Dukes Of Hazzard 75.00
Character, Elmer Fudd, Sheffield 100.00
Character, Lucy, 1962 . . . . 25.00
Character, Lucy, Peanuts Comic Strip, 1952 . . . . 95.00
Character, Mr. T, Nelsonic, Black Band, 1983 . . . . 18.00
Character, Mystery Sleuth 45.00
Character, Nolan Ryan 165.00
Character, Punky Brewster, Red Band, Watch-It, 1980s 20.00
Character, Rocketeer, Box 25.00
Character, Roger Rabbit, Digital 15.00
Character, Snoopy, Playing Tennis 35.00
Character, Spiderman, Waltham, Rubber Character Band, Gold Face, Metal Case 45.00
Character, Star Trek, Imitation Leather Band, 1980s 50.00
Character, Star Wars, Liquid Crystal Display, On Card 45.00
Character, Star Wars, Millennium Falcon, Brass, Leather Band, Adult 60.00
Character, Star Wars, Windup, 1958 . . . . 85.00
Character, Yogi Bear, Bradley, Box, 1963 . . . . 100.00
Character, Zorro, Box 350.00
CHIPS, TV, Wine, On Card, 1981 . . . . 24.00
Chronograph, 18K Gold, Enamel Dial, White Enamel Dial, 1935 . . . . 3740.00
Chronograph, 18K Gold, Tachometer, Enamel Dial, c.1925 . . . . 5465.00
Citrine & Diamond Bracelet, 18K Gold, 17 Jewel, Leather Box, 1940 . . . . 6900.00
Corum, 18 Jewel, Swiss Gold Ingot, Diamond Set Crown, 1975 . . . . 1725.00
Corum, 20 Dollar Gold Piece, 1928 Coin Movement, 18 Jewel, c.1970 . . . . 4000.00
Croton, Woman's, 17 Jewel, 18K Gold, Platinum & Diamond 110.00
Enicar, Triple Calendar, Moon Phase, Automatic 350.00
Geneve, Chronograph Calendar, 17 Jewel, Silvered Dial, 1980 . . . . 2530.00
Geneve, World Time, 19 Jewel, Gold, Blue Ground, 1990 . . . . 3220.00
Girard Perregaux, Steel Case, Engraved Enamel Painted Numbers, c.1930 . . . . 2100.00
Girard Perregaux, Woman's, 36 Single-Cut Diamonds On Case, Platinum 250.00
Golay Fils & Stahl, Woman's, Ring, Pave Diamond Lid, Gold, c.1960 . . . . 2530.00
Gruen, Art Deco, Round Diamonds, Platinum Mount, Cord Bracelet 258.00
Gruen, Woman's, Platinum & Diamond 1900.00
Gubelin, 18K Yellow Gold, Gold Tone Dial, Leather Speidel Strap 345.00
Hamilton, 14K White Gold, Silvered Face, 16 Small Cut Diamonds Bezel 230.00
Hamilton, Bates, 10K Yellow Gold Case, Grid Texture Dial, c.1955 . . . . 2000.00
Hamilton, Doctor's, Seckron, 17 Jewel, 10K Gold Filled, Ivory Color Dial, c.1930 . . . . . 1950.00
Hamilton, Electric, Ventura, 14K Yellow Gold, Futuristic Design, c.1957 . . . . 2500.00
Hamilton, Hidden Lugs, Diamond Dial, Gold Filled 125.00
Hamilton, Woman's, Driving, 14K Gold, c.1940 . . . . 1000.00
Hampden, CurveX Style, 14K Gold 190.00
Happy Diamonds, 18K Gold, Champagne Matte Dial, 1985 . . . . 2875.00
International, 17 Jewel, 18K Gold, Silvered Matte Dial, Arabic Numerals, 1935 . . . . 2300.00
Jean Renet, Woman's, 18K Gold, Malachite, Diamond & Sapphire 6250.00
Le Coultre, 18K White Gold, Tear Drop Lugs, c.1950 . . . . 1800.00
Le Coultre, Back Wind Bracelet, 3 Round Cut Diamonds, Snake Link Bracelet 1265.00
Le Coultre, Futurematic, 14K Gold, 2 Boxes, Papers 1200.00
Le Coultre, Mystery, 14K White Gold, Vacheron & Constantin, 1950s 2550.00
Le Coultre, Mystery, 18K Gold, Back Wind & Set, c.1970 . . . . 3450.00
Longines, 14K Gold, Engraved Oyster Tone Dial, Tonneau Case, c.1920 . . . . 3600.00
Longines, 14K Yellow Gold, Dial Flanked By Diamonds, Mesh Bracelet 230.00
Longines, 18K Gold, Silvered Dial, Round Case, 1945 . . . . 2330.00
Longines, Mystery Hand, 14K Gold 275.00
Longines, Woman's, 14K Gold, Art Deco 50.00

Lord Elgin, 14K Yellow Gold, Silvered Face, Gold Runes, Second Hand 175.00
Mappin, 18K Yellow Gold, Oval Case, Gray Dial, Elongated Numbers, c.1919 .... 2700.00
Movado, 18K Gold, Silvered Matte Dial, Curved Case, 1945 .... 2587.00
Movado, Bubble Back, 18K Gold 900.00
Movado, Calendar, 15 Jewel, 18K Gold Bracelet, Barrel Form Links, 1950 .... 2185.00
Movado, Enamel Face, 17 Jewel, 14K Yellow Gold, Gold Hands, Second Hand 460.00
Movado, Woman's, 14K Yellow Gold, 8 Diamonds. 210.00
Movado, Woman's, Face Set With Diamonds, Gold Mesh Band 690.00
Muller, 18K Gold, Silvered Matte Dial, Circular, Subsidiary Dials, 1995 .... 17250.00
Nivia, Square Dial, Diamond Rows, Iron Bracelet, 1936 .... 1840.00
Normandie, Tank Style, 17 Jewel, Swiss, Box 135.00
Omega, 14K Yellow Gold, Florentine Finish Mesh Bracelet 230.00
Omega, 18K 2-Tone Gold, Manual Wind 750.00
Omega, 18K Yellow Gold, Oyster-Tone Dial, Cord Bracelet, 1920s 2400.00
Omega, Automatic, Seamaster Deville 185.00
Omega, Black Runes, 14K Yellow Gold, Off-White Face, 6 1/4 In. 300.00
Omega, Calendar, Moon Phases, 17 Jewel, 18K Gold, Outer Rim Date, c.1945 ...... 3740.00
Omega, Chronograph, Commemorating 1969 Apollo Moon Landing, 1992 .... 5175.00
Patek Philippe, 18 Jewel, 18K Gold, Champagne Dial, Roman Numerals, 1970 ...... 2875.00
Patek Philippe, 18 Jewel, 18K Gold, Silvered Matte Dial, 1915 .... 4600.00
Patek Philippe, 18 Jewel, Silvered Dial, Roman Numerals, 1970 .... 3680.00
Patek Philippe, 18K 2-Tone Gold, Silvered Matte Dial, 1925 .... 7470.00
Patek Philippe, 18K Gold, 8 Adjustments, Silvered Matte Dial, c.1935 .... 4025.00
Patek Philippe, 18K Gold, Blue Matte Dial, Gold Baton Numerals, 1970 .... 3450.00
Patek Philippe, 18K Gold, Champagne Matte Dial, Roman Numerals, 1980 .... 4887.00
Patek Philippe, 18K Gold, Ricochet, Nickel Movement, Gold Textured Dial, 1965 .... 4887.00
Patek Philippe, 18K Gold, Silver Dial, Seconds Dial, Leather Strap, 1950s 4025.00
Patek Philippe, 18K Gold, Silvered Dial, Gold Baton Numerals, c.1953 .... 3450.00
Patek Philippe, 18K Gold, Silvered Matte Dial, Subsidiary Seconds 2875.00
Patek Philippe, 18K Pink Gold, Pink Dial, Gold, Disc Numerals, 1940 .... 3680.00
Patek Philippe, 18K Pink Gold, Silvered Dial, Gold Numerals, 1940 .... 9775.00
Patek Philippe, 18K Quartz, Blue Matte Dial, Gold Baton Numerals, Oval, 1980 ...... 3335.00
Patek Philippe, 18K Rose Gold, Scroll Form Lugs, Rose-Tone Dial, c.1946 .... 8300.00
Patek Philippe, 18K White Gold, Matte Dial, Woven Flexible Band, 1960s 2300.00
Patek Philippe, 18K White Gold, Silvered Matte Dial, Roman Numerals, 1990 .... 6325.00
Patek Philippe, 18K White Gold, White Matte Dial, Roman Numerals, 1985 .... 5750.00
Patek Philippe, 18K Yellow Gold, Enlongated Case, Silvered Dial, c.1942 .... 7700.00
Patek Philippe, 18K Yellow Gold, Off-White Dial, Minute Track, c.1948 .... 7800.00
Patek Philippe, 22K Gold, Skeletonized, Sapphire Crystals, Round Case 17250.00
Patek Philippe, 27 Jewel, 18K Gold, White Matte Dial, c.1980 .... 4900.00
Patek Philippe, 36 Jewel, Blue Textured Dial, Aperture For Date, 1980 .... 6037.00
Perle, 14K Gold, 11 Full Cut Diamonds, Band With Diamond Clasp, 8 3/4 In. 980.00
Piaget, 18 Jewel, 18K Gold, Champagne Matte Dial, Baton Numerals 1035.00
Piaget, 18 Jewel, 18K Gold, Malachite Dial, Round Case 2415.00
Piaget, 18K Yellow Gold, Quartz Movement, Solid Hinged Bracelet 4140.00
Piaget, Pave Diamond Face, Diamond Bezel, 18K Gold Bracelet 4255.00
Piguet, 18K Gold, Nickel Lever Movement, Black Dial, Roman Numerals, c.1980 .... 3450.00
Piguet, 18K Gold, Skeletonized, Bridge Engraved With Scrolls, 1985 .... 7475.00
Piguet, Woman's, 18 Jewel, 18K Gold, Diamond & Lapis Lazuli, c.1970 .... 5175.00
Piguet, Woman's, 22 Jewel, 18K Gold, Tigereye Dial, Surrounding Black Onyx, 1980 .. 2300.00
Rolex, 14K Gold, Silver Matte Dial, Gold Baton Numerals, 1960 .... 2990.00
Rolex, 14K Pink Gold, Pink Matte Dial, Rectangular Case, 1935 .... 7475.00
Rolex, 14K Rose Gold Case, Fluted Bezel, Hour Indicators, Rose Markers, c.1950 ...... 3300.00
Rolex, 14K Rose Gold, Fluted Bezel, Applied Rose Markers, c.1950s 3300.00
Rolex, 17 Jewel, 18K Pink Gold, Pink Dial, Gold Baton Numerals, 1955 .... 2645.00
Rolex, 18 Jewel, 18K Gold, Silver Matte Dial, Arabic Numerals, 1950 .... 1840.00
Rolex, 18 Jewel, 18K Gold, Silver Matte Dial, Round, 1950 .... 1840.00
Rolex, 18 Jewel, 18K Pink Gold, Pink Dial, Gold Baton Numerals, 1950 .... 2530.00
Rolex, 18K Gold, Lantern Form Clip, Pink Matte Dial, Baton Numerals, 1950 ...... 2875.00
Rolex, 18K Gold, Silvered Dial, Sapphire, Ruby Set Bird Resting On Branch 1725.00
Rolex, 18K Gold, Silvered Matte Dial, Disc Numerals, Sloping Case, 1937 .... 3162.00
Rolex, 18K Gold, Submarine Chronometer, Oyster Perpetual Date 6900.00
Rolex, 18K Pink Gold, Pink Dial, Applied Gold Baton Numerals, c.1950 .... 8912.00

Rolex, 18K Pink Gold, Silvered Matte Dial, Gold Baton Numerals, 1960 .... 4600.00
Rolex, 18K Pink Gold, Silvered Matte Dial, Roman Baton Numerals, 1950 .... 7360.00
Rolex, 18K Yellow Gold, Brushed Steel Dial, Ultra Slim Case, 1950s 3100.00
Rolex, 26 Jewel, 18K Pink Gold, Silvered Matte Dial, Aperture For Date, 1960 .... 3162.00
Rolex, Chronograph, 17 Jewel, Black Matte Dial, 1975 .... 7475.00
Rolex, Daytona, White Face, Stainless Steel, Box 7500.00
Rolex, Military, Black Matte Dial, Stainless Steel, 17 Jewel, c.1945 .... 5760.00
Rolex, Oyster Perpetual, Chronometer, Stainless Steel 330.00
Rolex, Oyster, 19 Jewel, Textured Dial, Self-Winding, 1950 .... 2875.00
Rolex, Oyster, Perpetual Date, Stainless Steel & Pink Gold Hands, c.1950 .... 2300.00
Rolex, Oyster, Silver Hexagonal, Silvered Turned Dial, 1928 .... 1150.00
Rolex, Oyster, Steel Case, Perpetual Date, Black Dial, Gold Hands, 1970 .... 3600.00
Rolex, Oyster, Steel Case, Perpetual Date, Yellow Gold Bezel, Black Dial, 1970 .... 3600.00
Rolex, Oyster, Steel Case, Screw-Off Back, Luminescent, c.1920 .... 2300.00
Rolex, Oyster, Woman's, 26 Jewel, Silvered Dial, Gold Baton Numerals, 1960 .... 2990.00
Rolex, Oyster, Woman's, 28 Jewel, Self-Winding, Perpetual Date, Bracelet, 1974 .... 6037.00
Rolex, Oyster, Woman's, Silvered Dial, Gold Baton Numerals, 1950 .... 4485.00
Rolex, Prince, 15 Jewel, Silvered, Pink Matte Dial, Rectangular, 1930 .... 5980.00
Rolex, Silvered Dial, Gold, Baton Numerals, 1945 .... 3450.00
Rolex, Woman's, 14K Yellow Gold, Mesh Band, Square Face 665.00
Rolex, Woman's, 18K Gold, Bracelet, Marked Dial & Movement 550.00
Rolex, Woman's, 27 Jewel, Silvered Dial, Gold Baton Numerals, 1975 .... 3105.00
S. Smith, Lever Movement, Enamel Dial, Second Hand, Blue Enamel Case 4887.00
Star Wars Millennium Falcon, Leather Band, Brass, Box 49.00
Ulysse Nardin, Chronometer, 17 Jewel, Marked Dial, Square 185.00
Universal, 17 Jewel, Chronograph, Memento Dial, 1950 .... 2070.00
Vacheron & Constantin, 17 Jewel, 18K Gold, Mono Metallic Balance, c.1980 .... 2590.00
Vacheron & Constantin, 17 Jewel, 18K Gold, Silvered Dial, Gold Baton Numerals ... 2070.00
Vacheron & Constantin, 17 Jewel, 18K Pink Gold, Lever Movement, 1950 .... 2875.00
Vacheron & Constantin, 17 Jewel, 18K Pink Gold, Pink Dial, 1945 .... 2185.00
Vacheron & Constantin, 18 Jewel, 18K Pink Gold, Silvered Dial, c.1950 .... 2300.00
Vacheron & Constantin, 18K Gold, Applied Gold Baton, Roman Numerals 2300.00
Vacheron & Constantin, 18K Gold, Silvered Matte Dial, 1950 .... 2530.00
Vacheron & Constantin, 18K Gold, White Dial, Gold Hands, Florentine Frame 1150.00
Vacheron & Constantin, 18K Pink Gold, Silvered Matte Dial, Baton Numerals 2875.00
Vacheron & Constantin, 18K White Gold, Silvered Dial, 1930 .... 3335.00
Vacheron & Constantin, Chronometer Royal, 29 Jewel, Regulator, c.1986 .... 4600.00
Wizard Of Oz, Yellow Brick Road Style Band, Blue, Yellow, Plastic, Box 10.00
Woman's, 18K Gold, Champagne Dial, Gold Baton Numerals, 1960 .... 1725.00
Woman's, 18K Gold, Roman Numerals, Round Case, 1970 .... 4025.00
Woman's, Open Face, 17 Jewel, 18K Gold, Lapis Lazuli Dial, Square Case, 1970 ...... 2185.00
X Files, Push Button & It Glows, England 60.00

YELLOWWARE is a heavy earthenware made of a yellowish clay. It
varies in color from light yellow to orange-yellow. Many nineteenth-
and twentieth-century kitchen bowls and jugs were made of yellowware. It was made in England and in the United States. Another
form of pottery that is sometimes classed as yellowware is listed in this
book in the Mocha category.

Batter Bowl 1200.00
Bottle, Ink, London, 6 In. 40.00
Bowl, 2 Brown Bands, 5 In. 10.00
Bowl, Brown & White Slip Design, 10 In. 75.00
Bowl, Brown Band, 8 In. 30.00
Bowl, Brown Band, 10 In. 35.00
Bowl, Brown Band, Embossed, 10 In. 85.00
Bowl, Cover, 8 In. 3200.00
Bowl, Feeding, Kitty 30.00
Bowl, Scalloped Rim, Horizontal Ribbing, 11 1/2 In. 80.00
Butter, Daisy & Trellis 45.00
Cookie Jar, Cover 80.00
Crock, Brown & White Slip, Banded 125.00
Crock, Lid, Blue & White Bands 225.00

Jar, Molasses	85.00
Jar, Preserve, Pair	85.00
Jug, Glazed, 8 1/2 In.	65.00
Jug, Handles, 4 In.	75.00
Match Holder, Man On Stump	215.00
Mold, Candy, 6 Different Shapes, 9 In.	275.00
Mold, Corn, Large	55.00
Mold, Fish	650.00
Mold, Parrot	650.00
Mold, Rabbit, Large	165.00
Mug, Afco Porter Malt Syrup, Stenciled In Black, c.1890, 4 1/2 In.	50.00
Mug, Cobalt Blue Bands	150.00
Pitcher, Blue Bands, Signed, 100% Buckeye Pure, c.1890, 8 In.	135.00
Pitcher, Brown & White Slip, Marked H	110.00
Pitcher, Cow Scene, Green	150.00
Pitcher, Light Blue Sponging, 10 In.	160.00
Pitcher, Lovebird	595.00
Pitcher, Molded Peacocks, Sponged Rockingham Glaze, 8 1/2 In.	95.00
Pitcher, Morning Glory Design, Basket Weave	225.00
Pitcher, Says Gesundheit Over Man's Picture	105.00
Pitcher, Soft Buff, Cobalt Blue Band, 9 1/4 In.	185.00
Pitcher, Soft Yellow, Blue, Brown Sponge Patterns, 9 5/8 In.	165.00
Plate, Armorial, Coat Of Arms, Work & Arms Of John Hancock, 8 In.	295.00
Salt, Footed	795.00
Salt Box, Ivory Bands	150.00
Sugar Sifter, Confectionery, Mug Shape	195.00

ZANE Pottery was founded in 1921 by Adam Reed and Harry McClelland in South Zanesville, Ohio, at the old Peters and Reed Building. Zane pottery is very similar to Peters and Reed pottery, but it is usually marked. The factory was sold in 1941 to Lawton Gonder.

Vase, Pink, Blue Ink Stamp, 5 In.	75.00
Vase, Shadow, Chocolate Drips, Medium Brown & Copper Dust Base, 8 In.	175.00

ZANESVILLE Art Pottery was founded in 1900 by David Schmidt in Zanesville, Ohio. The firm made faience umbrella stands, jardinieres, and pedestals. The company closed in 1962. Many pieces are marked with just the words *La Moro*.

LA MORO

Plate, Scalloped, Applied Open Flowers, Rose, 4 In.	40.00
Rose Bowl, Brown, 5 In.	135.00
Vase, Blue Drip Glaze, 1910, 8 In.	195.00
Vase, Lion & Ring Design, Mottled Green Over Pink, Marked, 21 In.	187.00

ZSOLNAY pottery was made in Hungary after 1862 and was characterized by Persian, Art Nouveau, or Hungarian motifs. A series of new Zsolnay figurines with green-gold luster finish is available in many shops today. Early Zsolnay was not marked, but by 1878 the tower trademark was used.

Bowl, Reticulated, Flower, Leaf Design, Steel Blue, Rust, Yellow, Pink, 5 x 7 1/2 In.	260.00
Ewer, 2 Women, 7 In.	175.00
Figurine, Deer, Green Iridescent Glaze, 1930	145.00
Figurine, Dog, Oryf, Bluish Luster	95.00
Figurine, Nude, Crying, Blue, Green Iridescent, Gold Stamp Steeple Mark, 10 In.	200.00
Figurine, Nude, Gold Stamp	225.00
Figurine, Nude, Seated, Golden Green Iridescent, 12 In.	360.00
Figurine, Nude, Strip-Tease, Green, 10 1/2 In.	195.00
Figurine, Polar Bear, Green, Pair	345.00
Pitcher, 2 Women	165.00
Urn, Blue Pecs Mark, 14 In.	450.00
Vase, Aqua Feather Pattern, Gold Iridescent, 7 1/2 In.	2415.00
Vase, Completely Reticulated, Double Walled, 13 In.	1500.00
Vase, Hungarian Design, 3 3/4 In.	30.00

INDEX

This index is computer-generated, making it as complete as possible. References in uppercase type are category listings. Those in lowercase letters refer to additional pages where the piece can be found. There is also an internal cross-referencing system used in the main part of the book, so if you look for a Kewpie doll in the Doll category, you will be told it is in its own category. There is additional information at the end of many paragraphs about where to find prices of pieces similar to yours.

A. WALTER, 1
ABC, 1, 47–48, 190, 399, 542, 624
ABINGDON, 1–2
ADAMS, 2, 150, 263, 766–768
ADVERTISING, 3–22, 24–25, 42, 48, 53–54, 100, 107, 120, 145–146, 218, 244–245, 445, 505, 546–547, 615, 619, 758, 763, 833, 839, 871
AGATA, 25, 551
Airplane, 24, 46, 114, 268, 462–463, 577, 794–795, 812, 815
AKRO AGATE, 26, 483
ALABASTER, 26, 146, 328, 450
Album, 160, 214, 542, 563, 581, 612, 619, 739
ALEXANDRITE, 26–27, 506
ALHAMBRA, 184, 186, 504, 711
Almanac, 542
ALUMINUM, 13, 25, 27, 51, 90, 112, 140, 254, 292, 294, 439, 441, 489, 618, 700, 775, 791, 870
Amber, see Jewelry
AMBER GLASS, 1, 3, 27–28, 180, 370, 453, 470
Amberette, see Pressed Glass, Amberette
AMBERINA, 28–29, 44, 123, 126, 245, 792
Ambrotype, 563
AMERICAN ART CLAY CO., 29
AMERICAN DINNERWARE, 29–32
AMERICAN ENCAUSTIC TILING CO., 33
AMETHYST GLASS, 33
Amos 'n' Andy, 358, 822
Amphora, see Teplitz
Andirons and related fireplace items, see Fireplace
ANIMAL TROPHY, 34
ANIMATION ART, 34–36
ANNA POTTERY, 36
Apothecary, 37, 73, 77, 84, 494, 657
Apple Peeler, see Kitchen, Peeler, Apple
ARC-EN-CIEL, 36
ARCHITECTURAL, 37–38, 173
AREQUIPA, 38
Argy-Rousseau, see G. Argy-Rousseau
ARITA, 38
ART DECO, 27, 37–38, 74, 77, 92, 96, 107, 112, 141, 149–151, 173, 177, 187, 194, 234, 281, 284, 287, 292, 305, 316, 328, 336, 340–341, 352, 355, 373, 378, 389, 396, 423, 427, 441, 450, 461–462, 464, 499, 522, 527, 553, 557–558, 562, 571, 615–616, 676, 870, 872
Art Glass, see Glass-Art
Art Nouveau, 38, 113, 148, 238, 256, 298, 302, 330, 375, 424, 426, 450, 456, 470, 479, 556, 560, 700, 717, 727, 772, 778, 793, 859
ART POTTERY, 38–39, 783
ARTS & CRAFTS, 39, 54, 96, 99, 113–114, 173, 257, 282, 284–286, 291–293, 296, 315–316, 321–322, 324, 328–329, 331, 337, 339, 341, 348, 416, 430, 462, 513, 515, 517, 538, 632, 783
Ashtray, 3, 26, 29, 38, 43, 57, 64, 69, 95, 97, 107, 128, 143–144, 158, 172–173, 175–176, 188–189, 192, 195–196, 201, 208, 239–240, 247, 261, 270, 272, 277, 279, 369, 373, 378–379, 384–385, 390, 392–395, 400, 404,

410, 432, 435, 446, 490, 494, 498, 505, 522–523, 525, 527, 530, 539, 554, 580–581, 586, 590, 616, 619, 626, 634, 636, 649, 653, 656, 669, 681, 689, 701, 708, 718, 726, 731, 736, 739, 746, 752, 755, 775–776, 793, 832, 852, 856, 869
Atomizer, 110, 446, 557
Aunt Jemima, 13–14, 46, 69–70, 72, 234, 440, 683
AURENE, 39–40, 556
Austria, see Porcelain; Royal Dux
AUTO, 40–42, 584
Autumn Leaf, 42–43
Avon, see Bottle, Avon

Babe Ruth, 737
Baby, 2, 12, 70, 217–223, 225–227, 230, 232–234, 373, 389, 394, 433, 699, 702, 749, 770, 795–796, 842
BACCARAT, 43–45, 556–557
Backbar, 37
BADGE, 45–46, 69, 101, 119, 207, 368, 396, 471, 536, 574, 738, 786, 795, 868
Banana Boat, 125, 129, 138, 183, 532, 593–594, 603, 619, 862
Banana Stand, 245, 393
BANK, 46–53, 55, 63, 66, 69, 104, 122, 133–134, 149, 158, 190, 208–209, 267, 272, 277, 372, 396, 399–400, 432, 458–459, 478, 490, 536, 572, 574, 580, 617, 620, 623, 625, 634, 647, 653–654, 689, 701, 746, 763, 830, 832–833, 842, 869
BANKO, 53, 163
Banner, 3, 55, 69, 142, 574, 740, 848
BARBED WIRE, 53
BARBER, 14, 53, 78, 245, 487
BAROMETER, 53–54, 518
Baseball, see Card, Baseball; Sports
BASKET, 28, 39, 54–55, 72, 75, 107, 114, 118, 123, 129–130, 157, 173, 178, 184, 187, 207, 239–241, 245–246, 256, 268, 280, 364, 370, 378, 390, 395, 400, 412, 435, 462, 488, 492, 496, 501–502, 507, 513, 521, 531–532, 541, 549, 558, 560, 567, 581, 633, 636–637, 652, 668, 671, 675, 688, 690, 695, 700, 711, 719, 722, 725–726, 731–733, 742, 746, 754, 761–762, 772, 776, 785, 836, 852, 856, 862
BATCHELDER, 55
Bathtub, 37
BATMAN, 55–57, 115
BATTERSEA, 57
BAUER, 57–60
BAVARIA, 60, 387, 557
Bayonet, 279, 443, 764
Beaded Bag, see Purse
BEATLES, 60–61
Bed Warmer, 95, 173, 784
BEEHIVE, 66, 61, 448, 584, 616, 621, 688, 749–750
Beer, 7, 9, 31, 79, 555, 650, 683, 725
Beer Bottle, see Bottle, Beer
BEER CAN, 61–62, 463, 615
BELL, 62, 66, 68–69, 72, 140, 164, 178, 182, 209, 253, 267, 272, 372, 404, 467, 487, 580, 587, 616, 649, 671, 719, 762, 771, 807, 811, 867, 869
BELLE WARE, 62
BELLEEK, 62–63

Belt Buckle, 154, 399, 648, 763, 786, 796
BENNINGTON, 63–64, 617, 755
BERLIN, 64, 444
BESWICK, 64–66
BETTY BOOP, 66
BICYCLE, 24, 56, 62, 66–67, 121, 212
Bin, 3, 760, 785
BING & GRONDAHL, 68
Binoculars, 68–69, 215, 397, 648, 796
BIRDCAGE, 69, 301, 514, 796, 830
Biscuit Barrel, 717, 852
Biscuit Jar, 97, 103, 180, 262, 409, 459, 465, 470, 511, 523, 527, 532, 553, 587, 633, 635, 652, 668, 675, 690, 706, 729, 742, 754, 847, 851–852
BISQUE, 55, 69–70, 93, 116, 187, 191, 211, 214–215, 217–228, 231–233, 235, 431, 433–434, 459, 465, 488–489, 526–527, 536, 567, 571, 667, 693
BLACK, 10, 18, 27, 52, 69–72, 229–230, 233–235, 530, 554, 557, 627, 684, 706, 708, 784, 798, 808
BLACK AMETHYST, 72, 506
Blanket, 287, 305–306, 412, 773, 830
BLOWN GLASS, 72–73, 82, 141, 422, 440, 449–450, 494–495, 553, 556, 580, 694, 749
Blue Glass, see Cobalt Blue
Blue Onion, see Onion
BLUE WILLOW, 74, 238, 454, 647, 759, 822, 854
BOCH FRERES, 74–75
BOEHM, 75
BOHEMIAN, 10, 75–76
BONE DISH, 76, 122, 262, 507, 532, 624
Book, 46, 60, 69–70, 94, 101, 104, 119, 158, 164, 190, 207–209, 241, 260, 279, 368, 397, 430, 434, 471, 490, 494, 508, 536, 542–543, 546, 555, 572, 574, 580, 616, 648, 697, 710, 736, 740, 763, 867, 869
BOOKENDS, 1, 26, 55, 66, 76–77, 95, 97, 109, 141, 145, 176, 269, 277, 280, 384, 392, 399–400, 404, 459, 484, 491, 505, 513, 528, 626, 634, 637, 669–670, 689, 701, 731, 776, 834, 837, 856
BOOKMARK, 3, 60, 77, 177, 368, 754, 781
BOTTLE, 5, 7, 27, 46, 63, 70, 72, 76–90, 110, 118, 136, 142, 158–162, 178, 184, 194, 209, 239, 241, 245, 268, 278–279, 356, 370, 372, 397, 420, 445, 467, 487, 505, 508, 532, 555–556, 597, 625, 684, 686–687, 692–693, 711, 717, 719, 732, 739, 755, 762, 786, 789, 793, 795, 834, 837, 850, 856, 866–868, 874
BOTTLE CAP, 15, 17, 90, 556, 774
BOTTLE OPENER, 90, 159, 175, 555
BOW, 90–91
BOX, 4, 8–9, 12, 30, 38–40, 56–57, 61, 66, 70, 90–94, 101, 109–111, 122, 133, 135, 142, 146, 151, 153, 155, 157, 161, 165, 173–174, 184, 188–191, 207, 209, 213, 235 241–244, 249, 253, 256, 258, 261, 267, 273, 287, 356, 374, 377–378, 382, 390, 413, 420, 422, 430, 433, 435, 445, 458, 463–465, 470–472, 478, 487, 494, 501, 504, 506, 508, 511, 513–514, 517, 526, 535–536, 541, 545–

546, 550, 553–554, 557–558, 560,
572–573, 580–582, 589, 626, 633,
638, 648–649, 652, 670, 672, 683–
684, 689, 691, 693–697, 700, 711,
719, 722, 725–728, 739, 752, 763,
770–771, 781, 784–787, 793, 830,
845, 847, 852, 862, 866–867, 869
BOY SCOUT, 49, 94–95
BRADLEY & HUBBARD, 95, 235, 462, 488
BRASS, 12, 19, 37, 39–40, 45, 53–54, 62,
66, 69–70, 77, 90–91, 93–96, 105,
112–113, 117, 119, 131, 142–143,
148, 150–151, 153, 175, 213, 236,
243, 253, 255–257, 259, 279, 291,
321–322, 343, 350, 354, 356, 368,
387, 399, 407–408, 416, 424, 427–
429, 434, 437, 441–442, 445, 449–
450, 452–454, 456–457, 462–463,
488–490, 495, 507, 514, 518–519,
530, 536, 547, 553, 557, 573, 577,
581, 589, 617, 670, 692, 694–695,
730, 739, 765, 774, 789–791, 817,
821, 831–832, 868, 874
Brastoff, see Sascha Brastoff
Bread Plate, see various silver
  categories, porcelain factories, and
  pressed glass patterns
Bread Tray, 30, 184, 387, 541, 719, 726
BRIDE'S BASKET, 96–97, 511, 725
BRIDE'S BOWL, 97, 470, 511, 521, 551
BRISTOL, 45, 97, 194, 477
Britannia, see Pewter
BRONZE, 16, 37, 62, 77, 90, 94–95,
97–100, 112–113, 148, 150, 235,
255–256, 326, 348, 366, 384, 390,
416–417, 439, 449–450, 452, 454,
456, 462, 485, 489, 519, 547, 622,
694, 696, 730, 736, 775–779, 843, 867
Broom, 256, 435, 437
BROWNIES, 1, 100
BRUSH, 56, 100–101, 190–191
Brush, McCoy, see McCoy
BUCK ROGERS, 101, 474
Bucket, 95, 101, 142, 173, 184, 253–254,
258, 284, 375, 381, 580, 700, 725,
785, 866
Buckle, 5, 424, 591
BUFFALO POTTERY, 102
BUFFALO POTTERY DELDARE, 102–103
Buggy, 131, 788
Bugle, 142, 514
Bugs Bunny, 24, 88, 146, 210, 231, 491,
556, 797, 872
BURMESE GLASS, 103–104, 377, 453,
637–638
BUSTER BROWN, 104–105, 584
BUTTER CHIP, 105, 263, 478, 527, 597,
614, 616, 653
Butter Mold, see Kitchen, Mold, Butter
BUTTON, 5, 56, 60, 101, 104–105, 142,
164, 175, 368, 467, 574–576, 580,
648, 710, 736, 738–739, 742, 798, 816
BUTTONHOOK, 105, 731, 776

Cabinet, 5, 37, 131, 195, 288–290, 349,
494, 563, 670, 760, 787, 789, 798,
830
Cake Set, 385, 551
Cake Stand, 72, 201, 205, 240, 268, 394,
411, 478, 501, 554, 582, 590–593,
595–604, 606, 652, 675, 719, 734, 747
CALENDAR, 105–107, 148, 151, 159
CALENDAR PLATE, 107
CAMARK, 107–108, 622
CAMBRIDGE GLASS, 108–110, 115, 618
CAMBRIDGE POTTERY, 110
CAMEO GLASS, 110–111
Camera, 5, 114, 207, 397, 399, 564, 648,
798, 829, 869
Campaign, see Political
CAMPBELL KIDS, 102, 111
Camphor glass, 111
CANDELABRUM, 44, 112, 449, 668, 776
CANDLESTICK, 26–27, 39, 44, 63, 72, 90,
102, 107, 109–110, 112–114, 128,
132, 139, 153, 176, 180, 184,

201–202, 205–206, 239, 269–271,
279–280, 370, 383, 388, 390, 392–
394, 431, 445, 462, 485, 504, 517,
521–523, 535–536, 541, 558–560,
562, 587, 614, 626, 638, 670–671,
688–689, 727, 752–753, 761–762,
768, 771, 776–777, 779, 781, 836,
841–842, 852, 862
Candlewick, see Imperial Glass; Pressed
Glass
CANDY CONTAINER, 56, 70, 114–116,
135, 139, 209, 381, 434, 536, 693
CANE, 117–118, 182, 185, 209, 564, 592,
781, 798, 810, 869
Canister, 5, 20, 22, 28, 30, 53, 57, 70,
72, 74, 273, 277, 379, 401, 494, 623,
743, 755, 784–785, 845
Canteen, 142, 277, 755, 833
CANTON, 118–119, 368
Cap Gun, 190, 368, 648, 798–799
CAPO-DI-MONTE, 119, 730
CAPTAIN MARVEL, 119
CAPTAIN MIDNIGHT, 119
Car, 5, 46, 119, 135, 207, 209, 215, 267,
544, 795, 799–803, 813, 865
Carafe, 57, 74, 126, 158, 184, 248, 356,
388, 528, 541, 620, 681, 747, 837–
838, 845
Caramel Slag, see Chocolate Glass
Carbine, 649
CARD, 4, 60, 91, 94, 100, 103, 120–122,
139, 159, 164, 177, 209–210, 260,
341, 358–359, 364, 397, 467, 471,
505, 508, 580, 616, 628, 710, 763,
779–780
Card Case, 38, 719, 727
Carder, see Aurene and Steuben
categories
CARLSBAD, 122
CARLTON WARE, 122–123
CARNIVAL GLASS, 123–129, 395, 410,
418, 422, 632
CAROUSEL, 130, 147, 701, 803
CARRIAGE, 130–131, 148, 268, 457, 710,
725, 803
Carte De Visite, 564
Cartridge, 458
CASH REGISTER, 11, 16, 131, 208, 803
Casserole, 2, 26, 30, 43, 57, 172, 200,
237, 248, 263, 273, 277, 279, 379–
381, 385, 401, 512, 527, 562, 587,
620, 625, 681–682, 701, 717, 747,
755, 766, 838, 845–846
CASTOR JAR, 131
CASTOR SET, 132, 599
Catalog, 40, 94, 258, 543–544
CAUGHLEY, 132, 747
Cauldron, 132, 263
Cel, see Animation Art
CELADON, 132, 639, 761
CELLULOID, 3, 11–12, 45, 66, 70, 77, 91,
133, 135, 139, 141, 175, 207, 210–
213, 217, 220, 241, 381, 424, 434,
462, 472, 489, 495, 527, 574–577,
579, 581, 609, 698–699, 710, 795,
797, 804, 810–811, 816, 820, 830, 844
Centerpiece, 28, 39, 119, 188, 240, 268,
370, 496, 502, 517, 535–536, 688,
717, 721, 724, 753–754, 776, 779
CERAMIC ART CO., 133
CERAMIC ARTS STUDIO, 133–134
Chair, 53, 142, 190, 195, 267, 292–302,
365, 397, 616, 804, 806, 865
Chalice, 76, 95, 369, 535, 542, 551, 721,
852, 856
CHALKWARE, 8, 48, 52, 71, 134–135,
209, 211, 434, 441, 471, 526, 571,
710, 728, 744
Chamber Pot, 238, 503, 755, 766
Chamberstick, 96, 280, 374, 383, 418,
485, 560, 623, 670, 785, 793, 842,
852
Charger, 39, 64, 97, 102, 132, 143, 153,
173, 176, 179–180, 192, 194, 237–
238, 244, 356, 369, 409, 466, 473,
478, 496, 498–499, 504, 523, 550,

552, 560, 562, 582, 587, 614, 623,
626, 635, 689, 691, 693, 696, 729,
735, 753, 834, 837, 841–842, 852,
856
CHARLIE CHAPLIN, 135, 438, 509–510,
666
CHARLIE McCARTHY, 135
CHELSEA, 135–136
CHELSEA GRAPE, 136
Cherry Pitter, 436
Chest, 7, 119, 305–310, 331, 420, 445,
494, 518, 787, 806, 830, 866
CHINESE EXPORT, 136–138, 306, 366,
765
CHINTZ, 138
CHOCOLATE GLASS, 138–139
Chocolate Pot, 96, 122, 192, 263, 367,
466, 473, 505, 532, 567, 626, 635,
638, 668, 672–673, 675, 719
Chocolate Set, 61, 367, 407, 466, 505,
523, 527, 532, 582, 671, 673
Chopper, 436
CHRISTMAS, 27, 61, 65–66, 68, 102, 115,
139–140, 164, 209, 278, 368, 373,
435, 443, 467, 470, 517, 543, 545,
578, 581, 635, 653, 655, 735, 854
Christmas Plate, see Collector Plate
CHRISTMAS TREE, 140–141, 167, 213,
396, 427, 451
CHROME, 90, 141, 149, 175, 253, 301,
436, 440, 463–464, 530–531, 617,
670, 771
Churn, 436, 620, 755
Cigar Cutter, 6, 418, 420, 695, 760, 844
CIGAR STORE FIGURE, 141–142
CINNABAR, 142
CIVIL WAR, 68, 142–143, 358, 494,
564–566, 588–589, 694, 752
CKAW, see Dedham
CLAMBROTH, 143, 483, 557
CLARICE CLIFF, 143–144
CLEWELL, 144
CLEWS, 145, 744
CLIFTON, 145
CLOCK, 40, 43, 56, 66, 100, 111, 114,
120, 136, 145–153, 159, 174, 184,
189–190, 210, 239, 243–244, 279,
397, 399, 401, 434, 436, 459, 466,
496, 507, 518, 555, 560, 589, 626,
648, 652, 682, 727–728, 734, 736,
738, 776, 852, 856, 869
CLOISONNE, 87, 153–154, 426, 484, 730,
831
CLOTHING, 154–157, 543, 791, 811
CLUTHRA, 157, 753
COALBROOKDALE, 157
COALPORT, 157, 416, 766
Coaster, 6, 26, 108, 196, 198, 201, 210,
240, 271, 377, 410, 717, 722, 766,
829, 869
COBALT BLUE, 38–39, 72, 76–77, 81–86,
89, 92, 101, 157–158, 172, 175, 188,
190, 193–194, 196, 203, 205–206,
238, 240, 247–253, 280, 376, 380,
388, 409, 411, 417, 431, 457, 462,
464–466, 470, 480, 488, 494, 504–
505, 516, 521, 523–525, 539, 541,
547, 551, 557–558, 596, 599, 618,
620, 622, 672, 674, 691, 705, 710–
711, 755, 757, 780, 835, 848
COCA-COLA, 158–161, 207, 241, 786
Cocktail Shaker, 38, 141, 198, 388, 393,
719, 725
COFFEE GRINDER, 161–162, 491
Coffee Set, 30, 173, 444, 491, 652, 708,
717, 719, 725, 764
Coffeepot, 2, 27, 30, 43, 58, 63, 68, 74,
96, 118, 137, 143, 168, 173, 248, 258,
263, 273, 375, 379–381, 387, 395,
401, 407, 420, 436, 441, 502, 527,
552, 554, 560–561, 582, 587, 614,
623, 638, 649, 652, 668, 673, 682,
717, 719, 722, 724, 727, 734, 743,
747, 756, 761, 764, 766, 784, 839,
864
COIN SPOT, 124, 162, 507, 534–535

COIN-OPERATED MACHINE, 159, 162–164, 177, 555
COLLECTOR PLATE, 164
Cologne, 184, 241, 556–558, 562, 687–688
Coloring Book, 189, 260, 368, 397, 471, 572, 580, 763
Columbian Exposition, 89, 869–871
COMIC ART, 164
COMMEMORATIVE, 164–165, 169, 464, 627, 647, 728, 752, 846, 853–854
COMPACT, 165, 278, 336, 868, 870
Compass, 6, 260, 279, 296, 518, 694–695, 786–787, 867
Condiment Set, 70, 367, 527, 535, 603, 675, 724
Console Set, 108, 143, 176, 240, 463, 541, 856
CONSOLIDATED GLASS, 166
Contemporary Glass, see Glass-Contemporary
COOKBOOK, 43, 166–167, 399, 728, 870
Cookie Cutter, 210, 381, 436, 784
COOKIE JAR, 1–2, 30, 56, 58, 66, 70, 94, 100–101, 122, 159, 167–172, 190, 205, 210, 249, 273, 368, 372, 374, 379, 381, 385, 388, 390, 395, 397, 399, 401, 459, 491–492, 504, 554, 572, 580, 620, 639, 670, 701–702, 763, 833, 846–847, 856, 862, 874
COORS, 172
COPELAND, 172, 789
COPELAND SPODE, 172–173
COPPER, 11, 69, 76–77, 173–174, 191, 235, 242–243, 254, 257, 268, 416, 423, 426, 437, 450–452, 457, 477, 515, 588, 669–670, 766–767, 789, 848–850
Copper Luster, see Luster, Copper
CORALENE, 174, 523–524, 552
CORDEY, 174–175
CORKSCREW, 175, 483
Cornucopia, 2, 109, 146, 158, 175, 195, 279, 377–378, 401, 541, 550, 569, 588, 622, 639, 669, 680, 705, 753, 856
CORONATION, 175, 199
COSMOS, 166, 175, 562, 636–638, 640, 642–643, 647
COVERLET, 175–176
COWAN, 148, 176–177
CRACKER JACK, 177, 536
CRACKLE GLASS, 131, 177–178, 280
CRANBERRY GLASS, 178, 180, 454, 506, 557
CREAMWARE, 179, 458, 467, 639, 642, 652, 744–745, 852, 854, 856, 859, 864
Crock, 63, 587, 620, 623, 686, 728, 735, 756–757, 846, 874
CROWN DERBY, 179
CROWN DUCAL, 138, 179–180
CROWN MILANO, 180
Crown Tuscan, see Cambridge Glass, Crown Tuscan
CRUET, 28, 103, 109, 138, 162, 178, 180–185, 198, 239, 245, 268–270, 376, 392, 394–395, 487, 496, 506, 511, 533, 551, 554, 590–595, 600, 602, 620, 675, 711, 727, 733, 754, 850–851, 862
Cuff Links, 6, 159, 210, 424–425, 576
CUP PLATE, 181, 190, 367, 458, 709, 731, 767
Cupboard, 312–315, 805
CURRIER & IVES, 31, 181–182, 593
Cuspidor, 6, 72, 96, 277, 369, 374, 395, 418–419, 478, 492, 623, 625, 735, 757, 760, 767, 842
CUSTARD GLASS, 182–183, 454, 792
CUT GLASS, 37, 44, 148, 180, 183–186, 450, 462–463, 506, 535, 557, 684, 726
CUT VELVET, 186, 511–512, 530
CYBIS, 187
CZECHOSLOVAKIA GLASS, 187–188, 609
CZECHOSLOVAKIA POTTERY, 188

D'ARGENTAL, 188
Dagger, 442, 868
Daguerreotype, 564–565
DANIEL BOONE, 14, 189
Darner, 39, 697
DAUM, 189–190
DAVENPORT, 190, 317, 512
DAVY CROCKETT, 190–191, 227, 474
DE MORGAN, 191
DE VEZ, 191
Decoder, 119, 207, 536
DECOY, 191–192
DEDHAM, 192–194
DEGENHART, 194
DEGUE, 194
DELATTE, 194
Deldare, see Buffalo Pottery Deldare
DELFT, 194–195
Demitasse Set, 122, 172, 466, 502, 614, 673, 719
DENTAL, 195
DENVER, 46, 195, 481, 616
DEPRESSION GLASS, 195–207
DERBY, 114, 207
Desk, 95–96, 142, 148–149, 151, 153, 243, 294, 316–319, 378, 384, 391, 434, 450, 452, 518, 549, 611, 753, 771, 774, 776
Desk Set, 95–96, 390, 484, 582, 670, 776
Dessert Set, 190, 445, 478, 502
DICK TRACY, 207–208
Dickens Ware, see Royal Doulton; Weller
Dinnerware, see American Dinnerware
DIONNE QUINTUPLETS, 208
Dipper, 436, 700
DISNEYANA, 208–217
Dispenser, 6–7, 159, 760
Doctor, see Dental; Medical
DOLL, 56, 60, 66, 70, 100–101, 111, 135, 159, 189–190, 207–208, 210–211, 217–234, 241–243, 260, 399, 413, 434–435, 441, 536, 563, 572, 580, 698, 700, 710, 739–740, 821
Dollhouse, 267, 806
Donald Duck, see Disneyana
Door Knocker, 37, 96–97, 173, 279, 419
Door Push, 8, 159, 556
Doorknob, 37, 465
DOORSTOP, 37, 95, 234–236, 740
DORCHESTER, 236–238
DOULTON, 238–239
Dr Pepper, 3, 6, 9, 13, 15, 88, 145, 584, 774
DRAGONWARE, 239, 856
DRESDEN, 239, 713
Dresser Box, 535, 830
Dresser Set, 33, 60, 174, 523, 776, 863
Drum, 94, 142, 148, 168, 211, 279, 346, 413, 424, 514, 806
DUNCAN & MILLER, 239–240
DURAND, 240–241

Earrings, 66, 70, 220, 222, 413, 425
Egg, 5–6, 55, 72–73, 115, 195, 296, 366, 435–436, 440, 531, 615, 692, 697, 699
Eggbeater, 437, 787
Eggcup, 31, 192–193, 249, 263, 274, 386, 395, 459, 501, 527, 530, 560, 582, 591–592, 594, 597–598, 601–602, 604, 627, 688, 709, 735, 748, 767, 793, 839, 853, 866
ELFINWARE, 241
Elizabeth II, 175, 462
ELVIS PRESLEY, 241–242, 619
ENAMEL, 38, 61, 149, 165, 242, 355, 387, 424–426, 461, 464, 557, 713, 726, 730, 750, 776, 854, 868
Epergne, 103, 110, 125, 178, 185, 242, 245, 501, 533, 717, 851, 863
ERICKSON, 242
ERPHILA, 242–243
ES GERMANY, 243
ESKIMO, 243
Extinguisher, 254

FABERGE, 243–244
FAIENCE, 244, 416, 653, 750
FAIRING, 244
Fairyland Luster, see Wedgwood
Famille Rose, see Chinese Export
FAN, 9, 39, 61, 70, 107, 157, 159, 166, 244–246, 256, 409, 428, 486, 493, 523, 533, 576, 596, 622, 629, 644, 753, 766, 859
FEDERZEICHNUNG, 245
Feeder, 762
Fence, 37, 61, 773
FENTON, 245–246, 453, 836
Fernery, 384, 433, 650, 673, 848
FIESTA, 67, 107, 247–253
Figurehead, 518
Finch, see Kay Finch
FINDLAY ONYX, 253
Fireback, 257
FIREFIGHTING, 253–255
FIREGLOW, 255, 512
FIREPLACE, 37, 147, 255–258, 451, 492, 518, 677
First Aid, 94, 472, 784
FISCHER, 258
FISHING, 19, 47, 147, 258–260, 762, 796
Flag, see Textile, Flag
Flagon, 560
FLASH GORDON, 260–261, 829
Flashlight, 9, 190, 421, 471–472, 731, 786–787, 808
Flask, 9, 36, 63, 81–82, 89–90, 115, 243, 279, 501, 516, 557, 576, 615, 623, 625, 686, 692, 719, 742, 757, 782
Flower Frog, 101, 107–110, 177, 246, 280, 378, 401, 485, 492, 511, 588, 621, 627, 634, 638, 640, 703, 834–835, 856–857
Flowerpot, 47, 58, 401, 492, 587, 703–704, 748, 757, 833, 839
Flue Cover, 257, 437
Flying Phoenix, see Phoenix Bird
FOLK ART, 267–268
FOOT WARMER, 268, 784, 866
Football, see Card; Football; Sports
Fork, 257, 712–714, 716–717, 719, 782
Fortune Teller, 163, 658
FOSTORIA, 268–272
Foval, see Fry
Frame, 13, 15–16, 18, 38, 69, 101, 106, 159, 173, 181–182, 243–244, 322, 363, 399, 408, 422, 466, 472, 480, 484, 539, 544, 549, 574, 578, 586, 606–608, 670, 690, 717, 722, 772, 776–777, 786, 791, 830, 864, 867
FRANCISCAN, 272–276
FRANCISWARE, 277
FRANKART, 277
FRANKOMA, 139, 277–278
FRATERNAL, 278–279
Fruit Jar, 82–83
FRY, 279–280
FRY FOVAL, 280
FULPER, 221, 280–281
Funnel, 437
FURNITURE, 267, 282–355

G. ARGY-ROUSSEAU, 355–356
GALLE, 283, 338, 356–357
GAME, 9, 56, 60, 70, 92, 100, 104, 135, 207, 212, 346–347, 358–364, 368, 397, 399, 466–467, 471–472, 480, 536, 580–581, 648, 718, 737, 741, 763, 868
GAME PLATE, 364
GAME SET, 364, 388
GARDEN FURNISHING, 364–366, 473, 480, 544, 772, 787
GAUDY DUTCH, 367
GAUDY IRONSTONE, 367
GAUDY WELSH, 367
GEISHA GIRL, 367, 549, 693

GENE AUTRY, 368
GIBSON GIRL, 226, 368
Ginger Jar, 137, 153, 240, 274, 389, 583
GIRL SCOUT, 368–369
GLASS-ART, 369
GLASS-CONTEMPORARY, 369
GLASS-MIDCENTURY, 369–370
GLASS-VENETIAN, 370–372
GLASSES, 159, 372
GOEBEL, 222, 372–373
GOLDSCHEIDER, 373–374
Golf, see Sports
GONDER, 52, 374
GOOFUS GLASS, 374
GOSS, 374
GOUDA, 374–375
GRANITEWARE, 375–376, 488
Grater, 375, 437, 440
GREENTOWN, 138–139, 376
Grill Plate, 31, 196–198, 200–201, 203, 270, 274, 647
Grinder, 437, 791
GRUEBY, 376–377
GUNDERSON, 377
GUSTAVSBERG, 377–378
GUTTA-PERCHA, 378, 490

HAEGER, 378–379
Hair Receiver, 505, 517, 650, 673, 857, 866
Half-Doll, see Pincushion Doll
HALL CHINA, 43, 296, 312, 379–381, 451, 575
HALLOWEEN, 381–383, 435
HAMPSHIRE, 383–384
HANDEL, 384
Handkerchief, 155, 159, 212, 241, 280, 347, 576, 617, 731, 847, 870
Hardware, see Architectural
HARKER, 189, 384–385, 440
HARLEQUIN, 385–387
Harmonica, 4, 61, 360, 514, 648, 810
Hat, 9, 45, 56, 92, 105, 114, 123, 135, 142, 155, 175, 191, 212, 245–246, 254, 360, 368, 373, 382, 399, 413, 576–577, 655, 688, 866
HATPIN, 387
HATPIN HOLDER, 125–126, 387, 434, 524, 650, 671, 673, 676, 693
HAVILAND, 387–388, 538
HAWKES, 388–389
HEAD VASE, 262, 277, 389, 399, 460
HEDI SCHOOP, 390
HEINTZ ART, 390–391
HEISEY, 391–394
Herend, see Fischer
HEUBACH, 115, 223, 394, 567
HIGBEE, 394
Historic Blue, see factory names, such as Adams, Clews, Ridgway, and Staffordshire
HOBNAIL, 78, 178, 239, 245–246, 370, 395, 411, 447–448, 501, 507, 533–535, 632, 733, 792
HOLLY AMBER, 395
HOLT HOWARD, 395–396
Honey Pot, 63, 172, 527, 711
HOPALONG CASSIDY, 396–398
HOWARD PIERCE, 398–399
HOWDY DOODY, 399–400
HULL, 400–403
Humidor, 10, 38, 96, 102, 126, 137, 242, 268, 289, 384, 390–391, 479, 517, 524, 527, 541, 560, 583, 587, 627, 665, 693, 729, 744, 777, 848, 853, 865
HUMMEL, 404–407
HUTSCHENREUTHER, 407

Ice Bucket, 10, 27–28, 108–109, 146, 185, 196, 198, 242, 268–270, 392, 394, 411, 536, 717, 721, 846
Ice Pick, 788
ICON, 407–409
IMARI, 409–410
IMPERIAL GLASS, 164, 401, 410–412, 728

Incense Burner, 38, 99, 382, 691
INDIAN, 45, 86, 115, 141–142, 233, 263, 266, 268, 278, 394, 412–415, 435, 473, 475, 484, 491, 507, 517, 530, 554, 585, 609, 634, 714, 729, 752, 778, 791, 811, 814, 843–844, 849
INDIAN TREE, 32, 39, 416
INKSTAND, 389, 416, 549, 614, 722
INKWELL, 44, 95, 238, 374, 416–417, 431, 470, 531, 548, 551, 614, 623, 731, 735, 777, 782, 793, 853
INSULATOR, 417–418
Irish Belleek, see Belleek
IRON, 37, 47–48, 77, 112–113, 234, 236, 256–257, 322, 326, 340–341, 347, 365–366, 416–419, 436–437, 439–442, 449, 453, 544, 546, 618, 694, 730, 761, 787, 789–790, 798, 806, 811, 814, 831, 849
Iron, 437
Ironing Board, 437, 811
IRONSTONE, 105, 172, 420, 507, 731
IVORY, 87, 93, 118, 245, 283, 311, 359, 366, 420–421, 425–426, 462, 520, 589, 610, 697, 730

JACK ARMSTRONG, 421
JACK-IN-THE-PULPIT, 29, 40, 104, 188, 245, 422, 433, 611, 754, 781
JADE, 87, 390, 422–423, 425–429, 494, 535, 553, 752–753
Japanese Woodblock Print, see Print, Japanese
JASPERWARE, 87, 173, 422, 429, 615, 693, 852–856
Jell-O, 19
JEWELRY, 56, 93, 133, 267, 289, 420, 422–430, 433, 541, 847–848
JOHN ROGERS, 430
JUDAICA, 430
JUGTOWN, 430–431
JUKEBOX, 66, 431

KATE GREENAWAY, 431, 517
KAUFFMANN, 431–432
KAY FINCH, 432–433
Kayserzinn, see Pewter
KELVA, 433
KEW BLAS, 433
KEWPIE, 433–435, 459, 584
Key, 12, 16, 151, 163, 389, 694
Kimball, see Cluthra
King's Rose, see Soft Paste
KITCHEN, 111, 149–151, 216, 289, 304, 314, 348, 435–442, 798
KNIFE, 66, 93–94, 142, 159, 172, 177, 191, 212, 243, 397, 414, 442–443, 472, 495, 552, 572, 581, 670, 715, 718, 720, 722, 731, 737, 763, 782, 786, 867–868
Knowles, Taylor & Knowles, see KTK; Lotus Ware
Korean Ware, see Sumida
KOSTA, 443
KPM, 444–445
KU KLUX KLAN, 445
KUTANI, 445

Label, 10–11, 21, 70, 84, 96, 100, 110, 212, 269, 397, 449, 467, 493, 557, 622, 654, 728, 737, 740, 786
LACQUER, 142, 331, 353, 445–446
Ladle, 27, 31, 264, 269, 274, 434, 438, 477, 502, 555, 560, 718, 720, 722–723, 725, 782, 863
Lady Head Vase, see Head Vase
LALIQUE, 446–447
LAMP, 1, 4, 26, 28, 33, 39, 44, 73–74, 95–96, 99, 103, 109, 111, 115, 119, 137–139, 143, 153, 158, 166, 175, 177–178, 185–189, 191, 212, 238, 240, 244, 249, 270, 277, 280–281, 355–356, 371, 378, 383–384, 390–391, 397, 399, 401, 410, 446–457, 461, 467, 484, 487, 491–492, 504, 511–513, 516, 522, 524, 528, 531,

533, 535–536, 538, 541–542, 549–550, 561–562, 581, 587, 611, 627, 633–635, 641, 654, 670–671, 680, 690, 693, 703, 727, 734, 753, 768, 777–778, 785, 821, 830–831, 835, 837, 842, 851, 853, 858, 863, 870
LANTERN, 69, 115, 140, 173, 366, 382–383, 456–457, 492, 518, 565, 577, 617, 648, 778, 811, 817
Lazy Susan, 31, 278, 410, 420, 621
LE VERRE FRANCAIS, 457–458
LEATHER, 6, 92, 94, 154–155, 242, 253–254, 296, 306, 330–331, 336, 340, 458, 577, 589, 609–610, 649, 739, 765, 810–811, 831, 868
LEEDS, 214, 216, 458
LEFTON, 433, 458–460
LEGRAS, 461
Lemonade Set, 201, 524
LENOX, 461–462, 557
LETTER OPENER, 244, 462, 713–714, 782, 831, 870
LIBBEY, 28–29, 212, 462–463
Light Bulb, 66, 140
LIGHTER, 159, 213, 279, 463–465, 531, 572, 665, 760, 868
LIGHTNING ROD, 465, 849
Li'l Abner, 48, 361
LIMOGES, 100, 105, 149, 429, 465–467, 538, 701
Lincoln, 40, 77, 167, 330, 465, 563, 732, 801, 826
LINDBERGH, 467
LITHOPHANE, 467, 750
LIVERPOOL, 467
LLADRO, 467–470
Lock, 37, 518, 617, 699
LOCKE ART, 470
LOETZ, 470–471
LONE RANGER, 471–472
LONGWY, 472–473
LONHUDA, 473
LOTUS WARE, 473–474
Loving Cup, 175, 279, 509, 641, 665
LOW, 59, , 110, 184, 246, 270, 272, 392, 474, 485, 504, 591–592, 596–598
Loy-Nel-Art, see McCoy
LUNCH BOX, 56, 61, 101, 111, 191, 207, 213, 397, 399, 472, 474–476, 581, 648, 737–739, 763
LUNCH PAIL, 213, 476–477
LUNEVILLE, 513
Lure, 258–259
LUSTER, 62, 122, 383, 477, 528, 537, 557, 583, 638, 673, 698, 731, 762–763, 767, 852–853, 856, 859
Luster, Fairyland, see Wedgwood
Luster, Sunderland, see Sunderland
Luster, Tea Leaf, see Tea Leaf Ironstone
LUSTRE ART GLASS, 477
LUSTRES, 477
Lutz, 483, 547

MAASTRICHT, 477
Magnifying Glass, 421, 694, 778, 786
Mailbox, 115, 760
MAIZE, 478
MAJOLICA, 105, 366, 478–481, 784, 853–854
MAP, 291, , 481–482, 509, 536, 617, 812, 870
MARBLE, 26, 63, 113, 150, 160, 177, 195, 212, 241, 312, 320, 334, 348, 359, 364–365, 397, 416, 449, 482–484, 572, 737, 763
MARBLE CARVING, 484–485
MARBLEHEAD, 485–486
Marionette, 213, 228, 399
MARTIN BROTHERS, 486–487
MARY GREGORY, 487
Masher, 438
Mask, 11, 56, 66, 96, 213, 243, 255, 260, 278, 382–383, 414, 471, 520, 549, 577, 583–584, 731, 741, 783, 812, 865
Masonic, see Fraternal
MASON'S, 83, 488

MASON'S IRONSTONE, 488
MASSIER, 488
MATCH HOLDER, 69, 177, 410, 479,
    488–489, 502, 507, 650, 693, 728,
    759, 848, 875
MATCH SAFE, 213, 489–490, 577, 776
MATSU-NO-KE, 490
MATT MORGAN, 490
Mayonnaise Set, 524, 527
McCOY, 190, 490–494
McKEE, 494, 618
Measure, 375, 503, 789
Mechanical Bank, see Bank, Mechanical
MEDICAL, 494–495
MEERSCHAUM, 495–496
MEISSEN, 496–498, 532
Melodeon, 515
MERCURY GLASS, 498
MERRIMAC, 498
METTLACH, 498–501
Mickey Mouse, 35, 208–217, 372
Microscope, 694, 812
MILK GLASS, 4, 72, 190, 395, 398, 451,
    456, 488, 501–502, 546, 557,
    562–563, 701, 763, 862–863
MILLEFIORI, 547–548
Minnie Mouse, 35, 209–214, 216–217
MINTON, 502–503
Mirror, 11, 37, 70, 99, 139, 165, 213,
    239, 241, 267, 309, 320, 322–328,
    397, 399, 446, 577, 697, 710, 720,
    727, 730, 778, 793, 830
MOCHA, 503
Mold, 96, 135, 139, 375, 419, 438–439,
    495, 561, 759, 784, 789, 866, 875
MONMOUTH, 504
Mont Joye, see Mt. Joye
MOORCROFT, 504–505
MORIAGE, 505, 772
Mortar & Pestle, 96, 495, 669, 853
MOSAIC TILE CO., 505
MOSER, 148, 505–506
MOSS ROSE, 387–388, 460, 507
MOTHER-OF-PEARL, 54, 131, 162, 165,
    174, 424, 426, 462–463, 507, 512,
    520, 535, 549, 554, 556, 566, 610,
    632, 650, 690, 697–698, 765, 850
MOTORCYCLE, 507–508, 581, 585, 805,
    813–814
Mount Washington, see Mt. Washington
MOVIE, 56, 397, 445, 472, 508–511,
    648
Moxie, 9, 17, 775
MT. JOYE, 511
MT. WASHINGTON, 511–512
Muffineer, 103, 511, 673, 690
MULBERRY, 512
MULLER FRERES, 512–513
MUNCIE, 513
Murano, see Glass-Venetian
MUSIC, 289, 298, 339, 513–516
MUSTACHE CUP, 388, 516, 532, 673
Mustard, 103, 138, 250, 254, 312, 367,
    391, 396, 402, 502–503, 577, 597,
    599, 673, 720, 723, 769, 772, 782,
    854
MZ AUSTRIA, 516

NAILSEA, 516
NAKARA, 516–517
NANKING, 517
NAPKIN RING, 274, 517, 527
Nappy, 58, 127, 138, 193, 198, 247–248,
    250, 269, 272, 386, 389, 392–393,
    411, 420, 463, 533, 590, 603, 634,
    846
NASH, 517–518
NAUTICAL, 117, 518–520, 703, 777, 848
NETSUKE, 520
NEW HALL, 521
NEW MARTINSVILLE, 521
New York World's Fair, 245, 573
NEWCOMB, 521–522
Nickelodeon, 163
NILOAK, 387, 522–523
NIPPON, 230, 523–525, 784

NODDER, 46–48, 51–53, 66, 69–70, 139,
    213, 434, 452, 525–527, 577, 683–685
NORITAKE, 527–528, 765
NORSE, 528
NORTH DAKOTA SCHOOL OF MINES,
    528–529
NORTHWOOD, 529–530
Nu-Art see Imperial Glass
NUTCRACKER, 530, 839
Nymphenburg, see Royal Nymphenburg

OCCUPIED JAPAN, 464, 530–531, 795,
    800, 803
OHR, 531
OLD IVORY, 532
Old Paris, see Paris
Old Sleepy Eye, see Sleepy Eye
ONION, 252, 276, 532
OPALESCENT GLASS, 78, 87, 92, 162, 178,
    240, 245, 280, 374, 395, 446, 462–
    463, 512, 529–530, 532–535, 557,
    606, 683, 792–793, 836–838, 864
OPALINE, 76, 384, 535
OPERA GLASSES, 535
Organ, 50, 298, 340, 514–515, 815
Ornament, 61, 66, 135, 139–141, 213,
    373, 434, 470, 834
ORPHAN ANNIE, 536
ORREFORS, 536–537
OTT & BREWER, 537
OVERBECK, 537–538
OWENS, 538
OYSTER PLATE, 479, 538, 833

PADEN CITY, 539
Pail, 70, 213, 375, 458, 561, 815
PAINTING, 539–541
PAIRPOINT, 541–542
Palmer Cox, Brownies, see Brownies
PAPER, 3, 6, 100, 105, 213, 245, 383,
    536, 542–545, 577, 729, 760, 798
Paper Clip, 778
PAPER DOLL, 207, 213, 434, 545–546,
    710
PAPERWEIGHT, 1, 33, 44, 63, 99, 177,
    187, 189, 193, 371, 376, 419, 434,
    443, 446–447, 463, 470, 487, 537,
    542, 546–548, 550, 577, 599, 617,
    624, 628, 718, 768, 778, 780, 834–
    835, 837, 841, 850, 868, 870
PAPIER-MACHE, 114–116, 139, 141, 209,
    215, 219, 230, 255, 289, 350–351,
    353, 381–383, 434, 526–527, 548–
    549, 573, 577, 730, 765, 804, 810–
    811, 817
Parasol, see Umbrella
PARIAN, 63, 172, 230, 549
PARIS, 452, 535, 549–550, 557–558,
    695
PATE-DE-VERRE, 1, 189, 550
PATE-SUR-PATE, 394, 503, 550–551, 635
PAUL REVERE POTTERY, 551, 716, 721
PEACHBLOW, 97, 110, 174, 181, 377,
    395, 454, 521, 551–552
PEARL, 191, 426, 430, 552, 848, 858
PEARLWARE, 458, 552–553, 589
PEKING GLASS, 553
PELOTON, 553
PEN, 70, 397, 399, 553–554, 737, 782,
    870
PEN & PENCIL, 554
PENCIL, 56, 93, 101, 115, 135, 160, 209,
    213, 397, 399, 434, 464, 554, 573,
    577, 581, 611, 737
PENCIL SHARPENER, 71, 135, 160, 213,
    554, 581
PENNSBURY, 554–555
PEPSI-COLA, 23, 555–556
PERFUME BOTTLE, 44, 66, 76, 111, 157,
    187, 373, 447, 455, 461, 487, 502,
    511, 516, 521, 524, 535–536, 553,
    556–558, 611, 683, 711, 770, 834,
    841–842, 845, 848, 850–851, 854
PETERS & REED, 558–559
Petrus Regout, see Maastricht
PEWABIC, 559–560

PEWTER, 53, 77, 150, 314–315, 449,
    454–456, 495, 520, 560–562, 730, 765
PHOENIX BIRD, 562
PHOENIX GLASS, 562–563
PHONOGRAPH, 550, 563, 816
PHONOGRAPH NEEDLE, 22
PHOTOGRAPHY, 563–567
Piano, 8, 52, 156, 285, 340, 384, 452,
    515–516, 704, 773, 816
PIANO BABY, 567
PICKARD, 567–569
PICTURE, 4, 38, 241, 399, 435, 467, 472,
    484, 569–570, 574, 722, 737, 775
Picture Frame, see Furniture, Frame
Pierce, see Howard Pierce
PIGEON FORGE, 570
PILKINGTON, 571, 787
Pillow, 122, 194, 236, 374, 563,
    644–645, 674, 773, 841, 861
Pin, 12, 61, 67, 95, 119, 135, 139, 160,
    207, 213–214, 221, 244, 255, 266,
    383, 389, 395, 397, 399, 414, 421,
    427–430, 445, 472, 507, 523, 556,
    573, 581, 594, 649, 723, 731–732,
    736, 742, 763, 781, 786, 844, 854–
    855, 867–870
Pinball, 163, 361–362
Pincushion, 214, 424, 698–699
PINCUSHION DOLL, 571
Pink Slag, see Slag Glass, Pink
PIPE, 17, 93, 374, 414, 464, 495–496,
    515, 531, 543, 571, 580–581, 792
PISGAH FOREST, 571–572
Pistol, 82, 101, 207, 260, 464
Plane, 732, 763, 789–790
PLANTERS PEANUTS, 572–573
PLASTIC, 6, 19, 46–48, 51–52, 101, 111,
    139, 145–146, 149, 151, 160–161,
    169, 171, 190–191, 207, 214, 216,
    382, 396–399, 435, 437, 440–441,
    472, 474, 476, 526–527, 573–575,
    577–578, 580, 610, 615–616, 698,
    710, 774, 795, 797–798, 801, 803,
    805–806, 808–809, 813, 817, 819,
    824, 829
PLATED AMBERINA, 573
PLIQUE-A-JOUR, 573
POLITICAL, 573–579
POMONA, 579–580, 716, 753
Pontypool, see Tole
POPEYE, 159, 382, 580–581, 829
PORCELAIN, 2, 8, 11, 13–19, 24–25, 42,
    51–52, 76, 87–88, 113, 119, 137, 148,
    150, 159–161, 181, 188, 211–212,
    327, 434–436, 440, 507, 516,
    530–531, 538, 581–584, 618, 633,
    687, 698–699, 701, 730–731,
    749–752, 760, 765, 771, 774–775,
    784–785, 819, 842
Porringer, 275, 551, 561, 720, 729,
    782
POSTCARD, 61, 71, 95, 105, 160, 207,
    214, 241, 445, 472, 578, 584–586,
    617, 729, 762, 870
POSTER, 13, 56, 61, 71, 160, 214, 241,
    260, 279, 383, 397, 399, 508–510,
    556, 578, 586, 649, 739–740, 763,
    867–869
Pot, 63, 195, 258, 414, 477, 480, 513,
    561, 572, 589, 624, 760, 762, 785,
    854–855, 858
POTLID, 586
POTTERY, 3, 10, 12–13, 47, 52–53, 62,
    66, 86, 104, 181, 209, 417, 495,
    526–527, 586–588, 750–751
POWDER FLASK, 588–589
POWDER HORN, 589
PRATT, 586, 589, 785
PRESSED GLASS, 417, 455, 589–606
PRINT, 13, 143, 435, 578, 606–609, 739,
    871
Projector, 216, 565–566, 816
Puppet, 24, 56, 135, 207, 214, 230–231,
    383, 581, 737, 763
PURSE, 156, 187, 214, 424, 557,
    609–611, 870

Puzzle, 56, 93, 101, 191, 207, 214, 261, 362–363, 399, 420, 467, 510, 578, 581, 587, 614, 633, 649, 744, 763, 793, 831

QUEZAL, 611–612
QUILT, 339, 448, 465, 612–614, 790
QUIMPER, 614–615

RADFORD, 615
RADIO, 13, 52, 56, 160, 210, 214, 397, 556, 573, 615–616, 786, 802, 811, 817
RAILROAD, 82, 616–617, 829, 843–844, 865
Rattle, 133, 383, 695
RAZOR, 396, 617–618, 870
REAMER, 74, 280, 494, 618–619, 622, 635, 709
RECORD, 56, 61, 160, 191, 214, 241, 368, 578, 581, 619
RED WING, 619–623
REDWARE, 571, 623–624, 729, 746
Reel, 71, 259, 817
Regina, 514
Regout, see Maastricht
RIDGWAY, 74, 262, 624
Ring Tree, 506, 535, 733
RIVIERA, 624–625, 800, 843
ROCKINGHAM, 625
Rockwell, 164
Rogers, see John Rogers
Rolling Pin, 116, 385, 440, 516, 784
ROOKWOOD, 626–632
Rosaline, see Steuben
ROSE BOWL, 103, 111, 121, 123–127, 129, 159, 174, 180, 186, 240, 246, 269, 389, 461, 470, 505, 507, 512, 523, 530, 534, 551, 553, 632–634, 641–642, 690, 723, 729, 733, 754, 836–837, 850–851, 875
ROSE CANTON, 633
ROSE MEDALLION, 633
Rose O'Neill, see Kewpie
ROSE TAPESTRY, 523, 633–634
ROSEMEADE, 634–635
ROSENTHAL, 635–636
ROSEVILLE, 636–647
ROWLAND & MARSELLUS, 647
ROY ROGERS, 647–649
ROYAL BAYREUTH, 6, 181, 634, 649–651, 762
ROYAL BONN, 652
ROYAL COPENHAGEN, 652–653
ROYAL COPLEY, 653–655
ROYAL CROWN DERBY, 655
ROYAL DOULTON, 175, 655–667
ROYAL DUX, 667
ROYAL FLEMISH, 667
Royal Haeger, see Haeger
Royal Ivy, see Pressed Glass, Royal Ivy
ROYAL NYMPHENBURG, 668
Royal Oak, see Pressed Glass, Royal Oak
Royal Rudolstadt, see Rudolstadt
Royal Vienna, see Beehive
ROYAL WORCESTER, 437–438, 668–669
ROYCROFT, 286, 300, 330, 339, 669–670
Rozane, see Roseville
ROZENBURG, 670
RRP, 670
RS GERMANY, 671
RS POLAND, 671
RS PRUSSIA, 671–675
RS SUHL, 675
RS TILLOWITZ, 675
RUBENA, 162, 675
RUBENA VERDE, 675
RUBY GLASS, 377, 675–676, 751
RUDOLSTADT, 676
RUG, 13, 34, 214, 414–415, 676–680
Ruler, 13, 214, 421, 617
RUMRILL, 622, 680
RUSKIN, 680–681
RUSSEL WRIGHT, 452, 681–683

SABINO, 683
Sadiron, 419, 437, 440

Sailor's Valentine, 519
SALOPIAN, 683
SALT & PEPPER, 32, 43, 59, 63, 65–66, 72, 74, 103, 108, 110–111, 132, 134, 160, 183, 193, 196–197, 199, 203–205, 214–215, 240, 251, 270–271, 276, 278, 373, 379–382, 385, 388, 396, 402, 411, 460, 507, 512, 524, 528, 530, 534, 568, 573, 581, 593, 595–597, 603, 606, 622, 634–636, 642, 651, 682–686, 704–705, 720, 725, 749, 768, 782, 835, 840, 847–848, 863, 871
SALT GLAZE, 417, 430–431, 583, 587, 620, 686, 743–745, 756–757, 855
Saltshaker, 13, 42, 143, 178, 196, 199, 205, 251, 380, 480, 512, 534, 556, 568, 589, 593, 601, 604, 635, 667, 675, 768, 847–848
Samovar, 96, 726
SAMPLER, 686–687
SAMSON, 687
SANDWICH GLASS, 181, 456, 687–688
Santa Claus, 1, 50, 52, 116, 139–140, 161, 170, 218, 231, 256, 268, 372, 395, 433, 436, 438, 527, 660
SARREGUEMINES, 688
SASCHA BRASTOFF, 689–690
SATIN GLASS, 96–97, 455, 507, 633, 685, 690–691, 850
SATSUMA, 691–692
Saturday Evening Girls, see Paul Revere Pottery
SCALE, 692, 819
Scarf, 156, 649, 773, 871
SCHAFER & VATER, 692–693
SCHNEIDER, 693
SCIENTIFIC INSTRUMENT, 497, 693–695
Scissors, 143, 440, 771, 782
Scoop, 160, 440
Screen, 257, 330–331, 583, 837
SCRIMSHAW, 695
Seat, 366, 419
SEBASTIAN MINIATURES, 695
SEG, see Paul Revere Pottery
SEVRES, 696
SEWER TILE, 696
SEWING, 296, 319, 330, 351–352, 697–700, 762, 821, 830
SHAKER, 197, 296, 300, 306, 310, 315, 319, 322, 330, 339–340, 352, 440, 460, 494, 512, 651, 700, 705, 833
SHAVING MUG, 202, 265, 524, 624, 651, 674, 693, 700–701, 705, 768
SHAWNEE, 399, 701–706
SHEARWATER, 706
SHEET MUSIC, 95, 135, 191, 215, 241, 368, 445, 467, 536, 578–579, 706–708, 711, 871
Sheffield, see Silver-English; Silver Plate
SHELLEY, 618, 708–709
SHIRLEY TEMPLE, 710–711
Shoehorn, 13, 96, 731, 776, 782, 791
Shriner, see Fraternal
Sideboard, 334–336, 806, 820
Sifter, 440
Sign, 13–19, 42, 53, 71, 105, 160–161, 177, 208, 255, 260, 278, 378, 435, 519, 556, 628, 642, 695, 698, 728–729, 738, 749, 771, 820, 869
Silent Butler, 419
Silhouette, 277, 569–570, 637–642, 645, 647, 712, 737, 849–850
SILVER DEPOSIT, 711
SILVER FLATWARE PLATED, 711–712
SILVER FLATWARE STERLING, 712–717
SILVER PLATE, 44, 52, 54, 112–113, 131, 158, 326, 416, 499–500, 509–510, 514, 517, 717–718, 730
Silver, Sheffield, see Silver Plate; Silver-English
SILVER-AMERICAN, 718–721
SILVER-AUSTRIAN, 721
SILVER-CHINESE, 721
SILVER-CONTINENTAL, 721

SILVER-DANISH, 721–722
SILVER-DUTCH, 722
SILVER-ENGLISH, 722–724
SILVER-FRENCH, 724–725
SILVER-GERMAN, 725
SILVER-HUNGARIAN, 725
SILVER-IRISH, 725
SILVER-ITALIAN, 725
SILVER-JAPANESE, 725
SILVER-MEXICAN, 725
SILVER-PERUVIAN, 725
SILVER-RUSSIAN, 725–726
SILVER-SCOTTISH, 726
SILVER-STERLING, 105, 108, 112–114, 148–149, 165, 210, 215, 387–388, 393, 414, 420, 423–430, 462, 464, 489, 554, 556, 609–611, 618, 697, 698, 726–727, 730, 732, 766, 843, 844
SILVER-SWEDISH, 727
SINCLAIRE, 727
Skiing, see Sports
Skimmer, 257, 440
Slag, Caramel, see Chocolate Glass
SLAG GLASS, 727
Sled, 140, 820
SLEEPY EYE, 17, 728–729
Sleigh, 62, 131, 283, 354
SLIPWARE, 729
Slot Machine, see Coin-Operated Machine
SMITH BROTHERS, 729
Smoking Set, 391, 651, 655
SNOW BABIES, 730
Snuff Bottle, see Bottle, Snuff
SNUFFBOX, 498, 723, 726, 730, 745
Soap, 19, 63, 215, 265, 375, 420, 435, 627, 743, 757, 764, 838
Soap Dish, 671, 760, 768
SOAPSTONE, 731
Socks, 764
Soda Fountain, 19, 37
SOFT PASTE, 1, 731, 744
SOUVENIR, 77, 183, 255, 368, 383, 592–594, 599, 705, 731–732, 840
SPANGLE GLASS, 732–733
SPANISH LACE, 733
Sparkler, 261
SPATTER GLASS, 733
SPATTERWARE, 733–734
SPELTER, 734
Spice Box, 31, 440, 561, 785
Spill, 553, 597–598, 602
SPINNING WHEEL, 734, 821
SPODE, 175, 734–735
SPONGEWARE, 2, 46, 735–736
Spoon, 19, 165, 193, 215, 252, 396, 415, 439–440, 495, 510, 561, 573, 579, 673, 716, 720–722, 726–727, 732, 738, 782, 871
Spoon Holder, 215, 400, 460
Spooner, 29, 110, 123, 126–128, 138, 158, 175, 178, 182–183, 186, 253, 266, 271, 376, 379, 393, 528, 530, 534, 551, 590–605, 674, 837
SPORTS, 736–742
Sprinkler, 366, 828
St. Louis World's Fair, 585
STAFFORDSHIRE, 1, 74, 86, 179, 262, 417, 742–746, 785
STANGL, 1, 746–749
Stationery, 61, 161, 400, 869
STEIN, 61, 63, 78, 119, 143, 193, 383, 493, 499–500, 524, 535, 550, 561, 628, 729, 749–752, 864
Stencil, 304, 312
STEREO CARD, 752
STEREOSCOPE, 752
Sterling Silver, see Silver-Sterling
STEUBEN, 39–40, 557, 752–754
STEVENGRAPH, 754
STEVENS & WILLIAMS, 754
Stickpin, 19, 215, 430, 579, 693
STIEGEL TYPE, 89, 140, 755
Still, 209
Stock Certificate, 545, 617

STONEWARE, 46, 52, 63, 81, 86, 89, 239, 417, 484, 492, 495, 558, 622, 670, 749–752, 755–760, 803
STORE, 11–12, 95, 453, 692, 760–761, 785
STOVE, 260, 536, 761, 806, 821
Strainer, 179, 195, 376, 441, 531, 722, 745, 867
STRETCH GLASS, 761
String Holder, 20, 71, 135, 140, 215, 396, 441, 695, 761, 866
SULPHIDE, 37, 43–44, 484, 548
SUMIDA, 761–762
SUNBONNET BABIES, 762
SUNDERLAND, 346, 762–763
Sundial, 99, 366, 380, 694
SUPERMAN, 763–764
SUSIE COOPER, 764
SWANKYSWIG, 764
Sweeper, 216, 821
SWORD, 117–118, 143, 279, 429, 462, 563–564, 764–765, 871
SYRACUSE, 532, 765

T-Shirt, 764
Tapestry, Porcelain, see Rose Tapestry
TEA CADDY, 68, 94, 118–119, 137, 157, 179, 195, 480, 589, 674, 720–721, 724, 727, 745, 765–766, 782, 793, 855, 864
TEA LEAF IRONSTONE, 516, 766–768
TECO, 768–769
TEDDY BEAR, 101, 433, 698, 703, 769–770
TELEPHONE, 161–162, 171, 215, 339, 353, 706, 764, 770–771, 822, 869
Telescope, 143, 520, 694–695, 786
TELEVISION, 452, 771–772
TEPLITZ, 772
TERRA-COTTA, 366, 624, 761, 772, 783–784
TEXTILE, 435, 579, 690, 732, 773–774
THERMOMETER, 15, 54, 111, 161, 215, 441, 495, 556, 694, 740, 774–775
Thermos, 40, 57, 72, 101, 207, 215, 400, 649, 764, 822
Thimble, 700
TIFFANY, 165, 747, 775–779, 843
TIFFANY GLASS, 779–781
TIFFANY GOLD, 781
TIFFANY POTTERY, 781
TIFFANY SILVER, 781–783
TIFFIN, 783
TILE, 29, 33, 38, 55, 72, 102, 191, 193, 195, 244, 276, 278–279, 281, 376–378, 396, 462, 466, 473–474, 480, 485, 487–488, 503, 505, 521, 538, 551, 559, 579, 614, 628, 666, 690, 780, 783, 841, 855, 863
Tin, 3–4, 6, 8, 13–19, 25, 40, 47–48, 50, 72, 135, 146, 160–161, 191, 209–210, 215, 217, 254, 358, 360, 383, 399–400, 436–437, 440, 449–450, 457, 474, 476, 488–489, 556, 577, 581, 617, 649, 700, 742, 771, 775, 794–798, 800–801, 804–808, 811–812, 814, 816–823, 825, 827, 829–830
Tintype, 566–567
TINWARE, 784
Toast Rack, 724
Toaster, 258, 441
Tobacco Cutter, 419
TOBACCO JAR, 177, 186, 195, 238, 390, 625, 772, 784, 848, 858
TOBY JUG, 238, 460, 462, 579, 589, 666, 785
TOLE, 697, 730, 785–786
TOM MIX, 786
Tongs, 258, 715, 721, 724–725, 791
TOOL, 96, 143, 520, 786–792
Toothbrush Holder, 215, 266, 472, 536, 583, 848
TOOTHPICK HOLDER, 25, 27, 29, 44, 72, 96, 103, 109, 125, 127, 139, 143, 166, 182–183, 187, 194, 215, 253, 269–

272, 383, 391–393, 395, 411, 431, 433, 435, 463, 466, 494, 498, 502, 506, 512, 517, 521, 524, 530–532, 542, 551, 573, 590–606, 622, 651, 666, 671, 674–676, 709, 718, 727–729, 762, 780, 782, 792–793, 836–837, 858, 863
TORQUAY, 793
TORTOISESHELL, 165, 288, 423, 429, 553, 688, 730, 766, 793
TORTOISESHELL GLASS, 794
Towel, 329, 774
TOY, 24, 72, 101, 119, 135, 140, 161, 208, 215–216, 261, 398, 400, 472, 536, 556, 581, 764, 782, 794–830, 871
Trade Stimulator, 24, 164
Train, 78–79, 140, 171, 216, 452, 556, 808, 823–824
TRAMP ART, 830
TRAP, 831
Tray, 1–2, 24–25, 27, 33, 61, 69, 72, 96, 99, 103, 108–110, 124, 141, 157, 161, 173–174, 182, 186, 198–201, 216, 240, 252, 266, 269, 276, 353, 356, 370, 376, 389–390, 399, 410–412, 415, 441, 446–447, 463, 466, 473, 477, 480, 498, 500, 505, 511, 524, 528, 542, 549, 551, 555–556, 569, 579, 587, 590, 593–595, 598, 603, 605, 615, 622, 628, 634, 642, 649, 651, 655, 666, 670, 674, 676, 683, 690, 709, 718, 721, 724–727, 735, 746, 749, 757, 778–780, 782, 785–786, 791, 793, 834, 848, 855, 863, 866, 871
Treen, see Wooden
TRENCH ART, 831
TRIVET, 33, 102, 137, 216, 278–279, 376, 381, 396, 419, 437, 439, 441, 473, 485–486, 521, 528, 551, 622, 628–629, 831
Truck, 24, 53, 88, 116, 161, 216, 556, 686, 825–828
TRUNK, 710, 831–832
TUTHILL, 832
TYPEWRITER, 554, 828, 832
TYPEWRITER RIBBON, 832

UHL, 832–833
UMBRELLA, 25, 84, 96, 216, 238, 340, 410, 417, 494, 736, 738, 828–829, 833, 871
Umbrella Stand, 174, 481, 558, 642, 858–859
Uncle Sam, 51–53, 65, 116, 135, 141, 164, 278, 389, 531, 576, 583
Uniform, 157, 177, 279, 566, 769, 868–869
UNION PORCELAIN WORKS, 833
University of North Dakota, see North Dakota School of Mines

VAL ST. LAMBERT, 833–834
Valentine, 209–210, 435, 489, 544–545, 666
VALLERYSTHAL, 834
VAN BRIGGLE, 834–836
VASA MURRHINA, 836
VASART, 836
VASELINE GLASS, 489, 836–837
Venetian glass, see Glass-Venetian
VENINI, 837
VERLYS, 837–838
VERNON KILNS, 838–840
VERRE DE SOIE, 558, 753–754, 841
Vienna, see Beehive
VIENNA ART, 841
VILLEROY & BOCH, 750, 841
Violin, 516, 623
VOLKMAR, 841
VOLKSTEDT, 842

Wahpeton Pottery, see Rosemeade
Wallace Nutting photographs are listed under Print, Nutting. His reproduction furniture is listed under Furniture.
Wallpaper, 37, 91, 94, 331
WALRATH, 842
Walt Disney, see Disneyana
Walter, see A. Walter
WARWICK, 263–265, 394, 842–843, 861–862
Wash Stick, 442
Washboard, 442, 829
Washbowl, 734, 768
Washing Machine, 11, 616, 829
Washstand, 355, 786, 829
Washtub, 25, 442
WATCH, 18, 105, 135, 137, 177, 217, 323, 424–425, 508, 536, 727, 738, 843–844
WATCH FOB, 217, 508, 556, 579, 786, 844
Water Cooler, 623, 833
WATERFORD, 206, 845
Watering Can, 78, 217, 494, 672, 705
WATT, 845–847
WAVE CREST, 847–848
WEAPON, 848
WEATHER VANE, 848–850
WEBB, 27, 116, 424, 850–851
WEBB BURMESE, 851
WEBB PEACHBLOW, 851
WEDGWOOD, 175, 480, 719, 764, 852–856
WELLER, 856–862
WEMYSS, 862
WESTMORELAND, 501, 862–863
WHEATLEY, 863–864
Wheelbarrow, 704, 791, 829
WHEELING POTTERY, 263–264, 266
WHIELDON, 864
Whirligig, 217, 268
Whisk Broom, 72, 403
Whistle, 19, 25, 96, 105, 177, 189, 218, 573, 588, 625, 829
WILLETS, 864
Willow, see Blue Willow
Windmill Weight, 419–420
WINDOW, 285, 488, 641, 781, 864
Windup, 24, 47, 101, 135, 145–146, 149, 216, 261, 268, 400, 513–514, 536, 581, 764, 794–823, 825, 829–830, 872
Wine Set, 129, 676
WOOD CARVING, 864–866
WOODEN, 3–7, 12, 16, 18, 20, 25, 42, 66–67, 69–70, 88, 90, 92–94, 130–131, 135, 142, 149, 191, 209, 212, 215–216, 221, 234, 242, 259, 268, 284, 328, 359, 417, 435–436, 440, 442, 457, 481, 495, 536, 557, 577, 579, 611, 618, 670, 695, 697–698, 700, 728, 738, 742, 752, 771, 774–775, 784, 788, 791, 797–798, 803–806, 810–811, 820–822, 825, 829, 850, 866
WORCESTER, 85–86, 544, 760, 789, 791, 866–867
WORLD WAR I, 463, 519, 707, 831, 867–868
WORLD WAR II, 45, 254, 546, 564, 787, 868–869
WORLD'S FAIR, 36, 249, 551, 586, 616, 798, 836, 869–871
WPA, 871
Wrench, 143, 791–792
WRISTWATCH, 119, 161, 191, 208, 217, 368, 398, 400, 472, 536, 573, 649, 764, 871–874

YELLOWWARE, 417, 874–875

ZANE, 875
ZANESVILLE, 33, 72, 90, 547, 875
ZSOLNAY, 875